Twenty-Sixth Edition
Blue Book
of Gun Values™
by S.P. Fjestad

$39.95
Publisher's Softcover Suggested List Price

Publisher's Limited Edition Hardcover
Suggested List Price - $54.95 (limited quantities)

NRA Special Limited Edition
Suggested List Price - $39.95 (limited quantities)

2

Publisher's Note:

This book is the result of continuous firearms research carried out by attending and/or participating in trade shows, gun shows, auctions, and also by communicating with contributing editors, gun dealers, collectors, company historians, and other knowledgeable industry professionals worldwide each year. This book represents an analysis of prices for which collectible firearms have actually been selling during that period at an average retail level. Although every reasonable effort has been made to compile an accurate and reliable guide, gun prices may vary significantly (especially auction prices) depending on such factors as the locality of the sale, the number of sales we were able to consider, and economic conditions. Accordingly, no representation can be made that the guns listed may be bought or sold at prices indicated, nor shall the author or publisher be responsible for any error made in compiling and recording such prices and related information.

All Rights Reserved
Copyright 2005
Blue Book Publications, Inc.
8009 34th Avenue South, Suite 175
Minneapolis, MN 55425 U.S.A.

Orders Only: 800-877-4867
Phone: 952-854-5229
Fax: 952-853-1486
Email: bluebook@bluebookinc.com
Website: http://www.bluebookinc.com

Published and printed in the United States of America

ISBN No. 1-886768-55-2

Library of Congress ISSN number - 1524-6043

TABLE OF CONTENTS

While many of you have probably dealt with our company for years, it may be helpful for you to know a little bit more about our operation, including information on how to contact us regarding our various titles, software programs, and other informational services.

Blue Book Publications, Inc.
8009 34th Avenue South, Suite 175
Minneapolis, MN 55425 USA
Phone: 952-854-5229 • Orders Only (domestic and Canada): 800-877-4867
Fax: 952-853-1486 (available 24 hours a day)
Website: http://www.bluebookinc.com
Email: bluebook@bluebookinc.com - we check our email at 9am, 12pm, and 3:30pm M - F
(excluding major U.S. holidays). Please refer to individual email addresses listed below with
phone extension numbers.

To find out the latest information on our products (including availability and pricing) and related consumer services, and up-to-date industry information (trade show recaps with photos/captions, upcoming events, feature articles, etc.), please check our website, as it is updated on a regular basis. Surf us - you'll have fun!

Since our phone system is equipped with voicemail, you may also wish to know extension numbers which have been provided below:

Ext. 10 - Beth Marthaler
(bethm@bluebookinc.com)
Ext. 11 - Katie Sandin
(katies@bluebookinc.com)
Ext. 12 - John Andraschko
(johnand@bluebookinc.com)
Ext. 13 - S.P. Fjestad
(stevef@bluebookinc.com)
Ext. 15 - Clint Schmidt
(clints@bluebookinc.com)

Ext. 16 - John Allen
(johna@bluebookinc.com)
Ext. 17 - Zach Fjestad
(zachf@bluebookinc.com)
Ext. 18 - Tom Stock
(toms@bluebookinc.com)
Ext. 19 - Cassandra Faulkner (cassandraf@bluebookinc.com)
Ext. 22 - Stacy Knutson
(stacyk@bluebookinc.com)

Office hours are: 8:30am - 5:00pm CST, Monday - Friday.

Additionally, an after-hours message service is available for ordering. All orders are processed within 24 hours of receipt, assuming payment and order information are correct. Shipping methods depend on the product, but we generally ship via Media Mail (equivalent to USPS 4th Class). Expedited shipping services, including UPS, First Class (USPS), and Priority Mail (USPS) are also available domestically for an additional charge. Please contact us directly for an expedited shipping quotation.

All correspondence regarding technical information/values on guns or guitars is answered on a first-come, first-served basis. That means that letters, faxes, and emails are answered in the order in which they are received, even though some people think that their emails take preference over everything else. Please refer to our Gun Questions/Appraisal Policy on page 19 for more information on telephone questions regarding firearms.

Online subscriptions and individual downloads for the *Blue Book of Gun Values*, *Blue Book of Modern Black Powder Arms*, *Blue Book of Airguns*, *Blue Book of Electric Guitars*, *Blue Book of Acoustic Guitars*, and the *Blue Book of Guitar Amplifiers* are available.

As this edition goes to press, the following titles/products are currently available, unless otherwise specified:

Blue Book of Gun Values, 26th Edition by S.P. Fjestad (ISBN 1-886768-55-2, 1,936 pages).
Parker Gun Identification & Serialization, compiled by Charlie Price and edited by S.P. Fjestad
    (ISBN 1-886768-37-4).
Blue Book of Modern Black Powder Arms, 4th Edition by John Allen & Dennis Adler (ISBN 1-886768-46-3).
Blue Book of Airguns, 5th Edition by Dr. Robert Beeman & John Allen (ISBN 1-886768-56-0, available April 30, 2005).
Blue Book 3-Pack CD-ROM (includes the databases from 26th Edition *Blue Book of Gun Values*, 4th Edition,
    Blue Book of Modern Black Powder Arms, and 5th Edition *Blue Book of Airguns* (available May 1, 2005).
Blue Book of Electric Guitars, 9th Edition, by Zach Fjestad, edited by S.P. Fjestad (ISBN 1-886768-57-9, available
    June 1, 2005).
Blue Book of Acoustic Guitars, 8th Edition, by Zach Fjestad, edited by S.P. Fjestad (ISBN 1-886768-58-7, available
    June 1, 2005).
Blue Book of Guitar Amplifiers, 2nd Edition, by Zach Fjestad, edited by S.P. Fjestad (ISBN 1-886768-42-0).
Blue Book of Guitars CD-ROM (IBM format only).
Blue Book of Guitar Amplifiers CD-ROM (IBM format only).

If you would like more information about any of the above publications/products, simply check our website: www.bluebookinc.com.

We would like to thank all of you for your business in the past - you are the reason we are successful. Our goal remains the same - to give you the best products, the most accurate and up-to-date information for the money, and the highest level of customer service available in today's marketplace. If something is right, tell the world over time. If something is wrong, please tell us immediately - we'll make it right.

MEET THE STAFF

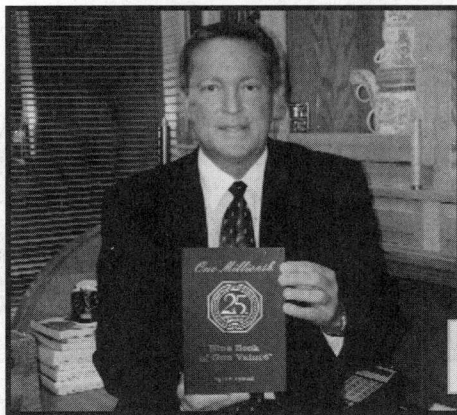

Many of you may want to know what the person on the other end of the telephone/fax/email looks like, so here are the faces that go with the voices.

S.P. Fjestad with one millionth
Blue Book of Gun Values.

John B. Allen – Author &
Associate Editor Arms Division

Cassandra Faulkner –
Executive Assistant Editor

MEET THE STAFF

Tom Stock – CFO

John Andraschko – Technology Director

Clint Schmidt – Art Director

Beth Marthaler – Operations Manager

Katie Sandin – Operations

Stacy Knutson – Proofreader/Operations

Zachary R. Fjestad – Author/Editor
Guitar & Amp Division

Bitey – Floor/wall/tight spaces Division
Manager (unseen by most employees)

Undoubtedly, one of the most frequently asked questions over the years has been "How do you come up with the prices for the book?" Almost all of the currently manufactured firearms values and information are obtained by attending firearms industry trade shows, gathering information from manufacturers, importers, and distributors, and checking websites. Remember, the Blue Book of Gun Values is the only firearms pricing guide that includes almost all of the firearms industry's new models within the same year. Because of this commitment, it is possible that some of the information you read after getting your new book is only weeks old, not months or even years.

On many collectible antique and discontinued guns, the professionals listed below typically specialize in a certain company, trademark, or configuration, and their expertise and knowledge obtained and shared within these specific areas has helped this publication tremendously over the years. These people are truly experts within their fields and deserve much of the credit on older makes/models. Despite using a PC since 1982 in writing each new manuscript, this scribe is proud to say that not once has a computer set a price in this text. Each new *Blue Book of Gun Values* is pretty much a fresh batch of cookies. While the publishing recipe stays the same, each year the ingredients get better. Very few other resources are used, since there seems to be nothing else that's as up-to-date or as useful. Every new entry/revision is put in knowing that the courtroom could be the final stop if it's wrong.

If you feel that you have an important correction, revision, or addition, please submit it by letter, fax, or email - sorry, we can't do this over the telephone. Once received, we will review the information, and, if accepted, it will be seen not only in the next edition of the *Blue Book of Gun Values*, but also online almost immediately. We rely on reader feedback to help make this publication stay accurate and up-to-date.

Once again, the people listed below are to be thanked for their contributions, and, more importantly, for sharing their knowledge. Without them, this new 26th Edition wouldn't even be close to 2,000 pages, and you wouldn't be as well-informed and up-to-date.

Leonardo M. Antaris, M.D.	Jay Hansen
David Kosowski	Mike Golembiewski
David Hartzell	Carol and the late Don Wilkerson
John Stimson, Jr.	Charles Layson
Lowell Pauli	Jean Verney-Carron
William R. Mook	Bertram O'Neill, Jr.
Frank Pycha III	Richard Spurzem
Rick Nahas	Gary Chatham
Anthony Vanderlinden & the Browning Collectors Association	Rodney Herrmann
	John Houchins
H.M. Shirley	Bob Ball
Steve Wang	Joe Pestana
Steve Engleson	Margaret Sheldon from Sturm, Ruger & Co.
John Gyde	Joe Prather from Griffin & Howe
Earl Sheehan, Jr.	Jim Jasken
James W. Whitcomb	LeRoy Merz
Don "Duck" Combs	Ian Skennerton
Robert Rayburn	Larry Stewart
Jim Supica	Joe Gillenwater
Edward King from ASI	John T. Callahan
Lynn Oliver	Leslee Dengler from Winchester Custom Shop
Glen Jensen of Browning	Ron McGhie from Browning Custom Shop
Keith Bernkrant from European American Armory	Roy Marcot (we missed you this year!)
Kevin Cherry	Kathleen Hoyt - Colt historian
Gurney Brown	Jack Heath - retired Remington historian
Elena Micheli	Paul Pluff from Smith & Wesson
Randy Shuman	Matt Bryant from GSI

James A. Buelow
John Lacy
Richard Machniak
Don Anderson
Charlie Price
David Avery, D.D.S.
Richard Skeuse of Parker Reproductions
John Kopec
Dr. Lance Christiansen
Larry Baer
Steve Barnett
J.B. Wood
Morris Hallowell IV
Martin J. Lane
Jim King
Dwight Van Brunt & Rande Simon from Kimber
Karl Lippard - First National Gun Banque
Keeva Segal
Cathy Williams from Beretta USA
Paul Roberts from J. Roberts & Sons
Dieter Krieghoff
Linda Powell from Remington
Kerby Smith from Para-Ordnance
R.L. Wilson
Orvin Olson
Tom Turpin
Jodi DePorter from Armalite
Brad Taylor
Robert (Doc) Adelman aka, "mad" rocket scientist
Daniel Sheil, Jr.
Ralph Hagan
Dr. Robert & Toshika Beeman (Honorary)
Paul Warden from America Remembers
Doug Turnbull
Jim Spacek
Marv Adams
Edmund Goldshinsky of Marlin Firearms
Paolo Amadi
T. Rees Day
Larry "Iron" Orr
Mims Reed
Bill Allen
George C. Carlson
Dave Wills
Charles Semmer
Thomas Mintner
Lt. Col. Mark Rendina
David M. Rachwal
Rick Crosier
Leon Weir
Mike Streitbeck

Jay Huber
Harold Pedersen
Richard Dee Hanks, Jon W. Miller, MD, Maylene Rabeneck, Arley J. Wallace, Jerry Watson & the High Standard Collectors Association
Gail Foster, Alvin Olson & the Minnesota Weapons Collectors Association
Roger Morris
Brook Davis
Ric Cameron
Peter Horn II - The Beretta Gallery
Barry Delong
Hal Hamilton
Dan Shuck
Richard Rohal
Rob Blank
Dietrich Apel
Axel Eichendorff
Tor Karstensen
The Buffalo Bill Historical Center in Cody, WY, including David Kennedy, Waddy Culvert, Warren Neuman, and Nathan Bender
Karen Gibbons (moral support and Cajun food in Cody)
F.E. "Pete" Wall
Tom Tompkins
David Noll
G. Brad Sullivan
Dean Rinehart
A.O. Salvo
Don Criswell
Dr. Joseph Eisenlauer
John Dougan
Jim Lutes
Harry Klein
Rick Maples
George Fram - Mossberg Collectors Association
Jim Foral
Jim Ellis
Nigel Beaumont, Peter Blaine and crew - J. Purdey & Sons
Daryl Greatrex, Roger Mitchell, Robert Pearson, David Winks (ret.), and Russell Wilkin - Holland & Holland
Peter Powell - William Powell & Son
Col. (ret.) R.D. Whittington
Richard Gomsrud
Lewis Yearout
Robert and Barb White
Ruger Collectors Association (RCA)
Colt Collectors Association (CCA)
Remington Society of America
Marlin Firearms Collectors Association, Ltd.

In Remembrance

Bob Allen, famed shooter and founder of the Bob Allen Company, and his wife Sari. Jerry Van Dijk, a trade show icon and original manager of the SHOT show. Don Nygord, an Olympic shooting champion and world record holder who founded Nygord Precision. Dave Vore, whose small but legendary gun shop in Fergus Falls, MN, more than anything else, helped me in developing and nurturing an early interest in firearms collecting.

FOREWORD

irst of all, every one of you is to be thanked who either purchased or read/used last year's Silver Anniversary Edition of the *Blue Book of Gun Values*. Not only was it the all-time, best selling book Blue Book Publications, Inc. has ever published, but the 25th edition also bears the distinction of being the edition in which the magical one millionth copy was sold. A million books, one title - I'm not aware of any other gun book title selling this many. Seven digits was my goal all along, but I never thought it would take almost a quarter century to achieve it. I was a 31 year old punk when getting involved in this project, and I'm now a middle aged man who is very grateful for the ride you have afforded me.

Dr. Ugo Gussalli Beretta (r), whose family owned business goes back to 1526, and the author/publisher, S.P. Fjestad, shown at the recent SCI show in Reno, NV.

A lot has changed in the past year. More than anything else, all of us need to realize how fortunate we are to have the NRA continue to help protect our constitutionally guaranteed gun rights. Today's outstanding NRA leadership and its support by the large majority of the membership are keys to the success of this continual battle for our gun rights. We're the only country left on the planet that offers its citizens this extraordinary freedom. I can't tell you how impressed I am with Executive Vice President Wayne LaPierre, who fights every day and consistently shoots down our anti-gun adversaries, or at the very least, neutralizes them. This guy can go one on one with anybody, and gets our point across effectively, without compromise. Kayne Robinson, the very approachable outgoing NRA President, who routinely walks gun and trade shows with his family, has also done a tremendous job. Sandra Froman, the incoming NRA President, is a natural for this most important position. It's always a pleasure seeing/talking to her at the trade and consumer shows. This gal likes her iron, and probably shoots it a lot more than you or I.

On September 9, 1994, the firearms industry took a big hit after some bad and unnecessary firearms legislation was passed. Many of us felt the Assault Weapons Ban portion of the Crime Bill was not only here to stay, but additional anti-gun laws might also start popping up on a regular basis on federal, state, and local levels. Cities were suing the firearms industry, and we spent millions fighting and stopping most of these frivolous lawsuits. Thanks to the NRA and the National Shooting Sports Foundation (NSSF), under the capable watches of Robert Delfay and Doug Painter, not only did most of these lawsuits get thrown out of court or reversed, but legisla-

tion has now been passed to prevent such lawsuits in the future.

But our most important achievements during this time period are that we voted a lot of anti-gun politicians out of office, or prevented them from getting elected. And we finally recovered our lost ground - a political landmark. It's now like the Assault Weapons Ban never existed. If you're an anti-gun politician these days, and are vocal about it, chances are, you won't get elected or re-elected. This advantage has helped us tremendously, but we need to watch our flanks for the continuing assault on our gun rights. Even though we are now in a favorable position of power in Congress, this is no time to get complacent, or to be less vigilant in aggressively protecting our Second Amendment freedoms.

So what's new in the 26th edition? A lot. Maybe the biggest change is that domestic companies like Armalite, Bushmaster, DPMS, Olympic Arms, etc. are once again able to make rifles and pistols with pre-ban features. Surprisingly, Colt has decided not to make its AR-15 in pre-ban configurations, and some pistol manufacturers have also decided against offering consumers high capacity magazines, since there are still a few states where they are banned (hopefully, not for long). In many cases, the pre-ban configuration is now less expensive than it was 11 years ago! Please read Tom Spithaler's article (pages 22-23) regarding what's currently happening in this segment of the firearms marketplace.

In the collectible marketplace, top condition original military pistols, rifles, and shotguns, in addition to Brownings, Colts, Marlins, Mausers, Remingtons, Savages, Winchesters, and other top trademarks have once again gone up in value, and this continuing pattern shows virtually no potential for downside risk - these are truly the firearms blue chip investments.

One thing that is coming up more with each edition is how gun auctions are affecting prices. Some of you have contacted us stating that the auction prices of common guns may be up to four times the values listed in the *Blue Book of Gun Values*. One of the contributing editors, who wishes to remain anonymous, has the following take on this recent phenomenon.

"Although many firearm aficionados and dealers follow auctions closely, the prices realized under this scenario cannot be used as an absolute indicator. On more than just a rare occasion, the emotional intensity and misguided need to "own at any price" may drive the price, even for relatively common collectibles, well outside the gravitational pull of the earth. Some of the more outrageous sales include $6,000 for a late CZ 27 with a silencer barrel, $4,500 for a S&W Model 1917 revolver w/ holster/lanyard/ammo pouches, $8,000 for a Walther PP NSKK rig, and $22K for a cased Luftwaffe Survival drilling w/ accessories. And these were hammer prices exclusive of the buyer's premium! While the condition of these guns was superior, none were prototypes or "one of a kind" to justify such financial outlays. Clearly, the bidders had not done their homework, for with just a little patience, the same guns in the same condition could have been bought for less than 50%, a situation that will become dishearteningly clear once the new owner looks to resell."

The recent flourish of firearms auctions has also resulted in another interesting development - it seems that refinished and restored firearms sell for more money at auctions than at gun shows or from dealer inventories. Please read the restoration editorials by Dr. Leonardo Antaris, Doug Turnbull, Mike Clark, Kevin Cherry, and Robert Simpson on pages 26-36, as they are very informative and some of the answers may surprise you.

Make sure you also read Anthony Vanderlinden's explanation of this edition's cover image, as it is a regal story. Many of you may remember Charles Priore's article in the 25th edition, and he has followed it up with another great story on firearms and academia, including the recent formation of a shooting team at Carleton College, in Northfield, MN. Youth is always the secret to any sport/discipline, and getting these younger shooters to pull the trigger on a regular basis has no substitute for instilling a pro-gun attitude the rest of their lives.

Once again, this edition has two completely different covers - this standard cover and a special NRA limited edition. There are only 500 of these special NRA limited editions, and every dime goes to the NRA Foundation to help sponsor our endowment for the National Firearms Museum in Fairfax, VA. If you've collected the previous four NRA limited editions, this will make a nice addition and keep your set intact. So far, Blue Book Publications, Inc. has contributed over $50,000 to the NRA Museum. If in the area, you need to stop by and spend at least a day looking at all the exhibits. Our display is entitled, Presidential Pieces and Regal Guns of Royal Houses, and contains firearms from such notables as Teddy Roosevelt, Napoleon, Prince Charles, and Dwight Eisenhower.

I still tell everyone this project is not an automatic annuity - each new edition has to be written with the same intensity and comprehensiveness as the earlier editions. In closing, thanks again for all your help and support over the years. Without it, this publication would not have received the notoriety and respect that it has earned throughout 26 editions. Our gun rights and inherent freedoms have never been more important - let's do whatever is necessary to keep and protect them.

Sincerely,

S.P. Fjestad
Author & Publisher
Blue Book of Gun Values

PS - If you have any extra time, tune in the *Guns & Ammo* TV program on the Outdoor Channel (check your cable/satellite listings). My segment is called "What's It Worth," and is typically at the end of the program.

HOW TO USE THIS BOOK

The prices listed in this 26th Edition of the *Blue Book of Gun Values* are based on national average retail prices for both modern and antique firearms, and some accessories/acoutrements. **This is not a firearms wholesale pricing guide. More importantly, do not expect to walk into a gun/pawn shop or gun show and think that the proprietor/dealer/collector should pay you the retail price listed within this text for your gun(s).** Resale offers on many models could be anywhere from near retail to 20%-50% less than the values listed, depending upon locality, desirability, dealer inventory, and profitability. In other words, if you want to receive 100% of the price (retail value), then you have to do 100% of the work (become the retailer, which also includes assuming 100% of the risk).

Percentages of original condition (with corresponding prices) are listed between 10%-100% for most antiques (unless configuration, rarity, and age preclude upper conditions), and 60%-100% on most modern firearms since condition below 60% is seldom encountered (or purchased). Please consult our revised, sixty-four-page Photo Percentage Grading System™ (PPGS) located on pages 49-111 to learn more about the condition of your firearm(s). Since condition is the overriding factor in price evaluation, study these photos and captions carefully to learn more about the condition of your specimen(s).

Please refer to the Abbreviations section (page 1,851) for a complete listing of abbreviations used within this text. Also, an expanded Glossary is now located on pages 1,844-1,850, explaining most firearms terminology. Updated ATF regional information is also provided in this edition – see page 1,918. You may also want to check out the Store Brand Cross-Over List on pages 1,865-1,871, since hundreds of makes and models are cross-referenced. A Proof Marks section located on pages 1,912-1,917 may also help you identify and date many European firearms. If you wish to contact current manufacturers, importers, and/or some distributors, please refer to the Trademark Index on pages 1,809-1,843 for listings and contact information, which includes websites and email addresses whenever possible.

Since the 26th Edition is now almost 2,000 pages, it may be easier to zero in on a particular manufacturer and category (pistols, rifles, shotguns, etc.) by referring to the updated Index on pages 1,920-1,935. For trademarks and companies with more than one configuration of firearms, individual category names are listed alphabetically. Alphabetical tabs are now located on the tops of the pages next to the page number and heading, making it easier to find the information you want quickly. Sidebar markers are also provided, enabling you to zero in on an alphabetical section quickly. As in previous editions, the NRA condition standards and grading criteria have been included to make the conversion to percentages easier (see page 47). This will be especially be helpful when evaluating antiques. Additionally, NRA condition standards are now represented in the PPGS. Note the NRA headings on these pages.

To find a model in this text, first look under the name of the manufacturer, trademark, brand name, and in some cases, the importer (please consult the Index if necessary). Next, find the correct category name(s) (Commemoratives, Pistols, Rifles, Shotguns, etc.). When applicable, antiques will appear before modern guns, and are typically listed in chronological sequence.

Once you find the correct model or sub-model under its respective subheading, determine the specimen's percentage of original condition (see the Photo Percentage Grading System™ on pages 49-111) and find the corresponding percentage column showing the price. Commemoratives or special/limited editions will generally appear last under a manufacturer's heading. For those of you who would like to make notes within this publication, there may be a Notes Page at the end of each alphabetical section allowing you room for notes and miscellaneous observations. For the sake of simplicity, the following organizational framework has been adopted throughout this publication.

1. Alphabetical names are located on the top of right-facing, odd-numbered pages and appear as follows:

S SECTION

2. Trademark, manufacturer, brand name, importer, or organization is listed in bold face type alphabetically, like this:

ASTRA, CHARLES DALY, HOLLAND & HOLLAND LTD., SKS

3. Manufacturer information is listed directly beneath the trademark heading:

    Current Swiss company (SIG) established during 1860 in Neuhausen, Switzerland. P210 pistols are currently imported and distributed by SIG Arms, established in 1985, and located in Exeter, NH.

4. Manufacturer notes may appear next under individual heading descriptions and can be differentiated by the following typeface:

    During 2003, Bushmater bought Professional Ordnance and the Carbon 15 trademark. Please refer to the Bushmaster section for currently manufactured Carbon 15 rifles and pistols (still manufactured in Lake Havasu City).

5. The next classification is the category name (normally, in alphabetical sequence) in uppercase lettering (inside a screened gray box) referring mostly to a firearm's configuration:

    CARBINES, PISTOLS, REPRODUCTIONS, REVOLVERS, RIFLES, SHOTGUNS

6. A further sub-classification may appear under a category name, as depicted below. These are sub-categories of a major category name, and, again, appear in alphabetical order whenever possible.

    Pricing of S&W Performance Center Handguns

7. Following a category or sub-category name, a category note may follow to help explain the category, and/or provide limited information on models and values. This appears as follows:

    Savage made a wide variety of inexpensive, utilitarian shotguns that, to date, have attracted mostly shooting interest, but little collector interest. A listing of these models may be found in the back of this text under "Serialization."

8. Model names appear flush left, are bold faced, and are in uppercase lettering either in chronological order (normally) or alphabetical order (sometimes, the previous model name and/or close subvariation will appear at the end in parentheses) and are listed under the individual category names. Examples include:

    # MODEL 82A1, CUSTOM HIGH COUNTRY, T-BOLT TT-1, FIELD III, SPORT KING

9. Model descriptions are denoted by the following typeface and usually include the following information:
    - calibers, gauges/bore, action type, barrel length(s), finish(es), weight, and other descriptive data are further categorized adjacent to model names in this typeface. This is where most of the information is listed for each specific model including identifiable features and possibly some production data, including quantity, date of manufacture, and discontinuance date, if known.

10. Variations (and possible production periods) within a model appear as sub-models – they are differentiated from model names by an artistic icon ✳ prefix, are indented, and are in uppercase and lowercase type, as follows:

    ✳ *Bisley Model, K15 Magnum, PXT LDA, Stainless Target II, SCIII Model*

    This is usually followed by a short description of that sub-model. These sub-model descriptions have the same typeface as the model descriptions:
    - additional sub-model information could include finishes, calibers, barrel lengths, special order features, and other production data specific for that sub-model.

11. Also included is yet another layer of model/information nomenclature differentiating sub-models from variations of sub-models or a lower hierarchy of sub-model information. These items are indented from the sub-models, and have the icon graphic >, for example:

    >Model 77 LR, Model 385 Sporting Clays Set, Polymer Gold Match

    A description for this level of sub-model information may appear next to the sub-entry, and uses the same typeface as model and sub-model descriptions shown above.

12. Manufacturer and other notes/information appear in smaller type, generally after the price line, and should be read since they contain important, critical, and/or up-to-date information, like the following:

    All Polymer Models were disc. in 2002 in favor of the new "Ten" Series, with improved Kimber made frame. Magazines are interchangeable.

13. Extra cost features/special value orders and other value added/subtracted features are placed directly under individual price lines or, in some cases, category names. These individual lines appear bolder than other descriptive typeface, like the following:

Add 15% for sel-opening action.
Subtract 20% for non-matching stock.

On many guns less than twenty years old, these add/subtract items indicate the original factory pricing for that model's option, either added or subtracted from the last MSR.

14. On many discontinued models/variations after 1985, and some newer models, a line may appear under the price line, indicating either the last or current manufacturer's suggested retail price flush right on the page, like this:

Last MSR was $1,850.

15. Grading lines normally appear at the top of each page, and in the middle if price lines change. If you are uncertain as to how to properly grade a particular firearm, please refer to the all-new, digital color Photo Percentage Grading System™ (PPGS) on pages 49-111 for more assistance. The most commonly encountered grading line (shown with typical price line underneath) in this text is from 100%-60%:

GRADING - PPGS™	100%	98%	95%	90%	80%	70%	60%
MSR $588	$470	$390	$295	$235	$205	$185	$165

Antique grading lines have additional values listed for 100%-10% and also 80%-10%. When "N/A" (Not Applicable) is listed instead of a value, this indicates that this particular model is not encountered enough in those condition factors. Examples (with price lines) are as follows:

100%	98%	95%	90%	80%	70%	60%	50%	40%	30%	20%	10%
$795	$700	$625	$575	$525	$475	$425	$375	$335	$300	$275	$250
N/A	N/A	$17,250	$14,750	$12,500	$10,000	$8,750	$7,900	$7,200	$6,800	$6,300	$5,800

Commemorative/limited edition grading and price lines will appear as follows:

GRADING - PPGS™	100%	Issue Price	Qty. Made
	$2,495	$1,450	250

In some cases, an organization's or company's listing (i.e. Ducks Unlimited, the National Wild Turkey Federation, etc.) of guns will appear as follows:

Manufacturer	Model	Quantity	Year	Issue Price
Winchester	Model 94 (.30-30) Babe Ruth Tribute	300	1994	$1,895 or N/A

16. Price line format is as follows – when the price line shown below (with proper grading line) is encountered,

GRADING - PPGS™	100%	98%	95%	90%	80%	70%	60%
MSR $1,399	$1,200	$995	$850	$750	$650	$550	$475

it automatically indicates that the gun is currently manufactured, and the MSR is shown left of the 100% column. A price range for an MSR indicates the importer's/distributor's pricing varies. Following this are the 100%-60% values. **This 100% price is the national average price a consumer will typically expect to pay for that model in NIB unfired condition.** 100% specimens without boxes, warranties, etc., that are currently manufactured may be discounted slightly (5%-20%, depending on the desirability of make and model). **This 100% price on currently manufactured guns also assumes not previously sold at retail. In a few cases, a "N/A" may appear for both the MSR and 100% values. This indicates that NIB and 100% pricing is currently either not available or not predictable on this model.**

17. A currently manufactured gun without a retail price published by the manufacturer/importer will appear as follows:

No MSR	$325	$295	$260	$230	$200	$180	$160

Obviously, the 100% price is the national average price a consumer will pay for a gun in new condition. Again, on currently manufactured guns, this assumes NIB condition, and not previously sold at retail.

GRADING - PPGS™	100%	98%	95%	90%	80%	70%	60%

18. When a currently manufactured stainless steel or limited mfg./special edition firearm with or without retail pricing is encountered, it will not have prices listed from 90%-60%, as these lower condition factors are seldom encountered below 90%. The price lines will appear as follows in this case:

MSR $649	$500	$425	$325				
No MSR	$3,350	$2,750	$1,950				

19. A price line with seven values listed, as represented below, indicates a discontinued, out-of-production model with values shown for 100%-60% conditions. Values are normally not listed for 50%-10% condition factors, since these lower conditions are seldom encountered on recently discontinued models. Examples include:

	$895	$775	$650	$525	$425	$350	$275
	N/A	$1,150	$1,000	$875	$750	$625	$500

Values for conditions under 60% will typically be no less than 50% (1/2) of the 60% price, unless the gun has been shot to a point where the action may be loose or questionable. Obviously, no "MSR" will appear in the left margin, but a last manufacturer's suggested retail price may appear flush right below the price line, automatically indicating a discontinued gun, like this:

Last MSR was $4,150.

20. Early Winchester lever action grading and price lines incorporate price ranges on certain Winchester models which are most frequently encountered in 50% or less condition. These grading and price range lines appear as follows:

Above Average	Average	Below Average
$1,950 - $2,500	$1,300 - $1,950	$700 - $1,300

An explanation of what to look for in these three condition ranges will precede this information in that section. The 26th Edition also includes a grading/price line that represents percentages and respective values for guns above 50% condition. This grading/value line appears as follows:

95% = $11,000	70% = $6,000	50% = $3,500

A complete listing of Reference Sources is arranged alphabetically by author on pages 1,859-1,861. Also, virtually every magazine available for the shooting industry worldwide is listed in the Periodicals section on pages 1,862-1,864, including current subscription price.

Enlarged and recently updated in the 26th Edition are the Trademark Index (pages 1,809-1,843), Model Serialization breakdown of major trademarks (pages 1,872-1,911), and a Store Brand Cross-Over List (pages 1,865-1,871). When using the expanded Model Serialization section, make sure your model is listed and find the serial number within the yearly range listings.

Since this publication is now 1,936 pages, you may want to take advantage of our new expanded Index (pages 1,920-1,935) as a speedy alternative to going through the pages alphabetically.

REVOLVER

SEMI-AUTO

1. Muzzle	11. Grip	21. Grip Medallion
2. Front Sight	12. Rear Grip Strap	22. Slide Address
3. Barrel	13. Grip Safety	23. Grip Screw
4. Frame	14. Hammer	24. Ejection Port
5. Slide (Serrated)	15. Rear Sight	25. Bolt
6. Trigger Guard	16. Safety Lever	
7. Trigger	17. Top Strap	
8. Magazine (Hidden)	18. Top Break Hinge	
9. Cylinder	19. Cylinder Flute	
10. Front Grip Strap	20. Rib	

SINGLE BARREL
TRAP

SEMI-AUTO

1. Buttplate	12. Breech/Chamber	23. Magazine Tube Cap
2. Buttstock	13. Boxlock Action	24. Front Sight Bead
3. Flat Grip	14. Receiver	25. Muzzle
4. Safety Button	15. Forearm & Slide	26. Ejection Port
5. Trigger Guard	16. Beavertail Forearm	27. Pistol Grip
6. Trigger	17. Barrel(s)	28. Vent Recoil Pad
7. Magazine Tube	18. Ventilated Rib	
8. Top Opening Lever	19. Breech Block/Bolt	
9. Frame	20. Toe	
10. Straight Grip	21. Heel	
11. Wrist of Stock	22. Comb (Fluted)	

LEVER ACTION

BOLT ACTION

1. Buttplate	13. Trigger	25. Lever (Curved)
2. Wrist of Stock	14. Magazine Release Lever	26. Hammer
3. Buttstock	15. Detachable Box	27. Receiver
4. Comb	Magazine	28. Forearm
5. Sling Swivel	16. Forend (Schnabel)	29. Magazine Tube
6. Full Pistol Grip	17. Barrel	30. Loading Port
7. Full Pistol Grip Cap	18. Bolt	31. Forearm Cap
8. Toe	19. Bolt Handle	32. Scope Rings
9. Heel	20. Cocking Indicator	33. Scope
10. Monte Carlo Stock with	21. Rear Sight	34. Scope Mounts
Rollover Checkpiece	22. Hooded-Ramp Front Sight	35. Folding Rear Sight
11. Skipline Checkering	23. Muzzle	
12. Trigger Guard	24. Rear Sight Elevator	

BUYING OR SELLING?

Over the course of many editions, we've had many referral requests for buying, selling, or trading firearms. As Blue Book Publications, Inc. is a publisher, not a gun shop, this service is designed to link you up with the right companies and/or individuals. There is no charge for this service, nor do we receive a commission (a thank you would be appreciated, however!). The goal is for you to get hooked up with the right people. Our established international network of reliable dealers and collectors allows your particular buy or sell request to be referred to the right company/individual based on both your region and area of collectibility. All replies are treated strictly confidentially.

Correspondence and replies should be directed to:

> **Blue Book Publications, Inc.**
> **Attn: John Allen**
> **8009 34th Ave. So., Ste. 175 • Minneapolis, MN 55425 USA**
> **Phone: 952-854-5229, ext. 16 • Fax: 952-853-1486**
> **Email: guns@bluebookinc.com**
> **Use "Referral" in the subject line or it may get deleted.**

Winchester Model 1892

GUN QUESTIONS/APPRAISALS POLICY

Whether we wanted it or not, Blue Book Publications, Inc. has ended up in the driver's seat as the clearinghouse for gun information. Because the volume of gun questions now requires full-time attention, we have developed a standardized policy that will enable us to provide you with the service you have come to expect from Blue Book Publications, Inc. To that end, we have extended all of these services to our website (www.bluebookinc.com).

To ensure that the research department can answer every gun question with an equal degree of thoroughness, a massive firearms library of well over 1,000 volumes, hundreds of both new and old factory brochures, price sheets, and dealer inventory listings are maintained and constantly updated. It's a huge job, and we answer every question like we could go to court on it.

POLICY FOR GUN QUESTIONS

The charge is $10 per gun question, payable by a major credit card. All gun questions are answered on a first-come, first-served basis, guaranteeing that everyone will be treated equally. All pricing requests will be given within a value range only. Gun question telephone/fax hours are 9:00 a.m. to 4:00 p.m., M-F, CST, no exceptions please. If we are not available by phone, please leave a voicemail. You must provide us with all the necessary gun information if you want an accurate answer. For email questions (firearms inquiries) please refer to www.bluebookinc.com. Letter questions (preferred, with photos) will also be answered in the order of arrival. Make sure you include the proper return address and phone number.

APPRAISAL INFORMATION

Written appraisals will be performed only if the following criteria are met:
We must have good quality photos with a complete description, including manufacturer's name, model, gauge/caliber, barrel length, and other pertinent information. On some firearms (depending on the trademark and model), a factory letter may be necessary. Our charge for a written appraisal is $20 per gun. Once the appraised amount for either a single gun or multiple guns reaches $500, the charge will be 2% of the appraised value. Please allow 2-3 weeks response time per appraisal request.

ADDITIONAL SERVICES

Individuals requesting a photocopy of a particular page or section from any edition for insurance or reference purposes will be billed at $5 per page, up to 5 pages, and $3.50 per page thereafter.

TURNAROUND TIME

Our goal is to answer most telephone, mail, email, or faxed gun questions in less than 5 business days, unless we're away attending trade/gun shows. This also assumes that all information needed to process the question(s) is initially provided, otherwise delays will occur.

Please direct all gun questions and appraisals to:
Blue Book Publications, Inc.
Attn: Research Dept.
8009 34th Ave. S., Suite 175
Minneapolis, MN 55425 USA
Phone: 952-854-5229, ext. 16
Fax: 952-853-1486 • www.bluebookinc.com
Email: guns@bluebookinc.com
Use "Firearm Inquiry" in the subject line or it may get deleted.

- COVER STORY -
KING ALBERT'S PRESENTATION PISTOL
by Anthony Vanderlinden

There was once a time when the entire world knew of King Albert. In the years of the Great War, journalists wrote about Albert and referred to him as "The Defender of Right," "The King Soldier," and "The King of Virtue." Here is a brief history on how Albert became one of the most respected kings in the world.

KING ALBERT, THE MAN

Prince Albert was born on April 8, 1875. He was not destined to become the next ruler of the small nation of Belgium because he was not a descendent of King Leopold II.

However, King Leopold II had lost his only son in 1869. Leopold had devoted himself to modernizing the country and expanding the riches of the nation of Belgium while, at the same time, profiting from his many enterprises. He was known for his tireless pursuit of colonial expansion, and, in fact, Leopold's often-ruthless pursuit of wealth made him unpopular among the Belgian people. This relentless desire resulted in his hiring of the explorer Stanley. Stanley's goal was to find wealth on the African continent, and specifically in the Congo.

Albert's father was an academic with little interest in royalty. He was said to be content with overseeing the Belgian cavalry. He had once been offered the throne of Romania, which he had turned down.

Albert was seventeen years old when his older brother passed away. With a father uninterested in taking the reign, and with no direct descendants of King Leopold, Albert, who was King Leopold's nephew, became the nation's only candidate for the throne.

Albert's unpretentious lifestyle made him popular with the Belgian people. He often visited with them, taking an interest in their work. He talked with miners, went down coal shafts, drove automobiles, and conducted train locomotives. This quality, which was in such stark contrast to Leopold, endeared Albert to the Belgian people.

Albert I was thirty-four in 1909 when Leopold's health started to fail. While on his deathbed, Leopold warned Albert of the German ideas of expansionism and urged Albert to expand the nation's defensive capabilities.

Albert ascended to the throne on December 23, 1909. It was only a few months later, while hosting Kaiser Wilhelm of Germany, that the new king realized that the warnings of Leopold were well-founded. The Kaiser's visit in 1910 had propelled Albert to begin reforming the nation's military. Although a monarchy, the country's affairs were managed by parliament. Parliament progressed slowly and the first reforms only started to take place in 1913.

THE GREAT WAR

The assassination of Archduke Franz Ferdinand of Austria in 1914 propelled the world into a global war. Russia declared war on Germany, and Germany declared war on Russia and its ally, France. Belgium was served an ultimatum by Germany, demanding the right of way to attack France through Belgium. The Belgian government rejected the ultimatum and mobilized its troops, and France and England were notified of the Belgian decision. Then, the German attack on Belgium on August 4, 1914 drew England into the war as Belgium's constitutional neutrality was guaranteed by England.

The Belgians resisted gallantly, but were no match for the enormous German invasion force. Indeed, the Belgians were often outnumbered five to one during the first month of the war. The Germans never anticipated the delays that they experienced due to the Belgian resistance. At the time there was little doubt that the Belgian campaign was responsible for failing the German Schlieffen plan, and these delays gave the French and British troops enough time to mobilize.

By November, King Albert had retreated with the remaining Belgian army behind the Yser River in the utmost western part of the country. He refused to be pushed into France (since such a move would result in Albert losing control of his forces), and the army stood its ground.

King Albert remained with his troops and had refused to move to Le Havre in France where the Belgian government had set up temporary functions. The king and his queen, Elisabeth, had taken residence near the trenches in La Panne, in a summerhouse on the beach.

The front stabilized and King Albert's priorities shifted from resisting the German invasion to supplying his troops. He relied heavily on the allies for equipment and supplies.

King Albert quickly adopted the habit of making anonymous rounds in the trenches. Most often he would wear a military overcoat without any insignia. There are numerous accounts of Belgian officers instructing him to do chores and of fellow soldiers who treated him as a grunt. Albert remained incognito and usually complied with the orders and requests.

It was common to see somebody at the door of the summerhouse to extend apologies. For most men in the trenches (enlisted men as well as officers), the realization of the identity of the man in the military overcoat usually came too late. King Albert's excursions into the trenches gave him the keen advantage of knowing firsthand the living conditions and needs of his soldiers.

Albert rarely traveled away from the Belgian trenches. On occasion he flew in a Belgian fighter plane to England for fundraising events. This marked the first time in history that a head of state traveled across borders in a plane. Aside from the risks of the front, Albert regularly insisted on flying war patrols, much to the dismay of Belgian aviators, who were more interested in protecting the king than placing him in harm's way.

While Albert commanded the troops, Elisabeth nursed the wounded. Although she was of German descent, she captured the admiration of the people when she converted the royal palaces into hospitals early on in the war. Throughout the war, she was known to work tiring hours in field hospitals.

THE PRESENTATION PISTOL

Albert's compassion and his willingness to live with his soldiers made him one of the most respected men of the day. The admiration for the king that walked the trenches soon caught up with people worldwide.

It is believed that Belgian officers made arrangements to have one new FN Browning 1900 pistol engraved as a gift to the King for his birthday in 1915. This gift may have had a practical function: many Belgian officers tried to convince Albert, who was known to walk through the trenches unarmed, to carry a weapon.

The FN Browning 1900 pistol was adopted in 1900 and was the standard service pistol of the Belgian army. Its reliability was legendary, but the scarcity of materials made obtaining a new pistol a difficult task. It is unknown where and how the Belgian staff found the new presentation pistol; it is also not known how the pistol and its case made it from the Fabrique Nationale factory to the front. The FN factory, located in Herstal near the city of Liege, had been under German control since the early days of the war.

It is known that FN employees had taken large quantities of warehoused pistols home in order to avoid having the weapons seized by the enemy. Residents of Liege had been harboring so many arms that the Germans imposed the death penalty on anybody caught possessing a firearm.

Factory records show that the presentation pistol for King Albert was one of the many that were removed from the factory by employees days before the German invasion. How the pistol made it behind Belgian lines remains a mystery. We do not know how the engraving was applied and it is not known where the work was performed. It is believed that the engraving was done behind enemy lines by one of the many artisans who were now in the trenches fighting for Belgium.

It is engraved and inlaid in 24 karat gold with the following: "La Panne 1915" and "Vaincre ou Mourir" "Victory or Death." The left side of the pistol is engraved with the Royal crest of King Albert.

MR. WOODBURY

By the end of 1915, King Albert had Belgian, British, French, as well as Senegalese soldiers under his command.

Mr. E. Woodbury, an Australian officer, was placed under command of King Albert in 1916 and worked as a liaison between King Albert and Commonwealth troops. Woodbury often visited the King and Queen for tea, and it did not take long for Woodbury to befriend the royal couple. He spent many hours talking to King Albert in his study. Apparently, Woodbury always marveled at the FN Browning 1900 pistol that was in its case near King Albert's worktable. Woodbury's fascination with the gun is not surprising, considering the reputation that Browning pistols had at that time. The sleek and compact design of the pistol must have been appealing to Woodbury, who carried a bulky British service revolver.

Albert did not carry the pistol as the Belgian officers had hoped; the pistol remained in its case, in Albert's small office in the beach house, for the duration of the war.

The war ended and the armistice was signed on November 11, 1918. Rumors started to spread that the working class was planning a revolt to take control of the nation, similar to a situation that had erupted in Russia just a year earlier. A socialist politician managed to convince Albert that a revolt had started in the capitol of Brussels.

Albert and Elisabeth took immediate action. The Belgian cavalry was summoned, and Albert and Elisabeth rode out immediately toward Brussels in order to quell the revolt and reclaim the capitol. Surprisingly, Elisabeth rode out ahead of the cavalry, an action rarely seen of a queen.

Because time was of importance, there was no practical way to pack and carry personal items from La Panne. Nurses were summoned to the house at La Panne to give away items belonging to the queen. Woodbury came to say farewell and was surprised to receive the pistol he had marveled at for years.

As Albert and Elisabeth rode through the Belgian countryside, they witnessed for the first time the devastation of the war. While the country was in shambles, the popularity of Albert and Elisabeth was still intact, as evidenced by the thousands of people who cheered them as they rode by. Many of the surviving photographs of their journey to Brussels show the king and queen on horseback entering the city of Ghent, the same city where, about a hundred years earlier, the treaty of Ghent was signed, ending the U.S. British war of 1812. When King Albert and Queen Elisabeth eventually made it with the cavalry to Brussels, they found no revolt - only cheers from a joyous population.

AFTER THE WAR

Woodbury returned to Australia after the war with his prized possession. In 1919, Woodbury traveled to California after learning that King Albert and Queen Elisabeth were visiting the United States to meet and thank all those who were involved with helping Belgium and the war effort.

The royal couple met Herbert Hoover, who later became the thirty-first president of the United States, and who had managed the Belgian relief organization during the war and had kept the Belgian population from starving. They also met with the Browning family in Utah, to applaud John Browning for his firearm designs. While on the West Coast, King Albert met with Woodbury. It is said that they took a walk near the beach. It is not known today what the men discussed, but Woodbury remained in touch with the Royal family for the remainder of his life. Every holiday season he would send Christmas wishes to the king and queen. The pistol remained a cherished souvenir of his friendship with Albert and Elisabeth. Woodbury's children and grandchildren recall the many stories, and attest that the pistol was kept in its open case on display in the Woodbury house. ∎

Anthony Vanderlinden has been a scholar of FN Browning firearms and the history of Fabrique Nationale for more than a decade. Vanderlinden has written several books and articles on these topics and can be reached via the following website: www.fn-browning.com.

THE PERFECT SUNSET!
VICTORY OVER ASSAULT WEAPONS POLITICS
by Thomas A. Spithaler

They say that time flies when you are having fun. This would intimate that time moves very slowly in moments of trouble or distress. Well, that seems to be true.

A little more than ten years ago, a piece of legislation passed in front of our Congress in Washington, DC, and became law. This legislation became known to the average American as the Assault Weapons Ban (AWB) of 1994. While the "official" agenda was to increase law enforcement for the "protection of America" and to "reduce crime," these portions of the legislation became lost in the shuffle as millions of Americans were put on alert that the government really does not trust them with firearms. The feds made it known that, in the government's opinion, you, the gun owner, are the real criminal menace to society. The gig was up, the gloves were off, and it was "us against them." America became instantly, and vehemently, divided into two segments: pro-gun and anti-gun.

This legislation, as you probably know, put into place laws that restricted the manufacture of semi-automatic firearms in certain configurations, as well as the manufacture of high capacity (more than 10 rounds) magazines. The law that was passed was set up with a "test period" of ten years, so that our government could monitor its effectiveness. At the end of ten years, if not renewed by an act of Congress, it simply would go away, or "sunset."

To the credit of Americans, we rose to this challenge against our rights by first complying with the regulations, and then taking a stand for what we thought of such legislation by voting the largest swing in Congressional and Senate seating in the history of this great nation. Ten years later, our legislators remembered that swing.

Ten years is a long time. And since we, as gun owners, collectors, and shooters, were not having fun, it went by very slowly. But now that this legislation has "sunset," or expired, as if it had never happened at all, we rejoice that our freedoms have been restored. For once in our lifetimes, we were able to see, through the power of our vote as individuals, that a piece of burden-some, garbage legislation would die a righteous death of starvation right before our eyes. What a glorious moment that was when September 10, 2004 rolled around. Legislative euthanasia at its best!

Why did it die, you ask? Well, the simple answer is that the legislation did not work! It was a useless piece of legislation passed by people who had no concept of what our constitutional rights are, and an even lesser idea of the true facts with regard to firearms ownership, its collective effect on crime, and the true statistics that bear out these facts.

What are the facts?
1. Bayonet lugs and flash suppressors have nothing to do with crime.
2. Collapsible stocks have nothing to do with crime.
3. Criminals do not need a flash suppressor, threaded muzzle, collapsible stock, or bayonet lug in order to commit a crime with a firearm.

With the ten-year "study period" over, the evidence, once argued by gun rights activist groups such as the NRA, Gun Owners of America, and the Second Amendment Foundation, is now proven fact: Guns don't kill people. People kill people, and it has always been against the law to kill people, unless your life is in danger, and being able to legally defend yourself is one of America's greatest guaranteed rights. It has been since before Cain whacked Abel (with something other than an AR style carbine with bayonet lug, flash suppressor, and collapsible stock) in the fields outside the Garden of Eden. This is not going to change anytime soon.

Some of these facts were released by a study commissioned by the Clinton administration and performed by the National Academy of Sciences. The results of this study were just released this past year. A separate and independent study was compiled by the U.S. Justice Department. Both studies were based on statistics collected during the ten-year period of the ban.

The NAS study resulted in the release of a 328-page report, 253 journal articles, 99 books, and 43 different government publications. This was no small study, and the information compiled, much to the dismay of the members of the panel (all of whom were known to be anti-gun proponents), was very clear.

The results of both studies showed that gun control does not equate to crime control, nor to reduced crime. In other words, legislation controlling the right to keep and bear arms has no effect on crime or the reduction thereof.

However, the AWB did have its effects on the industry. Once belittled for "circumventing the spirit of the law" for producing firearms without the banned features, thereby negating their assault weapon definition, arms manufacturers are now in full swing, shipping "evil assault weapons" the day after the expiration of the ban. Arms manufacturers are shipping guns in numbers that have not been seen since just before the enactment of the ban in 1994.

Rumors of major brand name manufacturers having been close to bankruptcy because of the ban, as well as mixed experience in dealing with such a drop in demand for product the year or so before the expiration of the ban in 2004, seemed to be true. Had it not been for the sunset of the AWB, some major brand name manufacturers would not have survived. Others thrived by diversifying their manufacturing. But when a manufacturing facility is, in reality, not much more than an assembly shop (which is the bulk of the AR-15 style rifle manufacturing marketplace), and all of the parts and components are being purchased rather than manufactured in-house, there is little that can be done to diversify and save a company's income. Riding high on the wave of enthusiasm, times are now good, and highly profitable for these same manufacturers. God bless America!

Another area that the AWB, and its subsequent sunset, has changed is the interest in these sorts of firearms. As expected, interest is up. But what is unique about this level of interest is that a great deal of it is from first-time buyers for this type of product.

Semi-automatic firearms have long had a loyal and enthusiastic following. But now, I see more young people, women, and first time buyers than ever before.

What I am most enthusiastic about is the young buyer. The young adults, who were only ten years old or less at the time that the AWB went into effect, are very enthusiastic and respectful. Both male and female, they never before had the opportunity to own a semi-automatic rifle in the currently legal configuration. They are excited, respectful, and reflective of the fact that their rights are always in jeopardy. We are now seeing the rise of a whole new younger generation of shooters that want to enjoy shooting semi-automatic rifles for sport, competition, hunting, or just plain fun.

Knowing what they know, these shooters will be the activists defending our Second Amendment rights far into the future. They will be able to pass on to a future generation (which those of us older than they will not have the opportunity to do) the importance of diligence, alertness, defending one's rights, and voting. Why? Because they have lived it. They have experienced a right taken away, and will forever remember the thrill of an inalienable right being restored. ■

They're back -- with a vengeance!

ACADEMIA AND FIREARMS:
STEPPING UP TO THE PLATE

By Charles F. Priore, Jr.

The editorials in the 25th Anniversary Edition of the *Blue Book of Gun Values* had a markedly different slant than those in previous editions. As a matter of fact, this new concept was hatched over my dinner table with S.P. Fjestad and R.L. Wilson in attendance. For that edition, editorials were written by a variety of people from different walks of life. There was a female documentary filmmaker, a minister, and even a guitar collector/expert. And then there was me, the academic librarian who, for twenty years, has been employed by two very elite *liberal* colleges - one the birthplace of the late Senator Paul Wellstone!

My 2004 article described the display/exhibit sponsored by the Carleton College Gould Library of famed firearms historian R.L. "Larry" Wilson (Carleton Class of 1961), who came to campus after a forty-year hiatus and gave a talk entitled "Annie Oakley and a History of Women at Arms." I mentioned also that, despite the worries of student or faculty protests or demonstrations, nothing happened - and the entire event was a smashing success.

The piece then went on to describe how faculty and staff in academia should try to reach out to undergraduates and get them involved in the hunting/shooting sports. And just as important, it was time for the industry to stop supporting these do-nothing Police Chief groups and "step up to the plate" by spreading some of their largesse on this future generation of young and highly educated shooters. With the recent legal setbacks to the anti-gunners, in which the courts have ruled that the firearms industry is not liable for gun crimes, now is a perfect time for the industry giants to re-channel their efforts.

Just a few weeks after the publication of the 25th edition, I casually scanned the front page of the Carletonian, our student-run newspaper. There, on page one, was an article entitled "Newly chartered gun club to educate, oppose legislation." Seldom do I jump up from my chair and yell (unless it's at my dog), but I did this day. I tracked down the president of the club and told him quite honestly, "I've been

waiting for you for 20 years!" Andrew Weiner, the founder and club president, is a junior and a philosophy major. He hails from Madison, Wisconsin, and comes from a family where firearms are just an accepted way of life. The club's charter is to educate and oppose anti-gun legislation, but, due to liability issues, the club cannot be funded by the college for any shooting activities.

I took it upon myself to invite Andrew and Ada (another student) out to my home for a relaxing hour or two of shooting. Although she had never even held a firearm before, Ada took to shooting like a duck to water. After some careful instruction, she started off with a .22 revolver, then a .38 Special, followed by a .357 Magnum, and, finally, a .45 Colt. Ada was enthralled, and hit a spinner target at twenty feet six consecutive times with the Magnum. "How about a rifle?" she asked. Well, it happens that I keep a Winchester Model 1894 .30-30 in my shop in order to pick off raccoons that try to take some of my prize laying hens. Before I could say "Chuck Connors," Ada was blasting away and hitting targets with such precision that I was dumbfounded. Then we took a breather and had the most interesting exchange.

The daughter of a police officer in Chicago, and born in Mexico, she was warned never to even consider shooting or owning a gun. But her internal logic led her to believe that she shouldn't condemn something without giving it at least a cursory examination. Ada told me repeatedly how much she loved shooting and how much she wanted to come back (she is currently in Germany pursuing her studies and reports that it is next to impossible for her to do any kind of shooting there!). With a club membership of sixty-five students, thirty percent of them women, it became obvious to me that some sort of sponsorship and a larger, much more accommodating location were needed in order to keep this club a viable and self-perpetuating organization.

Falling back on my article, I decided to approach the industry and to seek support from some of the local shooting clubs. In the words of the late William B. Ruger, "We are sometimes our own worst enemy." Right off the bat, I ran into a brick wall. The clubs were all eager for new members, but steadfastly refused to consider anything other than the status quo. For example, when I informed one club president that the students would only shoot a few times per year and certainly not in the summer when they all went home, my entreaties made no headway at all. No student or group discounts allowed, period. One club would not return my calls. Another insisted that all of the students, in addition to their dues, pay another $40 for membership to the NRA, which of course is a great idea, but not an affordable one.

I was beginning to get desperate. Why could I not find a simple gun club for these future shooters? After all, this was rural Minnesota. Then, a friend at the college recommended a small gun club just a few miles from my farm. I had not even known that it existed, but the Kenyon Sportsman's Club seemed to be the answer. After a few days of telephone tag, I finally made contact with one of the club officials. We had a most enjoyable conversation. The grounds would be perfect, the distance from campus very reasonable, and the dues only twenty dollars a year. I thought I had found the answer to this elusive issue when the bombshell was dropped. After forty-five minutes (long-distance, I might add), he finally informed me, "Oh, but we don't allow women members." I just about dropped the phone. When I tried to explain that I have two daughters ages eight and ten and that I wanted to join them up, I was informed that they could visit, and that they could shoot - but they could not join! Now, I am not a "liberal" person, but this sort of discrimi-

nation makes my blood boil. So much for these Neanderthals - I was back on the trail again.

Sometimes, when a door closes, a window opens. Just a few weeks before this article is going to press, the pieces of my quest are beginning to gel. I have kept in touch with R.L. "Larry" Wilson, and, dare I say, my daughters now think of him as "Uncle Larry." During one of our recent phone conversations, where I expressed my frustrations, he said he would start to "pull some strings" to help out our club. A few weeks had passed when, suddenly, I was overwhelmed by a $1,000 donation from the National Shooting Sports Foundation. Then, S.P. Fjestad, author and publisher of the *Blue Book of Gun Values*, made contact with Birchwood Casey. They are located in Minnesota and are the manufacturers of targets and cleaning supplies. They have "opened up" their catalog for us and they, too, are being quite generous. Cabela's, which needs no introduction, has given the club a gift certificate to get us going. And last, but not least, a small gun range (The Wanamingo Sportsman's Club) has enthusiastically embraced our organization, especially the women members, with $10 per year memberships! Talk about the rewards of perseverance.

Last year, I closed my article by writing that, if we wanted to preserve our shooting heritage, we needed to get the camel's nose into the tent. I think you will agree that we have succeeded!

For more information, or assistance, contact me at cpriore@carleton.edu. ∎

Enthusiastic shooters Jon Yue, Max Herzl-Betz, club president Andrew Weiner, Adam Sunderland and Charlie Priore brave the Minnesota cold to have some fun!

REFINISHED/RESTORED FIREARMS -
TRASH OR TREASURE?

by S.P. Fjestad

Maybe the best thing that ever happened to Bill Harrah was buying his first car, a 1959 Edsel with a non-original front bumper. Bill was the owner of Harrah's casinos, and, perhaps more importantly, he was famous for putting together the world's largest and most important automotive collection, located in Reno, Nevada. The weekend after buying his Edsel, Bill drove it to a local car show and swap meet. He was beaming as he drove into his reserved viewing place, and many people came over and immediately congratulated him on his foray into car collecting. The exception was one old, scruffy-looking guy, who slowly walked by, carefully inspected the car, and, afterward, casually commented to the owner, "Nice Edsel, Mr. Harrah, but it's got the wrong front bumper." Bill became instantly angry and defensive, and told the old geezer that he didn't know what he was talking about.

But the next day, still bitter about the bumper incident, Bill made a few phone calls, and finally ended up locating a retired Ford mechanic who had worked on many Edsels in the late '50s and early '60s. After lunch, Bill drove the car over to Sparks, and after a short introduction and car show recap, the guy walked out to the curb where the mint Edsel was parked. After taking a brief look at the bumper, he nodded his head, and, looking over to Bill, who was deadpanned, said "The old guy is right - this ain't the correct bumper for this car." After that, originality became Polar North whenever Bill Harrah bought and restored his automobiles. Because of Bill's influence in the world of collectible automobiles, this industry started out on the fast track, with professional restorations almost immediately achieving consumer acceptance, credibility, and, perhaps most importantly, predictable pricing for restored cars based on restoration quality levels. As a result, these restored cream puffs, in many cases, are now more desirable than the originals, and are priced accordingly.

Even though there are differences between how car and firearms collectors view restorations in their respective fields of interest, restored guns have certainly not been embraced with the same level of enthusiasm, nor supported with the same amount of money, that properly restored cars have been since Harrah bought his first Edsel. Why is this? Because thirty or forty years ago, most guns were refinished rather crudely, since their owners usually didn't care about correct restoration techniques or what might happen to any potential long-term collectibility - they just wanted the gun to somewhat resemble its original new appearance. A typical gun shop window sign of that era might have read "Will make your worn and shiny Model 12 look like new again for only $39.95!" Consumers who bit on offers like this usually got their gun(s) back within several weeks, complete with cheap, hot-dipped, reblued metal parts and overpolished and rounded receiver corners. This would be the equivalent of a "Maaco $199 special!" automotive paint job today.

In today's marketplace, while these older, down-and-dirty refinishes still retain a shooter base price, they have little or no collector interest or value. Yet, quality restorations of the right make, model, and gauge/caliber, can now approach up to seventy percent of the value of a mint original gun - a big change! While a frame-off car restoration has always been the most desirable to any car collector, a properly restored firearm has only recently become more acceptable to both gun dealers and collectors.

The following articles by Dr. Leonardo Antaris, Doug Turnbull from Turnbull Restorations, Mike Clark from Collectors Firearms, Robert Simpson from Simpson Ltd., and Kevin Cherry of Cherry's Fine Guns represent five different perspectives on how restored firearms are performing in today's marketplace, and offer unique viewpoints based on over a century of collective experiences. Perhaps the best insurance you can get to make sure you know exactly what you are buying is to deal with a known, reliable dealer/collector, and educate yourself as much as possible in your chosen field of collecting. Read all of these articles carefully so that you know the facts before buying, selling, or trading a refinished/restored firearm. ■

THE COMPLEX ART OF VALUING A RESTORED GUN

by Leonardo M. Antaris, MD

There can be no doubt that the vast majority of collectors prefer original condition firearms. But only up to a point. If the price becomes prohibitive or the condition is appalling, it becomes reasonable to consider a restoration.

The real problem in valuing a restoration is in determining the quality of the work. In the past, a restored gun was little more than a hastily performed reblue and, to a certain extent, the terminology remains interchangeable. For example, refinished guns are usually described as "restored" when being sold but "reblued" when being bought.

But what does "restoration" really mean? In the eyes of most collectors, a restored gun should be virtually identical in appearance to a freshly manufactured firearm. We all know that anything man has once made can be recreated. The problem, familiar to all collectors and restorers, is the issue of cost. For while we can rebuild the original machinery, use the same polishing compounds, mark the guns with the same stamps, and use the same method of bluing, doing a first-class job takes time and money. Unfortunately, as the restoration is likely being performed on a single firearm, the cost to do a really first-class job usually far outweighs the value of the restored arm.

So we usually have to contend with some degree of compromise. Will the surface finishing be sub-par? An approximation of the original stamps? Will the final bluing be a little bit off? And what about recutting the damaged engraving?

Perhaps the most straightforward issue is to re-weld and subsequently machine a badly pitted surface. These mechanics can be accomplished by any well-trained machinist. The matter of markings is a little trickier. Dies with the exact characters have to be replicated, then the firearm needs to be stamped in the original manner. Roll markings can be particularly difficult, and stampings, if amateurishly applied, are often off-center or double-struck (when the dies bounce). This assumes that the restorer is familiar with the specifics of the original gun - a big and often incorrect assumption. The finish may be the most difficult part of the process, for many of the original chemicals are no longer available. And, even if they can be located, there is a certain amount of oxidation, discoloration, and congealment that occurs over time. The vast majority of restorers fall down on this process, for the finish looks too fresh, too dark, or artificially aged. Putting a little wear and patina on a freshly restored gun, and in just the right places, is an art form unto itself.

The key concern in putting forth a "values guide" for restored guns is the lack of standardization. For example, if a restored gun is truly indistinguishable from the original, it would likely fetch close to the same price unless clearly denoted, a process that most honest vendors would favor. Placing a small set of initials under the grip or marking the guns inconspicuously, as does Colt and Smith & Wesson, would have merit. This would be particularly true for some of the top quality restorers whose guns may soon appreciate in their own right.

Second-rate restorations are another matter, for from the standpoint of values, they differ little from inconsequential reblues. Most of us are familiar with the "quick dip" restoration. While parts of the metal may have been freshened, the rounded corners and rust pits, now under the blue, remain as glaring telltales to the most casual collector. So, has the gun been "restored" (a term that connotes care and expertise), or "reblued?" The difference, whether real or imagined, may reflect a lot of money.

Mint Restored Mauser Broomhandle Carbine Flatside Cone Hammer, experimental variation, $20K if original, buy this for only $12.5K!

An even more important issue under the guise of "restoration" concerns the faking of guns. While everyone reading this article hopes to find an elusive and rare gun, no one, and I mean no one, wants to be defrauded. Unfortunately, once the gun has received a "fresh coat of paint," it may be difficult to determine its level of originality. When delving into this minefield, a particularly onerous tale comes to mind. Not that many years ago, a "creative" machinist started buying every nice-looking 1920 commercial Luger he could lay his hands on. The left receivers were "shaved" and restruck with German naval marks. The guns were then fitted with six inch 9mmP barrels and two-position rear sights. After a few extra marks and "restoration"... voila! A rare Navy Luger. More of these FAKES were sold as original or restored guns than you could possibly imagine. But this swindling is not limited to Lugers. Substitute Colt SAA, Winchester Model 70, Parker shotgun, Mauser 20-shot pistol, etc., and repeat the story. In fact, most dealers today will tell you that there are now more "rare" guns in circulation than ever left the factory!

But back to the original question: how to value a restored firearm, assuming it is truly a restoration and not a fake? Hands-on experience is indispensable, for it is critical to assess the degree and quality of the work. Just how good is it? Beauty is in the eye of the beholder, but if you are thinking of restoring or buying a restored gun, here are two general guidelines:

1) Common guns: A job worth doing is worth doing well. By and large, it is not worthwhile to restore a common gun. In today's market, a high-quality restoration that involves relatively little work will likely cost $500-$1,000. Extensive restorations may cost upwards of $5,000. So much for restoring a common WWII Luger that in near new original condition would only fetch $1,800. If you are a buyer, unless price is critical, you should only consider original finish guns.

2) Rare guns: Restoration is much more acceptable for truly rare specimens, particularly those that would be unavailable by other means or whose condition is so disgusting that the owner would only show the gun in a dark room or after a prolonged apology. And even then, originality may be king. After all,

what would Colt collectors prefer, a well-cared for Walker in 10% original condition or a "mint" restoration? Bet on the original condition gun!

So... finally... how much to pay? If you must buy a common refinished/restored gun, you would be well-advised to value the restoration at no more than 60% the value of an original gun in comparable condition. Of course, there are exceptions such as British shotguns, double rifles, and prototype firearms, but very few. Poor-quality restorations and reblues are worth considerably less, especially those with poor bores.

Over the past decade we have seen more and more restored guns for sale. Colts, Lugers, and Winchesters have been particularly popular. Unfortunately, a significant fraction of these guns are being passed off by the unscrupulous as originals. In many cases, the vendor pleads ignorance even though he/she may have been responsible for the work! This is a problem for the casual buyer/collector/investor who purchases these guns with the assumption that they are original, only to take a financial bloodbath when the truth is revealed, sometimes many years later, when reselling the item(s). Decidedly, a poor investment.

There will never be a more important time to do your homework than before buying a restored gun. As the years pass, restorations will definitely become more prevalent, and many of the better ones will be sold as "mint, original" guns - sucking ignorant buyers into the abyss of deception. The purchaser needs to be very familiar with all points of the original firearm to determine the quality of the restoration and sidestep any issues of fraudulence. Yes, restored guns will appreciate as much as the original guns, but only if they have been purchased for a price appropriate to their status.

Do your homework or get an opinion from a knowledgeable source before committing to purchase. It pays to know the difference! ∎

Leonardo M. Antaris, MD, is a long-time *Blue Book of Gun Values* contributing editor, and is the author of *Astra Automatic Pistols* and *Star Firearms*.

YOU CAN'T DO THAT, YOU'LL RUIN IT AND IT WON'T BE WORTH AS MUCH!

by Douglas Turnbull

We have all heard this statement when the discussion of restoring firearms comes up in conversation. The thought of restoring old guns to original condition has long been considered unacceptable. It has been believed that tampering with an original gun would detract from its value, even if time and heavy use had taken their toll. No one could possibly duplicate the craftsmanship, quality, and finishes of the original guns. Or, maybe people consider it a sign of disrespect to disturb the work of the original craftsmen.

While it is true that most collectors would prefer a high condition original, there are the problems of availability, condition, and, most of all, prices. The prices of 95% to 98% of original firearms have risen to the point where most mere mortals cannot afford them. Over the past twenty years, an ever-increasing number of collectors are using restored firearms as a way to own high condition firearms without having to sell their soul to afford the original.

While high-quality restoration work is expensive when you look at it on the surface, compare a Winchester Model 1886 deluxe rifle in 95% to 98% original condition to one that has been restored to 100% original condition. The price for the original rifle will start around $20,000 and could go as high as $40,000 or more. If you purchased the same rifle in 50% to 60% condition for $3,000 and then invested $5,000 to have it professionally restored, the rifle would be worth $15,000-$20,000 after restoration. Needless to say, this is a fairly good return on your money and a significant savings over purchasing the original.

There are a very small percentage of collectible firearms that remain in high condition today. The majority of collectible firearms today are in a condition commensurate with their age, while many more are in a state of decay, disrepair, and neglect. If the condition has degraded to a point where the "collectible value" is gone, then having the gun restored is a way to not only increase the value, but also to offer the owner or buyer the opportunity to have a firearm that looks, feels, and functions just as it did the day it left the factory.

A restoration might be performed on a firearm if the following characteristics exist:

- Rarity
- Unique or rare configuration
- Poor condition as compared to other arms in the same collection
- Sentimental value

With the first two, the cost of the restoration work will most likely be the determining factor in deciding if the restoration should be preformed. With the last two, the cost of the restoration will generally take a backseat to the owner's wishes and desires. While in most cases restoring a firearm will increase its value, the owner should be aware of the value before restoration, the cost of the restoration, and the value of the gun after restoration before making a decision.

Restoration work can be broken down into two basic categories: the quick-fix restoration (also known as a refinish) and the professional restoration. The quick fix is done with little or no concern for historical accuracy. We have all seen the rounded edges and washed out screw holes from spending too much time on a buffing wheel and the pitting still visible through what is, in most cases, the incorrect type of bluing. In most cases, we see this type of work on lower grade or non-collectible guns. However, when this technique is used on a rare or desirable firearm, it can make even the most seasoned collector walk away shaking their head in disgust.

A professionally restored firearm should be indistinguishable from the factory original; very few people possess the level of skill and knowledge needed to make that a reality. Restoration is the combination of so many different skills that it would be impossible to list them all. First and foremost, the restorer must be familiar with the techniques and materials used by the original maker as well as any and all changes the firearm underwent during production.

One of the best examples of the level of detail involved in restoration work is to look at the Colt Model 1911 automatic pistol produced for use in WWI. These pistols are still seen in moderate quantities and have enjoyed an increased interest over the last ten to fifteen years from collectors. From the start of production in 1912 to the final pistol produced in 1919, the changes made were quite dramatic. You are saying to yourself, "I've seen Colt 1911s from that time period, and they all look the same." To the untrained eye, yes, but look a little closer. The metal polish underwent five distinct changes alone and the slide and frame markings changed four major times with numerous minor changes intermixed. Several of the components, such as the hammer, slide safety, and magazine, all underwent changes during production. The bluing also changed several times. Altogether, the WWI era 1911 underwent over fifty changes throughout production, not to mention the fact that there were multiple manufactures such as Colt, Springfield Armory, and Remington-UMC. The ability to correctly identify and incorporate these details when performing a restoration is what sets the professional restoration apart from all other work. These details can be the difference between a selling price of $500 to $800 for a refinished 1911 to as much as $3,000 to $5,000 or more for a properly restored 1911 pistol.

It is much easier to sell a restored gun today than twenty years ago, due in large part to the quality of the restoration work being done today. This level of quality is the main reason why some of the most diehard collectors, who in the past would turn their noses up at restorations, have begun buying, selling, and even collecting restored firearms. One of the best examples of this change in thinking involves the recent sale of a restored Winchester rifle to an "old school collector" at a gun show. This collector had been looking at restored firearms for years and just could not bring himself to purchase a "redone gun." After seeing the work displayed at our table for several days and asking us every question he could think of about the rifle and the work that had been done, this old school collector walked over to the table and paid us the asking price for the rifle. After the transaction was complete, the collector shook our hands and told us that this was by far the finest Winchester he had seen.

One of the most difficult situations involving a restored firearm came about several years ago when a dealer misrepresented a high grade Parker 28 gauge GHE shotgun. Upon discovering that the gun was in fact a restoration, the purchaser of the shotgun came into my shop and demanded to know why we were faking guns. It never occurred to him that the dealer had misrepresented the gun. It turned out the dealer was the one who had the work done on the gun in the first place.

Professionally restored Winchester Model 1886 Deluxe rifle in rare .50 express cal. Why pay $35K for an original when you can buy this for ONLY $17.5K?

Pricing of restored firearms is sometimes a guessing game, but using the 75%-85% original condition value as listed in *Blue Book* will get you started in the right direction. You should also follow the prices at the major firearms auctions and on the Internet to determine the current prices for particular firearms. Deciding to purchase a restored firearm or having a firearm restored is a very complex and sometimes difficult decision. Before making a decision, you should seek out and talk to the experts and, most importantly, do your homework! It will pay off in the end and keep you from having a bad case of buyer's remorse.

If you can't bring yourself to purchase a restored firearm or have one of your own guns restored because you still believe that it will detract form the value, then ask yourself this question:

If the restoration is done by a professional using the identical techniques, materials, skill and attention to detail as the original maker, and the gun looks, feels, and functions exactly as it did the day it left the factory, then is restoration such a bad thing?

Anything less is the difference between refinishing and restoration. ∎

Doug Turnbull, founder of Doug Turnbull Restorations, Inc. is one of the finest restoration experts in the firearms industry today, and specializes in top quality, authentic restorations in major trademarks.

He can be contacted at:
Doug Turnbull Restorations, Inc.
6680 Rt. 5 & 20
Bloomfield, NY 14469-0471
Phone: 585-657-6338
Website: www.turnbullrestoration.com

FABULOUS OR FAKE?

A Restoration Perspective by Mike Clark from Collectors Firearms

Over the years, what has been your perspective on how to price a refinished versus an original gun? How much difference is there in value between a professionally restored gun and an average refinished gun?

A basic tenet of gun pricing has always been that a refinished gun is valued less than an identical make/model that is in original condition. There are many variables to be considered in making the price determination. Generally speaking, the refinished gun, if done poorly, might be 20-25% of the value of a non-finished gun, and may actually be so undesirable as to be almost non-saleable. If the refinished gun is very well done, it could be valued at 50%, or possibly as high as 75%, of the value of an identical, original make/model.

A good example might be a U.S. Martial Colt single action. An original, super condition, 95% or better, early U.S.-issued single action might sell for $30,000 to $50,000, or more, depending on the U.S. inspector markings. In the past twenty or thirty years, there have been several gunsmiths, legitimate restorers, and, unfortunately, some fakers, who have made some outstanding restorations and some equally outstanding fakes. The outright fakes aside, it is reasonable to say that a perfectly restored U.S. single action with no alterations of early production would be worth $5,000 to $10,000 in today's marketplace.

Do you think that, because many of the superior, top original condition makes/models have become so expensive in today's marketplace, many collectors today would rather opt for a professionally restored specimen instead?

I do not believe that many collectors would choose to buy a restored gun, but I think there are more than a few, and I think the number is growing.

Do you think gun collectors overall have come to view properly restored guns much more favorably today than they did twenty years ago?

Thirty years ago, restoration for the most part was regarded as "needed repair work" and was limited in scope. Fixing a splinter or chunk of wood out of a Winchester stock was considered acceptable, just as was replacing or welding notches in a single action hammer. At that time, restoration was called refinishing, rebluing, or faking. The word restoration has come to be more acceptable with people who are fairly new to collecting. Older, more established collectors still view restoration as a repugnant word, whereas "repairs" on a small scale are acceptable.

If you can remember, how have properly restored antiques performed as investments over the last ten to fifteen years compared to originals?

Restored guns have not been a good investment over the last ten to fifteen years when compared to an original gun. As I always advise my customers, "Buy it because you like it, first and foremost. If it turns out to be a good investment, that's great. If it turns out you owned it for years and broke even, that's okay too. If you lost money when you sold it, then that's the price you paid for the pleasure of ownership and enjoyment." The investment aspect should be secondary to a collector.

Is it true that the rarer and more desirable an original gun is, proportionately, a restored similar specimen is also worth more money?

This concept is generally true, but the reality of it is that the rare gun that has been restored, while not being more proportionately valuable, is more saleable. The downside of the restoration is that the cost of restoration may not be rewarded by enough of an increase in value to equal the cost!

What's the best experience you've had with a refinished/restored gun?

I have had good experiences with "repairing" collector guns to make them more saleable, and thus more valuable.

I think that large scale restoration, i.e. complete rebluing, restocking, etc., is overall less than desirable as it relates to value and saleability.

Winchester Pre-War Model 70 in .250-3000 Savage cal. Poorly refinished, but rare cal. Now only $795!

What's the worst experience you've ever had with restoration?

I can't think of a worst experience, but I've seen some real "hack" jobs done on decent guns that really needed only minor work, and were turned into something tragic.

Given the quality of some of the top restorations available today, do you think that these better restorations will appreciate in value as fast as the originals?

It would be illogical to say that quality restoration would appreciate in value as fast as originals.

Is it easier to resell a properly restored firearm today than it was twenty years ago?

It is my opinion that the connoisseurship of collecting has deteriorated in the last fifteen years. Newer collectors with less sophistication are more accepting of restored guns. This is especially true of the auction scene. I have observed badly refinished guns, described as such in the auction catalog, bring prices in excess of what a nice original gun would fetch. This can only be attributed to a lack of knowledge or a lack of care on the part of the buyer. This happens with such regularity that it can no longer be viewed as an anomaly, but rather a trend among some auction buyers.

Given the amount of both original and restored guns showing up at auctions recently, do you think pricing for refinished/restored guns has become more predictable?

The only predictable aspect of refinished guns sold at auction is that they fetch more at auction than they do in the hands of a dealer. Legitimate dealers tend to price refinished guns accordingly. At auction, two or more unsophisticated buyers might and do bid refinished guns to embarrassing levels.

Under what circumstances would you recommend restoration to a client/customer?

Restoration would be recommended only when it benefits the gun first and the owner secondarily. A broken wrist on a stock, a cracked tang on a rifle, removal of rust, and minor cosmetic help would be recommended. Full-scale restocking or refinishing would be a very isolated recommendation. In general, repairs are alright when they do not transform the gun so much as to move it into the area of fakery.

Can you always tell the difference between a restored gun and an original? If so, what do you look for in your area(s) of expertise?

Only the most experienced and well-seasoned person can spot the very best restoration or repair. It is very possible to overlook such fine work. I have owned guns with broken stocks, actual shattered stocks with chips and splinters missing, that were repaired. I have shown them to the most knowledgeable dealers and collectors and they were undetectable. A mediocre or poor repair or restoration is easily spotted.

Differences in finish, filing, fitting, etc. are things to look for, but nothing beats showing the gun(s) to a reliable expert. The ability to spot repairs and restoration comes over a long period of time, but even time and experience cannot help some "experts."

Are you in favor of top-quality restorations being marked somewhere indicating that the gun is a restoration? If so, do you think this would help stop restored guns from being passed off as originals?

Marking guns with a restorer's mark may be helpful, but remember that the unscrupulous faker or dealer could easily have such a mark removed.

The best advice to a collector is to deal with reputable people who guarantee what they sell and will state that guarantee in writing. Deal with people who have deep enough pockets to make good on a guarantee if it becomes necessary to do so. The customer doesn't want excuses such as "I'm short of money right now," or "I'll sell it on consignment for you."

Auction buyers should enlist the help of an experienced friend or pay a dealer for his knowledge and help. Auctioneers auction all sorts of things and guns may not be their forte, so don't rely on auction descriptions. ∎

Mike Clark is a gun dealer with decades of experience. His company, Collectors Firearms, typically has over 5,000 firearms in inventory. He can be contacted at:

Collectors Firearms
3301 Fondren Suite O
Houston, Texas 77063
Phone: (713) 781-1960
Fax: (713) 781-6407
Website: www.collectorsfirearms.com

FABULOUS OR FAKE?

A Restoration Perspective by Robert Simpson from Simpson Ltd.

Over the years, what has been your perspective on how to price a refinished vs. an original gun?

Typically the price is 33% to 50% of the price of guns with original finish.

How much difference is there in value between a professionally restored gun and an average refinished gun?

Much of the value depends upon the quality of the restoration. This is a quagmire of moral and ethical consideration. Too often, restored guns are sold as "original." This has created a stigma, which has caused colletors to avoid restored guns. The saleability of an item is reduced when it has been restored.

Do you think that, because many of the superior, top original condition makes/models have become so expensive in today's marketplace, many collectors today would rather opt for a professionally restored specimen instead?

Many? No, but a few collectors might opt for one.

Do you think gun collectors overall have come to view properly restored guns much more favorably today than they did twenty years ago?

Not "much more." Perhaps a little more favorably.

If you can remember, what did a restored common WWII Luger sell for ten years ago, as opposed to today?

The price ten years ago may have been in the $200-300 range. Today the price would be $500-800. Restorations are still less saleable than original finish.

Is it true that the rarer and more desirable an original gun is, proportionately, a restored similar specimen is also worth more money?

Yes.

What's the best experience you've had with a refinished/restored gun?

I just sold the only Imperial Navy Luger documented to a specific German officer. This was a restored gun.

What is the worst experience you've had?

I had a $30,000 Luger returned. It had been a consignment gun, and the consignee had long since been paid, so I mostly lost $30,000. This was a restored gun.

Rare 1904 Navy Luger with fat barrel and correct two digit ser. no. Looks original, but is older high quality restoration. $13.5K – will take partial trade.

Given the quality of some of the top restorations available today, do you think that these better restorations will appreciate in value as fast as the originals?

No.

Is it easier to resell a properly restored firearm today than it was twenty years ago?

Yes.

Given the amount of both original and restored guns showing up at auctions recently, do you think pricing for refinished/restored guns has become more predictable?

Slightly.

Under what circumstances would you recommend restoration to a client/customer?

I would recommend restoration if the item has historic significance or sentimental value to the customer.

Can you always tell the difference between a restored gun and an original? If so, what do you look for in your area(s) of expertise?

This comes from years of experience looking at 10,000 other identical guns. I look at machine marks on metal, the color of the finish, and the integrity of flats and corners. I would hope that, given my years of looking at Lugers in particular, I can tell if an item has been restored.

Are you in favor of top-quality restorations being marked somewhere indicating that the gun is a restoration? If so, do you think this would help stop restored guns being passed off as originals?

No to both of these questions. ∎

FABULOUS OR FAKE?

A Restoration Perspective by Kevin Cherry from Cherry's Fine Guns.

Over the years, what has been your perspective on how to price a refinished versus an original gun? How much difference is there in value between a professionally restored gun and an average refinished gun?

This is a very rough rule of thumb, but we start at half of the 100% *Blue Book* price and go from there.

How much difference is there in value between a professionally restored gun and an average refinished gun?

A lot of difference. Professionally restored guns we look at as a plus, and refinished guns we look at as a minus. A single action might have a restored value of, say, $4,500, while a refinished one might have a value of $1,500 to $2,500.

Do you think that, because many of the superior, top original condition makes/models have become so expensive in today's marketplace, many collectors today would rather opt for a professionally restored specimen instead?

I would not say "many" but I would say "some."

Do you think gun collectors overall have come to view properly restored guns much more favorably today than they did twenty years ago?

Yes, I think they look more favorably on restored guns now.

If you can remember, what did a restored Colt SAA sell for ten years ago, as opposed to today?

A Tommy Haas restored cavalry sold for about $2,500 to $3,000 ten years ago and was a very slow sell at that price. Today, a Turnbull restoration would probably bring twice that.

Is it true that the rarer and more desirable an original gun is, proportionately, a restored similar specimen is also worth more money?

Yes.

What's the best experience you've had with a refinished/restored gun?

Last year I sold a Singer 1911A1 that was professionally restored for around $17,000.

What's the worst experience you've had?

A Colt U.S. Cavalry that I bought as real but was restored back in the late 1980s.

Given the quality of some of the top restorations available today, do you think that these better restorations will appreciate in value

Early Colt U.S. Cavalry Model – looks great, but is early restoration. No factory records. Why spend $35K when you can own this for only $9,500?

as fast as the originals?

Restorations are growing in interest but they still have a limited appeal. Right now I do not think that their values will rise as fast as the originals.

Is it easier to resell a properly restored firearm today than it was twenty years ago?

Yes.

Given the number of both original and restored guns showing up at auctions recently, do you think pricing for refinished and restored guns has become more predictable?

Yes, because there is more documented information on the pricing.

Under what circumstances would you recommend restoration to a client/customer?

I never recommend restoration. In my eyes, original guns continue to get harder to find. However, if a customer wants to do it, we provide the name of a good restorer.

Can you always tell the difference between a restored gun and an original? If so, what do you look for in your area(s) of expertise?

Yes, we can usually tell a restored gun from an original. We take the stance that the gun is restored and we inspect the gun with the idea of proving that it is

restored. We look for things like sharpness of edges, clarity of markings, hue of the blue and case colors or brightness of the nickel, for starters.

Are you in favor of top-quality restorations being marked somewhere, indicating that the gun is a restoration? If so, do you think this would help stop restored guns from being passed off as originals?

Yes. If they could mark the guns it would be wonderful. They need not mark them on the external parts of the gun, but in places like under the grips or under the ejector rod assembly. Turnbull could look the number up on their computer system to see if the gun had been there, too.

Kevin Cherry is President of the Colt Collectors Association and a third generation owner of Cherry's Fine Guns in Greensboro, NC. His father, Robert Cherry, was responsible for the firearms industry's first commemorative gun, launched in 1961.

He can be contacted at:
Cherry's Fine Guns
3402-A W. Wendover Ave.
Greensboro, NC 27407
Phone: 336-854-4182
Website: www.cherrys.com

DEFENDING **YOUR** SECOND AMENDMENT RIGHT TO OWN GUNS, HUNT, SHOOT, PROTECT YOURSELF AND SO MUCH MORE...

For nearly 130 years the National Rifle Association has been the leader in defending our Second Amendment right to keep and bear arms as well as protecting our hunting rights and traditions. We're fighting the gun banners and animal rights fanatics on all fronts. By joining the NRA, or renewing your existing membership, you will help to keep our unique American traditions alive.

When you join NRA you will receive these great benefits:

- NRA Black and Gold Shooters Cap
- A no-annual-fee NRA Visa card (for qualified individuals)
- Your choice of NRA monthly publications, *America's 1st Freedom*, *American Hunter* or *American Rifleman*

- $10,000 Personal Accident Insurance
- $1,000 in ArmsCare Firearm Insurance
- Hotel, Car Rental and Interstate Moving Discounts
- Discounts at local Gun Stores and other Retail Outlets

And much, much, more...

- -

NATIONAL RIFLE ASSOCIATION

☐ 1 Year Regular.........$35   ☐ 3 Year Regular.........$85
☐ 5 Year Regular........$125   Date_____

NRA Recruiter #X012415

If renewal, give ID# ☐☐☐☐☐☐☐   Payment Information:

Mr./Mrs./Ms. _____   ☐ Check/Money Order

Street: _____ Apt.#: _____   Charge to: ☐ MC ☐ VISA ☐ Amex

City: _____ State: _____ Zip _____   ☐ Discover   Expiration Date ☐☐☐☐

Daytime Phone: (_____)_____   Credit Card#

Choose ONE Magazine: ☐ America's 1st Freedom   ☐☐☐☐☐☐☐☐☐☐☐☐☐☐☐☐

☐ American Rifleman   ☐ American Hunter   Member Signature _____

Contributions gifts or membership dues made or paid to the National Rifle Association of America are not refundable or transferable and are not deductible as charitable contributions for Federal Income Tax purposes.
Mail with payment to: NRA, 11250 Waples Mill Rd., Fairfax, VA 22030

38

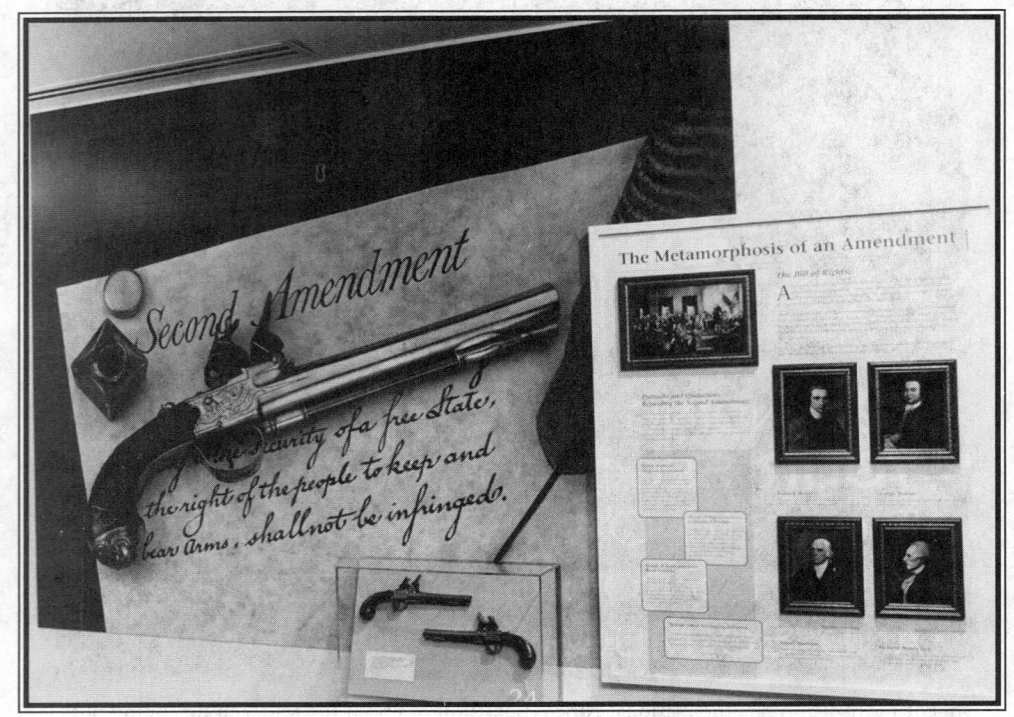

National Firearms Museum

The only museum dedicated to telling our story of freedom and the American experience through firearms…the NATIONAL FIREARMS MUSEUM

As a firearms owner, the National Firearms Museum accurately tells your story through 85 educational exhibits displaying over 2,000 historic and rare firearms.

Your TAX-DEDUCTIBLE GIFT to the NATIONAL FIREARMS MUSEUM ENDOWMENT will help guarantee that future generations will be able to learn of America's constitutional rights and firearms heritage.

For further information on how you can help permanently endow the National Firearms Museum's future contact: The NRA Foundation
11250 Waples Mill Road, Fairfax, VA 22030
or call 1-800-423-6894 • www.nrafoundation.org

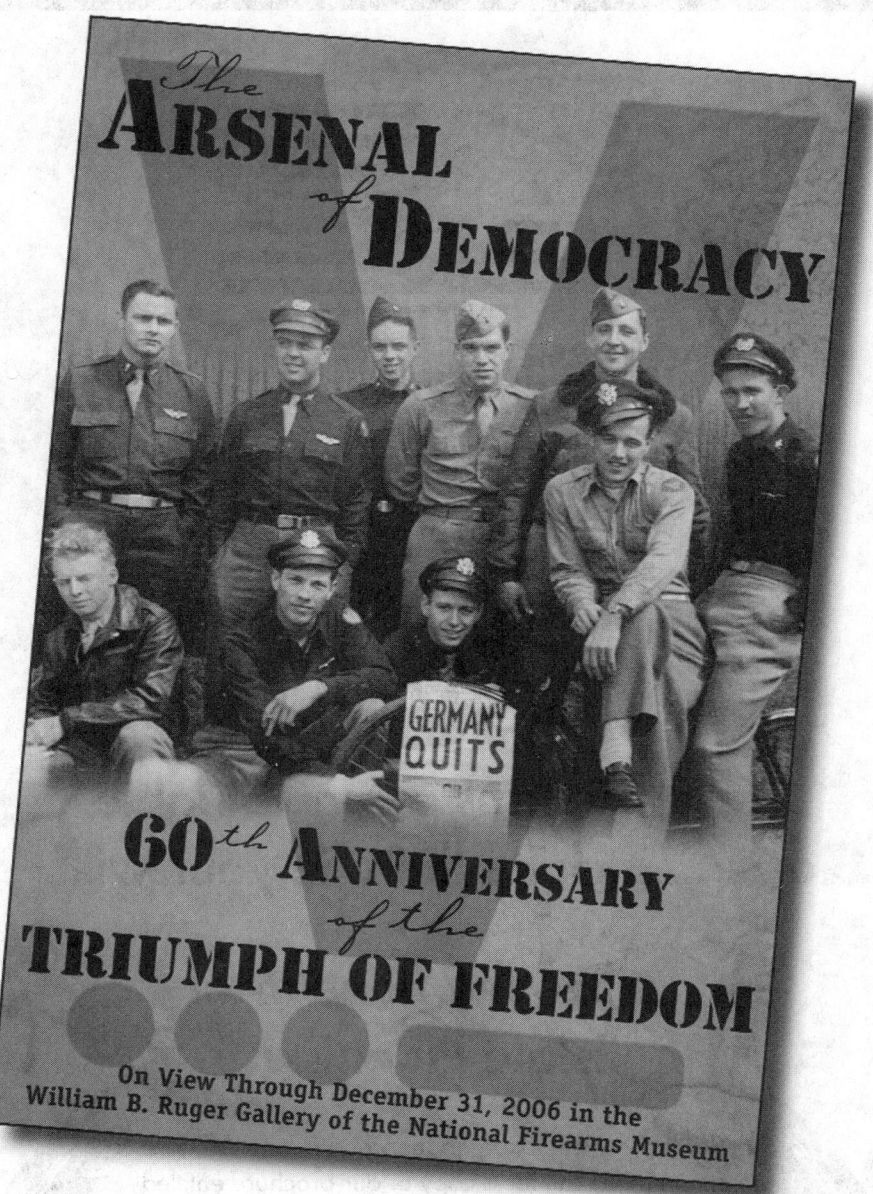

The
ARSENAL
of
DEMOCRACY

GERMANY QUITS

60th ANNIVERSARY
of the
TRIUMPH OF FREEDOM

On View Through December 31, 2006 in the
William B. Ruger Gallery of the National Firearms Museum

The National Firearms Museum is located at NRA National Headquarters in the
Washington, DC metro area of Virginia, off Interstate 66 (Exit 57A)
and can be reached by taxi from Dulles and Reagan Airports.
For further information call 703-267-1600 or E-mail nfmstaff@nrahq.org.

The **NRA** Foundation

Teach Freedom... ™

INVEST IN THE FUTURE OF THE SHOOTING SPORTS

The NRA Foundation is a 501(c)(3) charitable organization that supports a wide range of firearm-related public service activities of the National Rifle Association and other groups that promote the continuation of America's firearms heritage. Since 1990, the foundation has awarded 11,000 grants for $71 million nationwide. More than half have been invested in youth programs — the future of the shooting sports.

Through The NRA Foundation Endowment, you can make a gift to secure these traditions for generations. The endowment establishes a permanent base of funding for shooting sports programs, ensuring their continuation and expansion forever. The NRA Foundation National Firearms Museum Endowment is an example of a program that gun collectors might want to support through any one of a variety of charitable giving programs.

Your tax-deductible donation to The NRA Foundation is truly an investment in the future of the shooting sports. You are invited to join us in our commitment to promote safety and conservation, teach the responsible use of firearms, and protect our American firearms traditions by making a tax-deductible gift to The NRA Foundation.

For more information, please contact:

The NRA Foundation

11250 Waples Mill Road ★ Fairfax, VA 22030

www.nrafoundation.org ★ 800-423-6894

WHILE YOU'RE
CALLING THEM IN

we're WATCHING THE
POLITICAL
WATERS

While the politics of Washington, DC may seem a thousand miles from your favorite duck blind or tree stand, the decisions made by elected officials and government regulators have a direct impact on our ability to enjoy the great outdoors.

Influential in Washington, the Congressional Sportsmen's Foundation serves as the sportsman's link to Congress. With our communications channels and relationships in place, we ensure sportsmen have a seat at the table when decisions impacting fish and wildlife conservation funding and sportsmen's access are made.

CSF took the lead in coordinating a coalition of sportsmen's groups to ensure that conservation programs were a priority for Congress when the Farm Bill was debated in 2002. The result–$15 billion for programs important to sportsmen.

Our wins for sportsmen are made possible by the support of our partners–the outdoor industry and America's leading conservation organization–and our unique ability to effectively call into action over 300 members of Congress.

So remember, when you're in the field, we're "on the hill" working for you. To become a partner contact us at 202-543-6850 or www.sportsmenslink.org

Congressional Sportsmen's Foundation
KEEPING SPORTSMEN ON TOP OF THE HILL

A Salute To Its Contributors

Hunting & Shooting Sports Heritage Fund Supporters

AcuSport Corporation
ADCO Sales inc.
Adstar, Inc.
Allen Company, Inc.
Alliant Powder
Amateur Trapshooting Association
Anschutz
Armor Accessories
Aspen Packaging Corporation
ATK Ammunition
B Square Co.
Barnes Bullets, Inc.
Baron Technology, Inc.
Bass Pro Shops
Benelli USA Corporation
Beretta USA Corporation
Bianchi International
Big Rock Sports LLC
Bill Hicks Co. Ltd
Bismuth Cartridge Company
Blue Book Publications
Blue Trail Range & Gun Store
Boyt Harness Company/
Bob Allen Company
Break Free Inc.
Brodock Press Inc.
Brownells
Browning Arms Company
Bucks Hill Management LLC
Butler Creek
Camfour
Carters Country Outdoor Sales
CCI Ammunition
Champion Targets
Chicago Ridge Sports Guns and
Range
Chucks Gun Shop (TX)
Colt's Manufacturing Co.
COR-BON/Glaser LLC
Crimson Trace Lasers
CZ-USA
Davidsons, Inc.
Doug Turnbull Restoration, Inc.
Dunkin-Lewis Inc
Eldorado Cartridge Corporation

Ellett Brothers, Inc.
Environmetal, Inc. - Hevishot
Estate Cartridge
Fairfield County Fish & Game
Federal Capital Communication
Corp
Federal Cartridge Company
Field & Stream
Firearms Marketing Group
Fishing Hunting News
Flagler Productions, Inc.
Franchi USA
Freedom Arms, Inc.
G. A. Tolton Associates
G.B. Stumpp and Assocaties, Inc.
Gary Grant Sales Company, Inc.
Glenn Zanders Sporting Goods
Glock Inc.
Gun Week
GunBroker.com
H & G Marketing, Inc.
H & H Gun Range
H and R 1871, LLC.
Harris Publications
Hi-Point Firearms/M.K.S.Supply
Inc.
High Sierra Consulting
Hill Country Wholesale, Inc.
HMT Marketing
Hodgdon Powder Company
Hoppes
Hornady Manufacturing Co.
Huntington Die Specialties
International Cartridge Corp
Irlene Mandrell Celebrity Shoot
J. H. Nicholson, Inc.
J. Harding Associates
Jerrys Sport Center Inc
Jim Ferry and Associates
Jones and Company Inc
Joseph Chiarello & Company, Inc.
Kahr Arms
Kel-Tec CNC Industries, Inc.
Kittery Trading Post
Kleen-Bore Incorporated
L. H. French Company

Laser Max Inc
Laura Burgess, LLC
Leupold and Stevens Inc.
Lew Horton Distributing Company,
Inc.
Lipseys, Inc.
Ludwikoski and Associates, Inc.
Lyman Products Corporation
Marlin Firearms Company
Maryland Licensed Firearms
Dealers Association, Inc.
Maschmedt and Associates
McBrides, Inc.
Mega Sports Inc.
Michaels of Oregon Co.
National Skeet Shooting
Association
National Sporting Clays
Association
National Wild Turkey Federation
North American Arms
North American Hunter
North Country Marketing
Nosler, Inc.
Old Sacramento Armoury Inc.
Olympic Optical Company
Otis Technology, Inc.
Outdoor Empire Publishing
Outdoor Life
Outdoor Marketing Group LLC
Outers Guncare
Outers Trap
Owen J. Brown and Associates
Para-Ordnance Mfg. Inc.
Pesco, Inc.
Precision Arms of NM, Inc.
Presser Enterprises
Primedia Special Interest
Publications Progressive
Farmer/Rural Sportsman
RCBS
Redfield Mounts
Remington Ammunition
Remington Arms Company Inc.
Roachs Sporting Goods

Rohrbaugh Firearms Corporation
RSR Group, Inc
Savage Arms Inc.
Schueler, LaFond, Spry and
Associates, Inc.
Second Amendment Foundation
Shooting Sports Retailer
Sierra Bullets, LLC
SIGARMS Inc.
Sightron, Inc.
Simmons Mounts
Simpson Sales Company Inc.
Smith & Wesson
Speedfeed, Inc.
Speer Bullet
Sportco Marketing
Sporting Clays of America
Spragues Sports Inc.
St. Marks Powder Inc.
Stapel Knives
Stoeger Industries, Inc.
Stonewood LLC
Stoney Point
Sturm, Ruger and Company Inc.
Swanson Russell and Associates
Target Communications Corp.
Taurus International Firearms
Texas Jacks, Inc.
The Bean Agency
The Firearms Trade
The Outdoor Channel
The Outdoor Connection, Inc.
The Sportsman's Gazette
Tim Bailey and Associates Inc.
Tom Greshams Gun Talk
Trulock Tool
Tucker and Associates, Inc.
Turners Outdoorsman
U.S. Repeating Arms Company Inc.
Uberti USA
Uncle Mikes
W. L. Baumler Company
Walther USA LLC
Weaver Mounts
Williams Shooters Supply, Inc.
Women & Guns Magazine

WHEN THE COMPANY THAT MAKES YOUR HANDGUN SUP-
PORTS THE HERITAGE FUND, YOU'RE BUYING A REAL
ACTION PISTOL.

You *want* a beavertail grip safety, hand-checkered frame and a match barrel, and you *need* to make sure the maker of your next handgun is also protecting the future of your sport, by supporting the Hunting and Shooting Sports Heritage Fund. The Heritage Fund works for you, by advancing pro-gun legislation in Washington, D.C., by mobilizing sportsmen into a powerful voting bloc and by defending against junk lawsuits that threaten your traditions and firearm freedoms. So give your support to the companies that support the Heritage Fund, and you're sure to see the kind of action you want. To learn which manufacturers are actively promoting your rights to hunt and shoot, so you can give them your support, visit www.heritagefund.org.

Hunting &
Shooting Sports
Heritage Fund

GRADING CRITERIA

The old, NRA method of firearms grading – relying upon adjectives such as "Excellent" or "Fair" - has served the firearms community for many years. However, today's dealers/collectors, especially those who deal in modern guns, have turned away from the older, more subjective system. This is because there is too much variance within some of the older subjective grades, making accurate grading difficult.

Most dealers and collectors are now utilizing what is essentially an objective method for deciding the condition of a gun: THE PERCENTAGE OF ORIGINAL FACTORY FINISH(ES) REMAINING ON THE GUN. After looking critically at a variety of firearms and carefully studying the Photo Percentage Grading System™ (pages 49-111), it will soon become evident whether a gun has 98%, 90%, 70%, or less finish remaining. Remember, sometimes an older gun described as NIB can actually be 98% or less condition, simply because of the wear accumulated by taking it in and out of the box and being handled too many times. Commemoratives are especially prone to this problem. Of course, factors such as quality of finish(es), engraving (and other embellishments), special orders/features, historical significance and/or provenance, etc., can and do affect prices immensely. Also, it seems that every year bore condition becomes more important in the overall grading factor (and price) of both collectible and desirable major trademarks such as Winchester, Remington, Sharps, Schuetzens, older Springfields, etc. Because of this, bore condition must be listed separately for those guns for which it makes a difference in value. Never pay a premium for condition that isn't there. Remember, original condition still beats everything else to the bank.

Every gun's unique condition factor - and therefore price - is best determined by the percentage of original finish(es) remaining, with the key consideration being the overall frame/receiver finish. The key word here is "original," for if anyone other than the factory has refinished the gun, its value as a collector's item has been diminished, with the exception of rare and historical pieces that have been properly restored. Every year, top-quality restorations have become more accepted, and prices have gone up proportionally with the quality of the workmanship. Also popular now are antique finishes, and a new question has come up: "What is 100% antique finish on new reproductions?" The answer is that it is a gun that started out as new, and then was aged to a lower condition factor to duplicate natural wear and tear.

CAREFULLY STUDY THE HIGH-QUALITY DIGITAL IMAGES AND READ THE CAPTIONS ON PAGES 49-111. Note where the finishes of a firearm typically wear off first. These are usually places where the gun accumulates wear from holster/case rubbing and contact with the hands or body over an extended period of time. A variety of firearms have been shown in four-color to guarantee that your "sampling rate" for observing finishes with their correct colors is as diversified as possible.

It should be noted that, the older a collectible firearm is, the smaller the percentage of original finish one can expect to find. Also, some very old and/or very rare firearms are acceptable to collectors in almost any condition!

For your convenience, NRA Condition Standards are listed next door on page 47. Converting from this grading system to percentages can now be done accurately. Remember, the price is wrong if the condition factor isn't right!

CONVERTING TO NRA MODERN STANDARDS

When converting from NRA Modern Standards, the following rules generally apply:

New/Perfect	100% with or without box. Not mint - new (i.e., no excuses). 100% on currently manufactured firearms assumes NIB condition and not sold previously at retail.
Excellent	95% - 99% (typically)
Very Good	80% - 95% (should be all original)
Good	60% - 80% (should be all original)
Fair	20% - 60% (may or may not be original, but must function properly and shoot)
Poor	under 20% (shooting not a factor)

NRA CONDITION STANDARDS

The NRA conditions listed below have been provided as guidelines to assist the reader in converting and comparing condition factors to the Photo Percentage Grading System™ (see pages 49-111). NRA condition standards are now represented in the PPGS - please refer to pages 62-66 (handguns) and 94-97 (long guns). In order to use this book correctly, the reader is urged to examine these images of NRA condition standards. Once the gun's condition has been accurately assessed, values can be accurately ascertained.

NRA MODERN CONDITION DESCRIPTIONS

New - not previously sold at retail, in same condition as current factory production.

Perfect - in new condition in every respect.

Excellent - new condition, used very little, no noticeable marring of wood or metal, bluing near perfect (except at muzzle or sharp edges).

Very Good - in perfect working condition, no appreciable wear on working surfaces, no corrosion or pitting, only minor surface dents or scratches.

Good - in safe working condition, minor wear on working surfaces, no broken parts, no corrosion or pitting that will interfere with proper functioning.

Fair - in safe working condition, but well worn, perhaps requiring replacement of minor parts or adjustments which should be indicated in advertisement, no rust, but may have corrosion pits which do not render article unsafe or inoperable.

NRA ANTIQUE CONDITION DESCRIPTIONS

Factory New - all original parts; 100% original finish; in perfect condition in every respect, inside and out.

Excellent - all original parts; over 80% original finish; sharp lettering, numerals, and design on metal and wood; unmarred wood; fine bore.

Fine - all original parts; over 30% original finish; sharp lettering, numerals, and design on metal and wood; minor marks in wood; good bore.

Very Good - all original parts; up to 30% original finish; original metal surfaces smooth with all edges sharp; clear lettering, numerals, and design on metal; wood slightly scratched or bruised; bore disregarded for collectors firearms.

Good - some minor replacement parts; metal smoothly rusted or lightly pitted in places; cleaned or reblued; principal lettering, numerals, and design on metal legible; wood refinished, scratched, bruised or minor cracks repaired; in good working order.

Fair - some major parts replaced; minor replacement parts may be required; metal rusted; may be lightly pitted all over; vigorously cleaned or reblued; rounded edges of metal and wood; principal lettering, numerals, and design on metal partly obliterated; wood scratched, bruised, cracked or repaired where broken; in fair working order or can be easily repaired and placed in working order.

Poor - major and minor parts replaced; major replacement parts required and extensive restoration needed; metal deeply pitted; principal lettering, numerals, and design obliterated; wood badly scratched, bruised, cracked or broken; mechanically inoperative; generally undesirable as a collector's firearm.

Getting the Right Grade
The Price is Wrong if the Condition Isn't Right

The next sixty-four pages represent the most important section in this book. Most of you already know that the color Photo Percentage Grading System (PPGS)™ originally started in the 11th Edition. The first color PPGS™ was sixteen pages, and, somehow, was printed without page numbers! Even in its infancy, the PPGS™ quickly established standardized condition factors based on a firearm's percentage of original condition. For the 24th Edition, published in 2003, we decided it would be a good idea to provide a definitive, all-new, sixty-four-page PPGS™ with top-quality, digital color images. Everyone thought this was going to be a week's worth of work, but by the time the last laser proof was corrected, and color was approved, it had involved over a month of full-time attention by Cassandra and myself. Hundreds of images had to be thoroughly evaluated by individual condition characteristics, and, once the final images were selected, almost 10,000 words of very carefully written text needed to be generated.

After fifteen editions, the Photo Percentage Grading System™ has now become the industry standard for visibly ascertaining various condition factors based on a percentage system. This edition's PPGS™ has twenty-five percent new images and captions. As in the past, three primary categories of firearms have been visually included: handguns, rifles, and shotguns. We have also included images of NRA condition standards for handguns and long guns, as well as case colors. Please study the images and read the captions carefully to better understand the various condition percentages. The 26th Edition also retains the "PPGS-o-meters" whenever possible, so you can get a quick fix on condition factors.

Condition factors pictured (indicated by PPGS-o-meters), unless otherwise noted, refer to the percentage of a gun's remaining finish(es), including blue, case colors, nickel, or another type of original finish remaining on the frame/receiver. On older guns, describing the receiver/frame finish accurately is absolutely critical for providing a gun with a reliable and accurate grade. Typically, a long gun with 80% frame finish will have at least 95% barrel blue remaining, due to the way that these parts wear differently.

Additional percentages of condition may be used to describe other specific parts of a gun (i.e. barrel, wood finish, plating, magazine tube, etc.). Percentages of patina/brown or other finish discoloration factors must also be explained separately when necessary, and likewise be interpolated accurately. **With antiques, the overall percentage within this text is NOT an average of the various condition factors, but, again, refers to the overall original condition of the frame/receiver. Being able to spot original condition has never been more important, especially when the prices get into four, five, and six figures.** Remember, the price is wrong if the condition factor isn't right.

Computer savvy readers will be pleased to know that this updated 26th Edition PPGS™ is also included free of charge on our website at www.bluebookinc.com. Sections of the *Blue Book of Gun Values* continue to be available for purchase online via download anytime, anywhere. Good information never sleeps!

Now, more than ever, it takes a well-trained sense of sight, hearing, touch, and smell, and a corresponding connection to the most powerful computer ever built, a trained human brain, to accurately fingerprint a gun's correct condition factor. Regardless of how much knowledge you've accumulated from books, websites, auction catalogs, dealer listings, etc., you're still in potential danger as a buyer if you can't figure out a gun's condition factor(s) accurately. More than anything else, an older gun's overall condition must "add up" (i.e., a well-used Parker Bros. SxS with almost no case colors remaining should not have mint-looking barrels, and a crispy condition Luger should not have faded straw colors and/or worn grips).

While the 26th Edition's Photo Percentage Grading System™ certainly isn't meant to be the Last Testament on firearms grading, it hopefully goes a lot further than anything else published on the subject. Once you've accumulated the experience necessary to grade guns accurately, a ten-second "CAT scan" is usually all the time that is needed to zero in on each gun's unique condition factor.

S.P. Fjestad

S.P. Fjestad
Author & Publisher - *Blue Book of Gun Values*™

P.S. The publisher wishes to express his thanks and gratitude to Pat Hogan & Rock Island Auctions for authorizing the use of their digital catalog images for the Photo Percentage Grading System™ (PPGS™).

NIB condition, factory engraved Colt Python. .357 Mag. cal. 6 in. vent. rib. barrel, ser. no. 53117E - mfg. 1978. This older, engraved Python letters from Colt's Historical Department, confirming the D standard level factory engraving and blue finish – engraver is not listed. This revolver was shipped to Berns Wholesale Sporting Goods in Denver, CO on Feb. 14, 1978. Most engraved firearms, especially recently manufactured ones, are in 98% or better condition, since their owners seldom, if ever, shoot or use them. Note scuffed custom shop box indicating it has seen quite a bit of wear, probably due to either transporting or having been on the bottom of a stack of boxes. One of the best ways to determine a recently manufactured revolver's condition is to look for a vertical drag line between the cylinder lockup notches. Factory engraved major trademarks have always led the pack in terms of investment performance, and this revolver is no exception.

HANDGUNS: REVOLVERS, DA

Mint condition (99%+), early boxed Smith & Wesson .44 Magnum (Pre-Model 29), .44 Mag. cal., 6½ in. round barrel w/rib, ser. no. S171279 - mfg. 1957. 1957 was an interesting year. The Russians launched their Sputnik satellite, Chevrolet introduced its new Bel Air Coupe at $2,399, and S&W released the legendary Model 29 for $140. This pre-Model 29 is designated a 4-screw model with "S" series serial number without model designator. S&W collectors will always pay a few more C-notes for this type of condition. Only light vertical drag lines knock this gun out of the NIB condition. Observe pinned barrel, vivid case colors with no fading, and perfect grips. This revolver's value is aided immensely with its early vinyl covered hardwood box containing cleaning equipment and screwdriver. Normally seen in this condition factor in the $1,450-$1,650 price range, this revolver auctioned at over $3,700 several years ago! Is it worth it? No.

Photo Percentage Grading System™

98% condition, Smith & Wesson Model 10-5 Military & Police, .38 Spl. cal., 4 in. round barrel, ser. no. D479824 - mfg. 1972-73. This S&W revolver with nickel finish hasn't been used much. It may even be unfired, since many recently manufactured revolvers in their boxes have had little or no shooting. Observe strong case colors, minty grips, and older grey and blue S&W cardboard box. This gun retailed for $92 in 1972, and in today's marketplace, is valued in the $275 range – only a $183 increase after 33 years. So why is this revolver's investment performance so lackluster compared to the Pre-Model 29 on the preceding page? The answer can be easily summed up – overall desirability. Nobody really cares about another nickel plated Model 10 (even if it is older), while the early Model 29s have always been very desirable, collectible, and expensive.

HANDGUNS: REVOLVERS, DA

HANDGUNS: REVOLVERS, DA

Photo Percentage Grading System™

95% condition, Smith & Wesson Model 34, .22 LR cal., 4 in. barrel, ser. no. 191 - mfg. 1954. 95% on newer mfg. revolvers typically means minor barrel muzzle wear, indicating holster use and a more noticeable wear line between the cylinder lock cutouts. Flat latch cylinder release indicates early mfg., and is worth 25% more than later mfg. Note round butt grip configuration with S&W medallions inset in slightly worn walnut grips with diamond checkering. Careful observation also reveals slight wear on frame and cylinder edges. Bluing is still bright, with several small areas of slight discoloration – case colors on hammer/trigger are near perfect. Whenever a revolver in this condition is encountered, the bore should be near perfect, and the action tight and in tune. Overall, a nice example of early S&W quality that can still be used and purchased for a reasonable price.

Twenty-Sixth Edition *Blue Book of Gun Values*™

90% condition, Colt Model Police Positive (Second Issue), .38 Spl. cal., 6 in. barrel, ser. no. 260484 - mfg. 1928. Notice overall wear on this revolver compared to the Smith & Wesson Model 34 on the opposite page. As you can see, the main difference is more muzzle wear accumulated through holster use, light hammer pitting (especially on the spur), minor freckling (light rust) on the cylinder and barrel, and some shininess at the bottom of the crane (yoke). Black rubber grips with Colt logo are in excellent condition, and frame and grip screws appear to be original and untampered with. Early Colt DA enthusiasts will always be attracted to the mirror frame and barrel polishing found on all Colts during this era. Even though this revolver is 75 years old, the bore should be in excellent condition also, matching the overall condition factor.

HANDGUNS: REVOLVERS, DA

HANDGUNS: REVOLVERS, DA

80% condition, Smith & Wesson .455 Hand Ejector 2nd Model with Canadian proofmarks, .455 Mark II cal., 6½ in. barrel, ser. no. 54318 - mfg. circa 1916. This gun might have made 90% condition if it wasn't for the barrel wear next to frame. Closer examination reveals an earlier area of small barrel pitting that apparently someone overcleaned to the point where it wore off the bluing around the pitting. Also note some discoloration in the barrel bluing, scratches and nicks on barrel, frame, and cylinder, and four exposed frame screws. Checkered wooden grips with S&W medallions show some wear, but hammer/trigger case colors are excellent. Note the lanyard ring on the bottom of the grip frame, standard for this model. While unseen in image, this specimen has both the Commonwealth "BNP" (British Nitro Proof), and Canadian crossed flags, indicating military usage.

***Photo Percentage Grading System*™**

Twenty-Sixth Edition *Blue Book of Gun Values*™

Twenty-Sixth Edition *Blue Book of Gun Values*™

Photo Percentage Grading System™

70% condition, Smith & Wesson .38 Military & Police 1st Model (Model 1899 Navy), .38 military (U.S. Service) cal., 6 in. barrel, ser. no. 5504 - mfg. circa 1900. This specimen is a good example of an older, used revolver in above average condition, even though it has barrel and cylinder discoloration and pitting (brown areas) and worn grips (the diamond pattern around the screw is barely visible). This particular revolver is one of 1,000 that were purchased by the U.S. Navy. Inset photo of bottom of grip frame reveals seven line markings with U.S. Navy markings (note anchor) and "CAB" inspector marks. Considering this U.S. Navy Contract model was typically subjected to sea conditions, including salt corrosion, most specimens today are in this condition factor or worse. Even with this much finish wear, however, the action remains very tight, and the bore is still bright with very little corrosion.

Photo Percentage Grading System™

60% condition, engraved Spanish copy of Smith & Wesson .32-20 WCF Hand Ejector, .32-20 WCF cal. 6 in. barrel, ser. no. M12256 - mfg. circa 1920s. This revolver's condition factor is based on the amount of original gold plating remaining, which originally covered 100% of the metal surfaces. Observe areas which typically accumulate the least amount of wear on a revolver – the cylinder flutes, bottom of barrel underneath ejector housing, upper part of frame, and crane (yoke). Thin gold plating explains the wear on the barrel and lower frame. Mother-of-pearl grips are probably original, but notice the gap between the arched portion of the grip and the frame. If this was an original factory engraved S&W, someone would care, and pay accordingly, but as a Spanish copy with little or no collectibility, this gun gets priced as a fancy shooter.

Twenty-Sixth Edition _Blue Book of Gun Values™_

Twin-Sixth Edition *Blue Book of Gun Values*™

Photo Percentage Grading System™

50% condition, Smith & Wesson .38 Military & Police 1st Model (Model 1899 Navy), .38 S&W Spl. cal., 6 in. round barrel, ser. no. 5151 - mfg. circa 1900. Compare this slightly more used revolver to the one on page 55. Note that the overall appearance is darker, with the barrel showing more wear, and the rear frame scratching and pitting is very obvious. Even though the barrel, cylinder, and frame metal condition is less than the previous page, the case colors on the hammer and trigger are actually better on this revolver. Again, note the inset with USN and anchor signature. The checkered grips are also in worse condition. Nice, straight slots on frame screw heads on this and the previous revolver indicate this revolver has probably never been taken apart. Older original revolvers in this condition factor or less typically show more pitting and bluing discoloration.

HANDGUNS: REVOLVERS, DA

HANDGUNS: REVOLVERS, DA

40% condition, Smith & Wesson .38 Military & Police 1st Model (Model 1899 Navy), .38 S&W Spl. cal., 6 in. barrel, ser. no. 5043 - mfg. circa 1900. This Model 1899 Navy would be at least 70% overall, if it wasn't for the major finish deterioration on the rear of the frame – note the brown patina and pitting in back of the S&W logo. Barrel, frame, cylinder scratches, nicks, and gouges are also typical of this condition factor. The ejector rod has also turned a brown patina. As you can see, each gun is unique once you get down to these lower condition factors, and each revolver component (barrel, frame, cylinder, grips, case colors, trigger/hammer) has to be taken into consideration before the overall condition factor can be accurately established. In cases where finish wear is excessive on a single part, it is usually prudent to mention/describe that lower condition factor/problem separately.

Photo Percentage Grading System™

Twenty-Sixth Edition *Blue Book of Gun Values™*

Twenty-Sixth Edition Blue Book of Gun Values™

Photo Percentage Grading System™

HANDGUNS: REVOLVERS, DA

30% condition, U.S. Colt Alaskan Model 1878/1902, .45 LC cal., 6 in. round barrel, ser. no. 45317 - mfg. 1900. Notice how the overall condition of this revolver is approximately in 10% less condition than the S&W on the preceding page. This military marked specimen, which includes RAC on left side and JTT (John T. Thompson, of Thompson machine gun fame) inspector initials on right side, also has a U.S. property marking. Observe the smooth, overall brownish patina finish, while the barrel exhibits overall pitting, even though the bore is excellent. Note traces of bright barrel blue next to and in front of ejector rode assembly. Screw heads look original, and grips with rampant Colt inserts are worn proportionately with the rest of this gun's finish. Oversize trigger and trigger guard, in addition to the lanyard ring are distinguishing features of this U.S. military contract model, allowing soldiers to fire it with mittened or gloved hands.

20% condition, Colt Model 1901 New Army & Navy, .38 LC cal., 6 in. barrel, ser. no. 2822 - mfg. 1892. Compare the overall finish on this revolver to the one on page 59. This gun's finish has turned mostly brown patina, with the only bright bluing remaining in protected areas (cylinder flutes and front of frame). Note the rust inside of cylinder flutes and upper front portion of frame. Closer examination reveals that frame screws have been amateurishly removed. "RAC" marked grips show moderate wear, but are original, and free of major dings and cracks. This revolver's value is enhanced somewhat because it still has a very tight action and bright bore, which is very important to collectors of older revolvers. Many handgun collectors would rather have a no problem gun in this condition than one in 50% condition, but with major pitting, a dark bore, and other problems. The original holster and belt accompany this well-worn specimen.

Photo Percentage Grading System™

Photo Percentage Grading System™

HANDGUNS: REVOLVERS, DA

10%-20% condition, inscribed Colt Model 1878 DA Frontier Six Shooter, .44-40 WCF cal., 4¾ in. barrel, ser. no. 34108 - mfg. 1894. If the condition factor is less than this, it won't make much of a price difference anyway. Almost all metal surfaces have either no finish or a slight brown patina – note the exterior of cylinder was severely rusted in the past, but cylinder flutes retain a nice brown patina finish. This particular gun's salvation is the 17 pages of documentation that are provided, proving it belonged to "G.H. Ward Sheriff Vinta Co.," the sheriff who captured Butch Cassidy and delivered him to prison – note backstrap inscription. Any gun with a documented, sterling provenance has to be appraised individually. The auction estimate on this revolver was $1,500-$2,500, the Blue Book price range is $500-$625 (for a normal gun), and when the final auction gavel sounded, it sold for $3,450, including 15% buyer's premium!

Photo Percentage Grading System™

NRA Excellent (over 80% condition), inscribed Colt Model 1851 Navy, .36 cal. percussion, 7½ in. octagon barrel, ser. no. 127080/2 - mfg. 1862. This commercial Colt 1851 Navy was manufactured during the Civil War (1861-1865), and has the late New York barrel address. The frame, barrel, trigger guard, and backstrap all have matching 127080/2 serial numbers, indicating this gun was one of a two gun presentation set. The backstrap is inscribed "To Major Hill, 45th Reg't OVI" (Ohio Volunteer Infantry). Also verifying this revolver's authenticity is a tintype (older photograph) of Major Hill, his saber, and a Colt 1851 Navy. Note the barrel and loading lever retain most of the original finish, strong frame case colors, fire blued untampered frame screws, and excellent original wood grips, all adding up to the NRA Excellent condition factor this revolver deserves. Blue Book value w/o provenance – approx. $4,100. Auction price – $11,500.

Twenty-Sixth Edition *Blue Book of Gun Values*™

Twenty-Sixth Edition Blue Book of Gun Values™

Photo Percentage Grading System™

NRA Fine (30%-80% condition), Remington New Model Army, .44 cal. percussion, 8 in. octagon barrel, ser. no. 19329 - mfg. circa 1866. Overall, a nice, no problem Remington revolver retaining approx. 40%-50% original finish. Octagon barrel retains much of its bright bluing on the flats, while edges are shiny. Most of the frame and unfluted cylinder have turned a nice brown patina, while two-piece grips show normal handling marks with tiny chips. Action remains tight, and this revolver does not have the "New Model" markings used in later manufacture. While some of these guns were converted into .44 rimfire, this specimen retains its original percussion configuration. Also note the brass trigger guard and excellent condition of the screw heads. Since NRA Fine condition covers everything from 30%-80%, this revolver represents the middle of the NRA Fine condition range. Guns in better condition than this generally retain more bright blue, while guns in worse condition will have more patina.

REVOLVERS, SA - NRA GRADING STANDARDS

Photo Percentage Grading System™

NRA Very Good (0%-30% condition), U.S. Colt SAA Cavalry Model 1873, .45 Colt cal., ser. no. 17579 - mfg. 1875. Except for protected areas, this gun's original blue and case colored finishes have turned a smooth greyish-brown patina. One-piece walnut grips are fine, with only minor scratches, and matching serial numbers are on all visible components. Note how serial numbers are marked on the frame and trigger guard in the macro image. On 1st Generation SAAs, it always pays to inspect the numbers very carefully, since they were stamped with a rotating roll die. Not only should all the serial numbers look the same, but they should also retain the same vertical positioning in all three areas. Other macro image of "U.S." property stamp marking becomes very important, since revolvers in this serial range were probably issued as replacements to the 7th Cavalry after the Battle of Little Big Horn.

Twenty-Sixth Edition *Blue Book of Gun Values*™

Twenty-Sixth Edition Blue Book of Gun Values™

NRA Good, Colt Model 1849 Pocket, .31 cal. percussion, 6 in. octagon barrel, ser. no. 181985 - mfg. 1860. Note how the finish on this revolver (10%-20%) has turned an overall plum patina, as opposed to the bright bluing and case colors remaining on the 1851 Navy on page 62. Dark areas on barrel and frame indicate major areas of earlier pitting. Brass trigger guard and frame, originally silver plated, indicate that this revolver is a first type, as the second type has steel grip straps. The cylinder has been filed and renumbered to match the two line address, while the grips have been revarnished over the dents and scratches. Screws look good, and this gun's overall condition suggests that it was never abused during its shooting career. This revolver's operating mechanism still functions smoothly, even though the bore is somewhat dark and lightly pitted.

REVOLVERS, SA - NRA GRADING STANDARDS

REVOLVERS, SA - NRA GRADING STANDARDS

NRA Fair, Colt Model 1849 Pocket, .31 cal. percussion, 4 in. octagon barrel, ser. no. 186127 - mfg. 1861. The first thing you may note while comparing this gun to the one on page 65, is that the trigger guard and backstraps are steel instead of brass, indicating that this model is a second type of the 1849 Pocket Model. Finish has turned to a grey/brown patina overall, and metal surfaces have many dings, gouges, and scratches in addition to some previous pitting. While unseen, the backstrap has been filed to remove dents, and the grips are worn at the high spots, but retain almost half their varnish. Several frame screws have been replaced, and the action is in good condition overall. The only NRA condition factor worse than this is Poor, which means that both major and minor parts have been replaced, and metal surfaces are deeply pitted.

Photo Percentage Grading System™

Twenty-Sixth Edition *Blue Book of Gun Values*™

NIB condition, SIG Model P210-6, 9mm Para cal., 4¾ in. barrel, ser. no. P77929 - mfg. circa 1980s. The legendary SIG P210 has earned its reputation for being the Rolls Royce/Mercedes Benz of semi-auto pistols. Originally manufactured in Switzerland beginning in 1947, this model was originally designated the SP47/8, and became the standard military sidearm of the Swiss Army during 1949. Later redesignated the Model P210, this pistol has been manufactured continuously for 55 years. Rack the action and disassemble this model to fully understand the P210's glass like and butter smooth operating mechanism. Not known for selecting intermediate quality or choosing the lowest bid, Switzerland has always spared no expense on the guns for its military, law enforcement, and citizens. This commercial Model P210-6 with rear micrometer sights and checkered wood grips also has its original blue box, test target numbered to the gun, speed loader, and extra magazine.

Mint condition (99%+), Sturm Ruger Standard Model Red Eagle, .22 LR cal., 4¾ in. barrel, ser. no. 11903 - mfg. 1950. This early Ruger has the Red Eagle medallion in left grip, indicating this pistol was produced while Alexander Sturm was still alive, since the eagle went to a black color to honor his death in 1951. Every year a pistol like this gets a little more collectible, since fewer and fewer remain in this mint condition factor. Also, common guns like this are usually the hardest to find in this condition with box, since the great majority saw a lot of use, and perhaps, some abuse. Approximately 29,000 of this model were manufactured between 1949-1952, and early production featured "salt cod" wood boxes, which came from the fishing industry. While tempting to shoot, this pistol should remain in its box or shot very sparingly, so its investment potential is not negatively affected.

98% condition, Colt Woodsman Target Second Series Air Force Contract, .22 LR cal., 6 in. barrel, ser. no. 65518-S - mfg. late 1949. Previously, this pistol was described as a Colt Woodsman Second Series, and a contributing editor called in after getting his 24th edition, wondering why the caption hadn't included the information that this pistol was a rare Air Force Contract variation, based on its serial number. This variation has a fixed rear sight, different front sight, no automatic slide stop, and no provision for the usual grip adapter on the backstrap. Only 950 were manufactured circa 1949, 925 for the Air Force (issued for Arctic survival), and 25 for Rock Island. None were marked as U.S. Property or with other U.S. military markings/proofs – all were numbered in the 6XXXX-S range. The buyer who purchased it at auction paid just under $1,000, and got a bargain, since the auction reserve was $450-$600 for a standard Target Second Series, while this rare variation's value is closer to $1,750.

HANDGUNS: SEMI-AUTO PISTOLS

95% condition, Savage Model 1917, .380 ACP cal., 4¼ in. barrel, ser. no. 19646B - mfg. 1920. This early Savage pistol, without model designation, can also be identified by its caliber, hammer spur, and trapezoid grips. Notice there is more wear on the sharp metal edges, especially around lower front grip strap, compared to the 98% Colt Woodsman on the previous page. Case colors on trigger remain vivid and black rubber grips show light scratching. Manufactured during the first year of America's prohibition, the original black cardboard box helps this pistol's value. Clean, major trademark, no problem pistols like this one with its superior original condition, have traditionally been no downside risk investments for their owners. Maybe the best part about 95% condition is that you can actually enjoy shooting these guns once in a while, without negatively affecting the value, if properly maintained.

Photo Percentage Grading System™

90% condition, Japanese Baby Nambu, 7mm cal., 3 5/16 in. barrel, ser. no. 3865 - mfg. circa 1916. Originally designed by General Nambu of the Japanese Imperial Army around the turn of the 20th century, most people are initially surprised by this model's small size. Compare the bluing on this pistol against the 95% Savage Model 1917 – even though the Nambu has less edge wear overall, note how the bluing on the frame above the grips is thinning and slightly pitted. The barrel also shows signs of freckling and minor holster wear, while the checkered wooden grips with sharp points are near perfect. The Tokyo Artillery Arsenal manufactured the Baby Nambu from 1903-1923 (ser. no. range 1-5900), after which Tokyo Gas and Electric took over in late 1923 – until manufacture was discontinued in 1929. Approximately 6,500 Baby Nambus were manufactured total, and this gun's original holster will also add value to this gun.

HANDGUNS: SEMI-AUTO PISTOLS

HANDGUNS: SEMI-AUTO PISTOLS

Photo Percentage Grading System™

80% condition, Walther P.38 Pistol code AC-45 w/holster, 9mm Para. cal., 4 7/8 in. barrel, ser. no. 2622b. This P.38 double action pistol was manufactured towards the end of the war during 1945. The AC-45 code (not shown – left side of frame) designates Walther production (byf was Mauser, and cyq was Spreewerke), and the polishing, bluing, and overall finish were not up to par with earlier manufacture during 1938-1944. During the end of WWII, the Germans were taking quality control shortcuts to get pistols into the hands of the ever decreasing number of desperate German soldiers. Close examination reveals machine cutter lines on both the barrel and side of slide. Also note metal scratching and thinning of the blue in trigger guard area. Not visible in this image is the wear on front grip strap and lower trigger guard, retaining almost no original blue, which decreases this pistol's condition another 10%. Black grips are excellent, and original holster is stamped with the WaA36 code.

Twenty-Sixth Edition *Blue Book of Gun Values*™

70% condition, Remington UMC Model 1911, .45 ACP cal., 5 in. round barrel, w/o ser. no. - mfg. circa 1918. Production sample guns like this without serial numbers are often referred to as "lunchbox specials." This pistol is an original WWI Remington-UMC, except for the Colt hammer, trigger, and magazine. While the slide and upper frame would probably grade out at 90%, mostly due to edge wear, the grip strap bluing is mostly gone, having turned to a brownish patina. Also note scratching and scuffing on slide address, in addition to some checkering wear on lower portion of grips, which have a heavy coating of varnish. Even without a serial number (or perhaps because of it!) this WWI U.S. military pistol is very valuable, since relatively few were manufactured (approximately 21,500), compared to other larger U.S. government contracts for the Model 1911, including Colt and Springfield Armory.

HANDGUNS: SEMI-AUTO PISTOLS

60% condition, CZ Model 27 w/Holster, 7.65mm/.32 ACP cal., 3½ in. round barrel, ser. no. 139914 - mfg. circa 1941. While the upper frame of this well used, WWII CZ Model 27 is very clean, with only minor freckling and light pitting, the grip straps, trigger guard area, and lower front of frame have turned grey, indicating a lot of previous use. Close inspection above grip reveals a WaA76 Waffenamt proofmark. Condition of the black synthetic grips with checkering and CZ logo match the rest of this gun's overall condition factor. Unless a pistol is very rare, or has historical provenance, collectibility for 60% or less original condition is considerably lower than an original gun in 95%+ condition. The non-original, unmarked black leather holster doesn't add much value to this gun. This type of well cared for pistol in 60% condition is a lot more desirable than an 80% specimen with some serious pitting.

Photo Percentage Grading System™

Twenty-Sixth Edition Blue Book of Gun Values™

50% condition, Mauser Standard Pre-War Commercial Broomhandle w/Stock, 7.63mm Mauser cal., 5½ in. barrel, ser. no. 95950 - mfg. circa 1909. If only someone would have taken better care of this Broomhandle during its lifetime. The barrel shows a lot of serious pitting, and you can see what happens if you get the steel wool (maybe sandpaper in this case) out and get aggressive! Receiver rail is almost completely shiny, and magazine well housing in front of trigger guard is very scratched, and has serious pitting on the bottom. Grips are worn, but match this Broomhandle's overall condition factor. Stock is original, but has been broken and poorly repaired – also, it does not match. Action is mechanically tight, and bore is very good. This is a classic example of a very collectible pistol losing over 65% of its potential value because the owner(s) didn't give it some TLC when it needed it the most.

HANDGUNS: SEMI-AUTO PISTOLS

HANDGUNS: SEMI-AUTO PISTOLS

Photo Percentage Grading System™

40% condition, Colt Model 1905, 45 ACP cal., 4 7/8 in. barrel, ser. no. 1656 - mfg. early 1907. As you can see, this gun has problems. Note the original bright bluing on frame, but overall grey finish on slide, indicating that someone acid cleaned this gun thoroughly in the past, probably trying to clean up the heavy pitting on the right side (not shown). Since the frame is one condition factor (thinning blue), and the slide is a totally different condition (grey patina), this pistol's overall condition factor had to be interpolated based on the overall appearance. Note heavy frame scratching next to grips. Grip straps are also worn and grey, and left wood grip has a crack above the top screw. Action is mechanically good, and all parts are original. This gun has lost most of its collector value because of its altered condition and poor eye appeal.

Twenty-Sixth Edition *Blue Book of Gun Values*™

HANDGUNS: SEMI-AUTO PISTOLS

30% condition, Colt Model 1905, .45 ACP cal., 4 7/8 in. barrel, ser. no. 3730 - mfg. 1909. Most of this pistol's lifetime is behind it. Note how the original bluing has turned a dark grey patina, the front of the slide is shiny, and there is pitting throughout the slide. Frame has also turned to a mostly brown patina, and some bluing remains in protected areas. The grip straps are very worn and have turned grey, while the checkered, revarnished grips also show a lot of wear. Action is mechanically okay. This gun is a good example of when value is determined almost completely by collectibility, not shootability. 500 of this model were factory slotted for a shoulder stock – this rare configuration automatically adds 50% to the pistol's value, regardless of condition. Most pistols in this condition factor are not very collectible, but this rare Colt is an exception.

HANDGUNS: SEMI-AUTO PISTOLS

20% condition, Colt Model 1905, 45 ACP cal., 4 7/8 in. barrel, ser. no. 1840 - mfg. 1907. We know what you're thinking – how did the front of this gun become so pitted? Even CSI undergraduates will quickly figure out what happened in this case. At one point (maybe several), the gun and its holster got very wet. Unfortunately, the gun was stored in the wet holster, and witness the results. Serious pitting is an understatement to describe the wear on the front and rear of this unfortunate pistol. The only thing this gun still has going for it is that it can still claim originality and functionality. Grips are well-worn, and the points are long gone on the checkering. Rampant Colt logo is still visible on rear of slide. The only original finish remaining on this gun is in the protected area on the upper frame around the radiused grips.

Twenty-Sixth Edition *Blue Book of Gun Values*™

Twenty-Sixth Edition *Blue Book of Gun Values*™

Photo Percentage Grading System™

HANDGUNS: SEMI-AUTO PISTOLS

10% condition, Colt Model 1900 w/Sight Safety, .38 rimless cal., 6 in. barrel, ser. no. 2930 - mfg. 1902. We know what you're thinking – again. Why would anybody possibly buy any pistol in this kind of condition, regardless of its rarity and overall desirability factors? The answer from a Colt collector could be, "I didn't have one, and it was cheap!" (Cheap in this case means ten C-notes!). The answer from a shotgun dealer or a rifle shooter might be, "I don't care how rare it is, I'll give you one hundred and fifty bucks for it in trade-in." Entire pistol has turned into two-tone patina (slide is grey and frame is brown), with heavy previous pitting on both the frame and slide. Original Colt grips show proportionate wear. Condition lower than this doesn't matter, but if it is encountered, family members should be notified immediately, and sent directly to the hospital's ICU.

RIFLES

NIB condition, Winchester Model 9422 Boy Scouts of America Commemorative, .22 LR cal., 20 in. round barrel, ser. no. BSA3002 – mfg. 1985. With commemoratives, it is very important to have the box(es), paperwork (including warranty card), and any other accessories/accoutrements that came with the gun when it left the factory. Since most commemoratives are never used or shot, proper storage is the key to keeping them truly NIB – this becomes especially important on silver, gold, or bright nickel finishes, since they have a tendency to naturally tarnish. Commemoratives and limited editions that have been shot and don't have the original box or paperwork are nothing more than fancy shooters most of the time, and are priced accordingly with little or no premium. Because the commemorative consumer is now more in charge (consumers now own most of the guns since distributor/dealer inventories are depleted) than during the 1960s-1980s, commemorative firearms values are possibly as strong as they have ever been. When the supply side of commemorative economics has to be purchased from knowledgeable collectors or savvy dealers, and demand stays the same or increases slightly, prices have no choice but to go up. If and when the manufacturers crank up the commemorative production runs again (and it won't be like the good old days), the old marketplace characteristics may reappear. Until then, however, the commemorative market-place remains steady, with values having become more predictable. Two variations of this model, the Boy Scout (15,000 mfg. – original issue price was $495) and the Eagle Scout (1,000 mfg. – original issue price was $1,710), were manufactured to commemorate the Boy Scouts 75th Anniversary in 1985. Some well heeled Eagle Scouts at the time paid as much as $5,000 to get an Eagle Scout model! In today's marketplace, an NIB Boy Scout model is valued at $695, while the Eagle Scout is $3,750, more than double its original 1985 MSR.

***Photo Percentage Grading System*™**

Twenty-Sixth Edition *Blue Book of Gun Values*™

RIFLES

Mint condition, Engraved Savage Exhibition Model 1899 Lever Action, .303 Sav. cal., 26 in. round barrel, ser. no. 36390 - mfg. 1904. This Exhibition Model 1899 Savage is like-new with no wear or handling marks. It also comes with a letter from Savage's historian, John Callahan, stating that the engraving was done by Enoch Tue & Son, and additional provenance states that this rifle was displayed at the St. Louis World's Fair in 1903. Most long guns like this made for exhibitions are typically 95%+ original condition, as these guns were typically displayed several times a year, but never used. Note the deluxe Circassian walnut used for the stock and forearm of this gun also indicate that this specimen was destined to be a show gun, as American walnut was standard. Not many original 100 year old guns retain this condition factor, and the premium paid is up to the potential buyer.

RIFLES

98% condition, Savage Model 1899G Takedown Lever Action, .30-30 Win. cal., 22 in. barrel, ser. no. 374169 - mfg. 1938. The 98% condition factor for rifles typically means light receiver wear on the edges and some light muzzle wear on the barrel. Case colors on this takedown Savage are near perfect, as is the original stock and forearm finish. While this gun may have been used only infrequently, it always pays to check the front of the bolt face for noticeable amounts of primer ring impression – always a sign that the gun has been shot more than you think. Corrugated steel buttplate shows no wear, and checkering pattern indicates that it's a Model 1899G, manufactured from 1922-1941. A gun in this 98% condition factor can still be used for hunting, without deteriorating its condition – with a little caution in the field, and proper maintenance.

Photo Percentage Grading System™

Twenty-Sixth Edition *Blue Book of Gun Values*™

95% condition, Winchester Model 1903, .22 Win. Auto rimfire cal., 20 in. round barrel, ser. no. 11822 - mfg. 1929. In many cases, common models in major trademarks are the hardest guns to find in this condition factor. Most of these common guns saw a lot of use, and were originally not purchased as a potential investment for future generations. While some dealers and collectors might consider this Depression era rifle a 98% gun overall, the edge wear on the sharp corners of both sides of the receiver, in addition to the scratches on right side of stock, lower this rifle to 95% condition. Most experienced dealers and collectors have learned that when buying, selling, or trading, it's better to under evaluate a condition factor rather than overestimate. Deluxe checkered stock and forearm with most of the original varnish is always a big plus for Winchester collectors, especially when the condition is this good.

RIFLES

RIFLES

90% condition, Springfield M1903, .30-06 cal., 24 in. round barrel, ser. no. 404889 - mfg. 1910. This early Model 1903 was manufactured the same year that China abolished slavery. 20 years ago, not a lot of people cared about (or paid a lot of money for) this type of a common U.S. military rifle - that's not the case today. Note the blue and color case hardened metal finishes. It has nice original wood with no problems and "J.F.C." final inspector mark (for J.F. Coyle) in block letters inside rectangle in addition to script "P" in circle proof stamped on underside stock wrist. More than anything else, originality is the key when determining value on this type of 20th century U.S. military rifle - knowing what to look for in proofs/markings, how the original markings appear, and where to find them are absolutely critical when evaluating this rifle's value. Sling is an early RIA 1904 pattern.

***Photo Percentage Grading System*™**

***Twenty-Sixth Edition Blue Book of Gun Values*™**

RIFLES

80% condition, Deluxe Winchester Model 1886 Lever Action, .33 WCF cal., 24 in. round barrel, ser. no. 135850 - mfg. 1905. This Winchester is a good example of various condition factors adding up to an 80% overall condition factor. While barrel and magazine tube remain in 95% condition, the receiver metal is 60% overall – mostly due to normal usage when in the field. Side mounted Lyman sight also shows normal wear for this gun's overall condition factor. Most of the original varnish on checkered deluxe pistol grip walnut stock (with shotgun buttplate) and forearm remains, but note nicks, scratches, staining, and a few light gouges. Case colors on lever have mostly faded, but are still visible on the hammer. Action is mechanically tight, but rear barrel sight has been removed and the slot filled. Original bright bluing and plenty of stock/forearm varnish are what Winchester collectors and dealers always look (and pay extra) for.

RIFLES

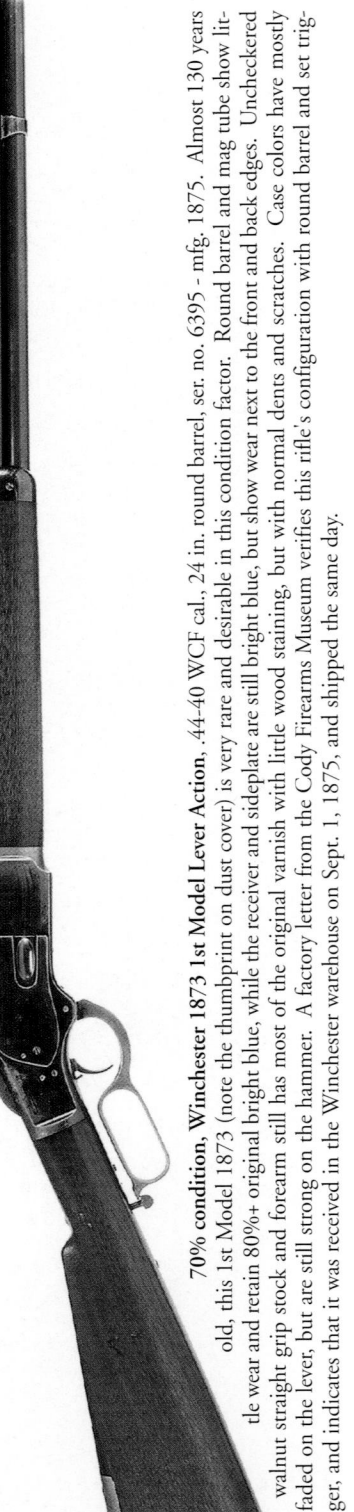

70% condition, **Winchester 1873 1st Model Lever Action**, 44-40 WCF cal., 24 in. round barrel, ser. no. 6395 - mfg. 1875. Almost 130 years old, this 1st Model 1873 (note the thumbprint on dust cover) is very rare and desirable in this condition factor. Round barrel and mag tube show little wear and retain 80%+ original bright blue, while the receiver and sideplate are still bright blue, but show wear next to the front and back edges. Uncheckered walnut straight grip stock and forearm still has most of the original varnish with little wood staining, but with normal dents and scratches. Case colors have mostly faded on the lever, but are still strong on the hammer. A factory letter from the Cody Firearms Museum verifies this rifle's configuration with round barrel and set trigger, and indicates that it was received in the Winchester warehouse on Sept. 1, 1875, and shipped the same day.

Photo Percentage Grading System™

Twenty-Sixth Edition Blue Book of Gun Values™

RIFLES

60% condition, Winchester Model 1892 Saddle Ring Carbine, .32-20 WCF cal., 20 in. round barrel, ser. no. 917231 – mfg. late 1922. Compare the overall condition of this Model 1892 to the Winchester Model 1873 on the preceding page, and you'll observe approximately 10% less original condition. Notice how top, bottom, front, and rear of receiver have worn, turning silver with light brown patina, while the receiver sides retain a lot of the original bright bluing. The receiver on this carbine was refinished some time ago (note slightly rounded edges), and helps to explain its current wear pattern. Saddle ring imprint on rear let side of receiver is normal, and barrel band has turned mostly grey. Uncheckered straight grip walnut stock shows signs of light cleaning, but is still flush with metal. Action remains mechanically perfect, and its overall good eye appeal help elevate its value to above that of a poor reblue.

RIFLES

50% condition, Winchester Model 1894 Deluxe Saddle Ring Carbine, .30-30 Win. cal., 20 in. round barrel, ser. no. 582407 - mfg. 1911. Even in this condition factor, this Model 1894 deluxe saddle ring carbine is very desirable, with a 2002 RIA auction estimate of $4,500-$7,500! Nickel steel barrel with ladder type rear sight and half magazine still has 95%+ original bluing, while the receiver has had much of its bluing flake off. Do not confuse receiver flaking with normal wear and usage – some Winchester lever action rifles can be almost unfired, but show similar frame wear as this specimen. Flaking occurred because the bluing did not adhere properly on guns with a high nickel content in the steel. Deluxe checkered walnut stock with steel shotgun buttplate, may have been resprayed at a later date, but the varnish is in excellent condition, and matches the condition of the forearm. Auction price – approx. $2,600.

Photo Percentage Grading System™

Twenty-Sixth Edition *Blue Book of Gun Values*™

40% condition, **Winchester Model 1894 Lever Action**, .32 Win. Spl. cal., 26 in. round barrel, ser. no. 875560 - mfg. 1920. In the gun business, this is what you call a gun's condition factors "adding up" correctly. This plain Jane Model 1894 with 26 in. barrel is a study on what to look for when evaluating an older rifle. Note how the nickel steel barrel still has much of its bright blue, while the mag tube has turned a brown patina overall. Metal forearm cap is mostly shiny, and matches the condition on the receiver and wood. Flat receiver sides still have a lot of bright bluing left, especially at rear – also note how the loading gate finish looks good. The original stock wood and varnish has darkened somewhat, especially next to the receiver (normal) and the forearm shows normal use in the right areas. The receiver screw heads look good, and again, this Winchester still has a lot of eye appeal.

RIFLES

RIFLES

30% condition, Savage Model 1899 Lever Action, .300 Sav. cal., 24 in. round barrel, ser. no. 324301 - mfg. 1929. If this rifle could talk, you'd probably be listening to a lot of interesting older deer hunting tales. Mostly shiny receiver shows previous polishing, while thinning barrel wear indicates this lever action has been on many previous hunting trips. Uncheckered straight grip walnut stock has turned somewhat dark due to oil staining and handling, and has some dings and scratches. While unseen, serious cracks in the stock have been repaired, and some pitting is present on both the frame and the barrel. Lever is also mostly shiny, attesting to the years of use. This rifle in this condition has now reached shooter status only, since most collectors want better condition in this type of common model. In other words, figure out its price as a shooter, and don't pay a penny more.

Photo Percentage Grading System™

RIFLES

Twenty-Sixth Edition Blue Book of Gun Values™

Photo Percentage Grading System™

20% condition, Winchester Model 1906 Slide Action, .22 S-L-R cal., 20 in. round barrel, ser. no. 256876 - mfg. 1926. Two of Winchester's most popular slide action .22 cal. rifles, the Models 1890 and 1906, enjoyed tremendous popularity between 1890-1932, with almost 1.7 million manufactured. Yet, a mint specimen of either model is very rare and only infrequently encountered. This Model 1906 is in below average condition, with the receiver having turned a dark brown patina, and showing major areas of pitting. Barrel has also turned an overall brown patina, while the mag tube and action bar are nickel plated. Stock and forearm have been revarnished, and do not match the rest of this gun's condition. Action remains tight, while bore is good. This rifle's value has bottomed out in this condition factor, and has limited desirability for Winchester collectors wanting better condition.

RIFLES

10% **condition,** Winchester 3rd Model 1873 Lever Action, .32-20 WCF cal., 24 in. octagon barrel, ser. no. 354761B - mfg. 1890. This Model 1873 is a good example of an antique rifle's original finish having turned a smooth grey brown patina overall (compare the finish on this gun to the one on page 88). Even though this gun has little original finish left, it does not have major problems like severe pitting, replaced non-original parts, or damaged/cracked wood, even though the stock and forearm have been previously revarnished. All markings remain sharp, the action is mechanically okay, and the bore is fair. Many Winchester collectors would still rather have a no problem, original rifle like this than a 40% overall specimen with major finish problems and alterations. This specimen would be considered an entry-level model for collecting, based on its condition and originality.

Photo Percentage Grading System™

Twenty-Sixth Edition *Blue Book of Gun Values*™

RIFLES

0%-10% condition (NRA Poor), Altered Winchester Model 1873 Lever Action, .32-20 WCF cal., 24 in. octagon barrel, ser. no. 167428 - mfg. 1884. Except for the forearm cap, there is no original finish remaining on either the receiver, barrel, or magazine tube. This gun has had all its metal surfaces polished and is also missing major parts such as the dust cover, receiver screws, and rear sight. Both the stock and the forearm are crude replacements, and fit poorly to the metal. This rifle (or what's left of it) constitutes 0% condition (NRA Poor). So what's it worth? The answer is, add up values for the individual parts, and don't include the stock or forearm. In this case, the total is approx. $400, still cheaper than a modern reproduction. Unfortunately, most guns in this condition factor never become more desirable (or expensive) as junk will always be junk, and gets priced accordingly!

RIFLES: CASE COLORS

NRA Excellent (over 80% condition), Marlin Model Model 1893 Takedown, .38-55 cal., 30 in. octagon barrel, ser. no. 136493 - mfg. 1896. This special order Marlin rifle, manufactured the same year as the introduction of the motion picture, had a base price of $13. Special features on this gun include a 30 in. octagon barrel ($5 up charge), take down feature ($4 up charge), and extra select walnut with B checkering ($20 up charge) - bringing the total up to $42! Note the vivid case colors on both sides of the receiver, featuring predominately mottled blues and greens. Barrel and magazine tube bluing are above 95%, and checkered Circassian walnut stock and forearm retain most of the original varnish. Once you start adding up what these special orders/features can do to a major trademark gun in this type of superior original condition in today's marketplace, the price tag gets turbo charged in a hurry!

Photo Percentage Grading System™

Twenty-Sixth Edition Blue Book of Gun Values™

RIFLES: CASE COLORS

NRA Fine (30%-80% condition), Engraved Marlin Model 1889 Deluxe Lever Action, .32-20 WCF cal., 24 in. octagon barrel, ser. no. 69896 - mfg. June 18, 1892. As a general rule of thumb, engraved guns appear to have less case colors than non-engraved standard models. Extensive engraving on any case colored rifle actually subdues the case colors somewhat, as the scrollwork tends to break up the overall pattern. Note how front and rear receiver edges have become shiny with light freckling, and how wood to metal fit is perfect. Also note that the case colored lever has coloration left only in the protected area where it pivots. Hammer case colors are nice, and match the overall condition factor of this fine rifle. While some dealers and collectors may refer to this condition as Very Fine, this term is not a proper NRA Antique condition factor.

RIFLES: CASE COLORS

NRA Fine (30%-80% condition), Sharps Conversion Carbine, .50-70 cal., 22 in. round barrel, ser. no. C18688 - mfg. circa 1868. Since different firearms companies had different "recipes" for their case coloring processes, many of which were proprietary, it is no surprise that the coloration and overall intensity of the case colors varied not only from manufacturer to manufacturer, but also from gun to gun. Compare the 30%-40% case colors on this carbine to the Marlins shown previously. Note the preliminary remaining color is blue, especially noticeable around the protected area of the pivoting hammer. It is normal on a Sharps rifle/carbine that the right side of the action looks better than the left. Also notice the overall greying of the outside metal surfaces. Hammer is still in good condition, and still retains some mottled case colors.

Twenty-Sixth Edition *Blue Book of Gun Values*™

Photo Percentage Grading System™

Twenty-Sixth Edition Blue Book of Gun Values™

Photo Percentage Grading System™

RIFLES: CASE COLORS

NRA Very Good (0%-30% condition), Winchester Model 1890, .22 WRF cal., 24 in. octagon barrel, ser. no. 44235 - mfg. circa 1896. This extremely popular Winchester second model slide action rifle kept its $16 retail price the same between 1890-1916, after which it went up to $32.75. The receiver's case covers have mostly faded, with some traces remaining on left side. Observe the wear on the sharp edges of barrel with wrench marks, and overall greyish color of magazine tube. The stock shows signs of staining, probably indicating earlier sanding and/or refinishing. As important as anything else on this rifle is the three individual finishes (i.e., stock/forearm varnish, case colored receiver, and barrel/mag. tube bluing), all "add up," meaning that no one finish is that much better or worse than the rest. Bore condition on antique rifles is getting to be more important to collectors every year.

Twenty-Sixth Edition
Blue Book of Gun Values™ *2005*

S	APRIL					S	S	MAY					S	S	JUNE					S
					1	2	1	2	3	4	5	6	7			1	2	3	4
3	4	5	6	7	8	9	8	9	10	11	12	13	14	5	6	7	8	9	10	11
10	11	12	13	14	15	16	15	16	17	18	19	20	21	12	13	14	15	16	17	18
17	18	19	20	21	22	23	22	23	24	25	26	27	28	19	20	21	22	23	24	25
24	25	26	27	28	29	30	29	30	31					26	27	28	29	30		

S	JULY					S	S	AUGUST					S	S	SEPTEMBER					S
					1	2	1	2	3	4	5	6					1	2	3
3	4	5	6	7	8	9	7	8	9	10	11	12	13	4	5	6	7	8	9	10
10	11	12	13	14	15	16	14	15	16	17	18	19	20	11	12	13	14	15	16	17
17	18	19	20	21	22	23	21	22	23	24	25	26	27	18	19	20	21	22	23	24
24	25	26	27	28	29	30	28	29	30	31				25	26	27	28	29	30	
31																				

S	OCTOBER					S	S	NOVEMBER					S	S	DECEMBER					S
						1		1	2	3	4	5					1	2	3
2	3	4	5	6	7	8	6	7	8	9	10	11	12	4	5	6	7	8	9	10
9	10	11	12	13	14	15	13	14	15	16	17	18	19	11	12	13	14	15	16	17
16	17	18	19	20	21	22	20	21	22	23	24	25	26	18	19	20	21	22	23	24
23	24	25	26	27	28	29	27	28	29	30				25	26	27	28	29	30	31
30	31																			

Twenty-Sixth Edition
Blue Book of Gun Values™ *2006*

S	JANUARY					S	S	FEBRUARY					S	S	MARCH					S
1	2	3	4	5	6	7			1	2	3	4				1	2	3	4
8	9	10	11	12	13	14	5	6	7	8	9	10	11	5	6	7	8	9	10	11
15	16	17	18	19	20	21	12	13	14	15	16	17	18	12	13	14	15	16	17	18
22	23	24	25	26	27	28	19	20	21	22	23	24	25	19	20	21	22	23	24	25
29	30	31					26	27	28					26	27	28	29	30	31	

Bergmann Model 1897 - ser. no. 258. Theodor Bergmann developed the Model 1897 pistol to compete with the Mauser C96 for military contracts. The new Bergmann, also known as the No. 5, was chambered for the bottlenecked 7.8mm Bergmann cartridge. This was the first Bergmann to have a detachable magazine, a clip that held two columns of cartridges, and could be loaded with a stripper clip or in the conventional manner.

Edward Ezell reported that approximately 800 Model 1897s were completed. Although several minor variations ensued, this pistol was typical of most examples. All were sold with a hollow shoulder stock that was leather wrapped over a metal frame and had the stock lug numbered to the pistol. In the background is a box of 7.8mm DWM ammunition contemporary to the gun. Collection: Leonardo M. Antaris, M.D.

NIB condition, Winchester Model 23 Cased Pigeon Grade Lightweight SxS, 20 ga., 25½ in. vent. rib barrels., ser. no. PKW 204779 - mfg. circa 1984. This Pigeon Grade SxS model was manufactured by Miroku in Japan until 1986. The good news is its NIB condition factor, short barrels with open choking (bored IC/M), English straight grip stock, and it's a 20 ga., not a 12. The bad news is that it doesn't have choke tubes, which became standard in 1986. Correct Winchester green canvas case with leather ends is also original to this gun, and adds approximately $150 of value. Small gauge shotguns, especially 28 ga. and .410 bore, have outperformed the rest of the gauges as an investment by a significant margin in recent times. Conversely, common makes/models in 12 ga. without choke tubes are getting less desirable each year, and one contributing editor recently commented that without choke tubes, it is the "kiss of death" when selling,

Photo Percentage Grading System™

Twenty-Sixth Edition *Blue Book of Gun Values™*

SHOTGUNS

Mint condition (99%+), Beretta BL-6 O/U, 12 ga., 28 in. VR barrels with fixed chokes, ser. no. A14931B, BL series mfg. 1968-1973. While the Browning Superposed Grade I - Midas are a lot more well-known and popular with American shooters than Beretta's competitive O/U models during the 1960s-1970s, the Beretta O/U shotguns were every bit as good in quality. In the case of this BL-6, Beretta's top-of-the-line standard production gun, it retailed during 1973 for approximately the same price as a Browning Superposed Lightweight 12 ga. – $485. Current value on a mint BL-6 is approx. $1,200, while the Superposed Grade I is now at $1,750. Perhaps as significant as anything else are the differences between Italian and American/Japanese manufactured styling/design, with the slim European styled forearm not that popular in the U.S. at the time. Beretta also had limited distribution through Garcia during this period. As with most discontinued shotguns, the most desirable gauge will be the 28 ga., followed by the .410 bore, then 20 ga., 16 ga., 10 ga., and finally 12 ga. How big of a difference? Huge on the 28 ga. and .410 bore – and getting bigger every year. For shotgun enthusiasts, unlike rifle shooters, who frequently get a variety of new calibers, there are only a relatively small number of gauges to shoot/collect.

SHOTGUNS

Photo Percentage Grading System™

98% condition, Boxed L.C. Smith Field Grade SxS Long Range Waterfowl, 12 ga., 32 in. round barrels, ser. no. 86110 - mfg. circa 1925. Even though this shotgun is also new and unfired, normal storage wear, cleaning, and occasional assembly have all accumulated enough wear to knock this gun's condition factor down to 98%. Original L.C. Smith case colors do not get any better than this – look at the vivid blues and greens surrounded by greyish/brown swirls. Also note unstained, light colored, checkered standard grade walnut stock and forearm, and tight wood to metal fit around sideplates. When a desirable gun's condition factor is this good, the value may double or even triple the 90% value. L.C. Smith only had one level of quality – the best, regardless of what the grade was. Stock and splinter forearm show virtually no wear. In many cases, a 98%+ condition specimen of a factory's most common model is the hardest to find, since most of them were heavily used. Original box is somewhat tattered, and has water staining.

Twenty-Sixth Edition *Blue Book of Gun Values*™

SHOTGUNS

95% condition, Belgian Browning A-5 Semi-Auto, 12 ga., 30 in. solid rib barrel, ser. no. 41914 - mfg. 1953. This 50 year old Belgian A-5 is still in great condition, with only minor wear on the receiver edges, and slight freckling in back of ejection port. Older style, checkered round pistol grip stock and 30 in. solid rib barrel also indicate earlier manufacture. Barrel address is marked, "Browning Arms Co, St, Louis, MO." When A-5 condition gets lower than this, prices fall off rapidly, as most Browning collectors prefer to have 98%+ condition, whenever possible. After almost 100 years of near continuous production, Browning finally discontinued the venerable Auto-5 shotgun in 1999. In today's A-5 marketplace, shorter barrels (26 or 28 in.) with open field chokes are worth considerably more than their 30-32 in. full choke counterparts.

SHOTGUNS

90% **condition,** Belgian Browning A-5 Sweet Sixteen, 16 ga., 28 in. barrel, ser. no. S14514 - mfg. 1954. Note the additional wear around the lower receiver edges on this Browning compared to the one on page 103. This Sweet Sixteen A-5 is referred to as a round knob, long tang variation, indicating that the pistol grip is rounded (mfg. 1952-1976), instead of flat, and the lower tang is longer than recent manufacture. Note blonde French walnut stock and forearm, typical for this period of production. This is a good example of what a rarer variation of a common model can do to the price tag. While the frequently encountered 12 ga. A-5 with 30 in. barrel on page 103 sold for approx. $625, this rarer Sweet Sixteen in less condition sold for over $800, and could have broken $1,300 if it had a ventilated rib and was in 98%+ original condition.

Photo Percentage Grading System™

Twenty-Sixth Edition *Blue Book of Gun Values*™

80% condition, Winchester Model 12 Trench Gun w/Bayonet, 12 ga., 20 7/8 in. round barrel, ser. no. 1014064 - mfg. 1943. U.S. military shotguns, like this specimen, were not as collectible (or expensive) as U.S. military handguns up to approximately 15 years ago – then things changed, in a hurry. Originality is Polar North for U.S. military long gun collectors, in addition to knowing exactly what proof marks should be present and where they are located. Note the "U.S." and ordnance "flaming bomb" proofs on right side of receiver, crisp stock cartouche, in addition to sling swivels. Compare receiver bluing to the 70%-75% and 60% condition Model 12s on the following pages. While the receiver on this gun is probably closer to 90%, the barrel, barrel shroud, and mag. tube lower this shotgun's condition factor down to 80% overall. Remington 1917 marked bayonet also adds some value to this original WWII U.S. military shotgun.

SHOTGUNS

70%-75% condition, Winchester Model 12 Slide Action, 12 ga., 28 in. round barrel, ser. no. 902723, mfg. 1941. Very few shotgun models are found in such a wide array of condition factors as the Model 12 Winchester. It's pretty hard for any shotgun enthusiast not to have a Model 12 somewhere in his/her gun vault. This particular shotgun shows normal wear, but no abuse. While some dealers and collectors might grade this gun at 80% based on the receiver and barrel bluing, the wear on the mag tube and ring at end of barrel assembly knock this shotgun's condition down to approx. 70%-75%. Stock has a Pachmayr rubber vent. replacement recoil pad with spacers, but has not been cut. Horizontal striations and dulling on breech block indicate this shotgun has pumped out more than a few ounces of lead (hopefully, no steel!) in its lifetime.

Twenty-Sixth Edition *Blue Book of Gun Values*™   ***Photo Percentage Grading System*™**

SHOTGUNS

60% condition, Winchester **Model 12 Slide Action,** 12 ga., 30 in. round barrel, ser. no. 219576 - mfg. early Jan., 1919. When a shotgun gets down to this condition factor, normally the barrel also shows visible wear, as seen on this shotgun. Note how receiver, barrel, and mag. tube have also started to turn a brownish patina. Scuffed breech block and horizontal wear line on mag tube tell this shotgun's shooting story. The stock has been sanded – note how light it is in the back, but gets dark where it joins the receiver (compare to Model 12 on page 106). Most of this gun's value must be determined by what it's worth as a reliable shooter, since the 12 ga./30 in. full choke barrel is the most common Model 12 configuration. The smaller gauges, especially the 28 ga. and .410 bore, are always more desirable than a 12 ga. in any shotgun model.

SHOTGUNS

50% condition, **Winchester Model 12 Slide Action**, 16 ga., 28 in. round barrel, ser. no. 886875 - mfg. 1941. This is a good example of a well used, no problem Model 12. All the major components (wood, receiver, barrel, and mag tube) are worn in all the right places, as well as not worn in all the right places. When barrel wear reaches this type of brown patina condition, the rest of the gun should look even more worn, as the barrel was normally not handled that much during usage. The mag tube is equally worn, and the original stock and forearm reveal the right amount of original varnish to match the rest of the gun. Recently, 16 ga. guns have made a comeback in terms of collectibility, and are now priced slightly above the 12 ga. – if original condition is 95% or better.

Twenty-Sixth Edition *Blue Book of Gun Values*™

***Photo Percentage Grading System*™**

SHOTGUNS

40% condition, Ithaca Model 4E Single Barrel Trap, 12 ga., 29½ in. round barrel, ser. no. 258371 - mfg. 1916. Compare the case colors on frame of this Ithaca Model 4E to the L.C. Smith Field Grade SxS on page 102, and note the coloration difference. Vent. rib barrel appears to have been shortened, since it now has an improved cylinder choke. Funky stock now has non-factory adj. comb, and a Morgan adj. recoil pad. One of the problems in modifying a gun like this to an individual's shooting dimensions and preferences, is that when it comes time to sell, the next person is probably going to want a different setup, including a different LOP on the stock. Frame sides show areas of case colors, but are mostly worn off on the nicely engraved bottom of the frame. If this gun hadn't been altered, the price would be considerably higher than the not quite $500 it brought at auction.

30% condition, Wells Fargo Remington Hammer Coach Gun, 12 ga., 20 in. ribbed barrels, ser. no. 78099 - mfg. 1897. Documented provenance guaranteeing this shotgun's colorful history, including a letter from the Railway Express Agency from New York, NY, is perhaps the most important single consideration when ascertaining its correct value. This hammer Remington has the new style "low circular hammers" and decarbonized steel barrels. Frame and barrel metal finishes have mostly turned an overall brownish patina, while stock and forearm still have most of the original varnish. Colt, Parker, Ithaca, Remington, and Whitney all produced coach guns during the late 1800s-early 1900s. Note how the "Wells Fargo & Co. 99" barrel marking has been hand cut over the top rib engraving. Be wary of "coach guns" that started out as long barrel sporting shotguns, but have had their barrels cut off - see explanation under the Coach Guns listing.

Photo Percentage Grading System™

Twenty-Sixth Edition *Blue Book of Gun Values*™

SHOTGUNS

20% or less condition, Parker GH Grade Hammerless damascus SxS, 12 ga., 30 in. barrels, ser. no. 115310 - mfg. 1903. This gun was new the same year the Wright Brothers took off from Kitty Hawk, NC. How do you grade this gun properly? No easy question, and no easy answer. Note that almost all the original frame case colors are gone, with the exception of some faded colors between the hinge pin and forearm. The rest of this gun's frame may have been previously polished, as some of the engraving has thinned out in areas. Stock and forearm have been refinished, but the damascus hammerless barrels still show great patterning, and double triggers are to be expected on the Model GH, which retailed for approximately $80 when new, $25 more with ejectors. Parker shotguns have continued to lead the domestic SxS marketplace price appreciation, with pricing for strong, original condition guns in smaller gauges (20 ga. and less) going well above auction reserve levels. Don't forget that originality has always been Polar North for Parker shotgun collectors.

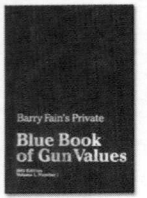

1st Edition (Vol. I, No. I)
1981

2nd Edition (Vol. II, No. I)
1982

3rd Edition (Vol. II, No. II)
1982

4th Edition
1983

5th Edition
1984

6th Edition
1985

7th Edition
1986

8th Edition
1987

9th Edition
1988

10th Edition
1989

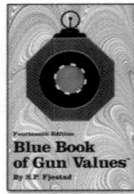

11th Edition
1990

12th Edition
1991

13th Edition
1992

14th Edition
1993

15th Edition
1994

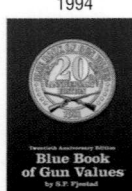

16th Edition
1995

17th Edition
1996

18th Edition
1997

19th Edition
1998

20th Edition
1999

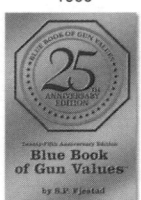

21st Edition
2000

22nd Edition
2001

23rd Edition
2002

24th Edition
2003

25th Edition
2004

For more information and availability on these older editions, please contact us at:

Blue Book Publications, Inc.
1-800-877-4867
www.bluebookinc.com

Good Information Never Sleeps!™

A SECTION

A.A.

Previously manufactured by Azanza & Arrizabalaga located in Eibar, Spain.

GRADING - PPGS™	100%	98%	95%	90%	80%	70%	60%

PISTOLS: SEMI-AUTO

A.A. - 7.65mm cal., semi-auto pistol, slide marked Azanza & Arrizabalaga Model 1916, A.A. in oval on frame.

$235	$200	$165	$135	$115	$85	$75

REIMS - 6.35mm or 7.65mm cal., semi-auto pistol, copies of M1906 Browning, marked 1914 Model.

$185	$150	$130	$110	$90	$70	$50

A.A.A.

Previously manufactured by Aldazabal located in Spain.

PISTOLS: SEMI-AUTO

M1919 - 7.65mm cal., semi-auto pistol.

$110	$100	$85	$70	$65	$60	$55

A.A. ARMS INC.

Previous manufacturer located in Monroe, NC until 1999.

CARBINES: SEMI-AUTO

AR9 CARBINE - similar action to AP9, except has carbine length barrel and side-folding metal stock. Banned 1994.

$750	$625	$550	$475	$400	$350	$300

PISTOLS: SEMI-AUTO

AP9 MINI-SERIES PISTOL - 9mm Para. cal., semi-auto blowback paramilitary design, phosphate/blue or nickel finish, 2 barrel lengths, 10 (C/B 1994) or 20* shot mag. Disc. 1999, parts cleanup during 2000.

$210	$185	$165	$150	$135	$125	$115

Last MSR was $245.

Add $20 for nickel finish.
Add $200 for AP9 long barrel Target Model (banned 1994).

A & B HIGH PERFORMANCE FIREARMS

Previous competition pistol manufacturer located in Arvin, CA.

PISTOLS: SEMI-AUTO

LIMITED CLASS - 9mm Para. or .38 Super cal., single action, competition M1911-styled action, STI frame, Ultimatch bull barrel, Caspian slide, Bo-Mar adj. rear sight, blue or chrome finish.

$1,875	$1,600	$1,375	$1,150	$925	$700	$550

Last MSR was $1,875.

GRADING - PPGS™	100%	98%	95%	90%	80%	70%	60%

OPEN CLASS - 9mm Para. or .38 Super cal., single action, competition M1911-styled action, STI frame, Ultimatch or Hybrid compensated barrel, Caspian slide, C-More scope, blue or chrome finish.

	$2,800	$2,300	$1,875	$1,600	$1,375	$1,000	$750

Last MSR was $2,800.

A.R. SALES

Previous manufacturer located in South El Monte, CA, circa 1968-1977.

PISTOLS: SEMI-AUTO

HANDGUN - .45 ACP cal., semi-auto patterned after Colt Model 1911 Govt., less weight than normal Colt .45.

	$295	$250	$225	$205	$175	$155	$145

RIFLES: SEMI-AUTO

RIFLE: MARK IV SPORTER - .308 Win. cal., semi-auto, M-14 style action, clip-fed, adj. sights. Approx. 200 mfg.

	$725	$650	$575	$500	$450	$400	$350

ADC

Current pistol manufacturer and customizer located in Gardone, Italy. Consumer direct sales.

ADC manufactures high quality custom pistols, mainly M1911 design. ADC also provides a complete range of customizing and gunsmithing services. Please contact the company directly for more information (see Trademark Index).

AFC

Previously manufactured by Auguste Francotte located in Liege, Belgium, 1912-1914.

PISTOLS: SEMI-AUTO

SEMI-AUTO PISTOL - 6.35mm cal., 6 shot mag., frame marked "Francotte Liege."

	$275	$250	$220	$165	$140	$110	$85

A. J. ORDNANCE

Previous manufacturer located in Covina, CA.

PISTOLS: SEMI-AUTO

THOMAS - .45 ACP cal., semi-auto, double action only, 6 shot, 3 1/2 in. barrel, fixed sights, checkered plastic grips, delayed blowback action, stainless steel barrel. Disc. mid 1970s.

	$600	$525	$450	$400	$350	$300	$250

Add 50% for chrome or stainless steel.

A K S (AK-47, AK-74, & AKM COPIES)

Select fire paramilitary design rifle originally designed in Russia (initials refer to Avtomat Kalashnikova, 1947). The AK-47 was officially adopted by Russia in 1949. Russian mfg. select fire AK-47s have not been mfg. since the mid 1950s. Semi-auto AK-47 and AKM clones are currently manufactured by several arsenals in China including Norinco and Poly Technologies, Inc. (currently illegal to import), in addition to other countries including the Czech Republic, Bulgaria, Russia, Egypt, and Hungary. On April 6th, 1998, recent "sporterized" variations (imported 1994-1998) with thumbhole stocks were banned by presidential order. Beginning 2000, AK-47s are being assembled in the U.S., using both new mfg. and older original military parts/components.

AK-47s are not rare – over 100 million have been manufactured by Russia and China since WWII.

AK/AK-47/AKM HISTORY & RECENT IMPORTATION

Since the early 1950s, the AK/AK-47/AKM series of select fire rifles has been the standard issue military rifle of the former Soviet Union and its satellites. It continues to fulfill that role reliably today. The AK series of rifles, from the early variants of the AK-47 through the AKM and AK-74, is undoubtedly the most widely used military small arms design in the world. Developed by Mikhail Kalashnikov (the AK stands for Avtomat Kalashnikova) in 1946, the AK went into full production in 1947 in Izhevsk, Russia. In 1953, the milled receiver was put into mass production. Since then, variants of the original AK-47 have been manufactured by almost every former Soviet bloc country and some free world nations, including Egypt. The AK action is the basis for numerous other weapons, including the RPK (Ruchnoy Pulemyot Kalashnikova).

The AK-47 was replaced in 1959 by the AKM, and retained the same basic design. The rifle was simply updated to incorporate easier and more efficient production methods, using a stamped, sheet metal receiver that was pinned and riveted in place, rather than a milled receiver. Other changes included a form of the beavertail forearm, muzzle compensator, and anti-bounce device intended to improve controllability and increase accuracy.

The AK was designed to be, and always has been, a "peasant-proof" military weapon. It is a robust firearm, both in design and function. Its record on the battlefields around the world is impressive, rivaled only by the great M1 Garand of the U.S. or bolt rifles such as the English Mark III Enfield. The original AK-47 prototypes are on display in the Red Army Museum in Moscow.

All of the current semi-auto AK "clones" are copies of the AKM's basic receiver design and internal components minus the full-auto parts. The Saiga rifle (see separate listing), manufactured by the Izhevsk Machining Plant, in Izhevsk, Russia, is the sole Russian entry in this market. It is available in the standard 7.62x39mm, 5.45x39mm (disc.) and in 20 ga. or .410 bore. Molot (hammer) OJSC also exports semi-auto AKs to the U.S. under the trade name Vepr. (see separate listing) – both the Saiga and Vepr. are imported and distributed by Robinson Armaments. Molot was the home of the PPSh-41 sub-machine gun during WWII, and also manufactured the RPK and the RPK-74. Other AK European manufacturers include companies in the Czech Republic, Bulgaria, as well as the former Yugoslavia. The Egyptian-made Maahdi AK clones were also available in the U.S. market.

Interest in the Kalashnikov design is at an all-time high due to the availability of high quality military AK-74, AKS-74, AKS-74U, and RPK-74 parts kits. Some models, such as those produced by Marc Krebs, are of very high quality. Currently, it is hard to go to a gun show or page through a buy/sell firearms magazine and not see a variety of parts, accessories, and high capacity magazines available for the variety of AK variants. For shooters, the value represented by these guns is undeniable for the price point.

Values for almost all of the imported AK clones are based solely on their use as sporting or target rifles. Fit and finish varies by country and importer. Most fall on the "low" side. Interest peaked prior to the passage of the 1994 Crime Bill and both AK clones and their "high capacity" magazines were bringing a premium for a short period of time in 1993 and 1994. However, interest waned during 1995-97, and the reduced demand lowered prices. In November of 1997, the Clinton Administration instituted an "administrative suspension" on all import licenses for these types of firearms in order to do a study on their use as "sporting firearms."

On April 6th, 1998, the Clinton Administration, in the political wake of the Jonesboro tragedy, banned the further import of 58 "assault-type" rifles, claiming that these semi-autos could not be classified as sporting weapons – the AK-47 and most related configurations were included. During 1997, firearms importers obtained permits to import almost 600,000 reconfigured rifles – approximately only 20,000 had entered the country when this bill took effect. When the ban occurred, applications were pending to import an additional 1,000,000 guns. Previously, thumbhole-stocked AK Sporters were still legal for import, and recent exporters included the Czech Republic, Russia, and Egypt.

RIFLES: SEMI-AUTO, AK-47, AK-74, & AKM MODELS

Also refer to separate listings under Poly Technologies, Inc., Norinco, Federal Ordnance, B-West, K.B.I., Sentinel Arms, American Arms, Inc., and others who have recently imported this configuration.

GRADING - PPGS™	100%	98%	95%	90%	80%	70%	60%

AK-47 (AKM) RECENT IMPORTS - 7.62x39mm (most common cal., former Russian M43 military), 5.45x39mm (Romanian mfg. or Saiga/MAK - recent mfg. only), or .223 Rem. cal., semi-auto Kalashnikov action, stamped (most common) or milled receiver, typically 16 1/2 in. barrel, 5, 10, or 30* (C/B 1994) shot mag., wood or synthetic stock and forearm except on folding stock model, recent importation (1994-early 1998) mostly had newer "sporterized" fixed stocks with thumbholes, may be supplied with bayonet, sling, cleaning kit, patterned after former military production rifle of China and Russia.

AK-47 technically designates the original select fire (semi or full-auto), Russian made military rifle with milled receiver. Recent semi-auto "clones" normally have stamped receivers and are technically designated AKMs. Recent mfg. AK-47 clones refer to rifles with milled receivers. Chinese importation stopped during late 1990.

Add 10-15% for 5.45x39mm cal. on Eastern European mfg. (non-recent import).

Add 20% for older folding stock variations.

	100%	98%	95%	90%	80%	70%	60%
Current U.S. assembly							
MSR N/A	$495	$425	$325	$295	$250	$230	$210
Chinese mfg.							
(usually poor quality)	$275	$225	$195	$165	$145	$120	$110
Egyptian mfg.							
(recent import)	$345	$275	$225	$185	$165	$130	$115
Romanian mfg.							
(recent import)	$335	$285	$260	$240	$220	$200	$180
Yugoslavian mfg.	$525	$425	$325	$275	$240	$220	$200
Hungarian mfg.	$525	$425	$325	$275	$240	$220	$200
Czech mfg.	$525	$425	$325	$275	$240	$220	$200
Bulgarian mfg.	$525	$425	$325	$275	$240	$220	$200

Recent U.S. assembly refers to an original stamped European (mostly FEG) or milled receiver with U.S. assembly, using either new parts or matched, older unused original Eastern European mfg. parts (BATF 922.R compliant). This newest generation of AK-47s is high quality overall, and cannot be sold in California. Check city and state laws regarding high capacity magazine compliance.

AK-74 - 5.45x39mm cal., semi-auto action based on the AKM, imported from Bulgaria and other previous Eastern bloc countries, in addition to recent assembly in the U.S., using FEG receivers, Bulgarian parts sets, and additional U.S. made components.

	100%	98%	95%	90%	80%	70%	60%
Bulgarian mfg.	$450	$375	$315	$275	$240	$220	$200
Recent U.S. assembly	$495	$425	$325	$295	$250	$230	$210

A M A C

See Iver Johnson section in this text. AMAC stands for American Military Arms Corporation manufactured in Jacksonville, AR. AMAC ceased operations early 1993.

AMP TECHNICAL SERVICE GmbH

Previous manufacturer located in Puccheim, Germany. Previous imported and distributed exclusively beginning 2001 by CQB Products, located in Tustin, CA.

RIFLES: BOLT ACTION

DSR-1 - .300 Win. Mag., .308 Win., or .338 Lapua cal., bolt action, bull pup design with in-line stock, receiver is made from aluminum, titanium, and polymers, internal parts are stainless steel, two-stage adj. trigger, 4 or 5 shot mag., 25.6 Lothar Walther fluted barrel with muzzlebrake and vent. shroud, includes bipod, ambidextrous 3 position safety, 13 lbs. Imported 2002-2004.

	100%	98%	95%	90%	80%	70%	60%
	$7,295	$6,300	$5,200	$4,100	$3,000	$2,500	$2,000

Last MSR was $7,795.

Add $100 for .300 Win. Mag. cal.

Add $300 for .338 Lapua cal.

GRADING - PPGS™	100%	98%	95%	90%	80%	70%	60%

A M T

Current trademark manufactured beginning late 2004 by Crusader Gun Company, Inc., located in Houston, TX. Previous trademark manufactured by Galena Industries Inc. located in Sturgis, SD, 1999-Jan., 2001. Previously located in Irwindale, CA until 1998. From 1998-2001, all AMTs manufactured by Galena Industries Inc. had a lifetime warranty, which is now void. Also see Irwindale Arms, Inc. and Auto-Mag for older discontinued models.

Galena Industries phased out the use of the AMT name, but continued to use individual model nomenclature until 2001.

During 2005, Crusader Gun Company Inc. acquired the previous tooling of AMT - Auto Mag., and plans to reintroduce the following models: Auto Mag II, Auto Mag III, the Back Up .380, and the Back Up .45. As this edition went to press, production on these models was just beginning. Please contact the company directly for more information and pricing on these models.

PISTOLS: SEMI-AUTO

From 1999-2001, AMT began using Millett sights exclusively. Between 1993-98, AMT changed from white outline Millett adj. sights to an adj. 3 dot (white) system mfg. by LPA in Italy. Early production pistols were made in El Monte, CA, and are marked "El Monte."

LIGHTNING - .22 LR cal., semi-auto, stainless steel only, 5 (bull only), 6 1/2, 8 1/2, 10 1/2, or 12 1/2 (disc. 1987) in. bull or tapered barrels, adj. sights and trigger, pistol based on semi-auto Ruger action, tapered barrels. 23,903 were mfg. 1984-87.

$350 $200 $150

Last MSR was $289.

This model featured a frame grooved for scope mounts, Clark trigger, Millett sights, and either Pachmayr rubber or Wayland wood grips as standard equipment.

* ***Bull's Eye Regulation Target*** - similar to 6 1/2 in. Lightning with bull barrel, except has vent. rib, wood grips, extended rear sight. Mfg. 1986 only.

$425 $350 $285

Last MSR was $436.

BABY AUTOMAG - .22 LR cal., semi-auto, stainless steel only, 8 1/2 in. vent. rib barrel, Millett adj. sights, smooth walnut grips, 1,001 mfg.

$750 $650 $550

AUTOMAG II - .22 Mag. cal., stainless steel only, 3 3/8 (Compact Model), 4 1/2, or 6 in. barrel, gas assisted action, white outline Millett adj. sights, grooved Lexan grips, 7 (Compact) or 9 shot mag., 24-32 oz. Mfg. 1987-2001, reintroduced late 2004.

MSR $429 $365 $255 $200

Add $60 for 4 1/2 in. barrel or $120 for 6 in. barrel.

AUTOMAG III - .30 Carbine or 9mm Win. Mag. (mfg. 1993 only) cal., stainless steel, 6 3/8 in. barrel, patterned after Colt Govt. Model, white outline Millett adj. sights, grooved Lexan grips, 8 shot mag., 43 oz. Mfg. 1992-2001, reintroduced mid-2005.

MSR N/A $530 $445 $335

Last MSR was $549.

This model is scheduled for manufacturing again shortly by Crusader Gun Company, Inc.

AUTOMAG IV - 10mm (disc. 1993) or .45 Win. Mag. cal., 6 1/2 (.45 Win. Mag. only) or 8 5/8 (disc. 1993) in. barrel, 7/8 shot mag., Millett adj. sights, stainless steel, 46 oz. Mfg. 1992-2001.

$530 $445 $325

GRADING - PPGS™	100%	98%	95%	90%	80%	70%	60%

AUTOMAG V - .50 AE cal., stainless steel, 6 1/2 in. barrel, gas venting system reduces recoil, 5 shot mag., 46 oz. Mfg. 1993-95.

	$815	$700	$625				

Last MSR was $900.

AUTOMAG 440 - .440 Cor-Bon cal., special order only. Mfg. 1999-2001.

	$775	$650	$550				

Last MSR was $899.

JAVELINA - 10mm cal., semi-auto, 7 in. barrel, 8 shot mag., Millett adj. sights, wraparound Neoprene grips, wide adj. trigger, long grip safety, 48 oz. Mfg. 1992 only.

	$560	$460	$360				

Last MSR was $676.

BACKUP PISTOL - .22 LR (disc. 1987), .357 Sig. (new 1996), .380 ACP, .38 Super (new 1995), 9mm Para. (new 1995), .40 S&W (new 1995), .400 Cor-Bon (new 1997), or .45 ACP (new 1995) cal., semi-auto, choice of traditional double action (disc. 1992) or double action only (new 1992), 2 1/2 (.22 LR or .380 ACP) or 3 in. barrel, stainless steel, Lexan grips, 5 (.380 ACP or .40 S&W), 6, or 8 (.22 LR) shot mag., 18 (.380 ACP only) or 23 oz. Older disc. walnut grip models are worth a slight premium. In 1992, AMT reengineered this model and removed all external levers, production resumed again late 2004.

* *.22 LR cal.* - .22 LR cal., limited production.

	$375	$275	$175				

* *.380 ACP cal.* - disc. 2000, reintroduced 2004.

MSR $350	$295	$225	$140				

* *9mm Para., .38 Super, .40 S&W, or .45 ACP cal.*

MSR $406	$350	$250	$195				

* *.357 Sig., .38 Super, or .400 Cor-Bon cal.*

MSR $459	$385	$295	$225				

BACKUP PISTOL II - .380 ACP cal., single action, semi-auto, stainless steel, 2 1/2 in. barrel, 5 shot finger extension mag., black carbon fiber grips, 18 oz. Mfg. 1993-98.

	$260	$190	$150				

Last MSR was $369.

.45 ACP STANDARD GOVERNMENT MODEL - .45 ACP cal., similar to Colt semi-auto Govt. Model, stainless steel, 5 in. barrel, fixed rear sight, loaded chamber indicator, adj. trigger, wraparound neoprene grips, 38 oz. Disc. 1999.

	$325	$275	$225				

Last MSR was $399.

HARDBALLER II - .45 ACP cal., similar to Colt Gold Cup Model, stainless steel, 5 in. barrel, adj. Millett rear sight, serrated rib, loaded chamber indicator, adj. trigger, wraparound neoprene grips, 38 oz. Disc. 2001.

	$400	$325	$250				

Last MSR was $499.

Add $280 for 7 in. Hardballer conversion kit (disc. 1997).

* *Hardballer Longslide* - similar to Hardballer, except 7 in. barrel, longer slide assembly, and also available in .400 Cor-Bon (named .400 Accelerator, new 1998), 46 oz. Disc. 2001.

	$425	$320	$250				

Last MSR was $549.

Add $50 for .400 Cor-Bon (.400 Accelerator) cal.
Add $300 for 5 in. Longslide conversion kit (disc. 1997).

GRADING - PPGS™	100%	98%	95%	90%	80%	70%	60%

COMMANDO - .40 S&W cal., 4 in. barrel. Mfg. 1998-2001.

	$400	$325	$250

Last MSR was $499.

SKIPPER - .45 ACP cal., re-released in 1991 with choice of .40 S&W or .45 ACP cal., similar to Hardballer, except approx. 1 in. shorter slide on pre-'84 mfg, 4 1/4 in. barrel, checkered walnut grips, matte finish stainless steel, Millett adj. rear sight, 7 shot mag., 33 oz. Disc. 1991.

	$350	$285	$250

Last MSR was $450.

COMBAT SKIPPER - similar to Skipper, only with fixed sights. Disc. 1984.

	$375	$330	$295

BULL'S EYE TARGET MODEL - .40 S&W cal., similar to Hardballer with 5 in. barrel, 8 shot mag., adj. Millett sights, wraparound neoprene grips, 38 oz. Mfg. 1991 only.

	$400	$340	$295

Last MSR was $500.

"ON DUTY" DOUBLE ACTION - 9mm Para., .40 S&W, or .45 ACP (new late 1994) cal., stainless steel slide and barrel, 4 1/2 in. barrel, 10 (C/B 1994), 15* (9mm Para.), 11* (.40 S&W), or 9 (.45 ACP) shot mag., 3-dot sighting system, anodized aluminum frame, trigger disconnect safety with inertia firing pin, carbon fiber grips, 32 oz. Mfg. 1991-94.

	$385	$295	$250

Last MSR was $470.

Add $60 for .45 ACP cal.

In 1992, this model became available with either traditional double action with decocking lever or double action only with safety.

RIFLES: BOLT ACTION

AMT rifles were discontinued in 1998.

BOLT ACTION STANDARD SINGLE SHOT - 11 various cals., post '64 push-feed action, pre '64 3-position side safety, cone breech, composite stock, cryogenic treated stainless steel barrel w/o sights, 8 1/2 lbs. Mfg. 1996-97.

	$825	$650	$450

Last MSR was $1,500.

✴ *Bolt Action Deluxe Single Shot* - 11 various cals., Mauser type controlled feeding, short, medium, or long right-hand or left-hand action, pre '64 3-position side safety and claw type extractor, cryogenic treated stainless steel barrel w/o sights, custom Kevlar stock, approx. 8 1/2 lbs. Mfg. 1996 only.

	$995	$800	$600

Last MSR was $2,400.

BOLT ACTION STANDARD REPEATER - 21 various cals., post '64 push-feed action, Mauser type mag., pre '64 3-position side safety, Model 70 type trigger, composite stock, cryogenic treated stainless steel barrel w/o sights. 8 1/2 lbs. Mfg. 1996 only.

	$800	$625	$500

Last MSR was $1,110.

✴ *Bolt Action Deluxe Repeater* - similar features to Bolt Action Deluxe Single Shot, except has Mauser type mag. Mfg. 1996 only.

	$1,000	$800	$650

Last MSR was $1,596.

GRADING - PPGS™	100%	98%	95%	90%	80%	70%	60%

RIFLES: SEMI-AUTO

LIGHTNING (25/22) - .22 LR cal., semi-auto based on Ruger 10-22 action, stainless steel, 30 shot mag., 17 1/2 in. bull or tapered barrel, nylon pistol grip handle and forearm, folding stock with recoil pad or youth stock, fixed sights, 6 lbs. Mfg. 1986-93.

$220 $175 $150

Last MSR was $296.

SMALL GAME HUNTER (SGH) - .22 LR cal., same mechanical action as Lightning, except has matte black nylon stock with checkered forearm and grip, 22 in. barrel, 10 shot mag., no sights, removable recoil pad allows storage in stock, 6 lbs. Mfg. 1986-93.

$230 $190 $160

Last MSR was $300.

SMALL GAME HUNTER II - similar to Small Game Hunter, except has match grade 22 in. heavyweight full-floating barrel, 10 shot rotary mag., black fiberglass nylon stock, no sights, 6 lbs. Mfg. 1993 only.

$230 $190 $160

Last MSR was $300.

Add $70 for 17 1/2 in. stainless steel barrel.
Add $150 for 22 1/2 in. stainless steel match grade barrel.

CHALLENGE EDITION (I, II, III) - .22 LR cal., semi-auto target variation featuring McMillan fiberglass stock, 16 1/4 (choice of 6 in. barrel weight extension or 3 in. muzzle brake, new 1997), 18, 20 (mfg. 1994-96), or 22 (mfg. 1994-96) in. floating stainless steel bull barrel, custom designed or Jewell (new 1997) trigger, custom order through AMT's Custom Shop. Mfg. 1994-98.

$800 $600 $450

Last MSR was $1,296.

Subtract $200 without Jewell trigger.
Add $144 for 16 1/4 barrel with 3 in. muzzle brake (Challenge Edition II, new 1997).
Add $85 for 16 1/4 barrel with 6 in. barrel extension (Challenge Edition III).

✱ *Challenge Edition Elite With Bloop Tube* - features 16 1/4 in. barrel with a 6 in. bloop tube extension enabling increased bullet velocity with muzzle heavy character- istics, McMillan fiberglass STC stock. Mfg. 1996-98.

$925 $700 $550

Last MSR was $1,498.

Subtract $255 if without compensator.

SPORTER EDITION - .22 LR cal., 16 1/2, 18, 20, or 22 in. tapered sporter barrel, McMillan fiberglass sporter stock. Mfg. 1996 only.

$650 $525 $400

Last MSR was $900.

HUNTER EDITION I - .22 LR cal., 18, 20, or 22 in. regular barrel with injection molded sporter stock. Mfg. 1996 only (replaced with Hunter Edition II).

$550 $425 $300

Last MSR was $800.

✱ *Hunter Edition II* - .22 LR cal., 22 in. tapered sporter barrel with 2 lb. Jewell trigger, McMillan synthetic sporter stock. Mfg. 1997-98.

$750 $575 $425

Last MSR was $1,354.

GRADING - PPGS™	100%	98%	95%	90%	80%	70%	60%

FLY SWATTER I - .22 LR cal., 16 1/2 in. regular barrel with injection molded (1996 only) or Hogue over-molded (new 1997) sporter stock. Mfg. 1996-97.

$575 $450 $325

Last MSR was $822.

✳ *Fly Swatter II* - similar to Fly Swatter I, except has 3 in. muzzle brake. Mfg. 1997 only.

$675 $475 $350

Last MSR was $936.

BR-50 ACCELERATOR EDITION - .22 LR cal., features 16 1/4 (new 1998) or 16 1/2 (disc. 1997) in. bull barrel with 3 in. muzzle brake (new 1998), McMillan bench rest stock, Hoehn barrel tuner (disc. 1997), and Jewell trigger. Mfg. 1997-98.

$795 $600 $450

Last MSR was $1,440.

ACCULITE EDITION RIFLE - .22 LR cal., features 18 in. Magnum Research graphite barrel with muzzle brake, thumbhole sporter stock, adj. Jewell trigger, 4 3/4 lbs. Mfg. 1998 only.

$750 $575 $425

Last MSR was $1,321.

INTIMIDATOR EDITION RIFLE - .22 LR cal., 16 1/4 Shilen select match grade barrel with 6 in. bloop tube, adj. Jewell trigger, 6 1/4 lbs. Mfg. 1998 only.

$875 $625 $475

Last MSR was $1,581.

MAGNUM HUNTER - .22 Mag. cal., semi-auto, 20 in. free-floating barrel, stainless steel, 10 shot straight stacked mag., w/o sights, drilled and tapped for Weaver 87-A scope base, black synthetic stock, 6 lbs. Mfg. 1995-98.

$375 $295 $225

Last MSR was $459.

TARGET RIFLE SEMI-AUTO - .22 LR cal., button rifled cryogenic treated barrel with target crown, choice of Fajen laminate or Hogue composite stock, 10 shot mag., 1-piece receiver with integral Weaver mount, 7 1/2 lbs. Mfg. 1997-98.

$425 $350 $275

Last MSR was $549.

Add $50 for Fajen laminate stock.

AR-7 INDUSTRIES, LLC

Current manufacturer established 1998, and currently located beginning 2004 in Geneseo, IL. Previously located in Meriden, CT 1998-early 2004. Dealer and distributor sales.

In February 2004, AR-7 Industries LLC was purchased by ArmaLite, Inc., and current manufacturer is located in Geneseo, IL.

RIFLES: BOLT ACTION

AR-7 TAKEDOWN - .22 LR cal., bolt action variation of the AR-7 Explorer rifle, similar takedown/storage configuration, 2 1/2 lbs. Advertised 2002 only.

While advertised during 2002, this model has yet to be manufactured.

GRADING - PPGS™	100%	98%	95%	90%	80%	70%	60%

RIFLES: SEMI-AUTO

AR-7 EXPLORER RIFLE - .22 LR cal., takedown barrelled action stores in synthetic stock which floats, 8 shot mag., aperture rear sight, 16 in. barrel (synthetic barrel with steel liner), black matte finish on AR-7, silvertone on AR-7S (disc. 2000), camouflage finish on AR-7C, two-tone (silver receiver with black stock and barrel) on AR-7T (disc. 2000), walnut finish on AR-W (mfg. 2001-2002), stowed length 16 1/2 in., 2 1/2 lbs. New late 1998.

MSR $150	$125	$100	$85	$75	$65	$55	$50

Add $15 for camo or walnut finish.

This model was also previously manufactured by Survival Arms, Inc. and Charter Arms – see individual listings for information.

AR-7 SPORTER (AR-20) - .22 LR cal., 16 1/2 in. steel barrel with vent. aluminum shroud, metal skeleton fixed stock with pistol grip, 8 (new 2001) or 16 shot "flip clip" (optional) mag., 3.85 lbs. New late 1998.

MSR $200	$170	$145	$120	$105	$95	$80	$70

Add $100 for sporter conversion kit (includes aluminum shrouded barrel, pistol grip stock, and 16 shot flip clip).

This model was also previously manufactured by Survival Arms, Inc. – see individual listing for information.

AR-7 TARGET - .22 LR cal., 16 in. bull barrel with 7/8 in. cantilever scope mount, tube stock with pistol grip, 8 shot mag., 3-9x40mm compact rubber armored scope is optional, 5.65 lbs. New 2002.

MSR $210	$175	$150	$125	$105	$95	$80	$70

Add $60 for compact scope.

ASAI AG (ADVANCED SMALL ARMS INDUSTRIES)

Previous manufacturer located in Solothurn, Switzerland 1994-2004. Previously imported until 2000 by Magnum Research, Inc. located in Minneapolis, MN.

PISTOLS: SEMI-AUTO

ONE PRO.45 - 9mm Para. (limited mfg. in Europe, never imported into the U.S.), .40 S&W (limited mfg. in Europe, never imported into the U.S.), .400 Cor-Bon (conversion only), or .45 ACP cal., SA or DA, 3 (disc. 1998) or 3 3/4 in. barrel with polygonal rifling, steel or alloy (not imported into U.S.) frame, black contoured synthetic grips, black or two-tone (less than 10 mfg.) finish, 10 shot mag., includes plastic case, extra 10 shot mag., and cleaning kit, 25 or 31 oz. Imported mid 1997-2000.

	$595	$485	$410	$360	$330	$300	$275

Last MSR was $699.

Add $209 for .400 Cor-Bon conversion kit without compensator.

Add $249 for .45 ACP or .400 Cor-Bon conversion kit with extended barrel, compensator, and recoil spring guide.

AWA USA

Current importer established during late 2004 and located in Hialeah, FL.

AWA USA purchased the remaining assets of American Western Arms, Inc. in late 2004. As this edition went to press, this company was just getting started as an importer of guns manufactured by AWA International, Inc. in Brescia, Italy. Please contact the company directly for more information, including current model lineup and retail pricing (see Trademark Index).

GRADING - PPGS™	100%	98%	95%	90%	80%	70%	60%

A-SQUARE COMPANY

Current firearms and ammunition manufacturer located in Jeffersonville, IN beginning 2003. A-Square Company is a wholly owned subsidiary of JISTA, LLC. Previously located in Bedford KY until 2002, Louisville, KY until 2000, and in Madison, IN until 1991.

A-Square also offers different grades of walnut, different metal finishes, and various sights/scope rings as special orders. Custom calibers are also available upon special order.

A-SQUARE

RIFLES: BOLT ACTION

Add $325 for A-Grade walnut, add $625 for AAA-Grade fancy walnut, add $500 for English walnut (disc.), add $100 for accent package (disc.), add $550 for black synthetic stock, add $600 for weather-impervious package (disc.), add $325 for 3-leaf steel express sights, add $300 for royal high gloss blue finish (disc. 1995), add $150 for high gloss polymer wood finish (disc. 2002), or $550 for .505 Gibbs or .577 Tyrannosaur cal.

HANNIBAL MODEL - most cals. available, bolt action built on a P-17 Enfield receiver, 22-26 in. barrel, deluxe oil finished walnut with pistol grip and recoil pad, Teflon coated metal, choice of barrel length and LOP, 9-11 1/4 lbs. New 1986.

MSR $3,625	$3,400	$2,850	$2,400	$2,100	$1,875	$1,725	$1,575

HAMILCAR MODEL - various cals. available, smaller variation of the Hannibal model featuring slimmer design gained by not needing the reinforcement for heavy Mag. cals., 4-7 shot mag., cocks on opening, 8-8 1/2 lbs. New 1994.

MSR $3,625	$3,400	$2,850	$2,400	$2,100	$1,875	$1,725	$1,575

CAESAR MODEL - most cals. available, bolt action built on a Remington M-700 receiver until 1993, Sako L-V actions were utilized beginning 1993, 22-26 in. barrel, select walnut with pistol grip and recoil pad, primarily a left-handed action with right-hand a special order, 9-10 3/4 lbs. New 1986.

MSR $3,625	$3,400	$2,850	$2,400	$2,100	$1,875	$1,725	$1,575

GENGHIS KHAN MODEL - .22-250 Rem., .243 Win., .25-06, or 6mm Rem. cal., features Winchester pre '64 Model 70 action, heavy tapered barrel, Coil-Chek stock helps reduce recoil, designed for varmint hunting. New 1995.

MSR $3,625	$3,400	$2,850	$2,400	$2,100	$1,875	$1,725	$1,575

ATCSA

Previously manufactured by Armas De Tiro Y Casa located in Spain.

REVOLVERS

COLT POCKET PISTOL COPY - revolver, .38 cal., 6 shot.

	$155	$140	$110	$100	$90	$75	$65

SINGLE SHOT REVOLVER - target pistol.

	$195	$165	$145	$110	$100	$90	$75

ATA ARMS

Current shotgun manufacturer located in Istanbul, Turkey. No current U.S. importation.

SHOTGUNS

ATA Arms manufactures a complete line of good quality semi-auto and slide action shotguns in various configurations. Please contact the factory directly for more information, including model availability and U.S. pricing.

GRADING - PPGS™	100%	98%	95%	90%	80%	70%	60%

AYA (AGUIRRE Y ARANZABAL)

Current manufacturer established in 1917, and located in Eibar, Spain. Currently imported and distributed by Fieldsport, located in Traverse City, MI; New England Custom Gun Service, Ltd. (NECG), located in Plainfield, NH; John F. Rowe, located in Enid, OK; and by Anglo American Sporting Agency, located in Corona del Mar, CA. Previously imported by William Larkin Moore 1969-1978 (with Agoura, CA import marking) and 1978-1986 (with West Lake, CA import marking). Diarm also manufactured AYAs circa 1986-1988 in Eibar, Spain. Retail and dealer sales by importer and AYA select distributors.

AYA manufactured shotguns can be denoted by serialization. Serial numbers over 600,001 with barrel flats marked Arms de Chasse or Scotia Group are post-1988 AYA manufactured while specimens under 600,000 may have been manufactured by Diarm - Diarm manufacture is not covered by the AYA warranty, nor is the resale the same as values listed below.

SHOTGUNS: O/U

Additionally, AYA manufactures a Coral boxlock, both in standard and deluxe configurations, the Excelsior sidelock model is also available. The MD2 and MD6 O/U models complete their European line. Please contact Anglo American Sporting Agency directly for more information on these guns (see Trademark Index).

Add 5% for gauges smaller than 12 ga.

Add 5% for 3 in. magnum chambers.

AUGUSTA - 12 ga. only, deluxe O/U sidelock, arabesque engraving in deep relief, select walnut.

This model has been imported off and on over the years and the importers should be contacted directly for current pricing information and availability.

CORAL "A" - 12 or 16 ga., boxlock action with Kersten cross bolt, vent. rib, ejectors, double triggers. Disc. 1985.

	$1,275	$1,050	$875	$775	$695	$625	$560

Last MSR was $2,195.

CORAL "B" - similar to Coral A, except for coin-wash engraved receiver. Disc. 1985.

	$1,395	$1,100	$925	$820	$720	$650	$595

Last MSR was $2,450.

MODEL 37 SUPER - 12, 16, or 20 ga., various barrel lengths and chokes, vent. rib, sidelock, auto ejector, elaborate engraving, high grade wood. Merkel style action. Prices below reflect older models. Disc.

12 ga.	$2,600	$2,350	$2,100	$1,900	$1,700	$1,500	$1,250
16 ga.	$2,550	$2,200	$2,000	$1,700	$1,500	$1,350	$1,150
20 ga.	$3,000	$2,500	$2,200	$1,900	$1,700	$1,600	$1,475

✱ **New Model 37 A/B/C** - game scene engraved, detachable sidelock action, nickel steel receiver. This model has been imported off and on over the years.

Please contact the importers directly for pricing information and availability on this model.

MODEL 77 - 12 ga. only, Merkel style O/U sidelock with Greener crossbolt, deluxe engraving checkering. Disc. 1985.

	$3,100	$2,750	$2,500	$2,255	$2,030	$1,805	$1,600

Last MSR was $4,100.

MODEL 79 "A" - 12 ga. only, boxlock with double locking lugs, sel. trigger, ejectors. Disc. 1985.

	$1,275	$1,075	$965	$880	$790	$705	$640

Last MSR was $1,595.

GRADING - PPGS™	100%	98%	95%	90%	80%	70%	60%

MODEL 79 "B" - similar to Model 79 "A," only more elaborate engraving. Disc. 1985.

	$1,395	$1,200	$1,085	$990	$890	$790	$695

Last MSR was $1,795.

MODEL 79 "C" - similar to Model 79 "B," only more elaborate engraving, double triggers on request. Disc. 1985.

	$2,050	$1,825	$1,605	$1,460	$1,315	$1,165	$1,000

Last MSR was $2,650.

SHOTGUNS: SxS

Current retail values on the AYA shotguns listed below could vary somewhat from importer to importer.

> On current models listed below, add 5% to values if other than 12 ga.
>
> Add $775 for SNT, or $905 for SST on currently manufactured guns.

BILL HANUS BIRDGUN - 16, 20, or 28 ga., similar wood, fit, checkering, and finish as the No. 53 sidelock, except is Anson & Deeley boxlock, individual frames proportionate to ga., 27 in. barrels with concave rib choked Sk. 1 & 2, case colored receiver with moderate engraving, SST, ejectors, includes leather covered handguard, splinter forearm, straight grip. Importation began 1997.

MSR $2,895	$2,550	$2,100	$1,725	$1,450	$1,100	$875	$700

Subtract $400 for DT.

> This model is available only through Bill Hanus Birdguns LLC. Stocks bent for cast-on and leather covered decelerator pads are also available at additional cost.

BOLERO - similar to Matador, with non-selective single trigger and extractors. Disc. 1984.

	$450	$395	$350	$300	$275	$250	$220

COUNTRYMAN GAME GUN - 12 or 20 ga. Imported 1998-2002.

	$2,050	$1,650	$675	$525	$450	$410	$365

Last MSR was $2,295.

IBERIA - 12 or 20 ga., 3 in., boxlock, double triggers, plain walnut. Disc. 1984.

	$495	$450	$395	$350	$300	$265	$230

IBERIA II - 12 or 16 ga., 28 in. barrels, 2 3/4 in. chamber only, double triggers, plain walnut. Mfg. 1984-85 only.

	$550	$475	$425	$365	$300	$265	$230

Last MSR was $570.

MATADOR - 10, 12, 16, 20, 28 ga., or .410 bore, 26, 28, or 30 in. barrel, various chokes, Anson & Deeley boxlock, auto ejectors, beavertail forearm, SST, checkered pistol grip stock. Mfg. 1955-63.

	$550	$475	$375	$325	$275	$225	$200

Add 10% for 20 ga. or 20% for .410 bore or 28 ga.

MATADOR NO. 2 - similar to Matador, with vent. rib, 12 or 20 ga. only. Disc.

	$675	$575	$475	$375	$300	$250	$200

Add 10% for 20 ga.

MATADOR NO. 3A - 12 or 20 ga., 3 in. chamber in 20 ga. only, boxlock, vent. rib, ejectors, SST. Disc. 1985.

	$795	$675	$575	$495	$440	$385	$335

Last MSR was $1,235.

Add 10% for 20 ga.

SENIOR - 12 ga. only, self-opener, engraved sidelock action, select walnut. Top-of-the-line quality, made to special order only. Lighter up-land version also available. Disc. 1987.

	$15,500	$12,000	$10,000	$8,000	$6,500	$5,500	$4,500

Last MSR was $21,000.

GRADING - PPGS™	100%	98%	95%	90%	80%	70%	60%

NO. 1 - 12, 16, 20, 28 ga. or .410 bore, full sidelock action, straight grip, ejectors, DTs, elaborate fine scroll engraving. Importation disc. 1987, resumed in 1991.

	MSR $8,895	$7,450	$6,250	$5,150	$4,000	$3,250	$2,750	$2,250

Add approx. $400 for rounded action.

Add approx. $2,640 for extra set of barrels.

✽ *No. 1 DeLuxe* - features bold foliate engraving.

	MSR $11,995	$9,250	$7,500	$6,250	$5,000	$4,000	$3,000	$2,500

Add approx. $300 for rounded action.

Add approx. $2,640 for extra set of barrels.

✽ *No. 1 DeLuxe English* - exhibition quality wood and engraved by Geoff Moore, English metal finish, custom order only.

This shotgun is specifically made for A.S.I., and is sold exclusively in the U.K. marketplace. Please contact A.S.I. for more information, including availability and prices (see Trademark Index).

NO. 2 - 12, 16, 20, 28 ga., or .410 bore, 3 in. chambers, English-style sidelock, ejector, cocking indicators, DTs. Importation disc. 1987, resumed 1991.

	MSR $4,395	$3,850	$3,200	$2,600	$2,000	$1,650	$1,275	$1,000

Add $200 for rounded action.

Add approx. $1,755 for extra set of barrels.

✽ *Bill Hanus Dreamgun No. 2 Sidelock* - features Boss rounded action and customer selected wood, one year delivery. Importation began 2003.

	MSR $4,850	$4,250	$3,525	$2,800	$2,300	$1,850	$1,500	$1,200

This model is only available from Bill Hanus Birdguns LLC.

NO. 3-A - 12, 16, 20, 28 ga., or .410 bore, boxlock, extractors, double triggers. Disc. 1985.

		$675	$575	$495	$450	$400	$375	$350

Last MSR was $850.

Add 25%-35% for 28 ga. or .410 bore.

NO. 4 - 12, 16, 20, 28 ga., or .410 bore, 3 in. chambers, English-style straight stock, boxlock action, ejectors, double trigger, straight grip stock, standard wood, Importation disc. 1987, resumed 1991.

	MSR $2,300	$2,000	$1,675	$1,250	$1,000	$850	$600	$500

Add $945 for extra set of barrels.

✽ *No. 4/53* - similar to No. 4, except has No. 53 wood upgrade. Importation disc. 1987, resumed 1991.

	MSR $2,795	$2,350	$1,950	$1,550	$1,250	$1,000	$875	$725

Add approx. $200 for No. 4/53S (includes wood upgrade, SNT, and round knob pistol grip, disc.)

NO. 4 DELUXE - 12, 20, 28 ga. or .410 bore, English-style, boxlock, ejector, stock, forearm, trigger to order. Importation disc. 1985, resumed 1991.

	MSR $3,360	$2,950	$2,500	$2,000	$1,650	$1,450	$1,200	$1,000

Add $962 for extra set of barrels.

XXV BOXLOCK (BL) - 12, 20, 28 ga. or .410 bore, similar to No. 4 Deluxe, except 25 in. barrels, Churchill rib. Importation disc. 1986, resumed 1991.

	MSR $2,950	$2,550	$2,175	$1,750	$1,450	$1,250	$1,000	$875

Add approx. $1,509 for extra set of barrels.

XXV SIDELOCK (SL) - 12, 16, 20 (disc. 1997), 28 (disc. 1997) ga., or .410 bore (disc. 1997), sidelock ejector, 25 in. barrels, Churchill rib. stock, forearm, trigger to order. Importation disc. 1986, resumed 1991.

✽ *12, 16, or 20 ga.*

	MSR $4,750	$4,000	$3,350	$2,550	$2,100	$1,650	$1,275	$1,000

Add approx. $1,720 for extra set of barrels.

GRADING - PPGS™	100%	98%	95%	90%	80%	70%	60%

NO. 53 - 12, 16 (disc. 1997), or 20 ga., engraved sidelock ejector, sideclips, third lock. Stock, forearm, trigger to order. Importation disc. 1986, resumed 1991.

MSR $5,695	$4,800	$3,900	$3,150	$2,650	$2,000	$1,500	$1,250

Add $1,733 for extra set of barrels.

NO. 56 - 12, 16 (disc. 1997), or 20 (disc. 1999) ga., sidelock action-engraved, ejectors, sel. trigger. Importation disc. 1985, resumed 1991.

MSR $8,500	$7,150	$6,000	$5,000	$4,000	$3,250	$2,750	$2,250

Add $2,850 for extra set of barrels.

NO. 106 - 12, 16, or 20 ga., English-style boxlock, double trigger, pistol grip, 28 in. barrels. Disc. 1985.

$550	$475	$400	$360	$320	$300	$275

Last MSR was $585.

Add 20% for 16 or 20 ga.

107-LI - 12 or 16 ga., English-style boxlock, double trigger, straight grip, light English scroll engraving. Disc. 1985.

$775	$650	$550	$495	$450	$400	$350

Last MSR was $745.

MODEL 116 - 12, 16, or 20 ga., 27-30 in. barrels, any choke, hand detachable H&H sidelocks, double triggers, engraved, select checkered walnut pistol grip stock. Disc. 1985.

$1,500	$1,275	$1,075	$925	$800	$700	$600

Last MSR was $1,125.

MODEL 117 - 10, 12, 16, or 20 ga., 3 in. chambers, 26-30 in. barrels, any choke, hand detachable H&H sidelocks, ejectors, SST, engraved, select checkered walnut pistol grip stock. Disc. 1986.

$1,750	$1,500	$1,225	$1,075	$925	$800	$700

Last MSR was $1,075.

MODEL 117 QUAIL UNLIMITED - 12 ga. only, 26 in. barrels choked IC/M with 3 in. chambers, upgraded wood and checkering, high gloss bluing, gold colored ST, engraved by Baron Technologies in PA, only 42 mfg. for Quail Unlimited of North America.

$1,650	$1,400	$1,150	$975	$875	$800	$725

This model had a retail price of $1,700 but was made available to Quail Unlimited members for approx. $1,200.

MODEL 210 - 12 or 16 ga., boxlock, exposed hammers, double triggers, plain walnut, light engraving. Disc. 1985.

$795	$675	$550	$475	$435	$395	$350

Last MSR was $900.

MODEL 711 SIDELOCK - sidelock action. Mfg. 1985 only.

$1,450	$1,250	$1,075	$925	$800	$700	$600

Last MSR was $1,250.

ABADIE

Previous trademark of Portuguese military revolvers manufactured by several Belgian makers.

REVOLVERS

MODEL 1878 (OFFICER'S MODEL) - 9.1mm cal., solid frame revolver, 6 shot, ejector rod, officer's issue A.

$220	$195	$165	$130	$120	$110	$100

GRADING - PPGS™	100%	98%	95%	90%	80%	70%	60%

MODEL 1886 (TROOPER'S MODEL) - similar to 1878, but larger, trooper issue A.

		$195	$175	$160	$120	$110	$100	$90

ABBEY, GEORGE T.

Previous manufacturer of percussion and breechloading firearms located in Utica, NY from 1845-1852, and Chicago, IL from 1852-1874.

100%	98%	95%	90%	80%	70%	60%	50%	40%	30%	20%	10%

RIFLES: PERCUSSION

PERCUSSION RIFLE

✱ *.44 cal.* - 32 in. octagon barrel.

$605	$550	$470	$415	$370	$340	$305	$275	$250	$220	$195	$165

✱ *.44 cal.* - octagon barrel, brass trimmed.

$770	$735	$695	$605	$550	$485	$450	$405	$365	$330	$275	$220

✱ *.44 cal.* - 31 in. side-by-side barrels.

$1,210	$1,100	$880	$770	$715	$650	$595	$550	$515	$475	$430	$360

✱ *.44 cal.* - O/U, brass trimmed.

$1,485	$1,295	$1,130	$990	$910	$855	$770	$715	$660	$605	$495	$330

ABBEY, F.J. & COMPANY

Previous manufacturer of muzzle and breech loading shotguns and rifles located in Chicago, IL, 1858-1878.

RIFLES: PERCUSSION

PERCUSSION RIFLE - several variations.

$605	$550	$470	$415	$360	$305	$275	$250	$210	$175	$145	$110

SHOTGUNS: PERCUSSION

PERCUSSION SHOTGUN - several variations.

$800	$715	$635	$550	$470	$415	$360	$320	$285	$250	$210	$155

ABBIATICO & SALVINELLI (FAMARS)

Please refer to the Famars di Abbiatico & Salvinelli srl listing.

ACCU-MATCH INTERNATIONAL INC.

Previous handgun and pistol parts manufacturer located in Mesa, AZ circa 1996.

GRADING - PPGS™	100%	98%	95%	90%	80%	70%	60%

PISTOLS: SEMI-AUTO

ACCU-MATCH PISTOL - .45 ACP cal., patterned after the Colt Govt. 1911, competition pistol features stainless steel construction with 5 1/2 in. match grade barrel with 3 ports, recoil reduction system, 8 shot mag., 3 dot sight system. Approx. 160 mfg. 1996 only.

	$795	$700	$625	$550	$450	$375	$325

Last MSR was $840.

ACCU-TEK

Current trademark manufactured by Excel Industries, Inc., located in Chino, CA. Distributor and dealer direct sales.

GRADING - PPGS™	100%	98%	95%	90%	80%	70%	60%

PISTOLS: SEMI-AUTO

MODEL AT-25 - .25 ACP cal., single action, 2 1/2 in. barrel, 7 shot mag. with finger extension, similar design to AT-32, stainless steel, aluminum, or alloy construction with choice of stainless, satin aluminum, or black finish, 11 (Model AT-25AL) or 18 (Model AT-25B, disc.) oz. Mfg. 1992-95.

	$150	$125	$105	$90	$80	$70	$60

Last MSR was $182.

This model was available in satin aluminum (Model AT-25AL) or black (Model AT-25SSB) finish.

MODEL AT-32SS - .32 ACP cal., single action design, 2 1/2 in. barrel, 5 shot mag. with finger extension, alloy (disc. 1991) or stainless steel (new 1992) construction, black synthetic grips, manual safety with firing pin block and trigger disconnect, side mag. release, exposed hammer, satin aluminum (disc. 1991) finish, 16 oz. Mfg. in U.S. 1990-2003.

	$190	$155	$120	$100	$80	$70	$60

Last MSR was $239.

Add $5 for black finish (Model AT-32SSB).

MODEL AT-380II (SS/SSB) - .380 ACP cal., similar to Model AT-32, except has 2 3/4 in. barrel, 6 shot mag., black grips, alloy (disc. 1991) or stainless steel construction, 23.5 oz. New 1990.

MSR $249	$195	$160	$120	$100	$90	$80	$70

Add $5 for black finish (Model AT-380SSB, disc. 1999).

BL-380 - .380 ACP cal., double action only, carbon steel, black finish, compact size, two 5 shot mags., lockable case. Mfg. 1997-99.

	$165	$140	$120	$100	$90	$80	$70

Last MSR was $199.

MODEL HC-380SS - .380 ACP cal., single action semi-auto, stainless steel, 2 1/2 in. barrel, 10 (C/B 1994) or 13* shot mag., manual safety with firing pin block and trigger disconnect, exposed hammer, 26 oz. Mfg. 1993-2003.

	$210	$155	$120				

Last MSR was $249.

Add $5 for black finish (Model HC-380B, mfg. 1995-99).

MODEL AT-9SS - 9mm Para. cal., double action only, stainless steel, 3.2 in. barrel, 8 shot mag., firing pin block with no external safety, black or brushed stainless finish, 3 dot sights adj. for windage, 28 oz. Mfg. 1995-96 only.

	$260	$205	$165				

Last MSR was $317.

BL-9 - 9mm Para. cal., double action only, carbon steel, black finish, ultra compact size, includes two 5 shot mags., and lockable case. Mfg. 1997-2002.

	$195	$150	$120	$100	$90	$80	$70

Last MSR was $232.

CP-9SS - 9mm Para. cal., double action only, stainless steel, black finish, compact size, 8 shot mag. Mfg. 1997-99.

	$220	$165	$125				

Last MSR was $265.

MODEL XL-9SS - 9mm Para. cal, double action only, stainless steel, 3 in. barrel, 5 shot mag., black pebble finished grips, 3 dot adj. sights, 24 oz. Mfg. 1999-2003.

	$215	$170	$125				

Last MSR was $267.

GRADING - PPGS™	100%	98%	95%	90%	80%	70%	60%

MODEL AT-40SS - .40 S&W cal., double action only, 3.2 in. barrel, 7 shot mag., firing pin block with no external safety, black or brushed stainless finish, 3 dot sights adj. for windage, 28 oz. Mfg. 1995-96 only.

	$260	$205	$165

Last MSR was $317.

CP-40SS - .40 S&W cal., 7 shot mag., otherwise similar to CP-9SS. Mfg. 1997-99.

	$220	$165	$125

Last MSR was $265.

MODEL AT-45SS - .45 ACP cal., similar to Model AT-40SS, except has 6 shot mag., stainless only, 28 oz. Mfg. 1996 only.

	$265	$210	$165

Last MSR was $327.

CP-45SS - .45 ACP cal., 6 shot mag., otherwise similar to CP-40SS. Mfg. 1997-99.

	$220	$165	$125

Last MSR was $265.

ACCURACY INTERNATIONAL LTD.

Current rifle manufacturer located in Hampshire, England since 1978. Currently imported and distributed by Accuracy International North America Inc., located in Oak Ridge, TN. Previously imported until 1998 by Gunsite Training Center, located in Paulden, AZ.

RIFLES: BOLT ACTION

In addition to the models listed below, Accuracy International also makes military and law enforcement rifles, including the SR98 Australian, G22 German, and the Dutch SLA.

AE MODEL - .308 Win. cal., similar to AWP Model, 5 shot mag., 24 in. stainless barrel, Harris bipod attachment point, four sling attachment points, Picatinny rail. New 2002.

MSR $2,493	$2,250	$1,950	$1,675	$1,425	$1,200	$1,050	$875

AW MODEL - .243 Win. (new 2000) or .308 Win. cal., precision bolt action featuring 26 in. 1:12 twist stainless steel barrel with muzzle brake, 3 lug bolt, 10 shot detachable mag., green synthetic folding (military/LE only) thumbhole adj. stock, AI bipod, 14 lbs. Importation began 1995.

MSR $4,712	$4,300	$3,350	$2,650	$2,150	$1,800	$1,500	$1,300

Add $376 for AW-F Model (disc. 2002).

AWP MODEL - similar to AW Model, except has 24 in. barrel w/o muzzle brake, 15 lbs. Importation began 1995.

MSR $4,410	$4,025	$3,150	$2,500	$2,000	$1,750	$1,450	$1,250

Add $310 for AWP-F Model (disc. 2002).

Subtract $639 if w/o bipod.

This model is available with many accessories – with everything, the MSR is approx. $6,775.

AWM MODEL (SUPER MAGNUM) - .300 Win. Mag. or .338 Lapua cal., 6 lug bolt, 26 or 27 in. 1:9/1:10 twist stainless steel barrel with muzzle brake, AI bipod, 5 shot mag., 15 1/2 lbs. Importation began 1995.

MSR $5,077	$4,675	$3,800	$2,950	$2,500	$2,000	$1,750	$1,500

Add $324 for AWM-F Model (disc. 2002).

Subtract $641 if w/o bipod.

GRADING - PPGS™	100%	98%	95%	90%	80%	70%	60%

PALMAMASTER - .308 Win. cal., available with either NRA prone or UIT style stock, 30 in. stainless steel fluted barrel, designed for competition shooting, laminate stock. Disc. 2002.

	$2,600	$2,350	$2,100	$1,900	$1,700	$1,500	$1,250

Last MSR was $2,850.

CISMMASTER - .22 BR, 6mm BR, .243 Win., .308 Win., 6.5x55mm, or 7.5x55mm cal., designed for slow and rapid fire international and military shooting competition, 10 shot mag., 2 stage trigger. Disc. 2002.

	$3,175	$2,850	$2,600	$2,350	$2,100	$1,900	$1,700

Last MSR was $3,480.

VARMINT RIFLE - .22 Middlested, .22 BR, .22-250 Rem., .223 Rem., 6mm BR, .243 Win., .308 Win., or 7mm-08 Rem. cal., features 26 in. fluted stainless steel barrel. Mfg. 1997-2002.

	$3,200	$2,725	$2,350	$1,950	$1,675	$1,475	$1,300

Last MSR was $3,650.

AW50 - .50 BMG, advanced ergonomic design, features built-in anti-recoil system, 5 shot mag., adj. third supporting leg, folding stock, 35 lbs. New 1998.

MSR $10,925	$10,250	$8,750	$7,500	$6,250	$4,950	$3,750	$2,900

ACHA

Previous manufacturer located in Eibar, Spain until 1936.

PISTOLS: SEMI-AUTO

MODEL 1916 - 6.35mm cal., semi-auto pistol, 7 shot mag., 1905 Browning copy.

	$250	$185	$130	$90	$80	$70	$60

ATLAS - 6.35mm cal., semi-auto pistol, 6 shot mag., slide marked ATLAS, 1905 Browning copy.

	$200	$165	$125	$95	$75	$65	$50

LOOKING GLASS - 6.35mm cal., semi-auto pistol, 6 shot mag., blue or nickel, 1905 Browning copy, slide marked "Looking Glass," many variations.

	$235	$170	$130	$100	$85	$70	$55

Add 50% for extended grip.

LOOKING GLASS - 7.65mm cal., semi-auto pistol.

	$245	$175	$140	$105	$90	$75	$65

ACME

Previous trade name of Davenport Arms Company Shotguns, Maltby Henley & Co. Revolvers, and Merwin Hulbert & Co. Owl Head Revolvers.

100%	98%	95%	90%	80%	70%	60%	50%	40%	30%	20%	10%

REVOLVERS

SEVEN SHOT REVOLVER - .22 short rimfire cal., single action.

$360	$310	$240	$185	$165	$150	$120	$110	$100	$90	$65	$55

FIVE SHOT REVOLVER - .32 short rimfire cal., single action.

$360	$320	$255	$200	$175	$160	$120	$110	$100	$90	$65	$55

ACME ARMS

Previous trade name for Cornwall Hardware Co., NY.

REVOLVERS

SEVEN SHOT - .22 short rimfire cal., single action.

$275	$250	$210	$185	$165	$155	$140	$125	$110	$90	$85	$75

100%	98%	95%	90%	80%	70%	60%	50%	40%	30%	20%	10%

FIVE SHOT - .32 short Rimfire cal., single action.

| $285 | $255 | $215 | $195 | $175 | $165 | $145 | $120 | $100 | $90 | $85 | $75 |

SHOTGUNS: SxS

SIDE-BY-SIDE - 12 ga., damascus barrel.

| $275 | $240 | $195 | $165 | $145 | $125 | $110 | $95 | $65 | $60 | $50 | $45 |

ACME HAMMERLESS

Previously manufactured by Hopkins & Allen, for Hulbert Brothers, 1893.

REVOLVERS

FIVE SHOT - .32 centerfire cal., double action, top break, non-ejecting.

| $145 | $125 | $100 | $90 | $80 | $70 | $60 | $50 | $40 | $30 | $20 | $15 |

    Also known as Forehand Model 1891, can be hammer or hammerless.

FIVE SHOT - .38 centerfire cal., double action, top break, non-ejecting.

| $145 | $125 | $100 | $90 | $80 | $70 | $60 | $50 | $40 | $30 | $20 | $15 |

    Also known as Forehand Model 1891, can be hammer or hammerless.

ACTION (M.S.)

Previously manufactured by Modesto Santos, located in Eibar, Spain.

GRADING - PPGS™	100%	98%	95%	90%	80%	70%	60%

PISTOLS: SEMI-AUTO

MODEL 1915 - 7.65mm cal., semi-auto pistol (French Military).

| | $245 | $175 | $140 | $105 | $90 | $75 | $65 |

MODEL 1920 - 6.35mm cal., semi-auto pistol, slide marked "Action."

| | $195 | $150 | $110 | $85 | $65 | $45 | $40 |

ACTION ARMS LTD.

Previous firearms importer and distributor until 1994, located in Philadelphia, PA.

Only Action Arms Models AT-84S, AT-88S, and the Model B Sporter will be listed under this heading. Galil, Timberwolf, and Uzi trademarks can be located in their respective sections.

CARBINES: SEMI-AUTO

MODEL B SPORTER - 9mm Para. cal., patterned after the original Uzi Model B Sporter, 16.1 in. barrel, closed breech, thumbhole stock with recoil pad, 10 shot mag., adj. rear sight, 8.8 lbs. Limited importation from China 1994 only.

| | $545 | $475 | $435 | $385 | $335 | $295 | $275 |

                                         Last MSR was $595.

PISTOLS: SEMI-AUTO

AT-84S - 9mm Para. cal., selective double action design, patterned after the CZ-75, 4.8 in. barrel, 15 shot mag., originally introduced in 1985.

| | $470 | $415 | $385 | $360 | $330 | $275 | $220 |

    The AT-84S Series was mfg. in Switzerland by Industrial Technology & Machines A.G. and was sold by Action Arms between June of 1987 and 1989. Serial number range is 01201-06000. No P or H models were ever mfg. in this series (2 or 3 prototypes only).

GRADING - PPGS™	100%	98%	95%	90%	80%	70%	60%

AT-88S - 9mm or .41 Action Express (available early 1990) cal., selective double action design patterned after CZ-75, 4.8 in. barrel, 15 shot (9mm) or 10 shot (.41 AE) mag., can be "cocked and locked," fixed sights, blue metal, walnut grips, 35.3 oz. Introduced in 1987 with limited production samples imported in 1989.

		$500	$450	$395	$360	$330	$275	$220

A very small quantity of AT-88Ss (various configurations) were made by I.T.M. of Switzerland and finishes included all blue, all chrome, or 2-tone. These pistols may exhibit both I.T.M. and A.A.L. markings. More recent manufacture was performed by Sphinx-Muller of Switzerland. These pistols were mfg. by Sphinx-Muller, renamed the AT-2000 Series and previously imported by Sile Distributors.

RIFLES: SLIDE ACTION

TIMBERWOLF - see separate listing in T section.

ACTION LEGENDS MFG., INC.

Current manufacturer, importer, and distributor established during 2004 and located in Houston, TX.

RIFLES

MODEL 888 M1 CARBINE - .22 LR or .30 Carbine cal., 18 in. barrel, mfg. from new original M1 parts and stock and unused GI parts, 10, 15, or 30 shot mag., choice of birch or walnut stock, parkerized finish, metal or wood handguard, 5.5 lbs.

MSR $650		$575	$425	$300	$225	$175	$150	$125

Add $11 for .22 LR cal.
Add $31 for walnut/metal forearm or $47 for walnut/wood forearm.

MODEL 1903 SPRINGFIELD - .30-06 cal. 24 in. barrel, bolt action, mfg. from new and original GI parts, 5 shot mag., parkerized finish, wood stock, canvas sling.

MSR $950		$850	$725	$625	$550	$500	$450	$375

ADAMS

Previously manufactured by Deane, Adams, & Deane, located in London, England.

100%	98%	95%	90%	80%	70%	60%	50%	40%	30%	20%	10%

REVOLVERS: PERCUSSION

MODEL 1851 - .38 cal., double action, 4 1/2 in. barrel.

$1,375	$1,265	$1,100	$990	$855	$745	$690	$605	$550	$440	$385	$330

MODEL 1851 - .44 cal., double action, 6 in. barrel.

$935	$880	$800	$690	$550	$495	$440	$395	$340	$305	$275	$255

MODEL 1851 - .50 cal., Dragoon, double action, 8 in. barrel.

$1,375	$1,265	$1,100	$990	$855	$715	$690	$605	$550	$385	$360	$340

MODEL 1851 - .38 cal., cased with accessories.

$1,760	$1,595	$1,375	$1,100	$990	$910	$825	$745	$660	$605	$550	$525

MODEL 1851 - .44 cal., cased with accessories.

$1,295	$1,155	$990	$880	$770	$690	$635	$550	$440	$385	$360	$330

MODEL 1851 - .50 cal., Dragoon, cased with accessories.

$1,680	$1,485	$1,210	$1,185	$990	$880	$800	$715	$635	$550	$495	$470

100%	98%	95%	90%	80%	70%	60%	50%	40%	30%	20%	10%

ADAMS, JOSEPH

Previous manufacturer located in Birmingham, England.

PISTOLS: FLINTLOCK

OFFICER MODEL - .65 cal., flintlock pistol, Brown Bess.

$2,850	$2,500	$2,250	$2,000	$1,800	$1,600	$1,400	$1,100	$900	$825	$725	$600

ADAMY, GEBR. JAGDWAFFEN

Current manufacturer established circa 1921 and located in Suhl, Germany. Currently imported by New England Custom Guns, Ltd., located in Plainfield, NH. The Adamy gunmaking tradition goes back to 1820, and sixth and seventh generation descendants are currently building guns.

Adamy Jadgwaffen currently specializes in custom-made break open rifles, drillings, and combination guns, SxS and O/U shotguns, and double rifles featuring an Anson & Deeley boxlock action or H&H type sidelocks. Since all guns are made to custom order, please contact New England Custom Gun Service (current importer) directly for more information.

ADCO SALES INC.

Current firearms importer of Diamond shotguns, CZ pistols (Strakonice mfg. only), and accessory manufacturer established circa 1981, and currently located in Woburn, MA. Dealer sales.

GRADING - PPGS™	100%	98%	95%	90%	80%	70%	60%

SHOTGUNS: SEMI-AUTO

All semi-auto shotguns are mfg. in Turkey.

GOLD SERIES - 12 ga., 3 in. chamber, gas operated, 24 (slug gun, non-rifled, includes open sights) or 28 in. VR barrel with 3 choke tubes, semi-humpback style, anodized alloy frame with gold etching, rotary bolt, grey trigger guard, choice of black synthetic or checkered Turkish walnut stock with recoil pad, and forearm. Importation began 2001.

MSR $549		$450	$375	$325	$295	$270	$235	$200

Subtract $50 for black synthetic stock and forearm.

DIAMOND IMPERIAL SERIES - 12 or 20 ga., 3 (20 ga.) or 3 1/2 (12 ga.) in. chamber, 24 (slug, 12 ga.), 26 (20 ga. only), or 28 in. VR barrel with 3 chokes (except slug), features rotary bi-lateral bolt, deluxe checkered stock and forearm. Imported 2003-2004.

		$425	$350	$300	$250	$225	$200	$175

Last MSR was $499.

Subtract $20 for slug variation.

DIAMOND ELITE SERIES - 12 ga., 3 in. chamber, gas operated, similar to Gold Series, except has engraved receiver with choice of 22 (slug), 24, 26, or 28 in. VR barrel with 3 choke tubes, deluxe checkered walnut stock and forearm. Importation began 2001.

MSR $449		$375	$330	$295	$260	$230	$200	$175

DIAMOND PANTHER SERIES - 12 ga., 3 in. chamber, gas operated, similar to Diamond Elite Series, except has black synthetic stock and forearm, 20 (slug), 20 regular, or 28 in. barrel with 3 choke tubes. Importation began 2002.

MSR $399		$335	$280	$260	$240	$225	$200	$175

Add $20 for walnut stock and forearm (new 2003).

GRADING - PPGS™	100%	98%	95%	90%	80%	70%	60%

MARINER MODEL (SILVER SERIES) - 12 ga., 3 in. chamber, gas operated, 20 (slug, new 2003) or 22 in. VR barrel, anodized alloy frame receiver with high strength satin silver metal finish, checkered walnut stock and forearm. Importation began 2002.

MSR $499	$425	$350	$300	$250	$225	$200	$175

SHOTGUNS: SLIDE ACTION

All Adco slide action shotguns are mfg. in Turkey.

GOLD ELITE SERIES - 12 ga., 3 in. chamber, 24 (slug gun, non-rifled, includes open sights) or 28 in. VR barrel with 3 choke tubes, semi-humpback style, anodized alloy frame, choice of black synthetic or checkered Turkish walnut stock with recoil pad, and forearm, 7 lbs. Importation began 2001.

MSR $379	$300	$250	$205	$175	$160	$145	$120

Subtract $60 for black synthetic stock and forearm.

DIAMOND IMPERIAL SERIES - 12 ga., 3 1/2 in. chamber, 28 in. VR barrel with 3 chokes, deluxe checkered stock and forearm. Importation began 2003.

MSR $399	$335	$280	$260	$240	$225	$200	$175

DIAMOND ELITE SERIES - 12 ga., 3 in. chamber, similar to Gold Elite Series, except has engraved receiver with choice of 20 (slug), regular 20 (disc. 2002), 24, or 28 in. VR barrel with 3 choke tubes, deluxe checkered walnut stock and forearm. Importation began 2001.

MSR $359	$280	$240	$200	$175	$160	$145	$120

DIAMOND PANTHER SERIES - 12 ga., 3 in. chamber, similar to Diamond Elite Series, except has black synthetic stock and forearm, 18 1/2 (slug), 20 (disc. 2002), 22 (slug, new 2003), or 28 in. barrel with 3 choke tubes. Importation began 2001.

MSR $239	$200	$165	$145	$135	$115	$105	$95

Subtract $30 for 18 1/2 in. slug variation.

MARINER MODEL - 12 ga., 3 in. chamber, choice of 18 1/2 plain or 22 in VR barrel with chokes, 5 shot mag., black synthetic stock and forearm. Importation began 2003.

MSR $319	$250	$225	$200	$175	$150	$135	$110

ADIRONDACK ARMS COMPANY

Previous manufacturer located in Plattsburgh, NY, 1870-1874.

Magazine loaded repeating rifle, .44 cal., brass or iron frame, later model, may also be marked A.S. Babbitt, Plattsburgh, N.Y., absorbed by Winchester in 1874, then disc.

This rifle was designed in 1870 and patented by Orvill M. Robinson in Upper Jay, NY. It was available in .38 and .44 cal. rimfire versions without a wood forend and had a high cyclic rate of fire. Original models were made in Plattsburgh, NY, at which time A.S. Babbitt became one of several additional partners. In 1872, Robinson was granted a patent for a second model rifle. It was similar to the Model 1870, except a wood forend was added and the operating mechanism was changed considerably. Following these improvements, Mr. Oliver Winchester contacted Mr. Robinson and purchased the entire Robinson company, discontinuing manufacture.

100%	98%	95%	90%	80%	70%	60%	50%	40%	30%	20%	10%

RIFLES

EARLY MODEL - finger holds on hammer.

$2,400	$2,100	$1,750	$1,450	$1,325	$1,200	$1,075	$975	$875	$775	$675	$600

LATE MODEL - action worked by buttons top of receiver mid-section.

$2,200	$1,950	$1,675	$1,300	$1,200	$1,100	$975	$875	$775	$675	$550	$495

GRADING - PPGS™	100%	98%	95%	90%	80%	70%	60%

ADLER

Previously manufactured by Engelbrecht & Wolff located in Blasii, Germany, 1905-1907.

PISTOLS: SEMI-AUTO

SEMI-AUTO PISTOL - 7mm Adler cal., 8 shot mag., cocking lever on top of frame.

	100%	98%	95%	90%	80%	70%	60%
	$5,000	$4,000	$3,000	$2,500	$2,000	$1,495	$1,100

ADVANTAGE ARMS USA, INC.

Previous manufacturer located in St. Paul, MN, and distributed by Wildfire Sports, Inc. also located in St. Paul, MN. Advantage Arms USA, Inc. was sold and moved to Tucson, AZ, with the new name of New Advantage Arms, Inc. (see separate listing).

DERRINGERS

MODEL 422 - .22 LR or 22 Mag. cal., 4 barrel double action derringer, rotating firing pin, this model is patterned after the Mossberg "Brownie," 2 1/2 in. barrel, high grade alloy frame and barrel, 4 shot, available in blue, nickel, or QPQ (heat treated but appears blue) finish, 15 oz. Mfg. 1986-87 only.

			$150	$135	$115	$105	$95	$85	$75

Last MSR was $166.

Add 15% for .22 Mag. cal.
Add $6 for nickel finish.
Add $11 for QPQ finish.

AETNA

Previous trademark manufactured by Harrington & Richardson located in Worchester, MA.

Type: single action revolvers, all of the same general size and configuration, solid frame, spur trigger, so-called "Suicide Specials" during their day.

100%	98%	95%	90%	80%	70%	60%	50%	40%	30%	20%	10%

REVOLVERS

AETNA NO. 2 - .32 rimfire cal., 5 shot.

100%	98%	95%	90%	80%	70%	60%	50%	40%	30%	20%	10%
$330	$275	$215	$185	$170	$155	$145	$120	$100	$85	$75	$55

AETNA NO. 2 1/2 - .32 rimfire cal., 5 shot.

100%	98%	95%	90%	80%	70%	60%	50%	40%	30%	20%	10%
$330	$275	$215	$185	$170	$155	$145	$120	$100	$85	$75	$55

MODEL 1876 - .22 rimfire cal., 7 shot.

100%	98%	95%	90%	80%	70%	60%	50%	40%	30%	20%	10%
$330	$275	$210	$195	$175	$165	$155	$130	$110	$95	$90	$65

MODEL 1876 - .32 rimfire cal., 5 shot.

100%	98%	95%	90%	80%	70%	60%	50%	40%	30%	20%	10%
$330	$275	$210	$175	$165	$155	$145	$120	$105	$90	$75	$55

MODEL 1876 - .38 rimfire cal., 5 shot.

100%	98%	95%	90%	80%	70%	60%	50%	40%	30%	20%	10%
$330	$275	$220	$205	$195	$175	$165	$145	$120	$105	$95	$85

AETNA ARMS COMPANY

Previous manufacturer located in New York, 1869-1883.

Single action pocket revolver, blue or nickel, birdshead grip, copy of S&W Models 1-3, models marked ALLING are worth a slight premium.

REVOLVERS

SEVEN SHOT - .22 rimfire cal.

100%	98%	95%	90%	80%	70%	60%	50%	40%	30%	20%	10%
$250	$235	$210	$195	$175	$165	$155	$130	$110	$95	$90	$65

100%	98%	95%	90%	80%	70%	60%	50%	40%	30%	20%	10%

FIVE SHOT - .32 rimfire cal.

$230	$220	$205	$175	$165	$155	$145	$120	$105	$90	$75	$55

AGNER

Previous trademark manufactured by Saxhoj Products Inc. in Denmark. Imported until 1986 by Beeman Arms, Inc. located in Santa Rosa, CA.

GRADING - PPGS™	100%	98%	95%	90%	80%	70%	60%

PISTOL: SEMI-AUTO

MODEL M 80 - .22 LR cal. only, stainless steel, semi-auto target pistol, new design features unique security key safety feature, adj. French walnut grips, dry fire mechanism, 5.9 in. barrel, 5 shot mag., limited production, 2.4 lbs. Imported 1981-86.

	$1,125	$1,040	$950

Last MSR was $1,295.

Add $100 for left-hand action.

AIR MATCH

Previously imported by Kendall International, located in Paris, KY.

PISTOLS: SINGLE SHOT

AIR MATCH 500 - .22 LR cal. match single shot pistol, target grips, adj. front counterweight, 10 1/2 in. barrel. Imported 1984-86.

$550	$495	$450	$425	$395	$360	$330

Last MSR was $788.

AJAX ARMY

Previously distributed by E.C. Meacham Co., maker unknown, circa 1880s.

100%	98%	95%	90%	80%	70%	60%	50%	40%	30%	20%	10%

REVOLVERS

SINGLE ACTION - .44 rimfire cal., spur trigger, solid frame.

$550	$440	$360	$315	$275	$255	$230	$210	$185	$170	$155	$140

AKRILL, E.

Previously manufactured in France, circa mid 1800s.

RIFLES: FLINTLOCK

FLINTLOCK RIFLE - .69 cal., breech loaded, damascus octagon barrel.

$3,300	$2,750	$2,200	$1,980	$1,460	$1,320	$1,240	$1,075	$935	$800	$745	$660

ALAMO RANGER

Previous manufacturer located in Spain.

GRADING - PPGS™	100%	98%	95%	90%	80%	70%	60%

REVOLVERS

REVOLVER - .38 Spl. cal., Spanish copy of Colt Model 1929.

	$140	$120	$110	$100	$90	$85	$75

ALASKA

Previous trademark manufactured by Hood Firearms Company, Norwich, CT, 1873-1884.

100%	98%	95%	90%	80%	70%	60%	50%	40%	30%	20%	10%

These inexpensive utilitarian revolvers were dubbed "Suicide Specials" in their day.

REVOLVERS

SINGLE ACTION - .22 rimfire cal, 7 shot, spur trigger, solid frame.

$275	$220	$195	$145	$140	$125	$110	$100	$90	$75	$70	$65

FIVE SHOT - .32 Short rimfire cal.

$220	$195	$160	$155	$150	$140	$125	$105	$95	$85	$75	$70

ALASKAN COMMEMORATIVES

The following is a complete chronological listing of Alaskan special and limited editions.

GRADING - PPGS™	100%	Issue Price	Qty. Made

COMMEMORATIVES, SPECIAL EDITIONS, & LIMITED MFG.

For additional information on some of these models, please contact Investment Arms, Inc. (see Trademark Index).

1967 ALASKAN PURCHASE CENTENNIAL WINCHESTER 94 CARBINE - see listing under Winchester Commemoratives.

1967 ALASKA PURCHASE CENTENNIAL CONTENDER - .22 Hornet and .357 Mag. cal., Thompson Contender with 2 barrels, Ser. no. range beginning with C0001.
Issue price is unknown and rarity precludes accurate secondary market pricing.

1976 ALASKA PIPELINE COMMEMORATIVE - .45 LC cal., Colt SAA, cased with Kershaw knife.

	$1,495	$800	801

1981 ALASKA STATE TROOPER 40TH ANNIVERSARY - .357 Mag. cal., Smith & Wesson Model 19-5, 4 in. barrel, cased with belt buckle and patch.

	$850	$500	250

1984 STATE OF ALASKA SILVER ANNIVERSARY EDITION - .44 Mag. cal., Smith & Wesson Model 29-3, 6 in. barrel, cased with bronze brown bear and ivory grips with scrimshaw AK state seal and silver engraving.

	$12,250	$10,000	10

1984 ALASKA SILVER ANNIVERSARY - .44 Mag. cal., Smith & Wesson Model 29-3, 6 in. barrel, cased with gold engraving.

	$1,500	$1,195	300

1984 ALASKA STATEHOOD 25TH ANNIVERSARY - .338 Win. Mag. cal., Winchester Model 70XTR, sterling silver engraving.

	$1,100	$1,080	500

1984 ALASKA 25TH ANNIVERSARY - .357 Mag. cal., Colt Python, 6 in. barrel, engraved brown bear with gold lettering and numbers, cased.

	$1,000	$500	200

1988 IDITAROD "1 OF 1,000" - .44 Mag. cal., Smith & Wesson Model 629-1, 6 in. barrel, cased with laser-etched box, while a thousand were planned, only 500 were mfg.

	$995	$775	500

1988 ALASKA SERIES "TOKLAT" SPECIAL - .45 Win. Mag. cal., LAR mfg. Grizzly Mag., mfg. for Great Northern Guns in Anchorage, AK, cased with plaque.

	$1,800	$1,195	20

GRADING - PPGS™	100%	Issue Price	Qty. Made

1990 ALASKA "GUIDE" SERIES - .454 Casull cal., Freedom Arms mfg. for Great Northern Guns in Anchorage, AK, 5 1/2 in. barrel, Custom Field Grade, engraved handle.

	$1,900	$1,300	25

1991 ALASKA "MASTER GUIDE" SERIES - .454 Casull cal., Freedom Arms mfg. for Great Northern Guns in Anchorage, AK, 5 1/2 in. barrel, Custom Premier Grade, engraved handle.

	$2,200	$1,600	26

1997 ALASKA IDITAROD TRAPPER SILVER ANNIVERSARY EDITION - .45 LC cal., Win. Mod. 94 Trapper rifle, 24Kt. gold engraving, extensive laser carved stock and forearm with musher and dog team, cased.

	$4,950	$2,495	149

1997 ALASKA IDITAROD SINGLE ACTION SILVER ANNIVERSARY EDITION - .45 LC cal., Colt SAA, 24Kt. gold engraving with Iditarod logo and trail scenes, cased.

	$4,950	$2,495	149

1998 ALASKA "KLONDIKE" COMMEMORATIVE GRADE I - .30-30 Win. cal., Winchester Model 94, 24 in. round barrel, roll engraved with Klondike scene on receiver, sponsored by the Alaskan Gun Collectors Association.

	$550	$550	450

✳ *1998 Alaska "Klondike" Commemorative Hi-Grade* - similar to Grade I, except has gold plated receiver.

	$1,000	$1,000	100

1998 ALASKA GOLD RUSH (1898-1998) CENTENNIAL - .38-55 WCF cal., Winchester Model 94 rifle, featuring 24Kt. gold engraving, serial numbered, silver medallion inlayed in stock, and extensive laser carving on stock and forearm, cased. New 1998.

	$6,500	$2,795	25

2000 ALASKA AMERICAN BALD EAGLE LIMITED EDITION - .45-70 Govt., Marlin Model 1895SS lever action rifle, 24Kt. gold etching of American eagle, extensive laser etched stock and forearm with Alaska and eagle scenes, includes special glass display case and leather carrying case.

	N/A	$2,750	10 per state

2000 ALASKA MILLENNIUM RIFLE - .45 LC cal., Winchester Model 1866 Sporting Rifle mfg. by Uberti, cased with silver and gold presentation numbered buckle, features 24Kt. gold engraving with symbols representing events in U.S. history.

	N/A	$2,495	10 per state

2000 ALASKA MILLENNIUM REVOLVER - .44 cal., Colt Model 1860 mfg. by Colt, cased, 24Kt. gold engraved with Statue of Freedom, "Don't Tread On Me" "One Nation, Under God, Indivisible with Liberty and Justice for All."

	N/A	$1,895	10 per state

2001 JOE REDDINGTON SR. "FATHER OF THE IDITAROD" - .45 LC cal., Winchester Model 1866 lever action carbine mfg. by Uberti, 24Kt. gold engraved map of the 1,049 mile Iditarod Trail, "Last Great Race."

	N/A	$2,750	82

2001 80th ANNIVERSARY ANCHORAGE POLICE DEPARTMENT - 12 ga., Remington Model 870 in riot configuration, mfg. by Remington, special combat sights, extended mag., 24Kt. gold engraved receiver, cased with officer's badge, personalized for owner officer, honors the fallen officers of the Anchorage Police Dept. from 1921-2001.

	N/A	$1,895	100

GRADING - PPGS™	100%	Issue Price	Qty. Made

2002 ALASKA TRIBUTE TO OLD GLORY LIMITED EDITION - .45 LC cal., Winchester Model 94, featuring 24Kt. gold engraving, extensive laser carved stock and forearm, commemorates history of American flag, cased.

	N/A	$2,995	10 per state

2002 ALASKA 9-11 LIBERTY RIFLE EDITION - .22 LR cal., semi-auto, featuring 24Kt. gold uncirculated NY quarter placed in buttstock, laser engraved stock with Twin Towers, the Pentagon, and bald eagle, mfg. by Sturm Ruger.

	N/A	$500	500 per state

ALCHEMY ARMS COMPANY

Current manufacturer established during 1999, and located in Auburn, WA. Dealer sales

GRADING - PPGS™	100%	98%	95%	90%	80%	70%	60%

PISTOLS: SEMI-AUTO

SPECTRE STANDARD ISSUE (SI) - 9mm Para., .40 S&W, or .45 ACP cal., single action full size design, hammerless firing mechanism, linear action trigger, keyed internal locking device, aluminum receiver with 4 1/2 in. match grade stainless steel barrel and slide, tactical rail, various silver/black finishes, lowered ejection port, 10 shot double column mag, 32 oz. New 2000.

MSR $749	$675	$585	$525	$465	$415	$350	$300

SPECTRE SERVICE GRADE (SG & SGC) - similar to Spectre Standard Issue, except does not have tactical rail and rounded trigger guard, SGC is Commander style with 4 in. barrel and weighs 27 oz. New 2000, SGC new 2001.

MSR $749	$675	$585	$525	$465	$415	$350	$300

SPECTRE TITANIUM EDITION (TI/TIC) - similar to Spectre Series, except features a titanium slide with aluminum receiver, 22 (TIC is Commander style) or 24 oz. New 2000.

MSR $999	$895	$775	$675	$575	$500	$450	$395

ALDAZABAL

Previously manufactured by Aldazabal, Leturiondo & Cia., located in Spain.

PISTOLS: SEMI-AUTO

SEMI-AUTOMATIC PISTOL - 7.65mm cal., 7 shot, Eibar style.

	$195	$165	$110	$100	$90	$75	$65

ALERT

Previous trademark manufactured by Hood Firearms Company, Norwich, CT, 1873-1881.

These revolvers were dubbed "Suicide Specials" in their day.

100%	98%	95%	90%	80%	70%	60%	50%	40%	30%	20%	10%

REVOLVERS

SINGLE ACTION - .22 rimfire cal., 7 shot, spur trigger, solid frame.

$220	$195	$165	$145	$130	$125	$110	$100	$90	$75	$70	$65

FIVE SHOT - .32 Short rimfire cal.

$170	$165	$160	$155	$150	$140	$125	$105	$95	$85	$75	$70

GRADING - PPGS™	100%	98%	95%	90%	80%	70%	60%

ALESSANDRI, LOU, AND SON

Previous custom rifle manufacturer located in Rehoboth, MA 1975-circa 1998.

Lou Alessandri and Son were noted for their top-quality custom rifles (bolt action and side-by-side). Double rifles started at $18,500, while Express bolt actions started at $5,600. All guns were custom built per individual specifications and a wide variety of special order options were available. In addition to building custom rifles, Lou Alessandri and Son also offered a complete line of high-quality cleaning kits and related accessories. To determine the used value of a Lou Alessandri & Son rifle, the configuration has to be evaluated carefully (caliber, grade of wood, embellishments, and overall desirability).

ALEXANDER ARMS LLC

Current manufacturer located in Radford, VA. Dealer and military sales.

RIFLES: SEMI-AUTO

.50 BEOWULF - .50 Beowulf cal., AR-15 styling, shoots 300-400 grain bullet at approx. 1,800 feet per second, forged upper and lower receiver, 7 shot mag., rotary locking bolt and gas delay mechanism, various configurations include Entry ($1,299 MSR), Over Match kit ($1,390 MSR), Over Match Plus kit ($1,500 MSR), Over Match Tactical kit ($1,605 MSR), Precision Entry ($1,341 MSR), Precision kit ($1,432 MSR), AWS ($1,548 MSR), and Law Enforcement (POR). New 2002.

✳ **Overwatch .50** - similar to .50 Beowulf, except has 24 in. stainless steel barrel, extended range model, shoots 334 grain bullet at approx. 2,000 feet per second, 9.25 lbs. New 2004.

MSR $1,789	$1,550	$1,350	$1,150	$950	$800	$700	$600

GENGHIS - 5.45x39mm cal., M-4 styling with 16 in. stainless steel barrel, forged upper and lower receiver, 10 shot mag., various configurations include Entry ($1,066 MSR), Over Match kit ($1,158 MSR), Over Match Plus kit ($1,267 MSR), Over Match Tactical kit ($1,372 MSR). New 2002.

6.5 GRENDEL - 6.5 Grendel cal., M-4 styling with 18.5 or 20 in. stainless steel barrel, 10 shot mag., various configurations include Entry ($1,471 MSR), Hunter ($1,362 MSR), and AWS ($1,704 MSR). New 2004.

✳ **Overwatch 6.5** - 6.5 Grendel cal., 24 in. stainless steel barrel with match chamber, extremely accurate, forged and hard anodized upper and lower receiver. New 2004.

MSR $1,752	$1,525	$1,325	$1,125	$925	$800	$700	$600

ALEXIA

Previous trademark manufactured by Hopkins & Allen, located in Norwich, CT, 1867-1915.

Also known as: Blue Jacket, Captain Jack, Chichester, Defender, Dictator, Monarch, Mountain Eagle, Hopkins & Allen, Towers Police Safety, and Universal.

100%	98%	95%	90%	80%	70%	60%	50%	40%	30%	20%	10%

REVOLVERS

The revolvers listed below are single action design, solid frame, spur trigger – they were an inexpensive vest pocket pistol issued under numerous names for private companies, octagon barrel.

.22 RIMFIRE - 7 shot.

$165	$160	$155	$145	$130	$125	$110	$100	$90	$75	$70	$65

.32 SHORT RIMFIRE - 5 shot.

$170	$165	$160	$155	$150	$140	$125	$105	$95	$85	$75	$70

100%	98%	95%	90%	80%	70%	60%	50%	40%	30%	20%	10%

SINGLE ACTION .38 SHORT RIMFIRE - 5 shot.

$195	$180	$170	$165	$160	$145	$140	$120	$110	$100	$90	$85

.41 SHORT RIMFIRE - 5 shot.

$220	$210	$205	$195	$180	$170	$160	$145	$125	$110	$100	$90

ALFA

Previous trademark manufactured by Armero Especialistas Reunidas, located in Eibar, Spain, circa 1920.

All revolvers are marked Alfa on grips.

GRADING - PPGS™	100%	98%	95%	90%	80%	70%	60%

REVOLVERS

EARLY MODEL - .32, .38, or .44 cal., copies of S&W No. 2 by O. Hermanos.

	$145	$130	$120	$110	$105	$95	$75

Add 50% for .44 cal.

LATE MODEL - .22 LR, .32 S&W, or .38 S&W cal., copies of Colt Police Positive and S&W Military and Police.

	$160	$150	$130	$120	$110	$100	$90

ALFA PROJ

Current handgun and starter revolver manufacturer established during 1993, and located in Brno, Czech Republic. No current U.S. importation.

Alfa Proj marked handguns are of good quality and utilitarian manufacture, and are currently available in both double action revolvers and semi-auto pistols.

ALKARTASUNA FABRICA DE ARMAS, S.A.

Previous manufacturer located in Guernica, Spain.

PISTOLS: SEMI-AUTO

ALKARTASUNA CARTRIDGE COUNTER - 6.35mm cal., 7 shot, left grip panel cartridge counter, loaded indicator, grip safety.

	$450	$350	$275	$225	$175	$150	$125

ALKARTASUNA RUBY AUTOMATIC - 7.65mm cal., 2 variations - more common is the "Ruby" type, 9 shot, 3 5/8 in. barrel, blue, fixed sights, checkered wood or hard rubber grips, used by French Army in WWI and WWII. Mfg. 1917-22.

	$265	$195	$165	$110	$65	$55	$45

Add 10% for extended barrel.

ALLEN & THURBER

Previous manufacturer/trademark originally located in Grafton, Mass. Ethan Allen started many plants to keep up with expanding business after 1832. Listed below is a chronological order of the firms constituting the family dynasty founded by Ethan Allen.

E. Allen - Grafton, Mass. 1832-1837
Allen & Thurber - Grafton, Mass. 1837-1842
Allen & Thurber - Norwich, Conn. 1842-1847
Allen & Thurber - Worcester, Mass. 1847-1854
Allen, Thurber, & Co. - Worcester, Mass. 1854-1856
Allen & Wheelock - Worcester, Mass. 1856-1865
E. Allen & Co. - Worcester, Mass. 1865-1871
Forehand & Wadsworth - Worcester, Mass. 1871-1890
Forehand Arms Co. - Worcester, Mass. 1890-1902

GRADING - PPGS™	100%	98%	95%	90%	80%	70%	60%

No other 19th-century American firm produced a wider variety of firearms than did Ethan Allen & subsidiaries. In 1902, Forehand Arms Co. was sold to Hopkins & Allen.

Please refer to the Hopkins & Allen section for approximate values.

ALLEN FIREARMS

Previous importer located in Santa Fe, NM importing A. Uberti Firearms until early in 1987. After Allen Firearms closed, Cimarron F.A. Mfg. Co. located in Houston, TX purchased the remaining inventory (in addition to ordering new products under their name).

Allen Firearms was formerly called Western Arms and manufactured both modern and black powder reproduction firearms and accessories patterned after famous older models. Only modern cartridge guns will be shown in this section.

Rather than provide a complete listing of Allen Firearms models, the following rules usually apply. Since Allen Firearms imported A. Uberti firearms, the Uberti section in this text should be referenced for current values regarding models with similar configurations. Collectibility to date has been limited on most Allen Firearms models, and as a rule, up-to-date values on this trademark are established by current importation prices of Uberti firearms. A complete listing of older Allen Firearms models can be found in Blue Book editions Eleven and Twelve. The models listed below are provided since Uberti is not currently manufacturing them.

RIFLES: REPRODUCTIONS

SHARPS/GEMMER SPORTING RIFLE - .45-70 Govt. cal. only, copy of the famous Sharps rifle. Introduced 1985.

	$575	$515	$430	$375	$320	$295	$270

Last MSR was $599.

1979 JUSTIN CENTENNIAL COMMEMORATIVE - includes specially engraved 1866 sporting rifle and 1873 single action revolver (7 1/2 in. barrel) with gold plated parts and inlay. Both guns are chambered for .44-40 cal. Also includes special hand signed pair of Justin boots, serial numbered belt buckle and presentation oak case. All serial numbers are matching.

GRADING - PPGS™	100%	Issue Price	Qty. Made

MODEL 1873 1 of 1,000 - .44-40 cal, special wood, only 1,000 manufactured. Disc. 1985.

	$1,350	$1,500	1,000

ALPHA ARMS INC.

Previous manufacturer located in Flower Mound, TX from 1983-1987.

Retail price included custom hard case.

GRADING - PPGS™	100%	98%	95%	90%	80%	70%	60%

RIFLES: BOLT ACTION

Many special order options including an octagonal barrel, various finishes, special sights, and deluxe wood were available at extra cost on the models listed below. These options, while not listed separately by price, will add value to the prices shown below. All Alpha Arms rifles were manufactured under stringent quality control.

ALPHA CUSTOM - available in most calibers from .222 Rem. through .338 Win. Mag., many other calibers available on special order, 3 position Model 70 type safety, 60 degree bolt, 20 to 24 in. Douglas barrel, limited production, right-hand or left-hand, deluxe checkered Claro walnut standard, approx. 6 lbs. Mfg. 1984-87.

	$1,525	$1,200	$975	$850	$725	$640	$560

Last MSR was $1,735.

GRADING - PPGS™	100%	98%	95%	90%	80%	70%	60%

ALPHA GRAND SLAM - same general specifications as the Alpha Custom, except comes standard with laminated wood stock, fluted bolt and non-glare matte finished metal parts, right-hand or left-hand, approx. 6 1/2 lbs. Mfg. 1985-87.

	$1,200	$950	$875	$750	$650	$600	$525

Last MSR was $1,465.

ALPHA ALASKAN - .308 Win., .350 Rem. Mag., .358 Win., or .458 Win. Mag. cal., action is similar to Alpha Grand Slam, except barrel, receiver, bolt and safety are stainless steel, right-hand or left-hand, Nitex coated small parts, approx. 6 3/4-7 1/2 lbs. Mfg. 1985-87.

	$1,525	$1,200	$975	$850	$725	$640	$560

Last MSR was $1,735.

ALPHA BIG-FIVE - .300 H&H thru .375 H&H or .458 Win. Mag. cal., reinforced stock and decelerator recoil pad. Mfg. 1987 only.

	$1,575	$1,250	$1,050	$895	$750	$640	$560

Last MSR was $1,795.

AMERICA REMEMBERS

Current organization located in Ashland, VA, that privately commissions historical, limited/special editions in conjunction with various manufacturers. Previously located in Mechanicsville, VA until 1999.

America Remembers is a private non-governmental organization dedicated to the remembrance of notable Americans and important historical American events. Along with its affiliates, the Armed Forces Commemorative Society®, American Heroes and Legends®, and the United States Society of Arms and Armour®, the company produces special issue limited edition firearms. America Remembers purchased the antique arms division of the U.S. Historical Society on April 1, 1994. Older U.S.H.S. firearms can be located in the U section of this text.

LIMITED/SPECIAL EDITIONS

Values listed below reflect America Remembers most recent issue prices. These do not necessarily represent secondary marketplace prices. No other values are listed since America Remembers limited edition firearms do not appear that frequently in the secondary marketplace. This is because America Remembers typically sells to consumers directly, without involving normal gun dealers and distributors. Because of this consumer direct sales program, many gun dealers do not have a working knowledge about what America Remembers firearms are currently selling for. The publisher suggests that those people owning America Remembers Limited/Special Editions contact America Remembers (See Trademark Index) for current information, including secondary marketplace liquidity.

Please refer to the *Blue Book of Modern Black Powder Arms* by John Allen & Dennis Adler (now online also) for more information and prices on America Remembers black powder models.

Manufacturer	Model	Edition Limit	Recent Issue Price

HANDGUNS

While not specifically mentioned, the handguns listed below all have various degrees of ornamentation and other embellishments (including some inscriptions).

REVOLVERS: SINGLE ACTION

Manufacturer	Model	Edition Limit	Recent Issue Price
Uberti	American Indian Tribute SAA .45 LC	300	$1,795
Uberti	Buffalo Bill Sesquicentennial SAA .45 LC	500	$1,500
Uberti	Doc Holliday SAA .45 LC	200	$1,795
Colt	Interpol SAA .45 LC	154	$4,500
Uberti	Gene Autry Cowboy Edition SAA	1,000	$1,695
Colt	Gene Autry Premier Colt SAA	100	$5,250

Manufacturer	Model	Edition Limit	Recent Issue Price
Uberti	George Jones SA .45 LC	950	$1,675
Uberti	Herb Jeffries Tribute .45 LC	500	$1,695
Uberti	Hopalong Cassidy Cowboy SAA	950	$1,695
Colt	Hopalong Cassidy Premier Colt SAA	100	$4,500
Colt	James Arness Colt Cowboy SA Revolver	250	$1,895
Colt	Roy Rogers & Dale Evans SAA	250	$3,195
Uberti	Seventh Cavalry SAA Tribute	500	$1,695
Colt	Sitting Bull Colt Cowboy SA Revolver .45 Colt	300	$1,995
Uberti	Tom Mix Tribute SAA .45 LC	200	$1,895
Colt	Tom Mix Premier Edition .45 LC	50	$3,195
Uberti	Travis Tritt SAA .45 LC	500	$1,695
Ruger	Ruger and His Guns Classic .44 Magnum	400	$1,995
Ruger	Ruger and His Guns Premier .44 Magnum	100	$3,595
Uberti	Clayton Moore SAA .45 LC	500	$1,695
Colt	Geronimo Colt Cowboy SA .45 LC	100	$1,995
Colt	Heroic Indian Leaders SAA .44 Spl.	50	$3,195
Navy Arms	Frank & Jesse James Tribute .45 LC Schofield Cavalry Model	100	$1,695
Colt	Elvis Western Tribute Colt Cowboy SA .45 LC	300	$1,995
Colt	Roy Rogers "Happy Trails to You" Colt Cowboy SA .45	250	$2,195
Colt	Texas Ranger Tribute Colt Cowboy SA .45 LC	300	$2,195
Colt	West Point Bicentennial Colt Cowboy SA .45	300	$2,195
Colt	Gene Autry Tribute Colt Cowboy	150	$2,195
Colt	U.S. Cavalry Association Tribute Colt Cowboy	300	$2,195
S&W	Native American Legends Tribute Model 3 Schofield .45	100	$3,195
Colt	Gen. George S. Patton, Jr. SA .45	500	$2,295

SEMI-AUTOS: .45 ACP

Manufacturer	Model	Edition Limit	Recent Issue Price
Colt	Army Air Corp. Tribute	300	$1,795
Colt	American Eagle Tribute	2,500	$2,195
Colt	American Patriot Tribute	N/A	$1,695
Colt	Army Air Forces Tribute	500	$1,500
Colt	Audie Murphy Tribute	1,000	$1,795
Colt	Chuck Yeager Tribute	1,000	$1,895
Colt	Ernie Irvan Tribute	250	$1,895
Colt	Leatherneck Tribute Pistol	300	$1,895
Colt	Navajo Code Talkers Yellowhorse (w/knife)	300	$3,000
Auto-Ordnance	Pacific Naval Tribute	500	$1,500
Colt	Pearl Harbor Tribute Pistol	500	$1,795
Colt	Purple Heart Tribute Pistol	250	$1,695
Colt	VJ-Day Tribute	250	$1,495
Colt	West Point Tribute	300	$1,995
Colt	West Point WWII Tribute Pistol	500	$1,995
Colt	Wings of Freedom-USAF 50th Anniversary Tribute	250	$1,695
Colt	VFW 100th Anniversary	500	$1,695
Colt	Special Operations Associations Tribute	250	$1,695
Colt	Spirit of America Tribute Pistol	911	$1,595
Colt	Berlin Airlift Golden Anniversary Tribute	250	$1,595
Colt	Elvis Tribute Pistol	300	$1,895
Colt	VFW Korean War Tribute	300	$1,695
Colt	NRA Tribute Pistol	300	$1,995
Colt	U.S. Army 20th Century Tribute	300	$1,995
Colt	VFW Vietnam War Tribute	300	$1,995
Colt	Colt Patriotic Tribute	500	$1,995

Manufacturer	Model	Edition Limit	Recent Issue Price
Colt	Gen. George S. Patton Jr. Tribute	500	$2,195
Colt	WWII Golden Anniversary Marine Pacific Tribute	500	$1,500
Beretta	Operation Iraqi Freedom Tribute 92FS Semi-Auto 9mm	300	$2,195
Browning	Special Operations Association Vietnam Tribute Browning Hi-Power Captain	250	$1,795
Colt	Colt Legacy Tribute	300	$1,995
Colt	Ranger Spirit Tribute	300	$1,995
Colt	Air Force Academy 50th Anniversary Tribute	300	$1,995
Colt	Navajo Code Talkers Tribute	300	$1,995

RIFLES

Manufacturer	Model	Edition Limit	Recent Issue Price
Winchester	Model 94 (.22 LR) King Richard Tribute	200	$1,495
Winchester	Model 94 (.30-30) American Eagle Tribute	500	$1,695
Winchester	Model 94 (.30-30) American Wildlife Tribute	300	$1,495
Winchester	Model 94 (.30-30)B. Bill Sesqui. Tribute	300	$1,895
Winchester	Model 94 (.30-30) Babe Ruth Tribute	300	$1,895
Winchester	Model 94 (.30-30) Bruce Boxleitner Tribute	100	$1,895
Winchester	Model 94 (.30-30) California Sesquicentennial	150	$1,495
Winchester	Model 94 (.30-30) C.M. Russell Tribute	300	$1,895
Winchester	Model 94 (.30-30) Cherokee Trail of Tears Tribute	300	$1,795
Winchester	Model 94 (.30-30) Cochise Tribute Rifle	300	$1,695
Winchester	Model 94 (.30-30) Dale Berry Tribute	300	$1,850
Winchester	Model 94 (.30-30) Davey Allison Tribute	500	$1,695
Winchester	Model 94 (.30-30) Deer Hunter Tribute	300	$1,795
Winchester	Model 94 (.30-30) Dennis Weaver Tribute	100	$1,895
Winchester	Model 94 (.30-30) Elvis and Graceland Tribute	1,000	$1,895
Winchester	Model 94 (.30-30) Field & Stream Tribute	300	$1,595
Winchester	Model 94 (.30-30) Wrangler Ft. Worth Tribute	300	$1,850
Winchester	Model 94 (.30-30) Gene Autry Tribute	300	$2,100
Winchester	Model 94 (.30-30) George Jones Tribute	300	$1,695
Winchester	Model 94 (.30-30) Great North American Rodeo	500	$1,595
Winchester	Model 94 (.30-30) Heroic Indian Leaders Tribute	300	$1,650
Winchester	Model 94 (.30-30) Hopalong Cassidy Tribute	500	$1,850
Winchester	Model 94 (.30-30) Leatherneck Sportsman Tribute	300	$1,895
Winchester	Model 94 (.30-30) Roy Rogers Tribute	300	$2,100
Winchester	Model 94 Roy Rogers & Gabby Hayes .45 LC	300	$1,795
Winchester	Model 94 (.30-30) Rusty Wallace Tribute	1,000	$1,895
Winchester	Model 94 (.30-30) Tennessee Ernie Ford Tribute	100	$1,895
Winchester	Model 94 (.30-30) Terry Labonte Tribute	1,000	$1,895
Winchester	Model 94 (.30-30) Texas Motor Speedway	500	$1,795
Winchester	Model 94 (.30-30) Ty Murray Tribute	500	$1,695
Winchester	Model 94 (.30-30) U.S. Cavalry Association Tribute	300	$1,850
Winchester	Model 94 (.30-30) Tribute to Yellowstone National Park	125	$1,695
Marlin	Model 336CS (.30-30) Whitetail Trophy	500	$1,595
Marlin	Model 336CS (.30-30) Whitetail Hunter Tribute	300	$1,395
Marlin	Model 336CS (.30-30) Whitetail Deer Trophy	300	$1,595
Marlin	Model 1894 (.45 LC) White Buffalo Spirit Tribute	300	$2,100
Winchester	Model 94 (.45 LC) American Cowboy Tribute	200	$3,195
Winchester	Model 94 (.45 LC) American Indian Tribute	300	$1,250
Winchester	Model 94 (.45 LC) Citation Bass Tribute	300	$1,495
Winchester	Model 94 (.45 LC) Darrell Waltrip 25th Anniversary	750	$1,795
Winchester	Model 94 (.45 LC) Monte Hale Tribute	300	$1,850
Winchester	Model 94 (.45 LC) Rex Allen Tribute	500	$1,595
Winchester	Model 94 (.45 LC) Clint Walker Tribute	300	$1,850

Manufacturer	Model	Edition Limit	Recent Issue Price
Winchester	Model 92 (.45 LC) Lawmen & Outlaws of the Wild West	300	$1,850
Marlin	Model 336CS (.30-30) American Hunter Tribute	300	$1,695
Uberti	Model 1873 (.44-40) Buffalo Bill's Wild West Tribute	300	$1,995
Uberti	Model 1873 (.44-40) Scouts of the Western Frontier	300	$1,995
Uberti	Model 1873 (.44-40) Wild West Exhibition Shooters Tribute	300	$1,795
Uberti	Model 1873 (.44-40) Wild West Frontier Tribute	125	$1,695
Winchester	Model 94 (.30-30) Wrangler Gene Autry, Smiley Burnette, & Pat Buttram Tribute	300	$1,895
Winchester	Model 94 (.30-30) Iron Eyes Cody Tribute	300	$1,795
Winchester	Mode 94 (.30-30) James Arness Tribute	250	$1,895
Winchester	Model 94 (.30-30) NRA Tribute	300	$1,850
Winchester	Model 94 (.30-30) Nolan Ryan Tribute	324	$1,850
Winchester	Model 94 (.30-30) Tribute to the Rough Riders	300	$1,695
Winchester	Model 94 (.30-30) Richard Boone Tribute	250	$1,895
Winchester	Model 94 (.30-30) Richard Farnsworth Tribute	100	$1,895
Winchester	Model 94 (.30-30) Texas Ranger 175th Anniversary Tribute	300	$1,950
Winchester	Model 94 (.30-30) Texas Trophy Hunters	250	$1,695
Uberti	Henry (.44-40) A Nation Reunited: Civil War Tribute	300	$1,895
Uberti	Model 1873 (.45 LC) Wyatt Earp Sesquicentennial Tribute	300	$1,995
Marlin	Model 1894 (.45 LC) Cowboy Limited Roy Rogers/Dale Evans & Dusty Rogers Tribute	300	$1,895
Winchester	Model 94 (.30-30) Audie Murphy Tribute	250	$1,895
Winchester	Model 94 (.30-30) Frederic Remington Art Museum Tribute	300	$1,695
Winchester	Model 94 (.30-30) National Cowboy Hall of Fame	300	$1,895
Winchester	Model 94 (.30-30) Travis Tritt Tribute	300	$1,850
Winchester	Model 94 (.30-30) 101 Ranch Western Tribute	300	$1,850
Uberti	Model 1873 (.44-40) Heroes of Texas Tribute	300	$2,195
Uberti	Model 1866 (.44-40) Yellow Boy American Buffalo Tribute	300	$1,995
Uberti	Henry Civil War Cavalry Leaders Tribute (.44-40)	300	$2,195
Uberti	Henry Mort Künstler Civil War Tribute (.44-40)	300	$2,195
Uberti	Henry Quanah Parker Red River War Tribute (.44-40)	300	$2,195
Uberti	Henry Sons of Confederate Veterans (.44-40)	300	$2,295
Uberti	Henry (.44-40) West Point Civil War Tribute	300	$1,995
Uberti	Henry (.44-40) West Point Civil War Union Leaders	500	$2,295
Uberti	Henry (.44-40) West Point Civil War Confederate Leader	500	$2,295
Winchester	Model 94 (.30-30) Progressive Farmer/Rural Sportsman Whitetail Deer Tribute	300	$1,695
Winchester	Model 94 (.30-30) Virginia Deer Hunters Whitetail Deer Tribute	50	$1,495
Uberti	Henry (.44-40) Gettysburg Tribute	500	$2,295
Uberti	American Indian Tribute Henry (.44-40)	500	$2,295
Uberti	Chisholm Trail Tribute Model 1873 Sporting	300	$2,195
Uberti	Legends of the Old West Tribute Model 1866 Yellow Boy (.44-40)	500	$1,995
Winchester	Red Man 100th Anniversary Tribute Model 94 (.30-30)	100	$1,895
Springfield Armory	NRA Tribute M1 Garand Rifle (.30-06)	300	$2,895
Browning	Mule Deer Foundation Tribute BAR (.30-06)	300	$2,195

Manufacturer	Model	Edition Limit	Recent Issue Price
Browning	BAR Semi-Auto (.30-06) Rocky Mt. Elk Tribute	300	$2,195
Winchester	Model 94 Frank McCarthy American West Tribute (.30-30)	300	$1,895
Winchester	Model 94 Clayton Moore Tribute (.30-30)	300	$1,995
Springfield Armory	Leatherneck Tribute M1 Garand (.30-06)	300	$2,895

SHOTGUNS

Manufacturer	Model	Edition Limit	Recent Issue Price
Remington	Model 870 Wingmaster (12 ga.) Ned & Dale Jarrett	750	$1,595
SIACE	Law & Order (12 ga.) double-hammered shotgun	100	$3,000
Remington	Model 870 (12 ga.) Remington Deer Hunter Tribute	300	$1,495
Remington	Model 870 (12 ga.) Remington Waterfowl Tribute	300	$1,795
Browning	Model BPS (12 ga.) Texas Sportsman Tribute	250	$1,495
Remington	Model 870 (12 ga.) Wingmaster Ducks Unlimited Tribute	300	$1,795
Remington	Model 11-87 (12 ga.) Ducks Unlimited Flyways Tribute	300	$1,995
Baikal	John Wayne Coach Shotgun (12 ga.)	2,500	$1,795
Ruger	Red Label (20 ga.) Wildlife Forever 15th Anniversary Tribute	100	$2,495
Remington	Nat'l Wild Turkey Fed. 30th Anniversary Tribute Model 11-87 Premier (12 ga.)	300	$1,995

AMERICAN ARMS

Previous manufacturer located in Garden Grove, CA.

GRADING - PPGS™	100%	98%	95%	90%	80%	70%	60%

PISTOLS: SEMI-AUTO

EAGLE 380 - .380 ACP cal. only, stainless steel semi-auto, copy of Walther PPK/S, 6 shot mag., 3 1/4 in. barrel, limited production, 20 oz.

	100%	98%	95%
	$400	$250	$215

Last MSR was $289.

Add $25 for case.
Add $50 for case and belt buckle.
Add $25 for black teflon finish (disc. 1985).

AMERICAN ARMS CO.

Previous manufacturer located in Boston, MA from 1870-1901 and Milwaukee, WI. from 1893-1904. American Arms Co. was acquired by Marlin in 1901.

100%	98%	95%	90%	80%	70%	60%	50%	40%	30%	20%	10%

DERRINGERS

O/U DESIGN - .22 Short R.F., .32 Short R.F., or .41 Short R.F. cal., Wheeler Pat. Action, brass frame, spur trigger.

100%	98%	95%	90%	80%	70%	60%	50%	40%	30%	20%	10%
$800	$750	$700	$650	$575	$500	$420	$360	$300	$225	$160	$110

SHOTGUNS: SxS

HAMMERLESS MODEL - 12 ga., semi-hammerless.

100%	98%	95%	90%	80%	70%	60%	50%	40%	30%	20%	10%
$600	$550	$500	$450	$350	$275	$225	$175	$150	$125	$100	$75

WHITMORE PATENT - 10 or 12 ga., hammerless, checkering.

100%	98%	95%	90%	80%	70%	60%	50%	40%	30%	20%	10%
$685	$625	$575	$520	$460	$400	$340	$270	$200	$150	$125	$100

Add 10% for 10 ga. (2 7/8 in. chambers).

SINGLESHOT - 12 ga., semi-hammerless, damascus barrel.

100%	98%	95%	90%	80%	70%	60%	50%	40%	30%	20%	10%
$260	$225	$200	$175	$150	$125	$90	$70	$50	$40	$30	$20

AMERICAN ARMS, INC.

Previous importer and manufacturer located in North Kansas City, MO, until 2000. American Arms imported various Spanish shotguns (Indesal, Lanber, Norica, and Zabala Hermanos), Italian shotguns including F. Stefano, several European pistols and rifles, and Sites handguns (1990-2000) mfg. in Torino, Italy. This company also manufactured several pistols in North Kansas City, MO. For more information and pricing on Norica airguns previously imported by American Arms, please refer to the *Blue Book of Airguns* by Dr. Robert Beeman & John Allen (now online also).

In late 2000, TriStar Sporting Arms, Ltd. acquired the parts inventory for some models previously imported by American Arms, Inc. Original warranties from American Arms do not apply to TriStar Sporting Arms, Ltd.

COMBINATION GUNS

RS COMBO - choice of .222 Rem. or .308 Win. rifle barrel under 12 ga. barrel, engraved boxlock frame with antique silver finish, DTs, 24 in. VR barrels with shotgun choke tubes, rifle sights, grooved for scope mounting, Monte Carlo stock, 7 lbs. 14 oz. Imported 1989 only.

$675	$595	$550	$495	$450	$420	$385

Last MSR was $749.

PISTOLS: SEMI-AUTO

MODEL TT-9MM TOKAREV - 9mm Para. cal., semi-auto single action, 4 1/2 in. barrel, 9 shot mag., hammer block external safety, 31 oz. Imported 1988-89 only.

$250	$230	$210	$195	$180	$170	$160

Last MSR was $289.

This model is patterned after the Tokarev action and was made from machined steel parts in Yugoslavia.

MODEL EP-380 - .380 ACP cal., semi-auto double action, stainless steel, 3 1/2 in. barrel, 7 shot mag., wood checkered grips, adj. rear sight, 25 oz. Imported 1988-90 only.

$375	$325	$250

Last MSR was $449.

This model was made in West Germany.

MODEL PK-22 CLASSIC - .22 LR cal., semi-auto double action, styled after Govt. .45 ACP, 3 1/3 in. barrel, 8 shot finger extension mag., black polymer grips, 22 oz. Mfg. 1988-96.

$165	$140	$115	$100	$90	$80	$70

Last MSR was $199.

This model was made in North Kansas City, MO. It has patented safety features such as external hammer block and internal blocking of the firing pin until the trigger is pulled.

MODEL CX-22 CLASSIC - .22 LR cal., style patterned after Walther PPK, 3 1/3 in. barrel, 8 shot finger extension mag., 22 oz. Mfg. 1990-95.

$175	$145	$125	$110	$100	$90	$80

Last MSR was $213.

This model was made in North Kansas City, MO. It has patented safety features such as external hammer block and internal blocking of the firing pin until the trigger is pulled.

✳ *CXC-22* - similar to CX-22 Classic, except has chrome slide. Mfg. in 1990 only.

$170	$150	$125	$110	$100	$90	$80

Last MSR was $189.

GRADING - PPGS™	100%	98%	95%	90%	80%	70%	60%

MODEL PX-22/25 CLASSIC - .22 LR or .25 ACP (mfg. 1991 only) cal., compact variation of the Model CX-22, 2 3/4 in. barrel, 7 shot finger extension mag., 15 oz. New 1989, PX-25 was mfg. 1991 only, PX-22 was disc. 1995.

	$175	$145	$125	$110	$100	$90	$80

Last MSR was $206.

This model was made in North Kansas City, MO. It has patented safety features such as external hammer block and internal blocking of the firing pin until the trigger is pulled.

MODEL P-98 CLASSIC - .22 LR cal., semi-auto double action patterned after Walther P.38, 5 in. barrel, 8 shot mag., blue/black finish, grooved wraparound grips, 26 oz. Mfg. 1990-96.

	$170	$145	$125	$110	$100	$90	$80

Last MSR was $209.

ESCORT - .380 ACP cal., double action only, 3 3/8 in. barrel, 7 shot mag., unique thin profile, matte stainless steel, soft polymer grips, polygonal rifling, 19 oz. Mfg. 1995-97.

	$285	$230	$200	$185	$170	$160	$150

Last MSR was $349.

SABRE - while this model was advertised, it was never mfg.

SPECTRE - 9mm Para., .40 S&W (mfg. 1991 only), or .45 ACP (new 1993) cal., semi-auto double action, 6 in. barrel with polygonal rifling, 30 shot mag., ambidextrous safety, decocking lever, adj. sights, 4 1/2 lbs., mfg. in Italy by Sites. Imported 1990-93.

	$500	$325	$275	$240	$200	$185	$170

Last MSR was $429.

Add $28 for .45 ACP cal.

This model was previously imported by F.I.E. located in Hialeah, FL (1989-1990).

AUSSIE SEMI-AUTO - 9mm Para. or .40 S&W cal., semi-auto double action, polymer frame with nickeled steel slide and 4 3/4 in. barrel, 10 shot mag., features 5 safeties, open slide after last shot, 23 oz. Limited importation from Spain 1996 only.

	$350	$250	$225	$200	$185	$170	$160

Last MSR was $425.

REVOLVERS: SAA

REGULATOR MODEL - .357 Mag., .44-40, or .45 LC cal., 4 3/4, 5 1/2 (new 1993), or 7 1/2 in. barrel, reproduction of the Colt Peacemaker, featuring brass trigger guard and back strap, fixed sights, half-cock and hammer block safeties, blade front, grooved rear sights, color case hardened frame and blue barrel/cylinder or nickel finish (imported 1999 only in .45 LC cal.), walnut grips, 35 oz. Mfg. by Uberti. Imported 1992-2000.

	$270	$230	$200	$185	$170	$160	$150

Last MSR was $320.

Add $55 for nickel finish (disc. 1999).
Add $40 for dual cylinder set (.44-40/.44 Spl. or .45 LC/.45 ACP). Disc. 1998.

✳ *Regulator Deluxe* - similar to Regulator Model, except .45 LC cal. only, all blue charcoal finish (mfg. 1996-97) or color case hardened frame (new 1998), case hardened (pre-1993) or blue (post-1993) steel trigger guard and back strap. Importation disc. 1992, resumed 1994-2000.

	$315	$260	$215	$190	$170	$160	$150

Last MSR was $365.

Add $70 for dual cylinder set (.44-40/.44 Spl. or .45 LC/.45 ACP). Disc. 1992.

GRADING - PPGS™	100%	98%	95%	90%	80%	70%	60%

❋ *Buckhorn* - .44 Mag cal., 4 3/4, 6, or 7 1/2 in. barrel, otherwise similar to Regulator Model, 44 oz. Imported 1993-96.

	$305	$255	$205	$185	$170	$160	$150

Last MSR was $379.

Add $10 for Target variation (flattop and adj. rear sight). Imported 1994 only.

❋ *Storekeeper* - .44-40 WCF or .45 LC cal., 4 in. barrel, smooth walnut curved grips, nickel or B/H nickel finish, 31 oz. Imported 1999 only.

	$320	$265	$215	$190	$170	$160	$150

Last MSR was $375.

Add $44 for B/H nickel finish.

UBERTI BISLEY - .45 LC cal., patterned after the Colt Bisley, case hardened steel frame, 4 3/4, 5 1/2, or 7 1/2 in. barrel with fixed sights, hammer block safety. Imported 1997-98 only.

	$425	$340	$275	$215	$190	$170	$160

Last MSR was $475.

UBERTI .454 SAA - .454 cal., 6 SR or 7 1/2 in. top-ported barrel, hammer block safety, satin nickel finish, custom hardwood grips, wide trigger, adj. rear sight. Imported 1996-97 only.

	$750	$625	$550	$495	$465	$435	$375

Last MSR was $869.

SILVERADO - .357 Mag., .44 Mag., or .45 LC cal., 4 3/4, 5 1/2, or 7 1/2 barrel, brushed nickel finish, unfluted cylinder, laminated charcoal grips. Mfg. by Uberti, imported 1999- 2000.

	$345	$285	$220	$195	$170	$160	$150

Last MSR was $409.

RIFLES: O/U

SILVER EXPRESS - 8x57JRS or 9.3x74R cal., O/U boxlock design, gold SNT, monoblock 28 in. separated barrels, manual safety, silver finished receiver with light engraving, skipline checkered walnut stock and forearm, approx. 7 3/4 lbs. Limited importation 1999-2000.

	$1,800	$1,625	$1,500	$1,375	$1,250	$1,125	$1,000

Last MSR was $1,949.

RIFLES: REPRODUCTIONS

MODEL 1860 HENRY REPLICA - .44-40 WCF or .45 LC cal., 24 1/4 in. blue or white finish (new 1999) barrel, 9 1/4 lbs. Mfg. by Uberti, importation disc. 2000.

	$835	$625	$525	$425	$360	$320	$260

Last MSR was $940.

Add $50 for white barrel finish.

❋ *Henry Trapper* - similar to the Henry Replica, except has 18 1/2 in. barrel, 8 lbs. Imported 1999-2000.

	$835	$625	$525	$425	$360	$320	$260

Last MSR was $940.

Add $50 for white barrel finish.

MODEL 1866 WINCHESTER REPLICA - .44-40 WCF or .45 LC cal., 19 (Carbine) or 24 1/4 (Rifle) in. barrel, approx. 8 lbs. Mfg. by Uberti, importation disc. 2000.

	$650	$550	$460	$375	$300	$250	$200

Last MSR was $730.

Subtract $20 for Carbine variation (Yellowboy).

GRADING - PPGS™	100%	98%	95%	90%	80%	70%	60%

MODEL 1873 WINCHESTER REPLICA - .44-40 WCF or .45 LC cal., 24 1/4 or 30 (new 1999) in. octagon barrel, case colored receiver, approx. 8 1/4 lbs. Mfg. by Uberti, importation disc. 2000.

	$775	$625	$525	$425	$360	$320	$260

Last MSR was $860.

Add $80 for 30 in. barrel.

* **Model 1873 Deluxe Winchester Replica** - similar to Model 1873 Winchester Replica, except has better quality checkered pistol grip stock and forearm. Disc. 1997.

	$1,100	$775	$625	$500	$425	$350	$275

Last MSR was $1,299.

MODEL 1885 SINGLE SHOT HIGH WALL - .45-70 Govt. cal., 28 in. round barrel, color case hardened frame, 8.82 lbs. Mfg. by Uberti, imported 1998-2000.

	$700	$575	$495	$395	$350	$300	$260

Last MSR was $810.

SHARPS CAVALRY CARBINE - .45-70 Govt. cal., 22 in. heavy round barrel, case colored action, blue barrel with adj. rear ladder sight, DST, unchecked walnut stock and forearm, 8 lbs. 3 oz. Imported 1999-2000.

	$625	$525	$450	$400	$360	$330	$300

Last MSR was $660.

SHARPS FRONTIER CARBINE - similar to Cavalry Carbine, except has regular barrel with barrel band and single trigger, 7 lbs. 13 oz. Imported 1999-2000.

	$615	$535	$450	$400	$360	$330	$300

Last MSR was $675.

SHARPS 1874 SPORTING RIFLE - .45-70 Govt. or .45-120 black powder cartridge, 28 in. octagon barrel, checkered walnut stock and forearm, DST, 9 lbs. 3 oz. Imported 1999-2000.

	$635	$535	$450	$400	$360	$330	$300

Last MSR was $685.

* **Sharps 1874 Deluxe Sporting Rifle** - similar to Sharps 1874 Sporting Rifle, except has brown barrel finish. Imported 1999-2000.

	$650	$545	$460	$410	$360	$330	$300

Last MSR was $705.

RIFLES: SEMI-AUTO

MODEL ZCY 308 - .308 Win. cal., gas operated semi-auto AK-47 type action, Yugoslavian mfg. Imported 1988 only.

	$775	$650	$550	$450	$400	$375	$350

Last MSR was $825.

MODEL AKY 39 - 7.62x39mm cal., gas operated semi-auto AK-47 type action, teakwood fixed stock and grip, flip up Tritium night front sight and rear, Yugoslavian mfg. Imported 1988-89 only.

	$650	$550	$495	$440	$395	$350	$300

Last MSR was $559.

This model was supplied with sling and cleaning kit.

* **Model AKF 39 Folding Stock** - 7.62x39mm cal., folding stock variation of the Model AKY-39. Imported 1988-89 only.

	$725	$625	$550	$475	$425	$375	$325

Last MSR was $589.

GRADING - PPGS™	100%	98%	95%	90%	80%	70%	60%

EXP-64 SURVIVAL RIFLE - .22 LR cal., semi-auto, takedown rifle stores in oversize synthetic stock compartment, 21 in. barrel, 10 shot mag., open sights, receiver grooved for scope mounting, cross bolt safety, 40 in. overall length, 7 lbs. Imported 1989-90 only.

	$150	$135	$125	$115	$105	$95	$85

Last MSR was $169.

MINI-MAX - .22 LR cal., semi-auto, 18 3/4 in. barrel, wood or black synthetic stock, 10 shot mag., adj. rear sight, 4 1/3 lbs. Imported in 1990 only.

	$85	$75	$65	$55	$45	$40	$35

Last MSR was $99.

Add $6 for wood stock.

SM 64 TD SPORTER - .22 LR cal., semi-auto, takedown barrel, 21 in. barrel, checkered walnut finished hardwood stock and forend, hooded front sight and adj. rear sight, 7 lbs. Imported 1989-90 only.

	$130	$115	$105	$95	$85	$75	$65

Last MSR was $149.

SHOTGUNS: O/U

American Arms imported Spanish shotguns manufactured by Zabala Hermanos, Lanber, and Indesal. Italian shotguns were also imported and mfg. by Stefano Fausti (Models Silver, Waterfowl, and Turkey Special). American Arms also imported Franchi Black Magic semi-auto and O/U shotguns until 1998. These shotguns will appear under the Franchi section in this text. Older Diarm models have been listed below.

LINCE - 12 or 20 ga., 3 in. chambers, boxlock with Greener crossbolt, various barrel lengths and chokings, available in either blue or shiny chrome finish, SST, VR, ejectors. Imported 1986 only.

	$510	$400	$380	$360	$340	$320	$300

Last MSR was $610.

Add $70 for choke tubes.

SILVER MODEL - 12 or 20 ga. only, similar to Lince Model, except has brushed aluminum finished receiver, no engraving. Imported 1986-87 only.

	$495	$450	$390	$360	$330	$300	$285

Last MSR was $545.

Add $50 for multi-chokes.

SILVER I - similar to Silver Model, except also available in 28 ga. or .410 bore (both new 1988), single selective trigger became standard in 1988, extractors, engraved frame, fixed chokes, recoil pad. Imported 1986-2000.

	$535	$430	$350	$300	$285	$270	$255

Last MSR was $649.

Add $30 for 28 ga. or .410 bore.
Engraved frame became standard in 1987.

SILVER II - similar to Silver I, except is supplied with choke tubes, deluxe walnut, and ejectors, 16 ga. new 1999. Imported 1987-2000.

	$660	$560	$475	$400	$360	$330	$300

Last MSR was $769.

Add $46 for 28 ga. or .410 bore (fixed chokes only).

✳ *Silver II Lite (Silver Upland Lite)* - 12, 20, or 28 ga. (disc. 1995), 3 in. chambers (except for 28 ga.), 26 in. VR barrels, with Franchoke tubes (except for 28 ga.), SST, ejectors, engraved frame with antique silver finish, checkered walnut stock and forearm, 5 3/4-6 1/4 lbs. Imported 1994-98.

	$800	$660	$550	$485	$440	$400	$360

Last MSR was $925.

GRADING - PPGS™	100%	98%	95%	90%	80%	70%	60%

✳ **Small Gauge Combo** - includes either 20/28 ga. (new 1997) or 28 ga./.410 bore barrels. Imported 1989-2000.

	$1,080	$925	$750	$625	$550	$495	$450

Last MSR was $1,239.

SILVER LITE - 12 or 20 ga., 2 3/4 in. chambers, boxlock action, 26 in. vent. barrels with VR and choke tubes, blue alloy receiver, SST, ejectors, gold trigger, checkered walnut stock and forearm, 5 lbs. 14 oz. or 6 (12 ga.) lbs., mfg. by Lanber. Imported 1990-92.

	$625	$535	$460	$400	$360	$330	$300

Last MSR was $749.

SILVER HUNTER - 12 or 20 ga., steel boxlock action, SST, extractors, monoblock VR 26 or 28 (12 ga. only) in. barrels with 2 choke tubes, checkered walnut stock and forearm. Imported 1999 only.

	$550	$450	$375	$315	$285	$270	$255

Last MSR was $629.

SILVER SPORTING - 12 ga. or 20 ga. (new 1996), Sporting Clay model, boxlock action, 28, 29 (new 1999), or 30 (new 1993) in. ported vent. barrels with channelled broadway VR, choke tubes, and elongated forcing cones, nickel finished engraved receiver, SST, ejectors, figured walnut stock and forearm with handcut checkering, 7 lbs. 6 oz. Mfg. by Lanber, imported 1990-2000. 1993 manufacture by Pedersoli.

	$835	$680	$550	$485	$440	$400	$360

Last MSR was $965.

SILVER SKEET - 12 ga. only, similar appearance to Silver Sporting, 26 or 28 (new 1993) in. ported vent. barrels with raised VR, 4 choke tubes, recoil pad, 7 lbs. 6 oz. Imported 1992-93 only.

	$790	$685	$575	$495	$450	$400	$360

Last MSR was $899.

SILVER TRAP - similar appearance to Silver Sporting, 30 in. ported barrels with raised VR, 4 choke tubes, recoil pad, trap stock dimensions, 7 3/4 lbs. Imported 1992-1993 only.

	$790	$685	$575	$495	$450	$400	$360

Last MSR was $899.

STERLING/BRISTOL - 12 or 20 ga., 3 in. chambers, boxlock with Greener crossbolt and false side plates, various barrel lengths and choke tubes, chrome finished receiver with moderate game scene engraving, SST, VR, ejectors. Imported 1986-89.

	$695	$550	$495	$450	$400	$375	$350

Last MSR was $825.

Until 1989, this model was designated the Bristol. In 1988, the engraving pattern was changed from game scene to elaborate scroll type.

SIR - 12 or 20 ga., 3 in. chambers, sidelock with Greener crossbolt, various barrel lengths and chokings, chrome finished receiver with game scene engraving, ST, VR, ejectors, deluxe checkered pistol grip stock and forearm. Imported 1986 only.

	$1,100	$900	$750	$675	$610	$565	$520

Last MSR was $1,090.

Add $75 for choke tubes.

ROYAL - 12 or 20 ga., 3 in. chambers, sidelock with Greener crossbolt, various barrel lengths and chokings, chrome finished receiver with elaborate scroll engraving, ST, VR, ejectors, oil finished deluxe checkered pistol grip and forearm. Imported 1986-87 only.

	$1,595	$1,310	$1,080	$960	$850	$750	$675

Last MSR was $1,730.

Add $65 for choke tubes.

GRADING - PPGS™	100%	98%	95%	90%	80%	70%	60%

EXCELSIOR - 12 or 20 ga., 3 in. chambers, sidelock with Greener crossbolt, various barrel lengths and chokings, chrome finished receiver with elaborate deep relief engraving and multiple gold inlays, ST, VR, ejectors, oil finished deluxe checkered pistol grip and forearm. Imported 1986-87 only.

	$1,775	$1,510	$1,250	$1,100	$975	$885	$780

Last MSR was $1,925.

Add $70 for choke tubes.

WS/WT - O/U (SILVER) 12 WATERFOWL/TURKEY SPECIAL - 12 ga. only, Mag. chambers (3 1/2 in. was added in 1989), 24 (Turkey - disc. 1996), 26 (Turkey) or 28 (Waterfowl) in. barrels with choke tubes, SST, ejectors, parkerized metal finish, matte finished stock and forearm, Mossy Oak Breakup camo pattern began 1997 for Turkey Special, sling swivels, recoil pad, approx. 7 lbs. Imported 1987-2000.

	$650	$550	$460	$395	$360	$330	$300

Last MSR was $799.

Add $86 for Camo Turkey Model (WT/OU Camo 12, Breakup camo pattern, new 1997).

✳ *10 ga. Waterfowl* - 10 ga. Mag., double triggers, extractors, matte finishes similar to 12 ga. Waterfowl, beavertail forearm. Imported 1988-89 only.

	$750	$625	$550	$495	$450	$390	$360

Last MSR was $829.

WT-O/U10 TURKEY SPECIAL - 10 ga., 3 1/2 in. Mag., 26 in. barrels with choke tubes, SST (became standard in 1990), extractors, recoil pad, non-glare metal finish, 9 lbs. 10 oz. Imported 1988-2000.

	$865	$695	$550	$500	$450	$390	$360

Last MSR was $995.

F.S. 200 - 12 ga., trap or skeet model, 26 or 32 in. separated barrels only, SST, ejectors, boxlock with Greener crossbolt, black or chromed receiver, checkered walnut stock and forearm. Imported 1986-87 only.

	$690	$560	$500	$450	$410	$375	$350

Last MSR was $835.

F.S. 300 - 12 ga., trap or skeet model, 26, 30, or 32 in. separated barrels only, SST, ejectors, boxlock with Greener crossbolt and false side plates lightly engraved, chromed receiver, checkered walnut stock and forearm. Imported 1986 only.

	$825	$675	$610	$555	$510	$470	$440

Last MSR was $995.

F.S. 400 - 12 ga., trap or skeet model, 26, 30, or 32 in. separated barrels only, ST, ejectors, sidelock with Greener crossbolt, lightly engraved chromed receiver, checkered walnut stock and forearm. Imported 1986 only.

	$1,145	$945	$860	$800	$740	$680	$620

Last MSR was $1,360.

F.S. 500 - same specifications as F.S. 400. Importation disc. 1985.

	$1,175	$950	$860	$795	$730	$660	$595

Last MSR was $1,360.

SHOTGUNS: SxS

American Arms imported Spanish shotguns manufactured by Zabala Hermanos and Grulla. Older discontinued Diarm models will also be shown in this section.

GENTRY/YORK - 12, 16 (disc. 1990), 20, 28 ga., or .410 bore, 3 in. chambers, boxlock, ejectors (extractors after 1986), double or SST (became standard in 1992), chromed receiver features fine scroll engraving, fixed chokes, pistol grip stock with recoil pad and beavertail forearm. Imported 1986-2000.

	$625	$475	$375	$300	$280	$260	$240

Last MSR was $750.

GRADING - PPGS™	100%	98%	95%	90%	80%	70%	60%

Add $45 for 28 ga. or .410 bore.

Before 1988 this model was designated York (case coloring began 1988, silver finish began 1993). DTs were supplied with 28 ga. or .410 bore 1990-2000.

BRITTANY - 12 or 20 ga., boxlock action, 25 (20 ga. only, disc. 1996), 26, or 27 (12 ga. only, disc. 1996) in. barrels, SST, ejectors, matted solid rib, choke tubes, engraved case colored frame, checkered walnut straight grip stock with recoil pad and semi-beavertail forearm, 6 1/2 or 7 lbs. Imported 1989-2000.

$725	$575	$485	$435	$400	$375	$350	

Last MSR was $885.

The wood finish was changed in this model from oil to semi-gloss in 1991.

SHOGUN - 10 ga., 3 1/2 in. chambers, boxlock, ejectors, double triggers, chromed receiver features fine scroll engraving. Imported 1986 only.

$440	$350	$325	$300	$280	$260	$240

Last MSR was $525.

DERBY - 12, 20, 28 (disc. 1991) ga., or .410 bore (disc. 1991) ga., 3 in. chambers, sidelock, ejectors, double (disc. 1989) or SNT, chromed receiver features fine scroll engraving, fixed chokes, straight grip walnut stock and forearm. Imported 1986-94.

$1,150	$975	$850	$750	$625	$500	$425

Last MSR was $1,039.

Add 10% for 28 ga. or .410 bore (disc. 1991).

Subtract 10% for DT.

Add approx. 50%-60% for 2-barrel set (20 and 28 ga. – approx. 300 sets mfg.) – disc. 1990.

This model featured a case-colored receiver between 1988-90 and was changed to coin finish in late 1991. At the same time, the wood finish was changed from oil to semi-gloss.

GRULLA NO. 2 - 12, 20, 28 ga., or .410 bore, hand fitted sidelock action, 26 or 28 in. barrels, DTs, ejectors, fixed chokes, concave rib, case colored receiver with elaborate engraving, deluxe English style straight stock and splinter forearm (checkered and hand rubbed), between 5 3/4-6 1/4 lbs. Imported 1989-2000.

This model was individually handcrafted with less than 800 mfg. each year. Before going to a special order basis, this model retailed for $3,099 (1994).

❋ *Small Gauge Set* - includes choice of 20/28 ga. or 28 ga./.410 bore barrel combination (26 in. fixed choke barrels). Imported 1989-95.

$3,600	$3,000	$2,375	$2,000	$1,650	$1,325	$1,150

Before going to a special order basis, this combination last retailed for $4,219 (1994/5).

WS/SS 10 WATERFOWL SPECIAL - 10 ga. only, 3 1/2 in. chambers, 32 in. barrels, DTs, parkerized finish, sling swivels and camouflaged sling, extractors, fixed chokes, recoil pad, 11 lbs. 3 oz. Imported 1987-93.

$560	$500	$440	$400	$375	$350	$325

Last MSR was $639.

WT/SS 10 - 10 ga. only, 3 1/2 in. chambers, similar to TS/SS 12, except as 28 in. barrels with multi-chokes. Imported 1998-2000.

$775	$650	$550	$450	$400	$375	$350

Last MSR was $860.

TS/SS 10/12 TURKEY SPECIAL - 10 (disc. 1995) or 12 ga., 3 or 3 1/2 in. chambers (3 1/2 in. 12 ga. introduced in 1989), 26 in. barrels only, double triggers, parkerized finish, dull finish stock and forearm, sling swivels, recoil pad, choke tubes, 7 lbs. 6 oz. or 10 lbs. 13 oz. (10 ga.). Imported 1987-2000.

$665	$550	$450	$400	$375	$350	$325

Last MSR was $799.

This model in 12 ga. was supplied with a SST.

GRADING - PPGS™	100%	98%	95%	90%	80%	70%	60%

SHOTGUNS: SEMI-AUTO

PHANTOM FIELD - 12 ga. only, 3 in. chamber, gas operated, 24, 26, or 28 in. VR barrel with 3 choke tubes, black synthetic or checkered walnut stock and forearm, blue finish. Imported 1999-2000.

$395	$360	$330	$275	$250	$225	$200

Last MSR was $439.

* *Phantom HP* - similar to Phantom Field with synthetic stock and forearm, except has 19 in. threaded barrels for external choke tubes, swivel studs, and extended mag. Imported 1999-2000.

$400	$365	$330	$275	$250	$225	$200

Last MSR was $449.

SHOTGUNS: SINGLE SHOT

SINGLE SHOT MODEL - 12, 20 ga., or .410 bore, 3 in. chamber non-exposed hammer, pistol grip stock, non-reflective finish. Imported 1988-89 only.

$90	$80	$70	$60	$55	$50	$45

Last MSR was $99.

* *Camper Special* - 12, 20 ga., or .410 bore, 3 in. chamber folding design, 21 in. barrel, pistol grip. Imported 1988-89 only.

$95	$80	$70	$60	$55	$50	$45

Last MSR was $107.

* *Slugger* - 12 or 20 ga., 24 in. slug shotgun barrel with adj. rear sight and blade front, recoil pad. Imported 1989 only.

$100	$85	$75	$65	$55	$50	$45

Last MSR was $115.

* *Youth* - 20 ga. or .410 bore, 26 in. barrel, 12 1/2 in. stock dimensions, recoil pad. Imported 1989 only.

$100	$85	$75	$65	$55	$50	$45

Last MSR was $115.

* *Combo* - interchangeable rifle and shotgun barrels, choice of .22 Hornet/12 ga. with 28 in. barrel or .22 LR/20 ga. with 26 in. barrel, includes fitted hard case. Imported 1989 only.

$195	$165	$130	$115	$100	$90	$80

Last MSR was $235.

* *10 Ga. Model* - 10 ga. only, 3 1/2 in. chambers, 26 in. multi-choke or 32 in. full fixed choke barrel, non-exposed hammer, non-reflective finish. Imported 1988-89 only.

$135	$115	$95	$80	$70	$60	$55

Last MSR was $149.

Add $30 for multi-chokes (26 in. barrel).

AMERICAN BARLOCK WONDER

Previous trademark manufactured by Crescent Arms for Sears Roebuck & Co.

SHOTGUNS: SxS

SIDE-BY-SIDE - various gauges, hammerless or outside hammer, damascus or steel barrels.

$240	$225	$200	$175	$140	$100	$75

Add 15% for steel barrels, smaller gauges.

SINGLE SHOT - various gauges, hammer, steel barrel.

$125	$115	$100	$90	$75	$60	$50

Add 35% for smaller gauges.

GRADING - PPGS™	100%	98%	95%	90%	80%	70%	60%

AMERICAN DERRINGER CORPORATION

Current manufacturer located in Waco, TX since 1980.
Distributor and dealer sales.

DERRINGERS: STAINLESS STEEL

MODEL 1 - available in over 55 cals. including .22 LR through .45-70 Govt., also 2 1/2 in.
.410 shot shell, O/U stainless steel derringer, top break action, satin or high polish finish,
3 in. barrels, automatic barrel selection, hammer block type safety, 15 oz., spur trigger,
rosewood grips. New 1980.

* **Regular Cals.** - most cals. between .22 LR and .40 S&W.

  MSR $390   **$300**   **$225**   **$160**
  Add $55 for high polish finish.
  Add approx. $140 for .22 Hornet (disc. 1989).
  Add $170 for .223 Rem. or $140 for .30-30 Win. cal. (disc. 2003).

* **Larger Cals.** - typically .44 Spl. - .45-70 Govt. cal.

  MSR $455   **$345**   **$275**   **$195**
  Add $55 for high polish finish.
  Add $75 for .41 Mag., .44 Mag., or .45 Win. Mag. cal.

  This model can be ordered with special ser. nos. and other custom features at additional
  cost(s).

* **Model 1 Engraved** - limited mfg., mostly special ordered.
  Please contact the factory regarding a price quotation for this special order model.

* **Model 1 Millennium 2000 Series** - .45 LC/.410 shotshell only, 3 in. barrel, 15,000 mfg.
  beginning 1998 in various configurations including Gambler and Cowboy.

                           The 2003 MSR on this model was $470.
  Please contact the factory regarding a price quotation for this special order model.

* **Model 1 United We Stand Commemorative** - .45 LC/.410 shotshell only, 3 in. barrel,
  choice of custom grips, includes red, white and blue presentation case. Limited
  mfg. 2002-2003.

             $355   **$285**   **$230**

                           Last MSR was $450.

  American Derringer Corporation donated a portion of the proceeds from this commemorative
  to the post-9/11 recovery effort.

LADY DERRINGER - available in various cals. between .22 LR - .45 LC, and .45 LC/.410
shotshell cal., O/U top break action, 3 in. barrel, high polish stainless steel, spur trigger,
scrimshawed synthetic ivory grips, handfitted action allowing easy cocking, with French
styled leatherette display case, 15 1/2 oz. New 1990.

  Please contact the factory regarding a price quotation for this model.

* **Deluxe Engraved** - similar to Deluxe Grade, except hand engraved with circa 1880
  patterns. Disc. 1994.

             $650   **$515**   **$400**

                           Last MSR was $750.

  Mother-of-pearl grips and personalized engraving were available as extra cost options on this
  model.

* **14Kt. Gold Engraved** - entire Derringer manufactured out of a 14Kt. gold bar (contains approx. 20 oz. of 14Kt. gold and 3 oz. of stainless steel), custom engraved
  with diamond sights, special order only until late 1993.

             N/A   **N/A**   **N/A**

                           Last MSR was $100,000.

GRADING - PPGS™	100%	98%	95%	90%	80%	70%	60%

✳ *Millenium Lady Derringer* - similar to Model 1 Millenium 2000 Series. Disc.

	$390	$290	$210				

Last MSR was $470.

LADY DERRINGER II - .22 LR (disc.), .32 ACP (disc.), .38 Spl., or .22 Mag. (disc.) cal., O/U pivot design with double action, aluminum frame, trigger guard stops at trigger bottom, 8 oz. Mfg. 1999-2003.

$395 $290 $210

Last MSR was $480.

GRADING - PPGS™	100%	Issue Price	Qty. Made

MODEL 1 TEXAS COMMEMORATIVE - .38 Spl., .44-40, or .45 LC cal., similar to Model 1 except has brass frame, stainless steel barrel, and stag grips.

	100%	Issue Price	Qty. Made
.44-40 cal.	$395	$440	N/A
.45 cal.	$415	$470	N/A
Add $25 for special serial number.			
.32 Mag.	$205	$255	500+
.38 Spl.	$340	$385	N/A
.22 LR (mfg. 1991-92)	$200	$238	500
.41 Rimfire (not shootable)	$235	$295	500
Fully engraved model	$695	$750	limited

American Derringer is making the Texas Commemorative on a limited basis - please contact the factory directly for a price quotation on this model.

125TH ANNIVERSARY - special edition 125th anniversary variation with pistol case. Disc. 1993.

	100%	Issue Price	Qty. Made
.44-40 or .45 cal.	$285	$320	500
.38 Spl.	$185	$225	500
Deluxe engraved model	$650	$750	limited

GRADING - PPGS™	100%	98%	95%	90%	80%	70%	60%

MODEL 3 - .32 Mag. (new 1990 - limited availability) or .38 Spl. cal., single shot, 2 1/2 in. barrel, 8 1/2 oz., spur trigger, rosewood grips. Disc. 1994.

$95 $70 $55

Last MSR was $120.

MODEL 4 - .357 Mag., .357 Max., .44 Mag. (disc. 2003), .45 ACP, .45-70 Govt. (disc. 2003), or .45 LC cal. on upper barrel, 3 in. .410 shotshell lower barrel, O/U derringer combination pistol, 4 1/10 in. barrel, rosewood grips, 16 1/2 oz. New 1985.

MSR $470 $400 $315 $230

Add $75 for oversized grips.

Add $105 for .44 Mag. cal. (oversized grips became standard 1997, disc. 2003).

Add $150 for .45-70 Govt. cal. in both barrels (disc. 2003).

This model was also available on special order in either .50-70 or .50 Saunders cal. (new 1989 – single shot only). MSR was $395.

✳ *Model 4 Engraved* - .45 LC/.410 shotshell cal., allow 12 weeks for delivery. New 1997.

Please contact the factory directly for a price quotation on this special order model.

✳ *Alaskan Survival Model* - similar to Model 4, except .45-70 Govt. cal. top barrel, and choice of .44 Mag. (disc.), .45 LC, or .45 LC/.410 shotshell lower barrel.

MSR $550 $450 $350 $295

Add $60 for high polish finish.

GRADING - PPGS™	100%	98%	95%	90%	80%	70%	60%

MODEL 6 - .22 Mag. (disc.), .357 Mag., .45 LC, .45 ACP, or .45 LC/.410 shotshell cal., O/U, 6 in. barrel, 21 oz. Available in high polish, satin, or grey matte finish (standard). New 1986.

> MSR $505 $390 $275 $215
>
> Add $25 for either .45 LC or .45 LC/.410 shotshell.
> Add $13 for satin finish (disc. 1994).
> Add $70 for high polish finish.
> Add $50 for oversized grips (disc. 1994, reinstated 1998-99).

> ✳ *Model 6 Engraved* - .45 LC/.410 shotshell cal., allow 12 weeks for delivery. New 1997.
>> Please contact the factory directly for a price quotation on this special order model.

MODEL 7 - .22 LR (disc.), .22 Mag. (mfg. 1992-2003), .32 H&R Mag. (disc.), .38 Spl., .38 S&W (disc. 1989), .380 ACP, (disc.) or .44 Spl. (disc.) cal., O/U, same basic specifications as Model 1, except ultra lightweight (7 1/2 oz.).

> MSR $400 $310 $215 $155

> ✳ *.44 Special Cal.* - .44 Spl. cal. only. Disc.
>> $500 $440 $370

Last MSR was $585.

MODEL 8 - .45 LC/.410 shotshell cal., O/U, 8 in. barrel, nickel finish, grooved grips, 24 oz. New 1997.

> MSR $595 $480 $375 $310
>
> Add $80 for high polish finish.

> ✳ *Model 8 Engraved* - .45 LC/.410 shotshell cal. Limited mfg. 1997-98 only.
>> $1,675 $1,300 $975

Last MSR was $1,917.

MODEL 10 - .38 Spl. (new 1995), .45 ACP, .45 LC, or .45 LC/.410 shotshell (disc. 1997), O/U, 3 in. stainless barrels, aluminum frame and barrel, matte grey finish, 7.5 oz. New 1988.

> MSR $390 $315 $235 $180
>
> Add approx. $60 for .45 LC or .45 ACP cal.

MODEL 11 - .22 LR (mfg. 1995-2003), .22 Mag. (mfg. 1995-2003), .32 H&R Mag. (mfg. 1995-2003), .380 ACP (mfg. 1995-2003), or .38 Spl. cal., same basic specifications as Model 1, matte grey finish, only 11 oz.

> MSR $390 $315 $235 $180

RIMFIRE DOUBLE ACTION - .22 LR or .22 Mag. cal., 3 1/2 in. O/U barrels, double action trigger, dual extraction, hammerless, blue finish with black synthetic grips, 11 oz. Mfg. 1990-95.

> $145 $115 $95

Last MSR was $170.

This O/U Derringer was patterned after the original High Standard design.

DS .22 MAG. - .22 Mag. cal., 3 in. barrel, stainless steel with blue finish, 11 oz. Special order beginning 1998.

> Please contact the factory directly for a price quotation on this model.

DA 38 DOUBLE ACTION - .22 LR (mfg. 1996-2003), .357 Mag. (new 1991), .38 Spl., 9mm Para., or .40 S&W (new 1993) cal., 3 in. O/U barrels, satin stainless steel with aluminum grip frame, double action trigger design, hammerblock thumb safety, choice of checkered rosewood, walnut, or other hardwood grips, 14.5 oz. New 1990.

> MSR $505 $395 $275 $210
>
> Add $25 for 9mm Para., .357 Mag., or for .40 S&W cal.
> Add $15 for Lady Derringer Model (scrimshawed synthetic ivory grips, .38 Spl. only. Mfg. 1992-94).

GRADING - PPGS™	100%	98%	95%	90%	80%	70%	60%

MINI-COP - .22 Mag. cal., 4 shot double action design, stainless steel construction, patterned after the original Mini-Cop mfg. in Torrance, CA. Mfg. 1990-94.

	$250	$220	$185				

Last MSR was $313.

4-BARREL DERRINGER - .22 LR, .38 Spl., or .357 Mag. cal., double action, similar design to Mini-Cop, semi-matte finish, 28 oz. While advertised beginning 1991 at $425, only a few prototypes were manufactured during 1997.

CUSTOM TARGET MODELS - .38 Spl. Wadcutter or 9mm Federal (disc.) cal., mfg. for End of Trail Derringer Match, limited production. Mfg. 1990-92.

	$695	$575	$475				

Last MSR was $750.

4 BARREL DERRINGER - while advertised, this model never went into production.

PISTOLS: PEN DESIGN

MODEL 2 PEN PISTOL - .22 LR, .25 ACP, or .32 ACP cal., unique hinged action allows pen to be converted into a legal pistol within two seconds, folding design, 2 in. barrel, cocks on opening action, firing pin block grip safety, brushed stainless finish, 5 oz. Mfg. 1993-94.

	$145	$120	$100				

Last MSR was $203.

Add $24 for .32 ACP cal.

PISTOLS: SEMI-AUTO

STANDARD MODEL

* *.25 Mag. Cal.* - .25 Mag., semi-auto single action, less than 100 manufactured in stainless steel only.

	$500	$400	$300				

* *.25 ACP Cal.* - .25 ACP, semi-auto single action, less than 400 manufactured in stainless steel, less than 50 in blue steel.

	100%	98%	95%
Stainless	$400	$300	$250
Blue	$550	$400	$325

LM-5 - .25 ACP, .32 Mag. (disc. 1997), or .380 ACP (mfg. 1998-99) cal., compact stainless semi-auto, single action, 2 1/4 in. barrel, hammerless, wood grips, 4 (.32 Mag. or .380 ACP) or 5 (.25 ACP) shot mag., 15 oz. Limited mfg. since 1997.

The 2003 MSR on this model was $353.

Please contact the factory directly for a price quotation on this model.

Add $27 for .32 Mag. cal. (disc. 1997).

* *LM-5 .380 ACP* - limited mfg., disc. 1999.

	$365	$295	$215				

Last MSR was $425.

PISTOLS: SLIDE-ACTION

LM-4 (SEMMERLING) - .45 ACP cal., 2 in. barrel, super compact, thumb activated slide mechanism, blue finish, 4 shot mag., 24 oz., very limited manufacture since 1998.

The 2003 MSR on this model was $2,655.

Please contact the factory directly for a price quotation on this special order model.

GRADING - PPGS™	100%	98%	95%	90%	80%	70%	60%

AMERICAN FIREARMS MANUFACTURING CO., INC.

Previous manufacturer located in San Antonio, TX between 1972-1974.

DERRINGERS

AMERICAN .38 SPL. - .38 Spl. cal., O/U configuration, approx. 3,000-4,000 mfg. between 1972-74.

	$200	$165	$135

AMERICAN .380 AUTOMATIC - .380 ACP cal., 8 shot, 3 1/2 in. barrel, stainless steel, smooth walnut grips, approx. 10 mfg. 1972-74.

	$700	$500	$300

PISTOLS: SEMI-AUTO

AMERICAN .25 AUTOMATIC - .25 ACP cal., 8 shot, 2 1/10 in. barrel, smooth walnut grips. Mfg. 1966-74.

	100%	98%	95%	90%	80%	70%	60%
Stainless	$195	$180	$165	N/A	N/A	N/A	N/A
Blue	$165	$150	$140	$120	$100	$90	$85

AMERICAN FRONTIER FIREARMS MFG., INC.

Previous manufacturer located in Aguanga, CA 1995-2000.

American Frontier Firearms Mfg., Inc. manufactured a line of replica metallic cartridge firing revolvers (black powder or smokeless). These revolvers were manufactured in .22 LR, .32 Spl., .38 Spl., .44 Russian, or .45 LC. During 2000, AFF developed a new cartridge, a .44 A.F.F. It can be used in revolvers firing .44-40 WCF, .44 Russian, .44 Spl., and .44 Mag. It also meets current S.A.S.S. specifications.

REVOLVERS: CARTRIDGE CONVERSIONS & OPEN TOPS

Production on these models was mid-1997 through 2000. Revolvers were supplied with standard finish high polish blue steel parts, color case hardened hammer and/or trigger, silver-plated or blue backstrap and trigger guard, and varnished walnut grips. Special orders were also available featuring simulated ivory grips, special finishes, and engraving options. Some models and variations had very limited production, due to problems procuring high quality parts.

1851 NAVY RICHARDS CONVERSION - .38 Spl., .38 LC, .44 Russian, or .44-40 WCF cal., 4 3/4, 5 1/2, or 7 1/2 in. octagon barrel, roll engraved cylinder, blue steel finish, varnished walnut grips. No ejector rod.

$695	$550	$375	$325	$295	$265	$235

Last MSR was $795.

1851 NAVY RICHARDS & MASON CONVERSION - .38 Spl., .38 LC, .44 Russian, or .44-40 WCF cal., 4 3/4, 5 1/2, or 7 1/2 in. octagon barrel with Mason ejector assembly, roll engraved cylinder, blue steel finish, varnished walnut grips.

$695	$550	$375	$325	$295	$265	$235

Last MSR was $795.

1858 REMINGTON NEW ARMY CAVALRY MODEL - .38 Spl., .44-40 WCF or .45 LC cal., 7 1/2 in. barrel with ejector assembly, blue steel finish, color case hardened hammer, varnished walnut grips.

$715	$575	$475	$375	$325	$275	$225

Last MSR was $795.

GRADING - PPGS™	100%	98%	95%	90%	80%	70%	60%

1858 REMINGTON NEW ARMY ARTILLERY MODEL - .38 Spl., .44-40 WCF and .45 LC cal., 5 1/2 in. barrel with ejector assembly, blue steel finish, color case hardened hammer, varnished walnut grips.

	$715	$575	$475	$375	$325	$275	$225

Last MSR was $795.

1858 REMINGTON ORIGINAL FACTORY-TYPE CONVERSION - .38 Spl., .44-40 WCF, or .45 LC cal., 5 1/2 or 7 1/2 in. barrels, original loading lever and no gate or ejector assembly, blue steel finish, color case hardened hammer, varnished walnut grips.

	$715	$575	$475	$375	$325	$275	$225

Last MSR was $795.

POCKET REMINGTON - .22 LR, .32 S&W Short, or .38 Spl. cal., 3.5 in. barrel with or without ejector rod or gate, blue steel finish, color case hardened hammer, varnished walnut grips.

	$425	$375	$325	$275	$225	$185	$165

Last MSR was $495.

1860 ARMY RICHARDS CONVERSION - .38 Spl., .38 LC, or .44-40 WCF cal., 4 3/4, 5 1/2, or 7 1/2 in. round barrel, with or without ejector assembly, roll engraved cylinder, blue steel finish, silver plated trigger guard, varnished walnut grips.

	$695	$550	$375	$325	$295	$265	$235

Last MSR was $795.

1861 NAVY RICHARDS CONVERSION - .38 Spl., or .38 LC cal., 4 1/2 or 7 1/2 in. round barrel with ejector assembly, blue steel finish, silver plated backstrap and trigger guard, varnished walnut grips.

	$695	$550	$375	$325	$295	$265	$235

Last MSR was $795.

POCKET NAVY RICHARDS & MASON CONVERSION - .32 S&W Short cal., 4 1/2 in. octagon barrel with ejector assembly, blue steel finish, silver plated backstrap and trigger guard, color case hardened trigger and hammer, varnished walnut grips.

	$465	$375	$325	$275	$225	$185	$165

Last MSR was $495.

1871-72 OPEN TOP FRONTIER MODEL - .38 Spl., .38 LC, or .44-40 WCF cal., 4 3/4, 5 1/2, or 7 1/2 in. round barrel with ejector assembly, blue steel finish, varnished walnut grips.

	$695	$550	$375	$325	$295	$265	$235

Last MSR was $795.

✱ *1871-72 Open-Top Tiffany Model* - similar to 1871-72 Standard Model, except has engraved gold/silver finished Tiffany grips and also available with 4 3/4 in. barrel. Mfg. 2001.

	$995	$895	$700	$525	$450	$395	$350

Last MSR was $1,200.

AMERICAN GUN CO.

Previous trademark manufactured by Crescent Firearms Co. and distributed by H. & D. Folsom Co.

REVOLVERS

REVOLVER - .32 S&W cal., 5 shot, double action, top break-open action.

	$175	$160	$140	$120	$95	$65	$50

GRADING - PPGS™	100%	98%	95%	90%	80%	70%	60%

SHOTGUNS: SxS

SxS - various gauges, hammer or hammerless, damascus or steel barrels.

	100%	98%	95%	90%	80%	70%	60%
	$240	$225	$200	$175	$140	$100	$75

Add 15% for small gauges or steel barrels.

AMERICAN HISTORICAL FOUNDATION, THE

Current organization which privately commissions historical commemoratives in conjunction with leading manufacturers and craftsmen around the world. The Foundation is located in Richmond, VA. Direct to consumer sales only, via phone, correspondence or personal visit to their headquarters and museums. Delivery to local FFL holder.

The Foundation's limited/special edition models are not all manufactured at one time. Rather, guns are fabricated as demand dictates. Limited editions include guns by Colt, Winchester, Browning, Dan Wesson, Auto-Ordnance/Thompson, Sturm Ruger, Holland & Holland, Walther, Smith & Wesson, Mauser, and Beretta.

LIMITED/SPECIAL EDITIONS

AHF consumers include members, history buffs, veterans, museums, and other interested parties who normally keep these items for a considerable time period, and very few are sold in the secondary marketplace annually. Because of this consumer direct sales program, many non-AHF consumers and gun dealers do not have a working knowledge on current pricing for AHF firearms.

The publisher suggests that those people who want more information about American Historical Foundation's Commemorative Issue firearms contact AHF directly (see Trademark Index), or visit their web site: www.ahfrichmond.com. Additionally, information on most AHF offerings manufactured between 1988-1997 can be found in the 20th Edition *Blue Book of Gun Values*.

AMERICAN HUNTING RIFLES, INC. (AHR)

Current rifle manufacturer established in 1998 and located in Hamilton, MT.

RIFLES: BOLT ACTION

CZ-550 actions are also available individually. Prices range from $450-$575.

CLASSIC 550 - standard and various Howell proprietary cals., CZ 550 double square bridge standard action, controlled feed claw extractor, 25 in. chrome-moly sporter barrel, also available in optional stainless steel, blue finish, black fiberglass or optional walnut stock with Decelerator recoil pad. New 1999.

MSR $1,495	$1,325	$1,050	$900	$775	$650	$550	$495

Add $75 for stainless steel barrel.

Add $150 for integral and removable muzzle brake, with protective cap.

VARMINT 550 PRO - .220 Howell, .220 Swift, .22-250 Rem., .30-06, or .308 Win. cal., CZ 550 double square bridge standard action, 26 in. stainless heavy barrel, SST, black fiberglass stock with Decelerator recoil pad. New 2001.

MSR $1,795	$1,625	$1,250	$1,050	$900	$725	$650	$500

SAFARI 550 - various Mag. cals., similar to Classic 550, except has Magnum action with integral scope mounts, oil finished fancy walnut stock, trigger guard safety. New 2001.

MSR $2,995	$2,675	$2,075	$1,725	$1,450	$1,175	$950	$825

GRADING - PPGS™	100%	98%	95%	90%	80%	70%	60%

SAFARI 550 DGR - various standard Mag. cals. from .404 Jeffery – .500 AHR, excluding special orders, similar to Safari 550, except has 3 position safety, extra fancy wood, and banded front sling attachment. New 2001.

MSR $3,495	$3,050	$2,550	$2,075	$1,625	$1,400	$1,125	$875

585 DGR - .585 AHR cal., otherwise similar to Safari 550 DGR. New 2002.

Please contact the factory directly for current pricing and availability.

AMERICAN INDUSTRIES

Please refer to the Calico section in this text.

AMERICAN INTERNATIONAL CORP.

Previous manufacturer and importer located in Salt Lake City, UT, circa 1972-1984. American International was a wholly owned subsidiary of ARDCO (American Research & Development). ARDCO's previous name was American Mining & Development. American International imported firearms from Voere, located in Kufstein, Austria. American Arms International (AAI) was another subsidiary of ARDCO.

In 1979, after American International Corp. had dissolved, AAI resumed production using mostly Voere parts. After running out of Voere parts, late production featured U.S. mfg. receivers (can be recognized by not having a pivoting barrel retainer slotted on the bottom of the receiver). American Arms International declared bankruptcy in 1984.

CARBINES: SEMI-AUTO

AMERICAN 180 AUTO CARBINE (M-1) - .22 LR cal., a specialized design for paramilitary use, 177 round drum mag., 16 1/2 in. barrel, aperture sight, high impact plastic stock and forearm, aluminum alloy reciever with black finish. Semi-auto variation mfg. 1979-c.1984. Total Voere production (denoted by A prefix serial number) between 1972-1979 was 2,300 carbines (includes both full and semi-auto versions). Later mfg. was marked either M-1 (semi-auto) or M-2 (fully auto). B ser. no. prefix was introduced in 1980, and barrel markings were changed to "Amer Arms Intl, SLC, UT."

	$725	$600	$475	$375	$350	$325	$295

Add $550 for Laser Lok System – first commercially available laser sighting system.
Add approx. $300 for extra drum mag. and winder (fragile and subject to breakage).

AMERICAN LEGENDS

Previous trademark of some handguns manufactured by IAI. Please refer to the IAI section in this text.

AMERICAN SPIRIT ARMS CORP.

Current rifle and components manufacturer established in 1998, and located in Scottsdale, AZ. Dealer and direct sales.

RIFLES: SEMI-AUTO

Add $25 for green furniture, $65 for black barrel finish, $75 for fluted barrel, $125 for porting, $119 for two-stage match trigger, and $55 for National Match sights on .223 cal. models listed below.

ASA 24 IN. BULL BARREL FLATTOP RIFLE - .223 Rem. cal., patterned after AR-15, forged steel lower receiver, forged aluminum flattop upper receiver, 24 in. stainless steel bull barrel, free floating aluminum handguard, includes Harris bipod. New 1999.

MSR $950	$850	$700	$625	$550	$500	$450	$400

ASA 24 IN. BULL BARREL A2 RIFLE - similar to ASA Bull Barrel Flattop, except features A2 upper receiver with carrying handle and sights. New 1999.

MSR $980	$875	$725	$650	$565	$500	$450	$400

GRADING - PPGS™	100%	98%	95%	90%	80%	70%	60%

OPEN MATCH RIFLE - .223 Rem. cal., 16 in. fluted and ported stainless steel match barrel with round shroud, flattop without sights, forged upper and lower receiver, two-stage match trigger, upgraded pistol grip, individually tested, USPSA/IPSC open class legal. New 2001.

MSR $1,500	$1,350	$1,100	$950	$825	$725	$650	$525

LIMITED MATCH RIFLE - .223 Rem. cal., 16 in. fluted stainless steel match barrel with round shroud with staggered hand grip, National Match front and rear sights, two-stage match trigger, upgraded pistol grip, individually tested, USPSA/IPSC open class legal. New 2001.

MSR $1,300	$1,175	$975	$825	$725	$650	$525	$475

DCM SERVICE RIFLE - .223 Rem. cal., 20 in. stainless steel match barrel with ribbed free floating shroud, National Match front and rear sights, two-stage match trigger, pistol grip, individually tested. New 2001.

MSR $1,300	$1,175	$975	$825	$725	$650	$525	$475

ASA 16 IN. M4 RIFLE - .223 Rem. cal., features non-collapsible stock and M4 handguard, 16 in. barrel with muzzlebrake, aluminum flattop upper receiver. New 2002.

MSR $905	$795	$700	$625	$525	$450	$400	$350

ASA 20 IN. A2 RIFLE - .223 Rem. cal., features A2 receiver and 20 in. National Match barrel. New 1999.

MSR $820	$765	$640	$565	$500	$425	$350	$300

ASA CARBINE WITH SIDE CHARGING RECEIVER - .223 Rem. cal., features aluminum side charging flattop upper receiver, M4 handguard, 16 in. NM barrel with slotted muzzlebrake. Mfg. 2002-2004.

	$865	$750	$650	$565	$500	$450	$400

Last MSR was $970.

C.A.R. POST-BAN 16 IN. CARBINE - .223 Rem. cal., non-collapsible stock, Wilson 16 in. National Match barrel. New 1999.

MSR $830	$775	$650	$575	$500	$450	$400	$350

ASA 16 IN. BULL BARREL A2 INVADER - .223 Rem. cal., similar to ASA 24 in. Bull Barrel rifle, except has 16 in. stainless steel barrel. New 1999.

MSR $955	$860	$725	$630	$550	$500	$450	$400

ASA 9MM A2 CAR CARBINE - 9mm Para. cal., forged upper and lower receiver, non-collapsible CAR stock, 16 in. Wilson heavy barrel w/o muzzlebrake, with birdcage flash hider (pre-ban) or muzzlebrake (post-ban), includes 9mm conversion block, 25 shot modified Uzi mag. New 2002.

MSR $950	$860	$725	$630	$550	$500	$450	$400

Add $550 per extra 25 shot mag.

ASA 9MM FLATTOP CAR RIFLE - 9mm Para. cal., similar to A2 CAR Rifle, except has is flattop w/o sights. New 2002.

MSR $950	$860	$725	$630	$550	$500	$450	$400

ASA 16 IN. TACTICAL RIFLE - .308 Win. cal., 16 in. stainless steel air gauged regular or match barrel, side charging handle, Hogue pistol grip, guaranteed 1/2 in. MOA, individually tested, 8 3/4 lbs. New 2002.

MSR $1,675	$1,475	$1,200	$995	$850	$750	$650	$525

Add $515 for Match Rifle (includes fluted and ported barrel, 2 stage trigger, and hard chromed bolt and carrier).

ASA 24 IN. MATCH RIFLE - .308 Win. cal., 24 in. stainless steel air gauged match barrel with or w/o fluting/porting, side charging handle, Hogue pistol grip, guaranteed 1/2 in. MOA, individually tested, approx. 12 lbs. New 2002.

MSR $1,675	$1,475	$1,200	$995	$850	$750	$650	$525

Add $515 for Match Rifle (includes fluted and ported barrel, 2 stage trigger, and hard chromed bolt and carrier).

AMERICAN WESTERN ARMS, INC.

Previous trademark and importer 1999-2004, and located in Delray Beach, FL. During late 2004, the remaining assets of this company were sold and a new company was established as AWA USA in Hialeah, FL. SAA revolver components were manufactured in the former Armi San Marco factory in Italy (now AWA International, Inc.), and assembled in the U.S. This plant was thoroughly updated during 2000 with all new tooling, stringent quality control, and now has bone colored case hardening in house. Dealer sales.

Please refer to AWA USA listing for current information.

AWA International Inc. purchased American Western Arms, Inc. in 2000, along with Classic Old West Styles (COWS) and Millenium Leather.

Please refer to the *Blue Book of Modern Black Powder Arms* by John Allen & Dennis Adler (now online also) for more information and prices on American Western Arms' lineup of modern black powder models.

REVOLVERS: CARTRIDGE CONVERSIONS & OPEN TOP

1851 NAVY RICHARDS-TYPE CARTRIDGE CONVERSION - .38 Spl., .38 LC, or .44-40 WCF, 5 1/2 or 7 1/2 in. octagon barrel, color case hardened frame and hammer. Disc. 2000.

$650	$525	$450	$375	$300	$225	$200

Last MSR was $750.

1860 ARMY RICHARDS-TYPE CARTRIDGE CONVERSION - .38 Spl., .38 LC, or .44-40 WCF, 5 1/2 or 8 in. round barrel, color case hardened frame and hammer. Disc. 2000.

$650	$525	$450	$375	$300	$225	$200

Last MSR was $750.

1861 NAVY RICHARDS-TYPE CARTRIDGE CONVERSION - .38 Spl., .38 LC, or .44-40 WCF, 5 1/2 or 7 1/2 in. round barrel, color case hardened frame and hammer. Disc. 2000.

$650	$525	$450	$375	$300	$225	$200

Last MSR was $750.

1872 OPEN TOP - .38 Spl., .38 LC, or .44-40 WCF, 5 1/2 or 7 1/2 in. round barrel, color case hardened frame and hammer. Disc. 2000.

$650	$525	$450	$375	$300	$225	$200

Last MSR was $750.

REVOLVERS: SINGLE ACTION

PEACEKEEPER (MODEL 1) - .32-20 WCF (special order), .38-40 WCF (special order), .357 Mag., .44 Spl. (special order), .44-40 WCF, or .45 LC cal., 3, 3 1/2 (Sheriff), 4, 4 3/4, 5 1/2, 7 1/2, 10 (Buntline), or 12 (Buntline) in. barrel, charcoal case colored receiver, blue finish, black powder or cross-pin frame, beveled cylinder, original hammer design w/o transfer bar safety, 2-line patent dates, 1st Generation Colt style hard rubber grips, assembled in America. While original prototypes were developed in 2000, actual importation was late 2000-2003.

$725	$600	$550	$500	$460	$430	$400

Last MSR was $835.

　　　　Add $35 for Sheriff, Thunderer, Birdshead, or Cavalry/Artillery configurations.
　　　　Add $165 for bright nickel finish.
　　　　Add $1,450 for grade A (25% coverage), $1,750 for grade B (50% coverage), $1,920 for grade C (75% coverage), or $2,240 for grade D (100% coverage) engraving – nickel finish only.
　　　　Add $90 for dual cylinder.

GRADING - PPGS™	100%	98%	95%	90%	80%	70%	60%

LONGHORN - .357 Mag., .44-40 WCF, or .45 LC cal., 3 1/2 (Sheriff), 4 3/4, 5 1/2, or 7 1/2 in. barrel, case colored receiver, blue finish, one-piece walnut grips, 2 line address, assembled in America. Imported 2001-2003.

	$435	$375	$340	$315	$285	$260	$230

Last MSR was $495.

> **Add $30 for Sheriff or Birdshead/Thunderer Model.**
> **Add $100 for nickel finish.**

CLASSIC - .357 Mag. or .45 LC cal. only, flat main spring, 4 3/4 or 5 1/2 in. barrel, blue frame, one piece smooth walnut grips, two line patent dates, 5-5 1/2 lb. trigger. Imported 2003-2004.

	$385	$340	$315	$285	$260	$230	$200

Last MSR was $440.

> **Add $125 for Turnbull case colors.**
> **Add $195 for nickel or hard chrome finish.**

* *Classic Bisley* - similar to Classic, except has Bisley configuration frame. Imported 2004 only.

	$450	$395	$350	$315	$285	$260	$230

Last MSR was $520.

> **Add $125 for Turnbull case colors.**
> **Add $195 for nickel or hard chrome finish.**

ULTIMATE - .32-20 WCF, .38-40 WCF, .357 Mag., .44-40 WCF, .44 Spl., or .45 LC cal., coil suspension main spring, 3, 3 1/2, 4, 4 1/2, 5 1/2, or 7 1/2 in. barrel, blue frame, one piece smooth walnut grips. Imported 2003-2004.

	$525	$450	$395	$350	$315	$285	$260

Last MSR was $600.

> **Add $125 for Turnbull case colors.**
> **Add $195 for nickel or hard chrome finish.**

RIFLES: LEVER ACTION

1892 CARBINE/RIFLE - .357 Mag., .44-40 WCF, or .45 LC cal., 20 (short rifle – octagon, carbine – round) or 24 1/2 octagon barrel, blue finish, uncheckered walnut stock and forearm. Limited importation from Italy late 2000 only.

	$625	$525	$450	$395	$350	$300	$250

Last MSR was $695.

LIGHTNING CARBINE/RIFLE - .32-20 WCF, .38 Spl., .38-40 WCF, .44-40 WCF, or .45 LC cal., patterned after the Colt Lightning rifle, firing pin block safety, blue finish, 20 (carbine) or 24 in. round or octagon barrel, engraved receiver with AWA logo, walnut stock and forearm. Imported 2003-2004.

	$745	$625	$575	$500	$460	$430	$400

Last MSR was $850.

> **Add $40 for octagon barrel.**
> **Add $350 for White Lightning Model (polished steel receiver.)**
> **Add $300 for case colored hardened finish.**

* *Lightning Carbine/Rifle Limited Edition* - similar to regular Lightning Carbine/Rifle, except has engraved chrome receiver and select walnut stock, only 500 mfg. Imported 2003-2004.

	$1,075	$900	$775	$650	$575	$500	$460

Last MSR was $1,200.

SHOTGUNS: SXS

HAMMERLESS COACHGUN - while initially advertised during 2000, this model never went into production.

GRADING - PPGS™	100%	98%	95%	90%	80%	70%	60%

AMTEC 2000, INC.

Previous trademark incorporating Erma Werke (German) and H & R 1871 (U.S.) companies located in Gardner, MA until 1999. Amtec 2000, Inc. previously imported the Erma SR 100 rifle (see listing in Erma Suhl section).

REVOLVERS

5 SHOT REVOLVER - .38 S&W cal., 5 shot double action, swing-out cylinder, 2 or 3 in. barrel, transfer bar safety, Pachmayr composition grips, high polish blue, matte electroless nickel, or stainless steel construction, fixed sights, approx. 25 oz., 200 mfg. 1996-99, all were distributed and sold in Europe only (no U.S. pricing).

ANCIENS ETABLISSEMENTS PIEPER

Please refer to the Bayard section in this text for Bayard Models 1908, 1923, and 1930. In addition, Bergmann-Bayard Models 1908 and 1910 mfg. in Gaggenau, Germany will appear under the Bergman heading.

ANGEL ARMS INC.

Previous manufacturer located in Hayward, CA, 1998-2001.

PISTOLS: SEMI-AUTO

The pistols listed below were designed to shoot a unique integrated case projectile (ICP). These projectiles were hollow, contained the powder charge, and since the case was the projectile, there was no ejection.

MODEL 1000 SE GUN ONE - .45 ICP (Integrated Case Projectile) cal., unique semi-auto design, mag tube is located on top of 6 in. fixed barrel.

While advertised, this model never went into production. $1,900 was the projected MSR.

MODEL QT 427 ZMR - .427 ICP (Integrated Case Projectile) cal., break open action, 5 shot tube or 10 shot staggered mag, 3 1/2 in. barrel, located underneath clear mag tube, 5 oz., compact size.

While advertised, this model never went into production. $900 was the projected MSR.

ANSCHÜTZ

Current manufacturer (J. G. Anschütz, GmbH & Co. KG) established in 1856 and currently located in Ulm, Germany. Sporting and certain models of target rifles are currently distributed by AcuSport since 1996, headquartered in Bellefontaine, OH, Zanders Sporting Goods (1997) located in Baldwin, IL, and Ellett Brothers, located in Chapin, SC,

DIE MEISTER MACHER

beginning 2000. Target rifles are imported by various distributors (please see Trademark Index for current listing). Beginning 2003, sporting rifles are distributed by Jerry's Sport Center, located in Forest City, PA, Outdoor Sports Headquarters, located in Dayton, OH, Bonitz Brothers, located in Harrisbug, PA, and Simmons Gun Specialties, located in Spring Hill, KS. Sporting rifles were imported 1996-2003 by Tristar Sporting Arms. Ltd., located in N. Kansas City, MO. Previously distributed until 2000 by Go Sportsmen's Supply, located in Billings, MT. Previously imported and distributed through 1995 in the U.S. by Precision Sales International Inc., located in Westfield, MA.

For more information and current pricing on both new and used Anschütz airguns, please refer to the *Blue Book of Airguns* by Dr. Robert Beeman & John Allen (now online also).

PISTOLS: BOLT ACTION

Anschütz also manufactured an MSP Pistol Series with ergonomic stock for the silhouette shooters. This series was designed for target shooting. All currently produced Anschütz pistols are delivered with a keyed security gun lock.

MODEL 1416P/1451P (EXEMPLAR)

.22 LR cal., bolt action, Match 64 left-hand action (for right-hand shooters), approx. 7 (original Silhouette Model, mfg. 1994-95) or 10 in. barrel, single shot (Model 1451P, new 1997) or repeater with 5 shot mag. (Model 1416P), two-stage trigger, adj. rear sight, receiver grooved for scope, contoured grip and forestock are stippled, 3 1/3 lbs., also available for left-hand shooters. Mfg. 1987-97.

	$395	$345	$295	$250	$225	$200	$180

Last MSR was $470.

Add $17 for single shot (Model 1451P).

Add $110 for right-hand action (for left-hand shooters).

This model was previously designated the Exemplar until 1996.

❊ *Exemplar Magnum* - while advertised in 1987, only one .22 Mag. was manufactured.

❊ *Exemplar XIV* - .22 LR cal., similar to Exemplar, except has 14 in. barrel, 4.15 lbs. Imported 1988-95.

	$450	$370	$300	$250	$225	$200	$180

Last MSR was $562.

❊ *Exemplar Hornet* - .22 Hornet cal., 5 shot mag., Match 54 left-hand action, 10 in. barrel, grooved and tapped w/o sights, 4.35 lbs. Imported 1988-95.

	$835	$685	$575	$525	$475	$415	$365

Last MSR was $995.

This model may also be marked M-1730MSPE Field.

❊ *Model 1416 MSPR/MSPE* - .22 LR cal., silhouette variation of the Exemplar pistol, MSPR designates repeater, MSPE designates single shot. Mfg. 1997 only.

	$1,100	$875	$750	$625	$525	$450	$375

Last MSR was $1,260.

MODEL 64P

.22 LR or .22 Mag. (disc. 2001) cal., right-hand Match 64 bolt action, 10 in. barrel drilled and tapped (sights not included), weather proof "Choate" Rynite stock with stippling, 2 stage trigger, 4 (.22 Mag.) or 5 shot mag., 3 1/2 lbs. Mfg. 1998-2003.

	$445	$385	$335	$285	$240	$200	$180

Last MSR was $509.

Add 10% for .22 Mag. cal. (Model 64P Mag., disc. 2001).

Add $73 for accessory sight set.

❊ *Model 64LP* - .22 LR cal., left-hand Match 64 bolt action, 12 in. drilled and tapped barrel (sights not included), "Choate" Rynite stock with stippling, two-stage trigger, 5 shot mag., approx. 3 1/2 lbs. Imported 2003-2004.

	$495	$400	$350	$300	$275	$235	$200

Last MSR was $602.

MODEL 17LP

.17 HMR cal., 4 shot mag., otherwise similar to Model 64LP. Imported 2003-2004.

	$535	$450	$400	$350	$300	$250	$225

Last MSR was $651.

RIFLES: BOLT ACTION, DISC.

Sile Distributors located in NY acted as an import agent during the early 1960s which can be identified by Sile barrel markings. Savage imported Anschütz rifles were available from 1963-1981 and also have Savage/Anschütz barrel markings. While some of those models might not be listed below, refer to models of similar caliber and quality that are listed to ascertain values.

During the period when Savage was importing Anschütz rifles, certain models in the Anschütz line were designated either "Savage-Anschütz" or "Anschütz-Savage" for sales by Savage in the U.S. Conversely, certain models manufactured by Savage were designated "Anschütz-Savage" for sale by Anschütz in Europe. Some of these models did not have any modifications but others were restocked, supplied with different sights, and had other different features from their origi-

GRADING - PPGS™	100%	98%	95%	90%	80%	70%	60%

nal counterparts. In most cases, the original model numbers were used.

Some "Anschütz-Savage" rifles have made their way into the U.S. While somewhat rare, these rifles are typically based on the Savage Model 110 action. They are not as desirable as those "Savage-Anschütz" marked rifles utilizing the superior Anschütz actions. Anschütz also manufactured between 1,000-2,000 rifles utilizing SAKO actions in .222 Rem. cal. in the late 50s-early 60s. These guns will approximate values shown on the discontinued centerfire models listed below.

Currently, Anschütz offers 3 different actions. The 1451 action is Anschütz's entry level action, which is lightweight in design, utilizes cam cocking, and has a lateral sliding safety. The 1451 action is currently used in the Models 1451 D KL, 1451 R Sporter Target, and 1451 Target. The Match 64 utilizes a cam cocking system with claw extractor and ejector, grooved receiver, and sliding safety on the right side behind the bolt. The Model 64 match action is used on the Model 1416 and variations, 1418, 64MP R, 1516, 1517 D Classic, 1517 D HB Classic, 1517 D Monte Carlo, 1517 M PR, and the Model 64 Target pistol. The Match 54 is Anschütz's top-of-the-line action, and features dual locking lugs on the bolt which are seated eccentricaly in the receiver, allowing more support for improved stock bedding. It also features a cam cocking bolt, 2 position pivot rear safety, and is drilled and tapped. The Match 54 action is currently utilized on the 1710 series, 1712D, 1717, 1720, 1730 series, 1733, and 1740 Models.

The models below have been listed in numerical sequence.

MARK 10 TARGET RIFLE - .22 LR cal., single shot. 26 in. heavy barrel, adj. sights, globe front, target stock with full pistol grip, adj. palm stop. Mfg. 1963-81.

	$425	$365	$335	$295	$260	$230	$210

MODEL 54 SPORTER - .22 LR cal., Match 54 action, 5 shot mag., 24 in. round tapered barrel, Monte Carlo roll-over cheekpiece, folding leaf sight, checkered pistol grip. Mfg. 1963-81.

	$750	$675	$625	$525	$450	$400	$360

MODEL 54M - similar to Model 54 Sporter, except .22 Mag. cal.

	$850	$750	$675	$575	$500	$435	$395

MODEL MATCH 64 - .22 LR cal., Match 64 action, single shot, 26 in. barrel, hardwood stock with stipled ergonomic pistol grip, adj. pad, grooved receiver, approx. 8 lbs. Disc.

	$575	$500	$450	$400	$350	$295	$250

Subtract $150 if w/o correct Anschütz micrometer sights (front and rear).

MODEL 141 - .22 LR cal., 5 shot mag., 23 in. round tapered barrel, Monte Carlo stock, folding leaf sight. Disc.

	$375	$325	$275	$225	$200	$180	$160

❋ *Model 141M (Mag.)* - similar to Model 141, except .22 Mag. cal.

	$450	$385	$325	$265	$225	$200	$180

MODEL 153 - .222 Rem. cal., 24 in. barrel, folding leaf rear sight, French walnut stock, rosewood forend tip and pistol grip cap. Mfg. 1963-81.

	$750	$675	$575	$475	$400	$375	$350

MODEL 153-S - similar to Model 153, 24 in. barrel, double set triggers.

	$850	$775	$625	$525	$425	$400	$375

MODEL 164 - .22 LR cal., 5 shot mag., 23 in. round tapered barrel, Monte Carlo stock, folding leaf sight. Mfg. 1963-81.

	$425	$375	$325	$300	$250	$200	$160

MODEL 164M - similar to Model 164, except .22 Mag. cal.

	$475	$425	$375	$325	$275	$210	$180

MODEL 184 - .22 LR cal., 21 1/2 in. barrel, Monte Carlo combination, checkered pistol grip, Schnabel forend, folding leaf sight. Mfg. 1963-1981.

	$495	$435	$375	$325	$275	$210	$180

GRADING - PPGS™	100%	98%	95%	90%	80%	70%	60%

MODEL 1400 - .22 LR cal., regular barrel, with sights. Disc.

	$350	$320	$290	$260	$230	$210	$195

MODEL 1407 I.S.U. MATCH 54 - .22 LR cal., heavy barrel, match two-stage trigger, stippled walnut stock and forearm with aluminum rail, aperture sights. Disc.

	$650	$550	$475	$400	$350	$300	$260

Last MSR was approx. $530.

MODEL 1408 - .22 LR cal., heavy barrel, no sights. Disc.

	$450	$375	$325	$275	$235	$210	$195

Add $150 for 1408 ED Model.

MODEL 1411 MATCH 54 - .22 LR cal., prone position target model, heavy barrel, aperture sights, side safety, fast lock time, adj. cheekpiece. Disc.

	$650	$550	$475	$400	$350	$300	$260

Last MSR was approx. $575.

Subtract $150 if w/o correct Anschütz micrometer sights (front and rear).

MODEL 1413 SUPER MATCH 54 - .22 LR cal., top-of-the-line free style international target rifle, adj. cheekpiece and curved buttplate, heavy target barrel with aperture sights. Disc.

	$825	$725	$625	$525	$425	$375	$325

Last MSR was approx. $875.

Subtract $150 if w/o correct Anschütz micrometer sights (front and rear).

MODEL 1418 - .22 LR cal., sporter variation, previous importation by Savage Arms.

	$375	$325	$275	$225	$200	$175	$150

MODEL 1418 MANNLICHER - .22 LR cal., hunting model, fine checkering, 5 shot mag.

	$825	$750	$650	$550	$450	$375	$325

MODEL 1450 - .22 LR cal., Sporter, 5 shot mag.

	$450	$375	$325	$275	$225	$200	$175

MODEL 1518 MANNLICHER - deluxe model of Model 1418.

	$950	$850	$725	$625	$525	$450	$350

MODEL 1574 SPORTER - .22 Mag., .222 Rem., .22-250 Rem., .223 Rem., .243 Win., or .308 Win. cal. Mfg. by Krico (Kriegeskorte) located at Stuttgart and distributed by Anschütz, approx. 1,000 imported during 1970-73.

	$795	$695	$595	$540	$485	$430	$375

MODEL 1807 - .22 LR cal., replacement for the Model 1407 Match 54, for I.S.U. and NRA shooting, 26 in. barrel, Match 54 action, 10 lbs. Disc.

	$495	$425	$350	$300	$250	$225	$200

RIFLES: BOLT ACTION SPORTER, .17 RIMFIRE - CURRENT MFG.

MODEL 1502D HB CLASSIC - .17 Mach 2 cal., features Model 64 action with single stage trigger, 5 shot mag., checkered walnut stock, choice of regular or grooved beavertail forend, heavy barrel w/o sights. Importation began 2005.

MSR $790		$695	$595	$550	$495	$450	$415	$385

Add $46 for beavertail forend.

MODEL 1517D CLASSIC - .17 HMR cal., features Model 64 action with single stage trigger, 4 shot mag., checkered walnut stock with or w/o Monte Carlo cheekpiece, 23 in. regular or heavy barrel, 5.5 or 6.2 (heavy barrel) lbs. Importation began 2003.

MSR $834		$720	$615	$565	$500	$450	$415	$385

Add $21 for Monte Carlo stock.
Add $51 for left-hand Match 64 action (new 2004).
Add $44 for Model 1517D HB with heavy barrel and grooved beavertail forend (new 2005).

GRADING - PPGS™	100%	98%	95%	90%	80%	70%	60%

✳ *Model 1517 MP R Multi-Purpose* - .17 HMR cal., 25.5 in. heavy match barrel, two-stage trigger, no sights, hardwood Monte Carlo stock with beavertail forend, 9 lbs. Importation began 2003.

	MSR $952	$815	$675	$585	$530	$470	$425	$395

MODEL 1702D HB CLASSIC - .17 Mach 2 cal., Match 54 action, 23 in. heavy barrel w/o sights, 5 shot mag., checkered walnut stock and forend, match grade single stage adj. trigger, 7.3 lbs. Importation began 2005.

	MSR $1,512	$1,300	$1,075	$875	$750	$650	$550	$450

MODEL 1717D KL (CUSTOM) - .17 HMR cal., features Match 54 action, 23 in. barrel, no sights, Monte Carlo stock with pistol grip cap and Schnabel forend, 7.3 lbs. Importation began late 2002.

	MSR $1,642	$1,365	$1,100	$925	$825	$725	$625	$525

Add $274 for Meistergrade (select walnut and gold etched trigger guard).

MODEL 1717D CLASSIC - .17 HMR cal., features Match 54 action, 4 shot mag., 23 in. regular or heavy barrel, no sights, 8 lbs. New 2002.

	MSR $1,539	$1,300	$1,175	$925	$800	$700	$600	$525

Add $274 for Meistergrade (select walnut and gold etched trigger guard).

RIFLES: BOLT ACTION SPORTER, .22 LR - RECENT MFG.

All currently produced Anschütz rifles are delivered with a keyed security gun lock.

Current manufactured Anschütz rifles use the following alphabetical suffixes when describing factory features and options. D = single stage trigger, G = threaded barrel, HB = heavy barrel, KL = folding leaf sight, KV = heavy tangent signt, L = left-hand action, MP = Multi-Purpose, R = repeater, and ST = double set trigger.

KADETT - .22 LR cal., bolt action, youth dimensions, 22 in. barrel, 5 shot clip mag., folding leaf rear sight, single stage trigger, grooved receiver, checkered hard-wood stock, 5 1/2 lbs. Mfg. 1987 only.

		$235	$200	$180	$165	$150	$135	$120

Last MSR was $265.

ACHIEVER - .22 LR cal., bolt action, 19 1/2 in. barrel, single shot, folding leaf rear sight, two stage trigger, grooved receiver, stippled hard-wood stock with vented forearm and adj. length of pull, 5 1/4 lbs. Mfg. 1987-95.

		$340	$280	$230	$205	$185	$165	$150

Last MSR was $399.

✳ *Achiever ST* - .22 LR cal., 2000 MK single shot action, slide safety, two stage trigger, adj. length of pull stock, target sights, approx. 6 1/2 lbs. Mfg. 1994-95.

		$415	$360	$315	$260	$230	$205	$185

Last MSR was $485.

MODEL WOODCHUCKER - .22 LR cal., similar to Model 1449D Youth, sold exclusively by R.S.R. Wholesale.

		$210	$185	$165	$150	$135	$120	$110

MODEL 64MP - .22 LR cal., repeater, 5 shot mag., 21.2 regular (disc. 2002) or 25.5 (new 2003) in. drilled and tapped heavy match steel or stainless steel (mfg. 2000-2003) barrel, two stage trigger, uncheckered walnut stained stock and beavertail forend, adj. rubber buttplate. Importation began 1999.

	MSR $916	$775	$625	$500	$400	$300	$240	$225

Add $79 for stainless steel barrel (disc. 2003).
Add $50 for left-hand action (disc. 2005).
Subtract approx. $75 if w/o swivel rail.

GRADING - PPGS™	100%	98%	95%	90%	80%	70%	60%

✳ *Model 64R Sporter Target* - .22 LR cal., repeater, Match 64 action, two-stage match trigger, match grade barrel, checkered hardwood stock, 10 shot mag., adj. butt-plate and stainless steel rail. Importation began 2004.

MSR $932	$785	$625	$500	$400	$300	$240	$225

This model replaced the Model 1451 Sport Target during 2004.

MODEL 1416D CUSTOM (LUXUS) - .22 LR cal., Match 64 action, 22.5 in. barrel, 5 or 10 shot mag., cam cocking system on recent mfg., checkered Monte Carlo walnut stock, folding leaf sight, 6 lbs. 2 oz.

MSR $819	$715	$575	$475	$375	$300	$250	$225

This model utilizes the Match 64 action, similar to the Anschütz Model 1403 Target.

✳ *Model 1416D Fiberglass* - similar to Model 1416D Custom, except has McMillan fiberglass stock in hunter brown color and includes roll-over cheekpiece and checkered Wundhammer swell pistol grip, 5 1/4 lbs. Imported 1991 only.

	$755	$650	$575	$525	$475	$415	$365

Last MSR was $842.

MODEL 1416D CLASSIC - same specifications as Model 1416D Custom, except straight hardwood stock.

MSR $768	$660	$525	$425	$365	$315	$260	$240

Add $66 for left-hand action (Model 1416LD).

Add $28 for iron sights.

✳ *1416D Classic Heavy Barrel* - similar to Model 1416D Classic, except has heavy barrel and no sights, grooved beavertail forend became standard 2005. Mfg. 2000-2001, reintroduced 2003.

MSR $813	$700	$550	$435	$375	$325	$260	$240

MODEL 1418D - .22 LR cal., Match 64 action, Mannlicher full stock, skipline checkering, 19 3/4 in. barrel, same action as Model 1416D, 5 lbs. 5 oz. Importation disc. 1995, resumed 1998-2003.

	$915	$800	$700	$575	$495	$425	$360

Last MSR was $1,014.

Add $40 for set trigger (mfg. 1985-89).

MODEL 1448D - .22 Clay Bird cal., Model 1451 action, 22 1/2 in. smooth bore barrel w/o sights, repeater, 5 shot mag., checkered walnut stained stock and forend. Imported 1999-2001.

	$295	$265	$240	$220	$200	$185	$170

Last MSR was $349.

MODEL 1449D YOUTH - .22 LR cal., bolt action design, youth dimensions, 16 1/4 in. tapered barrel with adj. rear sight, receiver is grooved for scope mounting, 5 shot mag. with single shot adapter available, European hardwood stock, 12 1/4 in. trigger pull, 3 1/2 lbs. Imported 1990-91 only.

	$210	$185	$165	$150	$135	$120	$110

Last MSR was $249.

MODEL 1451 E/R SPORTER/TARGET - .22 LR cal., single shot (Model 1451E) or 5 shot repeater (Model 1451R), Model 1451 action, sporter target model w/o front sight, 22 (new 1998) or 22 3/4 (disc. 1997) in. barrel w/o sights, stippled pistol grip wood stock and vent. forend (with or w/o beavertail), 6 1/2 lbs. Mfg. 1996-2001.

	$435	$395	$360	$330	$300	$280	$260

Last MSR was $485.

Subtract approx. $100 for Model 1451E (single shot).

Add $110 for Model 1451 Junior Super Target (single shot only).

✳ **Model 1451R Sporter Target Prisma** - .22 LR cal., 5 shot repeater, entry level cam cocking, claw extractor, and recessed bolt face, sliding safety, fully adj. stipled hardwood stock, 22 in. target barrel, grooved receiver, optional micrometer sights, 6.3 lbs. Imported 2001-2003.

	100%	98%	95%	90%	80%	70%	60%
	$455	$415	$385	$350	$325	$300	$275

Last MSR was $515.

This model was replaced by the Model 64R Sporter Target.

✳ **Model 1451ST-R** - .22 LR cal., repeater, 5 shot mag., drilled and tapped 22 in. barrel w/o sights, cam cocking system, 2 stage trigger, unchecked walnut stained hardwood stock. Imported 1999-2001.

	$435	$395	$360	$330	$300	$280	$260

Last MSR was $485.

✳ **Model 1451D Custom** - similar to Model 1451D Classic, except has walnut stock with Monte Carlo cheekpiece, Schnabel forend, and sling swivels, 5 lbs. Mfg. 1998-2001.

	$430	$395	$360	$330	$300	$280	$260

Last MSR was $480.

✳ **Model 1451D Classic (Super)** - .22 LR cal., 5 shot, 22 3/4 in. barrel with front sights, grooved receiver, walnut finished straight hardwood stock, 5 lbs. Mfg. 1996-2001.

	$335	$280	$245	$210	$175	$160	$150

Last MSR was $398.

This model was designated the 1451 Super during 1996-97.

MODEL 1466D REPEATER - .22 LR cal., 24 in. conically tapered barrel with open sights, grooved receiver, checkered Monte Carlo walnut stock and forend. Imported 1996 only.

	$660	$525	$435	$375	$315	$260	$235

Last MSR was $766.

MODEL 1710D CUSTOM (1700D) - .22 LR cal., bolt action, Match 54 action, 5 shot mag., 23 3/4 (new 1998) or 24 (disc. 1997) in. regular (new 1998) or heavy (disc. 1997) barrel, folding rear sight, single or two-stage trigger (Model 1710 KL, mfg. 2003 only), Monte Carlo stock with roll-over cheekpiece and skipline checkering, 6.5-7.25 lbs.

MSR $1,570	$1,315	$1,050	$825	$675	$575	$475	$400

Add $278 for Meistergrade (select walnut and gold etched trigger guard – disc. 1996, resumed 1998 w/o gold trigger guard).

This model was designated 1422D until 1989 when it was changed to the Model 1700D with some modifications. In 1996, model nomenclature changed from Model 1700D Custom to the Model 1710D Custom. The Model 1400D Meistergrade was disc. 1987 – the last advertised retail price was $930.

The Model 1700D Custom employs the Anschütz Match 54 action.

✳ **Model 1700D Graphite** - similar to Model 1700D Custom, except has McMillan black graphite reinforced stock with Monte Carlo roll-over cheekpiece, includes sling and swivels, 22 in. barrel, 7 1/4 lbs. Imported 1991-95.

	$1,130	$885	$760	$650	$550	$450	$375

Last MSR was $1,299.

1710D CLASSIC - same general specifications as 1700D/1710D Custom, regular straight stock, choice of regular (disc. 2003), heavy (new 1999), or heavy stainless (mfg. 2000-2003) barrel, open sights (disc. 1994), 7.3-8 lbs. Disc. 1994. Importation resumed 1998.

MSR $1,469	$1,235	$1,025	$875	$750	$650	$525	$425

Add $274 for Meistergrade (select walnut and gold etched trigger guard, disc. 1994, reintroduced 2000).

This model was also available as a 2000 Signature Series – includes high polish bluing, select American black walnut, "1 of 200" and "Dieter Anschütz 2000" signature in 24Kt. gold on bottom of trigger guard, aluminum case, and dated certificate at no extra charge.

This model was designated 1422DCL Classic until 1989 when it was changed to the Model 1700D Classic with some modifications. The Model 1422DCL Classic Meistergrade was disc. 1987 – the last advertised retail price was $875. In 1998, this model was reintroduced as the Model 1710D Classic.

MODEL 1700D FEATHERWEIGHT (FWT)
- similar to Model 1700D Custom, except has matte black McMillan fiberglass stock configured like the Custom Model, 22 in. barrel, no sights, 6 1/4 lbs. Imported 1989-95.

	100%	98%	95%	90%	80%	70%	60%
	$1,075	$895	$775	$650	$550	$450	$375

Last MSR was $1,230.

❋ *Model 1700D Featherweight Deluxe* - similar specification to the Model 1700D Featherweight, except has skip-line checkered Fibergrain synthetic stock with realistic wood grain. Imported 1990-95.

	100%	98%	95%	90%	80%	70%	60%
	$1,235	$1,050	$875	$775	$650	$550	$450

Last MSR was $1,460.

MODEL 1700D BAVARIAN
- .22 LR cal., 24 in. barrel, 5 shot mag., checkered European style stock with European Monte Carlo cheekpiece and schnabel forend, 7 1/2 lbs. Mfg. 1988-95.

	100%	98%	95%	90%	80%	70%	60%
	$1,165	$935	$775	$650	$550	$450	$375

Last MSR was $1,364.

Add $199 for Meistergrade variation (select walnut).

MODEL 1712D
- .22 LR cal., current top-of-the-line sporter rifle with deluxe walnut. Imported 1997-98 only.

	100%	98%	95%	90%	80%	70%	60%
	$1,300	$1,100	$895	$775	$650	$550	$450

Last MSR was $1,495.

MODEL 1712 SILHOUETTE SPORTER
- .22 LR cal., similar to Model 1712D, except has Monte Carlo stock with adj. LOP and two-stage trigger. Importation began 2003.

	100%	98%	95%	90%	80%	70%	60%
MSR $1,554	$1,295	$1,025	$850	$750	$625	$525	$425

DIE MEISTERMACHER
- .22 LR cal., Match 54 action, top-of-the-line model, limited edition of 25 guns, select wood, extra polish on metal parts, hand-lapped barrel, with numerous gold inlays including Olympic wreath. Mfg. 1985.

	100%	98%	95%	90%	80%	70%	60%
	$2,750	$2,000	$1,600				

Last MSR was $2,475.

This variation sold out in late 1988.

RIFLES: BOLT ACTION SPORTER, .22 MAG. - RECENT MFG.

All currently produced Anschütz rifles are delivered with a keyed security gun lock.

Current manufactured Anschütz rifles use the following alphabetical suffixes when describing factory features and options. D = single stage trigger, G = threaded barrel, HB = heavy barrel, KL = folding leaf sight, KV = heavy tangent signt, L = left-hand action, MP = Multi-Purpose, R = repeater, and ST = double set trigger.

MODEL 1516D CUSTOM (LUXUS)
- similar to Model 1416D, except .22 Mag. cal., 4 shot mag., 6 lbs. 2 oz. Importation disc. 2003.

	100%	98%	95%	90%	80%	70%	60%
	$630	$530	$465	$385	$335	$275	$250

Last MSR was $717.

This model utilizes the Match 64 action, similar to the Anschütz Model 1403 Target. In 1996, model nomenclature changed from the Model 1516D Custom to Model 1516D Luxus and during 1998, it changed back to Model 1516D Custom.

❋ *1516D/DCL Classic* - same specifications as Model 1516D Custom, except regular hardwood stained stock, regular or heavy (new 2000) barrel.

	100%	98%	95%	90%	80%	70%	60%
MSR $819	$715	$600	$500	$400	$325	$275	$250

MODEL 1518D (LUXUS) - .22 Mag. cal., otherwise similar to Model 1418D (Mannlicher stock), 4 shot mag., 5 1/2 lbs. Importation disc. 1995, reintroduced 1997, nomenclature was changed to Model 1518D in 1997, disc. 2001.

| | $895 | $795 | $675 | $550 | $440 | $375 | $325 |

Last MSR was $987.

Add $50 for set trigger (disc. 1995).

MODEL 1720D CUSTOM (1700D) - .22 Mag. cal., bolt action, 5 shot mag., 23 3/4 (new 1998) or 24 (disc. 1991) in. regular (new 1998) or heavy (disc. 1991) barrel, iron sights, Monte Carlo stock with skipline checkering, 6 lbs. 10 oz-7 1/4 lbs. Importation disc. 1991, resumed 1998, disc. 2001.

| | $995 | $875 | $750 | $650 | $550 | $450 | $375 |

Last MSR was $1,104 for the Model 1720D Custom.
Last MSR was $1,229 for the Model 1700D.

Add $174 for Meistergrade variation (select walnut).

This model was designated 1522D until 1989 and then reintroduced as the Model 1700D with some modifications. The Model 1522D Custom Meistergrade was disc. 1985 – last advertised retail price was $678. In 1998, this model was reintroduced as the 1720D Custom.

MODEL 1700D/1720D CLASSIC - same general specifications as 1700D Custom, straight regular stock, choice of heavy (new 1999), or regular diameter barrel. Importation disc. 1991, resumed 1998, disc. 2001.

| | $900 | $795 | $700 | $625 | $525 | $425 | $350 |

Last MSR was $1,021 for the Model 1720D Classic.
Last MSR was $1,199 for the Model 1700D Classic.

Add $174 for Meistergrade variation (select walnut).

This model was designated 1522DCL until 1989 and then reintroduced as the Model 1700D with some modifications. In 1998, this model was reintroduced as the 1720D Classic. The Model 1522DCL Classic Meistergrade was disc. 1985 – the last advertised retail price was $660.

MODEL 1700D BAVARIAN - .22 Mag. cal., 24 in. barrel, clip mag., checkered European style stock with European Monte Carlo cheekpiece and schnabel forend, 7 1/2 lbs. Mfg. 1988-95.

| | $1,165 | $935 | $775 | $650 | $550 | $450 | $375 |

Last MSR was $1,364.

Add $199 for Meistergrade variation (select walnut).

RIFLES: BOLT ACTION SPORTER, CENTERFIRE - RECENT MFG.

All currently produced Anschütz rifles are delivered with a keyed security gun lock.

Current manufactured Anschütz rifles use the following alphabetical suffixes when describing factory features and options. D = single stage trigger, G = threaded barrel, HB = heavy barrel, KL = folding leaf sight, KV = heavy tangent signt, L = left-hand action, MP = Multi-Purpose, R = repeater, and ST = double set trigger.

MODEL 1433D - .22 Hornet cal., special order only, Match 54 target action, Mannlicher full stock, 4 shot mag. Disc. 1986.

| | $995 | $840 | $740 | $640 | $525 | $425 | $350 |

Last MSR was $826.

Add 5% for set trigger (new 1985).

MODEL 1730D CUSTOM (1700D) - .22 Hornet cal., 24 in. barrel, folding leaf sight, Monte Carlo stock with skipline checkering and rosewood grip cap, 4 shot mag., 7.75 lbs. Model 1432D was disc. 1987, and the Model 1700D was introduced 1989.

| MSR $1,729 | $1,450 | $1,175 | $1,050 | $850 | $750 | $650 | $550 |

Add $270 for Meistergrade variation (select walnut).

This model was designated 1432D until 1987 and then reintroduced 1989 as the Model 1700D with some modifications. In 1996, model nomenclature changed from the Model 1700D Custom to the Model 1730D Custom. The Model 1432D Custom Meistergrade was disc. 1986 – the last advertised retail price was $770.

The 1700D Custom comes standard with the Anschütz Match 54 action.

✱ *1700D Graphite* - similar to Model 1700D Custom, except has McMillan black graphite reinforced stock with Monte Carlo roll-over cheekpiece, includes sling and swivels, 22 in. barrel, 7 1/4 lbs. Imported 1995 only.

	$1,235	$1,025	$840	$725	$625	$525	$425

Last MSR was $1,478.

MODEL 1730D CLASSIC (1700D) - .22 Hornet cal., same general specifications as 1700D Custom, except regular stock and 23 1/2 (1432DCL), 5 shot, 23 3/4 regular, heavy (new 1999) – 1730D, or heavy stainless (imported 2001-2002), or 24 (1700D) in. barrel. Disc. 1994, reintroduced 1998.

MSR $1,621	$1,395	$1,150	$925	$775	$675	$550	$450

Last MSR was $1,395 on the Model 1700D Classic.

Add $274 for Meistergrade variation (select walnut).
Add $77 for heavy stainless barrel (disc. 2002).

This model was designated 1432D until 1987 and then reintroduced 1989 as the Model 1700D with some modifications. In 1998, this model was reintroduced as the Model 1730D Classic. This model comes standard with the Anschütz Match 54 action.

MODEL 1700D BAVARIAN - .22 Hornet or .222 Rem. cal., 24 in. barrel, 5 shot mag., checkered European style stock with European Monte Carlo cheekpiece and schnabel forend, 7 1/2 lbs. Mfg. 1988-95.

	$1,325	$1,050	$900	$775	$650	$550	$425

Last MSR was $1,364.

Add approx. $200 for Meistergrade variation (select walnut).

MODEL 1733D - .22 Hornet cal., Mannlicher full stock featuring skipline checkering, European walnut, and rosewood Schnabel tip, 19 3/4 in. barrel with hooded front sight, 6 lbs. 6 oz. Imported 1993-95, reintroduced 1998-2002.

	$1,255	$1,025	$895	$760	$625	$500	$400

Last MSR was $1,416.

MODEL 1740D CUSTOM (1700D) - .222 REM. - .222 Rem. cal., 3 shot, otherwise similar to Model 1700D Custom, except is also available with 23.75 in. barrel.

MSR $1,729	$1,450	$1,175	$1,050	$850	$750	$650	$550

Last MSR was $909 on the Model 1532D.

Add $270 for Meistergrade variation (select walnut).

This model was designated 1532D until 1987 and then reintroduced 1989 as the Model 1700D with some modifications. In 1996, model nomenclature changed from the Model 1700D Custom to the Model 1740D Custom. The Model 1532D MG Custom Meistergrade was disc. 1986 – the last advertised retail price was $770.

MODEL 1740D CLASSIC (1700D) - similar to Model 1700D Custom, except regular stock. Disc. 1994, reintroduced 1998.

MSR $1,621	$1,375	$1,125	$900	$775	$675	$575	$475

Last MSR was $849 on the Model 1532DCL.
Last MSR was $1,395 on the Model 1700D Classic.

Add $274 for Meistergrade variation (select walnut).
Add $77 for heavy stainless barrel (disc. 2002).

This model was designated 1532DCL until 1987 and then reintroduced 1989 as the Model 1700D with some modifications. In 1998, this model was reintroduced as the 1740D Classic.

MODEL 1743D - .222 Rem. cal., Mannlicher full stock variation of the Model 1740D, 6.8 lbs. Imported 1997-2001.

	$1,225	$1,000	$850	$750	$625	$500	$400

Last MSR was $1,373.

MODEL 1533 - .222 Rem. cal., open sights, checkered walnut stock. Disc. 1994.

	$795	$725	$660	$600	$550	$475	$400

GRADING - PPGS™	100%	98%	95%	90%	80%	70%	60%

RIFLES: BOLT ACTION, SILHOUETTE

Currently imported Anschütz silhouette rifles can vary somewhat in price, depending on the distributor and inventory. All currently produced Anschütz rifles are delivered with a keyed security gun lock.

MODEL 2013 SUPER-MATCH FREE RIFLE (BR-50) - .22 LR cal., single shot, 20 in. heavy barrel, no sights, black synthetic stock with adj. cheekpiece and widened forend ("ANSCHÜTZ BR-50" is stenciled on sides), 15.4 lbs. Limited importation 1994-98.

	$2,225	$1,750	$1,375	$1,050	$900	$725	$625

Last MSR was $2,880.

Add $300 for color laminate stock (mfg. 1997-98 only).

Model nomenclature changed from the BR-50 to the Model 2013 in 1997.

MODEL 64S RIFLE - .22 LR cal., single shot, 26 in. round barrel, beavertail forearm, adj. single stage trigger, aperture sights, target stock with Wundhammer grip and adj. buttplate, checkered pistol grip. Mfg. 1963-81.

	$475	$425	$375	$325	$285	$240	$220

Subtract 15% if without sights (Model 64).

This model was available in left-hand or right-hand action.

MODEL 64MS/MP R - .22 LR cal., single shot (Model 64MS, disc. 1996) or 5 shot repeater (Model 64MS R), silhouette target model, 21 1/4 in. barrel, no sights, Wundhammer swell stippled pistol grip beechwood stock, adj. trigger, 8 lbs.

MSR N/A	$925	$800	$700	$600	$500	$400	$325

Add $50 for left-hand action (disc.).

This variation employs a Match 64 action. R suffix nomenclature started 1997, S suffix began 2003.

✳ *Model 64MS - FWT* - similar to Model 64MS, except single stage trigger, 6 1/4 lbs. Disc. 1988.

	$550	$475	$425	$350	$325	$260	$230

Last MSR was $596.

MODEL 54.18MS - .22 LR cal., silhouette target model, 22 in. barrel, Match 54 single shot action, walnut Wundhammer stock is stippled on pistol grip and entire forearm, no sights, 8 lbs. 6 oz. Disc. 1997.

	$1,295	$1,075	$895	$760	$650	$550	$475

Last MSR was $1,579.

Add $96 for left-hand action.

This model employs the Super Match 54 action.

✳ *Model 54.18MS ED* - same action as Model 54.18MS, except has 19 1/4 in. barrel 7/8 in. diameter) with 14 1/4 in. extension tube, 3 removable muzzle weights. Disc. 1988.

	$1,075	$900	$775	$675	$575	$485	$410

Last MSR was $1,215.

Add $100 for left-hand action.

MODEL 54.18MS REP - similar to Model 54.18MS, except has repeating action, 5 shot mag., regular beechwood plain stock with or w/o, thumbhole, vented forend, or black, grey, or tan-green swirl synthetic stock, 7 3/4 lbs.

MSR N/A	$1,750	$1,500	$1,250	$995	$875	$750	$625

Add $75 for synthetic stock.

Add approx. $175 for wood stock, with or w/o thumbhole.

This model features a Super Match 54 action with clip mag. This model was introduced in 1989 with a wood stock and a retail price of $1,650. In 1990, the stock was changed to a synthetic McMillan fiberglass finished in grey. Currently, it is available with beechwood or synthetic stock.

GRADING - PPGS™	100%	98%	95%	90%	80%	70%	60%

✳ *Model 54.18MS REP Deluxe* - deluxe version of the Model 54.18MS REP featuring Fibergrain McMillan stock with advanced thumbhole design and stippled checkering. Imported 1990-97.

	$2,035	$1,600	$1,275	$1,025	$915	$785	$695

Last MSR was $2,450.

RIFLES: BOLT ACTION MATCH, RECENT MFG.

All currently manufactured Anschütz match/target and biathlon rifles listed in the following sections are imported by Champion's Choice, Inc., Champions Shooter's Supply, and Gunsmithing, Inc., unless otherwise noted. These match/target models may vary somewhat in price, depending on the distributor and inventory. All currently produced Anschütz match rifles are delivered with a keyed security gun lock.

MODEL 2000 MK - .22 LR cal., single shot match, 26 in. barrel, aperture sights, 7 1/2 lbs. Disc. 1988.

	$340	$290	$250	$210	$180	$160	$145

Last MSR was $400.

MODEL 1403D - .22 LR cal., improved Model 64S match rifle, single shot, no sights, adj. trigger, 8 lbs. 6 oz. Importation disc. in 1990.

	$600	$525	$450	$360	$300	$260	$225

Last MSR was $700.

> Add $50 for left-hand action (disc. 1988).

MODEL 1803D - .22 LR cal., Match 64 action, 25 1/2 in. target barrel, single stage adj. trigger, blond finished wood with dark stippling on pistol grip and forearm, adj. cheekpiece and buttplate, 8.6 lbs. Imported 1987-93.

	$850	$725	$625	$525	$430	$365	$310

Last MSR was $1,012.

> Add $70 for left-hand action (disc. 1989).

MODEL 1808D RT/1808MS R (RUNNING TARGET) - .22 LR cal., single shot running target model, 19 (w/o barrel weights) – 32 1/2 in. barrel, adj. stock, cheekpiece, trigger, heavy beavertail forend, no sights, muzzle barrel weights, 9 1/4 lbs. Importation disc. 1998.

	$1,850	$1,400	$1,075	$950	$800	$695	$595

Last MSR was $2,220.

> Add $50 for left-hand action (disc. 1991).
> Subtract 20% for earlier models (Model 1808D RT and Model 1808 ED-Super).
> This model was previously designated Model 1808D RT from 1991-96, and also the Model 1808 ED-Super during 1990 and earlier mfg.

MODEL 1808MS R - .22 LR cal., 5 shot repeater designed for metallic silhouette shooting, 19.2 in. barrel w/o sights, thumbhole Monte Carlo stock with grooved forearm featuring "ANSCHÜTZ" in panel scene, approx. 8 lbs. Importation began 1998.

MSR $1,916		$1,695	$1,450	$1,175	$1,025	$900	$800	$700

> This sporting model is distributed by Acusport Corp., Zander's Sporting Goods, Inc., and Ellett Brothers.

MODEL 1813 SUPER MATCH - .22 LR cal., top-of-the-line competition model with sophisticated adj. cheekpiece, buttplate, trigger, pistol grip, and palm rest, Super Match 54 action, stippled walnut stock with thumbhole grip, 15.4 lbs. Mfg. 1979-88.

	$1,850	$1,600	$1,400	$1,200	$975	$875	$775

> This model previously held all the Olympic and world records. The model nomenclature was changed to Model 1913 Super Match in 1988.

MODEL 1903D
.22 LR cal., similar specifications to the Model 1803D, except has new improved target stock and adj. cheekpiece made from walnut finished European hardwood, color laminated stock mfg. 1995-98, full length stippled checkering on forend and contoured pistol grip, fully adj. new style buttplate, 9.9 lbs. New 1990.

MSR N/A	$925	$825	$725	$625	$525	$450	$375

Add $130 for color laminated stock (disc. 1998).

MODEL 1907
.22 LR cal., single shot match "I.S.U." model, 26 in. button-rifled barrel, prone and position shooting, removable cheekpiece, adj. buttplate, hand stippled stock with ventilated forearm and choice of beechwood (new 1997) walnut, blond laminated (disc.), or color laminated (mfg. 1995-96) wood stock, 10 1/2 lbs.

MSR N/A	$1,840	$1,575	$1,350	$1,100	$900	$775	$650

Add $125 for left-hand action.
Add $130 for stainless steel barrel.
Add $125 for quick adj. cheekpiece (disc.).
Add $125 for color laminated stock (disc.).

This model is also available with an Anschütz stock no. 2213 blue laminate (Alu Color), featuring the most recent technology in stock innovation – MSR is $2,062.
This variation was designated Model 1807 before 1989.

MODEL 1909
target variation of the Model 1910 Super Match II, limited importation 1997-98 only.

	$1,925	$1,550	$1,225	$1,025	$895	$785	$695

Last MSR was $2,480.

MODEL 1910 SUPER MATCH II
.22 LR cal., single shot, 27 1/4 in. barrel, diopter sights, thumbhole stock is fully adj., 12 lbs., model down from 1813 (or 1913), special order only – limited quantities imported until 1998.

	$2,150	$1,750	$1,475	$1,100	$900	$725	$625

Last MSR was $2,967.

Add $149 for left-hand action.
Subtract 20% for Model 1810.
This variation was designated as Model 1810 before 1988.

MODEL 1911 PRONE MATCH
.22 LR cal., single shot match prone rifle, 27 1/4 in. barrel, beechwood stock with adj. cheekpiece, buttplate, no sights, 11.9 lbs.

MSR N/A	$1,865	$1,550	$1,200	$995	$925	$825	$700

Add $99 for stainless steel barrel.
Add $100 for left-hand action (disc. 1993).
Subtract 20% for Model 1811.
This variation was designated Model 1811 before 1988.

MODEL 1912 LADIES SPORT RIFLE
.22 LR cal., designed for new ladies I.S.S.F. standards, features 1907 barreled action w/o sights, walnut stock with shorter dimensions, 11.4 lbs. Importation began 1999.

MSR N/A	$2,340	$1,975	$1,575	$1,350	$1,100	$975	$825

Add $336 for aluminum stock.
Add $135 for left-hand action.

MODEL 1913 SUPER MATCH FREE RIFLE
.22 LR cal., single shot, top-of-the-line match rifle, every possible refinement, international diopter sights, 27 1/4 in. button rifled barrel, hand and palm rest, wood or blue aluminum Alu Color (new 2000) stock, 15.5 lbs.

MSR N/A	$2,075	$1,750	$1,500	$1,225	$1,050	$925	$785

Add $130 for stainless steel barrel.
Add approx. $675 for aluminum stock.
This variation was designated Model 1813 before 1988 (see separate listing).

GRADING - PPGS™	100%	98%	95%	90%	80%	70%	60%

MODEL 2007 ISSF STANDARD

.22 LR cal., ISSF model, featuring 19 3/4 in. standard or heavy (new 2001) barrel with 8 in. detachable front tube allowing for different sights and counter-weights (total barrel length with tube is 27 1/4 in.), adj. cheekpiece and rubber buttplate, grooved and vented forearm, choice of blond (disc. 2000), walnut, or blue aluminum Alu Color (new 2001) stock, Match 54 action, 12 lbs. New 1992.

MSR N/A	$2,525	$2,250	$1,875	$1,550	$1,325	$1,100	$965

Add $135 for stainless steel barrel.

Add approx. $520 for Acu Color aluminum stock, right-or left-hand.

This model underwent significant engineering changes during 1994, including a heavier receiver.

MODEL 2012 LADIES SPORT RIFLE

.22 LR cal., utilizes 2007 rectangular receiver barreled action designed for new ladies ISSF rules, smaller dimensions, walnut stock, 11.4 lbs. Importation began 1999.

MSR N/A	$3,295	$2,850	$2,525	$2,100	$1,775	$1,475	$1,200

MODEL 2013 SUPER MATCH "SPECIAL"

.22 LR cal., top-of-the-line international target rifle featuring 19 3/4 in. standard or heavy (new 2001) barrel with 8 in. detachable front tube allowing for different sights and counter-weights (total barrel length with tube is 27 1/4 in.), top grain walnut, color laminate, or Acu-Color aluminum stock with adj. hand rest, palm rest, cheekpiece, and elaborate metal buttplate, Match 54 action, 15.4 lbs. New 1992.

MSR N/A	$3,000	$2,600	$2,275	$1,900	$1,600	$1,250	$1,025

Add $135 for stainless steel barrel.

This model underwent significant engineering changes during 1994.

✳ *Model 2013 BR-50 (Benchrest)* - .22 LR cal., developed especially for benchrest competition, trigger can be adjusted for either light single or two-stage action, 19.6 in. barrel, uncheckered walnut stock with wide forend, 10.3 lbs. Importation began 1999.

MSR N/A	$2,175	$1,825	$1,475	$1,250	$975	$850	$725

RIFLES: BOLT ACTION, BIATHLON

MODEL 64R BIATHLON

.22 LR cal., repeater, 5 shot mag., Match 64 action, 21.2 in. barrel, match trigger, hardwood stock with adj. cheekpiece and buttplate, right- or left-hand action, 7.9 lbs. Importation began 2004.

MSR $974	$925	$825	$750	$675	$600	$525	$450

MODEL 1450B

.22 LR cal., 2000 MK action, 19 1/2 in. barrel, European hardwood with vent. forearm and adj. buttplate, aperture sights, 5 lbs. Mfg. 1993 only.

	$650	$550	$450	$375	$300	$260	$230

Last MSR was $765.

MODEL 1403B

.22 LR cal., Match 64 action, 21 1/2 in. barrel, blonde finished European hardwood with stippled pistol grip, Biathlon design allows 4 mags. to be stored in a housing attached to the forend on right side, entry level Biathlon gun, 8 1/2 lbs. Mfg. 1990-92.

	$850	$730	$660	$525	$450	$375	$335

Last MSR was $998.

MODEL 1827B

.22 LR cal., biathlon rifle, carries four 5 shot mags. in stock, special biathlon features, 21 1/2 in. barrel, limited mfg.

	$1,875	$1,550	$1,225	$1,025	$895	$785	$695

Last MSR was $2,457.

Add $120 for left-hand action (disc. 1989).

In 1990, the stock design was changed permitting 8 mags. to be stored in two housings attached to both the stock and forend on right side.

GRADING - PPGS™	100%	98%	95%	90%	80%	70%	60%

✴ *Model 1827BT Fortner* - same general specifications as Model 1827B, except has Fortner straight pull-through bolt action, color laminated stock became available 1995, blue or stainless barrel, 8.8 lbs. New 1986.

MSR N/A	$2,425	$2,100	$1,800	$1,675	$1,425	$1,175	$925

Add $125 for stainless steel barrel.

In 1990, the stock design was changed permitting 8 mags. to be stored in two housings attached to both the stock and forend on right side.

RIFLES: SEMI-AUTO

MODEL 520/61 - .22 LR cal., semi-auto, 24 in. barrel, 10 shot mag., Monte Carlo stock, 6 1/2 lbs. Disc. 1983.

	$295	$250	$215	$175	$150	$130	$120

MARK 525 SPORTER RIFLE - .22 LR cal., semi-auto, 24 in. barrel, 10 shot mag., adj. rear sight, Monte Carlo stock, 6 1/2 lbs. Imported 1984-95.

	$495	$425	$365	$315	$265	$225	$185

Last MSR was $547.

✴ *Mark 525 Carbine* - similar to Mark 525 Rifle, except has 20 in. barrel. Importation disc. 1986.

	$425	$365	$325	$265	$225	$200	$175

SHOTGUNS: O/U

Anschütz marked O/U shotguns were manufactured by Miroku of Japan and distributed in Germany only. Several grades of these shotguns were manufactured and while rarely seen in the U.S., values approximate other Miroku O/Us of similar quality and features ($650-$1,000 assuming 95% or better condition).

ANZIO IRONWORKS CORP.

Current manufacturer established during 2000, and located in St. Petersburg, FL. Anzio Ironworks has been making gun parts and accessories since 1994. Dealer and consumer sales.

RIFLES: BOLT ACTION

.50 BMG SINGLE SHOT TAKEDOWN MODEL - .50 BMG cal., modified bullpup configuration, tube stock with 2 in. buttpad, 17 in. barrel with match or military chambering and muzzle brake, automatic ambidextrous safety and decocking mechanism, takedown action allowing disassembly in under 25 seconds, adj. target trigger, inclined mounting rail, cased, 25 lbs. Mfg. 2000-2002.

	$2,350	$2,000	$1,800	$1600	$1,400	$1,200	$1,000

Last MSR was $2,500.

Add $150 for 29 in. barrel or $1,050 for 29 in. barrel assembly.

.50 BMG SINGLE SHOT TITANIUM TAKEDOWN MODEL - .50 BMG cal., modified bullpup configuration, tube stock, 16 in. barrel with match or military chambering and muzzlebrake, automatic ambidextrous safety and decocking mechanism, interrupted thread lockup, takedown action allowing disassembly in under 12 seconds, adj. target trigger, Picatinny rail mount, cased, 11 lbs. Limited mfg. 2002 only.

	$2,995	$2,600	$2,350	$2,000	$1,800	$1600	$1,400

Last MSR was $3,200.

Add $250 for 29 in. barrel, $350 for custom barrel length to 45 in., or $1,050 for 29 in. barrel assembly.

GRADING - PPGS™	100%	98%	95%	90%	80%	70%	60%

.50 BMG SINGLE SHOT MODEL - .50 BMG cal., laminated wood stock, butter knife bolt handle, bolt complete with ejector and extractor, parkerized finish, inclined mounting rail, 17 in. barrel with match or military chambering and muzzle-brake, 21 lbs. Limited mfg. 2002 only.

		$2,500	$2,200	$1,950	$1,675	$1,400	$1,200	$1,000

Last MSR was $2,750.

    Add $150 for 29 in. barrel or $250 for custom barrel length to 45 in.

.50 BMG SINGLE SHOT MODEL - .50 BMG cal., 29 1/2 in. Lothar Walther match grade barrel, AR-15 trigger and safety, fixed metal buttstock with shrouded barrel and optional muzzle brake, 22 lbs. New 2003.

MSR $1,995		$1,800	$1,625	$1,400	$1,200	$1,000	$900	$800

.50 BMG SINGLE SHOT MODEL W/TAKEDOWN BARREL - .50 BMG cal., similar to single shot model, except features a 20 minute incline rail, heavier receiver, match grade stainless steel takedown barrel with clamshell muzzle brake, .5 MOA guaranteed. New 2005.

MSR $3,500		$3,150	$2,750	$2,400	$2,100	$1,900	$1,700	$1,500

.50 BMG LIGHTWEIGHT REPEATER MODEL - .50 BMG cal., lightweight model with 18 in. Lothar Walther fluted target barrel with 3 (standard) or 5 shot detachable mag., titanium muzzle brake, scope rail, bipod, and sling, 13.5 lbs. New 2003.

MSR $4,300		$3,950	$3,300	$2,775	$2,350	$2,125	$1,850	$1,675

.50 BMG STANDARD REPEATER MODEL - .50 BMG cal., 18 or 26 in. barrel, similar to .50 Lightweight Repeater Model, except does not have barrel/receiver fluting, and is not available with titanium muzzle brake/bolt handle. New 2004.

MSR $2,895		$2,675	$2,300	$1,975	$1,750	$1,500	$1,350	$1,200

APACHE

Previous trademark manufactured by Ojanguren Y Vidosa located in Eibar, Spain.

PISTOLS: SEMI-AUTO

SEMI-AUTO - 6.35mm cal., clip fed.

	$225	$190	$160	$140	$120	$95	$75

ARCUS CO.

Current trademark of handguns manufactured in Bulgaria and currently imported by Century International Arms, located in Boca Raton, FL. Previously imported until 2000 by Miltex, Inc., located in Waldorf, MD.

PISTOLS: SEMI-AUTO

MODEL 94/94 COMPACT - 9 mm Para. cal., SA or DA (disc. 2000), 4 (compact), 4 3/4 or 5 1/4 (disc. 2000) in. barrel, 10 shot mag., choice of blue (disc.), two-tone, or silver matte (disc.) metal finish, rubber or molded synthetic (disc. 2000) grips, 32-35 oz. Imported 1998-2000, reimported beginning 2003.

No MSR	$295	$250	$225	$200	$180	$160	$150

MODEL 98DA/98DAC - 9 mm Para. cal., SA/DA, duo-tone finish, 10 shot mag., soft rubber grips with finger grooves, 32 oz. Importation began 2002.

No MSR	$295	$250	$225	$200	$180	$160	$150

ARLINGTON ORDNANCE

Previous importer located in Westport, CT until 1996. Formerly located in Weston, CT.

GRADING - PPGS™	100%	98%	95%	90%	80%	70%	60%

CARBINES & RIFLES: SEMI-AUTO

M1 GARAND RIFLE - .30-06 cal., these Garands were imported from Korea in used condition, various manufacturers, with import stamp. Imported 1991-96.

	$475	$400	$360	$330	$300	$275	$250

Add $40 for stock upgrade (better wood).

✽ Arsenal Restored M1 Garand Rifle - .30-06 or .308 Win. cal., featured new barrel, rebuilt gas system, and reinspected components. Mfg. 1994-96.

	$550	$475	$400	$350	$315	$295	$265

Add 5% for .308 Win. cal.

TROPHY GARAND - .308 Win. cal. only, action was original mil-spec., included new barrel and checkered walnut stock and forend, recoil pad. Mfg. 1994-96.

	$725	$625	$525	$450	$375	$325	$275

Last MSR was $695.

T26 TANKER - .30-06 or .308 Win. cal., included new barrel and other key components, updated stock finish. Mfg. 1994-96.

	$650	$550	$450	$375	$325	$275	$250

.30 CAL. CARBINE - .30 Carbine cal., 18 in. barrel, imported from Korea in used condition, various manufacturers, with import stamp. Imported 1991-1996.

	$475	$400	$325	$275	$225	$200	$175

Add approximately $55 for stock upgrade (better wood).

MODEL FIVE CARBINE - while advertised, this model never went into production.

ARMALITE

Previous manufacturer located in Costa Mesa, CA, approx. 1959-1973.

RIFLES: SEMI-AUTO

AR-7 EXPLORER - .22 LR cal., 16 in. aluminum barrel with steel liner, aperture sight, take down action and barrel stores in hollow plastic stock in either brown (rare), black, or multi-color, gun will float, designed by Gene Stoner, mfg. 1959-73 by Armalite, 1973-90 by Charter Arms, 1990-97 by Survival Arms located in Cocoa, FL and current mfg. beginning 1997 by Henry Repeating Arms Co. located in Brooklyn, NY, and AR-7 Industries, LLC, located in Meriden, CT, starting 1998.

Black/Multi-color stock	$215	$190	$160	$140	$120	$100	$80
Brown stock	$375	$300	$240	$185	$165	$145	$125

Some unusual early Costa Mesa AR-7 variations have been observed with ported barrels, extendable wire stock, hooded front sight, and hollow pistol grip containing cleaning kit, perhaps indicating a special military contract survival weapon.

AR-7 CUSTOM - similar to AR-7 Explorer, only with custom walnut stock including cheekpiece, pistol grip. Mfg. 1964-70.

	$185	$150	$125	$100	$90	$80	$70

AR-180 - .223 Rem. cal., semi-auto, gas operated, 18 1/4 in. barrel, folding stock. Manufactured by Armalite in Costa Mesa, CA, 1969-1972, Howa Machinery Ltd., Nagoya, Japan 1972 and 1973, and by Sterling Armament Co. Ltd., Dagenham, Essex, England.

Sterling Mfg.	$1,250	$1,125	$950	$900	$850	$800	$750
Howa Mfg.	$1,650	$1,500	$1,350	$1,100	$975	$875	$775
Costa Mesa Mfg.	$1,700	$1,550	$1,375	$1,125	$1,000	$900	$800

SHOTGUNS: SEMI-AUTO

AR-17 - 12 ga., semi-auto, 24 in. barrel, interchangeable choke tubes, recoil operated, high strength aluminum barrel and receiver, plastic stock and forearm, either gold anodized or black finish. Only 2,000 mfg. 1964-65.

	$750	$575	$475	$400	$350	$295	$200

GRADING - PPGS™	100%	98%	95%	90%	80%	70%	60%

ARMALITE, INC.

Current manufacturer located in Geneseo, IL. New manufacture began in 1995 after Eagle Arms, Inc. purchased the ArmaLite trademarks. The ArmaLite trademark was originally used by Armalite (no relation to ArmaLite, Inc.) during mfg. in Costa Mesa, CA, approx. 1959-1973 (see Armalite listing above). Dealer direct sales.

RIFLES: BOLT ACTION

AR-30M - .300 Win. Mag., .308 Win., or .338 Lapua cal., scaled down AR-50, repeater, Shilen modified single stage trigger, w/o muzzle brake, 5 shot detachable mag., 26 in. barrel, 12 lbs. New 2003.

	MSR $1,460	$1,275	$1,100	$925	$825	$725	$600	$500

Add $155 for .338 Lapua cal.

AR-50 - .50 BMG cal., single shot bolt action with octagonal receiver integrated into a skeletonized aluminum stock with adj. cheekpiece and recoil pad, 31 in. tapered barrel w/o sights and sophisticated muzzle brake (reduces felt recoil to approx. .243 Win. cal.), removable buttstock, right or left-hand action, single stage trigger, 33.2 lbs. New 1999.

	MSR $2,885	$2,525	$2,125	$1,850	$1,650	$1,475	$1,250	$1,100

During 2004, this model was produced with a special commemorative stamp notation on the left side of the receiver.

RIFLES: SEMI-AUTO

All ArmaLite semi-auto rifles have a limited lifetime warranty.

Add $100 for stainless steel barrel on those AR-10 models which are available with that option.

Add $100 for National Match trigger where applicable.

Add $100 for black stock, forearm, and pistol grip where applicable.

Add $150 for 100% Realtree Hardwoods or Advantage Classic camo finish.

AR-10 SERIES - semi-auto paramilitary design, various configurations, with or w/o sights and carry handle, choice of standard green, black (new 1999), or camo finish, supplied with two 10 shot mags. (until 2004), current mfg. typically ships with one 10 round and one 20 round mag. New late 1995.

✳ **AR-10B Rifle** - .308 Win. cal., patterned after the early Armalite AR-10 rifle, featuring tapered M16 handguards, pistol grip, distinctive charging bolt on top inside of carry handle (cannot be scoped), original brown color, 20 in. barrel, 9 1/2 lbs. New 1999.

	MSR $1,698	$1,495	$1,225	$1,075	$975	$875	$750	$675

✳ **AR-10T Rifle** - .243 Win. (disc. 2003), .300 RSUM (new 2004, Ultra Mag Model), or .308 Win. cal., features 24 in. stainless 1:10 twist heavy barrel, two-stage NM trigger, smooth green or black fiberglass handguard tube, stock, and pistol grip, Picatinny rail, w/o sights or carry handle, 10.4 lbs.

	MSR $2,126	$1,860	$1,550	$1,300	$1,100	$995	$875	$750

Add $260 for AR-10T Ultra in .300 RSUM cal.

✳ **AR-10T Carbine (Navy Model)** - .308 Win. cal., similar to AR-10T Rifle, except has 16 in. stainless barrel and match trigger, 8 1/2 lbs. Disc. 2004.

	$1,825	$1,525	$1,275	$1,075	$995	$875	$750

Last MSR was $2,080.

GRADING - PPGS™	100%	98%	95%	90%	80%	70%	60%

* *AR-10A4 SPR (Special Purpose Rifle)* - .243 Win. (disc. 2003) or .308 Win. cal., features 20 in. chrome-lined 1:10 twist barrel, removable front sight, green or black furniture, Picatinny rail, w/o carry handle, approx. 9 lbs.

MSR $1,506	**$1,325**	**$1,075**	**$900**	**$800**	**$700**	**$600**	**$525**

* *AR-10A4 Carbine* - .308 Win. cal., similar to AR-10A4 Rifle, except has 16 in. barrel, 8.4 lbs.

MSR $1,506	**$1,325**	**$1,075**	**$900**	**$800**	**$700**	**$600**	**$525**

Add $414 for SIR system (modular receiver sleeving system, new 2004).

* *AR-10A2 Infantry Model Rifle* - .243 Win. (disc. 2003) or .308 Win. cal., features 20 in. chrome-lined 1:10 barrel, includes fixed sights and carry handle, 9.4 lbs.

MSR $1,506	**$1,325**	**$1,075**	**$900**	**$800**	**$700**	**$600**	**$525**

* *AR-10A2 Carbine* - .308 Win. cal., similar to AR-10A2 Rifle, except has 16 in. barrel, 8.7 lbs.

MSR $1,506	**$1,325**	**$1,075**	**$900**	**$800**	**$700**	**$600**	**$525**

Add $74 for 4-way quad rail on front of forearm (new 2004).

* *AR-10SOF (Special Operation Forces) Carbine* - .308 Win. cal., available in either A2 or A4 configurations, fixed tube stock, 16 in. barrel, black finish only. Mfg. 2003-2004.

	$1,250	**$1,075**	**$900**	**$800**	**$700**	**$600**	**$525**

Last MSR was $1,503.

Add $52 for A2 configuration (includes Picatinny rail).

M15 RIFLE/CARBINE VARIATIONS - .223 Rem. cal., various configurations, barrel lengths, sights, and other features.

* *M15A2 National Match Rifle* - features 20 in. stainless steel NM sleeved 1:8 twist barrel with National Match sights and NM two-stage trigger, grooved barrel shroud, 9 lbs.

MSR $1,472	**$1,255**	**$1,050**	**$875**	**$775**	**$675**	**$595**	**$525**

This model is also available with black stock, forearm, and pistol grip at no extra charge.

* *M15A2 Golden Eagle* - similiar to M15A2 National Match Rifle, except has 20 in. heavy barrel, 9.4 lbs. Limited mfg. 1998 only.

	$1,200	**$975**	**$850**	**$750**	**$675**	**$595**	**$525**

Last MSR was $1,350.

* *M15A2 Service Rifle* - includes 20 in. chrome-lined 1:9 twist barrel, fixed sights and carrying handle, 8.2 lbs.

MSR $1,100	**$950**	**$775**	**$675**	**$575**	**$500**	**$450**	**$415**

* *M15A2 Carbine* - similar to M15A2 Service Rifle, except has 16 in. barrel, 7 lbs.

MSR $1,100	**$950**	**$775**	**$675**	**$575**	**$500**	**$450**	**$415**

* *M15A4 SPR (Special Purpose Rifle)* - includes 20 in. chrome-lined H-Bar 1:9 twist barrel with National Match sights, Picatinny rail, detachable carry handle, grooved barrel shroud, 7.9 lbs.

MSR $1,100	**$950**	**$775**	**$675**	**$575**	**$500**	**$450**	**$415**

* *M15A4 Carbine* - similar to M15A4 Special Purpose Rifle, except has 16 in. barrel, 7 lbs.

MSR $1,100	**$950**	**$775**	**$675**	**$575**	**$500**	**$450**	**$415**

* *M15A4 SPR II (Special Purpose Rifle)* - similar to M15A4 SPR, except has triple lapped rifled barrel, strengthed floating barrel sleeve and two-stage match trigger, green or black furniture. New 2003.

MSR $1,472	**$1,250**	**$1,050**	**$875**	**$800**	**$700**	**$600**	**$500**

GRADING - PPGS™	100%	98%	95%	90%	80%	70%	60%

* **M4A1C Carbine** - features 16 in. chrome-lined 1:9 twist heavy barrel with National Match sights and detachable carrying handle, grooved barrel shroud, 7 lbs. Disc. 1997.

	$840	$725	$640	$560	$500	$450	$415

Last MSR was $935.

* **M4C Carbine** - similar to M4A1C Carbine, except has non-removable carrying handle and fixed sights, 7 lbs. Disc. 1997.

	$785	$675	$600	$550	$500	$450	$415

Last MSR was $870.

* **M15SOF (Special Operation Forces) Carbine** - .223 Rem. cal., available in either A2 or A4 configurations, fixed tube stock, 16 in. barrel, black finish only. Mfg. 2003-2004.

	$950	$775	$675	$600	$525	$475	$450

Last MSR was $1,084.

Add $69 for A2 configuration (includes Picatinny rail).

* **M15TN** - .223 Rem. cal., 20 in. stainless steel barrel, National Match trigger, green or black finish. New 2004.

MSR $1,322	$1,130	$925	$825	$700	$600	$500	$450

* **M15A4T Rifle (Eagle Eye)** - 24 in. stainless steel 1:8 twist heavy barrel, two-stage trigger, smooth green or black fiberglass hand guard, Picatinny front sight rail but w/o sights and carrying handle, 9.2 lbs.

MSR $1,504	$1,325	$1,075	$900	$800	$700	$600	$525

* **M15A4T Carbine (Eagle Eye)** - features 16 in. stainless steel 1:9 twist heavy barrel, picatinny rail, smooth fiberglass handguard tube, two-stage trigger, 7.1 lbs. Mfg. 1997-2004.

	$1,225	$995	$850	$775	$675	$595	$525

Last MSR was $1,383.

* **M15A4 Predator** - similar to M15A4T Eagle Eye, except has 1:12 twist barrel. Disc. 1996.

	$1,215	$985	$850	$750	$675	$595	$525

Last MSR was $1,350.

* **M15A4 Action Master** - includes 20 in. stainless steel 1:9 twist barrel, two-stage trigger, muzzle brake, Picatinny flattop design w/o sights or carrying handle, 9 lbs. Disc. 1997.

	$1,050	$900	$800	$700	$625	$565	$500

Last MSR was $1,175.

AR-180B - .223 Rem. cal., polymer lower receiver with formed sheet metal upper, standard AR-15 trigger group/magazine, incorporates the best features of the M15 (lower group with trigger and mag. well) and early AR-180 (gas system allowing operating gases to be kept outside the receiver) rifles, 19.8 in. barrel with integral muzzle brake, 6 lbs. New 2003.

MSR $750	$675	$600	$525	$475	$425	$400	$375

For more information on the original ArmaLite AR-180 and variations, please refer to the previous ArmaLite listing.

ARMAMENT TECHNOLOGY

Previous firearms manufacturer located in Halifax, Nova Scotia, Canada 1988-2003.

Armament Technology discontinued making bolt action rifles in 2003. Currently, the company is distributing optical rifle sights only.

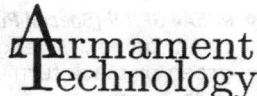

GRADING - PPGS™	100%	98%	95%	90%	80%	70%	60%

RIFLES: BOLT-ACTION

AT1-C24 TACTICAL RIFLE - .308 Win. or .300 Win. Mag. (disc. 2000) cal., similar to AT1-M24, except has detachable mag., adj. cheekpiece and buttstock for LOP, includes 3.5-10X 30mm tactical scope and Mil-Spec shipping case, 1/2" MOA guaranteed, 14.9 lbs. Mfg. 1998-2003.

	$4,095	$3,650	$2,775	$2,250	$1,825	$1,500	$1,275

Last MSR was $4,195.

AT1-C24B TACTICAL RIFLE - .308 Win. cal., similar to AT1-C24, except is not available in left-hand, 15.9 lbs. Mfg. 2001-2003.

	$4,250	$3,750	$2,850	$2,300	$1,850	$1,525	$1,300

Last MSR was $4,695.

AT1-M24 TACTICAL RIFLE - .223 Rem. (new 1998), .308 Win., or .300 Win. Mag. (disc. 2000) cal., bolt action, tactical rifle with competition tuned right-hand or left-hand Rem. 700 action, stainless steel barrel, Kevlar reinforced fiberglass stock, Harris bipod, matte black finish, competition trigger, 1/2" MOA guaranteed, 14.9 lbs. Disc. 2003.

	$4,350	$3,850	$2,850	$2,350	$1,900	$1,600	$1,350

Last MSR was $4,495.

ARMAMENT TECHNOLOGY CORP.

Previous manufacturer located in Las Vegas, NV between 1972-1978.

RIFLES: SEMI-AUTO

In addition to the models listed below, ATC also manufactured a select fire pistol named "Firefly II."

MODEL 4 POCKET RIFLE - .22 LR cal., semi-auto action (supplied by Mossberg), 5 in. barrel, shortened rifle (18 1/2 in. overall length) with cut stock, 7 shot mag., approx. 450 mfg., approx. 3 lbs.

	$350	$295	$260	$230	$195	$175	$150

MODEL 6 - full length variation of the Model 4, Mossberg Model 453-T with ATC trademarks, approx. 12 mfg., approx. 5 1/2 lbs.

	$125	$100	$85	$75	$65	$55	$45

M-2 FIREFLY - 9mm Para. cal., featured a unique gas delayed blowback action, paramilitary configuration, collapsible stock, very limited mfg., 4 3/4 lbs.

	$695	$625	$550	$475	$395	$350	$295

ARMAS AZOR, S.A.

Previous manufacturer of double rifles located in Eibar, Spain. Previously imported 1994-1997 by Armes De Chasse located in Hertford, NC.

RIFLES: SxS, SIDELOCK

The models listed below are English styled sidelock double rifles. Gold inlay and custom engraving prices were quoted per individual request.

AFRICA MARK I - available in most cals. between 9.3 X 74R and .375 H&H, nominal engraving and select grade wood.

Previous retail prices ranged between $8,000-$10,000.

AFRICA MARK II - available in most cals. between 9.3 X 74R and .375 H&H, African game scene engraving and superior grade wood.

Previous retail prices ranged between $10,000-$12,000.

AFRICA MARK III - available in most cals. between 9.3 X 74R and .470 NE Mag., intricate scroll engraving, cartridge trap, top tang, and superior quality grade wood.

Previous retail prices ranged between $13,000-$18,000.

GRADING - PPGS™	100%	98%	95%	90%	80%	70%	60%

SHOTGUNS: SxS, SIDELOCK

SIDELOCK MODEL - 12 ga.-.410 bore, English style sidelock game gun.

	100%	98%	95%	90%	80%	70%	60%
	$3,275	$2,700	$2,200	$1,750	$1,500	$1,250	$995

Last MSR was $3,500.

ARMES DE CHASSE LLC

Current importer and distributor located in Hertford, NC.

SHOTGUNS: SxS

ALBEMARLE GAME GUN SIDELOCK - 12, 16 (special order only), 20, 28 ga., or .410 bore (new 2001), H&H style detachable sidelock action, Purdey style bolt, DT with articulated front trigger, 26, 27, or 28 in. barrels with concave solid rib, ejectors, checkered oil finished walnut English or pistol grip stock and forearm (base price includes custom stock dimensions), extensive lockplate engraving, 5 3/4 (20 ga.) or 6 7/8 (12 ga.) lbs. Allow 6 months for delivery. Spanish importation began late 1999.

MSR $3,525	$3,100	$2,650	$2,195	$1,800	$1,500	$1,200	$995

Add 10% for 28 ga.or .410 bore.
Add $1,050 for extra set of barrels.
Add $1,525 for Grade A fine scroll engraving.
Add $1,330 for Grade A black and gold option (mfg. 2000-2003).
Add $1,310 for Grade B ribbon and scroll engraving.
Add $1,100 Grade C game scene engraving.
Add $135 for left-hand.

ALBEMARLE GAME GUN BOXLOCK - 12, 16 (special order only), 20, 28 ga., or .410 bore, H&H style boxlock action, DT, ejectors, old silver or case hardened action, beavertail or semi-beavertail forend available. Importation began 2003.

MSR $2,635	$2,350	$2,150	$1,875	$1,525	$1,200	$995	$875

Add $135 for left-hand.
Add 10% for 28 ga.or .410 bore.

ARMES PIERRE ARTISAN ETS. (P. CHAPUIS)

Current manufacturer located in St. Bonnet Le Chateau, France.

Armes Pierre Artisan manufactures high quality double rifles and shotguns on a custom order basis. Please contact the factory directly for more information, including a price quotation, delivery time, and available options.

ARMI SAN PAOLO

Previous manufacturer located in Concesio, Italy.

During 2002, Armi San Paolo changed its name to Euroarms Italia. Please refer to Euroarms Italia listing for current information.

REVOLVERS

Armi San Paolo manufactured double action .22 and .38 cal. revolvers in both 2 and 6 in. barrel lengths. These revolvers were manufactured in Concesio, Italy under license from J.P. Sauer & Sohn. Assuming 95%+ condition, these handguns are currently priced in the $150-$225 range.

ARMI SPORT

Current manufacturer established in 1958, and located in Brescia, Italy. Currently imported exclusively by Taylor's & Co., Inc., located in Winchester, VA.

Armi Sport also manufactures a complete line of percussion and flintlock blackpowder reproductions and replicas, including both pistols and rifles. For more information on these replicas, please refer to the *Blue Book of Modern Black Powder Arms* by John Allen & Dennis Adler.

RIFLES: REPRODUCTIONS

Armi Sport manufactures top quality reproductions of famous rifles/carbines, including the Model 1874 Deluxe Sharps Sporting rifle in various configurations and cals., including .45-70, the Model 1865 Spencer Carbine in .45 Schofield, .44 Russian, or .56-50 cal., and the Model 1892 lever action takedown rifle and carbine. Please refer to the Taylor's & Co., Inc. listing for current information on these models, including U.S. pricing and availability.

ARMINEX LTD.

Previous manufacturer located in Scottsdale, AZ.

PISTOLS: SEMI-AUTO

TRI-FIRE - .45 ACP cal., single action auto, interchangeable barrels allow caliber conversion. Available in 5, 6, or 7 (disc. 1984) in. stainless barrel lengths, no grip safety, steel frame construction, ambidextrous thumb safety (on Target and Presentation only), smooth walnut grips, 38 oz. Approx. 400 mfg. between 1981-85.

$750	$650	$475	$400	$375	$350	$325

Last MSR was $396.

Add $50 if presentation cased.
Add approx. $130/conversion unit.

✳ *Target Model* - same specifications as Tri-Fire, except has 6 or 7 (disc. 1984) in. barrel. Very limited mfg.

$850	$725	$550	$450	$400	$360	$330

Last MSR was $448.

ARMINIUS

Current trademark of revolvers manufactured by Weihrach, located in Mellrickstadt, Germany. No current U.S. importation. Previously manufactured in Zella-Mehlis, Germany beginning circa 1922-mid 1970s.

PISTOLS: SINGLE SHOT

MODEL 1 - .22 LR cal., target model, adj. sights.

$275	$210	$195	$165	$155	$140	$110

MODEL 2 - similar to Model 1, except has set trigger.

$340	$255	$225	$190	$170	$155	$140

REVOLVERS

Currently manufactured Arminius revolvers are not individually listed, since they are not currently imported into the U.S. There are however, many models, including combat, sport, and target variations. Calibers include .22 LR. .22 Mag., .32 S&W Wadcutter, .357 Mag., and .38 Spl.

MODEL 3 - .25 ACP cal., folding trigger, hammerless.

$175	$135	$125	$105	$100	$90	$80

MODEL 8 - .320 Revolver cal., folding trigger, hammerless.

$175	$135	$125	$105	$100	$90	$80

MODEL 9 - .32 ACP cal.

$185	$140	$130	$115	$105	$95	$85

MODEL 10 - .32 ACP cal., hammerless.

$165	$125	$120	$100	$95	$85	$75

GRADING - PPGS™	100%	98%	95%	90%	80%	70%	60%

TARGET - .22 LR cal.

	100%	98%	95%	90%	80%	70%	60%
	$90	$70	$65	$55	$50	$45	$45

ARMITAGE INTERNATIONAL, LTD.

Previous manufacturer until 1990 located in Seneca, SC.

PISTOLS: SEMI-AUTO

SCARAB SKORPION - 9mm Para. Cal., paramilitary design patterned after the Czech Model 61, direct blow back action, 4.63 in. barrel, matte black finish, 12 shot (standard) or 32 shot (optional) mag., 3.5 lbs. Mfg. in U.S. 1989-90 only.

	100%	98%	95%	90%	80%	70%	60%
	$625	$550	$475	$400	$350	$300	$260

Last MSR was $400.

Add $45 for threaded flash hider or imitation suppressor.
Only 602 Scarab Skorpions were manufactured during 1989-90.

ARMORY USA L.L.C.

Current manufacturer/importer located in Houston, TX. Previous company name was Arsenal USA LLC.

RIFLES: SEMI-AUTO

Armory USA, LLC produces a variety of AK-47/AKM/AK-74 semi-auto rifles. Early rifles used Bulgarian milled receivers, later versions were built using sheet metal receivers made in Hungary by FEG. During 2004, Armory USA began production of 1.6mm thick U.S. made AK receivers, which are sold as both receivers and complete rifles. Production of 1mm thick receivers began in Jan. 2005. Models not listed here may have been assembled by other manufacturers using these receivers.

During 2004, Armory USA began assembling rifles at a new factory in Kazanlak, Bulgaria. Some components are made in the U.S., in compliance with the BATF.

Please refer to the Arsenal USA listing for pre-2004 manufactured/imported rifles.

MODEL SSR-56-2 - 7.62x39mm cal., Armory USA made 1.6mm receiver wall thickness, Poly-Tec barrel assembly, Bulgarian internal parts. Approx. 400 mfg. during 2004.

	100%	98%	95%	90%	80%	70%	60%
	$450	$400	$325	$275	$225	$175	$125

Last MSR was $500.

MODEL AMD-63-2 UP - 7.62x39mm cal., Armory USA made 1.6mm receiver wall thickness, Hungarian parts, underfolding buttstock. Approx. 125 mfg. 2004.

	100%	98%	95%	90%	80%	70%	60%
	$500	$450	$400	$300	$250	$200	$150

Last MSR was $600.

MODEL SSR-85C-2 - 7.62x39mm cal., assembled in Bulgaria, marked "ISD Ltd," blond wood and black polymer furniture. Imported beginning 2004.

MSR $550	100%	98%	95%	90%	80%	70%	60%
	$500	$450	$400	$300	$250	$200	$150

Add $100 for sidefolding buttstock (Model SSR-85C-2 SF).

MODEL SSR-74-2 - 5.45x39mm cal., assembled in Bulgaria, marked "ISD Ltd," blond wood and black polymer furniture. Imported beginning 2005.

MSR $550	100%	98%	95%	90%	80%	70%	60%
	$500	$450	$400	$300	$250	$200	$150

ARMS CORPORATION OF THE PHILIPPINES

Please refer to the Armscor listing in this section.

GRADING - PPGS™	100%	98%	95%	90%	80%	70%	60%

ARMS MORAVIA, LTD.

Current European importer/exporter of firearms and accessories located in Ostrava, Czech Republic. Previously imported into the United States by Anderson & Richardson Arms Co., located in Ft. Worth, TX until 2001.

Arms Moravia Ltd. exports a wide variety of European trademarks, including their own line of pistols.

ARMS RESEARCH ASSOCIATES

Previous manufacturer until 1991, located in Stone Park, IL.

CARBINES: SEMI-AUTO

KF SYSTEM - 9mm Para. cal., paramilitary design carbine, 18 1/2 in. barrel, vent. barrel shroud, 20 or 36 shot mag., matte black finish, 7 1/2 lbs., select fire-class III transferable only.

	$395	$350	$300	$275	$250	$230	$210

Last MSR was $379.

ARMS TECH LTD.

Previous manufacturer located in Phoenix, AZ 1987-1998.

RIFLES: SEMI-AUTO

SUPER MATCH INTERDICTION POLICE MODEL - .243 Win., .300 Win. Mag., or .308 Win. (standard) cal., features 22 in. free floating Schnieder or Douglas air gauged stainless steel barrel, gas operation, McMillan stock, updated trigger group, detachable box mag., 13 1/4 lbs. Limited mfg. 1996-98.

	$3,950	$3,650	$3,300	$3,000	$2,750	$2,350	$2,000

Last MSR was $4,800.

ARMSCO

Current North American importer and distributor of Huglu shotguns located in Des Plaines, IL. Please refer to the Huglu section for more information.

ARMSCOR

Current trademark of firearms manufactured by Arms Corporation of the Philippines (manufacturing began 1952) established in 1995. Currently imported and distributed by Armscor

ARMSCOR ▰

Precision International (full line), located in Las Vegas, NV beginning 2001, and by K.B.I., Inc. located in Harrisburg, PA beginning 1995. Previously imported by Ruko located in Buffalo, NY until 1995 and by Armscorp Precision Inc. located in San Mateo, CA until 1991.

In 1991, the importation of Arms Corporation of the Philippines firearms was changed to Ruko Products, Inc., located in Buffalo, NY. Barrel markings on firearms imported by Ruko Products, Inc. state "Ruko-Armscor" instead of the older "Armscorp Precision" barrel markings. All Armscorp Precision, Inc. models were discontinued in 1991.

The models listed below also provide cross-referencing for older Armscorp Precision and Ruko imported models.

PISTOLS: SEMI-AUTO

M-1911-A1 FS (FULL SIZE STANDARD) - .45 ACP cal., patterned after the Colt Govt. Model, 7 shot mag. (2 provided), 5 in. barrel, parkerized (disc. 2001), blue (new 2002), two-tone (new 2002), or stainless steel (new 2002), skeletonized combat hammer and trigger, front and rear slide serrations, hard rubber grips, 38 oz. Imported 1996-97, reintroduced 2001.

MSR $399	$350	$300	$280	$260	$240	$220	$200

Add $31 for two-tone finish.

Add $75 for stainless steel.

This model is also available in a high capacity configuration (Model 1911-A2 HC, 13 shot mag., $519 MSR) for law enforcement only.

GRADING - PPGS™	100%	98%	95%	90%	80%	70%	60%

M-1911-A1 MS (COMMANDER) - .45 ACP cal., Commander configuration with 4 in. barrel, otherwise similar to M-1911 A1 Standard, rear slide serrations only. Importation began 2001.

	MSR $408	$360	$300	$280	$260	$240	$220	$200

Add $37 for two-tone finish.
Add $90 for stainless steel.

M-1911-A1 CS (OFFICER) - .45 ACP cal., officer's configuration with 3 1/2 in. barrel, checkered hardwood grips, 2.16 lbs. Importation began 2002.

	MSR $423	$370	$310	$285	$265	$245	$220	$200

Add $52 for two-tone finish.
Add $105 for stainless steel.

M-1911-A1 MEDALLION SERIES - 9mm Para., .40 S&W, or .45 ACP cal., 5 in. barrel, customized model including many shooting enhancements, match barrel, hand fitted slide and frame, choice of checkered wood or Pachmayr grips, available in either Standard or Tactical variation, blue, two-tone or chrome finish. Importation began 2002.

	MSR $539	$445	$350	$310	$285	$260	$240	$220

Add $129 for Tactical Model, add $198 for Tactical Model two-tone, or $203 for Tactical Model chrome.

REVOLVERS

MODEL 200 (DC) REVOLVER - .38 Spl. cal., 6 shot, double action, 2 1/2 (importation disc.), 4 (new 1998) or 6 (new 1998, importation disc.) in. barrel with shroud, transfer bar safety, combat style rubber grips, blue finish only, fixed rear sight, 26 oz. Imported 1996-99, reintroduced 2001.

	MSR $156	$145	$125	$105	$90	$75	$65	$60

Add approx. $6 for 4 in. barrel or $16 for 6 in. barrel (disc.)

MODEL 202 REVOLVER - similar to Model 200, except does not have barrel shroud. Importation began 2001.

	MSR $156	$135	$115	$100	$85	$75	$65	$60

MODEL 206 REVOLVER - similar to Model 200, except has 2 in. barrel, 24 oz. Importation began 2001.

	MSR $180	$160	$125	$105	$90	$75	$65	$60

MODEL 210 REVOLVER - similar to Model 200, except has 4 in. VR barrel, and adj. rear sight, 28 oz. Importation began 2001.

	MSR $196	$175	$150	$125	$105	$90	$75	$65

RIFLES: BOLT ACTION

M-12Y/12-TY - .22 LR cal., bolt action, single shot, youth model with 18 3/8 in. barrel. Imported 1997 only, reintroduced during 2001.

	$95	$80	$70	$60	$50	$40	$35

Last MSR was $109.

M-14P - .22 LR cal., bolt action, 10 shot mag., 23 in. barrel, open sights, hooded bead ramp front sight and leaf type rear sight, 6 lbs. Disc. 1997.

	$95	$75	$60	$50	$45	$40	$35

Last MSR was $129.

A youth model was also available with shorter dimensions at no extra charge (M-14Y).

GRADING - PPGS™	100%	98%	95%	90%	80%	70%	60%

✳ *M-14-D* - .22 LR cal., bolt action, similar to M-14P, except has adj. rear sight and checkered mahogany stock. Importation disc. 1995.

	$105	$85	$70	$60	$50	$45	$40

Last MSR was $139.

M-1400LW - .22 LR cal., similar action to M-14P, except has checkered stock and Schnabel forend, 10 shot mag., hard rubber pad, 6 lbs. Imported 1990-92.

	$185	$165	$150	$135	$120	$105	$95

Last MSR was $219.

✳ *M-1400S* - .22 LR cal., similar to M-1500(S), except has 10 shot mag., 6.7 lbs. Imported 1996-97.

	$175	$125	$100	$75	$65	$55	$50

Last MSR was $224.

✳ *M-1400 (SC-Super Classic)* - .22 LR cal., otherwise similar to M-1500SC, except has 10 shot mag. and 23 in. barrel, 6 lbs. Imported 1990-97, reintroduced 2001.

MSR $242	$200	$150	$110	$85	$70	$60	$55

Add $18 for stainless steel construction (new 2002).

✳ *M-1400E* - .22 LR cal., 6 or 10 shot mag., similar to M-1400, except has checkered stock and Scnabel forend, hard rubber pad, fiber optic front sight and adj. rear sight. Importation began 2004.

As this edition went to press, prices had yet to be established on this model.

✳ *M-1400 Sporster* - .22 LR cal., similar to M-1400E, except has competition type stock and scalloped forearm, Monte Carlo style butt with cheekpiece. Importation began 2004.

As this edition went to press, prices had yet to be established on this model.

M-1500S - .22 Mag. cal., deluxe bolt action, 5 shot mag., 21 1/2 or 22 5/8 in. barrel, checkered mahogany stock, open sights, 7 lbs. Disc. 1997, reintroduced 2001.

	$145	$125	$110	$95	$85	$75	$65

Last MSR was $160.

✳ *M-1500LW (Lightweight)* - similar to M-1500, except has lightweight classic European styled stock made of checkered American Walnut, with buttpad. Imported 1990-92.

	$190	$170	$150	$135	$120	$105	$95

Last MSR was $229.

✳ *M-1500 (SC-Super Classic)* - checkered American Walnut stock with hard rubber pad and Monte Carlo cheekpiece, hardwood forend tip, engine turned bolt, 7 lbs. Imported 1990-97, reintroduced 2001.

MSR $260	$215	$165	$120	$100	$85	$70	$60

Subtract $3 for stainless steel.

M-1800S (CLASSIC) - .22 Hornet cal., 5 shot mag., double locking lugs, checkered hardwood stock, adj. rear sight, 6.6 lbs. Imported 1996-97.

	$250	$225	$200	$180	$165	$150	$135

Last MSR was $358.

✳ *M-1800SC (Super Classic)* - similar to M-1800S, except has checkered walnut stock with forend tip, and high polish bluing, 7 1/4 lbs. Imported 1996-97, reintroduced during 2001.

	$285	$260	$240	$220	$200	$185	$170

Last MSR was $323.

RIFLES: SEMI-AUTO

M-1600 - .22 LR cal., semi-auto, 10 or 15 (disc.) shot mag., 18 in. barrel, copy of the Armalite M16, ebony stock, 5 1/4 lbs.

MSR $205	$170	$130	$100	$80	$65	$55	$50

GRADING - PPGS™	100%	98%	95%	90%	80%	70%	60%

✱ *M-1600R* - similar to M-1600, except has stainless steel retractable buttstock and vent. barrel hood, 7 1/4 lbs. Importation disc. 1995.

	$155	$115	$95	$75	$65	$55	$50

Last MSR was $199.

M-20 - .22 LR cal., 10 shot mag., deluxe checkered hardwood stock and forend, blue or stainless steel. Importation began 2002.

MSR $245	$205	$155	$110	$85	$70	$60	$55

Add $15 for stainless steel construction (new 2002).

M-20P - .22 LR cal., semi-auto, 15 shot mag., 20 3/4 in. barrel, open sights, 5 1/2 lbs. Disc. 1997, reintroduced during 2001

	$100	$80	$60	$50	$45	$40	$35

Last MSR was $120.

✱ *M-20C* - similar to M-20P, except has carbine style stock, barrel band, and curved steel buttplate, 16 1/2 in. barrel, 5 1/4 lbs. Previously available from K.B.I. only, disc. 2001.

	$130	$100	$80	$60	$50	$45	$40

Last MSR was $159.

✱ *M-20D* - .22 LR cal., 22 in. barrel, 10 or 15 shot mag., checkered hardwood stock and forend, 6 1/2 lbs. Importation began 2002.

MSR $245	$205	$155	$110	$85	$70	$60	$55

Add $15 for stainless steel construction (new 2002).

M-2000(S) - same specifications as M-20P, except has checkered mahogany stock and adj. rear sight. Disc. 1997.

	$140	$120	$95	$75	$60	$55	$50

Last MSR was $213.

✱ *M-2000SC (Super Classic)* - similar to M-2000, except has checkered American Walnut stock with cheekpiece and hardwood forend tip, engine turned bolt, 6 lbs. Imported 1990-97.

	$270	$215	$175	$140	$110	$95	$85

Last MSR was $340.

M-50S - .22 LR cal., semi-auto design, 16 1/2 in. shrouded barrel, 25 or 30 shot mag., uncheckered mahogany stock, 6 1/2 lbs. Disc. 1995.

	$155	$115	$95	$75	$65	$50	$45

Last MSR was $209.

M-AK22(S) - .22 LR cal., semi-auto, copy of the famous Russian Kalashnikov AK-47 rifle, 18 1/2 in. barrel, 10 or 15 (disc.) shot mag., mahogany stock and forearm, 7 lbs.

MSR $224	$185	$165	$145	$120	$95	$85	$80

✱ *M-AK22(F)* - similar to M-AK22, except has metal folding stock, and 30 shot mag. Disc. 1995.

	$275	$225	$185	$150	$115	$95	$80

Last MSR was $299.

SHOTGUNS: SLIDE ACTION

M-30 F (INTERCHANGEABLE CHOKES) - 12 ga. only, 28 in. plain barrel with 3 choke tubes, 5 shot mag., uncheckered stock and forearm. Disc. 1999.

	$225	$190	$160	$140	$120	$95	$85

Last MSR was $269.

✱ *M-30 D/IC (Deluxe)* - similar to Model M30 IC, except has checkered walnut stock and forearm with recoil pad. Importation reintroduced during 2001 only.

	$180	$155	$125	$110	$95	$85	$75

Last MSR was $208.

GRADING - PPGS™	100%	98%	95%	90%	80%	70%	60%

M-30 DG (DEER GUN) - 12 ga. only, law enforcement version of M-30, 20 in. plain barrel, iron sights, 7 shot mag., approx. 7 lbs. Disc. 1999, reintroduced during 2001.

	$165	$140	$120	$100	$85	$75	$70

Last MSR was $195.

M-30SAS1 - 12 ga. only, riot configuration with 20 in. barrel and vent. barrel shroud, and speedfeed 4 shot (disc.) or regular synthetic buttstock and forearm, 6 shot mag., matte finish, 8 lbs. Mfg. 1996-99, reintroduced 2001.

MSR $211	$180	$155	$130	$110	$95	$85	$75

Add $56 for Speedfeed stock (new 2002).

M-30 R6/R8 (RIOT) - 12 ga. only, similar to M-30DG, except has front bead sight only, 5 or 7 shot mag., cyl. bore. Disc. 1999, reintroduced 2001.

MSR $181	$155	$135	$110	$90	$80	$75	$70

Add $7 for 7 shot mag.

M-30BG - 12 ga. only, 18 1/2 in. barrel, 5 shot mag., polymer pistol grip and forearm. Importation began 2004.

As this edition went to press, prices had yet to be established on this model.

M-30F/FS - similar to M-30BG, except has additional folding metal stock unit.

MSR $211	$180	$155	$130	$110	$95	$85	$75

M30 C (COMBO) - 12 ga., 20 in. barrel, 5 shot mag., unique detachable black synthetic buttstock that separates, allowing pistol grip only operation. Disc. 1995.

	$210	$175	$145	$120	$100	$90	$80

Last MSR was $289.

M30 RP (COMBO) - 12 ga. only, same action as M-30 DG, interchangeable black pistol grip, 18 1/4 in. plain barrel w/front bead sight, 6 1/4 lbs. Disc. 1995.

	$210	$175	$145	$120	$100	$90	$80

Last MSR was $289.

ARMSCORP USA, INC.

Current manufacturer and importer located in Baltimore, MD. Dealer direct sales only.

PISTOLS: SEMI-AUTO

HI POWER - 9mm Para. cal., patterned after Browning design, 4 2/3 in. barrel, military finish, 13 shot mag., synthetic checkered grips, spur hammer, 2 lbs. mfg. in Argentina, imported 1989-90 only.

	$395	$350	$295	$275	$250	$225	$200

Last MSR was $450.

Add $15 for round hammer.

Add $50 for hard chrome finish w/combat grips (disc. 1989).

✱ *Compact Detective HP* - similar to Hi Power, except has 3 1/2 in. barrel, 1.9 lbs. Mfg. 1989 only.

	$395	$350	$295	$275	$250	$225	$200

Last MSR was $475.

SD-9 - 9mm Para. cal., double action only, blowback mechanism, 3.07 in. barrel, 6 shot mag., frame is fabricated mostly of heavy gauge sheet metal stampings, chamber indicator, limited Israeli mfg., 1 1/2 lbs. Imported 1989-90 only.

	$350	$250	$230	$210	$195	$180	$170

Last MSR was $350.

This pistol has also been manufactured by Sirkis Industries – refer to their section in this text.

GRADING - PPGS™	100%	98%	95%	90%	80%	70%	60%

P22 - .22 LR cal., patterned after the Colt Woodsman, 4 or 6 in. barrel, 10 shot mag., checkered wood grips, mfg. in Argentina. Imported 1989-90 only.

		$190	$150	$130	$115	$100	$95	$85

Last MSR was $225.

RIFLES: SEMI-AUTO

M-14 RIFLE (NORINCO PARTS) - .308 Win. cal., 20 shot mag., newly mfg. M-14 using Norinco parts, wood stock. Mfg. 1991-92 only.

	$925	$850	$750	$675	$575	$475	$375

Last MSR was $688.

M-14R RIFLE (USGI PARTS) - .308 Win. cal., 10 (C/B 1994) or 20* shot mag., newly manufactured M-14 using original excellent condition forged G.I. parts including USGI fiberglass stock with rubber recoil pad. New 1986.

MSR $1,895	$1,625	$1,375	$1,100	$975	$825	$700	$550

Add $80 for medium weight National Match walnut stock (M-14RNS).
Add $25 for G.I. buttplate (disc.).
Add $45 for USGI birch stock (M-14RNSB, disc.).

M-14 BEGINNING NATIONAL MATCH - .308 Win. cal., mfg. from hand selected older USGI parts, except for new receiver and new USGI air gauged premium barrel, guaranteed to shoot 1 1/4 in. group at 100 yards. Mfg. 1993-96.

	$1,750	$1,350	$1,050	$925	$825	$725	$625

Last MSR was $1,950.

M-14 NMR (NATIONAL MATCH) - .308 Win. cal., built in accordance with A.M.T.U. mil. specs., 3 different barrel weights to choose from, NM rear sight system, calibrated mag., leather sling, guaranteed 1" MOA. New 1987.

MSR $2,850	$2,425	$1,875	$1,500	$1,150	$950	$825	$700

M-21 MATCH RIFLE - .308 Win. cal., NM rear lugged receiver, choice of McMillan fiberglass or laminated wood stock, guaranteed 1" MOA.

MSR $3,595	$3,125	$2,550	$1,975	$1,650	$1,300	$995	$825

T-48 FAL ISRAELI PATTERN RIFLE - .308 Win. cal., mfg. in the U.S. to precise original metric dimensions (parts are interchangeable with original Belgium FAL), forged receiver, hammer forged chrome lined mil-spec. 21 in. barrel (standard or heavy) with flash suppressor, adj. front sight, aperture rear sight, 10 lbs. Imported 1990-92.

	$1,325	$1,150	$975	$825	$750	$650	$550

Last MSR was $1,244.

This model was guaranteed to shoot within 2.5 MOA with match ammunition.

* **T-48 FAL L1A1 Pattern** - .308 Win. cal., fully enclosed forend with vents, 10 lbs. Imported 1992 only.

	$1,325	$1,150	$975	$825	$750	$650	$550

Last MSR was $1,181.

Add $122 for wood handguard sporter model (limited supply).

T-48 BUSH MODEL - similar to T-48 FAL, except has 18 in. barrel, 9 3/4 lbs. Mfg. 1990 only.

	$1,225	$1,050	$925	$775	$625	$525	$465

Last MSR was $1,250.

FRHB - .308 Win. cal., Israeli mfg. with heavy barrel and bipod. Imported 1990 only.

	$1,725	$1,450	$1,150	$975	$875	$795	$725

Last MSR was $1,895.

GRADING - PPGS™	100%	98%	95%	90%	80%	70%	60%

FAL - .308 Win. cal., Armscorp forged receiver, 21 in. Argentinian rebuilt barrel, manufactured to military specs., supplied with one military 20 shot mag., aperture rear sight, 10 lbs. Mfg. 1987-89.

	$1,425	$1,200	$1,050	$875	$750	$650	$550

Last MSR was $875.

> **Subtract $55 if without flash hider.**
> **Add $75 for heavy barrel with bipod (14 lbs.).**
> **Add $400 (last retail) for .22 LR conversion kit.**
> This model was guaranteed to shoot within 2.5 MOA with match ammunition.

❊ *FAL Bush Model* - similar to FAL, except has 18 in. barrel with flash suppressor, 9 3/4 lbs. Mfg. 1989 only.

	$2,100	$1,900	$1,800	$1,700	$1,500	$1,250	$1,000

Last MSR was $900.

❊ *FAL Para Model* - similar to FAL Bush Model, except has metal folding stock, leaf rear sight. Mfg. 1989 only.

	$2,450	$2,150	$1,950	$1,800	$1,600	$1,475	$1,250

Last MSR was $930.

❊ *FAL Factory Rebuilt* - factory (Argentine) rebuilt FAL without flash suppressor in excellent condition with Armscorp forged receiver, 9 lbs. 10 oz. Disc. 1989.

	$1,475	$1,250	$995	$825	$750	$575	$495

Last MSR was $675.

> **Add 20% for heavy barrel variation manufactured in Argentina under license from F.N.**

M36 ISRAELI SNIPER RIFLE - .308 Win. cal., gas operated semi-auto, Bullpup configuration, 22 in. free floating barrel, Armscorp M14 receiver, 20 shot mag., includes flash suppressor and bipod, 10 lbs. Civilian offering 1989 only.

	$2,900	$2,500	$2,275	$2,050	$1,900	$1,775	$1,600

Last MSR was $3,000.

EXPERT MODEL - .22 LR cal., semi-auto, 20.9 in. barrel, 10 shot mag., wood stock with one-screw takedown, iron sights with grooved receiver, 5.1 lbs. New 1989.

	$195	$150	$125	$115	$105	$95	$85

Last MSR was $225.

ARM SPORT LLC

Current conversion manufacturer and customizer located in Eastlake, CO.

Gunsmith R.L. Millington specializes in authentic, hand-built conversions of Colt and Remington black powder pistols to metallic cartridge, custom engraving, refinishing, and antique refinishing.

CARTRIDGE CONVERSIONS

All prices listed are for conversion work only. Current calibers include .32 S&W Short, .38 S&W, .38 LC, .38 Spl., .44-40 WCF, and .45 LC. Antiquing and period-style engraving are options. Currently, Arms Sport LLC is charging $875 for converting the 1839 Texas Paterson, Colt Pocket Dragoon (Wells-Fargo Model), 1851 Navy, 1861 Navy, and 1862 Pocket Navy/1862 Pocket Police, $895 for the 1847 Walker/Dragoon Models and the 1860 Army, $565 for the 1858 Remington Army, $785 for the Remington Navy, and $365 for the Remington Pocket Pistol.

ARMSPORT, INC.

Previous importer and distributor located in Miami, FL. Armsport imported shotguns (various configurations, mfg by Emilio Rizzini of Italy, and Sarsilmaz of Turkey) until 2000. Armsport, Inc. imported a revolver and offered a complete line of accessories (snap caps, scope rings, and cleaning kits).

For a complete listing of older Armsport, Inc. models, please refer to the 20th – 21st Editions or the online version of the *Blue Book of Gun Values*.

ARNOLD ARMS CO., INC.

Previous rifle manufacturer located in Arlington, WA, 1994-2001.

In addition to making a series of accurate rifles built on their own Apollo action, Arnold Arms Co. also built rifles on Remington, Ruger, Sako, or Winchester actions. All Arnold Arms rifles had a written guarantee on accuracy (1/2 in. group or less at 100 yards with handloads), and a 5 year limited warranty. Any Arnold Arms warranty is now void. The company also made proprietary cartridges in 6mm Arnold, .257 Arnold, .270 Arnold, .300 Arnold, .338 Arnold, or .458 Arnold.

RIFLES: BOLT ACTION

Arnold Arms Co., Inc. made a wide variety of quality bolt action rifles, including the African Trophy, Grand African Rifle, Alaskan Series, Classic Hunter Series, Neutralizer Series, Varminter Series, and the Strike Viper Series. For a complete listing of older Arnold Arms models and current values, please refer to the online version of the *Blue Book of Gun Values* (no charge).

ARRIETA, S.L.

Current manufacturer located in Elgoibar, Spain. Currently imported by several importers including Wingshooting Adventures, Quality Arms, Griffin & Howe, William Larkin Moore, and Orvis (see separate listing). Previously imported by New England Arms.

More information can be obtained on the Arrieta models listed below by contacting the importers listed above.

RIFLES: SxS

R-1 - 7x65R, 8x57JRS, or 9.3x74R cal., true sidelock, ejectors, quarter rib barrel with express rear sight.

MSR $12,287	$11,000	$9,350	$7,400	$6,200	$5,250	$4,700	$4,000

R-2 - similar to R-1, except has more elaborate H&H style engraving, elongated tangs, and choice of English or reinforced pistol grip with metal cap, ejectors.

MSR $17,490	$15,500	$12,950	$10,450	$9,250	$7,950	$6,850	$5,900

R-3 - similar to R-1, except includes .375 H&H or .470 NE cal.

MSR N/A	N/A	$16,250	$13,250	$10,500	$9,250	$7,850	$6,850

SHOTGUNS: SxS

The models listed below are essentially custom ordered per individual specifications – delivery time is approx. 12 months.

All Arrieta shotguns have frames scaled to individual gauges. Standard gauges are 12 & 16. Most models are available with either color case hardened or coin finished frames. Many factory upgrades and custom options/special orders are available from the individual importers – please contact them directly for availability and current pricing on these special orders.

On the models listed below, there are four different types of sidelock actions. One is used on the Model 550. Another is used on Models 557, 578, and 871. A third is used on Models 590 and 595 (designed for heavy use). Finally, the best quality is used on Models 600-903, except for Model 900 (557 action), and Model 871. All Arrieta actions are assisted opening, except the Models 557, 570, 578, and 871.

Note that some of the MSRs include price ranges instead of a single price. This is due to the fluctuation in pricing from the various importers and distributors.

Add 10% for small gauges (20, 24, 28, 32 ga., or .410 bore).

GRADING - PPGS™	100%	98%	95%	90%	80%	70%	60%

Add approx. $1,000 for single trigger depending on action.
Add 10% for matched pair.
Add 5% for rounded action on standard models (except Models 871 and 872).
Extra barrels are priced from $1,500-$2,100/set depending on model.

557 - 12, 16, or 20 ga., Demi-Bloc steel barrels, detachable engraved sidelocks, double triggers, ejectors.

MSR $3,850	$3,350	$2,350	$1,750	$1,250	$925	$875	$675

570 - 12, 16, or 20 ga., similar to 560 (non-standard model), except has non-detachable sidelocks.

MSR $4,785	$4,175	$3,475	$2,450	$1,825	$1,375	$1,075	$850

578 - 12, 16, or 20 ga., similar to 570, except is fine English scrollwork engraved.

MSR $5,225	$4,550	$3,950	$3,000	$2,100	$1,525	$1,175	$950

600 - 12, 16, or 20 ga., top-of-the-line self-opening action, very ornate engraving throughout.

MSR $7,095	$6,175	$5,275	$4,150	$3,300	$2,550	$1,950	$1,575

601 - all gauges, sidelock action with nickel plating, ejectors, SST, self-opening action, border engraving.

MSR $8,055	$7,000	$6,000	$5,100	$4,300	$3,250	$2,450	$1,925

801 - all gauges, Holland-style detachable sidelocks, self-opening action standard, ejectors, coin-wash finish, finest Churchill style engraving.

MSR $10,700	$9,300	$8,300	$7,300	$6,325	$5,275	$4,400	$3,500

802 - 12, 16, or 20 ga., similar to 801 only non-detachable sidelocks, finest Holland-style engraving.

MSR $10,700	$9,300	$8,300	$7,300	$6,325	$5,275	$4,400	$3,500

"BOSS" ROUND BODY - all gauges, Boss pattern best quality engraving, includes $1,500 wood upgrade.

MSR N/A	N/A	$8,250	$7,150	$5,950	$5,200	$4,400	$3,600

803 - all gauges, similar to 801, finest Purdey-style engraving.

MSR $8,175	$7,100	$6,175	$5,300	$4,175	$3,500	$2,950	$2,500

871 - all gauges, rounded frame sidelock action with Demi-Bloc barrels, scroll engraved, ejectors, DTs.

MSR $5,895	$5,125	$4,500	$3,425	$2,750	$2,200	$1,750	$1,450

872 - all gauges, rounded frame sidelock action with Demi-Bloc barrels, elaborate scroll engraving with third lever fastener.

MSR $14,382	$12,500	$11,000	$9,500	$7,250	$6,000	$5,250	$4,500

873 - all gauges, sidelock action with Demi-Bloc barrels, game scene engraving, ejectors, SST.

MSR $10,725	$9,325	$8,300	$7,300	$6,325	$5,275	$4,400	$3,500

874 - all gauges, sidelock action with Demi-Bloc barrels, action is gold line engraved.

MSR $10,725	$9,325	$8,300	$7,300	$6,325	$5,275	$4,400	$3,500

875 - all gauges, top-of-the-line quality, built to individual customer specs. only, elaborate engraving with gold inlays.

MSR $19,940	$17,500	$14,550	$11,000	$9,250	$8,100	$7,250	$6,300

931 - all gauges, self-opening action, elaborate engraving, H&H selective ejectors.

MSR $18,590	$16,100	$13,250	$10,000	$8,500	$7,500	$6,750	$5,500

ARRIZABALAGA, PEDRO

Current manufacturer located in Eibar, Spain since 1940. Currently imported and distributed by Harry Marx Hi-Grade Imports located in Gilroy, CA, and by William Larkin Moore, located in Scottsdale, AZ. Previously imported by New England Arms Corp. located in Kittery Point, ME.

Arrizabalaga manufactures best quality guns only, carefully made to individual customer specifications. Shotguns listed below have demi-bloc, chopper lump barrels and self-opening hand-detachable locks as standard features. The models listed below are essentially custom ordered per individual specifications — delivery time is approx. 12-18 months.

Add 10% for matched pair.
Add $3,500 per extra barrels.
Add 10% for 28 ga.
Add 12% for .410 bore.
Add $1,000 for single non-selective trigger.
Add $450 for beavertail forearm.
Add $400 for pistol grip stock.

SHOTGUNS: SxS

HEAVY SCROLL MODEL - all gauges, sidelock action, elaborate engraving, deluxe oil finished stock and forearm.

	100%	98%	95%	90%	80%	70%	60%
MSR $11,350	$10,400	$7,550	$5,850	$5,000	$4,350	$3,850	$3,325

ENGLISH SCROLL MODEL - all gauges, sidelock action, English scroll engraving, deluxe oil finished walnut stock and forearm.

	100%	98%	95%	90%	80%	70%	60%
MSR $11,850	$11,250	$8,000	$6,050	$5,000	$4,500	$4,000	$3,450

MODEL DELUXE - all gauges, limited importation.

	100%	98%	95%	90%	80%	70%	60%
MSR $12,750	$11,650	$8,350	$6,250	$5,250	$5,000	$4,500	$4,000

BOSS STYLE ROUND ACTION MODEL - all gauges, features English Boss style scroll engraving.

	100%	98%	95%	90%	80%	70%	60%
MSR $12,600	$11,500	$9,200	$7,600	$6,050	$5,250	$4,500	$4,000

Add $450 for Luxe engraving.

SPECIAL MODEL - all gauges, sidelock top-of-the-line model, best quality wood and engraving.

	100%	98%	95%	90%	80%	70%	60%
MSR $17,250	$15,500	$10,350	$9,100	$8,000	$7,000	$6,000	$5,000

ARSENAL, BULGARIA

Current manufacturer located in Bulgaria. Currently imported by Arsenal, Inc., located in Las Vegas, NV. Previously imported exclusively 1994-96 by Sentinel Arms located in Detroit, MI. For currently imported models, please refer to the Arsenal, Inc. listing.

The artillery arsenal in Rousse began in 1878, and was managed by Russian officers until 1884, when a Bulgarian was appointed the director. In 1891, the factory was transferred to Sofia, and was renamed the Sofia Artillery Arsenal until the entire facility was moved to Kazanlak in 1924. At that point, the name was changed to the State Military Factory. After WWII, the arsenal diversified into civilian production, and its nickname was "Factory 10." In 1958, the first AK-47 under Russian license came off the assembly line, and in 1982, the one millionth AK-47 had been manufactured.

PISTOLS: SEMI-AUTO

MAKAROV MODEL - 9mm Makarov cal., 3 2/3 in. barrel, 8 shot mag., black synthetic grips, blue finish. Disc. 1996.

	98%	95%	90%	80%	70%	60%
$185	$165	$125	$115	$105	$95	$85

GRADING - PPGS™	100%	98%	95%	90%	80%	70%	60%

RIFLES: SEMI-AUTO

BULGARIAN SA-93 - 7.62x39mm cal., Kalashnikov milled action with hardwood thumbhole stock, 16.3 in. barrel, 5 shot detachable mag., 9 lbs. Disc. 1996.

	$525	$440	$350	$275	$225	$200	$175

✳ *Bulgarian SA-93L* - 7.62x39mm cal., similar to Bulgarian SA-93 except has 20 in. barrel, with or without optics, 9 lbs. Disc. 1996.

	$595	$525	$450	$395	$350	$295	$250

Add $145 with optics.

BULGARIAN SS-94 - 7.62x39mm cal., Kalashnikov action featuring single shot operation, thumbhole hardwood stock, 5 shot detachable mag., 9 lbs. Disc. 1996.

	$475	$395	$325	$275	$225	$190	$180

ARSENAL INC.

Current importer established during 2001 and located in Las Vegas, NV. Dealer and distributor sales.

RIFLES: SEMI-AUTO

Arsenal Inc. is the exclusive importer of various Arsenal Bulgaria AK style/design rifles in .223 Rem. (new 2003), 5.45x39.5mm or 7.62x39mm cal. Additionally, Arsenal Inc. manufactures a wide range of all U.S. made models conforming 100% to Arsenal Bulgaria specifications and manufacturing procedures. All models, either U.S. made or imported, feature forged and milled receivers, and hammer forged barrels.

SA M-5/SA M-5G/SA M-5S/SA M-5SG - .223 Rem. cal., patterned after the AK-47, 16.3 in. barrel, black (SA M-5) or green (SA M-5G) synthetic furniture with pistol grip, approx. 8.1 lbs. New 2003.

MSR $780	$695	$535	$450	$375	$325	$300	$275

Add $10 for SA M-5G.
Add $75 for SA M-5S with scope rail (limited edition).
Add $80 for SA M-5SG.

SA RPK-5 S - .223 Rem. cal., features blonde wood stock, pistol grip and forearm, 23 1/4 in. barrel with tripod and scope rail, approx. 11 lbs. Limited edition beginning 2003.

MSR $1,240	$1,075	$925	$800	$700	$625	$550	$495

SA M-7/SA M-7G/SA M-7S/SA M-7SG - 7.62x39mm cal., also available in carbine, otherwise similar to SA M-5. New 2003.

MSR $755	$675	$525	$450	$400	$350	$325	$295

Add $35 for SA M-7S with scope rail.
Add $5 for SA M-7G with OD green furniture.
Add $40 for SA M-7SG with scope rail.

SA M-7 CLASSIC - 7.62x39mm cal., features blonde wood stock, pistol grip and forearm, double stack magazine, less than 200 mfg. 2001-2002 only.

	$795	$650	$525	$400	$350	$325	$295

Last MSR was $1,200.

SA RPK-7 - 7.62x39mm cal., otherwise similar to SA RPK-5 S, except does not have scope rail. Limited edition beginning 2003.

MSR $1,130	$995	$875	$750	$650	$575	$515	$475

SLR 101 S - 7.62x39mm cal., similar to SA M-7, except has black thumbole synthetic stock, available in polymer black (SLR 101SB1) or polymer OD Green (SLR 101SG1). New 2003.

MSR $410	$335	$275	$240	$210	$185	$170	$155

Add $100 for SLR 101SB1.
Add $110 for SLR 101SG1.

GRADING - PPGS™	100%	98%	95%	90%	80%	70%	60%

SLR 101SB/SG - 7.62x39mm cal., double stack mag., features side mount scope rail, 16 in. barrel, standard military stock configuration. New 2004.

MSR $655	$525	$450	$375	$295	$250	$200	$185

Add $45 for SG Model with green polymer.

SAS M-7 - 7.62x39mm cal., U.S. mfg., authentic semi-auto version of Bulgarian model AR M1F with vertical gas block and ATF approved fixed metal underfolding style stock. Limited edition of 200 to be mfg. during 2004.

MSR $1,100	$975	$850	$725	$650	$575	$515	$475

SAS M-7 CLASSIC - 7.62x39mm cal., U.S. mfg., authentic semi-auto version of Russian 1953 Model AKS-47 with slant gas block and ATF approved fixed metal underfolding style stock. Limited edition of 200 to be mfg. beginning 2004.

MSR $1,150	$995	$850	$725	$650	$575	$515	$475

ARSENAL USA LLC

Previous manufacturer/importer from 1999-2004, and located in Houston, TX. During September 2004, Arsenal USA LLC changed its name to Armory USA L.L.C. Please refer to this listing for currently manufactured rifles.

RIFLES: SEMI-AUTO

MODEL SSR-99 - 7.62x39mm cal., Bulgarian milled receiver and parts, black polymer furniture. Less than 300 mfg. 1999-2000.

$525	$450	$400	$350	$300	$250	$200

Last MSR was $600.

MODEL K-101 - .223 Rem. cal., Bulgarian milled receiver and parts, black polymer furniture. Less than 200 mfg. 1999-2000

$525	$450	$400	$350	$300	$250	$200

Last MSR was $600.

MODEL SSR-99P - 7.62x39mm cal., Bulgarian milled receiver and parts, with rare Polish grenade launching variant parts, Polish wood furniture. Less than 500 mfg. 1999-2001

$525	$450	$400	$350	$300	$250	$200

Last MSR was $600.

MODEL SSR-85B - 7.62x39mm cal., Hungarian FEG receiver and Polish AKM parts, blond Hungarian wood furniture, small number produced using ITM U.S. made receiver. Approx. 1,200 mfg. 2000-2003

$400	$350	$300	$250	$200	$150	$125

Last MSR was $450.

MODEL AMD-63 - 7.62x39mm cal., Hungarian FEG receiver and Polish AKM parts, unique metal lower handguard with pistol grip. 200 mfg. 2000-2003.

$525	$450	$400	$350	$300	$250	$200

Last MSR was $600.

MODEL SSR-56 - 7.62x39mm cal., Hungarian FEG receiver, Poly-Tec barrel assembly and Bulgarian internal parts. Approx. 500 mfg. 2002-2003.

$400	$350	$300	$250	$200	$150	$125

Last MSR was $450.

ART MANIFACTTURA ARMI

Current longarm manufacturer located in Gardone, Italy. Currently imported beginning 2004 by William Larkin Moore, located in Scottsdale, AZ. Art Manifacttura Armi manufactures high quality custom long guns, including rifles and shotguns. Please contact the importer (see Trademark Index) directly for more information, including availability and pricing.

GRADING - PPGS™	100%	98%	95%	90%	80%	70%	60%

Currently imported models include a SxS Anson & Deely boxlock action with rose and scroll engraving - $15,000 MSR, a H&H type sidelock SxS shotgun with choice of H&H or Purdey style engraving - $24,000 MSR, and a SxS sidelock rifle in .375 H&H, .470 NE, or .500 NE cal., with rose and scroll engraving - $39,000 MSR.

ASP

Previously manufactured customized variation of a S&W Model 39-2 semi-auto pistol (or related variations) mfg. by Armament Systems and Procedures located in Appleton, WI.

PISTOLS: SEMI-AUTO

ASP - 9mm Para. cal., compact double action semi-auto, features see-through grips with cut-away mag. making cartridges visible, Teflon coated, re-contoured lightened slide, combat trigger guard, spurless hammer, and mostly painted Guttersnipe rear sight (no front sight), supplied with 3 mags., 24 oz. loaded. Approx. 3,000 mfg. until 1981.

$1,500	$1,275	$1,050	$875	$775	$695	$625

Add $200 for Tritium filled Guttersnipe.

This pistol is marked ASP on the magazine extension.

✳ ***ASP Quest For Excellence*** - special edition, marked "Quest for Excellence." included buffalo horn grips, presentation book case and letter opener. Approx. 100 mfg.

$3,150	$2,700	$2,400	$2,050	$1,775	$1,525	$1,275

REVOLVERS

ASP REVOLVER - .44 Spl. cal., conversion from a Ruger Speed or Security Six, 5 shot. Less than 100 mfg., unmarked.

$1,275	$1,075	$950	$875	$775	$700	$650

ASPREY

Previous long gun manufacturer located in London, England. While established in 1781, Asprey manufactured high quality shotguns and rifles 1990-99. During 1998, the name was changed to Asprey & Garrard. Guns are currently manufactured by William & Son, located in London, England.

Please refer to the William & Son listing for currently manufactured models.

ASTRA

Previous manufacturer located in Guernica, Spain. Astra was one of the oldest and most widely recognized trademarks in Spain, with a history dating back to 1908. Though arms were manufactured for many years by Unceta y Compania, S.A., located in Guernica, Spain, corporate reorganization resulted in renaming the same firm Astra Sport, S.A. (1995-1997), and Astra Sport Guerniquesa de Mecanizado Tratamiento y Montaje de Armas, S.A. (1997-1998).

Although Astra had hoped to acquire Star patents and relocate to a smaller facility, these efforts were not successful. Foreclosure sealed the factory doors in July, 1998, and all inventory, including the "factory collection," was released for sale in 1999.

PISTOLS: SEMI-AUTO

MODEL 1911 - .25 ACP or .32 ACP cal., semi-auto, may have external or internal hammer.

$365	$265	$175	$135	$115	$100	$85

Add 50% if with external hammer.

GRADING - PPGS™	100%	98%	95%	90%	80%	70%	60%

MODEL 1915/1916 - .32 ACP cal., semi-auto.

| | $350 | $265 | $175 | $135 | $115 | $100 | $85 |

Note: Models 1915/1916 were later referred to as Model 100 Special.

CAMPO GIRO 1913 - mfg. 1913-14. Ser. No. range 1-1,300.

| | $4,000 | $3,350 | $2,900 | $2,250 | $1,750 | $1,200 | $750 |

Add 10% for matching magazine.

CAMPO GIRO 1913-1916 - mfg. 1915-19. Ser. No. range 1-13,625.

| | $2,250 | $1,950 | $1,300 | $850 | $650 | $500 | $400 |

Add 10% if fit with horn logo grips.
Add 10% for matching magazine.

MODEL 200 FIRECAT AUTOMATIC PISTOL - .25 ACP cal., 2 1/4 in. barrel, 6 shot, blue, plastic grips. Mfg. 1920-68.

| | $250 | $190 | $165 | $145 | $125 | $110 | $100 |

100% prices assume N.I.B. condition.
Add 50% for engraved M-200.

MODEL 300 - .32 ACP or .380 ACP cal., semi-auto.

| | $850 | $650 | $450 | $325 | $225 | $180 | $150 |

Add 20% for Nazi-proofed .380 ACP pistols.
Add 100% for lightly engraved M-300.
Add 200% for deeply engraved M300 model with salesman sample grips.

MODEL 400 AUTOMATIC PISTOL - 9mm Bayard Long cal., 9 shot, 6 in. barrel, blue, fixed sights, plastic grips. Mfg. 1921-45.

| | $450 | $400 | $325 | $275 | $225 | $175 | $125 |

Add 200% for Navy variation.
Add 100% for Nazi accepted specimens.
Serial range of Nazi accepted specimens (no markings) is S/N 92,851-98,850.
This particular model in reworked configuration has recently been imported in large quantities.

✳ **"F. Ascaso" Marked Model 400 Copies** - close copy of the Astra Model 400, produced by the Spanish Republican forces during the later part of the Spanish Civil War, F. Ascaso marked (un-numbered) mags., salt blue, estimated production is approx. 8,000, has identifying logo on slide and grip panels, and base of magazine.

| | $750 | $500 | $425 | $310 | $280 | $255 | $225 |

✳ **R.E. (Republica Espagnola) Marked Model 400 Copies** - ser. range to approx. 15,000, has identifying logo on forward slide and grip panels.

| | $500 | $400 | $295 | $240 | $210 | $170 | $125 |

Add $200 if pistol is fit with wood serrated grips having brass RE medallion.

MODEL 600 MOD. AUTOMATIC - 9mm Para. cal., 8 shot, 5 1/4 in. barrel, blue, fixed sights, wood or plastic grips. Mfg. 1944-45.

| | $395 | $325 | $250 | $175 | $155 | $140 | $130 |

Add 100% for Nazi Waffenamt proofing (serial range 1-10,500).

MODEL 700 SPECIAL - .32 ACP cal., semi-auto.

| | $1,200 | $1,000 | $800 | $700 | $600 | $500 | $400 |

MODEL 800 CONDOR AUTOMATIC - 9mm Para. cal., similar to Model 600, except has exposed hammer. Mfg. 1958-65.

| | $1,500 | $1,250 | $1,000 | $900 | $800 | $700 | $600 |

Add 20% if NIB with accessories.

GRADING - PPGS™	100%	98%	95%	90%	80%	70%	60%

MODEL 900 - 7.63 Mauser cal., Broomhandle copy, parts non-interchangeable with Mauser. Mfg. from 1928-36.

	$2,950	$2,250	$1,750	$1,200	$900	$700	$500

Add $650 for non-matching shoulder stock.
Add $900 for matching stock.
Add 50% for early Bolo grip variation.
Add 20% for specimens with Japanese characters.

MODEL 902 - 7.63 Mauser cal., semi-auto, similar to Model 900 except 20 shot mag. Beware of fakes - usually created by welding up selective fire pistols.

	$15,000	$12,000	$9,500	$6,500	$3,500	$3,000	$2,500

Add $1,500 for original "booted" stock.
Subtract 60% for selective fire version.

MACHINE PISTOLS - class III, transferrable only, 10 or 20 shot detachable mag., several variations.

	$7,500	$6,000	$5,000	$4,500	$4,000	$3,000	$2,000

MODEL 3000 POCKET AUTOMATIC - .32 ACP or .380 ACP cal., 4 in. barrel, fixed sights, blue, plastic grips. Mfg. 1947-56.

	$700	$550	$400	$300	$250	$200	$150

Add 100% for engraved M3000.

MODEL 1000 OR 1000 SPECIAL - .32 ACP cal., semi-auto, extended frame to hold 12 shot mag.

	$750	$600	$425	$310	$280	$255	$225

MODEL 2000 CUB - .22 short or .25 ACP cal., 2 1/4 in. barrel, fixed sights, blue, plastic grips, also chrome finish, mfg. 1954-98, U.S. importation stopped by GCA 68. Astra also made 2000 Model 2000 Cubs for Colt called Jr. Model (see Colt section).

	$250	$190	$140	$115	$95	$85	$75

Add 25% for chrome finish.
Add 50% for engraved M-2000.

MODEL 2000 CAMPER - .22 short cal. only, similar to Model 2000 Cub, with 4 in. barrel. Mfg. 1955-1960.

	$350	$275	$200	$160	$125	$90	$70

Add 10% if in original box.

CONSTABLE - .22 LR (10 shot, disc. 1990), .32 ACP (8 shot, disc. 1984), or .380 ACP (7 shot) cal., double action, exposed hammer, 3 1/2 in. barrel, fixed sight, blue or chrome (disc.) finish, plastic grips. Imported 1965-91.

	$325	$295	$250	$225	$200	$175	$150

Last MSR was $380.

Add $10 for chrome finish or wood grips (disc. in 1990).
Add 10% for .22 LR cal.

* *Constable Stainless* - .380 ACP cal. only, stainless version of the Constable. Mfg. 1986 only.

	$450	$400	$350				

Last MSR was $345.

* *Constable Sport* - similar to Constable, except has 6 in. barrel, blue finish only, 35 oz. Mfg. 1986-87 only.

	$375	$325	$275	$225	$175	$165	$150

Last MSR was $330.

* *Blue Engraved Constable* - blue engraved. Importation disc. 1987.

	$450	$325	$250				

Last MSR was $375.

Add $20 for .22 LR or checkered wood grips.

GRADING - PPGS™	100%	98%	95%	90%	80%	70%	60%

❋ Chrome Engraved Constable - chrome engraved. Importation disc. 1987.

	$395	$320	$250				

Last MSR was $390.

Add $20 for .22 LR or checkered wood grips.

CONSTABLE A-60 - .380 ACP cal., double action, 3 1/2 in. barrel, 13 shot mag., ambidextrous safety, adj. rear sight, blue finish only. Imported 1986-91.

	$395	$325	$280	$245	$220	$185	$160

Last MSR was $475.

MODEL A-70 - 9mm Para. or .40 S&W cal., single action, 3 1/2 in. barrel, steel frame and slide, 7 (.40 S&W) or 8 (9mm Para.) shot mag., compact design, dual safeties, 3-dot sights, matte blue or nickel (new 1993) finish, 25 3/4 oz. Imported 1991-96.

	$275	$250	$225	$200	$185	$170	$160

Last MSR was $358.

Add $29 for nickel finish.

❋ Model A-70 Stainless - stainless steel variation of the Model A-70. Mfg. 1994 only.

	$365	$325	$275				

Last MSR was $435.

MODEL A-75 - 9mm Para., .40 S&W, or .45 ACP (new 1994) cal., action similar to Model A-70, except has selective double action with a decocking lever, steel or aluminum (9mm Para. only) frame. Importation began 1993.

❋ 9mm Para or .40 S&W. - choice of blue or nickel steel frame or lightweight aluminum frame (23 1/2 oz.), 7 (.40 S&W) or 8 (9mm Para.) shot mag. Disc. 1998.

	$295	$265	$240	$210	$185	$170	$160

Last MSR was $303.

Add $17 for nickel finish.
Add $20 for lightweight model (aluminum frame).

❋ .45 ACP - blue or nickel finish, 7 shot mag. Disc. 1998.

	$325	$260	$225	$200	$175	$160	$150

Last MSR was $358.

Add $23 for nickel finish.

❋ Model A-75 Stainless - stainless steel variation of the Model A-75. Mfg. 1994 only.

	$375	$325	$295				

Last MSR was $485.

MODEL A-80 - 9mm Para, .38 Super (disc.), or .45 ACP cal., double action, semi-auto, 15 shot mag. (9 for .45 ACP), 3 3/4 in. barrel. Imported 1982-89.

	$350	$320	$285	$265	$240	$210	$185

Last MSR was $425.

Add $35 for chrome finish (disc.).
.38 Super cal. in chrome finish will command a premium (10%-20%).

MODEL A-90 - 9mm Para. or .45 ACP cal., 1986 designation for Model A-80 with updated slide mounted safety and pushbutton mag. release, 3 3/4 in. barrel, 14 shot mag. (9mm), or 8 shot (.45 ACP), blue only, approx. 48 oz. Imported 1986-90, replaced by Model A-100.

	$425	$350	$295	$275	$245	$225	$200

Last MSR was $500.

MODEL A-100 - 9mm Para., .40 S&W, or .45 ACP cal., replaced the Model A-90 in 1990, with similar specifications, blue or nickel finish, re-engineered 1993 incorporating increased mag. capacity, 10 (C/B 1994), 17*/9mm, 12*/.40 S&W, or 9 shot/.45 ACP, approx. 29 oz. Imported 1990-97.

	$400	$325	$295	$275	$245	$225	$175

Last MSR was $351.

Add $22 for nickel finish.
A small number of pistols with an extended slide were made for the Turkish police - add 50%.

GRADING - PPGS™	100%	98%	95%	90%	80%	70%	60%

MODEL 4000 FALCON - .22 LR, .32 ACP, or .380 ACP cal., 4 in. barrel, fixed sights, blue, plastic grips, exposed hammer. Mfg. 1956-86.

	$550	$425	$330	$260	$235	$200	$150

Last MSR was $340.

Add 50% for .22 cal.
Add 10% for .380 ACP.
Add 100% for engraved Model-4000 Falcon.

* *Model 4000 Tri-cal. Kit* - includes frame and 3 barrels (.22 LR, .32 ACP, and .380 ACP cals.), may have rust blue, salt blue, or chromed (rare) finish, less than 200 mfg.

	$1,250	$950	$750	$650	$575	$500	$450

Subtract 15% if not in factory box.

REVOLVERS

CADIX DOUBLE ACTION REVOLVER - .22 LR cal., 9 shot, .38 Spl., 5 shot, 4 or 6 in. barrel, adj. sights, blue, plastic grips. Mfg. 1960-68.

	$195	$165	$140	$120	$110	$85	$55

.357 D/A REVOLVER - .357 Mag. cal., 6 shot, 3, 4, 6, or 8 1/2 in. barrel, adj. sights, blue, checkered wood grips. Mfg. 1972-88.

	$250	$215	$185	$170	$155	$140	$125

Last MSR was $295.

Add 50% for 8 1/2 in. barrel.

* *Stainless Steel* - 4 in. barrel only. Disc. 1987.

	$285	$245	$205				

Last MSR was $330.

LARGE CAL. D/A REVOLVER - .41 Mag. (disc. 1985), .44 Mag., or .45 LC (disc. 1987) cal., 6 shot, 6 or 8 1/2 in. (.44 Mag. only) barrels. Mfg. 1980-87.

	$280	$235	$210	$190	$180	$170	$160

Last MSR was $315.

* *Stainless Steel* - .44 Mag. cal. only, 6 in. barrel only, 2 1/2 lbs. Importation disc. 1993.

	$370	$300	$265				

Last MSR was $450.

CONVERTIBLE REVOLVER - 9mm Para. cal. with extra .357 Mag. cal. cylinder, 6 shot, 3 in. barrel, blue only, checkered walnut grips, 2 1/4 lbs. Imported 1986-1993.

	$375	$315	$250	$225	$200	$180	$160

Last MSR was $395.

TERMINATOR - .44 Mag. or .44 Spl. (disc.) cal., 6 shot, adj. rear sight, Roberts rubber grips, 2 3/4 in. shrouded barrel only. Inventories were depleted in 1989.

Blue finish	$295	$250	$200	$175	$160	$150	$140

Last MSR was $250.

Stainless steel	$325	$275	$225				

Last MSR was $275.

These models were distributed by Sile Distributors, Inc. located in New York, NY.

ATKIN, GRANT & LANG LTD.

Current gunmaker established in 1960, and located in Hertfordshire, England. Atkin, Grant & Lang is the parent company that owns the trademarks of Henry Atkin, Stephen Grant and Joseph Lang. Please refer to these individual trademarks listed separately.

GRADING - PPGS™	100%	98%	95%	90%	80%	70%	60%

ATKIN, HENRY

Current trademark established in 1877 and currently manufactured by Atkin Grant & Lang, Ltd. located in Hertfordshire, England. Henry Atkin Ltd. joined with Grant & Lang during 1960, forming Atkin Grant & Lang Ltd. No current U.S. importation.

Atkin Grant & Lang Ltd. provide a useful historical research service on older Henry Atkin shotguns and rifles. The charge for this service is £25 per gun, and the company will give you all pertinent factory information regarding the history.

SHOTGUNS: SxS

Prices on Henry Atkin shotguns do not include VAT or importation costs. Please contact the company directly (see Trademark Index) for more information, including availability, delivery time, and a price quotation.

Add 10% for matched pairs.

BOXLOCK MODEL - 28 (2 mfg.) or 20 (3 mfg.) ga., very limited millenium edition.
This model is POR from the factory, based on an individual custom order.

SIDELOCK MODEL - 12, 20 ga., or .410 bore, best quality sidelock ejector model with opening assist.
This model is POR from the factory, based on an individual custom order.

AUSTRALIAN AUTOMATIC ARMS PTY. LTD.

Previous manufacturer located in Tasmania, Australia. Previously imported and distributed by California Armory, Inc. located in San Bruno, CA.

PISTOLS: SEMI-AUTO

SAP - .223 Rem. cal., semi-auto paramilitary design pistol, 10 1/2 in. barrel, 20 shot mag., fiberglass stock and forearm, 5.9 lbs. Imported 1986-93.

$795	$700	$600	$550	$500	$475	$450

Last MSR was $799.

RIFLES: SEMI-AUTO

SAR - .223 Rem. cal., semi-auto paramilitary design rifle, 16 1/4 or 20 in. (new 1989) barrel, 5 or 20 shot M-16 style mag., fiberglass stock and forearm, 7 1/2 lbs. Imported 1986-89.

$850	$750	$650	$600	$550	$500	$475

Last MSR was $663.

Add $25 for 20 in. barrel.
This model was also available in fully auto version (AR).

SAC - .223 Rem. cal., semi-auto paramilitary design carbine, 10 1/2 in. barrel, 20 shot mag., fiberglass stock and forearm, 6.9 lbs. New 1986.
This model was available to class III dealers and law enforcement agencies only.

SP - .223 Rem. cal., semi-auto, sporting configuration, 16 1/4 or 20 in. barrel, wood stock and forearm, 5 or 20 shot M-16 style mag., 7.5 lbs. Imported late 1991-93.

$850	$750	$650	$600	$550	$500	$475

Last MSR was $879.

Add $40 for wood stock.

AUSTRALIAN INTERNATIONAL ARMS

Current exporter located in Brisbane, Australia. Australian Interntaional Arms works in cooperation with ADI Limited Lithgow, formerly Small Arms Factory, known for its SMLE No. I MKIII and L1A1 rifles. Previously imported and distributed until 2004 by Tristar Sporting Arms, Ltd., located in N. Kansas City, MO.

GRADING - PPGS™	100%	98%	95%	90%	80%	70%	60%

RIFLES: BOLT ACTION, ENFIELD SERIES

M10 ENFIELD - 7.62x39mm cal., features L42A1 improved action, all new components, teak stock with steel buttplate, 16.1 (short carbine), or 25.2 (.308 Win. cal.
only) in. barrel, AK-47 style mag., two-stage trigger, elevated Picatinny rail, CNC
milled receiver, 8.3 lbs. Imported 2003-2004.

	$575	$500	$425	$350	$300	$275	$250

Last MSR was $659.

NO.4 MK IV - .308 Win. cal., 25.2 in. barrel with full teak stock, with or w/o accessories, 9.1 lbs. Imported 2003-2004.

	$650	$550	$450	$375	$325	$295	$275

Last MSR was $759.

> **Add $440 for walnut stock, glass bedded target barrel, elevated Picatinny rail, and
> accessories.**

M 42 - .308 Win. cal., 27.6 in. barrel with mahogany stock and extra cheekpiece, blue
printed action, bright metal/barrel finish, includes Picatinny rail, 8.2 lbs. Imported
2003-2004.

	$1,125	$950	$800	$650	$550	$450	$350

Last MSR was $1,295.

SHOTGUNS: LEVER ACTION

MODEL 1887 - 12 ga., 2 3/4 in. chamber, reproduction of the Winchester Model 1887,
uncheckered oil finished walnut stock and forearm, blue finish, steel buttplate, 5
shot, exposed hammer with half cock, 22 in. barrel, 8 3/4 lbs. Limited importation
2003-2004.

	$995	$850	$750	$650	$600	$550	$500

Last MSR was $1,195.

AUTAUGA RIFLES, INC.

Previous manufacturer located in Prattville, AL 1996-2002. In 2000, Autauga Arms,
Inc. changed their name to Autauga Rifles, Inc.

PISTOLS: SEMI-AUTO

AUTAUGA MKII 32 - .32 ACP cal., double action only, 2 in. barrel, hammerless, blowback type action, 6 shot mag., stainless steel, black polymer grips, 12 oz. 3,200
mfg. 1996-2000.

	$325	$225	$185

Early guns did not have the MKII designation.

Last MSR was $399.

RIFLES: BOLT ACTION

Autauga Rifles, Inc. manufactured a complete line of precision bolt action rifles that were special
ordered per individual customer specifications. Configurations included hunting, long range
competition, law enforcement and military tactical rifles. Complete packages included rifle,
optics, hardware, and cleaning equipment. Standard rifle prices varied from $2,500-$3,500,
depending on options. Rifles were supplied with a Pelican 1750 case.

AUTO MAG

Previously manufactured (circa 1971-1982)
by Auto Mag. Corp. and TDE Corp. Recent
manufacture (Harry Sanford Commemorative) was produced by Galena Industries,
located in Sturgis, SD.

Less than 9,000 Auto Mags were produced by all manufacturers. All pistols originally had all stainless steel mags.

Short recoil rotary bolt system made entirely of stainless steel. Most pistols were sold in .44 AMP cal., although .357 AMP was also a popular factory option.

A unique handgun, the Auto Mag was never a commercial success due to high manufacturing costs and initial functioning problems (mostly attributed to hand loading all the ammo – once factory ammo became available, reliability improved significantly). Initial reaction to Dirty Harry's use of this weapon in the movie "Sudden Impact" (1983), as well as Burt Reynolds in "Malone" (1987) made prices escalate considerably, but most values appear to have stabilized since 1989. Be aware of fakes – especially of the XP variety (re-serialized, re-stamped, location of markings, etc.). Also, the ease of barrel swapping should be considered when deciding on a potential purchase. Auto Mags were never magna ported from the factory (only The Custom 100 Series). Non-original magna porting actually detracts from the values listed below, since it is a non-factory alteration.

Serial number ranges for the various models are as follows: Pasadena mfg. – A0000 through A03700. TDE North Hollywood – mostly A02500 through A05015, although some were marked with very low ser. numbers. TDE El Monte mfg. – A05016 through A08300. (Note: these numbers should only be used as a guideline – as the company named changed, serial numbers overlapped.)

High Standard was the national distributor for Auto Mag from 1974-1975. These guns were chambered in .44 AMP and .357 AMP. High Standard catalog numbers are: 9346 for .44 AMP, and 9347 for .357 AMP. High Standard sold 134 Auto Mags with an "H" prefix. Serial numbers between H1 and H198, with one at .44 AMP and 26 were .357 AMP. High Standard also sold 911 Auto Mags between serial numbers A05278-A07637. 777 of these were .44 AMP and 108 were .357 AMP. The "H" prefix guns remain a collectors' item and command a 25% premium over values listed below. It is estimated that an additional 300 barrels were marked High Standard.

TDE/OMC marked pistols - B00001 through B00370 are known as the "B" series or solid bolt models (only 370 manufactured). This "B" series also commands collector premiums.

AMT manufactured the last two lots of Auto Mags; the first was the "C" series and was basically the same as the "B" except that only 50 guns were fabricated. The "B" Series was manufactured in 1979. Ser. no. C00001-C00050 "C" Series was manufactured in 1979, and the "Last" Series was manufactured in 1982. The last Auto Mags made by AMT were appropriately serial numbered LAST 1 through LAST 50. These guns had the reputation of being the poorest quality but do carry collector premiums. One interesting variation is the North Hollywood "two-line" model. Also, the first .357 cal. pistols manufactured did not have the words AUTO MAG appearing on the gun. These are also collectors' items.

In addition to the above calibers, a very few non-factory .22, .25 and .30 LMP (Lomont Magnum Pistols) cal. prototypes were fabricated by Kent Lomont. These specimens will usually demand a premium over the values listed below. Also, some barrels and pistols were made in Covina, CA.

PISTOLS: SEMI-AUTO

ORIGINAL PASADENA - .44 AMP cal. only, 6 1/2 in. VR barrel, ser. no. A0001 – A3,300.

$2,500   **$2,300**   **$1,995**

This model is generally regarded as having the most quality, as all components were milled from Carpenter 455 stainless steel stock.

TDE NORTH HOLLYWOOD - ser. no. range A3,400 – A05015.

* *.44 AMP* - 6 1/2 in. VR barrel, initial guns were mfg. from existing Pasadena parts, later mfg. required new components made by TDE.

$2,275   **$1,850**   **$1,700**

Quality on this model goes down in later mfg. (some small parts are not stainless). Because of this, higher serial numbered guns in this model are less desirable.

GRADING - PPGS™	100%	98%	95%	90%	80%	70%	60%

❋ *.357 AMP* - two line address, there are no factory records verifying this caliber, and most were assembled with spare barrels.

$1,850 $1,600 $1,450

TDE EL MONTE - ser. no. range A05016-A08300.

❋ *.44 AMP* - 6 1/2 VR, 8 1/2, or 10 1/2 in. tapered barrel.

$2,000 $1,700 $1,600

❋ *.357 AMP* - 6 1/2 VR, 8 1/2, or 10 1/2 in. tapered barrel.

$1,750 $1,600 $1,450

HIGH STANDARD - "H" prefixed serial numbers, approx. 132 mfg. by TDE with High Standard markings.

$2,250 $2,100 $1,850

LEE JURRAS STANDARD MODELS - see listings below, custom features would vary from presentation grade polishing of barrel and frame to exotic wood or micarta grips.

❋ *LEJ Standard Automag* - .357 AMP or .44 AMP cal., 6 1/2 w/VR, 8 1/2, or 10 1/2 in. non-rib barrel, TDE markings, lion's head logo. 1,100-1,200 mfg. 1974-76 by Lee Jurras & Associates.

$2,225 $2,050 $1,775

Lee Jurras added his Lion's head logo (1974-1976) on TDE manufactured guns. There were also a very limited quantity of original shoulder stocks (less than 12), and were available for the International and Alaskan models only – extreme rarity precludes accurate price evaluation.

Several other calibers and variations were marketed through Lee Jurras including one-of-a-kind exotics like a .30 cal. Cougar with 12 in. barrel and highly polished metal.

LEE JURRAS CUSTOM MODELS - Lee Jurras Custom Models included the 100 (listed below), 200 International (12 mfg.), 300 Alaskan (9 mfg.), 400 Backpacker (5 mfg.), 500 Grizzly (5 mfg.), 600 Condor (2 mfg.), and Metallic Silouhette (2 mfg.). Because of the rarity factor, these models with 12 or less mfg. are difficult to price accurately, and must be evaluated and appraised individually.

❋ *LEJ Custom Model 100* - .357 AMP, .41 JMP (Jurras Magnum Pistol), or .44 AMP cal., 6 1/2 in. VR or 8 1/2 non-rib (only 10 mfg. in each cal.) polished magna-ported barrel, custom laminated wood grips, special carrying case. 100 mfg. in each cal.

$3,150 $2,850 $2,350

TDE/OMC "B" SERIES - 6 1/2 VR or 10 in. barrel, ser. no. range B00001-B00370.

$2,250 $2,100 $1,850

AMT "C" SERIES - 6 1/2 VR or 10 in. barrel, ser. no. range C00001-C00050.

$2,250 $2,100 $1,850

Note: guns were cased (plastic attache style) with accessories. Collector caution - over the years, the foam in these plastic cases can break down, and may cause discoloration and pitting on the gun. Original Auto-Mag ammo (only original mfg. by CDM in Mexico and Norma in Sweden) is currently selling for approx. $75-$95 a box. Starline now has .44 AMP brass, and Cor-bon loaded .44 AMP ammo also – new 2001.

HARRY SANFORD COMMEMORATIVE AUTO MAG - .44 AMP cal., Automag, Inc. commemorative reissue, "STURGIS, SD" barrel address with Harry Sanford signature on left rear of slide, cased. 1,000 pistols were scheduled to be mfg., but only approx. 300 actually completed by Galena Industries 1999-2000.

$2,750 $2,300 $1,995

Last MSR was $2,750.

GRADING - PPGS™	100%	98%	95%	90%	80%	70%	60%

AUTO-ORDNANCE CORP.

Current manufacturer with facilities located in Worcester, MA, and corporate offices in Blauvelt, NY. Auto-Ordnance Corp. became a division of Kahr Arms in 1999. Auto-Ordnance Corp. was a division of Gun Parts Corp. until 1999. Previously located in West Hurley, NY. Consumer, dealer and distributor sales.

Auto-Ordnance Corp. manufactures an exact reproduction of the original 1927 Thompson machine gun. They are currently available from Kahr Arms in semi-auto only since production ceased on fully automatic variations (Model 1928 and M1) in 1986 (mfg. 1975-1986 including 609 M1s). All guns currently manufactured utilize the Thompson trademark, are manufactured in the U.S. and come with a lifetime warranty.

PISTOLS: SEMI-AUTO

During 1997, Auto Ordnance discontinued all calibers on the pistols listed below, except for .45 ACP cal. or 9mm Para. slide kits were available for $179. Also, conversion units (converting .45 ACP to .38 Super or 9mm Para.) were available for $195.

All current Auto Ordnance 1911 Models include a spent case, plastic case, and cable lock.

1911 A1 STANDARD/COMPACT STANDARD - .38 Super (disc. 1996), 9mm Para. (disc. 1996), .40 S&W (mfg. 1991-93), 10mm (mfg. 1991-96), or .45 ACP cal., 4 1/4 (.45 ACP only, Compact Standard Model), 4 1/2 (.40 S&W cal. only) or 5 (Standard Model) in. barrel, 7 shot mag., single action, parts interchange with the original Colt Govt. Model, blue or nickel finish, checkered plastic grips, 39 oz.

MSR $592	$450	$370	$295	$255	$235	$225	$215

Add $28 for satin nickel (mfg. 1990-96) or $37 for duo-tone (mfg. 1992-96) finish (.45 ACP only).

* **WWII Parkerized 1911 A1** - .45 ACP cal., no frills variation of the 1911 A1, military parkerizing, G.I. detailing with military style roll stamp, plastic or checkered walnut (disc. 2001) grips, and lanyard loop. New 1992.

MSR $581	$445	$365	$295	$255	$235	$225	$215

* **1911 A1 "Standard 80"** - .45 ACP cal., features firing pin block in slide, otherwise similar to 1911 A1 Standard. New 2004.

MSR $592	$450	$370	$300	$255	$235	$225	$215

* **1911 A1 Deluxe** - .38 Super (disc. 1996), 9mm Para. (disc. 1996), or .45 ACP cal., 5 in. barrel, 3 dot sights, wraparound grips, 39 oz. New 1991.

MSR $597	$465	$375	$310	$255	$240	$225	$215

* **1911 A1 General** - .38 Super (mfg. 1996 only) or .45 ACP cal., 4 1/2 in. barrel with full length recoil guide system, 7 shot mag., blue finish, 3 dot fixed Millett sights, black rubber wraparound grips, Commander styling, 37 oz. Mfg. 1992-98.

$385	$315	$255	$235	$225	$215	$200

Last MSR was $465.

* **1911 A1 Custom High Polish** - .45 ACP cal., 8 shot mag., 5 in. barrel, custom combat hammer, beavertail grip safety, rosewood grips with medallions, 3-dot sights, flat mainspring housing, Videcki speed trigger, 39 oz. Mfg. 1997-99.

$485	$395	$325	$265	$235	$225	$215

Last MSR was $585.

* **Competition 1911** - .38 Super (1996 only) or .45 ACP cal., competition features include compensated barrel, commander hammer, flat mainspring housing, white 3- dot sighting system, beavertail grip safety, black textured wraparound grips. Mfg. 1993-96.

$530	$415	$375	$330	$300	$285	$270

Last MSR was $636.

Add $10 for .38 Super cal.

GRADING – PPGS™	100%	98%	95%	90%	80%	70%	60%

* ***Thompson Custom 1911*** - .45 ACP cal., stainless steel or aluminum (Lightweight model, new 2005) construction, Series 80 design, 5 in. barrel, Thompson bullet logo on left side of double serrated slide, 7 shot mag., grip safety, checkered laminate grips with medallion, skeletonized trigger, combat hammer, low profile sights, 39 oz. New 2004.

MSR $753	$660	$550	$475	$400	$350	$300	$275

MODEL ZG-51 "PIT BULL" - .45 ACP cal. only, compact variation of the 1911 A1, 3 5/8 in. standard (disc. 1996) or 4 3/8 in. compensated (new 1997) barrel, 7 shot mag., 36 oz. Mfg. 1988-99.

$385	$310	$255	$235	$225	$215	$200

Last MSR was $470.

RIFLES: SEMI-AUTO

The Auto-Ordnance Thompson replicas listed below are currently supplied with a 15, 20, or 30 shot stick mag. Tommy Guns are not currently legal in CA or CT.

Auto-Ordnance Corporation

1927 A-1 STANDARD - .45 ACP cal., 16 in. plain barrel, solid steel construction, standard military sight, walnut stock and horizontal forearm. Disc. 1986.

$570	$490	$430	$360	$315	$290	$270

Last MSR was $575.

1927 A-1 DELUXE CARBINE - 10mm (mfg. 1991-93) or .45 ACP cal., 16 1/2 in. finned barrel with compensator, includes one 30 shot original surplus mag., current mfg. accepts drum mags., solid steel construction, matte black finish, adj. rear sight, walnut stock, pistol grip, and finger grooved forearm grip, 13 lbs.

MSR $1,109	$825	$650	$525	$425	$325	$295	$275

Add $66 for current mfg. 30 shot stick mag.

Add $171 for current mfg. 10 shot X-drum mag. (they resemble the older 50 shot L-type drum) – new 1994.

Add $284 for 50* shot drum mag. or $350 for 100* shot drum mag. (mfg. 1990-93) on this model and other 1927 variations.

Add $129 for factory violin case or $139 for hard case.

* ***1927 A-1C Lightweight Deluxe*** - .45 ACP cal., similar to 1927 A-1 Deluxe, except receiver made of a lightweight alloy, current mfg. accepts drum mags., 9 1/2 lbs. New 1984.

MSR $958	$825	$675	$525	$425	$350	$295	$275

* ***1927 A-1 Presentation Walnut Carbine*** - .45 ACP cal., similar to 1927 A-1 Deluxe, except has presentation grade walnut buttstock, pistol grip, and foregrip, supplied with plastic case. Limited mfg. 2003.

$850	$675	$525	$425	$350	$325	$295

Last MSR was $1,121.

* ***1927 A-1 Deluxe .22 LR Cal.*** - .22 LR cal., very limited mfg., 30 shot mag. standard.

$1,100	$995	$925	$800	$700	$650	$575

1927 A-1 COMMANDO - .45 ACP cal., 16 1/2 in. finned barrel with compensator, 30 shot mag., black finished stock and forearm, parkerized metal, black nylon sling, 13 lbs. New 1997.

MSR $1,088	$875	$675	$525	$425	$350	$295	$275

Add $171 each for current mfg. 10 shot X-drum mags. (they resemble the older 50 shot L-type drums) – new 1994.

GRADING - PPGS™	100%	98%	95%	90%	80%	70%	60%

M1 CARBINE (.45 ACP CAL.) - .45 ACP cal., combat model, 16 1/2 in. smooth barrel w/o compensator, 30 shot original surplus mag., side-cocking lever, matte black finish, walnut stock, pistol grip, and grooved horizontal forearm, current mfg. will not accept drum mags., 11 1/2 lbs. New 1986.

	100%	98%	95%	90%	80%	70%	60%
MSR $1,041	$825	$675	$525	$400	$325	$285	$265

✳ *1927 M1-C Lightweight* - similar to M1 Carbine, except receiver is made of a lightweight alloy, current mfg. accepts drum mags., 9 1/2 lbs. Mfg. 2001-2002, reintroduced 2005.

	100%	98%	95%	90%	80%	70%	60%
MSR $890	$725	$600	$500	$400	$325	$295	$275

M1-CARBINE (.30 CAL.) - .30 Carbine cal., birch or walnut stock, 18 in. barrel, all new parts, parkerized reciever, metal handguard, apeture rear sight and bayonet lug, 15 shot mag., 5.4 lbs. New 2004.

	100%	98%	95%	90%	80%	70%	60%
MSR $639	$545	$485	$380	$330	$295	$275	$250

Add $46 for walnut stock.

THOMPSON SBR - .45 ACP cal., 10 1/2 in. finned barrel, closed bolt, blue metal finish, pistol grip forearm, 30 shot mag., 12 lbs. New 2004.

	100%	98%	95%	90%	80%	70%	60%
MSR $1,456	$1,275	$1,075	$900	$800	$700	$600	$500

This carbine model may only be shipped from the factory to a Class II manufacturer or Class III dealer.

THOMPSON M1 SBR - .45 ACP cal., 10 1/2 in. barrel, closed bolt, blue metal finish, regular forearm, 30 shot mag., 12 lbs. New 2004.

	100%	98%	95%	90%	80%	70%	60%
MSR $1,352	$1,200	$1,050	$875	$775	$675	$600	$500

This carbine model may only be shipped from the factory to a Class II manufacturer or Class III dealer.

1927 A5 PISTOL/CARBINE - .45 ACP cal., 13 in. finned barrel, alloy construction, overall length 26 in., 10 (C/B 1994) shot mag., 7 lbs. Mfg. disc. 1994.

	100%	98%	95%	90%	80%	70%	60%
	$1,050	$925	$825	$750	$650	$600	$500

Last MSR was $765.

1927 A3 - .22 CAL. - .22 LR cal., 16 or 18 in. finned barrel with compensator, alloy frame and receiver, fixed or detachable walnut stock, pistol grip, and forearm pistol grip, 7 lbs. Mfg. disc. 1994.

	100%	98%	95%	90%	80%	70%	60%
	$995	$875	$750	$650	$550	$500	$450

Last MSR was $510.

AUTO-POINTER

Previous trademark manufactured by Yamamoto Co. Formerly imported by Sloans.

SEMI-AUTO SHOTGUN - 12 or 20 ga., gas operated. Disc.

	100%	98%	95%	90%	80%	70%	60%
	$275	$240	$220	$195	$180	$160	$145

AXTELL RIFLE CO.

Current rifle manufacturer located in Sheridan, MT. Distributed by The Riflesmith Inc., located in Sheridan, MT. Consumer direct sales.

New Model 1877 Sharps reproductions are available for both long-range and sporting rifles listed below in the following black powder calibers: .40-50, .40-70, .40-90, .45-70 Govt., .45-90, and .45-100 cal. The Riflesmith Inc. should be contacted (see Trademark Index) directly for accessories and/or engraving options.

Add $275 for bull hide rifle case.

GRADING - PPGS™	100%	98%	95%	90%	80%	70%	60%

NUMBER ONE CREEDMOOR - features 34 in. Rigby style barrel, choice of high-grade black or English checkered walnut stock and forearm with ebony inlays. Long range sights. 10 lbs.

MSR $4,700		$4,700	$3,950	$3,500	$3,025	$2,500	$2,000	$1,575

C-EXPRESS - top-of-the-line model with double set triggers, 32 or 34 in. 1/2 round, 1/2 octagon barrel, select walnut checkered stock, deluxe front and rear sights, approx. 13 lbs.

MSR $5,200		$5,200	$4,300	$3,750	$3,150	$2,600	$2,100	$1,650

NUMBER TWO LONG RANGE - choice of 30-34 in. Rigby style barrel, select black or English checkered walnut stock and forearm. Long range sights.

MSR $4,200		$4,200	$3,250	$3,050	$2,525	$2,000	$1,650	$1,300

OVERBAUGH SCHUETZEN - features 26-30 in. octagon barrel, double-set triggers, Schuetzen buttplate with cheekpiece, palm rest, short-range sights, 11-14 lbs.

MSR $4,500		$4,500	$3,650	$3,350	$2,675	$2,125	$1,700	$1,300

LOWER SPORTER - 28 or 30 in. octagon barrel, double-set triggers, steel buttplate with straight grip, standard rifle weight of 9 lbs.

MSR $2,900		$2,900	$2,200	$1,725	$1,350	$995	$825	$700

LOWER BUSINESS - 28 in. contoured round barrel, double-set triggers, black walnut stock has steel shotgun buttplate with straight grip, hunter tang, blade front sights, approx. 8 1/2 lbs.

MSR $2,900		$2,900	$2,200	$1,725	$1,350	$995	$825	$700

NOTES

B SECTION

BSA GUNS LIMITED

Current manufacturer established in 1861 and located in Birmingham, England. BSA (Birmingham Small Arms) currently manufactures airguns only. BSA Imports, located in Ft. Lauderdale, FL, imports O/U, SxS, and semi-auto shotguns which are manufactured in Europe and utilize the BSA logo/trademark. English-made BSA firearms were imported until 1985 by Precision Sports from Ithaca, NY and 1986 by BSA Guns Ltd., located in Grand Prairie, TX. Imported and distributed until 1989 by Samco Global Arms, Inc., located in Miami, FL.

For more information and current pricing on both new and used BSA airguns, please refer to the *Blue Book of Airguns* by Dr. Robert Beeman & John Allen (also online).

GRADING - PPGS™	100%	98%	95%	90%	80%	70%	60%

RIFLES: BOLT ACTION

Importation of all BSA rimfire and centerfire rifles was disc. 1987.

MAJESTIC FEATHERWEIGHT DELUXE - .243 Win., .270 Win., .308 Win., or .30-06 cal., bolt action, 22 in. barrel, folding sight, checkered European style stock. Mfg. 1959-65.

	100%	98%	95%	90%	80%	70%	60%
	$395	$350	$220	$195	$180	$165	$145
.458 Mag.	$445	$375	$305	$275	$220	$210	$200

MAJESTIC DELUXE - .222 Rem., .22 Hornet, .243 Win., 7x57mm, .308 Win., or .30-06 cal., heavier barrel.

	100%	98%	95%	90%	80%	70%	60%
	$395	$300	$300	$275	$250	$165	$145

Add 100% for .22 Hornet cal.

MONARCH DELUXE - similar to Majestic Deluxe, but American design stock. Mfg. 1965-74.

	100%	98%	95%	90%	80%	70%	60%
	$395	$275	$250	$220	$195	$180	$165

MONARCH DELUXE VARMINT - similar to Monarch Deluxe, except .222 Rem. or .243 Win. cal., 24 in. heavy barrel. Disc.

	100%	98%	95%	90%	80%	70%	60%
	$395	$315	$275	$250	$210	$195	$180

MARTINI ISU MATCH .22 - .22 LR cal. only, single shot, bolt action, similar to CFT Model. Disc. 1985.

	100%	98%	95%	90%	80%	70%	60%
	$825	$700	$600	$530	$475	$435	$400

Last MSR was $1,000.

Add $100 for Mk. V.H.B. Model.

CF-2 ACTION - .222 Rem., .22-250 Rem., .243 Win., 6.5x55mm, 7x57mm, 7x64mm, 7mm Rem. Mag., .270 Win., .308 Win., .30-06, or .300 Win. Mag. cal., bolt action, barrel length 23-26 in., 7 1/2-8 lbs. CF-2 nomenclature designates an action rather than a model. The following are CF-2 actioned models.

Add $70 for double set trigger option on the following models.

✱ *Sporter/Classic* - same cals. as above, checkered oil finished walnut stock. Imported 1986-87.

	100%	98%	95%	90%	80%	70%	60%
	$395	$275	$250	$225	$210	$195	$180

Last MSR was $360.

Sporter Model features Monte Carlo stock, rosewood capped forearm and pistol grip stock, and swivels.

GRADING - PPGS™	100%	98%	95%	90%	80%	70%	60%

* *Classic Varminter* - .222 Rem. - .243 Win. cals. only, heavy barrel, matte finish, with swivels. Imported 1986 only.

	$395	$275	$250	$225	$210	$190	$175

Last MSR was $345.

* *Heavy Barrel Model* - .222 Rem., .22-250 Rem., or .243 Win. cal., approx. 9 lbs., no sights.

	$375	$300	$260	$240	$225	$210	$180

Last MSR was $410.

* *Carbine Model* - 20 in. barrel. Disc. 1985.

	$495	$375	$300	$270	$250	$225	$200

Last MSR was $480.

* *Stutzen Rifle* - Mannlicher style full length stock, same general specifications as Sporter/Classic, 20 1/2 in. barrel. Not available in 7mm Rem. Mag. or .300 Win. Mag. cal.

	$595	$400	$325	$300	$275	$250	$225

Last MSR was $385.

* *Regal Custom* - similar to Sporter Model, except has slim classic European style stock with Schnabel forend, deluxe walnut with extra checkering, ebony forend cap, engraved action and floorplate. Limited importation 1986 only.

	$875	$795	$685	$590	$550	$500	$450

Last MSR was $950.

This model was custom-made by special order only.

CFT TARGET RIFLE - 7.62mm cal., single shot, bolt action, globe front and aperture rear sights, 26 1/2 in. barrel, 11 lbs. Disc. 1987.

	$675	$590	$550	$500	$450	$400	$360

Last MSR was $780.

RIFLES: SINGLE SHOT

NO. 12 MARTINI - .22 LR cal., 29 in. barrel, target sights, straight stock, pre-WWII.

	$595	$495	$375	$300	$250	$200	$175

MILITARY MARTINI HENRY (MODELS 1871 & 1885) - various cals., pre-WWII mfg. many configurations and barrel lengths. Pricing takes into consideration most commonly encountered types with no engraving or special orders.

	100%	98%	95%	90%	80%	70%	60%
Post-1900 mfg.	$900	$700	$500	$450	$400	$365	$335
Pre-1899 mfg.	$550	$475	$400	$350	$300	$250	$200

MARTINI CADET - various cals., mostly military issue, many thousands previously imported into the U.S. from England, many have been sporterized or modified.

	$600	$450	$400	$350	$300	$275	$250

* *Martini Australian Junior Cadet* - .310 cal., mfg. by BSA and W.W. Greener, Francotte patent one-piece take out action, various rear sight configurations, some have been coverted to modern cartridges.

	$350	$325	$275	$235	$200	$180	$160

MODEL 15 - similar to No. 12 Martini, except pistol grip stock, better grade target sights, pre-WWII.

	$595	$495	$375	$300	$250	$200	$175

CENTURION MATCH RIFLE - similar to Model 15, except Centurion guarantee 1 1/2 in. grouping at 100 yards, 24 in. barrel, pre-WWII.

	$440	$385	$330	$275	$240	$220	$175

MATCH 12/15 - similar to Model 15, except made after WWII.

	$595	$495	$375	$300	$250	$200	$175

GRADING - PPGS™	100%	98%	95%	90%	80%	70%	60%

MODEL 12/15 - heavy barrel.

	$595	$495	$375	$300	$250	$200	$175

MODEL 13 - lighter version of No. 12 Martini.

	$595	$495	$375	$300	$250	$200	$175

MODEL 13 SPORTER - similar to Model 13, except has sport sights.

	$595	$495	$375	$300	$250	$200	$175
.22 Hornet	$795	$700	$575	$450	$375	$325	$275

MARTINI INTERNATIONAL MATCH - .22 LR cal., 29 in. heavy barrel, international sights. Mfg. 1950-53.

	$695	$600	$475	$400	$350	$325	$300

INTERNATIONAL LIGHT - 26 in. lightweight barrel.

	$600	$500	$450	$400	$350	$325	$300

INTERNATIONAL MKII - improved trigger, ejectors and stock design. Mfg. 1953-59.

	$700	$600	$550	$500	$450	$400	$350

INTERNATIONAL MKIII - longer action, floating barrel. Mfg. 1959-67.

	$800	$700	$650	$600	$550	$500	$450

INTERNATIONAL ISU - modeled to meet ISU standards, 28 in. barrel. Mfg. 1968-disc.

	$800	$700	$650	$600	$550	$500	$450

INTERNATIONAL MARK V - similar to ISU, but heavier barrel, mfg. 1976-disc.

	$800	$700	$650	$600	$550	$500	$450

SHOTGUNS

BSA also manufactured SxS boxlock shotguns in various grades. Normally encountered in 12 ga. with DTs and extractors, these shotguns are of good quality and are typically encountered in the secondary market in the $250-$500 range, assuming standard grade.

SILVER EAGLE O/U - 12 or 20 ga., 3 in. chambers, 26 or 28 in. barrels, multichokes, hand-checkered Turkish walnut stock, blue receiver, gold SST, extractors (Silver Eagle) or ejectors (Silver Eagle II). Importation began 2004.

MSR $489	$395	$360	$330	$295	$260	$230	$200

Add $100 for ejectors (Silver Eagle II).

FALCON O/U - 12 or 20 ga., 3 in. chambers, boxlock action, 26, 28, or 30 in. barrels, Beretta style multichokes, laser checkered field walnut stock with Schnabel forend, ejectors, case colored engraved receiver, gold SST. Importation began 2004.

MSR $1,199	$1,000	$900	$800	$700	$600	$500	$400

SPORTING O/U - 12 ga., 2 3/4 in. chambers, 28 or 30 in. ported barrels, multichokes, checkered walnut target stock, ejectors, silver finished engraved receiver, triggerguard, safety and opening lever, gold SST. Importation began 2004.

MSR $1,249	$1,025	$950	$825	$725	$625	$525	$425

CLASSIC SxS - 12, 16, 20, 28 ga. or .410 bore, 2 3/4 (16 or 28 ga.) or 3 in. chambers, 26 or 28 in. barrels with Beretta style choke tubes, checkered select walnut stock with Prince of Wales pistol grip, ejectors, case colored hardened receiver, gold SST, semi-beavertail forend. Importation began 2004.

MSR $1,299	$1,065	$975	$850	$750	$650	$550	$450

ROYAL SxS - 12 or 20 ga., 3 in. chambers, 26 or 28 in. barrels with Beretta style choke tubes, checkered select walnut stock. Importation began 2005.

MSR $1,499	$1,225	$1,075	$975	$850	$750	$650	$550

GRADING - PPGS™	100%	98%	95%	90%	80%	70%	60%

200/300 SERIES SEMI-AUTO - 12, 16, 20, 28 ga. or .410 bore, 2 3/4 (16, 28 ga. or .410 bore), 3 or 3 1/2 (Model 312 only) in. chamber, 24 (Model 312 only), 26 or 28 in. barrels, vent. rib, multichokes, synthetic or checkered Turkish walnut stock, blue receiver, gold trigger, drilled and tapped, firing pin block. Importation began 2004.

MSR $399	$325	$285	$250	$225	$200	$175	$150

Add $60 for wood stock.
Add $30 for 16 or 28 ga. or .410 bore.
Add $20 for 3 1/2 in. chamber.

This model is also available in a Youth Model - 20 ga. only, at no extra charge.

B-WEST

Previous importer/distributor located in Tucson, AZ, until 1997.

B-West previously imported rifles (including AK-47 clones, the Saiga, Dragunov, etc.), the IJ series .380 ACP Makarov pistol, and the Daewoo DP-51 semi-auto pistol.

LES BAER CUSTOM, INC.

Please refer to the L section of this text.

BAFORD ARMS, INC.

Previous manufacturer located in Bristol, TN. Previously distributed by C.L. Reedy & Associates, Inc. located in Melbourne, FL.

DERRINGERS

THUNDER DERRINGER - .44 Spl. cal./.410 shotshell, single shot, tip-up action, 3 in. barrel, blue finish steel finish, spur trigger, wood grips. Introduced late 1988 with limited mfg. until 1991, when production permanently ceased.

	$130	$110	$95	$90	$85	$80	$75

Last MSR was $130.

Add $90 for interchangeable barrel kit.

Interchangeable pistol barrels are chambered in various calibers between .22 Short and 9mm Para. There are two types: one fits flush while the other facilitates a scope mounting.

PISTOLS: SEMI-AUTO

MODEL 35 FIRE POWER - 9mm Para. cal., semi-auto single action, patterned after the Browning Hi-Power, total stainless steel construction, 4 3/4 in. barrel, combat hammer and safety, Pachmayr grips, removable barrel bushing, Millett Mk. II sights, 14 shot mag., 32 oz. Introduced late 1988 with limited mfg. until 1993.

	$500	$425	$350

Last MSR was $550.

BAIKAL

Current trademark of products manufactured by the Russian State Unitary Plant "Izhevsky Mechanichesky Zavod" (FSUP IMZ). Many Baikal SxS and O/U hunting guns (including air guns) were imported and distributed exclusively late 1998-2004 by European American Armory Corp., located in Sharpes, FL. Previously imported 1993-96 by Big Bear, located in Dallas, TX.

Baikal (name of a lake in Siberia) was one of the first state-run holdovers from the former Soviet Union to market firearms, ammunition, optics and other sporting goods from a variety of plants within Russia. Now Baikal is the state-licensed trademark of the Izhevsky Mechanichesky Zavod, a government-owned plant in Izhevsk, Russia.

The company was founded in 1942 as part of the Russian National Defense Industry. At that time, the plant produced world renowned Tokarev TT pistols. Upon conclusion of WWII, the company expanded its operation to include non-military weapons (O/U, SxS, and single barrel shotguns). FSUP IMZ is one of the world's largest manufacturers of mil-

GRADING - PPGS™	100%	98%	95%	90%	80%	70%	60%

itary and non-military weapons. The total amount of guns that are produced by the FSUP IMZ is 600,000 units per year. The products range from various smoothbore guns, including slide action and self-loading models, rifled and combination guns, to a full array of sporting, civil, and combat pistols, including the internationally famous Makarov pistol. Since 2000, Baikal has produced a new pistol for the Russian Army that was developed by the enterprise designers and named after the group's leader – the Yarygin pistol.

FSUP IMZ features efficient manufacturing capacity and unique intellectual potential of qualified engineers-and-technicians staff. The FSUP IMZ is also undertaking the task of reintroducing the world to the "Russian Custom Gunsmith." There is a gunsmith school at the factory area for custom, one-of-a-kind hand engraved shotguns and rifles. The guns produced by the school feature high-quality assembly, attractive appearance and high functional quality according to the best traditions of Russian gunmakers.

In the past, Baikal shotguns have had limited importation into the U.S. 1993 marked the first year that Baikals were officially (and legally) imported into the U.S. because of Russia's previous export restrictions domestically. In prior years, however, a few O/Us have been seen for sale and have no doubt been imported into this country one at a time. Currently produced Baikals are noted for their high quality at low-level costs.

N/As have replaced MSRs on certain models below, indicating recent importation by EAA.

COMBINATION GUNS

IZH-94 O/U - 12 or 20 (new 2001) ga. over various cals. (domestic and metric), 3 in. chamber, boxlock action, 24 in. separated barrels with express sights, DT, extractors, choke tube (shotgun barrel), checkered walnut stock and forearm, approx. 7 1/4 lbs.

	MSR N/A	$425	$375	$335	$300	$275	$250	$235

✱ **IZH-94 .410 Bore/Rimfire** - .410 bore with 3 in. chamber over choice of .17 HMR, .22 LR or .22 Mag. cal., single trigger, walnut stock and forearm. Importation began 2003.

	MSR N/A	$175	$140	$130	$125	$120	$115	$110

PISTOLS: SEMI-AUTO

IZH-35M - 22 LR cal., semi-auto target pistol featuring fully adj. walnut ergonomic target grip, 6 in. hammer forged barrel, adj. trigger assembly, integral grip safety, 5 shot mag., cocking indicator and detachable scope mount, 2.3 lbs. Importation began 2000.

	MSR N/A	$425	$385	$335	$300	$275	$250	$225

IJ-70 - .380 ACP or 9x18 Makarov cal., double action semi-auto, all steel blue construction, 4 in. barrel, slide mounted safety with decocking, fully adj. target sights, choice of two 8 shot (IJ- 70), two 10 (C/B 1994, Model IJ-70-HC), or two 12* shot mag., holster and cleaning rod, checkered plastic grips, 25 oz. Disc. 1996.

		$175	$150	$135	$120	$105	$95	$85

Last MSR was $199.

Add $40 for IJ-70-HC (High Capacity).
Add $50 for .380 ACP cal.
Add $10 for nickel finish (disc.).

RIFLES: O/U

IZH-94 EXPRESS - .222 Rem., .223 Rem., .30-06, .308 Win., 6.5x55mm, or 7.62x39mm cal., DT, extractors, mono bloc construction, 24 in. barrels with express sights, checkered walnut stock and forearm, 8.3 lbs. Importation began 2001.

	MSR N/A	$450	$395	$365	$335	$295	$280	$265

GRADING - PPGS™	100%	98%	95%	90%	80%	70%	60%

RIFLES: SxS

IZH-MP221 - .223 Rem., .270 Win., .30-06, .308 Win., .45-70 Govt., or 7.62x39mm cal., boxlock monobloc action, DT, adj. barrel regulation, 11mm scope rail, checkered walnut stock and forearm with sling swivels, extractors, vent. recoil pad, 7 1/2 lbs. Importation began 2003.

MSR N/A	$525	$425	$365	$335	$295	$280	$265

RIFLES: SINGLE BARREL

IZH-18MH - available in 11 cals. between .22 Hornet and .45-70 Govt., boxlock action, 23 1/2 in. barrel with extractor, underlever action next to triggerguard, checkered walnut stock with vent. recoil pad, sling swivels, iron sights or scope rail, 6.8 lbs. Importation began 2003.

MSR N/A	$190	$165	$145	$130	$120	$110	$105

SHOTGUNS: O/U, RECENT IMPORTATION

IZH-27 FIELD MODEL - 12 or 20 (new 1992) ga., double triggers, extractors, 26 or 28 in. barrels. Disc. 1996.

	$330	$275	$250	$225	$195	$180	$165

Last MSR was $399.

Add $40 for single trigger and automatic ejectors (Model IJ-27EIC).

IZH-27 - 12, 16 (new 2000), 20, 28 ga., or .410 bore, 3 in. chambers (2 3/4 in. on 16 or 28 ga.) boxlock action, 26 or 28 in. VR barrels with (standard on 12 and 20 ga.) or w/o chokes, monobloc receiver, walnut checkered stock (with or w/o Monte Carlo) and forearm, extractors (disc.) or ejectors, blue or nickel finish (new 2001), SST. Importation began 1999.

MSR N/A	$400	$350	$295	$265	$225	$200	$190

Add $10 for 16 or 20 ga.
Add $34 for 28 ga. or .410 bore.
Add $224 for 20 ga. 2 barrel set.
Add $24 for nickel finish.
Add $80 for nickel finish with barrel porting (12 ga. only, disc. 2003).

* **IZH-27 Sporting** - 12 or 20 ga., 3 in. chambers, SST, ejectors, ported 29.5 in. barrels with MC-3 chokes, nickel finished frame. Importation began 2004.

MSR N/A	$525	$450	$400	$350	$295	$265	$225

MP 233 SPORTING - 12 ga. only, 3 in. chambers, 26, 28, or 29 1/2 in. unported (disc.) or ported barrels with multi-chokes and wide VR, removable trigger group, SST, ejectors, checkered walnut stock and forearm, includes carrying case, 7.2 lbs. Importation began 1999.

MSR N/A	$775	$650	$575	$500	$460	$430	$395

SHOTGUNS: SxS, RECENT IMPORTATION

The following Bounty Hunters are available in either 12 or 20 ga., include 3 in. chambers, are designed for cowboy action shooting, with choice of hammers or hammerless action, SST, DT (disc.), or double selective triggers, 20 in. barrels with or w/o choke tubes, hardwood or walnut stock and forearm, engraved receiver, extractors, and weigh approx. 7 lbs.

IZH-43 FIELD MODEL - 12 or 20 ga., double triggers, extractors, 20, 26 (disc.), or 28 in. barrels. Disc. 1996.

	$235	$200	$160	$130	$105	$95	$75

Last MSR was $299.

Add $20 for 20 in. barrels bored C/C.

GRADING - PPGS™	100%	98%	95%	90%	80%	70%	60%

IZH-43 TRADITIONAL HUNTING MODEL - 12, 16 (new 2000), 20, 28 ga., or .410 bore, 3 in. chambers only on .410 bore, Anson & Deeley style boxlock action with monobloc, SST, 24, 26, or 28 in. barrels with or w/o (28 ga. and .410 bore) choke tubes, checkered walnut stock and forearm, approx. 7 lbs. Importation began 1999.

MSR N/A	$340	$295	$250	$220	$185	$165	$150

Add $30 for 16, 20, 28 ga., or .410 bore.
Add $20 for nickel finish (new 2004).

✱ *IZH-43 2 Barrel Set* - includes both 20 and 28 ga. barrels. Importation began 2000.

MSR N/A	$515	$465	$415	$375	$345	$315	$290

✱ *IZH-43 Traditional Bounty Hunter* -12, 20 ga., or .410 bore (mfg. 2001-2002), 2 3/4 in. chambers, hammerless, 20 in. barrels with choice of cyl./cyl. bore or multi-chokes, nickel receiver (new 2004), DT or SST, hardwood or walnut stock. Importation began 2000.

MSR N/A	$275	$235	$205	$185	$165	$150	$145

Add $20 for nickel receiver.
Add $40-$50 for walnut stock and forearm.
Add $50-$60 for SST.
Add $159 for .45-70 cal. barrel inserts (only if shotgun is 12 ga., has 2 3/4 in. chambers, and 20 in. barrels with choke tubes).

IZH-43K EXTERNAL HAMMER -12 or 20 (disc.) ga., similar to IZH-43 Hunting Model, except has engraved sideplates and external cocking hammers, approx. 6.3 lbs. Importation began 2000.

MSR N/A	$330	$290	$260	$235	$215	$200	$195

Add $20 for choke tubes.
Add $20 for external firing pins.

✱ *IZH-43K External Hammer 2 Barrel Set* - includes both 20 and 28 ga. barrels. Imported 2000 only.

	$550	$500	$460	$420	$395	$360	$330

Last MSR was $639.

✱ *IZH-43K Bounty Hunter Traditional* - 12 or 20 (disc. 2002) ga., 20 in. barrels with choice of cyl./cyl. bore or multichokes. Importation began 2000.

MSR N/A	$285	$260	$225	$200	$180	$165	$150

Add $40 for multichokes or $50 for multichokes and SST.
Add $10 for external firing pins and traditional sideplates.
Add $159 for .45-70 cal. barrel inserts (only if shotgun is 12 ga., has 2 3/4 in. chambers, and 20 in. barrels with choke tubes).

MP-213 - 12 ga. only, 3 in. chambers, hammerless, SST (disc. 2000) or double selective triggers, ejectors, removable trigger assembly, 20 (Coach Gun), 24, 26, or 28 in. monobloc barrels with choke tubes, checkered walnut stock and forearm, includes carrying case, approx. 7 lbs. Importation began 1999.

MSR N/A	$795	$675	$595	$525	$450	$400	$360

Add $159 for .45-70 cal. barrel inserts (only if shotgun is 12 ga., has 2 3/4 in. chambers, and 20 in. barrels with choke tubes).

SHOTGUNS: SEMI-AUTO, RECENT IMPORTATION

MP-151 - 12 ga., 3 in. chamber, 26 or 28 in. plain barrel with 2 choke tubes, black synthetic or checkered walnut Monte Carlo stock, tube or detachable box (available late 1999) mag., approx. 7.8 lbs. Imported 1999 only.

	$275	$235	$215	$195	$180	$165	$150

Last MSR was $310.

GRADING - PPGS™	100%	98%	95%	90%	80%	70%	60%

MP-153 - 12 ga. only, 3 1/2 in. chamber, 24 (new 2001), 26 or 28 in. VR barrel with choke tubes, black synthetic or walnut stock and forearm, approx. 8 lbs. Importation began 2000.

	MSR N/A	$395	$360	$320	$285	$235	$200	$190

Add $30 for MC-4 choke tubes (24 in. barrel only).
Subtract $110 for black synthetic stock and forearm.

SHOTGUNS: SINGLE SHOT, RECENT IMPORTATION

IZH-18M - 12, 16, 20 ga., or .410 bore, 26 or 28 in. barrel. Disc. 1996.

	$60	$50	$40	$35	$30	$30	$25

Last MSR was $74.

IZH-18 - 12, 16 (new 2000), 20 ga., or .410 bore, .410 bore has 3 in. chamber, hammerless, 26 or 28 in. barrel with fixed or multichokes (12 or 20 ga. only, new 2001), ejector, blue or nickel (new 2001) finish, decocking/cocking lever on rear of triggerguard, cocking indicator, hardwood or walnut (new 2001) stock and forearm, trigger block safety, approx. 5 1/2 lbs. Importation began 1998.

	MSR N/A	$90	$75	$65	$55	$45	$35	$30

Add $10 for Youth Model (20 ga. or .410 bore only).
Add $110 for nickel finished receiver (IZH-18 Max) with MC-3 multichokes and walnut stock and forearm.

✴ **IZH-18 Sporting** - 12 or 20 (new 2004) ga., 29 1/2 in. VR barrel with porting, rubber butt pad. Importation began 2002.

	MSR N/A	$235	$200	$160	$135	$110	$95	$80

SHOTGUNS: SLIDE ACTION, RECENT IMPORTATION

IZH-81 - 12 ga. only, 3 in. chamber, 5 shot box mag., 20, 26, or 28 in. plain or VR barrel with (26 or 28 in. barrel only) or w/o choke tubes, hardwood or walnut (disc. 1999) stock and corncob style forearm, blue finish. Imported 1999-2000.

	$235	$190	$170	$160	$145	$135	$125

Last MSR was $269.

Add $17 for walnut stock (disc.1999).
Add $68 for VR barrel (walnut stock only).

MP-133 - 12 ga., 3 1/2 in. chamber, 20, 24 (new 2001), 26, or 28 in. VR barrel with choke tubes (not available with 20 in. barrel), walnut stock and forearm, approx. 7 lbs. Importation began 2000.

	MSR N/A	$295	$230	$195	$185	$155	$145	$135

BAILONS GUNMAKERS LIMITED

Previous manufacturer located in Birmingham, England until 1993, when operations ceased. Inquiries regarding this trademark (including repairs) should be directed to Guthrie Consulting (see Trademark Index for listing).

RIFLES: BOLT ACTION

HUNTING RIFLE - various cals., modified Mauser bolt action, barrel length to suit from 18 to 30 in., set triggers or match, Habicht Telescope sight (magnification and reticle to suit), engraving, and types of finishes are at optional cost, prices below reflect standard rifle with no options. Imported 1986-1993.

	$2,495	$2,250	$1,995	$1,775	$1,625	$1,450	$1,300

Last MSR was $2,750.

GRADING - PPGS™	100%	98%	95%	90%	80%	70%	60%

BAKER, W.H. & CO.

Previous manufacturer located in Syracuse, NY circa 1878-1883.

Originally started by William H. and Ellis L. Baker circa 1878. During this time, Leroy H. and Lyman C. Smith financed the new company, W.H. Baker & Co. Circa 1880, L.C. Smith bought the interest from the two Baker partners and continued production with markings reading "L.C. Smith and Co., Maker of the Baker Gun" on the rib and "Baker Pat." on the locks. Smith decided to drop the Baker name in 1883, but continued to manufacture this gun and a shotgun/rifle combination gun in Syracuse, NY until 1888. At this point, the company was sold to the Hunter Brothers and this new company, Baker Gun & Forging Co., began making both the New Baker shotguns (see separate listing below) and the Ithaca gun. The company was sold to the Hunter Brothers circa 1888, and the Hunter Arms Company made L.C. Smith shotguns for approximately 60 years, at which point the Marlin Firearms Company bought the business during the early 1940s.

Baker guns were originally 10 or 12 ga., and unusual in that the opening mechanism was operated by pressing forward on the front trigger. While relatively rare, most original Baker guns (including the shotgun/rifle) do not have a lot of original finish remaining. Most specimens are priced in the $400-$850 range, assuming finish is less than 10%. If condition is better than 40%, guns have to be evaluated individually for accurate pricing.

BAKER GUN & FORGING CO.

Previous manufacturer located in Batavia, NY circa 1889-1933.

SHOTGUNS: SxS

Note: Original damascus guns in 80% or better condition with bright case colors will approach the values of steel barrel counterparts. Average original condition (0%-30%) receiver finish models are typically priced in the $275-$400 range, if working. Check for short chambers and chokes to make sure barrels haven't been shortened.

THE NEW BAKER - 10 or 12 ga., exposed hammers, damascus barrels, extractors.

	100%	98%	95%	90%	80%	70%	60%
	$350	$300	$260	$225	$195	$175	$150

BATAVIA SPECIAL - 12, 16, or 20 ga., 26, 28, 30, or 32 in. barrels, any standard choke, checkered pistol grip stock, sidelock, extractors.

	100%	98%	95%	90%	80%	70%	60%
	$385	$305	$275	$260	$250	$220	$200

BATAVIA LEADER - similar to Special, except has deluxe finish.

	100%	98%	95%	90%	80%	70%	60%
	$440	$360	$335	$305	$285	$265	$220
Auto ejectors	$525	$440	$415	$385	$370	$330	$305

BLACK BEAUTY - similar to Batavia Special with light engraving.

	100%	98%	95%	90%	80%	70%	60%
	$500	$440	$360	$335	$305	$285	$265

BLACK BEAUTY SPECIAL - similar to Leader, except has engraved, select wood.

	100%	98%	95%	90%	80%	70%	60%
	$745	$650	$615	$590	$550	$525	$495
Auto ejectors	$855	$760	$725	$700	$660	$635	$605

BATAVIA EJECTOR - similar to Leader, but finer finish.

	100%	98%	95%	90%	80%	70%	60%
	$880	$770	$745	$715	$690	$660	$635
Damascus barrels	$440	$330	$305	$275	$250	$220	$165

BAKER S GRADE - similar to Leader, but finer finish, better grade wood.

	100%	98%	95%	90%	80%	70%	60%
	$880	$775	$745	$715	$690	$650	$635
Auto ejectors	$1,100	$990	$965	$935	$910	$880	$745

BAKER R GRADE - similar to Leader, except scroll and game scene engraved, Krupp barrels, fancy wood.

	100%	98%	95%	90%	80%	70%	60%
	$1,100	$990	$965	$935	$910	$880	$745
Auto ejectors	$1,320	$1,210	$1,155	$1,100	$1,075	$1,045	$965
Damascus barrel	$550	$415	$385	$360	$330	$275	$230

GRADING - PPGS™	100%	98%	95%	90%	80%	70%	60%

PARAGON GRADE - custom order only to customer specifications.

	100%	98%	95%	90%	80%	70%	60%
	$1,650	$1,430	$1,320	$1,210	$1,155	$1,045	$770
Auto ejectors	$1,815	$1,595	$1,485	$1,375	$1,210	$1,100	$990

EXPERT GRADE - auto ejectors standard, overall finer grade wood and engraving.

	$2,500	$2,100	$1,850	$1,500	$1,250	$1,000	$750

DELUXE GRADE - best quality.

	$3,750	$3,250	$2,950	$2,650	$2,300	$2,000	$1,600

Add $200 for single trigger.

SHOTGUNS: SINGLE BARREL TRAP

Baker manufactured the Sterling, the Elite, and the Superba single barrel trap guns. These guns, although more rare than their side-by-side counterparts, are not as desirable. Typically, values will be 50%-75% less than for a side-by-side model, depending on condition.

BALLARD RIFLE, LLC

Current rifle manufacturer located in Cody, WY, since 1996. Dealer and consumer direct sales.

RIFLES: SINGLE SHOT

All Ballard rifles feature receivers milled from solid stock, hand polished barrels, and authentic "packed" case hardening. Many custom features are also available – contact the factory directly for availability and pricing. In addition to the standard models listed (up to 12 months delivery time), special order models include No. 1 Silhouette ($3,250 MSR), No. 2 Sporting ($3,450 MSR), No. 4 Perfection ($3,450 MSR), No. 5 1/2 Montana ($3,625 MSR), No. 6 Schuetzen ($3,960 MSR), No. 8 Union Hill ($3,795 MSR), Schoyen Schuetzen ($4,155 MSR), No. 3 Gallery ($3,200 MSR), and No. 3F Fine Gallery ($3,645 MSR). Allow up to 12 months for delivery.

BALLARD 1 1/2 HUNTER'S RIFLE - available in 7 cals. between .22 LR - .50-70, single trigger, uncheckered stock and forearm, S style lever action, 9 3/4 - 10 1/2 lbs.

MSR $3,100	$2,750	$2,400	$2,050	$1,875	$1,575	$1,325	$1,075

BALLARD 1 3/4 FAR WEST RIFLE - available in 8 cals. between .32-40 WCF - .50-90 SS, patterned after the original Ballard Far West Model, 30 or 32 in. standard or heavyweight octagon barrel, double set triggers, ring style lever, 9 3/4 - 10 1/2 lbs.

MSR $3,400	$3,000	$2,650	$2,250	$2,075	$1,750	$1,425	$1,150

BALLARD NO. 5 PACIFIC - available in 9 cals. between .32-40 WCF - .50-90 SS, includes under-barrel wiping rod, otherwise similar to No. 1 3/4 Far West Rifle.

MSR $3,600	$3,200	$2,750	$2,350	$2,100	$1,775	$1,450	$1,175

BALLARD NO. 4 1/2 MID RANGE - available in 5 cals. between .32-40 WCF - .45-110, configured for black powder cartridge silhouette, half-round, half-octagon 30 or 32 in. standard or heavyweight barrel, single or double set triggers, pistol grip stock, full loop lever, hard rubber Ballard buttplate, Vernier tang sight. 10 3/4 - 11 1/2 lbs.

MSR $3,475	$3,050	$2,675	$2,275	$2,075	$1,750	$1,425	$1,150

BALLARD NO. 7 LONG RANGE - available in 5 cals. between .40-65 Win. - .45-110, designed for long range shooting, half-round, half-octagon 32 or 34 in. standard or heavyweight barrel, other features similar to Ballard No. 4 1/2 Mid Range.

MSR $3,675	$3,250	$2,775	$2,350	$2,100	$1,775	$1,450	$1,175

WINCHESTER MODEL 1885 HIGH WALL - various cals., exact copy of original Winchester Model 1885 (parts interchange), 30 or 32 in. octagon barrel, ST with small lever, case colored receiver, uncheckered straight grip walnut stock and foream, approx. 9 lbs. New 2001.

MSR $3,200	$2,850	$2,500	$2,100	$1,900	$1,600	$1,325	$1,075

Add $250 for Special Sporting Model.
Add $800 for Helm Schuetzen Model.

GRADING - PPGS™	100%	98%	95%	90%	80%	70%	60%

✷ *Winchester Model 1885 High Wall Deluxe* - similar to Model 1885 High Wall, except has deluxe checkered pistol grip stock with shotgun buttplate and forearm, double set triggers, 32 in. No. 4 barrel, aperture sights, 11 lbs. New 2001.

	MSR $3,675	$3,250	$2,775	$2,350	$2,100	$1,775	$1,450	$1,175

Add $75 for Express Model.

BALTIMORE ARMS COMPANY

Previous manufacturer of SxS shotguns located in Baltimore, MD circa 1895-1902.

SHOTGUNS: SxS

STYLE 1 - this variation does not have the improved Hollenbeck barrel locking mechanism characterized by the eye-shaped hole in the top rib extension. Mfg. 1895-1900.

There are 4 grades of Baltimore Arms Company shotguns: Field, Grade A, Grade B, and Grade C. Prices generally range from $295-$1,500 depending on condition and grade.

STYLE 2 - this variation has the improved barrel locking mechanism and is patent date marked "FEB. 13, 1900" on the water table. Mfg. 1900-02.

There are 4 grades of Baltimore Arms Company shotguns: Field, Grade A, Grade B, and Grade C. Prices generally range from $295-$2,000 depending on condition and grade.

BANSNER'S ULTIMATE RIFLES, L.L.C.

Current custom rifle manufacturer established during 1981 and located in Adamstown, PA. In 2000, the company name changed from Bansner's Gunsmithing Specialities to Bansner's Ultimate Rifles, L.L.C. Consumer direct sales.

RIFLES: BOLT ACTION

All Bansner's UR rifles up to approx. June 1, 1999 have either Remington 700 or Winchester post-64 claw extractor actions. After this approx. date, Bansner's started using its own proprietary action, and during 2005, released the Sharpshooter model with Nesika Bay action.

ULTIMATE ONE - various cals. and configurations including different metal finishes and special orders, Rem. 700 (disc. 1999), Win. post-64 Model 70 (disc. 1999), Bansner's custom action beginning 2004, exclusive action was mfg. by McMillan Bros. Rifle Co., Inc. (steel or stainless steel, mfg. 2001-2003), Douglas premium air gauged (disc.) or Lilja fluted barrel with M-50 muzzle brake, large extractor, plunger ejector, 3 lbs. custom tuned trigger, custom color synthetic stock with Pachmayr decelerator pad, includes Talley custom scope bases and rings, various weights.

	MSR $4,995	$4,450	$3,475	$2,825	$2,350	$1,950	$1,700	$1,450

Add $325 for 3 position Model 70 style safety or Lazzeroni calibers.

SAFARI HUNTER - various dangerous game cals., Lilja Precision stainless steel 24 in. barrel, scalloped action based on the M-70 Classic, M-50 muzzle brake, synthetic stock with Pachmayr decelerator pad, matte black teflon metal finish. New 2003.

	MSR $5,495	$4,900	$3,550	$2,925	$2,300	$2,000	$1,700	$1,450

SHARPSHOOTER - various cals., Neskia Bay action, Lilja Precision medium to heavy weight match grade fluted barrel (customer choice of length), with recessed crown, Jewell trigger, brown wood laminate pillar bedded and reinforced fiberglass stock with palm swell, "Ti" polymer K-Kote metal finish, ebony forend tip, inletted swivel studs. New 2005.

	MSR $8,495	$7,800	$6,750	$5,850	$4,950	$4,000	$3,250	$2,750

GRADING - PPGS™	100%	98%	95%	90%	80%	70%	60%

SHEEP HUNTER X-TREME - various cals., Rem. 700 action, accurized, turned outside, fluted bolt, skeletonized bolt handle, alloy ADL trigger guard, Jewell trigger, Lilja Precision barrel, fiberglass stock, 5 1/4 lbs.

MSR $4,995	$4,450	$3,475	$2,825	$2,350	$1,950	$1,700	$1,450

VARMINT HUNTER - various cals., Rem. 700 action, accurized and polished, Jewell varmint trigger, Lilja Precision stainless steel barrel, Ti K-Kote metal finish, fully bedded fiberglass stock, Pachmayr Decelerator pad.

MSR $4,995	$4,450	$3,475	$2,825	$2,350	$1,950	$1,700	$1,450

ALPINE HUNTER - .300 WSM cal. only, Howa 1500 action, milled receiver, fluted barrel, muzzle brake, tuned trigger, fully bedded fiberglass stock, Pachmayr Decelerator pad, Ti K-Kote metal finish.

MSR $2,295	$2,075	$1,850	$1,625	$1,400	$1,200	$1,000	$800

ALASKAN HUNTER - various cals., Rem. 700 action, accurized, scalloped and polished receiver, fluted bolt, skeletonized handle, alloy ADL trigger guard, Lilja Precision barrel, fiberglass stock, Pachmayr Decelerator pad, approx. 5 lbs. Disc. 2004.

	$3,525	$2,900	$2,450	$2,050	$1,875	$1,675	$1,450

Last MSR was $3,895.

ULTIMATE RIFLE - various cals., Rem. 700 or Win. 70 action, accurized and polished, 3 lbs. trigger pull, Lilja Precision stainless steel barrel, fully bedded fiberglass stock, Pachmayr Decelerator pad. Disc. 2004.

	$2,995	$2,600	$2,300	$2,000	$1,800	$1,600	$1,400

Last MSR was $3,300.

HIGH TECH SERIES - various cals., Howa 1500 steel or stainless steel action with factory barrel and Bansner's synthetic stock with Pachmayr decelerator pad. Mfg. 1997-2004.

	$965	$835	$725	$625	$575	$500	$450

Last MSR was $1,050.

Add $100 for all stainless steel.

TRADITIONAL CLASSIC - various cals., custom Dakota 76 controlled round feed claw extract action with custom floorplate and inside bow release, Lilja Precision match grade hand lapped barrel, choice of matte blue or "Ti" polymer K-Kote metal finish, synthetic stock, Pachmayer decelerator pad. New 2005.

MSR $4,695	$4,250	$3,250	$2,800	$2,350	$1,950	$1,700	$1,450

LIMITED EDITION SERIES - various cals., customized Bansner's (new 2004) or Rem. 700 action with scalloped receiver, fluted bolt body and Jewell trigger, Gentry 3-position safety, synthetic stock with choice of black or silver coated teflon metal, 25-50 of each limited edition beginning 2003.

Currently, Bansner's is offering the Ultimate Classic Model (MSR $5,395, Bansner's action - 50 mfg.) and the Hunting Fool X-treme ($4,495, Rem. 700 action - 50 mfg.) Limited Editions.

BARRETT FIREARMS MANUFACTURING, INC.

BARRETT FIREARMS

Current manufacturer located in Murfreesboro, TN. Dealer direct sales.

RIFLES: BOLT ACTION

MODEL 90 - .50 BMG cal., bolt action design, 29 in. match grade barrel with muzzle brake, 5 shot detachable box mag., includes extendible bi-pod legs, scope optional, 22 lbs. Mfg. 1990-95.

	$3,450	$2,950	$2,400	$2,150	$1,875	$1,600	$1,500

Last MSR was $3,650.

Add $1,150 for Swarovski 10X scope and rings.

GRADING - PPGS™	100%	98%	95%	90%	80%	70%	60%

MODEL 95M - .50 BMG cal., bolt action design, 29 in. match grade barrel with high efficiency muzzle brake, 5 shot detachable box mag., includes extendible bi-pod legs, scope optional, 22.5 lbs. New 1995.

	MSR $5,540	$4,800	$3,850	$2,850	$2,425	$1,875	$1,600	$1,500

MODEL 99 - .50 BMG cal., single shot bolt action, 25-32 in. barrel with muzzle brake, straight through design with pistol grip and bi-pod, black or silver finish, 21-25 lbs. New 1999.

	MSR $3,675	$3,150	$2,550	$2,000	$1,825	$1,550	$1,250	$1,050

Add $250 for fluted barrel.

RIFLES: SEMI-AUTO

MODEL 82 RIFLE - .50 BMG cal., semi-auto recoil operation, 33-37 in. barrel, 11 shot mag., 2,850 FPS muzzle velocity, scope sight only, parkerized finish, 35 lbs. Mfg. 1985-87.

		$4,350	$3,950	$3,450	$2,700	$2,150	$1,800	$1,500

Last MSR for consumers was $3,180 in 1985.

This model underwent design changes since initial production. Only 115 were mfg. starting with ser. no. 100.

MODEL 82A1 - .50 BMG cal., paramilitary design, variant of the original Model 82, back-up iron sights provided and fitted hard case, 29 (new late 1989) or 33 (disc. 1989) in. barrel, 10 shot detachable mag., 32 1/2 lbs. for 1989 and older mfg., approx. 30 lbs. for 1990 mfg. and newer. Current mfg. includes Picatinny rail, watertight case and cleaning kit.

	MSR $7,775	$7,100	$6,150	$5,200	$4,375	$3,700	$3,150	$2,650

Add $360 for pack-mat backpack case (new 1999).
Add $275 for camo backpack carrying case (disc.).
Add $1,325 for Swarovski 10X scope and rings (disc.).

This model boasts official U.S. rifle status following government procurement during Operation Desert Storm. In 1992, a new "arrowhead" shaped muzzle brake was introduced to reduce recoil.

MODEL 98 - .338 Lapua Mag. cal., 10 shot box mag., 24 in. match grade barrel with muzzle brake, bi-pod, 15 1/2 lbs.

While advertised during mid-1999, this model was never produced.

MODEL M468 - 6.8 SPC cal., 16 in. barrel with muzzle brake, 5, 10, or 28 shot mag., dual spring extractor system, folding front sight, gas block, two-stage trigger, integrated rail system, folding rear sight, 7.3 lbs. New 2005.

	MSR $2,700	$2,400	$2,050	$1,675	$1,375	$1,175	$995	$875

Add $1,590 for Model M468 upper conversion kit.

BAR-STO

Previous manufacturer located in Palms, CA. Bar-Sto still manufactures barrels and firearms-related accessories.

PISTOLS: SEMI-AUTO

BAR-STO .25 ACP PISTOL - .25 ACP cal., patterned after the Baby Browning, brushed stainless steel finish, walnut grips, approx. 250 manufactured in circa 1974.

		$195	$165	$125

GRADING - PPGS™	100%	98%	95%	90%	80%	70%	60%

BATTAGLIA, MAURO

Current manufacturer established in 1992 and located in Ravenna, Italy. No current U.S. importation.

Mauro Battaglia manufactures custom order high quality SxS shotguns. He also manufactures a sidelock action with new, unique design. Please contact the factory directly for more information.

BAUER FIREARMS CORPORATION

Previous manufacturer located in Fraser, MI circa 1971-1984.

DERRINGERS

THE RABBIT - .22 LR cal. and .410 bore, combination gun, all metal construction, O/U configuration. Mfg. 1982-84.

	100%	98%	95%	90%	80%	70%	60%
	$125	$100	$90	$80	$70	$60	$50

PISTOLS: SEMI-AUTO

BAUER .25 ACP - .25 ACP cal., 2 1/2 in. barrel, 6 shot, fixed sights, checkered walnut or pearlite grips. Mfg. 1972-84.

	100%	98%	95%
	$150	$130	$110

Note: These guns are identical to the Baby Browning, except stainless steel.

✳ *Bauer .25 ACP Bicentennial Model* - .25 ACP cal., engraved with buckle in display case.

	100%	98%	95%
	$300	$200	$150

BAYARD

Previously manufactured by Anciens Etablissements Pieper located in Herstal, Belgium.

Even though Bayard Models 1908, both 1923s, and 1930 were manufactured only by Anciens Etablissements Pieper of Herstal, Belgium, these pistols are listed under this heading as they are most commonly referred to by this trademark designation.

PISTOLS: SEMI-AUTO

.25 ACP and .380 ACP cals. are more rare than the .32 ACP, and will command a 20%+ premium above values listed unless indicated differently.

MODEL 1908 POCKET AUTOMATIC - .25 ACP, .32 ACP, or .380 ACP cal., 6 shot, 2 1/4 in. barrel, fixed sights, blue, hard rubber grips.

	100%	98%	95%	90%	80%	70%	60%
	$350	$250	$165	$100	$85	$70	$55

Add 10% for .25 ACP cal.
Add 25% if marked with Imperial Eagle.
Add 200% if factory engraved.

MODEL 1923 POCKET AUTOMATIC - .25 ACP cal., 2 1/2 in. barrel, blue, fixed sights, checkered hard rubber grips.

	100%	98%	95%	90%	80%	70%	60%
	$350	$295	$225	$170	$140	$125	$95

BAYARD 1923 POCKET AUTOMATIC - .32 ACP or .380 ACP cal., 6 shot, 3 5/16 in. barrel, fixed sights, blue, checkered hard rubber grips.

	100%	98%	95%	90%	80%	70%	60%
	$375	$295	$225	$170	$140	$125	$95

Add 100% for .380 ACP cal.

BAYARD 1930 POCKET AUTOMATIC - slight modification of 1923.

	100%	98%	95%	90%	80%	70%	60%
	$350	$250	$200	$170	$145	$120	$95

BECAS

Current trademark of shotguns manufactured by Molot, JSC, located in the Kirov Region, Russia.

Becas semi-automatic and slide action shotguns have had little or no importation into the U.S. Please contact the factory for more information (see Trademark Index), including model availability and pricing.

BEEMAN OUTDOOR SPORTS

Previous importer and distributor located in Santa Rosa, CA.

On April 1, 1993, Beeman Precision Arms, Inc. was split into two independent companies: Beeman Precision Airguns, a division of S/R Industries (Maryland Corp.), located in Huntington Beach, CA retains worldwide distribution of Beeman airguns and accessories. Beeman Outdoor Sports, a Division of Robert's Precision Arms, Inc., located in Santa Rosa, CA distributed Feinwerkbau firearms until 1995.

Beeman Precision Arms, Inc. was a large importer, primarily specializing in high quality European air rifles and pistols. Firearms trademarks previously distributed in the U.S. include the following trademarks: Agner (disc. 1986), Erma (disc. 1985), FAS (disc. 1987), Fabarm (disc. 1985), Feinwerkbau, Korth (disc. 1990), Krico (disc. 1988), Unique (disc. 1991), and Weihrauch (disc.). These trademarks appear under their respective alphabetical headings.

For more information and current pricing on both new and used Beeman Precision Airguns, please refer to the *Blue Book of Airguns* by Dr. Robert Beeman & John Allen (also online).

The following firearms were manufactured to Beeman specifications, and are therefore listed under the Beeman Outdoor Sports heading.

PISTOLS: SEMI-AUTO

BEEMAN MP-08 - .380 ACP cal., Luger type toggle action, 3 1/2 in. barrel, 6 shot mag., blue, 1.4 lbs. Mfg. 1968-90.

	$395	$335	$275	$240	$185	$145	$115

Last MSR was $390.

In 1988, Beeman took over importation of these two models (MP-08 and P-08). These revised models have new Luger style checkered walnut grips and 3 1/2 in. barrel. Previous variations had plastic grips.

BEEMAN P-08 - .22 LR cal., Luger type toggle action, 8 shot mag., 3.8 in. barrel, blue, checkered walnut grips, 1.9 lbs. Mfg. 1969-90.

	$395	$335	$275	$240	$185	$145	$115

Last MSR was $390.

PISTOLS: SINGLE SHOT

MODEL SP/SPX - .22 LR cal., designed for silhouette shooting, 10 in. heavy bull barrel, blue metal parts, birchwood stocks and forearm, aperture sights, 3.9 lbs. Disc. 1994.

	$625	$550	$475	$425	$375	$330	$295

Last MSR was $700.

Only a few of these models were actually delivered.

* *Model SPX Deluxe* - similar to Model SPX, except has matte chrome metal finish, hand stippled walnut grips, and Anschütz rear sight. Limited mfg. 1993-94.

	$800	$725	$650	$575	$500	$425	$350

Last MSR was $900.

GRADING - PPGS™	100%	98%	95%	90%	80%	70%	60%

SP STANDARD - .22 LR cal., sidelever action, 8, 10, 12, or 15 in. barrel, adj. sights and walnut grips, single shot. Made in W. Germany. Imported 1985-86 only.

	$250	$220	$180	$170	$160	$150	$140

Last MSR was $250.

Add $10 or $30 for 12 or 15 in. barrel respectively.

SP DELUXE - similar to SP Standard, except has forearm, about 3 1/2 lbs. Made in W. Germany. Imported 1985-86 only.

	$275	$240	$200	$185	$170	$155	$145

Last MSR was $300.

Add $10 or $30 for 12 or 15 in. barrel respectively.

BEHOLLA PISTOL

Previously manufactured by Becker & Hollander located in Suhl, Germany.

PISTOLS: SEMI-AUTO

BEHOLLA POCKET AUTOMATIC - .32 ACP cal., 7 shot, 2.9 in. barrel, blue, serrated wood or rubber grips, mfg. 1915-20, from 1920-25 the same gun was mfg. by Stenda-Werke.

	$225	$170	$150	$135	$120	$100	$90

BENELLI

Current manufacturer established in 1972, and located in Urbino, Italy. Benelli USA was formed during late 1997, and is currently importing all Benelli shotguns and rifles. Benelli pistols (and air pistols) are currently imported by Larry's Guns, located in Portland, ME beginning 2003. Company headquarters are located in Accokeek, MD. Shotguns were previously imported 1983-1997 by Heckler & Koch, Inc., located in Sterling, VA. Handguns were previously imported until 1997 by European American Armory, located in Sharpes, FL, in addition to Sile Distributors, Inc., until 1995, located in New York, NY, and Saco, located in Arlington, VA.

For more information on Benelli air pistols, please refer to the *Blue Book of Airguns* by Dr. Robert Beeman and John Allen (also online).

PISTOLS: SEMI-AUTO

Models B-77, B-80, and MP3S were previously imported by Sile Distributors. Models MP90S and MP95E Atlanta were imported by Benelli USA until 2002. Beginning 2003, Benelli pistols are exclusively imported by Larry's Guns, located in Portland, ME.

MODEL B-76 - 9mm Para. cal., selective double action, all steel, 4 1/4 in. barrel, 8 shot mag., 34 oz. Importation disc. in 1990.

	$400	$375	$335	$295	$245	$225	$210

Last MSR was $428.

MODEL B-76S TARGET - 9mm Para. cal., similar to B-76, except has 5 1/2 in. barrel, target grips, and adj. rear sights. Importation disc. 1990.

	$550	$475	$425	$395	$350	$325	$300

Last MSR was $595.

MODEL B-77 - .32 ACP cal., selective double action, all steel, 4 1/4 in. barrel, 8 shot mag. Importation disc. 1995.

	$395	$350	$295	$255	$225	$200	$180

Last MSR was $385.

GRADING - PPGS™	100%	98%	95%	90%	80%	70%	60%

MODEL B-80 - .30 Luger cal., selective double action, all steel, 4 1/4 in. barrel, 8 shot mag., 34 oz. Importation disc. 1995.

	$395	$350	$295	$255	$225	$200	$180

Last MSR was $385.

MODEL B-80S TARGET - similar to B-80, except has 5 1/2 in. barrel, target grips, and adj. rear sights. Importation disc. 1995.

	$500	$450	$375	$325	$295	$275	$250

Last MSR was $572.

MODEL MP3S - .32 S&W Long Wadcutter cal., target variation with 5 1/2 in. barrel, high gloss bluing, target grips, and adj. rear sights. Importation disc. 1995.

	$550	$450	$375	$325	$295	$275	$250

Last MSR was $785.

MODEL MP90S WORLD CUP - .22 S (disc.), .22 LR, or .32 S&W Wadcutter (disc. 1999) cal., 4.4 in. barrel, blue finish, target pistol featuring forward assisted breech bolt mechanism, anatomic grips, and adj. weight, 5 (disc.), 6 or 9 (optional) shot mag., 2.4 lbs. Imported 1992-2002, and again beginning 2003.

MSR N/A	$1,050	$850	$725	$650	$600	$550	$500

Add $105 for .32 S&W Wadcutter cal.

Conversion kits were previously available for this model at an extra charge.

MODEL MP95E ATLANTA - .22 LR or .32 S&W Wadcutter (disc. 1999) cal., 4.4 in. barrel, features inertial recoiling mass system, integral Weaver style base mount, 5 (disc.), 6 or 9 (optional) shot mag., adj. trigger assembly, fully adj. sight, modular firing system, blue or matte chrome finish, smooth laminate (chrome finish only) or choice of checkered adj. (disc.) or non-adj. walnut grips, 2.5 lbs. Imported late 1994-2002, and again beginning 2003.

MSR N/A	$643	$575	$495	$450	$400	$375	$350

Add $57 for chrome finish.

Add $117 for .32 S&W Wadcutter cal.

This model was originally designated as Model MP95.

RIFLES: SEMI-AUTO

R1 STANDARD CARBINE/RIFLE - .270 WSM (new 2005), .30-06, .308 Win., .300 WSM (new 2005), or .300 Win. Mag. cal., features auto-regulating gas operated (ARGO) system and rotating 3 lug bolt, 20 (carbine, .30-06 or .300 Win. Mag. only), 22, or 24 (.300 Win. Mag. cal. only) in. barrel with cryogenic treatment and interchangeable rear rib, detachable 3 or 4 shot mag., no sights, forearm is fixed to the alloy receiver, drilled and tapped, Picatinny rail included, available in black or nickel plated (Europe only) receiver finish, checkered walnut Monte Carlo stock and forearm, recoil pad is cut into the stock (adj., with shims), ambidextrous safety, approx. 7 lbs. New 2002.

MSR $1,080	$885	$755	$625	$550	$495	$445	$375

SHOTGUNS: SEMI-AUTO, 1985-OLDER

Benelli semi-auto 3rd generation (inertia recoil) shotguns were imported starting in the late 1960s. The receivers were mfg. of light aluminum alloy - the SL-80 Model 121 had a semi-gloss, anodized black finish, the Model 123 had an ornate photo-engraved receiver, the Model Special 80 had a brushed, white nickel-plated receiver, and the Model 121 M1 had a matte finish receiver, barrel, and stock. All 12 ga. SL-80 Series shotguns will accept 2 3/4 or 3 in. shells, and all SL-80 Series 12 ga. Models have interchangeable barrels (except the 121 M1) with 4 different model receivers (121, 121 M1, 123, and Special 80). All 4 models had fixed choke barrels.

The SL-80 Series shotguns were disc. during 1985, and neither H&K nor Benelli USA has parts for these guns. There may be forearms, used barrels (from CDNN), and other misc. parts still available for the 12 ga. from Gun Parts Corp. (see Trademark Index for more information).

GRADING - PPGS™	100%	98%	95%	90%	80%	70%	60%

Approx. 50,000 SL-80 series shotguns were mfg. before discontinuance - choke markings (located on side or underneath barrel) are as follows: * full choke, ** imp. mod., *** mod., **** imp. cyl. SL-80 series guns used the same action (much different than current mfg.) and all had the split receiver design. Be aware of possible wood cracking where the barrel rests on the thin area of the forend and also on the underside of the buttstock behind trigger guard. When buying or selling a SL-80 Series shotgun, be aware that when comparing the SL-80 Series with the newer action Benellis (post 1985), there is a big difference between the action, design changes, and actual selling prices in today's marketplace. The SL80s are much lower priced than current production Benellis.

Since the late 1980s, the Benelli SL-80 series marketplace has dropped sharply, and relatively few guns have been traded during the new millennium. In the past five years, there have been an increasing number of SL-80 guns for sale which have had unresolved mechanical problems. Parts are scarce and high priced. Wood for most models are no longer available. Buyers would be well-sdvised to be cautious when considering buying a used SL-80 series Benelli.

100% values within this section assume NIB condition.

Subtract 5% for "SACO" importation (Saco was located in Arlington, VA).

SL-80 SERIES MODEL SL-121V - 12 ga., field grade, 26, or 28 in. fixed choke VR barrel, anodized and black semi-gloss finish on lower receiver. Disc. 1985.

$395	$340	$300	$275	$240	$185	$160

Last MSR was $397.

SL-80 SERIES MODEL SL-121/SL-122 SLUG - 12 ga., features Monte Carlo stock and flat bottom Trap Grade beavertail forearm, 21 1/16 cyl. bore barrel, fixed open ring rear iron sights and fixed front ramp, 5 shot mag., recoil pad, 7 lbs. 3 oz. Disc. 1985.

$385	$360	$325	$300	$230	$185	$160

Last MSR was $434.

SL-80 SERIES MODEL SL-123V - 12 ga., stylish field grade, receiver Ergal special aluminum alloy with photo engraving, 26 or 28 in. VR barrel with various chokes, approx. 6 lbs. 13 oz. Disc. 1985.

$420	$365	$350	$325	$225	$200	$185

Last MSR was $464.

Add $20 for trap stock, $10 for beavertail forearm and $25 for skeet barrel.

The only difference between the SL-123V and SL-121V is the photo engraved receiver. The SL-123V was at times referred to as the deluxe model when compared to with the SL-121V. Both models were field grade shotguns.

EX-L - 12 ga., similar in appearance to the Model SL123V, except has hand-engraved receiver, very limited mfg. with unpredictable premiums over Model SL123V.

SL-80 SERIES MODEL 121 M1 POLICE/MILITARY - 12 ga. only, similar in appearance to the Super 90 M1, hardwood stock, 7 shot mag., matte metal and wood finish, most stocks had adj. lateral sling attachment inside of buttstock, 18 3/4 in. barrel. Disc. 1985.

$395	$350	$300	$285	$250	$225	$195

Since many of this model were sold to the police and military, used specimens should be checked carefully for excessive wear and/or possible damage.

MODEL 80 SPECIAL SKEET/TRAP - 12 ga. only, 28 in. VR with mod. choke and phosphorescent bead sight, has trap/skeet Monte Carlo grade/style wood stock with recoil pad, lower receiver is nickel plated, 7 lbs. 10 oz. Disc. 1986.

$465	$395	$350	$295	$250	$225	$195

Last MSR was $531.

Trap guns should have high comb trap stock and trap grade forearm (not field grade/style wood). Trap guns should also be inspected carefully for internal wear before buying/selling.

GRADING - PPGS™	100%	98%	95%	90%	80%	70%	60%

SL-80 SERIES MODEL SL201 FIELD GRADE - 20 ga., 26 in. VR barrel bored mod., black anodized lower receiver, approx. 5 lbs. 10 oz., mfg. in France for Benelli. Disc. 1985.

	$385	$360	$340	$300	$240	$185	$165

Last MSR was $399.

BRI-BENELLI SL-80 123 SLUG GUN - 12 ga. only, custom designed, premium slug gun featuring SL-80 Series action and drilled and tapped rifle bored barrel by E. R. Shaw Barrel Co., assembled by BRI in the U.S., Monte Carlo stock with beavertail forend, approx. 25 guns total mfg. 1986-87.

	$1,895	$1,275	$1,025	$875	$750	$625	$525

Subtract 40% if w/o trap style beavertail forend and Monte Carlo stock.

Original issue price on this model was $750-$850. These specimens are marked "BRI-Benelli" on barrel. No warranties exist on this model.

SHOTGUNS: SEMI-AUTO, 1986-NEWER

Extra barrels (non-slug) for the currently manufactured models are typically priced in the $305-$385 range, depending on the model. Unless indicated otherwise, all currently manufactured Benelli shotguns utilize a red bar front sight, and are equipped with a patented Benelli keyed chamber lock.

M1 FIELD (SUPER 90) - 12 or 20 (new 2001) ga., 3 in. chamber, inertia recoil operating system, alloy receiver, 21 (new 1990, 12 ga. only), 24 (new 1990), 26, or 28 in. vent. rib barrel and 3-shot mag., includes 5 screw in choke tubes, satin walnut (new 1994), black polymer stock, Turkey Models include steady-grip with built-in stock pistol grip (new 2003) or regular pistol grip, red fiber optic front sight, 100% Realtree X-tra Brown (mfg. 1997-2001) or Advantage Timber HD (new 2001, 20 ga. only until 2002) camo coverage, approx. 5.8 (20 ga.) or 7.2 (12 ga.) lbs.

MSR $1,000	$800	$675	$575	$445	$375	$335	$300

Add $30 for 20 ga.

Add $15 for satin walnut stock (12 ga., 26 or 28 in. barrel only).

Add $100 for Advantage Timber HD camo finish in 12 ga., $20 in 20 ga.

Add $195 for Turkey configuration with 24 in. barrel, steady-grip and 100% Timber HD camo coverage.

Add $100 for Turkey configuration with 24 in. barrel and Timber HD camo finish (disc. 2004).

Add $95 for Realtree Xtra Brown camo finish (disc. 2001).

Add $45 for 11 oz. mercury recoil reducer (synthetic stock only).

Add $20 for left-hand action (mfg. 2000-2003, available in synthetic and camo, 12 ga. only).

During 2000, Benelli improved this model with a stepped VR and oversized safety.

This model was available with an extended magazine tube (26 or 28 in. barrel only).

M1 FIELD SLUG (SUPER 90) - 12 (disc. 2004) or 20 (new 2004) ga., 3 in. chamber, incorporates improvements on the Benelli action, including rotating Montefeltro bolt system, 19 3/4 cyl. bore (disc. 1997) or 24 (new 1998) in. rifled barrel with iron sights (disc. 1997, reintroduced 2001), drilled and tapped beginning 1998, 3 (new 1998) or 7 (disc. 1997) shot mag., Realtree Xtra Brown camo (mfg. 2000-2001), Advantage Timber HD (new 2002) camo, or black fiberglass stock and forearm, 6.5 - 7.6 lbs. New 1986.

MSR $1,105	$895	$700	$600	$475	$375	$335	$300

Add $110 for Advantage Timber HD camo finish.

Add $105 for Realtree Xtra brown camo finish (disc. 2001).

Subtract 15% for 19 3/4 cyl. bore barrel with iron sights.

GRADING - PPGS™	100%	98%	95%	90%	80%	70%	60%

M1 DEFENSE (SUPER 90) - similar to Super 90 Slug, except has pistol grip stock, 7.1 lbs. Disc. 1998.

	$685	$525	$395	$325	$300	$270	$250

Last MSR was $851.

Add $41 for ghost-ring sighting system.

M1 PRACTICAL (SUPER 90) - 12 ga. only, 3 in. chamber, 26 in. plain barrel with muzzle brake, designed for IPSC events, extended 8 shot mag. tube, oversized safety, speed loader, larger bolt handle, Milspec adj. ghost-ring sight and Picatinny rail, black regular synthetic stock and forearm, matte metal finish, includes 3 choke tubes, 7.6 lbs. Mfg. 1998-2004.

	$1,055	$875	$750	$625	$525	$450	$400

Last MSR was $1,285.

M1 TACTICAL (SUPER 90) - 12 ga. only, 3 in. chamber, 18 1/2 in. barrel, fixed rifle or ghost-ring sighting system, available with synthetic pistol grip or standard buttstock, includes 3 choke tubes, 5 shot mag., 6.7 - 7 lbs. Mfg. 1993-2004.

	$810	$675	$575	$450	$375	$335	$300

Last MSR was $975.

Add $50 for ghost-ring sighting system.
Add $50-$65 for pistol grip stock.

✷ *M1 Tactical M* - similar to M1 Tactical, except has military ghost-ring sights and standard synthetic stock, 7.1 lbs. Mfg. 1999-2000.

	$795	$595	$435	$375	$315	$275	$250

Last MSR was $960.

Add $10 for pistol grip stock.

M1 ENTRY (SUPER 90) - 12 ga. only, includes 14 in. barrel, choice of synthetic pistol grip or standard stock, choice of rifle or ghost-ring sights, 5 shot mag. (2 shot extension), approx. 6.7 lbs. New 1992.

MSR N/A	$810	$675	$585	$450	$395	$340	$310

Add $15 for synthetic pistol grip stock.
Add $65 for ghost-ring sighting system.

This model requires special licensing (special tax stamp) for consumers, and is normally available to law enforcement/military only.

M1 SPORTING SPECIAL (SUPER 90) - 12 ga., 18 1/2 in. barrel, matte black finish, includes ghost ring sighting system, 6 1/2 lbs. Mfg. 1993-97.

	$750	$650	$550	$450	$395	$340	$310

Last MSR was $924.

M2 FIELD - 12 ga. only, 3 in. chamber, similar operating system as the M1, redesigned receiver, trigger guard, and safety, 3 shot mag., red fiber optic front sight, short forearm with large magazine cap, includes ComforTech stock system with two gel pads that reduce recoil, 21 (Turkey), 24 (Turkey, with steady-grip), 26, or 28 in. VR barrel with cryo treatment, satin walnut, synthetic, or choice of 100% coverage Advantage Max-4 HD or Advantage Timber HD camo stock, 6.9 - 7.2 lbs. New 2004.

MSR $1,070	$885	$695	$600	$475	$375	$335	$300

Add $65 for black synthetic stock and forearm.
Add $185 for 100% camo coverage.
Add $175 for 24 in. barrel with steady-grip Turkey configuration (new 2005).
Add $185 for Turkey configuration with pistol grip and 100% Timber HD camo coverage.
Add $100 for left hand action.

✷ *M2 Field Super Slug* - 24 in. rifled barrel with open sights, choice of black synthetic stock and forearm, or 100% Advantage Timber HD camo coverage, 7.3 lbs. New 2004.

MSR $1,200	$975	$750	$650	$500	$400	$350	$300

Add $120 for Timber HD camo coverage.

GRADING - PPGS™	100%	98%	95%	90%	80%	70%	60%

M2 PRACTICAL - 12 ga. only, 3 in. chamber, 26 in. compensated barrel with ghost ring sights, designed for IPSC competition, 8 shot mag., Picatinny rail. New 2005.

MSR $1,335	$1,095	$900	$800	$650	$550	$475	$425

M2 TACTICAL - 12 ga. only, 3 in. chamber, 18.5 in. barrel with choice of pistol grip, regular stock, or ComforTech stock configuration, matte finish, 5 shot mag., AirTouch checkering pattern on stock and forearm, open rifle or ghost ring sights, 6.7-7 lbs. New 2005.

MSR $1,000	$800	$675	$575	$445	$375	$335	$300

Add $65 for ghost ring sights.
Add $135 for ComforTech stock configuration.

M3 CONVERTIBLE AUTO/PUMP (SUPER 90) - 12 ga. only, 3 in. chamber, defense configuration incorporating convertible (fingertip activated) pump or semi-auto action, 19 3/4 in. cyl. bore barrel with ghost ring or rifle sights, 5 shot mag., choice of standard black polymer stock or integral pistol grip (disc. 1996, reintroduced 1999), approx. 7.3 lbs. New 1989.

MSR $1,165	$965	$750	$650	$525	$450	$375	$325

Add approx. $20 for standard configuration stock.
Add $55 for open sights.
Add $110 for folding stock (mfg. 1990-disc.) - only available as a complete gun.
Add $340 for Model 200 Laser Sight System with bracket (disc.).

M4 TACTICAL - 12 ga. only, consumer version of the U.S. Military M4, 3 in. chamber, includes auto-regulating gas operating (ARGO) system, dual stainless self cleaning pistons, 4 shot mag., matte black phosphated metal and black standard, 18.5 in. barrel with ghost ring sights, pistol grip, or non-collapsible (disc. 2004) stock and forearm, includes Picatinny rail, approx. 7.8 lbs. Importation began late 2003.

MSR $1,465	$1,250	$1,000	$875	$800	$725	$650	$600

M1014 LIMITED EDITION - similar to M4, except only available with non-collapsible stock, U.S. flag engraved on receiver, 8 lbs. Limited edition of 2,500 mfg. 2003-2004.

	$1,375	$1,050	$875				

Last MSR was $1,575.

MONTEFELTRO STANDARD HUNTER (SUPER 90) - 12 or 20 (new 1993) ga., 3 in. chamber, aluminum alloy receiver, rotary bolt, 21 (disc. 1997), 24, 26, or 28 (12 ga. only) in. VR barrel with 5 choke tubes, matte black metal or 100% Realtree camo (20 ga. only, mfg. 1998-2000) finish, checkered walnut stock and forearm with choice of high gloss (disc. 1997) or satin finish, 4 shot mag., approx. 5.5 (20 ga.) or 7.1 lbs. New 1988.

MSR $1,070	$885	$735	$625	$525	$450	$395	$340

Add $100 for 100% Realtree camo finish on 20 ga. only (disc.).
Add $10 for left-hand action (12 ga., 26 or 28 in. barrel only).
Add $10 for shortened stock with 12 1/2 in. LOP, approx. 5.5 lbs. (20 ga. only, new 1999).

* *Montefeltro Grade II* - 12 or 20 ga., 26 in. VR barrel with 5 chokes, red fiber optic front sight, includes upgraded select walnut and gold accents, 5.5 (20 ga.) or 6.9 (12 ga.) lbs. New 2004.

MSR $1,220	$1,000	$850	$735	$600	$525	$450	$395

* *Montefeltro Limited Edition (Super 90)* - 20 ga. only, nickel plated lower receiver with etched gold highlights, 26 in. VR barrel. Limited mfg. 1995-96.

	$1,825	$1,525	$1,225	$995	$875	$750	$625

Last MSR was $2,080.

* *Montefeltro Turkey Gun* - similar to Montefeltro Standard Hunter except has 24 in. VR barrel with 3 choke tubes, satin finish wood only, 7 lbs. Imported 1989 only.

		$650	$575	$500	$450	$415	$365	$310

Last MSR was $675.

GRADING - PPGS™	100%	98%	95%	90%	80%	70%	60%

* *Montefeltro Uplander* - similar to Montefeltro Turkey Gun except has 21 or 24 in. VR barrel with 3 choke tubes, satin finish wood only, 7 lbs. Mfg. 1989-92.

	$650	$575	$500	$450	$415	$365	$310

Last MSR was $799.

* *Montefeltro Slug Gun* - deer gun configuration with 19 3/4 in. slug barrel. Disc. 1992.

	$650	$500	$475	$425	$400	$350	$310

Last MSR was $799.

CORDOBA - 12 ga. only, 3 in. chamber, 28 or 30 in. 10mm ported VR cyro barrel, 4 shot mag., matte black finish, black synthetic ComforTech stock, 7.2 lbs.   New 2005.

MSR $1,600	$1,350	$1,075	$925	$825	$725	$650	$600

SPORT MODEL - 12 ga., 3 in. chamber, one piece blued alloy receiver, 26 (disc. 1999, reintroduced during 2001 only) or 28 in. barrel with 5 choke tubes and 2 removable and interchangeable carbon fiber vent. ribs, 4 shot mag., adj. butt pad and buttstock, satin finished select checkered walnut stock and forearm, "Benelli" outlined in red on matte finished receiver side, approx. 7.1 lbs. Mfg. 1997-2002.

	$1,125	$895	$750	$575	$500	$450	$400

Last MSR was $1,375.

SPORT II - 12 ga., 3 in. chamber, one piece satin nickel finished alloy receiver, blued, 26 (disc. 2004), 28, or 30 (new 2005) in. cryogenically treated ported barrel with 5 extra long (not flush with barrel) choke tubes, twin bead sights, 4 shot mag., gel recoil pad with stock spacer kit provided, satin finished select checkered walnut stock and forearm, "Sport II" on receiver side, approx. 7 7/8 lbs. Importation began 2003.

MSR $1,470	$1,195	$950	$800	$600	$500	$450	$400

SUPERSPORT - 12 ga. only, 3 in. chamber, checkered black carbon fiber stock and forearm with AirTouch recoil reduction system, 4 shot mag., 28 or 30 in. ported VR barrel with Crio treatment and extended Crio choke tubes, twin bead sights, satin nickel receiver finish with "Supersport" on right side, 7.9 lbs. New 2004.

MSR $1,670	$1,335	$1,050	$895	$650	$600	$525	$475

LEGACY MODEL - 12 or 20 (new 1999) ga., 3 in. chamber, 24 (20 ga. only), 26 or 28 (12 ga. only) in. VR barrel with 5 choke tubes and red bar front sight with bead mid-sight, 4 shot mag., engraved nickel finished alloy lower or all alloy (20 ga. only) receiver, cartridge drop lever, select checkered walnut stock with vent. recoil pad and forearm, stock shim kit provided, mfg. to commemorate the 30th Anniversary of Benelli shotgun manufacturing, approx. 5.8 lbs. or 7.5 lbs. New 1998.

MSR $1,435	$1,175	$935	$780	$575	$500	$450	$400

Add $30 for 20 ga.

* *Legacy Limited Edition* - 12 or 20 ga., features acid etched engraving with gold filled game scenes, only 250 of each ga. mfg. for the new millennium only, deluxe checkered walnut stock and forearm. Limited mfg. 2000 only.

	$1,750	$1,475	$850	$675	$600	$500	$450

Last MSR was $1,600.

Add 20% to individual prices for a 2 gun set with matching serial numbers (NIB only).

EXECUTIVE SERIES - 12 ga. only, 3 in. chamber, features engraved all-steel greyed lower receiver by Giovanelli, mid-rib barrel bead, high polish upper receiver and barrel bluing, extra select grade walnut, 5 choke tubes, and other accessories, choice of 21 (disc.), 24 (disc.), 26, or 28 in. VR barrel, approx. 7 3/4 lbs. Special order only beginning 1996.

* *Grade/Type I*

MSR $5,500	$4,900	$3,825	$2,600

GRADING - PPGS™	100%	98%	95%	90%	80%	70%	60%
✱ *Grade/Type II*							
MSR $6,125	$5,375	$4,175	$3,075				
✱ *Grade/Type III*							
MSR $7,250	$6,350	$4,700	$3,550				

BLACK EAGLE - 12 ga., 3 in. chamber, Montefeltro action, similar to Montefeltro Super 90 Standard Hunter except has black synthetic regular or pistol grip stock and forearm, 21 (disc. 1990), 24 (disc. 1990), 26, or 28 (new 1990) in. VR barrel with 3 choke tubes, right-hand only. Originally imported 1989-90, resumed 1997 only.

	$825	$675	$550	$450	$375	$315	$285

Last MSR was $992.

This configuration changed to competition in 1991 (see Black Eagle Competition Model).

✱ *Black Eagle Competition Model* - 12 ga. only, designed for competition shooting with action adj. for lighter loads, silver finished etched lower receiver, 26 or 28 in. VR barrel with 5 choke tubes and wrench provided, includes buttstock drop adjustment kit. Mfg. 1991-97.

	$1,025	$795	$675	$550	$475	$375	$300

Last MSR was $1,229.

✱ *Black Eagle 1994 Limited Edition* - 12 ga. only, features 26 in. VR barrel with extra fancy grade checkered walnut and gold inlays on receiver sides, 1,000 mfg. 1994-95 only with special serialization.

	$1,775	$1,500	$1,225	$995	$875	$750	$625

Last MSR was $2,000.

✱ *Black Eagle Slug Gun* - 12 ga., 24 in. rifled barrel with receiver scope mount. Imported 1990-91 only.

	$735	$625	$500	$425	$365	$315	$285

Last MSR was $859.

SUPER BLACK EAGLE - 12 ga. only, 3 1/2 in. chamber, updated Montefeltro action accepts all 12 ga. loads, right or left-hand (new 1999) action, upper steel/lower alloy receiver, 24, 26, or 28 in. VR barrel with 5 choke tubes and wrench provided, 3 shot mag., choice of matte finish and satin wood stock, blue finish and high gloss wood finish (26 or 28 in. barrel only, disc. 2004), or 100% coverage Advantage Timber HD (new 2002) or Realtree X-tra Brown camo. (mfg. 1997-2001) finish on polymer stock and forearm, Turkey Models include steady-grip with built-in stock pistol grip (new 2003) or regular pistol grip with 24 in. barrel, red fiberoptic front sight with metal bead sight, black synthetic stock and forearm with matte metal finish was introduced in 1993, vent. recoil pad, includes buttstock drop adjustment kit, approx. 7.4 lbs. New 1991.

MSR $1,305	$1,075	$895	$775	$625	$525	$475	$425

Add $95 for Advantage Timber HD camo finish (Turkey Models).
Add $95 for 100% coverage Realtree camo wood/metal finish (disc. 2001).
Add $10 for satin walnut stock and forearm (26 or 28 in. barrel only).
Add $45 for 11 oz. mercury recoil reducer (synthetic stock only).
Add $75 for left-hand action for either black synthetic stock/forearm or full coverage camo finish (disc. 2004).
Add $180 for Turkey configuration with 24 in. barrel, steady-grip, and 100% Timber HD camo coverage.

✱ *Super Black Eagle Limited Edition* - 12 ga. only, features 26 in. VR barrel with extra fancy grade checkered walnut and gold inlays on nickel plated receiver sides, 1,000 mfg. beginning 1997 with special serialization, 7.4 lbs. Disc. 1999.

	$1,825	$1,500	$1,225	$995	$875	$750	$625

Last MSR was $2,095.

GRADING - PPGS™	100%	98%	95%	90%	80%	70%	60%

✻ Super Black Eagle Slug Gun - 12 ga., 3 in. chamber, includes 24 in. rifled barrel with adj. rifle sights, drilled and tapped receiver, choice of matte or camo metal finish, choice of black polymer (new 1993), satin finished wood, or 100% Advantage Timber HD (new 2002) or Realtree X-tra Brown camo (mfg. 2000-2001), 7.6 lbs. Mfg. 1992-2003.

	$1,110	$910	$775	$650	$575	$475	$425

Last MSR was $1,335.

Add $10 for wood stock.
Add $125 for Advantage Timber HD camo finish.
Add $100 for Realtree X-tra Brown camo finish (disc. 2001).

SUPER BLACK EAGLE I - 12 ga. only, 3 1/2 in. chamber, 24, 26, or 28 in. barrel, choice of satin walnut wood with matte metal finish, synthetic, Advantage Max-4 HD camo (100% coverage), Advantage Timber HD (100% coverage), or steady-grip (Turkey, 24 in. barrel only) with Advantage Timber HD, red fiberoptic front sight with bead metal sight, 3 shot mag. New 2005.

MSR $1,333	$1,100	$925	$800	$650	$550	$500	$450

Add $67 for satin walnut stock and forearm.
Add $120 for camo finish.
Add $200 for Turkey configuration with steady-grip stock.

✻ Super Black Eagle I Slug - 12 ga. only, 24 in. smoothbore barrel, satin walnut stock and forearm, matte metal finish, 3 shot mag., adj. rifle sights. New 2005.

MSR $1,465	$1,185	$950	$825	$700	$600	$475	$425

SUPER BLACK EAGLE II - 12 ga. only, 3 1/2 in. chamber, action similar to Super Black Eagle, includes ComforTech recoil reduction in stock with two gel pads, 3 shot mag., 24 (Turkey), 26, or 28 in. VR barrel with cryogenic treatment, larger trigger guard, AirTouch checkering on stock and shortened forearm, choice of satin finished walnut, black synthetic, or 100% coverage of Advantage Max-4 HD or Advantage Timber HD camo, approx. 7.2 lbs. New 2004.

MSR $1,465	$1,185	$950	$825	$700	$600	$475	$425

Add $35 for left-hand action.
Add $120 for camo.
Add $120 for Turkey configuration (right or left hand) with 100% Advantage Timber HD camo.

✻ Super Black Eagle II Slug - 12 ga. only, 24 in. barrel with rifled bore and open sights, includes Picatinny rail, choice of satin walnut stock and forearm, black synthetic, or 100% camo coverage of Timber HD, approx. 7.4 lbs. New 2004.

MSR $1,535	$1,250	$950	$825	$675	$575	$475	$425

Add $120 for 100% camo treatment.

✻ Super Black Eagle II Flyway Limited Edition - four variations include: the Atlantic, Mississippi, Central, and Pacific Flyways, roll engraved satin grey receiver finish with four gold duck/goose inlays (each Flyway has four different inlays), select checkered walnut stock and forearm, 7.2 lbs. 175 of each Flyway manufactured 2004.

	$1,795	$1,500	$1,275	$1,000	$875	$800	$725

Last MSR was $2,130.

SHOTGUNS: SLIDE-ACTION

All currently manufactured Benelli shotguns are equipped with a patented Benelli keyed chamber lock.

GRADING - PPGS™	100%	98%	95%	90%	80%	70%	60%

NOVA - 12 or 20 (new 2001) ga., 3 (20 ga. only) or 3 1/2 in. chamber, unique design allows stock and internal metal receiver "shell" to be molded in one unit, utilizing a glass polymer matrix, Montefeltro rotating bolt, dual action bars, 24 (Turkey only), 26, or 28 in. VR barrel with 3 choke tubes and red fiberoptic front sight, 3 (3 1/2 in. shells) or 4 shot mag., matte metal finish, choice of black synthetic, full coverage Realtree X-tra brown (disc. 2002), Advantage Max-4 HD, or Advantage Timber HD (new 2001, 20 ga. only until 2002) camo stock and forearm with grooved hand ribs, mag. shell stop button in bottom of forearm, approx. 6.5 (20 ga.) or 8 lbs. New 1999.

MSR $350	**$300**	**$265**	**$235**	**$215**	**$200**	**$185**	**$160**

> **Add $65 for Realtree X-tra brown full camo finish (12 ga. only, disc. 2002).**
> **Add $75 for full camo coverage.**
> **Add $75 for 24 in. barrel with 100% Timber HD camo coverage (Turkey Model).**
> **Add $15 for Youth Model with 13 in. LOP.**
> **Add $60 for 2 (12 ga.) or $45 for 4 (20 ga. only) shot magazine extension.**
> **Add $45 for recoil reducer - 10 oz. (disc.) or 14 oz. mercury, installed in stock with reduction tube operation.**

✴ ***Nova Tactical (Special Purpose Smooth Bore)*** - similar action to Nova, features 18.5 in. cyl. bore barrel with choice of rifle or ghost ring (new 2000) sights, black synthetic stock and forearm only, 7.2 lbs. New 1999.

MSR $315	**$270**	**$240**	**$215**	**$195**	**$175**	**$160**	**$145**

> **Add $35 for ghost ring sights.**

✴ ***Nova H₂O*** - 12 ga. only, 3 1/2 in. chamber, 18.5 in. matte nickel finished barrel, black synthetic stock and forearm, 4 shot mag., 7.2 lbs. Importation began 2003.

MSR $500	**$410**	**$360**	**$320**	**$290**	**$255**	**$225**	**$200**

✴ ***Nova Entry*** - 12 ga. only, 14 in. barrel, choice of ghost ring or open rifle sights, black synthetic stock and forearm, 4 shot mag., approx. 6.9 lbs. Importation began 2003.

MSR N/A	**$295**	**$265**	**$235**	**$220**	**$215**	**$200**	**$185**

> **Add $30 for ghost ring sights.**
> This model is available to law enforcement or military only.

✴ ***Nova Slug*** - 12 or 20 ga., features 24 in. rifled bore drilled and tapped barrel with open rifle sights, black synthetic or 100% coverage Advantage Timber HD camo stock and forearm, 8.1 lbs. New 2000.

MSR $520	**$435**	**$390**	**$355**	**$315**	**$285**	**$260**	**$240**

> **Add $80 for Advantage Timber HD camo.**
> **Add $25 for Slug & Field combo with extra 26 in. Field barrel.**

BENSON FIREARMS LTD.

Previous importer for guns manufactured by Aldo Uberti in Italy. Previously imported and distributed from 1987-1989 by Benson Firearms Ltd. located in Seattle, WA. Benson Firearms Ltd. combined with A. Uberti USA Inc. in early 1989 and discontinued importation.

Benson Firearms can be differentiated from other A. Uberti imports by the "Benson Firearms Seattle, WA" barrel marking.

Rather than provide a complete listing of Benson Firearms models, the following rules usually apply. Since Benson Firearms imported A. Uberti firearms, the Uberti section in this text should be referenced for current values regarding models with similar configurations. Collectibility to date has been limited on most Benson Fireams models, and as a rule, up-to-date values on this trademark are established by current importation prices of Uberti firearms. A complete listing of older Benson Firearms models can be found in the 11th and 12th Editions of the *Blue Book of Gun Values*.

BENTON & BROWN FIREARMS, INC.

Previous manufacturer located in Fort Worth, TX and Delhi, LA circa 1993-1996.

RIFLES: BOLT ACTION

MODEL 93 - available in 15 cals. between .243 Win. and .375 H&H Mag., patterned after the Model R-84 Blaser, takedown, free floating 22 or 24 in. barrels, right- or left-hand action, checkered walnut stock and forearm, 7-8 1/2 lbs. New 1993.

$1,875	$1,550	$1,225	$1,100	$995	$875	$750

Last MSR was $2,075.

Subtract $200 for fiberglass stock.
Add $450 per interchangeable barrel.

BERETTA, DR. FRANCO

Previous manufacturer located in Concesio (Brescia), Italy until 1994.

SHOTGUNS: O/U, BLACK DIAMOND SERIES

Black Diamond target guns were imported exclusively by Double M Shooting Sports until 1988.

FIELD MODEL - 12, 16, 20, 28 ga., or .410 bore, variety of chokes, coin finish receiver.

$595	$550	$495	$450	$395	$365	$335

Last MSR was $960.

GRADE ONE - 12, 16, 20, 28 ga., or .410 bore, variety of chokes, coin finish receiver with acid etched engraving, French walnut. Trap or skeet model also available, except in 16 ga.

$1,020	$900	$810	$720	$630	$570	$525

Last MSR was $1,440.

GRADE TWO - 12, 16, 20, 28 ga., or .410 bore, variety of chokes, coin finish receiver with moderate engraving, French walnut. Trap or skeet model also available, except in 16 ga.

$1,475	$1,320	$1,200	$1,080	$930	$815	$750

Last MSR was $2,040.

GRADE THREE - 12, 16, 20, 28 ga., or .410 bore, variety of chokes, coin finish receiver with scrollwork engraving, French walnut. Trap or skeet model also available, except in 16 ga.

$2,100	$1,920	$1,775	$1,560	$1,410	$1,200	$1,035

Last MSR was $3,000.

GRADE FOUR - 12, 16, 20, 28 ga., or .410 bore, variety of chokes, coin finish receiver with elaborate engraving, French walnut. Trap or skeet model also available, except in 16 ga.

$2,500	$2,250	$1,950	$1,650	$1,375	$1,125	$995

Last MSR was $3,960.

SKEET SET - includes 12, 20, 28 ga., and .410 bore barrels, available in Grades One through Four.

Multiply values on Grades One - Four by 275% for 4 ga. skeet sets.

SHOTGUNS: O/U, SxS, & SINGLE BARREL, RECENT MFG.

GAMMA STANDARD O & U - 12, 16, or 20 ga., 26 or 28 in. barrels, coin finish receiver with extensive engraving, Italian walnut. Imported 1984-88.

$400	$360	$330	$300	$275	$260	$240

Last MSR was $445.

Add $83 with single trigger and ejectors.

GRADING - PPGS™	100%	98%	95%	90%	80%	70%	60%

✳ *Gamma Standard* - with interchangeable choke tubes. Importation disc. 1993.

	$825	$695	$525	$425	$325	$250	$195

Last MSR was $1,000.

Add 20% for auto ejectors.
Add $100 for single trigger.
Add 36% for Gamma Trap or Skeet variation (ST).

GAMMA DELUXE O & U - 12, 16, or 20 ga., 26 or 28 in. barrels, coin finish receiver with extensive engraving, Italian walnut. Imported 1984-88.

	$445	$405	$370	$350	$325	$300	$275

Last MSR was $480.

Add $84 with single trigger and ejectors.

✳ *Gamma Deluxe* - with interchangeable choke tubes. Importation disc. 1988.

	$635	$570	$530	$490	$450	$420	$390

Last MSR was $685.

GAMMA TARGET O & U - 12 ga. only, SST, ejectors, Wundhammer swell pistol grip, English walnut stock and beavertail forearm. Imported 1986-88.

	$550	$505	$455	$410	$370	$350	$325

Last MSR was $595.

ALPHA STANDARD O & U - 12, 16, or 20 ga., 26 or 28 in. barrels, coin finish receiver with extensive engraving, Italian walnut. Imported 1984-88, resumed 1993.

	$720	$650	$525	$450	$375	$300	$250

Last MSR was $780.

Add 18% for auto ejectors.
Add $100 for single trigger.

ALPHA DELUXE O & U - 12, 16, or 20 ga., 26 or 28 in. barrels, coin finish receiver with extensive engraving, sling swivels, Italian walnut. Imported 1984-88.

	$395	$355	$330	$300	$275	$250	$230

Last MSR was $435.

Add $75 with single trigger and ejectors.
Add $80 for interchangeable choke tubes (disc. 1985).

AMERICA STANDARD O & U - .410 bore only, 26 or 28 in. barrels, coin finish receiver with extensive engraving, Italian walnut. Imported 1984-88.

	$305	$280	$265	$240	$215	$205	$190

Last MSR was $335.

Add $85 for Deluxe model.

EUROPA O & U - .410 bore only, 26 in. barrels, coin finish receiver with some engraving, Italian walnut. Imported 1984-88.

	$275	$250	$235	$220	$210	$200	$185

Last MSR was $295.

Add $95 for Deluxe model (disc. 1985).

FRANCIA STANDARD SxS - .410 bore only, double triggers, extractors, checkered walnut. Imported 1986-88.

	$235	$220	$210	$200	$185	$175	$160

Last MSR was $255.

Add $19 for Deluxe Model.

OMEGA STANDARD SxS - 12, 16, or 20 ga., 26 or 28 in. barrels, coin finish receiver with extensive engraving, Italian walnut. Imported 1984-93.

	$780	$695	$550	$450	$375	$300	$250

Last MSR was $880.

Add 32% for auto ejectors.
Add 10% for single trigger (disc. 1985).

GRADING - PPGS™	100%	98%	95%	90%	80%	70%	60%

MILANO O/U - 9mm Flobert, folding design. Imported 1993 only.

	100%	98%	95%	90%	80%	70%	60%
	$380	$330	$295	$250	$210	$180	$150

Last MSR was $420.

VERONA/BERGAMO SxS - 9mm Flobert, folding design, Bergamo model has hammers, Verona model is hammerless. Imported 1993 only.

	$270	$225	$180	$140	$115	$95	$75

Last MSR was $300.

BRESCIA SINGLE BARREL - 9mm Flobert, folding design. Imported 1993 only.

	$175	$150	$130	$110	$90	$70	$55

Last MSR was $200.

BETA SINGLE BARREL - 12, 16, 20, 24, 28, 32 ga., or .410 bore, single barrel field gun, VR, chrome finish receiver, folding design. Imported 1985-93.

	$215	$185	$160	$145	$135	$125	$115

Last MSR was $240.

Add 10% for VR.

SHOTGUNS: SEMI-AUTO

ARIETE STANDARD - 12 ga. only, gas operated, 2 3/4 or 3 in. chamber, various barrel lengths, with or without choke tubes, aluminum receiver, checkered stock and forearm, approx. 6.9 lbs. Imported 1993 only.

	$995	$795	$525	$425	$325	$250	$195

Last MSR was $1,180.

Add $20 for 3 in. mag. variation.

SHOTGUNS: SLIDE ACTION

ARIETE - 12 ga. only, 3 in. chamber, various barrel lengths without VR, twin action bars, matte finish, recoil pad. Imported 1993 only.

	$780	$695	$550	$450	$375	$300	$250

Last MSR was $880.

BERETTA

Current manufacturer located in Brescia, Italy, 1526-present - company name in Italy is Fabbrica d'Armi Pietro Beretta - in Accokeek, MD, 1978 to date. Beretta U.S.A. Corp. was formed in 1977 and is located in Accokeek, MD. Beretta U.S.A. Corp. has been importing Beretta Firearms exclusively since 1980. 1970-1977 manufacture was imported exclusively by Garcia. Distributor and dealer direct sales.

Beretta is one of the world's oldest family owned industrial firms, having started business in 1526. In addition to Beretta owning Benelli & Franchi, the company also purchased Sako and Tikka Companies in late 1999, Aldo Uberti & Co. in 2000, and Burris Optics in 2002. Beretta continues to be a continual leader in firearms development and safety, and shooters attest to the reliability of their weapons worldwide.

For more information and current pricing on both new and used Beretta precision airguns, please refer to the *Blue Book of Airguns* by Dr. Robert Beeman & John Allen (also online).

PISTOLS: SEMI-AUTO, PRE-WWII MFG.

MODEL 1915 - .32 or 9mm Glisenti cal., Beretta's first military pistol, exaggerated slide stop, safety on rear of tang, checkered wood grips, 7 shot mag., serial range 1-16,000.

	$950	$700	$550	$400	$325	$275	$225

9mm Para. cal. is not interchangeable and potentially dangerous if interchanged with 9mm Glisenti cal.

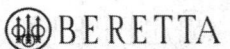

GRADING - PPGS™	100%	98%	95%	90%	80%	70%	60%

MODEL 1915-1917 - later 7.65mm cal. variation, 8 shot mag., exaggerated slide stops, wood grips, sold commercially and to the military. A few marked "RM" were issued to the Italian Navy, ser. no. range 16,000-72,000. Mfg. 1917-21.

	$550	$475	$400	$300	$250	$200	$165

Add 100% if Navy issue.

MODEL 1922 - successor to the Model 1915-1917, mfg. with more open slide and modern slide stop, wood or pressed metal grips, ser. no. range 200,000-243,000. Mfg. 1922-1932.

	$500	$425	$375	$275	$235	$195	$160

Add 100% if Navy issue.

MODEL 1923 - 9mm Glisenti cal., 8 shot, 4 in. barrel, fixed sights, usually with pressed steel grips, less frequently smooth wood with PB emblem, occasionally slotted for shoulder stock. Most were purchased by the Italian Army and marked "RE," ser. no. range 300,000-310,400. Mfg. 1923-26.

	$1,000	$850	$550	$400	$325	$275	$250

Add 25% if slotted for shoulder stock.

MODEL 1919 - .25 ACP cal., SA, 8 shot mag., offered in several variations. First type in serial range 100,000-156,000, subsequent improvement involved changing the disconnector and left panel in the range 156,000-185,000.

	$375	$325	$275	$225	$195	$165	$135

MODEL 1926 - similar to Model 1919, except fit with wood panels bearing an encircled PB. Approx. 11,000 pistols were mfg. in ser. no. range 187,000-198,000.

	$350	$315	$270	$220	$190	$160	$130

MODEL 1926-31 - similar to Model 1926, except has small modifications in the slide, grips are no longer impressed with the PB monogram, interrupted serial range from 198,000-200,000 and 600,000-601,000.

	$325	$310	$265	$215	$190	$160	$125

MODEL 318 - .25 ACP cal., 2 1/2 in. barrel, fixed sights, blue, modifications in the slide legend, grip configuration, and magazine floor plate. Limited production during 1936-37, in ser. no. range 609,000-615,000.

	$275	$240	$215	$180	$160	$140	$120

Add 50%-100% for engraved and plated variations if in 98%+ original condition.

Embellished variations of the Model 318 included the Model 319 (engraved/blue), Model 320 (engraved/nickel plated) and Model 321 (engraved/gold plated).

MODEL 418 - .25 ACP cal., fixed sights, similar to Model 318, but with loaded indicator and grip safety (early type is semi-circular, late type is curved), occasionally was made with an alloy frame, popular pistol mfg. 1937-1961 with minor modifications. Later guns are suffixed with the letters A, B, and C, 178,000 mfg.

	$250	$225	$200	$175	$155	$135	$120

Add 50%-100% for engraved and plated variations if in 98%+ original condition.

Embellished variations of the Model 418 included the Model 419 (engraved blue), Model 420 (engraved nickel), and Model 421 (engraved gold plated).

MODEL 1932 - 7.65mm cal., two variations including straight and curved rear grip strap, smooth wood grips bearing PB monogram (commercial) or RM monogram (Italian Navy). 8,000 mfg. in ser. no. range 400,000-408,000.

	$1,600	$1,250	$750	$550	$400	$350	$300

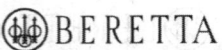

GRADING - PPGS™	100%	98%	95%	90%	80%	70%	60%

MODEL 1934 - 7.65mm or .380 ACP cal., (9mm Kurz cal.), 3 3/8 in. barrel, fixed sights, blue, plastic grips, Italy's service weapon in WWII, one of the most common Beretta pistols - over one million manufactured between 1934-80, many of the military pistols have a parkerized finish, usually fit with metal-backed grips, later guns have an alphabetical prefix. Post-war production (1946) serial numbers start with C00001.

	$395	$325	$275	$225	$195	$165	$135

Add 10% for high polish, unless post-war production.

Add 20% for Italian Air Force.

Add 300% for post-war commercial deluxe pistols which were engraved, gold plated, and cased with a spare mag. and cleaning brush.

MODEL 1935 - similar to the Model 1934, except 7.65mm cal., 3 1/2 in. barrel, fixed sights, blue, plastic grips, the wartime model had poor finish, a small number were fit with an experimental slide safety in the ser. no. range 500,xxx, military issue was often parkerized. 525,000 mfg. 1935-67.

	$350	$315	$270	$220	$190	$160	$130

Add 10% for high polish, unless post-war production.

Add 300% for post-war commercial deluxe pistols which were engraved, gold plated, and cased with a spare mag. and cleaning brush.

PISTOLS: SEMI-AUTO, POST WWII MFG.

100% values on below listed models assume NIB condition.

MODEL 948 - .22 LR cal., 3 1/2 or 6 in. barrel, fixed sights, hammer.

	$175	$150	$125	$100	$75	$60	$50

MODEL 949 OLYMPIC TARGET - .22 S or LR cal., 8 3/4 in. barrel, target sights, adj. barrel weights, blue, muzzle brake, checkered wood grips with thumbrest. Limited mfg. 1959-64.

	$660	$550	$495	$385	$305	$250	$195

MODEL 950CC MINX M2 - .22 short cal., hinged 2 3/8 in. barrel, fixed sights, blue, plastic grips. Mfg. 1955-disc.

	$135	$115	$105	$95	$85	$75	$70

MODEL 950CC SPECIAL MINX M4 - similar to M2, with 4 in. barrel.

	$135	$115	$105	$95	$85	$75	$70

MODEL 950B JETFIRE - similar to M2, in .25 ACP cal.

	$150	$120	$105	$95	$85	$75	$70

MODEL 951 BRIGADIER - 9mm Para. cal., 4 1/2 in. barrel, fixed sights, blue, plastic grips, current Italian service pistol and immediate predecessor to the M92 Series. Mfg. 1952-disc.

	$285	$235	$195	$175	$150	$130	$115

Add $350 for "Egyptian" (denoted by EC prefix) or "Israeli" Model.

MODEL 20 - .25 ACP cal., double action, alloy frame, 9 shot, 2 1/2 in. barrel, plastic or walnut grips, 10.9 oz. Disc. 1985.

	$160	$140	$125	$115	$95	$85	$75

Last MSR was $214.

MODEL 70 PUMA OR COUGAR - .32 ACP or .380 ACP cal., 3 1/2 in. barrel, fixed or adj. sights, blue, plastic grips, .32 Puma alloy frame, .380 Cougar steel frame. Disc.

	$215	$180	$165	$150	$130	$110	$90

Add 10% for .380 ACP cal.

MODEL 70T - .32 ACP cal., similar to Model 70, target sights. Disc.

	$275	$250	$220	$195	$165	$150	$140

GRADING - PPGS™	100%	98%	95%	90%	80%	70%	60%

MODEL 70S - .22 LR or .380 ACP cal., single action, 3 1/2 in. barrel, 9 shot, blue finish, plastic grips, weight .22 cal. - 18 oz., .380 ACP - 23 oz., steel frame, .22 LR has adj. rear sight. Disc. 1985.

	$240	$210	$185	$170	$155	$140	$125

Last MSR was $295.

MODEL 71 JAGUAR - .22 LR cal., version of Model 70, alloy frame. Disc.

	$220	$195	$180	$160	$150	$140	$110

MODEL 72 JAGUAR - similar to 71, with 6 in. barrel. Disc.

	$220	$195	$180	$160	$150	$140	$110

MODEL 76P-76W TARGET PISTOL - .22 LR cal., single action, 11 shot, steel frame, 6 in. barrel, adj. sights, blue finish, thumbrest plastic grips (76-P). Disc. 1985.

	$345	$300	$275	$245	$220	$195	$170

Last MSR was $395.

Add $40 for thumbrest wood grips (Model 76-W).

MODEL 80 - .22 short cal., target pistol with limited importation into the U.S.

	$750	$675	$595	$550	$495	$450	$395

MODEL 81P-81W - .32 ACP cal., double action, 13 shot, 3.8 in. barrel, fixed sights, blue. Imported 1976-84.

	$300	$250	$225	$195	$175	$155	$135

Add $90 for nickel finish.
Add $20 for wood grips (W suffix).

MODEL 82W - .32 ACP cal., double action, more compact than Model 81, 10 shot, walnut grips, 17 oz. Importation disc. 1984.

	$295	$250	$225	$195	$175	$155	$135

Add $75 for nickel finish.

MODEL 84B - .380 ACP cal., double action, brown wood or plastic grips, 13 shot mag., blue finish, fixed sights. Disc.

	$295	$250	$225	$195	$175	$155	$135

MODEL 84W-EL - similar to Model 84 but specially engraved, select walnut grips. Presentation case. Disc. 1984.

	$1,025	$770	$720	$615	$565	$520	$460

MODEL 86P-86W - .380 ACP cal. only, double action, tip-up 4 1/3 in. barrel, 8 shot mag., plastic or walnut grips, 23 oz. While this model was advertised, it was never released.
MSR was $480 in 1986, walnut grips were $80 extra (86-W).

MODEL 90 DOUBLE ACTION AUTOMATIC - .32 ACP cal., 3 5/8 in. barrel, fixed sights, blue, plastic grips. Mfg. 1969-83.

	$275	$195	$175	$155	$130	$110	$95

Add 25% if without external slide latch.

MODEL 100 - .32 ACP cal., fixed sights. Disc.

	$250	$220	$195	$165	$150	$140	$130

MODEL 101 - similar to Model 70T, except in .22 LR. Disc.

	$250	$220	$195	$165	$150	$140	$130

MODEL 102 - .22 LR cal., target pistol, single action, steel/alloy construction, plastic grips, 10 shot mag. with finger extension, adj. rear sight. Disc.

	$325	$250	$220	$195	$165	$150	$140

PISTOLS: SEMI-AUTO, RECENT AND CURRENT MFG.

On Beretta's large frame pistols, alphabetical suffixes refer to the following: F Model - double/single action system with external safety decocking lever, G Model - double/single action system with external decocking only lever, D Model - double action only without safety lever, DS Model - double action only with external safety lever.

The models in this section appear in numerical sequence.

MODEL 21(A)-W BOBCAT - .22 LR or .25 ACP cal., double action, alloy frame, 7 (.22 LR) or 8 (.25 ACP) shot mag., 2.4 in. barrel, plastic or walnut (EL Model, disc. 2000) grips, 11 1/2 oz.

❋ *Blue Finish*

	100%	98%	95%	90%	80%	70%	60%
MSR $315	$245	$195	$150	$130	$115	$95	$85

   Add approx. $75 for engraving and wood grips (EL Model, disc. 2000).

❋ *Nickel Finish* - disc. 2000.

	98%	95%	90%	80%	70%	60%
	$255	$215	$165	$140	$130	$115	$95

                                       Last MSR was $322.

❋ *Matte Finish* - matte finished metal, plastic grips. New 1992.

	100%	98%	95%	90%	80%	70%	60%
MSR $275	$215	$180	$145	$115	$95	$85	$80

   This model is manufactured by Beretta U.S.A. Corp. in Accokeek, MD.

❋ *Stainless Steel (Inox)* - similar to Model 21 Bobcat, except is .22 LR only, stainless steel with plastic grips, approx. 11.5 oz. New 2000.

	100%	98%	95%
MSR $340	$265	$220	$170

❋ *Lady Beretta* - .22 LR cal. only, similar to Model 21-W, except is specially serial numbered and has gold etching on top of frame and slide sides. Supplied with a blue velvet drawstring bag. 1990 issue.

	100%	98%	95%	90%	80%	70%	60%
	$245	$185	$160	$140	$130	$115	$100

                                       Last MSR was $285.

   This model was sold exclusively by Lew Horton Distributing Co.

MODEL U22 NEOS - .22 LR cal., single action, unique design features modular construction and modern styling, matte black finish, 10 shot mag., 4.5 or 6 in. barrel with sights incorporated into integral full length sight rail, various colored grips with interchangeable rubber inlays in aqua, grey, or blue (black standard), 31.5 or 36 oz. New 2002.

	100%	98%	95%	90%	80%	70%	60%
MSR $285	$230	$195	$170	$145	$120	$100	$90

   This model is also available in a carbine kit, which includes a 16 in. barrel and skeletonized buttstock. Current MSR is $282 (not legal in CA).

❋ *Model U22 Neos Inox* - similar to Model U22 Neos, except slide and barrel are stainless steel. New 2002.

	100%	98%	95%
MSR $335	$270	$220	$185

MODEL U22 NEOS DLX - .22 LR cal., similar to Model U22 Neos, except includes adj. trigger and interchangeable front and rear sights (six included), 6 or 7.5 in. barrel, laser engraved "U22 NEOS" on slide. New mid-2003.

	100%	98%	95%	90%	80%	70%	60%
MSR $355	$285	$230	$200	$170	$145	$125	$110

❋ *Model U22 Neos DLX Inox* - similar to U22 Neos DLX, except is stainless steel. New mid-2003.

	100%	98%	95%
MSR $395	$320	$255	$215

MODEL 71 - .22 LR cal., single action, 8 shot, 6 in. barrel, plastic grips with thumbrest, finger extension mag. Imported 1987 only.

	100%	98%	95%	90%	80%	70%	60%
	$190	$160	$140	$130	$115	$95	$85

                                       Last MSR was $215.

GRADING - PPGS™	100%	98%	95%	90%	80%	70%	60%

MODEL 84 CHEETAH

.380 ACP cal., single/double action semi-auto, 3.82 in. barrel, alloy frame, steel slide, 10 (C/B 1994) or 13* (reintroduced late 2004) shot staggered mag., firing pin block, ambidextrous manual safety (also used as a decocking lever), low profile 3 dot sights, curved trigger guard, plastic or wood (available with nickel finish) grips, blue (disc.), Bruniton, or nickel (disc. 2001, reintroduced 2004) finish, 23.3 oz.

MSR $625	$475	$380	$330	$275	$240	$210	$190

Add $30 for wood grips (Model 84W, disc. 2001).

Add $65 for nickel finish (Model 84FS, includes checkered wood grips).

✳ *Model 84F* - similar specifications to the Model 84P-84W, except patterned after the Model 92F Govt. Model, matte black Bruniton finish, squared off trigger guard, plastic or wood grips, 23 oz. Mfg. 1990 only.

		$395	$330	$300	$270	$240	$210	$190

Last MSR was $479.

MODEL 85 CHEETAH

.380 ACP cal., same general specifications as the Model 84, except slimmer profile because of 8 shot straight line mag., Model 85P has plastic grips, 21.9 oz.

MSR $590	$455	$355	$300	$250	$210	$190	$175

Add $75 for nickel finish (includes wood grips, disc. 2001, reintroduced 2004).

Add $33 for wood grips with blue finish (Model 85W – disc. 2000).

✳ *Model 85F* - similar specifications to the Model 85P-85W, except patterned after the Model 92F Govt. Model, matte black Bruniton finish, squared off trigger guard, plastic or wood grips, 21.8 oz. Mfg. in 1990 only.

		$375	$300	$270	$240	$210	$190	$175

Last MSR was $440.

Add $25 for wood grips.

MODEL 86 CHEETAH

.380 ACP cal., single/double action semi-auto with 4.4 in. tip-up barrel, 8 shot mag., checkered walnut grips, matte Bruniton finish, fixed sights, gold trigger, 23.3 oz. Imported 1991-2004.

		$500	$390	$320	$250	$225	$190	$175

Last MSR was $615.

MODEL 87 CHEETAH

.22 LR cal., single/double action semi-auto, 7 shot mag., 3.82 or 6 in. target barrel with counterweight (disc. 1994), blue finish, wood grips, 20 oz. (3.82 in. barrel). Importation began 1986.

MSR $625	$510	$395	$325	$250	$225	$190	$175

✳ *Model 87 Target* - single action only target variation of the Model 87 with 5.9 in. barrel, 10 shot mag., 23.3 (older mfg.) or 41 (new mfg.) oz. Disc. 1994, reintroduced 2000.

MSR $710	$600	$465	$380	$340	$290	$255	$215

This model was reintroduced in 2000, and now features adj. rear target sight, integral scope base rail that is machined on the aluminum barrel sleeve, and Bruniton finish with anodized aluminum frame.

MODEL 89 GOLD STANDARD

.22 LR cal., single action target semi-auto, matte Bruniton black finish on metal parts, 6 in. barrel, 10 shot mag., anatomical wood grips, adj. sights, 41 oz. Imported 1988-2000.

		$630	$510	$410	$360	$310	$275	$250

Last MSR was $802.

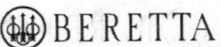
GRADING - PPGS™	100%	98%	95%	90%	80%	70%	60%

MODEL 950 JETFIRE (BS) - .22 Short (disc. 1992) or .25 ACP cal., single action, alloy frame, 8 shot (.25 cal. only) or 6 shot mag., tip-up 2 1/2 and 4 in. (.22 S only) barrel, plastic grips, thumb safety, matte (new 1992, plastic grips only), blue or nickel finish, 9.9 oz. Disc. 2002.

		$180	$140	$115	$100	$90	$80	$70

Last MSR was $226.

Add $22 for blue finish (disc. 1999).
Add $80 for nickel finish (disc. 1999).
This model is manufactured by Beretta U.S.A. Corp. in Accokeek, MD.

✳ *Model 950 Jetfire Stainless (Inox)* - similar to Model 950 BS, except is stainless steel. Mfg. 2000-2002.

$210	$150	$120

Last MSR was $267.

✳ *Model 950 EL* - same general specifications as Model 950 BS, only with wood grips and gold plated parts. Disc. 1999.

$275	$230	$200	$180	$165	$150	$135

Last MSR was $337.

MODEL 3032 TOMCAT - .32 ACP cal., similar to Model 21 Bobcat, except has 2.45 in. barrel, 7 shot mag., choice of matte or blue finish, plastic grips, regular or Tritium AO Big Dot Express (new 2002) sights, approx. 14.5 oz., mfg. by Beretta U.S.A. New 1996.

MSR $370	$285	$220	$170	$135	$115	$95	$85

Add $20 for blue finish.
Add $80 for Alley Cat package – includes Tritium AO Big Dot Express sights and in-the-pants Alcantara synthetic holster.

✳ *Model 3032 Tomcat Stainless (Inox)* - similar to Model 3032 Tomcat, except has stainless steel slide and barrel, grey anodized alloy frame, 15.8 oz. New 2000.

MSR $460	$350	$265	$200

✳ *Model 3032 Tomcat Titanium* - similar to Model 3032 Tomcat, except has titanium frame, blue finish only, 16.9 oz. Mfg. 2001-late 2002.

$460	$360	$310

Last MSR was $589.

MODEL 8000 COUGAR F/D - 9mm Para. cal., single/double (Model 8000 Cougar F) or DA (Model 8000 Cougar D, disc. 2000) only, short recoil system with 3.6 in. rotating barrel, 10 or 13 (became option late 2004) shot mag., fixed sights, anodized aluminum alloy frame, black plastic grips, Bruniton matte black finish, 32.6 oz. Mfg. 1995-2005.

$665	$575	$440	$385	$335	$300	$275

Last MSR was $800.

✳ *Model 8000 Mini Cougar* - similar to Model 8000 Cougar, except overall height has been reduced to 4 1/2 in. and weight is 27.6 oz. Mfg. 1998-2003.

$600	$545	$415	$375	$330	$300	$275

Last MSR was $709.

✳ *Model 8000L Cougar* - similar to Model 8000F Cougar, except has shortened grip, 10 or 13 (optional late 2004) shot double stack mag., 28.2 oz. Mfg. 2003-2005.

$665	$575	$440	$385	$335	$300	$275

Last MSR was $800.

✳ *Model 8000 Cougar (Inox)* - similar to Model 8000F Cougar, except is stainless steel. Limited mfg. 2004 only.

$715	$575	$450

Last MSR was $875.

GRADING - PPGS™	100%	98%	95%	90%	80%	70%	60%

MODEL 8040 COUGAR F/D

MODEL 8040 COUGAR F/D - .40 S&W cal., single/double (Model 8040 Cougar F) or DA (Model 8040 Cougar D, disc. 2000) only, short recoil system with 3.6 in. rotating barrel, 10 or 11 (became optional late 2004) shot mag., fixed sights, anodized aluminum alloy frame, Bruniton matte black finish, 32.4 oz. Mfg. 1995-2005.

	$665	$575	$440	$385	$335	$300	$275

Last MSR was $800.

✳ *Model 8040 Cougar (Inox)* - similar to Model 8040F Cougar, except is stainless steel. Limited mfg. 2004 only.

	$715	$575	$450				

Last MSR was $875.

✳ *Model 8040 Mini Cougar* - similar to Model 8040 Cougar, except overall height has been reduced to 4 1/2 in. and weight is 27.6 oz., supplied with 8 and extended 10 shot mag. Mfg. 1998-2003.

	$600	$545	$415	$375	$330	$300	$275

Last MSR was $709.

MODEL 8045 COUGAR F/D

MODEL 8045 COUGAR F/D - .45 ACP cal., 8 shot mag., otherwise similar to Models 8000 and 8040, 32 oz. Mfg. 1998-2004, D Model disc. 2002.

	$710	$560	$450	$395	$345	$300	$275

Last MSR was $860.

Subtract approx. $25 for Model 8045 Cougar D (DA only, disc. 2002).

✳ *Model 8045 Mini Cougar D/F* - similar to Model 8045 Cougar, except overall height has been reduced to 4 1/2 in. and weight is 27.6 oz, supplied with 6 shot mag. Importation began 1999, D Model disc. 2002, F disc. in 2003.

	$635	$515	$435	$385	$340	$300	$275

Last MSR was $764.

Subtract approx. $25 for Model 8045 Mini-Cougar D (DA only, disc. 2002).

MODEL 8357 COUGAR F

MODEL 8357 COUGAR F - .357 Sig cal., single/double action, 5.5 in. barrel, blue finish with plastic grips, 10 shot mag., 32.4 oz. Mfg. 2001-2004.

	$665	$575	$450	$395	$350	$300	$275

Last MSR was $800.

MODEL 9000S TYPE F/D

MODEL 9000S TYPE F/D - 9mm Para. or .40 S&W cal., single/double (Model 9000S Type F) or DA only (Model 9000S Type D, disc. 2003), 3.5 in. tilt barrel, 10 or 12 (9mm Para. only, optional late 2004) shot mag., spurless (Type D only) or external (Type F) hammer, ambidextrous safety with hammer decocking, sub-compact pistol utilizing state of the art ergonomic design by Giugiaro Design, matte black technopolymer frame, overmolded rubber grip, cased, approx. 26.5 oz. New 2000.

MSR $485	$410	$330	$285	$260	$240	$220	$200

Add $24 for B-Lok safety system using key lock (mfg. 2003, Type F only).

Pistols: Semi-Auto, Model 92 & Variations - 5.9 in. barrel

MODEL 92 COMBAT

MODEL 92 COMBAT - similar to Model 92, except has 5.9 in. target barrel, blue finish, plastic grips, only 50 imported into the U.S. for competition.

	$775	$625	$475	$300	$255	$240	$220

Pistols: Semi-Auto, Model 92 & Variations - 4.9 in. barrel

MODEL 92 (FIRST SERIES)

MODEL 92 (FIRST SERIES) - 4.9 in. barrel, early production Model 92s had a flat slide, frame mounted safety, and mag. release button at base of pistol grip. Production of the M92 was approx. 5,000 pistols. Originally mfg. 1976. Disc.

	$750	$600	$450	$300	$255	$240	$220

MODEL 92S (SECOND SERIES)

MODEL 92S (SECOND SERIES) - similar to Model 92, except has a slide mounted firing pin safety. Disc.

	$575	$475	$375	$300	$250	$240	$220

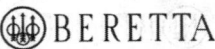
GRADING - PPGS™	100%	98%	95%	90%	80%	70%	60%

MODEL 92SB-P (THIRD SERIES) - 9mm Luger cal., double action, 15 shot mag., 4.9 in. barrel, fixed sights, alloy frame, high-polish blue finish, plastic grips (Model 92SB-P), conventionally located push button magazine release, ambidextrous safety, 34 1/2 oz. Mfg. 1980-85.

	$525	$425	$395	$350	$325	$295	$270

Last MSR was $600.

✳ *Model 92SB-W* - similar to above, only with wood grips. Disc. 1985.

	$550	$450	$400	$355	$330	$290	$260

Last MSR was $620.

MODEL 92D - 9mm Para. cal., double action only, otherwise similar to Model 92F, except does not have a manual safety lever, includes black plastic grips, 3 dot sights, 33.8 oz. Introduced 1992 - disc. 1998.

	$475	$400	$350	$300	$250	$210	$190

Last MSR was $586.

Add $90 for Tritium (new 1994) sight system.

Add 10% for Trijicon (disc.) sights.

MODEL 92FS & 92F - 9mm Para. cal., official U.S. military variation of 92 Series, 4.9 in. barrel, alloy frame, steel slide, 10 (C/B 1994), or 15* (reintroduced late 2004, optional) shot mag., chamber loaded indicator, matte black Bruniton or olive drab (mfg. 2004) finish, squared off trigger guard to facilitate two-hand shooting, extended mag. base, choice of regular or 3 dot sights (new 1991), approx 34.5 oz. Model 92F-P has plastic grips. Model 92F-W has wood grips. New 1984.

MSR $715	$595	$485	$430	$380	$340	$300	$275

Add $25 for olive drab finish (mfg. 2004 only).

Add $24 for B-Lok safety system using key lock (mfg. 2003 only).

Add $462 for .22 LR conversion kit (includes slide, barrel, spring, follower, and .22 LR mag., new 2002).

Add approx. $20 for checkered wood grips (Model 92F-W, disc. 1998).

Add approx. $80 for Tritium sight system (mfg. 1994-98).

Add 10% for Trijicon (disc.) sights.

Add approx. $175 for gold engraving/accenting (Model EL-3, 92F-W only, disc. 1998).

Add $395 for 9mm Competition Conversion Kit (mfg. 1992-98).

The Model 92FS incorporates a slide retaining pin engineering change not included in the Model 92F.

The U.S. military on January 15, 1985 announced that the M9 military variation of the commercial Model 92F would replace the Colt Govt. Model .45 ACP as the standard government issue sidearm. Because of domestic political pressures, Congress requested that a new sidearm competition be conducted again in 1988. The result of this second trial was that the Department of the Army announced on May 22, 1989 that Beretta had won again. This military contract with Beretta U.S.A. Corp. initially involved over 320,000 Model M9s (military designation for the commercial Model 92F) manufactured for U.S. military consumption in the 1990s. Actual delivery of commercial Model 92s began in January of 1986, while M9 delivery to U.S. Armed Forces exceeded 430,000 units, and was completed in 1999.

✳ *Model 92FS & 92F Stainless (Inox)* - similar to Model 92F/92FS, except is mfg. from stainless steel, satin finish with plastic grips, 3 dot sights, initially released to law enforcement agencies only, this model is now commercially manufactured in quantity.

MSR $795	$650	$525	$415				

Add $180 for laser grips (new 2004).

Add $24 for B-Lok safety system using key lock (mfg. 2003 only).

Add approx. $20 for wood grips (disc. 1998).

Add approx. $90 for Trijicon (1993 only) or Tritium (mfg. 1994-98) sight system.

GRADING - PPGS™	100%	98%	95%	90%	80%	70%	60%

MODEL 92FS BRIGADIER - similar to the Model 92FS, except has heavier slide to reduce felt recoil, wraparound rubber grips, and 3 dot sights, 35.3 oz. New 1999.

	100%	98%	95%	90%	80%	70%	60%
MSR $795	$650	$525	$425	$385	$335	$300	$275

✳ *Model 92FS Brigadier Stainless (Inox)* - similar to Model 92FS Brigadier, except is stainless steel, 35.3 oz. New 2000.

MSR $845	$690	$575	$475				

MODEL 92FS B.A.T.S. - 9mm Para. cal., 4.9 in. barrel, features black matte Bruniton finish and textured rubber wraparound grips with finger grooves, package includes both 10 and 15 shot mags., Airlight knife, aluminum carrying case, 34.4 oz. Limited mfg. late 2000 only.

		$665	$550	$465	$415	$360	$300	$275

Last MSR was $785.

MODEL 92FS VERTEC - 9mm Para. cal., single/double action, features vertical grip design, special short reach trigger, thin dual textured grip panels, and integral accessory rail on lower frame, removable front sight, beveled 10 shot mag., Bruniton finish, 32.2 oz. New 2002.

MSR $760	$635	$495	$440	$385	$340	$300	$275

Add $25 for B-Lok safety system using key lock (mfg. 2003).

✳ *Model 92FS Vertec Stainless (Inox)* - stainless variation of the Model 92FS Vertec. New 2002.

MSR $825	$670	$525	$425				

Add $170 for laser grips (new 2004).

Add $25 for B-Lok safety system using key lock (mfg. 2003).

MODEL 92 BLACK INOX - 9mm Para. cal., single/double action, features black stainless slide and stipled, finger groove plastic grips. Limited mfg. 2002 only.

	$610	$485	$390				

Last MSR was $734.

MODEL 92 BILLENIUM - 9mm Para. cal., single action only, frame mounted safety, contoured steel frame with checkered grip straps and contoured carbon fiber grips, interchangeable sights, oversize mag. release button, unique slide serrations and Billenium engraving, nickel alloy surface treatment finish, includes deluxe lockable carrying case, 43.3 oz. Limited mfg. in Italy of 2,000 during 2002-2003.

	$1,100	$900	$750	$650	$575	$500	$425

Last MSR was $1,429.

MODEL 92 STEEL I - 9mm Para. cal., single action only or SA/DA, plastic grips, features all-steel construction, frame mounted safety, nickel alloy finish, includes two 10 shot mags., 41.1 oz. New 2004.

MSR $1,600	$1,295	$1,150	$900	$825	$750	$675	$595

MODEL 92FS YEAR 2000 - 9mm Para. cal., 4.9 in. barrel, matte black Bruniton finish, features rosewood laminate grips with Beretta "trident" logo on brass medallions. 2,000 mfg. during 2000 only.

	$615	$500	$450	$400	$350	$300	$275

Last MSR was $726.

MODEL 92F-ELS - deluxe variation of the Model 92F featuring high polish stainless steel finish with gold highlights on trim, frame etchings, and small parts, plastic grips. Mfg. 1992-94.

	$685	$550	$425				

Last MSR was $790.

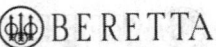
MODEL 92F/FS "UNITED WE STAND" LIMITED EDITION
- 9mm Para. cal., features laser etched gold American flag and "United We Stand" slide lettering, Bruniton finish, black plastic grips. Mfg. limited to 2001 (Model 92F) and 3,900 (Model 92FS) pistols in late 2001 - early 2002.

	100%	98%	95%	90%	80%	70%	60%
	$625	$560	$485	$425	$375	$300	$275

Last MSR $734.

Beretta USA made a donation from the proceeds of this model to the NYPD Foundation and the Survivor's Fund of the National Capitol Region.

MODEL 92FS 470th ANNIVERSARY LIMITED EDITION
- features stainless steel construction with mirror polished finish, smooth select walnut grips with inlaid gold plated medallions, gold filled engraving with Dr. Ugo Gussalli-Beretta's signature, 470th Anniversary logos, only 470 mfg. (with "1 of 470" gold filled on each gun) beginning 1999, lockable walnut case. Disc. 2004.

$1,950 $1,575 $1,100

Last MSR was $2,217.

MODEL 92F/FS "DESERT STORM" SPECIAL EDITION
- 9mm Para. cal., features U.S. Central Command seal, marked "Official Sidearm U.S. Armed Forces" on left side of slide, right side is marked "DESERT STORM", stamped "15 January 1991 - 11 April 1991", special ser. no. Approx. 8,000 mfg. 1991-92.

$625 $560 $485 $425 $375 $300 $275

Last MSR was $660.

MODEL 92F DELUXE
- deluxe model featuring gold or silver plating and elaborate engraving. Importation began 1993.

MSR $5,750 $4,950 $3,750 $2,500

This model is available at the Beretta Galleries or select Beretta Premium dealers only.

MODEL 92G
- 9mm Para. cal., identical to the Model 92F, except features a spring loaded decocking lever that safely lowers the hammer allowing fire-ready when unholstering the pistol. New 1990.

The Model 92G is sold to law enforcement agencies only and prices are slightly higher than the standard Model 92FS. This pistol has been used by French Gendarmes since 1987.

MODEL 92G-SD
- 9mm Para. cal., similar to Model 92G, except has an integral accessory rail machined into frame in front of trigger guard for sighting devices, Bruniton finish, 10 shot mag., Tritium sights, 35.3 oz. New 2003.

MSR $1,175 $955 $745 $585 $510 $450 $400 $350

MODEL 92F WITH U.S. M9 MARKED SLIDE/FRAME
- 9mm Para. cal., approx. 2,000 mfg. with special serial no. range, "BER" prefix, government assembly numbers on frame, slide, hammer, mag. etc. Mfg. for the Armed Forces Reserve shooters, identical to military M9, except for serial number.

$1,000 $900 $800 $725 $650 $575 $500

MODEL 92FS OPERATION ENDURING FREEDOM
- 9mm Para. cal., M9 U.S. Army edition, two 10 shot mags., "BER" prefix, 2,500 mfg. 2003 only.

$625 $500 $425

Last MSR was $712.

M9 LIMITED STANDARD EDITION
- commercial limited edition of the U.S. Govt. M9 military pistol, features gold inscribed slide legend "The First Decade 1985-1995", Air Force or Marine Corps emblems on right slide side, 10,000 mfg. during 1995-97.

$600 $475 $425

Last MSR was $643.

✳ ***M9 Limited Deluxe Edition*** - features checkered walnut grips, gold-plated hammer, grip screws, and mag. release button. Disc. 1997.

$695 $525 $475

Last MSR was $750.

GRADING - PPGS™	100%	98%	95%	90%	80%	70%	60%

M9 SPECIAL EDITION - patterned after the U.S. Armed Forces M9, special M9-XXXX ser. no. range, one 15 shot mag. (pre-1994 mfg.), dot and post sight system, M9 military packaging including Army operator's manual, Bianchi M12 holster, mag. pouch, and web pistol belt. Mfg. 1998-2000.

	$850	$700	$550				

Last MSR was $861.

Pistols: Semi-Auto, Model 92 & Variations - 4.7 in. barrel

MODEL 92FS INOX TACTICAL - 9mm Para. cal., 4.7 in. barrel, features satin matte finished stainless steel slide and alloy frame, rubber grips, Tritium sights. Mfg. 1999-2000.

	$695	$560	$480	$425	$375	$325	$295

Last MSR was $822.

MODEL 92FS BORDER MARSHAL - 9mm Para. cal., commercial equivalent of the I.N.S. (Immigration & Naturalization Service) government contract, 4.7 in. barrel, heavy duty steel slide, Tritium sights, Border Marshal engraving on the slide. Mfg. 1999-2000.

	$670	$560	$480	$425	$375	$325	$295

Last MSR was $802.

MODEL 92G ELITE IA (BRIGADIER) - 9mm Para. cal., similar to Model 92FS Brigadier, except has 4.7 in. stainless barrel and many standard I.D.P.A. competition features including front and rear serrated slide, skeletonized hammer, and removable 3 dot sighting system, plastic grips, includes Elite engraving on slide, 35.3 oz. New 1999.

MSR $875	$725	$585	$495	$425	$360	$300	$275

✴ *Model 92G Elite II (Brigadier)* - similar to Model 92G Elite, except has stainless steel slide with black "Elite II" markings, target barrel crown, extended mag. release, optimized trigger mechanism, front and back strap checkering, low profile Novak rear sight, 35 oz. New mid-2000.

MSR $985	$815	$635	$530	$450	$385	$325	$295

Pistols: Semi-Auto, Model 92 & Variations - 4.3 in. barrel

MODEL 92D CENTURION - 9mm Para. cal., compact variation with 4.3 in. barrel, plastic grips only, without safety, choice of 3 dot or Tritium sights. Mfg. 1994-98.

	$460	$360	$300	$250	$210	$190	$175

Last MSR was $586.

Add $90 for Tritium sights.

MODEL 92SB-P COMPACT - similar to Model 92SB, except has 4.3 in. barrel, 14 shot, plastic grips (Model 92SB-P), rarer when frontstrap has curved lip, 31 oz. Disc. 1985.

	$500	$440	$385	$345	$310	$285	$260

Last MSR was $620.

Add $60 for nickel finish.

✴ *Model 92SB-W Compact* - similar to above only with wood grips. Disc. 1985.

	$525	$465	$395	$355	$335	$300	$280

Last MSR was $635.

MODEL 92F/92FS COMPACT - similar to Model 92F, except has 4.3 in. barrel and 13 shot mag., plastic or wood grips, 31 1/2 oz. While temporarily suspended in 1986, production was resumed 1989-93.

	$550	$450	$415	$375	$335	$300	$275

Last MSR was $625.

Add $20 for checkered walnut grips (Model 92F Wood).
Add $65 for Trijicon sight system.

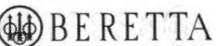
❋ *Model 92F Compact "M"* - similar to Model 92F Compact, except has 8 shot straight line mag., plastic grips only. Imported 1990-93.

$550	$450	$415	$375	$335	$300	$275

Last MSR was $625.

Add $65 for Trijicon sight system.
Approx. 1,200 92SBM Models were imported in the 1980s.

MODEL 92F & 92FS CENTURION - similar to Model 92F, except has compact barrel slide unit with full size frame, 4.3 in. barrel, choice of plastic or wood grips, 3 dot sight system, same length as Model 92F Compact, 10 (C/B 1994) or 15* shot mag., 33.2 oz. Mfg. 1992-98.

$525	$435	$395	$365	$335	$300	$275

Last MSR was $613.

Add approx. $20 for checkered walnut grips (Model 92F Wood).
Add $90 for Tritium sight system (mfg. 1994-98).
Add 10% for Trijicon sights (disc.).

MODEL 92FS COMPACT - 9mm Para. cal., similar to Model 92 Compact Type M, except has 10 shot staggered mag., 35.3 oz. Mfg. 1999-2003.

$575	$465	$415	$370	$335	$300	$275

Last MSR was $691.

❋ *Model 92FS Compact Stainless (Inox)* - similar to Model 92FS Compact, except is stainless steel. Mfg. 2000-2003.

$620	$490	$395

Last MSR was $748.

❋ *Model 92FS Custom Carry* - 9mm Para. cal., 4.3 in. barrel, shortened grip, low profile control levers, left side only safety lever, blue only, 10 shot staggered mag., plastic grips. Mfg. 1999-2000.

$550	$450	$400	$365	$335	$300	$275

Last MSR was $655.

❋ *Model 92FS Custom Carry II (Type M)* - 9mm Para. cal., similar dimensions as Custom Carry, except is stainless steel construction with black components and black slide markings, Novak low profile 3-dot sights, 8 shot single stack mag., 30.9 oz. Mfg. 2000.

$560	$455	$410

Last MSR was $669.

MODEL 92 TYPE M COMPACT - same features as the Model 92FS, except has 4.3 in. barrel, overall height is 5.3 in., Bruniton matte finish, choice of single/double or double action only (disc. 1998), plastic grips, single column 8 shot mag., 30.9 oz. Mfg. 1998-2003.

$575	$465	$415	$370	$335	$300	$275

Last MSR was $691.

Add approx. $90 for Tritium sight system (disc. 1998).
Subtract approx. $25 for double action only (disc. 1998).

❋ *Model 92 Type M Compact Stainless (Inox)* - similar to Model 92 Type M, except is stainless steel. Mfg. 2000-2003.

$615	$475	$395

Last MSR was $748.

Pistols: Semi-Auto, Model 96 & Variations, Recent Mfg.

The models in this section appear in approximate chronological sequence.

MODEL 96D - .40 S&W cal., 4.9 in. barrel, double action only variation of the Model 96F, no safety, 3 dot sight system, 33.8 oz. Introduced 1992 - disc. 1998.

$460	$360	$300	$250	$210	$190	$175

Last MSR was $586.

Add $90 for Tritium sight system (new 1994).
Add $65 for Trijicon sights (disc.).

GRADING - PPGS™	100%	98%	95%	90%	80%	70%	60%

❋ *Model 96D Centurion* - similar to Model 96D, except is compact variation with 4.3 in. barrel, 3 dot sights. Mfg. 1994-98.

	$460	$360	$300	$250	$210	$190	$175

Last MSR was $586.

Add $90 for Tritium sight system.

MODEL 96, 96F, & 96FS - .40 S&W cal., similar to Model 92F, 4.9 in. barrel, plastic grips only, flared grip with grip strap serrations, Bruniton matte black finish, 3 dot sight system, 10 or 11 (optional) shot mag., 34.4 oz. Introduced 1992.

MSR $715	$595	$475	$420	$380	$335	$300	$275

Add $24 for B-Lok safety system with key lock (mfg. 2003).
Add $91 for Tritium sight system (mfg. 1994-99).
Add 10% for Trijicon sights (disc.).
Current model nomenclature for this pistol is the Model 96.

❋ *Model 96, 96FS Stainless (Inox)* - stainless variation of the Model 96FS, rubber grips, 34.4 oz. Importation began 1999.

MSR $795	$650	$525	$425

Add $24 for B-Lok safety system with key lock (mfg. 2003).
Current model nomenclature for this pistol is the Model 96 Inox.

❋ *Model 96F Compact* - 4.3 in. barrel, 10 shot mag., 3 dot sights, plastic grips, approx. 32 oz. Mfg. 2000-2003.

	$580	$465	$415	$370	$335	$300	$275

Last MSR was $691.
While advertised during the 1990s, this gun finally went into production during 2000.

❋ *Model 96F Compact Stainless (Inox)* - similar to Model 96F Compact, except is stainless steel. Mfg. 2000-2003.

	$620	$500	$415

Last MSR was $748.

❋ *Model 96F Centurion* - similar to Model 96F, except has 4.3 in. barrel, 33.2 oz. Mfg. 1992-99.

	$525	$435	$395	$365	$335	$300	$275

Last MSR was $613.

Add $91 for Tritium sight system (new 1994).

❋ *Model 96 Stainless (Inox) "United We Stand" Limited Edition* - 40 S&W cal., features laser etched gold American flag and "United We Stand" slide lettering. Mfg. limited to 3,900 pistols in late 2001 - early 2002.

	$625	$560	$485

Last MSR $734.
Beretta USA made a donation from the proceeds of this model to the NYPD Foundation and the Survivor's Fund of the National Capitol Region.

❋ *Model 96FS B.A.T.S.* - .40 S&W cal., 4.9 in. barrel, features black matte Bruniton finish and textured rubber wraparound grips with finger grooves, package includes both 10 and 11 shot mags., Airlight knife, aluminum carrying case, 34.4 oz. Limited mfg. mid-2000 only.

	$665	$550	$465	$415	$360	$300	$275

Last MSR was $785.

❋ *Model 96G Elite IA (Brigadier)* - .40 S&W cal., similar to Model 96 Brigadier, except has 4.7 in. stainless barrel and many standard I.D.P.A. competition features including front and rear serrated slide, skeletonized hammer, and removable 3 dot sighting system, plastic grips, includes Elite engraving on slide. New 1999.

MSR $875	$725	$575	$480	$420	$350	$300	$275

GRADING - PPGS™	100%	98%	95%	90%	80%	70%	60%

✳ Model 96G Elite II (Brigadier) - similar to Model 96G Elite, except has stainless steel slide with black "Elite II" markings, target barrel crown, extended mag. release, optimized trigger mechanism, front and back strap checkering, low profile Novak rear sight, 35.3 oz. New mid-2000.

MSR $985	$815	$625	$525	$450	$385	$325	$295

MODEL 96G-SD - .40 S&W cal., similar to Model 92G that allows ready-fire, except has an integral accessory rail machined into frame in front of trigger guard for sighting devices, Bruniton finish, 10 shot mag., Tritium sights, 35.3 oz. New 2003.

MSR $1,175	$955	$725	$625	$525	$450	$400	$350

MODEL 96 STEEL I - .40 S&W cal., single action only or SA/DA, plastic grips, features all steel construction, nickel alloy frame, slim vertical grip, frame mounted safety, includes two 10 shot mags. New 2004.

MSR $1,600	$1,295	$1,140	$950	$825	$750	$675	$595

MODEL 96 COMBAT - .40 S&W cal., single action only, similar to Model 96 Stock, except has factory tuned trigger, 4.9 (new 1998) or 5.9 in. barrel with weight and fully adj. rear target sight, aluminum or plastic grips. Mfg. in Italy 1997-2001.

	$1,350	$1,060	$900	$775	$625	$550	$495

Last MSR was $1,735.

Add approx. $250 for 5.9 in. barrel (previously available as a Combat Combo).

MODEL 96 VERTEC - .40 S&W cal., single/double action, 4.9 in. barrel, features vertical grip design, special short reach trigger, thin dual textured grip panels, and integral accessory rail on lower frame, removable front sight, beveled 10 shot mag., Bruniton finish, 32.2 oz. New 2002.

MSR $760	$635	$495	$440	$385	$340	$300	$275

Add $25 for B-Lok safety system with key lock (mfg. 2003).

✳ Model 96 Vertec Stainless (Inox) - stainless variation of the Model 96 Vertec. New 2002.

MSR $825	$670	$530	$430

Add $25 for B-Lok safety system with key lock (mfg. 2003).

MODEL 96 BLACK INOX - .40 S&W cal., single/double action, features black stainless slide and stippled, finger groove plastic grips. Limited mfg. 2002 only.

$610	$485	$390

Last MSR was $734.

MODEL 96 BORDER MARSHAL - .40 S&W cal., commercial equivalent of the I.N.S. (Immigration & Naturalization Service) government contract, 4.7 in. barrel, heavy duty steel slide, Tritium sights, Border Marshal engraving on the slide. Mfg. 1999-2000.

$670	$560	$480	$425	$375	$325	$295

Last MSR was $802.

MODEL 96 BRIGADIER - similar to Model 96FS, except has heavier slide to reduce felt recoil, wraparound rubber grips, and 3 dot sights, 35.3 oz. New 1999.

MSR $795	$660	$510	$440	$385	$335	$300	$275

✳ Model 96 Brigadier Stainless (Inox) - similar to Model 96 Brigadier, except is stainless steel. New 2000.

MSR $845	$680	$530	$425

MODEL 96 CUSTOM CARRY - .40 S&W cal., 4.3 in. barrel, shortened grip, low profile control levers, left side only safety lever, blue only, 10 shot staggered mag., plastic grips. Mfg. 1999-2000.

$550	$450	$400	$365	$335	$300	$275

Last MSR was $655.

GRADING - PPGS™	100%	98%	95%	90%	80%	70%	60%

MODEL 96 STOCK

MODEL 96 STOCK - .40 S&W cal., designed for practical shooting competition, includes accurized barrel bushing, 4.9 in. barrel, competition frame mounted ambi-dextrous safety, 3 interchangeable front sights, checkered front and back grip straps, aluminum grips, beveled mag. well, cased with two mags. and tool kit, 35 oz. Mfg. 1997-99, limited quantities remained into 2000.

	$1,200	$995	$865	$725	$600	$550	$495

Last MSR was $1,407.

REVOLVERS: SINGLE ACTION

Beretta's SAA revolvers are manufactured in Italy by Aldo & C. Uberti S.r.l., which was purchased by Beretta in 2000.

STAMPEDE SAA - .357 Mag., .44-40 WCF (mfg. 2003), or .45 LC cal., patterned after the Colt SAA, transfer bar and half-cock safeties, 6 shot, 4 3/4, 5 1/2, or 7 1/2 in. barrel, various finishes, approx. 37 oz. Mfg. by Uberti beginning mid-2003.

✳ *Stampede Blue* - features blue finish with case colored frame and black polymer grips.

MSR $568		$450	$375	$315	$285	$255	$230	$210

✳ *Stampede Brushed Nickel* - features brushed nickel finish with smooth walnut grips with Beretta medallions and fire blued frame screws.

MSR $604		$475	$395	$335	$295	$265	$235	$215

✳ *Stampede Stainless (Inox)* - .45 LC cal. only, features stainless steel construction, otherwise similar to Stampede. New 2004.

MSR $744		$585	$495	$425

✳ *Stampede Marshal* - .357 Mag. or .45 LC cal., 3 1/2 in. barrel. New 2004.

MSR $604		$475	$395	$335	$295	$265	$235	$215

✳ *Stampede Deluxe* - features charcoal blue metal finish, case colored frame and deluxe smooth walnut grips.

MSR $744		$585	$495	$425	$365	$320	$275	$250

RIFLES: BOLT ACTION, RECENT MFG.

MODEL 500 CUSTOM

MODEL 500 CUSTOM - .222 Rem., .223 Rem., .243 Win., .270 Win., .30-06, or .308 Win. cal., 3 action lengths, 24 in. barrel, iron sights, checkered walnut stock with recoil pad. Importation was resumed 1988 only.

	$595	$530	$450	$395	$350	$315	$275

Last MSR was $725.

Add 10%-15% for .223 Rem. cal.

✳ *Model 500 S* - similar to Model 500, except is equipped with iron sights. Imported 1986 only.

	$615	$560	$460	$400	$350	$315	$275

Last MSR was $700.

✳ *Model 500 DL* - same specifications as Model 500, only better walnut and light engraving. Disc. 1986.

	$1,395	$1,260	$1,000	$875	$795	$725	$650

Last MSR was $1,595.

Add 10%-15% for .223 Rem. cal.

✳ *Model 500 DLS* - similar to Model 500 DL, except is equipped with iron sights. Imported 1986 only.

	$1,420	$1,285	$1,020	$875	$795	$725	$650

Last MSR was $1,625.

✴ Model 500 EELL - same specifications as Model 500 DL, only select walnut and more engraving. Disc. 1986.

	$1,550	$1,260	$1,150	$1,000	$875	$800	$725

Last MSR was $1,745.

Add 10%-15% for .223 Rem. cal.

✴ Model 500 EELLS - similar to Model 500 EELL, except is equipped with iron sights. Imported 1986 only.

	$1,575	$1,425	$1,200	$1,120	$875	$800	$725

Last MSR was $1,785.

MODEL 501 - .243 Win. or .308 Win. cal., medium bolt action, 6 shot, 23 in. barrel, no sights, checkered walnut stock. Disc. 1986.

	$595	$530	$465	$395	$350	$315	$275

Last MSR was $665.

✴ Model 501 S - similar to Model 501, except is equipped with iron sights. Imported 1986 only.

	$615	$560	$460	$400	$350	$315	$275

Last MSR was $700.

✴ Model 501 DL - same specifications as Model 501, only better walnut and light engraving. Disc. 1986.

	$1,395	$1,260	$1,000	$875	$795	$725	$650

Last MSR was $1,575.

✴ Model 501 DLS - similar to Model 501 DL, except is equipped with iron sights. Imported 1986 only.

	$1,420	$1,285	$1,020	$875	$795	$725	$650

Last MSR was $1,625.

✴ Model 501 EELL - same specifications as Model 501 DL, only select walnut and more engraving. Disc. 1986.

	$1,550	$1,260	$1,150	$1,000	$875	$800	$725

Last MSR was $1,745.

✴ Model 501 EELLS - similar to Model 501 EELL, except is equipped with iron sights. Imported 1986 only.

	$1,575	$1,425	$1,200	$1,120	$875	$800	$725

Last MSR was $1,785.

MODEL 502 - .30-06, .270 or 7mm Rem. Mag. cal., long bolt action, 5 or 6 shot, 24 in. barrel, no sights, checkered walnut stock. Disc. 1986.

	$625	$565	$490	$440	$395	$360	$330

Last MSR was $710.

✴ Model 502 S - similar to Model 502, except is equipped with iron sights. Imported 1986 only.

	$650	$595	$525	$460	$395	$360	$330

Last MSR was $745.

✴ Model 502 DL - same specifications as Model 502, only better walnut and light engraving. Also available in .375 H&H Mag. Disc. 1986.

	$1,495	$1,310	$1,175	$1,025	$900	$775	$695

Last MSR was $1,640.

✴ Model 502 DLS - similar to Model 502, except is equipped with iron sights. Imported 1986 only.

	$1,410	$1,325	$1,175	$1,025	$900	$775	$695

Last MSR was $1,660.

* *Model 502 EELL* - same specifications as Model 502 DL, only select walnut and more engraving. Also available in .375 H&H Mag. Disc. 1986.

	$1,575	$1,425	$1,200	$1,120	$875	$800	$725

Last MSR was $1,785.

* *Model 502 EELLS* - similar to Model 502 EELL, except is equipped with iron sights. Imported 1986 only.

	$1,575	$1,425	$1,200	$1,120	$875	$800	$725

Last MSR was $1,785.

MATO SYNTHETIC - .270 Win., .280 Rem., .30-06, .300 Win. Mag., .338 Win. Mag., .375 H&H, or 7mm Rem. Mag. cal., 23.6 in. barrel, composite black synthetic stock with integral bedding block, Mauser style 98 action with controlled round feeding, 3 position safety, ergonomic bolt handle, 3 or 4 shot detachable box mag., adj. trigger, black satin metal finish, mfg. in the U.S., 8 lbs. Mfg. 1997-2002.

	$975	$825	$750	$675	$575	$495	$400

Last MSR was $1,117.

Add $357 for .375 H&H cal. (includes muzzle brake and iron sights).

* *Mato Deluxe* - same cals. as the standard model, features deluxe checkered walnut with ebony forend tip, cased, 7.9 lbs. Mfg. 1997-2002.

	$2,025	$1,575	$1,150	$995	$825	$675	$600

Last MSR was $2,470.

Add $325 for .375 H&H cal. (includes muzzle brake and iron sights).

* *Mato Deluxe Safari Grade* - .375 H&H cal. only, elaborately hand engraved with best quality wood. Available through Beretta Premium dealers only. Disc. 2002.

	$14,750	$12,500	$10,250	$8,000	$6,750	$5,500	$4,350

Last MSR was $16,500.

RIFLES: SEMI-AUTO, RECENT MFG.

BM-59 M-1 GARAND - with original Beretta M1 receiver, only 200 imported into the U.S.

	$2,000	$1,850	$1,650	$1,500	$1,300	$1,100	$975

Last MSR was $2,080.

BM-62 - similar to BM-59, except has flash suppressor and is Italian marked.

	$2,000	$1,850	$1,650	$1,500	$1,300	$1,100	$975

AR-70 - .222 Rem. or .223 Rem. cal., semi-auto paramilitary design rifle, 5, 8, or 30 shot mag., diopter sights, epoxy finish, 17.72 in. barrel, 8.3 lbs.

	$1,925	$1,675	$1,375	$1,150	$1,025	$850	$750

Last MSR was $1,065.

1989 Federal legislation banned the importation of this model into U.S.

CX4 STORM CARBINE - 9mm Para., .40 S&W or .45 ACP cal., blowback single action, Giugiaro design featuring paramilitary styling with one-piece matte black synthetic stock with thumbhole, rubber recoil pad and stock cheekpiece, top, bottom, and side picatinny rails, ghost ring sights, 16.6 in. hammer forged barrel, reversible crossbolt safety, mag. button, bolt handle, and ejection port, 8 (.45 ACP cal.), 10 (disc.), 11 (8000 and 8040 models, new 2005), or 15 (92 or 96 carbine, new 2005) shot mag. (accepts Models 92, 96, 8000, 8040, and 8045 pistol mags.), 29.7 in. overall length, 5.75 lbs. New mid-2003.

MSR $775	$585	$485	$425	$385	$355	$325	$300

Add $70 for 92 Carbine package (includes scope).

This model is available in 6 variations - 8000 (9mm Para.), 8040 (.40 S&W), 8045 (.45 ACP), 92 (9mm Para.), 92 Carbine package (w/scope), and 96 Carbine (.40 S&W).

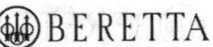
GRADING - PPGS™	100%	98%	95%	90%	80%	70%	60%

RIFLES: O/U, CUSTOM

Current high grade Beretta O/U and SxS rifles are sold only by premium grade franchised Beretta dealers. For a listing of these dealers, contact a Beretta Gallery (see Trademark Index).

MODEL S686/S689 SILVER SABLE - .30-06, 9.3x74R, or .444 cal. (disc. 1995), boxlock action, single or double (special order only) triggers. Importation began 1995.

	MSR $4,200	$3,500	$3,000	$2,700	$2,200	$2,000	$1,800	$1,550

Add $500 for 9.3x74R cal.

MODEL S689 GOLD SABLE - 9.3x74R or 30-06 cal., boxlock action, nickel (disc. 1985) or case hardened (new 1986) receiver, double triggers, 23 in. barrels, auto ejectors, sling swivels, 7.7 lbs.

	MSR $5,950	$4,875	$4,250	$3,750	$2,950	$2,350	$1,900	$1,600

Add $500 for 9.3x74R cal.

Add approx. $2,000 for scope and quick detachable claw mounts.

MODEL S686/S689 EELL DIAMOND SABLE - .30-06, 9.3x74R, or .444 Marlin cal., moderate engraving. New 1995.

	MSR $12,750	$10,500	$8,750	$7,750	$6,750	$5,975	$5,325	$4,700

Add $1,250 for an extra set of 20 ga. barrels with forearm.

Add approx. $2,000 for scope and quick detachable claw mounts.

SSO EXPRESS - .375 H&H or .458 Win. Mag. cal., sidelock action, case hardened receiver, double triggers, 23 in. barrels, auto ejectors, 11 lbs., cased. Importation disc. 1989.

	$12,500	$9,500	$8,250	$6,950	$6,100	$5,600	$4,875

Last MSR was $17,533.

Add $425 for claw mounts.

SSO5 EXPRESS - similar to SSO Express except has more elaborate engraving and better walnut.

	$14,250	$11,750	$8,750	$7,500	$6,750	$6,100	$5,600

Last MSR was $19,600.

SSO6 EXPRESS CUSTOM SIDELOCK - 9.3x74R, .375 H&H, or .458 Win. Mag. cal., next to top-of-the-line sidelock double rifle, individually built to the customer's specifications, cased. New 1990.

	MSR $39,500	$32,750	$21,850	$16,000	$12,250	$9,750	$8,750	$7,000

Add $6,750 for extra set of barrels.

Add approx. $600 for Cookleigh scope mounts or $1,400 for Zeiss 4x32mm scope.

✳ *SS06 EELL Gold Custom* - same cals. as SS06 Express, features multiple gold inlays and best quality wood.

	MSR $45,500	$37,250	$25,000	$18,500	$14,000	$11,500	$9,000	$7,500

Add $6,750 for extra set of barrels.

Add approx. $25,000-$45,000 for upgraded master engraving.

Add approx. $600 for Cookleigh scope mounts or $1,400 for Zeiss 4x32mm scope.

RIFLES: SxS, CUSTOM

MODEL 455 SIDE-BY-SIDE - .375 H&H, .416 Rigby, .458 Win. Mag., .470 NE, or .500 3 in. NE cal., top of the line sidelock double rifle, individually built to the customer's specifications, cased. New 1990.

	MSR $55,650	$46,250	$36,500	$28,500	$24,000	$19,250	$16,000	$13,000

Add approx. $600 for Cookleigh scope mounts or $1,400 for Zeiss 4x32mm scope.

GRADING - PPGS™	100%	98%	95%	90%	80%	70%	60%

✴ *Model 455 EELL* - similar cals. as Model 455 SxS, top-of-the-line custom sidelock double rifle featuring every refinement of the gunmaker's art, cased.

MSR on this model ranges from $76,500-$112,500, depending on amount of engraving and the engraver.

Add approx. $600 for Cookleigh scope mounts or $1,400 for Zeiss 4Xx32mm scope.

SHOTGUNS: O/U, DISC.

BL-1 - 12 ga., 26, 28, or 30 in. barrels with fixed chokes, blued receiver/barrel finish, boxlock, extractors, double triggers, checkered pistol grip stock, approx. 7 lbs. Mfg. 1968-73.

	$395	$350	$285	$245	$200	$185	$165

BL-2 - similar to BL-1, except with single selective trigger, more engraving.

	$450	$395	$350	$300	$275	$245	$200

BL-2 STAKE-OUT - riot configuration with 18 in. barrels, DT, blue finish, approx. 6,000 mfg.

	$400	$350	$285	$245	$200	$185	$165

BL-2/S - similar to BL-2, with vent. rib and speed trigger. Mfg. 1974-76.

	$475	$425	$365	$315	$285	$250	$215

BL-3 - also available in 20 or 28 ga., blued receiver/barrel finish, similar to BL-2, with more engraving and vent. rib., 6-7.25 lbs. Mfg. 1968-76.

	$600	$550	$525	$470	$440	$385	$350

Add 50% for 20 ga., if original condition is 90%+.

BL-3 SKEET

	$675	$615	$550	$500	$450	$400	$360

Subtract 10% for 26 in. barrels.

BL-3 TRAP

	$595	$550	$495	$450	$415	$375	$335

BL-4 - 12, 20, or 28 ga., 3 in. chambers (12 and 20 ga. only), blued receiver/barrel finish, deluxe version of BL-3, more engraving, better wood, and ejectors, 6-7.25 lbs.

	$900	$800	$725	$625	$550	$500	$450

Add 20% for 20 ga.
Add 50% for 28 ga.

BL-4 SKEET

	$795	$745	$675	$635	$550	$495	$450

Subtract 10% for 26 in. barrels.

BL-4 TRAP

	$625	$575	$525	$475	$425	$360	$325

BL-5 - 12, 20, or 28 ga., higher grade version of BL-4 with more engraving, matte grey reciever with blued barrels, full pistol grip stock.

	$1,050	$900	$825	$725	$650	$550	$475

Add 20% for 20 ga.
Add 50% for 28 ga.

BL-5 SKEET

	$925	$825	$750	$675	$600	$525	$450

Subtract 10% for 26 in. barrels.

BL-5 TRAP

	$850	$775	$695	$595	$525	$465	$400

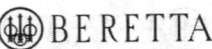

GRADING - PPGS™	100%	98%	95%	90%	80%	70%	60%

BL-6 - 12, 20, or 28 ga., boxlock with coin finished scroll engraved sideplates, deluxe checkered walnut stock with full pistol grip and slender forearm, ejectors, SST.

	$1,250	$1,075	$900	$800	$700	$600	$500

Add 20% for 20 ga.
Add 50% for 28 ga.

BL-6 SKEET

	$1,250	$1,075	$900	$800	$700	$600	$500

Subtract 10% for 26 in. barrels.

BL-6 TRAP

	$1,100	$950	$850	$750	$650	$575	$500

MODEL S55 B - 12 or 20 ga., 26, 28, or 30 in. barrels, various chokes, boxlock, extractors, selective trigger, checkered pistol grip stock. Disc.

	$600	$550	$495	$440	$385	$330	$300

Add 25% for 20 ga.

MODEL S56 E - similar to S55B, with engraved receiver and auto ejectors. Disc.

	$800	$750	$700	$650	$600	$550	$500

Add 25% for 20 ga.

MODEL S58 SKEET - similar to S56E, with 26 in. Bohler steel barrels, skeet bore, wide vent. rib, skeet.

	$800	$725	$650	$550	$495	$445	$395

Subtract 10% for 26 in. barrels.

MODEL S58 TRAP - similar to S58 Skeet, with 30 in. barrels, imp. mod. and full choke, Monte Carlo stock with pad.

	$650	$575	$525	$495	$450	$410	$365

SILVER SNIPE - 12, 20 or 28 ga., 26, 28, or 30 in. barrels, boxlock, extractors, trigger optional, checkered pistol grip stock. Mfg. 1955-67.

	$725	$650	$595	$550	$475	$425	$395

Add 20% for 20 ga.
Add 50% for 28 ga.

✳ *Silver Snipe SST* - with vent. rib and SST.

	$775	$695	$650	$595	$550	$495	$450

Add 20% for 20 ga.
Add 25% for ejectors.
Add 50% for 28 ga.

GOLDEN SNIPE - similar to Silver Snipe, with auto ejectors and vent. rib standard.

	$995	$875	$775	$700	$650	$600	$550

Add 20% for 20 ga.
Add 50% for 28 ga.

✳ *Golden Snipe SST* - with SST.

	$995	$875	$775	$700	$650	$600	$550

Add 20% for 20 ga.
Add 50% for 28 ga.

MODEL (S)57 E - higher quality version of Golden Snipe. Mfg. 1955-67.

	$825	$770	$660	$635	$550	$495	$450

Add 20% for 20 ga.
Add 50% for 28 ga.

✳ *Model (S)57 E SST* - with single selective trigger.

	$1,050	$950	$825	$750	$650	$550	$495

Add 50% for 20 ga.
Add 100% for 28 ga.

GRADING - PPGS™	100%	98%	95%	90%	80%	70%	60%

ASE MODEL - 12 or 20 ga., light border scroll engraving, mfg. approx. 1947-64.

	100%	98%	95%	90%	80%	70%	60%
12 ga.	$1,875	$1,600	$1,425	$1,175	$895	$750	$625
20 ga.	$2,800	$2,400	$2,075	$1,700	$1,450	$1,200	$850

ASEL MODEL - 12 or 20 ga., 26, 28, or 30 in. barrels, various chokes, single trigger, receiver moderately engraved, checkered pistol grip stock, auto ejectors. Mfg. 1947-1964.

12 ga.	$2,750	$2,375	$1,975	$1,600	$1,375	$1,050	$875
20 ga.	$4,650	$3,950	$3,500	$3,000	$2,475	$2,050	$1,675

ASEELL MODEL - 12 or 20 ga., full coverage engraving, very limited mfg.

12 ga.	$4,650	$3,950	$3,500	$3,000	$2,475	$2,050	$1,675
20 ga.	$8,150	$7,350	$6,500	$5,750	$5,000	$4,250	$3,500

GRADE 100 - 12 ga., 26, 28, or 30 in. barrels, any choke, sidelock, double trigger, auto ejectors, checkered pistol grip or straight stock.

$1,820	$1,550	$1,300	$1,100	$900	$775	$695

MODEL 200 - similar to 100, with chrome lined bores and action parts, higher quality engraving.

$2,310	$2,000	$1,870	$1,650	$1,375	$1,100	$875

MODEL 680 - 12 ga. only, competition trap and skeet model, boxlock, various chokes. Mono-trap model available. Silver finish receiver, hand engraved, premium walnut. Disc.

$995	$900	$800	$700	$600	$550	$500

Add approx. $300 for 2 barrel combo. package.

SHOTGUNS: O/U, FIELD - RECENT MFG.

All models listed in this category are field grade configuration regardless of model nomenclature.

BERETTA CHOKES AND THEIR CODES (ON REAR LEFT-SIDE OF BARREL)
* designates full choke (F).
** designates improved modified choke (IM).
*** designates modified choke (M).
**** designates improved cylinder choke (IC).
FK designates skeet (SK).
***** designates cylinder bore (CYL).

During 2003, Beretta introduced X-Tra Wood on stocks and forearms of select models. X-Tra Wood is a patented and exclusive Beretta wood enhancement finish where average wood is encapsulated with a waterproof film which resembles best quality Circassian walnut. Normal checkering is possible, and all X-tra Wood stocks are marked clearly on the bottom of the pistol grip cap. It can also be refinished through a special refinishing program available with Beretta USA.

Subtract 20% on the following factory multi-choke models if w/o newer Beretta Optima-chokes (12 ga. only, became standard 2003).

Note: values are for unaltered guns.

MODEL 685 - 12 or 20 ga. 2 3/4 or 3 in. chambers, matte chromed receiver, extractors, single trigger. Disc. 1986.

$595	$525	$460	$420	$360	$320	$295

Last MSR was $875.

MODEL 686 WHITE ONYX (ONYX) - 12, 20, or 28 (new 2003) ga., 2 3/4 (28 ga. only) or 3 in. chambers, boxlock action, 26 or 28 in. barrels with multi-chokes, matte blue metal (disc. 2003) or Dura-Jewel satin nickel alloy (new 2003, became standard 2004) frame, choice of standard pistol grip or English straight (disc. 1999) stock with gloss (new 1999), matte (disc. 2003) or X-Tra (standard beginning 2004) wood finish, single trigger, ejectors, approx. 6.2 or 6.8 lbs. New 1988.

MSR $1,795	$1,425	$1,000	$800	$650	$550	$480	$425

Add $154 for deluxe wood upgrade (mfg. 2001-2002, included case).
Subtract 10% for matte blue finish.

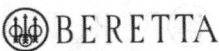

GRADING - PPGS™	100%	98%	95%	90%	80%	70%	60%

✳ Onyx Waterfowler Magnum - 12 ga. only, similar to Model S686 Onyx, except has 3 1/2 in. chambers, 28 in. barrels only, matte wood and metal finish. Mfg. 1993, reintroduced 1996-2003.

	$1,095	$950	$800	$675	$600	$550	$495

Last MSR was $1,648.

✳ Model 686 Essential - 12 ga. only, 3 in. chambers, 26 or 28 in. VR separated barrels with choke tubes, checkered high-gloss walnut stock and forearm, matte finished metal, 6.7 lbs. Mfg. 1994-96.

	$795	$700	$650	$600	$550	$500	$450

Last MSR was $1,186.

✳ Model S686 Silver Essential - 12 ga. only, 3 in. chambers, 26 or 28 in. VR separated barrels with choke tubes, checkered matte finished walnut stock and forearm, matte chrome finished receiver, 6.7 lbs. Imported 1997-98 only.

	$795	$700	$650	$600	$550	$500	$450

Last MSR was $1,070.

✳ Onyx Model 686 Quail Unlimited Covey Limited Edition - 12 (disc. 2002) 20, or 28 (new 2003) ga., similar to Model 686 Onyx, except includes 6 quail inlays in 24Kt. gold on receiver sides and Quail Unlimited logo on bottom of receiver, marked "1 of 750," deluxe checkered high gloss stock and forearm, cased with 5 choke tubes, 750 of each ga. Mfg. 2002-2004.

	$1,625	$1,375	$1,025	$825	$725	$625	$525

Last MSR was $2,000.

This model is available through Beretta Showcase Dealers only.

✳ Onyx Model 686 Ringneck Pheasants Forever Limited Edition - 12 or 20 ga., similar to Onyx Model 686 Quail Unlimited, except includes multiple ringneck pheasant inlays in 24Kt. gold on receiver sides and Pheasants Forever logo on bottom of receiver, marked "1 of 500," deluxe checkered high gloss stock and forearm, cased with 5 choke tubes, 500 of each ga. Mfg. 2003-2004.

	$1,625	$1,400	$1,050	$850	$750	$650	$550

Last MSR was $2,027.

ULTRALIGHT 686/687 (ONYX) - 12 ga. only, 2 3/4 in. chambers, Ergal alloy receiver reinforced with titanium plate, electroless nickel finish receiver with game scene engraving (new 1998, restyled 2002 with several gold inlays) or matte black finish on receiver (disc. 1997) and 26 (disc. 2001) or 28 in. VR barrels, choice of English (new 2001) straight or pistol grip checkered walnut stock and forearm, matte (new 2001, restyled) or gloss wood finish, choke tubes, gilded lettering and logo (disc. 1997), gold SST, ejectors, very light weight, 5 lbs. 11 oz. Importation began 1992.

MSR $1,995	$1,650	$1,400	$1,150	$875	$775	$650	$575

Add approx. $150 for deluxe wood upgrade (includes case, mfg. 2001 only).
Subtract approx. 10%-15% if with matte black finish, depending on condition.
This model is discontinued as a 686 Series.

✳ Ultralight Deluxe (Onyx) - 12 ga. only, 2 3/4 in. chambers, similiar to 1998 Model 686 Ultralight, except has gold game scene engraving and select walnut stock and forearm. Mfg. began 1998.

MSR $2,495	$1,985	$1,595	$1,275	$975	$885	$800	$695

ONYX PRO - 12, 20, or 28 ga., 2 3/4 (28 ga.only) or 3 in. chambers, matte blue finish with Dura-Jewel treatment on receiver, X-Tra wood finish on stock and forearm, Geltek recoil pad, gold trigger, TruGlo sights, includes case and 5 choke tubes, 6.8 lbs. (12 ga.). Importation began 2003.

MSR $1,895	$1,535	$1,295	$1,125	$950	$800	$650	$575

✳ Onyx Pro 3.5 - 12 ga., 3 1/2 in. chambers, otherwise similar to Onyx Pro, 6.9 lbs. Importation began 2003.

MSR $1,995	$1,550	$1,325	$1,150	$975	$825	$675	$595

GRADING - PPGS™	100%	98%	95%	90%	80%	70%	60%

WHITEWING - 12 or 20 ga., 3 in. chambers, 26 or 28 in. separated VR barrels and MC3 choke tubes, similar to Model 686 Silver Essential, except has checkered gloss finish walnut stock and silver polished receiver with game scene engraving, 6.7 lbs. Mfg. 1999-2003.

	$1,095	$950	$875	$750	$650	$525	$400

Last MSR was $1,332.

BLACKWING - similar to Whitewing, except has matte black receiver finish, lower stock dimensions, and Schnabel forearm. Mfg. 2002-2003.

	$1,095	$950	$875	$750	$650	$525	$400

Last MSR was $1,332.

MODEL 686(L) SILVER PERDIZ - 12 (disc. 1990), 20 (disc. 1990), or 28 ga., field model, boxlock action, various barrels/ chokes, ejectors, single trigger, engraved silver finished receiver, special walnut, pistol or straight grip stock, fixed chokes disc. 1987. Importation disc. 1994.

	$1,000	$850	$650	$575	$525	$460	$415

Last MSR was $1,355.

Subtract 20% with fixed chokes (disc.).

Add 20% for 28 ga.

✳ *Onyx Model 686 Silver Pigeon S & Silver Pigeon (Silver Perdiz)* - 12, 20, or 28 (mfg. 1995-2001, reintroduced 2004) ga. or .410 bore (new 2005), 3 in. chambers (except for 28 ga.), 26 or 28 in. VR barrels with choke tubes, choice of polished (new 1999) or regular nickel finished receiver with scroll engraving, gold trigger, gloss finish checkered pistol grip or straight grip (disc. 1999) walnut stock and forearm, supplied with carrying case, 5 choke tubes, recoil pad and sling swivels beginning 2004, includes hardshell case, 6.8 lbs. New 1992.

MSR $1,995	$1,600	$1,295	$1,175	$950	$775	$650	$575

Add $153 for deluxe wood upgrade (Silver Pigeon only, 12 or 20 ga. only, includes case, mfg. 2001-2002).

During 1996, the model nomenclature was changed from the Silver Perdiz to the Silver Pigeon.

✳ *Onyx Model 686/687 Silver Pigeon S (Silver Perdiz) and 686 Silver Pigeon Combo* - similar to Model 686 Onyx, except is supplied with 1 set each of 20 ga. (28 in.) and 28 ga. (26 in.) barrels, includes carrying case, 5 choke tubes, recoil pad, and sling swivels, polished receiver became standard 1999. Introduced 1986.

MSR $2,795	$1,995	$1,625	$1,325	$1,050	$875	$820	$775

This model is discontinued as a 686 Series.

MODEL S686 EL GOLD PERDIZ - 12 or 20 ga., 3 in. chambers, boxlock action with floral scroll engraved sideplates, silver receiver finish, 26 or 28 (20 ga. only beginning 1997) VR in. barrels with choke tubes, gold SST, checkered walnut stock and forearm, cased, approx. 6.8 lbs. Mfg. 1992-97.

	$1,600	$1,350	$1,150	$950	$875	$800	$695

Last MSR was $1,930.

Add 10% for 20 ga.

MODEL S687(L) SILVER PIGEON - 12 (disc. 1999) or 20 ga., 3 in. chambers, boxlock, various barrels/chokes, ejectors, game scene engraved nickel finished receiver, gloss finished select walnut stock and forearm, approx. 6.8 lbs., fitted case was optional. Disc. 2000.

	$1,500	$1,325	$1,200	$975	$875	$800	$695

Last MSR was $2,255.

Subtract 30% without multi-chokes (disc.).

The "L" suffix model nomenclature was disc. 1996.

GRADING - PPGS™	100%	98%	95%	90%	80%	70%	60%

S687 SILVER PIGEON II - 12 or 20 ga., similar to Model S687 Silver Pigeon, except has deep relief engraved game scenes on receiver sides and oil finished (matte) walnut stock and forearm, 26 or 28 in. VR barrels with MC3 choke tubes. New 1999.

	MSR $2,395	$1,915	$1,650	$1,475	$1,200	$975	$875	$750

✳ *Silver Pigeon II Combo* - includes 1 set each of 28 ga. and 20 ga. with 28 in. barrels, cased with 5 choke tubes. Importation began 2003.

	MSR $3,295	$2,650	$2,000	$1,850	$1,725	$1,500	$1,300	$1,075

687 SILVER PIGEON III - 12, 20, or 28 ga., 26 or 28 in. VR barrels, engraved box-lock action with game scenes, select checkered walnut stock and forearm, Gel-Tek recoil pad, gold SST, TruGlo front sight, 6.8 lbs. New 2004.

	MSR $2,495	$1,800	$1,675	$1,500	$1,225	$995	$900	$800

687 SILVER PIGEON IV - 12, 20, or 28 ga., 2 3/4 (28 ga. only) or 3 in. chambers, black metal finished receiver with full coverage scroll engraving and 4 gold bird inlays, 26 or 28 in. barrels, checkered oil finished walnut stock with Gel-Tek recoil pad, TruGlo front sight, includes molded case with 5 choke tubes, 6.8 lbs. (12 ga.). Importation began 2003.

	MSR $2,795	$2,000	$1,850	$1,600	$1,325	$1,050	$875	$825

687 SILVER PIGEON V - 12, 20, 28 ga., or .410 bore (new 2005), 26 or 28 in. barrels, case colored finished receiver with gold bird inlays, 28 ga. is on a true "baby frame," upgraded select oil finished checkered straight grip English (not available in 12 ga.) or pistol grip walnut stock and forearm, gold SST, Gel-Tek recoil pad, Schnabel forend, 6.8 lbs., includes hardshell case. New 2004.

	MSR $3,295	$2,650	$2,275	$1,875	$1,525	$1,300	$1,075	$925

MODEL 687 DU - 12 (1990 release) or 20 ga., mfg. for DU dinner gun auctions and membership, prices may vary significantly from region to region.

		$1,500	$1,300	$1,200	$1,100	$895	$725	$575

Add 10% for 20 ga.

MODEL 687 BLACK & GOLD TERCENTENNIAL - 12 ga. only, 2 3/4 in. chambers, 28 in. barrels with fixed F/M chokes, bottom of blued receiver features special 1680-1980 Tercentennial logo, inlaid (with gold) and engraved by Giovanelli (signed), ser. no. 001-300.

		$1,650	$1,400	$1,250	$1,100	$895	$725	$525

MODEL 687 TERCENTENNIAL COMMEMORATIVE - 12 ga. only, 2 3/4 in. chambers, 28 in. barrels, engraved and signed by Giovanelli, with ducks and woodcocks on sides of grey finished frame, oil finished walnut stock and forearm, ser. no. 001-200.

		$1,650	$1,400	$1,250	$1,100	$895	$725	$525

MODEL 687 L ONYX - 12 or 20 ga., 3 in. chambers, same game scene engraving as standard Model 687 L, except has Onyx blackened receiver, multi-chokes standard. Mfg. 1990 only.

		$1,375	$1,100	$900	$750	$650	$575	$525

Last MSR was $1,590.

Add 10% for 20 ga.

MODEL 687 GOLDEN ONYX - 12 or 20 ga., 3 in. chambers, similar to Model 686 Onyx, except has more engraving, better walnut, and several gold inlays. Imported 1988-89 only.

		$1,525	$1,275	$995	$825	$700	$650	$575

Last MSR was $1,800.

Add 15% for 20 ga.

GRADING - PPGS™	100%	98%	95%	90%	80%	70%	60%

MODEL S687 EL GOLD PIGEON

- same general specifications as Model 687L, except also available in 28 ga. (new 1990) or .410 (new 1990) bore, 20 ga. disc. 2001, 2 3/4 or 3 in. chambers, boxlock with gold inlaid game scene on sideplates, highly figured walnut, and more engraving, oval nameplate, approx. 6.8 lbs, cased. Disc. 2002.

	$3,000	$2,575	$1,950	$1,575	$1,350	$1,150	$1,000

Last MSR was $4,099.

Add $100 for 28 ga.

* *Model 687 EL DU* - 28 ga. or .410 bore, small frame, released 1992 for DU auctions and membership.

	$2,500	$2,200	$1,800	$1,550	$1,400	$1,200	$1,050

MODEL S687 EL GOLD PIGEON II

- 12, 20, 28 ga., or .410 bore, similar to EL Gold Pigeon, except features deep relief engraving on sideplates, 6.8 lbs., cased. New 2001.

MSR $4,795	$3,825	$3,400	$2,950	$2,525	$2,000	$1,800	$1,500

* *Gold Pigeon II Combo* - includes either 20 and 28 ga. barrels or 28 ga. and .410 bore barrels, cased with 5 choke tubes. Importation began 2003.

MSR $5,595	$4,525	$3,925	$3,350	$2,775	$2,250	$1,950	$1,650

MODEL 687 EL ONYX

- 12 or 20 ga., 3 in. chambers, simulated sidelock plates with classic scroll engraving. Mfg. 1990 only.

	$2,000	$1,850	$1,500	$1,350	$1,150	$1,000	$950

Last MSR was $2,660.

MODEL S687 EELL DIAMOND PIGEON

- 12, 20, 28 ga. or .410 bore (new 2003), boxlock action, silver receiver with full sideplates and hand engraved game scenes, 26 or 28 in. VR barrels, 3 in. (except 28 ga.) chambers and gold plated trigger, cased, multi-chokes introduced 1988, 6.8 lbs.

MSR $5,995	$4,200	$3,500	$3,250	$2,450	$2,150	$1,850	$1,500

Add 10%-20% for earlier mfg. with hand chased engraving (non-machine engraved), depending on condition.

Subtract 20% if without multi-chokes.

This model is also available with a straight grip English stock at no extra charge (20 ga. only). If hand engraved, the engraver's name will be next to the trigger guard.

* *Model S687 EELL Combo* - includes either 20 and 28 ga. or 28 ga. and .410 bore multi-choke 26 or 28 in. barrels, cased. Limited importation.

MSR $7,495	$6,025	$5,400	$4,750	$3,975	$3,350	$2,775	$2,375

Subtract 20% for fixed chokes.

Multi-chokes became standard in 1991.

* *Model S687 EELL Gallery Edition* - 12, 20, 28 ga., or .410 bore, available as a pair (optional) or 2 barrel sets, featuring special engraving and upgraded wood with oil finish. New 2000.

Prices range from $7,250 -$8,750 for single guns and 2 barrel sets, depending on ga. and options. Pairs start at $16,675. Available at Beretta Galleries only.

MODEL S687 EXTRA

- 12, 20, 28 ga., or .410 bore, available in pairs or 2 barrel sets (special order only), features special engraving and upgraded wood with oil finish. New 2001.

Prices start at $7,875 for Field Model, and vary depending on ga. and options. Pairs start at approx. $16,675. Available at Beretta Premium dealers only.

GRADING - PPGS™	100%	98%	95%	90%	80%	70%	60%

MODEL ASE 90 PIGEON - 12 ga. only, 28 in. fixed choke (IM/F) vent. barrels with VR, new design features nickel-chromium-molybdenum receiver with special hardening and cross bolt engaging 2 monobloc lugs, detachable trigger grouping, V-shaped main springs, cold hammered barrels, choice of silver or blue receiver with gold etching and no engraving, top quality checkered walnut stock and forearm with vent. recoil pad, choke tubes, 7 lbs. 13 oz., cased. Imported 1992-94.

	$3,995	$3,500	$3,250	$3,000	$2,850	$2,500	$2,150

Last MSR was $8,070.

SHOTGUNS: O/U, SKEET - RECENT MFG.

Full descriptions for the following models may be found under the corresponding model numbers in the Field Shotguns category.

Subtract 20% on the following factory multi-choke models if w/o newer Beretta Optima-chokes (12 ga. only, became standard 2003).

Note: values are for unaltered guns.

MODEL S682 GOLD SKEET - 12, 20 (disc. 1991), 28 ga. (disc. 1988), or .410 bore (disc. 1988), competition skeet model, 26 (disc.) or 28 in. barrels, boxlock, skeet chokes, silver finish (disc.) or Greystone (titanium nitrate) receiver, hand engraved, premium walnut, cased. Mfg. 1984-99.

	$1,595	$1,400	$1,275	$1,025	$900	$800	$700

Last MSR was $2,850.

Subtract 20% for 26 in. barrels.
Subtract 20% for fixed chokes.
Subtract 20% for silver finish.

✳ **Model S682 Gold Skeet With Adj. Stock** - similar to Model S682 Gold Skeet, except has fully adj. stock, allowing the comb, drop, and cast to be adjusted per shooter. Imported 1999-2000.

	$1,700	$1,600	$1,500	$1,350	$1,075	$950	$825

Last MSR was $3,515.

✳ **Model S682 Gold E Skeet** - 12 ga. only, 28 or 30 in. VR barrels with Optima-Bore and Optima-Choke, adj. stock with memory system, dual color finished receiver with engraved merging circular lines and gold highlights, including trigger, deluxe wide checkered stock and Schnabel forearm with gloss wood finish, 7.6 lbs. New 2001.

MSR $4,195	$3,100	$2,750	$2,425	$2,000	$1,650	$1,425	$1,225

✳ **Model 682 Super Skeet** - 12 ga. only, 28 in. VR barrels bored SK/SK featuring factory porting, stock has separate adj. comb cheekpiece. Mfg. 1991-95.

	$1,500	$1,300	$1,200	$1,100	$1,050	$900	$800

Last MSR was $3,006.

✳ **Model 682 Skeet Deluxe** - similar to Model 682, except deluxe walnut and elaborate engraving. Disc. 1986.

	$2,275	$1,850	$1,575	$1,250	$1,050	$900	$800

Last MSR was $3,000.

✳ **Model 682 2-Barrel Skeet Set** - 12 ga. only, two barrel set bored for skeet and sporting clays competition. Imported 1988 only.

	$2,500	$2,250	$2,000	$1,850	$1,600	$1,400	$1,300

Last MSR was $6,650.

Subtract 50% if w/o choke tubes.

✳ **Model 682 4-Ga. Skeet Set** - four barrel skeet set comes with interchangeable barrels (28 in.) in 12, 20, 28 gauges, and .410 bore. Imported 1985-95.

	$3,500	$3,250	$3,000	$2,850	$2,500	$2,175	$1,900

Last MSR was $6,037.

Subtract 10% for silver frame.

GRADING - PPGS™	100%	98%	95%	90%	80%	70%	60%

MODEL S686 SKEET SILVER PERDIZ/SILVER PIGEON
- 12 ga. only, 28 in. VR barrels bored SK/SK, checkered walnut stock and forearm, Silver Perdiz was disc. 1996 and featured silver finish, while Silver Pigeon nomenclature began 1997 and features nickel finish, 7.6 lbs. Imported 1994-98.

	$900	$800	$750	$725	$625	$550	$480

Last MSR was $1,795.

MODEL S687 EELL SKEET DIAMOND PIGEON
- 12 ga. only, fixed chokes, 28 in. barrels, elaborate game scene engraving on sideplates, cased. Disc. 2002.

	$3,250	$3,075	$2,550	$2,000	$1,800	$1,500	$1,250

Last MSR was $4,984.

* **Model S687 EELL Skeet Diamond Pigeon With Adj. Stock** - similar to Model S687 EELL Skeet Diamond Pigeon, except has fully adj. stock, allowing the comb, drop, and cast to be adjusted per shooter. Imported 1999-2004.

	$4,900	$4,400	$4,100	$3,750	$3,250	$2,600	$2,150

Last MSR was $6,207.

* **Model S687 EELL 4-Ga. Skeet Set** - 4 ga. skeet set, cased. Imported 1988-1998.

	$5,750	$5,500	$4,750	$3,900	$3,400	$2,900	$2,450

Last MSR was $8,405.

DT10 TRIDENT SKEET
- 12 ga. only, 3 in. chambers, 28 or 30 in. vent. barrels with target VR, specially designed skeet gun featuring removable adj. trigger group, massive crossbolt locking system, Optima-choke competition choke tubes, Optima-Bore internal barrel configuration, specific point of impact, and unique distribution of mass that helps target acquisition and eliminate muzzle rise, adj. walnut stock with memory system, carbon reinforced frame, 7.9 lbs. New 2000.

MSR $6,995	$5,625	$5,025	$4,525	$4,150	$3,600	$3,150	$2,550

MODEL ASE 90 GOLD SKEET
- 12 ga. only, 28 in. fixed choke vent. barrels with VR, similar action and specifications as the Model ASE 90 Pigeon, except has more elaborate hand scroll engraving and extra fine wood, 7.6 lbs., cased. Mfg. 1992-99.

	$3,995	$3,500	$3,250	$3,000	$2,750	$2,500	$2,250

Last MSR was $12,060.

SHOTGUNS: O/U, SPORTING CLAYS - RECENT MFG.

These variations have been specifically designed for sporting clay target shooting. All of the following models have 3 in. chambers, unless specified otherwise. Full descriptions for the following models may be found under the corresponding model numbers in the Field Shotguns category.

Sporting Clays models with 30 in. barrels are currently more desireable than either 26 or 28 in., and premiums of 5%-10% are being asked. Values are for unalterered guns.

> **Subtract 20% on the following factory multi-choke models if w/o newer Beretta Optima-chokes (12 ga. only, became standard 2003).**
>
> Note: values are for unaltered guns.

MODEL S682 CONTINENTAL COURSE
- 12 ga. only, 2 3/4 in. chambers, 28 or 30 (disc. 1995) in. VR barrels with multi-chokes, designed for English Sporting Clays courses, previously was Model Super Sport with tapered rib, cased. Mfg. 1993-97.

	$1,500	$1,400	$1,225	$975	$875	$775	$675

Last MSR was $2,345.

MODEL S682 GOLD SPORTING
- 12 or 20 (mfg. 1992-94) ga., similar specifications to Model 682 Skeet, 2 3/4 in. chambers, 28, 30 (new 1989), or 31 (new 1997) in. unported or ported (new 1995) VR barrels, except over-field stock dimensions and hand engraved silver (disc.) or Greystone (titanium nitrate) finished receiver, cased, 7.6 lbs. Multi-chokes are standard. Disc. 2000.

	$1,700	$1,600	$1,400	$1,075	$950	$875	$800

Last MSR was $3,100.

Add $500 for extra set of 12 ga. barrels (combo. package - mfg. 1990-94).

* **Model S682 Gold E Sporting** - 12 ga. only, 28, 30, or 32 in. VR barrels with Optima-Bore and Optima-Choke, adj. stock with memory system, dual color finished receiver with engraved merging circular lines and gold highlights, including trigger, select wide checkered stock and Schnabel forearm with gloss wood finish, approx. 7.6 lbs. New 2001.

MSR $3,595	$2,500	$2,350	$2,050	$1,850	$1,625	$1,425	$1,200

MODEL 682 SUPER SPORTING - 12 ga. only, 2 3/4 in. chambers, 28 or 30 in. VR ported (new 1993) barrels with multi-chokes and tapered rib, otherwise similar to Model 682 Sporting, cased, 7.6 lbs. Imported 1989-95.

	$1,500	$1,375	$1,250	$1,100	$950	$875	$800

Last MSR was $3,017.

Beginning 1993, this model featured a special fully adj. stock and LOP.

MODEL 686 SPORTING/SPECIAL SPORTING - 12 ga. only, 3 in. chambers, deluxe checkered walnut stock and forearm with over-field dimensions, 28 or 30 (new 1991) in. barrels only, multi-chokes standard. Mfg. 1987-92.

	$1,200	$1,100	$950	$825	$675	$625	$550

Last MSR was $1,940.

The Model 686 Special Sporting is marked "Model S686 Special," and the barrels are marked "Sporting."

* **Model S686 Silver Pigeon (Silver Perdiz) Sporting** - 12 or 20 (disc. 2000) ga., 28 or 30 in. VR barrels with multi-chokes, 7.7 lbs. Mfg. 1993-2002.

	$1,300	$1,175	$995	$850	$725	$650	$575

Last MSR was $1,931.

Add $139 for deluxe wood upgrade (includes case, mfg. 2001-2002).

Until 1994, this model was named the Model 686 Hunter Sport. Between 1994-95, this model was named the S686 Silver Perdiz, and beginning 1996, this model was again renamed to the 686 Silver Pigeon Sporting.

* **Model 686 E Sporting** - 12, 20 or 28 ga., 3 in. chambers, 28 (20 ga. only) or 30 in. VR barrels with 5 chokes, improved styling, oil finished walnut stock and Schnabel forearm, includes accessories, 5 choke tubes, and carrying case, 7.7 lbs. Mfg. 2001-2004.

	$1,625	$1,325	$1,100	$975	$850	$750	$650

Last MSR was $2,008.

* **Model 686 Silver Perdiz/S686 Silver Pigeon Sporting Combo** - 12 ga., includes extra set of 30 in. barrels. Model 686 Silver Perdiz was manufactured 1991-95, Model S686 Silver Pigeon was manufactured 1997-99.

	$1,925	$1,700	$1,475	$1,250	$1,025	$900	$800

Last MSR was $2,210.

Last MSR was $2,687 for the 686 Silver Perdiz Combo.

MODEL 686 COLLECTION SPORT - 12 ga. only, features multi-colored checkered wood stock and forearm, 28 in. VR barrels, 7.7 lbs. Mfg. 1996 only.

	$900	$800	$700	$625	$550	$500	$475

Last MSR was $1,499.

MODEL 686 ONYX SPORTING - 12 ga. only, 28 or 30 in. vent. fixed choke barrels with VR, high luster blue finish with gold lettering on receiver sides. Mfg. 1992 only.

	$900	$800	$700	$600	$525	$450	$400

Last MSR was $1,940.

* **Model 686 Onyx Sporting w/Multi-chokes** - 12 ga. only, 28 or 30 in. VR barrels with multi- chokes, matte wood finish, choice of semi-matte black (disc. 1998) or polished black receiver with "P. Beretta" engraved in gold, 7.7 lbs. Mfg. 1993-2002.

	$1,095	$985	$775	$595	$525	$460	$415

Last MSR was $1,639.

Add $139 for deluxe wood upgrade (includes case, mfg. 2001-2002).

GRADING - PPGS™	100%	98%	95%	90%	80%	70%	60%

✱ **Model 686 English Course** - 12 ga. only, features 28 in. VR barrels and special reverse tapered VR with special sighting plane designed for English courses. Mfg. 1991-92.

	$1,095	$1,000	$900	$800	$700	$600	$500

Last MSR was $2,015.

MODEL 686 WHITE ONYX SPORTING - 12 ga. only, 30 or 32 in. VR barrels, nickel alloy finish, gold SST, oil finished checkered select walnut stock and forearm, black rubber recoil pad, Schnabel forend, 7-8.5 lbs. New 2004.

MSR $1,995	$1,625	$1,175	$995	$825	$700	$600	$550

MODEL S687(L) SILVER PIGEON (SILVER PERDIZ) SPORTING - 12 or 20 ga. only, deluxe checkered walnut stock and forearm with over-field dimensions, game scene engraved, 28 or 30 (12 ga. only) in. barrels, multi-chokes standard. Mfg. 1987-2001.

	$1,500	$1,350	$1,215	$975	$875	$775	$675

Last MSR was $2,363.

✱ **Model 687 Silver Pigeon Sporting Combo** - 12 ga., includes set of 28 and 30 in. barrels. Mfg. 2002 only.

	$1,950	$1,750	$1,600	$1,400	$1,200	$1,000	$875

Last MSR was $3,151.

✱ **Model 687 English Course** - 12 ga. only, features 28 in. VR barrels and special reverse tapered VR with special sighting plane designed for English courses. Mfg. 1991-92.

	$1,500	$1,400	$1,300	$1,075	$975	$895	$800

Last MSR was $2,630.

MODEL S687 SILVER PIGEON II SPORTING - 12, 20 (new 2002), or 28 ga. (new 2002), features deep relief game scene engraving on receiver sides, matte oil finished select walnut stock and forearm, 28, 30, or 32 (12 ga. only, new 2002) in. barrels with choke tubes, Optima-Bore choking with extended Optima-chokes became standard on 12 ga. in 2003, 7.7 lbs. Importation began 1999.

MSR $2,695	$1,825	$1,650	$1,525	$1,275	$995	$875	$775

Subtract 20% if w/o Optima chokes.

MODEL S687 SILVER PIGEON III SPORTING - 12 ga. only, 30 or 32 in. VR barrels, select checkered walnut stock and forearm, game scene engraving on receiver sides, floral and scroll engraving on bottom of receiver and trigger guard, approx. 8 lbs. New 2004.

MSR $2,795	$2,225	$1,875	$1,575	$1,300	$995	$875	$775

MODEL S687 EL GOLD PIGEON SPORTING - 12 ga. only, 28 or 30 in. VR barrels with multi-chokes (non-Optima), 7.7 lbs. Mfg. 1993-2001.

	$3,000	$2,750	$2,500	$2,250	$1,850	$1,500	$1,250

Last MSR was $4,182.

MODEL S687 EL GOLD PIGEON II SPORTING - 12, 20 (new 2003), 28 ga., or .410 bore (new 2003), similar to Model S687 Gold Pigeon Sporting, except features deep relief engraving on sideplates, also available in 28 ga. and 32 in. barrels beginning 2002, Optima-Bore choking with flush Optima-chokes became standard on 12 ga. in 2003. New 2001.

MSR $4,995	$4,000	$3,550	$3,175	$2,775	$2,300	$2,000	$1,600

✱ **Model 687 EL Gold Pigeon II Sporting 20 ga./.410 Bore** - includes set of 20 ga. and .410 bore barrels, cased. Imported 2003 only.

	$5,000	$4,000	$3,250	$2,850	$2,350	$1,975	$1,625

Last MSR was $6,071.

✱ **Model 687 EL Gold Pigeon II Sporting Combo** - 28 ga. and .410 bore, includes set of 30 in. barrels. New 2002.

MSR $5,995	$4,800	$4,150	$3,850	$3,325	$2,800	$2,375	$1,925

GRADING - PPGS™	100%	98%	95%	90%	80%	70%	60%

MODEL S687 EELL DIAMOND PIGEON SPORTING - 12, 20 (disc. 1992, reintroduced 2003), 28 (new 2003) ga. or .410 bore (new 2003), features fine scroll engraving on receiver and sideplates, deluxe checkered walnut stock and forearm with over-field dimensions, 28, 30 (new 1995), or 32 (new 2002) in. barrels only, Optima-Bore choking with flush Optima-chokes became standard on 12 ga. in 2003 or with multi-chokes, cased, 7.6 lbs. New 1987.

	MSR $6,495	$4,475	$3,900	$3,525	$2,875	$2,225	$1,800	$1,550

Add $875 for extra set of barrels (combo. package - 1990 mfg. only).

Subtract 10% if w/o Optima-chokes.

DT10 TRIDENT SPORTING - 12 ga. only, 3 in. chambers, 28, 30, or 32 in. vent. barrels with target VR, specially designed sporting gun featuring removable adj. trigger group, massive crossbolt locking system, Optima-choke competition choke tubes, Optima-Bore internal barrel configuration, specific point of impact, and unique distribution of mass that helps target acquisition and eliminate muzzle rise, deluxe checkered walnut stock and Schnabel forearm, carbon reinforced frame, cased, approx. 8 lbs. New 2000.

	MSR $6,495	$4,500	$4,250	$3,900	$2,875	$2,225	$1,800	$1,550

✳ *DT10 Trident L Sporting* - 12 ga., 30 or 32 in. barrels, floral engraved receiver and trigger guard, palm swell, adj. trigger. New 2004.

	MSR $7,995	$6,400	$5,775	$5,000	$4,300	$3,750	$3,250	$2,750

✳ *DT10 Trident EELL Sporting* - 12 ga., 30 or 32 in. barrels, hand engraved, upgraded wood. New 2004.

	MSR $10,750	$9,250	$7,750	$6,500	$5,500	$4,750	$4,000	$3,350

This model is available by special order through Beretta Galleries only.

MODEL ASE 90 GOLD SPORTING CLAYS - 12 ga. only, 28, 30, or 31 (new 1997) in. vent. barrels with VR, similar action and specifications to Model ASE 90 Pigeon, 7.5 lbs., cased. Mfg. 1992-99.

		$4,000	$3,750	$3,500	$3,250	$3,000	$2,850	$2,500

Last MSR was $12,145.

SHOTGUNS: O/U, TRAP - RECENT MFG.

Full descriptions for the following models may be found under the corresponding model numbers in the Field Shotguns category.

Subtract 20% on the following factory multi-choke models if w/o newer Beretta Optima-chokes (12 ga. only, became standard 2003).

Note: values are for unaltered guns.

MODEL S682 GOLD TRAP (GOLD X) - 12 ga. only, competition trap model, Greystone (titanium nitrate) or Bruniton finish (matte black, disc.), 30 or 32 in. barrels with or w/o choke tubes (became standard 1996), adj. trigger, supplied with case, 8.8 lbs. Mfg. 1985-2000.

		$1,800	$1,450	$1,200	$1,050	$900	$775	$650

Last MSR was $3,100.

Subtract 15% for Bruniton finish.

Subtract 20% if w/o choke tubes.

✳ *Model S682 Mono/Top Combo (Gold X)* - 12 ga. only, supplied with mono under or upper single barrel and O/U barrel sets, multi-chokes became standard 1996. Otherwise same specifications as Model S682 Gold Trap. Cased. Disc. 2000.

		$2,200	$1,800	$1,700	$1,600	$1,400	$1,200	$1,000

Last MSR was $4,085.

Subtract 15% for Bruniton finish.

✳ **Model S682 Gold Trap Adjustable Stock** - 12 ga. only, features Monte Carlo style stock with adj. comb, 30 or 32 in. barrels, 8.8 lbs. Mfg. 1998-2000.

$1,800	$1,700	$1,650	$1,475	$1,250	$1,050	$895

Last MSR was $3,625.

Add $985 for combo package (includes extra set of 34 in. barrels).

✳ **Model 682 Mono** - single under-barrel trap model, high post vent. rib, 32 or 34 in. barrel. Imported 1985-88.

$1,395	$1,100	$1,000	$900	$800	$700	$600

Last MSR was $1,890.

✳ **Model S682 Gold Live Bird (Pigeon Trap)** - 12 ga. only, includes features for international style pigeon and competition shooters including international style stock, standard or flat (new 1995) VR, and mid-rib sights, Greystone (new 1991) or matte black (disc.) metal finish, semi-gloss American walnut stock, light scroll engraving, sliding trigger, includes multi-chokes, cased, 8.8 lbs. Imported 1990-98.

$1,800	$1,625	$1,325	$1,175	$950	$895	$800

Last MSR was $2,910.

Subtract 15% for matte black.

✳ **Model 682 Gold X Trap Mono (Top Single)** - 12 ga. only, single over-barrel trap model, 32 or 34 in. barrel. Imported 1986-95.

$1,550	$1,350	$1,150	$925	$850	$775	$675

Last MSR was $2,734.

Multi-chokes became standard in 1989.

✳ **Model 682 Unsingle** - 12 ga. only, single under-barrel trap model with 32 in. high post VR, optional choke tubes. Imported 1992-94.

$1,550	$1,350	$1,150	$925	$850	$775	$675

Last MSR was $2,650.

MODEL S682 (GOLD X) SUPER TRAP

- 12 ga. only, competition trap model, 30 in. barrels, step tapered rib, factory porting, LOP, and separate stock cheekpiece are adjustable, cased. Imported 1991-95.

$1,800	$1,650	$1,375	$1,050	$900	$800	$700

Last MSR was $2,907.

✳ **Model S682 Top Mono Super Trap (Gold X)** - 12 ga. only, single over-barrel trap model, 32 or 34 in. barrel with choice of fixed or multi-chokes. Imported 1991-95.

$1,550	$1,375	$1,200	$1,050	$900	$800	$700

Last MSR was $3,083.

Add $73 for multi-chokes (32 in. barrels only) or 34 in. barrels.

✳ **Model S682 Gold Super Trap Top Combo (Gold X)** - 12 ga. only, supplied with upper single barrel and O/U barrel sets. Otherwise same specifications as Model 682 Super Trap, multi-chokes became standard 1996, cased. Imported 1991-97.

$2,200	$1,950	$1,825	$1,650	$1,400	$1,125	$895

Last MSR was $4,040.

MODEL S682 GOLD E TRAP

- 12 ga. only, 30 or 32 in. VR barrel with Optima-Bore and Optima-Choke, adj. stock with memory system, dual color finished receiver with engraved merging circular lines and gold highlights, including trigger, deluxe wide checkered stock with gloss wood finish, 7.6 lbs. New 2001.

MSR $4,195	$2,900	$2,750	$2,400	$1,975	$1,600	$1,325	$1,100

✳ **Model S682 Gold E Trap Combo Top** - 12 ga. only, includes 30 (scarce, disc. 2001), 32 (disc. 2002) or 34 (new 2002) in. mono top barrel and choice of 30 or 32 in. O/U barrels, cased. New 2001.

MSR $5,295	$3,800	$3,650	$3,250	$2,625	$2,075	$1,750	$1,500

GRADING - PPGS™	100%	98%	95%	90%	80%	70%	60%

MODEL S686 SILVER PIGEON TRAP - 12 ga. only, low-profile action, 30 in. VR barrels with 3/8 in. flat rib, matte wood finish, choke tubes, nickel finished receiver with scroll engraving, 7.7 lbs. Mfg. 1997-99.

	$1,295	$1,000	$725	$600	$525	$460	$415

Last MSR was $1,795.

✱ *Model S686 Silver Pigeon Trap Top Mono* - 12 ga. only, single over-barrel trap model, 32 or 34 in. barrel with multi-chokes, gloss wood finish, 8.14 lbs. Mfg. 1998-2002.

	$1,300	$1,035	$735	$600	$525	$460	$415

Last MSR was $1,869.

MODEL 686 INTERNATIONAL - 12 ga. only, 30 in. VR barrels bored IM/F, checkered walnut stock and forearm. Imported 1994 only.

	$900	$800	$725	$650	$550	$500	$460

Last MSR was $1,300.

MODEL S687 EELL DIAMOND PIGEON (X TRAP) - 12 ga. only, boxlock action with engraved black (new 1992) or silver (disc. 1991) finished side plates, Monte Carlo stock with recoil pad, 30 in. barrels with choke tubes, cased, 8.8 lbs. Disc. 1999.

	$3,500	$3,175	$2,475	$2,050	$1,725	$1,500	$1,250

Last MSR was $4,815.

✱ *Model S687 EELL Diamond Pigeon Trap Top Mono* - 12 ga. only, single over-barrel trap model, 32 or 34 in. barrel, fixed chokes standard. Imported 1988-92, resumed 1996, disc. 1999.

	$2,500	$2,250	$2,000	$1,850	$1,700	$1,425	$1,150

Last MSR was $5,060.

    Subtract $20% for non-Optima multi-chokes.

✱ *Model S687 EELL Diamond Pigeon X Bottom Mono Trap Combo* - 12 ga. only, supplied with 30 or 32 in. O/U barrels and a mono trap bottom barrel. Imported 1986-1988, resumed 1994-95.

	$3,250	$3,000	$2,725	$2,500	$2,250	$2,000	$1,725

Last MSR was $4,984.

    Add 5% for multi-chokes.

✱ *Model S687 EELL Diamond Pigeon X Top Mono Trap Combo* - 12 ga. only, supplied with 30 or 32 in. O/U barrels and a mono trap upper barrel, multi-chokes became standard 1995. Mfg. 1988-97.

	$4,750	$4,275	$3,650	$3,325	$2,875	$2,500	$2,175

Last MSR was $6,070.

MODEL ASE 90 GOLD TRAP - 12 ga. only, 30 in. vent. barrels with VR, similar action and specifications to Model ASE 90 Pigeon, 8.2 lbs., cased with extra trigger group, multi-chokes became standard 1995. Mfg. 1992-99.

	$4,250	$4,000	$3,750	$3,250	$2,750	$2,450	$2,250

Last MSR was $12,145.

    Add $2,000 for Trap Combo package.

DT10 TRIDENT TRAP - 12 ga. only, 3 in. chambers, 30 or 32 in. vent. barrels with target VR, specially designed trap gun featuring removable adj. trigger group, massive crossbolt locking system, Optima-choke competition choke tubes, Optima-Bore internal barrel configuration, specific point of impact, and unique distribution of mass that helps target acquisition and eliminate muzzle rise, adj. walnut stock with memory system, carbon reinforced frame, 8.8 lbs., cased. New 2000.

MSR $6,995	$5,600	$5,025	$4,550	$4,275	$3,995	$3,750	$3,450

GRADING - PPGS™	100%	98%	95%	90%	80%	70%	60%

✳ *DT10 Trident Trap Top Single* - includes 34 in. top single barrel, cased. New 2000.

MSR $6,995	$5,600	$5,025	$4,550	$4,275	$3,995	$3,750	$3,450

✳ *DT10 Trident Trap Bottom Single* - includes 34 in. bottom single barrel, cased. New 2004.

MSR $7,495	$6,250	$5,225	$4,525	$3,950	$3,275	$2,750	$2,250

✳ *DT10 Trident Trap Combo* - includes choice of 30 or 32 in. O/U barrels and a 34 in. top single barrel, cased. New 2000.

MSR $8,995	$6,800	$6,400	$5,900	$5,500	$4,750	$4,000	$3,250

✳ *DT10 Trident Trap Bottom Single Combo* - includes 34 in. bottom single barrel and choice of 30 or 32 in. O/U barrels, rib on bottom single barrel is adj. for point of impact, cased. New 2001.

MSR $9,995	$7,025	$6,000	$5,650	$5,250	$4,950	$4,250	$3,300

SHOTGUNS: O/U, CUSTOM GRADE - RECENT MFG.

Current high grade Beretta O/U and SxS shotguns are sold only by premium grade franchised Beretta dealers. For a listing of these dealers, contact a Beretta Gallery (see Trademark Index).

Where applicable, Beretta's new SST, with selector switch built into safety, is more desirable than older manufacture utilizing the disc. single, non-selective trigger.

Add 10% for 28 or 30 in. barrels.

Subtract 10%-15% for older style non-selective single trigger.

ROYAL PIGEON (GALLERY SPECIAL) - 12 or 20 ga., non-sideplated Mode 600 action, hand engraved in the EELL style, upgraded wood, made especially for Beretta Galleries. 40 mfg. in each gauge beginning 2004.

MSR $5,950	$5,250	$4,550	$4,100	$3,550	$3,200	$2,800	$2,400

ASEL - 12 or 20 ga., best SO grade boxlock with vintage 1960s action, SO grade hand finished wood, Boehler Antinit steel barrels, 28 mfg. in 20 ga. (2004-2005), 300 mfg. in 12 ga. New 2004.

MSR $25,750	$22,250	$18,500	$14,000	$10,500	$9,500	$8,500	$7,500

Pairs on this model are available for $59,225.

JUBILEE - 12, 20, 28 ga., or .410 bore, choice of Field or Sporting Clays configuration, signed scroll or game scene engraving, upgraded wood, tru-oil finish, and hand polished details throughout, cased. New 1998.

MSR $13,750	$11,600	$7,750	$5,950	$4,650	$3,100	$2,780	$2,500

✳ *Jubilee Matched Pair* - available with consecutive serial numbers, made to special order, cased. New 2002.

MSR $31,650	$25,000	$20,000	$15,000	$11,750	$7,000	$6,500	$5,000

SO-2 - 12 ga., 26-30 in. barrels, sidelock, any chokes, vent. rib, auto ejectors, SST, checkered stock in various configurations (field, skeet, or trap), grades differ in wood, engraving, and finish, cased. SO series mfg. 1948-disc.

MSR $4,750	$3,995	$2,950	$2,350	$1,950	$1,675	$1,475	$1,250

SO-3 - 2nd grade of the SO series.

MSR $6,250	$4,500	$3,550	$3,200	$2,800	$2,400	$2,100	$1,850

SO-3 EL - grade-up from SO-3 with better wood and engraving.

MSR $7,750	$6,250	$4,250	$3,600	$3,050	$2,500	$2,200	$1,950

SO-3 EELL - best quality model, custom specifications, choice of engraving motifs.

MSR $11,995	$10,250	$8,000	$6,850	$5,850	$5,100	$4,250	$3,600

Add $2,000 for master engraving.

SO-4 - 12 ga., sidelock, available in field, skeet, or trap configurations, custom specs., fluorescent sights, wide rib, cased. Disc. 1987, reintroduced 2001.

MSR $5,950	$5,250	$4,550	$4,100	$3,550	$3,200	$2,800	$2,400

ASE GOLD - see individual models with descriptions under Skeet, Sporting Clays, and Trap category names.

ASE 90 DE LUXE - 12 ga. only, specifications furnished by customer, deep scroll engraving signed by the engraver, upgraded wood, Sporting or Field Model, cased. New 1996.

	100%	98%	95%	90%	80%	70%	60%
MSR $24,500	$20,500	$15,000	$10,750	$8,750	$7,250	$6,000	$5,000

SO-5 COMPETITION - best quality O/U, extensively engraved, top quality checkered walnut stock (semi-pistol grip) and forearm, available in either Trap, Skeet, or Sporting configurations, leather cased, limited importation.

	100%	98%	95%	90%	80%	70%	60%
MSR $22,500	$19,000	$11,000	$8,500	$7,000	$6,000	$5,200	$4,500

Add $5,900 for extra set of barrels.

Add $3,500 for Trap Combo set (disc.).

SO-5 EELL - next to top-of-the-line model, available in either Trap, Skeet, or Sporting Clays configuration, custom built to customer dimensions.

	100%	98%	95%	90%	80%	70%	60%
MSR $15,000	$13,750	$9,250	$7,750	$6,250	$5,250	$4,750	$3,950

SO-6 COMPETITION - 12 ga. only high quality O/U, extensively scroll engraved, top quality checkered walnut stock (semi-pistol grip) and forearm, choice of Field (reintroduced during 1998), Trap, Skeet, or Sporting Clays configuration, built to customer specifications, leather cased, limited importation. Disc. 2002.

	95%	90%	80%	70%	60%
	$16,650	$13,500	$10,750	$8,500	$7,450	$6,350	$5,100

Last MSR was $23,900.

Add $6,250 for extra set of barrels.

SO-6 EL FIELD GRADE - 12 ga. only, available with rose and scroll engraving, 28, 30, or 32 in. barrels. New 2003.

	100%	98%	95%	90%	80%	70%	60%
MSR $27,500	$24,250	$19,750	$15,000	$11,000	$9,750	$8,750	$7,500

SO-6 EELL - 12 ga., current next to top-of-the-line model, field dimensions, custom built to customer specifications, leather cased.

	100%	98%	95%	90%	80%	70%	60%
MSR $34,900	$27,500	$21,500	$16,750	$12,750	$10,750	$9,500	$8,500

Add $6,250 for extra set of barrels.

Special engraving options are available on this model for an additional charge - contact the Gallery directly for pricing.

SO-6 EESS - 12 ga., features green enamel sideplates with diamond inlays. New 1998.

	100%	98%	95%	90%	80%	70%	60%
MSR $84,000	$77,500	$65,000	$52,000	$45,000	$39,000	$32,000	$26,500

✳ **SO-6 EESS w/o Diamonds** - features red or blue enamel sideplates, w/o diamonds. New 1998.

	100%	98%	95%	90%	80%	70%	60%
MSR $51,000	$40,000	$35,000	$27,250	$21,250	$16,750	$12,750	$10,750

SO-9 - 12, 20, 28 ga., or .410 bore, top-of-the-line sidelock model until 2003, 1990 was the first time the SO series was offered in smaller gauges, 28 ga. or .410 bore models have smaller proportionate frames. New 1990.

	100%	98%	95%	90%	80%	70%	60%
MSR $46,725	$35,000	$27,500	$20,500	$16,000	$12,000	$9,200	$7,000

Add $6,275 for extra set of barrels.

Add 10%-25% for well-known engravers.

Subtract 10% for 12 ga. on used specimens.

✳ **SO-9 EELL Special** - top-of-the-line O/U model, retail prices range from $55,000-$110,000, depending on individual custom-order engraving options.

SO-10 - top-of-the-line O/U sidelock model, barrels made of nickel, chromium, and molybdenum steel. Limited availability beginning late 2003.

	100%	98%	95%	90%	80%	70%	60%
MSR $56,215	$45,000	$35,500	$27,500	$20,500	$16,000	$12,000	$9,200

Pairs are available for $129,294. Any level of engraving is available on this model in 20 ga. through 2005. 28 ga. or .410 bore models will be available in 2006. Please contact the Beretta Gallery directly for more information about this model.

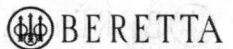

GRADING - PPGS™	100%	98%	95%	90%	80%	70%	60%

✳ **SO-10 EELL Special** - top-of-the-line O/U model, extra engraving.
This model starts at $64,500. Pairs are available for $148,500. Please contact the Beretta Gallery directly for more information regarding availability and options.

SHOTGUNS: SxS, RECENT MFG.

Subtract 20% on the following factory multi-choke models if w/o newer Beretta Optima-chokes (12 ga. only, became standard 2003).
Note: values are for unaltered guns.

MODEL 409 PB - 12, 16, 20, or 28 ga., 27, 28, and 30 in. barrels, various chokes, double triggers, plain extractors, checkered pistol grip stock. Mfg. 1934-64.

	$775	$675	$600	$550	$495	$440	$385

Add 25% for 20 ga.
Add 50% for 28 ga.

MODEL 410 E - higher quality, auto ejector version of 409 PB.

	100%	98%	95%	90%	80%	70%	60%
12 ga.	$1,275	$1,000	$895	$775	$675	$575	$475
20 ga.	$1,750	$1,550	$1,275	$1,000	$895	$775	$675
28 ga.	$3,775	$3,300	$2,800	$2,275	$1,800	$1,450	$1,100

MODEL 410 - similar to 410 E, except 10 ga. Mag., 32 in. barrel, full choke, heavier construction. Mfg. 1934-81.

	$1,200	$995	$880	$795	$700	$625	$550

MODEL 411 E - similar to 409 PB, with false sideplates and finer finishing. Mfg. 1934-64.

	100%	98%	95%	90%	80%	70%	60%
12 ga.	$2,000	$1,750	$1,350	$1,050	$895	$775	$675
20 ga.	$2,750	$2,325	$1,750	$1,300	$1,000	$895	$775
28 ga.	$4,250	$3,775	$3,300	$2,800	$2,275	$1,800	$1,450

MODEL 424-426 - 12 and 20 ga. (Model 426 only), 26 and 28 in. barrels, various chokes, boxlock, extractors, double triggers, light engraving, checkered straight stock.

	$1,475	$1,175	$975	$875	$750	$650	$600

Add $115 for Model 426.
Add 50% for 20 ga.

MODEL 426 E - similar to 424, with auto ejectors, SST, select wood and more intricate engraving, silver pigeon inlay. Disc. 1983.

	$1,950	$1,650	$1,325	$1,125	$850	$775	$675

MODEL 625 - 12 or 20 ga., 26-30 in. barrels, various chokes, boxlock, extractors, DTs or SST, light engraving, checkered straight stock. Imported 1984-86.

	$1,050	$950	$850	$775	$650	$600	$550

Last MSR was $835.

Add 50% for 20 ga.
Add 15% for SST.

MODEL GR-2 - 12 or 20 ga., 26 and 28 in. barrels, various chokes, boxlock, extractors, double triggers, checkered pistol grip stock. Mfg. 1968-76.

	$660	$605	$550	$495	$385	$330	$275

Add 50% for 20 ga.

MODEL GR-3 - similar to GR-2, with select wood and more engraving. Mfg. 1968-76.

	$770	$715	$640	$560	$475	$425	$375

Add 50% for 20 ga.

MODEL GR-4 - similar to GR-3, with auto ejectors. Mfg. 1968-76.

	$1,500	$1,275	$1,075	$900	$775	$675	$600

Add 50% for 20 ga.

GRADING - PPGS™	100%	98%	95%	90%	80%	70%	60%

SILVER HAWK - 12 ga. Mag. (3 in. chambers) & 10 ga. Mag. (3 1/2 chambers) with double triggers and extractors. Disc. 1967.

	100%	98%	95%	90%	80%	70%	60%
	$595	$495	$400	$350	$300	$275	$250

Subtract 10% for 10 ga.

SILVER HAWK FEATHERWEIGHT - 12, 16, 20, or 28 ga., 26-32 in. barrels, high solid rib, various chokes, single or double triggers, checkered pistol grip stock, beavertail forearm. Disc. 1967.

	100%	98%	95%	90%	80%	70%	60%
Double trigger	$650	$575	$500	$450	$400	$350	$300
Single trigger	$850	$750	$625	$550	$500	$450	$400

Add 50% for 20 ga.
Add 75% for 28 ga.

MODEL 470 SILVER HAWK (RECENT MFG.) - 12 or 20 ga., 3 in. chambers, 26 or 28 in. barrels with choice of fixed or multi-chokes (new 1999), satin chrome receiver finish, selector lever on forearm allows either automatic ejection or mechanical extraction, straight grip stock with matte finish, 5.9 or 6.5 lbs. Mfg. 1998-2002.

	100%	98%	95%	90%	80%	70%	60%
	$1,950	$1,700	$1,475	$1,300	$1,175	$1,025	$875

Last MSR was $2,596.

Add 15% for 20 ga.
Add $130 for multi-chokes (new 1999).

MODEL 470 EL - 12 or 20 ga., 3 in. chambers, 26 (20 ga. only) or 28 in. barrels with Optima-Chokes (12 ga. only) or MC3 multichokes, case colored boxlock receiver with 4 gold inlays (doves and ducks) on sideplates, selector lever on forearm allows either automatic ejection or mechanical extraction, deluxe straight grip stock and splinter forearm with oil finish, 5.9 or 6.5 lbs. New 2002.

		100%	98%	95%	80%	70%	60%
MSR $6,495		$4,500	$4,350	$4,000	$3,750	$3,550	$3,200	$2,800

This model is available only through select Beretta Showcase dealers.

MODEL 471 SILVER HAWK - 12 or 20 ga., 3 in. chambers, 26 or 28 in. barrels with multi-chokes or Optima-Chokes, engraved satin chrome or color case hardened receiver finish, selector lever on forearm allows either automatic ejection or mechanical extraction, ST, choice of straight grip or pistol grip stock with matte finish, beavertail or splinter forearm (fixed chokes only), 5.9 or 6.5 lbs. New 2003.

MSR $3,295		$2,250	$1,900	$1,675	$1,400	$1,100	$975	$800

Add $300 for color case hardened frame with straight grip stock and splinter forearm.

MODEL 471 EL - 12 or 20 ga., 3 in. chambers, 26 or 28 in. VR barrels, color case hardened receiver with gold accents, satin finished wood. New 2005.

MSR $6,495		$4,475	$3,900	$3,525	$2,875	$2,225	$1,800	$1,550

MODEL 626 FIELD - 12 or 20 (disc. 1987) ga., 2 3/4 in. chambers, 26 and 28 in. barrels, various chokes, boxlock, ejectors, single trigger, moderate engraving, pistol grip or straight checkered stock. Imported 1984-88.

	100%	98%	95%	90%	80%	70%	60%
	$1,450	$1,050	$875	$795	$675	$600	$550

Last MSR was $995.

Add 35% for 20 ga.

MODEL 626 ONYX - 12 or 20 ga., 3 in. chambers, 26 or 28 (new 1990) in. VR barrels with multi-chokes, matte finished metal parts, select checkered walnut stock and forearm. Imported 1988-93.

	100%	98%	95%	90%	80%	70%	60%
	$1,650	$1,250	$1,000	$925	$825	$750	$650

Last MSR was $1,870.

✳ *Model 626 Onyx Magnum* - 12 ga. only, 3 1/2 in. chambers. Mfg. 1990-92.

	100%	98%	95%	90%	80%	70%	60%
	$1,700	$1,300	$1,050	$925	$825	$750	$650

Last MSR was $1,870.

GRADING - PPGS™	100%	98%	95%	90%	80%	70%	60%

MODEL 627 EL FIELD

- 12 and 20 (disc. 1987) ga., 2 3/4 (disc. 1990) or 3 in. (became standard in 1991) chambers, 26 and 28 in. barrels, various chokes, box-lock, ejectors, single trigger, extensive engraving, pistol grip or straight checkered stock, cased. Imported 1985-93.

	$2,550	$2,150	$1,850	$1,500	$1,350	$1,150	$1,000

Last MSR was $3,270.

> **Subtract 5% for fixed chokes and 2 3/4 in. chambers.**
> **Add 25% for 20 ga.**

✳ *Model 627 EL Sport* - similar to Model 627 EL Field, except 12 ga. only, knurled rib, sporting clays dimensions. Importation disc. 1988.

	$2,750	$2,350	$1,925	$1,625	$1,475	$1,150	$1,000

Last MSR was $1,995.

> **Add 25% for 20 ga.**

MODEL 627 EELL

- 12 or 20 (disc. 1987) ga., 2 3/4 (disc.) or 3 (12 ga. only) in. chambers, 26 or 28 in. barrels, various chokes, boxlock, ejectors, single trigger, elaborate engraving, pistol grip or straight English checkered stock, cased. Imported 1985-93.

	$4,300	$3,675	$3,150	$2,800	$2,500	$2,175	$1,900

Last MSR was $5,405.

> **Add 20% for 20 ga.**
> **Add 10% for 28 in. barrels.**
> **Subtract 5% if fixed chokes only.**
> Multi-chokes became standard in 1991.

SHOTGUNS: SxS, CUSTOM GRADE

Current Custom grade Beretta O/U and SxS shotguns are sold only by premium grade franchised Beretta dealers. For a listing of these dealers, contact a Beretta Gallery (see Trademark Index).

> **Where applicable, Beretta's new SST, with selector switch built into safety, is more desirable than older manufacture utilizing the disc. single, non-selective trigger. Also, hand chased engraving on earlier mfg. (can be denoted by engraver's signature next to trigger guard) is more desirable, and may add a 10% premium, depending on condition.**

MODEL 450 SERIES

- 12 ga. only, built to individual customer order, various levels of engraving. Disc.

✳ *Model 450 EL* - incorporates H&H type sidelocks.

	$7,500	$6,950	$5,750	$5,250	$4,700	$4,200	$3,600

✳ *Model 450 EELL* - features third fastener with H&H type sidelocks.

	$8,000	$7,500	$6,000	$5,500	$4,850	$4,300	$3,750

SO-6

- same general specifications and embellishments as the SO series O/U guns, but SxS. Mfg. 1948-82.

	$7,250	$6,500	$5,925	$5,300	$4,700	$4,250	$3,850

SO-7

- top of the line SxS, finest quality wood, more elaborate engraving. Disc.

	$8,950	$7,950	$6,875	$6,000	$5,250	$4,600	$4,000

MODEL 451 SERIES

- 12 ga., totally hand-made, sidelock action, ejectors, scroll engraving. Custom made to order with fitted luggage case, various grades have increasing embellishments in EL Models.

✳ *Model 451* - disc. 1987.

	$6,250	$5,500	$4,875	$4,600	$4,300	$3,995	$3,600

Last MSR was $12,375.

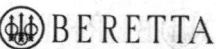
GRADING - PPGS™	100%	98%	95%	90%	80%	70%	60%

✳ *Model 451 E* - 12 ga. only, double triggers, specifications furnished by individual customer. Limited importation since 1989.

MSR $7,250	$6,750	$6,200	$5,500	$4,750	$4,000	$3,500	$2,750

Add approx. 40% for extra set of barrels.
Add $750 for SST (disc.).

✳ *Model 451 EL* - limited importation, temporarily disc. 1984.

MSR $15,250	$14,500	$7,750	$6,750	$5,600	$5,000	$4,500	$4,100

✳ *Model 451 EELL* - top-of-the-line for Model 451, choice of engraving motifs per customer specifications. Disc. 1987, reintroduced 1989.

MSR $18,500	$16,750	$8,500	$7,500	$6,500	$5,750	$5,150	$4,600

MODEL 452 CUSTOM - 12 ga. only, next to top-of-the-line side-by side shotgun featuring H&H style detachable locks, built to customer's specifications, leather cased. New 1990.

MSR $35,000	$28,750	$15,750	$11,750	$8,750	$6,650	$5,500	$4,500

Add $6,275 for extra set of barrels.

✳ *Model 452 EELL Custom* - 12 ga. only, top-of-the-line custom sidelock model featuring every refinement, built to customer's specifications, leather cased. Importation began 1992.

MSR $46,500	$38,950	$21,000	$15,750	$11,750	$9,000	$6,750	$5,600

Add $6,275 for extra set of barrels.
Add approx. $8,500-$43,500 for special master engraving options.

MODEL 470 EL CUSTOM - 12 or 20 ga., mfg. by Beretta's custom shop per individual order, custom case hardened frame with 24Kt. bird inlays, upgraded wood with oil finish. New 1999.

MSR $6,500	$5,225	$3,775	$2,825	$2,200	$1,725	$1,500	$1,200

MODEL JUBILEE II (MODEL 470 EELL) - 12 or 20 ga., scroll or game scene engraving signed by the engraver, select SO quality wood with Tru-oil finish, includes suede case, also available in pairs. New 1999.

MSR $15,250	$13,750	$9,250	$7,750	$6,250	$5,250	$4,750	$3,950

Pairs are available in this model for $35,075.

This model was designated the Model 470 EELL through 1999.

SHOTGUNS: SINGLE BARREL, DISC.

MARK II TRAP - 12 ga., 32 or 34 in. wide vent. rib, full choke, boxlock with auto ejector, Monte Carlo stock, recoil pad. Mfg. 1972-76.

	$550	$450	$400	$360	$330	$295	$260

MODEL FS-1 SINGLE BARREL - 12, 16, 20, 28 ga., or .410 bore, 26 or 28 in. barrels, full choke, checkered semi-pistol grip, under lever break open, folds to length of barrel (also known as Companion).

	$175	$150	$125	$110	$100	$90	$80

TR-1 TRAP - 12 ga., 32 in. full choke barrel, under lever break open, Monte Carlo pistol grip stock with pad, engraved. Mfg. 1968-71.

	$275	$250	$220	$195	$140	$110	$100

TR-2 TRAP - similar to TR-1, with high rib. Mfg. 1969-73.

	$290	$260	$230	$205	$150	$120	$110

MODEL 412 - 12, 20, 28 ga., or .410 bore, monobloc construction, folding action, sling swivels, checkered walnut stock and forearm, 5 lbs. Importation disc. 1988.

	$190	$170	$125	$100	$85	$70	$60

Last MSR was $215.

GRADING - PPGS™	100%	98%	95%	90%	80%	70%	60%

VANDALIA SPECIAL TRAP - 12 ga., sidelock action with crossbolt, fixed choke, coin finished receiver, light scroll hand engraving with borders, cased with accessories, never offically introduced or released commercially. 6 mfg. circa 1997.

	$4,600	$3,850	$3,150				

SHOTGUNS: SLIDE ACTION, DISC.

MODEL SL-2 - 12 ga., 26, 28, or 30 in. barrels, various chokes, vent. rib, checkered pistol grip stock. Mfg. 1968-71.

	$300	$275	$250	$220	$195	$165	$140

SILVER PIGEON - 12 ga., various chokes, light engraving.

	$250	$200	$175	$160	$150	$140	$130

GOLD PIGEON - 12 ga., various chokes, vent. rib, engraved.

	$475	$375	$310	$275	$240	$215	$195

Add $200 for deluxe models.

RUBY PIGEON - 12 ga., various chokes, vent. rib, elaborately engraved, special deluxe walnut.

	$600	$475	$395	$350	$295	$260	$230

SHOTGUNS: SEMI-AUTO

It is possible on some of the following models to have production variances occur including different engraving motifs, stock configurations and specifications, finishes, etc. These have occurred when Beretta changed from production of one model to another. Also, some European and English distributors have sold their excess inventory through Beretta U.S.A., creating additional variations/configurations that are not normally imported domestically. While sometimes rare, these specimens typically do not command premiums over Beretta's domestic models.

The following Beretta semi-auto models have been listed in numerical sequence, if possible, disregarding any alphabetical suffix or prefix.

BERETTA CHOKES AND THEIR CODES (ON REAR LEFT-SIDE OF BARREL)
* designates full choke (F).
** designates improved modified choke (IM).
*** designates modified choke (M).
**** designates improved cylinder choke (IC).
FK designates skeet (SK).
***** designates cylinder bore (CYL).

Subtract 10% on the following factory multi-choke models if w/o newer Beretta Optimachokes (12 ga. only, became standard 2003).

Note: values are for unaltered guns.

MODEL 60 - 12 ga., 2 3/4 in. chamber, gas operated with piston rod, 3 shot mag., 24, 26, or 28 in. plain barrel, approx. 7 lbs. Mfg. 1956-1960.

	$295	$260	$240	$220	$200	$185	$170

Add 10% for Model 60 Deluxe with special embellishments.

MODEL 61 - 12 ga., improved version of the Model 60 with recoil spring located in stock, chromium plated action and fine engraving, 24, 26, or 28 in. VR barrel. Mfg. approx. 1961-1965.

	$335	$295	$260	$235	$210	$195	$175

SILVER LARK - 12 ga., various chokes.

	$295	$260	$240	$220	$200	$185	$170

GOLD LARK - 12 ga., vent. rib, light scroll engraving, select walnut.

	$480	$400	$325	$260	$230	$210	$195

RUBY LARK - 12 ga., vent. rib, heavy engraving, deluxe walnut.

	$675	$550	$475	$395	$350	$295	$260

GRADING - PPGS™	100%	98%	95%	90%	80%	70%	60%

MODEL AL-1 - 12 and 20 ga., semi-auto gas operated, 26, 28, and 30 in. plain barrel, various chokes, checkered pistol grip stock. Mfg. 1971-73.

	$385	$360	$330	$305	$250	$195	$165

MODEL AL-2 - 12 or 20 ga., 26, 28, or 30 in. barrels, vent. rib, various chokes, gas operated, checkered pistol grip stock. Mfg. 1973-75.

	$330	$305	$275	$250	$220	$195	$165

MODEL AL-2 SKEET - similar to AL-2, with 26 in. wide rib skeet bored barrel. Mfg. 1973-75.

	$395	$360	$320	$275	$220	$200	$185

MODEL AL-2 TRAP - similar to AL-2, with 30 in. full choke barrel, wide rib, Monte Carlo stock, with recoil pad. Mfg. 1973-75.

	$375	$345	$315	$285	$250	$195	$165

MODEL AL-2 MAGNUM - 12 or 20 ga., 3 in. chamber, heavier action bar, 28 and 30 in. mod. or full choke. Mfg. 1973-75.

	$415	$385	$330	$275	$250	$230	$210

MODEL AL-3 - continuation of the AL-2 series. Mfg. 1975-1976.

	100%	98%	95%	90%	80%	70%	60%
Field grade	$395	$360	$330	$260	$240	$220	$190
Magnum grade	$425	$385	$330	$275	$250	$230	$210
Skeet grade	$400	$360	$330	$260	$240	$220	$190
Trap grade	$385	$350	$295	$250	$225	$210	$185

MODEL AL-3 DELUXE TRAP - similar to AL-3, with fully engraved receiver, premium grade wood. Mfg. 1975-76.

	$770	$715	$660	$605	$550	$495	$440

MODEL UGB25 XCEL - 12 ga., 2 3/4 in. chamber, unique two shot (second shell is located outside receiver on cartridge carrier), break open action featuring short recoil operating system, rising lock block system, light alloy black receiver with gold lettering, 30 or 32 in. three alloy steel barrel with Optima-Bore, competition front sight, laser checkered walnut stock with adj. comb, gold trigger, button safety, Gel-tek recoil pad, 7.7-9 lbs. New late 2004.

MSR $3,195	$2,850	$2,600	$2,400	$2,200	$2,000	$1,750	$1,500

MODEL ES100 PINTAIL (VITTORIA) - 12 ga., 3 in. chamber, uses Montefeltro short action, 24, 26, or 28 (new 1999) in. VR barrel, matte black metal finish, choice of matte finished wood (disc. 1998) or black synthetic stock and forearm (new 1999), includes sling swivels, 7.3 lbs. Mfg. 1993-2001, reintroduced 2003 only.

	$495	$425	$375	$350	$325	$275	$250

Last MSR was $682.

In 1999, this model was renamed the ES 100 Pintail (with synthetic stock).

✳ *Model ES100 Camouflage* - 12 ga. only, features 100% Advantage Wetlands, Realtree Hardwoods HD (new 2003), or Mossy Oak Shadowgrass (new 2003) coverage, 28 in. VR barrel only, 7.3 lbs. Mfg. 2000-2003.

	$495	$425	$375	$330	$280	$250	$230

Last MSR was $777.

✳ *ES100 Rifled Slug (Pintail Rifled Slug)* - 12 ga., 3 in. chamber, 24 in. rifled barrel with drilled and tapped upper receiver, barrel and upper receiver are permanently joined, anti-glare matte black metal finish, choice of matte finished wood (disc. 1998) or black synthetic (new 1999) stock and forearm, includes swivels, 7 lbs. Mfg. 1998-2001, reintroduced 2003 only.

	$495	$425	$375	$330	$280	$250	$230

Last MSR was $749.

Add $148 for combo package (includes extra 28 in. smooth bore barrel with MC3 choke, mfg. 2001).

In 1999, the model nomenclature changed from Pintail Rifled Slug to ES100 Rifled Slug.

GRADING - PPGS™	100%	98%	95%	90%	80%	70%	60%

✳ *Pintail Slug (Victoria)* - 12 ga. only, 24 in. slug barrel, includes rifle sights and rifle choke tubes, 7 lbs. Imported 1993-95.

	$495	$425	$375	$325	$280	$250	$230

Last MSR was $700.

✳ *Model ES100 NWTF Special Camouflage (Pintail)* - 12 ga. only, 24 in. VR barrel with 3 dot TruGlo fiberoptic sight system, includes Briley extended extra-full choke tube and 3 standard Mobilchoke tubes, features Mossy Oak Break-up treatment on synthetic stock and forearm, black matte anti-glare finish on metal components, includes nylon sling. Limited mfg. 1999, reintroduced 2002 only (limited mfg.).

	$600	$550	$475	$375	$325	$290	$265

Last MSR was $966.

MODEL 300/301 - continuation of the AL-3 series, scroll engraved receiver. Mfg. approx. 1968-82.

	100%	98%	95%	90%	80%	70%	60%
Field grade	$395	$360	$330	$260	$240	$220	$190
Magnum grade	$425	$385	$330	$275	$250	$230	$210
Skeet grade	$400	$360	$330	$260	$240	$220	$190
Trap grade	$385	$350	$295	$250	$225	$210	$185

Beretta changed model nomenclature rapidly during the Model 300 Series. In approx. 10 months, the evolution of this model had progressed from the 300 to 303 Series. Beginning with the Model 303, all receivers were milled with a 3 in. ejection port window.

MODEL 301 SLUG GUN - 22 in. barrel, with sights. Disc.

	$395	$360	$330	$305	$265	$230	$190

MODEL 302 - 12 or 20 ga., self-compensating gas operation semi-auto, designed for both 2 3/4 and 3 in. shells, available with interchangeable chokes, slug barrel, trap and skeet models (disc.), VR, mag. cut-off. Mfg. 1982-87. This model was superceded by the Model 303.

	$395	$365	$340	$310	$280	$255	$225

Last MSR was $480.

Add $30 for multi-choke set.

✳ *Model 302 Super Lusso* - same specifications as Model A302, but includes hand engraved receiver, many gold plated parts, and stock and forearm made from presentation grade walnut. Disc. 1986.

	$2,150	$1,950	$1,750	$1,550	$1,300	$1,050	$895

Last MSR was $2,500.

MODEL A-303 FIELD - 12 (disc. 1993) or 20 ga., 2 3/4 or 3 in. chambers, same gas operation as the Model 302, 26 or 28 in. VR barrel, high-strength alloy receiver, select wood with choice pistol grip or straight English stock, beavertail forearm, multi-chokes became standard 1987. Disc. 1996.

	$450	$400	$375	$335	$300	$270	$240

Last MSR was $799.

Subtract 20% without multi-chokes.
Subtract $20 for straight grip English stock.

✳ *A-303 Upland* - 12 (disc. 1993) or 20 ga., 2 3/4 or 3 in. chamber, 24 in. VR barrel with multi-chokes, English style straight stock, approx. 7 lbs. Importation began 1989. Disc. 1996.

	$450	$400	$380	$335	$300	$270	$240

Last MSR was $772.

✳ *A-303 Waterfowl/Turkey* - 12 ga. only, 3 in. chamber, choice of 24, 26, 28, or 30 in. VR barrel, matte finished wood and metal, multi-chokes are standard. Imported 1991 only.

	$495	$450	$395	$350	$300	$270	$240

Last MSR was $665.

GRADING - PPGS™	100%	98%	95%	90%	80%	70%	60%

✳ A-303 Sporting - 12 (disc. 1994) or 20 (new 1991) ga. only, 2 3/4 in. chambers, sporting clay dimensions, 28 or 30 (12 ga. only) in. VR barrel with multi-chokes. Mfg. 1988-96.

	$495	$450	$425	$375	$325	$300	$275

Last MSR was $822.

✳ A-303 Skeet - 12 (disc. 1994) or 20 ga., 26 in. VR barrel with fixed skeet choking. Importation disc. 1995.

	$400	$375	$350	$315	$275	$250	$225

Last MSR was $736.

✳ A-303 Super Skeet - 12 ga. only, 28 in. VR fixed choke barrel, features factory porting, adj. LOP, and adj. separate cheekpiece on stock. Mfg. 1991-92.

	$425	$375	$350	$315	$280	$240	$200

Last MSR was $1,160.

✳ A-303 Trap - 12 ga. only, 30 or 32 in. VR barrel with fixed choking or multi-chokes. Importation disc. 1994.

	$495	$450	$425	$400	$375	$350	$325

Last MSR was $735.

Add $40 for multi-chokes (with Monte Carlo stock).

✳ A-303 Super Trap - 12 ga. only, 30 or 32 in. VR multi-choke barrel with step tapered rib, features factory porting, adj. LOP, and adj. separate cheekpiece on stock. Mfg. 1991-92.

	$595	$550	$525	$500	$425	$365	$300

Last MSR was $1,210.

✳ A-303 Slug - 12 or 20 ga., 3 in. chamber (12 ga. only), 22 in. cylinder bore barrel, iron sights. Importation disc. 1991.

	$395	$350	$325	$300	$275	$265	$240

Last MSR was $665.

✳ A-303 Youth - 20 ga. only, 2 3/4 or 3 (disc.) in. chamber, 24 in. VR barrel with multi-chokes, shortened stock, approx. 6 lbs. Mfg. 1988-96.

	$495	$450	$375	$330	$300	$270	$240

Last MSR was $772.

MODEL A304 LARK

MODEL A304 LARK - 12 ga., 2 3/4 in. chamber, 20 (Silver Slug), 22 (Silver Slug), 24, 26, 28, or 30 in. barrel, vent. rib (except Silver Slug model), Mobilchoke or cylinder (Silver Slug) bore, ambidextrous safety, crossbolt, checkered walnut pistol grip stock and semi-beavertail forend, black recoil pad, black matte finished receiver with light scroll work, gold trigger, available in Silver Lark, Silver Slug, or Gold Lark. Mfg. 1994-disc.

	$450	$400	$375	$335	$300	$270	$240

Add 10% for Silver Lark with scroll engraved black receiver.

Add 20% for White or Black A304 Gold Lark Model with gold filled P. Beretta signature and game scene engraving.

MODEL AL390 FIELD SILVER MALLARD

MODEL AL390 FIELD SILVER MALLARD - 12 or 20 (new 1997) ga. only, 3 in. chamber, features new gas system that will accept all 2 3/4 and 3 in. shotshells, single stainless steel piston with self regulating valve, mag. cut-off on left side of receiver, 22 slug (12 ga. only, new 1994), 24, 26, 28, or 30 (12 ga. only) in. VR barrel with Mobilchoke system, choice of gloss or matte (includes sling swivels) wood finish on lightly engraved receiver, adj. checkered walnut stock, gold trigger, 6.4 (20 ga.) or 7.2 (12 ga.) lbs. Mfg. 1992-99.

	$495	$450	$415	$350	$300	$270	$240

Last MSR was $860.

Add $25 for 20 ga.

Subtract $25 for 24 in. barrel.

Beginning 1997, Beretta introduced the "AL" Series of the 390, which is the lightweight variation of the 390. Prior to 1997, this model was designated the A390 Series.

Model AL390 Field Deluxe Gold Mallard - similar to Model 390 Field, except has gold accents on receiver frame, including a gold inlaid snipe, setter, and P. Beretta signature, deluxe walnut, 7.2 lbs. Mfg. 1993-99.

$695	$575	$460	$400	$360	$320	$285

Last MSR was $1,025.

Add $30 for 20 ga.

Model AL390 Lioness Limited Edition - 12 ga. only, 28 in. VR barrel with MC3 choke tubes, deluxe checkered walnut stock and forearm. Limited mfg. 2002.

$2,450	$1,950	$1,600

Last MSR was $2,969.

Model AL390 Silver Mallard Synthetic - 12 ga. only, 3 in. chamber, 24, 26, 28, or 30 in. barrel with multi-choke, black synthetic stock and forearm with sling swivels, matte finish, approx. 7.2 lbs. Mfg. 1996-99.

$495	$450	$425	$350	$300	$270	$240

Last MSR was $885.

Model AL390 Silver Mallard Camouflage - 12 ga. only, 3 in. chamber, Advantage camo finish on entire gun, 24 or 28 in. VR barrel with choke tubes, synthetic stock and forearm, 7.2 lbs. Mfg. 1997-99.

$495	$450	$400	$375	$300	$270	$240

Last MSR was $1,020.

Model AL390 Silver Mallard Slug - 12 ga. only, 3 in. chamber, 22 in. non-rifled barrel with slug choke, gloss wood finish, adj. rear sight, approx. 6.8 or 7.4 (Model A390) lbs. Mfg. 1995-97.

$495	$450	$415	$350	$300	$270	$240

Last MSR was $860.

Model AL390 Silver Mallard Youth - 20 ga. only, 3 in. chamber, gloss wood finish, 24 in. VR barrel only with choke tubes, features youth stock dimensions, 6.4 lbs. Mfg. 1997-99.

$495	$450	$400	$350	$300	$270	$240

Last MSR was $885.

Model AL390 NWTF Special Camouflage - 12 ga. only, 3 in. chamber, 24 in. VR barrel with 3 dot TruGlo fiber optic sight system, includes Briley extended extra-full choke tube and 3 standard Mobilchoke tubes, full Realtree X-tra brown camo treatment (including synthetic stock and forearm), includes camo nylon sling. Special Edition released during 1999 only.

$595	$550	$525	$500	$475	$460	$425

Last MSR was $1,105.

> **Model AL390 NWTF Special Synthetic** - similar to NWTF Special Camouflage, except has matte black anti-glare finish. Mfg. 1999 only.

$495	$450	$400	$365	$315	$275	$240

Last MSR was $970.

Model AL390 NWTF Special Youth - 20 ga. only, 3 in. chamber, 24 in. barrel, shorter stock dimensions with 13 1/2 LOP, matte finished wood stock and forearm, matte black metal anti-glare finish. Mfg. 1999 only.

$595	$535	$425	$350	$300	$270	$240

Last MSR was $910.

MODEL AL390 SPORT SPORTING - 12 or 20 (new 1997) ga., 3 in. chamber, designed for sporting clays competition, similar to Model 390 Sport Skeet, 28 or 30 (12 ga. only) in. VR ported or unported barrel with choke tube, 6.8 (20 ga.) or 7.6 (12 ga.) lbs. Imported 1995-99.

$525	$475	$450	$400	$325	$275	$240

Last MSR was $925.

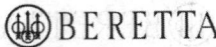

GRADING - PPGS™	100%	98%	95%	90%	80%	70%	60%

✳ Model AL390 Sport Sporting Collection - 12 or 20 (Youth Model) ga., 3 in. chamber, 26 (20 ga. only), 28 in. VR barrel with multi-choke, features multi-colored, gloss finished stock and forearm, 6.7 (20 ga.) or 7.6 (12 ga.) lbs. Mfg. 1998-99.

	$525	$475	$450	$400	$325	$275	$240

Last MSR was $965.

The 20 ga. in this model is a youth model with 13 1/2 LOP.

✳ Model AL390 Sport Gold Sporting - 12 ga. only, 28 or 30 in. VR barrel with multi-chokes, gloss finished wood, gold engraved receiver, 7.6 lbs. Mfg. 1997-99.

	$795	$725	$575	$525	$495	$460	$425

Last MSR was $1,145.

✳ Model AL390 Sport Diamond Sporting - 12 ga. only, 3 in. chamber, silver sided receiver with multiple gold inlays, EELL quality stock and forearm with oil finish, matte 28 or 30 in. barrel with multi-chokes, oval nameplate on stock, 7.6 lbs. Mfg. 1998-99.

	$2,000	$1,650	$1,450	$1,275	$1,200	$995	$825

Last MSR was $3,075.

✳ Model AL390 Sport Sporting Youth - 20 ga. only, 3 in. chamber, matte finished checkered stock and forearm, 26 in. VR barrel only with choke tubes, features youth stock dimensions (13 1/2 LOP), 6.7 lbs. Imported 1997-98 only.

	$500	$475	$450	$375	$300	$270	$240

Last MSR was $900.

MODEL AL390 SPORT SKEET
MODEL AL390 SPORT SKEET - 12 ga. only, 3 in. chamber, 26 (disc.) or 28 in. SK bored VR barrel, matte finish on wood and metal, black rubber recoil pad, 7.6 lbs. Imported 1995-99.

	$425	$400	$375	$350	$300	$270	$240

Last MSR was $890.

✳ Model AL390 Sport Super Skeet - 12 ga. only, 28 in. skeet choke VR ported barrels, includes adj. stock comb and LOP (using 3 different recoil pads) approx. 8.1 lbs. Mfg. 1993-99.

	$495	$450	$400	$375	$300	$270	$240

Last MSR was $1,160.

MODEL AL390 SPORT TRAP
MODEL AL390 SPORT TRAP - 12 ga. only, 3 in. chamber, 30 or 32 in. VR barrel, matte finish on wood and metal, black rubber recoil pad, 7.8 or 8 1/4 (A390) lbs. Imported 1995-99.

	$495	$450	$400	$375	$300	$270	$240

Last MSR was $890.

✳ Model AL390 Sport Super Trap - 12 ga. only, 30 or 32 in. VR multi-choke ported barrels, adj. stock comb and LOP, approx. 8 lbs. Mfg. 1993-97.

	$600	$500	$450	$400	$375	$325	$295

Last MSR was $1,215.

MODEL AL391 URIKA
MODEL AL391 URIKA - 12 or 20 ga., 3 in. chamber, features new self-compensating gas valve and receiver recoil absorber for internal shock reduction, satin finished checkered walnut stock and forearm, gas valve is located on the front bottom of the forearm, alloy receiver with thin design, cold hammer forged barrel, black anodized metal surfaces, gold trigger, beginning 2003, all 12 ga. AL391 Urika include Optima-Bore overbored barrels with flush Optima-Choke plus tubes, molded synthetic case included, 6.3-7.3 lbs. New 2000.

✳ Model AL391 Urika Standard - 12 or 20 ga., 24 (20 ga. only), 26, 28, or 30 (12 ga. only) in. VR barrel, available in synthetic stock beginning 2004 at no charge, approx. 5.95 (20 ga.) or 7.25 lbs. New 2000.

MSR $1,095	$795	$725	$615	$485	$400	$350	$300

Add $104 for Optima-Choke system (12 ga. only, disc. 2004).

GRADING - PPGS™	100%	98%	95%	90%	80%	70%	60%

✳ **Model AL391 Urika Synthetic Optima** - 12 ga. only, 24 (disc. 2003), 26, 28, or 30 (disc. 2003) in. VR barrel with matte finish, features black synthetic stock with over-sized grip area for a secure grip and recoil absorption and forearm, Optima-Chokes became standard in 2004, approx. 7.25 lbs. New 2000.

	MSR $1,095	$795	$725	$615	$485	$400	$350	$300

✳ **Model AL391 Urika Camouflage** - 12 ga. only, choice of 100% Hardwoods Green HD (mfg. 2003), RealTree Hardwoods HD (24 in. barrel only, turkey configuration), Max-4 HD (new 2004), or Advantage Wetlands camo (28 in. barrel only, water-fowl configuration, mfg. 2003) finish, with oversized stock grip, approx. 7.25 lbs. New 2000.

	MSR $1,195	$900	$825	$685	$530	$450	$400	$350

✳ **Model AL391 Urika Youth** - 20 ga. only, 24 in. VR barrel only, shortened walnut stock and regular forearm, 5.95 lbs. New 2000.

	MSR $1,095	$800	$725	$615	$485	$400	$350	$300

✳ **Model AL391 Urika Gold** - 12 or 20 ga., similar to Model AL391 Urika Standard, except has deluxe checkered walnut stock and forearm, choice of black (standard) or partial silver (lightweight configuration, 12 ga. only) receiver finish, multiple gold receiver inlays, 26 or 28 in. VR barrel, jewelled bolt, 5.9 (20 ga.), 6.6 (12 ga. lightweight), or approx. 7.25 lbs. Mfg. 2000-2002.

		$895	$725	$625	$495	$400	$350	$300

Last MSR was $1,213.

✳ **Model AL391 Covey Quail Unlimited** - 20 ga., matte black receiver with multiple gold quail inlays, deluxe checkered walnut stock and forearm, marked "1 of 1000." 1,000 mfg. 2003-2004.

		$1,075	$900	$825	$725	$625	$525	$425

Last MSR was $1,336.

✳ **Model AL391 Ringneck Pheasants Forever** - 12 ga., matte black receiver with multiple gold pheasant inlays, deluxe checkered walnut stock and forearm, includes Gel-Tek recoil pad and Optima-Bore chokes, marked "1 of 1000." 1,000 mfg. 2003-2004.

		$1,100	$995	$875	$775	$675	$550	$450

Last MSR was $1,377.

MODEL AL391 TEKNYS

MODEL AL391 TEKNYS - 12 or 20 ga., 3 in. chamber, multi-colored receiver with unique asymetrical patterns, X-tra Wood stock with Gel-Tek recoil pad, anti-glare receiver top, TruGlo Tru-bead front sight, choice of Optima-Bore or Mobilchokes (20 ga.), includes molded case with 5 choke tubes, 5.9 (20 ga.) or 7.3 (12 ga.) lbs. Importation began 2003.

	MSR $1,295	$1,050	$850	$750	$625	$525	$425	$375

✳ **Model AL391 Teknys Gold** - 12 or 20 ga., 3 in. chamber, receiver has engraved hunting scenes, jewelled breech bolt and carrier, checkered deluxe walnut stock and forearm with green colored enamel inserts in rear receiver and front of stock, includes Gel-Tek recoil pad, and stock recoil reducer. Importation began 2003.

	MSR $1,595	$1,285	$1,075	$935	$850	$750	$650	$550

✳ **Model AL391 Teknys Gold Sporting** - 12 or 20 ga., similar to Model AL391 Teknys Gold, except has two-tone dark grey receiver with blue enamel inserts on stock and receiver, interchangeable rib, improved forearm checkering pattern, includes Gel-Tek recoil pad and stock recoil reducer, deluxe checkered walnut stock and forearm, includes hard case, 6.6 (20 ga.) or 7.9 (12 ga.) lbs. Importation began 2003.

	MSR $1,795	$1,425	$1,175	$950	$800	$675	$550	$450

✳ **Model AL391 Teknys Gold Trap** - 12 ga. only, 30 or 32 in. VR barrel, oil finished checkered walnut stock, gold trigger, Gel-Tek recoil pad, includes hardshell case. Importation began 2004.

	MSR $1,895	$1,500	$1,175	$1,025	$850	$725	$625	$525

GRADING - PPGS™	100%	98%	95%	90%	80%	70%	60%

MODEL AL391 XTREMA2 3.5 - 12 ga. only, 3 1/2 in. chamber, features Gel-Tek recoil pad, spring mass and bolt travel recoil reducers lower felt recoil up to 20%, 24, 26, or 28 in. VR barrel with Optima-Choke Plus and Optima-Bore, gas operating system with rotating locking bolt, black synthetic stock and forearm with rubber inserts for firm control instead of traditional checkering, grooved receiver, removable trigger grip, includes carrying case, 7.8 lbs. New 2002.

	MSR $1,295	$1,035	$865	$775	$665	$550	$450	$350

    Add $200 for KO configuration (Kick-off recoil reduction).

    This model's nomenclature changed to Extrema2 during 2005.

✳ *Model AL391 Xtrema2 Camouflage* - 12 ga. only, similar operating system to Model AL391 Xtrema 3.5, choice of 100% RealTree Hardwoods HD (24 in. barrel only, turkey configuration), Max-4 HD (new 2004, 30 in. barrel only), Advantage Timber HD camo (26 in. barrel only, disc. 2004) or Advantage Wetlands (26 or 28 in. barrel, disc. 2004) finish, 7.8 lbs. New 2002.

	MSR $1,395	$1,000	$925	$850	$750	$650	$550	$450

    Add $200 for KO configuration (Kick-off recoil reduction).

✳ *Model AL391 Xtrema2 Slug* - 12 ga. only, 24 in. rifle bore barrel, Optima-Bore choke. New 2005.

	MSR $1,495	$1,100	$975	$875	$775	$675	$575	$475

    Add $100 for KO configuration (Kick-off recoil reduction).

MODEL AL391 URIKA SPORTING - 12 or 20 ga., 3 in. chamber, gas operating system the same as Model Al391 Urika Standard, 28 or 30 in. wide VR barrel with 2 beads, features special competition checkered walnut sporting stock with rounded solid rubber recoil pad, satin black receiver with silver markings, gold trigger, Mobilchoke tubes are standard on 20 ga., Optima-Bore chokes with flush Optima choke tubes became standard in 12 ga. during 2003 (AL391 Urika Sporting Optima), molded synthetic case included, 5.95 or 7.3 lbs. New 2000.

	MSR $1,195	$850	$795	$700	$600	$500	$400	$325

✳ *Model AL391 Urika Gold Sporting* - similar to Model AL391 Urika Gold, except has deluxe walnut stock and forearm, with choice of black (disc.) or silver receiver and gold accents. New 2000.

	MSR $1,395	$1,000	$950	$860	$750	$650	$550	$450

✳ *Model AL391 Diamond Sporting* - 12 ga. only, 3 in. chamber, silver sided receiver with multiple gold inlays, EELL quality stock and forearm with oil finish, matte 28 in. barrel with MC4 multi-chokes, oval nameplate on stock, 7.6 lbs. Mfg. 2002 only.

	$2,000	$1,850	$1,700	$1,525	$1,200	$995	$775

                      Last MSR was $3,139.

MODEL AL391 URIKA TRAP OPTIMA - 12 ga. only, 30 or 32 in. wide VR barrel with 2 beads, Monte Carlo stock with special trap recoil pad, satin black receiver with glossy side panels and silver markings, gold trigger, Optima-Bore chokes with flush Optima choke tubes became standard in 12 ga. during 2003, molded synthetic case included, 7.25 lbs. New 2000.

	MSR $1,195	$800	$725	$675	$600	$500	$400	$325

✳ *Model AL391 Urika Gold Trap* - similar to Model AL391 Urika Trap, except has black receiver with gold filled Beretta logo and P. Beretta signature, jewelled bolt and carrier, 7 1/4 lbs. Mfg. 2000-2002.

	$995	$850	$725	$565	$450	$415	$395

                      Last MSR was $1,254.

MODEL AL391 URIKA PARALLEL TARGET RL/SL - 12 ga. only, similar to Model AL391 Urika Trap, except features a Monte Carlo stock with parallel comb and reduced grip radius, RL suffix designates shorter LOP and slimmer grip, molded synthetic case included, 7.25 lbs. New 2000.

	MSR $1,195	$800	$725	$675	$600	$500	$400	$325

GRADING - PPGS™	100%	98%	95%	90%	80%	70%	60%

MODEL 1200 FIELD - 12 ga., inertia recoil system, 28 in. VR barrels with multi-chokes, checkered European walnut stock and forearm (pre-1989), matte black polymer stock and forearm (starting 1989), recoil pad, 4 shot mag., approx. 8 lbs. Imported 1984-1989.

	$375	$350	$300	$275	$250	$225	$200

Last MSR was $580.

❋ *Model 1200 Riot* - 12 ga. only, 2 3/4 or 3 in. chamber, 20 in. cyl. bore barrel with iron sights, extended mag. Imported 1989-90 only.

	$400	$375	$350	$295	$250	$225	$200

Last MSR was $660.

MODEL 1201 FIELD MAGNUM - 12 ga., 3 in. chamber, short recoil blowback action, 24, 26, or 28 in. VR barrel with multi-chokes (2), matte black polymer stock and forearm. Imported 1989-94.

	$500	$395	$340	$285	$250	$225	$200

Last MSR was $625.

The Model 1201 can be differentiated from the Model 1200 by stock spacers to adjust length.

❋ *Model 1201 FP (Riot)* - 12 ga., riot configuration featuring 18 (new 1997) or 20 (disc. 1996) in. cylinder bore barrel, 5 shot mag, choice of adj. rifle sights (disc.), Tritium sights (disc. 1998) or ghost ring (new 1999, Tritium front sight insert) sights, matte wood (disc.) or black synthetic stock and forearm, matte metal finish (disc.), 6.3 lbs. Mfg. 1991-2004.

	$725	$595	$500	$400	$300	$250	$200

Last MSR was $890.

Add $80 for Tritium sights (mfg. 1997-98).

Add $45 for pistol grip configuration (Model 1201 FPG3 - mfg. 1994 only).

MODEL AL3901 - 12 or 20 (new 2003) ga., 3 in. chamber, 24 (new 2003), 26 (new 2003), or 28 in. VR barrel with MC3 multi-chokes, choice of regular or shortened (Model AL3901RL) charcoal grey synthetic checkered wood, or Mossy Oak New Break-Up (new 2003), or Mossy Oak New Shadowgrass (new 2003) camo covered stock and forearm, gold trigger, matte metal finish, reversible crossbolt safety, 7 1/2 lbs. Mfg. 2002-2003.

	$450	$425	$375	$335	$280	$250	$230

Last MSR was $730.

Add $50 for camo finish.

This model was available through Beretta Showcase Dealers only.

MODEL 3901 PATRIOT - 12 or 20 ga., 3 in. chamber, 26 or 28 in. VR barrel with MC3 choke tubes, available in three configurations, including Citizen (synthetic stock), Statesman, or Ambassador (X-Tra wood), gas opertating system, 26 or 28 in. steel alloy hammer forged barrel, Mobilchoke, removable trigger group, mfg. in America. New 2005.

MSR $750	$625	$550	$475	$400	$350	$300	$250

Add $100 for Statesman configuration or $200 for Ambassador configuration.

COMMEMORATIVES

MODEL A-303 DUCKS UNLIMITED - 12 or 20 ga., D.U. serialization, 5,500 mfg. in 12 ga. 1986-87, 3,500 mfg. in 20 ga. 1987-88.

12 ga.	$575	$450	$350
20 ga.	$675	$475	$375

These D.U. Models had no retail pricing from Beretta. Rather, they were auctioned off at D.U. dinners, and as a result, prices could vary substantially from region to region.

MODEL 687 O/U SHOTGUN TERCENTENNIAL - 12 ga., SST and ejectors. Limited production, only 300 manufactured.

	$2,500	$1,950	$1,400

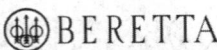

GRADING - PPGS™	100%	98%	95%	90%	80%	70%	60%

MODEL 84 PISTOL TERCENTENNIAL - commemorative, only 300 manufactured.
Fully engraved with gold inlays. Presentation case. Only 100 imported to U.S.

| | | | $1,450 | $1,100 | $850 | | |

BERGMANN

Previous manufacturer located in Gaggenau, Germany circa 1892-1944. Re-established in 1931 under Bergmann Erben.

100%	98%	95%	90%	80%	70%	60%	50%	40%	30%	20%	10%

PISTOLS: SEMI-AUTO

Prices established are for original guns with matching parts.

MODEL 1894 (ANTIQUE) - 8mm "Bergmann Schmeisser" cal. Extremely rare.

N/A	N/A	$18,500	$16,000	$12,000	$8,000	$7,500	$7,000	$6,500	$6,000	$5,500	$5,000

MODEL 1896-NO. 2 - 5mm cal., smaller type frame.

$2,400	$1,900	$1,600	$1,300	$1,100	$895	$715	$660	$610	$565	$515	$450

Add 50% for "folding trigger" version.

MODEL 1896-NO. 3 - 6.5mm cal. 80mm barrel.

$3,250	$2,750	$2,250	$1,800	$1,450	$925	$750	$700	$665	$630	$600	$565

Add 10% for early pistols without extractors and narrow grips.
Add 20% if hexagonal chamber.
Add 100% for target variation.

MODEL 1896-NO. 4 - 8mm cal., military contract. Rarely seen.

$4,950	$4,250	$3,500	$3,000	$2,200	$1,500	$900	$725	$665	$630	$600	$565

MODEL 1897-NO. 5 - 7.8mm cal., commercial manufacture. May be fit with shoulder stock.

$6,500	$5,000	$4,000	$3,000	$2,200	$1,500	$925	$750	$700	$665	$630	$600

Add 200% for long barrel carbine version.
Add 100% if fit with shoulder stock, add another 20% to total if matching stock.

BERGMANN MARS MODEL 1903 - .30 or 9mm Bergmann cal.

$5,500	$4,250	$3,000	$2,500	$2,000	$1,750	$1,500	$1,250	$1,000	$750	$600	$500

Add 100% if fit with shoulder stock.
Add 25% if .30 caliber (first 100 pistols).

MODEL 2 - .25 cal., small frame.

$350	$295	$260	$240	$215	$180	$160	$135	$115	$95	$80	$65

Add $100 for Model 2A.

MODEL 3 - .25 cal., small frame.

$350	$295	$260	$240	$215	$180	$160	$135	$115	$95	$80	$65

Add $100 for Model 3A.

ERBEN - .25 cal., Models I, II, and Special (.32 cal.).

$375	$325	$285	$260	$240	$215	$180	$160	$135	$115	$95	$80

PISTOLS: SEMI-AUTO - BERGMANN-BAYARD

Even though the below listed Bergmann-Bayard models were manufactured only by Anciens Etablissements Pieper of Herstal, Belgium, these pistols are listed under this heading as they are most commonly referred to by this trademark designation.

MODEL 1908 STANDARD COMMERCIAL - 9mm Bergmann/Bayard cal., identified by a mounted knight on the left magazine housing and is without finger cuts at base of magazine housing.

$1,900	$1,500	$1,100	$800	$625	$500	$400	$360	$335	$310	$285	$260

Add 25% if backstrap is slotted for shoulder stock.
Add $3,000 for excellent original leather/wood shoulder stock.

100%	98%	95%	90%	80%	70%	60%	50%	40%	30%	20%	10%

MODEL 1908 SPANISH CONTRACT - 9mm Bergmann/Bayard cal., total contract was for 3,000 pistols, can be identified from standard commercial pistols by the Spanish military acceptance stamp struck on the receiver.

$1,750	$1,400	$1,000	$750	$600	$450	$400	$360	$335	$310	$285	$260

MODEL 1910 STANDARD COMMERCIAL - 9mm Bergmann/Bayard cal., mechanically similar to Model 1908 Standard Commercial except has finger cuts in bottom of magazine housing, circular grooves are present on each side of magazine base.

$1,300	$1,000	$700	$600	$500	$400	$350	$315	$280	$265	$245	$225

MODEL 1910 DANISH GOVERNMENT CONTRACT - 9mm Bergmann/Bayard cal., Trolit grips were used for the original conversion, followed later by wood replacements, total contract was for 4,840 pistols with delivery mfg. 1911-1914. This variation can be identified from the usual commercial pistols by the Danish proof mark on the left receiver side and Danish inventory number on right side of receiver.

$1,500	$1,200	$900	$750	$600	$450	$400	$360	$335	$310	$285	$260

Subtract 20% if converted and overstamped M.1910/21.

MODEL 1910/21 TOJHUS - 9mm Bergmann/Bayard cal., these pistols are marked "Haerens Tojhus" and are numbered from 1-900, original grips were black Trolit, replacement grips are either all smooth or with checkered circles above and below grip screw.

$2,150	$1,800	$1,450	$1,100	$750	$600	$500	$400	$350	$310	$285	$260

This contract was manufactured by the Danish Royal Arsenal located in Copenhagen.

MODEL 1910/21 RUSTKAMMER - 9mm Bergmann/Bayard cal., pistols are marked "Haerens Rustkammer", and numbered 901-2204, grip replacements are the same as noted for Haerens Tojhus.

$1,950	$1,600	$1,200	$900	$600	$450	$400	$360	$335	$310	$285	$260

This contract was manufactured by the Danish Royal Arsenal located in Copenhagen.

WAYNE BERGQUIST CUSTOM PISTOLS

Current custom pistolsmith located in Naples, FL. The company should be contacted directly (see Trademark Index for current information) regarding its Bullseye, IPSC Tactical, and Defense/Carry models.

BERNARDELLI, VINCENZO

Current trademark with headquarters located in Brescia, Italy beginning mid-2002. No current U.S. importation. Previously manufactured from 1721 to August, 1997 in Gardone, VT, Italy. Previously imported and distributed until 1997 by Armsport, Inc. located in Miami, FL. Previously imported and distributed by Magnum Research, Inc. located in Minneapolis, MN (1989-1992), Quality Arms, Inc. located in Houston, TX, Armes De Chasse located in Chadds Ford, PA, Stoeger located in New York, NY, and Action Arms, Ltd. located in Philadelphia, PA.

There is some confusion on the Bernardelli trademark as there have been three different companies (Pietro Bernardelli, Vincenzo Bernardelli, and Santini Bernardelli) that have produced firearms. During the late 1980s, there were quite a lot of Pietro Bernardellis that were "dumped" in the American marketplace - these guns do not have the quality of Vincenzo Bernardelli and are not covered within the scope of this text.

The Vincenzo Bernardelli trademark was purchased in early 2002, and many of the older discontinued models are once again back into production, in addition to some new models. Please contact the company directly for more information, including domestic model availability, pricing, and current importation.

GRADING - PPGS™	100%	98%	95%	90%	80%	70%	60%

COMBINATION GUNS

MODEL 190 - 12, 16, or 20 ga. under .243 Win., .30-06, or .308 Win. cal., combination rifle/shotgun, boxlock action, DTs, extractors. Imported 1989 only.

	$1,295	$1,025	$895	$800	$700	$600	$525

Last MSR was $1,393.

Add $700 for extra set of 12 ga. O/U barrels.

MODEL COMB 2000 - 12, 16, or 20 ga. under choice of rifle cals., ejectors, set trigger. Imported 1990-97.

	$2,300	$1,550	$1,075	$875	$750	$675	$575

Last MSR was $2,920.

Add $621 for extra set of O/U shotgun barrels (Model COMB 2000S - disc.).

MODEL 120 - 12 ga. over choice of 12 cals., deluxe checkered walnut stock and forearm, iron sights, double triggers, vent. recoil pad, coin washed receiver with light engraving.

	$1,950	$1,585	$1,300	$1,050	$850	$760	$650

Last MSR was $2,411.

Add $130 for extra set of shotgun barrels.

PISTOLS: SEMI-AUTO

VEST POCKET MODEL - .25 ACP cal., 2 1/8 in. barrel, fixed sights, blue, bakelite grips. Mfg. 1945-48.

	$250	$195	$165	$140	$110	$90	$65

BABY SEMI-AUTO - .22 S or L cal., 2 1/8 in. barrel, fixed sights, blue, bakelite grips. Mfg. 1949-68.

	$250	$175	$150	$130	$100	$90	$80

SPORTER MODEL - .22 LR cal., 6, 8, or 10 in. barrels, target sights, blue, wood grips. Mfg. 1949-68.

	$305	$275	$220	$165	$140	$110	$85

MODEL 60 - .22 LR cal., .32 ACP, or .380 ACP cal., 3 1/2 in. barrel, fixed sights, blue, bakelite grips. Mfg. 1959-disc.

	$220	$195	$180	$165	$155	$135	$120

This model was not imported domestically.

MODEL 68 - .22 short or .22 LR cal., vest pocket model, 6 shot, bakelite grips, 8 1/2 oz. Disc.

	$140	$120	$110	$100	$90	$80	$70

This model was not imported domestically.

MODEL 80 - .22 LR or .380 ACP cal., 3 1/2 in. barrel, adj. sights, blue, thumbrest plastic grips. Imported 1968-88.

	$185	$160	$150	$140	$130	$115	$100

Add $5 for .380 ACP.

Note: This model was produced to conform to import regulations of GCA 1968. Importation of this model was disc. 1988.

MODEL USA - .22 LR, .32 ACP (disc.), or .380 ACP. cal., semi-auto, single action, steel frame, loaded chamber indicator, adj. sights, target bakelite grips, 7 shot (.380 ACP) or 10 shot (.22 LR) mag. Disc. 1997.

	$380	$295	$250	$215	$185	$165	$145

Last MSR was $425.

Add $60 for chrome finish.

This model has the same technical specifications as the Model 60.

GRADING - PPGS™	100%	98%	95%	90%	80%	70%	60%

MODEL AMR - .22 LR, .32 ACP (disc.), or .380 ACP cal., similar action to USA Model except has 6 in. barrel and adj. rear sight. Disc. 1994.

	$395	$325	$275	$225	$185	$165	$145

Last MSR was $445.

MODEL 90 SPORT TARGET - .22 LR cal. or .32 ACP, similar to Model 80, with 6 in. barrel. Imported 1968-88.

	$210	$185	$170	$155	$140	$120	$110

Last MSR was $245.

MODEL 69 TARGET - .22 LR cal., target semi-auto, single action, 5.9 in. heavy barrel, 10 shot mag., wraparound checkered wood grips, 38 oz.

	$575	$475	$400	$350	$275	$225	$185

Last MSR was $660.

This model was previously designated Model 100.

MODEL 100 TARGET - .22 LR cal., 5.9 in. barrel, adj. sight, blue, checkered wood, thumbrest grips, cased. Imported 1968-88.

	$395	$325	$295	$260	$225	$190	$175

Last MSR was $360.

P-ONE - 9mm Para. or .40 S&W cal., double action, 10 shot mag., choice of matte black or chrome finish. Imported 1993-97.

	$580	$495	$400	$360	$330	$295	$265

Last MSR was $684.

Add $36 for chrome finish.
Add $36 for wood grips.

✱ *P-One Compact* - compact variation of the P-One. Disc. 1997.

	$595	$500	$400	$360	$330	$295	$265

Last MSR was $702.

Add $48 for chrome finish.
Add $48 for wood grips.

MODEL P010 TARGET - .22 LR cal., single action, 5.9 in. barrel, adj. sights and trigger, matte black finish, large anatomic walnut stippled grips with thumbrest, 10 shot mag., 40.5 oz. Imported 1989-92, re-introduced 1995-97.

	$675	$575	$495	$425	$375	$325	$275

Last MSR was $768.

Add $132 for wood case and two sets of weights.

MODEL P018 - 7.65mm (disc. 1988), .380 ACP (mfg. 1993-94), or 9mm Para. cal., double action, semi- auto, steel construction, 4 7/8 in. barrel, 10 (C/B 1994) or 16* shot mag., black plastic (standard) or walnut checkered (disc. 1992) grips, blue (disc.), black (new 1994), or chrome finish, 36 oz. Imported 1985-96.

	$485	$400	$350	$300	$275	$250	$230

Last MSR was $560.

Add $40 for walnut grips (disc. 1992).
Add $60 for chrome finish.
Add $30 for carrying case w/combination lock (disc. 1989).
This model was extensively redesigned in 1989 and included a "cocked and locked" feature, thumb mag. release, loaded chamber indicator, as well as other improvements.

✱ *P018 Compact* - .380 ACP or 9mm Para. cal., similar to Model P018 except has 4 in. barrel and 10 (C/ B 1994) or 14* shot mag., approx. 2 lbs. Imported 1989-96.

	$545	$430	$375	$310	$275	$250	$230

Last MSR was $610.

Add $55 for chrome finish.
This model was also redesigned in 1989 to incorporate the same features as the Model P018.

GRADING - PPGS™	100%	98%	95%	90%	80%	70%	60%

PRACTICAL VB - 9x21mm cal., comp. gun built for IPSC competition, various configurations, black or matte chrome finish, 2, 4, or 6 port compensating system. Mfg. 1993-97.

	$1,100	$925	$775	$675	$575	$475	$400

Last MSR was $1,260.

Add $60 for 4 port compensator.
Add $60 for chrome finish.

* *Practical VB Customized* - state-of-the-art competition pistol featuring 4+2 port compensating system. Mfg. 1993-97.

	$1,775	$1,325	$1,100	$975	$850	$725	$600

Last MSR was $1,920.

Add $60 for chrome finish.

RIFLES: DOUBLE

EXPRESS VB - various cals., side-by-side sidelock action, ejectors, single or double triggers. Imported 1990-97.

	$5,475	$4,100	$3,400	$2,725	$2,275	$1,900	$1,600

Last MSR was $6,000.

Add $1,000 for Deluxe Model (double triggers).

EXPRESS 2000 - .30-06, 7x65R, 8x57JRS, or 9.3x74R cal., O/U boxlock design, single or double trigger, extractors, checkered walnut stock and forearm. Imported 1994-97.

	$2,600	$1,995	$1,600	$1,275	$1,100	$975	$875

Last MSR was $3,192.

Add $130 for single trigger.

MINERVA EXPRESS - various cals., exposed hammers, extractors, double triggers, moderate engraving. Imported 1995-97.

	$4,975	$3,850	$3,250	$2,725	$2,275	$1,900	$1,600

Last MSR was $5,850.

RIFLES: SEMI-AUTO

CARBINA .22 - .22 LR cal., blow back action. Imported 1990-97.

	$575	$375	$295	$210	$170	$150	$135

Last MSR was $720.

SHOTGUNS: FOLDING MODELS

SINGLE BARREL - 12, 16, 20, 24, 28, 32 ga., or .410 bore, gun folds in half. Importation disc. 1990.

	$230	$185	$150	$135	$125	$115	$100

Last MSR was $265.

DOUBLE BARREL - 12 and 16 ga., gun folds in half, double triggers. Previously available in Europe only.

	$570	$430	$370	$315	$285	$260	$230

SHOTGUNS: O/U

MODEL 115 HUNTING - 12 ga. only, boxlock action, monobloc frame, inclined plane lockings, blue receiver, single trigger, ejectors. Importation disc. 1989.

	$1,770	$1,425	$1,225	$1,000	$895	$750	$650

Last MSR was $1,915.

* *Model 115S* - similar to 115, except moderate engraving.

	$2,150	$1,925	$1,745	$1,500	$1,250	$1,025	$950

Last MSR was $2,500.

GRADING - PPGS™	100%	98%	95%	90%	80%	70%	60%

* *Model 115L* - similar to 115S, except extensive scroll engraving on silver finish receiver.

	$2,600	$2,375	$2,050	$1,750	$1,450	$1,100	$850

Last MSR was $3,170.

* *Model 115E* - sideplate, boxlock action, ejector, bulino game scene engraving.

	$4,650	$4,125	$3,600	$3,100	$2,650	$2,200	$1,800

Last MSR was $5,200.

MODEL 115 TARGET - 12 ga. only, same specifications as Model 115, except trap dimensions. Importation disc. 1989.

	$1,800	$1,595	$1,375	$1,175	$1,000	$895	$750

Last MSR was $2,160.

* *Model 115S* - same specifications as 115 Target, except light engraving. Importation disc. 1992.

	$3,275	$2,425	$1,825	$1,500	$1,250	$1,025	$895

Last MSR was $3,920.

This model was available in either Pigeon, Skeet, Sporting Clays, or Trap configuration.

* *Model 115L* - similar to 115S, except extensive scroll engraving on silver finish receiver. Importation disc. 1990.

	$3,700	$2,995	$2,600	$2,375	$2,050	$1,750	$1,450

Last MSR was $4,201.

* *Model 115E* - same specifications as 115S, except with extensively engraved sideplates. Importation disc. 1990.

	$5,950	$4,800	$4,125	$3,600	$3,100	$2,650	$2,200

Last MSR was $6,827.

* *Model 115S Trap/Skeet* - 12 ga. only, available in Trap or Skeet configuration, ejectors, single trigger. Disc. 1997.

	$3,250	$2,450	$1,825	$1,425	$995	$875	$725

Last MSR was $3,780.

* *Model 115S Sporting Clays* - 12 ga. only, SST, ejectors, choke tubes. Imported 1995-97.

	$3,875	$3,350	$2,775	$2,100	$1,750	$1,500	$1,350

Last MSR was $4,200.

MODEL 190 TARGET - 12 ga, SST, ejectors, engraved silver receiver, select checkered walnut stock and forearm. Imported 1986-89.

	$1,425	$1,095	$925	$800	$700	$600	$525

Last MSR was $1,572.

* *Model 190 MC* - similar to Model 190 Target except has Monte Carlo stock. Imported 1989 only.

	$1,000	$825	$700	$600	$525	$475	$450

Last MSR was $1,155.

* *Model 190 Special* - 12 ga. only, similar to Model 190 Target, except has better walnut and engraving. Imported 1988-89.

	$1,335	$1,000	$895	$800	$700	$600	$525

Last MSR was $1,456.

Add $75 for single trigger (Model 190 Special MS).
These variations are hunting models.

MODEL 192 FIELD - 12 ga. only, single or double triggers, ejectors, choke tubes optional. Imported 1995-97.

	$1,175	$895	$750	$650	$550	$450	$375

Last MSR was $1,425.

Add $65 for single trigger.
Add $200 for choke tubes.
Add $350 for 192 Special (includes double triggers, ejectors).

GRADING - PPGS™	100%	98%	95%	90%	80%	70%	60%

MODEL 192 MS COMPETITION - 12 ga. only, ejectors, selective or non-selective triggers, multi-chokes standard on Sporting Clays Model. Mfg. 1990-97.

	$1,725	$1,475	$1,150	$925	$775	$675	$575

Last MSR was $1,930.

Add $120 for SST.
Add $200 for choke tubes.
Add $485 for Special Sport.

This model was available in either Pigeon, Skeet, Sporting Clays, Special Sport, or Trap configuration.

MODEL 192 MS-MC HUNTING - 12 ga. only, boxlock action with engraved coin finished receiver, 3 in. chambers, ejectors, SST, 26 3/4 or 28 in. VR barrels with choke tubes, steel shot compatible. Imported 1990-1992.

	$1,400	$995	$825	$700	$600	$525	$475

Last MSR was $1,833.

❋ *Model 192 MS-MC-WF* - waterfowler variation which includes 3 1/2 in. chambers, 3 choke tubes, and SST. Imported 1990 only.

	$1,275	$950	$875	$775	$675	$575	$500

Last MSR was $1,444.

MODEL 200 LIGHTWEIGHT MS - 12 ga. only, silver grey finished receiver with game scene engraving, ejectors, DTs. Imported 1988-89, resumed 1993-97.

	$1,325	$975	$850	$725	$650	$550	$450

Last MSR was $1,525.

MODEL 220 MS HUNTING - 12 or 20 ga., silver grey finished receiver with engraving. Mfg. 1988-97.

	$1,350	$995	$850	$725	$650	$550	$450

Last MSR was $1,560.

Add $75 for SST.
Add $180 for 12 ga. slug variation with DTs (new 1994).
Add $700 for extra set of 12 ga. barrels (disc. 1990).

This model was available with either a pistol grip or English grip (straight) stock.

MODEL LUCK - 12 ga., ejectors, boxlock action, choice of double or single trigger. Imported 1994-97.

	$1,450	$995	$725	$650	$550	$450	$375

Last MSR was $1,795.

Add $275 for single trigger.

SATURNO MS-MC COMPETITION - 12 ga. only, sporter configuration, boxlock action with lightly engraved side plates, ejectors, DTs. Imported 1991-97.

	$2,325	$1,725	$1,150	$925	$775	$675	$575

Last MSR was $2,760.

This model was available in either Pigeon, Skeet, Sporting Clays, or Trap configuration.

SATURNO MS-MC HUNTING - 12 ga. only, boxlock action with lightly engraved side plates, ejectors, SST, includes multi-chokes. Imported 1991-92.

	$2,275	$1,525	$1,050	$875	$750	$695	$600

Last MSR was $2,609.

ORIONE S - 12 ga., double Purdey lock, VR, ejectors, engraved nickel finish receiver. Importation disc. 1989.

	$1,175	$1,025	$860	$760	$650	$560	$510

Last MSR was $1,425.

GRADING - PPGS™	100%	98%	95%	90%	80%	70%	60%

ORIONE L - similar to Orione S, single trigger, finer engraving, English or pistol type select walnut stock. Importation disc. 1989.

	$1,285	$1,125	$950	$840	$750	$650	$550

Last MSR was $1,550.

ORIONE E - top-of-the-line, deep relief engraving. Importation disc. 1989.

	$1,375	$1,200	$1,020	$900	$820	$710	$650

Last MSR was $1,660.

SHOTGUNS: SxS

Bernardelli side-by-side shotguns were manufactured with straight grip, English style stocks with pistol grip available as a special order. Importation of Bernardelli shotguns was inconsistent over the years.

A wide variety of special order options was available on these shotguns.

Barrel choke markings for V. Bernardelli shotguns are as follows; Full: *, Impr. Mod: **, Mod: ***, Impr. Cyl: ****, Cylinder: CL.

MODEL 110 - 12 ga., trap or skeet model, separated barrels, high post rib.

	$2,000	$1,500	$1,300	$1,100	$1,000	$900	$800

MODEL 110 EXTRA0 - similar to Model 110, except engraved.

	$3,021	$2,265	$1,970	$1,665	$1,510	$1,360	$1,210

S. UBERTO 1 GAMECOCK - 12, 16, 20, or 28 ga., 25 3/4 in. imp. cyl. and mod., 27 1/2 in. full and mod., hammerless, boxlock, extractors, two triggers, English style stock, checkered.

	$853	$635	$605	$550	$495	$440	$415

Add 20% for ejectors.

BRESCIA HAMMER DOUBLE BARREL - 12, 16, or 20 ga., 25 3/4, 27 1/2 and 29 1/2 in. mod. and full, 12 ga., 25 1/2 in. imp. cyl. and mod., sidelock, extractors, two triggers, straight English stock, splinter forearm, checkered. Importation disc.

	$2,050	$795	$600	$450	$425	$395	$350

Last MSR was $2,482.

ITALIA HAMMER DOUBLE BARREL - similar to Brescia, except higher grade engraving and wood. Importation disc.

	$2,275	$1,200	$900	$735	$650	$600	$550

Last MSR was $2,844.

ITALIA EXTRA HAMMER - 12, 16, or 20 ga., hammer double. Top-of-the-line hammer model. Importation disc.

	$6,400	$3,150	$2,200	$1,650	$1,375	$1,050	$800

Last MSR was $7,861.

MODEL 112 - 12 ga., entry-level model with extractors and DTs. Imported 1989 only.

	$850	$750	$675	$625	$550	$495	$450

Last MSR was $998.

Add $65 for single trigger (Model 112 M - disc.).

MODEL 112 E - 12 ga., Anson & Deeley action, light engraving. Importation disc. 1989.

	$995	$850	$775	$695	$625	$550	$495

Last MSR was $1,108.

MODEL 112 SI/S (EM) - similar to Model 112E, except has single or double triggers. Disc. 1997.

	$1,795	$1,000	$825	$725	$650	$550	$450

Last MSR was $2,100.

Add $174 for ejectors.
Add $138 for ST.
Add $420 for choke tubes.

GRADING - PPGS™	100%	98%	95%	90%	80%	70%	60%

✳ *Model 112 EM - MC* - similar to Model 112 EM, except has 3 in. chambers and 5 choke tubes. Imported 1990-92.

| | $1,600 | $1,000 | $850 | $775 | $675 | $575 | $495 |

Last MSR was $1,971.

✳ *Model 112 EM-MC-WF* - includes 3 1/2 in. chambers, waterfowl model with matte finish, single trigger and 3 choke tubes. Importation disc. 1990.

| | $1,275 | $975 | $850 | $775 | $675 | $575 | $495 |

Last MSR was $1,444.

S. UBERTO 1 - 12, 16, 20, or 28 ga., Anson & Deeley action, Purdey locks, light engraving, case hardened receiver, double triggers, extractors.

| | $1,050 | $900 | $800 | $700 | $625 | $550 | $495 |

Last MSR was $1,164.

Add $65 for single trigger (Model S. Uberto 1M).

✳ *S. Uberto 1E* - similar to S. Uberto 1, except with ejectors. Importation disc. 1990.

| | $1,175 | $950 | $850 | $740 | $650 | $565 | $495 |

Last MSR was $1,357.

Add $65 for single trigger (Model S. Uberto 1EM).

S. UBERTO 2 - 12, 16, 20, and 28 ga.'s, Anson & Deeley action, Purdey locks, light scroll engraving, silver finished receiver, double triggers, extractors. Importation disc. 1989, resumed 1993 -97.

| | $1,375 | $1,150 | $875 | $725 | $650 | $550 | $450 |

Last MSR was $1,580.

Add $35 for single trigger (Model S. Uberto 2M - disc.).

✳ *S. Uberto 2E* - similar to S. Uberto 2, except with ejectors. Disc. 1997.

| | $1,525 | $1,300 | $1,050 | $875 | $725 | $650 | $550 |

Last MSR was $1,710.

Add $80 for single trigger (Model S. Uberto 2EM - disc.).

S. UBERTO FS - 12, 16, 20, or 28 ga., Purdey locks, relief engraved with hunting scenes on silver finished receiver, double triggers, extractors. Importation disc. 1989, resumed 1993-97.

| | $1,695 | $1,450 | $1,125 | $895 | $750 | $675 | $575 |

Last MSR was $1,915.

Add $65 for single trigger (Model S. Uberto FSM - disc. 1989).

✳ *S. Uberto FSE* - similar to S. Uberto FS, except with ejectors. Importation disc. 1989.

| | $1,375 | $1,100 | $975 | $850 | $750 | $625 | $550 |

Last MSR was $1,537.

Add $65 for single trigger (Model S. Uberto FSEM).

ROMA 3 - similar to S. Uberto, double triggers, extractors, false sideplates, case hardened receiver. Importation disc. 1989, resumed 1993-97.

| | $1,425 | $1,200 | $895 | $775 | $675 | $575 | $475 |

Last MSR was $1,625.

Add $65 for single trigger (Model Roma 3M - disc.).

✳ *Roma 3E* - similar to Roma 3, except with ejectors. Disc. 1997.

| | $1,550 | $1,325 | $1,050 | $875 | $725 | $650 | $550 |

Last MSR was $1,770.

Add $80 for single trigger (Model Roma 3EM - disc.).

ROMA 4 - more deluxe model than Roma 3, false sideplates, scroll engraved, silver finished receiver. Importation disc. 1989.

| | $1,250 | $1,025 | $900 | $800 | $700 | $625 | $550 |

Last MSR was $1,439.

Add $65 for single trigger (Model Roma 4M).

GRADING - PPGS™	100%	98%	95%	90%	80%	70%	60%

✳ *Roma 4E* - similar to Roma 4, except with ejectors. Disc. 1997.

	$1,775	$1,475	$1,150	$925	$775	$675	$575

Last MSR was $2,000.

Add $80 for single trigger (Model Roma 4EM - disc.).

ROMA 6 - 12, 16, 20, or 28 ga., fully engraved sideplates with hunting scenes, Purdey locks, silver finish receiver, single trigger, finely figured English walnut. Importation disc. 1989.

	$1,395	$1,150	$975	$875	$775	$675	$600

Last MSR was $1,619.

Add $175 for single trigger (Model Roma 6M).

✳ *Roma 6E* - similar to Roma 6, except with ejectors, 16 ga. was disc. 1989. Disc. 1997.

	$2,400	$1,825	$1,475	$1,150	$925	$775	$675

Last MSR was $2,880.

Add $180 for single trigger (Model Roma 6EM).

ROMA 7 - 12 ga., ejectors, grade up from the Roma 6. Imported 1994-97.

	$3,200	$2,200	$1,675	$1,375	$995	$875	$750

Last MSR was $3,840.

ROMA 8 - 12 ga., ejectors, grade up from the Roma 7. Imported 1994-97.

	$3,700	$2,700	$1,950	$1,675	$1,375	$995	$875

Last MSR was $4,740.

ROMA 9 - 12 ga., ejectors, grade up from the Roma 8. Imported 1994-97.

	$4,550	$3,200	$2,500	$1,950	$1,675	$1,375	$995

Last MSR was $5,520.

ELIO - 12 ga. only, lightweight, extractors, fine English style scroll engraving on silver finish receiver. Importation disc. 1989.

	$1,125	$925	$850	$740	$650	$565	$475

Last MSR was $1,238.

Add $65 for single trigger (Model Elio M).

✳ *Elio E* - similar to Elio, except with ejectors. Importation disc. 1989.

	$1,200	$1,000	$895	$795	$695	$595	$500

Last MSR was $1,353.

Add $65 for single trigger (Model Elio EM).

SLUG GUN - 12 ga. only, 23 3/4 in. slug bored barrels, extractors, Anson & Deeley action, Purdey locks, lightly engraved, silver finish receiver. Importation disc. 1990.

	$1,325	$1,000	$895	$795	$695	$595	$500

Last MSR was $1,575.

Add $65 for single trigger (Model Slug M).

SLUG LUSSO - 12 ga. only, 23 3/4 in. slug bored barrels, sideplates, with extensive engraving featuring hunting scenes, cheekpiece, ejectors, silver finished receiver. Importation disc. 1992.

	$2,325	$1,550	$1,200	$995	$875	$750	$650

Last MSR was $2,793.

Add $80 for single trigger (Model Slug Lusso M).
This model was previously designated Slug Deluxe (1988 or earlier).

HEMINGWAY - 12, 20, or 28 (new 1992) ga., boxlock action, coin finished receiver with game scene engraving, 23 1/2 in. barrels, DTs, deluxe checkered walnut stock and forearm, 6 1/4 lbs. Disc. 1997.

	$2,050	$1,500	$1,050	$875	$750	$675	$575

Last MSR was $2,520.

Add $70 for single trigger.
Add $120 for single selective trigger.

GRADING - PPGS™	100%	98%	95%	90%	80%	70%	60%

HEMINGWAY DE LUXE - similar to Hemingway, except is also available in 16 ga. and has sideplates, better wood, and more engraving. Disc. 1997.

	$2,350	$1,750	$1,150	$925	$775	$675	$575

Last MSR was $2,874.

Add $126 for single trigger (Model Hemingway De Luxe M).

LAS PALOMAS PIGEON - 12 ga. live pigeon gun, single trigger, special dimensions for live pigeon shooting. Disc. 1997.

	$3,125	$2,550	$2,000	$1,700	$1,375	$995	$875

Last MSR was $3,700.

Add $750 for Pigeon Model (includes single trigger).

HOLLAND V.B. LISCIO - 12 ga. only, Holland type sidelocks, light engraving, silver finish receiver, single trigger, ejectors, select walnut. Disc. 1997.

	$10,350	$5,300	$4,450	$3,900	$3,350	$2,850	$2,400

Last MSR was $12,600.

HOLLAND V.B. INCISO - 12 ga. only, H&H sidelock action, Purdey locks, various barrel lengths, single trigger, ejectors, straight or pistol grip stock, 100% engraved on coin finished receiver. Importation disc. 1992.

	$10,700	$7,000	$5,500	$4,700	$4,200	$3,500	$3,000

Last MSR was $12,929.

HOLLAND V.B. LUSSO - 12 ga. only, H&H sidelock action, Purdey locks, various barrel lengths, single trigger, ejectors, straight or pistol grip stock, same features as Holland V.B. Inciso, only extra select wood and game scene engraving. Importation disc. 1992.

	$8,900	$7,900	$6,500	$5,200	$4,750	$4,000	$3,450

Last MSR was $14,377.

HOLLAND V.B. EXTRA - 12 ga. only, H&H style action, any barrel length and choke, double triggers, auto ejectors, straight or pistol grip stock, 100% engraved on coin finished receiver. Prices are completely dependent upon individual customer specifications. Values are for engraving pattern No. 3. Importation disc. 1992.

	$13,250	$9,700	$7,450	$6,150	$5,200	$4,600	$3,950

Last MSR was $16,549.

Add $1,034 for engraving pattern No. 4.
Add $4,551 for engraving pattern No. 12.
Add $8,895 for engraving pattern No. 20.
Add $621 for single trigger.

Older specimens ordered before 1992 could have values considerably lower than those listed.

HOLLAND V.B. GOLD - top-of-the-line model, made to individual order. Very limited production and ultra-rare. Importation disc. 1992.

	$47,500	$32,500	$24,000	$18,500	$13,000	$11,500	$9,950

Last MSR was $57,922.

Older specimens ordered before 1992 could have values considerably lower than those listed.

SHOTGUNS: SEMI-AUTO

MODEL 9MM FLOBERT - 9mm Flobert cal. (rimfire shot cartridge), 24.4 in. smooth bore barrel, 3 shot mag., steel receiver, walnut stock and forearm with sling and swivels, 5 lbs. 3 oz. Disc. 1997.

	$385	$265	$175	$150	$125	$105	$95

Last MSR was $474.

BERSA

Current manufacturer located in Ramos Mejia, Argentina. Currently distributed exclusively by Eagle Imports, Inc. located in Wanamassa, NJ. Previously imported and distributed before 1988 by Rock Island Armory located in Geneseo, IL, Outdoor Sports Headquarters, Inc. located in Dayton, OH, and R.S.A. Enterprises, Inc. located in Ocean, NJ. Distributor sales only.

PISTOLS: SEMI-AUTO

THUNDER 9 - 9mm Para. cal., double action semi-auto, 3 1/2 in. barrel, 10 (C/B 1994) or 14* shot mag., ambidextrous manual safety and decocking lever, automatic firing pin safety, 3-dot sights, aluminum frame, wraparound matte black polymer grips, link-free locked breech design, non-glare matte blue, satin nickel (new 1995), or duo-tone (new 1995) finish. Imported 1993-95.

$400	$335	$295	$265	$235	$210	$190

Last MSR was $475.

    Add $17 for duo-tone finish.
    Add $50 for satin nickel finish.

THUNDER 22 (MODEL 23) - .22 LR cal., double action semi-auto, 9 shot mag., 3 1/2 in. barrel, black polymer (new 1997) or walnut (disc. 1996) grips, 24 1/2 oz. Imported 1988-98.

$230	$195	$155	$125	$115	$105	$95

Last MSR was $265.

    Add $17 for satin nickel finish.

THUNDER 380 - .380 ACP cal., double action, 3 1/2 in. barrel, fixed sights, 7 shot mag., deep blue, satin nickel, or duo-tone (disc. 1995) finish, rubber grips, 25 3/4 oz. Imported 1995-98.

$235	$195	$155	$125	$115	$105	$95

Last MSR was $275.

    Add $16 for satin nickel.
    Add $16 for duo-tone finish (disc. 1995).

  ✹ ***Thunder 380 Deluxe*** - .380 ACP cal., 9 shot mag., black polymer grips, extended slide release and mag. bottom, polished blue, 3 dot sights, 23 oz. New 1997.

MSR $316	$260	$220	$170	$125	$115	$105	$95

  ✹ ***Thunder 380 Plus*** - similar to Thunder 380, except has 10 shot mag. Mfg. 1995-97.

$265	$210	$165	$130	$115	$105	$95

Last MSR was $316.

    Add $32 for satin nickel finish.
    Add $17 for duo-tone finish.

THUNDER SERIES (95) - .380 ACP cal., double action, 3 1/2 in. barrel, fixed sights, 7 shot mag., matte blue, satin nickel, or duotone (3,000 mfg. 2001 only) finish, black polymer grips, 23 oz. New 1995.

MSR $282	$230	$185	$145	$125	$115	$105	$95

    Add $10 for Concealed Carry Model (new 2005).
    Add $27 for satin nickel finish.

THUNDER 9MM ULTRA-COMPACT SERIES - 9mm Para. cal., double action, ultra-compact dimensions, choice of matte blue, nickel, or stainless steel, 9 or 17 shot mag. New 2004.

MSR $425	$355	$300	$270	$240	$220	$200	$185

    Add $42 for stainless steel.
    Add $17 for 17 shot mag.

GRADING - PPGS™	100%	98%	95%	90%	80%	70%	60%

THUNDER 40 ULTRA-COMPACT SERIES - .40 S&W cal., similar to Thunder 9mm, 10 or 13 shot mag. New late 2004.

| MSR $425 | $355 | $300 | $270 | $240 | $220 | $200 | $185 |

Add $42 for stainless steel.
Add $17 for 13 shot mag.

THUNDER 45 ULTRA-COMPACT SERIES - .45 ACP cal., double action, ultra compact configuration, 3.6 in. barrel, skeletonized hammer, loaded chamber indicator, 7 shot mag., choice of matte, duo tone (mfg. 2003 only), stainless steel (new 2004), or satin nickel finish, 27 oz. Importation began 2003.

| MSR $425 | $355 | $300 | $270 | $240 | $220 | $200 | $185 |

Add $25 for satin nickel finish.
Add $42 for stainless steel.
Add $24 for duo-tone finish (disc.)

MODEL 83 - .380 ACP cal., double action semi-auto, 3 1/2 in. barrel, blue or satin nickel finish, custom walnut grips, 6 shot mag., 24 1/2 oz. Imported 1988-94.

| | $235 | $180 | $150 | $125 | $115 | $105 | $95 |

Last MSR was $288.

Add $34 for satin nickel finish.

MODEL 85 - .380 ACP cal., similar specifications to Model 83 except has 12 or 13 shot mag., 30 1/2 oz. Imported 1988-94.

| | $285 | $245 | $220 | $195 | $170 | $150 | $130 |

Last MSR was $340.

Add $47 for satin nickel finish.

MODEL 86 - .380 ACP cal., blue matte or nickel finish, undercover model, wraparound rubber grips, 12 shot mag. Imported 1991-94.

| | $315 | $265 | $225 | $200 | $170 | $150 | $130 |

Last MSR was $375.

Add $29 for nickel finish.

MODEL 90 - 9mm Para. cal., single action, semi-auto, steel frame, checkered walnut grips, 13 shot mag., deep blue finish. Imported 1990-91 only.

| | $325 | $280 | $250 | $220 | $195 | $170 | $150 |

Last MSR was $384.

MODEL 223 - .22 LR cal., single action semi-auto, 10 shot mag., 3 1/2 in. barrel, blue finish, squared-off trigger guard, nylon grips. Importation disc. 1987.

| | $200 | $170 | $150 | $125 | $115 | $105 | $95 |

Last MSR was $239.

MODEL 224 - similar to Model 223, except has 4 in. barrel. Imported 1987 only.

| | $200 | $170 | $150 | $125 | $115 | $105 | $95 |

Last MSR was $239.

MODEL 225 - similar to Model 223, except has 5 in. barrel and 10 shot mag. Disc. 1987.

| | $155 | $135 | $125 | $115 | $105 | $95 | $85 |

Last MSR was $170.

MODEL 226 - similar to Model 225, except has 6 in. barrel. Importation disc. 1987.

| | $200 | $170 | $150 | $125 | $115 | $105 | $95 |

Last MSR was $239.

MODEL 323 - .32 ACP cal., single action semi-auto, 8 shot mag., thumbrest plastic grips, 25 oz. Disc. 1987.

| | $105 | $95 | $85 | $75 | $65 | $55 | $45 |

Last MSR was $125.

GRADING - PPGS™	100%	98%	95%	90%	80%	70%	60%

MODEL 383 - .380 ACP cal., single or double action semi-auto, 3 1/2 in. barrel, blue finish, nylon grips, 7 shot mag. Importation disc. 1988.

	$120	$95	$90	$80	$70	$60	$50

Last MSR was $188 for single action.
Last MSR was $239 for double action.

Add $15 for double action.

BERTUZZI, F.LLI

Current manufacturer located in Gardone, VT, Italy since 1886. No current U.S. importation. Previously imported and distributed by New England Arms Corp. located in Kittery Point, ME.

Bertuzzi makes only best quality sidelock O/U and SxS shotguns, both with and w/o external hammers. Only 40-50 guns are mfg. annually, and all are custom ordered per individual specifications. Please contact the factory directly for more information and current pricing.

SHOTGUNS: O/U

ZEUS - 12 ga., sidelock, auto ejector, deluxe engraving, deluxe wood checkering, SST. This model is available on special order only - contact the distributor for availability, prices, and options. Importation disc. 1994. Retail prices generally ranged from $18,500-$27,500.

ZEUS EXTRA LUSSO - 12, 16, or 20 ga., sidelock, auto ejector, deluxe wood, deluxe checkering and engraving, SST. This model was available on special order only. Prices generally ranged $35,000+. Disc. 2002.

ZEUS BOSS SYSTEM - 12 or 20 ga., features Boss locking system. Importation began 1995. Prices start at $45,000.

ZEUS SEAGULL WINGS - elaborate O/U model with hinged swing open locks, all internal surfaces polished and engraved, exhibition wood and finest Bulino style engraving are standard features. Prices start at $75,000.

SHOTGUNS: SxS

MODEL ORIONE - 12 , 16, 20, or 28 ga., round boxlock action, DT or ST, ejectors, base price includes full coverage engraving, deluxe Turkish walnut, and custom stock dimensions. Prices start at $18,950.

VENERE BEST QUALITY SIDELOCK - various gauges, best quality sidelock model with extensive engraving. Prices start at $20,000.

VENERE SEAGULL WINGS - elaborate model with hinged swing open locks, all internal surfaces polished and engraved, exhibition wood and finest Bulino style engraving are standard features. Prices start at $50,000.

ARIETE HAMMER GUN - all gauges, upper tang safety, double triggers, fine quality engraving. Prices start at $19,500. The self-cocking, auto-ejector mechanism is popular in this model and prices can vary between $20,000-$40,000.

BESCHI, MARIO

Previous manufacturer until circa 1983 located in Italy.

SHOTGUNS: O/U

BOXLOCK MODEL - 12 or 20 ga., standard model with light engraving.

	$3,000	$2,600	$2,300	$1,950	$1,600	$1,300	$995

GRADING - PPGS™	100%	98%	95%	90%	80%	70%	60%

SHOTGUNS: SxS

EXTRA LUSSO SIDELOCK - 12 or 20 ga., elaborate game scene engraving.

	100%	98%	95%	90%	80%	70%	60%
12 ga.	$12,000	$10,750	$9,250	$8,000	$6,750	$5,500	$4,250
20 ga.	$12,000	$10,750	$9,250	$8,000	$6,750	$5,500	$4,250

BOXLOCK MODEL - prices assume moderate engraving.

100%	98%	95%	90%	80%	70%	60%
$1,650	$1,475	$1,300	$1,050	$850	$650	$500

BETTINSOLI, TARCISIO, Srl

Current manufacturer located in Brescia, Italy. No current U.S. importation.

Bettinsoli manufactures fine quality O/U shotguns, express rifles, and combination guns. Please contact the factory directly for more information.

BIG BEAR ARMS & SPORT-ING GOODS INC.

Previous firearms importer located in Carrollton, TX 1992-1999, specializing in the importation of both Russian military surplus and new firearms. Limited inventories remained through 2000.

PISTOLS: SEMI-AUTO

IZH-70 MAKAROV - .380 ACP or 9mm Makarov cal., 8 shot mag., current mfg. from Russia. Imported 1994-99.

100%	98%	95%	90%	80%	70%	60%
$265	$185	$155	$135	$115	$100	$90

Last MSR was $325.

RIFLES: SEMI-AUTO

SAIGA SPORTER RIFLE - 7.62x39mm cal., semi-auto with improved Kalashnikov design, checkered hardwood (disc.) or synthetic stock and forearm, 5 or 10 (disc.) shot mag. Imported 1996-99.

100%	98%	95%	90%	80%	70%	60%
$575	$400	$325	$250	$225	$200	$175

Last MSR was $750.

Add $169 for 3.5X scope and mount.

SHOTGUNS

SAIGA SEMI-AUTO - .410 bore, 3 in. chamber, paramilitary configuration. Imported 1996-99.

100%	98%	95%	90%	80%	70%	60%
$425	$350	$295	$250	$200	$180	$165

Last MSR was $499.

IJ-27 O/U - 12 ga., 2 3/4 in. chambers. Imported 1995-99.

100%	98%	95%	90%	80%	70%	60%
$425	$350	$295	$250	$200	$180	$165

Last MSR was $499.

IJ-39E O/U - 12 ga., 2 3/4 in. chambers. Imported 1995-99.

100%	98%	95%	90%	80%	70%	60%
$760	$600	$495	$400	$360	$330	$295

Last MSR was $895.

IJ-43 SxS - 12 ga., 2 3/4 in. chambers. Imported 1995-99.

100%	98%	95%	90%	80%	70%	60%
$325	$250	$200	$175	$155	$145	$135

Last MSR was $399.

| GRADING - PPGS™ | 100% | 98% | 95% | 90% | 80% | 70% | 60% |

BIG HORN ARMS CORP.

Previous manufacturer located in Watertown, SD.

PISTOLS: SINGLE SHOT

TARGET PISTOL - .22 Short cal. only, unique action permitting auto. ejection, ambidextrous stock made of molded Tufflex with carvings, 26 oz. Approx. 1,200 mfg. Disc. in the late 1960s.

	$175	$150	$135	$125	$115	$105	$95

SHOTGUNS: SINGLE SHOT

LIL' MAGNUM SHOTGUN - .410 diameter reloadable shot cartridge, single shot open bolt operation, included reloading equipment, approx. 2,000 mfg. in the late 1960s.

	$125	$100	$75	$65	$55	$50	$45

BIGHORN RIFLE CO.

Previous manufacturer located in Orem, UT.

PISTOLS: BOLT ACTION

BIGHORN PISTOL - .22 LR cal., bolt action design.
Lack of information on this pistol precludes accurate pricing.

RIFLES: BOLT ACTION

BIGHORN RIFLE - Mauser action, choice of calibers, custom made bolt action of high quality, interchangeable barrels (gun was supplied with 2 barrels), adj. trigger, deluxe walnut stock, many custom options. Mfg. 1984 only.

	$2,100	$1,800	$1,600	$1,400	$1,200	$1,000	$850

BILL HANUS BIRDGUNS LLC

Current dealer located in Newport, OR. Bill Hanus currently sells a private label model from AYA (see listing under AYA), and previously had his own model manufactured by Armas Ugartechea (see separate listing) located in Eibar, Spain until 1997.

BINGHAM, LTD.

Previous manufacturer located in Norcross, GA circa 1976-1985.

RIFLES: BOLT ACTION

BANTAM - .22 LR or 22 Mag. cal., bolt action single shot, 18 1/2 in. barrel. Disc. 1985.

	$110	$90	$75	$65	$55	$45	$40

Last MSR was $120.

RIFLES: SEMI-AUTO

PPS 50 - .22 LR cal. only, blowback action, 50 round drum mag., standard model has Beechwood stock. Disc. 1985.

	$250	$225	$195	$180	$145	$135	$125

Last MSR was $230.

Add 15% for deluxe model with walnut stock.
Add 20% for Duramil model with chrome finish and walnut stock.
This model was styled after the Soviet WWII Model PPSh Sub Machine Gun.

AK-22 - .22 LR cal. only, blowback action, styled after AK-47, 15 shot mag. standard, 29 shot mag. available. Standard model has beechwood stock. Disc. 1985.

	$250	$225	$195	$180	$145	$135	$125

Last MSR was $230.

Add $20 for Deluxe model with walnut stock.

GRADING - PPGS™	100%	98%	95%	90%	80%	70%	60%

GALIL-22 - .22 LR cal. only, patterned after Galil semi-auto paramilitary design rifle. Disc.

	$250	$225	$195	$180	$145	$135	$125

FG-9 - 9mm Para. cal., blowback action, semi-auto paramilitary design carbine, 20 1/2 in. barrel.

> While advertised during 1984, this gun never went into production.

BITTNER

Previously manufactured by Gustav Bittner located in Vieprty, Bohemia (Austria, Hungary), circa 1893.

PISTOLS

BITTNER MODEL 1893 - 7.7mm Bittner cal., pistol with hand activated repeater mechanism, box magazine, checkered grips, limited manufacture circa 1893.

	N/A	$5,500	$4,250	$3,000	$2,400	$1,900	$1,500

BLAND, THOMAS & SONS GUNMAKERS LTD.

Current manufacturer located in England since 1840. This firm was purchased in 1990 by Woodcock Hill located in Benton, PA. Manufacturer direct sales only.

Woodcock Hill should be contacted directly (address listed in Trademark Index) for more information (including current models and prices) regarding Thomas Bland & Sons firearms. Prices will vary depending on the exchange rate between the pound/dollar.

Record checks by serial number on all Thomas Bland & Sons rifles and shotguns are also available.

RIFLES: CUSTOM

Double rifles are available in almost all calibers and specifications. Prices vary between $10,000-$75,000 depending upon configuration, finish, and accessories. Bolt action rifles are available in any type of action, most popular calibers, and other special options. The bolt action models are not manufactured in England. Prices begin at $1,500.

SHOTGUNS: CUSTOM

Boxlock, sidelock SxS and O/U best quality shotguns are available in all gauges with prices ranging between $14,500 -$40,000 depending upon configuration, finish, and accessories.

BLASER

Blaser

Currently manufactured by Blaser Jagdwaffen GmbH in Isny im Allgäu, Germany. Currently imported and distributed by SIG Arms located in Exeter, NH. Previously distributed approx. 1988-2002 by Autumn Sales Inc. located in Fort Worth, TX. Dealer sales.

The Blaser Company was founded in 1963 by Horst Blaser. In 1986, the company was taken over by Gerhard Blenk. During 1997, the company was sold to SIG. In late 2000, SIG Arms AG, the firearms portion of SIG, was purchased by SAN Swiss Arms AG, a newly formed company whose investors have a background in textiles. This new group includes 6 independently operational companies – Blaser Jadgwaffen GmbH, Hämmerli AG, Mauser, B.R. Rizzini (Aurora O/U shotguns), J.P. Sauer & Sohn GmbH, SIG-Sauer, and SAN Swiss Arms AG. The restructured Blaser group now includes the primary factories of Blaser (Germany) and SIG-Blaser (Switzerland), in addition to much outsourcing in the smaller Blaser operations located in Lichtenstein, Ungarn (Hungary), and Bulgaria. Blaser currently makes approx. 20,000 rifles annually, with most being sold in Europe to France, Austria, Italy, Spain, and Norway/Sweden. During 2003, Blaser manufactured the No. 100,000 R-93 Model, after producing this straight pull bolt action for less than a decade.

Current SAN Swiss Arms AG trademarks include: Blaser, Hämmerli, Mauser (pistols & rifles), B.R. Rizzini, Sauer rifles, and Sig-Sauer pistols. All trademarks are currently imported by SIG Arms, located in Exeter, NH. Please refer to these individual listings for current information and pricing.

Blaser Jagdwaffen also manufactures a large variety of rifles, drillings, and combination guns for the European market that are not imported domestically.

PISTOLS: BOLT ACTION

R-93 HHS (HUNTING HANDGUN SYSTEM) - various cals. between .222 Rem. - .375 H&H, features R93 right or left-hand straight pull bolt action, 14 in. hammer forged free floating barrel (interchangeable), matte black receiver with choice of wood, case colored, or game scene sideplates, Turkish walnut stock and pistol grip, 3-4 shot mag., 5 lbs. Importation began 2004.

MSR $2,900	$2,475	$2,050	$1,775	$1,500	$1,350	$1,200	$1,025

Add $200 for left-hand bolt assembly.
Add $900 per interchangeable barrel.

RIFLES: BOLT ACTION

Add approx. $141 for left-hand action available on most of the currently manufactured rifles.

R-84 - .22-250 Rem. (disc. 1993), .243 Win., 6mm Rem., .25- 06 Rem., .270 Win., .280 Rem., or .30-06 standard cals., .257 Wby. Mag., .264 Win. Mag., 7mm Rem. Mag., .300 Win. Mag., .300 Wby. Mag., .338 Win. Mag., or .375 H&H cal., 23 or 24 (Mag. cals. only) in. interchangeable barrel, scroll engraving on receiver, short bolt action with 60 degree rotation, checkered Turkish walnut stock and forearm, approx. 7 lbs. Mfg. 1988-94.

	$2,100	$1,575	$1,275	$1,050	$950	$850	$775

Last MSR was $2,300.

Add $50 for left-hand action.
Add $600 per interchangeable barrel (w/scope mounts).

This model has the scope mounted directly to the barrel (and not the receiver). Since the scope mounts are on the barrel extension, this takedown rifle is unique in that it does not require re- zeroing when the rifle is reassembled, regardless of caliber change.

* *R-84 Deluxe* - features a better grade of Turkish walnut with a North American game scene engraved on receiver, silver pistol grip cap with animal scene engraving.

	$2,375	$2,025	$1,650	$1,200	$1,000	$925	$825

Last MSR was $2,600.

Add $50 for left-hand action.

* *R-84 Super Deluxe* - best grade Turkish walnut with receiver featuring African game scene engraving (animals are in gold and silver), and silver pistol grip cap with gold animal engraving.

	$2,675	$2,225	$1,775	$1,300	$1,100	$975	$895

Last MSR was $2,950.

Add $50 for left-hand action.

R-93 CLASSIC - available in various domestic (.22-250 Rem. - .416 Rem. Mag.) and European (6.5x55mm and 7x57mm currently) calibers, 22, 24 (Mag. cals.), or 27 1/2 (disc.) in. barrel, unique patented rifle features straight pull bolt action (0 degree bolt lift), 360 degree radial locking system eliminates bolt rotation, unique safety offering cartridge in chamber capability, 3 shot mag, features interchangeable barrel system and newly designed bolt, searfree trigger mechanism, matte finished nickel receiver with engraving, non-glare "black velvet" barrel finish, integrated low scope mounts standard (1994-97 only), custom gun case with combination lock became standard 1998, 6 1/2 - 7 lbs. Importation began 1994, R-93 Classic introduced 1998, disc. May, 2002.

	$2,600	$2,200	$1,850	$1,675	$1,500	$1,375	$1,250

Last MSR was $2,950.

Add $595 per interchangeable barrel (w/o mounts).

IMPORTANT RECALL NOTICE - During 2002, Blaser issued an important recall on all R93 rifles due to a potential problem with the trigger assembly. All R93 rifles must be returned to

SIG Arms for inspection and possible trigger assembly replacement. Blaser request that consumers contact SIG Arms directly, not your local dealer. Please call 1-877-442-7671 for more information regarding this important safety recall on the Model R93 only.

During 1998, this model's nomenclature changed to the R-93 Classic. Scope mounts are no longer included. Between 1994-97, this model retailed for approx. $2,800 and a Deluxe Grade was available for $3,100, while the Super Deluxe Grade retailed for $3,500.

✳ *Model R-93 Classic Safari* - .416 Rem. Mag. cal., features 24 in. heavy barrel, open sights, large forearm, 9 1/2 lbs., this model was renamed the R-93 Classic in 1998. Imported 1994-2002.

	100%	98%	95%	90%	80%	70%	60%
	$3,575	$3,100	$2,650	$2,275	$1,825	$1,350	$1,150

Last MSR was $4,140.

R-93 LUXUS - available in 20 calibers from .222 Rem. - .375 H&H., similar to the R-93 Classic, except has higher quality walnut and ebony forend tip, available in right- or left-hand action, case not included. New 2002.

MSR $3,600	$3,100	$2,575	$2,100	$1,800	$1,525	$1,350	$1,200

Add $800 for 28 ga. shotgun barrel with replacement bolt head.

Add $600 for Luxus Plus Model with upgraded wood, black receiver and choice of color case hardened steel, wood, or animal sideplates (new 2005).

✳ *R-93 Luxus Safari* - .375 H&H or .416 Rem Mag. cal., similar to R-93 Classic Safari, except has higher quality walnut and ebony forend tip, available in right or left-hand action, case not included. New 2002.

MSR $4,000	$3,500	$2,925	$2,250	$1,950	$1,675	$1,500	$1,400

R-93 ATTACHE - various cals., features premium walnut stock and forearm with receiver wood panel inserts, wood bolt knob, ebony forearm tip, fluted barrel, includes case, approx. 6.5 lbs. New 1998.

MSR $5,000	$4,400	$3,700	$3,200	$2,600	$2,025	$1,675	$1,325

Add $1,162 per interchangeable barrel (w/o mounts).

Subtract $500 for standard non-fluted barrel.

R-93 GRAND LUXE - various cals., deluxe model with high grade checkered walnut stock and forearm, fully hand engraved receiver, 3 shot mag, 6.5 - 7 lbs. Mfg. 1999-2003.

	$4,350	$3,675	$2,800	$2,350	$1,850	$1,350	$1,150

Last MSR was $5,160.

R-93 LRS 2 (LONG RANGE SPORTER 2) - .22-250 Rem. (disc. 2004), .223 Rem., .308 Win., .300 Win. Mag. (new 2000), .338 Lapua (new 2000), 6.5x55mm (new 2005), or 6mm Norma BR (new 2005) cal., competition styled long range sporter with adj. trigger and stock, 5 or 10 (disc. 1999) shot removable box mag, free floating fluted barrel, many competition features, 10.4 lbs. New 1999.

MSR $3,400	$2,925	$2,500	$2,000	$1,675	$1,400	$1,200	$1,050

Add $500 for .338 Lapua cal.

Add $1,181 per interchangeable barrel (w/o mounts).

Add $1,600 for Package II or $2,600 for Package II in .338 Lapua cal. or Package III (includes Leupold scope, mounts, muzzle brake, bi-pod, and hard carry case).

R-93 SYNTHETIC - available in 21 cals. between .22-250 Rem. - .416 Rem. Mag., also available by special order in the same European cals. as the Model R-93 Repeater, features one-piece conventional black, wood grain (new 2004), or Mossy Oak camo (new 2004) synthetic stock, 22 or 26 in. barrel, without scope mounts and rings, 6.5 - 7 lbs. New 1998.

MSR $2,100	$1,800	$1,450	$1,150	$1,000	$875	$775	$675

Add $400 for black synthetic Safari Model in .375 H&H or .416 Rem. Mag.

Add $600 for wood grain or camo stock.

Add $400 for right-hand Professional Safari stock with palm swell or $600 for left-hand.

Add $800 for Professional Safari stock with heavy barrel and kickstop.

Add $700 per interchangeable barrel (w/o mounts) in standard cals.

GRADING - PPGS™	100%	98%	95%	90%	80%	70%	60%

R-93 LX - similar cals. as Model R-93 Synthetic, features checkered walnut stock and forearm, coin finished stippled receiver sides, without scope mounts and rings, 6 1/2 - 7 lbs. Mfg. 1998-2002.

	$1,750	$1,425	$1,195	$1,000	$875	$795	$695

Last MSR was $1,990.

Add $275 for Safari LX Model in .416 Rem. Mag. cal.

Add $595 per interchangeable barrel (w/o mounts).

R-93 PRESTIGE - similar to R-93 LX, except receiver has fine scroll engraving, and higher grade walnut, case not included. New 2002.

MSR $2,600	$2,200	$1,850	$1,475	$1,175	$975	$850	$750

Add $400 for Prestige Safari Model in .375 H&H or .416 Rem. Mag. cal.

ULTIMATE BOLT ACTION - .22-250 Rem., .243 Win., .25-06 Rem., .270 Win., .308 Win., .30-06, 7x57mm, 7x64mm, .264 Win. Mag., 7mm Rem. Mag., .300 Win. Mag., .338 Win. Mag., or .375 H&H cal., unique bolt action design with 60 degree bolt throw, interchangeable barrel capability, 3 locking lugs, safety lever cocks and uncocks the firing pin spring, exposed hammer, aluminum receiver, 22 or 24 in. barrel, single set trigger, silver finished receiver has light engraving, select checkered walnut stock and forearm, 6 3/4 lbs. Extra interchangeable barrels were $545 each, extra bolt heads were $175 each. Mfg. 1985-89.

	$1,350	$1,100	$975	$925	$825	$750	$675

Last MSR was $1,495.

All models were available in left-hand version at no extra charge.

ULTIMATE BOLT ACTION - SPECIAL ORDER - all of the following models may have been ordered with a buttstock cartridge trap - add $250-$500 depending on model. Mfg. was disc. 1989 on all models. Please contact SIG Arms for more information regarding Blaser's current extensive listing of special order rifles.

* *Ultimate Deluxe* - similar to Ultimate, except better wood and game scene engraving.

	$1,425	$1,175	$1,000	$950	$850	$775	$700

Last MSR was $1,595.

* *Ultimate Deluxe Carbine* - .243 Win. or .308 Win. cal. only, 19 1/2 in. barrel with full length forearm. New 1986.

	$1,600	$1,375	$1,150	$1,000	$900	$825	$750

Last MSR was $1,800.

* *Ultimate Super Deluxe* - similar to Ultimate Deluxe, except features better wood and game scene engraving. New 1986.

	$3,750	$3,250	$2,900	$2,600	$2,300	$2,100	$1,850

Last MSR was $4,030.

* *Ultimate Exclusive* - similar to Ultimate Super Deluxe, except features better wood and game scene engraving. New 1986.

	$4,850	$4,300	$3,500	$2,975	$2,600	$2,275	$1,975

Last MSR was $5,655.

Add $700 per interchangeable barrel.

* *Ultimate Super Exclusive* - similar to Ultimate Exclusive, except features better wood and game scene engraving. New 1986.

	$7,700	$6,800	$5,750	$4,700	$3,950	$3,450	$2,950

Last MSR was $8,905.

Add $950 per interchangeable barrel.

* *Ultimate Royal* - best quality Ultimate, featuring Bavarian cheekpiece and checkering/carving on stock and forearm, elaborate game scene engraving, gold plated hammer. New 1986.

	$9,000	$7,500	$6,750	$6,000	$5,375	$4,600	$4,000

Last MSR was $11,500.

Add $1,200 per interchangeable barrel.

GRADING - PPGS™	100%	98%	95%	90%	80%	70%	60%

RIFLES: SxS

S2 - various cals. between .222 Rem. - .500 NE, scalloped boxlock action false sideplates (higher grades only), 22.6 or 24 in. free floating barrels with quarter rib and iron sights, interchangeable barrels, easily regulated, tilting lock block, manual cocking safety, checkered Turkish walnut stock and forearm, approx. 7.7 lbs for standard cals, 10.1-11.2 lbs. for .375 H&H and larger cals. Importation began 2004.

MSR $8,500	$7,850	$6,750	$5,850	$4,950	$4,000	$3,250	$2,750

Add $3,000 for extra set of standard cal. barrels, or $5,300 for Safari cal. barrels.

This model is also available in higher grades, including the S2 Luxus ($9,500 MSR), S2 Super Luxus ($13,000 w/sideplates), S2 Exclusive ($17,000), S2 Super Exclusive ($21,000), and the S2 Royal ($29,000).

RIFLES: SINGLE SHOT

MODEL BL 820 - various American and European cals., falling block action, adj. trigger, 26 1/2 in. barrel, available in Standard to Royal configurations. Mfg. 1982-89.

Standard Model	$1,550	$1,300	$1,075	$925	$800	$700	$600

Last MSR was 2,900 DM.

Add 30% for Royal configuration.

MODEL K77 A - .22-250 Rem., .243 Win., 6.5x55mm, .270 Win., 7x57R, 7x65R, or .30-06 standard cals., 7mm Rem. Mag., .300 Win. Mag. or .300 Wby. Mag. cal., break open action, 23 or 24 in. barrel, 3 piece take down, upper tang safety, checkered walnut stock and forearm, engraved silver finished receiver, sling swivels, 5 1/2 lbs. Imported 1988-90.

	$2,000	$1,675	$1,475	$1,300	$1,100	$925	$800

Last MSR was $2,280.

Add $50 for Mag. calibers.
Add $730-$778 per interchangeable barrel.

K95 PRESTIGE - .222 Rem. (disc.), .243 Win., .270 Win., .308 Win., .30-06, 7mm Rem. Mag., .300 Win. Mag., or .300 Wby. Mag. cal., break open action, 22 (standard cals.) or 25 (Mag. cals.) in. barrel, upper tang safety/cocking lever, 3 piece takedown, checkered walnut stock and forearm, scroll engraved sideplates, sling swivels. Importation began 2000.

MSR $3,500	$3,075	$2,425	$1,950	$1,725	$1,500	$1,375	$1,250

Add $1,000 per interchangeable barrel.

K95 LUXUS - similar to Prestige, except has high grade checkered stock and forearm, engraved sideplates and receiver. Importation began 2000.

MSR $4,000	$3,500	$2,850	$2,250	$1,875	$1,650	$1,475	$1,350

Add $1,000 per interchangeable barrel.

K95 STUTZEN - various cals., features engraved aluminum frame, 20 in. octagon barrel and full length forearm, deluxe checkered Turkish walnut, iron sights, 6 lbs. Importation began 2004.

MSR $5,500	$4,950	$4,300	$3,800	$3,250	$2,700	$2,150	$1,850

BLEIKER, HEINRICH

Current rifle manufacturer located in Buetschwil, Switzerland.

RIFLES: BOLT ACTION

Please contact the factory directly for more information, including current U.S. pricing and availability (see Trademark Index).

GRADING - PPGS™	100%	98%	95%	90%	80%	70%	60%

CHALLENGER - .22 LR cal., Bleiker action featuring minimum firing pin resonance and precise head space clearance, super match trigger, match barrel, many options available. New 2002.

MSR $2,900	$2,750	$2,250	$1,775	$1,400	$1,100	$875	$725

MATCH RIFLE - 6mm BR, .308 Win., or 7.5x55mm Swiss cal., Bleiker alloy action featuring titanium hardening/coating, integrated magazine, super match trigger, match barrel, many options available, including different colors. New 2002.

MSR $2,900	$2,750	$2,250	$1,775	$1,400	$1,100	$875	$725

BLUEGRASS ARMORY

Current rifle manufacturer located in Richmond, KY. Consumer direct sales.

RIFLES: BOLT ACTION

VIPER MODEL - .408 Cheyenne (limited mfg.) or .50 BMG cal., single shot action with 3 lug bolt, 29 in. chrome moly steel barrel with muzzle brake, one-piece frame with aluminum stock incorporates Picatinny rail, includes detachable bi-pod, approx. 24 lbs. New 2003.

MSR $2,895	$2,500	$2,150	$1,900	$1,700	$1,550	$1,400	$1,250

BOBCAT WEAPONS INC.

Current manufacturer established in April, 2003 and located in Mesa, AZ.

RIFLES: SEMI-AUTO

BW-5 MODEL - 9mm Para cal., paramilitary design, stamped steel or polymer (Model BW-5 FS) lower receiver, roller lock bolt system with delayed blowback, 16 1/2 in. stainless steel barrel, choice of black, desert tan, OD green, or camo stock, pistol grip, and forearm, Model BW-5 FS has fake supressor, paddle mag. release and 8 7/8 in. barrel, 10 shot mag., approx. 6.4 lbs. New 2003.

MSR $1,350	$1,175	$995	$875	$800	$725	$650	$575

Add $275 for Model BW-5 FS.

BOHICA

Previous manufacturer and customizer located in Sedalia, CO, circa 1993-94.

RIFLES: SEMI-AUTO

M16-SA - .223 Rem., .50 AE, or various custom cals., AR-15 style, 16 or 20 in. barrel, A- 2 sights, standard handguard, approx. 950 were mfg. through September 1994.

	$1,375	$1,225	$1,000	$850	$725	$600	$525

Add $100 for flat-top receiver with scope rail.

Add $65 for two-piece, free floating handguard.

In addition to the rifles listed, Bohica also manufactured a M16-SA Match variation (retail was $2,295, approx. 10 mfg.), a pistol version of the M16-SA in both 7 and 10 in. barrel (retail was $1,995, approx. 50 mfg.), and a limited run of M16-SA in .50 AE cal. (retail was $1,695, approx. 25 mfg.).

BOITO

Previous manufacturer located in Brazil. Previously imported by F.I.E. Corp. located in Hialeah, FL.

Boito shotguns were inexpensive, utilitarian shotguns that are shootable, but not collectible. Because of this, prices typically range between $75 - $175, depending on the gauge and condition.

GRADING - PPGS™	100%	98%	95%	90%	80%	70%	60%

BOND ARMS, INC.

Current manufacturer located in Granbury, Texas beginning 1998.

DERRINGERS: O/U

A key entry internal safety locking device was introduced for all Defender models beginning in 2000. This device locks the preexisting crossbolt safety in the on-safe position.

TEXAS DEFENDER - 9mm Para., .32 H&R Mag., .357 Mag., .357 Max, .40 S&W, .44 Mag., .45 ACP, or .45 LC/.410 shot shell cals., O/U design, 3 in. barrels with spring loaded extractors, stainless steel, removable trigger guard, rebounding hammer, crossbolt safety, spring loaded cammed locking lever, 21 oz. New 1998.

MSR $379	$305	$250	$195

Add $139 per extra barrels.

Add $15 for left-hand model.

CENTURY 2000 DEFENDER (C2K) - .410 bore/.45 LC cal. with 2 1/2 in. chambers and 3 in. barrels, or .410 bore with 3 in. chambers and 3 1/2 in. barrels. New 1999.

MSR $394	$320	$265	$200

Add $15 for left-hand model.

COWBOY DEFENDER - similar cals. as Texas Defender, designed specifically for cowboy action shooting, w/o trigger guard. New 2000.

MSR $379	$305	$250	$195

Add $15 for left-hand model.

SUPER DEFENDER - .450 AutoBond cal., 3 in. barrels, rosewood grips, stainless steel construction, 20 oz. Limited mfg. 2003-2004.

	$300	$245	$195

Last MSR was $369.

SNAKE SLAYER - .410 bore/.45 LC cal. with 3 in. chambers and 3 1/2 in. barrels, features larger grip frame. New 2005.

MSR $445	$375	$300	$250

PISTOLS: SEMI-AUTO

.450 AUTOBOND - .450 AutoBond/.45 ACP cal., based on Colt 1911 design, full size frame, 5 in. barrel.

While advertised during 2003, this model never went into production.

BORCHARDT

Previous pistol design originating in Germany circa 1894-1897.

PISTOLS: SEMI-AUTO

Prices below assume matching parts and original condition.

MODEL 1893 - 7.65mm Borchardt cal., original Luger design, 6 1/2 in. barrel, blue finish with fire-blue small parts, checkered walnut grips, 8 shot mag., distinguished by elongated spring mechanism housing located behind the toggle assembly, may include accessories (mags., holster, stock) and/ or case.

✳ *Ludwig Loewe Mfg.* - serial numbered 1-1104.

	$12,000	$10,500	$9,000	$7,500	$6,250	$4,950	$3,750

Original stocks (with attached leather holster) are priced starting at $3,500.

>**Cased With Accessories** - original cased gun was supplied with matching shoulder stock, detachable cheekpiece, leather holster, 3 regular mags. and a hold-open mag.

	$25,000	$18,500	$13,500	$10,000	$8,000	$6,500	$5,000

GRADING - PPGS™	100%	98%	95%	90%	80%	70%	60%

✳ *DWM Mfg.* - starting approx. 1895, serial numbered 1105-3000.

	100%	98%	95%	90%	80%	70%	60%
	$11,250	$9,995	$8,500	$7,000	$5,750	$4,350	$3,250

Original stocks (with attached leather holster) are priced starting at $3,500.

>**Cased With Accessories** - original cased gun was supplied with unnumbered shoulder stock, detachable cheekpiece, leather holster, 3 regular mags. and a hold-open mag.

	100%	98%	95%	90%	80%	70%	60%
	$22,500	$18,000	$12,500	$10,000	$8,000	$6,500	$5,000

BOSIS, LUCIANO

Current manufacturer located in Travagliato, Italy. Currently imported by British Sporting Arms Ltd., located in Millsbrook, NY. Previously imported by Old Friends Hunting & Shooting Co., located in Livingston, MT, New England Arms, located in Kittery Point, ME and by William Larkin Moore & Co., located in Scottsdale, AZ.

All Luciano Bosis guns are manufactured on a custom order only basis. Annual production is approx. 25 best quality guns. Please contact the importers directly for current availability and pricing.

SHOTGUNS

Add 20% for 28 ga. or .410 bore, 1,375 euros for single trigger.

MICHAELANGELO O/U - 12, 16, 20, 28 ga., or .410 bore, Boss style sidelock action, 28 in. chopper lump barrels. Prices reflect base value in the white w/o engraving.

Prices start in the 44,000 euro range, w/o engraving, and go up according to special orders. Used values start at approx. $30,000.

HAMMER GUN SxS - 12 ga., sidelock action.

Please contact the importers directly for a price quotation on this model.

QUEEN SxS - 12, 16, 20, 28 ga., or .410 bore, H&H type sidelock action, 27 in. chopper lump barrels, fine and elaborate engraving.

Prices start in the 22,000 euro range and go up according to special orders.

COUNTRY SxS - 12, 16, 20, 28 ga., or .410 bore, Anson & Deeley type scalloped boxlock action, 27 in. chopper lump barrels, DT, checkered deluxe English straight grip stock and forearm.

Prices start in the 12,000 euro range and go up according to special orders.

BOSS & CO., LTD.

Current manufacturer located in London, England 1812 to date. Direct sales from the manufacturer only.

Boss manufactures some of the world's finest shotguns and rifles (best quality guns only). Their shotguns and rifles have always been custom built per individual order. Approximately 10,000 have been manufactured to date. The following are basic models (does not include special orders, optional engraving patterns, and other possible options). Prices indicated below for manufacturer's suggested retail and 100% condition factors are listed in English pounds. All new prices do not include English VAT. Delivery time for new guns is approx. 3 years. Values for used guns in 98%-60% condition factors are priced in U.S. dollars.

RIFLES: BOLT ACTION

BOSS BOLT ACTION - .270 Win. or .275 Rigby (disc.) cal., Mauser action with Walther premium sporter barrel, Win. Model 70 three position side safety, box mag., includes mounts and Zeiss scope.

	100%	98%	95%	90%	80%	70%	60%
MSR N/A	N/A	$13,000	$11,500	$7,750	$6,500	$5,500	$4,500

This model has very limited manufacture, and Boss should be contacted directly for a firm price quotation.

GRADING - PPGS™	100%	98%	95%	90%	80%	70%	60%

RIFLES: O/U & SxS, CUSTOM

Boss Express O/U double rifles are quoted per individual request only. Current base price for the .375 H&H cal. starts at £130,000 (w/o VAT), larger calibers up to .700 NE are also available at additional cost. Approx. 12 1/2 lbs. Older double rifles must be appraised individually. The Boss SxS rifle starts at £90,000 (w/o VAT). These models have had very limited manufacture.

SHOTGUNS: CUSTOM

BOSS O/U - 12, 16, 20, 28 ga., or .410 bore standard, barrel lengths and chokes to specifications, shell-framed sidelock, auto ejectors, double triggers or single non-selective, English straight stock standard to specifications, VR or pistol grip stock optional, best English bouquet & scroll fine engraving, limited production.

MSR £75,000	£75,000	$78,000	$55,500	$38,750	$32,500	$27,500	$22,500

Add £5,000 for 28 ga. or .410 bore.

Note: above values represent base gun only and are w/o VAT. Any additional engraving (tight bouquet and scroll is the traditional standard) and/or special orders will add considerably to the above prices.

BOSS SxS - all gauges, barrel lengths and chokes to specifications, bar- action side-lock, easy open/close action (not self-opening), square or rounded action, check-ered stock, pistol grip (optional) or straight grip stock, single (patented 3 pull system) or double triggers, splinter or beavertail (optional) forearm, best English bouquet & scroll engraving, limited production.

MSR £55,000	£55,000	$57,000	$46,500	$35,000	$27,750	$21,500	$18,000

Add £5,000 for 28 ga. or .410 bore.

Note: above values represent base gun only, and are w/o VAT. Any additional engraving (tight rose and scroll is the traditional standard) and/or special orders will add considerably to the above prices.

ROBERTSON O/U - 12 or 20 ga., boxlock action, fitted sideplates, single trigger, 28 or 30 in. rota-hammer forged monobloc barrels, available with or w/o top rib, oil fin-ished French walnut stock six point multi-locking feature, hand engraved, color case hardened receiver. New 2005.

MSR £8,000	£8,000	N/A	N/A

Note: above values represent base gun only and are w/o VAT.

ROBERTSON SxS - 12 or 20 ga., Anson & Deeley boxlock action, fitted sideplates, top tang safety, ejectors, single trigger, 28 or 30 in. barrels, Boss style concave rib, oil finished French walnut stock with splinter forearm, hand engraved, color case hardened receiver. New 2005.

MSR £6,000	£6,000	N/A	N/A

Note: above values represent base gun only and are w/o VAT.

BOSWELL, CHARLES

Previous trademark manufactured in London, England and Charlotte, NC.

In 1988, Charles Boswell was purchased by U.S. interests and Cape Horn International (previously Cape Horn Outfitters) located in Charlotte, NC, was retained to sell and manu-facture the Boswell Guns in the U.S. In addition to acquiring their entire inventory of English manufactured firearms, Charles Boswell fabricated new shotguns and double rifles in the U.S. using the best materials including English lock mechanisms and retained the Charles Boswell Co. trademark. Every gun was custom ordered to an individual cli-ent's requirements/specifications. Previously imported by Saxon Arms, Ltd., located in Clearwater, FL.

GRADING - PPGS™	100%	98%	95%	90%	80%	70%	60%

RIFLES: SxS

BOXLOCK RIFLE - .300 Express, .375 H&H, .458 Win. Mag., or .500 NE cal., made to individual order, choice of game scene engraving, Anson & Deeley boxlock actions, select European hybrid walnut, double triggers, leather cased. Disc. 1996.

	$17,500	$14,750	$11,750	$9,500	$8,500	$7,500	$6,500

Last MSR was $35,000.

 * **.600 Nitro Express**
  This model was priced by quotation only. A .600 NE sold for $123,000 in 1991. Disc. 1996.

SIDELOCK RIFLE - .300 Express, .375 H&H, or .458 Win. Mag. cal., made to individual order, choice of game scene engraving, H&H sidelock action, select European hybrid walnut, double triggers, leather cased. Disc. 1996.

	$35,000	$29,500	$25,000	$20,000	$16,500	$13,250	$10,750

Last MSR was $65,000.

 * **.600 Nitro Express**

	$65,000	$55,000	$45,000	$37,500	$30,000	$25,000	$19,950

Last MSR was $125,000.

SHOTGUNS: SxS

BOXLOCK MODEL - previously made to individual order, choice of engraving - including game scenes with gold, Anson & Deeley boxlock actions, select European hybrid walnut, double triggers, leather cased. While each shotgun was priced per individual special order, the below listed prices represented standard features and embellishments. Disc. 1996.

 * **Best Quality**

	$5,500	$4,750	$4,150	$3,550	$3,150	$2,650	$2,000

Last MSR was $9,500.

 * **Deluxe Grade** - game scene engraved.

	$6,750	$5,250	$4,500	$4,000	$3,550	$3,000	$2,500

Last MSR was $10,500.

   Add $900 for single trigger.
   Add $2,800 for extra set of barrels.
   Add $2,200 for 28 ga. or .410 bore.

FEATHERWEIGHT MONARCH GRADE - lavishly engraved with gold game scenes, lightweight model, specifications per individual customer special order. Mfg. 1989-96.

 * **Boxlock Model**

	$9,750	$7,350	$6,000	$5,000	$4,400	$3,750	$3,150

Last MSR was $12,500.

 * **Sidelock Model**

	$16,500	$14,000	$12,000	$9,750	$8,500	$7,250	$6,250

Last MSR was $25,000.

SIDELOCK MODEL - previously made to individual order, choice of game scene engraving, H&H sidelock action, select European hybrid walnut, double triggers, leather cased, while each shotgun was priced per individual special order, the below listed values represented standard features and embellishments.

	$11,750	$9,450	$8,250	$7,000	$6,000	$5,000	$4,000

Last MSR was $17,500.

   Add $4,000 for smaller gauges except .410 bore - add $5,000.
   Add $2,800 for extra set of barrels.
   Add $2,800 for extra set of .410 bore barrels.

BOWEN, BRUCE & COMPANY

Current shotgun manufacturer established 1996 and located in Sturgis, SD. Consumer direct sales only. Bruce Bowen & Company is a division of NIP Manufacturing, Inc.

SHOTGUNS: SINGLE SHOT

BOWEN TRAP GUN - 12 ga. only, unique break open action similar to Seitz trap gun, 32, 33, 34, or 35 in. fixed full choke barrel with four different rib configurations, allowing for four different points of impact, both release and pull triggers included, deluxe checkered walnut with either regular or Monte Carlo stock, individually made per customer's specifications, 9 lbs.

The base price for the Bowen Trap Gun is $16,500. Please contact the factory directly for a firm price quotation with various options and a delivery date.

BRAZIER, JOSEPH, LTD.

Current manufacturer established in circa 1700 and currently located in West Sussex, England. Currently represented in the U.S. by First National Gun Banque Corp., located in Colorado Springs, CO.

This firm was founded in approx. 1700 by William Brazier, Gunmaker, London (1700-1720), and was continued by his son, John Brazier, also of London, from 1740-1800. Benjamin Brazier was established in Wolverhampton from 1818-1835. Joseph Brazier was listed as a gun and lock maker at the same address (9 Brick Kiln Street) during 1827. From 1834 to 1887, the address as "The Ashes" on Great Brick Kiln Street, Wolverhampton. By 1838, the firm was also making implements, and had been appointed lock makers to the East India Company and the Board of Ordnance. In 1849, Joseph's elder son, also named Joseph, was made a partner, and the firm became known as Joseph Brazier & Son. By 1851, younger son Richard Brazier was made a partner, and the firm was renamed J & R Brazier. This company exhibited locks and accessories at the Great Exhibition of 1851.

During this same time, J & R Brazier was making gun furniture, sights, bullet, moulds, and breech loading actions. In 1855, Joseph Brazier patented a lever ramrod for Adams self-cocking pistols (No. 760) (single action later converted to double action), and to the Adams revolvers, which he made under license. During 1858, Richard Brazier patented a loading device (No. 1593), and at least one revolver using this patent was made; the name engraved on the revolver known was "Joseph Brazier & Son", which implied that Richard had died, and the firm's name had reverted.

By 1859, Joseph Brazier Jr. registered two designs, the first (No. 1056) was for a spring clamp, and the second (No. 1068) was for a lock vice. In 1864, Joseph Brazier Jr. reportedly patented a snap action breech loading mechanism (patent not traced). By 1872, the firm was classified as gun barrel makers, and in 1874 (as well as 1879-1880), the firm was recognized as gunmakers - breech loading. After 1874, the firm changed its name to Joseph Brazier & Sons, most likely indicating Joseph Sr. had retired after taking his sons into the business as partners. During 1876, the firm purchased a license to manufacture Anson & Deeley's famous patent boxlock. In 1887, William Mansfield Jr. became a senior partner, and the company moved from "The Ashes Works" to Lord Street. Mansfield was a lock maker on Lord Street from 1875-1896 and during 1887 under the name J. Brazier & Sons, patented the "Galwey Brazier Improved Game Scorer", which fitted into the forend or stock of a shotgun. By 1896, William Mansfield either retired or died, and G. Brazier together with W. Cashmore patented a safety for a hammerless gun.

It appears that after 1896, the Brazier family regained control of their family's business. Around 1920, the firm, which had approx. 26 employees, was bought by Edwin Chilton of Wolverhampton, and Brazier named locks continued to be made until 1978, when Chilton closed down the company. After 1978, Joseph Brazier, Ashes, was registered by Magnum Arms Company Ltd. at 46 Newhampton Rd. West, Wolverhampton, West Midlands. In 1983, Joseph Brazier Ltd. was registered as a limited company, and by 1993 was

GRADING - PPGS™	100%	98%	95%	90%	80%	70%	60%

acquired and incorporated.

Today, Joseph Brazier manufactures complete guns, gunlocks for the HMS Victory, firearms locks, parts, accessories, and new technology Solid Steel Barrels for the trade. The firm also offers state of the art engineering services to the English gunmaking trade and is an egineering consultant to 14 major firearms manufacturers.

For more information on the current line of Joseph Brazier Ltd. guns, please contact the U.S. representative directly, including information about importation, availability and pricing.

HANDGUNS

Joseph Brazier manufactures .357 Mag. cal. revolvers in stainless steel starting at $750. Semi-auto 1911 A1 style pistols are available in a variety of configurations and begin at $1,750.

RIFLES

A boxlock double rifle in .470 NE cal. is available starting at $13,500.

SHOTGUNS

Brazier boxlock SxS shotguns are available in 20 or 28 ga., with DTs, ejector and full hand engraving for $10,500.

A sidelock O/U Best gun is available in 12, 20, or 28 ga. and start at $22,500. Add $7,500 for solid barrels.

BREDA MECCANICA BRESCIANA

Current manufacturer located in Brescia, Italy. Previous company name was Ernesto Breda. Currently imported beginning 2002 by Tristar, located in No. Kansas City, MO. Previously imported 2000-2001 by Gryphon International, located in Kansas City, MO, and by Diana Imports Co., located in San Francisco, CA.

SHOTGUNS: O/U

VEGA SPECIAL - 12 or 20 ga., boxlock action, 26 or 28 in. barrels, single trigger, ejectors, blue only.

$575	$495	$460	$440	$400	$375	$350

Last MSR was $650.

VEGA SPECIAL TRAP - 12 ga. only, boxlock action, triggers and locks designed for competition shooting, 30 or 32 in. barrels, single trigger, ejectors, blue only.

$885	$820	$760	$720	$675	$635	$575

Last MSR was $1,114.

VEGA LUSSO - 12 ga. only, scalloped boxlock action, 3 in. chambers, SST, ejectors, 26 or 28 in. VR barrels, coin finished receiver with light perimeter engraving, deluxe checkered Circassian walnut stock and forearm. Imported 2001-2002.

$1,695	$1,375	$1,100	$975	$850	$725	$600

Last MSR was $1,858.

SIRIO STANDARD - 12 or 20 ga., boxlock action, 26 or 28 in. barrels, single trigger, ejectors, blue only, action extensively engraved. Also available in skeet model (28 in. barrels).

$2,000	$1,850	$1,630	$1,480	$1,320	$1,200	$1,050

Last MSR was $2,225.

GRADING - PPGS™	100%	98%	95%	90%	80%	70%	60%

PEGASO HUNTER - 12 or 20 ga., boxlock action, 3 in. chambers, 26, 28 (12 ga. only), or 30 (Sporting Clays only) in. VR barrels with 7mm (Hunter) or 11mm (Sporting Clays) rib, 5 interchangeable chokes, removable trigger group, engraved silver steel (Hunter Model) or blue finished (Sporting Clays), inertia SST, oil finished deluxe walnut stock and forearm, approx. 7-7.5 lbs. Imported 2004 only.

	$2,400	$2,050	$1,850	$1,650	$1,425	$1,200	$950

Last MSR was $2,739.

* *Pegaso Sporting Clays* - features upgraded wood, Breda logos in 24Kt. gold, removable trigger group, supplied with ABS fitted case. Imported 2004 only.

	$3,300	$2,875	$2,400	$2,050	$1,700	$1,450	$1,200

Last MSR was $3,644.

SHOTGUNS: SxS

ANDROMEDA SPECIAL - 12 ga. only, single trigger, ejectors, select checkered walnut, satin finish receiver with elaborate engraving.

	$640	$550	$480	$420	$365	$300	$250

Last MSR was $685.

SHOTGUNS: SEMI-AUTO

Add approx. 5% for vent. rib on those discontinued models below where applicable.
Add approx. 10% for choke tubes on discontinued models.

GOLD SERIES - 12 or 20 (lightweight) ga., 2 3/4 in. chamber, 25 or 27 in. barrels, recoil operated, interchangeable choke tubes on recent mfg., vent. rib is standard.

* *Antares Standard* - all steel construction. Importation disc. 1988.

	$440	$375	$340	$310	$285	$260	$240

Last MSR was $495.

* *Argus* - lightweight standard, weighs only 6.6 lbs. Importation disc. 1988.

	$450	$380	$340	$310	$285	$260	$240

Last MSR was $510.

* *Aries* - Magnum, 3 in. chambers, 7.9 lbs. Importation disc. 1988.

	$460	$395	$350	$320	$295	$270	$250

Last MSR was $525.

STANDARD - 12 ga., 2 3/4 in. chamber, recoil operated, 25 or 27 in. barrel, lightly engraved, interchangeable choke tubes on recent mfg. Disc.

	$300	$275	$255	$230	$215	$200	$180

GRADE 1 - 12 ga., similar to standard, except with fancier wood and engraving.

	$575	$530	$485	$440	$410	$380	$350

GRADE 2 - 12 ga., exceeds Grade 1 on embellishments.

	$685	$620	$560	$500	$460	$420	$375

GRADE 3 - 12 ga., top-of-the-line semi-auto.

	$850	$790	$700	$640	$590	$540	$480

MAGNUM MODEL - 12 ga. only, chambered for 3 in. shells.

	$470	$415	$380	$350	$315	$290	$265

ALTAIR SPECIAL - 12 ga., 2 3/4 in. chamber, gas operated, 25 or 27 in. barrel, alloy construction, interchangeable choke tubes on recent mfg., vent. rib is standard, choice of blue or chromed receiver.

	$440	$375	$340	$310	$285	$260	$240

Last MSR was $495.

GRADING - PPGS™	100%	98%	95%	90%	80%	70%	60%

ASTRO - 12 (disc. 2002) or 20 ga., 3 in. chamber, inertia movement action, 22 (slug), 24, 26, 28, or 30 in. VR barrel with choke tube, choice of black synthetic, Advantage camo, or Circassian walnut stock (recoil pad on 20 ga. only) and forearm. Importation began 2001.

MSR $1,215	$1,050	$825	$675	$600	$525	$450	$425

Add $100 for Advantage camo coverage (disc. 2002).

ASTROLUX - similar to Astro, except has two-tone receiver with engraving and deluxe checkered Circassian walnut stock and forearm. Imported 2001-2002.

	$1,475	$1,200	$995	$875	$750	$625	$550

Last MSR was $1,665.

ERMES SERIES (2000/2000 L) - 12 ga., 3 in. chamber, inertia recoil operating system, aluminum alloy receiver, nickel plated or blue (lower receiver only) finish, 24, 26, or 28 in. barrel with choke tube, deluxe checkered Circassian walnut stock and forearm. Importation began 2001.

MSR $1,339	$1,100	$925	$800	$700	$600	$500	$400

Add $417 for Ermes 2000 L with nickel finished receiver.

✳ *Ermes Silver* - similar to Ermes 2000, except has engraved nickel plated silver finish on lower receiver. Importation began 2002.

MSR $1,834	$1,550	$1,200	$975	$825	$700	$575	$495

✳ *Ermes Gold* - similar to Ermes 2000, except has nickel plated silver finish with engraving and 24Kt. animal gold inlays on lower receiver. Importation began 2002.

MSR $2,060	$1,650	$1,325	$1,075	$900	$775	$650	$550

MIRA - 12 ga. only, 3 in. chamber, gas operated, Ergal aluminum alloy receiver, choice of annodized black metal or Advantage camo finish, 22 (slug), 24, 26, 28, or 30 in. VR barrel with choke tube, Circassian walnut or black synthetic (disc. 2002) stock and forearm. Importation began 2001.

MSR $938	$815	$700	$625	$550	$450	$375	$325

Subtract 10% for black synthetic stock and forearm.
Add $12 for Sporting Clays configuration.

GRIZZLY MAG - 12 ga., 3 1/2 in. chamber, inertia operation with rotary bolt, 28 in. VR barrel with choke tubes, choice of matte black receiver/barrel finish or 100% Advantage Timber HD camo, sling swivels, includes fitted case, 7.5 lbs. Imported 2004 only.

	$1,195	$995	$850	$750	$625	$525	$425

Last MSR was $1,420.

ARIES 2 - 12 ga. only, 2 3/4 in. chamber, gas operated, engraved two-tone receiver, 28 or 30 in. VR barrel, deluxe checkered Circassian walnut stock and forearm. Limited importation 2001 only.

		$815	$725	$595	$550	$495	$445	$395

Last MSR was $925.

BREEDING, RYAN

Current custom rifle manufacturer located in Palmdale, CA.

RIFLES: BOLT ACTION

Ryan Breeding specializes in making high quality, custom built rifles in .22-.585 cal. On his safari rifles in larger cals., he features a 4 shot mag. and shorter barrel (19 in. - 24 in.) with optional muzzle brake. Please contact Ryan Breeding directly for more information, including pricing and availability.

GRADING - PPGS™	100%	98%	95%	90%	80%	70%	60%

BREN 10

Previous trademark manufactured 1983-1986 by Dornaus & Dixon Ent., Inc., located in Huntington Beach, CA.

Bren 10 magazines played an important part in the failure of these pistols to be accepted by consumers. Originally, Bren magazines were not shipped in some cases until a year after the customer received his gun. The complications arising around manufacturing a reliable dual caliber magazine domestically led to the downfall of this company. For this reason, original Bren 10 magazines are currently selling for $125-$150 if new (watch for fakes).

PISTOLS: SEMI-AUTO

Note: the Bren 10 shoots a Norma factory loaded 10mm auto. cartridge. Ballistically, it is very close to a .41 Mag. Bren pistols also have unique power seal rifling, with five lands and grooves. While in production, Bren pistols underwent (4) engineering changes, the most important probably being re-designing the floorplate of the magazine, thus preventing mag. shifting while undergoing recoil.

100% values in this section assume NIB condition. Subtract 10% without box/manual.

BREN 10 STANDARD MODEL - 10mm cal. only, semi-auto selective double action design, blue slide/silver frame finish, 5 in. barrel, 11 shot, stainless steel frame, usually supplied with two mags. although early mfg. did not include a mag. because of design problems, "83SM" ser. no. prefix. Mfg. 1984-86.

$1,575	$1,150	$750	$650	$550	$475	$395

Last MSR was $500.

Add $600 for .45 conversion unit.
Be wary of Standard Models with wooden cases and conversion kits – they are fakes!

BREN 10 MILITARY/POLICE MODEL - 10mm cal. only, identical to standard model, except has all black finish, "83MP" ser. no. prefix. Mfg. 1984-86.

$1,575	$1,150	$750	$650	$550	$475	$395

Last MSR was $550.

BREN 10 SPECIAL FORCES MODEL - 10mm cal. only, commercial version of the military pistol submitted to the U.S. gov't. Model D has dark finish. Model L has light finish, "SFD" ser. no. prefix on Model D, "SFL" ser. no. prefix on Model L. Disc. 1986.

Dark finish - Model D	$1,595	$1,150	$750	$650	$550	$475	$395
Light finish - Model L	$1,895	$1,550	$995	$825	$700	$575	$475

Last MSR was $600.

BREN 10 DUAL-MASTER PRESENTATION MODEL - 10mm and .45 ACP cal., supplied with extra slide and barrel (numbered to gun) to accommodate the .45 ACP, same mags. (two) for both cals., extra fine finish, light scroll engraving, with wood presentation case, "83DM" ser. no. prefix, less than 50 mfg. Disc. 1986.

$3,900	$3,000	$2,000	$1,000	$800	$500	$300

Last MSR was $800.

BREN 10 JEFF COOPER COMMEMORATIVE - 10mm cal. only, while 2,000 were annnounced for mfg., sources believe that approx. 13 were actually made, 22Kt. gold plated detailing, laser engraved stocks, special presentation chest. Disc. 1986.

$4,800	$4,500	$3,200	$2,950	$1,500	$750	$500

Last MSR was $2,000.

MARKSMAN MODEL - .45 ACP cal., 250 mfg. (in its own ser. range) for a retail shop in Chicago called "The Marksman," action similar to Bren 10 Standard Model, "MSM" ser. no. prefix.

$1,200	$895	$695	$500	$350	$200	$150

Add $650 for 10mm conversion unit.
Add $100 for original nylon carrying case marked "Marksman."

GRADING - PPGS™	100%	98%	95%	90%	80%	70%	60%

BRETTON

Current manufacturer located in Saint-Etienne, France. Previously imported and distributed by Mandall Shooting Supplies, Inc. located in Scottsdale, AZ.

SHOTGUNS: O/U

All Bretton shotguns are extremely lightweight and well balanced because of their unique design (permitting total disassembly including barrels) and use of various composition alloys.

BABY STANDARD (SPRINT MODEL) - 12 or 20 ga. only, sliding breech action allows barrels to move straight forward, 27 1/2 in. separated barrels, double triggers, side opening lever, blue action and barrels, recoil pad, checkered walnut stock and forearm, 4.8 lbs. Importation disc.

	$995	$885	$700	$625	$575	$475	$430

Prices reflect most recent importation information.

SPRINT DELUXE - 12, 16 (disc.), or 20 ga., action similar to Baby Standard, engraved coin finished receiver, 27 1/2 in. separated barrels, deluxe checkered walnut stock and forearm, extremely lightweight, 4.8 lbs. Importation disc. 1994.

	$895	$725	$625	$575	$475	$430	$395

Last MSR was $975.

FAIR PLAY MODEL - 12 or 20 ga., differs from Sprint Models in that action pivots like normal O/U, 27 1/2 in. separated barrels, lightweight construction, 4.8 lbs. Importation disc.

	$966	$850	$675	$625	$575	$475	$430

Add $64 for Fair Play Limited Model.

BRILEY

Current trademark manufactured by Briley Manufacturing Inc., and located in Houston, TX. Briley produces both pistols and rifles, in addition to manufacturing a complete line of top quality shotgun barrel tubes and chokes since 1976 - please contact the factory directly (see Trademark Index) for more information on these shotgun accessories.

PISTOLS: SEMI-AUTO

FANTOM - 9mm Para., .38 Super, .40 S&W, or .45 ACP cal., features Caspian aluminum wide body frame, Briley match barrel, and many competition features, hot blue slide finish and armor coated frame, 8 or 10 shot mag, black synthetic grips, approx. 22-24 oz. Mfg. 1998-2003.

	$1,675	$1,300	$1,075	$875	$750	$625	$575

Last MSR was $1,900.

Add $95 for hard chrome finish.
Add $75 for night sights.
Add $350 for 2 port barrel compensator.

ADVANTAGE - 9mm Para., .40 S&W, or .45 ACP cal., features 5 in. Briley match barrel, checkered walnut grips and front grip strap, hot blue finish. Mfg. 1998-2004.

	$1,495	$1,250	$1,050	$875	$750	$625	$575

Last MSR was $1,650.

Add $175 for hard chrome finish.
Add $100 for stainless steel (new 2000).

VERSATILITY PLUS - 9mm Para., .40 S&W, or .45 ACP cal., features steel or stainless steel (new 2000) 1911 Govt. length modular or Caspian frame, 5 in. barrel, checkered black synthetic grips and front grip strap, squared off trigger guard, hot blue finish. Mfg. 1998-2004.

	$1,625	$1,300	$1,050	$875	$725	$600	$550

Last MSR was $1,850.

Add $175 for hard chrome finish.
Add $175 for stainles steel (new 2000).

SIGNATURE SERIES - .40 S&W cal. only, similar to Versatility Plus. Mfg. 1998-2004.

	100%	98%	95%	90%	80%	70%	60%
	$1,975	$1,650	$1,325	$1,125	$900	$775	$625

Last MSR was $2,250.

Add $175 for hard chrome finish.

PLATE MASTER - 9mm Para. or .38 Super cal., features 1911 Govt. length frame, Briley TCII titanium barrel compensator, Briley scope mount, and other competition features, hot blue finish. Mfg. 1998-2004.

	100%	98%	95%	90%	80%	70%	60%
	$1,675	$1,325	$1,075	$895	$775	$625	$575

Last MSR was $1,895.

Add $175 for hard chrome finish.

EL PRESIDENTE - 9mm Para. or .38 Super cal., top-of-the-line competition model with Briley quad compensator with side ports, checkered synthetic grips and front grip strap, squared off trigger guard. Mfg. 1998-2004.

	100%	98%	95%	90%	80%	70%	60%
	$2,250	$1,925	$1,625	$1,325	$1,075	$875	$750

Last MSR was $2,550.

Add $175 for hard chrome finish.

RIFLES: BOLT ACTION

TRANS PECOS - .22-250 Rem., .243 Win., .260 Rem., .308 Win., or 7mm-08 Rem. cal., solid aluminum frame fits metal to metal with barreled action, bench rest grade Jewell trigger, match grade L. Walther barrel, 3 lug 45 degree one-piece bolt, choice of black synthetic (single shot) or checkered high gloss stock and forearm (repeater). Mfg. 1998-2002.

	100%	98%	95%	90%	80%	70%	60%
	$3,200	$2,750	$2,275	$1,950	$1,775	$1,525	$1,250

Last MSR was $3,495.

Subtract $500 for single shot action.

This model is guaranteed to shoot 1/2 in. groups at 100 yards with factory ammo.

RIFLES: SEMI-AUTO

HUNTER - .22 LR cal., utilizes Ruger 10/22 action, 21 1/2 in. tapered match stainless steel barrel with crown, Hogue rubber or wood stock, 10 shot mag., includes Briley integral scope mount, approx. 6 1/4 - 6 5/8 lbs.

MSR $600		$550	$475	$395	$360	$330	$300	$285

Add $250 for wood stock.

Add $100 for fluted barrel.

* *Hunter Magnum* -.22 Mag. cal., similar to Hunter, except is 9 shot mag. and 21 1/2 in. bull barrel. Disc. 2003.

		$750	$575	$475	$425	$375	$325	$295

Last MSR was $850.

Add $250 for walnut or laminate stock.

Add $100 for fluted barrel.

SPORTER - .22 LR cal., similar to Hunter, except has 18 1/2 or 21 1/2 in. match stainless steel bull barrel with crown, Hogue rubber, brown laminate, or unchecked-ered walnut sporter stock, 10 shot mag., approx. 6 1/2 lbs.

MSR $600		$550	$475	$395	$360	$330	$300	$285

Add $250 for laminate or sporter style walnut stock.

Add $100 for fluted barrel.

BMG - .22 LR cal., 17 in. match stainless steel bull barrel with target crown, includes 3 1/2 lbs. adj. match barrel weights, choice of Hogue rubber, brown laminate sporter, or walnut sporter stock, 10 shot mag., designed for match grade ammunition only.

MSR $750		$675	$600	$525	$465	$425	$385	$350

Add $250 for laminate or sporter style walnut stock.

GRADING - PPGS™	100%	98%	95%	90%	80%	70%	60%

BRITARMS

Previous trademark manufactured by Berdan Gunmakers Ltd. located in England. Previously imported and distributed until 1994 by Mandall Shooting Supplies, Inc. located in Scottsdale, AZ. Previously by Action Arms Ltd. (1982-1983) located in Philadelphia, PA.

Britarms Target Pistols had very limited importation into the U.S. While Britarms manufactured other models, only the Model 2000 is listed since it was formally imported through U.S. firms.

PISTOLS: SEMI-AUTO

MODEL 2000 (MK II) - .22 LR cal., standard fire target semi-auto pistol, adj. trigger and rear sight, anatomical adj. grips, 5.82 in. barrel, 5 shot mag., 3 lbs., limited importation, including approx. 2000 through Action Arms Ltd.

$995	$825	$700	$625	$550	$495	$450

Last MSR was $1,295.

This model features a bolt hold-open mechanism which serves as a manual safety to allow importation.

BRNO ARMS (ZBROJOVKA BRNO)

Currently manufactured by Zbrojovka Brno located in Brno, Czech Republic (formerly Czechoslovakia) since 1918. No current U.S. importation. Brno 98 bolt action rifles and actions were imported by EAA Corp, located in Sharpes, FL until 2002. Also previously imported and distributed by Euro-Imports, located in El Cajon, CA until 2001 and by Bohemia Arms located in Fountain Valley, CA until 1997. Brno rifles, shotguns, and combination guns produced at the Brno factory were previously imported and distributed by Magnum Research Inc. located in Minneapolis, MN (c. 1994-1996). In the early '50s, Brno rifles were imported by Continental Arms Corp. located in New York City. Pragotrade located in Ontario, Canada also imports this trademark for Canada currently (and exclusively). Previously imported by T.D. Arms located in New Baltimore, MD.

As more history is becoming available on this important European trademark, the following biographical sketch will provide some information. Circa 1918, some military personnel took over the controlling interest of the Austro-Hungarian armament shop in Brno, Czechoslovakia, renaming it The State Armament and Engineering Works. Approximately a year later, the name was changed to Czechoslovak State Armament Works. The former provinces of Bohemia and Moravia had long been firearms manufacturing centers within their regions. Prior to 1924, this firm was involved mainly with Mauser Model 98 type rifles (both assembly and mfg.).

Pistol manufacture was tranferred from Brno to Ceská Zbrojovka, located in Strakonice, Czechoslovakia, circa 1923. During 1964-1966, the Czech government transferred the production of long guns from Zbrojovka Brno to Ceská Zbrojovka Uhersky Brod. During the 1970s & 1980s, the arms production of Zbrojovka Brno accounted for less than 3% of its total capacity. The activities of this company were deverted into the production of typewriters, diesel motors, and automatic machine tools. While many firearm designs originated in Brno, Zbrojovka Brno was not the manufacturer. Because of this, the long guns manufactured in the mid-1960s, including the ZKK 600 - 602 series and ZKM rimfires, were manufactured in CZ Uhersky Brod. Because of the Czech government's decision to merge manufacture within both companies, the Brno trademark was also used by Ceská Zbrojovka Uhersky Brod.

This relationship was terminated in 1983, when both companies became part of the Agrozet conglomerate. While confusing, the arms utlizing the Brno trademark were not produced in Brno during this time. All firearms exported from Czechoslovakia at the time carried the Brno logo, and most of them were manufactured by Ceská Zbrojovka Uhersky Brod.

Since many of the models listed below have not been imported since 2002, N/As will appear in place of MSRs on those recent imports.

CZ PISTOLS & RIFLES

See separate listing under CZ in this text.

PISTOLS: SEMI-AUTO

MODEL ZBP-99 - 9mm Para. or .40 S&W cal., double action.
While advertised in 1998, this gun never went into production.

REVOLVERS

ZKR 551 - .32 S&W Long or .38 Spl. cal., double action, fixed access 6 shot cylinder, adj. sights, checkered wood grips with thumb rest, 6 in. barrel, approx. 2 lbs. Importation began 1999.

MSR N/A	$1,375	$1,100	$978	$875	$775	$675	$600

RIFLES: BOLT ACTION

The Brno Lightweight Sporter was introduced in the late 1930s. A small quantity was manufactured during pre-war and WWII. Most production occured between 1946-1955. Total production of this model was approx. 40,000+ units. A design change was implemented at approximately serial number 23,000, at which time the receiver was changed to a double square bridge dovetailed to accept scope mounts.

Earlier mfg. had a rounded receiver and some had claw type scope mounts installed. These guns were referenced as Models 21 and 22 domestically, but no model designation appears on the gun. Available cals. were 6.5x57mm, 7x57mm, 7x64mm, 8x57mm, or 8x60mm. Configuration was small ring Mauser 98 receiver with double set trigger(s), butterknife bolt, checkered walnut pistol grip stock (half or full length), with cheekpiece and sling swivels, late production incorporated four variations and two barrel lengths (20.5 or 23.6 in.).

All currently manufactured Brno firearms have a 3 year guarantee.

Brno rifles may be dated by the two digit date beside their proofmarks.

HORNET SPORTER (MODEL ZKW 465) - .22 Hornet cal., miniature Mauser action, 22 3/4 in. barrel, 5 shot clip mag., 3-leaf express sight, double set trigger(s), checkered pistol grip stock, also called Z-B Mauser, serial range noted is 00,111-37,393, approx. 40,000 mfg. between 1948-1973.

	$1,200	$925	$750	$625	$500	$400	$295

There are few examples in .218 Bee and .222 Rem. cal. - premiums can be added.
This model was redesigned with a subsequent designation of ZKB 680 Fox in approx. 1975.

MODEL ZG-47 - .270 Win., .30-06, 7x57mm, 7x64mm, 8x64S, 8x57mm, 9.3x62mm, or 10.75x68mm cal., large ring Mauser 98 action with 20mm dovetails on receiver ring and bridge, single trigger, hinged floorplate, rollover type safety and bolt handle designed for low scope mounting, 23 1/2 in. barrel, checkered pistol grip walnut stock with sling swivels and Schnabel forend, approx. serial range is 0-20,000, mfg. and exported world-wide between 1956-62 (approx.).

	$1,125	$895	$725	$600	$495	$395	$295

Early specimens of this model are marked "BRNO MADE IN CZECHOSLOVAKIA". This model is generally regarded as being one of the finest rifles that Brno has manufactured.

MODEL G 33-40 - 8mm cal., mfg. between 1940-42, prices below assume sporterized condition.

	$350	$295	$260	$230	$200	$175	$150

GRADING - PPGS™	100%	98%	95%	90%	80%	70%	60%

MODEL 21H - 6.5x57mm, 7x57mm, 7x64mm (scarce), 8x57mm, or 8x60mm cal., featherweight style design of the small ring Mauser type action, with (post-1949) or without 20mm dovetails on receiver ring and bridge, 20 1/2 or 23 in. barrel, butterknife style bolt handle, double set triggers, 2-leaf rear sight, checkered pistol grip walnut stock with cheekpiece and plastic buttplate/grip cap, small Schnabel forend, sling swivels included, noted serialization is 14,410-40,098, mfg. approx. 1946-55.

	$1,200	$925	$750	$625	$500	$400	$295

This model was available in 4 different variations: short barrel/short stock, short barrel/full length stock, long barrel/short stock, long barrel/full length stock. The left receiver rail on these models is marked "ZBROJOVKA BRNO, NARODNI PODNIK".

MODEL 22F - similar to 21H, with full length stock. Disc.

	$1,400	$1,100	$925	$800	$675	$550	$475

MODEL 1 - .22 LR cal., 22 3/4 in. barrel, 3-leaf sight, 5 shot clip mag., checkered pistol, 6 lbs. Mfg. 1946-57.

	$595	$540	$485	$405	$375	$320	$265

MODEL 2 - similar to Model 1, with checkered deluxe walnut stock.

	$635	$570	$515	$430	$405	$350	$295

MODEL 3 - .22 LR cal., target rifle model with 27 1/2 in. heavy barrel, adj. click target sights, 5 shot clip mag., plain target style stock with large swivels, 9 1/2 lbs. Mfg. 1949-56.

	$635	$570	$515	$430	$405	$350	$295

MODEL 4 - similar to Model 3, except has improved trigger design and safety. Mfg. 1957-62.

	$700	$635	$570	$515	$430	$405	$350

MODEL 5 - similar to Model 1, except has improved trigger design and safety. Mfg. 1957-73.

	$650	$570	$515	$430	$405	$350	$295

BRNO 98 STANDARD - .243 Win., .270 Win., .30-06, .308 Win., .300 Win. Mag., 7mm Rem. Mag. (new 2000), 7x64mm, or 9.3x62mm cal., Mauser 98 style action, 23.6 in. barrel with or without iron sights, checkered walnut stock with Bavarian cheekpiece, or synthetic stock and forearms (new 2002) single or set trigger, 7 1/4 lbs. Importation began 1998.

MSR N/A	$295	$275	$260	$240	$225	$210	$195

Add approx. $150 for checkered walnut stock with Bavarian cheekpiece.
Add $48 for Mag. cals.
Add $117 for single set trigger.

✻ Brno 98 Mannlicher - similar to Brno 98 Standard, except has full length stock. New 1998.

MSR N/A	$675	$540	$475	$385	$350	$315	$295

Add $46 for Mag. cals.

MODEL ZKB-110 SINGLE SHOT - .22 Hornet, .222 Rem., 5.6x52R, 5.6x50R Mag., 6.5x57R (disc. 1999), 7x57R (disc. 1999), or 8x57JRS (disc. 1999) cal., single shot break open rifle/shotgun, top lever opening, 23.6 in. barrel, uncheckered (Standard Model) or checkered walnut stock with Bavarian cheekpiece and forearm (Lux Model), includes sling swivels, 6 lbs. Importation began 1998.

MSR N/A	$225	$185	$160	$140	$120	$110	$100

Add $77 for ZKB-110 Lux Model.
Add $205 for ZKB-110 Super Lux Model (new 2000).
Add $48 for 7x57R or 8x57JRS cal. (disc. 1999).
Add $132 (standard) or $142 (Lux) for an interchangeable 12 ga. shotgun barrel.

GRADING - PPGS™	100%	98%	95%	90%	80%	70%	60%

MODEL ZOM-451 - .22 LR cal., straight pull bolt action, limited importation by Century International Arms during 1998.

MODEL ZKM-451 - .22 LR cal. Importation began 1995.

MSR N/A	$215	$200	$185	$170	$155	$140	$125

Add $62 for Lux Model (deluxe checkered wood).

MODEL ZKM-452 - please refer to the CZ listing in this text for current information (current mfg. is by CZ).

MODEL ZKM-456 LUX SPORTER - .22 LR cal., bolt action, 5 or 10 shot mag., 24.4 in. barrel, folding rear sight, blue finish, beechwood stock with pistol grip, 6.8 lbs. Imported 1992-98.

	$315	$260	$215	$175	$155	$135	$120

Last MSR was $370.

Add $18 for micrometer rear sight (ZKM-456 MI).

* *Model 456 L/LK Target* - .22 LR cal., Target variation of the ZKM-456 Lux featuring 25 or 28 in. barrel with adj. front and rear sights, 10.1 lbs. Imported 1992-98.

	$305	$250	$210	$170	$150	$130	$115

Last MSR was $358.

Add $7 for 25 in. barrel.

* *Model 456 Match Single Shot* - .22 LR cal., designed for UIT competition at 50 M, features 27 1/2 in. barrel, adj. cheekpiece and buttplate, aperture sights, 9.9 lbs. Imported 1992-98.

	$375	$335	$280	$250	$215	$175	$155

Last MSR was $459.

ZKK 600 - please refer to the CZ listing in this text for current information (current mfg. is by CZ).

ZKK 601 - please refer to the CZ listing in this text for current information (current mfg. was by CZ).

ZKK 602 - please refer to the CZ listing in this text for current information (current mfg. is by CZ).

ZKB 680 (FOX II) - .22 Hornet or .222 Rem. (disc.) cal., 23 1/2 in. barrel, 5 shot mag., set triggers, 5 lbs. 12 oz. Importation disc. 1991.

	$445	$380	$340	$295	$255	$230	$200

Last MSR was $499.

RIFLES: O/U

ZH-344, 348, & 349 - 7x57R (Model ZH-344), 7x65R (Model ZH-348), or 8x57JRS (Model ZH-349) cal., 23.6 in. VR barrels, double triggers, skip line checkering, sling swivels, approx. 7 1/2 lbs. Importation began 1998.

MSR N/A	$1,100	$978	$875	$775	$675	$600	$550

Add $324-$357 per additional set of shotgun barrels, $418 per additional rifle barrel, and $829 for additional Mag. cal. rifle barrels.

SUPER EXPRESS - 7x65R, 9.3x74R, .375 H&H, or .458 Win. Mag. (disc.) cal., sidelock action with Kersten breech crossbolt, hand engraved, skipline checkering, approx. 9 lbs. Importation disc. 1992.

	$3,450	$2,875	$2,300	$1,875	$1,600	$1,375	$1,200

Last MSR was $3,900.

This model previously could be ordered with 6 different types of engraving options. They were: Grade I - add $2,060, Grade II - add $1,030, Grade III - add $1,545, Grade IV - add $1,030, Grade V - add $620, Grade VI - add $660.

GRADING - PPGS™	100%	98%	95%	90%	80%	70%	60%

SUPER SAFARI - 7x64R, .375 H&H Mag., or 9.3x74R cal., action derived from the Super Express, sidelock, DT with set trigger built in, adj. point of impact, 23.6 in. barrels with open sights, deluxe skipline checkered walnut stock and forearm with vent. recoil pad, approx. 9 lbs. Imported 1992-disc.

	$2,375	$1,975	$1,675	$1,450	$1,225	$1,000	$900

RIFLES: SEMI-AUTO

ZKM-611 - .22 Mag. cal., 20 1/2 in. barrel, 6, 10 (C/B 1994), or 12* shot mag., black metal finish, beechwood (new 1996) or checkered walnut stock and forend, grooved receiver, 6.2 lbs. Importation began 1992.

MSR N/A	$395	$350	$300	$265	$230	$200	$185

Add $70 for walnut stock (disc. 1999).

MODEL 581 - .22 LR cal., semi-auto, select walnut stock, adj. sights, 5 shot mag. Disc.

	$600	$540	$495	$440	$395	$350	$295

RIFLES: SINGLE SHOT

ZK 99 - various cals., break open action with top lever, quarter rib on barrel, checkered walnut stock with cheekpiece and Schnabel forearm, includes swivels and slings, 5 3/4 lbs. Importation began 2000.

MSR N/A	$875	$725	$625	$550	$500	$450	$400

SHOTGUNS/COMBINATIONS GUNS: O/U

The following models were imported and distributed by Euro-Imports, located in El Cajon, CA.

ZH-300 SHOTGUN - 12 ga. only, double triggers with rear trigger doubling as single trigger, 27 1/2 in. barrels, 7 lbs. Imported 1986-92.

	$530	$430	$395	$360	$330	$300	$275

Last MSR was $599.

This model was available in skeet, trap, or field configuration.

ZH-301 FIELD SHOTGUN - 12 or 16 ga. field, 27 1/2 in. barrels, optional Monte Carlo stock (disc.).

MSR N/A	$600	$475	$375	$315	$240	$200	$180

Add $20 for Monte Carlo stock.

ZH-302 SKEET SHOTGUN - 12 ga., skeet model, 26 in. barrels, optional Monte Carlo stock (disc.).

MSR N/A	$650	$515	$375	$300	$250	$225	$195

Add $20 for Monte Carlo stock.

ZH-303 TRAP SHOTGUN - 12 ga., trap model, 30 in. barrels, optional Monte Carlo stock (disc.).

MSR N/A	$650	$515	$375	$300	$250	$225	$195

Add $20 for Monte Carlo stock.

ZH-300 SERIES COMBINATION GUNS - 7x57R x 12 ga. (ZH-304), 6x52R x 12 ga. (ZH-305), 6x50R Mag. x 12 ga. (ZH-306), .22 Hornet x 12 ga. (ZH-307), 7x65R x 12 ga. (ZH-308), 8x57JRS x 12 ga. (ZH-309), 7x57R x 16 ga. (ZH-324), 7x65R x 16 ga. (ZH-328), combination rifle/shotgun, optional adj. trigger and Monte Carlo stock. Importation disc. 1994 - reintroduced 1999.

MSR N/A	$695	$575	$425	$350	$300	$250	$195

Add $73 for cheekpiece and set trigger.
Add $35 for adj. trigger (disc.).
Add $20 for Monte Carlo stock (disc.).

ZH 300 Series over and unders are unique in that they permit 8 different interchangeable barrels including rifle and shotgun sets, interrupter on double trigger, blue action, engraved, diamond checkered walnut.

GRADING - PPGS™	100%	98%	95%	90%	80%	70%	60%

MODEL ZH-300 COMBO SET - Model ZH-300 style engraving and features, equipped with 8 interchangeable barrels that include various O/U configurations including shotgun/shotgun and shotgun/rifle configurations in various gauges and cals. Imported 1986-91.

	$2,950	$2,600	$2,250	$2,000	$1,800	$1,600	$1,450

Last MSR was $3,500.

MODEL 500/501 SHOTGUN - 12 ga. only, 28 in. VR barrels, double or single (disc. 1999) trigger.

MSR N/A	$845	$725	$625	$525	$425	$350	$295

Add $50 for single trigger (disc. 1999).

* *Model 500 Combo Set* - shotgun/rifle set comprised of 4 barrels including 12 ga. over barrels with choice of 5.6x52R (disc.), 7x57R, 7x65R, or 12 ga. under barrels (in either field, skeet, or trap chokings), sling swivels, set trigger on rifle/shotgun combo, chemically engraved, about 7 1/2 lbs. Imported 1987-91.

	$1,925	$1,625	$1,400	$1,200	$1,075	$950	$825

Last MSR was $2,169.

This model was available in limited quanitity.

MODEL 502 SERIES COMBINATION GUN - 12 ga. only, ejectors, combination shotgun/rifle available in .222 Rem., .243 Win., .30-06, .308 Win., and 4 metric cals., fixed choke, acid etched engraving, skipline checkering and cheekpiece. New 1986.

MSR N/A	$1,050	$850	$695	$600	$525	$425	$350

Add $699 for interchangeable 12 ga. shotgun barrels (new 1998).

BS-571/572 SHOTGUN/COMBINATION GUN - 12 ga. only, boxlock action with ejectors, 6x65R (disc.) or 7x65R rifle cal. only. Limited importation 1992-95.

	$825	$700	$600	$550	$475	$425	$375

Last MSR was $995.

Add approx. $115 for rifle/shotgun (12 ga. only) combination (Model 572).

MODEL 571 SUPER SERIES - 12 ga. field, skeet, and trap configuration as well as combination shotgun/rifle in 12 ga. x 7x57R or 7x65R cal. Importation disc. 1991.

	$800	$700	$640	$590	$550	$515	$475

Last MSR was $899.

Add $70 for single trigger or trap/skeet configuration (disc.).
Add $700 for extra set of 12 ga. field barrels.
Add $1,101 for hand engraving.

* *Super Combo* - 3 barrel set including 12 ga., 7x57R, and 7x65R barrels. Imported 1987-90.

	$1,925	$1,640	$1,425	$1,250	$1,100	$1,000	$925

Last MSR was $2,169.

SHOTGUNS: SxS

ZP-49 - 12 ga. only, ejectors, double triggers, true sidelock, Purdey-type top bolt, cocking indicators, walnut stock, swivels. Imported 1986-91.

	$535	$460	$420	$385	$350	$320	$290

Last MSR was $589.

Add $20 for engraving.

ZP-149 - similar to ZP-49, except has game scene engraving on sideplates, choice of English or pistol grip stock. Imported 1986-98.

	$575	$495	$425	$350	$300	$250	$225

Last MSR was $676.

Add $23 for pistol grip stock.

GRADING - PPGS™	100%	98%	95%	90%	80%	70%	60%

ZP-349 - 12 ga. only, extractors, double triggers, true sidelock, Purdey-type top bolt, cocking indicators, walnut stock with cheek piece, beavertail forearm, swivels, 7.3 lbs. Imported 1986 only.

	$450	$390	$360	$325	$300	$270	$250

Last MSR was $520.

Add $20 for engraving.

SHOTGUNS: SINGLE SHOT

ZBK 100 - 12 or 20 ga., 3 in. chamber, walnut stock and forearm. Importation began 1999.

MSR N/A	$180	$160	$140	$120	$105	$95	$85

BROCKMAN'S CUSTOM GUNSMITHING

Current custom rifle manufacturer and gunsmith established in 1986, and located in Gooding, Idaho. Consumer direct sales only.

Brockman's Custom Gunsmithing manufactures a wide variety of custom bolt action rifles typically based on Win. Model 70, Rem. Model 700, Dakota, or Nesika action. Please contact the company directly to find out more about their wide variety of custom rifles and gunsmithing services.

RIFLES: BOLT ACTION

Specific models and/or configurations include the Universal Hunter (complete gun base price $2,625), Dangerous Game (last MSR $2,450, disc. 2001), Premier Practical (base price $3,295), Model 70 Classic Practical (base price $2,695), Working Rifle (base price $2,895), Ladies rifles (base price was $2,100-$2,895 – disc. 2000), Scout rifles (last MSR $1,995 – disc. 2000), .50 Beowulf-Brockman (base price $995, includes case), and other handcrafted custom bolt action rifles.

RIFLES: LEVER ACTION

Brockman's modifies general purpose lever action rifles based on the Marlin 1895G/SS actions, including the Beast (base price $2,195), the SOB (is based on shorter and lighter Beast, disc. 2004, last MSR was $1,995), and the Master Guide Package (base price $1,062).

BROLIN ARMS, INC.

Previous importer of handguns (FEG mfg.), rifles (older Mauser military, see Mauser listing), shotguns (Chinese mfg.), and airguns from 1995-1999. Previously located in Pomona, CA, until 1999, and in La Verne, CA until 1997.

PISTOLS: SEMI-AUTO, SINGLE ACTION

LEGEND SERIES MODEL L45 - .45 ACP cal., patterned after the Colt 1911 Government Model, features include throated match 5 in. barrel, polished feed ramp, flared ejection port, beveled mag. well, flattop slide, flat mainspring housing, front strap high relief cut, aluminum lightweight extended trigger, high visibility sights, 7 shot mag., commander style hammer and checkered walnut grips, 38 oz. Mfg. 1995-98.

	$425	$365	$325	$295	$275	$250	$225

Last MSR was $500.

* *Legend Series Model L45C (Compact)* - similar to Model L45, except has 4 in. barrel, 35 oz. Mfg. 1995-98.

	$440	$380	$330	$295	$275	$250	$225

Last MSR was $520.

* *Legend Series Model L45T* - features standard frame with compact slide, 4 in. barrel, 36 oz. Mfg. 1997-98.

	$440	$380	$330	$295	$275	$250	$225

Last MSR was $520.

GRADING - PPGS™	100%	98%	95%	90%	80%	70%	60%

PATRIOT SERIES MODEL P45 COMP - .45 ACP cal., similar to Legend Series Model L45, except has one-piece match 4 in. barrel with integral dual port compensator, 7 shot mag., Millett or Novak combat sights (new 1997), test target provided, choice of blue or satin (frame only) finish, 38 oz. Mfg. 1996-97 only.

	$585	$475	$415	$365	$325	$285	$250

Last MSR was $649.

Add $70 for Novak combat sights (new 1997).
Add $20 for T-tone finish (frame only).

* *Patriot Series Model P45C (Compact)* - .45 ACP cal., similar to Model P45 Comp, except has 3 1/4 in. barrel with integral conical lock-up system, 34.5 oz. Mfg. 1996-97.

	$610	$495	$425	$375	$325	$285	$250

Last MSR was $689.

Add $70 for Novak combat sights.
Add $20 for T-tone finish (frame only).

* *Patriot Series Model P45T* - features standard frame with compact slide, 3 1/4 in. barrel, 35.5 oz. Mfg. 1997 only.

	$620	$500	$425	$375	$325	$285	$250

Last MSR was $699.

Add $60 for Novak combat sights (new 1997).
Add $10 for T-tone finish (frame only).

PRO STOCK MODEL COMPETITION PISTOL - .45 ACP cal., competition pistol featuring most state-of-the-art competitive improvements, 5 in. barrel, 8 shot mag., blue or satin (frame only) finish, signature wood grips, 40 oz. Mfg. 1996-97.

	$685	$550	$475	$415	$360	$295	$260

Last MSR was $779.

Add $20 for T-tone finish (frame only).

* *Pro Comp Model Competition Pistol* - similar to Pro Stock Model, except has 4 in. dual port compensated heavy match barrel, blue or satin (frame only) finish, 40 oz. Mfg. 1996-97.

	$800	$650	$525	$435	$375	$325	$295

Last MSR was $919.

Add $10 for T-tone finish (frame only).

TAC 11 - .45 ACP cal., 5 in. conical barrel w/o bushing, beavertail grip safety, 8 shot mag., T-tone or blue finish, Novak low profile combat or Tritium sights, black rubber contour grips, 37 oz. Mfg. 1997-98.

	$595	$485	$425	$365	$325	$285	$250

Last MSR was $670.

Add $90 for Tritium sights (disc. 1997).

* *Tac 11 Compact* - similar to Tac 11, except has shorter barrel. Mfg. 1998 only.

	$610	$495	$435	$365	$325	$285	$250

Last MSR was $690.

Add $60 for hard-chrome finish.

GOLD SERIES - .45 ACP cal., 5 in. barrel w/o barrel bushing and supported chamber, IPSC configuration with many features, adj. aluminum trigger, front and rear slide serations, stainless steel construction with choice of natural stainless or blue stainless finish. Limited mfg. 1998 only.

	$715	$625	$525				

Last MSR was $800.

PISTOLS: SEMI-AUTO, DOUBLE ACTION

The following models had limited manufacture 1998 only.

GRADING - PPGS™	100%	98%	95%	90%	80%	70%	60%

TAC SERIES SERVICE MODEL - .45 ACP cal., full sized double action service pistol, single/double action, 8 shot single column mag., front and rear slide serations, combat style trigger guard, royal or satin blue finish, low profile 3-dot sights. Mfg. 1998 only.

	$360	$315	$285	$260	$240	$220	$200

Last MSR was $400.

Add $20 for royal blue finish.

TAC SERIES FULL SIZE MODEL - 9mm Para., .40 S&W, or .45 ACP cal., similar to Tac Series Service Model, except longer barrel, checkered walnut or plastic grips, 8 (.45 ACP only) or 10 shot mag. Mfg. 1998 only.

	$360	$315	$285	$260	$240	$220	$200

Last MSR was $400.

Add $20 for royal blue finish.

TAC SERIES COMPACT MODEL - 9mm Para. or .40 S&W cal., shortened barrel/slide with full size frame, 10 shot mag. Mfg. 1998 only.

	$360	$315	$285	$260	$240	$220	$200

Last MSR was $400.

Add $20 for royal blue finish.

TAC SERIES BANTAM MODEL - 9mm Para. or .40 S&W cal., super compact size, single/double action with concealed hammer, all steel construction, 3-dot sights. Mfg. 1998 only.

	$360	$315	$285	$260	$240	$220	$200

Last MSR was $399.

BANTAM MODEL - 9mm Para. or .40 S&W cal., single or double action, super compact size, concealed hammer, all steel construction, 3-dot sights, royal blue or matte finish. Limited mfg. by FEG 1999 only.

	$360	$315	$285	$260	$240	$220	$200

Last MSR was $399.

PISTOLS: CUSTOM

Brolin Arms manufactured a small quantity of high performance M1911 based custom combat and competition pistols during 1998 only. The Formula Z Model Custom Combat Model retail price range was $1,300-$1,600, the Formula One RS Limited Class Competition Model was priced at $2,000-$2,300, and the Formula One RZ Competition Race Gun Model topped the line at $2,450-$2,750.

SHOTGUNS: SEMI-AUTO

MODEL BL-12 - 12 ga. only, 3 in. chamber, 18 1/2 (security) or 28 (field) in. VR barrel with 3 choke tubes (Beretta compatible), satin blue finish, choice of wood or synthetic stock and forearm. Mfg. 1998 only.

	$375	$325	$300	$280	$260	$240	$220

Last MSR was $430.

MODEL SAS-12 - 12 ga. only, 2 3/4 in. chamber, 24 in. barrel with IC choke tube, 3 (standard) or 5 shot (disc. late 1998) detachable box mag., synthetic stock and forearm, gas operated. Mfg. 1998-99.

	$445	$385	$335	$300	$280	$260	$240

Last MSR was $499.

Add $39 for extra 3 or 5 (disc.) shot mag.

SHOTGUNS: SLIDE ACTION

Brolin shotguns were manufactured in China through Hawk Industries, and were unauthorized copies of the Remington Model 870. Most of these slide action models were distributed by Interstate Arms, and it is thought that Norinco or China North Industries were connected to the manufacturer during the importation of these shotguns.

FIELD SERIES - 12 ga. only, 3 in. chamber, 24, 26, 28, or 30 in. VR barrel with mod. choke tube, steel receiver and aluminum trigger guard, choice of black synthetic or wood stock, bead sights, 5 shot mag., matte finish, 7.3 lbs. Mfg. 1997-98.

$195 $170 $155 $140 $130 $120 $110

Last MSR was $240.

✱ *Field Combo* - includes choice of extra 12 ga. 18 1/2 or 22 in. barrel, choice of regular or pistol grip stock. Mfg. 1997-98.

$230 $195 $175 $155 $140 $130 $120

Last MSR was $270.

Add approx. $25 for rifled deer barrel.

LAWMAN MODEL - 12 ga. only, 3 in. chamber, action patterned after the Rem. Model 870 (disc. 1998) or the Ithaca Model 37 (new 1999) 18 1/2 in. barrel, choice of bead, rifle (disc. 1998), or ghost ring (disc. 1998) sights, matte (disc. 1998), nickel (disc. 1997), royal blue (new 1998), satin blue (new 1998) or hard chrome finish, black synthetic or hardwood stock and forearm, 7 lbs. Mfg. in China 1997-99.

$165 $155 $145 $135 $125 $115 $105

Last MSR was $189.

Add $20 for nickel finish (disc. 1997).
Add $20 for hard chrome finish.
Add $20 for ghost ring sights.

SLUG SPECIAL - 12 ga. only, 3 in. chamber, choice of 18 1/2 or 22 in. barrel with either rifle sights, ghost ring, or cantilevered scope mount, wood or synthetic stock, choice of fixed IC choke, 4 in. extended rifled choke, or fully rifled barrel, 5 shot mag. Mfg. 1998 only.

$230 $180 $165 $150 $140 $130 $120

Last MSR was $270.

Add $10 for rifled barrel.
Add $20 for cantilevered scope mount.

SLUGMASTER - 12 ga. only, 3 in. chamber, action patterned after the Model 37 Ithaca, bottom ejection, choice of royal blue metal finish with wood stock or satin blue metal with synthetic stock, rifle sights, mfg. in China. Limited importation 1999 only.

$165 $155 $145 $135 $125 $115 $105

Last MSR was $189.

TURKEY SPECIAL - 12 ga. only, 3 in. chamber, 22 in. VR barrel with extra-full extended turkey choke, choice of wood or synthetic stock. Mfg. 1998 only.

$215 $165 $155 $145 $135 $125 $115

Last MSR was $250.

BRONCO

Previous trademark manufactured by Echave Y Arizmendi, located in Eibar, Spain.

PISTOLS: SEMI-AUTO

MODEL 1918 POCKET AUTOMATIC - 7.65mm cal., 6 shot, 2 1/2 in. barrel, fixed sights, blue, hard rubber grips. Mfg. 1918-25.

$175 $150 $100 $80 $70 $60 $50

VEST POCKET AUTOMATIC - 6.35mm cal., small frame. Disc.

$160 $125 $110 $95 $80 $60 $40

GRADING - PPGS™	100%	98%	95%	90%	80%	70%	60%

A.A. BROWN & SONS

Current long gun manufacturer established in 1930 and located in Birmingham, England.

A.A. Brown & Sons manufactures high quality SxS English sidelock ejector shotguns in all gauges with many options available. For more information, including pricing, VAT, customer options, availability and delivery time, please contact the company directly (see Trademark Index).

DAVID MCKAY BROWN (GUNMAKERS) LTD.

Current long gun manufacturer established in 1967 and located in Bothwell, Glasgow, Scotland.

Makers of Scottish Round Action SxS and O/U shotguns and rifles (approx. 30 guns mfg. annually). David McKay Brown apprenticed with Alex Martin Ltd. and John Dickson & Son before establishing his own gunmaking company. All guns made to customer order on round sidelock actions. Delivery approximately 12 months, depending on the configuration. Available through U.S. agent, Griffin & Howe, New York City and Bernardsville, NJ or the manufacturer directly.

Prices indicated below for manufacturer's suggested retail and 100% condition factors are listed in English pounds. Values for used guns in 98%-60% condition factors are priced in U.S. dollars.

RIFLES: CUSTOM, SxS

David McKay Brown should be contacted directly for a firm quotation on a SxS double rifle.

SHOTGUNS: CUSTOM

Add £250 for Pistol/Prince of Wales grip.
Add £1,000 for .410 bore.
Add £750 for single trigger.

SxS SHOTGUN - 12, 16, 20, 28 ga., or .410 bore, features rounded case colored action, double triggers, full scroll engraving, custom order only.

MSR £28,000	£28,000	$31,450	$25,250	$19,250	$15,750	$13,000	$11,000

O/U SHOTGUN - 12, 16, 20, 28 ga., or .410 bore, features rounded case colored action, double triggers, full scroll engraving, custom order only.

MSR £35,000	£35,000	$41,250	$34,000	$28,750	$23,250	$19,000	$14,750

ED BROWN CUSTOM, INC.

Current rifle manufacturer located in Perry, MO.

RIFLES: BOLT ACTION

*Ed Brown
Custom Rifles*

The following MSRs represent each model's base price, with many options available at additional charge.

MODEL 702 BUSHVELD - .338 Win. Mag., .340 Wby., .375 H&H, .416 Rem. Mag., .458 Lott, or .458 Win. Mag. cal., dangerous game rifle utilizing Ed Brown custom action, match grade 24 in. medium or heavyweight barrel, McMillan fiberglass stock with cheekpiece and recoil pad, approx. 8.5-9 lbs.

MSR $2,895	$2,895	$2,350	$1,800	$1,500	$1,200	$975	$725

Add $300 for .416 Rem. Mag. or .458 Lott cal.

MODEL 702 SAVANNA - various long and short action cals., hunting rifle utilizing Ed Brown Model 702 custom action, McMillan checkered fiberglass stock with steel trigger guard and floor plate, Talley rings and bases, 24 or 26 in. match grade barrel, approx. 7.5-8 lbs.

MSR $2,795	$2,795	$2,275	$1,775	$1,475	$1,200	$975	$725

Add $100 for muzzle brake.

GRADING - PPGS™	100%	98%	95%	90%	80%	70%	60%

MODEL 702 DENALI - various short and long action cals., designed as lightweight mountain hunting rifle, 22, 23 (disc.), or 24 in. lightweight barrel, glass bedded McMillian sporter stock with checkering and recoil pad, 3 position safety, 7.75 lbs. Mfg. 2002-2004.

	$2,895	$2,350	$1,800	$1,500	$1,200	$975	$725

Last MSR was $2,895.

MODEL 702 OZARK - various cals., lightweight hunting rifle utilizing Ed Brown custom short action, steel trigger guard and floorplate, 3 position safety, checkered lightweight fiberglass stock, match grade, hand lapped 21 in. barrel, approx. 6 1/2 lbs. Disc. 2003.

	$2,800	$2,300	$1,775	$1,500	$1,200	$975	$725

Last MSR was $2,800.

MODEL 702 DAMARA - various cals., including WSM, lightweight hunting rifle with Ed Brown short repeater action, 22 in. barrel and ultra-lightweight McMillan graphite stock with Pachmayr Decelerator pad, includes Talley mounts, 6.1 lbs. New 2004.

MSR $2,795	$2,795	$2,275	$1,775	$1,475	$1,200	$975	$725

Add $200 for Mag. cals.

MODEL 702 VARMINT - various varmint cals., features Ed Brown short single shot action with steel trigger guard and adj. trigger., match grade 24 or 26 (optional) barrel, hand bedded McMillian fiberglass stock and recoil pad, approx. 9 lbs.

MSR $2,495	$2,495	$2,000	$1,650	$1,350	$1,100	$925	$825

MODEL 702 LIGHT TARGET (TACTICAL) - .223 Rem. or .308 Win. cal., features Ed Brown short repeater action, aluminum trigger guard and floorplate, 21 in. match grade barrel, includes Talley scope mounts, approx. 8.75 lbs.

MSR $2,495	$2,495	$2,000	$1,650	$1,350	$1,100	$925	$825

MODEL 702 TARGET (TACTICAL) - .308 Win. or .300 Win. Mag. cal., top-of-the-line sniper weapon, 26 in. heavyweight match grade hand lapped barrel, McMillian fiberglass A-3 tactical stock, includes Leupold Mark IV scope mounts, 11.25 lbs.

MSR $2,495	$2,495	$2,000	$1,650	$1,350	$1,100	$925	$825

MODEL 702 M40A2 MARINE SNIPER - .30-06 or .308 Win. cal., 24 in. match grade barrel, special McMillian GP fiberglass tactical stock with recoil pad, Woodlands camo is molded into stock, this model is a duplicate of the original McMillian Marine Sniper rifle used in Vietnam, except for the Ed Brown action, with Leupold Mark IV or Nightforce scope mounts, 9 1/4 lbs. New 2002.

MSR $2,495	$2,495	$2,000	$1,650	$1,350	$1,100	$925	$825

ED BROWN PRODUCTS, INC.

Current pistol manufacturer located in Perry, MO.

PISTOLS: SEMI-AUTO

Add $100 for stainless steel frame and blue slide, $200 for 100% stainless steel construction (new 2002, .45 ACP cal. only), or $75 for ambidextrous safety on the following models.

CLASSIC CUSTOM - .45 ACP cal., M1911 style, top-of-the-line model with highest level of cosmetic finishing, 5 in. barrel, incorporates all custom Ed Brown features, including slide and frame, all blue or stainless steel frame, Hogue exotic checkered cocobolo wood grips, adj. Bo-Mar rear sight, custom made per individual order, 39 oz.

MSR $2,895	$2,750	$2,250	$1,725	$1,475	$1,175	$950	$725

GRADING - PPGS™	100%	98%	95%	90%	80%	70%	60%

CLASS A LIMITED - available in 8 cals., M1911 style, basic custom pistol and features all custom Ed Brown accessories, including slide and frame, 7 shot mag., 4.25 (Commander) or 5 in. barrel length, Hogue exotic grips, 34 or 39 oz. Disc. 2003.

	$2,250	$1,900	$1,550	$1,300	$1,050	$825	$700

Last MSR was $2,250.

Add $100 for stainless steel frame and all lower parts.
Add $100 for Novak night sights.

COMMANDER BOBTAIL - various cals., M1911 style, carry configuration, features round butt variation of the Class A Limited frame, incorporating frame and grip modifications, including a special housing w/o checkering, 4 1/4 in. barrel, Hogue exotic wood grips, 34 oz. Disc. 2003.

	$2,350	$1,900	$1,550	$1,325	$1,075	$850	$725

Last MSR was $2,350.

EXECUTIVE ELITE - .45 ACP cal., M1911 style, 5 in. barrel, choice of all blue, stainless blue, or full stainless slide/barrel, features Hardcore components, flared and lowered ejection port, Commander style hammer, 25 LPI checkering on front and rear grip strap, beveled mag. well, Novak low mount sights, checkered cocobolo wood grips, 34 oz. New 2004.

MSR $2,195	$2,195	$1,775	$1,500	$1,200	$995	$850	$675

EXECUTIVE CARRY - .45 ACP cal., similar to Executive Elite, except has 4 1/4 in. barrel and Bobtail grip, 34 oz. New 2004.

MSR $2,295	$2,295	$1,850	$1,550	$1,225	$995	$850	$675

KOBRA - .45 ACP cal., M1911 style, 7 shot, 5 in. barrel, features metal "snakeskin" treatment on frame, mainspring housing and slide, fixed Novak low mount night sights, Hogue exotic wood grips, 39 oz. New 2002.

MSR $1,995	$1,995	$1,650	$1,300	$1,025	$900	$750	$600

KOBRA CARRY - .45 ACP cal., M1911 style, 4 1/4 in. barrel, features round butt (Bobtail) and metal "snakeskin" treatment on frame, mainspring housing and slide, fixed Novak low mount night sights, 34 oz. New 2002.

MSR $2,095	$2,095	$1,725	$1,350	$1,050	$900	$750	$600

BROWN PRECISION, INC.

Current manufacturer established in 1968, and located in Los Molinos, CA. Previously manufactured in San Jose, CA. Consumer direct sales.

Brown Precision Inc. manufactures rifles primarily using Remington or Winchester actions and restocks them using a combination of Kevlar, Fiberglass and Graphite (wrinkle finish) to save weight. Stock colors are green, brown, grey, black, camo brown, camo green, or camo grey. Chet Brown pioneered the concept of the fiberglass rifle stock in 1968.

Brown Precision is also offering custom hand loaded ammunition for all rifles manufactured by Trophy Ammo of Chico, CA.

PISTOLS: BOLT ACTION

CUSTOM XP-100 HIGH COUNTRY - various cals., includes highly tuned XP-100 single shot action with Shilen stainless match grade barrel, electroless nickel or Teflon finish, fiberglass stock. Limited mfg. 1993-96.

	$1,550	$1,375	$1,150	$950	$775	$650	$525

Last MSR was $1,690.

GRADING - PPGS™	100%	98%	95%	90%	80%	70%	60%

RIFLES: BOLT ACTION

Brown Precision also manufactures a High Country Rifle from a customer supplied action. This conversion includes a Brown Precision stock, custom glass bedding, recoil pad, stock finish, etc. Prices range from $845-$945.

CUSTOM HIGH COUNTRY - various cals. within those factory barreled actions, choice of Rem. 700 ADL/BDL, Model 7, Ruger 77 (disc.), or Win. Model 70 push feed (disc.) or Winchester Model 70 Classic with controlled round feeding action and custom trigger guard, fiberglass/Kevlar stock (various colors), electroless nickel or Teflon metal finish, sling swivels and pad. Mfg. 1975-present.

MSR $3,495	$3,000	$2,600	$2,150	$1,750	$1,475	$1,250	$1,125

Add $200 for Rem. 700 BDL or Model 7 action.
Add $300 for stainless steel Rem. 700 BDL action.
Add $400 for Win. Model 70 Classic action with controlled round feeding.
Add $300 for left-hand action.
Subtract $500 if action is supplied by customer.
Add $100 for cryogenic barrel treatment.

✳ *Custom High Country ES II* - similar to Custom High Country, except includes cryogenic barrel treatment and speed lock firing pin spring, includes 60 rounds of custom ammo. Disc. 2003.

	$3,400	$2,650	$2,100	$1,725	$1,400	$1,125	$995

Last MSR was $3,995.

Add $100 for Rem. 700 BDL or Model 7 action.
Add $300 for stainless steel Rem. 700 BDL action.
Add $500 for Win. Model 70 Classic action with controlled round feeding.
Add $300 for left-hand action.
Subtract $700 if action is supplied by customer.

HIGH COUNTRY YOUTH RIFLE - various cals., choice of Rem. Model 7 or 700 factory barreled action, fiberglass stock. Mfg. 1993-2000.

	$1,250	$1,050	$825	$700	$550	$495	$440

Last MSR was $1,435.

Add $145 for lengthening stock.

BROWN PRECISION WINCHESTER 70 - .270 Win. or .30-06 cal., 22 in. featherweight barrel, camo stock in four colors with black recoil pad, 6 1/4 lbs. Mfg. 1989-92.

	$650	$575	$475	$425	$385	$325	$300

Last MSR was $750.

Add $20 for 7mm Rem. Mag. (24 in. sporter barrel).

BLASER BOLT ACTION RIFLE - standard Camex Blaser cals. and action, fiberglass stock and nickel plated barrel. Disc. 1989.

	$1,395	$1,150	$995	$875	$750	$675	$600

Last MSR was $1,395.

MODEL 7 SUPER LIGHT - .223 Rem., .243 Win., 6mm Rem., 7mm-08 Rem., or .308 Win. cal., Model 7 action, 18 in. factory barrel, no sights, 5 lbs. 4 oz. Disc. 1992.

	$995	$900	$750	$650	$575	$500	$450

Last MSR was $1,059.

This model could have been special ordered with similar options from the Custom High Country Model, with the exception of left-hand action.

LAW ENFORCEMENT SELECTIVE TARGET - .308 Win. cal., Model 700 Varmint action with 20, 22, or 24 in. factory barrel, O.D. green camouflage treatment. Disc. 1992.

	$995	$900	$750	$650	$575	$500	$450

Last MSR was $1,086.

This model could have been special ordered with similar options from the Custom High Country Model, with the exception of left-hand action.

GRADING - PPGS™	100%	98%	95%	90%	80%	70%	60%

TACTICAL ELITE - various cals. and custom features, customized per individual order. New 1997.

MSR $3,995	$3,500	$3,000	$2,500	$2,000	$1,650	$1,350	$1,200

Add $675 for 3 way adj. buttplate.
Subtract $700 if action is supplied by customer.

PRO VARMINTER - various cals., includes custom tuned Rem. Model 700 ADL action, Shilen match stainless steel barrel. New 1993.

MSR $3,295	$2,775	$2,450	$2,000	$1,750	$1,500	$1,250	$1,100

Add $300 for left-hand action.
Add $600 for optional Rem. Model 40-XB action with target trigger.
Subtract $500 if action is supplied by customer.

PRO HUNTER - available in over 25 cals., Model 700 ADL action is standard, match grade stainless steel barrel, dull electroless nickel, blue, or teflon finish, express sights, synthetic stock (four different colors). New 1988.

MSR $4,295	$3,550	$3,000	$2,550	$2,150	$1,775	$1,500	$1,350

Add $100 for left-hand action.
Subtract $500 if action is supplied by customer.

 ✳ *Pro Hunter Elite* - various cals., custom tuned Winchester Model 70 Super Grade action with controlled feed claw extractor, includes many custom order features. New 1993.

MSR $4,995	$4,375	$3,600	$2,825	$2,350	$1,900	$1,650	$1,350

Add $695 for drop box trigger guard (allows additonal round in mag.).
Subtract $700 if action is supplied by customer.
In late 1991, improvements were made including decelerator recoil pad, barrel band swivel, and speed lock firing pin spring.

THE UNIT - .270 Win., .300 Win. Mag., .300 Wby. Mag., .338 Win. Mag., 7mm-08 Rem., 7mm Rem. Mag., or 7mm STW cal., Rem. 700 BDL or Win. Mod. 70 controlled feed action, various lengths match grade stainless steel barrel with cryogenic treatment, Teflon or electroless nickel finish, Brown Precision Kevlar or graphite reinforced fiberglass stock, include 60 rounds of custom ammo. Limited mfg. 2001 only.

	$3,225	$2,500	$2,000	$1,650	$1,350	$1,125	$995

Last MSR was $3,795.

Add $500 for Win. Model 70 Super Grade action with controlled round feeding.
Add $200 for left-hand action.
Subtract $600 if action is supplied by customer.

SUPER BOLT RIMFIRE - .22 LR or .22 Mag. cal., modified Ruger 77/22 action, 20 in. heavy Shilen match grade steel or stainless steel barrel, extended mag. release, choice of lightweight fiberglass or Kevlar stock, blue or silver metal finish, 6 1/2 lbs.

MSR $1,895	$1,600	$1,200	$925	$825	$675	$600	$550

Add $100 for stainless steel barrel.
Add $200 for stainless steel action & barrel.

RIFLES: SEMI-AUTO

CUSTOM TEAM CHALLENGER - .22 LR cal., modified Ruger 10/22 action, 20 in. heavy Shilen match grade steel or stainless steel barrel, extended mag. release, choice of lightweight fiberglass or Kevlar stock, blue or silver metal finish.

MSR $1,595	$1,350	$1,075	$825	$675	$550	$450	$400

Add $100 for stainless steel barrel.
Add $200 for stainless steel barrel & action.

BROWNING

Current manufacturer with U.S. headquarters located in Morgan, UT. Browning guns originally were manufactured in Ogden, UT, circa 1880. Browning firearms are manufactured by Fabrique Nationale in Herstal and Liege, Belgium. Since 1976, Browning has also contracted Miroku of Japan and A.T.I. in Salt Lake City, UT to manufacture both long arms and handguns. In 1992, Browning (including F.N.) was acquired by GIAT of France. During late 1997, the French government received $82 million for the sale of F.N. Herstal from the Walloon business region surrounding Fabrique Nationale in Belgium.

The category names within the Browning section have been arranged in an alphabetical format: - PISTOLS (& variations), RIFLES (& variations), SHOTGUNS (& variations), SPECIAL EDITIONS, COMMEMORATIVES & LIMITED MFG.

The author would like to express his sincere thanks to the Browning Collector's Association, including members Anthony Vanderlinden, Richard Spurzem, Jim King, Bert O'Neill, Jr., Gary Chatham, and Rodney Herrmann for continuing to make their important contributions to the Browning section.

BROWNING HISTORY

The Browning firm, first known as J.M. Browning & Bro., was established in Ogden, Utah about 1880. Later known as Browning Brothers and Browning Arms Company (BAC), the firm actually manufactured only one gun - the Model 1878 Single Shot which was John M.'s first patent. Winchester bought the production and distribution rights to this gun in 1883, bringing it out as the Winchester M1885. From that time until 1900, Mr. Browning sold Winchester the exclusive rights to 31 rifles and 13 shotguns, of which Winchester produced only 7 rifles (M1885SS: the lever actions M1886, 1892, 1894 and 1895: and the slide action .22s M1890 and 1906) and 3 shotguns (M1887, M1893 and M1897). The other models were bought from Browning simply to keep them out of the hands of other arms makers.

John M. Browning, perhaps the greatest firearms inventor the world has ever known, was directly responsible for an estimated 80 separate firearms that evolved from his 128 patents. During his most prolific period from 1894 to 1910, Browning sold the rights to his rifles, semi-auto pistols, shotguns and machine guns to Winchester, Remington, Colt and Stevens in this country and to Fabrique Nationale (Belgium) for sale outside the U.S. Every Colt and F.N. semi-auto pistol is based on a Browning patent. In 1902, Browning broke off relations with Winchester when the company refused to negotiate a royalty arrangement for his new semi-auto shotgun (A-5). Browning took the prototype to F.N. F.N. has produced numerous automatic pistols, 3 rifles and 2 shotguns designed by John M. Browning and is still a major producer of arms sold by Browning in the U.S. and by F.N. distributors worldwide.

Our American military was armed for many years with Browning designed weaponry, not the least of which is the venerable "Old Slabside" 1911 Govt. Model .45 ACP. Today, the firm that bears the Browning name still stands at the forefront with the other makers of fine sporting firearms.

BROWNING FACTS

Note: Between 1966-1971 Browning used a salt-curing process to speed the drying time needed for their walnut stock blanks. Unfortunately, the salt would be released from the wood and oxidize the metal surface(s) after a period of time. These guns, especially bolt action rifles in all grades, some BARs, Superposed shotguns, and T-bolt models should be examined carefully around the edges of the wood for signs of freckling and rust. Discount values on guns which show tell-tale characteristics of salt corrosion 15%-50%, depending on how bad rusting has occurred. Check screws and wood under buttplate as well. Original Superposed owners of salt wood guns who still have their warranty card are still eligible for Browning factory refurbishing of affected parts only without charge. Otherwise, Browning has a standardized charge for each model.

Since the inception and standardization of steel shot for hunting purposes, the desirability factor of shotguns has changed considerably. On newer manufactures, choke tubes are now expected for most shooters, and shotguns without choke tubes must be discounted somewhat. Browning does not recommend using steel shot in any Superposed (B-25) or older Belgian Auto-5 barrels.

BROWNING VALUES INFORMATION

Editor's Note: It is important to note the differences in values of Browning firearms manufactured in Belgium by F.N. and those made recently in Japan by Miroku. We feel that these values are somewhat higher because of collector interest in Belgian guns, and not as the result of any inferiority of the quality of Browning guns made anywhere else.

AS A FINAL NOTE: Most post-war Brownings are collectible only if in 95% or better condition as most models have relatively high mfg. and are not that old. Condition under 95% is normally very shootable, but not as collectible and values for 95% or less condition could be lower than shown in some areas.

All add-ons or deductions on Browning's currently manufactured models reflect retail pricing without any discounting. On higher grade Browning firearms that are engraved, signed specimens by FN's master engravers Funken, J. Baerten, Vrancken, and Watrin will command premiums over the values listed.

BROWNING SERIALIZATION

In addition to the Belgian Browning serialization listed in the back of this text, the following codes will determine the year and origin of those guns made from 1975 to date. The 2 letters in the middle of the serial number are the code designations for year of manufacture. They represent the following: RV - 1975, RT - 1976, RR - 1977, RP - 1978, RN - 1979, PM - 1980, PZ - 1981, PY - 1982, PX - 1983, PW - 1984, PV - 1985, PT -1986, PR - 1987, PP - 1988, PN - 1989, NM - 1990, NZ - 1991, NY - 1992, NX - 1993, NW - 1994, NV - 1995, NT - 1996, NR - 1997, NP - 1998, NN - 1999, MM - 2000, MZ - 2001, MY - 2002, MX - 2003, MW - 2004, MV - 2005, MU - 2006, MT - 2007, and MS - 2008.

Since most Brownings use a 3-digit model identification code (appearing first on European or U.S. mfg. guns and last on Japanese mfg.), both where and when the specimen was made can easily be determined (i.e. ser. no. 611RP2785 would be a Model B-2000 made in Belgium, and assembled in Portugal during 1978 with 2785 being the ser. no.- ser. no. 01479PX368 indicates a B-SS 20 ga. mfg. in Japan in 1983).

BROWNING CUSTOM SHOP

Browning's Custom Shop in Herstal, Belgium, continues to make a wide variety of firearms, a number of which have limited importation into the U.S. Current Custom Shop Superposed prices and model information have been provided in the Superposed section. For more information on the Browning Custom Shop's additional offerings, please look under the various category names availability and current pricing. Please refer to Browning's web site at www.browning.com for more information on the wide variety of firearms available from the Browning Custom Shop in Belgium, or contact Browning directly.

PISTOLS: SEMI-AUTO, F.N. PRODUCTION UNLESS OTHERWISE NOTED

Currently, the Browning Custom Shop in Belgium is making the following Hi-Power custom shop models: Renaissance Dore ($6,066 MSR), Renaissance Nickel ($5,970 MSR), L1 ($4,163 MSR), I1 ($5,250 MSR), and B2 ($4,350 MSR).

MODEL 1899-FN - 7.65mm cal., first Belgian Browning, 4 in. barrel, similar to later M-1900 but w/o safety markings or lanyard ring, serial range 1-10,000, 10,000 mfg. 1899-1901.

	$695	$645	$600	$500	$450	$400	$350

Add 15% for guns manufactured in 1899 (ser. nos. 1-3900, without "A" prefix or suffix).
Add 50% for factory nickel finish (nickel finish with blue trigger and blue safety lever) – if 95% condition or better.
Add $400 for factory presentation case with accessories.

GRADING - PPGS™	100%	98%	95%	90%	80%	70%	60%

MODEL 1900-FN - 7.65mm cal., 4 in. barrel. 724,500 mfg. 1900-14.

	100%	98%	95%	90%	80%	70%	60%
	$495	$445	$395	$295	$195	$175	$150

Add 50% for factory nickel finish (nickel finish with blue trigger and safety lever) – if 95% condition or better.

Add $400 for factory presentation case with accessories.

Add $500 for Imperial Russian contract (crossed rifles marking on blue or nickel guns).

Add $100 for Imperial German contracts with German safety markings (Feuer & Sicher).

Add $100 minimum for special contract markings.

MODEL 1903-FN - 9mm Browning Long cal., 5 in. barrel. 58,400 mfg. 1903-27.

	$600	$500	$425	$375	$325	$275	$225

Add 50% if slotted to accept shoulder stock - beware of fakes.

Add $150 minimum for special contract markings.

This variation was also manufactured with a detachable shoulder stock. This accessory is rare and can add $1,000-$1,250 (shoulder stock w/o extended magazine) or $1,650-$1,850 (shoulder stock with extended magazine) to the values listed.

MODEL 1905-FN (VEST POCKET) - 6.35mm cal. (.25 ACP), dubbed "Vest Pocket" model, 2 in. barrel, manufactured by Fabrique Nationale, Herstal, Belgium. 1,086,133, mfg. 1906 to circa 1949.

* **First Variation** - no slide lock/safety lever.

	$475	$425	$375	$325	$275	$225	$175

Add 50% for factory nickel finish (nickel finish with blue trigger and blue safety lever) – if 95% condition or better.

Add $300 for factory presentation case.

Add $500 for Imperial Russian contract (crossed rifles marking on blue or nickel guns).

* **Second Variation** - post 1908, with slide lock/safety lever.

	$395	$325	$275	$225	$175	$125	$100

Add 50% for factory nickel finish (nickel finish with blue trigger and blue safety lever) – if 95% condition or better.

Add $300 for factory presentation case.

Add $500 for Imperial Russian contract (crossed rifles marking on blue or nickel guns).

Add $100 minimum for special contract markings.

MODEL 1907 HUSQVARNA MFG. - 9mm Browning Long cal., identical to FN Browning 1903, mfg. by Husqvarna in Sweden to supply the Swedish military. Mfg. started in 1917 because the FN Browning 1903 was not available from Belgium during WWI, produced 1917-1942. Many were imported into the U.S. and converted to .380 ACP cal. in the U.S.

	$350	$300	$240	$220	$200	$175	$150

Add 40% for early factory high polish blue finish.

Add 20% for early "Browning's Patent" slide legend.

Add 10% for "System Browning" slide legend.

Subtract 30% for .380 ACP conversion.

MODEL 1910-FN (MODEL 1955) - 7.65mm (.32 ACP) or Browning 9mm short (.380 ACP) cal., 4 in. barrel. FN manufacture. 701,266 mfg. 1912-1983.

	$425	$395	$300	$275	$250	$195	$150

Add 20% if BAC marked and 7.65mm cal., or if FN marked and .380 ACP cal.

Add $100 minimum for special contract markings.

This model is also referred to as the Model 1910/55. BAC marked pistols were imported 1954-1968. Importation ceased after the 1968 GCA.

MODEL 1922 OR 10/22 FN - 7.65mm (.32 ACP) or .380 ACP cal., 4 1/2 in. barrel, Model 10/22 and 1922 are the same. The Model 1910 was modified by FN technicians for sale to the Yugoslav military in 1922, includes a longer barrel, larger frame and magazine. Made primarily for police and military contracts, it was also sold in France, Holland, Greece, Germany, Turkey, and many other nations. Several hundred thousand were mfg. during the Nazi occupation of FN during 1940-44.

	$300	$275	$250	$225	$200	$175	$150

Add 150% if .380 ACP and WaA613 marked on triggerguard.
Add 30% if .32 ACP and WaA613 marked.
Add 20% if WaA103 marked.
Add 15% for post liberation "A" prefix ser. no.
Add at least $100 for special prewar contract markings.

FN "BABY" MODEL - 6.35mm (.25 ACP) cal., 2 in. barrel, w/o grip safety or slide lock lever, imported under BAC trademark from 1954-68+ in standard blue finish, lightweight nickel and alumnium frame, and engraved Renaissance models. Over 510,000 mfg. 1931-83.

* ***FN Marked*** - slide marked Fabrique Nationale, blue finish standard.

	$500	$440	$375	$295	$225	$200	$150

Add 10% for pre-war production (ser. no. 1-50140).
Add $100 for original cardboard or plastic box with extras.

* ***BAC Marked*** - slide marked Browning Arms Co., blue finish standard.

	$325	$275	$225	$195	$180	$165	$150

Add $50-$100 for original box and manual, or $25-$50 for original BAC pouch and manual.

* ***Lightweight Model*** - nickel or aluminum (introduced 1954) frame, with pearl grips.

	$450	$365	$325	$280	$245	$225	$200

* ***Renaissance Model*** - engraved, satin grey finish.

	$975	$750	$550

FN/BROWNING MODEL 10/71 - .380 ACP cal., 4 1/2 in. barrel, modified version of Model 1922 (10/22)in .380 ACP cal., grip safety, includes target sights and grips in addition to incorporating a magazine finger tip extension designed to comply with GCA of 1968. Sold in U.S. by BAC 1970-1974 as the "Standard .380," still mfg. by FN as Model 125.

	$395	$300	$250	$220	$205	$190	$160

* ***Renaissance Model***

	$975	$775	$625

MODEL 1935 HI-POWER (HP) - 9mm Para. cal., 13 shot mag., 4 21/32 in. barrel, Browning's last pistol design, over one million mfg. 1935 to date in variations for commercial, military, and police use in over 68 countries, first imported under BAC trademark in 1954.

Please refer to the Fabrique Nationale section of this book for pre-1954 variations (including pre-WWII, WWII, and earlier commercial models), as well as contemporary production of those variations not imported by BAC.

HI-POWER: POST-1954 MFG. - 9mm Para. or .40 S&W (new 1995) cal., similar to FN model 1935, has BAC slide marking, 10 (C/B 1994) or 13* shot mag., 4 3/4 in. barrel, polished blue finish, checkered walnut grips, fixed sights, molded grips were introduced in 1986 (disc. in 2000), ambidextrous safety was added to all models in 1989, approx. 32 (9mm Para.) or 35 (.40 S&W) oz., mfg. by FN in Belgium, imported 1954-2000, reintroduced 2002.

GRADING - PPGS™	100%	98%	95%	90%	80%	70%	60%

* Hi-Power Standard - Polished Blue Finish - includes fixed sights.

MSR $804	$635	$485	$410	$350	$310	$275	$250

Subtract $30 for molded grips (disc. 1990).

Add 25% for ring hammer and internal extractor.

Add 10% for ring hammer and external (more recent) extractor.

Major identifying factors of the Hi-Power are as follows: the "Thumb-Print" feature was mfg. from the beginning through 1958. Old style internal extractor was mfg. from the beginning through 1962, the "T" SN prefix (T-Series start visible extractor) was mfg. 1963-mid-1970s for all U.S. imports by BAC, 69C through 77C S/N prefixes were mfg. 1969-1977. Rounded type Ring Hammers with new external extractor were mfg. from 1962-1972 (for U.S. imports by BAC, much later on FN marked pistols). Spur Hammers have been mfg. 1972-present, and the "245" S/N prefix has been mfg. 1977-present. Some "215" ser. no. prefixes are scarce, these models were originally intended for military contracts only.

Older specimens in original dark green, maroon, or red/black plastic boxes were mfg. 1954-1965 and are very scarce - add $100+ in value. Black pouches (circa 1965-1968, especially with gold metal zipper) will also command a $25-$50 premium, depending on condition.

* Adj. sights

MSR $861	$665	$495	$415	$360	$325	$290	$265

* Mark III Matte Blue Finish - 9mm Para. or .40 S&W (mfg. 1994-2000, reintroduced 2003) cal., non-glare matte finish, ambidextrous safety, tapered dovetail rear fixed sight, two-piece molded grips, Mark III designation became standard in 1994, approx. 35 oz. Imported 1985-2000, reintroduced 2002.

MSR $781	$620	$475	$400	$350	$310	$275	$250

This model's finish may be confused with some recent imports which have a "black" finish. These black finish guns are painted rather than blue, and some parties have been selling them as original military FNs.

* Silver Chrome Finish - 9mm Para. or .40 S&W (new 1995) cal., entire gun finished in silver chrome, includes adj. sights and Pachmayr rubber grips, 36 (9mm Para.) or 39 (.40 S&W) oz. Assembled in Portugal, and imported 1991-2000.

	$570	$435	$370	$330	$300	$280	$255

Add 50% for circa 1980 Belgian model marked "Made in Belgium."

Last MSR was $718.

* Practical Model - 9mm Para. or .40 S&W (new 1995) cal., features blue slide, silver-chromed frame finish, wraparound Pachmayr rubber grips, round style serrated hammer, and choice of adj. sights (new 1993) or removable front sight, 36 (9mm Para.) or 39 (.40 S&W) oz. Imported 1990-2000, reintroduced 2002.

MSR $846	$650	$480	$400	$360	$325	$290	$265

Add $58 for adj. sights (disc. 2000).

* Nickel/Silver Chrome Finish - not to be confused with stainless steel (never offered in the Hi-Power), this nickel/silver chrome finish is different from the silver chrome finish released in 1991, gold trigger, checkered walnut grips. Approx. 11,609 mfg. 1980-85.

	$700	$550	$425	$375	$360	$340	$315

Add 50% for circa 1980 Belgian model marked "Made in Belgium."

Last MSR was $525.

* .30 Luger Hi-Power - .30 Luger cal., mfg. for European sales (most are marked BAC on slide), approx. 1,500 imported late 1986-89, similar specifications as 9mm Para. model.

	$675	$575	$450	$400	$365	$345	$315

This model was never cataloged for sale by BAC in the U.S. A few earlier specimens have been noted with F.N. markings and ring hammer.

GRADING - PPGS™	100%	98%	95%	90%	80%	70%	60%

✴ *GP Competition* - 9mm Para. cal., competition model with 6 in. barrel, detent adj. rear sight, rubber wraparound grips, front counterweight, improved barrel bushing, decreased trigger pull, approx. 36 1/2 oz.

	$950	$850	$650	$500	$450	$425	$400

The original GP Competition came in a black plastic case w/accesories and is more desirable than later imported specimens which were computer serial numbered and came in a styrofoam box. Above prices are for older models - subtract 10% if newer model (computer serial numbered). This model was never cataloged for sale by BAC in the U.S., and it is not serviced by Browning.

✴ *Tangent Rear Sight* - 9mm Para. cal., manufactured from 1965-78. Adj. rear sight to 500 meters. A total of approx. 7,000 were imported by Browning Arms Co. Early pistols are designated by "T" prefix and were mfg. 1964-69, later pistols mfg. 1972-76, had spur hammers and followed the 69C-76C ser. no. prefixes.

	$775	$650	$550	$450	$400	$370	$340

Add $100 for "T" prefix.
Add $50 for original pouch and instruction manual.

✴ *Tangent Capitan Polished Blue Finish* - 9mm Para. cal., features 50-500 meter tangent rear sight, blue finish with walnut grips, slide is marked "Made in Belgium, Assembled in Portugal," 32 oz. Imported 1993-2000.

	$600	$500	$400	$350	$300	$280	$260

Last MSR was $764.

✴ *Tangent Rear Sight & Slotted* - 9mm Para. cal., variation with grip strap slotted to accommodate shoulder stock. Early pistols had "T" prefixes. Later pistols had spur hammers and are in the serial range 73CXXXX-74CXXXX.

	$1,250	$975	$775	$650	$525	$440	$400

Add $150 if with "T" prefix.
Add $50 for original pouch and instruction booklet.

This variation will command a premium; beware of fakes, however (carefully examine slot milling and look for ser. no. in 3 places).

Vektor Arms in N. Salt Lake, UT, has imported this model again recently, with both the "245" and seldolm seen "511" (includes wide trigger, loaded chamber indicator and external spring mags.) ser. no. prefixes. These guns are not arsenal refinished or refurbished, and are sold in NIB condition, with two 13 shot mags. Pricing is $895 for the "245" prefix, and $995 for the "511" prefix.

BCA EDITION HI-POWER - 9mm Para. cal., limited edition made specifically for the Browning Collectors Association in 1980, approx. 100 were delivered.

	$750	$600	$500				

GOLD LINE HI-POWER - 9mm Para. cal., blue finish with gold line perimeter engraving.

	$5,000	$3,500	$2,500				

Add 10% for Ring Hammer.
Check this model carefully for factory originality - including the ring hammer, engraving and bluing, as most models encountered are reproductions.

RENAISSANCE HI-POWER - 9mm Para. cal., extensive scroll engraving on grey silver receiver, synthetic pearl grips, gold plated trigger. Disc. approx. 1978.

Round Hammer/fixed sights	$1,425	$1,025	$825				
Spur Hammer/fixed sights	$1,300	$950	$775				

Add $200 for internal extractor.
Add $100 for "Thumb Print."
Add $50 for original pouch and booklet.
Add $500 for older individual blue leatherette European case.
Add $300-$500 for coin finish, depending on condition.
Target sights do not affect the value of this model significantly.
Currently, the Browning Custom Shop in Belgium is making the following Renaissance models: Dore ($6,066 MSR), Nickele ($5,970 MSR), L1 ($4,163 MSR), I1 ($5,250 MSR), and the B2 ($4,350 MSR).

GRADING - PPGS™	100%	98%	95%	90%	80%	70%	60%

CASED GRADE I (BLUE) SET - one pistol each in .25 ACP, .380 ACP, and 9mm Para. cal., Hi-Power Grade I Models in walnut or black vinyl case, ser. no. not related to other calibers.

	$1,700	$1,350	$895				

Add $100 for walnut presentation case.
Add $100 for thumbprint.
Add $100 for "St. Louis" slide address.
Add $100 for old style extractor.
All original Grade I blue cased sets had a Ring Hammer 9mm Para. Hi-Power.

CASED RENAISSANCE SET - one pistol each in .25 ACP, .380 ACP, and 9mm Para. cal., Hi-Power Renaissance models in walnut or black vinyl case, ser. no. not related to other calibers. Offered 1954-69.

	$5,250	$4,500	$3,500				

Add 20% for coin finish in early walnut case.
Add $100 for "St. Louis" slide address.
Add $100 for old style extractor.
All original Renaissance cased sets had a Ring Hammer 9mm Para. Hi-Power.

CENTENNIAL MODEL HI-POWER - similar to fixed sight Hi-Power, chrome plated with inscription "Browning Centennial/1878-1978", engraved on side, checkered walnut grips with "B" in circle, cased, 3,500 mfg. in 1978. Original issue price was $495.

	$825	$650	$450				

CENTENAIRRE MODEL HI-POWER 1 OF 100 - 9mm Para. cal., unique pattern chemically etched, checkered walnut grips with border. 100 mfg. during 1989 – approx. half were sold in U.S., the other half in Europe.

	$4,000	$3,000	$2,000				

LOUIS XVI MODEL - 9mm Para., chemically etched throughout in leaf scroll patterns, satin finish, checkered grips, walnut case. Disc. 1984.

	$995	$850	$625				

Add 5% for adj. sights.

CLASSIC HI-POWER SERIES - 9mm Para. cal., less than 2,500 manufactured in Classic model and under 350 manufactured in Gold Classic. Both editions feature multiple engraved scenes, and a special silver grey finish, presentation grips, cased. Mfg. 1984-86.

	$950	$675	$495				

Last MSR was $1,000.

✳ *Gold Classic Hi-Power* - 5 gold inlays, select walnut grips are both checkered and carved. Less than 500 mfg. 1984-86.

	$1,850	$1,500	$1,150				

Last MSR was $2,000.

125th ANNIVERSARY HI-POWER - 9mm Para. cal., silver nirtride finish with scroll engraving, gold enhanced 125th Browning Anniversary logo with image of John M. Browning in gold on slide, 10 shot mag., fixed sights, smooth oil finished walnut grips. 125 mfg. 2003-2004 only.

	$1,450	$1,125	$850				

Last MSR was $1,516.

BROWNING DOUBLE ACTION - this model was first listed in the Browning catalog in 1985 but was never imported commercially. The advertised 1985 retail price was $494.

GRADING - PPGS™	100%	98%	95%	90%	80%	70%	60%

BDM/BPM/BRM SINGLE/DOUBLE ACTION - 9mm Para. cal., double mode design featuring slide selector allowing choice between pistol (true double action operation) or revolver mode (full hammer decocking after each shot), available in double mode, single mode (BPM-D decocker, mfg. 1997), or double action only (BRM-DAO, mfg. 1997), dual purpose decocking lever/safety, 4.73 in. barrel, 10 (C/B 1994) or 15* shot mag., matte blue finish, black molded wraparound grips, unique breech block allows visible cartridge inspection, adj. rear sight, 31 oz, mfg. in U.S. 1991-97.

	$465	$395	$365	$330	$300	$280	$260

Last MSR was $551.

This model features hammer block and firing pin block safeties.

❋ *BDM Practical* - similar to Standard BDM, except has matte blue slide and silver chrome frame. Mfg. 1997-98.

	$480	$400	$365	$330	$300	$280	$260

Last MSR was $571.

❋ *BDM Silver Chrome* - similar to Standard BDM, except has silver chrome finish. Only 119 mfg. in 1997 only.

	$480	$400	$365	$330	$300	$280	$260

Last MSR was $571.

FN DA 9 - 9mm Para. cal., choice of double action or double action only, 4 5/8 in. barrel, molded rubber grips, 10 shot mag., 31 oz. Mfg. by FN. While advertised in 1996, this model was never imported commercially - the retail price was listed at $613.

PRO-9/PRO-40 - 9mm Para or .40 S&W cal., double action, 4 in. barrel, 10, 14 (.40 S&W cal. only), or 16 (9mm Para. cal. only) shot mag., ambidextrous decocking and safety, black polymer frame with satin stainless steel slide, under barrel accessory rail, interchangeable backstrap inserts, fixed sights only, 30 (9mm Para.) or 33 oz. Mfg. in the U.S. New 2003.

MSR $628		$495	$425	$365	$315	$285	$265	$240

BDA-380 - .380 ACP cal., double action, 10 (C/B 1994) or 14* shot, 3 13/16 in. barrel, fixed sights, smooth walnut grips, 23 oz., introduced 1978 - recent production was by Beretta. Disc. 1997.

	$450	$345	$260	$220	$175	$150	$125

Last MSR was $564.

Nickel finish	$480	$360	$275	$230	$180	$150	$125

Last MSR was $607.

BDA MODEL - 9mm Para. (9 shot, 2,740 mfg.), .38 Super (752 mfg.), or .45 ACP (7 shot) cal., mfg. from 1977-80 by Sig-Sauer of W. Germany (same as Sig-Sauer 220).

9mm Para.	$550	$450	$375	$295	$250	$225	$200
.38 Super	$650	$575	$495	$450	$390	$350	$300
.45 ACP	$550	$450	$375	$295	$250	$225	$200

BDA SPECIAL LIMITED EDITION - .380 ACP, DA, blue or nickel finish, wood grips, 10 shot, includes extra magazine.

MSR $630	$525	$425	$375	$295	$250	$225	$200

This model is available exclusively from Davidson's.

NOMAD MODEL - .22 LR cal., 10 shot, 4 1/2 and 6 3/4 in. barrels, steel or alloy frame, adj. sights, blue finish, black plastic grips. Mfg. 1962-74 by FN.

	$295	$245	$185	$140	$125	$100	$85

Add 10% for alloy frame.

CHALLENGER MODEL - .22 LR cal., 10 shot, 4 1/2 and 6 3/4 in. barrels, steel frame, adj. sights, checkered walnut or plastic (mfg. 1974 only) wraparound grips, gold plated trigger. Mfg. 1962-75 by FN.

	$375	$315	$265	$215	$190	$170	$155

Add 10% for late production plastic grips.

GRADING - PPGS™	100%	98%	95%	90%	80%	70%	60%

✳ *Renaissance* - engraved satin nickel finish, 437 mfg. total (121 with 4.5 in. barrel, and 316 with 6.75 in. barrel).

	$1,625	$1,375	$900				

✳ *Gold Line* - blue finish, gold line border on perimeter of frame surfaces, 293 mfg. total (147 with 4.5 in. barrel, and 146 with 6.75 in. barrel).

	$1,625	$1,375	$900				

CHALLENGER II - .22 LR cal., Salt Lake City mfg., 6 3/4 in. barrel, steel frame, plastic impregnated hardwood grips, 38 oz. Mfg. 1975-82.

	$230	$180	$170	$145	$135	$120	$110

✳ *Challenger II BCA Commemorative* - .22 LR cal., mfg. to commemorate BCA's fourth anniversary.

	$295	$240	$175				

CHALLENGER III - .22 LR cal., Salt Lake City mfg., 5 1/2 in. bull barrel, 11 shot, alloy frame, adj. sights, 35 oz. Mfg. 1982-85.

	$220	$190	$170	$145	$135	$120	$110

Last MSR was $240.

CHALLENGER III SPORTER - similar to Challenger III, except 6 3/4 in. round barrel, wide trigger, 29 oz. Mfg. 1982-85.

	$220	$190	$170	$145	$135	$120	$110

Last MSR was $240.

MEDALIST MODEL - .22 LR cal., 6 3/4 in. barrel, vent. rib, adj. target sights and barrel weights (3 supplied), blue finish, target walnut grips with thumbrest, dry-fire mechanism, 46 oz., cased. Mfg. 1964-75 by FN.

	$900	$750	$595	$500	$425	$375	$325

Subtract 15% if without case and accessories.

Gold Line (407 mfg. 1963)	$1,950	$1,400	$950	
Renaissance Model	$2,350	$1,750	$1,250	

11 pistols were mfg. 1962-67 with full coverage engraving, and 382 were mfg. 1970-75 w/o full coverage engraving, early production guns were coin finished and later ones were satin chrome. Mfg. by FN 1964-75.

BAC Edition

Engraved (60 mfg.)	$2,450	$1,900	$1,400

This BAC edition was a special order (not regular production), featured full coverage engraving, and was sold in 1986.

INTERNATIONAL MEDALIST - target variation model manufactured 1977-80, 5.9 in. barrel, only 681 made with BAC markings and blue finish. Currently manufactured by FN in the parkerized international configuration.

	$650	$550	$475	$410	$350	$300	$275
Early Model	$850	$700	$550	$425	$360	$330	$280

BUCK MARK STANDARD .22 - .22 LR cal., 10 shot mag., 5 1/2 in. bull barrel, aluminum frame, composite grips with skipline checkering (disc. 1990) or molded rubber grips (new 1991), adj. sights, gold trigger, matte blue finish, 34-36 oz. New 1985.

MSR $319	$230	$190	$165	$125	$110	$100	$90

Add $58 for nickel finish (new 1991).

Buck Mark models are manufactured in Salt Lake City, UT.

✳ *Buck Mark Standard Stainless* - similar to Buck Mark Standard, except stainless steel, 34 oz. New 2005.

MSR $345	$250	$210	$180

GRADING - PPGS™	100%	98%	95%	90%	80%	70%	60%

❋ *Buck Mark Micro Standard* - similar to Buck Mark Standard, except has 4 in. barrel, choice of standard or nickel finish, 32 oz. New 1992.

MSR $319	$230	$190	$165	$125	$110	$100	$90

Add $58 for nickel finish.

>**Buck Mark Micro Standard Stainless** - similar to Buck Mark Micro Standard, except stainless steel, 34 oz. New 2005.

MSR $345	$250	$210	$180

❋ *Buck Mark Micro Plus* - similar to Micro Buck Mark, except has ambidextrous contoured laminated wood grips, nickel (new 1996) or blue finish. Disc. 2001.

	$265	$210	$155	$135	$120	$110	$100

Last MSR was $350.

Add $33 for nickel finish.

❋ *Buck Mark Challenge* - features smaller grip circumference for smaller hands, smooth (disc.) or checkered walnut grips with medallions, matte blue finish, 5 1/2 in. lightweight barrel, Pro-Target sights, 25 oz. New 1999.

MSR $356	$260	$210	$165	$125	$110	$100	$90

❋ *Buck Mark Micro Challenge* - similar to Buck Mark Challenge, except has 4 in. barrel. 23 oz. Mfg. 1999-2000.

	$230	$180	$140	$120	$110	$100	$90

Last MSR was $311.

❋ *Buck Mark Camper* - features 5 1/2 in. heavy barrel, ambidextrous molded black composite grips, matte blue or satin nickel finish, Pro-Target sights, 34 oz. New 1999.

MSR $287	$220	$180	$145	$115	$100	$95	$85

Add $33 for satin nickel finish.

>**Buck Mark Camper Stainless** - similar to Buck Mark Camper, except stainless steel, 34 oz. New 2005.

MSR $310	$230	$190	$165

❋ *Buck Mark Camper Special Edition* - same features as Buck Mark Camper, available in matte black or Mossy Oak Breakup Camo.

MSR $310	$230	$190	$165

Add $45 for camo.

This model is available exclusively through Davidson's.

❋ *Buck Mark Hunter* - features 7.25 in. round heavy barrel with integral scope base, Truglo front sight, smooth cocobolo target grips, matte blue finish, 38 oz. New 2005.

MSR $360	$265	$215	$165	$125	$110	$100	$90

❋ *Buck Mark Plus* - similar to Buck Mark Standard, except has uncheckered laminated wood grips, Tru-Glo Marble front sight (new 2002), and choice of high polish blue or nickel (new 1996), 34 oz. New 1987.

MSR $390	$285	$225	$165	$135	$120	$110	$100

Add $37 for nickel finish.

❋ *Buck Mark Classic Plus* - similar to Buck Mark Plus, except has rosewood grips and Tru-Glo Marble front sight. New 2002.

MSR $390	$285	$225	$165	$135	$120	$110	$100

This model is available from Full-Line dealers only.

❋ *Buck Mark Bullseye Standard* - similar to Buck Mark Bullseye Target, except has molded composite ambidextrous grips, 36 oz. New 1996.

MSR $468	$355	$280	$220	$175	$150	$135	$120

GRADING - PPGS™	100%	98%	95%	90%	80%	70%	60%

❋ *Buck Mark Bullseye Target* - Bullseye model featuring 16 click per turn Pro-Target rear sight, 7 1/4 in. fluted barrel, matte blue finish, adj. trigger pull, contoured rosewood target or wraparound finger groove (disc.) grips, 10 shot mag., 36 oz. New 1996.

	100%	98%	95%	90%	80%	70%	60%
MSR $604	**$440**	**$325**	**$260**	**$200**	**$165**	**$140**	**$125**

❋ *Buck Mark 5.5 Target* - same action as Buck Mark, 5 1/2 in. barrel with serrated top rib allowing adj. sight positioning, target sights, matte blue finish, choice of contoured walnut (disc. 2004), cocobolo (became standard 2005), or walnut wraparound finger groove grips (new 1992-disc.), 35 oz. New 1990.

	100%	98%	95%	90%	80%	70%	60%
MSR $511	**$375**	**$300**	**$245**	**$195**	**$160**	**$140**	**$125**

Add $54 for nickel finish (mfg. 1994-2000).

❋ *Buck Mark 5.5 Field* - same action and barrel as the Target 5.5, except sights are designed for field use, anodized blue finish, contoured walnut grips, choice of contoured walnut, cocobolo (became standard 2005), or walnut wraparound finger groove grips (new 1992-disc.), 35 1/2 oz. New 1991.

	100%	98%	95%	90%	80%	70%	60%
MSR $511	**$375**	**$300**	**$245**	**$195**	**$160**	**$140**	**$125**

❋ *Buck Mark 5.5 Gold Target* - similar to 5.5 Target, except has gold anodized frame and top rib. Mfg. 1991-99.

			95%	90%	80%	70%	60%
	$355	**$275**	**$220**	**$180**	**$160**	**$140**	**$125**

Last MSR was $477.

❋ *Buck Mark Commemorative* - features 6 3/4 in. Challenger style tapered barrel, white bonded ivory grips with scrimshaw style patterning including "1 of 1,000 Commemorative Model" on sides, matte blue finish, gold trigger, 30 1/2 oz. 1,000 mfg. 2001 only.

		98%	95%				
	$335	**$275**	**$225**				

Last MSR was $437.

❋ *Buck Mark Varmint* - same action as Buck Mark, 9 7/8 in. barrel with serrated top rib allowing adj. sight positioning, laminated wood grips, choice of contoured walnut or walnut wraparound finger groove grips (new 1992), optional detachable forearm, matte blue, 48 oz. Mfg. 1987-99.

		98%	95%	90%	80%	70%	60%
	$315	**$255**	**$200**	**$175**	**$155**	**$135**	**$120**

Last MSR was $403.

❋ *Buck Mark Silhouette* - silhouette variation of the Buck Mark, 9 7/8 in. bull barrel with serrated top rib allowing adj. sight positioning, hooded target sights, laminated wood stocks and forearm, choice of contoured walnut or walnut wraparound finger groove grips (new 1992), matte blue, 53 oz. Mfg. 1987-99.

		98%	95%	90%	80%	70%	60%
	$360	**$285**	**$230**	**$195**	**$170**	**$150**	**$135**

Last MSR was $448.

❋ *Buck Mark Unlimited Silhouette (Match)* - similar to Silhouette Model featuring 14 in. barrel with set back front sight, choice of contoured walnut or walnut wraparound finger groove grips (new 1992), 64 oz. Mfg. 1991-99.

		98%	95%	90%	80%	70%	60%
	$425	**$330**	**$270**	**$230**	**$195**	**$170**	**$150**

Last MSR was $536.

RIFLES: BOLT ACTION

MODEL 52 LIMITED EDITION - .22 LR cal., virtually identical to the original Winchester Model 52C Sporter, except for minor safety enhancements, bolt action, 24 in. drilled and tapped barrel, 5 shot detachable mag., pistol grip walnut stock with oil style finish, deep blue finish, adj. trigger, two position safety, 7 lbs. 5,000 mfg. 1991-92.

		98%	95%				
	$525	**$450**	**$395**				

Last MSR was $500.

GRADING - PPGS™	100%	98%	95%	90%	80%	70%	60%

MODEL BBR - .25-06 Rem., .270 Win., .30-06, 7mm Mag., .300 Win. Mag. or .338 Win. Mag. cal., short action available in .22-250 Rem., 243 Win., 257 Roberts, 7mm-08 Rem., or 308 Win. cal., 24 in. standard or heavy barrel, 60 degree throw, fluted bolt, adj. trigger, hidden detachable mag., no sights, checkered pistol grip, Monte Carlo stock. Mfg. 1978-84 by Miroku.

| | $500 | $375 | $335 | $310 | $250 | $220 | $200 |

Some rare production calibers will add premiums to the values listed (i.e., add 50% for .243 Win. cal.).

BBR RIFLE ELK ISSUE - 7mm Rem. Mag. cal., bolt action rifle, 1,000 manufactured, deeply blue receiver which has multiple animals gold inlaid, high grade walnut stock and forearm feature skipline checkering. Disc. 1986.

| | $1,275 | $950 | $795 |

Last MSR was $1,395.

T-BOLT T-1 - .22 LR cal., straight pull bolt action, 5 shot mag., 22 in. barrel, adj. rear sight, 5 1/2 lbs., plain pistol grip stock. Mfg. 1965-74 by FN.

| | $425 | $350 | $295 | $255 | $210 | $180 | $160 |

Add 10%-15% for left-hand model (mfg. 1967-74 only).

An aperture rear sight was standard for the first nine years of production.

T-BOLT T-2 - similar to T-1, only with select checkered walnut stock (lacquer finished), pinned front sight blade, 24 in. barrel, 6 lbs.

| | $600 | $450 | $350 | $295 | $240 | $200 | $180 |

Add 10%-15% for left-hand model (mfg. 1969-74 only).

* **Late production T-2** - features oil finished stock, press fit plastic front sight, and Browning computerized serialization.

| | $425 | $350 | $295 | $255 | $190 | $175 | $150 |

FN HIGH-POWER BOLT ACTION MODEL - .222 Rem. (Sako action), .222 Rem. Mag. (Sako action), .22-250 Rem. (Sako action), .243 Win., .257 Roberts, .264 Win. Mag., .270 Win., .284 Win. (Sako action), .30-06, .308 Win., 7mm Mag., .300 Win. Mag., .308 Norma Mag., .300 H&H, .338 Win. Mag., .375 H&H, or .458 Win. Mag. cal., standard Mauser type action with either short or long (more desirable) extractor, 22 or 24 in. (heavy available) barrel, folding leaf sight, checkered pistol grip stock. Mfg. 1960- 1974 by FN.

The .243 Win. and .308 Win. cals. were built on the small ring Mauser action prior to using the Sako medium action.

Note: Grades differ in engraving, finish, checkering, and grade of wood. It should be noted that the salt wood problem is more common in these high powered models. Guns should be checked carefully for rust below wood surfaces.

* **Safari Grade** - basic model with blue finish.

Standard cals.	$895	$725	$550	$450	$400	$350	$325
Mag. cals.	$1,000	$850	$650	$595	$525	$450	$400
.257 Roberts	$1,295	$1,050	$825	$700	$600	$525	$450
.284 Win.	$1,550	$1,200	$950	$800	$700	$600	$500
.308 Norma Mag.	$1,150	$850	$700	$600	$525	$450	$400
.338 Win. Mag.	$1,150	$950	$850	$735	$650	$595	$525
.375 H&H	$1,200	$1,000	$800	$700	$600	$525	$450
.458 Win. Mag.	$1,095	$995	$895	$750	$625	$525	$450

Add 15% for Magnum long extractor models.

Between 1963 and 1974, Browning also offered short and medium barrelled actions in the Safari, Medallion and Olympian Grades. These models have Sako barrelled actions and were stocked by FN. Medium weight barrels could also be ordered.

* **Safari Grade** - Short Sako Action - short action, .222 Rem. or .222 Rem. Mag. cal.

| | $900 | $775 | $550 | $450 | $400 | $350 | $325 |

GRADING - PPGS™	100%	98%	95%	90%	80%	70%	60%

✳ *Safari Grade* - Medium Sako Action - medium action, .22-250 Rem., .243 Win., .284 Win. or .308 Win. cal.

	100%	98%	95%	90%	80%	70%	60%
	$850	$725	$550	$450	$400	$350	$325

Add 100% for .284 Win. cal. (mfg. 1965-76).

In .284 Win. cal., only 162 rifles were mfg. in Safari Grade, 29 in Medallion Grade, and 10 in Olympian Grade.

✳ *Medallion Grade* - features select figured walnut with skipline checkering, rosewood grip and forearm caps, blue/black lustre bluing, receiver and barrel portion scroll engraved, ram's head engraved on floor plate.

	$1,450	$1,195	$995	$895	$800	$700	$600

Add 10%-50% for rare calibers.

Add 15% for Mag. cals. with long extractor.

Caliber rarity is as follows: .30-06 (least rare), .300 H&H, .375 H&H long extractor, .222 Rem./.222 Rem. Mag., .284 Win. (rarest). This model was also available with a Sako short or medium action - cals. are the same as listed for the Sako Safari.

✳ *Olympian Grade* - top-of-the-line model featuring highly figured walnut stock that is both checkered and carved. Receiver, floor plate, and trigger guard are chrome plated in a satin finish that has deep relief animal scenes engraved, as well as deep scroll work on other metal parts.

	$3,250	$2,850	$2,225	$1,850	$1,650	$1,450	$1,275

Add 10%-50% for rare calibers.

Add 15% for Mag. cals. with long extractor.

Caliber rarity is as follows: .30-06 (least rare), .300 H&H, .375 H&H long extractor, .222 Rem./.222 Rem. Mag., .284 Win. (rarest). This model was also available with a Sako short or medium action - cals. are the same as listed for the Sako Safari.

ACERA MODEL - .30-06 or .300 Win. Mag. cal., features straight pull action, Teflon coated breech block face, 7 lug bolt, 22 or 24 (.300 Win. Mag.) in. barrel, available w/o sights, with sights (disc. 1999), or with BOSS, detachable box mag., checkered walnut stock, gloss metal finish, 7 lbs. 3 oz. – 7 lbs. 9 oz. Mfg. 1999-2000, reintroduced during 2002 only.

	$820	$745	$660	$600	$550	$495	$450

Last MSR was $896.

Add $34 for .300 Win. Mag. cal.

Add $24 for iron sights (disc. 1999).

Add $80 for barrel BOSS (.30-06 cal. mfg. 2002 only).

RIFLES: BOLT ACTION, CENTERFIRE A-BOLT SERIES

A-BOLT HUNTER MODEL - available in .25-06 Rem., .270 Win., .280 Rem. (new 1988), .30-06, 7mm Rem. Mag., .300 Win. Mag., or .338 Win. Mag. cal. in long action, short action available in .223 Rem. (new 1988), .22-250 Win., .243 Win., .257 Roberts, .284 Win. (new 1989), 7mm-08 Rem., or .308 Win. cal., 3 or 4 shot mag., matte blue finish, 3 lug rotary bolt locking, 22 (short action only), 24 in. (disc. 1987), or 26 in. barrel (new 1988 - long action Mag. cals. only), 60 degree bolt throw, adj. trigger, hidden detachable mag., with or without sights, top tang thumb safety, checkered pistol grip stock, 6 lbs. 3 oz. - 7 lbs. 11oz. Mfg. 1985-93 by Miroku. Replaced by A-Bolt Model II in 1994.

	$415	$340	$295	$265	$240	$225	$210

Last MSR was $510.

Add $65 for open sights.

✱ **Medallion Model** - same A-Bolt specifications, except also available in .375 H&H cal., features better grade walnut stock with rosewood pistol grip and forend cap, synthetic floor plate, high lustre bluing, no sights. Disc. 1993. Replaced by A-Bolt Medallion Model II in 1994.

	$475	$385	$330	$290	$265	$250	$235

Last MSR was $597.

Add $25 for left-hand action (avail. in long action cals. only).

Add $100 for .375 H&H cal. (open sights only).

Left-hand action available in .25-06 Rem., .270 Win., .280 Rem., .30-06, 7mm Rem. Mag., .300 Win. Mag., .338 Win. Mag., or .375 H&H cal.

✱ **Micro Medallion Model** - .223 Rem. (new 1988), .22-250 Rem., .243 Win., .257 Roberts, .284 Win., .308 Win., or 7mm-08 Rem. cal., scaled down variation of the A-Bolt Hunter Model, 20 in. barrel, short action only, 13 5/16 in. LOP, 3 shot mag., no sights, 6 lbs. 3 oz. for short action. Mfg. 1988-93. Replaced by A-Bolt Micro Medallion Model II in 1994.

	$475	$385	$330	$290	$265	$250	$235

Last MSR was $597.

✱ **Gold Medallion Model** - .270 Win., .30-06, .300 Win. Mag. (new 1993), or 7mm Rem. Mag. cal., similar to Medallion Model, except has extra select walnut stock with continental style cheekpiece, gold lettering and light engraving, no sights. Mfg. 1988-93. Replaced by A- Bolt Gold Medallion Model II in 1994.

	$670	$535	$430	$360	$330	$300	$265

Last MSR was $810.

✱ **Euro-Bolt** - .22-250 Rem., .243 Win., .270 Win., .30-06, .308 Win., or 7mm Rem. Mag. cal., features European styling including Schnabel style forearm, rounded rear receiver, Mannlicher style bolt, European cheekpiece on satin finished checkered stock, low-lustre bluing, hinged floor plate with removable mag., cocking indicator, upper tang thumb activated safety, 6 lbs. 14 oz. - 7 lbs. 6 oz. (Mag.). Mfg. 1993-96.

	$600	$475	$395	$350	$300	$265	$250

Last MSR was $700.

✱ **Stainless Stalker** - .22-250 Rem. (left-hand only, new 1993), .25-06 Rem., .270 Win., .280 Rem., .30- 06, 7mm Rem. Mag., .300 Win. Mag., .338 Win. Mag. or .375 H&H (new 1990) cal., action and barrel are stainless steel, matte black graphite fiberglass composite stock, dull stainless finish, no sights, 6 lbs. 11 oz. - 7 lbs. 3 oz. Mfg. 1987-93. Replaced by Stainless Stalker II in 1994.

	$575	$430	$350				

Last MSR was $665.

Add $100 for .375 H&H cal.

Add $20 for left-hand action.

Originally, this model was offered in .270 Win., .30-06, or 7mm Rem. Mag. cal. only.

✱ **Camo Stalker** - .270 Win., .30-06, or 7mm Rem. Mag. cal., laminated black and green wood stock, matte finish on metal parts, no sights. Mfg. 1987-89.

	$400	$340	$310	$285	$250	$230	$215

Last MSR was $483.

✱ **Composite Stalker** - .25-06 Rem., .270 Win., .280 Rem., .30-06, 7mm Rem. Mag., .300 Win. Mag., or .338 Win. Mag. cal., black graphite fiberglass composite stock, matte non-glare metal finish, 6 lbs. 11 oz. - 7 lbs. 3 oz. Mfg. 1988-93. Replaced by Composite Stalker II in 1994.

	$410	$340	$295	$265	$240	$225	$210

Last MSR was $525.

A-BOLT BIGHORN SHEEP ISSUE - .270 Win. cal. only, 22 in. barrel, high grade walnut stock with gloss finish and skipline checkering, deep relief engraving on

GRADING - PPGS™	100%	98%	95%	90%	80%	70%	60%

receiver barrel, floorplate, and trigger guard, two 24Kt. inlays depicting bighorn sheep. 600 mfg. 1986-87 only.

	$975	**$750**	**$625**

Last MSR was $1,365.

A-BOLT PRONGHORN ISSUE - .243 Win. cal., presentation grade walnut with ski-pline checkering and pearl borders, receiver and barrel engraving, multiple gold inlays on receiver top and floor plate. 500 mfg. 1987 only.

	$925	**$725**	**$600**

Last MSR was $1,302.

RIFLES: BOLT ACTION, CENTERFIRE A-BOLT II SERIES

The A-Bolt II Series was introduced in 1994, and differs from the original A-Bolt variations (disc. 1993) in that a new anti-bind bolt featuring a non-rotating bolt sleeve has been incorporated in addition to an improved trigger system. Consumers also may have their name/inscription engraved on the flat bolt-face on any A- Bolt II Series variation for an additional $25. Browning introduced the BOSS (ballistic optimizing shooting system) in 1994 as an option on A-Bolt rifles, except Micro-Medallion models. It is available with ported BOSS (results in approx. 30% less recoil) or unported (designated BOSS-CR, for conventional recoil) muzzle brake.

A-BOLT HUNTER MODEL II - available in various cals. between .22-250 Rem. - .338 Win. Mag., .270 WSM and 7mm WSM cals. (new 2002), .300 WSM (new 2001), or .325 WSM (new 2005) cal., 22, 23 (.300 WSM cal. only), 24, or 26 in. barrel with (disc. 1998) or w/o open sights, walnut stock with gloss finish, top tang safety, low lustre bluing, 60 degree bolt throw, 6 lbs. 7 oz. – 7 lbs. 3 oz.

MSR $705	**$550**	**$445**	**$375**	**$300**	**$250**	**$225**	**$210**

Add $29 for Mag. cals.
Add $30 for left-hand action (various cals., new 2003).
Add approx. $60 for open sights (available in 8 cals., disc. 1998).

✳ *Hunter Model II WSSM* - .223 WSSM, .25 WSSM (new 2004), or .243 WSSM cal., 3 shot mag., super short action, 21 or 22 (new 2004) in. barrel, walnut stock with satin finish and smaller dimensions, 6.25 lbs. New 2003.

MSR $755	**$600**	**$495**	**$425**	**$375**	**$325**	**$280**	**$240**

✳ *Hunter Model II with BOSS* - same cals. as Hunter Model II until 1999, available only in .22- 250 Rem., .243 Win., .270 Win., .280 Rem., .30-06, or .308 Win. cal. during 1999, features 22 or 26 (Mag. cals. only, disc. 1998) in. barrel with BOSS. Mfg. 1994-99.

	$525	**$435**	**$365**	**$300**	**$260**	**$235**	**$215**

Last MSR was $617.

A-BOLT HUNTER FIELD (CLASSIC HUNTER) - .270 Win. (disc. 2001), .270 WSM (new 2002), .30-06 (disc. 2001), .300 Win. Mag. (disc. 2001), .300 WSM (new 2002), .325 WSM (new 2005) 7mm Rem. Mag. (disc. 2001), or 7mm WSM (new 2002) cal., 22 (disc. 2001), 23 (new 2002, WSM cals. only), or 26 (disc. 2001) in. barrel, 3-5 shot mag., features low-lustre bluing and select checkered satin finished Monte Carlo walnut stock and forend, approx. 6 1/2 - 7 1/4 lbs. New 1999.

MSR $808	**$655**	**$540**	**$445**	**$375**	**$315**	**$275**	**$250**

This model is available to Full-line and Medallion dealers only.

✳ *Hunter Field WSSM (Classic Hunter)* - .223 WSSM, .25 WSSM (new 2004), or .243 WSSM cal., 3 shot mag., super short action, 22 in. barrel, satin finished Monte Carlo walnut stock with palm swell and double bordered checkering, low lustre bluing, 6.25 lbs. New 2003.

MSR $829	**$660**	**$530**	**$450**	**$375**	**$325**	**$290**	**$265**

This model is available to Full-line and Medallion dealers only.

GRADING - PPGS™	100%	98%	95%	90%	80%	70%	60%

A-BOLT MICRO HUNTER

- .22 Hornet, .22-250 Rem., .223 Rem. (new 2000), .243 Win., .260 Rem. (disc. 2001), .270 WSM (new 2003), 7mm WSM (new 2003), .300 WSM (new 2003), .325 WSM (new 2005), .308 Win., or 7mm-08 Rem. cal., 3 shot mag., features shorter LOP and 20 or 22 in. barrel w/o sights, checkered walnut stock and forend, approx. 6.25 lbs. New 1999.

MSR $684	$525	$425	$350	$295	$245	$225	$210

Add $30 for .270 WSM, .300 WSM, or 7mm WSM cal.

Add $30 for left-hand action (new 2003).

A-BOLT MEDALLION MODEL II

- available in various cals. between .22-250 Rem. - .375 H&H, .260 Rem. (new 1999), .223 Rem. (disc. 2000), .300 WSM, .300 Rem. Ultra Mag., .325 WSM (new 2005) and .338 Rem. Ultra Mag. (new 2001), .270 WSM, 7mm WSM (new 2002), similar to Medallion Model with A-Bolt II improvements, without sights, except for .375 H&H cal. (open sights standard), gloss finished walnut stock with rosewood grip and forend caps, 6 lbs. 7 oz. – 7 lbs. 1 oz. New 1994.

MSR $805	$645	$535	$440	$365	$300	$275	$250

Add $30 for all Mag. cals.

Add $32 for left-hand action w/o sights.

Browning has introduced many left-handed action cals. in this model.

* ❋ *Medallion Model II WSSM* - .223 WSSM, .25 WSSM (new 2004), or .243 WSSM cal., 3 shot mag., super short action, 22 in. barrel, engraved receiver, Monte Carlo gloss finished walnut stock with rosewood pistol grip and forend caps, palm swell and double bordered checkering, no sights, low lustre bluing, 6.25 lbs. New 2003.

MSR $856	$740	$600	$475	$425	$385	$365	$335

* ❋ *Medallion Model II with BOSS* - similar to Medallion Model II, .25 WSSM (new 2005), .223 WSSM (new 2004), .243 WSSM (new 2004), .270 WSM and 7mm WSM cals (new 2003), .25-06 Rem., .260 Rem., .280 Rem., and .308 Win. cals. were disc. 1999, 22, 23 (new 2002, WSM cals. only) or 26 in. BOSS barrel. New 1994.

MSR $885	$730	$595	$475	$425	$385	$365	$335

Add $30 for normal Mag. and WSM cals. or $51 for WSSM cals.

Add $32 for left-hand action.

Browning has introduced many left-handed action cals. in this model.

* ❋ *Micro Medallion Model II* - .22 Hornet, .22-250 Rem., .223 Rem., .243 Win., 7mm-08 Rem., .284 Win. (disc. 1997), or .308 Win. cal., similar to Micro Medallion Model with A-Bolt II improvements, 20 or 22 (.22 Hornet only) in. barrel without sights, 6 lbs. Mfg. 1994-98.

	$525	$465	$400	$350	$300	$275	$250

Last MSR was $636.

A-BOLT CUSTOM TROPHY

- .270 Win., .30-06, .300 Win. Mag., or 7mm Rem. Mag. cal., features 24 or 26 (Mag. cals. only) in. octagon barrel with gold band at muzzle, no sights, gold outlines on barrel and receiver, checkered select American walnut stock with shadowline cheekpiece and skeleton pistol grip, approx. 7 1/2 lbs. Mfg. 1998-2000.

	$1,150	$925	$800	$660	$525	$450	$375

Last MSR was $1,428.

A-BOLT GOLD MEDALLION MODEL II

- .270 Win., .30-06, .300 Win. Mag. or 7mm Rem. Mag. cal., similar to Gold Medallion Model, except has A-Bolt II improvements, 22 or 26 in. barrel, approx. 7 1/2 lbs. Mfg. 1994-98.

	$695	$595	$450	$375	$335	$300	$265

Last MSR was $855.

* ❋ *Gold Medallion Model II with BOSS* - mfg. 1994-97.

	$750	$625	$525	$450	$375	$325	$285

Last MSR was $916.

A-BOLT WHITE GOLD MEDALLION - .270 WSM (new 2004), .270 Win., .30-06, .300 Win. Mag., .300 WSM (new 2004), .325 WSSM (new 2005), 7mm WSM (new 2004), or 7mm Rem. Mag. cal., stainless steel receiver and 22, 23 (new 2004), or 26 in. barrel, gold engraving, checkered high gloss Monte Carlo walnut stock with rosewood cap on forend and pistol grip, 6 lbs. 6 oz. - 7 lbs. 11 oz. New 1999.

MSR $1,155	$940	$725	$585				

Add $28 for Mag. cals.

✳ *White Gold Medallion RMEF* - 7mm Rem. Mag. cal. only, similar to White Gold Medallion, includes RMEF logo on pistol grip cap, gold engraved, stainless steel receiver and 26 in. barrel, select walnut stock, contrasting spacers and rosewood caps on forend and pistol grip, continental style cheekpiece and sling swivels, 7 lbs., 11 oz. Limited edition beginning 2003.

MSR $1,261	$1,000	$775	$625				

✳ *White Gold Medallion with BOSS* - similar to White Gold Medallion, except has barrel with BOSS, and not available in WSM cals.

MSR $1,235	$985	$765	$610				

Add $28 for non-WSSM Mag. cals.

A-BOLT ECLIPSE HUNTER WITH BOSS - .22-250 Rem. (disc. 1999), .243 Win. (disc. 1997), .270 Win., .30-06, .308 Win. (disc. 2000), or 7mm Rem. Mag. cal., features laminated thumbhole wood stock with cheekpiece, long action, 22 or 26 (7mm Rem. Mag. only) in. barrel with BOSS, approx. 7 1/2 lbs. New 1996.

MSR $1,134	$900	$725	$575	$480	$375	$325	$285

Add $28 for Mag. cal.

✳ *Eclipse Varmint with BOSS* - .22-250 Rem., .223 Rem., or .308 Win. cal., 24 in. heavy barrel with BOSS, 4 shot mag., otherwise similar to Eclipse Model, approx. 9 lbs. Mfg. 1996-99.

	$810	$655	$535	$455	$375	$325	$285

Last MSR was $969.

✳ *Eclipse M-1000 with BOSS* - .300 Win. Mag. cal., features special 26 in. heavy target barrel, refined trigger system, 9 lbs. 13 oz.

MSR $1,168	$945	$740	$595	$475	$385	$335	$285

✳ *Eclipse M-1000* - .270 WSM, 7mm WSM, .300 WSM, features 26 in. heavy blue or stainless steel bull barrel, 3 shot mag., 9 lbs. 14 oz. New 2004.

MSR $1,086	$870	$695	$565	$460	$375	$315	$275

Add $206 for stainless steel bull barrel.

A-BOLT VARMINT II WITH BOSS - .22-250 Rem., .223 Rem., or .308 Win. (new 1995) cal., features A-Bolt II improvements, 22 in. heavy barrel with BOSS, blue/gloss or satin/matte (new 1995, .223 Rem. disc. 1999) finish, black laminated wood stock with checkering, palm swell, and solid recoil pad, without sights, 9 lbs. Mfg. 1994-2000.

	$715	$600	$465	$380	$335	$300	$265

Last MSR was $879.

A-BOLT EURO-BOLT II - .243 Win., .270 Win., .30-06, .308 Win., or 7mm Rem. Mag. cal., similar to Euro-Bolt with A-Bolt II improvements, 22 or 26 (7mm Rem. Mag. only) in. barrel w/o sights, 6 lbs. 7 oz. - 7 lbs. 3 oz. (Mag.). Mfg. 1994-96.

	$625	$510	$410	$355	$300	$265	$250

Last MSR was $824.

✳ *Euro-Bolt II with BOSS* - .243 Win., .270 Win., or .308 Win. cal., 22 in. barrel with BOSS, 6 lbs. 7 oz.

	$725	$600	$500	$425	$350	$325	$295

Last MSR was $922.

A-BOLT STAINLESS STALKER II
similar to Stainless Stalker with A-Bolt improvements, available in various cals, between .22-250 Rem. - .375 H&H, .223 Rem. reintroduced during 2004 in SSA only, no sights, 6 lbs. 1 oz. - 7 lbs. 3 oz. New 1994.

MSR $897	$740	$535	$390

Add $29 for normal Mag. or WSM cals.

Add $27 for left-hand action.

Browning has introduced many left-handed action cals. in this model.

✹ ***Stainless Stalker II WSSM*** - .223 WSSM, .25 WSSM (new 2004), or .243 WSSM cal., 3 shot mag., super short action, 21 (disc.) or 22 in. barrel, walnut stock with satin finish and smaller dimensions, 6 lbs., 1 oz. New 2003.

MSR $947	$780	$575	$415

✹ ***Stainless Stalker II with BOSS*** - various cals. between .22-250 Rem. and .375 H&H, 22, 23 (new 2002, .300 WSM cal. only), 24 (.375 H&H cal. only) 26 (Mag. cals. only) in. barrel with BOSS.

MSR $977	$800	$595	$470

Add $29 for normal Mag. or WSSM cals., or $50 for WSSM cals. (new 2004).

Add $28 for left-hand action.

Browning has introduced many left-handed action cals. in this model.

A-BOLT CARBON FIBER STAINLESS STALKER
.22-250 Rem. or .300 Win. Mag. cal., features Christensen lightweight 22 or 26 in. carbon fiber barrel with steel liner, stainless steel action, black synthetic stock, 4 or 5 shot mag., approx. 6 1/4 or 7 1/4 lbs. Mfg. 2000-2001.

$1,475	$1,225	$975

Last MSR was $1,750.

A-BOLT COMPOSITE STALKER II
similar to Composite Stalker with A-Bolt II improvements, also available in .223 Rem. (SSA only beginning 2004), .22-250 Rem., .243 Win., .260 Rem. (mfg. 1999 only), .270 WSM (new 2002), 7mm-08 Rem., .308 Win., .300 WSM (new 2001), 325 WSM (new 2005), or 7mm WSM (new 2002) cal., 22, 23 (WSM cals. only), 24, or 26 (Mag. cals. only) in. barrel without sights, 6 lbs. 1 oz. - 7 lbs. 3 oz. New 1994.

MSR $705	$535	$415	$340	$285	$240	$225	$210

Add $31 for all Mag. cals.

✹ ***Composite Stalker II WSSM*** - .223 WSSM, .25 WSSM (new 2004), or .243 WSSM cal., 3 shot mag., super short action, 21 (disc.) or 22 in. barrel, black composite stock with matte blued metal and smaller dimensions, 6.1 lbs. New 2003.

MSR $755	$610	$495	$435	$380	$335	$295	$260

✹ ***Composite Stalker II with BOSS*** - .22-250 Rem. (disc. 1997), .223 Rem. (disc. 1999), .223 WSSM (new 2004), .243 Win. (disc. 2001), .243 WSSM (new 2004), .25 WSSM (new 2005), .25-06 Rem., .260 Rem. (disc. 1999), 7mm-08 Rem. (disc. 1999), .270 Win., .270 WSM (new 2003), .280 Rem. (disc. 1999), .30-06, .308 Win. (disc. 2001), 7mm Rem. Mag., 7mm WSM (new 2003), .300 Win. Mag., .300 WSM (new 2002), .338 Win. Mag., 22, 23 (WSM cals. only) or 26 (Mag. cals. only) in. barrel with BOSS.

MSR $785	$635	$525	$410	$345	$290	$250	$225

Add $29 for standard Mag. and WSM cals., or $50 for WSSM cals. (new 2004).

✹ ***Varmint Stalker*** - .22-250 Rem. or .223 Rem. (SSA only beginning 2004) cal., 24 or 26 (.22-250 Rem. cal. only) in. heavy barrel, features Dura-Touch armor coated composite stock with slight palm swell, matte blue metal, 4 or 6 shot mag., approx. 8-8 1/4 lbs. New 2002.

MSR $860	$685	$545	$435	$360	$300	$255	$230

GRADING - PPGS™	100%	98%	95%	90%	80%	70%	60%

✱ Varmint Stalker WSSM - .223 WSSM, .25 WSSM (new 2004), or .243 WSSM cal., 3 shot mag., super short action, 21 (mfg. 2003 only) or 24 (new 2004) in. barrel, features Dura-Touch armor coated composite stock with slight palm swell, matte blue metal, 7 lbs., 13 oz. New 2003.

	MSR $913	$735	$575	$475	$395	$335	$295	$275

A-BOLT MOUNTAIN TI - .270 WSM, .300 WSM, 7mm WSM, .223 WSSM (new 2005), .243 WSSM (new 2005), or .25 WSSM (new 2005) cal., features titanium short action receiver with composite bolt sleeve and stainless steel 23 in. barrel, fiberglass Bell & Carlson stock with Mossy Oak New Break-Up camo and Dura-Touch armor coating, Pachmayr Decelerator recoil pad, 5.25 lbs. New 2004.

	MSR $1,669	$1,430	$1,075	$865

Add $21 for WSSM cals.

A-BOLT GREYWOLF - .25-06 Rem., .270 Win., .280 Rem., .30-06, .300 Win. Mag., .338 Win. Mag., or 7mm Rem. Mag. cal., stainless steel, classic sporter with select walnut stock. Limited mfg. during 1994 only.

		$850	$675	$595

Last MSR was $935.

RIFLES: BOLT ACTION, RIMFIRE A-BOLT SERIES

A-BOLT GRADE I RIMFIRE - .22 LR or .22 Mag. (new 1989) cal., 60 degree bolt throw, 22 in. barrel, checkered walnut stock and forearm or laminated stock (scarce - approx. 1,500 mfg., 390 had no sights), 5 or 15 (optional) shot mag., adj. trigger, available with or without open sights, 5 lbs. 9 oz. Mfg. 1986-96.

✱ .22 LR cal.

	$320	$255	$195	$175	$160	$145	$130

Last MSR was $425.

Add $14 for open sights.

A 15 shot mag. was also available for this model at $45 retail.

✱ .22 Win. Mag. cal.

	$375	$295	$225	$195	$175	$160	$150

Last MSR was 493.

Add $21 for open sights.

A-BOLT GOLD MEDALLION RIMFIRE - .22 LR cal. only, similar to A-Bolt, except has high grade select walnut stock checkered 22 lines per inch, rosewood pistol and forend cap, high gloss finish, gold filled lettering and moderate engraving, solid recoil pad. Mfg. 1988-96.

	$455	$365	$310	$270	$240	$225	$210

Last MSR was $567.

RIFLES: LEVER ACTION

BL-17 - .17 Mach 2 cal., otherwise similar to the BL-22, 5 lbs., 2 oz. New 2005.

✱ BL-17 Grade I - uncheckered stock with choice of blued or nickel (BL-17 Field) receiver, blued trigger. New 2005.

	MSR $484	$390	$275	$225	$175	$140	$110	$100

Add $32 for nickel.

✱ BL-17 Grade II - features choice of engraved blued or nickel (Field) receiver, gold trigger, checkered stock and forearm. New 2005.

	MSR $524	$410	$315	$250	$200	$175	$150	$125

Add $53 for nickel.

✱ BL-17 Grade II Field Octagon - similar to BL-22 Classic/Field octagon, 5 lbs., 6 oz. New 2005, mfg. by Miroku.

	MSR $744	$600	$525	$465	$410	$355	$300	$250

GRADING - PPGS™	100%	98%	95%	90%	80%	70%	60%

BL-22 GRADE I - .22 S, L, and LR cal., 20 in. barrel, short throw (33 degree) lever, folding leaf sight, 15 shot (LR) mag., blue finish, exposed hammer, Western style gloss finished uncheckered stock and forearm, 5 lbs. Mfg. 1970-2003 by Miroku.

		$340	$245	$200	$160	$130	$110	$100

Last MSR was $436.

✳ *BL-22 Classic/Field* - similar to BL-22 Grade I, except has satin finished stock and forearm, blue or nickel (new 2005) receiver. New 1999, mfg. by Miroku.

MSR $462	$365	$260	$210	$165	$135	$110	$100

Add $32 for nickel (Field, new 2005).

This model is available through Full-Line and Medallion dealers only.

BL-22 GRADE II - same general specifications as BL-22, except scroll engraved blue receiver and deluxe high gloss checkered walnut stock and forearm. Disc. 2003.

		$385	$295	$225	$180	$140	$125	$115

Last MSR was $494.

✳ *BL-22 Grade II (Classic/Field)* - similar to BL-22 Grade II, except has satin finished stock and forearm, engraved blue or nickel (new 2005) receiver. New 1999, mfg. by Miroku.

MSR $524	$410	$310	$235	$190	$145	$125	$115

Add $31 for nickel (Field, new 2005).

This model is available through Full-Line and Medallion dealers only.

✳ *BL-22 Grade II Classic/Field Octagon* - features 24 in. octagon barrel and nitride finished receiver with scroll engraving, adj. buckhorn rear sight, 5 1/4 lbs. New 2004, mfg. by Miroku.

MSR $726	$590	$510	$450	$400	$350	$300	$250

MODEL 53 DELUXE LIMITED EDITION - .32-20 WCF cal. (round nose or hollow point bullets only), patterned after the original Winchester Model 53 (redesigned Model 1892), 7 shot tube mag., high polished blue metal, open sights, 22 in. tapered barrel, high grade checkered walnut stock featuring full pistol grip cap and shotgun style metal buttplate, 6 1/2 lbs. Only 5,000 mfg. in 1990.

		$795	$525	$425

Last MSR was $675.

MODEL 65 GRADE I LIMITED EDITION - .218 Bee cal., patterned after the Winchester Model 65, round tapered 24 in. barrel, open sights (hooded front), blue metal finish, 7 shot tube mag., uncheckered pistol grip stock and semi-beavertail forearm, metal buttplate, 6 3/4 lbs. 3,500 total mfg. for Grade I in 1989 only, inventory depleted in 1990.

		$550	$425	$375

Last MSR was $550.

✳ *Model 65 High Grade* - greyed receiver (and lever) with scroll engraving and gold plated animals, gold plated trigger, deluxe checkered walnut stock and semi-beavertail forearm. 1,500 total mfg. in 1989, inventory depleted in 1990.

		$850	$775	$700

Last MSR was $850.

MODEL 71 LIMITED EDITION CARBINE - .348 Win. cal., reproduction of the Winchester Model 71 Carbine, 20 in. barrel, open sights, 4 shot mag., 8 lbs. New 1987 with inventory depleted in 1990.

✳ *Grade I* - uncheckered satin finished walnut stock and forearm. 4,000 mfg. 1986-87 only.

		$600	$475	$400	$350	$325	$300	$275

Last MSR was $600.

* **High Grade** - deluxe checkered walnut stock and forearm with high gloss finish, scroll engraved- grey receiver with gold inlays and trigger. 3,000 mfg. 1986-87 only.

	$825	$625	$500

Last MSR was $980.

MODEL 71 LIMITED EDITION RIFLE - .348 Win. cal., reproduction of the Winchester Model 71 Rifle, 24 in. barrel, open sights, 4 shot mag., 8 lbs. 2 oz. Mfg. 1986-87 only with inventory depleted in 1990.

* **Grade I** - uncheckered satin finished walnut stock and forearm. 3,000 mfg. 1986-87 only.

$675	$525	$425	$375	$350	$300	$275

Last MSR was $600.

* **High Grade** - deluxe checkered walnut stock and forearm with high gloss finish, scroll engraved- grey receiver with gold inlays and trigger. 3,000 mfg. 1986-87 only.

$895	$675	$525

Last MSR was $980.

MODEL 81/BLR SHORT ACTION - .22-250 Rem., .222 Rem. (disc. 1989), .223 Rem., .243 Win., .257 Roberts (disc. 1992), 7mm-08 Rem., .284 Win. (disc. 1994), .308 Win., or .358 Win. (disc. 1992) cal., steel receiver, rotary bolt locking lugs, 20 in. barrel with band, 3 (.284 Win. only) or 4 shot detachable mag., adj. rear sight, checkered straight grip stock, recoil pad, approx. 7 lbs, no sights optional 1988-89. .243 Win. and .308 Win. cals. are the most popular in this model.

* **Model BLR USA** - .243 Win. or .308 Win. cal., this model was originally scheduled to be manufactured by TRW in Cleveland, OH for Browning. Originally assembled in 1966, these rifles are considered prototypes as they were never sold through regular channels and at one time were scheduled to be destroyed. Approx. 50-250 of these rifles exist, some still NIB.

$995	$895	$750	$600	$550	$500	$450

This variation has a 2-line legend on the right side marked "MADE IN USA" and "PATENT PENDING".

* **Model BLR Belgian** - .243 Win. or .308 Win. cal., mfg. was moved to FN in Belgium with original assembly beginning 1969 and concluding in 1973. This FN model included a number of small dimensioning and engraving changes.

$575	$500	$425	$375	$350	$315	$275

* **Model BLR Japan** - cals. as noted above, mfg. was moved to Miroku in Japan 1974-1980. Early guns during 1974 had stocks with impressed checkering. By 1975, cut checkering and gloss wood finish was used on stocks and forearms.

$480	$375	$325	$275	$250	$210	$180

Last MSR was $550.

    Add $40 without sights (scarce).
* **Model BLR 81 Short Action** - cals. as noted above, mfg. 1981-95 by Miroku in Japan.

	100%	98%	95%	90%	80%	70%	60%
.257 Roberts	$650	$575	$450	$325	$250	$200	$165
Standard cals.	$480	$400	$350	$265	$225	$175	$150
.284 Win./.358 Win.	$650	$550	$450	$325	$250	$200	$165
.222 Rem.	$850	$750	$600	$550	$425	$350	$300

Last MSR was $550.

MODEL BLR 81 LONG ACTION - .270 Win., .30-06, or 7mm Rem Mag. cal., incorporates distinct design changes, 22 or 24 in. barrel, approx. 8 1/2 lbs. Mfg. 1991-95 by Miroku.

$500	$425	$350	$280	$230	$200	$170

Last MSR was $580.

GRADING - PPGS™	100%	98%	95%	90%	80%	70%	60%

NEW MODEL LIGHTNING BLR (SHORT ACTION) - .22-250 Rem., .223 Rem. (disc. 1998), .243 Win., 7mm-08 Rem., or .308 Win. cal., rotary bolt locking lugs, 20 in. barrel w/o barrel band, similar action as the BLR 81, but features aluminum alloy receiver, checkered pistol grip stock and forearm, rack and pinion geared slide, fold down hammer, trigger travels with lever, 3-5 shot detachable mag., adj. rear sight, approx. 6 1/2 lbs. Mfg. by Miroku late 1995 - 2002.

	$525	$400	$340	$290	$220	$195	$165

Last MSR was $681.

NEW MODEL LIGHTNING BLR (LONG ACTION) - .270 Win., .30-06, .300 Win. Mag. (new 1997), or 7mm Rem. Mag. cal., 22 or 24 (Mag. cals.) in. barrel, approx. 7 1/4 - 7 3/4 lbs. Mfg. by Miroku 1995-2002.

	$550	$415	$335	$280	$230	$200	$170

Last MSR was $721.

BLR LIGHTWEIGHT '81 (SHORT ACTION) - .22-250 Rem., .243 Win., .270 WSM (new 2004), 7mm-08 Rem., .325 WSM (pistol grip only, new 2005), .300 WSM (new 2004), 7mm WSM (new 2004), .308 Win., .358 Win., .450 Marlin cal., 20 or 22 (WSM cals. only) in. barrel with barrel band, aluminum alloy receiver, choice of checkered Model 81 styled straight grip and forearm with gloss finish or checkered, gloss finished pistol grip with Schnabel forearm w/o barrel band (new 2005) stock, sling swivels (pistol grip only), rack and pinion geared slide with rotating breech head, fold down hammer, trigger travels with lever, 3-4 shot detachable mag., adj. rear sight, approx. 6 1/2 - 7 lbs. Mfg. by Miroku beginning 2003.

MSR $731		$550	$415	$330	$275	$225	$200	$170

Add $71 for WSM cals. (new 2004).

Add $34 for checkered pistol grip stock and Schnabel forearm (new 2005).

BLR LIGHTWEIGHT '81 (LONG ACTION) - .270 Win., .30-06, .300 Win. Mag., or 7mm Rem. Mag. cal., 22 or 24 in. barrel, 7 1/4 or 7 3/4 lbs. Mfg. by Miroku beginning 2003.

MSR $775		$585	$440	$350	$295	$235	$200	$170

Add $34 for checkered pistol grip stock and Schnabel forearm (new 2005).

MODEL 1886 LIMITED EDITION GRADE I RIFLE - .45-70 Govt. cal. only, patterned after the Winchester Model 1886, blue receiver, 26 in. octagon barrel, full mag., crescent buttplate, open sights. 7,000 mfg. 1986 only.

	$1,225	$950	$750				

Last MSR was $578.

✱ *Model 1886 Limited Edition High Grade Rifle* - same general specifications as Model 1886, except has checkered high grade walnut stock and forearm, greyed steel receiver, with game scene engraving including elk and American Bison, gold accenting with "1 of 3,000" engraved on top of barrel. 3,000 mfg. 1986 only.

	$1,795	$1,350	$995				

Last MSR was $935.

✱ *Model 1886 Montana Centennial Rifle* - similar to Model 1886 High Grade. 2,000 mfg. 1986 only to commemorate Montana Centennial.

	$1,795	$1,350	$995				

Last MSR was $935.

MODEL 1886 LIMITED EDITION GRADE I CARBINE - .45-70 Govt. cal. only, saddle ring carbine, patterned after the Winchester Model 1886 Carbine, blue receiver, 22 in. round barrel, 8 shot full mag., crescent buttplate, open sights. 7,000 total mfg. 1992-93.

	$750	$575	$450				

Last MSR was $750.

GRADING - PPGS™	100%	98%	95%	90%	80%	70%	60%

✻ **Model 1886 Limited Edition High Grade Carbine** - same general specifications as Model 1886, except has checkered high grade walnut stock and forearm, greyed steel receiver, with game scene engraving including bear and elk, gold accenting, 3,000 total mfg. 1992-93.

	$1,250	$925	$675

Last MSR was $1,175.

B-92 CARBINE - .357 Mag. or .44 Rem. Mag. cal., 20 in. barrel, patterned after the Winchester Model 92, 11 shot mag. (tubular), blue finish. Disc. 1986.

	$475	$375	$295	$200	$175	$160	$150

Last MSR was $342.

✻ **B-92 Centennial** - .44 Mag. cal., 6,000 mfg. in 1978.

	$495	$395	$350

Last MSR was $220.

✻ **B-92 BCA Commemorative** - mfg. to commemorate BCA's third anniversary.

	$495	$395	$350

MODEL 1895 LIMITED EDITION GRADE I - .30/40 Krag or .30-06 cal. only, patterned after the Winchester Model 1895, blue receiver, 24 in. barrel, 4 shot mag.(box type), select walnut, rear buckhorn sight, 8 lbs. Mfg. 1984 only.

	100%	98%	95%	90%	80%	70%	60%
.30/40 Krag	$550	$475	$375	$325	$300	$280	$260
.30-06	$600	$525	$400	$350	$325	$300	$280

Production totaled 6,000 in the .30-06 cal. and 2,000 in .30/40 Krag for this model.

✻ **Model 1895 Limited Edition High Grade** - same general specifications as Model 1895, except gold plated game scenes on satin finish receiver, gold trigger, and finely checkered select French walnut.

	$1,200	$975	$850

Production totaled 1,000 in the .30-06 cal. and 1,000 in .30/40 Krag for this model.

RIFLES: O/U

Currently, the Browning Custom Shop in Belgium is making the following B-25 double rifles: CCS Herstal ($10,386 MSR), CCS25 B2E ($15,116 MSR), CCS Africa ($15,266 MSR), Bavarian ($18,016 MSR), CCS25 D5G ($32,999 MSR), and the M1 ($45,265 MSR).

EXPRESS RIFLE - .270 Win., .30-06 cal., or 9.3x74R cal., Superposed Superlight style action. 24 in. barrels, checkered straight grip stock and forearm, auto ejectors, Fleur-de-lis engraving, single trigger, folding leaf rear sight, 6 lbs. 14 oz., cased. Disc. 1986.

	$3,500	$3,200	$2,750	$2,450	$2,150	$1,950	$1,750

Last MSR was $3,125.

GRADE I CONTINENTAL SET - includes .30-06 O/U rifle barrels with extra set of 20 ga. O/U shotgun barrels (26 1/2 in.), rifle barrels are 24 in., 20 ga. frame, SST, ejectors, blue receiver with scroll engraving, straight grip checkered stock and forearm, supplied with 2 barrel takedown case. Mfg. 1978-86.

	$4,750	$4,250	$3,850	$3,450	$3,150	$2,950	$2,750

RIFLES: SEMI-AUTO, .22 LR

Currently, the Browning Custom Shop in Belgium is making the following .22 LR cal. semi-auto models: Grade II ($2,920 MSR), and the Grade III ($4,546 MSR).

AUTO RIFLE GRADES I - VI - .22 LR or .22 short (disc.) cal., takedown design, 11 shot (16 for .22 short) tube mag. in buttstock, 19 1/4 in. barrel for all .22 LR, .22 shorts had various barrel lengths according to mfg. year: 19 1/4 in. for 1956, 22 3/8 in. for 1957, and 22 in. from 1958 until general production was disc. in 1983, checkered pistol grip stock, semi-beavertail forearm, stock has hole machined halfway to allow partial filling of tube mag., adj. folding rear or earlier wheel sight, Grades differ in finish, amount of engraving, and grade of wood, 4 3/4-5 3/4 lbs. Early top loaders were mfg. from 1914 until approx. 1955. Modern loader mfg. 1956 to 1974 by FN Belgium. Mfg. 1976-present by Miroku in Japan.

GRADING - PPGS™	100%	98%	95%	90%	80%	70%	60%

✳ *Grade I - FN*

	$575	$475	$375	$300	$250	$225	$200

Add 50% for wheel sight guns in .22 Short cal., if in 95% or better condition.
Add 50% for wheel sight guns in .22 LR cal., if in 95% or better condition.
Add at least $50 for original box and manual.
FN Postwar Grade Is have a lightly engraved blue steel receiver, checkered walnut, blue trigger, and a variety of rear sights.

✳ *Grade I - Miroku* - approx. 5.25 lbs.

MSR $535	$410	$325	$265	$225	$185	$160	$140

Miroku manufactured .22s can be determined by year of manufacture in the following manner: RV suffix - 1975, RT - 1976, RR - 1977, RP - 1978, RN - 1979, PM - 1980, PZ - 1981, PY - 1982, PX - 1983, PW - 1984, PV - 1985, PT - 1986, PR - 1987, PP - 1988, PN - 1989, NM - 1990, NZ - 1991, NY - 1992, NX - 1993, NW - 1994, NV - 1995, NT - 1996, NR - 1997, NP - 1998, NN - 1999, MM - 2000, MZ - 2001, MY - 2002, MX - 2003, MW - 2004, MV - 2005, MU - 2006.

✳ *Grade II - FN*

	$1,100	$900	$675	$450	$375	$350	$300

Add $100 for guns initialed by the engraver.
Add $200 for guns fully signed by the engraver.
Add 15% for Grade II with wheel sight.
FN Grade IIs have grey receiver, deluxe wood with finer checkering, gold plated trigger, and engraving depicting two squirrels and two prairie dogs. Unsigned, signed, or initialed by engraver.

✳ *Grade II - Miroku* - disc. 1984.

	$575	$500	$325	$225	$200	$175	$150

✳ *Grade III - FN*

	$2,625	$2,150	$1,650	$1,250	$850	$775	$725

Add 15% for guns signed by the engraver.
FN Grade IIIs have coin finish or grey chromed receiver, extra deluxe walnut with skipline checkering, gold plated trigger, and more elaborate game scene engraving usually featuring a dog flushing ducks or upland game. Signed or unsigned by engraver (Funken, J. Baerten, Vrancken, and Watrin will command premiums over values listed). A few were also special ordered with blue finish and special engraving - these command an extra premium.

✳ *Grade III - Miroku* - disc. 1983.

	$1,000	$700	$700	$500	$475	$425	$400

Add 15% for guns signed by the engraver.
Add 30% for "transition" guns signed by FN engravers with barrels and boxes marked "Made in Japan."

✳ *Grade VI - Miroku* - game scene engraved with gold plating, choice of blue or greyed receiver, deluxe walnut. New 1987.

MSR $1,145	$800	$625	$495	$415	$350	$300	$275

Add at least 50% for small run of .22 Short Grade VI mfg. during 2003.

✳ *Grade VI 125th Anniversary Miroku* - features silver nitride receiver with gold enhanced 125th Anniversary logo and delicate scroll engraving. 500 mfg. 2003-2004.

	$1,100	$950	$725				

Last MSR was $1,271.

BAR-22 - .22 LR cal., 20 1/4 in. barrel, 15 shot tube mag., folding leaf sight, high polish alloy receiver, checkered pistol grip stock, 5 lbs. 13 oz. Mfg. 1977-85 by Miroku.

	$400	$325	$275	$200	$175	$150	$125

Last MSR was $245.

BAR-22 GRADE II - engraved model of BAR-22 featuring game scenes on silver greyed alloy receiver, select French walnut. Disc. 1985.

	$600	$500	$425	$350	$200	$175	$150

Last MSR was $350.

GRADING - PPGS™	100%	98%	95%	90%	80%	70%	60%

BUCK MARK RIFLE - .22 LR cal., Buck Mark pistol blowback action, 18 in. tapered barrel with Hi-Viz fiber optic sights (Sporter Rifle), heavy barrel w/o sights (Target Rifle), or Classic Carbon Rifle (new 2003) with carbon composite barrel, includes intergral scope rail, uncheckered walnut or grey laminate (new 2002, no sights, Classic Target Rifle) Monte Carlo stock that attaches to non-detachable, one-piece skeletonized and enclosed rear grip assembly, 3 lbs., 10 oz. (Classic Carbon), 4 lbs. 6 oz. (Sporter) or approx. 5 lbs. 6 oz. (Target & Classic Target) New 2001.

	MSR $572	$440	$320	$275	$235	$200	$160	$150

    Add $17 for Buck Mark Classic/Field Target Rifle (new 2002).

    Add $80 for Classic/Field Carbon Rifle (new 2003).

    The Buck Mark Classic/Field Target & Classic/Field Carbon Rifles are available through Full-Line and Medallion dealers only.

RIFLES: SEMI-AUTO, BAR SERIES

Currently, the Browning Custom Shop in Belgium is making the following BAR custom shop rifles: Grade 4 VB ($6,283 MSR), Grade 4 PH ($7,441 MSR), and the Grade D ($6,543 MSR).

BROWNING PATENT 1900 - .35 Rem. cal. only, features most often matted rib barrel and checkered stock and forearm, similar to Remington Model 8 auto-loading rifle. 4,913 mfg. 1910-1929 by FN.

		$1,250	$1,000	$850	$800	$750	$600	$450

    Add 15% if rifle has plain barrel with tangent leaf rear sight.

BAR SEMI-AUTO - .243 Win., .270 Win., .280 Rem. (new 1990), .308 Win., or .30-06 cal. available in standard model, Mag. cals. include 7mm Rem., .300 Win., and .338 Win. Mag. (reintroduced 1990), gas operated, blued steel receiver, 22 or 24 (Mag. only) in. barrel, rotary bolt with seven lugs, folding leaf sight, walnut stock. Grades differ in engraving, finish, and grade of wood, in 1993, to celebrate the 25th Anniversary of the BAR, Browning introduced the BAR MK II Safari (see model listing), approx. 7 lbs. 6 oz. Mfg. 1967-present (includes BAR MK II).

    Add 20% for FN mfg. and assembled BARs (marked "Made in Belgium").

    Add 10% for .338 Win. Mag. cal. (FN mfg. only).

    Note: Original .338s were limited production, mostly seen in the deluxe Grade II only. During the last year of FN .338 production, several were delivered in a Grade I by FN. Although being rarer than the Grade II, it is not as desirable. The following prices are for Portugese assembled guns, manufactured by FN, and are so stamped on the barrel.

✳ *Grade I* - standard grade without engraving, blue finish. Ordering this model without sights became an option in 1988. Disc. 1992.

		$550	$475	$400	$350	$325	$300	$280
							Last MSR was $633.	

    Subtract $16 without sights.

    FN mfg. and assembled Grade Is can be denoted by light scroll engraving on the receiver.

✳ *Grade I Magnum* - standard grade without engraving, with recoil pad, 8 lbs. 6 oz. Disc. 1992.

		$575	$495	$425	$375	$350	$330	$310
							Last MSR was $680.	

    Subtract $16 without sights.

    Ordering this gun without sights became an option in 1988.

✳ *Grade II* - blue receiver, engraved with big game heads. Mfg. 1967-74.

		$695	$625	$575	$525	$470	$440	$415

This model was previously designated Deluxe.

✳ *Grade II Magnum* - magnum version of Grade II. Mfg. 1967-74.

		$750	$675	$625	$550	$510	$475	$450

GRADING - PPGS™	100%	98%	95%	90%	80%	70%	60%

✻ *Grade III* - features antelope and deer game scenes etched on greyed steel receiver, select checkered stock and forearm. Disc. 1984.

	$925	$800	$675	$625	$595	$550	$525

✻ *Grade III Magnum* - magnum version of Grade III, features elk and moose game scenes. Disc. 1984.

	$1,025	$850	$700	$660	$620	$595	$580

✻ *Grade IV* - engraved satin finish greyed receiver depicts big game animal scenes and trigger guard, carved borders on checkering. Disc. 1989.

	$1,475	$1,300	$1,150	$1,000	$900	$825	$750

Last MSR was $1,670.

✻ *Grade IV Magnum* - magnum version of Grade IV. Disc. 1984.

	$1,675	$1,495	$1,225	$1,050	$950	$850	$775

Last MSR was $1,720.

✻ *Grade V* - more elaborate engraving than Grade IV, with gold inlays. Mfg. 1971-74.

	$3,000	$2,600	$2,250	$1,850	$1,600	$1,450	$1,250

✻ *Grade V Magnum* - magnum version of Grade V.

	$3,650	$2,900	$2,400	$1,950	$1,700	$1,595	$1,400

BAR NORTH AMERICAN DEER RIFLE ISSUE - .30-06 cal. only, BAR style action with silver grey finish and engraved action, 600 total production, walnut cased with accessories. Disc. 1983 but were sold through 1989.

	$2,950	$2,300	$1,850

Last MSR was $3,550.

BAR MK II SAFARI - .22-250 Rem. (mfg. as prototype only during 1997), .25-06 Rem. (new 1997), .243 Win., .270 Win., .30-06, .308 Win., .270 Wby. Mag. (mfg. 1996-2000), 7mm Rem. Mag., .300 Win. Mag., or .338 Win. Mag. cal., improved BAR action featuring redesigned bolt release, new gas operating system, and reduced recoil, removable trigger assembly, 22, 23 (WSM cals. only), or 24 (Mag. cals. only) in. barrel with (adj. for windage and elevation) or without sights, BOSS became optional 1994, and is available with ported BOSS, which results in approx. 30% less recoil, or unported (designated BOSS-CR, for conventional recoil) muzzle brake, blue finish with scroll engraved receiver, checkered walnut stock and forearm, gold trigger, detachable 3 (.300 WSM cal. only), 4 (Mag. cals. only) or 5 shot box mag., approx. 7 lbs. 6 oz. except for Mag. cals. (8 lbs. 6 oz.). Mfg. by FN in Belgium. New 1993.

MSR $889	$725	$550	$465	$395	$360	$330	$310

Add $83 for Mag. cals.

Add $19 for open sights (not available in .270 Wby. Mag., disc.).

The new BAR MK II Safari does not have interchangeable magazine capability with the older pre-1993 BARs.

✻ *BAR Classic Mark II Safari* - .270 Win. (disc. 2001), .270 WSM (new 2003), .30-06 (disc. 2001), 7mm Rem. Mag., (disc. 2001), 7mm WSM (new 2003), .300 Win. Mag. (disc. 2001), or .300 WSM (new 2002) cal., similar to BAR Mark II Safari, except has satin finished checkered stock and forearm, 7 lbs. 6 oz. or 8 lbs. 6 oz. Mfg. 1999-2003.

	$785	$610	$520	$430	$380	$335	$310

Last MSR was $908.

Subtract approx. 10% for non-Mag. cals.

Add $17 for open sights (disc. 2000).

This model is available to Full-line and Medallion dealers only.

GRADING - PPGS™	100%	98%	95%	90%	80%	70%	60%

❋ BAR Mark II Safari with BOSS - .243 Win. (disc. 1999), .308 Win. (disc. 1999), .270 Win., .270 WSM (new 2003), .30-06, 7mm Rem. Mag., 7mm WSM (new 2003), .300 Win. Mag., .300 WSM (new 2003), .338 Win. Mag. cal., similar to BAR MK II Safari, with BOSS (ballistic optimizing shooting system) accurizing adj. assembly on barrel end, no sights, 7 1/2 or 8 1/2 lbs. New 1994.

MSR $988	$835	$650	$550	$450	$395	$350	$310

Add $83 for Mag. cals.

❋ BAR Mark II Lightweight - .243 Win., .270 Win., .30-06, .308 Win., 7mm Rem. Mag. (new 1999), .300 Win. Mag. (new 1999), or .338 Win. Mag. (new 1999) cal., features alloy receiver and 20 or 24 (Mag. cals. only) in. barrel, matte wood and barrel finish, open sights, 7 lbs. 2 oz. or 7 lbs. 12 oz. Mfg. 1997-2003.

	$710	$545	$450	$395	$355	$330	$310

Last MSR was $850.

Add $77 for Mag. cals. (new 1999).

❋ BAR MK II Lightweight with BOSS - 7mm Rem. Mag., .300 Win. Mag., or .338 Win. Mag. (disc. 1999) cal., similar to BAR Mark II Lightweight, except has 24 in. barrel with BOSS, 8 lbs., 6 oz. Mfg. 1999-2000.

	$800	$625	$525	$445	$385	$350	$310

Last MSR was $939.

❋ BAR MK II Lightweight Stalker - .243 Win., .270 Win., .270 WSM (new 2003), .30-06, .308 Win., 7mm Rem. Mag. (disc. 2004), 7mm WSM (new 2003), .300 Win. Mag., .300 WSM (new 2002), or .338 Win. Mag. cal., similar to BAR Mark II Safari, except has aluminum alloy receiver and checkered black synthetic stock and forearm, matte metal finish, 20, 22, 23 (new 2002, WSM cals. only), or 24 (Mag. cals. only) in. barrel with open sights, 7 lbs. 2 oz. – 7 lbs. 12 oz. New 2001.

MSR $883	$725	$575	$465	$395	$365	$330	$310

Add $131 for Mag. cals.

>BAR MK II Lightweight Stalker with BOSS - .270 WSM (new 2003), 7mm Rem. Mag., 7mm WSM (new 2003), .300 Win. Mag., .300 WSM (new 2002), or .338 Win. Mag. cal., similar to BAR Mark II Stalker, except has 23 (new 2002, WSM cals. only) or 24 in. barrel with BOSS, approx. 7 3/4 lbs. Mfg. 2001-2003.

	$835	$650	$540	$450	$395	$350	$325

Last MSR was $981.

❋ BAR MK II High Grade - .270 Win., .30-06, .300 Win. Mag., or 7mm Rem. Mag. cal., satin finished receiver with either whitetail/mule deer or moose/elk etched game scenes and gold border, checkered high grade gloss finished walnut stock and forearm, no sights, 7 lbs. 6 oz. or 8 lbs. 6 oz. Mfg. 2001-2003.

	$1,475	$1,015	$795	$675	$565	$465	$415

Last MSR was $1,856.

Add $58 for Mag. cals.

❋ BAR MK II Grade III - features Grade III engraving pattern. Mfg. by the FN custom shop 1996-99.

	$3,100	$1,875	$1,375	$1,000	$775	$675	$575

Last MSR was $3,754.

❋ BAR MK II Grade IV - features Grade IV engraving pattern. Mfg. by the FN custom shop beginning 1996.

	$3,180	$1,930	$1,400	$1,025	$795	$675	$575

Last MSR was $3,859.

GRADING - PPGS™	100%	98%	95%	90%	80%	70%	60%

BAR SHORTTRAC - .243 Win., .270 WSM, .300 WSM, .308 Win., or 7mm WSM cal., features new styling with aluminum alloy gas operated short action receiver and composite trigger guard and mag. floorplate, 22 or 23 in. hammer forged barrel w/o sights, mfg. in Belgium, drilled and tapped, checkered satin finished walnut stock supplied with 6 adj. shims and squared off forearm, 3 or 4 shot detachable mag., 6 lbs., 10 oz (regular cals.) or 7.25 lbs. (WSM cals.). New 2004.

	100%	98%	95%	90%	80%	70%	60%
MSR $885	$735	$575	$475	$410	$365	$330	$310

Add $80 for WSM cals.

BAR LONGTRAC - .270 Win., .30-06, .300 Win. Mag., or 7mm Rem. Mag. cal., similar to BAR Shorttrac, except has long action, 7 - 7.5 lbs. New 2004.

	100%	98%	95%	90%	80%	70%	60%
MSR $885	$735	$575	$475	$410	$365	$330	$310

Add $80 for WSM cals.

RIFLES: SEMI-AUTO, FAL SERIES

The following semi-auto FALs were imported by BAC in limited numbers, and can be identified by a sear slot in the receiver. Current production FALs can be found under the Fabrique Nationale heading.

FAL G SERIES STANDARD - 7.62mm cal., paramilitary design rifle, wood buttstock, wood or nylon forearm, milled receiver.

	$3,500	$3,100	$2,500	$2,150	$1,775	$1,450	$1,100

✳ *G Series Heavy Barrel* - wood furniture, milled receiver with special bipod.

	$6,500	$5,550	$4,900	$4,300	$3,725	$3,200	$2,725

✳ *G Series Lightweight* - lightweight variation of the FAL.

	$4,250	$3,700	$3,150	$2,600	$2,150	$1,900	$1,650

The Lightweight Model had the trigger frame, magazine, and return spring tube made out of aluminum.

✳ *Browning Arms Co. Import* - milled receiver, wood or nylon furniture.

	$2,400	$2,000	$1,700	$1,550	$1,400	$1,275	$1,150

✳ *CAL Model* - please refer to the FN section in this text for this listing.

Above Average	Average	Below Average

RIFLES: SINGLE SHOT

MODEL 1878 STANDARD - various cals., J.M. Browning's first patent, fewer than 600 made (highest known ser. no. is 542) by Browning Brothers in Ogden, Utah between 1878-1883, octagon barrel marked "Browning Bros. Ogden, Utah USA" plain wood stock and forearm with and without pistol grips, crescent steel buttplate, with or without ramrod, several receiver configurations, a very few were made in the deluxe model, seldom found in better than average used condition, with or w/o serial number. Approx. only 100 have survived – Browning Arms Co. & the Winchester Museum have no factory records on this model.

$25,000 - $30,000	$20,000 - $25,000	$15,000 - $20,000

Add 50% for Deluxe Rifle (checkered stock and forearm), 10% for Early Rifle with Sharps Borchardt type lever, 40% for Early Rifle stamped "Ogden, U.T.", 20% for any caliber other than .40-70 SS or .45-70 Govt., 25% for Late Model with rammer rod under barrel held by two thimbles (known as "Montana Model").

Subtract 20% if the original sights have been removed or replaced incorrectly.

Please refer to the grading explanation for Winchester lever actions regarding descriptions for the above condition factors.

Calibers in this model are listed from rarest to most commonly encountered: .50-70 Govt., .45 Sharps, .44 Rem., .40-90 Sharps, .44-77 Sharps, .45-70 Govt., and .40-70 Sharps Straight.

This model is rare since approx. only 550 were mfg. (approx. ser. range 1-550). This patent was sold to Winchester, which became their Model 1885 single shot. To date, less than 100 original Model 1878s have been encountered indicating a high mortality rate (most remaining specimens are in poor original condition). An inherent weakness of the original design was the way the stock attached to the action - Winchester later corrected this design flaw. A few remaining examples are not serial numbered. Barter guns are rifles that have Browning stamped actions and barrels of an older gunsmith's identity.

MODEL B-78 - .22-250 Rem., 6mm Rem., .243 Win., .25-06 Rem., 7mm Mag., .30-06, or .45-70 Govt. cal., 24 or 26 in. round or octagon barrel, lever activated falling block, no sights except .45- 70 Govt., checkered walnut stock, approx. 24,000 mfg. 1973-82.

	100%	98%	95%	90%	80%	70%	60%
	$695	$595	$465	$325	$295	$275	$250
.45-70 Govt. cal.	$795	$650	$475	$325	$295	$275	$250

The Model B-78 was reintroduced as the Model 1885 in 1985.

MODEL 1885 HIGH WALL - .22-250 Rem., .223 Rem. (disc. 1994), .270 Win., .30-06, 7mm Rem. Mag., .45-70 Govt., or .454 Casull (new 1998) cal., falling block action, sear safety, 28 in. octagonal barrel, adj. trigger, no sights, checkered walnut stock and Schnabel forearm, exposed hammer, gold trigger, approx. 8 3/4 lbs. Mfg. 1985-2001.

$775	$585	$455	$365	$330	$295	$275

Last MSR was $1,027.

This model is equipped with open sights in .45-70 Govt. and .454 Casull cals.

MODEL 1885 LOW WALL - .22 Hornet, .223 Rem. (disc. 2000), .243 Win. (disc. 2000), or .260 Rem. (new 1999) cal., action patterned after the Winchester Low Wall receiver, 24 in. barrel, adj. trigger, features thinner 24 in. barrel, 6 1/4 lbs. Mfg. 1995-2001.

$755	$575	$450	$360	$330	$295	$275

Last MSR was $997.

MODEL 1885 HIGH WALL TRADITIONAL HUNTER - .30-30 Win., .38-55 WCF or .45-70 Govt. cal., High-Wall action, 30 in. octagon barrel with ejector, blue receiver, rear tang aperture sight, crescent buttplate, checkered stock and forearm, approx. 9 lbs. Mfg. 1997-2000.

$1,075	$780	$585	$450	$360	$330	$295

Last MSR was $1,220.

✳ *Model 1885 High Wall Traditional Hunter 125th Anniversary* - .45-70 Govt. cal., features delicate scroll receiver engraving and gold enhanced 125th anniversary logo with gold border. 500 mfg. 2003-2004 only.

$1,450	$1,125	$850

Last MSR was $1,516.

MODEL 1885 LOW WALL TRADITIONAL HUNTER - .357 Mag., .44 Mag., or .45 LC cal., 24 in. half-round, half-octagon barrel, case colored receiver and buttplate, gold bead front, semi-buckhorn rear, and upper tang aperture sights, 6 1/2 lbs. Mfg. 1998-2001.

$1,130	$800	$615	$450	$375	$330	$295

Last MSR was $1,289.

MODEL 1885 BPCR (BLACK POWDER CARTRIDGE) - .40-65 Win. (black powder only) or .45-70 Govt. (black powder or smokeless) cal., case colored high wall action, 30 in. half-round, half-octagon barrel, checkered pistol grip stock with shotgun butt, w/o ejector system and shell deflector, vernier tang rear sight and globe front sight with spirit level, approx. 11 lbs. Mfg. 1996-2001.

$1,595	$1,275	$1,085	$925	$800	$700	$600

Last MSR was $1,766.

✳ *Model 1885 BPCR Creedmoor* - .45-90 cal., blue receiver, 34 in. half-round, half- octagon barrel with globe front and aperture rear tang sights, 11 3/4 lbs. Mfg. 1998-99.

$1,595	$1,285	$1,090	$925	$800	$700	$600

Last MSR was $1,764.

GRADING - PPGS™	100%	98%	95%	90%	80%	70%	60%

RIFLES: SLIDE ACTION

BPR - .243 Win., .270 Win., .30-06, .308 Win., .300 Win. Mag., or 7mm Rem. Mag. cal., 7 lug rotary bolt, blue alloy receiver, 22 or 24 (Mag. cals. only) in. barrel with open sights, features downward camming slide action assembly, checkered walnut stock and forend, cross-bolt safety, 3 or 4 shot mag., approx. 7 lbs. 3 oz. Mfg. 1997-2001.

	100%	98%	95%	90%	80%	70%	60%
	$635	$565	$510	$455	$400	$360	$330

Last MSR was $725.

Add $55 for Mag. cals.

BPR-22 - .22 LR or .22 Mag. cal., short-stroke action, 20 1/4 in. barrel, 11 shot tube mag., mfg. 1977-82.

	100%	98%	95%	90%	80%	70%	60%
	$275	$195	$170	$160	$140	$130	$100

✹ *BPR-22 Grade II* - similar to BPR-22, only engraved action, select walnut.

	100%	98%	95%	90%	80%	70%	60%
	$450	$350	$295	$260	$230	$200	$175

Add 10% for .22 Mag. cal.

TROMBONE MODEL - .22 LR cal. only, slide action with tube mag., fixed sights, takedown, 24 in. barrel, hammerless, with either FN or U.S. (rare) barrel address.

✹ *FN Barrel Address*

	100%	98%	95%	90%	80%	70%	60%
	$795	$695	$550	$450	$375	$295	$275

✹ *BAC Barrel Markings*

	100%	98%	95%	90%	80%	70%	60%
	$950	$795	$625	$550	$450	$395	$350

Over 150,000 "Trombones" were mfg. by FN from 1922-1974. About 3,200 were imported by BAC in late 1960s. Very rare with factory engraving.

BCA GRADE III FN TROMBONE - only 60 manufactured for the Browning Collectors Association 1985-86, silver engraved frame with deluxe walnut.

	100%	98%	95%
	$2,500	$2,100	$1,650

SHOTGUNS: BOLT ACTION, A-BOLT SERIES

A-BOLT MODEL - 12 ga. only, 3 in. chamber, 2 shot mag., same bolt system as A-Bolt II Rifle, 22 or 23 in. barrel (rifled or Invector with rifled tube), available in Stalker Model with graphite fiberglass composite stock or Hunter Model with select satin finished walnut stock, dull matte finished barrel and receiver, top tang safety, choice of no sights (new 1996) or adj. rear sight, drilled and tapped receiver, approx. 7 lbs. Mfg. by Miroku 1995-98.

✹ *Stalker Model*

	100%	98%	95%	90%	80%	70%	60%
	$435	$335	$300	$275	$260	$240	$220

Last MSR was $720.

Add $25 for open sights.
Add $100 for rifled barrel.

✹ *Hunter Model*

	100%	98%	95%	90%	80%	70%	60%
	$425	$325	$295	$275	$260	$240	$220

Last MSR was $805.

Add $24 for open sights.
Add $100 for rifled barrel.

SHOTGUNS: O/U

CYNERGY SERIES - 12, 20 (new 2005), or 28 (new 2005) ga., silver nitride finished receiver with clay pigeon motif, features new MonoLock hinge system, allowing low receiver profile, stock has adj. comb with built in Inflex recoil pad system allowing LOP adjustment, SST includes a striker based mechanical trigger system (also includes triple trigger), backbored and ported vent. barrels with VR, Invector Plus chokes, choice of wood or composite (12 ga. only) stock and forearm, impact ejectors. New 2004.

GRADING - PPGS™	100%	98%	95%	90%	80%	70%	60%

* **Cynergy Field** - 2 3/4 (28 ga. only) or 3 in. chambers, 26 or 28 in. non-ported barrels with 5/16 in. slanted VR, flush choke tubes, checkered Grade I walnut or non-glare black composite stock and forearm, approx. 6.25 - 7.5 lbs.

MSR $2,048	**$1,575**	**$1,200**	**$950**	**$875**	**$775**	**$700**	**$625**

Add $14 for 20 or 28 ga.

Subtract $62 for composite stock and forearm.

* **Cynergy Sporting** - 2 3/4 in. chambers, 28, 30, or 32 in. ported barrels with tapered VR (non-tapered 5/16 in. rib on 28 ga.), checkered walnut or black composite (12 ga. only) stock and forearm, extended choke tubes, approx. 6.5 - 8 lbs.

MSR $3,046	**$2,350**	**$1,900**	**$1,525**	**$1,275**	**$1,050**	**$875**	**$800**

Add $34 for 20 or 28 ga.

Subtract $200 for composite stock and forearm.

SHOTGUNS: O/U, CITORI HUNTING SERIES

All Citori shotguns which incorporate the Invector choke tube system may be used with steel shot. Invector Plus choke tubes are designed for backbored barrels. DO NOT USE Standard Invector choke tubes in barrels marked for the Invector Plus choking system.

CITORI HUNTING MODELS - 12, 16 (mfg. 1986-89), 20, 28 ga. (disc. 1994) or .410 bore (disc. 1994), 26, 28, or 30 in. barrels, various chokes, boxlock, auto ejectors, SST, vent. rib, features checkered semi-pistol grip stock with grooved semi-beavertail forearm, grades differ in amount of engraving, finish, and wood. Invector chokes became standard in 1988, Invector Plus chokes became standard 1995 on 12 or 20 ga., 6 lbs. 9 oz. - 8 lbs. 5 oz. Mfg. 1973-2001 by Miroku.

* **Grade I 12 or 20 ga.** - blue finish with light scroll engraving beginning 1978.

>**Earlier Mfg. without Invector Choking**

	$750	$675	$575	$525	$475	$425	$395

Add 15% for 16 ga. if in 90%+ original condition.

>**Grade I Hunter Model** - recent Mfg. with Invector Choking - 12 or 20 ga., 3 in. chambers, 20 ga. available with Standard Invector or Invector Plus (new 1994) choking system, Invector Plus choking standard on recently mfg. 12 and 20 ga., 6 lbs. 9 oz. - 8 lbs. 5 oz. Disc. 2001.

	$1,110	$795	$675	$525	$465	$395	$350

Last MSR was $1,486.

* **Grade I Smaller Gauges**

>**28 ga. or .410 bore** - without Invector choking. Disc. 1994.

	$850	$700	$575	$495	$450	$395	$350

Last MSR was $1,097.

* **Grade II** - 12, 20, 28 ga., or .410 bore. Mfg. 1978-1983.

	$995	$810	$740	$685	$610	$570	$540

* **Grade III** - 12, 16 (mfg. 1986-89), 20, 28 ga. (disc. 1994), or .410 bore (disc. 1994), greyed steel receiver with engraved game scenes featuring grouse (20 ga.) and ducks (12 ga.), Invector chokes standard, Invector Plus became standard in 12 ga. in 1994. Mfg. 1985-95.

	$1,425	$1,025	$835	$725	$625	$585	$550

Last MSR was $1,875.

Add 15% for 16 ga. if in 90%+ original condition.

Add 15%-25% for 28 ga. or .410 bore (both disc. 1989).

* **Grade V** - 12, 20, 28 ga., or .410 bore, extensive deep relief engraving with game scenes on satin grey receiver. Disc. 1984.

	$1,550	$1,265	$1,100	$990	$880	$795	$695

GRADING - PPGS™	100%	98%	95%	90%	80%	70%	60%

✳ **Grade VI** - 12, 16 (mfg. 1986-89), 20, 28 ga. (disc. 1992), or .410 bore (disc. 1989), blue or greyed receiver with extensive engraving including multiple gold inlays, Standard Invector (12 ga. disc. 1993) or Invector Plus chokes. Mfg. 1985-95.

	$2,100	$1,500	$1,225	$1,000	$895	$795	$695

Last MSR was $2,715.

Add 15% for 16 ga. if in 90%+ original condition.
Add 15%-25% for 28 ga.

✳ **3 1/2 in. Magnum Model** - 12 ga., 3 1/2 in. chambers, 28 or 30 in. VR barrels with back-bored Invector plus choke tubes, with recoil pad, approx. 8 1/2 lbs. 9 oz. Mfg. 1989-2000.

	$1,250	$950	$825	$695	$600	$550	$495

Last MSR was $1,563.

✳ **Sporting Hunter** - 12 or 20 ga., 3 or 3 1/2 (12 ga. only) in. chambers, 26, 28, or 30 (12 ga. only) in. barrels with Invector Plus choking, configured for both hunting and sporting clays shooting, Superposed style forearm, contoured recoil pad, front and center bead sights, gloss or satin (3 1/2 in. only) wood finish, 6 lbs. 9 oz. - 8 lbs. 9 oz. Mfg. 1998-2001.

	$1,250	$895	$725	$585	$475	$425	$375

Last MSR was $1,607.

Add $102 for 3 1/2 in. Mag. (wood satin finish only).

✳ **Satin Hunter** - 12 ga. only, 3 or 3 1/2 (disc. 2000) in. chambers, 26, 28, or 30 (3 1/2 in. Mag. only, disc. 1998) in. VR backbored barrels with Invector Plus choking, features satin wood finish, approx. 8 1/4 lbs. Mfg. 1998-2001.

	$1,150	$825	$650	$535	$445	$400	$350

Last MSR was $1,535.

✳ **Upland Special** - 12, 16 (mfg. 1989 only), or 20 ga. (2 3/4 in. chambers), short-ened checkered straight grip walnut stock (14 in. LOP) and Schnabel forearm, 24 in. barrels, blue finish, Invector (12 ga. disc. 1993) or Invector Plus choking, 6-6 3/4 lbs. Mfg. 1984-2000.

	$1,125	$850	$660	$550	$450	$425	$395

Last MSR was $1,514.

Add 15% for 16 ga. if in 90%+ original condition.
Subtract $125 for Invector choking.

✳ **White Upland Special** - 12 or 20 ga., 2 3/4 in. chambers, similar to Upland Special, except features silver nitride finished receiver, 6 1/8 or 6 1/2 lbs. Mfg. 2000-2001.

	$1,185	$885	$785	$575	$465	$440	$400

Last MSR was $1,583.

CITORI SUPERLIGHT MODELS - 12, 16, 20, 28 ga., or .410 bore, 2 3/4 in. chambers except for .410 bore, English stock, oil finish, Invector chokes became standard in 1988, Invector Plus became standard 1995 for 12 or 20 ga., approx. 5 lbs., 11 oz. - 6 3/4 lbs. Mfg. 1983-present.

✳ **Grade I 12, 16, or 20 ga.**

>**Earlier Mfg. without Invector Choking**

	$795	$700	$600	$550	$495	$445	$395

>**Grade I** - recent Mfg. with Invector Choking - 12 or 20 ga., 20 ga. available with Standard Invector or Invector Plus (new 1994, became standard 1995) choking system, Invector Plus choking standard on recently mfg. 12 ga. Disc. 2002.

	$1,175	$875	$675	$575	$475	$425	$395

Last MSR was $1,590.

Subtract $125 for Standard Invector choking in 20 ga.

GRADING - PPGS™	100%	98%	95%	90%	80%	70%	60%

✳ Grade I Smaller Gauges

>28 ga. or .410 bore - without Invector choking until 1993, Invector choking became an option in 1994 and standard in 1995. Disc. 2002.

	$1,325	$925	$775	$675	$550	$495	$450

Last MSR was $1,666.

Subtract 10% if without Invector choke tubes.

✳ Superlight Feather - 12 or 20 (new 2002) ga., greyed alloy receiver, 26 in. Invector choked VR barrels, straight grip English stock and scaled down Schnabel forearm, 5.75 or 6.25 lbs. New 1999.

MSR $1,938	$1,475	$1,050	$825	$675	$535	$460	$425

✳ Grade III - same gauges as Grade I, Standard Invector on 12 or 20 (disc.) ga. or Invector Plus (standard in 12 ga. beginning 1994) chokes. Mfg. 1986-2002.

	$1,750	$1,275	$975	$825	$675	$600	$550

Last MSR was $2,300.

Add $270 for 28 ga. or .410 bore (disc. 1997).
Subtract 10% if without Invector choke tubes.

✳ Grade V - sideplate available. Disc. 1984.

	$1,550	$1,265	$1,100	$990	$880	$795	$695

✳ Grade VI - older mfg. has Invector chokes standard (option on 28 ga. or .410 bore beginning 1994) or Invector Plus (standard and available in 12 or 20 ga. only) chokes, choice of blue or grey (new 1996) receiver finish. Mfg. 1983-2002.

	$2,625	$1,875	$1,425	$1,250	$1,025	$850	$700

Last MSR was $3,510.

Subtract 10% for 28 ga. or .410 bore without choke tubes.
Add $270 for 28 ga. or .410 bore with Standard Invector choking.

✳ Grade VI Sideplate - 20 ga. only. Disc.

	$2,950	$2,250	$1,950	$1,775	$1,650	$1,400	$1,175

CITORI SPORTER MODELS - similar to Citori Superlight, except with 3 in. chambers, 26 in. barrels, various chokes, straight grip stock, Schnabel forearm. Disc. 1983.

	$875	$740	$600	$550	$495	$440	$385

Add $50 for 28 ga. or .410 bore.

✳ Sporter Grade II - 12, 20, 28 ga., or .410 bore.

	$1,250	$1,075	$1,020	$965	$880	$770	$715

✳ Sporter Grade V - 12, 20, 28 ga., or .410 bore.

	$1,575	$1,395	$1,225	$1,100	$990	$880	$825

CITORI LIGHTNING MODELS - 12, 16 (disc. 1989), 20, 28 ga., or .410 bore, 2 3/4 (28 ga. only), or 3 in. (standard on 12 ga., 20 ga., and .410 bore) chamber, 26, 28, or 30 (disc.) in. barrels, Invector chokes standard on newer mfg. smaller ga.'s, Invector Plus became standard 1995 for 12 or 20 ga., boxlock, auto ejectors, SST, vent. rib, features checkered round knob pistol grip stock and slimmer forearm, grades differ in amount of engraving, finish, and quality of wood, approx. 6.5-8 lbs. Introduced 1988.

✳ Grade I 12, 16 or 20 ga.

>Earlier Mfg. - without Invector Choking.

	$795	$700	$600	$550	$495	$445	$395

Add 15% for 16 ga.

>Grade I - current mfg. with Invector Choking - 12 or 20 ga., Invector (disc. 1994) or Invector Plus choking (became standard on 12 ga. in 1994, 20 ga. in 1995).

MSR $1,645	$1,210	$895	$750	$650	$550	$500	$460

Subtract 10% for Standard Invector choking.

This model was supplied with scroll engraving with rosette design until 2004. Beginning 2004, standard engraving is high relief, intricate, sculpted.

GRADING - PPGS™	100%	98%	95%	90%	80%	70%	60%

✴ *Grade I Smaller Gauges*

>28 ga. or .410 bore - without Invector choking until 1993, Invector choking became an option in 1994, standard in 1995.

MSR $1,709	$1,295	$1,025	$850	$725	$650	$600	$550

Subtract 10% if without Standard Invector choking.

✴ *Grade III* - 12, 16 (disc. 1989), or 20 ga., greyed steel receiver with engraved game scenes (mallards/pheasants on 12 ga., quail/grouse on 20 ga.), older mfg. may or may not have Invector choking, Invector Plus choking is now standard on 12 or 20 ga. Mfg. 1988-2004.

	$1,865	$1,350	$1,035	$850	$675	$600	$550

Last MSR was $2,464.

Subtract 10% if without Invector choking.
Add 15% for 16 ga. (disc. 1989).

>28 ga. or .410 bore- features quail and grouse scene engraving. Disc. 2004.

	$2,375	$1,995	$1,850	$1,600	$1,375	$1,175	$995

Last MSR was $2,754.

✴ *Grade IV* - 12 or 20 ga., high relief engraving on grey receiver (pheasants on left, mallards on right on 12 ga., quail and grouse on 20 ga.) triggerguard and tang screws, high gloss finished walnut stock and forearm. New 2005.

MSR $2,608	$1,975	$1,400	$1,075	$875	$725	$625	$550

>28 ga. or .410 bore- features quail and grouse inlays.

MSR $2,920	$2,500	$2,100	$1,900	$1,650	$1,400	$1,200	$995

✴ *Grade VI* - 12, 16 (disc. 1989), 20 ga., blue or greyed receiver with extensive deep relief engraving with 7 gold inlays, including mallards/pheasants on receiver sides. Disc. 2004.

	$2,825	$2,000	$1,475	$1,275	$1,025	$850	$700

Last MSR was $3,797.

Add 15% for 16 ga. (disc. 1989).

>28 ga. or .410 bore - disc. 2004.

	$3,075	$2,150	$1,575	$1,325	$1,175	$1,025	$950

Last MSR was $4,090.

✴ *Grade VII* - 12 or 20 ga., deep relief engraving on grey or blue receiver, triggerguard, top tang, takedown lever and bracket, 24Kt. gold bird inlays (two flushing ringnecks and pointer on right side with three mallards on left side on 12 ga., quail and grouse on 20 ga.), high gloss finished walnut stock and forearm. New 2005.

MSR $4,146	$3,175	$2,200	$1,600	$1,350	$1,200	$1,025	$950

>28 ga. or .410 bore- features quail and grouse inlays.

MSR $4,466	$3,325	$2,350	$1,700	$1,450	$1,275	$1,075	$975

CITORI MODEL 525 FIELD

CITORI MODEL 525 FIELD - 12, 20, 28 (new 2003) ga. or .410 bore (new 2003), 3 in. chambers, engraved silver nitride receiver, 26 or 28 in. unported barrels featuring VR with forward angled posts, pronounced walnut pistol grip stock with European comb, flush fit Invector Plus choke tubes, oil finished European checkered stock with vent recoil pad, Schnabel forearm, 6 lbs. 6 oz. – 8 lbs. New 2002.

MSR $1,981	$1,535	$1,075	$825	$675	$525	$475	$450

Add $29 for 28 ga. or .410 bore.

CITORI ESPRIT

CITORI ESPRIT - 12 ga. only, 3 in. chambers, 28 in. barrels with VR and 3 choke tubes, features removable and interchangeable sideplates, satin finished receiver, choice of scroll or pointer engraving scenes, gold enhancements are optional, 8 1/4 lbs. Mfg. 2002-2003.

	$1,935	$1,425	$1,075	$875	$725	$625	$575

Last MSR was $2,502.

GRADING - PPGS™	100%	98%	95%	90%	80%	70%	60%

CITORI PRIVILEGE - 12 or 20 (new 2001) ga., 3 in. chambers, boxlock with extensively hand engraved sideplates, silver finished receiver, 26 or 28 in. barrels with 5/16 in. VR and Invector Plus choking, approx. 8 lbs. Mfg. 2000-2003.

	$4,775	$4,075	$3,450	$2,875	$2,475	$2,025	$1,750

Last MSR was $5,537.

CITORI LIGHTNING FEATHER - 12 or 20 (new 2000) ga., 3 in. chambers, greyed alloy receiver with dovetailed steel breechface and steel hinge pin, 26 or 28 in. Invector choked VR barrels, select checkered round knob walnut stock and forearm with gloss finish, approx. 6.25 - 7 lbs. New 1999.

MSR $1,869	$1,450	$1,050	$800	$675	$525	$475	$450

* *Citori Lightning Feather Combo* - includes set of 27 in. 20 ga. (3 in. chambers) and 28 ga. barrels with Invector Plus (20 ga.) and standard Invector (28 ga.) chokes, includes luggage case, approx. 6.25 lbs. New 2000.

MSR $3,037	$2,575	$2,075	$1,875	$1,625	$1,375	$1,175	$995

CITORI GRAN LIGHTNING (GL) MODEL - 12, 20, 28 ga. (new 1994), or .410 bore (new 1994) only, 2 3/4 (28 ga. only) or 3 in. chambers, similar to Lightning Model, except has Grade V/VI walnut stock and forearm with satin/oil finish, includes recoil pad, 26 or 28 in. barrels, Invector chokes standard on newer mfg. smaller ga.'s, Invector Plus became standard 1995 for 12 or 20 ga., 6.25 - 8 lbs. New 1990.

MSR $2,429	$1,915	$1,350	$1,075	$950	$775	$675	$575

Add $128 for 28 ga. or .410 bore.

Add 15% for standard Invector chokes.

Beginning 2004, high relief intricate sculpted engraving replaced rosette, scroll type engraving.

CITORI WHITE LIGHTNING - 12, 20, 28 (new 2000) ga., or .410 bore (new 2000), 3 in. chambers, silver nitride receiver with engraving, satin wood finish with round pistol grip stock and vent recoil pad, 26 or 28 in. VR barrels with Invector Plus choking, 6 lbs. 7 oz - 8 lbs. 2 oz. New 1998.

MSR $1,714	$1,335	$995	$825	$675	$600	$550	$500

Add $76 for .28 ga. or .410 bore (new 2000).

Beginning 2004, high relief intricate sculpted engraving replaced rosette, scroll type engraving.

CITORI MICRO LIGHTNING - 20 ga. only, 2 3/4 in. chambers, 24 in. VR barrels, Invector (disc. 1993) or Invector Plus (new 1994) choking, 13 3/4 LOP (1/2 in. shorter), 6 lbs. 3 oz. Mfg. 1991-2001.

* *Grade I*

	$1,250	$945	$785	$650	$600	$550	$500

Last MSR was $1,591.

Subtract 10% for standard Invector choking.

* *Grade III* - Invector (disc. 1993) or Invector Plus choking. Mfg. 1993-94.

	$1,415	$1,050	$850	$750	$625	$585	$550

Last MSR was $1,850.

* *Grade VI* - Mfg. 1993-94.

	$2,025	$1,575	$1,225	$1,025	$895	$795	$695

Last MSR was $2,680.

Subtract $267 for standard Invector choking.

CITORI CLASSIC LIGHTNING GRADE I - 12 or 20 ga., 3 in. chambers, 26 or 28 in. vent. rib barrels, Invector Plus chokes, silver nitride receiver with Grade I Superposed engraving, Grade II/III oil finished slender lightning style walnut stock and forearm, 6 lbs. 10 oz. - 8 lbs., 2 oz. New 2005.

MSR $1,891	$1,475	$1,075	$850	$725	$650	$550	$475

CITORI CLASSIC LIGHTNING FEATHER GRADE I - 12 or 20 ga., 3 in. chambers, 26 or 28 in. vent. rib barrels, Invector Plus chokes, lightweight alloy receiver with high relief sculpted engraving, Grade II/III satin finished lightning style stock and Schnabel forearm, 6 lbs. 3 oz. - 7 lbs. New 2005.

MSR $1,952	$1,525	$1,125	$900	$750	$675	$575	$500

CITORI SUPER LIGHTNING GRADE I - 12 or 20 ga., 3 in. chambers, 26 or 28 in. vent. rib barrels, Invector Plus chokes, deep blue receiver with gold border accents, Grade II/III gloss finished lightning style stock and Schnabel forearm, 6 lbs. 7 oz. - 8 lbs. 2 oz. New 2005.

MSR $1,866	$1,450	$1,050	$850	$725	$650	$550	$475

SHOTGUNS: O/U, CITORI SKEET

Subtract 10%-15% for all Skeet models with 26 in. barrels.

CITORI SKEET/SPECIAL SKEET MODELS - 12, 20, 28 ga., or .410 bore, same action as Citori Field, only with high post target rib (standard 1985), 26 and 28 in. skeet barrels, recoil pad, Invector chokes became standard in 1990 in 12 and 20 ga., Invector Plus chokes with ported barrels were an option during 1992 and became standard on the 12 ga. in 1994, new Special Skeet models were introduced during 1995 with decreased weight (1/4 lb. lighter) and better swing/balance characteristics.

❊ *Grade I*

> **>12 or 20 Ga.** - Invector Plus choking, high-post target rib, and ported barrels became standard in 1994, 7 1/4 - 8 lbs. Disc. 2000.

	$1,295	$1,095	$995	$800	$625	$575	$500

Last MSR was $1,742.

Add $100 for factory adj. comb (mfg. 1995-98).

Subtract 10% if without Invector Plus chokes.

Subtract 30% for fixed chokes.

Earlier mfg. skeet guns had a low profile, wide VR.

> **> Smaller Guages**- 28 ga. or .410 bore, 6 lbs. 15 oz. Disc. 1999.

	$1,300	$950	$775	$650	$550	$500	$450

Last MSR was $1,627.

Subtract 20% if without Invector chokes.

❊ *Grade II* - 12, 20, 28 ga., or .410 bore, high rib. Disc. 1983.

	$1,000	$850	$800	$740	$690	$650	$600

❊ *Grade III* - 12, 20, 28 ga., or .410 bore, Invector chokes originally in 12 and 20 ga. and became an option on 28 ga. and .410 bore in 1994. Mfg. 1986-99.

> **>12 or 20 Ga.** - Invector Plus choking, high-post target rib, and ported barrels became standard in 1994. Disc. 1999.

	$1,600	$1,300	$975	$795	$650	$550	$495

Last MSR was $2,310.

Add $100 for factory adj. comb (mfg. 1995-98).

> **> Smaller Gauges**- 28 ga. or .410 bore. Disc. 1999.

	$1,795	$1,325	$975	$825	$675	$595	$550

Last MSR was $2,316.

Subtract 20% if without standard Invector choking (new 1994).

❊ *Grade V* - 12, 20, 28 ga., or .410 bore, high rib. Disc. 1984.

	$2,000	$1,800	$1,600	$1,500	$1,250	$795	$650

Add 20% for 20 ga. or 30% for 28 ga.or .410 bore.

❊ *Grade VI* - Skeet gauges, choice of blue or grey finished receiver with multi gold inlays, deluxe walnut. Disc. 1995.

GRADING - PPGS™	100%	98%	95%	90%	80%	70%	60%

>12 Ga - Invector Plus choking, high-post target rib, and ported barrels became standard in 1994.

	$2,025	$1,600	$1,325	$1,100	$960	$875	$825

Last MSR was $2,555.

>Smaller Gauges - 20, 28 ga., or .410 bore, 20 ga. available with standard Invector choking, 28 ga. and .410 bore are choked SK/SK.

	$2,000	$1,600	$1,325	$1,100	$960	$875	$825

Last MSR was $2,518.

✳ *Skeet Golden Clays (GC)* - 12, 20, 28 ga., or .410 bore, 26 or 28 in. ported VR barrels, Invector Plus choking, Skeet features, satin grey receiver with Grade VI level of engraving and gold inlays depicting a transitional hunting to clay pigeon scene. Disc. 1993-99.

> 12 or 20 Ga. - Invector (disc. 1995) or Invector Plus choking, high-post target rib, and ported barrels (12 ga. only).

	$2,600	$2,400	$2,250	$2,000	$1,800	$1,500	$1,000

Last MSR was $3,434.

Add $100 for factory adj. comb (mfg. 1995-98).
Subtract approx. 20% if without Invector Plus choking.

> Smaller Gauges - 28 ga. or .410 bore, standard Invector or fixed SK/SK choking.

	$2,725	$2,500	$2,250	$2,000	$1,250	$950	$850

Last MSR was $3,356.

Subtract approx. 20% with fixed choking.

CITORI XS SKEET - 12 or 20 (new 2001) ga., ported 28 or 30 in. vent. barrels with 5/16 in. VR and Invector Plus choking, silver nitride receiver with gold accents, checkered walnut stock available with or without adj. comb, features similar to the Ultra XS Sporting Model, includes triple trigger system, approx. 7-8.25 lbs. New 2000.

MSR $2,434	$1,800	$1,600	$1,400	$1,200	$1,000	$675	$575

Add $274 for adj. comb.

This model's nomenclature was changed from Ultra XS Skeet to Citori XS Skeet in 2002.

CITORI 3 GAUGE SKEET SETS - supplied with one 20 ga. frame, 1 removable forearm, and 3 barrels consisting of 20, 28 ga. and .410 bore, cased. Mfg. 1987-96.

✳ *Grade I* - with high post target rib, standard Invector choking became standard 1994.

	$2,525	$2,075	$1,675	$1,450	$1,275	$1,050	$975

Last MSR was $3,100.

✳ *Grade III* - with high post target rib, available with standard Invector choking (new 1994) or fixed SK/SK chokes.

	$3,100	$2,350	$1,875	$1,550	$1,395	$1,250	$1,125

Last MSR was $3,900.

Subtract 20% for fixed SK/SK chokes.

✳ *Grade VI* - with high post target rib, fixed SK/SK chokes only. Disc. 1994.

	$3,250	$2,500	$2,000	$1,775	$1,600	$1,400	$1,275

Last MSR was $3,990.

✳ *Golden Clays* - features Golden Clays accents and engraving, standard Invector choking. Mfg. 1994-95 only.

	$4,250	$3,075	$2,600	$2,100	$1,900	$1,750	$1,600

Last MSR was $5,100.

CITORI 4 GAUGE SKEET SETS - supplied with one 12 ga. frame, 1 removable forearm, and 4 barrels consisting of 12, 20, 28 ga., and .410 bore, cased. Imported 1985 only.

GRADING - PPGS™	100%	98%	95%	90%	80%	70%	60%

* *Grade I* - with high post target rib, choice of standard Invector (new 1994) or fixed SK/SK choking.

| | $3,750 | $2,850 | $2,400 | $1,975 | $1,800 | $1,775 | $1,600 |

Last MSR was $4,450.

Subtract 10% for fixed SK/SK choking.

* *Grade III* - with high post target rib, choice of standard Invector (new 1994) or fixed SK/SK choking.

| | $4,575 | $3,250 | $2,700 | $2,250 | $1,950 | $1,800 | $1,700 |

Last MSR was $5,450.

Subtract 20% for fixed SK/SK choking.

* *Grade VI* - with high post target rib, fixed SK/SK choking only. Disc. 1994.

| | $4,600 | $3,350 | $2,775 | $2,300 | $2,100 | $2,000 | $1,900 |

Last MSR was $5,225.

* *Golden Clays* - features Golden Clays accents and engraving, standard Invector choking. Mfg. 1994 only.

| | $5,650 | $4,100 | $3,300 | $2,600 | $2,350 | $2,100 | $1,975 |

Last MSR was $6,750.

SHOTGUNS: O/U, CITORI SPORTING CLAYS

All sporting clays models mfg. after 1994 have the Triple Trigger System which includes 3 interchangeable trigger shoes.

MODEL 325 - 12 or 20 ga., 28, 30, or 32 (12 ga. only) in. 10mm VR barrels with Invector Plus choking, 12 ga. has ported barrels, European styling featuring checkered walnut stock and Schnabel forearm, greyed nitrous finished receiver, top tang safety, SST, ejectors, 6 lbs. 12 oz. - 7 lbs. 15 oz. Mfg. 1993-94.

| | $1,095 | $995 | $850 | $715 | $575 | $495 | $450 |

Last MSR was $1,625.

* *Model 325 Golden Clays* - 12 or 20 ga., 28, 30, or 32 in. ported (12 ga. only) or unported (20 ga. only) VR barrels, Invector Plus choking, Model 325 Grade II features, satin grey receiver with engraving and gold inlays depicting a transitional hunting to clay pigeon scene. Mfg. 1994 only.

| | $2,000 | $1,850 | $1,450 | $1,150 | $975 | $875 | $825 |

Last MSR was $3,030.

MODEL 425 SPORTING CLAYS GRADE I - 12 or 20 ga., 28, 30, or 32 (disc. 2000 - 12 ga. only, adj. comb) in. 10mm VR barrels with Invector Plus choking, 12 ga. has ported barrels, with or without adj. comb (disc. 2000), European styling featuring checkered walnut stock and Schnabel forearm, mono-bloc action with greyed nitrous finished receiver, top tang safety, SST, ejectors, solid pad, approx. 6 3/4 - 8 lbs. Mfg. 1995-2001.

| | $1,400 | $1,200 | $1,000 | $825 | $725 | $625 | $525 |

Last MSR was $2,006.

Add $231 for adj. comb.

* *Model 425 Golden Clays (GC)* - 12 or 20 ga., 28, 30, or 32 (disc. 1999) in. ported (12 ga. only) or unported (20 ga. only) VR barrels, with (disc. 1998) or without adj. comb, Invector Plus choking, Model 325 Grade II features, satin grey receiver with engraving and gold inlays depicting a transitional hunting to clay pigeon scene, 6 lbs., 13 oz. - 7 lbs., 14 oz. Mfg. 1995-2001.

| | $2,500 | $2,275 | $1,675 | $1,325 | $1,100 | $995 | $875 |

Last MSR was $3,977.

Add $100 for factory adj. comb (disc. 1998).

* *Model 425 WSSF* - 12 ga. only, special dimensions for Women's Shooting Sports Foundation, features painted turquoise finish with WSSF logo on stock or natural walnut finish (new 1997), 7 1/4 lbs. Mfg. 1995-99.

| | $1,550 | $1,075 | $895 | $725 | $575 | $495 | $450 |

Last MSR was $1,855.

MODEL 525 SPORTING

- 12, 20, 28 (new 2003) ga., or .410 bore (new 2003), 2 3/4 in. chambers, 28, 30, or 32 (new 2003) in. vent. barrels with 8-11 mm (12 ga. only) or 10 mm (20 ga. only) width canted VR and porting (12 or 20 ga. only), Hi-Viz Pro-Comp sights, redesigned stock, includes full set of Midas Grade Invector Plus choke tubes (non-flush), oil finished European style checkered Grade III/IV walnut stock with palm swell and forearm, 7–8 1/4 lbs. New 2002.

	MSR $2,778	$2,150	$1,725	$1,350	$1,000	$895	$775	$675

Add $9 for 28 ga. or .410 bore.

Add $280 for adj. comb stock (new 2004, 12 or 20 ga.).

✽ *Model 525 Sporting Grade I* - 12 ga. only, 3 in. chambers, 28, 30, or 32 in. barrels, silver nitride receiver with light 525 style field engraving, Grade I American walnut stock and Schnabel forearm, right hand palm swell, tapered floating rib, triple trigger system, three Invector Plus choke tubes, Hi-Viz Pro-Comp sight, approx. 8 lbs. New 2005.

	MSR $2,319	$1,850	$1,375	$1,050	$900	$775	$675	$575

MODEL 525 GOLDEN CLAYS

- 12, 20, 28 (new 2003) ga. or .410 bore (new 2003), similar features to the Model 525 Sporting, except has oil finished Grade V/VI walnut stock and forearm, engraving pattern that depicts the transistion of a game bird into a clay bird in 24Kt. gold, includes 5 Midas Grade Invector Plus choke tubes (non-flush), 7-8.5 lbs. New 2002.

	MSR $4,450	$3,475	$2,475	$1,800	$1,375	$1,100	$995	$875

Add $203 for 28 ga. or .410 bore.

XS GOLDEN CLAYS

- 12 or 20 ga. only, similar to Model 525 Golden Clays, except has traditional checkering pattern and 1/2 - 3/8 in. width VR, includes 3 choke tubes. Mfg. 2002-2003.

		$2,295	$1,995	$1,650	$1,325	$1,100	$995	$875

Last MSR was $3,914.

MODEL 802 EXTENDED SWING (ES) SPORTING

- 12 ga. only, 2 3/4 in. chambers, features 28 in. ventilated ported VR barrels (low post, 6.2mm wide) which accept either Invector Plus 2 or 4 stainless steel extension tubes (extends barrels to 30 or 32 in.), adj. pull trigger, slimmer checkered and Schnabel forearm, 7 lbs. 5 oz. Mfg. 1996-2001.

		$1,295	$1,095	$975	$800	$700	$600	$550

Last MSR was $2,063.

GTI GRADE I

- 12 ga. only, 28 or 30 in. barrel with 13mm vent. rib and barrels, red lettering on receiver during 1989 only - changed to gold lettering and borders with Browning logo in 1990, checkered stock and semi-beavertail forearm, ported barrels were introduced 1990 and became standard 1992, Invector chokes standard, back-bored Invector plus chokes became standard in 1990, approx. 8 lbs. Mfg. 1989-94.

		$950	$850	$750	$600	$525	$495	$450

Last MSR was $1,450.

Subtract $100 for standard chokes.

Add $35 for Signature Painted Model.

The Signature Painted Model includes special paint treatment on stock and forearm featuring Browning logos and trademark - new 1993.

✽ *GTI Golden Clays* - 12 ga. only, 28, 30, or 32 in. ported VR barrels, Invector Plus choking, GTI features, satin grey receiver with Grade VI level of engraving and gold inlays depicting a transitional hunting to clay pigeon scene. Mfg. 1993-94.

		$2,000	$1,800	$1,450	$1,150	$975	$875	$825

Last MSR was $2,930.

GRADING - PPGS™	100%	98%	95%	90%	80%	70%	60%

GRADE I SPECIAL SPORTING - 12 ga. only, 2 3/4 in. chambers, target dimensions, high-post tapered rib, 28, 30, or 32 in. barrels, full pistol grip with palm swell, adj. comb became optional in 1994, approx. 8 lbs. 3 oz. Mfg. 1989-99.

	$1,095	$925	$775	$635	$525	$495	$450

Last MSR was $1,636.

> **Add $100 for factory adj. comb.**
>
> **Add $35 for Signature Painted Model (disc. 1994).**
>
> **Add $800 for 2 barrel set (28 and 30 in. barrels), disc. 1990.**
>
> The Signature Painted Model includes special paint treatment on stock and forearm featuring Browning logos and trademark - mfg. 1993-94.
>
> Ported barrels were new in 1990 and became standard in 1992.
>
> In 1990, the Grade I designation was added to this model. Changes include back-bored barrels with Invector plus choke tubes.

* ✳ *Special Sporting Golden Clays (GC)* - 12 ga. only, 28, 30, or 32 in. ported barrels with high- post VR, Invector Plus choking, Special Sporting features, satin grey receiver with Grade VI level of engraving and gold inlays depicting a transitional hunting to clay pigeon scene. Mfg. 1993-98.

	$2,000	$1,800	$1,500	$1,175	$995	$875	$825

Last MSR was $3,203.

> **Add $100 for factory adj. comb.**

GRADE I SPECIAL SPORTING PIGEON GRADE - 12 ga. only, Vector Plus choking and ported barrels, higher grade of Special Sporting model featuring higher grade walnut and gold line receiver accents. Mfg. 1993-94.

	$1,200	$975	$850	$700	$575	$495	$450

Last MSR was $1,630.

ULTRA SPORTER - 12 ga. only, 28, 30, or 32 in. barrels with vent rib separating barrels, low tapered 13- 10mm VR, blue or grey (new 1996) receiver with gold accents, satin finished checkered pistol grip stock and forearm, Invector Plus choking, 7 lbs. 10 oz. - 8 lbs. 4 oz. Mfg. 1995-99.

	$1,525	$1,050	$875	$750	$575	$495	$450

Last MSR was $1,800.

> **Add $210 for adj. comb (disc. 1998).**
>
> This model was designated GTI until 1995.

* ✳ *Ultra Sporter Golden Clays (GC)* - 12 ga. only, features better wood and satin finished engraved receiver with gold inlays clay target scene. Mfg. 1995-99.

	$2,000	$1,800	$1,575	$1,200	$1,000	$875	$825

Last MSR was $3,396.

> **Add $210 for adj. comb (disc. 1997).**

CITORI FEATHER XS SPORTING - 12, 20, 28 ga., or .410 bore, 2 3/4 in. chambers (3 in. standard on .410 bore), 28 or 30 in. vent. barrels with tapered VR (12 ga. only) and Invector Plus choking on 12 and 20 ga. (standard Invector on 28 ga. and .410 bore, 28 in. barrels), alloy receiver with dovetailed steel breechface and hinge pin, satin finished checkered walnut pistol grip stock with Schnabel forearm, Hi-Viz comp. sighting system (includes 8 interchangeable colored light pipes), Nitex receiver finish, includes triple trigger system (3 interchangeable trigger shoes), 6 lbs. (28 ga. or .410 bore) - approx. 7 lbs. (12 ga., 30 in. barrels). Mfg. 2000-2002.

	$1,700	$1,375	$1,150	$995	$875	$775	$675

Last MSR was $2,311.

GRADING - PPGS™	100%	98%	95%	90%	80%	70%	60%

CITORI XS SPORTING (ULTRA) - 12, 20, 28 ga. (disc. 2003) or .410 bore (disc. 2003), greyed steel receiver with silver nitride finish, 24Kt. gold accents and light engraving, 28, 30, or 32 (new 2003) in. barrels, with or w/o (30 in. barrels only) barrel porting, 12 ga. features flush Invector Plus choking and right-hand palm swell, Hi-Viz Pro-Comp sight, triple trigger system, select checkered walnut stock with satin finish and Schnabel forearm, 6 lbs. 5 oz. – 7 lbs. 14 oz. New 1999.

	MSR $2,472	$1,650	$1,400	$1,150	$995	$875	$750	$650

> **Add 10% for 28 ga. or .410 bore.**

CITORI LIGHTNING SPORTING (GRADE I) - 12 ga. only, features 3 in. chambers, rounded pistol grip, Lightning style forearm, choice of high or low post VR, standard or adj. (new 1995) comb stock, "Lightning Sporting Clays Edition" inscribed and gold-filled on receiver, triple trigger system, 28 in. ported or 30 in. ported or unported (disc.) barrels, approx. 8 1/2 lbs. Mfg. 1989-2004.

	$1,300	$1,045	$885	$765	$650	$550	$495

> *Last MSR was $1,794.*

> **Add $100 for adj. comb (disc. 1998).**

> **Subtract $100 for low rib.**

The Signature Painted Model includes special paint treatment on stock and forearm featuring Browning logos and trademark - mfg. 1993-94.

Ported barrels were new in 1990 and became standard in 1992.

Between 1990-2000, the Grade I designation was added to this model. Changes include back-bored barrels with Invector plus choke tubes.

✱ *Lightning Sporting Golden Clays (GC)* - 12 ga. only, 28, 30, or 32 (disc.) in. ported barrels with choice of low or high-post VR, standard or adj. (new 1995) comb stock, Invector Plus choking, Lightning Sporting features, satin grey receiver with Grade VI level of engraving and gold inlays depicting a transitional hunting to clay birds scene, approx. 8 1/2 lbs. Mfg. 1993-98.

	$2,000	$1,850	$1,475	$1,150	$995	$875	$825

> *Last MSR was $3,092.*

> **Add $100 for factory adj. comb.**

> **Subtract $100 for low post rib.**

GRADE I LIGHTNING SPORTING PIGEON GRADE - 12 ga. only, higher grade model featuring higher grade walnut and gold line receiver accents. Mfg. 1993-94.

	$1,195	$950	$850	$700	$575	$495	$450

> *Last MSR was $1,566.*

> **Subtract $100 for low post rib.**

SPORTING HUNTER - please refer to description and pricing under Shotguns: O/U Citori Hunting Series category.

SHOTGUNS: O/U, CITORI TARGET

CITORI XS SPECIAL - 12 ga. only, 2 3/4 in. chambers, 30 or 32 in. vent. barrels, silver nitride receiver with XS Special engraving, adj. comb, floating 8-11mm tapered rib, includes triple trigger system and 5 Midas Grade Invector Plus chokes (non-flush), approx. 8.75 lbs. New 2004.

	MSR $2,727	$2,000	$1,725	$1,375	$1,075	$950	$850	$750

SHOTGUNS: O/U, CITORI TRAP

CITORI TRAP MODELS - 12 ga., similar to Standard Citori, 30 or 32 in. barrels, trap chokes, Monte Carlo stock, recoil pad. Invector chokes became standard in 1988, Invector Plus chokes with ported barrels became an option in 1992, and were made standard in 1993, new Special Trap models were introduced during 1995 with decreased weight (1/4 lb. lighter) and better swing/balance characteristics. Mfg. 1974-current.

GRADING - PPGS™	100%	98%	95%	90%	80%	70%	60%

❋ *Grade I* - w/o choke tube, mfg. 1974-78.

	$900	$800	$750	$650	$525	$495	$450

❋ *Grade I Special Trap* - approx. 8 1/2 lbs. Mfg. 1995-99.

	$1,295	$975	$795	$650	$525	$495	$450

Last MSR was $1,658.

Add $100 for factory adj. comb.
Subtract 20% without Invector chokes or high rib.

❋ *Trap Combination Set* - Grade I only, 32 in. O/U and 34 in. single barrel, cased. Disc.

	$1,295	$1,100	$975	$900	$825	$775	$725

❋ *Grade I Plus Trap* - features adj. rib and stock, back-bored barrels, Invector Plus choke system. Mfg. 1990-94.

	$1,560	$1,200	$940	$800	$700	$600	$500

Last MSR was $2,005.

Add 5% for ported barrels.

In 1991 this model included a travel vault gun case at no extra charge. Subtract $50 for older mfg. without travel case.

❋ *Grade I Plus Trap Combo* - includes ported barrels with Invector Plus choking and extra standard single ported barrel, luggage case. Mfg. 1992-94.

	$2,500	$2,425	$2,100	$1,900	$1,700	$1,500	$1,250

Last MSR was $3,435.

❋ *Plus Trap Golden Clays* - 12 ga. only, 30 or 32 in. ported VR barrels, Invector Plus choking, Trap features, satin grey receiver with Grade VI level of engraving and gold inlays depicting a transitional hunting to clay birds scene. Mfg. 1993-94.

	$2,400	$2,275	$1,900	$1,600	$1,400	$1,200	$995

Last MSR was $3,435.

❋ *Plus Trap Golden Clays Combo* - includes O/U ported barrels with Invector Plus choking and extra standard single ported barrel, luggage case. Mfg. 1993-94.

	$4,425	$3,300	$2,775	$2,250	$1,925	$1,800	$1,700

Last MSR was $5,200.

❋ *Citori XT Trap* - 12 ga. only, features greyed receiver with 24Kt. gold accents and light engraving, triple trigger system (includes 3 interchangeable triggers for 1/8 in. adj. on LOP), 30 or 32 in. vent. backbored barrels with high-post VR, checkered high gloss Monte Carlo walnut stock and forearm, right hand palm swell, waffle-style recoil pad, approx. approx. 8 3/8 lbs. New 1999.

MSR $2,275	$1,600	$1,400	$1,200	$1,000	$800	$700	$500

Add $274 for adj. comb.

❋ *Citori XT Trap Gold* - 12 ga. only, 2 3/4 in. chambers, features intricate "Golden Clays" engraving with game bird/clay bird, Grade V/VI American walnut stock and semi-beavertail forearm, vented 30 or 32 in. ported barrels with high post VR and Invector Plus choke system with five flush Midas Grade chokes, adj. comb, adj. GraCoil recoil reduction system, triple trigger system, Hi-Viz Pro-Comp sight with mid-bead, approx. 9 lbs. New 2005.

MSR $4,221	$3,500	$2,525	$1,850	$1,475	$1,150	$995	$875

❋ *Pigeon Grade* - 12 ga. only, features extra deluxe walnut, Invector Plus ported barrels, and receiver gold accents. Mfg. 1993-94.

	$1,715	$1,250	$950	$800	$700	$600	$500

Last MSR was $2,225.

❋ *Signature Painted* - 12 ga. only, features painted red/black stock with Browning logos on stock and forearm, Invector Plus ported barrels. Mfg. 1993-94.

	$1,595	$1,200	$940	$800	$700	$600	$500

Last MSR was $2,065.

GRADING - PPGS™	100%	98%	95%	90%	80%	70%	60%

✳ *Grade II* - high post rib. Mfg. 1978-1983.

	$1,000	$850	$800	$740	$690	$650	$600

✳ *Grade III* - 12 ga. only, high post rib, Invector Plus choking and ported barrels became standard in 1994. Mfg. 1986-99.

	$1,795	$1,250	$950	$795	$625	$550	$495

Last MSR was $2,310.

Add $100 for factory adj. comb.

Subtract 10% if without Invector Plus chokes or ported barrels.

✳ *Grade V* - high post rib. Mfg. 1978-1984.

	$1,475	$1,150	$990	$880	$795	$710	$620

✳ *Grade VI* - 12 ga. only, Invector chokes became standard in 1985, Invector Plus chokes became standard in 1994. Disc. 1994.

	$1,925	$1,525	$1,225	$1,100	$960	$875	$825

Last MSR was $2,555.

Subtract $150 if without Invector Plus chokes or ported barrels.

✳ *Trap Golden Clays (GC)* - 12 ga. only, 30 or 32 in. ported VR barrels, Invector Plus choking, Trap features, Monte Carlo or regular stock, satin grey receiver with Grade VI level of engraving and gold inlays depicting a transitional hunting to clay pigeon scene. Mfg. 1993-99.

	$2,600	$2,300	$2,000	$1,750	$1,500	$1,250	$825

Last MSR was $3,434.

Add $220 for adj. comb (new 1995).

CITORI XS PRO-COMP - 12 ga. only, 2 3/4 in. chambers, 28 or 30 in. vent. and ported VR barrels with spreader chokes, adj. comb, beavertail forearm, GraCoil recoil reduction system, right-hand palm swell, triple trigger system, features removable tungsten alloy forearm weight which approximates the same weight as barrel tubes, also has removable/removable front barrel weight to adj. the swing through, approx. 9 lbs. Mfg. 2002-2004.

	$3,350	$2,400	$1,750	$1,425	$1,100	$975	$850

Last MSR was $4,027.

SHOTGUNS: O/U, SUPERPOSED GENERAL INFO & CHOKE CODES

SUPERPOSED MODEL - 12, 20 (introduced circa 1948-49), 28 ga. (introduced 1960) or .410 bore (introduced 1960), 26 1/2, 28, 30, or 32 in. barrels, various chokes, boxlock, auto ejectors, various trigger combinations (single & double), checkered pistol grip stock, mfg. 1931-40 and 1948-76 by FN, grades differ in amount of engraving, inlays, general quality of workmanship and wood.

NOTE: The use of steel shot is NOT recommended in any Superposed Series manufactured in Belgium (B-25 variations).

BROWNING CHOKES AND THEIR CODES (MARKED NEXT TO EJECTORS)

* designates full choke (F).

*- designates improved modified choke (IM).

** designates modified choke (M).

**- designates improved cylinder choke (IC).

**$ designates skeet (SK).

*** designates cylinder bore (CYL).

SKEET MODELS were available in every ga. and grade.

TRAP MODELS were available in every grade in 12 ga. only.

BROADWAY TRAP MODELS (mfg. 1961-75) featured a 5/8 in. wide vent. rib and were also available in every grade.

Please refer to the new expanded Browning Superposed serialization section in this text for determining year of manufacture.

GRADING - PPGS™	100%	98%	95%	90%	80%	70%	60%

SUPERPOSED: 1931-1940 MFG. (PRE-WWII)

Early pre-war guns had long slender forearms with a metal plate at the front called a horseshoe plate. Approx. circa 1936, the forearm was changed to the one used post war – smaller with a transverse bolt to hold the forearm on. The earlier forearm had a long bolt that ran from front to back through the metal plate to hold the forearm on. The earlier transverse bolts were recessed into the sides of the forearms. Later the head and fastener on the other side of the forearm were flush with the wood.

Pre-war cases were manufactured in black or brown, with a textured surface called elephant hide, in leather or tex leather. Insides were lined with grey or blue cloth, and the Browning brass label was on the inside top of the case, not the outside. Depending on original condition, these cases sell in the $200-$400 range – single barrel cases are more common than multi-barrel ones.

Extra barrels (same ga. only) could be ordered with the original gun, and were supplied in a Browning hard case.

Very few pre-war Pigeon, Diana, and Midas Grades were signed by the engraver.

Add approx. 35%-50% per extra set of barrels (same ga. only), depending on condition.

Subtract 10%-25% for recoil pad (depending on originality, deterioration, and condition).

STANDARD GRADE/GRADE I/LIGHTNING - 12 ga. only, boxlock action, blue w/border receiver engraving until 1938, when a simple small center rosette engraving pattern was introduced, 4 trigger options until 1938, when the barrel selector was moved to the top tang, trigger options included: double normal, selective single with the selector on the bottom next to the trigger, twin single, and non- selective single, Standard model nomenclature was changed to Grade I during 1938, in addition to changing the trigger to SST with the barrel selector on the top tang, raised hollow or ventilated rib, Lightning Model introduced during 1936 in Standard grade with striped barrels – ribs were extra cost. Original buttplates featured intertwined twin circles and were made of horn.

	12 ga.	N/A	$2,200	$1,650	$1,325	$1,050	$900	$825

Original buttplates with unaltered (uncut) stock are very important to collectors for this period of Superposed manufacture.

First year production Superposed will command a premium (approx. ser. no. range 1-2,000). The twin single trigger is also very desirable for collectors.

Recoil pads were an extra option during this time, and even though they might be factory installed, they are not desirable to collectors, and as a result, prices could be reduced substantially based on pad deterioration. Pad makers included: Jostam, Hawkins, Noshoc, D&W, and Black Diamond – these pads were $5 options pre-WWII.

PIGEON GRADE - grey receiver with 2 pigeons on either side, these earlier guns had larger engraved pigeons than later production (1960 and later). Mfg. 1931-40.

	12 ga.	N/A	$4,350	$3,700	$2,950	$2,250	$1,600	$1,400

The Pigeon Grade style of engraving is the only pre-war style that was continued after WWII.

DIANA GRADE - grey receiver with lighter style, delicate European style engraving, boars and stags were pictured in the 1931 catalog, but dogs and birds could also be special ordered at no additional cost until 1936, after which it became extra cost, dogs and birds engraving are more common than boars and stag. Mfg. 1931-40.

	12 ga.	N/A	$6,500	$5,250	$4,000	$3,375	$2,750	$2,000

The Diana Grade was changed dramatically in post-WWII production.

MIDAS GRADE - featured gold inlaid pigeons with outstretched wings on blue frame sides and bottom plus trigger guard. This Germanic syle engraving also exhibited multiple gold escutcheons and gold lining, ejector trip rods, ejector hammers and firing pins are also 18Kt. gold plated, finest checkered walnut.

	12 ga.	N/A	$7,750	$6,500	$5,250	$3,650	$3,000	$2,450

The Midas Grade was changed dramatically in post-WWII production.

SUPERPOSED: 1948-1960 MFG. (POST-WWII)

Model nomenclature was changed from pre-war designations to Grades I-VI. During this period, extra barrels could only be ordered in the same gauge as the original gun. Hardshell cases from this era are referred to as Tolex cases – they have blue velvet lining, and a brass Browning label on the outside top.

Engraved guns signed by Browning's top engravers (Funken, Vrancken, Watrin, Doyen, Müller, & Magis) will command a premium over unsigned guns. Felix Funken retired in 1960, and died in 1966.

On most Superposed with added recoil pads, the stock has usually been cut to keep the LOP the same. The correct LOP on a Superposed is 14 1/4 inches, with or w/o a recoil pad.

The twin circle buttplate was always horn, and was used on very early post war guns until 1949-1950.

Barrel addresses appeared as follows: circa 1947-1958 "St. Louis, M.O." (earliest BAC markings) or "St. Louis, Missouri", 1959-1968 "St. Louis, Missouri and Montreal P.Q.", 1969-1975 "Morgan, Utah and Montreal, P.Q.". Make sure barrel address date matches year of mfg. (see listings in the back of this text).

The original factory configuration of almost all Superposed shotguns can be verified by grade, gauge/bore, and barrel length. To obtain information on a specific Belgian Superposed serial number, please contact the Browning historian directly (refer to Trademark Index for more information).

> Add approx. 35%-50% per extra set of barrels (same ga. only), depending on condition.
> Add $200-$300 for correct Tolex hardshell case with paperwork.
> Subtract $150-$500 for non-original recoil pads on Grade I models, depending on condition.
> Subtract $250-$750 for non-original recoil pads on the higher grades, depending on condition.
> Special order Superposed with non-standard factory engraving, checkered buttstocks, 3 piece forearms, and other special orders will command premiums over standard configurations.

GRADE I STANDARD WEIGHT - 12 or 20 ga. (3 in. chambers were introduced in the 12 ga. during 1955, and in 20 ga. during 1957), otherwise similar to pre-war mfg., blue finish and triggers until 1955, gold trigger(s) became standard in 1955, raised (standard until 1959) or vent. rib only beginning in 1959, round knob long tang (RKLT) stock configuration, this earlier period of mfg. also featured smaller, narrower forearms and thinner pistol grip stock with horn buttplate (can be determined by the rounded "g" in Browning, not square), early post-war production had similar pre-WWII minimal engraving until circa 1952-53, more standard engraving continued through 1955, when Grade I models featured considerably more engraving, post-war 12 ga. serialization began at approx. 17,100, and with 200 on 20 ga. Mfg. 1948-60.

	100%	98%	95%	90%	80%	70%	60%
12 ga.	$1,995	$1,550	$1,100	$950	$825	$750	$700
20 ga.	$3,300	$2,875	$2,200	$1,600	$1,275	$1,100	$995

Grade I models had 3 levels of standard engraving coverage.

✳ *Grade I Lightning Hunting Model* - 12 or 20 ga., 6 oz. lighter than Standard Weight. Introduced in all Grades beginning 1956.

	100%	98%	95%	90%	80%	70%	60%
12 ga.	$1,995	$1,550	$1,100	$950	$825	$750	$700
20 ga.	$3,300	$2,875	$2,200	$1,600	$1,275	$1,100	$995

✳ *Grade I Magnum* - 12 ga. only, 3 in. chambers, 28, 30, or 32 in. barrels with raised or vent. rib, recoil pad standard, introduced in all Grades in 1955.

	100%	98%	95%	90%	80%	70%	60%
	$1,995	$1,650	$1,300	$1,075	$875	$800	$725

This model with 30 in. barrels is now popular again, as Sporting Clays shooters like this desirable configuration.

GRADING - PPGS™	100%	98%	95%	90%	80%	70%	60%

✳ Grade I Trap Standard Weight Model - 12 ga. only, various configurations, Introduced 1952.

	100%	98%	95%	90%	80%	70%	60%
	$1,995	$1,650	$1,300	$1,075	$850	$750	$700

Pre-war trap guns and those manufactured post-war until approx. 1955 were virtually indistinguishable from field guns as they had field style forearms, round knob (semi-pistol grip) and long tangs. The only way to tell the difference is they had a longer LOP (14 1/2 in.) and a shorter drop at the heel – 1 3/4 in. vs. 2 1/2 in. for field stocks. These early trap guns did not come with recoil pads. Between 1956-1960, trap guns had the forearm changed to semi- beavertail. These late guns with semi-beavertail forearms are very desirable today due to their rarity and overall desirability.

GRADE II - featured pre-war Pigeon Grade engraving with large pigeons, some early post- war mfg. were signed by Funken.

	100%	98%	95%	90%	80%	70%	60%
12 ga.	$3,750	$3,150	$2,600	$1,900	$1,650	$1,550	$1,450
20 ga.	$6,500	$5,800	$4,850	$3,900	$3,200	$2,500	$1,850

GRADE III - 12 or 20 ga., European style engraving, commonly referred to as "fighting cocks," pheasants on right side, fighting cocks on left, most were signed by the engraver.

	100%	98%	95%	90%	80%	70%	60%
12 ga.	$4,500	$3,600	$2,850	$2,150	$1,850	$1,650	$1,550
20 ga.	$8,950	$7,750	$6,500	$5,750	$4,500	$3,650	$2,750

GRADE IV - 12 or 20 ga., features deeper European style engraving with dogs and foxes, most were signed by the engraver.

	100%	98%	95%	90%	80%	70%	60%
12 ga.	$7,000	$6,000	$5,000	$3,500	$1,850	$1,700	$1,625
20 ga.	$11,500	$10,000	$8,000	$6,500	$4,500	$3,200	$2,800

GRADE V - 12 or 20 ga., features deeper engraving than pre-war Diana Grade, pheasants and ducks on reciever, most were signed by the engraver – Doyen was prevalant on this model.

	100%	98%	95%	90%	80%	70%	60%
12 ga.	$7,000	$6,000	$5,000	$3,500	$2,500	$1,800	$1,700
20 ga.	$9,500	$8,000	$6,500	$5,000	$3,750	$2,950	$2,450

GRADE VI - 12 or 20 ga., engraving pattern similar to later production Midas Grade, almost all of these were signed by Müller. Introduced in July, 1957, changed in 1960, limited production, and rarest of the 6 grades.

	100%	98%	95%	90%	80%	70%	60%
12 ga.	$7,650	$6,400	$5,250	$3,750	$2,625	$1,950	$1,750
20 ga.	$22,000	$16,500	$11,000	$6,500	$4,500	$3,950	$3,600

SUPERPOSED:1960-1976 MFG.

In early 1960, a major change was made in the manner in which the various grades of Superposed were designated. The Roman numerals used in the 1950s were dropped, and Browning once again returned to names. The Pigeon, Diana, and Midas names used for pre-war designations were brought back and replaced the Grade II, Grade V, and Grade VI respectively. Grades III & IV were dropped and replaced by the Pointer. The Grade I remained unchanged.

The Broadway Trap Model was introduced in 1961. Browning's lifetime Superposed warranty began in 1963. During 1965, the Hydro Coil stock (1 year only) and barrel Super Tubes were introduced. During 1966, a major change was implemented to save money when Browning switched from a long tang to short tang. During 1970-71, the stock configuration was once again changed to a full pistol grip (referred to as flat knob), and the long tang was brought back. Also at this time, mechanical triggers were implemented vs. the older inertial design, and silver solder vent. ribs vs. tin solder. As a result, this period of Superposed manufacture was mechanically better and more reliable. The Superlight Model was introduced in 12 ga. during 1967, 20 ga. during 1969, and became available in all Grades beginning in 1971. All gauge Skeet sets became available in all Grades during 1972.

During late 1966, Browning's salt wood problems began to emerge, and continued until 1972. Most experts have never seen a long tang salt gun, and therefore believe that almost 100% of the salt guns had short tangs. Depending on the damage (it can vary a lot), values for salt damaged guns can be reduced as much as 50% (heavy pitting and original salt wood). Those salt guns that have been restocked by Browning are accepted by the shooting fraternity, and can command as much as 90% of the value of non-salt original guns. To determine if a Superposed has salt damage, examine carefully any gun where the serial number is within the 1966-71 production range (please refer to the Browning Superposed serialization section), and carefully inspect the wood around the buttplate, forearm, and where the wood joins the receiver metal for any telltale rusting or pitting.

Engraved guns signed by Browning's top engravers (Funken, Vrancken, Watrin, Magis, Müeller, and J. Baerten) will command a premium over unsigned guns. Also, more and more Superposed models are appearing with Angelo Bee's signature (while non-factory, Mr. Bee's work is universally recognized. He engraved in Belgium at FN from 1951-74.) Louis Vrancken & Andre Watrin took over as heads of the engraving department in 1960.

The following values are for 1960-76 Superposed production non-salt damaged guns. Most desirable period of mfg. is 1960-66 (round knob, long tang, pre-salt). Guns made during 1970-76 (FKLT) are worth more than RKST, but probably less than RKLT. Lowest values are for 1966-71 mfg. (round/flat knob, short tang and potential salt problems).

Barrel addresses appeared as follows: circa 1947-1958 "St. Louis, M.O." (earliest BAC markings) or "St. Louis, Missouri", 1959-1968 "St. Louis, Missouri and Montreal P.Q.", 1969-1975 "Morgan, Utah and Montreal, P.Q." Make sure barrel address date matches year of mfg. (see listings in the back of this text).

The original factory configuration of almost all Superposed shotguns can be verified by grade, gauge/bore, and barrel length. To obtain information on a specific Belgian Superposed serial number, please contact the Browning historian directly (refer to Trademark Index for more information).

   Subtract approx. 15%-50% for salt wood (depending on extent of damage).

   Subtract 10% for new style Skeet configuration on models.

   Subtract $150-$500 for non-original recoil pads on Grade I models, depending on condition.

   Subtract $250-$750 for non-original recoil pads on the higher grades, depending on condition.

   Special order Superposed with non-standard factory engraving, checkered buttstocks, 3 piece forearms, and other special orders will command premiums over standard configurations.

Superposed with Extra Barrel(s) or Super-Tubes

The Superposed could be special ordered from the factory in the following combinations: 12 or 20 ga. with one extra set of barrels in same ga., 12 ga. with one extra set in 20 ga., 12 or 20 ga. with two extra barrel sets of same ga., 20 ga. with one extra set in either 28 ga. or .410 bore, 20 ga. with both 28 ga. and .410 bore barrel sets, and 28 ga. with extra set of .410 bore barrels. Super-Tubes were adaptable on 12 ga. guns only; came from the factory cased with accessories, 16 1/2 in. long, factory installation.

   Add 40-50% of the gun's value for each Grade I extra barrel set(s). For higher grades, add approx. $1,000-$2,500 per barrel set, depending on grade.

   Add $250 for Super-Tubes - available for 12 ga. only, introduced in 1965.

   Add $400 for Super-Tube Set - 3 ga. set (20, 28 ga., and .410 bore).

   Subtract $150-$500 for non-original recoil pads on Grade I models, depending on condition.

   Subtract $250-$750 for non-original recoil pads on the higher grades, depending on condition.

Superposed Variations

On most Superposed with added recoil pads, the stock has usually been cut to keep the LOP the same. The correct LOP on a Superposed is 14 1/4 inches (14 1/2 in. on Trap & New Style Skeet), with or w/o a factory recoil pad, unless special ordered from the factory. Except for the Superlight Model, individual configurations have not been broken out on the Pigeon, Pointer, Diana, and Midas grades, but values will be similar to each other in most cases.

GRADE I STANDARD WEIGHT & LIGHTNING - 12, 20, 28 ga., or .410 bore (the 28 ga. & .410 bore were not cataloged until 1960), 28 ga. and .410 bore were built on a 20 ga. frame, the buttplate was changed from horn to plastic during 1961, 12 and 20 ga. Lightning Models were approx. 6 oz. lighter than Standard Weight.

	100%	98%	95%	90%	80%	70%	60%
12 ga.	$1,850	$1,450	$1,050	$900	$825	$750	$700
20 ga.	$3,200	$2,700	$2,200	$1,550	$1,275	$1,100	$995
28 ga.	$5,500	$4,700	$3,800	$3,000	$2,500	$2,250	$2,100
.410 Bore	$4,250	$3,500	$3,000	$2,200	$1,475	$1,225	$1,100

Subtract 10%-15% for Grade I Standardweight (12 ga. only).

Add 20%-25% for round knob, long tang stock variations (pre-1966), unless Skeet choked.

✳ *Grade I Magnum* - 12 ga. only, 3 in. chambers, 28, 30, or 32 in. barrels with vent. rib, recoil pad standard.

12 ga.	$1,850	$1,500	$1,100	$1,000	$825	$775	$725

This model with 30 in. barrels is now popular again, as Sporting Clays shooters like this desirable configuration.

✳ *Grade I Superlight* - 12 (mfg. 1967-76), 20 (1969-76), 28 (very rare) ga. or .410 bore (mfg. 1970-76) features lightweight construction and straight grip stock. During 1971, the Superlight was offered in all Grades.

Add 10%-30% over Standardweight and Lightning values, depending on condition and overall desirability.

A Quail Unlimited limited edition was also available in the Superlight Series, add 10%-15% if in 98%+ original condition.

✳ *Grade I Skeet/New Model Skeet* - 12, 20, 28 ga. or .410 bore, 26 1/2 or 28 in. VR barrels with fixed SK/SK chokes, New Model Skeet was introduced during 1968, and was available in both Standard and Lightning weights in 12 and 20 ga., this New Model featured a flat bottom pistol grip stock with factory vent. recoil pad and beavertail forearm, pre-'68 mfg. was basically a hunting model with skeet chokes. Mfg. circa 1950s-1976.

12 ga.	$1,575	$1,328	$1,050	$900	$825	$750	$700
20 ga.	$2,250	$1,975	$1,600	$1,200	$950	$850	$775
28 ga.	$3,950	$3,350	$2,650	$2,200	$1,550	$1,275	$1,100
.410 bore	$2,500	$2,250	$1,850	$1,400	$1,100	$925	$850

Add approx. 10%-15% for pre 1968 mfg. (w/o beavertail forearm and recoil pad.)

Subtract 20% for 26 in. (New Skeet style) barrels.

✳ *Grade I Four Gauge Skeet Set* - includes 12, 20, 28 ga. and .410 bore barrels, 26 1/2 or 28 in. VR barrels, 12 ga. frame, single removable beavertail forearm, includes fitted luggage case. Mfg. 1972-76.

	$5,500	$5,100	$4,800	$4,150	$3,650	$2,750	$2,250

Subtract 20% for 26 in. (New Skeet style) barrels.

✳ *Grade I Trap Model (Lightning and Broadway)* - 12 ga. only, FKLT, Trap dimension stock with recoil pad, semi-beavertail forearm, 30 or 32 in. barrels with either standard 5/16 in. VR (Lightning) or 5/8 in. Broadway VR, first cataloged in 1961, this new Lightning Model Trap was approx. 6 oz. lighter than previous mfg., front and center ivory bead sights standard, 14 3/8 in. LOP, Broadway is approx. 1 lbs. heavier than Lightning with same length barrels.

	$1,850	$1,500	$1,100	$1,000	$825	$750	$700

BROWNING.

PIGEON GRADE -12, 20, 28 ga. or .410 bore, features a silver grey receiver with 2 smaller flying pigeons surrounded by fine scroll engraving on each side of the frame, receiver bottom and tangs also exhibit fine scroll work. Disc. 1974.

	100%	98%	95%	90%	80%	70%	60%
12 ga.	$4,000	$3,500	$2,800	$1,900	$1,700	$1,570	$1,485
20 ga.	$7,000	$6,000	$4,500	$3,200	$2,200	$1,995	$1,850
28 ga.	$8,500	$7,500	$5,500	$4,200	$3,500	$2,500	$2,250
.410 bore	$6,500	$4,800	$3,600	$3,100	$2,500	$2,150	$1,900

Add 20%-25% for round knob, long tang stock variations (pre-1966), unless Skeet choked.
Subtract 20% for newer Skeet style model with beavertail forearm and recoil pad.
Between 1948-1960, this model was designated the Grade II.

* *Pigeon Grade Superlight* - 12 (mfg. 1967-76), 20 (1969-76), 28 (very rare) ga. or .410 bore (mfg. 1970-76) features lightweight construction and straight grip stock. During 1971, the Superlight was offered in all Grades.

Add 15%-30% over standard **Pigeon Grade** values, depending on condition and overall desirability.

POINTER GRADE - features engraved silver grey receiver with a pointer on one side, and a setter on the other, select checkered walnut, early production was engraved by Funken, while the final design was executed by Vrancken. Mfg. 1959-disc. 1966, except for special orders.

	100%	98%	95%	90%	80%	70%	60%
12 ga.	$7,000	$6,000	$4,750	$3,500	$2,800	$2,000	$1,625
20 ga.	$10,000	$7,500	$6,500	$5,500	$4,500	$3,200	$2,700
28 ga. (rare)	$14,000	$12,500	$10,500	$6,500	$4,200	$3,500	$3,150
.410 bore (rare)	$10,500	$8,750	$7,750	$5,200	$4,200	$3,100	$2,850

Add 20%-25% for round knob, long tang stock variations (pre-1966), unless Skeet choked.
Subtract 20% for newer Skeet style model with beavertail forearm and recoil pad.

* *Pointer Grade Superlight* - this model was available by special order only, and was never cataloged by BAC.

Add 25%-35% over standard **Pointer Grade** values, depending on condition and overall desirability.

DIANA GRADE - deeper engraving with duck and pheasant game scenes - similar to 1948-60 mfg. Grade V. Disc. 1976.

	100%	98%	95%	90%	80%	70%	60%
12 ga.	$6,500	$5,750	$3,000	$2,200	$2,000	$1,800	$1,700
20 ga.	$9,500	$7,000	$5,000	$4,000	$3,500	$3,150	$2,800
28 ga.	$14,000	$11,000	$7,000	$6,200	$5,200	$4,000	$3,650
.410 bore	$8,500	$6,750	$5,500	$4,200	$3,700	$3,250	$2,950

Add 25% for round knob, long tang stock variations (pre-1966).
Subtract 20% for newer Skeet style model with beavertail forearm and recoil pad.
Between 1948-1960, this model was designated the Grade V.

* *Diana Grade Superlight* - 12 (mfg. 1967-76), 20 (1969-76), 28 (very rare) ga. or .410 bore (mfg. 1970-76) features lightweight construction and straight grip stock. During 1971, the Superlight was offered in all Grades.

Add 20%-30% over standard **Diana Grade** values, depending on condition and overall desirability.

MIDAS GRADE - features new design by Vrancken with deep relief scroll engraving with gold inlaid ducks and pheasants on frame sides and a quail on the bottom, ejector trip rods, ejector hammers, and firing pins are also 18Kt. gold plated, best quality walnut with fine checkering. Disc. 1976.

	100%	98%	95%	90%	80%	70%	60%
12 ga.	$8,000	$7,000	$5,500	$4,250	$3,750	$3,250	$2,500
20 ga.	$13,000	$9,500	$6,800	$6,200	$4,600	$4,000	$3,650
28 ga.	$16,500	$12,500	$9,000	$7,000	$5,700	$5,000	$4,650
.410 bore	$10,500	$8,500	$6,200	$5,000	$4,000	$3,500	$3,150

Add 25% for round knob, long tang stock variations (pre-1966), unless Skeet choked.
Subtract 20% for newer Skeet style model with beavertail forearm and recoil pad.
Between 1948-1960, this model was designated the Grade VI.

GRADING - PPGS™	100%	98%	95%	90%	80%	70%	60%

✳ *Midas Grade Superlight* - 12 (mfg. 1967-76), 20 (1969-76), 28 (very rare) ga. or .410 bore (mfg. 1970-76) features lightweight construction and straight grip stock. During 1971, the Superlight was offered in all Grades.

Add 20%-30% over standard Midas Grade values, depending on condition and overall desirability.

BICENTENNIAL SUPERPOSED SUPERLIGHT - specially engraved limited edition Model, 51 mfg. - one for each state and Washington, D.C. Left side has U.S. Flag, bald eagle and state emblem inlaid in gold. Right side has gold inlaid hunter and turkey. Blue receiver, fancy checkered English stock, Schnabel forend, velvet lined wood case. Made 1976 by FN.

$11,000 $8,500 $7,000

EXPOSITION/EXHIBITION MODEL - this specially manufactured Superposed saw limited production from pre-WWII through 1976. There are true exhibition models and a "C" series. Most "C" series did not have carved stocks, and were a special BAC sale of FN guns which did not sell well in Europe. True exhibition guns had gold lettering on the barrels in most cases, and many also had carved stocks. These guns were made for a very special reason, purpose, or person. Prices usually start in the 5 digit level – the C Series is typically priced between $17,500 - $25,000, and true Exhibition guns can get much more expensive, depending on how elaborate the embellishments are.

SUPERPOSED PRESENTATION MODELS (P1-P4) - custom made versions of the Lightning Field, Super Light, Trap, and Skeet guns, specifications the same as Standard models, with differences in finish, engraving and inlay(s), and grade of wood and checkering. These guns were introduced by FN in 1977 and were disc. after 1984. Gauge premiums below refer to Models P1-P3.

Add 50% for 20 ga.
Add 75% for 28 ga.
Add 40% for .410 bore.
Add $1,000 of the gun's value for each P1 extra barrel set(s). For higher grades, add approx. $1,000-$2,500 per barrel set, depending on grade.
Subtract 25% for P Series Trap Models.
Subtract 25% for P Series Broadway Trap Models.
Subtract 20% for P Series Skeet 12 and 20 ga. guns.

Since P Series Superposed were disc. in 1985, collector interest has increased substantially. Interestingly, the P series models are rarer than most of the pre-1976 high grade Superposed models.

✳ *Presentation 1* - silver grey or blue receiver, oak leaf and fine scroll engraved, choice of 6 different animal scenes.

	$3,300	$2,500	$2,100	$1,850	$1,500	$1,250	$1,000

✳ *Presentation 1 w/gold inlays* - similar to Presentation 1, only with gold inlays.

	$4,750	$3,500	$3,000	$2,100	$1,825	$1,700	$1,500

✳ *Presentation 2* - silver grey or blue receiver, high relief engraving, choice of 3 different sets of game scenes.

	$4,800	$4,000	$2,750	$2,050	$1,825	$1,700	$1,500

✳ *Presentation 2 w/gold inlays* - similar to Presentation 2, only with gold inlays.

	$7,000	$6,000	$4,200	$2,150	$1,925	$1,750	$1,550

✳ *Presentation 3* - silver grey or blue receiver, more elaborate high relief engraving with choice of partridges, mallards, or geese depicted on frame sides in 18Kt. gold.

	$9,000	$7,500	$5,500	$3,750	$3,200	$2,875	$2,300

✳ *Presentation 4* - features engraved side plates in either silver grey or blue finish, hand engraved game scenes include waterfowl on right frame side, 5 pheasants on left frame side, 2 quail on receiver bottom, and a retriever's head on trigger guard. Extra figure walnut stock and forearm.

	$8,000	$6,900	$5,250	$4,000	$3,350	$2,950	$2,375

Add 30% for 20 ga., 70% for 28 ga., or 50% for .410 bore.

GRADING - PPGS™	100%	98%	95%	90%	80%	70%	60%

✳ *Presentation 4 w/gold inlays* - similar to Presentation 4, only with game scenes inlaid in 18Kt. gold.

	100%	98%	95%	90%	80%	70%	60%
	$12,000	$10,500	$8,700	$6,000	$4,250	$3,650	$2,950

Add 50% for 20 ga., 75% for 28 ga., or 50% for .410 bore.

P SERIES SUPERLITE - available in various configurations including multi-barrel sets.

✳ *Presentation I Superlite w/Gold* - G, H, I, J, K, or L style engraving.

	100%	98%	95%	90%	80%	70%	60%
12 ga.(25 mfg.)	$5,000	$4,500	$3,750	$2,750	$2,500	$2,200	$2,000
20 ga.(80 mfg.)	$7,000	$6,700	$5,750	$4,750	$3,500	$2,900	$2,500
28 ga.(38 mfg.)	$9,000	$8,750	$8,000	$7,000	$5,500	$3,750	$3,000
.410 bore (47 mfg.)	$7,000	$6,700	$5,750	$4,750	$3,500	$2,900	$2,500

Add $1,500 per extra barrel.
Add 40% for an all option gun (checkered buttstock, oil finish, three piece forend, rare).
Add 15% for J. Baerten signed gun (rare).
Subtract 35% for Trap or Skeet Models.
Subtract 25% for regular, no option FKLT models with gold.
Subtract 30% for A, B, C, D, E, or F models w/o gold.

✳ *Presentation II Superlite* - P, Q, or R style engraving.

	100%	98%	95%	90%	80%	70%	60%
12 ga.(23 mfg.)	$7,000	$6,500	$5,750	$5,000	$4,000	$3,000	$2,000
20 ga.(93 mfg.)	$10,000	$9,000	$8,000	$6,000	$5,000	$4,000	$3,000
28 ga.(57 mfg.)	$12,000	$11,000	$8,500	$7,500	$6,500	$5,500	$4,500
.410 bore (44 mfg.)	$10,000	$9,000	$8,000	$6,000	$5,000	$4,000	$3,000

Add $1,500 per extra barrel.
Add 30% for an all option gun (checkered buttstock, oil finish, three piece forend, rare).
Add 15% for J. Baerten signed gun (rare).
Subtract 35% for Trap or Skeet Models.
Subtract 25% for regular, no option FKLT models with gold.
Subtract 30% for M, N, or O models w/o gold.

✳ *Presentation III Superlite* - S, T, or U style engraving.

	100%	98%	95%	90%	80%	70%	60%
12 ga.(16 mfg.)	$9,500	$9,000	$7,500	$6,000	$4,500	$4,000	$3,500
20 ga.(85 mfg.)	$13,000	$12,000	$10,000	$8,000	$6,500	$5,500	$4,500
28 ga.(36 mfg.)	$16,000	$15,000	$13,000	$10,500	$8,500	$7,000	$6,000
.410 bore (37 mfg.)	$11,500	$10,500	$9,000	$7,000	$6,000	$5,000	$4,000

Add $2,000 per extra barrel.
Add 25%-30% for an all option gun (checkered buttstock, oil finish, three piece forend).
Add 25% for an all option FKLT gun (very rare).
Add 15% for J. Baerten signed gun (rare).
Subtract 35% for Trap or Skeet Models.
Subtract 25% for regular, no option FKLT models.

✳ *Presentation IV Superlite w/Gold* - W style engraving.

	100%	98%	95%	90%	80%	70%	60%
12 ga.(14 mfg.)	$15,000	$13,000	$11,000	$9,000	$7,000	$5,500	$4,000
20 ga.(44 mfg.)	$17,500	$16,000	$13,000	$10,000	$8,500	$6,500	$5,000
28 ga.(20 mfg.)	$20,000	$18,000	$16,000	$12,500	$10,500	$8,000	$7,000
.410 bore (35 mfg.)	$15,000	$13,000	$11,000	$9,000	$7,000	$5,500	$4,000

Add $2,500 per extra barrel.
Add 25%-30% for an all option gun (checkered buttstock, oil finish, three piece forend).
Add 25% for an all option FKLT gun (very rare).
Add 15% for J. Baerten signed gun (rare).
Subtract 35% for Trap or Skeet Models.
Subtract 25% for regular, no option FKLT models.
Subtract 35% for plain models w/o gold.

GRADING - PPGS™	100%	98%	95%	90%	80%	70%	60%

LIEGE - 12 ga., 26 1/2, 28 or 30 in. barrels, various chokes, boxlock, auto ejectors, non- selective single trigger, vent. rib, checkered pistol grip stock. Approx. 10,000 mfg. 1973-75 by FN.

| | $850 | $700 | $600 | $500 | $425 | $400 | $375 |

This model is also known as the B-26.

GRAND LIEGE - similar to Liege, except has deluxe checkered walnut stock and forearm, and engraved receiver. Disc.

| | $1,150 | $875 | $750 | $675 | $600 | $550 | $495 |

B-26 - with BAC markings. Mfg. 1973-75.

| | $750 | $625 | $575 | $500 | $425 | $400 | $375 |

B-27 - F.N. manufactured modified B-26, imported into the U.S. in 1984, same action as Liege (B 26), blue or satin finished receiver with light engraving, no BAC markings and never cataloged.

✳ *Standard Game* - 28 in. barrels, 9/32 in. vent. rib, pistol grip stock, Schnabel forearm, SST, blue receiver, choking M/F only.

| | $850 | $700 | $600 | $500 | $425 | $400 | $375 |

Also available in Skeet model with gold "Browning" logo on blue receiver. Prices are the same.

✳ *Deluxe Game (Grade II)* - similar to Standard Grade, except has 30 in. barrels, better wood and English scroll engraved satin finished receiver, choking M/F only.

| | $875 | $725 | $625 | $575 | $510 | $475 | $445 |

✳ *Grand Deluxe Game* - 28 in. IC/IM & M/F choked barrels, game scene engraved, signed by the engraver, 90% receiver coverage.

| | $1,100 | $850 | $775 | $700 | $640 | $580 | $520 |

This model was also available in a Trap configuration - values are about the same as above.

✳ *Deluxe Skeet* - similar to Deluxe Game (Grade II), except is designed for skeet shooting.

| | $850 | $725 | $625 | $575 | $510 | $475 | $445 |

International Skeet is also available at same price; hand fit pistol grip with stippling and International Type recoil pad.

✳ *Deluxe Trap* - similar to Deluxe Game (Grade II), except is configured for trap shooting.

| | $750 | $650 | $560 | $530 | $500 | $475 | $445 |

✳ *City of Liege Commemorative* - limited edition of 250 units manufactured to commemorate the 1,000th anniversary of the city of Liege, cased. Only 29 imported into the U.S.

| | $1,125 | $975 | $910 | $850 | $775 | $700 | $600 |

ST-100 - 12 ga., Belgian mfg., O/U trap configuration with separated barrels and adj. point of impact, manufactured 1979-81 for European sale mostly, floating VR, ST, deluxe checkered walnut stock and forearm, non-BAC model.

| | $3,500 | $2,750 | $2,000 | $1,850 | $1,200 | $975 | $825 |

WATERFOWL SUPERPOSED SHOTGUN SERIES - 12 ga., 500 made of each issue, 7 gold inlays with extensive engraving on French Grey receiver, lightning action, 28 in. barrels, checkered buttstock, full-length walnut case, factory inventories were depleted on Mallard, Pintail, and Black Duck Issues in 1989.

Add 20% for 3 gun set with same serial number.

✳ *1981 Mallard Issue*

| | $7,250 | $6,000 | $4,200 |

Last MSR was $7,000.

This issue was sold out in 1988.

GRADING - PPGS™	100%	98%	95%	90%	80%	70%	60%

❋ 1982 Pintail Issue

	$7,250	$6,000	$4,200				

Last MSR was $7,000.

❋ 1983 Black Duck Issue

	$7,250	$6,000	$4,200				

Last MSR was $8,800.

SUPERPOSED SHOTGUN: 1983-86 MFG. - 12 or 20 ga. In 1983, Browning announced renewed production of the famous Belgian "Superposed" O/U in Grade I only. Available in Lightning or Superlight models, 3 in. chambers in Lightning 20 ga., 26 1/2 or 28 in. barrels. Belgian manufactured from 1983-86.

❋ Grade I - limited mfg., not compatible with steel shot.

	100%	98%	95%	90%	80%	70%	60%
Lightning	$2,500	$1,975	$1,450	$950	$800	$675	$550
Superlight	$3,300	$2,750	$1,850	$1,400	$1,000	$850	$675

Last MSR was $1,995.

Add 25% for 20 ga.

OVER/UNDER CLASSIC SERIES SHOTGUN - 20 ga. only, 26 in. barrels, less than 2,500 manufactured in Classic model and under 350 manufactured in Gold Classic. Both editions feature multiple engraved scenes and a special silver grey finish. Select American walnut featuring oil finish. Available 1986 only.

	$2,750	$2,200	$1,800				

Last MSR was $2,000.

❋ Gold Classic - 8 gold inlays, select walnut forearm and stock are both checkered and carved, many were shipped back to Belgium due to poor sales domestically. Available 1986 only.

	$5,995	$4,150	$3,150				

Last MSR was $6,000

SHOTGUNS: O/U, SUPERPOSED HIGH GRADES: 1985-PRESENT

Browning, in 1985, resumed production of the Superposed in Pigeon, Pointer, Diana, and Midas grades. They were available in 12 and 20 ga. only, in either a Lightning or Superlight configuration. These higher grades were custom ordered from the factory with delivery ranging from 8 to more than 12 months. Custom options could be special ordered on each grade with corresponding prices being higher than shown below. B-25 engraving patterns on these various grades will nearly duplicate those styles manufactured before 1976. Skeet models were not available.

Superposed: Custom Shop Current Pricing & Models

In 2000, Browning changed the nomenclature of their B-25 shotgun Series. Prices reflect current custom shop MSRs. These new boxlock grades include: Special Woodcock $16,466, Special Duck $17,233, Special Pigeon $18,249, Trap Evolution 2 $19,333, Sporting 207 Gold 25 $17,233, US Model B $18,249, Diana UK $23,416, and Grades B11 - $9,590 (disc. 2003), B12 - $9,680 (disc. 2003), B2G - $18,333 (disc. 2003, reintroduced 2004), C11 - $22,132, C12 - $22,999, C2G - $23,166, D11 - $30,982, D12 - $30,499, D2L $30,765, D4G $35,582, D5G - $35,715, Special Automn - $35,715, Cheverny - $35,715.

Additionally, the Browning Custom Shop also offers the following shotguns in various grades with engraved sideplates: Grade II - $23,234 (disc. 2003), C2S - $32,582, Grade E1 - $43,265, Grade F1 - $44,165, Grade I1 - $43,498, Grade M1 - $46,565, Grade M2 - $44,332, Special Perdrix - $58,998, Windsor Or - $56,164, Chenonceau - $59,748, and Cheverny - $60,331. These new grades are special order only through the Browning Custom Shop.

Grade I Traditional, Pigeon Grade, Pointer Grade, Diana Grade, and Midas Grade Superposed are listed separately under the B-25 model listing.

Add 20% for 20 ga. on previously owned models.
Add approx. $1,250 for a previously owned extra set of barrels.
Add $6,479 - $11,954 per extra set of barrels on currently manufactured Superposed models, depending on the grade.

B-25 - 12 or 20 ga. only, original Superposed Model manufactured entirely from parts fabricated in Herstal, Belgium. Also available in Superlight configuration. This older nomenclature series was discontinued domestically in 1999, but the Custom Shop is still producing these grades.

✳ *Grade I Traditional*

MSR $16,999	$13,600	N/A	N/A

✳ *Pigeon Grade*

MSR $16,033	$13,500	N/A	N/A

✳ *Pointer C Grade*

MSR $20,416	$16,335	N/A	N/A

✳ *Diana C Grade*

MSR $20,882	$16,700	N/A	N/A

✳ *Midas D Grade*

MSR $25,082	$20,000	N/A	N/A

B-25 125th ANNIVERSARY - 12 ga. only, 2 3/4 in. chamber, 28 in. VR barrels with fixed M/F chokes and 8mm rib, Lightning style stock and forearm with oil finish and black buttplate, case colored receiver with gold border and gold enhanced 125th Anniversary logo. 10 mfg. 2003 only.

$13,750	$5,250	$3,750	$2,850	$2,300	$2,000	$1,750

Last MSR was $15,219.

B-125 - 12 or 20 ga. only, retains all the features of the original Superposed, except parts are subcontracted worldwide to decrease production costs and are assembled "in the white" at Herstal's Custom Gun Shop in Belgium, choice of three different engraving styles and two receiver finishes. Mfg. 1988-2003.

✳ *Hunting Model* - available in either Hunting Lightning or Superlight configuration.

> *"A" Style Engraving* - blue frame with border engraving featuring Browning logo engraved on each side.

$3,400	$2,750	$2,150	$1,700	$1,450	$1,275	$1,050

Last MSR was $3,925.

> *"B" Style Engraving* - coin finished frame with smaller game scene engravings.

$3,700	$3,100	$2,250	$1,800	$1,500	$1,300	$1,100

Last MSR was $4,360.

> *"C" Style Engraving* - coin finished frame with elaborate scroll work and game scene engraving.

$4,100	$3,475	$2,450	$1,900	$1,600	$1,400	$1,200

Last MSR was $4,903.

✳ *Sporting Clays Model* - 12 ga. only, designed for sporting clays competition and includes Invector plus choke tube system.

> *"A" Style Engraving*- blue frame with border engraving featuring Browning logo engraved on each side.

$3,400	$2,750	$2,150	$1,700	$1,450	$1,275	$1,050

Last MSR was $3,925.

> *"B" Style Engraving* - coin finished frame with smaller game scene engravings.

$3,700	$3,100	$2,250	$1,800	$1,500	$1,300	$1,100

Last MSR was $4,360.

> *"C" Style Engraving* - coin finished frame with elaborate scroll work and game scene engraving.

$4,100	$3,475	$2,450	$1,900	$1,600	$1,400	$1,200

Last MSR was $4,903.

✳ *Trap Model* - standard F-1 style engraving.

$4,950	$3,550	$2,325	$1,750	$1,450	$1,275	$1,050

Last MSR was $5,452.

GRADING - PPGS™	100%	98%	95%	90%	80%	70%	60%

SHOTGUNS: SxS

The Browning Custom Shop in Herstal, Belgium currently offers several SxS sidelock models manufactured by Lebeau-Courally. Models include the LC1 (blued receiver, $18,566 MSR), and LC2 (coin finished receiver, $21,916 MSR).

B-SS - 12 or 20 ga., 26, 28, or 30 in. barrels, various chokes, engraved boxlock action, auto ejectors, checkered pistol grip walnut stock, beavertail forearm, SST. Mfg. 1971-88 by Miroku.

	100%	98%	95%	90%	80%	70%	60%
12 ga.	$1,000	$850	$725	$650	$550	$450	$350
20 ga.	$2,000	$1,775	$1,525	$1,300	$1,100	$950	$800

Last MSR was $775.

Early guns had a single non-selective trigger (silver plated) - subtract 10%.

✳ *Grade II* - satin greyed steel receiver featuring an engraved pheasant, duck, quail, and dogs. Disc. 1983.

	100%	98%	95%	90%	80%	70%	60%
	$2,950	$2,550	$2,175	$1,775	$1,350	$1,100	$925

B-SS SPORTER - has straight grip stock and slim forearm, oil finish, 26 or 28 in. barrels. Disc. 1988.

	100%	98%	95%	90%	80%	70%	60%
	$1,850	$1,625	$1,400	$1,150	$950	$800	$650

Last MSR was $775.

Add 50% for 20 ga., if in 95%+ condition.

✳ *B-SS Sporter Grade II* - satin greyed steel receiver featuring an engraved pheasant, duck, quail and dogs. Disc. 1983.

	100%	98%	95%	90%	80%	70%	60%
	$2,950	$2,550	$2,175	$1,775	$1,350	$1,100	$925

Add 50% for 20 ga., if in 95%+ condition.

✳ *B-SS "Bottle" Sporter Set* - 12 and 20 ga., wild turkey and wood duck inlays on 12 ga., wood ducks only on 20 ga., straight grip sporter stock, shoulders are sculpted and engraved, Exhibition grade walnut, engraving was done in Belgium by custom shop, cased in Browning Airways case. Less than 100 mfg. circa 1976.

	100%	98%	95%	90%	80%	70%	60%
Set	$6,950	$6,500	$5,850	$5,250	$4,600	$4,000	$3,450
12 ga.	$2,750	$2,400	$2,100	$1,850	$1,600	$1,400	$1,200
20 ga.	$3,250	$2,950	$2,650	$2,300	$2,000	$1,800	$1,600

This model got its nickname from a Mr. Bottles Sporting Goods store in Wichita, KS, who special ordered 100 sets of these guns circa 1976.

B-SS SIDELOCK - 12 or 20 ga., engraved sidelock action in satin grey finish, ST, 26 or 28 in. barrels, English select walnut stock, splinter forend. Mfg. 1983-88 in Miroku in Japan.

	100%	98%	95%	90%	80%	70%	60%
12 ga.	$3,500	$3,100	$2,600	$2,275	$1,875	$1,500	$1,250
20 ga.	$4,750	$4,100	$3,500	$2,875	$2,300	$1,875	$1,500

Last MSR was $2,000.

SHOTGUNS: SEMI-AUTO, DISC.

BROWNING CHOKES AND THEIR CODES (ON REAR LEFT-SIDE OF BARREL)
* designates full choke (F).
*- designates improved modified choke (IM).
** designates modified choke (M).
**- designates improved cylinder choke (IC).
**$ designates skeet (SK).
*** designates cylinder bore (CYL).
The publisher would like to thank Mr. H.M. Shirley, Jr. for his contributions to the A-5 section.
Add $145-$295 per additional barrel, depending on the condition and configuration.

GRADING - PPGS™	100%	98%	95%	90%	80%	70%	60%

AUTO-5 STANDARD - 1903-1940 MFG.
12 ga. (introduced in Sept., 1903, Browning discontinued imports Dec., 1903), 16 ga. (introduced in 1909, but not in the U.S.), in 1923, Browning resumed importing both 12 and 16 ga. in four grades that differ in engraving, inlays, and grade of wood, both gauges were available with 26-32 in. barrel, recoil operated, 4 shot mag. with cutoff, various chokes, checkered pistol grip stock, horn buttplate, also available in a 3 shot version with shorter magazine tube to limit capacity to 3 rounds from 1932-1940. Importation temporarily ceased in 1940 with the German occupation of Belgium, ser. no. range 1-224,596 (12 ga.) and 1-126,175 (16 ga.).

	100%	98%	95%	90%	80%	70%	60%
Grade 1	$675	$575	$475	$375	$325	$285	$250
Solid matte rib	$750	$675	$575	$475	$375	$325	$285
With vent. rib	$825	$725	$650	$575	$465	$375	$325
Grade 2 (disc.1937)	$1,350	$1,100	$925	$825	$725	$650	$575
Solid matte rib	$1,525	$1,350	$1,100	$925	$760	$685	$625
With vent. rib	$1,695	$1,500	$1,250	$1,025	$825	$775	$675
Grade 3 (disc. 1940)	$2,625	$2,350	$2,100	$1,900	$1,600	$1,375	$1,095
Solid matte rib	$2,800	$2,500	$2,250	$2,050	$1,750	$1,500	$1,195
With vent. rib	$3,195	$2,795	$2,475	$2,225	$2,000	$1,700	$1,350
Grade 4 (disc. 1940)	$3,995	$3,655	$3,300	$2,995	$2,550	$2,050	$1,650
Solid matte rib	$4,350	$3,995	$3,655	$3,300	$2,975	$2,350	$2,050

Early models with safety mounted in front of trigger guard are not as desirable as there are potential safety problems inherent in the design.

Pre-WWII 16 ga. A-5s could be chambered for 2 9/16 in. shells. These shotguns are considerably less desirable than 16 ga. A-5s chambered for 2 3/4 in. modern shotshells. Since some guns have been modified to 2 3/4 in., careful inspection is advised before purchasing or shooting. The 2 9/16 chambered guns can be modified by the Browning Service Dept. to accept 2 3/4 in. shells if so desired.

AUTO-5 POLICE CONTRACT
12 ga. only, 5 or 8 (factory extended) shot mag., black enamel finish on receiver and barrel, can be recognized by the European "POL" police markings below serial number, 24 in. barrel. Imported in limited quantities during 1999.

	100%	98%	95%	90%	80%	70%	60%
5 shot mag.	N/A	$550	$525	$495	$450	$400	$375
8 shot mag.	N/A	$1,200	$995	$895	$795	$750	$650

"AMERICAN BROWNING" AUTO-5
12, 16, or 20 ga., Remington-produced model of the Auto-5, very similar to the Remington Model 11, except with Browning logo, mag. cut-off, and different engraving, over 38,000 mfg. in 12 ga. (ser. no. range B5000- B43129), over 14,000 in 16 ga. (ser. no. range A5000-A19450), and 11,000 in 20 ga. (ser. no. range C5000- C16152), stocks have Remington style round knob pistol grip. Mfg. 1940-47.

100%	98%	95%	90%	80%	70%	60%
$495	$395	$350	$325	$295	$250	$225

Add 10% for vent. rib and/or 20 ga.

An easy way to identify this configuration is to look for the "A", "B", or "C" prefix on the left side of receiver.

SHOTGUNS: SEMI-AUTO, RECENT MFG.

BROWNING CHOKES AND THEIR CODES (ON REAR LEFT-SIDE OF BARREL)

* designates full choke (F).

*- designates improved modified choke (IM).

** designates modified choke (M).

**- designates improved cylinder choke (IC).

**$ designates skeet (SK).

*** designates cylinder bore (CYL).

INV. designates barrel is threaded for Browning Invector choke tube system.

INV. PLUS designates back-bored barrels.

GRADING - PPGS™	100%	98%	95%	90%	80%	70%	60%

Miroku manufactured A-5s can be determined by year of manufacture in the following manner: RV suffix - 1975, RT - 1976, RR - 1977, RP - 1978, RN - 1979, PM - 1980, PZ - 1981, PY - 1982, PX - 1983, PW - 1984, PV - 1985, PT - 1986, PR - 1987, PP - 1988, PN - 1989, NM - 1990, NZ - 1991, NY - 1992, NX - 1993, NW - 1994, NV - 1995, NT - 1996, NR - 1997, NP - 1998.

Browning resumed importation from F.N. in 1946.   On November 26, 1997, Browning announced that the venerable Auto-5 would finally be discontinued. Final shipments were made in February, 1998. Over 3 million A-5s were mfg. by F.N. in all configurations between 1903-1976. 1976-1998 mfg. was by Miroku.

NOTE: Barrels are interchangeable between older Belgian A-5 models and recent Japanese A-5s mfg. by Miroku, if the gauge and chamber length are the same. A different barrel ring design and thicker barrel wall design might necessitate some minor sanding of the inner forearm on the older model, but otherwise, these barrels are fully interchangeable.

NOTE: The use of steel shot is recommended ONLY in those recent models manufactured in Japan - NOT in the older Belgian variations.

Recoil operation, scroll engraved receiver, 1946-1951 mfg. has safety in front of triggerguard, 1951-1976 mfg. has crossbolt safety behind the trigger, post-war 16 ga. imports by Browning are chambered for 2 3/4 in., horn (to 1964) to plastic (1962-1976) buttplate, high luster finish (to 1962) and glossy lacquer (1962-1976) finish, buttstock has either round knob pistol grip (to 1967) or flat knob (new 1967).

Add 10-15% for the round knob (rounded pistol grip knob on stock) variation on FN models only. Add $195-$375 per additional barrel, depending on the condition and configuration.

AUTO-5 STANDARDWEIGHT - 12 (disc. 1970) or 16 (disc. 1964) ga., 26-32 in. barrel, various chokes, checkered walnut stock and forearm, between 7 1/3-8 lbs. Browning resumed importation from F.N. in 1946.

	100%	98%	95%	90%	80%	70%	60%
Plain barrel	$495	$425	$375	$325	$295	$270	$240
Matted rib(solid)	$650	$550	$450	$400	$350	$300	$275
Vent rib	$795	$650	$550	$500	$450	$400	$375

Add 20% for NIB condition.

Add 10% for round knob.

Note: Watch for cracked forearms on all A-5 models (due to barrel recoil.)

Barrel addresses appeared as follows: circa 1930-1958 "St. Louis, M.O.", 1959-1968 "St. Louis, Missouri and Montreal P.Q.", 1969-1976 "Morgan, Utah and Montreal, P.Q.". Barrels are serial numbered to the gun until 1953. Make sure barrel address date matches year of mfg. (see listings in the back of this text).

AUTO-5 LIGHTWEIGHT (LIGHT 12 & LIGHT 20) - 12 (new 1947) or 20 (new 1958) ga., recoil operated, 26, 28, or 30 in. barrel, various chokes, gold plated trigger, checkered pistol grip round knob (disc. 1967) or flat knob (mfg. 1967-1976) stock, approx. 10 oz. lighter than Standard weight.

	100%	98%	95%	90%	80%	70%	60%
FN model	$650	$550	$450	$400	$375	$350	$325
FN-vent. rib	$950	$795	$645	$575	$465	$435	$395

Add 10% for NIB condition.

Add 40% for 20 ga. with VR.

✳ *Light 12 Miroku* - 12 ga. only, 22, 26, 28, or 30 in. VR (became standard 1986) barrel with Invector choke system, approx. 8-8 1/2 lbs. Mfg. 1976-Feb. 1998.

	100%	98%	95%	90%	80%	70%	60%
	$775	$595	$525	$465	$415	$365	$315

Last MSR was $840.

Subtract 10% without Invector chokes.

✳ *Light 20 Miroku* - 20 ga. only, 2 3/4 in. chamber, similar to original Belgian Light 20, VR, 22 (new 1995), 26, or 28 in. barrel, Invector chokes standard until 1993, Invector Plus choking became standard 1994, 6 lbs. 12 oz - 7 lbs. 2 oz. Mfg. 1987-97.

	100%	98%	95%	90%	80%	70%	60%
	$825	$625	$550	$495	$435	$385	$335

Last MSR was $840.

GRADING - PPGS™	100%	98%	95%	90%	80%	70%	60%

AUTO-5 MAGNUM - 12 (new 1958) or 20 (new 1967) ga., 3 in. chamber, 26, 28, 30, or 32 in. barrels, various chokes, VR or etched, 8 1/2 - 9 lbs. Mfg. 1958-76 by FN, 1976-Feb. 1998 by Miroku.

FN model.	$725	$650	$550	$450	$400	$375	$350
FN-vent. rib.	$925	$795	$695	$645	$575	$465	$415

Add 10% for NIB condition.

Add 15% for 20 ga. with VR if NIB.

Between 1976-1985 approx. 2,000 Belgian 12 ga. A-5 Mags. were imported into the U.S. These late models can be differentiated by serialization - also, slight premiums may be asked.

✳ **A-5 Mag. Miroku** - 12 or 20 ga., VR barrel with Invector choke system until 1993, Invector Plus choking became standard 1994, 8 1/2 - 9 lbs. Disc. 1997.

	$825	$650	$595	$525	$465	$400	$350

Last MSR was $866.

Subtract $87 for 20 ga. Mag.

Subtract 10% without Invector chokes.

AUTO-5 STALKER - 12 ga. only, 2 3/4 (Light-12) or 3 (Mag. Stalker) in. chamber, 22 (Light-12 only), 26, 28, or 30, or 32 (Mag. only) in. VR barrel with Invector chokes, black matte finish graphite-fiberglass stock and forearm, matte finished metal, recoil pad, 8 lbs. 1 oz. - 8 lbs. 13 oz. Mfg. 1992-97.

	$775	$595	$525	$465	$415	$365	$315

Last MSR was $840.

Add $26 for Mag. Stalker.

AUTO-5 BUCK SPECIAL - 12, 16, or 20 ga., included Lightweight, Standardweight, and Magnum Models, 24 in. barrel, slug bore, adj. sight, optional sling studs and sling, between 1985-88, Buck Special barrels were available at additional cost. Introduced in 1962, mfg. by F.N. until 1976, and by Miroku from 1976-1984, and again in 1989.

✳ **FN Mfg.**

	$850	$665	$625	$575	$465	$415	$365

This model was made in Light 12, Standard 12, 3 in. Mag. 12, Sweet 16, Standard 16, Lightweight 20 and Lightweight 20 Mag. (new 1967) configurations.

✳ **Miroku model** - mfg. 1989-97.

	$725	$575	$525	$475	$395	$355	$315

Last MSR was $829.

Add $35 for Buck Special on 3 in. Mag. receiver.

AUTO-5 SKEET - 12, 16, or 20 ga., Lightweight models with 26 or 28 in. skeet bored, vent. rib barrel. Pre 1976 mfg. by F.N., 1976-1983 mfg. by Miroku.

✳ **FN Mfg.**

	$725	$575	$495	$445	$375	$325	$285

Add 20% for vent. rib.

✳ **Standard Miroku**

	$775	$595	$525	$465	$415	$365	$315

AUTO-5 TRAP MODEL - 12 ga. only, similar to Standard, 30 in. full vent. rib barrel, 8 1/2 lbs., mfg. by FN until 1970.

	$850	$665	$625	$575	$465	$415	$365

AUTO-5 SWEET 16 - 16 ga., 2 9/16 in. chamber from 1937-1940, and 2 3/4 in. chamber from 1947-1975, similar configuration to Lightweight, 12 and 20 ga., gold plated trigger, 10 oz. lighter than Standardweight Model 16 ga., 1937-1940 mfg. Sweet Sixteens were available in pre-war Grades I, III, and IV. Mfg. 1937-1975 by F.N.

Plain Barrel	$850	$665	$625	$575	$465	$415	$365
Solid Matte Rib	$1,295	$995	$825	$775	$650	$575	$475
Vent. Rib	$1,595	$1,295	$950	$825	$700	$625	$550

GRADING - PPGS™	100%	98%	95%	90%	80%	70%	60%

✳ *Sweet 16 Miroku* - 16 ga. only, similar to original Belgian Sweet 16, VR, Invector choke standard. Mfg. 1987-92.

	$1,095	$925	$850	$725	$625	$525	$450

Last MSR was $720.

AUTO-5 TWO MILLIONTH COMMEMORATIVE - 12 ga., 2,500 mfg., 1971-74 mfg., special walnut, engraving, high-lustre bluing, cased with Browning book. Issue price was $550-$700, serial range 2,000,000-1 to 2,000,000-2,500.

	$1,650	$1,295	$995

A-5 CLASSIC SERIES SHOTGUN - 12 ga., 5,000 mfg. in Classic model, 500 mfg. in Gold Classic. Both editions feature game scenes, John M. Browning's profile, and other inscriptions, special silver grey finished receiver. Introduced 1984.

✳ *Classic Model* - no inlays. Factory inventories were depleted in 1987.

	$1,195	$945	$725

Last MSR was $1,260.

✳ *Gold Classic Model* - features 5 inlays depicting duck hunting scenes. Mfg. 1986 with inventory depleted 1989.

	$4,195	$3,495	$2,495

Last MSR was $6,500.

A-5 BCA COMMEMORATIVE - 12 ga., 3 in. Mag., round knob, Belgian mfg., 1984 issue price was $595.

	$995	$795	$650

A-5 DU 50TH ANNIVERSARY

✳ *A-5 DU Light 12* - 12 ga. only, 5,500 mfg. in 1987 only for Ducks Unlimited chapters throughout North America. Prices will fluctuate greatly from chapter to chapter as these guns were auctioned to the highest bidder. Receiver is specially engraved and has "Fiftieth Year" depicted on right side of receiver, deluxe checkered stock and forearm, high gloss blue.

	$1,095	$850	$650

✳ *A-5 DU Sweet 16* - 16 ga. only, companion 1988-89 DU auction gun, 4,500 mfg. 1988 only.

	$1,675	$1,375	$975

✳ *A-5 DU Light 20* - 20 ga. only, companion 1990 DU auction gun, 4,500 mfg. 1990 only.

	$1,395	$1,195	$850

A-5 FINAL TRIBUTE - 12 ga. only, limited edition of 1,000 guns, features elaborate engraving on white receiver, the last of the A-5 semi-autos. Mfg. 1999 only, sellout occurred during 2000.

	$1,795	$1,395	$1,095	$950	$825	$700	$575

Last MSR was $1,330.

STANDARD DOUBLE AUTO - 12 ga. only, short recoil action, 2 shot, 26, 28, or 30 in. barrel, various chokes, checkered pistol grip stock, blue steel receiver was disc. approx. 1960, frame engraving is gold foil filled (and can flake). Mfg. 1952-71.

	$650	$525	$450	$400	$350	$300	$260
w/vent. rib	$750	$650	$575	$525	$475	$425	$350

TWELVETTE DOUBLE AUTO - similar to Double Auto, except hiduminum (aircraft alloy) frame and color anodized in royal or light blue, satin grey, maroon red, light brown, several shades of green, gold, jet, and dragon black, approx. 7 lbs. without rib. Approx. 67,000 (all variations) mfg. 1952-71.

	$650	$525	$450	$400	$350	$300	$260
w/vent. rib	$750	$650	$575	$525	$475	$425	$350

Add 20-25% for brown or gold colored receiver.
Add 50%+ for maroon red or royal blue receiver (rare, only a few mfg.).

TWENTYWEIGHT DOUBLE AUTO - similar to Twelvette, but 3/4 pound lighter, jet black finish with engraving accented with gold foil, 26 1/2 in. barrel only. Mfg. 1952-71.

	100%	98%	95%	90%	80%	70%	60%
	$650	$525	$450	$400	$350	$300	$260
w/vent. rib	$825	$725	$625	$575	$525	$475	$395

B/2000 STANDARD - 12 or 20 ga. (new 1975), 26, 28, or 30 in. barrel, various chokes, vent. rib, gas operated, checkered pistol grip stock, Belgian manufactured but assembled in Portugal, approx. 115,000 imported (approx. 95,000 in 12 ga., and 20,000 in 20 ga.) into the U.S. between 1974-83.

$380	$345	$315	$295	$265	$240	$210

Last MSR was $475.

This model could be converted to accept 3 in. Mag. shotshells by simply installing a barrel chambered for 3 in. shells.

Even though production on this model ceased in 1979, assembly and sales were not discontinued until 1983.

B/2000 MAGNUM - similar to B/2000 Auto Shotgun, except with 3 in. chambered barrel (all receivers were the same), recoil pad, vent. rib.

$410	$360	$330	$305	$275	$250	$220

B/2000 SKEET - similar to Standard, with 26 in. skeet bored barrel, floating vent. rib, skeet stock, pad.

$400	$345	$315	$295	$265	$240	$210

B/2000 TRAP - similar to Standard, with 30 or 32 in. barrel bored F or IM, floating rib, Monte Carlo trap stock.

$400	$345	$315	$295	$265	$240	$210

B/2000 BUCK SPECIAL - 12 or 20 ga., barrel sights on 24 in. barrel.

$400	$345	$315	$295	$265	$240	$210

1976 CANADIAN OLYMPICS B2000 - 12 ga., 100 manufactured in 1976 for Canadian sales only, high polish blue with multiple gold inlays including Olympic crest, 30 in. barrel, cased. Issue price was $1,295.

$1,395	$995	$695

MODEL B-80 - 12 or 20 ga., 3 in. capability by changing barrel, gas operation, 4 shot, hunting models use choice of steel or aluminum receiver, anodized aluminum was used in the Superlight (12 ga. mfg. 1984 only), 6 to 8 lbs. 1 oz. Buck special disc. 1984. Components manufactured by Beretta of Italy and finished and assembled FN's plant in Portugal. Mfg. 1981-late 1988, final inventory was sold in 1991. Invector chokes became standard in 1985.

$450	$375	$325	$295	$275	$250	$230

Last MSR was $562.

Steel frames were reintroduced into production again in 1988.

* *Model B-80 Upland Special* - 12 or 20 ga., 2 3/4 in. chamber, 22 in. vent. rib barrel, straight grip stock, Invector chokes. Mfg. 1986-88.

$475	$390	$340	$305	$280	$260	$240

Last MSR was $562.

MODEL B 80 DU COMMEMORATIVE - mfg. for American DU Chapters (The Plains and others), price fluctuates greatly as collector support is sometimes limited. Unless new, this model's values approximate those of the regular Model B-80. If NIB, values recently have been in the $700-$995 range.

A-500 (R) HUNTING - 12 ga. only, 3 in. chamber, new design utilizing short recoil system with a four- lug rotary bolt design, capable of shooting all 12 gauge loads interchangeably, magazine cut-off, 26, 28, or 30 in. VR barrel with Invector chokes standard, 24 in. barrel on Buck Special (fixed choke), high polished blue finish with red accents on receiver sides, gold trigger, checkered semi-pistol grip walnut stock with vent. recoil pad, 7 lbs. 11 oz. - 8 lbs. 1 oz. Mfg. 1987-93.

	$475	$425	$375	$325	$295	$275	$250

Last MSR was $560.

Add $33 for Buck Special variation (Invector chokes).

This model features fewer moving parts than many other semi-auto shotguns due to the short recoil operating system. From 1987-90, this model was the Model A-500 – R suffix was added in 1991.

A-500G HUNTING - similar to A-500, except is gas operated, distinguishable by "A-500G" in gold accents on receiver, capable of shooting all 2 3/4 or 3 in. shells inter-changeably, approx. 8 lbs. Mfg. 1990-93.

	$555	$425	$375	$325	$295	$275	$250

Last MSR was $653.

A Buck Special variation was mfg. until 1992. No premiums currently exist.

❋ *A-500G Sporting Clays* - 12 ga. only, Sporting Clays variation with 30 in. VR barrel, 8 lbs. 2 oz. Mfg. 1992-93.

	$555	$425	$375	$325	$295	$275	$250

Last MSR was $653.

GOLD 3 IN. HUNTER - 12 or 20 ga., 3 in. chamber, self-cleaning piston rod gas action with self-regulation, alloy receiver with non-glare black finish and "Gold Hunter" on receiver side, 26, 28, or 30 (12 ga. only, disc. 2001) in. VR Invector Plus (12 ga. only) or Invector (20 ga. only) choked barrel with high polish bluing, cross-bolt safety, gloss finish checkered walnut stock and forearm with recoil pad (vent on 12 ga.), includes 3 choke tubes, 6 lbs. 12 oz. - 7 lbs. 10 oz. Parts mfg. in Belgium and final assembly in Portugal. New 1994.

MSR $1,025	$825	$575	$450	$375	$300	$275	$250

Do not use 12 ga. 3 1/2 in. chambered barrels on a either 2 3/4 or 3 in. receiver, or vice versa.

GOLD 3 1/2 IN. HUNTER - 12 ga., 3 1/2 in. chamber, 24 (mfg. 2002-2003), 26, 28, or 30 (disc. 2003) in. VR barrel with Invector Plus choking, otherwise similar to Gold Hunter, 3-4 shot mag., approx. 7 .75 lbs. New 1998.

MSR $1,190	$985	$775	$650	$550	$450	$375	$335

❋ *Gold 3 1/2 In. Turkey/Waterfowl Hunter* - similar to Gold 3 1/2 in. Hunter, full coverage (including barrel) Mossy Oak Break-Up camo finish, 24 in. VR barrel with extra full choke tube, 7 1/4 lbs. Mfg. 1999-2000.

	$875	$695	$600	$500	$425	$375	$335

Last MSR was $1,038.

❋ *Gold 3 1/2 In. Mossy Oak Break-Up/Shadow Grass* - similar to Gold 3 1/2 in. Hunter, choice of full coverage (including barrel) Mossy Oak Break-Up, New Break-Up (standard beginning 2004) or Shadow Grass camo finish, 24 (Mossy Oak Break-Up only, disc. 2001), 26 (Mossy Oak Shadow Grass only), or 28 (Mossy Oak Shadow Grass only) in. VR backbored barrel with Invector Plus choke tubes, Dura-Touch armor coating became standard 2003, approx. 7 1/2 lbs. New 1999.

MSR $1,332	$1,085	$825	$700	$600	$500	$400	$350

❋ *Gold 3 1/2 In. NWTF Mossy Oak Break-Up* - 12 ga. only, 3 1/2 in. chamber, 24 in. VR barrel with 4 chokes tubes and Hi-Viz sight, full coverage Mossy Oak Break-Up camo pattern, Dura Touch armor coating became standard 2003, 7 1/4 lbs. Mfg. 2001-2002.

	$1,025	$800	$660	$545	$450	$385	$335

Last MSR was $1,221.

GRADING - PPGS™	100%	98%	95%	90%	80%	70%	60%

✳ *Gold NWTF Ultimate Turkey Gun* - 12 ga. only, similar to Gold NWTF Mossy Oak Break-Up, except has extended full strut turkey tube and neoprene sling, 7.25 lbs. New 2003.

MSR $1,440	$1,175	$950	$825	$675	$575	$500	$450

GOLD FIELD HUNTER (CLASSIC)

- similar to Gold Hunter, except has semi-hump back receiver design, magazine cutoff, adj. comb, and satin finished wood, 26 or 28 in. VR barrel. New 1999.

MSR $1,025	$825	$575	$450	$375	$300	$275	$250

This model is available through Full-line and Medallion dealers only.

✳ *Gold Classic High Grade Hunter* - 12 (disc. 2001) or 20 ga. (new 2002), similar to Gold Classic Hunter, except has nickel finished receiver featuring multiple gold inlays with ducks and dogs (disc.) or doves and quail (current) and light scroll engraving, deluxe checkered gloss finished walnut stock and forearm, 28 in. barrel only, 6 lbs. 14 oz. New 1999-2004.

	$1,575	$1,250	$1,050	$875	$725	$625	$550

Last MSR was $1,838.

This model is available through Full-line and Medallion dealers only.

>*Gold Upland Special* - 12 or 20 ga., 3 in. chamber, 24 or 26 (20 ga. only) in. VR barrel, checkered satin finsihed straight grip stock, 6.75 (20 ga.) or 7 lbs. New 2001.

MSR $1,025	$825	$575	$450	$375	$300	$275	$250

>*Gold Micro* - 20 ga. only, 3 in. chamber, 24 (new 2002) or 26 in. VR barrel, features shorter stock (13 7/8 LOP) and lighter weight, 6 lbs., 10 oz. New 2001.

MSR $1,025	$825	$575	$450	$375	$300	$275	$250

✳ *Gold Turkey/Waterfowl Hunter Camo* - similar to Gold Hunter, full coverage (including barrel) Mossy Oak Break-Up camo finish, 24 in. VR barrel with Hi-Viz sights and extra full choke tube, 7 lbs. Mfg. 1999-2000.

	$715	$500	$400	$350	$295	$275	$250

Last MSR was $867.

✳ *Gold Mossy Oak New Break-Up/Shadow Grass* - similar to Gold Hunter, choice of full coverage (including barrel) Mossy Oak New Break-Up or New Shadow Grass camo finish (New became standard in 2004), 24 (Mossy Oak Break-Up only, disc. 2004), 26, or 28 in. VR back-bored barrel with Invector Plus choke tubes, Dura-Touch armor coating became standard 2003, approx. 7.25 - 7.75 lbs. New 1999.

MSR $1,127	$900	$625	$500	$425	$325	$285	$250

✳ *Gold NWTF Mossy Oak New Break-Up* - 12 ga. only, 3 in. chamber, drilled and tapped receiver, 24 in. VR barrel with 4 chokes tubes and Hi-Viz sight, full coverage Mossy Oak New Break-up camo pattern, Dura-Touch armor coating became standard 2003, 7 lbs. New 2001.

MSR $1,202	$950	$700	$575	$450	$375	$300	$250

GOLD EVOLVE

- 12 ga. only, 3 in. chamber, features updated engraved receiver, magazine cap, and canted VR design, 26, 28, or 30 in. barrel, includes shim adj. stock system, newly designed checkered satin finished walnut stock and forearm, alloy mag. tube, Hi-Viz pro-comp sight system, 6.5 - 7.25 lbs. New 2004.

MSR $1,196	$950	$650	$525	$425	$335	$285	$250

GOLD FUSION

- 12 or 20 (new 2002) ga., 3 in. chamber, 26, 28, or 30 (12 ga. only, new 2002) in. wide profile lightweight VR barrel with 5 Invector Plus chokes and Hi-Viz pro-comp sight system, checkered oil finished Turkish walnut stock and forearm with adj. comb system, alloy mag. tube, includes hardshell case, 6.25 - 7 lbs. New 2001.

MSR $1,129	$895	$625	$500	$400	$350	$295	$260

GRADING - PPGS™	100%	98%	95%	90%	80%	70%	60%

✴ *Gold Fusion High Grade* - 12 or 20 ga., 3 in. chamber, silver nitride receiver with engraving and gold inlays (mallards and lab on 12 ga., quail and pointer on 20 ga.), 26, 28, or 30 in. barrel with five interchangeable Invector Plus chokes, high grade Turkish walnut stock and forearm, shim adj. stock system with .25 in. adj. range, Hi-Viz TriComp sight system, includes hard case, 6 lbs., 6 oz. - 7 lbs. New 2005.

MSR $2,095	$1,750	$1,350	$1,125	$950	$850	$725	$625

GOLD DEER HUNTER - 12 or 20 (new 2001) ga., 3 in. chamber, 22 in. barrel with choice of 5 in. rifled Invector choke (disc. 1998) or rifled plain barrel, cantilevered scope mount, sling swivels, 6.75 (20 ga.) or 7.75 lbs. New 1997.

MSR $1,131	$900	$625	$500	$400	$325	$285	$250

Subtract approx. 10% for rifled choke tube (disc. 1998).

✴ *Gold Deer Hunter with Mossy Oak Break-Up Camo* - 12 ga., similar to Gold Deer Hunter, except has full Mossy Oak Break-Up or New Break-Up (standard 2004) camo coverage, rifled barrel standard. New 1999.

MSR $1,218	$1,000	$775	$640	$550	$450	$365	$335

GOLD 3 IN. STALKER - similar to Gold Hunter (3 in. chamber), except has checkered black composite stock and forearm with sling swivels, approx. 7 3/8 lbs. New 1998.

MSR $981	$800	$575	$475	$375	$300	$275	$250

✴ *Gold Stalker Field (Classic)* - similar to Gold Stalker, except has semi-hump back receiver design, magazine cutoff and adj. comb, 26 or 28 in. VR barrel. New 1999.

MSR $981	$800	$575	$475	$375	$300	$275	$250

This model is available through Full-line and Medallion dealers only.

✴ *Gold Turkey/Waterfowl Stalker* - similar to Gold Stalker, except has 24 in. VR barrel with extra full choke tube, Hi-Viz sights, matte non-glare wood and finish, 7 lbs. Mfg. 1999-2000.

	$710	$525	$425	$350	$300	$275	$250

Last MSR was $850.

✴ *Gold NWTF Stalker* - 12 ga. only, 3 in. chamber, 24 in. VR barrel with 3 chokes tubes and Hi-Viz sight, 7 lbs. Mfg. 2001-2002.

	$635	$475	$415	$350	$295	$275	$250

Last MSR was $744.

✴ *Gold Rifled Deer Stalker* - 12 ga. only, 22 in. rifled barrel, cantilevered scope mount, sling swivels, 7.75 lbs. New 1997.

MSR $1,086	$875	$600	$475	$395	$340	$295	$265

GOLD 3 1/2 IN. STALKER - 12 ga., 3 1/2 in. chamber, 26, 28, or 30 (disc. 2002) in. VR barrel with Invector Plus choking, otherwise similar to Gold Stalker, 3-4 shot mag., approx. 7 lbs. 10 oz. New 1998.

MSR $1,148	$950	$725	$625	$525	$425	$375	$335

✴ *Gold 3 1/2 Turkey/Waterfowl Stalker* - similar to Gold 3 1/2 Stalker, except has 24 in. VR barrel with extra full choke tube, matte non-glare wood and finish, 7 1/4 lbs. Mfg. 1999-2000.

	$860	$685	$595	$500	$420	$375	$335

Last MSR was $1,022.

GOLD SPORTING CLAYS - 12 ga. only, similar specs as the Gold Hunter, except has 2 3/4 in. chamber, 28 or 30 in. ported barrel with Invector Plus choking, gloss finished walnut stock and forearm, adj. stock shims, Hi-Viz front sight, approx. 7.75 lbs. New 1996.

MSR $1,105	$875	$595	$475	$375	$325	$285	$260

This model is supplied standard with 2 interchangeable gas pistons for light or heavy loads.

* *Gold Golden Clays* - 12 ga. only, 2 3/4 in. chamber, nickel finished engraved receiver with gold accents and game birds, new scroll motif was introduced during 2005, deluxe satin finished checkered walnut stock and forearm, 28 or 30 in. VR ported barrel with Hi-Viz tri-comp front sight and mid-bead, approx. 7.75 lbs. New 1999.

MSR $1,812	$1,450	$1,175	$925	$850	$750	$650	$550

  Subtract approx. 10% if with older engraving motif (non-scroll, disc. 2004).

* *Gold Sporting Ladies/Youth* - similar to Gold Sporting Clays, except has shorter 13 1/2 in. LOP stock, 28 in. barrel only, approx. 7.5 lbs. New 1999.

MSR $1,105	$875	$595	$475	$375	$325	$285	$260

  >**Gold Golden Clays Ladies/Youth** - similar to Gold Sporting Ladies/Youth, except features coin finished receiver with "golden clays" rose motif and gold enhancements, satin finished select walnut stock and forearm. New 2005.

MSR $1,812	$1,450	$1,275	$1,000	$875	$750	$625	$550

BSA 10 - while advertised, this gun had its model nomenclature changed to the Gold 10 Ga. before mfg. started.

GOLD LIGHT 10 GA. HUNTER/STALKER

GOLD LIGHT 10 GA. HUNTER/STALKER - 10 ga. Mag., 3 1/2 in. chamber, short stroke self-cleaning gas action, 4 shot mag., steel (disc. 2000) or aluminum (new 2001) receiver, choice of high polish (Hunter Model, disc. 2000), dull finish (Stalker Model, disc. 1999, reintroduced 2000) bluing, 24 (NWTF Model only with Break-Up, new 2001), 26, 28, or 30 (disc. 2001) in. VR standard Invector choke barrel, available with either high-gloss checkered walnut (Hunter, disc. 2002) stock/forearm, matte black fiberglass (Stalker, disc. 1998, reintroduced 2000-2003) stock/forearm, or choice of 100% camo treatment in Shadow Grass (disc. 2003), Break-Up (mfg. 2001-2003), New Shadow Grass (new 2005) or New Break-Up (new 2004), vent recoil pad, Dura-Touch armor coating became standard for camo finishes during 2003, approx. 9.5 lbs. (aluminum reciever) or 10 lbs. 10 oz. (steel receiver), mfg. by Miroku, Japan. New 1994.

MSR $1,336	$1,100	$865	$735	$625	$525	$450	$400

Add $111 for the NWTF Model with Mossy Oak New Break-Up.

Add 10% for extra 24 in. turkey barrel.

Subtract approx. 10% for matte black fiberglass stock and forearm.

Subtract 10% for steel receiver.

During 1999-2001, this model was packaged to include an extra 24 in. turkey barrel.

SHOTGUNS: SINGLE BARREL, BT-99 & BT-100

BT-99 STANDARD TRAP GUN - 12 ga., 32 or 34 in. vent. rib barrel, mod., imp. mod., or full choke, boxlock, auto ejector, checkered pistol grip with Monte Carlo or conventional style stock, beavertail forearm. Invector chokes became standard in 1986 and ported barrel with Invector Plus chokes and back boring became standard in 1992. Values below assume Invector Plus choking with ported barrel. Mfg. 1968-94 by Miroku.

		$895	$700	$550	$460	$400	$360	$330

  Last MSR was $1,288.

  Subtract $125 without Invector chokes or ported barrels.

* *BT-99 2 Barrel Set* - without Invector choking or barrel porting. Disc. 1983.

		$1,050	$850	$750	$700	$650	$600	$550

* *BT-99 Stainless* - features all stainless construction with Invector Plus ported 32 or 34 in. black VR barrel. Mfg. 1993-94.

		$1,325	$995	$850	$700	$575	$495	$450

  Last MSR was $1,738.

GRADING - PPGS™	100%	98%	95%	90%	80%	70%	60%

✱ *Current Mfg. BT-99* - choice of 32 or 34 in. back bored unported barrel with 11/32 in. high post rib and one full Invector Plus choke tube, conventional or adj. comb stock, beavertail forearm, ejector only, 8 lbs. 5 oz. New 2001.

MSR $1,329	$1,100	$850	$725	$600	$500	$425	$395

Add $255 for factory adj. comb stock.

✱ *BT-99 Micro* - 30 or 32 in. high post VR barrel, similar to BT-99, except has short-ened 13 3/4 LOP, approx. 7.75 lbs. New 2004.

MSR $1,329	$1,100	$850	$725	$600	$500	$425	$395

✱ *Pigeon Grade* - features higher grade walnut and gold receiver accents, Invector chokes and ported barrels. Mfg. 1993-94.

	$1,225	$895	$715	$600	$525	$495	$450

Last MSR was $1,505.

1978-1985 mfg.	$1,700	$1,500	$1,200	$1,100	$650	$575	$525

Older Pigeon Grade guns featured a satin grey receiver with deep relief, engraved pigeons in a fleur-de-lis background.

✱ *Signature Painted* - features painted red/black stock with Browning logos on stock and forearm, Invector Plus ported barrels. Mfg. 1993-94.

	$1,015	$900	$800	$700	$600	$500	$330

Last MSR was $1,323.

✱ *BT-99 Golden Clays* - features high-grade wood and gold outline receiver and inlays depicting a transitional hunting to clay pigeon scene, current mfg. includes ported barrel, adj. comb and LOP, and GraCoil recoil reduction, approx. 9 lbs. Mfg. 1994, reintroduced 2003.

MSR $3,509	$2,650	$1,950	$1,450	$1,150	$975	$875	$795

Subtract 15% for older mfg. w/o current features.

GRADE I BT-99 PLUS - similar to BT-99, except has adj. rib to control point of impact and new recoil reduction system that reduces felt recoil by 50%, stock has adj. comb and buttplate (recoil pad), back-bored barrel, Invector chokes, 8 3/4 lbs. Mfg. 1989-94.

	$1,400	$1,300	$1,200	$1,100	$1,000	$800	$700

Last MSR was $1,835.

Add 5% for ported barrel.

In 1990, the Grade I designation was added to this model. In 1991, this model was supplied with a travel vault gun case as standard equipment. Older mfg. will not have these cases as an original accessory.

Beginning 1991, a Micro Plus Model was introduced that incorporates smaller dimensions (shorter stock and choice of shorter barrel). Values are the same as listed.

✱ *BT-99 Plus Stainless* - features all stainless construction with Invector Plus ported 32 or 34 in. black VR barrel. Mfg. 1993-94.

	$1,710	$1,245	$975				

Last MSR was $2,240.

Beginning 1991, a Micro Plus Model was introduced that incorporates smaller dimensions (shorter stock and choice of shorter barrel). Values are the same as listed.

✱ *BT-99 Plus Pigeon Grade* - features higher grade walnut and gold receiver accents, Invector chokes and ported barrels. Mfg. 1993-disc.

	$1,595	$1,200	$925	$800	$700	$600	$500

Last MSR was $2,065.

Beginning 1991, a Micro Plus Model was introduced that incorporates smaller dimensions (shorter stock and choice of shorter barrel). Values are the same.

GRADING - PPGS™	100%	98%	95%	90%	80%	70%	60%

✳ **BT-99 Plus Signature Painted** - features painted red/black stock with Browning logos on stock and forearm, Invector Plus ported barrels. Mfg. 1993-94.

	$1,500	$1,150	$915	$800	$700	$600	$500

Last MSR was $1,890.

Beginning 1991, a Micro Plus Model was introduced that incorporates smaller dimensions (shorter stock and choice of shorter barrel). Values are the same.

✳ **BT-99 Plus Golden Clays** - features high-grade wood and gold outline receiver and inlays depicting a transitional hunting to clay pigeon scene. Mfg. 1994 only.

	$2,700	$2,350	$2,050	$1,850	$1,700	$1,550	$1,395

Last MSR was $3,205.

Beginning 1991, a Micro Plus Model was introduced that incorporates smaller dimensions (shorter stock and choice of shorter barrel). Values are the same.

BT-99 MAX - 12 ga. only, choice of blue steel with engraving or stainless steel barrel, receiver, and trigger guard, 32 or 34 in. high post VR ported barrel, thin forearm with finger grooves, select walnut pistol grip stock (regular or Monte Carlo) with high gloss finish, ejector/ extractor selector, no safety, approx. 8 lbs. 10 oz. Mfg. 1995-96.

	$1,250	$925	$725	$600	$525	$495	$450

Last MSR was $1,496.

Add $400 for stainless steel.

BT-100 STANDARD TRAP GUN - 12 ga. only, 32 or 34 in. steel high-post ported Invector Plus or fixed choked (F) barrel, without safety, choice of blue or stainless steel receiver, removable trigger assembly, ejector selector (either ejects or extracts) adj. comb and thumbhole stock (disc. 1999) are optional, approx. 8 lbs. 10 oz. Mfg. 1995-2002.

	$1,835	$1,225	$985	$780	$575	$495	$450

Last MSR was $2,266.

Subtract approx. 10% for fixed choke.
Add $100 for adj. comb.
Add $558 for replacement trigger assembly (blue or stainless).

✳ **Stainless BT-100** - features stainless steel barrel, receiver, trigger guard and top lever. Disc. 2002.

	$2,310	$1,475	$1,125				

Last MSR was $2,742.

Subtract approx. 10% for fixed choke.
Add $100 for adj. comb.
Add $558 for replacement trigger assembly (blue or stainless).

BT-100 SATIN (LOW LUSTRE) - features 32 or 34 in. Invector Plus barrel, satin/ low lustre metal/wood finish, conventional type stock without Monte Carlo, quick removable trigger with adj. trigger pull, 8 lbs. 10 oz. Mfg. 1998-2000.

	$1,365	$1,100	$935	$750	$650	$575	$495

Last MSR was $1,684.

SHOTGUNS: SINGLE BARREL, RECOILLESS TRAP

RECOILLESS SINGLE BARREL TRAP - 12 ga., special bolt action design that eliminates 72% of felt recoil, 27 (also available in Micro Model) or 30 in. high-post vent. rib Invector Plus choked back-bored barrel, rib adjusts for 3 points of impact (3, 6, or 9 in.), stock has adj. pull (2 sizes) and comb height, anodized receiver, no safety, approx. 8 1/2 lbs. Mfg. 1994-96.

	$700	$600	$550	$525	$500	$450	$400

Last MSR was $1,995.

The Micro Model features a 27 in. barrel and shorter length of pull.

GRADING - PPGS™	100%	98%	95%	90%	80%	70%	60%

* **Signature Painted** - features painted red/black stock with Browning logos on stock and forearm, Invector Plus ported barrels. Mfg. 1994 only.

		$1,000	$900	$700	$650	$500	$450	$400

Last MSR was $1,900.

SHOTGUNS: SLIDE ACTION

Do not use BPS barrels chambered for 3 1/2 in. shotshells on a BPS 3 in. receiver or vice versa.

BPS HUNTER/FIELD MODEL - 12, 20, or 28 (new 1994) ga. or .410 bore (new 2000), 2 3/4 (28 ga. only) or 3 in. chamber, bottom ejection, double action bars, top tang safety, 5 shot capacity, vent. rib, all steel receiver with variety of finishes, receiver engraving became standard 1991 and was disc. during 1998, 20 and 28 ga. are approx. 1/2 lb. lighter than 12 ga. Field Models, Invector or Invector Plus (new 1994 in 20 ga.) choking, various barrel lengths, Invector Plus choking became standard 1995 (except 28 ga.), back bored barrels on 12 and 20 ga. BPS Models (except Game guns) became standard during 2003, 6 3/4 lbs. - 8 lbs. 3 oz. Mfg. by Miroku 1977-to-date.

MSR $509	$375	$325	$275	$225	$200	$185	$170

Add $35 for 28 ga. or .410 bore.

Subtract 10% if without Invector Plus choke tubes.

* **Stalker Model** - 12 ga. only, 3 in. chamber, all metal parts have a dull matte finish, non-glare black synthetic composite stock and forearm, 24 (mfg. 1999-2000), 26, 28, or 30 in. VR barrel, approx. 8 lbs. New 1987.

MSR $492	$360	$315	$265	$225	$200	$185	$170

* **BPS Camouflage** - 12 or 20 (NWTF Model, new 2003) ga., 3 in. chamber, features Mossy Oak Shadow Grass, Mossy Oak Break-Up (mfg. 2000-2003), or New Break-Up (new 2004) full camo treatment, 24 (standard model disc., or NWTF Model with Mossy Oak Break-Up camo – new 2001), 26, or 28 in. barrel, Dura-Touch armor coating became standard during 2003, approx. 8 lbs. New 1999.

MSR $605	$415	$365	$335	$300	$275	$245	$215

Add $31 for NWTF Model with 24 in. barrel with New Mossy Oak Break-Up camo treatment.

Add $69 for 20 ga. NWTF Break-Up Model.

* **Pigeon Grade** - 12 ga. only, 3 in. chamber, features high grade walnut and gold trimmed receiver, 26 or 28 in. VR barrel with Invector chokes, 7 lbs. 10 oz. Mfg. 1992-98.

	$500	$465	$395	$350	$310	$290	$275

Last MSR was $603.

* **Upland Special** - 12 or 20 ga., 3 in. chamber, 22 in. VR barrel, straight grip stock, Invector (pre-1994) or Invector Plus (new 1994, standard 1995) choking, 6.75 - 7.5 lbs. Mfg. 1985-current.

MSR $509	$360	$325	$275	$225	$200	$185	$170

Subtract 10% if without Invector Plus choke tubes.

* **Turkey Special** - 12 ga. only, 3 in. chamber, 20 1/2 in. lightened barrel, non-glare walnut stock, matte finished barrel and receiver, receiver is drilled and tapped for scope base, rifle-style stock dimensions, sling swivels, new extra-full Invector choke tube, 7 lbs. 8 oz. Mfg. 1992-2001.

	$400	$340	$275	$240	$215	$190	$175

Last MSR was $500.

* **Micro Model** - 20 ga. only, 22 in. vent. rib barrel, pistol grip stock (13 1/4 LOP), Invector Plus choking (includes 3 chokes), 6.75 lbs. New 2001.

MSR $509	$360	$325	$275	$225	$200	$185	$170

GRADING - PPGS™	100%	98%	95%	90%	80%	70%	60%

✻ *Micro - Youth and Ladies Model* - 20 ga. only, 22 in. vent. rib barrel, straight grip shortened stock (13 1/4 LOP), Invector (pre-1994) or Invector Plus (new 1994, standard 1995) choking, 6 3/4 lbs. Mfg. 1986-2002.

	$385	$300	$260	$225	$200	$185	$170

Last MSR was $473.

Subtract 10% if without Invector Plus choke tubes.

✻ *Deer Hunter/Special (DG, DS or DH)* - 12 ga. only, 3 in. chamber, 20 1/2 (disc. 2000) or 22 in. barrel with 5 in. rifled choke tube or rifled barrel (DH, cantilever scope mount with satin finish only, new 1997), iron sights, scope mount base, choice of gloss (DG, disc. 1997) or satin (DS, disc. 2000) finish checkered stock with recoil pad and forearm, sling swivels, polished or matte finished metal, approx. 7.5 lbs. New 1992.

MSR $624	$485	$395	$315	$255	$220	$195	$175

Subtract approx. 10% for rifled choke tube.

✻ *Buck Special* - 12 or 20 (disc. 1984) ga., 3 in. chamber, 24 in. cyl. bore barrel, iron sights, 7 lbs. 10 oz. Reintroduced 1988-disc. 1998.

	$335	$275	$230	$200	$185	$175	$160

Last MSR was $409.

BPS MAGNUM HUNTER/STALKER 12 GA.

- 12 ga., 3 1/2 in. chamber, 24 (disc. 1997, reintroduced 1999-2000 - Stalker only), 26, 28, or 30 (disc. 1997) in. barrel with Invector chokes and vent. rib, 4 shot mag., 7.75 lbs. Hunter 3 1/2 in. Model disc. 2002.

MSR $579	$465	$390	$345	$315	$275	$245	$215

In 1990, the back-bored Invector plus choke tube system became standard in 12 ga. 3 1/2 in. chamber only.

✻ *Camo Magnum Hunter 3 1/2 In.* - 12 ga., similar to Magnum Hunter or Stalker, features Mossy Oak Shadow Grass or Mossy Oak Break-Up (new 2000) full camo treatment, 24 (standard model disc., or NWTF Model with Mossy Oak Break-Up camo – new 2001), 26, or 28 in. VR barrel, Dura-Touch armor coating became standard during 2003, approx. 7.75 - 9.25 lbs. New 1999.

MSR $688	$565	$475	$415	$355	$310	$290	$275

Add $50 for NWTF Model with 24 in. barrel (12 ga., available in Mossy Oak Break-Up only beginning 2000).

✻ *Magnum Hunting Waterfowl* - 10 ga., 3 1/2 in. Mag. with choice of 28 or 30 in. matte finished VR barrel with standard Invector choking, features higher grade walnut and gold trimmed receiver with Waterfowl outlined, approx. 9 lbs. 6 oz. Mfg. 1993-98.

	$615	$525	$450	$400	$350	$315	$285

Last MSR was $750.

✻ *3 1/2 In. Buck Special* - 10 or 12 (disc. 1994) ga., 3 1/2 in. chambers, 24 in. cyl. bore barrel, 7 lbs. 10 oz. Mfg. 1990-97.

	$570	$460	$410	$370	$335	$310	$290

Last MSR was $677.

BPS MAGNUM HUNTER/STALKER 10 GA.

- 10 ga., 3 1/2 in. chamber, currently available in either Stalker (black synthetic stock and forearm), or camo (choice of Mossy Oak New Break-Up or New Shadowgrass with Dura-Touch coating) configuration, 10.5 lbs. Disc. 2001, reintroduced 2004.

MSR $579	$465	$390	$345	$315	$275	$245	$215

Add $109 for camo.

✻ *BPS 10 ga. NWTF* - features 24 in. VR barrel with Hi-Viz Tri-Viz fiber optic sights and extra full XF extended turkey choke tube, 100% Mossy Oak New Break-Up camo coverage, NWTF logo on synthetic stock, 10 lbs., 3 oz.

MSR $738	$550	$475	$425	$375	$325	$275	$225

GRADING - PPGS™	100%	98%	95%	90%	80%	70%	60%

BPS TRAP MODEL - 12 ga., 30 in. barrel. Disc. 1984 but trap barrels were available separately for several years.

	$360	$300	$270	$230	$210	$190	$170

BPS WILD TURKEY FEDERATION COMMEMORATIVE - only 500 manufactured. Disc. 1991.

	$495	$395	$325

BPS PACIFIC EDITION DU - limited mfg., DU serialization, cased.

	$595	$475	$350

BPS COASTAL DU - limited mfg., DU serialization, cased.

	$595	$475	$350

BPS WATERFOWL DELUXE - 12 ga. Mag., gold trigger and etching, Invector chokes, limited mfg.

	$625	$525	$450

MODEL 12 LIMITED EDITION SERIES

* *Grade I 20 Ga.* - 20 ga. only, 2 3/4 in. chamber only, reproduction of the famous Winchester Model 12 with slight design improvements, 26 in. VR barrel bored modified, 5 shot mag., high post floating rib, walnut stock and forearm with semi-gloss finish, take down, serialization format similar to 28 ga., 7 lbs. 1 oz. 8,000 mfg. in 1988 with inventory depleted 1990.

	$450	$400	$300

Last MSR was $735.

* *Grade V 20 Ga.* - similar specifications to Grade I, except has select walnut checkered 22 lines per inch with high gloss finish, extensive game scene engraving including multiple gold inlays serialization format similar to 28 ga. Mfg. 1988 only.

	$795	$695	$575

Last MSR was $1,187.

Browning Arms Company limited manufacture to 4,000 Grade V 20 Ga.'s.

* *Grade I 28 Ga.* - 28 ga. only, similar to Grade I 20 Ga., except in 28 ga., 26 in. VR modified choke barrel, 5 digit ser. no. with NM872 suffix. 7,000 mfg. 1991-92.

	$450	$400	$300

Last MSR was $772.

* *Grade V 28 ga.* - 28 ga. only, similar to Grade V 20 ga., except in 28 ga., 26 in. VR modified choke barrel, 5 digit ser. no. with NM972 suffix. 5,000 mfg. 1991-92.

	$795	$695	$575

Last MSR was $1,246.

MODEL 42 LIMITED EDITION

* *Model 42 Grade I* - .410 bore, 3 in. chamber, reproduction of the Winchester Model 42 with slight design improvements, 26 in. VR full choke barrel, select walnut stock, 5 digit ser. no. with NZ882 suffix, 6 lbs. 12 oz. 6,000 mfg. late 1991-1993.

	$495	$400	$300

Last MSR was $800.

* *Model 42 Grade V* - .410 bore, engraving and embellishments similar to the Model 12 Grade V, 5 digit ser. no. with NZ982 suffix, 6,000 mfg. late 1991-1993.

	$795	$695	$575

Last MSR was $1,360.

SPECIAL EDITIONS, COMMEMORATIVES, & LIMITED MFG.

Please refer to the *Blue Book of Modern Black Powder Arms* by John Allen & Dennis Adler (now online also) for more information and prices on Browning black powder rifles.

GRADING - PPGS™	100%	98%	95%	90%	80%	70%	60%

BICENTENNIAL 1876-1976 SET - .45-70 Govt. cal., Model 78 rifle with specially engraved receiver, silver finish, fancy wood, cased, with engraved knife and medallion, 1,000 sets mfg. in 1976. Issue price - $1,500.

$1,750	$1,300	$850	

CENTENNIAL O/U RIFLE/SHOTGUN - 20 ga. O/U shotgun w/extra set of .30-06 O/U rifle barrels. Shotgun barrels are 26 1/2 in., rifle barrels are 24 in., SST, ejectors, elaborate scroll engraved receiver with 2 gold inlays, straight grip special oil finished walnut stock and forearm, deluxe walnut full-length case. 500 mfg. 1978 only.

$6,250	$5,750	$4,950	$4,450	$3,900	$3,500	$2,975

Last MSR was $7,000.

CENTENNIAL SET - complete Browning set mfg. in 1978, includes the Centennial O/U rifle/shotgun, 9mm Hi-Power, B92 .44 Mag., Mountain Rifle, and a set of three knives.

$8,250	$7,000	$5,750

1 OF 50 BICENTENNIAL RIFLE - .30-06 cal., Model 78 single shot with 26 in. octagon barrel, includes special engraving by Neil Hartliep (non-factory), extra fine walnut, 4X wide angle scope, special luggage case. 50 mfg. (one for each state) during 1976 only and sold by silent mail order bidding (minimum bid was $3,100 in 1976).

As very few specimens are bought or sold each year, pricing is rather unpredictable. A few specimens have been sold in the $5,000 range recently. Remember, the work on this gun was subcontracted by Centennial Guns (division of Frigon Guns located in Clay Center, KS).

BUCK MARK COMMEMORATIVE PISTOL - features 6 3/4 in. Challenger style tapered barrel, white bonded ivory grips with scrimshaw style patterning including "1 of 1,000 Commemorative Model" on sides, matte blue finish, gold trigger, 30 1/2 oz. 1,000 mfg. 2001-2002.

$335	$275	$225

Last MSR was $437.

BRUCHET

Current manufacturer located in Saint Etienne, France. Distributed exclusively from 1982- 1989 by Wes Gilpin located in Dallas, TX. In 1989, Bruchet was able to get permission to use the older Darne trademark and all new manufacture will be entered under the Darne listing.

Paul Bruchet has been manufacturing his shotguns patterned after the Darne action since 1981, following his tenure at Darne as line foreman until 1979 (at which time the Darne plant closed). These new Bruchet Models were designated "A" or "B". All shotguns were totally hand made with approx. 50 guns being mfg. each year.

Since Paul Bruchet was able to retain the Darne trademark in 1989, please refer to the Darne section in this text for current manufacture.

SHOTGUNS: SxS

MODEL A - 12, 16, 20, 28 ga., or .410 bore, small key opening, ejectors, double triggers only, basically 4 variations (1, 1A, 2, and 2A), wide assortment of customer specified special orders.

Retail values were as follows: Model 1A started at under $2,000, the Model 2 started at $3,000, and the Model 2A started at $3,500. Each additional grade represented more embellishments and better grade of walnut. Magnum chambers could be ordered at a small surcharge. Importation began 1982, values represent the last published retail prices from 1989.

MODEL B - 12, 16, 20, 28 ga., or .410 bore, large key opening, self-opening (assisted) action, ejectors, double triggers only, basically special ordered to individual customer specifications.

Retail values were as follows: Model B starts at $5,800 and included deluxe carrying case. Each additional upgrade represented more embellishments and a better grade of walnut. Magnum chambers could be ordered at a small surcharge. Importation began 1982, values represent the last published retail prices from 1989.

GRADING - PPGS™	100%	98%	95%	90%	80%	70%	60%

BRYCO ARMS

Current manufacturer located in Irvine, CA. Distributed by Jennings Firearms, Inc. located in Carson City, NV. Distributor sales only.

PISTOLS: SEMI-AUTO, SINGLE ACTION

MODEL T-22 - while advertised during 1997 at a retail price of $179, this model was never produced.

MODEL J-25 - .25 ACP cal., aluminum alloy frame, 2.5 in. barrel, single action, synthetic ivory, walnut, or black combat grips, positive safety, 11 oz. Mfg. 1988-95, reintroduced 1999.

MSR $79	$65	$55	$45	$40	$35	$30	$30

    This model is available in either satin nickel, bright chrome, or black teflon finish.

MODEL M-32/M-38 - .22 LR (disc.), .32 ACP, or .380 ACP cal., semi-auto single action, 2.8 in. barrel, pressure cast fabrication using non-ferrous alloy, chrome or blue finish, black combat grips, 16 oz. New 1991.

MSR $79	$65	$50	$40	$35	$30	$30	$30

    Add $20 for .380 ACP cal.

MODEL M-48 - .22 LR, .32 ACP, or .380 ACP cal., semi-auto single action, 4 in. barrel, larger frame variation of the M-38, chrome or blue finish, black combat grips, 24 oz. Mfg. 1991-95.

		$85	$75	$65	$55	$50	$45	$40

    Last MSR was $96.

MODEL M-5 - .380 ACP or 9mm Para. cal., 3 1/4 in. barrel, 10 or 12 shot mag., blue or nickel finish, black synthetic grips, 36 oz. Disc. 1995.

		$85	$75	$65	$55	$50	$45	$40

    Last MSR was $100 for the .380 ACP, $119 for 9mm Para.

    Add $15 for 9mm Para. cal.

MODEL M-59 - .380 ACP or 9mm Para. cal., 4 in. barrel, 10 shot mag., blue or nickel finish, black synthetic grips, 36 oz. Disc. 1995.

	$95	$85	$75	$70	$65	$60	$55

    Last MSR was $119.

    Add $15 for 9mm Para. cal.

JENNINGS NINE - 9mm Para. cal., single action, redesigned model 59, frame mounted ejector, contour grips, loaded chamber indicator, 30 oz. New 1997.

MSR $145	$120	$100	$85	$75	$65	$55	$50

BUDISCHOWSKY

Previous manufacturer located in Mt. Clemens, MI.

PISTOLS: SEMI-AUTO

TP-70 - .22 LR cal., double action, 2 1/2 in. barrel, stainless steel, fixed sights, plastic grips. Mfg. 1973-77.

	$440	$385	$330

TP-70 - similar to TP-70, except .25 ACP cal. Mfg. 1973-77.

	$330	$275	$220

    Note: In 1977, Norton Arms marketed this pistol. Quality of workmanship is not on par with the early Budischowsky and values are approx. 35% less.

SEMI-AUTO PISTOL - .223 Rem. cal., 11 5/8 in. barrel, 20 or 30 shot mag., fixed sights, a novel paramilitary designed type pistol.

	$470	$415	$385	$360	$305	$250	$220

GRADING - PPGS™	100%	98%	95%	90%	80%	70%	60%

RIFLES: SEMI-AUTO

PARAMILITARY DESIGN RIFLE - .223 Rem. cal., semi-auto, 18 in. barrel, wood paramilitary stock.

	100%	98%	95%	90%	80%	70%	60%
	$505	$440	$415	$385	$330	$275	$250

PARAMILITARY DESIGN RIFLE W/FOLDING STOCK

	100%	98%	95%	90%	80%	70%	60%
	$575	$500	$450	$425	$395	$360	$330

BULLARD ARMS

Previous manufacturer located in Springfield, MA, circa 1880s.

Designed by prolific inventor James Bullard, the design, quality, and workmanship of Bullard rifles rivaled those of any competitor during the 1880s. Bullard made two basic rifles: a lever action repeater and a single shot. The repeater was made in two frame styles: large and small. The single shot was also made in two basic styles; solid frame and detachable-interchangeable barrel model.

100%	98%	95%	90%	80%	70%	60%	50%	40%	30%	20%	10%

RIFLES: LEVER ACTION

LEVER ACTION REPEATER - rack and pinion style lever activated mechanism, mag. mounted under barrel, loaded through underside of action while lever was opened, blue finish with various parts (including receiver) sometimes case hardened, approx. 2,800 mfg.

✳ *Large Frame* - .40-60, .45-60, .45-70 Govt., .45-75, .50-95, .40-70 Bullard, .40-90 Bullard, .45-85 Bullard or .50-115 Bullard cal., 26 or 28 in. round, octagon, or part round barrel, crescent steel or hard rubber buttplates with elk motif, ser. no. range 1-1,500 and 2,000-3,000.

100%	98%	95%	90%	80%	70%	60%	50%	40%	30%	20%	10%
N/A	N/A	$2,800	$2,450	$1,950	$1,750	$1,625	$1,450	$1,275	$1,150	$975	$850

Add 25% for .40-90 Bullard, .50-95, or .50-115 Bullard cal.

Add 25% for deluxe checkered wood with pistol grip.

Various military and experimental models are found in this frame size and will command significant premiums.

✳ *Small Frame* - .32-40 Bullard or .38-45 Bullard cal., (other calibers cataloged, but essentially unknown), 24, 26, or 28 in. round, octagon or part round barrel, crescent steel or hard rubber buttplates with turkey motif, ser. no. range 1,500-2,000.

100%	98%	95%	90%	80%	70%	60%	50%	40%	30%	20%	10%
N/A	N/A	$2,400	$2,000	$1,750	$1,550	$1,375	$1,175	$1,025	$900	$825	$750

Add 25% for deluxe checkered wood with pistol grip.

Add 40% for any caliber other than .32-40 and .38-45.

Although the small frame saw less production and is scarcer than the large frame repeater, it is not as desirable among collectors, and is typically priced less than a large frame model.

RIFLES: SINGLE SHOT

SINGLE SHOT MODEL - thin receiver with full lever, similar in appearance to small frame repeater action, except shorter (several parts including lever will interchange), 26, 28, or 30 in. round, octagon, or part round barrel, blue finish with various parts sometimes case hardened (including receiver), crescent steel or hard rubber buttplates, ser. no. range 3,500-4,100.

✳ *Solid Frame* - wide variety of cals. from .22 rimfire to .50 cal., (.22 and .32-40 are most common), essentially one frame size, except the .22 was somewhat smaller.

100%	98%	95%	90%	80%	70%	60%	50%	40%	30%	20%	10%
N/A	N/A	$2,500	$2,200	$1,850	$1,575	$1,450	$1,375	$1,250	$1,125	$995	$900

100%	98%	95%	90%	80%	70%	60%	50%	40%	30%	20%	10%

* ✳ **Detachable-interchangeable Barrel Model** - same cals. as small frame model with two frame sizes - small (.38 cal. and smaller) and large (.40 cal. and larger), interchangeable barrels could not be switched between the two frame sizes, barrel and breech detach from action.

N/A	N/A	$2,500	$2,200	$1,850	$1,575	$1,450	$1,375	$1,250	$1,125	$995	$900

Add 20% for large frame.
Add 30% for .50 cals.
Add 30% for extra barrel with forend (numbers matching).
Add 30% for Schuetzen model.
Add 25% for deluxe checkered wood with pistol grip.

BUL TRANSMARK LTD.

Current manufacturer located in Tel Aviv, Israel. Currently imported beginning 2003 by K.B.I., located in Harrisburg, PA. Previously imported and distributed in North America during 2002 by EAA Corp., located in Sharpes, FL. Previously imported and distributed 1997-2001 by International Security Academy (ISA) located in Los Angeles, CA, and from 1996-1997 by All America Sales, Inc. located in Memphis, TN. Dealer sales only.

GRADING - PPGS™	100%	98%	95%	90%	80%	70%	60%

PISTOLS: SEMI-AUTO

Please refer to the Charles Daly section in this text for current information and prices on Bul Transmark pistols (marked Charles Daly beginning 2004.)

M-5 frame kits were previously available at $399 retail.

BUL IMPACT - while advertised during 1999, this model was never produced.

BUL STORM & COMPACT - while advertised during 1999, this model was never produced.

BUL 1911 GOVERNMENT (M-5 STANDARD) - .38 Super (disc.), 9mm Para. (disc.), .40 S&W (disc.), or .45 ACP cal., single action, 5 in. barrel, polymer double column frame, steel slide, aluminum speed trigger, checkered front and rear grip straps, blue or chrome (new 2000) finished slide, 10 shot staggered mag., 31-33 oz. Imported 1995-2000, reintroduced 2002-2003.

			$525	$450	$375	$325	$295	$275	$250

Last MSR was $559.

Add 10% for .38 Super or .40 S&W cal.

* ✳ **Bul Commander (M5 Standard)** - similar to M-5 Government, except has 3.8 (disc.), 4 1/3 (new 2004) or 4 1/4 (disc.) in. barrel, 29-30 oz. Imported 1998-2000, reintroduced 2002-2003.

			$525	$450	$375	$325	$295	$275	$250

Last MSR was $559.

Add 10% for .38 Super or .40 S&W cal.
Add $40 for matte chrome finished slide.

* ✳ **Bul M5 Stinger** - similar to Bul 1911 Government, except has 10 shot mag., 3 in. barrel, 24 oz. Imported 2002-2003.

			$525	$450	$375	$325	$295	$275	$250

Last MSR was $559.

* ✳ **Bul M-5 Standard Street Comp.** - similar to M-5 Standard Commander, except has single port compensated 4 1/4 in. barrel, 32 oz. Imported 1998-99.

			$960	$825	$700	$600	$500	$450	$375

Last MSR was $1,060.

Add $28 for .38 Super or .40 S&W cal.

GRADING - PPGS™	100%	98%	95%	90%	80%	70%	60%

❊ *Bul M-5 Multi Caliber* - similar cals. as the M-5 Standard Government, includes 3 upper-ends including Commander length, another with adj. sights, and a third with a single port compensator, cased. Imported 1999-2000.

	$1,575	$1,275	$1,050	$850	$725	$625	$525

Last MSR was $1,768.

BUL M-5 STANDARD IPSC - .38 Super, 9mm Para., .40 S&W, or .45 ACP cal., configured for IPSC competition, with custom slide to frame fit and match grade barrel bushing. Imported 1998-2001, reintroduced 2003.

	$925	$825	$725	$625	$525	$425	$375

Last MSR was $990.

Add $111 for .38 Super or .40 S&W cal. (disc. 2001).
Add $70 for chrome finish (mfg. 2000-2001).

BUL M-5 STANDARD MATCH - IPSC custom race gun, includes multi-port compensator system. Imported 1998-99.

	$1,200	$1,000	$825	$700	$600	$500	$425

Last MSR was $1,655.

Add $24 for .38 Super or .40 S&W cal.

BUL M-5 JET - same cals. as the M-5 Standard IPSC, features Commander length with 4 1/4 in. barrel and 4 port compensator on top of barrel, 31 oz. Imported 1999-2000.

	$875	$725	$625	$525	$475	$400	$350

Last MSR was $1,158.

Add $51 for .38 Super or .40 S&W cal.

BUL M-5 MODIFIED - 9mm Para., .38 Super, .40 S&W, or .45 ACP cal., designed for Modified class competition, features new Optima 2000 optical sight fitted to slide, 5 port compensation on top of barrel, includes carrying case, 38 oz. Imported 1998-2001.

	$1,075	$925	$800	$675	$550	$500	$450

Last MSR was $1,430.

BUL M-5 TARGET - same cals. as the M-5 Modified, features 6 in. slide and barrel, choice of sights, and match grade oversize barrel bushing, includes 3 mags and carrying case, 38 oz. Imported 1999-2001.

	$895	$775	$700	$600	$500	$450	$400

Last MSR was $1,196.

Add $315 for Aristocrat Tri-state sights.

BUL M-5 ULTIMATE RACER - top-level IPSC competition gun, includes 3 mags. and carrying case, 38 oz. Imported 1998-2001.

	$1,050	$925	$800	$700	$600	$525	$450

Last MSR was $1,573.

Add $306 for fitted C-more optical sight.

BUSHMASTER FIREARMS

Currently manufactured by Bushmaster Firearms/Quality Parts Company located in Windham, ME. Older mfg. was by Gwinn Arms Co. located in Winston-Salem, NC 1972-1974. The Quality Parts Co. gained control in 1986. Distributor, dealer, or consumer direct sales.

During 2003, Bushmaster purchased Professional Ordnance, previous maker of the Carbon 15 Series of semi-auto pistols and rifles/carbines. Carbon 15s are still made in Lake Havasu City, AZ, but are now marked with Bushmaster logo. For pre-2003 Carbon 15 mfg., please refer to the Professional Ordnance section in this text.

GRADING - PPGS™	100%	98%	95%	90%	80%	70%	60%

PISTOLS: SEMI-AUTO

BUSHMASTER PISTOL - .223 Rem. cal., top bolt (older models with aluminum receivers) or side bolt (most recent mfg.) operation, steel frame (current mfg.), 11 1/2 in. barrel, parkerized finish, adj. sights, wood stock, 5.25 lbs.

	$650	$550	$450	$400	$375	$350	$300

Last MSR was $375.

Add $40 for electroless nickel finish (disc. 1988).
This model uses a 30 shot M-16 mag. and the AK-47 gas system.

CARBON-15 TYPE 21 - .223 Rem cal., ultra lightweight carbon fiber upper and lower receivers, 7.25 in. "Profile" stainless steel barrel, quick detachable muzzle compensator, ghost ring sights, 10 or 30 (new late 2004) shot mag., A2 pistol grip, also accepts AR-15 type mags., Stoner type operating sytem, tool steel bolt, extractor and carrier, 40 oz. New 2003 (Bushmaster mfg.).

MSR $825		$750	$675	$600	$550	$500	$450	$395

Add $170 for Type 21S with full length barrel shroud and Picatinny rail.

CARBON-15 TYPE 97 - similar to Carbon 15 Type 20, except has fluted barrel, Hogue overmolded pistol grip and chrome plated bolt carrier, 46 oz. New 2003 (Bushmaster mfg.).

MSR $892		$795	$725	$625	$575	$525	$475	$425

Add $143 for Type 97S with full length barrel shroud, upper and lower Picatinny rail.

RIFLES: SEMI-AUTO

All currently manufactured Bushmaster rifles are shipped with a hard plastic lockable case. Most Bushmaster barrels are marked "5.56 NATO", and can be used safely with either 5.56 NATO (higher velocity/pressure) or .223 Rem. cal. ammo.

BUSHMASTER RIFLE - .223 Rem. cal., semi-auto, top bolt (older models with aluminum receivers) or side bolt (current mfg.) operation, steel frame (current mfg.), 18 1/2 in. barrel, parkerized finish, adj. sights, wood stock, 6 1/4 lbs., base values are for folding stock model.

	$675	$625	$550	$500	$475	$425	$400

Last MSR was $350.

Add $40 for electroless nickel finish (disc. 1988).
Add $65 for fixed rock maple wood stock.
This model uses a 30 shot M-16 mag. and the AK-47 gas system.

✱ Rifle Combination System - includes rifle with both metal folding stock and wood stock with pistol grip.

	$400	$360	$330	$300	$275	$250	$230

Last MSR was $450.

XM15-E2S/A-2/A-3 TARGET RIFLE - .223 Rem. cal., semi-auto patterned after the Colt AR-15, 20, 24, or 26 in. Govt. spec. match grade chrome lined or stainless steel (new 2002) barrel, 10 or 30 shot mag., manganese phosphate or Realtree Camo (20 in. barrel only, new late 2004) barrel finish, rear sight adj. for windage and elevation, cage flash suppressor (disc. 1994), approx. 8.3 lbs. Mfg. began 1989 in U.S.

MSR $995		$840	$715	$650	$595	$535	$475	$425

Add $50 for fluted barrel or $60 for stainless steel barrel (new 2002).
Add $10 for 24 in. or $25 for 26 in. (disc. 2002) barrel.
Add $100 for A-3 removable carry handle.
Add $60 for Realtree Camo finish.

✳ *XM15-E2S/A-2/A-3 Shorty Carbine* - similar to above, except with fixed or telescoping buttstock and 11 1/2 (disc. 1995), 14 (disc. 1994), or 16 in. barrel with (disc. 1994) or w/o suppressor, approx. 7.4 lbs. Mfg. began 1989.

MSR $985	$830	$715	$650	$595	$535	$475	$425

Add $50 for fluted barrel.
Add $100 for A-3 removable carry handle.
Add $30 for XM15 E2S AK Carbine with 30 shot mag.
Add $10 for dissipator models (features lengthened handguard).
This model does not have the target rear sight system of the XM15-E2S rifle.

✳ *M4 Post-Ban Carbine* (***XM15-E2S***) - 16 in. barrel, features fixed or telestock (new late 2004) tubular stock, pistol grip, phosphate or desert camo (stock, pistol grip, and forearm only) finish, M4 carbine configuration with permanently attached Izzy muzzle brake, 30 shot mag. became standard in late 2004. New 2003.

MSR $1,065	$895	$775	$700	$625	$550	$475	$425

Add $100 for A3 removable carrying handle.
Subtract $55 for M4 Patrolman Carbine with A2 birdcage flash supressor, collapsible stock and 30 round magazine.
Add $35 for desert camo finish.

✳ *Limited Edition 20th Anniversary Rifle* - 20 in. barrel, features 20th Anniversary engraving on upper and lower receiver, special medallion in buttstock, includes hardwood presentation case. Limited mfg. 1998-99.

	$1,495	$1,300	$1,125	$975	$875	$800	$725

✳ *Limited Edition 25th Anniversary Carbine* - features skeletonized tubular stock, pistol grip, A-3 type flatop with flip-up sights, laser engraved 25th anniversary crest on lower magwell, nickel plated ejection port. Limited mfg. of 1,500 during 2003.

	$1,495	$1,300	$1,125	$975	$875	$800	$725

Last MSR was $1,695.

✳ *E2 Carbine* - .223 Rem. cal., features 16 in. match chrome barrel with new M16A2 handguard and short suppressor, choice of A1 or E2 sights. Mfg. 1994-95.

	$895	$825	$725	$650	$600	$550	$500

Add approx. $50 for E2 sighting system.

DISSIPATOR CARBINE - .223 Rem. cal., 16 in. heavy barrel with full length forearm and special gas block placement (gas block system is located behind the front sight base and under the rifle length handguard), A2 or A3 style with choice of solid buttstock or six-position telestock, 30 shot mag., lockable carrying case. New late 2004.

MSR $995	$840	$715	$650	$595	$535	$475	$425

Add $50 for fluted barrel.
Add $100 for A3 removable carrying handle.

SUPERLIGHT CARBINE - .223 Rem. cal., 16 in. lightweight barrel, choice of fixed, tele-style, or stub stock with finger groove pistol grip, A2 or A3 type configuration, black finish, 5.8 - 6.25 lbs. New 2004.

MSR $985	$830	$715	$650	$595	$535	$475	$425

Add $25 for fixed tele-style stock.
Add $100 for A-3 removable carry handle.

MODULAR CARBINE - .223 Rem. cal., 16 in. barrel with flash suppressor, includes many Bushmaster modular accessories, such as skeleton stock and four-rail free floating tubular forearm, rear flip up and detachable sight, 10 or 30 (new late 2004) shot mag., 6.3 lbs. New 2004.

MSR $1,650	$1,475	$1,175	$1,000	$900	$800	$725	$650

GRADING - PPGS™	100%	98%	95%	90%	80%	70%	60%

V-MATCH COMPETITION RIFLE - .223 Rem. cal., top-of-the line match/competition rifle, flattop receiver with extended aluminum barrel shroud, choice of 20, 24, or 26 (disc. 2002) in. barrel, 8.3 lbs. New 1994.

	MSR $1,055	$955	$860	$730	$650	$575	$515	$465

Add $50 for fluted barrel.
Add $10 for 24 in. or $25 for 26 (disc. 2002) in. barrel.
Add $100 for A-3 removable carry handle.

✳ *V-Match Commando Carbine* - similar to V-Match Competition Rifle, except has 16 in. barrel. New 1997.

	MSR $1,045	$945	$850	$725	$650	$575	$515	$465

Add $50 for fluted barrel.
Add $100 for A-3 removable carry handle.

VARMINTER - .223 Rem. cal., includes DCM 24 in. extra heavy fluted or stainless steel varmint barrel, competition trigger, rubberized pistol grip, flattop receiver with mini-risers (add 1/2 in. height for scope mounting), free floating vented tube forearm, 5 shot mag, controlled ejection path. New 2002.

	MSR $1,245	$1,025	$900	$775	$675	$600	$550	$500

The stainless variation includes an adj., ergonomic pistol grip.

DCM COMPETITION RIFLE - .223 Rem. cal., includes DCM competition features such as modified A2 rear sight, 20 in. extra heavy 1 in. diameter competition barrel, custom trigger job, and free-floating hand guard. New 1998.

	MSR $1,495		$1,375	$1,125	$975	$875	$800	$725	$650

M17S BULLPUP - .223 Rem. cal., semi-auto bullpup configuration featuring gas operated rotating bolt, 10 (C/B 1994) or 30* shot mag., 21.5 plain or 22 (disc.) in. barrel with flash-hider (disc.), glass composites and aluminum materials, phosphate coating, 8.25 lbs. New 1992.

	MSR $765		$700	$650	$525	$475	$425	$400	$385

CARBON-15 TYPE 21 - .223 Rem. cal., ultra lightweight carbon fiber upper and lower receivers, 16 in. "Profile" stainless steel barrel, quick detachable muzzle compensator, Stoner type operating system, tool steel bolt, extractor and carrier, optics mounting base, fixed tube stock, 10 or 30 (new late 2004) shot mag., also accepts AR-15 type mags., 3.9 lbs. New 2003 (Bushmaster mfg.).

	MSR $916		$850	$775	$675	$575	$500	$450	$400

✳ *Carbon-15 Lady* - .223 Rem. cal., 16 in. barrel, includes overall tan finish (except for barrel) and webbed tube stock with recoil pad, chrome/nickel plating on small parts, supplied with soft case, 4 lbs. New 2004.

	MSR $989		$875	$775	$675	$575	$500	$450	$400

CARBON-15 TYPE 97/97S - .223 Rem. cal., ultra lightweight carbon fiber upper and lower receivers, Stoner type operating system, hard chromed tool steel bolt, extractor and carrier, 16 in. fluted stainless steel barrel, quick detachable muzzle compensator, optics mounting base, 10 or 30 (new late 2004) shot mag., quick detachable stock, also accepts AR-15 type mags., 3.9 or 4.3 (Model 97S) lbs. New 2003 (Bushmaster mfg.).

	MSR $1,039		$900	$825	$750	$675	$600	$550	$500

Add $153 for Model 97S (includes Picatinny rail and "Scout" extension, double walled heat shield foregrip, ambidextrous safety, and multi-carry silent sling).

CARBON-15 .22 LR - .22 LR cal., similar to Carbon-15 Type 21, 16 in. barrel, Picatinny rail, 10 shot tube mag. fixed stock, approx. 4.4 lbs.

	MSR $746		$650	$550	$475	$400	$350	$300	$265

Bushmaster also makes a Carbon-15 .22 rimfire upper receiver/barrel assembly that is dedicated to Bushmaster lower receivers - current MSR is $387 (new 2005).

CARBON-15 MODEL 4 CARBINE - .223 Rem. cal., features carbon composite receiver, collapsible tube stock, 16 in. barrel with compensator, 30 shot mag., semi-auto design styled after the military M4, 5.5 lbs. New 2005.

	MSR $1,035	$900	$825	$750	$675	$600	$550	$500

BUSHMASTER .308 SERIES - .308 Win. cal., 16 or 20 in. phosphate coated heavy alloy steel barrel with Izzy compensator, 20 shot mag., solid buttstock or skeletonized stock, available in A2 or A3 style with a variety of configurations, including muzzle brakes, flash suppressors, and sighting options. New late 2004.

	MSR $1,750	$1,495	$1,250	$1,050	$825	$725	$625	$550

Add $25 for A3 removable carry handle.
Add $10 for 20 in. barrel.
Add $50 (16 in. barrel) or $60 (20 in. barrel) for skeletonized stock.
Add approx. $100 for free-floating foream.

C SECTION

CETME

Previous manufacturer located in Madrid, Spain. CETME is an abbreviation for Centro Estudios Technicos de Materiales Especiales.

GRADING - PPGS™	100%	98%	95%	90%	80%	70%	60%

RIFLES: SEMI-AUTO

AUTOLOADING RIFLE - 7.62x51mm NATO cal., 17 3/4 in. barrel, delayed blowback action, utilizing rollers to lock breech, similar to HK-91 in appearance, wood military style stock, aperture rear sight.

$2,950	$2,650	$2,350	$2,000	$1,725	$1,500	$1,350

The H&K G3 is the next generation of this rifle, and many parts are interchangeable between the CETME and the the G3.

C Z (CESKÁ ZBROJOVKA)

Current manufacturer located in Uhersky Brod, Czech Republic, 1936-current. Previous manufacture was in Strakonice, Czechoslovakia circa 1923-late 1950s. Newly manufactured CZ firearms are currently imported exclusively by CZ USA located in Kansas City, KS. Previously imported by Magnum Research, Inc. located in Minneapolis, MN until mid-1994. Previously imported before 1994 by Action Arms Ltd. located in Philadelphia, PA. Dealer and distributor sales.

Ceská Zbrojovka simply means Czech weapons factory. CZ's full name is Ceská Zbrojovka a.s. Uhersky Brod, often abbreviated to CZUB a.s., meaning joint stock company. Uhersky Brod is the town the factory is located in. Zbrojovka Brno means weapons or arms factory located in Brno.

Zbrojovka Brno was built in 1916-1918, as a subsidiary of the Vienna Arsenal. After WWI, this factory was given the responsibility of providing the newly formed Czechoslovakian military with infantry weapons, specifically rifles and light machine guns. Circa 1923, pistol manufacture was transferred from Brno to Ceská Zbrojovka, located in the town of Strakonice, southwest of Bohemia. Since the location change, Zbrojovka Brno has never produced pistols on any great scale (please refer to the Brno section in this text for more information).

Ceská Zbrojovka Strakonice began developing many innovative and revolutionary pistol designs. These models, including the CZ-24, CZ-27, and CZ-52 are certainly well-known throughout the world. During the mid-1950s, CZ's facilities were converted to making motorcycles and precision engineering products.

Ceská Zbrojovka, located in the town of Uhersky Brod, was founded in 1936, as a subsidiary of Ceská Zbrojovka Strakonice, in a government decision designed to move firearms production further away from the German border, and out of the reach of German bombers. Uhersky Brod is located approx. 60 miles east of Brno. Before WWII, the factory produced aircraft machine guns (LK-30), the military pistol (CZ-38 in 9mm Para.), and rifle Models Z242-Z247. During WWII, the factory was taken over by the Germans, and the facilities were used for the production of aircraft machine guns (German designed MG 17s) and related components for other models of military weapons.

Shortly after WWII, Ceská Zbrojovka Uhersky Brod resumed production of firearms for the civilian marketplace, including the CZ 241 semi-auto shotgun, and some O/U shotguns. The production of pistols commenced during the mid-1950s, with the introduction of the Model CZ-50 and other small pistol models named DUO in 6.35mm cal. Up to this point, the main pistol producer in Czechoslovakia was CZ Strakonice as stated above. The CZ-52 pistol was the last model they produced. Since the end of the 1950s, Ceská Zbrojovka Uhersky Brod has become the sole producer of pistols.

After WWII, the Ceská Zbrojovka Uhersky Brod became massively involved in other types of production besides sporting and hunting firearms. Production reached a high during the 1980s, when hunting/sporting firearms manufacture resulted in approx. 30% of total production. The balance of manufacture was devoted to the production of power hydraulics for tractors, while gears and accessory drive boxes for speed reduction in turbo prop airplane engines made up the rest.

During 1964-1966, the Czech government transferred the production of long guns from Zbrojovka Brno to Ceská Zbrojovka Uhersky Brod. During the 1970s & 1980s, the arms production of Zbrojovka Brno accounted for less than 3% of its total capacity. The activities of this company were diverted into the production of typewriters, diesel motors, and automatic machine tools. While many firearm designs originated in Brno, Zbrojovka Brno was not the manufacturer. Because of this, the long guns manufactured in the mid-1960s, including the ZKK 600-602 series and ZKM rimfires, were manufactured in CZ Uhersky Brod. Because of the Czech government's decision to merge manufacture within both companies, the Brno trademark was also used by Ceská Zbrojovka Uhersky Brod.

This relationship was terminated in 1983, when both companies became part of the Agrozet conglomerate. While confusing, the arms utlizing the Brno trademark were not produced in Brno during this time. All firearms exported from Czechoslovakia at the time carried the Brno logo, and most of them were manufactured by Ceská Zbrojovka Uhersky Brod.

During 1975, Ceská Zbrojovka Uhersky Brod designed and began manufacture of the famous CZ-75 pistol. Production in quantity began in 1977. To date, over 700,000 CZ-75s have been produced. This semi-auto has been made in many variations and/or modifications to suit many military and commercial contracts. During the mid-1980s, the CZ factory released the CZ-85, basically a CZ-75 with ambidextrous safety and slide stop. In the mid-1990s, production of the CZ-100 began - this new model featured a polymer frame. The CZ 550 line of rifles was also introduced at this same time.

For more information and current pricing on both new and used CZ airguns, please refer to the *Blue Book of Airguns* by Dr. Robert Beeman & John Allen (also online).

COMBINATION GUNS

CZ 584 SOLO - 12 ga. over choice of 7x57mm Mauser (importation disc. 1999), 7x57R, 7x65R, .222 Rem. (importation disc. 1999), .223 Rem. (imported 1994-99), .243 Win. (imported 1994-99), .30-06 (new 1994), 7mm Mauser (imported 1994-99), and .308 Win. (importation disc. 1999) cals. also available, 24 1/2 in. barrels, similar action to CZ 581 O/U shotgun, extractors or ejectors, rifle sights, approx. 7.4 lbs. Importation disc. 1986, resumed 1994. Disc. 1995, importation resumed 1999. Disc. 2003.

	$775	$655	$595	$515	$450	$385	$350

Last MSR was $917.

Add 20% for ejectors.

PISTOLS: SEMI-AUTO, DISC.

The models listed below were made in Ceská Zbrojovka Strakonice, with the exception of some models manufactured in Ceská Zbrojovka Prague during the Nazi occupation of Czechoslovakia. The VZ38 was also produced in Uhersky Brod.

"DUO" POCKET AUTOMATIC - .25 ACP cal., 6 shot, 2 1/8 in. barrel, fixed sights, blue or nickel, plastic grips. Mfg. 1926-present (current Z pistol by Brno).

	$225	$190	$170	$150	$125	$100	$75

Add 40% for WWII years.

This model was manufactured by Dushek and is similar to the Z pistol equivalent by Brno.

CZ 22 - .380 ACP cal., derived from Mauser variation and manufactured under license from Mauser. Mfg. 1923 only.

	$550	$400	$350	$325	$300	$295	$250

CZ 24 - .380 ACP cal.

* ***Standard Frame*** - 8 shot mag. Over 175,000 mfg. 1924-38. Over half issued to Czech Army. Same general design as CZ 22 except no gap between trigger and frame. Production continued to 1941.

	$425	$375	$325	$300	$275	$235	$200

Add $50 if Nazi proofed.

Add 200% if Kriegsmarine proofed (scarce, be wary of counterfeit markings).

* ***Long Frame*** - 9 shot mag.

	$1,750	$1,500	$1,250	$1,000	$900	$800	$700

Add $750 if fit with stock slot (either standard frame or long frame).

CZ 27 - .32 ACP cal.

* ***"CESKA" Slide Legend Variation*** - slanted slide grooves, high polish, available as Pre-war Commercial, DR proofed, or Nazi proofed. Ser. no. range 16,000-21,500.

	$550	$450	$350	$300	$250	$200	$150

* ***"BÖHMISCHE" Slide Legend Variation*** - vertical slide grooves, high or medium polish, Nazi Police pistols dated 1941, 1942, or 1943 marked with Eagle/K on left trigger guard web, ser. no. range 21,500-261,000.

	$350	$300	$250	$200	$150	$135	$100

Add 125% if 1941 dated.

Add 100% if 1942 or 1943 dated.

Add 200% if Kriegsmarine proofed (beware of counterfeit markings).

* ***"fnh" Slide Legend Variation*** - medium polish or phosphate. Ser. no. range 261,000-476,000.

	$300	$250	$200	$175	$150	$125	$100

Add 20% for late phosphate war finish.

* ***Sound Suppressor Barrel Variation*** - a small number of phosphate pistols were fitted with an extended barrel for suppressor attachment. Usually in 450,000-460,000 ser. no. range.

	$2,000	$1,750	$1,500	$1,300	$1,250	$1,100	$1,000

* ***Post WWII mfg.*** - dated 1945, 1946, 1947, 1948, 1949, 1950, 1951. These models will have the "NARODNI PODNIK" inscription on slide.

Currently, these variations average $250 in 95%+ condition while reworks (very common) average under $200.

VZ 38 DOUBLE ACTION AUTOMATIC - .380 ACP cal., 9 shot, double action only, 4 5/8 in. barrel, fixed sights, blue, plastic grips. Mfg. 1938-39.

	$500	$425	$350	$300	$250	$200	$150

Add $1,200 for Waffenampt proofed (E/WaA76 on barrel and left frame), usually phosphate finished and either unnumbered or in B291,000-B293,000 ser. no. range.

Changed to Model 39T after 1939.

VZ 38 "BULGARIAN CONTRACT" - .380 ACP cal., 9 shot, single or double action, prominent safety on left frame. Usually in 420,000-423,000 ser. no. range.

	$2,500	$1,800	$1,400	$1,000	$800	$600	$500

MODEL 1945 DOUBLE ACTION AUTOMATIC - .25 ACP cal., 8 shot, 2 1/2 in. barrel, fixed sights, blue, plastic grips. Double action only. Mfg. between 1945-52.

	$250	$200	$165	$150	$140	$130	$120

PISTOLS: SEMI-AUTO, RECENT MFG.

The CZ-52 was manufactured in Strakonice.

CZ P-01 - 9mm Para cal., based on CZ-75 design, but with metallurgical improvements, aluminum alloy frame, hammer forged 3.8 in. barrel, 10 or 13 (new 2005) shot mag., decocker, includes M3 rail on bottom of frame, checkered rubber grips, matte black polycoat finish, 27.2 oz. Importation began 2003.

MSR $586	$465	$395	$340	$305	$265	$235	$210

CZ-40B -.40 S&W cal. only, CZ-75B operating mechanism in alloy M1911 style frame, single/double action, black polycoat finish, 10 shot double column mag., fixed sights, firing pin block safety. Limited importation 2002 only.

$420	$350	$315	$290	$275	$250	$225

Last MSR was $494.

✳ *CZ-40 P Compact* - .40 S&W cal., limited edition, 1,500 imported 2004.

$325	$285	$265	$245	$225	$200	$175

Last MSR was $380.

CZ-50/70 - .32 ACP cal., double action, blowback action, 3 3/4 in. barrel, loaded chamber indicator, 8 shot mag.

$150	$125	$110	$100	$90	$80	$70

Used models are currently imported by Century International Arms, Inc. located in St. Albans, VT.

CZ-52 - 7.62 Tokarev or 9mm Para. cal., single action semi-auto, roller locking breech system, 4.9 in. barrel, 8 shot mag.

$180	$150	$135	$125	$95	$85	$75

Add $40 for extra 9mm Para. barrel.

Currently imported used CZ-52 models are priced in the $115-$135 range, depending on condition, and will have the current importer's mark visible on the gun.

CZ-70 - 7.65mm/.32 ACP cal., double action, similar to Walther PP, 8 shot mag., 1 lb. 9 oz. Disc.

$400	$350	$300	$275	$250	$225	$200

A very limited quantity of this model was imported.

CZ-75, CZ-75 B, CZ-75 BD - 9mm Para. or .40 S&W (disc. 1997, reintroduced 1999) cal., Poldi steel, selective double action, double action only, or single action only, frame safety, 4 3/4 in. barrel, 10 (C/B 1994, standard for .40 S&W cal.) or 15* shot mag., currently available in black polycoat/polymer (standard, DA and SA only), matte blue (disc. 1994), high polish (disc. 1994), glossy blue (new 1999), dual tone (new 1998), or satin nickel (new 1994) finish, black plastic grips, non-suffix early guns did not have a firing pin block safety, reversible mag. release, ambidextrous safety, and were usually shipped with two mags., B suffix model nomenclature was added 1998, and designated some internal mechanism changes, BD suffix indicates decocker mechanism, 34.3 oz.

MSR $509	$430	$355	$310	$275	$225	$210	$195

Add $16 for .40 S&W cal.

Add $9 for Model CZ-75 BD (decocker).

Add $16 for glossy blue or dual tone finish.

Add $16 for satin nickel finish.

Add $299 for CZ Kadet .22 LR adapter (includes .22 LR upper slide assembly and mag., new 1998).

Add $9 for single action only (black polymer frame).

"First Model" variations, mostly imported by Pragotrade of Canada, are identifiable by short slide rails, no half-cock feature, and were mostly available in high polish blue only. These early pistols sell for $1,000 if NIB condition, chrome engraved $1,500 (NIB), factory competition $1,350 (NIB).

✳ *CZ-75 B Military* - 9mm Para. cal. Importation 2000-2002.

$365	$315	$270	$250	$225	$210	$195

Last MSR was $429.

GRADING - PPGS™	100%	98%	95%	90%	80%	70%	60%

* CZ-75 B Tactical - similar to CZ-75 B, except has OD green frame and matte black polymer slide, includes CZ knife. Limited importation during 2003.

	$425	$355	$305	$270	$225	$210	$195

Last MSR was $499.

* CZ-75 Semi-Compact - 9mm Para. cal. only, 13 shot mag., choice of black polymer, matte, or high polish blue finish. Imported 1994 only.

	$350	$300	$275	$250	$230	$250	$200

Last MSR was $519.

Add $20 for matte blue finish.
Add $40 for high polish blue finish.

* CZ-75 Compact - 9mm Para. or .40 S&W (new 2005) cal. only, otherwise similiar to CZ-75, full-size frame, except has 3.9 in. barrel, 10 (C/B 1994) or 13* shot mag., checkered walnut grips, 33 oz. New 1993.

MSR $539	$440	$370	$345	$295	$255	$230	$210

Add $15 for glossy blue, dual tone, or satin nickel finish.
Add $55 for .40 S&W cal.
Add $299 for CZ Kadet .22 LR adapter (includes .22 LR upper slide assembly and mag., new 1998).

* CZ-75 D PCR Compact - 9mm Para. cal., similar to CZ-75 Compact, except has black polymer frame, decocker, 1.7 lbs. Importation began 2000.

MSR $554	$445	$380	$335	$300	$265	$235	$210

* CZ-75 Kadet - .22 LR cal., black polymer finish, 10 shot mag, 4.88 in. barrel. Mfg. 1999-2004.

	$400	$340	$305	$280	$255	$235	$215

Last MSR was $495.

* CZ-75 25th Anniversary - 9mm Para. cal., features include 25th Anniversary markings. Limited mfg. 2000 only.

	$625	$450	$375				

Last MSR was $699.

* CZ-75 Champion - 9mm Para. (new 2000) or .40 S&W cal., dual tone finish, IPSC competition features including 3 port compensator, finger grooved synthetic grips, target trigger and sights, 4 1/2 in. barrel, approx. 2.2 lbs. Imported 1999-2004.

	$1,410	$1,150	$1,025	$875	$725	$600	$500

Last MSR was $1,598.

* CZ-75 Standard IPSC - .40 S&W cal., IPSC features, 5.4 in. barrel, dual tone finish, checkered wood grips, 10 or 16 (new 2005) shot mag., 45 oz. New 1999.

MSR $1,152	$1,000	$900	$750	$625	$550	$450	$350

* CZ-75 Modified - similar to Standard, except has dual port compensator and red dot reflex sight, approx. 2.8 lbs. Imported 2001-2002.

	$1,385	$1,135	$1,000	$875	$735	$600	$500

Last MSR was $1,567.

* Model CZ-75 Special Editions - 9mm Para. cal., similar to CZ-75, except has optional special edition finishes including all matte nickel, bright nickel frame, matte chrome, all brushed chrome, bright chrome, or gold frame, choice of matching finish slide, master blue slide, gold small parts, or master blue slide with gold small parts, price line refers to all matte nickel finish. Imported 1993-94 by Action Arms only.

	$525	$465	$415	$375	$335	$310	$285

Last MSR was $699.

Add approx. $120 for matte nickel frame with master blue small parts.
Add approx. $180 for matte nickel with gold small parts, matte nickel frame with master blue slide and gold small parts, master blue with gold small parts, or gold frame with master blue slide.

GRADING - PPGS™	100%	98%	95%	90%	80%	70%	60%

✳ Model CZ-75 30th Anniversary - 9mm Para. cal., features special 30th anniversary engraving with 24Kt. gold plated controls and accents, 10 or 15 shot mag., high gloss blue finish, birch grips with carved "30." 1,000 mfg. (ser. no. 1-1,000) beginning 2005.

As this edition went to press, prices had not been established on this model.

CZ-82 - 9x18mm Makarov cal., current Czech military sidearm, most recent exportation was to W. Germany in Makarov chambering.

This model is similar to the CZ-83 except for cal. Prices are similar to the model CZ-83.

CZ-83 - .32 ACP (disc. 1994, reintroduced 1999-2002) or .380 ACP (new 1986), or 9mm Makarov (mfg. 1999-2001) cal., modern design, 3 dot sights, 3.8 in. barrel, choice of carry modes, blue (disc. 1994), glossy blue (new 1998), satin nickel (new 1999, not available in .32 ACP), or black polymer (disc. 1997) finish, black synthetic grips, 10 (C/B 1994), 12* (.380 ACP) or 15* (.32 ACP) shot mag., 26.2 oz. Mfg. began 1985, but U.S. importation started in 1992.

MSR $420	$340	$270	$235	$195	$180	$170	$160

✳ CZ-83 Special Editions - .380 ACP cal. only, similar to CZ-83, has optional special edition finishes including all matte nickel, master high polish blue, bright nickel frame, matte chrome, all brushed chrome, bright chrome, or gold frame, choice of matching finish slide, master blue slide, gold small parts, or master blue slide with gold small parts, price line refers to all matte nickel or high polish blue finish. Importation disc. 1994.

	$425	$375	$335	$295	$250	$225	$200

Last MSR was $569.

Add approx. $90 for matte nickel frame with master blue small parts.

Add approx. $175 for matte nickel with gold small parts, matte nickel frame with master blue slide and gold small parts, master blue with gold small parts, or gold frame with master blue slide.

CZ-85, CZ-85 B - 9mm Para. or 9x21mm (imported 1993-94 only) cal., variation of the CZ-75 with ambidextrous controls, new plastic grip design, sight rib, available in black polymer, matte blue (disc. 1994), glossy blue (mfg. 2001 only), or high-gloss blue (9mm Para. only, disc. 1994) finish, includes firing pin block and finger rest trigger, plastic grips, 15 shot mag. new 2005, B suffix model nomenclature was added during 1998, approx. 2.2 lbs.

MSR $536	$445	$365	$325	$290	$255	$230	$210

Add $291 for CZ Kadet .22 LR adapter (includes .22 LR upper slide assembly and mag., mfg. 1998 only).

✳ CZ-85 Combat - similar to CZ-85B, except has fully adj. rear sight, available in black polymer, matte blue (disc. 1994), glossy blue (new 2001), dual-tone, satin nickel, or high-gloss blue finish, walnut (disc. 1994) or black plastic (new 1994) grips, extended mag. release, and free dropping mag., 15 shot mag. new 2005. Importation began 1992.

MSR $599	$475	$410	$365	$335	$295	$265	$240

Add $24 for glossy blue, satin nickel, or dual-tone finish.

Add $291 for CZ Kadet .22 LR adapter (includes .22 LR upper slide assembly and mag., mfg. 1998 only).

✳ CZ-85 Champion - .40 S&W or 9x21mm cal., similar to CZ-75 Champion, except has 3 port compensator. Imported 1999 only.

	$1,325	$1,100	$975	$850	$725	$600	$500

Last MSR was $1,484.

✳ Model CZ-85 Special Editions - 9mm Para. cal., similar to CZ-85, has optional special edition finishes including all matte nickel, bright nickel frame, matte chrome, all brushed chrome, bright chrome, or gold frame, choice of matching finish slide, master blue slide, gold small parts, or master blue slide with gold small parts, price line refers to all matte nickel finish. Imported 1993-94 only.

	$575	$495	$450	$395	$350	$325	$285

Last MSR was $749.

Subtract $60 for matte nickel frame with master blue slide.

Add $130 for matte nickel frame with master blue small parts, matte nickel with gold small parts, matte nickel frame with master blue slide and gold small parts, master blue with gold small parts or gold frame with master blue slide.

✳ Model CZ-85 Combat Special Editions - 9mm Para. cal., similar finishes to Model CZ-85 Special Editions, price line refers to all matte nickel finish. Limited importation 1994-95.

	$775	$725	$650	$595	$525	$450	$375

Last MSR was $1,049.

Subtract $125 for matte nickel frame with master blue small parts.

Add $245 for matte nickel with gold small parts, matte nickel frame with master blue slide and gold small parts, master blue with gold small parts, or gold frame with master blue slide.

CZ-97 B - .45 ACP cal., single or double action, manual safety with firing pin block safety, 4.84 in. barrel with short recoil system, black polymer or glossy blue finish, checkered wood grips, double column 10 shot mag., last shot hold open slide, 40 oz. New 1998.

MSR $663	$555	$480	$400	$345	$295	$260	$240

Add $17 for glossy blue finish.

CZ-100 - 9mm Para. or .40 S&W cal., double action only with firing pin block and locked breech, w/o external manual safety, black polymer finish, 3 dot sights, high impact plastic frame, 10 or 12 (new 2005, 9mm Para. cal. only) shot mag., 3.9 in. barrel, approx. 24 oz. New 1996.

MSR $449	$380	$320	$275	$245	$210	$195	$180

CZ-122 B SPORT - .22 LR cal., semi-auto, single action only, 6 in. solid ribbed barrel with adj. rear sight, manual and firing pin block safety, last shot hold open slide, steel frame and slide with two-tone finish, ribbed black polymer grips, 10 shot mag., 30 oz. Limited mfg. 1998 only.

	$225	$190	$175	$160	$150	$140	$135

Last MSR was $259.

CZ-2075 RAMI - 9mm Para. or .40 S&W cal., SA/DA operation, 3 in. barrel, double stack 8 (.40 S&W cal.), 10 (9mm Para. cal., flush fit) or 14 (9mm Para. cal.) shot mag. with finger extension, snag free sights, black polycoat finish with black checkered grips, alloy frame, 25 oz. New 2005.

MSR $576	$460	$390	$340	$300	$265	$235	$210

RIFLES: BOLT ACTION, COMMERCIAL MFG.

Ceská Zbrojovka began manufacturing rifles circa 1936. Long gun production was discontinued between 1948-1964, with the exception of the massive military contracts during that time period.

CZ USA MODEL 3 - .270 WSM, 7mm WSM, or .300 WSM, Mauser style claw extractor, adj. M-70 type trigger, bottom floorplate with 3 shot fixed mag., three position safety, blue or stainless matte finished action and 24 in. barrel, right- or left-hand action, drilled and tapped, American black walnut stock with fleur-de-lis, no sights, mfg. in the U.S., 7.9 lbs. New 2005.

MSR $872	$725	$600	$550	$495	$450	$400	$350

Add $10 for left-hand action.

Add $21 for stainless steel action and barrel.

GRADING - PPGS™	100%	98%	95%	90%	80%	70%	60%

MODEL CZ-452 STYLE (ZKM-452)

MODEL CZ-452 STYLE (ZKM-452) - .22 LR or .22 Win. Mag. (disc. 1998) cal., bolt action, 5, 6 (.22 Mag. only), or 10 shot mag., 24.8 in. barrel, choice of black synthetic stock and matte nickel metal finish (new 1999) or uncheckered hardwood stock with Schnabel forend and blue metal finish (disc. 1998), adj. rear sight, 6.6 lbs. Importation began 1995 from CZ, earlier mfg. was by Brno.

	MSR $389	$310	$260	$215	$175	$150	$135	$120

Add $50 for .22 Win. Mag. cal. (disc. 1998).

* **Model CZ-452D Deluxe/Lux (ZKM-452D)** - similar to ZKM-452 only with checkered walnut stock. Importation began 1995.

	MSR $389	$310	$260	$215	$175	$150	$135	$120

Add $30 for .22 Win. Mag. cal.

* **Model CZ-452 American Classic (ZKM-452)** - .17 HMR (new 2003), .17 Mach 2 (new 2005), .22 LR or .22 Win. Mag. cal., 5 shot mag., American style walnut stock. Importation began 1999.

	MSR $389	$310	$260	$215	$175	$150	$135	$120

Add $30 for .22 Win. Mag. cal.
Add $44 for .17 HMR cal.

* **Model CZ-452 FS** - .17 HMR (new 2005), .22 LR or .22 Win. Mag. cal., 5 shot detachable mag., 21 in. barrel, features full length walnut Mannlicher stock, tangent rear adj. sight, 6.4 lbs. New 2004.

	MSR $449	$380	$330	$280	$245	$215	$195	$180

Add $9 for .22 Win. Mag. or .17 HMR cal.

* **Model CZ-452 Silouhette** - similar to CZ-452 American Classic, except has black synthetic stock and blue metal, 5.3 lbs. New 2003.

	MSR $389	$310	$260	$215	$175	$150	$135	$120

* **Model CZ-452 Scout (ZKM-452)** - .22 LR cal. only, youth configuration with shorter 16.2 in. barrel and uncheckered hardwood stock, 5 shot mag., 5 lbs. Importation began 2000.

	MSR $249	$195	$160	$135	$115	$95	$75	$65

* **Model CZ-452 Training Rifle** - .22 LR cal., military training rifle configuration with beechwood stock and 5 shot mag., 5.3 lbs. New 2002.

	MSR $280	$220	$175	$150	$120	$100	$80	$70

* **Model CZ-452 Varmint (ZKM-452)** - .17 HMR (new 2005), .17 Mach 2 (new 2005), .22 LR or .22 Win. Mag. (new 2004) cal. only, similar to Model ZKM-452D, except has 21 in. heavy barrel and no sights, 6.8 lbs. Importation began 1998.

	MSR $419	$340	$280	$240	$190	$170	$150	$140

Add $24 for .17 HMR, .17 Mach 2, or .22 Win. Mag. cal.

CZ 513 HUNTER

CZ 513 HUNTER - .22 LR cal., entry level bolt action, 5 shot detachable mag., beechwood stock. Imported 1994 only.

		$195	$175	$150	$125	$95	$80	$65

Last MSR was $225.

Add $30 for Farmer Model.
This model was imported exclusively by Action Arms.

CZ 513 BASIC

CZ 513 BASIC - .22 LR cal., 5 shot detachable mag., 20.9 in. barrel, non-adj. trigger, uncheckered beechwood stock, iron sights, 5.75 lbs. New 2004.

	MSR $247	$195	$165	$135	$115	$95	$80	$65

CZ 527 (LUX)

CZ 527 (LUX) - .22 Hornet, .222 Rem., .223 Rem. cal., Mauser style bolt action with silent safety, 21.9 in. barrel with open sights, 5 shot detachable mag., hardwood (disc.) or checkered walnut stock and forend, 6.2 lbs. Importation began 1995.

	MSR $599	$500	$420	$385	$340	$300	$275	$250

Add $91 for Model CZ-527 FS with checkered Mannlicher style walnut stock and forend.

GRADING - PPGS™	100%	98%	95%	90%	80%	70%	60%

CZ 527 America Classic - similar to CZ 527 Lux, also available in .221 Fireball cal. (new 2004), various wood stock configurations, scope rings included. New 1999.

MSR $599	$500	$420	$385	$340	$300	$275	$250

Add $9 for .204 Ruger or .221 Fireball cal.
Add $34 for maple, brown laminate, spring camo laminate, or sunset camo laminate stock (new 2005).
Add $174 English walnut stock or $204 for fancy American walnut stock.

CZ 527 Prestige - .22 Hornet or .223 Rem. cal., similar to CZ 527 Lux, except has deluxe checkered walnut stock and forend, no sights, jewel bolt, SST, scope rings included. 6.3 lbs. Limited mfg. beginning 2001.

MSR $	$755	$520	$410	$380	$330	$285	$260

CZ 527 Varmint - .17 Rem. (new 2005), .204 Ruger (new 2005), or .223 Rem. cal., configuration with heavy barrel and no sights, choice of walnut (.204 Ruger only), maple (.223 Rem. cal. only), laminated (new 2002), or H-S Precision Kevlar (new 2002) black stock, approx. 8 lbs. Importation began 2001.

MSR $	$500	$420	$380	$340	$300	$275	$250

Add $ for grey laminate stock (.223 Rem. cal. only) or $202 for H-S Precision Kevlar Accuracy stock.

CZ 527 Carbine - .223 Rem. (new 2001) or 7.62x39mm cal., carbine configuration with shorter barrel, 6 lbs. New 1999.

MSR $06	$510	$425	$385	$345	$300	$275	$250

.243 Win., .270 Win., .30-06, .308 Win., or 7x57mm cal., detachable 4 shot mag. (.30-06 and .308 Win. cals. only) or 5 shot fixed mag., choice of regular or Mannlicher (.30-06 or .308 Win. cal. only) stock, hooded ramp front sight, 7 1/4 lbs. Importation 1995 only.

	$495	$425	$370	$330	$300	$275	$250

Last MSR was $649.

Add $100 for Mannlicher style stock.

CZ 537 Mountain Carbine - .243 Win. only, 19 in. barrel, 5 shot detachable mag., includes ring mounts, 7.1 lbs. Imported 1994 only.

	$525	$450	$375	$330	$300	$275	$250

Last MSR was $669.

CZ 550 STANDARD - various cals. have been imported to date, 4 shot detachable mag. (.243 Win. or .308 Win. only) or internal 5 shot, 23.6 in. barrel, receiver drilled and tapped for Remington 700 style scope base, no sights, checkered walnut stock and forearm, 7 1/4 lbs. Imported 1995-2000.

	$475	$395	$340	$310	$285	$260	$240

Last MSR was $561.

Add $21 for .243 Win. or .308 Win. cal. with detachable mag.

CZ 550 Lux - various cals., similar to CZ 550 Standard, except has deluxe checkered walnut stock with Bavarian style cheekpiece and vent. recoil pad. Mfg. 1998-2004.

	$495	$415	$350	$315	$285	$260	$240

Last MSR was $588.

Add $20 for detachable mag. (.22-250 Rem., .243 Win., or .308 Win. cal., disc.).

>CZ 550 Battue Lux - similar to CZ 550 Lux, except has 20 1/2 in. barrel with integral barrel fixed rear sight. Limited mfg. 1998 only.

	$450	$375	$330	$300	$280	$260	$240

Last MSR was $519.

Add $30 for .243 Win. or .308 Win. cal. with removable mag.

GRADING - PPGS™	100%	98%	95%	90%	80%	70%	60%

✳ **CZ 550 Magnum Standard** - .300 Win. Mag., .375 H&H, .416 Rem. Mag. (disc. 1998), .416 Rigby, .458 Win. Mag., or 7mm Rem. Mag. (importation disc. 1997) cal., 3-5 shot fixed mag., 25 in. barrel with express rear sight, checkered hardwood stock, 9 1/4 lbs. Limited mfg. 1998 only.

	$525	$475	$440	$400	$375	$350	$335

Last MSR was $595.

Add $40 for .416 Rem. Mag., .416 Rigby, or .458 Win. Mag. cal.

➤**CZ 550 Magnum Standard Lux** - similar to CZ 550 Magnum, except has select checkered walnut, 7.7-9.4 lbs. New 1998.

MSR $690	$600	$500	$445	$395	$350		$300

Add $185 for .300 Win. Mag. (disc.), .375 H&H, .416 Rigby, or .458 Win. Mag. cal.

✳ **CZ 550 American Safari Field Magnum** - .375 H&H, .416 Rigby, .458 Win., or .458 Lott cal., choice of field grade wood or laminate stock, 9.9 lbs. New 2004.

MSR $875	$725	$595	$540	$475	$425	$350	$350

Add $45 for .458 Lott cal.

Add $299 for brown laminate, spring camo laminate, or sunset camo laminate stock.

✳ **CZ 550 American Safari Deluxe Magnum** - .375 H&H, .416 Rigby, .458 Win., or .458 Lott cal., similar to Field Grade, except has deluxe walnut stock. New 2004.

MSR $1,593	$1,350	$1,125	$975	$875	$800	$725	

✳ **CZ 550 Custom Grade Safari Magnum** - .404 Jeffery, .450 Rigby, or .505 Gibbs cal., custom Magnum action with two-position safety, single set trigger set., individual requirements, glossy or matte blue metal finish, checkered grade American walnut stock and forend, express sights, built per individual custom order. New 2005.

MSR $1,750	$1,575	$1,275	$1,075	$925	$850	$775	

Add $100 for .505 Gibbs cal.

✳ **CZ 550 Prestige** - .270 Win. or .30-06 cal., similar to CZ 550 Lux, except has deluxe checkered walnut stock and forend, no sights, scope rings included. Imported 2001, reintroduced 2003-2005.

	$740	$510	$405	$380	$325	$285	$260

Last MSR was $854.

✳ **CZ 550 American Classic** - .22-250 Rem., .243 Win., .270 Win., .30-06, .308 Win., 6.5x55mm (new 2001), 7x57mm (disc. 2004), or 9.3x62mm cal., features American style walnut stock, fixed or detachable mag., scope rings included, no sights, approx. 8 lbs. New mid-1999.

MSR $606	$510	$420	$355	$315	$285	$260	$240

Add $17 for detachable 4-5 shot mag. (.22-250 Rem., .243 Win. and .308 Win. only).

✳ **CZ 550 Varmint** - .22-250 Rem. (new 2002) or .308 Win. cal., 25.6 in. barrel w/o sights, 4 shot detachable mag., checkered walnut (.308 Win. cal. only), H-S Precision Kevlar (new 2005), or laminated (new 2002) stock with vent. recoil pad, 9.3 lbs. Importation began 2000.

MSR $652	$535	$435	$375	$320	$285	$260	$240

Add $97 for laminated stock (new 2002).

Add $171 for H-S Precision Kevlar stock (new 2005).

✳ **CZ 550 FS Mannlicher** - similar to CZ 550 American Classic, except has Mannlicher stock and 20.5 in. barrel, not available in .22-250 Rem. cal., fixed 5 shot or 4 shot detachable mag. (.243 Win. or .308 Win. cal. only), 7.4 lbs. Imported 1996-98, reintroduced 2001.

MSR $705	$575	$500	$435	$385	$355	$335	$300

GRADING - PPGS™	100%	98%	95%	90%	80%	70%	60%

✴ *CZ 550 Battue FS Mannlicher* - similar to CZ 550 FS Mannlicher, except has integral barrel fixed rear sight. Limited mfg. 1998 only.

	$525	$465	$425	$395	$360	$330	$300

Last MSR was $609.

Add $30 for .243 Win. or .308 Win. cal. with removable mag.

✴ *CZ 550 Minnesota* - similar to CZ 550 Lux, except has select walnut stock w/o cheekpiece, and barrel has no sights. Limited mfg. 1998 only.

	$445	$375	$330	$300	$280	$260	$240

Last MSR was $505.

Add $30 for .243 Win. or .308 Win. cal. with removable mag.

ZKK 600 - .270 Win., .30-06, or 7x57mm cal., improved Mauser type action, 23 1/2 in. barrel, checkered walnut stock, 5 shot internal mag., thumb safety, 7.2 lbs. Importation disc. 1995.

	$500	$425	$370	$330	$300	$275	$250

Last MSR was $589.

ZKK 601 - .243 Win. or .308 Win. cal., otherwise similar to ZKK 600. Importation disc. 1995.

	$500	$425	$370	$330	$300	$275	$250

Last MSR was $589.

ZKK 602 - .300 Win. Mag. (disc.), .375 H&H, .416 Rigby (new 1996), .416 Rem. (new 1996), 8x68mm (disc.), or .458 Win. Mag. cal., similar to ZKK 600, except has 25.2 in. barrel and 3 leaf express rear sight, 9.3 lbs. Disc. 1997.

	$675	$575	$495	$450	$395	$350	$310

Last MSR was $799.

CZ-700 SNIPER - .308 Win. cal., sniper design features forged billet receiver with permanently attached Weaver rail, 25.6 in. heavy barrel w/o sights, 10 shot detachable mag., laminated thumbhole stock with adj. cheekpiece and buttplate, large bolt handle, fully adj. trigger, 11.9 lbs. Limited importation 2001 only.

	$1,875	$1,575	$1,250	$1,025	$895	$775	$650

Last MSR was $2,097.

RIFLES: O/U

CZ-589 STOPPER - .458 Win. Mag. cal. only, Kersten style boxlock action with Blitz type trigger, checkered Turkish walnut stock and forearm, fixed iron sights, includes sling swivels, 9.3 lbs. Approx. 5 mfg. and imported 2001 only.

	$2,695	$2,300	$2,000	$1,750	$1,500	$1,250	$1,050

Last MSR was $2,999.

Add $1,000 for sideplates and special engraving/checkering.

RIFLES: SEMI-AUTO

CZ-M52 (1952) - 7.62x45mm Czech cal., semi-auto, 20 2/3 in. barrel, 10 shot detachable mag., tangent rear sight, this model was also imported briefly by Samco Global Arms, Inc. located in Miami, FL.

	$550	$450	$350	$300	$250	$200	$150

CZ-M52/57 (1957) - 7.62x39mm cal., later variation of the CZ-M52.

	$425	$375	$325	$300	$250	$200	$150

CZ-511 - .22 LR cal., blowback action, 22.2 in. barrel, uncheckered beechwood stock, flip-up rear sight, receiver top slotted for scope mounts, 8 shot mag., approx. 5 1/2 lbs. Previously disc. 1986, importation resumed 1998-2001.

	$295	$245	$210	$190	$175	$160	$150

Last MSR was $351.

GRADING - PPGS™	100%	98%	95%	90%	80%	70%	60%

CZ-712/720 - 12 (Model 712) or 20 (Model 720) ga., 3 in. chamber, gas operated, checkered Turkish walnut stock, 26 or 28 in. vent. barrel, matte black chrome, aluminum receiver, Mossy Oak Shadow Grass or Mossy Oak Obsession camo treatment, multichokes, jeweled bolt, single trigger. New 2005.

MSR $399	$350	$295	$265	$235	$195	$175	$150

Add $27 for 20 ga.
Add $61 for 100% camo coverage.

CZ-712 MAGNUM - 12 ga. only, 3 1/2 in. chamber, 24 or 28 in. barrel, matte black chrome, checkered walnut, Mossy Oak Shadowgrass (28 in. barrel) or Mossy Oak Obsession (24 in. barrel) camo treatment, single trigger, vent. rib., 7.5 lbs. New 2005.

MSR $499	$425	$375	$325	$295	$265	$235	$200

Add $100 for 100% camo coverage.

SHOTGUNS: O/U

CZ 581 SOLO - 12 ga., 2 3/4 in. chambers, boxlock action with Kersten upper locking mechanism, ejectors, checkered walnut stock and forearm, approx. 7.4 lbs. Importation disc. 1995, resumed during 1999.

MSR $872	$740	$625	$570	$490	$425	$385	$350

Add 10% for single trigger (disc.).

MALLARD - 12 or 20 ga., DT, extractors, 28 in. VR barrels with multichokes, coin finished alloy receiver, checkered Turkish walnut stock and forearm. New 2005.

MSR $475	$425	$375	$335	$300	$275	$250	$225

CANVASBACK 103D - 12 or 20 ga., 3 in. chambers, 26 or 28 in. VR barrels with choke tubes, extractors, blued frame with light perimeter engraving, SST, stock/forearm similar to Redhead. New 2005.

MSR $695	$625	$550	$495	$450	$400	$350	$300

REDHEAD DELUXE 103DE - 12 or 20 ga., boxlock action, SST, ejectors, checkered round knob Turkish walnut pistol grip stock and Schnabel forearm, coin finished frame and triggerguard, 26 or 28 in. VR barrels with screw-in chokes. New 2005.

MSR $795	$725	$650	$575	$525	$475	$425	$395

✹ *Redhead 103 D Mini* - 28 ga. or .410 bore, scaled down frame, otherwise similar to Redhead Deluxe, but w/o ejectors. New 2005.

MSR $825	$750	$675	$600	$550	$500	$450	$425

WOODCOCK DELUXE 103FE - 12 or 20 ga., ejectors, SST, 26 or 28 in. barrels with screw-in chokes, color case hardened boxlock frame with sideplates and triggerguard, hand engraving, checkered round knob Turkish walnut stock and Schnabel forearm. New 2005.

MSR $1,056	$895	$775	$650	$575	$500	$450	$395

✹ *Woodcock 103F Mini* - 28 ga. or .410 bore, scaled down frame, otherwise similar to Woodcock Deluxe, but w/o ejectors. New 2005.

MSR $1,129	$975	$850	$750	$675	$600	$550	$500

SHOTGUNS: SxS

DURANGO - 12 or 20 ga., hammerless countroured boxlock action with color case hardened frame, 20 in. barrels, single trigger, multichokes, checkered Turkish walnut round knob stock and splinter forearm. New 2005.

MSR $795	$725	$625	$525	$425	$350	$300	$250

AMARILLO - similar to Durango, except has double triggers. New 2005.

MSR $695	$625	$550	$475	$375	$300	$250	$200

GRADING - PPGS™	100%	98%	95%	90%	80%	70%	60%

BOBWHITE 202B - 12, 20, 28 ga. or .410 bore, 26 or 28 in. barrels with multichokes (N/A in .410 bore), color case hardened engraved boxlock action with sideplates, DT, checkered Turkish walnut straight grip English style stock and semi-beavertail forearm. New 2005.

MSR $695	$625	$550	$475	$375	$300	$250	$200

Add $174 for 28 ga. or .410 bore.

RINGNECK 201A - similar to Bobwhite, except has single trigger. New 2005.

MSR $869	$775	$725	$650	$575	$500	$450	$395

✳ *Ringneck 201A Mini* - 28 ga. or .410 bore, proportional frame to gauge, extractors, otherwise similar to Ringneck 201A. New 2005.

MSR $1,045	$895	$750	$675	$600	$525	$450	$375

CZ (STRAKONICE)

Current manufacturer established in 1919 and located in Strakonice, Czech Republic. Currently imported by Adco Sales, Inc., located in Woburn, MA.

EXPLAINING THE CZ MYSTERY

An aspect of the post-communist Czech economy is that there are now two rival manufacturing firms bearing the name of CZ (Ceska Zbrojovka). This company was started in Plzen in 1919, and moved to Strakonice in 1921, near the western border of Bohemia. The factory at Straconice remained the primary center for Czech handgun manufacture until the 1960s. Additionally, pistols (and a great many rifles) were made at another CZ - Czeskoslovenska Zbrojovka of Brno. However, the manufacture of pistols was transferred at an early date to the CZ factory at Strakonice.

During the rise of Hitler and the Nazis, the Czechs were justifiably alarmed at having so much of their arms industry within easy reach of the Nazis. Consequently, the two CZs collaborated in opening a joint manufacturing facility in 1936, far from the German border at Uhersky Brod. While Czechoslovakia was united, Uhersky Brod was in the very middle of the country; now it is located only a few kilometers west of the Czech Republic's border with Slovakia.

The CZ facility at Uhersky Brod eventually took over most of Czechoslovakia's firearms manufacturing during the postwar years although handgun manufacture continued on a reduced scale at the plant at Strakonice.

The dismemberment of the state-owned communist economy in the early 1990s has resulted in the existence of the two competitive CZ firms - one based in Uhersky Brod, the other at the older plant at Strakonice. The Brno operation also retains the name "CZ." The CZ based in Uhersky Brod is represented in the U.S. by CZ-USA, based in Kansas City, KS. The CZ based in Strakonice is represented by Adco Sales, Inc., located in Woburn, MA.

Information appears courtesy of Jan Liberoul and Gun World *magazine.*

PISTOLS: SEMI-AUTO

Older Strakonice manufacture can be found in the C Z (Ceska Zbrojovka) section.

CZ-75 - 9mm Para. cal., single/double action, 4 3/4 in. barrel, steel frame, 10 shot mag., blue finish only. Limited importation 2004 only.

$475	$425	$375	$325	$295	$275	$225

Last MSR was $569.

CZ-TT - 9mm Para., .40 S&W, or .45 ACP cal., single/double action, polymer frame, 3.77 in. ported or unported barrel, matte finish, 10 shot mag., 26.1 oz. Importation began 2004.

MSR $479	$415	$375	$325	$295	$275	$250	$225

Add $30 for ported barrel (disc.).
Add $40 for ported barrel and slide serrations (disc.).
Add $399 for conversion kit with one mag.

GRADING - PPGS™	100%	98%	95%	90%	80%	70%	60%

CZ-T POLYMER COMPACT - similar to CZ-TT, except has shorter barrel. Limited importation 2004 only.

	$475	$425	$375	$325	$295	$275	$225

Last MSR was $559.

ADCO/CZ 1911-A1 - .38 Super or .45 ACP cal., standard size government model with 5 in. barrel, black matte finish. Limited importation 2004.

	$475	$425	$375	$325	$295	$275	$225

Last MSR was $559.

    Add $10 for .38 Super cal.

CABANAS

Previous trademark manufactured by Industrias Cabanas, S.A. in Aguilas, Mexico 1949-1999. Previously imported and retailed by Mandall Shooting Supplies, Inc. located in Scottsdale, AZ.

Cabanas manufactured a unique single shot bolt action rifle which shot oversized .177 pellets/BBs powered by .22 blanks at 1,150 feet per second. There were at least 8 variations, and secondary market prices today for 95%+ original condition ranges from approx. $65-$120. Transfer requires FFL. This trademark had limited U.S. importation.

CABELA'S INC.

Current sporting goods dealer and catalog company headquartered in Sidney, NE. Consumer direct (store or mail order catalog) sales only.

In addition to the models listed below, Cabela's also imports black powder cartridge Sharps replicas, revolvers, and other reproductions, mostly manufactured in Italy by A. Uberti, Pedersoli, and Pietta (please see individual sections for more info).

Cabela's also has a wide variety of black powder muzzleloading rifles and pistols, in addition to replicas of popular older Colt and Winchester firearms.

Please refer to the *Colt Blackpowder Reproductions & Replicas* by Dennis Adler and the *Blue Book of Modern Black Powder Arms* (also online) by John Allen & Dennis Adler for more information and prices on Cabela's lineup of modern black powder models.

Cabela's should be contacted directly (see Trademark Index) to receive the most recent information on their complete firearms and black powder line-ups, including related accessories.

SHOTGUNS: SxS

HEMINGWAY MODEL - mfg. for Cabela's by V. Bernardelli located in Italy, ST, ejectors. Disc. 1994.

	$925	$775	$700	$640	$575	$525	$465

Last MSR was $975.

AYA GRADE II CUSTOM - mfg. for Cabela's by AYA located in Eibar, Spain, ST, ejectors, similar to AYA Model II with Model 53 engraving and trim. Disc. and sold out.

	$3,650	$3,100	$2,500	$2,000	$1,650	$1,275	$1,000

CAEM, RENATO

Current manufacturer of small gauge, SxS shotguns located in Marcheno Val Trompia, Italy. No current importation.

Renato Caem manufactures approx. 5 best quality scalloped boxlock SxS shotguns annually, only in 20 ga., 28 ga., or .410 bore. Please contact the factory directly for more information regarding specifications, delivery, and current prices (see Trademark Index).

CAESAR GUERINI, s.r.l.

Current manufacturer located in Marcheno, Italy. Currently imported beginning 2003 by Caesar Guerini USA LLC.

SHOTGUNS: O/U, FIELD

FLYWAY - 12 ga., 3 in. chambers, 28 or 30 in. barrels, beavertail forend, multichokes, blued boxlock receiver with satin finish and gold mallard on bottom, parallel 10mm top rib, shipped with hard case, 7 lbs. 14 oz. - 8 lbs.

MSR $2,295	$1,795	$1,495	$1,295	$1,095	$895	$800	$725

WOODLANDER - 12, 20 or 28 ga., 2 3/4 (28 ga.) or 3 in. chambers, 26 or 28 in. barrels, case hardened boxlock receiver with Bulino style engraved (ruffed grouse in gold on bottom of receiver), Prince of Wales grip and Schnabel forend, 6mm top rib, multichokes, shipped with hard case, 6 lbs. 2 oz.-6 lbs. 14 oz.

MSR $2,295	$1,795	$1,495	$1,295	$1,095	$895	$800	$725

TEMPIO - 12, 20 or 28 ga., 2 3/4 (28 ga.) or 3 in. chambers, 26 or 28 in. barrels, grey "Tinaloy" boxlock receiver featuring gold grouse, quail, and pheasant game scenes surrounded by scroll, Prince of Wales grip and Schnabel forend, oil finished wood, multichokes, factory hard case, 6 lbs. 4 oz.-7 lbs.

MSR $2,450	$2,095	$1,795	$1,595	$1,395	$1,195	$995	$850

MAGNUS LIGHT - 12, 20 or 28 ga., 2 3/4 (28 ga.) or 3 in. chambers, 26 or 28 in. barrels, case hardened sideplated boxlock alloy receiver with gold grouse, pheasant, and quail game scenes, Prince of Wales grip, Schnabel forend, oil finished wood, multichokes, factory hard case, 5 lbs. 4 oz.-6 lbs.

MSR $2,995	$2,295	$2,095	$1,895	$1,495	$1,295	$1,095	$900

 ❋ *Magnus* - similar to Magnus Light, except has steel receiver, 6 lbs. 4 oz.-7 lbs.

MSR $2,995	$2,295	$2,095	$1,895	$1,495	$1,295	$1,095	$900

FORUM - 12, 20 or 28 ga., 2 3/4 (28 ga.) or 3 in. chambers, 26 or 28 in. barrels, side-plated, coin finished boxlock receiver, blind sideplates with no visible screws, Bulino style engraving with game scenes and floral scroll, Prince of Wales grip, Schnable forend, checkered stock with oil finish, multichokes, factory hard case, 6 lbs. 5 oz.-7 lbs.

MSR $6,695	$4,000	$3,750	$3,295	$2,995	$2,495	$2,095	$1,850

SHOTGUNS: O/U, SPORTING CLAYS

SUMMIT SPORTING - 12, 20 or 28 ga., 30, 32, or 34 (12 ga. only) in. barrels, grey "Tinaloy" boxlock receiver with neo-modern engraving, 10mm parallel top rib with vent. side ribs, adj. trigger, pistol grip stock, Schnabel forend, right hand palm swell, extended choke tubes, factory case, 7 lbs. 4 oz.-8 lbs. 2 oz.

MSR $2,650	$2,250	$1,995	$1,695	$1,495	$1,295	$1,000	$895

 ❋ *Summit Limited Sporting* - similar to Summit Sporting, except has case hardened receiver.

MSR $2,995	$2,295	$2,095	$1,895	$1,495	$1,295	$1,095	$900

MAGNUS SPORTING - 12, 20 or 28 ga., 30, 32, or 34 (12 ga. only) in. barrels, side-plated grey "Tinaloy" boxlock receiver featuring gold grousek, quail, and phesant game scenes, 10mm parallel top rib with vent. side ribs, pistol grip stock and Schnabel forend, adj. trigger, extended choke tubes, factory hard case, 7 lbs. 4 oz.-8 lbs. 2 oz.

MSR $3,395	$2,795	$2,495	$2,195	$1,695	$1,495	$1,295	$1,100

FORUM SPORTING - 12, 20 or 28 ga., 30, 32, or 34 (12 ga. only) in. barrels, coin finished sideplated boxlock receiver, Bulino style game scene engraving, blinid side-plates with no screws showing, specs are available by request.

MSR $6,695	$4,000	$3,750	$3,295	$2,995	$2,495	$2,095	$1,850

CALICO LIGHT WEAPONS SYSTEMS

Previous manufacturer established during 1986, and located in Sparks, NV 1998-2001. Previously located in Bakersfield, CA.

A complete line of accessories was available for all Calico carbines and pistols.

CARBINES

LIBERTY 50-100 - 9mm Para. cal., 16.1 in. barrel, downward ejection, aluminum alloy receiver, synthetic stock with pistol grip (some early post-ban specimens had full wood stocks with thumbhole cutouts), 50 or 100 shot helical feed mag., ambidextrous safety, 7 lbs. Mfg. 1995-2001.

| $850 | $675 | $550 | $500 | $450 | $400 | $350 |

Last MSR was $860.

Add $125 for 100 shot helical feed mag.

M-100 - .22 LR cal., semi-auto carbine, paramilitary design with folding buttstock, 100 shot helical feed mag., alloy frame, ambidextrous safety, 16.1 in. shrouded barrel with flash suppressor/muzzle brake, 4.2 lbs. empty. Mfg. 1986-94.

| $625 | $550 | $450 | $400 | $350 | $300 | $275 |

Last MSR was $308.

✳ *M-100 FS* - similar to M-100, except has solid stock and barrel does not have flash suppressor. Mfg. 1996-2001.

| $550 | $450 | $400 | $360 | $315 | $275 | $250 |

Last MSR was $650.

M-101 - while advertised, this model never went into production.

M-105 SPORTER - similar to M-100, except has walnut distinctively styled buttstock and forend, 4 3/4 lbs. empty. Mfg. 1989-94.

| $400 | $350 | $280 | $235 | $200 | $175 | $160 |

Last MSR was $335.

M-106 - while advertised, this model never went into production.

M-900 - 9mm Para. cal., retarded blowback action, paramilitary design with collapsible buttstock, cast aluminum receiver with stainless steel bolt, static cocking handle, 16 in. barrel, fixed rear sight with adj. post front, 50 (standard) or 100 shot helical feed mag., ambidextrous safety, black polymer pistol grip and forend, 3.7 lbs. empty. Mfg. 1989-90, reintroduced 1992-93.

| $875 | $775 | $675 | $575 | $475 | $400 | $350 |

Last MSR was $618.

✳ *M-900S* - similar to M-900, except has non-collapsible shoulder stock. Disc. 1993.

| $650 | $550 | $475 | $400 | $350 | $300 | $275 |

Last MSR was $632.

✳ *M-901 Canada Carbine* - 9mm Para. cal., similar to M-900, except has 18 1/2 in. barrel and sliding stock. Disc. 1992.

| $675 | $595 | $550 | $475 | $350 | $300 | $285 |

Last MSR was $643.

This model was also available with solid fixed stock (Model 901S).

M-951 TACTICAL CARBINE - 9mm Para. cal., 16.1 in. barrel, similar appearance to M-900 Carbine, except has muzzle brake and extra pistol grip on front of forearm, 4 3/4 lbs. Mfg. 1990-94.

| $525 | $450 | $395 | $350 | $300 | $275 | $250 |

Last MSR was $556.

GRADING - PPGS™	100%	98%	95%	90%	80%	70%	60%

✳ M-951S - similar to M-951, except has synthetic buttstock. Mfg. 1991-94.

	$525	$450	$395	$350	$300	$275	$250

Last MSR was $567.

PISTOLS: SEMI-AUTO

M-110 - .22 LR cal., same action as M-100 Carbine, 6 in. barrel with muzzle brake, 100 round helical feed mag., includes notched rear sight and adj. windage front sight, 10 1/2 in. sight radius, ambidextrous safety, pistol grip storage compartment, 2.21 lbs. empty. Mfg. 1989-2001.

	$475	$395	$315	$260	$230	$200	$180

Last MSR was $570.

M-950 - 9mm Para. cal., same operating mechanism as the M-900 Carbine, 6 in. barrel, 50 (standard) or 100 shot helical feed mag., 2 1/4 lbs. empty. Mfg. 1989-94.

	$450	$375	$325	$285	$260	$240	$225

Last MSR was $518.

Many accessories were also available for this model.

CAMEX-BLASER USA, INC.

Previous importer/distributor of Blaser Jagdwaffen Gmbh rifles.

Previously imported Camex-Blaser rifles can be located in the Blaser section in this text.

CAPRINUS

Previous shotgun manufacturer located in Varberg, Sweden.

SHOTGUNS: O/U

CAPRINUS SWEDEN - 12 ga., boxlock action, ejectors, ST, stainless steel receiver, unique design incorporates breaking down without forearm disassembly, 29 1/2 in. barrels with choke tubes, limited mfg. during early 1980s.

	$3,750	$3,250	$2,850	$2,400	$2,000	$1,600	$1,200

Last MSR was approx. $5,955.

CARBON 15

Please refer to Professional Ordnance (discontinued mfg.) and the Bushmaster (current mfg.) for more information on this trademark.

CARL GUSTAF

Previous manufacturer located in Eskilstuna, Sweden. No current importation. Previously imported by Hansen & Co. located in Southport, CT during 1994-95, and by Precision Sales International located in Westfield, MA during 1991-1993.

RIFLES: BOLT ACTION

MODEL CG 2000 STANDARD GRADE - 6.5x55mm, 7x64mm, 9.3x62mm, .243 Win., .270 Win., .30-06, .308 Win., 7mm Rem. Mag., or .300 Win. Mag. cal., bolt action, Monte Carlo walnut stock with checkering and Wundhammer grip, 24 in. barrel, detachable 3 or 4 shot mag., with or without sights, cold-swaged barrel and receiver, 60 degree bolt, 3-way slide safety, 7 1/2 lbs. Imported began 1991-95.

	$1,325	$1,050	$875	$725	$575	$475	$375

Last MSR was $1,535.

Add $540 for Mag. cals.

This model was supplied with individual 80 meter signed test targets. This model was also been imported as the Fairfax 2000 series.

GRADING - PPGS™	100%	98%	95%	90%	80%	70%	60%

✳ *Model 2000 Luxe Grade* - .270 Win., .30-06, .308 Win., or 6.5x55mm cal., features choice of regular or Mannlicher deluxe walnut stock. Imported 1995 only.

	$1,695	$1,400	$1,200	$975	$825	$650	$475

Last MSR was $1,935.

A Model 2000 Super-Luxe was also available in 6.5x55mm or .30-06 cal. - retail was $4,250.

MODEL 3000 - various cals., features Sauer action with non-rotating bolt. Previously imported by Aimpoint.

	$675	$575	$475	$400	$375	$350	$325

STANDARD BOLT ACTION RIFLE - 6.5x55mm, 7x64mm, .270 Win., 7mm Rem. Mag., .308 Win., .30-06, or 9.3x62mm cal., 24 in. barrel, folding rear sight, checkered classic style stock. Mfg. 1970-77.

	$375	$325	$300	$275	$250	$225	$200

✳ *Monte Carlo stock*

	$450	$395	$350	$300	$275	$250	$225

GRADE II - similar to Monte Carlo Standard, in .22-250 Rem., .25-06 Rem., 6.5x55mm, .270 Win., 7mm Rem. Mag., .308 Win., .30-06, or .300 Win. Mag. cal., select stock and rosewood pistol grip cap, and forearm tip.

	$500	$425	$375	$325	$295	$275	$250

GRADE III - similar to Grade II, except fancy wood, deluxe high gloss finish.

	$575	$475	$425	$350	$325	$300	$275

DELUXE - similar to Grade III, except engraved floorplate and trigger guard, Deluxe French walnut, and jeweled bolt.

	$675	$575	$475	$400	$375	$350	$325

VARMINT TARGET MODEL - .222 Rem., .22-250 Rem., .243 Win., bolt action, fast lock time, or 6.5x55mm cal., 27 in. barrel, no sights, large bakelite bolt knob, target type stock. Mfg. 1970. Disc.

	$550	$495	$440	$385	$360	$320	$290

GRAND PRIX SINGLE SHOT TARGET - .22 LR cal., fastest lock time bolt action, 27 in. heavy barrel with adj. weight, no sights, target stock, adj. buttplate. Mfg. 1970. Disc.

	$550	$495	$440	$385	$360	$320	$290

CASARTELLI, CARLO

Previous manufacturer located in Brescia, Italy until 2000. Previously imported and distributed until 1999 by New England Arms Corp. located in Kittery Point, ME.

Casartelli rifles and shotguns were available through special order only. Virtually any custom gun configuration could be manufactured to the customer's exact specifications and requirements.

RIFLES

AFRICA MODEL - BOLT ACTION - various heavy and Mag. cals., action is square bridge type Mauser, full coverage game scene engraving appropriate to caliber, takedown, limited production.

	$10,200	$7,500	$5,900	$5,300	$4,700	$4,100	$3,600

Last MSR was $12,000.

SAFARI MODEL - BOLT ACTION - standard cals., regular Mauser action, full coverage game scene engraving, limited production.

	$6,250	$5,900	$5,250	$4,950	$4,150	$3,650	$3,150

Last MSR was $8,250.

GRADING - PPGS™	100%	98%	95%	90%	80%	70%	60%

KENYA - DOUBLE RIFLE - most standard and Mag. cals., sidelock action, elaborate game scene and/or scroll engraving, limited production.

	$24,250	$21,500	$17,750	$14,750	$12,000	$9,950	$8,250

Last MSR was $35,000.

SHOTGUNS: SxS

SIDELOCK MODEL - various gauges, elaborate game scene and/or scroll engraving, limited production.

	$13,000	$9,750	$7,900	$6,500	$5,200	$4,250	$3,750

Last MSR was $17,000.

CASPIAN ARMS, LTD.

Current parts manufacturer located in Wolcott, VT. Dealer direct sales only.

Caspian Arms currently fabricates high quality steel, stainless steel, titanium (new 2002), and alloy frames for the Colt Government Model 1911/A1, both in standard and high capacity frames. Frame sizes include the Government, Commander, and Officer's. Caspian Arms Ltd. also manufactures slides, including a damascus variation ($525), and related small parts, in addition to having many special order machine operations available. Please contact them directly for current information on their extensive line of pistol-related components.

PISTOLS: SEMI-AUTO

VIETNAM COMMEMORATIVE - .45 ACP, total production was 1,000, hand engraved by J.J. Adams, nickel plated, branch service medallion installed in grips. Limited mfg. 1986-93.

	$1,450	$995	$795

Last MSR was $1,500.

Add $350 for gold plating.
Add $200 for serial numbers below RVN100.

This Vietnam Commemorative was also available in 24Kt. gold hand inlay edition for $14,000 - very limited production.

CASULL ARMS CORPORATION

Current manufacturer and distributor located in Afton, WY, since 1996. Consumer direct and dealer sales.

PISTOLS: SEMI-AUTO

CA-3800 - .38 Casull cal., single action, 6 in. match barrel, 8 shot mag., blue or stainless finish, checkered exotic wood grips, 2 piece guide rod, fully adj. rear sight and Casull mfg. adj. front sight, hand fitted slide to frame, slide features Dick Casull signature on left side, includes locking aluminum carrying case and 2 mags., 40 oz. New 2001.

MSR $2,495		$2,395	$2,150	$1,975	$1,825	$1,675	$1,550	$1,425

Add $300 for 6 in. .45 ACP barrel.
Add $400 for all stainless model.
Add $100 for either stainless steel frame and blue slide or vice versa.
Add $900 for both cals. with custom fitted extra slides.
Add $400 for compensator.

GRADING - PPGS™	100%	98%	95%	90%	80%	70%	60%

REVOLVERS

CA2000 MINI-FRAME REVOLVER - .22 LR or .32 ACP cal., double-action, fold up trigger, hammerless, manual safety, hardwood grips. New 1997.

MSR $395	$350	$295	$250	$225	$200	$185	$170

CA3000 SMALL FRAME REVOLVER - while advertised during 1997 (MSR - $1,495), this model never went into production.

CA4000 LARGE FRAME REVOLVER - while advertised during 1997 (MSR - $1,995), this model never went into production.

RIFLES: BOLT ACTION

CAC5000 CONVENTIONAL - standard cals. include .270 Win., .300 Win. Mag., .375 H&H, .458 Win. Mag., or 7mm Rem. Mag. cal., features improved bolt action with conventional extraction, box mag. Limited mfg. 1997-99.

			$2,275	$1,950	$1,600		

Last MSR was $2,495.

CRS7000 CASULL RIFLE SYSTEM - .30 Casull or 6.5 Casull cal., patented bolt and extraction system, features new, all-metal bedding system allowing take-down and reassembly without affecting accuracy, box mag., stainless barrel without sights, unchecked-ered walnut stock, sporter or benchrest configuration. Limited mfg. 1997-99.

			$2,700	$2,350	$2,000		

Last MSR was $2,995.

CAVALRY ARMS CORPORATION

Current manufacturer located in Gilbert, AZ. Previously located in Mesa, AZ.

Cavalry Arms Corporation manufactures the CAV-15 Series rifle, styled after the AR-15. Base price is $775-$800. Additionally, many options and accessories are available. Cavalry Arms also makes paramilitary conversions for select slide action shotguns. Please contact the company directly for more information, including a price quotation (see Trademark Index).

CENTURION ORDNANCE, INC.

Previous importer located in Helotes, TX. Centurion Ordnance imports Aguila ammunition.

SHOTGUNS: SLIDE ACTION

POSEIDON - 12 ga., 1 3/4 in. chamber (shoots "mini-shells" and slugs), 18 1/4 in. smoothbore barrel, 13 in. LOP, black synthetic stock and forearm, 6 shot mag., adj. rear sight, 5 lbs., 5 oz. Limited importation 2001.

$285	$250	$225	$200	$185	$170	$155

While prototypes of this model were imported briefly during 2001, this gun never made it into the consumer marketplace.

Mini-shells retailed for $12.60 for a box of 20 (shot sizes include 7, #4 & #1 buckshot).

CENTURY ARMS

Previous manufacturer circa 1996-1998 located in Balwyn, Victoria, Australia.

RIFLES: SINGLE SHOT

REWA RIFLE - 4 bore ball, break open action, massive single shot with case colored and engraved action, deluxe checkered stock and forearm with ebony tip, iron sights, production limited to a few prototypes only (a convertible shotgun barrel was also planned).

Extreme rarity precludes accurate pricing on this model.

GRADING - PPGS™	100%	98%	95%	90%	80%	70%	60%

CENTURY INTERNATIONAL ARMS, INC.

Current importer and distributor with corporate offices located in Delray Beach, FL. Century International Arms, Inc. was previously headquartered in St. Albans, VT until 1997, and Boca Raton, FL from 1997-2004.

CENTURY INTERNATIONAL ARMS INC.

Century International Arms, Inc. imports a wide variety of used military rifles and pistols. Current rifle importation includes: British Enfields (various configurations), various German Mauser rifle contract models, Italian Carcanos, Russian Mosin-Nagants, various Czech military, including the CZ-24, CZ-98/22, and VZ-24, Yugoslavian Model 59/66, Austrian Mannlicher and Steyr Mannlicher models, Russian/Romanian/Hungarian Model 44s, Swiss Schmidt-Rubin K31s, and many others. Current pistol importation includes: Walther P1, Ballester Rigaud (Argentina), and CZ Model 50 and 52s. For more information on these recent imports, please contact the company directly regarding availability and pricing.

In the past, Century International Arms has also imported French Lebels and MAS models, F.N. Model 49s, Hakims, Egyptian Rashids, Swedish Ljungman Model 42Bs, Chinese and Russian SKSs, and M-1 Carbines/Garands. Imported pistols have included various WWI and WWII used military pistols including Mauser Broomhandles, Lugers, P.38s, Argentine mfg. M1911s, French PA 35s, and recently, models from both FEG and Republic Arms, located in South Africa.

Additionally, Century International Arms imports a wide range of accessories, including bayonettes, holsters, stocks, magazines, grips, mounts, scopes, misc. parts, new and surplus ammunition, etc., and should be contacted directly (see Trademark Index) for a copy of their most recent catalog, or check their web site for current offerings.

PISTOLS: SEMI-AUTO

Century International Arms Inc. also imports Arcus pistols from Bulgaria and Daewoo pistols from South Korea. Please refer to the individual sections for more information.

M-1911 STYLE PISTOLS - .45 ACP cal., patterned after the Colt Govt. Model 1911, choice of 4 1/4 (Blue Thunder Commodore, Commodore 1911, or GI-Officer's Model) or 5 (SAM Elite/SAM Standard or SAM Chief/Falcon) ported (disc. 2002) or unported barrel, 7 shot mag., various configurations and finishes, many target features are standard on most models. Importation from Phillippines began 2001.

No MSR	$315	$265	$235	$215	$195	$180	$165

Add $35 for Commodore Blue Thunder Model with squared off triggerguard.

RIFLES: SEMI-AUTO

G-3 SPORTER - .308 Win. cal., mfg. from genuine G3 parts, and American made receiver with integrated scope rail, includes 20 shot mag., 19 in. barrel, pistol grip stock, matte black finish, refinished condition only, 9.3 lbs. New 1999.

No MSR	$585	$500	$450	$425	$395	$375	$350

FAL SPORTER - .308 Win. cal., U.S. mfg., new barrel receiver, synthetic furniture, 20 shot mag. New 2004.

No MSR	$650	$600	$550	$500	$465	$435	$400

CETME SPORTER - .308 Win. cal., new mfg. Cetme action, 19.5 in. barrel, 20 shot mag., choice of blue or Mossy Oak Break-Up camo (disc.) metal finish, wood (disc.) or synthetic stock, pistol grip, and vent. forearm, refinished condition only, 9.7 lbs. New 2002.

No MSR	$395	$350	$295	$265	$245	$230	$215

GRADING - PPGS™	100%	98%	95%	90%	80%	70%	60%

S.A.R. 1 - 7.62x39mm cal., AK-47 styling, 16.5 in. barrel, wood stock and forearm, scope rail mounted on receiver, includes one 10 and two 30 shot double stack mags., 7.08 lbs. Mfg. by Romarm of Romania. Importation disc. 2003.

	$395	$350	$295	$265	$245	$230	$215

S.A.R. 2 - 5.45x39mm cal., AK-47 styling, 16 in. barrel, wood stock and forearm, includes one 10 and one 30 shot double stack mags., 8 lbs. Mfg. by Romarm of Romania. Importation disc. 2003.

	$395	$350	$295	$265	$245	$230	$215

S.A.R. 3 - .223 Rem. cal., AK-47 styling, 16 in. barrel, wood stock and forearm, includes one 10 and one 30 shot double stack mags., 8 lbs. Mfg. by Romarm of Romania. Importation disc. 2003.

	$395	$350	$295	$265	$245	$230	$215

WASR-10 LO-CAP - 7.62x39mm cal., AK-47 styling, 16.25 in. barrel, wood stock and forearm, includes one 5 and one 10 shot single stack mags., 7.5 lbs. Mfg. by Romarm of Romania.

No MSR	$269	$215	$170	$145	$130	$115	$105

WASR-10 HIGH-CAP - 7.62x39mm cal., AK-47 styling, 16.25 in. barrel, wood stock and forearm, includes two 30 shot double stack mags., 7.5 lbs. Mfg. by Romarm of Romania.

No MSR	$399	$330	$290	$270	$250	$230	$215

Add $130 for 75 shot drum mag.

L1A1 SPORTER - .308 Win. cal., current mfg. receiver patterned after the Browning L1A1, includes carrying handle, synthetic furniture, 20 shot mag., 22.5 in. barrel, fold over aperture rear sight, 9.5 lbs. Mfg. in U.S.

No MSR	$485	$395	$350	$325	$295	$275	$250

DRAGUNOV - 7.62x54R cal., new CNC milled receiver, Dragunov configuration stock with thumbole, 26 1/2 in. barrel, supplied with scope and cleaning kit. Mfg. in Romania.

No MSR	$875	$750	$650	$600	$500	$450	$395

RIFLES: SLIDE ACTION

PAR 1 OR 3 - 7.62x39mm (PAR 1) or .223 Rem. (PAR 3) cal., AK receiver styling, 10 shot mag., accepts double stack AK magazines, wood stock, pistol grip, and forearm, 20.9 in. barrel, 7.6 lbs. Mfg. by PAR, and importation began 2002.

No MSR	$360	$300	$275	$250	$225	$200	$175

SHOTGUNS

ARTHEMIS (SUPER ARTHEMIS) O/U - 12, 20, 28 (new 2004) ga. or .410 bore, 3 in. chambers, 28 in. VR barrels, SST, extractors, checkered walnut stock and forearm, 5.3-7.4 lbs. Mfg. by Khan in Turkey, importation disc.

	$450	$395	$350	$325	$285	$250	$225

Add $25 for 20 ga. or 28 ga.
Add $50 for .410 bore.

PHANTOM SEMI-AUTO - 12 ga. only, 3 in. chamber, 24, 26, or 28 in. VR barrels with 3 choke tubes, black synthetic stock and forearm. Mfg. in Turkey, importation disc.

	$265	$225	$200	$185	$175	$165	$155

SAS-12 SEMI-AUTO - 12 ga. only, 2 3/4 in. chamber, detachable 3 (Type II) or 5 shot mag., black synthetic stock and forearm, 22 or 23.5 in. barrel. Mfg. by PRC in China.

No MSR	$225	$185	$165	$155	$145	$135	$125

Add approx. $25 for ghost ring rear with blade front or bead sight.

GRADING - PPGS™	100%	98%	95%	90%	80%	70%	60%

COACH SxS - 12, 20 ga., or .410 bore, exposed hammers, 20 in. barrels, DTs, steel construction, checkered walnut stock and forearm, includes sling swivels. Mfg. in China.

	No MSR	$240	$195	$175	$165	$155	$145	$135

MODEL IJ2 SLIDE ACTION - 12 ga. only, 2 3/4 or 3 in. chamber, 19 in. barrel with ghost ring sights or fiber optic front sights, fixed choke only, 7.2 lbs. Mfg. in China.

	No MSR	$199	$170	$150	$125	$100	$90	$80

CENTURY MFG., INC.

Previous manufacturer located in Knightstown, IN, Feb. 2002-late 2004. Previously manufactured in Evansville and Greenfield, IN 1973-circa 1999. Consumer direct and dealer sales.

This revolver design was originally manufactured in 1972 by Russell Wilson, who sandcasted the bronze frame (cloned from the Colt SAA configuration) in Evansville, IN. Gene Phelps purchased the manufacturing rights for this gun and formed a partnership with Earl Keller to produce a redesigned frame, also using sandcast bronze.

The original Century revolver was made in Evansville, IN beginning in 1973 (1973 was the 100th anniversary of the .45-70 Govt. cartridge - hence the term Century) and production was halted in 1976 at ser. no. 524. In late 1976, Phelps and Keller (the two original partners on the venture) dissolved their partnership and each began manufacturing their own version of the .45-70 revolver. Gene Phelps completely redesigned the gun's interior and began manufacturing the Heritage I, with an investment-cast steel frame, and without the Century's novel cross-bolt safety. Keller's Century Manufacturing, Inc. continued to produce the original Century, with some design refinements, and in 1985 the company was purchased by Dr. Paul Majors, who died in Dec. of 2001.

The most recent Century revolver featured a manganese bronze frame and other components in addition to having a cross-bolt safety. They were produced in .45-70 and various other cals., in Greenfield, IN. Earl Keller died in 1986. The second series was made in Greenfield, IN with limited production resuming in 1986. Earlier handmade "Evansville" Model 100s (disc.) are currently selling for between $2,500-$3,500, depending on the region.

In Feb., 2002, Century Mfg. was purchased by Dave Lukens & Jeff Yelton and moved to Knightstown, IN. New production guns also included a revolving rifle built on the Model 100 frame. These new production guns carried a limited lifetime guarantee.

REVOLVERS

Less than 3,000 Model 100s were manufactured 1976-2001. The following values below are for .45-70 Govt. cal. Other calibers were priced from $2,000 on up.

MODEL 100 - .30-30 Win. (new 1987), .375 Win. (new 1986), .444 Marlin (new 1986), .45-70 Govt., .50-70 Govt. (new 1987), or .50-110 cal., single action 6 shot, manganese bronze frame, steel cylinder, 6 1/2, 8, 10, or 12 (disc.) in. round or octagon barrel, unique crossbolt safety that locks the hammer, adj. sights, walnut grips, 5 lbs. 14 oz. Disc. 2000, reintroduced 2002-2004.

✳ **.45-70 Govt. and other cals.** - includes all cals. except .50-110.

	$1,295	$1,100	$995	$900	$850	$800	$750

Last MSR (2002-2004) was $1,295.
Previous mfg. last MSR was $2,000.

Add $200 for calibers other than .45-70 Govt.
Add $110 for normal octagon barrel.
Add $200 for stainless steel fabrication.

✳ **.50-110 cal.**

	$2,895	$2,350	$1,950	$1,700	$1,500	$1,250	$1,025

Last MSR was $2,895.

CHAMPLIN FIREARMS, INC.

Current custom manufacturer, gunsmith, and importer located in Enid, OK. Champlin Firearms was established in 1966. Direct sales only.

Champlin Firearms, Inc. manufactures handcrafted rifles built around a patented bolt action of their own design and manufacture. Most guns are built per individual customer order and specifications. Values will vary greatly depending on the configuration, desirability, and special order specifications. All Champlin rifles are built along classic lines with best quality wood and exemplary workmanship. They have been used successfully on safaris and have shot dangerous game throughout the world.

Champlin Firearms, Inc. also inventories a wide selection of high grade, top-quality shotguns and rifles (especially top trademark doubles and bolt actions). Contact George Caswell (owner) directly for a current listing (please refer to Trademark Index). Additional services include a complete gunsmithing service for all grades of English double rifles and shotguns. Custom stocks are also built to individual customer specifications. All double rifles are test fired and checked thoroughly upon completion of manufacture or repair. Again, Champlin Firearms should be contacted for consultation and quotation regarding this additional work.

RIFLES: BOLT ACTION

BOLT ACTION RIFLE - various cals., round or octagon barrel, adj. trigger, each rifle is built to customer specifications. Values below represent base gun with standard wood, no options, and no engraving.

MSR $8,500	$8,500	$8,000	$7,000	$6,750	$6,000	$5,250	$4,500

Many additional special order options are available on this model and Champlin Firearms should be contacted directly for price quotations.

CHAPUIS ARMES

Current manufacturer located in St. Bonnet Le Chateau, France. Currently imported by William Larkin Moore, located in Scottsdale AZ, and by Chadick's, Ltd. (limited importation) located in Terrell, TX. Previously imported by GSI, Inc. located in Trussville, AL until 1995 and Armes De Chasse located in Chadds Ford, PA until 1993.

Chapuis rifles and shotguns are manufactured on a limited basis. Most of their emphasis is on high-quality double rifles and shotguns. For further information regarding this respected French trademark, please contact the importer.

RIFLES: O/U

SUPER ORION C15 MODEL - .300 Win. Mag. or .375 H&H cal., notched boxlock action with ejectors, coin finish only, 23.6 in. barrels with quarter rib, engraved action, approx. 8 lbs. Imported 1995-96.

$8,250	$7,150	$6,250	$5,400	$4,200	$3,500	$3,150

Last MSR was $9,195.

Add $2,900 for .375 H&H cal.

RIFLES: SxS

William Larkin Moore also has The Artisan Express ($11,200) and the Imperial Express ($20,000) Models available. Please contact them directly for more information.

RGEX EXPRESS MODEL - .30-06, .300 Win. Mag., 7x65R, 8x57JRS, or 9.3x74R cal., double rifle, ejectors, boxlock action, 23.6 in. barrels, deluxe checkered walnut stock with cheekpiece, full line of options are available, 7 lbs. 6 oz. Limited importation beginning 1998-1999.

Values below assume metric or .30-06 cal.

MSR $6,900	$6,275	$5,800	$5,350	$4,900	$4,450	$3,850	$3,250

GRADING - PPGS™	100%	98%	95%	90%	80%	70%	60%

Add approx. $700 for .300 Win. Mag. cal.

Add approx. 60% for HGEX Express Supreme Model (engraved, not avail. in .300 Win. Mag. cal.).

Add 110% for HGEX Express Imperial Model (scroll engraved, not avail. in .300 Win. Mag. cal.).

UGEX UTILITY GRADE EXPRESS - similar to RGEX, except has select walnut. New 1998.

	MSR $5,500	$5,000	$4,500	$3,950	$3,500	$2,950	$2,550	$2,100

Add $500 for .300 Win. Mag. cal.

AFRICAN P.H. (PROFESSIONAL HUNTER) GRADE I - .30-06, .300 Win. Mag., .375 H&H, .416 Rigby, 9.3x74R, or .470 NE cal., notched boxlock action with English scroll border engraving, case colored receiver, selective ejectors, deluxe walnut stock with English cheekpiece.

Values below are for .375 H&H or .300 Win. Mag cal.

	MSR N/A	$9,350	$8,475	$7,500	$6,500	$5,650	$4,600	$4,000

Add $2,825 for .470 NE cal.

Add $4,000 for .416 Rigby cal.

Subtract $1,500 for .30-06 or 9.3x74R.

This model was previously designated Express Agex Brousse.

✳ *African PH Grade II* - similar to Grade I, except has master signed scroll engraving with game scene on bottom of coin finished receiver.

	MSR N/A	$18,500	$15,250	$12,000	$10,000	$8,000	$7,000	$6,000

Values above assume .470 NE cal. Subtract for smaller cals.

BROUSSE MODEL (SAFARI EXPRESS) - .300 Win. Mag., .375 H&H, .416 Rigby, or .470 NE cal., similar to Grade I Professional Hunter, except has full rose and scroll engraving coverage on coin finished receiver. New 1998.

	MSR $10,800	$9,950	$8,950	$7,750	$6,600	$5,500	$4,500	$3,500

Add $3,000 for .416 Rigby cal.

Add $3,100 for .470 NE cal.

Add apprximately 100% for Safari Deluxe Express in .470 NE cal.

SAVANA MODEL - .30-06, .300 Win. Mag., .375 H&H, .416 R Chapuis (disc.), .416 Rigby, .470 NE, or 9.3x74R cal., deluxe version of the Agex Jungle, except has hand-engraved game scenes on action sides and Cape Buffalo head on floorplate of action, case colored (disc.) or coin finish.

Values below are for .375 H&H cal.

	MSR N/A	$20,250	$17,350	$15,300	$13,000	$10,500	$8,750	$7,500

Add $2,000 for .470 NE cal.

Add $3,000 for .416 Rigby cal.

Subtract $2,500 for .30-06 or 9.3x74R.

Subtract $2,000 for .300 Win. Mag. cal.

JUNGLE MODEL - .30-06, .300 Win. Mag., .375 H&H, .416 R Chapuis (mfg. 1993-96), .470 NE (new 1992), or 9.3x74R cal., boxlock action, case colored (disc.) or coin finish, special reinforced receiver with double underbites, 25 5/8 in. barrels, fine English scroll engraving with 3 African animals, ejectors, select French walnut with compartment in pistol grip cap.

Values below are for .375 H&H cal.

	MSR N/A	$11,850	$9,950	$8,150	$7,200	$6,250	$5,400	$4,350

Add $2,500 for .470 NE cal.

Add $3,500 for .416 Rigby cal.

Subtract $2,000 for .30-06 or 9.3x74R.

Subtract $1,000 for .300 Win. Mag. cal.

GRADING - PPGS™	100%	98%	95%	90%	80%	70%	60%

✴ *Jungle Second Grade* - features elaborate engraving and best quality wood. Disc. 1996.

	$26,000	$22,500	$19,000	$16,000	$13,000	$10,000	$8,750

Last MSR was $29,395.

Add $3,900 for .470 NE cal.

EXPRESS AGEX AFRICA - same cals. as AGEX Jungle, notched boxlock action, master signed scroll engraving and African game scenes, selective ejectors, cased. Importation disc. 1994.

	$19,250	$17,750	$15,250	$13,500	$11,250	$10,000	$9,000

Last MSR was $20,954.

Add $2,896 for .470 NE cal.
Add $5,626 for .416 R Chapuis cal.

EXPRESS AGEX SAFARI - similar to AGEX Africa, except has top-of-the-line engraving and wood. Importation disc. 1994.

	$29,000	$26,550	$22,350	$19,150	$16,950	$14,000	$12,000

Last MSR was $30,375.

Add $2,040 for .470 NE cal.
Add $5,134 for .416 R Chapuis cal.

RIFLES: SINGLE SHOT

OURAL EXEL MODEL - .270 Win., .300 Win. Mag., 7mm Rem. Mag. cal., notched boxlock action, English scroll engraving, extractors, 23 5/8 in. barrel, fitted and engraved scope mounts. Importation disc. 1994, reintroduced 1999, current pricing is POR.

MSR N/A	$4,875	$4,200	$3,775	$3,250	$2,800	$2,400	$1,775

Add approx. 20% for Oural Luxe Model (features better engraving and wood).
Add approx. 58% for Oural Elite Model (features game scene engraving and presentation walnut).

SHOTGUNS

SPORTING CLAYS MODEL O/U - 12 or 20 (3 in. Mag.) ga., scalloped boxlock action, 27 1/2 or 30 in. VR barrels, ST, case colored receiver with English scroll engraving. Limited importation 1997-98.

	$3,675	$3,300	$2,900	$2,500	$2,100	$1,675	$1,300

Last MSR was $3,995.

ST. BONETT MODEL SxS - 12, 16, or 20 (3 in. Mag.) ga., boxlock with case colored (disc.) or coin finished sideplates featuring fine English scroll (disc.) or game scene engraving, 27 1/2 in. monobloc barrels, DTs, ejectors, checkered straight grip walnut stock and forearm, hardshell case. Limited importation began 1997.

MSR N/A	$2,675	$2,300	$2,000	$1,675	$1,300	$1,000	$850

RGP/BLE MODEL SxS - 16 or 20 ga., boxlock action, semi-beavertail foream, concave rib, coin finished receiver with fine rose and scroll engraving. Importation began 2005 by William Larkin Moore.

MSR $3,250	$2,950	$2,600	$2,275	$2,000	$1,800	$1,600	$1,400

Add $250 for 20 ga.

CHAPUIS, P. ETS

Current manufacturer located in Saint-Bonnet le Chateau, France.

P. Chapuis specializes in custom order rifles and shotguns. Recently, this company has developed a process to color the receiver sideplates while using traditional engraving techniques - this results in a unique 3-D scene. Currently, this manufacturer has no U.S. importation and should be contacted directly (see Trademark Index) for more model information and current pricing. This is a different company than Chapuis Armes.

CHARLES DALY

See Daly, Charles.

CHARLIN ARMS

Previous manufacturer located in St. Etienne, France.

Charlin Arms previously made shotguns which were patterned after Darne firearms. Typically, they are very high quality and values seem to approximate the Darne guns. Once you have determined the comparable model in Darne, please refer to the Darne section in this book.

CHARTER 2000, INC.

Current manufacturer located in Shelton, CT established during 1998.

Charter 2000, Inc. acquired the rights to reproduce the original Charter Arms Undercover Model. Otherwise, it is not affiliated with Charter Arms in any way, nor is it responsible for repair or service on older Charter Arms handguns.

DERRINGERS

DIXIE DERRINGER - .22 LR or .22 Mag. cal., 5 shot, 1 1/8 in. barrel, stainless construction, spur trigger, hardwood grips, 5 oz. New 2002.

	MSR $189		$165	$130	$110

Add $10 for .22 Mag. cal.

REVOLVERS

BULLDOG - .44 Spl. cal., 5 shot, 2 1/2 in. barrel, steel or stainless steel construction, hammer block safety, choice of standard or pocket hammer, round butt with finger groove grips, 21 oz. New late 1999.

MSR $320	$270	$235	$210	$185	$170	$150	$130

Add $20 for stainless steel.

POLICE BULLDOG - .38 Spl. cal., 5 shot, large frame, 4 in. tapered or bull barrel, exposed ejector rod, full rubber grips, approx. 23 oz. New 2002.

MSR $320	$270	$235	$210	$185	$170	$150	$130

UNDERCOVER - .38 Spl. cal., regular double action or DAO, 5 shot, 2 in. barrel, steel or stainless steel construction, checkered compact round butt (standard hammer) or super compact (concealed hammer) synthetic grips (full rubber of boot compact) with finger grooves, 18 oz. New late 1998.

MSR $279	$240	$205	$180	$165	$145	$135	$115

Add $20 for stainless steel.

OFF DUTY - .38 Spl. cal., DAO, 5 shot, 2 in. barrel, aluminum frame, hammerless, combat synthetic grips, 12 oz. New 2002.

MSR $349	$295	$260	$225	$200	$185	$160	$140

MAG. PUG - .357 Mag./.38 Spl., 5 shot, 2.2 in. ported barrel, blue or stainless steel, full rubber grips, 24 oz. New 2001.

MSR $320	$270	$230	$195	$175	$160	$145	$130

Add $8 for stainless steel.

PATHFINDER - .22 LR or .22 Mag. cal., 6 shot, 2 in. barrel, stainless construction, checkered walnut grips, 19 oz. New 2002.

	MSR $265		$230	$200	$180

GRADING - PPGS™	100%	98%	95%	90%	80%	70%	60%

RIFLES: BOLT ACTION

FIELD KING - .243 Win. (disc. 2000), .25-06 Rem., .270 Win., or .30-06 cal., blue or stainless Mauser long action, 4 shot mag., blue or stainless 22 in. E.R. Shaw barrel, checkered black fiberglass reinforced stock with recoil pad, 6 3/4 lbs. Mfg. 2000-2002.

| | $300 | $250 | $215 | | | | |

Last MSR was $345.

Subtract $46 for non-stainless standard blue rifle.

✻ *Field King Carbine* - .308 Win. only, similar to Field King, except is available in 18 in. barrel with compensator only, blue finish or stainless steel. Mfg. 2000-2002.

| | $300 | $250 | $215 | $200 | $185 | $175 | $165 |

Last MSR was $345.

CHARTER ARMS

Previously manufactured by Charco, Inc. located in Ansonia, CT 1992-1996. Previously manufactured by Charter Arms located in Stratford, CT 1991-earlier.

PISTOLS: SEMI-AUTO

MODEL 40 - .22 LR cal. only, double action semi-auto, 3.3 in. barrel, 8 shot mag., 21 1/2 oz., fixed sights, stainless steel. Mfg. 1984-86.

| | $265 | $240 | $220 | | | | |

Last MSR was $319.

MODEL 79K - .32 or .380 ACP cal., double action semi-auto, 3.6 in. barrel, 7 shot mag., 24 1/2 oz., fixed sights, stainless steel. Mfg. 1984-86.

| | $325 | $300 | $280 | | | | |

Last MSR was $390.

EXPLORER II & S II PISTOL - .22 LR cal., semi-auto survival pistol, barrel unscrews, 8 shot mag., black, gold (disc.), silvertone, or camouflage finish, 6, 8, or 10 in. barrels, simulated walnut grips. Disc. 1986.

| | $90 | $80 | $70 | $60 | $55 | $50 | $45 |

Last MSR was $109.

This model uses a modified AR-7 action.
Manufacture of this model was by Survival Arms located in Cocoa, FL.

MODEL 42T (COMPETITION II TARGET) - .22 LR cal. only, single action, 5.9 in. barrel, target model with checkered walnut grips, adj. sights, blue finish only. Mfg. 1984-85 only.

| | $490 | $450 | $395 | $350 | $300 | $260 | $220 |

Last MSR was $599.

REVOLVERS: DOUBLE ACTION

All Charter Arms revolvers had a hammer block safety system, 8 groove rifling, unbreakable beryllium copper firing pin, triple safety features, no sideplate, steel frames, and lifetime warranty to the original owner.

BONNIE & CLYDE SET - .32 H&R Mag. (Bonnie) and .38 Spl. (Clyde) cal., matched pair, 6 shot, 2 1/2 in. fully shrouded barrel, wood laminate grips (color coordinated), blue finish, pistols individually marked "Bonnie" or "Clyde" on barrels, supplied with gun rugs. Mfg. 1989-91.

| | $425 | $365 | $335 | $295 | $260 | $240 | $220 |

GRADING - PPGS™	100%	98%	95%	90%	80%	70%	60%

LADY ON DUTY - .32 S&W or .38 Spl. cal., 5 (.38 Spl.) or 6 shot, 2 in. shrouded barrel, fixed sights, rose neoprene grips, cased. Mfg. 1995-96.

	$195	$165	$145	$130	$115	$100	$85

Last MSR was $219.

PATHFINDER - .22 LR or .22 Mag. (disc. 1989) cal., 6 shot, 2, 3, or 6 (disc. 1985) in. barrels, round butt, adj. sights, walnut grips, wide trigger and spur hammer. Disc. 1990.

	$185	$150	$125	$110	$90	$70	$50

* *Pathfinder - Square Butt* - .22 LR or .22 Mag. (disc. 1989) cal., 6 in. barrel, square butt, otherwise similar to Pathfinder. Disc. 1990.

	$190	$155	$125	$110	$90	$70	$50

* *Pathfinder Stainless* - .22 LR or .22 Mag. (disc. 1989) cal., stainless variation, 3 1/2 in. shrouded barrel. Disc. 1990.

	$185	$150	$130

UNDERCOVER - .32 S&W (disc. 1989) or .38 Spl. cal., 5 shot in .38 Spl., 6 shot in .32 S&W, 2 (.38 Spl.) or 3 in. barrel, wide trigger and spur hammer, fixed sights, .38 Spl. can also be ordered with pocket hammer. Disc. 1991.

	$175	$145	$115	$100	$90	$85	$80

* *Undercover Stainless* - 2 in. shrouded barrel only. Disc. 1994.

	$260	$195	$140

Last MSR was $304.

UNDERCOVERETTE - .32 S&W Long cal., similar to Undercover, 6 shot, 2 in. barrel, blue. Disc.

	$155	$140	$110	$100	$90	$70	$55

BULLDOG - .44 Spl. cal., 5 shot, 2 1/2 or 3 (disc. 1988) in. barrels, wide trigger and spur or pocket hammer, checkered bulldog grips (walnut or neoprene), blue or electroless nickel finish. Disc. 1991, reinstated 1994. Disc.1996.

	$225	$195	$155	$125	$110	$90	$70

Last MSR was $268.

Add $22 for electroless nickel finish.

* *Bulldog Stainless* - 2 1/2 in. bull or 3 (disc. 1989) in. regular barrel. Disc. 1991.

	$195	$155	$125

* *Target Bulldog* - .357 Mag. or .44 Spl. cal., 5 shot, 4 in. shrouded barrel, adj. sights, square butt only, blue finish. Mfg. 1980-88.

	$225	$150	$125	$110	$100	$90	$80

Last MSR was $255.

Subtract $10 for .357 Mag. cal.

* *Target Bulldog Stainless* - 9mm Federal, .357 Mag. or .44 Spl. cal., 5 shot, 5 1/2 in. shrouded VR barrel, adj. sights, square butt target grips only, matte finished, 28 oz. Mfg. 1989-91.

	$250	$175	$125

BULLDOG PUG - .44 Spl. cal., 5 shot, 2 1/2 in. shrouded barrel, fixed sights, walnut or neoprene grips. Mfg. 1986-93.

	$240	$195	$160	$130	$110	$100	$90

Last MSR was $279.

* *Bulldog Pug Stainless* - 2 1/2 in. shrouded barrel. Mfg. 1987-93.

	$300	$235	$175

Last MSR was $334.

BULLDOG TRACKER - .357 Mag. (.38 Spl.) cal., 5 shot, 2 1/2, 4 (disc. 1989), and 6 (disc. 1989) in. bull barrels, adj. sights, blue only, checkered bulldog grips, square butt on 4 or 6 in. barrel only. Disc. 1986, reintroduced 1989-91.

| | $185 | $150 | $125 | $110 | $100 | $90 | $80 |

MAGNUM PUG - .357 Mag. cal., 5 shot, fixed sights, 2.2 in. shrouded barrel, blue finish. Mfg. 1995-96.

| | $225 | $195 | $155 | $125 | $110 | $90 | $70 |

Last MSR was $268.

POLICE BULLDOG - .32 H&R Mag., .38 Spl. or .44 Spl. cal., 5 (.44 Spl. only) or 6 shot, fixed sights, blue only, 3 1/2 or 4 in. barrel, Neoprene grips or square butt (.44 Spl. only). Disc. 1991.

| | $175 | $140 | $120 | $105 | $95 | $85 | $75 |

Add $20 for either .44 Spl. cal or 3 1/2 in. shrouded barrel.

* **Stainless Police Bulldog** - .32 Mag., .357 Mag. (new 1989), .38 Spl. (disc. 1988 - reintroduced 1990) or .44 Spl. (new 1989) cal., 5 (.357 Mag. or .44 Spl.) or 6 (.32 Mag. or .38 Spl.) shot, square butt, 3 1/2 or 4 in. shrouded barrel. Mfg. 1987-91.

| | $195 | $160 | $150 | $140 |

Add $20 for .357 Mag. or .44 Special cal.

Neoprene grips are standard on these models except for the .357 Mag. (square butt).

POLICE UNDERCOVER - .32 H&R Mag. or .38 Spl. cal., 6 shot, spur or pocket hammer, 2.2 in. shrouded barrel, checkered walnut grips, fixed sights, blue or electroless nickel (new 1994) finish. Disc. 1996.

| | $205 | $175 | $145 | $120 | $100 | $85 | $75 |

Last MSR was $238.

Add $14 for electroless nickel finish.

* **Stainless Police Undercover** - similar to Police Undercover. Disc. 1993.

| | $240 | $185 | $150 |

Last MSR was $276.

OFF DUTY - .22 LR (new 1993), .22 Mag. (new 1994), or .38 Spl. cal., 5 (.38 Spl.) or 6 (.22 LR) shot, 2 in. barrel, fixed sights, conventional or DA only, blue, matte black (disc.), or electroless nickel (new 1994) finish. Disc. 1996.

| | $170 | $145 | $120 | $105 | $90 | $85 | $80 |

Last MSR was $200.

Add $39 for electroless nickel finish.

Add $7 for double action only.

* **Stainless Off Duty** - similar to Off Duty. Disc. 1993.

| | $235 | $180 | $145 |

Last MSR was $268.

PIT BULL - 9mm Federal (rare), .357 Mag. (disc. 1989), or .38 Spl. (disc. 1989) cal., 5 shot, 2 1/2, 3 1/2, or 4 (disc. 1989) in. full shrouded barrel, Neoprene grips, approx. 26 oz. Mfg. 1989-91.

| | $230 | $180 | $150 | $125 | $115 | $100 | $90 |

* **Stainless Pit Bull** - 2 1/2 or 3 1/2 in. shrouded barrel. Disc. 1991.

| | $240 | $190 | $155 |

GRADING - PPGS™	100%	98%	95%	90%	80%	70%	60%

RIFLES: SEMI-AUTO

AR-7 EXPLORER RIFLE - .22 LR cal., takedown, barreled action stores in Cycolac synthetic stock, 8 shot mag., adj. sights, 16 in. barrel, black finish on AR-7, silvertone on AR-7S. Camouflage finish new 1986 (AR-7C). Mfg. until 1990.

	$125	$100	$85	$75	$65	$55	$50

Last MSR was $146.

> In 1990, the manufacturing of this model was taken over by Survival Arms located in Cocoa, FL. Current mfg. AR-7 rifles will be found under the Henry Repeating Arms Company and AR-7 Industries.

CHEYTAC

Current manufacturer located in Arco, ID.

RIFLES: BOLT ACTION

Cheytac currently manufactures an advanced 5 shot bolt action design in .408 Cheyenne Tactical cal. The Intervention Model 200 Military has an MSR of $11,000, weighs 27 lbs., and includes an advanced ballistic computer to help with accuracy. It also offers an Intervention Model M310 Target Model for $4,095 MSR. Please contact the company directly for more information, including pricing and commercial availability (see Trademark Index).

CHIPMUNK RIFLES

Current trademark manufactured by Rogue Rifle Co., Inc., located in Lewiston, ID, beginning 2001. Previously located in Prospect, OR from 1997-2001. Previously manufactured by Oregon Arms, Inc. located in Prospect, OR 1988-1996. Previously manufactured by Chipmunk Manufacturing located in Medford, OR until 1988. Dealer sales.

PISTOLS: SINGLE SHOT

SILHOUETTE PISTOL - .22 LR cal., bolt action design with 14 7/8 in. barrel, iron sights, rear grip walnut stock. Mfg. 1984-88.

	$135	$115	$95	$80	$70	$60	$50

Last MSR was $150.

SILHOUETTE/HUNTER - .17 HMR, .17 Mach 2, .22 LR, or .22 Mag. cal., 10 in. barrel, drilled and tapped, left-handed bolt, Truglo sights, target style stock with ergonomic grip. New 2005.

MSR $175	$140	$120	$100	$85	$75	$65	$55

Add $10 for walnut stock or $15 for camo laminate stock.
Add $15 for .17 HMR, .17 Mach 2, or .22 Mag.

RIFLES: BOLT ACTION, SINGLE SHOT

Add approx. $20 for stainless steel action/barrel on current models (new 2005).

CHIPMUNK STANDARD RIFLE - .17 HMR (new 2002), .17 Mach 2 (new 2005), .22 LR or .22 Mag. (disc. 1987, reintroduced 1999) cal., manually cocked single shot, youth model with 16 1/8 in. barrel and 11 1/2 LOP, choice of black or brown laminate (new 1999), camo (new 2002, various colored woods), synthetic (new 2004), or uncheckered Monte Carlo walnut stock, iron sights (adj. aperture rear) or Truglo sights (new 2005), 30 in. overall length, 2 1/2 (standard barrel) or 4 (bull barrel) lbs.

MSR $140	$110	$100	$90	$80	$70	$60	$50

Add $10 for .22 Mag. cal.
Add $10 for .17 HMR or .17 Mach 2 cal.
Add $20 for walnut stock.
Add $35 for black/brown laminate or camo stock.

GRADING - PPGS™	100%	98%	95%	90%	80%	70%	60%

Subtract approx. 10% for black coated wood stock.

* **Bull Barrel Model** - similar to Chipmunk Single Shot rifle, features 16 1/8 in. bull barrel, 4 lbs. New 1999.

MSR $175	$145	$125	$100	$90	$80	$70	$60

Add $15 for .22 Mag., .17 HMR or .17 Mach 2 cal.
Add $15 for laminate or camo stock.

* **Deluxe Rifle** - similar to standard rifle, except has upgraded deluxe hand checkered Monte Carlo walnut stock. New 1987.

MSR $190	$155	$130	$115	$100	$85	$75	$65

Add $10 for .22 Mag. cal., .17 HMR, or .17 Mach 2 cal.

* **Target Rifle** - similar to Chipmunk rifle, except has 18 in. heavy barrel, micrometer target sights, target stock with adj. accessory rail and buttplate, 5 lbs. New mid-2002.

MSR $350	$295	$255	$215	$185	$165	$150	$135

* **Chipmunk Special Edition** - similar to Deluxe Model, except has hand engraving.
  Please contact the company directly for pricing and availability on this model.

BARRACUDA CHIPMUNK - unique design thumbhole stock, pistol grip, floating barrel, also available in bull barrel. New 2005.

MSR $200	$165	$145	$120	$100	$85	$75	$65

SHOTGUNS: SINGLE SHOT

CHIPMUNK .410 SHOTGUN - .410 bore, 18.25 in. smoothbore barrel, single shot, manual cocking, blue only, 11 1/2 in. LOP, walnut stock, approx. 3.25 lbs. New mid-2002.

MSR $190	$155	$130	$100	$90	$80	$70	$60

CHRISTENSEN ARMS

Current rifle manufacturer established in 1995, and currently located in Fayette, UT. Previously located in St. George, UT during 1995-99. Direct sales only.

PISTOL

CARBON ONE PISTOL - various cals., graphite barrel lengths up to 14 in., uses Thompson Center Encore or Contender pistol frame, less than 1 in. grouping for 3 shots at 100 yards, satin nickel receiver, approx. 2.5-3 lbs. Limited mfg. beginning 1999.

This model is basically a special order, please contact the company directly.

RIFLES: BOLT ACTION

In addition to the models listed below, Christensen Arms also offers the Carbon One Custom barrel installed on a customer action (any caliber) for $995 ($825 if short chambered by competent gunsmith), as well as providing a Carbon Wrap conversion to an existing steel barrel ($599).

Add $400 for Remington titanium action, $195 for titanium muzzle brake, $225 for Jewel trigger, $135 for Teflon coated action, $100 for camo stock (Realtree, Mossy Oak, or Natural Gear), and $75 for lightened action on the models listed below.

CARBON ONE CUSTOM - most popular cals., features Remington 700 BDL short action or Winchester Model 70 action, barrel (up to 28 in. long) features a match grade Shilen/Christensen precision 416R stainless steel barrel liner inside a larger diameter graphite/epoxy barrel casing with crown, black synthetic stock, Shilen trigger, 5.5-6.5 lbs. New 1996.

MSR $3,650	$3,250	$2,875	$2,425	$2,000	$1,650	$1,425	$1,225

Variations include the Carbon Lite (5 lbs.), Carbon King (6-7 lbs., .25-.308 cal.), Carbon Cannon (includes muzzle brake, 6 1/2-7 1/2 lbs., Magnum series), or Carbon Tactical (includes muzzle brake, 6 1/2 lbs., new 1997), or Carbon Conquest (new 1998).

GRADING - PPGS™	100%	98%	95%	90%	80%	70%	60%

CARBON ONE HUNTER - various popular cals., features Remington M700 (regular or stainless) or Winchester Model 70 stainless action, available with HS Precision or synthetic stock, large diameter graphite barrel with stainless steel barrel liner, 6.5-7 lbs. New 1999.

	100%	98%	95%	90%	80%	70%	60%
MSR $1,599	$1,400	$1,200	$950	$825	$700	$600	$500

CARBON RANGER CONQUEST - .50 BMG cal., single shot or repeater (5 shot), McMillian stainless steel bolt action, max barrel length is 32 in. with muzzle brake, Christensen composite stock with bipod, approx. 16 (single shot) - 20 lbs. New 2001.

	100%	98%	95%	90%	80%	70%	60%
MSR $5,500	$4,950	$4,075	$3,500	$3,000	$2,625	$2,200	$1,900

Subtract $650 if single shot.

CARBON RANGER - .50 BMG cal., large diameter graphite barrel casing (up to 36 in. long), no stock or forearm, twin rails extending from frame sides are attached to recoil pad, Omni Wind Runner action, bipod and choice of scope are included, 25-32 lbs. Limited mfg. 1998-2000 only.

	100%	98%	95%	90%	80%	70%	60%
	$9,950	$8,900	$8,000	$7,100	$6,200	$5,300	$4,400

Last MSR was $10,625.

RIFLES: SEMI-AUTO

Christensen Arms also offers a Carbon One Challenge drop-in barrel (16 oz.) for the Ruger Model 10/22. MSR for the .22 LR is $450, $475 for .22 Mag.

CARBON ONE CHALLENGE (CUSTOM) - .22 LR or .22 Mag. (disc. 2002) cal., features Ruger 10/22 Model 1103 action with modified bolt release, synthetic bull barrel with precision stainless steel liner, 2 lb. Volquartsen trigger, Fajen brown laminated wood (disc.) or black synthetic stock with thumbhole, approx. 3.5-4 lbs. New 1996.

	100%	98%	95%	90%	80%	70%	60%
MSR $1,500	$1,325	$1,150	$975	$850	$725	$600	$500

Add $350 for .17 HMR or .22 Mag. cal.

The 100% price represents the base model, with no options.

✳ *Carbon One Challenge* - .22 LR cal., non-custom shop variation, 4 lbs. New 1999.

	100%	98%	95%	90%	80%	70%	60%
	$550	$495	$440	$400	$365	$330	$295

Last MSR was $599.

CARBON CHALLENGE II - similar to Carbon Challenge I, except has AMT stainless receiver and trigger, black synthetic stock, approx. 4 1/2 lbs. Limited 1997-98 only.

	100%	98%	95%	90%	80%	70%	60%
	$1,150	$975	$875	$800	$725	$650	$525

Last MSR was $1,299.

E.J. CHURCHILL GUNMAKERS

Current manufacturer established in 1891, and located in High Wycombe, England since 1996. Previously imported until 2001 by Aspen Outfitters, located in Aspen, CO. Previously manufactured in London, England. This company underwent various trading forms until Churchill, Atkin, Grant & Lang Ltd. closed in 1981. Currently, Churchill Gunmakers' rifles and shotguns are manufactured in High Wycombe, England.

Churchill Guns are very fine quality, and can be ordered with many custom features. We will list both discontinued and current models and approximate values, but strongly urge competent appraisal if purchase or sale is contemplated.

Prices indicated below for manufacturer's suggested retail and 100% condition factors are listed in English pounds. All new prices do not include English VAT. Values for used guns in 98%-60% condition factors are priced in U.S. dollars.

GRADING - PPGS™	100%	98%	95%	90%	80%	70%	60%

RIFLES: BOLT ACTION

"ONE OF ONE THOUSAND RIFLE" - .270 Win., 7mm Rem. Mag., .308 Win., .30-06, .300 Win. Mag., .375 H&H, or .458 Win. Mag. cal., Mauser type bolt action, 5 shot standard, 3 shot mag. Magnum, 24 in. barrel, classic French walnut stock, swivel recoil pad with trap, trap pistol grip cap. Mfg. 1973 for Interarms 20th Anniversary, only 100 mfg.

	100%	98%	95%	90%	80%	70%	60%
	$3,995	$3,500	$2,950	$2,500	$2,000	$1,650	$1,350

Add 50% for .375 H&H or .458 Win. Mag. cal.

BARONET RIFLE - various cals. from .30-06 to .375 H&H cal., standard Mauser 98 action with swept bolt handle, fully adj. trigger and 3 position side safety, border engraving, deluxe checkered European walnut stock and forearm, custom order only, allow 8-10 months for delivery, approx. 8.5-9 lbs. New 2001.

MSR £11,500	£11,500	$15,000	$12,500	$10,000	$7,500	$5,000	$3,250

Add £3,500 for Magnum Mauser action.
Add £2,535 for detachable scope mounts.

RIFLES: SxS

PREMIERE MODEL - various cals. up to .600 NE, pinless sidelock ejector mechanism with cocking indicators, 24 or 26 in. chopper lump barrels, double triggers, extended top tang, square or rounded body, full traditional fine scroll engraving, color case hardened action, allow 20-24 months for delivery, 9.5-12.5 lbs. Mfg. resumed 1998.

MSR £52,500	£52,500	$65,000	$55,000	$45,000	$35,000	$27,500	$20,000

Add £650 for hand detachable sidelocks.
Add £3,000 for .300-.500 NE cals. (cals. over .500 NE are P.O.R.)

SHOTGUNS: O/U

PREMIERE MODEL - 12, 16 (limited mfg.), 20, 28 ga., or .410 bore, 2 3/4 in. chambers, similar barrels and bores as Premiere SxS Model engraved, pinless sidelock ejector with cocking indicators, choice of monobloc (disc.) or chopper lump barrels, mechanical ST, auto ejectors, checkered pistol grip or straight stock, allow 18-24 months for delivery, 6.5 (20 ga.) or 7 (12 ga.) lbs.

MSR £46,500	£46,500	$52,500	$45,000	$37,500	$30,000	$22,500	$16,500

Add £2,000 for 28 ga. or .410 bore.
Add £650 for hand detachable sidelocks.
Add £12,675 for extra set of barrels.
Add approx. 10% for ordering pair of matched guns.
Subtract approx. £1,500 for DT. (disc.).

SHOTGUNS: SxS

All models below were built or finished to customer specifications pertaining to choking, chambers, barrel lengths, stock measurements, weight, engraving patterns. Standardized patterns did exist, however, for each model. The "XXV" designation referred to the 25 in. barrel length, which was a Churchill specialty and was also a registered trademark.

PREMIERE MODEL - most gauges, 2 3/4 in. chambers, best quality, easy opening or standard opening, 25 (XXV), 28, 30, or 32 (disc.) in. chopper lump barrels, any choke, sidelock, pinless sidelock ejector with cocking indicators, double triggers standard, engraved, color case hardened action, checkered, straight or pistol grip stock, allow 18-24 months for delivery, 5 lbs. 14 oz. (20 ga.) or 6 lbs. 6 oz. (12 ga.).

MSR £39,500	£39,500	$44,500	$37,500	$31,250	$24,750	$20,750	$16,500

Add £2,000 for 28 ga.
Add £8,950 for extra set of barrels.
Add £3,445 for ST.
Add approx. 10% for ordering pair of matched guns.

GRADING - PPGS™	100%	98%	95%	90%	80%	70%	60%

IMPERIAL MODEL - most gauges, most barrel lengths, second quality sidelock model, ejectors, mostly standard opening, a few made as easy opening. Also mfg. in some double rifles. Disc.

	100%	98%	95%	90%	80%	70%	60%
	$13,500	$11,500	$9,500	$7,500	$6,500	$5,250	$4,000

Add 20% for 20 ga., 40% for 28 ga., and $1,000 for SST, or 35% for double rifle. Subtract 10% for 16 ga.

FIELD MODEL - 12 ga. only, most barrel lengths, third quality sidelock model. Disc.

	$9,000	$8,000	$7,000	$6,000	$5,000	$4,500	$3,500

HERCULES MODEL - most gauges, 25-30 in. barrels, best quality boxlock model, ejectors, easy opening or standard opening. Also made in some double rifles in .22 Hornet and similar cals.

	$9,000	$8,000	$7,000	$6,000	$5,000	$4,500	$3,500

Add 20% for 20 ga., 40% for 28 ga., $1,000 for SST, and 35% double rifle. Subtract 10% for 16 ga.

UTILITY MODEL - all gauges (mostly encountered in 12 ga.), 25-30 in. barrels, second quality boxlock model, ejectors, checkered straight or pistol grip stock. Disc.

	$6,250	$4,500	$3,500	$3,000	$2,500	$2,000	$1,800

Add 20% for 20 ga., 40% for 28 ga., 60% for .410 bore, and $500 for SST. Subtract 10% for 16 ga.

CROWN MODEL - 12, 16, 20 ga., or .410 (rare) bore, third quality boxlock model, various barrel lengths. Disc.

	$4,500	$3,500	$3,000	$2,500	$2,000	$1,600	$1,200

Add 20% for 20 ga., 40% for 28 ga., 60% for .410 bore, and $500 for SST. Subtract 10% for 16 ga.

REGAL MODEL - 12, 16, 20, 28 ga., or .410 bore, second quality boxlock model introduced after WWII, released after Utility Model was disc. Premium for 28 ga. or .410 bore.

	$6,000	$4,300	$3,750	$3,100	$2,500	$2,000	$1,800

Add 20% for 20 ga., 40% for 28 ga., 60% for .410 bore, and $500 for SST. Subtract 10% for 16 ga.

* *Regal Grade* - 12, 20, 28 ga., or .410 bore, best quality boxlock model, ejectors, standard opening, limited production.

	$4,800	$4,000	$3,500	$3,000	$2,500	$2,000	$1,800

Last MSR was $5,625.

CHURCHILL

Previous trademark imported and distributed by Ellett Brothers located in Chapin, SC until 1993. Previously imported (until 1988) by Kassnar Imports, Inc. located in Harrisburg, PA. Not affiliated with E.J. Churchill Gunmakers, Ltd.

In late 1988, the Churchill trademark was sold to Ellett Brothers located in Chapin, SC.

RIFLES: BOLT ACTION

HIGHLANDER - .25-06 Rem., .243 Win., .270 Win., .308 Win., .30-06, 7mm Rem. Mag., or .300 Win. Mag. cal., bolt action, 22 in. barrel, thumb safety, no sights, 3 or 4 shot mag., checkered walnut stock, 7 1/2 lbs. Importation disc. 1991.

	$395	$350	$330	$300	$270	$240	$215

Last MSR was $460.

Add $30 for iron sights (disc).

GRADING - PPGS™	100%	98%	95%	90%	80%	70%	60%

REGENT - same cals. as Highlander, deluxe checkered walnut with Monte Carlo comb and cheekpiece. Last imported by Kassnar in 1988.

	$555	$455	$385	$340	$300	$280	$260

Last MSR was $610.

Add $30 for iron sights.

RIFLES: SEMI-AUTO

ROTARY 22 - .22 LR cal, beginners rifle, bolt hold-open device, adj. rear sight, 10 shot rotary mag. Imported 1989 only.

	$120	$105	$95	$85	$75	$65	$55

Last MSR was $130.

SHOTGUNS: O/U

MONARCH - 12, 20, 28 (disc.) ga., or .410 (disc.) bore, 25 (disc.), 26, or 28 in. vent. rib barrels, SST, extractors, boxlock action, DT, silver finish receiver with fine scroll engraving, checkered European walnut stock and forearm, 6 1/2-7 1/2 lbs.

	$460	$370	$340	$300	$250	$230	$210

Last MSR was $520.

Add $67 for .410 bore with 26 in. barrels (disc.).
Subtract $40 without SST.

✳ *Monarch Turkey Gun* - 12 ga. only, 24 in. barrels with matte finish. Imported 1990-91 only.

	$460	$370	$340	$300	$250	$230	$210

Last MSR was $529.

SPORTING CLAYS MODEL - 12 ga. only, designed for sporting clays competition with 28 in. VR ported barrels with choke tubes, ejectors, raised target style VR, checkered high gloss finish stock and forearm, 7 lbs. 6 oz. Imported 1992 only.

	$800	$725	$650	$575	$500	$450	$395

Last MSR was $900.

WINDSOR III - 12, 20 ga., or .410 bore (disc.), 27 or 30 in. barrels, double bottom lock, antique silver finish receiver with fine scroll engraving, extractors, SST, vent. rib, checkered pistol grip and forend. Importation disc. 1991.

	$550	$495	$450	$380	$340	$300	$280

Last MSR was $625.

Add $140 for Flyweight Model or choke tubes (disc.).
Add $75 for .410 bore.

NEW WINDSOR IV - 12 or 20 ga., 3 in. chambers, boxlock action, silver receiver with full scroll engraving, 26 or 28 (12 ga. only) VR barrels with choke tubes, ejectors, SST, checkered walnut pistol grip stock with black rubber vent. recoil pad, finger grooved forearm, gloss finish, gold trigger, 5 year warranty. Mfg. 1992 only.

	$625	$525	$450	$375	$325	$295	$275

Last MSR was $690.

WINDSOR IV - DISC. - 12, 20, 28 ga., or .410 bore, 26-30 in. barrels, double bottom lock, antique silver finish receiver with fine scroll engraving, ejectors, SST, vent. rib, checkered pistol grip and forend. Interchangeable chokes became standard in 1989. Importation disc. 1991.

	$725	$640	$530	$470	$430	$395	$360

Last MSR was $852.

Subtract $52 for 28 ga. or .410 bore.
Subtract $100 if without choke tubes.

REGENT V - 12 or 20 ga., 27 in. barrels, double bottom lock, antique silver finish receiver with extra fine scroll engraving, ejectors, single trigger, vent. rib, checkered pistol grip and forend. Interchangeable choke tubes standard. Disc. 1986, reintroduced 1990, disc. 1993.

		$895	$795	$700	$620	$560	$510	$470

Last MSR was $1,100.

This model was previously designated Regent VII until 1989 when it changed to the Regent V.

REGENT TRAP AND SKEET - 12 or 20 ga., 26 or 30 in. barrels, double bottom lock, antique silver finish receiver with sideplates engraved in fine scroll, ejectors, SST, vent. rib, checkered pistol grip and forend. Importation disc. 1991.

		$795	$650	$575	$540	$485	$440	$390

Last MSR was $963.

Add $40 for trap variation.

REGENT GRADE SHOTGUN/RIFLE COMBINATION - 12 ga. over either .222 Rem., .223 Rem., .243 Win. (disc.), .270 Win., .30-06, or .308 Win. cal., 25 in. barrels, double bottom lock, antique silver finish receiver with extra fine scroll engraving, ejectors, single trigger, vent. rib, checkered pistol grip and forend. Importation disc. 1991.

		$800	$700	$635	$560	$510	$475	$440

Last MSR was $927.

SHOTGUNS: SxS

WINDSOR I - 10 (disc. 1988), 12, 16, 20, 28 ga., or .410 bore, double barrel, 23-32 in. barrels, Anson and Deeley boxlock, antique silver finish receiver with fine scroll engraving, extractors, double triggers, checkered pistol grip and forend. Importation disc. 1991.

		$550	$465	$450	$385	$300	$250	$230

Last MSR was $653.

Add $150 for 10 ga.
Add $55 for 28 ga. or .410 bore.
Add $30 for Flyweight Models (25 in. barrels - disc. 1988).

WINDSOR II - 12 or 20 ga., 26-30 in. barrels, Anson and Deeley boxlock, antique silver finish receiver with fine scroll engraving, ejectors, double triggers, checkered pistol grip and forend. Add $100 for 10 ga. (disc.). Importation disc. 1987.

		$595	$485	$415	$350	$315	$270	$240

Last MSR was $638.

WINDSOR VI - 12 or 20 (disc.) ga., 25 or 28 in. barrels, sidelock, antique silver finish receiver with fine scroll engraving, ejectors, double triggers, checkered pistol grip and forend. Disc. 1987.

		$840	$700	$600	$550	$510	$460	$420

Last MSR was $900.

ROYAL - 10, 12, 20, 28 ga., or .410 bore, DTs, extractors, checkered walnut stock and forearm, case hardened receiver. Imported late 1988-91.

		$485	$405	$370	$310	$275	$250	$230

Last MSR was $540.

Add $20 for 28 ga.
Add $74 for .410 bore.

SHOTGUNS: SEMI-AUTO

STANDARD MODEL - 12 ga. only, gas operated and shoots different loads interchangeably without alterations, 24, 26, 28 in. VR barrel, magazine cut-off, hand checkered walnut with satin finish, matte metal finish, includes ICT choke tubes. New 1990.

		$495	$415	$375	$310	$275	$250	$230

Last MSR was $550.

GRADING - PPGS™	100%	98%	95%	90%	80%	70%	60%

✱ *Turkey Model* - similar to Standard Model, except has 24 in. barrel only. New 1990.

	$510	$425	$380	$315	$275	$250	$230

Last MSR was $570.

WINDSOR GRADE - 12 ga. only, 26, 28, or 30 in. barrels, gas operation, anodized alloy receiver, vent. rib, checkered pistol grip and forend, 7 1/2 lbs. Deluxe model includes polished receiver with etching.

	$380	$320	$300	$275	$250	$225	$200

Last MSR was $420.

> Add $35 for choke tubes.
> Add $55 for Deluxe model.

REGENT GRADE - 12 ga. only, 26, 28, or 30 in. barrels, gas operation, anodized alloy receiver, vent. rib, checkered pistol grip and forend, 7 1/2 lbs. Deluxe model includes polished receiver with etching. Disc. 1986.

	$440	$365	$340	$320	$300	$285	$270

Last MSR was $495.

> Add $35 for choke tubes.
> Add $55 for Deluxe model.

SHOTGUNS: SLIDE ACTION

WINDSOR GRADE - 12 ga. only, 26, 27, 28, or 30 in. barrels, double slides, anodized alloy receiver, vent. rib, checkered pistol grip and forend, 7 1/2 lbs. Disc. 1986.

	$385	$330	$310	$275	$250	$225	$200

Last MSR was $430.

CIMARRON F.A. CO.

Current importer, distributor, and retailer located in Fredricksburg, TX. Cimarron is currently importing A. Uberti, D. Pedersoli, and Armi-Sport firearms and black powder reproductions and replicas. Previous company name was Old-West Co. of Texas. Dealer sales only.

Please refer to the *Blue Book of Modern Black Powder Arms* by John Allen & Dennis Adler (also online) for more information and prices on Cimarron's lineup of modern black powder models.

REVOLVERS: REPRODUCTIONS, COLT

The Cimarron Arms reproductions of the 1873 Colt Peacemaker, mostly mfg. by Uberti, with the exception of previous limited production by Armi San Marco, are available in two configurations listed below. Beginning in 1984, Cimarron arms reproductions began incorporating many of the features of the 1st Generation Colt SAAs. These SAA revolvers are extremely accurate reproductions of the original Colt pre-war Peacemaker and are marked (and machined) the same as the originals, including serial numbers on frames, backstrap, trigger guard, and cylinder. Barrels are radiused and cylinders are beveled. Frames are color case hardened, stocks are walnut - choice of 4 3/4, 5 1/2, or 7 1/2 in. barrel. All Cimarron SAAs are currently barrel marked "-CIMARRON F.A. MFG. Co. FREDERICKSBURG, TX. U.S.A. -".

The "Old Model" configuration has the older style black powder frame, screw-in cylinder pin retainer, and circular "bullseye" ejector head. The Standard Model includes the post-1890 style frame with spring loaded cross-pin cylinder retainer and "half-moon" ejector head. Only the Old Model is available in the authentic old style "charcoal blue" finish (sometimes referred to as fire-bluing).

During 1998, Cimarron introduced an Original Finish (antiqued) that resembles the older, worn finish seen on many of the well-used, original Colt revolvers. This distressed finish is a greyish-brown patina color, and certain areas of these guns (end of barrel, grip straps, frame/cylinder edges, and grips) have been artifically aged to give them an authentic "been carried and used for 100 years" appearance.

Add $40 for Original Finish on SAAs listed below (disc. 2002). Add $40 for charcoal blue finish on SAAs listed below (disc. 2002). Add $150 for antique custom nickel or custom nickel finish. Add $350 for silver plating. Add $250 for U.S. Armory finish utilizing bonemeal case coloring. Add $295 for old style color case hardening and Carbona blue finish (disc. 2003). Add $45 for hand checkered walnut grips (disc. 2003). Add $60 for ivory polymer grips, stag grips, fleur-de-lis grips, black hard rubber grips, or aged ivory polymer grips. Add $225 Izit ivory grips. Add $325 for Izit ivory steer head grips (new 2004). Add $175 for Micarta grips. Add $595 for geniune ivory grips. Add $326 for mother-of-pearl grips. Add $850 for "A" style engraving (30% coverage) on SAAs listed below (disc 2004). Add $850 for "B" style engraving (50% coverage) on SAAs listed below. Add $1,800 for "C" style engraving (70% coverage) on SAAs listed below (disc. 2004). Add $2,400 for "Texas Cattle Brands" or full (100% coverage) engraving pattern (disc. 2004). Add $875 for Patton engraving. Add $1,500 for Teddy Roosevelt engraving. Add $1,350 for Open Top Standard engraving. Add $500 for percussion engraving on Pocket models, or $725 for regular models. Add $2,500 for Judge Roy Bean engraving. Add $2,400 for Wild Bill conversion engraving.

1871-72 OPEN TOP - .38 Long Colt, .38 S&W Spl., .44-40 WCF, .44 Russian, or .45 Schofield cal., 4 3/4 (new 2004), 5 1/2 (Navy size grips) or 7 1/2 (Army size grips) in. barrel, patterned after the Colt 1871-1872 Open Top, Navy grip frame is available in brass or silver plated. Mfg. by A. Uberti beginning 1999.

MSR $529	$435	$315	$265	$230	$200	$175	$160

Add $40 for charcoal blue finish.
Add $50 for original finish.
Add $25 for silver plated backstrap and trigger guard on Navy model only.

FRONTIER SIX SHOOTER - .22 LR (disc. 1995), .22 Mag. (disc.), .357 Mag., .38 Spl. (disc.), .38-40 WCF, .44 Spl. (new 1998), .44-40 WCF, or .45 LC cal., 4 3/4, 5 1/2, and 7 1/2 in. barrel lengths, steel backstraps and trigger guard. Importation disc. 1999.

✳ *Standard or Old Model*

		$395	$300	$250	$220	$195	$175	$160

Last MSR was $469.

Add $30 for convertible .45 ACP cylinder.

✳ *Sheriff's Model* - .44-40 WCF or .45 LC cal., w/o ejector, 3 or 4 (disc. 1992) in. barrel, steel backstraps and trigger guard. Disc. 1998, reintroduced 2000-2001.

		$395	$300	$250	$220	$195	$175	$160

Last MSR was $469.

✳ *New Sheriff Model* - .357 Mag., .44-40 WCF, .44 Spl., or .45 LC cal., 3 1/2 in. barrel with ejector, Old Model frame only. Importation began 1995.

MSR $499	$415	$315	$265	$225	$195	$175	$160

Add $40 for charcoal blue finish.
Add $45 for checkered walnut grips.

✳ *Target Model* - similar to Standard Model, except has fully adj. target rear sight, brass or steel backstrap. Importation disc. 1991.

		$355	$280	$255	$220	$195	$175	$160

Last MSR was $400.

Add $40 for .357 Mag. cal.
This variation was available in the Standard Model configuration only and with standard finish.

BADLANDS SAA MODEL - .357 Mag. or .45 LC cal., 4 3/4 in. barrel, brass backstrap and trigger guard, flat black receiver and barrel finish, steel frame, smooth wood grips, case colored hammer. New 2005.

MSR $325	$275	$245	$220	$200	$185	$160	$150

MODEL P SAA - .32-20 WCF, .38-40 WCF, .357 Mag., .44-40 WCF, .44 Spl., or .45 LC cal., features either pinched frame (.45 LC cal. with 7 1/2 in. barrel only) or pre-war configuration, standard finish or charcoal blue, 4 3/4, 5 1/2, or 7 1/2 in. barrel. Importation began 1996.

MSR $499	$415	$325	$275	$235	$200	$180	$160

Add $50 for convertible .45 ACP cylinder.
Add $50 for original finish.
Add $40 for charcoal blue finish.
Add $50 for target model with adj. sights and flattop frame (7 1/2 in. barrel with .45 LC or .44-40 WCF cal. only).
Add $100 for stainless steel construction in .357 Mag. or .45 LC cal. only (new 2004).

✳ *Model P Jr. SAA* - .38 Colt/S&W Spl. cal., features smaller size frame (20% less) proportioned from the SAA, but with standard single action grip frame, 3 1/2, 4 3/4, or 5 1/2 in. barrel. Mfg. by A. Uberti 2000-2001, reintroduced 2004.

MSR $489	$410	$320	$270	$230	$200	$180	$160

Add $40 for charcoal blue.
Add $45 for checkered walnut grips.
Add $60 for dual cylinder (.32-20 WCF/.32 H&R Mag. cal., new 2004).

EVIL ROY SAA - .357 Mag., .44-40 WCF, or .45 LC cal., 4 3/4 or 5 1/2 in. barrel, features wide square notch rear sight and constant with front sight, smooth or checkered slim grips, lightened trigger and hammer springs, color case hardened finish on frame, Evil Roy signature on bottom of grip strap. New 2005.

MSR $719	$575	$500	$425	$385	$340	$310	$275

WYATT EARP LIMITED EDITION BUNTLINE - .45 LC cal., only, 10 in. barrel, sterling silver plaque inlaid into wood grips, case colored receiver. Importation began 2002.

MSR $759	$625	$525	$425	$385	$340	$310	$275

Add $40 for original finish.

BISLEY SAA - .357 Mag., .44 Spl., .44-40 WCF, or .45 LC cal., 4 3/4, 5 1/2, or 7 1/2 in. barrel, Bisley configured grips, case colored receiver, smooth walnut grips, flattop target model available with 7 1/2 in. barrel in .44-40 WCF or .45 LC cal. only. Importation began 2002.

MSR $525	$450	$375	$320	$280	$260	$240	$220

EL PISTOLERO - .357 Mag. or .45 LC cal., similar to the Model P, except has brass backstrap and trigger guard, 4 3/4, 5 1/2, or 7 1/2 in. barrel, case hardened frame with blue barrel and cylinder. Mfg. 1997 only.

	$320	$275	$250	$225	$210	$195	$180

Last MSR was $359.

BUNTLINE MODEL - .357 Mag., .44-40 WCF, or .45 LC cal., 18 in. barrel, brass or steel backstrap cut for shoulder stock. Disc. 1989.

	$355	$280	$255	$220	$195	$175	$160

Last MSR was $400.

Add $10 for target sights.

BUNTLINE CARBINE - similar cals. to Buntline Model, except also includes .22 LR/.22 Mag. (convertible cylinders), 18 in. barrel, includes non-detachable shoulder stock with brass hardware and finger extension trigger guard. Importation disc. 1991.

	$380	$295	$260	$225	$195	$175	$160

Last MSR was $440.

Add $20 for target sights.
Add $20 for .22 LR/.22 Mag. combo.

GRADING - PPGS™	100%	98%	95%	90%	80%	70%	60%

BUCKHORN - .44 Spl. or .44 Mag. cal., reinforced variation of the Cimarron SAA designed for more powerful cartridges, 4 3/4, 6 or 7 1/2 in. barrel, brass or steel backstrap. Disc. 1993.

	$355	$285	$260	$220	$195	$175	$160

Last MSR was $400.

✹ *Buckhorn Convertible Model* - .44 Mag./.44-40 WCF cylinders are included, 4 3/4, 6 or 7 1/2 in. barrel. Disc. 1989.

	$375	$295	$265	$220	$195	$175	$160

Last MSR was $427.

Add $12 for target sights.

✹ *Buckhorn Target Model* - .44 Spl. or .44 Mag. cal., 4 3/4, 6 or 7 1/2 in. barrel, adj. rear sight. Importation disc. 1991.

	$370	$290	$265	$225	$195	$175	$160

Last MSR was $420.

✹ *Buckhorn Buntline* - .44-40 WCF, .44 Spl., or .44 Mag. cal., 18 in. barrel, fixed or target sights. Disc. 1989.

	$370	$285	$265	$220	$195	$175	$160

Last MSR was $419.

Add $30 for target sights.

✹ *Buckhorn Carbine* - .44-40 WCF, .44 Spl., or .44 Mag. cal., 18 in. barrel, includes non-detachable shoulder stock with brass hardware and lanyard ring. Disc. 1990.

	$375	$290	$265	$220	$195	$175	$160

Last MSR was $429.

Add $30 for target sights.

THUNDERER - .357 Mag., .44 Spl., .44-40 WCF or .45 LC cal., patterned after Colt's Thunderer Model, 3 1/2, 4 3/4, or 5 1/2 (new 2000) in. barrel with full ejector rod housing, birdshead grips, choice of case colored or nickel finish. Importation began 1994.

MSR $519	$430	$325	$265	$220	$195	$175	$160

Add $45 for checkered walnut grips.
Add $50 for convertible .45 ACP cylinder (3 1/2 or 4 3/4 in. only).

✹ *Thunderer Long Tom* - .357 Mag., .44-40 WCF or .45 LC cal., 7 1/2 in. barrel. New 1997.

MSR $519	$430	$325	$265	$220	$195	$175	$160

Add $45 for checkered walnut grips.

U.S. 7TH CAVALRY CUSTER MODEL - authentic reproduction of original Colt military cavalry contract, 7 1/2 in. barrel, marked U.S. on lower left frame, one piece walnut grips with military cartouche.

MSR $549	$465	$385	$335	$285	$265	$240	$220

Add $40 for charcoal blue finish.
Add $50 for original finish.

U.S. CAVALRY MODEL P (A.P. CASEY) - .45 LC cal. only, 7 1/2 in. barrel, Old Model frame. Mfg. 1996-97.

	$430	$365	$315	$280	$260	$240	$220

Last MSR was $499.

U.S. ARTILLERY MODEL - Renaldo A. Carr 1895 U.S. Artillery Model Commemorative, 5 1/2 in. barrel. Limited mfg.

	$430	$365	$315	$280	$260	$240	$220

Last MSR was $499.

U.S. ARTILLERY ROUGH RIDER - .45 LC cal. only, 5 1/2 in. barrel, Old Model frame. New 1996.

MSR $549	$465	$385	$335	$285	$265	$240	$220

Add $40 for charcoal blue finish.
Add $50 for original finish.

GRADING - PPGS™	100%	98%	95%	90%	80%	70%	60%

7TH CAVALRY CASED SET - U.S. Cavalry Model in case with accessories. Disc. 1990.

	$695	$625	$550	$500	$460	$420	$385

Last MSR was $780.

WILD BILL ELLIOT TEXAS CATTLEBRAND - .45 LC cal. Mfg. 1994-96.

	$1,225	$1,025	$875	$750	$625	$550	$475

Last MSR was $1,395.

JUDGE ROY BEAN COMMEMORATIVE - mfg. to commemorate Judge Roy Bean's Texas cattlebrand. Disc. 1996.

	$1,500	$1,175	$995	$875	$750	$625	$550

Last MSR was $1,695.

LIGHTNING - .38 Colt (disc.) and .38 S&W Spl. cal., patterned after the original Colt Lightning, 3 1/2, 4 3/4 or 5 1/2 in. barrel, birdshead grips. Mfg. by A. Uberti 1999-2001, reintroduced 2003.

MSR $499	$415	$325	$275	$235	$200	$180	$160

Add $40 for charcoal blue.
Add $60 for dual cylinder (.32-20 WCF/.32 H&R Mag. cal., new 2004).
Add $45 for checkered walnut grips.

REVOLVERS: REPRODUCTIONS, COLT CONVERSIONS

1851 NAVY RICHARDS-MASON CONVERSION - .38 Spl. cal., patterned after the original Richards-Mason 1851 Navy Conversion, 4 3/4, 5 1/2 or 7 1/2 in. barrel, available in standard, charcoal blue, or original finish. Mfg. by Uberti. Importation began 2003.

MSR $529	$425	$365	$310	$275	$250	$210	$180

Add $40 for charcoal blue finish.
Add $50 for original finish.
Add $25 for silver plated backstrap and triggerguard.

1860 ARMY RICHARDS-MASON CONVERSION - .44 WCF and Russian or .45 Schofield cal., patterned after the original Richards-Mason 1860 Conversion, 4 3/4, 5 1/2 or 8 in. barrel, available in standard, charcoal blue or original finish. Mfg. by Uberti. Importation began 2003.

MSR $529	$425	$365	$310	$275	$250	$210	$180

Add $40 for charcoal blue finish.
Add $50 for original finish.

1868 THUER CONVERSION TO 1860 ARMY - .44-40 WCF cal., Thuer conversion ring and cylinder, cartridge loading tool, all other specifications same as 1860 Army. Disc. 2002.

	$350	$275	$250	$225	$200	$185	$160

Last MSR was $418.

This model requires a special hand-loaded round in .44 cal for the Thuer Conversion.

REVOLVERS: REPRODUCTIONS, REMINGTON

These guns are reproductions of the Models 1875 and 1890.

Add $90 for nickel plating, $10 for charcoal blue finish on models listed below.

MODEL 1875 - .357 Mag., .44-40 WCF, or .45 LC cal., 7 1/2 barrel. Disc. 1993.

	$340	$250	$200	$170	$155	$140	$120

Last MSR was $390.

❋ *Model 1875 Carbine* - same cals. as Model 1875, 18 in. barrel, includes non-detachable shoulder stock with brass hardware and lanyard ring. Importation disc. 1990.

	$410	$340	$300	$265	$230	$200	$180

Last MSR was $460.

GRADING - PPGS™	100%	98%	95%	90%	80%	70%	60%

MODEL 1890 - .357 Mag., .44-40 WCF, or .45 LC cal., 5 1/2 or 7 1/2 in. barrel. Disc. 1993.

	$340	$250	$210	$175	$160	$145	$125

Last MSR was $390.

1871 ROLLING BLOCK TARGET PISTOL - .22 LR, .22 Hornet (new 1990), .22 Mag., or .357 Mag. cal., 9 1/2 in. barrel. Importation disc. 1990.

	$250	$200	$180	$160	$140	$125	$110

Last MSR was $280.

* *1871 Rolling Block Baby Carbine* - same cals. as Target Pistol, has 22 in. barrel and walnut stock and forearm, brass trigger guard and buttplate. Importation disc. 1990.

	$310	$245	$205	$170	$155	$140	$120

Last MSR was $340.

REVOLVERS: REPRODUCTIONS, SMITH & WESSON

SCHOFIELD MODEL NUMBER THREE - .38 Spl. (disc. 1997), .38-40 WCF (disc. 1997), .44 Russian/Spl., .44-40 WCF, .45 Schofield, .45 ACP (disc.), or .45 LC cal., available in 7 (Civilian or Military) or 5 (Wells Fargo only) in. barrel. Mfg. by Armi San Marco 1996-99.

	$730	$640	$570	$515	$450	$400	$360

Last MSR was $849.

Add $100 for nickel finish.
Add $150 for custom nickel finish.
This model was also available as a "Little Big Horn" variation with sub-inspector markings and "SBL" cartouche.

RIFLES: REPRODUCTIONS, REMINGTON ROLLING BLOCK

Add $200 for AA select wood, $400 for AAA premium select wood, or $600 for super premium (fine European walnut). Add $150 for fine hand oil finish or $200 for super fine stock finish.

ROLLING BLOCK SPORTING RIFLE - .45-70 cal., 30 in. barrel, walnut stock and forearm. Imported 1989-90 only.

	$625	$565	$430	$395	$350	$320	$300

Last MSR was $620.

* *Deluxe Rolling Block Sporting Rifle* - similar to standard model, except has select wood. Importation disc. 1990.

	$725	$640	$485	$450	$375	$340	$320

Last MSR was $720.

REMINGTON ROLLING BLOCK LONG RANGE CREEDMOOR - .45-70 Govt. cal., 30 in. tapered octagon barrel, deluxe checkered walnut stock. Importation began 1997.

	$1,125	$825	$700	$625	$550	$500	$450

Last MSR was $1,295.

"ADOBE WALLS" ROLLING BLOCK - .45-70 Govt. cal., 30 in. octagon barrel, hand checkered walnut stock, case hardened receiver, German silver nose cap, optional Creedmore sight. Mfg. by Pedersoli. Importation began 2004.

MSR $1,415	$1,195	$925	$850	$750	$650	$550	$450

RIFLES: REPRODUCTIONS, SHARPS

Add $200 for AA select wood, $400 for AAA premium select wood, or $600 for super premium (fine European walnut). Add $150 for fine hand oil finish or $200 for super fine stock finish.

GRADING - PPGS™	100%	98%	95%	90%	80%	70%	60%

SPORTING #1 RIFLE - .40-65 Win. or .45-70 Govt. cal., 32 in. octagon barrel, pistol grip stock. Mfg. by Pedersoli. Imported 2000-2002.

	$975	$800	$675	$600	$525	$475	$375

Last MSR was $1,095.

SPORTING #1 SILHOUETTE RIFLE - .45-70 Govt. or .50-70 cal., 32 in. octagon barrel with silhouette sights, pistol grip stock. Mfg. by Pedersoli. Importation began 2003.

MSR $1,350	$1,160	$925	$765	$650	$550	$475	$375

ARMI-SPORT BILLY DIXON MODEL 1874 SPORTING RIFLE - .45-70 Govt., .45-90 Win., .45-110 (new 2003), or .50-90 (new 2003) cal., 32 in. barrel, nickel silver front blade and forearm cap, checkered deluxe walnut stock, double set triggers. Mfg. by Armi-Sport. Importation began 1997.

MSR $1,349	$1,160	$925	$765	$650	$550	$475	$375

PEDERSOLI BILLY DIXON MODEL 1874 SPORTING RIFLE - .45-70 Govt., .45-90 Win., or .50-70 (new 2004) cal., 32 in. barrel, nickel silver front blade and forearm cap, checkered deluxe walnut stock, double set triggers. Mfg. by Pedersoli. Importation began 1997.

MSR $1,620	$1,425	$1,150	$875	$775	$675	$575	$475

Add $30 for .45-70 Govt. cal. or $50 for .45-90 Win. cal.

ARMI-SPORT QUIGLEY II MODEL 1874 SPORTING RIFLE - .45-70 Govt., .45-90 Win., .45-110 (new 2004), .45-120 Sharps, or .50-90 (new 2002) cal., 34 in. octagon barrel with storage compartment in stock. Mfg. by Armi-Sport. Importation began 2000.

MSR $1,430	$1,200	$875	$750	$650	$550	$500	$450

PEDERSOLI QUIGLEY MODEL 1874 SPORTING RIFLE - .45-70 Govt., .45-90 Win., .45-120 Sharps, .50-70 (new 2004), or .50-90 (new 2002) cal., 34 in. octagon barrel with storage compartment in stock. Mfg. by Pedersoli. Importation began 2000.

MSR $1,725	$1,500	$1,200	$925	$800	$700	$600	$500

Add $20 for .45-90 Win. cal., $50 for .45-110 or .45-120 cal., or $80 for .50-70 or .50-90 cal.

SHARPS BIG 50 LONG RANGE MODEL 1874 SPORTING RIFLE - .50-90 cal., 34 in. barrel, double set triggers, apeture rear sight, checkered stock and forearm. Mfg. by Pedersoli. Importation began 2004.

MSR $1,888	$1,600	$1,275	$950	$825	$725	$625	$525

SHARPS "PRIDE OF THE PLAINS" MODEL 1874 - .45-70 Govt. cal., 32 in. matte black octagon barrel, hand checkered walnut stock, nickel receiver, Creedmore rear sight. Mfg. by Pedersoli. Importation began 2004.

MSR $1,620	$1,425	$1,150	$875	$775	$675	$575	$475

SHARPS PROFESSIONAL HUNTER MODEL 1874 - .45-70 Govt. cal. Importation began 2005.

MSR $1,159	$985	$735	$600	$500	$400	$350	$300

SHARPS TEXAS RANGER CARBINE MODEL 1874 - .45-70 Govt. or .50-70 cal., 22 in. round blue barrel, American black walnut stock, case colored receiver, marked with TS initials with Lone Star in between on barrel. Mfg. by Armi Sport. Importation began 2004.

MSR $1,199	$1,025	$800	$700	$600	$500	$400	$350

RIFLES: REPRODUCTIONS, SPENCER

1865 SPENCER REPEATING RIFLE - .56-60 cal., case colored receiver, 20 in. barrel, straight grip stock, inlcudes slings. Importation began 2005.

MSR $1,149	$975	$725	$625	$550	$475	$400	$350

RIFLES: REPRODUCTIONS, WINCHESTER

Add $200 for AA select wood, $400 for AAA premium select wood, or $600 for super premium (fine European walnut). Add $150 for fine hand oil finish or $200 for super fine stock finish.

HENRY RIFLE/CARBINE - .44-40 WCF, .44 Spl. (mfg. 1993-95), or .45 LC (new 1993) cal., brass or case colored steel (.44-40 WCF and .45 LC cal. only, new 2002) frame, 24 1/4 in. barrel on rifle, 22 (disc. 1995, .44-40 WCF cal. only) in. barrel on carbine.

MSR $1,149	$975	$725	$625	$550	$475	$400	$350

Add $65 for charcoal blue or $50 for in-the-white finish.

Add $80 for original finish.

Add $91 for steel frame model.

Add approx. $900 for standard engraving.

Add $2,150 for Lincoln Presentation engraving.

Previous to 1997, this model could also be special ordered with Grade A engraving ($450 extra), Grade B engraving ($550 extra), and Grade C engraving ($725 extra).

CIVIL WAR HENRY RIFLE - .44-40 WCF or .45 LC (new 1998) cal., 24 1/4 in. barrel, patterned after the U.S. issue original inspected by Chas. G. Chapman (C.G.C.) with military inspector's marks and cartouche, military sling swivels became standard in 1996. Importation began 1993.

MSR $1,199	$1,025	$775	$675	$575	$475	$400	$350

Add $65 for charcoal blue or in-the-white finish.

Add $80 for original finish.

1866 SPORTING RIFLE (YELLOWBOY) - .22 LR (disc. 1993), .22 Mag. (disc. 1993), .32-20 WCF (new 2002), .38 Spl. (new 1995), .38-40 WCF (new 2002), .44-40 WCF, or .45 LC (new 1993) cal., brass receiver, 20 (new 2000, Short Rifle) or 24 in. octagon barrel.

MSR $965	$815	$615	$500	$425	$350	$300	$250

Add $65 for charcoal blue finish (new 1997).

Add $80 for original finish (.44-40 WCF or .45 LC cal. only).

Add $875 for standard engraving (new 1997).

Add $2,700 for Mexican Eagle engraving (new 1997) or $2,450 for Red Cloud engraving (new 2005).

Add $500 (retail) for A engraving, $650 for B engraving, $1,175 for C engraving. Disc. 1996.

1866 YELLOWBOY CARBINE - .32-20 WCF, .38 Spl., .44 Spl., .44-40 WCF, or .45 LC cal., similar to Model 1866 Sporting Rifle, except has 19 in. round barrel with 2 bands, saddle ring, uncheckered walnut stock and forearm.

MSR $925	$800	$640	$530	$430	$350	$300	$250

Add $65 for charcoal blue finish (new 1997).

Add $80 for original finish (available in .44-40 WCF or .45 LC cal.).

Add $25 for saddle ring.

✳ *1866 Trapper Carbine* - .38 Spl. (new 2002), .44-40 WCF, or .45 LC (new 2005) cal., 16 in. round barrel. Importation disc. 1990, reintroduced 2002.

MSR $925	$800	$640	$530	$430	$350	$300	$250

✳ *1866 Yellowboy Indian Carbine* - .22 LR, .22 Mag., .38 Spl., or .44-40 WCF cal., 19 in. round barrel. Disc. 1989.

	$575	$475	$400	$350	$300	$260	$220

Last MSR was $649.

This model had a photo engraved brass frame and brass tacks in stock and forearm.

GRADING - PPGS™	100%	98%	95%	90%	80%	70%	60%

✳ *Red Cloud Commemorative Carbine* - same cals. as Yellowboy Indian Carbine, includes special engraving representing Oglalla Indian tribe symbols, brass tacks in forearm and stock. Disc. 1989.

		$575	$475	$400	$350	$300	$260	$220

Last MSR was $649.

1873 SPORTING RIFLE - .22 LR (disc. 1993), .22 Mag. (disc. 1993), .32-20 WCF (new 2002), .357 Mag., .38-40 WCF (new 2002), .44 Spl. (new 2002), .44-40 WCF, or .45 LC cal., 24 1/4 in. octagon barrel, case hardened receiver, full mag., iron sights.

MSR $1,149	$975	$725	$600	$500	$400	$350	$300

Add $65 for charcoal blue finish (new 1997, not available in .32-20 WCF or .38-40 WCF cal.).

Add $425 for old style color case hardening.

Add $80 for original finish (.44-40 WCF or 45 LC cal. only).

Add $71 for Deluxe Model with pistol grip.

Add $895 for standard engraving or $1,800 for 1 of 1,000 engraving.

Add $500 (retail) for A engraving, $650 for B engraving, $1,075 for C engraving (disc. 2002).

✳ *1873 Evil Roy Rifle* - .357 Mag. or .45 LC cal., 20 in. barrel, features Evil Roy shooting improvements. Importation began 2005.

MSR $1,800	$1,500	$1,175	$900	$800	$700	$600	$500

✳ *1873 Larry Crow Signature Series Rifle* - .357 Mag. or .45 LC cal., 20 in. barrel, features Larry Crow shooting improvements and signature. Importation began 2005.

MSR $2,275	$1,850	$1,525	$1,175	$900	$800	$700	$600

✳ *1873 Short Rifle* - .32-20 WCF (new 2002), .357 Mag. (new 2000), .38-40 WCF (new 2002), .44 Spl. (new 2002), .44-40 WCF or .45 LC cal., features 20 in. octagon barrel, case hardened receiver, iron sights. Importation began 1990.

MSR $1,149	$975	$725	$600	$500	$400	$350	$300

Add $65 for charcoal blue finish (not available in .32-20 WCF or .44 Spl cal.).

Add $80 for original finish (.44-40 WCF or .45 LC only).

Add $71 for Deluxe Border Model with pistol grip.

✳ *1873 Long Range Rifle* - .44-40 WCF or .45 LC cal., includes 30 in. octagon barrel with full mag., case hardened receiver, iron sights. New 1990.

MSR $1,120	$930	$700	$600	$500	$400	$350	$295

Add $65 for charcoal blue finish (new 1997).

Add $95 for Deluxe Model with pistol grip.

Add $895 for standard engraving or $1,800 for 1 of 1,000 engraving.

✳ *1873 Saddle Ring Carbine* - .22 LR (disc. 1993), .22 Mag. (disc. 1993), .32-20 WCF (new 2002), .357 Mag., .38-40 WCF (new 2002), .44 Spl. (new 2002), .44-40 WCF, or .45 LC cal., blue steel receiver, with or w/o saddle ring, 19 in. round barrel.

MSR $1,045	$890	$685	$555	$450	$375	$325	$295

Add $25 for saddle ring and case colored frame.

Add $65 for charcoal blue finish (new 1997).

Add $80 for original finish (.44-40 WCF or 45 LC cal. only).

Add $90 for nickel plating (disc.).

✳ *1873 Trapper Carbine* - .357 Mag. (new 1990, reintroduced 2004), .44-40 WCF (disc. 1990, reintroduced 2005), or .45 LC (mfg. 1990, reintroduced 2005) cal., 16 in. barrel, blue finish only. Importation disc. 1990, reintroduced 2004.

MSR $1,045	$890	$685	$555	$450	$375	$325	$295

GRADING - PPGS™	100%	98%	95%	90%	80%	70%	60%

1885 HI-WALL RIFLE - .30-40 Krag (new 2004), .348 Win. (new 2004), .38-55 WCF (new 2000), .40-65 WCF, .45-70 Govt., .45-90 WCF (new 2000), .45-120 WCF (mfg. 2002-2004) cal., 28 (disc.) or 30 in. octagon barrel, case hardened finish on frame, iron sights (standard) or optional aperture rear and globe front sight (new 2002). New 1998.

	MSR $995	$850	$675	$575	$475	$375	$325	$295

Add $180 for engraved reciever, adj. sights, and pistol grip (new 2002).

Add $775 for standard engraving, $1,500 for deluxe engraving, or $3,250 for deluxe gold line engraving.

1885 LOW WALL RIFLE - .22 LR, .22 Hornet, .22 Mag., .30-30 Win., .32-20 WCF, .357 Mag., .38-40 WCF, .44 Mag., .38-55, .44-40 WCF, or .45 LC cal., 30 in. barrel, hand checkered walnut stock, single or double set trigger. Importation began 2005.

	MSR $995	$850	$675	$575	$475	$375	$325	$295

Add $180 for engraved reciever, adj. sights, and pistol grip.

Add $775 for standard engraving, $1,500 for deluxe engraving, or $3,250 for deluxe gold line engraving.

MODEL 1892 RIFLE - .357 Mag., .44 Mag., .44-40 WCF, or .45 LC, 20 or 24 in. barrel, available in either solid or takedown frame, unchecked walnut stock and forearm, case colored receiver. Importation began 2005.

	MSR $849	$725	$600	$500	$400	$350	$250	$200

Add $126 for takedown frame.

CLARIDGE HI-TEC INC.

Previous manufacturer located in Northridge, CA 1990-1993. In 1990, Claridge Hi-Tec, Inc. was created and took over Goncz Armament, Inc.

All Claridge Hi-Tec firearms utilized match barrels mfg. in-house that were button-rifled. The Claridge action is an original design and does not copy other actions. Claridge Hi-Tec models can be altered (Law Enforcement Companion Series) to accept Beretta 92F or Sig Model 226 magazines.

PISTOLS

Add $40 for polished stainless steel frame construction.

L-9 PISTOL - 9mm Para., .40 S&W, or .45 ACP cal., semi-auto paramilitary design, 7 1/2 (new 1992) or 9 1/2 (disc. 1991) in. shrouded barrel, aluminum receiver, choice of black matte, matte silver, or polished silver finish, one piece grip, safety locks firing pin in place, 10 (disc.), 17, or 30 shot double row mag., adj. sights, 3 3/4 lbs. Mfg. 1991-93.

		$595	$525	$375	$300	$265	$225	$200

Last MSR was $598.

Add $395 for a trigger activated laser sighting scope was available in Models M, L, C, and T new mfg.

S-9 PISTOL - similar to L-9, except has 5 in. non-shrouded threaded barrel, 3 lbs. 9 oz. Disc. 1993.

		$695	$625	$550	$475	$350	$280	$250

Last MSR was $535.

T-9 PISTOL - similar to L-9, except has 9 1/2 in. barrel. Mfg. 1992-93.

		$550	$495	$375	$300	$265	$225	$200

Last MSR was $598.

M PISTOL - similar to L Model, except has 7 1/2 in. barrel, 3 lbs. Disc. 1991.

		$575	$515	$375	$300	$265	$225	$200

Last MSR was $720.

GRADING - PPGS™	100%	98%	95%	90%	80%	70%	60%

RIFLES: CARBINES

C-9 CARBINE - same cals. as L and S Model pistols, 16.1 in. shrouded barrel, choice of composite or uncheckered walnut stock and forearm, 5 lbs. 12 oz. Mfg. 1991-93.

	$650	$595	$525	$450	$395	$350	$300

Last MSR was $675.

Add $74 for black graphite composite stock.

Add $474 for integral laser model (with graphite stock).

This model was available with either gloss walnut, dull walnut, or black graphite composite stock.

LAW ENFORCEMENT COMPANION (LEC) - 9mm Para., .40 S&W, or .45 ACP cal., 16 1/4 button rifled barrel, black graphite composition buttstock and foregrip, buttstock also provides space for an extra mag., available in either aluminum or stainless steel frame, matte black finish, available with full integral laser sighting system. Limited mfg. 1992-93.

	$750	$650	$575	$495	$425	$375	$325

Last MSR was $749.

Add $400 for integral laser sighting system.

CLARK CUSTOM GUNS, INC.

Current custom gun maker and gunsmith located in Princeton, LA. Clark Custom Guns, Inc. has been customizing various configurations of handguns, rifles, and shotguns since 1950. It would be impossible to list within the confines of this text the many conversions this company has performed. It is recommended to contact this company directly (see Trademark Index) for an up-to-date price sheet and catalog on their extensive line-up of high quality competition pistols and related components. Custom revolvers, rifles, and shotguns are also available in addition to various handgun competition parts, related gunsmithing services, and a firearms training facility called The Shootout.

The legendary James E. Clark, Sr. passed away during 2000. In 1958, he became the first and only full-time civilian to win the National Pistol Championships.

PISTOLS: SEMI-AUTO

Clark Custom Guns currently manufactures a wide variety of M1911 style handguns, including the Bullseye Pistols (MSR $1,420-$1,985), the Custom Combat (MSR $1,560-$2,260), the Meltdown (MSR $1,380-$1,680), Millennium Meltdown (features damascus slide, only 50 mfg. during 2000 - MSR was $3,795), .460 Rowland Hunter LS (MSR $2,295), and the Unlimited (disc. 2003, last MSR was $2,020-$2,405). Clark will also build the above configurations on a customer supplied gun – prices are less, please contact the company directly regarding more information on these pistol conversions (see Trademark Index).

CLASSIC DOUBLES

Previous trademark manufactured in Tochigi City, Japan until 1987. Previously imported and distributed by Classic Doubles International, Inc. located in St. Louis, MO.

The factory closed in 1987, and all Classic Doubles remaining in inventory were sold to GU Wholesalers located in Omaha, NE in 1990. To date, there has been little collectibility in the Classic Doubles trademark. As a result, values are determined by the shooting value each model has to offer against other competing models in the same configuration. Also, in some regions of the country, 98% condition or less specimens may be priced lower than values shown in this section.

In late 1987, Winchester/Olin discontinued importation of their Japanese shotgun models (Models 101 and 23). At that point, Classic Doubles International, Inc. became the sole importer of these shotguns. There were very few changes made during this changeover of importation. The late manufacture Classic Double shotguns (Models 101 and 201) do

GRADING - PPGS™	100%	98%	95%	90%	80%	70%	60%

not have the Winchester trademark or definitive Winchester proofmark stamped on the barrels. The Model 201 was a new model designation.

SHOTGUNS: O/U, MODEL 101 - FIELD MODELS

The late manufacture Classic Doubles have an interchangeable choke tube system compatible with the older Winchester manufactured models. Prices listed include a luggage style carrying case.

100% values listed below for the Classic Doubles Shotguns assume NIB condition - subtract 10%-15% if without box, warranty card, and original shipping container (with packing materials).

CLASSIC FIELD GRADE I - 12 or 20 ga., 3 in. chambers, vent. rib, 25 1/2 or 28 in. vent. barrels with choke tubes, blue receiver with moderate scroll engraving, ejectors, checkered pistol grip or English stock and forearm, 6 1/4-7 lbs.

	$1,400	$1,250	$1,100	$1,000	$900	$825	$750

Last MSR was $1,905.

WATERFOWL MODEL - 12 ga. only, 3 in. chambers, 30 in. barrels with vent. rib and choke tubes, matte blue receiver with moderate engraving, low gloss walnut stock with vent. recoil pad, 7 3/4 lbs.

	$1,150	$995	$895	$800	$700	$600	$500

Last MSR was $1,520.

CLASSIC SPORTER - 12 ga. only, made for Sporting Clays competition, 28 or 30 in. vent. barrels and rib with choke tubes, quick detachable stock system, border engraved coin finished receiver with non-reflective matte surface on top frame and lever, checkered walnut stock and forearm, 7 3/4 lbs.

	$1,995	$1,500	$1,295	$1,150	$1,000	$900	$775

Last MSR was $1,980.

Add $965 for extra barrel.

CLASSIC FIELD GRADE II - 12, 20, 28 ga., or .410 bore, 28 in. VR barrels with choke tubes, deluxe walnut with round knob pistol grip stock and forearm with fine fleur-de-lis checkering, coin finished receiver (different sizes) with game scene engraving featuring hunting motifs on receiver sides and bottom, .410 bore bored M/F only, 6 1/4-7 lbs.

	$1,795	$1,475	$1,275	$1,100	$1,000	$900	$795

Last MSR was $2,190.

Add 15% for .410 bore (baby frame).
Add 50% for 28 ga. (baby frame).

The lack of supply of the Winchester/Olin Model 101 28 ga. small frame has caused a significant increase in demand for the .410 bore or 28 ga. The Grade II .410 bore is the only round knob pistol grip produced in both Winchester and Classic Doubles manufacture.

CLASSIC FIELD GRADE II TWO BARREL SET - 12 and 20 ga. barrels, both with Winchokes, 26 in. barrels - 20 ga., 28 in. barrels - 12 ga., coin finished receiver with game scene engraving and borders, 6 1/2 (20 ga.) or 7 (12 ga.) lbs.

	$2,695	$2,175	$1,825	$1,550	$1,375	$1,200	$1,075

Last MSR was $3,420.

SHOTGUNS: O/U, MODEL 101 - TARGET MODELS

CLASSIC TRAP SINGLE - 12 ga. only, over single 32 or 34 in. VR barrel with choke tubes, blue receiver with light engraving, choice of Monte Carlo or regular stock, recoil pad, 8 1/2 lbs.

	$1,425	$1,250	$1,100	$1,000	$900	$825	$750

Last MSR was $2,070.

GRADING - PPGS™	100%	98%	95%	90%	80%	70%	60%

CLASSIC TRAP - 12 ga. only, 30 or 32 in. vent. barrels and rib with choke tubes, finish and engraving similar to Classic Trap Single, choice of Monte Carlo or standard stock with recoil pad, 8 3/4 or 9 lbs.

	$1,300	$1,125	$1,000	$900	$825	$750	$675

Last MSR was $1,905.

CLASSIC TRAP COMBO - includes one set of O/U barrels (30 or 32 in.) and one over single barrel (32 or 34 in.), choke tubes, choice of Monte Carlo or standard stock, 8 3/4 or 9 lbs.

	$2,125	$1,875	$1,600	$1,475	$1,300	$1,175	$995

Last MSR was $2,825.

CLASSIC SKEET - 12 or 20 ga., 27 1/2 in. vent. barrels and rib, choke tubes on 12 ga. only, smaller gauges are bored SK/SK, similar metal finish to Classic Trap models, 7 1/4 or 7 3/4 lbs.

	$1,695	$1,375	$1,175	$1,025	$900	$825	$750

Last MSR was $1,905.

* *Classic Skeet 4 ga. Set* - similar to Classic Skeet except has 4 barrels (12, 20, 28 ga., or .410 bore), 12 ga. has choke tubes, smaller gauges are bored SK/SK.

	$3,900	$3,500	$3,100	$2,875	$2,600	$2,300	$1,995

Last MSR was $4,765.

SHOTGUNS: SxS

MODEL 201 CLASSIC - 12 or 20 ga., 3 in. chambers, forged steel monobloc with improved lug design, 26 in. choke tube barrels with vent. rib, high lustre bluing, no engraving, SST, ejectors, premium walnut stock and beavertail forearm with fancy checkering pattern, solid red rubber recoil pad, 6 3/4-7 lbs.

	$2,150	$1,875	$1,650	$1,400	$1,200	$995	$775

Last MSR was $2,190.

Add $120 for 20 ga.

The 12 ga. could be ordered with choke tubes at no extra charge. Only 63 were mfg. with choke tubes and slight premiums are being asked.

* *Model 201 Classic Small Bore Set* - 28 ga. and .410 bore two barrel set, similar to Model 201 Classic except has smaller frame and overall dimensions, 28 in. VR barrels only bored IC/M on 28 ga. and M/F on .410 bore, very limited importation, 6 or 6 1/2 lbs.

	$4,250	$3,650	$3,250	$2,800	$2,400	$1,950	$1,475

Last MSR was $3,675.

CLERKE ARMS, LTD.

Previous manufacturer located in Raton, New Mexico 1997-2001.

PISTOLS: SINGLE SHOT

COMPETITOR PISTOL - available in 16 centerfire and 2 rimfire cals., 10, 12, 14, 16, or 20 (.410 bore only) in. barrel, features new uplifting C Breech gun system, Xtender slide can be fitted to all Colt .45 ACPs and replicas with no frame modification, matte finish, checkered wood grips. Mfg. 1998-2001.

	$300	$285	$265	$240	$220	$200	$185

Last MSR was $325.

Add $135-$155 per interchangeable barrel, depending on length.

CLERKE PRODUCTS

Previous manufacturer located in Santa Monica, CA.

GRADING - PPGS™	100%	98%	95%	90%	80%	70%	60%

REVOLVERS: DOUBLE ACTION

DOUBLE ACTION REVOLVER - .22 S, L, LR, or .32 S&W Long cal., inexpensive double action revolvers that sold to dealers for $15 in 1971.

RIFLES: SINGLE SHOT

HI-WALL - single shot rifle, falling block replica of Winchester 1885 High Wall, lever operated, case hardened receiver, 26 in. barrel, available in most modern calibers, no sights, checkered walnut pistol grip stock, Schnabel forearm. Mfg. 1972-74.

	$250	$225	$185	$175	$150	$140	$125

DELUXE HI-WALL - similar to Hi-Wall, except half octagon barrel, select wood and recoil pad.

	$300	$275	$235	$210	$180	$160	$145

CLIFTON ARMS

Previous manufacturer of custom rifles from 1992-1997 located in Medina, TX. Clifton Arms specialized in composite stocks (with or without integral, retractable bipod).

Clifton Arms manufactured composite, hand laminated stocks that were patterned after the Dakota 76 stock configuration.

RIFLES: BOLT ACTION

CLIFTON SCOUT RIFLE - .243 Win. (disc. 1993), .30-06, .308 Win., .350 Rem. Mag., .35 Whelen, 7mm-08 Rem. (disc. 1993), or .416 Rem. Mag. cal., choice of Dakota 76, pre-64 Winchester Model 70, or Ruger 77 MK II (standard) stainless action with bolt face altered to controlled round feeding, Shilen stainless premium match grade barrel, Clifton synthetic stock with bipod, many other special orders were available. Mfg. 1992-97.

	$3,000	$2,350	$1,650

This model was available as a Standard Scout (.308 Win. cal. with 19 in. barrel), Pseudo Scout (.30-06 cal. with 19 1/2 in. barrel), Super Scout (.35 Whelen or .350 Rem. Mag. with 20 in. barrel), or African Scout (.416 Rem. Mag. with 22 in. barrel).

COACH GUNS

A coach gun is a SxS shotgun with short barrels, and was used extensively in the American West for the protection of horse-drawn coach passengers, hence the name. They were also called guard guns, as they were used for guard duty and other security purposes.

SHOTGUNS: SxS, COACH/GUARD GUNS

The author wishes to express his thanks to Jon Vander Bloomen for compiling much of the following information.

Extensive research indicates that three American gun companies made coach guns in the late 1800s and early 1900s – Colt, Parker, and Ithaca. Remington and Whitney may also have produced some, but there are no factory records to prove it. W.W. Greener of Birmingham, England may have made some short double barrel shotguns for guard use, but no one has seen any factory documentation to support this.

An "original" coach gun, properly called a guard gun, is a double barrel (SxS) shotgun that was made with short barrels, not a long barreled sporting gun that was cut off (see muzzle diagram). However, the muzzles of an original coach gun and a gun whose barrels have been cut off look the same. On both, there is a gap between the muzzles that is filled in with lead. The reason for this is because shotgun barrels are tapered. In order for the muzzles to touch on a 26 inch or shorter gun, the barrel walls would need to be thicker at the muzzle to eliminate the gap.

Some original coach guns may also have original factory markings, identification letters/numerals on the stock and other distinguishing features that indicate that the gun was originally made and marked to identify it as company property. However, don't think that there's "safety in numbers." There are a lot more Wells Fargo marked guns today than there were 85 years ago.

The real question is, how can you tell an original coach gun from a sporting arm whose barrels have been cut down to potentially "enhance" its desirability factor? Hopefully, by obtaining factory documentation. To find out if a coach gun is an original or a "cut" gun, it is recommended that you contact the factory for documentation (if possible), giving the serial number of the gun and asking for the proper barrel length at the time the gun left the factory. Unfortunately, no Remington records exist. Parker records can be found in Vols. I & II of *The Parker Story*. W.W. Greener is still in business, and will look up a serial number, but it will take some time.

Colt records show that several double barrel shotguns left the factory with short barrels. Most of them were the Model 1878 hammer guns with 18 inch barrels. There where only three Model 1883 hammerless, boxlock guns made with short barrels; the lengths are as follows, 18, 22, and 24 inches. All of the Colt Damascus barrels were made in Belgium and shipped to the Colt factory in an unfinished state, so they were just Damascus tubes. Therefore when Colt got an order for a coach/guard gun, the barrels were custom made to length just as the longer barreled guns. These short barreled Colts are "original coach/guard guns." The extreme rarity of a Colt factory coach gun precludes accurate pricing evaluation.

Parker records show that several guns were made with short barrels. Not all short Parkers were made for guard use however, since some hunters preferred short barrels in the field (for fast upland birds). Parker purchased different grades of steel tubes and made their own barrels. When Parker received an order for a guard gun, the barrels were custom made to length. It would have been more costly for Parker to cut a long barreled choked gun, except in the case of used sporting arms that were cut for guard use. It is likely that the lower grade 10 and 12 ga. guns that left the Parker factory with short barrels are "original" coach/guard guns. The extreme rarity factor of a Parker factory coach gun precludes accurate pricing evaluation.

Ithaca records show that 750 hammer doubles were made for Wells Fargo between 1909 and 1917. The first 200 guns had 26 in. barrels, and the remaining 550 had 24 in. barrels. Wells Fargo, as well as other express companies, used various makes of shotguns, mostly used lower grade models that were cut to a shorter length. There is no proof that any company other than Ithaca made guard guns for Wells Fargo. It is recommeded that a buyer get original documentation when considering a purchase of a Wells Fargo coach gun or any other gun that is claimed to have been used by a famous person. Average condition Wells Fargo coach guns are typically priced in the $4,000-$4,500 range, regardless if they are manufactured by Ithaca or are another trademark that had barrels cut. What's important to the buyer is that the gun is a documented Wells Fargo gun, and should have some paperwork specifying that.

What's important to remember is that if there is no original documentation, there's no proof. And if there's no proof, the shotgun may or may not be an original coach gun. It is recommended that when buying, selling, or trading coach guns, the price tag should be proportional to the gun's originality and provenance. Anything less could result in an unwarranted premium for a tired out, "reconfigured" SxS plain Jane shotgun, with some added non-original markings/carvings.

Older sawed-off double barrel shotguns with no documentation as being an express company gun, or a gun used by a famous person are valued in the $200 to $2,000 range, depending on trademark and condition, condition being most important. A good guide for pricing sawed-off doubles is to check the value of the same gun that has not been cut and then deduct 5% to 50%. If no price guide is available for that particular make, then consider availability. For example, tens of thousands of Belgian doubles were made in the 1800s. Because of the increase in collectibility of American western artifacts, original coach guns and all express company guns are highly prized and sought after, but the buyer must always be wary.

Muzzles

Cut Off
or Made Short

Sporting Arm
Not Cut

COBB MANUFACTURING, INC.

Current rifle manufacturer located in Dallas, GA.

RIFLES: BOLT ACTION

MODEL FA50 (T) - .50 BMG cal., straight pull bolt action, lightweight tactical rifle, standard a2 style stock, ergonomic pistol grip, parkerized finish, Lothar-Walther 30 in. barrel, recoil reducing Armalite muzzle brake, padded Mil-spec sling, includes two 10 shot mags., detachable M60 bipod, watertight case, 29 lbs.

MSR $6,000	$5,500	$4,750	$4,000	$3,250	$2,500	$2,000	$1,750

Many options are available for this model - please contact the company directly for more information (see Trademark Index).

COBRA ENTERPRISES OF UTAH, INC.

Current pistol manufacturer established in 2001, with headquarters in Salt Lake City, UT. During 2004, the name was changed from Cobra Enterprises to Cobra Enterprises of Utah, Inc.

DERRINGERS

COBRA DERRINGER - .22 LR, .22 Win Mag., .25 ACP, or .32 ACP standard cal., 2.4 (Standard Series), 2.75 (Big Bore Series) or 3.5 (Long Bore Series) in. barrel, tip-up action, spur trigger, internal hammer block safety, pearl, black, or laminated wood grips, chrome, black powder coat, or satin chrome finish, 9.5 oz.

MSR $116	$85	$70	$60	$50	$40	$35	$35

Add $24 for .22 Mag., .32 H&R Mag., .38 Spl., or 9mm Para cal. with 2 3/4 in. barrel.

Add $24 for .22 Mag., .38 Spl., or 9mm Para cal. with 3 1/2 in. barrel.

PISTOLS: SEMI-AUTO

CA (COBRA) SERIES - .32 ACP (CA32 Model) or 380 ACP (CA380 Model) cal., blowback single action, 2.8 in. barrel, 5 or 6 shot mag., chrome, black powder coat, or satin chrome finish, 22 oz.

MSR $124	$95	$75	$65	$55	$45	$40	$35

FREEDOM SERIES - .32 ACP (FS32 Model) or 380 ACP (FS380 Model) cal., blowback single action, 3 1/2 in. barrel, 7 (.380 ACP) or 8 (.32 ACP) shot mag., bright chrome, black powder coat, or satin nickel finish, 2.1 lbs. New 2004.

MSR $134	$105	$85	$75	$65	$55	$45	$35

PATRIOT SERIES - .380 ACP or 9mm Para. cal., DAO, 3.3 in. barrel, polymer frame, 10 shot mag., loaded indicator, also available with black melonite coated slide, 20.5 oz.

MSR $279	$220	$195	$170	$150	$125	$110	$100

Add $10 for 9mm Para. cal.

✷ *Patriot 45* - .45 ACP cal., DAO, black polymer frame with stainless steel slide, 3 in. barrel, 6 shot mag., 20 oz.

MSR $316	$260	$220	$195	$175	$150	$135	$120

COBRAY INDUSTRIES

See listing under S.W.D. in the S section of this text.

GRADING - PPGS™	100%	98%	95%	90%	80%	70%	60%

COGSWELL & HARRISON (GUNMAKERS), LTD.

Current manufacturer established durng 1770, and located in London, England. Previously imported by British Game Guns, located in Kent, WA.

In 1993, Cogswell & Harrison came under new management and have concentrated on building best quality guns utilizing Beesley or Purdey type sidelocks, Woodward styled O/Us, and a round action boxlock. The company also provides a serialization service (free of charge), that provides the exact date of manufacture. A Certificate of Origin is also available for $60 per gun, and indicates the original specifications and configuration – weights, dimensions, materials, points of choke, and original owner (including price paid). Cogswell & Harrison also offers a full repair and restoration service.

RIFLES: SxS

Prices indicated below are for manufacturer's suggested retail and 100% condition factors are listed in English pounds. All new prices do not include VAT. Values for used guns in 98%-60% condition factors are priced in U.S. dollars. Allow 12-14 months for delivery on boxlocks, 18-24 months on sidelocks.

BOXLOCK MODEL - various cals. from .300 H&H - .600 NE, boxlock action, custom order only. New 1999.

> Currently, a standard boxlock double rifle in .300 H&H cal. retails for £20,800, and £30,500 for .600 NE, with standard fine engraving, and w/o case.

SIDELOCK MODEL - standard cals. include .300 H&H, .375 H&H, .465, .470 NE, .577, and .600 NE, Beesley or Purdey type action standard, also available with H&H type system, individually made per customer specifications, 8 lbs. 10 oz.-14 lbs. 6 oz., depending on caliber. New 1999.

MSR £40,800	£40,800	$50,000	$42,000	$36,000	$30,000	$24,000	$18,000

Add £1,100 for .375 H&H cal.
Add £3,100 for .465 or .470 NE cal.

✳ *Cals. .577 & .600 NE*

MSR £50,500	£50,500	$60,000	$50,000	$42,000	$36,000	$30,000	$24,000

SHOTGUNS: O/U, SIDELOCK

WOODWARD TYPE - Woodward style action, finest materials, each gun custom-built for individual specifications, delivery time approx. 18-23 months.

MSR £31,770	£31,770	$47,250	$41,000	$36,000	$29,500	$22,350	$16,750

Add £1,250 for 20 ga.
Add £3,500 for 28 ga.

SHOTGUNS: SxS, OLDER MFG.

REGENCY - 12, 16, or 20 ga., 26, 28, or 30 in. barrels, any choke combination, hammerless Anson & Deeley system, boxlock, double triggers, auto ejectors, straight English stock.

	$4,275	$3,750	$3,450	$3,125	$2,750	$2,500	$2,250

> Last MSR was $3,200.

AMBASSADOR MODEL - same gauges and barrels as Regency, boxlock with ornamental strengthening sideplates, auto ejectors, double triggers, engraved game scene or scroll rose motif, English stock.

	$5,500	$4,950	$4,450	$3,950	$3,500	$3,100	$2,850

> Last MSR was $4,000.

GRADING - PPGS™	100%	98%	95%	90%	80%	70%	60%

MARKOR - 12, 16, or 20 ga., 27 1/2 or 30 in. barrel and choke, boxlock, double trigger, English stock. Disc.

	$1,675	$1,475	$1,300	$1,050	$975	$825	$700

Add 20% for auto ejectors.

HUNTIC MODEL - 12, 16, or 20 ga., 25, 27, or 30 in. barrels, any choke, sidelock, auto ejectors, English style stock. Disc.

	$3,900	$3,500	$3,200	$3,000	$2,800	$2,500	$2,175

Add $400 for SST.

AVANT TOUT SERIES - 12, 16, or 20 ga., 25, 27 1/2, or 30 in. barrels, boxlock, ornamental strengthening sideplates, straight English stock, auto ejectors, series disc.

	$2,550	$2,250	$1,925	$1,700	$1,495	$1,350	$1,200

REX OR AVANT TOUT III - no sideplates.

	$2,150	$1,800	$1,650	$1,500	$1,350	$1,200	$1,075

SANDHURST OR AVANT TOUT II

	$2,800	$2,500	$2,300	$2,150	$2,000	$1,750	$1,500

KONOR OR AVANT TOUT I

	$3,275	$2,850	$2,500	$2,250	$2,000	$1,750	$1,500

Add $400 for SST.
Add 20% for 20 ga.
Subtract 10% for 16 ga.

BEST QUALITY - 12, 16, or 20 gauges, 25, 26, 28, or 30 in. barrels, any choke, hand detachable sidelock, auto ejectors, double triggers standard, English stock.

✻ *Primic Model* - disc.

	$6,200	$5,750	$4,650	$4,150	$3,650	$3,050	$2,500

✻ *Victor Model*

	$9,250	$8,500	$7,250	$6,250	$5,000	$4,350	$3,740

Add $400 for SST.
Add 20% for 20 ga.
Note: Degree of engraving and grade of wood are the basic differences among models.

SHOTGUNS: SxS, BOXLOCK & SIDELOCK - CURRENT MFG.

Prices indicated below are for manufacturer's suggested retail and 100% condition factors are listed in English pounds. All new prices do not include VAT. Values for used guns in 98%-60% condition factors are priced in U.S. dollars. Allow 9-12 months for delivery on boxlocks, 18-23 months on sidelocks.

All models below are available in 12, 20, or 28 ga.

REGENCY - scalloped boxlock action, DTs, 100% large scroll engraving coverage on receiver and tangs, light barrel engraving, checkered straight grip stock with teardrop. Introduced 1970 to commemmorate C&H's bicentennial.

MSR £9,760	£9,760	$14,750	$12,250	$10,000	$8,000	$6,500	$4,950

Add £310 for 20 ga.
Add £510 for 28 ga.

VICTORIA - features scalloped round body boxlock action with 100% medium scroll engraving coverage on receiver and tangs, moderate barrel engraving, select checkered stock and forearm.

MSR £11,770	£11,770	$16,950	$14,500	$12,250	$10,000	$7,800	$6,100

Add £360 for 20 ga.
Add £585 for 28 ga.

GRADING - PPGS™	100%	98%	95%	90%	80%	70%	60%

EXTRA QUALITY VICTORIA - similar to Victoria Model, except has better quality wood and more engraving.

MSR £13,180	£13,180	$18,750	$16,250	$14,000	$11,750	$8,900	$7,350

Add £440 for 20 ga.
Add £890 for 28 ga.

EXTRA QUALITY (SPECIAL) VICTORIA - top-of-the-line round boxlock action with best quality walnut and chopperlump barrels, removable crosspin, and other refinements.

MSR £15,180	£15,180	$22,350	$19,450	$16,350	$13,150	$10,250	$8,400

Add £440 for 20 ga.
Add £810 for 28 ga.

SELF-OPENING SLE SxS - sidelock action, best quality Beesley action and engraving, each gun custom-built per individual specifications, delivery time approx. 18-23 months.

MSR £27,170	£27,170	$41,000	$36,000	$29,500	$22,350	$16,750	$12,500

Add £1,250 for 20 ga.
Add £3,500 for 28 ga.

COLT'S MANUFACTURING COMPANY, INC.

Current manufacturer with headquarters located in West Hartford, CT.

Manufactured from 1836-1842 in Paterson, NJ; 1847-1848 in Whitneyville, CT; 1854-1864 in London, England; and from 1848-date in Hartford, CT. Colt Firearms became a division of Colt Industries in 1964. In March 1990, the Colt Firearms Division was sold to C.F. Holding Corp. located in Hartford, CT, and the new company is called Colt's Manufacturing Company, Inc. The original Hartford plant was closed during 1994, the same year the company was sold again to a new investor group headed by Zilkha Co., located in New York, NY.

In late 1999, Colt discontinued many of their consumer revolvers, but have recently reintroduced both the Anaconda and Python Elite through the Custom Shop. Production on both models is now suspended, but has not permanently ended. The semi-auto pistols remaining in production are now referred to as Model "O."

For more information and current pricing on both new and used Colt airguns, please refer to the *Blue Book of Airguns* by Dr. Robert Beeman & John Allen (also online).

REVOLVERS: PERCUSSION

Prices shown for percussion Colts are for guns only. Original cased guns with accessories will bring a healthy premium over non-cased models (200-350% over a gun only is common). Be very careful when buying an "original" cased gun, as many fake cases have shown up in recent years.

If possible, it is advisable to procure a factory letter (available only within the following ser. no. ranges) before buying, selling, or trading Models 1851 Navy (ser. range 98,000-132,000), 1860 Army (ser. range 1,000-140,000), or 1861 Navy (ser. range 1-12,000). These watermarked letters are available by writing Colt Archive Properties LLC in Hartford, CT, with a charge of $300 or more per serial number (if they can research it). Include your name and address, Colt model name, serial number, and check or credit card information to: COLT ARCHIVE PROPERTIES LLC, P.O. Box 1868, Hartford, CT 06144-1868. Please allow 90-120 days for a response.

Prices shown on the following pages for extremely rare Colt's firearms might not include values in the 90%, 95%, 98%, and 100% condition columns. Prices are very hard to establish since these excellent to mint specimens are seldom seen or sold.

100%	98%	95%	90%	80%	70%	60%	50%	40%	30%	20%	10%

Revolvers: Percussion, Paterson Variations

POCKET MODEL PATERSON NO. 1 - also known as "Baby Paterson," .28 cal., 5 shot, 2 1/2 in. to 4 3/4 in. octagon barrels, blue metal, varnished walnut grips. Serial range 1 to approx. 500. Standard bbl. marking "Patent Arms M'g Co. Paterson N.J.-Colt's Pt." Centaur scene with four horse head trademark and "COLT" on 1 1/16 in. cylinder of round or square type. Mfg. 1837-1838.

> This and all other Paterson models have 5 shot cylinders and serial numbers are not commonly in evidence externally. Disassembly of the arm is usually necessary to determine the serial number.

> The Pocket Model Paterson No. 1 (Baby Paterson) is the first production-made handgun in Colt's Paterson, N.J. facility. It is very small in size, almost appearing as a toy or miniature.

✳ *Standard Production Model* - without attached loading lever.

N/A	N/A	$37,000	$29,000	$22,000	$19,250	$15,300	$13,250	$11,750	$10,250	$9,000	$8,000

✳ *Late Production Ehlers Model* - with attached loading lever, 31/32 round back cylinder and recoil shield milled for ease of capping. Barrel marked "Patent Arms Paterson N.J.-Colt's Pt." Approx. 500 mfg. including the Ehlers Model under Belt Model No. 2 Mfg. 1840-1843.

N/A	N/A	$41,000	$32,500	$24,650	$20,000	$15,825	$13,750	$12,250	$10,750	$9,500	$8,500

BELT MODEL PATERSON NO. 2 - .31 or .34 cal., 5 shot, 2 1/2 in. to 5 1/2 in. octagon barrels, blue metal, varnished walnut grips. Serial range 1-approx. 850 which includes the Belt Model No. 3. All standard production Belt Models No. 2 have straight bottom style grips. Standard bbl. markings "Patent Arms M'g Co. Paterson N-J. Colt's Pt." Centaur scene with four horse head trademark and "COLT" on cylinder of round or square backed type. Mfg 1837-40. Somewhat heavier than the Pocket No. 1 revolver.

✳ *Standard Production Model* - without attached loading lever.

N/A	N/A	$37,000	$29,250	$22,500	$19,450	$15,300	$13,250	$11,750	$10,250	$9,000	$8,000

✳ *Ehlers Model* - with attached loading lever, 1 1/16 in. round back cylinder, recoil shield milled for ease of capping. Barrel marked "Patent Arms Paterson N-J. Colt's Pt." Approx. 500 mfg. including the Ehlers Model under Pocket Model No. 1. Mfg. 1840-43.

N/A	N/A	$45,000	$35,500	$27,750	$23,650	$19,380	$15,500	$13,500	$12,000	$10,600	$9,500

BELT MODEL PATERSON NO. 3 - .31 or .34 cal., 5 shot, 3 1/2 in. to 5 1/2 in. octagon barrels, blue metal, a few having case hardened hammers. Varnished walnut grips. Serial range 1-approx. 850 which includes the Belt Model No. 2. All standard production Belt Models No. 3 have the flared bottom style grips. Standard barrel markings "Patent Arms M'g Co. Paterson N-J. Colt's Pt." The square backed cylinder is seen less often than the more common round back, both bearing the Centaur scene with four horse head trademark and "COLT," with both Belt Models, revolvers exhibiting attached loading levers are less common than those without a lever. Mfg. 1837-40.

✳ *Standard Model w/o Lever* - without attached loading lever.

N/A	N/A	$37,000	$29,250	$22,500	$19,450	$15,300	$13,250	$11,750	$10,250	$9,000	$8,000

✳ *Standard Model With Lever* - with attached loading lever and recoil shield milled for ease of capping (scarce).

N/A	N/A	$40,600	$33,500	$27,150	$23,500	$20,150	$17,500	$15,250	$13,500	$12,000	$10,750

HOLSTER MODEL NO. 5 - also known as "Texas Paterson" - .36 cal., 5 shot, 4 in. to 12 in. octagon barrels, blue metal with case hardened frame and hammer. All cylinders bear the stage coach hold-up scene. Varnished walnut grips of flared bottom style. Serial range 1 to approx. 1,000. As with all models of Patersons, the serial number usually cannot be seen without disassembly of the revolver. Very large and heavy compared to the other Paterson models. Enjoys more popularity with collectors because of its military and frontier use. Mfg. 1838-40.

100%	98%	95%	90%	80%	70%	60%	50%	40%	30%	20%	10%

Many specimens encountered in this variation show extreme use. Consequently, fine to mint specimens are quite rare and highly prized by collectors. Values are given for non-military marked specimens. Any specimen bearing an authenticated martial marking is truly a rarity and should be appraised individually. NOTE: Watch for fakes here. There are now many times more faked martial markings, often times on non-original Patersons, than there are originals.

* **Standard Production Model w/o Lever** - without attached loading lever, round or square backed cylinder.

N/A	N/A	$152,000	$113,250	$87,000	$69,500	$58,150	$49,000	$42,000	$37,000	$32,500	$28,000

* **Standard Production Model With Lever** - with attached loading lever, round backed cylinder and recoil shield milled for ease of capping.

N/A	N/A	$164,500	$119,000	$93,500	$77,000	$64,775	$55,000	$47,500	$41,500	$37,000	$32,500

Revolvers: Percussion, Walker Model

WALKER MODEL REVOLVER - .44 cal., 6 shot, 9 in. part round, part octagon barrel, blue metal with case hardened frame, lever and hammer. Cylinder left without finish, brass trigger guard. One piece walnut grips. Mfg. 1847; total production approx. 1,100. Ser. numbers beginning with no. 1 were applied for each of five different military companies (A,B,C,D, & E). The total for the military issue Walkers was approx. 1,000 revolvers; the remaining approx. 100 revolvers were produced for civilian distribution. Barrels marked "Address SamL Colt New-York City," found on right side of barrel lug is "US" over "1847," cylinder bears Texas Ranger/Indian fight scene. Various metal parts and walnut grips stamped with Govt. Inspectors'. marks.

Because of these arms being subjected to great extremes of use, they will exhibit high degrees of wear, often to the extent that most or all markings will be worn off. Replaced parts are common and many badly worn and damaged specimens have been extensively rebuilt and restored. NOTE: Use great caution when contemplating the purchase of a Walker. A multitude of out-and-out fakes and "antiqued" reproduction Walkers have been fed into the market over the past few decades. Some of these are old enough (and have aged enough naturally) to almost resemble an authentic specimen. Enlist the services of a qualified expert before your dollars are spent. Only 10-12% of the original production of approx. 1,100 specimens have been accounted for. The acquisition of an authenticated Walker revolver is the ultimate goal of serious Colt collectors.

* **Standard Military Issue Model**

N/A	N/A	N/A	$272,000	$195,000	$160,000	$134,000	$100,000	$87,500	$77,500	$67,500	$57,500

* **Limited Civilian Issue Model** - serial range 1001 to approx. 1100. Similar to military model except Govt. inspectors' marks were not applied. Pricing is difficult on the civilian issue arms. They tend to be in considerably better condition than the much more common military specimens. The factors of scarcity and condition will often bring higher prices from the advanced collector of means, especially in the finer grades of condition. On the other hand, the collector appreciating military usage will pay more for military marked examples. This publication tries to reflect the latest trends on purchase of civilian models.

N/A	N/A	N/A	$267,000	$193,000	$155,000	$130,000	$96,000	$85,000	$75,000	$65,000	$50,000

Revolvers: Percussion, Dragoon Series

WHITNEYVILLE HARTFORD DRAGOON - .44 cal., 6 shot, 7 1/2 in. part octagon, part round barrel, some of the left-over Walker parts were used in Dragoons, blue metal with case hardened frame, lever, hammer, brass trigger guard and steel cylinder bears Texas Ranger and Indian battle scene. Mfg. 1847. Total production approx. 240. Serial range approx. 1,100 to 1,340 in sequence following civilian Walkers.

* **Rear frame cut out for grips**

N/A	N/A	$146,500	$115,250	$91,000	$75,000	$63,000	$53,000	$47,000	$42,000	$38,000	$35,000

100%	98%	95%	90%	80%	70%	60%	50%	40%	30%	20%	10%

* Straight rear frame

100%	98%	95%	90%	80%	70%	60%	50%	40%	30%	20%	10%
N/A	N/A	$108,000	$80,000	$57,000	$48,500	$38,000	$30,000	$25,000	$22,000	$20,000	$18,500

FIRST MODEL DRAGOON - .44 cal., 6 shot, 7 1/2 in. round and octagon barrel, blue metal with case hardened frame, lever, hammer, brass grip straps, silvered straps for civilian market, serial range numbered after Hartford Dragoon, 1341 to around 8000. Mfg. 1848-50. Total production approx. 7,000. Oval cyl. slots, square back trigger guard, Texas Ranger and Indian fight scene on cylinder.

* Military Model

100%	98%	95%	90%	80%	70%	60%	50%	40%	30%	20%	10%
N/A	N/A	$52,150	$42,000	$29,500	$22,000	$17,075	$14,250	$11,000	$9,000	$8,000	$7,000

* Civilian Model

100%	98%	95%	90%	80%	70%	60%	50%	40%	30%	20%	10%
N/A	N/A	$43,500	$28,250	$23,500	$18,000	$13,750	$10,500	$8,000	$6,500	$6,000	$5,500

FLUCK MODEL DRAGOON - basically a First Model Dragoon, with 7 1/2 in. altered Walker barrels and fully martially marked, should be extensively checked over, used to replace defective Walkers. Mfg. 1848. Total production 300. Serial range approx. 2,216 to 2,515.

100%	98%	95%	90%	80%	70%	60%	50%	40%	30%	20%	10%
N/A	N/A	$48,900	$37,750	$32,000	$24,000	$19,375	$17,000	$15,000	$11,000	$10,000	$9,500

SECOND MODEL DRAGOON - .44 cal., 6 shot, 7 1/2 in. round and octagon barrel, serial range following the First Model Dragoon 8,000-10,700. Mfg. 1850-51. Texas Ranger and Indian fight scene on cylinder.

* Military Model

100%	98%	95%	90%	80%	70%	60%	50%	40%	30%	20%	10%
N/A	N/A	$42,375	$33,000	$25,250	$18,750	$15,050	$12,000	$10,000	$8,500	$7,500	$6,500

* Civilian Model

100%	98%	95%	90%	80%	70%	60%	50%	40%	30%	20%	10%
N/A	N/A	$37,500	$28,000	$21,500	$17,750	$14,000	$11,500	$9,500	$7,750	$6,500	$5,500

* New Hampshire or Massachusetts - notice state markings on front portion of trigger guard.

100%	98%	95%	90%	80%	70%	60%	50%	40%	30%	20%	10%
N/A	N/A	$46,175	$34,350	$26,500	$20,500	$16,075	$13,250	$11,250	$9,500	$8,500	$7,750

THIRD MODEL DRAGOON - .44 cal., 6 shot, 7 1/2 in. round or octagon barrel, same basic features as earlier models, but with round trigger guard and rectangular cylinder slots, serial range approx. 10,200-19,600, some overlapping of numbers, with approx. 10,500 mfg. from 1851-61. Texas Ranger and Indian fight scene on cylinder.

* Third Model Dragoon

100%	98%	95%	90%	80%	70%	60%	50%	40%	30%	20%	10%
N/A	N/A	$35,300	$23,850	$15,650	$13,000	$10,450	$8,900	$7,800	$6,900	$6,250	$5,750

* Martially marked U.S.

100%	98%	95%	90%	80%	70%	60%	50%	40%	30%	20%	10%
N/A	N/A	$38,000	$27,250	$21,000	$15,500	$13,000	$11,000	$9,500	$8,250	$7,250	$6,500

* Third Model - 8 in. barrel.

100%	98%	95%	90%	80%	70%	60%	50%	40%	30%	20%	10%
N/A	N/A	$40,250	$32,500	$28,750	$23,700	$19,900	$16,500	$14,000	$11,500	$9,500	$8,000

* First and Second Variation - shoulder stock model.

100%	98%	95%	90%	80%	70%	60%	50%	40%	30%	20%	10%
N/A	N/A	$40,750	$31,450	$24,450	$20,000	$17,000	$14,000	$11,750	$9,750	$8,250	$7,250

* Third Variation

100%	98%	95%	90%	80%	70%	60%	50%	40%	30%	20%	10%
N/A	N/A	$39,125	$31,000	$23,000	$19,500	$16,075	$13,250	$11,000	$9,000	$7,500	$6,500

* C.L. Dragoon

100%	98%	95%	90%	80%	70%	60%	50%	40%	30%	20%	10%
N/A	N/A	$52,700	$39,750	$30,250	$25,250	$21,250	$17,250	$14,750	$12,500	$10,500	$8,500

ENGLISH HARTFORD DRAGOON - basically a Third Model Dragoon, assembled at Colt's London factory, with unique serial range 1-700, some were assembled from earlier parts inventories, easy to spot with British proofs of crown over V and crown over GP, the blue was of the English type, many were engraved.

100%	98%	95%	90%	80%	70%	60%	50%	40%	30%	20%	10%
N/A	N/A	$34,250	$23,950	$17,250	$13,750	$11,150	$9,300	$8,200	$7,300	$6,600	$6,000

1848 BABY DRAGOONS - .31 cal., 5 shot, 3, 4, 5, or 6 in. octagon barrels, most without loading lever, serial range 1-15,500, a scaled down version of the .44 caliber Dragoons, early ones with Texas Ranger scene and later ones with the holdup scene.

100%	98%	95%	90%	80%	70%	60%	50%	40%	30%	20%	10%

* *Type I* - left-hand barrel stamping, Texas Ranger and Indian scene, approx. serial range 1-150.

| N/A | N/A | $16,300 | $12,750 | $10,450 | $9,000 | $7,750 | $6,500 | $5,750 | $5,250 | $4,850 | $4,350 |

* *Type II* - with Texas Ranger and Indian scene, 11,600 serial range, without loading lever.

| N/A | N/A | $12,500 | $8,950 | $7,600 | $6,000 | $4,850 | $3,950 | $3,300 | $3,000 | $2,800 | $2,600 |

* *Type III* - with Stagecoach scene and oval cylinder slots, serial range 10,400-12,000.

| N/A | N/A | $12,500 | $8,950 | $7,600 | $6,000 | $4,850 | $3,950 | $3,300 | $3,000 | $2,800 | $2,600 |

* *Type IV* - with Stagecoach holdup scene, rectangle cylinder slots, serial range 11,000-12,500.

| N/A | N/A | $12,500 | $8,950 | $7,600 | $6,000 | $4,850 | $3,950 | $3,300 | $3,000 | $2,800 | $2,600 |

* *Type V* - with Stagecoach holdup scene, rectangle cylinder slots and loading lever, serial range 11,600-15,500.

| N/A | N/A | $13,150 | $9,150 | $7,750 | $5,700 | $4,700 | $3,900 | $3,300 | $2,950 | $2,650 | $2,350 |

Revolvers: Percussion, Models 1849, 1851, 1855, 1860, 1861, & 1862

1849 POCKET MODEL - .31 cal., 5 or 6 shot, 3, 4, 5, and 6 in. octagon barrels, most with loading levers, blue metal with case hardened frame, lever and hammer, grip straps of brass (silver plated), or steel (silver plated or blue), stagecoach hold-up scene on cylinder, serial range 12,000 to 340,000. Mfg. 1850-73.

* *First Type* - 4, 5, or 6 in. barrel, loading lever and small or large brass trigger guard.

| N/A | N/A | $3,550 | $2,750 | $2,125 | $1,700 | $1,375 | $1,000 | $750 | $600 | $550 | $475 |

* *Second Type* - 4, 5, or 6 in. barrel, loading lever and steel grip straps.

| N/A | N/A | $4,275 | $3,350 | $2,550 | $2,000 | $1,675 | $1,150 | $850 | $700 | $650 | $575 |

* *Wells Fargo Model* - 3 in. barrel, without loading lever and with small round trigger guard.

| N/A | N/A | $11,275 | $8,025 | $5,565 | $3,875 | $2,700 | $2,000 | $1,700 | $1,525 | $1,375 | $1,150 |

1849 LONDON POCKET MODEL - London pistols were of the same general configuration, but of better finish, serial range 1-11,000. Mfg. 1853-57.

* *Early Type* - serial numbered under 1500, with small trigger guard and brass grip straps.

| N/A | N/A | $5,725 | $4,675 | $3,800 | $3,025 | $2,400 | $1,850 | $1,450 | $1,150 | $1,000 | $875 |

* *Late Type* - oval trigger guard and steel grip straps.

| N/A | N/A | $3,675 | $2,900 | $2,350 | $1,900 | $1,500 | $1,175 | $950 | $825 | $725 | $625 |

1851 NAVY - .36 cal., 6 shot, 7 1/2 in. octagon barrel and loading lever, blue metal with case hardened frame, lever and hammer, one piece walnut finished grips, cylinder scene of Texas Navy battle with Mexico, serial range 1-highest recorded number was 215,348, three barrel addresses 1-74,000 (ADDRESS SAML COLT, NEW YORK CITY), 74,000-101,000 (ADDRESS SAML COLT, HARTFORD, CT.) 101,000-215,348 (ADDRESS COL. SAML COLT, NEW YORK, U.S. AMERICA). Mfg. 1850-73.

* *First Model* - square back trigger guard, bottom wedge screw, serial range 1-1,250.

| N/A | N/A | $22,575 | $18,475 | $14,875 | $12,375 | $9,385 | $7,700 | $6,300 | $5,200 | $4,400 | $3,400 |

* *Second Model* - square back trigger guard, top wedge screw, serial range 1,250-4,000.

| N/A | N/A | $14,700 | $10,250 | $8,000 | $6,650 | $5,560 | $4,600 | $3,900 | $3,300 | $2,800 | $2,300 |

* *Third Model* - small round brass trigger guard, serial range 4,200-85,000.

| N/A | N/A | $6,925 | $5,525 | $4,275 | $3,500 | $2,850 | $2,300 | $1,900 | $1,550 | $1,250 | $995 |

100%	98%	95%	90%	80%	70%	60%	50%	40%	30%	20%	10%

❋ *Fourth Model* - large round brass trigger guard, serial range 85,000-215,348.

100%	98%	95%	90%	80%	70%	60%	50%	40%	30%	20%	10%
N/A	N/A	$6,175	$5,025	$4,135	$3,275	$2,650	$2,125	$1,750	$1,425	$1,175	$900

❋ *Iron Gripstrap Model* - most often seen in fourth model.

N/A	N/A	$7,775	$6,300	$5,125	$4,300	$3,500	$2,750	$2,200	$1,750	$1,425	$1,125

❋ *Martially Marked U.S. Navys* - brass or iron gripstrap.

N/A	N/A	$11,300	$7,875	$6,250	$4,900	$3,825	$2,900	$2,325	$1,875	$1,500	$1,200

❋ *Cut for shoulder stock* - first and second type (like third model Dragoon).

N/A	N/A	$14,175	$9,450	$7,275	$5,675	$4,600	$3,750	$3,000	$2,450	$1,950	$1,475

❋ *Third Type* - four screw frame.

N/A	N/A	$9,075	$7,600	$6,250	$5,000	$3,925	$3,100	$2,500	$2,000	$1,650	$1,325

51 NAVY LONDON MODEL - basically the same gun as the Hartford piece with London barrel address, with British proof marks in serial range 1-42,000. Mfg. 1853-57.

❋ *Early First Model* - serial range below 2000, brass grip straps and small trigger guard.

N/A	N/A	$7,875	$6,300	$5,225	$4,350	$3,550	$2,800	$2,250	$1,800	$1,475	$1,175

❋ *Late Second Model* - balance of production, large round trigger guard, steel grip straps, all London parts.

N/A	N/A	$7,275	$5,900	$4,925	$4,100	$3,350	$2,575	$2,000	$1,650	$1,375	$1,100

1855 SIDEHAMMER POCKET MODEL (ROOT MODEL) - .28 cal., had 3 1/2 in. octagon barrel, .31 cal. usually had 3 1/2 in. or 4 1/2 in. round barrel. Blue with case hardened lever and hammer, one piece wraparound style walnut grips.

Commonly called the "Root" Model by collectors, manufactured 1855 through 1870. The .28 cal. model serial numbered 1 through approx. 30,000. The .31 cal. round barrel model serial numbered 1 through approx. 14,000. Total production approx. 44,000.

Easily recognizable by its side mounted hammer and cylinder rotation ratchet at rear of frame.

❋ *Model 1 and 1A* - .28 cal., 3 7/16 in. octagonal bbl., oct. load lever, Indian/cabin cyl. scene, Hartford barrel address. Serial range 1 to 384.

N/A	N/A	$6,050	$3,885	$3,225	$2,775	$2,350	$2,000	$1,825	$1,650	$1,400	$1,100

❋ *Model 2* - .28 cal., 3 1/2 in. oct. bbl., Indian/cabin cyl. scene, Hartford barrel address with pointed hand. Serial range 476 to 25,000.

N/A	N/A	$2,250	$1,400	$1,075	$900	$775	$665	$595	$535	$485	$425

❋ *Model 3* - .28 cal., 3 1/2 in. oct. bbl., full fluted cylinder, Hartford barrel address with pointed hand. Serial range 25,001 to 30,000.

N/A	N/A	$2,275	$1,450	$1,100	$950	$850	$750	$650	$585	$535	$485

❋ *Model 3A* - .31 cal., 3 1/2 in. oct. bbl., full fluted cylinder, Hartford barrel address. Serial range 1 to 1,350.

N/A	N/A	$2,325	$1,375	$1,150	$995	$895	$775	$675	$595	$535	$485

❋ *Model 4* - .31 cal., 3 1/2 in. oct. bbl., full fluted cylinder, Hartford barrel address. Serial range 1,351 to 2,400.

N/A	N/A	$2,325	$1,375	$1,150	$995	$895	$775	$675	$595	$535	$485

❋ *Model 5* - .31 cal., 3 1/2 in. round bbl., full fluted cylinder, "COL. COLT NEW-YORK" barrel address. Serial range 2,401 to 8,000.

N/A	N/A	$2,325	$1,375	$1,150	$995	$895	$775	$675	$595	$535	$485

❋ *Model 5A* - .31 cal., 4 1/2 in. round bbl., included in same serial range as Model 5.

N/A	N/A	$3,675	$2,200	$1,825	$1,400	$1,225	$1,075	$975	$875	$775	$695

❋ *Model 6* - .31 cal., 3 1/2 in. round bbl., stage coach hold-up cylinder scene, "COL. COLT NEW-YORK" barrel address. Serial range 8,001 through 11,074.

N/A	N/A	$2,325	$1,375	$1,150	$995	$895	$775	$675	$595	$535	$485

100%	98%	95%	90%	80%	70%	60%	50%	40%	30%	20%	10%

✳ **Model 6A** - .31 cal., 4 1/2 in. round bbl., included in same serial range as Model 6.

| N/A | N/A | $2,325 | $1,375 | $1,150 | $995 | $895 | $775 | $675 | $595 | $535 | $485 |

✳ **Model 7** - .31 cal., 3 1/2 in. round bbl., stage coach hold-up cylinder scene, "COL. COLT NEW-YORK" barrel address. Cylinder pin retained by screw-in cylinder. Serial range 11,075 through 14,000.

| N/A | N/A | $3,375 | $1,925 | $1,400 | $1,225 | $1,125 | $995 | $900 | $800 | $725 | $650 |

✳ **Model 7A** - .31 cal., 4 1/2 in. round bbl., including same cylinder scene, barrel address and serial range as Model 7.

| N/A | N/A | $4,225 | $2,600 | $1,825 | $1,400 | $1,275 | $1,150 | $1,025 | $925 | $825 | $750 |

1860 MODEL ARMY - .44 cal., 6 shot, 7 1/2 and 8 in. round barrels with loading lever, blue metal with case hardened frame, lever and hammer, one piece walnut grips, normally blue steel back strap and brass trigger guard, barrel markings were "ADDRESS SAM COLT, HARTFORD, CT." on early productions and "ADDRESS COL. SAM COLT, NEW YORK, U.S. AMERICA" on balance, serial range 1-about 200,500, Texas Navy scene on round cylinder model. Mfg. 1860-73.

✳ **Fluted Cylinder Model** - Fluted Cylinder Model, full length cylinder flutes and no cylinder scene, 7 1/2 or 8 in. barrel, grips of Navy (very rare) or Army size, usually 4 screw frames.

| N/A | N/A | $13,650 | $10,400 | $8,075 | $6,650 | $5,500 | $4,550 | $3,850 | $3,250 | $2,750 | $2,350 |

✳ **Round Cylinder Model** - roll engraved Texas Navy scene, some with early Hartford address, Army grips, four screw frame to about 50,000 range, most were sold to the U.S. Government and will be martially marked.

| N/A | N/A | $10,175 | $7,625 | $6,250 | $5,000 | $3,925 | $3,100 | $2,500 | $2,000 | $1,650 | $1,375 |

✳ **Civilian Model** - same general configurations as Round Cylinder Model, but with 3 screw frame, no shoulder stock cuts and better blue finish than military pieces, late New York barrel address.

| N/A | N/A | $9,975 | $6,950 | $5,600 | $4,525 | $3,600 | $2,825 | $2,275 | $1,850 | $1,500 | $1,225 |

1861 MODEL NAVY - .36 cal., 6 shot, 7 1/2 in. round barrel with loading lever, blue metal with case hardened frame, lever and hammer, silver plated brass grip straps, the barrel address was "ADDRESS COL. SAM COLT, NEW YORK, U.S. AMERICA", serial range 1-38,843, cylinder scene of Texas Navy and Mexico Battle, mfg. 1861-73.

✳ **Fluted Cylinder Navy** - in serial range 1-100, with fluted cylinder and without rolled cylinder scene.

| N/A | N/A | $28,100 | $20,750 | $16,900 | $13,650 | $10,975 | $8,750 | $7,250 | $6,250 | $5,550 | $4,875 |

✳ **Regular production model**

| N/A | N/A | $11,550 | $8,725 | $6,350 | $5,100 | $4,000 | $3,275 | $2,600 | $2,150 | $1,725 | $1,475 |

✳ **Martially Marked Navys** - will bear the U.S. stamp and inspector's marks, those marked U.S.N. on butt were of a 650 piece order for the Navy.

| N/A | N/A | $13,125 | $9,025 | $6,875 | $5,100 | $4,125 | $3,350 | $2,775 | $2,300 | $1,900 | $1,550 |

✳ **London Marked Navy** - with "ADDRESS COL. COLT, LONDON", for barrel address.

| N/A | N/A | $9,925 | $7,900 | $6,175 | $4,925 | $3,975 | $3,225 | $2,675 | $2,225 | $1,850 | $1,475 |

✳ **Shoulder Stock Cut Navy** - 4 screw frames in serial range 11,000-14,000, made for third style stock (see Dragoon stocks).

| N/A | N/A | $17,325 | $11,025 | $8,320 | $6,700 | $5,600 | $4,650 | $3,950 | $3,350 | $2,850 | $2,375 |

1862 POLICE MODEL - .36 cal., 5 shot half fluted and rebated cylinder, 4 1/2, 5 1/2, and 6 1/2 in. round barrels (also 3 1/2 in. bbl. but quite rare) and loading lever. Mfg. 1861-73. Serial numbered with Model 1862 Pocket Navy, approx. 28,000 1862 Police Models were produced. Blue with case hardened frame, lever and hammer, grip straps silver plated, one piece walnut grips. Serial range 1 through approx. 47,000. Standard barrel marking "ADDRESS COL. SAML COLT NEW-YORK U.S. AMERICA" "COLTS/PATENT" on left side of frame, "PAT SEPT. 10TH 1850" stamped in cyl. flute.

100%	98%	95%	90%	80%	70%	60%	50%	40%	30%	20%	10%

Many Model 1862 Police and 1862 Pocket Navy revolvers were converted to cartridge with the advent of the metallic cartridge. Consequently these models in their original cap and ball chambering are quite desirable to collectors.

* ❉ *Early Model* - "ADDRESS SAM COLT/HARTFORD CT" barrel address, silvered iron grip straps.

N/A	N/A	$10,175	$6,825	$5,300	$4,375	$3,525	$2,750	$2,200	$1,750	$1,375	$1,075

* ❉ *Early Model* - same but silvered brass grip straps.

N/A	N/A	$9,450	$6,450	$4,950	$3,975	$3,075	$2,300	$1,875	$1,535	$1,235	$1,000

* ❉ *Standard Production Model* - with New York barrel address.

N/A	N/A	$8,400	$4,425	$3,225	$2,475	$2,025	$1,675	$1,400	$1,175	$925	$775

* ❉ *Export Production Model* - with "L" below serial numbers (for export to England), steel grip straps. Most often but not always bearing British proofs.

N/A	N/A	$8,925	$4,700	$3,450	$2,675	$2,175	$1,810	$1,525	$1,275	$1,050	$875

* ❉ *London Marked Model* - similar to above, except with "ADDRESS, COL. COLT/LONDON" address on barrel.

N/A	N/A	$12,075	$8,925	$6,750	$5,250	$4,125	$3,250	$2,750	$2,400	$2,150	$1,800

1862 POCKET MODEL NAVY (1865 POCKET PISTOL) - .36 cal., 5 shot rebated cylinder, 4 1/2 in., 5 1/2 in., and 6 1/2 in. octagonal barrels with loading lever. Mfg. 1861-73. Serial numbered with Model 1862 Police Model, approx. 19,000 Model 1862 Pocket Navy Revolvers produced. Blue with case hardened frame, lever and hammer, grip straps silver plated brass, one piece walnut grips. Serial range 1 through approx. 47,000. Standard barrel markings "ADDRESS COL. SAML COLT NEW-YORK U.S. AMERICA" "COLTS/PATENT" on left side of frame, stage coach hold-up scene on cylinder.

This model has been identified for decades to collectors as the Model 1853 or the Model 1862 Pocket Model Navy. Recent research indicates that a more correct model name for this revolver is the 1865 Pocket Pistol.

Because of being produced during the advent of the metallic cartridge, the number remaining in the original cap and ball configuration is rather few; scarce with any serial number, but particularly so in numbers over approx. 19,800.

* ❉ *Standard Model* - 4 1/2, 5 1/2 and 6 1/2 in. barrel lengths.

N/A	N/A	$8,925	$6,475	$4,950	$3,975	$3,075	$2,300	$1,875	$1,535	$1,235	$1,000

* ❉ *Export Production Model* - with "L" below serial numbers (for export to England), steel grip straps. Often found with British proofs.

N/A	N/A	$9,450	$7,875	$6,250	$4,900	$3,850	$3,025	$2,475	$2,000	$1,650	$1,375

* ❉ *London Marked Model* - similar to above but "ADDRESS COL. COLT/LONDON" address on barrel.

N/A	N/A	$14,900	$11,200	$8,575	$6,750	$5,625	$4,650	$3,950	$3,350	$2,850	$2,375

REVOLVERS: PERCUSSION CONVERSIONS

Colt Thuer Conversions

COLT THUER CONVERSIONS (c. 1868-1872) - .31, .36, and .44 CF cal., less than 5,000 produced in all models. This was Colt's first commercial attempt at converting percussion revolvers to fire fixed ammo. Standard features: usually threaded inside rammer for a Thuer loading tool, a hardened flat face on hammer, deepened loading cutout on right side of lug, Thuer ring and back of cylinder have matching assembly numbers. Beware of fakes! Only non-experimental Colt models are listed. Rarity by barrel length will not be considered here. Serial numbers are often missing on cylinder.

Prices for Colt Conversions reflect values for blue and case hardened examples. Nickel plated specimens are rarely seen, but typically sell for 20%-40% less than blue finish.

Any defects, excessive wear, or dulled blue will affect value. Nickeled conversions that have lost their translucence (become cloudy) should be discounted more than usual 20%-40% from blue and case hardened examples, especially on near-mint to mint specimens.

100%	98%	95%	90%	80%	70%	60%	50%	40%	30%	20%	10%
✳ *1849 Pocket*											
$25,000	$22,500	$17,500	$15,000	$13,000	$11,000	$9,500	$8,500	$7,500	$6,750	$6,000	$5,000
✳ *1851 Navy*											
$23,000	$21,000	$16,000	$14,000	$12,000	$10,000	$8,500	$7,750	$7,000	$6,500	$5,750	$4,750
✳ *1860 Army* - the most common Thuer, but popular because it's a large frame model.											
$27,000	$24,000	$19,000	$16,000	$14,000	$12,000	$11,000	$10,000	$9,500	$8,500	$7,500	$6,500
✳ *1861 Navy*											
$25,000	$22,500	$19,000	$16,000	$14,000	$11,000	$9,500	$8,500	$7,500	$6,700	$6,000	$5,000
✳ *1862 Police*											
$20,000	$18,000	$15,000	$13,000	$11,000	$8,500	$7,500	$6,750	$6,000	$5,500	$5,000	$4,500
✳ *1862 Pocket Navy*											
$20,000	$18,000	$15,000	$13,000	$11,000	$8,500	$7,500	$6,750	$6,000	$5,500	$5,000	$4,500

Richards Conversions: All Variations

RICHARDS CONVERSION, COLT 1860 ARMY REVOLVER - .44 CF cal., produced circa 1870s, special machining to barrel and breech of cylinder for conversion to a cartridge weapon. Produced in two serial ranges: one numbered under 10,000 and a separate group generally in the 190,000 to 200,000 range.

✳ *1860 Army First Model Richards* - quick ID: integral rear sight on breech plate. Floating firing pin in breechplate. Front edge of barrel lug is same as 1860 percussion Army. Breechplate extends over rear edge of cylinder.

$24,000	$20,000	$16,000	$13,000	$9,000	$7,000	$6,000	$5,250	$4,500	$4,000	$3,500	$3,000

✳ *1860 Army Second Model Richards* - quick ID: standard Richards type barrel. A space between face of conversion ring and rear of cylinder when viewed from the side. No integral sight on breechplate, cut away at top allowing hammer to directly strike the cartridge.

$24,000	$22,000	$17,000	$14,500	$9,500	$7,500	$6,500	$6,000	$5,250	$4,500	$4,000	$3,500

✳ *1860 Army Twelve Stop Cylinder Variation Richards* - quick ID: generally the same as standard model Richards except cylinder has extra "safety" notches between the locking notches. This variation was usually produced in the 100-300, 1,000-1,700 and 200,000 serial ranges. Cylinder locking notches over chambers often broken through. Watch for alterations.

$27,500	$24,000	$19,000	$15,000	$12,500	$8,500	$7,000	$6,500	$6,000	$5,500	$5,000	$4,500

✳ *1860 Army U.S. Marked Richards* - quick ID: generally the same as 1st Model Richards (many minor differences). Has "U.S." stamped on left barrel lug and "A" (Ainsworth) inspector marks in several places. They are converted 1860 percussion Armys, so original numbers are typically in 23,000-144,000 range plus a second set of assembly numbers. Oiled grips, military soft blue finish.

$30,000	$27,000	$22,500	$17,500	$13,000	$9,500	$7,750	$7,000	$6,500	$6,000	$5,500	$4,500

Richards-Mason Conversions: All Variations

1860 ARMY RICHARDS-MASON - .44 CF cal., overall, much rarer than Richards Army Conversions, circa 1870s, approximately 2100 produced. A rare variation has an 1860 Army rebated cylinder and a barrel with a lug shaped similar to 1861 Navy Conversion.

✳ *1860 Army Richards-Mason* - quick ID: breechplate without integral rear sight, cutout at top so hammer can strike primer directly. A space can be seen between breechplate and rear of cylinder. Rear of lug is a vertical line instead of the bullet shape cutout seen on Richards models.

$25,000	$20,000	$15,000	$12,500	$9,000	$8,000	$7,500	$7,000	$6,250	$5,500	$4,500	$3,750

100%	98%	95%	90%	80%	70%	60%	50%	40%	30%	20%	10%

1851 NAVY RICHARDS-MASON - .38 CF and RF cal., circa 1870s. Produced in two different serial ranges. Has improved Richards-Mason breechplate that is flush with diameter of recoil shield. Difficult to locate in prime condition.

❊ *1851 Navy Civilian Model Richards-Mason* - quick ID: Richards-Mason breechplate which is same diameter as recoil shield, octagon barrel, mirrored civilian blue. Nickel finish commonly seen.

$11,000	$10,000	$7,500	$6,500	$5,500	$4,500	$4,000	$3,500	$3,000	$2,500	$2,000	$1,500

❊ *1851 U.S. Navy Richards-Mason* - quick ID: Richards-Mason breechplate, oiled grips, soft blue military finish, produced in US. percussion range of 40,000-90,000 ranges. Inconsistent "U.S.N." and other inspector markings. Iron straps, "U.S." on frame.

$15,000	$13,000	$10,000	$7,500	$6,000	$5,000	$4,500	$4,000	$3,500	$3,000	$2,250	$1,750

1861 NAVY RICHARDS-MASON - produced in civilian and military versions, circa 1870s, made in RF and CF cal. in two serial ranges. Round 7 1/2 in. barrel.

❊ *1861 Navy Civilian Model Richards-Mason* - quick ID: Richards-Mason breechplate, round 7 1/2 in. barrel with attached ejector housing, unrebated cylinder. When blue, has a commercial high gloss finish.

$13,000	$11,000	$8,500	$6,500	$4,750	$4,250	$3,750	$3,400	$3,000	$2,400	$2,000	$1,500

❊ *1861 Navy U.S. Navy Richards-Mason* - soft military blue finish, oiled grips, converted from percussion U.S. Navy revolvers, inconsistent military markings, centerfire, set of extra serial numbers often seen on cylinder.

$17,500	$15,000	$11,000	$8,500	$5,500	$5,000	$4,500	$4,000	$3,500	$3,000	$2,500	$2,000

COLT 1862 POLICE & POCKET NAVY RICHARDS-MASON CONVERSIONS (circa 1870s) - .38 RF and CF cal., parts for 1862 Police, 1862 Pocket Navy, as well as 1849 Pockets are often intermixed. As parts bins were depleted, Colt used whatever components that would fit, resulting in a tremendous amount of minor variations. Some barrels were converted from percussion models while others were newly made as cartridge barrels without rammer plugs and loading slots in the lug. There are three different serial ranges (1849, 1862 Police/Pocket Navy, Conversion). 3 1/2 to 6 1/2 in. barrels, again not all features available on all models.

Nickel plated conversions will bring 20%-40% less than blue and case hardened specimens.

❊ *4 1/2 in. Octagon Barrel Model* - quick ID: 4 1/2 in. octagon barrel without ejector. Rebated Pocket Navy Cylinder.

$7,000	$6,000	$5,000	$4,000	$3,000	$2,500	$1,750	$1,350	$1,150	$950	$750	$650

❊ *Round (Percussion) Barrel Pocket Navy with Ejector* - quick ID: plug in rammer slot; ejector housing, loading cutout in right side of lug, barrel remachined from Pocket Navy percussion barrel, Pocket Navy rebated cylinder. Similar appearance to cartridge barrel variation.

$7,250	$6,250	$5,250	$4,250	$3,000	$2,500	$2,000	$1,750	$1,500	$1,200	$1,000	$850

1862 POLICE AND POCKET (1865 POCKET MODEL) NAVY CONVERSION - 4 1/2, 5 1/2, or 6 1/2 in. barrels with 1862 Police percussion profile and added ejector housing. Has rebated Pocket Navy cylinder or rarer half fluted 1862 Police cylinder. 6 1/2 in. barrel will bring a premium.

❊ *1862 Police/Pocket Navy with Rebated Pocket Navy Cylinder* - quick ID: 1862 Police profile barrel with ejector housing and rebated 1862 Pocket Navy cylinder.

$7,500	$6,500	$4,500	$4,000	$2,750	$2,250	$1,750	$1,400	$1,100	$900	$650	$550

❊ *1862 Police/Pocket Navy with Half Fluted Cylinder* - quick ID: 1862 Police profile barrel with ejector housing and 1/2 fluted Police cylinder.

$9,000	$7,500	$5,000	$4,500	$3,250	$2,750	$2,000	$1,600	$1,300	$1,100	$850	$700

100%	98%	95%	90%	80%	70%	60%	50%	40%	30%	20%	10%

Conversions with Round Cartridge Barrel

ROUND CARTRIDGE BARREL WITH EJECTOR - .38 RF and CF cal. 4 1/2, 5 1/2, or 6 1/2 in. barrels produced as a cartridge component without rammer slots and lug cutouts inherent to a percussion barrel.

❋ *1862 Pocket Navy Round Cartridge Barrel* - quick ID: much shorter lug area than similar model converted from percussion barrel. No slots or loading cutouts on barrel. With ejector housing and Pocket Navy rebated cylinder. Often called the "Baby Open Top," very scarce.

$9,500	$7,250	$5,750	$5,000	$4,250	$3,250	$2,800	$2,500	$2,000	$1,750	$1,450	$1,250

3 1/2 IN. ROUND CARTRIDGE BARREL CONVERSION - .38 RF or CF cal., sometimes seen with serial numbers that are from 1849 Pocket Model (300,000 range). Barrel newly made for cartridges, not converted from a percussion barrel.

❋ *3 1/2 in. Round Cartridge Barrel* - quick ID: only type conversion with 3 1/2 in. barrel. No ejector, no loading lever slot or loading cutout in lug area. Pocket Navy rebated cylinder.

$5,000	$4,000	$2,400	$1,800	$1,400	$1,100	$975	$875	$800	$700	$600	$500

REVOLVERS: "OPEN TOP" MODELS

If possible, it is advisable to procure a factory letter before buying/selling this Open Top Revolver. These watermarked letters are available by writing Colt Archive Properties LLC in Hartford, CT, with a charge of $200 or more per serial number (if they can research it). Send your name and address, Colt model name, serial number, and check or credit card information to: COLT ARCHIVE PROPERTIES LLC, P.O. Box 1868, Hartford, CT 06144-1868. Please allow 90-120 days for a response.

1871-72 OPEN TOP MODEL RIMFIRE - .44 cal. rimfire, 6 shot, 7 1/2 in. barrel, without frame topstrap, blue metal with casehardened hammer, serial range 1-approx. 7,000, barrel address "ADDRESS COL. SAM COLT, NEW YORK, U.S. AMERICA", forerunner of the single action Army, quite desirable. Mfg. 1871-72.

> **Add 20% for blue finish on models listed below.**

❋ *Regular Production Model* - 7 1/2 in. barrel, New York address, Navy grips.

N/A	N/A	$27,500	$22,750	$18,500	$15,000	$12,750	$8,750	$6,750	$6,000	$5,300	$4,850

❋ *Regular Production* - with Army grips.

N/A	N/A	$24,000	$18,750	$15,000	$12,500	$10,250	$7,000	$5,750	$5,000	$4,450	$4,250

❋ *Late Production* - with address "COLT PT. F. A. MANUFACTURING CO., HARTFORD, CT., U.S.A."

N/A	N/A	$21,000	$16,000	$13,000	$10,750	$7,500	$6,000	$5,200	$4,650	$4,150	$3,700

> **Add 40% for models with 8 in. barrel or COLTS/PATENT frame markings.**

REVOLVERS: PERCUSSION, 2ND & 3RD GENERATION BLACK POWDER SERIES

To learn more about the 2nd & 3rd Generation Percussion Black Powder Series, it is recommended to purchase *Colt Black Powder Reproductions & Replicas - A Collector's & Shooter's Guide* and the *Blue Book of Modern Black Powder Arms* by John Allen & Dennis Adler. The 2nd Edition contains more information on the Colt 2nd Generation Black Powder Series than anything else previously published. These definitive books are available from Blue Book Publications, Inc. To order, please call, fax, email, or visit www.bluebookinc.com.

DERRINGERS

FIRST MODEL DERRINGER - .41 rimfire cal., single shot, 2 1/2 in. barrel, scroll engraving standard, blue, nickel, or silver plated barrel, downward pivoting barrel, no grips, serial numbered 1-6,500. Mfg. approx. 1870-1890.

$3,325	$2,500	$2,150	$1,925	$1,700	$1,450	$1,275	$1,075	$875	$750	$675	$650

100%	98%	95%	90%	80%	70%	60%	50%	40%	30%	20%	10%

SECOND MODEL DERRINGER - .41 rimfire or centerfire cal., single shot, 2 1/2 in. barrel, scroll engraving standard, blue, nickel, or silver plated barrel, downward pivoting barrel, checkered and varnished walnut grips, "No 2" marked on top of barrel, serial numbered 1-9,000. Mfg. approx. 1870-1890.

100%	98%	95%	90%	80%	70%	60%	50%	40%	30%	20%	10%
$1,775	$1,475	$1,275	$1,100	$950	$850	$750	$650	$585	$535	$500	$475

Add 100% for .41 centerfire cal.

THIRD MODEL DERRINGER (THUER MODEL) - .41 rimfire or centerfire (rare) cal., single shot, side pivoting 2 1/2 in. barrel, varnished walnut grips, blue barrels, bronze frames were either nickel or silver plated, engraving optional, Colt-barrel address, spur trigger, serial numbered approx. 1-45,000. Mfg. approx. 1875-1910.

100%	98%	95%	90%	80%	70%	60%	50%	40%	30%	20%	10%
$1,500	$1,275	$950	$825	$725	$625	$550	$495	$450	$415	$385	$360

Add 30%-50% for .41 centerfire cal. Early models are worth considerably more.

GRADING - PPGS™	100%	98%	95%	90%	80%	70%	60%

FOURTH MODEL DERRINGER (FIRING) - .22 Short cal., single shot similar in appearance to the 3rd Model, 2 1/2 in. barrel, approx. 112,000 mfg. between 1959-1963 with either D or N suffix. A few were put in books (sometimes as pairs), picture frames, penholders, bookends, etc. (these will command premiums).

	100%	98%	95%
Gun only	$100	$85	$65
Gun w/accessories	$375	$275	$175

✱ *Fourth Model Derringer (non-firing)* - this variation was normally used for decoration and is normally encountered in books, picture frames, penholders, bookends, etc. Values below assume all factory materials intact - if not, prices are reduced to $50-$75 for gun only.

	100%	98%	95%
	$375	$250	$150

Non-firing guns usually do not have the barrel notch, thus preventing the hammer from striking the cartridge.

LORD DERRINGER - .22 Short cal. only, side pivoting Thuer action, gold plated with black chrome barrel and walnut grips. Mfg. 12,000 approx. 1959-1963 by Colt, cased.

	100%	98%	95%
	$175	$140	$100

LADY DERRINGER - .22 Short cal. only, side pivoting Thuer action, full gold plated finish with pearlite grips. Mfg. 3,000 approx. 1959-1963 by Colt, cased.

	100%	98%	95%
	$175	$140	$100

LORD & LADY CASED SET - one each of the Lord & Lady Derringers or combinations, consecutive serial numbers, numbered 1,001-up, with DER suffix.

	100%	98%	95%
	$495	$375	$275

LADY CASED SET - cased pair of Lady Derringers.

	100%	98%	95%
	$495	$375	$275

LORD CASED SET - cased pair of Lord Derringers.

	100%	98%	95%
	$495	$375	$275

BOOKCASE DERRINGER PAIR - .22 Short cal., consecutively numbered Derringers with synthetic ivory grips and nickel finish, cased inside unique hardcover "Colt Derringers" labeled book with red velvet lining, limited mfg. in early 1960s.

	100%	98%	95%
	$350	$275	$200

REVOLVERS: POCKET MODELS

If possible, it is advisable to procure a factory letter before buying/selling this variation (open top only). These watermarked letters are available by writing Colt Archive Properties LLC in Hartford, CT, with a charge of $200 or more per serial number (if they can research it). Send your name and address, Colt model name, serial number, and check or credit card information to: COLT ARCHIVE PROPERTIES LLC, P.O. Box 1868, Hartford, CT 06144-1868. Please allow 90-120 days for a response.

100%	98%	95%	90%	80%	70%	60%	50%	40%	30%	20%	10%

CLOVERLEAF HOUSE PISTOL - .41 Short or L rimfire cal., cloverleaf configured 4 shot cylinder, spur trigger, 1 1/2 or 3 in. barrel, blue or nickel plated, approx. 7,500 mfg. in ser. no. range 1-8,300 during 1871-76.

| $2,550 | $2,300 | $1,850 | $1,600 | $1,400 | $1,200 | $1,100 | $925 | $825 | $725 | $650 | $600 |

Add 30% for blue finish.

Add 80% for 1 1/2 in. barrel.

This model is sometimes referred to as the Jim Fisk model, as he was murdered by Edward Stokes with a Cloverleaf.

✱ **5-shot Cloverleaf** - similar to 4-shot model, except has round 5-shot cylinder and 2 5/8 in. barrel only, approx. 2,500 mfg. in ser. no. range 6,160-9,950 during 1871-76.

| $2,175 | $1,900 | $1,600 | $1,325 | $1,150 | $975 | $850 | $750 | $650 | $600 | $550 | $500 |

OPEN TOP REVOLVER (OLD LINE) - .22 Short or L rimfire cal., 2 3/8 or 2 7/8 in. barrel, without topstrap on frame, with or without integral ejector, blue or nickel plated, varnished walnut grips, approx. 114,200 mfg. 1871-77.

| $1,450 | $1,250 | $1,150 | $950 | $850 | $750 | $700 | $600 | $550 | $450 | $375 | $325 |

Add 30% for blue finish.

Add 120% for Early Model with ejector and high hammer spur.

REVOLVERS: NEW LINE SERIES & VARIATIONS

If possible, it is advisable to procure a factory letter before buying/selling New Line Revolvers. These watermarked letters are available by writing Colt Archive Properties LLC in Hartford, CT, with a charge of $100 or more per serial number (if they can research it). Send your name and address, Colt model name, serial number, and check or credit card information to: COLT ARCHIVE PROPERTIES LLC, P.O. Box 1868, Hartford, CT 06144-1868. Please allow 90-120 days for a response.

Add 30% for blue finish on models listed below.

1ST MODEL - .22, .30, .32, .38, or .41 cal. rim and centerfire, mfg. 1873-1876, 7 (.22 cal. only) or 5 shot, short cylinder flutes, cylinder stop slots cut on exterior of cylinder, 1 3/4, 2 1/4, or 4 in. barrel, full nickel or blue/case hardened finish, spur trigger. Many thousands mfg. 1873-1884.

| $1,250 | $1,050 | $925 | $825 | $750 | $675 | $600 | $550 | $450 | $350 | $300 | $250 |

2ND MODEL - similar to 1st Model, except has longer cylinder flutes and cylinder stop slots are on the back of cylinder, may or may not have loading gate. Mfg. 1876-1884.

| $1,125 | $995 | $875 | $800 | $725 | $650 | $575 | $500 | $400 | $325 | $275 | $235 |

Caliber rarity on both models from highest mfg. to lowest is: .22, .32, .30, .41, and .38.

NEW HOUSE MODEL - .38 or .41 cal. centerfire, 5 shot, 2 1/4 in. barrel, spur trigger, checkered hard rubber grips. Approx. 4,000 mfg. 1880-1886 starting at ser. no. 10,300.

| $1,475 | $1,150 | $1,000 | $875 | $775 | $675 | $600 | $485 | $425 | $360 | $325 | $310 |

NEW POLICE MODEL - .32, .38, or .41 cal. centerfire, 5 shot, 2 1/4, 4 1/2, 5, or 6 in. barrel, spur trigger, with or without ejector, stamped or etched "NEW POLICE" on barrel. Approx. 4,000 mfg. 1882-1886.

| $1,800 | $1,525 | $1,275 | $1,100 | $925 | $800 | $725 | $650 | $600 | $550 | $525 | $495 |

REVOLVERS: SAA, 1873-1940 MFG. (SER. NOS. 1-357,000)

The author wishes to express thanks to Charles Layson for making the following information available and reformatting the Colt 1st Generation SAA section.

The Colt SAA was produced in 36 calibers with many special order features or combinations available directly from the Colt factory. These factory special order features can greatly enhance the value of the revolver. The Single Action Colt, or "Peacemaker," as it is often called, is undoubtedly the most collectible handgun in the world, and as such, can command very high prices.

100%	98%	95%	90%	80%	70%	60%	50%	40%	30%	20%	10%

It is prudent to secure several professional opinions as to originality when contemplating an expensive purchase, since many SAAs have been altered or "improved" over the decades. Before he died, Keith Cochran, author of the *Colt Peacemaker Encyclopedia*, Vol. II, guesstimated that over 1/2 of all pre-WWII revolvers were no longer factory original. Because of this, it is advisable to procure a factory letter when buying or selling older or recently manufactured Colt Single Actions (hence guaranteeing original configuration and value credibility). These watermarked letters are based on the original factory handwritten shipping ledgers and are available by contacting Colt Archive Properties LLC in Hartford, CT. While not totally infallible, these letters are normally very accurate. If Colt cannot provide you with proper documentation after conducting research, they will issue a partial refund. No fee will be charged for SAAs serialized under 343,000 that are non-records guns.

Colt's new policy on 1st Generation SAAs is to call Colt Archive Properties, and a charge of $150 or more will be assessed (ser. no. range 354,000 - 357,859 cannot be researched). This service also includes a factory document which will follow in 2-3 weeks. Additionally, historical research premiums exist for factory engraving ($50-$175), unique shipping destination and company executive provenance ($50), and famous Western personalities or Colt family members ($100-$200). For just the date of manufacture, the charge is $25, while identification service providing general information is $50. The phone number is 860-244-1343. Ask for the Archive Dept. between the hours of 1-4 P.M. EST. Once contacted, they will tell you what the historical research charge will be. The address is COLT ARCHIVE PROPERTIES LLC, P.O. Box 1868, Hartford, CT 06144-1868.

Values shown below are for guns without special order features. Factory engraving, ivory grips, very rare special order barrel lengths, and special finishes would add considerably to the values shown below. One final word on single action Colts: Black Powder Colts (pre 165,000 serial range) should be scrutinized carefully for potential problems, including refinishing (including aging), replacement parts, restamped serial numbers, and added, non-factory special order features. This makes a major difference in pricing the SAA, since a genuine, original SAA's price tag will vary immensely from a non-original, made-up "parts gun."

SAA - 1st Generation Civilian/Commercial (Mfg. 1873-1940)

SINGLE ACTION ARMY - STANDARD MFG. - over 30 cals., six shot single action revolver, 4 3/4, 5 1/2, or 7 1/2 in. standard barrel lengths – 5 1/2 and 7 1/2 have the one-line barrel address, 4 3/4 has a two-line barrel address, blue with color case hardened frame or full nickel finish standard, one-piece, varnished walnut grips standard until 1882, when black, gutta percha (hard rubber) grips were introduced with eagle motif. Eagle-less grips became standard circa 1893. One-piece wood available upon request until approx. 1903. Rarely seen, two-piece, oil finished, walnut available thereafter. Mfg. 1873-1940.

* *Pinch Frame SAA (ser. no. range 1-160)* - .45 LC cal., 7 1/2 in. barrel, frame pinched to form rear sight. Mfg. 1873.

N/A	N/A	N/A	$65,000	$60,000	$55,000	$47,500	$42,000	$37,000	$32,000	$26,000	$20,000

Be aware! There are many counterfeits in this variation.

* *Early Black Powder SAA (ser. no. range 160-22,000)* - .45 LC cal., 7 1/2 in. barrel standard, blue or nickel finish, distinctive italic script style lettering used in barrel address, 5 1/2 in. barrels introduced in 1875, ser. nos. shared with early martial production. Mfg. 1873-76.

N/A	$48,000	$40,000	$32,000	$25,000	$18,000	$15,000	$12,000	$10,000	$8,000	$6,000	$4,000

Subtract 40% for nickel finish.

100%	98%	95%	90%	80%	70%	60%	50%	40%	30%	20%	10%

❋ *Intermediate Black Powder SAA (ser. no. range 22,000-130,000)* - .44-40 WCF (.44 WCF) cal. introduced in 1878 as a companion to the Winchester 1873 rifle, other calibers follow, 4 3/4 or 5 1/2 in. barrel became popular during this era, at appox. 52,000 ser. no. range the round ejector head was changed to an oval shape. During this same time period, Colt gradually abandoned the practice of placing the ser. nos. on the cylinders and barrels of civilian revolvers. Nickel plated guns seldom have ser. nos. on cylinders and barrels after 70,000, but are occasionally seen as high as the 100,000 range. Blued guns usually have numbers on barrels and cylinders up to 100,000 range, but only occasionally thereafter. Mfg. 1876-90.

N/A	$35,000	$32,000	$25,000	$17,000	$15,000	$12,000	$8,000	$7,000	$6,000	$4,000	$3,000

Subtract 30% for nickel finish.
Add 25% for original box.
Add 10% for 4 3/4 in. barrel.

❋ *Late Black Powder SAA (ser. no. range 130,000-165,000)* - three line patent date format changes to two line, circled rampant colt stamped on frame. Mfg. 1890-96.

N/A	$26,000	$22,000	$16,000	$12,000	$9,000	$7,500	$6,200	$5,800	$4,800	$3,700	$2,800

Subtract 20% for nickel finish.
Add 25% for original box.
Add 10% for 4 3/4 in. barrel.
Add 20% for one-piece wood or eagle grips.

❋ *Early Smokeless Powder SAA (Ser. no. range 165,000-300,000)* - several important physical characteristics were changed during this transition period. Most notably, in 1896 the vertical screw retaining the cylinder pin was eliminated in favor of the horizontal latch. This was similar to what had already been used on the double action models since 1877. The knurling pattern on the hammer spur began a two step revision in 1906. Up until this time, the knurling was enclosed in a border with a line underneath. Beginning in 1906, for approx. 2 years, the border remained, but the line underneath was eliminated. By late 1908, the border around the knurling was also eliminated, and thereafter, the knurling ran to the very edges of the hammer spur. Although Colt advertised their improved smokeless powder single action as early as 1897, they did not add the "VP" proofmark (verified proof, Colt's guarantee for smokeless powder use) to the trigger guard until 1904. Also, the company continued to use black powder rifling (wide grooves and narrow lands) and black powder front sights (small and low) until approx. 1911, when inventories were depleted. While the highest production figures were reached during this period, quality did not suffer. Many collectors feel that the polish, fit, and finish work performed during this 12 year span was at least as good, if not better, than before or since this period. Mfg. 1896-1908.

N/A	$15,000	$12,000	$8,500	$7,000	$6,000	$5,000	$4,200	$3,500	$3,000	$2,500	$2,000

Subtract 10% for nickel finish.
Add 20% for original box.
Add 25% for checkered walnut grips w/o medallions.
Add 30% for pre-1900 period mfg. (transitional range 1896-1900).

❋ *Intermediate Smokeless Powder SAA (ser. no. range 300,000-339,000)* - transitional changes to front sight and rifling were completed by 1914, the Bisley model was discontinued, the first Colt medallions were found in pearl and ivory grips starting in 1909, the new .44 Special caliber was introduced, the method of bluing was changed, the circled rampant colt gradually lost its circle as the die stamp began to wear. WWI came and went, and SAA sales began to decline. 1920 is significant to Colt SAA collectors since this was the year the company completed the relocation of the serial numbers. Those numbers on the trigger guard and backstrap were moved under the grips beginning in the late 338,000 ser. no. range

100%	98%	95%	90%	80%	70%	60%	50%	40%	30%	20%	10%

(1919), leaving only the ser. no. on the frame visible. This brought to a close the original ser. no. stamping location which began with the percussion revolvers. Many collectors regard this as the end of the "cowboy" period. Mfg. 1908-20.

$15,000	$12,000	$9,000	$7,000	$6,000	$4,800	$4,000	$3,200	$2,500	$2,000	$1,800	$1,500

Add 15% for original box.

Add 15% for smooth, two-piece walnut grips.

Add 25% for checkered, varnished walnut grips with deep set medallions.

* *Late Smokeless Powder SAA (ser. no. range 339,000-357,000)* - complete ser. no. visible only on frame, many cylinders are stamped at rear with the last two digits of ser. no., caliber marking on side of barrel was changed in 1928 to "Colt Single Action Army", followed by caliber, finish on hammer was changed from case hardening to blue with polished sides in 1935, and "V" notch rear sight was replaced with square groove to match wider front sight configuration during 1930. Mfg. 1920-40.

$8,500	$7,200	$5,750	$4,250	$3,500	$3,200	$2,800	$2,400	$2,000	$1,800	$1,600	$1,500

Add 15% for original box.

Add 20% for checkered, oil finished grips with flush medallions, post-1923.

Add 25% for checkered, varnished grips with deep set medallions, pre-1924.

It is important to remember that while special order grips such as pearl, ivory, or checkered wood may add as much as 25% to an SAA's value, they must be factory original to that particular gun, and be recorded as such in the factory records. Later add-ons enhance a gun's value by much less.

SAA 1st Generation Commercial, Non-Standard Mfg.

SINGLE ACTION ARMY, NON-STANDARD MFG. - throughout the 1873-1940 period of production, Colt manufactured several distinct types or configurations of SAAs that varied from the standard and therefore, have special significance to the collector.

* *.22 Rimfire SAA* - 5 1/2 or 7 1/2 in. barrel, both blue and nickel finishes, mfg. in two distinct runs, slightly less than 100 converted from unsold .44 rimfire revolvers on hand in the late 1880s, and in 1891, approx. 20 were mfg. as new guns.

N/A	N/A	$25,000	$18,000	$16,000	$14,500	$12,500	$11,000	$10,000	$8,500	$7,500	$6,500

Subtract 10% for those converted from .44 rimfire.

* *.44 Rimfire SAA* - .44 Henry rimfire cal., 7 1/2 in. barrel, most were shipped to Mexico and saw hard use, rare with any condition remaining, serial numbered in their own range, 1-1,863. Mfg. 1875-80.

N/A	N/A	N/A	$30,000	$25,000	$18,000	$15,000	$13,500	$12,500	$11,000	$9,500	$8,000

Beware! Many have been found with cut and/or stretched barrels.

* *Buntline Special Model SAA* - .45 LC cal., 12 or 16 in. non-standard barrel, rear adj. sight, long hammer screw for attachment of shoulder stock, very rare.

N/A	N/A	$135,000	$120,000	$100,000	$85,000	$75,000	$60,000	$50,000	$42,000	$35,000	$28,000

It is believed only 28 were produced in the 28,800 ser. no. range. Although other standard frame SAAs were mfg. with barrels over 7 1/2 in. long, and these will command higher than normal prices.

* *Etched Panel .44-40 SAA* - during 1878, soon after Colt began offering the .44 WCF cal., the new model nomenclature was changed to "Frontier Model." This may have been changed due to some persuasion from one of Colt's largest wholesalers, B. Kittredge & Co., of Cincinatti, OH. Kittredge had already begun advertising the .45 as the "Peacemaker" in 1876. Starting in the 41,000 ser. no. range, an acid etching process was used to mark the barrels "COLT FRONTIER SIX SHOOTER". Barrels so marked were continued until approx. the 129,000 ser. no. range (circa 1890).

N/A	$40,000	$30,000	$25,000	$18,000	$15,000	$12,000	$9,000	$7,500	$6,500	$5,000	$4,000

Add 30% for 5 1/2 in. barrel or 20% for 4 3/4 in. barrel.

Add 20% for one piece wood grips.

Subtract 50% for nickel finish.

This variation continues to be very sought-after amongst Colt SAA collectors. Beware of re-etched barrel logos.

100%	98%	95%	90%	80%	70%	60%	50%	40%	30%	20%	10%

✳ *Sheriff's Model SAA* - .44-40 WCF or .45 LC cal., 2 1/2, 3, 4, 4 3/4 (rare) or 7 1/2 (rare) in. barrel, configuration denotes barrel w/o ejector rod housing. According to single action collector and researcher Wynn Paul, the first short barrel, ejectorless Sheriff's or Storekeeper's model was shipped from the Colt factory on Feb. 22, 1882 to Hibbard, Spencer, Bartlett & Co., Chicago, IL, one of a shipment of ten. Most had either a 3 1/2 or 4 in. barrel. Mfg. throughout production until 1927.

N/A	$50,000	$40,000	$32,000	$25,000	$19,000	$16,000	$14,000	$12,000	$10,000	$8,000	$7,000

Add 30% for 2 1/2 or 7 1/2 in. barrels.

Add 30% for etched barrel panel.

Add 20% for one piece wood grips.

Subtract 40% for nickel finish.

Beware of fakes! The *Blue Book of Gun Values* strongly recommends getting a historical letter from Colt, then checking the authenticity of the serial numbers. Many guns have had numbers altered to match records.

✳ *Flat-top Target Model SAA* - various cals. from .22 to .476 Eley, 7 1/2 in. barrel, all blue finish, two-piece smooth walnut or rubber grips standard, occasionally with checkered walnut. Approx. 925 mfg. 1888-96.

N/A	$20,000	$18,000	$15,000	$12,000	$10,000	$8,000	$7,000	$6,000	$5,000	$4,000	$3,000

While rare, this model has limited collector appeal.

✳ *Long Flute Series SAA* - .32 WCF, .38 WCF, .41 LC, .44 S&W Spl., or .45 LC cal., during 1913, Colt decided to make use of approx. 1,500 DA model cylinders remaining in inventory. Since it was necessary to add a bolt lock notch and lead-in on these longer flute cylinders, they looked ahead of current production and blocked off ser. nos. 330,000-331,480 for this special treatment. Shipped 1913-15.

According to Hull & Radcliffe, whose survey includes 114 long flutes, no .44 WCF long flutes have been found. Quite possibly, the true number of long flutes mfg. slightly exceeds 1,500, and while rare, sell for only 5%-10% more than other SAAs of this period.

✳ *Pre-war parts/Post-war Mfg. SAAs* - .30 Carbine, .357 Mag., .38 Spl., .44 Spl., .44-40 WCF, or .45 LC cal., 5 1/2 in. barrel is the most common, as is blue barrel with case colors on frame, nickel finish is rare, many given as gifts to dignitaries and retiring Colt employees, shipping cartons were both brown and black, 338 SAAs were assembled from pre-war parts and shipped 1947-61.

Subtract 10%-20% from Late Smokeless Powder SAA values.

These SAAs shipped post-war are usually encountered in 95%+ condition.

✳ *Factory Engraved SAAs* - slightly less than 1% (approx. 3,200) SAAs are thought to have been engraved at the factory or elsewhere by authority from Colt 1873-1940. Colt offered 3 basic grades of engraving and since many of these guns carried special inscriptions, initials, grips, etc., the value ranges are very wide. Factory engraved black powder SAAs typically sell in the $2,500-$50,000 range, while factory engraved smokeless powder models usually peak in the $25,000 range. Very special or one-of-a-kind pieces, such as the 5 known "panel" engraved guns may bring upward of $300,000, depending on conditions and particulars. The Colt Historical Dept. can document most factory work.

✳ *Non-factory Engraved SAAs* - value depends upon when and where the engraving was done. Early "New York" or "dealer" engraved guns done outside the factory were usually shipped from Colt in the "soft" or w/o finish. The majority of these were done in the early 1880s, and condition being equal, are generally priced at 25%-50% of factory original specimens. Later guns, well done by a known contemporary artist, are usually priced by adding the values of the gun and the cost of engraving. Poor execution may actually lower the value of a plain, but original gun, as much as refinishing would. Here again, a factory letter can make a big difference. The notation of "soft" in the finish column is desirable, since the large wholesalers in the northeast used many of the same engravers as Colt.

100%	98%	95%	90%	80%	70%	60%	50%	40%	30%	20%	10%

* *Bisley Model SAA* - features more curved and longer grip strap, smaller hammer raked backward, this model was designed with the target shooter in mind, and named after Bisley, England, location of the international shooting matches during the late 19th and early 20th century. Approx. 45,000 were mfg. 1894-1913.

| N/A | $8,500 | $6,800 | $5,000 | $3,750 | $3,000 | $2,300 | $2,000 | $1,800 | $1,500 | $1,200 | $1,000 |

* *Flat-top Target Bisley SAA* - all standard SAA cals., similar to the Flat-top SAA, usually found with 7 1/2 in. barrel with all blue finish, two-piece walnut or rubber grips. 976 mfg. 1894-1913.

| N/A | $13,500 | $11,000 | $8,500 | $6,500 | $5,250 | $4,500 | $3,500 | $3,200 | $3,000 | $2,750 | $2,000 |

* *Battle of Britain SAA* - fearing invasion by Germany in 1940, the British Purchasing Commission began securing all types of firearms from many sources. A total of 163 single actions, mostly .38s and .45s in both blue and nickel, were sent to England by Colt. These guns were fully inspected and proofed by the British, in many cases showing the exact specifications of the cartridge on the bottom of the barrel. Most, if not all, were unissued, and remain today in 90% condition.

| $7,500 | $6,750 | $6,000 | $5,000 | $4,000 | $3,300 | $3,000 | $2,800 | $2,400 | $2,000 | $1,800 | $1,500 |

SAA U.S. Military, Mfg. 1873-1903

Since many of the military models listed below are frequently encountered with no original finish remaining, prices for original no condition specimens will be approx. three quarters of the 10% prices listed below. With original specimens getting harder and harder to find, many guns are now observed with major parts replacements, including barrels, cylinders, grips, etc.

Beware of restorations that are purported to be original! One expert believes that as many as 90% of Colt SAA Cavalry & Artillery models currently offered for sale, especially at gun shows, have been intentionally faked, or "enhanced" in some way. Likewise, many "questionable" guns have been consigned to the auction houses for disposal. Many have been altered in the last 40 years in all inspector serial ranges. Some have now been skillfully "aged" to look more original. When making a substantial purchase, a letter of authentication from a reliable source is suggested in addition to a factory historical letter. Also ask for a guarante of originality in writing from the seller. No factory information is available on U.S. Cavalry revolvers below ser. no. 30,600.

Blue Book Publications, Inc. would be happy to refer you to a credible source for authenticating the military revolvers listed below (very important). While a factory letter (if possible) verifies the configuration, it does not verify originality and/or authenticity. All inquiries are treated confidentially.

SINGLE ACTION ARMY (CAVALRY) - U.S. MILITARY CONTRACT - the Colt SAA was the primary sidearm of the U.S. military forces between 1873 and 1892, carried by all commissioned officers and mounted troops. While sometimes identified as the "Cavalry" model, this revolver was issued to all branches of service and state militia units. A total of 37,063 were purchased by the U.S government at an average cost of $12.50. Specifications called for 7 1/2 in. barrel, .45 LC cal., blue & color case hardened finish, one-piece, oil finished walnut grips. Each gun was stamped with the initial(s) of a U.S. ordnance principal sub-inspector and finally, with the letters "U.S." on the frame after being approved for delivery to the National Armory at Springfield, MA.

* *Early U.S. Model SAA* - principal sub-inspectors of this early period of military mfg. were O.W. Ainsworth (A), S.B. Lewis (L), A.P. Casey (C), and W.W. Johnson (J), examples with ser. nos. below 20,000 are most desirable and command premium prices, these guns are marked with only the single letter of the last name and were mfg. before 1876, ser. nos. are mixed with civilian sales up to ser. no. 20,000. There are no known sales to the U.S. government between the 20,000-30,000 ser. no. range.

| N/A | $75,000 | $65,000 | $50,000 | $35,000 | $25,000 | $18,000 | $16,000 | $14,000 | $13,000 | $12,000 | $10,000 |

Of this group, early Ainsworth inspected guns are the most valuable.

Be very careful when purchasing "Custer" serial range SAAs, as many non-original, made up SAAs have surfaced recently. Revolvers with serial numbers between 4,507-6,516 are considered to be within the "prime" Custer range. Unfortunately, no factory information is available on SAAs below 30,600. A letter of authentication is advisable.

100%	98%	95%	90%	80%	70%	60%	50%	40%	30%	20%	10%

* ***Mid-Range U.S. Model SAA*** - the primary ordnance sub-inspectors of this group were John T. Cleveland (J.T.C.), Henry Nettleton (H.N.), and David F. Clark (D.F.C.), these guns fall between ser. nos. 30,693-121,147. Mfg. 1876-87.

N/A	$60,000	$45,000	$37,000	$30,000	$22,000	$18,000	$15,000	$13,000	$12,000	$10,000	$8,000

* ***Late U.S. Model SAA*** - all inspected by Rinaldo A. Carr (R.A.C.) from 1890-1891, ser. no range 131,208-140,361. The last SAA purchased by the U.S. government was shipped from the factory on April 29, 1891.

N/A	$30,000	$25,000	$20,000	$18,000	$15,000	$13,000	$12,000	$10,000	$9,000	$8,000	$6,000

* ***Artillery Model SAAs*** - refers to U.S. government model SAA revolvers with 5 1/2 in. barrels and mismatched numbered parts. In response to growing dissatisfaction with the stopping power of the newly adopted (1892) Colt .38 cal. double action revolvers, the U.S. government directed Springfield Armory to draw all remaining quantities of .45 cal. Colt Cavalry revolvers from storage. After having the barrels shortened to 5 1/2 inches and being refurbished, these models were to be reissued to the troops soon to be involved in the Spanish-American War. This work was completed at Colt during 1895-96, and every effort was made to keep all serial numbers matching. These guns were to be issued to all units of the U.S. Army, and only by chance they were sent to several artillery companies. Many of these same revolvers were returned to Colt during 1900-1903 for refurbishing, but this time without regard for matching component serial numbers. This shortcut minimized precious time and saved the government $1.50 per gun. A few artillery models are believed to have been redone at various government arsenals, and this could explain the existence of several known artillery revolvers with blue frame. Regardless, the artillery model has now become one of the most studied and interesting types of single action Colts.

N/A	N/A	$14,000	$11,500	$8,500	$7,500	$6,000	$4,500	$3,700	$3,500	$3,000	$2,800

Only rarely will one be found with all the matching serial numbers, indicating that it escaped the last refinish - these guns will bring a premium price.

Artillery models with desirable low-numbered frames are currently being re-converted back into all matching Cavalry models with 7 1/2 in. barrels.

* ***New York State Militia SAA*** - in 1895, before work began on the artillery models, Colt refurbished 800 SA revolvers supplied by Springfield Armory to honor a request from the state of New York. These guns retained their 7 1/2 in. barrels and all original parts wherever possible (replacement parts were serial numbered to match). All were stamped on the bottom of the grips with the initials of Rinaldo A. Carr (R.A.C.). They were given a high polish blue and case hardened civilian finish with blue hammers. Since all other cavalry models in the government's possession were cut to 5 1/2 in. shortly thereafter, these 800 are quite possibly the only quantity of original 7 1/2 in. guns remaining that could actually have seen service on the frontier. All other 7 1/2 in. cavalry models that are seen today were most likely originally issued to state militias rather than to U.S. government miltary forces. These 800 revolvers therefore occupy a very significant position in the history of Colt firearms.

N/A	$18,500	$15,250	$13,750	$10,000	$9,000	$8,000	$7,200	$6,500	$5,000	$4,500	$4,000

REVOLVERS: SAA, 2ND GENERATION: 1956-1975 MFG.

The author wishes to express his thanks to Charles Layson, Carol & the late Don Wilkerson for their generous contributions and helping to reformat the 2nd & 3rd Generation Colt SAA information.

Popular demand brought back the Single Action Army in 1956 with minor modifications, most not detectable except to experts. Serial numbers began at 0001SA, and continued to 73,000SA before the "New Model" was introduced in 1976 (ser. no. 80,000SA). Premiums are paid for rare production variances in NIB condition. It should be noted "premium niches" exist in this model as collectors are establishing premiums paid for rarer production variances (the interrelation of barrel length, caliber, frame type, finish quality, year of manufacture, and other special features). The order of desirability on standard 2nd Generation SAAs is as follows: 4 3/4 in. barrels are the

GRADING - PPGS™	100%	98%	95%	90%	80%	70%	60%

most desirable, followed by 7 1/2 in., and then 5 1/2 in. Caliber desirability is as follows: .45 LC has the most demand, followed by .44 Spl., .38 Spl., and then .357 Mag. It follows that desirable calibers found with desirable barrel lengths will command healthy premiums if production was unusually low for a particular configuration. Reference books specifically on the post-war SAA are a must when determining the rarity factors on these multiple production combinations. Buntlines, Sheriff's Models, and special orders through the Custom Gun Shop are in a class by themselves, and have to be evaluated one at a time.

It is advisable to procure a factory letter when buying or selling older or recently manufactured Colt single actions (hence, guaranteeing authenticity and value credibility). These watermarked letters are based on the original factory handwritten shipping ledgers and are available by contacting Colt Archive Properties LLC in Hartford, CT. While not totally infallible, these letters are normally very accurate. If Colt cannot provide you with proper documentation after conducting research, they will issue a $50 refund. Colt's new policy on 2nd Generation SAAs is to call Colt Archive Properties, and a charge of $200 or more will be assessed. This service also includes a factory document which will follow in 2-3 weeks. Additionally, historical research premiums exist for factory engraving ($50-$175), unique shipping destination, or unique inscription ($50). For just the date of manufacture, the charge is $25, while identification service providing general information is $50. The phone number is 860-244-1343. Ask for the Archive Dept. between the hours of 1-4 P.M. EST. Once contacted, they will tell you what the exact historical research charge will be. The address is COLT ARCHIVE PROPERTIES LLC, P.O. Box 1868, Hartford, CT 06144-1868.

SINGLE ACTION ARMY (2ND GENERATION) - .357 Mag., .38 Spl., .44 Spl., or .45 LC cal., denoted by SA suffix, 3 (Sheriff's Model), 4 3/4, 5 1/2, 7 1/2, or 12 (Buntline) in. barrel length–5 1/2, 7 1/2, and 12 in. barrels have the one-line barrel address, all blue, blue/case hardened, or nickel finish. 2nd Generation SAAs have been grouped into the following 3 categories.

* *Early 2nd Generation* - ser. no. range 0001SA to approx. 39,000SA, shipped in one-piece black box similar to pre-war box. Mfg. from 1956-65.

.45 LC cal.	$2,750	$1,875	$1,500	$1,200	$1,000	$900	$800
.44 Spl. cal.	$2,600	$1,750	$1,350	$1,050	$900	$800	$700
.38 Spl. cal.	$2,300	$1,995	$1,600	$1,200	$900	$800	$700
.357 Mag. cal.	$2,300	$1,795	$1,350	$1,000	$800	$700	$600

Add 30% for original black box in good condition.
Add 20% for original nickel finish.
Add 15% for original 4 3/4 in. barrel.

* *Mid-range 2nd Generation* - ser. no. range 39,000SA to 70,055SA, shipped in a red and white, two-piece, stagecoach box. Mfg. from 1965-73.

.45 LC cal.	$1,800	$1,350	$1,100	$1,000	$900	$800	$700
.44 Spl. cal.	$1,700	$1,500	$1,225	$1,000	$900	$800	$700
.357 Mag. cal.	$1,700	$1,295	$975	$800	$700	$600	$550

Add 30% for original stagecoach box.
Add 10% for original nickel finish.
Add 15% for original 4 3/4 in. barrel.

* *Late 2nd Generation* - ser. no. range 70,055SA to 73,205SA, shipped in a brown, wood grain cardboard shell with 2 styrofoam inserts. Mfg. from 1973-76.

.45 LC cal.	$1,395	$1,150	$1,000	$900	$800	$700	$600
.357 Mag. cal.	$1,295	$950	$800	$750	$700	$650	$600

Add 15% for original brown/styrofoam box.
Add 10% for original nickel finish.
Add 10% for original 4 3/4 in. barrel.

2nd Generation SAAs in stagecoach box w/o eagle black grips (ser. numbered under approx. 52,000SA) are more desirable than those with eagle. Also, flat-top hammers are more desirable than round top hammers found between ser. no. range 27,012SA-61,575SA (mfg. mid-1959-1972).

GRADING - PPGS™	100%	98%	95%	90%	80%	70%	60%

Colt manufactured approximately 100 screwless frames during the 1970s, and assembled approximately 50 guns at the time. The other 50 sat in the warehouse for a while until Colt started assembling the screwless frames again during the 1990s. Most of these recent guns are engraved and in .38-40 WCF or .45 LC cal., and have either a 4 3/4 or 5 in. barrel. Typically, the engraver's name is part of the serial number. Bangor's distributed most of these guns, and in today's marketplace are priced in the $8,500-$10,000+ range.

SHERIFF'S MODEL (1961 MODEL) - .45 LC cal., distinictive configuration with 3 in. barrel and no ejector rod housing, ser. no. followed by SM suffix, 503 were mfg. for Centennial Arms Corp. - 478 had a blue/case hardened finish and 25 were done in nickel.

	$2,000	$1,600	$1,400	$1,200	$1,000	$800	$700

Add 25% for original two-piece box.
Add 200% for original nickel finish.
Add approx. 300% for nickel finish on 100% condition guns.

BUNTLINE SPECIAL (2ND GENERATION) - .45 LC cal. only, 12 in. barrel, blue/case hardened finish, rubber (early mfg.) or walnut grips. Over 3,900 mfg. between 1957-75.

	$1,695	$1,275	$1,000	$900	$850	$800	$750

Add 100% for original nickel finish (rare, watch for refinishing).
Add 30% for original black box in good condition.

NEW FRONTIER (2ND GENERATION) - .357 Mag., .38 Spl. (rare), .44 Spl., or .45 LC cal., denoted by flat-top frame, adj. rear sight, and "NF" after the serial number, 4 3/4 (scarce), 5 1/2 (scarce), or 7 1/2 (most common) in. barrel, case hardened frame/blue finish and smooth walnut grips were standard. Approx. 4,200 mfg. 1961-1975.

	$1,250	$950	$900	$850	$800	$750	$700

Add 15% for later brown/styrofoam box.
Add 20% for stagecoach or black box (must be in correct ser. no. range).
Add 35% for early black and gold box.
Add 50% for 4 3/4 in. barrel.
Add 25% for 5 1/2 in. barrel.
Add 200% for .38 Spl. cal. with 5 1/2 in. barrel, 600% for 7 1/2 in. barrel.

NEW FRONTIER BUNTLINE (2ND GENERATION) - .45 LC cal. only, 12 in. barrel, flat-top frame and adj. rear sight. Approx. 72 mfg. 1962-67.

	$2,500	$2,150	$1,650	$1,400	$1,200	$1,100	$1,000

Add 50% for original black or tan box (must be serial numbered to the gun).

FACTORY ENGRAVED 2ND GENERATION SAAs - approx. 350 revolvers were factory engraved with 90% being in .45 LC cal. Values range from 75%-100% higher than non-engraved specimens, with additional premiums paid for rare styles and configurations and/or for the notoriety of the engraver. Those SAAs done by Albert Herbert, A.A. White, Robert Burt, Leonard Francolini, and Dennis Kiesler are probably the highest-priced examples. Always check authenticity when buying, selling, or trading engraved 2nd Generation SAAs with the Colt Archive Dept. The charge for a factory letter per engraved gun is $150. $50 will be refunded if Colt cannot provide historical documentation.

Factory engraved 2nd Generation SAAs are at least 10 times rarer than engraved 3rd Generation pistols.

REVOLVERS: SAA, 3RD GENERATION: 1976-CURRENT MFG.

After a short break in production, Colt Firearms announced the resumption of full-scale production of the Single Action on Feb. 4th, 1976, at the N.S.G.A. (National Sporting Goods Association) Bi-Centennial show in Chicago.

The "New Model Colt Single Action Army" or the "Colt Post-War Single Action Army - New Model," as it was commonly referred to at the time, is known today to collectors as the "3rd

GRADING - PPGS™	100%	98%	95%	90%	80%	70%	60%

Generation Colt Single Action Army." Minor changes include a modified, thin front sight contour, and a return to back to the cylinder pin bushing in late 2002, plus a few other "minor, modern manufacturing techniques that have not changed the appearance, feel, action, or performance of this historic handgun...," according to Colt's press release at the time.

Production began with ser. no. 80,000SA, and reached 99,999SA in 1978. At this point, the SA suffix changed to a prefix beginning with SA01001. Serialization reached SA99,999 during 1993, and began over, this time separating the letters SA, and starting with S02001A. As this edition went to press, serial numbers had reached S37000A (excludes custom serial numbers). For whatever reasons, a few writers have erroneously referred to this current production run as "4th Generation Single Actions." This is an incorrect description, as these revolvers are mechanically identical to those produced since 1976, and should still be considered 3rd Generation guns.

For a listing of Colt's "P-Codes" (referring to the factory's model number designations specifying frame type, caliber, finish, and barrel length), please refer to the Colt Single Action Model Numbers section in the back of this book (located in Colt Serialization).

As with 1st and 2nd Generation Single Actions, a factory letter authenticating configuration and shipping destination can be obtained for $100 by writing to: COLT ARCHIVE PROPERTIES LLC, P.O. Box 1868, Hartford, CT 06144-1868. If Colt cannot provide proper documentation after conducting research, they will issue a refund of $50. Please allow 60-90 days for proper response.

POPULAR SAA CUSTOM SHOP SPECIAL ORDER OPTIONS

Add $115-$177 for special barrel length, add $312-$332 for caliber change, add $125 for custom-tuned action, add $228 (available in .45 LC only beginning 2000) for extra regular fluted or unfluted cylinder, add $308 for extra long fluted cylinder, add $65 for beveled front of cylinder, add $200 for mirror brite finish (disc.) or nickel finish, add $425 for gold or silver plating, add $80 for black eagle grips, add $15 for grip medallions, add $85 for smooth walnut grips, add $275 for North American elkhorn grips, add $225 for buffalo horn grips, add $375 for mother-of-pearl grips, add $575 for plain ivory grips, add $250 for imitation ivory, approx. 10% for grip checkering, add $155 for scrimshaw engraving (3 initials only), add $115 for consecutive serial numbers (pair), add $310 for individual unique serial number, add $105 to modify and shorten ejector housing, add $155 (per set) for heat blue small parts, add $255 for birdshead and $390 for extended butt frame, $350 for screwless frame. While a very few screwless frame SAAs have been mfg. to date, the Custom Shop now lists this option as a standard custom order feature.

Please contact the Colt Custom Shop for a written quotation ($25) regarding a custom built SAA with special options/features. Their address is: Colt Manufacturing Company, Inc. P.O. Box 1868, Hartford, CT 06101, ATTN: Custom Shop.

STANDARD/CUSTOM SINGLE ACTION ARMY (3RD GENERATION) - .32-20
WCF (new 2005), .357 Mag. (disc. approx. 1983, reintroduced 2005), .38 Spl. (reintroduced 2005), .38-40 WCF (reintroduced 2005), .44 Spl. (disc. approx. 1983), .44-40 WCF, or .45 LC cal., 4 (disc. 1988), 4.75, 5 (disc. 1987), 5 1/2, or 7 1/2 (limited production since 1992) in. barrel, 5 1/2 and 7 1/2 in. barrels have the one-line barrel address, standard finishes include color case hardened/blue or nickel, plastic black eagle or walnut grips (used mostly during 1991-92) standard, most recent mfg. has blue shipping box with white slip cover. Mfg. 1976 to date. Original 1976 issue price was approx. $242.

MSR $1,380	$1,295	$950	$800	$700	$650	$600	$550

Add $150 for nickel finish.

Add 10% for original .38-40 WCF cal.

Add 25% for original .38 Spl. cal.

Add 20% for black powder frame (disc. 1995).

Add $700 for original two-piece ivory grips with screw.

Add $700 for original one-piece ivory grips w/o screw.

Add 5% for original brown box with styrofoam inserts (mfg. 1976-93).

Through 2001, Colt offered the SAA as both Standard and Custom Models. The difference is that single actions that are further customized with engraving, special barrel lengths, stocks, etc., are packaged more eloquently because of the added value of the customizing.

Beginning 2001, all orders for SAA models are processed through the Colt Custom Shop. The

2001 Custom Shop MSR for the Custom SAA was $2,100.

Various custom order barrel lengths have been available on this model for some time.

The .357 Mag. and .44 Spl. cals. were mostly discontinued by 1983.

Colt manufactured approximately 100 screwless frames during the 1970s, and assembled approximately 50 guns at the time. The other 50 sat in the warehouse for a while until Colt started assembling the screwless frames again during the 1990s. Most of these recent guns are engraved and in .38-40 WCF or .45 LC cal., and have either a 4 3/4 or 5 in. barrel. Typically, the engraver's name is part of the serial number. Bangor's distributed most of these guns, and in today's marketplace they are priced in the $8,500-$10,000+ range.

To reference factory coding for the various Standard Model P (SAA) configurations, please refer to the Colt Single Action Model Numbers within the Colt Serialization section in the back of this text.

COLT COWBOY SINGLE ACTION ARMY - .45 LC cal., 4 3/4 (disc. 1999, reintroduced 2002), 5 1/2, or 7 1/2 (disc. 1999) in. barrel marked "COLT COWBOY .45 COLT" on left side, transfer bar safety, all steel construction, frame assembly done in the U.S., charcoal case colors on frame with blue metal parts, rampant Colt black competition grips similar in design to those used on 1st generation SAAs, 40 oz. Not mfg. in U.S. While advertised beginning 1998, this model was not manufactured until 1999-2003.

$595	$475	$450	$400	$375	$350	$335

Last MSR was $670.

✴ ***Cowboy Collection Set*** - includes SAA in .45 LC cal., with 5 1/2 in. barrel, stag (very limited) or imitation ivory (more common) grips, blue/color case hardened finish, accessories include collector's Bowie knife, silver medallion and collector's case. Limited mfg. 2000 only.

$1,250	$750	$625	$500	$425	$400	$400

Last MSR was approx. $1,600.

SHERIFF'S MODEL (3RD GENERATION) - .44-40 WCF or .45 LC cal., 3 in. barrel w/o ejector rod, blue/case colored, nickel, or royal blue finish. Approx. 4,560 guns mfg. 1980-85.

.45 LC cal. (blue/CH)	$1,395	$1,150	$900	$850	$800	$750	$700

Add 10% for extra convertible cylinder.

Add 10% for original nickel finish.

Add $400 for original ivory grips.

Subtract 20% for .44-40 WCF cal. or all blue finish.

BUNTLINE MODEL (3RD GENERATION) - .44-40 WCF or .45 LC cal. only, 12 in. barrel, blue/case hardened finish, walnut grips.

$1,395	$995	$800	$750	$700	$650	$600

Add 10% for original nickel finish.

Add $400 for original ivory grips.

NEW FRONTIER (3RD GENERATION) - .357 Mag., .44-40 WCF (rare), .44 Spl., or .45 LC cal., denoted by "NF" serial suffix, 4 3/4, 5 1/2, or 7 1/2 in. barrel, blue/case hardened finish, flattop frame, adj. rear sight, plain two-piece walnut grips. Mfg. 1978-81.

.44-40 WCF/.45 LC cal.	$1,050	$900	$800	$750	$700	$650	$600
.44 Spl. cal.	$795	$650	$500	$450	$425	$400	$400
.357 Mag. cal./7 1/2 in. nickel							
	$1,050	$900	$800	$750	$700	$650	$600

Subtract 10% for 5 1/2 in. barrel.

Subtract 15% for 7 1/2 in. barrel.

Add 5% for original brown box with styrofoam inserts.

Serial numbers on the New Frontier started at 01001NF, but during 1980 a few New Frontiers with 5 1/2 in. barrels were produced in the 7000NF serial range, where 2nd Generation New Frontiers left off. Therefore, a 3rd Generation New Frontier will either have a ser. no. starting with "0" or will have a higher number than 7288NF with no "0" prefix.

GRADING - PPGS™	100%	98%	95%	90%	80%	70%	60%

NEW FRONTIER BUNTLINE SPECIAL (3RD GENERATION) - .45 LC cal. only, 12 in. barrel, flat-top frame, adj. rear sight, limited mfg. as the New Buntline Commemorative during 1979. Please refer to the Colt Commemorative section for value information.

STOREKEEPER'S MODEL (3RD GENERATION) - .45 LC cal. only, black powder frame, 4 in. barrel w/o ejector rod, full nickel or royal blue/case hardened finish, ivory grips. Approx. 280 mfg. 1984-85.

	$1,700	$1,450	$1,300	$1,100	$900	$800	$750

Add 10% for original nickel finish.

CUSTOM & SPECIAL ENGRAVED EDITIONS (3RD GENERATION) - beginning in 1976, with the introduction of the "New Model" SAA (3rd Generation), the Colt Custom Shop produced many custom and special edition engraved Single Army Action revolvers. According to Mr. Don Wilkerson, author of *The Post-War Single Action Revolver 1976-1986*, "the term custom edition is defined as a group of identical revolvers assembled under the direction of the Custom Gun Shop at Colt's and sold through the normal distribution system. A custom edition differs from a special edition in that special editions are a group of revolvers made up to a customer's unique specifications, and sold as a group to one purchaser...." While the exact number is not known, it is thought that approx. 3,500 SAAs have been engraved since 1976. Since each edition is unique, values vary widely, depending upon the notability of the engraver, the amount and type of coverage, and the number produced. Models listed below are recent Colt Custom Editions.

✳ *Engraved European Model* - 9mm Para. cal., nickel finish only, 4 3/4, 5 1/2, or 7 1/2 in. barrel, rosewood grips with silver medallions, 40-43 oz. Mfg. 1991-92 only.

	$1,650	$1,395	$1,195

Last MSR was $1,990.

✳ *Engraved U.S. Model* - .45 ACP cal., royal blue finish only, 4 3/4, 5 1/2, or 7 1/2 in. barrel, walnut grips, 40-43 oz. Mfg. 1991-92 only.

	$1,750	$1,295	$1,095

Last MSR was $1,960.

✳ *Old World Engravers Sampler* - .45 LC cal., 5 1/2 in. barrel, nickel finish, buffalo horn grips, includes four unique styles of engraving. Mfg. 1997-98, reintroduced 2001-2002.

	$2,975	$2,450	$2,000

Last MSR was $3,445.

✳ *Legend Rodeo II SAA* - disc. 1998.

	$1,950	$1,500	$1,250

Last MSR was $2,450.

✳ *125th Anniversary Edition* - 2 line frame address, "45 COLT" barrel address marked barrel, beveled cylinder, oven blue finish. 1,000 mfg. 1997-2002.

	$1,600	$1,150	$825

Last MSR was $2,070.

FACTORY ENGRAVED SAAs (3RD GENERATION) - the rarity of the SAA configuration in addition to the notability of the engraver will make the difference on the premiums commanded. 3rd Generation factory engraved SAAs were produced in much greater numbers than were 2nd Generation SAAs. Over 80% of engraved 3rd Generation SAAs are .45 LC caliber, the majority have 7 1/2 in. barrels, and some variation of blue finish. Grade "C" (41% of engraved mfg.) and Grade "D" (24% of engraved mfg.) dominate production.

During 1978-79, Colt engraved as many as 300-500 guns on a single factory order. Unfortunately, the quality on many SAAs during this period was substandard, and as a result, these guns usually cap at approx. $2,000. If the level of quality is similar to today's SAAs, the price will also be similar. Today's Custom Shop is once again producing excellent quality engraved SAAs, and Class C engraved revolvers (with ivory grips) are currently priced in the $3,750 range.

Use the following add-ons as general guidelines for values on recently manufactured 3rd Generation SAAs.

Add approx. 10% for original nickel finish.

Add 25% for 4 3/4 in. barrel.

Add 15% for 5 1/2 in. barrel.

Add 10% for calibers other than .45 LC.

Add 30% for factory ivory grips.

Add 10% for original blue cardboard or plastic box.

SAA CUSTOM SHOP ENGRAVING PRICES - PRE-1997 - values below represent 1995 published SAA Custom Shop A-D engraving options before the company started separate Standard, Expert, and Master level pricing during 1997. For current Colt Custom Shop engraving prices, please refer to the "Colt Custom Shop Engraving - Current Mfg." section below.

Add $1,163 for Class "A" engraving (25% metal coverage).

Add $2,324 for Class "B" engraving (50% metal coverage).

Add $3,487 for Class "C" engraving (75% metal coverage).

Add $4,647 for Class "D" engraving (100% metal coverage).

Add an additional 13% (approx.) for buntline engraving.

Standard Engraving was performed mostly by standard level factory engravers and engraving options generally include A-D style coverage. Typically, gold work was not performed by these engravers and specimens are mostly unsigned. Expert Engravers executed classic American style scroll, no gold, and may be signed.

COLT CUSTOM SHOP ENGRAVING - CURRENT MFG.

The chart below indicates current Custom Shop engraving prices for the various frame sizes, amount of engraving coverage, and the three levels of engraving execution (i.e., Standard, Expert, and Master levels). SAAs are considered large frame, revolvers and full-size Government Models are considered medium frame, and Government Model 380s are considered small frame.

Most buyers of engraved Colt SAAs today are very knowledgeable, and many of them are no longer satisfied with Standard types of patterns and styles. As a result, those engraved guns with the rarest production variances coupled with unique engraving done at an Expert or better level are currently more desireable than their counterparts with Standard engraving patterns. Colt currently employs three full-time engravers at the factory, in addition to several outside sources (at all engraving levels).

The name of the engraver is available only when ordering either the Expert or the Master level of engraving. Currently, most collectors would rather have the Expert level of engraving.

Large Frame Size

ENGRAVING COVERAGE	STANDARD LEVEL	EXPERT LEVEL	MASTER LEVEL
A	$990	$900 (disc.)	$1,200 (disc.)
B	$1,320	$1,870	$3,465
C	$1,540	$2,750	$5,038
D	$1,760	$3,960	$6,930

Add 20% to large frame pricing for Buntline Models.

Other Custom Shop options are priced on request, including a wide variety of gold/silver inlays, panel scenes, color enamel inlays, gold/silver frame outlines, etc.

Medium Frame Size

Medium frame engraving is discontinued.

A	$900	N/A	N/A
B	$1,200	$1,700	$3,150
C	$1,400	$2,500	$4,580
D	$1,600	$3,600	$6,300

GRADING - PPGS™	100%	98%	95%	90%	80%	70%	60%

Small Frame Size

Factory small frame engraving was disc. 1998.

ENGRAVING COVERAGE	STANDARD LEVEL	EXPERT LEVEL	MASTER LEVEL
A	$400	$600	$800
B	$600	$800	$1,000
C	$800	$1,100	$1,500
D	$1,100	$1,300	$1,900

Subtract 20% from small frame pricing for Mustang Models.

REVOLVERS: SAA, SCOUT MODEL

100% values below assume NIB condition. Subtract 10% without box.

FRONTIER SCOUT (Q or F SUFFIX) - .22 LR or .22 Mag. (introduced after 1960) cal., "Q" or "F" suffix, blue with bright alloy frame, all blue, or duotone ("Q" models only) finish (rare), 4 3/4 or 9 1/2 (Buntline) in. barrel, available with interchangeable cylinders after 1964, black composition or walnut grips, approx. 246,000 mfg. 1957-70.

	$600	$425	$325	$250	$200	$175	$150

Add 10% for extra cylinder.
Add 20% for Buntline model.
Add 25% for "Q" suffix with duo-tone finish (mfg. 1957-58 only).
Add 10% for original box.

FRONTIER SCOUT (K SUFFIX) - Zamac alloy frame version of "Q" Model with "K" suffix, blue or nickel finish with walnut stocks, approx. 44,000 mfg. 1960-70.

	$600	$425	$325	$250	$200	$175	$150

Add 100% for double cased Scout set.
Add 150% for double cased Scout Buntline set.
Add 10% for original box.
This model used the alloy Zamac for manufacture (as opposed to aluminum in the "Q" and "F" suffix models), and specimens are 6 oz. heavier as a result.

FRONTIER SCOUT '62 (P SUFFIX) - blue finish version of "K" Model, except has "P" suffix, staglite grips, approx. 68,000 mfg. 1962-70.

	$600	$450	$375	$275	$225	$175	$160

Add 20% for Buntline.
Add 10% for original box.
Add 50% with extra cylinders.
Add 100% for double cased Scout set.
Add 150% for double cased Scout Buntline set.

PEACEMAKER - .22 LR/.22 Mag. cal., color case hardened steel frame, 4.4, 4 3/4, 6, or 7 1/2 (nicknamed Buntline Model but may be marked Peacemaker or Buntline) in. barrel, black composition grips, furnished with interchangeable .22 LR/.22 Mag. cylinders, approx. 190,000 mfg. 1970-77.

	$550	$400	$350	$275	$225	$175	$150

Add 20% for 4.4 in. barrel.
Add 30% for 4 3/4 in. barrel.
Add 10% for original box.
Subtract 10% if without extra cylinder.
This model can be denoted by a "G" or "L" prefix.

NEW FRONTIER - similar features as Peacemaker Model, except with flattop frame, ramp front and adj. rear sight, mfg. 1970-1977. Reintroduced in 1982 without convertible .22 Mag. cylinder and added cross bolt safety, available in Coltguard finish, all blue finish became standard in 1985. Mfg. disc. 1986.

	$500	$375	$300	$250	$200	$175	$150

Last MSR was $181.

Add 15% for Buntline model or 4 3/4 in. barrel.

GRADING - PPGS™	100%	98%	95%	90%	80%	70%	60%

PISTOLS: SEMI-AUTO, DISC.

Most of the semi-auto pistol models listed in the various pistol categories can have their original configuration confirmed with a Colt factory letter. To receive a letter, write: COLT ARCHIVE PROPERTIES, LLC, P.O. Box 1868, Hartford, CT, 06144. The research fee for these pistols is typically either $75 or $100, depending on the model. If they cannot obtain additional information on the variation you request, they will refund $50.

Until several years ago, the Single Action Army revolver commanded the most attention among Colt handgun collectors. Since 1987, Colt Semi-Autos have been in tremendous demand and have out-accelerated many other areas of Colt collecting. Because condition and originality play such a key role in determining Colt Semi-Auto prices, many variations have had their values pushed upward to the point where it is difficult to accurately determine a realistic price, especially on those models in 98% original condition or better. As a result, some of the rarer models seldomly encountered in true 100% original condition have had their values deleted since extreme rarity precludes accurate price evaluation. As always, the hardest prices to ascertain when firearms market conditions are bullish are the 98-100% values.

MODEL 1900 - .38 ACP cal., 6 in. barrel, blue, plain walnut grips - checkered hard rubber grips after S/N 2,450, high spur hammer, sight safety. Mfg. 1900-03.

	$12,000	$9,000	$7,000	$5,600	$4,000	$3,000	$2,000

    Add 60%+ for USN marked.

    Add 50% for US marked with inspector initials.

    Subtract 30%-50% for sight safety altered (factory refinished).

This model is serial numbered approx. between 1-4,274.

Somewhere between serial number 2,200 and 2,450, Colt began altering the sights to fixed sights in the production process, shipping both types. By approx. serial number 3,300, most guns shipped were altered during production. Guns altered during production are not refinished. Altered guns below serial number 2,200 were refinished, or at least had the slides refinished.

MODEL 1902 SPORTING - .38 ACP, 6 in. barrel, blue, fixed sights, checkered hard rubber grips, no safety, high spur hammer and round hammer. Mfg. 1902-08.

	N/A	$4,500	$3,250	$2,500	$1,750	$1,750	$900

This model is serial numbered approx. 4,275-11,000 and 30,000-30,190.

MODEL 1902 MILITARY - .38 ACP cal., 6 in. barrel, blue, similar to 1902 Sporting, hammer changed to spur type in 1908, checkered black hard rubber grips, lanyard swivel on bottom rear of left grip. Mfg. 1902-29.

	N/A	$4,500	$3,750	$2,500	$1,250	$900	$750

    Add 30% for front slide checkering.

    Add 20% with original box and instructions.

This model is serial numbered approx. 11,000-16,000 and 30,200-43,266.

MODEL 1902 MILITARY-U.S. ARMY MARKED - similar specifications to 1902 Military, only serial number range 15,001-15,200.

	N/A	$8,500	$6,500	$5,500	$4,250	$3,250	$2,500

MODEL 1903 POCKET (.38 ACP) - .38 ACP cal., 3 3/4 or 4 1/2 in. barrel, blue finish standard, checkered black hard rubber grips, similar to 1902 Sporting, but 4 1/2 in. barrel, 7 1/2 in. overall. Mfg. 1903-29.

	$1,850	$1,550	$1,250	$1,000	$750	$650	$500

    Add 30% for early round hammer.

    Add 20% with original box and instructions.

This model is serial numbered approx. 16,000-47,226.

GRADING - PPGS™	100%	98%	95%	90%	80%	70%	60%

MODEL 1903 POCKET (MODEL M .32 ACP)
.32 ACP cal., 4 in. barrel, charcoal blue, checkered hard rubber grips, hammerless, slide lock and grip safety, barrel lock bushing. Mfg. 1903-46.

	$800	$600	$450	$400	$350	$275	$225

Add 20% for nickel finish (mostly w/pearl grips).

Add 60% for first model (Type I) mfg. 1903-1911 if in 100%-98% condition. If lower than 98%, add 20%.

Add 30% for Type II if in 100%-98% condition.

Add 10% with original box and instructions.

Type I - 32 ACPs have a 4 in. barrel, barrel bushing, no magazine safety, and are serial numbered 1-71,999.

Type II - 32 ACPs still retain their barrel bushing but have a 3 3/4 in. barrel and were mfg. from 1908-1910. They are serial numbered 72,000-105,050.

Type III - 32 ACPs do not have a barrel bushing and were mfg. from 1910-1926. They are serial numbered 105,051-468,096.

Type IV - 32 ACPs have the added magazine safety (of which there are both the commercial and "U.S. Property" variations). They are serial numbered 468,097-554,446.

* *Model 1903 Parkerized* - U.S. Property, 3 1/4 in. barrel, no barrel bushing, magazine safety, serial numbered 554,447-572,214.

	$1,200	$1,000	$775	$600	$450	$350	$325

Add 50% for blue U.S. Property S/N 554,447 - approx. 562,000.

Add 20% with original box and instructions.

The 100% value on this model assumes NIB condition.

* *Model 1903 General Officer's Pistol* - .32 ACP cal., blue (mfg. until 1942) or parkerized (mfg. started 1942) finish.

* *Parkerized*	N/A	$1,800	$1,500	$1,250	$975	$875	$775
* *Blue Finish*	N/A	$2,500	$2,000	$1,850	$1,500	$1,300	$1,100

Values above assume issue to a General, and there must be paperwork to link the gun to the recipient. Otherwise, these values do not apply - see U.S. Property above for applicable values.

MODEL 1905
.45 ACP cal., 5 in. barrel, blue, fixed sights, checkered walnut stocks, similar to 1902 .38 ACP. Mfg. 1905-11.

	N/A	$5,500	$3,250	$2,150	$1,750	$1,500	$1,250

Add 50% for factory slotted specimens (500 manufactured).

Add 250% for 1907 U.S. Military Contract variation (205 manufactured).

The shoulder stock option for this pistol is exceedingly rare. Depending on the condition, this accessory can add $7,500-$10,000 to the price of the gun.

MODEL 1908 POCKET (MODEL M .380 ACP)
.380 ACP cal., first issue, 3 3/4 in. barrel only, similar to Pocket Model .32 ACP (32 ACP), except chambered for .380 ACP. Mfg. 1908-40.

	$1,000	$800	$650	$450	$350	$300	$275

Add 15% for Type I (see explanation below).

Add $100 for nickel finish.

Add 15% for pearl grips.

100% values assume NIB condition. Subtract 15% if without cardboard box. Pearl grips are normally encountered with nickel finish on this model.

Type I - 380 ACPs with barrel bushing and were mfg. 1908-1910 (6,251 mfg.). They are serial numbered 1-6,251.

Type II - 380 ACPs do not have a barrel bushing and were mfg. 1910-1926. They are serial numbered 6,252-92,893.

Type III - 380 ACPs have the added magazine safety (of which there are both the commercial and "U.S. Property" variations). They are serial numbered 92,894-134,499.

GRADING - PPGS™	100%	98%	95%	90%	80%	70%	60%

＊ Model 1908 "U.S. Property" - blue finish only, U.S. Property. Serial numbered 134,500-138,000.

	$2,500	$1,750	$925	$750	$650	$500	$350

＊ Model 1908 General Officer's Pistol - .380 ACP cal., blue finish only.

	$2,950	$2,400	$2,100	$1,850	$1,600	$1,400	$1,200

Values above assume issue to a General, and there must be paperwork to link the gun to the recipient. Otherwise, these values do not apply - see U.S. Property above for applicable values.

VEST POCKET MODEL 1908-HAMMERLESS

- .25 ACP cal., 2 in. barrel, fixed sights, checkered hard rubber grips on early models, walnut on later, magazine disconnect added on guns made after 1916. Mfg. 1908-46.

＊ Blue finish

	$600	$550	$400	$275	$225	$200	$155

＊ Nickel finish

	$850	$600	$435	$375	$325	$250	$200

Add 15% for pearl grips.

100% values assume NIB condition. Subtract 15% if without cardboard box in 95% or better condition only. This model was also supplied with a suede purse - add $150-$200, depending on condition.

Add 200% if "U.S. Property" marked.

MODEL 1909

- .45 ACP cal., straight handle design, 5 in. barrel, checkered walnut grips, approx. 22 mfg., ultra rare.

Extreme rarity factor precludes accurate price evaluation by individual condition factors. Specimens that are original and over 90% have sold for over $35,000 recently.

MODEL 1910

- .45 ACP cal., while not a production model, this gun is probably the most desirable semi-auto Colt pistol.

A nice specimen at a recent auction was gavelled down at $195,000.

GENERAL OFFICER'S PISTOL

- issued not only to Generals, but also to the OSS, U.S. Navy, and other government agencies, .32 ACP cal. U.S. Properties were blue until 1942, after which the parkerized finish became standard (most went to England and exhibit British proofmarks), .380 cal. U.S. Properties were always blue, 1911A1 WWII specimens have standard military finish, and the Rock Island Arsenal .45s were all issued to Generals - see listing below.

M15 (RIA mfg.)

	$6,500	$5,500	$4,500	$3,400	$2,900	$2,200	$1,750

Please refer to separate Model 1903, Model 1908, and Model 1911A1 Military General Officer's Model listings.

PISTOLS: SEMI-AUTO, GOVT. MODEL 1911 COMMERCIAL VARIATIONS

MODEL 1911 COMMERCIAL

- .45 ACP cal., 5 in. barrel, fixed sights, 7 shot mag., flat main spring housing, polished blue finish only (commercial and original military), checkered walnut grips. Denoted by "C" preceding serial number, approx. ser. no. range C1-C138,532. Watch for fakes. Colt licensed other companies to manufacture under government contracts, 39 oz. Mfg. 1912-1925.

Most M1911 variations listed below are not as collectible if under 60% original condition. However, they are still very desirable as shooters, and values (if in original condition) will approximate the 60% prices if in good mechanical condition.

Colt Model 1911s continue to enjoy high demand as of this writing and prices continue to be strong in the 95%-100% condition factors. Be careful on the 98%+ condition specimens, especially the rarer variations. Some collectors are now requiring a potential high-dollar Model 1911 to pass a metallurgical X-ray examination before purchasing.

＊ Model 1911 High Polish Blue - mfg. 1912 through ser. no. 4,500.

	$12,000	$10,000	$7,500	$5,000	$3,000	$1,500	$1,000

GRADING - PPGS™	100%	98%	95%	90%	80%	70%	60%

✱ Model 1911 Regular Finish - pistols mfg. after ser. no. 4,500.

	$4,500	$3,000	$2,200	$1,400	$900	$700	$600

Subtract 15% if without cardboard box in 100% condition only.
Approx. 138,532 were mfg. between 1912-25.
100% values assume NIB condition.

PISTOLS: SEMI-AUTO, GOVT. MODEL 1911 MILITARY VARIATIONS

All pistols in this section are .45 ACP (11.25mm) cal., unless otherwise noted.

COLT MFG. MODEL 1911 MILITARY - right side of slide marked "MODEL OF 1911 U.S. ARMY", blue finish only (NOT parkerized unless reworked).

	100%	98%	95%	90%	80%	70%	60%
✱ 1912 mfg.	$5,250	$4,500	$3,500	$2,300	$1,500	$900	$700
✱ 1913 mfg.	$4,750	$3,950	$2,950	$2,100	$1,450	$875	$700

Add 100% for the first 114 pistols with oversize "United States Property" marking.
Add 75% for pistols in the ser. no. range 115-2,400.

	100%	98%	95%	90%	80%	70%	60%
✱ 1914-1925 mfg.	$3,750	$3,000	$2,500	$1,850	$1,325	$925	$700
✱ 1918 mfg. - can be determined by black Army finish.	$3,500	$2,750	$2,350	$1,700	$1,200	$825	$600

Over 2,550,000 M1911 pistols were ordered for WWI and WWII by the U.S. Government, but approx. 650,000 were mfg. between 1911-25. Those pistols with a parkerized finish will indicate post-WWI reworking, usually marked with an arsenal code (ie. AA-AUGUSTA ARSENAL, SA-SPRINGFIELD ARSENAL, etc.). These reworks do not have the same values as original, unaltered specimens and prices generally are in the $325-$550 range.

NORTH AMERICAN ARMS COMPANY - less than 100 mfg. in Quebec, Canada during 1918 only, blue finish. Be very aware of fakes, as this variation is perhaps the most desirable Colt WWI Govt. semi-auto.

	N/A	N/A	$27,500	$25,000	$18,500	$15,000	$12,000

Note: a characteristic of the North American is the poor finish. The very best condition specimens will be in the 80%-90% range. All mint 100% specimens encountered in this model appear to have been refinished.

REMINGTON - UMC - over 21,500 mfg. (ser. numbered 1-21,676) in 1918-1919 only, blue finish.

	N/A	$3,500	$2,500	$1,500	$975	$725	$600

Most mint 100% specimens encountered in this model have been refinished - be careful.

SPRINGFIELD ARMORY - approx. 30,000 mfg. between 1914-1915, blue finish.

	N/A	$3,500	$2,500	$1,500	$975	$725	$600

Serialization is 72,751-83,855, 102,597-107,596, 113,497-120,566, and 125,567-133,186.
Most mint 100% specimens encountered in this model have been refinished - be careful.

U.S. NAVY - over 31,000 mfg. for U.S. Navy contract between 1911-1914 in defined serial ranges, blue finish. Marked "MODEL OF 1911 U.S. NAVY" on right slide side.

	$6,000	$4,800	$3,600	$2,500	$1,800	$1,200	$900

Add 100% for specimens under ser. no. 3,500.
U.S. Navy specimens are seldom found in over 80% original condition because of the corrosive factor encountered while at sea.

U.S. MARINE CORPS. - approx. 13,500 mfg. between 1911-13 and 1916-18 in defined serial ranges, blue finish, right side of slide marked "MODEL OF 1911 U.S. ARMY".

	$5,000	$4,000	$3,000	$2,000	$1,275	$1,050	$750

WWI BRITISH SERIES - .455 cal., serialized W19,000-W110,695, marked "CALIBRE 455", blue finish, proofed with broad arrow British Ordnance punch. Mfg. 1915-19.

	$3,500	$2,750	$2,100	$1,400	$975	$775	$650

Many WWI British-series M1911s were exported back to the U.S. following WWI and were converted to .45 ACP. Usually, a "5" has been crossed out of the original cal. designation.

GRADING - PPGS™	100%	98%	95%	90%	80%	70%	60%

BRITISH RAF REWORK - this variation is the WWI British series re-issued to RAF officers in the early 1920s, blue finish, differentiated by hand-stamped "RAF" or "R.A.F." on left side of frame.

| | $2,750 | $2,100 | $1,400 | $975 | $775 | $600 | $495 |

A.J. SAVAGE MUNITIONS CO. - mfg. slides only, blue finish, marked in middle on left side of slide with flaming ordnance bomb with "S" in center.

| | $1,850 | $1,500 | $1,100 | $875 | $725 | $625 | $550 |

NORWEGIAN TRIAL MODEL 1911 COLT - 11.25mm cal., approx. 300 mfg. with "C" prefix in 1913-14 only, usually encountered in 90% or less condition.

| | $2,750 | $2,100 | $1,400 | $975 | $775 | $625 | $525 |

These guns were ordered for Norwegian service evaluation and were mfg. by Colt in Hartford, CT.

NORWEGIAN MODEL 1912 11.25MM - 11.25mm cal., mfg. under license from Colt's during 1917, "M1912" slide designation. Approx. 95 mfg.

| | $6,000 | $5,000 | $4,000 | $3,500 | $3,000 | $2,600 | $2,200 |

NORWEGIAN 1914 11.25MM - this model has a distinctive extended slide release, all parts should be serial numbered and have numerous matching numbers, approx. 32,750 mfg. between 1918-1947, mostly military contract, commercial production was very limited.

| | $1,400 | $1,100 | $900 | $695 | $525 | $475 | $425 |

Add 250% for Waffenamt Nazi mfg. (mfg. 1945 only).

Serial ranges with corresponding year of manufacture on this model are as follows: 96-600 - 1918, 601-1,150 - 1919, 1,151-1,650 (Naval Artillery) - 1920, 1,651-2,200 - 1921, 2,201-2,950 - 1922, 2,951-4,610 - 1923, 4,611-6,700 - 1924, 6,701-8,940 - 1925, 8,941-11,820 - 1926, 11,821-15,900 - 1927, 15,901-20,100 - 1928, 20,101-21,440 - 1929, 21,441-21,940 - 1932, 21,941-22,040 - 1933, 22,041-22,141 - 1934, 22,142-22,211 - 1936, 22,212-22,311 - 1939, 22,312-22,361 - 1940, 22,362-26,460 - 1941, 26,461-29,614 - 1942, 29,615-32,335 (Waffenamt Nazi proofed) - 1945, 32,336-32,854 - (last original production) 1947.

Nazi production of the M1914 began in 1941. Between 1941-42, approx. 7,000 pistols were mfg. without Waffenamt stampings. Nazi proofed guns (all 1945 dated) began in the mid-29,000 serial range, and 920 were mfg. with the Nazi Eagle.

ARGENTINE CONTRACT MODEL 1916 - identified by the Argentine seal on top of slide, 1,000 mfg. in ser. range C20,001-C21,000, mfg. 1916.

| | $1,400 | $1,000 | $725 | $575 | $450 | $410 | $350 |

Most specimens of this model have been refinished.

RUSSIAN CONTRACT - approx. 51,000 mfg. in U.S. as commerical guns with random serial numbers approx. C23000-C89000, blue finish, identified by cyrillic inscription on left side of frame (translates to English Order). Mfg. 1916-17.

| | $5,000 | $4,250 | $3,750 | $2,500 | $1,800 | $1,500 | $1,000 |

This contract is seldolm encountered - beware of fakes.

PISTOLS: SEMI-AUTO, GOVT. MODEL 1911A1 COMMERCIAL VARIATIONS

All pistols in this section are .45 ACP cal., unless otherwise noted.

MODEL 1911A1 - blue or parkerized, checkered walnut grips, plastic on later military guns, checkered arched mainspring housing and longer grip safety spur. As in the Model 1911, Colt licensed other companies to produce under govt. contract during WWII. Mfg. 1925-70.

Inspect carefully for arsenal reworks (so marked by proofing, normally on left side of frame above or behind trigger), and reparkerizing.

Most M1911A1 variations listed below are not as collectible if under 60% original condition. However, they are still very desirable as shooters, and values (if in original condition) will approximate the 60% prices if in good mechanical condition.

GRADING - PPGS™	100%	98%	95%	90%	80%	70%	60%

MODEL 1911A1 PRE-WWII COLT COMMERCIAL - "C" preceding serial number, mfg. 1925-42. Approx. ser. no. range C138,533-C215,000.

	100%	98%	95%	90%	80%	70%	60%
	$3,000	$2,400	$1,750	$1,350	$900	$750	$550

Add 50% for nickel finish.

Add 20% with original box and instructions.

MODEL 1911A1 1946-1969 COLT COMMERCIAL - 5 in. barrel, fixed sights, "C" prefix until 1950 when changed to "C" suffix. Approx. 196,000 mfg. 1946-70.

* *1946-1950 Mfg.* - "C" Prefix with serial numbers C221,000-C240,227.

	100%	98%	95%	90%	80%	70%	60%
	$1,450	$1,175	$900	$750	$675	$550	$475

* *1950-1970 Mfg.* - "C" Suffix with serial numbers 240,228C-336,169C.

	100%	98%	95%	90%	80%	70%	60%
	$1,250	$1,000	$850	$745	$675	$550	$475

Add 10% for nickel finish.

SUPER .38 AUTOMATIC PISTOL - identical to Govt. Model .45, except chambered for .38 Super cal., blue or nickel finish. Mfg. 1928-70.

	100%	98%	95%	90%	80%	70%	60%
* *Pre-War*	$4,500	$3,200	$2,875	$1,750	$1,250	$875	$750
* *2nd Model*	$1,650	$1,200	$1,000	$875	$775	$600	$550
* *3rd Model*	$1,400	$875	$725	$660	$575	$500	$435
* *4th Model*	$1,300	$1,100	$900	$675	$575	$500	$450
* *CS Prefix*	$1,300	$1,100	$900	$675	$550	$475	$415

Add approx. 50% for nickel finish.

Pre-war variations are serialized below approx. 37,000.

The 2nd Model may be differentiated by noticing the heavier barrel and Rampant Colt on right side. The 3rd Model has a fat barrel with Rampant Colt on left side. The 4th Model has a thin barrel and Rampant Colt on left side.

SUPER MATCH .38 - similar to Super .38, but hand honed action, match grade barrel. Mfg. 1929-1946. Examine carefully for fakes.

	100%	98%	95%	90%	80%	70%	60%
* *Fixed sights*	$6,000	$5,000	$4,000	$3,000	$2,000	$1,500	$1,200

Add 35% for adj. sights (be cautious of fixed sight Super Matches converted to adj. sights).

A Colt historical letter is available for this model for $100.

MATCH .38 AMU - .38 rimless Spl. cal. (cartridges were mfg. by Win.), this variation was mfg. by Colt from a .38 Super frame (and has .38 Super serialization) with a .38 AMU conversion kit slide, the Army took .45 frames and assembled their guns using .38 AMU kits, blue finish.

	100%	98%	95%	90%	80%	70%	60%
* *Colt mfg. (unmodified)*	$3,500	$2,700	$2,200	$1,900	$1,675	$1,400	$1,100
* *Army modified*	$1,400	$1,200	$995	$800	$650	$550	$495
* *AMU kit only*	$750	$600	$500	$400	$350	$325	$295

On this configuration, the barrel, slide, and mag. were marked ".38 AMU".

SUPER MATCH .38 MS - .38 Super cal., 1961 mfg., serial numbered 101MS - 855MS, 754 total mfg, same configuration as the .38 Midrange.

	100%	98%	95%	90%	80%	70%	60%
	$4,500	$3,500	$2,250	$1,750	$1,500	$1,250	$1,100

1968-1969 BB TRANSITIONAL - denoted by BB prefix on serial number.

	100%	98%	95%	90%	80%	70%	60%
	$1,400	$1,100	$950	$750	$650	$550	$475

.45 ACP TO .22 LR CONVERSION UNIT - consists of slide assembly, barrel, bushing, floating chamber, ejector, recoil spring and guide, fitted with Stevens adj. rear sight, mfg. 1938 to 1947. Colt Master adj. sight 1947-54.

	100%	98%	95%	90%	80%	70%	60%
	$600	$550	$495	$350	$275	$200	$175

Add 100% for prewar mfg. ("U" prefix S/N on top of slide).

Add 200% for pre-war documented Marine Corp units.

GRADING - PPGS™	100%	98%	95%	90%	80%	70%	60%

.22 LR TO .45 ACP CONVERSION UNIT - converted service Ace .22 to .45 ACP cal. Mfg. 1938-1942. Very rare - 112 mfg.

	$4,500	$3,500	$2,500	$1,750	$1,100	$800	$700

Add 50% for original box and instructions.

These units have "U" prefixed serial numbers on top of slide.

PISTOLS: SEMI-AUTO, GOVT. MODEL 1911A1 MILITARY VARIATIONS

All pistols in this section are .45 ACP (11.25mm) cal., unless otherwise noted.

COLT MFG. MODEL 1911A1 MILITARY - approx. 1,643,068 mfg. between 1924-1945, ser. nos. 700,000 - on up, right side of frame marked "M1911A1 U.S. ARMY", bright blue finish up to approx. ser. no. 780,000, parkerized finish after that.

	$1,600	$1,400	$1,200	$925	$775	$675	$400

Add 200% for 1937 Navy (S/N 710,001 - 712,345) Blue.
Add 250% for 1938 Army (S/N 712,350 - 713,645) Blue.
Add 200% for 1939 Navy (S/N 713,646 - 717,281) Blue.
Add 150% for Blue guns outside these serial ranges.
Add 150% for 1942 Navy (S/N 793,658 - 797,639) Parkerized.
Add 150% for early 1911A1 military models with bright blue finish, if in 95%+ original condition.

A large grouping of over 7,000 Commercial 1911A1s was transferred to the U.S. government. These pistols had their commercial serial numbers crudely removed (in ser. range 860,000 - 866,000) and renumbered with a new military serial number. Some of these guns are unusual as the frames and slides have been cut for the Schwartz safety. This variation is rare, and a 20%-30% premium exists depending on the condition.

✴ *Model 1911A1 General Officer's Pistol* - standard military finish (WWII mfg.).

	$3,000	$2,500	$2,000	$1,500	$1,250	$875	$650

Values above assume issue to a General, and there must be paperwork to link the gun to the recipient.

DRAKE NATIONAL MATCH - Drake made slides only for use by the U.S. Army Marksmanship Unit to allow assembly of match guns.

	$1,500	$1,275	$1,000	$800	$625	$550	$400

GOVERNMENT NATIONAL MATCH REWORKS - assembled by government armorers, all parts marked "NM". parkerized finish. Most will be "S.A." marked.

	$1,500	$1,275	$1,000	$700	$625	$550	$400

Add 25% for Air Force pistols marked "AFPG" on slide.

These pistols were made specifically for the U.S. shooting team at Camp Perry.

ITHACA - approx. 369,129 mfg. 1943-1945 in Ithaca, NY, ser. no. ranges 856,405-916,404, 1,208,674-1,279,673, 1,441,431-1,471,430, 1,743,847-1,890,503, 2,075,104-2,134,403, and 2,619,014-2,693,613. Parkerized finish.

	$1,500	$1,300	$950	$725	$625	$550	$450

Add 20% with original shipping carton.

UNION SWITCH AND SIGNAL - approx. 55,000 mfg. 1943 only in Swissvale, PA, ser. no. range 1,041,405-1,096,404. Sandblast and blue finish.

	$2,650	$2,250	$1,750	$1,000	$700	$500	$450

REMINGTON RAND - approx. 1,086,624 mfg. 1943-1945 in Syracuse, NY, ser. no. ranges 916,405-1,041,404, 1,279,649-1,441,430, 1,471,431-1,609,528, 1,743,847-1,816,641, 1,890,504-2,075,103, 2,134,404-2,244,803, and 2,380,014-2,619,013. Parkerized finish.

	$1,400	$1,200	$900	$700	$600	$550	$450

Add 20% with original shipping carton.

GRADING - PPGS™	100%	98%	95%	90%	80%	70%	60%

SINGER MFG. CO. - 500 mfg. 1942 in Elizabeth, NJ, ser. no. range S800,001-S800,500. Blue finish with plastic grips.

	N/A	$24,000	$18,500	$15,000	$11,500	$10,000	$8,500

The Singer 1911A1 variation is one of the most sought-after Colt models. In recent years, values have increased significantly, and as a result, many fakes have emerged. Therefore, be very cautions when contemplating a purchase. Most specimens are now recognized by ser. no. and be very cautious when contemplating a purchase. Some collectors unsure of authenticity are now requiring X-ray testing to determine originality (slide restampings, ser. no. changes, etc.).

MEXICAN CONTRACT - mfg. approx. 1921-27 with "C" prefix ser. nos., frames marked "EJERCITO MEXICANO", most surviving examples show much use.

		$3,500	$2,500	$1,900	$1,500	$1,200	$900	$775

BRAZILIAN CONTRACT

		$5,500	$4,500	$3,000	$2,000	$1,250	$900	$700

ARGENTINE CONTRACT MODEL 1927 - serial numbered 1-10,000 under the mainspring housing and on the top of slide (should be matching), must have Argentine crest and "Model 1927" on right side of slide, external serial number applied to top of slide by the Argentine Arsenal, most have been Arsenal refinished.

		$1,150	$950	$750	$625	$550	$495	$450

Add 50% if original finish.

ARGENTINE MFG. - in 1927, the Argentina Arsenal "DGFM-FMAP" began manufacturing the Model 1911A1. The slide marking is two lines and reads "EJERCITO ARGENTINO SIST.COLT.CAL. 11.25mm MOD.1927".

		$750	$650	$500	$450	$400	$350	$325

Add 50% if original finish.

Add 20% for Argentine Navy "ARMADA NACIONAL" (small shipments between 1912-1948). Markings vary on different types.

This variation is not to be confused with the Ballester Molina/Rigaud Models (sold by Hispano Argentino Fábrica de Automóviles S.A., in Buenos Aires, Argentina - also known as the HAF-DASA). Please refer to the Hispano Argentino Fábrica de Automóviles S.A. section of this text.

ARGENTINE SERVICE MODEL ACE - .22 LR cal., conversion of the 1927 Argentine Contract Model, bottom right side of slide is marked "TRANSE A CAL .22 POR EST. VENTURINI S.A." Originally imported during 1996, this model was arsenal refinished and most pistols were in the 70%-95% condition range.

		$575	$525	$475	$425	$400	$375	$350

PISTOLS: SEMI-AUTO, ACE MODELS, 1931-1947 MFG.

COMMERCIAL ACE - .22 LR cal., similar to Government .45 ACP, but in .22 LR cal., 4 3/4 in. barrel, blue, adj. sights, checkered walnut grips, almost 11,000 mfg. (ser. no. range 1-10,935) 1931-41 and 1947.

		$3,000	$2,500	$1,750	$1,300	$900	$750	$500

Add 20% with original box and instructions.

SERVICE MODEL ACE - .22 LR cal., 5 in. barrel, blue or parkerized finish, similar to .45 ACP National Match except for caliber, has floating chamber to simulate .45 ACP recoil, limited mfg. 1935-45.

		$4,500	$3,500	$2,300	$2,000	$1,500	$1,000	$700

Add 20% with original box and instructions.

Subtract 10% for parkerized finish.

This variation is marked "SERVICE MODEL" on left frame, serial numbers have "SM" prefix and have ranges to approx. 13,800. Other markings such as "U.S. PROP'Y" or "R.S." (inspectors' marks) have also been observed on this model, and can add a premium if original condition is 95% or more.

GRADING - PPGS™	100%	98%	95%	90%	80%	70%	60%

PISTOLS: SEMI-AUTO, NATIONAL MATCH MODELS - PRE-WWII

NATIONAL MATCH - .45 ACP cal., similar to Government Model, except has hand-honed action, match grade barrel, blue. Mfg. 1933-41 within ser. no. range C164,800-C215,000.

Add 10% with original box and instructions.

		100%	98%	95%	90%	80%	70%	60%
✳	*Fixed sights*	$4,500	$3,500	$2,500	$1,500	$1,200	$900	$650
✳	*Adj. sights*	$8,000	$6,500	$5,000	$3,500	$1,750	$1,200	$850

PISTOLS: SEMI-AUTO, NATIONAL MATCH MODELS - WWII & POST-WWII

Add 10% for NIB condition on models listed below.

NATIONAL MATCH - .45 ACP cal., match grade barrel, new design bushing, flat or arched (mfg. approx. 1959-64) mainspring housing, long adj. stop trigger, hand fitted slide with enlarged ejection port, adj. target sights, gold medallions in grips, "NM" suffix. Mfg. 1957-70.

$1,400	$1,200	$900	$750	$700	$625	$600

Note: This model was the first Gold Cup National Match Model manufactured following WWII.

MKIII NATIONAL MATCH - .38 Spl. cal., similar to National Match, except chambered for .38 Spl., mid-range wadcutter, "NMR" or "MR" suffix. Mfg. 1961-74.

$1,450	$1,200	$900	$750	$700	$600	$500

MKIV/SERIES 70 GOLD CUP NATIONAL MATCH - .45 ACP cal., flat mainspring housing, Colt blue finish accurizer barrel and bushing, adj. trigger, target hammer, solid rib, Colt-Eliason sight. Mfg. 1970-83.

$1,150	$895	$700	$575	$500	$450	$400

MKIV/SERIES 70 GOLD CUP 75TH ANNIVERSARY NATIONAL MATCH - similar to Gold Cup, except was mfg. for commemorative aspect of Camp Perry, 1978, 200 mfg. 1978 only.

$1,250	$995	$750	$650	$550	$450	$425

GOLD CUP MKIV SERIES 80 NATIONAL MATCH - .45 ACP cal., 5 in. barrel flat mainspring housing, 7 or 8 shot mag., accurizer barrel and bushing, wide grooved adj. target trigger, target hammer, solid rib, Colt-Eliason rear sight, 39 oz. Mfg. 1983-96.

$950	$775	$600	$475	$425	$375	$350

Last MSR was $937.

In 1992, this model was updated to accept an 8 shot mag. During 1997, this updated model was designated the Gold Cup Trophy.

✳ *Stainless Gold Cup National Match* - similar to Gold Cup, only manufactured from stainless steel, matte finish. Mfg. late 1986-96.

$950	$775	$600

Last MSR was $1,003.

Add $70 for "Ultimate" bright stainless steel finish.
Add 10% for NIB condition.

✳ *Elite IX Gold Cup National Match* - 9mm Para. cal., stainless steel and blue, marked "GCNM" on right side, and "ELITE IX – 9mm Luger" on left side, "IX" prefix in ser. no.

$895	$725	$575	$450	$400	$365	$335

Add 10% for NIB condition.

✳ *.38 Super Elite National Match* - two-tone gun (stainless slide and blue frame), special edition by Accu-Sports.

$1,150	$925	$700

GRADING - PPGS™	100%	98%	95%	90%	80%	70%	60%

✳ *Bullseye National Match* - .45 ACP cal., hand-built, tuned, and adjusted by Colt's custom gunsmiths for precise match accuracy, includes factory-installed Bo-Mar sights, equipped with carrying case and 2 extra mags. Mfg. 1991-92.

	$1,325	$1,075	$895	$800	$725	$650	$600

Last MSR was $1,500.

✳ *Presentation Gold Cup* - .45 ACP cal., similar to regular Gold Cup Series 80 National Match, except has a deep blue-mirror bright finish accented by custom jeweled hammer, trigger, and barrel hood. Supplied with oak and velvet custom case. Mfg. 1991-92.

	$1,075	$895	$800	$725	$650	$600	$550

Last MSR was $1,195.

PISTOLS: SEMI-AUTO, SINGLE ACTION - RECENT MFG.

SEMI-AUTO CUSTOM SHOP ENGRAVING PRICING - PRE-1991

Values below represent pre-1991 factory semi-auto Custom Shop A-D engraving options, before they started separate Standard, Expert, and Master level pricing (1997). It should also be understood that, in most cases, the quality of the engraving and notoriety of the engraver can be as important as the amount of coverage.

Small Frame Engraving Options: includes Mustang, .380 ACP Government, Detective Special, and Diamondback models.

Add $776 for Class "A" Engraving (1/4 Metal Coverage).
Add $959 for Class "B" Engraving (1/2 Metal Coverage).
Add $1,426 for Class "C" Engraving (3/4 Metal Coverage).
Add $1,814 for Class "D" Engraving (Full Metal Coverage).

Medium Frame Engraving Options: includes .45 ACP Gold Cup, Government Model, Officer's ACP, Python, Combat Commander, King Cobra, Trooper MKV, Lawman MKV, and Delta Elite models.

Add $969 for Class "A" Engraving (1/4 Metal Coverage).
Add $1,199 for Class "B" Engraving (1/2 Metal Coverage).
Add $1,783 for Class "C" Engraving (3/4 Metal Coverage).
Add $2,289 for Class "D" Engraving (Full Metal Coverage).
Add 7% for 6 in. barrel, 14% for 8 in. barrel, or 25% for stainless steel construction.

Special engraving/options include inlays, seals, custom grips, and lettering. Prices were quoted upon request. Smooth ivory grips were $215 extra (1990 retail).

Beginning in 1991, Colt began shipping all models in a distinctive blue plastic carrying case/shipping container.

SEMI-AUTO CURRENT CUSTOM SHOP ENGRAVING PRICING

Please refer to the "Colt Custom Shop Engraving - Current Mfg." listing earlier in this section for current semi-auto engraving options and pricing. Semi-auto custom-order quotations from Colt are available at $25 each (deductible from work order).

JUNIOR POCKET MODEL - .22 S or .25 ACP cal., 2 1/4 in. barrel, blue, checkered walnut grips, made by Astra in Spain from 1958-68.

.22 Short	$350	$320	$250	$230	$190	$160	$140
.25 ACP	$300	$275	$225	$200	$165	$140	$130

Add 10% for nickel finish.

A very few conversion kits were offered for this model. They are rare and asking prices are $250-$325 if in mint condition.

COLT AUTOMATIC CALIBER .25 - .25 ACP cal., mfg. by Firearms International for Colt between 1970-73.

	$325	$300	$250	$210	$175	$150	$130

GRADING - PPGS™	100%	98%	95%	90%	80%	70%	60%

COMMANDER (PRE-70 SERIES)
- 9mm Para, .38 Super, or .45 ACP cal., 4 1/4 in. barrel, full size grips, alloy (Lightweight Model) variations. Mfg. 1950-76.

	100%	98%	95%	90%	80%	70%	60%
9mm Para.	$995	$775	$650	$550	$450	$400	$350
.38 Super/.45 ACP	$1,095	$950	$875	$750	$550	$495	$450

Add 50% for Springfield Armory test pistols.

This model has "LW" suffix.

GOVERNMENT MODEL MKIV/SERIES 70
- .45 ACP, .38 Super, 9mm Para., or 9mm Steyr cal., 5 in. barrel, checkered walnut grips/medallion. Series 70 models were serial numbered with "SM" prefixes (approx. 3,000 mfg.), "70G" prefixes 1970-76, "70L" and "70S" prefixes also (see Serialization section for more information), "G70" suffixes 1976-80, "B70" suffixes 1979-81, and "70B" prefixes 1981-83. Mfg. 1970-83.

	100%	98%	95%	90%	80%	70%	60%
Blue finish	$925	$700	$525	$425	$350	$315	$285
Nickel finish	$1,000	$750	$550	$450	$350	$315	$285

Add 10% if in NIB condition, 20% for NIB with early two-piece box.

9mm Steyr was made for European exportation only. However, a few specimens have found their way into the United States. Prices for NIB specimens are in the $750 range.

✳ *Series 70 Combat Govt.* - .45 ACP cal., bluish-black metal finish, features modifications for combat shooting, forerunner to the Combat Elite.

	100%	98%	95%	90%	80%	70%	60%
	$995	$775	$650	$550	$475	$395	$335

Add 10% for NIB condition.

✳ *Series 70 Lightweight Commander* - 7.65mm (.30 Luger), 9mm Para, .38 Super, or .45 ACP cal., 4 1/4 in. barrel, full size grips, this model is denoted by a "CLW" prefix. Mfg. 1970-83.

	100%	98%	95%	90%	80%	70%	60%
9mm Para.	$950	$750	$650	$525	$450	$375	$315
.38 Super/.45 ACP	$995	$775	$675	$550	$450	$375	$315
7.65mm	$2,500	$2,000	$1,575	$1,250	$995	$875	$750

Add 10% for NIB condition.

500 Lightweight Commanders were mfg. in 7.65mm cal. during 1971. While most of these were mfg. for export trade, 5 were sold in the U.S.

✳ *Series 70 Combat Commander*

	100%	98%	95%	90%	80%	70%	60%
	$875	$725	$625	$525	$450	$375	$300

Add 10% for NIB condition.

This model was also available in satin nickel finish (scarce).

✳ *Conversion Unit* - converts .45 ACP to .22 LR, mfg. 1954-84 with either Accro adj. rear sight or fixed sight.

	100%	98%	95%	90%	80%	70%	60%
Adj. Sight	$550	$500	$350	$300	$250	$200	$175
Fixed Sight	$650	$550	$400	$325	$250	$200	$175

Add 50% for conversion units in bright nickel finish (very scarce).

GOVERNMENT MODEL SERIES 70 MODEL O
- .45 ACP cal., patterned after the original Series 70 pistol, high polish blue finish or stainless steel (new 2005), new release from the Custom Shop beginning 2002.

	100%	98%	95%	90%	80%	70%	60%
MSR $1,100	$950	$825	$750	$650	$575	$495	$400

Add $100 for stainless steel (new 2005).

POST-WAR ACE SERVICE MODEL
- .22 LR cal., similar specifications to previous pre-WWII manufacture, blue (most common) or electroless nickel from Custom Shop finish, "SM" prefix (most common) or "B 70" suffix, approx. 30,000 mfg. between 1978-1982.

	100%	98%	95%	90%	80%	70%	60%
	$995	$795	$675	$575	$525	$450	$425

Add 10% for NIB condition.

This model is serial numbered approx. SM14,001-SM43,830.

GRADING - PPGS™	100%	98%	95%	90%	80%	70%	60%

GOVERNMENT MODEL MKIV/SERIES 80

.38 Super, 9mm Para. (disc. 1992), or .45 ACP (disc. 1996) cal., single action, 5 in. barrel, 7 or 8 (new 1992) shot mag. in .45 ACP, approx. 38 oz., action has firing pin safety, checkered walnut (pre-1991 mfg.) or rubber combat style grips with medallion (new 1991). Production started in 1983 with ser. no. FG01000.

* *Blue Finish* - this finish was disc. in 1997.

	$775	$650	$525	$425	$350	$325	$300

Last MSR was $600.

Add 5% for 9mm Para. (disc. 1992) cal.
Add 10% for NIB condition.

* *Nickel Finish* - .45 ACP (disc. 1986) or .38 Super (disc. in 1987) cal.

	$825	$575	$550	$450	$375	$325	$300

Last MSR was $735.

Add 10% for NIB condition.

* *Satin Nickel/Blue* - is supplied with Colt-Pachmayr grips. Disc. 1986.

	$800	$700	$525	$425	$350	$310	$290

Last MSR was $557.

Add 10% for NIB condition.

* *Stainless Steel* - 9mm Para. (mfg. 1991-92), .38 Super (new 1990), .40 S&W (new 1992) or .45 ACP cal. Disc. 1998.

	$750	$650	$525				

Last MSR was $813.

Add 5% for 9mm Para. (disc. 1992) cal.
Add 10% for NIB condition.

* *"Ultimate" Bright Stainless Steel* - .38 Super (new 1991) or .45 ACP cal., high polish stainless finish. Mfg. 1986-96.

	$850	$725	$600				

Last MSR was $863.

Add 10% for NIB condition.

* *Limited Class Model .45 ACP* - .45 ACP cal., designed for tactical competition, includes parkerized matte finish, lightweight composite trigger, ambidextrous safety, upswept grip safety, beveled mag. well, accurized, includes signed target. Mfg. 1994-97.

	$850	$700	$575	$525	$400	$375	$350

Last MSR was $936.

* *Custom Compensated Model .45 ACP* - .45 ACP cal., designed for serious competitive shooting, blue slide with full profile BAT Compensator, Bo-Mar rear sight, flared funnel mag. well. Mfg. by Custom Shop 1994-98.

	$1,900	$1,500	$1,250	$1,000	$875	$750	$625

Last MSR was $2,428.

MODEL M1911A1 CUSTOM TACTICAL GOV'T - LEVEL I

.45 ACP cal., designed for tactical competition, Commander style hammer, beveled/contoured mag. well, nylon flat mainspring housing, ambidextrous safety, long nylon trigger with over-travel stop, available in Officer's or Commmander's length. Mfg. 1998-2001.

	$640	$560	$495	$450	$400	$360	$330

Last MSR was $730.

In late 1999, this model was redesignated the Model O Custom Tactical Gov't.

* *Custom Tactical Gov't. Model - Level II* - similar to Level I, except has Videcki long aluminum trigger with over-travel stop, Heine fixed combat sights, Colt match grade barrel bushing, high-ride grip safety with palm swell, double diamond stocks. Mfg. 1998-2001.

	$825	$750	$650	$575	$495	$400	$300

Last MSR was $935.

GRADING - PPGS™	100%	98%	95%	90%	80%	70%	60%

* ***Custom Tactical Gov't. Model - Level III*** - similar to Level II, except has Bo-Mar adj. rear sight, super match hammer. Mfg. 1998-2001.

	$1,150	$1,025	$875	$750	$650	$575	$495

Last MSR was $1,350.

COMBAT GOVERNMENT SERIES 80 - .45 ACP cal., dark matte metal finish, features modifications for combat shooting, successor to the Series 70 Combat Govt. Disc.

	$850	$700	$550	$425	$375	$325	$300

Add 10% for NIB condition.

* ***Special Combat Government Competition Model*** - .38 Super (new 2005) or .45 ACP cal., competition model featuring skeletonized trigger, custom tuning, polished ramp, 5 in. throated barrel, flared ejection port, and cut-out hammer. Supplied with two 8 shot mags., two-tone (new 2004) or hard chrome slide and receiver, Bo-Mar rear and Clark dovetail front sight, flared mag. well, shipped with certified target. Mfg. by the Custom Shop. New 1992.

MSR $2,000	$1,675	$1,350	$1,050	$925	$800	$650	$575

* ***Special Combat Government (Carry Model)*** - similar to Special Combat Government, except has royal blue finish, bar-dot night sights, and ambidextrous safety. Mfg. 1992-2000.

	$1,125	$925	$750	$650	$575	$495	$400

Last MSR was $1,365.

* ***Combat Elite*** - .38 Super or .45 ACP cal., similar to Gold Cup, only with wraparound rubber grips, beveled magazine well, stainless steel receiver with carbon steel slide, and Accro adj. sighting system. Disc. 1996.

	$850	$725	$550	$470	$430	$400	$370

Last MSR was $895.

* ***Conversion Unit - Series 80*** - converts Series 80 Govt. Model only to .22 LR or 9mm Para., mfg. 1984-86, 1995, and 1998, with Accro adj. rear sight.

9mm Para.	$725	$650	$500	$400	$325	$250	$200
.22 LR (mfg. 1984-86)	$750	$650	$500	$400	$325	$250	$200

Last MSR was $305.

.22 LR (mfg. 1995 only, rare)							
	$775	$675	$525	$425	$325	$250	$200

> Colt Ace II Conversion Unit - similar to above, except features an aluminum slide and barrel w/o floating chamber, does not have hold open feature. Mfg. 1998.

	$350	$295	$275	$225	$190	$175	$150

COMBAT TARGET MODEL SERIES 80 - .45 ACP cal. only, 5 in. barrel, adj. sights, matte finish. Mfg. 1997 only.

	$700	$580	$485	$435	$405	$385	$365

Last MSR was $768.

* ***Combat Target Model Stainless*** - similar to Combat Target Model, except stainless steel finish. Mfg. 1997 only.

	$745	$625	$500				

Last MSR was $820.

COMMANDER LIGHTWEIGHT SERIES 80 - 9mm Para, .38 Super, or .45 ACP cal., 4 1/4 in. barrel, similar to Government Model, except shorter and lighter alloy frame, fixed sights, round spur hammer, 27 1/2 oz. Mfg. 1983-97.

	$750	$625	$525	$475	$420	$400	$380

Last MSR was $735.

Add 10% for .38 Super or 9mm Para. (disc.) cals.

Some pistols are marked "Super Lite Commander - .38 Super - " on left side, and "Lightweight Commander Model" on right side. There may be an "M" on magazine floorplate, with the Colt logo.

GRADING - PPGS™	100%	98%	95%	90%	80%	70%	60%

COMBAT COMMANDER SERIES 80 - .38 Super (disc.), 9mm Para. (disc. 1992), or .45 ACP cal., similar to Lightweight, except has steel frame.

* *Blue Finish* - disc. 1996.

	$695	$575	$485	$440	$415	$395	$375

Last MSR was $735.

Add $20 for 9mm Para. (disc.) or .38 Super (disc.) cal.

* *Blue Slide/Stainless Steel Receiver* - .45 ACP cal., two-tone matte finish, upswept grip safety, lightweight perforated trigger, black Hogue grips, 8 shot mag., 35 oz. Mfg. 1998 only.

	$750	$600	$495	$440	$415	$395	$375

Last MSR was $813.

* *Stainless Steel* - .38 Super (mfg. 1992-97) or .45 ACP cal. Mfg. 1990-98.

	$850	$675	$550

Last MSR was $813.

* *Satin Nickel* - disc. 1986.

	$850	$675	$550	$450	$425	$395	$375

Last MSR was $550.

* *Gold Cup Commander* - .45 ACP cal., features custom shop alterations including heavy duty adj. target sights, beveled mag. well, serrated front strap, checkered mainspring housing, wide grip safety, and Palo Alto wood grips. Mfg. 1991-93.

	$865	$715	$595	$550	$495	$440	$395

Last MSR was $936.

* *Gold Cup Commander Stainless* - stainless variation of the Gold Cup Commander. Mfg. 1992-disc.

	$870	$715	$595

Last MSR was $949

OFFICER'S MODEL SERIES 80 - .45 ACP cal. only, 3 1/2 in. barrel, 34 oz., 6 shot mag., short version of the Government Model. Mfg. 1985-disc.

* *Blue Finish* - disc. 1996.

	$700	$600	$495	$400	$365	$345	$325

Last MSR was $735.

* *Matte Blue Finish* - disc. 1991.

	$675	$575	$500	$380	$330	$300	$275

Last MSR was $625.

* *Officer's Stainless Steel* - matte stainless steel finish. Mfg. 1986-97.

	$700	$600	$495

Last MSR was $813.

Add $74 for "Ultimate" bright stainless steel finish (mfg. 1987-96).

* *Officer's Lightweight* - similar to Officer's ACP, except has alloy frame and weighs 24 oz. Mfg. 1986-97.

	$675	$575	$500	$340	$315	$295	$275

Last MSR was $735.

* *Concealed Carry Officer* - .45 ACP cal., features matte stainless steel slide with matte blue aluminum alloy receiver, 7 shot mag., black contoured Hogue grips, upswept grip safety, lightweight perforated trigger, 26 oz. Mfg. 1998 only.

	$650	$525	$450	$410	$380	$350	$325

Last MSR was $813.

* *Officer's Satin Nickel* - disc. 1985.

	$725	$575	$525	$375	$295	$260	$235

Last MSR was $513.

* *General Officer's Model* - bright stainless steel with rosewood grips, special edition. Disc. 1996.

	$700	$600	$500

Last MSR was $750.

COLT Z 40 - .40 S&W cal., DAO, alloy frame, double column mag., firing pin safety, 3 dot sights, blue finish with black checkered synthetic grips and silver trigger, straight backstrap, marked "Colt Z40" on top of slide, while approx. 750-800 pieces were mfg. 1998-99 by CZ for a Colt subcontract, they were never shipped, and as a result, very few have made it into the U.S. to date from the Czech Republic.

$595	$525	$475	$425	$400	$375	$350

DEFENDER MODEL O - .40 S&W (mfg. 1999 only) or .45 ACP cal., 3 in. barrel with 3 dot sights, 7 shot mag., rubber wrap-around grips with finger grooves, lightweight perforated trigger, stainless steel slide and frame - frame finished in matte stainless, firing pin safety, 22.5 oz. New 1998.

MSR $950	$800	$675	$575

* *Defender Plus* - .45 ACP cal., similar to Defender Model O, except has aluminum receiver and 8 shot mag. Mfg. 2002-2003.

	$750	$625	$500

Last MSR was $876.

XSE SERIES MODEL O - .45 ACP cal., 4 or 5 (Govt. Model only) in. barrel, stainless brushed finish, front and rear slide serrations, checkered double diamond rosewood grips, 3 dot sights, new roll marking and enhanced tolerances, extended ambidextrous thumb safeties. New 2000.

* *Government* - 5 in. barrel, blue (new 2002) or stainless brushed (SS Model) finish, 8 shot mag.

MSR $1,100	$925	$800	$650

* *Concealed Carry Officers SS* - features lightweight aluminum alloy frame, 4 1/4 in. barrel and 7 shot mag. Limited mfg. 2000 only.

	$650	$550	$450

Last MSR was $750.

* *Commander SS* - .38 Super cal., features 4 1/4 in. barrel and 8 shot mag.

MSR $1,100	$925	$800	$650

* *Lightweight Commander SS* - features lightweight aluminum alloy frame, 4 1/4 in. barrel and 8 shot mag.

MSR $1,100	$925	$800	$650

GOLD CUP NATIONAL MATCH MKIV/SERIES 80 - please refer to listing under Pistols: Semi-Auto, National Match Models - WWII and Post-WWII.

GOLD CUP TROPHY (MODEL O) - .45 ACP cal., flat mainspring housing, 7 (disc.) or 8 shot mag., accurizer barrel and bushing, round top slide, adj. aluminum trigger, target hammer, Bo-Mar Elliason style rear sight, checkered black wrap-around rubber grips, shipped with test target, 39 oz. New 1997.

MSR $1,300	$1,025	$850	$700	$600	$500	$450	$400

This model replaced the MKIV/Series 80 Gold Cup National Match in 1997, and is only available from the Colt Custom Shop.

* *Stainless Gold Cup Trophy* - similar to Gold Cup Trophy, only manufactured from stainless steel, matte finish, 39 oz. New 1997.

MSR $1,400	$1,100	$900	$750

GRADING - PPGS™	100%	98%	95%	90%	80%	70%	60%

1991 SERIES MODEL O (MKIV SERIES 80) - 9mm Para. (disc. 2001) or .45 ACP cal., similar to original WWII issue pistols with government issue parkerized matte finish, fixed sights, and black composite grips, 5 in. barrel, 7 shot mag., 38 oz., includes brown molded case. New 1991.

MSR $870	$725	$595	$475	$385	$325	$295	$275

This model is serialized consecutively with the last batch of Govt. models manufactured during 1945.

* *Model 1991 Stainless Steel* - features matte stainless steel frame and slide. New 1996.

MSR $920	$750	$625	$500				

* *Model 1991 Commander* - .45 ACP cal., 4 1/4 in. barrel, full size grip, 7 shot mag., parkerized finish, 36 oz. New 1993.

MSR $870	$725	$595	$475	$385	$325	$295	$275

>**Model 1991 Commander SS** - similar to Model M1991 A1 Commander, except is stainless steel. New 1999.

MSR $920	$750	$625	$500				

* *Model 1991 Officer's Compact* - similar to Model M1991 A1, except has 3 1/2 in. barrel, 6 shot mag., 34 oz. Mfg. 1992-99.

	$500	$400	$350	$325	$300	$250	$225

Last MSR was $556.

>**Model 1991 Officer's Stainless Compact** - similar to Model M1991 A1 Officer's Compact, except is stainless steel. Mfg. 1999 only.

	$510	$440	$355				

Last MSR was $610.

.38 SUPER MODEL O - .38 Super cal., 5 in. barrel, M1911 (bright stainless only) or M1911A1 style frame, Govt. Model, choice of blue, stainless steel, or bright stainless steel frame/slide, 3 dot sights, checkered rubber or double diamond walnut (bright stainless only) grips, 9 shot mag., beveled mag. well. New 2003.

MSR $950	$795	$635	$525	$450	$415	$385	$350

Add $30 for stainless steel, or $250 for bright stainless steel.

GUNSITE MODEL O - .45 ACP cal., M1911 style frame, Series 70 firing system, 4.25 (Commander configuration) or 5 in. barrel, checkered thin rosewood grips, blue or stainless steel, many shooting features are included, such as serrated flat mainspring housing, Gold Cup front strap serrations, Heine front and Novak rear sights, two 8 shot Wilson mags., McCormick hammer and sear, slide marked with Gunsite logo. New 2003.

MSR $1,400	$1,250	$1,050	$850	$725	$650	$575	$525

M1911 MODEL O SERIES 70 - .45 ACP cal., 5 in. barrel, accurate reproduction of the Model 1911 U.S. military sidearm, original style checkered walnut grips, carbonia blue finish, 7 shot mag., original WWI roll marks, original style packaging (cardboard box with wax paper), mfg. by the Custom Shop, 38 oz. New 2003.

MSR $990	$875	$775	$675	$575	$475	$425	$375

M1911A1 MODEL O - .45 ACP cal., 5 in. barrel, incorporates pre-Series 70 firing system, accurate reproduction of the Model 1911A1 U.S. military sidearm, original style composite grips, parkerized finish or stainless steel construction, 7 shot mag., original WWII roll marks, lanyard loop on arched serrated mainspring housing, wide spur hammer, safety and slide stop with original serrations, 38 oz., original style packaging (cardboard box with wax paper), approx. 4,000 mfg. by the Custom Shop. Mfg. 2001-2004.

	$835	$750	$650	$550	$450	$400	$350

Last MSR was $940.

Add $25 for stainless steel (new 2004).

GRADING - PPGS™	100%	98%	95%	90%	80%	70%	60%

DELTA ELITE - 10mm cal., 5 in. barrel, black neoprene grips, high profile 3 dot sights, blue finish, 8 shot mag., 38 oz. Mfg. 1987-96.

| | $800 | $650 | $525 | $450 | $400 | $300 | $275 |

Last MSR was $807.

The first 500 guns of this model (mfg. 1985) were called the Delta Elite First Edition, and featured laser engraving with gold-fill, smooth wood grips, and were furnished with presentation cases. Current pricing is in the $795-$995 range.

* *Stainless Steel* - matte stainless steel finish. Mfg. 1989-96.

| | $750 | $550 | $455 |

Last MSR was $860.

Add $78 for "Ultimate" brite stainless steel finish (disc. 1993).

The first 1,000 guns of this model (mfg. 1988) were called the Delta Elite First Edition, and featured stamped lettering on slide, ebony grips, and did not have display cases. Current pricing is in the $795-$850 range.

DELTA GOLD CUP STAINLESS - 10mm cal., target variation, includes Accro adj. rear sight and trigger (serrated also), wraparound combat grips. Mfg. 1989-93, re-released 1995-96.

| | $900 | $650 | $525 |

Last MSR was $1,027.

* *Delta Gold Cup Blue* - similar to Delta Gold Cup Stainless, except has blue finish. Mfg. 1991 only.

| | $775 | $600 | $500 | $450 | $400 | $360 | $330 |

Last MSR was $870.

.380 GOVERNMENT MODEL SERIES 80 - .380 ACP cal. only, single action, 3 1/4 in. barrel, 7 shot mag., fixed sights, composition stocks, 21 3/4 oz. New 1985.

* *Blue Finish* - finish disc. in 1997.

| | $550 | $450 | $395 | $325 | $250 | $215 | $200 |

Last MSR was $474.

* *Nickel Finish* - bright polish nickel finish with white composite grips. Disc. 1994.

| | $595 | $495 | $425 | $350 | $275 | $235 | $215 |

Last MSR was $504.

* *Coltguard Finish* - employs a high-strength electroless matte nickel finish. Mfg. 1986-89.

| | $595 | $495 | $425 | $350 | $275 | $235 | $215 |

Last MSR was $406.

* *Stainless Steel* - mfg. 1989-97.

| | $595 | $495 | $425 |

Last MSR was $508.

GOVT. POCKETLITE L.W. - similar to .380 Series 80 Govt. Model, except frame is mfg. with alloy, blue or nickel/stainless (mfg. 1992-93) finish only, black composition grips, 14 3/4 oz. Mfg. 1991-97.

| | $495 | $425 | $350 | $300 | $265 | $235 | $200 |

Last MSR was $462.

Add $30 for nickel/stainless finish (disc. 1993).

* *Govt. Pocketlite Teflon Nickel/Stainless* - similar to Govt. Pocketlite L.W., except has combination of Teflon nickel, stainless steel finish. Mfg. 1997-98.

| | $550 | $450 | $350 |

Last MSR was $508.

MUSTANG - similar to .380 Series Govt., except has 2 3/4 in. barrel, single action, 5 or 6 (new 1992) shot mag., blue finish only, 18 1/2 oz. Mfg. 1986-97.

| | $550 | $475 | $400 | $325 | $275 | $225 | $195 |

Last MSR was $462.

GRADING - PPGS™	100%	98%	95%	90%	80%	70%	60%

* ✱ *Nickel finish* - bright polish nickel finish with white composite grips. Mfg. 1987-94.

	$595	$495	$425	$350	$275	$235	$215

Last MSR was $504.

* ✱ *Stainless Steel* - stainless steel variation of the Mustang. Mfg. 1990-97.

	$595	$495	$425				

Last MSR was $508.

* ✱ *Coltguard finish* - employs a high-strength electroless matte nickel finish. Mfg. 1987.

	$595	$495	$425	$350	$275	$235	$215

Last MSR was $406.

MUSTANG PLUS II - .380 ACP cal. only, 2 3/4 in. barrel, blue finish, black composition grips, 7 shot mag., 20 oz. Mfg. 1988-96.

	$550	$475	$400	$325	$275	$225	$195

Last MSR was $462.

This model has the full grip length of the .380 Government Model.

* ✱ *Stainless Steel* - stainless steel variation of the Mustang Plus II. Mfg. 1990-97.

	$595	$495	$425				

Last MSR was $508.

MUSTANG POCKETLITE L.W. - similar to Mustang, except has aluminum alloy receiver and stainless slide, blue (disc. 1997) or nickel/stainless finish, black composite grips, 12 1/2 oz. Introduced 1987.

	$550	$475	$400	$325	$275	$225	$195

Last MSR was $462.

* ✱ *Nickel/Stainless Steel Finish* - similar to Mustang Pocketlite, except has nickel finish frame and stainless steel slide. Mfg. 1991-96.

	$595	$495	$425	$350	$275	$235	$215

Last MSR was $493.

* ✱ *Mustang Pocketlite Teflon Nickel/Stainless* - similar to Mustang Pocketlite L.W., except has combination of Teflon nickel, stainless steel finish. Mfg. 1997-99.

	$595	$495	$425				

Last MSR was $508.

* ✱ *Lady Elite* - features hard chrome receiver, blue slide with silver painted rollmark, finger extension mag., soft carrying case, limited mfg. 1995-96.

	$595	$495	$425	$350	$275	$235	$215

Last MSR was $612.

* ✱ *Nite Lite .380* - .380 ACP cal., features bar-dot glowing night sight, Teflon coated alloy receiver with stainless slide, finger extension mag., includes carrying case. Mfg. 1994 only.

	$595	$495	$425	$350	$275	$235	$215

Last MSR was $577.

PISTOLS: SEMI-AUTO, DOUBLE ACTION - RECENT MFG.

DOUBLE EAGLE SERIES 90 I & II - 9mm Para. (mfg. 1991 only), .38 Super (mfg. 1991 only), .45 ACP, or 10mm (disc. 1993) cal., double action semi-auto that operates on the Browning/Colt short recoil, link pivot locking system used by the Govt. Model, 5 in. barrel, matte stainless steel only, 3 dot sighting system or Accro adj. rear sight (disc. 1994), checkered synthetic Xenoy grips, 8 shot mag. (9 shot in 9mm Para. or .38 Super cal.), decocking lever, squared off combat trigger guard, 39 oz. Mfg. 1990-96.

	$850	$650	$500				

Last MSR was $727.

Add $50 for 9mm Para. or .38 Super cal.
Add $20 for 10mm cal.
Add 10% for NIB condition.

The first edition (1,000 mfg. in 1989) on this model did not have a decocking lever - retail was $916.

✳ Double Eagle Combat Commander - .40 S&W (new 1992) or .45 ACP cal., 4 1/4 in. barrel, 8 shot mag., white dot sights, 36 oz. Mfg. 1991-96.

	100%	98%	95%
	$850	$650	$500

Last MSR was $727.

✳ Officer's Model - .45 ACP cal., 3 1/2 in. barrel, 8 shot mag., 35 oz. Mfg. 1991-disc.

	$850	$650	$500

Last MSR was $727.

✳ Officer's Lightweight Model - .45 ACP cal. only, 3 1/2 in. barrel, alloy frame with blue finish only, white dot sights, 25 oz. Mfg. 1991-93.

	100%	98%	95%	90%	80%	70%	60%
	$900	$700	$500	$400	$365	$330	$295

Last MSR was $696.

ALL AMERICAN MODEL 2000 - 9mm Para. cal. only, double action semi-auto, new design features roller-bearing mounted trigger allowing double action only trigger pull every shot, utilizes a recoil operated rotary action featuring integral locking lugs similar to the military M-16 rifle, hammerless, 4 1/2 in. barrel, matte finished steel slide and polymer receiver, 15 shot mag., 3-dot sighting system, ambidextrous mag. release, black synthetic checkered grips, internal striker block safety, checkered trigger guard and front grip strap, 29 oz. Manufacturing difficulty forced discontinuance and design and tooling were returned to Reed Knight. Mfg. 1991-93.

✳ Model 2000 - Polymer Frame

	100%	98%	95%	90%	80%	70%	60%
	$750	$650	$525	$450	$375	$325	$275

Last MSR was $575.

   Add 10% for NIB condition.
   This model could also be converted to a shorter version using a 3 3/4 in. barrel/bushing kit (no tools or other components were needed - $75 retail during 1993 only).

✳ Model 2000 - Aluminum Frame - similar to polymer Model 2000, except frame is aluminum, serial numbered RK00001-RK03000 to commemorate the designer (Reed Knight). Mfg. 1993.

	$850	$700	$550	$465	$375	$325	$275

Last MSR was $575.

   Add 10% for NIB condition.

PONY SERIES 90 - .380 ACP cal., double action only, 2 3/4 in. barrel, bobbed hammer, 6 shot mag., stainless construction, brushed finish, fixed sights, black composition grips, 19 oz. Mfg. 1997 only.

	$495	$350	$295

Last MSR was $529.

✳ Pony Pocketlite Lightweight - .380 ACP cal., similar to Pony Series 90, except utilizes aluminum and stainless steel construction, brushed finish, 13 oz. Mfg. 1997- 99.

	$495	$350	$295

Last MSR was $529.

POCKET NINE - 9mm Para. cal., double action only, 2 3/4 in. barrel, aluminum frame, ultra slim profile, 6 shot mag, matte/brushed stainless steel, wraparound rubber grips, 3-dot sights, 17 oz. Mfg. 1999 only.

	$595	$425	$350

Last MSR was $615.

PISTOLS: SEMI-AUTO, .22 CAL. - WOODSMAN SERIES

The publisher wishes to once again express his thanks to Major (ret.) Robert J. Rayburn for his continued generous contributions of information regarding the Colt Woodsman Series.

The Colt Woodsman was made for 62 years, and included a multitude of variations/options in models, sights, barrels, grips, markings, etc. Many of the variations are quite scarce and desirable, but generally known only to specialized collectors. The following price guidelines are for standard production models, and only for those specimens in unmodified, factory original condition.

Over 690,000 Woodsmans with variations were mfg. between 1915-1977.

Factory engraved and special order Woodsmans are relatively rare and very desirable. Prices can fluctuate greatly, and auctions can sometimes be the only source of supply for these seldomly encountered pistols.

Note: All 100% condition Woodsmans with the original serial numbered box, test target, instruction folder, hang tag, and screw driver typically command a 10-25% premium, depending on the model's age and rarity.

PRE-WOODSMAN - .22 LR cal., 6 5/8 in. barrel. 10 shot mag., blue only, bottom mag. release, checkered wood grips, adj. front and rear sights, this model was officially named "Colt Automatic Pistol, Caliber .22 Target Model," magazine base has 2-line legend "CAL .22" "COLT". Standard velocity ammo. only. Approx. 54,000 mfg. 1915-27.

	$1,395	$1,195	$750	$475	$375	$300	$275

Add 10% for pencil barrels (1915-1922 mfg. only, ser. nos. below 31000).

This model was manufactured to use standard velocity ammunition only (not high speed). Colt did offer a conversion kit for high velocity ammo. after the transition to high velocity in 1931. Woodsmans mfg. between 1915-1922 had a lightweight pencil barrel (approx. serial range 1-31,000). The medium barrel was introduced in 1922 and was retained until the 90,000 serial range (approx. mfg. 1922-1934).

WOODSMAN 1ST SERIES - .22 LR cal., 10 shot mag., blue only, bottom mag. release, checkered wood grips, marked "The Woodsman" on receiver, adj. sights, mfg. from 1927-47, total production was approx. 112,000.

Note: Guns made prior to 1931 were designed for standard velocity .22 LR ammunition only. The new style main spring housing, designed for high velocity ammunition, began appearing at approx. ser. no. 80,000 and was completely phased in by approx. ser. no. 85,000. Later guns, INCLUDING ALL PISTOLS MADE AFTER WWII, were designed for high velocity ammunition.

Between 1934 and 1947 a tapered barrel was standard production (approx. ser. range 90,000-187,423).

✳ *Sport Model* - 4 1/2 in. barrel, this model was introduced in 1933.

	$1,295	$1,095	$700	$550	$450	$395	$350

Add 10% for adj. front sight (available beginning 1937).

Add 50% for medium weight barrel (1933-34 mfg. only), and an additional 50% for semi-circular "half moon" front sight (1933 mfg. only).

Approx. serial range on this variation is 86,105-187,423 from 1933 to 1947.

✳ *Target Model* - 6 5/8 in. barrel.

	$1,150	$950	$600	$400	$325	$275	$250

Note: Colt discontinued the 1st series in 1947. These guns are quite different from the 2nd series started later in 1947. Both the front and rear sights are adjustable.

WOODSMAN 1ST SERIES MATCH TARGET - .22 LR cal. only, 6 5/8 in. heavy barrel, commonly called "Bullseye" Match Target, mfg. 1938-44, production totaled around 16,000. Difficult to find in mint condition. Values listed assume original one-piece extended walnut grips.

	$2,595	$1,995	$1,295	$750	$650	$600	$550

The correct magazine on this model has a 3-line legend "COLT WOODSMAN", "CAL. 22 L.R.", and "MATCH TARGET MOD".

✳ *"U.S. Property" Marked* - approx. 4,000 Match Target Woodsmans were sold to the U.S. Army and U.S. Navy during WWII. Most have serial numbers above MT12500, although some were shipped out of sequence with lower numbers. The wartime guns had elongated plastic stocks and standard blue finish, although some of them are now parkerized as the result of arsenal refinishing or other non-factory modifications. They are marked with either "US PROPERTY" or the ordnance wheel with crossed cannon, as well as the initials of the govt. inspector. Some also have additional markings.

	$2,695	$2,195	$1,595	$1,150	$925	$750	$575

Check parkerized finish carefully for originality on this variation, as some "recent parkerizing" has been observed.

GRADING - PPGS™	100%	98%	95%	90%	80%	70%	60%

WOODSMAN 2ND SERIES

- .22 LR cal. only, slide stop and hold open, push button mag. release on this model is located on the left side of frame, Coltwood plastic grips (mfg. 1947-1950) or brown plastic grips (mfg. 1950-55), total production on all 2nd Series was (not including the Challenger) approx. 146,000, serialization has "S" suffix. Mfg. 1947-1955.

* *Sport Model* - 4 1/2 in. barrel.

	100%	98%	95%	90%	80%	70%	60%
	$895	$750	$550	$395	$350	$295	$250

* *Target Model* - 6 in. barrel.

	$795	$650	$495	$350	$325	$275	$225

* *Match Target Model* - 4 1/2 in. heavy barrel.

	$1,295	$995	$695	$550	$475	$450	$425

* *Match Target Model* - 6 in. heavy barrel.

	$1,095	$895	$600	$450	$400	$350	$300

WOODSMAN 3RD SERIES

- .22 LR cal. only, slide stop and hold open, black plastic grips (mfg. 1955-60) or walnut grips (1960-77), 3rd Models can be differentiated from 2nd Models by their bottom mag. release. Total production of all 3rd series Woodsman models (not including the Huntsman or Targetsman) exceeded 100,000, serialization has "S" suffix. Mfg. 1955-1977.

* *Sport Model* - 4 1/2 in. barrel.

	$795	$695	$495	$325	$300	$275	$250

* *Target Model* - 6 in. barrel.

	$750	$650	$450	$275	$250	$235	$225

* *Match Target Model* - 4 1/2 or 6 in. heavy barrel.

	$950	$850	$600	$450	$375	$350	$295

Add $100 for a 4 1/2 in. barrel if condition is 95% or better.

CHALLENGER MODEL

- similar to Woodsman 2nd Series, only with fixed sights, without hold open, and bottom mag. release, 4 1/2 and 6 in. barrels, mfg. between 1950-1955 with total production reaching approx. 77,000. Plastic grips.

	$650	$495	$325	$250	$225	$210	$180

HUNTSMAN MODEL

- .22 LR cal. only, fixed sights and no hold open, 4 1/2 and 6 in. barrels, black plastic grips to serial number 141094-C - walnut grips after that cut-off. Mfg. between 1955-77 with total production reaching over 100,000.

	$595	$495	$350	$250	$200	$180	$160

The Huntsman is very similar to the Challenger Model, except is built on a 3rd series frame.

* *Huntsman Model S Master Series* - approx. 400 Model S Masters were sold in 1983. This was a parts clean-up by Colt, using Huntsman frames leftover from the last days of production. They were equipped with automatic slide stop and Elliason rear sight, gold etching on the slide, and a French fitted walnut case marked "1 of 400". Approx. 285 had straight, non-tapered Huntsman barrel, while the remainder had the tapered Woodsman Sport barrel with pinned front sight.

	100%	98%	95%	90%	80%	70%	60%
Huntsman barrel	$1,295	$895	$500	$425	$350	$325	$295
Woodsman barrel	$1,395	$800	$600	$500	$425	$350	$325

Above values assume original walnut case included. Values for this model in 98%-60% original condition are hard to compute, as most are mint or new.

TARGETSMAN MODEL

- similar to the Huntsman, except has adj. rear sight and thumbrest on left grip, 6 in. barrel only, approx. 65,000 mfg. 1959-77.

	$650	$495	$350	$260	$240	$220	$200

GRADING - PPGS™	100%	98%	95%	90%	80%	70%	60%

CADET - .22 LR cal., 4 1/2 in. barrel, stainless steel, 10 shot mag., predecessor to the Colt 22 Model, originally introduced in 1994, fixed sights, this model was disc. by 1995 because of litigation involving the trademarked model name, 33 1/2 oz.

	$450	$350	$300

COLT 22 - .22 LR cal., 4 1/2 in. VR barrel, stainless steel, fixed sights, 10 shot mag., one-piece black Pachmayr rubber grips, 33 1/2 oz. Mfg. 1994-98.

	$350	$295	$250

Last MSR was $248.

* ***Colt 22 Target*** - .22 LR cal., 6 in. VR barrel with full length grooved sight rib, adj. rear sight, 40 1/2 oz. Mfg. 1995-99.

	$350	$295	$250

Last MSR was $377.

100%	98%	95%	90%	80%	70%	60%	50%	40%	30%	20%	10%

REVOLVERS: DOUBLE ACTION

Most of the double action revolvers listed can have their original configuration confirmed with a Colt factory letter. To receive a letter, write: COLT ARCHIVE PROPERTIES, LLC, P.O. Box 1868, Hartford, CT, 06144. The research fee for these revolvers is typically either $75 or $100, depending on the model. If they cannot obtain additional information on the variation you request, they will refund $50.

In Oct. of 1999, Colt announced that all double action revolvers would be discontinued, including any custom shop manufacture. After over 120 years of continuous production, the series of swing out double action revolvers finally ended. As a result, interest and prices for this discontinued revolver configuration have already increased, even on recently discontinued models/configurations. During 2002, Colt announced that the Custom Shop would make both the Anaconda and the Python Elite, and these two double action revolvers are the only ones currently produced by Colt.

Prices on top condition Colt DAs have continued to remain strong, particularly for correctly boxed/cased guns. Be aware of ill-matched or wrong vintage boxes being mated to an unmatched gun. Original boxes will enhance the values of all Colt DAs.

MODEL 1877 LIGHTNING - .38 Colt or .32 Colt (very rare) cal., 2, 2 1/2, 3 1/2, 4 1/2, or 6 in. barrels without ejector, 4 1/2, 5, 6, 7, or 7 1/2 in. barrels with ejector, 6 shot double action, long cylinder fluting, blue finish with case hardened frame and hammer, full nickel plating also available. Over 166,000 mfg. from 1877-1910.

$1,775	$1,500	$1,200	$950	$875	$775	$700	$650	$575	$475	$350	$295

Subtract approx. 15% for nickel plating.

Shorter barrel lengths w/o ejector rod will bring a 10%-15% premium, depending on condition.

Also, an etched barrel will command a 10%-15% over a roll marked barrel, depending on condition.

This model has a fragile mechanism - values are for working guns.

MODEL 1877 THUNDERER - .41 Colt cal. only, otherwise same general specifications as Model 1877 Lightning.

$1,800	$1,600	$1,150	$975	$875	$775	$675	$600	$525	$450	$325	$285

MODEL 1878 DA - .22 LR (very rare), .32-20 WCF (scarce), .38 Colt, .38-40 WCF (scarce, approx. 1,600 mfg.), .41 LC (scarce), .44 Russian, .44 German, .44 S&W, .44-40 WCF (Colt Frontier Six Shooter), .45 LC, .450 Eley, .455 Eley, or .476 Eley cal., 2 1/2 (scarce), 3 1/2, or 4 in. barrels without ejector, 4 3/4, 5 1/2, or 7 1/2 in. with ejector. Mfg. 1878-1905. Over 51,000 made.

$5,250	$4,750	$3,750	$3,000	$2,500	$1,750	$1,500	$950	$850	$750	$625	$500

This model in .44-40 WCF was called the Colt Frontier Six Shooter, and this inscription is either etched or roll marked on the barrel.

This model had a weak operating mechanism, and should be carefully inspected to make sure the cylinder turns and locks up properly. Since original parts are scarce, at least $500 must be deducted for a non-working action.

100%	98%	95%	90%	80%	70%	60%	50%	40%	30%	20%	10%

Many original 1878 barrels have "found their way" on the front end of a SAA frame since the barrels are interchangable. Because of this, many "original" Model 1878 DAs may have an incorrect and/or later SAA Colt barrel attached. Watch yourself here!

MODEL 1889 "NAVY" (NEW NAVY DA, MODEL OF 1889)

- .38 Short and Long Colt, and .41 Short and Long Colt cal., 3, 4 1/2, and 6 in. barrel, blue (military and civilian) or nickel (civilian only) finish, wood (military) or hard rubber (civilian) grips, the first solid frame, swing out cylinder with no visible locking latches (rotates counter-clockwise), sideplate is also on the right-hand side of frame, Colt produced approx. 31,000 mfg. 1889-1894, 1st 5,000 were ordered by U.S. Navy, with some additional orders later in production - hence name.

| $1,750 | $1,550 | $1,350 | $1,150 | $950 | $750 | $650 | $575 | $500 | $425 | $350 | $300 |

Add 40% for 3 in. barrel.

Add 35% for .38 Short or Long Colt cal.

Add 65%-100% for U.S. Navy Contract (ser. no. 1-5,000), U.S.N. on butt (.38 LC cal. only), depending on condition.

MODEL 1892 "NEW ARMY & NAVY" (2ND ISSUE)

- similar to 1889 Navy, but double cylinder notches, double locking bolt, and shorter flutes, square cyl. release thumb catch, hard rubber (commercial models) or plain uncheckered wood (military models) grips, .32-20 WCF cal. (uncommon) added in 1905. Mfg. 1892-1907.

| $1,450 | $1,200 | $950 | $800 | $500 | $400 | $300 | $250 | $225 | $210 | $195 | $180 |

Add $100-$750 for U.S.N. markings, depending on condition.

Add 25% for 3 in. barrel.

Models made before 1898 will bring a premium.

* **Models 1892, 1894, 1895, 1896, 1901, 1903** - these were variations of the Model 1892, military model (.38 Long Colt only) values will approximate those shown above, while civilian models will be approx. 10%-25% less, depending on condition.

MODEL 1902/1904 (ALASKAN/PHILLIPINES)

- .45 LC cal., oversized trigger guard and long trigger, 6 shot cylinder with long flutes, pinched frame, removable trigger guard, 6 in. barrel, blue finish, checkered walnut stocks, later guns have hard black rubber, inspector markings and a small U.S. ordnance proof on right side. Approx. 50 Model 1904 mfg. in the low 51,000 ser. no. range. late 1904, and shipped to Springfield Armory.

| N/A | N/A | $4,650 | $4,375 | $4,150 | $3,850 | $3,550 | $3,175 | $2,850 | $2,500 | $2,150 | $1,675 |

Extreme rarity factor on M-1904 precludes accurate pricing.

OFFICER'S MODEL TARGET (FIRST ISSUE)

- .38 Spl. or .38 Long Colt cal., 6 in. barrel, cylinder rotates counter-clockwise and sideplate is on right-hand side of frame, adj. front - adj. rear type sights, high luster blue, flat-top, last patent date 1901. Mfg. 1904-08.

| $1,500 | $1,250 | $950 | $775 | $625 | $550 | $495 | $395 | $295 | $275 | $250 | $225 |

OFFICER'S MODEL TARGET (SECOND ISSUE)

- .32 Colt or .38 Spl. cal., 4, 4 1/2, 5, 6, or 7 1/2 in. barrel, cylinder rotates clockwise, high luster blue through 1916, adj. front - adj. rear type sights, checkered walnut grips, deep set medallions in grips were standard from 1913-1923. Mfg. 1908-1926. Last patent date July 4, 1905.

| $1,150 | $1,000 | $850 | $515 | $450 | $395 | $330 | $290 | $250 | $225 | $210 | $195 |

Add 60% for .32 Colt cal.

Add 60% for 4, 4 1/2, or 5 in. barrel.

OFFICER'S MODEL TARGET (THIRD ISSUE)

- similar design to the Second Issue, .22 cal. was added beginning 1930, heavy barrel was introduced in 1935. Mfg. 1927-1949. Last patent date Oct. 5, 1926.

| $825 | $750 | $650 | $550 | $450 | $375 | $325 | $295 | $265 | $245 | $225 | $205 |

Add 10% for .22 LR cal. (mfg. started 1930).

100%	98%	95%	90%	80%	70%	60%	50%	40%	30%	20%	10%

MODEL 1905 MARINE CORPS

.38 Short or Long, similar to New Navy Second Issue, except has a round butt, checkered wood grips w/o medallion, and 6 in. barrel only. Mfg. 1905-1909 in approx. ser. no. range 10,001-10,926, about 926 mfg.

$2,650	$2,350	$2,050	$1,750	$1,625	$1,425	$1,250	$1,000	$895	$795	$695	$595

Add 30% for Military issue marked "USMC" on butt.

ARMY SPECIAL MODEL

.32-20 WCF, .38 (various), and .41 Colt cals., 4, 4 1/2, 5, and 6 in. barrels, hard rubber grips standard through 1923 - checkered wood with medallions beginning about 1924, blue finish, fixed sights, rounded checkered cylinder release thumb catch, smooth trigger, has heavier frame than New Navy, approx. ser. no. range 291,000-540,000, last patent date on barrel was July 4, 1905. Mfg. 1908-27.

$750	$675	$500	$400	$325	$295	$275	$250	$225	$200	$185	$175

Add 15% for nickel finish.

NEW SERVICE MODEL

.38 Spl., .357 Mag., .38-40 WCF, .44-40 WCF, .44 Russian, .44 Spl., .45 ACP, .45 LC, .450 Eley, .455 Eley, or .476 Eley cals., 4, 5, or 6 in. barrels in .357 Mag. and .38 Spl., 4 1/2, 5 1/2, and 7 1/2 in. barrel in all others, blue or nickel finish, bright blue finish was used through circa 1916, originally hard rubber (until approx. late '20s), with later guns having walnut grips with medallions. Mfg. 1898-1942.

New Service Models marked "NEW SERVICE 45 COLT" in .45 ACP cal. with shorter cylinder for rimmed cartridge are rare. Early models (first type) have flat latches. Later models (second type) have rounded cylinder latches.

Approx. 356,000 Colt New Service revolvers were mfg., but only approx. 122,800 were Commercial variations. 95% were mfg. with blue finish, while 5% were nickel plated (approx. 6,140 revolvers). Colt also mfg. a very limited number (probably less than 10) of New Service revolvers with smooth bores. When encountered, it is important to get a Colt factory letter confirming the smooth bore barrel. Prices can range $6,500-$10,000+, depending on original condition.

Rare cals. (.450 and .476 Eley cals.) and 4 in. barrels will command premiums over values listed below.

* **Commercial**

$1,975	$1,650	$1,375	$1,250	$995	$875	$775	$650	$500	$425	$375	$295

Add 35% for nickel finish.

Add 50% for factory pearl, ivory or walnut grips.

* **1909 Army Model**

$1,995	$1,350	$1,175	$1,000	$925	$850	$775	$680	$590	$510	$435	$375

* **RNWMP & RCMP Model** - .45 LC or .455 Eley cal., contract for Royal Canadian Northwest Mounted Police.

$1,995	$1,350	$1,175	$1,000	$925	$850	$775	$680	$590	$510	$435	$375

* **1909 Navy Model** - shortest production run of the Model 1909 variations.

$3,000	$2,550	$2,100	$1,500	$1,150	$1,000	$895	$775	$725	$650	$525	$500

* **1909 - USMC**

$3,350	$2,650	$2,175	$1,775	$1,500	$1,250	$975	$850	$775	$675	$550	$500

* **1917 Army**

$1,375	$1,050	$895	$700	$610	$525	$455	$390	$335	$295	$250	$200

* **1917 Civilian/Commercial (1917 C/CM)** - .45 ACP cal., 5 1/2 in. barrel only, last patent date is Oct. 5, 1926, checkered walnut grips with medallions, left side of barrel marked "Colt Model 1917 Auto Ctge". Approx. 1,000 mfg. during 1932, serialized 335,000-336,000.

$1,500	$1,275	$1,050	$850	$650	$525	$450	$415	$385	$350	$325	$295

* **1917 Civilian/Commercial (Piece Parts Model)** - .38-40 WCF, .44-40 WCF, or .45 LC cal., 4 1/2 or 5 1/2 in. barrel, hard rubber grips, or checkered walnut with medallions, last patent date is July 4, 1905, approx. 1,000 mfg. serialized 336,450- 337,500.

$1,375	$1,050	$925	$800	$625	$495	$415	$380	$360	$330	$300	$275

100%	98%	95%	90%	80%	70%	60%	50%	40%	30%	20%	10%

* ***New Service Target*** - similar to New Service Model, flattop frame, hand-honed action and adj. front - adj. rear type sights, 6 (scarce) or 7 1/2 in. barrel, square butt, round butt available after 1930, checkered grip straps, checkered walnut grips with medallion after 1913, blue or nickel (scarce) finish. Mfg. 1900-40.

100%	98%	95%	90%	80%	70%	60%	50%	40%	30%	20%	10%
$3,150	$3,000	$2,575	$2,100	$1,750	$1,500	$1,250	$900	$750	$635	$550	$460

     Add 40% - 60% for 6 in. barrel, depending on original condition.

* ***Shooting Master*** - various cals. from 38 Spl. through .45 LC, 6 in. barrel, checkered walnut grips with Colt Medallion, machined grip straps, trigger, hammer, and ejector rod head, round or square butt, approx. ser. no. range 333,000-350,000.

     >Regular cals.

100%	98%	95%	90%	80%	70%	60%	50%	40%	30%	20%	10%
$1,350	$1,150	$1,025	$900	$825	$755	$665	$575	$500	$435	$395	$375

     >.357 Mag.

100%	98%	95%	90%	80%	70%	60%	50%	40%	30%	20%	10%
$2,500	$2,300	$2,100	$1,850	$1,600	$1,475	$1,300	$1,100	$995	$825	$750	$650

     >.38 Spl.

100%	98%	95%	90%	80%	70%	60%	50%	40%	30%	20%	10%
$2,500	$2,300	$2,100	$1,850	$1,600	$1,475	$1,300	$1,100	$995	$825	$750	$650

     >.45 ACP or .45 LC cals.

100%	98%	95%	90%	80%	70%	60%	50%	40%	30%	20%	10%
N/A	N/A	$3,850	$3,425	$3,050	$2,500	$2,050	$1,675	$1,350	$1,000	$750	$600

     >.44 Spl. cal.

100%	98%	95%	90%	80%	70%	60%	50%	40%	30%	20%	10%
N/A	N/A	$4,600	$4,050	$3,500	$3,000	$2,500	$2,000	$1,575	$1,250	$1,000	$850

     The Shooting Master could be ordered with a square butt after 1933.

OFFICIAL POLICE PRE-WAR

- .32-20 WCF (disc. 1942), .38-200 (British), .41 long (disc. 1930), .38 Spl., or .22 LR (introduced 1930 - 4 or 6 in. barrel only, 4 in. scarce) cal., blue finish, 6 shot, round (very scarce) or square butt, 4, 5, or 6 in. barrels, 2 in. barrel (scarce) in .38 Spl., checkered walnut grips, fixed sights, last patent date on barrel was Oct. 5, 1926. Mfg. 1927-46.

100%	98%	95%	90%	80%	70%	60%	50%	40%	30%	20%	10%
$650	$550	$450	$350	$325	$300	$275	$250	$210	$185	$165	$145

     Add 100% for round butt with factory verified letter.
     Add 15% for nickel finish.
     Add 15% for .22 LR cal.

OFFICIAL POLICE POST-WAR

- .22 LR or .38 Spl. cal., 2, 4, 5, or 6 in. barrel, Colt-wood plastic grips 1947-1954 - checkered walnut thereafter, fixed sights, no patent dates on barrel. Mfg. 1947-69.

100%	98%	95%	90%	80%	70%	60%	50%	40%	30%	20%	10%
$550	$450	$375	$350	$265	$235	$210	$185	$165	$145	$135	$125

     Add 15% for nickel finish.
     Add 15% for .22 cal.
     On this model, the 2 in. barrel in .38 Spl. cal. is scarce. .22 cal. was available with 4 or 6 in. barrel only.

MARSHAL MODEL

- .38 Spl. cal., 2 (less common) or 4 in. barrel, round butt, differentiated by "M" suffix and "COLT MARSHAL" on barrel, about 2,500 mfg. 1954-1956 in approx. ser. no. range 833350-M through 845320-M.

100%	98%	95%	90%	80%	70%	60%	50%	40%	30%	20%	10%
$875	$775	$675	$500	$395	$335	$305	$275	$245	$215	$180	$160

     Add 60% for 2 in. barrel.
     Add 50% for nickel finish.

COMMANDO MODEL

- .38 Spl. cal., 2 in. (less common), 4 in. (common), or 6 in. (rare) barrel, should have plastic grips, parkerized finish, about 50,000 mfg. between 1942-1945, 32 oz., marked "COLT COMMANDO" on barrel, last patent date on barrel was Oct. 5, 1926.

100%	98%	95%	90%	80%	70%	60%	50%	40%	30%	20%	10%
$850	$750	$600	$375	$350	$315	$280	$260	$240	$220	$195	$180

     Add 15% for 2 in. barrel.

OFFICIAL POLICE MKIII

- .38 Spl. cal., 4, 5, or 6 in. barrels, no patent dates on barrel. Mfg. 1969-75.

100%	98%	95%	90%	80%	70%	60%	50%	40%	30%	20%	10%

✶ Blue finish

| $400 | $325 | $250 | $150 | $135 | $125 | $115 | $105 | $100 | $95 | $90 | $85 |

✶ Nickel finish

| $395 | $295 | $200 | $175 | $165 | $155 | $145 | $135 | $125 | $115 | $105 | $100 |

METROPOLITAN MK III - .38 Spl. cal., similar to Official Police, except heavier and 4 in. heavy barrel only, blue finish. Mfg. 1969-72.

| $495 | $395 | $300 | $250 | $200 | $180 | $160 | $140 | $120 | $110 | $100 | $90 |

OFFICER'S MODEL SPECIAL (FOURTH ISSUE) - .22 LR or .38 Spl. cal., 6 in. barrel, blue, similar to Third Issue, only heavier non-tapered barrel, new style hammer and "Coltmaster Sight," checkered plastic grips, no patent dates on barrel. Mfg. 1949-52.

| $700 | $575 | $500 | $375 | $325 | $295 | $265 | $245 | $225 | $205 | $190 | $175 |

Add $75 for .22 LR cal.

OFFICER'S MODEL MATCH (FIFTH ISSUE) - .22 LR, .22 Mag, or .38 Spl. cal., 6 in. barrel, single (rare) or double action, tapered heavy barrel, nickel finish is scarce in this model, wide spur hammer, Accro sight, large target grips (walnut). Mfg. 1953-69.

| $575 | $525 | $425 | $325 | $300 | $275 | $250 | $225 | $200 | $185 | $170 | $155 |

Add $75 for .22 LR cal.

Add 100% for .22 Mag. cal. (approx. 850 mfg.).

✶ Officer's Model Match Single Action only - limited mfg.

| $1,325 | $1,200 | $995 | $925 | $850 | $775 | $700 | $650 | $600 | $550 | $475 | $425 |

OFFICER'S MODEL MATCH MK III (SIXTH ISSUE) - .38 Spl. cal. only, 6 in. shrouded VR barrel, wide spur hammer, Accro sights, target grips. 496 mfg. 1969-70 only.

| $1,450 | $1,275 | $1,050 | $925 | $850 | $775 | $700 | $650 | $600 | $550 | $475 | $425 |

NEW POCKET - .32 Short and LC, or .32 Colt New Police cal., 2 1/2, 3 1/2, 5, or 6 in. barrel, rubber grips, blue or nickel finish, round butt, last patent date on barrel was Nov. 6, 1888. Mfg. 1895-1905.

| $750 | $650 | $550 | $400 | $300 | $275 | $250 | $215 | $190 | $170 | $150 | $140 |

Subtract $50-$75 for chipped hard rubber grips (commonly found on this model).

POCKET POSITIVE (FIRST ISSUE) - similar to New Pocket, except has positive lock feature, also chambered for .32 Colt, .32 S&W, and .32 Colt New Police cals., last patent date on barrel was July 4, 1905. Mfg. 1905-27.

| $600 | $525 | $425 | $350 | $325 | $295 | $265 | $235 | $210 | $185 | $165 | $145 |

Add 15%-20% for nickel finish.

Add 15% for 90%+ condition early transitional guns that are double marked with "NEW POCKET" on frame.

Subtract $50-$75 for chipped hard rubber grips (commonly found on this model).

POCKET POSITIVE (SECOND ISSUE) - similar to Pocket Positive First Issue, except has stippled and matted top strap, last patent date on barrel was Oct. 5, 1926. Mfg. 1927-40.

| $600 | $525 | $425 | $350 | $325 | $295 | $265 | $235 | $210 | $185 | $165 | $145 |

Add 15%-20% for nickel finish.

Subtract $50-$75 for chipped hard rubber grips (commonly found on this model).

NEW POLICE - .32 Colt and .32 Colt New Police cal., 2 1/2, 4, and 6 in. barrels, fixed sights, same frame as New Pocket, except larger, square butt grips, rubber grips, last patent date on barrel was Nov. 6, 1888. Mfg. 1896-1907.

| $750 | $650 | $550 | $375 | $325 | $275 | $215 | $185 | $170 | $160 | $150 | $145 |

Add 25% for nickel finish.

Subtract $25-$50 for chipped hard rubber grips (commonly found on this model).

100%	98%	95%	90%	80%	70%	60%	50%	40%	30%	20%	10%

NEW POLICE TARGET - .32 Colt cal., 6 in. barrel, blue, late models use New Police frame, but include transitional improvements from later Police Positive Target Model (First Issue), last patent date on barrel was Nov. 6, 1888. Approx. 5,000 mfg. 1897-1907.

| $1,450 | $1,250 | $950 | $900 | $475 | $395 | $350 | $300 | $275 | $250 | $225 | $200 |

POLICE POSITIVE (FIRST ISSUE) - .32 Colt, .32 New Police, .38 New Police, or .38 S&W cals., 2 1/2 in. (.32 only), 4, 5, or 6 in. barrels, improved "positive lock" version of the New Police, hard rubber grips standard through 1923, checkered walnut grips became standard 1924, denoted by 1905 last patent date and smooth top strap. Mfg. 1907-27.

| $550 | $450 | $375 | $295 | $275 | $250 | $225 | $205 | $185 | $170 | $160 | $150 |

Add 15% for nickel finish.

Add 10% for 90%+ condition early transitional guns that are double marked with "NEW POLICE" on frame.

POLICE POSITIVE (SECOND ISSUE) - similar to Police Positive First Issue, except has 1926 last patent date, serrated top strap, and slightly heavier frame, walnut grips standard. Mfg. 1928-1947.

| $550 | $450 | $375 | $295 | $275 | $250 | $225 | $205 | $185 | $170 | $160 | $150 |

Add 15% for nickel finish.

POLICE POSITIVE TARGET MODEL (FIRST ISSUE, MODEL "G") - .22 LR, .22 WRF, .32 Colt, or .32 New Police cals., 6 in. barrel, blue, adj. sight, hard rubber grips standard through 1923, checkered walnut grips thereafter, last patent date on barrel was July 4, 1905, 22 oz. Mfg. 1907-1925.

| $900 | $750 | $675 | $575 | $475 | $425 | $390 | $360 | $325 | $285 | $250 | $210 |

Add 40% for .32 cal.

POLICE POSITIVE TARGET MODEL (SECOND ISSUE, MODEL "C") - similar to First Issue, except has slightly heavier frame and a last patent date of Oct. 5, 1926, 26 oz. Mfg. 1926-41.

| $900 | $750 | $675 | $575 | $475 | $425 | $390 | $360 | $325 | $285 | $250 | $210 |

Add 40% for .32 cal.

POLICE POSITIVE SPECIAL (FIRST ISSUE) - .32-20 WCF, .32 New Police, .38 New Police, or .38 Spl. cals., 4, 5, or 6 in. barrels, fixed sights, frame longer to permit longer cylinder, denoted by 1905 last patent date on top of barrel, longer frame and smooth top strap, rubber grips. Mfg. 1907-27.

| $650 | $550 | $450 | $325 | $300 | $275 | $250 | $225 | $200 | $185 | $170 | $155 |

POLICE POSITIVE SPECIAL (SECOND ISSUE) - similar to Police Postive Special (First Issue), except has 1926 last patent date on top of barrel, wood grips only, smooth (early mfg.) or checkered (later mfg.) trigger, and serrated top strap. Mfg. 1928-46.

| $650 | $550 | $450 | $325 | $300 | $275 | $250 | $225 | $200 | $185 | $170 | $155 |

CAMP PERRY MODEL - .22 LR cal., 8 in. (less common) or 10 in., Officer's Model frame modified to accept a flat single shot chamber. The model name was stamped on the left side of the chamber, the only single shot Colt on a revolver frame, last patent date on barrel was Oct. 5, 1926. 2,488 mfg. between 1926-41.

| $2,100 | $1,650 | $1,450 | $950 | $875 | $775 | $715 | $645 | $575 | $495 | $425 | $365 |

Add 25% for 8 in. barrel.

BANKER'S SPECIAL - 2 in. barrel, blue, square butt standard through 1933, round butt standard 1934-40, last patent date on barrel was Oct. 5, 1926. Mfg. 1926-40.

❋ *.38 cal.* - available in .38 Colt Police Positive (New Police) or .38 S&W cal.

| $1,500 | $1,100 | $900 | $595 | $495 | $395 | $325 | $275 | $235 | $205 | $185 | $165 |

Add 45% for nickel finish.

100%	98%	95%	90%	80%	70%	60%	50%	40%	30%	20%	10%

✳ .22 LR cal.

| $2,250 | $2,000 | $1,650 | $1,100 | $750 | $650 | $550 | $475 | $425 | $385 | $355 | $325 |

Add 30%-50% for nickel finish, depending on original condition.

COURIER - .22 S, L, & LR. or .32 New Police (S&W) cals., double action, 6 shot, 3 in. barrel. Approx. 3,053 mfg. 1953-56.

| $950 | $850 | $750 | $550 | $475 | $425 | $395 | $350 | $325 | $295 | $260 | $230 |

Add 10% for .22 cal.

Even though fewer .22 cal. Couriers were mfg. than Banker's Specials, the Banker's Specials are still more desirable, as they are less frequently encountered in 95-100% condition.
Some .32 New Police (S&W) cal. models can be found with alloy or steel cylinders.

AIRCREWMAN SPECIAL - .38 Spl. cal., double action, aluminum frame and cylinder, 2 in. barrel, 11 oz., fixed sights, checkered walnut grips overlapping at top of frame, inset with silver Air Force buttons, mfg. 1951 mostly.

| $4,000 | $3,500 | $2,750 | $2,100 | $1,700 | $1,350 | $1,075 | $950 | $850 | $750 | $675 | $595 |

Approx. 1,200 mfg. within ser. no. range 2,900LW-7,775LW. Most were ordered destroyed. Perhaps less than 25 have survived.

BORDER PATROL (FIRST ISSUE) - .38 Spl. cal., double action, 6 shot, 4 in. heavy barrel, should have plastic grips, 400 mfg. during 1952 only in 823,000 ser. no. range.

| $4,000 | $3,500 | $3,000 | $1,400 | $1,125 | $995 | $875 | $775 | $675 | $595 | $525 | $475 |

This model is built on the Official Police Model frame.

DETECTIVE SPECIAL PRE-WAR (FIRST ISSUE) - .38 Spl. cal., 2 in. barrel, blue, wood grips, square butt standard through 1933, round butt standard thereafter, last patent date on barrel was Oct. 5, 1926. Mfg. 1927-46.

| $900 | $825 | $725 | $450 | $375 | $325 | $275 | $250 | $225 | $205 | $190 | $175 |

Add 15% for nickel finish.
Add 20% for square butt.

DETECTIVE SPECIAL POST-WAR (SECOND ISSUE) - .32 NP, .38 NP, or .38 Spl. cal., 2 or 3 (scarce) in. barrel, plastic grips 1947-54 - wood grips thereafter, wrap-under wood grips started in 1966. Mfg. 1947-72.

| $550 | $450 | $375 | $275 | $250 | $200 | $185 | $170 | $160 | $150 | $140 | $120 |

Add 15% for nickel finish.
Add 15% for 3 in. barrel.

COBRA (FIRST ISSUE) - .22 LR, .32 Colt NP, .38 Colt NP, or .38 Spl. cal., first issue, 2, 3, or 4 (square butt on early model, later models had round butt) in. barrel, blue or nickel finish, similar to Detective Special, only alloy frame and available in .22 LR, very early guns had plastic grips with silver medallions, changed to plastic w/o medallions, and finally changed to wood grips. Mfg. 1950-72.

| $575 | $500 | $425 | $250 | $225 | $200 | $185 | $170 | $160 | $150 | $140 | $120 |

Add 20% for .22 LR cal.
Add 15% for nickel finish.
Add 15% for .38 cal. with 3 in. barrel.
The .22 LR cal. is available in 3 in. barrel only.

AGENT (FIRST ISSUE) - .38 Spl. cal., similar to Cobra first issue, except shorter grip frame. Mfg. 1955-72.

| $550 | $475 | $375 | $275 | $235 | $180 | $160 | $145 | $130 | $120 | $110 | $100 |

AGENT L.W. (SECOND ISSUE) - .38 Spl. cal., similar to First Issue, except shrouded ejector rod, alloy frame, matte finish since 1982. Mfg. 1973-86.

| $500 | $425 | $350 | $215 | $195 | $175 | $150 | $135 | $125 | $115 | $105 | $100 |

Last MSR was $260.

100%	98%	95%	90%	80%	70%	60%	50%	40%	30%	20%	10%

COBRA (SECOND ISSUE) - .38 Spl. cal., similar to Cobra first issue, except shrouded ejector rod, some were shipped with factory installed hammer shroud. Mfg. 1973-81.

| $500 | $425 | $350 | $250 | $225 | $200 | $190 | $175 | $160 | $150 | $140 | $120 |

DETECTIVE SPECIAL (THIRD ISSUE) - .38 Spl. cal., similar to Second Issue, shrouded ejector rod, 2 or 3 (scarce) in. barrel, fixed sights, wraparound wood grips. Mfg. 1973-86.

| $450 | $425 | $400 | $300 | $260 | $230 | $200 | $185 | $175 | $160 | $150 | $140 |

Last MSR was $429.

Add $50 for nickel.
Add 15% for 3 in. barrel.
Also available with class A engraving - add $590 if in 98% condition or better.

COMMANDO SPECIAL - .38 Spl. cal., similar to Detective Special with steel frame, shrouded ejector rod, 2 in. barrel, matte parkerized finish, rubber grips. Mfg. 1984-86.

| $425 | $325 | $265 | $225 | $195 | $185 | $155 | $140 | $125 | $115 | $105 | $100 |

Last MSR was $260.

POLICE POSITIVE SPECIAL (THIRD ISSUE) - .38 Spl. cal., similar to Detective Special Second Issue, except 4, 5, or 6 in. barrel. Mfg. 1947-76.

| $475 | $400 | $350 | $225 | $195 | $185 | $165 | $140 | $125 | $115 | $105 | $100 |

POLICE POSITIVE SPECIAL (FOURTH ISSUE) - .38 Spl. cal., shrouded ejector rod housing only, steel frame, blue or nickel finish. Mfg. 1977-78 and 1994-95.

| $450 | $375 | $350 | $220 | $195 | $175 | $165 | $135 | $125 | $115 | $105 | $100 |

Last MSR was $400.

Add 10% for nickel finish.

VIPER MODEL - .38 Spl. cal., similar to Police Positive Special (Fourth Issue), alloy frame, 4 in. ejector rod housing only. Mfg. 1977 only.

| $475 | $425 | $375 | $250 | $225 | $200 | $190 | $175 | $160 | $150 | $140 | $120 |

Add 30% for nickel finish.

DIAMONDBACK - .22 LR, .22 Mag. (limited mfg.), or .38 Spl. cal., 2 1/2 (scarce in .22 LR), 4, or 6 in. VR barrel, adj. sights, steel frame, checkered walnut grips. Mfg. 1966-86.

| $750 | $650 | $575 | $425 | $350 | $285 | $260 | $230 | $210 | $190 | $175 | $160 |

Last MSR was $461.

Add 20% for nickel finish.
Add 20% for .22 LR cal. or 30% for .22 LR or .22 Mag. cal. with 2 1/2 in. barrel.
Note: Approx. 2,200 Diamondbacks were made with 6 in. barrels and nickel finish in .22 cal. - made 1979. Add additional $150 for 95+% specimens.

COLT .357 MAG - 4 in. or 6 in. barrel, heavy frame, Accro sight, blue or nickel finish, checkered walnut grips. Mfg. 1953-61.

❋ *Standard hammer*

| $600 | $525 | $450 | $300 | $275 | $265 | $255 | $245 | $230 | $220 | $210 | $200 |

❋ *Wide hammer w/target grips*

| $600 | $525 | $450 | $300 | $285 | $265 | $255 | $245 | $235 | $225 | $215 | $205 |

Add 15% for nickel finish.
In 1962, this model was absorbed into the Trooper line.

TROOPER - .22 LR (4 in. only, scarce), .357 Mag., or .38 Spl. cal., 4 or 6 in. barrel, blue or nickel finish, quick draw ramp front sight, adj. rear sight, checkered walnut grips. Mfg. 1953-69.

❋ *Standard hammer*

| $525 | $425 | $375 | $210 | $200 | $190 | $180 | $170 | $165 | $160 | $155 | $150 |

100%	98%	95%	90%	80%	70%	60%	50%	40%	30%	20%	10%

✳ Wide hammer and target grips

| $525 | $450 | $375 | $225 | $210 | $200 | $190 | $180 | $170 | $165 | $160 | $155 |

Add $75-$125 for .22 LR cal. (4 in. barrel only), depending on condition.

Add 15% for nickel finish.

GRADING - PPGS™	100%	98%	95%	90%	80%	70%	60%

TROOPER MK III - .22 LR, .22 Mag., .357 Mag., or .38 Spl. cal., 4, 6, or 8 in. solid rib barrel, adj. sights, walnut target grips, redesigned lock work to reduce amount of hand fitting needed on earlier predecessors. Mfg. 1969-83.

	100%	98%	95%	90%	80%	70%	60%
Blue finish	$450	$325	$225	$180	$170	$160	$150
Nickel finish	$475	$350	$250	$200	$185	$170	$160

TROOPER MK V - .357 Mag. cal. only, 4, 6, or 8 in. barrel, adj. sights, walnut target grips, improved version of Mark III action, vent. rib barrel, a few made with solid rib, redesigned 1982. Disc. 1986.

	100%	98%	95%	90%	80%	70%	60%
Blue finish	$450	$350	$275	$215	$185	$170	$160

Last MSR was $362.

	100%	98%	95%	90%	80%	70%	60%
Nickel finish	$475	$400	$300	$235	$200	$185	$170

Last MSR was $396.

LAWMAN SKY MARSHALL - .38 Spl. cal., 2 in. barrel, experimental revolver with a replaceable plastic cylinder preloaded with plastic bullets, blue finish, checkered walnut grips, this model was designed to be carried on airliners by Federal Marshals during the 1970s.

	100%	98%	95%	90%	80%	70%	60%
	$925	$850	$775	$700	$625	$550	$475

LAWMAN MK III - .357 Mag. cal., 2 in. and 4 in. barrel, unshrouded or shrouded ejector rod for 2 in. barrel, fixed sights, checkered walnut grips. Mfg. 1969-83.

	100%	98%	95%	90%	80%	70%	60%
Blue finish	$425	$375	$300	$180	$170	$160	$150
Nickel finish	$450	$400	$325	$250	$200	$180	$170

LAWMAN MK V - .357 Mag. cal., 2 or 4 in. barrel, shrouded ejector rod for 2 in. barrel, fixed sights, checkered walnut grips, improved version of MK III action. Mfg. 1984 and 1985 only.

	100%	98%	95%	90%	80%	70%	60%
Blue finish	$450	$375	$325	$180	$165	$150	$140

Last MSR was $309.

	100%	98%	95%	90%	80%	70%	60%
Nickel finish	$475	$400	$350	$250	$200	$180	$170

Last MSR was $328.

BORDER PATROL (SECOND ISSUE) - .357 Mag. cal., 4 in. heavy barrel, similar to Trooper Mark III frame, less polishing to frame. Limited mfg. 1970-75.

✳ Blue Finish - 5,356 mfg.

	100%	98%	95%	90%	80%	70%	60%
	$625	$495	$375	$275	$235	$200	$180

✳ Nickel Finish - 1,152 mfg.

	100%	98%	95%	90%	80%	70%	60%
	$725	$625	$500	$400	$325	$275	$235

PEACEKEEPER - .357 Mag. cal. only, similar to Trooper MK V, 4 or 6 in. barrel, matte blue finish, rubber combat grips, adj. rear sight, about 42 oz. Mfg. 1985-87.

	100%	98%	95%	90%	80%	70%	60%
	$395	$325	$275	$225	$195	$180	$165

Last MSR was $330.

BOA - .357 Mag. cal., deep blue polish, full length ejector shroud with Mark V action, 600 each mfg. in 4 and 6 in. barrel lengths. Entire production run was purchased by Lew Horton Distributing Co., Inc. located in Southboro, MA. 1985 retail was $525.

	100%	98%	95%	90%	80%	70%	60%
	$750	$675	$550	$425	$375	$350	$325

GRADING - PPGS™	100%	98%	95%	90%	80%	70%	60%

✱ *Boa Set* - 100 sets mfg. including 4 and 6 in. barrels with fully shrouded ejector rod housing, consecutive serial numbers, cases were supplied by Lew Horton. 1985 retail was $1,200.

	$1,650	$1,300	$950

POLICE POSITIVE MK V (FIFTH ISSUE) - .38 Spl. cal., full shrouded 4 in. barrel, steel frame, blue finish, rubber grips. Mfg. 1994-95.

	$425	$350	$295	$250	$195	$180	$165

DETECTIVE SPECIAL (FOURTH ISSUE) - .38 Spl. cal., 6 shot, 2 in. barrel, steel frame, blue finish, black composition grips with gold medallions, 21 oz. Reintroduced 1993, disc. 1995.

	$425	$350	$295	$250	$195	$180	$165

Last MSR was $400.

✱ *Bobbed Detective Special* - .38 Spl. cal., double action only with bobbed hammer, night front sight, honed action, choice of hard chrome or standard blue finish. Mfg. 1994-95.

	$595	$500	$375	$300	$250	$200	$175

Last MSR was $599.

Add $30 for hard chrome finish.

COLT .38 SF-VI - .38 Spl. cal., 6 shot, 2 or 4 in. barrel, transfer bar safety, choice of matte (2 in.), bright polished (4 in.), or black (4 in.) finish, stainless steel, regular or bobbed (4 in. barrel only) hammer, fixed sights, black composition combat grips, 21 oz. Mfg. 1995-96.

	$425	$350	$295

Last MSR was $408.

✱ *Colt Special Lady* - while advertised during 1996, this model had very limited mfg.

COLT .38 DSII - .357 Mag. (new 1998) or .38 Spl. cal., 6 shot, 2 in. barrel, stainless steel, service hammer, rubber combat style checkered grips, 21 oz. Mfg. 1997-98.

	$450	$365	$300

Last MSR was $435.

This model features a redesigned trigger grouping and is capable of shooting .38+P ammo.

COLT MAGNUM CARRY - .357 Mag. cal., 6 shot, 2 in. barrel, transfer bar safety, satin stainless steel, wraparound rubber grips with finger grooves, ramp front sight, 21 oz. Mfg. 1999 only.

	$475	$360	$295

Last MSR was $460.

COMBAT COBRA - .357 Mag. cal., 2 1/2 in. barrel, special edition for Lew Horton with "CC" prefix and stainless steel construction.

	$575	$475	$400

KING COBRA - .357 Mag. cal., blue metal, black neoprene round butt grips, 2 1/2 (new 1990), 4 or 6 in. solid rib barrel only, outline sights, approx. 42 oz. (4 in. barrel). Mfg. 1986-92.

	$495	$350	$300	$250	$210	$200	$185

Last MSR was $410.

KING COBRA STAINLESS - .357 Mag. cal., stainless steel construction, black neoprene round butt grips, 2 (mfg. 1988-94), 4, 6, or 8 (mfg. 1990-94) in. solid rib barrel, white outline sights, approx. 36 oz. (2 1/2 in. barrel). Mfg. late 1987-92, production resumed 1994, disc. 1998.

	$550	$425	$325

Last MSR was $485.

✳ King Cobra "Ultimate" Bright Stainless - similar to King Cobra, except for bright stainless steel, 2 1/2 (new 1990), 4, 6, or 8 (new 1991) in. barrel. Mfg. 1988-92.

		$595	$400	$300			

Last MSR was $470.

PYTHON - .357 Mag. cal., 2 1/2 (disc. 1994), 3 (a.k.a Combat Python, disc., very scarce), 4, 6, or 8 in. barrel with vent rib, Royal Blue finish, full shrouded ejector rod, adj. rear sight, checkered walnut grips (prior to 1991), rubber Hogue monogrips (2 1/2 or 4 in. barrel), or rubber target (6 or 8 in. barrel) grips, 38-48 oz. Mfg. 1955-96.

✳ Blue or Royal Blue Finish (Mfg. 1955-1969) - includes no letter prefix or suffix in ser. no., pre 1968-69.

	$950	$850	$700	$600	$500	$395	$350

Add 10% for NIB condition.

Add 50% for very early production (circa 1950s) with high polish finish and correct full checkered, non-varnished grips.

Add 25% for 3 in. barrel.

✳ Blue or Royal Blue Finish (Mfg. circa 1970-1996)

	$875	$775	$675	$600	$500	$395	$350

Last MSR was $815.

Add 10% for NIB condition.

Add 25% for 3 in. barrel.

The standard Python was manufactured 1955-1996, and 1997-recent production is through the Colt Custom Shop by special order only (see Python Elite listing).

During 2001-2002, Colt shipped some Pythons production to dealers with prices in $1,100 - $1,200 retail range. These guns had a slightly different (rougher) line checkering pattern on the cylinder release and hammer parts.

There were also a few Pythons mfg. in .256 Win. Mag. (circa 1961), .38 Spl. (Python Target), .41 Mag., and .44 Spl. cals. While the .22 LR and the .22 WMR (.22 Mag.) were advertised in earlier factory catalogs, they were never mass-produced - only a few prototypes exist. At least one known example of a .22 cal. Python was found at an auction, but it had only a special factory barrel sleeve for photographic purposes, and was not a shootable gun. The amount of premium on these cals. depends on how serious (and deep-pocketed) the Python collector is.

A California distributor special ordered a quantity of the first 3 in. barreled Pythons, which at the time were not available. Colt probably utilized made-up 8 in. guns and either had them modified or re-barreled, with special marking. These guns are an unusual variant (sometimes referred to as a Combat Python), and are priced similarly to later factory 3 in. barrel Pythons.

✳ Nickel finish - available in polished or satin nickel, disc. 1985.

$1,150	$825	$675	$575	$475	$395	$300

Last MSR was $693.

Add 10% for NIB condition.

Add 60% for very rare 3 in. barrel.

Add 10% for satin nickel finish.

Satin nickel finish is so designated on original boxes as "Royal Coltguard" or "E NICK" (electroless nickel).

✳ Stainless Steel - stainless steel construction, matte finish, neoprene target or combat stocks, 2 1/2 (disc. 1994), 4, 6, or 8 (new 1989) in. barrel. Mfg. 1983-96.

	$975	$800	$650				

Last MSR was $904.

Add 10% for NIB condition.

The 6 in. barrel includes neoprene target stocks.

✳ "Ultimate" Bright Stainless Steel - deluxe, highly polished stainless model, 2 1/2 (disc.), 4, 6, or 8 in. VR barrel. Mfg. 1985-disc.

	$1,150	$825	$675				

Last MSR was $935.

Add 10% for NIB condition.

GRADING - PPGS™	100%	98%	95%	90%	80%	70%	60%

PYTHON ELITE - .357 Mag. cal., 4 or 6 in. VR barrel, choice of Royal Blue (mfg. 1997 only) or stainless steel, Colt-Elliason adj. rear sight, rubber service style (disc.) or smooth walnut finger groove grips, 38 or 43 1/2 oz. New 1997, disc. 1998, reintroduced 1999, again during 2002.

MSR $1,150	$975	$875	$750	$650	$550	$475	$395

This model is available by custom order only through the Colt Custom Shop.

* *Python Elite Stainless* - similar to Python Elite, except is stainless steel. Mfg. 1997-99, reintroduced in 2002.

MSR $1,150	$975	$875	$750	

This model is available by custom order only through the Colt Custom Shop.

ULTIMATE PYTHON - .357 Mag. cal., specially tuned by the custom shop, supplied with both Colt-Elliason target and Accro white outline sighting systems, walnut and rubber grips also included, choice of Colt Royal Blue or Ultimate Stainless finish, 6 in. barrel only. Mfg. 1991-93.

	$1,175	$975	$795	$695	$595	$495	$450

Last MSR was $1,140.

Add $120 for Ultimate Stainless Model.

PYTHON HUNTER - .357 Mag. cal., 8 in. barrel, includes Leupold 2X scope, Halliburton aluminum case and accessories. Mfg. 1981 only.

	$1,450	$1,300	$1,100	$850	$725	$650	$600

Last MSR was $995.

Add 10% for NIB condition.

PYTHON SILHOUETTE - .357 Mag. cal., 8 in. barrel, includes Leupold 2X scope, similar to Python Hunter, except barrel is roll marked with Silhouette name and scope position has been moved rearward, black luggage type case. Mfg. circa 1983.

	$1,500	$1,325	$1,100	$850	$700	$650	$600

Add 10% for NIB condition.

PYTHON .38 SPECIAL - 8 in. barrel, blue or nickel finish. Disc.

	$950	$775	$675	$550	$500	$400	$350

Add 10% for NIB condition.

GRIZZLY - .357 Mag. cal., 6 in. barrel, matte stainless finish, approx. 500 mfg.

	$800	$675	$575	

Add 10% for NIB condition.

This model was mfg. by the Colt Custom Shop.

WHITETAILER - .357 Mag. cal., 8 in. barrel, matte stainless finish, aluminum hard shell cased with 2X scope.

	$1,095	$950	$750	

Add 10% for NIB condition.

* *Whitetailer II* - similar to Whitetailer, except has high polish finish.

	$1,050	$875	$750	

Add 10% for NIB condition.

KODIAK - .44 Mag. cal., 4 or 6 in. Magna-ported barrel with non-fluted cylinder, stainless steel, Pachmayr grips, built on Anaconda frame, "Colt Kodiak .44 Magnum" with outline of bear's footprint on left side of barrel, ser. nos. start with CKA. Approx. 2,000 mfg. in 1993 by Custom Shop.

	$900	$625	$525	

ANACONDA - .44 Mag. or .45 LC (mfg. 1992-99) cal., double action, 4 (new 1991), 6, or 8 in. VR barrel, transfer bar safety system, 6 shot, choice of matte (disc. 2003), Realtree Grey camo (.44 Mag. with 8 in. barrel only, mfg. 1996 only) finish, or stainless steel, black neoprene combat grips with Colt medallion, red ramp front sight, full length ejector rod housing, white outline rear adj. sight, approx. 47-59 oz. Mfg. 1990-99, reintroduced 2002.

GRADING - PPGS™	100%	98%	95%	90%	80%	70%	60%

✳ Anaconda Current Mfg. - beginning 2002, the Anaconda is only available through the Colt Custom Shop.

MSR $1,000 $850 $475 $400

Add $50 for 8 in. barrel.

✳ Anaconda 1990-99 Mfg. - standard production, this period of production was not mfg. by the Colt Custom Shop.

$750 $600 $500

Add 10% for .45 LC cal.

✳ Anaconda with scope - .44 Mag. cal. only, 8 in. barrel, Realtree Grey camo finish on gun and scope. Mfg. 1996 only.

$900 $750 $575

Last MSR was $999.

✳ Anaconda Hunter - .44 Mag. cal., supplied with Leupold 2X scope, carrying case, cleaning accessories, and both walnut and rubber grips, 8 in. barrel only. Mfg. 1991-93.

$1,095 $895 $725

Last MSR was $1,200.

✳ Custom Ported Anaconda - .44 Mag. cal., features 6 (disc.) or 8 in. Magna-ported barrel and Colt-Elliason rear sight, contoured trigger, and Pachmayr rubber grips, brushed stainless steel. Mfg. 1992-93, re-released 1995-96, again in 2002-2003.

$875 $600 $495

Last MSR was $1,050.

✳ Anaconda 1st Edition - .44 Mag. cal., Ultimate Stainless finish, special rollmark on left side of barrel reads "Colt Anaconda First Edition", with aluminum carrying case, ser. no. range MM00001-MM01000, 1,000 mfg. 1990 only.

$950 $750 $625

100%	98%	95%	90%	80%	70%	60%	50%	40%	30%	20%	10%

RIFLES: PRE-1904

A Colt letter of provenance for the Lightning models listed below is $100 per gun (limited records). Colt-Burgess model factory letters are also available at $100 per gun.

FIRST MODEL RING LEVER - .34, .36, .38, .40, or .44 cal., 8 or 10 shot revolving cylinder, 32 in. octagon barrel, walnut stock, no forend, 200 mfg., Percussion. Mfg. 1837-1838.

✳ Standard Model

N/A	N/A	N/A	$37,500	$28,000	$21,500	$16,500	$13,500	$11,000	$9,000	$7,500	$6,500

✳ Improved Model - attached loading lever.

N/A	N/A	N/A	$41,000	$29,650	$22,750	$17,500	$14,500	$12,000	$10,000	$8,500	$7,500

SECOND MODEL RING LEVER - similar to First Model, w/o top strap over cylinder, .44 caliber only, Percussion, 5,000 mfg., 1838-1841.

✳ Standard Model

N/A	N/A	N/A	$33,500	$24,500	$17,000	$13,000	$11,000	$8,780	$7,200	$6,300	$5,650

✳ Improved Model

N/A	N/A	N/A	$34,750	$26,000	$17,750	$13,300	$11,200	$8,900	$7,325	$6,390	$5,725

MODEL 1839 CARBINE - .52 smooth bore cal., 6 shot cylinder, 24 in. barrel, exposed hammer for cocking, blue, walnut stock, percussion, approx. 950 mfg., 1838-1841.

✳ Early Model

N/A	N/A	N/A	$38,500	$29,000	$22,000	$17,500	$14,750	$11,500	$9,350	$7,750	$6,750

100%	98%	95%	90%	80%	70%	60%	50%	40%	30%	20%	10%

* *Standard Model* - no loading lever.

| N/A | N/A | N/A | $31,000 | $22,500 | $17,000 | $13,500 | $11,250 | $9,000 | $7,500 | $6,600 | $6,000 |

MODEL 1855 REVOLVING
- .36, .44, or .56 cal., various barrel lengths and stock styles, 5 or 6 shot cylinder, blue with walnut buttstock, no forend, percussion. Mfg. 1856- 1864.

* *1/2 Stock Sporter* - 24, 27, or 30 in. barrel, approx. 1,500 mfg.

| N/A | N/A | N/A | $11,500 | $9,000 | $7,850 | $7,000 | $6,500 | $6,000 | $5,500 | $5,100 | $4,750 |

* *Full Stock Sporter* - 21, 24, 27, 30, or 31 in. barrel, approx. 2,000 mfg.

| N/A | N/A | N/A | $13,500 | $11,275 | $9,150 | $8,250 | $7,500 | $6,950 | $6,500 | $6,100 | $5,750 |

* *Military Model, U.S.* - marked, 21-37 in. barrel, 9,310 mfg.

| N/A | N/A | N/A | $17,500 | $14,650 | $11,900 | $10,500 | $9,800 | $9,050 | $8,450 | $7,900 | $7,475 |

* *.36 Caliber Carbine Model* - 15, 18, or 21 in. barrel, 4,400 mfg.

| N/A | N/A | N/A | $17,150 | $14,350 | $11,660 | $10,525 | $9,600 | $8,875 | $8,275 | $7,750 | $7,300 |

* *.56 Caliber Artillery Carbine* - 5 shot, 21 in. barrel with bayonet lug and forestock, approx. 64 mfg.

| N/A | N/A | N/A | $19,000 | $16,500 | $13,500 | $10,875 | $9,850 | $9,100 | $8,400 | $7,950 | $7,500 |

* *Shotgun Model* - .60 or .75 cal., smooth bore, 27, 30, 33, or 36 in. barrels, 1,100 mfg.

| N/A | N/A | N/A | $12,750 | $11,000 | $9,000 | $8,000 | $7,250 | $6,750 | $6,300 | $6,000 | $5,600 |

BERDAN
- .42 bottle-necked CF cal., abreech loading, approx. 30,000 mfg. 1866- circa 1870. Scarce since most were sent to Russia and have Russian barrel markings, approx. 50-100 are Hartford marked.

* *Berdan Rifle* - .32 1/2 in. barrel, approx. 10 lbs.

| N/A | N/A | N/A | $3,250 | $2,750 | $2,250 | $1,850 | $1,650 | $1,450 | $1,325 | $1,250 | $1,175 |

* *Berdan Carbine* - half stock, 18 1/4 in. barrel, approx. 50 mfg., both Russian and Hartford marked.

| N/A | N/A | N/A | $8,300 | $7,600 | $6,725 | $6,100 | $5,500 | $4,750 | $3,950 | $3,275 | $2,750 |

MODEL 1861 MUSKET
- .58 cal., percussion, muzzle loader, 40 in. barrel, with 3 bands, metal parts, white walnut stock. 75,000 mfg., 1861-65.

| N/A | N/A | N/A | $1,895 | $1,750 | $1,650 | $1,500 | $1,350 | $1,250 | $1,150 | $1,000 | $850 |

COLT-BURGESS LEVER ACTION
- .44-40 WCF cal., 25 1/2 in. barrel, 15 shot tube mag., blue with case hardened lever and hammer, walnut stock. 6,400 mfg., 1883-85.

| N/A | N/A | N/A | $5,500 | $4,900 | $4,465 | $4,170 | $3,930 | $3,700 | $3,525 | $3,350 | $3,100 |

COLT-BURGESS CARBINE
- similar to Rifle, with 20 in. barrel.

| N/A | N/A | N/A | $7,900 | $7,300 | $6,725 | $6,250 | $5,850 | $5,500 | $5,200 | $4,950 | $4,750 |

COLT-BURGESS BABY CARBINE
- similar to Carbine, with lightened frame.

| N/A | N/A | N/A | $9,720 | $8,975 | $8,275 | $7,695 | $7,200 | $6,765 | $6,395 | $6,100 | $5,850 |

LIGHTNING SLIDE ACTION - SMALL FRAME
- .22 S or L cal., 24 in. barrel, open sights, walnut straight stock, round or octagon barrel, approx. 90,000 mfg. 1887-1903.

| N/A | N/A | N/A | $1,000 | $795 | $650 | $575 | $535 | $495 | $450 | $400 | $375 |

LIGHTNING SLIDE ACTION - MEDIUM FRAME
- .32-20 WCF, .38-40 WCF, or .44-40 WCF cal., similar to small frame, except with 26 in. barrel and larger frame. Approx. 90,000 mfg. 1884-1904.

| N/A | N/A | N/A | $1,775 | $1,475 | $1,175 | $950 | $775 | $650 | $550 | $495 | $450 |

LIGHTNING SLIDE ACTION - LARGE FRAME
- .38-56 WCF, .40-60 WCF, .45-60 WCF, .45-65 WCF, .45-85 WCF, or .50-95 Express cal., large version of previously described Lightnings, approx. 6,500 mfg. 1887-1894.

| N/A | N/A | N/A | $3,250 | $2,750 | $2,250 | $1,850 | $1,650 | $1,450 | $1,325 | $1,250 | $1,175 |

Add 25% for .50-95 Express cal.

100%	98%	95%	90%	80%	70%	60%	50%	40%	30%	20%	10%

LIGHTNING CARBINE MEDIUM FRAME - similar to Rifle, with 20 in. barrel.

N/A	N/A	N/A	$2,850	$2,450	$2,150	$1,950	$1,750	$1,450	$1,175	$1,050	$950

LIGHTNING CARBINE LARGE FRAME - 22 in. barrel.

N/A	N/A	N/A	$6,250	$5,350	$4,850	$4,375	$3,925	$3,625	$3,375	$3,150	$2,975

LIGHTNING BABY CARBINE MEDIUM FRAME - lightened version of Carbine.

N/A	N/A	N/A	$4,000	$3,450	$2,950	$2,450	$2,100	$1,850	$1,650	$1,425	$1,350

LIGHTNING BABY CARBINE LARGE FRAME - lightened version.

N/A	N/A	N/A	$8,500	$7,750	$6,850	$6,300	$5,825	$5,425	$5,075	$4,775	$4,350

Add 50% for .50-95 Express cal.

DOUBLE RIFLE SxS - various cals. in the .45 range, hammers, very limited production between 1878-1880. Most guns were owned by friends of Caldwell Colt - Sam Colt's son, the original designer. Colt Double Rifles are extremely rare and desirable, and should be examined carefully. Prices typically range between $15,000-$25,000, if all original.

GRADING - PPGS™	100%	98%	95%	90%	80%	70%	60%

COLTEER 1-22 - .22 LR or .22 Mag. cal., single shot bolt action, 20, 22, or 24 (.22 Mag. only, w/o sights) in. round barrel, adj. rear sight (20 or 22 in. barrel), plain walnut stock. Approx. 50,000 mfg. 1957-66.

	$275	$215	$175	$140	$110	$95	$80

Add 10% for .22 Mag. cal.

STAGECOACH - .22 LR cal., semi-auto, 16 1/2 in. barrel, 13 shot mag., deluxe walnut, saddle ring w/ leather thong, roll-engraved hold-up scene. Over 25,000 mfg. 1965-mid '70s.

	$325	$275	$215	$175	$140	$110	$90

COLTEER - .22 LR cal., similar to Stagecoach, except 19 3/8 in. barrel, 15 shot mag., no engraving and plain walnut. Over 25,000 mfg. 1965-mid '70s.

	$275	$215	$175	$140	$110	$95	$80

COURIER - similar to Colteer semi-auto, except pistol-grip stock and enlarged forearm. Mfg. 1970-mid '70s.

	$275	$215	$175	$140	$110	$95	$80

RIFLES: BOLT ACTION, CENTERFIRE

COLT "57" - .243 Win. or .30-06 cal., FN Mauser action, mfg. by Jefferson Mfg. Co. in N. Haven, CT during 1957, approx. 5,000 mfg. starting at ser. no. 1, checkered American Monte Carlo walnut stock, rear aperture and wraparound front sight, drilled and tapped for scope.

	$595	$550	$500	$450	$400	$350	$325

This model was also available in a deluxe version with deluxe hand checkered walnut stock - add 15%.

COLTSMAN STANDARD RIFLE - .223 Rem., .243 Win., .264 Win. Mag., .30-06, .300 Win. Mag., or .308 Win. cal., mfg. by Kodiak, Mauser or Sako-action, 22 in. or 24 in. (.300 Win. Mag.), 5 or 6 shot mag. Approx. 10,000 (both models) mfg. 1958-66.

	$495	$450	$425	$400	$350	$325	$300

COLTSMAN CUSTOM RIFLE - deluxe variation including deluxe walnut with skipline checkering and rosewood forearm cap.

	$695	$650	$600	$550	$500	$450	$400

GRADING - PPGS™	100%	98%	95%	90%	80%	70%	60%

COLT SAUER RIFLE (STANDARD ACTION) - .25-06 Rem., .270 Win. or .30-06 cal., non-rotating bolt action, manufactured in Germany by J. P. Sauer & Sohn, 24 in. barrel, 4 round mag., no sights, checkered walnut stock with rosewood forend tip and pistol grip cap, recoil pad. Mfg. 1974-85.

	$1,300	$1,100	$950	$850	$700	$650	$600

Last MSR was $1,257.

> **Add 10% for .25-06 Rem. cal.**

COLT SAUER SHORT ACTION - similar to the standard except in .22-250 Rem., .243 Win. cal. or .308 Win. cal. Mfg. 1976-85.

	$1,400	$1,200	$1,000	$850	$700	$650	$600

Last MSR was $1,257.

> **Add 25% for .308 Win. cal.**

COLT SAUER MAGNUM - similar to the standard except in 7mm Rem. Mag., 300 Win. Mag., or 300 Weatherby Mag. cal. Mfg. 1974-85.

	$1,550	$1,300	$1,100	$900	$800	$700	$600

Last MSR was $1,300.

COLT SAUER GRADE IV - similar to the Magnum except has silver receiver, each caliber features a different engraved animal.

	$3,000	$2,800	$2,000	$2,400	$2,200	$2,000	$1,500

> **Add 10% for Magnum cals.**

COLT SAUER GRAND ALASKAN - heavier version in .375 H&H cal., adj. sights. Mfg. 1978-85.

	$1,600	$1,400	$1,200	$1,100	$900	$800	$750

COLT SAUER GRAND AFRICAN - .458 Win. Mag. cal., 4 round capacity, 9 lb. 12 oz. Mfg. 1974-85.

	$1,600	$1,400	$1,200	$1,000	$820	$740	$690

Last MSR was $1,400.

COLT LIGHT RIFLE - .243 Win., .260 Rem., .270 Win., .280 Rem., .25-06 Rem., .30-06, .308 Win., 7x57mm, .300 Win. Mag., 7mm-08, or 7mm Rem. Mag. cal., short or long action, matte black synthetic stock, matte metal finish, adj. trigger, 3 position side safety, approx. 5.4 lbs. in short action, manufactured by Saco Defense in the U.S. New 2000.

MSR $779	$675	$550	$500	$450	$400	$350	$295

RIFLES: SINGLE SHOT, CENTERFIRE

COLT-SHARPS RIFLE - .17 Bee, .22-250 Rem., .243 Win., .25-06 Rem., 7mm Rem. Mag., .30-06, or .375 H&H cal., Sharps falling block action, high-gloss bluing, deluxe checkered walnut stock and forearm. Approx. 500 mfg. 1970-77.

	$2,295	$1,950	$1,650	$1,200	$1,000	$800	$650

DRILLINGS

COLT SAUER DRILLING - 12 ga./.30-06, 16 ga./.30-06 (rare), or .243 Win. cal., 25 in. barrels, engraved receiver, 8 lbs. Disc. 1985.

	$3,300	$3,000	$2,600	$2,300	$2,000	$1,800	$1,500

Last MSR was $4,228.

RIFLES: SEMI-AUTO, AR-15 & VARIATIONS

The AR-15 rifle and variations are the civilian versions of the U.S. armed forces M-16 model, which was initially ordered by the U.S. Army in 1963. Colt's obtained the exclusive manufacturing and marketing rights to the AR-15 from the Armalite division of the Fairchild Engine and Airplane Corporation in 1961.

GRADING - PPGS™	100%	98%	95%	90%	80%	70%	60%

Factory Colt AR-15 receivers are stamped with the model names only (Sporter II, Government Model, Colt Carbine, Sporter Match H-Bar, Match Target), but are not stamped with the model numbers (R6500, R6550, R6521, MT6430, CR6724). Because of this, if an AR-15 rifle/carbine does not have its original box, the only way to determine whether the gun is pre-ban or not is to look at the serial number and see if the configuration matches the features listed below within the two pre-ban subcategories.

AR-15 production included transition models, which were made up of obsolete and old stock parts. These transition models include: blue label box models having large front takedown pins, no internal sear block, 20 in. barrel models having bayonet lugs, misstamped nomenclature on receivers, and having green label bolt assemblies.

Rifling twists on the Colt AR-15 have changed throughout the years, and barrel twists are stamped at the end of the barrel on top. They started with a 1:12 in. twist, changed to a 1:7 in. twist (to match with the new, longer .223 Rem./5.56mm SS109-type bullet), and finally changed to a 1:9 in. twist in combination with 1:7 in. twist models as a compromise for bullets in the 50-68 grain range. Current mfg. AR-15s/Match Targets have rifling twists/turns incorporated into the model descriptions.

Colt's never sold pre-ban lower receivers individually. It only sold completely assembled rifles. A Colt letter of provenance for the AR-15 models listed below is $100 per gun.

AR-15, Pre-Ban, 1963-1989 Mfg. w/ Green Label Box

Common features of 1963-1989 mfg. AR-15s are bayonet lug, flash hider, large front takedown pin, no internal sear block, and w/o reinforcement around the magazine release button.

AR-15 boxes during this period of mfg. had a green label with serial number affixed on a white sticker. Box is taped in two places with brown masking tape. NIB consists of the rifle with barrel stick down the barrel, plastic muzzle cap on flash hider, factory tag hanging from front sight post, rifle is in plastic bag with ser. no. on white sticker attached to bag, cardboard insert, accessory bag with two 20 round mags., manual, sling, and cleaning brushes. Cleaning rods are in separate bag.

Pre-ban parts rifles are rifles that are not assembled in their proper factory configuration. Counterfeit pre-ban rifles are rifles using post-ban receivers and assembled into a pre-ban configuration (it is a felony to assemble or alter a post-ban rifle into a pre-ban configuration). Unstamped L.E. only rifles are a felony to possess, and can be sold only to sworn law enforcement officers.

> **Add $100 for NIB condition.**
> **Add $300 for early green label box models with reinforced lower receiver.**

SP-1 (R6000) - .223 Rem. cal., original Colt paramilitary configuration without forward bolt assist, 20 in. barrel with 1:12 in. twist, identifiable by the triangular shaped handguards/forearm, no case deflector, A1 sights, finishes included parkerizing and electroless nickel, approx. 6 3/4 lbs. Mfg. 1963-84.

	$1,850	$1,750	$1,700	$1,600	$1,400	$1,200	$995

> **Early mfg. will command substantial premiums, especially for very low ser. nos. - ser. range is SP00001 (1963)-SP55301 (1976).**
> Pre-ban serialization is ser. no. SP360,200 and lower.
> Early SP-1s were packaged differently than later standard green box label guns.

* **SP-1 Carbine (R6001)** - similar to SP-1, except has 16 in. barrel, ribbed handguards, and collapsible buttstock with high gloss finish.

	$2,000	$1,825	$1,650	$1,500	$1,350	$1,150	$975

> Pre-ban serialization is ser. no. SP360200 and lower.
> Early SP-1s were packaged differently than later standard green box label guns.

SPORTER II (R6500) - .223 Rem. cal., various configurations, receiver stamped "Sporter II", 20 in. barrel, 1:7 twist, A1 sights and forward assist, disc.

	$1,475	$1,275	$1,100	$950	$800	$725	$650

> Serial numbers SP360200 and below are pre-ban.

GRADING - PPGS™	100%	98%	95%	90%	80%	70%	60%

✳ Sporter II Carbine (R6420) - similar to Sporter II, except has 16 in. barrel, A1 sights and collapsible buttstock.

	$1,500	$1,350	$1,200	$1,050	$900	$800	$700

Serial numbers SP360200 and below are pre-ban.

GOVERNMENT MODEL (R6550)
- .223 cal., receiver is stamped Government Model, 20 in. barrel with 1:7 in. twist, A2 sights, forward assist and brass deflector, very desirable because this model has the closest configurations to what the U.S. military is currently using.

	$2,000	$1,850	$1,700	$1,550	$1,400	$1,250	$1,050

In 1987, Colt replaced the AR-15A2 Sporter II Rifle with the AR-15A2 Govt. Model. This new model has the 800 meter rear sighting system housed in the receiver's carrying handle (similar to the M-16 A2).

Serial numbers GS008000 and below are pre-ban.

✳ Government Model (6550K) - similar to R6550, except does not have bayonet lug, originally supplied with .22 cal. conversion kit.

	$2,000	$1,850	$1,700	$1,550	$1,400	$1,250	$1,050

Subtract $300 w/o conversion kit.
Serial numbers GS008000 and below are pre-ban.

✳ Government Model (R6550CC) - similar to R6550, except has Z-Cote tiger striped camo finish, very scarce (watch for cheap imitation paint jobs).

	$3,500	$3,350	$3,100	$2,800	$2,600	$2,400	$2,000

Serial numbers GS008000 and below are pre-ban.

H-BAR MODEL (R6600)
- H-Bar model with 20 in heavy barrel, 1:7 twist, forward assist, A2 sights, brass deflector, 8 lbs. New 1986.

	$1,800	$1,650	$1,500	$1,350	$1,200	$1,050	$925

Serial numbers SP360200 and below are pre-ban.

✳ H-Bar (R6600K) - similar to R6600, except has no bayonet lug, supplied with .22 LR cal. conversion kit.

	$1,800	$1,650	$1,500	$1,350	$1,200	$1,050	$925

Subtract $300 w/o conversion kit.
Serial numbers SP360200 and below are pre-ban.

✳ Delta H-Bar (R6600DH) - similar to R6600, except has 3-9X rubber armored variable scope, removable cheekpiece, adj. scope mount, and black leather sling, range selected, aluminum cased. Mfg. 1987-91.

	$2,300	$2,150	$1,925	$1,775	$1,575	$1,375	$1,125

Last MSR was $1,460.

Serial numbers SP360200 and below are pre-ban.

AR-15, Pre-Ban, 1989-Sept. 11, 1994 Mfg. w/Blue Label Box

Common features of 1989-1994 AR-15 production include a small front takedown pin, internal sear block, reinforcement around the mag. release button, flash hider, no bayonet lug on 20 in. models, A2 sights, brass deflector, and forward bolt assist. Models R6430 and 6450 do not have A2 sights, brass deflector, or forward bolt assist.

Blue label boxed AR-15s were mfg. between 1989-Sept. 11, 1994. Please refer to box description under Pre-1989 AR-15 mfg.

Pre-ban parts rifles are rifles that are not assembled in their proper factory configuration. Counterfeit pre-ban rifles are rifles using post-ban receivers and assembled into a pre-ban configuration (it is a felony to assemble or alter a post-ban rifle into a pre-ban configuration). Unstamped L.E. only rifles are a felony to possess, and can be sold only to sworn law enforcement officers.

Add $100 for NIB condition.

GRADING - PPGS™	100%	98%	95%	90%	80%	70%	60%

AR-15A3 TACTICAL CARBINE (R-6721)

.223 Rem. cal., M4 flattop with 16 in. heavy barrel, 1:9 twist, pre-ban configuration with flash hider, bayonet lug, and 4-position, A2 sights, collapsible stock, removable carry handle, 134 were sold commercially in the U.S., most collectible AR-15. Mfg. 1994 only.

	$5,000	$4,775	$4,500	$4,300	$4,100	$3,850	$3,600

On the R-6721, serial numbers BD000134 and below are pre-ban.

Please note the serial number cutoff on this model, as Colt shipped out a lot of unstamped post-ban law enforcement only "LEO" rifles before finally stamping them as a restricted rifle.

GOVERNMENT CARBINE (R6520)

receiver is stamped Government Carbine, two-position collapsible buttstock, 800 meter adj. rear sight, 16 in. barrel bayonet lug, 1:7 twist, shortened forearm, 5 lbs. 13 oz. Mfg. 1988-94.

	$1,975	$1,850	$1,700	$1,550	$1,400	$1,250	$1,050

Last MSR was $880.

On the R6520, serial numbers GC018500 and below are pre-ban.

Please note the serial number cutoff on this model, as Colt shipped out a lot of unstamped post-ban law enforcement only "LEO" rifles before finally stamping them as a restricted rifle. This model was manufactured in both green and blue label configurations.

COLT CARBINE (R6521)

stamped Colt Carbine, similar to R6520, except has no bayonet lug, 16 in. barrel, 1:7 twist. Disc. 1988.

	$2,200	$2,050	$1,900	$1,750	$1,600	$1,525	$1,375

Last MSR was $770.

Serial numbers CC001616 and below are pre-ban.

SPORTER LIGHTWEIGHT (R6530)

.223 Rem., receiver is stamped Sporter Lightweight, 16 in. barrel, 1:7 twist, similar to R6520, except does not have bayonet lug and collapsible stock.

	$1,500	$1,350	$1,200	$1,050	$900	$800	$700

Last MSR was $740.

Serial numbers SI027246 and below are pre-ban.

9mm CARBINE (R6450)

9mm Para. cal., carbine model with 16 in. barrel and bayonet lug with 1:10 twist, w/o forward bolt assist and brass deflector, two-position collapsible stock, with 20 shot mag., 6 lbs. 5 oz.

	$1,800	$1,675	$1,500	$1,350	$1,200	$1,050	$925

Last MSR was $696.

On the R6450, serial numbers TA010100 are pre-ban.

Please note the serial number cutoff on this model, as Colt shipped out a lot of unstamped post-ban law enforcement only "LEO" rifles before finally stamping them as a restricted rifle. This model was manufactured with either a green or blue label configurations.

9mm CARBINE (R6430)

9mm Para. cal., similar to R6450 Carbine, except does not have bayonet lug or collapsible stock. New 1992.

	$1,500	$1,350	$1,200	$1,050	$925	$825	$725

Serial numbers NL004800 are pre-ban.

7.62x39mm CARBINE (R6830)

7.62x39mm cal., 16 in. barrel w/o bayonet lug and 1:12 twist, fixed buttstock. New 1992.

	$1,400	$1,250	$1,050	$900	$775	$675	$575

Serial numbers LH011326 are pre-ban.

TARGET COMPETITION H-BAR RIFLE (R6700)

.223 Rem. cal., features flat-top upper receiver for scope mounting, 20 in. H-Bar barrel (1:9 in. twist), quick detachable carry handle which incorporates a 600-meter rear sighting system, dovetailed upper receiver is grooved to accept Weaver style scope rings, 8 1/2 lbs.

	$1,700	$1,550	$1,400	$1,250	$1,050	$875	$725

Serial numbers CH019500 and below are pre-ban.

GRADING - PPGS™	100%	98%	95%	90%	80%	70%	60%

COMPETITION H-BAR CUSTOM SHOP (R6701) - .223 Rem. cal., similar to the R6700, but is equipped with detachable scope mount, custom shop enhancements added to trigger and barrel, 2,000 mfg. from Colt Custom Shop.

	$1,800	$1,650	$1,500	$1,350	$1,200	$1,050	$900

MATCH H-BAR (R6601) - heavy 20 in. H-Bar barrel with 1:7 twist, fixed buttstock. 8 lbs.

	$1,500	$1,350	$1,200	$1,050	$900	$800	$700

✱ *Delta H-Bar (R6601DH)* - similar to R6601, except has 3-9X rubber armored variable scope, removable cheekpiece, adj. scope mount, and black leather sling, range selected, aluminum cased. Mfg. 1987-91.

	$2,000	$1,850	$1,700	$1,550	$1,400	$1,250	$1,100

Last MSR was $1,460.

Serial numbers MH086020 and below are pre-ban.

SPORTER TARGET (R6551) - similar to R6601, except has 20 in. barrel which tapers down underneath handguard, 7 1/2 lbs.

	$1,500	$1,350	$1,200	$1,050	$900	$800	$700

On the R6551, serial numbers ST038100 and below are pre-ban.

AR-15, Post-Ban, Mfg. Sept. 12, 1994-Present

Add $368 for Colt Scout C-More Sight on current mfg.
Add $444 for Colt Tactical C-More Sight on current mfg.

MATCH TARGET COMPETITION H-BAR RIFLE (MT6700) - .223 Rem. cal., features flattop upper receiver for scope mounting, 20 in. barrel (1 turn in 9 in.), quick detachable carry handle which incorporates a 600-meter rear sighting system, counterbored muzzle, dovetailed upper receiver is grooved to accept Weaver style scope rings, supplied with two 5, 8, or 9 (new 1999) shot mags., cleaning kit, and sling, matte black finish, 8 1/2 lbs. New 1992.

MSR $1,315		$1,075	$925	$825	$725	$650	$575	$525

Add $55 for compensator (MT6700C, new 1999).

TACTICAL ELITE MODEL (TE6700) - .223 Rem. cal., 20 in. heavy barrel, 1:8 in. barrel rifling twist, Hogue finger groove pistol grip, Choate buttstock, fine tuned for accuracy, includes scope and mount, approx. 1,000 rifles made by the Custom Shop circa 1996-97.

	$1,650	$1,450	$1,250	$1,025	$900	$800	$700

COLT ACCURIZED RIFLE (CR6724) - .223 Rem. cal., 24 in. stainless match barrel, matte finish, accurized AR-15, 8 (disc. 1998) or 9 (new 1999) shot mag., 9.41 lbs. New 1997.

MSR $1,470		$1,180	$1,025	$850	$795	$725	$650	$575

MATCH TARGET COMPETITION H-BAR II (MT6731) - .223 Rem. cal., flattop, 16.1 in. barrel (1:9 in.), matte finish, 7.1 lbs. New 1995.

MSR $1,290		$1,050	$925	$850	$725	$625	$575	$525

MATCH TARGET LIGHTWEIGHT (MT6430, MT6530, or MT6830) - .223 Rem. (MT6530, 1:7 in. twist), 7.62x39mm (MT6830, disc. 1996, 1:12 in. twist), or 9mm Para. (MT6430, disc. 1996, 1:10 in. twist) cals., features 16 in. barrel (non-threaded per C/B 1994), initially shorter stock and handguard, adj. rear sight for windage and elevation, includes 2 detachable 5, 8, or 9 (new 1999) shot mags., approx. 7 lbs. Mfg. 1991-2002.

	$925	$795	$725	$665	$600	$550	$495

Last MSR was $1,111.

Add $200 for .22 LR conversion kit (disc. 1994).

GRADING - PPGS™	100%	98%	95%	90%	80%	70%	60%

TARGET GOVT. MODEL RIFLE (MT6551) - .223 Rem. cal., semi-auto version of the M-16 rifle with forward bolt assist, gas operated, 20 in. barrel (1:7 in.), straight line black nylon stock, aperture rear, post front sight, 5, 8, 9 (new 1999), 7 1/2 lbs. Disc. 2002.

	$950	$825	$750	$675	$600	$550	$495

Last MSR was $1,144.

Add $200 for .22 LR conversion kit (mfg. 1990-94).

MATCH TARGET M4 RIFLE (MT6400C) - .223 Rem. cal., similar to current U.S. armed forces M4 model, except semi-auto, 10 shot mag., 16.1 in. barrel with 1:7 in. twist, matte black finish, fixed tube buttstock, A3 detachable carrying handle, 7.3 lbs. New 2002.

MSR $1,420	$1,150	$950	$850	$750	$650	$575	$525

MATCH TARGET H-BAR (MT6601) - features heavy 20 in. H-Bar barrel, 1:7 in. twist, A2 sights, 8 lbs. New 1986.

MSR $1,300	$1,075	$925	$825	$725	$650	$575	$525

Add $200 for .22 LR conversion kit (mfg. 1990-94).

This model is available with a compensator at no additional charge (MT6601C, new 1999).

AR-15 SCOPE (3X/4X) AND MOUNT - initially offered with 3X scope, then switched to 4X. Disc.

	$300	$250	$185

Last MSR was $344.

SHOTGUNS: O/U

ARMSMEAR - 12 ga. only, 2 3/4 in. chambers, a few prototypes were mfg. by Worshipful Co. Gunmakers of London, boxlock action with engraved sideplates, checkered high-grade European walnut stock and forearm, 28 (HE) or 30 (LE) in. VR barrels with screw-in chokes, choice of light (Armsmear 12 LE) or heavy (Armsmear 12 HE) engraving, 7 1/2 lbs. This model was originally advertised in 1995.

While advertised, this model was never manufactured.

100%	98%	95%	90%	80%	70%	60%	50%	40%	30%	20%	10%

SHOTGUNS: SxS, DISC.

Strong, original case colors and vivid damascus barrel patterning will make the difference when determining values on the Models 1878 and 1883. Remember, the models listed below were designed to shoot black powder loads only, not smokeless powder.

A Colt letter of provenance for the models listed below is $100 per gun.

MODEL 1878 HAMMER SHOTGUN - 10 or 12 ga., 28-32 in. blue or browned damascus barrels, double triggers, sideplates, case hardened breech, extractors, semi-pistol grip stock, 22,683 mfg. between 1878-89. Many of these guns were ordered with special features - these original guns command premiums above the prices listed below.

$3,750	$3,250	$2,950	$2,675	$2,200	$1,925	$1,650	$1,485	$1,100	$990	$880	$725

MODEL 1883 HAMMERLESS - 8, 10, or 12 ga., 28-32 in. damascus barrels, many deluxe custom orders occur in this model. Mfg. from 1883-95. Approx. serial range is 1-3,050 and 4,055-8,365. Seldom encountered in mint condition.

$4,250	$3,750	$3,350	$2,995	$2,675	$2,200	$1,925	$1,650	$1,485	$1,100	$990	$875

Add 200% for 8 ga.

This model was generally a custom order gun with no standard grades being designated. Quality was extremely high, and the high cost of manufacture is a large reason why the gun never sold in large numbers commercially. The Model 1883 was discontinued after only 12 years of manufacture (it was one of the most expensive shotguns during its day). Values above assume moderate engraving and above average walnut.

GRADING - PPGS™	100%	98%	95%	90%	80%	70%	60%

SxS SHOTGUN MFG. 1961-62 - 12 ga. or 16 ga., various barrel lengths, DTs, checkered stock and forearm, mfg. in France 1961-62 by Fabrication Mechanique, estimated total between 25-50 guns in serial range 467,000-469,000.

	$675	$595	$525	$450	$400	$360	$320

SHOTGUNS: SEMI-AUTO

STANDARD AUTO SHOTGUN - 12 or 20 ga. (also available in Mags.), mfg. by Franchi of Italy, aluminum frame, 26, 28, 30, or 32 in. plain or VR barrel almost 5,300 mfg. (both models) 1962-66.

	$375	$350	$325	$295	$260	$230	$200

Add $50 for VR barrel.

CUSTOM AUTO SHOTGUN - similar to Standard Model, except deluxe walnut, hand engraved receiver. Mfg. 1962-1966.

	$475	$425	$375	$350	$325	$295	$260

SHOTGUNS: SLIDE ACTION

COLTSMAN PUMP SHOTGUN - 12, 16, or 20 ga., Manufrance frame assembled by both Kodiak and Montgomery Wards, 26 or 28 in. plain barrel, aluminum frame. Approx. 2,000 mfg. 1961-1965.

	$325	$295	$260	$230	$200	$180	$165

Add 30% for Riot model with extended magazine and 20 in. barrel (not cataloged).

COMMEMORATIVES, SPECIAL EDITIONS, & LIMITED MFG.

During the course of a year, we receive many phone calls and letters on Colt special editions and limited editions that do not appear in this section. It should be noted that a factory commemorative issue is a gun that has been manufactured, marketed, and sold through the auspices of the specific trademark (in this case Colt). There have literally been hundreds of special and limited editions which, although mostly made by Colt (some were subcontracted), were not marketed or retailed by Colt. These guns are NOT Colt commemoratives and, for the most part, do not have the desirability factor that the factory commemoratives have. Your best alternative to find out more information about the multitude of these special/limited editions is to write: COLT ARCHIVE PROPERTIES, LLC, P.O. Box 1868, Hartford, CT, 06144. If anyone could have any information, it would be the factory. Their research fee is $100 per gun, with a premium charge for factory engraving. If they cannot obtain additional information on the variation you request, they will refund $50. Unfortunately, in some cases, a special/limited edition may not be researchable. In situations like this, do not confuse rarity with desirability.

Typically, special and limited editions are made for distributors. These subcontracts seem to be mostly made to signify/commemorate an organization, state, special event or occasion, personality, etc. These are typically marketed and sold through a distributor to dealers, or a company/individual to those people who want to purchase them. These special editions may or may not have a retail price and often times, since demand is regional, values decrease rapidly in other areas of the country. In some cases, if the distributor/wholesaler who ordered the initial special/limited edition is known (and still in business), you may be able to find more information by contacting them directly. Desirability is the key to determining values on these editions.

Because the commemorative consumer is now more in charge (consumers now own most of the guns since distributor/dealer inventories are depleted) than during the 1980s, commemorative firearms are possibly as strong as they have ever been. When the supply side of commemorative economics has to be purchased from knowledgable collectors or savvy dealers and demand stays the same or increases slightly, prices have no choice but to go up. If and when the manufacturers crank up the commemorative production runs again (and it won't be like the good old days), the old marketplace characteristics may reappear. Until then, however, the commemorative marketplace remains steady, with values having become more predictable.

As a reminder on commemoratives, I would like to repeat a few facts, especially for the beginning collector, but also for all manufacturers of commemoratives. Commemoratives are current

GRADING - PPGS™	100%	Issue Price	Qty. Made

production guns designed as a reproduction of a historically famous gun model, or as a tie-in with historically famous persons or events. They are generally of very excellent quality and often embellished with select woods and finishes such as silver, nickel, or gold plating. Obviously, they are manufactured to be instant collectibles and to be pleasing to the eye. As with firearms in general, not all commemorative models have achieved collector status, although most enjoy an active market. Consecutively-numbered pairs as well as collections based on the same serial number may bring a premium. Remember that handguns usually are in some type of wood presentation case, and that rifles may be cased or in packaging with graphics styled to the particular theme of the collectible. The original factory packaging and papers should always accompany the firearm, as they are necessary to realize full value at the time of sale, and become more important every year.

NIB commemorative firearms should be absolutely new, unfired, and as issued, since any obvious use or wear removes it from collector status and lowers its value significantly. Many owners have allowed their commemoratives to sit in their boxes while encased in plastic wrappers for years without inspecting them for corrosion or oxidation damage. This is risky, especially if stored inside a plastic wrapper for long periods of time, since any accumulated moisture cannot escape. Periodic inspection should be implemented to ensure no damage occurs - this is important, since even light "freckling" created from touching the metal surfaces can reduce values significantly. A mint or unfired gun without its original packaging can lose as much as 50% of its normal value - many used commemoratives get sold as "fancy shooters" with little, if any, premiums being asked.

A final note on commemoratives: One of the characteristics of commemoratives/special editions is that over the years of ownership, most of the originals stay in the same, NIM condition. Thus, if supply always is constant and in one condition, demand has to increase before price appreciation can occur. After 44 years of commemorative/special edition production, many models' performance records can be accurately analyzed and the appreciation (or depreciation) can be compared against other purchases of equal vintage. You be the judge.

1961 GENESEO, ILLINOIS 125TH ANNIVERSARY DERRINGER

	$650	$28	104

1961 SHERIFF'S MODEL - blue and case hardened, 3 in. barrel, "SM" suffix.

	$2,250	$130	478

1961 SHERIFF'S MODEL - nickel, 3 in. barrel, "SM" suffix.

	$6,000	$140	25

1961 125TH ANNIVERSARY MODEL SAA

	$1,395	$150	7,390

1961 KANSAS STATEHOOD CENTENNIAL SCOUT

	$450	$75	6,201

1961 PONY EXPRESS CENTENNIAL SCOUT

	$475	$80	1,007

1961 CIVIL WAR CENTENNIAL PISTOL .22 SHORT

	$175	$33	24,114

1962 ROCK ISLAND ARSENAL CENTENNIAL MODEL

	$250	$39	550

1962 COLUMBUS, OHIO SESQUICENTENNIAL SCOUT

	$550	$100	200

1962 FORT FINDLAY, OHIO SESQUICENTENNIAL SCOUT

	$650	$90	110

1962 FORT FINDLAY CASE PAIR - .22 LR and .22 Mag. cals.

	$2,500	$185	20

GRADING - PPGS™	100%	Issue Price	Qty. Made
1962 NEW MEXICO GOLDEN ANNIVERSARY SCOUT			
	$450	$80	1,000
1962 FORT MCPHERSON, NEBRASKA CENTENNIAL DERRINGER			
	$395	$29	300
1962 WEST VIRGINIA STATEHOOD CENTENNIAL SCOUT			
	$450	$75	3,452
1963 WEST VIRGINIA STATEHOOD CENTENNIAL SAA .45			
	$1,495	$150	600
1963 ARIZONA TERRITORIAL CENTENNIAL SCOUT			
	$450	$75	5,355
1963 ARIZONA TERRITORIAL CENTENNIAL SAA .45			
	$1,495	$150	1,280
1963 CAROLINA CHARTER TERCENTENARY SCOUT			
	$450	$75	300
1963 CAROLINA CHARTER TERCENTENARY 22/45 COMBO			
	$1,895	$240	251
1963 H. COOK "1 TO 100" 22/45 COMBO			
	$1,995	$275	100
1963 FORT STEPHENSON, OHIO SESQUICENTENNIAL SCOUT			
	$550	$75	200
1963 BATTLE OF GETTYSBURG CENTENNIAL SCOUT			
	$450	$90	1,019
1963 IDAHO TERRITORIAL CENTENNIAL SCOUT			
	$450	$75	902
1963 GEN. JOHN HUNT MORGAN INDIANA RAID SCOUT			
	$650	$75	100
1964 CHERRY'S SPORTING GOODS 35TH ANNIVERSARY 22/45 COMBO			
	$1,995	$275	100
1964 NEVADA STATEHOOD CENTENNIAL SCOUT			
	$450	$75	3,984
1964 NEVADA STATEHOOD CENTENNIAL SAA .45			
	$1,795	$150	1,688
1964 NEVADA STATEHOOD CENTENNIAL 22/45 COMBO			
	$1,895	$240	189
1964 NEVADA ST. CENT. 22/45 COMBO W/EXTRA ENGR. CYLS.			
	$1,995	$350	577
1964 NEVADA "BATTLE BORN" SCOUT			
	$450	$85	981
1964 NEVADA "BATTLE BORN" SAA .45			
	$1,495	$175	80
1964 NEVADA "BATTLE BORN" 22/45 COMBO			
	$2,595	$265	20
1964 MONTANA TERRITORIAL CENTENNIAL SCOUT			
	$450	$75	2,300

GRADING - PPGS™	100%	Issue Price	Qty. Made

1964 MONTANA TERRITORIAL CENTENNIAL SAA .45
	$1,495	$150	851

Approx. 100-200 sets (including the Scout) were sold with matching ser. numbers.

1964 WYOMING DIAMOND JUBILEE SCOUT
	$450	$75	2,357

1964 GENERAL HOOD CENTENNIAL SCOUT
	$450	$75	1,503

1964 NEW JERSEY TERCENTENARY SCOUT
	$450	$75	1,001

1964 NEW JERSEY TERCENTENARY SAA .45
	$1,495	$150	250

1964 ST. LOUIS BICENTENNIAL SCOUT
	$450	$75	802

1964 ST. LOUIS BICENTENNIAL SAA .45
	$1,495	$150	200

1964 ST. LOUIS BICENTENNIAL 22/45 COMBO
	$1,895	$240	250

1964 CALIFORNIA GOLD RUSH SCOUT
	$475	$80	500

1964 PONY EXPRESS PRESENTATION SAA .45
	$1,495	$250	1,004

1964 CHAMIZAL TREATY SCOUT
	$450	$85	450

1964 CHAMIZAL TREATY SAA .45
	$1,395	$170	50

1964 CHAMIZAL TREATY 22/45 COMBO
	$1,995	$280	50

1964 COL. SAM COLT SESQUI. PRESENTATION SAA .45
	$1,495	$225	4,750

1964 COL. SAM COLT SESQUI. DELUXE PRES. SAA .45
	$2,500	$500	200

1964 COL. SAM COLT SESQUI. SPEC. DELUXE PRES. SAA .45
	$4,000	$1,000	50

1964 WYATT EARP BUNTLINE SAA .45
	$2,750	$250	150

1965 OREGON TRAIL SCOUT
	$450	$75	1,995

1965 JOAQUIN MURIETTA 22/45 COMBO
	$1,995	$350	100

1965 FORTY-NINER MINER SCOUT
	$450	$85	500

1965 OLD FT. DES MOINES RECONSTRUCTION SCOUT
	$475	$90	700

1965 OLD FT. DES MOINES RECONSTRUCTION SAA .45
	$1,495	$170	100

GRADING - PPGS™	100%	Issue Price	Qty. Made
1965 OLD FT. DES MOINES RECONSTRUCTION 22/45 COMBO			
	$1,995	$290	100
1965 APPOMATTOX CENTENNIAL SCOUT			
	$450	$75	1,001
1965 APPOMATTOX CENTENNIAL SAA .45			
	$1,495	$150	250
1965 APPOMATTOX CENTENNIAL 22/45 COMBO			
	$1,895	$240	250
1965 GENERAL MEADE CAMPAIGN SCOUT			
	$450	$75	1,197
1965 ST. AUGUSTINE QUADRACENTENNIAL SCOUT			
	$475	$85	500
1965 KANSAS COWTOWN SERIES - Wichita Scout.			
	$450	$85	500
1966 KANSAS COWTOWN SERIES - Dodge City Scout.			
	$450	$85	500
1966 COLORADO GOLD RUSH SCOUT			
	$475	$85	1,350
1966 OKLAHOMA DIAMOND JUBILEE			
	$450	$85	1,343
1966 DAKOTA TERRITORY SCOUT			
	$450	$85	1,000
1966 GENERAL MEADE SAA .45			
	$1,395	$165	200
1966 ABERCROMBIE & FITCH "TRAILBLAZER" - New York.			
	$1,295	$275	200
1966 KANSAS COWTOWN SERIES - Abilene Scout.			
	$450	$95	500
1966 INDIANA SESQUICENTENNIAL SCOUT			
	$450	$85	1,500
1966 PONY EXPRESS .45 SAA 4-SQUARE SET (4 GUNS)			
	$5,995	$1,400	unknown
1966 CALIFORNIA GOLD RUSH SAA .45			
	$1,495	$175	130
1966 ABERCROMBIE & FITCH "TRAILBLAZER" - Chicago.			
	$1,295	$275	100
1966 ABERCROMBIE & FITCH "TRAILBLAZER" - San Francisco.			
	$1,295	$275	100
1967 LAWMAN SERIES - Bat Masterson Scout.			
	$475	$90	3,000
1967 LAWMAN SERIES - Bat Masterson SAA .45.			
	$1,500	$180	500
1967 ALAMO SCOUT			
	$450	$85	4,250

GRADING - PPGS™	100%	Issue Price	Qty. Made

1967 ALAMO SAA .45

| | $1,495 | $165 | 750 |

1967 ALAMO 22/45 COMBO

| | $1,895 | $265 | 250 |

1967 KANSAS COWTOWN SERIES - Coffeyville Scout.

| | $450 | $95 | 500 |

1967 KANSAS TRAIL SERIES - Chisolm Trail Scout.

| | $450 | $100 | 500 |

1967 WWI SERIES - .45 ACP cal., Chateau Thierry.

| | $795 | $200 | 7,400 |

1967 WWI SERIES - Chateau Thierry Deluxe.

| | $1,350 | $500 | 75 |

1967 WWI SERIES - Chateau Thierry Spec. Deluxe.

| | $2,750 | $1,000 | 25 |

1968 NEBRASKA CENTENNIAL SCOUT

| | $450 | $100 | 7,001 |

1968 KANSAS TRAIL SERIES - Pawnee Trail Scout.

| | $450 | $110 | 501 |

1968 WWI SERIES - .45 ACP cal., Belleau Wood.

| | $795 | $200 | 7,400 |

1968 WWI SERIES - Belleau Wood Deluxe.

| | $1,350 | $500 | 75 |

1968 WWI SERIES - Belleau Wood Special Deluxe.

| | $2,750 | $1,000 | 25 |

1968 LAWMAN SERIES - Pat Garrett Scout.

| | $475 | $110 | 3,000 |

1968 LAWMAN SERIES - Pat Garrett .45 SAA.

| | $1,495 | $220 | 500 |

1969 GEN. NATHAN BEDFORD FORREST SCOUT

| | $450 | $110 | 3,000 |

1969 KANSAS TRAIL SERIES - Santa Fe Trail Scout.

| | $450 | $120 | 501 |

1969 WWI SERIES - .45 ACP cal., 2nd Battle of the Marne.

| | $795 | $220 | 7,400 |

1969 WWI SERIES - 2nd Battle of the Marne Deluxe.

| | $1,350 | $500 | 75 |

1969 WWI SERIES - 2nd Battle of the Marne Spec. Deluxe.

| | $2,750 | $1,000 | 25 |

1969 ALABAMA SESQUICENTENNIAL SCOUT

| | $450 | $110 | 3,001 |

1969 ALABAMA SESQUICENTENNIAL .45 SAA

| | $15,000 | unknown | 1 |

1969 GOLDEN SPIKE SCOUT

| | $475 | $135 | 11,000 |

GRADING - PPGS™	100%	Issue Price	Qty. Made

1969 KANSAS TRAIL SERIES - Shawnee Trail Scout.

| | $450 | $120 | 501 |

1969 WWI SERIES - .45 ACP cal., Meuse-Argonne.

| | $795 | $220 | 7,400 |

1969 WWI SERIES - Meuse-Argonne Deluxe.

| | $1,350 | $500 | 75 |

1969 WWI SERIES - Meuse-Argonne Spec. Deluxe.

| | $2,750 | $1,000 | 25 |

1969 ARKANSAS TERRITORIAL SESQUICENTENNIAL SCOUT

| | $450 | $110 | 3,500 |

1969 LAWMAN SERIES - .45 SAA Wild Bill Hickok.

| | $1,495 | $220 | 500 |

1969 LAWMAN SERIES - Wild Bill Hickok Scout.

| | $475 | $117 | 3,000 |

1969 CALIFORNIA BICENTENNIAL SCOUT

| | $450 | $135 | 5,000 |

1970 KANSAS FORT SERIES - Ft. Larned Scout.

| | $450 | $120 | 500 |

1970 WWII SERIES - European Theatre.

| | $795 | $250 | 11,500 |

1970 WWII SERIES - Pacific Theatre.

| | $795 | $250 | 11,500 |

Note: A complete set of the WWI and WWII Series standard grade models (6 guns) with matching serial numbers in NIB condition is currently selling in the $4,500 range.

1970 TEXAS RANGER SAA .45

| | $2,250 | $650 | 1,000 |

1970 TEXAS RANGER GRADE I (95% ENGRAVING COVERAGE)

| | $6,000 | N/A | 90 |

1970 TEXAS RANGER GRADE II (75% ENGRAVING COVERAGE)

| | $5,500 | $2,250 | 80 |

1970 TEXAS RANGER GRADE III (50% ENGRAVING COVERAGE)

| | $5,000 | $2,950 | 90 |

1970 KANSAS FORTS - Ft. Hays Scout.

| | $450 | $130 | 500 |

1970 MAINE SESQUICENTENNIAL SCOUT

| | $450 | $120 | 3,000 |

1970 MISSOURI SESQUICENTENNIAL SCOUT

| | $450 | $125 | 3,000 |

1970 MISSOURI SESQUICENTENNIAL .45 SAA

| | $1,495 | $220 | 900 |

1970 KANSAS FORTS - Ft. Riley Scout.

| | $450 | $130 | 500 |

1970 LAWMAN SERIES - Wyatt Earp Scout.

| | $495 | $125 | 3,000 |

1970 LAWMAN SERIES - Wyatt Earp .45 SAA.

| | $2,750 | $395 | 500 |

GRADING - PPGS™	100%	Issue Price	Qty. Made
1971 NRA CENTENNIAL .45 SAA			
	$1,495	$250	5,000
1971 NRA CENTENNIAL .357 SAA			
	$1,395	$250	5,000
1971 NRA CENTENNIAL GOLD CUP .45 ACP			
	$1,295	$250	2,500
1971 1851 NAVY - U.S. Grant.			
	$595	$250	4,750
1971 1851 NAVY - Robert E. Lee.			
	$595	$250	4,750
1971 1851 NAVY - Lee-Grant Set.			
	$1,350	$500	250
1971 KANSAS SERIES - Ft. Scott Scout.			
	$450	$130	500
1972 FLORIDA TERRITORY SESQUICENTENNIAL SCOUT			
	$450	$125	2,001
1972 ARIZONA RANGER SCOUT			
	$450	$135	3,001
1975 PEACEMAKER CENTENNIAL .45			
	$1,495	$300	1,500
1975 PEACEMAKER CENTENNIAL 44.40			
	$1,495	$300	1,500
1975 PEACEMAKER CENT. CASED PAIR			
	$3,250	$625	500

USS TEXAS BATTLESHIP SPECIAL EDITION (1975) - .45 ACP cal., Model 1911A1 with special embellishments, nickel finish, this model is not a factory commemorative.

	$995	unknown	500

USS ARIZONA BATTLESHIP SPECIAL EDITION (1975) - .45 ACP cal., Model 1911A1 with special embellishments, nickel finish, this model is not a factory commemorative.

	$995	unknown	500

1976 U.S. BICENTENNIAL SET - includes SAA .45, Python .357 Mag., and black powder Dragoon in walnut display case with drawers.

	$2,995	$1,695	1,776

1976 BICENTENNIAL SAA FREEDOM COLTS - consisted of A, B, and C sets, set As were engraved, Bs had gold work and accessories, Cs were similar to Bs, but had shoulder stock. Set A prices averaged $1,500-$3,000 in 1976, set B prices varied between $3,500-$20,000, and set C prices started at $5,000. Total mfg. was 4 set As, 6 set Bs, and 1 set C. These sets in today's marketplace are too rare to accurately evaluate and pricing is literally "what the market will bear."

These guns were all engraved by Dwain Wright located in Applegate, OR.

1977 2ND AMENDMENT .22

	$450	$195	3,020

1977 U.S. CAVALRY 200TH ANNIVERSARY SET

	$1,250	$995	3,000

GRADING - PPGS™	100%	Issue Price	Qty. Made

1978 STATEHOOD 3RD MODEL DRAGOON
$6,995 — $12,500 — 52

1979 NED BUNTLINE .45 SAA
$1,295 — $895 — 3,000

OHIO PRESIDENT'S SPECIAL EDITION (1979) - .45 ACP cal., Model 1911A1 with special Ohio embellishments, this is not a factory commemorative.
$995 — unknown — 250

1979 TOMBSTONE CENTENNIAL .45 SAA - .45 LC cal., 7 1/2 in. barrel, nickel finish, two-piece walnut stocks, P-1876 Model, etched with scroll engraving and Western scenes. 300 mfg. (200 singles and 50 pairs).
$1,495 — $995 — 300

This model was not sold retail through the auspices of Colt.

1980 DRUG ENFORCEMENT AGENCY (DEA) .45 AUTO
$1,100 — $550 — 910

This model was not sold retail through the auspices of Colt.

1980 OLYMPICS ACE MODEL SPECIAL EDITION
$1,195 — $1,000 — 200

This model was not sold retail through the auspices of Colt.

1980 HERITAGE-WALKER .44 PERCUSSION
$950 — $1,475 — 1,847

1981 "JOHN M. BROWNING" .45 ACP SEMI-AUTO
$995 — $1,100 — 3,000

1980-81 .45 ACP GOVT. SIGNATURE SERIES - .45 ACP cal., blue finished Govt. slide with gold auroplated slide or nickel finish. 250 mfg. in both finishes.
$995 — $833 — 250

Add $50 for blue finish.

1980-81 ACE SIGNATURE SERIES - .22 LR cal., featured Cocobolo grips with medallions, blue finish with photo engraving, cased. 1,000 mfg.
$1,195 — $955 — 1,000

1981 BUFFALO BILL SPECIAL EDITION - .44-40 WCF cal., 7 1/2 in. barrel, gold and silver plating, Class C engraved, scrimshaw ivory grips featuring Buffalo Bill and his TE Wyoming Ranch brand, leather cased, 250 mfg. serialized 1BB-250BB.
$4,975 — $4,200 — 250

This model was a special edition (not commemorative) that was made specifically for the Buffalo Bill Historical Center.

1982 JOHN WAYNE SAA STANDARD
$2,250 — $2,995 — 3,100

While advertising literature indicated 3,100 were mfg., 3,041 were sold.

1982 JOHN WAYNE SAA DELUXE
$7,500 — $10,000 — 500

While advertising literature indicated 500 were mfg., only 90 were sold.

1982 JOHN WAYNE SAA PRESENTATION
$12,000 — $20,000 — 100

While advertising literature indicated 100 were mfg., only 47 were sold.

Note: Each grade of the above John Wayne commemoratives has its own serial number range.

1983 BUFFALO BILL WILD WEST SHOW CENTENNIAL SAA .45
$1,595 — $1,350 — 500

GRADING - PPGS™	100%	Issue Price	Qty. Made

1983 CCA LIMITED EDITION SAA - .44-40 WCF cal., 4 3/4 in. barrel, nickel finish, fleur-de-lis checkered walnut grips, two line barrel address and Colt Frontier Six Shooter roll marking. 250 mfg. in 1983 to commemorate Colt Collector's Assn.

	$1,595	$825	250

This model was not sold at retail through the auspices of Colt.

1983 "ARMORY MODEL" SAA .45 ACP - this model had limited production, and should not be confused as being a commemorative. So-called because it was shipped with extra .45 long Colt cylinder and the "Colt Armory Edition" book by E. Grant. Presentation cased.

	$1,795	$1,125	500

20 Armory model commemoratives were available with class A engraving - $2,595, B engraving - $2,995, C engraving - $3,500, D engraving - $3,995.

1983 PYTHON SILVER SNAKE SPECIAL EDITION - .357 Mag. cal., 6 in. barrel, black chrome stainless steel, Pachmayr grips with custom shop pewter medallions, etched engraving, includes custom gun pouch.

	$1,495	$1,150	250

1984 1ST EDITION GOVT. MODEL .380 ACP

	$550	$425	1,000

Serial range RC00000-RC01000.

1984 JOHN WAYNE "DUKE" FRONTIER .22

	$795	$475	5,000

1984 COLT/WINCHESTER SET - 1 ea. of the Model 1894 Winchester carbine and Colt Peacemaker, serial numbered 1WC-4440WC, .44-40 WCF cal., elaborate gold etching, cased. Pistol became available for sale individually in 1986 - see individual listing below for values.

Please refer to 1984 Winchester/Colt Set in the Winchester Commemorative section in this text.

WINCHESTER/COLT SAA - .44-40 WCF cal., 7 1/2 in. barrel, gold etching, this commemorative was originally made as part of the 1984 Winchester/Colt rifle-pistol set, but was later able to be purchased individually. Originally mfg. 1984.

	$1,495	N/A	4,000

1984 USA EDITION SAA - .44-40 WCF cal., 7 1/2 in. barrel, old style black powder frame, bullseye ejector rod head, 3 line patent date, high polished blue with gold line engraving. 100 guns total mfg. - 1 for each state and its capitol.

	$3,500	$4,995	100

1984 KIT CARSON .22 NEW FRONTIER - 6 in. barrel, color case hardened frame, gold artwork, serial numbered KCC0001-KCC1000, cased.

	$450	$550	1,000

1984 SECOND EDITION GOVT. MODEL .380 ACP - serial numbered 00000RC-01000RC.

	$550	$525	1,000

1984 OFFICER'S COMMENCEMENT ISSUE - Officer's ACP with Marine Corps emblem, rosewood grips, silver plated oak leaf scroll, cased.

	$995	$700	1,000

This model was not sold retail through the auspices of Colt.

1984 THEODORE ROOSEVELT COMMEMORATIVE SAA - .44-40 WCF cal., 7 1/2 in. barrel, black powder frame, case colored receiver, factory "B" hand engraving, ivory stocks, cased.

	$1,995	$1,695	500

GRADING - PPGS™	100%	Issue Price	Qty. Made

1984 NORTH AMERICAN OILMEN SAA BUNTLINE - .45 LC cal., 12 in. barrel, non-fluted cylinder, elaborate gold etching, ebony grips with ivory inlays, stand-up glass case, ser. nos. 1-100 mfg. for Canada, 101-200 for the U.S.

	$3,250	$3,900	200

This model was not sold retail through the auspices of Colt.

1985 TEXAS 150th SESQUICENTENNIAL SAA - .45 cal., Sheriff's model, 4 3/4 in. barrel, mirror bright blue, gold etching, 24Kt. gold plated backstrap and trigger guard, smooth ivory grips, French fit oak presentation case. Mfg. 1985 only.

* *Standard Model* - 1,000 mfg.

	$1,495	$1,836	1,000

* *Premier Model* - elaborate engraving, 75 mfg.

	$4,995	$7,995	75

1986 150th ANNIVERSARY SAA - .45 LC cal., 10 in. barrel, 50% engraved, royal blue finish, Goncalo Alves smooth grips, 150th anniversary logo in stocks, cherry-wood case. 490 mfg. 1986 only.

	$1,995	$1,595	490

1986 150th ANNIVERSARY ENGRAVING SAMPLER SAA - various cals., 4 different engraving styles on metal surfaces, 75% coverage, ivory grips, signed by the engraver, available with either blue or nickel finish. New 1986.

	$3,250	$1,613	unknown

1986 150th ANNIVERSARY ENGRAVING SAMPLER .45 M1911A1 - .45 ACP cal., 4 different engraving styles on metal surfaces, 75% coverage, ivory grips, signed by the engraver, available with either blue or nickel finish. New 1986.

	$1,495	$1,155	unknown

Add $60 for nickel.

1986 MUSTANG FIRST EDITION - .380 ACP cal., 1,000 manufactured serialized MU00001-MU01000 (the first thousand of production), rosewood stocks, walnut presentation case. Mfg. 1986 only.

	$550	$475	1,000

OFFICER'S ACP HEIRLOOM EDITION - .45 ACP cal., personalized with individual's choice for serial number (ie. John Smith 1), mirror brite bluing, jeweled barrel, hammer, and trigger, ivory grips, with historical letter and mahogany case. New 1986.

	$1,550	$1,643	open

1986 DOUBLE DIAMOND SET - set is comprised of a Python Ultimate .357 Mag. revolver and Officer's Model .45 ACP, both guns in stainless steel, smooth rosewood grips, presentation cased. 1,000 sets mfg. 1986 only, serial numbered 1-1,000 (matched).

	$1,750	$1,575	1,000

DELTA MATCH H-BAR RIFLE - AR-15 A2 H-Bar rifle selectively chosen and equipped with 3x9 variable power rubber armored scope, leather sling, shoulder stock cheekpiece, cased. Mfg. 1987.

	$1,500	$1,425	open

12TH MAN-'SPIRIT OF AGGIELAND' - .45 ACP cal., mfg. to commemorate Texas A&M University, serial numbered TAM001-TAM999, 24Kt gold plating including wreaths on left frame and inscription on right, cherrywood glass top presentation case, includes personalized class graduation inscription. Available 1987 only.

	$950	$950	999

This model was not sold retail through the auspices of Colt.

KLAY-COLT 1851 NAVY - .36 cal., cased reproduction of the 3rd Model 1851 Navy, special fabrication insuring old world quality, charcoal bluing, heat treated screws and accessories, cased. Introduced 1986.

GRADING - PPGS™	100%	Issue Price	Qty. Made

✳ *Standard Edition* - no engraving.

	$1,850	$1,850	150

✳ *Engraved Edition* - choice of engraving.

	$3,150	$3,150	50

Optional engraving patterns with or without gold inlays available at extra cost.

COMBAT ELITE CUSTOM EDITION - .45 ACP cal., with ambidextrous thumb safety, wide grip safety, hand honed action, and carrying case, ser. numbered CG00001-CG00500. Mfg. 1987.

	$1,095	$900	500

1987 SHERIFF'S EDITION - set of 5 SAA Sheriff's configuration revolvers in .45 LC cal., barrel lengths include 2, 2 1/2, 3, 4, and 5 1/2 in., royal blue finish, smooth rosewood grips with medallions, supplied with glass top display case which displays the revolvers in a circle around a brass sheriff's badge. Serialization has 3 numeral prefix (which is the same in each set), followed by the letters "SE," followed by 1 or 2 numerals (indicating barrel length) - i.e. serial number 002SE25 indicates the second set built, Sheriff's Edition (SE), and a barrel length of 2 1/2 inches.

	$6,500	$7,500	200 sets

1989 SNAKE EYES LIMITED EDITION - includes two Python revolvers (2 1/2 in. barrels), one finished in brite stainless steel and the other in Royal Blue finish, grips are ivory-like with scrimshaw "snake eyes" dice on left side and royal flush poker hand on right, includes chips and playing cards, 500 sets only of consecutive serial numbers. New 1989.

	$1,950	$2,950	500

1990 SAA HEIRLOOM II EDITION - .45 LC cal., 7 1/2 in. barrel, color case hardened frame and hammer, balance of metal finished in Colt Royal Blue, one piece American Walnut grips with cartouche on lower left side, personalized inscription on backstrap, walnut cased. Available 1990 only.

	$1,595	$1,600	open

1990 JOE FOSS LIMITED EDITION .45 ACP GOVT. MODEL - .45 ACP cal., first limited edition in Colt's All American Hero Series, commemorates Joe Foss, famous American WWII Marine Fighter Pilot, gun features gold etched scenes on slide sides, smooth walnut grips. While 2,500 were advertised, only 300+ were mfg. Serial numbered beginning with JF 0001. French fitted walnut presentation case, 38 oz. Mfg. 1990 only.

	$1,850	$1,375	300+

1911A1 50th ANNIVERSARY BATTLE OF THE BULGE - .45 ACP cal., special edition commemorating the Battle of the Bulge, silver plated with gold inlays, 300 mfg. serialized BB001-BB300.

	$1,495	$1,250	300

Add $150 for deluxe presentation case.

This special edition was sold exclusively by Cherry's located in Greensboro, NC.

1993 CCA LIMITED EDITION SAA - .38-40 WCF cal., 4 3/4 in. barrel, nickel finish, walnut grips, CCA markings on grip strap. 150 mfg. in 1993.

	$1,500	$1,165	150

This model was not sold at retail through the auspices of Colt.

COMANCHE

Current trademark manufactured in South America beginning 2001. Currently distributed (master distributor) beginning 2002 by SGS Importers, located in Wanamassa, NJ. Distributor sales.

GRADING - PPGS™	100%	98%	95%	90%	80%	70%	60%

PISTOLS: SINGLE SHOT

SUPER COMANCHE - .45 LC cal./.410 bore, 10 in. rifled barrel, blue, duo-tone (new 2004) or satin nickel finish, black rubber grips and forearm, barrel release lever on front of trigger guard, adj. rear sight, transfer bar and manual safeties, 47 oz. New 2002.

MSR $175	$145	$125	$100	$85	$70	$60	$50

Add $17 for satin nickel finish.

This model is not available for sale in some states.

REVOLVERS: SA

COMANCHE I - .22 LR cal., 6 in. full lug barrel, 9 shot, blue or stainless, adj. sights, rubber grips, 39 oz. New 2002.

MSR $242	$195	$175	$160	$145	$130	$120	$110

Add $25 for stainless steel construction.

COMANCHE II - .38 Spl. +P cal., 3 (new 2004) or 4 in. full lug barrel, 6 shot, blue or stainless, adj. sight, approx. 30 oz. New 2002.

MSR $225	$185	$165	$150	$135	$120	$110	$95

Add $17 for stainless steel construction.

COMANCHE III - .357 Mag. cal., 3, 4, or 6 in. full lug barrel, 6 shot, blue or stainless, adj. sight, 29-39 oz. New 2002.

MSR $259	$220	$185	$165	$150	$140	$130	$100

Add $25 for stainless steel construction.

COMANCHE IV - .44 Mag. cal., 6 in. barrel only with adj. sights, blue or stainless steel. Mfg. 2004.

$250	$205	$180	$165	$150	$140	$130

Last MSR was $308.

Add $25 for stainless steel construction.

COMBINATION GUNS

Combination guns were originally European in origin, and are either SxS or O/U configuration, consisting of a rifle and a shotgun barrel.

Many imported combination guns designed for the U.S. have been known as turkey guns in the past, typically with a .22 rimfire/medium cal. centerfire rifle barrel over a 12 ga., 20 ga., or .410 bore shotgun barrel. European guns typically have metric rifle cals., and the shotgun barrel is usually 12 or 16 ga. European combination guns (see configurations below) need to be evaluated individually, since values will depend on the desirability of the gun's configuration in the U.S. (i.e., metric vs. American cals., gauge, type of lock, engraving, quality of wood, etc.). Most non-custom European boxlock combination guns with metric cals. in average condition are currently priced in the $395-$1,250 range, while American combination guns (the Savage Model 24 and others) are priced in the $175-$450 range.

GRADING - PPGS™	100%	98%	95%	90%	80%	70%	60%

COMMANDO ARMS

Previous manufacturer located in Knoxville, TN.

Commando Arms became the new name for Volunteer Enterprises in the late 1970s.

RIFLES: CARBINES

MARK 45 - .45 ACP cal., carbine styled after the Thompson sub-machine gun, 16 1/2 in. barrel.

$495	$425	$350	$315	$280	$225	$195

COMPETITOR CORPORATION

Current manufacturer established in 1988 and located in Jaffrey, NH. Previously located in New Ipswich, NH until 2001, and in West Groton, MA from 1988-1995. Dealer direct or distributor sales.

PISTOLS: SINGLE SHOT

COMPETITOR - available in over 400 cals. from .17 LR - .50 AE, ranging from small rimfire to large belted Magnums, 14 in. barrel standard, rotary cannon action, cocks on opening, dual sliding thumb and trigger safety, rotary style ejector, click adj. sights, matte blue or optional electroless nickel finish, choice of synthetic, laminated, or natural wood grips (ambidextrous), extractor or ejector. Approx. 59-73 oz. New 1988.

MSR $480	$410	$375	$320	$290	$255	$225	$200

Add $20 for laminated wood stock.

Add approx. $50 for walnut grips (disc.).

Add $60 for electroless nickel finish (barreled action only).

Add $175 for extra 14 in. standard cal. barrel with sights.

Add $40 for 10 1/2-16 in. standard cal. barrel with sights.

Add $70 for 17-23 in. barrel.

Add $60 for factory-installed muzzle brake.

Add $220 for rimfire or centerfire conversion kit.

CONCO ARMS

Current importer located in Emmaus, PA.

RIFLES: SxS

PRO HUNTER BOXLOCK SxS - various cals. through .700 NE, Anson & Deeley action with double underlocking lugs and scalloped frame, ejectors, standard scroll engraving, H&H style frame reinforcement, checkered Circassian walnut stock and forearm, custom order only, mfg. by Hambrusch in Ferlach, Austria. Importation disc. 2004.

$23,611	$18,750	$15,950	$12,500	$10,000	$8,700	$7,500

Last MSR was $23,611.

Add $673 for .375 H&H, $1,061 for .470 NE cal., $1,987 for .500 NE, $12,816 for .577/.600 NE or $30,318 for .700 NE cal.

PRO HUNTER SIDELOCK SxS - various cals. through .700 NE, full sidelock action with standard scroll engraving, ejectors, hinged DT, checkered Circassian walnut stock and forearm, custom order only, mfg. by Hambrusch in Ferlach, Austria.

MSR $29,600	$29,600	$24,750	$19,750	$16,150	$13,750	$11,000	$9,995

Add $889 for .375 H&H, add $1,061 .470 NE cal., $1,987 for .500 NE, $14,761 for .577/.600 NE or $35,058 for .700 NE cal.

GRADING - PPGS™	100%	98%	95%	90%	80%	70%	60%

CONNECTICUT SHOTGUN MANUFACTURING CO.

Current rifle and shotgun manufacturer established during 1995, and located in New Britain, CT.

Connecticut Shotgun Manufacturing Co. has already established itself as one of America's premier gunmakers, specializing in best quality O/U and SxS shotguns, in addition to a SxS double rifle. Please contact the company directly for more information, including pricing and availability.

RIFLES: SxS

MODEL 22 - various rimfire and centerfire calibers, based on the Model 21 action, Grand American styling and features, 4 game animals inlayed in 24Kt. gold, frame scaled proportionately to the caliber, iron sights, SST. Limited mfg. beginning 2002.

Each gun is custom-built to the customer's exact specifications and prices are POR.

SHOTGUNS: O/U, SIDELOCK

A. GALAZAN MODEL - 12, 16, 20, 28 ga., or .410 bore, features strong, low profile sidelock action with Boss-style metal reinforced forearm, top-of-the-line model utilizing best quality materials and U.S. workmanship, wide choice of custom features and engraving options.

Each gun is custom-built to the customer's exact specifications and prices start at $38,000 without engraving.

A. GALAZAN ROUND BODY MODEL - 12, 16, 20, 28 ga., or .410 bore, round body, wide choice of custom features and engraving options.

Each gun is custom-built to the customer's exact specifications and prices start at $43,000 without engraving.

SHOTGUNS: SxS

MODEL 21 - 12, 16, 20, 28 ga., or .410 bore, 4 frame sizes (12, 16, 20, and 28/.410 bore), various barrel lengths up to 32 in. with either matte solid or vent. rib and fixed chokes, best quality checkered wood, wide choice of custom features and engraving options, new mfg. not associated with Winchester production. Limited mfg. beginning 2002.

Each gun is custom-built to the customer's exact specifications.

* **Model 21-1** - features frame light scroll engraving patterned after Winchester's No. 1 style, A fancy wood. New 2002.

MSR $9,995	$9,995	$8,750	$7,250	$6,500	$5,750	$5,000	$4,250

Add $2,005 for 28 ga. or $3,505 for .410 bore.

* **Model 21-5** - features both scroll and three hunting scenes engraving patterned after Winchester's No. 5 style on frame and barrels, AA fancy wood. New 2002.

MSR $12,900	$12,900	$9,950	$8,750	$7,250	$6,500	$5,750	$5,000

Add $2,100 for 28 ga. or $2,600 for .410 bore.

* **Model 21-6** - features both tight scroll and dog/game bird engraving patterned after Winchester's No. 6 style on frame and barrels, AAA fancy wood. New 2002.

MSR $13,900	$13,900	$11,250	$9,250	$8,250	$7,000	$6,000	$5,250

Add $2,100 for 28 ga. or $2,600 for .410 bore.

* **Model 21 Grand American** - top-of-the-line standard model with 2 sets of barrels, elaborate scroll engraving on barrels and frame, 5 gold inlays, including dogs and birds, B carved stock and forearm, AAA full fancy feather crotch American walnut. New 2002.

MSR $16,995	$16,995	$14,250	$11,650	$9,000	$7,500	$6,250	$5,500

GRADING - PPGS™	100%	98%	95%	90%	80%	70%	60%

* ❋ **Model 21 Royal Exhibition** - top-of-the-line model with 2 sets of barrels, numerous engraving and gold inlay options, best quality wood. New 2002.
  This model is built to customer's specifications and priced on request only.

A. GALAZAN ROUND BODY MODEL - 12, 16, 20, 28 ga., or .410 bore, round body, top-of-the-line model utilizing best quality materials and U.S. workmanship, no visible pins or screws, wide choice of custom features and engraving options.

Each gun is custom-built to the customer's exact specifications and price is by individual special order only.

CONNECTICUT VALLEY CLASSICS, INC.

Previous trademark manufactured by Cooper Arms, located in Stevensville, MT 1996-1998.

CVC, Inc. was a division of CVC Sports, Inc. Previous sales and marketing offices were located in Holyoke, MA until 1996 and in Westport, CT 1993-95.

SHOTGUNS: O/U

The models listed below have receiver dimensions built to the exact specifications of the original Classic Doubles Model 101. The only difference is that the tang spacer has been made an integral part of the frame.

Add $1,350 for each additional barrel set.

CLASSIC 101 SPORTER - 12 ga. only, boxlock action, monoblock, 28, 30, or 32 in. VR barrels with multi-chokes, SST, ejectors, nickel finished receiver with light engraving, checkered American black walnut stock and forearm with low luster finish, approx. 7 3/4 lbs.

$1,875	$1,550	$1,225	$1,000	$825	$700	$600

Last MSR was $2,195.

CLASSIC SPORTER SB - 12 ga. only, boxlock action, entry level sporter model. Mfg. 1997-98.

$2,250	$1,875	$1,575	$1,175	$950	$775	$650

Last MSR was $2,495.

GRADE I CLASSIC SPORTER - 12 ga. only, boxlock action, monobloc, 28, 30, or 32 in. vented barrels with VR, lengthened forcing cones, and 2 3/8 in. multi-chokes, SST, ejectors, stainless steel receiver with light engraving, checkered 20 LPI AA American black walnut stock and forearm with low luster finish, approx. 7 3/4 lbs. Disc. 1998.

$2,695	$2,100	$1,675	$1,250	$1,000	$825	$700

Last MSR was $2,995.

* ❋ **Women's Classic Sporter** - similar to Grade I Classic Sporter, except has smaller stock dimensions and 28 in. barrels only, 7 1/2 lbs. Mfg. 1996-98.

$2,695	$2,100	$1,675	$1,250	$1,000	$825	$700

Last MSR was $2,995.

This model was also available in Grade II or Grade III Women's Classic Sporter.

* ❋ **Grade II Classic Sporter** - similar to Grade I Classic Sporter, except has AAA American or Claro walnut with 22 LPI hand-checkering, 30 in. barrels only.

$3,100	$2,350	$1,800	$1,325	$1,050	$850	$725

Last MSR was $3,5(

* ❋ **Grade III Classsic Sporter** - similar to Grade II Classic Sporter, except has fleu checkering patterns and gold accents. Disc. 1998.

$3,600	$2,750	$1,975	$1,450	$1,175	$925	

Last MSR w

GRADING - PPGS™	100%	98%	95%	90%	80%	70%	60%

GRADE I CLASSIC FIELD - 12 ga. only, similar to Grade I Classic Sporter, except has solid rib and standard flush-mounted choke-tubes, 27 1/2 in. barrels, 7 1/2 lbs. Mfg. 1996-98.

$2,695	$2,100	$1,675	$1,250	$1,000	$825	$700

Last MSR was $2,995.

✳ *Classic Waterfowler* - 12 ga. only, 30 or 32 (disc. 1995) in. VR barrels, non-reflective surfaces, bird scene engraving, overbored barrels with lengthened forcing cones and four standard CVC chokes, 8 lbs. Mfg. 1993-98.

$2,495	$2,000	$1,575	$1,175	$950	$775	$650

Last MSR was $2,795.

✳ *Grade II Classic Field* - similar to Grade I Classic Field, except has AAA American or Claro walnut with 22 LPI hand-checkering.

$3,025	$2,250	$1,750	$1,300	$1,050	$850	$725

Last MSR was $3,495.

✳ *Grade III Classic/English Field* - similar to Grade II Classic Field, except has fleur-de-lis checkering patterns and gold accents, choice of straight English (25 1/2 in. VR barrels only) or pistol grip stock. Disc. 1998.

$3,575	$2,850	$2,025	$1,500	$1,200	$925	$750

Last MSR was $4,195.

Add $100 for straight English stock.

✳ *Classic Skeet* - 12 ga. only, 29 in. vented barrels with 9mm VR, otherwise similar to Grade I Classic Sporter, 7 1/2 lbs. Mfg. 1996-98.

$2,695	$2,100	$1,675	$1,250	$1,000	$825	$700

Last MSR was $2,995.

✳ *Classic Flyer* - 12 ga. only, live bird gun featuring AAA walnut and 22 LPI checkering, oil finish, 30 in. vented overbored barrels with 11mm tapered top rib and lengthened forcing cones, scroll engraving with pigeon scene on bottom, 8 lbs. Mfg. 1996-98.

$3,100	$2,350	$1,800	$1,325	$1,050	$850	$725

Last MSR was $3,595.

CONQUEST

Current trademark of guns manufactured by various companies in Spain, Turkey, Germany, and Italy. No current U.S. importation.

The Conquest trademark currently includes shotguns in O/U, SxS, slide action, and semi-auto configuration. Please contact the company directly for more information (see Trademark Index).

CONTENTO/VENTURA

Previously imported by Ventura Imports in Seal Beach, CA. Ventura also imported Bertuzzi and Piotti.

SHOTGUNS: O/U

CONTENTO O/U - 12 ga., 32 in. barrels, boxlock, optional screw in choke tubes, high vent. rib, SST, auto ejectors, hand checkered Monte Carlo trap stock.

$1,045	$990	$935	$880	$770	$690	$635

MK 2 - includes O/U barrels, with extra single barrel.

$1,375	$1,320	$1,265	$1,210	$1,100	$1,020	$965

MK 2 - leather cased, combination set.

$1,705	$1,650	$1,595	$1,540	$1,430	$1,350	$1,295

MK 3 - engraved, O/U.

$1,650	$1,570	$1,485	$1,375	$1,295	$1,185	$1,100

GRADING - PPGS™	100%	98%	95%	90%	80%	70%	60%

MK 3 - includes O/U barrels, with extra single barrel.

	$2,200	$2,035	$1,925	$1,815	$1,650	$1,595	$1,515

MK 3 - leather cased, combination set.

	$2,750	$2,420	$2,200	$2,090	$1,955	$1,815	$1,760

SHOTGUNS: SxS

MODEL 51 - 12, 16, 20, 28 ga., or .410 bore, 26-32 in. barrels, various chokes, extractors, boxlock, double triggers, checkered straight stock.

	$385	$360	$330	$305	$250	$220	$165
Auto ejectors	$495	$440	$385	$360	$305	$275	$220

MODEL 52 - 10 ga., double triggers only, otherwise similar to Model 51.

	$525	$495	$470	$415	$360	$305	$250

MODEL 53 - deluxe version of Model 51, scalloped frame, auto ejectors.

	$470	$440	$415	$385	$330	$275	$220
SST	$605	$550	$525	$495	$440	$385	$330

MODEL 61 - 12 or 20 ga., 26, 27, 28, or 30 in. barrels, H&H sidelocks, various chokes, floral engraved, hand detachable locks, cocking indicators, select walnut pistol grip stock, auto ejectors.

	$880	$825	$770	$745	$690	$605	$550
SST	$1,020	$965	$910	$855	$800	$715	$660

MODEL 65 - similar to Model 61, with elaborate engraving and quality hand finishing.

	$1,100	$1,045	$990	$965	$880	$825	$770

CONTINENTAL ARMS CORPORATION

Previous importer that imported high quality shotguns and rifles (usually Belgian), circa mid-1950s-mid-1970s.

RIFLES

BOLT ACTION - mostly large cals., typically custom Mauser action, makers include Defourney and Dumoulin.

> Specimens should be evaluated individually due to the many configurations and embellishments encountered. This model is rarely seen in today's marketplace.

DOUBLE RIFLE - .270 Win., .303 British, .30-40 Krag, .348 Win., .30-06, .375 H&H, .400 Jeffreys, .470, .475, .500, or .600 Nitro Express cal., 24 or 26 in. barrels, Anson & Deeley boxlock system, although some sidelocks were mfg., double triggers, checkered stock.

	$4,950	$4,350	$3,850	$3,300	$2,970	$2,750	$2,500

Add 10% for boxlock with sideplates.
Add 15% for ejectors.
Add 30%-50% for .375 H&H and larger cals., depending on the size of the cal.

SHOTGUNS: O/U

Add 20% for .410 bore.
Add 30% for 28 ga.
Add 10% for Defourney mfg.

CENTAURE BOXLOCK - 12, 20, 28 ga., or .410 bore, ejectors, light er chopper lump barrels with cross-bolt, double underlocks, SST, 3-piece for'

	$2,000	$1,675	$1,500	$1,250	$1,025	$87'	

GRADING - PPGS™	100%	98%	95%	90%	80%	70%	60%

CENTAURE LIEGE ROYAL CROWN GRADE - similar to Centaure Boxlock, except has game scene engraving, better figured wood and silver crown inlay.

	100%	98%	95%	90%	80%	70%	60%
	$3,150	$2,850	$2,600	$2,250	$1,900	$1,600	$1,400

CENTAURE IMPERIAL CROWN GRADE - similar to Royal Crown Grade, except has higher grade wood, extensive game scene engraving, oak leaf engraving on barrels, and gold inlay on top lever.

	$4,500	$4,150	$3,750	$3,500	$3,200	$2,900	$2,700

SHOTGUNS: SxS

Add 20% for .410 bore.
Add 30% for 28 ga.
Add 10% for Defourney mfg.

CENTAURE - all gauges, basic boxlock action with double triggers and extractors.

	$1,050	$950	$895	$850	$700	$500	$400

Add 35% for ejectors.

CENTAURE ROYAL CROWN GRADE - all gauges, single trigger, ejectors, checkered stock and forearm, game scene engraving, can be identified by silver crown inlaid on top lever.

	$3,400	$3,150	$2,800	$2,600	$2,325	$2,100	$1,950

CENTAURE IMPERIAL CROWN GRADE - similar to Royal Crown, except gold inlay on top lever, extensive game scene engraving on receiver and barrels.

	$4,275	$3,850	$3,500	$3,150	$2,850	$2,575	$2,300

COOEY, H.W., MACHINE & ARMS CO. LTD.

Previous manufacturer located in Cobourg, Ontario, Canada 1903-1961. During 1961, Cooey was sold to the Olin Corporation and placed under the supervision of the Winchester Western Division. At that point, the manufacture of Winchesters (primarily for Winchester Canada) began and continued through the mid-1970s (see Iver Johnson).

To date, there is limited collector demand for most models in this trademark and values should be based on the shooting utility rather than collector premiums due to rarity. Values for average condition guns will typically range between $75-$150.

RIFLES

Cooey manufactured a wide number of rifles, including bolt actions, single shots, and semi-autos. During the late 1920s-early 1930s, Cooey manufactured the Model X and 2X for Iver Johnson (please refer to Iver Johnson section).
Pre-1961 Cooey mfg. models include: 25, 35, 39, 55, 60, 62, 75, 78, 82, Ace, Ace 1, Ace 2, Ace 3, Ace Repeater, Ace Special, Bisley Sport, Canuck, Canuck 25, Canuck Junior, Canuck Western, Cooey Repeater, HWC, Mohawk, and several unnumbered single shot and repeating sporter rifles. Post-1961 Cooey firearms made by Winchester include: Model 10, Model 39, Model 60, Model 600, Model 64, Model 64 Deluxe, Model 64A, 64B, Model 71, 71 Carbine, Model 75, 750, and 750 Deluxe, Model 710, and Ranger.

SHOTGUNS

Cooey manufactured both double and single barrel shotguns for Iver Johnson (Hercules and Champion) during the late 1920s-early 1930s (see Iver Johnson section). Cooey also manufactured single shot shotguns. Pre-1961 Cooey mfg. models include: .22 rimfire smoothbore, 37A, 84, Canuck 25, and Canuck 410. Post-1961 Cooey firearms made by Winchester include: Models 84 and 840.

COONAN ARMS

Previous manufacture by Dan Coonan, and distributed from November 1994-September 1998 by JS Worldwide Distribution Co. located in Maplewood, MN. Previously located in St. Paul, MN, approx. 1983-1996.

During 1985, Dan Coonan sold Coonan Arms to Bill Davis. In 1990, Dan Coonan left the company, and during July 1994, the company filed for Chapter 11. Coonan Arms was incorporated by JS Worldwide Distribution in November 1994. On Sept. 25, 1998, Coonan Arms and JS Worldwide Distribution was dissolved by the state of MN.

PISTOLS: SEMI-AUTO

COONAN .357 MAG. MODEL B - .357 Mag. cal. only, stainless steel and alloy construction, single action, semi-auto, design based on the Colt Model 1911, 7 shot mag., 5 or 6 (new 1989) in. barrel, smooth or checkered (new 1996) walnut grips, Teflon finish options new 1996, 42 oz. Mfg. 1983-99.

$685 $535 $425

Last MSR was $735.

Add $40 for checkered walnut grips.
Add $33 for 6 in. barrel (new 1989).
Add $140 for Millett adj. rear sight.
Add $165 for Bo-Mar sight.
Add $45 for .38 Spl. conversion kit (new 1986).

This model could be differentiated from the Model A in that it had an extended grip safety lever, linkless barrel system, enclosed trigger bar slot, and recontoured rear grip strap. This model became standard in 1985.

✳ *Coonan .357 Cadet Model* - similar to .357 Mag. Model B, except is compact variation with 3.9 in. barrel and 6 shot mag., 39 oz. Mfg. 1993-99.

$785 $630 $500

Last MSR was $855.

Options were similar to those listed for the Model B.

✳ *Coonan .357 Cadet II* - features standard grip with 7/8 shot mag. Mfg. 1996-99.

$785 $630 $500

Last MSR was $855.

Options were similar to those listed for the Model B.

✳ *Model B Compensated* - 6 in. barrel with compensator. Mfg. 1990-99.

$900 $795 $650

Last MSR was $1,015.

Options were similar to those listed for the Model B.

✳ *Model Classic Compensated* - features 5 in. barrel with integral compensator, Millett white/orange outline sights, checkered black walnut grips, Teflon black and matte stainless two-tone finish, 42 oz. Mfg. 1996-99.

$1,275 $1,025 $825 $675 $595 $525 $450
Last MSR was $1,400.

COONAN .357 MAG. MODEL A - original model without above listed improvements, special order only, inventory depleted in 1991. Serialization is under 2,00 for this model (less than 1,200 were mfg.).

$1,150 $775 $550

Last MSR was $

Add approx. $350 for early variations with engraved slide.
This variation will also shoot .38+P loads. The first 25 Model As were engraved o' of slide.

GRADING - PPGS™	100%	98%	95%	90%	80%	70%	60%

COONAN .41 MAGNUM - .41 Mag. cal., 5 in. barrel, smooth or checkered walnut grips. Mfg. 1997-99.

	$760	$625	$500

Last MSR was $825.

Options were similar to those listed for the .357 Mag.

COOPER FIREARMS OF MONTANA, INC.

Current manufacturer located in Stevensville, MT since 1991. Available through Cooper Arms registered dealers only.

RIFLES: BOLT ACTION

Approx. 15,000 Cooper rifles have been manufactured in over 50 calibers to date.

Add $150 for left-hand action (custom order only) on the models listed below.

MODEL 21 SINGLE SHOT - various medium size cals., 3 front locking lugs.

* *Model 21 Classic* - various cals., single shot, 24 in. chrome moly match grade barrel, stock is AA Claro walnut with 20 LPI hand checkering and hand rubbed oil finish, machined aluminum trigger guard, matte metal finish, approx. 7-7 1/4 lbs. New 1999.

MSR $1,100	$950	$800	$650	$550	$495	$450	$400

* *Model 21 Custom Classic* - includes Brownell No. 1 checkering pattern, ebony forend tip, and steel grip cap.

MSR $1,995	$1,725	$1,300	$975	$750	$650	$550	$475

* *Model 21 Western Classic* - various cals., features octagon barrel and case hardened action and metal work. New 1997.

MSR $2,595	$2,250	$1,800	$1,550	$1,275	$995	$875	$750

* *Model 21 Varminter* - various cals., 24 in. stainless steel match grade barrel, stock is AA Claro walnut with 20 LPI hand checkering and hand rubbed oil finish, machined aluminum trigger guard, approx. 7-7 1/4 lbs. New 1999.

MSR $995	$875	$750	$625	$550	$495	$450	$400

* *Model 21 Varmint Extreme* - various cals. between .17 Rem.-.223 Rem. (including metric cals.), features stainless barrel, checkered stock. New 1994.

MSR $1,795	$1,650	$1,425	$1,200	$995	$825	$600	$475

Add $465 for Benchrest Model with Jewell trigger (mfg. 1995-96).

* *Model 21 Montana Varminter* - various cals. New 2000.

MSR $1,295	$1,150	$975	$825	$650	$550	$475	$425

MODEL 22 - various mid-action cals., larger scale action of the Model 21.

* *Model 22 Classic* - various mid-action cals., 24 in. chrome moly match grade barrel, stock is AA Claro walnut with 20 LPI hand checkering and hand rubbed oil finish, machined aluminum trigger guard, matte metal finish, approx. 7-7 1/4 lbs. New 1999.

MSR $1,295	$1,150	$975	$825	$650	$550	$475	$425

* *Model 22 Custom Classic* - includes Brownell No. 1 checkering pattern, ebony forend tip, and steel grip cap.

MSR $2,195	$1,900	$1,400	$1,050	$775	$675	$575	$475

* *Model 22 Western Classic* - various cals., features octagon barrel and case hardened action and bolt. New 1997.

MSR $2,795	$2,375	$1,950	$1,675	$1,375	$1,050	$925	$825

* *Model 22 Varminter* - various cals., otherwise similar to the Model 21 Varminter. New 2000.

MSR $1,199	$1,025	$850	$700	$600	$525	$450	$400

GRADING - PPGS™	100%	98%	95%	90%	80%	70%	60%
✳ *Model 22 Montana Varminter* - various cals. New 2000.							
MSR $1,495	$1,300	$1,075	$900	$700	$600	$500	$425

✳ *Model 22 Pro-Varmint Extreme* - .220 Swift, .22 BR (new 1996), .22-250 Rem., .243 Win., .25-06 Rem., .308 Win., 6mm PPC, 6.5x55mm (new 1996) or 7.62x39mm (new 1996) cal., available in either Pro-Varmint, Benchrest, or Black Jack (black synthetic stock) configuration. New 1995.

MSR $1,995	$1,725	$1,300	$975	$750	$650	$550	$475

Add $400 for Benchrest Model.

MODEL 22 CLASSIC REPEATER - .22-250 Rem., .243 Win., .308 Win., or 7mm-08 Rem. cal., 3 shot mag. While advertised during 1996 only at $2,400 retail, this model was never mfg.

MODEL CUSTOM CLASSIC - .22 LR, .22 Mag., .22 Hornet or .222 Rem. cal., features Anschutz Match 54 action with deluxe walnut stock with American features and smaller trigger guard. Mfg. 1996-99.

	$1,750	$1,375	$1,075	$900	$725	$600	$500

Last MSR was $1,995.

MODEL CUSTOM MANNLICHER - .22 LR, .22 Mag., .22 Hornet, or .222 Rem. cal., features newest Anschutz Match 54 action with deluxe Mannlicher walnut stock and other special features. Mfg. 1996-99.

	$1,975	$1,625	$1,425	$1,225	$975	$850	$700

Last MSR was $2,195.

MODEL 36 SPORTSMAN - .22 LR, .17 CCM, or .22 Hornet cal., without Shilen barrel, standard wood with rubber recoil pad. Mfg. 1994 only.

	$675	$575	$495	$450	$400	$350	$295

Last MSR was $750.

MODEL 36 MARKSMAN - .22 LR, .17 CCM, or .22 Hornet cal., 4 shot mag., 23 in. chrome moly barrel, AA Claro walnut with 22 LPI checkering, 45 degree bolt, sling swivels, hand rubbed oil finish, 7 lbs. Mfg. 1992-94.

	$975	$750	$625	$550	$495	$450	$400

Last MSR was $1,125.

✳ *Model 36 Montana Trail Blazer* - .22 LR cal. only, lightweight field gun with sporter barrel. Mfg. 1996 only.

	$1,300	$1,025	$775	$650	$575	$475	$425

Last MSR was $1,475.

✳ *Model 36 Classic* - .22 LR cal. only, features choice of AAA Claro or AA French walnut with Monte Carlo cheekpiece. Disc. 1996.

	$1,500	$1,175	$875	$700	$625	$525	$450

Last MSR was $1,695.

✳ *Model 36 Varmint Extreme* - various cals., heavy Varmint stainless barrel, checkered stock. Mfg. 1997 only.

	$1,525	$1,175	$875	$700	$625	$525	$450

Last MSR was $1,695.

✳ *Model 36 Western Classic* - various cals., features octagon barrel and case hardened action and bolt. Mfg. 1997-99.

	$1,900	$1,400	$1,000	$775	$650	$550	$475

Last MSR was $2,195.

✳ *Model 36 Custom Classic* - includes Brownell No. 1 checkering pattern, ebony forend tip, and steel grip cap. Disc. 1999.

	$1,625	$1,325	$1,050	$825	$700	$600	$50

Last MSR was $1,850.

* *Model 36 TRP-1* - target variation of the Model 36 with ISU synthetic stock and adj. cheekpiece, 23 in. Wiseman/McMillan stainless steel or chrome moly barrel, single shot, fully adj. single stage trigger, vent. forearm. Mfg. 1992-93.

$950	$795	$625	$525	$475	$425	$375

Last MSR was $1,095.

* *Model MS-36 (TRP-1S)* - silhouette variation of the Model 36 TRP-1, clear epoxy finish, silhouette style stock, Pachmayr buttpad. Mfg. 1992-93.

$895	$725	$625	$550	$495	$450	$400

Last MSR was $995.

* *Model 36 BR-50* - .22 LR cal., benchrest variation featuring black synthetic stock and heavy stainless barrel. Mfg. 1993-99.

$1,675	$1,250	$950	$750	$650	$550	$475

Last MSR was $1,950.

* *Model 36 IR-50/50* - .22 LR cal. only, lightweight sporter style competition rifle with heavy 20 in. barrel. Mfg. 1996-99.

$1,675	$1,250	$950	$750	$650	$550	$475

Last MSR was $1,950.

* *Model 36 Featherweight* - .17 CCM, .22 LR, or .22 Hornet cal., features matte black synthetic stock and metal, Jewell trigger. Mfg. 1994-99.

$1,600	$1,225	$900	$700	$625	$525	$450

Last MSR was $1,795.

MODEL 38 SPORTER - .17 CCM, or .22 CCM cal., 3 shot mag., 24 in. chrome moly barrel, AA Claro walnut with 22 LPI checkering, 45 degree bolt, sling swivels, hand rubbed oil finish, 8 lbs. Mfg. 1992-93.

$965	$750	$625	$550	$495	$450	$400

Last MSR was $1,095.

Add $100 for Standard Grade (AA Claro walnut).
Add $200 for Custom Grade.
Add $300 for Custom Classic Grade.

The custom grade includes choice of AAA Claro or AA French walnut with Monte Carlo cheekpiece. The .17 CCM and .22 CCM cartridges designate Cooper Centerfire Magnum. Basically, the .22 CCM is a centerfire derivative of the .22 Mag. cal., and the .17 CCM is simply a necked down variation.

* *Model 38 Repeater (Deluxe)* - deluxe variation of the Model 38 Sporter. 650 mfg. 1992-1994.

$1,750	$1,400	$1,000	$775	$650	$550	$475

MODEL 38 SINGLE SHOT - small, mostly rimmed cals., 3 front locking lugs. New 1998.

* *Model 38 Classic* - various cals., single shot, 20 in. chrome moly match grade barrel, stock is AA Claro walnut with 20 LPI hand checkering and hand rubbed oil finish, machined aluminum trigger guard, matte metal finish, approx. 7-7 1/4 lbs. New 1999.

MSR $1,100	$950	$800	$650	$550	$495	$450	$400

* *Model 38 Custom Classic* - includes Brownell No. 1 checkering pattern, ebony forend tip, and steel grip cap.

MSR $1,995	$1,735	$1,325	$975	$750	$650	$550	$475

* *Model 38 Western Classic* - various cals., features octagon barrel and case hardened action and bolt. New 1997.

MSR $2,595	$2,250	$1,800	$1,550	$1,275	$995	$875	$750

* *Model 38 Varminter* - various cals., single shot, 24 in. stainless steel match grade barrel, stock is AA Claro walnut with 20 LPI hand checkering and hand rubbed oil finish, machined aluminum trigger guard, approx. 7-7 1/4 lbs. New 1999.

MSR $995	$875	$750	$625	$550	$495	$450	$400

GRADING - PPGS™	100%	98%	95%	90%	80%	70%	60%

✳ *Model 38 Varmint Extreme* - various cals. including the new .19-223, heavy stainless steel barrel w/o sights, checkered stock. New 1997.

	100%	98%	95%	90%	80%	70%	60%
MSR $1,795	$1,650	$1,425	$1,200	$995	$825	$600	$475

✳ *Model 38 Montana Varminter* - various cals. New 2000.

	100%	98%	95%	90%	80%	70%	60%
MSR $1,295	$1,150	$975	$825	$650	$550	$475	$425

MODEL 40 - .17 CCM (disc. 1995), .17 Ackley Hornet, .22 CCM (disc. 1995), .22 Hornet, or .22 K Hornet cal., 3 lug action, incorporates Anschütz mag., choice of Classic, Custom Classic, or Classic Varminter configuration. Mfg. 1995-96.

	98%	95%	90%	80%	70%	60%
	$1,600	$1,200	$950	$750	$650	$550	$475

Last MSR was $1,825.

Add $200 for Custom Classic or Classic Varminter (disc.) Model.

MODEL 57 CLASSIC - .17 HMR (new 2002), .22 LR or .22 Mag. (new 2001) cal., 3 rear locking lugs, various configurations, barrel lengths, and features. New 2000.

Add approx. $100 for .17 HMR or .22 Mag. cal. on the following models.

	100%	98%	95%	90%	80%	70%	60%
MSR $1,149	$965	$815	$675	$550	$495	$450	$400

✳ *Model 57 Custom Classic* - new 2000.

	100%	98%	95%	90%	80%	70%	60%
MSR $1,895	$1,650	$1,275	$900	$725	$625	$525	$450

✳ *Model 57 Western Classic* - new 2000.

	100%	98%	95%	90%	80%	70%	60%
MSR $2,495	$2,250	$1,650	$1,175	$825	$725	$650	$575

MODEL 72 MONTANA PLAINSMAN - various cals., single shot featuring case colored Win. Model 1885 action with heavy octagon barrel, double set triggers, deluxe checkered straight grip stock and forearm, no sights. While advertised during 1997 at a retail price of $2,195, this model never went into production.

RIFLES: SINGLE SHOT

MODEL 7 PEREGRINE FALLING BLOCK - various cals., falling block action with under lever, choice of varmint extreme or custom sporter configuration, 24 in. barrel, deluxe checkered walnut stock, tang mounted safety, approx. 6 lbs. Limited production 2001 only.

	100%	98%	95%	90%	80%	70%	60%
	$1,750	$1,400	$1,100	$925	$800	$675	$550

Last MSR was $1,995.

Add $300 for custom sporter variation.

COP

Previous Derringer manufacturer located in Torrance, CA.

DERRINGERS

COP DERRINGER - .357 Mag. cal., 4 shot, 3 in. barrel, stainless steel mfg., double action, wood grips, 28 oz. COP stands for Compact Off-Duty Police. Disc.

	95%	90%	80%
	$350	$325	$285

COSMI, AMERICO & FIGLIO

Current semi-auto shotgun manufacturer established during 1930, and located in Ancona, Italy. No current importation. Previously imported 2003-2004 by Old Friends Hunting & Shooting Co., from 1985-2003 by New England Arms Co., and from 2001-2002 by Autumn Sales, Inc., located in Fort Worth, TX. Please contact the factory directly for more information and model availability (see Trademark Index).

Cosmi

Approximately 7,200 Cosmi shotguns have been manufactured since 1930 (the design dates back to 1925). They are known for their unique mechanism and high-quality fabrication techniques. Since each gun's parts are made separately (and individually serial numbered), most components are not interchangeable from one gun to another.

GRADING - PPGS™	100%	98%	95%	90%	80%	70%	60%

SHOTGUNS: SEMI-AUTO

Subtract 15% w/o choke tubes on models below.

STANDARD MODEL - 12, 16, or 20 ga., (a 28 ga. and .410 bore will be available 2004), 2 3/4 (16 ga. only) or 3 in. chamber, semi-auto, unique pivoting break open action loads cartridges into stock chamber from inside of receiver, 8 shot mag. with 3 shot option reducer, steel, alloy, or titanium frame, Boehler Antinit steel barrel (moves when shooting) available with or without choke tubes, all internal parts are mfg. from special chrome-nickel steel or titanium (new 1990), custom order gun only with dimensions specified by individual customer (approx. 6 month delivery time on 12 and 20 ga.).

* *Standard Grade* - barrel and attached receiver assembly are blue, frame is chromed-nickel steel or aluminum, w/o engraving.

MSR N/A	$12,000	$9,000	$7,500	$6,000	$4,500	$3,750	$3,350

* *Aluminum Model* - 12 or 20 ga., receiver made out of machined aluminum, approx. 7 lbs. in 12 ga., approx. 5.9 lbs. in 20 ga.

MSR N/A	$14,000	$11,000	$9,250	$7,500	$5,000	$4,275	$3,750

* *Titanium Model* - 12 or 20 ga., receiver made out of machined titanium, approx. 6.8 lbs. in 12 ga., approx. 5.7 lbs. in 20 ga. New 1990.

MSR N/A	$16,500	$13,000	$11,250	$9,000	$7,000	$5,250	$4,250

* *Engraved Models*

Cosmi offers various engraving styles/patterns on the De Luxe, Extra De Luxe, and Prestige models, with prices depending on the amount and style of coverage. Please contact the importer directly for more information, availability, and current pricing on these engraving options.

COUNTY, S.A.L.

Previous shotgun manufacturer located in Eibar, Spain.

SHOTGUNS: O/U

County manufactured a wide variety of both boxlock and sidelock O/Us, which had very limited U.S. importation.

CRESCENT FIRE ARMS CO. & CRESCENT-DAVIS ARMS CO.

Previous manufacturers and trademarks manufactured circa 1888-1931 in Norwich, CT.

In 1888, George W. Cilley bought out the defunct Bacon Arms Co. of Norwich, CT. He then formed an alliance with Frank Foster, and borrowed enough money to form the Crescent Fire Arms Company. Cilley and Foster each held several firearms patents, and both were highly qualified in firearms design and manufacture. Production began with single shot tip-up shotguns that had an external side hammer. Double barrel shotgun production was started in 1891. In 1893, they began making bicycle chains, and that same year, H&D Folsom took over the company's financial control. Early in the 1890s, Crescent built a rifle that resembled the Remington No. 4. A very rare Crescent was the .410 bore shotgun pistol, which was introduced in the 1920s. In 1929, N.R. Davis Firearms Co., then owned by Warner Arms Corp., merged with Cresent to become Crescent-Davis Arms Co. Because of financial crisis, business continued to decline, and they were forced to sell out. Savage Arms Co. acquired Davis-Cresent in 1931, assembled guns from the remaining parts, and these guns were sold under the Crescent name only. In 1932, the city of Norwich, CT, took over the Crescent property for non-payment of back taxes. After the Norwich facility was closed, manufacture was moved to Chicopee Falls.

It is unknown whether or not Crescent did any high grade or custom work. However, a very well engraved SxS, with the Crescent logo, is known to exist in a private collection.

GRADING - PPGS™	100%	98%	95%	90%	80%	70%	60%

Crescent Fire Arms Company remains best known as a manufacturer of "house brand" shotguns (i.e., Crescent private labeled guns for retailers, distributors, mail-order houses, etc.). Over 100 different trademarks have been observed to date, manufactured by Crescent. Almost all the remaining specimens today are priced as shooters and have no collector value.

SHOTGUNS

SINGLE SHOT MODEL - 12, 16, 20, 28 ga., or .410 bore, exposed hammer, various barrel lengths, walnut stock and forearm. Disc.

	100%	98%	95%	90%	80%	70%	60%
	$125	$100	$85	$70	$60	$45	$30

Add 15% for 16 or 20 ga., 50% for 28 ga. or .410 bore.

SxS MODEL - values below assume standard models with double triggers, extractors, original finish, and 100% working order. Sidelock actions were also available and will command premiums from prices listed below. Shotguns with exposed hammers can equal their hammerless counterparts if condition is 80% or better.

	100%	98%	95%	90%	80%	70%	60%
12 ga.	$295	$265	$230	$200	$170	$150	$125
16 ga.	$195	$175	$150	$125	$100	$85	$65
20 ga.	$295	$265	$230	$200	$170	$150	$125
28 ga.	$375	$325	$280	$250	$200	$150	$100
.410 bore	$400	$350	$300	$250	$200	$150	$100

KNICKERBOCKER - 20 ga., 14 in. nickel-plated barrels, case-hardened receiver, pistol grip, mfg. circa 1900s.

Extreme rarity factor precludes accurate pricing information.

VICTOR EJECTOR - .410 bore, 12 in. single barrel, total production unknown, possibly prototype for Crescent Certified Shotgun.

Extreme rarity factor precludes accurate pricing information.

NEW EMPIRE - hammerless .410 smooth bore or 20 ga., 12 1/4 in. barrels, extremely rare firearm whose total production and years of manufacture are unknown at this time (only known documentation is mentioned as an "Auto Burglar Gun" in an advertisement by "Saul Ruben, The Gun Store, 68 E. Long St., Columbus, OH" of the October 1932 issue of *Hunter-Trader-Trapper*, which lists a $14.75 retail price). The receiver is marked "New Empire". At this time, 5 specimens are known in .410 smooth bore, with ser. nos. scattered throughout the S-1 to S-19 range. The ser. no. appears on the metal under the forearm. The Crescent Auto & Burglar Gun may have been distributed by the H.&D. Folsom Arms Co. of New York City through its manufacturing division, the Crescent Firearms Co., Norwich, CT. Crescent's sellers included the Belknap Hardware Co., Louisville, KY and Hibbard-Spencer-Bartlett Co., Chicago, IL.

	100%	98%	95%	90%	80%	70%	60%
	$1,200	$1,000	$900	$800	$700	$600	$500

CRESCENT CERTIFIED SHOTGUN - .410 smooth bore, 12 1/2 in. barrel, approx. 4,000 mfg. from approx. 1930-32 by the Crescent-Davis Arms Corp., and possibly thereafter until 1934 by the J. Stevens Arms Co., left receiver side is stamped "Crescent Certified Shotgun/Crescent-Davis Arms Corp./Norwich, Conn. U.S.A." Also termed the "Ever-Ready" Model 200 and advertised with a blue frame, but specimens with "tiger stripe" and regular case coloring have been observed, guns not currently registered with ATF cannot be legally owned and are subject to seizure.

	100%	98%	95%	90%	80%	70%	60%
	$1,200	$1,000	$900	$800	$700	$600	$500

Add $100-$300 for original cardboard box.

CRICKET RIFLE

Please refer to the Keystone Sporting Arms, Inc. section in this text.

CROSSFIRE LLC

Previous manufacturer located in La Grange, GA 1998-2001.

COMBINATION GUNS

CROSSFIRE MK-I - 12 ga. (3 in. chamber) over .223 Rem. cal., unique slide action O/U design allows stacked shotgun/rifle configuration, 18 3/4 in. shotgun barrel with invector chokes over 16 1/4 in. rifle barrel, detachable 4 (shotgun) and 5 (rifle) shot mags., open sights, Picatinny style rail scope mount, synthetic stock and forearm, choice of black (MK-I) or RealTree 100% camo (MK-1RT) finish, single trigger with ambidextrous fire control lever, 8.6 lbs. Mfg. mid-1998-2001.

$1,750	$1,550	$1,350	$1,175	$995	$895	$825

Last MSR was $1,895.

Add $100 for camo finish.

CUMBERLAND MOUNTAIN ARMS, INC.

Previous manufacturer located in Winchester, TN early 1993-99.

RIFLES: SINGLE SHOT

PLATEAU RIFLE - .40-65 or .45-70 Govt. cal., patterned after the Browning High Wall single shot, various barrel lengths up to 32 in., manual safety, blue receiver and barrel, Marble's style buckhorn rear sight, receiver drilled for scope mounts. Mfg. 1993-99.

$1,075	$825	$675	$575	$500	$450	$400

Last MSR was $1,295.

Add approx. $200-$350 for deluxe wood.

CUSTOM GUN GUILD

Previous manufacturer located in Doraville, GA.

WOOD'S MODEL IV SINGLE SHOT - various cals., custom manufactured, falling block type single shot, lightweight, only 5 1/2 lbs. Mfg. 1984 only.

$2,975	$2,500	$2,000	$1,850	$1,700	$1,500	1,250

D SECTION

D.C. INDUSTRIES, INC.

Current manucturer and gunsmithing services located in Blaine, MN.

As this edition went to press, D.C. Industries, Inc. (Dan Coonan, Inc.) had plans to begin manufacturing the Expert .357 Coonan Magnum. Please contact the company directly for more information, including availability and pricing (see Trademark Index).

DGS, INC.

Current custom rifle gunsmith located in Casper, WY.

Custom gunsmith Dale A. Storey manufactures a variety of bolt action rifles built per individual customer order only. They include the Storey Custom and Storey Lightweight, as well as other variations. Please contact the company directly for more information and current prices on these quality custom rifles.

CUSTOM GUNSMITHING

DPMS, INC.

Current manufacturer established in 1986 and located in St. Cloud, MN. Previously located in Becker, MN. DPMS (Defense Procurement Manufacturing Services, Inc.) manufactures high quality AR-15 style rifles, barrel assemblies (including a new conversion for .22 cal.), related parts and components. Distributor, dealer, and consumer direct sales.

GRADING - PPGS™	100%	98%	95%	90%	80%	70%	60%

PISTOLS: SEMI-AUTO

DPMS .45 - .45 ACP cal., patterned after the Colt M1911A-1, 7 shot mag., 5 in. barrel, 38 oz. Limited mfg. 2001 only.

	$475	$425	$360	$330	$300	$275	$250

Last MSR was $519.

PISTOLS: SLIDE ACTION

PANTHER PUMP PISTOL - .223 Rem. cal., slide action paramilitary design, 10 1/2 in. threaded heavy barrel, aluminum handguard incorporates slide action mechanism, pistol grip only (no stock), carrying handle with sights, 5 lbs.

MSR $1,595	$1,475	$1,200	$1,025	$925	$825	$700	$575

PANTHER .22 LR PISTOL - .22 LR cal., 8.5 in. heavy chrome-moly steel barrel, 10 shot mag., black aircraft aluminum flattop upper receiver, black forged aircraft aluminum lower receiver, blowback action, phosphate and hard chrome finished bolt and carrier, aluminum trigger guard, ribbed aluminum free float tube hand guard, no sights, 4.25 lbs. New 2005.

MSR $735	$675	$625	$550	$475	$425	$375	$335

RIFLES: BOLT ACTION

DPMS also distributes Evolution USA bolt action rifles. Please refer to the Evolution USA section for current models and pricing.

RIFLES: SEMI-AUTO

Each new DPMS rifle/carbine comes equipped with two mags. (high cap where legal), a nylon web sling, and a cleaning kit. Post-crime bill manufactured DPMS rifles may have pre-ban features, including collapsible stocks, high capacity mags, and a flash hider/compensator. Models with these features are not available in certain states.

The Panther AR-15 Series was introduced in 1993 with the following features: 223 Rem., 5.56x45mm, or 7.62x39mm Russian (new 2000) cal., semi-auto or slide action, paramilitary design, various barrel lengths and configurations, 10 or 30 shot mag., black synthetic stock and forearm, various weights.

PANTHER CLASSIC - 5.56x45mm cal., 16 or 20 in. heavy barrel, ribbed barrel shroud, includes carrying handle with sights, 8 lbs.

MSR $809	$730	$625	$550	$475	$425	$375	$335

Add $76 for left-hand variation (Southpaw Panther).

✱ *Panther Bulldog* - 20 in. stainless fluted bull barrel, flattop, adj. buttstock, vented free float handguard, 11 lbs. Disc. 1999.

$1,150	$835	$725	$625	$550	$475	$425

Last MSR was $1,219.

PANTHER 7.62x39mm - 7.62x39mm Russian cal., 20 in. heavy barrel, black Zytel buttstock with trapdoor. New 2000.

MSR $849	$765	$650	$575	$495	$440	$385	$335

PANTHER DCM - .223 Rem. cal., 20 in. stainless steel heavy barrel, National Match sights, two-stage trigger, black Zytel composition buttstock, 9 lbs. Mfg. 1998-2003.

$975	$795	$675	$595	$525	$460	$415

Last MSR was $1,099.

PANTHER LITE 16 - 5.56x45mm cal., 16 in. 1x9 twist post-ban chrome moly barrel, non-collapsible fiberite CAR stock, forged A1 upper with forward bolt assist, black Teflon finish, 5.75 lbs. New 2002.

MSR $709	$655	$595	$550	$475	$425	$375	$335

PANTHER CLASSIC SIXTEEN - 5.45x45mm cal., 16 in. heavy barrel, adj. sights, black Zytel composition buttstock, 6 1/2 lbs. New 1998.

MSR $799	$720	$630	$550	$475	$425	$375	$335

Add $55 for Panther Free Float Sixteen with free floating barrel and vent. handguard.

PANTHER LO-PRO CLASSIC - .223 Rem. cal., 16 in. bull barrel, features flattop lo-pro upper receiver with push pin. New 2002.

MSR $699	$650	$595	$550	$475	$425	$375	$335

PANTHER TUBER - 5.56x45mm cal., features 16 in. post-ban heavy barrel with full length 2 inch aluminum free float handguard, adj. A2 rear sights. New 2002.

MSR $746	$675	$625	$565	$485	$435	$375	$335

PANTHER A2 TACTICAL - 5.56x45mm cal., features 16 in. heavy manganese phosphated barrel, standard A2 handguard, 9.75 lbs. New 2004.

MSR $809	$705	$625	$550	$475	$425	$375	$335

PANTHER AP4 CARBINE - 5.56x45mm cal., features 16 in. M4 contour barrel with A2 flash hider, permanently attached Miculek compensator, fixed fiberglass reinforced polymer M4 stock, 7.25 lbs. New 2004.

MSR $899	$815	$725	$600	$525	$450	$400	$360

✱ *Panther Carbine* - 6.8x43mm SPC or 5.56x45mm cal., 11.5 or 16 in. barrel, collapsible stock, includes carrying handle, 6.5 lbs.

MSR $849	$765	$650	$575	$495	$440	$385	$335

The 11.5 in. barrel model is available for law enforcement only.

GRADING - PPGS™	100%	98%	95%	90%	80%	70%	60%

PRAIRIE PANTHER - 20 in. heavy fluted barrel, flat-top, vented free float handguard, 8 3/4 lbs. Disc. 1999.

	$875	$750	$635	$550	$475	$425	$375

Last MSR was $959.

PANTHER BULL - .223 Rem. cal., features 16, 20 (standard), or 24 in. stainless free floating bull barrel, flattop, aluminum forearm, 10 lbs.

MSR $915	$835	$725	$600	$525	$450	$400	$360

Subtract $30 for 16 in. barrel (Panther Bull Sweet Sixteen).
Add $30 for 24 in. barrel (Panther Bull Twenty-Four).

✳ *Panther Bull Classic* - .223 Rem. cal., features 20 in. long, 1 in. bull barrel, adj. sights, 10 lbs. New 1998.

MSR $905	$825	$725	$600	$525	$450	$400	$360

Add $200 for SST lower.

✳ *Panther Deluxe Bull Twenty-Four Special* - .223 Rem. cal., features 24 in. stainless fluted barrel, adj. A2 buttstock with sniper pistol grip. New 1998.

MSR $1,189	$1,075	$825	$700	$600	$525	$460	$415

✳ *Panther Super Bull* - .223 Rem. cal., 16, 20, or 24 in. extra heavy bull barrel, flat-top receiver, free float handguard, approx. 11 lbs. Mfg. 1997-98, 24 in. model reintroduced during late 2004.

MSR $1,199	$1,075	$835	$725	$600	$525	$460	$415

✳ *Panther Extreme Super Bull* - features 24 in. extra heavy stainless steel bull barrel (1 1/8 in. diameter barrel), flat-top, hi-rider upper receiver, skeletonized A2 buttstock, 11 3/4 lbs. Mfg. 1999-2004.

	$1,075	$835	$715	$600	$525	$460	$415

Last MSR was $1,199.

ARTIC PANTHER - .223 Rem. cal., similar to Panther Bull, except has white powder coat finish on receiver and handguard, 10 lbs. New 1997.

MSR $1,099	$995	$795	$675	$595	$525	$460	$415

PANTHER RACE GUN - .223 Rem. cal., 24 in. stainless steel barrel with Hot Rod hand guard, IronStone steel and aluminum stock with rubber buttplate and brass weights, 16 lbs. New 2001.

MSR $1,719	$1,565	$1,250	$1,050	$950	$850	$725	$600

PANTHER SINGLE SHOT - 5.56x45mm cal., 20 in. barrel, A2 black Zytel stock and handguard, single shot only w/o magazine, 9 lbs.

MSR $814	$725	$640	$560	$485	$435	$375	$335

PANTHER .22 RIFLE - .22 LR cal., AR-15 style receiver, 16 in. bull barrel, black Teflon metal finish, Picatinny rail, black Zytel A2 buttstock, 7.8 lbs. New 2003.

MSR $649	$595	$550	$475	$425	$375	$335	$300

PANTHER DCM .22 LR RIFLE - .22 LR cal., features 20 in. fluted stainless steel H-Bar barrel with 1:16 rate of twist, A2 upper receiver with National Match sights, black teflon finish, A2 stock and handguards, also available with optional DCM handguard system. New 2004.

MSR $749	$675	$600	$525	$450	$400	$350	$325

PANTHER AP4 .22 LR RIFLE - .22 LR cal., features 16 in. M4 contoured barrel with 1:16 rate of twist, M4 handguards and pinned carstock, A3 flattop upper receiver, detachable carry handle with A2 sights and black teflon finish, 6.5 lbs. New 2004.

MSR $799	$700	$625	$550	$475	$425	$375	$335

This model is also available in a pre-ban configuration for law enforcement.

GRADING - PPGS™	100%	98%	95%	90%	80%	70%	60%

PANTHER .300 LONG RANGE RIFLE - .300 RSUM cal., features 20 in. fluted steel bull barrel with 1:10 rate of twist, vented standard length aluminum handguard, aircraft grade aluminum alloy upper and lower receiver, black teflon finish, A2 skeletonized buttstock, 12.5 lbs. New 2004.

MSR $1,250	$1,075	$925	$825	$725	$650	$600	$550

PANTHER .308 LONG RANGE RIFLE - .308 Win. cal., 24 in. bull barrel with 1:10 rate of twist, ribbed free-floating aluminum forearm tube, aircraft alloy upper/lower, A2 buttstock, black Teflon finish. New mid-2003.

MSR $1,149	$1,025	$850	$750	$650	$575	$500	$450

✱ *Panther .308B* - similar features as the Long Range Rifle, except has 18 in. chromemoly bull barrel and carbine length aluminum handguard. New late 2003.

MSR $1,149	$1,025	$850	$750	$650	$575	$500	$450

✱ *Panther .308T* - similar features as the .308B, except has 16 in. H-Bar barrel. New 2004.

MSR $1,149	$1,025	$850	$750	$650	$575	$500	$450

RIFLES: SLIDE ACTION

PANTHER PUMP - .223 Rem. cal., paramilitary design, 20 in. threaded heavy barrel with flash hider, aluminum handguard incorporates slide action mechanism, carrying handle with sights, bayonet lug, designed by Les Branson, 8 1/2 lbs.

MSR $1,695	$1,525	$1,275	$1,050	$925	$775	$650	$575

DSA INC.

Current manufacturer, importer, and distributor of semi-auto rifles and related components located in Barrington, IL. Previously located in Round Lake and Grayslake, IL.

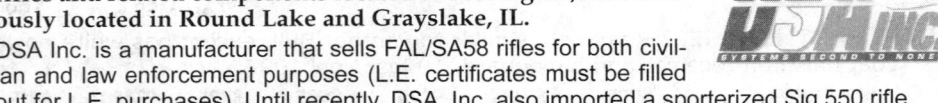

DSA Inc. is a manufacturer that sells FAL/SA58 rifles for both civilian and law enforcement purposes (L.E. certificates must be filled out for L.E. purchases). Until recently, DSA, Inc. also imported a sporterized Sig 550 rifle.

RIFLES: BOLT ACTION

DS-MP1 - .308 Win. cal., 22 in. match grade barrel, Rem. 700 action with Badger Ordnance precision ground heavy recoil lug, trued bolt face and lugs, hand lapped stainless steel barrel with recessed target crown, black McMillan A5 pillar bedded stock, Picatinny rail, includes test target guaranteeing 1/2 MOA at 100 yards, black or camo Duracoat finish, 11.5 lbs. New 2004.

MSR $2,800	$2,500	$2,150	$1,800	$1,550	$1,250	$1,000	$850

RIFLES: SEMI-AUTO

The SA-58 rifles listed below are available in either a standard DuraCoat solid (OD Green or GrayWolf), or optional camo pattern finishes - add $250 for camo. Patterns include: Underbrush, Woodland, Winter Twig, Tiger Stripe, Urban Camo, Belgian Camo, Afghan Camo or Mossy Oak Breakup. DSA Inc. makes three types of forged steel receivers, and they are distinquished by the machining cuts on Types I and II, and no cuts on Type III.

SA58 STANDARD RIFLE - .308 Win. cal., FAL design using high precision CNC machinery, 21 (standard or bull) or 24 in. (bull only) steel or stainless steel cyrogenically treated barrel, black synthetic stock, pistol grip (standard 2001) attached to frame, 10 or 20 shot mag., 8.7-11lbs.

MSR $1,475	$1,300	$1,075	$950	$800	$675	$600	$525

Add $250 for stainless steel 21 or 24 in. bull barrel.
Add $270 for bull barrel.

GRADING - PPGS™	100%	98%	95%	90%	80%	70%	60%

✳ **SA58 Predator** - .243 Win., .260 Rem., or .308 Win. cal., Type 1 or Type 3 receiver, 16 or 19 in. barrel with target crown, green fiberglass furniture, Picatinny scope rail, 5 or 10 shot mag., approx. 9 lbs. New 2003.

MSR $1,595	$1,395	$1,150	$950	$800	$675	$575	$500

Add $100 for .260 Rem. or .243 Win. cal.

✳ **SA58 Graywolf** - .300 WSM (disc. 2005) or .308 Win. cal., Type 1 or Type 3 receiver, 21 in. bull barrel with target crown, gray aluminum handguard, synthetic stock and adj. pistol grip, Picatinny scope rail, 5 or 10 shot mag., approx. 13 lbs. New 2003.

MSR $2,120	$1,800	$1,550	$1,325	$1,125	$950	$800	$675

✳ **SA58 Standard/Tactical Carbine** - similar to SA58 Standard Rifle, except has 16.25 in. barrel, 8.25 lbs. New 1999.

MSR $1,395	$1,225	$1,025	$900	$775	$650	$575	$500

Add $80 for Tactical Carbine with fluted barrel and w/o muzzle brake (new 2003).
Add $200 for SA58 Lightweight Carbine with aluminum receiver components (disc. 2004).
Add $250 for SA58 Stainless Steel Carbine (included scope mount through 2000).

✳ **SA58 Collectors Series** - .308 Win. cal., configurations include the Congo ($1,695 - MSR), Para Congo ($1,995 - MSR), and the G1 ($1,695 - MSR). New 2003.

✳ **SA58 T48 Replica** - .308 Win. cal., 10 or 20 shot fixed mag., stripper clip top cover, cryogenic barrel, wood furniture, replica Browning flash hider. Importation began 2002.

MSR $1,795	$1,500	$1,275	$1,050	$850	$725	$625	$525

DS-S1 - .223 Win. cal., 16, 20, or 24 in. match chamber stainless steel bull barrel, A2 buttstock with free float aluminum handguard, Picatinny gas block sight base, forged lower receiver, NM two-stage trigger, forged flattop upper receiver, optional fluted barrel, variety of Duracoat solid or camo finishes available, 8-10 lbs. New 2004.

MSR $950	$850	$775	$675	$600	$525	$450	$400

DS-CV1 CARBINE - 5.56 NATO cal., 16 in. chrome moly D4 barrel with press on mock flash hider, fixed Shorty buttstock, D4 handguard and heatshield, forged front sight base, forged lower receiver, forged flattop upper receiver, variety of Duracoat solid or camo finishes available, 6.25 lbs. New 2004.

MSR $850	$775	$700	$625	$550	$500	$450	$400

DS-LE4 CARBINE - 5.56 NATO cal., 14.5 or 16 in. chrome moly D4 barrel with threaded A2 flash hider, collapsible CAR buttstock, D4 handguard with heatshield, forged lower receiver, forged front sight base with bayonet lug, forged flattop upper receiver, Duracoat solid or camo finish, 6.15 or 6.25 lbs. New 2004.

The 14.5 in. model is for law enforcement only. Please contact the factory directly for pricing on this model.

DWM

Previous manufacturer located in Berlin, Germany circa 1900-1930. DWM (Deutsche Waffen und Munitions Fabriken) manufactured Lugers are listed in the Luger section.

PISTOLS: SEMI-AUTO

POCKET AUTOMATIC - 7.65mm cal., 3 1/2 in. barrel, blue, hard rubber grips. Mfg. 1921-31.

	$700	$630	$580	$500	$420	$380	$330

DAEWOO

Current manufacturer located in Korea. Current

limited importation by Century International Arms, located in Boca Raton, FL. Previous importation included Kimber of America, Inc. until 1997, Daewoo Precision Industries, Ltd., until mid-1996, located in Southampton, PA, and previously distributed by Nationwide Sports Distributors 1993-96. Previously imported by KBI, Inc. and Firstshot, Inc., both located in Harrisburg, PA, and B-West located in Tucson, AZ.

Daewoo makes a variety of firearms, most of which are not imported into the U.S.

PISTOLS: SEMI-AUTO

DH380 - .380 ACP cal., double action design. Imported 1995-96.

	100%	98%	95%	90%	80%	70%	60%
	$330	$285	$260	$235	$210	$185	$165

Last MSR was $375.

DH40 - .40 S&W cal., otherwise similar to DP51, 32 oz. Imported beginning 1995.

No MSR	$325	$270	$245	$225	$200	$185	$170	$160

DP51 STANDARD/COMPACT - 9mm Para. cal., double action enabling lowering hammer w/o depressing trigger, 3 1/2 (DP51 C or S, disc.) or 4.1 (DP51) in. barrel, 10 (C/B 1994), 12* (.40 S&W), or 13* (9mm Para.) shot mag., 3-dot sights, tri-action mechanism (SA, DA, or fast action), ambidextrous controls, alloy receiver, polished or sand-blasted black finish, 28 or 32 oz., includes lockable carrying case with accessories. Imported in various configuration beginning in 1991.

No MSR	$315	$265	$240	$220	$200	$185	$170	$160

Add 10% for DP51 Compact (disc.).

DP52 - .22 LR cal., double action, 3.8 in. barrel, alloy receiver, 10 shot mag., blue finish, 23 oz. Imported 1994-96.

	$320	$275	$225	$200	$180	$165	$150

Last MSR was $380.

RIFLES: SEMI-AUTO

MAX II (K2) - .223 Rem. cal., paramilitary design rifle, 18 in. barrel, gas operated rotating bolt, folding fiberglass stock, interchangeable mags. with the Colt M16, 7 lbs. Importation disc. 1986.

	$950	$875	$800	$725	$625	$550	$475

Last MSR was $609.

✻ **MAX I (K1A1)** - similar to above, except has retractable stock. Importation disc. 1986.

	$1,050	$925	$850	$750	$650	$575	$500

Last MSR was $592.

DR200 - .223 Rem. cal., paramilitary configuration with sporterized stock, 10 shot mag. Imported 1995-96.

	$650	$550	$475	$425	$395	$375	$350

Last MSR was $535.

DR300 - 7.62x39mm cal., paramilitary configuration with or w/o thumbhole stock. Importation disc.

	$550	$475	$425	$395	$375	$350	$325

DAISY

Current airgun manufacturer with headquarters located in Rogers, AR.

For more information and current pricing on both new and used Daisy airguns, please refer to the *Blue Book of Airguns* by Dr. Robert Beeman & John Allen (also online).

GRADING - PPGS™	100%	98%	95%	90%	80%	70%	60%

RIFLES: SINGLE SHOT, DISC.

As the V/L ammunition availability diminishes, values listed below may fluctuate.

V/L STANDARD RIFLE - .22 V/L cal. (caseless air ignited cartridge), 1,100 FPS, 18 in. barrel, plastic stock, not particularly accurate. Approx. 19,000 mfg. 1968-69.

	$250	$225	$195	$150	$125	$95	$80

V/L PRESENTATION - similar to Collector's Kit, except does not have owner's name inscribed on buttplate, walnut stock. 4,000 mfg. for dealers.

	$325	$295	$265	$235	$195	$160	$130

Last MSR was $125.

V/L COLLECTOR'S KIT - comes with case, gun cradles, 300 rounds of ammo, and a gold plated brass buttplate with owner's name and serial number of gun. Approx. 4,000 mfg., available only by direct factory order.

	$545	$495	$425	$350	$275	$225	$165

Last MSR was $125.

Note: The Daisy .22 V/L was discontinued because the BATF ruled that the gun constituted a firearm, and since Daisy was federally licensed to manufacture air weapons only, the factory decided to discontinue manufacture.

RIFLES: BOLT ACTION, DISC.

All Legacy models have a removable trigger, slings and swivels, takedown barrel, dovetail receiver for scope mounting, rifled inner steel barrel with 12 lands and grooves, and an adj. rear sight. Weight is between 6 1/2-7 lbs.

MODEL 8 - .22 S or LR cal., single shot, 16 in. barrel, black synthetic stock, 30,000 mfg. for Wal-Mart only 1987-88.

	$175	$150	$125	$95	$80	$70	$55

During 1987, Daisy assembled this model using left-over Iver Johnson parts.

LEGACY MODELS 2201/2211 - .22 LR cal., single shot, bolt action, plastic (2201) or walnut finished hardwood (2211) stock, models vary in features, prices range from $150-$175. Mfg. 1988-91.

LEGACY MODELS 2202/2212 - .22 LR cal., bolt action repeater, 10 shot rotary mag., plastic (2202) or walnut finished hardwood (2212) stock, models vary in features, prices range from $150-$175. Mfg. 1988-91.

Model 2202 has copolymer stock with adj. buttplate.

RIFLES: SEMI-AUTO

LEGACY MODELS 2203/2213 - .22 LR cal., 7 shot box mag., models vary in features, prices range from $165-$190. Mfg. 1988-91.

Model 2203 has copolymer stock with adj. buttplate. Model 2213 has American hardwood stock.

DAKIN GUN CO.

Previous importer located in San Francisco, CA circa 1960s.

SHOTGUNS: O/U

MODEL 170 - 12, 16, 20 ga., or .410 bore, boxlock, light engraving, double triggers, vent rib.

	$495	$400	$325	$275	$245	$220	$195

SHOTGUNS: SxS

MODEL 100 - 12 or 20 ga., boxlock, engraved, double trigger.

	$425	$350	$275	$240	$205	$190	$170

GRADING - PPGS™	100%	98%	95%	90%	80%	70%	60%

MODEL 147 - 12 or 20 ga., boxlock, engraved, vent. rib, double trigger.

	$495	$385	$300	$265	$235	$215	$195

MODEL 160 - 12 or 20 ga., boxlock, single trigger, ejectors, vent. rib.

	$825	$700	$595	$495	$450	$395	$360

MODEL 215 - 12 or 20 ga., sidelock, heavy engraving, special walnut, single trigger, ejectors, vent. rib.

	$2,250	$1,900	$1,675	$1,300	$1,100	$925	$775

DAKOTA ARMS, INC.

Current manufacturer and importer established in 1987, located in Sturgis, SD. Dealer and direct sales through manufacturer only. This company is not affiliated with Dakota Single Action Revolvers.

Dakota Arms Inc. also owns the rights to Miller Arms and Nesika actions. Please refer to these individual sections for more information.

Dakota Arms models listed below are also available with many custom options - please contact the factory directly for availability and pricing. Left-hand rifles are also available at no extra charge on all models. Actions (barreled or unbarreled) may also be purchased separately. Please contact the manufacturer directly for individual quotations.

RIFLES: BOLT ACTION

DAKOTA .22 RIFLE - .17 HMR (new 2004) .22 LR, .22 Win Mag. (new 2004) or .22 Hornet (disc.) cal., combines features of the Win. Model 52 Sporter and Dakota 76, full sized receiver, trigger and striker block safety similar to Dakota 76, 5 shot mag., 22 in. chrome moly barrel, checkered XX walnut stock, no sights, 6 1/2 lbs. Mfg. 1992-98, reintroduced 2003-2004.

	$2,650	$2,250	$1,750	$1,350	$950	$750	$550

Last MSR was $3,000.

DAKOTA 76 TRAVELER - various cals. between .25-06 Rem. - .450 Dakota, in addition to Dakota proprietary calibers, almost seamless take down rifle based on the Dakota 76 design, threadless disassembly ensuring scope stability and accuracy, in addition to no possibility of increasing the head space during repeated disassembly, wood stock, right- or left-hand action. New 1999.

MSR $4,995	$4,500	$3,850	$3,150	$2,625	$2,200	$1,750	$1,450

Add $1,000 for Safari Traveler.
Add $1,800 for African Traveler.
Add $1,850 (standard cals.) or $2,150 (Safari cals.) per interchangeable barrel.

DAKOTA 76 CLASSIC GRADE - available in various cals. (short, standard, or long action), custom frame incorporating many Win. Model 70 features, 21 or 23 in. barrel, Mauser type extractor, checkered X English walnut stock, 7 1/2 lbs. Left-hand action available at no extra charge. New 1987.

MSR $4,295	$3,750	$3,100	$2,500	$2,000	$1,650	$1,350	$1,125

This Model is also available with a composite stock at no extra charge.

DAKOTA 76 VARMINT GRADE - available in 9 cals. between .17 Rem. and 6mm PPC, single shot bolt-action, heavy barrel. Mfg. 1994-97.

	$2,275	$1,775	$1,425	$1,175	$990	$880	$770

Last MSR was $2,500.

GRADING - PPGS™	100%	98%	95%	90%	80%	70%	60%

DAKOTA 76 SAFARI GRADE - available in various cals., 23 in. barrel, one-piece drop trigger guard assembly with hinged floor plate, checkered XXX English walnut stock with ebony forearm tip. Left-hand action available at no extra charge, 8.5 lbs. New 1987.

	100%	98%	95%	90%	80%	70%	60%
MSR $4,995	$4,500	$3,850	$3,150	$2,625	$2,200	$1,750	$1,450

Subtract $400 (retail) if ordered with composite stock (disc.).

DAKOTA 76 AFRICAN GRADE - .404 Jeffery, .416 Dakota, .416 Rigby, or .450 Dakota cal., 4 shot mag., select wood with cross bolts in the stock, other features similar to Safari Grade Model, 24 in. barrel, "R" prefix on serial number, 9.5 lbs. New 1989.

	100%	98%	95%	90%	80%	70%	60%
MSR $5,795	$5,100	$4,300	$3,600	$3,250	$2,850	$2,400	$1,995

DAKOTA 76 ALPINE GRADE - .22-250 Rem., .243 Win., 6mm Rem., .250-3000 Savage, 7mm-08 Rem., .308 Win., or .358 Win. cal., short action variation of the Classic Grade, 21 or 23 in. barrel, lighter weight model featuring a blind 4 shot mag., checkered X English walnut slimmer stock and barrel, serial numbered with a "K" prefix, 6.5 lbs. Mfg. 1989-92.

	98%	95%	90%	80%	70%	60%
	$1,850	$1,495	$1,300	$1,075	$925	$800	$700

Last MSR was $1,995.

Other calibers were available on a special order basis.

DAKOTA LONGBOW TACTICAL E.R. (T-76) - .300 Dakota Mag., .330 Dakota Mag., or .338 Lapua Mag. cal., 28 in. stainless barrel, tactical designed for long range, black synthetic stock with adj. comb, includes Picatinny optical rail, Model 70 style trigger, matte finish metal, controlled round feeding, includes deployment kit, 13.7 lbs. New 1997.

	100%	98%	95%	90%	80%	70%	60%
MSR $4,500	$4,050	$3,475	$2,900	$2,500	$2,050	$1,675	$1,375

DAKOTA MODEL 97 LIGHTWEIGHT HUNTER - available in most popular cals. between .22-250 Rem. and .308 Win., features fiberglass stock with black recoil pad, right hand only, 6 lbs. Mfg. 1998-2004.

	98%	95%	90%	80%	70%	60%
	$1,925	$1,625	$1,250	$995	$875	$750	$650

Last MSR was $2,195.

Add $300 for Wood Hunter 97 (includes semi-fancy wood and blind mag.).

* *Dakota Model 97 Deluxe Hunter* - available in short or long action, matte blue finish, checkered AAA claro stock with cheekpiece, controlled round feed, three position safety, cloverleaf tang, 24 or 26 in. precision match chromolly blue or stainless barrel, right or left hand.

	100%	98%	95%	90%	80%	70%	60%
MSR $3,295	$2,995	$2,500	$2,150	$1,775	$1,500	$1,250	$1,000

Add $200 for stainless barrel.

* *Dakota Model 97 All Weather Outfitter* - available in short or long action, matte blue finish, precision sand-colored composite stock, aluminum pillar bedding, controlled round feed, three position safety, cloverleaf tang, 24 or 26 in. precision match chromolly stainless barrel, right or left hand. New 2005.

	100%	98%	95%	90%	80%	70%	60%
MSR $2,995	$2,650	$2,300	$1,900	$1,625	$1,375	$1,100	$995

DAKOTA MODEL 97 LONG RANGE HUNTER - available in 13 popular cals. between .25-06 Rem. and .375 Dakota Mag., composite black H-S Precision stock, 24 or 26 in. barrel, adj. match trigger, Model 76 ejector system, approx. 7.7 lbs. New 1997.

	100%	98%	95%	90%	80%	70%	60%
MSR $2,495	$2,175	$1,825	$1,475	$1,150	$975	$850	$750

Add $300 for Wood Hunter 97 (includes semi-fancy wood and blind mag., disc. 2004).

Add $800 for Deluxe Hunter 97 (includes semi-fancy wood and point panel checkering with floorplate, disc. 2004).

GRADING - PPGS™	100%	98%	95%	90%	80%	70%	60%

DAKOTA CLASSIC PREDATOR - various cals., special select checkered claro walnut sporter style stock with cheekpiece, 22 in. match grade stainless steel barrel, swivel studs. New 2005.

| | MSR $2,695 | $2,325 | $1,900 | $1,450 | $1,125 | $950 | $775 | $650 |

✱ Dakota Serious Predator - similar to Classic Predator, except has varmint type stock with semi-beavertail forend.

| | MSR $2,495 | $2,175 | $1,825 | $1,475 | $1,150 | $975 | $850 | $750 |

✱ Dakota All-Weather Predator - similar to Serious Predator, except has precision composite varmint stype stock with semi-beavertail forend.

| | MSR $1,995 | $1,800 | $1,600 | $1,275 | $1,000 | $875 | $725 | $625 |

RIFLES: SxS

DOUBLE RIFLE - .470 NE, .500 NE, and most rimmed cals., round boxlock action similar to Dakota shotgun, 25 in. chopper lump barrels, selective ejectors, supplied with Americase, mfg. in conjunction with Ferlib. New 2001.

| | MSR POR | N/A | $19,250 | $16,750 | $13,500 | $11,250 | $9,250 | $7,850 |

RIFLES: SINGLE SHOT

DAKOTA MODEL 10 - available in most rimmed and rimless commercially loaded standard and Mag. cals., standard or enlarged Magnum (new 1994) action, 23 in. round barrel, top tang safety, deluxe checkered XX English walnut stock and forearm, 6 lbs. New 1990.

| | MSR $4,495 | $3,925 | $3,350 | $2,800 | $2,450 | $1,800 | $1,450 | $1,225 |

DAKOTA MODEL 97 VARMINT HUNTER - various varmint cals., rounded short action, 24 in. chrome-moly barrel, adj. trigger, black fiberglass stock standard, right-hand only, approx. 8 lbs. New 1998.

| | | $1,600 | $1,375 | $1,100 | $950 | $750 | $650 | $550 |

Last MSR was $1,795.

Add $700 for Wood Varmint Hunter 97 (includes semi-fancy wood and blind mag.).
Add $1,200 for Deluxe Varmint Hunter 97 (includes semi-fancy wood and point panel checkering with floorplate).

LITTLE SHARPS RIFLE - various cals. between .22 LR and .38-55 WCF, features scaled-down frame for smaller cals. (20% smaller than original Sharps), 26 in. octagon barrel, approx. 8 lbs. New 1998.

| | MSR $3,500 | $3,150 | $2,875 | $2,600 | $2,250 | $1,850 | $1,550 | $1,275 |

Add $100+ for English walnut wood upgrade.
Add $250 for set trigger.

SHOTGUNS: SxS

CLASSIC GRADE - 20 ga. only, case colored round boxlock action, 27 in. barrels with fixed chokes, DTs, straight grip checkered English walnut stock and splinter forearm, no engraving, 6 lbs. Mfg. 1996-98.

| | | $7,450 | $6,750 | $6,000 | $5,400 | $4,800 | $4,200 | $3,450 |

Last MSR was $7,950.

PREMIER GRADE - 20, 28 ga. (new 2000), or .410 bore (new 2000), similar to Dakota Classic Field Grade, 27 in. barrels, exhibition grade English walnut, French grey metal finish, 50% engraving coverage, straight grip, splinter forend, DT, hand-rubbed oil finish stock, game rib with gold bead, ejectors, choice of chokes. Mfg. in conjunction with Ferlib.

| | MSR $13,950 | $13,950 | $10,250 | $8,300 | $6,950 | $5,650 | $4,850 | $4,000 |

Add 10% for 28 ga. or .410 bore.

GRADING - PPGS™	100%	98%	95%	90%	80%	70%	60%

DAKOTA AMERICAN LEGEND - 20, 28 ga., or .410 bore, fully scroll-engraved coin finish round boxlock action with gold inlays, French grey metal finish, special select English walnut mfg. to customer dimensions, 27 in. barrels with game rib and gold bead, straight grip, DT, round action, ejectors, choice of chokes, oak and leather trunk case, 6 lbs. New 1996.

MSR $18,000	$16,000	$13,000	$11,000	$9,250	$7,500	$6,250	$5,000

Add 10% for 28 ga. or .410 bore.

Only 100 guns are scheduled to be mfg. Also offered in a 12 ga. and .410 bore/28 ga. set.

DAKOTA CLASSIC FIELD GRADE KNOCKABOUT - 12, 16, 20, 24 (new 2005), 28, 32 (new 2005) ga., or .410 bore, Anson & Deeley boxlock action, monobloc (12, 20, or 28 ga.) or chopper lump (16 ga. or .410 bore only) 28 or 30 in. barrels, ejectors, DT, custom dimensions, checkered Turkish walnut stock and splinter forearm with oil finish, includes scroll and border engraving. New 2004.

MSR $4,500	$4,100	$3,625	$3,100	$2,600	$2,200	$1,650	$1,350

Add $600 for 16, 32 ga. or .410 bore.

Add $1,501 for Express Gun with rifled 24.5 in. barrels with quarter rib and folding leaf express sights (12 or 20 ga. only, disc. 2004).

DAKOTA CLASSIC GRADE II - similar to Field Grade, except has extra fancy Turkish walnut and game scene engraving. New 2004.

MSR $5,500	$5,000	$4,500	$3,950	$3,500	$3,000	$2,550	$2,200

Add $700 for 16, 32 ga. or .410 bore.

Add $1,501 for Express Gun with rifled 24.5 in. barrels with quarter rib and folding leaf express sights (12 or 20 ga. only, disc. 2004).

DAKOTA CLASSIC GRADE III - similar to Grade II, except has XXX Turkish walnut and scroll and gold game scene engraving. New 2004.

MSR $6,500	$5,950	$5,450	$4,750	$4,150	$3,500	$3,000	$2,500

Add $800 for 16, 32 ga. or .410 bore.

Add $1,501 for Express Gun with rifled 24.5 in. barrels with quarter rib and folding leaf express sights (12 or 20 ga. only, disc. 2004).

DAKOTA SINGLE ACTION REVOLVERS

Dakota revolvers are currently manufactured in Italy by Uberti, and imported and distributed by E.M.F. Co., Inc. located in Santa Ana, CA. Dealer direct sales only.

Other firearms imported by E.M.F. Co., Inc. will be found in the E section of this book.

REVOLVERS: REPRODUCTIONS

Until 2000, most Dakota SAAs were manufactured by Armi San Marco. Beginning 2001, all current SAAs are manufactured by Uberti and Pietta.

Add $105 for combo cylinder on the model listed below (.45 ACP cal. only on Remingtons, .44-40 WCF, .44 Spl., or .45 ACP on Peacemaker SAAs).

OLD MODEL SAA - .22 LR, .32-20 WCF, .357 Mag., .38-40 WCF, .44 Spl., .44-40 WCF, or .45 LC cal., copy of the Colt SAA, 4 5/8, 5 1/2, or 7 1/2 in. barrels, blue finish, case hardened frame, 1-piece walnut grips, solid brass backstrap and trigger guard. Importation disc. 1991.

$325	$250	$200	$175	$150	$135	$120

Last MSR was $600.

Add $100 for nickel finish (disc.).

Add $110 for convertible cylinders.

GRADING - PPGS™	100%	98%	95%	90%	80%	70%	60%

✳ *Engraved Old Model* - .32-20 WCF, .357 Mag., .38-40 WCF, .44-40 WCF, or .45 cal., 4 3/4, 5 1/2, or 7 1/2 in. barrel. Disc. 1993, reintroduced 1996, disc. 1998.

	$695	$500	$425	$350	$325	$300	$275

Last MSR was $840.

Add $160 for nickel finish (disc).

✳ *Cattlebrand Engraved* - .44-40 WCF or .45 LC cal., 5 1/2, or 7 1/2 in. barrel, patterned after the famous Colt Cattlebrand variation (features various cattlebrands engraved on the barrel, frame and cylinder). Imported 1992-93, reintroduced 1996, disc. 1998.

	$695	$500	$425	$350	$325	$300	$275

Last MSR was $840.

Add $140 for silver-plating.

NEW DAKOTA SAA - .357 Mag., .44-40 WCF, or .45 LC cal., features forged steel frame, black nickel backstrap and trigger guard, 4 (.45 LC cal. with standard grips), 4 3/4, 5 1/2, or 7 1/2 in. barrel, choice of case hardened or nickel frame, one piece walnut grips, original Colt type hammer (without transfer bar safety). Imported 1991-2004.

	$335	$290	$255	$215	$175	$150	$135

Last MSR was $375.

Add $85 for combo. cylinder (disc. 2002).
Add $135 for satin nickel (disc.) or $175 for bright satin nickel finish.

✳ *Sheriff Model* - cals. similar to New Model, 3 1/2 in. barrel. Imported 1997-99.

	$340	$285	$230	$175	$150	$135	$120

Last MSR was $435.

DAKOTA PREMIER SAA - .45 LC cal., black powder frame, initial mfg. was with 4 5/8 or 5 1/2 in. barrel, set screw cylinder pin release, steel backstrap and trigger guard, one-piece grips. This model was the predecessor to the New Hartford Model.

	$375	$295	$250	$190	$170	$160	$150

Last MSR was $520.

HARTFORD 1873 SAA (NEW OR OLD STYLE FRAME) - .22 LR (disc. 1992), .32-20 WCF, .357 Mag., .38-40 WCF, .44-40 WCF, .44 Spl., or .45 LC cal., features forged steel frame, backstrap, and trigger guard, exact reproduction of Colt's 1st or 2nd generation SAA, choice of black powder (with base pin frame set screw) or 2nd generation (push button cylinder pin release) frame, case hardened frame, original Colt markings, 4 (.45 LC cal. with standard grips), 4 3/4, 5 1/2, or 7 1/2 in. barrel. Importation began 1991.

MSR $410	$365	$335	$300	$270	$240	$210	$180

Add $135 for satin nickel (disc.) or $175 for bright satin nickel finish.
Add $105 for combo cylinder (.45 ACP cal. only).

✳ *Old West (Antique) Finish* - .45 LC cal. only, black powder frame, finish has been aged for older appearance. Mfg. 2001-2003, reintroduced 2005.

MSR $430	$375	$325	$265	$230	$185	$155	$125

✳ *Pinkerton Model* - .357 Mag., .38-40 WCF (disc. 1999), or .45 LC cal., birdshead grips, 4 or 4 3/4 in. barrel. New 1994.

MSR $415	$365	$335	$300	$270	$240	$210	$180

✳ *Deputy Model* - .45 LC cal., 3 1/2 (new 2003) or 4 (disc. 2000) in. barrel with full length ejector shroud, standard SAA grips. Imported 2000, reimported 2003.

	$415	$335	$300	$265	$225	$175	$150

Last MSR was $480.

GRADING - PPGS™	100%	98%	95%	90%	80%	70%	60%

* *Express Model* - .45 LC cal., features "Lightning" grips, 4 or 4 3/4 in. barrel, New Model. Imported 1999-2000.

	$340	$300	$265	$225	$175	$150	$125

Last MSR was $375.

* *Cavalry Model* - .45 LC cal., 7 1/2 in. barrel, faithful reproduction of the original Colt Cavalry Model, one-piece walnut grips with inspector cartouche, case hardened frame and hammer. Importation began 1991.

MSR $415	$370	$340	$300	$270	$240	$210	$180

* *Artillery Model* - .45 LC cal., similar to Cavalry Model, except has 5 1/2 in. barrel. Importation began 1991.

MSR $415	$370	$340	$300	$270	$240	$210	$180

* *Stallion Model* - .38 Spl. cal., 3 1/2 (bird's head grips only) or 4 3/4 in. (walnut grips only) barrel with ejector rod housing, case colored frame, steel backstrap and trigger guard. Importation began 2005.

MSR $375	$340	$310	$285	$250	$220	$195	$160

Add $25 for 3 1/2 in. barrel with bird's head grips.

* *Texas Sesquicentennial* - .45 LC cal., 4 3/4 in. barrel, 50 mfg. for Texas Sesquicentennial with special engraving, includes numbered belt buckle and presentation case. Disc. 1991.

	$1,200	$925	$725

Original list price was $4,550.

* *Target Model* - .357 Mag., .44-40 WCF, or .45 LC cal., 5 1/2, or 7 1/2 in. barrel, case hardened frame, brass backstrap. Imported 1987-90.

	$325	$240	$185	$150	$140	$130	$120

Last MSR was $500.

* *Buntline Model* - .357 Mag. (disc.), .44-40 WCF (disc.), or .45 LC cal., blue only, 10 (mfg. 1997-2002) or 12 in. barrel. Importation disc. 1990, reintroduced 1997.

MSR $430	$380	$350	$310	$275	$240	$210	$180

Add $175 for bright or satin (disc.) nickel finish, $110 for ultra ivory or stag grips (disc.).

* *Buckhorn Model* - 16 1/4 in. barrel, otherwise similar to Buntline. Importation disc. 1987.

	$295	$250	$180	$170	$160	$150	$140

Last MSR was $495.

HARTFORD PREMIER 1873 SA - .357 Mag., .32-20 WCF, or .45 LC cal., 4 3/4, 5 1/2, or 7 1/2 in. barrel, charcoal bone case colored frame, high polish blue, choice of black Colt style checkered or ultra stag grips, tuned action with light hammer pull. Imported 1999-2004.

	$550	$475	$425	$375	$325	$275	$240

Last MSR was $625.

FRONTIER MARSHAL SA - .357 Mag., .44-40 WCF (disc. 2004), or .45 LC cal., 4 3/4, 5 1/2, or 7 1/2 in. barrel, case colored frame, brass backstrap and triggerguard, blue barrel/cylinder. Importation began 2003.

MSR $360	$330	$295	$270	$240	$210	$180	$160

GREAT WESTERN II CUSTOM 1873 SA - .357 Mag., .44-40 WCF, or .45 LC cal., 4 3/4, 5 1/2, or 7 1/2 in. barrel, four metal finishes include all blue, blue w/case colored frame, bright nickel, or satin nickel, ultra ivory grips, mfg. by Pietta. Importation began 2003.

MSR $625	$550	$475	$425	$375	$325	$275	$240

Add $110 for ultra stag grips or $960-$1,300 for engraving options.

* *Great Western II Californian* - similar to Great Western II, except has standard charcoal case colored frame and blue finish. Importation began 2003.

MSR $435	$385	$350	$315	$280	$250	$215	$180

Add $150 for custom bone case coloring or $175 for bright nickel finish.
Add $110 for ultra ivory or ultra stag fitted grips.

GRADING - PPGS™	100%	98%	95%	90%	80%	70%	60%

SHERIFF'S OLD/NEW MODEL SAA - .32-20 WCF (disc.), .357 Mag. (disc. 2000), .38-40 WCF (disc.), .44 Spl. (disc.), .44-40 WCF (disc. 2000), or .45 LC cal., 3 1/2 in. barrel only. Importation disc. 1991, resumed 1994-2000, again in 2003.

	$415	$335	$300	$265	$225	$175	$150

Last MSR was $480.

U.S. ARMY SAA - variety of cals., premium quality construction. Disc. 1985.

	$300	$205	$180	$165	$155	$145	$135

Last MSR was $395.

✳ **U.S. Army Commemorative** - .45 LC cal., 7 1/2 in. barrel, serial numbered 1-500, blue finish, case hardened frame, steel backstrap and trigger guard, 1-piece walnut grips. Importation disc. 1987.

	$350	$265	$185	$170	$160	$150	$135

Last MSR was $495.

CONVERTIBLE MODEL SAA - available with .22 LR/.22 Mag., .32-20 WCF/.32 H&R Mag., .357 Mag./9mm Para., .44-40 WCF/.44 Spl. cal., or .45 LC/.45 ACP double cylinders. Imported 1986-90.

	$380	$310	$260	$220	$195	$170	$150

Last MSR was $580.

FAST DRAW MODEL SAA - .22 LR, .22 Mag., .32-20 WCF, .32 H&R Mag., .357 Mag., .38-40 WCF, 9mm Para., .44 Spl., .44-40 WCF, .45 ACP, or .45 LC cal., case hardened frame, 4 5/8 in. barrel. Importation disc. 1990.

	$340	$295	$225	$165	$150	$135	$125

Last MSR was $480.

BISLEY MODEL SAA - .22 LR (disc.), .22 Mag.(disc.), .32-20 WCF (disc.), .32 H&R Mag. (disc.), .38-40 WCF, .357 Mag. (disc. 1999), 9mm Para. (disc.), .44 Spl. (disc.), .44-40 WCF, .45 ACP (disc.), or .45 LC (current mfg.) cal., 4 3/4 (disc. 1994, reintroduced 2001-2003 in .44-40 WCF cal. only), 5 1/2, or 7 1/2 in. barrel lengths. Imported 1986-91, reintroduced 1993-disc. 1995, reintroduced 1997.

MSR $435	$385	$350	$315	$280	$250	$215	$180

Add $175 for bright or satin (disc.) nickel finish.
Add $112 for combo. cylinder (.45 ACP - disc.).

✳ **Engraved Bisley** - .32-20 WCF, .38-40 WCF, .357 Mag., .44-40 WCF, or .45 LC cal. (disc. 1990), 4 3/4, 5 1/2, or 7 1/2 in. barrel, action engraved throughout. Imported 1987-91.

	$425	$350	$275	$250	$225	$200	$180

Last MSR was $570.

Add $100 for nickel finish.

1873 FRONTIER MODEL SAA - .22 LR cal., 4 3/4 in. barrel, case colored frame, black nickel backstrap and trigger guard. Mfg. by IAR, imported 1999-2002.

	$275	$250	$225	$175	$150	$135	$120

Last MSR was $315.

Add $125 for bright nickel finish.

REMINGTON 1875 SA ARMY/FRONTIER - .357 Mag., .44-40 WCF (disc. 2003) or .45 LC (disc. 2003) cal., available in either 5 1/2 (Frontier) or 7 1/2 (Army, disc. 2003) in. barrel, blue and case colored metal finishes, walnut grips. Mfg. by A. Uberti.

MSR $435	$385	$335	$275	$230	$200	$180	$160

Add $215 for engraving with custom patina finish.
Add $15 for steel trigger guard (disc.).
Add $160 for bright or satin (disc. 2000) nickel plating.
Add $250 for engraving (disc.).
Add $85 for convertible cylinder (.45 LC/.45 ACP, disc.).

GRADING - PPGS™	100%	98%	95%	90%	80%	70%	60%

REMINGTON MODEL 1890 SA POLICE - .45 LC cal., standard blue or engraved frame with custom patina finish, 5 1/2 in. barrel, lanyard ring in buttstock, blue frame, walnut grips, mfg. by A. Uberti. New 1986.

	MSR $450	$395	$340	$280	$235	$200	$180	$160

Add $210 for laser engraving with custom patina finish.
Add $10 for steel trigger guard (disc.).
Add $160 for bright or satin (disc. 2000) nickel plating.
Add $85 for convertible cylinder (.45 LC/.45 ACP, disc.).
Add $260 for engraving (disc.).

SCHOFIELD MODEL - .45 LC cal., replica of the original S&W Schofield, choice of 3 1/2 (Hideout), 5 (Wells Fargo) or 7 in. (Civilian/Cavalry) barrel, blue finish. Mfg. by Uberti. Imported 1999-2003.

	$575	$500	$450	$415	$385	$360	$340

Last MSR was $625.

DALVAR OF USA

Current importer of recently manufactured Radom pistols located in Henderson, NV. Please refer to the Radom listing in this text.

DALY, CHARLES: PRUSSIAN MFG.

Previous trademark manufactured in Prussia, England, Belgium, and the U.S. circa 1875-pre-WWII.

Charles Daly was a gentleman (not a company) whose goal was to give the U.S. shotgun consumer a European-manufactured gun of similar quality to the premier American shotguns of the same era. Accordingly, he had various European firms fabricate shotguns with American shooting features and preferences. Many "Prussian" Dalys were built by various firms in Suhl, Germany. Importation ceased prior to WWII. These Prussian Charles Dalys utilized the finest materials and best workmanship of their time.

In 1865, Charles Daly was one of two partners who founded the sporting goods business named Schoverling & Daly. They were importers and dealers located in New York City. In 1873, the company reorganized to include a third partner, and the corporate name was changed to Schoverling, Daly & Gates.

Marking the Charles Daly name on firearms began some time around 1875. Daly's name was chosen because it had an appealing sound and would likely influence potential buyers to choose their firearms. Schoverling, Daly & Gates established their lofty reputation by dealing in top-quality merchandise. Because they were known for their high standard of excellence, the Charles Daly brand garnered much esteem.

Schoverling, Daly & Gates made every effort to select only the finest quality firearms for sale in the United States. Initially, manufacturers in Prussia, such as Schiller and Lindner, and later Heym and Sauer of Germany, were selected for their suberbly constructed shotguns. Early manufacturers also included J&W Tolley of England, Newmann of Belgium, and even Lefever Arms of New York.

Schoverling, Daly & Gates changed ownership several times throughout the years. Eventually, the company's primary asset was the Charles Daly trademark. In 1910, Henry Modell bought the company, and controlled it for several years. In the 1920s, he sold out to the Walzer family, owners of Sloan's Sporting Goods of Ridgefield, CT. The Walzers established a branch of Sloan's in New York known as Charles Daly & Company. Sloan's imported quality shotguns from many companies, including Italian gun makers Beretta and Vincenzo Bernardelli, Miroku of Japan, and Garbi of Spain.

GRADING - PPGS™	100%	98%	95%	90%	80%	70%	60%

DRILLINGS

DRILLING MODEL - 12, 16, or 20 gauges and .25-20 WCF, .25-35 WCF, or .30-30 WCF cal., 3 barrel combination gun, extractors, double triggers, engraved action, select walnut, mfg. by both Linder and Sauer. Linder mfg. guns are extremely rare - very few specimens are to be found domestically. Sauer guns were not marked for grade, but rather had three levels of engraving which determined the grade. Most Sauer guns had a tang mounted aperture rear sight and a separate rifle cock and were sidelocks. Disc. 1933.

* *Superior Quality* - borderline engraving only.

	100%	98%	95%	90%	80%	70%	60%
Sauer mfg.	$3,000	$2,600	$2,300	$2,000	$1,700	$1,500	$1,200

* *Diamond Quality* - full scroll engraving.

	100%	98%	95%	90%	80%	70%	60%
Sauer mfg.	$5,500	$4,800	$4,400	$4,000	$3,500	$3,000	$2,200

* *Regent Diamond Quality* - top-of-the-line model featuring full game scene coverage.

	100%	98%	95%	90%	80%	70%	60%
Linder mfg.	$12,000	$11,000	$10,000	$9,000	$7,000	$6,000	$5,000
Sauer mfg.	$8,000	$7,000	$6,700	$6,000	$5,000	$4,000	$3,000

RIFLES

BOLT ACTION GRADE I - .22 Hornet cal., mfg. by F. Jaeger & Co. of Suhl, Germany, 5 shot mag., 24 in. barrel, miniature Mauser bolt action, deluxe walnut. Disc.

100%	98%	95%	90%	80%	70%	60%
$820	$615	$535	$455	$410	$370	$330

SHOTGUNS

In the higher grade Prussian Daly variations, there is quite a bit of difference in their manufacture, including engraving options, levels of wood embellishment, and other extra cost features at the time. H.A. Linder produced approx. 2,500 guns (ser. numbered accordingly), and many of the higher grades show a noticeable difference in the amount of engraving (from minimal to considerable game scene engraving). These guns can be either case colored only or have gold inlaid birds and animals (the number of which can also vary) and barrels can have various levels of engraving on both the breech and muzzle ends. All of these factors have considerable impact on the overall value of a particular specimen. It is estimated that it took three craftsmen one year to produce a single Diamond Regent gun.

COMMANIDER O&U - 12, 16, 20, 28 ga., or .410 bore, Anson & Deeley boxlock action, single or double triggers, ejectors. Mfg. in Belgium circa 1939.

* *Model 100*

100%	98%	95%	90%	80%	70%	60%
$500	$375	$325	$275	$250	$225	$200

Add $100 for single trigger.

* *Model 200* - similar to Model 100, except has deluxe walnut.

100%	98%	95%	90%	80%	70%	60%
$650	$490	$425	$360	$325	$300	$260

Add 10%-30% for 28 ga. and .410 bore.

EMPIRE O&U - 12, 16, or 20 ga., various barrel lengths, Anson & Deeley boxlock, ejectors and double triggers, fine engraving, deluxe walnut. Disc. 1933.

100%	98%	95%	90%	80%	70%	60%
$4,000	$3,400	$2,750	$2,375	$2,000	$1,825	$1,625

DIAMOND O&U - similar to Empire model, only finer workmanship and materials.

100%	98%	95%	90%	80%	70%	60%
$5,000	$4,300	$3,475	$3,000	$2,600	$2,300	$2,000

SUPERIOR SxS - 10, 12, 20, 28 ga., or .410 bore, Anson & Deeley boxlock, various barrel lengths, extractors. Disc. 1933.

100%	98%	95%	90%	80%	70%	60%
$1,050	$790	$690	$580	$525	$475	$420

EMPIRE SxS - similar to Superior, only more engraving and better wood.

	100%	98%	95%	90%	80%	70%	60%
Linder mfg.	$5,000	$4,400	$3,900	$3,500	$2,800	$2,200	$1,500
Sauer mfg.	$4,200	$3,500	$3,100	$2,800	$2,200	$1,800	$1,400

GRADING - PPGS™	100%	98%	95%	90%	80%	70%	60%
DIAMOND SxS - similar to Empire model, only more elaborate and with gold inlays.							
Linder mfg.	$10,000	$9,000	$8,500	$8,000	$7,000	$6,000	$4,500
Sauer mfg.	$7,000	$6,200	$5,500	$5,000	$4,000	$3,000	$2,000

Subtract 20%-25% if without gold inlays.

DIAMOND REGENT SxS - top-of-the-line Prussian side-by-side and with gold inlays.							
Linder mfg.	$16,000	$13,500	$12,000	$11,000	$8,500	$7,000	$5,000
Sauer mfg.	$8,500	$7,700	$7,000	$6,500	$5,000	$4,000	$3,000

EMPIRE SINGLE BARREL TRAP - 12 ga., 30-34 in. barrel, Anson & Deeley boxlock, ejector, vent. rib, finely engraved with select walnut, chopper lump extension, top quality. Disc. 1933.

	100%	98%	95%	90%	80%	70%	60%
Linder mfg.	$3,995	$3,500	$3,100	$2,800	$2,200	$1,800	$1,400
Sauer mfg.	$2,150	$1,675	$1,475	$1,100	$960	$850	$750

SEXTUPLE SINGLE BARREL TRAP - 12 ga., 30-34 in. barrel, six locking bolts, ejector, vent. rib, elaborately engraved and checkered. Regent Diamond Model has better engraving and wood.

✳ *Empire Quality*

	100%	98%	95%	90%	80%	70%	60%
Linder mfg.	$4,600	$4,150	$3,650	$3,100	$2,800	$2,200	$1,800
Sauer mfg.	$2,600	$2,100	$1,700	$1,400	$1,100	$900	$750

✳ *Regent Diamond Quality*

	100%	98%	95%	90%	80%	70%	60%
Linder mfg.	$5,000	$4,400	$3,900	$3,500	$2,800	$2,200	$1,500
Sauer mfg.	$3,300	$2,850	$2,400	$1,950	$1,650	$1,350	$995

DALY, CHARLES: JAPANESE MFG.

Previously manufactured by B.C. Miroku, located in Kochi, Japan until 1976.

SHOTGUNS: O/U

In the early sixties, C. Daly guns were manufactured by the firm of B.C. Miroku in Kochi, Japan. This Japanese gun manufacturing company has produced guns for many companies, Browning being the biggest current customer. Miroku guns are high quality with excellent fit and finish. Many of them are highly engraved and are fine examples of the gunmaker's art. Charles Daly Miroku Guns are becoming quite collectible in some areas (smaller gauges with open chokes). Their production ceased in 1976.

O/U MODELS - 12, 20, 28 ga., or .410 bore, 26, 28, or 30 in. vent. rib barrels, various chokes, boxlock, auto ejectors, SST, select walnut checkered pistol grip stock, Superior and Diamond Grade Trap have Monte Carlo stocks, the grades differ in amount of engraving and wood. Mfg. 1963-1976 by Miroku.

Approx. 1,000 28 ga. Lightweight guns were manufactured. All 28 ga. Lightweights (approx. observed ser. range 230020-230998) have barrel spacing 3/4 in. center to center, while the normal 28 ga. has a measurement of 7/8 in. After the Charles Daly line of O/Us were mechanically redesigned, both the 28 ga. and .410 bore were only made on the new 20 ga. frame. To date, no one has observed a .410 bore Lightweight Charles Daly.

Add 20% for 20 ga. on models listed below.
Add 50% for 28 ga. on models listed below.
Add 60% for .410 bore on models listed below.
Add 200% for original 28 ga. Lightweight models in 98%+ condition (rare).

✳ *Field Grade* - 12 or 20 ga., light engraving.

	100%	98%	95%	90%	80%	70%	60%
	$750	$650	$595	$550	$475	$400	$350

✳ *Venture Grade* - all gauges, moderate engraving.

	100%	98%	95%	90%	80%	70%	60%
	$700	$600	$550	$500	$450	$400	$350

✳ *Venture Skeet* - 26 in. barrels choked skeet and skeet.

	100%	98%	95%	90%	80%	70%	60%
	$725	$625	$575	$525	$475	$425	$375

GRADING - PPGS™	100%	98%	95%	90%	80%	70%	60%

✳ **Venture Trap** - 30 in. imp. mod. and full.

	100%	98%	95%	90%	80%	70%	60%
	$650	$550	$500	$475	$425	$375	$350

✳ **Superior Grade** - all gauges, select checkered walnut stock with round knob, scroll engraving similar to Grade I Browning Superposed.

	$950	$850	$750	$700	$650	$600	$550

✳ **Superior Trap**

	$850	$675	$575	$550	$500	$440	$390

This model had an optional selective ejection system enabling the shooter to deactivate the ejectors.

✳ **Diamond Grade** - all gauges, extensive engraving with better quality wood.

	$1,550	$1,275	$1,100	$995	$895	$775	$700

✳ **Diamond Grade Skeet**

	$1,600	$1,325	$1,125	$1,000	$900	$775	$700

✳ **Diamond Grade Trap**

	$1,200	$995	$850	$775	$700	$625	$550

✳ **Wide Rib Diamond Grade Flattop Trap**

	$1,200	$995	$850	$775	$700	$625	$550

✳ **Diamond Regent Grade** - mostly 12 ga., extensive frame engraving with gold inlays, rare.

	$3,150	$2,750	$2,250	$1,950	$1,750	$1,500	$1,250

SHOTGUNS: SxS

EMPIRE SHOTGUN - 12, 16, or 20 ga., 26, 28, or 30 in. barrels, various chokes, boxlock, extractors, single trigger, checkered pistol grip stock. Mfg. 1968-71.

	$545	$495	$470	$415	$360	$305	$250
Vent. rib	$595	$535	$500	$450	$400	$350	$300

Add 25% for 20 ga.

MODEL 500 - 20 ga., raised rib, DT, extractors.

	$350	$315	$285	$260	$230	$210	$195

1974 WILDLIFE COMMEMORATIVE - duck scene engraved, Diamond Grade, Trap, or Skeet, limited to 500 guns. Mfg. 1974 only.

	$1,800	$1,625	$1,425	$1,250	$995	$875	$775

SHOTGUNS: SINGLE BARREL, TRAP

SUPERIOR GRADE SINGLE BARREL TRAP - 12 ga., 32 or 34 in. vent. rib, full choke barrel, auto ejector, Monte Carlo stock with recoil pad. Mfg. 1968-76.

	$600	$550	$525	$495	$440	$385	$330

DALY, CHARLES: 1976 TO PRESENT

Currently manufactured trademark imported since late 1996 by KBI, Inc. located in Harrisburg, PA. Previously imported by Outdoor Sports Headquarters, Inc. located in Dayton, OH until 1995.

In 1976, Sloan's Sporting Goods sold the Daly division to Outdoor Sports Headquarters, Inc., a sporting goods wholesaler located in Dayton, OH. OSHI continued the importation of high-grade Daly shotguns, primarily from Italy and Spain. By the mid-1980s, the Charles Daly brand was transformed into a broad consumer line of excellent firearms and hunting accessories.

In 1996, OSHI was sold to Jerry's Sports Center, Inc. of Forest City, PA, a major wholesaler of firearms and hunting supplies. Within a few months of Jerry's acquisition of OSHI, K.B.I., Inc. of Harrisburg, PA, purchased the Charles Daly trademark from JSC. As it turned out,

GRADING - PPGS™	100%	98%	95%	90%	80%	70%	60%

Michael Kassnar, president of K.B.I., Inc., had produced almost all of the Charles Daly products for OSHI from 1976-1985 in his capacity of president of Kassnar Imports, Inc. K.B.I., Inc. resurrected the complete line of O/U and SxS shotguns in early 1997.

In 1998, the line expanded to include rimfire rifles and the first pistol produced under the Daly name, a Model 1911-A1 in .45 ACP cal. In 1999, semi-auto and slide action shotguns were also reintroduced. In 2000, the additions included 3 1/2 in. slide actions and semi-autos, Country Squire .410 bore shotguns, bolt action centerfire rifles, and the DDA 10-45, the first double action pistol produced under the Charles Daly name.

COMBINATION GUNS

SUPERIOR COMBINATION MODEL - 12 ga. (multi-chokes became standard in 2001) over choice of .22 Hornet, .22-250 Rem. (disc. 1998), .223 Rem., .243 Win. (disc. 1998), .270 Win. (disc. 1998), .30-06, or .308 Win. (disc. 1998) cal., boxlock action with dovetailed receiver (accepts scope mounts and iron sights), 23.5 in. barrels with iron sights, approx. 7 5/8 lbs. Importation began 1997.

MSR $1,479	$1,260	$1,000	$825	$700	$575	$475	$375

EMPIRE COMBINATION MODEL - 12 ga. (multi-chokes became standard in 2001) over choice of .22 Hornet, .22-250 Rem. (disc. 1998), .223 Rem., .243 Win. (disc. 1998), .270 Win. (disc. 1998), .30-06, or .308 Win. (disc. 1998) cal., boxlock action, 23.5 in. barrels, engraved with choice checkered walnut stock and forearm. Importation began 1997.

MSR $2,189	$1,800	$1,525	$1,225	$1,000	$850	$725	$600

PISTOLS: SEMI-AUTO

During 2001, the nomenclature on these 1911 models was changed to include a new "E" prefix. The new "E" stands for enhanced, and features include extended high-rise beavertail grip safety, combat trigger, combat hammer, beveled magwell, flared and lowered ejection port, dovetailed front and low profile rear sights, and hand checkered double diamond grips.

GOVERNMENT 1911-A1 FIELD EFS/FS - .38 Super (new 2005), .40 S&W (new 2005), .45 ACP cal., steel frame, single action, skeletonized combat hammer and trigger, ambidextrous safety, 8 or 10 shot mag., extended slide release and beavertail grip safety, oversized and lowered ejection port, 5 in. barrel with solid barrel bushing, matte blue (Field FS), stainless slide/blue frame (Superior FS, mfg. 1999-2002), or all stainless (Empire EFS, new 1999) finish, includes two 8 or 10 shot mags. and lockable carrying case. New 1998.

MSR $529	$435	$375	$350	$325	$300	$280	$260

Add $50 for Superior EFS Model (disc. 2002).

Add $199 for .22 LR conversion kit with adj. sight (disc. 1999).

＊ Stainless Empire EFS - similar to Field FS, except is stainless steel.

MSR $629	$500	$425	$375

GOVERNMENT 1911-A1 TARGET EFST/FST - similar to Government 1911-A1 Field FS, except has target sights. Importation began 2000.

MSR $619	$525	$425	$375	$350	$325	$300	$275

Add $40 for Superior FST Model (disc. 2000).

Add $65 for Empire FST Model (disc. 2000).

＊ Stainless Empire EFST - .45 ACP cal. only, similar to Target EFST, except is stainless steel. New 2001.

MSR $724	$590	$485	$380

＊ Field EFSTC - .45 ACP cal., 5 3/4 in. compensated barrel with 3 ports, blue or stainless steel, 44.5 oz. Limited importation 2001 only.

	$550	$450	$395	$360	$330	$300	$265

Last MSR was $679.

Add $100 for stainless steel (Empire EFSTC).

GRADING - PPGS™	100%	98%	95%	90%	80%	70%	60%

EMPIRE ECMT CUSTOM MATCH - .45 ACP cal., 5 in. barrel, match features, high polish stainless steel, 38.5 oz. Importation began 2001.

MSR $799	$665	$585	$480				

COMMANDER 1911-A1 FIELD EMS/MS - similar to Government 1911-A1, except has 4 in. Commander barrel and features. Importation began 1999.

MSR $529	$435	$375	$350	$325	$300	$280	$260

Add $40 for Superior MS Model (includes stainless steel slide and blue frame, disc. 2000).

* *Stainless Empire EMS* - .45 ACP cal. only, similar to Field EMS/MS, except is stainless steel. New 1999.

MSR $629	$500	$425	$375				

* *Field EMSCC* - carry comp., similar to Commander Field EMS, except has single port compensator, blue or stainless. Imported 2001 only.

	$540	$435	$395	$360	$325	$295	$260

Last MSR was $619.

OFFICER'S 1911-A1 FIELD ECS/CS - similar to Commander, except has 3.5 in. barrel and Officer's Model features. Importation began 1999.

MSR $529	$435	$375	$350	$325	$300	$280	$260

Add $40 for Superior CS Model (includes stainless steel slide and blue frame, disc. 2000).

* *Stainless Empire ECS* - .45 ACP cal. only, similar to Field ECS/CS, except is stainless steel. New 1999.

MSR $629	$500	$425	$375				

* *Field ECSCC* - carry comp., similar to Officer's Field ECS, except has single port compensator, blue or stainless. Importation began 2001.

	$540	$435	$395	$360	$325	$295	$260

Last MSR was $619.

Add $100 for Empire ECS Model (full stainless steel construction).

COMMANDER 1911-A1 POLYMER FRAME PC - .45 ACP only, features polymer frame, 4 in. barrel, available in matte blue (Field PC) or stainless slide/blue frame (Superior PC). Imported 1999-2000.

	$460	$400	$360	$330	$295	$280	$260

Last MSR was $530.

Add $25 for Superior PC Model (includes stainless steel slide and blue frame).

GOVERNMENT 1911-A2 FIELD EFS HC - .40 S&W or .45 ACP cal., 5 in. barrel, similar to Government 1911 A-1 Field EFS, 13 (.45 ACP cal.), or 15 (.40 S&W cal.) shot mag., blue finish only. Importation began 2005.

MSR $699	$575	$475	$400	$350	$325	$300	$275

Add $90 for Target Model (.45 ACP cal. only, new 2005).

MODEL DDA 10-45 FS (DOUBLE ACTION) - .40 S&W (disc. 2001) or .45 ACP cal., single or double action, 4 3/8 in. barrel, polymer frame with checkering, double stacked 10 shot mag. with interchangeable base plate (allowing for extra grip length), matte black or two-tone (new 2001) finish, 28 1/2 oz. Imported 2000-2002.

	$450	$395	$360	$325	$300	$280	$260

Last MSR was $519.

Add $40 for two-tone finish.

* *Model DDA 10-45 CS* - similar to Model DDA 10-45 FS, except has 3 5/8 in. barrel, 26 oz. Imported 2000-2002.

	$450	$395	$360	$325	$300	$280	$260

Last MSR was $519.

Add approx. $10 for colored frame (yellow, OD green, or fuschia, new 2001) and compensated barrel.

GRADING - PPGS™	100%	98%	95%	90%	80%	70%	60%

FIELD HP HI-POWER - 9mm Para cal., single action, 3 5/8 in. barrel, patterned after the Browning Hi-Power, blue or hard chrome (new 2005) finish, 10 or 13 shot mag., mfg. in U.S. Mfg. beginning late 2003.

MSR $549	$460	$400	$365	$325	$295	$275	$250

Add $120 for hard chrome finish.

M-5 STANDARD (BUL 1911 GOVERNMENT) - .40 S&W or .45 ACP cal., single action, 5 in. barrel, polymer double column frame, steel slide, aluminum speed trigger, checkered front and rear grip straps, blue or chrome finished slide, 10, 14 (.45 ACP cal.), or 17 (.40 S&W cal.) shot staggered mag., 31-33 oz. Mfg. by Bul Transmark in Israel. Importation began 2004.

MSR $719	$590	$485	$410	$355	$325	$300	$275

❋ *M-5 Standard Commander* - similar to M-5 Standard, except has 4 1/3 in. barrel, 29-30 oz. Mfg. by Bul Transmark in Israel. Importation began 2004.

MSR $719	$590	$485	$410	$355	$325	$300	$275

❋ *M-5 Ultra-X* - 9mm Para. or .45 ACP cal., 10 or 12 (9mm Para. cal. only) shot mag., compact variation with 3.15 in. barrel. Importation began 2005.

MSR $719	$590	$485	$410	$355	$325	$300	$275

M-5 IPSC - .40 S&W, or .45 ACP cal., configured for IPSC competition, 5 in. barrel, with custom slide to frame fit and match grade barrel bushing. Mfg. by Bul Transmark in Israel. Importation began 2004.

MSR $1,499	$1,275	$995	$850	$700	$625	$550	$475

ZDA MODEL - 9mm Para. or .40 S&W cal., DA, 4 1/8 in. barrel, 12 (.40 S&W cal.) or 15 (9mm Para. cal.) shot mag., mfg. by Zastava. Importation began 2005.

MSR $589	$490	$425	$385	$340	$300	$275	$250

REVOLVERS: SA

MODEL 1873 CLASSIC - .357 Mag. or .45 LC cal., 4.75, 5.5 or 7.5 in. barrel, case hardened frame, blue finish, choice of brass or steel backstrap, and trigger guard. Importation began 2004.

MSR $449	$375	$350	$300	$275	$250	$225	$200

Add $30 for steel backstrap and trigger guard.

❋ *Model 1873 Stainless Classic* - similar to Model 1873, except has matte finish, stainless construction with steel backstrap and trigger guard. Importation began 2004.

MSR $659	$575	$525	$450	$400	$350	$300	$250

RIFLES: BOLT ACTION

K.B.I. also imports a wide variety of Mauser and Mini-Mauser actions. MSRs range between $319-$659.

MAUSER 98 - various cals., Mauser 98 action, 22 (new 2001) or 23 (disc.) in. barrel, 3-5 shot, hinged floorplate, fiberglass/graphite composite (Field Grade) or checkered European walnut (Superior Grade) stock, open sights, drilled and tapped receiver, side safety. Importation began 1998, and resumed during 2001.

❋ *Field Grade* - features fiberglass/graphite composite stock, matte blue finish or matte stainless steel.

MSR $459	$395	$350	$315	$285	$255	$225	$200

Add $90 for stainless steel.
Add $30 for current Mag. cals. (.330 Win. Mag. or 7mm Rem. Mag.).
Add 50% for .375 H&H or .458 Win. Mag. cal. (disc.).

GRADING - PPGS™	100%	98%	95%	90%	80%	70%	60%

✳ *Superior Grade* - features checkered European walnut stock and high polish blue finish.

MSR $599	$525	$450	$395	$350	$325	$295	$275

Add $190 for .375 H&H or .458 Win. Mag. cal.

Add $30 for current Mag. cals. (.300 Win. Mag. or 7mm Rem. Mag.).

Add $30 for left-hand action (.30-06 cal. only).

MINI-MAUSER 98 - .22 Hornet, .22-250 Rem. (disc.), .223 Rem., or 7.62x39mm cal., similar to Mauser 98, except has 18.1 (new 2001) or 19 1/4 (disc.) in. barrel, 5 shot.

✳ *Field Grade* - features fiberglass/graphite composite stock.

	$345	$295	$265	$230	$200	$185	$170

Last MSR was $399.

✳ *Superior Grade* - features checkered European walnut stock.

MSR $599	$525	$450	$395	$350	$325	$295	$275

Add $30 for left-hand action (.223 Rem. cal. only).

FIELD HUNTER - .22 Hornet, .223 Rem., .243 Win., .270 Win., .30-06, .308 Win., .300 Rem. Ultra Mag., .330 Win. Mag., .338 Win. Mag., or 7mm Rem. Mag. cal., 22 or 24 (Mag. cals. only) barrel w/o sights, detachable mag. on short action cals. (.22 Hornet, .223 Rem., or .243 Win.), high polish bluing, checkered walnut stock and forend, right- or left-hand action, gold trigger, approx. 7 1/3 lbs. Imported 2000 only.

	$475	$425	$375	$350	$325	$280	$240

Last MSR was $565.

Add approx. $31 for left-hand action (.223 Rem., .243 Win., .270 Win., .30-06, .300 Rem. Ultra Mag., or 7mm Rem. Mag.).

✳ *Field Hunter Stainless/Polymer* - similar to Field Hunter, except has stainless steel barrel and action, black polymer stock with checkering. Imported 2000 only.

	$495	$450	$395

Last MSR was $580.

FIELD GRADE .22 LR CAL. - .22 LR cal., 16 1/4 (True Youth Standard), 17 1/2 (Youth), or 22 5/8 (Standard) in. barrel, single shot (True Youth Standard) or 6 shot mag., all steel shrouded action, grooved receiver, walnut finished hardwood stock. Imported 1998-2002.

	$110	$95	$80	$70	$60	$55	$50

Last MSR was $135.

Add $14 for repeater Youth Model (6 shot, new 2000).

Add $20 for single shot True Youth Standard with shortened dimensions.

✳ *Field Grade Polymer/Hardwood* - similar to Field Grade, except has stainless steel action and barrel with black polymer (disc.) or hardwood (new 2001) checkered stock, 6 1/3 lbs. Imported 2000-2002.

	$120	$100	$85	$70	$60	$55	$50

Last MSR was $149.

✳ *Superior Grade* - .22 LR (disc. 2001), .22 Mag., or .22 Hornet cal., 22 5/8 in. barrel, 5 or 6 shot mag., features checkered walnut finished stock with adj. rear sight. Imported 1998-2002.

	$175	$135	$105	$90	$80	$70	$60

Last MSR was $209.

Add $160 for .22 Hornet cal.

Subtract $20 for .22 LR cal. (disc. 2001).

GRADING - PPGS™	100%	98%	95%	90%	80%	70%	60%

✳ Empire Grade - similar to Superior Grade, except has checkered California walnut stock with rosewood grip and forend caps, high polish bluing and damascened bolt. Imported 1998-2001.

	$290	$260	$230	$215	$195	$180	$170

Last MSR was $349.

Add $20 for .22 Mag. cal.
Add $130 for .22 Hornet cal.

SUPERIOR II RIMFIRE - .17 HMR, .22 LR, or .22 Mag., 22 in. barrel, walnut stock. New 2005.

MSR $259	$215	$185	$165	$135	$120	$110	$100

Add $40 for .22 Mag. or $75 for .17 HMR cal.

RIFLES: O/U

SUPERIOR EXPRESS - .30-06 cal., 23.5 in. barrels with quarter rib and leaf sights, dovetailed receiver for scope mounting, silver finished boxlock receiver, gold SST, checkered walnut stock and forearm, 7.75 lbs. Importation began 2000.

MSR $2,259	$1,900	$1,625	$1,400	$1,225	$1,075	$950	$875

EMPIRE EXPRESS - .30-06, .375 H&H (new 2005), or .416 Rigby (new 2005) cal., 23.5 in. barrels with quarter rib and leaf sights, dovetailed receiver for scope mounting, silver finished boxlock receiver with shoulders, gold SST, checkered European style walnut stock with Bavarian cheekpiece and forearm, 7.75 lbs. Importation began 2000.

MSR $2,949	$2,525	$2,000	$1,675	$1,350	$1,100	$950	$875

Add $710 for .375 H&H or .416 Rigby cal.

RIFLES: SEMI-AUTO

SEMI-AUTO RIFLE - .22 LR cal., steel receiver, 20 3/4 in. barrel with adj. rear sight, 10 shot mag. Mfg. 1998-2002.

✳ Field Grade - features unchecked walnut finished hardwood stock.

	$110	$95	$80	$70	$60	$55	$50

Last MSR was $135.

✳ Field Grade Polymer/Hardwood - similar to Field Grade, except has stainless steel action and barrel with black polymer (disc.) or hardwood checkered stock, 6 1/8 lbs. Mfg. 2000-2002.

	$120	$100	$85				

Last MSR was $149.

✳ Superior Grade - features checkered walnut finished stock. Disc. 2001.

	$175	$130	$100	$90	$80	$70	$60

Last MSR was $209.

✳ Empire Grade - features checkered California walnut stock. Disc. 2001.

	$275	$245	$220	$195	$180	$170	$160

Last MSR was $334.

RIFLES: SINGLE SHOT

FIELD GRADE - .22 Hornet, .223 Rem., .243 Win., or .270 Win. cal., single shot break open action, 22 in. barrel with mount base, drilled and tapped, adj. or no sights, checkered hardwood stock and forearm. Limited importation 2001 only.

	$165	$140	$110	$95	$80	$70	$60

Last MSR was $189.

Add $10 for adj. sights.

This model is also available in a Youth configuration at no extra charge.

GRADING - PPGS™	100%	98%	95%	90%	80%	70%	60%

SHOTGUNS: O/U

Current O/U production is from Italy.

PRESENTATION MODEL - 12 or 20 ga., with choke tubes, Purdey double underlug locking action with decorative engraved sideplates, French walnut, single trigger, ejectors. Disc. 1986.

	100%	98%	95%	90%	80%	70%	60%
	$995	$840	$750	$670	$615	$560	$520

Last MSR was $1,165.

COUNTRY SQUIRE MODEL - .410 bore only, 3 in. chambers, case colored boxlock action, gold DT, 25 1/2 in. vent. barrels with VR and F/F chokes, checkered straight grip stock and Schnabel forearm, approx. 6 lbs. Disc. 2002.

	$640	$575	$525	$475	$425	$375	$350

Last MSR was $715.

FIELD II HUNTER - 12, 16 (new 2001), 20, 28 ga., or .410 bore, similar to DeLuxe Model except has fixed chokes, extractors, machine stock checkering, and blue receiver, 5.5-7 lbs., depending on ga./barrel lengths. New 1989.

MSR $1,029	$850	$675	$575	$475	$375	$315	$285

Add $100 for 28 ga. or .410 bore.

✳ *Field II Hunter with Ejectors* - similar to Field II Hunter, except has ejectors and multi-chokes (not available on 28 ga. or .410 bore), Monte Carlo stock. Importation began 1997.

MSR $1,279	$1,065	$900	$800	$675	$575	$475	$375

✳ *Field II Hunter Ultra-Light* - 12 or 20 ga., alloy frame, 26 in. VR barrels only with fixed IC/M (disc. 2000) or multi-chokes (new 2001), thin forearm, approx. 5.5 lbs. Importation began 1999.

MSR $1,199	$965	$840	$725	$625	$525	$425	$325

DELUXE MODEL - 12, 20, 28 ga. (disc. 1995), or .410 bore (disc. 1995), boxlock with self adj. crossbolt, 26 or 28 in. chrome lined VR barrels with internal choke tubes, SST, ejectors, antique silver finish on receiver, deluxe hand checkered walnut stock and forearm. Imported 1989-96.

	$650	$525	$475	$425	$400	$375	$350

Last MSR was $770.

SPORTING CLAYS MODEL - 12 ga. only, SST, ejectors, silver engraved receiver, checkered walnut stock and forearm, screw-in chokes, 28 (disc.) or 30 (new 1996) in. VR ported barrels. Imported 1995-96.

	$775	$700	$625	$550	$475	$395	$350

Last MSR was $895.

SUPERIOR II - 12 or 20 ga., various chokes, boxlock action, single trigger, ejectors, engraved. Disc. 1988.

	$675	$575	$475	$425	$395	$375	$350

Last MSR was $875.

Add $35 for 12 ga. Mag. (disc. 1987).

FIELD III - 12 or 20 ga., various chokes, boxlock action, single trigger. Disc. 1989.

	$395	$370	$340	$315	$285	$260	$230

Last MSR was $450.

SUPERIOR II HUNTER - 12, 20, 28 ga. (new 1998), or .410 bore, 3 in. chambers (except 28 ga.), boxlock action, ejectors, 26, 28, or 30 in. VR barrels with multi-chokes (except 28 ga. and .410 bore), barrel porting became standard during 2000, select checkered walnut stock and forearm, 6 1/8-7 lbs. Importation began 1997.

MSR $1,519	$1,325	$1,075	$900	$800	$675	$575	$475

Subtract $70 for 28 ga. or .410 bore.

GRADING - PPGS™	100%	98%	95%	90%	80%	70%	60%

* **Superior II Sporting** - 12 or 20 ga. (disc. 1998), 26 (disc. 1998), 28, or 30 (12 ga. only) in. 10mm VR barrels with multi-chokes and ported barrels. Importation began 1997.

MSR $1,659	$1,400	$1,150	$950	$825	$725	$625	$525

* **Superior II Trap** - 12 ga. only, 30 or 32 (disc. 2001) in. VR barrels with choice of fixed chokes or multi-chokes, regular or Monte Carlo stock. Importation began 1997.

MSR $1,699	$1,450	$1,175	$950	$825	$725	$625	$525

Subtract 10% if w/o multi-chokes with Monte Carlo stock.

* **Superior Skeet** - 12 or 20 ga., 26 in. VR barrels with choice of Skeet fixed chokes or multi-chokes, regular or Monte Carlo stock. Imported 1997-98.

		$935	$800	$700	$600	$500	$450	$375

Last MSR was $1,039.

Add $120 for multi-chokes with Monte Carlo stock.

EMPIRE DL HUNTER - 12, 20, 28 ga., or .410 bore, boxlock action, silver receiver with game scene engraving, ejectors, SST, 26 or 28 (12 or 20 ga. only) in. VR barrels with multi-chokes (except 28 ga. and .410 bore). Imported 1997-98.

		$1,025	$875	$750	$650	$550	$475	$395

Last MSR was $1,159.

Add $65 for 28 ga. or $110 for .410 bore.

EMPIRE II EDL HUNTER - similar to Empire DL Hunter, except has engraved sideplates featuring game scenes. New 1998.

MSR $2,029	$1,675	$1,250	$1,000	$875	$775	$675	$575

Subtract $10 for 28 ga. or .410 bore.

* **Empire II Sporting** - 12 or 20 ga. (disc. 1999), 26 (disc. 1999), 28, or 30 (12 ga. only) in. VR barrels with multi-chokes. Importation began 1997.

MSR $2,049	$1,675	$1,250	$1,100	$875	$775	$675	$575

* **Empire II Trap** - 12 ga. only, 30 or 32 (disc. 2000) in. VR barrels with choice of fixed chokes (32 in. barrel only) or multi-chokes, regular (disc. 1998) or Monte Carlo stock. Importation began 1997.

MSR $2,099	$1,700	$1,275	$1,050	$925	$800	$700	$600

Subtract 10% if w/o multi-chokes.

* **Empire II Mono Trap** - features 30 or 32 in. single top barrel, standard or adj. Monte Carlo stock. Importation began 1999.

MSR $3,249	$2,825	$2,400	$2,150	$1,800	$1,425	$1,150	$925

Subtract approx. 20% if w/o adj. Monte Carlo stock.

* **Empire II Trap Combo** - includes mono 32 in. barrel and extra set of 30 in. O/U barrels, standard or adj. Monte Carlo stock. Importation began 1999.

MSR $3,919	$3,500	$3,150	$2,700	$2,250	$1,925	$1,625	$1,375

Subtract approx. 20% if w/o adj. Monte Carlo stock.

* **Empire Skeet** - 12 or 20 ga., 26 in. VR barrels with choice of Skeet fixed chokes or multi-chokes, regular or Monte Carlo stock. Imported 1997-98.

		$1,050	$875	$750	$650	$550	$475	$395

Last MSR was $1,189.

Add $125 for multi-chokes with Monte Carlo stock.

DIAMOND FIELD - 12 or 20 ga. (disc. 1986) Mag., with choke tubes. Same action as Presentation Model without sideplates, engraved, select walnut, single trigger, ejectors. Disc. 1986.

		$695	$600	$550	$510	$460	$420	$380

Last MSR was $895.

GRADING - PPGS™	100%	98%	95%	90%	80%	70%	60%

✳ Diamond Trap or Skeet - 12 ga. only, 26 or 30 in. barrels only. Disc. 1986.

	100%	98%	95%	90%	80%	70%	60%
	$850	$700	$550	$500	$475	$450	$425

Last MSR was $1,050.

Subtract $50 for Skeet Model.

DIAMOND GTX DL HUNTER - 12, 20, 28 ga., or .410 bore, sidelock action, ejectors, SST, elaborate engraving with select checkered walnut stock and forearm, 26, 28 (12 or 20 ga. only), or 30 (12 ga. only) in. VR barrels with multi-chokes (except 28 ga. and .410 bore). Imported 1997 only.

	100%	98%	95%	90%	80%	70%	60%
	$11,250	$9,000	$7,000	$5,700	$4,900	$4,200	$3,750

Last MSR was $12,399.

✳ Diamond GTX EDL Hunter - more elaborate variation of the Diamond GTX DL Hunter. Imported 1997 only.

	100%	98%	95%	90%	80%	70%	60%
	$13,750	$11,250	$9,000	$7,000	$5,700	$4,900	$4,200

Last MSR was $15,999.

DIAMOND GTX SPORTING - 12 or 20 (disc. 1998) ga., boxlock Boss action with light perimeter engraving, 28 or 30 (12 ga. only) in. VR barrels with multi-chokes and porting. Imported 1997-2001.

	100%	98%	95%	90%	80%	70%	60%
	$5,260	$4,750	$4,275	$3,675	$3,150	$2,750	$2,175

Last MSR was $5,849.

DIAMOND GTX TRAP - 12 ga. only, boxlock Boss action with light perimeter engraving, 30 in. VR barrels with choice of fixed (disc. 1999) or multi-chokes with barrel porting, regular or adj. (new 1999) Monte Carlo stock. Imported 1997-2001.

	100%	98%	95%	90%	80%	70%	60%
	$5,865	$4,900	$4,400	$3,825	$3,175	$2,750	$2,175

Last MSR was $6,699.

Subtract 10% w/o fixed chokes.

DIAMOND GTX MONO TRAP - features single top barrel, adj. Monte Carlo stock. Imported 1999-2001.

	100%	98%	95%	90%	80%	70%	60%
	$5,795	$4,850	$4,400	$3,825	$3,150	$2,750	$2,175

Last MSR was $6,619.

✳ Diamond GTX Trap Combo - includes 32 in. mono barrel and extra set of 30 in. O/U barrels, adj. Monte Carlo stock. Imported 1999-2001.

	100%	98%	95%	90%	80%	70%	60%
	$6,775	$5,775	$4,825	$4,325	$3,775	$3,150	$2,750

Last MSR was $7,419.

DIAMOND GTX SKEET - 12 or 20 ga., 26 or 28 (20 ga. only with Monte Carlo stock) in. VR barrels with choice of Skeet fixed chokes or multi-chokes, regular or Monte Carlo stock. Imported 1997-98.

	100%	98%	95%	90%	80%	70%	60%
	$4,700	$4,100	$3,800	$3,400	$2,975	$2,700	$2,100

Last MSR was $5,149.

Add $140 for multi-chokes with Monte Carlo stock.

DIAMOND REGENT GTX DL HUNTER - 12, 20, 28 ga., or .410 bore, sidelock action, ejectors, SST, best quality engraving with premium checkered walnut stock and forearm, 26, 28 (12 or 20 ga. only), or 30 (12 ga. only) in. VR barrels with multi-chokes (except 28 ga. and .410 bore). Imported 1997 only.

	100%	98%	95%	90%	80%	70%	60%
	$19,750	$16,250	$13,750	$11,250	$9,000	$7,000	$5,700

Last MSR was $22,299.

✳ Diamond Regent GTX EDL Hunter - top-of-the-line model incorporating best quality engraving and premium walnut. Imported 1997 only.

	100%	98%	95%	90%	80%	70%	60%
	$23,000	$19,500	$16,000	$13,750	$10,500	$8,750	$7,700

Last MSR was $26,429.

GRADING - PPGS™	100%	98%	95%	90%	80%	70%	60%

SHOTGUNS: SxS

FIELD III - 12 or 20 ga., various chokes, boxlock action, single trigger. Disc.

	$350	$315	$285	$260	$230	$210	$195

COUNTRY SQUIRE MODEL - .28 ga. or .410 bore, 3 in. chambers, case colored boxlock action, gold DT, 26 in. barrels with fixed chokes, checkered stock and splinter forearm, approx. 6 lbs. Disc. 2000.

	$600	$550	$500	$450	$400	$360	$330

Last MSR was $680.

FIELD II HUNTER MODEL - 10 (disc. 2002), 12, 16 (new 2005), 20, 28 ga., or .410 bore, boxlock action, 26, 28, 30 (12 ga. only), or 32 (10 ga. only) in. barrels, fixed (disc. 2000) or multi-chokes (12 or 20 ga. only), 6-7 3/ 8 lbs., or 11 1/4 (10 ga.) lbs. Importation began 1997.

MSR $1,189	$975	$875	$750	$650	$550	$450	$375

Subtract $90 for 16 ga., 28 ga. or .410 bore (extractors only).
Subtract approx. 15% if w/o ejectors and multi-chokes (not available in 28 ga. or .410 bore).

SUPERIOR - 12 or 20 ga., boxlock action, various chokes, single trigger. Disc. 1985.

	$550	$470	$405	$345	$315	$280	$250

Last MSR was $624.

SUPERIOR HUNTER - 12, 20, or 28 (new 1999) ga. or .410 bore (new 2000), 26 or 28 in. barrels with fixed (disc. 2000) or multi-chokes (new 2001, 12 or 20 ga. only), 5 7/8-6 3/4 lbs. Importation began 1997.

MSR $1,659	$1,395	$1,150	$975	$850	$725	$625	$525

Subtract $30 for 28 ga. or .410 bore.

LUXE MODEL - 12 (disc. 1991) or 20 ga., boxlock action, SST, ejectors, 26 in. barrels with choke tubes, checkered pistol grip walnut stock with semi-beavertail forearm, recoil pad. Imported 1990-94.

	$575	$450	$395	$350	$315	$285	$260

Last MSR was $650.

This model was manufactured by Hermanos located in Spain.

EMPIRE HUNTER - 12, 20, or 28 (disc. 1998) ga., 26 or 28 in. barrels with fixed or multi-chokes (new 2001), 6-6 7/8 lbs. Importation began 1997.

MSR $2,119	$1,700	$1,300	$1,050	$925	$825	$700	$600

DIAMOND DL - 12, 20, 28 ga., or .410 bore, case colored sidelock action with 3rd lever fastener, scroll engraving, select checkered walnut stock and splinter forearm, 26 or 28 in. barrels with fixed chokes. Importation began 1997.

	$6,060	$4,950	$4,375	$3,775	$3,200	$2,750	$2,175

Last MSR was $6,999.

DIAMOND REGENT DL - 12, 20, 28 ga., or .410 bore, sidelock action with best quality engraving and premium checkered walnut stock and forearm, 26 or 28 in. barrels with fixed chokes. Imported 1997 only.

	$18,950	$15,750	$13,250	$10,750	$8,900	$6,900	$5,600

Last MSR was $21,659.

SHOTGUNS: SEMI-AUTO

The Charles Daly "Novamatic" shotguns were produced in 1968 by Breda in Italy. The Novamatic series was not imported by Outdoor Sport Headquarters, Inc.

GRADING - PPGS™	100%	98%	95%	90%	80%	70%	60%

NOVAMATIC LIGHTWEIGHT MODEL - 12 ga., 26 or 28 in. barrel, various chokes, available with quick choke interchangeable tubes, checkered pistol grip stock, similar to the Breda shotgun. Mfg. 1968 only.

	$305	$275	$250	$220	$195	$165	$140

Add $25 for vent. rib.

Add $15 for quick choke.

NOVAMATIC SUPER LIGHTWEIGHT - 12 or 20 ga., similar to Lightweight, except approx. 1/2 lb. lighter.

	$330	$305	$275	$250	$220	$195	$165

Add $25 for vent. rib.

Add $15 for quick choke.

NOVAMATIC MAGNUM - 12 or 20 ga. with 3 in. chambers, similar to Lightweight, 28 or 30 in. vent rib barrel, full choke.

	$330	$305	$275	$250	$220	$195	$165

NOVAMATIC TRAP - similar to Lightweight, with 30 in. full vent. rib barrel, Monte Carlo stock.

	$360	$330	$305	$275	$250	$220	$195

CHARLES DALY AUTOMATIC - 12 ga., 2 3/4 or 3 in. chambers, gas operation, alloy frame, pistol grip (high gloss) or English stock, vent. rib, 5 shot mag. Also available as slug gun with iron sights. Invector chokes became standard in 1986. Disc. 1988.

	$320	$275	$235	$205	$190	$170	$150

Last MSR was $365.

Add $15 for oil finished English stock.

MULTI-XII - 12 ga. only, 3 in. chamber, 27 in. VR multichoke barrel, self-adjusting gas operation, deluxe checkered walnut stock with recoil pad and forearm. Imported 1987-88 only.

	$425	$360	$320	$285	$250	$225	$195

Last MSR was $498.

FIELD HUNTER - 12, 20 (new 2002), or 28 (new 2002) ga., 3 in. chamber (12 or 20 ga.), gas operated, aluminum receiver, 22 (Youth or smoothbore slug), 24, 26, 28, or 30 in. VR barrel with multi-chokes, choice of standard wood/black metal or 100% Advantage (disc. 2001), Advantage Timber HD (new 2002), Realtree (disc. 2001), Realtree Hardwoods HD, Advantage Max-4 HD (12 ga. only, new 2004), Advantage Wetlands (mfg. 2001-2003), or Advantage Classic (disc. 2001) camo coverage, synthetic stock and forearm, 6 7/8-7 1/8 lbs. Importation began 1999.

MSR $389	$340	$300	$275	$250	$225	$200	$175

Add $70 for 100% camo coverage.

Add $70 for 28 ga.

Add $100 for left-hand action (12 ga. only).

✴ *Field Hunter Maxi-Mag* - 12 ga. only, 3 1/2 in. chamber, 24, 26 (new 2001), or 28 in. VR barrel with multi-choke, 7mm VR rib, choice of wood/metal or 100% camo coverage similar to Field Hunter, 6 7/8-7 1/8 lbs. Importation began 2000.

MSR $469	$425	$390	$360	$330	$300	$275	$250

Add $70 for 100% camo coverage.

✴ *Field Hunter Maxi-Mag Turkey Hunter* - 12 ga. only, includes 24 in. barrel, Hi/Tri-Viz fiber optic sights and XX full ported turkey choke tube, Advantage Timber or Realtree Hardwoods HD camo treatment, Uncle Mike's camo sling and sling swivels. New 2002.

MSR $609	$545	$465	$395	$350	$300	$275	$250

GRADING - PPGS™	100%	98%	95%	90%	80%	70%	60%

❊ *Field Slug* - 12 ga. only, 22 in. cyl. bore barrel with adj. sights, black synthetic stock and forearm, nickel (disc. 2002) or black chrome finish, adj. open sights. Imported 1999-2003.

	$355	$320	$290	$275	$250	$225	$200

Last MSR was $409.

Add $20 for satin nickel finish (disc. 2002).

Add $40 for fully rifled barrel with adj. sights (new 2002).

SUPERIOR II HUNTER - similar to Field Hunter, except has 20 LPI checkered Turkish walnut stock and forearm, gold highlights and trigger. Importation began 1999.

MSR $539	$465	$415	$360	$330	$295	$275	$250

Add $60 for 28 ga.

Add $100 for left-hand action (12 ga. only).

❊ *Superior II Sporting* - 12 ga. only, similar to Superior Hunter, except has 28 or 30 in. ported 10mm VR barrels. Importation began 1999.

MSR $569	$495	$450	$395	$350	$310	$285	$255

❊ *Superior II Trap* - 12 ga. only, 30 or 32 in. ported barrel with front and mid bead sights. Importation began 1999.

MSR $589	$510	$450	$400	$350	$310	$285	$255

SHOTGUNS: SLIDE ACTION

FIELD HUNTER - 12 or 20 (new 2001) ga., 3 in. chamber, 22 (Youth, 20 ga. only), 24, 26, 28, or 30 in. VR barrel with multi-choke, synthetic stock and forearm, choice of standard wood/metal or 100% Advantage Timber HD (new 2002), Realtree Hardwoods HD 12 ga. only, (new 2002) or Advantage Classic (disc. 2001) camo coverage, 5 5/8-6 7/8 lbs. Importation began 1999.

MSR $219	$185	$165	$155	$145	$135	$125	$110

Add $70 for camo coverage.

Add $20 for Youth model.

❊ *Field Hunter Maxi-Mag.* - 12 ga. only, 3 1/2 in. chamber, 24, 26 (new 2001), or 28 in. VR barrel with multi-choke, 7mm VR rib, choice of wood/metal or 100% camo coverage similar to Field Hunter, including Advantage Wetlands (new 2003) and Advantage Max-4 HD, approx. 6.75 lbs. Importation began 2000.

MSR $259	$215	$185	$165	$135	$120	$110	$100

Add $60 for 100% camo finish.

Add $130 for camo Turkey Model with Hi/Tri-Viz fiber optic sights and XX full ported turkey choke tube – also includes sling and sling swivels (new 2002).

❊ *Field Slug* - 12 ga. only, 18 1/2 in. cyl. bore or 22 in. fully rifled (new 2002) barrel with adj. sights, black synthetic stock and forearm, black chrome or dull nickel finish. Imported 1999-2003.

	$210	$190	$180	$165	$150	$135	$125

Last MSR was $229.

Subtract 15% for 18 1/2 in. barrel.

❊ *Field Tactical* - 12 ga. only, 18 1/2 in. cyl. bore barrel with front sight, black synthetic stock and forearm, matte blue metal finish, 6 lbs. Importation began 2000.

MSR $199	$175	$160	$150	$135	$125	$115	$100

Add $40 for nickel finish and adj. sights.

DAN ARMS OF AMERICA

Previous trademark of shotguns manufactured in Italy by Silma. Previously imported by Dan Arms of America located in Allentown, PA and by Dan Arms of North America (previously called Sportsman's Emporium Ltd.) located in Fort Washington, PA.

All shotguns listed below were discontinued in early 1988.

GRADING - PPGS™	100%	98%	95%	90%	80%	70%	60%

SHOTGUNS: O/U

LUX GRADE I - 12 or 20 ga., 3 in. Mag. chambers, 26, 28, or 30 in. barrels, vent. rib, extractors, pistol grip, double trigger, European walnut.

	$280	$220	$210	$200	$190	$180	$170

Last MSR was $350.

LUX GRADE II - 12 ga. only, 3 in. Mag. chambers, 26, 28, or 30 in. barrels, vent. rib, extractors, pistol grip, single trigger, European walnut.

	$320	$250	$240	$230	$215	$200	$190

Last MSR was $395.

LUX GRADE III - 12 or 20 ga., 3 in. Mag. chambers, 26, 28, or 30 in. barrels, vent. rib, ejectors, pistol grip, single trigger, checkered European walnut.

	$375	$300	$285	$270	$255	$240	$220

Last MSR was $450.

LUX GRADE IV - 12 ga. only, 3 in. Mag. chambers, 28 in. barrels, vent. rib, ejectors, pistol grip, single trigger, checkered European walnut, multi-chokes with 5 tubes.

	$460	$390	$350	$310	$285	$265	$245

Last MSR was $550.

SKEET MODEL - 12 ga. only, 26 1/2 in. barrels, 10mm vent. rib, anatomical pistol grip.

	$550	$450	$400	$355	$320	$300	$285

Last MSR was $650.

TRAP MODEL - 12 ga. only, 30 in. barrels, 10mm vent. rib, anatomical pistol grip.

	$550	$450	$400	$355	$320	$300	$285

Last MSR was $650.

SILVERSNIPE - 12 or 20 ga., made to customer specifications, sideplates, select high grade walnut, name engraving upon request.

	$1,300	$1,200	$1,050	$900	$800	$700	$600

Last MSR was $1,475.

SHOTGUNS: SxS

FIELD MODEL - 12, 16, 20, 28 ga., or .410 bore, double triggers, extractors, 26 or 28 in. barrels.

	$285	$220	$210	$200	$190	$180	$170

Last MSR was $350.

DELUXE FIELD MODEL - 12 or 20 ga., single triggers, ejectors, 26 or 28 in. barrels.

	$440	$375	$340	$310	$290	$260	$230

Last MSR was $500.

DARDICK

Previous manufacturer located in Hamden, CT.

CARBINES

DARDICK CARBINE CONVERSION - .22 or .38 Dardick Tround cal., 23 in. barrel (interchangeable), walnut stock. Limited mfg.

	$1,275	$1,075	$900	$825	$750	$700	$650

PISTOLS: SEMI-AUTO

SERIES 1100 - .38 Dardick Tround cal., double action, 11 shot mag.

	$1,500	$1,300	$1,100	$950	$875	$795	$700

Dardick ammunition in itself is collectible - currently, individual "Trounds" are selling in the $5-$10 range.

GRADING - PPGS™	100%	98%	95%	90%	80%	70%	60%

SERIES 1500 - .22, .30, or .38 Dardick Tround cal., double action, 15 shot mag.

	$1,200	$1,000	$900	$800	$700	$600	$500

Subtract 40% for .30 cal.

DARNE S.A.

Current manufacturer producing shotguns 1881-1979 and 1990 to date in Saint Etienne, France. Darne also began making double rifles circa 1996. Currently imported by The Drumming Stump, Inc. located in Circle Pines, MN beginning 1996. Previously imported by Wes Gilpin located in Dallas, TX until 1992.

For F. Darne Fils Aîné please refer to the F Section. Also, please refer to the Bruchet section for 1982-1990 mfg. utilizing the Darne action.

RIFLES: DOUBLE

MODEL R EXPRESS SxS - 8x57 JRS or 9.3x74R cal., double rifle version of the Darne Model R Series shotgun, many options available, including style of rib, sights, stock configuration, etc. Importation began 1996.

MSR POR	N/A	$9,750	$8,100	$7,000	$6,000	$5,000	$4,000

EXPRESS SUPERPOSEÉ - .30-06, 8x57 JRS, or 9.3.74R cal., double rifle version of the Darne O/U shotgun, boxlock with false sideplates, straight grip stock, many options available. Importation began 1996.

MSR POR	N/A	$5,300	$4,500	$3,800	$3,300	$2,900	$2,650

SHOTGUNS: SxS, PRE-1980 MFG.

DARNE SLIDING BREECH SHOTGUN - 12, 16, 20, or 28 ga., SxS, unique action utilizes sliding breech lock-up, high quality mfg., 27 1/2 in. barrel standard with other lengths available, any choke combination, either straight grip or pistol grip stock, checkered, models differ in amount of engraving and grade of wood.

* *Bird Hunter Model R11*

	$1,500	$1,350	$1,100	$950	$825	$700	$600

* *Pheasant Hunter Model R15*

	$2,250	$2,000	$1,800	$1,625	$1,500	$1,425	$1,300

* *Magnum Model R16*

	$3,500	$3,150	$2,650	$2,300	$2,000	$1,750	$1,500

* *Quail Hunter Model V19*

	$4,500	$4,150	$3,700	$3,350	$2,850	$2,400	$1,950

* *Model V22*

	$5,750	$5,300	$4,600	$4,150	$3,650	$3,000	$2,500

* *Hors Series No. 1 Model V*

	$6,350	$5,750	$5,250	$4,500	$3,850	$3,150	$2,600

SHOTGUNS: 1989-CURRENT MFG.

In 1990, Paul Bruchet (the old Darne plant superintendent) obtained permission to once again use the Darne trademark. Hence, all 1990 and later mfg. has been produced by Paul Bruchet.

All new mfg. Darnes can be choked to the customer's choice. All models listed below have automatic ejectors, are oil finished by hand, and may be barreled to any length (except for Models R 11, 12, and 13). All prices are subject to change without notice.

O/U Models

SB1 - similar to SB3, traditional European O/U, DT, extractors, straight or semi-pistol grip stock. Importation began 1998.

MSR POR	N/A	$2,000	$1,650	$1,450	$1,100	$950	$825

GRADING - PPGS™	100%	98%	95%	90%	80%	70%	60%

SB2 - similar to SB3, except has scroll engraving, wood upgrade, and 28 in. barrels. Importation began 1996.

MSR POR	N/A	$2,400	$1,975	$1,625	$1,250	$1,000	$875

SB3 - 12 or 20 ga., scalloped boxlock action, extractors, 26 in. barrels, DTs, choice of English straight grip stock or semi-pistol grip. Importation began 1996.

MSR POR	N/A	$2,900	$2,300	$1,925	$1,800	$1,650	$1,375

SxS Sliding Breech Models

R 11 - 12 or 16 ga., half pistol grip stock, light engraving. Disc. 1999.

	$4,000	$2,825	$2,275	$1,925	$1,775	$1,650	$1,375

Last MSR was $4,500.

      Add 10% for R 11 Slug (includes duck bill rib).

R 12 - similar to R 11, except with better engraving.

MSR POR	N/A	$3,625	$2,775	$2,250	$1,925	$1,775	$1,650

R 13 - 12, 16, or 20 ga., straight or pistol grip stock, traditional action with bouquet engraving and obturator discs.

MSR POR	N/A	$4,250	$3,375	$2,675	$2,250	$1,950	$1,760

R 14 - 12, 16, or 20 ga., slug gun, choice of forearms, light engraving, and optional cheek rest pistol grip stock is also available.

MSR POR	N/A	$4,300	$3,400	$2,675	$2,250	$1,950	$1,760

R 15 - 12, 16, 20, 24, 28 ga., or .410 bore, select walnut stock and forearm with fine checkering, large scroll engraving, obturator disks.

MSR POR	N/A	$4,500	$3,550	$2,850	$2,400	$1,975	$1,825

R 16 - same as R 15, except has 3 in. chambers.

MSR POR	N/A	$4,600	$3,625	$2,900	$2,450	$1,975	$1,825

R 17 - 12 (including Mag.), 16, 20, 24, 28 ga., or .410 bore., Magnum model (3 in. chambers), customer's choice engraving patterns, superior quality wood finish.

MSR POR	N/A	$6,900	$5,900	$4,950	$3,625	$2,950	$2,575

V 19 - all gauges, easy opening large key action, top quality walnut and checkering, full coverage rose and scroll engraving with chiseled fences.

MSR POR	N/A	$8,500	$7,300	$6,100	$5,150	$4,200	$3,150

V 20 - similar to V 19, except has deep relief rosace engraving and chiseled fences.

MSR POR	N/A	$8,950	$7,600	$6,275	$5,350	$4,200	$3,150

V 21 - similar to V 19, except has 100% coverage English rose and scroll engraving and chiseled fences.

MSR POR	N/A	$10,250	$8,650	$7,425	$6,150	$5,250	$4,200

V 22 - similar to V 21, except has 100% engraving coverage featuring bouquet patterns and deeply chiseled fences, sculpted shoulders, best quality walnut.

MSR POR	N/A	$13,500	$11,000	$9,775	$8,500	$7,225	$6,000

VHS - all gauges, top-of-the-line model incorporating customer's choice of engraving style, type of inlays, and checkering pattern, best quality wood. Due to the unique nature of this model, each specimen must be appraised individually. New guns are priced per individual customer order.

DAVID MILLER CO.

Current custom rifle manufacturer located in Tucson, AZ since 1973.

The David Miller Co., composed of David Miller and Curt Crum, is a custom rifle shop building best quality bolt action rifles only. All guns are built per individual custom order and the company should be contacted directly for more information and price quotations.

All currently crafted rifles from the David Miller Co. are made using highly modified and finished Winchester Model 70 Super Grade actions or, on rare occasion, a Weatherby Mark V action. Two models of rifles are crafted in the Miller shop, the Classic and the Marksman. The Classic is the top-of-the-line in custom bolt action rifles available today and is priced starting at $38,000. The Marksman is equally well constructed but without many of the very labor-intensive features and is standard with a laminated wood stock rather than top quality walnut. The Marksman is intended as a serious hunting rifle and has a starting price of $18,000. The waiting period for either the Classic or the Marksman is about 2 1/2 years. Please contact the David Miller Co. directly for a quotation on a new rifle (see Trademark Index).

Used rifles should be individually appraised to ascertain current values. Very few genuine Miller rifles ever appear on the used gun market. At the 2004 Safari Club International annual convention, an early David Miller Co. custom rifle, crafted around a much modified and refined Mauser G33/40 action and chambered for the .30-06 cartridge, equivalent to today's Classic rifle, sold used for $24,000.

DAVIDSON FIREARMS

Previously manufactured by Fábrica de Armas, located in Eibar, Spain.

SHOTGUNS: SxS

MODEL 63B - 12, 16, 20, 28 ga., or .410 bore, 25, 26, 28, or 30 in. barrels, Anson & Deeley boxlock, engraved and nickel plated frame, various chokes, walnut checkered stock. Mfg. 1963-disc.

	100%	98%	95%	90%	80%	70%	60%
	$275	$260	$220	$200	$175	$165	$155

✳ *Model 63B Magnum* - similar to 63B, except 10 ga. Mag., 12, or 20 ga. Mag., 32 in. barrel.

	100%	98%	95%	90%	80%	70%	60%
12 or 20 ga.	$360	$340	$310	$275	$230	$195	$165
10 ga.	$385	$370	$340	$305	$250	$220	$195

MODEL 69SL - 12 or 20 ga., true detachable sidelock action, engraved nickel plated action, 26 in. and 28 in. barrels, imp. cyl. and mod., mod. and full, checkered walnut stock. Mfg. 1963-76.

	100%	98%	95%	90%	80%	70%	60%
	$415	$395	$375	$340	$320	$290	$260

MODEL 73 STAGECOACH - 12 or 20 ga., detachable sidelock exposed hammers, 3 in. chambers, 20 in. mod. and full barrels, checkered walnut stock. Mfg. 1976-disc.

	100%	98%	95%	90%	80%	70%	60%
	$275	$260	$220	$200	$175	$165	$155

DAVIS N.R.

Please refer to the Crescent Fire Arms Co. listing.

DAVIS INDUSTRIES

Previous manufacturer located in Chino, CA 1995-2001. Previously located in Mira Loma, CA until 1995. Distributor sales only.

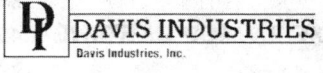
DAVIS INDUSTRIES
Davis Industries, Inc.

Davis Industries provided a lifetime warranty on all products, which is now void.

DERRINGERS

D-SERIES DERRINGER - .22 LR, .22 Mag., .25 ACP, .32 ACP, .32 H&R Mag. (new 1995), .38 Spl. (new 1992), or 9mm Para. cal., O/U steel construction, 2.4 or 2 3/4 (.38 Spl. only) in. vent. rib barrel, 9 1/2 or 11 1/2 oz., black Teflon or chrome finish. Disc. 2001.

	100%	98%	95%	90%	80%	70%	60%
	$65	$55	$45	$40	$35	$30	$30

Last MSR was $75.

Add $23 for Big-Bore series (larger frame) in .22 Mag., .32 H&R Mag., .38 Spl., or 9mm Para. cal.
Add $29 for Long-Bore cals. (.22 Mag., .32 H&R Mag. - disc., .38 Spl., or 9mm Para.).
In this series, the .25 ACP cal. is the Model D-25 and the .32 ACP cal. is the Model D-32.

GRADING - PPGS™	100%	98%	95%	90%	80%	70%	60%

LONG BORE DERRINGER - .22 Mag., .32 H&R Mag. (disc. 1998), .38 Spl., or 9mm Para. cal., similar to D Series, except has 3 3/4 in. barrel, 13 oz. Mfg. 1995-2001.

	$90	$75	$65	$55	$45	$40	$35

Last MSR was $104.

PISTOLS: SEMI-AUTO

P-32 - .32 ACP cal., single action, 6 shot mag., 2.8 in. barrel, black Teflon or chrome finish, laminated wood grips, 22 oz. Mfg. 1987-2001.

	$75	$65	$55	$50	$45	$35	$35

Last MSR was $88.

P-380 - .380 ACP cal., single action, similar to P-32, 5 shot mag., 2.8 in. barrel, bright chrome or black Teflon finish, internal shock resister for recoil, wood (disc.) or black synthetic grips, 22 oz. Mfg. 1989-2001.

	$85	$75	$65	$55	$45	$35	$35

Last MSR was $98.

DEFOURNEY

Current long gun manufacturer located in Belgium. No current U.S. importation.

Defourney specializes in both quality sidelock and boxlock (with or w/o sideplates) shotguns. Prices range from $750-$3,250 for boxlock shotguns and start in the $2,500 range for sidelock models, assuming 80% or better original condition.

DEMAS, ETS

Current manufacturer located in St. Etienne, France since 1967. Currently imported beginning 2004 by Verney-Carron USA, Inc., located in Clay Center, KS. Previously imported by The Drumming Stump, located in Circle Pines, MN.

During 2004, Verney-Carron S.A., located in St. Etienne, France (please refer to separate listing) purchased Demas, which manufactures a full line of quality O/U and SxS rifles and shotguns. Prices vary according to configuration, engraving options, and quality of wood. Please contact Verney-Carron for more information, including current model availability and U.S. pricing (see Trademark Index).

DEMRO

Previous manufacturer located in Manchester, CT.

RIFLES: SEMI-AUTO

T.A.C. MODEL 1 RIFLE - .45 ACP or 9mm Luger cal., blow back operation, 16 7/8 in. barrel, open bolt fire combination, lock-in receiver must be set to fire, also available in carbine model.

	$650	$595	$525	$475	$425	$395	$360

XF-7 WASP CARBINE - .45 ACP or 9mm Luger cal., blow back operation, 16 7/8 in. barrel.

	$650	$595	$525	$475	$425	$395	$360

Add $45 for case.

DEPAR

Previous manufacturer located in Istanbul, Turkey.

Depar manufactured both semi-auto and O/U shotguns.

SHOTGUNS

ATAK O/U - 12 ga. only, 2 3/4 in. chambers, ejectors, SST.

	$350	$295	$250	$225	$200	$185	$170

Last MSR was $350.

Add approx. 30% with scroll engraving and walnut stock and forearm.

GRADING - PPGS™	100%	98%	95%	90%	80%	70%	60%

ATILGAN SEMI-AUTO - 12 ga. only, 3 in. chamber, gas operated, includes multi-chokes.

	$170	$150	$135	$125	$115	$105	$95

Last MSR was $195.

* *Atilgan Semi-Auto De Luxe* - similar to Atilgan Semi-Auto, except has engraved receiver and deluxe walnut stock and forearm.

	$350	$295	$250	$225	$200	$185	$170

Last MSR was $350.

SAFARI SLIDE ACTION - 12 ga. only, 3 in. chamber, synthetic stock standard.

	$170	$150	$135	$125	$115	$105	$95

Last MSR was $170.

Add 10% for walnut stock and forearm.
Add approx. 50% for nickel chrome receiver finish and light scroll engraving.

DESERT INDUSTRIES, INC.

Previous manufacturer located in Las Vegas, NV 1991-1996. See listing under Steel City Arms, Inc. for older models.

In 1990, Desert Industries, Inc. was created - this new company was the same as Steel City Arms, Inc. More recently manufactured guns will have the Las Vegas slide address.

PISTOLS: SEMI-AUTO

THE DOUBLE DEUCE - .22 LR cal., double action, 2 1/2 in. barrel, matte stainless steel construction, 6 shot mag., rosewood grips, 15 oz. Limited mfg. 1991-96.

	$350	$295	$275

Last MSR was $400.

TWO BIT SPECIAL - .25 ACP cal., double action, 2 1/2 in. barrel, similar to Double Deuce, except has 5 shot mag., 15 oz. Approx. 12 protoypes mfg. 1991-96.

	$375	$350	$295

Last MSR was $400.

DETONICS FIREARMS INDUSTRIES

Previous manufacturer located in Bellevue, WA 1976-1988. Detonics was sold in early 1988 to the New Detonics Manufacturing Corporation, a wholly owned subsidiary of "1045 Investors Group Limited."

Please refer to the New Detonics Manufacturing Corporation in the "N" section of this text for complete model listings of both companies.

DETONICS USA

Current manufacturer located in Pendergrass, GA.

Detonics USA has recently introduced the CombatMaster .45 and is planning to introduce the Model 9-11-01. Please contact the company directly for availability and pricing (see Trademark Index).

DIAMOND SHOTGUNS

Please refer to the Adco Sales Inc. listing.

DIARM S.A.

Previous manufacturing conglomerate (25 companies) located in Deba, Spain 1986-1989. Previously imported and distributed by American Arms, Inc. located in North Kansas City, MO. Older Diarm models can be found under the American Arms, Inc. heading in this publication.

GRADING - PPGS™	100%	98%	95%	90%	80%	70%	60%

DIAWA

Previous U.S. firearms importer and distributor.

Diawa imported various firearms circa 1960s-early 1970s. Configurations included semi-auto shotguns mfg. by Singer Nikko, Ltd. of Japan, and bolt action rifles. Values are based on the current utilitarian value, since there is little collectibility on these guns.

DICKSON & MACNAUGHTON

Current trading company established in 1996, and located in Edinburgh, Scotland.

During 1999, the directors of James MacNaughton & Sons acquired the whole share capital of John Dickson & Son, from whom they purchased the MacNaughton manufacturing rights in 1996. The two companies now trade under the name of Dickson & MacNaughton, and trademarks currently owned are: John Dickson & Son, Dan'l Fraser, Alex Henry, James MacNaughton & Sons, Alex Martin, and Thomas Mortimer.

JOHN DICKSON & SON

Current trademark purchased during 1999 by James MacNaughton & Sons, located in Edinburgh, Scotland. Both trademarks are currently traded under the name Dickson & MacNaughton.

Please contact the company directly for more information on this trademark (see Trademark Index).

DIXIE GUN WORKS

Current importer, distributor, and catalog retailer established 1954, and located in Union City, TN.

In addition to importing a variety of firearms, Dixie Gun Works has also established itself as one of the leaders in black powder reproductions and replicas, related shooting accessories, and acoutrements. For more information regarding black powder reproductions and replicas and related shooting accessories, please contact the company directly and request a catalog. Please refer to the *Blue Book of Modern Black Powder Arms* by John Allen & Dennis Adler for more information on Dixie Gun Work's black powder reproductions and replicas.

RIFLES: REPRODUCTIONS

REMINGTON ROLLING BLOCK LONG RANGE RIFLE - .40-65 or .45-70 Govt. cal., 30 in. tapered octagon barrel, case colored receiver and buttplate, vernier tang sight.

	MSR $900	$775	$695	$595	$500	$400	$350	$325

Add $150 for .45-70 Govt. cal.

1874 SHARPS LIGHTWEIGHT HUNTER - .45-70 Govt. cal., reproduction of the Sharps No. 3 sporting rifle, 32 in. blued tapered octagon barrel, straight stock, case colored receiver and buttplate, vernier tang sight. Disc. 2004.

	$865	$725	$600	$500	$400	$350	$300

Last MSR was $975.

1874 SHARPS SILHOUETTE RIFLE - .40-65 or 45-70 Govt. cal., reproduction of the Sharps No. 1 sporting rifle, 30 in. blued tapered octagon barrel, pistol grip stock, case colored receiver and buttplate.

	MSR $1,100	$950	$800	$650	$550	$475	$400	$325

Add $900 for engraving with in-the-white receiver and buttplate.

HENRY RIFLE - .44-40 WCF or .45 LC cal., iron, brass or case colored steel (.44-40 WCF cal. only) frame, 24 1/4 in. blued barrel, 12 shot integral mag., blue finish, 9.25 lbs.

	MSR $1,050	$875	$775	$675	$525	$425	$360	$320

Add $450 for engraving (.44-40 WCF cal. only).
Subtract $25 for case hardend iron frame.

GRADING - PPGS™	100%	98%	95%	90%	80%	70%	60%

✳ ***Henry Trapper*** - similar to above, except has 16 1/2 in. barrel, 7 shot integral mag., 7 3/4 lbs. Disc. 2004.

	$775	$650	$525	$450	$400	$360	$320

Last MSR was $950.

1866 CARBINE - .44-40 WCF, or .45 LC cal., brass receiver, 10 shot tube mag., 19 in. tapered round barrel, 7.5 lbs.

MSR $835	$750	$650	$550	$450	$375	$350	$300

1873 CARBINE - .44-40 WCF or .45 LC cal., blued metal finish, 19 in. tapered round barrel, 9 shot tube mag., elevator rear sight, 7.25 lbs.

MSR $835	$750	$650	$550	$450	$375	$350	$300

1873 RIFLE - .44-40 WCF or .45 LC cal., blued metal finish, 24 in. octagon barrel, available with either full or half mag., checkered pistol grip or straight grip stock, 8.25 lbs.

MSR $1,015	$850	$750	$650	$550	$450	$375	$350

✳ ***1873 Deluxe Sporting Rifle*** - similar to 1873 Rifle, except has checkered stock with straight or pistol grip stock, full or half mag.

MSR $1,015	$850	$750	$650	$550	$450	$375	$350

Add $410 for engraving (.44-40 WCF cal. only).

1873 TRAPDOOR CARBINE/RIFLE - .45-70 Govt. cal., blued furniture, oil finished American walnut stock, 7 or 9 lbs.

MSR $875	$765	$675	$600	$500	$425	$350	$275

Add $225 for Officer's Model, with case colored lock and trigger guard, single set trigger.
Add $100 for Rifle.

KODIAK MARK IV DOUBLE EXPRESS SxS RIFLE - .45-70 Govt. cal., back action, browned 24 in. barrels with triple leaf express sights, color case hardened frame, trigger guard and hammers.

MSR $3,250	$2,825	$2,450	$2,150	$1,850	$1,600	$1,400	$1,200

DLASK ARMS CORP.

Current manufacturer located in British Columbia, Canada. Sales offices are located in Blaine, WA. Direct sales.

PISTOLS: SEMI-AUTO

Dlask Arms Corp. manufactures custom M-1911 style custom guns for all levels of competition. Previous non-custom standard models included the TC Tactical Carry at $1,200 last MSR, Gold Team at $2,000 last MSR, Silver Team L/S at $1,700 last MSR, and the Master Class at $3,500 last MSR. In addition, Dlask also manufactures a wide variety of custom parts for the M-1911. For more information on a custom-built competition gun, please contact the company directly (see Trademark Index).

DOMINGO, ACHA

Please refer to Acha section.

DOMINO, IGI

Previous Italian company absorbed during 1990 by FAS (see separate listing in F section). Previously imported by Mandall Shooting Supplies located in Scottsdale, AZ.

PISTOLS: SEMI-AUTO

MODEL OP 601 MATCH PISTOL - .22 Short cal., 5 shot, 5.6 in. barrel, match sights, full target grips, vent. barrel and slide to reduce recoil, adj. and removable trigger.

	$1,300	$1,000	$715	$635	$550	$495	$440

Last MSR was $1,495.

GRADING - PPGS™	100%	98%	95%	90%	80%	70%	60%

MODEL SP 602 MATCH PISTOL - .22 LR cal., 5 1/2 in. barrel, similar to 601, but .22 LR and slightly different trigger.

	100%	98%	95%	90%	80%	70%	60%
	$1,300	$1,100	$800	$700	$600	$550	$495

Last MSR was $1,495.

DOUBLESTAR CORP.

Current rifle manufacturer located in Winchester, KY. Dealer sales only.

RIFLES/CARBINES: SEMI-AUTO

DSC STARCAR CARBINE - .223 Rem. cal., AR-15 design, fixed post-ban CAR type stock, 16 in. barrel, A2 or flattop upper receiver, 7 lbs.

MSR $775	$695	$625	$550	$485	$440	$400	$365

Add $80 for detachable carrying handle.

DSC STAR M4 CARBINE - .223 Rem. cal., AR-15 M4 carbine design, fixed M4 style post-ban buttstock, 16 in. barrel, M4 handguard, 6.76 lbs.

MSR $895	$795	$715	$640	$565	$500	$465	$430

Add $70 for detachable carrying handle.

DSC STAR DISSIPATOR - .223 Rem. cal., AR-15 design, 16 in. dissipator barrel with full length handguard, A2 or CAR buttstock.

MSR $875	$775	$695	$625	$550	$500	$465	$430

Add $65 for detachable carrying handle.

DSC STAR-15 LIGHTWEIGHT TACTICAL - .223 Rem. cal., AR-15 design, 16 in. fluted H-Bar barrel with attached muzzle brake, shorty A2 buttstock, A2 or flattop upper receiver, 6.25 lbs. Disc. 2004.

	$775	$695	$625	$550	$500	$465	$430

Last MSR was $880.

Add $70 for detachable carrying handle.

DSC STAR-15 RIFLE - .223 Rem. cal., AR-15 design, 20 in. match barrel, ribbed forearm, A2 or flattop upper receiver, 8 lbs.

MSR $775	$695	$625	$550	$485	$440	$400	$365

Add $80 for flattop with detachable carrying handle.

DSC STAR-15 9MM CARBINE - 9mm Para cal., AR-15 design, 16 in. barrel, ribbed forearm, A2 or flattop upper receiver, 7 1/2 lbs. Mfg. 2004 only.

	$875	$775	$675	$575	$525	$475	$425

Last MSR was $995.

DSC CRITTERSLAYER - .223 Rem. cal., AR-15 design, 24 in. fluted Shaw barrel, full length Picatinny rail on receiver and Badger handguard, two-stage match trigger, palmrest, ergonomic pistol grip with finger grooves, includes Harris LMS swivel bipod, flattop or high rise upper receiver, 11.5 lbs.

MSR $1,300	$1,185	$1,000	$875	$800	$700	$625	$550

Add $40 for ported barrel.

✳ *DSC CritterSlayer Jr.* - similar to CritterSlayer, except has 16 in. barrel and fully adj. A-2 style buttstock, DSC flattop or high rise upper receiver.

MSR $1,000	$875	$750	$650	$550	$450	$375	$325

Add $70 for detachable carrying handle or $40 for removable front sight.

DSC EXPEDITION CARBINE/RIFLE - .223 Rem. cal., AR-15 design, 16 or 20 in. lightweight contour barrel, A2 or flattop upper receiver, 8 lbs.

MSR $825	$725	$650	$575	$500	$450	$400	$365

DSC STAR-15 DCM SERVICE RIFLE - 5.56 NATO cal., AR-15 design, 20 in. match

GRADING - PPGS™	100%	98%	95%	90%	80%	70%	60%

barrel, National Match front and rear sights, two-stage match trigger, DCM free-floating handguard, 8 lbs.

MSR $1,000	$895	$825	$725	$650	$550	$485	$440

DSC TARGET CARBINE - .223 Rem. cal., AR-15 design, features 16 in. dissipator barrel with full length round one-piece National Match handguard, flip-up sights, Picatinny rail, flattop upper receiver.

MSR $1,175	$1,000	$875	$775	$695	$625	$550	$485

DSC SUPER MATCH RIFLE - .223 Rem. cal., AR-15 design, 16, 20, 22, or 24 in. stainless steel Super Match barrel, flattop or high rise upper receiver, includes Picatinny rail and one-piece National Match free-floating handguard.

MSR $875	$775	$695	$625	$550	$500	$465	$430

DOWNSIZER CORPORATION

Current pistol manufacturer established in 1994, and located in Santee, CA. Dealer sales only.

DERRINGERS

MODEL WSP (WORLD'S SMALLEST PISTOL) - 9mm Para. (disc. 1999), .357 Mag., .357 Sig. (disc. 1999), .40 S&W (disc. 1999), or .45 ACP cal., single shot pistol, tip-up 2.1 in. barrel with push-button release, internal firing pin block, double action only, synthetic grips, stainless steel, overall size is smaller than a playing card, 11 oz. New 1997.

MSR $499	$415	$300	$235

DREYSE PISTOL

Previously manufactured by Rheinische Metallwaren and Machinenfabrik, located in Sommerda, Germany.

PISTOLS: SEMI-AUTO

MODEL 1907 AUTOMATIC - 7.65mm/.32 ACP cal., 8 shot, 3 1/2 in. barrel, blue, fixed sights, hard rubber grips. Mfg. 1907-14.

$250	$185	$150	$120	$95	$75	$50

MODEL 1910 - 9mm Para. cal., mfg. 1912-1915. Production estimated at 1,000 pistols, usually found in the 12xx-13xx ser. no. range. Seldom encountered.

$6,500	$5,500	$4,500	$3,500	$2,500	$2,000	$1,500

VEST POCKET AUTOMATIC - .25 ACP cal., 6 shot, 2 in. barrel, blue, fixed sights, hard rubber grips. Mfg. 1912-15.

$325	$235	$150	$130	$100	$75	$65

Add 100% for early version with double extractors.

DRILLINGS

A Drilling is a three-barrel combination gun (two shotgun barrels and a rifle barrel, vice versa, or three shotgun barrels). Normally, two triggers fire the shotgun barrels and one of them activates the rifle barrel when the barrel selector is moved forward (usually located on the upper tang). Most well-made Drillings in above average condition are surprisingly accurate when using the rifle barrel(s), because of the stiffness gained with three barrels fixed together.

DRILLING CONFIGURATIONS & EXPLANATIONS

Please refer to illustrations below depicting the most commonly encountered Drilling configurations.

Illustration No. 1 - Normal Drilling configuration with 2 shotgun barrels over a rimmed, centerfire rifle (most are 16 ga. x 16 ga. by either 9.3x72R or 8x57JR cal.).

Illustration No. 2 - Two rifle barrels over a shotgun. This configuration will normally command twice the price as No. 1. German designation is "Doppelbüchsdrilling".

Illustration No. 3 - Three barrels with no two being the same gauge or caliber. This configuration is very collectible, especially if the smallest caliber is .22 LR. Again, price will be double of No. 1.

Illustration No. 4 - Sometimes called a Bock Drilling with one shotgun and two rifle barrels. This variation brings a good premium over No. 1.

Illustration No. 5 - Rib Drilling with rifle caliber generally small (.22 LR or .22 Hornet). German designation is "Schienendrilling".

Illustration No. 6 - Three shotgun barrels with the same gauge or three rifle barrels with different calibers. This configuration is quite rare and healthy premiums are charged over No. 1.

Illustration No. 7 - A variation of No. 3, this configuration features shotgun O/U barrels with a rifle barrel on the side. German designation is "Bock-Doppelflinte mit seitlichem Kleinkaliberlauf".

Illustration No. 8 - Very unusual - a 3-barrel drilling in vertical design - 2 rifle barrels under a shotgun barrel. This configuration is seldomly encountered.

> The following German nomenclatures apply as follows: single barrel rifle = Büchse; SxS double rifle = Doppelbüchse; O/U double rifle = Bock-Doppelbüchse; SxS double shotgun = Doppelflinte; O/U double shotgun = Bock-Doppelflinte; SxS double shotgun, rifle bbl. under = Drilling; SxS double shotgun, rifle bbl. on top = Schienendrilling; single shotgun, rifle bbl. under = Bock-Büchsflinte; single shotgun, rifle bbl. at side = Büchsflinte; single shotgun, rifle bbl. under and at side = Bock-Drilling; double rifle, shot bbl. under = Doppelbüchsdrilling; O/U double shotgun, rifle bbl. at side = Bock-Doppelflinte mit seitlichem Kleinkaliberlauf; SxS double shotgun, plus two rifle bbls. = Vierling.

DRILLING HISTORY

For over 140 years Drillings have been the classic hunting gun of many European countries, especially Germany and Austria. Because a single hunting trip may require shooting both wildfowl and animals (often times within several hours), Europeans have long favored a single longarm that could afford both rifle and shotgun shooting, be reliable, and not wear the hunter out while transporting it in the field. Americans, on the other hand, have not placed as much emphasis on this combination gun principle, and more often than not have chosen to buy both a rifle and shotgun for each specific hunting application. Since Drillings are becoming more popular, collectibility has improved in this country for those collectors who see the utility and functionality of these mostly hand-assembled weapons. Very few Drillings manufactured before WWII are alike today in configuration and condition.

DRILLING CALIBERS

Some people may be confused as to how the European metric calibers compare to domestic cartridges in terms of overall performance. This comparison has been added to assist you when contemplating what type of field performance, velocity, and killing power you can expect in these European calibers: 9.3x74 is similar to .375 Win. Mag., 9.3x72R is similar to .44 Mag. or .44-40 WCF, 8x57JRS is similar to .30-06, .30-30 Win. is 7.62x51R, 8x57JR is similar to .30-06, 7x65R is similar to .280 Rem., 7x57R is similar to .257 Roberts, 6.5x57R is similar to .243 Win., 5.6x52R is a .22 Savage Hi-Power, 5.6x34R is similar to .22 Hornet. Drillings can also be encountered in American calibers such as .270 Win., .30-06, .30-30 Win., .38-55 WCF, or .32-20 WCF.

DRILLING VALUES AND CONDITION FACTORS

Rather than list the various manufacturers of Drillings (there are hundreds), it should be noted that guns with major trademarks and established provenances (i.e. Charles Daly, Colt Sauer, Ferlach addressed, Heym, Krieghoff, J.P. Sauer, Berlin [rare] and Suhl addressed, etc.) will usually be more collectible than other, lesser-known brands, even if the quality of workmanship is similar. The overall quality, condition, engraving, wood type/fanciness, and carving all have to be taken into consideration when evaluating a Drilling. Some Drillings were assembled from manufactured parts by skilled and crafted gunsmiths and are sometimes better quality than factory specimens. Pre-war specimens are generally more desirable to collectors (even though less expensive than post-war variations) and to date, have outperformed post-war specimens in price appreciation. Many older pre-war specimens were designed for rimmed cartridges with lower breech pressures and should not be re-bored or reloaded for the "hotter" cartridges/loads available today. It should be noted that since Drillings are more complex than a typical shotgun, most of the manufacture has been done by hand - some guns have taken individual craftsmen over a year to fabricate! Ordering a new Drilling today would be a very expensive proposition, and buying a good used specimen will save you thousands of dollars (and maybe a year wait). For these reasons, many collectors feel Drillings today are under-priced since they can be purchased at a fraction of the cost for a new one (and may well be better quality also).

Condition is another major consideration. A gun that shows much use and is not operationally intact/correct may bring several thousand dollars less than another similar specimen showing little wear and excellent original finish (including the case colors or coin finish).

Most above average condition boxlock Drillings in the above mentioned trademarks start in the $1,750 range and can go to $10,000 and higher if the configuration, features, and condition are all desirable. Average condition Drillings usually sell in the $1,350 - $2,750 range assuming moderate engraving, metric calibers, and a few features. Also, while not many Drillings are available in the secondary marketplace, they have become increasingly popular due to shooting sports magazines and other gun publications. For these reasons, Drillings have to be evaluated one at a time and a COMPETENT appraisal/evaluation should be procured before buying or selling a specimen.

Drillings with original claw-mounted scopes (rail-mount or swing-off) are worth 50%-80% premiums.

FEATURES THAT ADD VALUE TO DRILLINGS

Drillings with American calibers and smaller gauges will sometimes be more desirable (depending on engraving, case colors, or coin finish) than the European metric calibers (i.e. a gun configured 20 ga. x 20 ga. by .243 Win. will sell for more than a similar gun in 16 ga. x 16 ga. by 9.3 x 72R cal.). The most commonly encountered gauges and calibers are 16 ga. (most pre-war guns are chambered for 2 9/16 in.). In addition, a sidelock action will be more desirable than a boxlock, and a lot more expensive if the locks are also detachable.

Drilling aficionados will mention there are four main things to look for when contemplating a drilling purchase - beauty, condition, quality, and features. Features and embellishments become very critical in ascertaining Drilling values also. A gun with deep relief engraving, carved stock, claw mounts w/ scope, buffalo horn trigger guard and buttplate, cocking indicators, two position front sight (i.e. night sight), middle set of express sights, adj. trigger, concealed upper tang peep sight, a non-Greener safety system, lightweight (under 6 1/2 lbs.), separate rifle cocking, shotgun barrel inserts in .22LR or .22 Mag. cal. (approx. 8 or 11 in. long), cartridge trap, etc. is going to be A LOT more collectible than a plain-Jane hammer model with a loose action.

FEATURES THAT DETRACT VALUE FROM DRILLINGS

If it isn't beautiful, it probably won't sell. Beauty sells.

OBSERVATIONS ON DRILLING COLLECTIBILITY

Condition determines whether a Nitro-proofed Drilling's value is comparable to its black powder or damascus barrel counterparts.

DRULOV

Previous handgun manufacturer located in North Bohemia.

PISTOLS: SINGLE SHOT

PAV - .22 LR cal., single shot, 9 3/4 in. barrel, all steel construction. Imported 1986 only.

$95	$85	$75	$65	$60	$55	$50

Last MSR was $105.

DRULOV 70 - .22 LR cal., single shot. Add $30 for set trigger. Disc. 1986.

$105	$95	$85	$75	$70	$65	$60

Last MSR was $115.

DRULOV 75 - .22 LR cal., single shot with set trigger & micrometer sights. Also available in left-hand. Importation disc. 1991.

$300	$250	$215	$185	$155	$140	$120

Last MSR was $349.

DRULOV 78 - .22 LR cal., similar to Drulov 75. Imported 1986 only.

$275	$240	$200	$175	$150	$130	$110

Last MSR was $180.

DUBIEL ARMS COMPANY

Previous manufacturer located in Sherman, TX. Dubiel Arms made custom bolt action rifles from 1975-approx. 1990.

RIFLES: BOLT ACTION

BOLT ACTION RIFLE - .22-250 Rem.-.458 Win. Mag. cals., custom made bolt action, barrel length and weight to order, no sights, Canjar trigger, all steel parts, custom made rifle stocks available in five styles. Disc.

$2,000	$1,750	$1,500	$1,275	$1,125	$975	$825

Last MSR was $2,500.

DUCKS UNLIMITED, INC.

National wildlife organization with headquarters located in Memphis, TN.

SHOTGUNS: DINNER GUNS (GUN-OF-THE-YEAR)

The makes and models listed below reflect "dinner guns" only. Dinner guns (Gun-of-the-Year) refer to those shotguns sold at the various annual banquets held by Ducks Unlimited chapters. Dinner guns do not have a retail price. Rather, banquet auction prices can vary substantially from chapter to chapter, as can secondary market values.

Manufacturer	Model	Quantity	Year
Remington	Model 1100 12 ga.	500	1973
Remington	Model 870 12 ga.	600	1974
Winchester	Model 12 12 ga.	800	1975
Winchester	Model Super X-1 12 ga.	900	1976
Ithaca	Model 37 12 ga. (40th Ann'y)	1,125	1977
Ithaca	Model 51 12 ga.	1,250	1978
Weatherby	Model Patrician 12 ga.	1,600	1979
Weatherby	Model Centurion 12 ga.	2,000	1980
Remington	Model 1100 12 ga. Mag.	2,400	1981
Remington	Model 870 12 ga. Mag.	3,000	1982
Browning	Model B-80 12 ga.	3,400	1983
Browning	Model BPS 12 ga.	3,800	1984
Remington	Model 1100 12 ga.	4,500	1985
Beretta	Model A303 12 ga.	5,500	1986
Beretta	Model A303 20 ga.	3,500	1987
Browning	Model A5 12 ga. (50th Ann'y)	5,000	1987
Browning	Model A5 16 ga.	4,500	1988
Browning	Model A500 12 ga.	4,500	1989
Browning	Model A5 20 ga.	4,500	1990
Beretta	Model A390 12 ga.	4,200	1991
Franchi	Model Semi-Auto 12 ga.	4,200	1992
Winchester	Model 12 20 ga.	3,800	1993
Browning	Model A500R 12 ga.	3,300	1994
Browning	Model 12 Repro. 28 ga.	1,000	1995
Browning	Model BPS 12 ga.	3,500	1996
Browning	Model Gold Hunter	2,500	1997

This model commemorated DU's 60th anniversary.

Manufacturer	Model	Quantity	Year
Remington	Model 11-87 12 ga.	3,500	1998
Browning	Model BPS 20 ga.	3,500	1999
Beretta	Model AL390 12 ga.	3,500	2000

This dinner gun is the Gold Mallard variation of the Model Al390.

Manufacturer	Model	Quantity	Year
Fabarm	Model Red Lion 12 ga.	3,600	2001
Browning	Model BPS 28 ga.	3,500	2002
Beretta	Model AL391	3,500	2003
Winchester	SX2	2,800	2004

DUMOULIN, ERNEST S.P.R.L.

Current manufacturer located in Herstal, Belgium. No current U.S. importation. Previously imported 1998-2000 by Armes De Chasse LLC, located in Hertford, NC. Previously imported and retailed on a very limited basis by Midwest Gun Sport located in Zebulon, NC until 1990 (formerly from Ellisville, MO). Older importation was by Abercrombie & Fitch located in New York, NY.

Most Ernest Dumoulin (son of Henri) drillings, rifles, and shotguns are essentially custom ordered firearms with a long list of options available which, in some cases, can easily double the values of models shown below. Because of this, these options are not listed individually. Please contact the factory directly for more information regarding current models and pricing.

GRADING - PPGS™	100%	98%	95%	90%	80%	70%	60%

COMBINATION GUNS

EAGLE MODEL - O/U configuration (shotgun barrel on bottom), 12 or 20 ga., .22 Hornet, .222 Rem., .222 Rem. Mag., 6mm Rem., .243 Win., .25-06 Rem., .30-06, 6.5x57R, 7x57R, 8x57JRS, or 9.3x74R cal., boxlock action. 1989-disc.

$2,700	$2,400	$2,175	$1,850	$1,595	$1,400	$1,195

Last MSR was $2,700.

RIFLES: BOLT ACTION

E. Dumoulin has had very limited importation since 1989. Beginning in 1998, some bolt action models have been imported into the U.S.

BAVARIA DELUXE - .243 Win. through .458 Win. cals., 21 1/2, 24, or 25 1/2 in. octagonal barrel, French walnut stock with rosewood forend tip and pistol grip cap, no sights, custom made essentially with Sako (disc.) or Mauser action. Many engraving options available from $510-$1,900. Disc. 1985.

Series I	$995	$890	$775	$650	$575	$530	$460

Last MSR was $1,080.

Add 15% for .375 H&H or .458 Win. Mag. cal.

RIFLE MOUSQUETON - .243 Win. through .338 Win. cals., 20 in. barrel, Mannlicher style, French walnut stock and pistol grip cap, no sights, custom made essentially with Sako or Mauser action. Many engraving options available from $510-$1,900. Disc.

$720	$620	$560	$510	$470	$420	$360

CENTURION MODEL - .270 Win. through .458 Win. cals., 21 1/2, 24, or 25 1/2 in. barrels, French walnut stock with rosewood forearm tip and pistol grip cap, no sights, custom made essentially with Sako or Mauser action. Many engraving options available from $510-$1,900. Importation disc. 1986.

$660	$590	$535	$480	$425	$390	$360

Last MSR was $740.

CENTURION CLASSIC - standard cals. only, similar to Centurion, Mauser 98 action only and has better wood.

$1,525	$1,375	$1,175	$975	$800	$700	$600

Last MSR was $1,525.

These models were also available in Mag. cals. that are divided into 4 groups - 1, 2, 3, and 4 Mag. Series. These options retailed in the $50-$300 price range.

❋ *Diane* - grade up from Centurion Classic, 22 in. barrel, Mauser 98 action, M-70 safety, adj. steel trigger.

$1,450	$1,250	$1,000	$825	$700	$600	$500

Last MSR was $1,450.

❋ *Amazone* - grade up from Diane, 20 in. barrel, full stock.

$1,750	$1,525	$1,325	$1,075	$865	$750	$600

Last MSR was $1,750.

❋ *Bavaria Deluxe* - .243 Win. through .458 Win. cals., 21 1/2, 24, or 25 1/2 in. octagonal barrel, French walnut stock with rosewood forend tip and pistol grip cap, no sights, custom made essentially with Sako (disc.) or Mauser action. Many engraving options available from $510 - $1,900.

$1,900	$1,675	$1,450	$1,200	$995	$775	$650

Last MSR was $1,900.

❋ *Safari* - Mag. cals. only.

$2,350	$1,775	$1,475	$1,200	$995	$775	$650

Last MSR was $2,350.

GRADING - PPGS™	100%	98%	95%	90%	80%	70%	60%

MANNLICHER MODEL - various cals., Mauser type bolt action, full stocked. Disc. 1985.

	$730	$660	$580	$520	$470	$430	$395

Last MSR was $825.

✳ *Mannlicher Classic* - similar to basic Mannlicher, except has better walnut. Disc. 1985.

	$995	$890	$775	$650	$575	$530	$460

Last MSR was $1,065.

MATCH MODEL - match target rifle, adj. sights and stock. Disc. 1985.

	$1,640	$1,490	$1,300	$1,050	$900	$800	$700

Last MSR was $1,860.

✳ *Match NATO* - 7.62 cal. match rifle. Disc. 1985.

	$2,640	$2,400	$2,175	$1,850	$1,595	$1,400	$1,195

Last MSR was $3,000.

ST. HUBERT MODEL - Sako action, various cals. and barrel lengths. Disc. 1985.

	$1,900	$1,700	$1,495	$1,300	$1,150	$995	$850

Last MSR was $2,125.

SAFARI SPORTSMAN - .416 Rigby, .375 H&H, .505 Gibbs, or .404 Jeffreys cal., Mauser 98 action, 4 shot mag., limited availability in 1986.

	4,000	$3,550	$3,250	$2,800	$2,400	$2,000	$1,750

Last MSR was $4,000.

Add $300 for .505 Gibbs cal.

SAFARI PROFESSIONAL - various Mag. cals., prices below reflect rifle w/o engraving. Limited importation.

MSR POR	N/A	$9,100	$8,150	$7,400	$6,500	$5,500	$4,500

AFRICAN PRO - similar to Safari Sportsman except has ebony or buffalo horn forend tip, tilting hood for the front sight, multiple folding rear sight.

	$4,800	$4,000	$3,550	$3,250	$2,800	$2,400	$2,000

Last MSR was $4,800.

GRAND CLASSIC - various cals., prices below reflect rifle w/o engraving. Limited importation.

MSR POR	N/A	$7,300	$6,500	$5,500	$4,500	$3,750	$3,000$

RIFLES: SxS

EUROPA I - .22 Hornet, .222 Rem., .222 Rem. Mag., 6mm Rem., .243 Win., .25-06 Rem., .30-06, 6.5x57R, 7x57R, 8x57JRS, or 9.3x74R cal., Anson & Deeley boxlock action, moderate engraving. 1989-disc.

	$4,800	$4,200	$3,800	$3,500	$3,250	$2,995	$2,700

Last MSR was $4,800.

CONTINENTAL I - same calibers as Europa I, sidelock action, 12 engraving options to choose from, many options available on special order. 1989-disc.

	$8,600	$7,700	$6,995	$6,400	$5,600	$4,750	$4,150

Last MSR was $8,600.

"PIONNIER" EXPRESS MODEL - assorted cals. from .22 Hornet through .600 Nitro Express, SxS configuration, heavily engraved, select walnut. Limited production, Anson & Deeley triple lock action, sideplates available at extra charge.

✳ *P-I and P-II* - English style scroll or bouquet (P-II) engraving.

	$7,850	$6,500	$5,825	$5,200	$4,650	$4,160	$3,700

Last MSR was $7,850.

Add $400 for P-II engraving.

GRADING - PPGS™	100%	98%	95%	90%	80%	70%	60%

✳ P III - English style lace engraving (tapestry style).

	100%	98%	95%	90%	80%	70%	60%
	$8,640	$7,750	$7,000	$6,400	$5,600	$4,750	$4,150

Last MSR was $8,640.

✳ P-IV through P-VIII - various styles of royal engraving with or without hunting scenes.

	$9,100	$7,995	$7,450	$6,800	$6,000	$5,000	$4,350

Last MSR was $9,100.

    Add $400 for gold inlays.

✳ P-IX through P-XII - Louis XVI style engraving.

	$9,540	$8,600	$7,800	$7,250	$6,400	$5,250	$4,500

Last MSR was $9,540.

✳ Pionnier Magnum - .338 Win. Mag., .375 H&H, .416 Rigby, .416 Hoffman, .458 Win. Mag., .577 Nitro Express, or .600 Nitro Express cal. Boxlock action with Greener crossbolt.

	$10,900	$9,400	$8,650	$7,800	$7,000	$6,450	$5,825

Last MSR was $10,900.

PIONNIER RECENT IMPORTATION - .300 H&H, .300 Win. Mag., .338 Win. Mag., .375 H&H, .416 Rigby, .458 Win. Mag., or .470 NE cal., similar action as described above with or w/o sideplates, prices below reflect rifle w/o engraving. Limited importation.

MSR POR	N/A	$15,000	$12,250	$9,975	$8,500	$7,500	$6,500

    Add $1,800 for sideplates.
    Add $2,800 for .375 H&H, .470 NE, or .500 NE cal.

ARISTOCRATE MODEL - available in all cals. up to .375 H&H (also in 20 ga.), single shot action with low profile, exhibition oil finished walnut stock and forearm. Values below assume standard model (12 engraving options available). Imported 1987-88 only.

	$9,100	$8,450	$7,775	$7,000	$6,450	$5,825	$5,275

Last MSR was $10,400.

PRESTIGE SIDELOCK - similar cals. as the Pionnier Model, best quality sidelock, triple locking, 10 different presentation options available, values below reflect standard model without options. Custom order only, 1 year waiting period. Mfg. began 1986, limited importation.

MSR POR	NA	$37,500	$31,000	$25,000	$21,750	$19,250	$16,250

FLEURON SIDELOCK - 6.5x57R, 7x57R, 7x65R, .30 Blaser, 8x57 JRS, 8x57 RS, or 9.3x74R cal., made per individual customer specifications. Limited importation.

MSR POR	N/A	$26,000	$21,750	$19,250	$16,750	$14,000	$11,750

SHOTGUNS: O/U

BOSS ROYAL SUPERPOSED - 12, 20 or 28 ga., full sidelock, exhibition grade walnut, double triggers, top-of-the-line quality, built to special order. Values listed assume standard gun (12 engraving options available). 1987-disc.

	$18,500	$16,000	$13,750	$11,000	$9,775	$8,000	$6,950

Last MSR was $18,500.

    Add 6% for 28 ga.

SUPERPOSED EXPRESS "INTERNATIONAL" - O/U shotgun, includes extra set of rifle barrels, 20 ga., 7 choices of rifle cals., deluxe walnut. Elaborate engraving patterns available at extra charge, limited production. Disc. 1985.

	$2,400	$2,000	$1,800	$1,575	$1,400	$1,200	$1,050

Last MSR was $2,490.

GRADING - PPGS™	100%	98%	95%	90%	80%	70%	60%

SHOTGUNS: SxS

EUROPA MODEL - 12, 20, 28 ga., or .410 bore, Anson & Deeley boxlock action, single or double trigger, moderately engraved, oil finished stock and forearm, choice of 6 engraving options. 1989-disc.

	$3,300	$2,750	$2,350	$2,000	$1,800	$1,575	$1,400

Last MSR was $3,300.

LIEGE MODEL - 12, 16 (disc. 1986), 20, or 28 ga., Anson & Deeley locking action, elaborate engraving, deluxe walnut. 1986-disc.

  ✳ *Luxe Model*

	$5,300	$4,600	$3,900	$3,300	$2,900	$2,600	$2,300

Last MSR was $5,900 (disc. 1988).

  ✳ *Grand Luxe*

	$6,900	$6,000	$5,000	$4,300	$3,600	$3,200	$2,875

Last MSR was $6,900.

  Add 15% for 28 ga.
  Add 15% for sideplates.

  Many engraving options and other special order features can be added to the above models.

CONTINENTAL MODEL - 12, 20, 28 ga., or .410 bore, sidelock action, double or single trigger, deluxe oil finished walnut stock, choice of 6 engraving options. 1989-disc.

	$7,400	$6,250	$5,200	$4,400	$3,700	$3,200	$2,875

Last MSR was $7,400.

ETENDARD MODEL - 12, 20, 28 ga., or .410 bore, full sidelock, exhibition grade walnut, double triggers, top-of-the-line quality, built to special order. Values listed assume standard gun (many engraving options available). Mfg. began 1987, limited importation.

MSR POR	N/A	$25,750	$21,750	$19,250	$16,750	$14,000	$11,750

  Add $890 for 20, 28 ga. or .410 bore.

DUMOULIN, HENRI & FILS

Current manufacturer located in Herstal, Belgium. No current importation. Previously imported and distributed by New England Arms Corp. located in Kittery Point, ME.

H. Dumoulin has manufactured quality firearms in Liege/Herstal, Belgium since 1947. They specialize in big-bore, high quality bolt action rifles, generally built on Mauser 98 or commercial Mauser actions. The improved double square bridge Imperial Magnum action was developed and introduced in 1987.

RIFLES: BOLT ACTION

GRAND LUXE BOLT ACTION - .300 Wby. Mag., .338 Win. Mag., .375 H&H, .378 Wby. Mag., .404 Jeffrey, .416 Rigby, .460 Wby. Mag., or .505 Gibbs cal., 24, 25.6, or 26 in. barrel, European walnut stock with ebony forend tip and pistol grip cap, folding leaf sights with hooded front, custom made on the Dumoulin Imperial Magnum double square bridge action. Many engraving options available.

MSR POR	N/A	$7,995	$7,525	$6,700	$5,750	$5,100	$4,400

  Add $750 for left-hand action.
  Add $1,150 for extended top and bottom tang.
  Add $1,000 for claw mounts.
  Add $1,000 for .505 Gibbs cal.

SOVEREIGN - available in same cals. as Grand Luxe Bolt Action, except with a higher quality finish, knurled bolt handles, gold inlayed lettering. Many engraving options available.

  Pricing on this model depends on engraving, wood and other options. Imperial Magnum is also available in various stages of completion, barreled actions, actions in the white, etc. Please contact the factory directly for quotation (see Trademark Index).

RIFLES: SxS CUSTOM

BOXLOCK RIFLE - boxlock action, best quality double rifle, highly figured European walnut, finely hand checkered with standard scroll engraving. Custom ordered to customer's dimensions. Prices start at $15,000.

SIDELOCK RIFLE - sidelock action, best quality hand detachable locks, top quality European walnut, finely hand checkered with standard scroll engraving. Additional engraving or deluxe wood quoted on request. Prices start at $20,000.

SHOTGUNS: SxS, CUSTOM

BOXLOCK MODEL - available in most gauges, individually built per customer special order. The factory should be contacted directly for more information and a price quotation.

SIDELOCK MODEL - available in most gauges, individually built per customer special order. The factory should be contacted directly for more information and a price quotation.

DUMOULIN HERSTAL S.A.

Current manufacturer established in 1997 and located in Herstal, Belgium. This manufacturer's sister company is Ernest Dumoulin S.P.R.L. Currently imported by Empire Rifle Company, LLC, located in Meriden, NH. Previously imported by Arms De Chasse, LLC, located in Hertford, NC.

Dumoulin Herstal manufactures a complete line of quality bolt action rifles in many configurations and calibers. They also produce their own A2000 LM (Long Magnum) action, based on the 1930s Mauser Oberndorf design, which is available separately. Dumoulin manufactures 100-150 guns annually. Please contact the importer directly regarding current information, including model availability and prices.

RIFLES: BOLT ACTION

The following models employ the A2000 Dumoulin action featuring forged flattop receiver, 3 locking lugs with claw extractors, and one-piece bolt, handle, and knob.

ADVENTURER SERIES - various cals. from .25-06 Rem. - .458 Win. Mag., configurations include Euro 2000 and Euroforest. Limited importation began 1999.

Depending on variation and caliber, prices for this series range from $1,510-$1,936.

GENTLEMAN HUNTER SERIES (LIEGE MODEL) - various cals. from .25-06 Rem. - .458 Win. Mag., including some additional Safari cals., configurations include Liege, Liege Safari, Liege Full Stock (Mannlicher), or Liege Thumbhole. Limited importation began 1999.

Depending on variation and caliber, prices for this series range from $2,368-$3,268.

TRADITIONAL LIEGE CRAFTSMAN SERIES (HERSTAL MODEL) - various cals. from .25-06 Rem. - .458 Win. Mag., including many Safari cals., configurations include Herstal, Herstal Full Stock (Mannlicher), or Herstal Safari (5 shot mag.). Limited importation began 1999.

Depending on variation and caliber, prices for this series range from $5,950-$7,500.

MODEL WHITE HUNTER SAFARI SPECIAL - .375 H&H, .416 Rigby, .416 Wby. Mag., .500 Jeffery, or .505 Gibbs cal., other cals. available upon request, this model features the proprietary Dumoulin Herstal A2000/LM (Long Magnum) action, hinged floorplate, express sights, deluxe checkered walnut stock with ebony forend. Limited importation began 1999.

Prices for this model start at $12,700.

E SECTION

E.D.M. ARMS

Current manufacturer established in 1997 and located in Redlands, CA. Dealer and consumer direct sales.

GRADING - PPGS™	100%	98%	95%	90%	80%	70%	60%

RIFLES: BOLT ACTION

WINDRUNNER MODEL 96 (XM107) - .338 Lapua (new 2002) or .50 BMG cal., takedown repeater action, EDM machined receiver, fully adj. stock, match grade 28 in. barrel that removes within seconds, allowing exact head space every time the barrel is reinstalled, includes two 5 (.50 BMG cal.) or 8 (.338 Lapua) shot mags., Picatinny rail, and bipod, 24 (Lightweight Tactical Takedown) or 36 lbs.

MSR $7,500	$7,500	$6,850	$6,200	$5,500	$5,000	$4,500	$4,000

✱ *Windrunner Model 96 SS99* - similar to Windrunner, except is single shot, w/o mag., includes bipod and sling, 32 lbs. New 2002.

MSR $5,850	$5,850	$5,150	$4,450	$3,850	$3,250	$2,850	$2,450

MODEL XM04 CHEYENNE TACTICAL - .408 CheyTac cal., takedown repeater, tactical bolt action configuration, 5 shot mag., 30 in. fluted barrel with suppressor, desert camo finish, retractable stock, effective range is 2,500+ yards, 27 lbs. New 2002.

MSR $7,500	$7,500	$6,850	$6,200	$5,500	$5,000	$4,500	$4,000

Subtract $1,400 for single shot action (disc.).

MODEL 50 - .50 BMG cal., bolt action, single shot, twin rail adj. skeletonized stock, Picatinny rail and bipod. Mfg. 2003.

$4,250	$3,750	$3,250	$2,850	$2,450	$2,050	$1,650

Last MSR was $4,250.

MODEL 98 - .338 Lapua cal., takedown repeating bolt action, single rail adj. stock, pistol grip. New 2003.

MSR $7,500	$7,500	$6,850	$6,200	$5,500	$5,000	$4,500	$4,000

E.M.F. CO., INC.

Current importer and distributor established circa 1960 and located in Santa Ana, CA. Distributor and dealer sales.

For information on Dakota Single Action Revolvers imported by E.M.F., please refer to the Dakota Single Action Revolvers section. Please refer to the *Blue Book of Modern Black Powder Arms* by John Allen & Dennis Adler (also online) for more information and prices on E.M.F.'s lineup of modern black powder models.

DERRINGERS: REPRODUCTIONS

STANDARD MODEL - .22 Short cal., copy of Colt Model Lord or Lady Derringer, blue, nickel, gold (disc.), or silver (disc.) gold finish. Importation disc. 1992.

$95	$80	$70	$60	$55	$50	$45

Last MSR was $125.

1872 STANDARD MODEL - .22 Short cal., copy of Colt Model Lord or Lady Derringer, nickel or silver/gold frame finish, hardwood grips, 7 oz.

MSR $90	$75	$65	$60	$55	$50	$45	$40

Add $30 for case, $95 for cased set with two Derringers.

GRADING - PPGS™	100%	98%	95%	90%	80%	70%	60%

PISTOLS: REPRODUCTIONS

REMINGTON ROLLING BLOCK PISTOL - .357 Mag. cal., rolling block design. Disc. 1992.

	$300	$225	$185	$165	$155	$145	$135

Last MSR was $395.

REVOLVERS: REPRODUCTIONS

Please refer to the Dakota Single Action Revolvers section in this text for a complete listing of reproductions.

RIFLES: SxS

KODIAK MARK IV DOUBLE EXPRESS SXS RIFLE - .45-70 Govt. cal., back action, browned 24 in. barrels with triple leaf express sights, color case hardened frame, trigger guard and hammers. Importation disc. 2004.

	$2,650	$1,950	$1,625	$1,400	$1,200	$1,050	$895

Last MSR was $2,995.

RIFLES: SEMI-AUTO, REPRODUCTIONS

These models are authentic shooting reproductions previously mfg. in Italy.

AP 74 - .22 LR or .32 ACP cal., copy of the Colt AR-15, 15 shot mag., 20 in. barrel, 6 3/4 lbs. Importation disc. 1989.

	$350	$295	$250	$200	$175	$155	$145

Last MSR was $295.

Add $25 for .32 cal.

* **Sporter Carbine** - .22 LR cal. only, wood sporter stock. Importation disc. 1989.

	$375	$325	$275	$225	$195	$175	$160

Last MSR was $320.

* **Paramilitary Paratrooper Carbine** - .22 LR cal. only, folding wire stock, black nylon on paramilitary design model. Importation disc. 1987.

	$395	$350	$300	$260	$215	$175	$165

Last MSR was $325.

Add $10 for wood folding stock.

* **"Dressed" Military Model** - with Cyclops scope, Colt bayonet, sling, and bipod. Disc. 1986.

	$395	$350	$300	$265	$240	$220	$200

Last MSR was $450.

GALIL - .22 LR cal. only, reproduction of the Israeli Galil. Importation disc. 1989.

	$350	$295	$250	$200	$175	$155	$145

Last MSR was $295.

KALASHNIKOV AK-47 - .22 LR cal. only, reproduction of the Russian AK-47, semi-auto. Importation disc. 1989.

	$350	$295	$250	$200	$175	$155	$145

Last MSR was $295.

FRENCH M.A.S. - .22 LR cal. only, reproduction of the French Bull-Pup Combat Rifle, with carrying handle, 29 shot mag. Importation disc. 1989.

	$375	$325	$265	$240	$220	$200	$185

Last MSR was $320.

M1 CARBINE - .30 cal. only, copy of the U.S. Military M1 Carbine. Disc. 1985.

	$225	$175	$150	$140	$130	$120	$110

Last MSR was $205.

Add $43 for Paratrooper variation.

GRADING - PPGS™	100%	98%	95%	90%	80%	70%	60%

RIFLES: REMINGTON REPRODUCTIONS

ROLLING BLOCK CARBINE/RIFLE - .45-70 Govt. cal., authentic reproduction of the Remington Rolling Block Rifle, standard (disc. 2003) or target model, 26 (carbine) or 30 in. octagon barrel. Mfg. by Pedersoli. Importation began 1991.

	MSR $950	$825	$725	$625	$575	$525	$450	$415

Subtract $60 for carbine model (new 2005).
Subtract approx. $100 for standard model.

✴ *Deluxe Rolling Block Rifle* - .45-70 Govt. cal., similar to Rolling Block Rifle, except has 32 in. barrel, checkered pistol grip stock, and German silver forearm cap. Imported 2000-2002.

$900	$700	$500	$450	$400	$365	$330

Last MSR was $1,125.

BABY ROLLING BLOCK CARBINE - .357 Mag. cal. Mfg. 1992 only.

$395	$300	$260	$220	$185	$160	$140

Last MSR was $490.

REVOLVING CARBINE - .357 Mag., .44-40 WCF (disc.), or .45 LC cal., 18 in. barrel, case colored frame, walnut grips, Model 1875 Army Single Action design, 5 lbs. Importation disc. 1995, reintroduced 2003.

$450	$375	$315	$265	$230	$200	$185

Last MSR was $560.

TEXAS CARBINE (1858 REMINGTON) - .22 LR cal., action patterned after Remington revolving carbine, 21 in. octagon barrel, wood stock and forearm, brass frame. Also available with extra .22 Mag. cylinder. Importation disc. 1998.

$295	$225	$175	$150	$135	$125	$110

Last MSR was $400.

RIFLES: SHARPS REPRODUCTIONS

1874 SHARPS HARTFORD SPORTING OR MILITARY RIFLE - .45-70 Govt., .45 LC (new 2004) or .45-120 cal., copy of the Sharps Single Shot, 28 or 30 in. octagonal barrel, case hardened frame, single or double set triggers. Importation disc. 1999, reintroduced 2003.

	MSR $780	$685	$625	$550	$495	$450	$425	$400

Add $120 for checkered stock.
Add $180 for in-the-white (no metal finish).
Add $95 for .45-70 Govt. cal.
Add $120 for brown finish.
Add $45 for target variation with 1/2 round, 1/2 octagon barrel.
Add $300 for 1874 Business Rifle configuration in .45-70 Govt. cal. only.

✴ *1874 Deluxe Rifle* - .45-70 Govt. or .45-120 (disc.) cal., blue or brown finish, 32 in. tapered octagon barrel, double set triggers, checkered pistol grip and forearm, case hardened frame, silver forend tip.

	MSR $1,320	$1,200	$1,025	$875	$775	$695	$625	$565

An engraved version of this model is also available for $2,220, and Super Deluxe with gold inlays is $2,990.

✴ *1874 Military Carbine* - saddle ring carbine with 22 in. round barrel, single trigger. Disc. 2005.

$695	$625	$550	$495	$450	$425	$400

Last MSR was $760.

GRADING - PPGS™	100%	98%	95%	90%	80%	70%	60%

QUIGLEY SHARPS MODEL 1874 SPORTING RIFLE - .45-70 Govt., .45-90, or .45-120 (disc. 2003) cal., 34 in. heavy octagon barrel with storage compartment in stock. Importation began 2000.

MSR $1,800	$1,550	$1,300	$1,050	$875	$750	$625	$550

RIFLES: SPRINGFIELD REPRODUCTIONS

SPRINGFIELD 1873 TRAPDOOR CARBINE/RIFLE - .45-70 Govt. cal., trapdoor single shot action, 22 (carbine), 26 (Officer's Model), or 32 (Rifle) in. barrel, blue action, walnut stock. Mfg. by Pedersoli.

MSR $1,020	$900	$800	$725	$650	$575	$495	$425

Add $170 for Rifle or $300 for Officer's Model.

RIFLES: WINCHESTER REPRODUCTIONS

DELUXE 1860 HENRY RIFLE - .44-40 WCF or .45 LC cal. only, brass or case colored steel frame, deluxe walnut, reproduction of New Haven Arms Co.'s Henry Rifle, 24 in. blue or white barrel. New 1987.

MSR $1,045	$925	$750	$525	$400	$350	$300	$275

Add $105 for in-the-white barrel or for case colored steel (.45 LC cal. only) frame.

* ❋ *Engraved Henry Rifle* - similar to deluxe Henry Rifle except has hand engraved receiver. Imported 1987-90.

	$1,350	$975	$700	$525	$400	$340	$295

Last MSR was $1,598.

1866 YELLOWBOY CARBINE - .22 LR (disc. 2002), .22 Mag. (mfg. 2000-2002), .32-20 WCF (mfg. 2000-2002), .38 Spl., .38-40 WCF (mfg. 2000-2002, reintroduced 2005), .44-40 WCF, or .45 LC (new 1993) cal., 19 in. barrel, brass frame, saddle ring carbine. Disc. 2003, reintroduced 2005.

MSR $790	$675	$550	$450	$325	$265	$235	$200

* ❋ *1866 Rifle* - same cals. as 1866 Yellowboy Carbine, 20 (Border model short rifle, new 1999) or 24 1/4 in. barrel.

MSR $850	$715	$575	$465	$335	$275	$235	$200

Add $25 for in-the-white barrel.

* ❋ *Engraved Yellowboy Carbine* - .38 Spl. or .44-40 WCF cal. Importation disc. 1990.

	$875	$575	$440	$330	$295	$260	$230

Last MSR was $1,080.

1873 CARBINE - .22 Mag. (disc.), .32-20 WCF (mfg. 1999-2000, reintroduced 2005), .357 Mag. (disc. 2000, reintroduced 2003, and again in 2005), .38-40 WCF (mfg. 2000, reintroduced 2005), .44 Spl. (mfg. 2000, reintroduced 2005), .44-40 WCF (disc. 2000, reintroduced 2005), or .45 LC cal., 19 in. barrel, copy of the Winchester Model 1873, blue (disc. 2000) or case hardened steel receiver. Disc. 2003, reintroduced 2005.

MSR $960	$825	$650	$500	$400	$325	$275	$235

* ❋ *1873 Rifle* - similar cals. as Carbine, 20 (Border model short rifle, new 1999), 24 1/4, or 30 (limited importation 2000 only) in. barrel, case hardened receiver.

MSR $985	$850	$675	$525	$425	$325	$275	$235

Add $50 for 30 in. barrel (disc.).
Add $115 for Deluxe Border model.
Add $120 for Deluxe model with checkered pistol grip stock (.357 Mag. or .45 LC cal. only, disc. 2003).

* ❋ *1873 "Young Boy" Carbine/Rifle* - .22 LR cal., blue steel, 19 or 24 1/4 in. barrel. Imported 1995-96.

	$800	$600	$450	$330	$295	$260	$230

Last MSR was $1,050.

Add $50 for rifle barrel.

GRADING - PPGS™	100%	98%	95%	90%	80%	70%	60%

✳ Engraved Rifle - .357 Mag. or .44-40 WCF cal. only. Importation disc. 1987.

	$895	$635	$500	$450	$400	$360	$325

Last MSR was $850.

PREMIER 1873 CARBINE & RIFLE - .45 LC cal., case hardened frame, uncheckered walnut stock and forearm, full mag., rifle has 24 1/4 in. barrel, carbine has 19 in. barrel. Imported 1988-1989 only.

	$850	$595	$450	$330	$295	$260	$230

Last MSR was $1,160.

1885 HIGH WALL RIFLE - .38-55 WCF (new 2000), .40-65 (new 2005), .45-70 Govt., or .45-90 (new 2005) cal., action patterned after the Winchester Model 1885 High Wall, 30 or 32 (mfg. 2003 only) in. barrel, checkered walnut stock. Mfg. by Uberti. Imported 1998-2003, reintroduced 2005.

MSR $875	$775	$665	$550	$450	$375	$325	$295

Add $85 for checkered pistol grip stock.
Add $50 for checkered stock and forearm (disc.).

HARTFORD 1892 CARBINE - .357 Mag., .44 Mag. (disc. 2003, reintroduced 2005), .45 LC cal., or .44-40 WCF (disc. 2003) cal., case hardened, blued, brass, or stainless steel frame, 20 in. round barrel with or w/o saddle ring, buckhorn sights, standard stock with crescent buttplate and forearm. Importation began 2003.

MSR $381	$330	$290	$260	$235	$200	$185	$170

Add $12 for saddle ring, brass frame, or color case hardened frame.
Add $49 for stainless steel (.357 Mag. cal. only).

HARTFORD 1892 RIFLE - .357 Mag., .44-40 WCF, .44 Mag., or .45 LC cal., case hardened, blued, brass, or stainless steel frame, 20 (short rifle) or 24 octagon barrel with buckhorn sights, standard stock with crescent buttplate and forearm. Importation began 1998.

MSR $443	$390	$345	$290	$255	$220	$200	$185

Add $12 for brass or color case hardened frame, or $37 for stainless steel frame.
Add $20 for Target Model with case hardened receiver, and 1/2 round, 1/2 octagon barrel (disc. 2003).
This model is also packaged with the Great Western II 1873 SA revolver - combination sets range from $950-$1,200.

SHOTGUNS: SxS

HARTFORD MODEL STAGECOACH SHOTGUN - 12 ga., exposed hammers, 20 in. barrels, checkered walnut stock and forearm, color case hardened frame, mfg. in Spain by Aral. Limited importation 2001-2005.

	$575	$500	$450	$420	$375	$340	$325

Last MSR was $650.

STAGECOACH MODEL - 12 ga. only, features exposed hammers and 20 in. brown barrels, mfg. by S.I.A.C.E. Imported 2000-2002.

	$1,175	$900	$700	$500	$450	$400	$365

Last MSR was $1,375.

SHOTGUNS: SEMI-AUTO

MARK V CONQUEST - 12 ga. only, 28 in. barrel with choke tubes. Limited importation 2003.

	$385	$325	$275	$240	$220	$200	$185

Last MSR was $460.

84 GUN CO.

Previous manufacturer located in Eighty Four, PA. Circa early 1970s.

RIFLES: BOLT ACTION

CLASSIC RIFLE - various calibers. Grades 1-4.

	100%	98%	95%	90%	80%	70%	60%
Grade 1	$420	$315	$275	$235	$210	$190	$170
Grade 2	$780	$585	$512	$430	$390	$355	$315
Grade 3	$860	$645	$560	$475	$430	$390	$345
Grade 4	$1,580	$1,185	$1,030	$870	$790	$715	$640

LOBO RIFLE - various calibers. Grades standard, 1-4.

	100%	98%	95%	90%	80%	70%	60%
Standard	$415	$315	$270	$230	$210	$190	$170
Grade 1	$540	$405	$355	$300	$270	$245	$220
Grade 2	$795	$600	$520	$440	$400	$360	$320
Grade 3	$1,600	$1,200	$1,040	$880	$800	$720	$640
Grade 4	$2,350	$1,765	$1,530	$1,295	$1,175	$1,060	$940

PENNSYLVANIA RIFLE - various calibers. Grades standard, 1-4.

	100%	98%	95%	90%	80%	70%	60%
Standard	$420	$315	$275	$235	$210	$190	$170
Grade 1	$540	$405	$355	$300	$270	$245	$220
Grade 2	$795	$600	$520	$440	$400	$360	$320
Grade 3	$1,600	$1,200	$1,040	$880	$800	$720	$640
Grade 4	$2,350	$1,765	$1,530	$1,295	$1,175	$1,060	$940

EAGLE ARMS, INC.

Current manufacturer located in Geneseo, IL. Previous division of ArmaLite, Inc. 1995-2002, located in Geneseo, IL. Manufacture of pre-1995 Eagle Arms rifles was in Coal Valley, IL.

During 1995, Eagle Arms, Inc. reintroduced the ArmaLite trademark. The new company was organized under the ArmaLite name. In 2003, Eagle Arms became a separate company, and is no longer a division of ArmaLite.

RIFLES: SEMI-AUTO, RECENT MFG.

On the following M-15 models manufactured 1995 and earlier, A2 accessories included a collapsible carbine type buttstock (disc. per 1994 C/B) and forward bolt assist mechanism. Accessories are similar, except also have national match sights. The A2 suffix indicates rifle is supplied with carrying handle, A4 designates a flattop receiver, some are equipped with a detachable carrying handle.

AR-10 MATCH RIFLE - .308 Win. cal., very similar to the Armalite AR-10 A4 rifle, 20 or 24 (Match rifle) in. chrome moly barrel, A2 (Service rifle) or A4 style flattop upper receiver (no sights), black stock with pistol grip and forearm, 10 shot mag., 9.6 lbs. New 2001.

MSR $1,000	$925	$850	$775	$700	$650	$600	$550

Add $65 for Service rifle with A2 front/rear sights.
Add $480 for 24 in. barrel and aluminum free-floating handguard.

MODEL M15 A2/A4 RIFLE (EA-15 E-1) - .223 Rem. or .308 Win. cal., patterned after the Colt AR-15A2, 20 in. barrel, A2 sights or A4 flattop, with (pre 1993) or w/o forward bolt assist, 7 lbs. Mfg. 1990-1993, reintroduced 2002.

MSR $795	$725	$600	$525	$450	$400	$375	$350

Add $40 for .223 cal. flattop (Model E15A4B).
Add $205 for .308 Win. cal. flattop.

GRADING - PPGS™	100%	98%	95%	90%	80%	70%	60%

✳ **M15 A2/A4 Carbine (EA9025C/EA9027C)** - features collapsible (disc. per C/B 1994) or fixed (new 1994) buttstock and 16 in. barrel, 5 lbs. 14 oz. Mfg. 1990-95, reintroduced 2002.

	MSR $795	$725	$600	$525	$450	$400	$375	$350

Add $40 for flattop (Model E15A4CB).

1997 retail for the pre-ban models was $1,100 (EA9396).

Beginning 1993, the A2 accessory kit became standard on this model.

✳ **M15 A2 H-BAR Rifle (EA9040C)** - features heavy Target barrel, 8 lbs. 14 oz., includes E-2 accessories. Mfg. 1990-95.

	$825	$725	$600	$525	$450	$400	$375

Last MSR was $895.

1997 retail for this pre-ban model was $1,100 (EA9200).

✳ **M15 A4 Eagle Spirit (EA9055S)** - includes 16 in. premium air gauged national match barrel, fixed stock, full length tubular aluminum hand guard, designed for IPSC shooting, includes match grade accessories, 8 lbs. 6 oz. Mfg. 1993-95, reintroduced 2002 only.

	$725	$650	$550	$500	$450	$395	$350

Last MSR was $850.

The 1995 pre-ban variation of this model retailed at $1,475 (EA9603).

✳ **M15 A2 Golden Eagle (EA9049S)** - similar to M15 A2 H-BAR, except has (N.M.) National Match accessories and two-stage trigger, 20 in. extra heavy barrel, 12 lbs. 12 oz. Mfg 1991-95, reintroduced 2002 only.

	$995	$850	$725	$650	$550	$500	$450

Last MSR was $1,125.

The 1997 pre-ban variation of this model retailed at $1,300 (EA9500).

✳ **M15 A4 Eagle Eye (EA9901)** - includes 24 in. free floating 1 in. barrel with tubular aluminum hand guard, weighted buttstock, designed for silhouette matches, 14 lbs. Mfg. 1993-95.

	$1,325	$1,075	$875	$725	$600	$525	$450

Last MSR was $1,495.

✳ **M15 Action Master (EA9052S)** - match rifle, flattop, solid aluminum handguard tube that allows for free floating 20 in. barrel with compensator, N.M. accessories, fixed stock, 8 lbs. 5 oz. Mfg. 1992-95, reintroduced 2002 only.

	$725	$650	$550	$500	$450	$395	$350

Last MSR was $850.

The 1995 pre-ban variation of this model retailed at $1,475 (EA5600).

✳ **M15 A4 Special Purpose Rifle (EA9042C)** - 20 in. barrel, flattop (A4) or detachable handle receiver. Disc. 1995.

	$850	$725	$600	$525	$450	$400	$375

Last MSR was $955.

The 1995 pre-ban variation of this model retailed at $1,165 (EA9204).

✳ **M15 A4 Predator (EA9902)** - post-ban only, 18 in. barrel, National Match trigger, flattop (A4) or detachable handle receiver. Mfg. 1995 only.

	$1,125	$895	$725	$600	$525	$450	$400

Last MSR was $1,350.

EFFEBI SNC

Current manufacturer located in Concesio, Italy since 1994. Currently imported and distributed beginning 2004 by American Outdoor Adventures, located in Leesburg, GA. Previously named Dr. Franco Beretta until 1994. Also refer to the Dr. Franco Beretta listing.

Effebi manufacturers a variety of good quality shotguns in O/U, SxS, and single barrel configurations, including the top quality SxS sidelock Gemini model. Effebi's full line of shotguns is available from the importer. The importer should be contacted directly (see Trademark Index) for more information regarding current pricing and shotgun model availability.

EGO ARMAS, S.A.

Current manufacturer established circa 1953 and located in Eibar, Spain. No current U.S. importation.

Ego Armas manufactures high quality sidelock double rifles ranging in price from approx. 5,000-8,850 euros in cals. up to .375 H&H, and 13,100 euros for the .416 Rigby or .470 NE., in addition to a boxlock express model for 3,000 euros. Mounted scopes are also available. Boxlock and sidelock shotguns are also available ranging in price from 770-1,050 euros for a boxlock (hammer model also available), and 1,475-2,200 euros for sidelock action with ejectors and English wood finish. More information, including current models and approximate U.S. pricing, can be obtained by contacting this manufacturer directly (see Trademark Index).

EMPIRE RIFLE COMPANY LLC

Current rifle manufacturer located in Meriden, NH.

RIFLES: BOLT ACTION

Empire Rifle Company manufactures a complete line of high quality custom Mauser bolt action rifles, with barrel lengths and caliber specified by the customer.

LEGACY MODEL - various cals. from .257 Roberts to .500 Jeffrey, imported Mauser action from Europe, stainless match grade barrel, checkered walnut or Kevlar stock and forearm with cheekpiece, right hand only.

MSR $3,795	$3,450	$3,150	$2,850	$2,500	$2,150	$1,850	$1,600

    Add $200 for Guide Model with X walnut stock.
    Add $1,100 for Professional Grade with AAA walnut stock.
    Add $2,000 for Express Grade with all options included.

LIBERTY MODEL - over 40 various cals., similar action as Legacy Model, scaled down design for women shooters, walnut or Kevlar stock, stainless steel match grade barrel. New 2005.

MSR $3,795	$3,450	$3,150	$2,850	$2,500	$2,150	$1,850	$1,600

    Add $1,100 for Professional Grade with AAA walnut stock.
    Add $2,000 for Express Grade with all options included.

STANDARD MODEL - various Magnum cals., features Empire 98S Mauser action, stainless match grade barrel, checkered walnut or Kevlar stock and forearm, recoil pad, available in right or left hand. New 2005.

MSR $4,495	$4,100	$3,750	$3,375	$3,000	$2,650	$2,300	$1,900

    Add $200 for Guide Model with X walnut stock.
    Add $1,100 for Professional Grade with AAA walnut stock.
    Add $2,000 for Express Grade with all options included.

EMPRE EAST AFRICA MODEL - various cals. up to .505 Gibbs, Mauser Magnum action, right or left hand, checkered walnut or Kevlar pistol grip stock with recoil pad, straight bolt handle, integral box mag.

MSR $6,495	$5,995	$5,400	$4,850	$4,300	$3,850	$3,350	$2,750

    Add $1,100 for Professional Grade with AAA walnut stock.
    Add $2,000 for Express Grade with all options included.

GRADING - PPGS™	100%	98%	95%	90%	80%	70%	60%

ENFIELDS

Previously manufactured by the Royal Small Arms Factory located in the northern outskirts of London, in Middlesex, England. The Enfield rifles, carbines and revolvers were produced by other British factories as well as Australia (from 1913), Canada (from 1941), the United States (from 1941), India (from 1905), and Pakistan (from 1959). The publisher would like to thank Mr. Ian Skennerton for making the following information available.

REVOLVERS

450 ENFIELD REVOLVER Mk I & II - often called the .476. 6 shot, hinged barrel with exposed knuckle joint axis at front, a top break action with forward-sliding chamber for extraction. Mk I model (checkered grips) introduced in 1880 with an Mk II variant (plain wooden grips) in 1882. Designed by American Owen Jones and made at Enfield R.S.A.F., it was not liked due to sliding chamber extraction and cumbersome proportions.

$800	$725	$600	$550	$500	$450	$375

.455 WEBLEY REVOLVER - made by Webley & Scott, purchased privately by officers as well on War Office contracts. Mk I model approved in 1887, Mk II in 1894, Mk III in 1897, Mk IV in 1899, Mk V in 1913, and the Mk VI in 1915. The Mark number is stamped on the revolver frame. Composition grips. Enfield made the Mk VI Webley during 1921-1926. Earlier Marks can sell at a 30% plus premium over the Marks V and VI, as well as more scarce Enfield production (1921-26).

$750	$650	$550	$500	$450	$375	$260

NO. 2 MK. I REVOLVER - .380 Enfield (based on .38 S&W with a 200 grain bullet) cal., double action, 6 shot, fixed sights, blue or black finish, wood or composition grips, top break action, Enfield made copy of the .380 Mk IV Webley. Introduced in 1932.

$600	$500	$400	$300	$250	$200	$150

NO. 2 MK. I*/MK I REVOLVER** - .380 Enfield with hammer spur removed and other manufacturing concessions applied. Wartime production by Albion in England with a very few by Howard Auto Cultivators (H.A.C.) in Australia (which bring a sizeable premium due to the short run of 355 revolvers). Enfield & Albion production only.

$500	$400	$325	$275	$250	$200	$150

RIFLES

.577 ENFIELD PATTERN 1853 RIFLE/CARBINE/MUSKET - adopted from 1853 as the general service issue, percussion lock marked "Tower, Enfield, B.S.A., L.S.A., Windsor" on lockplate, available in 3-band long rifle, 2-band short rifle, engineer (Lancaster), artillery, and cavalry carbine configurations, many supplied to the Confederacy during America's Civil War.

$1,200	$1,000	$875	$750	$675	$600	$475

.577 SNIDER-ENFIELD RIFLE/CARBINE - adopted in 1866 as a breech-loading conversion of the .577 Enfield, single shot, swing-over breech block, modified percussion lock, the Mk III improved locking breech in 1869 was new manufacture.

$1,000	$850	$750	$675	$600	$500	$375

.450 MARTINI-HENRY - Britain's first purpose built breech-loader in 1871, hinged falling block action with internal lock mechanism, early Mk I rifle had a safety catch, Mk II rifle introduced in 1876, Cavalry Carbine in 1877, Artillery Carbine in 1879, Mk III rifle in 1879 and the long lever "humpback" Mk IV in 1887 which was sent to India & Nepal.

$900	$750	$675	$600	$550	$450	$325

GRADING - PPGS™	100%	98%	95%	90%	80%	70%	60%

.303 MARTINI-ENFIELD - conversion of .450 M.-H., the converted markings are stamped on the left side of the receiver. Artillery & cavalry carbines are more prolific than the rifles, artillery models are marked "A.C." with the Mark number on the left side of the receiver and cavalry models are marked "C.C.", followed by the Mark number.

	$850	$700	$650	$550	$500	$450	$325

.303 MAGAZINE LEE-METFORD - introduced in 1888 with 7-groove Metford segmental rifling and 8-round detachable magazine, rifles proceeded through Marks I, I*, II, & II* which is marked on the right side of the action body below the factory and year, underneath the closed bolt handle, rifles have 30.2 in., carbines have 20.75 in. barrels. Mk I & I* rifle have single-row 8 round magazine, carbines are 6 round, Mk II & II* rifles are 10 round staggered box.

	$2,000	$1,800	$1,700	$1,600	$1,450	$1,250	$995

Add 50%+ for Mk I and I* models.

.303 MAGAZINE LEE-ENFIELD - introduced in 1895 with 5-groove Enfield rifling for cordite loads. Fitted with safety catch on the cocking piece, rifles and carbines went through Marks I and I*, Mk I* has no cleaning rod provision in forend or nosecap.

	$1,800	$1,650	$1,300	$1,100	$950	$850	$625

.303 CHARGER LOADING LEE-ENFIELD - M.L.M. and M.L.E. rifles with 30.2 in. barrels, modified for clip charger loading, after 1907 fitted with improved sights and foresight protector, conversions marked on left of receiver butt socket with factory and year.

	$1,450	$1,350	$1,200	$1,050	$950	$850	$600

.303 S.M.L.E. Mk I (SHORT, MAGAZINE LEE-ENFIELD) - features a sliding charger guide on the bolthead, bone inserts on the rear sight slide and incurving nosecap foresight protector wings, 10 round staggered row detachable mag with magazine cut-off provision in the receiver. Introduced 1903, made at Enfield, BSA, and LSA until 1907.

	$1,500	$1,300	$1,100	$950	$800	$650	$500

.303 S.M.L.E. Mk III (RIFLE NO. 1 Mk III) - improved rearsight and rear handguard over the S.M.L.E. Mk I, still retains the magazine cut-off and volley sights of the Mk I S.M.L.E. model., approved in 1907, also made by Lithgow and Ishapore.

	$750	$650	$550	$500	$475	$400	$350

.303 RIFLE NO. 1 Mk III* - incorporates production shortcuts, no magazine cut-off, long range volley sights, or backsight windage adjustment. Made by Enfield, BSA, LSA, SSA, Lithgow and Ishapore, introduced in 1915.

	$400	$350	$300	$275	$250	$195	$150

.303 RIFLE NO. 1 Mk III* H.T. SNIPER - factory fitted telescopic sight and heavy barrel, converted at Lithgow, Australia at the end of WWII, special bedding of furniture, some were also fitted with a cheekpiece, British & Lithgow actions.

	$2,750	$2,250	$1,900	$1,700	$1,450	$1,300	$1,050

Buyer beware - check for authentic ser. nos., as there have been some fakes on this model.

.22 PATT 1914 NOS. 1 & 2 - single-shot WW1 conversions by the British gun trade. No. 1 model is from S.M.L.E. Mk I, No. 2 is from S.M.L.E. Mk III.

	$550	$475	$425	$375	$325	$290	$240

The .22 Patt. 1914 No. 1 will bring a 30% premium due to its earlier S.M.L.E. Mk I configuration.

.22 NO. 2 Mk IV* - converted No. 1 rifle (S.M.L.E.) to single-loading trainer, modified in Britain, Lithgow (Australia) and Ishapore (India).

	$450	$350	$300	$275	$250	$200	$150

GRADING - PPGS™	100%	98%	95%	90%	80%	70%	60%

.303 NO. 3 (PATTERN 1914 RIFLE) - U.S. manufactured British modified Mauser action during WWI, made by Winchester, Remington & Eddystone, very similar to the U.S. .30 Model 1917, and shares many interchageable component parts.

	$600	$525	$400	$325	$250	$200	$125

Add 40% for Winchester Mk I*(F) with fine adj. backsight.

.303 NO. 3 Mk I* (T) (PATTERN 1914 SNIPER) - converted in England by Periscope Prism Co. (1918) & B.S.A. (1938) from Winchester rifles, the Pattern 1918 telescope on crawfoot mounts was fitted.

	$3,500	$3,000	$2,500	$2,250	$2,000	$1,850	$1,500

.303 NO. 3 Mk I* (T) A SNIPER - converted in England by Alex Martin in WWII from Winchester MK I* (F) rifles, Great War Aldis & P.P. Co. telescopes (ex-SMLE snipers) were fitted, original SMLE rifle engraved number is usually visible, usually off-set (left).

	$2,750	$2,500	$2,300	$2,100	$1,950	$1,750	$1,500

Add 30% for overhead mount.

.303 NO. 4 Mk I & II* - WWII production Lee-Enfield, British R.O.F. Fazakerley, Maltby and BSA Shirley (M47C) from 1941, Britain only made the Mk I model, wartime U.S. Lend-Lease production marked "US PROPERTY", serial number contains letter "S" while Canadian Long Branch rifles contain an "L", U.S. and Canada made both Mk I and Mk I* models.

	$400	$350	$300	$250	$200	$150	$100

Rare 1933 trials No. 4 rifles made at Enfield will bring a 50%+ premium.

.303 NO. 4 Mk II, Mk 1/2 & 1/3 - postwar Fazakerley [ROF(F)] production with the "hung" trigger and better quality fittings than wartime production, Mk 1/2 and 1/3 converted from Mk I and Mk I* rifles respectively, the No. 4 Mk 2 was of new manufacture, also made in the early 1970s at Wah Cantt, Pakistan on ex-Fazakerley machinery.

	$600	$500	$450	$400	$350	$250	$150

.303 NO. 4 Mk I (T) - converted by Holland & Holland (S51) during WWII in England, also by Long Branch in Canada from indigenous production, the No. 32 telescopic sight was generally fitted, made in England or by R.E.L. in Canada.

	$3,000	$2,750	$2,500	$2,250	$2,000	$1,750	$1,375

✳ *W/o telescope sight but with original mounts*

	$950	$850	$750	$650	$550	$450	$375

Add $150-$250 for original green painted rifle chest, with telescope carrier case.

.303 NO. 5 MK. I JUNGLE CARBINE - 20.5 in. barrel with flash hider, lightened action body and shortened furniture. From 1944, for service in the Far East.

	$500	$450	$400	$350	$300	$250	$200

Indian service issues have a transverse wood screw in the forend which is less desirable.

.22 NO. 7 - postwar rimfire trainer on No. 4 action, British model has magazine feed, the Long Branch is designated "C No. 7" and is single shot only, but originally issued in chest. Mfg. in England by BSA and in Canada by Long Branch.

	$750	$700	$625	$550	$500	$450	$300

Add $100-$200 for original marked Canadian chest.

.22 NO. 8 Mk I - postwar rimfire trainer, half-stock target rifle style made by BSA (M47C) and Fazakerley on a modified No. 4 action body.

	$700	$600	$525	$475	$400	$350	$300

.22 NO. 9 Mk I - single shot only, full length rifle resembling the No. 4, British conversion of the No. 4 Mk I rifle by Parker Hale for the Royal Navy.

	$550	$500	$450	$400	$350	$275	$200

GRADING - PPGS™	100%	98%	95%	90%	80%	70%	60%

7.62mm L42A1 SNIPER - Enfield conversion and extensive rebuild of the No. 4 Mk I(T) sniper rifle, fitted with an upgraded No. 32 telescopic sight to L1A1, half-stocked furniture, 7.62mm magazine with integral ejector, with heavy target barrel.

	$4,500	$4,000	$3,750	$3,250	$2,950	$2,600	$2,200

.230 FRANCOTTE CADET MARTINI - turn of the century British empire trainer with Belgian Francotte patent, small size modular Martini action.

	$600	$500	$450	$350	$300	$275	$200

.310 CADET MARTINI - later production small Francotte action on Australian contract by W.W. Greener and BSA, circa 1910.

	$600	$450	$350	$300	$275	$250	$200

ENFIELD AMERICA, INC.

Previous manufacturer located in Atlanta, GA.

PISTOLS: SEMI-AUTO

MP-9 - 9mm Para. cal., paramilitary design, similar to MP-45. Mfg. 1985.

	$550	$475	$425	$350	$295	$260	$240

Add $150 for carbine kit.

MP-45 - .45 ACP cal., paramilitary design, 4 1/2, 6, 8, 10, or 18 1/2 in. shrouded barrel, parkerized finish, 10, 30, 40, or 50 shot mag., 6 lbs. Mfg. 1985 only.

	$550	$475	$425	$350	$295	$260	$240

Last MSR was $350.

ENTRÉPRISE ARMS INC.

Current manufacturer located in Irwindale, CA, since 1996. Dealer and consumer sales.

PISTOLS: SEMI-AUTO

The models listed below are patterned after the Colt M1911, but have "Widebody" frames.

ELITE SERIES - .45 ACP cal., 3 1/4 in. barrel, features steel 1911 Widebody frame, flat mainspring housing, flared ejection port, 10 shot mag., bead blasted black oxide finish, tactical sights, 36 oz. New 1997.

* *Elite P325*

MSR $700		$625	$565	$500	$450	$400	$360	$330

* *Elite P425* - similar to Elite P325, except has 4 1/4 in. barrel, 38 oz. New 1997.

MSR $700		$625	$565	$500	$450	$400	$360	$330

* *Elite P500* - similar to Elite P325, except has 5 in. barrel, 40 oz. New 1997.

MSR $700		$625	$565	$500	$450	$400	$360	$330

TACTICAL SERIES - .45 ACP cal., 3 1/4 in. barrel, features Tactical Widebody with "De-horned" slide and frame allowing snag-free carry, narrow ambidextrous thumb safety, 10 shot mag., low profile Novak or ghost ring sights, squared trigger guard, flat main spring housing, matte black oxide finish, 36 oz. New 1997.

* *Tactical P325*

MSR $979		$875	$750	$650	$575	$500	$450	$395

* *Tactical P325 Plus* - similar to P325, except has short officer's length slide/barrel fitted onto a full government frame, designed as concealed carry pistol. New 1998.

MSR $979		$875	$750	$650	$575	$500	$450	$395

* *Tactical P425* - similar to Tactical P325, except has 4 1/4 in. barrel, 38 oz. New 1997.

MSR $979		$875	$750	$650	$575	$500	$450	$395

GRADING - PPGS™	100%	98%	95%	90%	80%	70%	60%

✳ *Tactical P500* - similar to Tactical P325, except has 5 in. barrel, 40 oz. New 1997.

MSR $979	$875	$750	$650	$575	$500	$450	$395

MEDALIST SERIES (TITLEIST, P500 NATIONAL MATCH) - .40 S&W or .45 ACP cal., 5 in. barrel, features tighter tolerances and numerous custom features, 10 shot mag., front and rear slide serrations, blue slide, includes Bo-Mar low mount rear adj. sight, 40 oz. New 1997.

MSR $979	$875	$750	$675	$575	$525	$475	$425

Add $120 for .40 S&W cal.

During 1999, this model's nomenclature changed from the Titleist Series to the Medalist Series.

BOXER SERIES - similar to Titleist Series, except has fully machined "high mass" and flattop slide. New 1998.

MSR $1,399	$1,200	$995	$850	$750	$625	$550	$500

Add $100 for .40 S&W cal.

TOURNAMENT SHOOTER MODEL (TSM I-III) - .40 S&W or .45 ACP cal., 5, 5 1/2 (TSM III only), or 6 (.45 ACP only) in. barrel, blue finish, designed for IPSC competition, 10 shot mag., TSM II is standard, 40-44 oz. New 1997.

MSR $2,000	$1,800	$1,550	$1,325	$1,100	$950	$875	$750

Add $300 for TSM I.

Add $700 for TSM III.

RIFLES: CARBINES, SEMI-AUTO

STG58C CARBINE - .308 Win. cal., paramilitary design, 16 1/2 in. barrel with muzzle brake, synthetic pistol grip stock, last shot bolt hold open, adj. gas system, mil-spec black oxide finish, 20 shot mag., 200-600 meter apeture sights, supplied with black nylon sling, various configurations, approx. 9 lbs. New 2000.

✳ *STG58C Scout Carbine* - Entreprise Type 03 receiver, integral bipod, includes carry handle. New 2000.

MSR $1,199	$1,075	$875	$750	$625	$575	$500	$450

✳ *STG58C Carbine* - Entreprise Type 01 receiver, machined aluminum free-floating handguards, carry handle. New 2000.

MSR $1,399	$1,200	$995	$850	$750	$625	$550	$500

RIFLES: SEMI-AUTO

STG58C RIFLE - .308 Win. cal., paramilitary design, choice of 16 1/2, 21, or 24 in. barrel with muzzle brake, synthetic pistol grip stock, last shot bolt hold open, adj. gas system, mil-spec black oxide finish, 20 shot mag., 200-600 meter aperture sights, supplied with black nylon sling, various configurations, 8 1/2-13 lbs. New 2000.

✳ *STG58C Lightweight Model* - 16 1/2 in. barrel, Entreprise Type 03 receiver, 8 1/2 lbs. New 2000.

MSR $1,199	$1,050	$900	$800	$725	$650	$600	$550

✳ *STG58C Standard Model* - 21 in. barrel, Entreprise Type 03 receiver, integral bipod, 9.8 lbs. New 2000.

MSR $999	$895	$775	$675	$575	$525	$475	$425

✳ *STG58C Government Model* - 21 in. barrel, Entreprise Type 01 receiver, integral bipod, 9.5 lbs. New 2000.

MSR $1,199	$1,050	$900	$800	$725	$650	$600	$550

✳ *STG58C Target Model* - 21 in. barrel, Entreprise Type 01 receiver, with aluminum free-floating handguards, 11 1/2 lbs. New 2000.

MSR $1,399	$1,200	$995	$850	$750	$625	$550	$500

GRADING - PPGS™	100%	98%	95%	90%	80%	70%	60%

✳ *STG58C Match Target Model* - 24 in. match heavy barrel, Entreprise Type 01 receiver, with aluminum fee-floating handguards, 13 lbs. New 2000.

	100%	98%	95%	90%	80%	70%	60%
MSR $1,999	$1,825	$1,650	$1,475	$1,200	$1,000	$850	$750

ERA

Previous manufacturer located in Brazil.

SHOTGUNS

ERA O/U - 12 or 20 ga., 28 in. vent. rib barrel, full and mod., double triggers, extractors, checkered hardwood stock.

	100%	98%	95%	90%	80%	70%	60%
	$275	$250	$225	$200	$170	$150	$125
Trap version	$300	$275	$250	$225	$200	$175	$150
Skeet version	$300	$275	$250	$225	$200	$175	$150

ERA SxS - 12, 20 ga., or .410 bore, 26, 28, or 30 in. barrels, various chokes, double triggers, extractors, checkered pistol grip stock.

$165	$150	$135	$125	$110	$100	$85

ERA RIOT SxS - 12 or 20 ga., 18 in. barrels.

$185	$175	$150	$140	$125	$110	$95

ERA QUAIL SxS - 12 or 20 ga., 20 in. barrels.

$185	$175	$150	$140	$125	$110	$95

ERMA SUHL, GmbH

Current manufacturer located in Suhl, Germany, since January 1998. No current U.S. importation. Erma Suhl purchased the remaining assets from Erma-Werke, and production was once again resumed.

RIFLES: BOLT ACTION

SR100 SNIPER RIFLE - .300 Win. Mag., .308 Win., or .338 Lapua Mag. cal., bolt action, tactical rifle featuring brown laminated wood stock with thumbhole, adj. buttplate/cheekpiece, and vent. forend, forged aluminum receiver, 25 1/2 or 29 1/2 in. barrel, muzzle brake, adj. match trigger, approx. 15 lbs. Limited importation 1997-98 only.

$6,500	$5,750	$5,000	$4,350	$3,750	$3,000	$2,350

Last MSR was $8,600.

This model was imported exclusively by Amtec 2000, Inc., located in Gardner, MA. Most recent importation was in .300 Win. Mag., and included a Steyr scope mount.

ERMA-WERKE

Previous manufacturer located in Dachau, Germany (Erma-Werke production) until bankruptcy occurred in October of 1997. Pistols were previously imported and distributed by Precision Sales International, Inc. located in Westfield, MA, Nygord Precision Products located in Prescott, AZ, and Mandall's Shooting Supplies, Inc. located in Scottsdale, AZ. Previously distributed by Excam located in Hialeah, FL.

Erma-Werke also manufactured private label handguns for American Arms Inc. (refer to their section for listings).

PISTOLS: SEMI-AUTO

MODEL LA 22 - .22 LR cal., action patterned after the Luger. Mfg. 1964-67.

$395	$335	$275	$240	$200	$175	$140

GRADING - PPGS™	100%	98%	95%	90%	80%	70%	60%

ERMA KGP68A/BEEMAN MP-08 - .32 ACP or .380 ACP cal., Luger type toggle action, 3 1/2 (Beeman) or 4 in. barrel, 6 shot mag., blue, 1.4 lbs. Mfg. 1968-disc.

	$450	$400	$335	$275	$240	$185	$145

Last MSR was $500.

This model was imported exclusively by Mandall's Shooting Supplies, Inc. located in Scottsdale, AZ. From 1988-90, Beeman took over importation of this model in .380 ACP cal. only with new Luger style checkered walnut grips and 3 1/2 in. barrel. Previous models had plastic grips.

ERMA KGP69/BEEMAN P-08 - .22 LR cal., Luger type toggle action, 8 shot mag., 3 3/4 in. barrel, blue, plastic (disc.) or checkered walnut grips. Mfg. 1969-disc.

	$335	$275	$240	$185	$145	$115	$95

Last MSR was $390.

Beeman was the sole importer of this model between 1988-90.

MODEL ESP 85A SPORT/MATCH PISTOL - .22 LR or .32 S&W Long Wadcutter cal., blow back semi-auto, 6 in. barrel, 5 or 8 (.32 S&W only) shot mag., choice of sporting or adj. stippled match grips with thumbrest, fully adj. and interchangeable sights, gun is supplied with 1 extra weight, extra mag., sights, disassembly tools, and attaché style case ($134 option) with foam rubber cut-outs, 2 1/2 lbs. Imported 1989-97.

	$1,225	$925	$800	$650	$550	$495	$450

Last MSR was $1,785.

Subtract $315 for Junior Model.
Add $215 for .32 S&W cal.
Add $110 for Match Model (with anatomical grips).
Add $980-$1,390 for conversion unit.
Add approx. $215 for chrome finish.
Add $24 for left-hand action (Match Model only - disc. 1994).

ESP 85 refers to Junior Model (new 1995). The ESP 85 series was distributed by Precision Sales International, Inc. and Mandall Shooting Supplies, Inc.

❋ *Model ESP 85A Complete Set* - includes both .22 LR and .32 S&W Long Wadcutter barrels and mags., cased with accessories, complete set was disc. 1991.

	$1,525	$1,350	$1,125	$950	$825	$750	$625

Last MSR was $1,995.

EP-22 - similar to Model LA 22.

	$395	$335	$275	$240	$200	$175	$140

ET-22 LUGER CARBINE - .22 LR cal., 11 3/4 in. barrel, blue rear ramp sight, checkered walnut grips and uncheckered forearm, adj. artillery type rear sight, rarely seen.

	$425	$365	$330	$275	$240	$200	$175

Add 20% for leatherette case.

REVOLVERS: DOUBLE ACTION

These models were distributed by Precision Sales International, Inc. only.

ER-772 STANDARD/MATCH - .22 LR cal., standard or match gun with special adj. contoured grips with stippling, 6 in. barrel, action similar to ER-777, fully adj. and extended rear sight, interchangeable front sight, 3 lbs. Imported 1990-94.

	$1,100	$875	$725	$625	$550	$495	$450

Last MSR was $1,371.

ER-773 STANDARD/MATCH - .32 S&W Long Wadcutter cal., otherwise similar to ER-772 Match, 2.9 lbs. Imported 1990-95.

	$925	$825	$695	$525	$475	$425	$385

Last MSR was $1,068.

GRADING - PPGS™	100%	98%	95%	90%	80%	70%	60%

ER-777 STANDARD - .357 Mag. cal., 6 shot, 4 or 5 1/2 in. barrel, solid rib and full barrel shroud, adj. target rear sight, blue steel, checkered sport grips, 2 3/4 lbs. Imported 1990-95.

	$875	$775	$650	$475	$425	$385	$350

Last MSR was $1,019.

RIFLES

Models listed below were available from Mandall Shooting Supplies, unless otherwise noted.

EM-1 .22 CARBINE - .22 LR cal., M1 copy, 10 or 15 shot mag., 18 in. barrel, rear adj. aperture sight, 5.6 lbs. Mfg. 1966-97.

	$365	$295	$250	$215	$190	$175	$160

Last MSR was $400.

EGM-1 - similar to EM-1 except for unslotted buttstock, 5 shot mag.

	$260	$230	$195	$175	$150	$125	$100

Last MSR was $295.

EG-72 PUMP - .22 LR cal., outside hammer, 15 shot mag., 18 1/2 in. barrel. Mfg. 1970-76.

	$125	$95	$90	$75	$70	$65	$60

EG-712 LEVER-ACTION - .22 LR cal., Win. Model 94 copy, tube mag., 18 1/2 in. barrel. Mfg. 1976-97.

	$260	$230	$195	$175	$150	$125	$100

Last MSR was $295.

EG-73 - .22 Mag. cal., similar to EG-712 12 shot mag. Mfg. 1973-97.

	$265	$230	$195	$175	$150	$125	$100

Last MSR was $300.

ESCALADE

Current trademark of slide action shotguns imported by Mitchell's Mausers, located in Fountain Valley, CA.

SHOTGUNS: SLIDE ACTION

ESCALADE MODEL - 12 ga. only, 18 1/2, 22 or 28 in. chrome lined barrel with choke tubes (except Home Defense model), dual action bars, Turkish walnut checkered stock and grooved forearm, available in Home Defense (18 1/2 in.) or Hunting (22 or 28 in.) configurations. Importation from Turkey began 2004.

MSR $295	$250	$225	$195	$175	$150	$125	$100

ESCORT

Current trademark of semi-auto and slide action shotguns manaufactured by Hatsan Arms Co., located in Izmir, Turkey, and imported beginning 2002 by Legacy Sports International, located in Alexandria, VA.

SHOTGUNS: SEMI-AUTO

Beginning 2004, all models have a round back receiver with 3/8 in. dovetail milled along top for mounting sights.

GRADING - PPGS™	100%	98%	95%	90%	80%	70%	60%

ESCORT SERIES - 3 IN. - 12 or 20 (new 2005) ga., 3 in. chamber, gas operated action with 2 position adj. screw (disc. 2003), 20, 22 (AS Youth & PS Slug, new 2005), 24, 26 (new 2005), or 28 in. VR barrel with 3 multi-chokes, blue finish, vent recoil pad, gold trigger, checkered walnut (Model AS) or polymer (Model PS) black or 100% camo coverage Mossy Oak Break Up (disc. 2004), Mossy Oak Obsession (new 2005), or Shadowgrass camo stock and forearm, 6.4-7 lbs. Importation began 2002.

	MSR $399	$345	$295	$275	$250	$230	$215	$195

Add $22 for walnut stock and forearm.

Add $44 for 100% camo coverage.

Add $81 for 24 in. barrel with Model PS TriViz sights and Mossy Oak Break Up camo coverage (disc. 2004).

As this edition went to press, prices had yet to be determined on the PS Slug Combo.

✳ *Aimguard* - similar to Escort model, except has black chrome finish, black polymer stock, 20 in. barrel, cylinder bore. Importation began 2004.

	MSR $392	$340	$295	$275	$250	$230	$215	$195

✳ *Waterfowl/Tukey Combo* - includes camo stock and forearm, 24 in. barrel with HiViz and TriViz sights and 28 in. barrel with HiViz Spark sight, hard case. Importation began 2003.

	MSR $574	$475	$400	$365	$330	$300	$280	$260

ESCORT SERIES - 3 1/2 IN. - 12 ga., 3 1/2 in. chamber, polymer stock and forearm, blued steel or Mossy Oak Obsession camo coverage, 24 or 28 in. barrel with choke tubes, standard or choice of Spark front sight or TriViz sights, 7.6 lbs. Importation began 2005.

	MSR $465	$385	$325	$295	$275	$250	$230	$215

Add $43 for camo and Spark front sight.

Add $59 for 24 in. barrel with Model PS TriViz sights and camo coverage.

SHOTGUNS: SLIDE ACTION

ESCORT SERIES - 12 or 20 (new 2005) ga., 3 in. chamber, matte blue finish or 100% camo coverage with polymer stock and forearm, 18 (Aimguard or Marine-Guard Model), 22 (Field Slug, new 2005), 24 (Turkey, includes extra turkey choke tube and FH TriViz sight combo with Mossy Oak Break Up [disc. 2004] or Obsession camo coverage), 26 (new 2005, Field Hunter) or 28 (Field Hunter) in. barrel, alloy receiver with 3/8 in. milled dovetail for sight mounting, trigger guard safety, 5 shot mag. with cut off button, two stock adj. shims, 6.4-7 lbs. Importation began 2003.

✳ *Aimguard* - 18 in. barrel with black synthetic stock, fixed cyl. bore choke, 6.4 lbs.

	MSR $392	$340	$295	$275	$250	$230	$215	$195

✳ *MarineGuard* - 12 ga., 18 in. barrel with black synthetic stock, nickel receiver, fixed cyl. bore choke, 6.4 lbs.

	MSR $211	$165	$140	$125	$110	$100	$90	$80

✳ *Field Hunter* - 24 or 28 in. barrel, 100% camo coverage or matte blue finish, includes 3 choke tubes.

	MSR $247	$190	$165	$140	$120	$105	$90	$80

Add $65 for camo stock.

Add $23 for combo in 12 ga.

Add $116 for FH TriViz sight combo.

As this edition went to press, prices had yet to be determined on the Field Hunter Slug Combo in 12 and 20 ga.

EUROARMS OF AMERICA

Current black powder importer and distributor located in Winchester, VA. Manufactured by Euroarms Italia Srl, established 1970, and located in Concesio, Italy. The factory was previously named Armi San Paolo until 2002.

GRADING - PPGS™	100%	98%	95%	90%	80%	70%	60%

Euroarms imported a variety of firearms, including revolvers and rifles, mfg. by Armi San Paolo between 1970-1996. Values are currently in the $135-$835 range, depending on configuration and condition.

Please refer to the *Blue Book of Modern Black Powder Arms* by John Allen & Dennis Adler (also online) for more information and prices on Euroarms of America's quality lineup of modern black powder reproductions and replicas.

EUROARMS ITALIA Srl

Current black powder manufacturer and importer/exporter located in Concesio, Italy.

Euroarms Italia is the new name for Armi San Paolo, and was established during 2002. Euroarms Italia exports its black powder reproductions and accessories through Euroarms of America, Dixie Gun Works, Cabela's, and Navy Arms.

EUROPEAN AMERICAN ARMORY CORP.

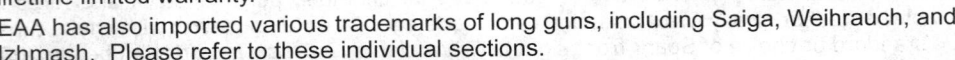

Current importer and distributor located in Sharpes, FL beginning late 1990. Distributor and dealer sales.

EAA currently imports its handguns from Tanfoglio, located in Italy, and from H. Weihrauch, located in Germany. All guns are covered by EAA's lifetime limited warranty.

EAA has also imported various trademarks of long guns, including Saiga, Weihrauch, and Izhmash. Please refer to these individual sections.

PISTOLS: SEMI-AUTO, EUROPEAN SERIES

MODEL EA220 - .22 LR cal., 3.88 in. barrel, 10 shot mag., single action, steel frame, 26 oz., blue, chrome or blue/chrome, wood grips. Importation disc. 1992.

$185	$150	$120	$100	$95	$85	$75

Last MSR was $225.

Add approx. $20 for chrome or blue/chrome finish.

MODEL EA22-T - .22 LR cal., 6 in. barrel, cocking indicator and grip safety, 5 or 12 shot mag., adj. trigger and grip, single action, steel frame, target model, 40 oz. Imported 1991-93.

$375	$295	$260	$220	$185	$165	$150

Last MSR was $450.

EUROPEAN 32 (320) - .32 ACP cal., 3.88 in. barrel, 7 shot mag., single action, steel frame, 26 oz., blue, chrome or blue/chrome, wood grips. Importation 1991-95.

$130	$110	$95	$85	$80	$75	$70

Last MSR was $161.

Add $14 for chrome finish.

EUROPEAN 380 - .380 ACP cal., single (new 1994) or double (disc. 1994) action, 3 7/8 in. barrel, blue, brushed chrome (disc. 1996), Wonder finish (new 1997), matte blue/chrome (disc. 1993), or blue/gold plated Duo-Tone (European Lady, disc. 1995) finish, 7 shot bottom release mag., steel construction, firing pin safety, external hammer, smooth wood or ivory rose polymer (European Lady) grips, 26 oz. Imported 1992-2001.

$145	$115	$95	$85	$75	$70	$65

Last MSR was $179.

Add $9 for Wonder finish (new 1997).
Add $67 for European Lady model (disc. 1995).
Add $32 for double action design (disc. 1994).
Add $14 for brushed chrome or matte blue/chrome (disc. 1993) finish.
This model employed a unique patented magazine gun lock system.

GRADING - PPGS™	100%	98%	95%	90%	80%	70%	60%

PISTOLS: SEMI-AUTO, WITNESS SERIES

The following Witness pistols also have a .22 LR conversion kit available for $229.

EA 38 SUPER SERIES - .38 Super cal., action patterned after the CZ-75, selective double action, 4 1/2 in. barrel, steel or polymer frame/steel slide (mfg. 1997-2004), 10 (C/B 1994), 18 (new late 2004) or 19* shot mag., choice of Wonder (heat treated grey satin finish, new 1997), stainless steel (disc. 1996) or blue, blue/chrome (disc. 1994), or brushed chrome (disc. 1996) finish, combat sights, black neoprene grips, 33 oz. Importation began 1994.

MSR $459	$375	$315	$255	$225	$200	$185	$180

Subtract $20 for polymer frame.

✴ *Model EA 38 Stainless* - similar to EA 38, except is stainless steel. Imported 1994-96.

$525	$435	$350

Last MSR was $595.

✴ *Model EA 38 Compact* - similar to EA 38 Super Series, except has 3 5/8 in. unported or ported barrel, choice of matte blue or Wonder finish, 30 oz. Mfg. 1999-2004.

$370	$310	$255	$225	$200	$185	$180

Last MSR was $449.

Subtract $20 for polymer frame.
Add $20 for Wonder finish or ported barrel (polymer frame only).

EA 9 SERIES - 9mm Para. cal., action patterned after the CZ-75, selective double action, 4 1/2 in. unported or ported (polymer, New Frame only, new 2002) barrel, steel or polymer frame/steel slide (new 1997), 10 (C/B 1994), 16*, or 18 (new late 2004) shot mag., choice of Wonder (new 1997), stainless steel (disc. 1996) or blue, blue/chrome (disc. 1993), or brushed chrome (disc. 1996) finish, combat sights, black neoprene grips, 33 oz. Importation began late 1990.

MSR $459	$375	$315	$255	$225	$200	$185	$180

Subtract $20 for polymer frame, $30 for polymer New Frame.

✴ *Model EA 9 Stainless* - similar to EA 9, except is stainless steel. Imported 1992-96.

$420	$350	$295

Last MSR was $480.

✴ *Model EA 9 (L) Compact* - similar to EA 9, except has 3 5/8 in. unported or ported (polymer frame only, new 2002) barrel and 10 (C/ B 1994), 12 (new late 2004), or 13* shot mag., 27 oz.

MSR $459	$375	$315	$255	$225	$200	$185	$180

Subtract $30 for polymer frame.
Add $10-$20 for ported barrel (polymer frame only).

EA 40 SERIES - .40 S&W cal., action patterned after the CZ-75, selective double action, 4 1/2 in. barrel, steel or polymer frame/steel slide (new 1997), 10 (C/B 1994), 12*, or 15 (new late 2004) shot mag., choice of Wonder (new 1997), stainless steel (disc. 1996) or blue, blue/chrome (disc.), or brushed chrome (disc. 1996) finish, combat sights, black neoprene grips, 33 oz. Importation began late 1990.

MSR $459	$375	$315	$255	$225	$200	$185	$180

Subtract $30 for polymer frame.
Subtract $20 for polymer New Frame.
Add $10-$20 for Wonder finish.

✴ *Model EA 40 Stainless* - similar to EA 40, except is stainless steel. Imported 1992-96.

$455	$365	$295

Last MSR was $509.

GRADING - PPGS™	100%	98%	95%	90%	80%	70%	60%

✳ Model EA 40 (L) Compact - similar to EA 40, except has 3 5/8 in. unported or ported barrel, 9 or 12 (new late 2004) shot mag.

MSR $459	$375	$315	$255	$225	$200	$185	$180

Subtract $30 for polymer frame.
Add $10-$20 for Wonder finish.
Add $10-$20 for ported barrel (polymer frame only).

EA 10 SUPER SERIES - 10mm cal., action patterned after the CZ-75, selective double action, 4 1/2 in. barrel, steel frame, 10, 12*, or 15 (new late 2004) shot mag., choice of stainless steel (disc.), blue, chrome (disc.), or Wonder (new 1999) finish, combat sights, black neoprene grips, 33 oz. Imported 1994 only, resumed 1999.

MSR $459	$375	$315	$255	$225	$200	$185	$180

Add $10 for Wonder finish.
Add $30 for chrome finish (disc.).
Add $65 for stainless steel (disc.).

✳ Model EA 10 Stainless - similar to EA 10, except is stainless steel.

	$495	$425	$350				

Last MSR was $566.

✳ Model EA 10 Carry Comp - similar to EA 10, except has 4 1/2 in. compensated barrel, blue or Wonder (new 2005) finish. New 1999.

MSR $489	$415	$350	$285	$240	$215	$190	$180

Subtract $20 for blue finish.

✳ Model EA 10 Compact - similar to EA 10, except has 3 5/8 in. barrel, 8 or 12 (new late 2004) shot mag.

MSR $459	$375	$315	$255	$225	$200	$185	$180

Add $10 for Wonder finish.

EA 41 SERIES - .41 Action Express cal., action patterned after the CZ-75, selective double action, 4 1/2 in. barrel, steel frame, 11 shot mag., blue, blue/chrome, or brushed chrome finish, combat sights, black neoprene grips, 33 oz. Importation disc. 1993.

	$450	$375	$325	$275	$250	$225	$200

Last MSR was $595.

Add $40 for blue/chrome or brushed chrome finish.

✳ Model EA 41 Compact - similar to EA 41, except has 3 1/2 in. barrel and 8 shot mag.

	$495	$425	$375	$325	$295	$260	$230

Last MSR was $625.

Add $40 for blue/chrome or brushed chrome finish.

EA 45 SERIES - .45 ACP cal., action patterned after the CZ-75, selective double action, 4 1/2 in. standard or compensated (new 1998) barrel, steel frame, polymer full size frame (new 2004), or polymer frame/steel slide (new 1997), 10 (C/ B 1994) or 11* shot mag., choice of Wonder (new 1997), stainless steel (disc. 1996) or blue, blue/chrome (disc. 1993), or brushed chrome (disc. 1996) finish, combat sights, walnut grips, 35 oz. Importation began late 1990.

MSR $429	$355	$300	$255	$225	$200	$185	$180

Add $30 for Wonder finish.
Add $40 for carry configuration with compensator.
Add $40 for ported barrel (steel only, with Wonder finish, disc. 2004).

✳ Model EA 45 Stainless - similar to EA 45, except is stainless steel. Imported 1992-96.

	$510	$430	$350				

Last MSR was $595.

GRADING - PPGS™	100%	98%	95%	90%	80%	70%	60%

✱ Model EA 45 (L) Compact - similar to EA 45, except has 3 5/8 in. unported or ported barrel and 8 shot mag.

MSR $429	$355	$300	$255	$225	$200	$185	$180

Add $30 for Wonder finish.

Add $30 for ported barrel (polymer frame only, disc. 2004).

Add $50 for single port barrel compensator or carry configuration with compensator (disc.).

WITNESS CARRY COMP GUN - .38 Super (disc. 1997), 9mm Para. (disc. 1997), .40 S&W cal. (disc. 1997), 10mm (disc. 1994, reintroduced 1999), or .45 ACP cal., full size frame with compact slide and 1 in. compensator, 10 (C/B 1994), 12* (.40 S&W), or 16* (9mm Para.) shot mag., Wonder (new 1997), blue or Duo-Tone (disc. 1994) finish. Imported 1992-2004.

	$425	$360	$310	$270	$235	$210	$195

Last MSR was $479.

Add $10 for Wonder finish.

WITNESS SPORT - .38 Super, 9mm Para., .40 S&W, 10mm (disc. 1994), or .45 ACP cal., 4 1/2 in. barrel, full size frame, standard slide length, Duo-Tone finish, extended safety and high capacity mag., target sights. Imported 1994-95.

	$535	$470	$400	$375	$350	$325	$295

Last MSR was $616.

Add $86 for .38 Super, 10mm, or .45 ACP cal.

WITNESS SPORT LONG SLIDE - .38 Super, 9mm Para., .40 S&W, 10mm (disc. 1994), or .45 ACP cal., long slide variation of the EA Series, except has 4 3/4 in. ported or unported barrel and slide, Duo-Tone finish, extended safety and high capacity mag., competition sights, 34 1/2 oz. Importation disc. 1995.

	$595	$500	$450	$395	$350	$325	$295

Last MSR was $681.

Add $79 for .38 Super, 10mm, or .45 ACP cal.

WITNESS LIMITED CLASS - .38 Super, 9mm Para., .40 S&W, or .45 ACP cal., match frame, competition grips, high capacity mag., single action trigger, long slide with match barrel and super sight, extended safety, blue finish only. Imported 1994-98.

	$855	$715	$610	$500	$450	$400	$375

Last MSR was $967.

✱ Witness Limited - 9mm Para., 10mm, .38 Super, .40 S&W or .45 ACP cal., 4.75 in. barrel, competition hard chrome frame, 10 (.45 ACP), 15 (.40 S&W or 10mm) or 18 (9mm Para. or .38 Super) shot mag., square trigger guard, full length dust shroud, cone slide lock up, checkered frame and back strap, skeletonized hammer, low profile checkered walnut grips, 39 oz. Importation began 2005.

MSR $999	$875	$725	$625	$525	$475	$425	$395

WITNESS COMBO PACKAGE - includes one built up frame and 9mm Para./.40 S&W complete conversion kits, blue, chrome, or Duo-Tone (disc. 1994) finish, full size variation with 4 1/2 in. barrel. Imported 1992-97.

	$515	$460	$400	$375	$350	$325	$295

Last MSR was $588.

Add $29 for chrome or Duo-Tone finish.

✱ Witness Combo Package (L) Compact - similar to Witness Combo Package, except has 3 5/8 in. barrels, blue only. Imported 1994-97.

	$515	$460	$400	$375	$350	$325	$295

Last MSR was $588.

GRADING - PPGS™	100%	98%	95%	90%	80%	70%	60%

WITNESS MULTI-CLASS PISTOL PACKAGE - .38 Super, 9mm Para., 9x21mm, .40 S&W, or .45 ACP cal., consists of one Witness Limited Class Pistol and complete Unlimited Class top half (slide and barrel), dual chamber steel compensator, blue finish only. Imported 1994 only.

	$1,450	$1,200	$1,025	$895	$775	$650	$525

Last MSR was $1,638.

WITNESS TRI-CALIBER PACKAGE - includes one built up frame and caliber conversions (9mm Para., .40 S&W, and .41 AE) that include slide, barrel, recoil guide, and spring, matte blue or chrome finish, compact or full size variations, includes carry case. Imported 1992-1993 only.

	$975	$825	$700	$575	$495	$425	$375

Last MSR was $1,195.

Add $40 for chrome finish.

WITNESS SILVER TEAM - .38 Super, 9mm Para., 9x21mm, 10mm (disc. 1994), .40 S&W, or .45 ACP cal., dual comp. chambers, SA trigger, super sight and drilled and tapped for scope mount, competition features include hammer, extended safety, paddle mag. release, black rubber grips, double-dip blue finish, high capacity mag. Imported 1992-98.

	$855	$710	$600	$500	$425	$375	$325

Last MSR was $967.

WITNESS GOLD TEAM - .38 Super, 9mm Para., 9x21mm, 10mm (disc. 1994), .40 S&W, or .45 ACP cal., triple comp. chambers, SA trigger, super sight and drilled and tapped for scope mount, top-of-the-line competition model featuring hand-fitted major components and 25 LPI checkering, hard chrome finish. Imported 1992-98.

	$1,875	$1,525	$1,250	$995	$825	$700	$575

Last MSR was $2,150.

This model was also available as a frame only - retail was $389.

✳ *Witness Gold* - 9mm Para., .38 Super, .40 S&W or .45 ACP cal., 5.25 in. barrel, triple chamber compensator, 15 (.40 S&W or .45 ACP) or 18 (9mm Para. or .38 Super) shot mag., competition hard chrome frame, cone slide lock up, checkered frame and back strap, competition hammer safety, super sight, aluminum grips, 44 oz. Importation began 2005.

MSR $1,699		$1,475	$1,250	$1,050	$925	$800	$675	$550

WITNESS STOCK - 9mm Para., 10mm, .40 S&W or .45 ACP cal., 4.5 in. barrel, competition hard chrome frame, 10 (.45 ACP), 15 (.40 S&W or 10mm) or 18 (9mm Para.) shot mag., tapered cone slide lock up, checkered frame and back strap, extended safety, adj. sights, diamond checkered walnut grips, heart shaped hammer, 33 oz. Importation began 2005.

MSR $779	$675	$575	$475	$425	$375	$325	$275

WITNESS HUNTER - 10mm or .45 ACP cal., 6 in. barrel, competition hard chrome frame, 10 (.45 ACP) or 15 (10mm) shot mag., checkered frame, blue or camo finish, tapered cone barrel, drilled and tapped, single action trigger, extended manual safety, low profile heavy duty adj. front sight, 41 oz. Importation began 2005.

MSR $909	$750	$650	$575	$500	$425	$375	$300

Add $30 for camo finish.

F.A.B. 92 - 9mm Para. or .40 S&W cal., double action featuring hammer drop safety and decocker (Witness style), 4 1/2 in. barrel, 16* (9mm Para.) or 12* (.40 S&W), or 10 (C/B 1994) shot mag., all steel construction, blue, chrome (disc. 1993), or Duo-Tone (disc. 1993) finish, smooth wood grips, 33 oz. Imported 1992-95.

	$335	$280	$235	$210	$190	$170	$155

Last MSR was $386.

Add $40 for chrome or Duo-Tone finish.
Add $29 for .40 S&W cal.
F.A.B. designates Foreign American Brands.

GRADING - PPGS™	100%	98%	95%	90%	80%	70%	60%

✳ **F.A.B. 92 Compact** - similar to F.A.B. 92, except has 3 5/8 in. barrel, 13* (9mm Para.), 10 (9mm only, C/B 1994), or 9 (.40 S&W) shot mag., 30 oz. Imported 1992-95.

		$335	$280	$235	$210	$190	$170	$155

Last MSR was $386.

Add $40 for chrome or Duo-Tone finish.
Add $29 for .40 S&W cal.

PISTOLS: SINGLE SHOT

THOR RAPTOR - .223 Rem., .270 Win., .30-06, .300 Win. Mag., .308 Win., .375 Win., .44 Mag., .45-70 Govt., .50 S&W, 7mm-08 Rem., or 7mm Rem. cal., blue steel frame, 14 in. barrel with polygonal rifling, single action, rubber grips, auto ejectors, integral sight base, 5 lbs. Importation began 2005.

MSR $1,099	$895	$775	$700	$625	$550	$475	$395

REVOLVERS: DOUBLE ACTION, WINDICATOR SERIES

STANDARD GRADE - .22 LR (disc.), .22LR/.22 Mag. combo. (disc.), .22 Mag. (disc.), .32 H&R (disc. 1993), .357 Mag. (new 1994), or .38 Spl. (alloy frame only) cal., 2 (.32 H&R, .357 Mag., or .38 Spl. only), 4 (new 1997), or 6 (disc.) in. squared off barrel, blue or chrome (.38 Spl. only, new 1994) finish, steel or alloy frame, 6 (.38 Spl.), 7 (.32 H&R), or 8 (.22 LR/.22 Mag.) shot, finger grooved rubber grips. Importation from Germany began 1992.

MSR $249	$205	$170	$145	$125	$110	$85	$75

Add $10 for steel frame in .357 Mag. cal.
Add $10 for 4 in. barrel.
Add $78 for .22 LR/.22 Mag. combo. (disc.).

TACTICAL GRADE - .38 Spl. cal. only, fixed sights, 6 shot, 2 in. (bobbed hammer) or 4 in. compensated barrel, blue finish only. Imported 1992-93.

	$220	$190	$165	$145	$130	$115	$105

Last MSR was $295.

Add $80 for 4 in. compensated barrel.

TARGET GRADE - .22 LR, .357 Mag., or .38 Spl. cal., 6 or 8 (.22 LR) shot, 6 in. squared off barrel, finger grooved hardwood stocks, adj. trigger pull and rear sight, blue finish only, 3.1 lbs. Imported 1992-1993.

	$425	$325	$260	$220	$200	$185	$170

Last MSR was $550.

REVOLVERS: SAA, BOUNTY HUNTER SERIES

MODEL EASAB - .22 LR cal., single action revolver, 6 shot, 4 3/4 in. barrel, blue or chrome (disc. 1991) finish, wood grips. Importation disc. 1995.

	$70	$55	$50	$45	$40	$35	$30

Last MSR was $85.

Add $20 for chrome finish.

MODEL EASAMB COMBO - includes .22 LR and .22 Mag. cal. cylinders, 4 3/4 (standard), 6, or 9 in. barrel, blue finish, wood grips. Importation disc. 1995.

	$85	$75	$65	$55	$50	$45	$40

Last MSR was $100.

Add $14 for 9 in. barrel.
Add $40 for gold backstrap and trigger guard (disc.).

GRADING - PPGS™	100%	98%	95%	90%	80%	70%	60%

BIG BORE BOUNTY HUNTER - .357 Mag., .44-40 WCF (new 2005), .44 Mag., or .45 LC cal., 4 1/2 (new 1994), 5 1/2 (disc. 1993), or 7 1/2 in. barrel, 6 shot, choice of blue, chrome (mfg. 1994-95), nickel (new 1998), or case colored finish, gold trigger guard/backstrap (disc. 1994), or gold (disc.) finish, 32-41 oz. New 1992.

MSR $369	$315	$255	$205	$175	$165	$155	$150

Add $10 for .44 Mag. or .45 LC cal. or $20 for .44-40 WCF cal.
Add $30 for nickel finish.
Add $20 for chrome finish (disc.).
Add $15 for gold-plated grip strap and trigger guard (disc.).
Add approx. $100 for gold plated finish (disc.)

✳ *Small Bore Bounty Hunter Combo* - includes .22 LR/.22 Mag. cal. cylinders, 4 3/4 or 6 3/4 in. barrel, half cock mechanism and transfer bar safety, choice of 6 or 8 shot, blue or nickel (new 1998) finish. New 1997.

MSR $269	$210	$175	$150	$130	$110	$95	$85

Add $30 for nickel finish.

RIFLES

EAA rifles were manufactured by Sabatti in Italy (est. 1674), Lu-Mar in Italy, and H. Weihrauch in Germany (see separate listing in the H. Weihrauch section). Imported 1992-96.

SP1822 SPORTER - .22 LR cal., semi-auto, 18 1/2 in. barrel, wood stock and forearm, adj. sights, 10 shot box mag., 5 1/4-6 1/2 lbs. Imported 1994-96.

$180	$145	$120	$100	$90	$80	$70

Last MSR was $206.

✳ *SP1822 Thumbhole* - similar to Sporter, except has one-piece Bell & Carlson green synthetic thumbhole stock, without sights. Importation disc. 1995.

$310	$260	$230	$200	$175	$150	$135

Last MSR was $358.

ROVER 870 - .22-250 Rem., .243 Win., .25-06 Rem., .270 Win., .30-06, .308 Win., 7mm Rem. Mag., .300 Win. Mag., or .338 Win. Mag. cal., bolt action rifle featuring all-steel construction with 22 in. hammer-forged rifled barrel, staggered 5 shot internal mag., open sights. Imported 1993 only.

$795	$695	$600	$550	$495	$450	$395

Last MSR was $995.

SHOTGUNS: O/U

SCIROCCO BASIC - 12 ga. only, single trigger, extractors, 26 or 28 in. fixed choke VR barrels, boxlock action, nickel engraved frame. Imported 1994-95.

$425	$350	$315	$285	$260	$240	$220

Last MSR was $478.

This model was mfg. by Lu-Mar located in Italy.

SCIROCCO SPORTING CLAYS - 12 ga. only, 28 or 30 in. barrels with 5 choke tubes and wide VR, SST, ejectors, Raybar front sight, nickel engraved frame. Imported 1994-95.

$650	$550	$495	$450	$400	$350	$315

Last MSR was $734.

This model was mfg. by Lu-Mar located in Italy.

FALCON - 12, 20 ga., or .410 bore, 3 in. chambers, 26, 28, or 30 in. fixed choke VR barrels, boxlock action, single or double trigger, extractors or ejectors, checkered pistol grip and forend. Imported 1993 only.

$650	$525	$450	$375	$325	$295	$260

Last MSR was $795.

Add $80 for .410 bore.
Add $100 for SST and ejectors.

GRADING - PPGS™	100%	98%	95%	90%	80%	70%	60%

SPORTING CLAYS PRO GOLD - 12 ga. only, 2 3/4 in. chambers, 28 or 30 in. screw-in choke barrels with wide VR, boxlock action, SST, ejectors, blue frame with engraving, recoil pad with custom carry case. Imported 1993-94.

	$850	$725	$650	$575	$525	$475	$425

Last MSR was $978.

SHOTGUNS: SxS

SABA - 12, 20, 28 ga., or .410 bore, 3 in. chambers, boxlock action with scrolled nickel finish, DT or SST, 26 or 28 in. fixed choke barrels with raised matted rib, ejectors, checkered stock and forearm with sling swivels. Imported 1993 only.

	$950	$825	$700	$575	$495	$425	$375

Last MSR was $1,195.

Add $100 for SST.

SHOTGUNS: SEMI-AUTO

BUNDA SERIES - 12 ga. only, 2 3/4 or 3 in. chamber (depending on barrel) gas operated, 19, 26, 28 or 30 in. barrel with 4 choke tubes, choice of black synthetic or Turkish walnut stock and forearm, aluminum receiver. Limited importation 1998 only.

	$360	$300	$275	$250	$225	$200	$185

Last MSR was $406.

Add $9 for Turkish walnut stock and forearm.

SHOTGUNS: SLIDE ACTION

MODEL PM2 - 12 ga. only, slide action, unique 7 shot detachable mag., 20 in. barrel, black wood stock and composite forearm, dual action bars, cross-bolt safety on triggerguard, available in matte blue or chrome finish, 6.81 lbs. Imported 1992 only.

	$550	$450	$395	$335	$295	$260	$230

Last MSR was $695.

Add $200 for night sights.
Add $75 for matte chrome finish.

EVANS, WILLIAM, GUN & RIFLE MAKERS

Please refer to the W section in this text.

EVOLUTION USA

Current rifle manufacturer located in White Bird, ID since 1993. Distributor and dealer sales.

RIFLES: BOLT ACTION

ARGALI - most short action cals., trued Rem. Model 700 action, Krieger ultra light barrel, synthetic stock, 5 1/2 lbs. Mfg. 2000-2004.

	$2,000	$1,700	$1,450	$1,225	$950	$775	$675

Last MSR was $2,450.

COYOTE - available in various cals., blue printed Rem. Model 700 action, Grand Master (disc. 1999) or Kreiger match barrel with cryogenic treatment, Kevlar/graphite stock. Mfg. 1996-2004.

	$1,900	$1,600	$1,325	$1,100	$900	$825	$725

Last MSR was $2,296.

COYOTE II - various cals., trued Remington M 700 action and customized trigger, matte black metal parts, HS Precision Kevlar graphite tactical stock with aluminum and fiberglass reinforced bedding. New 2001.

MSR $2,295	$1,900	$1,600	$1,325	$1,100	$900	$825	$725

GRADING - PPGS™	100%	98%	95%	90%	80%	70%	60%

PHANTOM II - various cals., trued and blue printed custom Evolution repeater action, match stainless steel barrel, Timney match trigger, McMillian A2 or A3 tactical stock, matte black metal, 11 1/2 lbs. New 1999.

	100%	98%	95%	90%	80%	70%	60%
MSR $2,736	$2,250	$1,925	$1,650	$1,350	$1,050	$875	$725

PHANTOM III - .50 BMG cal., single shot, 28 in. contoured barrel with muzzle brake, larger but similar to the contour and specs of the Phantom II, 22 lbs. New 2001.

MSR $4,690	$4,250	$3,500	$3,050	$2,750	$2,350	$2,000	$1,650

YELLOW WOLF - available in various cals., designed for big game, blue printed Rem. Model 700 action, Kreiger match barrel, Kevlar/graphite stock. New 1996.

MSR $2,549	$2,075	$1,675	$1,325	$1,075	$900	$775	$650

IMPALA - most popular cals., Rem. Model 700 trued action w/o floor plate, lightweight sporter, Kevlar graphite stock. Mfg. 1998-99.

	$1,275	$1,050	$950	$750	$650	$575	$500

Last MSR was $1,456.

KUDU - most standard length cals., Winchester Pre-64 Model 70 action, stainless steel match barrel, sporter style Kevlar graphite stock. New 1998.

MSR $2,579	$2,150	$1,850	$1,650	$1,350	$1,050	$875	$725

Add $2,500 for presentation walnut stock.

SHI-AWELA - various cals., medium weight sporter, Evolution M1000 stainless action, stainless match barrel, Kevlar/graphite stock. Mfg. 1999-2002.

	$2,600	$2,000	$1,750				

Last MSR Was $3,052.

MBOGO - .375 H&H, .416 Rem., or .458 Win. Mag. cal., choice of Sako (disc.), Dakota (disc.), Rem. Model 700, Win. Pre-64 Model 70, or stainless steel Evolution M1000 action, stainless steel match barrel, express style Kevlar graphite stock. New 1998.

This rifle with Evolution action requires 11% federal excise tax.

✳ *Sako or Remington Action* - disc.

	$1,550	$1,325	$1,100	$925	$750	$650	$575

Last MSR was $1,828.

✳ *Win. Pre-64 Model 70 or Evolution Stainless Action*

MSR $2,650	$2,300	$2,000	$1,725	$1,500	$1,250	$1,050	$875

Add $2,500 for presentation walnut stock.

✳ *Dakota Action*

	$2,775	$2,400	$2,000	$1,750	$1,500	$1,250	$1,000

Last MSR was $3,142.

BOLT ACTION SNIPER/VARMINT SERIES - various cals., 3 different configurations included Sniper, Informal Target Varmint, and Field Grade Varmint, featured match barrel, action, and tuned trigger. Prices for the Sniper rifle started at approx. $3,000 while the Varmint guns started at approx. $2,000. Disc. 2000.

RIFLES: SxS

NYATI - .375 H&H, .416 NE, .470 NE, or .500 NE (disc. 2000) cal., reinforced Anson & Deeley action, choice of color case hardened or coin finished engraved receiver, blue chrome moly barrels, various wood grades available, express sights. New 1999. Custom order only.

MSR $8,595	$7,800	$6,850	$5,750	$4,750	$4,150	$3,525	$3,000

NYALA - various standard cals., including .300 Win. Mag., 3 grades available, 7 lbs., 9 oz. New 2001.

MSR $4,895	$4,500	$4,000	$3,600	$3,150	$2,750	$2,350	$2,000

GRADING - PPGS™	100%	98%	95%	90%	80%	70%	60%

RIFLES: SEMI-AUTO

WOLVERINE - .22 LR cal., Grand Master barrel, Kevlar/graphite stock. Mfg. 1996-2000.

	$730	$650	$565	$515	$455	$400	$360

Last MSR was $850.

GRENADA - .223 Rem. cal., paramilitary design based on the AR-15 with flat upper receiver, 17 in. stainless steel match barrel with integral muzzle brake, NM trigger. Disc. 2000.

	$985	$825	$675	$600	$525	$465	$400

Last MSR was $1,195.

DESERT STORM - similar to Grenada, except has 21 in. match barrel. Disc. 2003.

	$975	$825	$665	$560	$500	$450	$400

Last MSR was $1,189.

IWO JIMA - features carrying handle incorporating iron sights, 20 in. stainless steel match barrel, A2 HBAR action, tubular handguard. Limited mfg.

	$1,000	$875	$775	$700	$600	$475	$425

RIFLES : SINGLE SHOT

IMPALA - various standard cals., including .300 Win. Mag., 5 grades available, similar appearance and handling as Nyala. New 2001.

Please contact Evolution USA directly regarding more information and current pricing on this model.

PHANTOM III SINGLE SHOT - .50 BMG cal., Evolution M-2000 stainless single shot action, Lilja match barrel with flutes and muzzle brake. New 2000.

MSR $4,650	$4,225	$3,550	$3,175	$2,750	$2,375	$2,000	$1,850

EXCAM

Previous importer and distributor located in Hialeah, FL that went out of business late 1990. Excam distributed Dart, Erma, Tanarmi, Targa, & Warrior exclusively for the U.S. These trademarks will appear under Excam only in this book. All importation of Excam firearms ceased in 1990.

All Targa and Tanarmi pistols were manufactured in Gardone V.T., Italy. All Erma and Warrior pistols and rifles were manufactured in W. Germany. Senator O/U shotguns were manufactured by A. Zoli located in Brescia, Italy.

HANDGUNS: TANARMI MFG.

TA 38SB O/U DERRINGER - .38 Spl. cal. only, O/U Derringer-copy of Rem. Model 41, 3 in. barrels, 14 oz., with safety, blue finish only, checkered nylon grips. Importation disc. 1985.

	$150	$125	$110	$90	$75	$65	$55

Last MSR was $80.

MODEL TA 22 SAA - .22 LR cal., 6 shot, 4 3/4 in. barrel, brass trigger guard and grip straps, blue finish, wood grips, 34 oz.

	$85	$70	$60	$55	$50	$45	$40

Last MSR was $99.

MODEL TA 76 SAA - .22 LR cal., single action revolver, 4 3/4 in. barrel, 6 shot, blue finish only, wood grips, 32 oz.

	$85	$65	$55	$50	$45	$40	$35

Last MSR was $95.

Add $4 for chrome finish or brass backstrap and trigger guard.

GRADING - PPGS™	100%	98%	95%	90%	80%	70%	60%

✳ **Model TA 76M Combo** - includes .22 LR and .22 Mag. cal. cylinders, 4 3/4 (standard), 6, or 9 in. barrel, blue finish, wood grips.

	$125	$115	$95	$75	$65	$60	$55

Last MSR was $105.

    Add $6 for chrome plated finish (4 3/4 in. barrel only).
    Add $10 for 6 (Model TA 766) or 9 (Model TA 769) in. barrel.
    Add $16 for brass backstrap and trigger guard (N/A in 9 in. barrel).

TA 41 SERIES SEMI-AUTO - .41 Action Express cal., action similar to TA 90 Series, 11 shot mag., matte blue (Model TA 41B) or matte chrome (Model TA 41C) finish, combat sights, black neoprene grips, 38 oz. Imported 1989-90.

	$450	$390	$360	$330	$295	$265	$240

Last MSR was $490.

    Add $70 for adj. target sights (Model TA 41BT).

✳ **Model TA 41C** - matte chrome finish.

	$485	$430	$395	$360	$330	$295	$270

Last MSR was $550.

    Add $50 (retail) for adj. target sights (Model TA 41CT).

✳ **Model TA 41 SS** - .41 AE cal., compensated variation of the Model TA 41 except has 5 in. ported barrel and slide, blue/chrome finish, competition sights, 40 oz. Import 1989-90.

	$575	$450	$420	$385	$350	$325	$300

Last MSR was $650.

TA 90 SERIES SEMI-AUTO - 9mm Para. cal., double action, copy of the CZ-75, 4 3/4 in. barrel, steel frame, 15 shot mag., matte blue (Model TA 90B) or matte chrome finish (Model TA 90C), combat sights, wood (disc. 1985) or neoprene grips, 38 oz. New 1985.

	$365	$300	$260	$225	$205	$190	$180

Last MSR was $415.

    Add $85 for adj. target sights (TA 90BT).
    Earlier models featured a polished blue finish and nickel steel alloy frame (35 oz.).

✳ **Model TA 90C** - matte chrome finish.

	$380	$315	$270	$235	$210	$190	$180

Last MSR was $430.

    Add $95 for adj. target sights (TA 90CT).

✳ **Model BTA 90B and C** - 9mm Para. cal., smaller version of TA 90, 3 1/2 in. barrel, 12 shot mag., neoprene grips. Imported 1986-90.

	$380	$315	$270	$235	$210	$190	$180

Last MSR was $430.

    Add $20 for chrome finish (BTA 90C).

✳ **Model TA 90 SS** - 9mm Para. cal., compensated variation of the Model TA 90 except has 5 in. ported barrel and slide, blue/chrome finish, competition sights, 40 oz. Imported 1989-90.

	$575	$450	$420	$385	$350	$325	$300

Last MSR was $650.

✳ **TA 90BK** - convertible kit including 2 barrels (9mm and .41 AE) and 2 mags. While advertised, this combination never saw production.

PISTOLS: SEMI-AUTO, ERMA MFG.

RX 22 - .22 LR cal. only, double action-Walther copy, 3 1/4 in. barrel, 8 shot mag., blue only, plastic grips, 17 oz. Assembled in the U.S. Disc. 1986.

	$140	$125	$105	$95	$90	$85	$80

Last MSR was $139.

GRADING - PPGS™	100%	98%	95%	90%	80%	70%	60%

KGP 22 - .22 LR cal. only, Luger type toggle action, 3.78 in. barrel, 8 shot mag., blue only, plastic grips, 29 oz. Importation disc. 1986.

	$220	$195	$175	$155	$135	$120	$105

Last MSR was $220.

KGP 380 - .380 ACP cal. only, Luger type toggle action, 3 1/2 in. barrel, 5 shot mag., blue only, plastic grips, 23 oz. Disc. 1986.

	$250	$215	$185	$160	$145	$135	$125

Last MSR was $230.

PISTOLS: SEMI-AUTO, TARGA MFG.

GT 22 SERIES - .22 LR cal., 3.88 in. barrel, 10 shot mag., single action 26 oz., steel frame, either satin chrome (GT 22C) or standard blue (GT 22B) finish, wood grips became standard in 1986. GT 22T is 6 in. barrel target version (12 shot mag.).

	$170	$140	$125	$110	$95	$80	$70

Last MSR was $200.

Add $15 for chrome finish (Model GT 22C).

GT 26 and GT 27B OR C - .25 ACP cal., 2 1/2 in. barrel, 6 shot mag., single action, 13 oz., available in standard blue alloy, satin chrome alloy (GT 27B or C), or steel frame (GT 26S), wood grips became standard in 1986.

	$50	$45	$35	$30	$30	$25	$25

Last MSR was $56.

Add $59 for steel frame (Model GT 26S).
Add $13 for chrome alloy (Model GT 27C).

GT 28 SERIES - .25 ACP cal., 2 1/2 in. barrel, 5 shot mag., single action, blue alloy, wood grips. Imported 1990 only.

	$45	$35	$30	$30	$25	$25	$20

Last MSR was $51.

Add $18 for chrome finish (Model GT 28C).

GT 32 SERIES - .32 ACP cal., 3.88 in. barrel, 7 shot mag., single action, steel frame, 26 oz., either satin chrome (GT 32C) or standard blue (GT 32B), wood grips became standard in 1986.

	$170	$140	$125	$110	$95	$80	$70

Last MSR was $200.

Add $15 for chrome finish (Model GT 32C).

GT 380 ACP SERIES - .380 ACP cal., 3.88 in. barrel, 6 shot mag., single action, steel frame, 26 oz., either satin chrome (GT 380C) or standard blue (GT 380B), wood grips became standard in 1986.

	$175	$145	$135	$125	$115	$105	$95

Last MSR was $212.

Add $8 for chrome finish (Model GT 380C).

* **GT 380 LW** - similar to GT 380 Series except has light alloy receiver and 3 1/4 in. barrel.

	$100	$85	$70	$60	$55	$50	$45

Last MSR was $119.

* **GT 380 BE or CE** - engraved models, either blue (BE) or chrome (CE) finish, wood grips. Importation disc. 1989.

	$180	$155	$145	$135	$125	$115	$105

Last MSR was $220.

Add $25 for chrome finish (Model GT 380 CE).

GT 380 XE - .380 ACP cal., 3.88 in. barrel, 11 shot mag., blue only, wood grips, 28 oz.

	$190	$165	$155	$145	$135	$125	$115

Last MSR was $235.

GRADING - PPGS™	100%	98%	95%	90%	80%	70%	60%

❋ **GT 32 XEB** - .32 ACP cal., similar to GT 380 XE, 12 shot mag. Disc. 1985.

	$165	$145	$135	$125	$115	$100	$95

Last MSR was $189.

REVOLVERS

RX 38 B - .38 Spl. cal., double action, 6 shot, 2 in. barrel, blue finish only. Imported 1990-disc.

	$150	$125	$100	$85	$65	$55	$50

Last MSR was $95.

ALDO UBERTI CATTLEMAN SA REVOLVER - .357 Mag., .44 Mag., or .45 LC cal., 6 shot, single action, 5 1/2, 6, or 7 1/2 in. barrels, target sights, wood grips, blue finish. Mfg. 1985-86.

	$295	$250	$195	$165	$150	$140	$130

Last MSR was $222.

Add 10% for .44 Mag. or .45 LC cal.

ALDO UBERTI DA INSPECTOR - .38 Spl., double action, 3 or 4 in. barrel, blue finish, wood grips, 6 shot. Disc. 1986.

	$325	$250	$200	$180	$165	$150	$140

Last MSR was $240.

Add $17 for adj. sights.

WARRIOR DOUBLE ACTION MODEL W 722 (B) - .22 LR or .22 Mag. cal. only, double action, 6 in. barrel, 8 shot, blue only, plastic grips, 35 oz. Disc. 1986.

	$100	$80	$70	$65	$60	$55	$50

Last MSR was $98.

Add $50 for .22 Mag. extra cyl.

WARRIOR DOUBLE ACTION MODEL W 384 (B) - .38 Spl. cal. only, double action, 4 or 6 in. barrels, 6 shot, blue only, plastic grips, 30 oz. Vent. rib standard. Disc. 1986.

	$135	$110	$100	$90	$80	$70	$65

Last MSR was $125.

Add $5 for 6 in. barrel (W 386 B).

WARRIOR DOUBLE ACTION MODEL W 357 - .357 Mag. cal. only, double action, 4 or 6 in. barrels, 6 shot, blue only, plastic grips, 36 oz. Vent. rib standard. 6 in. barrel (W 3576). Disc. 1986.

	$190	$165	$145	$135	$130	$125	$120

Last MSR was $185.

RIFLES: ERMA MFG.

EG 712 - .22 LR cal. only, lever action copied after the Win. Model 92, 18 1/2 in. barrel, 15 shot, iron sights. Disc. 1985.

	$180	$160	$140	$125	$115	$100	$90

Last MSR was $204.

EG 712L - .22 LR cal. only, lever action copied after the Win. Model 92, 18 1/2 in. octagonal barrel, deluxe walnut silver plated receiver and barrel bands, 15 shot, iron sights. Disc.

	$300	$241	$220	$180	$150	$130	$115

EG 73 - .22 Mag. cal. only, lever action copied after the Win. Model 92, 19 1/4 in. barrel, 12 shot, iron sights, blue only. Disc. 1985.

	$205	$185	$160	$140	$130	$120	$105

Last MSR was $229.

GRADING - PPGS™	100%	98%	95%	90%	80%	70%	60%

EG 722 - .22 LR cal. only, slide action, 18 1/2 in. barrel, 15 shot, iron sights, blue only. Disc. 1985.

	$180	$160	$140	$125	$115	$100	$90

Last MSR was $204.

EM 1 CARBINE - .22 LR or .22 Mag. cal., gas semi-auto, copy of the original M1 carbine, 19 1/2 in. barrel, 15 shot, iron sights, blue only. ESG 22 is .22 Mag. (12 shot). Disc. 1985.

	$175	$155	$140	$125	$115	$100	$90

Last MSR was $195.

Add $100 for ESG 22, .22 Mag.

SHOTGUNS: O/U

SENATOR MODEL - 12, 20 ga., or .410 bore, 3 in. chambers, 26 or 28 in. F/M barrels, folding action, double triggers, extractors, vent. barrels and rib, checkered walnut stock and forearm, engraved silver finished receiver, mfg. by Antonio Zoli. Imported 1986-87.

	$235	$200	$180	$165	$150	$140	$130

Last MSR was $275.

EXCEL ARMS

Trademark of pistols and rifles manufactured by Excel Industries, Inc., located in Chino, CA.

PISTOLS: SEMI-AUTO

ACCELERATOR MP - .17 HMR (MP-17) or .22 Mag. (MP-22) cal., 8.5 in. barrel, polymer frame with stainless steel slide, adj. sights, 9 shot mag., 54 oz. New 2005.

MSR $385	$340	$295	$260	$230	$200	$180	$160

RIFLES: SEMI-AUTO

MR17/MR22 - .17 HMR (MR17) or .22 Mag. (MR22) cal., black composite stock with large thumbhole, fluted 18 in. stainless steel barrel and receiver with shroud, fully adj. sights, 9 shot mag., 8 lbs. New 2004.

MSR $465	$425	$385	$335	$285	$240	$200	$180

EXEL ARMS OF AMERICA, INC.

Previous importer located in Gardener, MA. Exel Arms previously imported Lanber (Series 100), Ugartechea (Series 200), and Laurona (Series 300) shotguns. Please refer to the appropriate sections for more information on this series.

F SECTION

F. DARNE FILS AINÉ

Previous manufacturer located in St. Etienne, France.

Francisque Darne was the eldest son of Regis Darne, who developed the sliding breech gun. In 1910, Francisque left his father's company to form his own, "F. Darne Fils Ainé," producing high quality versions of the original 1894 patent R model Darne. Regis Darne updated most of his designs in 1909 and allowed the older patents to become public domain.

Francisque Darne died in 1917, but his company remained in production until 1955 under at least four different owners. SIFARM, a combination of the manufacturers Berthon Freres, Francisque Darne, Didier-Drevet, Gerest, and Ronchard-Cizeron, was absorbed in 1963 by Verney-Carron, along with the famous Canonnerie (barrel makers) Jean Breuil.

As is usually the case, the earlier production guns are by far the highest quality. Wide variations in quality exist in this marque, depending on the financial health of the owners at the time of production.

GRADING - PPGS™	100%	98%	95%	90%	80%	70%	60%

SHOTGUNS: SxS, PRE-WAR MODELS

CLASSIC MODEL - 12 or 16 ga., an exact copy of the first Darne patent of 1894. Available in four grades.

* *Type A* - standard French proof barrels, very light engraving, color case hardened, no quality stamps on barrel flats.

	100%	98%	95%	90%	80%	70%	60%
	$1,200	$1,000	$800	$700	$600	$500	$450

* *Type B* - French gray hardened or color case hardened, somewhat more engraving, 1 quality stamp on barrel flats.

	100%	98%	95%	90%	80%	70%	60%
	$1,700	$1,400	$1,200	$900	$700	$600	$500

* *Type C* - French gray hardening over modern or old English engraving, double proofed barrels with two quality stamps on barrel flats.

	100%	98%	95%	90%	80%	70%	60%
	$2,000	$1,650	$1,350	$1,000	$800	$650	$550

* *Type E* - French gray hardening over elaborate engraving. Better quality wood in either English or semi-pistol grip. Double proof barrels with four quality stamps on barrel flats.

	100%	98%	95%	90%	80%	70%	60%
	$2,400	$2,000	$1,600	$1,300	$1,000	$900	$800

MODEL T - 12 or 16 ga., stylistic improvements to the 1894 patent R model. Two-piece stock, barrels removed by holding a button on forend, 4 grades, all were originally color case hardened, never blue.

Both the T 32 and T 34 were available in 10 ga. with 70mm or 75mm chambers and 72cm or 76cm barrels on special order. The barrels would carry triple proof in 10 ga.

* *Type T 32* - lightly engraved, 3 quality stamps on barrel flats.

	100%	98%	95%	90%	80%	70%	60%
	$1,950	$1,700	$1,250	$950	$700	$600	$500

Add 30% for 10 ga.

* *Model T 34* - better engraving and wood, 5 quality stamps on barrel flats.

	100%	98%	95%	90%	80%	70%	60%
	$2,100	$1,800	$1,500	$1,100	$850	$675	$575

Add 30% for 10 ga.

* *Model T 35* - mono bloc barrels of superior French proof steel, better engraving and wood, 6 quality stamps on barrel flats.

	100%	98%	95%	90%	80%	70%	60%
	$2,500	$2,200	$1,800	$1,400	$1,200	$1,000	$800

GRADING - PPGS™	100%	98%	95%	90%	80%	70%	60%

* ❋ *Model T 36* - mono bloc barrels of superior French proof steel, top-of-the-line T model, 7 quality stamps on barrel flats.

	$2,800	$2,500	$2,100	$1,700	$1,400	$1,200	$850

MODEL FIXED - 12 or 16 ga., further tinkering with the 1894 R model, these located the barrels in a rectangular block cut near the flats. Two grades.

* ❋ *Type No. 3* - color case hardened or French gray hardened. Good quality engraving and wood. For pricing, see Type T 34.
* ❋ *Type No. 4* - better wood and engraving. For pricing, see Type T 35.

MODEL PLATINUM - 12 or 16 ga., based on the model Fixed, these were top-of-the-line sliding breech guns. Four grades.

* ❋ *Type No. 5* - mono bloc barrels, English or art nouveau style engraving, chisled fences.

	$3,100	$2,800	$2,500	$2,200	$1,700	$1,400	$1,100

* ❋ *Type No. 6* - mono bloc barrels, English rose and scroll engraving or game scene or art nouveau style, high grade wood.

	$3,400	$2,900	$2,600	$2,350	$1,900	$1,600	$1,200

* ❋ *Type No. 7* - mono bloc barrels of top quality French proof steel, engraved in English rose and scroll or deep chisled art nouveau style, superior wood. Pigeon model.

	$3,800	$3,500	$3,000	$2,800	$2,200	$1,900	$1,500

* ❋ *Type No. 8* - mono bloc barrels of top quality French proof steel. Top-of-the-line model with all details to customer's wishes. Very rare in any condition. Rarity precludes accurate pricing.

SHOTGUNS: SxS, POST-WAR MODELS

Note: the model name of the following post-war guns is usually engraved on the side of the gun in front of the safety lever.

CLASSIC MODEL - 12 or 16 ga. with modified and full choke on 70 cm barrels, simple case colored gun with no engraving and plain wood in semi-pistol grip or straight stock, 2 quality stamps.

	$1,250	$1,000	$850	$700	$600	$525	$400

BARONNET-BROUSSARD - 12, 16, or 20 ga. with 70 cm barrels (two-piece stock on 12 and 16 ga.), lightly engraved with satin chrome receiver finish, Broussard model featured 80 cm barrels but was essentially the same, 3 quality stamps.

	$1,400	$1,200	$1,000	$800	$675	$550	$475

   Add 20% for Broussard model.

GOUVERNEUR MODEL - 12, 16, or 20 ga., better engraving and one-piece stock of select walnut, French gray receiver, choice of barrel lengths in 12 ga. (70 cm, 72 cm, or 74 cm.) classic or modern style engraving, 5 quality stamps.

	$1,800	$1,650	$1,200	$1,000	$750	$600	$550

GOUVERNEUR PLUME AND PLUME MAGNUM - same as above, but with plume (swamped rib) on Plume Model, plume rib and 76mm chambers included on Plume Magnum Model. Prices about 10% higher than previous models due to these having six quality stamps on flats of barrels in spite of being the same basic gun.

RAMBOUILLET MODEL - 12 or 16 ga., double sears in a large key action somewhat similar to the Darne V models stylistically, one-piece stock of select walnut, in semi-pistol grip or straight style, light engraving on color case hardening, choice of rib, 8 quality stamps.

	$1,500	$1,300	$1,100	$900	$700	$650	$575

GRADING - PPGS™	100%	98%	95%	90%	80%	70%	60%

AMBASSADEUR MODEL - 12 or 16 ga., large key model with double sears. French gray finish on breech with excellent engraving, one-piece stock of good quality walnut, top-of-the-line production model, 10 quality stamps.

	$2,700	$2,400	$2,200	$1,800	$1,500	$1,100	$850

PRESTIGE MODEL - top-of-the-line custom gun, mono bloc barrels of Jacob Holtzer steel with plume swamped rib. Large key action with silent operation and double sears, one-piece stock of best quality walnut, in straight style only, 72 cm barrels, excellent full coverage engraving, eight month minimum wait, 12 quality stamps.

	$3,500	$3,100	$2,900	$2,600	$2,200	$1,700	$1,200

F.A.I.R. S.r.l.

Current manufacturer established in 1971 (F.A.I.R. stands for Fabbrica Armi Isidoro Rizzini) and located in Marcheno, Italy (owned by Isidoro Rizzini). In 2003, the name changed from F.A.I.R. Tecni-Mec I. Rizzini to F.A.I.R. S.r.l. Previously imported and distributed exclusively by New England Arms Corp. located in Kittery Point, ME.

Please contact the factory directly for more information, including current model availability and pricing.

RIFLES: SINGLE SHOT

KIPPLAUF MODEL 500/500 DELUXE - various cals., single barrel stalking rifle. New 2002.

MSR N/A	$1,825	$1,650	$1,350	$1,050	$900	$750	$700

SHOTGUNS: O/U

F.A.I.R. manufactures a wide variety of shotguns, rifles, and combination guns, including O/Us and single shots in assorted models. Some models, however, are not being imported into the U.S. at this time. For more information on the complete F.A.I.R. model line-up, please contact New England Arms Corp.

Beginning 1999, Models 500, 600, 702, and 900 in 16 ga. have their own size frame (approx. 6 1/4 lbs). A unique, smaller 28 ga. frame was introduced in 2000 (also used for .410 bore), and weighs approx. 5 3/4 lbs. Numerous options are available, including custom dimensions.

MODEL PREMIERE EM DELUXE/SPORTING - 12, 20, 28 ga., or .410 bore, standard model with ST, ejectors, vent. rib barrels, blue frame. Importation began 1998.

MSR N/A	$850	$700	$675	$525	$450	$400	$360

MODEL 500 - 12, 16, 20, 28 ga., or .410 bore, boxlock action with case colored frame and scroll engraving, choke tubes (5) except for .410 bore. Importation began 1998.

MSR N/A	$2,000	$1,750	$1,525	$1,275	$1,075	$950	$825

Add $275 for Model 500 Gold (includes gold inlays on receiver).

MODEL 600 GOLD - same gauges as Model 500, features case colored or coin finished receiver with engraved and gold inlaid sideplates. Importation began 1998.

MSR N/A	$2,650	$2,225	$1,900	$1,675	$1,400	$1,150	$925

MODEL S 610 - 10 ga., 3 1/2 in. Mag., O/U boxlock action, double underlug locking, 32 in. VR barrels, SST, ejectors, checkered walnut stock and forearm. Imported 1991-97.

	$925	$825	$750	$675	$595	$525	$450

Last MSR was $1,000.

MODEL SPL 640 - 12, 16, 20, 28 ga., or .410 bore, folding O/U design, DT, 26 in. VR barrels. Importation disc. 1997.

	$465	$390	$325	$260	$215	$180	$160

Last MSR was $500.

GRADING - PPGS™	100%	98%	95%	90%	80%	70%	60%

MODEL 702 - 12, 16, 20, 28 ga., or .410 bore, O/U boxlock with sideplates, standard interchangeable chokes available, case colored receiver with hand inlaid 24Kt. gold wire outlines on sideplates, frame, and triggerguard, SST, ejectors. Importation began 1995.

MSR N/A	$3,500	$2,450	$2,000	$1,750	$1,500	$1,350	$1,225

MODEL 900 - similar to Model 702, except has hand executed Bulino/scroll engraving on coin finished receiver, game scenes vary with each ga., case colored receiver available upon request. Importation began 1995.

MSR N/A	$3,500	$2,450	$2,000	$1,750	$1,500	$1,350	$1,225

❋ **Model 900 EL** - same general specifications as the Model 900, except has full engraving coverage with individually signed Bulino game scene engraving and higher quality wood. Importation began 2001.

MSR N/A	$5,500	$4,500	$4,000	$3,500	$2,450	$2,000	$1,750

❋ **Model 900 EELL** - same general specifications as Model 900 EL, top-of-the-line model with highly figured Turkish walnut, extensive engraving, cased. Importation began 2001.

MSR N/A	$6,875	$6,000	$5,500	$4,500	$4,000	$3,500	$2,450

MODEL 902 - similar to Model 900, except has sideplates. Importation began 2001.

MSR N/A	$4,275	$3,250	$2,650	$2,100	$1,825	$1,500	$1,350

❋ **Model 902 EL** - same general specifications as the Model 902, except has full engraving coverage on sideplates and upgraded wood. Importation began 2001.

MSR N/A	$6,275	$5,300	$4,500	$3,900	$2,700	$2,300	$2,100

❋ **Model 902 EELL** - same general specifications as Model 902 EL, top-of-the-line model with highly figured Turkish walnut, extensive Bullino game scene engraving with signature, cased. Importation began 2001.

MSR N/A	$8,350	$7,500	$6,500	$5,600	$4,600	$3,600	$2,750

F.A.V.S. di FRANCESCO GUGLIELMI-NOTTI

Current manufacturer established in 1957, and located in Villar Focchiardo, Italy. No current U.S. importation. F.A.V.S. is an abbreviation for Fabbrica Armi Valle Susa.

RIFLES: SINGLE SHOT

STRADIVARI - various cals., unique "shorty" bullpup configuration utilizing a break open single shot action and pivoting wood buttstock that opens/closes breech, finger grooved pistol grip wood stock with short forend, scope is mounted on front portion of barrel, 19 3/4 in., 24 in., or 29 in. barrel with muzzleweight.

Please contact the manufacturer directly regarding U.S. importation and current pricing (see Trademark Index).

FAS

Current pistol manufacturer located in Milan, Italy. No current U.S. importation. Previously imported and distributed by Nygord Precision Products located in Prescott, AZ, and Mandall Shooting Supplies, located in Scottsdale, AZ, by Beeman Precision Arms, Inc. located in Santa Rosa, CA and Osborne's located in Cheboygan, MI.

PISTOLS: SEMI-AUTO

MODEL OP601 - .22 Short cal. only, competition pistol, 5.9 in. barrel, 5 shot mag., wraparound match wood grips, 41 1/2 oz.

MSR N/A	$1,025	$875	$695	$640	$565	$500	$450

GRADING - PPGS™	100%	98%	95%	90%	80%	70%	60%

MODEL 602 - .22 LR cal. only, competition pistol, 5.6 in. barrel, 5 shot mag., ergonomically designed match wood grips, 40 oz. Importation disc. 1994.

	$895	$800	$625	$600	$525	$475	$425

Last MSR was $1,100.

MODEL CF603 - .32 S&W Wadcutter cal. only, competition pistol, 5.3 in. barrel, 5 shot mag., ergonomically designed adj. or non-adj. match wood grips, 40 oz.

MSR N/A	$975	$875	$695	$640	$565	$500	$450

MODEL SP607 (LADY) - .22 LR cal. only, semi-auto competition pistol, similar to Model 602, except has removable barrel weights, 5.6 in. barrel.

MSR N/A	$975	$875	$695	$640	$565	$500	$450

FEG

Current manufacturer located in Hungary (FEG stands for Fegyver es Gepgyar) since circa 1900. Currently imported by Century International Arms located in Delray Beach, FL (see additional information under the Century International Arms in this text). Previously imported and distributed by K.B.I., Inc. located in Harrisburg, PA, and distributed until 1998 by Interarms located in Alexandria, VA.

PISTOLS: SEMI-AUTO, INTERARMS IMPORTED

All FEG pistols were supplied with two mags.

MARK II AP22 - .22 LR cal., double action, 3.4 in. barrel, 8 shot mag., blue finish, black plastic grips, 23 oz. Imported 1997-98.

	$235	$200	$175	$160	$145	$130	$115

Last MSR was $269.

MARK II AP - .380 ACP cal., double action, patterned after the Walther PP, 3.9 in. barrel, 7 shot mag., blue finish, black plastic grips, 27 oz. Imported 1997-98.

	$235	$200	$175	$160	$145	$130	$115

Last MSR was $269.

MARK II APK - .380 ACP cal., similar to Mark II AP, except is patterned after the Walther PPK/S, 3.4 in. barrel, 7 shot mag., blue finish, black plastic grips, 25 oz. Imported 1997-98.

	$235	$200	$175	$160	$145	$130	$115

Last MSR was $269.

PISTOLS: SEMI-AUTO, RECENT IMPORTATION

In addition to the following imported models, FEG also makes additional models available mostly in Europe. Currently, these pistols include the RL61 (.22 LR cal.), the P9R/P9RK (9mm Para. cal.), AP9/APK9 (.380 ACP cal.), P9RZ Compact (9mm Para cal.), and the AC/ACK (.45 ACP cal.).

MODEL PMK-380 - .380 ACP cal., patterned after Walther PP, alloy frame, double action, 4 in. barrel, plastic grips with thumbrest, blue finish, 21 oz. Importation by K.B.I. 1992-2003.

	$205	$180	$160	$135	$120	$110	$100

Last MSR was $239.

MODEL SMC-380 - .380 ACP cal., double action semi-auto, patterned after Walther PPK, alloy frame, 3 1/2 in. barrel, 6 shot mag., plastic grips with thumbrest, blue finish, 18 1/2 oz. Importation by K.B.I. 1993-2003.

	$205	$180	$160	$135	$120	$110	$100

Last MSR was $239.

GRADING - PPGS™	100%	98%	95%	90%	80%	70%	60%

✱ *Model SMC-22* - .22 LR cal., 8 shot mag., otherwise similar to Model SMC-380. Importation disc. 1997.

	$210	$195	$180	$165	$150	$135	$115

Last MSR was $235.

MODEL SMC-918 - 9x18 Makarov cal., double action, semi-auto, 7 shot mag. Importation disc. 1997.

	$175	$150	$130	$110	$95	$85	$75

Last MSR was $235.

MODEL PA-63 - 9x18 Makarov cal., single or double action, 3.93 in. barrel, blue or bright aluminum anodized frame with blued steel slide, fixed sights, plastic grips, decocking safety. Previously imported by Century International Arms.

	$175	$150	$130	$110	$95	$85	$75

MODEL R-9 - 9mm Para. cal., patterned after Browning Hi-Power, double action, 13 shot mag., blue finish, steel construction, checkered wood grips. Imported 1986-87 only.

	$275	$230	$200	$180	$165	$155	$145

Last MSR was $375.

MODEL PPH - .380 ACP cal., patterned after Walther PP, alloy frame, double action, plastic grips with thumbrest, blue finish. Imported 1986-87 only.

	$200	$170	$140	$125	$115	$105	$95

Last MSR was $225.

MODEL MBK-9HP - 9mm Para. cal., patterned after Browning Hi-Power, double action, 4 2/3 in. barrel, 14 shot mag., blue finish, steel construction, checkered wood grips, 36 oz. Imported 1992 only.

	$315	$270	$250	$225	$200	$185	$170

Last MSR was $349.

✱ *Model MBK-9HPC* - compact variation of the Model MBK-9HP with 4 in. barrel, 34 oz. Imported 1992 only.

	$325	$275	$250	$225	$200	$185	$170

Last MSR was $359.

MODEL PJK-9HP - 9mm Para. cal., patterned after Browning Hi-Power, single action, all steel construction, 4 3/4 in. barrel, thumb safety, 10 (C/B 1994) or 13* shot mag. and cleaning rod, 32 oz. Importation by K.B.I. 1992-2003.

	$250	$225	$195	$175	$150	$130	$120

Last MSR was $295.

Add approx. $60 for industrial hard chrome finish (Model PJK-9HPC - includes Uncle Mike's rubber grips, disc. 1999).

MODEL GKK-92C - 9mm Para. cal., double action semi-auto, 4 in. barrel, 14 shot mag., improved variation of MBK models, includes same accessories as PJK-9H, 34 oz. Importation disc. 1993.

	$315	$280	$255	$230	$200	$185	$170

Last MSR was $369.

MODEL GKK-40C - .40 S&W cal., 9 shot mag., otherwise similar to GKK-45. Imported 1995-96.

	$300	$265	$230	$200	$180	$160	$145

Last MSR was $349.

MODEL GKK-45 - .45 ACP cal., double action semi-auto, all steel, 4 1/4 in. barrel, blue (disc. 1994) or chrome (Model GKK-45C) finish checkered walnut grips, 8 shot mag., approx. 37 oz. Imported 1993-96.

	$300	$265	$230	$200	$180	$160	$145

Last MSR was $349.

GRADING - PPGS™	100%	98%	95%	90%	80%	70%	60%

RIFLES: SEMI-AUTO

MODEL SA-85M - 7.62x39mm cal., sporter rifle utilizing AKM action, 16.3 in. barrel, 6 shot detachable mag., thumbhole stock, 7 lbs. 10 oz. Imported 1991, banned 1998.

	$350	$315	$280	$250	$225	$200	$185

Last MSR was $429.

SA-2000M - .223 Rem. or 7.62x39mm cal., sporter rifle with skeletonized Choate synthetic stock, 17 3/4 in. barrel with muzzle brake, 10 shot detachable mag. Imported 1999-2000.

	$330	$285	$250	$225	$200	$185	$170

Last MSR was $365.

Add approx. $100 for .223 Rem. cal.

FIAS

Previous long gun and related components manufacturer located in Brescia, Italy. FIAS is an abbreviation for Fabbrica Italiana Armi Sabatti.

FIAS became part of the Sabatti Armi group circa 2002, and is based in Gardone VT, Brescia. Please refer to Sabatti for current information, including any domestic importation.

F.I.E.

Previous importer (F.I.E. is the acronym for Firearms Import & Export) located in Hialeah, FL until 1990.

F.I.E. filed bankruptcy in November of 1990 and all models are discontinued. Some parts or service for these older firearms may be obtained through NumrichGun Parts Corp. (see Trademark Index), even though all warranties on F.I.E. guns are void.

DERRINGERS

MODEL D38 - .38 Spl. cal., O/U, chrome finish only, no transfer bar. Disc. 1985.

	$70	$60	$55	$45	$40	$35	$30

Last MSR was $82.

Add $17 for walnut grips.

MODEL D86 - .38 Spl. cal., single shot, 3 in. barrel, internal transfer bar safety, ammo storage compartment, blue or Dyna-chrome finish, 11 oz. Mfg. 1986-disc.

	$80	$65	$55	$50	$45	$40	$35

Last MSR was $95.

Add $9 for Dyna-chrome finish.
Add $25 for deluxe model (walnut stocks).
Add $60 for Misty Gold finish (disc.).

PISTOLS: SEMI-AUTO, TITAN SERIES

TITAN II (E32 SERIES) - .32 ACP (disc. 1988), or .380 ACP, single action, blue (standard) or chrome finish. Mfg. in U.S. - disc.

	$195	$160	$135	$120	$105	$95	$85

Last MSR was $220.

Add $25 for walnut grips.
Add $10 for chrome finish.

This series was redesigned in 1988 to be shorter and more compact. Older series Titans are worth approx. $50 less than values shown above.

GRADING - PPGS™	100%	98%	95%	90%	80%	70%	60%

SUPER TITAN - .380 ACP cal., proofed AH, otherwise similar to Super Titan II. Mfg in Italy by Tanfoglio.

	$215	$185	$155	$135	$120	$105	$95

SUPER TITAN II - .32 ACP (disc. 1988), or .380 ACP cal., single action, 12 shot mag. in .32 ACP, 11 for .380 cal., walnut grips, standard blue only. Mfg. in U.S.-disc.

	$215	$185	$155	$135	$120	$105	$95

Last MSR was $260.

.22 TITAN II (E22) - .22 LR cal., single action, 10 shot mag., blue finish only. Walnut grips standard. Mfg. 1990 only.

	$130	$105	$90	$80	$70	$65	$60

Last MSR was $161.

✳ *Lady .22* - similar to .22 TITAN II except has combination blue/gold finish with scrimshawed red rose on ivory polymer grips. New 1990.

	$185	$155	$130	$120	$105	$95	$85

Last MSR was $208.

THE BEST (A27) - .25 ACP cal., single action, blue only, deluxe finish, walnut grips, steel frame, 6 shot mag. Mfg. in Spain by Astra. Importation disc. 1988.

	$125	$105	$90	$80	$70	$65	$60

Last MSR was $155.

.25 TITAN (E27 SERIES) - .25 ACP cal., single action, blue (disc. 1989) or Dyna-chrome finish (standard 1990).

	$60	$50	$45	$40	$35	$30	$30

Last MSR was $77.

> Subtract $5 for blue finish.
> Add $26 for gold trim (new 1986).
> Add $62 for Misty Gold finish (1988 only).

✳ *Titan Tigress* - similar to .25 Titan except is entirely gold plated and cased, ladies pistol. Imported 1989-90 only.

	$130	$110	$95				

Last MSR was $153.

.25 TITAN (E38 SERIES) - .25 ACP cal., similar to E27 series except has standard blue finish. Mfg. 1990 only.

	$50	$45	$40	$35	$30	$30	$25

Last MSR was $59.

> Add $9 for Dyna-chrome finish.

SSP SERIES - .32 ACP or .380 ACP cal., single action semi-auto, 3 1/8 in. barrel, 5 shot mag., blue or chrome finish, composition grips, 25 oz. Mfg. in US, 1990 only.

	$120	$95	$85	$75	$65	$60	$55

Last MSR was $146.

> Add $19 for chrome finish.

✳ *Lady SSP* - similar to SSP except has gold trimmed parts, scrimshawed red rose on ivory polymer grips, and gold case. Mfg. 1990 only.

	$210	$180	$155	$135	$120	$105	$95

Last MSR was $250.

TZ-75 - 9mm Para. cal., double action, 4.72 in. barrel, steel frame and slide, 15 shot mag., patterned after the CZ-75 action, 35 oz. Imported 1982-1989. This model was updated in 1988 (Series 88).

	$375	$325	$290	$270	$250	$235	$220

Last MSR was $440.

> Add $20 for satin chrome finish (new 1986).
> Add $20 for black rubber grips.

TZ-75 SERIES 88 - 9mm Para. or .41 Action Express cal., improved TZ-75 action, 4.72 in. barrel, steel frame and slide, 11 (.41 AE) or 17 (9mm Para.) shot mag., fixed removable rear sight, choice of matte blue, satin chrome, or blue slide/chrome frame finish, updated CZ-75 action, 35 oz. Mfg. 1988-90.

	$435	$360	$330	$295	$280	$260	$240

Last MSR was $519.

Add $97 for .41 Action Express cal.
Add $20 for satin chrome on 9mm Para., $29 on .41 AE.
Add $14 for black rubber grips.

This model was also available with a blue slide/chrome frame (I.P.S.C. configuration) at no extra charge.

The TZ-75 Series 88 was re-engineered in 1988 to include: frame mounted sear locking safety (cocked and locked), Colt style firing pin safety block, improved recessed slide serrations, muzzle barrel swell, bobbed hammer design, elongated combat style slide stop, new mag. release, and removable rear sight.

✱ *TZ-75 Combo* - includes both .41 Action Express and 9mm Para. barrels. Mfg. 1990 only.

	$615	$535	$475	$430	$395	$370	$350

Last MSR was $709.

Add $29 for satin chrome or blue slide/chrome frame finish.

✱ *TZ-75 Series 88 Govt. Model* - 9mm Para. cal. only, compact variation of the TZ-75 Series 88, 3 3/5 in. barrel, 12 shot mag., checkered walnut grips, 33 1/2 oz. Mfg. 1990 only.

	$435	$360	$330	$295	$280	$260	$240

Last MSR was $519.

Add $20 for satin chrome or blue slide/chrome frame finish.

✱ *TZ-75 Series 88 with ported barrel* - similar to the TZ-75 Series 88 except has 5 in. ported barrel and slide. Mfg. 1990 only.

	$615	$535	$475	$430	$395	$370	$350

Last MSR was $709.

✱ *Compensated TZ-75 Series 88* - similar to the TZ-75 Series 88 except has 5 3/4 in. compensated barrel, 42 oz. Mfg. 1990 only.

	$700	$615	$535	$475	$430	$395	$370

Last MSR was $804.

MODEL 722 TP SILHOUETTE PISTOL - .22 LR cal., bolt action target pistol, 10 in. free-floating barrel, 4-way adj. trigger, micro adj. rear sight, 6 or 10 shot mag., stippled pistol grip and forearm, supplied with 2-piece scope mount, 3.4 lbs. Mfg. 1990 only.

	$220	$190	$160	$140	$125	$115	$100

Last MSR was $263.

SPECTRE PISTOL - 9mm Para. or .45 ACP cal., double action, unique triple action blowback system with two piece bolt, 6 in. barrel, military style configuration, adj. sights, 30 or 50 (optional with unique 4 column configuation) shot mag., 4.8 lbs. Mfg. 1989-90 only.

	$675	$600	$525	$480	$440	$400	$360

Last MSR was $718.

Add $14 for mag. loading tool.

KG-99 - 9mm Para. cal., paramilitary design pistol, 36 shot mag. Mini-99 also available with 20 shot mag. and 3 in. barrel. Disc. 1984.

	$550	$475	$440	$400	$365	$330	$300

This model was not manufactured but sold by F.I.E.

REVOLVERS: DOUBLE ACTION, ARMINIUS SERIES

All pistols under this heading were manufactured in W. Germany under the trademark Arminius. .22 cal. is 8 shot, .32 S&W is 7 shot, all others 6 shot.

GRADING - PPGS™	100%	98%	95%	90%	80%	70%	60%

MODEL 522TB - .22 LR cal., blue finish, 4 in. barrel, 8 shot.

	100%	98%	95%	90%	80%	70%	60%
	$130	$100	$85	$75	$70	$65	$60

Last MSR was $174.

     Add $23 for walnut grips.

722 SERIES - .22 LR cal., blue (standard) or chrome finish (disc. 1985), 6 in. barrel, 8 shot.

	$125	$100	$90	$80	$70	$65	$60

Last MSR was $161.

     Add $23 for walnut grips.
     Add $49 for .22 LR/.22 Mag. combo.
     Add $15 for chrome finish.

STANDARD REVOLVER - .22 LR, .22 Mag., .32 Mag. or .38 Spl. cal., 2 or 4 in. barrel, blue finish, fixed sights, without ejector assembly. Mfg in US 1989-90.

	$80	$70	$65	$60	$55	$50	$45

Last MSR was $101.

     Add $19 for chrome finish (2 in. barrel only).
     Add $38 for gold plated finish (2 in. barrel only).
     Add $23 for .22 Combo package (2 cylinders - 4 in. barrel only).
     Models with 4 in. barrels were available in blue finish only.

MODEL 532TB - .32 S&W cal., blue (standard) or chrome finish (disc. 1985), adj. sights, 4 in. barrel, 7 shot.

	$145	$120	$100	$80	$75	$70	$65

Last MSR was $183.

     Add $23 for walnut grips.
     Add $15 for chrome finish.

MODEL 732B - similar to Model 532TB, except has 6 in. barrel and fixed sights. Imported 1988 only.

	$120	$100	$90	$80	$70	$65	$60

Last MSR was $140.

MODEL N-38 (TITAN TIGER) - .38 Spl. cal., blue (standard) or chrome finish (disc. 1985), 2 or 4 in. barrel, fixed sights. Disc. 1990.

	$130	$110	$95	$80	$75	$65	$60

Last MSR was $176.

     Add $23 for walnut grips.
     Add $15 for chrome finish.

ZEPHYR - .38 Spl. cal., 5 shot, aluminum construction, 2 in. barrel, blue finish, checkered grips, 14 oz. Mfg. 1990 only.

	$145	$120	$100	$80	$75	$70	$65

Last MSR was $189.

     ✳ *Lady Zephyr* - similar to Zephyr, except has gold trimmed parts, scrimshawed red rose on ivory polymer grips, and gold case. Mfg. 1990 only.

	$250	$210	$180	$155	$135	$115	$95

Last MSR was $295.

MODEL 384TB - .38 Spl. cal., blue (standard) or chrome finish (disc. 1985), 6 shot, 4 in. barrel.

	$150	$125	$105	$85	$80	$70	$65

Last MSR was $195.

     Add $23 for walnut grips.
     Add $13 for chrome finish.

GRADING - PPGS™	100%	98%	95%	90%	80%	70%	60%

MODEL 386TB - .38 Spl. cal., blue (standard) or chrome finish (disc. 1985), 6 shot, 6 in. barrel.

	$150	$125	$105	$85	$80	$70	$65

Last MSR was $195.

Add $23 for walnut grips.
Add $13 for chrome finish.

.357 MAG. SERIES - .357 Mag. cal., blue (standard) or chrome finish (disc. 1985), 6 shot, 3 (Model 3573TB), 4 (Model 3574TB), or 6 (Model 3576TB) in. barrels.

	$200	$170	$135	$120	$110	$100	$90

Last MSR was $255.

Add $23 for walnut grips.
Add $15 for chrome finish.

Revolvers: Double Action, Snub-Nose

Previously manufactured 2 in. snub-nosed revolvers are listed in the previous category under Standard Revolver, Titan Tiger, and Zephyr.

222 SERIES - .22 LR & .22 Mag. cal., blue (standard) or chrome finish, 2 in. snub-nose barrel. Disc. 1985.

	$135	$115	$90	$85	$75	$65	$60

Last MSR was $120.

Add $15 for walnut grips.
Add $45 for .22 LR/.22 Mag. combo.

✳ *222B Series* - .22 LR cal. only 1989, similar to 222 Series. Reintroduced 1987-1989.

	$150	$120	$105	$85	$80	$70	$65

Last MSR was $185.

Add $45 for .22 LR/.22 Mag. combo (disc. 1988).

232 SERIES - .32 S&W cal., blue (standard) or chrome finish, 2 in. barrel. Disc.

	$120	$90	$85	$75	$65	$60	$55

Add $15 for walnut grips.
Add $14 for adj. sights.
Add $28 for chrome finish.

✳ *232B SERIES* - similar to 232 Series, 2 in. barrel. Reintroduced 1987-1989.

	$150	$125	$110	$95	$85	$75	$70

Last MSR was $185.

Add $5 for adj. sights.

MODEL 382TB - .38 Spl. cal., blue (standard) or chrome finish, 2 in. barrel. Disc. 1985.

	$125	$110	$100	$90	$80	$75	$65

Last MSR was $145.

Add $15 for walnut grips.
Add $16 for chrome finish.

MODEL 3572 - .357 Mag. cal., blue (standard) or chrome finish, 2 in. barrel. Disc. 1984.

	$223	$170	$160	$135	$125	$115	$100

Add $15 for walnut grips.
Add $17 for chrome finish.

REVOLVERS: SINGLE ACTION

Combo designations on the following models indicate 2 cylinders (.22 LR/.22 Mag.).

GRADING - PPGS™	100%	98%	95%	90%	80%	70%	60%

COWBOY - .22 LR or .22 LR/Mag. cal. combo, 3 1/4 or 6 in. barrel, blue finish, square butt grip, without ejector tube, fixed sights. U.S. mfg. 1989-90.

	$75	$65	$50	$45	$40	$35	$30

Last MSR was $95.

Add $23 for combo.

GOLD RUSH - .22 LR or .22 LR/Mag. cal. combo, 3 1/4, 4 3/4, or 6 1/2 in. barrel, round (3 1/4 in. barrel only) or square butt grip, gold band on barrel and cylinder, ivory-tex grips. Mfg in U.S. 1989-90.

	$155	$125	$110	$95	$85	$75	$70

Last MSR was $189.

Add $47 for combo.

TEXAS RANGER (TEX 22 SERIES) - .22 LR or .22 Mag. cal. (combo only), 3 1/4 (new 1986), 4 3/4, 6 1/2 (new 1989), 7, or 9 in. barrel, 6 shot, blue only. Mfg in U.S.-disc.

	$80	$70	$60	$50	$45	$40	$35

Last MSR was $108.

Add $23 for combo.
Add $6 for 9 in. barrel.
This model with a 3 1/4 in. barrel is called the Little Ranger.

BUFFALO SCOUT (E15 SERIES) - .22 LR or .22 Mag. cal., blue (standard) or chrome finish, 4 3/4 in. barrel. Mfg. in Brescia, Italy - disc.

	$75	$55	$45	$35	$35	$30	$30

Last MSR was $98.

Add $23 for walnut grips.
Add $23 for combo.
Add $9 for chrome or blue/gold finish.

✴ *The Yellow Rose Combo* - all metal parts 24Kt. gold plated, smooth walnut grips. Mfg. 1986-90.

	$130	$110	$95				

Last MSR was $161.

Add $151 for scrimshawed ivory polymer grips - walnut cased (new 1989).

LEGEND SAA (PL-22 SERIES) - .22 LR or .22 Mag. cal., blue only. Mfg. in Brescia, Italy. Disc. 1984.

	$120	$90	$85	$75	$65	$60	$55

Add $3 for walnut grips.
Add $17 for combo.

HOMBRE MODEL - .357 Mag., .44 Mag., or .45 LC cal., color case hardened receiver, 5 1/2 (disc. 1985), 6, or 7 1/2 in. barrel, 45 oz., smooth walnut grips. Previously mfg. W. Germany.

	$220	$180	$145	$130	$120	$110	$100

Last MSR was $265.

Add $25 for brass back strap and trigger guard (disc.).

✴ *Golden Hombre* - same general specifications as Hombre, except all metal surfaces are plated in 24Kt. gold.

	$300	$210	$145				

Last MSR was $350.

Add $65 for ivory polymer grips (new 1989).

GRADING - PPGS™	100%	98%	95%	90%	80%	70%	60%

RIFLES: BOLT-ACTION

MODEL 122 - .22 LR cal., 6 or 10 shot box mag., 21 in. tapered barrel, Monte Carlo walnut stock, adj. sights. Mfg. by Hamilton & Hunter. Mfg. 1986-disc.

	$100	$80	$70	$60	$55	$50	$45

Last MSR was $115.

MODEL 322 - .22 LR cal., competition model, 26.2 in. floating barrel, adj. trigger, 6 or 10 shot mag., stippled pistol grip, 7 lbs. Mfg. 1990-disc.

	$580	$425	$380	$340	$295	$260	$230

Last MSR was $665.

MODEL 422 - similar to Model 322 except has heavy barrel, 9 lbs. Mfg. 1990-disc.

	$580	$425	$380	$340	$295	$260	$230

Last MSR was $665.

RIFLES: SEMI-AUTO

GR-8 BLACK BEAUTY - .22 LR cal., 14 shot, 19 1/2 in. barrel, 64 oz., tubular feed, black nylon stock, patterned after Rem. Nylon 66. Mfg. by C.B.C. of Brazil. F.I.E. Importation disc. 1988.

	$90	$75	$70	$65	$60	$55	$50

Last MSR was $100.

PARA RIFLE - .22 LR cal., paramilitary designed rifle with tube stock (is also magazine), includes green cloth case with white stenciled letters, takedown, 11 shot mag., matte black receiver finish, approx. 4 lbs. Mfg. by L. Franchi between 1979-84. Imported into the U.S. from 1985-88.

	$325	$275	$225	$195	$155	$130	$110

Last MSR was $225.

> 8,000 of this model were manufactured by L. Franchi. 5,000 went to the Italian Government and were used as training rifles (with German scopes). The remainder were imported by F.I.E. (without scopes).

SPECTRE CARBINE - 9mm Para. cal., same action as Spectre pistol, paramilitary design carbine, collapsible metal butt stock, 30 or 50 (opt.) shot mag., adj. rear sight, with pistol and forearm grip. Mfg. 1989-disc.

	$550	$450	$375	$300	$275	$250	$225

Last MSR was $700.

SHOTGUNS

All currently manufactured Franchi shotguns can be located in the Franchi section of this text.

S.O.B. - 12, 20 ga., or .410 bore, 18 1/2 in. single barrel, pistol grip only. Disc. 1984.

	$100	$90	$80	$70	$60	$55	$50

THE STURDY O/U - 12 or 20 ga., 3 in. chambers, 28 in. barrels, vent. rib and barrels, engraved silver finish receiver, double triggers, extractors, manufactured by Maroccini of Italy. Imported 1985-1988.

	$300	$275	$250	$235	$220	$205	$190

Last MSR was $350.

⁕ *Sturdy Deluxe Priti* - similar to The Sturdy model except has deluxe walnut. Importation disc. 1988.

	$325	$290	$260	$240	$225	$205	$195

Last MSR was $380.

Add $70 for ejectors, SST, and choke tubes.

GRADING - PPGS™	100%	98%	95%	90%	80%	70%	60%

✳ *Model 12 Deluxe* - 12 ga. only, SST, auto ejectors, multi-choked barrels, select walnut. Imported 1988 only.

	$320	$290	$260	$240	$225	$205	$195

Last MSR was $380.

THE BRUTE - 12, 20 ga, or .410 bore, 19 in. barrels, 30 in. overall length. Side-by-side action, disc. 1984.

	$195	$150	$140	$120	$110	$100	$90

SPAS-12 - this model appears under the Franchi heading in the F section.

SAS-12 - this model appears under the Franchi heading in the F section.

LAW-12 - this model appears under the Franchi heading in the F section.

FMJ

Previous manufacturer located in Copperhill, TN, until circa 1998.

Little information is available regarding FMJ firearms (including short barrel derringers and pistols), except they were inexpensive shooters and are not collectible. Their production records were turned in to the BATF during 1998.

FNH USA, INC.

Current importer located McLean, VA.

FNH USA, Inc. imports a complete line of commercial, law enforcement, and military style firearms, including pistols (mfg. by FN in Belgium), rifles (some models are made by U.S Repeating Arms), and shotguns (mfg. by FN Manufacturing).

HANDGUNS

FNH USA currently imports the following semi-auto pistols: the Five-seveN USG (new 2005), FNP9, FNP 9m, FNP 40, HP-SA, and the HP-SFS. Please contact the importer directly for more information, including availability and pricing (see Trademark Index).

RIFLES: BOLT ACTION

FNH USA currently imports the Patrol Bolt rifle, and a series of long range precision rifles, including the FN A1, FN A1a, FN A2, FN A3 G, and the FN A4. FNH USA also imports a line of modular system rifles, including the Ultima Ratio Intervention, the Ultima Ratio Commando II, and the .338 Lapua Model. Additionally, FNH USA imports a wide range of tactical rifles for military and law enforcement only. Please contact the company directly for more information, including availability and pricing.

SHOTGUNS

FNH USA imports tactical style shotguns, including the FN Police Shotgun, FN Self-Loading Police Shotgun, and the FN Tactical Police Shotgun. Please contact the company directly for more information, including availability and pricing.

FTL

Previously manufactured by Wilkinson Arms located in Covina, CA for the FTL Marketing Corp. located in N. Hollywood, CA.

PISTOLS: SEMI-AUTO

FTL AUTO NINE - .22 LR cal., single action, hammerless, blowback action, 8 shot mag., checkered plastic grips, fixed sights. Disc.

	$200	$160	$125	$105	$95	$85	$75

GRADING - PPGS™	100%	98%	95%	90%	80%	70%	60%

FABARM, S.p.A.

Current manufacturer established in 1900 and located in Brescia, Italy. Currently imported by SIG Arms, located in Exeter, NH. Previously imported and distributed by Heckler & Koch, Inc. 1998-2004. Certain models had limited importation by Ithaca Acquisition Corp. located in King Ferry, NY during 1993-1995. Previously imported and distributed (1988-1990) by St. Lawrence Sales, Inc. located in Lake Orion, MI. Previously imported until 1986 by Beeman Precision Arms, Inc. located in Santa Rosa, CA.

Fabarm currently manufactures approx. 35,000 long guns annually. Many models are not currently imported into the U.S.

SHOTGUNS: O/U

FIELD MODEL - 12 ga. only, 29 1/8 in. VR barrels, single trigger, ejectors, silver finished receiver, also available in Skeet and Trap models. Disc. 1985.

	$695	$595	$550	$500	$460	$420	$390

Last MSR was $795.

SKEET/TRAP COMBINATION SET - 12 ga. only, is supplied with both skeet and trap barrel assemblies, cased. Disc. 1986.

	$1,050	$900	$840	$780	$720	$670	$600

Last MSR was $1,195.

Add $39 for high gloss wood finish.

Add $30 for auto safety.

The following models have boxlock actions with coin finished receivers and light engraving.

GAMMA FIELD - 12 or 20 (disc.) ga., SST, ejectors, 26, 28, 29, 30, or 32 in. VR barrels, fixed or innerchokes, checkered walnut stock and forearm, 6 1/2 lbs. Imported 1989-95.

	$840	$715	$660	$600	$550	$450	$375

Last MSR was $1,044.

Add $28 for 5 innerchokes with wrench (3 in. chambers in 12 ga.).

Add $50 for 20 ga. (3 in. chambers).

✳ *Gamma AL Superlight* - 12 ga. only, similar to Gamma Field except receiver is made from Ergal light alloy, 6 lbs. Imported 1989-90.

	$875	$760	$695	$625	$550	$450	$375

Last MSR was $970.

Add $41 for 5 innerchokes with wrench.

Add $66 for 20 ga. with 3 in. chambers. New 1990.

This model is chambered for 2 3/4 in. shells only.

GAMMA SPORTING CLAYS COMPETITION - 12 ga. only, designed for sporting clays competition, SST, 28, 29, or 30 in. VR, (10mm) and barrels supplied with 5 innerchokes, special recoil pad, ejectors, checkered walnut stock and forearm. Imported 1989-95.

	$950	$825	$725	$650	$575	$495	$400

Last MSR was $1,175.

Add $17 for trap stock and forearm (disc. - includes 28 in. barrels with 5 choke tubes).

GAMMA SKEET - 12 ga. only, 27 1/2 or 28 in. VR barrels, SST, ejectors, supplied with 5 innerchokes, special recoil pad, checkered walnut stock and forearm, reversed Skeet chokes new 1994. Imported 1989-95.

	$875	$735	$695	$635	$550	$450	$375

Last MSR was $1,107.

GAMMA TRAP - 12 ga. only, 29 or 30 in. VR barrels with special trap chokes and 10mm rib, SST, ejectors, checkered Monte Carlo stock and forearm, 7 1/2 lbs. Imported 1989-95.

	$875	$735	$695	$635	$550	$450	$375

Last MSR was $1,107.

GRADING - PPGS™	100%	98%	95%	90%	80%	70%	60%

GAMMA PARADOX - 12 ga. only, 25 in. VR barrels with top barrel rifled and lower barrel supplied with 3 innerchokes, SST, ejectors, checkered walnut stock and forearm, 6 lbs. 6 oz. Imported 1989-90.

	$850	$750	$695	$625	$550	$450	$375

Last MSR was $945.

✳ *Gamma Paradox AL Superlight* - similar to Gamma Paradox except receiver is made from Ergal light alloy, 5 lbs. 7 oz. Imported 1989-90.

	$875	$760	$695	$625	$550	$450	$375

Last MSR was $960.

GAMMA 2 FIELD - 12 ga., 3 in. chambers, boxlock action, 26 or 28 in. VR barrels with 5 titanium Innerchokes, ejectors, light grey satin or case colored forged steel receiver with light engraving, gold trigger, checkered walnut stock and Schnabel forearm, approx. 6.6 lbs. Importation began 2005.

MSR $1,675	$1,395	$1,150	$875	$775	$675	$575	$525

GAMMA 2 SPORTING - 12 ga., 3 in. chambers, boxlock action, similar to Field except has 30 or 32 in. barrels with choke tubes. Importation began 2005.

MSR $1,795	$1,500	$1,250	$950	$850	$750	$650	$575

WATERFOWLER - 12 ga., 3 1/2 in. chambers, 28 or 30 in. barrels, 100% Max 4 camo coverage on stock and forearm. Importation began 2005.

MSR $1,595	$1,350	$1,100	$825	$725	$625	$525	$475

STL VS - 12 ga. only, 3 in. chambers, 30 or 32 in. barrels with extended choke tubes, available in Sporting (with HiViz sights) or Trap configuration, adj. comb, checkered deluxe walnut stock and foream, grey chrome receiver with light engraving, gold trigger, approx. 7.7 lbs. Importation began 2005.

MSR $2,295	$1,900	$1,675	$1,350	$1,050	$875	$775	$675

EURALFA - 12 ga., 2 3/4 in. chambers, 26 or 28 in. VR barrels with fixed chokes, DT or SNT, extractors, blue receiver with photo engraving, 6 1/2 lbs. Imported 1989-90.

	$495	$460	$420	$390	$350	$310	$275

Last MSR was $571.

✳ *Euralfa AL Superlight* - 12 ga., similar to Euralfa except receiver is made from Ergal light alloy, 6 lbs. Imported 1989-90.

	$515	$475	$430	$400	$360	$320	$285

Last MSR was $603.

✳ *Euralfa Trap* - 12 ga. only, 3 in. chambers, 30 in. barrels bored IM/F. Imported 1990.

	$550	$495	$460	$430	$400	$360	$320

Last MSR was $636.

✳ *Euralfa Magnum* - 12 ga., 3 in. chambers, 26, 28, or 29 in. VR (10mm wide) barrels with fixed chokes, rubber recoil pad. Imported 1989-90.

	$515	$475	$430	$400	$360	$320	$285

Last MSR was $587.

✳ *Euralfa Innerchoke* - 12 ga. only, 3 in. chambers, 28 in. barrels. Imported 1990 only.

	$560	$500	$460	$430	$400	$360	$320

Last MSR was $652.

✳ *Euralfa Slug* - 12 ga. only, 24 in. barrels bored cyl./cyl. Imported 1990.

	$500	$475	$430	$400	$360	$320	$285

Last MSR was $571.

EURALFA PARADOX - 12 ga. only, similar to Euralfa except 25 in. VR barrels with top barrel rifled and lower barrel supplied with 3 innerchokes, 6 lbs. 6 oz. Imported 1989-90.

	$550	$495	$460	$430	$400	$360	$320

Last MSR was $636.

GRADING - PPGS™	100%	98%	95%	90%	80%	70%	60%

✳ *Euralfa Paradox AL Superlight* - similar to Euralfa Paradox except receiver is made from Ergal light alloy, 5 lbs. 7 oz. Imported 1989-1990.

	$550	$495	$460	$430	$400	$360	$320

Last MSR was $636.

SILVER LION - 12 or 20 ga., similar to Max Lion, except has standard wood and lockable hard plastic case, ported 26 in. TriBore barrels became optional during 1999, standard in 2000, 6.8-7.7 lbs. Imported 1998-2004.

	$1,165	$975	$850	$750	$625	$525	$425

Last MSR was $1,349.

Subtract 10% if w/o TriBore system barrels.

✳ *Silver Lion Cub Model* - similar to Silver Lion, except has youth dimensions (12 1/2 LOP), steel receiver, ported 24 in. TriBore vent. barrels standard, mid rib bead, approx. 6 lbs. Imported 1999-2004.

	$1,135	$950	$850	$750	$625	$525	$425

Last MSR was $1,315.

ULTRA MAG LION - 12 ga. only, 3 1/2 in. chambers, 28 in. standard or ported TriBore (new 1999) barrels, choice of non-glare matte metal finish (disc. 2000) or 100% Advantage Wetlands camo coverage, black colored walnut stock and forearm, non-automatic ejectors, 7.9 lbs., includes lockable plastic case. Imported 1998-2004.

	$1,165	$975	$850	$750	$625	$525	$425

Last MSR was $1,349.

CAMO TURKEY MODEL - 12 ga. only, 3 1/2 in. chambers, 20 in. separated barrels, unique Picatinny rail on top of receiver allows convenient scope mounting, 100% Advantage extra brown camo coverage, includes two ultra-full ported choke tubes, locking fitted luggage case, approx. 7 1/2 lbs. Imported 1999-2000, reintroduced 2002-2004.

	$1,025	$900	$800	$725	$625	$550	$500

Last MSR was $1,235.

SUPER LIGHT LION - 12 ga. only, 3 in. chambers, lightweight alloy receiver, blue finish, 24 in. vent. standard (disc. 1999) or ported TriBore (new 1999, standard 2000) barrels with VR, standard checkered walnut stock and forearm, includes lockable hard plastic case, 6 1/2 lbs. Imported 1998-2000.

	$975	$850	$775	$700	$600	$550	$500

Last MSR was $1,159.

Subtract $100 if w/o ported TriBore barrels (disc. 1999).

✳ *Super Light Lion Cub (Youth) Model* - similar to Silver Lion Youth Model, except has Ergal 55 aluminum receiver, approx. 5 3/4 lbs. Imported 1999-2000.

	$925	$825	$765	$685	$600	$550	$500

Last MSR was $1,099.

SPORTING CLAYS COMPETITION LION - 12 or 20 ga., 3 in. chambers, 28 or 30 (12 ga. only, new 2000) in. vent. ported TriBore barrels with 10mm VR, recoil reducer in buttstock, checkered walnut stock and forearm, adj. SST, includes locking fitted luggage case. Importation began 1999.

	$1,185	$1,025	$875	$745	$630	$525	$425

Last MSR was $1,419.

GRADING - PPGS™	100%	98%	95%	90%	80%	70%	60%

* ***Sporting Clays Competition Lion Extra*** - 12 ga. only, 28, 30, or 32 (new 2003) in. unported (mfg. 2001-current) or ported (mfg. 2000 only) TriBore VR barrels, regular walnut or black competition checkered stock and forearm, adj. cheekpiece, case colored receiver or 100% carbon fiber metal finish, includes 8 choke tubes, locking fitted luggage case, approx. 7.8 lbs. Mfg. 2000-2004.

	$1,700	$1,450	$1,200	$975	$850	$750	$675

Last MSR was $1,925.

Add $74 for case colored receiver with gold inlays and set of 8 choke tubes (mfg. 2004).

BLACK LION COMPETITION
- 12 or 20 ga., competition model featuring blue receiver, 26, 28, or 30 (12 ga. only) in. vent. standard or ported TriBore (new 1999) barrels with VR, deluxe checkered wood, 6.8-7.8 lbs. Imported 1998-99.

	$1,300	$1,025	$875	$775	$675	$600	$550

Last MSR was $1,529.

Add $66 for ported TriBore barrels.

MAX LION
- 12 or 20 ga., 3 in. chambers, engraved boxlock action with nickel finish, 26, 28, or 30 (12 ga. only) in. vent. standard (disc. 1999) or ported TriBore (new 1999, standard 2000) barrels with VR, rebounding hammers, deluxe checkered stock and forearm, with vent. recoil pad, choke tubes, gold SST, non-automatic safety, includes locking fitted luggage case, 6.8-7.8 lbs. Importation 1998-2003.

	$1,625	$1,350	$1,150	$950	$850	$750	$675

Last MSR was $1,799.

Subtract $100 if w/o ported TriBore barrels (disc. 1999).

* ***Max Lion Light*** - 12 or 20 (new 2001) ga., similar to Max Lion, except has 24 (disc. 2000, reintroduced 2002) or 26 (mfg. 2001 only) in. barrels with TriBore system and gold game birds on satin finished receiver sides, 7-7.2 lbs. Mfg. 2000-2003.

	$1,625	$1,350	$1,150	$950	$850	$750	$675

Last MSR was $1,799.

* ***Max Lion Sporting Clays*** - 12 or 20 ga., includes adj., enhanced walnut competition stock, case hardened receiver, 32 in. Tribore barrels with 8 chokes, 7.9 lbs. Imported 2003.

	$1,625	$1,350	$1,150	$950	$850	$750	$675

Last MSR was $1,799.

* ***Max Lion Paradox*** - 12 or 20 ga., features 24 in. upper smoothbore barrel with Tri-Bore and lower barrel with paradox rifling, VR on 20 ga., case colored receiver, select walnut, sling studs on lower barrel, 7.6 lbs. Mfg. 2002-2003.

	$975	$875	$775	$700	$625	$550	$500

Last MSR was $1,129.

SHOTGUNS: SxS

The following models have boxlock actions with added sideplates.

BETA MODEL
- 12 ga. only, 2 3/4 in. chambers, standard model with checkered walnut stock and forearm, ST, ejectors. Imported 1989 only.

	$695	$625	$550	$450	$375	$300	$250

Last MSR was $920.

This model was replaced by the Beta Lux in 1990.

BETA LUX
- 12 ga. only, 3 in. chambers, SST, ejectors, boxlock action, 24, 26, 28, or 30 in. barrels bored F/M, 6.6 lbs. Imported 1990-95.

	$1,100	$875	$725	$625	$550	$475	$400

Last MSR was $1,270.

Add $30 for 5 Innerchokes.
Add $114 for competition trap/pigeon model (disc.).

GRADING - PPGS™	100%	98%	95%	90%	80%	70%	60%

BETA EUROPE - 12 ga. only, deluxe model with coin finished game scene engraved sideplates, 26 1/2 or 27 1/2 in. barrels with fixed chokes, ejectors, DT or SST, checkered English stock and splinter forearm, 6 lbs. 6 oz. Imported 1989-90.

	$1,400	$1,100	$850	$700	$575	$495	$450

Last MSR was $1,711.

Add $33 for semi-beavertail forend.
Add $130 for competition trap/pigeon model.

CLASSIC LION - 12 ga. only, 3 in. chambers, boxlock action, SST or DT, ejectors, Tri-Bore barrels with 5 choke tubes, approx. 7 lbs. Importation began 1998.

* *Grade I* - features standard grade wood, 26, 28, or 30 in. VR barrels, English (DT) or pistol grip (disc.) stock, engraved nickel finished receiver, gold SST. Importation disc. 2004.

	$1,375	$1,125	$850	$750	$650	$550	$500

Last MSR was $1,649.

* *Grade II* - features deluxe wood and removable sideplates with engraving, SST, fitted luggage case.

	$1,875	$1,525	$1,200	$950	$850	$750	$675

Last MSR was $2,325.

>**Grade II Bill Hanus Birdgun Model** - similar to Grade II, except has best quality wood. Importation disc. 2000.

	$2,275	$1,925	$1,550	$1,225	$995	$875	$800

Last MSR was $2,599.

This model was available through Bill Hanus Birdguns, LLC only.

* *Classic Lion Elite* - features case colored receiver, DT, select checkered straight grip stock and splinter forearm, 26 or 28 in. fixed choke barrels, 7 3/4 lbs. Importation disc. 2003.

	$1,395	$1,150	$875	$775	$650	$550	$500

Last MSR was $1,689.

SHOTGUNS: SEMI-AUTO

The following models are gas operated, self compensating, have 4 shot mags., aluminum receivers, twin action bars, blue receiver with photo etched game scene engraving, and checkered walnut stock and forearm.

Add $25 for De Luxe engraving or camouflage wood finish.

DEER GUN - 12 ga. only, 3 in. chamber, 24 in. rifled barrel with front and rear rifle sights, 5 shot mag., 7 lbs. Limited importation 1994-95.

	$695	$475	$425	$375	$325	$300	$285

Last MSR was $775.

ELLEGI STANDARD - 12 ga. only, 28 in. VR barrel with fixed choke, blue receiver, gold trigger, 6 lbs. 9 oz. Imported 1989-90.

	$525	$450	$375	$325	$300	$275	$250

Last MSR was $619.

* *Ellegi Multichoke* - similar to Ellegi Standard except 5 different choke tubes extend length of barrel up to 6 in., average weight is 6 lbs. 9 oz. Imported 1989-90.

	$540	$475	$395	$350	$325	$300	$265

Last MSR was $644.

The standard barrel length on this model is 24 1/2 in. (30 1/2 in. with full extra-long choke tube).

* *Ellegi Innerchoke* - 12 ga. only, 3 in. chamber, 28 in. VR barrel with 5 innerchokes supplied, 7 lbs. Imported 1989-90.

	$540	$475	$395	$350	$325	$300	$265

Last MSR was $644.

GRADING - PPGS™	100%	98%	95%	90%	80%	70%	60%

✳ *Ellegi Magnum* - 12 ga. only, 3 in. chamber, 30 in. VR barrel with fixed choke, recoil pad, 7 1/4 lbs. Imported 1989-90.

	$525	$450	$375	$325	$300	$275	$250

Last MSR was $619.

✳ *Ellegi Super Goose* - 12 ga. only, 3 in. chamber, 35 1/2 in. VR (12mm wide) barrel with fixed choke, adj. rifle rear sight, supplied with rail for mounting scope rings, rubber recoil pad, designed especially for long range shooting, 7 1/2 lbs. Imported 1989-90.

	$625	$495	$425	$375	$340	$315	$280

Last MSR was $734.

✳ *Ellegi Slug* - 12 ga. only, 24 1/2 in. barrel, adj. rear sight and bead front, 6 lbs. 9 oz. Imported 1989-90.

	$545	$475	$395	$350	$325	$300	$265

Last MSR was $652.

Add $200 for combo set (includes innerchoked 28 in. barrel).

✳ *Ellegi Police* - 12 ga. only, 20 in. cylinder bored barrel, matte black receiver, non-glare stock and forearm. Imported 1989-90.

	$495	$425	$360	$300	$275	$250	$225

Last MSR was $587.

TACTICAL SEMI-AUTO - 12 ga. only, 3 in. chamber, 20 in. barrel with TriBore choke system with cylinder choke, tactical configuration with large cocking handle, over-sized safety, black polymer stock and forearm, pistol grip stock design new 2003, choice of Picatinny rail with either integral rear or fixed front and ghost ring (new 2003) sight, 5 shot mag., 6.6 lbs. Imported 2001-2004.

	$875	$775	$650	$575	$515	$450	$400

Last MSR was $1,025.

RED LION MARK II - 12 ga. only, 3 in. chamber, gas operated, alloy receiver, 24, 26, or 28 in. VR standard (disc. 1999) or ported TriBore (standard 2000) barrel, matte finish, reversible safety (oversize beginning 2000), checkered walnut stock and forearm, red receiver logo, lockable plastic case, approx. 7 lbs. Imported 1998-2000.

	$710	$635	$550	$500	$450	$400	$360

Last MSR was $820.

During 2000, the model nomenclature changed to Red Lion Mark II.

GOLD LION MARK II - similar to Red Lion, except has select walnut stock with olive wood pistol grip cap, ported barrel, gold trigger and receiver logo. Imported 1998-2002.

	$750	$675	$595	$550	$500	$450	$400

Last MSR was $849.

During 2000, the model nomenclature changed to Gold Lion Mark II.

GOLD LION MARK III - 12 ga. only, improved Mark II action with Ergal 55 alloy receiver, rubber buffer in gas operating system, 26 or 28 in. VR barrel with TriBore choke system, includes stock shim kit and hardshell case, 7.2 lbs. Imported 2003 only.

	$815	$700	$625	$575	$495	$450	$395

Last MSR was $939.

REX LION - 12 ga. only, limited edition of the Gold Lion Mark II, features black and silver finished receiver with gold medallions, checkered Turkish walnut stock, 26 or 28 in. barrel, 7 3/4 lbs. New 2002.

	$900	$775	$700	$625	$550	$500	$450

Last MSR was $1,049.

GRADING - PPGS™	100%	98%	95%	90%	80%	70%	60%

CAMO LION - 12 ga. only, 3 in. chamber, 20, 24, 26, or 28 in. ported TriBore VR barrel, features 100% Advantage Wetlands camo coverage, approx. 7 lbs. Imported 1999-2002.

	$850	$725	$650	$575	$510	$450	$400

Last MSR was $979.

SPORTING CLAYS LION - 12 ga. only, 28 in. ported TriBore VR barrel, deluxe checkered walnut stock and forearm with olive wood pistol grip cap, matte finish with gold accents on receiver sides, approx. 7.2 lbs. Imported 1999-2000.

	$865	$745	$645	$565	$510	$450	$400

Last MSR was $999.

✳ ***Sporting Clays Lion Extra*** - similar to Sporting Clays Lion, 28 or 30 in. barrel, except has carbon fiber metal finish, stock recoil reducer, adj. cheekpiece on checkered walnut or black (new 2002) stock and forearm, includes 6 choke tubes and locking fitted luggage case. Imported 2000-2004.

	$1,100	$950	$825	$725	$625	$550	$500

Last MSR was $1,375.

LION H35 TITAN - 12 ga. only, 26, 28, or 30 in. barrel with choke tubes, 3 or 5 shot mag., sling swivels, interchangeable recoil pad, grey alloy receiver with light engraving, gold trigger, checkered pistol grip walnut stock and forearm with TriWood finish, features titanium protection coating on receiver and new gas system with pulse piston utilizing Zirconium metallurgy. Approx. 6.6 lbs.

MSR $1,175	$1,050	$950	$850	$750	$650	$550	$450

LION H368 - 12 ga. only, 3 in. chamber, gas operated, alloy receiver, 24 (Turkey Model, new 2005), 26 (new 2005), 28, or 30 (new 2005) in. VR barrel with TriBore choke system (includes 3 choke tubes), composite synthetic stock with soft touch coating stock and forearm, matte black or 100% Realtree Hardwoods HD (disc. 2004) or Max 4 (new 2005) camo coverage. 7.2 lbs. Importation began 2003.

MSR $825	$750	$675	$600	$525	$450	$375	$325

Add $50 for camo stock and forearm.

SHOTGUNS: SINGLE BARREL

The following models have receivers made out of aluminum alloy, rear trigger guard safety, and matte black finish metal surfaces.

OMEGA STANDARD - 12, 20 ga., or .410 bore, 3 in. chamber, 26 or 28 (12 ga. only) in. barrel, checkered beech stock and forearm, approx. 5 lbs. 5 oz. Imported 1989-90.

	$120	$95	$80	$70	$60	$55	$50

Last MSR was $139.

✳ ***Goose Gun*** - 12 ga. only, similar to Omega Standard, except has a 35 1/2 in. barrel, 6 lbs. Imported 1989-90.

	$135	$115	$90	$80	$70	$60	$55

Last MSR was $156.

MONOTRAP SHOTGUN - 12 ga. only, 2 3/4 in. chamber, lightweight 20 ga. frame with nickel finish, 30 (disc. 2001) or 34 (ported, new 2001) in. over single VR barrel with TriBore system and 3 competition choke tubes, adj. trigger, checkered walnut stock and forearm with adj. cheekpiece, recoil system, 6 or 6.9 lbs. Imported 2000-2003.

	$1,625	$1,375	$1,150	$950	$825	$725	$625

Last MSR was $1,799.

SHOTGUNS: SLIDE ACTION

The following models are variations of the same action based on a twin bar slide system, alloy receiver with anti-glare finish (including barrel), rear trigger guard safety, and 2 3/4 or 3 in. shell interchangeability.

Add $25 for camouflage wood finish on the following models.

MODEL S.D.A.S.S. - 12 ga. only, 3 in. chamber, originally designed for police and self defense use, 8 shot tube mag., 20 or 24 1/2 in. barrel threaded for external choke tubes, approx. 6 lbs. 6 oz. Imported 1989-90.

$325	$285	$260	$230	$195	$160	$140

Last MSR was $415.

This model with 24 1/2 in. barrel is threaded for external multi-chokes which can add up to 6 in. to the barrel length - available for a $17 extra charge.

* **Special Police** - similar to Model S.D.A.S.S. except has special heavy 20 in. cylinder bored barrel, VR, cooling jacket, 6 shot mag., rubber recoil pad. Imported 1989-90.

$340	$295	$265	$230	$195	$160	$140

Last MSR was $440.

* **Martial** - 12 ga. only, 18, 20, 28, 30, or 35 1/2 (disc. 1989) in. barrel, fixed sights and choke, approx. 6 1/4 lbs. Imported 1989-90.

$330	$290	$260	$225	$190	$160	$140

Last MSR was $424.

Add $41 for VR.
Add $20 for 35 1/2 (disc. 1989) in. barrel.
Add $33 for multi-choke (plain rib with 1 choke and wrench).
Add $65 for innerchoke (includes 1 choke and wrench - VR barrel only).

FP6 - 12 ga. only, 3 in. chamber, 20 or 28 (new 2001) in. shrouded barrel (non-ported TriBore system became standard 2000) with vent. heat shield, with or w/o Picatinny rail, with (new 2003) or w/o ghost ring rear sight, camo (new 2001), matte, or carbon fiber (new 2000) finished metal, 100% Mossy Oak camo (mfg. 2001-2003) or black synthetic stock and forearm, pistol grip stock design new 2003, various security configurations, includes locking plastic case, 6 1/2-7 lbs. Importation began 1998.

MSR $549	$460	$400	$365	$325	$295	$265	$240

Subtract $30 for 100% Mossy Oak Break-up camo coverage (disc. 2003).

FABBRI s.n.c.

Current manufacturer established during 1965, and currently located in Concesio, Italy (previously located in Brescia). The factory should be contacted directly (see Trademark Index) for more information regarding current information and prices on the following models.

Ivo Fabbri and Daniel Perazzi were partners in the shotgun manufacturing business beginning in 1960 - these guns are ser. no. 5001-5339. Circa 1965, Fabbri and Perazzi split up and formed their own individual companies. Fabbri s.n.c. relocated from Brescia to Concesio during 1969 and underwent a name change from Armi Fabbri to Fabbri s.n.c. during 1989. The first CNC machine was installed during 1974. Currently, Fabbri s.n.c. engravers include Creative Art, Pedersoli, Torcoli, and Francassi. Fabbri manufactures perhaps the highest quality shotguns available in today's marketplace - approx. 20-30 guns are mfg. annually. Delivery times range from 2-4 years.

SHOTGUNS: CUSTOM

SxS SHOTGUN - 12 or 20 ga., one of the world's best sidelock SxS shotguns, ejectors, full engraving, "E" prefix ser. no., two types of back action. Disc.

Currently, Fabbri SxS shotguns manufactured recently with type II actions and in mint condition are priced in the $31,750-$40,000 range. Subtract $10,000 for scroll engraving, and/or approx. 50% for type I action.

GRADING - PPGS™	100%	98%	95%	90%	80%	70%	60%

O/U SHOTGUN - 12 or 20 ga., top-of-the-line quality with advanced CNC metal fabrication, steel or stainless steel (new 2002) construction, any combination of engraving, wood, and other options. Both the type/style of engraving and the engraver will make a big difference on the current value of a custom ordered Fabbri O/U shotgun. Because engraving alone can add $50,000+ to the cost of a new shotgun, a qualified appraisal from a reputable dealer/collector is advised when buying or selling recently manufactured Fabbri O/U shotguns.

> **Current retail starts at approx. $78,500 FOB Italy, w/o engraving.**
>
> **Mint guns mfg. 1967-1983 are currently priced in the $36,500-$40,000 range, guns mfg. between 1983-1989 are priced in the $52,500-$57,500 range, and mfg. within the last 10 years are currently priced in the $67,500-$75,000 range.**

FABRIQUE NATIONALE

Current manufacturer located in Herstal, near Liege, Belgium. The current company name is "Group Herstal," however, the company is better known by "Fabrique Nationale" or "Fabrique Nationale d'Armes de Guerre." FN established their first contract with John M. Browning in 1897 for the manufacture of their first pistol, the FN 1899 Model. Additional contracts were signed and the relationship further blossomed with the manu- facture of the A-5 shotgun. FN was acquired by GIAT of France in 1992. In late 1997, the company was purchased by the Walloon government of Belgium. Additional production facilities are located in Portugal (assembly) and Japan.

Also See: Browning Arms under Rifles, Shotguns, and Pistols.

The author would like to express his sincere thanks to Anthony Vanderlinden from the Browning Collector's Association for making FN contributions to this edition.

PISTOLS: SEMI-AUTO

For FN Models 1900, 1903, 1905, 1910, 1922 (10/22), Baby Model, and the Model 10/71, please refer to the Browning Pistol section in this text.

PISTOLS: SEMI-AUTO, HI-POWER VARIATIONS

The F.N. Hi-Power (also known as P-35) was Browning's last pistol design. A 9mm Para., single action, semi-auto pistol, it was the first to incorporate a staggered high capacity magazine. It has a 4 21/32 in. barrel, 13 shot mag., hammer and mag. safeties, a wide variety of finishes and sight options. It's probably the most widely used military pistol in the world.

PRE-WAR COMMERCIAL HP - 9mm Para. cal., single action, blue, wood grips, tangent rear sight, slotted (original) for stock with tangent rear sight, 13 shot mag. Mfg. 1935-disc.

	100%	98%	95%	90%	80%	70%	60%
Tangent sight & slotted	$1,875	$1,200	$995	$850	$600	$450	$375

Add $600 for original pre-war flat board stock with attached holster.

PRE-WAR FOREIGN MILITARY CONTRACTS - mfg. under military contract for various countries.

	100%	98%	95%	90%	80%	70%	60%
Lithuanian Crest	N/A	$2,000	$1,500	$995	$700	$650	$550
Estonian Contract ("E.V." or "K.L.")	N/A	$2,100	$1,500	$995	$800	$700	$600
Finnish Contract ("SA" marked)	N/A	$1,750	$1,250	$985	$750	$650	$550
Chinese refinished imports	$700	$650	$575	$500	$450	$400	$350

Add $600 for original (Finnish contract) pre-war flat board stock with attached holster.
Add $550 for original Finnish contract stock (ser. no. 11,000-15,000) with removed holster.
Add $800 for original Belgian military shoulder stock.

GRADING - PPGS™	100%	98%	95%	90%	80%	70%	60%

Note: Belgian military stocks did not have attached holsters, these shoulder stocks were numbered to the guns and have one small Belgian Military proof stamped on the wood.

Pre-war Belgian military HPs are priced similarly to the pre-war Commercial Model. Most Finnish contract guns can be identified by the "SA" stamp on frame and/or slide, and/or magazine, in addition to known serial number range. 2,400 pistols were shipped to Finland in 1940. All pistols fall in the 11,000–15,000 serial number range.

Chinese contract pistols can sometimes be identified by Chinese added inventory markings. Chinese contract pistols are in the 5,000–10,000 and 20,000–21,000 ser. no. range. Some Chinese contract pistols have been refinished, and all are relatively recent imports.

WWII PRODUCTION: WAFFENAMT PROOFED

There is a range of finishes during Nazi production that varies from the excellent pre-war commercial finish on early guns assembled from captured parts to the roughly milled, poorly finished specimens mfg. late in the war. Values listed assume all major parts (slide, barrel, and frame) are matching with original magazine.

In recent years, some Nazi production Hi-Powers have had the rear grip strap milled out and slotted to accept a shoulder stock. Careful observation is advised before purchasing a "rare" (and expensive) slotted and tangent sight specimen. Many HPs have been restored, since the restoration is easily accomplished by professionals.

* **Type I: Tangent sights** - slotted - taken from existing pre-war Belgian army pistols, quality is excellent, correct ser. range is quite limited, approx. 40,000-47,000. Ser. range for production under German occupation is 50,001-53,000. All are proofed WaA 613.

	N/A	$2,750	$2,400	$2,000	$1,500	$1,250	$995

Beware of restorations.

* **Type II** - tangent rear sight only, approx. 90,000 mfg. with generally good quality finish, pistols are proofed WaA613, WaA103, some are WaA140.

	N/A	$1,500	$1,100	$750	$550	$450	$400

Add 25% if pistol is marked WaA613.
Add 15% if pistol is marked WaA103.

* **Type III Standard Fixed Sights** - most common HP pistol produced during the war.

$750	$625	$500	$395	$325	$300	$200

Add 15% for late war Bakelite/synthetic grips.
Add 20% for eagle N proof instead of WaA140 proof, or for no WaA140 proof.

POST-OCCUPATION PRODUCTION
- commercial mfg. began 1944, first imported with BAC markings in 1954 (see Browning HP section). Military mfg. from Sept. 1944-present. Early (1944) models are identifiable by an "A" serial number prefix and are not fitted with a magazine safety. In 1947, the rear slide bushing became hardened by a new heat treatment process. Other design modifications were added in 1950. Many thousands manufactured under various government contracts, many will have a "T" prefix.

Add $50 if round hammer.
Add $200-$2,000 for military pistols with crests, depending on condition and variation.

* **Tangent sight only**

$700	$600	$500	$400	$350	$325	$300

Add $100 for "T" prefix.
Values above are for BACo. imported models that are not slotted.

* **Tangent sight** - slotted for stock, military or commercial mfg.

$1,200	$1,050	$950	$700	$600	$500	$400

Add $150 for "T" prefix.
Add $150 for internal extractor.

* **Fixed sight** - most common variation.

$600	$500	$450	$400	$350	$325	$300

Add $100 for ring hammer.
Add 10% for "A" prefix, but only in 98%+ condition.

SULTAN OF MUSCAT AND OMAN CONTRACT

* *First Model* - matte finish, reverse crest, scarce.

	100%	98%	95%
	$4,500	$3,500	$2,500

* *Second Model* - high polish finish, standard crest.

	100%	98%	95%
	$4,000	$2,950	$1,750

INGLIS MANUFACTURED HI-POWERS - SEE INGLIS SECTION.

RIFLES: BOLT ACTION

F.N. MAUSER SPORTER DELUXE - available in popular American and European calibers, 24 in. barrel, adj. sight, checkered pistol grip stock. Mfg. 1947-63.

100%	98%	95%	90%	80%	70%	60%
$650	$550	$495	$450	$395	$350	$295

F.N. PRESENTATION GRADE - similar to Deluxe, except engraved and select wood.

100%	98%	95%	90%	80%	70%	60%
$1,350	$1,150	$935	$855	$750	$625	$500

F.N. SUPREME - .243 Win., .270 Win., 7mm Rem. Mag., .308 Win. cal., or .30-06, 24 in. barrel, peep sight, checkered pistol grip stock. Mfg. 1957-75.

100%	98%	95%	90%	80%	70%	60%
$725	$625	$575	$495	$450	$400	$375

F.N. SUPREME MAGNUM - .264 Win. Mag., 7mm Rem. Mag., .300 Win. Mag., or .375 H&H cal. Mfg. beginning circa 1953.

100%	98%	95%	90%	80%	70%	60%
$775	$675	$600	$525	$475	$425	$395

Add 100% for .375 H&H cal.

F.N. SNIPER RIFLE (MODEL 30) - .308 Win. cal., this model was a Mauser actioned Sniper Rifle equipped with 20 in. extra heavy barrel, flash hider, separate removable diopter sights, Hensoldt 4X scope, hardcase, bipod, and sling. 51 complete factory sets were imported into the U.S., with additional surplus rifles that were privately imported.

100%	98%	95%	90%	80%	70%	60%
$3,550	$3,300	$2,800	$2,500	$2,200	$2,000	$1,800

Subtract 15% if removable diopter sights or bipod is missing.
Subtract 10% if scope is not marked with F.N. logo.
Values assume complete factory outfit with all accessories.

RIFLES: SEMI-AUTO

MODEL 1949 - 7x57mm Mauser, 7.65mm Mauser, 7.92mm Mauser, or .30-06 cal., (.308 Win. cal. for Argentine conversion rifles), gas operated, 10 shot box mag. (20 round detachable mag. for Argentine conversions), 23 in. barrel, military rifle, tangent rear sight.

	100%	98%	95%	90%	80%	70%	60%
Columbia	$1,200	$1,100	$950	$850	$750	$650	$600
Luxemborg	$1,000	$900	$850	$750	$650	$550	$500
Venezuela	$800	$775	$750	$700	$600	$500	$450
Argentina	N/A	$825	$775	$750	$650	$600	$500
Egyptian	$850	$700	$650	$550	$500	$400	$350

Subtract 30% for U.S. rebuilt, non-matching rifles with reproduction stocks.
FN-49 contract rifles not listed above are very rare in the U.S. and will demand a premium. Carefully inspect black paint finish for factory originality, as all FN-49s were factory painted. Original sniper rifles are extremely rare and can bring $2,000+. Beware of U.S. assembled "sniper" configurations, and Belgian military "ABL" scopes mounted on other contract rifles and sold as original sniper configurations.

RIFLES: SEMI-AUTO, FAL/LAR/FNC SERIES

After tremendous price increases between 1985-88, Fabrique Nationale decided in 1988 to discontinue this series completely. Not only are these rifles not exported to the U.S. any longer, but all production has ceased in Belgium as well. The only way FN will produce these models again is if they are given a large military contract - in which case a "side order" of commercial guns may

GRADING - PPGS™	100%	98%	95%	90%	80%	70%	60%

be built. 1989 Federal legislation regarding this type of paramilitary design also helped push up prices to their current level. FAL rifles were also mfg. in Israel by I.M.I.

F.N. FAL - semi-auto, French designation for the F.N. L.A.R. (light automatic rifle), otherwise similar to the L.A.R.

	$2,375	$2,050	$1,750	$1,550	$1,375	$1,200	$1,025

✳ *F.N. FAL G* - most desirable FAL model.

	$3,750	$3,000	$2,600	$2,375	$2,050	$1,750	$1,550

F.N. L.A.R. COMPETITION (50.00, LIGHT AUTOMATIC RIFLE) - .308 Win. (7.62x51mm) cal., semi-auto, competition rifle with match flash hider, 21 in. barrel, adj. 4 position fire selector on automatic models, wood stock, aperture rear sight adj. from 100-600 meters, 9.4 lbs. Mfg. 1981-83.

	$2,750	$2,500	$2,400	$2,250	$2,100	$2,000	$1,950

This model was designated by the factory as the 50.00 Model.
Mid-1987 retail on this model was $1,258. The last MSR was $3,179 (this price reflected the last exchange rate and special order status of this model).

✳ *Heavy barrel rifle (50.41 & 50.42)* - barrel is twice as heavy as standard L.A.R., includes wood or synthetic stock, short wood forearm, and bipod, 12.2 lbs. Importation disc. 1988.

	$3,250	$2,750	$2,500	$2,350	$2,200	$2,000	$1,900

Add $400 for walnut stock.

There were 2 variations of this model. The Model 50.41 had a synthetic buttstock while the Model 50.42 had a wood buttstock with steel buttplate incorporating a top extension used for either shoulder resting or inverted grenade launching.
Mid-1987 retail on this model was $1,497 (Model 50.41) or $1,654 (Model 50.42). The last MSR was $3,776 (this price reflected the last exchange rate and special order status of this model).

✳ *Paratrooper rifle (50.63 & 50.64)* - similar to L.A.R. model, except has folding stock, 8.3 lbs. Mfg. 1950-88.

	$3,300	$2,650	$2,300	$2,150	$1,900	$1,700	$1,500

There were 2 variations of the Paratrooper L.A.R. Model. The Model 50.63 had a stationary aperture rear sight and 18 in. barrel. The Model 50.64 was supplied with a 21 in. barrel and had a rear sight calibrated for either 150 or 200 meters. Both models retailed for the same price.
Mid-1987 retail on this model was $1,310 (both the Model 50.63 and 50.64). The last MSR was $3,239 (this price reflected the last exchange rate and special order status of this model).

CAL - originally imported in 1980, FN's .223 CAL military rifle succeeded the .308 FAL and preceeded the .223 FNC, at first declared illegal but later given amnesty, only 20 imported by Browning.

	$7,750	$6,500	$5,250	$4,500	$3,850	$3,200	$2,650

G series FALs were imported between 1959-62 by Browning Arms Co. This rifle was declared illegal by the GCA of 1968 and was exempted 5 years later. Total numbers exempted are: Standard model-1822, Heavy Barrel model-21, Paratrooper model-5

FNC MODEL - .223 Rem. (5.56mm) cal., lightweight combat carbine, 18 1/2 in. barrel, NATO approved, 30 shot mag., 8.4 lbs. Disc. 1987.

	$2,150	$1,775	$1,425	$1,250	$1,050	$950	$825

Add $200 for Paratrooper model (16 or 18 1/2 in. barrel).

While rarer, the 16 in. barrel model incorporated a flash hider that did not perform as well as the flash hider used on the standard 18 1/2 in. barrel.
Mid-1987 retail on this model was $749 (Standard Model) and $782 (Paratrooper Model). The last MSR was $2,204 (Standard Model) and $2,322 (Paratrooper Model) - these prices reflected the last exchange rate and special order status of these models.

GRADING - PPGS™	100%	98%	95%	90%	80%	70%	60%

FALCO, S.R.L.

Current shotgun manufacturer established circa 1960, and located in Marcheno, Italy. No current U.S. importation. Some models were imported by K.B.I. until 2002.

Falco manufactures a variety of good quality, small gauge shotguns (20 ga., 28 ga., or .410 bore only) in various configurations, including O/U, SxS, and single shot. Falco is well-known for their folding action design. Please contact the factory directly for information on availability and pricing (see Trademark Index).

FALCON FIREARMS

Previous manufacturer located in Northridge, CA from 1986-1990.

PISTOLS: SEMI-AUTO

PORTSIDER - .45 ACP cal., patterned after Colt M 1911 A-1, stainless steel, fixed sights, 5 in. barrel, 7 shot mag., available in left-hand only. Mfg. 1986-90.

$500 $425 $375

Last MSR was $580.

* **Portsider Set** - features right- and left-hand models with matching serial numbers. Only 100 sets mfg. 1986-87.

$1,300 $1,100 $895

Last MSR was $1,400.

GOLD FALCON - .45 ACP cal., machined receiver made from solid 17Kt. gold alloy, stainless steel slide, diamond sighting system, choice of grips, standard or personalized engraving options. Only 50 mfg.

$25,000 $17,500 $11,500

Last MSR was $30,500.

FAMARS di ABBIATICO & SALVINELLI SRL

Current manufacturer established 1967 by Mario Abbiatico and Remo Salvinelli, and located in Gardone, Italy. Distributed by William Larkin Moore, located in Scottsdale, AZ, in the east coast by Robin Hollow Outfitters, located in Addieville, RI, and in the middle west by Fieldsport, located in Traverse City, MI. Previously distributed by The First National Gun Banque, located in Colorado Springs, CO. Previously imported by A&S of America, located in Jefferson Boro, PA.

A&S Famars manufactures some of the world's finest rifles and shotguns - approx. 100 are fabricated annually. Most Famars guns include a lifetime warranty. Because every A&S Famars longarm is an individual custom order, each Famars firearm must have its value ascertained on an individual appraisal basis.

All A&S Famars shotguns incorporate a patented A&S Famars mechanism, and many are available in Hunting, Trap, Skeet, Sporting Clays, and Pigeon configurations. All models except the Excalibur O/U have chopper lump barrels.

RIFLES: SxS, CUSTOM MFG.

Boxlock and sidelock rifles are all best quality and range in calibers between .22 LR and .600 Nitro Express. Each gun is manufactured per individual customer special order. Further information and price quotations are available by contacting the distributors directly.

A&S Famars models currently manufactured and listed below are broken down into three basic grades. The Extra grade is English scroll, Purdey style engraving, with quality 4 wood, and includes leather case. The Prestige grade is game scene or full English scroll engraving, with quality 4 wood and includes leather case. The De Luxe grade includes very detailed, deep ornamental or ornamental and game scene engraving, exhibition quality wood, and leather case.

GRADING - PPGS™	100%	98%	95%	90%	80%	70%	60%

EXCALIBUR EXPRESS - various cals. up to .375 H&H cal.

	MSR N/A	$17,500	$15,000	$13,000	$11,000	$9,500	$8,500	$7,500

Add $1,584 for Extra.
Add $3,180 for Prestige.
Add $7,200 for De Luxe.

AFRICA EXPRESS STANDARD, EXTRA, PRESTIGE, & DE LUXE

Current MSR on this model is $34,320.
Add $2,191 for Africa Extra.
Add $5,280 for Africa Express Prestige.
Add $10,480 for Africa Express De Luxe.
Add approx. 15% for .500 NE-.600 NE cal.

VENUS EXPRESS EXTRA, PRESTIGE, DE LUXE

Current MSR on this model is $49,300.
Add $6,600 for Venus Express Prestige.
Add $15,380 for Venus Express De Luxe.
Add approx. 10% for .500 NE-.600 NE cal.

VENUS EXPRESS EXTRALUSSO - top-of-the-line model.

Please contact the importers directly regarding a price quotation on this very limited model.

SHOTGUNS: O/U, CUSTOM MFG.

O/U SIDELOCK MODELS

✳ *Jorema* - 12 or 20 ga. Disc. 1999.

	$25,000	$19,750	$13,500	$10,250	$8,750	$7,500	$6,250

Last MSR was $25,650.

Add 10% for 20 ga.

✳ *Sovereign Extra, Prestige, De Luxe (Jorema Royal, Aries)*
Current MSR on this model is $50,622.
Add $3,102 for Prestige.
Add $11,880 for De Luxe.
Add 10% for 28 ga. or .410 bore, depending on the grade.
This model was originally called the Jorema Royal, then renamed the Aries in 2000, and renamed the Sovereign in 2002.

✳ *Royale SH* - 12, 20, 28 ga., or .410 bore, bar action. Disc. 2002.

	$34,000	$23,750	$17,750	$13,000	$10,000	$8,500	$7,250

Last MSR was $38,875.

Add 20% for 28 ga. or .410 bore.

CASTORE EXTRA, PRESTIGE, DE LUXE

MSR $33,528	$30,250	$26,900	$22,000	$17,000	$13,000	$10,500	$8,500

Add $3,168 for Prestige.
Add $11,880 for De Luxe.

PEGASUS EXTRA, PRESTIGE, DE LUXE - features Famars patented sidelocks.

MSR N/A	$26,750	$21,750	$16,500	$12,500	$10,000	$8,500	$7,250

Add $2,820 for Prestige.
Add $10,800 for De Luxe.
Add 10% for 28 ga. or .410 bore.

O/U COMPETITION MODELS - 12, 20, 28 ga. or .410 bore, current models include the BL, BLE (Extra), BLP (Prestige), BLX (sideplate), BLXE, BLXP, SL (sidelock), SLE, and SLP.

Add approx. 10% for 28 ga. or .410 bore.

GRADING - PPGS™	100%	98%	95%	90%	80%	70%	60%

❋ *Excalibur BL* - detachable locks, monobloc barrels.

MSR $11,297	$10,250	$9,450	$8,250	$7,150	$6,000	$4,950	$4,250

Add $1,507 for BL Extra.
Add $2,563-2,651 for BL Extra with round action, depending on model.
Add $2,959 for Prestige.
Add $10,340 for De Luxe.

❋ *Excalibur BL Round Titanium* - titanium round action.

MSR $24,816	$21,750	$19,000	$17,000	$14,500	$11,250	$9,750	$8,500

Add $2,376 for Extra.
Add $10,692 for De Luxe.

❋ *Excalibur BLX* - detachable trigger mechanism with sideplates and monobloc barrels.

MSR $15,576	$14,000	$12,000	$9,950	$8,750	$7,650	$6,550	$5,550

Add $1,056 for BLX Extra.
Add $4,082 for Prestige.
Add $14,863 for De Luxe.

❋ *Excalibur SL* - sidelock action, monobloc barrels. Disc. 2002.

	$21,000	$17,500	$13,250	$9,750	$8,200	$7,500	$6,750

Last MSR was $23,750.

ROMBO

❋ *Rombo Extra, Prestige, De Luxe Quattrocanne* - 28 ga. or .410 bore, Anson & Deeley locking system with sideplates, side opening lever, four barrels are arranged in a quad pattern. Limited mfg.

MSR $57,222	$52,750	$45,000	$39,000	$33,750	$27,250	$22,750	$18,750

Add $3,102 for Prestige.
Add $11,880 for De Luxe.

POSEIDON BL - 12, 20, 28 ga. or .410 bore., round action with monobloc or demibloc barrels.

MSR $19,020	$17,000	$15,000	$13,000	$11,000	$9,250	$8,250	$7,000

Add approx. 10% for 28 ga. or .410 bore.
Add $1,164 for BL Extra.
Add $2,208 for Prestige.
Add $9,480 for De Luxe.
Add approx. $5,000 for demibloc barrels.

❋ *Poseidon BL Round Titanium* - titanium round action with demibloc barrels.

MSR N/A	$29,750	$25,750	$21,000	$17,250	$14,750	$13,000	$11,750

Add $2,160 for BL Extra.
Add $9,720 for De Luxe.

❋ *Poseidon BLX* - monobloc or demibloc barrels.

MSR N/A	$18,350	$16,000	$13,750	$11,500	$9,650	$8,500	$7,250

Add $1,200 for BLX Extra.
Add $3,480 for Prestige.
Add $13,172 for De Luxe.
Add $4,380 for demibloc barrels.

SHOTGUNS: SxS

Add 20% for 28 ga. or .410 bore.

CASTORE PRESTIGE/DE LUXE HAMMER GUN - various gauges, double barrel, exposed hammers, double triggers.

MSR $33,528	$30,000	$26,250	$23,000	$19,750	$16,750	$14,650	$12,000

Add $3,168 for Prestige.
Add $11,880 for De Luxe.

GRADING - PPGS™	100%	98%	95%	90%	80%	70%	60%

BOXLOCK MODELS - various gauges, available with Anson-Deeley boxlock action, scalloped or rounded frame, various engraving patterns available.

* ✵ *Zeus Extra, Prestige, De Luxe* - 12 or 20 ga., features round action, side lever release, DT, limited mfg.

MSR $24,244	$22,000	$19,750	$14,500	$10,850	$8,950	$7,600	$6,500

  Add $3,938 for Prestige.
  Add $8,162 for De Luxe.
  Add approx. 50% for 28 ga. or 20% for .410 bore.

* ✵ *Tribute Extra, Prestige, De Luxe* - 12 (disc.), 20 (disc.), 28 ga., or .410 bore (disc.), scalloped back drop lock action, 7.25 lbs., limited mfg.

MSR N/A	$27,750	$24,250	$20,750	$15,250	$12,350	$10,750	$9,250

  Add $3,600 for Prestige.
  Add $11,640 for De Luxe.
  Add approx. 20% for 28 ga. or 10% for .410 bore.

SIDELOCK MODELS

* ✵ *Highline (Veneri)* - various gauges, round body, back action, very limited mfg. Disc. 1999.

$27,000	$20,000	$16,000	$12,250	$10,000	$8,500	$7,250

  Last MSR was $30,000.

* ✵ *Venus Extra/Prestige/De Luxe* - features patented Famars sidelocks, back action. Current MSR on this model is $40,876.

  Add $3,366 for Prestige.
  Add $11,880 for De Luxe.
  Add 10% for 28 ga. or .410 bore.

FANZOJ, JOHANN

Current long gun manufacturer located in Ferlach, Austria.

Johann Fanzoj is the 9th generation in his family to manufacture top quality long arms. Today's configurations include double rifles in all possible calibers, double shotguns, bolt action rifles, stalking rifles, combination guns, drillings, and the new Tri-Bore three barrel shotgun. Fanzoj was also a member of the Ferlach Guild, which was dissolved in 2004. Prices range from $15,000-$150,000, and almost anything is possible through custom order. Please contact the factory directly for current model availability, pricing, and to order a catalog. (see Trademark Index)

FAUSTI STEFANO SRL

Current manufacturer located in Marcheno, Italy. Currently imported beginning in 2000 by Traditions, located in Old Saybrook, CT.

S. Fausti manufactures a variety of good quality shotguns in O/U, SxS, and single shot configurations. Please refer to the Traditions section for current information on recent Fausti importation. New importation by Traditions can be determined by the Fausti Stefano SRL markings. Previously imported until 1999 by American Arms located in N. Kansas City, MO (Fausti, Cav., Stefano & Figlie snc.).

FAUSTI° STEFANO s.r.l.

GRADING - PPGS™	100%	98%	95%	90%	80%	70%	60%

FEATHER INDUSTRIES, INC.

Previous manufacturer located in Boulder, CO until 1995.

DERRINGERS

GUARDIAN ANGEL CENTERFIRE - 9mm Para. or .38 Spl. cal., O/U design, stainless steel, double action backup derringer. Mfg. 1988-89 only.

$130	$95	$75

Last MSR was $140.

This model has interchangeable loading blocks that allow shooting 9mm Para. or .38 Spl. There is no exposed hammer and trigger is totally enclosed.

GUARDIAN ANGEL RIMFIRE - .22 LR or .22 Mag. cal., design is similar to 9mm Para./.38 Spl. model, loading block breech, 2 in. barrel, fixed sights, 12 oz. Mfg. 1990-95.

$100	$75	$60

Last MSR was $120.

Add $30 for individual extra loading blocks.

This model has interchangeable loading blocks that allow shooting .22 LR or .22 Mag. There is no exposed hammer and the trigger is totally enclosed.

PISTOLS: SEMI-AUTO

MINI-AT - .22 LR cal., pistol variation of the AT-22, 5 1/2 in. shrouded barrel, 20 shot mag., approx. 2 lbs. Mfg. 1986-89.

$195	$165	$145	$135	$130	$125	$115

Last MSR was $220.

RIFLES: SEMI-AUTO

AT-22 - .22 LR cal., semi-auto blowback action, 17 in. detachable shrouded barrel, collapsible metal stock, adj. rear sight, with sling and swivels, 20 shot mag., 3 1/4 lbs. Mfg. 1986-95.

$225	$175	$155	$145	$135	$125	$115

Last MSR was $250.

F2 - similar to AT-22, except is equipped with a fixed polymer buttstock. Mfg. 1992-95.

$245	$190	$165	$150	$135	$125	$115

Last MSR was $280.

AT-9 - 9mm Para. cal., semi-auto blowback action, 16 in. barrel, paramilitary design, available with 10 (C/B 1994), 25*, 32 (disc.), or 100 (disc. 1989) shot mag., 5 lbs. Mfg. 1988-95.

$700	$625	$550	$495	$450	$400	$350

Last MSR was $500.

Add $250 for 100 shot drum mag.

F9 - similar to AT-9, except is equipped with a fixed polymer buttstock. Mfg. 1992-95.

$575	$525	$450	$395	$335	$295	$260

Last MSR was $535.

SATURN 30 - 7.62x39mm Kalashnikov cal., semi-auto, gas operated, 19 1/2 in. barrel, composite stock with large thumbhole pistol grip, 5 shot detachable mag., drilled and tapped for scope mounts, adj. rear sight, 8 1/2 lbs. Mfg. in 1990 only.

$650	$550	$475	$425	$375	$325	$280

Last MSR was $695.

KG-9 - 9mm Para. cal., semi-auto blowback action, 25 or 50 shot mag., paramilitary configuration. Mfg. 1989 only.

$750	$675	$600	$550	$500	$450	$400

Last MSR was $560.

Add $100 for 50 shot mag.

GRADING - PPGS™	100%	98%	95%	90%	80%	70%	60%

SAR-180 - .22 LR cal., semi-auto blowback action, 17 1/2 in. barrel, 165 shot drum mag., fully adj. rear sight, walnut stock with combat style pistol grip and forend, 6 1/4 lbs. Mfg. 1989 only.

	$495	$425	$375	$325	$275	$240	$200

Last MSR was $500.

    Add $250 for 165 shot drum mag.
    Add $200 for retractable stock.
    Add $395 for laser sight.

This variation was also manufactured for a limited time by ILARCO (Illinois Arms Company), previously located in Itasca, IL.

KG-22 - .22 LR cal., similar to KG-9, 20 shot mag. Mfg. 1989 only.

	$295	$250	$200	$175	$155	$145	$135

Last MSR was $300.

FEATHER USA

Current rifle manufacturer located in Eaton, CO.

RIFLES: SEMI-AUTO

Feather USA currently manufactures the following paramilitary styled rifles with steel wire stocks: RAV22 (.22 LR cal., $399 MSR), RAV9 (9mm Para. cal. - $599 MSR), RAV40 (.40 S&W cal. - $699), and the RAV45ACP ($759 MSR). High accuracy variations (HA suffix) with tapered bull barrels are also available for approx. $160 extra. Many options are available. Please contact the company directly for more information, including availability (see Trademark Index).

FEDERAL ENGINEERING CORPORATION

Previous manufacturer located in Chicago, IL.

RIFLES: SEMI-AUTO

XC-220 - .22 LR cal., semi-auto paramilitary design rifle, 16 5/16 in. barrel, 28 shot mag., machined steel action, 7 1/2 lbs. Mfg. 1984-89.

	$495	$450	$400	$350	$320	$295	$275

XC-450 - .45 ACP cal. only, semi-auto paramilitary design carbine, 16 1/2 in. barrel length, 30 shot mag., fires from closed bolt, machined steel action, 8 1/2 lbs. Mfg. 1984-89.

	$950	$825	$750	$675	$600	$550	$500

XC-900 - 9mm Para. cal., semi-auto paramilitary design carbine, 16 1/2 in. barrel length, 32 shot mag., fires from closed bolt, machine steel action, 8 lbs. Mfg. 1984-89.

	$950	$825	$750	$675	$600	$550	$500

FEDERAL ORDNANCE, INC.

Previous manufacturer, importer, and distributor located in South El Monte, CA from 1966-1992. Brickley Trading Co. bought the remaining assets of Federal Ordnance, Inc. in late 1992, and continued to import various firearms until circa 1998.

Federal Ordnance imported and distributed both foreign and domestic military handguns and rifles until 1992. In addition, they also fabricated firearms using mostly newer parts.

PISTOLS: SEMI-AUTO

In addition to the following Broomhandle models, Federal Ordnance also manufactured other special editions. These models include the British Model, Cut-Away, Cartridge Counter, Para La Guerra, and others. Prices are in the $800-$950 range (retail).

GRADING - PPGS™	100%	98%	95%	90%	80%	70%	60%

MODEL 714 BROOMHANDLE

MODEL 714 BROOMHANDLE - 7.63 Mauser or 9mm Para. cal., 5 1/2 in. barrel, new frame, exterior completely refinished, 10 shot detachable mag., "fair" bore, adj. rear sight. Mfg. 1986-91.

	$550	$500	$450	$400	$350	$325	$300

Last MSR was $820.

Add $100 for new barrel.

* **Model 714 Para La Guerra** - 7.63 Mauser or 9mm Para. cal., remanufactured to duplicate Spanish Civil War configuration Broomhandle, includes 10 in. barrel with "Para La Guerra" engraved on side. Mfg. 1990-91 only.

	$575	$525	$450	$400	$350	$325	$300

Last MSR was $890.

* **Model 714 Bolo** - similar to Model 714 Broomhandle, except has smaller grips, 3.9 in. barrel, 10 shot mag. standard. Mfg. 1988 only.

	$550	$500	$450	$400	$350	$325	$300

Last MSR was $890.

STANDARD BROOMHANDLE - 7.63 Mauser or 9mm Para. cal., refurbished (new barrels, completely refinished, etc.) C-96 pistols, replaced springs, includes original Chinese shoulder/holster stock. Disc. 1991.

	$525	$485	$450	$420	$390	$380	$360

Last MSR was $735.

Subtract $150 without shoulder/holster stock.

* **Standard Bolo** - similar to Standard Broomhandle, except Bolo configuration (3.9 in. barrel and smaller grips). Includes original Chinese shoulder/holster stock. Mfg. 1990-91 only.

	$480	$450	$420	$390	$380	$370	$360

Last MSR was $530.

RANGER 1911A1 GI - .45 ACP cal., 5 in. barrel, 7 shot mag., steel construction throughout, checkered walnut grips, 40 oz. Mfg. 1988-92.

	$385	$350	$310	$280	$260	$240	$200

Last MSR was $440.

Add $20 for Ranger Extended Model (40 oz. - new 1990).
Add $40 for Ranger Ambo (ambidextrous safety, 40 oz. - new 1990).
Add $15 for lightweight Ranger Lite Model (32 oz. - new 1990).
These pistols are patterned after the Colt 1911A1 Govt. Model.

* **Ranger Ten** - 10mm cal., otherwise similar to regular Ranger 1911A1. Mfg. 1990-91 only.

	$675	$525	$475	$450	$420	$395	$370

Last MSR was $780.

RANGER SUPERCOMP - .45 ACP or 10mm cal., compensated variation of the Ranger 1911A1 with 6 in. compensated barrel, slide, tuned trigger, and other competition features, 42 oz. Mfg. 1990-91 only.

	$1,250	$875	$775	$675	$600	$550	$495

Last MSR was $1,390.

Add $10 for 10mm cal.

THE RANGER ALPHA - .38 Super, 10mm, or .45 ACP cal., 5 or 6 in. barrel, patterned after the Colt Govt. Model. Mfg. 1990-91 only.

	$895	$775	$675	$575	$475	$425	$380

Last MSR was $1,000.

Add $16 for 10mm cal.
Add $16 for 6 in. barrel.
Add $9-$25 for ported 5 or 6 in. barrel depending on cal.

GRADING - PPGS™	100%	98%	95%	90%	80%	70%	60%

RIFLES/CARBINES

ALL AMERICAN SPORTER BOLT ACTION - .30-06 cal., Springfield M1903 receiver, new sporter stock, drilled and tapped for scope base (included), blue finish. Mfg. late 1991-92.

	$165	$145	$120	$100	$90	$80	$75

MODEL 713 DELUXE MAUSER SEMI-AUTO CARBINE - 7.63 Mauser or 9mm Para. cal., 16 in. barrel, detachable stock, one 10 shot and one 20 shot detachable mag., deluxe walnut, leather case with accessories, adj. sights to 1,000 meters, 5 lbs. 1,500 mfg. 1986-92.

	$1,495	$1,250	$1,050				

Last MSR was $1,986.

✱ *Field Grade Mauser Carbine* - 7.63 Mauser or 9mm Para. (new 1989) cal., 16 in. barrel, 10 shot fixed mag., nondetachable walnut stock. Mfg. 1987-92.

	$750	$675	$600	$525	$475	$425	$400

Last MSR was $1,200.

M-14 SEMI-AUTO - .308 Win. cal., legal for private ownership (no selector), 20 shot mag., refinished original M-14 parts, available in either filled fiberglass, G.I. fiberglass, refinished wood, or new walnut stock. Mfg. 1986-91.

	$825	$750	$695	$650	$595	$550	$475

Last MSR was $700.

Add $50 for filled fiberglass stock.
Add $110 for refinished wood stock.
Add $190 for new walnut stock with handguard.
During the end of production, Chinese parts were used on this model. Values are the same.

TANKER GARAND SEMI-AUTO - .30-06 or .308 Win. cal., original U.S. GI parts, 18 in. barrel, new hardwood stock, parkerized finish. Mfg. began late 1991.

	$825	$750	$695	$650	$595	$550	$475

CHINESE RPK 86S-7 SEMI-AUTO - 7.62x39mm cal., semi-auto version of the P.R.C.-RPK light machine gun, 75 shot drum mag., 23 3/4 in. barrel, with bipod. Imported 1989 only.

	$1,000	$875	$725	$650	$575	$525	$475

Last MSR was $500.

Add $100 for 75 shot drum mag.

FEINWERKBAU

Current manufacturer established circa 1951, and located in Oberndorf, Germany. Feinwerkbau firearms are currently being imported by Nygord Precision, located in Prescott, AZ.

Feinwerkbau manufactures some of the world's finest quality target rifles and pistols (.22 LR rimfire and airgun). Target rifles and pistols have had limited importation into the U.S. Feinwerkbau also manufactures world championship winning airguns and a black powder pistol. For more information and current pricing on both new and used Feinwerkbau airguns, please refer to the *Blue Book of Airguns* by Dr. Robert Beeman & John Allen (also online). For more information on the black powder pistol, please refer to the *Blue Book of Modern Black Powder Arms* by John Allen & Dennis Adler (also online).

PISTOLS: SEMI-AUTO, RIMFIRE

MODEL AW-93 - .22 LR cal., 6 in. barrel, 5 shot mag., ergonomically designed stippled walnut grips with adj. heel, unique damper prevents muzzle jump and recoil, satin receiver finish, bolt burnished, top-of-the-line Target pistol, current mfg. includes plastic case, approx. 2 1/2 lbs. New 1993.

MSR $1,945		$1,825	$1,575	$1,375	$1,150	$950	$850	$750

GRADING - PPGS™	100%	98%	95%	90%	80%	70%	60%

* **Model AW-93 Lightweight** - similar to standard Model AW-93, except has lightened frame, 2 1/3 lbs. Limited importation began 2004.

MSR $1,945	$1,825	$1,575	$1,375	$1,150	$950	$850	$750

RIFLES: BOLT ACTION, RIMFIRE

MODEL 2000 - .22 LR cal. only, single shot, match target bolt action rifle, fully adj. trigger, walnut stocks, four variations featuring different specifications. Importation disc. 1988.

* **Universal Model** - 26 3/8 in. barrel, aperture sights, stippled pistol grip and forearm, 9 3/4 lbs.

	$1,150	$925	$850	$735	$650	$595	$550

Last MSR was $1,395.

Add $350 for electronic trigger.
Add $160 for left-hand variation.

* **Mini 2000 (Junior)** - 22 in. barrel, aperture sights, stippled pistol grip, 9 1/8 lbs.

	$1,025	$875	$825	$700	$625	$575	$525

Last MSR was $1,225.

Add $350 for electronic trigger.
Add $150 for left-hand variation.

* **Match Model** - 26 1/4 in. barrel, adj. cheekpiece on stock, stippled pistol grip and forearm, aperture sights.

	$1,075	$895	$825	$700	$625	$575	$525

Last MSR was $1,285.

Add $390 for electronic trigger.
Add $113 for left-hand variation.

* **Running Target** - adj. cheekpiece on stock, thumbhole stippled pistol grip, no sights, for running boar competition.

	$1,150	$925	$850	$735	$650	$595	$550

Last MSR was $1,398.

Add $142 for left-hand variation.

MODEL 2600 UNIVERSAL - .22 LR cal. only, similar design to Model 600 air rifle, single shot, 26.3 in. barrel, aperture sights, 10.6 lbs. Imported 1986-94.

	$1,425	$1,125	$925	$850	$735	$650	$595

Last MSR was $1,695.

Add $160 for left-hand variation.

MODEL 2600 ULTRA MATCH FREE RIFLE - .22 LR cal., single shot match gun based on Model 2600 action, 26.1 in. barrel, laminated stock with thumbhole, fully adj. aperture sights, 14 lbs. 1 oz. Mfg. 1986-94.

	$2,175	$1,750	$1,400	$1,150	$925	$850	$735

Last MSR was $2,498.

Add $250 for electronic trigger (disc. 1988).
Add $152 for left-hand variation.

MODEL 2602 UNIVERSAL (UIT) RIFLE - .22 LR cal., designed for Match competition, state-of-the-art Target rifle with different color wood laminations possible, adj. cheekpiece, short or long barrel, two-stage trigger. New 1997.

MSR $1,615	$1,450	$1,275	$1,125	$975	$850	$725	$600

Add $125 for left-hand action.

MODEL 2602 FREE RIFLE - .22 LR cal., standard Match rifle with red and blue anodized aluminum stock with adj. cheekpiece and buttplate, and adj. hand rest, 16 3/4 or 26 1/2 in. barrel with unique 13 3/4 in. squared-off barrel sleeve with sight, diopter sights, top-of-the-line competition rifle, approx. 13.86 lbs. New 1997.

MSR $2,365	$2,035	$1,800	$1,575	$1,350	$1,175	$1,000	$850

Add $155 for left-hand action.

GRADING - PPGS™	100%	98%	95%	90%	80%	70%	60%

MODEL 2602 SUPER MATCH - .22 LR cal., Super Match variation featuring state-of-the-art design, adj. stock, comb, LOP, and trigger pull.

	MSR $2,995	$2,550	$2,175	$1,800	$1,575	$1,350	$1,175	$1,000

Add $130 for left-hand action.

Subtract $130 for Model 2602 Sport RT.

MODEL 2602 SPORT - .22 LR cal., sporter variation of the Model 2602, short or long barrel, right- or left-hand action, two-stage trigger, laminated wood stock with red stripes and thumbhole, adj. cheekpiece and buttplate, approx. 12.75 lbs. New 2000.

	MSR $2,240	$1,950	$1,750	$1,525	$1,325	$1,175	$1,000	$850

FEMARU

Previously manufactured by Femaru-Fegyver-es Gepgyar R.T. located in Budapest, Hungary.

PISTOLS: SEMI-AUTO

MODEL 1910 - 7.65mm Roth/Steyr cal., rare and only infrequently encountered. Estimated serial range 1-10,000.

		$2,500	$2,000	$1,500	$1,150	$975	$850	$725

MODEL 1929 (29M) - .380 ACP cal., 3.93 in. barrel, 8 shot mag., identifiable by squared-off rear slide with vertical serrations, 2 piece walnut grips, approx. 50,000 mfg.

		$400	$340	$275	$215	$185	$165	$145

MODEL 1937 (37M) - .32 ACP or .380 ACP cal., 3.93 in. barrel, 8 shot mag., commercial blue finish, left slide marking "FEMARU FEGYVER ES GEPGYAR RT. 37M", vertically grooved 2-piece walnut grips, approx. 200,000 mfg. (.380 ACP cal.) for Hungarian service before Nazi variations began (dubbed "Pistole Modell 37 (ung)," circa 1941), Nazi marked "jhv 41" or "jhv 44", 27 oz.

		$500	$400	$300	$250	$225	$200	$175

Add 50% for Waffenamt proofing (.32 ACP only).

Add another 100% if with holster and 2 matching mags.

FROMMER STOP POCKET AUTO - .32 ACP or .380 ACP cal., 6 or 7 shot, 3 7/8 in. barrel, fixed sights, blue, rubber grips, locked breech, outside hammer. Mfg. 1912-1920.

		$350	$300	$250	$225	$200	$175	$150

Add 50% for .380 ACP cal.

FROMMER BABY POCKET AUTO - similar to Stop Pocket Auto, except 2 in. barrel, 5 or 6 shot.

		$250	$215	$180	$150	$115	$90	$70

FROMMER LILIPUT AUTO - .25 ACP cal., blowback action, 6 shot, 2.14 in. barrel, blue, hard rubber grips. Mfg. in early 1920s.

		$400	$300	$200	$145	$115	$90	$75

FERLACH GUNS

Includes those firearms manufactured in Ferlach, Austria from 1558 to present. The Ferlach Guild (Genossenschaft) represented most of Ferlach's gunmakers until it was dissolved in 2004.

Many people mistakenly believe that Ferlach is a trademark - it is not. Rather, it is a small village in Austria where a gun guild was started as early as 1558. At that time, it was absolutely necessary that all the people involved in fabricating a firearm were located together in close proximity. This enabled the barrel maker, the stock maker, and the lock mechanism maker to work together closely to ensure that everyone was performing their task(s) correctly, effectively and efficiently. As the individual skills became better and more refined, more and more firearms were manufactured. Eventually, individual gunsmiths began to put their name on the barrel or frame of those guns which they had either manufactured solely or with the help of their fellow Ferlach craftsmen. Since all Ferlach firearms are essentially hand made per individual special order, very few are exactly alike. In the past, the gunsmiths of Ferlach have produced almost every type of shoulder arm imaginable, including such modern weapons as superposed and juxtaposed rifles and shotguns, hammerless drillings, repeating rifles, 3 barrel rifles, combination guns, 4 barrel rifles/shotguns/combination guns (called Vierlings), hammer guns of every type, etc. Some of these specimens represent the highest refinement in the gunmakers trade. Because of the almost unlimited variety of Ferlach variations, it is recommended that a COMPETENT appraisal is procured before buying or selling a specimen.

As is the case with many other European weapons, those models with desirable American features will generally outperform those with European specifications (i.e. a Ferlach sidelock combination gun that is 20 ga. x .243 Win. will be more valuable than a similar specimen chambered for 16 ga. x 5.6 by 50Rmm with sling swivels). Original condition and overall beauty are the primary factors to consider when contemplating buying or selling a Ferlach longarm. Other considerations include: type of action, difficulty of fabrication (Vierlings are very complicated to construct), caliber/gauge desirability, notoriety of gunsmith on barrel legend, elaborateness of embellishments, condition, rarity, accessories, and any provenance a specimen might have.

Today's master gunsmiths of Ferlach carry on the Old World tradition of quality in every respect. Most guns manufactured today are by individual special order with a wide range of calibers/gauges and other special features and options. As of this writing, these gunsmiths in alphabetical order are: Ludwig Borovnik, Johann Fanzoj, Wilfried Glanznig, Josef Hambrusch, Karl Hauptmann, Gottfried Juch, Josef Just, Jakob Koschat, Peter Michelitsch, Johann & Walter Outschar, Herbert Scheiring, Benedikt Winkler, And Josef Winkler. Anyone wishing to contact these master gunmakers should contact the indivudal gunmaker.

FERLIB

Current manufacturer established circa late 1940s, and located in Gardone V.T., Italy. SxS rifles have been imported and distributed by Dakota Arms, Inc. since late 1999, and they are located in Sturgis, SD. Previously distributed until 1999 by Hi-Grade Imports located in Gilroy, CA.

Ferlib currently manufactures approx. 20 best quality guns annually. All are special order, and all engraving is quoted individually.

RIFLES: SxS

Please refer to the listing in Dakota Arms for more information this model, as it is imported exclusively by Dakota Arms.

SHOTGUNS: O/U

BOSS MODEL - features Boss style action, custom order gun, many engraving options.

Prices for this model start at $29,500, w/o engraving (quoted separately).

SHOTGUNS: SxS

The following models are available in 10, 12, 16, 20, 24, 28, 32 ga., or .410 bore. Also available for an additional charge are extra quality wood and upgraded engraving.

Add 10% for 24, 28, 32 ga., or .410 bore.

Add $250 for single trigger.

Add $650 for leather case.

MIGNON HAMMER MODEL - back action, exposed hammers, extensive scroll engraving, deluxe checkered walnut stock and forearm.

Prices for this model start at $19,000.

GRADING - PPGS™	100%	98%	95%	90%	80%	70%	60%

MODEL F.VI - 12, 16, 20, 28 ga., or .410 bore, Anson & Deeley scalloped boxlock action, ejectors, double triggers, case hardened frame, select checkered stock and forearm. Disc. 1992.

	$3,500	**$2,950**	**$2,275**	**$1,975**	**$1,600**	**$1,250**	**$1,000**

Last MSR was $3,250.

MODEL 7 (F.VII) - 12, 16, 20, 28 ga., or .410 bore, Anson & Deeley scalloped boxlock action, ejectors, double triggers, coin finish, full coverage English scroll or game scene engraving, select checkered stock and forearm.

MSR N/A	**$9,950**	**$8,750**	**$7,600**	**$6,500**	**$5,400**	**$4,500**	**$3,400**

* *Model 7 Rex* - similar to Model 7, except has sideplates with extensive engraving. Importation began 2000.

MSR N/A	**$13,300**	**$10,650**	**$9,150**	**$8,100**	**$7,000**	**$6,000**	**$5,000**

* *Model 7 Premier* - top-of-the-line boxlock model, similar to Model 7 Rex, except more extensive engraving with gold inlays, best quality walnut. Importation began 2000.

MSR N/A	**$15,000**	**$12,750**	**$10,950**	**$9,250**	**$8,100**	**$7,100**	**$6,100**

MODEL F.VII/SC - 12, 16, 20, 28 ga., or .410 bore, Anson & Deeley scalloped boxlock action, ejectors, double triggers, coin finish, game scene with scroll accent engraving with gold inlays, select checkered stock and forearm. Importation disc. 1999.

	$6,200	**$5,500**	**$5,000**	**$4,500**	**$3,800**	**$3,300**	**$2,750**

Last MSR was $7,800.

SIDE PLATE MODEL (F.VII SIDEPLATE) - 12, 16, 20, 28 ga., or .410 bore, Anson & Deeley boxlock action with sideplates, ejectors, single trigger, coin finish, extensive English scroll or game scene and scroll accent engraving, select checkered stock and forearm.

MSR N/A	**$12,950**	**$10,500**	**$9,000**	**$8,000**	**$7,000**	**$6,000**	**$5,000**

Subtract $400 if English scroll engraved.

* *F.VII/SC Gold* - similar to F.VII Sideplate, except with gold inlays.

MSR N/A	**$13,450**	**$10,950**	**$9,250**	**$8,100**	**$7,100**	**$6,100**	**$5,100**

PRINCE MODEL - various gauges, contoured Anson & Deeley action with rounded frame, choice of top or side lever opening, DT, deluxe checkered walnut stock and forearm. Importation began 2000.

MSR N/A	**$10,600**	**$9,250**	**$8,100**	**$6,800**	**$5,550**	**$4,600**	**$3,500**

Add $2,550 for side lever opening.

SIDELOCK MODEL - various models and gauges, full H&H sidelock action, special order to customer specifications. Importation began in 2000.

Prices for this model start at $20,000 w/o engraving. The Esposizione & L'Inglesina models retail for $25,500, and the Model E Fantasy currently lists at $39,500 (including engraving).

FIALA ARMS AND EQUIPMENT CO.

Previous manufacturer located in New Haven, CT. Fiala Arms and Equipment Co. was founded circa 1920, and went bankrupt shortly thereafter. Fiala Outfits, Inc. of New York City, NY reportedly bought the remaining guns, parts, and inventory and sold them between circa 1922 until approximately 1930. Also see Schall & Co.

The author would like to thank Mr. John Stimson for making the following information available.

PISTOLS: SLIDE ACTION

FIALA REPEATING PISTOL - .22 LR cal., similar to Colt Woodsman, manual operation, blue finish, interchangeable 3, 7 1/2 (fixed or smoothbore) or 20 (smoothbore optional) in. barrel, optional detachable buttstock, smooth or ribbed walnut grips, rear sight is square notched blade that tips up into an elevated adj. aperture sight, marked "Fiala Arms and Equipment Co. Inc./New Haven Conn./Patents Pending" on

GRADING - PPGS™	100%	98%	95%	90%	80%	70%	60%

right side of frame behind the grip, and "MODEL 1920/Made in U.S.A." on the right side of the frame above the triggerguard, left side of frame marked "FIALA ARMS" above the image of a polar bear with "TRADE MARK" below polar bear in area above the triggerguard.

* *Cased with all 3 barrels and stock*

	$2,500	$2,400	$2,250	$2,100	$1,250	$1,100	$975

Add 15% for dovetail vs. screw stock/frame attachment.

Add $100 for smooth bore 20 in. barrel.

* *Gun only*

	$525	$475	$400	$350	$300	$290	$280

This model was available with three different case variations - canvas, black or tan leatherette (velvet lined and fitted with a lock). Some pistols are also marked "Columbia Arms Company" or Botwinik Brothers."

This model has been classified by the ATF as a "Curio" or "Relic" and is collectible when in a complete state with all accoutrements.

FINNISH LION

Previous trademark manufactured by Valmet (now Tikka) located in Sweden. Limited importation into the U.S. by Mandall's Shooting Supplies, Inc. in Scottsdale, AZ.

RIFLES: BOLT ACTION

MATCH MODEL - .22 LR cal., bolt action, single shot, 29 in. barrel, extended aperture sight, globe front sight, thumbhole stock, adj. hook butt. Mfg. 1937-72.

	$495	$415	$360	$305	$250	$210	$195

CHAMPION FREE MODEL - .22 LR cal., bolt action, single shot, 29 in. barrel, double set trigger, full target stock and accessories. Mfg. 1965-72.

	$580	$495	$440	$385	$330	$290	$265

STANDARD ISU TARGET MODEL - .22 LR cal., bolt action, single shot, 27 in. barrel, full target stock and accessories. Mfg. 1966-1977.

	$330	$275	$250	$205	$180	$165	$150

TARGET MODEL - .22 LR cal., target rifle with adj. stock and trigger, bolt action, single shot, aperture sights.

	$725	$595	$495	$440	$385	$340	$295

Last MSR was $795.

FIOCCHI OF AMERICA, INC.

Previous firearms importer and distributor located in Ozark, MO.

Fiocchi of America imported Pardini target pistols until 1990, and continues to manufacture a wide variety of ammunition domestically. Fiocchi also imported Antonio Zoli shotguns until 1988. These trademarks can be found in their respective sections of this text.

FIREARMS INTERNATIONAL (F.I.)

Previous importer and assembler located in Washington, D.C.

F.I. manufactured and imported various shotguns and pistols including the Star D and Iver Johnson Pony handguns. F.I. sold less than 100 .380 ACPs that were marked Colt before the Mustang was introduced - these are rare. While some models are relatively rare, collectability to date has been minimal and most models sell in the $125-$250 range.

GRADING - PPGS™	100%	98%	95%	90%	80%	70%	60%

FIREARMS INTERNATIONAL, INC.

Current manufacturer established in 1998, and located in Houston, TX. Dealer sales.

In September, 2004, a new company called Crusader Group Gun Company, Inc. was formed, and includes the assets of Firearms International, Inc., High Standard Manufacturing Co., AMT-Auto Mag, and Arsenal Line Products.

While IAI (Israel Arms International) was originally established to market firearms manufactured by Israel Arms, Ltd. through Firearms International, Inc., IAI defaulted on this agreement without any sales being made.

PISTOLS: SEMI-AUTO

During 1999, Firearms International, Inc. obtained permission to use older High Standard model nomenclature (Crusader & Supermatic Trophy) for use with their M-1911 pistols. Currently manufactured pistols are marked Firearms International Inc. on the frame, and High Standard on the slide.

Sharpshooter .45 ACP to .22 LR cal. conversion units are also available - fixed sight model retails for $280, adj. rear sight model retails for $340.

MODEL 1911 CRUSADER (CUSTOM SERIES) - 38 Super (new 2002, Two-tone finish only) or .45 ACP cal., 5 in. barrel, 7 or 9 (.38 Super cal. only) shot mag., many shooting enhancements are standard, stainless steel, blue, or Tu-tone (new 2001) finish, adj. sights, 40 oz. New 2000.

MSR $645	$585	$525	$475	$425	$400	$375	$350

Add $50 for stainless steel.
Add $30 for Two-tone finish.
Add $50 for .38 Super cal.

* **Crusader Combat** - similar to M-1911 Crusader, except has 4 1/4 in. barrel and choice of fixed or adj. (disc. 2000) sights, 38 oz. New 2000.

MSR $645	$585	$525	$475	$425	$400	$375	$350

Add $50 for stainless steel.
Add $30 for Two-tone finish.

* **Crusader Compact** - 4 in. barrel, similar to Crusader Combat, except has shorter grip frame, 6 shot mag., 36 oz. Limited mfg. 2000 only.

	$715	$600	$500	$475	$425	$375	$325

Last MSR was $775.

STR-5S SUPERMATIC TROPHY MATCH (MATCH MODEL) - similar to M-1911 Crusader, except has National Match 5 or 6 in. barrel and bushing, polished feed ramp and throated barrel, lowered/flared ejection port, 40 oz. New 2000.

MSR $895	$795	$700	$600	$525	$475	$425	$375

Subtract $100 for blue finish (disc. 2001).
Subtract $80 if w/o sights and no finish (disc.).

CAMP PERRY MODEL (TX5870FS/AS) - .45 ACP cal., 5 in. barrel, mil-spec slide, barrel and barrel bushing, blue or Tu-Tone (mfg. 2001 only) finish only, competition tuned, beveled mag. well, 40 oz. New 2000.

MSR $749	$650	$600	$550	$495	$450	$400	$350

Add $46 for adj. sights.

G-MAN - .45 ACP cal., 5 in. barrel, special tolerances, including frame to slide fit, match grade stainless barrel and National Match bushing, polished feed ramp, throated barrel, slotted hammer, lightweight trigger, lowered and flared ejection port, beveled mag. well, checkered American walnut grips, black Teflon finish, includes two 8 shot mag., 39 oz. New 2001.

MSR $1,225	$1,075	$900	$825	$750	$675	$600	$550

GRADING - PPGS™	100%	98%	95%	90%	80%	70%	60%

GI MODEL - .45 ACP cal., 5 in. barrel, parkerized finish, fixed sights, classic WWII style (1911A1 frame), 7 shot mag. Introduced 2002.

	MSR $549	$475	$425	$375	$335	$300	$285	$270

ARMY SPECIAL - .45 ACP cal., 5 in. barrel, blue or parkerized finish, 7 shot mag., fixed sights, 39 oz. Limited mfg. 2000.

	$485	$435	$395	$365	$330	$300	$285

Last MSR was $549.

NAVY MODEL - similar to Army Special, except is stainless steel, 39 oz. Limited mfg. 2000.

	$535	$465	$425	$395	$350	$325	$300

Last MSR was $599.

AIR CREW MODEL - similar to Army Special, except is titanium, 26 oz. New 2000.

While advertised, this model never went into production.

RIFLES: SEMI-AUTO

M1 CARBINE - .30 Carbine cal., 18 in. barrel, parkerized finish, wood stock, adj. rear sight, 10 shot mag., mfg. in the U.S., and patterned after the WWII design, 5 1/2 lbs. Limited mfg. 2001-2003.

	$500	$425	$375	$335	$300	$275	$250

Last MSR was $575.

P50 RIFLE/CARBINE - .50 BMG cal., designed by Robert Pauza, gas operation, 24 or 29 in. barrel, MOA accuracy at 1,000 yards, includes two 5 shot mags. and hard case, 25 (carbine) or 30 lbs. Limited mfg. 2001-2003.

	$7,500	$6,750	$5,750	$5,000	$4,500	$4,000	$3,500

Last MSR was $7,950.

FIRESTORM

Current trademark of pistols manufactured by Industria Argentina and Fabrinor, S.A.L. Distributed (master distributor) beginning late 2000 by SGS Imports, International Inc., located in Wanamassa, NJ.

PISTOLS: SEMI-AUTO

Beginning 2004, all Firestorm pistols are available with an integral locking system (ILS).

FIRESTORM SERIES (.22 LR & .380 ACP) - .22 LR or .380 ACP cal., double action, 3 1/2 in. barrel, matte or duo-tone finish, 7 (.380 ACP) or 10 (.22 LR) shot mag., 3 dot combat sights, anatomic rubber grips with finger grooves, 23 oz. Importation began 2001.

	MSR $284	$240	$205	$175	$155	$145	$135	$125

Add $8 for duo-tone finish.

MINI-FIRESTORM - 9mm Para., .40 S&W, or .45 ACP (new 2002) cal., double action, 3 1/2 in. barrel, nickel, matte or duo-tone finish, 7 (.45 ACP cal.) or 10 shot mag., 3 dot sights, polymer grips, safeties include manual, firing pin, and decocking, 24.5-27 oz. Importation began 2001.

	MSR $400	$335	$285	$255	$220	$195	$180	$165

Add $9 for duo-tone finish.
Add $9 for .45 ACP cal.
Add $25 for nickel finish.

FIRESTORM 45 GOVERNMENT - .45 ACP cal., single action, 5 1/8 in. barrel, matte or duo-tone finish, 7 shot mag., anatomic rubber grips with finger grooves, 36 oz. Importation began 2001.

	MSR $309	$260	$230	$200	$180	$165	$150	$135

Add $8 for duo-tone finish.

GRADING - PPGS™	100%	98%	95%	90%	80%	70%	60%

* *Firestorm 45 Compact* - .45 ACP cal., 4 1/4 in. barrel, otherwise similar to Firestorm 45 Government, 34 oz. Importation began 2001.

MSR $309	$260	$230	$200	$180	$165	$150	$135

Add $8 for duo-tone finish.

* *Firestorm Mini Compact* - .45 ACP cal., 3 1/8 in. barrel, chrome or matte or duo-tone finish, 10 shot staggered mag., polymer grips, 31 oz. Imported 2001 only.

	$280	$245	$215	$195	$180	$170	$155

Last MSR was $324.

Add $17 for chrome finish.

FIRESTORM GOVERNMENT SPECIAL EDITION - .38 Super cal., single action, 5 1/8 in. barrel, blue finish, 9 shot, fixed 3-dot sights, skeletonized combat hammer, extended beavertail grip safety.

MSR $334	$280	$250	$220	$190	$175	$165	$155

This model is available exclusively through Davidson's.

FLODMAN GUNS

Current manufacturer established in 1978 and located in Järsta, Sweden. In 1992, Skullman Enterprise AB took over Flodman Guns. No current U.S. importation.

O/U: LONG GUNS

Flodman manufactures a variety of high quality shotguns, combination guns, and double rifles. They offer three designs – hunting, sporting, and luxury. All Flodman O/Us utilize a low profile, boxlock, stainless steel self-opening action, patented ejector (allows dry firing w/o ejector movement), and have no hammer, but a primed firing pin which moves perpendicularly, allowing 2/1000 of a second detonation time. Barrels are available in either titanium or Sandvik steel, and are equipped with choke tubes. Prices for the Standard Model start at $9,800, while Titanium barrels start at $15,500. Please contact the factory directly for more information regarding an individual price quotation and delivery time (see Trademark Index).

FORT WORTH FIREARMS

Previous manufacturer located in Fort Worth, TX 1995-2000.

PISTOLS: SEMI-AUTO, RIMFIRE

MATCH MASTER STANDARD - .22 LR cal., 3 7/8, 4 1/2, 5 1/2, 7 1/2, or 10 in. bull barrel, double extractors, includes upper push button and standard mag. release, beveled mag. well, angled grip, flared slide, low profile frame. Mfg. 1995-2000.

	$310	$265	$230	$200	$185	$170	$160

Last MSR was $389.

Add $84 for 10 in. bull barrel.

* *Match Master Dovetail* - similar to Match Master Standard, except has 3 7/8, 4 1/2, or 5 1/2 barrel with dovetail rib. Mfg. 1995-2000.

	$385	$325	$285	$240	$215	$190	$170

Last MSR was $473.

* *Match Master Deluxe* - similar to Match Master Standard, except has Weaver rib on barrel. Mfg. 1995-2000.

	$450	$365	$315	$280	$240	$215	$190

Last MSR was $538.

Add $92 for 10 in. barrel.

SPORT KING - .22 LR cal., 4 1/2 or 5 1/2 in. barrel, blue finish, military grips, drift sight, 10 shot mag. Mfg. 1995-2000.

	$275	$245	$225	$200	$185	$170	$160

Last MSR was $313.

GRADING - PPGS™	100%	98%	95%	90%	80%	70%	60%

CITATION - .22 LR cal., 5 1/2 in. bull or 7 1/4 in. fluted barrel, military grips, 10 shot mag. Mfg. 1995-2000.

	$310	$265	$230	$200	$185	$170	$160

Last MSR was $389.

TROPHY - .22 LR cal., 5 1/2 or 7 1/4 in. bull barrel, blue finish, military grips, 10 shot mag. Mfg. 1995-2000.

	$330	$285	$240	$200	$185	$170	$160

Last MSR was $411.

Add $41 for left-hand action (5 1/2 in. barrel only).

VICTOR - .22 LR cal., 3 7/8, 4 1/2 (VR or Weaver rib), or 5 1/2 (VR or Weaver rib), 8 (Weaver rib), or 10 (Weaver rib) in. barrel, blue finish, military grips, 10 shot mag. Mfg. 1995-2000.

	$385	$325	$285	$240	$215	$190	$170

Last MSR was $473.

Add $65 for 4 1/2 or 5 1/2 in. Weaver rib barrel.
Add approx. $148 for 8 or 10 in. Weaver rib barrel.

OLYMPIC - .22 LR or Short cal., 6 3/4 in. fluted barrel, blue finish, military grips, 10 shot mag. Mfg. 1995-2000.

	$525	$465	$415	$360	$330	$295	$265

Last MSR was $600.

SHARP SHOOTER - .22 LR cal., 5 1/2 in. bull barrel, blue finish, military grips, 10 shot mag. Mfg. 1995-2000.

	$300	$260	$230	$200	$185	$170	$160

Last MSR was $380.

RIFLES: BOLT ACTION

YOUTH RIFLE - .22 LR cal., bolt action, single shot, shortened stock dimensions. Mfg. 1995-96.

	$120	$105	$90	$80	$70	$60	$50

Last MSR was $138.

SHOTGUNS: SLIDE ACTION

GL 18 - 12 ga. only, security configuration with 18 in. barrel with perforated shroud, thumb operated laser/xenon light built into end of 7 shot mag. tube, ammo storage. Mfg. 1995-96.

	$295	$265	$240	$210	$190	$170	$160

Last MSR was $347.

FOX, A.H.

Current manufacturer located in New Britain, CT. The A.H. Fox trademark was brought to life once again during 1993 when the Connecticut Shotgun Manufacturing Company began producing an A.H. Fox 20 gauge in 5 different grades. Previously manufactured in Philadelphia, PA 1903-1930, and in Utica, NY from 1930-approx. 1946. Manufactured by Savage 1930-1988.

Depending on the remaining A.H. Fox factory data, a factory letter authenticating the configuration of a particular Fox shotgun (not to be confused with the more recent Savage/Stevens designed Fox doubles) may be obtained by contacting John T. Callahan (see Trademark Index for listings and address). If a model number is not known, please include a photo, the ser. no., gauge, barrel length and style, stock and forearm style, markings, patent dates, inspector stamps, etc. The charge for this service is $25.00 for the Sterlingworth Model, and $35.00 for graded models A-F and single barrel trap guns. Please allow 2-4 weeks for an adequate response.

Mr. Ansley H. Fox first started manufacturing shotguns in circa 1896. This first company was called the Fox Gun Co. and was located in Baltimore, MD. Relatively few guns were made and surviving specimens today are very rare. After this venture, Mr. Fox was employed by the Baltimore Gun Co. for several years (circa 1900-1903). Following this period, he formed the Philadelphia Gun Co. where the predecessors to the A.H. Fox Gun Co. models were manufactured. These Philadelphia Gun Co. models (circa 1904) were the same as the newer Fox shotguns except that the hinge pin was removed. Sources indicate that the lowest grade was an A with the highest being an E (fully engraved and ultra rare). Following this tenure, Mr. Fox went on to form the A.H. Fox Gun Co. that was started approx. 1905. In addition to being an entrepreneur and trend setter, Mr. Fox also had the reputation of being an expert shot in his own right, winning more than a few events on the East Coast around the turn of the century.

The A.H. Fox Gun Company of Philadelphia, Pennsylvania, began production in 1905 and produced high quality double barrel shotguns until 1930. The Savage Arms Company, then of Utica, New York, acquired the Fox Company and produced these guns until 1942, when all but the utilitarian model B series guns were discontinued.

A.H. Fox guns are considered an American classic comparable to L.C. Smith, Parker, and others. Collector interest is high and will undoubtedly grow. The guns do not command quite as high a price as the Smith and Parker guns, but represent a fine investment collectible value.

> **Savage-made guns from 1930-1942 are usually valued similarly to the early A.H. Fox guns. The recent production B series are just not in the same class and are obviously not intended to be. They are lower priced by today's standards and are designed as a utility grade hunting gun.**

FOX COMPANY CHRONOLOGY

1906 - Company formed January 1906, A, B & C Grades introduced in 12 ga. only. D and F Grades introduced in 12 ga. in 1907. Ejector guns introduced in 1908. 1910 saw the introduction of the 12 ga. Sterlingworth - William H. Gough takes over as Chief of Engraving. Ansley Fox resigns in 1911 - first catalog showing Sterlingworth Model (called Model 1911). A-F Grades released in 16 and 20 ga. during 1912, as well as the addition of a 20 ga. Sterlingworth. 16 ga. Sterlingworth introduced in 1913. Fox/Kautsky single trigger introduced in 1914 - engineering transition complete. During 1915, the XE Grade was introduced. The B Grade was dropped in 1918. Single barrel trap guns (J, K, and L Grades) were introduced in 1919. 1920 saw the introduction of the M Grade single barrel trap. In 1922, both the G and HE Grades were released. Beavertail forend and vent. rib were introduced in 1927. 1929 was the Savage buy-out (November), GE Grade dropped. Company moved from Philadelphia, PA to Utica, NY in 1930. Skeeter Grade introduced in 1931 while the 20 ga. HE Grade was disc. 1932 saw the introduction of both the Trap Grade Double and SP Grade. Wildfowl Grade was introduced in 1934. 1935 was the last year of the K and L single barrel trap guns. 1937 was the last year for the J Grade single barrel trap gun. The last 16 and 12 ga. Sterlingworths were built in 1939. The outbreak of the war in 1941 saw the last FE Grade shipped, the Wildfowler Grade dropped, and the introduction of the Model B. 1942 was the last retail catalog. Factory records indicate that the last 12 ga. was shipped in 1945 and the last 20 ga. was shipped during 1946 (SP Grade shipped in December, 1946). However, guns continued to be assembled from left-over parts as late as the 1960s.

FOX SERIAL NUMBER ASSIGNMENTS

The publisher wishes to express his thanks to Mr. John Callahan and Mr. Gurney Brown for providing the model serialization and years of mfg. in this section.

- Ser. # range 1-35,285 - 12 ga. A-F Grades
- Ser. # range 200,000-203,975 - 20 ga., Grades A-F
- Ser. # range 300,000-303,875 - 16 ga., Grades A-F
- Ser. # range 50,000-161,556 - 12 ga. Sterlingworth
- Ser. # range 250,000-271,304 - 20 ga. Sterlingworth
- Ser. # range 300,000-378,481 - 16 ga. Sterlingworth
- Ser. # range 400,000-450,568 - 12 ga. Single Barrel Traps, Grades J,K,L,M

GRADING - PPGS™	100%	98%	95%	90%	80%	70%	60%

FOX MODELS BY YEARS IN MFG.

Sterlingworth - 1910-1942 mfg.
Wildfowler - 1934-1940 mfg.
Trap Double - 1932-1936 mfg.
Skeeter - 1931 mfg.
SP - 1932-1946 mfg.
A - 1906-1942 mfg.
B - 1905-1918 mfg.
C - 1905-1942 mfg.
D - 1907-1942 mfg.
F - 1907-1940 mfg.
G - 1922-1929 mfg.
H - 1923-1942 mfg.
J - 1919-1939 mfg.
K - 1919-1934 mfg.
L - 1919-1934 mfg.
M - 1919-1936 mfg.
X - 1915-1942 mfg.

SHOTGUNS: SxS, CURRENT MFG.

Delivery time for custom orders is currently 10-14 months, depending on gauge and grade.

The following models are manufactured by the Connecticut Manufacturing Co. located in New Britain, CT. These finely made shotguns have the following standard features: automatic safety, auto ejectors, DTs, Chromox 26, 28, or 30 in. barrels, individual barrel chokings, 2 3/4 in. chambers, scalloped receiver, Turkish Circassian walnut with hand-rubbed oil finish, choice of straight, semi-pistol or full-pistol grip stock with custom dimensions, splinter forearm, ivory bead sights. Special order options are as follows: Krupp steel barrels ($200), Fox SST ($1,200), walnut upgrades ($300-$2,200), custom initials ($200-$350), personalized gold inlays on barrel ($500), skeleton steel buttplate ($650), beavertail forearm ($650), and traditional leather trunk case with accessories ($850). Multi-barrel sets (same or multi-gauge) are also available with prices ranging from $4,500-$8,200, depending on the grade.

Add $1,500 for 28 ga. and .410 bore guns on the following models (except Exhibition Grade).

CE GRADE - 16 (new 1995), 20, 28 ga. (new 1995), or .410 bore (new 1995), engraved with fine scroll and game scenes, Grade I Turkish Circassian walnut. New 1993.

	100%	98%	95%	90%	80%	70%	60%
MSR $11,000	$11,000	$8,500	$6,250	$5,250	$4,500	$3,350	$2,700

XE GRADE - gauges similar to CE Grade, scroll work and engraved game scenes, Grade II Turkish Circassian walnut. New 1993.

	100%	98%	95%	90%	80%	70%	60%
MSR $12,500	$12,500	$9,250	$6,500	$5,500	$4,750	$3,500	$3,000

DE GRADE - gauges similar to CE Grade, intricate and extensive engraving, Grade III highly figured Turkish Circassian walnut. New 1993.

	100%	98%	95%	90%	80%	70%	60%
MSR $15,000	$15,000	$11,500	$9,500	$7,750	$6,250	$5,000	$4,000

FE GRADE - gauges similar to CE Grade, gold inlays surrounded by different types of scroll work, Grade IV highly figured Turkish Circassian walnut with finest checkering. New 1993.

	100%	98%	95%	90%	80%	70%	60%
MSR $20,000	$20,000	$16,500	$12,750	$9,750	$8,000	$6,250	$4,750

EXHIBITION GRADE - gauges similar to CE Grade, individually built per customer specifications on a "cost-no-object" basis, includes best-quality leather trunk case with full accessories, Exhibition Grade Turkish Circassian walnut. New 1993.

This model is a special order only, and the base price is $30,000. Please contact the company directly for an individual price quotation and available options.

100%	98%	95%	90%	80%	70%	60%	50%	40%	30%	20%	10%

SHOTGUNS: SxS, DISC.

STERLINGWORTH - 12, 16, or 20 ga., 26, 28, or 30 in. barrels, various chokes, box-lock, extractors, double trigger, checkered pistol grip stock. Mfg. 1905-30.

N/A	$1,475	$1,250	$975	$875	$750	$575	$500	$450	$395	$350	$300

Add 33% for auto ejectors.
Add 50% for 20 ga.
Add 20% for 16 ga.
Add 25% for single trigger.
Ser. no. range on 12 ga. Sterlingworths is 50,000-161,556, 16 ga. is 300,000-378,481, and 20 ga. is 250,000-271,304.

STERLINGWORTH DELUXE - similar to Sterlingworth, with recoil pad and ivory bead, 32 in. barrel available.

N/A	$1,875	$1,475	$1,100	$950	$850	$750	$650	$550	$475	$425	$395

Add 33% for auto ejectors.
Add 50% for 20 ga.
Add 20% for 16 ga.
A single trigger was not an option on this model.

STERLINGWORTH SKEET - similar to Sterlingworth, with 26 or 28 in. skeet boring, straight grip stock.

This model is very scarce (only several are known) and the extreme rarity factor precludes accurate price evaluation.

SUPER HE GRADE - 12 ga., 2 3/4 (very rare) or 3 in. chambered long range gun, 30 and 32 in. full choke, auto ejectors, otherwise similar to Sterlingworth.

N/A	$5,200	$4,800	$4,400	$3,950	$3,400	$2,850	$2,300	$1,900	$1,625	$1,475	$1,300

Add 10% for SST.
Original 3 in. chambered HE grades are marked "not warranted, see instruction tag" on barrel flats. The HE grade was also manufactured in 20 ga. but is extremely rare. 2 3/4 in. chambers are rarer than 3 in. guns in this model.

HIGHER GRADE MODELS (A-F) - the following higher grade Fox shotguns are similar to the Sterlingworth in configuration. The grades differ in engraving and inlays, grade of wood and general workmanship. The E designation means auto ejectors.

Early A and B grades have very little engraving and are much less desirable than later models. The following values are for later guns.
VALUES ARE FOR 12 GA.
Add 50% for 16 ga. (made on same frame as 20 ga.).
Add 75% for 20 ga.
Add $200-$1,000 for SST, depending on grade.
Add $200-$1,000 for beavertail forearm, depending on grade.
Note: These guns were disc. in 1942 by Savage Arms after they mfg. them for 12 years. Pre-1930 guns were made by A.H. Fox Company.

✳ *A Grade*

N/A	$2,175	$1,875	$1,625	$1,375	$1,075	$900	$825	$725	$650	$600	$525

✳ *AE Grade (ejectors)*

N/A	$2,700	$2,400	$2,075	$1,675	$1,400	$1,150	$1,000	$900	$850	$825	$725

✳ *BE Grade (ejectors)*

N/A	N/A	$4,450	$3,950	$3,475	$2,950	$2,500	$2,250	$1,975	$1,800	$1,675	$1,550

This model is rarely encountered.

✳ *CE Grade (ejectors)*

N/A	N/A	$5,200	$4,650	$4,150	$3,750	$3,300	$3,000	$2,700	$2,425	$2,150	$1,875

✳ *XE Grade (ejectors)*

N/A	N/A	$7,350	$6,750	$5,950	$5,225	$4,625	$4,100	$3,650	$3,200	$2,750	$2,400

100%	98%	95%	90%	80%	70%	60%	50%	40%	30%	20%	10%
✳ DE Grade (ejectors)											
N/A	N/A	$11,650	$9,675	$8,750	$7,500	$6,750	$6,000	$5,300	$4,750	$4,300	$3,750
✳ FE Grade (ejectors) - top-of-the-line model, only infrequently encountered.											
N/A	N/A	$19,500	$16,450	$14,150	$12,000	$10,500	$9,750	$9,150	$9,000	$8,750	$8,250

SINGLE BARREL TRAP - 12 ga., 30 or 32 in. vent. rib barrel, full choke, boxlock, auto ejector, checkered trap style stock and recoil pad. The grades differ in wood, engraving, and overall quality. ME grade is custom built and extremely high quality with gold inlays. These models were disc. 1942. 568 single barrel trap guns were mfg. between 1932-42 and have a ser. range of 400,000-400,568, with Monte Carlo stock.

Even though trap guns may be rarer than their SxS counterparts, to date their desirability is less since there are simply fewer collectors.

✳ JE Grade											
N/A	$3,860	$3,550	$3,200	$2,800	$2,500	$2,100	$1,800	$1,600	$1,500	$1,425	$1,325
✳ KE Grade											
N/A	$5,200	$4,650	$4,000	$3,500	$3,200	$2,800	$2,600	$2,400	$2,250	$2,100	$1,975
✳ LE Grade											
N/A	N/A	$6,500	$5,750	$5,000	$4,500	$4,100	$3,750	$3,300	$3,000	$2,650	$2,300
✳ ME Grade											

Extreme rarity factor precludes accurate percentage pricing on this model.

GRADING - PPGS™	100%	98%	95%	90%	80%	70%	60%

MODEL B DOUBLE BARREL - 12, 16, 20 ga., or .410 bore, 24-30 in. barrels, various chokes, vent rib on newer models, boxlock, extractors, double triggers, handcut or pressed checkered pistol grip stock and forearm. Mfg. 1940-86.

	$395	$350	$295	$265	$235	$200	$180

Last MSR was $250.

Add 20% for 20 ga., 35% for .410 bore.

MODEL B-ST - similar to model B, with single trigger. Mfg. 1955-66.

	$500	$425	$350	$315	$290	$260	$230

Add 20% for 20 ga., 35% for .410 bore.

MODEL B-DL - similar to model B-ST, with satin chrome frame, select wood. Mfg. 1962-65.

	$600	$475	$425	$350	$315	$275	$250

Add 20% for 20 ga., 35% for .410 bore.

MODEL B-DE - similar to B-DL, with less checkering. Mfg. 1965-66.

	$550	$450	$400	$325	$300	$275	$250

Add 20% for 20 ga., 35% for .410 bore.

MODEL B-SE - 12, 20 ga., or .410 bore, single trigger, selective ejectors, vent. rib, beavertail forearm, select walnut with press checkering. Mfg. 1966-88.

	$750	$675	$600	$550	$475	$400	$325

Last MSR was $525.

Add 20% for 20 ga., 35% for .410 bore.

Even though there were multiple series designations assigned to this model, there seems to be little difference in desirability. For that reason, other designations will be priced similarly to values shown above.

FRANCHI, LUIGI

Current manufacturer established during the mid-1860s, and located in Brescia, Italy. This trademark has been imported for approx. the past 50 years. Cur-

GRADING - PPGS™	100%	98%	95%	90%	80%	70%	60%

rently imported exclusively by Benelli USA, located in Accokeek, MD, since 1998. Previously imported and distributed by American Arms, Inc. located in North Kansas City, MO. Some models were previously imported by FIE firearms located in Hialeah, FL. Also see Sauer/Franchi heading in the S section.

RIFLES: SEMI-AUTO

CENTENNIAL MODEL - .22 LR cal., 21 in. barrel, open sight to commemorate Franchi's 100th anniversary. Mfg. 1968 only.

	$330	$250	$220	$195	$165	$150	$140

* *Engraved deluxe model*

	$415	$330	$305	$275	$240	$200	$165

* *Gallery model*

	$220	$195	$160	$120	$100	$80	$60

SHOTGUNS: O/U

Currently manufactured Franchi O/U shotguns are supplied with a custom-fitted hard case, and use choke tubes that are compatible with both Beretta and Benelli.

DE LUXE MODEL PRITI - 12 or 20 ga., boxlock action, ST, ejectors, 26 or 28 in. VR barrels with fixed chokes. Imported 1988-89 only.

	$395	$350	$315	$285	$240	$215	$185

Last MSR was $460.

This model was imported exclusively by FIE Firearms located in Hialeah, FL.

ALCIONE MODEL - 12 ga., 28 in. barrels, less engraving than Alcione SL, separated barrels. Importation disc. 1989.

	$675	$550	$495	$460	$430	$380	$335

Last MSR was $800.

Previously designated Diamond Model.
This model was imported exclusively by FIE Firearms located in Hialeah, FL.

ALCIONE SL - 12 ga., 27 or 28 in. barrels, 6 lbs. 13 oz., separated barrels, ejectors, single trigger, silver finished frame engraved with luggage case. Importation disc. 1986.

	$1,150	$995	$875	$800	$725	$640	$550

Last MSR was $1,595.

ALCIONE 2000 SX (FIELD MODEL) - 12 ga., 3 in. chambers, 28 in. barrels, SST, separated barrels, ejectors, single trigger, engraved silver finished frame with gold accents, with case, 7 lbs. 4 oz. Imported 1997 only.

	$1,675	$1,495	$1,275	$1,025	$875	$750	$650

Last MSR was $1,895.

ALCIONE FIELD - 12 ga. only, 3 in. chambers, blue (Classic Field, new 2004), polished steel (silver) alloy frame with game bird etching, SST, ejectors, 26 or 28 in. interchangeable barrels with choke tubes, checkered satin finished walnut stock and forearm, also available in left-hand, 7.4 lbs. New 1998.

MSR $1,310		$1,125	$960	$825	$725	$600	$500	$425

This model was previously designated 97-12 IBS.

Add $90 for Classic Field Model with blue receiver, gold trigger, and Schnabel forearm.

* *Alcione LF* - 12 or 20 ga., 3 in. chambers (20 ga. only), lightweight alloy receiver with etching and gold fill, approx. 6.8 lbs. Mfg. 2000-2002.

	$1,150	$975	$875	$775	$650	$550	$425

Last MSR was $1,305.

GRADING - PPGS™	100%	98%	95%	90%	80%	70%	60%

ALCIONE CLASSIC - 12 ga. only, 3 in. chambers, blue non-engraved reciever, SST, ejectors, 26 or 28 in. VR barrels with choke tubes, checkered satin finished walnut stock and forearm. 7.5 lbs. New 2004.

MSR $1,320	$1,125	$960	$825	$725	$600	$500	$425

Add $475 for extra set of 12 or 20 ga. barrels.

ALCIONE SL SPORT - 12 ga. only, 2 3/4 in. chambers (can also be fitted for barrels with 3 in. chambers), polished stainless steel receiver, blue barrels, SST, manual safety, ejectors, 30 in. target rib ported barrels with choke tubes, detachable side-plates, available in left-hand, 7.7 lbs.

MSR $1,700	$1,435	$1,200	$950	$850	$725	$625	$475

This model was previously designated SL IBS.

ALCIONE SP - 12 ga. only, 3 in. chambers, satin silver finished boxlock action with engraved sideplates including mallard and pheasant gold inlays, gloss finished AA Grade checkered walnut pistol grip stock and Schnabel forearm, 28 in. VR barrels with choke tubes, 20 ga. barrels can be ordered w/o additional gunsmithing, 7.5 lbs. Importation began 2003.

MSR $2,780	$2,325	$2,000	$1,750	$1,500	$1,275	$1,100	$975

Add $490 for extra set of 20 ga. barrels.

ALCIONE SX - 12 ga. only, 3 in. chambers, 26 or 28 in. interchangeable vent. barrels with VR and 3 choke tubes, deluxe walnut, removeable sideplates with etched game scenes, gold trigger, approx. 7.4 lbs. Importation began 2001.

MSR $1,855	$1,535	$1,350	$1,050	$925	$800	$700	$575

Add $490 for extra set of barrels.

Add $125 for Alcione Classic SX with blued receiver (new 2004).

ALCIONE TITANIUM (T) - 12 or 20 ga., 3 in. chambers, features receiver manufactured from aluminum alloy coupled with titanium inserts, 26 or 28 in. interchangeable vent. barrels with VR and 3 choke tubes, deluxe walnut, removable sideplates with etched game scenes, gold trigger with selector switch, approx. 6.8 lbs. Importation began 2002.

MSR $1,470	$1,260	$1,050	$950	$875	$800	$750	$695

Add $460 for 2 barrel set (includes extra 20 ga. barrels).

VELOCE - 20 or 28 ga., 3 in. chambers on 20 ga., 26 or 28 (20 ga. only) in. vent. barrels with 3 choke tubes, aluminum frame with steel reinforcement, etched game scene receiver with gold filled inlays, skeletonized opening lever, deluxe oil finished checkered pistol grip or English (new 2002) stock and forearm, mechanical gold SST, 5.5 (28 ga.) or 5.8 (20 ga.) lbs. Importation began 2001.

MSR $1,470	$1,260	$1,050	$950	$875	$800	$750	$695

Add $75 for 28 ga.

✳ *Veloce Grade II* - similar to Veloce Model, except has semi-pistol grip deluxe walnut stock. Limited importation 2004 only.

	$1,750	$1,500	$1,250	$1,050	$925	$825	$725

Last MSR was $2,000.

Add $75 for 28 ga.

✳ *Veloce Squire Limited Edition* - includes one set of 26 in. 20 ga. and one set of 26 in. 28 ga. barrels, cased, 5.7 lbs. Importation began 2003.

MSR $2,470	$2,050	$1,750	$1,450	$1,125	$975	$875	$775

BLACK MAGIC SPORTING HUNTER - 12 ga. only, 3 in. chambers, 28 in. separated barrels with VR and Franchokes, black frame with gold accents and trigger, SST, ejectors, checkered walnut stock and forearm, 7 lbs. Imported 1989-91.

	$995	$875	$800	$725	$650	$575	$495

Last MSR was $1,249.

The Black Magic Model Series was imported exclusively by American Arms, Inc. located in North Kansas City, MO.

GRADING - PPGS™	100%	98%	95%	90%	80%	70%	60%

✳ Black Magic Lightweight Hunter - similar to Black Magic Sporting Hunter except 2 3/4 in. chambers only, 26 in. separated barrels with VR and Franchokes, alloy frame, 6 lbs. Imported 1989-91.

	$975	$850	$775	$700	$625	$550	$475

Last MSR was $1,209.

SPORTING 2000 - 12 ga. only, design for sporting clays or hunting, 28 in. vent. ported (disc. 1993) or unported (new 1997) barrels with target VR and choke tubes, SST, ejectors, select walnut with checkering, solid pad, hard case, 7 3/4 lbs. Imported 1992-1993, resumed 1997, disc. 1998.

	$1,275	$1,025	$875	$750	$650	$575	$500

Last MSR was $1,495.

ARISTOCRAT FIELD - 12 ga., 26, 28, or 30 in. barrels, various chokes, vent. rib, auto ejectors, boxlock, selective single trigger, checkered pistol grip stock. Mfg. 1960-69.

	$660	$470	$440	$395	$375	$340	$310

ARISTOCRAT MAGNUM - similar to Field, except 32 in. barrel, 3 in. chamber, full choke, pad. Mfg. 1962-65.

	$660	$470	$440	$395	$375	$340	$310

ARISTOCRAT SKEET - similar to Field, but 26 in. vent. rib, bored skeet no. 1 and no. 2. Mfg. 1960-69.

	$715	$525	$495	$450	$430	$395	$365

ARISTOCRAT TRAP - 30 in. vent. rib barrel, bored mod. and full, trap stock Mfg. 1960-69.

	$745	$550	$525	$480	$455	$415	$380

ARISTOCRAT SILVER KING - select wood, engraved coin finished frame. Mfg. 1962-69.

	$750	$560	$535	$485	$470	$430	$400

ARISTOCRAT DELUXE - finer wood, more engraving. Mfg. 1960-66.

	$990	$870	$835	$810	$770	$715	$660

ARISTOCRAT SUPREME - gold inlaid game birds. Mfg. 1960-66.

	$1,430	$1,265	$1,155	$1,075	$990	$935	$880

ARISTOCRAT IMPERIAL - high grade wood, more engraving. Mfg. 1967-69.

	$2,640	$2,200	$2,090	$1,925	$1,815	$1,650	$1,430

ARISTOCRAT MONTE CARLO - highest grade wood, elaborate engraving and inlay, mfg. 1967-69.

	$3,520	$3,080	$2,915	$2,640	$2,420	$2,090	$1,870

FALCONET S - 12 ga., lightweight model of the Alcione SL, 27 or 28 in. barrels, 6 lbs. 1 oz., separated barrels, moderate engraving on silver finish frame. Disc. 1985.

	$895	$765	$660	$560	$510	$460	$410

Last MSR was $1,015.

FALCONET FIELD - 12, 16, 20, 28 ga., or .410 bore, 24-30 in. barrels, various chokes, auto ejectors, select single trigger, engraved alloy frame, checkered walnut stock. Mfg. 1968-75.

	100%	98%	95%	90%	80%	70%	60%
Buckskin (light)	$550	$495	$470	$440	$415	$385	$360
Ebony (black)	$550	$495	$470	$440	$415	$385	$360
Silver	$605	$550	$525	$495	$470	$415	$385

Add 25% for 28 ga. or .410 bore.

GRADING - PPGS™	100%	98%	95%	90%	80%	70%	60%

FALCONET SKEET - 26 in. barrels, bored skeet no. 1 and no. 2, wide vent. rib, case hardened steel frame. Mfg. 1970-74.

	$935	$855	$825	$770	$715	$690	$650

FALCONET INTERNATIONAL SKEET - higher grade wood, more engraving. Mfg. 1970-74.

	$1,045	$935	$865	$825	$770	$745	$700

FALCONET STANDARD TRAP - 12 ga., 30 in. mod. and full, wide vent. rib, trap stock, pad. Mfg. 1970-74.

	$935	$855	$825	$770	$715	$690	$650

FALCONET INTERNATIONAL TRAP - higher grade wood, more engraving. Mfg. 1970-74.

	$1,045	$935	$865	$825	$770	$745	$700

FALCONET 2000 - 12 ga. only, boxlock with alloy frame featuring silver finish with gold plated game scenes, 26 in. separated barrels with VR and choke tubes, SST, ejectors, select checkered walnut stock and forearm, hard case, 6 lbs. Imported 1992-97.

	$1,245	$975	$850	$725	$650	$575	$500

Last MSR was $1,375.

FALCONET 97-12 IBS - 12 ga. only, 2 3/4 in. chambers, ultra light alloy frame with gold inlays, scroll engraving, and nickel finish, SST, ejectors, 26 in. barrels with Franchokes, checkered walnut stock and forearm, includes hard case. Imported 1998-2000.

	$875	$750	$625	$550	$500	$450	$400

Last MSR was $965.

PEREGRINE MODEL 451 - 12 ga., 26-28 in. barrels, various chokes, vent. rib, auto ejectors, alloy frame, selective single trigger, checkered pistol grip stock. Mfg. 1975.

	$605	$550	$525	$495	$440	$415	$360

PEREGRINE MODEL 400 - similar to 451, except steel frame. Mfg. 1975.

	$660	$605	$570	$540	$495	$460	$385

MODEL 2003 TRAP - 12 ga., 30 or 32 in. barrels, imp. mod. and full, or full and full, boxlock, auto ejectors, single selective trigger, high vent. rib, trap style stock, pad, cased. Mfg. 1976. Disc.

	$1,205	$1,090	$1,045	$910	$855	$770	$660

MODEL 2004 TRAP - similar to 2003, except single barrel, cased. Mfg. 1976. Disc.

	$1,205	$1,090	$1,045	$910	$855	$770	$660

MODEL 2005 COMBINATION TRAP - two sets of barrels, one single, one O/U, cased. Mfg. 1976. Disc.

	$1,815	$1,595	$1,515	$1,320	$1,210	$1,075	$935

MODEL 2005/3 COMBINATION TRAP - three sets of barrels, cased. Mfg. 1976. Disc.

	$2,420	$2,090	$1,980	$1,705	$1,515	$1,485	$1,320

UNDERGUN MODEL 3000 - radical competition trap, very high rib separated barrels, under single and O/U, drop in set screw chokes (hex drive), set aluminum cased. Disc.

	$2,750	$2,530	$2,310	$2,090	$1,980	$1,870	$1,760

SHOTGUNS: SxS

AIRONE - 12 ga., choice of barrel length and chokes, box lock, Anson & Deeley, auto ejectors, double triggers, checkered English style stock, engraved. Mfg. 1940-50.

	$1,320	$1,100	$935	$825	$745	$715	$660

GRADING - PPGS™	100%	98%	95%	90%	80%	70%	60%

ASTORE - similar to Airone, except less engraving, extractors. Mfg. 1937-60.

	100%	98%	95%	90%	80%	70%	60%
	$990	$910	$770	$715	$635	$580	$550

ASTORE 5 - similar to Astore, except higher grade wood, more engraving, auto ejectors. Disc.

	$2,200	$1,925	$1,650	$1,540	$1,460	$1,375	$1,320

ASTORE II - similar to Astore 5, except less elaborate, currently mfg. in Spain for Franchi.

	$1,210	$1,045	$935	$880	$800	$715	$660

HIGHLANDER - 12, 20, or 28 ga., 3 in. chambers except for 28 ga., English style straight grip walnut stock and splinter forearm, scalloped coin finished boxlock receiver, SST, extractors, 26 in. barrels with fixed chokes, includes fitted hardcase, 5.7-6.4 lbs. Limited importation 2003.

	$1,575	$1,275	$1,075	$950	$825	$700	$600

Last MSR was $1,800.

SIDELOCK DOUBLE BARREL - 12, 16, or 20 ga., barrels and choke custom order, stock to order, hand detachable side lock, self-opening action, auto ejectors, six grades offered, they differ only in overall quality and ornamentation, and grade of wood used.

	100%	98%	95%	90%	80%	70%	60%
Condor	$7,700	$6,600	$6,050	$5,720	$5,500	$4,620	$3,960
Imperial	$10,450	$9,350	$8,800	$8,250	$7,480	$6,600	$5,720
Imperiales	$10,670	$9,570	$9,020	$8,470	$7,700	$6,820	$5,940

SIDE-LOCK DOUBLE BARREL - the following models are available through the Beretta Galleries and selected premium dealers only (see Trademark Index).

✴ *No. 5 Imperial Monte Carlo*

MSR $27,500	N/A	$13,750	$11,000	$9,900	$8,900	$7,750	$6,500

✴ *No. 17 Imperial Monte Carlo*

MSR $35,000	N/A	$15,250	$12,500	$10,500	$9,350	$8,000	$7,000

✴ *Imperial Monte Carlo Extra*

Note: Imperial Monte Carlo Extra is currently being mfg. on special order only. Prices range from $53,000-$90,000.

SHOTGUNS: SEMI-AUTO

BLACK MAGIC GAME - 12 ga. only, 3 in. chamber with gas metering system, interchangeable shell handling without adjustments, two-tone black alloy receiver with gold accents and trigger, 24, 26, or 28 in. VR barrel with Franchokes, checkered walnut stock and forearm, 7 lbs. Imported 1989-91.

	$550	$450	$395	$330	$300	$270	$240

Last MSR was $659.

✴ *Black Magic Skeet* - skeet variation of the Black Magic Game, 2 3/4 in. chamber, 26 in. ported VR barrel with fixed Tula skeet choke, skeet dimensioned stock, 7 1/4 lbs. Imported 1989-91.

	$580	$475	$425	$350	$325	$295	$265

Last MSR was $699.

✴ *Black Magic Trap* - trap variation of the Black Magic Game, 2 3/4 in. chamber, 30 in. VR barrel with Franchoke system, trap dimensioned stock, 7 1/2 lbs. Imported 1989-91.

	$615	$495	$430	$350	$325	$295	$265

Last MSR was $739.

GRADING - PPGS™	100%	98%	95%	90%	80%	70%	60%

48 AL FIELD MODEL - 12 (disc. 2001), 20, or 28 (new 1996) ga., 2 3/4 in. chamber, 24, 26, 28, or 30 (disc. in 1990) in. VR barrel with (beginning 1989) or w/o choke tubes, long recoil operation, alloy receiver, checkered pistol grip walnut stock and forearm, VR standard, standard choke tubes became available in 1989, 12 ga., 6 lbs. 9 oz. and 20 ga., 5 lbs. 6 oz. Mfg. 1950-present.

	MSR $735	$600	$550	$450	$350	$300	$265	$235

    Add $115 for 28 ga.

    Add $30 for 12 ga. 24 in. slug barrel (disc. 1994).

    Subtract 10% if without choke tubes.

    This model is also available as a Youth Model (12 1/2 LOP, 20 ga. only). Starting in 1990, black receiver, gold accents, and choke tubes became standard.

✴ *48 AL Deluxe* - 20 or 28 ga., 26 in. barrel, similar to AL 48 Field, except has a high polish blue finish and upgraded walnut pistol grip or English (new 2002) stock and forearm, gold trigger and receiver accents, approx. 5.5 lbs. New 2000.

	MSR $970	$795	$650	$550	$425	$350	$300	$265

    Add $50 for 28 ga.

STANDARD MAGNUM (48/AL) - similar to Standard, except has 3 in. chamber with 28 in. (disc. 1988) or 32 in. VR barrel, recoil pad. Mfg. 1954-90.

	$415	$360	$300	$270	$250	$230	$210
							Last MSR was $482.

    This model was slated to be replaced with the Combo S/T - however, while advertised, the Combo S/T was never mfg.

HUNTER MODEL (48/AL) - similar to Standard, except etched receiver, better wood, VR standard, Franchokes became available in 1989. Mfg. 1950-90.

	$415	$360	$300	$270	$250	$230	$210
							Last MSR was $482.

    Add $35 for internal Franchokes (3).

    This model was imported exclusively by FIE Firearms located in Hialeah, FL.

HUNTER MAGNUM - mfg. 1954-73.

	$430	$380	$370	$340	$315	$290	$275

PRESTIGE MODEL - 12 ga. only, gas operated, vent. rib, various barrel lengths, alloy receiver, Franchokes became available in 1989. Imported 1985-89.

	$575	$475	$395	$325	$310	$295	$275
							Last MSR was $720.

    Add $40 for internal Franchokes (3).

    This model was imported exclusively by FIE Firearms located in Hialeah, FL.

✴ *Turkey Model* - similar to Prestige Model except has dull matte black finish, Franchokes standard. Imported 1989 only.

	$615	$515	$425	$350	$320	$300	$280
							Last MSR was $760.

    This model was imported exclusively by FIE Firearms located in Hialeah, FL.

ELITE MODEL - same general specifications as the Prestige Model, only etched receiver, Franchokes became available in 1989. Imported 1985-89.

	$595	$500	$425	$350	$320	$300	$280
							Last MSR was $740.

    Add $45 for internal Franchokes (3).

    This model was imported exclusively by FIE Firearms located in Hialeah, FL.

GRADING - PPGS™	100%	98%	95%	90%	80%	70%	60%

MODEL 610 VS - 12 ga., incorporates gas-operated Variopress System, adjusts for both 2 3/4 and 3 in. shells, 4 lug rotating breech bolt, alloy receiver, non-glare finish, 26 or 28 in. VR barrels with Franchokes, checkered walnut stock and forearm. Imported 1997 only.

	$650	$550	$425	$325	$275	$250	$225

Last MSR was $750.

Add $45 for engraved receiver and bolt (Model 610 VSL).

MODEL 612/620 (VS) - 12 (Model 612) or 20 (Model 620) ga., 3 in. chamber, features VarioSystem/Variomax gas operation utilizing reversible gas adjustment collar on mag. tube, advanced safety system, black receiver with (disc. 2001) or w/o gold borders (new 2002), 24, 26, or 28 in. barrel with choke tubes, last shot hold open, choice of checkered satin walnut, black synthetic (not available in 20 ga.) stock and forearm, 100% Realtree X-tra brown (disc. 1999), Realtree HD Timber (new 2002), Max-4 HD (new 2004, not available in 20 ga.), or Advantage (mfg. 2000-2002) camo coverage, 5.9-7 lbs. New 1998-2004.

	$550	$475	$415	$350	$325	$300	$275

Last MSR was $660.

Add $15 for satin finished walnut stock and forearm.
Add $105 for 100% camo coverage (Models 612/620 VS Camo).
Add $15 for 20 ga. or for Youth Model (20 ga. only, 12 1/2 LOP stock).
This model was previously designated the Variopress 612/620.

* *Model 612 Sporting* - 12 ga. only, features blue receiver with gold logo (new 2002), or silver receiver with black border and gold small parts (disc. 1998), matte black receiver with green logo (mfg. 2000-2002), or matte black top/polish sides receiver with gold lettering (new 2003), 28 (disc. 1998) or 30 (new 2000) in. ported target rib barrel with extended 4 in. forcing cone and elongated Franchokes, select checkered walnut stock and forearm, 7.1 lbs. Limited mfg. 1998, reintroduced 2000-2004.

	$825	$750	$625	$525	$450	$375	$325

Last MSR was $975.

This model was previously designated the Variopress 612 Sporting.

MODEL 612 DEFENSE - 12 ga. only, 18 1/2 in. barrel with cyl. bore, matte finish metal with black synthetic stock and forearm, 6 1/2 lbs. Imported 2000-2002.

	$525	$450	$375	$325	$285	$265	$245

Last MSR was $635.

This model was previously designated the Variopress 612 Defense.

MODEL 712 - 12 ga. only, 3 in. chamber, Benelli inertia recoil system with rotating bolt head, aluminum receiver, 24, 26, or 28 in. VR barrel, 5 shot mag., choice of synthetic, Weathercoat walnut, or 100% Advantage Timber HD or Max-4 HD camo coverage, recoil pad, approx. 7 lbs. Limited importation 2004 only.

	$650	$575	$500	$450	$375	$325	$275

Last MSR was $750.

Add $65 for walnut stock and forearm with Weathercoating.
Add $105 for camo finish.

* *Model 712 Raptor* - features 30 in. ported VR barrels with extended choke tubes, satin nickel receiver with green Franchi logo insert on right side, checkered Weathercoat pistol grip stock with recoil pad, blue finish, 5 shot mag., Benelli rotary bolt design, approx. 7 lbs. New 2005.

MSR $850	$725	$640	$525	$475	$395	$350	$325

MODEL 720 - 20 ga. only, 3 in. chamber, similar to Model 712, except is not available with synthetic stock, also available with short LOP, approx. 6 lbs. New 2004.

MSR $700	$575	$500	$425	$350	$325	$300	$275

Add $90 for 100% camo finish.

GRADING - PPGS™	100%	98%	95%	90%	80%	70%	60%

❋ *Model 720 Raptor* - features 28 in. barrels with Weathercoat stock, blue finish, 5 shot mag. New 2005.

MSR $850	$725	$640	$525	$475	$395	$350	$325

MODEL 912

12 ga. only, 3 1/2 chamber, VarioSystem/Variomax gas operation utilizing reversible gas adjustment collar on mag. tube, lightweight alloy receiver, 24, 26, 28, or 30 in. VR barrel with 3 choke tubes, choice of satin walnut stock (new 2002), black synthetic or 100% Advantage Timber HD or Max-4 HD (new 2004) camo coverage, magazine cutoff, includes hard case, 7.5-7.8 lbs. Importation began 2001.

MSR $790	$665	$575	$500	$450	$375	$325	$275

Add $110 for camo coverage.

Add $60 for satin finished walnut stock and forearm.

Add $60 for Model 912 steady-grip with 24 in. barrel and 100% Timber HD camo coverage.

This model was previously designated the Variopress 912.

MODEL I-12

12 ga. only, 3 in. chamber, 24, 26, or 28 in. VR barrel, inertia operating system with free floating bolt which compresses an inertia spring upon recoil, choice of synthetic or satin walnut stock and forearm, blued, matte blue, Max-4 HD or Timber HD camo coverage. New 2005.

MSR $660	$550	$475	$415	$350	$325	$300	$275

Add $70 for 100% camo coverage.

Add $100 for walnut stock and forearm.

SPAS-12

12 ga., 2 3/4 in. chamber, combat shotgun that offers pump or semi-auto operation, 5 (new 1991) or 8 (disc.) shot tube mag., alloy receiver, synthetic stock with built-in pistol grip (limited quantities were also mfg. with a folding stock or metal fixed stock), one-button switch to change from semi-auto to slide action operation, 21.5 in. barrel, 8.75 lbs. Importation disc. 1994.

	$675	$575	$475	$400	$350	$300	$280

Last MSR was $769.

This model was imported exclusively by FIE Firearms located in Hialeah, FL until 1990.

SPAS-15

12 ga. only, 2 3/4 in. chamber, operates as either semi-auto or slide action that is convertible with a one-button switch, 6 shot detachable box mag., 21.5 in. barrel, lateral folding skeleton stock, carrying handle, 10 lbs. Limited importation 1989 only.

This model had very limited importation (less than 200) as the BATF disallowed further importation almost immediately. Even though the retail was in the $700 range, demand and rarity have pushed prices past the $2,000 level.

SAS-12

12 ga. only, 3 in. chamber, slide action only, synthetic stock with built-in pistol grip, 8 shot tube mag., 21 1/2 in. barrel, 6.8 lbs. Imported 1988-90 only.

	$415	$360	$300	$270	$250	$230	$210

Last MSR was $473.

This model was imported exclusively by FIE Firearms located in Hialeah, FL.

LAW-12

12 ga. only, 2 3/4 in. chamber, gas operated semi-auto, synthetic stock with built-in pistol grip, 5 (new 1991) or 8 (disc.) shot tube mag., 21 1/2 in. barrel, 6 3/4 lbs. Imported 1988-94.

	$570	$485	$400	$360	$320	$300	$280

Last MSR was $719.

TURKEY GUN

12 ga., similar to Standard Mag., 3 in. chamber only, turkey scene engraved. Mfg. 1963-65.

	$415	$385	$370	$340	$315	$290	$275

SLUG GUN

22 in. plain barrel, and rifle sights.

	$360	$330	$315	$295	$275	$255	$240

GRADING - PPGS™	100%	98%	95%	90%	80%	70%	60%

SKEET GUN - 26 in. skeet choke, vent. rib, select wood. Mfg. 1972-74.

	$385	$370	$350	$330	$310	$285	$265

ELDORADO - fancy wood and gold filled engraved receiver. Mfg. 1954-75.

	$450	$420	$395	$380	$360	$340	$320

CROWN GRADE - engraved hunting scene. Mfg. 1954-75.

	$1,540	$1,320	$1,210	$1,045	$965	$910	$855

DIAMOND GRADE SILVER INLAID SCROLL - mfg. 1954-75.

	$1,980	$1,735	$1,540	$1,430	$1,210	$1,045	$965

IMPERIAL GRADE - gold inlaid hunting scene.

	$2,420	$2,090	$1,925	$1,760	$1,595	$1,485	$1,320

Note: Standard, Skeet and Slug with steel frame mfg. 1965-1972, designated "Dynamic" 12 ga., values are the same.

MODEL 500 STANDARD - 12 ga., 26 or 28 in. barrel, various chokes, vent. rib, gas operated, checkered pistol grip stock. Mfg. 1976-disc.

	$330	$310	$305	$265	$230	$195	$165

MODEL 520 DELUXE - engraved receiver.

	$385	$365	$330	$290	$260	$220	$195

MODEL 520 ELDORADO GOLD - fine wood, engraved gold, inlaid receiver. Mfg. 1977-disc.

	$990	$770	$715	$660	$580	$525	$470

MODEL 530 AUTO TRAP - similar to 500, except 30 or 32 in. full choke barrels, very high rib, special trap stock, pad.

	$660	$550	$525	$440	$415	$385	$330

FRANCOTTE, AUGUSTE & CIE. S.A.

Previous manufacturer located in Leige, Belgium 1805-2002. Previously imported until 1999 by Armes De Chasse located in Hertford, NC, VL&D between 1900-1930s, and Abercrombie & Fitch until approx. 1962.

It is important to note that original A. Francotte SxS rifles and shotguns should exhibit the "crown over AF" maker's mark amongst the proofmarks.

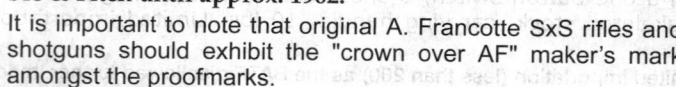

REVOLVERS

Francotte manufactured Pryse-type revolvers at the end of the 19th century, and these revolvers bore the name of the well-known British retailer. Encountered only infrequently domestically, these specimens found overseas are usually priced in the $150-$650 range.

RIFLES

All recently mfg. rifles in this section were custom made to the purchaser's individual specifications. Francotte took advantage of 5 different frame sizes for its double rifles.

BOLT ACTION MODEL - many calibers between .18 Bee and .505 Gibbs Mag., select checkered walnut stock, engraved mag. floor plate, gold inlays optional, the following values assume engraving.

* *Short Bolt Action* - cals. with shorter cartridges.

	$9,400	$7,350	$6,000	$4,950	$4,100	$3,300	$2,700

Subtract $3,250 if without engraving.

* *Standard Model* - cals. with medium cartridge lengths.

	$7,825	$6,100	$4,975	$4,100	$3,300	$2,700	$2,000

Subtract $2,675 if without engraving.

GRADING - PPGS™	100%	98%	95%	90%	80%	70%	60%

* *Magnum Action* - cals. with longer cartridge lengths.

	100%	98%	95%	90%	80%	70%	60%
	$13,750	$10,850	$9,350	$7,750	$6,400	$4,950	$3,950

Subtract $7,850 if without engraving.

SINGLE SHOT MOUNTAIN RIFLE - variety of cals., boxlock or sidelock action, custom order only.

* *Boxlock Mountain Rifle* - 6.5x50R, 7x57R, or 7x65R cal.

	100%	98%	95%	90%	80%	70%	60%
	$13,900	$11,000	$9,450	$7,850	$6,500	$5,000	$4,000

Subtract $4,800 if without engraving.
Add 10% for optional sideplates.

* *Sidelock Mountain Rifle* - 7x65R or 7mm Rem. Mag. cal.

	100%	98%	95%	90%	80%	70%	60%
	$24,800	$20,350	$16,650	$13,000	$10,500	$9,000	$8,000

BOXLOCK SxS RIFLE - .30-06, .375 H&H, .470 NE, .500-3 in. or 9.3x62mm cal., ejectors, case colored frame with border engraving (including screws), quarter rib on barrel, deluxe checkered pistol grip walnut stock and forearm. Mfg. 1997-disc.

	100%	98%	95%	90%	80%	70%	60%
	$11,850	$9,700	$8,500	$7,250	$6,000	$4,950	$4,100

SIDELOCK SxS RIFLE - .30-06, .375 H&H, .470 NE, .500-3 in. or 9.3x62mm cal., ejectors, case colored frame with border engraving (including screws), quarter rib on barrel, deluxe checkered pistol grip walnut stock and forearm. Mfg. 1997-disc.

	100%	98%	95%	90%	80%	70%	60%
	$16,250	$14,250	$12,500	$10,250	$8,750	$7,250	$6,500

Add 50% for .375 H&H cal.

STANDARD SxS BOXLOCK RIFLE - variety of cals., custom order only.

	100%	98%	95%	90%	80%	70%	60%
	$18,650	$15,500	$11,350	$8,750	$6,950	$5,750	$5,000

Subtract $7,600 if without engraving.
Add $1,449 for optional sideplates.
Add 15% for .375 H&H, .458 Win. Mag. cal., or other larger calibers upon request.

STANDARD SxS SIDELOCK RIFLE - variety of cals., custom order only.

	100%	98%	95%	90%	80%	70%	60%
	$29,450	$25,000	$20,250	$16,500	$13,000	$10,500	$9,000

Subtract $7,000 if without engraving.

SHOTGUNS: SxS

All recently manufactured shotguns in this section were custom made to purchaser's individual specifications. Basic types listed were also available in 24 or 32 ga. upon special order. Francotte took advantage of 5 different action sizes, one for each gauge. Auguste Francotte did not manufacture guns by model - all guns were custom order.

Original A. Francotte SxS shotguns must have the "Francotte Choke Bore" marking on the water table. Be wary of fake barrel and frame markings, as some guns have recenty surfaced that are not Francotte, but have the Francotte name.

Add 10% for 20 ga. or 15% for 28 ga. or .410 bore.

BOXLOCK MODEL - 12, 16, 20, 28 ga., or .410 bore, premium grade Belgium side-by-side, double triggers standard, auto ejectors, English scroll engraving, Anson & Deeley boxlock action.

	100%	98%	95%	90%	80%	70%	60%
	$15,450	$11,250	$8,000	$6,250	$5,000	$4,000	$3,250

Subtract $5,925 if without engraving.
Add $1,159 for sideplates with engraving.

* *Deluxe Anson & Deeley* - gold inlaid game scenes, and engraving was by customer's personal preference.

SIDELOCK MODEL - 12, 16, 20, 28 ga., or .410 bore, true sidelock action, Arabesque scroll engraving, various chokes and barrel lengths, custom order only.

	100%	98%	95%	90%	80%	70%	60%
	$27,300	$22,000	$18,750	$15,150	$12,000	$9,000	$7,750

Subtract $4,850 if without engraving.

GRADING - PPGS™	100%	98%	95%	90%	80%	70%	60%

✱ Deluxe Sidelock - gold inlaid game scenes and engraving are by customer's personal preference.

JUBILEE MODEL - case colored frame with hand engraving, VL&D or A&F manufacture. Mfg. circa 1920-1970.

	100%	98%	95%	90%	80%	70%	60%
	$2,250	$1,875	$1,525	$1,325	$1,100	$975	$850
No. 14	$2,750	$2,250	$1,975	$1,775	$1,600	$1,450	$1,150
No. 18	$2,950	$2,550	$2,250	$1,925	$1,700	$1,550	$1,225
No. 20	$3,450	$2,900	$2,575	$2,275	$1,900	$1,725	$1,375
No. 25	$4,000	$3,500	$3,000	$2,500	$2,150	$1,925	$1,575
No. 30	$5,450	$4,975	$4,500	$4,000	$3,500	$2,500	$2,200

KNOCKABOUT MODEL - disc. circa 1975.

	100%	98%	95%	90%	80%	70%	60%
	$2,350	$1,850	$1,575	$1,265	$1,100	$935	$825

Add 75% for 20 ga.
Add approx. 200%-250% for 28 ga. or .410 bore.

NO. 45 EAGLE GRADE MODEL - this model can be identified by the gold eagle on frame bottom, disc. circa 1977.

	100%	98%	95%	90%	80%	70%	60%
	$7,650	$6,700	$5,850	$4,950	$4,250	$3,800	$3,000

FRASER, DANL. & CO.

Current trademark owned by Dickson & MacNaughton located in Edinburgh, Scotland. Previously imported and distributed by Flying G Ranch, located in Carrizo Springs, TX.

Danl. Fraser & Co. has manufactured rifles since 1873 (originally located in Edinburgh, Scotland).

RIFLES: SINGLE SHOT

HIGHLANDER SINGLE SHOT - .22 LR or .22 Hornet cal., underlever falling block action (color case hardened), 24 in. (1/2 round, 1/2 octagon) barrel, folding express-style sights, pistol grip walnut stock with fine checkering. Disc.

$415	$335	$300	$280	$260	$240	$220

Last MSR was $475.

✱ Royal Highlander - .22 LR or .22 Hornet cal., mfg. in Scotland, rose and scroll engraving with 18Kt. inlays. Special order only.

FRASER FIREARMS CORP.

Previously manufactured by R.B. Industries, Ltd. until 1990. Previously distributed by Fraser Firearms Corp. located in Fraser, MI.

PISTOLS: SEMI-AUTO

FRASER 25 CAL. - .25 ACP cal. only, copy of the Bauer semi-auto pocket model, 6 shot mag., 2 1/4 in. barrel, stainless steel construction.

$120	$100	$90

Last MSR was $133.

Add $17 for Model 2 (black nylon grips).
Add $115 for Model 3 (24 Kt. gold plated).

FREEDOM ARMS

Current manufacturer established during 1983, and located in Freedom, WY. Distributor and dealer sales.

REVOLVERS: MINI, STAINLESS STEEL

Because Freedom Arms' manufacturing capacity has been maximized due to the success of the .454 Casull revolver, the mini-revolver series was discontinued beginning 1989.

FA-S-22LR (PATRIOT) - .22 LR cal., 5 shot, 1, 1 3/4 (disc. 1988), or 3 (disc. 1988) in. barrel, Hi-Gloss finish. Disc. 1989.

	$175	$135	$100

Last MSR was $153.

Add $15 for 3 in. barrel model (FA-BG-22LR, Minute-Man, disc. 1988).

FA-S-22M (IRONSIDES) - .22 Mag. cal., 4 shot, 1, 1 3/4 (disc. 1988), or 3 in. barrel, Hi Gloss finish. Disc. 1989.

	$200	$150	$110

Last MSR was $177.

Add $43 for 3 in. barrel model (Bostonian).

FA-S-22-LR BUCKLE/REVOLVER COMBINATION - .22 LR cal., 1 in. barrel, pistol is housed in belt buckle. Disc. 1989.

	$295	$225	$185

Last MSR was $193.

✳ **.22 Mag. cal.**

	$350	$250	$200

Last MSR was $216.

REVOLVERS: SA, STAINLESS STEEL

Freedom Arms also offers a complete line of accessories and factory installed options. The factory should be contacted directly for an up-to-date listing and prices. Beginning in 1999, all revolvers are equipped with a locking safety device which slides into the muzzle and locks into the chamber under the firing pin, making it impossible to either load the top chamber or turn the cylinder.

Add $272 per interchangeable cylinder in different cals. on most of the following centerfire models.

Add $144 for 4 port Mag-na-ported barrel.

Add $109 for 2 port Mag-na-ported barrel.

Add $468 for octagon barrel.

Add $78 for non-standard barrel length.

MODEL 83 FIELD GRADE - .22 LR, .357 Mag., .41 Mag., .44 Mag., .45 LC (disc. 1990), .454 Casull, .475 Linebaugh, or .50 AE (disc. 2004) cal., 5 shot, 4 3/4, 6, 7 1/2, 9 (.357 Mag. only), or 10 in. barrel, fixed or aluminum base adj. rear sight with replaceable blade front sight, matte stainless steel construction, manual sliding-bar safety system, Pachmayr presentation grips, 56 oz. (.454 Casull cal. with 7 1/2 in. barrel). New 1988.

MSR $1,573	$1,355	$1,025	$775

Add $66 for .454 Casull, .475 Linebaugh, or .50 AE cal.

Add $26 for .454 Casull cal. with fixed sight.

Add $230 for .22 LR cal. with match chamber and 10 in. barrel.

GRADING - PPGS™	100%	98%	95%	90%	80%	70%	60%

MODEL 83 HUNTER PAK FIELD GRADE

- .357 Mag., .44 Rem. Mag., or .454 Casull cal., 7 1/2 in. barrel, plastic grips, field grade low profile adj. sight or no front sight base, sling and studs, locking aluminum carrying case with cleaning kit and tool. Mfg. 1990-93.

           $1,075   **$925**   **$775**

Last MSR was $1,333.

Add $76 for low profile adj. sight and Pachmayr grips.

✳ *Model 83 Hunter Pak Premier Grade* - .357 Mag., .44 Rem. Mag., or .454 Casull cal., 7 1/2 in. barrel, ebony micarta grips, no sights or premier grade adj. sight, sling and studs, locking aluminum carrying case with cleaning kit and tool. Mfg. 1990-93.

           $1,395   **$1,025**   **$850**

Last MSR was $1,611.

Add $100 for adj. sights.

MODEL 83 PREMIER GRADE

- .357 Mag., .41 Mag., .44 Mag., .454 Casull, .475 Linebaugh, or .50 AE cal., 5 shot, 4 3/4, 6, 7 1/2, 9 (.357 Mag. only) or 10 in. barrel, fixed or steel base adj. rear sight and replaceable blade front sight, stainless steel construction, bright brushed finish, manual sliding-bar safety system, and impregnated hardwood grips, 52.8 oz. New 1983.

   MSR $2,035   **$1,700**   **$1,275**   **$875**

Add $3 for .454 Casull cal. with fixed sight (4 3/4 or 6 in. barrel only).

Add $85 for .454 Casull, .475 Linebaugh, or .50 AE cal. with adj. sight.

MODEL 83 VARMINT GRADE

- .22 LR cal., 5 shot, dual firing pins, choice of 5 1/8 or 7 1/2 in. barrel, steel base adj. V notch rear sight and replaceable brass bead front sight, stainless steel construction, matte finish, manual sliding bar-safety system, pre-set trigger stop, impregnated hardwood grips, 58 oz. Disc. 2005.

           $1,525   **$1,125**   **$825**

Last MSR was $1,828.

Add $264 for extra .22 Mag. cylinder.

MODEL 83 CENTERFIRE SILHOUETTE

- .357 Mag., .41 Mag., or .44 Mag. cal., 5 shot, 9 (.357 Mag. only) or 10 in. barrel, Pachmayr presentation grips, Iron Sight Gun Works silhouette rear sight and replaceable adj. front sight blade with hood, stainless steel construction, matte finish, manual sliding-bar safety system.

   MSR $1,684   **$1,425**   **$1,050**   **$795**

✳ *Model 83 (.454 Casull Silhouette Model)* - .454 Casull cal., includes 10 in. barrel, Pachmayr grips, field grade finish, silhouette competition sights, and trigger over travel screw.

           $1,600   **$1,150**   **$850**

Last MSR was $1,958.

✳ *Model 83 Silhouette Pak* - .44 Mag. cal., includes 10 in. barrel, silhouette competition sight, honed action with 3 lb. trigger pull, plastic grips, locking aluminum carrying case with cleaning kit and tool. Mfg. 1990 only.

           $1,000   **$850**   **$750**

Last MSR was $1,242.

✳ *Model 83 .454 Casull Silhouette Pak* - .454 Casull cal., includes 10 in. barrel, silhouette competition sight, honed action with 3 lb. trigger pull, hardwood grips, locking aluminum carrying case with cleaning kit and tool. Mfg. 1990 only.

           $1,275   **$995**   **$850**

Last MSR was $1,522.

MODEL 83 .22 CAL. SILHOUETTE CLASS

- .22 LR cal., 5 shot, 10 in. barrel, black micarta grips, Iron Sight Gun Works silhouette rear sight and replaceable adj. front sight blade with hood, stainless steel construction, matte finish, manual sliding-bar safety system, dual firing pins, lightened hammer for fast lock time, pre-set trigger stop, 63 oz. New 1991.

   MSR $1,914   **$1,625**   **$1,185**   **$875**

GRADING - PPGS™	100%	98%	95%	90%	80%	70%	60%

MODEL 97 PREMIER GRADE - .17 HMR (new 2004), .22 LR (new 2002), .357 Mag., .32 H&R Mag. (new 2004), .41 Rem. Mag. (new 2000), .44 Spl. (new 2003), .45 LC (new 1999) cal., 5 (.41 Mag., .44. Spl., or .45 LC cal.) or 6 (.17 HMR, .22 LR or .357 Mag. cal.) shot, 3 1/2 (new 2004), 4 1/2 (new 2000), 5 1/2, 7 1/2, or 10 in. barrel, fixed or steel base adj. rear sight and replaceable blade front sight, stainless steel construction, bright brushed finish, automatic transfer bar safety system, optional round butt grip, impregnated hardwood grips. New 1997.

MSR $1,718	**$1,460**	**$1,075**	**$795**				

Add $66 for .17 HMR or .22 LR cal. with sporting chambers.
Add $215 for 3 1/2 in. barrel (disc.).
Add $162 for optional round butt grip.
Subtract $94 for fixed sights (.32 H&R Mag., .357 Mag. or .45 LC cal. only).

U.S. DEPUTY MARSHAL - 3 in. barrel only with no ejector, fixed or adj. sights, U.S. Marshal medallion in left hardwood grip. Mfg. 1990-93.

	$1,325	**$900**	**$750**				

Last MSR was $1475 (fixed sights).
Last MSR was $1,558 (adj. sights).

Add approx. $80 for adj. sights.

SIGNATURE EDITION - .454 Casull cal., high polish stainless steel, 7 1/2 in. barrel only, rosewood grips, cased with accessories, only 93 of 100 were actually mfg.

	$2,300	**$1,750**	**$1,300**				

Last MSR was $2,684.

PRIMUS INTER PARES - 1 of every 1,000 guns were made in this variation, includes octagonal barrel, ivory grips, 7 1/2 in. barrel, and cased. Disc. 1993.
Rarity factor precludes accurate pricing.

FRENCH MILITARY

Various configurations manufactured in several locations in France.

PISTOLS: SEMI-AUTO

MODEL 1935A AUTO PISTOL - 7.65mm French Long cal., 8 shot, 4.3 in. barrel, fixed sights, blue, checkered wood grips, French service sidearm. Mfg. 1935-45.

	$275	**$225**	**$180**	**$135**	**$110**	**$100**	**$90**

Add 50% if Nazi proofed.

✽ *MODEL 1935S* - .32 ACP or .380 ACP cal., 4 1/3 in. barrel, enamel finish, Colt Govt. Model locking system, 26 oz.

	$325	**$295**	**$260**	**$225**	**$195**	**$170**	**$150**

M.A.B. MODEL C - .32 ACP cal., design based on FN Browning Model 1910, 6.1 in. barrel. Introduced 1933.

	$250	**$220**	**$190**	**$170**	**$150**	**$125**	**$110**

M.A.B. MODEL D - .32 ACP cal., 3.96 in. barrel, single action, similar to Model C, mfg. commercially 1933-1940, many thousands mfg. for the German military during WWII (marked "Pistole MAB Kaliber 7.65mm").

	$275	**$225**	**$200**	**$175**	**$150**	**$125**	**$110**

MODEL M.A.B. PA - 15 - 9mm Para. cal., single action, 16 shot, currently used by French military.

	$550	**$500**	**$450**	**$400**	**$365**	**$335**	**$300**

Subtract 10% for phosphate.

MODEL M.A.B. PA - 15 TARGET - rare target variation of PA-15, adj. sight, 6 in. barrel, cased.

	$1,250	**$1,000**	**$750**	**$675**	**$600**	**$550**	**$500**

GRADING - PPGS™	100%	98%	95%	90%	80%	70%	60%

RIFLES: BOLT ACTION

MODEL 1886 LEBEL - 8mm Lebel cal., 32 in. barrel, adj. sight, military stock. Mfg. 1886-WWII.

	$125	$100	$75	$65	$50	$40	$25

1936 MAS MILITARY RIFLE - 7.5mm MAS cal., 22 in. barrel, adj. sight, military stock, bayonet in forearm. Mfg. 1936-1940.

	$300	$225	$175	$145	$125	$100	$80

MODEL 45 - .22 LR cal., may have Mauser parts, aperture rear sight, post-war mfg.

	$400	$360	$330	$275	$235	$200	$175

FRIGON GUNS, INC.

Previously manufactured by Marocchi in Italy. Previously imported by Frigon Guns, Inc. located in Clay Center, KS.

SHOTGUNS

FT-I - 12 ga. only, single barrel trap gun, blue finish, 32 or 34 in. VR barrel, quick-change stock. Mfg. 1986-94.

	$925	$675	$525	$435	$375	$350	$295

Last MSR was $1,100.

FT-C - 12 ga. only, quick-change stock, trap combination gun includes 1 single barrel and 1 set of O/U barrels, cased. Mfg. 1986-94.

	$1,700	$1,325	$1,050	$875	$775	$685	$620

Last MSR was $1,975.

FS-4 - 4-barrel skeet set including 12, 20, 28 ga., or .410 bore, individual forearms, quick-change stock, vent. barrels (except for .410 bore), cased. Mfg. 1986-94.

	$2,575	$1,975	$1,675	$1,475	$1,350	$1,250	$1,150

Last MSR was $2,890.

FROMMER PISTOLS

Previously manufactured by Femaru-Fegyver-es Gepgyar R.T., Budapest, Hungary. Please refer to the Femaru listing in this section.

FURR ARMS

Current manufacturer located in Orem, UT. Please refer to the Gatling Gun listing in this text.

FULTON ARMORY

Current rifle manufacturer and parts supplier located in Savage, MD. Dealer sales.

RIFLES: SEMI-AUTO

Fulton Armory makes a comprehensive array of the four US Gas Operated Service Rifles: M1 Garand, M1 Carbine, M14 and AR-15-type, including corresponding commercial versions and upper receiver assemblies and related parts and components. Current Fulton Armory FAR-15 models include: Legacy, a 60s semi-auto M16 replication - $800-900 MSR, Classics, mirroring current military M16A2/A4 and M4 models - $800-$1000 MSR, Guardian Carbines - $1,000-$1,100 MSR, Liberator and Phantom Tactical Carbines and Enhanced Battle Rifles - $1,000-$1,200 MSR, Mirage NRA/DCM National Match Rifles - $1400-$1,800 MSR, Predator Varmint Rifles - $1,300-$1,800 MSR, Accutron NRA Match Rifles - $1,300-$2,200 MSR, Hornet Lightweight Rifle - $750 MSR, disc. 2003, and the Millennial Lightweight Rifle and Carbine - $750-$850 MSR, disc. 2002.

Current Fulton Armory M14-type rifles using Fulton Armory's semi-auto M14 receiver include:

the M14 Service Rifle - $1,800-$2,000 MSR, M14 Competition Rifle (NRA/CMP Service Rifle Match-Legal) - $2,200-$2,500 MSR, M14 JSSW with Sage Stock/Accuracy System - $2,500-$2,900 MSR, and the M14 Peerless Rifle (NRA/CMP Service Rifle Match-Legal) - $2,600-$3,000 MSR.

Additionally, Fulton Armory manufactures U.S. military and enhanced civilian configurations of the M1 Garand and M1 Carbine, using genuine U.S.G.I. receivers. Models include: the M1 Garand Service Rifle - $1,300-$1,500 MSR, M1 Garand Competition Rifle (John C. Garand Match-Legal) - $1,600 MSR, M1 Garand Peerless Rifle (NRA/CMP Service Rifle Match-Legal) - $2,000 MSR, and the M1 Carbine Service Rifle in Cals. .30 Carbine and 5.7 MMJ Spitfire - $1,000-$1,100 MSR.

Please contact the factory directly for more information, including current availability and pricing (see Trademark Index).

NOTES

F IS FOR FROSTBITE...

... or the town named after it, Frostbite Falls! And frostbitten is what this newly formed Carleton College shooting team was when they were photographed on one of the sub-zero Minnesota days in Jan. Maybe the girls were the smartest – they stayed at home until the deep freeze was over.

G SECTION

GALAZAN

Current trademark established in 1995, and manufactured by Connecticut Shotgun Manufacturing Co., located in New Britain, CT. Consumer direct sales.

The Galazan trademark has established itself as one of the premier names in best quality O/U shotguns and double rifles. All guns are custom order. For more information regarding current firearms manufacturing, please refer to the Connecticut Shotgun Manufacturing Co. listing in this text.

GALEF SHOTGUNS

Previous importer of Zabala Hermanos (Spanish) and Antonio Zoli (Italian) shotguns.

GRADING - PPGS™	100%	98%	95%	90%	80%	70%	60%

SHOTGUNS

COMPANION FOLDING SINGLE BARREL - 12, 16, 20, 28 ga., or .410 bore, 28 in. barrel, full choke, 30 in. full, 12 ga. only, hammerless, underlever, checkered pistol grip stock.

	100%	98%	95%	90%	80%	70%	60%
	$155	$125	$100	$85	$75	$65	$55

MONTE CARLO TRAP SINGLE BARREL - 12 ga., 32 in. full vent. rib, hammerless, underlever, recoil pad, checkered pistol grip Monte Carlo stock. Disc.

	100%	98%	95%	90%	80%	70%	60%
	$225	$185	$175	$150	$135	$125	$100

SILVER SNIPE O/U - 12 or 20 ga., 3 in. chambers, 26, 28, or 30 in. barrels, imp. cyl. and mod. or full and mod. vent. rib, checkered pistol grip stock, boxlock, extractors, single trigger. Mfg. by Angelo Zoli, disc.

	100%	98%	95%	90%	80%	70%	60%
	$525	$500	$475	$400	$375	$325	$275

GOLDEN SNIPE O/U - similar to Silver Snipe, except has auto ejectors.

	100%	98%	95%	90%	80%	70%	60%
	$595	$525	$500	$475	$375	$350	$300

SILVER HAWK SxS - 12 or 20 ga., 3 in. chambers, 26, 28, or 30 in. barrels, imp. cyl. and mod. or mod. and full, boxlock, extractors, checkered pistol grip and beavertail forearm. Mfg. by Angelo Zoli, 1968-72.

	100%	98%	95%	90%	80%	70%	60%
	$450	$400	$375	$350	$300	$275	$250

GALEF ZABALA SxS - 10, 12, 16, or 20 ga., 22, 26, 28, or 30 in. barrels, boxlock, extractors.

	100%	98%	95%	90%	80%	70%	60%
10 gauge	$250	$230	$200	$175	$150	$140	$125
Other gauges	$200	$175	$150	$130	$120	$110	$100

GALENA INDUSTRIES INC.

Please refer to the AMT and Automag listings.

GALIL

Current trademark manufactured by Israel Military Industries (IMI). No current consumer importation. Recent Galil semi-auto sporterized rifles and variations with thumbhole stocks were banned in April, 1998. Beginning late 1996, Galil rifles and pistols were available in selective fire mode only (law enforcement, military only) and are currently imported by UZI America, Inc., a subsidiary of O.F. Mossberg & Sons, Inc. Previously imported by Action Arms, Ltd. located in Philadelphia, PA until 1994. Previously imported by Springfield Armory located in Geneseo, IL and Magnum Research, Inc., located in Minneapolis, MN.

Magnum Research importation can be denoted by a serial number prefix "MR", while Action Arms imported rifles have either "AA" or "AAL" prefixes.

GRADING - PPGS™	100%	98%	95%	90%	80%	70%	60%

RIFLES: SEMI-AUTO

Models 329, 330 (Hadar II), 331, 332, 339 (sniper system with 6x40 mounted Nimrod scope), 361, 372, 386, and 392 all refer to various configurations of the Galil rifle.

MODEL AR - .223 Rem. cal. or .308 Win. cal., semi-auto paramilitary design rifle, gas operated - rotating bolt, 16.1 in. (.223 Rem. cal. only) or 19 in. (.308 Win. cal. only) barrel, parkerized, folding stock. Flip-up Tritium night sights. 8.6 lbs.

	$2,500	$2,100	$1,875	$1,700	$1,500	$1,375	$1,250

Last MSR was $950.

MODEL ARM - similar to Model AR, except includes folding bipod, vented hardwood handguard, and carrying handle.

	$2,750	$2,350	$2,100	$1,900	$1,700	$1,550	$1,325

Last MSR was $1,050.

GALIL SPORTER - similar to above, except has one-piece thumbhole stock, 4 (.308 Win.) or 5 (.223 Rem.) shot mag., choice of wood (disc.) or polymer hand guard, 8 1/2 lbs. Imported 1991-93.

	$1,200	$1,050	$950	$850	$750	$675	$600

Last MSR was $950.

HADAR II - .308 cal., gas operated, paramilitary type configuration, 1 piece walnut thumbhole stock with pistol grip and forearm, 18 1/2 in. barrel, adj. rear sight, recoil pad, 4 shot (standard) or 25 shot mag., 10.3 lbs. Imported 1989 only.

	$1,295	$1,025	$975	$875	$750	$675	$600

Last MSR was $998.

SNIPER OUTFIT - .308 Win. cal., semi-auto, limited production, sniper model built to exact I.D.F. specifications for improved accuracy, 20 in. heavy barrel, hardwood folding stock (adj. recoil pad and adj. cheekpiece) and forearm, includes Tritium night sights, bipod, detachable 6x40mm Nimrod scope, two 25 shot mags., carrying/storage case, 14.1 lbs. Imported 1989 only.

	$6,500	$5,750	$5,000	$4,350	$3,750	$3,250	$2,850

Last MSR was $3,995.

GAMBA, RENATO

Current manufacturer established in 1748, and located in Gardone V.T., Italy. Currently imported by Renato Gamba U.S.A. Corp. - U.S. service center located in Bernardsville, NJ. Gamba of America, a subsidiary of Firing Line, located in Aurora, CO, was the exclusive importer and distributor for Renato Gamba long guns from 1996-2000. Pistols were previously imported and distributed (until 1990) by Armscorp of America, Inc. located in Baltimore, MD. Shotguns were previously (until 1992) imported by Heckler & Koch, Inc. located in Sterling, VA.

RENATO GAMBA

Filli Gamba (Gamba Brothers) was founded in 1946. G. Gamba sold his tooling to his brother, Renato, in 1967 when Renato Gamba left his brothers and S.A.B. was formed. Filli Gamba closed in 1989 and the Zanotti firm was also purchsed the same year.

Renato Gamba firearms have had limited importation since 1986. In 1989, several smaller European firearms companies were purchased by R. Gamba and are now part of the Renato Gamba Group. The importation of R. Gamba guns changed in 1990 to reflect their long term interest in exporting firearms to America. Earlier imported models may be rare but have not enjoyed much collectibility to date.

PISTOLS: SEMI-AUTO

All the following models were discontinued for importation approx. 1990, and importation on certain models began again during 2005.

GRADING - PPGS™	100%	98%	95%	90%	80%	70%	60%

MAUSER HSc SUPER - for more information, please refer to the Mauser Pistols: HSc Post-WWII Mfg. section.

SAB G90 STANDARD - .30 Luger/7.65 Para. (disc.), 9x18mm Ultra (disc.), 9x21mm (new 2005), or 9mm Para. (disc.) cal., double action, 4.72 in. barrel, 10 (C/B 1994) or 15* shot side release mag., blue or chrome (disc.) finish, hammer drop safety on frame, smooth walnut grips, fixed rear sight, 2.2 lbs.

MSR $783	$675	$575	$465	$335	$295	$275	$250

Add $145 for chrome finish.

❋ *SAB G90 Competition* - 9mm Para. cal., similar to SAB G90 Standard, except has adj. rear sight, "cocked and locked" operation, and checkered walnut grips. Imported 1990 only.

$1,175	$425	$375	$325	$300	$275	$250

Last MSR was $1,364.

Add $205 for stainless steel (SAB G90 Service Competition).

SAB G91 COMPACT - similar to SAB G90, except has 3.54 in. barrel, 12 shot mag., 1.87 lbs.

$625	$375	$325	$295	$275	$250	$225

Last MSR was $736.

Add $65 for chrome finish (disc.).

❋ *SAB G91 Competition* - 9mm Para. cal., similar to SAB G91 Compact, except has adj. rear sight, "cocked and locked" operation, and checkered walnut grips. Imported 1990 only.

$450	$395	$330	$300	$275	$250	$225

Last MSR was $575.

SAB G2001 - .380 ACP cal., double action, mfg. from forged and milled steel, high polish blue, neoprene grips, slide mounted manual safety with firing pin block, 10 shot mag.

$615	$395	$325	$295	$275	$250	$225

Last MSR was $699.

REVOLVERS

The following models were discontinued for importation approx. 1990, and certain models were imported again beginning 2005.

TRIDENT FAST ACTION - .32 S&W or .38 Spl. cal., 2 1/2 or 3 in. barrel, double action, blue frame with checkered walnut grips, 6 shot, 23 oz.

$550	$425	$360	$330	$295	$270	$245

Last MSR was $630.

TRIDENT SUPER - .32 S&W or .38 Spl. cal., 4 in. vent. rib barrel, 6 shot, double action, checkered walnut grips, 25 oz.

$585	$450	$375	$340	$310	$280	$250

Last MSR was $683.

TRIDENT MATCH 900 - .32 S&W Long W.C. (disc.) or .38 Spl. cal., double action, 6 shot, match gun featuring 6 in. heavy barrel and anatomically compatible checkered walnut (disc.) or rubber (new 2005) grips, adj. sights, 2.2 lbs.

MSR $1,210	$1,050	$800	$700	$600	$500	$450	$400

TRIDENT MATCH 901 - .32 S&W cal., similar to Trident Match 900.

MSR $1,210	$1,050	$800	$700	$600	$500	$450	$400

GRADING - PPGS™	100%	98%	95%	90%	80%	70%	60%

RIFLES

SAFARI EXPRESS SxS - 7x65R, 9.3x74R, or .375 H&H cal., 25 in. barrels with open sights, underlug locking with Greener crossbolt, ejectors except on .375 H&H, coin finished frame with scroll work and game scene engraving, DTs, deluxe checkered walnut stock with cheekpiece and recoil pad, 9.9 lbs.

	$5,685	$4,575	$3,950	$3,575	$3,175	$2,850	$2,500

Last MSR was $6,630.

CONCORDE EXPRESS O/U - .30-06, 8x57JRS, or 9.3x74R cal., 23 3/4 in. barrels, monoblock frame, Boss type action, ejectors, cased.
Current MSR on this model is $21,950.

DAYTONA SL EXPRESS O/U - .30-06, .375 H&H, or 9.3x74R cal., monoblock frame with Boss type improved action, 23 3/4 in. barrels, detachable Gamba trigger assembly, hand engraved sideplates with game scenes and English scroll.
Current MSR on this model is $27,045.

EXPRESS MAXIM SxS - .375 H&H, .458 Win. Mag., .470 NE, or .458 Lott (new 1995) cal., sidelock action, fine engraving with big game scenes signed by the master engraver, includes leather case.
Current MSR on this model is $96,390.

MUSTANG EXTRA SINGLE SHOT - 5.6x50mm (disc.), 5.6x57R (disc.), 6.5x57R, 7x65R, .222 Rem. (disc.), .243 Win., .270 Win., or .30-06 cal., single 25 1/2 in. barrel configuration with highly engraved sidelock action featuring triple-bite double Purdey locking system with Greener crossbolt, extra fine vine leaf Renaissance engraving (game scene upon request), double-set triggers, best quality checkered walnut stock and forearm, 6.17 lbs.
Current MSR on this model is $49,572.

RGZ 1000 BOLT ACTION - 7x64mm, .270 Win., 7mm Rem. Mag., or .300 Win. Mag. cal., modified Mauser K-98 action, 20 1/2 in. barrel, pistol grip stock with cheekpiece, 7 lbs.

	$1,100	$885	$825	$760	$700	$640	$575

Last MSR was $1,310.

✻ *RGX 1000 Express* - similar to RGZ 1000, except has 23 3/4 in. barrel and double set triggers, 7.7 lbs.

	$1,255	$960	$875	$795	$725	$650	$575

Last MSR was $1,475.

SHOTGUNS: O/U

Most of the following O/U models (except for the Daytona Trap and Concorde Model) were discontinued in 1990 when H&K became the exclusive importer for R. Gamba shotguns.
Add on values for the following models represent the manufacturer's suggested retail on those items, not necessarily the value in the secondary marketplace.

EUROPA 2000 - 12 ga. only, engraved, silver finished boxlock action with sideplates, vent. rib, single trigger, ejectors, deluxe checkered stock and forearm, 6.84 lbs.

	$1,250	$995	$895	$835	$775	$715	$650

Last MSR was $1,475.

EDINBURGH SUPER SLUG - 12 ga. only, trap model, SST, ejectors, engraved action, deluxe checkered stock and forearm.

	$1,225	$980	$895	$835	$775	$715	$650

Last MSR was $1,425.

GRADING - PPGS™	100%	98%	95%	90%	80%	70%	60%

GRIFONE SPORTING TRAP - 12 ga. only, trap model, SST, ejectors, moderately engraved action, deluxe checkered stock and forearm.

	$975	$900	$850	$800	$750	$700	$650

Last MSR was $1,425.

GRINTA TRAP/SKEET - 12 ga. only, trap/skeet model, SST, ejectors, medium engraving coverage.

	$900	$825	$725	$650	$575	$500	$450

Last MSR was $1,710.

VICTORY TRAP/SKEET - similar to Grinta Model, except has better walnut and more engraving.

	$1,200	$1,075	$950	$850	$750	$650	$550

Last MSR was $1,905.

EDINBURG MATCH - similar to Victory Model, except has different style of engraving.

	$1,200	$1,075	$950	$850	$750	$650	$550

Last MSR was $1,930.

MONTREAL MODEL 90/91 - 12 ga. only, boxlock, interchangeable trigger assembly, select walnut, vent. rib. Available in International Trap, American Skeet, Sporting, and Field models.

	$2,650	$2,275	$1,700	$1,400	$1,100	$1,000	$900

Add $200 for single selective trigger.

The Model 90 has a flat-sided receiver, while the Model 91 has a Daytona sculpted receiver.

MONTREAL 90/91 AMERICAN TRAP COMBO - 12 ga. only, 32 in. barrels and adj. impact, single 34 in. barrel, interchangeable trigger assembly.

	$2,800	$2,100	$1,820	$1,540	$1,400	$1,260	$1,120

SINGLE BARREL TRAP-MODEL 496 - 12 ga. only, boxlock, vent. rib.

	$1,150	$865	$750	$635	$575	$520	$460

HUNTER II - 12 ga. only, boxlock action with alloy frame, reinforced barrels including 5 choke tubes, SST, ejectors, 23.5 (Woodcock), 26 or 27 (Game) in. barrels, checkered walnut stock and forearm, approx. 6 lbs. Limited importation beginning 2002.

Current MSR on this model is $2,204.

LE MANS SPORTING/TRAP - 12 ga. only, boxlock action with steel frame, reinforced barrels including 5 choke tubes, single trigger (Trap) or SST (Sporting), ejectors, checkered walnut stock and forearm, approx. 6 lbs. Limited importation beginning 2002.

Current MSR on this model is $2,892.

CONCORDE GAME MODEL - 12 or 20 ga., Boss type improved locking system, ejectors, 26 3/4 or 28 in. VR barrels, available in Hunting, Trap, Skeet, and Sporting configurations, 2nd generation Concorde with fixed single trigger group started 2002. Importation began 1995.

MSR $8,759		$7,500	$4,500	$3,350	$2,850	$2,350	$2,000	$1,750

Add $500 for SST.

Add $1,129 for Sporting Model.

Add $3,350 for Concorde SL with game scene engraved sideplates (disc.).

Add $2,000 for Trap combo (disc.).

❋ *Concorde SSLL* - features sideplates, engraved with game scenes, fixed trigger group, ejectors, select walnut stock, 30 in. barrels. Importation began 2005.

Current MSR on this model is $26,439.

❋ *Grade 7* - includes engraving featuring game scenes and English scroll. Disc.

	$12,400	$7,750	$5,950	$5,000	$4,400	$3,850	$3,250

Last MSR was $13,540.

Add $1,070 for Sporting Clays Model.

GRADING - PPGS™	100%	98%	95%	90%	80%	70%	60%

✳ *Grade 8* - features top-of-the-line English scroll engraving. Disc.

	$9,500	$6,650	$5,000	$4,250	$3,600	$2,925	$2,400

Last MSR was $10,650.

Add $1,070 for Sporting Clays Model.

CARRERA SPORTING MODEL - 12 ga., features similar to Daytona Model, 28, 30, or 32 in. barrels, SST, 5 chokes, upgraded wood, gold woodcock engraved on action. Importation began 2005.

Current MSR on this model is $14,707.

DAYTONA (2K NEW SERIES) & VARIATIONS - 12 ga. only, monolithic boxlock action, SST, ejectors, detachable trigger group, blue or chrome finish standard, available in either Hunting, Skeet, Pigeon, Sporting Clays, Olympic Trap, or American Trap configuration, deluxe walnut with fine English scroll engraving with game scenes. New Daytona series started in 2000. Importation began 1990.

MSR $10,356	$9,100	$8,500	$6,000	$4,300	$3,700	$2,950	$2,400

Add $1,102 for Sporting Clays Model.
Add approx. $1,600 for removable trigger group.
Add $1,530 for New American Trap configuration (disc.).
Add $2,000 for Daytona combo package (disc.).
Add $4,160-$4,958 for extra set of O/U barrels.

✳ *Grade 4 Daytona Model* - most elaborately engraved numbered Daytona model, choice of eagle panel scene or fine scroll engraving.

MSR $24,980	$22,250	$18,250	$15,000	$11,750	$9,950	$8,900	$7,750

Add $430 for Luxe game scene and fine English scroll engraving.

✳ *Grade 5/5E Daytona Model* - one grade below Grade 4.

MSR $24,182	$21,500	$18,000	$15,000	$11,750	$9,950	$8,900	$7,750

✳ *Grade 6/6 SCE Daytona Model* - one grade below Grade 5, choice of duck game scene or tight scroll engraving.

MSR $21,482	$19,250	$17,000	$14,000	$10,450	$8,750	$7,750	$6,750

Add $3,498 for game scene engraving (Grade 6 SCE).

✳ *Grade 7 Daytona Model* - one grade below Grade 6, oval game scene engraving with English scroll on perimeter.

MSR $19,416	$17,250	$15,500	$12,750	$9,750	$7,500	$6,250	$5,000

✳ *Grade 8 Daytona Model* - features English scroll engraving.

MSR $17,819	$15,750	$13,750	$11,500	$8,950	$7,250	$6,000	$4,750

DAYTONA SL - deluxe variation of the Daytona Model, except has sideplates with extensive engraving, new mfg. has detachable trigger group, available in the same configurations as the Daytona Model, includes case. Limited importation 1990-94, reintroduced 2000-2005.

	$26,000	$18,000	$11,500	$10,500	$9,000	$7,200	$5,500

Last MSR was $29,310.

✳ *Grade 1 SL* - elaborate engraving with 24Kt. gold game scene engraving.

MSR $50,895	$46,250	$40,000	$26,750	$17,500	$14,500	$12,000	$9,750

✳ *Grade 2 SL* - elaborate scroll and game scene engraving, w/o gold inlays.

MSR $38,832	$34,000	$28,250	$21,000	$13,500	$11,500	$9,500	$7,750

✳ *Grade 3 SL* - features hand engraved sideplates with English scroll and game scenes. Importation began 1995.

MSR $33,737	$29,250	$26,000	$18,750	$11,750	$10,250	$8,250	$7,250

✳ *Grade Royale* - top-of-the-line Daytona Model.

MSR $37,539	$33,450	$28,000	$20,000	$12,500	$10,750	$9,150	$7,400

✳ *Grade Purdey* - features Purdey locking system, English scroll engraving.

MSR $36,602	$32,500	$27,000	$19,000	$12,000	$10,250	$8,950	$7,300

GRADING - PPGS™	100%	98%	95%	90%	80%	70%	60%

DAYTONA SLE BEST - features elaborate scroll and 24Kt. gold game scene inlays.

MSR $58,551	$53,000	$47,000	$31,000	$20,000	$17,000	$13,500	$10,750

DAYTONA SLE VENUS - features elaborate scroll and game scene engraving.

MSR $53,456	$47,750	$42,500	$28,500	$18,750	$15,500	$12,950	$10,250

* *SLE Tiger* - features sideplates with African game scenes.

MSR $50,895	$45,500	$40,500	$27,500	$17,950	$14,950	$12,950	$10,250

DAYTONA SLHH - 12 or 20 ga., H&H style sidelock action with Boss improved lock-up, top-of-the-line model, game or competition configuration, includes leather case. Importation began in 1990.

> Current MSR on this model is $67,473.

* *Grade 1* - similar to Grade 2, except has better engraving.

> Current MSR on this model is $80,721.

* *Grade 2* - available in either Hunting (12 ga. only), Skeet, Trap, Pigeon, or Sporting Clays configuration.

> Current MSR on this model is $74,056.

* *Grade 3* - features elaborate scroll and game scene engraving.

> Current MSR on this model is $66,096.

DAYTONA VENUS SLEHH - boxlock action with engraved sideplates featuring relief scroll and Goddess of the Hunt engraving.

> Current MSR on this model is $87,688.

DAYTONA SLHH "THE BEST" - sidelock action with elaborate engraving and multiple 24Kt. gold game scene inlays.

> Current MSR on this model is $94,656.
>
> Renato Gamba also offers a Triptych set of 3 SLHH models (Diamond Collection) in 12, 20, and 28 ga. Current MSR is $358,020 (includes show case).

ONE OF THOUSAND - top-of-the-line model with every possible refinement, Boss action, individually special ordered only.

> Current MSR on this model is $123,930.

BAYERN 88 COMBINATION GUN - 12 ga. over same cals. listed for Mustang Model, coin finished boxlock action with game scene engraving, DTs, extractors, deluxe checkered walnut stock with recoil pad, 7 1/2 lbs.

	$1,000	$875	$775	$700	$650	$600	$550

> Last MSR was $1,595.

SHOTGUNS: SxS

Previous to 1989, an optional 28 ga. on a 28 ga. frame was available for most of the following models .

> **Add 20%+ for 28 ga. on the following models.**

HUNTER SUPER - 12 ga. only, Anson & Deeley engraved boxlock action with silver finish, DTs, extractors, 6.84 lbs.

	$1,750	$1,275	$895	$760	$630	$575	$525

> Last MSR was $1,506.

PRINCIPESSA - 12 or 20 ga., similar to Hunter Super except has English straight grip stock and better engraving, 6.62 lbs. Importation disc. 1994.

	$2,750	$1,900	$1,525	$1,250	$995	$800	$625

> Last MSR was $2,495.

> **Add $200 for single trigger.**

S. VINCENT 580 EXTRA DELUXE - 12 ga. only, custom made to individual preferences, very high quality, sidelock action, engraving coverage 100%.

	$4,950	$4,250	$3,500	$2,750	$2,125	$1,775	$1,625

GRADING - PPGS™	100%	98%	95%	90%	80%	70%	60%

OXFORD 90 - 12 or 20 ga., boxlock action with Purdey locking system, DTs, ejectors, scroll engraving on sideplates, deluxe checkered straight grip walnut stock with recoil pad or checkered butt, 6.84 lbs. Disc. 1998.

	$2,750	$2,250	$1,925	$1,600	$1,250	$1,025	$875

Last MSR was $4,300.

Add $245 for single trigger.

OXFORD EXTRA - 12 or 20 ga., double Purdey locking system, includes elegantly engraved sideplates, ejectors, and better quality hand checkered stock and forearm. Importation began 1992.

MSR $7,658	$6,950	$6,250	$5,750	$3,950	$2,975	$2,475	$2,100

Add $633 for single trigger.

MODEL 624 PRINCE - 12 or 20 ga. (disc.), boxlock action, ejectors, choice of English scroll or with woodcock (Model 624 Prince Beccaccia) on bottom of frame, hand checkered walnut stock and forearm. Importation began 1992.

MSR $7,960	$7,250	$6,350	$5,750	$3,950	$2,975	$2,475	$2,100

Add $769 for single trigger.
Add $496 for Model 624 Prince Beccaccia.

MODEL 624 PRINCE EXTRA - similar to Model 624 Prince, except has deep floral hand engraving.

MSR $14,321	$12,950	$11,000	$9,995	$6,750	$4,250	$3,150	$2,750

NEW LONDON GOLD - 12 or 20 ga., H&H side-lock system, ejectors, DT or SST, demibloc chopper lump barrels, English scroll engraving, deluxe checkered straight grip stock and forearm, 6.84 lbs.

MSR $20,105	$17,250	$15,250	$9,250	$5,750	$3,750	$3,100	$2,500

Add $1,101 for single trigger.

LONDON ROYAL - similar to London Model except has less extensive game scene engraving.

	$9,000	$8,000	$7,000	$5,750	$4,750	$3,950	$3,475

Last MSR was $6,730.

ZANOTTI 1625 MAXIM - 12 or 20 ga., H&H sidelock system, ejectors, demibloc barrels, coin finished action with royal English scroll engraving, cased. New 2002.
Current MSR on this model is $50,949.

AMBASSADOR MODEL - 12 or 20 ga., H&H sidelock system, available with either gold-line engraving on barrels and frame with blue receiver (Gold and Black Model) or English scroll engraving (English Engraved Model), single trigger, ejectors, deluxe checkered walnut stock and forearm, cased, 6.4 lbs.
Current MSR on this model is $56,457.
Add $1,377 for English scroll engraving.
Subtract 25% for 12 ga. in used condition only.
This model is also available in either Field or Sporting versions upon special request.

AMBASSADOR EXECUTIVE - 12 or 20 ga. only, top-of-the-line model, made to individual order only, every possible refinement.
Current MSR on this model is $74,358.
A matched pair of Ambassador Executive models is also available for $179,010.
Subtract 25% for 12 ga. in used condition only.

SHOTGUNS: SLIDE ACTION

MODEL 2100 - 12 ga., 3 in. chamber, 19 1/2 in. barrel, 7 shot mag., law enforcement configuration with matte black metal and wood, 6.62 lbs. Limited importation.

	$450	$375	$325	$295	$275	$250	$225

Last MSR was $715.

GRADING - PPGS™	100%	98%	95%	90%	80%	70%	60%

GARBI, ARMAS

Current manufacturer located in Eibar, Spain. Imported and distributed exclusively by W.L. Moore & Co. located in Scottsdale, AZ. Distributor sales.

Currently, Garbi is mfg. 100-125 shotguns per year.

RIFLES: SxS

Garbi also manufactures a deluxe SxS double rifle in 7x65R, 8x57JRS, 9.3x74R, .300 H&H, or .375 H&H cal. Currently, the base retail price for this Express Rifle is $27,500. Please contact the importer or factory directly for more information (including special orders and prices) on this model.

SHOTGUNS: SxS, DISC.

MODEL 120 - 12, 16, 20, or 28 ga., Holland-pattern sidelock ejector double with chopper lump barrels of nickel-chrome steel, H&H type easy opening mechanism, game scene engraving - 3 patterns available. Well figured walnut stock. Importation disc. 1994.

	$7,500	$6,000	$4,875	$4,125	$3,375	$2,600	$2,200

Last MSR was $9,400.

SPECIAL WLM - 12, 16, 20, or 28 ga., top-of-the-line Holland-pattern sidelock ejector double with chopper lump barrels, full coverage large scroll engraving, fancy-figured walnut stock. Importation disc. 1994.

	$7,500	$6,000	$4,875	$4,125	$3,375	$2,600	$2,200

Last MSR was $9,400.

SPECIAL AG - 12, 16, 20, or 28 ga., top-of-the-line Holland-pattern sidelock ejector double with chopper lump barrels, large scroll engraving patterned after Lebeau-Courally, fancy figured walnut stock. Disc.

	$8,000	$6,350	$5,200	$4,300	$3,550	$2,750	$2,300

Last MSR was $9,200.

SHOTGUNS: SxS, RECENT MFG.

On the following models, add $300 for 28 ga., $1,750 for single trigger, $600-$2,500 for English or Turkish walnut wood upgrade, $700 for beavertail forearm, $2,150-$4,750 per extra set of barrels (depending on grade), $225 for barrels over 28 in., and $250 for Churchill style level file-cut rib.

MODEL 100 - 12, 16, or 20 ga., Holland-pattern detachable sidelock ejector double, Purdey style scroll engraving, chopper lump barrels, oil finish, select walnut, articulated trigger.

MSR N/A	$4,500	$3,800	$3,250	$2,350	$1,700	$1,450	$1,200

MODEL 101 - 12, 16, or 20 ga., round body action and smooth wood now standard, Holland-pattern sidelock ejector double with chopper lump barrels, scroll engraving, selected walnut stock.

MSR N/A	$5,850	$4,900	$4,100	$3,025	$2,375	$1,900	$1,650

MODEL 103A - 12, 16, 20, or 28 ga., Holland-pattern sidelock ejector double with chopper lump barrels, fine scroll and rosette engraving, selected walnut stock.

MSR $10,300	$9,250	$8,100	$6,100	$5,000	$3,575	$2,800	$2,350

✳ **Model 103A Royal** - deluxe variation of the Model 103A, features engraving patterned after the H&H royal styles, extra fancy walnut, gold stock oval plate and matted concave rib.

MSR N/A	$10,500	$9,200	$7,400	$6,825	$5,350	$4,350	$3,500

GRADING - PPGS™	100%	98%	95%	90%	80%	70%	60%

MODEL 103B - 12, 16, 20, or 28 ga., Holland-pattern sidelock ejector double with chopper lump barrels of nickel-chrome steel, H&H type easy opening mechanism, fine scroll and rosette engraving, well figured walnut stock.

	100%	98%	95%	90%	80%	70%	60%
MSR $16,000	$14,750	$12,000	$8,850	$7,100	$6,150	$4,950	$3,950

✳ *Model 103B Royal* - deluxe variation of the Model 103B, features engraving patterned after the H&H "Royal" styles, extra fancy walnut, gold stock oval plate and matted concave rib.

	100%	98%	95%	90%	80%	70%	60%
MSR N/A	$14,500	$12,300	$10,000	$8,850	$6,750	$5,350	$4,350

MODEL 200 - 12, 16, 20, or 28 ga., Holland-pattern sidelock ejector double with chopper lump barrels of nickel-chrome steel, heavy-duty locks, magnum proofed, very fine Continental style floral scroll engraving, well figured walnut stock.

	100%	98%	95%	90%	80%	70%	60%
MSR $13,000	$11,250	$8,500	$6,500	$5,950	$4,750	$3,750	$3,100

GARRAY RIFLES LTD.

Current rifle manufacturer with headquarters located in Kelowna, British Columbia, Canada. Direct sales only.

RIFLES: BOLT ACTION

GARRAY RIFLE - calibers range from .243 to .458, with other calibers available by special order, all factory calibers and proprietary BGA (Big Game Adventures) calibers on standard length actions are available, features exhibition grade, deluxe checkered, modified European style Turkish walnut stock based on the FN Mauser design, with Schnabel forend, rounded pistol grip, Dakota style swivel mount, Continental cheekpiece, Pro-Custom finish, client's initials in medallion on buttstock, 3 shot mag., 23 in. chrome-moly barrel, no sights, Pachmayr Decekerator recoil pad, approx. 7 lbs.

> GarRay rifles are custom built by Serengeti Rifle Co. in Kalispell, MT. Current MSR is $5,995, and includes custom leather case. Less than 100 are built annually, and each rifle includes a custom leather case. Please contact the headquarters directly for more information, including options, delivery time, and a price quotation.

GASTINNE RENETTE

Previous manufacturer and retailer 1812-2003, and located in Paris, France.

On Jan. 1, 2003, Gastinne Renette closed its doors at its famous location on Franklin D. Roosevelt Avenue in Paris. Gastinne Renette had limited U.S. importation and distribution, and most guns were subcontracted to other European manufacturers.

RIFLES: BOLT ACTION

Values listed are base prices for each model - since all guns were made to individual order. Wood, level of engraving, and other special features were available at additional cost.

STANDARD MODEL MAUSER ACTION

	100%	98%	95%	90%	80%	70%	60%
	$5,150	$4,450	$3,850	$3,150	$2,550	$1,900	$1,500

Last MSR was $6,000.

DELUXE MAUSER ACTION

	100%	98%	95%	90%	80%	70%	60%
	$9,950	$7,850	$6,850	$5,750	$4,750	$3,900	$2,750

Last MSR was $12,000.

RIFLES: SxS, DOUBLE

BOXLOCK MODEL - variety of cals., features Anson & Deeley boxlock mechanism, color case hardened frame. Imported 1993-2002.

	100%	98%	95%	90%	80%	70%	60%
	$8,950	$7,750	$6,950	$5,850	$4,950	$4,100	$3,200

Last MSR was $10,000.

GRADING - PPGS™	100%	98%	95%	90%	80%	70%	60%

EUROPEAN SIDELOCK

	$31,000	$27,000	$22,500	$18,750	$15,000	$12,500	$10,000

Last MSR was $36,000.

AFRICAN SIDELOCK - various Mag. cals. Imported 1993-2002.

	$33,000	$28,750	$23,500	$19,250	$15,500	$12,750	$10,000

Last MSR was $40,000.

STANDARD TYPE G - 9.3x74R, 7.65R, .30-06, or .375 H&H cal., double bolt action, ejectors, reinforced stock, 23 3/4 in. barrels, bouquet style engraving with deluxe walnut stock and forearm, 7 lbs. 6 oz.

	$2,995	$2,500	$2,150	$1,700	$1,560	$1,480	$1,340

DELUXE TYPE R - 9.3x74R, 7.65R, .30-06, or .375 H&H cal., double bolt action, true sideplates, ejectors, reinforced stock, 23 3/4 in. barrels, animal engraving with deluxe walnut stock and forearm, 7 lbs. 6 oz.

	$3,875	$3,325	$2,700	$2,175	$1,850	$1,700	$1,525

PRESIDENT TYPE PT - 9.3x74R, 7.65R, .30-06, or .375 H&H cal., double bolt action, true sideplates, ejectors, reinforced stock, 23 3/4 in. barrels, light engraving with gold line inlays, best quality walnut, 7 lbs. 6 oz.

	$4,250	$3,725	$3,200	$2,650	$2,250	$1,825	$1,600

RIFLES: SINGLE SHOT

FALLING BLOCK MODEL

	$9,750	$8,250	$6,750	$5,900	$5,000	$4,000	$3,000

Last MSR was $14,000.

SIDELOCK MODEL - features breakdown action. Imported 1993-2002.

	$25,750	$21,250	$18,000	$14,750	$11,350	$9,250	$7,000

Last MSR was $34,000.

SHOTGUNS: SxS

MODEL 105 - 12 or 20 ga., Anson and Deeley type triple bolt action, ejectors, double triggers, case hardened frame, 6 lbs. 8 oz.

	$2,250	$1,800	$1,400	$1,250	$1,125	$1,000	$900

MODEL 98 - 12 and 20 ga., Purdey type triple bolt action, ejectors, double triggers, case hardened frame, 6 lbs. 8 oz.

	$2,995	$2,500	$2,000	$1,850	$1,580	$1,430	$1,260

MODEL 202 - 12 or 20 ga., Purdey type triple bolt action, sidelocks, fine English engraving, first grade French walnut, ejectors, double triggers, coin finished frame, 6 lbs. 10 oz.

	$4,500	$3,950	$3,250	$2,500	$2,175	$1,875	$1,650

Last MSR was $5,250.

MODEL 353 - 12 or 20 ga., Purdey type triple bolt action, hand detachable sidelocks, Chopper lump barrels, fine English engraving, first grade French walnut, ejectors, double triggers, case hardened frame, best quality, 6 lbs. 10 oz.

	$17,500	$13,650	$11,000	$8,900	$6,700	$6,250	$5,750

Last MSR was $19,950.

GATEWAY PRECISION ARMS

Current manufacturer located in Affton, MO. Dealer direct sales.

The XL Hunter model was previously manufactured by RPM until 2004.

GRADING - PPGS™	100%	98%	95%	90%	80%	70%	60%

PISTOLS: SINGLE SHOT

XL HUNTER - over 40 cals., tip-up action, stainless steel frame, 5 1/16 in. under-lug, 12 or 14 in. Douglas chrome-moly (new 2004) or stainless steel barrel, ISGW rear and Patridge or hooded front sight, with (became standard 2000) or w/o external positive extractor. New 1995.

	MSR $1,350		$1,225	$995	$750

Add $200 for stainless steel barrel.
Add $160 for muzzle brake.
Add $50 for left-hand action.
Add $407-$547 per extra barrel, depending on length.

GATLING GUN COMPANY

Currently manufactured and distributed by Furr Arms, established 1961, and located in Orem, UT.

The Furr Arms-Gatling Gun Company manufactures high quality 1/6, 1/3, 1/2, 3/4, and full scale brass reproductions of famous, antique Gatling guns and cannons. Model Gatling guns include various models and scales from 1874 to 1893. Model cannons include the British Naval Cannon and the James Six Pounder. Prices vary according to the complexity of each model and are available by contacting Furr Arms.

Since the factory currently is not manufacturing any of the following reproductions, current prices could be 10%-25% over the 100% values, based on limited availability. 100% values represent the current manufacturer's suggested retail.

REPRODUCTIONS: CANNONS

GATLING GUN - CANNONS

* James Six Lb. Cannon 1/6

	$900	$750	$575

* James Six Lb. Cannon 1/5

	$2,200	$1,850	$1,400

* James Six Lb. Cannon 1/3

	$3,200	$2,550	$2,000

* H.M.S. Victory Naval Cannon 1/10

	$500	$375	$325

* H.M.S. Victory Naval Cannon 1/10 - this cannon is mounted on an oak ship deck section complete with planking, port lid, and working block and tackle.

	$900	$750	$575

* H.M.S. Victory Naval Cannon 1/3

	$3,200	$2,550	$2,000

REPRODUCTIONS: GATLING GUNS

REPRODUCTION GATLING GUNS

* 1874 Carriage 1/6

	$5,000	$4,000	$3,500

* 1874 Carriage Gatling 1/3

	$11,000	$8,750	$6,500

* 1876 Carriage Gatling 1/2

	$15,000	$11,500	$8,575

* 1876 Carriage Gatling 3/4

	$19,000	$15,000	$12,000

* 1874 Camel Tripod 1/6

	$4,000	$3,000	$2,500

GRADING - PPGS™	100%	98%	95%	90%	80%	70%	60%
✳ 1874 Camel Tripod 1/3							
	$4,500	$3,500	$2,800				
✳ 1876 Camel Tripod 1/2							
	$8,000	$6,500	$5,250				
✳ 1876 Camel Tripod 3/4							
	$12,000	$9,000	$7,500				
✳ 1876 Camel Tripod (Full)							
	$18,000	$14,500	$11,500				
✳ 1893 Police Gatling 1/6							
	$2,500	$2,100	$1,650				
✳ 1893 Police Gatling 1/3							
	$3,200	$2,550	$2,000				
✳ 1883 Carriage Gatling 1/6							
	$5,000	$4,000	$3,500				
✳ 1883 Carriage Gatling 1/3							
	$6,500	$5,250	$4,250				

GAUCHER

Current manufacturer located in St. Etienne, France. No current U.S. importation. Previously imported and distributed by Mandall Shooting Supplies located in Scottsdale, AZ.

Gaucher 🅖 *Armes*

During 1997, Gaucher released four shooting rifles with unique sound suppression (approx. 71 dB) in 9mm Para., 12mm cal., or .410 bore - prices are in the $311-$372 range. Additionally, Gaucher manufactures rifles (O/U and SxS double, bolt action rimfire, and semi-auto rimfire), shotguns (SxS, single shot), and 22 LR cal. target pistols. To date, there has been little importation of Gaucher firearms. Please contact the Gaucher factory directly (see Trademark Index) for more information and up-to-date pricing regarding their current lineup of firearms.

PISTOLS: SINGLE SHOT, TARGET

MODEL GN1 - .22 LR cal., single shot silhouette pistol featuring 10 in. barrel, adj. sights, anatomically shaped grips, monobloc lever cocking, 2.42 lbs. Limited importation.

$360	$325	$290	$260	$230	$200	$185

Last MSR was $380.

MODEL GP - similar to Model GN1, except has forearm integrated into grip. Limited importation.

$300	$275	$250	$225	$200	$185	$160

Last MSR was $323.

GAZELLE ARMS

Current trademark established circa 1970, and manufactured by Hisar Avcilik & Doga Sporlasi San Ve Tic. Ltd. Sti., located in Konak-Izmir, Turkey. Currently imported and distributed by Ema Distributors LLC, located in Pineville, NC.

Gazelle Arms currently manufactures a line of good quality, inexpensive shotguns, including semi-autos, SxSs, single shots, and O/Us. Current MSRs on the semi-auto shotguns range from $345-$390, while the O/U is priced at $500. Please contact the distributor directly for more information (see Trademark Index).

GAVAGE

Previous manufacturer located in Liege, Belgium circa 1936-1943.

GRADING - PPGS™	100%	98%	95%	90%	80%	70%	60%

PISTOLS: SEMI-AUTO

GAVAGE PISTOL - .32 ACP/7.65mm cal., patterned after the Clement, fixed barrel, limited mfg.

	100%	98%	95%	90%	80%	70%	60%
	$375	$325	$250	$200	$175	$150	$125

This pistol is very rare if encountered with Waffenamt proofmarks - healthy premiums are being asked.

GENTRY, DAVID - CUSTOM GUNMAKER

Current custom rifle maker located in Belgrade, MT.

David Gentry is a current custom rifle builder who usually fabricates rifles to individual custom order requests. Current models include Gentry's Black Beauty, Mountain "70," Gray Ghost, and the Outfitter's Rifle. The Rough Rider Model was disc. 1994. David Gentry also manufactures top quality muzzle brakes, stainless steel Featherlight scope rings (1 in. and 30mm), and performs custom metalwork. Mr. Gentry should be contacted directly (see Trademark Index) for more information on options/prices.

GERMAN P.38 MILITARY & COMMERCIAL PISTOLS

Previously manufactured P.38s from various German companies, circa 1938-1946.

Also See: Fabrique Nationale, Luger, Mauser, and Walther for other military pistols.

PISTOLS: SEMI-AUTO

P.38 - 9mm Para. cal., double action, 5 in. barrel, 8 shot mag., fixed sights, brown or black composite grips, blue finish. Many variations exhibiting a variety of metal finishes and codings, 34 oz. Over 1,000,000 manufactured during WWII.

Based on the prototype "Armee Pistole" from 1936, this model was adopted as the standard service pistol of the German Military in 1938. The P.38 was manufactured by Walther - code "ac" (mfg. 1939-1945), Mauser - code "byf" (mfg. Nov. of 1942-1945), and Spreewerke - code "cyq" (mfg. 1943-1945). The finish on most WWII 1942 and later P.38s is not of the same quality as the pre-war and early war Walther guns with the Spreewerke (cyq) models being the poorest. Pre-war Walther commercial manufactured P.38s (Models AP and Walther Banner HPs) are comparable to Zero Series - 3rd Issue values listed.

AP "ARMEE PISTOLE" - 9mm Para. cal., concealed hammer prototype from 1936, approx. 50 handmade examples, each one different in some details, walnut checkered grips.

Extreme rarity precludes accurate pricing on this model. However, examples seen at auctions have been priced at $35K-$45K.

  Add 30% for dural finish.

  Add 15% for matching mag.

  Add 30% for slotted milling for stock.

HP "HEERES PISTOLE" - 9mm Para. cal., early Walther commercial production, high polish until approx. 13,000 ser. no. range, approx. 24,000 mfg. from 1938-1944.

It is recommended that early variations are evaluated and priced by an expert. Watch for fakes.

✳ *Experimental "Concealed Extractor" HP* - 7.65mm or 9mm Para., first experimental production ser. range 1026-approx. 1080, handmade glossy finish, approx. 20 mfg. Rarely seen in U.S. market.

	N/A	$12,000	$10,000	$8,000	$7,000	$6,000	$5,000

  Add 20% for 7.65mm Para. cal.

  Add 30% for dural aluminum frame.

✳ *"Swedish" HP* - experimental first production HP for Swedish trials, ser. range H1,001-H2,065, "H" prefix, rectangular firing pin and crown/N proofs, thin sight, thick safety lever, superb polish, handmade craftsmanship.

	$3,300	$3,000	$2,500	$2,100	$1,700	$1,500	$1,100

GRADING - PPGS™	100%	98%	95%	90%	80%	70%	60%

* ***Standard HP Production*** - ser. range 2,080-approx. 24,000, high gloss finish until approx. ser. no. 13,000 - then changed to military blue (1944).

	$2,250	$1,750	$1,500	$1,350	$1,200	$1,100	$995

Add 20% for Nazi "359" military proof (scarce).
Add 10% for matching mag.
Add 20% for high polish finish.

* ***7.65mm Para HP Production*** - 7.65mm Para cal., single or double action, very limited mfg., rarest collector category for standard production P.38s.

	N/A	$10,500	$9,500	$8,000	$7,000	$6,000	$5,000

Add 100% for single action.

* ***Late War HP Production*** - marked "MOD P38" on left slide, rough military blue finish, some frames show heavy tool marks, ser. range 24,000-25,990, w/o matching mags.

	$1,850	$1,500	$1,300	$1,000	$800	$600	$500

ZERO-SERIES - 9mm Para. cal., features Walther banner, high polish finish, 5-digit number w/o suffix. Mfg. 1940.

Add 10% for matching mag.

* ***Zero Series*** - 1st Issue - internal extractor, square firing pin, ser. range 01-01,000.

	$10,000	$8,000	$6,000	$4,000	$3,000	$2,500	$2,000

* ***Zero Series*** - 2nd Issue - external extractor, square firing pin, ser. range 02,001-03,445, more difficult to find than 1st Issue.

	$6,500	$5,000	$3,500	$2,500	$1,900	$1,300	$1,000

* ***Zero Series*** - 3rd Issue - external extractor, round firing pin, 03,446-013,725, after ser. no. 10,000, some models had brown military style grips.

	$3,250	$2,500	$2,000	$1,750	$1,600	$1,250	$1,000

* ***480 code*** - "480" appears on slide, first military contract P.38, approx. 7,200 mfg. with ser. range 1-7,665, rare in any condition above 90%.

	$6,000	$4,000	$3,000	$2,500	$2,000	$1,500	$1,250

ac-NO DATE (UNDATED) - 9mm Para. cal., "ac" (Walther code) appears on slide without date, "ac" on triggerguard, 2,800 mfg. with ser. range 7,356-9,691, rarest military coded P.38, rarely encountered in 90% or better original condition.

	$6,000	$4,000	$3,000	$2,500	$2,000	$1,500	$1,250

Add 20% for matching mag.

* ***ac-40 Surcharge*** - hand-stamped "40" before regular ac-40 production, ser. range 9,691-9,978 A, 10,000 mfg., high polish, rare in any condition above 90%.

	$4,000	$3,500	$3,000	$2,500	$2,000	$1,500	$1,000

Add 20% for matching mag.

ac-40 CODE - 9mm Para. cal., indicates 1940 mfg., the 480 code was dropped in October of 1940, and the "ac" code was started, approx. 10,000 mfg. with ser. range 1B-9,900B.

	$2,450	$2,200	$1,900	$1,575	$1,250	$1,000	$850

Add 20% for matching mag.

* ***ac-41 1st and 2nd Variation*** - last military high polish guns, only 1st var. (ser. range 1-4,833 B) has "ac" on left triggerguard, 2nd var. continues to ser. no. 4,527 I.

	$1,800	$1,500	$1,000	$800	$700	$550	$500

Add 20% for matching mag.

ac-41 3RD VAR. or ac-42 CODE - 9mm Para. cal., dull military finish, ser. range (approx.) ac-41, 4,500 I to ac-42, 9,200 K. Matching magazines stop at approx. ac-42, 2,000 B.

	$1,250	$1,100	$900	$700	$600	$500	$450

Add 20% for matching mag.

GRADING - PPGS™	100%	98%	95%	90%	80%	70%	60%

"byf" CODED 42 - 9mm Para. cal., dull military finish, approx. 15,000 mfg.

	100%	98%	95%	90%	80%	70%	60%
	$1,250	$1,100	$900	$700	$600	$500	$400

Add 30% for early "135" proofed parts.

"byf" POLICE CODED 43 or 44 - 9mm Para. cal., eagle F or L.

	100%	98%	95%	90%	80%	70%	60%
	$2,000	$1,500	$1,000	$750	$650	$550	$450

Add 20% for "dual tone" phosphate finish.

"ac" or "byf" CODED 43-45 - 9mm Para. cal., letters are followed by two digit code corresponding to year of mfg. 1943-45. Two line codes are more desirable than single line models. Highest P.38 production occurred in 1943 and 1944.

	100%	98%	95%	90%	80%	70%	60%
	$700	$600	$550	$500	$450	$425	$400

Add up to 50% for "dual tone" (blue and phosphate finish - byf-44 date) if in 95%+ or better condition.

"cyq" CODE AND "ac-45" MISMATCH - 9mm Para. cal., cyq variation typically exhibits rough machining with visible circular milling marks, mismatched slide and frame on ac-45 model.

	100%	98%	95%	90%	80%	70%	60%
	$475	$400	$375	$350	$325	$300	$275

Add 30% for A or B prefix on serialization.

LATE WAR (1945) - 9mm Para. cal., Zero Series with rough milled finish, ser. range 025,960-027,659.

	100%	98%	95%	90%	80%	70%	60%
	$1,500	$1,200	$1,000	$800	$700	$600	$500

1945 "svw" CODE - 9mm Para. cal., Nazi proofed only, most dual tone finish, some all blue or all grey.

	100%	98%	95%	90%	80%	70%	60%
	$1,200	$1,100	$900	$700	$600	$500	$400

Add 20% for all blue or all grey.
Subtract 50% for French production (Star proof).

1946 "svw" CODE - 9mm Para. cal., Mauser mfg. 1946 with French controlling production.

	100%	98%	95%	90%	80%	70%	60%
	$550	$425	$360	$330	$295	$270	$245

Lower condition prices for this model are usually based on shooting value.

GEVARM

Previous manufacturer located in Saint Etienne, France.

RIFLES: SEMI-AUTO

E-1 AUTOLOADING RIFLE - .22 LR cal., 19 in. barrel, open sights, walnut pistol grip stock.

	100%	98%	95%	90%	80%	70%	60%
	$300	$250	$225	$195	$180	$165	$150

GIANI, VITTORIO

Current manufacturer located in Brescia, Italy.

Vittorio Giani specializes in bolt action rifles, but also manufactures SxS rifles and shotguns. Please contact the factory directly for more information, including pricing and availability (see Trademark Index).

GIB

Previous trademark manufactured in Spain.

SHOTGUNS: SxS

10 GAUGE MAGNUM - 10 ga., 3 1/2 in. chambers, 32 in. full choke barrel, case hardened frame, matted rib, rubber pad, checkered pistol grip walnut stock. Disc.

	100%	98%	95%	90%	80%	70%	60%
	$275	$250	$235	$220	$200	$175	$150

GRADING - PPGS™	100%	98%	95%	90%	80%	70%	60%

GIBBS GUNS, INC.

Previously manufactured by Volunteer Enterprises in Knoxville, TN and previously distributed by Gibbs Guns, Inc. located in Greenback,TN.

CARBINES

MARK 45 CARBINE - .45 ACP cal. only, based on M6 Thompson machine gun, 16 1/2 in. barrel, 5, 15, 30, or 90 shot mag. U.S. mfg. Disc. 1988.

	$575	$495	$450	$375	$330	$300	$285

Last MSR was $279.

Add $150 for 90 shot mag.
Add $60+ for nickel plating.

GIBBS RIFLE COMPANY, INC.

Current manufacturer, importer, and distributor located in Martinsburg, WV. Gibbs manufactured rifles with the Gibbs trademark in Martinsburg, WV 1991-94, in addition to importing Mauser-Werke firearms until 1995. Dealer and distributor sales.

In the past, Gibbs Rifle Company, Inc. imported a variety of older firearms, including British military rifles and handguns (both original and refurbished condition), a good selection of used military contract pistols and rifles, in addition to other shooting products and accessories, including a bipod patterned after the Parker-Hale M-85.

Gibbs Rifle Company, Inc. currently imports and manufactures military collectibles, historical remakes, and special sporting rifles. All rifles are carefully inspected, commercially cleaned and boxed to ensure their quality, and all have a limited lifetime warranty. Gibbs Rifle Company, Inc. also offers membership in the Gibbs Military Collectors Club, an organization dedicated to military firearms collectors. Please contact them directly for more information, including membership (refer to Firearms Associations listing).

RIFLES: BOLT ACTION

M-71/84 MAUSER - 11mm Mauser cal., 31 1/2 in. barrel, available in good original or refurbished condition, 10 lbs. Imported 1999-2004.

	$165	$135	$120	$110	$100	$90	$85

Last MSR was $190.

Add $110 for refurbished condition (all parts are historically correct and have been cleaned and hand inspected).
This rifle cannot be safely shot with modern ammunition.

M-1888 MAUSER - 8mm Mauser (7.92x57mm) cal., good original condition, 30 in. barrel, 10 lbs. Imported 1999-2004.

	$85	$75	$65	$55	$45	$40	$35

Last MSR was $100.

This rifle cannot be safely shot with modern ammunition.

M-98K ISRAELI MAUSER - .308 Win. cal., rebarreled by the Israeli Arsenal Ha'as, various makers, 23.6 in. barrel, original condition (offered in 3 grades), 9 lbs. Imported 1999-2003.

	$150	$125	$115	$105	$95	$90	$85

Last MSR was $170.

Add $10 for Grade 2, or $20 for Grade 1.

M-98 MAUSER SPORTER - .270 Win. or .30-06 cal., Mauser M-98 type action, blue finish, sporterized checkered hardwood stock and forend, 24 in. Wilson barrel. Mfg. in Martinsburg, WV 1998-99.

	$295	$265	$245	$225	$210	$195	$180

Last MSR was $330.

GRADING - PPGS™	100%	98%	95%	90%	80%	70%	60%

2A HUNTER RIFLE/CARBINE - .308 Win. cal., sporterized action features black enamel refinish, synthetic stock, 12 shot mag, and choice of 18 (carbine) or 22 1/2 (rifle) in. barrel with Parker-Hale muzzle brake, approx. 10 lbs. Mfg. 1999 only.

	$235	$200	$180	$165	$155	$145	$140

Last MSR was $275.

ENFIELD NO. 5 JUNGLE CARBINE - .303 British cal., older No. 4 Enfield barrel action with newly manufactured stock, bayonet lug and flash hider have been added, 20 in. barrel, 7 3/4 lbs. Imported 1999-2004.

	$175	$155	$125	$115	$105	$95	$90

Last MSR was $205.

ENFIELD NO. 7 JUNGLE CARBINE - .308 Win. cal., older 2A action with reconfigured original wood, flash hider and bayonet lug have been added, 20 in. barrel, 8 lbs. Imported 1999-2004.

	$170	$150	$125	$115	$105	$95	$90

Last MSR was $200.

QUEST EXTREME CARBINE - .303 British cal., updated No. 5 Enfield action with 20 in. barrel with compensator and flash hider, electroless nickel metal finish, new buttstock with survival kit packaged in butt trap, 7.75 lbs. Imported 2000-2004.

	$215	$185	$170	$160	$150	$140	$130

Last MSR was $250.

QUEST II - .308 Win. cal., modern 2A Enfield barreled action, mfg. from chrome vanadium steel, 20 in. barrel with compensator/flash-hider and adj. rear sight, front sight protector, pre-fitted see-through scope mount accepts all Weaver based optics and accessories, electroless nickel finish, hardwood stock with survial kit included, 12 shot mag., 8 lbs. Imported 2001-2004.

	$235	$200	$185	$170	$160	$155	$150

Last MSR was $280.

QUEST III - .308 Win. cal., similar to Quest II, except has black syntetic stock, w/o survival kit. Imported 2002-2004.

	$250	$220	$200	$185	$170	$160	$155

Last MSR was $300.

SUMMIT FRONTIER .45-70 CARBINE - .45-70 Govt. cal., remanufactured No. 4 Enfield action, new 21 in. button rifled barrel with front sight, blue action and barrel, checkered hardwood sporting stock, 3 shot mag., 8 1/2 lbs. Importation began 2000.

MSR $385	$330	$280	$255	$230	$210	$195	$180

GIBBS ECONOMY SPORTER - 8mm Mauser cal., sporterized military action with good barrel and sporting sights, walnut finished checkered hardwood stock. Mfg. 1993-94.

	$185	$150	$135	$120	$100	$85	$70

Last MSR was $205.

GIBBS MAUSER SPORTER - .243 Win., .270 Win., .30-06, or .308 Win. cal., features M-98 action, walnut finished checkered hardwood stock, action is drilled and tapped, flip-up rear sight and ramp front. Mfg. 1993-94.

	$250	$220	$195	$175	$150	$135	$120

Last MSR was $295.

MODEL 81 CLASSIC - available in 11 cals. between .22-250 Rem. and 7mm Rem. Mag., 24 in. barrel, open sights, 4 shot mag., select checkered walnut with sling swivels, 7 3/4 lbs.

	$795	$595	$475	$395	$340	$300	$280

Last MSR was $900.

✱ *Model 81 African* - .375 H&H or 9.3x62mm cal., similar specifications as Model 81 Classic with quarter rib and express sights, engraved action, Pachmayr recoil pad, 9 lbs.

	$925	$725	$600	$500	$425	$360	$330

Last MSR was $1,050.

GRADING - PPGS™	100%	98%	95%	90%	80%	70%	60%

MODEL 85 SNIPER RIFLE - .308 Win. cal., bolt action, 24 in. heavy barrel, 10 shot mag., camo green synthetic McMillan stock with stippling, built in adj. bipod and recoil pad, enlarged contoured bolt, adj. sights, 12 lbs. 6 oz.

	$1,825	$1,450	$1,275	$1,050	$875	$750	$625

Last MSR was $2,050.

MODEL 87 TARGET - .243 Win., 6.5x55mm, .308 Win., .30-06, or .300 Win. Mag. cal., target stock, aperture sights. Mfg. disc. 1992.

	$1,375	$1,100	$900	$775	$650	$550	$495

Last MSR was $1,500.

MODEL 1000 STANDARD - .22-250 Rem., .243 Win., 6mm Rem., 6.5x55mm, 7x57mm, 7x64mm, .270 Win., .30-06, or .308 Win. cal., 22 in. barrel, 4 shot built in mag., checkered walnut stock with cheekpiece, open sights, 7 1/4 lbs.

	$425	$375	$325	$290	$260	$240	$220

Last MSR was $495.

✳ *Model 1000 Clip* - similar to Model 1000 Standard, except has detachable 4 shot mag.

	$460	$395	$350	$300	$270	$240	$220

Last MSR was $535.

MODEL 1100 LIGHTWEIGHT - available in 9 cals. between .22-250 Rem. and .308 Win., 22 in. barrel, open sights, 4 shot mag., 6 1/2 lbs.

	$435	$380	$325	$290	$260	$240	$220

Last MSR was $510.

✳ *Model 1100M African* - .375 H&H, or .458 Win. Mag. cal., 24 in. barrel, 4 shot mag., 9 1/2 lbs.

	$825	$650	$575	$500	$450	$425	$400

Last MSR was $930.

MODEL 1200 SUPER - .22-250 Rem., .243 Win., 6mm, 6.5x55mm, 7x64mm, .270 Win., .30-06, or .308 Win. cal., bolt action, Mauser type action, 24 in. barrel, folding sight, skip checkered walnut stock, pad swivels, rosewood pistol grip cap and forend tip.

	$495	$400	$350	$325	$285	$270	$255

Last MSR was $595.

✳ *Model 1200 Super Clip* - similar to Model 1200 Super, except has detachable 4 shot box mag.

	$525	$425	$375	$350	$300	$280	$265

Last MSR was $640.

MODEL 1300S SCOUT - .243 Win. or .308 Win. cal., 20 in. barrel with muzzle brake, internal 5 shot or detachable 5/10 shot mag., laminated checkered birchwood stock, sling swivels, 8 1/2 lbs.

	$425	$375	$325	$290	$260	$240	$220

Last MSR was $495.

Add $30 for detachable mag. (Model 1300C).

MODEL 1500S SURVIVOR - .308 Win. cal., bolt action, matte stainless construction, black composite (Kevlar/fiberglass) stock, 22 in. barrel, 4 shot mag., 7 lbs. Mfg. began 1993. Disc.

	$395	$350	$300	$270	$240	$210	$185

Last MSR was $450.

Add $30 for detachable mag. (Model 1500C).

This model was made for the Gibbs Rifle Co. by Bell & Carlson, Inc.

RIFLES: BOLT ACTION, MIDLAND SERIES

MODEL 2100 MIDLAND DELUXE - similar to Model 2600 Midland, except has checkered walnut stock and pistol grip cap.

	$335	$280	$235	$210	$190	$180	$170

Last MSR was $390.

GRADING - PPGS™	100%	98%	95%	90%	80%	70%	60%

MODEL 2600 MIDLAND - .22-250 Rem., .243 Win., 6mm Rem. (disc. 1994), 6.5x55mm (disc. 1994), 7x57mm (disc. 1994), 7x64mm (disc. 1994), .270 Win., .30-06, or .308 Win. cal., 22 in. barrel, 4 shot mag., checkered hardwood stock with Monte Carlo cheekpiece, open sights, drilled and tapped action, 7 lbs. Disc. 1997.

		$350	$275	$225	$200	$180	$165	$150

Last MSR was $400.

This model was re-introduced during late 1996, utilizing a 1903 Springfield action with choice of 5 shot fixed mag. with hinged floorplate or 3 shot detachable mag.

MIDLAND 2700 LIGHTWEIGHT - lightweight variation of the Model 2100 Midland Deluxe featuring tapered barrel, anodized aluminum trigger housing and lightened stock with full pistol grip and recoil pad, Schnabel forend, 6 1/2 lbs.

		$350	$285	$245	$225	$200	$190	$180

Last MSR was $415.

MIDLAND 2800 - similar to Model 2600 Midland, except has laminated birchwood stock, re-introduced during late 1996, utilizing a 1903 Springfield action, 7 lbs. Disc. 1997.

		$360	$295	$250	$215	$195	$185	$175

Last MSR was $430.

SHOTGUNS: SINGLE SHOT

MIDLAND STALKER - 12 ga., trigger bar safety, unique squeeze break open action and cocking system, 28 1/2 in. barrel bored F, hardwood stock and forearm, 6 lbs.

		$90	$65	$55	$45	$35	$30	$25

Last MSR was $110.

GIL, ANTONIO & CO.

Current manufacturer located in Eibar, Spain. Limited U.S. importation. Previously imported and distributed exclusively late 2000-2004 by New England Arms Corp., located in Kittery Point, ME.

All Antonio Gil shotguns are handmade, and can be built to each customer's exact measurements at no extra cost. All models are equipped with chopper lump barrels as a standard feature. Please contact the company directly for more information, including current U.S. pricing and availability (see Trademark Index).

SHOTGUNS: SxS

All models are sidelock only.

Add 10% for 20, 28 ga. or .410 bore.
Add $500-$1,500 for wood upgrade.
Add $1,000-$1,250 per extra set of barrels.
Add $500 for non-selective trigger.

LAGA - 12, 16, 20, 28 ga. or .410 bore, sidelock action with color case hardened receiver and scroll engraving, demi-bloc barrels, DT, deluxe checkered walnut stock and forearm. Importation began 2001.

MSR N/A		$2,250	$1,750	$1,500	$1,350	$1,200	$1,100	$995

OLIMPIA - 12, 16, 20, 28 ga. or .410 bore, sidelock action, features traditional rose and scroll engraving on coin finished receiver. Importation began 2001.

MSR N/A		$2,575	$2,250	$1,750	$1,500	$1,350	$1,200	$1,050

ALHAMBRA - 12, 16, 20, 28 ga. or .410 bore, sidelock action, features elaborate full coverage floral scroll engraving on coin finished receiver and wood upgrade. Importation began 2001.

MSR N/A		$3,625	$3,150	$2,575	$2,250	$1,750	$1,500	$1,350

DIAMOND - 12, 16, 20, 28 ga. or .410 bore, sidelock action, top-of-the-line model with best engraving and best quality wood. Importation began 2001.

MSR N/A		$5,475	$4,650	$4,125	$3,625	$3,050	$2,500	$2,000

GLISENTI

Please refer to the Italian Military Arms section in this text.

GLOCK

Currently manufactured by Glock GmbH in Austria beginning 1983.
Exclusively imported and distributed by Glock, Inc., located in
Smyrna, GA. Distributor and dealer sales.

All Glock pistols have a "safe action" safety system (double action only)
which includes trigger safety, firing pin safety, and drop safety. Glock pistols have only 35
parts for reliability and simplicity of operation.

PISTOLS: SEMI-AUTO

Add $25 for internal locking system (ILS) on most currently manufactured models listed
below (new 2004).

Add $95 for tactical light or $284 for tactical light with laser for most currently manufactured pistols listed below.

MODEL 17/17C SPORT/SERVICE - 9mm Para. cal., double action, polymer frame,
mag., trigger and other pistol parts, 4.49 in. steel hexagonal rifled barrel with (Model
17C, new 1999) or w/o ports, steel slide and springs, 10 (C/B 1994), 17* (reintroduced
late 2004), or 19* (reintroduced late 2004) shot mag., adj. (Sport Model) or fixed (Service Model) rear sight, includes lockable pistol box, cable lock, cleaning rod, and other
accessories, extra mag. and spare rear sight, 24.75 oz. Importation began late 1985.

MSR $599	$475	$425	$395	$365	$335	$295	$250

Add $18 (Model 17) for adj. rear sight.
Add $22 for Model 17C with fixed (new 2004) or adj. (disc. 2003) rear sight.
Add $22 for steel sight or $47 for night sights (new 2004).
Add $80 for fixed Meprolight sight or $105 for fixed Trijicon sight (disc. 2003).
Add $119 for competition model w/ adj. sights (Model 17CC, mfg. 2000-2003).

✻ *Model 17L Competition Model* - 9mm Para. cal., competition version of the Model 17,
includes internally compensated 6.02 in. barrel, recalibrated trigger pull (3 1/2 lb.
pull), adj. rear sight, 26.3 oz. Mfg. 1988-1999.

$650	$545	$425

Last MSR was $795.

Add $28 for adj. sight.
Early models with barrel ports matched to relieved slide will command a small premium.

✻ *Glock 17 Desert Storm Commemorative* - 9mm Para. cal., features coalition forces listing on top of barrel, inscription on side of slide "NEW WORLD ORDER". 1,000
mfg. in 1991 only.

$995	$825	$600

Last MSR was $795.

MODEL 19/19C COMPACT SPORT/SERVICE - 9mm Para. cal., similar to Model
17, except has scaled down dimensions with 4.02 in. ported (Model 19C, new 1999)
or unported barrel and serrated grip straps, 10 (C/B 1994), 15* (reintroduced late
2004), or 17* (reintroduced late 2004) shot mag., fixed (Service Model) or adj.
(Sport Model) rear sight, 23 1/2 oz. New 1988.

MSR $599	$475	$425	$395	$365	$335	$295	$250

Add $18 (Model 19) for adj. rear sight.
Add $22 for Model 19C with fixed (new 2004) or adj. (disc. 2003) rear sight.
Add $22 for steel sight or $47 for night sights (new 2004).
Add $80 for fixed Meprolight sight or $105 for fixed Trijicon sight (disc. 2003).
Add $119 for competition model w/ adj. sights (Model 19CC, mfg. 2000-2003).

During 1996, AcuSport Corp. commissioned Glock to make a special production run of matching 9mm Para. cal. sets. Each set consists of a Model 19 and 26 with serialization as follows:
Model 19 (ser. range AAA0000-AAA0499) and Model 26 (ser. range AAB0000-AAB0499).

GRADING - PPGS™	100%	98%	95%	90%	80%	70%	60%

MODEL 20/20C SPORT/SERVICE - 10mm Norma cal., similar action to Model 17, features 4.6 in. ported (Model 20C, new 1999) or unported barrel, 10 (C/B 1994) or 15* (reintroduced late 2004) shot mag., larger slide and receiver, fixed (Service Model) or adj. (Sport Model) rear sight, 30 oz. New 1990.

MSR $637	$500	$440	$410	$375	$350	$325	$295

Add $18 for adj. rear sight, $22 for steel sight or $47 for night sight (new 2004).
Add $80 for fixed Meprolight sight or $105 for fixed Trijicon sight (disc. 2003).
Add $39 for compensated barrel (Model 20C).
Add $145 for competition model w/ adj. sights (Model 20CC, mfg. 2000-2003).

MODEL 21/21C SPORT/SERVICE - .45 ACP cal., similar to Model 20, except has octagonal profile and rifling, right hard twist, 10 (C/B 1994) or 13* (reintroduced late 2004) shot mag., 29 oz. Introduced May 1991.

MSR $637	$500	$440	$410	$375	$350	$325	$295

Add $18 for adj. rear sight, $22 for steel sight or $47 for night sight (new 2004).
Add $80 for fixed Meprolight sight or $105 for fixed Trijicon sight (disc. 2003).
Add $39 for compensated barrel (Model 21C).
Add $145 for competition model w/ adj. sights (Model 21CC, mfg. 2000-2003).

MODEL 22/22C SPORT/SERVICE - .40 S&W cal., similar to Model 17, except has locking block pin above trigger guard, 4.49 in. barrel, 10 (C/B 1994) or 15* (reintroduced late 2004) shot mag., 25.5 oz. Introduced 1990.

MSR $599	$475	$425	$395	$365	$335	$295	$250

Add $34 for Model 22C with adj. (disc. 2003) or fixed (new 2004) rear sight.
Add $18 (Model 22) for adj. rear sight or $22 for steel sight (new 2004).
Add $80 for fixed Meprolight sight or $105 for fixed Trijicon sight (disc. 2003).
Add $22 for compensated barrel (Model 22C).
Add $119 for competition model w/ adj. sights (Model 22CC, mfg. 2000-2004).

200 Model 22s were originally shipped with serial numbers beginning with "NY-1." Somehow, they probably were erroneously numbered at the factory (probably thinking that they somehow were part of the New York State Troopers shipment of Model 17s) during 1990. Premiums will occur on this variation.

MODEL 23/23C COMPACT SPORT/SERVICE - .40 S&W cal., compact variation of the Model 22 with 4.02 in. ported (Model 23C, new 1999) or unported barrel and 10 (C/B 1994) or 13* (reintroduced 2004) shot mag., 23 1/2 oz. New 1990.

MSR $599	$475	$425	$395	$365	$335	$295	$250

Add $18 for adj. rear sight, $22 for steel sight or $47 for night sight (new 2004).
Add $80 for fixed Meprolight sight or $105 for fixed Trijicon sight (disc. 2003).
Add $22 for compensated barrel (Model 23C).
Add $145 for competition model w/ adj. sights (Model 23CC, mfg. 2000-2003).

During 1996, AcuSport Corp. commissioned Glock to make a special production run of matching .40 S&W cal. sets. Each set consists of a Model 23 and 27 with serialization as follows: Model 23 (ser. range AAC0000-AAC1499) and Model 27 (ser. range AAD0000-AAD1499).

MODEL 24/24C - .40 S&W cal., similar to Model 17L Competition, choice of standard or ported (Model 24C) barrel and fixed or adj. rear sight. Mfg. 1994-99.

		$665	$525	$415			

Last MSR was $795.

Add $40 for compensated barrel.
Add $28 for adj. rear sight.

MODEL 25 - .380 ACP cal., similar to Model 19 with 4.02 in. barrel, 10 shot mag., 22.5 oz. New 1999.

This model is available for law enforcement only.

GRADING - PPGS™	100%	98%	95%	90%	80%	70%	60%

MODEL 26 - 9mm Para. cal., sub-compact variation of the Model 19, except has shortened grip, 3.5 in. barrel, 10 shot mag., 21.75 oz. New 1995.

	MSR $599	$475	$425	$395	$365	$335	$295	$250

Add $18 for adj. rear sight.
Add $22 steel sight or $47 for night sight.
Add $80 for fixed Meprolight sight or $105 for fixed Trijicon sight (disc. 2004).

MODEL 27 - .40 S&W cal., sub-compact variation of the Model 23, except has shortened grip, 3.5 in. barrel, 9 shot mag., 21.75 oz. New 1995.

	MSR $599	$475	$425	$395	$365	$335	$295	$250

Add $18 for adj. rear sight.
Add $22 steel sight or $47 for night sight.
Add $80 for fixed Meprolight sight or $105 for fixed Trijicon sight (disc. 2004).

MODEL 28 - .380 ACP cal., similar to Model 26/27/33, except has scaled down dimensions with 3.46 in. barrel, approx. 20 oz. New 1999.

This model is available for law enforcement only.

MODEL 29 - 10mm Norma cal., sub-compact model featuring 3.78 in. barrel, 10 shot mag., 27 oz. Mfg. 1997-2002.

	MSR $637	$500	$440	$410	$375	$350	$325	$295

Add $18 for adj. rear sight.
Add $22 steel sight or $47 for night sight.
Add $80 for fixed Meprolight sight or $105 for fixed Trijicon sight (disc. 2004).

MODEL 30 - .45 ACP cal., compact Model 21, 3.75 in. barrel, 10 shot mag., features octagonal profile rifling, and extension on mag., 26.5 oz. New 1997.

	MSR $637	$500	$440	$410	$375	$350	$325	$295

Add $18 for adj. rear sight.
Add $22 steel sight or $47 for night sight.
Add $80 for fixed Meprolight sight or $105 for fixed Trijicon sight (disc. 2004).

MODEL 31/31C - .357 SIG cal., similar to Model 17, 4.49 in. ported (Model 31C, new 1999) or unported barrel, fixed sights, 10 shot mag., 26 oz. New 1998.

	MSR $599	$475	$425	$395	$365	$335	$295	$250

Add $18 for adj. rear sight.
Add $22 steel sight or $47 for night sight.
Add $80 for fixed Meprolight sight or $105 for fixed Trijicon sight (disc. 2004).
Add $22 for compensated barrel (Model 31C).
Add $119 for competition model w/ adj. sights (Model 31CC, mfg. 2000-2004).

MODEL 32/32C - .357 SIG cal., similar to Model 19, 4.02 in. ported (Model 32C) or unported barrel, 24 oz. New 1998.

	MSR $599	$475	$425	$395	$365	$335	$295	$250

Add $18 for adj. rear sight.
Add $22 steel sight or $47 for night sight.
Add $80 for fixed Meprolight sight or $105 for fixed Trijicon sight (disc. 2004).
Add $22 for compensated barrel (Model 32C).
Add $119 for competition model w/ adj. sights (Model 32CC, mfg. 2000-2004).

MODEL 33 - .357 SIG cal., compact variation of Models 31 & 32, features 3.5 in. barrel with shortened frame and magazine housing, 10 shot mag., 22 oz. New 1998.

	MSR $599	$475	$425	$395	$365	$335	$295	$250

Add $18 for adj. rear sight.
Add $22 steel sight or $47 for night sight.
Add $80 for fixed Meprolight sight or $105 for fixed Trijicon sight (disc. 2004).

GRADING - PPGS™	100%	98%	95%	90%	80%	70%	60%

MODEL 34 - 9mm Para. cal., similar construction to Model 17, except has 5.32 in. barrel, extended slide stop lever and magazine catch, fixed sights, target grips with finger grooves, thumbrest, receiver has rails for mounting accessories, 10 shot mag., 25.75 oz. New 1998.

	100%	98%	95%	90%	80%	70%	60%
MSR $679	$525	$450	$375	$325	$295	$260	$225

MODEL 35 - .40 S&W cal., 27.5 oz., otherwise similar to Model 34. New 1998.

	100%	98%	95%	90%	80%	70%	60%
MSR $679	$525	$450	$375	$325	$295	$260	$225

MODEL 36 - .45 ACP cal., similar to Model 30, except has single column 6 shot mag., 22 1/2 oz. New 1999.

	100%	98%	95%	90%	80%	70%	60%
MSR $637	$500	$440	$410	$375	$350	$325	$295

Add $18 for adj. rear sight.
Add $22 steel sight or $47 for night sight.
Add $80 for fixed Meprolight sight or $105 for fixed Trijicon sight (disc. 2004).

MODEL 37 - .45 G.A.P. (Glock Automatic Pistol) cal., 4.6 in. barrel, similar to Model 21, except has extended slide stop lever, wider and heavier slide, changed locking block and ejector. New 2003.

	100%	98%	95%	90%	80%	70%	60%
MSR $615	$535	$450	$375	$325	$295	$260	$225

Add $18 for adj. sights or $22 for steel sight.
Add $47 for night sights.

GOLAN

See KSN Industries Ltd. listing.

GOLDEN EAGLE

Previous trademark of rifles/shotguns produced by Nikko Limited located in Tochigi, Japan, circa 1975-1981.

Please refer to the Nikko Firearms Limited listing in this text for a complete chronological history of Nikko - Japan's previous long gun manufacturer.

RIFLES: BOLT ACTION

MODEL 7000 GRADE I - bolt action, all popular American calibers, including .270 Win., and .300 Wby. Mag., 24 or 26 in. barrels, select skipline checkered walnut stock, rosewood forend tip, golden eagle head engraved in pistol grip cap, recoil pad. Mfg. 1976-81.

$600	$550	$525	$450	$375	$340	$290

MODEL 7000 GRADE I AFRICAN - .375 H&H and .458 Win. Mag. cal., similar to 7000, open sights.

$650	$590	$555	$480	$400	$365	$315

MODEL 7000 GRADE II - scroll engraving, better grade wood.

$690	$625	$590	$510	$430	$395	$340

SHOTGUNS: O/U

MODEL 5000 GRADE I (FIELD) - 12 or 20 ga., 26, 28, or 30 in. barrels, various chokes, vent. rib, engraved frame, gold eagle head inlay, auto ejectors, SST, checkered pistol grip beavertail stock. Mfg. 1975-81.

$850	$775	$700	$625	$560	$510	$440

MODEL 5000 GRADE I SKEET - similar to 5000 Field, except 26 or 28 in. skeet bored, wide rib.

$875	$800	$725	$650	$580	$510	$440

GRADING - PPGS™	100%	98%	95%	90%	80%	70%	60%

MODEL 5000 GRADE I TRAP - similar to 5000 Field, except 30 or 32 in. barrel, mod. and full, imp. mod. and full, or full and full choke, wide rib, trap stock with pad.

	$875	$800	$725	$650	$580	$510	$440

MODEL 5000 GRADE II - available in Field, Trap, and Skeet, more engraving, better grade wood, with screaming eagle on frame in gold.

	$950	$875	$790	$710	$630	$540	$460
Skeet	$975	$895	$810	$725	$640	$540	$460
Trap	$975	$895	$810	$725	$640	$540	$460

GRANDEE GRADE III - similar to 5000 Grade II, except elaborate engraving, inlays, and better grade wood.

	$2,500	$2,200	$1,900	$1,575	$1,250	$1,000	$850

GOLDEN STATE ARMS

Previous importer located in Pasadena, CA. Golden State Arms imported and subcontracted various firearms constructed by European and Japanese manufacturers - achieving private label status on some guns.

Most firearms previously imported by Golden State Arms (including private labels) are not that collectible. In many cases, the shooting value will determine the price of a specimen. In some models or configurations which are currently desirable, however, premiums may exist.

GONCZ ARMAMENT, INC.

Previous manufacturer located in North Hollywood, CA circa 1984-1990.

While advertised, BATF records indicate very few Goncz pistols or carbines were actually produced. All of these guns were prototypes or individually hand-built and none were ever mass produced through normal fabrication techniques.

In 1990, Claridge Hi-Tec, Inc. purchased Goncz Armament, Inc.

GRANGER, G.

Current manufacturer established during 1902, and located in Saint Etienne, France. Current U.S. agent is Jean-Jacques Perodeau, located in Enid, OK.

All guns are made on a custom order basis. Please contact the U.S. agent directly for more information (please refer to Trademark Index).

SHOTGUNS: SxS, SIDELOCK

GRANGER SxS - 12, 16, 20, or 28 ga., case hardened receiver, Granger sidelock mechanism and plates, DT or SNT, choice of pistol or straight grip, deluxe French walnut stock and forearm, prices will vary per older customer specifications and appointments, delivery time is 12-36 months. Limited mfg.

MSR N/A	N/A	$25,000	$21,000	$18,000	$15,000	$12,000	$9,000

Add $4,767 for fine English engraving.
Add $1,783 for Aiglon fastening action.

GRANITE MOUNTAIN ARMS, INC.

Current action manufacturer located in Phoenix, AZ. Previously located in Prescott, AZ. Consumer and dealer sales.

Granite Mountain Arms, Inc. manufactures a double square bridge Mauser magnum action, available in four sizes, in both left and right hand. Sizes range from Short Magnum, Standard Magnum, Express Magnum, and the African Express Magnum for the largest of calibers such as the .505 Gibbs and the .585 cal. Barreled actions are also available, and custom rifles can be ordered from a select list of builders. Please contact the company directly for more information, including availability and pricing (see Trademark Index).

GRANT, STEPHEN

Current trademark manufactured by Atkin, Grant & Lang, established in 1867, and located in Hertfordshire, England.

The Stephen Grant trademark is responsible for mostly custom order SxS rifles and shotguns. Shotguns can be top or side lever and are equipped with sidelocks and a self-opening mechanism. Please contact the company directly for current information, availability, delivery time, and custom order pricing.

Atkin, Grant & Lang provide a useful historical research service on older Stephen Grant shotguns and rifles. The charge for this service is £25 per gun, and the company will give you all pertinent factory information regarding the history.

RIFLES: SxS

Prices on current custom order rifles and shotguns do not include VAT or importation costs.

SIDELOCK MODEL - various cals. between .300 H&H - .577 NE, best quality sidelock, individually made per customer specifications.

MSR N/A	N/A	$39,250	$35,000	$31,000	$27,000	$24,000	$20,500

SHOTGUNS: O/U

Prices on current custom order rifles and shotguns do not include VAT or importation costs.

SIDELOCK MODEL - 12, 16, 20, 28 ga., or 410 bore, best quality sidelock ejector, individually made per customer specifications.

MSR N/A	N/A	$18,500	$15,000	$12,000	$10,000	$8,850	$7,500

Add 20% for 20 ga.
Add 30% for 28 ga. and .410 bore.

SHOTGUNS: SxS

Prices on current custom order rifles and shotguns do not include VAT or importation costs.

SIDELOCK MODEL - 12, 16, 20, 28 ga., or .410 bore, best quality sidelock ejector, top or side lever opening, individually made per customer specifications.

MSR N/A	N/A	$12,000	$9,900	$8,700	$7,500	$6,250	$5,000

Add 20% for 20 ga.
Add 30% for 28 ga. and .410 bore.

GREAT WESTERN ARMS COMPANY

Previous company founded by Mr. William R. Wilson and located in CA.

Originated probably in early 1953, when Colt Firearms Company ceased production of what is known today as "First Generation Single Action Army Revolvers." After several trips to the Colt factory to ascertain Colt's intent of reviving their production of the S.A. Army, and being assured it would never be revived, he founded the G.W. Arms Co. The main change between the Colt S.A. and the G.W. Frontier was removing the firing pin from the hammer and the design of a rebounding firing pin inserted in the revolver frame. This firm also redesigned the Remington Double Derringer and produced a derringer in 2 cals., .38 S&W and .38 S&W Special. Approx. 2,000 of these were mfg. Production of the Frontier probably did not exceed 23,000. When the Colt Company resumed production of their 2nd Generation S.A. 1873 Revolver, it rang the death knell of Great Western Arms Co. products, and the G.W. Arms Co. soon disappeared with its last sales of their "Frontier" being sold as unassembled "Kit Guns" to be assembled by the purchaser.

DERRINGERS

GREAT WESTERN DERRINGER - .38 S&W or .38 S&W Spl. cal. (not interchangeable). Basically an improved version of the Remington Double Derringer frame.

$350	$300	$250	$225	$200	$180	$175

GRADING - PPGS™	100%	98%	95%	90%	80%	70%	60%

REVOLVERS: SINGLE ACTION

FRONTIER MODEL SAA - .45 LC, .44-40 WCF, .44 Mag., .44 Spl., .357 Atomic, .357 Mag., .38 S&W Spl., .32-20 WCF, .22 Hornet, or .22 Rimfire cal., 3 1/2, 5 1/2, or 7 1/2 in. barrel, blue with case hardened colors on frame, gate and hammer, all blue, satin blue, nickel, black nickel, copper plated black oxide, gold, silver, gold and silver and parkerizing, grips were imitation stag (plastic), wood, pearl, ivory and sterling silver on special order. Unfinished "Kit Guns" were also sold, allowing buyer to assemble and finish.

	$800	$750	$700	$600	$450	$400	$350

Add 50% for flattop model.

Great Western Arms Company had a wide variety of factory special order features and options. They will act both independently and interdependently to determine the premiums on values listed.

GREENER, W.W., LIMITED

Current manufacturer established in 1829 and located in Hagley, England, with sales and administration offices located in Wiltshire, England. No current U.S. importation. Until 1994, Gibbs Rifle Co. located in Martinsburg, WV was the U.S. agent.

RIFLES: SxS, CURRENT MFG.

Boxlock and sidelock rifle quotations may be obtained by writing the company directly (see Trademark Index). A complete choice of calibers, engraving options, and walnut selection are available on a special order basis only.

SHOTGUNS: SINGLE SHOT

GENERAL PURPOSE - 12 ga., improved Martini action, single shot, 26, 30, or 32 in. barrel, full or mod., auto ejectors, straight checkered stock.

	$330	$305	$275	$220	$195	$165	$160

GP MK II - 12 ga. only, famed general purpose (GP) English shotgun configuration featuring Greener Martini action, 28 or 30 in. barrel, walnut stock and forearm. Mfg. resumed in 1991.

MSR N/A	$522	$450	$400	$350	$300	$250	$195

Older, used military contract variations of this model have been imported recently - typically seen in the $165-$200 range.

SHOTGUNS: SxS, DISC.

FARKILLER GRADE F35 - 12 ga., 28, 30, or 32 in. barrels, hammerless boxlock, checkered straight or semi-pistol grip stock.

	$2,420	$2,200	$2,090	$1,870	$1,760	$1,650	$1,540
Auto ejectors	$3,300	$3,025	$2,750	$2,475	$2,035	$1,925	$1,650

FARKILLER GRADE F35 LARGE BORE - 8 or 10 ga., similar to F35.

	$2,750	$2,585	$2,310	$2,090	$1,980	$1,815	$1,650
Auto ejectors	$3,575	$3,300	$3,080	$2,860	$2,640	$2,090	$1,925

HAMMERLESS EJECTOR MODELS - 12, 16, 20, 28 ga., or .410 bore, 26, 28, or 30 in. barrels supplied with any choke combination, auto ejectors, single or double triggers, straight or semi-pistol grip stock, grades differ as follows:

✳ *Jubilee Grade DH35*

	$2,420	$2,255	$2,090	$1,925	$1,650	$1,540	$1,375

✳ *Sovereign Grade DH40*

	$2,860	$2,695	$2,420	$2,200	$1,980	$1,815	$1,595

GRADING - PPGS™	100%	98%	95%	90%	80%	70%	60%
✳ *Crown Grade DH55*							
	$3,300	$3,080	$2,915	$2,750	$2,420	$2,035	$1,760
✳ *Royal Grade DH75*							
	$4,400	$4,180	$3,850	$3,300	$3,080	$2,915	$2,640

Add $400 for SST.

Note: Degree of engraving and grade of wood are the basic differences between models.

EMPIRE - 12 ga. only, 2 3/4 or 3 in., any choke, 28, 30, or 32 in. barrel, hammerless, boxlock, straight stock or semi pistol grip.

	100%	98%	95%	90%	80%	70%	60%
	$1,760	$1,540	$1,320	$1,100	$935	$825	$770
Auto ejectors	$1,980	$1,760	$1,540	$1,320	$1,155	$1,045	$990

EMPIRE DELUXE - similar to Empire, only better grade wood.

	100%	98%	95%	90%	80%	70%	60%
	$1,980	$1,760	$1,540	$1,320	$1,155	$1,045	$990
Auto ejectors	$2,200	$1,980	$1,760	$1,540	$1,375	$1,265	$1,100

SHOTGUNS: SxS, CURRENT MFG.

Various hard and soft cases are available for the following models with prices ranging from $500 up to $3,200.

NO. 5 NEEDHAM EJECTOR - 12, 16, 20 ga., or .410 bore, scalloped boxlock action, DT, any barrel length.

MSR N/A	$4,470	$3,750	$3,175	$2,750	$2,250	$1,825	$1,475

This model has been re-introduced to commemorate the takeover of J. V. Needham by W.W. Greener in 1874.

DH 40 - similar to No. 5 Needham Ejector, except has better engraving and deluxe walnut stock and forearm.

MSR N/A	$6,705	$5,900	$5,000	$4,250	$3,500	$2,850	$2,100

DH 75 - 12 ga. only, 2 3/4 in. chambers, Greener "Facile Princeps" scalloped boxlock action 27, 28, or 30 in. barrels, case hardened receiver, choice of engraving (game scene or fine scroll work).

MSR N/A	$11,175	$9,950	$8,450	$7,250	$6,000	$4,950	$3,875

DOH 90 - 12, 16, 20 ga., or .410 bore, 2 1/2, 2 3/4 or 3 in. Mag. chambers, best boxlock featuring Anson & Deeley scalloped boxlock action with Greener easy-opening device, French walnut stock, DT.

MSR N/A	$14,900	$12,500	$9,750	$8,250	$7,000	$5,850	$4,675

L 120 - 12, 16, 20 ga., or .410 bore, best sidelock ejector model with dovetail lump barrels, fine scroll engraving with choice of bright or color case hardened frame finish.

MSR N/A	$22,350	$19,500	$16,000	$13,000	$10,000	$7,850	$6,000

L 150 - 12, 16, 20 ga., or .410 bore, 2 1/2 or 3 in. chambers, very best sidelock ejector model with chopper lump barrels and easy-opening device, bright or color case hardened frame finish.

MSR N/A	$29,800	$24,000	$21,000	$17,000	$14,000	$11,000	$8,500

L 500 - 12, 16, 20 ga., or .410 bore, new St. George sidelock ejector model incorporating top-of-the-line carved engraving, walnut, and workmanship.

Because this model is entirely custom ordered per individual choice, a price quotation is necessary on every order.

GREIFELT AND COMPANY

Previous manufacturer located in Suhl, E. Germany.

COMBINATION GUNS

COMBINATION MODEL - 12, 16, 20, 28 ga., or .410 bore, shotgun barrel, rifle in any rimmed caliber, 24 or 26 in. solid rib barrel, pre-WWII.

	$5,200	$4,800	$4,400	$4,000	$3,600	$3,150	$2,800

Add $700 for auto ejectors.
Subtract 10% for 16 ga.
Add 20% for 28 ga. or .410 bore.
Subtract 40-50% for obsolete rifle caliber.
Above values for 12 or 20 ga. over obtainable rifle cartridge.

DRILLINGS

DRILLING MODEL - 12, 16, or 20 ga., SxS shotgun over rimmed rifle caliber, 26 in. barrels, boxlock, extractors, double triggers, rifle sight activated by barrel selector, pre-WWII.

	$3,500	$3,000	$2,750	$2,550	$2,300	$2,000	$1,750

Subtract 10% for 16 ga.
Subtract 40-50% for obsolete cals.
Above values for 12 or 20 ga. over obtainable rifle cartridge.

SHOTGUNS: O/U

GRADE NO. 1 - 12, 16, 20, 28 ga., or .410 bore, O/U, any barrel 26-32 in., choke, vent. or solid rib, Anson & Deeley boxlock, auto ejectors, checkered pistol grip or English stock, pre-war.

12 or 20 ga.	$3,600	$3,200	$2,850	$2,500	$2,100	$1,750	$1,500

Subtract 10% for 16 ga.
Add 30% for 28 ga. or .410 bore.
Add $300 for vent. rib.
Add $400 for SST.

GRADE NO. 3 - similar to No. 1, except less elaborate engraving, pre-WWII.

12 or 20 ga.	$2,850	$2,500	$2,200	$2,000	$1,650	$1,350	$1,200

Subtract 10% for 16 ga.
Add 20% for 28 ga. or .410 bore.
Add $300 for vent. rib.
Add $400 for SST.

MODEL 143E - similar to No. 1, except not as high quality as pre-war model, not available in 28 ga. or .410 bore. Mfg. post-WWII.

	$2,400	$2,150	$1,850	$1,550	$1,350	$1,175	$1,000

Add 10% for vent. rib and SST.

SHOTGUNS: SxS

MODEL 22 - 12 or 20 ga., 28 or 30 in. mod. and full, hammerless, boxlock, false side-plates, extractors, checkered pistol grip or English style stock, post-WWII.

	$2,200	$1,760	$1,595	$1,320	$1,100	$990	$825

MODEL 22E - similar to Model 22, except has auto ejectors.

	$2,750	$2,200	$1,980	$1,760	$1,540	$1,430	$1,265

GRADING - PPGS™	100%	98%	95%	90%	80%	70%	60%

MODEL 103 - 12 or 16 ga., 28 or 30 in. mod. and full, extractors, double triggers, checkered pistol grip or English stock, post-war.

		100%	98%	95%	90%	80%	70%	60%
		$1,980	$1,650	$1,485	$1,210	$990	$880	$715

MODEL 103E - similar to Model 103, except has auto ejectors.

	100%	98%	95%	90%	80%	70%	60%
	$2,200	$1,760	$1,595	$1,320	$1,100	$990	$825

GRENDEL, INC.

Previous manufacturer located in Rockledge, FL, circa 1990-95.

PISTOLS: SEMI-AUTO

MODEL P-10 SERIES - .380 ACP cal., blowback double action, 10 shot mag., small dimensions, hammerless, matte blue finish, 15 oz. Mfg. disc. 1991.

	100%	98%	95%	90%	80%	70%	60%
	$140	$125	$115	$105	$95	$90	$85

Last MSR was $155.

Add $15 for electroless nickel finish.
Add $15 for nickel green finish.
Green finish was available at no extra charge.

MODEL P-12 - .380 ACP cal., double action only, 3 in. barrel, steel construction with polymer grip area, no external safety, 11 shot Zytel mag., blue or electroless nickel finish, 11 lb. trigger pull, 13 oz. Mfg. 1992-95.

	100%	98%	95%	90%	80%	70%	60%
	$155	$135	$120	$110	$100	$90	$80

Last MSR was $175.

Add $20 for nickel finish.
Add $50 for threaded barrel with muzzle brake parts option.

MODEL P-30 - .22 Mag. cal., blowback similar action to P-12, 5 in. barrel, hammerless, matte black finish, 10 (C/B 1994) or 30* shot mag., 21 oz. Mfg. 1990-95.

	100%	98%	95%	90%	80%	70%	60%
	$240	$200	$175	$155	$140	$125	$115

Last MSR was $225.

Add $25 for electroless nickel finish (disc. 1991).
Add $35 for scope mount (Weaver base).

✱ *Model P-30M* - similar to Model P-30, except has 5.6 in. barrel with removable muzzle brake. Mfg. 1990-95.

	100%	98%	95%	90%	80%	70%	60%
	$250	$210	$180	$160	$140	$125	$115

Last MSR was $235.

Add $25 for electroless nickel finish (disc. 1991).

MODEL P-30L - similar to Model P-30, except has 8 in. barrel with removable muzzle brake, 22 oz. Mfg. 1991-92.

	100%	98%	95%	90%	80%	70%	60%
	$275	$235	$200	$180	$160	$140	$125

Last MSR was $280.

Add $15 for Model P-30LM that allows for fitting various accessories.

MODEL P-31 - .22 Mag. cal., same action as P-30, except has 11 in. barrel, enclosed synthetic barrel shroud and flash hider, 48 oz. Mfg. 1990-95.

	100%	98%	95%	90%	80%	70%	60%
	$350	$315	$275	$240	$215	$185	$160

Last MSR was $345.

RIFLES & CARBINES

MODEL R-31 - similar design to Model P-31, except has 16 in. barrel and telescoping stock, 64 oz. Mfg. 1991-95.

	100%	98%	95%	90%	80%	70%	60%
	$365	$325	$275	$235	$210	$185	$165

Last MSR was $385.

GRADING - PPGS™	100%	98%	95%	90%	80%	70%	60%

SRT-20F COMPACT - .243 Win. or .308 Win. cal., bolt action based on the Sako A-2 action, 20 in. match grade finned barrel with muzzle brake, folding synthetic stock, integrated bipod rest, no sights, 9 shot mag., 6.7 lbs. Disc. 1989.

		$575	$525	$475	$395	$365	$340	$320

Last MSR was $525.

Grendel previously manufactured the SRT-16F, SRT-20L, and SRT-24 - all were disc. 1988. Values are approx. the same as the SRT-20F.

GRIFFIN & HOWE

Current custom gunsmith, rifle manufacturer, and importer established 1923, with store locations in Bernardsville, NJ (gunsmithing also), and Greenwich, CT. Griffin & Howe also had a NY City store location until April, 2003.

Founded in 1923 by Seymour Griffin and James Howe, Griffin & Howe continues to build its custom rifles as well as providing the full spectrum of gunsmithing services and importation of fine English guns.

Griffin & Howe has been building custom rifles since 1923. They also perform a variety of custom gunsmithing services. Prices may vary greatly depending on configuration, desirability, condition and special features. Most used Griffin & Howe Custom Rifles in average condition and without special engraving start at $3,150+ and rise according to condition and nature of the individual gun. Since 1923, fewer than 2,800 have been made. In 1930, Griffin & Howe became a subsidiary of Abercrombie & Fitch and remained with them until 1976, when it became a privately held company. Because all Griffin & Howe rifles are essentially special ordered, accurate pricing can be ascertained only by examining each individual gun. Elaborate specimens by this maker trademark will command over $10,000. Engraving by Joseph Fugger, Winston Churchill, Robert Swartley or Rudolph Kornbrath will add considerably to the value.

Pricing on new custom rifles, with a wide selection of options, is available directly from Griffin & Howe.

RIFLES: BOLT ACTION

Values represent a standard gun with no upgrades or options.

G&H CLASSIC FRENCH WALNUT STOCK - most popular cals., custom honed action with lapped lugs, Douglas premium barrel, hand engraving, French walnut sporter stock with ebony forend tip, G&H pistol grip cap, "Griffin & Howe, New York" barrel address, custom order.

Current MSR on this model is $15,000.

WIN M70 STANDARD ACTION - for .243 Win., .270 Win., .30-06, or .308 Win. cal.

	$6,500	$6,050	$5,350	$4,600	$3,900	$3,300	$2,750

WIN M70 MEDIUM - .300 Win. Mag., 7mm Rem. Mag., or .338 Win. Mag. cal.

	$6,750	$6,250	$5,500	$4,750	$4,000	$3,450	$2,950

WIN M70 MAGNUM - .375 H&H or .416 Rigby cal.

	$7,000	$6,500	$5,650	$4,850	$4,100	$3,550	$3,000

WIN M52 - .22 LR cal.

	$4,350	$4,000	$3,700	$3,400	$3,100	$2,700	$2,400

WIN HIGHWALL

	$3,800	$3,500	$3,150	$2,850	$2,500	$2,100	$1,850

SPRINGFIELD 1903

	$3,800	$3,450	$3,250	$3,000	$2,700	$2,450	$2,100

GRADING - PPGS™	100%	98%	95%	90%	80%	70%	60%
SPRINGFIELD 1922							
	$3,650	$3,300	$3,050	$2,850	$2,500	$2,250	$2,000
MAUSER STANDARD							
	$5,250	$4,750	$4,250	$3,750	$3,300	$3,000	$2,650
MAUSER MAGNUM							
	$9,850	$9,000	$8,500	$7,850	$6,850	$5,950	$4,950
SAVAGE 99							
	$2,850	$2,550	$2,250	$2,000	$1,850	$1,600	$1,350

G&H PRE-'64 MODEL 70 CLASSIC SYNTHETIC STOCK - most popular cals., features glass bedded synthetic classic sporter stock in black or woodgrain finish, Douglas premium barrel, "Griffin & Howe, New York" barrel address, custom order. Disc. 2002.

	$4,750	$4,450	$4,000	$3,700	$3,500	$3,300	$3,100

Last MSR was $2,250.

SHOTGUNS: O/U

MADISON - 12, 20, 28 ga., or .410 bore, case hardened frame, 26 1/2, 28, or 30 in. VR barrels, scroll engraved with gold accents. Mfg. by the Belgian Browning custom shop using a B25 action beginning 1999.

MSR $9,750	$9,000	$8,250	$7,750	$7,150	$6,450	$5,500	$4,500

CLAREMONT - 12 ga. only, case hardened frame, shallow frame BOSS style lock-up, 30 in. VR barrels standard length, scroll engraving with gold accents. Mfg. by Gamba beginning 1999.

MSR $8,750	$8,000	$7,500	$7,100	$6,250	$5,750	$5,000	$4,300

EXTRA FINISH CLAREMONT - similiar to Claremont, except has coin finished frame with full coverage acanthus scroll engraving and drop out trigger group. Importation began 1999.

MSR $11,500	$10,800	$9,950	$8,500	$7,300	$6,500	$5,700	$5,200

CLAREMONT LUSSO - similar to Extra Finish Claremont, except has fully engraved sideplates. Importation began 2000.

MSR $18,000	$17,250	$16,750	$14,800	$12,000	$10,250	$9,000	$8,000

BROADWAY - 12 or 20 ga., case hardened frame, 26, 28, or 30 in. VR barrels, scroll engraving with gold accents. Mfg. by the Belgian Browning custom shop using a B125 action 1999-2003.

	$5,750	$5,250	$4,600	$4,150	$3,650	$2,950	$2,550

Last MSR was $5,750.

SUPERBRITTE - 12 or 16 ga., unique side opening design, built by Britte company in Liege, Belgium before WWII, purchased by G&H in 2001.

MSR $25,000	$23,500	$21,250	$18,500	$16,750	$14,950	$12,750	$11,500

SHOTGUNS: SxS

ROUND BODY GAME GUN - 12, 16, 20, 28 ga., or .410 bore, features case colored round frame with sidelock action, "SAFE" in gold, H&H style selective ejectors, 25-30 in. barrels, double triggers, checkered straight grip stock and splinter forearm, G&H name gold inlaid, cased (optional 2004). Mfg. by Arrieta, importation began 1989.

MSR $5,950	$5,500	$5,100	$4,750	$4,150	$3,600	$3,100	$2,500

Add $500 for 20 ga., $900 for 28 ga. or .410 bore.
Add $1,150 for single trigger.

GRADING - PPGS™	100%	98%	95%	90%	80%	70%	60%

✳ *Pair of Round Body Game Guns* - 12, 16, 20, 28 ga. or .410 bore, scroll engraved with case colored hardened finish, "SAFE" in gold, round sidelock action, H&H style selective ejectors, 25-30 in. barrels, double triggers, checkered straight grip and splinter forearm, G&H name inlaid in gold, built as a pair, and gold numbered 1 & 2 on barrels, forend, and top lever. Mfg. by Arrieta.

MSR $12,950	$11,950	$10,500	$9,500	$8,500	$7,650	$6,850	$6,000

Add $1,000 for pair of 20 ga.

Add $3,000 for assisted opening.

EXTRA FINISH ROUND BODY GAME GUN - same action as Round Body Game Gun, except has coin finished frame and game scene engraving with gold accents, upgraded wood. Importation began 1999.

MSR $8,950	$8,300	$7,850	$7,200	$6,400	$5,600	$4,900	$4,000

Add $800 for 20 ga. or $1,000 for 28 ga. or .410 bore.

Add $1,150 for single trigger.

✳ *Pair of Extra Finish Round Body Game Guns* - built as a pair, gold numbered 1 & 2 on barrels, forend, and top lever.

MSR $19,750	$18,500	$16,500	$14,750	$13,500	$11,500	$9,750	$8,500

Add $2,000 for pair of 20 ga.

Add $3,000 for assisted opening.

BRITTE - 12 ga. only, best quality sidelock ejector, built by Britte company in Liege, Belgium before WWII, purchased by G&H in 2001.

MSR $15,000	$13,750	$12,900	$11,700	$10,500	$9,250	$8,400	$7,500

CONTINENTAL SIDELOCK - 12 ga. only, best quality Britte action, finished by current Belgium gunmakers such as Lebeau-Courally, various scroll patterns, case colored or bright finish, finest European walnut stock.

MSR $18,500	$17,000	$15,000	$13,100	$11,000	$9,250	$8,300	$6,900

✳ *Pair of Continental Sidelocks* - 12 ga. only, built as a pair, gold numbered 1 & 2 on barrels, forend, and top lever.

MSR $38,500	$35,500	$31,400	$28,750	$26,750	$23,500	$19,500	$17,750

GRIFFON

Currently manufactured by Continental Weapons (Pty) Ltd. established in 1996, and located in Midrand, Johannesburg, South Africa. No current U.S. importation. Previously imported and distributed by Griffon USA, Inc., a subsidiary of 21st Century Technologies, Inc., located in Ft. Worth, TX, and by First Defense International located in San Clemente, CA.

GRIFFON

Values represent the most recent U.S. pricing.

GRIFFON 1911 A1 COMBAT - .45 ACP cal., patterned after the Colt M1911, single action, 4.13 in. barrel, 7 shot mag., ported barrel/slide, black Teflon finish, Commander hammer, Tritium sights, 36.5 oz. New 1997.

MSR N/A	$445	$375	$335	$300	$275	$250	$225

GRIFFON CW 11 - 9mm Para. cal., 8 shot mag., 4 in. barrel without porting, combo blue/chrome finish, perforated trigger, 3 dot sighting system. New 1997.

MSR N/A	$445	$375	$335	$300	$275	$250	$225

GRADING - PPGS™	100%	98%	95%	90%	80%	70%	60%

GRULLA ARMAS

Current manufacturer located in Eibar, Spain since 1932. Currently imported and distributed by Hi-Grade Imports, located in Gilroy, CA, Fieldsport, located in Traverse City, MI, GSI, located in Trussville, AL, Lion Country Supply, located in Port Matilda, PA, and by Dale's Decoy Den, located in Nelsonville, OH.

Grulla Armas manufactures a complete line of quality SxS shotguns in addition to both SxS and double rifles.

RIFLES

C-95 BOLT ACTION - .338 Win. Mag. or .375 H&H cal., deluxe bolt action featuring extensively scroll engraved square bridge receiver with elongated upper tang, octagon barrel with quarter rib and express sights, deluxe checkered wood with ebony forend tip, custom made per individual order. New 1996.

MSR $7,500	$6,950	$6,400	$5,750	$4,950	$4,300	$3,600	$2,750

E-95 SxS DOUBLE RIFLE - 9.3x74R or .375 H&H cal., top-of-the-line double rifle utilizing H&H type sidelocks with scroll engraving, skeleton steel buttplate, regulated barrels, beavertail forend, custom-made per individual order. New 1996.

MSR $20,000	$18,000	$15,750	$13,250	$11,750	$9,650	$8,500	$7,250

SHOTGUNS: SxS, SIDELOCK

The following models are currently available in 12, 16, 20, 28 ga., or .410 bore. All guns have double triggers with hinged front, selective auto-ejectors, and straight grip stock with splinter forearm. Values represent standard models with no options.

MODEL 209 - HOLLAND - choice of case colored, antique silver, or coin finished receiver, scroll engraving with hand rubbed oil finish, 27 or 28 in. chopper lump barrels, gas escape valves.

MSR $3,450	$2,950	$2,525	$2,125	$1,800	$1,500	$1,325	$1,100

MODEL 215 - similar to Model 209, except has rose and scroll engraving and nicer wood.

MSR $4,050	$3,600	$3,000	$2,500	$2,100	$1,800	$1,500	$1,325

MODEL 216 - similar to Model 215, except features Purdey style scroll hand engraving.

MSR $4,550	$4,000	$3,550	$2,975	$2,475	$2,100	$1,800	$1,500

MODEL 216RB - round body version of the Model 216, features Purdey style scroll hand engraving, drop points absent, upgraded wood, deluxe finish.

MSR $4,950	$4,200	$3,675	$3,050	$2,500	$2,000	$1,800	$1,650

MODEL 216RL - 12, 20, or 28 ga., round body, H&H style sidelocks, deluxe checkered straight grip walnut stock and forearm, 28 in. chopper lump barrels, 6-7.1 lbs. Importation began 2004.

MSR $7,495	$6,950	$6,200	$5,400	$4,600	$3,800	$3,000	$2,450

This model is sold exclusively through GSI, Inc.

MODEL 219 - features morte elaborate engraving and better wood.

	$5,325	$4,950	$4,000	$3,550	$2,950	$2,475	$1,995

Last MSR was $6,050.

CONSORT - features easy-opening H&H style action, upgraded wood, approx. 50% floral pattern engraving, deluxe finish, 27 or 28 in. chopper lump barrels, gas escape valves.

MSR $6,475	$5,875	$5,150	$4,575	$3,850	$3,275	$2,650	$2,200

GRADING - PPGS™	100%	98%	95%	90%	80%	70%	60%

WINDSOR - similar to Consort Model, except has approx. 70% engraving, round action, drop points absent, deep relief engraving with upgraded wood, deluxe finish, 27 or 28 in. chopper lump barrel.

	MSR $6,995	$6,225	$5,600	$4,975	$4,350	$3,750	$3,000	$2,400

MODEL 219-P

	MSR $7,750	$7,050	$6,225	$5,600	$4,850	$4,100	$3,200	$2,600

SUPER MH - best quality sidelock with Purdey style engraving, seven pin H&H lock, H&H style assisted opening, chrome nickel steel barrels, fitted leather case, select XXX walnut stock, deluxe hand rubbed oil finish.

	MSR $12,395	$11,400	$9,500	$8,475	$7,425	$6,200	$5,000	$4,150

NUMBER 1 - next to the top-of-the-line gun with best quality features.

	MSR $15,550	$13,175	$10,625	$8,800	$7,575	$6,350	$5,150	$4,200

ROYAL - 12 or 20 ga., top-of-the-line model with H&H style scroll engraving, seven pin H&H lock, H&H style assisted opening, chrome nickel steel barrels, fitted leather case, select XXX walnut stock, deluxe hand rubbed oil finish.

	MSR $22,995	$20,500	$16,750	$13,000	$10,500	$8,750	$7,575	$6,350

GRÜNIG & ELMIGER AG

Current rifle manufacturer located in Malters, Switzerland. Currently represented in the U.S. by Gunsmithing, Inc., located in Colorado Springs, CO, and by Brenzovich Firearms Training Center, located in Ft. Hancock, TX.

Grünig & Elmiger AG manufacture high quality competition and sporting rifles. Please contact the factory directly for current U.S. availability and pricing (see Trademark Index).

GUN WORKS, LTD.

Previous manufacturer and distributor located in Buffalo, NY. Early guns were made in Tonawanda, NY.

HANDGUNS

X-CALIBER - .44 Mag. cal., single shot, tip up pistol, 8 in. barrel, matte type blue finish, ergonomic hardwood grips, probably used older Sterling Arms parts and restamped the barrel address. Limited mfg.

	$350	$300	$260	$230	$200	$175	$150

MODEL 9 - .357 Mag., 9mm Para., .38 Super, or .38 Spl. cal., O/U derringer, electroless nickel finish, 2 1/2 in. barrel, wood grips, Millett sights, 15 oz. Disc. 1986.

	$135	$120	$105	$95	$65	$55	$50

Last MSR was $149.

GUSTAF, CARL

See listing under Carl Gustaf.

GYROJET

See MBA Gyrojet listing in the M Section of this text.

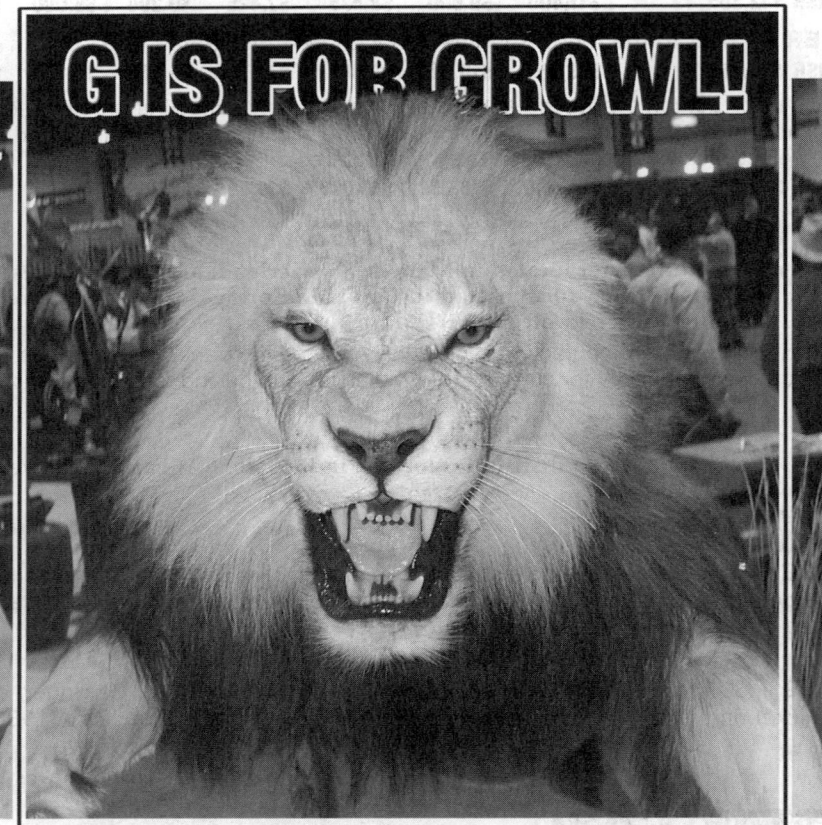

You could almost hear the roar out of this beautiful lion from the recent Safari Club International show in Reno, NV.

H SECTION

HHF

Please refer to the Huglu section.

H.J.S. INDUSTRIES, INC.

Previous manufacturer located in Brownsville, TX.

GRADING - PPGS™	100%	98%	95%	90%	80%	70%	60%

DERRINGERS

FRONTIER FOUR - .22 LR cal., 4 shot derringer, stainless steel construction, 5 1/2 oz.

	$115	$90	$80				

LONE STAR - .38 S&W cal., single shot derringer, stainless steel construction, 6 oz.

	$137	$105	$95				

H & R 1871, LLC. (HARRINGTON & RICHARDSON)

Current manufacturer and holding company located in Gardner, MA since 1991. During 2000, Marlin Firearms Co. purchased the assets of H&R 1871, Inc., and the name was changed to H&R 1871, LLC. Production of H&R products will continue at the factory located in Gardner, MA.

H & R 1871 LLC utilizes the original H & R trademark and does not accept warranty work for older (pre-1986 mfg.) Harrington & Richardson, Inc. firearms. Distributor sales only.

The use of the original Harrington & Richardson trademark was permitted during 1991. All new manufacture will use this trademark, but older H & Rs manufactured by Harrington & Richardson, Inc. are not the responsibility of H & R 1871, LLC.

REVOLVERS

Additional revolvers using the New England Firearms trademark may be located in the N section of this text. During 1997-99, all H & R 1871, Inc. revolvers were supplied with a lockable plastic case.

929 SIDEKICK - .22 LR cal., 9 shot, blue metal, swing-out cylinder, 4 in. heavy barrel, square butt with brown laminate grips, fixed sights, 30 oz. Mfg. 1996-99.

	$150	$120	$100	$85	$75	$65	$55

Last MSR was $173.

✳ ***929 Sidekick Trapper Edition*** - similar to 929 Sidekick, except has grey laminate grips and special barrel markings, limited mfg. 1996 only, distributed through 1996.

	$150	$115	$95	$85	$75	$65	$55

Last MSR was $175.

939 PREMIER WESTERN TARGET - .22 LR cal., 9 shot, blue metal, swing-out cylinder, target model with ribbed 6 in. heavy barrel and adj. rear sight, hardwood grips, 36 oz. Mfg. 1995-99.

	$150	$125	$105	$90	$75	$65	$55

Last MSR was $190.

FOURTY-NINER (WESTERN 949) - .22 LR cal., 9 shot fixed cylinder, case colored frame, 5 1/2 or 7 1/2 in. barrel, hardwood grips, fixed sights, approx. 37 oz. Mfg. 1995-99.

	$150	$125	$105	$90	$75	$65	$55

Last MSR was $190.

GRADING - PPGS™	100%	98%	95%	90%	80%	70%	60%

SPORTSMAN 999 - .22 LR cal., single or double action, top break action with auto shell ejection, 9 shot, 4 or 6 in. barrel with fluted solid rib, smooth hardwood stocks, transfer bar safety, blue finish, adj. sights, 30-34 oz. Mfg. 1991-99.

	$230	$180	$145	$125	$115	$100	$90

Last MSR was $285.

RIFLES: SINGLE SHOT

H&R 1871 began providing the Trigger Guardian trigger locking system beginning Dec. 1, 1999 at no extra charge.

ULTRA MODEL - .22 Mag. (new 2002), .22-250 Rem. (disc. 1994), .223 Rem. (disc. 1997, reintroduced 2002), .25-06 Rem. (new 1995), .243 Win., .270 Win. (new 2005), .30-06 (new 2005), .308 Win. (new 1995), .357 Rem. Max. (mfg. 1996-98), .450 Marlin (mfg. 2001-2004), 7x57mm (mfg. 1997 only), or 7x64mm (mfg. 1997 only) cal., single shot break-open action with ejector, side-lever release, 22 in. heavy (.22-250 Rem. or .223 Rem.), 22 in. normal (.22 Mag., .308 Win. or .450 Marlin), or 26 in. (.25-06 Rem.) barrel with scope mount rail, checkered curly maple (disc. 1994) or laminated cinnamon hardwood Monte Carlo stock with black line recoil pad, sling swivel studs, 7-8 lbs. New 1993.

MSR $349	$275	$220	$160	$120	$110	$95	$85

Subtract $30 for metric cals. (disc.).

This model features a scope rail on .25-06 Rem. and .308 Win. cals.

❋ *Ultra .22 Mag.* - .22 Mag. cal. only, 22 standard or 24 in. heavy (disc.) in. barrel.

MSR $203	$160	$130	$105	$90	$85	$80	$75

❋ *Ultra Varmint Model* - .204 Ruger (new 2005), .22-250 Rem. (new 2005), .223 Rem. or .243 Win. (disc. 2004) cal., features heavy 24 in. fluted (new 2005) or unfluted (disc. 2004) barrel, blue finish, natural finish cinnamon laminate Monte Carlo (disc. 2004) or synthetic (new 2005) stock, includes scope mount rail. New 1998.

MSR $396	$315	$245	$180	$150	$125	$110	$95

Subtract approx. 15% if w/o fluted barrel.

❋ *Ultra Comp. Model* - .270 Win. or .30-06 cal., features 23 in. barrel with integral compensator, blue finish, multi-color checkered laminate wood stock and forearm. Approx. 7-8 lbs. Mfg. 1997-2003.

	$310	$240	$195	$150	$125	$105	$95

Last MSR was $376.

❋ *Rocky Mountain Elk Foundation Commemorative 1st Ed.* - .280 Rem. cal., 26 in. blue barrel, features RMEF medallion in stock, high gloss bluing, 7-8 lbs. Mfg. 1995-96.

	$220	$175	$135				

Last MSR was $270.

❋ *Rocky Mountain Elk Foundation Commemorative 2nd Ed.* - .35 Whelen cal., 26 in. blue barrel, features RMEF medallion in multi-color laminate stock and forearm, high gloss bluing, 7-8 lbs. Mfg. 1996-97.

	$260	$215	$160				

Last MSR was $300.

WHITETAILS UNLIMITED COMMEMORATIVE RIFLE - .30-30 (new 1998) or .45-70 Govt. cal., Topper style break-open action, 22 in. barrel, blue frame with special etching, checkered American walnut stock (with medallion) and forearm. 7 lbs. Mfg. 1997-98.

	$250	$210	$170				

Last MSR was $290.

HARRINGTON & RICHARDSON BUFFALO CLASSIC

HARRINGTON & RICHARDSON BUFFALO CLASSIC - .45-70 Govt. cal., top lever break open action, 32 in. barrel, case hardened frame, checkered walnut stock and forearm, 8 lbs. New 1995.

	MSR $438		$365	$280	$230			

This model was also produced under the Wesson & Harrington trademark.

HARRINGTON & RICHARDSON TARGET RIFLE - .38-55 WCF cal., 28 in. barrel, target sights, blue finish 7 1/2 lbs. New 1998.

	MSR $438		$365	$280	$230			

This model was also produced under the Wesson & Harrington trademark.

SHOTGUNS: O/U

PINNACLE - 12 or 20 ga., 3 in. chambers, 26 (12 ga.) or 28 (20 ga.) in. vent. rib barrels with choke tubes, SST, ejectors, checkered walnut finished pistol grip stock with fluted comb, vent. recoil pad, bead front sight, 6.75 lbs. New 2005.

	MSR $886		$675	$525	$450	$400	$365	$335	$295

SHOTGUNS: SEMI-AUTO

EXCELL AUTO 5 - 12 ga., 3 in. chamber, 28 in. VR barrel with choke tubes, 5 shot mag., black synthetic, walnut, or Realtree Advantage Wetlands 100% camo covered pistol grip stock with fluted comb, vent. recoil pad, bead front sight, approx. 7 lbs. New 2005.

	MSR $415		$325	$275	$235	$200	$180	$160	$140

Add $46 for walnut stock or $80 for 100% camo coverage.

✱ *Excell Auto 5 Turkey* - 12 ga., 3 in. chamber, fiber optic sights, 5 shot mag., 22 in. vent. rib barrel with choke tubes, Realtree Advantage Hardwoods camo covered pistol grip stock and barrel, 7 lbs. New 2005.

	MSR $495		$425	$375	$335	$295	$265	$230	$195

✱ *Excell Auto 5 Combo* - includes 24 in. rifled slug barrel and 28 in. regular barrel, synthetic stock only. New 2005.

	MSR $583		$485	$400	$360	$320	$290	$260	$230

SHOTGUNS: SINGLE SHOT

H&R 1871 began providing the Trigger Guardian trigger locking system beginning Dec. 1, 1999 at no extra charge.

TOPPER (098) - 12, 16 (new 1992), 20, 28 (mfg. 1992-95, reintroduced 1998) ga., or .410 bore, 2 3/4 (16 and 28 ga.) or 3 in. chamber, 26 or 28 in. barrel, break open side lever release action, transfer bar safety, ejector, satin nickel frame with blue barrel, black finish hardwood stock with full pistol grip and forearm, 5-6 lbs. Mfg. began 1991.

	MSR $149		$110	$90	$80	$70	$60	$50	$40

✱ *Topper Deluxe* - 12 ga. only, 3 1/2 in. chamber, satin nickel frame with blue barrel, 28 in. barrel with 1 choke tube, black finish hardwood stock (with recoil pad) and forearm, 5-6 lbs. New 1991.

	MSR $175		$135	$115	$95	$80	$70	$60	$50

✱ *Topper Deluxe Classic* - 12 or 20 (new 2005) ga., 3 in. chamber, 26 (20 ga. only, new 2005) or 28 (12 ga. only) in. VR barrel with choke tube, matte nickel plated receiver, checkered American walnut pistol grip stock and forearm with recoil pad. New 2004.

	MSR $220		$180	$160	$135	$120	$95	$80	$70

GRADING - PPGS™	100%	98%	95%	90%	80%	70%	60%

* ✹ **Topper Deluxe Rifled Slug Gun** - 12 ga. only, 3 in. chamber, 24 in. compensated barrel, rifle sights, dark American hardwood stock and forearm, satin nickel frame, approx. 5 1/2 lbs. Mfg. 1996-99.

	$150	$115	$95	$85	$75	$65	$55

Last MSR was $170.

* ✹ **Topper Jr.** - 20 ga. or .410 bore, smaller variation of the Topper 098 with youth dimensions including 22 in. barrel and shortened stock with recoil pad, satin nickel frame with blue barrel, 12 1/2 in. LOP, 5-6 lbs. Mfg. began 1991.

MSR $156	$110	$95	$80	$70	$60	$50	$40

* ✹ **Topper Jr. Classic** - 20, 28 (disc. 2004) ga., or .410 bore, 22 in. barrel, checkered American black walnut stock and forearm, recoil pad, 12 1/2 in. LOP. Mfg. began 1991.

MSR $193	$160	$120	$95	$80	$70	$65	$60

* ✹ **NWTF Turkey Mag.** - 10 (mfg. 1996 only) or 12 (mfg. 1991-95) ga., 3 1/2 in. chamber, 24 in. drilled and tapped barrel with 1 choke tube, entire gun is covered in Mossy Oak camo, includes sling and swivels, 6 lbs. Mfg. 1991-96.

	$145	$120	$100	$85	$75	$65	$55

Last MSR was $180.

This model was part of the National Wild Turkey Federation (NWTF) sponsorship program.

* ✹ **1994 NWTF Youth Turkey Gun** - 20 ga., 3 in. chamber, 22 in. full choke barrel, features Realtree camo finish and sling, limited mfg. 1994-95.

	$140	$110	$95	$85	$75	$65	$55

Last MSR was $160.

* ✹ **2000 NWTF/Youth Edition** - 12 or 20 ga., 3 in. chamber, 20 ga. is NWTF Youth Edition with 22 in. barrel, camo finished laminate stock and forend with NWTF laser engraved frame, includes sling and swivels. Mfg. 2000-2004.

	$175	$130	$115	$95	$80	$70	$60

Last MSR was $207.

Add $9 for NWTF Edition - 12 ga. with 24 in. barrel.

THE TAMER - .410 bore, 3 in. chamber, synthetic thumbhole stock is designed to hold 4 shells, transfer bar system, 19 in. full choke barrel, electroless nickel finish, 6 lbs. New 1994.

MSR $169	$130	$110	$90	$80	$70	$60	$50

SB1-920 ULTRA SLUG HUNTER - .20 ga. only, utilizes 12 ga. action and barrel that has been under-bored to 20 ga. and fully rifled, hardwood Monte Carlo stock and forearm, matte black frame. Mfg. 1996-Disc.

	$190	$155	$125	$100	$85	$75	$65

Last MSR was $225.

ULTRA SLUG HUNTER - 12 or 20 ga., 3 in. chamber, 22 (20 ga., Youth Model) or 24 in. fully rifled heavy barrel, side-release lever, black Monte Carlo hardwood stock with recoil pad, matte finished frame, 8-9 lbs. New 1995.

MSR $266	$220	$170	$135	$105	$90	$75	$65

* ✹ **Ultra Slug Hunter Deluxe** - similar to Ultra Slug Hunter, except has checkered camo laminate wood and scope mount rail, adj. rear sight. New 1997.

MSR $328	$270	$215	$170	$130	$105	$90	$80

WHITETAILS UNLIMITED RIFLED SLUG GUN - 12 ga., 3 in. chamber, 24 in. fully rifled heavy barrel, hand checkered Monte Carlo black laminate stock and forend, Whitetails medallion, hammer extension, swivels and sling. Mfg. 1998-99.

	$220	$185	$145	$120	$100	$85	$75

Last MSR was $255.

H-S PRECISION, INC.

Current custom pistol and rifle manufacturer established 1990 and located in Rapid City, SD. H-S Precision, Inc. also manufactures synthetic stocks and custom machine barrels as well. Dealer and consumer direct sales.

H-S Precision introduced the aluminum bedding block for rifle stocks in 1981, and has been making advanced composite synthetic stocks and custom ballistic test barrels for almost two decades.

In addition to the following models, H-S Precision, Inc. also built rifles using a customer's action (mostly Remington 700 or Winchester Post 64 Model 70). 2004 MSRs ranged from $1,520-$1,830.

PISTOLS: SINGLE SHOT

PRO-SERIES 2000 VP/SP - various cals., stainless steel receiver, 15 in. fluted stainless steel barrel, 3 position safety, laminated composite Pro-Series stock, Teflon coated receiver and barrel, choice of varmint (VP, no sights) or silhouette (SP, drilled and tapped for sights) configuration, choice of stock colors. New late 1997.

MSR $1,875	$1,725	$1,500	$1,250	$1,075	$995	$875	$750

RIFLES: BOLT ACTION, PRO-SERIES 2000

All H-S Precision rifles feature Kevlar/graphite laminate stocks, cut rifle barrels, and other high tech innovations including a molded aluminum bedding block system. Beginning in 1999, H-S Precision began utilizing their H-S 2000 action, and model nomenclature was changed to begin with Pro-Series 2000.

Add $150-$175 for left-hand action.

PRO-SERIES 2000 VARMINT TAKEDOWN (VTD) - .22-250 Rem., .270 Win., .308 Win., or .300 Win. Mag. cal., accurized Remington Model 700 receiver (disc. 1999) or H-S 2000 action (new 2000), H-S stainless steel cut rifled and fluted barrel, 5 or 10 shot detachable mag, Teflon coated metal finish. New 1997.

MSR $3,500	$3,150	$2,650	$2,250	$1,875	$1,550	$1,300	$1,150

Add $100 for extended barrel port (Model VTD EP, disc.).
Add $1,750-$1,950 for extra barrel, depending on head size.

PRO-SERIES 2000 SPORTER/VARMINT (VAR/SPR) - various short and long action cals., Remington ADL action only, each rifle is built per individual specifications. New 1990.

MSR $2,175	$1,995	$1,775	$1,525	$1,225	$900	$750	$650

Add $100 for 2000 Varmint VAR Model.
Add $125 for fluted barrel.
Add $100 for extended barrel port (Model VAR/SPR EP, disc.).
Add $880 for extra stainless barrel (disc.).

PRO-SERIES 2000 PRO-HUNTER RIFLE (PHR) - available in 10 Safari cals., 24 or 26 in. fluted stainless steel barrel with cut rifling, Teflon finish, Pro-Series sporter stock, long action only.

MSR $2,375	$2,100	$1,725	$1,375	$1,025	$800	$675	$575

Add $1,225 for Pro-Hunter takedown rifle (PTD).

PRO-SERIES 2000 PRO-HUNTER LIGHTWEIGHT (PHL) - short action only, various cals. including WSM, 20 or 22 in. fluted barrel, Teflon coated action and barrel, green/tan camo stock, 5.5 lbs. New 2004.

MSR $2,475	$2,195	$1,775	$1,450	$1,050	$850	$700	$600

GRADING - PPGS™	100%	98%	95%	90%	80%	70%	60%

PRO-SERIES 2000 LONG RANGE (HEAVY TACTICAL MARKSMAN, HTR) - various cals., stainless fluted barrel standard, Remington BDL (disc. 1999) or Pro-Series 2000 (new 2000) action. New 1990.

	MSR $2,400	$2,100	$1,825	$1,550	$1,275	$950	$775	$650

Add $100 for extended barrel port (Model HTR EP, disc.).

PRO-SERIES 2000 SHORT TACTICAL (STR) - .308 Win. cal., 20 in. fluted barrel, matte Teflon finished action and barrel, 20 in. fluted barrel with standard porting, Pro Series Tactical stock. New 2004.

	MSR $2,375	$2,075	$1,800	$1,525	$1,275	$950	$775	$650

PRO-SERIES 2000 TAKEDOWN TACTICAL LONG RANGE (TTD) - various short and long action cals., stainless steel barrel, Remington BDL takedown action, matte blue finish. New 1990.

	MSR $3,800	$3,475	$2,950	$2,500	$2,000	$1,650	$1,375	$1,200

Add $1,750-$1,950 for extra barrel, depending on head size.
Add $100 for extended barrel port (Model TTD EP, disc.).

PRO SERIES 2000 RAPID DEPLOYMENT RIFLE (RDR) - .308 Win. cal., Pro-Series 2000 stainless steel short action only, 20 in. fluted barrel, black synthetic stock with or w/o thumbhole, black teflon metal finish, approx. 7.5 lbs. New 2000.

	MSR $2,275	$2,075	$1,825	$1,550	$1,225	$900	$750	$650

Add $125 for PST60A Long Range stock (disc.).

TAKEDOWN LONG RANGE (TACTICAL MARKSMAN) - .223 Rem., .243 Win., .30-06, .308 Win., 7mm Rem. Mag., .300 Win. Mag., or .338 Win. Mag. cal., includes "kwik klip" and stainless fluted barrel. Mfg. 1990-97.

		$2,895	$2,225	$1,675	$1,350	$995	$850	$750

Last MSR was $2,895.

A complete rifle package consisting of 2 calibers (.308 Win. and .300 Win. Mag.), scope and fitted case was available for $5,200 retail.

HWP INDUSTRIES

Previous manufacturer located in Milwaukee, WI circa 1989.

REVOLVERS

THE SLEDGEHAMMER - .500 HWP Mag. cal., 5 shot revolver, double action, stainless steel, full shrouded 4 in. barrel (quick change), Pachmayr grips. Limited mfg. 1989 only.

	$1,150	$895	$750

Last MSR was $1,295.

HAENEL, C.G.

Previous manufacturer located in Suhl, Germany. Haenel mfg. many varieties of firearms between 1925-circa 1940. Currently, Haenel continues to manufacture airguns, mostly for Europe. Presently not imported into the U.S.

During 1925-WWII, C.G. Haenel manufactured a variety of sporting longarms, mostly concentrating on bolt action rifles, drillings, and SxS shotguns. Some of these guns are extremely well executed, and must be appraised individually. If quality, condition, and overall desirability are at a level similar to pre-war Sauers, Krieghoffs, etc., Haenel values could be similar to the trademarks just mentioned. However, a standard grade Haenel rifle/shotgun/drilling, in an obscure metric caliber with no engraving in 70% or less original condition, gets priced for its utilitarian shooting value as opposed to adding a collector premium.

For more information and current pricing on both new and used Haenel, C.G., airguns, please refer to the *Blue Book of Airguns* by Robert Beeman & John Allen (also online).

GRADING - PPGS™	100%	98%	95%	90%	80%	70%	60%

PISTOLS: SEMI-AUTO

SCHMEISSER MODEL 1 & 2 - .25 ACP cal., similar to Baby Browning.

	$500	$400	$300	$275	$230	$200	$180

MODELS 200-205 - see Hämmerli-Walther.

RIFLES: BOLT ACTION

MAUSER-MANNLICHER SPORTING RIFLE - 7x57mm, 8x57R, or 9x57R cal., M/88 Mauser type action, 22 or 24 in. octagon barrel, Mannlicher box mag., double set triggers, raised rib on barrel, leaf sight, sporter stock.

	$440	$360	$330	$275	$250	$220	$165

88 MAUSER SPORTER - similar to Mauser-Mannlicher, with Mauser 5 shot mag.

	$525	$450	$375	$325	$275	$240	$200

HAMBRUSCH JAGDWAFFEN GmbH

Current manufacturer established in 1752, and located in Ferlach, Austria. Currently imported and distributed exclusively by CONCO Arms, located in Emmaus, PA.

Hambrusch Jagdwaffen was a member of the Ferlach Gun Guild until it was dissolved in 2004. This company manufactures many types of high-grade long arms, including SxS shotguns, combination guns, drillings, double rifles, and single shot rifles. The combinations of these configurations are almost endless. During 2002, Hambrusch introduced a new proprietary big game cartridge, the .600/538 MM (Mega Magnum with 722 grain bullet). Please refer to the Conco Arms section for more information on select Hambrusch models, or contact Conco Arms directly for more information, availability, and current pricing.

HÄMMERLI AG

Current manufacturer located in Lenzburg, Switzerland. Currently imported and distributed by SIG Arms Inc. located in Exeter, NH, Larry's Guns, located in Portland, ME, Gunsmithing Inc., located in Colorado Springs, CO, and **HÄMMERLI** Champion's Choice, located in LaVergne, TN. Previously imported until 1995 by Hämmerli Pistols USA, located in Groveland, CA, and by Beeman Precision Arms located in Santa Rosa, CA.

For more information and current pricing on both new and used Hämmerli airguns, please refer to the *Blue Book of Airguns* by Dr. Robert Beeman & John Allen (also online).

PISTOLS: SINGLE SHOT, RIMFIRE

FP-10 FREE PISTOL - .22 LR cal., current top-of-the-line Hämmerli pistol. Importation began 2000.

MSR N/A	$1,525	$1,200	$950	$850	$750	$650	$575

MODEL 33MP - .22 LR cal., similar to the Model 100, except not available in a deluxe model. Mfg. 1933-49.

	$925	$725	$650	$550	$470	$440	$385

MODEL 100 FREE PISTOL - .22 LR cal., 11 1/2 in. octagon barrel, blue, martini action single shot, set trigger, micro rear sight, walnut stock and forearm. Mfg. 1950-56.

	$880	$660	$605	$550	$470	$440	$385

Add 15%-20% for Olympic rings, "London," and "1948" markings (indicative of Swiss shooting team).

GRADING - PPGS™	100%	98%	95%	90%	80%	70%	60%
✳ *Deluxe model* - carved stock.							
	$990	$770	$715	$660	$580	$550	$495

MODEL 101 - similar to Model 100, but heavy round barrel, improved action and sights, matte finish. Mfg. 1956-60.

	$880	$660	$605	$550	$470	$440	$385

MODEL 102 - similar to Model 101, except high polished finish. Mfg. 1956-60.

	$880	$660	$605	$550	$470	$440	$385
✳ *Deluxe model*	$990	$770	$715	$660	$580	$550	$495

MODEL 103 FREE PISTOL - similar to Model 101, except lighter octagon polished barrel. Mfg. 1956-60.

	$935	$715	$660	$605	$580	$550	$495

MODEL 104 MATCH PISTOL - similar to Model 103, except lighter round barrel, redesigned stock, mfg. 1961-65.

	$760	$660	$550	$495	$470	$440	$385

MODEL 105 MATCH PISTOL - similar to Model 103, except redesigned action and stock, octagon barrel. Mfg. 1962-65.

	$935	$715	$660	$605	$580	$550	$495

MODEL 106 MATCH PISTOL - similar to Model 105, except improved trigger.

	$910	$690	$580	$525	$495	$470	$415

MODEL 107 MATCH PISTOL - similar to Model 105, except improved trigger.

	$990	$770	$660	$550	$525	$495	$440
✳ *Deluxe model* - engraved and carved wood.							
	$1,320	$990	$880	$660	$635	$605	$550

MODEL 120-1 SINGLE SHOT FREE PISTOL - .22 LR cal., bolt action, 9.9 in. barrel, blue barrel and receiver, side lever operated, anodized aluminum lever and frame, walnut checkered grips.

	$600	$540	$475	$425	$375	$325	$295

MODEL 120-2 - similar to 120-1, except stocks hand contoured.

	$600	$540	$475	$425	$375	$325	$295

MODEL 120 HEAVY BARREL - similar to 120-1, with 5.7 in. bull barrel.

	$600	$540	$475	$425	$375	$325	$295

MODEL 150 FREE PISTOL - .22 LR cal., 11.3 in. barrel, improved Martini-type action, set trigger, innovative design incorporating many unusual features. Disc. 1989.

	$1,850	$1,495	$1,275	$1,120	$980	$900	$850

Last MSR was $1,980.

Add $113 for left-hand variation.
The Model 150 was replaced by the Model 151.

MODEL 151 FREE PISTOL - replacement for the Model 150 Free Pistol. Imported 1990-93.

	$1,850	$1,495	$1,275	$1,120	$995	$900	$800

Last MSR was $1,980.

MODEL 152 FREE PISTOL - .22 LR cal., 11.3 in. barrel. improved Martini-type action, electronic trigger release, innovative design incorporating many unusual features. State-of-the-art target pistol. Disc. 1992.

	$1,995	$1,600	$1,350	$1,195	$1,090	$990	$895

Last MSR was $2,105.

Add $57 for left-hand variation.

GRADING - PPGS™	100%	98%	95%	90%	80%	70%	60%

MODEL 160 FREE PISTOL - .22 LR cal., similar to Model 150, except has poly-carbon fiber forend, includes carrying case. Mfg. 1993-2002.

	$1,725	$1,475	$1,175	$900	$800	$700	$595

Last MSR was $1,850.

Add $290 for smaller adj. grips.

MODEL 162 FREE PISTOL - .22 LR cal., replacement for the Model 152 Free Pistol, includes poly-carbon fiber forend, includes carrying case. Imported 1993-2000.

	$2,150	$1,700	$1,375	$1,125	$900	$800	$700

Last MSR was $2,410.

Add $290 for smaller adj. grips.

PISTOLS: SEMI-AUTO

MODELS 200-205 - see Hämmerli-Walther.

INTERNATIONAL MODEL 206 - .22 Short or .22 LR cal., semi-auto, 7 1/16 in. barrel with muzzle brake, adj. sights, walnut grips, blue. Mfg. 1962-69.

	$675	$625	$525	$450	$395	$365	$330

INTERNATIONAL MODEL 207 - similar to 206, except adj. grip heel.

	$725	$650	$550	$475	$425	$375	$350

INTERNATIONAL MODEL 208 - .22 LR cal., 9 shot, 6 in. barrel, blue, adj. sights, checkered walnut grips with adj. heel. Mfg. 1966-88.

	$2,000	$1,700	$1,450	$1,150	$925	$825	$725

Last MSR was $1,755.

This model was replaced by the Model 208S.

✱ *Model 208S* - similar to Model 208, except has redesigned triggerguard and safety with interchangeable rear sight element. Imported 1988-2000.

	$2,450	$2,150	$1,750	$1,450	$1,150	$925	$825

Last MSR was $2,021.

Add $125 for factory scope mount.
Add $180 for smaller adj. grips.

✱ *Model 208 Deluxe* - similar to Model 208, except has carved grips and elaborate engraving. Importation disc. 1988.

	$2,995	$2,500	$1,995				

Last MSR was $3,250.

✱ *Model 208C (Commemorative)* - limited edition commemorative. Disc. 1987.

	$2,100	$1,750	$1,400				

Last MSR was $2,225.

INTERNATIONAL MODEL 209 - .22 Short cal., semi-auto, 5 shot, 4 3/4 in. barrel, muzzle brake, adj. sights, blue, walnut stock. Mfg. 1966-70.

	$800	$690	$635	$550	$525	$485	$440

INTERNATIONAL MODEL 210 - similar to 209, but grips have adj. heel. Mfg. 1966-70.

	$800	$715	$660	$590	$540	$525	$495

MODEL 211 - .22 LR cal., semi-auto, 9 shot, 6 in. barrel, adj. sights, blue, similar to Model 208 except non-adj. walnut stocks. Importation disc. 1990.

	$1,550	$1,275	$1,050	$950	$880	$835	$770

Last MSR was $1,669.

MODEL 212 HUNTER - .22 LR cal., semi-auto, hunter's pistol, 9 shot, 5 in. barrel, adj. sights, blue, walnut stocks. Importation disc. 1993.

	$1,250	$1,000	$875	$775	$675	$575	$475

Last MSR was $1,395.

GRADING - PPGS™	100%	98%	95%	90%	80%	70%	60%

MODEL 215 - .22 LR cal., semi-auto, Model 208 specs on commercial target model, 9 shot, 5 in. barrel, adj. sights, blue, walnut stocks. Importation disc. 1990.

	$1,395	$1,050	$895	$775	$695	$650	$600

Last MSR was $1,505.

MODEL 230 RAPID FIRE PISTOL - .22 S cal., semi-auto, 5 shot, 6.3 in. barrel, blue, adj. sights, smooth walnut grips. Mfg. 1970-83.

	$705	$635	$580	$530	$485	$450	$415

MODEL 230-2 - similar to 230, except checkered grips with adj. heel. Mfg. 1970-83.

	$735	$655	$605	$570	$515	$485	$470

MODEL 232-1 RAPID FIRE PISTOL - .22 S cal., semi-auto, 6 shot, 5.1 in. barrel, blue, adj. sights, contoured walnut grips. Importation disc. 1993.

	$1,395	$1,125	$950	$850	$750	$700	$650

Last MSR was $1,505.

Add $25 for wraparound grips sizes S-M-LG (Model 232-2).

MODEL 280 - .22 LR or .32 S&W Wadcutter cal., new modular pistol design utilizing carbon fiber synthetic material to replace frame and other critical parts, adj. grips, trigger, and rear sight, 4.6 in. barrel, 5 or 6 shot mag., approx. 2.2 lbs. Imported 1988-2000.

	$1,450	$1,125	$900	$800	$675	$575	$475

Last MSR was $1,643.

Add $200 for .32 S&W Wadcutter cal.

Add $765 (.22 LR) or $965 (.32 S&W Wadcutter) for conversion kit.

Add $200 for smaller adj. grips.

A package is also available with both calibers, magazines, and hard case for $2,595.

MODEL SP 20 - .22 LR or .32 S&W Wadcutter cal., replacement for Model 280, features low-level sight line, colored alloy receiver (blue, red, gold, violet, or black), adj. "JPS" buffer system that varies recoil characteristics per individual preference, black Hi-Grip anatomical grips. Mfg. 1998-2002.

	$1,325	$1,075	$925	$800	$700	$600	$500

Last MSR was $1,450.

Add $110 for .32 S&W Wadcutter cal.

Add $499 for .22 LR conversion, $599 for .32 S&W Wadcutter conversion.

MODEL SP 20 RRS - .22 LR or .32 S&W Wadcutter cal., state-of-the-art target pistol featuring composite frame with redesigned ergonomic grips, RRS designates recoil reducing system, fully hand adj. rear sight, various slide colors available. New 2002.

MSR $1,450	$1,395	$1,250	$1,125	$1,025	$925	$825	$725

Add $110 for .32 S&W Wadcutter cal.

This model is available only from Larry's Guns.

MODEL P-240 - see SIG-Hämmerli for this model.

TRAILSIDE - .22 LR cal., single action, 4 1/2 or 6 in. barrel, two-tone finish, choice of ultralight polymer composite grips or target variation which includes wood grips and adj. rear sight, 10 shot mag., cased with trigger lock, 28 or 30 oz. New 1999.

MSR $455	$395	$350	$300	$275	$250	$225	$200

Add $79 for 4 1/2 in. barrel with target sights, or $95 for 6 in. barrel with target sights.

This model was also available as one of SIG Arms' limited editions in Jan. 2004 - it included a BSA 30mm red dot optical sight with integrated mount and 6 in. barrel. Last MSR was $709.

✴ *Trailside Competition* - includes 6 in. barrel with blue anatomical stipled grips and adj. bottom rest, cased with trigger lock, 37.2 oz. New 2000, limited importation to date.

MSR $710	$580	$500	$400	$350	$300	$265	$225

GRADING - PPGS™	100%	98%	95%	90%	80%	70%	60%

X-ESSE - .22 LR cal., European variation of the Trailside, available in Sport, Long, and Short configurations, polymer or anatomic stipled polymer target grips, adj. hand rest, 10 shot mag. Limited mfg. and importation beginning 2004.

Due to limited importation, this model does not have a current MSR.

RIFLES: BOLT ACTION, TARGET

OLYMPIC 300 METER - .30-06 cal., bolt action, single shot free rifle, U.S.A. import, 7x57mm overseas, 20 1/2 in. heavy barrel, double set trigger, aperture rear sight, globe front, free rifle stock with thumbhole pistol grip, beavertail forearm, Swiss style target butt. Mfg. 1945-59.

	$880	$745	$605	$550	$470	$440	$415

HÄMMERLI-TANNER 300 METER FREE RIFLE - similar to Olympic 300, except 7.5mm standard, also was available in other calibers. Mfg. 1962-disc.

	$895	$825	$770	$715	$660	$580	$520

Last MSR was $935.

MODEL 45 SMALLBORE MATCH RIFLE - .22 LR cal., bolt action, single shot, 27 1/2 in. heavy barrel, same sights and stock type as Hämmerli-Tanner. Mfg. 1945-57.

	$660	$550	$470	$440	$385	$360	$330

MODEL 54 SMALLBORE MATCH RIFLE - similar to 45 Smallbore, except adj. butt. Mfg. 1954-57.

	$670	$560	$480	$450	$395	$370	$340

MODEL S 205 - 6mm BR, 7.5x55mm, or .308 Win. cal., designed for 300 meter competition, adj. blue aluminum stock, 5 shot mag., Hammerli apeture rear sight, Sauer produced 205 action with 26 in. heavy free floating barrel, 12 lbs. New 2004.

As this edition went to press, prices had yet to be established on this model.

MODEL 503 SMALLBORE FREE RIFLE - similar to 54 Smallbore, except free style stock.

	$660	$550	$470	$440	$385	$360	$330

MODEL 505 MATCH RIFLE - match stock with aperture sights.

	$690	$580	$495	$470	$415	$385	$360

MODEL 506 SMALLBORE MATCH RIFLE - similar to 503 Smallbore. Mfg. 1963-66.

	$690	$580	$495	$470	$415	$385	$360

SPORTING RIFLE - various calibers, set triggers, Mauser repeating action.

	$725	$650	$490	$425	$360	$325	$300

HÄMMERLI-WALTHER

Previously manufactured semi-auto target pistols made under joint effort from Hämmerli and Walther.

PISTOLS: SEMI-AUTO, RIMFIRE

MODEL 200 OLYMPIA - .22 Short or LR cal., 7 1/2 in. barrel, 1952 type, adj. sights, barrel weight, blue, checkered walnut grips. Mfg. 1952-58.

	$660	$605	$550	$440	$415	$385	$360

MODEL 200 OLYMPIA - 1958 type, similar to 1952 type, except has muzzle brake. Mfg. 1958-63.

	$715	$605	$550	$495	$470	$415	$385

MODEL 201 - similar to 200, 1952 type, except 9 1/2 in. barrel. Mfg. 1955-57.

	$660	$605	$550	$440	$415	$385	$360

GRADING - PPGS™	100%	98%	95%	90%	80%	70%	60%

MODEL 202 - similar to 201, except adj. heel grips. Mfg. 1955-57.

	100%	98%	95%	90%	80%	70%	60%
	$715	$605	$550	$495	$470	$415	$385

MODEL 203 - similar to 200, except has adj. heel grip.

✳ *1955 Type* - no muzzle brake.

	$715	$605	$550	$495	$470	$415	$385

✳ *1958 Type* - muzzle brake.

	$770	$660	$605	$550	$525	$470	$440

MODEL 204 - similar to 200, except .22 LR cal. only.

✳ *1956 Type* - no muzzle brake.

	$745	$635	$580	$525	$495	$470	$440

✳ *1958 Type* - muzzle brake.

	$800	$690	$635	$550	$525	$495	$470

MODEL 205 - .22 LR cal., similar to 204, except adj. heel grips.

✳ *1956 Type* - no muzzle brake.

	$800	$690	$635	$550	$525	$495	$470

✳ *1958 Type* - muzzle brake.

	$855	$745	$715	$635	$580	$525	$495

HARRINGTON & RICHARDSON, INC.

Previous manufacturer located in Gardner, MA - formerly from Worchester, MA. Successors to Wesson & Harrington, manufactured from 1871 until January 24, 1986. H & R 1871, LLC was formed during 1991 (see their listing in the front of this section). H & R 1871, LLC is not responsible for the warranties or safety of older pre-1986 H & R firearms.

A manufacturer of utilitarian firearms for over 115 years, H & R ceased operation on January 24, 1986. Even though new manufacture (under H & R 1871, LLC) is utilizing the H & R trademark, the discontinuance of older models in either NIB or mint condition may command slight asking premiums, but probably will not affect values on those handguns only recently discontinued. Most H & R firearms are still purchased for their shooting value rather than collecting potential.

Please refer to H & R listing in the Serialization section for alphabetical suffix information on how to determine year of manufacture for most H & R firearms between 1940-82.

COMBINATION GUNS: SINGLE SHOT

MODEL 058 - 20 ga./.30-30, .22 Rem. Jet, .22 Hornet, .357 Mag., or .44 Mag. cal. combination, 2 separate barrels supplied, blue only. Disc. 1985.

	$155	$130	$110	$95	$85	$75	$65

Last MSR was $145.

MODEL 258 COMBINATION HANDY GUN II - supplied with 20 ga., 22 in. barrel and 22 in. rifle barrel in .22 Hornet, .30-30 Win., or .357 Mag. cal., electroless, matte nickel finish, side lever action release, cased, 6 1/2 lbs. Disc. 1985.

	$175	$155	$140	$130	$120	$100	$95

Last MSR was $195.

COMMEMORATIVES, SPECIAL EDITIONS, & LIMITED MFG.

ABILENE ANNIVERSARY .22 REVOLVER - 300 mfg. 1967.

	$150	$115	$75

Last MSR was $83.50 (1967).

GRADING - PPGS™	100%	98%	95%	90%	80%	70%	60%

H&R 100TH ANNIVERSARY OFFICER'S MODEL - 1871-1971, Commemorative Officer's Model, Springfield 1873 Replica, Trapdoor, .45-70 Govt. cal., engraved metal work, 26 in. barrel, anniversary plaque on stock, 10,000 mfg. in 1971.

	$595	$550	$500

Last MSR was $250.

MODEL 171 AND 171 DELUXE - please refer to listings under Rifles section.

MODEL 172 CARBINE - .45-70 Govt. cal., 22 in. barrel, Trapdoor action, walnut stock, silver plated grip cap, tang sight. Mfg. 1978-82.

	$1,250	$1,000	$750

MODEL 173 RIFLE - .45-70 Govt. cal., similar to Officer's Model, no plaque on stock. Mfg. 1972-83.

	$495	$425	$325

MODEL 174 CARBINE (LITTLE BIG HORN) - .45-70 Govt. cal., Little Big Horn Commercial Carbine. Quantity unknown.

	$395	$325	$250

Last MSR was $220 (1972).

MODEL 178 - .45-70 Govt. cal., Infantry Musket Replica, 32 in. barrel. Mfg. 1973-84.

	$375	$325	$250

1873 SPRINGFIELD TRAPDOOR - .45-70 Govt. cal., unknown quantities mfg. 1973.

	$450	$350	$275

Last MSR was $250.

CUSTER MEMORIAL ISSUE - .45-70 Govt. cal., limited production, deluxe walnut stock, highly engraved, gold inlaid, mahogany display case and two volumes on Custer history. Each weapon bears the name of one who fell at Little Big Horn.

✻ *Officer's Model* - 25 mfg., must be new with original box/accessories.

	$3,995	$3,150	$2,400

Last MSR was $3,000 (1973).

✻ *Enlisted Men's Model* - 243 mfg., must be new with original box/accessories.

	$1,995	$1,400	$900

Last MSR was $2,000 (1973).

HANDGUNS: PRE-1942

MODEL 4 - .32 S&W Long 6 shot, or .38 S&W Long 5 shot cal., (1904), double action, 2 1/2, 4 1/2, and 6 in. barrels, blue or nickel, hard rubber grips, solid frame, fixed sights. Mfg. 1904-41.

	$95	$85	$70	$55	$45	$35	$30

MODEL 5 - .32 S&W Long cal., 5 shot only, (1905), double action, same as Model 4. Mfg. 1905-39.

	$95	$85	$70	$55	$45	$35	$30

MODEL 6 - .22 LR cal., 7 shot only, (1906), double action, similar to Model 4. mfg. 1906-41.

	$95	$85	$70	$55	$45	$35	$30

AMERICAN - .32 S&W, .32 Colt New Police, .38 S&W, .38 Colt New Police, or .44 Webley cal., 5 or 6 (.32 S&W cal.) shot, double action, 2 1/2, 4, or 6 in. barrel, fixed sights, blue or nickel.

	$95	$85	$70	$55	$45	$35	$30

GRADING - PPGS™	100%	98%	95%	90%	80%	70%	60%

YOUNG AMERICAN - .22 Long, 7 shot, or .32 S&W, 5 shot cal., double action, 2, 4 1/2, or 6 in. barrel, fixed sights, blue or nickel. Mfg. 1887-1941.

	$135	$105	$95	$80	$65	$55	$45

VEST POCKET - double action, 1 1/8 in. barrel, blue or nickel, solid frame, spurless hammer.

	$95	$85	$70	$55	$45	$35	$30

HUNTER - .22 LR cal., double action, 10 in. octagon barrel, 9 shot, checkered walnut grips.

	$140	$110	$100	$85	$65	$55	$45

TRAPPER - .22 LR cal., double action, 7 shot, 6 in. octagon barrel, checkered walnut stocks.

	$175	$135	$100	$85	$65	$55	$45

MODEL 922 - .22 LR cal., first issue, 9 shot, 10 in. octagon barrel on early models, 6 in. round barrel on later models, checkered walnut grips.

	$195	$170	$155	$140	$125	$110	$95

Some early guns were marked "22 SPECIAL" on left barrel.

AUTOMATIC EJECTING - .32 S&W cal., 6 shot, .38 S&W, 5 shot, double action, 3 1/4, 4, 5, or 6 in. barrels, hinged top break, blue or nickel finish, fixed sights, black rubber grips. Mfg. 1896-disc.

	$160	$150	$105	$90	$75	$65	$55

PREMIER - .22 LR, 7 shot, or .32 S&W, 5 shot cal., double action, break open, small frame.

	$95	$85	$70	$55	$45	$35	$30

HAMMERLESS - .22 LR, 7 shot, or .32 S&W, 5 shot cal., double action, 2, 3, 4, 5, or 6 in. barrels, small frame, top break, blue or nickel, black rubber grips.

	$125	$110	$100	$85	$65	$55	$45

HAMMERLESS - .32 S&W, 6 shot, or .38 S&W, 5 shot cal., double action, 3 1/4, 4, 5, or 6 in. barrels, large frame, break open.

	$125	$110	$100	$85	$65	$55	$45

TARGET MODEL - .22 LR, or .22 WRF cal., 7 shot, double action, 6 in. barrel, fixed sights, break open, small frame, blue only, walnut grips.

	$140	$120	$100	$85	$70	$60	$50

.22 SPECIAL - .22 LR, or .22 WRF cal., 9 shot, double action, 6 in. barrel, break open, large frame, blue only, gold plated front sight, walnut grips.

	$165	$140	$120	$100	$85	$70	$60

EXPERT - double action, similar to .22 Special, except 10 in. barrel.

	$150	$140	$120	$100	$85	$70	$60

SPORTSMAN NO. 199 - .22 LR cal., 9 shot, single action, 6 in. barrel, adj. target sights, break open, blue only, checkered walnut grips.

	$275	$250	$200	$165	$140	$110	$90

DEFENDER - .38 S&W cal., double action, 4 or 6 in. barrel, fixed sights, blue, break open, black plastic grips, made during WWII for police reserves and major corporation guards.

	$140	$120	$110	$100	$85	$65	$55

ULTRA SPORTSMAN - .22 LR cal., 9 shot, single action, 6 in. barrel, blue, break open, adj. sights, walnut grips, short cylinder action, wide hammer spur.

	$220	$200	$180	$150	$120	$100	$85

GRADING - PPGS™	100%	98%	95%	90%	80%	70%	60%

NEW DEFENDER - .22 LR cal., 9 shot, double action, 2 in. barrel, break open, adj. sights, blue, round butt, checkered walnut grip.

	$220	$200	$180	$150	$120	$100	$85

USRA SINGLE SHOT TARGET - please refer to this listing in the U.S.R.A. section.

.25 CAL. SELF LOADING PISTOL - .25 ACP cal., 6 shot, 2 in. barrel, blue, black rubber grips. 16,630 mfg. 1912-16.

	$375	$330	$305	$250	$195	$165	$140

.32 CAL. SELF LOADING PISTOL - .32 ACP cal., 8 shot, 3 1/2 in. barrel, fixed sights, black rubber grips. Mfg. 1916-24.

	$330	$305	$250	$195	$165	$140	$110

> **Add 20% for type I models if in 90%+ original condition.**
>
> Type I models with 12 slide pull grooves are serialized 1-3,025. Type II (more common) are serialized 3,026-34,500.

HANDY-GUN - smooth bore (mfg. 1921-1934) or rifled barrel (mfg. 1931-1934) pistol, single shot, top lever break open, available in either 8 or 12 1/4 in. choked or unchoked barrel in either .410 bore or 28 ga., case colored (Tiger stripe colors resulting from hot cyanide method) or blue frame. Rifled barrel (.22 LR in blue frame or .32-20 WCF cal. in case colored frame, 12 1/4 in. barrel only) is rare. Early smooth bore guns bear only manufacturer's name, later blue and case-colored guns are stamped H & R "Handy-Gun" on left side and manufacturer's name on right side, as are all rifled barrel models. Ser. nos. on barrel lug and frame should match. Smooth bore Handy-Guns (more than 50 variations have been documented) not currently registered with ATF cannot be legally owned and are subject to seizure. Rifled barrels are exempt if not w/shoulder stock.

✳ *Smooth bore* - ser. no. range is 1-53,933.

	$595	$495	$400	$350	$295	$250	$200

✳ *.22 Rimfire* - ser. no. range is 1-approx. 223.

	$900	$750	$650	$550	$500	$450	$350

✳ *.32-20 WCF* - ser. no. range is approx. 43,851-43,937.

	$1,200	$1,000	$800	$650	$550	$500	$450

> **Add $50-$250 for original box, and $75-$200 for original H&R holster.**
>
> Values for smooth bore are for the most common variation (.410 with 12 1/4 in. choked barrel), premiums of 25%-200% or more for rare variations (8 in. barrel, 28 ga., hooked trigger guard, optional detachable shoulder stock), rarest (just a few were made) is a .410 bore with 18 in. choked barrel mfg. in 1934. "Private branded" or "trade-branded" variations command 25%-100% premiums.
>
> An optional detachable wire stock was available, but not commonly ordered. Most smooth bore variations were not drilled for a shoulder stock.

REVOLVERS: RECENT MFG.

MODEL 504 SQUARE BUTT - .32 H&R Mag. cal., 5 shot, 4 or 6 in. bull barrels, adj. rear sight, swing out cylinder, blue, black plastic and walnut grips. Mfg. 1984-85.

	$165	$145	$135	$120	$110	$100	$90

Last MSR was $185.

✳ *Model 504 Round Butt* - compact design available with 3 or 4 in. barrel only. Disc. 1985.

	$165	$145	$135	$120	$110	$100	$90

Last MSR was $185.

MODEL 532 - .32 H&R Mag. cal., 5 shot, 2 1/2 and 4 in. barrels, solid frame revolver, blue, pull pin cylinder, black plastic and walnut grips. Mfg. 1984-85.

	$100	$90	$80	$70	$60	$50	$45

Last MSR was $115.

GRADING - PPGS™	100%	98%	95%	90%	80%	70%	60%

MODEL 586 - .32 H&R Mag. cal., 5 shot, Western-style revolver, double action, 4 1/2, 5 1/2, 7 1/2, or 10 in. barrels, adj. rear sight, fixed cylinder, antique finish, black plastic or walnut grips. Mfg. 1984-85.

	$175	$155	$135	$120	$110	$100	$90

Last MSR was $195.

MODEL 603 - .22 Mag. cal., 6 in. barrel, double action. Disc.

	$159	$120	$110	$95	$90	$80	$70

MODEL 604 - same specifications as the Model 603, only has 6 in. bull barrel.

	$170	$130	$115	$95	$90	$80	$70

MODEL 622 - .22 Short, Long, or LR cal., solid frame, 6 shot, 2 1/2, 4, or 6 in. barrels, blue, plastic grips. Mfg. 1957-85.

	$95	$82	$70	$60	$55	$50	$45

Last MSR was $104.

MODEL 623 - same basic specifications as the Model 622, nickel finish only. Disc.

	$115	$95	$75	$60	$55	$50	$45

MODEL 632 GUARDSMAN - .32 S&W cal., 6 shot, 2 1/2 or 4 in. barrel, solid frame, checkered tenite grips, blue. Mfg. 1953-84.

	$104	$82	$70	$60	$55	$50	$45

MODEL 633 - same basic specifications as the Model 632, only nickel finish. Disc.

	$115	$95	$75	$60	$55	$50	$45

MODEL 642 - .22 Mag cal., 2 1/2 or 4 in. barrel. Disc.

	$95	$70	$65	$60	$50	$45	$40

MODEL 649 CONVERTIBLE - .22 LR or .22 Mag. cal., furnished with extra cylinder, Western style, double action, side loading, 5 1/2 or 7 1/2 in. barrel, 6 shot, walnut grips, blue finish. Mfg. 1976-1985.

	$140	$120	$110	$95	$90	$80	$70

Last MSR was $160.

MODEL 650 CONVERTIBLE - similar to Model 649, except with nickel finish and only available with 5.5 in. barrel. Disc. 1985.

	$150	$130	$115	$100	$90	$80	$70

Last MSR was $175.

MODEL 660 GUNFIGHTER - similar to Model 650, except with blue finish, 5.5 in. barrel.

	$150	$130	$115	$100	$90	$80	$70

MODEL 666 - .22 LR or .22 Mag. cal., 6 shot, 6 in. barrel, blue, plastic grips, convertible. Mfg. 1976-82.

	$100	$90	$70	$50	$45	$35	$30

MODEL 676 - .22 LR or .22 Mag. cal., 6 shot, 4 1/2, 5 1/2, 7 1/2, or 12 in. barrel, side load and eject, convertible (includes .22 LR/.22 Mag. cylinders), blue, case hardened frame, one piece walnut stock. Mfg. 1976-82.

	$140	$120	$100	$85	$60	$45	$35

MODEL 686 CONVERTIBLE - .22 LR or .22 Mag. cal., furnished with extra cylinder, Western style, double action, side loading, 5 1/2, 7 1/2, 10 or 12 in. barrel, 6 shot, walnut grips, color case hardened frame, adj. rear sight, 12 in. barrel. Disc. 1984.

	$185	$160	$140	$125	$110	$90	$80

MODEL 732 - .32 S&W or .32 H&R Mag. cal., 6 shot, 2 1/2 and 4 in. barrels, fixed sights, swing out cylinder, blue, black plastic grips. Add $15 for .32 H&R Mag. cal. Mfg. 1958- disc.

	$127	$100	$85	$75	$65	$55	$45

GRADING - PPGS™	100%	98%	95%	90%	80%	70%	60%

MODEL 733 - similiar to the Model 732, only nickel finish and available only with 2 1/2 in. barrel.

    Add $15 for .32 H&R Mag. cal.

	$140	$125	$110	$85	$75	$60	$50

MODEL 900 - .22 S, L, or LR cal., 9 shot, 2 1/2, 4, or 6 in. barrels, snap out cylinder, blue, black plastic grips. Mfg. 1962-73.

	$90	$85	$70	$55	$50	$40	$30

MODEL 901 - similar to 900, but chrome with white tenite grips. Mfg. 1962-63.

	$110	$100	$90	$70	$50	$40	$30

MODEL 904 - .22 S, L, LR cal., double action, 4 or 6 in. bull barrel, target grade, 9 shot. Disc. 1985.

	$150	$135	$120	$105	$95	$80	$70

Last MSR was $168.

MODEL 905 - similar to Model 904, except with nickel finish and 4 in. barrel only. Disc. 1985.

	$160	$140	$125	$105	$95	$80	$70

Last MSR was $185.

MODEL 922 - .22 LR cal., Second Issue, 9 shot, 2 1/2, 4, or 6 in. barrels, solid frame, blue, plastic grips. Mfg. 1950-82.

	$85	$70	$60	$45	$40	$30	$25

MODEL 923 - similar to 922, only nickel.

	$90	$75	$65	$50	$45	$35	$30

MODEL 925 DEFENDER - .38 S&W cal., 5 shot, 2 1/2 in. barrel, blue, break open, adj. sight, wraparound one piece grip. Mfg. 1964-1984.

	$130	$120	$100	$85	$70	$60	$50

MODEL 935 - similar to Model 925, except with nickel finish.

	$145	$135	$115	$100	$70	$60	$50

MODEL 926 - .22 LR or .38 S&W cal., 5 (.38 S&W) or 9 (.22LR) shot, 4 in. barrel, blue, adj. rear sight, break open, walnut grips. Mfg. 1968-82.

	$130	$120	$100	$85	$70	$60	$50

   ✱ *Model 926 Abilene Kansas Centennial* - .22 LR cal., barrel is marked "Abilene Kansas" and "1869 Centennial 1969", mfg. 1969 only.

	$175	$155	$125	$105	$90	$80	$70

MODEL 929 SIDEKICK - .22 LR cal., 9 shot, 2 1/2, 4, or 6 in. barrels, swing out cylinder, plastic grips, blue. Mfg. 1956-85.

	$115	$100	$70	$55	$45	$35	$30

Last MSR was $127.

MODEL 930 SIDEKICK - similar to 929 Sidekick, only nickel finish and not available with 6 in. barrel. Disc. 1985.

	$125	$110	$80	$65	$55	$45	$40

Last MSR was $140.

MODEL 939 ULTRA SIDEKICK - .22 S, L, or LR cal., 9 shot, 6 in. barrel, swing out cylinder, vent rib, adj. sights, blue. Mfg. 1958-82.

	$110	$100	$85	$70	$55	$45	$30

MODEL 940 ULTRA SIDEKICK - similar to 939, only round barrel. Disc.

	$105	$95	$75	$65	$50	$40	$30

GRADING - PPGS™	100%	98%	95%	90%	80%	70%	60%

MODEL 949 "FORTY NINER" - .22 S, L, or LR cal., 5 1/2 in. barrel, double action, solid frame, 9 shot, side load and Western style ejection, adj. rear sight, walnut grips. Mfg. 1960-85.

	$115	$100	$85	$70	$55	$50	$45

Last MSR was $127.

MODEL 950 - similar to Model 949, except with nickel finish. Disc. 1985.

	$125	$105	$90	$70	$55	$50	$45

Last MSR was $145.

MODEL 976 - similar to 949, only color case hardened frame. Disc.

	$100	$90	$85	$70	$60	$50	$35

MODEL 999 SPORTSMAN - 22 LR cal., Second Issue, 9 shot, 4 or 6 in. vent. rib barrel, top-break action, adj. sights, walnut grips. Mfg. 1950-85.

	$195	$170	$155	$140	$125	$110	$95

This model was also made in a Sportsman Centennial Commemorative. Add 15%-25% if NIB.

MODEL 999 ENGRAVED - similar to 999, only engraved throughout, 6 in. barrel only. Disc. 1985.

	$425	$375	$300	$260	$225	$190	$175

Last MSR was $525.

RIFLES

REISING MODEL 60 - .45 ACP cal., semi-auto, 12 or 20 shot detachable mag., 18 1/4 in. barrel, plain wood stock with sling swivels. Approx. 3,500 mfg. 1944-46.

	N/A	N/A	$2,750	$2,350	$2,150	$1,950	$1,775

MODEL 65 MILITARY - .22 LR cal., 10 shot mag., 23 in. barrel, Redfield aperture rear sight. Mfg. 1944-46 for USMC.

	$250	$230	$200	$165	$145	$130	$110

MODEL 150 - .22 LR cal., semi-auto, 5 shot. Mfg. 1949-53.

	$95	$85	$70	$55	$40	$35	$30

MODEL 155 - .44 Mag. or .45-70 Govt. cal., single shot, break open. Mfg. 1972-disc.

	$150	$130	$115	$95	$75	$55	$45

MODEL 157 - .22 Mag., .22 Hornet, or .30-30 cal., single shot, break open, Mannlicher stock. Mfg. 1976-84.

	$165	$150	$135	$100	$80	$65	$45

MODEL 158 - .22 Jet, .22 Hornet, .30-30, .357 Mag., or .44 Mag. cal., single shot break open, 22 in. barrel, side or top lever action release, ejector, case hardened frame. Disc. 1985.

	$150	$135	$125	$90	$80	$60	$50

Last MSR was $115.

✻ *Model 158 Combination* - supplied with rifle barrel and 20 ga., 26 in. barrel. Disc. 1985.

	$195	$175	$150	$135	$115	$100	$90

Last MSR was $145.

MODEL 165 - .22 LR cal., 10 shot. Mfg. 1945-61.

	$120	$110	$95	$85	$70	$55	$50

MODEL 171 - .45-70 Govt. cal., Model 1873 Trapdoor copy, 22 in. barrel, Model 174 is the deluxe model. Disc.

	$350	$300	$270	$250	$230	$210	$195

MODEL 171-DL - .45-70 Govt. cal., single shot, Springfield copy, 22 in. barrel. Mfg. 1984-85.

	$400	$350	$295	$250	$225	$200	$185

Last MSR was $385.

GRADING - PPGS™	100%	98%	95%	90%	80%	70%	60%

MODEL 174

	$400	$375	$325	$300	$250	$210	$195

MODEL 300 ULTRA - .22-250 Rem., .243 Win., .270 Win., .30-06, .308 Win., 7mm Mag., or .300 Win. Mag. cal., bolt action, 22 or 24 in. barrel. Mfg. 1965-78.

	$495	$450	$425	$400	$350	$325	$295

MODEL 301 CARBINE - similar to 300, but 18 in. barrel, full length Mannlicher stock, N/A .22-250 Rem. cal.

	$440	$415	$360	$305	$250	$220	$195

MODEL 317 ULTRA WILDCAT - .17 Rem., .17-223, .222 Rem., or .223 Rem. cal., short action Sako, 20 in. barrel, no sights. Mfg. 1968-76.

	$550	$525	$500	$450	$400	$350	$325

MODEL 317P PRESENTATION - similar to Model 317, but deluxe wood basketweave checkering. Mfg. 1968-76.

	$625	$550	$495	$440	$400	$360	$305

MODEL 322 - .222 Rem. cal., short throw bolt action, 6 shot mag., 24 in. barrel, checkered hardwood Monte Carlo stock with cheekpiece, drilled and tapped, approx. 6 3/4 lbs. Mfg. circa 1973-80.

	$325	$275	$245	$220	$200	$180	$165

MODEL 333 - 7mm Mag. cal., similar to Model 300, plainer version. Mfg. 1974 only.

	$250	$230	$215	$180	$160	$140	$120

MODEL 340 - .243 Win., .270 Win., .30-06, .308 Win., or 7mm Mauser cal., bolt action, 5 shot, 22 in. barrel, checkered walnut. Mfg. 1982-84.

	$395	$300	$275	$240	$220	$200	$180

MODEL 360 ULTRA AUTOMATIC - .243 Win. or .308 Win. cal., 3 shot, 22 in. barrel. Mfg. 1965-78.

	$395	$350	$325	$300	$275	$250	$225

MODEL 370 ULTRA MEDALIST TARGET - .22-250 Rem., .243 Win., or 6mm Rem. cal., Varmint Rifle, 5 shot mag., 24 in. varmint weight barrel, uncheckered target stock with rollover cheekpiece and semi-beavertail forearm, 9 1/2 lbs. Mfg. 1968-73.

	$475	$425	$385	$360	$340	$325	$295

MODEL 422 - .22 S, L, or LR cal., slide action. Mfg. 1956-58.

	$110	$100	$85	$65	$45	$40	$30

❋ *Model 450* - similar to Model 451 Medalist only no sights.

	$150	$140	$120	$110	$95	$70	$55

MODEL 451 MEDALIST - .22 LR cal., bolt action, 5 shot, 26 in. barrel. Mfg. 1948-61.

	$165	$150	$140	$110	$100	$85	$55

MODEL 700 - .22 Mag. cal., semi-auto, 5 shot, clip mag., 22 in. barrel. Mfg. 1977-85.

	$275	$250	$225	$200	$175	$150	$125

Last MSR was $210.

MODEL 700DL - similar to Model 700 except deluxe checkered walnut. 4-power scope is standard, recoil pad. Disc. 1985.

	$395	$350	$325	$300	$275	$250	$200

Last MSR was $360.

MODEL 750 - .22 LR cal. single shot bolt action, 22 in. barrel, open sights, youth stock dimensions. Disc. 1985.

	$85	$75	$60	$50	$45	$40	$35

Last MSR was $95.

GRADING - PPGS™	100%	98%	95%	90%	80%	70%	60%

MODEL 865 - .22 LR cal. bolt action, 5 shot mag., 22 in. barrel. Disc. 1985.

	$90	$80	$65	$55	$50	$45	$40

Last MSR was $105.

MODEL 5200 TARGET - .22 LR cal. target rifle, heavy 28 in. barrel, adj. trigger, no sights, single shot. 11 lbs. Disc. 1985.

	$475	$450	$400	$350	$300	$275	$250

Last MSR was $450.

MODEL 5200 SPORTER - .22 LR cal., bolt action, 5 shot, 24 in. barrel, adj. sights, checkered walnut. Disc. 1983.

	$595	$550	$500	$475	$450	$400	$350

SHOTGUNS

HARRICH NO. 1 - 12 ga., single barrel Trap Gun, 32 or 34 in. full choke, high quality, engraved, vent. rib. Mfg. by Ferlach of Austria from 1971-75.

	$1,650	$1,595	$1,485	$1,320	$1,100	$880	$770

MODEL 3 HAMMERLESS - similar to Model 8, but no visible external hammer. Mfg. 1908-42.

	$85	$75	$70	$55	$45	$40	$30

MODEL 5 LIGHTWEIGHT - 24, 28 ga., or .410 bore only. Mfg. 1908-42.

	$95	$90	$75	$65	$55	$40	$35

MODEL 6 HEAVY BREECH - similar to Model 8, only 10 ga. - 20 ga., heavier barrels. Mfg. 1908-42.

	$95	$85	$75	$60	$50	$45	$35

MODEL 7 OR 9 BAY STATE - similar to Model 8, only 12, 16, 20 ga., or .410 bore, rounded pistol grip. Mfg. 1908-42.

	$85	$75	$70	$55	$45	$40	$30

MODEL 8 STANDARD - 12, 16, 20, 24, 28 ga., or .410 bore, 26-32 in. barrel, plain pistol grip stock, auto ejector, break open. Mfg. 1908-42.

	$150	$125	$95	$75	$65	$60	$55

   Add 100% for 28 ga. or .410 bore.

FOLDING GUN - 12, 16, 20, 28 ga., or .410 bore, single shot, hinged frame, barrel folds against stock. Mfg. 1908-42.

	$225	$195	$160	$125	$100	$85	$60

   Add 75% for 28 ga. or .410 bore.

TOPPER - 12, 16, 20 ga., or .410 bore, single shot, top or side lever break open action, 10 different variations of this shotgun, all are very similar and values run too close to differentiate, with ejector. Mfg. 1946-disc.

	$145	$125	$100	$85	$70	$55	$45

   Add 15% for Topper Deluxe (Model 488, chrome finish).

   This model was also designated the Model 48, Model 158 (not in 28 ga.), Model 162 Buck gun with open sights, and Model 198 (28 ga. or .410 bore only).

MODEL 088 - 12, 16, 20, 28 ga., or .410 bore, single shot, hammer model, ejector, top or side lever break open action, blue barrel finish with case hardened frame. Disc. 1985.

	$85	$75	$55	$50	$45	$40	$35

Last MSR was $95.

MODEL 099 - 12, 16, 20 ga., or .410 bore, similar to Model 088, only electroless nickel finish, ejector, top or side lever break open action. Disc. 1984.

	$95	$80	$60	$55	$50	$45	$40

GRADING - PPGS™	100%	98%	95%	90%	80%	70%	60%

MODEL 162 - 12 or 20 ga., single shot, 24 in. slug barrel with rifle sights, case hardened frame, top or side lever break open action. Disc. 1984.

	$115	$105	$90	$80	$65	$55	$45

MODEL 176 - 10 (3 1/2 in.), 12, or 20 ga., Mag., single shot, 32-36 in. heavy barrel, top or side lever break open action. Mfg. 1977-85.

	$110	$95	$80	$70	$60	$50	$45

Last MSR was $125.

MODELS 348/349 BOLT ACTION - 12 or 16 ga., 3 shot tube mag., 28 in. barrel (Model 349 has adj. vari-choke), walnut stock, 7 1/2 lbs. Disc.

	$115	$90	$75	$60	$50	$45	$40

MODEL 400 PUMP ACTION - 12, 16, or 20 ga., 28 in. full choke. Mfg. 1955-67.

	$155	$145	$125	$110	$90	$75	$55

MODEL 401 PUMP - similar to 400, but H&R variable choke. Mfg. 1956-63.

	$165	$155	$140	$120	$100	$90	$65

MODEL 402 PUMP - .410 bore, similar to 400, lightweight. Mfg. 1959-67.

	$175	$165	$150	$140	$110	$100	$85

MODEL 403 AUTOLOADER - .410 bore, 26 in. full choke, takedown. Mfg. 1964 only.

	$195	$180	$165	$155	$120	$100	$85

MODEL 404 - 12, 20 ga., or .410 bore, double barrel, SxS, 26 or 28 in. barrel, boxlock, extractors, double triggers. Mfg. by Rossi of Brazil 1969-72.

	$185	$175	$165	$145	$110	$90	$70

MODEL 404C - similar to 404, only checkered stock.

	$200	$185	$175	$155	$120	$100	$85

MODEL 440 - 12, 16, or 20 ga., pump action, 26, 28, or 30 in. barrels, available in various chokes, plain pistol grip and slide. Mfg. 1968-73.

	$145	$130	$110	$100	$85	$70	$55

MODEL 442 - pump action, similar to 440, only vent. rib, checkered stock. Mfg. 1969-73.

	$175	$165	$155	$140	$100	$85	$65

MODEL 490 - 20 ga. or .410 bore, made for junior shooters, Greenwing finish - add $10. Disc. 1984.

	$85	$65	$60	$50	$45	$40	$40

MODEL 1212 - 12 ga., O/U, Field, 2 3/4 in., 28 in. vent. rib barrels, various chokes, checkered walnut stocks. Mfg. by Lanber Arms, Spain, from 1976-disc.

	$310	$295	$275	$250	$200	$175	$155

MODEL 1212 WATERFOWL - 12 ga., 3 in. chamber, similar to Model 1212, 30 in. barrel.

	$320	$310	$285	$260	$210	$185	$165

HARRIS GUNWORKS

Previous firearms manufacturer located in Phoenix, AZ 1995-March 31, 2000. Previously named Harris-McMillan Gunworks and G. McMillan and Co., Inc. (please refer to the M section for more information on these two trademarks).

RIFLES: BOLT ACTION

BENCHREST COMPETITOR - .222 Rem. (disc.), .243 Win., 6mm Rem., 6mm PPC, 6mm BR, or .308 Win. cal., benchrest configuration. Mfg. 1993-2000.

	$2,675	$2,425	$1,950	$1,675	$1,425	$1,200	$1,025

Last MSR was $3,050.

GRADING - PPGS™	100%	98%	95%	90%	80%	70%	60%

NATIONAL MATCH COMPETITOR - .308 Win., or 7mm-08 Rem. cal. Mfg. 1993-2000.

	100%	98%	95%	90%	80%	70%	60%
	$3,125	$2,675	$2,300	$1,875	$1,650	$1,325	$1,100

Last MSR was $3,500.

LONG RANGE TARGET MODEL - .300 Win. Mag., .300 Phoenix, .30-378 Wby. Mag., .30-416 Rigby, .338 Lapua, or 7mm Rem. Mag. cal., black synthetic fully adj. stock, w/o sights, grey barrel finish. Mfg. 1996-2000.

	$3,225	$2,700	$2,325	$1,900	$1,650	$1,325	$1,100

Last MSR was $3,620.

TALON SPORTER - available in various cals. between .22-250 Rem. and .416 Rem., receiver available in either 4340 chrome molybdenum or 17-4 stainless steel, drilled and tapped, match grade barrel. Mfg. 1992-2000.

	$2,600	$2,075	$1,725	$1,375	$1,050	$895	$800

Last MSR was $2,900.

The Talon action is patterned after the Winchester pre-64 Model 70. It features a cone breech, controlled feed, claw extractor, and 3 position safety.

SIGNATURE CLASSIC SPORTER - various cals. available between .22-250 Rem. and .416 Rem., premium wood stock, matte metal finish, buttoning used on rifling for 22 or 24 in. stainless steel barrel, McMillan action made from 4340 chrome moly steel (either left- or right-handed), 3 or 4 shot mag. supplied with 5 shot test target. Mfg. 1988-2000.

	$2,450	$2,000	$1,675	$1,325	$1,000	$895	$800

Last MSR was $2,700.

SIGNATURE VARMINTER - similar to Signature Model, except is available in 12 cals. between .22-250 Rem. and .350 Rem. Mag., hand bedded fiberglass stock, adj. trigger, 26 in. heavily contoured barrel. Mfg. 1988-2000.

	$2,450	$2,000	$1,675	$1,325	$1,000	$895	$800

Last MSR was $2,700.

SIGNATURE TITANIUM MOUNTAIN RIFLE - .270 Win., .280 Rem., .30-06, .300 Win. Mag., .338 Win. Mag., or 7mm Rem. Mag. cal., lighter weight variation with shorter stainless steel or graphite/steel composite barrel, 5 3/4 (w/graphite barrel), or 6 1/2 lbs. Mfg. 1990-2000.

	$2,950	$2,575	$2,300	$1,925	$1,650	$1,325	$1,100

Last MSR was $3,300.

Add $400 with graphite barrel.

SIGNATURE ALASKAN - available in many cals. between .270 Win. and .458 Win. Mag. Mfg. 1990-2000.

	$3,425	$2,725	$2,275	$1,650	$1,250	$1,125	$900

Last MSR was $3,800.

TALON SAFARI - available in many cals. between .300 Win. Mag. and .460 Wby. Mag., hand bedded fiberglass stock, 4 shot mag., 24 in. stainless steel barrel, matte black finish, 9 1/2 lbs. Mfg. 1988-2000.

	$3,650	$2,850	$2,500	$2,150	$2,000	$1,850	$1,700

Last MSR was $3,900.

Add $300 for .300 Phoenix, .30-416 Rigby, .30-378 Wby. Mag., .338 Lapua, .335-378, .338-378, .378 Wby. Mag., .416 Wby. Mag. or Rigby, or .460 Wby. Mag. cal.

The Talon action is patterned after the Winchester pre-64 Model 70. It features a cone breech, controlled feed, claw extractor, and 3 position safety. Older Signature action rifles do not have this new Talon action.

M-40 SNIPER RIFLE - .308 Win. cal., Remington action with McMillan match grade heavy contour barrel, fiberglass stock with recoil pad, 4 shot mag., 9 lbs. Mfg. 1990-2000.

	$1,825	$1,450	$1,125	$925	$800	$700	$600

Last MSR was $2,000.

GRADING - PPGS™	100%	98%	95%	90%	80%	70%	60%

M-86 SNIPER RIFLE - .300 Phoenix (disc. 1996), .30-06 (new 1989), .300 Win. Mag. or .308 Win. cal., fiberglass stock, variety of optical sights. Mfg. 1988-2000.

	$2,450	$2,000	$1,675	$1,325	$1,000	$895	$800

Last MSR was $2,700.

Add $300 for .300 Phoenix cal. with Harris action (disc. 1996).
Add $200 for takedown feature (mfg. 1993-96).

.300 PHOENIX - available in most popular .30 cals., special fiberglass stock with adj. cheekpiece and buttplate, right- or left-hand action, 12 1/2 lbs. Mfg. 1997-2000.

	$3,025	$2,650	$2,325	$1,925	$1,675	$1,325	$1,100

Last MSR was $3,380.

M-87 LONG RANGE SNIPER RIFLE - .50 BMG cal., stainless steel bolt action, 29 in. barrel with muzzle brake, single shot, camo synthetic stock, accurate to 1500 meters, 21 lbs. Mfg. 1988-2000.

	$3,450	$2,800	$2,375	$2,000	$1,850	$1,700	$1,575

Last MSR was $3,885.

✳ *M-87R* - similiar specs. as Model 87, except has 5 shot fixed box mag. Mfg. 1990-2000.

	$3,725	$2,950	$2,550	$2,200	$2,000	$1,850	$1,700

Last MSR was $4,000.

M-88 U.S. NAVY - .50 BMG cal., reintroduced U.S. Navy Seal Team shell holder single shot action with thumb hole stock (one-piece or breakdown two-piece), 24 lbs. Mfg. 1997-2000.

	$3,250	$2,600	$2,200	$1,625	$1,250	$1,125	$900

Last MSR was $3,600.

Add $300 for two-piece breakdown stock.

M-89 SNIPER RIFLE - .308 Win. cal., 28 in. barrel with suppressor (also available without), fiberglass stock adj. for length and recoil pad, 15 1/4 lbs. Mfg. 1990-2000.

	$2,875	$2,525	$2,250	$1,875	$1,650	$1,325	$1,100

Last MSR was $3,200.

Add $425 for muzzle suppressor (disc. 1996).

M-92 BULL PUP - .50 BMG cal., bullpup configuration with shorter barrel. Mfg. 1993-2000.

	$4,300	$3,250	$2,750	$2,300	$2,050	$1,850	$1,700

Last MSR was $4,770.

M-93 - .50 BMG cal., similar to M-87, except has folding stock and detachable 5 or 10 shot box mag. Mfg. 1993-2000.

	$3,800	$3,250	$2,750	$2,300	$2,000	$1,850	$1,700

Last MSR was $4,150.

Add $300 for two-piece folding stock or dovetail combo. quick disassembly fixture.

M-95 TITANIUM/GRAPHITE - .50 BMG cal., features titanium alloy M-87 receiver with graphite barrel and steel liner, single shot or repeater, approx. 18 lbs. Mfg. 1997-2000.

	$4,650	$4,175	$3,475	$2,875	$2,300	$2,050	$1,850

Last MSR was $5,085.

Add $165 for fixed mag.
Add $315 for detachable mag.

M-96 SEMI-AUTO - .50 BMG cal., gas-operated with 5 shot detachable mag., carry handle scope mount, steel receiver, 30 lbs. Mfg. 1997-2000.

	$6,200	$5,625	$5,075	$4,650	$4,175	$3,475	$2,875

Last MSR was $6,800.

GRADING - PPGS™	100%	98%	95%	90%	80%	70%	60%

RIFLES SxS

BOXLOCK MODEL - various cals. from .270 Win. - .500 NE, engraved boxlock action, 3 leaf express rear sights, AAA wood, high polish barrel blue, equipped with aluminum case and chain, custom order. Mfg. 1998-2000.

			100%	98%	95%	90%	80%	70%	60%
			$12,000	$10,000	$8,500	$7,000	$6,000	$5,000	$4,000

Last MSR was $12,000.

Add $1,000 for quick detachable claw scope mounts.
Add $6,000 for additional set of rifle barrels.
Add $5,000 for additional set of shotgun barrels.

SIDELOCK MODEL - various cals. from .375 H&H - .577 NE, engraved sidelock action, 3 leaf express rear sights, AAA wood, high polish barrel blue, equipped with aluminum case and chain, custom order. Mfg. 1998-2000.

			100%	98%	95%	90%	80%	70%	60%
			$18,200	$15,750	$12,000	$10,000	$8,500	$7,000	$6,000

Last MSR was $18,200.

Add $1,000 for quick detachable claw scope mounts.
Add $6,000 for additional set of rifle barrels.
Add $5,000 for additional set of shotgun barrels.

HARRISON & HUSSEY LTD.

Current trademark founded in 1919 and currently owned by Cogswell & Harrison, located in Slough, England.

Harrison & Hussey Ltd. was founded in 1919 and purchased by Stephen Grant & Joseph Lang Ltd. in 1930. Boss & Co. took over Harrison & Hussey's original 41 Albermarle Street location and remained there until 1961.

Harrison & Hussey guns are best quality English longarms. It is recommended that an appraisal be obtained before purchase. Harrison & Hussey records have remained intact, and Cogswell & Harrison can provide owners with a date of manufacture free of charge, providing there is a serial number. A full repair and restoration service is also offered. Please contact Cogswell & Harrison for more information about these services (see Trademark Index).

HARTFORD ARMORY

Current manufacturer located in Collinsville, CT beginning 2003. Distributed exclusively by Taylor's & Co, Inc., located in Winchester, VA.

REVOLVERS: REPRODUCTIONS

MODEL 1875 - .357 Mag., .44 Mag., .44-40 WCF, or .45 LC cal., reproduction of original Remington Model 1875 with reinforced barrel, 5 3/4 or 7 1/2 in. barrel, blue metal finish standard (optional frame case colors by Doug Turnbull), or stainless steel construction, includes wooden presentation box with six brass snap caps. New 2004.

MSR $1,495		$1,325	$1,100	$875	$700	$600	$500	$450

MODEL 1890 - .357 Mag., .44 Mag., .44-40 WCF, or .45 LC cal., reproduction of original Remington Model 1890, 5 3/4 or 7 1/2 in. barrel, blue metal or stainless steel, includes wooden presentation box with six brass snap caps. New 2004.

MSR $1,495		$1,325	$1,100	$875	$700	$600	$500	$450

HARTFORD ARMS & EQUIPMENT COMPANY

Previous manufacturer located in Harford, CT 1925-1932. Established in 1925, this firm was bankrupt when purchased by the High Standard Company in 1932.

GRADING - PPGS™	100%	98%	95%	90%	80%	70%	60%

PISTOLS: SEMI-AUTO, RIMFIRE

HARTFORD AUTOMATIC TARGET MODEL 1925 - .22 LR cal., 6 3/4 in. round barrel, checkered black hard rubber or ribbed walnut grips, 10 shot, frame marked "Manfd. by/the Hartford Arms and Equip. Co./Hartford, Conn./Patented/.22 cal./Long Rifle" on left side in front of breech. Approx. 5,000 mfg. 1925-1930.

	$550	$500	$450	$400	$310	$300	$280

Add $150 for guns in original Hartford Arms box numbered to gun.

HARTFORD REPEATING PISTOL

The existence of this pistol is in doubt. If encountered, please have the gun checked for authenticity by an expert. The interrelationship of Fiala, Hartford, and Schall through the common gun designer suggests that if this gun exists, then it is probably a Hartford marked repeater like the Fiala and Schall models. Numerous examples of unmarked Schall pistols exist, and some have confused the Schall as a Hartford repeater.

PISTOLS: SINGLE SHOT

HARTFORD SINGLE SHOT TARGET - .22 LR cal., single shot, manual operation, 6 3/4 in. round barrel, fixed sights, ribbed walnut or composition grips, frame marked "Manfd. by/the Hartford Arms and Equip. Co./Hartford, Conn./Patented/.22 cal./Long Rifle" on the left side in front of the breech, resembles a semi-auto, no mag.

	$600	$550	$500	$425	$350	$310	$300

Add $150 for guns in original Hartford Arms box numbered to gun.

Add $250 for guns in original High Standard box numbered to gun.

High Standard produced a number of these models in 1933. These guns were mfg. from Hartford parts and carried the Hartford markings. The box for High Standard manufactured guns carry the High Standard and Hartford names. Hartford production is unknown, but probably less than 800. High Standard production less than 900 pistols.

HARTMANN & WEISS GmbH

Current manufacturer established during 1965 and located in Hamburg, Germany.

Hartmann and Weiss manufactures only top quality longarms, including sidelock SxS shotguns and rifles, O/U shotguns and rifles, falling block single shot rifles (including the Heeren and Hagn action), and bolt action rifles with three lengths of action. Please contact the manufacturer directly for more information and/or a price quotation (see Trademark Index).

HASKELL MANUFACTURING

Previous manufacturer of .45 ACP cal. semi-auto pistols located in Lima, OH. Previously distributed by MKS Supply located in Mansfield, OH.

Refer to listing under Hi-Point Firearms.

HATFIELD GUN CO., INC.

Previous manufacturer located in St. Joseph, MO. The following shotguns were previously manufactured until 1996 by the Hatfield Gun Co., Inc. (designated Hatfield Rifle Works until 1986).

SHOTGUNS: O/U

BOXLOCK - 20 ga. only, boxlock action with satin grey finished receiver, maple stock. Mfg. 1995-96.

	$3,350	$2,950	$2,550	$2,175	$1,725	$1,450	$1,100

Last MSR was $3,749.

Add $1,425 for extra 28 ga. barrels.

GRADING - PPGS™	100%	98%	95%	90%	80%	70%	60%

SHOTGUNS: SxS

In addition to Grades I and II, Hatfield also offered custom order shotguns built per individual special order - prices started at $3,000.

GRADE I UPLANDER - 20 or 28 ga., 3 in. chambers, 26 in. IC/M, matted rib barrels, case hardened boxlock action, single trigger, ejectors, deluxe checkered straight grip maple stock and forearm, 5 3/4 lbs, cased. Mfg. 1987-96.

	$1,975	$1,700	$1,500	$1,325	$1,150	$900	$725

Last MSR was $2,249.

Add $800 for extra 28 ga. barrels.

✷ *Collector's Grade I* - mfg. 1990-92.

	$1,475	$1,200	$1,000	$875	$700	$550	$475

Last MSR was $1,625.

Add $400 for extra 28 ga. barrels.

GRADE II PIGEON - similar to Grade I, except has scroll engraving on top lever, sides, floor plate, and triggerguard, cased. Mfg. 1987-96.

	$2,650	$2,250	$1,825	$1,475	$1,100	$900	$775

Last MSR was $2,995.

Add $995 for extra 28 ga. barrels.

✷ *Collector's Grade II* - mfg. 1990-92.

	$2,675	$2,000	$1,600	$1,250	$1,050	$875	$775

Last MSR was $3,025.

Add $400 for extra 28 ga. barrels.

GRADE III SUPER PIGEON - includes heavy relief scroll engraving (total coverage) on frame, top lever, floor plate, and triggerguard, leather cased. Mfg. 1987-disc.

	$2,350	$1,900	$1,495	$1,200	$1,025	$900	$775

Last MSR was $3,500.

Add $900 for extra 28 ga. barrels.

✷ *Collector's Grade III* - mfg. 1990-disc.

	$3,000	$2,500	$2,000	$1,750	$1,400	$1,175	$995

Last MSR was $4,375.

Add $900 for extra 28 ga. barrels.

GRADE IV GOLDEN QUAIL - more extensive engraving including six 24Kt. gold inlays on frame and floor plate, 2 gold barrel bands, leather cased. Mfg. 1987-disc.

	$3,995	$3,575	$2,900	$2,350	$1,900	$1,600	$1,300

Last MSR was $5,500.

Add $900 for extra 28 ga. barrels.

✷ *Collector's Grade IV* - mfg. 1990-disc.

	$4,475	$3,900	$3,300	$2,650	$2,175	$1,800	$1,500

Last MSR was $6,625.

Add $1,350 for extra 28 ga. barrels.

GRADE V WOODCOCK - previous top-of-the-line model with best quality engraving and multiple gold inlays, leather cased. Mfg. 1987-disc.

	$4,600	$4,400	$3,350	$2,700	$2,175	$1,800	$1,500

Last MSR was $6,900.

Add $1,500 for extra 28 ga. barrels.

✷ *Collector's Grade V* - mfg. 1990-disc.

	$6,200	$5,700	$4,475	$3,900	$3,300	$2,650	$2,200

Last MSR was $8,500.

Add $2,000 for extra 28 ga. barrels.

GRADING - PPGS™	100%	98%	95%	90%	80%	70%	60%

GRADE VI BLACK WIDOW - mfg. 1990-disc.

	$5,200	$4,875	$3,700	$3,000	$2,500	$2,100	$1,800

Last MSR was $7,900.

GRADE VII ROYALE - mfg. 1990-disc.

	$5,200	$4,875	$3,700	$3,000	$2,500	$2,100	$1,800

Last MSR was $7,900.

GRADE VIII TOP HAT - top-of-the-line model with best quality wood and extensive engraving with gold inlays. Built to individual customer specifications. Mfg. 1990-disc.

	$12,000	$9,750	$8,750	$7,500	$6,500	$5,500	$4,500

Last MSR was $17,500.

SIDELOCK MODEL - 20 ga. only, satin grey finished receiver, full engraving. Mfg. 1995-96.

	$10,750	$8,750	$7,500	$6,250	$5,000	$4,850	$3,600

Last MSR was $12,000.

✳ *Grade II Sidelock* - features high relief full coverage engraving, color case hardened receiver, multiple gold and silver inlays.

	$15,000	$12,000	$10,750	$8,750	$7,000	$5,750	$4,650

Last MSR was $17,500.

HATFIELD'S

Current manufacturer established during 2003, and located in St. Joseph, MO.

SHOTGUNS: SxS

UPLANDER 28 - 28 ga., small scalloped boxlock frame, extractors, SST or DT, 26 in. monobloc barrels with matte rib, checkered Circassian walnut straight grip stock and splinter forearm, case colored frame, 4 lbs. New 2004.

MSR $1,499	$1,350	$1,200	$1,000	$875	$700	$550	$475

Add $100 for single trigger.

KARL HAUPTMANN JAGDWAFFEN

Current manufacturer located in Ferlach, Austria. Consumer direct sales.

Karl Hauptmann was a member of the Ferlach Guild until is was dissolved in 2004. His son Gerd Hauptmann is currently the managing director of the company. Hauptmann Jagdwaffen manufactures high quality shotguns, combination guns, and double rifles, and a very unique, three barrel SxSxS rifle. Since every gun is custom made according to each customer's specifications, please contact the factory directly for an individual price quotation and delivery time (see Trademark Index).

HAWES FIREARMS

Previously manufactured by J.P. Sauer & Sohn in Eckernforde, Germany. Previously imported by Hawes Firearms in Van Nuys, CA.

Rather than give an individual listing of the various single action and double action (including Medallion models) revolvers that have been imported, a generalized price range is as follows: centerfire single actions usually are in the $150-$275 range, centerfire double actions are $175-$295, while .22 rimfire models are typically valued between $60-140.

HECKLER & KOCH

Current manufacturer established in 1949, and located in Oberndorf/Neckar, Germany. Currently imported and distributed by Heckler & Koch, Inc. (U.S. headquarters) located in Sterling, VA (previously located in Chantilly, VA). During 2004,

GRADING - PPGS™	100%	98%	95%	90%	80%	70%	60%

H & K built a new plant in Columbus, GA, primarily to manufacture guns for American military and law enforcement. In early 1991, H & K was absorbed by Royal Ordnance, a division of British Aerospace (BAE Systems) located in England. During December 2002, BAE Systems sold Heckler & Koch to a group of European investors. Heckler & Koch, Inc. and HKJS GmbH are wholly owned subsidiaries of Suhler Jag- und Sportwaffen Holding GmbH and the sole licensees of Heckler & Koch commercial firearms technology.

PISTOLS: SEMI-AUTO, RECENT MFG.

Add $53 for ambidextrous control lever (safety/decocking lever on right side), and $387 for laser sighting device BA-6 (new 2002) on currently manufactured USP and USP Compact models. Also add $25 for any USP/USP Compact variant other than Variant 1.

USP and USP Compact (with bobbed hammer) Models are divided into 9 variations. They include: USP Variant 1 (DA/SA with control safety decocking lever on left), USP Variant 2 (DA/SA with control safety decocking lever on right), USP Variant 3 (DA/SA with control safety decocking lever on left), USP Variant 4 (DA/SA with control safety decocking lever on right), USP Variant 5 (DAO with control safety decocking lever on left), USP Variant 6 (DAO with control safety decocking lever on right), USP Variant 7 (DAO with no control lever), USP Variant 9 (DA/SA with safety control lever on left), and USP Variant 10 (DA/SA with safety control lever on right).

HK4 - .380 ACP, .32 ACP, .25 ACP, and .22 LR cals., double action auto, available with all caliber conversion units, 3 1/3 in. barrel, blue, plastic grips. Disc. 1984.

	100%	98%	95%	90%	80%	70%	60%
.25 ACP or .32 ACP cal.	$295	$260	$230	$215	$180	$150	$130
.22 LR or .380 ACP cal.	$375	$325	$300	$250	$195	$160	$140

This model was also available as a H & K commemorative model with gold tone plaque on slide and came in a plastic presentation box. Add approx. 25% to .22 LR or .380 ACP cal. prices if NIB.

✳ *.380 ACP with .22 LR conversion*

	$480	$385	$350	$325	$310	$290	$280

✳ *.380 ACP with all conversions*

	$650	$550	$450	$420	$390	$375	$360

This model was also mfg. in a French model in .22 LR and/or .32 ACP (about 500 imported).

P9S - .45 ACP or 9mm Para. cal., double action combat model, 4 in. barrel, phosphate finish, sculptured plastic grips, fixed sights. Although production ceased in 1984, limited quantities were available until 1989.

	$850	$775	$650	$525	$450	$375	$300

Last MSR was $1,299.

Add 25% for .45 ACP.

P9S TARGET - .45 ACP or 9mm Para. cal., 4 in. barrel, phosphate finish, adj. sights and trigger. Although production ceased in 1984, limited quantities were available until 1989.

	$1,000	$800	$600	$540	$500	$465	$430

Last MSR was $1,382.

P9S COMPETITION KIT - 9mm Para. or .45 ACP (rare) cal., similar to P9S Target, except extra 5 1/2 in. barrel and weight, competition walnut grip, 2 slides. Disc. 1984.

	$1,150	$950	$875	$800	$720	$640	$550

Last MSR was $2,250.

P7 PSP - 9mm Para. cal., older variation of the P7 M8, without extended trigger guard, ambidextrous mag. release (European style), or heat shield. Standard production ceased 1986. A reissue of this model was mfg. in 1990, with approx. 150 produced. Limited quantities remained through 1999.

	$850	$750	$650	$550	$460	$410	$390

Last MSR was $1,111.

Add $200 for European Model with larger frame.

GRADING - PPGS™	100%	98%	95%	90%	80%	70%	60%

P7 M8 - 9mm Para. cal., unique squeeze cocking single action, extended square combat type trigger guard with heat shield, 4.13 in. fixed barrel with polygonal rifling, 8 shot mag., ambidextrous mag. release, fixed 3-dot sighting system, stippled black plastic grips, black phosphate or nickel (mfg. 1992-2000) finish, includes 2 mags., 28 oz. Disc. 2005.

	MSR $1,515	$1,125	$950	$775	$650	$550	$500	$450

Add $102 for Tritium sights (various colors, new 1993).
Add $566 for .22 LR conversion kit (barrel, slide, and two mags., disc. 1999).
This model had limited availability through 2005.

P7 M13 - similar to P7 M8, only with staggered 13 shot mag., 30 oz. Disc. 1994.

		$1,575	$1,250	$1,050	$825	$700	$575	$525
						Last MSR was $1,330.		

Add $85 for Tritium sights (various colors, new 1993).
Add 10% for factory wood grips.

P7 M10 - .40 S&W cal., similar specifications as P7 M13, except has 10 shot mag., 39 oz. Mfg. 1991-94.

		$1,125	$950	$775	$650	$550	$500	$450
						Last MSR was $1,315.		

Add $85 for Tritium sights (various colors, new 1993).

P7 K3 - .22 LR or .380 ACP cal., uses unique oil-filled buffer to decrease recoil, 3.8 in. barrel, matte black or nickel (less common) finish, 8 shot mag. (includes 2), 26 1/2 oz. Mfg. 1988-94.

		$1,295	$850	$715	$600	$525	$450	$410
						Last MSR was $1,100.		

Add $525 for .22 LR conversion kit.
Add $228 for .32 ACP conversion kit.
Add $85 for Tritium sights (various colors, new 1993).

P2000 - 9mm Para., .357 SIG (new 2005), or .40 S&W cal., SA/DA, compact design, patterned after USP Compact Model, features pre-cocked hammer system with very short trigger rest distance, lockout safety device, 3 dot sights, 3.62 in. barrel with polygon rifling, 10 shot mag. with finger extension, or optional 13 shot mag. (new late 2004), with or w/o decocker, interchangeable rear grip panels, black finish, approx. 22 oz.

	MSR $887	$775	$675	$550	$475	$400	$350	$300

Add $33 for magazine disconnect.

✱ **P2000 SubCompact** - similar to P2000, features LEM (Law Enforcement Modification) trigger system, 2.48 in. barrel, 9 (.40 S&W cal.) or 10 (9mm Para.) shot mag., approx. 27 oz. Importation began 2005.

	MSR $929	$795	$695	$550	$475	$400	$350	$300

USP 9 - 9mm Para. cal., available in regular DA/SA mode or DA only (10 variants), 4.13 in. barrel with polygonal rifling, Browning-type action with H & K recoil reduction system, polymer frame, all metal surfaces specially treated, can be carried cocked and locked, stippled synthetic grips, bobbed hammer, 3-dot sighting system, multiple safeties, 10 (C/B 1994), 15 (optional late 2004), or 16* shot polymer mag., 26.5 oz. New 1993.

	MSR $769	$670	$540	$485	$430	$365	$330	$295

Add $102 for Tritium sights (various colors, new 1993).

✱ **USP 9 SD** - similar to USP 9, except has target sights and 4.56 threaded barrel, approx. 27 oz. Importation began 2004.

	MSR $939	$825	$700	$625	$550	$500	$450	$400

GRADING - PPGS™	100%	98%	95%	90%	80%	70%	60%

✷ *USP 9 Stainless* - similar to USP 9, except has satin finished stainless steel slide. Mfg. 1996-2001.

	$700	$565	$475				

Last MSR was $817.

USP 9 COMPACT - 9mm Para. cal., compact variation of the USP 9 featuring 3.58 in. barrel, 10 or 13 (optional beginning late 2004) shot mag., 25.5 oz. New 1997.

MSR $799	$690	$550	$475	$430	$375	$335	$300

✷ *USP 9 Compact Stainless* - similar to USP 9 Compact, except has satin finished stainless steel slide. Mfg. 1997-2004.

	$735	$595	$500				

Last MSR was $849.

✷ *USP 9 Compact LEM* - LEM designates law enforcement modification, DAO, unique trigger mechanism decreases trigger pull to 7.5-8.5 lbs, blue only, approx. 24.5 oz. Imported 2003-2004.

	$695	$575	$495	$450	$400	$350	$315

Last MSR was $799.

USP 40 - .40 S&W cal., similar to USP 9, 9 variants of DA/SA/DAO, 10 (C/B1994), 13* (optional, reintroduced late 2004), or 16 (optional, new 2005, needs jet funnel modification) shot mag., 27.75 oz. New 1993.

MSR $769	$675	$550	$485	$430	$365	$330	$295

Add $102 for Tritium sights (various colors, new 1993).

A desert tan finish became available during 2005 at no extra charge.

✷ *USP 40 Stainless* - similar to USP 40, except has satin finished stainless steel slide. Mfg. 1996-2003.

	$700	$565	$470				

Last MSR was $817.

USP 40 COMPACT - .40 S&W cal., compact variation of the USP 40 featuring 3.58 in. barrel, 10 or 12 (optional beginning late 2004) shot mag., 27 oz. New 1997.

MSR $799	$695	$575	$495	$450	$400	$350	$315

A desert tan finish became available during 2005 at no extra charge.

✷ *USP 40 Compact Stainless* - similar to USP 40 Compact, except has satin finished stainless steel slide. Mfg. 1997-2004.

	$735	$595	$500				

Last MSR was $849.

✷ *USP 40 Compact LEM* - LEM designates law enforcement modification, DAO, unique trigger mechanism decreases trigger pull to 7.5-8.5 lbs, blue only, approx. 24.5 oz. Importation began 2002.

MSR $799	$695	$575	$495	$450	$400	$350	$315

USP 40 TACTICAL - .40 S&W cal., enhanced variation of the USP 40, 4.92 in. threaded barrel with rubber o-ring, 10 (standard) or 13 (optional) shot mag., adj. target type sights and trigger, New 2005.

MSR $1,019	$895	$775	$675	$575	$500	$450	$400

USP 45 - .45 ACP cal., similar to USP 9, 9 variants of DA/SA/DAO, 10 (C/B 1994), 12 (optional, new late 2004) or 13* shot mag., 27.75 oz. New 1995.

MSR $839	$730	$595	$500	$450	$395	$350	$315

Add $102 for Tritium sights (various colors, new 1993).

A desert tan finish became available during 2005 at no extra charge.

✷ *USP 45 Stainless* - similar to USP 45, except has satin finished stainless steel slide. Mfg. 1996-2003.

	$760	$600	$500				

Last MSR was $888.

GRADING - PPGS™	100%	98%	95%	90%	80%	70%	60%

✵ *USP 45 Match Pistol* - .45 ACP cal., features 6.02 in. barrel with polygonal rifling, micrometer adj. high relief and raised rear sight, raised target front sight, 10 shot mag., barrel weight, fluted, and ambidextrous safety, choice of matte black or stainless steel slide, supplied with additional o-rings and setup tools, 38 oz. Mfg. 1997-98.

	$1,275	$1,025	$825	$750	$675	$550	$500

Last MSR was $1,369.

Add $72 for stainless steel slide model.

USP 45 COMPACT - .45 ACP cal., compact variation of the USP 45, featuring 3.8 in. barrel, 8 shot mag., 28 oz. New 1998.

MSR $874	$760	$595	$500	$450	$400	$350	$315

✵ *USP 45 Compact Stainless* - similar to USP 45 Compact, except has satin finished stainless steel slide. Mfg. 1998-2004.

	$775	$615	$510

Last MSR was $894.

✵ *USP 45 Compact 50th Anniversary* - commemorates the 50th year of H & K (1950-2000), 1 of 1,000 special edition featuring high polish blue slide with 50th Anniversary logo engraved in gold and silver, supplied with presentation wood case and commemorative coin. Limited mfg. 2000 only.

	$1,150	$895	$795

Last MSR was $999.

USP 45 TACTICAL PISTOL - .45 ACP cal., enhanced variation of the USP 45, 4.92 in. threaded barrel with rubber o-ring, 10 or 12 (optional beginning late 2004) shot mag., adj. target type sights and trigger, limited availability, 36 oz. New 1998.

MSR $1,115	$995	$875	$775	$675	$600	$525	$495

A desert tan finish became available during 2005 at no extra charge.

USP 357 - .357 SIG cal., available in 4.25 (Standard, disc. 2004) or 3.58 (Compact) configuration, 10 or 12 (optional beginning 2004) shot mag., black finish, approx. 24.5 oz. Importation began 2001.

MSR $799	$695	$560	$500	$450	$395	$350	$300

Subtract $30 for Standard Model (disc. 2004).

USP EXPERT - 9mm Para. (new 2003), .40 S&W (new 2002) or .45 ACP cal., features new slide design with 5.2 in. barrel, 10 (standard) or optional 12 (.45 ACP), 13 (.40 S&W), or 15 (9mm Para.) shot mag., match grade SA or DA trigger pull, recoil reduction system, reinforced polymer frame, adj. rear sight, approx. 30 oz. New 1999.

MSR $1,356	$1,200	$1,025	$900	$800	$700	$625	$525

USP ELITE - 9mm Para. or .45 ACP cal, long slide variation of the USP, 6.2 in. barrel, match trigger parts, target sights, ambidextrous control levers, blue finish, includes two 10 shot mags. or optional 12 (.45 ACP) or 15 (9mm Para.) shot mag. Importation began 2003.

MSR $1,356	$1,200	$1,025	$900	$800	$700	$625	$525

MARK 23 SPECIAL OPERATIONS PISTOL - .45 ACP cal., 5.87 in. threaded barrel, polymer frame and integral grips, 3-dot sighting, 10 or 12 (optional beginning late 2004) shot mag., squared off trigger guard, 2.6 lbs., limited availability. New 1996.

MSR $2,412	$2,150	$1,850	$1,600	$1,275	$1,000	$850	$725

"MK23" is the official military design. Not available to civilians.

A desert tan finish became available during 2005 at no extra charge.

SP 89 - 9mm Para. cal., recoil operated delayed roller-locked bolt system, 4.5 in. barrel, 15 shot mag., adj. aperture rear sight (accepts HK claw-lock scope mounts), 4.4 lbs. Mfg. 1990-93.

	$3,000	$2,750	$2,500	$2,250	$2,000	$1,750	$1,500

Last MSR was $1,325.

GRADING - PPGS™	100%	98%	95%	90%	80%	70%	60%

VP 70Z - 9mm Para. cal., 18 shot, double action only, 4.5 in. barrel, parkerized finish, plastic receiver/grip assembly. Disc. 1984.

		$550	$475	$400	$350	$325	$275	$250

   Add 125% if frame cut for shoulder stock (Model VP 70M, NFA Class III).

   The majority of pistols that were cut for shoulder stock are the Model VP 70M, and are subject to NFA Class III regulation.

RIFLES: BOLT ACTION

BASR - .22 LR, .22-250 Rem., 6mm PPC, .300 Win. Mag., .30-06, or .308 Win. cal., Kevlar stock, stainless steel barrel, limited production. Special order only. Mfg. 1986 only.

	$5,750	$5,000	$4,500	$4,000	$3,650	$3,300	$2,600

Last MSR was $2,199.

   Less than 135 of this variation were manufactured and they are extremely rare. Contractual disputes with the U.S. supplier stopped H & K from receiving any BASR models.

RIFLES: SEMI-AUTO

Most of the models listed, being of a paramilitary design, were disc. in 1989 due to Federal legislation. Sporterized variations mfg. after 1994 with thumbhole stocks were banned in April, 1998. In 1991, the HK-91, HK-93, and HK-94 were discontinued. Last published retail prices (1991) were $999 for fixed stock models and $1,199 for retractable stock models.

In the early '70s, S.A.C.O. importers located in Virginia sold the Models 41 and 43 which were the predecessors to the Model 91 and 93, respectively. Values for these earlier variations will be higher than values listed.

SR-9 - .308 Win. cal., semi-auto sporting rifle, 19.7 in. barrel, Kevlar reinforced fiberglass thumbhole stock and forearm, 5 shot mag., diopter adj. rear sight, accepts H & K claw-lock scope mounts. Mfg. 1990-93.

	$1,875	$1,525	$1,200	$1,025	$875	$750	$650

Last MSR was $1,199.

   While advertised again during 1998, this model was finally banned in April, 1998.

SR-9T - .308 Win. cal., precision target rifle with adj. MSG 90 buttstock and PSG-1 trigger group, 5 shot mag. Mfg. 1992-93.

	$2,595	$2,175	$1,850	$1,575	$1,175	$995	$850

Last MSR was $1,725.

   While advertised again during 1998, this model was finally banned in April, 1998.

SR-9TC - .308 Win. cal., similar to SR-9T except has PSG-1 adj. buttstock. Mfg. 1993 only.

	$3,150	$2,725	$2,400	$2,075	$1,725	$1,275	$1,050

Last MSR was $1,995.

   While advertised again during 1998, this model was finally banned in April, 1998.

PSG-1 - .308 Win. cal. only, high precision marksman's rifle, 5 shot mag., adj. buttstock, includes accessories and case (Hensholdt illuminated 6x42mm scope), 17.8 lbs. Importation disc. 1998.

	$10,500	$9,500	$8,500	$7,500	$6,500	$5,500	$4,500

Last MSR was $10,811.

MODEL 41 A-2 - .308 Win. cal., predecessor to the Model 91 A-2, originally imported by Golden State Arms.

	$3,000	$2,750	$2,500	$2,250	$1,850	$1,600	$1,350

MODEL 43 A-2 - predecesor to the Model 93 A-2. Disc.

	$3,000	$2,750	$2,500	$2,250	$1,850	$1,600	$1,350

GRADING - PPGS™	100%	98%	95%	90%	80%	70%	60%

MODEL 91 A-2 - .308 Win. cal., semi-auto paramilitary design rifle, delayed roller lock bolt system, antennuated recoil, black cycolac stock, 17.7 in. barrel, 20 shot mag., 9.7 lbs. Importation disc. 1989.

  * *Fixed stock model*

	$2,500	$2,350	$2,100	$1,950	$1,825	$1,700	$1,525

Last MSR was $999.

> **Add $200 for desert camo finish.**
> **Add $275 for NATO black finish.**

  * *Model 91 SBF (Semi-Beltfed)* - supplied with bipod and M60 link (200 shot with starter tab) and MG42 modified belt (49 shot with fixed starter tab), limited mfg. Disc.

	$8,950	$7,750	$6,500

  * *Model 91 A-3* - with retractable metal stock.

	$2,650	$2,500	$2,375	$2,150	$2,000	$1,875	$1,750

Last MSR was $1,114.

> Add $775 for .22 LR conversion kit.

  * *Model 91 A-2 Package* - includes A.R.M.S. mount, B-Square rings, Leupold 3x9 compact scope with matte finish. Importation disc. 1988.

	$3,000	$2,600	$2,250	$2,000	$1,750	$1,550	$1,325

Last MSR was $1,285.

> **Add 30% for retractable stock.**

MODEL 93 A-2 - .223 Rem. cal., smaller version of the H & K 91, 25 shot mag., 16.14 in. barrel, 8 lbs.

  * *Fixed stock model*

	$2,650	$2,500	$2,375	$2,150	$2,000	$1,875	$1,750

Last MSR was $946.

> **Add 10% for desert camo finish.**
> **Add 15% for NATO black finish.**

  * *Model 93 A-3* - with retractable metal stock.

	$2,950	$2,725	$2,575	$2,375	$2,100	$1,950	$1,825

Last MSR was $1,114.

  * *Model 93 A-2 Package* - includes A.R.M.S. mount, B-Square rings, Leupold 3x9 compact scope with matte finish. Importation disc. 1988.

	$3,150	$2,750	$2,500	$2,200	$2,050	$1,900	$1,800

Last MSR was $1,285.

> **Add 10% for retractable stock.**

MODEL 94 CARBINE A-2 - 9mm Para. cal., semi-auto carbine, 16.54 in. barrel, aperture rear sight, 15 shot mag. New 1983.

  * *Fixed stock model*

	$3,650	$3,400	$3,150	$3,000	$2,750	$2,450	$2,100

Last MSR was $946.

  * *Model 94 Carbine A-3* - retractable metal stock.

	$3,850	$3,600	$3,350	$3,150	$2,875	$2,575	$2,350

Last MSR was $1,114.

  * *Model 94 A-2 Package* - includes A.R.M.S. mount, B-Square rings, Leupold 3x9 compact scope with matte finish. Importation disc. 1988.

	$4,150	$3,775	$3,500	$3,250	$2,950	$2,575	$2,200

Last MSR was $1,285.

> **Add 10% for retractable stock.**

GRADING - PPGS™	100%	98%	95%	90%	80%	70%	60%

* ***Model 94 SGI*** - 9mm Para. cal., target rifle, aluminum alloy bi-pod, Leupold 6X scope, 15 or 30 shot mag. Imported 1986 only.

	$3,250	**$2,900**	**$2,600**	**$2,300**	**$2,075**	**$1,875**	**$1,700**

Last MSR was $1,340.

MODEL 270 - .22 LR cal., sporting rifle, 19.7 in. barrel with standard or polygonal rifling, 5 or 20 shot mag., high luster blue, plain walnut stock, approx. 5.7 lbs. Disc. 1985.

	$625	**$550**	**$475**	**$400**	**$350**	**$300**	**$275**

Last MSR was $200.

MODEL 300 - .22 Mag. cal., 5 or 15 shot, polygonal rifling standard, otherwise similar to H & K 270 with checkered walnut stock. Importation disc. 1989.

	$1,200	**$900**	**$775**	**$625**	**$550**	**$450**	**$400**

Last MSR was $608.

Add $350-$400 for factory H & K scope mount system.

* ***Model 300 Package*** - includes A.R.M.S. mount, B-Square rings, Leupold 3x9 compact scope with matte finish. Importation disc. 1988.

	$1,475	**$1,125**	**$925**	**$725**	**$650**	**$550**	**$450**

Last MSR was $689.

MODEL 630 - .223 Rem. cal., delayed roller lock bolt system, 17.7 in. barrel with or w/o muzzle brake (early mfg.), reduced recoil, checkered walnut, 4 or 10 shot mag., 7.04 lbs. Importation disc. 1986.

	$1,450	**$1,150**	**$975**	**$850**	**$750**	**$650**	**$575**

Last MSR was $784.

Add $350-$400 for factory H & K scope mount system.

The .222 Rem. cal. was also available in this model. Most were French contracts.

MODEL 770 - .308 Win. cal., 3 or 10 shot mag., 19.7 in. barrel with or w/o muzzle brake (early mfg.), otherwise similar to Model 630, 7.92 lbs. Importation disc. 1986.

	$2,000	**$1,750**	**$1,500**	**$1,275**	**$1,050**	**$950**	**$850**

Last MSR was $797.

Add $350-$400 for factory H & K scope mount system.

Significant price increases stopped the importation of this model.

Approx. 6 Model 770s were imported in .243 Win. cal. during 1984. Values for the .243 Win. cal. will be considerably higher than listed for the .308 Win. cal.

MODEL 911 - .308 Win. cal., earlier importation. Disc.

	$1,750	**$1,550**	**$1,350**	**$1,175**	**$950**	**$850**	**$725**

MODEL 940 - .30-06 cal., 21.6 in. barrel with or w/o muzzle brake (early mfg.), otherwise same as Model 770, 8.62 lbs. Importation disc. 1986.

	$1,950	**$1,750**	**$1,500**	**$1,250**	**$995**	**$875**	**$750**

Last MSR was $917.

Add $350-$400 for factory H & K scope mount system.

Cals. 7x64mm and 9.3x62mm were also available in this model.

Significant price increases stopped the importation of this model.

* ***Model 940K*** - similar to Model 940, except has 16 in. barrel and higher cheekpiece. Two imported 1984 only.

Rarity precludes accurate price evaluation.

SLB 2000 - .30-06 or .308 Win. (new 2003) cal. (same bolt system allows cartridge changeability), short stroke piston actuated gas operating system, alloy receiver with black weather resistant coating, gold accents on receiver, 19.69 in. barrel (interchangeable), checkered walnut stock and specially angled pistol grip, tang mounted safety blocks hammer and trigger, 2, 5, or 10 shot mag., iron sights, 7.28 lbs. Imported 2001-2003.

	$1,150	**$995**	**$895**	**$825**	**$775**	**$700**	**$650**

Last MSR was $1,299.

GRADING - PPGS™	100%	98%	95%	90%	80%	70%	60%

MODELS SL6 & SL7 CARBINE - .223 Rem. or .308 Win. cal., 17.71 in. barrel, delayed roller lock bolt system, reduced recoil, vent. wood hand guard, 3 or 4 shot mag., 8.36 lbs., matte black metal finish, HK-SL6 is .223 Rem. cal., HK-SL7 is .308 Win. cal. Importation disc. in 1986.

	$1,150	$950	$800	$675	$575	$500	$425

Add $250-$300 for factory H & K scope mount system.

These models were the last sporter variations H & K imported into the U.S. - no U.S. importation since 1986.

MODEL SL8-1 - .223 Rem. cal., short stroke piston actuated gas operating system, advanced grey carbon fiber polymer construction based on the German Army G36 rifle, thumbhole stock with adj. cheekpiece and buttstock, 10 shot mag., modular and removable Picatinny rail sight, removable sights from rail, 20.8 cold hammer forged heavy barrel, adj. sights, 8.6 lbs. Imported 2000-2003.

	$1,195	$975	$875	$800	$750	$700	$650

Last MSR was $1,249.

Add $338 for carrying handle with 1.5X-3X optical sights.

Add $624 for carrying handle with 1.5X-3X optical sights and red dot reflex sight.

MODEL USC .45 ACP CARBINE - .45 ACP cal., similar design/construction as the Model SL8-1, except is blowback action, and has 16 in. barrel and grey skeletonized buttstock, 10 shot mag., 6 lbs. Imported 2000-2003.

	$1,085	$950	$875	$800	$750	$700	$650

Last MSR was $1,249.

SHOTGUNS: SEMI-AUTO

Previously imported H & K Benelli shotguns can be found under their own heading.

MODEL 512 - 12 ga. only, mfg. by Franchi for German military contract, rifle sights, matte finished metal, walnut stock, fixed choke pattern diverter giving rectangular shot pattern. Importation disc. 1991.

	$1,500	$1,300	$1,100	$925	$800	$700	$600

Last Mfg.'s Wholesale was $1,895.

SLS 2002 - 12 ga. only, 3 in. chamber, IQ-port gas operation (excess gas is vented forward through forearm cap), various barrel lengths, including slug barrel, double slide rails, deluxe checkered walnut stock and forearm, phosphate black finish, approx. 6 3/4 lbs. European introduction 2002.

While advertised during 2002, this gun has not been imported into the U.S.

HEINIE SPECIALTY PRODUCTS

Current pistol and related components manufacturer established in 1973, and located in Quincy, IL.

Heinie manufactures both scratch built personal defense and tactical/carry 1911 packages in a wide variety of chamberings. Almost any combination of special orders and features are available. Please contact the factory directly for information regarding current pricing and availability (see Trademark Index).

HELWAN

Previous trademark imported by Navy Arms Co. and Interarms until 1995.

PISTOLS: SEMI-AUTO

BRIGADIER - 9mm Para. cal., single action, 4.5 in. barrel, all steel construction, 8 shot mag. with finger extension, black plastic grips, 32.6 oz. Imported 1988-94.

	$195	$150	$125	$115	$105	$95	$85

Last MSR was $260.

This model is patterned after the Beretta Model 951 Brigadier. They were manufactured at the Helwan arsenal in Egypt.

GRADING - PPGS™	100%	98%	95%	90%	80%	70%	60%

HENDRY, RAMSAY & WILCOX

Current manufacturer located in Perth, Scotland.

Hendry, Ramsay & Wilcox manufactures top quality shotguns and rifles which are priced per individual quotation. Please contact the factory directly (see Trademark Index) for more information on this trademark.

HENRY, ALEX

Current trademark owned and manufactured by Dickson & MacNaughton, located in Edinburgh, Scotland.

Please contact Dickson & MacNaughton directly for more information regarding this trademark, including current availability and pricing (see Trademark Index).

HENRY REPEATING ARMS COMPANY

Current rifle manufacturer established during 1997, and located in Brooklyn, NY. Distributor and dealer sales.

RIFLES

HENRY MINI-BOLT - .22 LR cal., single shot, stainless steel receiver and barrel, Williams fire sights, manual safety, 11 1/2 in. LOP, black synthetic stock, 3 1/4 lbs. New 2002.

MSR $205	$175	$145	$125	$110	$95	$90	$85

HENRY ACU-BOLT - .17 HMR, .22 LR or .22 Mag. cal., scaled down action, includes scope. New 2004.

MSR $335	$270	$240	$200	$180	$160	$140	$120

HENRY LEVER ACTION - .22 LR or .22 Mag. (new 2000) cal., side ejection, blue steel receiver, 18 1/4 (.22 LR only) or 19 1/4 (.22 Mag. only) in. barrel, 11 (.22 Mag.) or 15 (.22 LR) shot mag., deluxe American walnut stock and forearm, adj. rear sight and hooded front, 5.5 lbs. New 1997.

MSR $280	$225	$195	$175	$150	$140	$130	$120

Add $120 for .22 Mag. cal.

This model is also available as a Youth Model, with 13 in. LOP and shorter barrel.

✳ *Henry Carbine* - similar to Henry Lever Action, except has shorter barrel and large loop lever. New 1998.

MSR $290	$230	$200	$175	$150	$140	$130	$120

✳ *Henry Varmint Express* - .17 HMR cal., similar to Henry Lever Action, except has 20 in. barrel, includes scope mount, 11 shot tube mag., Monte Carlo stock, 5.75 lbs. New 2003.

MSR $475	$395	$335	$275	$230	$195	$175	$150

✳ *Henry Golden Boy Lever Action* - .17 HMR, .22 LR, or .22 Mag. cal., features brasslite receiver, buttplate, and rear sight, 20 in. octagon barrel, 16 shot mag. New mid-1999.

MSR $410	$355	$290	$230	$195	$175	$160	$140

Add $75 for .22 Mag. cal. (new 2002).
Add $80 for .17 HMR cal. (new 2005).
Add $20 for large loop lever (new 2004).

✳ *Henry Golden Boy Deluxe* - .22 LR cal., features hand engraved gold and silver brasslite receiver, deluxe uncheckered walnut stock and forearm. New 2004.

MSR $1,200	$1,075	$975	$850	$725	$600	$525	$450

HENRY "BIG BOY" - .44 Mag./.44 Spl. or .45 LC (new 2004) cal., brass receiver, buttplate, and barrel band, 20 in. octagon barrel with 10 shot tube mag., buckhorn rear sight, straight grip walnut stock and forearm, 8.68 lbs. New 2003.

MSR $775	$690	$615	$530	$450	$400	$350	$300

GRADING - PPGS™	100%	98%	95%	90%	80%	70%	60%

HENRY PUMP ACTION - .22 LR cal., blue grooved receiver, 18.25 in. barrel, walnut straight grip stock and forearm, 15 shot mag., adj. rear sight, approx. 5 1/2 lbs. New 1999.

	MSR $310		$250	$210	$175	$160	$140	$130	$120

HENRY U.S. SURVIVAL .22 SEMI-AUTO - .22 LR cal., patterned after the Armalite AR-7 with improvements, takedown design enables receiver, 2 mags., and barrel to stow in ABS plastic stock, 100% Mossy Oak Break-Up camo (new 2000) or weather resistant silver or black (new 1999) stock/metal finish, two 8 shot mags., adj. sights, 16.5 in. long when disassembled and stowed in stock, approx. 2.5 lbs. New 1997.

	MSR $205		$175	$150	$130	$120	$105	$95	$90

Add $55 for 100% camo finish (new 2000).

HENRY RIFLE

Please refer to the Winchester section in this text for this model.

HERITAGE MANUFACTURING, INC.

Current manufacturer located in Opa Locka, FL since 1992. Dealer and distributor sales.

Heritage Manufacturing, Inc.

PISTOLS: SEMI-AUTO

H-25/25S - .25 ACP cal., 6 shot mag. with finger extension, single action, exposed hammer, choice of blue or blue/gold finish, 13 1/2 oz. Mfg. 1995-99.

	$125	$95	$80	$65	$55	$50	$45

Last MSR was $150.

Add $10 for nickel steel.

Add $10 for Model H-25G (blue/gold finish with checkered grips).

STEALTH SHADOW COMPACT - 9mm Para. or .40 S&W cal., striker firing mechanism, stainless steel slide and 3.9 in. barrel, black all polymer frame, manual safety, 10 shot mag. with finger extension, fixed sights, choice of stainless slide, two-tone stainless slide, or all black (Shadow) finish, 20.5 oz. Mfg. 1996-2000.

	$255	$220	$190	$165	$150	$135	$110

Last MSR was $300.

Add $30 for .40 S&W cal.

REVOLVERS

Rough Rider SAA models are made in the U.S.A.

ROUGH RIDER SAA SERIES - .17 HMR (new 2003), .22 LR or .22 LR/.22 Mag. cal. combo, SAA design with choice of alloy (33.4 oz.) or steel (35 oz., new 2000) frame, hammer block safety, blue, nickel (disc. 2001), black satin (new 2002), satin (new 2001), or silver satin (new 2005) finish, 4 3/4, 6 1/2, or 9 (combo only) in. barrel, fixed or adj. (new 2001) rear sight, smooth or camo (new 2003) wood grips, approx. 33 1/2 oz. New 1993.

✷ *Rough Rider SAA Steel Frame Series* - available in blue, black satin (mfg. 2003), or case hardened (mfg. 2003) finish, includes extra .22 Mag. cylinder.

	MSR $190		$160	$125	$95	$80	$70	$60	$50

Add $51 for nickel finish (combo package only, disc. 2001).

Add $50 for .17 HMR cal. with adj. sights (new 2003, not available in 4 3/4 in. barrel).

Add $20 for 9 in. barrel (available with combo package only).

Subtract $50 for alloy frame with combo package (disc. 2002).

GRADING - PPGS™	100%	98%	95%	90%	80%	70%	60%

✳ *Rough Rider SAA Fixed Sight Series* - .22 LR/.22 Mag. cal. combo only, 4 3/4, 6 1/2, or 9 in. barrel.

MSR $160	$130	$110	$95	$80	$70	$60	$50

Add $40 for satin or black satin finish.
Add $25 for faux mother-of-pearl grips.
Add $5 for 9 in. barrel.

✳ *Rough Rider SAA Adjustable Sight Series* - .22 LR/.22 Mag. cal. combo only, 4 3/4, 6 1/2, or 9 in. barrel.

MSR $190	$155	$135	$110	$95	$80	$70	$60

Add $30 for satin or black satin finish.
Add $30 for steel frame (disc. 2002).
During 2004, a Williams red ramp front sight and Millett adj. microclick rear sight became available on the 6 1/2 in. barrel.

✳ *Rough Rider SAA Illuminator Series* - .22 LR/.22 Mag. cal. combo only, features Adco-Hot Shot Red Dot frame mounted sight, 6 1/2 in. barrel only.

MSR $190	$155	$135	$110	$95	$80	$70	$60

✳ *Rough Rider SAA with Birds Head Grip* - .22 LR/.22 Mag. cal. combo only, choice of 2 3/4 (disc. 1997), 3 (disc. 1994), 3 1/2, or 4 3/4 in. barrel. New 1993.

MSR $160	$135	$110	$95	$85	$75	$65	$60

Add $40 for satin finish or $25 for faux mother-of-pearl grips.
Add $30 for nickel finish (disc. 2001).

SENTRY DA SERIES - .22 Mag. (disc. 1996), .32 Mag. (disc. 1996), .38 Spl., or 9mm Para. (disc. 1996) cal., snubnose design, with 2 or 4 (.22 LR or .38 Spl.) in. barrel, 6 (centerfire) or 8 (rimfire) shot, transfer bar safety, blue or nickel finish, black polymer grips, ramp front sight. Mfg. 1993-97.

	$110	$85	$70	$55	$50	$45	$40

Last MSR was $130.

Add $10 for nickel finish.

HEROLD RIFLE

Previously manufactured by Franz Jaeger, located in Suhl, Germany.

RIFLES: BOLT ACTION

SPORTING RIFLE - .22 Hornet cal., miniature Mauser action, 24 in. barrel, leaf sight, double set trigger, select checkered stock, imported by Daly & Stoeger, pre-WWII.

	$990	$880	$825	$770	$660	$550	$495

HERTERS

Previous importer, distributor, and retailer headquartered in Waseca, MN from early 1960s - 1979. Herters also had additional retail stores scattered throughout the upper Midwest.

Herters subcontracted various manufacturers (mostly European) to fabricate Powermag revolvers, U-9/J-9 rifles, and shotguns which were mostly patterned after more famous original models. Most of these copies were designed to undersell the competition at the time and while quality in most cases was quite good, consumer sales were not strong enough to continue production. While many Herters models are relatively rare, collectibility to date has been minimal. Herters model values are usually under the original trademarks from which they were derived and to date have been based more on the shooting utility than the collector potential.

HESSE ARMS

Previous manufacturer located in Inver Grove Heights, MN.

Hesse Arms manufactured very limited quantities of semi-auto pistols, bolt action and semi-auto rifles. Because of this and due to space considerations, individual models have not been individually listed and priced as in previous editions.

GRADING - PPGS™	100%	98%	95%	90%	80%	70%	60%

HEYM WAFFENFABRIK GmbH

Current manufacturer established in 1865 and located in Gleichamberg, Germany since 1995. Limited importation beginning 1999 by New England Custom Gun Service, Ltd., located in Plainfield, NH. The Ivory Hunter SxS double rifle is imported exclusively by PSI, located in Fayetteville, WV. During 1998, Heym underwent a management change. Previously manufactured in Muennerstadt, Germany circa 1952-1995 and Suhl, Germany between 1865-1945. Originally founded in 1865 by F.W. Heym. Previously imported by JagerSport, Ltd. located in Cranston, RI 1993-94 only, Heckler & Koch, Inc. (until 1993) located in Sterling, VA, Heym America, Inc. (subsidiary of F.W. Heym of W. Germany) located in Fort Wayne, IN, and originally by Paul Jaeger, Inc. 1970-1986.

Please contact the importers for more information, current pricing and domestic model availability (see Trademark Index).

Pre-war guns in 95%+ original condition will bring a premium over values listed.

COMBINATION GUNS

MODEL 22 S2 O/U - rifle/shotgun combination, 12, 16, or 20 ga. (3 in.), under rifle (17 cals. available), single set trigger, takedown feature (standard 1990), coin finish with engraving, 5 1/2 lbs.

$3,675	$3,000	$2,450	$1,875	$1,575	$1,325	$1,100

Last MSR was $4,125.

Subtract $380 without engraving.

This model featured a dampened rifle barrel which prevents the "climbing" of groups, thereby enhancing accuracy.

MODEL 25 O/U - rifle/shotgun combination, 12, 16, or 20 ga. over various rifle cals., 23 3/4 in. barrels with iron sights, checkered walnut stock and forearm, 5.9 lbs.

MSR N/A	$2,425	$1,725	$1,350	$1,125	$950	$800	$700

Add $800 for deluxe game scene engraving.

MODEL 55 BF O/U - rifle/shotgun combination, popular U.S. and European cals., shotgun barrels interchangeable in 12 (disc.), 16, or 20 ga., 25 or 28 in. barrels, boxlock, auto ejectors, silver finish, fine German engraving, folding leaf sight, checkered pistol grip stock.

$6,500	$5,400	$4,950	$4,525	$3,950	$3,615	$3,210

Last MSR was $7,485.

Add $3,250 for O/U rifle and $2,250 for O/U shotgun or shotgun/rifle combination extra barrels.

MODEL 88 BF SxS - 2 barrel set with 20 ga. barrels and an extra set of rifle barrels available in cals. .375 H&H Mag., .458 Win. Mag., .470 N.E., or .500 N.E.

$13,100	$10,750	$9,600	$8,150	$6,900	$5,850	$4,850

Last MSR was $15,060.

This model is a larger frame variation of the Model 88 B.

* *Model 88B/F Safari* - includes set of rifle and shotgun barrels, choice of .375 H&H, .458 Win. Mag., .470 NE, or .500 NE cal. and extra set of 20 ga. 3 in. chamber barrels.

$16,150	$14,100	$11,950	$10,250	$8,950	$6,750	$5,250

Last MSR was $18,530.

MODEL 88 F SxS - available in various cals. and 20 ga. with 2 3/4 or 3 in. chambers.

$13,300	$11,250	$10,100	$9,400	$8,000	$6,950	$5,800

Last MSR was $14,650.

DRILLINGS

MODEL 33 BOXLOCK STANDARD - 16 or 20 ga., boxlock, Arabesque engraving, shotgun barrels over popular European cals., and .222 Rem., .243 Win., .270 Win., .308 Win., and .30-06 cal. rifle barrel, 25 in. full and mod. barrels, set trigger on rifle, checkered pistol grip stock.

	100%	98%	95%	90%	80%	70%	60%
MSR N/A	$6,075	$5,300	$4,525	$3,950	$3,350	$2,750	$2,150

✳ *Model 33 Deluxe* - similiar specifications as Standard Model, only hunting scene engraved.

	100%	98%	95%	90%	80%	70%	60%
MSR N/A	$6,450	$5,425	$4,650	$4,025	$3,400	$2,750	$2,150

MODEL 35 STANDARD - 3 barrels, (two rifle and one shotgun), choice of cals. with top barrel either 16 or 20 ga., light border engraving, 8 1/4 lbs.

	100%	98%	95%	90%	80%	70%	60%
	$13,650	$11,000	$9,250	$8,000	$6,850	$5,700	$4,600

Last MSR was $15,100.

Add $2,430 for hunting scene engraving.

MODEL 37 SIDELOCK STANDARD - shotgun barrels (12, 16, or 20 ga.) over rifle, detachable sidelocks, select French walnut, border engraving, 8 lbs.

	100%	98%	95%	90%	80%	70%	60%
MSR N/A	$8,650	$7,850	$6,950	$6,000	$5,000	$4,000	$2,950

✳ *Model 37 Deluxe* - similar to Model 37 Standard, except has large engraved hunting scenes.

	100%	98%	95%	90%	80%	70%	60%
MSR N/A	$9,650	$8,700	$7,600	$6,500	$5,400	$4,300	$3,200

MODEL 37 B STANDARD - rifle barrels over shotgun (20 ga.), sidelock, border engraved, about 8.6 lbs.

	100%	98%	95%	90%	80%	70%	60%
	$13,250	$10,875	$9,500	$8,400	$7,550	$6,500	$5,650

Last MSR was $15,065.

✳ *Model 37 B Deluxe* - similar to Model 37 B Standard, except has large hunting scene engraving.

	100%	98%	95%	90%	80%	70%	60%
	$15,600	$12,750	$10,700	$9,450	$8,200	$7,050	$5,750

Last MSR was $17,620.

RIFLES: BOLT ACTION

On most of the models listed, the "N" suffix in the model denotes standard calibers, whereas "G" refers to Mag. cals. Heym currently manufactures approx. 100 bolt actions per month, with 54 company personnel.

MODEL SR 10 SPORTER - various cals., originally mfg. by H & K. Limited mfg.

	100%	98%	95%	90%	80%	70%	60%
	$1,325	$1,100	$950	$850	$750	$650	$550

MODEL SR 20N & CLASSIC - available in 18 cals., Mauser type bolt action, single trigger, French walnut, 24 in. Krupp steel barrel except Mag. (25 in.). Importation disc. 2001.

	100%	98%	95%	90%	80%	70%	60%
	$1,825	$1,425	$1,100	$900	$800	$700	$600

Last MSR was $2,100.

Subtract $70 without iron sights.
Add $430 for left-hand variation.
Add $300 for Mag. cals. (G suffix).
Add $1,140 for .375 H&H cal. (Model SR20 G Etoscha).
Add $260 for Classic Model.
Add $300 for carbine Classic Model.

✳ *Model SR 20 Hunter* - similar to Model SR 20N, except has classic style fiberglass stock with either matte blue or parkerized metal finish. Imported 1988-90.

	100%	98%	95%	90%	80%	70%	60%
	$1,500	$1,225	$1,050	$900	$800	$700	$600

Last MSR was $1,750.

GRADING - PPGS™	100%	98%	95%	90%	80%	70%	60%

✱ *Model SR 20L* - Mannlicher style stock, European configuration, 18 in. barrel, 7 lbs.

	$1,475	$1,225	$985	$895	$785	$720	$650

Last MSR was $1,700.

SR 20 TROPHY - available in all SR 20 cals., bolt action, 22 or 24 (Mag. cals. only) in. octagonal barrel, classic stock configuration with cheekpiece and recoil pad. Importation began 1989.

	$2,550	$2,100	$1,800	$1,500	$1,250	$985	$895

Last MSR was $2,815.

> Add $120 for Mag. cals.
> This model was also available in either right-hand or left-hand action.

SR 20G CLASSIC SPORTER - available in various cals., bolt action, 22 or 24 in. round barrel, steel grip cap. Importation began 1989.

	$1,875	$1,600	$1,300	$1,050	$900	$785	$720

Last MSR was $2,235.

> Subtract $70 without iron sights.
> This model was also available in either right-hand or left-hand action.

SR 20 ALPINE - available in standard cals. between .243 Win. and 9.3x62mm, mountain style rifle with Mannlicher forend and classic buttstock, supplied with mounted open sights. Importation began 1989.

	$1,900	$1,650	$1,325	$1,075	$925	$800	$750

Last MSR was $2,165.

This model was also available in either right-hand or left-hand action.

SR 20 MATCH - .308 Win. cal., 24 in. heavy barrel, target stock with accessory rail, large bolt handle, supplied without sights, 9 lbs. Imported 1991-94.

	$1,860	$1,600	$1,300	$1,050	$900	$785	$720

Last MSR was $2,200.

SR 20 CLASSIC SAFARI - .375 H&H, .404 Jeffery (disc.), .425 Express, or .458 Win. Mag. cal., 24 in. barrel only, express rear sight and large front post sights, tight grained walnut. Imported 1989-94.

	$2,150	$1,650	$1,250	$1,050	$875	$800	$700

Last MSR was $2,530.

This model was also available in either right-hand or left-hand action.

SR 21 N - 26 standard and metric cals., traditional bolt action that is bascially a Mauser M90 design with modern extractor recessed in the bolt face, single set trigger, unique interchangeable barrel/receiver, detachable mag., 3 position side safety, right- or left-hand action, iron sights, approx. 7 lbs. New 2001.

MSR N/A	$1,950	$1,500	$1,175	$950	$825	$725	$625

> Add $325 for carbine (Model SR 21 N Classic).
> Add $1,325 for Model SR 21 N Concorde.
> Add $110 for Model SR 21 N Keiler.

SR 30 N - various cals., straight pull bolt with lock in the receiver head, iron sights, deluxe checkered walnut stock with rosewood pistol grip cap and forend tip, sling swivels, available in various configurations, 7-7 1/2 lbs.

MSR $2,795	$2,350	$1,950	$1,500	$1,225	$950	$850	$750

> Add $264 for SR 30 N Classic Model (carbine).
> Add $1,505 for SR 30 N Concorde Model.
> Add $155 for SR 30 N Wild Boar Model.

GRADING - PPGS™	100%	98%	95%	90%	80%	70%	60%

EXPRESS SERIES RIFLE - .338 Lapua Mag., .375 H&H, .378 Wby. Mag., .404 rimless Jeffery (disc. 1992), .416 Rigby, .450 Ackley, .460 Wby. Mag., .500 NE (new 1994), .500 A-Square, or .505 Gibbs cal., express sights, Timney single trigger. New 1989.

MSR N/A	$5,500	$4,800	$4,050	$3,150	$2,500	$2,150	$1,875

Add $525 for .460 Wby. Mag. - .505 Gibbs cal.
Add $375 for muzzle brake (includes installation).
Add $555 for left-hand action (disc. 1992).

✷ **.577 NE & .600 NE Cals.** - .577 NE or .600 NE cal., 24 in. barrel, reinforced action, 2 shot mag. New 1991.

MSR N/A	$9,550	$8,350	$7,250	$6,100	$5,000	$3,750	$2,950

Add $1,125 for .600 NE cal.

RIFLES: O/U

MODEL 55 BOXLOCK - various cals., engraving similar to Model 55 BF.

MSR N/A	$6,350	$5,400	$4,500	$3,750	$3,250	$2,750	$2,450

Add $500 for deluxe game scene engraving.

MODEL 55 SIDELOCK - O/U rifle only with different caliber for each barrel, double set triggers, "Bergstutzen" design.

MSR N/A	$9,350	$8,000	$6,850	$5,950	$5,125	$4,500	$3,975

Add $1,000 for Deluxe Model.

RIFLES: SxS

MODEL 80 B - various cals., modified boxlock action with top sear bars, regular or manual cocking, 23 3/4 in. barrels with quarter rib and iron sights, DT or ST, deluxe checkered walnut stock and forearm, 6.6 lbs.

MSR N/A	$6,025	$5,300	$4,550	$3,950	$3,350	$2,750	$2,150

Add $600 for ST with hand cocking, $700 for DT with hand cocking.

MODEL 88 B SAFARI CLASSIC - available in most safari cals. between .300 Win. Mag. - .458 Win. Mag. boxlock action, Krupp steel barrels, double underlocking lugs with Greener crossbolt, ejectors, checkered circassian walnut, built to customer specifications, 7 1/2 lbs.

MSR N/A	$11,650	$9,750	$8,600	$7,100	$6,125	$5,420	$4,575

Add $550 for .416 Rigby - .500 NE cal.

✷ **Model 88 B Safari Classic Sidelock (BSS)** - sidelock model with interceptor sears.

MSR N/A	$15,500	$13,000	$10,250	$8,750	$7,425	$6,300	$5,175

This model is also available in both .577 NE and .600 NE cal. Prices start at $28,575 for the .577 NE, and $32,500 for .600 NE.

✷ **Model 88 B Safari Classic Boxlock** - available in various safari cals., double safety bar, 24 in. barrels, 9.9 lbs.

MSR N/A	$9,850	$8,600	$7,400	$6,300	$5,175	$4,500	$3,750

Add $1,150 for .300 Win. Mag. - .500 NE cal.

✷ **Model 88 B Safari Sidelock** - sidelock model with interceptor sears.

MSR N/A	$12,250	$10,250	$8,850	$7,500	$6,300	$5,175	$4,250

IVORY HUNTER - large dangerous game cals. only, sidelock model, custom order only.
Please contact PSI, the exclusive importer, for more information on this model (see Trademark Index).

GRADING - PPGS™	100%	98%	95%	90%	80%	70%	60%

RIFLES: SINGLE SHOT

MODEL HR 30N - available in many cals., Ruger No. 1 falling block action, 24 in. barrel, French walnut with Bavarian cheekpiece, round barrel, Sporter or full length carbine style French walnut stock, engraved coin finished receiver, 6.6 lbs.

	$3,500	$2,975	$2,350	$1,950	$1,675	$1,350	$1,175

Last MSR was $4,040.

Add $440 for Mag. cals.

Add $1,710 for Mannlicher stocked Carbine Model.

Add $850 for hunting scene engraving (minimum extra charge).

MODEL HR 38 N - available in many cals., Ruger No. 1 falling block action 24 in. barrel, octagon barrel, French walnut with Bavarian cheekpiece, Sporter or full length carbine style French walnut stock, engraved coin finished receiver, 6.6 lbs.

	$4,150	$3,450	$2,875	$2,300	$1,950	$1,675	$1,350

Last MSR was $4,835.

Add $235 for Mag. cals.

Add $2,400 for sideplates with engraved large game hunting scenes.

MODEL 44 B - various standard and metric cals., single lock action with thumbpiece and sideplates, open sights with barrel quarter rib, deluxe checkered stock and forearm, 6.6 lbs.

MSR N/A	$4,900	$4,350	$3,550	$3,025	$2,350	$2,000	$1,750

Add $1,100 for Deluxe Model.

SHOTGUNS: O/U

MODEL 55 F - 16 or 20 ga., ejectors, engraved, 6.6 lbs. Importation disc. 1992.

	$5,100	$4,525	$3,950	$3,615	$3,200	$2,775	$2,300

Last MSR was $5,500.

MODEL 55 SS - sidelock version of Model 55 F, large engraved hunting scenes.

	$4,500	$3,825	$3,300	$2,850	$2,400	$2,000	$1,700

Last MSR was $4,890.

MODEL 200 - 20 ga., 3 in. chambers, boxlock action, DTs, 28 in. VR barrels, light engraving, previous importation.

	$895	$795	$700	$650	$600	$550	$500

VIERLINGS

MODEL 37 V - 4 barrel configuration, various cals. and gauges, special order only. Limited mfg.

MSR N/A	$14,500	$11,000	$9,000	$7,750	$6,500	$5,500	$4,500

Add $1,700 for Deluxe Model.

HI-POINT FIREARMS

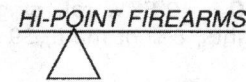

HI-POINT FIREARMS

Current trademark marketed by MKS Supply, Inc. located in Dayton, Ohio. Hi-Point firearms have been manufactured since 1988. Dealer and distributor sales.

Prior to 1993, trademarks sold by MKS Supply, Inc. (including Beemiller, Haskell Manufacturing, Inc., Iberia Firearms, Inc., and Stallard Arms, Inc.) had their own separate manufacturers' markings. Beginning in 1993, Hi-Point Firearms eliminated these individualized markings and chose instead to have currently manufactured guns labeled "Hi-Point Firearms".

GRADING - PPGS™	100%	98%	95%	90%	80%	70%	60%

CARBINES

MODEL 995/4095 - 9mm Para. or .40 S&W (Model 4095, new late 2003) cal., 16.5 or 17.5 (.40 S&W cal. only) in. barrel, one-piece camo or black polymer stock features pistol grip, 10 shot mag., aperture rear sight, parkerized or chrome finish. New 1996.

	MSR $199	$170	$135	$115	$95	$85	$75	$70

Add $21 for .40 S&W cal.
Add $10 for chrome finish.
Add $11 for camo stock (new 2002).
Add $81 for detachable compensator, laser, and mount (new 1999).
This model is manufactured by Beemiller, located in Mansfield, OH.

PISTOLS: SEMI-AUTO

Beginning 2000, all compact models feature magazine disconnect safety and last shot hold open, and all pistols are shipped with a rear adj. aperture sight (which can replace the standard rear adj. sight).

MODEL CF-380 POLYMER - .380 ACP cal., single action, 3.5 or 4 (new 2002) in. barrel, polymer frame, 3-dot adj. sights, 8 shot mag. with thumb activated release, chrome slide (disc.) or two-tone black satin finish, 29 oz. New 1995.

	MSR $120	$100	$85	$75	$65	$55	$50	$45

Add $15 for 4 in. barrel with compensator and two mags. (Model 380 Comp).
This model is manufactured by Beemiller, located in Mansfield, OH.

JS-9 - 9mm Para. cal., single action, 4.5 in. barrel, thumb safety, fixed (disc. 1999) or adj. (new 2000) sights, 8 shot mag., non-glare military blue finish (early mfg.) or black satin finish (new 1991), copolymer synthetic grips, 39 oz. Mfg. 1990-2000.

	$140	$110	$95	$80	$70	$65	$60

Last MSR was $159.

Add 10% for nickel finish (disc.).
This model was manufactured by Beemiller, Inc. located in Mansfield, OH.

✳ **JS-9 Compact (Model C-9)** - compact variation of the Model JS-9 with 3.5 in. barrel and 8 shot mag., choice of alloy or polymer (new 1994, various slide/frame finishes) frame, 3-dot adj. sights became standard in 2000, 32 (polymer) or 29 oz. New 1993.

	MSR $140	$110	$90	$80	$70	$65	$60	$55

This model is manufactured by Beemiller, Inc. located in Mansfield, OH.

✳ **JS-9 Comp** - features 4 in. barrel with compensator, with (new 1999) or w/o laser sight package, adj. sights, 10 shot mag. New 1998.

	MSR $169	$140	$115	$100	$90	$80	$75	$70

Add $75 for laser sights and mount.

JS-40 - .40 S&W cal., single action, steel frame, black finish, 4.5 in. barrel, 3-dot adj. sights, 8 shot mag., 39 oz. Mfg. 1992-2002.

	$135	$110	$100	$90	$80	$75	$70

Last MSR was $159.

This model was manufactured by Iberia Firearms, Inc. located in Iberia, OH.
Add $7 for nickel finish (disc. 1994).

JC-40 - .40 S&W cal., single action, polymer frame, black finish, 4.5 in. barrel, 3-dot adj. sights, accessory rail (new 2004), 10 shot mag., 32 oz. New 2002.

	MSR $179	$145	$120	$100	$90	$80	$75	$70

This model is manufactured by Iberia Firearms, Inc. located in Iberia, OH.

GRADING - PPGS™	100%	98%	95%	90%	80%	70%	60%

JS-45 - .45 ACP cal., single action, steel frame, similar to JS-9, except has 7 shot mag. and 4 1/2 in. barrel, adj. sights, 39 oz. Mfg. 1991-2002.

	$135	$110	$100	$90	$80	$75	$70

Last MSR was $159.

Add $10 for nickel finish (disc. 1994).

This model was manufactured by Haskell Mfg., Inc. located in Lima, OH.

JH-45 - .45 ACP cal., single action, polymer frame, similar to JS-9, except has 9 shot mag. and 4.5 in. barrel, accessory rail (new 2004), adj. sights, 32 oz. New 2003.

MSR $179		$145	$120	$100	$90	$80	$75	$70

This model is manufactured by Haskell Mfg., Inc. located in Lima, OH.

HIGGINS, J.C.

Previous trademark used on Sears & Roebuck rifles and shotguns manufactured between 1946-1962.

The J.C. Higgins trademark has appeared literally on hundreds of various models (shotguns and rifles) sold through the Sears & Roebuck retail network. Most of these models were manufactured through subcontracts with both domestic and international firearms manufacturers. Typically, they were "spec." guns made to sell at a specific price to undersell the competition. Most of these models were derivatives of existing factory models (i.e., Browning, High Standard, Marlin, Mossberg, Savage, Stevens, Winchester, etc.) with less expensive wood and perhaps missing the features found on those models from which they were derived.

To date, there has been minimal interest in collecting J.C. Higgins guns, regardless of rarity. Rather than list J.C. Higgins models, a general guideline is that values generally are under the models of their "1st generation relatives" (listed above). The Ranger trademark was also used by Sears & Roebuck - it is not any more desirable than those guns marked "J.C. Higgins". As a result, prices are ascertained by the shooting value of the gun, rather than its collector value.

For converting J.C. Higgins models to the subcontracted manufacturers, please refer to the Store Brand Crossover List before the Serialization section.

HIGH STANDARD

Previous manufacturer located in New Haven, Hamden, and East Hartford, CT. High Standard Mfg. Co. was founded in 1926. They entered the firearms business when they purchased Hartford Arms and Equipment Co. in 1932. The original plant was located in New Haven, CT. During WWII High Standard operated plants in New Haven and Hamden. After the war, the operations were consolidated in Hamden. In 1968, the company was sold to the Leisure Group, Inc. A final move was made to East Hartford, CT in 1977 where they remained until the doors were closed in late 1984. In early 1978, the Leisure Group sold the company to the management and the company became High Standard, Inc.

Many collectors have realized the rarity and quality factors this trademark has earned. 13 different variations (Models C, A, D, E, H-D, H-E, H-A, H-B First Model, G-380, GB, GD, GE, and Olympic, commonly called the GO) had a total production of less than 43,000 pistols. For these reasons, top condition High Standard pistols are getting more difficult to find each year.

As a final note on High Standard pistols, the following High Standard semi-auto pistols have been reformatted into the following new category names: Letter Series, Letter Series w/ Hammer, Lever Letter Series, Lever Name Series, 100 Series, 101 Series, 102 Series, 103 Series, 104 Series, 105 Series, 106 Series - Military Models, 107 Series, Conversion Kits, and SH Series.

Note: catalog numbers were not always consistent with design series, and in 1966-1967 changed with accessories offered, but not design series.

GRADING - PPGS™	100%	98%	95%	90%	80%	70%	60%

The approx. ser. number cut-off for New Haven, CT marked guns is 442,XXX.

The approx. ser. number range for Hamden, CT marked guns is 431,XXX-2,500,811, G 1,001-G 13,757 (Shipped) or G15,650 (Packed) or ML 1,001-ML 23,065. One exception is a 9211 Victor serial number 3,000,000 shipped 1 March, 1974.

The first gun shipped 16 June, 1977 from E. Hartford was a Victor 9217 serial number EH0001.

The approx. ser. number ranges for E. Hartford, CT manufacture is ML 25,000 and ML 86,641 and SH 10,001 and SH 34,034. One exception is a single gun numbered ML90,000.

Original factory boxes have become very desirable. Prices can range from $50-$100 for a good condition Model 106 or 107 factory box to over $150 for an older box of a desirable model.

DERRINGERS

DERRINGER MODELS - .22 or .22 Mag. cal., double action only O/U, 2 shot, 3 1/2 in. barrels.

The first derringer was mfg. about 1962, at the approximate serial number 1,261,903 in Hamden, CT. The serial numbers continued in the handgun serial number series until serial number 2,500,464 in 1975, when the derringers were put into a separate serial number group with a D prefix, D 1,001 through D 96,098 V. Serial number D 12,047 was the last Hamden made gun, with E. Hartford production beginning with D 13,000. After 1976, the guns were made in East Hartford.

Three different styles of roll marking methods were used during production.

The First style is marked with the caliber and "D-100" or "DM-101" on left side of frame, "Hi-Standard Derringer" with eagle logo on left side of barrel.

The Second style is marked with the caliber and "D-100", "D-101", or "DM-101" on left side of frame, "Hi-Standard Derringer" with trigger logo on left side of barrel. Both the first and second types were marked "HIGH STANDARD MFG. CORP./-HAMDEN, CONN. U.S.A.-"

The Third style is marked with the caliber and "D-101" or "DM-101" on left side of frame, "Derringer" on left side of barrel. The third style was marked with different addresses and company names on the right side of the barrel. Style 3A is marked on the right side of the barrel the same as types one and two. Type 3B is marked with "HIGH STANDARD MFG. CORP./-E. HARTFORD, CONN. US.A.-" and type 3C is marked "HIGH STANDARD INC./-E. HARTFORD, CONN. U.S.A.-" Later third style is not marked with the "D-101" or "DM-101". The early derringers had a grooved back grip strap, which changed to a smooth grip strap just before the move to E. Hartford.

Near the end of production, a "V" suffix was added to some visually impaired guns, which were sold at discount. These guns were guaranteed to function properly, but the company would not allow them to be returned for appearance reasons. Numerous guns' earlier serial numbers, held back because of visual flaws, were also marked with the "V" and were shipped in 1984. The earliest V suffix gun found to date is D 25,945V.

✱ ***Blue Finish*** - .22 LR or .22 Mag. cal., blue, white or black grips.

	100%	98%	95%	90%	80%	70%	60%
	$275	$225	$200	$165	$140	$110	$100

Values assume First series.

Subtract 10% for Second or Third series.

Subtract 20% for Third series with black grips.

  .22 LR D-100 First series, catalog #9193, mfg. 1962-67, ser. no. 1,261,903.
  .22 LR D-100 Second series, catalog #9193, mfg. 1967-1969, ser. no. 1,6XX,XXX.
  .22 LR D-101 Second series, catalog #9193, mfg. 1969-1970, ser. no. 2,1XX,XXX.
  .22 LR D-101 Third series, catalog #9193, mfg. 1970-75, ser. no. 2,497,125.
  .22 LR Third series, catalog #9193, mfg. 1975-77, ser. no. D 02,809-D 13,319.
  .22 LR Third series, catalog #9193, mfg. 1982-84, ser. no. D 73,100-D 96,098 V.
  .22 Mag. DM-101 First series, catalog #9194, mfg. 1963-67, ser. no. 1,301,611.
  .22 Mag. DM-101 Second series, catalog #9194, mfg. 1967-1970, ser. no. 1,6XX,XXX.
  .22 Mag. DM-101 Third series, catalog #9193, mfg. 1970-1975, ser. no. 2,500,464.
  .22 Mag. Third series, catalog #9193, mfg. 1975-1982, ser. no. D 01,001.
  .22 Mag. Third series, catalog #9193, mfg. 1982-84, ser. no. D95,217 V.

GRADING - PPGS™	100%	98%	95%	90%	80%	70%	60%

✳ ***Nickel Finish*** - .22 LR or .22 Mag. cal., nickel, black grips, ivory grips were used on some early models, introduced 1970.

	$280	$230	$205	$170	$140	$110	$100

.22 LR D-101 Third series, catalog #9305, mfg. 1970-75, ser. no. 2,182,780-2,476,0XX.
.22 LR Third series, catalog #9305, mfg. 1975-77, ser. no. D05,543-D 13,426.
.22 Mag. DM-101 Third series, catalog #9306, mfg. 1970-75, ser. no. 2,182,380-2,500,464.
.22 Mag. Third series, catalog #9306, mfg. 1975-1984, ser. no. D 01,001-D 95,217 V.

✳ ***Gold plated*** - .22 LR or .22 Mag. cal., with black grips, includes presentation case, introduced 1964.

	$550	$475	$400

Add $75 for derringers with 1-3 digit serial numbers.

Subtract $50 if w/o presentation case.

#9195 derringers found in the regular serial number series around 1,339,002-1,339,080 beginning the end of 1963. #9196 found in regular serial number series around 2,366,556-2,366,561, 2,398,810-2,397,819 in 1973, and D 81,122 in 1982. Others are in a separate serial number series running from 1 through 123 which contains about 25 #9195 and 30 #9196 derringers.

.22 LR D-100 First Series, catalog #9195, mfg. 1963-1973.
.22 Mag. DM-101 First Series, catalog #9196, mfg. 1964-1973.
.22 LR D-100 First Series, cased pair, catalog #9197.
.22 Mag. DM-101 First Series, cased pair, catalog #9198.

While matched sets did have factory catalog numbers, rarity and lack of known sales preclude accurate valuation.

PRESIDENTIAL DERRINGER -.22 Mag. cal., gold plated, smooth walnut grips, includes walnut case marked "PRESIDENTIAL DERRINGER".

	$500	$425	$375

Subtract $50 if w/o presentation case.

Third series, catalog #9196, mfg. 1974-78. Serial numbers DM1 through DM 416 (353 guns) and HDM153 through HDM160 (7 guns) and a few special prefixes on about 10 guns.

PRESENTATION DERRINGER

✳ ***Gold Plated*** - .22 Mag. cal., smooth walnut grips, includes presentation case marked "PRESENTATION DERRINGER", ser. no GP0 through GP1000, approx. 917 produced in 1980 in E. Hartford.

	$450	$395	$350

Subtract $50 if w/o presentation case.

Third series, catalog #9196, mfg. 1980 only.

✳ ***Electroless Nickel Finish*** - . 22 LR or .22 Mag. cal., checkered walnut grips.

	$300	$260	$225

.22 LR Third series, catalog #9421, mfg. 1981-83, ser. no. D 74,351 - D 87,705.
.22 Mag Third series, catalog #9420, mfg. 1981-83, ser. no. D 63.390 - D 93,632.

✳ ***Silver Plated*** -.22 Mag. cal., faux mother-of-pearl grips, includes presentation case marked "PRESENTATION DERRINGER", ser. nos. SP0 through SP500, 501 were mfg. 1981.

	$500	$450	$400

Subtract $50 if w/o presentation case.

Third series, catalog #9341.

PISTOLS: SEMI-AUTO, LETTER SERIES

These were the first models made and used letters to designate the various models. A few guns from this series were sold after WWII. Catalog numbers for this series were assigned after the war in order to utilize the record keeping system of that time. This design series utilized three different takedowns. Types I-A and I-B takedowns have the takedown lever on the left side of the frame. Type I-A takedown has a round retracting rod protruding through the rear of the slide off center to the left side. Type I-B takedown is an improved, more durable design with a rectangular retracting rod. Type II takedown has the takedown lever in the right side of the frame with a round pick-up button on the top of the slide. Type I-A takedown was utilized from 1932 to February 1938 and the type I-B

GRADING - PPGS™	100%	98%	95%	90%	80%	70%	60%

takedown was utilized from that time until August 1939. Models B and C are the only models with the Type I-A takedown. The Model B and other Letter Models utilized type I-B and II takedowns. Guns with original boxes and original papers can add significant premiums but, like the guns, the condition is very important as is the requirement that the box be numbered to the gun. Those guns listed as a Curio or Relic by BATF are noted in this text with a C-R abbreviation at the end of the model description. Serial number ranges are best estimates as of this printing and may change with further research. All serial numbers are located on the front gripstrap.

Add approx. 15% for original box with papers on the following models.

MODEL B - .22 LR cal., original High Standard pistol, basically the same gun as Hartford Arms 1925 Automatic, small frame, 4 1/2 or 6 3/4 in. lightweight barrel (approx .63" diameter at frame), fixed Patridge type front and rear sights, checkered hard rubber grips (later production versions have checkered grips impressed with the High Standard monogram), 10 shot mag. Beginning ser. no. 5,000. Approx. 65,000, early production utilized Hartford front sight, safety and takedown levers. Post War models have the frame contour of the B-US. C-R.

	100%	98%	95%	90%	80%	70%	60%
	$600	$450	$375	$275	$175	$140	$100

Add $75 for I-B Type takedown.
Add $75 for early models with Hartford Arms parts.
Add $50 for post-war versions (ser. nos. greater than 146,000).

4 1/2 in. barrel	#9000	1932 - 1942 & 1946
6 3/4 in. barrel	#9001	1932 - 1942 & 1946

Most guns found in serial number ranges from 5,000 to about 95,894 and from about 148,198 to about 151,021.

MODEL B-US - a version of the Model B with slight contour modification to the back of the frame. 4 1/2 in. barrel only. 14,000 made for the US government during 1942-1943. Most are marked "PROPERTY OF U.S." on the top of the barrel and on the right side of the frame above trigger guard. Crossed cannon ordnance stamp usually found on the right side of the frame. Monogrammed hard rubber grips. Type II takedown only. Note the early Model Bs shipped to the government and marked "PROPERTY OF U.S." had the original frame contour .22 LR cal., 10 shot mag.

	$825	$700	$575	$475	$375	$250	$150

Most guns found in serial number range from about 92,344 to about 111,631.

MODEL S - .22 LR cal., chambered for .22 LR shot shell cartridge, essentially a Model B with a 6 3/4 in. smooth bore barrel only without choke, ivory bead front sight, left side of slide is stamped "HI-STANDARD MODEL S .22 LR SHOT ONLY", this variation was never a production model, ten are registered as Model S. Additional five with Model C slides are registered, Model C/S. Others may exist but only 15 are registered with BATF (see serial numbers below). Manufactured in 1939 and 1940. Values for both variations are equal. 6 3/4 in. barrels. C-R.

	$4,750	$4,250	$3,750	$3,250

Serial numbers: Model S - 48,142, 48,143, 48,144, 48,145, 48,146, 59,474 , 59,496, 59,458, 59,459, 59,493, Model C/S: 59,279, 59,460, 59,469, 59,473, 59,478. S/N 59,484 is listed as a Model S in the factory records but is not currently registered with the BATF.

MODEL C - .22 Short cal. only, identical to Model B in appearance, small frame, 4 1/2 or 6 3/4 in. light weight barrel, fixed rear sight, checkered hard rubber grips with or without H.S. monogram, this action was adapted for the decreased power of the .22 Short cartridge. Early production in separate serial number series beginning with 500 and continuing through 3,116. Joined regular serial number series at 42,806. There are numerous Model Cs in the regular serial number series earlier that 42,806 around 25,600 which shipped a date later than the Model Bs in the same serial number range. C-R.

	$900	$725	$500	$400	$300	$200	$150

Add $75 for I-A takedown.
Add $175 for I-B takedown.

GRADING - PPGS™	100%	98%	95%	90%	80%	70%	60%

This model was used primarily for plinking and gallery shooting. The Model C was made in all 3 variations of takedowns - I-A, I-B, and Type II.

4 1/2 in. barrel		#9061	1936 -1942	
6 3/4 in. barrel		#9062	1936 -1942	

Most guns found in serial number ranges from 500 to 3,116 and from about 42,806 to about 86,249.

MODEL A - .22 LR cal., similar to Model B, except grip part of frame is lengthened with a squared-off butt, 4 1/2 or 6 3/4 in. light weight barrel, adj. rear sight, checkered walnut grips, Checkered thumbrest walnut grips optionally available separately, automatic slide lock, 10 shot mag. Approx. 7,300 mfg. C-R.

	100%	98%	95%	90%	80%	70%	60%
	$750	$650	$500	$400	$300	$200	$150

Add $175 for I-B takedown.

4 1/2 in. barrel		#9005	1938 - 1942	
6 3/4 in. barrel		#9006	1938 - 1942	

Most guns found in serial number range from about 33,209 to about 97,734.

MODEL D - .22 LR cal., identical to Model A except 4 1/2 or 6 3/4 in. medium weight barrel (approx .79" diameter at frame), adj. sights, walnut grips, checkered thumbrest walnut grips optionally available separately, slide lock, trigger stop, 10 shot mag. Approx. 2,500 mfg. C-R.

	100%	98%	95%	90%	80%	70%	60%
	$950	$725	$550	$440	$310	$200	$150

Add $175 for I-B takedown.

4 1/2 in. barrel		#9063	1938 - 1942	
6 3/4 in. barrel		#9064	1938 - 1942	

Most guns found in serial number range from about 33,216 to about 95,206.

MODEL E - .22 LR cal., high quality, deluxe model of the hammerless series, adj. sight, 4 1/2 or 6 3/4 in. heavy bull barrel (approx .90" diameter at frame), checkered walnut target grips with thumbrest, automatic slide lock, trigger stop, 10 shot mag. Approx. 2,600 mfg. C-R.

	100%	98%	95%	90%	80%	70%	60%
	$1,125	$925	$775	$650	$500	$350	$200

Add $175 for I-B takedown.

4 1/2 in. barrel		#9067	1938 - 1942	
6 3/4 in. barrel		#9068	1938 - 1942	

Most guns found in serial number range from about 34,419 to about 98,306.

PISTOLS: SEMI-AUTO, LETTER SERIES W/HAMMER

Second series of models made, like the letter models with external hammers. Letters were still used to designate the various models. Most were produced before the war, but a few models were produced after the war. Catalog numbers for this series were assigned after the war in order to utilize the record keeping system of that time. Type II takedown only. Guns with original boxes and original papers can add significant premiums but, like the guns, condition is very important, as is the requirement that the box be numbered to the gun. Those guns listed as a Curio or Relic by BATF are noted - C-R. Serial number ranges are best estimates as of this printing and may change with further research. All ser. numbers are located on forestrap of frame.

Add approx. 15% for original box with papers on the following models.

MODEL H-D - .22 LR cal., first exposed hammer model, similar to Model D, 4 1/2 or 6 3/4 in. medium weight barrel, adj. sight, trigger stop, slide lock, checkered walnut grips, (checkered thumbrest walnut grips optionally available separately), no external safety, 10 shot mag, pistols in the 135,990 to 145,439 range have a safety and are marked "Model HD" but do not have the adjustable sight or trigger overtravel screw. Approx. 6,900 mfg. C-R.

	100%	98%	95%	90%	80%	70%	60%
	$1,200	$950	$700	$500	$400	$300	$200

4 1/2 in. barrel		#9065	1940 - 1941 & 1945	
6 3/4 in. barrel		#9066	1940 - 1941	

Most guns found in serial number ranges from about 45,463 to about 93,164 and from about 135,990 to about 145,439.

GRADING - PPGS™	100%	98%	95%	90%	80%	70%	60%

USA-MODEL-HD - .22 LR cal., this model was developed because the government needed a training pistol similar to the Colt Model 1911 .45 ACP, the result was a Model HD with external safety and fixed sight, 4 1/2 in. medium weight barrel, the barrel is marked "Property of USA", black checkered hard rubber grips, first models mfg. had high gloss blue finish, changed to a parkerized finish near ser. no. 130XXX. Approx. 44,000 mfg. 1943-45. C-R.

	$775	$700	$625	$525	$400	$300	$200

  Add 20% for early blue finish.

  Most guns found in serial number range from about 103,863 to about 145,700.

MODEL USA-HD-MS - .22 LR cal., variation of the USA-Model-HD with integral silencer, mfg. for U.S. Government for the OSS during 1944 and 1945, ownership requires NFA transfer, approx. 2,000 mfg. Only a few registered with BATF for civilian ownership.

	$6,000	$5,600	$5,250	$4,850	$4,450	$4,100	$3,750

  Most guns found in serial number range from about 110,074 to about 130,040.

MODEL H-D MILITARY -.22 LR cal., though called H-D Military, this model was not mfg. for the government, essentially a Model H-D with an external safety, 4 1/2 or 6 3/4 in. barrel, plastic (early mfg.) or checkered walnut grips (later mfg,) trigger stop (later manufacture), 10 shot mag. Approx. 150,000 mfg. C-R.

	$575	$475	$400	$330	$230	$150	$125

  4 1/2 in. barrel   #9050   1945 - 1950
  6 3/4 in. barrel   #9051   1945 - 1950

  Most guns found in serial number range from about 145,196 to about 334,751.

MODEL H-E - .22 LR cal., deluxe model of exposed hammer series, 4 1/2 or 6 3/4 in. heavy barrel, adj. sight, trigger stop, slide lock, deluxe hand checkered walnut grips with thumbrests, no external safety, 10 shot mag. Rare - approx 1,000 mfg. 1941-42. C-R.

	$1,950	$1,600	$1,300	$975	$700	$575	$450

  4 1/2 in. barrel   #9026   1940 - 1942
  6 3/4 in. barrel   #9027   1940 - 1942

  Most guns found in serial number range from about 51,802 to about 90,588.

MODEL H-A - .22 LR cal., similar to Model A, 4 1/2 or 6 3/4 in. lightweight barrel, adj. sight, slide lock, plain checkered walnut grips, no external safety, 10 shot mag. Rare - approx. 1,000 mfg. C-R.

	$1,050	$900	$750	$575	$400	$300	$200

  4 1/2 in. barrel   #9007   1940 - 1942
  6 3/4 in. barrel   #9008   1940 - 1942

  Most guns found in serial number range from about 53,176 to about 92,816.

MODEL H-B - .22 LR cal., duplicate of Model B with external hammer, 4 1/2 or 6 3/4 in. lightweight barrel, fixed sight, checkered hard rubber grips with or w/o H.S. monogram, no external safety, 10 shot mag. Approx. 2,100 mfg. C-R.

	$775	$650	$510	$385	$275	$225	$175

  4 1/2 in. barrel   1940 - 1941
  6 3/4 in. barrel   1940 - 1941

  Most guns found in serial number range from about 52,405 to about 86,155.

✳ *Model H-B Second Model* - reintroduced as an H-B second model similar to first model, except with external safety. C-R.

	$600	$525	$425	$325	$225	$185	$150

  4 1/2 in. barrel   #9003   1948 - 1949   274,197 - 311,535
  6 3/4 in. barrel   #9004   1948 - 1949   274,996 - 311,520

PISTOLS: SEMI-AUTO, LEVER LETTER SERIES

These were the third design models made, which incorporate interchangeable barrels with a lever takedown. The .22 caliber guns evolved from the Model G-380, High Standard's first production removable barrel gun which is included in this section. Like the letter models with external hammers, these .22 caliber models still use letters to designate the various models. New to this series was the adjustable Davis sight. Also introduced in this series was a breech face shrouded by the slide. Significant premiums can be asked for guns with the combination of both barrels, if verified by factory records that the gun shipped as a combination. (Buyer beware - many "combinations" have been created after leaving the factory). Non-factory combinations should have additional value equal to the value of an extra barrel. Guns with original boxes and papers can add significant premiums but, like the guns, the condition is very important, as is the requirement that the box be numbered to the gun. Those guns listed as a Curio or Relic by BATF are noted - C-R. Serial number ranges are best estimates, and may change with further research. Ser. numbers are on the right side of slide and rear right side of frame. Mfg. 1949-50.

Add approx. 15% for original box with papers on the following models.

MODEL G-380 CENTERFIRE
- .380 ACP cal., only in-house production of a center-fire pistol, transition model to the G-series using a lever takedown, exposed hammer, fixed sights, checkered black plastic grips, external safety, 5 in. barrel only, 6 shot mag. Approx. 7,400 mfg. in a serial number series of its own but a few examples exist in the regular serial number range around 329,337. C-R.

	$550	$450	$400	$325	$245	$210	$180
5.00" barrel		#9060	1947 - 1950		123 - 7,551		

MODEL GB
- .22 LR cal., similar to Model B with light barrel, small frame, external safety, fixed sight, monogrammed checkered brown plastic grips, interchangeable 4 1/2 or 6 3/4 in. barrel with lever takedown, 10 shot mag., last short frame model produced. Approx. 4,900 mfg. C-R.

	$600	$450	$375	$300	$225	$175	$150

Add $225 for factory combination.

4 1/2 in. barrel	#9110	1949 - 1950	310,449 - 335,278
6 3/4 in. barrel	#9111	1949 - 1950	309,578 - 335,095
Combination with both barrels	#9112	1949 - 1950	311,001 - 335,066

MODEL GD
- .22 LR cal., large frame, medium weight, interchangeable 4 1/2 or 6 3/4 in. barrel with lever takedown, adj. Davis sight (named for designer G.F. Davis), sight is adj. for both windage and elevation, trigger stop, slide lock, grips avail. in plain checkered walnut or deluxe with thumbrest, 10 shot mag. Approx. 3,300 mfg. C-R.

	$975	$825	$675	$525	$400	$300	$225

Add $325 for factory combination.

Add $50 for factory target grips.

4 1/2 in. barrel standard walnut grips	#9020	1949 - 1950	315,445 - 335,279
6 3/4 in. barrel standard walnut grips	#9021	1949 - 1950	311,804 - 335,300
Combination with both barrels and standard walnut grips	#9022	1949 - 1950	312,001 - 335,247
4 1/2 in. barrel thumbrest walnut grips	#9023	1949 - 1950	316,623 - 326,850
6 3/4 in. barrel thumbrest walnut grips	#9024	1949 - 1950	311,804 - 335,222
Combination with both barrels and thumbrest walnut grips	#9025	1949 - 1950	317,914 - 335,278.

MODEL GE
- .22 LR cal., deluxe top-of-the-line model, large frame, interchangeable 4 1/2 or 6 3/4 in. heavy bull barrel with lever takedown, Davis adj. sight, deluxe walnut hand checkered grips with thumbrest, trigger stop, slide lock, 10 shot mag. Approx. 2,900 mfg. C-R.

	$1,400	$1,200	$975	$725	$450	$350	$250

Add $375 for factory combination.

4 1/2 in. barrel	#9030	1949 - 1950	314,050 - 335,275
6 3/4 in. barrel	#9031	1949 - 1950	314,027 - 335,198
Combination with both barrels	#9032	1949 - 1950	312,002 - 335,200.

GRADING - PPGS™	100%	98%	95%	90%	80%	70%	60%

OLYMPIC (G-O) - .22 Short cal., adaptation of Model GE in .22 Short cal., also known as First Model Olympic, first fired in Olympic competition in 1948, deluxe top-of-the-line quality, interchangeable 4 1/2 or 6 3/4 in. heavy bull barrel with lever takedown, Davis adj. sight, deluxe hand checkered walnut grips with thumbrests, trigger stop, slide lock, grooved fore and rear strap, first High Standard large production gun with aluminum slide, special curved magazine, a few guns exist which will utilize a magazine with a straight back, the majority of these Olympics use the curved magazine with a humped back, grooved surface on top of barrel and slide. Rare - approx. 1,200 mfg. C-R.

	100%	98%	95%	90%	80%	70%	60%
	$1,800	$1,500	$1,150	$825	$550	$425	$325

Add $375 for factory combination.
Add $300 for the straight back magazine variation.

4 1/2 in. barrel	#9040	1949 - 1950	325,929 - 334-735
6 3/4 in. barrel	#9041	1949 - 1950	307,734 - 334,979
Combination with both barrels	#9042	1949 - 1950	329,590 - 334,399.

PISTOLS: SEMI-AUTO, LEVER NAME SERIES

These models were the fourth design evolving from the lever letter series with slight changes. This series followed the precedent of naming the models instead of utilizing letters set by the Olympic (G-O). The upscale models, the Supermatic and Olympic, incorporated a rib dovetailed to the top of the barrel and a dovetail slot on the bottom of the barrel for mounting balance weights. This series continued the breech face shrouded by the slide. Significant premiums can be asked for guns with the combination of both barrels, if verified by factory records that the gun shipped as a combination. (Buyer beware - many "combinations" have been created after leaving the factory). Non-factory combinations should have additional value equal to the value of the extra barrel. Adjustable sight models continued to use the Davis sight. No guns in this series were offered with barrels incorporating the integral stabilizer but stabilizer barrels were offered in 1954 after the series ended. Most guns in this series utilized a single screw to retain the grips. However, the earliest Olympics used a screw for each side before changing to a single screw. Guns with original boxes and original papers can add significant premiums but, like the guns, the condition is very important, as is the requirement that the box be numbered to the gun. Serial number ranges are best estimates, and may change with further research.

Add approx. 15% for original box with papers on the following models.

SPORT-KING (FIRST MODEL) - .22 LR cal., 10 shot mag., similar to Field-King except has fixed sight and lightweight interchangeable 4 1/2 or 6 3/4 in. barrel featuring lever takedown, early models did not have a slide hold back when the magazine became empty, early variation w/o hold back was produced in about twice the quantity as the later models incorporating this feature.

	100%	98%	95%	90%	80%	70%	60%
	$425	$350	$300	$250	$200	$150	$100

Add $25 for guns with hold back.
Add $200 for factory combination.

4 1/2 in. barrel	#9080	1950 - 1954	335,001 - 442,604
6 3/4 in. barrel	#9081	1950 - 1954	335,012 - 442,081
Combination with both barrels	#9082	1951 - 1953	337,699 - 442,570

FIELD-KING (FIRST MODEL) - .22 LR cal., plain version of Supermatic, 10 shot mag., interchangeable 4 1/2 or 6 3/4 in. barrels with lever takedown, Davis adj. sight, trigger stop, slide lock, 10 shot mag., no rib on barrels or provisions for weights.

	100%	98%	95%	90%	80%	70%	60%
	$625	$550	$450	$340	$275	$225	$175

Add $225 for factory combination.

4 1/2 in. barrel	#9090	1951 - 1953	342,703 - 428,939
6 3/4 in. barrel	#9091	1951 - 1953	341,751 - 414,203
Combination with both barrels	#9092	1951 - 1953	348,762

GRADING - PPGS™	100%	98%	95%	90%	80%	70%	60%

SUPERMATIC (FIRST MODEL) - .22 LR cal., 4 1/2 or 6 3/4 in. interchangeable barrel with lever takedown, Davis adj. sight, trigger stop, 10 shot mag., slide lock, front and back straps grooved, brown plastic thumb rest grips, serrated rib between front and rear sight, adj. 2 oz. and 3 oz. weights which dovetail into and beneath barrel, a filler strip was provided for when the weights were not used.

	$750	$625	$500	$400	$320	$225	$175

Add $250 for factory combination.

4 1/2 in. barrel with provisions for weights	#9070	1951 - 1953	340,103 - 438,698
6 3/4 in. barrel with provisions for weights	#9071	1951 - 1953	338,210 - 443,411
Combination with both barrels	#9072	1951 - 1953	340,101 - 439,924

OLYMPIC (SECOND MODEL) - .22 Short cal., identical in all respects to the Supermatic, except has aluminum slide for rapid recoil, 10 shot mag., interchangeable 4 1/2 or 6 3/4 in. barrel with lever takedown, also available as combination with both barrels, Davis adj. sight, ribbed barrels and provisions for weights, 2 oz. and a 3 oz. weight were provided with this model, as was a filler strip for when the weights were not used, grooved front and back straps on frame.

	$1,050	$875	$725	$600	$500	$400	$300

Add $250 for factory combination.

Note: Conversion kits for converting from .22 LR to .22 Short became available in 1956 (see the information at the end of the 101 section).

4 1/2 in. barrel with provisions for weights	#9043	1951 - 1953	341,795
6 3/4 in. barrel with provisions for weights	#9044	1951 - 1953	341,788 - 438,561
Combination with both barrels	#9045	1951 - 1953	348,505

PISTOLS: SEMI-AUTO, 100 SERIES

The 100 Series firearms were the fifth design models evolving from the Lever Name Series designs. This series introduced the small, push button barrel release takedown, and deleted the shrouded breech. This series featured slanted plastic grips as standard issue. The upscale models continued with the ribbed barrel and a dovetail slot on the bottom of the barrel for mounting balance weights. Adjustable sight models continued to use the Davis sight. New to this series was the introduction of an aluminum frame on the Flite King and the Sport King Lightweight. Also included in this series was a new striker fired design called the Dura-Matic, designated as a low cost plinker. Significant premiums can be asked for guns with the combination of both barrels, if verified by factory records that the gun shipped as a combination. Buyer beware - many "combinations" have been created after leaving the factory. Non-factory combinations should have additional value equal to the value of the extra barrel. Guns with original boxes and original papers can add significant premiums but, like the guns, the condition is very important, as is the requirement that the box be numbered to the gun. Serial number ranges starting points are best estimates, and may change with further research.

Add approx. 10% for original box with papers on the following models.

DURA-MATIC - .22 LR cal., 4 1/2 or 6 1/2 in. barrels, fixed sight, striker fired, oversized plastic grips, M-100 stamped on right side of slide, unique thumb screw takedown, pushbutton release for the thumb screw, push-button mag. release and oversized trigger guard. Mfg. 1954.

	$325	$275	$225	$175	$150	$125	$100

Add $150 for factory combination.

4 1/2 in. barrel	#9124	1954 - 1954	458,801 - 47X,XXX
6 1/2 in. barrel	#9125	1954 - 1954	458,802 - 47X,XXX
Combination with both barrels	#9126	1954 - 1954	459,675 - 47X,XXX

GRADING - PPGS™	100%	98%	95%	90%	80%	70%	60%

SPORT-KING (SECOND MODEL) - .22 LR cal., similar to Flite-King but with steel slide and frame, SK 100 stamped on right side of slide, front and rear grip straps on this model are smooth, slide lock, fixed rear sight.

	100%	98%	95%	90%	80%	70%	60%
	$400	$350	$275	$200	$175	$150	$100

Add $200 for factory combination.

Add $250 for ARMAMEX version.

In late 1958, Col. Rex Applegate imported about three hundred into Mexico. These guns are marked with his company's name, ARMAMEX. Marked "ARMAMEX, MEXICO" on the right side of the barrel and "SPORT KING / CAL. 22 L.R." on the left side of the barrel. Customary "HI-STANDARD" marking on the left side of the slide. Serial numbers around 870,084-870,383. Note that the Applegate guns were made after the 102 series was in production. Armamex catalog number 1910.

4 1/2 in. barrel	#9100	1954 - 1957	436,311 - 804,081
6 3/4 in. barrel	#9101	1954 - 1957	436,308 - 804,080
Combination with both barrels	#9102	1954 - 1957	443,651 - 804,075

SPORT-KING LIGHTWEIGHT - .22 LR cal., similar to standard Sport-King, except has forged aluminum alloy frame, "Lightweight" is inscribed in script on the left side of frame, also available in nickel.

	100%	98%	95%	90%	80%	70%	60%
	$500	$400	$325	$250	$175	$150	$100

Add $150 for nickel finish.

Add $200 for factory combination.

4 1/2 in. barrel blue	#9156	1955 - 1964	506,248
6 3/4 in. barrel blue	#9157	1955 - 1964	506,243
Combination with both barrels blue	#9158	1956 - 1959	506,320
4 1/2 in. barrel nickel	#9167	1957 - 1960	726,752
6 3/4 in. barrel nickel	#9168	1957 - 1960	726,745
Combination with both barrels nickel	#9169	1957 - 1959	726,909

FLITE-KING (FIRST MODEL) - .22 Short cal., 10 shot mag., blued finish with black anodized aluminum frame and slide, 4 1/2, 6 3/4 in. barrel, or a combination with both barrel lengths, brown plastic checkered thumb rest grips, fixed sights.

	100%	98%	95%	90%	80%	70%	60%
	$575	$475	$400	$340	$260	$180	$135

Add $200 for factory combination.

4 1/2 in. barrel	#9103	1953 - 1957	431,297
6 3/4 in. barrel	#9104	1953 - 1957	431,286
Combination with both barrels	#9105	1954 - 1957	431,532

FIELD-KING (SECOND MODEL) - .22 LR cal., 4 1/2 or 6 3/4 in. interchangeable barrel with push-button takedown, FK 100 stamped on right side of slide, 10 shot mag., front and rear grip straps on this model are smooth, slide lock, trigger stop, adj. rear sight. Mfg. briefly in 1954.

	100%	98%	95%	90%	80%	70%	60%
	$750	$625	$525	$425	$350	$250	$150

Add $225 for factory combination.

4 1/2 in. barrel	#9106	1954 - 1954	446,645
6 3/4 in. barrel	#9107	1954 - 1954	446,595
Combination with both barrels	#9108	1954 - 1954	446,601

SUPERMATIC (SECOND MODEL) - .22 LR cal., 4 1/2 or 6 3/4 in. interchangeable barrel with push-button takedown, "S-100" stamped on right side of slide, 10 shot mag., adj. 2 oz. or 3 oz. weights, slide lock, trigger stop, adj. rear sight, grooved front and back straps on frame, a 2 oz. and a 3 oz. weight were provided with this model as was a filler strip for when the weights were not used. Mfg. briefly in 1954.

	100%	98%	95%	90%	80%	70%	60%
	$825	$725	$625	$500	$350	$250	$150

Add $250 for factory combination.

4 1/2 in. barrel with provisions for weights	#9109	1954 - 1954	446,516 -
6 3/4 in. barrel with provisions for weights	#9110	1954 - 1954	446,445 -
Combination with both barrels	#9111	1954 - 1954	446,705 -

GRADING - PPGS™	100%	98%	95%	90%	80%	70%	60%

OLYMPIC (THIRD MODEL) - .22 Short cal., 4 1/2 or 6 3/4 in. interchangeable barrel with push-button takedown, 10 shot mag., "O-100" stamped on right side of alloy slide, adj. 2 oz. or 3 oz. weights, adj. rear sight, slide lock, trigger stop, grooved front and back straps on frame, a 2 oz. and a 3 oz. weight were provided with this model as was a filler strip for when the weights were not used. Mfg. briefly in 1954.

	$1,175	$925	$750	$575	$425	$300	$200

Add $250 for factory combination.

Note: Conversion kits for converting from .22 LR to .22 Short became available in 1956 - see the information at the end of the 101 section.

4 1/2 in. barrel with provisions for weights	#9112	1954 - 1954	447,209
6 3/4 in. barrel with provisions for weights	#9113	1954 - 1954	447,210
Combination with both barrels	#9114	1954 - 1954	447,205

PISTOLS: SEMI-AUTO, 101 SERIES

The 101 Series were the sixth design models evolving from the 100 Series. This series continued the small push button barrel release takedown. The ribbed barrel was dropped from the upscale models, but the dovetail slot on the bottom of the barrel for mounting balance weights continued. Adjustable sight models continued to use the Davis sight (Note: the Flight King, Sport King, and Sport King Lightweight did not upgrade to this series). Significant premiums can be asked for guns with the combination of both barrels, if verified by factory records that the gun shipped as a combination. Buyer beware - many "combinations" have been created after leaving the factory. Non-factory combinations should have additional value equal to the value of the extra barrel. Guns with original boxes and papers can add significant premiums, but like the guns, the condition is very important, as is the requirement that the box be numbered to the gun. Serial number ranges are best estimates and may change with further research.

Add approx. 10% for original box with papers on the following models.

DURA-MATIC - .22 LR cal., 4 1/2 or 6 1/2 in. barrel, fixed sight, oversized plastic grips, "M-101" stamped on right side of slide (mfg. 1954 to 1970), later appeared renamed "Plinker" M-101 during 1971 to 1973.

	$300	$235	$200	$160	$125	$100	$80

Add $150 for factory combination.

Add $80 for Plinker with case in original box.

The Plinker was not available with both barrel combination. During the first year, the Plinker came with a zippered carrying case. The Dura-matic was sold by Sears Roebuck & Co. as the J.C. Higgins Model 80. This Sears variation had some minor exterior differences but, mechanically it was the same - including a unique thumb screw takedown, push-button mag. release and oversized trigger guard.

A slightly modified version was sold by Sears Roebuck & Co. as the J. C. Higgins M-80.

Dura-Matic

4 1/2 in. barrel	#9124	1955 - 1970	47X,XXX
6.50" barrel	#9125	1955 - 1970	47X,XXX
Combination with both barrels	#9126	1955 - 1959	47X,XXX

Sears M-80

4 1/2 in. barrel	#9133	1955-1962	477,292
6.50" barrel	#9134	1955-1962	477,649
Combination with both barrels	#9135	1955-1962	477,303

Plinker

4 1/2 in. barrel	#9214		1971 - 1973
6 3/4 in. barrel	#9215		1971 - 1973

FIELD-KING (THIRD MODEL) - .22 LR cal., 4 1/2 or 6 3/4 in. interchangeable barrel with push-button takedown, FK 101 stamped on right side of slide, 10 shot mag., front and rear grip straps on this model are smooth, adj. rear sight, slide lock, trigger stop, brown plastic thumb rest grips, 6 3/4 in. barrel incorporates a muzzle brake with one slot either side of the front sight.

	$650	$550	$475	$425	$350	$235	$175

Add $225 for factory combination.

GRADING - PPGS™	100%	98%	95%	90%	80%	70%	60%
4 1/2 in. barrel		#9115	1954 - 1957	447,149			
6 3/4 in. barrel		#9116	1954 - 1957	447,146 - 799,260			
Combination with both barrels		#9117	1954 - 1957	- 799,259			

SUPERMATIC (THIRD MODEL)

- .22 LR cal, 4 1/2 or 6 3/4 in. interchangeable barrel with push-button takedown, "S 101" stamped on right side of slide, 10 shot mag., adj. 2 oz. or 3 oz. weights and a filler strip for when the weights were not used, 6 3/4 in. barrel incorporates a muzzle brake with one slot either side of the front sight, slide lock, trigger stop, adj. rear sight, brown plastic thumb rest grips, grooved front and back straps on frame, also produced with U.S. marking for the military.

	$750	$675	$550	$475	$350	$235	$175

Add $250 for factory combination.

4 1/2 in. barrel with provisions for weights		#9118	1954 - 1957	447,586 -			
6 3/4 in. barrel with provisions for weights and integral stabilizer		#9119	1954 - 1957	446,511 -			
Combination with both barrels		#9120	1954 - 1957	447,595 -			

OLYMPIC (FOURTH MODEL)

- .22 Short cal., 4 1/2 or 6 3/4 in. interchangeable barrel with push-button takedown, "O-101" stamped on right side of alloy slide, 10 shot mag., adj. 2 oz. or 3 oz. weights and a filler strip for when the weights were not used, 6 3/4 in. barrel incorporates a muzzle brake with one slot either side of the front sight, adj. rear sight, slide lock, trigger stop, brown plastic thumb rest grips, grooved front and back straps on frame.

	$1,050	$875	$700	$575	$450	$325	$200

Add $250 for factory combination.

4 1/2 in. barrel with provisions for weights		#9121	1954 - 1957	447,230 -			
6 3/4 in. barrel with provisions for weights and integral stabilizer		#9122	1954 - 1957	447,214 -			
Combination with both barrels		#9123	1954 - 1957	447,227 -			

✳ *Conversion kits* - kits for converting .22 LR guns to .22 Short were announced in both the 1956 catalog and in a 1956 brochure. Kits include a barrel, an aluminum slide, and magazine (.22 short to .22 LR conversion had a steel slide).

	$525	$435	$375

Values are for kits in original boxes.
Cat.# 9150 Supermatic/Field King to 22 short, 4 1/2 Bbl.
Cat.# 9151 Supermatic/Field King to 22 short, 6 3/4 Bbl.
Cat.# 9152 Olympic to Supermatic 22 L.R., 4 1/2 Bbl.
Cat.# 9153 Olympic to Supermatic 22 L.R., 6 3/4 Bbl.
Cat.# 9154 Olympic to Field King 22 L.R., 4 1/2 Bbl.
Cat.# 9155 Olympic to Field King 22 L.R., 6 3/4 Bbl.
Kits were also offered for the earlier lever name series and the 100 Series guns. Catalog numbers are unknown for conversion kits for lever name series or the the 100 series guns.

PISTOLS: SEMI-AUTO, 102 SERIES

The 102 Series was a major design change, incorporating a new frame with a large push button takedown release, and a superb adjustable sight. There is little difference between the two series. Pistols in this series are marked Model 102 on right side of the slide. Three variations of ejectors were utilized during the 102 Series. No premiums exist for these variations. Significant premiums can be asked for guns with the combination of both barrels, if verified by factory records that the gun shipped as a combination. Buyer beware - many "combinations" have been created after leaving the factory. Non-factory combinations should have additional value equal to the value of the extra barrel. The 102 Series was produced from 1958 to 1960, ending at approx. ser. no. 1,12X,XXX. Guns with original boxes and papers can add significant premiums but, like the guns, the condition is very important as is the requirement that the box be numbered to the gun.

Original cased 102 Series Trophy, Olympic Citation models, and Special Presentation combinations in 98%+ condition are currently in great demand and are bringing asking prices in the $1,500-$2,600 range.

Add approx. 10% for original box with papers on the following models.

GRADING - PPGS™	100%	98%	95%	90%	80%	70%	60%

SPORT-KING - .22 LR cal., 10 shot mag., 4 1/2 or 6 3/4 in. lightweight, round and tapered barrels, blued finish, fixed sights, checkered plastic grips, smooth grip straps, also available as a combination with both barrel lengths.

	$365	$300	$250	$215	$160	$120	$90

Add $100 for nickel finish
Add $200 for factory combination.

4 1/2 in. tapered barrel blued	#9200	1958 - 1960	778,028
6 3/4 in. tapered barrel blued	#9201	1958 - 1960	778,021
Combination with both barrels	#9202	1958 - 1959	778,026

FLITE-KING - .22 Short cal., otherwise similar to the Sport King Models 102 and 103, steel frames with an alloy slide.

	$500	$415	$360	$310	$240	$170	$120

Add $200 for factory combination.

4 1/2 in. tapered barrel blued	#9220	1958 - 1960	791,149
6 3/4 in. tapered barrel bluled	#9221	1958 - 1960	791,150
Combination with both barrels	#9222	1958 - 1959	791,169

SUPERMATIC TOURNAMENT - .22 LR cal., 10 shot, 4 1/2 or 6 3/4 in. tapered barrel, brown diamond checkered plastic slant grips, adj. sight, push button takedown, smooth front and back grip straps.

	$660	$580	$475	$375	$300	$220	$150

Add $200 for factory combination.

4 1/2 in. tapered barrel	#9270	1958 - 1960	796,555
6 3/4 in. tapered barrel	#9271	1958 - 1960	796,536
Combination with both barrels	#9272	1958 - 1959	

The U.S. Govt. ordered the Model 102 Tournaments to use for training. These models were marked "U.S." on left side of frame.

SUPERMATIC CITATION - .22 LR cal., 10 shot, 6 3/4, 8, and 10 in. tapered barrels, diamond checkered plastic slant grips, adj. sight, push-button takedown, one grade above Tournament, grooved front and back grip straps, trigger stop, trigger pull adjustment, adj. sight located on 8 and 10 in. barrel, detachable stabilizer and 2 or 3 oz. barrel weights available.

	$760	$625	$510	$430	$340	$250	$180

Add $100 for 8 in. barrel.
Add $200 premium for 10 in. barrel.

6 3/4 in. tapered barrel with provisions for weights and stabilizer	#9260	1958 - 1960	803,303
8 in. tapered barrel with provisions for weights and stabilizer	#9261	1958 - 1960	795,726
10 in. tapered barrel with provisions for weights and stabilizer	#9262	1958 - 1960	771,275

The U.S. Govt. ordered a quantity of Model 102 Citations to be used for training, marked "U.S." on left side of frame.

SUPERMATIC TROPHY - .22 LR cal., 10 shot, 6 3/4 in., 8 in. and 10 in. tapered barrels, 5 1/2 bull and 7 1/4 in. fluted barrels became avail. in 1962, detachable barrel weights and stabilizer also available, walnut checkered thumbrest grips, grooved front and back grip straps, trigger stop, trigger pull adjustment, gold trigger, gold safety button and gold inlaid lettering, adj. sight and push-button takedown.

	$1,150	$915	$815	$650	$475	$350	$225

Add $125 for 8 in. barrel.
Add $225 for 10 in. barrel.

6 3/4 in. tapered barrel with provisions for weights and stabilizer	#9250	1958 - 1960	812,641
8 in. tapered barrel with provisions for weights and stabilizer	#9251	1958 - 1960	791,247
10 in. tapered barrel with provisions for weights and stabilizer	#9252	1958 - 1960	791,246

GRADING - PPGS™	100%	98%	95%	90%	80%	70%	60%

OLYMPIC - .22 Short cal., similar to Citation, adj. sight located on 8 and 10 in. barrel and on the slide of the 6 3/4 in barrel, early models marked "Olympic Citation", then changed to "Olympic" only about 1960, grooved front and back straps on frame, checkered plastic grips, trigger stop, trigger pull adjustment.

	100%	98%	95%	90%	80%	70%	60%
	$1,150	$925	$675	$450	$325	$275	$225

Add $125 for 8 in. barrel.
Add $225 for 10 in. barrel.
Add $200 for "Olympic Citation" marked guns.

6 3/4 in. tapered barrel with provisions for weights and stabilizer	#9280	1958 - 1960	812,365
8 in. tapered barrel with provisions for weights and stabilizer	#9281	1958 - 1960	796,924
10 in. tapered barrel with provisions for weights and stabilizer	#9282	1958 - 1960	796,930

PISTOLS: SEMI-AUTO, 103 SERIES

The 103 Series was a major design change incorporating a new frame with a large push button takedown release. There is little difference between the two Series. This Series is marked Model 103 on right side of the slide. Significant premiums can be asked for guns with the combination of both barrels, if verified by factory records that the gun shipped as a combination. Buyer beware - many "combinations" have been created after leaving the factory. Non-factory combinations should have additional value equal to the value of the extra barrel. The 103 Series was produced 1960 to 1963, except for the Sport King, the Flite King, the Supermatic Tournament, and the Sharpshooter - see date ranges of the individual models below. After mid-1975, the Sport King and the Sharpshooter appeared in the "G" prefix serial numbered series - see serial number chart. Guns with original boxes and papers can add significant premiums but, like the guns, the condition is very important as is the requirement that the box be numbered to the gun.

Original cased 103 Series Trophy, Olympic Trophy, Olympic Citation models, and Special Presentation combinations in 98%+ condition are currently in great demand, with asking prices in the $1,500-$2,600 range.

Add approx. 10% for original box with papers on the following models.

SPORT-KING - .22 LR cal., 4 1/2 or 6 3/4 in. lightweight, round and tapered barrel, 10 shot mag., blue finish, fixed sights, checkered plastic grips, smooth grip straps, available as a combination with both barrel lengths.

	100%	98%	95%	90%	80%	70%	60%
	$355	$300	$250	$200	$150	$120	$90

Add $100 for nickel finish.
Add $200 for factory combination.

4 1/2 in. tapered barrel blued	#9200	1960 - 1970 & 1973 - 1977
6 3/4 in. tapered barrel blued	#9201	1960 - 1970 & 1973 - 1978
4 1/2 in. tapered barrel nickel	#9220	1973 - 1977
6 3/4 in. tapered barrel nickel	#9221	1973 - 1977

Note that later production models were not marked 103. 254 Sport Kings (#9200 & #9201) shipped in May, 1977 with serial numbers between G160,000 - G162,590. 116 guns, #9201 Sport Kings, shipped April and May 1978 serial numbers G20,106 - G20,223.

FLITE-KING - .22 Short cal., similar to Sport King Model 103, steel frame with an alloy slide.

	100%	98%	95%	90%	80%	70%	60%
	$500	$415	$360	$310	$240	$170	$120

Add $200 for factory combination.

4 1/2 in. bull barrel	#9220	1960 - 1965
6 3/4 in. fluted barrel	#9221	1960 - 1965

SUPERMATIC TOURNAMENT - .22 LR cal., 4 1/2, 5 1/2 bull (avail. 1963), or 6 3/4 in. tapered barrel, 10 shot mag., brown diamond checkered plastic slant grips, adj. sight, push button takedown, this model featured smooth front and back grip straps.

	100%	98%	95%	90%	80%	70%	60%
	$645	$550	$475	$375	$300	$220	$150

Add $200 for factory combination.

GRADING - PPGS™	100%	98%	95%	90%	80%	70%	60%

4 1/2 in. tapered barrel	#9270	1960 - 1962		
6 3/4 in. tapered barrel	#9271	1960 - 1965		
5 1/2 in. bull barrel with provisions for weights and stabilizer	#9275	1962 - 1965		

SHARPSHOOTER - .22 LR cal., 5 1/2 in. bull barrel, 10 shot mag., blue finish, adj. sights, checkered plastic grips, smooth grip straps, some mfg. with Model 103 marked slides.

	100%	98%	95%	90%	80%	70%	60%
	$350	$300	$270	$240	$200	$160	$125

5 1/2 in. bull barrel	#9205	1971 - 1977

Although the Model 103 marked guns have 1969 and later serial numbers, they were shipped after the introduction of the Sharpshooter in 1971, and were probably converted from unsold Sport Kings. Some early Sharpshooters have "Sport King" on the left side of the frame.

SUPERMATIC CITATION - .22 LR cal., 6 3/4, 8, or 10 in. tapered barrels, 10 shot, diamond checkered plastic slant grips, adj. sight, push-button takedown, one grade above Tournament, grooved front and back grip straps, trigger stop, trigger pull adjustment, adj. sight located on 8 and 10 in. barrel (a 5 1/2 in. target bull barrel became avail. in 1962), detachable stabilizer and 2 or 3 oz. barrel weights available.

	100%	98%	95%	90%	80%	70%	60%
	$760	$625	$510	$430	$340	$250	$180

Add $100 for 8 in. barrel.
Add $200 for 10 in. barrel.

6 3/4 in. tapered barrel with provisions for weights and stabilizer	#9260	1960 - 1964
8 in. tapered barrel with provisions for weights and stabilizer	#9261	1960 - 1964
10 in. tapered barrel with provisions for weights and stabilizer	#9262	1960 - 1963
5 1/2 in. bull barrel	#9263	1962 - 1963

The U.S. Govt. ordered a quantity of Model 103 Citations to be used for training, marked "U.S." on left side of frame.

SUPERMATIC TROPHY - .22 LR cal., 6 3/4 in., 8 or 10 in. tapered barrels, 5 1/2 bull and 7 1/4 in. fluted barrels became avail. in 1962, 10 shot, detachable barrel weights and stabilizer were also available, walnut checkered thumbrest grips, grooved front and back grip straps, trigger stop, trigger pull adjustment, gold trigger, gold safety button and gold inlaid lettering, adj. sight and push-button takedown.

	100%	98%	95%	90%	80%	70%	60%
	$1,100	$925	$815	$650	$475	$350	$225

Add $125 for 8 in. barrel.
Add $225 for 10 in. barrel.

6 3/4 in. tapered barrel with provisions for weights and stabilizer	#9250	1960 - 1962
8 in. tapered barrel with provisions for weights and stabilizer	#9251	1960 - 1962
10 in. tapered barrel with provisions for weights and stabilizer	#9252	1960 - 1962
5 1/2 in. bull barrel	#9253	4/62 - 1962
5 1/2 in. bull barrel with provisions for weights and stabilizer	#9254	1963 - 1963
7 3/4 in. fluted barrel with provisions for weights and stabilizer	#9255	4/63 - 1963

ISU OLYMPIC - .22 Short cal., 6 3/4 in. barrel with integral stabilizer, 10 shot, grooved grip straps, checkered walnut thumbrest grips, trigger stop, trigger pull adjustment, high luster finish, alloy slide.

	100%	98%	95%	90%	80%	70%	60%
	$1,125	$925	$700	$475	$330	$260	$180

Add $1,000 for Model 9289 marked "Olympic Trophy" if in 98% or better condition.

6 3/4 in. tapered barrel with integral stabilizer - with accessories	#9299	1961 - 1963
6 3/4 in. tapered barrel with integral stabilizer - with accessories	#9289	1961 - 1962
5 1/2 in. bull barrel	#9294	1963 - 1963

There was also an Olympic ISU with a Supermatic Trophy finish (catalog number 9289) - fewer than 500 were produced.

GRADING - PPGS™	100%	98%	95%	90%	80%	70%	60%

OLYMPIC - .22 Short cal., similar to Citation, adj. sight located on 8 in and 10 in. barrel and on the slide of the 6 3/4 in barrel, grooved front and back straps on frame, checkered plastic grips, trigger stop, trigger pull adjustment.

	100%	98%	95%	90%	80%	70%	60%
	$1,150	$950	$675	$450	$325	$275	$225

Add $125 for 8 in. barrel.

Add $225 for 10 in. barrel.

Add $150 for "Olympic Citation" marked guns.

6 3/4 in. tapered barrel with provisions for weights and stabilizer	#9280	1960 - 1963	
8 in. tapered barrel with provisions for weights and stabilizer	#9281	1960 - 1963	
10 in. tapered barrel with provisions for weights and stabilizer	#9282	1960 - 1963	

PISTOLS: SEMI-AUTO, 104 SERIES

The 104 Series is the last of the slant grip gun designs. Early production marked "Model 104". Later production is unmarked. The trigger stop screw moved from the right side of the frame to the trigger on the up scale models with that feature. During the production of this series, the accessories were deleted in lieu of a price increase. The serial numbers of later guns produced after mid-1975 utilized a new serial numbering system with the slant grip models utilizing a "G" prefix on the serial number. This series was produced from 1963 to 1978. Guns with original boxes and papers can add significant premiums but, like the guns, the condition is very important as is the requirement that the box be numbered to the gun.

Add approx. 10% for original box with papers on the following models.

SUPERMATIC CITATION - .22 LR cal., similar to Model 102/103 Series, 10 shot mag., blue finish, adj. sights, brown plastic grips were standard on the 6 3/4, 8, and 10 in. guns, or thumbrest walnut checkered grips standard on the 5 1/2 in. model, grooved front and back straps.

	100%	98%	95%	90%	80%	70%	60%
	$725	$625	$500	$430	$340	$250	$180

Add $150 for 8 in. barrel.

Add $250 for 10 in. barrel.

103 guns, #9244 Citations, shipped March-May, 1978 serial numbers G20,000-G-20,105.

6 3/4 in. tapered barrel with provisions for weights and stabilizer	#9260	1963 - 1965
8 in. tapered barrel with provisions for weights and stabilizer	#9261	1963 - 1965
10 in. tapered barrel with provisions for weights and stabilizer	#9262	1963 - 1963
5 1/2 in. bull barrel with extra magazine	#9263	1963 - 1966
5 1/2 in. bull barrel w/o extra magazine	#9244	1967 - 1978

SUPERMATIC TROPHY - .22 LR cal., similar to Model 102/103 Series, top-of-the-line target model, 5 1/2 in. bull, or 7 1/4 in. fluted barrel, extra mag., muzzle brake and weights were supplied with gun, grooved front and back straps, checkered walnut grips, super polished blue finish, adjustable sights, 2 and 3 oz. adjustable weights, checkered walnut thumb rest grips, grooved front and back straps on frame. Mfg. 1964-65.

	100%	98%	95%	90%	80%	70%	60%
	$1,050	$900	$675	$450	$375	$250	$175

Add $150 for high polish blue finish.

5 1/2 in. bull barrel with accessories	#9254	1963 - 1965
7.25" fluted barrel with accessories	#9255	1963 - 1965

OLYMPIC - .22 LR cal., similar to Model 102, grooved front and back straps, checkered plastic grips, the 5 1/2 in. bull barrel was supplied with muzzle brake and weights.

	100%	98%	95%	90%	80%	70%	60%
	$1,050	$925	$700	$500	$300	$225	$150
8 in. barrel	#9281	1963 - 1963					

GRADING - PPGS™	100%	98%	95%	90%	80%	70%	60%

ISU OLYMPIC - .22 Short cal., similar to Model 102, grooved front and back straps, 6 3/4 in. barrel with integral muzzle brake, wts. avail., walnut checkered thumbrest grips standard, 5 1/2 in. barrel introduced 1964.

	$1,050	$900	$725	$500	$350	$225	$150

5 1/2 in. barrel w/accessories	#9295	1964 - 1965
6 3/4 in. tapered barrel with integral stabilizer - with accessories	#9299	1963 - 1966
6 3/4 in. tapered barrel with integral stabilizer - w/o accessories	#9237	1967 - 1977

Catalog and price lists refer to #9295 as both the Olympic and Olympic ISU. This model met ISU regulations and included a removable muzzlebrake and weights.

THE VICTOR (SLANT GRIP) - .22 LR cal., 10 shot mag. 4 1/2 in. or 5 1/2 in. slab sided barrels with either ventilated or solid ribs, adj. sights are integral with the rib, blue finish, barrel tapped for weight, checkered walnut thumb rest grips, grooved front and back straps on frame, trigger is adj. for both pull force and over travel, probably fewer that 700 of these slant grip Victors were mfg. in all configurations, and probably fewer than 40 each of the 4 1/2 in. guns. Most guns are in the ser. no. range above 2,401,XXX, with a few in the ML serial number series.

	$2,500	$2,000	$1,400	$850	$550	$250	$200

Add $75 for steel rib.
Add $200 for solid rib.
Add $300 for 4 1/2 in. barrel

4 1/2 in. slabbed barrel with ventilated steel rib	#9218	1973 - 1973
5 1/2 in. slabbed barrel with ventilated steel rib	#9219	1973 - 1973
4 1/2 in. slabbed barrel with solid aluminum rib	#9226	1974 - 1974
5 1/2 in. slabbed barrel with solid aluminum rib	#9229	1974 - 1974
4 1/2 in. slabbed barrel with ventilated aluminum rib	#9218	1973 - 1974
5 1/2 in. slabbed barrel with ventilated aluminum rib	#9219	1973 - 1974

Note the early vent. rib. barrels were steel, and the later ones were aluminum - w/o a change in the catalog numbers. Buyer beware - fakes exist.

CONVERSION KITS MODEL 102/103/104

	$500	$450	$400	$325	$275	$200	$150

Add $250 for Trophy Conversions.
Add $125 for 8 in. barrel.
Add $225 for 10 in. barrel.

Cat. # 9266 Olympic to Supermatic Citation, 6 3/4 Bbl.,
Cat. # 9264 Olympic to Supermatic Citation, 8 Bbl.,
Cat. # 9265 Olympic to Supermatic Citation, 10 Bbl.,
Cat. # 9283 Supermatic Citation to Olympic, 6 3/4 Bbl.,
Cat. # 9284 Supermatic Citation to Olympic, 8 Bbl.,
Cat. # 9285 Supermatic Citation to Olympic, 10 Bbl.,
Cat. # 9286 Supermatic Trophy to Olympic, 6 3/4 Bbl.,
Cat. # 9287 Supermatic Trophy to Olympic, 8 Bbl.,
Cat. # 9288 Supermatic Trophy to Olympic, 10 Bbl.

PISTOLS: SEMI-AUTO, 105 SERIES

Note: High Standard designed the Model 105 but did not produce it. The 105 Series was to have been a 104 Series gun with the bridge style sight that appeared on the 106 series.

PISTOLS: SEMI-AUTO, 106 SERIES, MILITARY MODELS

Referred to as military models, this series was designed to provide same grip angle and feel of the Colt Military Model 1911. This design was introduced in 1965, and continued through most of 1968. The design utilized the tooling of the 104 Series guns, which resulted in the occasional

GRADING - PPGS™	100%	98%	95%	90%	80%	70%	60%

appearance of a bullet shaped brass design in the rear grip strap when the spring hole was not properly plugged. This design appears as both a full bullet shape or only the outline. There is no premium for this feature. The magazines in this series have a red plastic bottom. The right side of the frame is marked "MODEL 106"/"MILITARY". During the production of this series, the accessories were deleted in lieu of a price increase. This resulted in two catalog numbers for each model. Guns with original boxes and papers can add significant premiums but, like the guns, the condition is very important as is the requirement that the box be numbered to the gun.

Add approx. 10% for original box with papers on the following models.

SUPERMATIC TOURNAMENT MILITARY - .22 LR cal., entry level target pistol, early guns had smooth front and back straps and no trigger stop, later models had stippled grip straps and a trigger stop, slide mounted rear sight instead of bridge sight, 5 1/2 in. bull or 6 3/4 in. tapered barrel with military grips.

	100%	98%	95%	90%	80%	70%	60%
	$625	$475	$375	$250	$200	$150	$125

Add $125 for guns with boxes and accessories if factory records verify model numbers.

5 1/2 in. bull barrel with accessories	#9230	1965 - 1966	1,484,801 - 1,602,XXX
6 3/4 in. fluted barrel with accessories	#9231	1965 - 1966	1,484,817 - 1,599,XXX
5 1/2 in. bull barrel w/o accessories	#9232	1966 - 1968	1,594,XXX - 1,93X,XXX
6 3/4 in. fluted barrel w/o accessories	#9233	1966 - 1968	1,598,XXX - 1,94X,XXX

SUPERMATIC CITATION MILITARY - .22 LR cal., 5 1/2 in. bull or 7 1/4 in. fluted barrel, mid-level target pistol, trigger stop, trigger pull adjustment, stippled front and back straps, new rear bridge type sight.

	$675	$575	$475	$375	$275	$200	$175

Add $150 for guns with boxes and accessories if factory records verify model numbers.

5 1/2 in. bull barrel with accessories	#9240	1965 - 1966	1,465,195 - 1,595,XXX
7.25" fluted barrel with accessories	#9241	1965 - 1966	1,467,353 - 1,595,XXX
5 1/2 in. bull barrel w/o accessories	#9242	1966 - 1968	1,595,XXX - 1,98X,XXX
7.25" fluted barrel w/o accessories	#9243	1966 - 1968	1,592,XXX - 1,98X,XXX

SUPERMATIC TROPHY MILITARY - .22 LR cal., 5 1/2 bull or 7 1/4 in. fluted barrel, top-of-the-line target pistol, trigger stop, trigger pull adjustment, stippled front and back straps, gold plated trigger, safety and magazine release, gold filled lettering, new rear bridge type sight.

	$975	$850	$650	$500	$375	$225	$175

Add $100 for high polish blue finish.

Add $200 premium for guns with boxes and accessories if factory records verify model numbers.

5 1/2 in. bull barrel with accessories	#9245	1965 - 1966	1,436,172 - 1,595,XXX
7.25" fluted barrel with accessories	#9246	1965 - 1966	1,436,170 - 1,595,XXX
5 1/2 in. bull barrel w/o accessories	#9247	1966 - 1968	1,595,XXX - 1,97X.XXX
7.25" fluted barrel w/oaccessories	#9248	1966 - 1968	1,595,XXX - 1,97X,XXX

OLYMPIC MILITARY - listed in catalog but not in shipping records.
Catalog number #9235 for 5 1/2 in. barrel.

OLYMPIC ISU MILITARY - .22 Short cal., target pistol, 6 3/4 in. tapered barrel with integral stabilizer, trigger stop, trigger pull adjustment, stippled front and back straps, rear bridge type sight, military grips, supplied with extra mag. and weights.

	$1,075	$850	$675	$475	$350	$250	$175

6 3/4 in. tapered barrel with integral stabilizer - with accessories	#9238	1965 - 1966	
6 3/4 in. tapered barrel with integral stabilizer - w/o accessories	#9236	1966 - 1968	1,511,284

PISTOLS: SEMI-AUTO, 107 SERIES

The 107 Series was the evolutionary successor to the 106 Series. This Series had the frame redesigned to eliminate the plugging of the spring hole produced with the old tooling. During the time of this series' production, the "MODEL 107" and the "MILITARY" marking on the frame was removed at about serial number 2,330,000. Then later the "MILITARY" marking reappeared at about serial number 2,4XX,XXX and remained until the end of the traditional serial number series.

GRADING - PPGS™	100%	98%	95%	90%	80%	70%	60%

The "MILITARY" marking is absent from the guns with the "ML" prefixed serial numbers. There is no premium associated with these variations. These marking changes were not a change in design series, but rather only a change in markings. The traditional serial number series ran until August of 1975. The serial numbers on guns produced beginning July 1975 utilized a new serial numbering system. The Military models utilized an "ML" prefix on the serial number. Early production utilized the red bottomed magazines. Later guns had magazines with blued steel bottoms. The 107 Series was produced from 1968 until Sept 1981. Production was at Hamden, CT from 1968 to 1976 (S/N ML23,065), and at East Hartford 1977 (S/N ML25,000) to 1981 (S/N ML 86,641).

The desirability factor for Hamden guns is higher than for East Hartford guns. Guns with original boxes and papers can add significant premiums, but like the guns, the condition is very important as is the requirement that the box be numbered to the gun.

Add approx. 10% for original box with papers on the following models.
Subtract about 7% for East Hartford mfg.

SPORT KING - .22 LR cal., similar to previous Sport Kings, except has military grips, labeled "SPORT KING-M." Mfg. in East Hartford only.

	$325	$250	$200	$175	$150	$125	$100
4 1/2 in. barrel	#9258	1978 - 1981	ML35,454 - ML86,493
6 3/4 in. barrel	#9259	1978 - 1981	ML35,453 - ML86,488
6 3/4 in. barrel (123 guns)	#9259	1980 - 1980	MLG20,224 - MLG20,408

SHARPSHOOTER - .22 LR cal., models with military grips were labeled "SHARP-SHOOTER-M." Mfg. in East Hartford only.

	$425	$365	$300	$250	$200	$150	$125
5 1/2 in. bull barrel	#9210	1977 - 1981	ML29,215 - ML86,641

✱ * *Sharpshooter Survival Pack* - introduced 1981, includes Sharpshooter-M pistol, electroless nickel, 5 1/2 in. bull barrel, push-button takedown, packaged in canvas carrying case with extra nickel magazine.

	$625	$550	$450	$350	$250	$200	$150

Subtract $100 for guns without the case.
Subtract $65 for guns without the extra magazine for guns in exc. condition.

5 1/2 in. bull barrel	#9424	1981 - 1981	ML 85,635 - ML86,044

SUPERMATIC TOURNAMENT MILITARY - .22 LR cal., similar to Model 106 Series, last of the Tournament pistols, adj. sight mounted on slide, smooth front and back straps on frame.

	$550	$475	$375	$300	$250	$150	$125
5 1/2 in. bull barrel	#9232	1968 - 1971
6 3/4 in. barrel	#9233	1968 - 1971

SUPERMATIC CITATION MILITARY - .22 LR cal., similar to Model 106 Series, 7 1/4 fluted and 5 1/2 in. bull barrel available, mid-level target pistol.

	$625	$525	$425	$325	$275	$225	$175
5 1/2 in. bull barrel	#9242	1968 - 1981
7.25" fluted barrel	#9243	1968 - 1981

SUPERMATIC TROPHY MILITARY - .22 LR cal., similar to Model 106 Series, top-of-the-line target pistol.

	$900	$750	$575	$450	$325	$250	$175
5 1/2 in. bull barrel	#9247	1968 - 1981
7.25" fluted barrel	#9248	1968 - 1981

1972 OLYMPIC COMMEMORATIVE - .22 LR cal., highly engraved version of a Supermatic Trophy Military Model 107, high polish blue finish, 5 1/2 in. bull barrel, has 5 Olympic gold rings on right side of receiver, ser. no. has a "T" prefix, came with a lined presentation case, early models were marked "MODEL 107", and were not high polished. C-R.

	$5,500	$4,500	$4,000

Last MSR was $605.

Values assume guns in original presentation cases.

5 1/2 in. bull barrel	#9207	1972 - 1975	T0,000,000 - T0,000,999

GRADING - PPGS™	100%	98%	95%	90%	80%	70%	60%

This model was a limited edition with 1,000 guns planned, but only 108 guns were listed in the shipping records, plus one frame manufactured due to their high price. A couple of prototypes are believed to exist in the regular serial number series. The original Issue price was $550. One fully engraved gun is known. Buyer beware - fakes may exist.

OLYMPIC ISU MILITARY - .22 Short cal., target pistol for Olympic Style Rapid Fire Events, 6 3/4 in. fluted barrel with integral stabilizer and two detachable weights.

	$1,050	$875	$675	$575	$475	$325	$250
6 3/4 in. barrel	#9238	1968 - 1977					

1980 OLYMPIC COMMEMORATIVE - engraved, right side of slide has the five gold ring Olympic logo, "USA" prefix on serial numbers from 0001 to 1000, lined presentation case, a limited edition of the Model 107 Olympic ISU with 1000 being produced. C-R.

	$1,350	$1,000	$875

Values assume complete guns with box, papers, and presentation case - subtract $250 for guns in exc. condition.

6 3/4 in. barrel	#9239	1980 - 1980	USA 0001 - USA 1000

THE VICTOR - .22 LR cal., 4 1/2 or 5 1/2 in. slab sided barrels with either ventilated or solid ribs, 10 shot mag., adjustable sights are integral with the rib, blue finish, barrel tapped for weight, checkered walnut thumb rest grips, stippled front and back straps on frame, earliest ventilated steel ribs (1971) were smooth on top, later steel ventilated ribs were grooved, aluminum replaced the steel on later ventilated ribs, still later a clearance groove was added for spent shell ejection behind the barrel, solid aluminum ribs introduced 1973, early models marked "THE VICTOR" on the left side of the barrel, later guns marked simply "VICTOR" on the left side of the frame, a few transition guns are marked in both locations, early wts. are rectangular with round bottoms, later weights were flat bottomed with three grooves.

	$725	$575	$525	$400	$300	$200	$150

Add $150 for smooth topped vent. steel rib from first year of production.
Add $125 for steel ribs.
Add $150 for solid rib guns.
Add $100 for 4 1/2 in. barrel.
Add $140 for Hamden guns (7digit serial numbers and ML prefix serial numbers below ML 23,066).

4 1/2 in. slabbed barrel with ventilated steel rib	#9216	1971 - 1973
5 1/2 in. slabbed barrel with ventilated steel rib	#9217	1971 - 1973
4 1/2 in. slabbed barrel with solid aluminum rib	#9206	1973 - 1977
5 1/2 in. slabbed barrel with solid aluminum rib	#9211	1973 - 1977
4 1/2 in. slabbed barrel with ventilated aluminum rib	#9216	1973 - 1979
5 1/2 in. slabbed barrel with ventilated aluminum rib	#9217	1973 - 1981

10X - .22 LR cal., 5 1/2 in. bull barrel, push-button takedown. Specifically designed for top flight shooting, hand-picked parts and precisely assembled by one of only five High Standard Master Gunsmiths (with his initials under the left grip of each gun), black matte finish, black painted checkered walnut grips, stippled front and back straps. Mfg. in East Hartford.

	$2,660	$2,150	$1,850	$1,275	$950	$725	$575

Values are for guns with box and papers including test target - subtract $150 if missing.

5 1/2 in. bull barrel	#9372	1980 - 1981	ML71,116 - ML86,123

GRADING - PPGS™	100%	98%	95%	90%	80%	70%	60%

PISTOLS: SEMI-AUTO, CONVERSION KITS

These kits for the conversion of .22 LR cal. to .22 Short cal. contained an aluminum slide, the barrel and accessory listed below, and two Short mags., and comes in "gun size box" set in styrofoam. Manufactured in E. Hartford 1979-1982

VICTOR KIT - includes 5 1/2 in. barrel with aluminum vent rib and barrel weight, designated #9370 when mfg.

$550	$450	$350

TROPHY/CITATION KIT - includes 5 1/2 in. bull barrel and a stabilizer, designated #9371 when mfg.

$550	$450	$350

PISTOLS: SEMI-AUTO, SH SERIES

This was the final series of High Standard pistols and can be differentiated from the 107 Series by the new barrel release in place of the push button takedown. An allen head screw attached the frame to the barrel. This was a cost reduction design change. Shipped from late May 1981-August 1984. Serial No. range was SH10,001-SH34,034. Near the end of production, a "V" suffix was added to some visually impaired guns which were sold at discount. These guns were guaranteed to function properly, but the company would not allow them to be returned for appearance reasons. A few guns were made in this Series with an "SH" prefix serial number with the Model 107 pushbutton takedown. Serial number ranges are best estimates, and may change with further research.

Add approx. 10% for original box with papers on the following models.

SPORT KING - .22 LR cal., similar to ML series, except has allen screw takedown, 4 1/2 or 6 3/4 in. barrel, electroless nickel finish also available, also called the "SPORT KING-M."

$275	$235	$215	$185	$150	$125	$100

Add 15% for the electroless nickel guns.
Values are for the blued guns.

4 1/2 in. barrel blued	#9258	1981 - 1984	SH10,889 - SH33,964
6 3/4 in. barrel blued	#9259	1981 - 1983	SH10,001 - SH28,232
4 1/2 in. barrel electroless nickel	#9450	1983 - 1983	SH27,003 - SH31,436
6 3/4 in. barrel electroless nickel	#9451	1983 - 1983	SH27,004 - SH31,054

SHARPSHOOTER - .22 LR cal., "SH" prefix serial no. with allen screw takedown, military grips, electroless nickel version utilized in some survival kits.

$350	$285	$240	$200	$175	$150	$125

This model was also sometimes called "SHARPSHOOTER-M."

5 1/2 in. bull barrel	#9210	1981 - 1982	SH10,8XX - SH25,074

SUPERMATIC CITATION MILITARY - .22 LR cal., similar to previous Citation model, except with allen screw takedown and military grips.

$500	$435	$350	$275	$225	$175	$150

5 1/2 in. bull barrel	#9242	1981 - 1982	SH10,550 - SH25,166
7.25" fluted barrel	#9243	1981 - 1982	SH10,513 - SH25,167

CITATION II - .22 LR cal., 10 shot, new variation of the Supermatic Citation, 5 1/2 or 7 1/4 in. slab sided barrel, checkered military-type wood grips, allen screw takedown, SH prefix serial no., slab sided barrel, rear sight mounted on slide, electroless nickel model also available in the survival pack, this model replaced the Sharpshooter and the Supermatic Citation.

$450	$375	$325	$275	$225	$175	$150

5 1/2 in. slab sided barrel	#9348	1982 - 1984	SH25,326 - SH31,495
7.25" slab sided barrel	#9349	1982 - 1984	SH25,575 - SH31,496

GRADING - PPGS™	100%	98%	95%	90%	80%	70%	60%

SUPERMATIC TROPHY MILITARY - .22 LR cal., similar to previous Trophy Model with "SH" prefix, except has allen screw takedown, military grips.

	$550	$475	$375	$300	$250	$200	$150

5 1/2 in. bull barrel	#9247	1981 - 1984	SH10,865 - SH32,630
7.25" fluted barrel	#9248	1981 - 1984	SH10,492 - SH33,828

VICTOR - .22 LR cal., similar to previous Victor, new allen screw takedown, "SH" prefix, military grips, 5 1/2 in. vent. barrel only mfg. in this Victor Series, some Victor ser. numbers had a "V" suffix.

	$525	$450	$350	$275	$225	$175	$150

5 1/2 in. slabbed barrel with vent. aluminum rib	9217	1984 - 1984	SH10,321 - SH34,034

10X - .22 LR cal., top-of-the-line model similar to previous 10X, but with allen screw takedown, also available with 7 1/4 in. fluted barrel and a 5 1/2 in. ribbed barrel like a Victor.

	$2,100	$1,750	$1,425	$1,000	$775	$675	$575

Add $1000-$900 for ribbed barrel model.
Add $500-$600 for fluted barrel.
Values are for guns with box and papers including test target - subtract $150 if missing.

5 1/2 in. bull barrel	#9372	1981 - 1983	SH10,200 - SH29,640
7.25" fluted barrel	#9249	1983 - 1983	SH27,536 - SH29,641
5 1/2 in. Slabbed barrel w/vent. rib	#9434	1983 - 1983	SH26,657 - SH29,601

SURVIVAL PACK - .22 LR cal., Sharpshooter "M" or Citation II electroless nickel, allen screw takedown, packaged in canvas carrying case with extra nickel magazine (two different fabrics utilized during production).

	$500	$450	$375	$300	$250	$200	$175

Subtract $100 for guns without the case and $65 for guns without the extra magazine for guns in exc. condition.

Sharpshooter version	#9424	1981 - 1982	SH10,048 - SH25,XXX
Citation II version	#9424	1982 - 1984	SH25,XXX - SH31,312

REVOLVERS: POLICE STYLE

The Sentinel revolvers begin with the R-100 design series, and continue through the R-109 design series. Later steel framed Sentinels carry no design series markings. A change of design series designation indicates design changes to the guns. The only R-105 known to date is a private labeled gun made for Sears. The design series designations and the associated catalog numbers which follow are best estimates, and may require further research. Earliest Sentinels in 1955 were in a separate serial number series from 1 through approximately 45,000. Then they were included in a serial number series common to all handguns. In 1974, they were again put in a separate serial number series with a prefix - S101 through S79946. Many of the later guns had a "V" suffix which indicates it was visually impaired, but guaranteed to work properly.

High Standard private labeled the aluminum framed Sentinels for both Sears and Western Auto. A few were also provided to Col. Rex Applegate for his ARMAMEX company in Mexico.

Add 20% for extra convertible cylinder (.22 LR/.22 Mag.) on those models listed that apply.

SENTINEL - .22 S, L, or LR cal., aluminum frame, nine shot, SA or DA, swing out cylinder, 2 3/8, 3, 4, 5, or 6 in. barrel, fixed sights, return spring on ejector beginning with R-102 Series, until 1960 the 2 3/8 in. barrel model had a bobbed hammer, beginning in 1961 this changed to a standard spur hammer with no change in Cat. No.

✳ *Blue finish*

	$180	$155	$115	$95	$85	$70	$55

✳ *Nickel finish*

	$200	$175	$130	$105	$95	$85	$65

Subtract $15 for early models without spring return ejector.

R-100, R-101, R-102 Series 3 in. bbl., brown sq. butt, plastic grips, blue, #9127, mfg. 1955-1960.
R-100, R-101, R-102 Series 3 in. bbl., brown sq. butt, plastic grips, nickel #9136, mfg. 1956-1960.
R-100 Series 5 in. bbl., brown sq. butt, plastic grips, blue, #9128, mfg. 1955 only.

GRADING - PPGS™	100%	98%	95%	90%	80%	70%	60%

R-100, R-101, R-102 Series 6 in. bbl.
Brown sq. butt, plastic grips, blue,   #9128   mfg. 1956-1964.
White sq. butt, plastic grips, nickel   #9137   mfg. 1956-1964.
R-102, R-103 Series 4 in. bbl.
Brown sq. butt, plastic grips, blue   #9159   mfg. 1957-1964.
White sq. butt, plastic grips, nickel   #9160   mfg. 1957-1964.
R-102, R-103 Series 2 3/8 in. bbl, faux ivory round butt, plastic grips
Blue   #9144   mfg. 1957-1966.
Nickel   #9145   mfg. 1957-1966.

✳ *Sentinel w/Dura-Tone colors* - 2 3/8 in. barrel, offered in three different color anodized frames, featured nickel plated cylinders, triggers, and hammers, round butt ivory colored plastic grips, mahogany finished case.

Add $40 for R-102 models.

✳ *Turquoise finish*

	$500	$400	$300	$220	$170	$140	$110

✳ *Pink finish*

	$500	$400	$300	$220	$170	$140	$110

✳ *Gold finish*

	$475	$375	$295	$210	$170	$140	$110

R-101, R-102 Series   #9161   mfg. 1957-1962   710,397 - 1,221,102
R-101, R-102 Series   #9162   mfg. 1957-1962   710,463 - 1,221,101
R-101, R-102 Series   #9163   mfg. 1957-1962   710,393 - 1,160,442

SENTINEL IMPERIAL - similar to Sentinel, except has adj. sights, two piece walnut grips, mfg. 1962-64.

✳ *Blue finish*

	$210	$190	$170	$125	$110	$95	$85

✳ *Nickel finish*

	$220	$200	$180	$135	$110	$100	$90

R-104 Series 4 in. bbl., blue   #9187   mfg. 1962-1964.
R-104 Series 6 in. bbl., blue   #9188   mfg. 1962-1964.
R-104 Series 4 in. bbl., nickel   #9191   mfg. 1962-1964.
R-104 Series 6 in. bbl., nickel   #9192   mfg. 1962-1964.

SENTINEL DELUXE - similar to Sentinel, except has two piece walnut square butt grips and fixed sights, wide trigger, 24 or 26 oz.

✳ *Blue finish*

	$200	$175	$160	$115	$95	$85	$75

✳ *Nickel finish*

	$220	$195	$160	$115	$100	$90	$80

R-106, R-107 Series 4 in. bbl., blue   #9146   mfg. 1965-69, 1972-73.
R-106, R-107 Series 4 in. bbl., nickel   #9148   mfg. 1965-1973.
R-106, R-107 Series 6 in. bbl., blue   #9147   mfg. 1965-69, 1972-73.
R-106, R-107 Series 6 in. bbl., nickel   #9149   mfg. 1965-1973.

SENTINEL SNUB - similar to Sentinel Deluxe, except has checkered bird's-head grip, blue or nickel finish, 2 3/8 in. barrel, 20 oz.

✳ *Blue finish*

	$200	$165	$140	$110	$100	$90	$80

✳ *Nickel finish*

	$220	$175	$150	$120	$110	$95	$85

R-108 Series, brown round butt, plastic grip
Blue   #9344   mfg. 1967-69, 1972-73.
Nickel   #9345   mfg. 1967-69, 1972-73.

KIT GUN - 22 LR cal., swing out cylinder, 9 shot, 4 in. barrel, adj. sights, blue finish, aluminum frame, round butt walnut grips.

	$215	$170	$140	$120	$110	$100	$90

R-109 Series   #9304   mfg. 1971-1973.

GRADING - PPGS™	100%	98%	95%	90%	80%	70%	60%

CAMP GUN - 22 LR or .22 Mag. cal., 6 in. barrel, blue, adj. rear sight, checkered walnut grips, also available as a combination with both cylinders.

	100%	98%	95%	90%	80%	70%	60%
	$220	$195	$175	$155	$120	$110	$100

Add $50 for combination with both cylinders.

R-109 Series, .22 S/L/LR	#9342	mfg. 1976-77.
R-109 Series, .22 Mag.	#9343	mfg. 1976-77.
R-109 Series, Combination	#9393	mfg. 1977-1984.

SENTINEL MARK I - .22 S, L, or LR cal., SA or DA, swing out cylinder, 2, 3, or 4 in. barrel, steel frame, fixed sights, blue or nickel finish, adj. sights on 3 or 4 in. barrel, smooth wood, square butt grips.

* *Blue finish*

	100%	98%	95%	90%	80%	70%	60%
	$225	$200	$175	$155	$120	$105	$95

* *Nickel finish*

	100%	98%	95%	90%	80%	70%	60%
	$250	$225	$200	$155	$130	$110	$100

$25 premium for adj. sights.

2 in. bbl., fixed sights, blue	#9350	mfg. 1974-77.
2 in. bbl., fixed sights ,nickel	#9351	mfg. 1974-77.
3 in. bbl., fixed sights, blue	#9352	mfg. 1974 only.
3 in. bbl., fixed sights, nickel	#9354	mfg. 1974 only.
3 in. bbl., adj. sights, blue	#9353	mfg. 1974 only.
3 in. bbl., adj. sights, nickel	#9355	mfg. 1974 only.
4 in. bbl., fixed sights, blue	#9356	mfg. 1974-77.
4 in. bbl., fixed sights, nickel	#9358	mfg. 1974-77.
4 in. bbl., adj. sights, blue	#9357	mfg. 1974-77.
4 in. bbl., adj. sights, nickel	#9359	mfg. 1974-77.

SENTINEL MARK IV - similar to Sentinel Mark I, except .22 Mag. cal.

* *Blue finish*

	100%	98%	95%	90%	80%	70%	60%
	$235	$215	$190	$165	$130	$110	$100

* *Nickel finish*

	100%	98%	95%	90%	80%	70%	60%
	$255	$225	$205	$185	$150	$130	$110

Add $25 for adj. sights.

2 in. bbl., fixed sights, blue	#9360	mfg. 1974-77.
2 in. bbl., fixed sights, nickel	#9361	mfg. 1974-77.
3 in. bbl., fixed sights, blue	#9362	mfg. 1974-77.
3 in. bbl., fixed sights, nickel	#9363	mfg. 1974-77.
3 in. bbl., adj. sights, blue	#9364	mfg. 1974-77.
3 in. bbl., adj. sights, nickel	#9365	mfg. 1974-77.
4 in. bbl., fixed sights, blue	#9366	mfg. 1974-77.
4 in. bbl., fixed sights, nickel	#9367	mfg. 1974-77.
4 in. bbl., adj. sights, blue	#9368	mfg. 1974-77.
4 in. bbl., adj. sights, nickel	#9369	mfg. 1974-77.

POWER PLUS - .38 Spl. cal., 5 shot, SA or DA, swing out cylinder, blue finish, steel frame, serial numbers between PG 1010 and PG1273, only 177 mfg. 1983-84.

	100%	98%	95%	90%	80%	70%	60%
	$550	$500	$425	$360	$250	$200	$150

Catalog number 9438.

SENTINEL - similar to Mark I Sentinel, except without the Mark I markings, steel frame, blue finish, offered as a combination with cylinders for .22 LR and .22 Mag.

	100%	98%	95%	90%	80%	70%	60%
	$260	$245	$235	$215	$205	$195	$185

Add $25 for adj. sights.

Subtract $50 for guns with only one cylinder.

Values are for guns with both cylinders.

2 in. bbl., fixed sights	#9390	mfg. 1978-1984.
4 in. bbl., adj. sights	#9392	mfg. 1978-1984.

GRADING - PPGS™	100%	98%	95%	90%	80%	70%	60%

SENTINEL MARK II - .357 Mag. cal., SA or DA, 6 shot, swing out cylinder, blue finish, steel frame, fixed sights, produced by Dan Wesson for High Standard from 1974-75.

	$265	$230	$195	$180	$150	$140	$130

Serial numbers had an "H" prefix H10001 to H35100. A few preproduction guns were sold to employees (H1 to about H28).

2 1/2 in. bbl., #9401, 4 in. bbl., #9402.
6 in. bbl., #9403.

SENTINEL MARK III - similar to Mark II, except adj. sights, mfg. by Dan Wesson.

	$300	$260	$230	$200	$165	$150	$140

2 1/2 in. and 6 in. bbl.   #9407
4 in. bbl.   #9408
6 in. bbl.   #9409

CRUSADER - planned production only in .357 Mag., .44 Mag. or .45 Colt cal., swing-out cylinder, unique geared action, adj. sights.

.357 Mag., 4 1/4 in. barrel, catalog   #9458   advertised 1979-1980.
.357 Mag., 6 1/2 in. barrel, catalog   #9459   advertised 1979-1980.
.44 Mag., 4 1/4 in. barrel, catalog   #9452   advertised 1979-1980.
.44 Mag., 6 1/2 in. barrel, catalog   #9453   advertised 1979-1980.
.44 Mag., 8 3/4 in. barrel, catalog   #9454   advertised 1979-1980.
.45 Colt, 4 1/4 in. barrel, catalog   #9455   advertised 1979-1980.
.45 Colt, 6 1/2 in. barrel, catalog   #9456   advertised 1979-1980.
.45 Colt, 8 3/4 in. barrel, catalog   #9457   advertised 1979-1980.

Only a few prototypes with "EX" prefix serial numbers of this model exist, and pre-production Crusaders with serial numbers C1001 and C1002 exist.

CRUSADER 50TH ANNIVERSARY - .44 Mag. or .45 LC cal., 51 mfg. for each cal. in 8 3/8 in. barrel with 1/3 coverage engraving (ser. no. 0-50), double action employing gear assembly, blue with a gold crusader figure on the side plate, and an anniversary rollmark to commemorate High Standard's 50th anniversary, cased.

* *Standard Model w/o engraving*

	$725	$600	$500

* *8 3/8 in. barrel*

	$1,350	$1,100	$950

Add 25% for single digit serial number.

Limited availability might affect asking prices considerably. Two gun sets with matching serial numbers were also available - current asking prices are over $3,250.

Advertising materials at the time listed 450 revolvers of each cal. in a 6 1/2 in. barrel (ser. no. 51-500). Serial numbers for the 8 3/4 in. barrels are 44M0 through 44M50 (shipped 1979 through 1981) and 45C0 through 45C50 (shipped in 1981). Serial numbers 44M51 through 44M500 (approx 425 guns shipped 1978 through 1983). Serial numbers 45C51 through 45C487 (approx 339 guns shipped 1981 through 1983).

.44 Mag., 8 3/4 in. bbl.,
first 51 of 501 commemoratives   #9601   mfg. 1979-981.
.44 Mag., 6 1/2 in. bbl.,
balance of 501 commemoratives   #9603   mfg. 1978-983.
.45 Colt, 8 3/4 in. bbl.,
first 51 of 501 commemoratives   #9600   mfg. 1981 only.
.45 Colt, 6 1/2 in. bbl.,
balance of 501 commemoratives   #9602   mfg. 1981-1983.

REVOLVERS: WESTERN STYLE

The Western style revolvers begin with the W-100 design series and continue through the W-106 design series. The changes of design series designations indicate design changes to the guns. The design series designations and the associated catalog numbers which follow are best estimates. Early western revolvers were in the serial number series common to all handguns. In 1972, they were put in a separate serial number series with an "M" prefix – M 1001 through M90916. Many of the later guns had a "V" suffix which indicated the gun signified visually impaired but guaranteed to work properly. High Standard private labeled the aluminum frame Western style revolvers for both Sears and Western Auto.

GRADING - PPGS™	100%	98%	95%	90%	80%	70%	60%

DURANGO - .22 S, L, or LR cal., single/double action, 9 shot, blue or nickel finish, aluminum or steel frame, 4 1/2 or 5 1/2 in. barrel, fixed or adj. sights, square butt walnut grips, two models have their grip straps and trigger guard nickel plated.

✹ *Blue finish*

	100%	98%	95%	90%	80%	70%	60%
	$200	$175	$155	$120	$85	$70	$55

✹ *Nickel finish*

	100%	98%	95%	90%	80%	70%	60%
	$220	$195	$175	$130	$95	$85	$65

    Add $25 for steel frame.

    Add $25 for adj. sights.

    Values assume aluminum frames.

W-105 Series, aluminum frame
4 1/2 in. bbl., blue with brass trim   #9302   mfg. 1970-73.

W-105 Series, aluminum frame
5 1/2 in. bbl., blue   #9307   mfg. 1971-73.

W-105 Series, aluminum frame
5 1/2 in. bbl., nickel   #9308   mfg. 1971-73.

W-106 Series, steel frame
5 1/2 in. bbl., blue with nickel trim,   #9316   mfg. 1974 only.

W-106 Series, steel frame
5 1/2 in. bbl., nickel   #9317   mfg. 1974 only.

W-106 Series, steel frame
5 1/2 in. bbl., adj. sights, blue/nickel   #9318   mfg. 1974 only.

HOMBRE - similar to Double Nine aluminum frame, but no ejector rod housing, 4 1/2 in. barrel, fixed sights and square butt walnut grips.

✹ *Blue finish*

	100%	98%	95%	90%	80%	70%	60%
	$200	$175	$155	$120	$85	$70	$65

✹ *Nickel finish*

	100%	98%	95%	90%	80%	70%	60%
	$220	$195	$175	$130	$95	$85	$65

W-105 Series, blue   #9300   mfg. 1970-1972.
W-105 Series, nickel   #9301   mfg. 1970-1972.

LONGHORN - .22 LR or .22 Mag. cal., DA, 4 1/2, 5 1/2, or 9 1/2 in. barrel, 9 shot, swing out cylinder, fixed sights except for one model.

✹ *1958-1970 Mfg.* - .22 S, L, or LR cal., SA or DA, aluminum frame guns, blue finish, fixed sights, square butt grips, one model has grip straps and trigger guard with gold plating contrasting with the blue frame.

	100%	98%	95%	90%	80%	70%	60%
	$250	$230	$195	$170	$125	$90	$80

These guns are found in the W-100, W-101, W-102, W-103, and W-104 design series.

ALUMINUM FRAME:
4 1/2 in. bbl., faux ivory plastic grips   #9175   mfg. 1961 only.
5 1/2 in. bbl., faux ivory plastic grips   #9176   mfg. 1961 only.
9 1/2 in. bbl., ivory colored plastic grips   #9177   mfg. 1961 only.
4 1/2 in. bbl., pearl style plastic grips   #9178   mfg. 1961-65.
5 1/2 in. bbl., stag style plastic grips   #9179   mfg. 1961-65.
9 1/2 in. bbl., walnut grips   #9180   mfg. 1961-65.
Sears version   #9184
9 1/2 in. bbl., walnut grips,
gold colored trim   #9199   mfg. 1966 only.
9 1/2 in. bbl., walnut grips   #9399   mfg. 1967-1970.

✹ *1971-1984 Mfg.* - .22 S, L, LR, or .22 Mag. cal., steel frame, or a combination with both cylinders.

	100%	98%	95%	90%	80%	70%	60%
	$315	$270	$245	$200	$140	$105	$90

    Add $45 for combination models.

    Add $25 for adj. sights

W-106 SERIES
9 1/2 in. bbl., .22 S/L/LR   #9397   mfg. 1984 only.
9 1/2 in. bbl., .22 Mag.   #9327   mfg. 1971-74.
9 1/2 in. bbl., combination   #9326   mfg. 1971-76.
9 1/2 in. bbl., combination, adj. sights   #9328,   mfg. 1976-1984.

GRADING - PPGS™	100%	98%	95%	90%	80%	70%	60%

DOUBLE NINE

✳ *1958-1970 Mfg* - .22 S, L, or LR cal., SA or DA, aluminum frame, one model has grip straps and trigger guard with gold plating contrasting with the blue frame.

>**Blue finish**

	$200	$175	$155	$120	$100	$80	$70

>**Nickel finish**

	$245	$205	$180	$135	$95	$80	$70

These guns are found in the W-100, W-101, W-102, W-103, and W-104 design series. Catalog Nos.

Blue with faux ivory plastic grip	#9169	mfg. 1958-1965.
Nickel with black plastic grips	#9170	mfg. 1958-1970.
Sears version, Blue, "Ranger"	#9171.	
Sears version, Nickel, "Ranger"	#9174	
Blue/gold colored trim, stag style grips	#9129,	mfg. 1966 only.
Blue, stag style grips	#9329	mfg. 1967-1970.

✳ *1971-1984 Mfg.* - steel frame, walnut grips.

>**Blue finish**

	$260	$230	$205	$165	$130	$100	$90

>**Nickel finish**

	$280	$235	$210	$165	$135	$100	$90

Add $45 for combination models.

W-106 Series, blue, combination	#9320	mfg. 1971-79.
W-106 Series, blue, .22 Mag.	#9321	mfg. 1971-73.
W-106 Series, nickel, combination	#9322	mfg. 1971-73.
W-106 Series, nickel, .22 Mag.	#9323	mfg. 1971-76.
W-106 Series, blue, combination, adj. sights	#9324	mfg. 1971-1984.
W-106 Series, blue, .22 Mag., adj. sights	#9325	mfg. 1971-73.

THE GUN/HIGH SIERRA - .22 S, L, LR cal., single/double action, 9 shot, available as a combination model with a second cylinder in .22 Mag., blue finish with gold plated grip straps and trigger guard, steel frame, 7 in. octagon barrel, fixed or adj. sights and square butt walnut grips, gold plated grip frame.

	$315	$270	$245	$200	$150	$120	$100

Add $40 for presentation case.

Add $45 for combination models.

Add $25 for adj. sights.

This gun was introduced as "The Gun" in the February 1973 price list and the name changed to "High Sierra" by the November 1973 price list. Note that the early production had neither "High Sierra" markings nor any other name. The name High Sierra was the result of a "name the gun" contest after the gun was introduced.

.22 S, L, LR, in a case	#9313	mfg. 1973-74.
Combination, in a case	#9314	mfg. 1973-74.
Combination, in a case, adj. sights	#9315	mfg. 1973-74.
Combination, without a case	#9374	mfg. 1975 only.
Combination, without a case, adj. sights	#9375	mfg. 1975-1984.
.22 S, L, LR, without a case	#9379	mfg. 1984 only.

POSSE - similar to Double Nine aluminum, except has 3 1/2 in. barrel, blue, brass grip frame, fixed sights, walnut grips.

	$200	$175	$155	$120	$90	$80	$70

W-104 and W-105 Series	#9181	mfg. 1961-1965.
Sears version	#9183	

NATCHEZ - .22 S, L, LR cal., SA or DA, 9 shot, blue finish, aluminum frame, 5 1/2 in. barrel, fixed sights, square butt stag style plastic grips.

	$300	$250	$215	$185	$135	$100	$80

W-104 and W-105 Series	#9182	mfg. 1961-1965.
Sears version	#9186	

GRADING - PPGS™	100%	98%	95%	90%	80%	70%	60%

MARSHAL - .22 S, L, LR cal., SA or DA, 9 shot, blue finish, aluminum frame, fixed sights, 5.5 in. long barrel, square butt stag style plastic grips.

	$200	$175	$150	$120	$110	$90	$80

Values are for gun alone. Add $40 if box, papers and accessories are present and in excellent condition.

Catalog number 9330, mfg. 1971-73.

Offered in a special promotion package with a holster, trigger lock, and spray can of G-96 gun scrubber.

RIFLES/CARBINES

SPORT KING FIELD SEMI-AUTO RIFLE - .22 S, L, or LR cal., 22 1/4 in. barrel, walnut stock, open sights, 15, 17, or 21 shot tube mag.

	$165	$145	$120	$90	$70	$60	$50

A-100, A-103. Catalog number   #8000   mfg. 1960-1965.

SPORT KING SPECIAL - similar to Field Model, except has beavertail forearm and Monte Carlo stock.

	$185	$165	$145	$125	$100	$80	$60

A-100, A-103. Catalog number   #8001   mfg. 1960-1965.

SPORT KING SEMI-AUTO CARBINE - .22 S, L, or LR cal., 18 1/4 in. barrel, straight grip walnut stock with barrel band and sling, open sights, 12, 14, or 17 shot tube mag.

	$195	$175	$155	$140	$110	$80	$60

A-101, A-102. Catalog number   #8002   mfg. 1962-1971.

SPORT KING DELUXE / SPORT KING SEMI-AUTO RIFLE - revised nomenclature for the Sport King Special, catalog number 6005 is also the same gun but called Sport King, a special promotional package (catalog number 8007) was offered which included the Sport King rifle, a zippered gun case, a plastic trigger lock, and G-96 gun lubricant.

	$215	$180	$160	$140	$110	$80	$60

Add 10% for complete 8007 package in original box.

A-1041 Sport King Deluxe Catalog number #8005   mfg. 1966-1971.
Sport King Catalog number   #8007   mfg. 1971 only.
Sport King Catalog number   #6005   mfg. 1973-1976.

HI-POWER FIELD CENTERFIRE BOLT ACTION - .270 Win. or .30-06 cal., Mauser type action, 4 shot mag., 22 in. barrel, folding rear sight, plain stock.

	$350	$325	$295	$250	$225	$175	$150

H-100   .30-06 Catalog number   #8507   mfg. 1962-1965
H-100   .270 Catalog number   #8509   mfg. 1962-1965

HI-POWER DELUXE - similar to Field, except has checkered Monte Carlo stock and sling swivels.

	$400	$375	$350	$320	$275	$225	$175

H-100   .30-06 Catalog number   #8506   mfg. 1962-1965.
H-100   .270 Catalog number   #8508   mfg. 1962-1965.
H-100   .308 Catalog number   #8511   mfg. 1965-1965.
H-100   .243 Catalog number   #8513   mfg. 1965-1965.

SPORT KING/FLITE KING SLIDE ACTION RIFLE - .22 S, L, or LR cal., 24 in. barrel, tube mag., hammerless, Patridge sight, Monte Carlo stock with pistol grip, semi beavertail forearm.

	$175	$150	$120	$100	$80	$65	$50

P-100   Sport King Catalog number   #8004   mfg. 1963-1965.
P-1011 Sport King Catalog number   #8006   mfg. 1966-1971.
Flite King Catalog number   #6006   mfg. 1973-1976.

GRADING - PPGS™	100%	98%	95%	90%	80%	70%	60%

SHOTGUNS: BOLT ACTION

MODEL 514 - some of the Sears versions of this shotgun were recalled for safety considerations in the late 1990s.

	$135	$120	$90	$70	$60	$50	$40

CATALOG NUMBERS

	Series	Barrel	Full Choke	Adj Choke	Single shot	Full Choke	Date Range
12 Ga	514	Plain	8370	8373	8376		Unknown
16 GA	514	Plain	8371	8374	8377		Unknown
20 Ga	514	Plain	8372	8375	8378		Unknown

The catalog numbers shown are from a parts book which does not provide production dates.

SHOTGUNS: SEMI-AUTO

High Standard began making shotguns for Sears Roebuck in the late 1940s. In 1960, High Standard began marketing shotguns under their own name and the approximately 200 models in the following listing is derived from the High Standard catalogs and price lists of that time. A redesign of the shotgun line occurred with new models introduced in 1966. In 1973, High Standard introduced their new "Trophy Line" of shotguns and this marked a change in catalog numbers from the number beginning with the numeral 8 to the number beginning with the numeral 6. At this time the previous catalog numbers were referred to as the "Regular Line". Some regular line guns were cataloged in 1973, but this was the last year for them except the Police models. The 12 gauge pumps in the Trophy line were the guns which had interchangeable barrels. Serial numbers began appearing on the High Standard shotguns during mid to late 1967. Beginning about 1958, many of the shotguns had a two letter date code.

Additionally, there are over 150 catalog numbers for both semi-auto and slide action shotguns not listed here which represent models with High Standard markings but with special roll marking or other features which High Standard produced for several large distributors. Many of these distributor specials had their own model names which included Point Right, Pointer, Birdwing, NATO Pintail, Model 200 (J.C. Penney 20 ga. semi-auto), and Sport Deluxe. These distributor label guns are not listed in the following data.

The choke markings used by High Standard are: * Full, ** Modified, *** Improved Cylinder, and **** Skeet Bore. Cylinder Bore has no mark.

SUPERMATIC FIELD - 12 or 20 ga., 2 3/4 (12 ga.) or 3 (20 ga.) chambers, 28 or 30 in. barrel, full or modified choke, improved cylinder, gas operated, blue finish, plain pistol grip walnut stock and forearm, 4 shot mag. capacity.

	$225	$210	$185	$170	$150	$140	$120

Add 5% for 20 gauge.

Supermatic Field models were superceded by models in the Supermatic Deluxe group beginning in 1966.

SUPERMATIC FIELD CATALOG NUMBERS

	Series	Barrel	30 in.Full	28 in. Modified	26 in.Imp. Cyl.	27 in. Adj.	Date Range
12 ga.	C-100	Plain	8203	8200	8201	8202	1960-1965
20 ga.	C-200	Plain	8270	8271	8273		1963-1965

SUPERMATIC SPECIAL - 12 or 20 ga., similar to the Supermatic Field except has 27 in. barrel with 6 position click stop adjustable choke, 2 3/4 (12 ga.) or 3 in. (20 ga.) chambers.

	$225	$205	$190	$175	$150	$140	$120

Supermatic Special models were superceded by models in the Supermatic Deluxe group beginning in 1966.

C-100 catalog	#8250	mfg. 1961-65.
C-200 catalog	#8272	mfg. 1963-65.

SUPERMATIC DELUXE - 12 or 20 ga., 2 3/4 (12 ga.) or 3 (20 ga.) in. chambers, gas operated, blue finish, 26, 27, 28, or 30 in. barrel, checkered pistol grip, walnut stock

GRADING - PPGS™	100%	98%	95%	90%	80%	70%	60%

and forearm, 4 shot mag., recoil pad (new 1966).

	$265	$240	$205	$175	$150	$140	$130

Add $20 for vent rib versions.

SUPERMATIC DELUXE CATALOG NUMBERS

12 Ga	Series	Barrel	30" Full	28" Full	28" Modified	26" Imp Cyl	27" adj.	Date Range
	C-100	Plain	8213	8210	8211	8212		1960-1965
	C-100	Vent Rib	8214	8215	8216			1960-1965
	C-1200	Plain	8207	8204	8205	8206	8251	1966-1972
	C-1200	Vent Rib	8224	8225	8226	8227		1966-1973
	Late	Plain	6207	6205				1973-1975
	Late	Vent Rib	6224	6225	6226	6232		1973-1976
20 Ga	Series	Barrel		28" Full	28" Modified	26" Imp Cyl	27" adj.	Date Range
	C-200	Plain		8274	8276	1963-1965		
	C-2011	Plain		8280	8283	8279	8275	1966-1973
	C-2011	Vent Rib		8284	8285	8282		1966-1974
	Late	Plain		6280	6283	6279		1973-1975
	Late	Vent Rib		6284	6285	-	6282	1973-1976

SUPERMATIC CITATION - similar to Supermatic Trophy model except w/o vent. rib, 2 3/4 in. chambers, 6 click stop adjustable choke.

	$240	$225	$205	$190	$160	$140	$115

Catalog #8220 has a compensator integral with the adjustable choke.

12 ga., 27 in. barrel, adjustable catalog   #8220   mfg. 1960.
C-100, 12 ga., 27 in. barrel,
adjustable catalog   #8221   mfg. 1961-62.

SUPERMATIC TROPHY - 12 or 20 ga., 2 3/4 (12 ga.) or 3 (20 ga.) in. chamber, gas operated, blue finish, checkered walnut stock and forend, 4 shot mag., 6 click stop adjustable choke.

	$250	$235	$210	$190	$165	$145	$120

Catalog #8230 has a compensator integral with the adjustable choke.

12 ga., 27 in. barrel,
Adjustable Vent Rib, catalog   #8230   mfg. 1960.
C-100, 12 ga., 27 in. barrel,
Adjustable Vent Rib, catalog   #8231   mfg. 1961-65.
C-200, 20 ga., 27 in. barrel,
Adjustable Vent Rib, catalog   #8281   mfg. 1963-65.

SUPERMATIC DUCK - 12 ga., 3 in. magnum chamber, (also fits 2 3/4 in. shells), blue finish, checkered pistol grip walnut stock and forearm, 5 (2 3/4 in. shells) or 4 (3 in. shells) shot mag.

	$285	$255	$205	$175	$145	$125	$110

Add $20 for vent rib.

C-101, 12 ga., 3 in., 30 in. barrel,
Full Choke Vent Rib, catalog   #8240   mfg. 1960 only.
C-101, 12 ga., 3 in., 30 in. barrel,
Full Choke, catalog   #8241   mfg. 1961-62.
12 ga., 3 in., 30 in. barrel, F
ull Choke Vent Rib, catalog   #8242   mfg. 1961-65.
12 ga., 3 in., 30 in. barrel,
Full Choke, catalog   #8243   mfg. 1963-65.
C-1211, 12 ga., 3 in., 30 in. barrel, F
ull Choke, catalog   #8244   mfg. 1966-1973.
C-1211, 12 ga., 3 in., 30 in. barrel,
Full Choke Vent Rib, catalog   #8247   mfg. 1966-1973.
12 ga., 3 in., 30 in. barrel,
Full Choke Vent Rib, catalog   #6247   mfg. 1973-75.

SUPERMATIC DEER GUN - similar to Supermatic Deluxe, except has 22 in. cylinder bore barrel, rifle sights, checkered stock and forearm, recoil pad.

	$245	$220	$190	$175	$150	$125	$115

Receiver tapped for aperture sight on cat no. 8246.

12 ga., 22 in. barrel,
Cylinder Bore, catalog   #8245   mfg. 1965 only.
C-1200, 12 ga. , 22 in. barrel,
Cylinder Bore, catalog   #8246   mfg. 1966-1972.

SUPERMATIC SKEET - similar to Supermatic Deluxe, except has select American walnut stock and forearm, 2 3/4 (12 ga.) or 3 (20 ga.) in. chamber.

	$290	$270	$240	$210	$180	$160	$140

C-100, 12 ga., 26 in. barrel,
Skeet Choke, Vent Rib, catalog #8260 mfg. 1962-63.
12 ga., 26 in. barrel,
Skeet Choke, Vent Rib, catalog #8262 mfg. 1964-65.
C-1200, 12 ga., 26 in. barrel,
Skeet Choke, Vent Rib, catalog #8264 mfg. 1966-72.
12 ga., 26 in. barrel,
Skeet Choke, Vent Rib, catalog #6264 mfg. 1973-75.
20 ga. , 26 in. barrel,
Skeet Choke, Vent Rib, catalog #8277 mfg. 1964-65.
C-2011, 20 ga., 26 in. barrel,
Skeet Choke, Vent Rib, catalog #8287 mfg. 1964-1972.
20 ga., 26 in. barrel,
Skeet Choke Vent Rib, catalog #6287 mfg. 1973-75.

SUPERMATIC TRAP - similar to Supermatic Deluxe, except has select American walnut stock and forearm and recoil pad.

	$275	$250	$230	$200	$180	$160	$140

Catalog number 8266 is the Executive Trap model with Fajen Monte Carlo stock and 2 3/4 in. chamber.

C-100, 12 ga., 30 in. barrel,
Full Choke, Vent Rib, catalog #8261 mfg. 1962-63.
12 ga., 30 in. barrel,
Full Choke, Vent Rib, catalog #8263 mfg. 1964-65.
C-1200, 12 ga., 30 in. barrel,
Full Choke, Vent Rib, catalog #8265 mfg. 1966-1972.
12 ga., 30 in. barrel,
Full Choke, Vent Rib, catalog #8266 mfg.1970-72.
12 ga., 30 in. barrel,
Full Choke, Vent Rib, catalog #6265 mfg. 1973-75.

SHOTGUNS: SLIDE ACTION

FLITE KING FIELD - 12, 16, 20 ga. or .410 bore, 2 3/4 (12 or 16 ga.) or 3 (20 ga. or .410 bore) in. chamber, blued finish, 4 or 5 shot mag., plain pistol grip walnut stock and forend.

	$200	$175	$150	$130	$115	$105	$95

Add 50% for .410 bore.

FLITE KING FIELD CATALOG NUMBERS

	Series	Barrel	30" Full	28" Full	28" Modified	26" Imp Cyl	Date Range
12 Ga	K-100	Plain	8103	8100	8101	8102	1960-1965
16 Ga	K-160	Plain	-	8300	8301	8302	1960-1965
20 Ga	K-200	Plain	-	8400	8401	8402	1960-1965
.410 bore		Plain	-	-	-	8450	1962-1965

FLITE KING SPECIAL - 12, 16, or 20 ga., 2 3/4 (12 or 16 ga.) or 3 (20 ga.) in. chamber, 5 shot mag., blued finish, 27 in. barrel, 6 click adj. choke, walnut stock and forend.

	$200	$175	$150	$130	$115	$105	$95

K-100, K-10, 12 ga., catalog #8110 mfg. 1961-65.
K-160, 16 ga., catalog #8310 mfg. 1961-64.
K-200, 20 ga., catalog #8410 mfg. 1961-65.

FLITE KING DELUXE - 12, 16, 20, 28 ga., or .410 bore, 2 3/4 (12, 16, 28 ga.) or 3 (20 ga. or .410 bore) chamber, blued finish, checkered walnut pistol grip stock and forearm, 5 shot mag., 6 click adj. choke, available with and without a vent rib, recoil pad beginning 1966 except .410 models.

	$205	$185	$160	$140	$120	$100	$90

GRADING - PPGS™	100%	98%	95%	90%	80%	70%	60%

Add $20 for vent rib.

Add 50% for plain barrel in 28 ga. or .410 bore.

Add 55% for ribbed barrel in 28 ga. or .410 bore.

Add $25 for catalog numbers 6135-6142 with interchangeable barrels capability.

Catalog nos. 8411 and 6411 were the Converta Pump sold with two stocks - one youth sized and one adult size. The 12 ga. models with catalog nos. 6115 through 6142 are models with provisions for interchangeable barrels.

FLITE KING DELUXE CATALOG NUMBERS

	Series	Barrel	30" Full	28" Full	28" Modified	26" Imp Cyl	27" Adj.	Date Range
12 Ga	K-100	Plain	8123	8120	8121	8122		1961-1962
	K-100	Vent Rib	8127	8124	8125	8126		1961-1965
	K-121/1221	Plain	8135	8132	8133	8134	8115	1966-1972
	K-121/1221	Vent Rib	8136	8137	8138		8142	1966-1972
	Late	Plain	6135	6132	6133	6134	6115	1973-1975
	Late	Vent Rib	6136	6137	6138		6142	1973-1975
16 Ga	Series	Barrel		28" Full	28" Modified	26" Imp Cyl		Date Range
	K-160	Plain		8320	8321	8322		1961-1962
	K-160	Vent Rib		8324	8325	8326		1961-1965
20 Ga	Series	Barrel		28" Full	28" Modified	26" Imp Cyl	27" adj.	Date Range
	K-200	Plain		8400	8401	8402		1961-1962
	K-200	Vent Rib		8425	8426	8427		1961-1965
	K-2011	Plain		8403	8404	8405		1966-1972
	K-2011	Vent Rib		8429	8430	8443	8442	1966-1972
	Late	Plain		6403	6404			1973-1975
	Late	Vent Rib		6429	6430	6443	6442	1973-1975
28 Ga	Series	Barrel		26" Full	26" Modified	Date Range		
	K-2800	Plain		8332	8333	1966-1972		
	K-2800	Vent Rib		8334	8335	1966-1972		
	Late	Plain		6332	6333	1973-1975		
	Late	Vent Rib		6334	6335	1973-1975		
.410 Bore	Series	Barrel		26" Full	26" Skeet	Date Range		
	K-411	Vent Rib		8451	8452	1963-1965		
	Plain Vent Rib							
	K-4111	Plain		8453	8454	1966-1972		
	Late	26" Full		6453	6454	1973-1975		

MODEL 200

MODEL 200 - 12 ga., also sold as part of a promotional package beginning in 1971, which included the Model 200, a zippered gun case, a plastic trigger lock, and G-96 gun lubricant.

$175	$160	$140	$120	$105	$95	$90

Add $20 premium for entire promotional package in original box.

Model 200 Catalog Numbers

	Series	Barrel	30" Full	28" Full	28" Modified	26" Imp Cyl	Date Range
12 Ga	Series	Barrel	30" Full	28" Full	28" Modified	26" Imp Cyl	Date Range
		Plain	8196	8197	8198	8199	-
		Plain	8167 - cat no for promo pkg				1971

FLITE KING CITATION

FLITE KING CITATION - 12 or 16 ga., 2 3/4 in. chamber, similar to Flite King Trophy, except does not have vent rib.

$205	$190	$170	$150	$120	$100	$90

Catalog #8130 has a compensator integral with the adjustable choke.

K-100, 12 ga., 26 1/2 in. barrel, 6 click stop adjustable, catalog #8130 mfg. 1960.

K-10, 12 ga., 27 in. barrel, 6 click stop adjustable, catalog #8131 mfg. 1961-62.

K-160, 16 ga., 27 in. barrel, 6 click stop adjustable, catalog #8331 mfg. 1961-62.

FLITE KING TROPHY

FLITE KING TROPHY - 12, 16, or 20 ga., 2 3/4 (12 or 16 ga.) or 3 (20 ga.) in. chamber, blued finish, walnut stock and forend, 5 shot mag, vent. rib.

$215	$205	$175	$160	$130	$110	$100

Catalog #8140 has a compensator integral with the adjustable choke.

K-100, 12 ga., 26 1/2 in. barrel, 6 click stop adjustable, vent rib, catalog #8140, mfg. 1960.

K-10, 12 ga., 27 in. barrel, 6 click stop adjustable, vent rib, catalog #8141, mfg. 1961-65.

K-160, 16 ga., 27 in. barrel, 6 click stop adjustable, vent rib, catalog #8341, mfg. 1961-64.

K-200, 20 ga., 27 in. barrel, 6 click stop adjustable, vent rib., catalog #8441, mfg. 1962-65.

GRADING - PPGS™	100%	98%	95%	90%	80%	70%	60%

FLITE KING BRUSH

FLITE KING BRUSH - 12, ga., 2 3/4 in. chamber, similar to the Flite King Field, except has adjustable rifle sights, receiver is tapped for the Williams sight and provisions exist for sling swivels, deluxe models have Williams receiver sight, a leather sling and a recoil pad.

	$225	$200	$175	$150	$120	$100	$90

Add $10 for deluxe model.

Add $25 for catalog no. 6166 with interchangeable barrel capability.

K-102, K-101, 12 ga., 20 in. barrel, cylinder bore, catalog #8105 mfg. 1962-65.
K-102, 12 ga., 20 in. barrel, Cylinder Bore Deluxe, catalog #8106 mfg. 1964-65.
K-101, 12 ga., 26 in. barrel, Cylinder Bore, catalog #8107 mfg. 1962-63.
K-102, 12 ga., 26 in. barrel, Cylinder Bore Deluxe, catalog #8108 mfg. 1964-65.
K-102, 12 ga., 18 in. barrel, Cylinder Bore, catalog #8109 mfg. 1964-65.
K-120, K-1200, 12 ga., 20 in. barrel, Cylinder Bore, catalog #8116 mfg. 1966 - 1972.
K-120, K-1200, 12 ga., 20 in. barrel, Cylinder Bore Deluxe, catalog #8117 mfg. 1966 - 1972.
12 ga., 20 in. barrel, Improved Cylinder, catalog #6116 mfg. 1973-75.

FLITE KING SKEET

FLITE KING SKEET - 12, 20, 28 ga. or .410 bore, 2 3/4 (12 or 28 ga.) or 3 (20 ga. or .410 bore) in. chamber, similar to Flite King Deluxe except has select American walnut stock and forearm and no recoil pad.

	$290	$260	$230	$185	$150	$120	$100

Add 35% for 28 ga. or .410 bore.

Cat #6164 is a model with provisions for interchangeable barrels - add $25.

K-10, 12 ga., 26 in. barrel, Skeet Bore, Vent Rib, catalog #8160, mfg. 1962-63.
12 ga., 26 in. barrel, Skeet Bore, Vent Rib, catalog #8162, mfg. 1964-65.
K-121, K-1211, 12 ga., 26 in. barrel, Skeet Bore, Vent Rib, catalog # 8164, mfg. 1966 - 1972.
12 ga., 26 in. barrel, Skeet Bore, catalog #6164, mfg. 1973-75,
K-200, 20 ga., 26 in. barrel, Skeet Bore, catalog #8428, mfg. 1964-65.
K-2011, 20 ga., 26 in. barrel, Skeet Bore, catalog #8431, mfg. 1966 -1972.
20 ga., 26 in. barrel, Skeet Bore, catalog #6431, mfg. 1973-75.
K-2800, 28 ga., 26 in. barrel, Skeet Bore, catalog #8336, mfg. 1968 - 1972.
28 ga., 26 in. barrel, Skeet Bore, catalog #6336, mfg. 1973.
.410 bore , 26 in. barrel, Skeet Bore, catalog #8452, mfg. 1964 -65.
K-4111, .410 bore, 26 in. barrel, Skeet Bore, catalog #8455, mfg. 1968 - 1972.
.410 bore, 26 in. barrel, Skeet Bore, catalog #6455, mfg. 1973.

FLITE KING TRAP

FLITE KING TRAP - 12 ga., 2 3/4 in. chamber, similar to Flite King Deluxe, except has select American Walnut stock and forearm and recoil pad, 30 in. barrel.

	$275	$225	$195	$175	$150	$130	$110

Add $25 for Fajen Monte Carlo stock.

Cat. #8166 is the Executive trap model with Fajen Monte Carlo stock. Add $25 for Cat. #6165 - a model with provisions for interchangeable barrels.

K-10, 12 ga., 30 in. barrel, Full Choke, Vent Rib, catalog #8161, mfg. 1962-63.
12 ga., 30 in. barrel, Full Choke, Vent Rib, catalog #8163, mfg. 1964-65.
K-121, K-1211, 12 ga. 30 in. barrel, Full Choke, Vent Rib, catalog #8165, mfg. 1966 - 1972.
12 ga. , 30 in. barrel, Full Choke, Vent Rib, catalog #8166, mfg. 1970-71.
12 ga., 30 in. barrel, Full Choke, Vent Rib, catalog #6165, mfg. 1973-75.

SHOTGUNS: IMPORTED

SUPERMATIC SHADOW INDY O/U

SUPERMATIC SHADOW INDY O/U - 12 ga., boxlock, selective auto ejectors, single trigger, fully engraved receiver, skipline checkered walnut stock with pistol grip, vent. forearm, recoil pad, special "Airflow" rib.   Imported from Nikko in Japan.

	$860	$820	$770	$720	$625	$550	$500

12 ga., 2 3/4 in., 271/2 in. barrel, Skeet / Skeet Choke, catalog #54230, imported 1974-75.
12 ga., 2 3/4 in., 29 3/4 in. barrel, Full / Full Choke, catalog #54231, imported 1974-75.
12 ga., 2 3/4 in., 29 3/4 in. barrel, Imp.Mod / Full Choke, catalog #54232, imported 1974-75.

GRADING - PPGS™	100%	98%	95%	90%	80%	70%	60%

SUPERMATIC SHADOW SEVEN - similar to Shadow Indy, except has a standard size vent. rib, conventional forearm, no recoil pad, standard checkering, and less engraving. Imported from Nikko in Japan.

	$695	$660	$620	$575	$480	$430	$390

12 ga., 2 3/4 in., 27 1/2 in. barrel, Skeet / Skeet Choke, catalog #54220, imported 1974-75.
12 ga., 2 3/4 in., 27 1/2 in. barrel, Mod./ Imp. Choke, catalog #54221, imported 1974-75.
12 ga., 2 3/4 in., 27 1/2 in. barrel, Full / Mod. Choke, catalog #54222, imported 1974-75.
12 ga., 2 3/4 in., 29 3/4 in. barrel, Full / Full Choke, catalog #54223, imported 1974-75.
12 ga., 2 3/4 in., 29 3/4 in. barrel, Imp. Mod./ Full Choke, catalog #54224, imported 1974-75.

SUPERMATIC SHADOW AUTOMATIC - 12 or 20 ga., semi-auto, gas operated, interchangeable barrels, checkered walnut stock and forearm, special "Airflow" rib. Imported from Nikko in Japan.

	$395	$365	$340	$270	$200	$175	$150

12 ga., 2 3/4 in., 28 in. barrel, Imp. Mod. Choke, catalog #54200, imported 1974-75.
12 ga., 2 3/4 in., 28 in. barrel, Mod. Choke, catalog #54201, imported 1974-75.
12 ga., 2 3/4 in., 26 in. barrel, Skeet Choke, catalog #54203, imported 1974-75.
12 ga., 2 3/4 in., 28 in. barrel, Full Choke, catalog #54204, imported 1974-75.
12 ga., 2 3/4 in., 30 in. barrel, Full Choke, catalog #54205, imported 1974-75.
12 ga., 2 3/4 in., 30 in. barrel, Trap Choke, catalog #54206, imported 1974-75.
12 ga., 2 3/4 in., 30 in. barrel, Imp. Mod. Choke, catalog #54207, imported 1974-75.
20 ga., 3 in., 28 in. barrel, Imp. Mod. Choke, catalog #54210 , imported 1974-75.
20 ga., 3 in., 28 in. barrel, Mod. Choke, catalog #54211, imported 1974-75.
20 ga., 3 in., 26 in. barrel, Imp. Choke, catalog #54212, imported 1974-75.
20 ga., 3 in., 26 in. barrel, Skeet Choke, catalog #54213, imported 1974-75.
20 ga., 3 in., 28 in., barrel, Full Choke, catalog #54214 , imported 1974-75.

SHOTGUNS: DEFENSE & LAW ENFORCEMENT

SEMI AUTOMATIC MODEL - 12 ga., 20 in. cylinder bore barrel, 4 shot mag., recoil pad walnut stock and forearm.

	$250	$205	$180	$160	$130	$110	$100

C-1200, 12 ga., 20 in. barrel, cylinder bore, Riot 20-5, catalog #8294, mfg. 1969.
C-1200, 12 ga., 20 in. barrel, cylinder bore, rifle sights, Riot 20-5, catalog #8295, mfg. 1969.

MODELS 10A/10B SEMI-AUTO - 12 ga., combat model, 18 in. barrel, semi-auto, unique bullpup design incorporates raked pistol grip in front of receiver and metal shoulder pad attached directly to rear of receiver, black cycolac plastic shroud and pistol grip, very compact size (28 in. overall). Disc.

✴ *Model 10-A* - 4 shot mag., fixed carrying handle and integral flashlight.

	$775	$725	$665	$600	$475	$400	$350

12 ga., 18 in. barrel, cylinder bore, catalog #8290, mfg. 1967-69.

✴ *Model 10-B* - 12 ga., folding carrying handle, provisions made for attaching a Kel-lite flashlight to receiver top, extended blade front sight, 4 shot mag., carrying case.

	$695	$650	$600	$575	$450	$375	$325

Add 15% for flashlight.
Cat. No. 50284 optional carrying case and attachable flashlight; Cat. No. 50285 sold optionally.
12 ga., 18.13 in. barrel, cylinder bore, catalog #8291, mfg. 1970-77.

SLIDE ACTION RIOT SHOTGUN - 12 ga. only on the Flite King Action, 18 or 20 in. barrel, police riot gun, available with or w/o rifle sights, plain pistol grip oiled walnut stock & forearm forearm, changed to walnut stained and lacquered birch in the mid-1970s.

	$230	$200	$175	$150	$125	$115	$105

Catalog #8111/#8113 magazine capacity 6. # 8104/#8129 magazine capacity 5. A 1963 flyer mentions the #8105 Flite King Brush 20 in. and the #8107 Flite King Deluxe 20 in. as riot guns. The data on the #8105 and #8107 is listed under the Flite King Brush.
K-101, K-120, K-1200, 12 ga., 20 in. barrel, cylinder bore, Riot 20-6, catalog #8104, mfg. 1963-1977.
K-120, K-1200, 12 ga., 18 1/8 in. barrel, cylinder bore, Riot 18-7, catalog #8111, mfg. 1964-1978.
K-120, K-1200,12 ga., 18 in. barrel, cylinder bore, rifle sights, Riot 18-7, catalog #8113, mfg. 1965-1978.
K-120, 12 ga., 18 1/8 in. barrel, cylinder bore, rifle sights, Riot 18-6, catalog #8118, mfg. 1968.
12 ga., 20 in. barrel, cylinder bore, rifle sights, catalog #8129, mfg. 1976-77.
K-102, 12 ga., 20 in. barrel, cylinder bore, catalog #8112, 1964-65.
12 ga., 18 in. barrel, cylinder bore, rifle sights, catalog #8128, mfg. 1976-77.

GRADING - PPGS™	100%	98%	95%	90%	80%	70%	60%

HIGH STANDARD MANUFACTURING CO.

High Standard is a current trademark of firearms manufactured by Firearms International Inc., established in 1993 and located in Houston, TX.

This company was formed during 1993, utilizing many of the same employees and original material vendors that the original High Standard company used during their period of manufacture (1926-1984). During 2004, Crusader Group Gun Company, Inc. was formed, and this new company includes the assets of High Standard Manufacturing Co, Firearms International Inc., AMT-Auto Mag, and Arsenal Line Products.

PISTOLS: SEMI-AUTO, RIMFIRE

SPORT KING - .22 LR cal., 4 1/2 or 6 3/4 in. barrel, blue finish, military grips, 10 shot mag.

> While advertised during 1996, this model was produced in very limited quantites.

PLINKER - .17 High Standard or .22 LR cal., same design as former Ram-Line pistol, 4, 6, or 8 in. barrel with adj. rear sight, uses many plastic materials, interchangeable barrels, 10 shot mag., 14.25 oz.

> While advertised during late 2003, this model has yet to be manufactured.

SUPERMATIC CITATION - .22 LR cal., 5 1/2 or 7 1/4 (disc. 1995) in. barrel, matte blue (disc. 1996) or parkerized finish, military grips, open sights (disc. 2001) or universal scope base, 9 shot mag., 44 oz. Mfg. 1994-2003.

$415	$325	$260	$225	$200	$185	$170

Last MSR was $490.

> **Add $317 for .22 Short conversion kit (includes barrel, slide, and 2 mags.).**

SUPERMATIC CITATION MS - .17 High Standard (new 2003) or .22 LR cal., features 10 in. barrel, mounting bracket with scope base, designed for the Metallic Silhouette shooter, 54 oz. New 1997.

MSR $775	$675	$575	$500	$425	$375	$300	$265

> **Add approx. $119 for RPM sights (scope base only, disc).**

SUPERMATIC CITATION 10X - .22 LR cal., 5.5 in. barrel, blue finish, military grips, High Standard's most accurate pistol, choice of either factory or Shea custom tuning, 10 shot mag., approx. 45 oz., custom shop only. New 1994.

❊ *Factory Tuned 10X*

MSR $1,095	$950	$875	$775	$675	$575	$475	$375

❊ *Custom Shea 10X* - limited mfg. (approx. 150 pistols annually), hand-built by Bob Shea. New 1995.

MSR $1,295	$1,100	$975	$850	$750	$650	$550	$450

SUPERMATIC TOURNAMENT - .22 LR cal., choice of 4 1/2 (disc. 1995), 5 1/2, or 6 3/4 (disc. 1995) in. barrel, matte blue, non-adj. trigger, approx. 44 oz. Mfg. 1995-97, reintroduced 2004 through the custom shop.

MSR $795	$675	$595	$550	$475	$375	$300	$250

SUPERMATIC TROPHY - .17 High Standard (new 2003) or .22 LR cal., 5 1/2 or 7 1/4 in. barrel, blue finish, scope base became standard on 5 1/2 in. barrel in 2000, 2002 for 7 1/4 in. barrel, with or w/o iron sights, military grips, 10 shot mag., 44 or 46 oz. New 1994.

MSR $745	$650	$575	$525	$450	$350	$275	$225

> **Add $50 for iron sights.**
> **Add $50 for 7 1/4 in. barrel.**
>
> **Add $317 for .22 Short conversion kit (includes barrel, slide, and 2 mags.).**

GRADING - PPGS™	100%	98%	95%	90%	80%	70%	60%

VICTOR - .17 High Standard (new 2003) or .22 LR cal., 4 1/2 or 5 1/2 in. barrel, blue or parkerized (new 1995, 5 1/2 in. barrel only) finish, military grips, with open sight rib or universal mount (HSUM, blue only, new 1996), 10 shot mag., approx. 45 oz., custom shop only. New 1994.

MSR $745	$650	$575	$525	$450	$350	$275	$225

    Add $50 for open sights (5 1/2 in. barrel only).

    Add $317 for .22 Short conversion kit (includes VR barrel, slide, and 2 mags.).

✳ *Victor 10X* - factory tuned and individually tested, includes test target signed by the gunsmith, 46 oz. New 1997.

MSR $1,195	$1,050	$900	$800	$725	$625	$525	$425

✳ *Victor 10X Shea* - parkerized finish, 5 1/2 in. barrel only, 150 built by Bob Shea annually, 46 oz. New 1996.

MSR $1,395	$1,125	$975	$850	$750	$650	$550	$425

LIMITED EDITIONS - during 1996, High Standard offered several limited editions. They included the Victor (fully engraved, 6 mfg., $1,862 MSR), the Tournament (non-engraved, 26 mfg., $608 MSR), and the engraved Tournament (50% engraved, 6 mfg. $1,062 MSR). Additionally, only 5 sets were mfg. with 4 guns included – the Olympic 8 in. Space Gun, Tournament, Flite King, and Victor. Retail was $3,200 (non-engraved) or $7,200 (engraved). A 3 gun set was also available (w/o Olympic) for $2,150 (non-engraved) or $5,150 (engraved).

    Extreme rarity of these guns precludes accurate pricing.

OLYMPIC I.S.U. - .22 Short cal., 6 3/4 in. fluted barrel with integral muzzle brake, blue finish, military grips, 10 shot mag. Mfg. 1994-95 only.

	$550	$450	$385	$315	$250	$200	$185

    Last MSR was $625.

OLYMPIC MILITARY - .22 Short cal., 5 1/2 in. fluted bull barrel with removable stabilizer, aluminum alloy slide with steel frame, scope base or open sights. New 1995.

MSR $795	$675	$575	$475	$400	$350	$300	$250

    Subtract approx. $60 if w/o open sights.

OLYMPIC RAPID FIRE - .22 Short cal., 4 in. VR barrel with integral muzzle brake and forward mounted compensator, gold-plated small parts, matte finish, special grips with rear support, adj. trigger, 46 oz., custom shop only. New 1996-2003.

	$925	$725	$625	$525	$425	$375	$325

    Last MSR was $1,027.

HIGH TECH CUSTOM RIFLES

Current manufacturer of bolt action rifles located in Colorado Springs, CO.

High Tech Custom Rifles manufactures a complete line of custom built, high quality bolt action rifles, including the Shadow, Shadow II, Falcon Series, Varmint Hunter, Alaskan Pro Hunter and Mountain Hunter. They also manufacture and install their own proprietary muzzle brake (60%-80% recoil reduction). Please contact the company directly for more information, including pricing, availability and a custom quotation.

HILL COUNTRY RIFLE COMPANY

Current manufacturer of bolt action rifles located in New Braunfels, TX. Consumer direct sales.

RIFLES: BOLT ACTION

Hill Country Rifles currently manufactures a complete line of custom built, high quality bolt action rifles, including the Custom Hunter (MSR - $2,250), Custom Sheep, (MSR - $2,250) Custom Varmint (MSR - $2,450), Hill Country Classic (MSR - $2,400), Dangerous Game (MSR - $5,400), Semi-Custom (MSR - $1,595), and American Classic (MSR - $15,000). All synthetic cus-

GRADING - PPGS™	100%	98%	95%	90%	80%	70%	60%

tom rifles are built on a customer provided Rem. 700 or Win. Model 70 Classic action. Hill Country Rifles also accurizes rifles and performs complete gunsmithing services. For current model availability, features, special orders, and pricing information (including a custom quotation and delivery time), please contact the factory directly (see Trademark Index).

HISPANO ARGENTINO FABRICA DE AUTOMOVILES SA (HAFDASA)

Previous car manufacturer located in Buenos Aires, Argentina.

This company accepted and sold both commercial and military pistols manufactured by Ballester-Rigaud initially, followed by Ballester-Molina.

PISTOLS: SEMI-AUTO

BALLESTER-MOLINA/RIGAUD - .45 ACP or .22 LR cal., 5 in. barrel, patterned after the Colt M-1911A1 except has pinned trigger, is without grip safety, has different sear mechanism, and distinctive pattern retracting grooves in slide. Circa 1930-mid-1940s. Probably an unauthorized copy at the time.

	$500	$400	$360	$330	$300	$275	$225

Add 100% for .22 LR.

GEORGE HOENIG, INC.

Current custom rifle builder located in Boise, ID.

LONG GUNS

George Hoenig builds a unique patented rotary round action O/U rifle, shotgun, or combination gun. Opening is achieved by rotating barrels quarter turn to the right, then sliding barrel assembly forward. Because of this, there is no top opening lever. Standard features include double triggers, extractors, rotary safety on stock, and coin finished scroll engraved frame. Prices for a 28 or 20 ga. game gun start at $19,980 (approx. 6-6 1/4 lbs., 12 month delivery time), while the double rifle (approx. 7 1/3 - 8 1/3 lbs.) and combination guns have a base price of $24,975. For more information, delivery time, and current pricing, please contact George Hoenig directly (see Trademark Index).

HOFER-JAGDWAFFEN, PETER

Current master gunsmith located in Ferlach, Austria. Custom order only, best quality rifles (most configurations) and shotguns (O/U and SxS) made per individual order. Prices usually start in the $20,000 range, and can go up to over $600,000! Information (including an individualized quotation) can be obtained by contacting Mr. Hofer directly (see Trademark Index).

P.L. HOLEHAN, INC.

Current custom rifle manufacturer located in Tucson, AZ. Consumer direct sales.

P.L. Holehan, Inc. is a custom rifle maker fabricating best quality bolt action rifles only. The company is also known for its integral return to zero scope mounting system. All guns are essentially built per individual custom order and the company should be contacted directly for more information, including special order options/features (see Trademark Index).

RIFLES: BOLT ACTION

Subtract approx. $500-$750 for fiberglass stock, depending on the model (disc.).

GRADING - PPGS™	100%	98%	95%	90%	80%	70%	60%

SAFARI HUNTER - various Safari cals., features Win. M-70 controlled feed claw extractor, double square bridge action, premium grade barrel, satin blue metal finish, choice of fiberglass or oil finished English walnut stock with ebony forend tip, Pachmayr decelerator pad, hinged floor plate, 9.5 lbs.

	MSR $7,050	$7,050	$6,250	$5,000	$4,500	$3,750	$3,250	$2,650

AFRICAN HUNTER - various Safari cals., similar to Safari Hunter, except features Dakota Magnum action, 10.25 lbs. New 2002.

	MSR $9,050	$9,050	$8,000	$7,000	$6,000	$5,000	$4,000	$3,000

CLASSIC HUNTER - available in most popular non-Safari cals., hinged floor plate, standard or blind box mag., 7.5 - 8 lbs.

	MSR $5,950	$5,950	$5,200	$4,450	$3,850	$3,300	$2,800	$2,300

Add $200 for standard box mag.

LONG RANGE HUNTER - various cals., action similar to Classic Hunter, except has 26 in. fluted barrel, satin blue or matte Teflon metal finish, 8.75 lbs.

	MSR $5,900	$5,900	$5,250	$4,500	$3,900	$3,300	$2,800	$2,300

LIGHTWEIGHT CLASSIC HUNTER - various cals., features short action, Win. M-70 controlled feed claw extractor, lightweight 22 in. barrel, standard or blind box mag., 6.5-7 lbs.

	MSR $5,750	$5,750	$5,000	$4,350	$3,750	$3,200	$2,700	$2,200

Add $200 for standard box mag.

ALPINE HUNTER - various cals., Win. M-70 short or standard length action with controlled feeding, blind box mag., fiberglass (disc.) or Kevlar stock, approx. 6-6.75 lbs. New 2000.

	MSR $4,050	$4,050	$3,350	$2,750	$2,450	$2,150	$1,750	$1,350

HOLLAND & HOLLAND LTD.

Current manufacturer established in 1835 and located in London, England since 1835, with gun showrooms currently located in New York City, London, England and Paris, France.

Holland & Holland over the years has justly earned the reputation of producing some of the finest firearms ever manufactured, exhibiting outstanding quality and superior craftsmanship.

HOLLAND & HOLLAND
Established 1835

Most of these fine arms were made to order for the famous, wealthy, or royalty of their day. Because of the individual nature of each firearm, these early guns, as with any high grade item, must be individually appraised.

All H&H long guns are built per individual special order. Orders may be placed directly with the office in England or through their Paris showroom. Please refer to these listings in the Trademark Index for address, telephone, or fax information

The early double rifles were proofed and regulated with the black powder ammunition of their day. These exposed hammer rifles were almost exclusively sold cased with accessories by Holland & Holland, and are seldom encountered today. Purchase of these as well as any high grade firearm should include trusted appraisal.

RIFLES: MODERN

During 2003, H&H released two new large proprietary cartridges. They are: .400 H&H Mag. Belted Rimless (400 grain bullet with 400 H&H headstamp), and .465 H&H Belted Rimless (480 grain bullet with 465 H&H headstamp).

All currently manufactured H&H rifles are priced in English pounds, and 98%-60% values are not included. All older and recently manufactured used rifles are priced in dollars.

GRADING - PPGS™	100%	98%	95%	90%	80%	70%	60%

ROOK RIFLE - .250, .295/.300, .360, .380 black powder cals., single shot, break-open action, various levels of embellishment - Royal Models were made but most Rook rifles were base models with few extra features. Disc.

> Values today range from $600 (average condition, small cal.) to $2,500 (larger cal., engraving, better wood, perhaps cased).

BEST QUALITY MAGAZINE RIFLE - Mauser 98 (current mfg.) or Enfield (disc.) action, various cals., built per individual customer specifications, checkered French walnut stock available in traditional configuration or with Monte Carlo pattern.

* *Current Mfg.*

MSR £14,300	£14,300	N/A					

Add £1,450 for calibers .375 H&H and greater.

Add £2,200 for full length carbine stock.

Add £1,550+ for deluxe grade walnut.

The values listed represent the standard model without additional options or engraving (of which there are a wide array).

* *Older & Recent Mfg.*

	N/A	$17,750	$15,250	$11,750	$9,000	$7,750	$6,500

Subtract 25% for Enfield action.

DE LUXE MAGAZINE RIFLE - similar to Best Quality, except with deluxe grade walnut and various engraving options, very limited mfg.

> There is no standard base price on this model - rather, individual options are custom ordered and are individually priced.

DOMINION GRADE NO. 2 MODEL DOUBLE RIFLE SxS - various British and American cals., 24-28 in. barrels, sidelock, folding leaf sight, checkered French walnut stock, auto ejectors.

	$15,000	$13,000	$11,000	$10,000	$9,000	$7,000	$6,500

Add 25% for dangerous game cals.

ROYAL DOUBLE SxS RIFLE - OLDER & RECENT MFG. - similar to No. 2, except has deluxe finish and more engraving.

	100%	98%	95%	90%	80%	70%	60%
.300 H&H cal. or less	N/A	$47,500	$40,000	$36,000	$30,000	$25,000	$22,000
Up to .375 H&H cal.	N/A	$54,000	$45,000	$40,000	$34,000	$28,500	$25,000
Up to .470 NE cal.	N/A	$66,000	$55,000	$50,000	$37,500	$31,500	$27,500
Up to .600 NE cal.	N/A	$72,000	$60,000	$55,000	$50,000	$45,000	$40,000

Subtract 15% if w/o ejectors.

Subtract 25% if w/o reinforced action.

ROYAL DE LUXE SxS RIFLE - CURRENT MFG. - same cals. as the Royal Double SxS, except also available in .700 H&H cal., top-of-the-line model, every refinement, 22-26 in. chopper lump barrels, traditional royal scroll engraving, color case hardened frame or bright finish, built to individual order only with almost any option possible, includes aluminum travel case, 8 3/4 lbs. (.300 H&H cal.).

* *.240 H&H, 7mm H&H, or 8mm cal.*

MSR £68,400	£68,400	N/A					

* *.275 H&H, .300 H&H, or 9.3mm cal.*

MSR £70,500	£70,500	N/A					

* *.375 H&H or .465 H&H cal.*

MSR £75,750	£75,750	N/A					

* *.577 NE or .600 NE cal.*

MSR £82,750	£82,750	N/A					

H&H .700 BORE SxS DOUBLE RIFLE - .700 H&H cal., 1,000 grain jacketed bullet, approx. 19 lbs. with 26 in. barrels chambered 3 1/2 in. This is the largest caliber rifle available in the world today.

GRADING - PPGS™	100%	98%	95%	90%	80%	70%	60%

✳ *Royal Model* - this model is not currently mfg. 1997 retail was $115,920.

✳ *Royal De Luxe Model*

MSR £120,450   £120,450   N/A

ROUND ACTION SIDELOCK SxS DOUBLE RIFLE - available in standard flanged cals., rounded back action sidelock with DT, 24 in. chopper lump barrels, English rose and fine scroll and border engraving, color case hardened or bright finish frame. New 2004.

MSR £35,200   £35,200   N/A

Add £5,200 for optional calibers.

SHOTGUNS: O/U

All currently manufactured H&H shotguns are priced in English pounds, and 98%-60% values are not included. All older and recently manufactured used rifles are priced in dollars.

ROYAL OLD MODEL - 12 ga., customer specifications as to barrel length and choke, hand detachable sidelocks, auto ejectors, checkered straight grip stock. Mfg. until 1951. Very rare, very few mfg.

	$37,500	$32,000	$28,000	$23,500	$20,000	$18,000	$16,500

Add 5% for single trigger.

ROYAL NEW MODEL - similar to Old Model, with improved narrow action. Mfg. until 1960, fewer than 30 mfg.

	$36,000	$31,000	$27,000	$22,500	$19,000	$17,000	$15,500

ROYAL SIDELOCK GAME GUN - 12, 20, 28 (new 1997) ga., or .410 bore (new 1997), somewhat similar to New Model, with improved cocking, striking and ejection, slimmer action body, DT, 25 to 30 in. game or VR barrels, 2 3/4 in. chambers, finest checkered walnut straight hand or pistol grip stock, scroll engraved receiver with color case hardened or bright finish, prototype testing has finished and guns are available for demonstration, includes aluminum case, 5 lbs. 1 oz - 7 lbs. 8 oz. Written quotations on this re-released model are available by contacting H&H directly (see Trademark Index). Values listed are for base models only and reflect the most recent factory information.

Add £1,250 for single trigger.

Add £10,900-£11,950 per extra set of barrels, depending on bore.

✳ *12 or 20 ga.*

MSR £54,300   £54,300   N/A

Add £2,900 for 28 ga. or £4,200 for .410 bore.

ROYAL DE LUXE MODEL - similar to Royal Sidelock Game Gun, except choice of more elaborate engraving and exhibition wood.

This model is quoted per individual special order only.

SPORTING MODEL - 12, 16, 20, or 28 ga., 2 3/4 or 3 in. chambers, designed with a trigger plate action, Game or Sporting Clays configuration featuring detachable SST mechanism, 25 to 32 in. game or VR barrels, medium scroll engraving, bright finish only. Options on specifications to include screw-in chokes, 12 ga. - 7 1/4-8 lbs., 28 ga. - 6 lbs. New 1993. Values listed reflect most recent factory information.

MSR £31,850   £31,850   N/A

Add £1,250 for color case hardened action with gold name inlay.

Add £8,300-£8,650 per extra set of barrels, depending on bore.

SPORTING DE LUXE MODEL - similar to Sporting O/U Model, except with choice of more elaborate engraving and exhibition wood. New 1993.

This model is quoted per individual special order only.

GRADING - PPGS™	100%	98%	95%	90%	80%	70%	60%

SHOTGUNS: SxS

Holland & Holland currently manufactures the Royal De Luxe Game Gun and Royal Game Gun (limited mfg.) models in sidelock configuration. In addition to the sidelock models, H&H also manufactured the boxlock models Cavalier, Cavalier De Luxe, Northwood, and Northwood De Luxe until recently. The following values assume standard model with double triggers, game rib, standard walnut, or casing. Additional special order features will add considerable value to the price of a new custom order.

In 1988, Holland & Holland absorbed W & C Scott and manufactured the Chatsworth, Bowood, and Kinmount boxlock models until they were discontinued in late 1990. H&H has phased this trademark out, and more information can be found in the W & C Scott section of this text.

All currently manufactured H&H shotguns are priced in English pounds, and 98%-60% values are not included. All older and recently manufactured used rifles are priced in dollars.

NORTHWOOD SxS BOXLOCK - 12, 16 (disc. 1992), 20, or 28 (disc. 1992) ga., 28 or 30 in. barrels, scalloped-case colored receiver, boxlock, auto ejectors, double triggers, border engraving, checkered pistol grip or straight stock. The values shown are for standard model. Disc. 1993.

	$5,950	$5,200	$4,450	$3,850	$3,300	$2,800	$2,300

Last MSR was $6,705.

   Add approx. 10% for 20 ga.
   Add approx. 20% for 28 ga.

＊ *Northwood De Luxe* - 12, 16, 20, or 28 ga., scalloped-case colored receiver with moderate engraving and select walnut, double triggers. Disc. 1993.

	$6,375	$5,450	$4,600	$3,950	$3,350	$2,850	$2,400

Last MSR was $7,450.

   Add approx. 10% for 20 ga.
   Add approx. 20% for 28 ga.

CAVALIER SxS BOXLOCK - 12, 20, or 28 (disc. 1992) ga., best quality model boxlock with scalloped frame, double triggers, ejectors, and case colored receiver. Disc.

	$9,500	$7,750	$6,350	$5,500	$4,850	$4,100	$3,500

Last MSR was $11,175.

   Add approx. 10% for 20 ga.
   Add approx. 20% for 28 ga.

＊ *Cavalier De Luxe* - similar to Cavalier Model, except has deluxe walnut and better engraving. Disc. 1993.

	$9,950	$8,000	$6,500	$5,600	$4,950	$4,200	$3,600

Last MSR was $11,920.

   Add approx. 10% for 20 ga.
   Add approx. 20% for 28 ga.

DOMINION GAME GUN - 12, 16, or 20 ga., 25-30 in. barrels, any choke, sidelock, auto ejectors, double triggers, checkered straight grip stock. Disc. 1990.

	$6,750	$6,150	$5,650	$4,750	$4,150	$3,650	$3,250

   Add 20% for 20 gauge.

ROUND ACTION SIDELOCK - 12 or 20 ga., 2 3/4 in. chambers, rounded frame with back action sidelock, DT, 28 in. chopper lump barrels with game rib, scroll and border engraving, color case hardened or bright finish. New 2004.

MSR £25,250	£25,250	N/A

   Add £5,200 for traditional English rose and fine scroll engraving pattern.

GRADING - PPGS™		100%	98%	95%	90%	80%	70%	60%

ROYAL HAMMERLESS EJECTOR SIDELOCK (OLDER & RECENT MFG.) - 12, 16, 20, 28 ga., or .410 bore, non-self (disc.) or self-opening (recent mfg.), customer specifications as to barrel length and chokes, hand detachable sidelocks, stocked in pistol grip or straight style to specifications. Mfg. 1885-disc.

		100%	98%	95%	90%	80%	70%	60%
12 ga.	N/A	$17,500	$14,750	$12,500	$10,000	$9,000	$8,000
20 ga.	N/A	$23,500	$20,750	$17,500	$14,750	$12,500	$10,000
28 ga.	N/A	$27,050	$24,500	$21,000	$17,500	$14,500	$12,500
.410 bore	N/A	$31,000	$27,750	$23,750	$19,500	$16,250	$14,000

Add 15% for self-opening action.

Add 10%-15% if cased with accessories.

Subtract approx. 10%-15% on 12 ga. with 2 1/2 in. chambers.

Values listed are for older, previously manufactured specimens.

ROYAL GAME GUN (CURRENT MFG.) - 12, 16, 20, 28 ga., or .410 bore, best quality sidelock self-opening game gun. Mfg. per individual customer specifications, includes aluminum travel case. The following values reflect most recent factory information. Mfg. 1922 to date.

✷ *12, 16, or 20 ga.*

MSR £44,500	£44,500	N/A		

Add £3,100 for 28 ga. or .410 bore.

Add £3,730 for ST.

Add £9,350-£10,150, per extra set of barrels, depending on bore.

Add $3,100 for VR (disc.).

ROYAL DE LUXE GAME GUN - 12, 16, 20, 28 ga., or .410 bore, top-of-the-line sidelock self-opening shotgun. Mfg. per individual customer specifications. Current production.

This model is quoted per individual special order only.

Older mfg. is sometimes referred to as the De Luxe Model.

BADMINTON SIDELOCK - 12, 16, or 20 ga., similar to Royal model, except has traditional rose and scroll engraving and does not have self-opening action. Disc.

		100%	98%	95%	90%	80%	70%	60%
12 ga.	N/A	$9,000	$8,000	$7,000	$6,000	$5,000	$4,000
20 ga.	N/A	$10,800	$9,600	$8,400	$7,200	$6,000	$4,800

Add $1,000 for SST.

✷ *Badminton Game Gun* - 12 or 20 ga., double or single trigger. Disc. 1988.

		100%	98%	95%	90%	80%	70%	60%
	N/A	$17,000	$14,500	$12,250	$10,000	$8,500	$6,750

Last MSR was $28,000.

RIVIERA SIDELOCK - similar to Badminton model, with two sets of barrels. Mfg. until 1967.

		100%	98%	95%	90%	80%	70%	60%
12 ga.	N/A	$11,500	$9,500	$7,950	$7,100	$6,350	$5,600
20 ga.	N/A	$13,800	$11,750	$9,000	$8,250	$7,200	$6,450

CENTENARY SIDELOCK - 12 ga., 2 in. chambers, lightened version of Royal, Badminton, and Dominion grades. The values would be the same as for the standard models, mfg. until 1962.

SHOTGUNS: SINGLE SHOT

SINGLE BARREL TRAP GUN - 12 ga., 30 or 32 in. full choke barrel, vent. rib, boxlock, auto ejector, Monte Carlo pistol grip stock, pad. Disc.

		100%	98%	95%	90%	80%	70%	60%
	N/A	$9,250	$8,000	$6,750	$5,800	$4,750	$3,950

Last MSR was $28,420.

✷ *Trap Guns - Older Mfg.*

		100%	98%	95%	90%	80%	70%	60%
Standard Grade	N/A	$4,500	$4,000	$3,250	$2,500	$2,250	$2,000
De Luxe Grade	N/A	$7,000	$6,250	$5,000	$4,500	$3,750	$3,000
Exhibition Grade	N/A	$8,950	$7,500	$6,000	$5,500	$5,000	$4,250

HOLLOWAY & NAUGHTON

Current trade name of long guns manufactured since the late 1800s in England. No current U.S. importation.

Please contact the factory directly (see Trademark Index) for more information including individual quotations. Holloway & Naughton makes 7-10 best quality, custom order only guns annually. They also perform all services, including engraving, in-house.

RIFLES: CUSTOM

O/U DOUBLE RIFLE - custom order, Boss style, best quality. New 2005.

Entry price for a O/U double rifle starts at £75,000, and increases according to customer's specifications.

SxS DOUBLE RIFLE - custom order, Boss style, best quality. New 2005.

Entry price for a SxS double rifle starts at £65,000, and increases according to customer's specifications.

SHOTGUNS: CUSTOM

BOXLOCK O/U MODEL - 12 or 20 ga., Anson & Deeley boxlock action, moderate engraving, special order only. Disc. 2003.

Last MSR was approx. $14,000.

SIDELOCK SPORTING O/U MODEL - 12, 16, 20, 28 ga. or .410 bore (special order only), various configurations including field and sporting clays, features lightweight true Boss case colored action (semi-bright or muted colors) with reinforced forearm, SST, exhibition grade wood, engraving per customer specifications (choice of medium scroll or bouquet and scroll), special order only, approx. 12 month delivery time, 6-7 1/2 lbs.

Prices for this model start at £55,000 (Sporting Clays, 12 or 20 ga.), fully engraved, and includes leather case with accessories and tools.

BOXLOCK SxS MODEL - 12 or 20 ga., Anson & Deeley boxlock action, moderate engraving, special order only. Disc.

Last MSR was $18,000.

HOLLOWAY ARMS CO.

Previous manufacturer located in Fort Worth, TX.

Holloway firearms did not make many rifles or carbines before operations ceased.

RIFLES: SEMI-AUTO

HAC MODEL 7 RIFLE - .308 Win. cal., gas operated semi-auto paramilitary design rifle, 20 in. barrel, adj. front and rear sights, 20 shot mag., side folding stock, right or left-hand action. Mfg. 1984-85 only.

100%	98%	95%	90%	80%	70%	60%
$1,800	$1,650	$1,600	$1,500	$1,400	$1,300	$1,200

Last MSR was $675.

✳ *Model 7C Carbine* - 16 in. carbine, same general specifications as Model 7. Disc. 1985.

100%	98%	95%	90%	80%	70%	60%
$1,950	$1,750	$1,700	$1,500	$1,400	$1,300	$1,200

Last MSR was $675.

Also available from the manufacturer were the Models 7S and 7M (Sniper and Match models).

HOLMES FIREARMS

Previous manufacturer located in Wheeler, AR. Previously distributed by D.B. Distributing, Fayetteville, AR.

GRADING - PPGS™	100%	98%	95%	90%	80%	70%	60%

PISTOLS: SEMI-AUTO

These pistols were mfg. in very limited numbers, most were in prototype configuration and exhibit changes from gun to gun. These models were open bolt and subject to 1988 federal legislation regulations.

MP-83 - 9mm Para. or .45 ACP cal., paramilitary design pistol, 6 in. barrel, walnut stock and forearm, blue finish, 3 1/2 lbs.

	$700	$600	$500	$450	$400	$375	$350

Last MSR was $450.

Add 10% for deluxe package.
Add 40% for conversion kit (mfg. 1985 only).

MP-22 - .22 LR cal., 2 1/2 lbs., steel and aluminum construction, 6 in. barrel, similar appearance to MP-83. Mfg. 1985 only.

	$395	$360	$320	$285	$250	$230	$210

Last MSR was $400.

SHOTGUNS

COMBAT 12 - 12 ga., riot configuration, cylinder bore barrel. Disc. 1983.

	$795	$720	$650	$595	$550	$500	$450

Last MSR was $750.

HOPKINS & ALLEN ARMS COMPANY, 1902-1914

Previous manufacturer located in Norwich, CT. H&A started their firearms business in 1867, manufacturing percussion revolvers. Before 1870, they were producing rimfire cartridge guns and eventually centerfire handguns and long guns. Prior to 1896, H&A guns were marked "HOPKINS & ALLEN MANUFG. CO. NORWICH CONN." or other private tradenames, including Merwin, Hulbert & Company. Hopkins & Allen guns are about equally priced with Stevens, N.R. Davis, Crescent Firearms Co., etc. There are many exceptions due to the numerous limited production guns, examples of which are the AA GRADE double shotgun and the "PARROT BEAK" Derringer. Hopkins & Allen also manufactured firearms which were not described in their catalogs.

Compiled from Hopkins & Allen catalogs by Charles E. Carder.

HANDGUNS

Most H&A handguns were nickel plated, with blue finish originally costing $.50 extra, grips were hard rubber, wood or pearl. Some had engraving from low to very good quality. Revolver barrel lengths varied from 1 3/4-6 in. Calibers were .22 rimfire (.22 S, L, or LR) up to .38-40 WCF. Specific calibers have not been listed in this section.

FOREHAND MODEL - .32 cal., top break, double action, five shot.

	$190	$160	$140	$120	$100	$85	$75

FOREHAND MODEL - similar to above except hammerless. (This model was offered in large and small frame).

	$190	$160	$140	$120	$100	$85	$75

FOREHAND MODEL - large frame as above in .32 and .38 centerfire cal. with full hammer or "bobbed" hammer.

	$190	$160	$140	$120	$100	$85	$75

FOREHAND MODEL - solid frame and hard rubber grips, otherwise as above in small frame.

	$170	$140	$120	$100	$85	$75	$65

GRADING - PPGS™	100%	98%	95%	90%	80%	70%	60%

FOREHAND MODEL - similar to above models, with "folding hammer." .22 rimfires were seven shot, while .32 and .38 centerfires were five shot. By 1909, the Forehand logo was dropped from these revolvers.

	$170	$140	$120	$100	$85	$75	$65

H&A NEW MODEL AUTOMATIC HAMMER REVOLVER - similar to top break with hammer, produced in small and large frame, in .22 rimfire, .32 and .38 centerfire cal.

	$170	$140	$120	$100	$85	$75	$65

H&A SOLID FRAME - .32 and .38 centerfire cal., five shot, double action, hammer or "bobbed" hammer.

	$175	$140	$120	$100	$85	$70	$55

H&A XL MODEL - similar to above in .22, .32 and .38 cal.

	$160	$140	$120	$100	$85	$70	$55

H&A RANGE MODEL - .22, .32 and .38 cal., solid frame, loading gate on right side, wood target style grips, single or double action (two models, large and small frames).

	$200	$175	$140	$120	$100	$85	$70

H&A TRIPLE ACTION SAFETY POLICE REVOLVER - .22, .32 and .38 cal., top break with newly designed locking mechanism, hard rubber or pearl grips (considered to be one of the best designed breaktops in its time). Other options for this model included hammerless, engraved, and wood target or pearl grips.

	$240	$210	$175	$140	$120	$100	$85

H&A NEW VEST POCKET DERRINGER - .22 Short rimfire cal., single shot, tip up, single action, 3 1/2 in. overall length, folding trigger, blue or nickel finish, wood or pearl grips with golden monograms. This model was first listed about 1910 and known as the "Parrot Beak." It is estimated that less than one thousand were produced, and they are very rare.

	$2,375	$2,100	$1,800	$1,550	$1,250	$950	$650

H&A NEW MODEL TARGET PISTOL - .22 rimfire cal., single shot top break with the same new locking mechanism as the Safety Police Revolver, wood target grips with golden monograms, blue finish and 6, 8, or 10 in. barrels.

	$565	$495	$440	$375	$325	$285	$250

H&A NEW MODEL SKELETON STOCK TARGET PISTOL - similar to above, with rounded hard rubber grips with logo, detachable "skeleton metal stock," 18 in. barrel, and blue finish.

	$850	$775	$675	$600	$550	$500	$465

RIFLES

Hopkins & Allen started building "falling block" rifles circa 1887-1914 with the buy-out of the Baystate Arms Company. Most commonly seen is the "Junior" model, known after 1902 as 922, 925, and 932. These numbers were in reference to the catalog numbers, not model numbers. In the very late 1890s or early 1900s, the Number 722, 822, and 832 rifles were added. In 1906, a "bolt action" repeater was added to their line, followed in 1909 by a "bolt action" single shot "military." Specific calibers have not been listed in this section.

Add $60-$75 for Lyman tang sights on the following models.

NUMBER 922 - falling block, lever operated, .22 cal. rimfire, with round bbl.

	$310	$245	$195	$195	$165	$125	$110

NUMBER 925 - similar to above in .25 cal. rimfire.

	$390	$310	$245	$195	$150	$110	$95

GRADING - PPGS™	100%	98%	95%	90%	80%	70%	60%

NUMBER 932 - similar to above in .32 cal. rimfire.

	100%	98%	95%	90%	80%	70%	60%
	$310	$245	$195	$150	$110	$95	$80

NUMBER 938 - similar to above in .38 S&W centerfire.

	$440	$350	$285	$225	$200	$175	$150

NUMBER 1922 - similar to above in .22 cal. rimfire with octagon bbl.

	$310	$250	$200	$180	$165	$150	$125

NUMBER 1932 - similar to above in .32 cal. rimfire.

	$310	$250	$200	$165	$125	$110	$90

NUMBER 2922 - similar to above in .22 cal. rimfire, with checkering.

	$420	$335	$265	$225	$195	$175	$150

NUMBER 2932 - similar to above in .32 cal. rimfire.

	$420	$335	$265	$225	$195	$175	$150

NUMBER 3922 - similar to above in .22 cal. rimfire, "SCHUETZEN RIFLE," nickeled Swiss buttplate, octagon barrel (Schuetzen rifles in good cond. are somewhat rare).

	$775	$620	$495	$450	$400	$365	$325

NUMBER 3925 - similar to above in .25-20 WCF (this caliber rifle is more rare than the .22 cal. rimfire).

	$1,010	$810	$650	$600	$550	$500	$450

NUMBER 44XL - chambered for the 44XL shotshell, similar to Number 922, except has smooth bore (referred to as "TAXIDERMIST'S" or "LADIES GUN").

	$530	$430	$350	$325	$275	$235	$200

NUMBER 722 - .22 cal. rimfire, rolling block, thumb operated.

	$300	$240	$195	$165	$125	$110	$90

SCOUT MILITARY RIFLE - similar to above with military style stock and with a "Bonneted Indian" stamped on the left side of frame (these are somewhat rare).

	$505	$405	$325	$285	$250	$200	$175

NUMBER 822 - .22 cal. rimfire, rolling block, lever operated.

	$300	$240	$195	$175	$150	$125	$100

NUMBER 832 - .32 cal. rimfire, otherwise similar to Model 822 (this model was offered first with "pig tail" type levers and later with "loop" type levers. The "loop" levers are somewhat rare).

	$350	$280	$225	$200	$175	$150	$125

NUMBER 4922 - .22 rimfire cal., bolt action, repeater.

	$260	$205	$165	$135	$120	$100	$80

NUMBER 5022 - similar to above with deluxe checkering.

	$340	$270	$215	$175	$150	$135	$100

MILITARY RIFLE - similar to above, except single shot with military style stock and sling (in good condition, these are somewhat rare).

	$490	$395	$315	$250	$225	$200	$185

NOISELESS - .22 rimfire, similar to the Number 922, except for checkered wood and the addition of a noise suppressor attached to the muzzle, by means of mating threads inside of suppressor and outside of barrel. The job is so well fitted, that it is difficult to recognize the suppressor. The front sight is attached to a dovetail slot in the suppressor. These rifles are listed under the National Firearms Act of 1934 and must have proper licensing. Very rare.

	$690	$625	$575	$500	$450	$395	$325

GRADING - PPGS™	100%	98%	95%	90%	80%	70%	60%

SHOTGUNS: SxS

Hopkins & Allen purchased Forehand Arms Co. and W.H. Davenport and continued to produce their line of firearms, and after a few years dropped the Forehand name. In 1902, they offered the Forehand double boxlocks with or without outside hammers. Most models were offered in 12, 16 & 20 gauge. Sidelocks were added 1906-09. In 1902, the AA GRADE, a very high quality boxlock, was offered for $100 to $125. It had fine damascus barrels, straight grip, plain or automatic ejectors, fine wood, and engraving, and was competitive with some Remingtons, L.C. Smiths, Bakers and other fine guns of that era. This gun was very short lived and today is rare. One feature found on all H&A double barrel guns is the "rib extension" or "doll's head."

BOXLOCK - Anson & Deeley type frame, damascus, twist, and steel barrels.

	$315	$275	$235	$195	$160	$130	$95

BOXLOCK - similar to above, except with outside hammers.

	$315	$275	$235	$195	$160	$130	$95

SIDELOCK - hammerless, damascus, twist, and steel barrels.

	$315	$275	$235	$195	$160	$130	$115

SIDELOCK - similar to above, except with outside hammers.

	$315	$275	$235	$195	$160	$130	$95

SHOTGUNS: SINGLE SHOT

H&A produced a "falling block" shotgun in most gauges circa 1887-early 1900s. Falling Blocks (FBs) in 12 ga. were built on heavy frames with the 20 and 16 gauges sharing a medium frame. Prior to 1902, some FBs were chambered for .45-70 shotshells and, today, these are rare if in good condition. From the 1890s through 1914, 38XL, 44XL shotshell guns were periodically offered in the Junior frame. After 1902, "tip-over" single shotguns were offered in Forehand designs and, later, the Davenport designs.

FALLING BLOCK - lever operated, outside hammer.

	$275	$235	$210	$180	$160	$145	$125

BOXLOCK - with outside hammer, damascus, twist, and steel barrels.

	$190	$170	$150	$130	$110	$95	$80

BOXLOCK - hammerless, top safety.

	$190	$170	$150	$130	$110	$95	$80

GOOSE GUNS - outside hammer, 8, 10, or 12 ga., were offered with barrels up to 40 inches long.

	$250	$225	$190	$170	$150	$135	$115

"SAFETY SINGLE GUN" - engraved with outside hammer and top safety. Was offered in 1911 and recommended for trap shooting for $15.00.

	$250	$225	$195	$175	$155	$140	$125

HORTON, LEW, DIST. CO.

See Lew Horton Dist. Co. listing.

HOWA

Current manufacturer established in 1967, and located in Tokyo, Japan. Howa sporting rifles are currently imported beginning Oct., 1999 by Legacy Sports International, LLC, located in Alexandria, VA. Previously imported until 1999 by Interarms/Howa, located in Alexandria, VA, Weatherby (Vanguard Series only), Smith & Wesson (pre-1985), and Mossberg (1986-1987).

RIFLES: BOLT ACTION

Howa also manufactures barreled actions in various configurations. Current MSRs range from $385-$523.

GRADING - PPGS™	100%	98%	95%	90%	80%	70%	60%

MODEL 1500 HUNTER - various cals., 3 (Mag. or WSM cals. only) or 5 shot, 22 or 24 in. barrel, adj. rear sight and trigger, checkered walnut stock, blue metal finish or stainless steel (new 1999) construction, approx. 7.6 lbs. Imported by Interarms 1988 only, reintroduced by Legacy during 1999.

MSR $574	$460	$345	$295	$250	$215	$175	$160

Add $21 for Mag. cals.
Add $108 for stainless steel.

MODEL 1500+/1500 LIGHTNING - various cals., lightweight variation of the Model 1500 Hunter featuring lightweight regular or Carbolite (disc.) black synthetic stock with cheekpiece and pressed checkering, or 100% Realtree camo coverage (new 2005), 22 or 24 in. barrel, no sights, 3 or 5 shot mag., blue or stainless steel, approx. 7-7.6 lbs. Imported 1988-1991, reimportation began 1993.

MSR $508	$410	$335	$280	$240	$210	$175	$160

Last MSR was $539 when disc. in 1991.

Add $23 for Mag. cals., including WSMs.
Add $112 for stainless steel.
Add $37 for camo.
Subtract approx. 10% if w/o Nikko scope package.
During 2005, a Nikko scope package became standard on this model.
The Model 1500+ was introduced during 2005, and features a three position safety.

MODEL 1500+/1500 ULTRALIGHT - .243 Win., .308 Win. (new 2003), or 7mm-08 Rem. (new 2003) cal., 20 in. barrel, short bolt throw, non-glare blue, blue/black metal, or stainless steel finish, black finished hardwood stock, 5 shot mag., w/o sights, Youth model with 12 5/8 in. LOP introduced 2003, 6.4 lbs. Importation began 2002.

MSR $539	$445	$335	$295	$260	$230	$190	$170

Add $119 for stainless steel.
Add $21 for Nikko 3-9X x 42mm scope, flip up covers, rings, and bases - blue finish only.
The Model 1500+ was introduced during 2005, and features a three position safety.

MODEL 1500 VARMINT - .22-250 Rem., .223 Rem., .243 Win. (new 2005), or .308 Win. (mfg. 1990-92, reintroduced 2001) cal., 24 in. heavy barrel without sights, 5 shot mag., blue steel or stainless steel (new 1999) construction, black polymer (new 1999), 100% Realtree camo (new 2005), or walnut stock, approx. 9.3 lbs. Imported 1988-92, reintroduced 2001.

MSR $546	$450	$365	$310	$245	$210	$175	$160

Add $64 for wood stock.
Add $36 for camo.
Add $173 for stainless steel.

MODEL 1500+/1500 SUPREME - available in various standard and Mag. cals. between .22-250 Rem. - .338 Win. Mag., 22 or 24 in. barrel, 3 or 5 shot mag., choice of JRS Classic, black (Varminter only), Thumbhole Sporter, Varminter, or Thumbhole Varminter stock configuration available in either pepper or nutmeg finish, blue metal finish or stainless steel, 8-9.9 lbs. Importation began 2003.

The Model 1500+ was introduced during 2005, and features a three position safety.

✳ *Model 1500+/1500 Supreme JRS Classic* - standard stock configuration, w/o sights, 8 lbs. Importation began 2003.

MSR $646	$515	$395	$340	$300	$265	$240	$220

Add $109 for stainless steel.
Add $29 for Mag. cals.

✳ *Model 1500+/1500 Varminter Supreme* - .22-250 Rem., .223 Rem., .243 Win. (new 2005) or .308 Win. cal., nutmeg, pepper, or black synthetic stock, 9.3 lbs. Importation began 2003.

MSR $711	$565	$410	$350	$315	$275	$250	$225

Add $109 for stainless steel.

✳ *Model 1500+/1500 Thumbhole Varminter Supreme* - similar to Supreme Varminter, except has thumbhole stock configuration. Importation began 2003.

MSR $733	**$585**	**$425**	**$365**	**$325**	**$275**	**$250**	**$225**

Add $109 for stainless steel.

✳ *Model 1500+/1500 Thumbhole Sporter Supreme* - similar to Thumbole Varminter, except has 22 in. barrel, 8 lbs. Importation began 2003.

MSR $704	**$560**	**$400**	**$350**	**$310**	**$275**	**$250**	**$225**

Add $109 for stainless steel.
Add $29 for Mag. cals.

MODEL 1500 CUSTOM - .300 Win. Mag. or .300 WSM cal., 22 or 24 (.300 Win. Mag. cal. only) in. barrel, black polymer or laminate wood in either the Classic JRS or thumbhole configuration, 3 shot mag., blue (.300 Win. Mag. cal. only) or stainless steel barrel and action, 7.6–8.1 lbs. Imported 2002-2004.

$775	**$695**	**$625**	**$550**	**$500**	**$465**	**$435**

Last MSR was $858.

Add $30 for JRS nutmeg finish stock and blued finish.
Add $102 for JRS laminate stock.
Add $131 for thumbhole laminate stock in pepper finish.

MODEL 1500 TEXAS SAFARI - .270 Win. or .300 Win. Mag. cal., features Howa M-1500 barreled action with Bill Wiseman recontoured bolt sleeve and receiver, bolt release, and 3-position safety, 3 or 5 shot mag., non-glare blue Teflon metal finish, brown laminate glass bedded stock, individually test fired, approx. 7.8 lbs. Imported 2002-2003.

$1,350	**$1,150**	**$950**	**$825**	**$675**	**$575**	**$500**

Last MSR was $1,580.

Add $240 for .300 Win. Mag. cal.
This model was also available as a complete custom rifle with many options and special orders.

MODEL 1500 PCS - .308 Win. cal., police counter sniper rifle featuring 24 in. barrel, choice of blue metal or stainless steel, black synthetic or checkered walnut stock, no sights, approx. 9.3 lbs. Imported 1999-2000.

$385	**$315**	**$265**	**$225**	**$195**	**$175**	**$160**

Last MSR was $465.

Add $20 for wood stock.
Add $60 for stainless steel.

MODEL 1500 TROPHY - .22-250 Rem., .223 Rem., .243 Win., .270 Win., .308 Win., .30-06, .300 Win. Mag., .338 Win. Mag. or 7mm Rem. Mag. cal., 3 (Mag. cals. only) or 5 shot, 22 or 24 in. barrel, adj. rear sight and trigger, select Monte Carlo stock with skipline checkering. Imported 1988-92.

$528	**$410**	**$335**	**$290**	**$260**	**$240**	**$225**

Last MSR was $528.

Add $20 for Mag. cals.

LIGHTNING WOODGRAIN - .243 Win., .270 Win., .30-06, .308 Win., or 7mm Rem. Mag. cal., features lightweight Carbolite synthetic stock with simulated wood grain and checkering, 22 in. barrel, 5 shot mag., no sights, 7.5 lbs. Imported 1994 only.

$450	**$395**	**$365**	**$320**	**$275**	**$250**	**$225**

Last MSR was $537.

Add $19 for 7mm Rem. Mag. cal.

REALTREE CAMO RIFLE - .270 Win. or .30-06 (disc. 1993) cal., 22 in. barrel, 5 shot mag., monobloc receiver, drilled and tapped, thumb safety, entire rifle is coated with a Realtree brown leaf camo pattern, no sights, 8 lbs. Imported 1993-94.

$495	**$400**	**$350**	**$325**	**$300**	**$280**	**$260**

Last MSR was $620.

GRADING - PPGS™	100%	98%	95%	90%	80%	70%	60%

HUG-SAN

Previous shotgun manufacturer located in Huglu, Turkey until 2000.

Hug-San manufactured slide action, semi-auto, and O/U shotguns, in various configurations and gauges.

HUGLU

Current shotgun manufacturer established in 1962, and located in Huglu, Turkey. Currently imported beginning 2002 by Armsco Firearms Corp., located in Des Plains, IL. Previously imported 1999-2002 by Huglu USA, located in Rigby, ID.

Huglu makes a wide variety of quality O/U, semi-auto, and SxS shotguns available in all gauges, and are now imported exclusively by Armsco. Some Huglu models were imported 1999-2002 by Huglu USA, and are stamped "Huglu USA, Rigby, ID" on the barrel. Huglu USA Ltd. Co. was reorganized in January 2003 as H-Legacy Shotguns Ltd. Co., and is now a Huglu dealer. For more information, including current models, prices, and U.S. availability, please contact Armsco directly (see Trademark Index).

SHOTGUNS: O/U

Armsco previously imported the 103 Series. Models with last MSRs included: 103D - $679 MSR, 103D Mini (28 ga. or .410 bore) - $849 MSR, 103DE (ejectors) - $849 MSR, 103C (case colored receiver) - $799 MSR, 103C Mini - MSR $999, 103CE - $949 MSR, 103F - $949, 103F Mini - $1,199 MSR, 103FE - $1,099 MSR, 103FEC - $1,199 MSR, 103FC Mini - $1,299 MSR., 104A $499 - MSR, and 104A Mini - $699 MSR.

Current O/U models include: Canvasback - $799 MSR, Canvasback Small Gauge - $949 MSR, Canvasback Deluxe - $899 MSR, Redhead - $799 MSR, Redhead Small Gauge - $949 MSR, Redhead Youth - disc. 2004, last MSR was $799, Redhead Deluxe - $899 MSR, Pintail - $1,049 MSR, Pintail Small Gauge - $1,299 MSR, Pintail Deluxe - $1,199 MSR, Mallard - $549 MSR, American Trap - disc. 2004, last MSR was $1,899, American Trap Combo - disc. 2004, last MSR was $2,199, and the English Sporter - $1,899 MSR.

SHOTGUNS: SxS

Armsco's previous lineup of Huglu SxS shotguns through 2003 with last MSRs included: 201A - $899 MSR, 201AC (choke tubes) - $999 MSR, 201A Mini - $1,099, 201AC Mini - $1,199, 202B - $599 MSR, 202B Mini - $799 MSR, 202BCB - $599 MSR, and the 200ACB - $799 MSR.

Current SxS models include: the Bobwhite - $699 MSR, Bobwhite Silver - $899 MSR, Ringneck - $999 MSR, Ringneck Small Gauge - $1,199 MSR, Woodcock - disc. 2004, last MSR was $1,049, Woodcock Small Gauge - disc. 2004, last MSR was $1,299, Woodcock Deluxe - disc. 2004, last MSR was $1,199, Amarillo - $699 MSR, and the Durango - $849 MSR.

SHOTGUNS: SEMI-AUTO

Armsco previous lineup of Huglu's semi-auto shotguns through 2003 with last MSRs included: 501GA - $499 MSR, 501GB - $499 MSR, 601GA - $499 MSR, 601GB - $499 MSR, 601GM (3 1/2 in. chamber) - $599 MSR, 701GA - $499 MSR, and the 701GB - $499 MSR.

Current semi-auto models include: Sharptail - $549 MSR, Teal - $549 MSR, and the Canadian - $649 MSR.

SHOTGUNS: SINGLE SHOT

Armsco imported the Model 301A. MSR was $199. Currently, the Cottontail Model is $199 MSR.

HUNTER ARMS COMPANY

Previous manufacturer located in Fulton, NY circa 1891-1945.

The Hunter Arms Company was formed to manufacture L.C. Smith shotguns. Please refer to the L.C. Smith section in this text for further information regarding this manufacturer (including Fulton, Fulton Special, and Hunter Special models).

GRADING - PPGS™	100%	98%	95%	90%	80%	70%	60%

HUSQVARNA

Previous manufacturer located in Husqvarna, Sweden.

Also see: Lahti Pistols.

RIFLES: BOLT ACTION

HI-POWER - .220 Swift, .270 Win., or .30-06 cal., Mauser type action, open sight, checkered beech wood. Mfg. 1946-51, early models found in 6.5x55mm, 8x57R, 9.3x57mm cals.

	$480	$440	$395	$365	$330	$295	$265

MODEL 1951 - similar to Hi-Power, except high profile stock.

	$500	$465	$425	$385	$340	$300	$270

SERIES 1100 DELUXE - similar to Model 1951, except has European walnut and jeweled bolt. Mfg. 1952-56.

	$520	$480	$440	$360	$330	$310	$290

SERIES 1000 SUPER GRADE - similar to Model 1951, has walnut Monte Carlo stock. Mfg. 1952-56.

	$520	$480	$440	$360	$330	$310	$290

SERIES 3100 CROWN GRADE - .243 Win., .270 Win., .30-06, 7x57mm, or .308 Win. cal., improved HVA Mauser action, 24 in. barrel, walnut stock, black forend tip and pistol grip cap. Mfg. 1954-72.

	$575	$525	$475	$400	$360	$330	$315

SERIES 3000 CROWN GRADE - similar to 3100, except has Monte Carlo stock.

	$660	$595	$525	$475	$400	$360	$330

SERIES 4100 LIGHTWEIGHT - HVA Mauser action, calibers same as 3100, 20 1/2 in. barrel, open sights, lightweight walnut stock, pistol grip, Schnabel forend. Mfg. 1954-72.

	$575	$525	$475	$400	$360	$330	$315

SERIES 4000 LIGHTWEIGHT - similar to 4100, except has Monte Carlo stock, no sights.

	$660	$595	$525	$475	$400	$360	$330

MODEL 456 LIGHTWEIGHT - similar to 4000/4100, except full length stock. Mfg. 1959-70.

	$600	$550	$495	$415	$385	$360	$330

SERIES 6000 IMPERIAL GRADE - similar to 3100, except has select wood, 3 leaf folding sight. Mfg. 1968-70.

	$695	$625	$575	$495	$470	$440	$395

SERIES 7000 IMPERIAL LIGHTWEIGHT - similar to 6000 Imperial, except 20 1/2 in. barrel, lightweight stock.

	$775	$695	$625	$575	$495	$470	$440

SERIES P-3000 PRESENTATION - similar to Crown, except engraved action, special wood. Mfg. 1968-70.

	$925	$850	$775	$675	$575	$500	$450

MODEL 9000 CROWN GRADE - cals. similar to Model 3100 Crown Grade, except also available in .300 Win. Mag. cal., Husqvarna action, 23 1/2 in. barrel, adj. trigger, adj. sight, walnut stock. Mfg. 1971-72.

	$575	$525	$475	$400	$360	$330	$315

GRADING - PPGS™	100%	98%	95%	90%	80%	70%	60%

MODEL 8000 IMPERIAL - similar to 9000, but jeweled bolt, engraved floor plate, no sights and deluxe stock. Mfg. 1971-1972.

	$750	$675	$595	$525	$495	$470	$415

HY-HUNTER INC. FIREARMS MANUFACTURING CO.

Previous trademark imported by Hy-Hunter Inc., located in Hollywood, CA.

Hy-Hunter Inc. imported single action revolvers in various calibers and O/U derringers manufactured in West Germany. Typically, prices are determined by their shooting value rather than their collector value. Prices generally range from $100-$175 depending on caliber and finish.

HYPER

Previous manufacturer located in Jenks, OK.

RIFLES: SINGLE SHOT

SINGLE SHOT RIFLE - all calibers, all standard lengths and contours, falling block trigger guard lever activated, adj. trigger, no sights, stocked to customer specifications, in AA grade walnut. Disc. 1984.

	$2,200	$1,980	$1,925	$1,870	$1,650	$1,540	$1,375

Add $75 for stainless barrel.
Add $85 for octagon barrel.

I SECTION

I.A.B. srl

Current manufacturer (Industria Armi Bresciane) of modern firearms, black powder replicas and historical Sharps rifles located in Gardone, Valtrompia, Brescia, Italy. Currently imported by Kiesler's, located in Jeffersonville, IN, E.M.F., located in Santa Ana, CA, Dixie Gun Works, located in Union City, TN, and Tristar Sporting Arms, located in Kansas City, MO. Previously imported by American Arms, located in Kansas City, MO. Previously distributed by Sporting Arms International, Inc. located in Indianola, MS.

Please refer to indiviual importers for model information and pricing.

I.A.B. also manufactures shotguns (O/U and single barrel trap or skeet) in various styles and configurations including combo sets. These guns employ a boxlock action, have ejectors, and various amounts of engraving. Prices for 100% condition usually start in the $650-$1,000 price range. I.A.B. shotguns are not being imported currently - values for older models will be determined by the prices shooters, not collectors, are willing to pay for them.

IAI

Please refer to Intrac Arms International LLC listing.

IAI INC. – AMERICAN LEGEND

Previous manufacturer, importer, and distributor located in Houston, TX. Firearms were manufactured by Israel Arms International, Inc., located in Houston, TX. IAI designates Israel Arms International, and should not be confused with Irwindale Arms, Inc. (also IAI).

The models listed were part of an American Legend Series that are patterned after famous American and Belgian military carbines/rifles and semi-auto pistols.

GRADING - PPGS™	100%	98%	95%	90%	80%	70%	60%

CARBINES/RIFLES

MODEL 888 M1 CARBINE - .22 LR or .30 Carbine cal., 18 in. barrel, mfg. from new original M1 parts and stock by IAI (barrel bolt and receiver) and unused GI parts, 10 shot mag., choice of birch or walnut stock, parkerized finish, metal or wood handguard, 5 1/2 lbs. Mfg. by IAI in Houston, TX 1998-2004.

	100%	98%	95%	90%	80%	70%	60%
	$475	$395	$365	$335	$295	$260	$240

Last MSR was $556.

Add $11 for .22 LR cal.

Add $31 for walnut/metal forearm or $47 for walnut/wood forearm.

MODEL 333 M1 GARAND - .30-06 cal., patterned after the WWII M1 Garand, 24 in. barrel, 8 shot en-bloc mag., parkerized finish, 9.5 lbs. Mfg. 2003-2004.

	100%	98%	95%	90%	80%	70%	60%
	$850	$775	$675	$575	$475	$375	$325

Last MSR was $972.

PISTOLS: SEMI-AUTO

MODEL 2000 - .45 ACP cal., patterned after the Colt Govt. 1911, 5 or 4 1/4 (Commander configuration, Model 2000-C) in. barrel, parkerized finish, plastic or rubber finger groove grips, 36-38 oz. Mfg. in South Africa 2002-2004.

	100%	98%	95%	90%	80%	70%	60%
	$415	$365	$325	$295	$275	$250	$225

Last MSR was $465.

I A I

Please refer to the Irwindale Arms, Inc. heading in this section.

IAR, Inc.

Current importer and distributor since 1995 located in San Juan Capistrano, CA.

IAR, Inc. imports and distributes a wide variety of firearms, including revolvers (MSR $435 for .45 LC cal.), baby rolling block carbines (MSR $500), rifle reproductions (MSR $500-$800), and exposed hammer shotguns (MSR $470). IAR, Inc. also imports black powder reproductions and replicas, plus a complete lineup of blank firing arms and ammunition, including pistols, revolvers, and rifles. Please contact the factory directly regarding their current product lineup and consumer pricing (see Trademark Index).

I G A SHOTGUNS

Current trademark with manufacturing facilities located in Veranopolis, Brazil (O/U and SxS shotguns only), and by Vursan Manufacturing (semi-auto shotguns only) beginning in 2000, located in Istanbul, Turkey. Currently imported by Stoeger Industries, Inc. located in Accokeek, MD. Previously located in Wayne, NJ.

During 2000, Stoeger Industries was purchased by Beretta USA Corp., located in Accokeek, MD.

SHOTGUNS: O/U

CONDOR MODEL - 12 ga. only, single trigger, ejectors, presentation walnut, chrome lined bores. Disc. 1985.

	$580	$500	$450	$410	$375	$350	$325

Last MSR was $667.

CONDOR I SINGLE TRIGGER - 12, 20 ga. or .410 bore (new 2005), 3 in. chambers, boxlock action, deluxe checkered walnut, extractors, 26 or 28 in. VR separated barrels with chokes tubes (standard beginning 1992), 7.7 lbs.

MSR $350	$315	$265	$230	$210	$195	$180	$160

Add $150 for Condor combo, including set of 12 ga. and 20 ga. barrels (new 2004).
This model is also available in a Youth model with 22 in. barrels and 13 LOP stock.

CONDOR II DOUBLE TRIGGER - 12 or 20 (disc.) ga., boxlock action, VR, checkered walnut, separated barrels. Disc. 1997.

	$350	$295	$260	$230	$195	$170	$150

Last MSR was $459.

CONDOR I SPECIAL - similar to Condor I, except features matte stainless steel receiver, oil finished hardwood stock and forearm. Importation began 2002.

MSR $415	$365	$325	$275	$235	$215	$195	$180

Add $135 for Condor combo, including set of 12 ga. and 20 ga. barrels (new 2004).

CONDOR SUPREME - 12 or 20 ga., boxlock action, single trigger, ejectors, 26 or 28 in. VR barrels with choke tubes, deluxe checkered walnut stock and forearm. Imported 1995-2000.

	$500	$450	$395	$360	$320	$280	$240

Last MSR was $629.

CONDOR SUPREME DELUXE - 12 or 20 ga., 3 in. chambers, 24 (20 ga. only), 26, or 30 (disc. 2001) in. VR barrels with choke tubes, high polish blue, gold SST, AE, checkered high gloss American walnut stock and forearm, approx. 7.7 lbs. Importation began 2000.

MSR $500	$455	$400	$360	$330	$300	$285	$265

Add $100 for Condor combo, including set of 12 ga. and 20 ga. barrels (new 2004).

GRADING - PPGS™	100%	98%	95%	90%	80%	70%	60%

HUNTER CLAYS MODEL - 12 ga. only, ST, ejectors, 28 in. barrels with choke tubes, deluxe checkered stock and forearm, gold trigger. Mfg. 1997-99.

	$595	$515	$435	$375	$335	$300	$270

Last MSR was $699.

CONDOR COMPETITION - 12 or 20 ga., 3 in. chambers, 30 in. ported barrels, checkered select American walnut stock and forearm. New 2005.

MSR $579	$495	$425	$375	$350	$315	$295	$275

TURKEY SERIES - 12 ga. only, 3 in. chambers, 26 in. VR barrels with choke tubes, ST, ejectors, Advantage camo on wood and metal (except receiver). Mfg. 1997-2000.

	$615	$525	$450	$380	$335	$300	$270

Last MSR was $729.

WATERFOWL SERIES - 12 ga. only, 3 in. chambers, similar to Turkey Series, except has 30 in. barrels. Mfg. 1998-2000.

	$615	$525	$450	$380	$335	$300	$270

Last MSR was $729.

TRAP SERIES - 12 ga., features SST, ejectors, 30 in. VR barrels with choke tubes, deluxe checkered Monte Carlo stock and forearm. Mfg. 1998-99.

	$595	$515	$435	$375	$335	$300	$270

Last MSR was $699.

ERA 2000 MODELS - 12 ga. only, 26 or 28 in. VR barrels with choke tubes, single trigger. Imported 1992-94.

	$585	$375	$315	$250	$215	$195	$180

Last MSR was $710.

SHOTGUNS: SxS

UPLANDER MODEL - 12, 16 (new 1996), 20, 28 ga., or .410 bore, 3 in. chambers, 24 (English style stock only), 26, or 28 in. barrels with extractors, DT, underlug lockup, checkered pistol grip or straight English (20 ga. or .410 bore only) stock, Youth Model also available in 20 ga. and .410 bore.

MSR $335	$300	$235	$185	$150	$130	$115	$100

Add $15 for choke tubes (12 or 20 ga.).

UPLANDER SPECIAL - 12, 20, or 28 ga., 3 in. chambers (not available in 28 ga.), 24 or 26 in. barrels, fixed chokes on 28 ga., features straight grip Brazilian hardwood checkered English stock and forearm, DT, approx. 7.3 lbs. New 2002.

MSR $375	$340	$300	$260	$230	$200	$165	$125

UPLANDER SUPREME - 12 or 20 ga., 3 in. chambers, 24 (20 ga. only), 26, or 28 in. barrels with choke tubes, AE, gold SST, high gloss checkered walnut stock and forearm. Importation began 2000.

MSR $445	$395	$355	$300	$265	$230	$200	$175

Add $154 for combo package (includes 12 and 20 ga. or 20 and 28 ga. barrels, new 2005).

DELUXE MODEL - 12, 20, 28 ga., or .410 bore, features better quality checkered walnut stock and forearm, gold triggers, 12 and 20 ga. have choke tubes, 28 ga. and .410 bore have fixed chokes. Mfg. 1997-99.

	$425	$365	$310	$270	$230	$195	$170

Last MSR was $559.

Subtract $40 for 28 ga. or .410 bore (fixed chokes only).

GRADING - PPGS™	100%	98%	95%	90%	80%	70%	60%

COACH GUN MODEL - 12, 20 ga., or .410 (new 1991) bore, hammerless, choice of blue or nickel (new 1996) finish, 20 in. fixed choke barrels only (IC/M), choice of dark (nickel finish only) or light hardwood stock, 6 1/2 lbs.

	MSR $320	$280	$240	$195	$165	$135	$110	$100

Add $55 for nickel finish.

Add $64 for engraved stagecoach scene on stock (mfg. 1996-99).

✳ *Coach Deluxe* - similar to Coach Gun Model, includes deluxe checkered walnut stock and forearm, fixed (IC/M) or choke tubes (new 1998), gold triggers. Mfg. 1997-99.

			$385	$325	$290	$260	$230	$195	$170

Last MSR was $499.

SILVERADO COACH GUN - similar to Coach Gun, except features a matte nickel metal finish and oil finished hardwood pistol grip or straight English (not available in .410 bore) stock and forearm. Imported 2002-2004.

			$320	$270	$215	$180	$150	$130	$110

Last MSR was $375.

COACH GUN SUPREME - 12, 20 ga. or .410 bore, blue, polished nickel, or stainless steel receiver, blue or polished nickel 20 or 24 in. barrels with choke tubes (except for .410 bore), checkered walnut stock with recoil pad and beavertail forearm, DT, extractors. Importation began 2004.

	MSR $370		$325	$275	$215	$180	$150	$130	$110

Add $20 for stainless steel receiver or $40 for polished nickel receiver and barrels.

Add $10 for 20 ga. or .410 bore.

TURKEY SERIES MODEL - 12 ga. only, 3 in. chambers, 24 in. barrels, DT, choke tubes. Mfg. 1997-2000.

			$425	$365	$310	$270	$230	$195	$170

Last MSR was $559.

SHOTGUNS : SEMI-AUTO

MODEL 2000 - 12 ga. only, 3 in. chamber, Benelli licensed inertia recoil operating system, 26, 28, or 30 in. VR barrel with 5 choke tubes, checkered walnut or black synthetic (new 2002) stock and forearm, matte metal, 100% Advantage Timber HD camo (new 2002), or Max-4 camo (new 2004) finish, approx. 7.1 lbs. Mfg. by Vursan Manufacturing located in Istanbul, Turkey, with importation beginning 2001.

	MSR $400		$340	$300	$270	$245	$225	$195	$175

Add $75 for 100% camo coverage.

Add $10 for checkered walnut stock and forearm.

Add $121 for Model 2000 Deluxe with upgraded wood and floral etched receiver trim (disc. 2003).

This model is also available as a combo package which includes a smoothbore slug barrel with screw-in IC choke and rifle sights - MSR is $589 in synthetic, $689 with camo, and $580 with walnut (disc. 2002).

✳ *Model 2000 Slug* - 12 ga. only, 3 in. chamber, available with walnut or synthetic with 100% Advantage Timber HD finish, 24 in. smoothbore barrel with adj. rifle sights, 6.7 lbs. Imported 2003-2004.

			$365	$320	$285	$250	$225	$195	$175

Last MSR was $430.

Add $15 for walnut stock and forearm.

Add $75 for 100% camo coverage.

GRADING - PPGS™	100%	98%	95%	90%	80%	70%	60%

SHOTGUNS : SINGLE BARREL

REUNA SINGLE BARREL - 12, 20 ga., or .410 bore, exposed hammer with half-cock, extractor. Disc. 1998.

	$95	$70	$60	$50	$45	$40	$35

Last MSR was $120.

Add $22 for choke tubes (12 ga. new 1992, 20 ga. new 1993).

✳ *Reuna Single Barrel Youth* - 20 ga. or .410 bore, 22 in. barrel, features rubber recoil pad. Imported 1993-98.

	$100	$75	$60	$50	$45	$40	$35

Last MSR was $132.

SINGLE BARREL CLASSIC - 12, 20 ga., or .410 bore, 3 in. chamber, break open action activated by moving triggerguard rearward, exposed hammer or hammerless (new 2003), 26 or 28 in. barrel with (new 2003) or w/o VR (disc. 2003), hardwood stock and forend, matte metal finish, Youth Model also available in 20 ga. or .410 bore (13 in. LOP), approx. 5.5 lbs. New 2002.

MSR $119	$95	$80	$65	$55	$45	$40	$35

Add $6 for Special Model with matte finished stainless steel receiver (new 2004).

SHOTGUNS : SLIDE ACTION

MODEL P350 - 12 ga. only, 3 1/2 in. chamber, 18.5 (Home Security), 24, 26, or 28 in. barrel, includes 5 screw-in chokes, choice of black synthetic, Timber HD, or Max-4 HD camo coverage. New 2005.

MSR $269	$230	$200	$180	$160	$140	$120	$100

Add $60 for 100% camo coverage.
Add $45 for 14 oz. recoil reducer.

IBERIA FIREARMS

Current manufacturer of .40 S&W cal. pistols located in Iberia, OH. Distributed by MKS Supply located in Dayton, OH. Distributor sales only.

Please refer to the Hi-Point section in this text.

IMPERIAL GUN CO. LTD

Previous manufacturer located in Surrey, Great Britain circa 1992-1995. The Imperial Gun Co. Ltd. had limited importation into the U.S.

Imperial Gun secondary marketplace values must be based realistically on their competitive shooting value, not collectibility.

INDIAN ARMS

Previous trademark manufactured by Indian Arms Corporation located in Detroit, MI.

PISTOLS: SEMI-AUTO

INDIAN ARMS .380 - .380 ACP cal., patterned after Walther PPK, stainless steel, 3 1/4 in. barrel, 6 shot mag., natural or blue finish, with (early specimens) or without key lock safety, with or without VR barrel, walnut grips, 20 oz. Mfg. 1975-77.

	$395	$285	$230

This model had limited manufacture with approx. 1,000 guns being made.

GRADING - PPGS™	100%	98%	95%	90%	80%	70%	60%

INDUSTRIA ARMI GALESI

Previous manufacturer located in Brescia, Italy.

PISTOLS: SEMI-AUTO

GALESI MODEL 6 POCKET AUTO - .22 LR or .25 ACP cal., 6 shot, 2 1/4 in. barrel blue, fixed sights, plastic grips. Mfg. 1930-disc.

$130	$120	$105	$90	$75	$65	$55

Add 100% if chrome engraved.

GALESI MODEL 9 POCKET AUTO - .22 LR, .32 ACP, or .380 ACP cal., 8 shot, 3 1/4 in. barrel, blue, fixed sights, plastic grips. Mfg. 1930-disc.

$165	$130	$110	$100	$85	$65	$55

Add 100% if chrome engraved.

INFALLIBLE

Previous trademark manufactured by Warner Arms Corp. located in Norwich, CT, and Davis-Warner Arms Corp. located in Assonet, MA.

PISTOLS: SEMI-AUTO

INFALLIBLE PISTOL - .32 ACP cal., 3.2 in. barrel, 7 shot mag., 24.7 oz.

* *Type I* - mfg. and marked "Warner Arms Corp., Norwich, Conn.", serial range is 501-2,299.

$325	$295	$270	$250	$225	$200	$180

* *Type II* - marked "Davis-Warner Arms Corporation, Assonet, Massachusetts", serial range is 2,300-5,299.

$295	$270	$250	$225	$195	$170	$150

* *Type III* - marked "Warner Arms Corporation, Norwich, Connecticut", serial range is 5,300-7,400.

$295	$270	$250	$225	$195	$170	$150

INFINITY FIREARMS

Current trademark manufactured by Strayer-Voight Inc. since 1994 and located in Grand Prairie, TX. Currently distributed by JP Enterprises, located in White Bear Lake, MN. Distributor and dealer sales.

PISTOLS: SEMI-AUTO

Strayer-Voight manufactures a complete line of custom high quality M1911-based semi-auto pistols in a wide variety of finishes, materials (including titanium), options, and special orders. Their curent lineup includes the Tiki Pistol, Titanium Model, Bushing Pistol, Comp. Gun, Hybricomp, IED 1911, Duotone 1911, PPC Masterpiece, and Competition Gun. Please contact JP Enterprises directly for more information on pricing and availability regarding Infinity firearms (see Trademark Index).

INGLIS HI-POWERS

Previously manufactured by John Inglis Co. Limited of Toronto, Canada. Over 151,000 Inglis Hi-Powers were manufactured between February 1944 and September 1945 under military contractual agreements.

PISTOLS: SEMI-AUTO

CHINESE CONTRACT PATTERN 35

* *Chinese No. 1* - 9mm Para. cal., large Chinese characters (6) on left slide, slotted for stock and tangent sights, can be denoted by no numerical prefix before the "CH" in serial number.

$3,500	$3,000	$2,350	$1,500	$1,000	$750	$600

Add approx. $350 for original wood holster stock (beware of reproductions).
Add $350-$450 for early front sight (approx. first 100 pistols only).

GRADING - PPGS™	100%	98%	95%	90%	80%	70%	60%

CH SERIES MILITARY

* **MK 1-No. 1 Inglis** - 9mm Para. cal., tangent sight, slotted, contracts included Canadian, Chinese, and other countries.

	$1,325	$1,050	$875	$725	$650	$550	$450

Add 10%-20% for decal on front strap.

Add approx. $350 for original wood holster stock. Beware of reproductions.

This model has been recently imported again. Most recent imports have been painted black or refinished, and are priced in the $350-$575 range.

T SERIES CANADIAN MILITARY

* **MK 1-No. 2 Inglis** - 9mm Para. cal., fixed sight, without slot, numerical prefix references (0-10) the number of guns in increments of 10,000. Scarcer variations include: 0, 9, and 10.

	$1,000	$750	$600	$400	$350	$295	$275

Add 10%-20% for original decal on front strap.

Add 15% for 0 variation prefix.

Add 10% for 9 variation prefix.

Add 30% for 10 variation (ser. no.) prefix.

Since the original decals are very fragile, most are observed with approx. 10%-90% of the decal remaining.

This model has been recently imported again. Most recent imports are priced $350-$650.

* **Inglis "DIAMOND" logo** - refers to Inglis trademark in diamond shaped logo on left side of slide, only a few prototypes were mfg. 1946-47.

	$3,000	$2,750	$2,000	$1,500	$1,200	$800	$600

Add 50% for polished steel (parkerized finish is more common).

Add 50% for 5 CH Series.

All Inglis diamond variations are in the 5CH or 9T ser. no. range.

Be careful of fakes!

* **MK 1-No. 2 Inglis** - fixed sight, slotted. Inspect slot very carefully, and provenance verification is advised.

	$1,950	$1,250	$1,100	$900	$800	$650	$500

INGRAM

Previously manufactured until late 1982 by Military Armament Corp. (MAC) located in Atlanta, GA.

PISTOLS: SEMI-AUTO

MAC 10 - .45 ACP or 9mm Para. cal., open bolt, semi-auto version of the sub machine gun, 10 (.45 ACP cal.), 16 (9mm Para cal.), 30 (.45 ACP cal.), or 32 (9mm Para cal.) shot mag., compact all metal welded construction, rear aperture and front blade sight. Disc. 1982.

	$850	$775	$700	$650	$600	$550	$495

Add approx. $160 for accessories (barrel extension, case, and extra mag.).

MAC 10A1 - similar to MAC 10 except fires from a closed bolt.

	$295	$275	$250	$230	$215	$200	$190

MAC 11 - similar to MAC 10 except in .380 ACP cal.

	$650	$595	$550	$525	$500	$480	$460

INTERARMS

Previous importer and distributor located in Alexandria, VA, from circa 1962-1999.

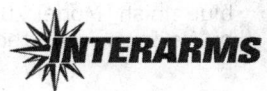

Interarms imported a multitude of trademarks and models since the early 1960s. Most of the models listed were recent imports.

The FEG, Howa, Rossi, and Walther trademarks will be found in their own sections listed alphabetically in this text.

PISTOLS: SEMI-AUTO, FEG & HELWAN MFG.

Please refer to the FEG & HELWAN sections in this text.

REVOLVERS: SA, VIRGINIAN SERIES

Virginian Revolvers were previously manufactured in Europe by various manufacturers (including Hämmerli of Switzerland). They were also manufactured in Midland, VA from 1976-1984. Older models with exceptional quality (including Hämmerli guns) are worth a premium over values listed.

VIRGINIAN DRAGOON STANDARD - .41 Mag., .44 Mag., or .45 LC (mfg. 1982-84) cal., improved action patterned after Colt SAA design, 6 shot, 6, 7 1/2, 8 3/8, or 12 (Buntline) in. barrel, blue finish, smooth walnut grips, adj. rear sight, 51 oz. with 7 1/2 in. barrel.

	$255	$225	$205	$190	$180	$170	$160

Last MSR was $315.

Add 15% for Buntline Model.

* ***Dragoon Standard Stainless*** - .41 Mag., .44 Mag., or .45 LC cal., 6 (disc.), 7 1/2 (disc.), or 8 3/8 in. barrel, same general specifications as Standard Dragoon.

	$265	$230	$210

Last MSR was $315.

DRAGOON SILHOUETTE - .357 Mag. or .44 Mag. cal., stainless steel, 7 1/2, 8 3/8, or 10 1/2 in. (standard on .357 Mag.) barrel, special sights and grips.

	$365	$320	$275

Last MSR was $425.

DRAGOON ENGRAVED - .44 Mag. cal. only, choice of stainless steel or blue finish, 6 or 7 1/2 in. barrel., "Sic Semper Tyrannis" inscription on butt with a 5 point star.

	$545	$470	$430	$395	$360	$320	$285

Last MSR was $625.

Add $75 for presentation case.

DRAGOON "DEPUTY" - .357 Mag. or .44 Mag. cal., blue barrel, case hardened frame, 5 in. barrel only.

	$250	$215	$195	$180	$165	$155	$145

Last MSR was $295.

* ***Stainless Deputy*** - similar to above, except .44 Mag. available in 6 in. barrel only, stainless steel.

	$255	$225	$205

Last MSR was $295.

VIRGINIAN .22 CONVERTIBLE - .22 LR/.22 Mag. cal. cylinders, 5 1/2 in. barrel only, adj. rear sight, 38 oz.

	$185	$155	$145	$135	$125	$115	$105

Last MSR was $219.

* ***Virginian .22 Convertible Stainless*** - stainless steel fabrication, otherwise similar to above.

	$200	$170	$155

Last MSR was $239.

RIFLES: BOLT ACTION, DISC.

MODEL JW-15 - .22 LR cal., 5 shot detachable mag., 23.8 in. barrel, open sights, blue finish, Model 70 style safety, patterned after the Brno Model ZKM, 5.5 lbs. Mfg. by Norinco. Imported 1990-96.

	$85	$70	$60	$50	$40	$35	$30

Last MSR was $109.

GRADING - PPGS™	100%	98%	95%	90%	80%	70%	60%

ENFIELD NO. 4 - .303 British cal., genuine British Commonwealth issue, 25 1/4 in. barrel, 10 shot box mag., 9 lbs. Importation disc. 1996.

| | $75 | $60 | $50 | $40 | $35 | $35 | $35 |

Last MSR was $86.

RIFLES: BOLT ACTION, HOWA MFG.

Please refer to the Howa section in this text.

RIFLES: BOLT ACTION, MAUSER ACTIONS

Whitworth rifles were mfg. in England. Mark X rifles were mfg. in Yugoslavia by Zastava Arms until late 1997.

MARK X VISCOUNT - .22-250 Rem. (disc. 1993), .243 Win. (disc. 1993), .25-06 Rem. (disc. 1993), .270 Win. (disc. 1993), 7x57mm (disc. 1993), 7mm Rem. Mag. (disc. 1994), .308 Win. (disc. 1994), .30-06, or .300 Win. Mag. (disc. 1994) cal., 5 shot, 3 shot mag., 24 in. barrel, adj. rear sight and trigger, classic style Monte Carlo stock. Disc. 1983, re-introduced 1985, disc. 1996.

| | $375 | $300 | $265 | $240 | $225 | $205 | $190 |

Last MSR was $471.

Add $15 for 7mm Rem. Mag. or .300 Win. Mag. cal.

This model is often referred to as the Viscount. Early manufacture was done in Manchester, England. Recent manufacture is in Yugoslavia. Earlier Manchester guns (before approx. 1980) will bring a slight premium over the values listed.

✳ *Mini Mark X* - .223 Rem. or 7.62x39mm (new in 1990) cal., miniature M98 Mauser System action, 20 in. barrel with iron sights, checkered hardwood stock, 5 shot mag., adj. trigger, 6.35 lbs. Imported 1987-94.

| | $360 | $295 | $265 | $240 | $225 | $205 | $190 |

Last MSR was $455.

✳ *Lightweight Mark X* - .22-250 Rem. (new 1994), .270 Win. (disc.), .30-06 (disc. 1994), or 7mm Rem. Mag. (disc.) cal., similar to Mark X Viscount, except has Carbolite (synthetic) stock and 20 in. barrel, 7 lbs. Imported 1988-90, reintroduced 1994-97.

| | $350 | $290 | $265 | $240 | $225 | $205 | $190 |

Last MSR was $438.

CAVALIER - similar to Viscount, except modern style stock, roll-over cheekpiece, rosewood pistol grip cap and forend tip, recoil pad. Disc.

| | $365 | $330 | $305 | $290 | $265 | $230 | $195 |

MANNLICHER STYLE CARBINE - similar to Cavalier, except 20 in. barrel, full length stock, no Magnum or varmint calibers. Disc.

| | $365 | $330 | $305 | $290 | $265 | $230 | $195 |

CONTINENTAL CARBINE - similar to Mannlicher Style, except with double set trigger. Disc.

| | $395 | $365 | $330 | $310 | $285 | $255 | $220 |

THE MARQUIS - .243 Win., .270 Win., .308 Win., 7x57mm, or .30-06 cal., 20 in. barrel, adj. trigger. Mannlicher style carbine. Disc. 1984.

| | $430 | $325 | $300 | $275 | $250 | $230 | $215 |

ALASKAN - similar to Mark X, except .375 H&H or .458 Win. Mag. cal., recoil pad and extra stock crossbolt. Disc. 1984.

| | $460 | $350 | $330 | $310 | $290 | $250 | $210 |

MARK X REALTREE - .270 Win. or .30-06 cal., features Realtree Camo finish. Imported 1994-96.

| | $460 | $390 | $365 | $320 | $275 | $250 | $225 |

Last MSR was $549.

GRADING - PPGS™	100%	98%	95%	90%	80%	70%	60%

MARK X WHITWORTH - .270 Win., .30-06, and .300 Win. Mag. cals, Mauser action, 24 in. barrel, open sights, 5 shot mag. (.300 Win. Mag. is only 3), checkered deluxe walnut with ebony forearm tip, thumb safety with sling swivels, adj. trigger, rubber recoil buttplate, 7 lbs. Imported 1984-96.

	$475	$400	$365	$320	$275	$250	$225

Last MSR was $565.

Add $19 for 7mm Rem. Mag. (disc.) or .300 Win. Mag. cal.

This model was the Whitworth American Field Series until 1987. Early manufacture was done in Manchester, England. Later manufacture was by Zastava located in Yugoslavia. Earlier Manchester guns (before approx. 1980) will bring a slight premium over the values listed.

WHITWORTH MANNLICHER STYLE CARBINE - .243 Win., .270 Win., .308 Win., 7x57mm, or .30-06 cal., bolt action with full length walnut Mannlicher style stock, open sights, sling swivels, thumb safety, 20 in. barrel, 5 shot mag., 7 lbs. Imported 1984-87.

	$570	$495	$455	$410	$375	$340	$310

Last MSR was $675.

WHITWORTH EXPRESS RIFLE - .375 H&H (disc. 1993) or .458 Win. Mag. cal., 3 shot, 24 in. barrel, 3 leaf express sight, English style walnut stock, checkered pistol grip and forend, 8 1/2 lbs. Imported 1974-96.

	$600	$540	$465	$425	$395	$375	$350

Last MSR was $703.

RIFLES: SEMI-AUTO

22-ATD - .22 LR cal. only, patterned after the Browning Semi-Auto, 19.4 in. barrel, 11 shot mag. in stock, blue finish, checkered hardwood stock, take-down design, adj. rear sight, 4.6 lbs. Mfg. by Norinco 1987-96.

	$110	$95	$90	$80	$75	$70	$65

Last MSR was $121.

Add $16 for camo case (disc.).

INTERCONTINENTAL ARMS INC.

Previous importer located in Los Angeles, CA circa 1970s.

Intercontinental Arms Inc. imported a variety of SA revolvers, an AR-15 type semi-auto rifle, a derringer, a rolling block single shot rifle, and a line of black powder pistol reproductions and replicas. While these firearms were good, utilitarian shooters, they have limited desirability in today's marketplace. The single action revolvers are typically priced in the $125-$275 range, the derringer is priced in the $95-$150 range, the AR-15 copy is priced in the $375-$650 range, and the single shot rolling block rifle is priced in the $125-$175 range, depending on condition.

INTERDYNAMIC OF AMERICA, INC.

Previous distributor located in Miami, FL 1981-84.

PISTOLS: SEMI-AUTO

KG-9 - 9mm Para. cal., 3 in. barrel, open bolt, paramilitary design pistol. Disc. approx. 1982.

	$750	$700	$650	$600	$575	$550	$525

KG-99 - 9mm Para. cal., 3 in. barrel, semi-auto paramilitary design pistol, closed bolt, 36 shot mag., 5 in. vent. shroud barrel, blue only, a stainless steel version of the KG-9. Mfg. by Interdynamic 1984 only.

	$375	$325	$275	$230	$200	$180	$160
KG-99M, mini pistol	$450	$400	$350	$285	$235	$200	$180

GRADING - PPGS™	100%	98%	95%	90%	80%	70%	60%

INTERSTATE ARMS CORP.

Current importer located in Billerica, MA.

Interstate Arms Corp. imports a variety of cowboy action shotguns and reproductions.

SHOTGUNS: SxS

MODEL 99 COACH GUN - 12 ga. only, 2 3/4 in. chambers, exposed hammers, 20 in. barrels with F/M fixed chokes, blue finish with checkered stock and forearm, 7.2 lbs. Limited importation beginning 1999.

MSR $300	$245	$215	$190	$175	$155	$145	$130

SHOTGUNS: LEVER ACTION

MODEL 87L - 12 ga. only, 2 3/4 in. chamber, patterned after the Winchester Model 1887, 20 in. barrel, walnut stock and forearm. Importation began mid-2003.

MSR $480	$385	$335	$275	$235	$200	$180	$165

SHOTGUNS: SLIDE ACTION

MODEL 97W HAMMER - 12 ga. only, patterned after the Win. Model 97, hammer, 20 in. plain barrel with cylinder bore fixed choke, solid frame, hardwood stock with grooved "corn cob" forearm. Importation began 2001.

MSR $359	$285	$250	$220	$190	$175	$160	$145

MODEL 97T WWI TRENCH GUN - 12 ga. only, authentic reproduction of the original Winchester WWI Trench Gun, complete with shrouded barrel, proper markings, finish, and wood. Importation began mid-2002.

MSR $425	$345	$295	$265	$225	$195	$175	$160

MODEL 372 - 12 ga., 3 in. chamber, 18.5 in. barrel with heat shield and ghost ring sights, bottom ejection port, cylinder choke, black synthetic stock and forearm. Importation began 2005.

As this edition went to press, prices had yet to be established on this model.

MODEL 981/982T - 12 ga. only, 3 in. chamber, defense configuration with 18 1/2 in. cylinder bore barrel with fixed choke, black synthetic stock and forearm, matte black metal finish. Importation began 2001.

MSR $235	$200	$170	$150	$125	$115	$95	$85

Add $15 for ghost ring sights (Model 982T).

INTRAC ARMS INTERNATIONAL INC.

Current importer located in Knoxville, TN. Intrac imports trademarks manufactured by Arsenal Bulgaria, and by IM Metal Production facility in Croatia beginning late 2000. Currently imported by HS America, located in Knoxville, TN. Distributor and dealer sales.

PISTOLS: SEMI-AUTO

HS 2000 - 9mm Para., .357 SIG, or .40 S&W cal., short recoil locked breech mechanism, polymer frame, trigger and grip safety, 3 dot low profile sights, loaded chamber indicator, black finish, 23 oz. Importation from Croatia began 2000.

MSR $419	$350	$295	$250	$225	$200	$185	$175

MAKAROV - .380 ACP or 9x18mm cal., double action, black phosphate finish, black grips, supplied with two 8 shot mags. and holster. Importation began 2002.

MSR $159	$145	$125	$110	$95	$85	$80	$75

GRADING - PPGS™	100%	98%	95%	90%	80%	70%	60%

RIFLES: SEMI-AUTO

ROMAK 1 & 2 - 7.62x39mm (Romak 1) or 5.45x39mm (Romak 2) cal., AK-47 copy with 16 1/2 in. barrel and scope mount on left side of receiver, wood thumbhole stock, includes 5 and 10 shot mags., and accessories. Importation began 2002.

MSR $329	$285	$250	$215	$190	$175	$160	$145

SLR-101 - similar to Romak, except has 17 1/4 in. cold hammer forged barrel and black polymer stock and forearm, includes 2 mags. and accessories. Importation began 2002.

MSR $359	$310	$265	$220	$195	$180	$165	$145

ROMAK 3 - 7.62x54R cal., based on current issue PSL/FPK sniper configuration, 5 or 10 shot mag., last shot bolt hold open, 26 1/2 in. barrel with muzzle brake, mil-spec scope with range finder, bullet drop compensator and illuminated recticle. Importation began 2002.

MSR $899	$800	$725	$650	$600	$550	$500	$450

INTRATEC

Previous manufacturer circa 1985-2000 located in Miami, FL.

PISTOLS: SEMI-AUTO

PROTEC-25 - .25 ACP. cal., double action only, 2 1/2 in. barrel, 8 shot mag., 13 oz. Disc. 2000.

	$110	$80	$65	$45	$35	$30	$25

Last MSR was $137.

Add $5 for Tec-Kote finish or black slide/frame finish (disc.).

TEC-DC9 - 9mm Para. cal., paramilitary design pistol, 5 in. shrouded barrel, matte black finish, 10 (C/B 1994) or 32* shot mag. Mfg. 1985-94.

$275	$230	$175	$155	$140	$130	$120

Last MSR was $269.

✳ **TEC-9DCK** - similar to TEC-9, except has new durable Tec-Kote finish with better protection than hard chrome. Mfg. 1991-94.

$295	$250	$185	$160	$140	$130	$120

Last MSR was $297.

✳ **TEC-DC9S** - matte stainless version of the TEC-9. Disc. 1994.

$350	$275	$200

Last MSR was $362.

Add $203 for TEC-9 with accessory package (deluxe case, 3-32 shot mags., paramilitary design grip, and recoil compensator).

TEC-DC9M - mini version of the Model TEC-9, including 3 in. barrel and 20 shot mag. Disc. 1994.

$295	$245	$185	$160	$140	$130	$120

Last MSR was $245.

✳ **TEC-DC9MK** - similar to TEC-9M, except has Tec-Kote rust resistant finish. Mfg. 1991-94.

$325	$275	$200	$165	$145	$130	$120

Last MSR was $277.

✳ **TEC-DC9MS** - matte stainless version of the TEC-9M. Disc. 1994.

$375	$295	$225

Last MSR was $339.

GRADING - PPGS™	100%	98%	95%	90%	80%	70%	60%

TEC-22 "SCORPION" - .22 LR cal., paramilitary design, 4 in. barrel, ambidextrous safety, military matte finish, or electroless nickel, 30 shot mag., adj. sights, 30 oz. Mfg. 1988-94.

	$225	$190	$165	$150	$135	$120	$100

Last MSR was $202.

Add $20 for TEC-Kote finish.

✳ *TEC-22N* - similar to TEC-22, except has nickel finish. Mfg. 1990 only.

	$240	$200	$175	$160	$140	$125	$105

Last MSR was $226.

Add $16 for threaded barrel (Model TEC-22TN).

TEC-22T - threaded barrel variation of the TEC-22 "Scorpion." Mfg 1991-94.

	$175	$145	$125	$110	$100	$90	$80

Last MSR was $161.

Add $23 for Tec-Kote finish.

SPORT-22 - .22 LR cal., 4 in. non-threaded barrel, 10 shot Ruger styled rotary mag., matte finish, adj. rear sight, 29 1/2 oz. New 1995.

	$140	$110	$95	$80	$65	$55	$45

Last MSR was $170.

Add $15 for stainless steel barrel.

CAT-9, CAT-45, CAT-380 - .380 ACP (new 1995), 9mm Para., or .45 ACP (new 1995) cal., double action only, black finish, polymer frame with top sight channel, only 27 parts, blowback action on 9mm Para., locked breech on .45 ACP, 6 (.45 ACP cal.) or 7 (.380 ACP or 9mm Para.) shot mag., 3 or 3 1/4 (.45 ACP only) in. barrel, 18-21 oz. Mfg. 1993-2000.

	$215	$180	$155	$135	$120	$100	$90

Last MSR was $260.

Subtract $25 for .380 ACP cal.
Add $20 for .45 ACP cal.
Add $15 for Fire Sights.
This series was designed by N. Sirkis of Israel.

AB-10 - 9mm Para. cal., design similar to Luger, 2 3/4 in. non-threaded barrel, choice of 32* (limited supply) or 10 shot mag., black synthetic frame, firing pin safety block, black or stainless steel finish, 45 oz. Mfg. 1997-2000.

	$235	$200	$180	$160	$150	$135	$120

Last MSR was $225.

Add $20 for stainless steel (new 2000).
Add $75 for 32 shot mag.

INTRATEC U.S.A.

Previous manufacturer located in Miami, FL.

DERRINGERS

TEC-38 DERRINGER - .22 Mag., .32 H&R Mag., or .38 Spl. cal., O/U, 3 in. barrel, blue frame, double action, 13 oz. Mfg. 1986-88.

	$110	$95	$85	$75	$65	$60	$55

Last MSR was $125.

PISTOLS: SEMI-AUTO

PROTEC-22 - while advertised for $112 MSR during 1993, this model never went into production.

TEC-9 - 9mm Para. cal., paramilitary design, 5 in. shrouded barrel, 32 shot mag. Disc.

	$450	$400	$350	$315	$275	$235	$195

TEC-9C - 9mm Para. cal., carbine variation with 16 1/2 in. barrel, 36 shot mag. Only 1 gun mfg. 1987 - extreme rarity precludes pricing.

INVESTARM, s.p.a.

Current manufacturer located in Marcheno, Italy. Currently distributed by Kimber, located in Yonkers, NY.

Investarm manufactures a wide variety of shotguns in various configurations, including folding single shots, folding O/Us, a range of high quality competition and hunting models (including the new Sydney Models), in addition to muzzle loading black powder rifles and pistols. Please contact the distributor directly for more information, including pricing and availability (see Trademark Index).

INVESTMENT ARMS INC.

Current company specializing in limited/special editions located in Fort Collins, CO.

Investment Arms Inc. subcontracts various gun manufactures to produce their own limited editions/special editions. These guns are typically limited by county or state, and feature various engraving motifs, configurations, and other embellishments. Please contact the company directly for more information on quantities, original issue prices, and dates of manufacture (refer to Trademark Index). Secondary marketplace liquidity is difficult to determine, based on relative rarity and limited collectibility.

IRWINDALE ARMS, INC. (IAI)

Previous manufacturer located in Irwindale, CA 1988-1991.

PISTOLS: SEMI-AUTO

In June, 1991, AMT reacquired the manufacturing rights to all IAI models. Please refer to the AMT section for recent models.

AUTOMAG III - .30 Carbine or 9mm Win. Mag. (mfg. 1990-92) cal., stainless steel only, 6 3/8 in. barrel, patterned after Colt Govt. Model, Millett adj. sights with white outline, grooved Lexan grips, 8 shot mag., 43 oz. Mfg. 1989-91.

$550 $475 $395

Last MSR was $606.

AUTOMAG IV - .45 Win. Mag., or 10mm cal., semi-auto, 6 1/2 or 8 5/8 (mfg. 1991) in. barrel, 7 shot mag., Millett adj. sights, stainless steel only, 46 oz. Mfg. 1990-91.

$565 $485 $500

Last MSR was $630.

JAVELINA - 10mm cal., semi-auto, 5 (disc. 1991) or 7 in. barrel, 8 shot mag., Millett adj. sights, wraparound Neoprene grips, stainless steel, wide adj. trigger, long grip safety, 48 oz. Mfg. 1990-91.

$525 $450 $375

Last MSR was $570.

BACKUP PISTOL - .380 ACP cal., semi-auto action, 2 1/2 in. barrel, stainless steel, Lexan grips, 5 shot mag., 18 oz. Older disc. walnut grip models are worth a slight premium. Disc. 1989.

$200 $165 $135

Last MSR was $243.

ISRAEL ARMS INTERNATIONAL, INC.

Previous importer (please refer to IAI listing) and manufacturer located in Houston, TX, 1997-2004.

GRADING - PPGS™	100%	98%	95%	90%	80%	70%	60%

ISRAEL ARMS LTD.

Previous manufacturer located in Kfar Saba, Israel. Imported and distributed exclusively by Israel Arms International, Inc. located in Houston, TX 1997-2001.

PISTOLS: SEMI-AUTO

MODEL 1500 HI POWER - 9mm Para. cal., single action, 3.85 (Compact) or 4.64 (Standard, disc. 1998) in. barrel, two-tone finish, rubberized grips, regular or Meprolite sights, 10 shot mag., 33.6 oz. Imported 1997-98 only.

$360	$305	$255	$225	$200	$185	$170

Last MSR was $413.

Add approx. $160 for two-tone finish with Meprolite sights.

❈ *Model 1500/1501 Hi-Power Compact* - 9mm Para. or .40 S&W cal., compact variation with 3.85 in. barrel, choice of two-tone (Model 1500) or blue (Model 1501) finish, 32.2 oz. Imported late 1999-2000.

$360	$305	$255	$225	$200	$185	$170

Last MSR was $412.

MODEL 2500 - 9mm Para. or .40 S&W cal., single or double action, ambidextrous safety with decocking feature, steel slide with alloy frame, 3 7/8 in. barrel, 10 shot mag., matte black finish, 34 oz.

While advertised during 1999, this model had very limited importation.

MODEL 3000 - 9mm Para cal., double action. Limited importation 2000-2001.

$335	$295	$260	$230	$200	$175	$150

Last MSR was $374.

MODEL 4000 - .40 S&W cal., double action. Limited importation 2000-2001.

$335	$295	$260	$230	$200	$175	$150

Last MSR was $374.

MODEL 5000/5001 COMBAT - .45 ACP cal., single action, 4 1/4 in barrel, combat configuration with ambidextrous safety, competition trigger, hammer, and slide stop, front and rear slide serrations, blue (Model 5001) or two-tone (Model 5000) finish, wraparound rubber grips, 42 oz., mfg. in Philipines. Imported 1999-2001.

$395	$365	$330	$295	$265	$235	$210

Last MSR was $448.

MODEL 6000/6001 STANDARD - .45 ACP cal., single action, 5 in. stainless steel barrel, features beveled feed ramp, extended slide stop, safety and magazine release, ambidextrous safety, beavertail grip safety and combat style hammer, blue (Model 6001) or two-tone (Model 6000, disc. 2000) finish, 38 oz., mfg. in Philipines. Imported 1999-2001.

$395	$365	$330	$295	$265	$235	$210

Last MSR was $448.

MODEL 7000/7001 WIDE FRAME - .45 ACP cal., single action, similar to Model 6000/6001, except has double stack mag., blue (Model 7001) or two-tone (Model 7000) finish, 40 oz. Imported 1999-2000.

$445	$395	$350	$300	$255	$225	$200

Last MSR was $490.

RIFLES

MODEL 333 M1 GARAND - .30-06 cal., 24 in. barrel, parts remanufactured to meet GI and mil specs, parkerized finish, 8 shot en-bloc mag., 9 1/2 lbs. Mfg. 2000-2001.

$640	$550	$495	$450	$400	$365	$335

Last MSR was $852.

GRADING - PPGS™	100%	98%	95%	90%	80%	70%	60%

MODEL 444 FAL - .308 Win. cal., patterned after the FN FAL model. Mfg. by Imbel, located in Brazil, 2000-2001.

	$675	$595	$535	$475	$425	$375	$350

Last MSR was $897.

ISRAELI MILITARY INDUSTRIES (IMI)

Current manufacturer established during 1933, and located in Israel. Limited importation currently.

IMI manufactured guns (both new and disc. models) include Galil, Jericho, Magnum Research, Timberwolf, Uzi, and others, and can be located in their respective sections.

ITALIAN MILITARY ARMS

Previous Italian popular military models mfg. since 1891.

PISTOLS: SEMI-AUTO

GLISENTI MODEL 1910 - 9mm Glisenti cal., 4 in. barrel, 7 shot mag., checkered wood grips, official Italian service pistol of both WWI and WWII, 32 oz.

	$1,200	$900	$750	$600	$500	$400	$300

Warning: 9mm Para. ammunition (9x19mm) cannot be used in this pistol - only 9mm Glisenti, as it is approx. 25% less powerful than the 9mm Para.

BRIXIA - similar to Glisenti Model 1910, except utilizes simplified mfg. techniques, mostly sold to civilians.

	$1,350	$1,000	$750	$600	$500	$400	$300

SOSSO - 9mm Para. cal., large experimental semi-auto, early pistols were double action and marked "Sosso", late guns were single action and built by FNA. All Sosso pistols feature a unique continuous "chain link" 19 or 21 shot mag. Approx. 5 guns mfg.

Extreme rarity factor precludes accurate price evaluation.

RIFLES: BOLT ACTION

MODEL 1891 MANNLICHER-CARCANO - 6.5x52mm Carcano cal., 6 shot, 31 in. barrel, straight handle, adj. sight, military stock.

	$120	$100	$85	$70	$55	$40	$30

MODEL 38 TERNI MILITARY RIFLE - 7.35x52mm Carcano cal., similar to 1891, except turned down bolt handle, 21 in. barrel and folding bayonet.

	$120	$100	$85	$70	$55	$40	$30

ITHACA CLASSIC DOUBLES

Previous importer and SxS shotgun manufacturer 1998-2003, and located in Victor, NY from 1999-2003 and Mendon, NY until 1999.

RIFLES: SxS

DOUBLE RIFLE - many popular cals., including .45-70 Govt., also available in 20 ga. with 26 in. fully rifled barrels, express sights, German claw type scope mounts, DT, ejectors, exhibition walnut standard, many options were available. Limited importation only.

Advertised MSR was $8,500, w/o engraving or other special orders/features.

SHOTGUNS: SxS

All Ithaca Classic Doubles shotguns were handmade to order in the U.S. Frames were made from the traditional forgings and internal parts from solid steel. Barrels were hammer forged from geniune Krupp steel. Metal finishing, checkering, oil finish, and engraving were done completely by hand. All guns were fitted to customer's specifications and wood selection. Guns

GRADING - PPGS™	100%	98%	95%	90%	80%	70%	60%

were available in .410 bore through 12 ga., with full rifle barrels available in 12 or 20 ga and .45-70 Govt. cal. Each gauge has its own frame size, and serial numbers were continued from the last gun Ithaca manufactured in 1948 (ser. no. 469,999).

The Ithaca custom shop manufactured custom orders, including special options and features.

> **For Special Combination Sets - add $3,000 (4E, 5E, 6E) and $3,750 (Grades 7E & Sousa) for extra set of 16 (20 ga. frame) or 28 (.410 bore frame) ga. barrels.**
>
> **Add $600-$2,150 for canvas, canvas and leather, leather, or oak and leather cases.**
>
> **Add $1,125 for SST or vent. rib.**
>
> **Add $950 for VR.**

SKEET GRADE (SPECIAL FIELD) - 16 (new 2001), 20, 28 ga., or .410 bore, designed for field and clay shooting, DT, ejectors, 26, 28, or 30 in. barrels with fixed chokes, light perimeter hand engraving with metal stippling on shoulders and in front of top opening lever, Turnbull bone and charcoal case colors, checkered pistol grip or English feather crotch walnut stock and forearm, 5lbs. 5 oz.–6 lbs. 6 oz. Mfg. late 1998-2002.

$5,500	$4,750	$3,750	$3,250	$2,650	$2,175	$1,775

Last MSR was $5,999.

> **Add 20% for SST or vent. rib option.**

CLASSIC COMPETITION GRADE - all gauges, competition features. Mfg. 2002-2003.

$5,500	$4,750	$3,750	$3,250	$2,650	$2,175	$1,775

Last MSR was $5,995.

GRADE 4E CLASSIC - 16 (new 2001), 20, 28 ga., or .410 bore, features gold plated triggers, jewelled barrel flats, hand tuned locks, hand engraved three game scenes with floral scroll, deluxe walnut stock and forearm with fleur-de-lis pattern and 22 LPI checkering, other specifications similar to Special Field/Skeet Grade. Mfg. 1998-2003.

$6,750	$5,750	$4,900	$4,100	$3,300	$2,500	$1,850

Last MSR was $7,500.

STAR MODEL COMPETITION - competition model. Limited mfg. 2003.

$6,750	$5,750	$4,900	$4,100	$3,300	$2,500	$1,850

Last MSR was $7,500.

GRADE 5E CLASSIC - step up from Grade 4E, with more elaborate frame engraving and gold inlays on frame sides, upgraded walnut. Mfg. 2002-2003.

$7,500	$6,500	$5,750	$4,850	$4,100	$3,500	$2,500

Last MSR was $8,500.

GRADE 6E CLASSIC - step up from Grade 5E, with fine scroll engraving and gold dog inlays on frame sides, upgraded walnut. Mfg. 2002-2003.

$8,500	$7,500	$6,500	$5,750	$4,950	$4,150	$3,250

Last MSR was $9,999.

GRADE 7E CLASSIC - 16 (new 2001), 20, 28 ga., or .410 bore, features hand engraved oak leaf scroll on frame and barrels, and 24Kt. flat gold game scene inlays, including a bald eagle on floor plate, exhibition grade American walnut with 12 checkered panels in fleur-de-lis pattern, other specifications similar to Special Field/Skeet Grade. Mfg. 1998-2003.

$9,250	$8,250	$7,250	$6,150	$5,350	$4,450	$3,500

Last MSR was $11,000.

SOUSA SPECIAL - 16 (new 2001), 20, 28 ga., or .410 bore, top-of-the-line model with every possible refinement, each gun individually hand fitted, jewelled, and polished, includes famous 24Kt. Sousa mermaid on trigger guard, other specifications similar to Special Field/Skeet Grade. Special order only, limited mfg. 1998-2003.

$16,750	$14,000	$12,000	$10,000	$8,250	$7,000	$5,750

Last MSR was $18,000.

GRADING - PPGS™	100%	98%	95%	90%	80%	70%	60%

SUPERLATIVE CLASS - custom order, best quality model with a wide choice of engraving options and inlays, exhibition grade walnut, approx. 10-15 guns were mfg. annually. Limited mfg. 2002-2003.

   Prices for this model started at $20,000.

SHOTGUNS: SINGLE SHOT

KNICKERBOCKER SINGLE BARREL TRAP - limited mfg. of 100 guns during 2003.

   Prices for this model started at $9,000, w/o engraving.

ITHACA GUN COMPANY LLC

Current manufacturer established during 1996 and located in King Ferry, NY. Ithaca Gun Company, LLC has resumed production on the Model 37 slide action shotgun and variations. Previously manufactured in Ithaca, NY, 1883 to Nov. of 1986. In the past, Ithaca also absorbed companies including Syracuse Arms Co., Lefever Arms Co., Union Fire Arms Co., Wilkes-Barre Gun Co., as well as others.

COMBINATION GUNS

LSA-55 TURKEY GUN - O/U shotgun-rifle combo, 12 ga., .222 Rem., 24 1/2 in. ribbed barrel, exposed hammer, folding rear sight, checkered Monte Carlo stock. Mfg. by Tikka, Finland 1970-81.

	$650	$575	$475	$450	$425	$385	$330

HANDGUNS

ITHACA WWII MILITARY MFG. - .45 ACP cal., mfg. for WWII military M1911A1 contracts, 7 shot mag. 5 in. barrel, ser. no. ranges 856,405-916,404, 1,208,674-1,279,673, 1,441,431-1,471,430, 1,743,847-1,890,503, 2,075,104-2,134,403, and 2,619,014-2,693,613. Parkerized finish.

	$800	$600	$500	$450	$375	$350	$325

   Add 20% with original shipping carton.

   For more information on other WWI and WWII M1911/A1 military contracts, please refer to the Colt's Manufacturing section Pistols: Semi-Auto, Govt. M1911/1911A1 Military Variations in this text.

ITHACA 50TH SEMI-AUTO ANNIVERSARY MODEL - .45 ACP cal., 5 in. match barrel with bushing, blue polished or tactical matte finish, checkered diamond pattern walnut grips, extended beavertail grip safety, includes plastic case and certificate, only 125 mfg. with special serialization 1995-97. Disc.

	$695	$625	$550	$500	$450	$400	$360

                  Last MSR was $795.

  This model was offered exclusively by All American Sales, Inc. located in Memphis, TN.

X-CALIBER SINGLE SHOT - .22 LR or .44 Mag. cal., break open action with contoured wood grip and forearm, 8, 10 or 15 in. barrel, unique dual firing pin detonates both rimfire and centerfire cartridges. While advertised in 1988, Models 20 and 30 were never sold, even though approx. 300 units were mfg. in 22 cal. only.

   While only infrequently encountered, the current price range for this model is in the $125-$295 range.

RIFLES: BOLT ACTION

LSA-55 STANDARD - .222 Rem., .22-250 Rem., 6mm Rem., .243 Win., or .308 Win. cal., Mauser type action, 22 in. barrel, leaf sight, 3 shot mag., checkered Monte Carlo stock. Mfg. in Finland by Tikka from 1969-77.

	$400	$375	$350	$310	$275	$250	$230

   The LSA Model designation stands for Light, Strong, Accurate.

GRADING - PPGS™	100%	98%	95%	90%	80%	70%	60%

LSA-55 DELUXE - similar to Standard, except rollover cheekpiece, rosewood pistol grip cap and forend tip, skipline checkering, no sights, scope mounts furnished.

	$495	$450	$425	$400	$365	$345	$325

LSA-55 HEAVY BARREL - similar to LSA-55, except .222 Rem. or .22-250 Rem. cal. only, target heavy barrel, special beavertail stock 8 1/2 lbs.

	$450	$425	$400	$375	$350	$325	$300

LSA-65 - similar to LSA-55, except long action for calibers .25-06 Rem., .270 Win., or .30-06. Mfg. 1969-77.

	$400	$375	$350	$310	$275	$250	$230

LSA-65 DELUXE - similar to LSA-55, except has deluxe checkered walnut stock, .25-06 Rem., .270 Win., or .30-06.

	$495	$450	$425	$400	$365	$345	$325

RIFLES: LEVER ACTION

MODEL 49 SADDLEGUN - .22 LR or .22 Mag. cal., lever action, single shot. Mfg. 1961-78. Martini-style action.

	$145	$130	$110	$80	$65	$50	$40

    Add 15% for .22 Mag. cal.
    Add 20% for Deluxe Model.

MODEL 49R - similar to Model 49 Saddlegun, except is slide action repeater. Mfg. 1965-1971.

	$265	$250	$235	$200	$175	$150	$125

    Add 15% for .22 Mag. cal.

MODEL 49 PRESENTATION - similar to Model 49 Saddlegun, except gold-plated trigger, hammer, engraved receiver, fancy walnut. Mfg. 1962-1974.

	$295	$275	$250	$235	$200	$165	$135

MODEL 49 ST. LOUIS BICENTENNIAL - like Deluxe Model 49, except inscription on receiver. 200 mfg. 1964.

	$325	$255	$215

Last MSR was $35.

MODEL 72 SADDLEGUN - .22 or .22 Mag. cal., lever action, 18 1/2 in. barrel, hooded front sight. Mfg. 1973-78 by Erma Werke, W. Germany.

	$325	$275	$225	$175	$145	$130	$120

MODEL 72 DELUXE - similar to Model 72, except has silver finished engraved receiver, deluxe walnut, octagon barrel. Mfg. 1974-76.

	$395	$325	$250	$225	$175	$145	$130

RIFLES: SEMI-AUTO

MODEL X5-C - .22 LR cal., 7 shot mag., grooved forearm, Model X5-T has tube mag. Mfg. 1958-64.

	$195	$165	$125	$100	$80	$70	$60

MODEL X-15 - .22 LR cal., similar to X5-C, except forearm is not grooved. Mfg. 1964-67.

	$195	$165	$125	$100	$80	$70	$60

RIFLES: SINGLE SHOT

MODEL 89 - .243 Win., .30-06, .375 H&H, .416 Rigby, or 7x57mm cal., falling block action, 26 or 28 in. Shilen barrel, full-length uncheckered walnut stock.

    While advertised at $658 MSR during 1994, this model never went into production.

GRADING - PPGS™	100%	98%	95%	90%	80%	70%	60%

SHOTGUNS: O/U, PREVIOUS IMPORTATION

Note: Ithaca was the sole importer for Perazzi in the '70s. All new and used models will be in the P section under Perazzi. Perazzi currently distributes their own firearms.

Note: Please refer to the Fabarm section in this text for those models previously imported by Ithaca (imported 1994-95).

Note: Previously imported SKB O/U shotguns can be found under the SKB heading.

SHOTGUNS: SxS, PREVIOUS IMPORTATION

Note: Previously imported SKB SxS shotguns can be found under the SKB heading.

SHOTGUNS: SxS, 1880-1948 MFG.

AUTO & BURGLAR SxS - 20 ga. smooth bore with 10 in. double barrels, case hardened finish, pistol grip, Model A (approx. 2,500 mfg.) has grip spur, Model B (approx. 2,000 mfg.) has squared grip; both were mfg. in lots of about 100 according to demand, and serial numbers are mixed with those of regular Ithaca shotguns. Guns not currently registered with BATF cannot be legally owned and are subject to seizure. Mfg. 1922-34.

* **Model A** - serial no. range is 343,336-398,365.

$1,850	$1,450	$1,200	$975	$775	$675	$575

* **Model B** - serial no. range is 425,000-464,699.

$1,450	$1,200	$975	$775	$675	$575	$465

Add $300-$500 for original holster (very rare). Prototype or special order guns (in 16, 28 ga., or .410 bore) are extremely rare and command premiums of 100%+.

ITHACA HAMMERLESS - 12, 16, 20, 28 ga., or .410 bore, 26-32 in. fluid steel or damascus barrels, boxlock, extractors, double triggers, any standard choke, checkered pistol grip stock and forearm, grades shown differ in overall quality, ornamentation, grade of wood, and style of checkering. In 1925, the rotary bolt and stronger frame were adapted (ser. numbers after 400,000 - commonly referred to as NID or New Ithaca Double). Values are the same as for pre-400,000 serial range shotguns. Ithaca doubles incorporated a number of design changes made on the action - they are referred to as the Lewis, Crass, Flues, and Minier frame variations.

Values below are for guns mfg. between 1925-1948.

Add $200 for SST.

Add $150 for SNT.

Add $350 for VR on Grades 4, 5, 7, and $2,000 Grade.

Add $200 for VR - lower grades.

Add $175 for beavertail forearm.

Add 33% for auto ejectors on Grades No. 1, 2, and 3.

Subtract 33% if without ejectors on Grades 4E-7E.

Early hammer doubles in average condition are approx. valued between $175-$450. However, if 60% condition remains (including original case colors), values can approximate those listed.

100%	98%	95%	90%	80%	70%	60%	50%	40%	30%	20%	10%

FIELD GRADE

* **10 ga. Mag.**

N/A	N/A	$1,500	$1,400	$1,300	$1,200	$1,100	$950	$825	$775	$675	$630

3 1/2 in. chambered 10 ga. Mags. are serial numbered over 500,000. Total mfg. was approx. 850 guns for all grades. 2 7/8 in. chambered 10 gauges are priced the same as a 12 ga. A 12 ga., 3 in. model was also made on the 10 ga. frame - only 87 were mfg. and specimens are noted in the 500,000 serial range.

* **12 ga.**

$1,000	$800	$600	$550	$500	$450	$415	$380	$350	$325	$300	$280

100%	98%	95%	90%	80%	70%	60%	50%	40%	30%	20%	10%
✳ **16 ga.**											
$1,100	$900	$800	$750	$700	$650	$600	$550	$500	$425	$375	$340
✳ **20 ga.**											
$1,400	$1,200	$1,000	$900	$850	$800	$750	$700	$600	$550	$500	$440
✳ **28 ga.**											
N/A	N/A	$2,850	$2,600	$2,400	$2,300	$2,250	$2,200	$2,100	$2,050	$2,025	$2,000
✳ **.410 bore**											
N/A	N/A	$2,850	$2,600	$2,400	$2,300	$2,250	$2,200	$2,100	$2,050	$2,025	$2,000

GRADE NO. 1 - manufactured in both Flues and NID models, similar to Field Grade.

100%	98%	95%	90%	80%	70%	60%	50%	40%	30%	20%	10%
✳ **12 ga.**											
$1,225	$1,000	$800	$600	$550	$500	$450	$415	$380	$350	$325	$315
✳ **16 ga.**											
$1,375	$1,150	$925	$825	$750	$700	$650	$600	$550	$500	$425	$395
✳ **20 ga.**											
$1,700	$1,400	$1,200	$1,000	$900	$850	$800	$750	$700	$600	$550	$525
✳ **28 ga.**											
N/A	N/A	$2,750	$2,200	$2,000	$1,800	$1,700	$1,600	$1,500	$1,400	$1,200	$1,125
✳ **.410 bore**											
N/A	N/A	$2,850	$2,250	$2,000	$1,800	$1,700	$1,600	$1,500	$1,400	$1,200	$1,125

GRADE NO. 2

100%	98%	95%	90%	80%	70%	60%	50%	40%	30%	20%	10%
✳ **10 ga. Mag.**											
$2,400	$2,000	$1,800	$1,600	$1,400	$1,300	$1,200	$1,100	$950	$900	$800	$735

3 1/2 in. chambered 10 ga. Mags. are serial numbered over 500,000. Total mfg. was approx. 850 guns for all grades. 2 7/8 in. chambered 10 gauges are priced the same as a 12 ga.

100%	98%	95%	90%	80%	70%	60%	50%	40%	30%	20%	10%
✳ **12 ga.**											
$1,500	$1,200	$1,000	$800	$600	$550	$500	$450	$415	$380	$350	$335
✳ **16 ga.**											
$1,500	$1,200	$1,000	$900	$800	$750	$700	$650	$600	$550	$500	$475
✳ **20 ga.**											
$1,800	$1,500	$1,200	$1,100	$1,000	$900	$850	$800	$750	$700	$650	$580
✳ **28 ga.**											
N/A	N/A	$3,250	$2,500	$2,000	$1,950	$1,850	$1,750	$1,650	$1,550	$1,450	$1,350
✳ **.410 bore**											
N/A	N/A	$3,250	$2,500	$2,000	$1,950	$1,850	$1,750	$1,650	$1,550	$1,450	$1,350

GRADE NO. 3

100%	98%	95%	90%	80%	70%	60%	50%	40%	30%	20%	10%
✳ **10 ga. Mag.**											
$3,500	$2,900	$2,300	$1,850	$1,600	$1,400	$1,300	$1,200	$1,100	$950	$825	$735

3 1/2 in. chambered 10 ga. Mags. are serial numbered over 500,000. Total mfg. was approx. 850 guns for all grades. 2 7/8 in. chambered 10 gauges are priced the same as a 12 ga.

100%	98%	95%	90%	80%	70%	60%	50%	40%	30%	20%	10%
✳ **12 ga.**											
$2,300	$2,075	$1,850	$1,500	$1,200	$1,000	$800	$750	$700	$650	$600	$550
✳ **16 ga.**											
N/A	N/A	$1,500	$1,275	$1,175	$1,000	$900	$850	$800	$750	$700	$650
✳ **20 ga.**											
N/A	N/A	$1,875	$1,675	$1,475	$1,300	$1,200	$1,100	$1,000	$900	$850	$800

✳ **28 ga.** - only 5 mfg.

Extreme rarity factor precludes accurate pricing evaluation.

✳ **.410 bore** - only 7 mfg.

Extreme rarity factor precludes accurate pricing evaluation.

100%	98%	95%	90%	80%	70%	60%	50%	40%	30%	20%	10%

GRADE NO. 4E - auto ejectors.

* *10 ga. Mag.*

| $5,800 | $5,350 | $4,650 | $4,100 | $3,350 | $2,650 | $2,100 | $1,975 | $1,875 | $1,750 | $1,650 | $1,550 |

3 1/2 in. chambered 10 ga. Mags. are serial numbered over 500,000. Total mfg. was approx. 850 guns for all grades. 2 7/8 in. chambered 10 gauges are priced the same as a 12 ga.

* *12 ga.*

| N/A | $3,750 | $3,325 | $3,000 | $2,500 | $2,100 | $1,700 | $1,550 | $1,325 | $1,200 | $1,100 | $995 |

* *16 ga.*

| N/A | N/A | $3,750 | $3,325 | $3,000 | $2,400 | $2,000 | $1,875 | $1,650 | $1,550 | $1,450 | $1,325 |

* *20 ga.*

| N/A | N/A | $4,625 | $4,250 | $3,725 | $3,525 | $3,300 | $3,100 | $2,950 | $2,700 | $2,300 | $1,975 |

* *28 ga.*

Extreme rarity factor precludes accurate pricing evaluation.

* *.410 bore*

Extreme rarity factor precludes accurate pricing evaluation.

GRADE NO. 5E - auto ejectors.

* *10 ga. - only 9 mfg.*

Extreme rarity factor precludes accurate pricing evaluation.

* *12 ga.*

| N/A | N/A | $3,200 | $3,000 | $2,700 | $2,200 | $1,875 | $1,650 | $1,325 | $1,200 | $1,100 | $1,050 |

* *16 ga.*

| N/A | N/A | $2,800 | $2,500 | $2,200 | $1,875 | $1,750 | $1,550 | $1,425 | $1,325 | $1,200 | $1,150 |

* *20 ga.*

| N/A | N/A | $4,000 | $3,700 | $3,300 | $3,000 | $2,875 | $2,650 | $2,325 | $2,100 | $1,875 | $1,700 |

* *28 ga.*

Extreme rarity factor precludes accurate pricing evaluation.

* *.410 bore*

Extreme rarity factor precludes accurate pricing evaluation.

GRADE NO. 7E - auto ejectors, only 22 mfg. in all gauges.

Extreme rarity factor precludes accurate pricing evaluation on this model.

$2,000 GRADE - 12 ga., top-of-the-line model, auto ejectors, single selective trigger.

| N/A | N/A | $8,450 | $7,400 | $6,500 | $5,650 | $4,750 | $4,000 | $3,250 | $2,600 | $2,100 | $1,700 |

Rarity on 16 or 20 ga. precludes accurate pricing.

PRE-WAR $1,000 GRADE - 12 ga., top-of-the-line models, auto ejectors, single selective trigger.

| N/A | N/A | $9,500 | $8,450 | $7,400 | $6,500 | $5,650 | $4,750 | $4,000 | $3,250 | $2,600 | $2,250 |

Rarity on 16 or 20 ga. precludes accurate pricing.

SOUSA GRADE - has mermaids on trigger guard in gold, only 11 manufactured (including one .410 bore). This model is very rare and prices are hard to establish. Recently, the price range has been approx. $15,000-$40,000, depending on gauge and original condition.

The famous band director and composer, John Phillip Sousa, assisted in the development of this model.

GRADING - PPGS™	100%	98%	95%	90%	80%	70%	60%

SHOTGUNS: SEMI-AUTO

MODEL 51A FEATHERLIGHT STANDARD - 12 or 20 ga., 30 in. full, 28 in. full or mod., 26 in. imp. cyl., gas operated, autoloading, checkered pistol grip stock. Vent. rib became standard during late production. Mfg. 1970-1985.

	100%	98%	95%	90%	80%	70%	60%
Older models w/o VR	$250	$230	$200	$180	$165	$150	$130
Recent production (w/VR)	$295	$265	$235	$210	$190	$175	$165

Last MSR with VR was $477.

MODEL 51A MAGNUM - similar to 51 Standard, except 3 in. shells only, blue finish, recoil pad, VR became standard in 1984. Disc. 1985.

	100%	98%	95%	90%	80%	70%	60%
Older models w/o VR	$265	$235	$220	$205	$180	$165	$150
Vent. rib	$325	$275	$250	$225	$200	$185	$170

MODEL 51A MAGNUM WATERFOWLER - similar to 51 Standard, except 3 in. shells only, matte finished metal & flat finished walnut, recoil pad. Vent. rib standard. Mfg. 1984-86.

100%	98%	95%	90%	80%	70%	60%
$325	$295	$275	$250	$230	$200	$180

Last MSR was $625.

Add $40 for camouflaged exterior finish (mfg. 1986 only).

MODEL 51A SUPREME TRAP - similar to 51 Standard, except 12 ga. only, 30 in. barrel, 7 post rib, full choke, select wood, pad, trap style stock. Add $36 for Monte Carlo. Mfg. 1970-86.

100%	98%	95%	90%	80%	70%	60%
$450	$375	$325	$295	$270	$250	$230

Last MSR was $869.

MODEL 51A SUPREME SKEET - similar to 51 Standard, except 26 in. VR barrel, skeet choke, select wood. Mfg. 1970-present. 20 ga. was available 1983. Disc. 1986.

100%	98%	95%	90%	80%	70%	60%
$465	$395	$340	$300	$280	$260	$240

Last MSR was $858.

MODEL 51A DEERSLAYER - similar to 51 Standard, with 24 in. slug barrel, rifle sights, recoil pad, no rib. Mfg. 1972-83.

100%	98%	95%	90%	80%	70%	60%
$350	$300	$260	$230	$195	$180	$165

Last MSR was $477.

MODEL 51A TURKEY GUN - 12 ga. Mag. only, 26 in. barrel, matte finish, sling and swivels included. Mfg. 1984-86.

100%	98%	95%	90%	80%	70%	60%
$360	$305	$275	$265	$250	$230	$210

Last MSR was $625.

MODEL 51 DUCKS UNLIMITED - similar to 51 Deluxe, with D/U emblem on receiver.

100%	98%	95%	90%	80%	70%	60%
$425	$375	$335	$300	$280	$260	$230

MODEL 51 PRESENTATION - 12 ga., blue, engraved, gold engraved receiver with deluxe walnut. Mfg. 1984-86.

100%	98%	95%	90%	80%	70%	60%
$1,325	$1,050	$875	$700	$575	$450	$325

Last MSR was $1,658.

MODEL XL 300 - 12 or 20 ga., gas operated, various barrel lengths with or w/o VR. Mfg. 1973-76.

100%	98%	95%	90%	80%	70%	60%
$250	$230	$200	$180	$165	$150	$130

Add 15% for VR barrel.

MODEL XL 900 - 12 or 20 ga., gas operated, various barrel lengths with VR. Mfg. 1973-78.

100%	98%	95%	90%	80%	70%	60%
$295	$275	$245	$210	$185	$170	$150

Add 10% for skeet, trap, or slug variations.

Shotguns: Semi-Auto, Mag-10 Series

All Ithaca Mag-10s were disc. 1986.

MAG-10 - 10 ga., 3 1/2 in. Mag., various barrel lengths, stainless steel breech block assembly, gas operated, various chokes, plain barrel, 11 lb. Mfg. 1975-86.

100% values assume NIB condition - if without, subtract 10%.

* *Standard Grade* - no checkering, ribless barrel, dull finished wood.

$600	$550	$500	$460	$430	$395	$375

Last MSR was $726.

* *Standard Grade with VR* - available in 22, 26, 28, or 32 in. barrel lengths - otherwise similar to Standard Grade.

$625	$550	$495	$450	$400	$360	$330

Last MSR was $781.

Add $60 for camouflaged exterior finish.
Add $60 for interchangeable choke tubes (3) - became available in 1986.

* *Deluxe Vent* - select checkered walnut stock and forearm, 22, 26, 28, or 32 in. barrels, high lustre wood finish.

$675	$600	$550	$495	$450	$400	$350

Last MSR was $924.

* *Supreme Grade* - extra-select checkered walnut stock and forearm, otherwise similar to Deluxe Vent.

$795	$725	$675	$595	$550	$495	$450

Last MSR was $1,124.

* *Mag. 10 Roadblocker* - 22 in. cylinder bored ribless barrel, parkerized finish.

$750	$625	$575	$500	$460	$430	$400

Last MSR was $741.

* *National Wild Turkey Fed. Special Edition* - mfg. in 1985 only.

$950	$795	$625

MAG-10 PRESENTATION OR CENTENNIAL - 10 ga. Mag., blue, engraved, gold inlaid receiver, extra fancy walnut. Limited production. Approx. 200 mfg. in Presentation Grade 1983-86.

$1,875	$1,550	$1,300	$1,050	$915	$830	$745

Last MSR was $1,727.

This configuration was also offered as a 3 gun set - a NIB set is currently selling in the $4,750 range.

SHOTGUNS: SINGLE SHOT, LEVER ACTION

MODEL 66 - 12, 20 ga., or .410 bore single shot lever action, field gun only. Mfg. 1963-78.

$125	$95	$90	$75	$70	$65	$55

Add 33% to .410 bore.
Add 25% for VRs that were also available on special order.

* *Model 66 RS* - 20 ga. slug gun with 22 in. barrel and rifle type sights, recoil pad.

$195	$165	$135	$115	$90	$80	$70

Add 25% for special order VR.

SHOTGUNS: SINGLE BARREL TRAP

CENTURY TRAP - please refer to the SKB section.

CENTURY II TRAP - please refer to the SKB section.

GRADING - PPGS™	100%	98%	95%	90%	80%	70%	60%

SINGLE BARREL TRAP - 12 ga., 30, 32, or 34 in. barrels, VR, boxlock, auto ejector, checkered pistol grip and forearm, grades differ in engraving, overall workmanship, and grade or wood and checkering. Values on these models sometimes vary greatly depending on originality of finish, customer alterations, and other variations trap shooters might use to alter dimensions for their particular shooting requirements. Values represent trap guns in original, unaltered condition.

> Note: Flues model mfg. prior to 1921 with serial numbers under 400,000 generally have better engraving than NID (New Ithaca Double) models over serial number 400,000 (also referred to as Knick models).
>
> Trap guns under 60% original condition will be within 25% of the value shown in the 60% column.

✳ *Victory Grade* - disc. 1938.

	100%	98%	95%	90%	80%	70%	60%
	$995	$850	$775	$675	$575	$495	$440

✳ *No. 4E* - disc. 1976.

	100%	98%	95%	90%	80%	70%	60%
	$2,450	$2,200	$2,000	$1,825	$1,625	$1,475	$1,350

✳ *No. 5E* - 12 ga., 32 or 34 in. barrel, custom order only, elaborate engraving, quality worksmanship throughout. Originally mfg. 1925-86, mfg. resumed 1988-91.

	100%	98%	95%	90%	80%	70%	60%
	$2,950	$2,550	$2,175	$1,900	$1,725	$1,495	$1,300

Last MSR was $7,500.

✳ *No. 6E* - this model was available by special order only. Rarity factor precludes accurate pricing.

✳ *No. 7E* - disc. 1964.

	100%	98%	95%	90%	80%	70%	60%
	$5,500	$4,700	$4,000	$3,500	$3,000	$2,500	$2,200

✳ *Dollar Grade* - 12 ga., 32 or 34 in. barrel. Top-of-the-line model custom built to customer specifications. Original mfg. was stopped 1986 and resumed 1988-91.

	100%	98%	95%	90%	80%	70%	60%
	$5,950	$5,200	$4,600	$3,850	$3,250	$2,775	$2,250

Last MSR was $10,000.

✳ *$5,000 Grade* - similar to Pre-War $1,000 grade.

	100%	98%	95%	90%	80%	70%	60%
	$9,500	$8,900	$8,175	$7,650	$6,725	$5,825	$4,950

✳ *Sousa Grade* - extremely rare.

> Extreme rarity factor precludes accurate pricing evaluation. Prices will be higher than the $5,000 Grade.

SHOTGUNS: SLIDE ACTION

During late 1996, Ithaca Gun Co., LLC resumed manufacture of the Model 37, while discontinuing the Model 87. In 1987, Ithaca Acquisition Corp. reintroduced the Model 37 as the Model 87. Recently manufactured Model 87s are listed in addition to both new and older Model 37s (produced pre-1986).

Over 2 million Model 37s have been produced to date.

Model 37s with ser. nos. above 855,000 will accept both 2 3/4 and 3 in. chambered barrels interchangeably. Earlier guns have incompatible threading for the magnum barrels.

MODEL 37 TRENCH AND RIOT GUNS - see separate listing under Trench Guns in the T Section.

MODEL 37 DS POLICE SPECIAL - 12 ga. only, 18 1/2 in. barrel with rifle sights, Parkerized finish on metal, oil finished stock, typically subcontracted by police departments or law enforcement agencies, with or without unit code markings.

	100%	98%	95%	90%	80%	70%	60%
	$325	$275	$235	$200	$185	$170	$160

MODEL 37 FEATHERLIGHT STANDARD - 12, 16, or 20 ga., bottom ejection, 4 shot mag., 26, 28, or 30 in. barrel, hammerless, take down, any standard choke. Mfg. 1937-disc.

	100%	98%	95%	90%	80%	70%	60%
	$250	$225	$195	$175	$160	$140	$125

Add 25% for 16 or 20 ga.

GRADING - PPGS™	100%	98%	95%	90%	80%	70%	60%

MODEL 37 $1000 GRADE - all gauges, deluxe engraving and checkering, gold inlaid, select figured walnut, hand-finished parts. Mfg. 1937-40.

| | $5,750 | $5,200 | $4,750 | $4,250 | $3,750 | $3,250 | $2,650 |

MODEL 37 $5000 GRADE - similar to $1000 Grade, post-war designation. Mfg. 1947-67.

| | $5,250 | $4,850 | $4,250 | $3,850 | $3,250 | $2,850 | $2,250 |

MODEL 37V - similar to 37, except VR. Mfg. 1962-disc.

| | $315 | $260 | $240 | $195 | $180 | $170 | $165 |

All currently manufactured Model 37s have the Featherlight designation. Prices are for older manufactured Model 37s.

MODEL 37D - similar to 37, except recoil pad, beavertail forearm, checkered. Mfg. 1954-81.

| | $295 | $275 | $235 | $200 | $185 | $175 | $160 |

MODEL 37DV - similar to 37D, except VR. Mfg. 1962-81.

| | $375 | $325 | $265 | $225 | $200 | $185 | $170 |

MODEL 37 ULTRA FEATHERLIGHT - 20 ga. only, bottom ejection, 4 shot mag., 26 or 28 in. VR barrel, standard choke, approx. 4 3/4 lbs. Disc.

| | $395 | $340 | $275 | $235 | $210 | $190 | $175 |

ULTRA FEATHERLIGHT RUFFED GROUSE SOCIETY SPECIAL EDITION - 20 ga. only, bottom ejection, aluminum receiver, 22 or 24 in. barrel, English style American walnut stock. Limited mfg. 2003-2004.

| | $715 | $565 | $435 | $375 | $300 | $260 | $230 |

Last MSR was $840.

MODEL 37 FIELD GRADE MAGNUM - 12 or 20 ga., 3 in. chambers, VR, walnut stock and corncob forearm, supplied with three choke tubes. Mfg. 1984-86.

| | $300 | $240 | $195 | $180 | $170 | $165 | $150 |

Last MSR was $428.

MODEL 37 FIELD GRADE STANDARD - 12 or 20 ga., economy model, corncob forearm, 26, 28, or 30 in. barrel. Mfg. 1983-85 only.

| | $245 | $225 | $195 | $175 | $160 | $140 | $120 |

Last MSR was $298.

MODEL 37 ULTRALIGHT - 12 (disc.) or 20 ga., new manufacture features checkered pistol grip (with Sid Bell red grip cap) and forearm, most recent mfg. was in deer configuration, 20 ga. only with 20 or 25 in. smooth bore barrel. Mfg. 1996-2002.

| | $475 | $380 | $340 | $300 | $275 | $250 | $225 |

Last MSR was $600.

MODEL 37 ENGLISH ULTRALIGHT DELUXE - 12 (disc.), 16 or 20 ga., 24, 25 (disc.), 26 or 28 in. barrels, choice of English straight grip stock with checkered forearm or pistol grip stock and grooved forearm, aluminum receiver, world's lightest pump, 20 ga. weighs 4 3/4 lb., 12 ga. weighs 5 1/2 lbs., checkered straight stock. Mfg. 1983-1986, reintroduced 1999.

| MSR $659 | $520 | $410 | $300 | $250 | $225 | $200 | $185 |

* *Model 37 Classic Ultralight Deluxe* - 16 or 20 ga., choice of pistol grip or English straight grip deluxe checkered walnut stock and forearm, 24, 26, or 28 in. VR barrel with three choke tubes, 5 1/4 lbs.

| MSR $834 | $700 | $555 | $425 | $375 | $300 | $260 | $230 |

MODEL 37R - 12, 16, or 20 ga., solid rib. Mfg. 1937-67.

| Plain stock | $295 | $200 | $175 | $145 | $130 | $110 | $90 |
| Checkered stock | $335 | $245 | $200 | $175 | $165 | $145 | $120 |

Add 20% for 16 or 20 ga.

GRADING - PPGS™	100%	98%	95%	90%	80%	70%	60%

MODEL 37R DELUXE - similar to 37R, except fancy wood. Mfg. 1937-1955.

	$425	$350	$275	$250	$225	$195	$165

MODEL 37 PROTECTION SERIES - 12 ga. only, 18.5 or 20 in. smoothbore barrel w/o chokes, 5 or 8 shot tube mag., approx. 6.75 lbs. New 2005.

MSR $482	$425	$375	$325	$275	$250	$225	$195

Add $27 for 20 in. barrel.

TURKEYSLAYER - 12 (Storm) or 20 (new 2000, Storm Light)) ga., 3 in. chamber, choice of matte blue or 100% camo coverage in Realtree Hardwoods (disc. 2002), Realtree Hardwoods HD (new 2003), Realtree Timber (disc. 2002), or Advantage (disc. 2001) pattern, 22 (disc. 2002) or 24 in. barrel with extended choke tube, Tru-glo fiber optic sights standard beginning 2003, 7 lbs. Mfg. 1996-2004.

	$375	$335	$300	$275	$250	$225	$200

Last MSR was $459.

Add $20 for ported choke tube (disc.).

* *Youth Turkeyslayer* - 20 ga. only, features 22 in. barrel and shortened youth dimension stock. Mfg. 1998-2003.

	$500	$375	$295	$225	$175	$160	$145

Last MSR was $615.

TUREYSLAYER II GUIDE SERIES - 12 ga. only, 3 in. chamber, 20 in. interchangeable barrel with turkey choke, choice of Realtree Hardwoods Green or 100% Mossy Oak Break Up camo coverage, pistol grip stock, includes 30mm red dot scope and sling, fiber optic sights. New 2005.

MSR $599	$500	$425	$365	$330	$300	$275	$250

WATERFOWLER - 12 (Storm) or 20 (Storm Light) ga., features black finish or Wetlands (disc.), Realtree Hardwoods HD Green, or Realtree Max 4 camo treatment, 24, 26, 28 (standard) or 30 in. barrel designed for shooting steel shot. Mfg. 1998-2004.

	$425	$375	$335	$300	$275	$250	$225

Last MSR was $499.

Add $50 for Realtree Max 4 camo.

MODEL 37 DELUXE W/VR - 12, 16 (Featherlight, new 1999), or 20 ga., similar to Model 87 Field Grade except has cut checkering, 26, 28, or 30 (disc. 2002) in. VR barrel, high gloss lacquer finish, and gold trigger, newer mfg. includes 3 choke tubes. New 1996.

MSR $627	$500	$380	$285	$230	$175	$160	$145

Add $30 for 20 ga. Youth Model.

* *Model 37 Deluxe English* - 12 (new 2000) or 20 ga., features 24, 26, or 28 in. English style vent. rib barrel, approx. 7 lbs. Mfg. 1998-2003.

	$485	$365	$275	$225	$175	$160	$145

Last MSR was $600.

Add $30 for 20 ga.

MODEL 37 CLASSIC - 12, 16 (Featherlight, new 1999), or 20 ga., features knuckle cut receiver, corn cob forearm, hand checkering, and sunburst recoil pad, 26 or 28 in. VR barrel with choke tubes, choice of pistol grip or English straight grip deluxe checkered walnut stock and forearm, 6 1/2 - 7 lbs. Limited production beginning 1998.

MSR $812	$680	$540	$425	$375	$300	$260	$230

* *Model 37 NRA Women's* - 16 or 20 ga., 24 in. VR barrel with three choke tubes, 5 1/4 or 6 1/2 lbs. Mfg. 2003-2004.

	$715	$565	$435	$375	$300	$260	$230

Last MSR was $840.

GRADING - PPGS™	100%	98%	95%	90%	80%	70%	60%

MODEL 37 SUPREME - 12, 16, or 20 ga., deluxe checkered walnut stock and fore-arm, 28 or 30 in. VR barrel, engraved receiver, approx. 7 3/4 lbs. Originally mfg. 1967-1986, reintroduced late 1996, disc. 1997, reintroduced 2003-2004.

	100%	98%	95%	90%	80%	70%	60%
	$895	$650	$550	$450	$400	$350	$425

Last MSR was $1,185.

| 1967-1997 Mfg. | $675 | $575 | $495 | $425 | $375 | $325 | $295 |

MODEL 37S SKEET GRADE - similar to 37, except Knicker VR, large forearm, fancy wood. Mfg. 1937-55.

	$495	$445	$375	$335	$300	$275	$250

Add 20% for 16 or 20 ga.

MODEL 37 SPORTING CLAYS - 12 ga. only, 24 (disc.), 26 (disc.), 28, or 30 (disc.) in. VR ported (standard 2001) or unported (disc. 2000) barrel with 3 Briley choke tubes, similar in appearances and features to Model 37 Trap. New 2000-2004.

	$1,275	$1,075	$925	$800	$650	$525	$450

Last MSR was $1,495.

MODEL 37T TRAP GRADE - similar to 37S, except trap stock, select walnut, recoil pad. Mfg. 1937-55.

	$475	$425	$375	$325	$295	$275	$250

Add 20% for early models with fleur-de-lis checkering.

MODEL 37 TRAP - 12 ga. only, 30 in. VR ported (standard 2001) or unported (disc. 2000) barrel with 3 Briley choke tubes, antique silver finished receiver with scroll style engraving and gold inlays on receiver sides, optional adj. cheekpiece stock. Mfg. 2000-2004.

	$1,275	$1,075	$925	$800	$650	$525	$450

Last MSR was $1,495.

MODEL 37T TARGET GRADE - replaced 37S and 37T. Mfg. from 1955-61.

	$475	$425	$375	$325	$295	$275	$250

MODEL 37 DEERSLAYER - 12, 16, or 20 ga., original Deerslayer, smooth bore with fixed choke only, rifle sights. Mfg. circa 1962-86.

	$300	$240	$195	$180	$170	$165	$150

MODEL 37 SUPER DELUXE DEERSLAYER - similar to Model 37 (87) Deerslayer, except Williams aperture rear sight and fancy wood. Mfg.1962-1985.

	$375	$335	$300	$270	$235	$210	$185

Last MSR was $447.

MODEL 37 DEERSLAYER DELUXE - 12, 16 (new 1999 - smooth bore only, rifled beginning 2000) or 20 ga., 20, 24, or 25 (disc.) in. smooth bore (disc.) or rifled bar-rel, current manufacture has choice of 100% Realtree Hardwoods 20/200 camo (mfg. 2000-2002, 12 ga. only) or walnut stock and forearm with cut checkering, light receiver engraving. Mfg. 1959-present.

MSR $591	$495	$410	$330	$285	$240	$210	$185

Add $50 for Hardwoods camo (disc.).

DEERSLAYER II - 12, 16 (new 2001), or 20 ga., 20, 24 (new 2003) or 25 (disc.) in. barrel with 1:34 rifling (also available with fast twist 1:25 rifling, 12 ga. only, disc.), Monte Carlo stock and forearm with cut checkering, receiver is drilled and tapped for scope mounting, 6.25-7 lbs. New 1996.

MSR $642	$520	$390	$310	$230	$175	$160	$145

✳ *Model 37 Deerslayer II Storm* - 12 or 20 (Storm Light) ga., 24 in. smooth bore barrel with choke tube and open rifle sights, 100% DSS treatment on stock, approx. 6 1/2 lbs. Mfg. 2003-2004.

	$350	$300	$275	$250	$225	$200	$185

Last MSR was $399.

GRADING - PPGS™	100%	98%	95%	90%	80%	70%	60%

DEERSLAYER II GUIDE SERIES - 12 or 20 ga., 20 or 24 in. rifled barrel with fiber optic sights, 3 in. chamber, blued metal, grey camo laminate pistol grip stock and forearm. New 2005.

	100%	98%	95%	90%	80%	70%	60%
MSR $599	$500	$415	$330	$285	$240	$210	$185

DEERSLAYER III - 12 ga., 26 in. smooth bore barrel with DSR-1 choke tube, 11 lbs. Mfg. 2003-2004.

		$750	$675	$600	$525	$450	$375	$300

Last MSR was $900.

MODEL 37 BICENTENNIAL - 12 ga., engraved, fancy wood, cased with pewter buckle, 1,776 mfg. 1976, 100% value assumes NIB condition with case and belt buckle.

		$595	$450	$325

MODEL 37 2500 SERIES CENTENNIAL - 12 ga., customized version of the Model 37 commemorating Ithaca's 100th year anniversary, silver plated, etched antique finish receiver, deluxe walnut. Mfg. 1980-84.

		$775	$625	$450

Last MSR was $919.

LIMITED EDITION MODEL 37 60TH ANNIVERSARY - 20 ga., scroll engraving by A&A Engraving on both sides of nickel receiver with dog game scene/eagle motif, supreme grade wood, includes case. 200 mfg. 1997 only.

		$1,450	$850	$475

Last MSR was $2,000.

MODEL 37 PRESENTATION - 12 ga., blue, engraved, gold mounted receiver with extra-fancy walnut, cased, limited production. Mfg. 1981-86.

		$1,500	$1,245	$1,080	$915	$830	$745	$665

Last MSR was $1,658.

A 3 gun set was also available - an NIB set is currently priced in the $1,750 range.

MODEL 37 DUCKS UNLIMITED - 12 ga., VR.

		$385	$305	$275

MODEL 37 60TH ANNIVERSARY - 20 ga., 3 in. chamber, 26 in. VR barrel, checkered Supreme wood, engraved, cased. 200 mfg. 1997 only.

		$1,750	$1,250	$850

MODEL 87 FIELD (BASIC) - 12 or 20 ga., 3 in. chamber, economy model, walnut stock and forearm with pressed checkering, 26, 28, or 30 (disc.) in. barrel with 3 choke tubes standard. Reintroduced 1987-96.

		$360	$290	$240	$195	$170	$160	$145

Last MSR was $477.

✳ *Model 87 Basic Field Combo* - 12 or 20 ga., includes 20/25 in. deer barrel with special bore and 28 in. VR multi-choke field barrel, unchecked walnut stock and corncob forearm, 7 lbs. Mfg. 1989-92.

		$400	$315	$275	$235	$210	$190	$170

Last MSR was $459.

Add $32 for rifled bore barrel.
Add $104 for laminated wood (includes rifle bored barrel).

✳ *Model 87 Camo Field* - 12 ga. only, 3 in. chamber, 24, 26, or 28 in. VR barrel, camoseal rust resistant finish on exterior parts. Available in either green or brown camo finish. Mfg. began 1986, resumed 1988, disc. 1996.

		$425	$315	$260	$200	$175	$160	$145

Last MSR was $542.

✳ *Model 87 Turkey Field* - 12 ga. only, 24 in. VR barrel with choice of fixed full choke or full choke tube, camo or matte blue finish. Mfg. 1989-96.

	100%	98%	95%	90%	80%	70%	60%
	$365	$285	$235	$190	$170	$160	$145

Last MSR was $466.

Add $85 for camo finish. Add $43 for full choke tube.

MODEL 87 ULTRALITE FIELD - 12 or 20 ga., 3 in. chamber, aluminum receiver, 20 (disc. 1988), 24, 25 (disc. 1988), or 26 in. barrel. 20 ga. weighs 5 lbs., 12 ga. weighs 5 3/4 lbs, multi-chokes (3) became standard in 1989. Originally mfg. 1985-86, reintroduced 1988-90.

	100%	98%	95%	90%	80%	70%	60%
	$445	$375	$295	$240	$210	$190	$170

Last MSR was $481.

Add $50 for slim grip model (12 1/2 in. stock - disc. 1985).
Subtract $42 if without multiple choke feature.
The 20 and 25 in. barrels were disc. when mfg. was resumed 1988.

✳ *Model 87 Ultra Deluxe* - similar to Ultralite Field except has cut checkering, high gloss lacquer finish, and gold trigger. Mfg 1989-91.

	100%	98%	95%	90%	80%	70%	60%
	$425	$360	$300	$250	$220	$190	$170

Last MSR was $514.

MODEL ENGLISH 87 - 20 ga. only, 3 in. chamber, 24 or 26 in. VR barrel with 3 choke tubes, steel receiver, checkered walnut stock and forearm, recoil pad, 6 3/4 lbs. Mfg. 1991-96.

	100%	98%	95%	90%	80%	70%	60%
	$425	$315	$260	$200	$175	$160	$145

Last MSR was $545.

MODEL 87 DELUXE - similar to Model 87 Field Grade except has cut checkering, 26, 28, or 30 in. VR barrel, high gloss lacquer finish, and gold trigger, newer mfg. includes 3 choke tubes. Mfg. 1989-96.

	100%	98%	95%	90%	80%	70%	60%
	$415	$310	$255	$200	$175	$160	$145

Last MSR was $533.

Add $54 for combo package (includes 20 in. special bore deer barrel, disc. 1992).
Add $87 for combo package with 20 or 25 in. rifled bore deer barrel, disc. 1992.

✳ *Model 87 Deluxe Magnum* - 12 or 20 ga., 3 in. chambers, VR, deluxe wood with checkered forearm. Mfg. 1981-86, production resumed 1988 only.

	100%	98%	95%	90%	80%	70%	60%
	$320	$270	$230	$210	$200	$185	$165

Last MSR was $395.

Add $77 for Combo package (extra 28 in. barrel).
New mfg. 20 ga. shotguns were available with a 25 in. barrel only (with choke tubes).

MODEL 87 SUPREME GRADE - 12 or 20 ga., presentation walnut, high luster blue, limited production, previously available in either trap, skeet, or field models, fixed chokes. Mfg. 1988-96.

	100%	98%	95%	90%	80%	70%	60%
	$640	$475	$395	$325	$295	$270	$250

Last MSR was $809.

BASIC DEERSLAYER - 12 ga. only, 20 or 25 in. special bore or rifled barrel, oil finished stock and corncob forearm with no checkering, iron sights, matte metal finish, 7 lbs. Mfg. 1989-96.

	100%	98%	95%	90%	80%	70%	60%
	$345	$280	$240	$195	$175	$160	$145

Last MSR was $425.

Add $40 for rifled barrel.

MODEL 87 FIELD DEERSLAYER - 12 or 20 ga., rifle slug barrel, 20 or 25 in. special smooth bore barrel with open sights. Mfg. 1959-86, reintroduced 1988-93.

	100%	98%	95%	90%	80%	70%	60%
	$300	$250	$210	$180	$160	$150	$140

Last MSR was $364.

GRADING - PPGS™	100%	98%	95%	90%	80%	70%	60%

MODEL 87 DELUXE DEERSLAYER - similar to Field Deerslayer except has cut checkering, high gloss lacquer finish, and gold trigger. Mfg. 1989-96.

	$365	$285	$235	$190	$170	$160	$145

Last MSR was $465.

> **Add $34 for rifled bore.**
>
> **Add $120 for combo package (28 in. multi-choke barrel).**

✳ *Model 87 Ultra Deerslayer* - similar to Deluxe Deerslayer except has aluminum frame. Mfg. 1989-90 only.

	$350	$285	$245	$200	$175	$160	$145

Last MSR was $444.

MONTE CARLO DEERSLAYER II - 12 ga. only, 20 or 25 in. barrel with rifling, Monte Carlo stock and forearm with cut checkering, receiver is drilled and tapped for scope mounting, 7 lbs. Mfg. 1989-96.

	$445	$335	$270	$210	$175	$160	$145

Last MSR was $567.

DEERSLAYER II FAST TWIST - 12 ga. only, 25 in. rifled permanently fixed barrel, Monte Carlo stock with checkering, receiver is drilled and tapped. Mfg. 1992-93.

	$440	$385	$325	$275	$235	$200	$180

Last MSR was $550.

MODEL 87 MILITARY & POLICE - 12 (3 in.) or 20 (new 1989) ga., short barrel Model 37 w/ normal stock or pistol grip only, 18 1/2, 20, or 24 3/4 (scarce) in. barrel, choice of front bead or rifle sights, front blade was usually a flourescent orange plastic, 5, 8, or 10 shot. Originally disc. 1983, reintroduced 1989-95.

	$265	$230	$200	$180	$170	$160	$150

Last MSR was $323.

> **Add $104 for nickel finish (mfg. 1991-92 only).**

IVER JOHNSON ARMS, INC.

Current manufacturer established during 2004 and located in Rockledge, FL.

The new Iver Johnson Arms, Inc. company was formed during 2004, and currently manufactures the Raven Series, based on the M1911 design, in both .22 LR (MSR $550) and .45 ACP cals. (MSR is $525-$550), the Target Eagle Series (MSR $600), and the Model PM 30G M1 Carbine (MSR is N/A). Additionally, Iver Johnson Arms, Inc. plans on releasing the X-300 Pony pistol in .380 ACP cal., in addition to a Frontier 4-barrel derringer during 2005. Please contact the company directly for more information, including availability and pricing (see Trademark Index).

IVER JOHNSON ARMS, INC.

Previously manufactured in Fitchburg, MA, 1883-1984 and Jacksonville, AR 1984-1993. Formerly Johnson Bye & Co. 1871-1883. Renamed Iver Johnson & Co. in 1871 until 1891. Renamed Iver Johnson's Arms & Cycle Works in 1891 with manufacturing moving to Fitchburg, MA. In 1975 the name changed to Iver Johnson's Arms, Inc., and two years later, company facilities were moved to Middlesex, NJ. In 1982, production was moved to Jacksonville, AR under the trade name Iver Johnson Arms, Inc. In 1983, Universal Firearms, Inc. was acquired by Iver Johnson Arms, Inc.

Iver Johnson Arms was sold in March of 1987 and was acquired by American Military Arms Corporation (AMAC). AMAC ceased operations in early 1993.

PISTOLS: SEMI-AUTO

AMAC also manufactured Delta 786 9mm Para. (disc. 1989), the Super Enforcer .30 Carbine, and the M-2 machine gun in .30 Carbine which are not listed in this text.

GRADING - PPGS™	100%	98%	95%	90%	80%	70%	60%

TRAILSMEN PISTOL - .22 LR cal. only, all steel construction, 4 1/2 or 6 in. barrel, blue finish, black checkered composition grips, 10 shot mag., approx. 30 oz. Mfg. 1985-86 and reintroduced 1990 only.

	100%	98%	95%	90%	80%	70%	60%
	$200	$165	$145	$130	$120	$110	$100

Last MSR was $230.

Add $20 for hardwood stocks and high polish blue (disc. 1990).

PONY PISTOL (PO380 SERIES) - .380 ACP cal. only, semi-auto single action, 3 in. barrel, 6 shot mag., all steel construction, blue or matte blue finish, 20 oz. Mfg. 1985-1986 (by Firearms International) and reintroduced 1990 only.

	100%	98%	95%	90%	80%	70%	60%
	$290	$245	$210	$185	$170	$155	$140

Last MSR was $330.

* **Pony .380 Stainless** - similar to Pony Pistol, except is stainless steel construction. New 1990 only.

	100%	98%	95%
	$315	$280	$240

Last MSR was $365.

* **Nickel Pony** - with nickel finish. Mfg. 1985 only.

	100%	98%	95%	90%	80%	70%	60%
	$260	$230	$215	$200	$185	$170	$160

Last MSR was $290 for nickel finish.

POCKET PISTOL (TP SERIES) - .22 LR or .25 ACP cal., semi-auto, double action, 3 in. barrel, 7 shot finger tip extension mag., black plastic grips, fixed sights, blue or matte finish, 15 oz. Previously mfg. 1985-86, reintroduced 1988-90.

	100%	98%	95%	90%	80%	70%	60%
	$145	$125	$110	$100	$90	$80	$70

Last MSR was $165.

Add $15 for nickel finish (disc. 1989).

AMAC-22/25 COMPACT - .22 Short (disc.) or .25 ACP cal., semi-auto, single action, 5 shot mag., 2 in. barrel, all steel construction, plastic grips, 9.3 oz. Disc. 1993.

	100%	98%	95%	90%	80%	70%	60%
	$165	$135	$115	$100	$90	$80	$70

Last MSR was $200.

Add $10 for nickel finish (disc. 1990).

* **Compact Elite Engraved** - similar to .25 ACP Compact, except has extensive engraving. Mfg. 1991-93.

	100%	98%	95%
	$850	$600	$475

Last MSR was $1,000.

SILVER HAWK - .22 LR or .25 ACP cal., double action semi-auto, similar to TP-22 Series, except is stainless steel. Mfg. 1990-93.

	100%	98%	95%
	$215	$185	$160

Last MSR was $250.

SUPER ENFORCER (MODEL 3000) - .30 Carbine cal. only, pistol version of the Carbine with 11 in. shrouded barrel. Mfg. 1985-1986 only.

	100%	98%	95%	90%	80%	70%	60%
	$400	$350	$325	$300	$200	$175	$160

Last MSR was $255.

Add $40 for stainless steel (disc. for 1986).

* **Enforcer** - similar to Super Enforcer model, except has 10 1/2 in. barrel. Reintroduced 1988, disc. 1993.

	100%	98%	95%	90%	80%	70%	60%
	$450	$400	$300	$275	$225	$200	$175

Last MSR was $417.

REVOLVERS

CATTLEMAN MAGNUM - .357 Mag., .44 Mag., or .45 LC cal., single action, 6 shot, Colt replica, 4 3/4, 5 1/2, or 7 1/2 in. barrel, case color frame, blue barrel, and brass grip frame, smooth walnut grips, fixed sights. Mfg. in Italy. Disc. 1984.

	100%	98%	95%	90%	80%	70%	60%
	$250	$200	$190	$150	$140	$130	$125
.44 Mag.	$275	$240	$200	$175	$165	$145	$135

GRADING - PPGS™	100%	98%	95%	90%	80%	70%	60%

BUCKHORN MAGNUM - similar to Cattleman, except flattop, adj. sights.

	$275	$225	$200	$175	$165	$145	$140

BUNTLINE BUCKHORN MAGNUM - similar to Buckhorn, only 18 in. barrel, detachable stock.

	$375	$335	$310	$275	$260	$250	$225
.44 Mag.	$400	$350	$325	$295	$280	$275	$250

TRAIL BLAZER - .22 LR, or .22 Mag. cal., interchangeable cylinder, 5 1/2 or 6 1/2 in. barrel, blue.

	$175	$145	$130	$120	$110	$100	$80

MODEL 1900 - .22 L, S, LR, .32 S&W, or .38 S&W cal., double action, 2 1/2, 4 1/2, or 6 in. barrel, fixed sights, blue or nickel, rubber grips. Mfg. 1900-47.

	$125	$80	$70	$60	$55	$45	$40

MODEL 1900 TARGET - .22 LR cal., 6 shot, 6 or 9 1/2 in. barrel, blue, fixed sights. Mfg. 1925-42.

	$140	$90	$80	$70	$65	$55	$50

TARGET SEALED 8 - .22 LR cal., 8 shot, 6 or 10 in. barrel, blue, fixed sights, rubber grips. Mfg. 1931-57.

	$150	$100	$95	$80	$75	$65	$60

Add 50% for 10 in. barrel.

TARGET 9 SHOT - similar to Target Sealed 8, except 9 shot. Mfg. 1929-46.

	$145	$90	$80	$70	$65	$55	$50

SAFETY HAMMER MODEL - .22 LR, .32 S&W, or .38 S&W cal., 2 or 3 in. barrel standard, 4, 5, or 6 in. available at extra cost, fixed sights, blue (standard) or nickel, break open. Mfg. 1892-50.

	$125	$80	$70	$60	$55	$45	$40

SAFETY HAMMERLESS - .32 S&W or .38 S&W cal., 2, 3 (.32 only), 3 1/4, 4, 5, or 6 in. barrel, double action only, break open, fixed sights, rubber grips, blue or nickel. Mfg. 1895-50.

	$125	$100	$95	$80	$75	$65	$60

.22 SUPERSHOT - .22 LR cal., 6 in. barrel, blue, fixed sights, checkered wood grips, break open, no counterbore. Mfg. 1929-49.

	$150	$80	$70	$60	$55	$45	$40

TRIGGER COCKING SINGLE ACTION - .22 LR cal., 8 shot, 6 in. barrel, break open, counterbored, blue, checkered wood grips, first pull on trigger cocks, second fires. Mfg. 1940-47. Rare in 100% condition.

	$350	$300	$250	$175	$100	$85	$75

.22 TARGET SINGLE ACTION - .22 LR cal., 8 shot, 6 in. barrel, break open, counterbored, checkered wood, adj. grips and sights. Mfg. 1938-48.

	$300	$250	$225	$200	$150	$125	$100

SUPERSHOT SEALED 8 - .22 LR cal., 8 shot, break open, blue, adj. sights, checkered wood grips. Mfg. 1931-57.

	$175	$130	$120	$110	$90	$85	$75

SUPERSHOT 9 - similar to Sealed 8, only 9 shot, not counterbored. Mfg. 1929-49.

	$135	$90	$80	$75	$60	$50	$40

PROTECTOR SEALED 8 - .22 LR cal., 8 shot, 2 1/2 in. barrel, break open, fixed sights, blue, wood grips. Mfg. 1933-49.

	$175	$135	$125	$110	$90	$80	$75

GRADING - PPGS™	100%	98%	95%	90%	80%	70%	60%

SUPERSHOT MODEL 844 - .22 LR cal., 8 shot, 4 1/2 or 6 in. barrel, adj. sights, break open, blue, wood grips. Mfg. 1955-56.

	$100	$90	$85	$80	$75	$60	$50

ARMSWORTH MODEL 855 - .22 LR cal., single action, 8 shot, 6 in. barrel, break open, blue, adj. sights, wood grips, adj. finger rest. Mfg. 1955-57.

	$300	$250	$225	$200	$150	$125	$100

MODEL 55A TARGET - .22 LR cal., 8 shot, 4 1/2 or 6 in. barrel, solid frame, blue, fixed sights, wood grips, loading gate. Mfg. 1955-84.

	$100	$75	$65	$50	$40	$35	$25

CADET - .22 LR, .22 WRM, .32 S&W, .38 S&W, or .38 Spl. cal., 2 1/2 in. barrel, blue, fixed sights, plastic grips. Mfg. 1955-84.

	$110	$90	$80	$75	$65	$55	$50

MODEL 57A TARGET - .22 LR cal., 8 shot, 4 1/2 or 6 in. barrel, solid frame, blue, adj. sights, wood grips. Mfg. 1955-75.

	$100	$80	$75	$65	$55	$45	$40

MODEL 66 TRAILSMAN - .22 LR cal., 6 in. barrel, break open, blue, adj. sights, rebounding hammer, wood grips. Mfg. 1958-75.

	$110	$90	$85	$75	$65	$55	$50

SIDEWINDER - .22 LR cal., 6 or 8 shot, 4 3/4 or 6 in. barrel, solid frame, blue, nickel, or case hardened finish, plastic grips, wood on case color model. Mfg. 1961-disc. 8 shot pre-1975.

	$110	$90	$85	$75	$65	$55	$50

SIDEWINDER S - similar to Sidewinder, except .22 WMR, interchangeable cylinder.

	$125	$100	$95	$85	$75	$65	$60

MODEL 67 VIKING - .22 LR cal., 8 shot, 4 1/2 or 6 in. barrel, break open, blue, adj. sights, wood grips with thumbrest. Mfg. 1964-75.

	$135	$110	$100	$95	$85	$75	$65

MODEL 67S VIKING - .22 LR, .32 S&W, or .38 S&W cal., 8 shot in .22, 5 shot in .32 or .38, 2 3/4 in. barrel, break open, adj. sights, plastic grips. Mfg. 1964-75.

	$130	$100	$95	$85	$75	$60	$50

AMERICAN BULLDOG - .22 LR, .22 WRM, or .38 Spl. cal., 6 shot in .22, 5 shot in .38, 2 1/2 or 4 in. barrel, blue or nickel, adj. sights, plastic grips. Mfg. 1974-76.

	$135	$110	$100	$90	$80	$65	$60

ROOKIE - .38 Spl. cal., 5 shot, 4 in. barrel, solid frame, blue or nickel, plastic grips. Mfg. 1975-84.

	$135	$110	$100	$90	$80	$65	$60

SPORTSMAN - .22 LR cal., 6 shot, 4 3/4 or 6 in. barrel, solid frame, blue, fixed sights, plastic grips. Mfg. 1974-76.

	$100	$80	$75	$65	$55	$45	$35

DELUXE TARGET - similar to Sportsman, adj. sights. Mfg. 1975-76 only.

	$110	$90	$85	$75	$65	$55	$40

SWING OUT - .22 LR, .22 WRM, .32 S&W, or .38 S&W cal., 6 shot in .22, 5 shot in .32 or .38, 2, 3, or 4 in. barrel, VR, 4 or 6 in., blue or nickel, fixed or adj. sights. Mfg. 1977-84.

	$130	$110	$100	$90	$80	$75	$65

✳ *VR Barrel* - 4 or 6 in. VR barrel, adj. sights.

	$170	$150	$140	$130	$125	$120	$100

GRADING - PPGS™	100%	98%	95%	90%	80%	70%	60%

RIFLES

MODEL X - .22 Short, Long, or LR cal., bolt action, single shot, 22 in. barrel, open sight, pistol grip with knob forend. Mfg. 1928-32.

	$150	$140	$125	$100	$75	$50	$40

This model was mfg. both in the U.S. and Canada (by Cooey). Canadian models generally have birch stocks.

* *Model XA* - same as Model X, except equipped with Lyman No. 55J receiver peep sight, ivory bead, swivels and leather sling strap, scarce. Mfg. 1928-32.

	$250	$200	$175	$150	$100	$75	$60

MODEL 2X - improved Model X, 24 in. heavy barrel, larger stock, adj. sights. Mfg. 1932-55.

	$175	$150	$135	$125	$75	$50	$40

* *Model 2XA* - sames as the Model 2X, except equipped with Lyman No. 55J receiver peep sight, ivory bead, swivels and leather sling, scarce. Mfg. 1932-45.

	$300	$250	$225	$175	$120	$125	$100

Add 25% for factory checkered stock.

LI'L CHAMP - .22 LR cal. only, single shot bolt action, 16 1/4 in. barrel, black molded stock, nickel plated bolt, youth dimensions, (32 1/2 in. overall length), 3 lbs. Introduced 1986, reintroduced 1988 only.

	$75	$60	$50	$45	$40	$35	$35

Last MSR was $92.

LONG RANGE RIFLE - .308 Win. (new 1991) or .50 BMG cal., bolt action design, single shot, 29 in. stainless steel fluted barrel with muzzle brake, adj. trigger pull, built-in bipod, adj. rail stock, includes Leupold M-1 Ultra 20X scope, 36 lbs. Limited mfg. between 1988-93.

	$3,150	$2,750	$2,400	$2,100	$1,800	$1,600	$1,400

Last MSR was $5,000.

9MM PARA. CARBINE (JJ9MM SERIES) - 9mm Para. cal. only, copy of U.S. military M1, 16 in. barrel, blue finish only, 20 shot mag. Mfg. 1985-86 only.

* *Hardwood Stock Model* - disc. 1986.

	$230	$200	$180	$170	$160	$150	$140

Last MSR was $255.

* *Standard Model* - with plastic stock. Disc. 1985.

	$225	$200	$180	$170	$160	$150	$140

Last MSR was $250.

* *Folding Plastic Stock Model* - disc. 1985.

	$350	$300	$265	$230	$200	$180	$170

Last MSR was $281.

DELTA-786 CARBINE - 9mm Para. cal., semi-auto, patterned after the U.S. military M1 Carbine, 16 in. barrel, matte black finish. Mfg. 1989 only.

	$575	$425	$360	$325	$295	$260	$230

Last MSR was $665.

.30 CARBINE CAL. - .30 Carbine or 9mm Para. (new 1991) cal., semi-auto, 18 or 20 (new 1991) in. barrel, available in various stock configurations, hardwood stock. Mfg. 1985-1986, reintroduced 1988, disc. 1993.

	$285	$215	$190	$165	$150	$140	$130

Last MSR was $350.

Add $16 for 9mm Para. cal.
Add $35 for walnut stock, Parkerized finish (disc. 1990), or 20 in. barrel (new 1991).

GRADING - PPGS™	100%	98%	95%	90%	80%	70%	60%

✳ Paratrooper Model - similar to standard model, except has folding synthetic stock. Disc. 1993.

	$400	$345	$270	$225	$195	$165	$150

Last MSR was $433.

✳ Stainless Steel Variation - disc. 1985.

	$230	$200	$180				

Last MSR was $250.

✳ 5.7mm Johnson (Spitfire) Cal. - remilled, add $30 for stainless steel.

	$195	$175	$165	$155	$145	$135	$125

Last MSR was $219.

.22 CAL. U.S. CARBINE - .22 LR or .22 Mag. cal., 18 1/2 in. barrel, except for Mag. (19.3 in.), 5.8 lbs., 15 shot mag., sling swivels. Mfg. in Germany by Erma 1985-1986, reintroduced 1988 only.

	$150	$120	$110	$100	$90	$85	$80

Last MSR was $166 for .22 LR cal.

Last MSR was $183 for .22 Mag. cal.

Add $120 for .22 Mag. model (gas operated - disc. 1986).

TARGETMASTER SLIDE ACTION - .22 LR or .22 Mag. (disc. 1986) cal., 18 1/2 in. barrel, 12 shot (LR) tube mag., 5 3/4 lbs. Mfg. in Germany by Erma 1985 only, reintroduced 1988-90.

	$175	$140	$125	$115	$100	$90	$80

Last MSR was $209.

This model was designated EW.22 HBP previously.

MODEL EW.22 HBL LEVER ACTION (WAGONMASTER) - .22 S, L, and LR or .22 Mag. cal., 18 1/2 in. barrel, walnut finish, hardwood stock, blue finish, 5 3/4 lbs., grooved for scope mounts. Mfg. in Germany by Erma 1985-1986, reintroduced 1988-90.

	$175	$140	$125	$115	$100	$90	$80

Last MSR was $209.

Add $23 for .22 Mag. cal. (19 in. barrel).

This model was also available in a Junior variation with smaller dimensions; values same as listed.

TRAIL BLAZER SEMI-AUTO (MODEL IJ.22 HB) - .22 LR cal. only, 10 shot mag., 18 1/2 in. barrel, 5.8 lbs. Mfg. 1985 only.

	$115	$100	$90	$85	$80	$75	$70

Last MSR was $125.

SHOTGUNS

CHAMPION - 10, 12, 16, 20, 24, 28, 32 ga., or .410 bore, also available in .44, .45, 12mm, or 14mm rifle cal., single barrel shotgun or rifle, 26-32 in. full barrel, exposed hammer, auto ejector, plain pistol grip stock. Mfg. 1909-56.

	$175	$150	$125	$100	$75	$50	$40

Subtract 25% for birch stock (12 ga. only, 1970s mfg.).

Values on both smaller gauge shotguns and rifles would be considerably higher than those listed. A mint 32 ga. might command 400% more than the listed values. Rifles will also bring premiums over values listed.

Iver Johnson Champion models were mfg. for Montgomery Ward's during the 1930s-1940s under the "Western-Field" name. These models were also manufactured in Canada by Cooey during the late 1920s-early 1930s. Values are similar to above.

MATTED RIB GRADE - similar to Champion, except not available in 10, 24, 28, or 32 ga., solid rib, checkered stock. Mfg. 1909-48.

	$200	$175	$150	$125	$100	$75	$60

This model has either a semi-octagon (with top matted) or jacketed breech.

GRADING - PPGS™	100%	98%	95%	90%	80%	70%	60%

TRAP GRADE - similar to Matted Rib, except 32 in. full barrel, super select wood, 12 ga., vent rib. Mfg. 1926-42.

	100%	98%	95%	90%	80%	70%	60%
	$350	$300	$250	$200	$150	$125	$100

HERCULES GRADE - 12, 16, 20, 28 ga., or .410 bore, 26-32 in. barrels, hammerless, boxlock, various chokes, extractors and double triggers standard, checkered pistol grip or straight stock. Mfg. 1918-43.

	100%	98%	95%	90%	80%	70%	60%
	$895	$625	$550	$525	$475	$335	$310

Add $200 for auto ejectors.
Add $200 for Miller SST.
Add 10% for 16 ga.
Add 20% for 20 ga.
Add 200% for 28 ga.
Add 100% for .410 bore.
Add 200%+ for rare factory engraved specimens.

The Hercules Model was mfg. in both USA and Canada by Cooey. The Hercules name was dropped in 1936 and became known as the "Iver Johnson Hammerless" until the end of production. Case colored frames were standard until 1936, blue frames were standard 1937-1943. A special run of Hercules Doubles was built in the 1930s for Montgomery Ward under the "Western Field" Model 53 nomenclature. All Western Field guns had a beavertail forearm, twin ivory sights, and recoil pad. Hercules 28 ga. SxSs are extremely rare.

SKEET-ER MODEL - 12, 16, 20, 28 ga., or .410 bore, similar to Hercules Model, except has blue receiver, super select wood and beavertail forearm, many Skeet-ers were special order guns with options including selective or non-selective Miller trigger, custom stock, barrel chokes, chamber lengths, checkering and wood finishes, sling swivels, extra barrels, recoil pad, checkered butt, VR, and various engraving patterns. Approx. 1,200 mfg. 1933-42.

	100%	98%	95%	90%	80%	70%	60%
	$1,695	$1,398	$1,000	$900	$800	$700	$600

Add 20% for auto ejectors.
Add 40% for SST.
Add 50% for factory VR.
Add 20% for 20 ga.
Add 100% for 16 ga., 28 ga. or .410 bore.
Add 200% for rare factory engraving (be wary of upgrades).
Add 50% for scarce factory case colors (be wary of new colors).

.410 bore is the most commonly encountered gun and was made on a special small frame. This model was probably responsible for more Skeet records than any other American .410 bore SxS shotgun.

✷ *Skeet-er Model (Italian Mfg.)* - .410 bore, straight grip, DT, Arkansas address, extractors, figured wood, a few were imported during the late 1970s-early 1980s as a possible reintroduction of the Skeet-er Model, not cataloged, rare.

Values are approx. 25% less than U.S. mfg. models.

SUPER TRAP - 12 ga. only, 32 in. full VR, boxlock, extractors, checkered pistol grip stock, beavertail forend and recoil pad. Mfg. 1928-42. Scarce.

	100%	98%	95%	90%	80%	70%	60%
	$1,095	$750	$550	$475	$415	$395	$370

Add $100 for auto ejectors.
Add $100 for SST.

SILVER SHADOW - O/U, 12 ga., 26 or 28 in. barrels, various chokes, extractors, vent rib, checkered pistol grip stock, Italian mfg. Disc.

	100%	98%	95%	90%	80%	70%	60%
	$375	$325	$300	$275	$225	$185	$175

IZHMASH

Current manufacturer located in Russia. Previously imported and distributed until 2004 by European American Armory (certain models only), located in Sharpes, FL.

GRADING - PPGS™	100%	98%	95%	90%	80%	70%	60%

Other models were also imported by Kalashnikov USA, located in Port St. Lucie, FL. Previously distributed by Interstate Arms Corp., located in Billerica, MA, and by L.A. Austin International, Inc., located in Surprise, AZ.

Other Izhmash trademarks include Saiga, Hesse-Saiga, Krebs-Saiga, Romak, Sobol (not imported) , Korshun (not imported), LOS, Maral (not imported), and Dragunov.

RIFLES: BOLT ACTION

URAL 5.1 MATCH RIFLE - .22 LR cal., single shot, competition model with eccentric bolt, adj. cheekpiece, trigger, and buttplate, 26 1/2 in. barrel with aperture sights, 11.3 lbs. Importation 2000.

MSR N/A	$1,075	$950	$825	$700	$600	$500	$425

URAL 6-1 MATCH RIFLE - .22 LR cal., U.I.T. configuration with adj. buttplate and 26 3/4 in. barrel, aperture sights, various accessories included, 10 2/3 lbs. Imported 2000-2002.

	$550	$500	$450	$400	$360	$330	$300

Last MSR was $625.

URAL 6-2 MATCH RIFLE - .22 LR cal., features laminated stock. Imported 2000-2002.

	$1,000	$875	$750	$650	$550	$450	$350

Last MSR was $1,125.

BIATHLON BASIC - .17 HMR (new 2003), 22 LR, or .22 Win. Mag. (new 2003) cal., entry level biathlon model, beech stock, heavy barrel with Weaver rail, 6.1 lbs. Importation began 2002.

MSR N/A	$315	$275	$240	$195	$175	$160	$145

Add $10 for .22 Mag. or $20 for .17 HMR cal.
Add $50 for adj. sights.

BIATHLON 7-4 - .22 LR cal., features pivoting crank action, extra mags. that can be stored on the stock, 19.7 in. barrel with aperture sights, includes biathlon harness, spare mags., and counter weights, 9.1 lbs. Importation began 2000.

MSR N/A	$895	$725	$650	$550	$450	$350	$300

CM-2 - .22 LR cal., light match rifle, similar overall to Ural 6-1, 19.8 in. (Youth) or 26.7 in. barrel. Imported 2000-2002, reinitroduced 2003.

MSR N/A	$365	$325	$285	$250	$225	$200	$180

LOS 7-1 SPORTER - .223 Rem., .308 Win., or 7.62x39mm cal., 21.8 in. hammer forged barrel with two lug bolt lockup, detachable 5 shot mag., adj. trigger, checkered hardwood stock with vent. recoil pad, 7.3 lbs. Imported 2000-2002.

	$360	$330	$300	$270	$240	$210	$190

Last MSR was $395.

Add $99 if w/o scope.

SHOTGUNS

Please refer to the Saiga section for more information about these models.

J SECTION

J.C. HIGGINS

Please refer to listing in the H section.

J.O. ARMS

Previous importer of KSN Industries, Ltd. pistols until 1997.

J.L.D. ENTERPRISES, INC.

Current rifle manufacturer located in Farmington, CT. Represented by Vincent A. Pestilli & Associates, located in Brownfield, ME.

GRADING - PPGS™	100%	98%	95%	90%	80%	70%	60%

RIFLES: SEMI-AUTO

All models include polymer case, trigger lock, and one 20 shot mag.

MODEL PTR-91 - .308 Win. cal., CNC machined scope mounts, front sight blade, German style rear sight, 18 in. heavy target match grade barrel with 1:12 twist, 20 shot mag. one piece forged cocking handle, parkerized finish, matte black coated.

MSR $995	$895	$800	$700	$600	$500	$450	$400

Add $500 for Match Target Rifle.

* **Model PTR-91T** - .308 Win. cal., similar to Model PTR-91, except has green furniture and original H&K flash hider. New 2005.

MSR $995	$895	$800	$700	$600	$500	$450	$400

MODEL PTR-91 A1 - .308 Win. cal., match grade rifle with polymer trigger group, front sight blade, German style rear sight with 4-position aperture diopter, 20 shot mag., steel bipod, hardguard bipod recesses into original H&K flash hider. New 2005.

MSR $1,295	$1,150	$925	$825	$725	$600	$500	$425

MODEL PTR-91 K - .308 Win. cal., Kurz law enforcement carbine with 16 in. barrel, front sight blade, German style rear sight with 4-position aperture diopter, 20 shot mag., tropical green furniture, wide handguard with bipod recesses, includes flash hider or muzzle brake. New 2005.

MSR $1,095	$950	$850	$750	$650	$550	$500	$400

MODEL PTR-91 KP - .308 Win. cal., Kurz paratrooper carbine, 16 in. barrel, front sight blade, German style rear sight with 4-position aperture diopter, 20 shot mag., tropical green furniture, wide handguard with bipod recesses, original H&K collapsible stock and flash hider. New 2005.

MSR $1,295	$1,150	$925	$825	$725	$600	$500	$425

JMC FABRICATION & MACHINE, INC.

Previous manufacturer located in Rockledge, FL 1997-99.

RIFLES: BOLT ACTION

MODEL 2000 M/P - .50 BMG cal., rapid takedown, 30 in. barrel, matte black finish, cast aluminum stock with Pachmayr pad, fully adj. bipod, 10 shot staggered mag., two-stage trigger, includes 24X U.S. Optics scope, prices assume all options included, 29 1/2 lbs. Limited mfg. 1998-99.

	$7,950	$7,400	$6,800	$6,150	$5,500	$4,900	$4,200

Last MSR was $8,500.

Subtract $2,800 if w/o options.

GRADING - PPGS™	100%	98%	95%	90%	80%	70%	60%

JP ENTERPRISES, INC.

Current manufacturer and customizer established in 1978, and located in White Bear Lake, MN since 2000, Vadnais Heights, MN 1998-2000, and in Shoreview, MN 1995-98. Distributor, dealer, and consumer sales.

JP Enterprises is a distributor for Infinity pistols, and also customizes Remington shotgun models 11-87, 1100, and 870, the Remington bolt action Model 700 series, Glock pistols, and the Armalite AR-10 series. Please contact the company directly or refer to their website (www.jprifles.com) for more information regarding these customizing services.

PISTOLS: SEMI-AUTO

Level I & Level II custom pistols were manufactured 1995-97 using Springfield Armory slides and frames. Only a few were made, and retail prices were $599 (Level I) and $950 (Level II).

RIFLES: SEMI-AUTO

BARRACUDA 10/22 - .22 LR cal., features customized Ruger 10/22 action with reworked fire control system, choice of stainless bull or carbon fiber superlight barrel, 3 lb. trigger, color laminated "Barracuda" skeletonized stock. Mfg. 1997-2003.

$1,075	$950	$775	$650	$575	$475	$400

Last MSR was $1,195.

A-2 MATCH - .223 Rem. cal., JP-15 lower receiver with JP fire control system, 20 in. JP Supermatch cryo-treated stainless barrel, standard A-2 stock and pistol grip, DCM type free float tube, Mil-Spec A-2 upper assembly with Smith National Match rear sight. Mfg. 1995-2003.

$1,525	$1,300	$1,100	$925	$825	$700	$600

Last MSR was $1,695.

JP15 (GRADE I A-3 FLAT TOP) - .223 Rem. cal., features Eagle Arms (disc. 1999), DPMS (disc. 1999) or JP15 lower assembly with JP fire control system, Mil-spec A-3 type upper receiver with 18 or 24 in. JP Supermatch cryo-treated stainless barrel, synthetic modified thumbhole or laminated wood thumbhole (disc. 2002) stock, JP vent. two-piece free float tube, JP adj. gas system and recoil eliminator. New 1995.

MSR $1,795	$1,600	$1,350	$1,125	$925	$825	$700	$600

Add $400 for NRA Hi-Power version with 24 in. bull barrel and sight package (disc. 2002).

Add $200 for laminated wood thumbhole stock (disc. 2002).

* *Grade I IPSC Limited Class* - similar to Grade I, except has quick detachable match grade iron sights, Versa-pod bipod. Mfg. 1999-2004.

$1,675	$1,400	$1,150	$995	$775	$625	$550

Last MSR was $1,795.

* *Grade I Tactical/SOF* - similar to Grade I, all matte black non-glare finish, 18, 20, or 24 in. Supermatch barrel. Mfg. 1999-2003.

$1,425	$1,225	$1,050	$925	$800	$700	$600

Last MSR was $1,595.

Add $798 for Trijicon A-COG sight with A-3 adapter.

GRADE II - .223 Rem. cal., features Mil-spec JP lower receiver with upper assembly finished in a special two-tone color anodizing process, JP fire control and gas system, 18-24 in. cryo treated stainless barrel, composite skeletonized stock, Harris bipod, choice of multi-color or black receiver and handguard, includes hard case. Mfg. 1998-2002.

$1,750	$1,450	$1,200	$1,025	$825	$700	$600

Last MSR was $1,895.

Add $200 for laminated wood thumbhole stock.

GRADING - PPGS™	100%	98%	95%	90%	80%	70%	60%

GRADE III (THE EDGE) - .223 Rem. cal., RND machined match upper/lower receiver system, 2-piece free floating forend, standard or laminated thumbhole wood stock, 18 to 24 in. barrel (cryo treated beginning 1998) with recoil eliminator, includes Harris bipod, top-of-the-line model, includes hard case. Mfg. 1996-2002.

	$2,550	$2,125	$1,750	$1,450	$1,150	$875	$750

Last MSR was $2,795.

> Add $250 for laminated thumbhole stock.

MODEL AR-10T - .243 Win. or .308 Win. cal., features Armalite receiver system with JP fire control, flat-top receiver, vent. free floating tube, 24 in. cryo treated stainless barrel, black finish. Mfg. 1998-2004.

	$2,175	$1,825	$1,600	$1,450	$1,150	$875	$750

Last MSR was $2,399.

> Add $150 for anodized upper assembly in custom color.
> Add $350 for laminated wood thumbhole stock.

✳ *Model AR-10LW* - lightweight variation of the Model AR-10T, includes 16-20 in. cryo treated stainless barrel, composite fiber tube, black finish only, 7-8 lbs. Mfg. 1998-2004.

	$2,175	$1,825	$1,600	$1,450	$1,150	$875	$750

Last MSR was $2,399.

> Add $200 for detachable sights.

CTR-02 COMPETITION TACTICAL RIFLE - .223 Rem. cal., state-of-the-art advanced AR design with many improvements, integral ACOG interface, various stock configurations, available with two different types of operating systems, depending on use, JP recoil eliminator and fire control system, 1/4 MOA possible, Trijicon advanced combat optical sight. New 2002.

MSR $2,295	$2,075	$1,650	$1,275	$1,025	$825	$750	$650

Add $500 for presentation grade finish.

J R DISTRIBUTING

Current manufacturer located in Moorpark, CA. J R Distributing is a division of J R Sports Distribution Corporation. Dealer and consumer sales.

RIFLES: SEMI-AUTO

.22 MAG. CUSTOM RIFLE - .22 Mag. cal., choice of Ruger 10/22 or AMT action, 20 in. bull barrel with laminate or synthetic stock, 9 shot rotary mag., supplied with hard case. New 1998.

MSR $795	$725	$650	$550	$500	$450	$400	$360

JSL (HEREFORD)

Previous manufacturer located in Hereford, England. Imported until 1994 by Specialty Shooters Supply, Inc. located in Fort Lauderdale, FL.

PISTOLS: SEMI-AUTO

SPITFIRE (G1) - 9mm Para. or 9x21mm cal., patterned after the Czech CZ-75/85, 3.7 in. barrel, ambidextrous safety, commander style hammer, black non-slip rubberized grip panels, investment cast stainless steel fabrication, 10 (C/B 1994) or 15* shot mag., 2.2 lbs. Imported 1992-94.

✳ *Spitfire Standard* - includes fixed rear sight, 2 mags., presentation case, and allen key.

	$1,332	$1,100	$925

Last MSR was $1,332.

> Add $81 for adj. rear sight (Sterling Model).

JACKSON HOLE FIREARMS

Previous manufacturer located in Jackson Hole, WY circa mid-70s.

RIFLES: BOLT ACTION

STANDARD RIFLE - various cals., Mauser 98 action utilizing patented system for interchangeable barrels, checkered walnut stock.

	100%	98%	95%	90%	80%	70%	60%
	$1,050	$875	$800	$725	$650	$575	$495

Jackson Hole Firearms manufactured a limited quantity of their unique interchangeable barrel bolt action rifles. Collectibility to date has been minimal, and values are affected by the J.P. Sauer Models 90 and 200 which also feature the interchangeable barrel design.

JAGD-UND SPORTWAFFEN SUHL GmbH

Current manufacturer located in Suhl, Germany since 1535.

Currently, the famous Merkel trademark (mfg. by Jagd-Und Sportwaffen Suhl GmbH) is imported by Heckler & Koch, located in Sterling, VA, and distributed by Gun South Inc. located in Trussville, AL. Please refer to the Merkel listing in this text for current information regarding this older European trademark. See the Trademark Index in this text for current factory information.

JANZ GmbH

Current revolver manufacturer established in 2000, and located in Malente, Germany. Currently imported beginning 2003 by Rocky Mountain Armoury, located in Silverthorne, CO.

REVOLVERS

JTL-E - .22 LR, .357 Mag./.38 Spl., .44 Mag., .45 Win. Mag., .454 Casull/.45 LC cal., DA, 6 or 7 (.357 Mag.) shot, 4–10 in. barrel with full lug, ergonomic stippled wood grips, target sights. New 2000.

Prices on this model start at $6,000.

Add $505 for .44 Mag. cal.

Add $800 for .45 Win. Mag., .45 LC, or .454 Casull cal.

Add $60 for 5 in. barrel, $180 for 6 in. barrel, $290 for 7 in. barrel, $430 for 8 in. barrel, or $355-$410 for 10 in. barrel (not available in .357 Mag. cal.).

JTL-S - .22 LR, .357 Mag./.38 Spl., .44 Mag., .45 Win. Mag., .454 Casull/.45 LC cal., DA, 6 or 7 (.357 Mag.) shot, unique interchangeable barrels and cylinders allows cals. to be changed rapidly, 4–10 in. barrel with full lug, ergonomic stippled wood grips, target sights. New 2003.

Prices on this model start at $6,000.

Add $450 for .44 Mag. cal.

Add $750 for .45 LC or .454 Casull cal.

Add $120 for 5 in. barrel, $210 for 6 in. barrel, $295 for 7 in. barrel, $390 for 8 in. barrel, or approx. $400-$410 for 10 in. barrel (not available in .357 Mag. cal.).

This model is also available as a package with .357 Mag., .44 Mag., and .454 Casull barrels (6 in. only - MSR is $5,850).

JAPANESE MILITARY

Previously manufactured prior to and during WWII in Japan by various manufacturers.

PISTOLS: SEMI-AUTO

Please refer to the Nambu section for further information on Nambus and variations.

GRADING - PPGS™	100%	98%	95%	90%	80%	70%	60%

HAMADA VARIATIONS

✷ *Type I* - .32 ACP cal., similar to FN Model 1910, except has 9 shot mag., early production pistols have chrysanthemum and Japanese characters on left slide, salt blue. Mfg. estimated at 5,000, but examples are scarce and usually in the 2,000-3,000 ser. range.

	$4,000	$3,250	$2,600	$2,200	$1,850	$1,500	$1,250

Add 10% for early variation.

✷ *Type II* - 8mm cal., designed to replace the Type 94 Nambu, larger than Type I and with a more squared profile, essentially a pre-production gun, all known examples are roughly finished in the white and are serial numbered 1-50.

	$5,000	$4,000	$3,250	$2,800	$2,500	$2,200	$1,900

REVOLVERS

1893 REVOLVER (MODEL 26) - 9mm Japanese cal., double action only, 4.7 in. barrel, blue, wood grips. Approx. 59,000 mfg. 1893-1925.

	$850	$600	$400	$200	$150	$135	$120

Subtract 25% for arsenal rework.
Add 150% for early mfg. with internal numbers (approx. first 300 revolvers).

RIFLES: MILITARY

Subtract 20% if National Crest (chrysanthemum flower) has been ground off front receiver ring.
Subtract 20% if serial numbers are not matching (does not apply to sniper rifles, as they are only rarely found with matching scopes and mounts).
Subtract 10%-40% for training rifles of each type.

MODEL 38 ARISAKA RIFLE - 6.5X51R Arisaka cal., Jap. Mauser type action, 31 in. barrel, adj. sight, adopted 1905.

	$625	$525	$400	$300	$225	$125	$75

MODEL 38 A & B CAVALRY CARBINE - 6.5x51R Arisaka cal., similar to Model 38 Rifle, except has 19 in. barrel. Mfg. 1911.

	$625	$550	$450	$325	$225	$125	$75

Add 300% for paratrooper variation with hinged stock (often referenced as Type I, has crude construction and cast iron hinge).

MODEL 44 CAVALRY ARISAKA CARBINE - 6.5x51R Arisaka cal., similar to T38 Carbine, features 19 in. barrel and folding bayonet.

	$750	$600	$500	$400	$325	$240	$135

MODEL 97 SNIPER RIFLE - based on Model 38.

	$3,500	$2,750	$2,200	$1,950	$1,650	$1,375	$1,100

Add $1,000 if complete with scope.

MODEL 99 SERVICE RIFLE - 7.7x58mm Arisaka cal., WWII version of Model 38, mostly encountered with shorter barrels than the Model 38 Arisaka Rifle.

	$375	$275	$225	$195	$150	$90	$65

Add 20% for monopod.
Add 500% for sniper variation with 4X scope.
Add $1,500 for externally adjustable scope.
Add 75% for long barrel.

PARATROOPER TAKEDOWN VERSION - 7.7x58mm Arisaka cal., adopted 1940, crossbolt barrel lock.

Type 2	$2,200	$1,850	$1,425	$1,125	$850	$700	$600

GRADING - PPGS™	100%	98%	95%	90%	80%	70%	60%

JARRETT RIFLES, INC.

Current manufacturer established in 1979, and located in Jackson, SC. Direct custom order sales only.

HANDGUNS

CUSTOM XP-100 HUNTER - various cals., re-machined Remington XP-100 action, Jarrett match grade stainless steel barrel, McMillan fiberglass stock, various options. Limited mfg.

MSR N/A	$3,450	$2,650	$2,150	$1,750	$1,350	$1,050	$995

ULTIMATE REDHAWK - .44 Mag. cal., features Hogue grips and muzzle brake. Mfg. 1995-2000.

	$1,150	$1,025	$850	$675	$575	$500	$450

Last MSR was $1,150.

RIFLES: BOLT ACTION

Jarrett rifles are justifiably famous for their well-known Beanfield rifles (refers to shooting over a beanfield at long range targets). A Jarrett innovation is the Tri-Lock receiver, which has 3 locking lugs, and a semi-integral recoil lug. Jarrett blueprints every action for proper dimensioning and rigid tolerances, and this explains why their rifles have set rigid accuracy standards.

A wide variety of options are available for Jarrett custom rifles (holders of 16 world records in rifle accuracy). The factory should be contacted directly (see Trademark Index) for pricing and availability regarding these special order options. Custom gunsmithing services for Jarrett rifles are also available and the manufacturer should be contacted directly for gunsmith quotations.

STANDARD HUNTING RIFLE - various cals., Remington Model 700 right-hand or left-hand action, McMillan fiberglass stock, blue receiver, Jarrett satin finish match grade barrel, sling studs and leather sling, rings and base, weights vary. Disc. 2003.

	$4,625	$4,150	$3,650	$3,150	$2,750	$2,150	$1,750

Last MSR was $4,625.

WALK ABOUT - various cals. in short action only, features Remington Model 7 action (left-hand utilizes Rem. Model 700 short action), weights vary. Mfg. 1995-2003.

	$4,625	$4,150	$3,650	$3,150	$2,750	$2,150	$1,750

Last MSR was $4,625.

TRUCK GUN - various small bore cals., 19-20 in. barrel, black synthetic stock. Mfg. 1999-2003.

	$4,625	$4,150	$3,650	$3,150	$2,750	$2,150	$1,750

Last MSR was $4,625.

BENCHREST/YOUTH/TACTICAL - various cals., various configurations depending on application. New 1999.

	$4,625	$4,150	$3,650	$3,150	$2,750	$2,150	$1,750

Last MSR was $4,625.

SERIES RIFLE - various cals., various configurations, only 100 made of each series. Mfg. 1993-2003.

❋ *Standard Series Rifle* - various cals.

	$5,025	$4,450	$3,850	$3,250	$2,850	$2,250	$1,850

Last MSR was $5,025.

❋ *Coup de Grace* - various cals. Mfg. 1996-99.

	$3,295	$2,750	$2,300	$1,800	$1,500	$1,250	$995

Last MSR was $3,495.

❋ *Nombre Unique Series* - various cals., 100 mfg. 1999 only.

	$3,495	$2,900	$2,400	$1,850	$1,550	$1,250	$995

Last MSR was $3,695.

GRADING - PPGS™	100%	98%	95%	90%	80%	70%	60%

SIGNATURE SERIES - various cals., Jarrett tri-lock stainless steel receiver, fiberglass, wood laminate, or deluxe walnut stock, helical fluted bolt with three lugs, built to special order only. New 2004.

MSR $6,880	$6,880	$5,500	$4,750	$4,000	$3,325	$2,850	$2,250

WIND WALKER SERIES - various cals. up to .30 cal., Rem. M-700 ADL action only, lightweight design, 24 in. tapered barrel with muzzle brake, Brown Precision stock, 7 1/4 lbs. New 1999.

MSR $6,650	$6,650	$5,375	$4,700	$4,000	$3,300	$2,850	$2,250

Current MSR does not include excise tax on this model.

ORIGINAL BEANFIELD RIFLE - built on customer supplied action, choice of caliber, stock style, color, barrel length and finish, with or w/o muzzle brake, supplied with 20 rounds of ammo and test target. New 2005.

MSR $4,850	$4,850	$4,250	$3,825	$3,400	$3,000	$2,600	$2,200

Current MSR does not include excise tax on this model.

PROFESSIONAL HUNTER - Mag. cals. to customer's specifications, starting with .375 H&H, features Winchester controlled round feed Model 70 action with claw extractor and 3 position bolt shroud safety, Jarrett match grade stainless steel barrel, McMillan stock, quarter rib with iron sights, includes 2 sets of detachable rings and two 1.75X-6X x 32mm Leupold scopes, takedown action, includes custom built Americase.

MSR $9,390	$9,390	$8,040	$6,450	$5,250	$4,300	$3,600	$3,000

Current MSR does not include excise tax on this model.

.50 CAL. - .50 BMG cal., McMillan custom receiver, choice of repeater or single shot, 30 or 34 in. barrel with muzzle brake, 28-45 lbs. Mfg. 1999-2003.

	$8,050	$6,500	$5,300	$4,350	$3,650	$3,000	$2,500

Last MSR was $8,050.

Add $300 for repeater action.

CLASSIC SERIES - various cals., 100 mfg. 1989 only.

	$3,195	$2,650	$2,100	$1,650	$1,375	$1,150	$875

INVESTOR SERIES - various cals., 100 mfg. 1989 only.

	$3,195	$2,650	$2,100	$1,650	$1,375	$1,150	$875

ACCURACY LEGEND SERIES - various cals., similar to Jarrett Custom Rifle, except has many accuracy tune-ups incorporated as well as muzzle brake. 100 mfg. 1993 only.

	$3,495	$2,850	$2,300	$1,850	$1,500	$1,250	$995

Last MSR was $3,495.

COUP de MAIM - various cals., similar to the Jarrett Custom Rifle, includes muzzle brake, matte black or olive drab finish, Model 70 style bolt release. 100 mfg. 1995 only.

	$2,750	$2,300	$1,800	$1,500	$1,250	$995	$775

Last MSR was $3,495.

PRIVATE COLLECTION - various cals., similar quality as the Jarrett Custom Rifle, except many extra cost special order options are included, ser. numbered 1-100. Mfg. 1994 only.

	$3,495	$2,850	$2,300	$1,850	$1,500	$1,250	$995

Last MSR was $3,495.

SILENT PARTNER SERIES - various cals., only 10 mfg. 1994 only.

	$3,495	$2,850	$2,300	$1,850	$1,500	$1,250	$995

ULTIMATE HUNTER SERIES - various cals., 100 mfg. 1989 only.

	$3,495	$2,850	$2,300	$1,850	$1,500	$1,250	$995

GRADING - PPGS™	100%	98%	95%	90%	80%	70%	60%

RIFLES: RIMFIRE, SEMI-AUTO

SQUIRREL KING - .22 LR cal., reworked Ruger 10/22 action, 18 in. barrel, McMillan or Brown Precision synthetic stock. Mfg. 1999-2003.

	100%	98%	95%	90%	80%	70%	60%
	$1,650	$1,300	$1,050	$900	$700	$575	$475

Last MSR was $1,800.

Add $195 for Target King variation.

SHOTGUNS: SLIDE ACTION

JARRETT ULTIMATE SHOTGUN - 12 ga., Remington Model 870 action with 21 in. hand lapped barrel with interchangeable chokes, 8 shot mag. extension, matte black or olive drab green finish. Disc. 1999.

	100%	98%	95%	90%	80%	70%	60%
	$900	$825	$675	$550	$450	$350	$295

Last MSR was $1,000.

JEFFERY, W.J. & CO. LTD

Current trademark manufactured by J. Roberts & Son (Gunmakers) Ltd., located in London, England. Previous manufacture was also in London, England.

J. Roberts & Son (Gunmakers) Ltd. currently manufactures W.J. Jeffery shotguns, bolt action and double rifles. Many options are available, including calibers, special engraving, etc. Please contact the company directly for more information, including pricing, delivery time and availability (see Trademark Index).

In addition to making a complete line of their own shotguns and rifles, W.J. Jeffery also was subcontracted by many other exporters, distributors, and retailers (including London's famous Army & Navy department store). Many models were produced and, rather than list them individually, a generalized format has been adopted for determining values on both discontinued rifles and shotguns.

RIFLES, CURRENT MFG.

W.J. Jeffery bolt action rifles are available in all standard and Magnum chamberings, and prices range from £5,500 - £14,000, depending on configuration and features. Delivery time is approx. 6-15 months.

W.J. Jeffery boxlock ejector rifles are available in calibers from .375 H&H - .500NE, and prices start at £20,000+, depending on configuration and features. A sidelock ejector rifle is available in 9.3x74R cal., and prices range from £30,000 - £40,000, depending on features and configuration.

RIFLES, DISC.

SINGLE SHOT - various cals., falling block action, checkered walnut stock and forearm, usually multiple folding leaves rear sight (also tangent), excellent quality. Prices start in the $600 range for poor condition specimens in obsolete or undesirable cals. and can go up to $5,000 for 100% condition in .600 Nitro Express.

    Subtract substantially for the Martini action variation.

BOXLOCK DOUBLE RIFLE - many cals., various engraving patterns, top or under (usually large cals.) lever opening, multiple folding leaves rear sight, checkered walnut stock and forearm. Prices usually start in the $1,500 range for poor condition in undesirable cals. and can exceed $8,000 if encountered with elaborate engraving in .475 Express or larger cals.

    Subtract approx. 40% if with hammers, over 50% if with damascus barrels.

SIDELOCK DOUBLE RIFLE - various cals., available in No. 1 or No. 2 grade, top-lever opening, best quality engraving, deluxe checkered walnut stock and forearm, almost any custom order could be filled. Prices start in the $3,250 range for 60% condition in smaller cals. and can easily go to $12,000+ when found in excellent condition in the larger cals.

    Subtract approx. 40% if with hammers, over 50% if with damascus barrels.

GRADING - PPGS™	100%	98%	95%	90%	80%	70%	60%

SHOTGUNS, CURRENT MFG.

SxS best sidelock shotguns start at £30,000, with Beesley or Purdey style actions. Please contact the company directly (see Trademark Index) for more information on currently manufactured W.J. Jeffery shotguns, including the sidelock ejector models, and the London finished SxS and O/U Italian and Spanish shotguns manufactured under J. Roberts & Son patterns.

SHOTGUNS: SxS, DISC.

BOXLOCK SHOTGUN - most ga., many combinations of options available, top-lever opening, many ranges of engraving, high quality and worksmanship. Values usually start in the $650 range if in poor condition and can go to $4,500+ if in a small ga. in near new condition ($1,750 for 12 ga.).

> **Subtract approx. 40% if with hammers, over 50% if with damascus barrels.**

SIDELOCK SHOTGUN - most ga., many combinations of options available, top-lever opening, many ranges of engraving, high quality and worksmanship. Values usually start in the $1,250 range if in poor condition and can go to $8,500+ if in a small ga. in near new condition ($3,950 for 12 ga.).

JENNINGS, B.L., INC.

Previous manufacturer until 1985 located in City of Industry, CA. Currently, Jennings is the exclusive distributor for Bryco. Jennings also distributed Sundance and Accu-Tek. The Jennings trademark is now owned by Bryco Arms.

PISTOLS: SEMI-AUTO

MODEL J-22 - .22 LR cal., 6 shot, single action, 2 1/2 in. barrel, positive safety locks sear, satin nickel, bright chrome or black teflon finish, 13 oz. Disc. 1985.

	$65	$50	$40	$35	$30	$30	$30

Last MSR was $79.

JERICHO

Previous trademark of Israeli Military Industries (I.M.I.). Previously imported by K.B.I., Inc. located in Harrisburg, PA.

PISTOLS: SEMI-AUTO

JERICHO 941 - 9mm Para. cal. or .41 Action Express (by conversion only) cal., semi-auto double action or single action, 4.72 in. barrel with polygonal rifling, all steel fabrication, 3 dot Tritium sights, 11 or 16 (9mm Para.) shot mag., ambidextrous safety, polymer grips, decocking lever, 38 1/2 oz. Imported 1990-92.

	$550	$475	$425	$375	$325	$295	$260

Last MSR was $649.

> **Add $299 for .41 AE conversion kit.**
> Industrial hard chrome or nickel finishes were also available for all Jericho pistols.

* ✳ *Jericho 941 Pistol Package* - includes 9mm Para. and .41 AE conversion kit, cased with accessories. Mfg. 1990-91 only.

	$850	$775	$700	$625	$575	$495	$450

Last MSR was $775.

JOHANNSEN RIFLES

Currently manufactured by Reimer Johannsen GmbH, located in Germany. No current U.S. importation. Previously imported until 2003 by Johannsen, Inc., located in Plainfield, NH.

GRADING - PPGS™	100%	98%	95%	90%	80%	70%	60%

RIFLES: BOLT ACTION

Johannsen rifles feature high quality reproduction Mauser Magnum actions in 5 caliber group-ings and are manufactured by Orth, using sophisticated CAD and CNC technology, in addition to Old World gunsmithing techniques. Mauser Magnum actions start at $3,250, while standard actions start at $1,398.

Johannsen take down express rifles are unique in that the bolt locks into the barrel with the same precision every time. This design ensures that point of impact remains identical after each assembly/disassembly. Please contact the manufacturer directly for more information, including current pricing and domestic availability.

Add $4,490 for take down action on the models listed.

BASIC SQUARE BRIDGE RIFLE - various cals. between .375 H&H - .505 Gibbs, double square bridge, various options available, deluxe checkered walnut stock.

MSR N/A	$8,490	$7,700	$6,600	$5,550	$4,750	$4,000	$3,300

Subtract $500 if not finished (in-the-white).

CLASSIC SAFARI - various cals., single square bridge action with thumbcut, 8 lbs. 3 oz.

MSR N/A	$9,500	$7,850	$6,750	$5,600	$4,800	$4,000	$3,300

SAFARI RIFLE - various cals., features double square bridge action w/o thumbcut, 8 lbs. 6 oz.

MSR N/A	$10,250	$8,350	$7,000	$5,750	$4,900	$4,100	$3,400

TRADITION RIFLE - various cals., top-of-the-line model, 8 lbs.

MSR N/A	$10,550	$8,550	$7,150	$5,800	$4,950	$4,100	$3,400

JOHNSON AUTOMATICS, INC.

Previous manufacturer located in Providence, RI. Johnson Automatics, Inc. moved many times during its history, often with slight name changes. M.M. Johnson, Jr. died in 1965, and the company continued production at 104 Audubon Street in New Haven, CT as Johnson Arms, Inc. mostly specializing in sporter semi-auto rifles in .270 Win. or 30-06.

RIFLES: SEMI-AUTO

MODEL 1941 - .30-06 or 7x57mm cal., 22 in. removable air cooled barrel, recoil operated, perforated metal handguard, aperture sight, military stock. Most were made for Dutch military, some used by U.S. Marine Paratroopers, during WWII all .30-06 and 7x57mm were ordered by South American governments.

	$4,500	$3,950	$3,250	$2,650	$2,000	$1,450	$995

MilTech offers a restored version of this model, and inspect this model carefully for originality before considering a possible purchase. Values are somewhat lower for restored guns.

JUNG, WAFFEN, GMBH

Please refer to Waffen Jung GmbH.

JURRAS, LEE E.

Custom pistolsmith previously located in Hagerman, New Mexico. Howdah pistols were distributed by J & G Sales located in Prescott, AZ.

Ammunition for Jurras pistols was manufactured by Robert Davis, Jr. located in Athens, TN. Lee Jurras was the founder and president of Super Vel Cartridge Corporation. Mr. Jurras also made custom AutoMags (see AutoMag section). He established the Outstanding American Handgunner Awards, and was a pioneer of the first metallic silhouette shooting matches.

GRADING - PPGS™	100%	98%	95%	90%	80%	70%	60%

PISTOLS

100 LEJ Howdah pistols were custom built in the late 1970s. The action was based on the Thompson/Center Contender receiver. Almost any caliber, barrel length, finish, and stock was available by special order. Original MSR was approx. $800.

HOWDAH - most common in .375, .416, .460, .475, .500, or .577 Jurras cals., action based on Thompson/Center Contender receiver, 12 in. bull barrel, satin nickel, nickel, or blue finish, adj. rear sights, ebony, mesquite, or walnut stocks, special order serial number range from 001-100, limited mfg. (100).

* *Custom Grade*

	$1,150	$925	$800	$725	$650	$575	$500

* *Presentation Grade* - .375 Jurras or .460 Jurras cals. standard, deluxe Claro walnut stock and forearm.

	$2,000	$1,750	$1,500	$1,250	$1,050	$950	$825

Special order .416, .475, .500, or .577 Jurras calibers command a premium on this model.

JUST, JOSEF

Current custom long gun manufacturer and gunsmith established in 1790, and located in Ferlach, Austria.

Josef Just was a member of the Ferlach Guild until it was dissolved in 2004, and manufactures a variety of high quality long gun configurations (including SxSs, O/Us, drillings, vierlings, combination guns, and single shot), all to custom order. Please contact Mr. Just directly for more information and an individual price quotation (see Trademark Index).

NOTES

K SECTION

K.B.I., INC.

Current importer and distributor located in Harrisburg, PA. Distributor sales.

K.B.I., Inc. currently imports Charles Daly semi-auto pistols and shotguns and Bul Transmark semi-auto pistols. K.B.I. has imported Armscor (Arms Corp. of the Philippines), FEG pistols, and Liberty revolvers and SxS coach shotguns. These models may be found within their respective alphabetical sections. K.B.I. previously imported the Jericho pistol manufactured by I.M.I. from Israel. The Jericho pistol may be found under its own heading in this text.

GRADING - PPGS™	100%	98%	95%	90%	80%	70%	60%

RIFLES: BOLT ACTION

KASSNAR GRADE I - available in 9 cals., thumb safety that locks trigger, with or w/o deluxe sights, 22 in. barrel, 3 or 4 shot mag., includes swivel posts and oil finished standard grade European walnut with recoil pad, 7 1/2 lbs. Imported 1989-93.

	$445	$385	$325	$275	$225	$195	$175

Last MSR was $499.

NYLON 66 - .22 LR cal., patterned after the Remington Nylon 66. Imported until 1990 from C.B.C. in Brazil, South America.

	$125	$110	$95	$85	$75	$70	$65

Last MSR was $134.

MODEL 122 - .22 LR cal., bolt action design with mag. Imported from South America until 1990.

	$125	$110	$95	$85	$75	$70	$65

Last MSR was $136.

MODEL 522 - .22 LR cal., bolt action design with tube mag. Imported from South America until 1990.

	$130	$115	$100	$85	$75	$70	$65

Last MSR was $142.

BANTAM SINGLE SHOT - .22 LR cal., youth dimensions. Imported 1989-90 only.

	$110	$90	$85	$75	$70	$65	$60

Last MSR was $120.

SHOTGUNS

GRADE I O/U - 12, 20, 28 ga., or .410 bore, gold plated SST, extractors, vent. rib, checkered walnut stock and forearm. Imported 1989-93.

	$525	$425	$350	$295	$265	$240	$220

Last MSR was $599.

Add $70 for 28 ga. or .410 bore.
Add $50 for choke tubes (12 and 20 ga. only).
Add $150 for automatic ejectors (with choke tubes only).

GRADE II SxS - 10, 12, 16, 20, 28 ga., or .410 bore, boxlock action, case hardened receiver, English style checkered European walnut stock with splinter forearm, chrome barrels with concave rib, extractors, double hinged triggers. Imported 1989-90 only.

	$515	$435	$375	$325	$275	$250	$225

Last MSR was $575.

Add $95 for 28 ga. or .410 bore.
Add $85 for 10 ga.

GRADING - PPGS™	100%	98%	95%	90%	80%	70%	60%

KDF, INC.

Current manufacturer and custom riflesmith specializing in restocking and installing muzzle brakes, in addition to supplying specialized rifle parts. Located in Seguin, TX. KDF utilized Mauser K-15 actions imported from Oberndorf, Germany for many rifle models. Previously, KDF rifles were manufactured by Voere (until 1987) in Vöhrenbach, W. Germany.

Older KDF rifles were private labeled by Voere and marked KDF. Since Voere was absorbed by Mauser-Werke in 1987, model designations changed. Mauser-Werke does not private label (i.e. newer guns are marked Mauser-Werke), and these rifles can be found under the Mauser-Werke heading in this text.

RIFLES: BOLT ACTION, U.S. MFG.

KDF also builds custom rifles on Remington & Winchester actions, in addition to converting Rem. M700 and Winchester M70 rifles into custom rifles. Please contact the company directly for more information and pricing.

In 1989, KDF announced the release of a new American built redesigned Model K15 with many improvements. While advertised, approximately only 25 were manufactured in various cals.

K15 - .22-250 Rem. (disc. 1992), .243 Win., 6mm Rem., .25-06 Rem., .270 Win., .280 Rem., .30-06 cal. or .308 Win. cal., 60 degree short lift bolt action with 3 lugs, Kevlar composite or laminate walnut stock, adj. single stage competition trigger, box magazine, thumb activated slide safety, satin blue finish, 24 in. match grade barrel, deluxe checkered walnut stock with ebony accents and Pachmayr Decelerator recoil pad, approx. 8 lbs. Limited mfg. in U.S. starting 1989.

$1,750	**$1,375**	**$1,150**	**$950**	**$750**	**$650**	**$575**

Last MSR was $1,950.

✱ **K15 Magnum** - .270 Wby. Mag., .300 Win. Mag. (disc.), .300 Wby. Mag., 7mm Rem. Mag., .338 Win. Mag., .340 Wby. Mag. (disc.), .375 H&H, .411 KDF, .416 Rem. Mag. (disc.), or .458 Win. Mag. cal., similar to K15, except has 26 in. barrel. Mfg. in U.S. starting in 1989. Disc.

$1,795	**$1,400**	**$1,175**	**$975**	**$775**	**$675**	**$600**

Last MSR was $2,000.

KDF CLASSIC - cals. similar to K15, custom tuned Remington 700 action, bench rest barrel, Brown Precision stock, KDF accurizing, Arnold jewell custom trigger, matte blue finish, Pachmayr Decelerator pad, includes rings and bases.

$1,750	**$1,375**	**$1,150**	**$950**	**$750**	**$650**	**$575**

Last MSR was $1,950.

Add $50 for Mag. cals.

KDF FRONTIER - cals. similar to KDF Classic, custom tuned Winchester Model 70 action, bench rest barrel, Brown Precision stock, KDF accurizing, Arnold jewell custom trigger, matte blue finish, Pachmayr Decelerator pad, includes rings and bases.

$1,750	**$1,375**	**$1,150**	**$950**	**$750**	**$650**	**$575**

Last MSR was $1,950.

Add $50 for Mag. cals.

Add $150 for action with positive feeding claw extractor.

KDF VARMINT - varmint cals., custom tuned Remington 700 or XP action, bench rest heavy contour barrel, Brown Precision stock, KDF accurizing, Arnold jewell custom trigger, matte blue finish, Pachmayr Decelerator pad, includes rings and bases.

$2,000	**$1,725**	**$1,425**	**$1,200**	**$950**	**$750**	**$650**

Last MSR was $2,250.

Add $250 for Rem. XP action.

GRADING - PPGS™	100%	98%	95%	90%	80%	70%	60%

KDF MAUSER 98 - .22-250 Rem. (new 2000), .243 Win. (new 2000), .25-06 Rem. (new 2000), .270 Win., .30-06, .308 Win. (new 2000), or 6.5x55mm (new 2000) cal., sporterized action, Wilson, Adams, or Bennett barrel, Butler Creek black synthetic stock, 7.5 lbs. New 1998.

MSR N/A	$325	$275	$250	$225	$200	$185	$170

Add $80 for adj. trigger.
Add $160 for adj. trigger with thumb safety and custom bolt shroud.
Add $89 for walnut stock with Schnabel forend.
Subtract $40 for 6.5x55mm cal.

KDF CUSTOM MAUSER PACKAGE - various cals., features custom bolt shroud, adj. trigger, glass bedding, 1 in. rings, and KDF slimline muzzle brake. Mfg. 1998-99.

	$675	$550	$500	$450	$400	$360	$330

Last MSR was $750.

RIFLES: OLDER VOERE MFG. (PRE-1988)

TITAN SPORTER SERIES - various cals., 24 or 26 in. barrel, select walnut, pistol grip stock.

This series was available with either European Monte Carlo high-luster stock or in classic featherweight configuration with Schnabel forend - add $50-$200.

✳ *Titan Menor* - .222 Rem. or .223 Rem. cal. Importation disc. 1987.

	$675	$615	$560	$495	$450	$395	$350

Last MSR was $765.

Add $100 for Match or Competition model (.223 Rem. cal.).

✳ *Titan II Standard* - many cals., between .243 Win. and .30-06. Disc. 1988.

	$950	$825	$725	$625	$550	$500	$450

Last MSR was $1,075.

Add $100 for Match or Competition model (.308 Win. cal.).

✳ *Titan II Magnum* - available in cals. between 7mm Rem. Mag. and .375 H&H. Disc. 1988.

	$995	$875	$750	$650	$575	$520	$475

Last MSR was $1,125.

✳ *Titan .411 KDF Mag.* - .411 KDF cal., 26 in. barrel with recoil arrestor, 3 shot mag., blue or electroless nickel finish, 9 1/4 lbs. Imported 1986-88.

	$1,175	$965	$810	$725	$650	$575	$520

Last MSR was $1,300.

MODEL 2005 - .22 LR cal. only, semi-auto, 19 1/2 in. barrel, Monte Carlo stock, 5 shot mag., iron sights, 6 lbs. Imported 1986 only.

	$235	$215	$195	$175	$160	$145	$135

Last MSR was $165.

This model was ruled no longer importable by the BATF.

✳ *Model 2005 Deluxe* - similar to Model 2005, except has deluxe checkered walnut. Mfg. 1986-87 only.

	$260	$230	$210	$185	$165	$145	$135

Last MSR was $185.

MODEL 2107 - .22 LR or .22 Mag. cal., bolt action, 19 1/2 in. barrel, 5 shot mag., adj. iron sights, 6 lbs. Imported 1986-87 only.

	$175	$150	$125	$105	$95	$85	$80

Last MSR was $197.

Add $42 for .22 Mag. cal.

✳ *Model 2107 Deluxe (Mauser 107)* - similar to Model 2107, except has deluxe checkered walnut. Imported 1986-88.

	100%	98%	95%	90%	80%	70%	60%
	$185	$165	$140	$125	$110	$105	$100

Last MSR was $219.

Add $50 for .22 Mag. cal.

This model was redesignated KDF-Mauser Model 107 when Voere distributor/dealer inventories were depleted.

MODEL 2112 - .22 LR or .22 Mag. cal., similar to Model 2107, except has extra select walnut. Imported 1988 only.

	100%	98%	95%	90%	80%	70%	60%
	$235	$200	$180	$160	$145	$135	$125

Last MSR was $279.

Add $50 for .22 Mag. cal.

K-14 INSTA FIRE RIFLE - .22-250 Rem., .270 Win., .300 Wby. Mag., or .458 Win. Mag. cal., 24 or 26 in. barrel, no sights, ultra fast lock time, hidden detachable mag., checkered Monte Carlo stock, recoil pad. Imported 1971-78.

	100%	98%	95%	90%	80%	70%	60%
	$725	$650	$575	$525	$475	$425	$375
K15 (.22 cal.)	$235	$205	$175	$150	$135	$120	$105

K-15 (MODEL 225) - available in 13 cals. between .243 Win. and .300 Wby. Mag., bolt action, 60 degree bolt lift with 3 locking lugs, ultra fast lock time, adj. trigger, 24 or 26 (Mag. only) in. barrel, 3 or 5 shot mag., no sights, guaranteed 1/2 in. accuracy at 100 yards, many stock options available at extra cost. Left-handed action available in certain cals. at a $50 charge.

✳ *Deluxe Standard Sporter* - standard model available in 6 regular cals. and 9 Mag. cals. Disc. 1988.

	100%	98%	95%	90%	80%	70%	60%
	$1,075	$950	$810	$700	$625	$550	$495

Last MSR was $1,275.

Add $50 for Magnum action.
Add $525 for .411 KDF cal.

In addition to the 15 regular cals., it was also possible to order various other factory cals. as a $200 option.

This model was redesignated KDF-Mauser Model 225 when Voere distributor/dealer inventories were depleted.

✳ *K-15 Fiberstock Pro-Hunter* - similar to the K-15, except is supplied with fiberglass stock (various colors), choice of parkerized, matte blue, or electroless nickel metal finish, and recoil arrestor installed. Imported 1986-88.

	100%	98%	95%	90%	80%	70%	60%
	$1,420	$1,200	$950				

Last MSR was $1,680.

Add $50 for Magnum action.

This model was redesignated KDF-Mauser Model 225 when Voere distributor/dealer inventories were depleted.

✳ *K-15 Dangerous Game* - .411 KDF Mag. (new cartridge 1985) cal., choice of finishes, oil finished deluxe American walnut stock. Imported 1986-88.

	100%	98%	95%	90%	80%	70%	60%
	$1,895	$1,500	$1,150				

Last MSR was $2,100.

This model was redesignated KDF-Mauser Model 225 when Voere distributor/dealer inventories were depleted.

✳ *K-15 Swat Rifle* - .308 Win. cal. standard, 24 or 26 in. barrel, parkerized metal, oil finished target walnut stock, 3 or 4 shot detachable mag., 10 lbs. Importation disc. 1988.

	100%	98%	95%	90%	80%	70%	60%
	$1,475	$1,250	$1,000	$850	$725	$650	$575

Last MSR was $1,725.

GRADING - PPGS™	100%	98%	95%	90%	80%	70%	60%

K-16 - available in 6 standard cals. between .243 Win. and .300 Win. Mag. in addition to optional cals., modified Remington Model 700 action, standard features include KDF accurizing and Insta Fire ignition, single stage adj. trigger, Dupont Rynite stock (camel or grey), choice of finishes (high-gloss blue standard), recoil pad and quick detachable sling swivels, many options available. Imported 1988 only.

			$765	$675	$615	$560	$495	$450	$395

Last MSR was $876.

> **Add $120 for KDF muzzle brake.**
> **Add $250 for optional cals.**
> **Add $350 for .411 KDF Mag. cal.**

K-22 (MAUSER 201) - .22 LR or .22 Mag. cal., bolt action, free floating 21 in. barrel, 5 shot mag., adj. trigger, scaled down version of the K-15, unusual action incorporates two front-located locking lugs on bolt face that engage Stellite inserts on the front receiver portion, guaranteed 1 in. groupings at 100 yards, blue only, no sights, select walnut stock with cheekpiece, standard model disc. 1987.

$310	$285	$260	$240	$225	$210	$195

Last MSR was $345.

> **Add $50 for .22 Mag. cal.**

✻ **K-22 Deluxe (Mauser 201)** - better walnut and stock options. Model notation changed in 1988.

$410	$360	$295	$275	$250	$235	$210

Last MSR was $495.

> **Add $50 for .22 Mag. cal.**

This model was redesignated KDF-Mauser Model 201 when Voere distributor/dealer inventories were depleted.

✻ **K-22 Deluxe Custom** - richly layered walnut and stock options. Importation disc. 1987.

$655	$595	$550	$495	$450	$395	$350

Last MSR was $725.

> **Add $50 for .22 Mag. cal.**

✻ **K-22 Deluxe Special Select** - top-of-the-line bolt action, double set triggers. Importation disc. 1987.

$1,060	$950	$850	$750	$695	$650	$595

Last MSR was $1,225.

> **Add $50 for .22 Mag. cal.**

SHOTGUNS

CONDOR O/U - 12 ga., 28 in. barrel, various chokes, selective single trigger, auto ejectors, wide VR, boxlock, checkered pistol grip stock, Italian made.

$660	$635	$605	$580	$525	$470	$415

BRESCIA SxS - 12 ga., 28 in. barrel, full and mod., double triggers, engraved, checkered pistol grip stock.

$330	$305	$275	$250	$195	$165	$140

K.F.C.

Previously manufactured by Kawaguchiya Firearms Co., Ltd. Previously imported and distributed by La Paloma Marketing, Inc. located in Tucson, AZ.

SHOTGUNS

MODEL 250 SEMI-AUTO - 12 ga. only, semi-auto incorporating a patented, cushioned piston assembly, 26, 28, or 30 in. barrel, matte blue finish, vent. rib standard, checkered premium walnut, 7 lbs. Manufactured 1980-86.

$360	$290	$270	$250	$235	$220	$205

Last MSR was $485.

> **Add $60 for multi-chokes.**

GRADING - PPGS™	100%	98%	95%	90%	80%	70%	60%

✳ *Model 250 Deluxe Semi-Auto* - same specifications as Model 250, except has scrolled acid etching panels on both sides of normally black receiver. Disc. 1986.

	$395	$310	$290	$270	$250	$225	$210

Last MSR was $520.

FIELD GUN O/U - 12 ga. only, VR, premium grade walnut, semi pistol grip stock, F&IC chokes. Disc. 1986.

	$645	$565	$530	$495	$470	$445	$410

Last MSR was $748.

E-1 TRAP OR SKEET O/U - 12 ga. only, VR, oil finished premium grade walnut, semi pistol grip stock, engraved. Disc. 1986.

	$935	$800	$750	$700	$625	$550	$495

Last MSR was $1,070.

E-2 TRAP OR SKEET O/U - 12 ga. only, VR, oil finished premium grade walnut, semi pistol grip stock, detailed engraving. Disc. 1986.

	$1,450	$1,250	$1,075	$950	$850	$750	$650

Last MSR was $1,660.

KSN INDUSTRIES LTD.

Previous distributor (1952-1996) located in Houston, TX. Previously imported until 1996 exclusively by J.O. Arms, Inc. located in Houston, TX. Currently mfg. Israel Arms, Ltd. pistols may be found under their individual listing.

PISTOLS: SEMI-AUTO

The pistols listed below were mfg. by Israel Arms, Ltd.

KAREEN MK II - 9mm Para. or .40 S&W (new late 1994) cal., single action, 3.85 (Compact) or 4.64 (Standard) in. barrel, two-tone finish, rubberized grips, regular or Meprolite sights, 10 (C/B 1994), 13*, or 15* shot mag., 33 oz. Imported 1993-96.

	$360	$305	$255	$225	$200	$185	$170

Last MSR was $411.

Add approx. $160 for two-tone finish with Meprolite sights.

✳ *Kareen Mk II Compact* - compact variation with 3.85 in. barrel. Imported 1993-96.

	$415	$360	$315	$255	$225	$200	$185

Last MSR was $497.

GOLAN MODEL - 9mm Para. or .40 S&W cal., single or double action, ambidextrous safety with decocking feature, steel slide with alloy frame, 3 7/8 in. barrel, matte black finish, 29 oz. Imported 1994-96.

	$565	$515	$460	$410	$360	$330	$295

Last MSR was $650.

Add $35 for .40 S&W cal.

KAHR ARMS

Current manufacturer established 1993, with headquarters located in Blauvelt, NY, and manufacturing in Worchester, MA. Distributor and dealer sales.

PISTOLS: SEMI-AUTO

All Kahr pistols are supplied with two 7 shot mags., hard polymer case, trigger lock, and lifetime warranty.

GRADING - PPGS™	100%	98%	95%	90%	80%	70%	60%

CW9 - 9mm Para. cal., black polymer frame, matte stainless steel slide, 7 shot mag., DAO, 3 1/2 in. barrel, textured polymer grips, adj. rear sight, pinned in polymer front sight, white dot combat sights, 15.8 oz. New 2005.

MSR $533	$450	$410	$375	$325	$295	$275	$250

E9 - 9mm Para. cal., economized version of the K9, matte black finish or duo-tone (new 2003), supplied with one mag. Mfg. 1997 only, reintroduced 2003 only.

	$425	$365	$335	$300	$280	$265	$250

Last MSR was $490.

K9 COMPACT - 9mm Para. cal., trigger cocking, double action only with passive striker block, locked breech with Browning type recoil lug, steel construction, 3 1/2 in. barrel with polygonal rifling, 7 shot mag., wraparound black polymer grips, matte black, black titanium (Black-T, mfg. 1997-98), or electroless nickel (mfg. 1996-99) finish, 25 oz. Mfg. 1993-2003.

	$560	$485	$435	$385	$340	$315	$285

Last MSR was $648.

Add $74 for electroless nickel finish (disc.).
Add $126 for black titanium finish (Black-T, disc.).
Add $103 for tritium night sights (new 1996).

❉ *Economy K9* - features black matte finish, shipped with one mag. only. Limited mfg. 1999 only.

	$350	$300	$275	$250	$230	$210	$190

Last MSR was $399.

❉ *K9 Stainless* - similar to Kahr K9, except is matte finished stainless steel. New 1998.

MSR $719	$615	$525	$450				

Add $109 for tritium night sights.
Add $31 for matte black finish (new 2004).

❉ *K9 Elite 98 Stainless* - similar to K9, except has high polish slide and specially designed combat trigger utilizing shorter trigger stroke. New 1998.

MSR $783	$665	$575	$475				

Add $109 for tritium night sights.

❉ *K9 Wilson Custom Package* - includes Wilson customizing with Metalloy hard chrome frame, black slide, checkered front strap and beveled mag. well. Limited quantities mfg. 1998.

	$1,175	$995	$875	$775	$700	$625	$550

Last MSR was $1,310.

❉ *Kahr Lady K9* - similar to Kahr K9, except has lightened recoil spring, not available in black titanium finish, 25 oz. Mfg. 1997-99.

	$480	$435	$395	$365	$315	$285	$250

Last MSR was $545.

Add $74 for electroless nickel finish.
Add $85 for tritium night sights (new 1996).

P9 POLYMER COMPACT - 9mm Para cal., similar to Kahr K9, except has lightweight polymer frame, 7 shot mag., matte stainless slide, 17.9 oz. New 1999.

MSR $676	$575	$485	$425	$365	$325	$285	$250

Add $108 for tritium night sights (new 2000).
Add $31 for matte black finish (new 2004).

❉ *P9 Polymer Covert* - similar to Kahr K9 Polymer Compact, except has 1/2 in. shorter frame, supplied with one 6 and one 7 (with grip extension) shot mag., 16.9 oz. Limited mfg. 1999, reintroduced 2002.

MSR $676	$575	$485	$425	$365	$325	$285	$250

Add $108 for tritium night sights (new 2000).

GRADING - PPGS™	100%	98%	95%	90%	80%	70%	60%

MK9 MICRO SERIES - 9mm Para. cal., micro compact variation of the K9 featuring 3 in. barrel, double action only with passive striker block, overall size is 4 in. H x 5 1/2 in. L, duo-tone finish with stainless frame and black titanium slide, includes two 6 shot flush floor plate mags. Mfg. 1998-99.

	$650	$575	$515	$465	$425	$395	$375

Last MSR was $749.

Add $85 for tritium night sights.

✴ *MK9-Box* - similar to MK9, matte stainless steel frame with steel matte black slide, duo-tone finish. Limited mfg. 2003, reintroduced 2004.

MSR $475	$400	$325	$285

Add $100 for tritium night sights (disc.).

✴ *MK9 Stainless* - similar to MK9, except is stainless steel, supplied with 6 and 7 shot mag., 24 oz. New 1998.

MSR $719	$595	$495	$425

Add $108 for tritium night sights.

✴ *MK9 Elite 98 Stainless* - similar to Kahr MK9, except has high polish slide and specially designed combat trigger utilizing shorter trigger stroke, 24 oz. New 1998.

MSR $783	$650	$545	$460

Add $109 for tritium night sights.

✴ *MK9 Elite 2000 Stainless* - similar to MK9 Elite 98 Stainless, except features black stainless frame and slide, black Roguard finish. Mfg. 2001-2002.

	$575	$485	$425

Last MSR was $694.

PM9 MICRO POLYMER COMPACT - 9mm Para cal., 3 in. barrel with polygonal rifling, black polymer frame, trigger cocking DAO, blackened stainless steel slide, 6 or 7 (with mag. grip extension, disc.) shot mag., 16 oz. New 2003.

MSR $707	$600	$510	$430	$385	$340	$300	$275

Add $107 for tritium night sights.
Add $30 for matte black finish (new 2004).

MP9 COMPACT POLYMER - 9mm Para cal., features lightweight polymer frame and matte stainless steel slide, 3 in. barrel, DAO with passive striker block, supplied with 6 and 7 shot mag with grip extension, includes hard case and trigger lock, 15.9 oz. Mfg. 2002-2003.

	$565	$485	$415	$380	$340	$300	$275

Last MSR was $660.

Add $101 for tritium night sights.

T9 - 9mm Para cal., 4 in. barrel with polygonal rifling, matte stainless steel construction, checkered Hogue Pau Ferro wood grips, 8 shot mag., Elite 98 trigger, MMC or Novak low profile night sights, 28 oz. New 2002.

MSR $836	$715	$600	$485

TP9 - 9mm Para cal., similar to T9, except has black polymer frame and standard sights, 20 oz. New 2004.

MSR $719	$615	$500	$425

Add $117 for Novak night sights.

T40 - .40 S&W cal., 4 in. barrel with polygonal rifling, matte stainless steel construction, checkered Hogue Pau Ferro wood grips, 7 shot mag., Elite 98 trigger, MMC or Novak low profile night sights, 29 oz. New 2004.

MSR $719	$615	$500	$425

GRADING - PPGS™	100%	98%	95%	90%	80%	70%	60%

K40 COMPACT - .40 S&W cal., similar to Kahr K9, except has 6 shot mag., matte black or electroless nickel finish (disc. 1999), 26 oz. Mfg. 1997-2003.

	$560	$485	$435	$385	$340	$315	$285

Last MSR was $648.

Add $103 for tritium night sights (new 1997).
Add $74 for electroless nickel finish (disc. 1999).
Add $126 for black titanium finish (Black-T, disc. 1998).

❊ *K40 Stainless* - similar to Kahr K40, except is stainless steel. New 1997.

MSR $719	$615	$525	$450

Add $108 for tritium night sights.
Add $31 for matte black finish (new 2004).

❊ *K40 Elite 98 Stainless* - similar to Kahr K40, except has high polish slide and specially designed combat trigger utilizing shorter trigger stroke. New 1998.

MSR $783	$650	$545	$460

Add $109 for tritium night sights.

❊ *K40 Wilson Custom Package* - includes Wilson customizing with Metalloy hard chrome frame, black slide, checkered front strap and beveled mag. well. Limited quantities mfg. 1998.

	$1,175	$995	$875	$775	$700	$625	$550

Last MSR was $1,310.

❊ *K40 Covert Stainless (KS40 Small Frame)* - .40 S&W cal., similar to Kahr K40, except grip is 1/2 in. shorter, supplied with 5 and 6 shot mags., 25 oz. Mfg. 1998-2000.

	$500	$440	$400

Last MSR was $580.

Add $88 for tritium night sights.

P40 COMPACT POLYMER - .40 S&W cal., similar to P9 Compact, 6 shot mag., 18.9 oz. New 2001.

MSR $676	$575	$485	$420	$370	$325	$285	$250

Add $108 for tritium night sights.
Add $31 for matte black finished slide (new 2004).

❊ *P40 Polymer Covert* - similar to Kahr P40 Compact Polymer, except has 1/2 in. shorter frame, matte stainless slide, supplied with one 6 and one 7 (with grip extension) shot mag., 16.9 oz. New 2002.

MSR $676	$575	$485	$420	$370	$325	$285	$250

Add $108 for tritium night sights.

MK40 MICRO - .40 S&W cal., micro compact variation of the Kahr K40, featuring 3 in. barrel, matte stainless frame and slide, supplied with one 5 shot and one 6 shot (with grip extension) mag., 25 oz. New 1999.

MSR $719	$595	$495	$425

Add $109 for tritium night sights.

❊ *Kahr MK40 Elite Stainless* - similar to Kahr MK40, except has high polish slide and specially designed combat trigger utilizing shorter trigger stroke. New 2000.

MSR $783	$650	$545	$460

Add $109 for tritium night sights.

PM40 COMPACT POLYMER - .40 S&W cal., black polymer frame, 3 in. barrel, supplied with one 5 shot and one 6 shot (with grip extension) mag., matte finished stainless slide, 17 oz. New 2004.

MSR $707	$595	$500	$425

Add $108 for tritium night sights.
Add $30 for matte black finished slide (new 2005).

GRADING - PPGS™	100%	98%	95%	90%	80%	70%	60%

P45 POLYMER - .45 ACP cal., DAO, black polymer frame with matte stainless steel slide, 3.54 in. barrel, 6 shot mag., low profile, white barrel combat sights, 18.5 oz. New 2005.

	MSR $737	$625	$515	$435

KASSNAR IMPORTS, INC.

Previous importer and distributor located in Harrisburg, PA. Kassnar Imports operations ceased April, 1989.

Kassnar also imported Churchill and Omega shotguns which can be found in their individual section.

PISTOLS: SEMI-AUTO

PJK-9HP - 9mm Para. cal., single action, patterned after the Browning Hi-Power, 4 3/4 in. barrel, 13 shot mag., cone hammer, checkered walnut grips, 32 oz.

	$225	$200	$185	$175	$165	$155	$145

Add $15 for VR barrel.

This pistol was imported from Hungary. Approx. 18,000 (including the MBK-9HP) were imported until importation was disc. because of Federal ramifications.

MBK-9HP - 9mm Para. cal., double action, patterned after the Browning Hi-Power, 4 2/3 in. barrel, spur hammer, blue metal, checkered walnut grips, 14 shot mag., 36 oz. Limited importation was stopped in late 1985.

	$295	$260	$230	$190	$175	$165	$155

PMK-380 - .380 ACP cal., double action, patterned after the Walther PP, plastic grips with thumbrest, 4 in. barrel, 7 shot mag., 21 oz. Limited importation.

	$275	$235	$200	$185	$175	$165	$155

This model was imported in very limited quantities before Interarms began exclusive importation.

KEBERST INTERNATIONAL

Previously manufactured and distributed by Kendall International located in Paris, KY.

RIFLES: BOLT ACTION

KEBERST MODEL 1A - .338 Lapua Mag., .338-416 Rigby, or .338-06 cal., muzzle brake and unique recoil pad, camouflaged synthetic stock, package includes 3-9 power Leupold scope, stainless steel cleaning rod, custom designed case, built to special order only. Mfg. 1987-88 only.

	$3,475	$2,850	$2,475	$2,100	$1,750	$1,400	$1,150

Last MSR was $3,750.

Add $275 for 10X Ultra scope.

KEL-TEC CNC INDUSTRIES, INC.

Current manufacturer established in 1991, and located in Cocoa, FL. Dealer and distributor sales.

CARBINES/RIFLES: SEMI-AUTO

SUB-9/SUB-40 CARBINE - 9mm Para. or .40 S&W cal., unique pivoting 16.1 in. barrel rotates upwards and back, allowing overall size reduction and portability (16 in. x 7 in.), interchangeable grip assembly will accept most popular, double column, high capacity handgun mags., tube stock with polymer buttplate, matte black finish, 4.6 lbs. Mfg. 1997-2000.

	$325	$295	$265	$240	$215	$195	$180

Last MSR was $700.

Add $25 for .40 S&W cal.

GRADING - PPGS™	100%	98%	95%	90%	80%	70%	60%

SUB-2000 CARBINE - 9mm Para or .40 S&W (new 2004) cal., similar to Sub-9, choice of blue, parkerized (new 2003) or hard chrome (new 2003), 4 lbs. New 2001.

	MSR $391	$330	$300	$265	$240	$215	$195	$180

Add $27 for parkerized finish or $37 for hard chrome finish.

SU-16 RIFLE/CARBINE - .223 Rem. cal., unique downward folding stock, forearm folds down to become a bipod, 16 (new 2005) or 18.5 in. barrel, Picatinny receiver rail, M16 breech locking and feeding system, black synthetic stock (stores extra mags.) and forearm, approx. 4.7 lbs. New 2003.

	MSR $640	$575	$500	$450	$400	$350	$300	$265

Add $50 for lightweight variation.
Add $100 for carbine.

PISTOLS: SEMI-AUTO

P-3AT - .380 ACP cal., developed from the P-32, 2.76 in. barrel, 6 shot mag., black composite frame with parkerized steel slide, 7.3 oz. New 2003.

	MSR $311	$260	$210	$175	$160	$150	$135	$125

Add $41 for parkerized finish.
Add $56 for hard chrome finish.

P-11 - 9mm Para. cal., double action only, locked breech design, 3.1 in. barrel, composite frame with steel slide, transfer bar safety, matte blue, parkerized (new 1997), hard chrome (new 1999), or electroless nickel (disc. 1995) finish, black, grey, or green (disc. 1998) synthetic grips, 10 shot double column mag., 14.4 oz. New 1995.

	MSR $320	$270	$215	$180	$165	$150	$135	$125

Add $80 for night sights (mfg. 1997-2003).
Add $42 for parkerized finish (choice of grips).
Add $55 for hard chrome finish (new 1999).
Add $30 for electroless nickel finish (disc. 1995).
Add $175 for 9mm Para. to .40 S&W cal. conversion kit (disc. 2002).

✳ **P-11 Stainless** - similar to P-11, except is stainless steel, available with black (P-11SB), grey (P-11SGY), or green (P-11SGN) grips. Mfg. 1996-98.

				$350	$275	$230		

Last MSR was $408.

P-32 - .32 ACP cal., double action only with internal hammer block safety, composite frame with steel slide, 2.68 in. barrel, choice of parkerized, blue, or hard chrome finish, choice of light blue, dark blue, grey, green or full ivory grips, 6.6 oz. New 1999.

	MSR $306	$255	$200	$175	$160	$150	$135	$125

Add $41 for parkerized finish.
Add $56 for hard chrome finish.

P-40 - .40 S&W cal., double action only with internal hammer block safety, composite frame with steel slide, 3.3 in. barrel, choice of parkerized, blue, or hard chrome finish, 9 or 10 shot mag., 15.8 oz. Mfg. 1999-2001.

		$275	$225	$190	$175	$160	$140	$130

Last MSR was $331.

Add $41 for parkerized finish.
Add $58 for hard chrome finish.

KEMEN

Current competition shotgun manufacturer established in 1990, and located in Elgoibar, Spain. Currently imported exclusively by Fieldsport (all models), located in Traverse City, MI. Previously imported by Target Shotguns, located in Arden, NC, American Shooting Centers, located in

Houston, TX, by Fly and Field, located in Bend, OR, and by New England Custom Gun Service (Model KM-4 only), located in Plainfield, NH. Gun service is available through Briley.

SHOTGUNS: O/U

Kemen shotguns are built to individual customer specifications. 250-300 special order guns are made annually – delivery time is 4-6 months. Their unique metal finish makes them almost impervious to any type of oxidation or rust.

Add 7% for 20 ga. or 28 ga. on models listed below.

KM-4 STANDARD - 12 or 20 ga., boxlock action, competition shotgun various length vent. or separated barrels with VR and Briley choke tubes, detachable trigger group, blue receiver with gold accents, checkered walnut stock and forearm, wood upgrades available, cased, 8-8 1/2 lbs.

MSR $7,995	$7,450	$5,900	$5,000	$4,425	$3,800	$3,400	$2,850

✳ *KM-4 Combo* - includes 20 and 28 ga. barrels. New 2004.

MSR $12,995	$11,250	$9,450	$8,550	$6,650	$5,950	$4,950	$4,000

KM-4 LUXE A/B - similar to KM-4 Standard, except has nickel finished frame with choice of fine scroll or game scene engraving.

MSR $14,995	$13,500	$9,950	$8,250	$7,300	$6,200	$5,300	$4,475

Subtract $1,000 for KM-4 Luxe B.

KM-4 SUPER LUXE A/B/C - similar to KM-4 Luxe A/B, except has nickel finished frame with more elaborate game scene engraving, "A" suffix features game scene engraving, "B" suffix includes gold line engraving, "C" suffix has high relief scroll work and gold trigger.

MSR $15,795	$14,000	$10,250	$8,450	$7,550	$6,450	$5,500	$4,600

Add $700 for Super Luxe A variation.
Add $2,200 for Super Luxe B variation.

KM-4 EXTRA LUXE A/B/C - similar to KM-4 Super Luxe, except has nickel finished frame with sideplates and choice of Purdey style fine scroll (Extra Luxe A), extra fine game scene (Extra Luxe B), or gargoyle motif (Extra Luxe C) engraving.

MSR $16,995	$14,850	$11,000	$9,000	$8,000	$7,000	$6,000	$5,000

Add $3,000 for Extra Luxe B variation.
Add $8,000 for Extra Luxe C variation.

KM-4 EXTRA GOLD A/B - 12 or 20 ga., features engraved sideplate action with multiple gold inlays, select wood.

MSR $25,595	$22,750	$18,250	$15,000	$12,000	$9,950	$8,750	$7,500

Add $1,000 for Extra Gold B variation.

SUPREMA AX/BX/CX - 12 or 20 ga., top-of-the-line model, sidelock action, Suprema AX features English fine scroll engraving, custom ordered to individual specifications.

MSR $38,995	$35,000	$29,500	$25,000	$22,000	$18,000	$14,500	$11,000

Add $1,000 for BX Model or $3,000 for AX Model.

SHOTGUNS: SxS

KM-4 PARALELAS FIELD - sidelock action with blued frame, fixed chokes, checkered buttstock.

MSR $10,995	$9,995	$8,750	$7,500	$6,250	$5,000	$4,000	$3,000

IMPERIAL AX/BX - best quality sidelock model, many options available.

MSR $17,995	$15,750	$12,500	$9,950	$8,750	$7,500	$6,500	$5,750

Add $4,200 for Imperial BX Model.

GRADING - PPGS™	100%	98%	95%	90%	80%	70%	60%

SHOTGUNS: SINGLE BARREL

KM-4 TRAP - 12 ga., 34 in. single barrel with 20mm tapered step VR. New 2004.

MSR $9,495	$8,650	$7,450	$5,900	$5,000	$4,425	$3,800	$3,200

Add $2,500 for set of 32 in. O/U barrels with 20mm tapered step rib VR.

KENDALL INTERNATIONAL

Previous importer and distributor located in Paris, KY. Kendall International also imported Australian Automatic Arms, and the Keberst Rifle, Air rifles can be found in the *Blue Book of Airguns* by Dr. Robert Beeman & John Allen (also online).

KENTUCKY RIFLES

U.S. flintlock/percussion long rifle configuration originating in Pennsylvania. Kentucky rifles are a field unto themselves, and should be evaluated by an experienced and known source for accurate identification and/or price evaluation.

KENTUCKY RIFLES INDENTIFICATION & PRICING

The author wishes to express his thanks once again to Mr. James Buelow for updating the following information.

The Kentucky rifle was the creation of early settlers from Europe. This new American configuration combined the architectural elements of the English Fowler with the ornamental features of the German Jaeger.

The earliest recorded use of the term "Kentucky rifle" was in a ballad written after the battle of New Orleans. The battle was won by the American Long Rifle, in the hands of 2,000 frontiersmen. During that period, the area west of the 13 colonies was known as Kentucky; hence the name Kentucky rifle.

Kentucky rifles began appearing around the middle of the 18th century and disappeared by the middle of the 19th century. Their origin is credited to eastern Pennsylvania, but soon spread to many other states, including Maryland, Virginia, Tennessee, North Carolina, and areas where the rifle maker found a market for his skills.

The styles vary, but they have two things in common: they are long, and most had curly maple stocks. The bores are found both rifled and smooth. The rifles most prized by the collector are the ones that have relief or incised carving. Carved Kentucky rifles are considered one of America's earliest art forms and are now considered Americana personified. Present values may range from as low as $1,000 all the way up to $50,000+! Non-carved or plain Kentuckys are most often encountered.

The present value of an uncarved, original flintlock Kentucky rifle in average condition is approx. $3,000. An uncarved percussion specimen in average original condition is approx. $2,000. These prices diminish when the Kentucky rifle lacks a maker's name, usually found on the top of the barrel, or if it does not have a patch box. Kentucky rifle values vary greatly, due to maker popularity, quality of carving, condition, rifle style, and a mulititude of other factors.

During the past several decades, many fine contemporary Kentucky rifles have been built by craftsmen who understand the trade. Many of these guns are now available in the secondary marketplace. A large percentage have outstanding craftsmanship, and are highly sought after. These specimens sell in the $2,000-$10,000 range, depending on the notoriety of the builder and the sophistication of the work. Because of this, these guns have to be evaluated one at a time.

The best way to find out the value of a Kentucky rifle is to seek out a knowledgeable Kentucky rifle collector. To find such a person in your area, contact the Kentucky Rifle Association's Administrative Assistant: Ruth Collis, 2319 Sue Ann Dr., Lancaster, PA, 17602.

For information regarding contemporary Kentucky rifles makers (with some contact information), visit the Contemporary Longrifle Association at www.longrifle.ws, or see their listing under Firearms Associations.

GRADING - PPGS™	100%	98%	95%	90%	80%	70%	60%

KEPPELER - TECHNISCHE ENTWICKLUNGEN GmbH

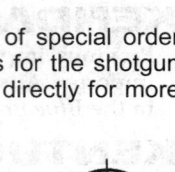

Current rifle manufacturer located in Fichtenberg, Germany. No current U.S. importation.

Keppeler manufactures a wide variety of top quality rifles, in many target configurations (including UIT-CISM, Prone, Free, and Sniper Bullpup). Both metric and domestic calibers are available as well as a variety of special order options. Keppeler also manufactures precision caliber conversion tubes for the shotgun barrel(s) on combination guns and drillings. Please contact the factory directly for more information and current pricing (see Trademark Index).

KEPPLINGER, ING. HANNES

Please refer to the Kufsteiner Waffenstube section.

KESSLER ARMS CORPORATION

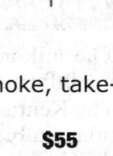

Previous manufacturer located in Silver Creek, NY.

SHOTGUNS

LEVERMATIC MODEL - 12, 16, or 20 ga., lever action, 26 or 28 in. full choke, takedown, plain pistol grip stock. Disc. 1953.

	$175	$150	$125	$100	$85	$65	$55

BOLT ACTION MODEL - 12, 16, or 20 ga., 26 or 28 in. full, takedown, plain stock. Mfg. 1951-53.

	$90	$65	$50	$45	$35	$35	$35

KEYSTONE SPORTING ARMS, INC.

Current rifle manufacturer established 1996, and located in Milton, PA. Distributor and dealer sales.

RIFLES: BOLT ACTION

CRICKETT SPORTER - .22 Short, .22 LR or .22 Mag. (mfg. 2001-2004) cal., manually cocked single shot, 16 1/8 in. barrel with adj. rear aperture sight, steel or stainless steel (new 1999) construction, 11 1/2 in. LOP (youth dimension), choice of walnut, colored laminate, camo synthetic, or molded black synthetic stock, stainless or blue barrel and receiver, 30 in. overall length, 2 1/2 lbs. New 1997.

MSR $165	$150	$135	$120	$105	$95	$85	$75

Add $20 for solid walnut stock.
Add $45-$60 for color laminated stock (various colors).
Add $35 for stainless steel, and $20 for bull barrel.
Add $25 for .22 Mag. cal. (disc. 2004).

✱ **Crickett Custom/Deluxe Sporter** - features deluxe hand checkered stock. Mfg. 1998-2000.

	$225	$195	$175	$150	$135	$120	$105

Last MSR was $250.

Add $10 for deluxe configuration.

KHAN

Current trademark of shotguns imported beginning late 2004 by Legacy Sports International, LLC, located in Alexandria, VA.

GRADING - PPGS™	100%	98%	95%	90%	80%	70%	60%

SHOTGUNS: O/U

ARTHEMIS ELITE FIELD/DELUXE - 12, 20, 28 ga. or .410 bore, 3 in. chambers (except for 28 ga.), 26 or 28 in. VR barrels with multichokes (fixed chokes on .410 bore), extractors, SST, matte blue (Field) or bright blue (Deluxe) metal finish, light engraving, choice of satin finish (Field) or polished select finish (Deluxe) walnut stock, 5.7-7.9 lbs. Importation began 2004.

MSR $617	$500	$450	$400	$350	$300	$265	$235

Add $15 for 20 ga.

Add $22 for 28 ga. or .410 bore.

Add $174 for Deluxe Model with bright blue metal and polished select wood stock (12 or 20 ga. only).

✳ **Arthemis Elite Sporting Clays** - 12 ga., 2 3/4 in. chambers, ejectors, 28 in. barrels, ST, otherwise similar to Arthemis Field, 8 lbs. Importation began 2004.

MSR $1,104	$925	$825	$725	$650	$575	$495	$425

SHOTGUNS: SxS

COACH GUN - 12 ga., 2 3/4 in. chamber, bright blue metal, hammerless boxlock action, extractors, polished select wood stock and forearm, 20 in. barrels with fixed cyl. bore chokes, 6.9 lbs. Importation began 2005.

MSR $784	$675	$595	$525	$450	$375	$300	$225

KIMAR srl

Current manufacturer located in Brescia, Italy. Currently imported by Valor Corporation, located in Sunrise, FL, Collector's Armoury, located in Alexandria, VA, and by IAR, located in San Juan Capistrano, CA.

Kimar is well known for its starter/signal revolvers and pistols in many popular configurations. Additionally, the company also manufactures a single shot, folding barrel shotgun in small hunting calibers. Please contact the importers directly for more information and U.S. availability (see Trademark Index).

J. KIMBALL ARMS CO.

Previous manufacturer located in Detroit, MI circa 1958.

PISTOLS: SEMI-AUTO

AUTOMATIC PISTOL - .30 Carbine or .22 Hornet (very rare) cal., 7 shot, 3 in. (Combat Model) or 5 in. (Target Model) barrel, approx. 32 oz. Less than 300 mfg. in 1958 only.

$1,200	$1,000	$850	$725	$550	$425	$300

Add 50% for .22 Hornet cal.

Functional weaknesses of this pistol caused discontinuance. Surviving specimens should be checked carefully for slide failures and other potential problems. Values assume no operational damage to the pistol.

KIMBER

Current trademark manufactured by Kimber Mfg., Inc., established during 1997, with company headquarters and manufacturing located in Yonkers, NY. Previous rifle manufacture was by Kimber of America, Inc., located in Clackamas, OR circa 1993-97. Dealer sales.

PISTOLS: SEMI-AUTO

Kimber pistols, including the very early models marked "Clackamas, Oregon", have all been manufactured in the current plant in Yonkers, NY. Prior to the 1998 production year, the "Classic" model pistols were alternately roll-scrolled "Classic", "Classic Custom" or "Custom Classic". During 1997-98, the "Classic" moniker was dropped from Kimber pistol nomenclature as a specific model.

All Kimber pistols are shipped with lockable high impact synthetic case with cable lock and one mag., beginning 1999.

Beginning in 2001, the "Series II" pistol, incorporating the Kimber Firing Pin Safety System, was, again, phased into almost all centerfire models. All pistols incorporating the firing pin block have the Roman Numeral "II" following the name of the pistol presented on the slide directly under the ejection port. This conversion was completed by February, 2002, and almost all subsequent Kimber centerfire pistols were Series II. There was no "Series I" pistol per se, but pre-series II models are often referred to in that manner.

During 2003, external extractors were phased into all .45 ACP models.

All three changes (disuse of the term "Classic" for pistols, Series II safety system, and external extractor) were "phased in" throughout normal production cycles. Therefore, no distinctive cut-off dates or serial numbering series were established to identify specific product runs or identify when these features were incorporated.

> **Add $280 for .22 LR cal. conversion kit for all mil-spec 1911 pistols (includes complete upper assembly, lightweight aluminum slide, premium bull barrel, and 10 shot mag.). Available in satin black and satin silver. Kimber began manufacture of these kits in early 2003. Prior to that, they were mfg. by a vendor.**

CUSTOM II - .45 ACP cal., patterned after the Colt Government Model 1911, 5 in. barrel, various finishes, 7 shot mag., forged steel frame, match grade barrel, bushing and trigger group, dovetail mounted sights, frame machined from steel forgings, high ride beavertail grip safety, choice of rubber, laminated wood (new 2002), walnut or rosewood (new 1999) grips, 38 oz. New 1995.

MSR $745	$620	$530	$445	$375	$335	$300	$275

> Add $22 for walnut or rosewood (disc.) grips.
> Add $140 for night sights.
> Add $159 for Royal II finish (polished blue and rosewood grips).
> This series' nomenclature added the Roman numeral "II" during 2001.

✳ *Custom Target II* - similar to Custom II, except features Kimber adj. rear sight. New 1998.

MSR $854	$730	$600	$525	$455	$395	$340	$300

✳ *Stainless II* - .38 Super (advertised in 1999, never mfg.), 9mm Para (advertised in 1999, never mfg.), .40 S&W (new 1999), or .45 ACP cal., similar to Custom II, except has stainless steel slide and frame.

MSR $848	$710	$595	$475

> Add $141 for night sights.
> Add $80 for 9mm Para or 10mm cal.
> Subtract $49 for .40 S&W cal.
> Subtract $27 for Stainless Limited Edition marked "Stainless LE" (disc. 1998).

✳ *Stainless Target II* - similar to Stainless II, except is available in .38 Super (new 2002), 9mm Para., or 10mm (new 2003) cal., features Kimber adj. rear sight. New 1998.

MSR $964	$800	$650	$550

> Add $30 for .40 S&W cal. (disc. 2002).
> Add $30 for .38 Super cal.

GOLD MATCH II - .45 ACP cal., features Kimber adj. sight, stainless steel match barrel and bushing, premium aluminum match grade trigger, ambidextrous thumb safety became standard in 1998, 8 shot mag., fancy checkered rosewood grips in double diamond pattern, hand fitted, high polish blue, hand fitted in the Kimber Custom Shop, 38 oz.

MSR $1,192	$1,050	$885	$750	$635	$525	$450	$400

> This series' nomenclature added the Roman numeral "II" during 2001.

GRADING - PPGS™	100%	98%	95%	90%	80%	70%	60%

✳ *Stainless Gold Match II* - .38 Super (advertised in 1999, never mfg.), 9mm Para (advertised in 1999, never mfg.), .40 S&W (new 1999), or .45 ACP cal., similar to Gold Match, except is stainless steel, 38 oz.

MSR $1,342	$1,150	$985	$790

Add $31 for .40 S&W cal.

TEAM MATCH II - .45 ACP or .38 Super (limited mfg. 2003-2004) cal., same pistol developed for USA Shooting Team (2004 Olympics Rapid Fire Pistol Team) competition, satin finish stainless steel frame and slide, 5 in. match grade barrel, 30 LPI front strap checkering, match grade trigger, Tactical Extractor system, extended magazine well, 8 shot mag., laminated red/white/blue grips, 38 oz. New 2003.

MSR $1,310	$1,095	$950	$775

Add $70 for .38 Super cal.

GOLD COMBAT II - .45 ACP cal. only, 5 in. barrel, full size carry pistol based on the Gold Match, steel frame and slide, stainless steel match grade barrel and bushing, KimPro finish, tritium night sights, checkered walnut grips, 38 oz, mfg. by Custom Shop. New 1999.

MSR $1,716	$1,485	$1,125	$965	$825	$675	$575	$400

This series' nomenclature added the Roman numeral "II" during 2001.

✳ *Gold Combat Stainless II* - similar to Gold Combat, except is all stainless steel. New 1999.

MSR $1,657	$1,425	$1,065	$925

✳ *Gold Combat RL II* - similar to Gold Combat, except is has Picatinny rail machined into the frame to accept optics and other tactical accessories. New 2003.

MSR $1,758	$1,500	$1,150	$995	$875	$775	$675	$575

SUPER MATCH II - .45 ACP cal. only, 5 in. barrel, top-of-the-line model, two-tone stainless steel construction, KimPro finish on slide, match grade trigger, custom shop markings, 38 oz. New 1999.

MSR $1,966	$1,530	$1,150	$980

This series' nomenclature added the Roman numeral "II" during 2001.

LTP II - .45 ACP cal., designed for Limited Ten competition, Tactical Extractor, steel frame and slide, KimPro finish, 20 LPI front strap checkering, 30 LPI checkering under trigger guard, tungsten guide rod, flattop serrated slide, beveled mag. well, ambidextrous thumb safety, adj. sight. Mfg. by Custom Shop beginning 2002.

MSR $2,078	$1,830	$1,600	$1,300	$1,000	$875	$750	$625

RIMFIRE TARGET - .17 Mach 2 (new 2004) or .22 LR cal., aluminum frame and slide in silver or black anodized finish, 5 in. barrel, black synthetic grips, Kimber adj. rear sight, 23 oz. New 2003.

MSR $760	$635	$530	$455	$375	$335	$300	$275

Add $18 for .17 Mach 2 cal.

✳ *Rimfire Super* - similar to Rimfire Target, except has flattop slide with agressive fluting on upper sides, premium aluminum trigger, ambidextrous safety, rosewood grips with logo inserts, guaranteed to fire a sub-1.5 in. 5 shot group at 25 yards, test target included, 23 oz., mfg. by Kimber Custom Shop. New 2004.

MSR $1,072	$915	$810	$730	$650	$575	$500	$450

POLYMER MODEL - .45 ACP cal., features widened black polymer frame offering larger mag. capacity, choice of fixed (Polymer Model) or adj. Kimber target (Polymer Target Model, disc. 1999) rear sight, matte black slide, 10 shot mag., 34 oz. Mfg. 1997-2001.

	$675	$575	$525	$475	$425	$375	$330

Last MSR was $795.

Add $88 for Polymer Target Model.

All Polymer Models were disc. in 2002 in favor of the new "Ten" Series with improved Kimber made frame. Magazines are interchangeable.

GRADING - PPGS™	100%	98%	95%	90%	80%	70%	60%

✳ *Polymer Stainless* - .38 Super (advertised in 1999, never mfg.), 9mm Para (advertised in 1999, never mfg.), .40 S&W (mfg. 1999 only), or .45 ACP cal., similar to Polymer Model, except has satin finish stainless steel slide. Mfg. 1998-2001.

$745 $625 $550

Last MSR was $856.

Add $88 for Polymer Stainless Target Model (disc. 1999).

✳ *Polymer Gold Match* - .45 ACP cal. only, similar to Gold Match, except has polymer frame, supplied with 10 shot double stack mag., 34 oz. Mfg. 1999-2001.

$925 $850 $725 $650 $550 $450 $400

Last MSR was $1,041.

>*Polymer Gold Match Stainless* - similar to Gold Match, except has polymer frame and stainless steel slide, 34 oz. Mfg. 1999-2001.

$1,025 $900 $750

Last MSR was $1,177.

✳ *Polymer Pro Carry* - .45 ACP cal. only, 4 in. bushingless bull barrel, steel slide, 32 oz. Mfg. 1999-2001.

$725 $650 $575 $485 $435 $375 $330

Last MSR was $814.

>*Polymer Pro Carry Stainless* - similar to Polymer Pro Carry, except has stainless steel slide. Mfg. 1999-2001.

$755 $625 $550

Last MSR was $874.

✳ *Ultra Ten* - .45 ACP cal., black polymer frame with aluminum frame insert, stainless slide, 3 in. barrel, 10 shot staggered mag., low profile sights, lighter version of the Polymer Series frame, Kimber Firing Pin Safety, 24 oz.

While advertised during 2001 with an MSR of $896, this model never went into production.

COMPACT II - .45 ACP cal., features 4 in. barrel, .4 in. shorter aluminum or steel frame, 7 shot mag., Commander style hammer, single recoil spring, low profile combat sights, checkered black synthetic grips, 28 (aluminum) or 34 (steel) oz. Mfg. 1998-2001.

$635 $535 $455 $395 $365 $325 $295

Last MSR was $764.

✳ *Compact Stainless II* - .40 S&W (mfg. 1999-2001) or .45 ACP cal., features stainless steel slide, 4 in. bull barrel, 4 in. shorter aluminum (disc.) or stainless (new 2002) frame, 7 shot mag., Commander style hammer, single recoil spring, low profile combat sights, black synthetic grips, 28 oz. New 1998.

MSR $889 $740 $595 $485

Add $32 for .40 S&W cal. (disc. 2001).

This model's nomenclature added the Roman numeral "II" during 2001.

✳ *Compact Aluminum Stainless II* - .40 S&W or .45 ACP cal., features aluminum frame and stainless steel slide, 28 oz. Mfg. 1999-2001.

$700 $575 $475

Last MSR was $837.

Add $36 for .40 S&W cal.

COMBAT CARRY - .40 S&W or .45 ACP cal., 4 in. barrel, carry model featuring aluminum frame and trigger, stainless steel slide, tritium night sights, and ambidextrous thumb safety, 28 oz. Limited mfg. 1999 only.

$940 $815 $675 $600 $500 $450 $400

Last MSR was $1,044.

Add $30 for .40 S&W cal.

GRADING - PPGS™	100%	98%	95%	90%	80%	70%	60%

PRO CARRY II - .40 S&W (disc. 2001) or .45 ACP cal., 4 in. barrel, features full length grip similar to Custom Model, aluminum frame (except Pro Carry HD), steel slide, 7 or 8 shot mag., 28 oz. New 1999.

	MSR $789	$655	$555	$450	$395	$355	$325	$295

Add $35 for .40 S&W cal. (disc.).

Add $104 for night sights.

This series' nomenclature added the Roman numeral "II" during 2001.

❋ *Stainless Pro Carry II* - similar to Pro Carry, except has stainless steel slide. New 1999.

	MSR $862	$725	$610	$480

Add $38 for .40 S&W cal.

Add $104 for night sights (.45 ACP cal. only).

❋ *Pro Carry HD II* - .38 Super (new 2002) or .45 ACP cal., similar to Pro Carry Stainless, except has heavier stainless steel frame, 35 oz. New 2001.

	MSR $897	$760	$635	$490

Add $39 for .38 Super cal.

ULTRA CARRY II - .40 S&W (disc. 2001) or .45 ACP cal., 3 in. barrel, aluminum frame, 7 shot mag., 25 oz. New 1999.

	MSR $783	$655	$555	$500	$445	$395	$350	$325

Add $39 for .40 S&W cal. (disc. 2001).

Add $104 for night sights.

This series' nomenclature added the Roman numeral "II" during 2001.

❋ *Stainless Ultra Carry II* - .40 S&W and .45 ACP cal., similar to Ultra Carry, except has stainless steel slide. New 1999.

	MSR $858	$735	$620	$480

Add $45 for .40 S&W cal.

Add $104 for night sights (.45 ACP cal. only).

ECLIPSE II SERIES - 10mm (Eclipse Custom II, new 2004) or .45 ACP cal., stainless steel slide and frame, matte finish with brush polished flat surfaces for elegant two-tone finish, Tritium night sights, target models have adj. Bar/Dot sights, silver/grey laminated double diamond grips, black small parts, 30 LPI front strap checkering, include Eclipse Ultra II (3 in. barrel, short grip), Eclipse Pro II and Eclipse Pro-Target II (4 in. barrel, standard grip), Eclipse Custom II, and Eclipse Target II (full size). New 2002.

	MSR $1,074	$990	$845	$730	$640	$525	$450	$400

Add $20 for Eclipse Custom II.

Add $103 for Eclipse Target II or Eclipse Pro-Target II.

Add $114 for Eclipse Custom II in 10mm cal.

The initial Custom Shop version of these pistols was mfg. during late 2001, featuring an ambidextrous thumb safety, and "Custom Shop" markings on left side of slide, 7,931 were mfg.

CUSTOM TLE II SERIES - .45 ACP cal., tactical law enforcement pistol with exactly the same features as the Kimber pistols carried by LAPD SWAT, black oxide coated stainless steel frame and slide. New 2003.

	MSR $914	$815	$725	$635

❋ *Stainless TLE II* - similar to Custom TLE II, except has stainless steel slide and frame. New 2004.

	MSR $1,052	$940	$810	$655

❋ *Custom TLE/RL II* - similar to Custom TLE II, except has Picatinny rail machined into the frame to accept optics and other tactical accessories. New 2003.

	MSR $1,038	$925	$800	$650

* *Stainless TLE/RL II* - similar to Custom TLE/RL II, except is stainless. New 2004.

  MSR $1,167 ... **$1,025** ... **$875** ... **$675**

* *Pro TLE/RL II* - similar to Custom TLE/RL II, except has 4 in. bushingless barrel. New 2004.

  MSR $1,061 ... **$945** ... **$800** ... **$650**

* *Stainless Pro TLE/RL II* - similar to Stainless TLE/RL II, except has 4 in. bushingless barrel. New 2004.

  MSR $1,197 ... **$1,050** ... **$875** ... **$675**

TACTICAL II SERIES - 9mm Para (Tactical Pro II, new 2004) or .45 ACP cal., lightweight tactical pistol, grey anodized frame with black carbon steel slide, external extrator, fixed tritium Meprolight 3-dot night sights, extended magazine well, 30 LPI front strap checkering, black/grey laminated logo grips, 7 shot mag. with bumper pad, available in Tactical Ultra II (3 in. barrel, short grip, 25 oz.), Tactical Pro II (4 in. barrel, standard grip, 28 oz.), and Tactical Custom II (5 in. barrel, standard grip, 31 oz.). New 2003.

> **MSR $1,080** ... **$995** ... **$850** ... **$725**
>
> **Add $25 for Tactical Pro II in 9mm Para. cal.**
>
> A Custom Shop version of the Pro Tactical II was manufactured in 2002, but w/o external extractor, checkering and night sights.

TEN II SERIES - .45 ACP cal., high capacity polymer frame, stainless steel slide with satin finish, impressed front grip strap checkering and serrations under trigger guard, textured finish, polymer grip safety and mainspring housing, 10 round double stack mag., includes Ultra Ten II (3 in. barrel, short grip, disc. 2003), Pro Carry Ten II (4 in. barrel, standard grip), Stainless Ten II (full size), and Gold Match Ten II (stainless steel barrel, polished stainless steel slide flats, hand fitted barrel/bushing to slide, adj. sight), 14 (pre-ban) round mags. also available, accepts magazines from older Kimber mfg. Polymer pistols. New 2002.

> **MSR $771** ... **$685** ... **$605** ... **$515** ... **$450** ... **$395** ... **$360** ... **$320**
>
> **Add $15 for Pro-Carry Ten II, $35 for Ultra Ten II (disc. 2003), or $290 for Gold Match Ten II.**

* *BP Ten II* - similar to Stainless Ten II, except has black oxide carbon steel slide, and aluminum subframe for lighter weight. New 2003.

  MSR $623 ... **$545** ... **$455** ... **$380** ... **$325** ... **$300** ... **$275** ... **$250**

* *Pro BP Ten II* - similar to Pro Carry Ten II, except has black oxide carbon steel slide, and aluminum subframe for lighter weight. New 2003.

  MSR $636 ... **$550** ... **$460** ... **$385** ... **$335** ... **$300** ... **$275** ... **$250**

CDP II (CUSTOM DEFENSE PACKAGE) - .40 S&W or .45 ACP cal., Custom Shop pistol featuring tritium night sights, stainless steel slide with black anodized aluminum frame, 3 in. (Ultra CDP II, 25 oz.), 4 in. (Pro CDP II and Compact CDP II, 28 oz.), or 5 in. (Custom CDP II, 31 oz.) barrel, carry bevel treatment, ambidextrous thumb safety, double diamond pattern checkered rosewood grips, 30 LPI checkered front strap and under trigger guard (new 2003), two-tone finish. New 2000.

> **MSR $1,165** ... **$1,010** ... **$860** ... **$730** ... **$650** ... **$525** ... **$450** ... **$400**
>
> **Add $38 for .40 S&W cal., available in Ultra CDP II configuration only.**
>
> The Pro CDP II has a full length grip frame.
>
> This series' nomenclature added the Roman numeral "II" during 2001.

ULTRA TEN II CDP - .45 ACP cal., tritium night sights, stainless steel slide with black polymer frame, 3 in. barrel, carry bevel treatment, standard manual safety, 10 shot mag., 24 oz. Mfg. 2003 only.

> $825 ... $725 ... $635 ... $525 ... $450 ... $400 ... $365
>
> *Last MSR was $926.*

Pistols: Kimber Non-Cataloged Models

Kimber has over the past several years, manufactured a number of pistols that did not appear in their catalog. To help identify non-cataloged models, pistols are listed in three categories: Custom Shop/Special Edition Pistols, Limited Edition Pistols, and Mid-Year Introduction Pistols.

Pistols: Kimber Custom Shop/Special Editions

Beginning in 1998, the Kimber Custom Shop began producing special edition pistols. Special edition models have been issued in either fixed numbers, or time limited. Where available, time limited models show the actual number produced. All models are .45 ACP caliber unless otherwise specified.

ROYAL CARRY - compact aluminum frame, 4 in. bushingless barrel, highly polished blue, night sights, ambidextrous safety, hand checkered rosewood grips, 28 oz. 600 mfg. 1998.

Last MSR was $903.

GOLD GUARDIAN - highly polished stainless steel slide and frame, hand fitted 5 in. match barrel and bushing, tritium night sights, ambidextrous safety, extended magazine well, skeletonized match trigger, hand checkered rosewood grips, 38 oz. 300 mfg. 1998.

Last MSR was $1,350.

ELITE CARRY - black anodized compact aluminum frame, stainless slide, 4 in. barrel, meltdown treatment on slide and frame, tritium night sights, 20 LPI checkered front strap, ambidextrous safety, aluminum match trigger, hand checkered rosewood grips, 28 oz. 1,200 mfg. 1998.

Last MSR was $1,019.

STAINLESS COVERT - meltdown stainless slide and frame finished in silver KimPro, 4 in. barrel, 30 LPI front strap checkering, 3-dot tritium night sights, hand checkered rosewood grips, 34 oz. 1,000 mfg. 1999.

Last MSR was $1,135.

PRO ELITE - aluminum frame with silver KimPro finish, stainless slide with black KimPro finish, full meltdown treatment on slide and frame, 4 in. barrel, 30 LPI front strap checkering, 3-dot tritium night sights, hand checkered rosewood grips, 28 oz. 2,500 mfg. 1999.

Last MSR was $1,140.

ULTRA ELITE - aluminum frame with black KimPro finish, satin stainless slide, full meltdown treatment on slide and frame, 3 in. barrel, 30 LPI front strap checkering, 3-dot tritium night sights, hand checkered rosewood grips, 25 oz. 2,750 mfg. 1999.

Last MSR was $1,085.

HERITAGE EDITION - black oxide steel frame and slide, 30 LPI front strap checkering, ambidextrous safety, premium aluminum trigger, NSSF Heritage medallion and special markings on slide, ser. no. begins with KHE, 38 oz. 1,041 mfg. 2000.

Last MSR was $1,065.

STAINLESS GOLD MATCH SE II - .38 Super or .45 ACP cal., stainless steel frame and slide, 5 in. barrel, serrated flat-top slide, 30 LPI front strap checkering, hand checkered rosewood grips, ambidextrous safety, polished flats, ser. no. begins with KSO, 38 oz. 260 (.38 Super) and 294 (.45 ACP) mfg. 2001.

Last MSR was $1,487.

  Add $88 for .38 Super cal.

ULTRA SHADOW II - black steel slide and anodized aluminum frame, 3 in. barrel, fixed tritium night sights, 30 LPI front strap checkering, grey laminate grips, silver grip and thumb safeties and mainspring housing, ser. no. begins with KUSLE, 25 oz.

Last MSR was $949.

PRO SHADOW II - black steel slide and anodized aluminum frame, 4 in. barrel, fixed tritium night sights, 30 LPI front strap checkering, grey laminate grips, silver grip and thumb safeties and mainspring housing, ser. no. begins with KPSLE, 28 oz.

Last MSR was $949.

ULTRA CDP ELITE II - .45 ACP cal., first Kimber .45 pistols with ramped match grade barrels, black anodized aluminum frame, black oxide carbon steel slide, 3 in. barrel, carry melt treatment for rounded and blended edges, Meprolight 3-dot tritium night sights, 30 LPI checkering on front strap and under trigger guard, ambidextrous thumb safety and charcoal/ruby laminated logo grips, 25 oz. Mfg. 2002-Jan., 2003.

Last MSR was $1,216.

ULTRA CDP ELITE STS II - .45 ACP cal., first Kimber .45 pistols with ramped match grade barrels, silver anodized aluminum frame, satin stainless steel slide, 3 in. barrel, carry melt treatment for rounded and blended edges, Meprolight 3-dot tritium night sights, 30 LPI checkering on front strap and under trigger guard, ambidextrous thumb safety and charcoal/ruby laminated logo grips, 25 oz. Mfg. 2002-Jan., 2003.

Last MSR was $1,155.

ULTRA RCP II - .45 ACP cal., refined carry pistol, black annodized frame, meltdown treatment with bobbed heel, 3 line ball milled front strap and bobbed grip safety, Kimpro finished, melted 3 in. trench cut slide (no sights), carbon steel barrel, bobbed spur hammer, black micarta call milled slim grips, bobbed magazine catch, 25 oz. New 2003.

	MSR $1,228	$1,075	$950	$825	$750	$675	$600	$525

* *Ultra SP II* - special anodized frame colors (black/blue, black/red, and black/silver) with black oxide slide, 7 shot mag., 3 in. bushingless barrel, 3-dot sights, carry melt, ball milled micarta grips, standard fixed sights, 25 oz. New 2003.

	MSR $1,175	$1,025	$900	$800	$725	$625	$575	$495

25th ANNIVERSARY CUSTOM LIMITED EDITION - .45 ACP cal., black oxide frame and slide, 5 in. barrel, premium aluminum trigger, fancy walnut anniversary logo grips, "1979-2004" engraving on slide, Series I safeties and traditional extractor, ser. no. range is KAPC0001-KAPC1911. Limited production of 1,911 beginning 2004.

	MSR $923	$825	$725	$650	$575	$500	$425	$350

* *25th Anniversary Gold Match* - blued frame and slide, deep polish on flats, 5 in. stainless barrel, premium aluminum trigger, ambidextrous safety, adj. sights, fancy walnut anniversary logo grips, "1979-2004" engraving in slide, Series I safeties and traditional extractor, ser. no. range KAPG0001-KAPG0500, 38 oz. Limited production of 500 beginning 2004.

	MSR $1,357	$1,175	$995	$875	$775	$700	$625	$550

* *25th Anniversary Limited Edition Pistol Set* - includes one Custom (ser. no. range KMSC0001-KMSC250) and one Gold Match (ser. no. range KMSG0001 - KMSG250), matched ser. nos., wood presentation case. Limited production of 250 beginning 2004.

	MSR $2,620	$2,250	$2,000	$1,775	$1,525	$1,300	$1,100	$900

RAPTOR II - .45 ACP cal., full size carbon steel frame with "scales" on front strap, continuing on slide in lieu of standard serrations, black oxide finish, back cut flattop, 5 in. stainless barrel with engraved "Raptor II" and "Custom Shop", black anodized trigger, ambidextrous safety, scaled Zebra wood grip panels with Kimber logo, fixed slant night sights, 38 oz. New 2004.

	MSR $1,204	$1,050	$875	$675	$575	$475	$400	$325

GRADING - PPGS™	100%	98%	95%	90%	80%	70%	60%

PRO RAPTOR II - .45 ACP cal., full size stainless steel frame with "scales" on front strap, continuing on carbon steel slide in lieu of standard serrations, black oxide finish, back cut flattop, 4 in. stainless barrel with engraved "Pro Raptor II" and "Custom Shop", black anodized trigger, ambidextrous safety, scaled Zebra wood grip panels with Kimber logo, fixed slant night sights, 38 oz. New 2004.

	MSR $1,089	$945	$800	$650	$550	$450	$375	$300

Pistols: Kimber Limited Editions

Kimber has produced limited runs of pistols for dealer groups, NRA Events, sporting goods stores, law enforcement agencies, special requests, etc. Limited run pistols can be as small as 25 mfg.

PRO CARRY SLE - all stainless steel slide and frame, 4 in. barrel, identicial to Stainless Pro Carry Model, except has stainless frame, mfg. for Kimber Master Dealers, cataloged in 2001, later production known as Pro Carry HD II, 1,329 mfg. during 2000.

Last MSR was $815.

PRO COMBAT - black oxide stainless steel frame and slide, 4 in. barrel, ambidextrous safety, tritium 3-dot night sights, match grade aluminum trigger, 30 LPI front strap checkering, hand checkered rosewood grips, 35 oz. Marketed by RGuns. 52 mfg. 2000.

Last MSR was $860.

TARGET ELITE II - two-tone stainless frame and slide, black oxide coating on frame, slide natural stainless, adj. rear sight, rosewood double diamond grips, sold through stores affiliated with Sports Inc. buying group, 38 oz. 220 mfg. 2001.

Last MSR was $950.

CUSTOM DEFENDER II - two-tone stainless frame and slide, black oxide coating on frame, slide natural stainless, fixed low profile rear sight, double diamond rosewood grips, sold only through stores affiliated with National Buying Service, 38 oz. 290 mfg. 2001.

Last MSR was $839.

CUSTOM ECLIPSE II - stainless slide and frame, 5 in. barrel, black oxide finish brush polished on the flats, 30 LPI front strap checkering, adj. night sights, laminated grey grips, ser. no. begins with KEL, 38 oz. 4,522 mfg. 2001.

Last MSR was $1,121.

PRO ECLIPSE II - stainless steel frame and slide, 4 in. barrel, black oxide finish brush polished on the flats, 30 LPI front strap checkering, fixed 3-dot night sights, laminated grey grips, ambidextrous safety, ser. no. begins with KRE, 35 oz. 2,207 mfg. 2001.

Last MSR was $1,065.

ULTRA ECLIPSE II - stainless steel frame and slide, 3 in. barrel, black oxide finish brush polished on the flats, 30 LPI front strap checkering, fixed 3-dot night sights, laminated grey grips, ambidextrous safety, 34 oz. 1,202 mfg. 2001.

Last MSR was $1,054.

STRYKER TEN II - Ultra Ten II with black polymer frame and frame insert and small parts, natural stainless slide, 25 oz. 200 mfg. 2002.

Last MSR was $850.

LAPD SWAT - black oxide coated stainless frame and slide, 5 in. barrel, low profile Meprolight 3-dot night sights, 30 LPI front strap checkering, black rubber double diamond grips, 38 oz. 300 mfg. 2002.

> Following extensive testing to select a duty pistol, LAPD SWAT chose a Kimber Stainless Custom II and had it enhanced to their specifications. This model was made strictly for law enforcement and not sold to the public. A civilian version called the Tactical law Enforcement (TLE) Series went into production in 2003.

GRADING - PPGS™	100%	98%	95%	90%	80%	70%	60%

NRA EPOCH II - stainless slide and frame, 5 in. barrel, black oxide finish brush polished on flats, 30 LPI front strap checkering, standard safety, fixed tritium night sights, laminated grey grips, ser. no. begins with KNRAE, Friends of NRA pistol available only at NRA banquets, 38 oz. 58 mfg. 2002.

This model had no established MSR.

THE BOSS II - limited edition to commemotate Blythe Sports 50th anniversary, stainless steel slide and frame, carry melt treatment, fixed white dot sights, premium aluminum 2 hole trigger, 5 in. carbin barrel, engraved "The BOSS II" on ejection port side, and "SPECIAL EDITION", black and sliver laminate grips with Blythe 50th anniversary logo in center on white insert, ser. no. KBSS000-KBSS024, 25 mfg.

This model had no established MSR.

ECLIPSE CLE II - 5 in. barrel, Eclipse Custom II finish on slide with black over stainless frame (no front strap checkering), charcoal/ruby Kimber logo grips, sold only through stores affiliated with National Buying Service, 38 oz. 271 mfg. 2003.

Last MSR was $917.

✷ *Eclipse PLE II* - similar to Eclipse CLE II, except has 4 in. bushingless barrel, sold only through stores affiliated with Sports Inc. buying group, 35 oz. 232 mfg. 2003.

Last MSR was $877.

✷ *Eclipse ULE II* - Eclipse Ultra II finish on slide with black over stainless frame (no front strap checkering), 3 in. bushingless barrel, charcoal/ruby Kimber logo grips, sold only through stores affiliated with National Buying Service, 34 oz. 227 mfg. 2003.

Last MSR was $890.

TEAM MATCH II - .38 Super cal., identical to original Team Match II, with .38 Super ramped barrel, match grade chamber, bushing and trigger group, special Team Match features, including 30 LPI checkered front strap, adj. sight, extended magazine well, premium aluminum trigger and red, white, and blue USA Shooting Team logo grips, 38 oz. Mfg. 2003-2004.

	100%	98%	95%	90%	80%	70%	60%
	$1,150	$995	$875	$775	$675	$575	$475

Last MSR was $1,352.

MCSOCOM ICQB (2004) - .45 ACP cal., at the request of the Marine Corps Special Operations Command (MCSOCOM) Detachment 1 (Det. 1), Kimber produced Interim Close Quarters Battle (ICQB) 1911 patterned pistols in accordance with very high specific requirements: steel frame and slide finished in matte black, internal extractor, GI length, guide rod and plug, light rail, bumped grip safety and ambidextrous manual safety, lanyard loop, Simonich G-10 "Gunner" grips, Novak low mount night sights.

There was no MSR on this model, as it was not available for sale to the general public. The civilian version of this pistol is called the Warrior.

Pistols: Kimber Mid-Year Introductions

Kimber occasionally chooses to introduce new pistols at times other than at the beginning of each model year in order to respond to customer demand. Models introduced normally transfer to successive model years with major features intact, but minor changes may be made to improve aesthetics or the function of the pistol.

ULTRA CDP - black anodized aluminum frame, satin stainless slide, full meltdown treatment, 3 in. barrel, 30 LPI front strap checkering, 3-dot tritium night sights, ambidextrous safety, hand checkered rosewood grips, 25 oz. Introductory run 2000, became part of standard Kimber lineup during 2001.

Last MSR was $1,086.

PRO CDP - similar to Ultra CDP, except has 4 in. barrel and full sized frame, 28 oz. Introductory run 2000, became part of standard Kimber lineup during 2001.

Last MSR was $1,086.

COMPACT CDP - similar to Pro CDP, except grip frame is .400 inches shorter, 28 oz. Introductory run 2000, became part of standard Kimber lineup during 2001.

Last MSR was $1,086.

PRO TACTICAL II - grey anodized aluminum frame, black carbon steel slide, 4 in. barrel, fixed white dot sights, extended steel magazine well, black/grey laminated logo grips, 7 shot mag. with bumper pad, 25 oz. 335 mfg. 2002-Jan., 2003.

Last MSR was $917.

ULTRA TACTICAL II - grey anodized frame, black carbon steel slide, 3 in. barrel, fixed white dot sights, extended aluminum mag. well, black/grey laminated logo grips, 7 shot mag. with bumper pad, 25 oz. 335 mfg. 2002.

Last MSR was $917.

CUSTOM TLE II - tactical law enforcement pistol similar to LAPD SWAT, black oxide coated stainless frame and slide, 5 in. barrel, low profile Meprolight 3-dot night sights, 30 LPI front strap checkering, black rubber double diamond grips, 38 oz. Mfg. 2002-Jan., 2003.

Last MSR was $910.

TEAM MATCH II - exact replica of USA Shooting Team (2004 Olympic Rapid Fire Pistol Team) training .45 ACP cal. pistol, satin finish stainless steel frame and slide, 5 in. barrel, 30 LPI front strap checkering match grade trigger and stainless barrel, external extractor, extended magazine well, 8 shot mag., laminated red/white/blue USA Shooting Team grips, 38 oz. Mfg. 2002.

Last MSR was $1,420.

BP TEN II - full size polymer pistol with black anodized aluminum rail insert, 5 in. carbin slide and barrel, external extractor, standard fixed sights, 10 shot mag., 34 oz. Mfg. 2003.

Last MSR was $619.

✷ *Pro BP Ten II* - similar to BP Ten II, except has 4 in. bushing less barrel, 32 oz. Mfg. 2003.

Last MSR was $633.

STAINLESS TARGET 10MM - first Kimber chambered for 10mm, ramped 5 in. match grade barrel, match grade chamber and bushing, 8 shot mag., dovetail mounted adj. sight, 38 oz. Mfg. 2003.

$925	**$800**	**$650**	

Last MSR was $1,026.

✷ *Stainless Target II 9mm* - similar to 10mm model, except is 9mm Para. cal., 9 shot mag., beavertail grip safety, extended thumb safety, slightly extended magazine release button standard, 38 oz. Mfg. 2003.

$925	**$800**	**$650**	

Last MSR was $1,026.

GOLD COMBAT RL II - carbon steel slide and frame, integral Picatinny light rail, 5 in. barrelm 30 LPI front strap and under triggerguard checkering, black KimPro finish, extended mag. well, ambidextrous safety, fixed 3 dot sights, premium aluminum trigger and double diamond rosewood grips, 38 oz. Mfg. 2003.

Last MSR was $1,749.

CUSTOM TLE/RL II - carbon steel slide and frame with integral Picatinny light rail, 5 in. barrel, 30 LPI front checkering and all black oxide finish, fixed 3 dot sights, standard aluminum trigger, black rubber grips, 38 oz. Mfg. 2003.

Last MSR was $1,033.

WARRIOR - production began following adoption of this pistol by the Marine Expeditionary Unit (MEU) Special Operations Capable (SOC), Detachment 1 (DEAT 1), civilian version with 5 in. barrel, Series I (no firing pin block), carbon steel slide and frame, integral Picatinny light rail, internal extractor, lanyard loop, bumped grip safety, G-10 material grip (coyote brown), wedge night sights, ambidextrous safety, GI length guide rod finished in black KimPro, 38 oz. New 2004.

MSR $1,250		$1,050	$925	$800	$700	$600	$500	$400

GRADING - PPGS™	100%	98%	95%	90%	80%	70%	60%

RIFLES: BOLT ACTION

Repeating and Single Shot

A three position Win. Model 70 type safety became a standard feature on all Kimber .22 LR and .17 Mach 2 cal. rifles in early 2004.

HUNTER - .22 LR cal., similar to Classic, except has lower grade walnut and different barrel contour, 6.7 lbs. New 2002.

MSR $809	$675	$575	$500	$450	$400	$350	$300

YOUTH - .22 LR cal., similar to Hunter, except has 12 1/4 in. LOP.

While this model was cataloged during 2002-2003 with an MSR of $746, it never went into production.

CLASSIC - .22 LR cal., Mauser claw extractor with 2 position Model 70 type safety, unique eccentric bolt that allows a "centerfire-type" firing pin for faster lock time and greater strength, AA walnut sporter stock with 20 LPI 4-point panel checkering and hand rubbed oil finish, 22 in. match grade sporter barrel with match chamber and Custom Sporter contour, 5 shot mag., steel grip cap, pillar bedding, bead blasted blue finish, adj. trigger, approx. 6 1/2 lbs. New 1999.

MSR $1,147	$975	$850	$750	$650	$550	$450	$350

Through 2002, all Kimber .22 cal. Classic rifles had an A grade claro walnut stock, 2-point checkering pattern, urethane finish, and straight barrel taper contour.

* **Classic Varmint** - .17 Mach 2 (new mid-2004) or .22 LR cal., similar to Classic, except has A walnut and 20 in. stainless fluted barrel in a heavy sporter contour. New 2003.

MSR $1,055	$925	$800	$700	$600	$500	$425	$375

* **Pro Varmint** - .17 Mach 2 (new mid-2004) or .22 LR cal., similar to Classic Varmint, except has grey laminate uncheckered stock, brush polished stainless 20 in. barrel with black flutes. New 2004.

MSR $1,108	$950	$825	$750	$650	$550	$450	$350

* **Custom Classic** - .22 LR cal., similar to Classic, except has 24 LPI wrap checkering, ebony forend tip and AAA walnut stock, 6.5 lbs. New 2003.

MSR $1,507	$1,300	$1,100	$875	$750	$650	$550	$475

SUPERAMERICA MODEL - .22 LR cal., top-of-the-line model with AAA claro walnut with 24 LPI full wrap checkering, hand rubbed oil finish, Custom Sporter barrel contour, ebony forend tip, cheekpiece and black recoil pad, 5 shot mag., 6 1/2 lbs. Limited mfg. beginning 2001.

MSR $1,865	$1,575	$1,300	$1,050	$900	$800	$700	$600

Through 2001, all Superamerica rifles had urethane finish and straight taper barrel contour.

* **Custom Match 25th Anniversary Ltd. Ed.** - .22 LR cal., similar to SuperAmerica model, except has AAA French walnut stock, black oxide matte finish barrel and receiver, steel buttplate, engraved grip cap, specially marked barrel and jeweled bolt. Limited production of 300 sequentially numbered rifles during 2004.

MSR $2,852	$2,325	$2,000	$1,700	$1,400	$1,100	$900	$750

SVT (SHORT VARMINT/TARGET) MODEL - .17 Mach 2 (new mid-2004) or .22 LR cal., 18 in. fluted stainless steel bull barrel, unwheckered grey laminate wood stock with high comb target design, matte blue action and satin stainless steel barrel, 5 shot mag., no sights, 7 1/2 lbs. New 1999.

MSR $1,007	$900	$775	$675	$575	$475	$375	$300

GRADING - PPGS™	100%	98%	95%	90%	80%	70%	60%

HS (HUNTER SILHOUETTE) MODEL

.22 LR cal., features 24 in. half-fluted medium sporter match grade barrel w/o sights, checkered walnut high comb Monte Carlo stock with hand rubbed oil finish, adj. trigger, matte blue finish, 7 lbs. New 1999.

MSR $915	$800	$675	$575	$500	$425	$350	$275

Through 2001, all HS Models had urethane finish.

MODEL 82C CLASSIC

.22 LR cal., 22 in. drilled and tapped receiver, repeater with 4 shot mag., checkered A claro walnut stock, polished and blue metal, 6 1/2 lbs. Mfg. 1995-99.

$775	$625	$550	$475	$400	$360	$330

Last MSR was $917.

The C suffix on this model designates manufacture by Kimber of America.

✳ **Stainless Classic** - .22 LR cal., features stainless steel barrel with matte blue action. Approx. 600 mfg. 1997-98.

$800	$650	$565

Last MSR was $968.

✳ **Varmint Stainless** - .22 LR cal., features 20 in. fluted stainless steel barrel, A claro walnut with 18 LPI side panel checkering. Approx. 1,000 mfg. 1995-98.

$825	$675	$575

Last MSR was $1,002.

MODEL 82C SVT

.22 LR cal., single shot, features 18 in. fluted heavy stainless barrel with uncheckered high comb target style walnut stock, matte blue action, 7 1/2 lbs. Mfg. 1997 only.

$675	$550	$495

Last MSR was $825.

SVT designates Short Varmint/Target.

MODEL 82C HS

while advertised during 1997, this model never went into production.

MODEL 82C SUPERAMERICA

.22 LR cal., 22 in. drilled and tapped barrel, 4 shot mag., AAA claro checkered walnut stock with steel pistol grip cap, polished and blue metal, 6 1/2 lbs. Mfg. 1993-99.

$1,275	$995	$875	$750	$650	$575	$400

Last MSR was $1,488.

MODEL 82C CUSTOM MATCH

.22 LR cal., features AA French walnut with 22 LPI wraparound checkering, steel Neidner-style buttplate, matte rust blue finish. Mfg. 1995-99.

$1,900	$1,525	$1,225	$975	$775	$650	$525

Last MSR was $2,158.

MODEL 82C SUPER CLASSIC

.22 LR cal., features AAA claro walnut with 18 LPI side panel checkering, polished and blue metal. Mfg. 1995-96.

$975	$875	$775	$675	$600	$550	$450

Last MSR was $1,090.

Centerfire Models

The models below feature a Mauser style action with controlled round feeding and extraction.

MODEL 84C SINGLE SHOT CLASSIC

while advertised during 1996-97, this model never went into production.

MODEL 84C SINGLE SHOT SUPERAMERICA

while advertised during 1996-97, this model never went into production.

MODEL 84C SINGLE SHOT VARMINT STAINLESS

while advertised during 1997, this model never went into production.

MODEL 84C SINGLE SHOT VARMINT - .17 Rem. or .223 Rem. cal., features 24 (first 200 rifles only), or 25 in. stainless match grade fluted barrel with recess crown, matte blue receiver finish, checkered A claro walnut stock with beavertail forend, 7 1/2 lbs. Mfg. 1997-99.

	$895	$765	$625

Last MSR was $1,032.

Add $150 for .17 Rem. cal. (less than 100 mfg.).

MODEL 84M - .22-250 Rem., .204 Ruger (new 2004), .223 Rem. (new 2004), .243 Win. (new 2004), .260 Rem., .308 Win., or 7mm-08 Rem. cal., true Mauser action, much improved version of the Model 84C, longer and stronger receiver, 2 position Model 70 type safety, 22 in. light sporter (Classic), 24 in. heavy stainless steel fluted (.308 Win. cal., LongMaster Classic, new 2002), 26 in. heavy stainless steel fluted sporter (Varmint), or 26 in. stainless bull (.22-250 Rem. cal., LongMaster VT) match grade barrel, match grade trigger, 5 shot mag. with sculpted steel floorplate), grey/black laminate target stock with high comb and extended pistol grip (LongMaster VT) or checkered walnut stock and forend, 5 lbs., 10 oz. (Sporter), 7 lbs., 5 oz. (Varmint and LongMaster Classic), or 10 lbs (LongMaster VT). New 2001.

A three position Win. Model 70 type safety became a standard feature on all Kimber 84M rifles in early 2004.

✷ **Model 84M Classic** - .243 Win., .260 Rem., .308 Win. or 7mm-08 Rem. cal.

MSR $945	$850	$725	$625	$525	$450	$400	$350

✷ **Model 84M Longmaster Classic** - .223 Rem., .243 Win., or .308 Win. cal.

MSR $1,038	$925	$775	$675	$575	$500	$450	$400

✷ **Model 84M Longmaster VT** - .22-250 Rem. cal. only.

MSR $1,162	$985	$850	$725	$625	$525	$450	$400

✷ **Model 84M Varmint** - .204 Ruger or .22-250 Rem. cal., features 26 in. heavy stainless steel fluted barrel.

MSR $1,001	$895	$775	$675	$575	$500	$450	$400

✷ **Model 84M Pro Varmint** - .22-250 Rem., .223 Rem., or .204 Ruger cal., similar to Model 84M Repeater, except has grey laminate uncheckered stock, brush polished 24 in. stainless steel barrel with black flutes. New 2004.

MSR $1,115	$950	$850	$750	$650	$550	$450	$350

MODEL 84M SUPERAMERICA - .223 Rem., .243 Win., .260 Rem., 7mm-08 Rem., or .308 Win. cal., similar to Model 84M Repeater, except has 24 LPI wrap checkering, ebony forend tip, AAA walnut, highly polished blue action and barrel. New 2003.

MSR $1,828	$1,575	$1,350	$1,150	$925	$825	$725	$625

MODEL 84M MONTANA - .243 Win., .260 Rem., 7mm-08 Rem., or .308 Win. cal., similar to Model 84M Repeater, except has synthetic stock and satin stainless steel barreled action, 5 lbs. 2 oz. New 2003.

MSR $1,124	$975	$850	$675

MODEL 84M LONGMASTER PRO - .22-250 Rem. or .308 Win. cal., similar to Longmaster VT, except has synthetic stock, 24 (.308 Win. cal.) or 26 (.22-250 Rem. cal.) in. brush polished stainless bull barrel with black flutes.

While this model was cataloged during 2003 with an MSR of $1,189, it never went into production.

MODEL 8400 CLASSIC - .270 WSM, 7mm WSM, .300 WSM, or .325 WSM (new 2005) cal., A walnut stock, 20 LPI panel checkering, 3-position Model 70 type safety, 24 in. sporter match grade blue barrel, match grade adj. trigger, also available in left-hand. New 2003.

MSR $1,080	$925	$750	$650	$550	$450	$400	$350

While a left-hand version of this model was cataloged during 2003, they were never produced.

GRADING - PPGS™	100%	98%	95%	90%	80%	70%	60%

✳ *Model 8400 SuperAmerica* - .270 WSM, 7mm WSM, .300 WSM, or .325 WSM (new 2005) cal., similar to Model 8400 Classic, except has AAA walnut stock, 24 LPI panel checkering, ebony forend tip, highly polished blue action, and 24 in. custom sporter barrel. New 2003.

MSR $2,023	$1,675	$1,450	$1,200	$950	$850	$725	$625

✳ *Model 8400 Montana* - .270 WSM, 7mm WSM, .300 WSM, or .325 WSM (new 2005) cal., similar to Model 8400 Classic, except has synthetic stock and 24 in. satin stainless steel custom sporter barrel, 6 lbs., 2 oz. New 2003.

MSR $1,220	$995	$850	$725

MODEL K770 CLASSIC - while advertised during 1997, this model never went into production. Prototypes only.

MODEL K770 SUPER AMERICA - while advertised during 1997, this model never went into production. Prototypes only.

Mauser 96 Sporters

MODEL 96 SPORTER - .308 Win. cal., features M-96 action with stainless steel fluted heavy barrel. Mfg. 1995-97.

	$450	$415	$365

Last MSR was $520.

During 1995-96, Kimber began sporterizing the Swedish Mauser Model 96 military surplus rifles. They featured stainless steel fluted barrels and a black synthetic Ramline stock, receivers were drilled and tapped to accept Weaver scope mounts, bead blasted bluing, and original reprofiled military bolt. The Sporter configuration included .243 Win., 6.5x55mm, or .308 Win. cal., while the heavy fluted barrel models were available in .22-250 Rem. or .308 Win. (Varmint or Heavy Barrel). Retail prices ranged from $340-$415 for the Standard Sporter, while the Varmint/Heavy barrel variation was priced at approx. $510. Sporter variations were also available as a combo package with scope and hardshell case - add approx. $30.

Mauser 98 Sporters

MODEL 98 SPORTER - .220 Swift (100 mfg.), .257 Roberts (100 mfg.), .270 Win., .280 Rem. (100 mfg.), .30-06, .300 Win. Mag., .338 Win. Mag., or 7mm Rem. Mag. cal., features Mauser M-98 action with stainless match grade fluted barrel, choice of synthetic or claro walnut stock, and Warne bases, matte black finish receiver. Mfg. 1996-98.

	$465	$425	$375

Last MSR was $535.

Add $25 for Mag. cals.
Add $100 for Claro walnut stock.

✳ *Mauser Model 98 Sporter Matte* - .300 Win. Mag., .338 Win. Mag., or 7mm Rem. Mag. cal., features 25 in. non-fluted sporter barrel, synthetic stock, and Weaver style bases. Disc. 1998.

$275	$250	$225	$200	$185	$170	$155

Last MSR was $339.

SHOTGUNS: O/U

AUGUSTA SERIES - 12 ga., 2 3/4 (Trap & Skeet) or 3 (Sporting & Field) in. chambers, BOSS type boxlock action with shallow frame, blue (Trap & Skeet) or polished metal (Field & Sporting) frame, ejectors, SST, tang safety with ejector, 26-34 in. vent. barrel lengths with VR backbored to .736 in., available in Field, Sporting, Skeet, and Trap variations, beavertail or Schnabel forend, Pachmayr decelerator recoil pad, 7 lbs., 2 oz-7 lbs., 13 oz. Mfg. in Italy by Investarm beginning 2002, limited delivery began early 2003.

MSR $5,676	$4,750	$4,250	$3,750	$3,250	$2,750	$2,250	$1,850

GRADING - PPGS™	100%	98%	95%	90%	80%	70%	60%

SHOTGUNS: SxS

VALIER SERIES - 20 ga., sidelock, 26 or 28 in. barrels, hand checkered Turkish walnut straight grip English stock, DT, fixed chokes, hand engraved blue or case colored finish, extractors (Grade I) or ejectors (Grade II), mfg. in Turkey. Importation began 2005.

MSR $4,200	$3,750	$3,300	$2,950	$2,500	$2,100	$1,650	$1,300

Add $800 for Grade II model.

KIMBER OF OREGON, INC.

Previous manufacturer located in Clackamas, OR circa 1980-1991.

Kimber of Oregon went out of business with its final sale in 1991. Rare models are starting to attract premiums already. In some models, magazines for these fine quality rifles are getting extremely hard to find with healthy premiums being asked. Once "B" suffix models were introduced, older manufacture started being referred to as "A" models.

PISTOLS: BOLT ACTION

PREDATOR MODEL - .221 Fireball, .223 Rem., 6mm TCU (disc. 1987), 7mm TCU, or 6x45mm (disc. 1987) cal., single shot Model 84 action with shortened 14 7/8 in. barrel, scope use only, one piece deluxe walnut stock with contoured pistol grip, 5 1/4 lbs., rare cals. will command a premium. Approx. 200 mfg. 1987-88 only.

* **Hunter Grade** - AA Claro walnut without checkering. Disc. 1988.

	$1,995	$1,750	$1,500	$1,250	$950	$800	$700

Last MSR was $995.

* **Super Grade** - similar to Hunter Grade, except has select French walnut with ebony forend tip and 22 lines/in. checkering. Disc. 1988.

	$3,000	$2,650	$2,250	$2,000	$1,750	$1,400	$1,250

Last MSR was $1,195.

RIFLES: BOLT ACTION

Note: No suffix in Kimber models denotes pre-1986 action design, "B" suffix models incorporate the new action with improved cocking system, faster lock time, swept-back bolt design, improved recoil lug, and are right-handed. Pre '83 rifles had no bolt release.

Add $175 for skeleton grip cap on models listed below.
Add $275 for skeleton buttplate on models listed below.
Add $100 for checkered bolt handle on models listed below.
Add $300 for raised quarter rib.
Add $100 for forend tip.
Extra fancy walnut on any Kimber will always command a premium.

Model 82, .22 Cal. Series

Add $200-$500 for .22 Hornet or .22 Mag. cal. on the models listed below, depending on the variation.

STANDARD MODEL 82 - .22 LR, .22 Mag., or .22 Hornet cal., Mauser type rear locking bolt action, 3 (.22 Hornet), 4 (.22 Mag.), or 5 (.22 LR) shot mag., 22 in. (Sporter) or 24 in. (Varmint) barrel, deluxe claro walnut, steel buttplate, rocker style safety, right or left-hand action, 6 1/2 lbs.

* **Classic Model** - disc. 1988.

	$885	$745	$650	$525	$450	$375	$335

Last MSR was $750.

GRADING - PPGS™	100%	98%	95%	90%	80%	70%	60%

✳ *Cascade Model* - Monte Carlo cheekpiece, disc. 1988.

	100%	98%	95%	90%	80%	70%	60%
	$885	$745	$650	$525	$450	$375	$335

Add $350 for Custom Cascade Model, with higher grade walnut, ebony forend tip, and Niedner style buttplate (34 mfg).

✳ *Custom Classic Model* - higher grade claro walnut, ebony forearm tip, Niedner style steel buttplate. Disc. 1988.

	100%	98%	95%	90%	80%	70%	60%
	$1,050	$900	$750	$675	$500	$475	$425

Last MSR was $995.

Add 25% for .218 Bee cal. (approx. 130 standard mfg.).

Add 10% for .22 Mag. cal.

Add 100% for .218 Mashburn mfg.

Also available in .25-20 (approx. 200 mfg. single shot only) cals. Mfg. 1985 only (retail price was $695).

✳ *Deluxe Grade* - .22 LR cal. only, similar to Custom Classic Model, AA walnut, 5 or 10 (optional) shot mag., 6 1/2 lbs. Mfg. 1989-90 only.

	100%	98%	95%	90%	80%	70%	60%
	$1,050	$925	$725	$625	$525	$450	$395

Last MSR was $1,195.

A left-hand variation was also available at no extra charge, but had limited mfg. in 1990.

SPORTER MODEL

SPORTER MODEL - .17 Ackley Hornet (approx. 9 mfg.), .17 K. Hornet (approx. 88 mfg.), or .22 LR cal., includes Model 82A action, 22 in. sporter weight barrel, 4 shot mag., round top receiver with bases, checkered stock and forend, 6 1/2 lbs. Mfg. 1991 only.

	100%	98%	95%	90%	80%	70%	60%
	$940	$785	$675	$575	$500	$450	$395

Last MSR was $995.

Add approx. 100% for .17 K Hornet or .17 Ackley Hornet cals.

RIMFIRE VARMINTER - .22 LR cal. only, Model 82A action, free floating 25 in. medium heavy barrel, laminated stock, 5 or optional 10 shot mag., rubber buttpad, 8 1/4 lbs. Mfg. 1990-91 only.

	100%	98%	95%	90%	80%	70%	60%
	$895	$775	$650	$575	$500	$450	$400

Last MSR was $795.

HUNTER GRADE - .22 LR cal. only, similar to Rimfire Varminter with Super America configured barrel and action with low glare metal finish. Mfg. 1990 only.

	100%	98%	95%	90%	80%	70%	60%
	$785	$625	$535	$455	$395	$340	$295

Last MSR was $895.

MINI CLASSIC - .22 LR cal. only, Model 82 action, 18 in. barrel, steel buttplate, sling swivels. Mfg. 1988 only.

	100%	98%	95%	90%	80%	70%	60%
	$700	$550	$500	$450	$400	$500	$300

Last MSR was $795.

GOVERNMENT MODEL 82A TARGET - .22 LR cal. only, specifically designed for U.S. Army training, 25 in. heavy target barrel including scope blocks, oversized stock, some rifles are "star" marked indicating an accuracy guarantee, 10 3/4 lbs. Mfg. 1987-91.

	100%	98%	95%	90%	80%	70%	60%
	$735	$600	$515	$460	$410	$350	$325

Last MSR was $595.

20,000 rifles were mfg. 1987-1989 to fill the initial U.S. government contract. U.S. property marked guns do exist in private hands - all within a low serial number range (watch markings carefully). Commercial guns were manufactured for the private sector with values listed.

ALL AMERICAN MATCH - .22 LR cal. only, precision rifled 25 in. free floating target grade barrel, stock is adj. both vertically and for length of pull, fully adj. single stage trigger, approx. 9 lbs. Mfg. 1990-91 only.

	100%	98%	95%	90%	80%	70%	60%
	$790	$625	$540	$465	$400	$340	$295

Last MSR was $895.

GRADING - PPGS™	100%	98%	95%	90%	80%	70%	60%

CONTINENTAL - .22 LR, .22 Mag., or .22 Hornet cal., Sporter action only, full length Mannlicher stock, open sights, deluxe walnut. Add $200 for .22 Mag. or .22 Hornet cal. New 1987.

This model was only available as a special order with prices on request from the factory.

✽ **Super Continental** - similar to Continental, except has AAA claro walnut with 22 lines/in. checkering. Mfg. 1987-88.

	$1,695	$1,500	$1,375	$1,250	$1,000	$875	$750

Last MSR was $1,465.

Add 100% if model is one of three known laminated stock variations with cheekpieces that were mfg., all in .22 LR cal.

S SERIES - .22 LR (535 mfg.), .22 Hornet (354 mfg.) or .22 Mag. (88 mfg.) cal., top-of-the-line limited production model, grooved for scope mounting, Neidner check-ered steel buttplate, best quality walnut, continental cheekpiece, ebony forend tip, Sporter configuration only. Mfg. early 1980s.

	$1,400	$1,200	$1,000	$825	$675	$550	$450

SUPER AMERICA - top-of-the-line model, includes detachable scope mounts, Nied-ner checkered steel buttplate and best quality walnut, cheekpiece and ebony forend tip added after 1983, available in Sporter configuration only. This model was disc. 1988, and reintroduced 1990-91.

	$1,400	$1,200	$1,000	$825	$675	$550	$450

Last MSR was $1,295.

✽ **Super Grade** - similar to Super America, AAA walnut, beaded cheekpiece, 5 or 10 (optional) shot mag., 6 1/2 lbs. Mfg. 1989 only.

	$1,250	$1,000	$900	$750	$675	$550	$500

Last MSR was $1,295.

Add a small premium for 10 shot mag.

CUSTOM MATCH - .22 LR or .22 Mag. cal., limited edition of 217 rifles, match dimension chamber, French walnut stock with 22 L.P.I. checkering, rust blue finish, other custom rifle features. Introduced 1984.

	$2,500	$2,000	$1,500	$1,250	$1,000	$850	$750

Add $500 for .22 Mag. cal.

BROWNELL - .22 LR cal., only 500 mfg. to commemorate the late Leonard Brownell, Mannlicher style extra deluxe claro walnut stock. Mfg. 1986 only.

	$2,000	$1,800	$1,500				

Last MSR was $1,500.

CENTENNIAL - .22 LR cal. only, limited edition (100 rifles) to commemorate centen-nial of .22 LR cal., includes hand-picked checkered walnut, moderate engraving, special Wilson Arms match barrel, skeleton buttplate and other refinements, serial numbered C1-C100. Mfg. 1987 only.

	$2,875	$2,500	$1,875				

Last MSR was $2,950.

TENTH ANNIVERSARY ISSUE - .22 LR cal., limited edition, French walnut stock featuring slim forend design with shadowed cheekpiece, Neidner steel buttplate and other refinements. Mfg. 1989 only.

	$1,800	$1,600	$1,400				

Add $100 for matte finish.

Model 84 Centerfire Series

Model 84 caliber rarity is as follows: .222 Rem. and .223 Rem. are common. 6x45mm or 47mm, .221 Fireball, .17 Rem., and .17 Mach IV are less common and more desirable. .223 Rem. Mag. is rare, while 5.6x50mm is extremely rare.

GRADING - PPGS™	100%	98%	95%	90%	80%	70%	60%

Add $75 for forend tip - option A. Add $300 for iron sights - option B. Add $100 for checkered bolt handle - option C. Add $200 for skeleton grip cap - option D. Add $300 for skeleton buttplate - option G. Add $250-$300 for 3-position safety in this series.

STANDARD MODEL 84 - .17 Rem., .17 Mach IV (disc. 1987), 6x45 or 47mm (disc. 1987), 5.6x50mm (disc. 1987), .221 Fireball, .222 Rem., .222 Rem. Mag. (disc. 1987), or .223 Rem. cal., "Mini-Mauser" type head locking bolt action, 5 shot mag., 22 (Sporter) or 24 (Varmint) in. barrel, deluxe Claro walnut, steel buttplate, rocker style safety, 6 1/2 lbs.

* *Classic Model* - disc. 1988.

	$1,095	$1,000	$875	$750	$600	$500	$400

Last MSR was $885.

Add $55 for disc. Cascade Model (Monte Carlo cheekpiece).
Add 20% for left-hand action.

Also available in left hand action in .22 Hornet, .222 Rem., .223 Rem., 6x45mm, 6x47mm, .17 Rem., and .17 Mach IV (very limited mfg.).

CUSTOM CLASSIC MODEL - higher grade Claro walnut, ebony forearm tip, Niedner style steel buttplate. Disc. 1988.

	$1,400	$1,200	$1,000	$825	$675	$550	$450

Last MSR was $1,130.

* *Deluxe Grade Sporter* - .17 Rem., .221 Rem., or .223 Rem. cal., Mauser action, AA walnut, similar to Custom Classic Model, 6 1/4 lbs. Mfg. 1989-90.

	$1,400	$1,200	$1,000	$825	$675	$550	$450

Last MSR was $1,295.

Also available in left-hand action (.223 Rem. cal. only), limited mfg.

CONTINENTAL - .221 Fireball (extremely rare, mfg. 1988 only) .222 Rem. or .223 Rem. cal., Sporter action only, full length Mannlicher stock, open sights, deluxe walnut. New 1987.

Extreme rarity precludes accurate price evaluation on this model.

* *Super Continental* - similar to Continental (same cals.), except has AAA Claro walnut with 22 lines/in. checkering. Mfg. 1987-88.

	$2,100	$1,850	$1,500	$1,250	$1,000	$800	$700

Last MSR was $1,600.

Add 100% if model is one of three known laminated stocks that were mfg. in .223 Rem. cal.

HUNTER GRADE - .17 Rem., .222 Rem., or .223 Rem. cal., laminated stock, Super America configured action and barrel with low glare metal finish. Mfg. 1990 only.

	$995	$875	$750	$650	$550	$475	$400

Last MSR was $995.

SPORTER - .17 Rem., .22 Hornet, .222 Rem., .22-250 Rem., or .223 Rem. cal., 22 in. sporter weight barrel, A grade Claro walnut, round top receiver with bases, 4 shot mag., hand checkering. Mfg. 1991 only.

	$1,020	$850	$725	$625	$550	$500	$495

Last MSR was $1,095.

This model was available in either right or left-hand action.

* *Big Bore Sporter* - .250 Savage or .35 Rem. cal., similar action to Sporter Model, except has 3/4 in. red Pachmayr Decelerator recoil pad. Mfg. 1991 only.

Extreme rarity precludes accurate price evaluation on this model - consult an expert when buying/selling this model. This model was available in either right or left-hand action.

Last MSR was $1,095.

GRADING - PPGS™	100%	98%	95%	90%	80%	70%	60%

SUPER AMERICA/SUPER GRADE - .17 Rem., .17 MK IV, .221 Fireball, .22 Hornet, .222 Rem., .222 Rem. Mag., .22-250 Rem., .223 Rem., 5.6x56mm, or 6x47mm cal., 22 in. sporter weight barrel, top-of-the-line, with detachable scope mounts, available in Sporter configuration only, cheekpiece and ebony forend tip added after 1983, 4 shot mag., right or left hand action. Disc. 1988, reintroduced 1990-91.

	$1,695	$1,500	$1,250	$1,000	$850	$725	$675

Last MSR was $1,495.

Be careful when buying rare cals. and/or options on this model.

✳ *Big Bore Super America* - .250 Savage or .35 Rem. cal., similar action to Super America Model, except has 3/4 in. red Pachmayr Decelerator recoil pad. Mfg. 1991 only.

	$2,100	$1,775	$1,425	$1,125	$925	$800	$700

Last MSR was $1,495.

CUSTOM MATCH - .222 Rem. or .223 Rem. cal., limited edition of 200 rifles, match dimension chamber, French walnut stock with 22 L.P.I. checkering, rust blue finish, other custom rifle features. Introduced 1986.

	$2,500	$2,000	$1,800	$1,500	$1,100	$1,000	$750

TENTH ANNIVERSARY ISSUE - .223 Rem. cal., limited edition, French walnut stock featuring slim forend design with shadowed cheekpiece, 22 in. barrel, roundtop receiver with mounts, Neidner steel buttplate and other refinements. Mfg. 1989 only.

	$1,995	$1,650	$1,250

Add $100 for matte finish.

ULTRA VARMINTER - .17 Rem., .22 Hornet (rare, new 1991), .221 Rem. (disc. 1990), .222 Rem., .22-250 Rem. (rare), or .223 Rem. cal., 24 in. medium weight stainless steel barrel, laminated birch stock, plain buttstock, right- or left-hand action, 7 3/4 lbs. Mfg. 1989-91 only.

	$1,600	$1,300	$1,175	$1,000	$850	$750	$675

Last MSR was $1,295.

✳ *Super Varminter* - similar to Ultra Varminter except has steel barrel, AAA walnut stock with beaded cheekpiece, 7 1/4 lbs. Mfg. 1989-91 only.

	$2,000	$1,850	$1,500	$1,200	$975	$775	$675

Last MSR was $1,495.

Model 89 Centerfire, Big Game Series

Fewer than 5,000 Model 89 BGRs were mfg. Note: fancy wood is harder to find in Model 89s.

MODEL 89 BGR - .270 Win., .280 Rem., 7mm Rem. Mag., .30-06, .300 Win. Mag., .338 Win. Mag., or .375 H&H cal., new action incorporates features from both Mauser 98 and Win. pre-64 Model 70, three position safety, 22 or 24 in. barrel, matte blue finish will command a premium. Introduced late 1988.

✳ *Classic Model* - deluxe Claro walnut checkered 18 lines/in. with steel buttplate. Disc. 1988.

	$875	$725	$600	$500	$415	$350	$300

Last MSR was $985.

Add $200 for .375 H&H cal.
Add $100 for matte finish.

✳ *Custom Classic Model* - higher grade Claro walnut, ebony forearm tip, Niedner style steel buttplate. Disc. 1988.

	$1,125	$950	$775	$650	$525	$450	$375

Last MSR was $1,230.

Add $200 for .375 H&H cal.

GRADING - PPGS™	100%	98%	95%	90%	80%	70%	60%

DELUXE GRADE - similar to Custom Classic Model, round top receiver with Model 70 scope mount hole configuration, AA walnut stock with ebony forend tip and rubber recoil pad (no cheekpiece), 22 or 24 in. barrel, 7 1/2-8 1/2 lbs. New 1989.

* *Featherweight Barrel Model* - .257 Roberts (rare), .25-06 Rem., 7x57mm (rare, disc. 1990), .270 Win., .280 Rem., or .30-06 cal., 5 shot mag., 22 in. Featherweight barrel, right-hand action only, 7 1/2 lbs. Disc. 1990.

	$1,600	$1,225	$1,000	$850	$700	$600	$525

Last MSR was $1,795.

> **Add 25% for 7x57mm cal.**
> **Add $470 for Super America Grade with square bridge, dovetail receiver.**
> **Add $100 for matte finish.**
> The Super America Grade will accept Kimber double lever scope mounts and has one grade better wood than the Deluxe Grade with beaded cheekpiece.

* *Medium-weight Barrel Model* - .300 Win. Mag., .300 H&H (rare, disc. 1990), .300 Wby. Mag. (very rare, new 1991), .338 Win. Mag., .35 Whelen (rare, disc. 1990), or 7mm Rem. Mag. cal., 3 shot mag., 24 in. medium-weight barrel, right-hand action only, 7 3/4-8 1/2 lbs. Disc. 1990.

	$1,675	$1,250	$1,025	$875	$725	$625	$550

Last MSR was $1,895.

> **Add a premium for rare cals.**
> **Add $495 for Super America Grade with square bridge, dovetail receiver.**
> **Add $100 for matte finish.**
> The Super America Grade will accept Kimber double lever scope mounts and has one grade better wood than the Deluxe Grade with beaded cheekpiece.

* *Heavy-weight Barrel Model* - .375 H&H Mag. cal., 3 shot mag., 24 in. heavy weight barrel, right-hand action only, 9 lbs. Disc. 1990.

	$2,000	$1,750	$1,500	$1,250	$1,000	$800	$700

Last MSR was $1,995.

> **Add $495 for Super America Grade with square bridge, dovetail receiver.**
> **Add $100 for matte finish.**
> The Super America Grade will accept Kimber double lever scope mounts and has one grade better wood than the Deluxe Grade with beaded cheekpiece.

SPORTER MODEL - same cals. as Deluxe/Super America Models, 22 in. featherweight or 24 in. medium or heavy barrel, double square bridge dovetail receiver, A grade Claro walnut stock with 3/4 in. red Pachmayr Decelerator recoil pad (Mag. cals. only with 24 in. barrel). Mfg. 1991 only.

	$1,395	$1,050	$900	$775	$650	$500	$450

Last MSR was $1,595.

> **Add $100 for medium Magnum action.**
> **Add $200 for heavy Magnum action (.375 H&H and .458 Win. Mag. cals.).**

HUNTER GRADE - .270 Win., .30-06, .300 Win. Mag., .338 Win. Mag., or 7mm Rem. Mag. cal., laminated stock, Super America configured action and barrel with low glare metal finish. Mfg. 1990-91 only.

	$1,325	$1,025	$895	$750	$625	$525	$450

Last MSR was $1,495.

> **Add $100 for Mag. cals.**

SUPER GRADE - similar to Super America Model, square top frame, AAA walnut, 22 or 24 in. barrel, plain buttstock, 7 1/2-8 1/2 lbs. Mfg. 1989 only.

	$1,575	$1,325	$995	$825	$695	$550	$500

Last MSR was $1,495.

> **Add $100 for .375 H&H cal.**
> **Add $100 for matte blue metal finish.**
> The 24 in. barrel was available in Mag. cals. only.

GRADING - PPGS™	100%	98%	95%	90%	80%	70%	60%

LIMITED WILDLIFE EDITION SERIES - series of 5 guns, includes .257 Roberts (Whitetail Deer Edition), .270 Win. (Mule Deer Edition), .338 Win. Mag. (Rocky Mt. Elk Edition), 7mm Rem. Mag. (Big Horn Sheep Edition), and .375 H&H (Grizzly Bear Edition) cals. included, hand select walnut, special Shilen Rifle barrel, gold plated trigger, receivers are stamped "Wildlife Edition," special prefix serialization, only 25 sets were to be manufactured in 1991 only, includes rings, swivels, and hard case.

> While advertised, only one .270 Win. Mule Deer model was mfg. Retail price was scheduled to be $3,595.

MODEL 89 AFRICAN - .375 H&H (rare), .416 Rigby (most common) cal., or .505 Gibbs (rare) cal., Magnum action, 24 in. heavy barrel, AA English walnut stock with beaded cheekpiece and rubber recoil pad, includes twin recoil cross bolts, express sights on quarter rib, drop box magazine, 10-10 1/2 lbs. Mfg. 1990-91 only.

		$5,500	$4,500	$4,000	$3,500	$2,750	$2,250	$1,650

Last MSR was $3,595.

.375 H&H or .505 Gibbs cal. will command a premium.

KIMEL INDUSTRIES, INC.

Previously manufactured until late 1994 by A.A. Arms located in Monroe, NC. Previously distributed by Kimel Industries, Inc. located in Matthews, NC.

CARBINES

AR-9 CARBINE - 9mm Para. cal., carbine variation of the AP-9 with 16 1/2 in. barrel, 20 shot mag., and steel rod folding stock. Mfg. 1991-94.

	$550	$475	$425	$365	$315	$275	$220

Last MSR was $384.

PISTOLS: SEMI-AUTO

AP-9 PISTOL - 9mm Para. cal., paramilitary design, blowback action with bolt knob on left side of receiver, 5 in. barrel with vent. shroud, front mounted 10 (C/B 1994) or 20* shot detachable mag., black matte finish, adj. front sight, 3 lbs. 7 oz. Mfg. 1989-94.

	$425	$365	$325	$275	$250	$225	$200

Last MSR was $279.

* *Mini AP-9* - compact variation of the AP-9 Model with 3 in. barrel, blue or nickel finish. Mfg. 1991-94.

	$475	$425	$350	$295	$275	$250	$225

Last MSR was $273.

* *Target AP-9* - target variation of the AP-9 with 12 in. match barrel with shroud, blue finish only. Mfg. 1991-94.

	$495	$462	$375	$325	$295	$275	$250

Last MSR was $294.

* *P-95* - similar to AP-9, except without barrel shroud and is supplied with 5 shot mag., parts are interchangeable with AP-9. Mfg. 1990-91 only.

	$350	$295	$265	$235	$195	$165	$13

Last MSR was $250.

KING'S GUN WORKS, INC.

Current custom handgun and accessories manufacturer established during 1949 and currently located in Glendale, CA. Dealer and consumer direct sales.

King's Gun Works manufactures a complete line of custom pistols patterned after Colt M-1911, in addition to many related accessories and/or after-market parts. Please contact the company directly for current information and prices (see Trademark Index listing).

GRADING - PPGS™	100%	98%	95%	90%	80%	70%	60%

KINTREK, INC.

Previous rifle manufacturer located in Owensboro, KY.

RIFLES: SEMI-AUTO

BULLPUP MODEL - .22 LR cal., bullpup configuration, hinged dust cover, clear Ram-Line type coil spring mag., black synthetic thumbhole stock, A-2 type front/rear sight. Disc.

	$275	$225	$200	$180	$160	$140	$120

KLEINGUENTHER FIREARMS CO.

Previous custom rifle manufacturer located in Seguin, TX until circa 2001. The original KDF Co. was started by Mr. Robert Kleinguenther and sold in the early 1980s. Mr. Kleinguenther then started a new company called Kleinguenther Firearms Co.

RIFLES: BOLT ACTION

Values listed below are for base model only with no additional customer special order options. Mr. Keinguenther also custom built rifles utilizing customer actions.

BOLT ACTION RIFLE - various cals., individual customer special order rifle with a variety of options, guns are guaranteed to shoot 1/2 M.O.A., choice of actions, various weights.

* **Winchester Model 70 Custom**

	$975	$800	$675	$575	$500	$450	$400

Last MSR was $975.

* **Sako Action** - various cals., newer guns feature the ballistic recoil muzzle brake system (60-70% recoil reduction), most newer stocks are mfg. out of high tech laminated wood with 28-32 resin coated panels.

	$1,550	$1,325	$1,100	$950	$825	$725	$625

Last MSR was $1,750.

    Add $155 for ballistic recoil muzzle brake system.

* **K-15**

	$1,375	$1,100	$950	$800	$675	$575	$500

Last MSR was $1,375.

KNIGHT'S MANUFACTURING COMPANY

Current manufacturer established in 1993, and located in Titusville, FL. Previously located in Vero Beach, FL. Dealer and consumer direct sales.

RIFLES: SEMI-AUTO

Some of the models listed below were also available in pre-ban configurations. Current mfg. is shipped with 9 shot (.308 Win. cal.) or 10 shot (.223 Rem. cal.) mag.

STONER SR-15 M-5 RIFLE - .223 Rem. cal., 20 in. standard weight barrel, flip-up low profile rear sight, two-stage target trigger, 7.6 lbs. New 1997.

MSR $1,705	$1,500	$1,225	$1,025	$900	$825	$725	$650

* **Stoner SR-15 M-4 Carbine** - similar to SR-15 rifle, except has 16 in. barrel, choice of fixed synthetic or non-collapsible buttstock. New 1997.

MSR $1,575	$1,400	$1,175	$950	$850	$775	$700	$650

    Add $100 for non-collapsible buttstock (SR-15 M-4 K-Carbine, disc. 2001).

* **Stoner SR-15 URX E3 Carbine** - features 16 in. free floating barrel with URX forearm, E3 type rounded lug improved bolt. New 2004.

MSR $1,939	$1,750	$1,525	$1,225	$995	$875	$775	$675

GRADING - PPGS™	100%	98%	95%	90%	80%	70%	60%

STONER SR-15 MATCH RIFLE - .223 Rem. cal., features flattop upper receiver with 20 in. match grade stainless steel free floating barrel with RAS forend, two-stage match trigger, 7.9 lbs. New 1997.

MSR $1,850	$1,650	$1,425	$1,150	$950	$850	$750	$700

STONER SR-25 SPORTER - .308 Win. cal., 20 in. lightweight barrel, AR-15 configuration with carrying handle, 5, 10, or 20 (disc. per C/B 1994) shot detachable mag., less than 2 MOA guaranteed, non-glare finish, 8.8 lbs. Mfg. 1993-97.

	$2,650	$2,250	$1,900	$1,600	$1,300	$1,000	$850

Last MSR was $2,995.

* **RAS Stoner Carbine (SR-25 Carbine)** - 16 in. free floating barrel, grooved non-slip handguard, removable carrying handle, 7 3/4 lbs. New 1995.

MSR $3,495	$3,025	$2,550	$2,125	$1,750	$1,500	$1,250	$1,000

Subtract 10% if w/o RAS.

In 2003, the Rail Adapter System (RAS) became standard on this model.

SR-25 RAS MATCH - similar to SR-25 Standard, except has 24 in. free floating match barrel and flat-top receiver, less than 1 MOA guaranteed, RAS became standard 2004, 10 3/4 lbs. New 1993.

MSR $3,629	$3,125	$2,625	$2,175	$1,775	$1,500	$1,250	$1,000

Subtract approx. $50 if w/o Rail Adapter System (RAS).

Over 3,000 SR-25s have been made to date.

* **SR-25 Lightweight Match** - features 20 in. medium contour free floating barrel, 9 1/2 lbs. Mfg. 1995-2004.

	$2,875	$2,450	$2,125	$1,750	$1,500	$1,250	$1,000

Last MSR was $3,244.

Add $51 for Rail Adapter System (RAS).

SR-25 MK11 MOD O CIVILIAN DELUXE SYSTEM PACKAGE - .308 Win. cal., consumer variation of the Navy Model Mark Eleven, Mod O, w/o sound supressor, includes Leupold 3.5-10X scope, 20 in. military grade match barrel, backup sights, cell-foam case and other accessories. New 2003.

MSR $8,245	$7,500	$6,825	$6,150	$5,550	$5,000	$4,500	$4,000

SR-25 MK11 MATCH RIFLE - .308 Win. cal., includes MK11 Mod O features and 20 in. heavy barrel. New 2004.

MSR $5,825	$5,175	$4,775	$4,400	$3,750	$3,150	$2,700	$2,350

SR-25 MK11 CARBINE - .308 Win. cal., includes MK11 Mod O features and 16 in. match grade stainless steel barrel with muzzle brake, URX 4x4 rail forend, 4-position buttstock. New 2005.

MSR $6,099	$5,500	$4,950	$4,550	$3,875	$3,250	$2,800	$2,450

SR-25 BR CARBINE - .308 Win. cal., similar to SR-25 MK11 Carbine, except has chrome lined steel barrel. New 2005.

MSR $5,845	$5,225	$4,775	$4,400	$3,750	$3,150	$2,700	$2,350

"DAVID TUBB" COMPETITION MATCH RIFLE - .260 Rem. or .308 Win. cal., incorporates refinements by David Tubb, top-of-the-line competition match rifle, including adj. and rotating buttstock pad. Mfg. 1998 only.

	$5,200	$4,000	$3,600	$3,150	$2,700	$2,300	$1,995

Last MSR was $5,995.

STONER SR-50 - .50 BMG cal., features high strength materials and lightweight design, fully locked breech and two lug rotary breech bolt, horizontal 5 shot box mag., tubular receiver supports a removable barrel, approx. 31 lbs. Limited mfg. 2000, non-commercial sales only.

Last MSR was $6,995.

KODIAK CO.

Previous manufacturer located in North Haven, CT circa 1963-66.

Kodiak Co. was in business for only a short time. They produced the first .22 Mag. semi-auto rifle (Model 260), as well as a centerfire bolt action (Model 158 Deluxe), and a slide action shotgun (Model 458). While Kodiak long guns are rare and extremely well made, collectability to date has been minimal with most specimens selling at a slight premium over similar quality trade name counterparts of that era. Prior to 1963, Kodiak firearms were marketed under the trade name of Jefferson.

KOLAR ARMS

Current manufacturer located in Racine, WI. Dealer direct sales.

SHOTGUNS

Kolar Arms manufactures fine quality O/U and single barrel boxlock shotguns in Skeet, Sporting Clays, and Trap configurations. Many options are available, including custom orders and engraving. Please contact the company directly for more information, including model availability, delivery time, and pricing.

KOLIBRI

Previous trademark manufactured 1914-1925 by Georg Grabner located in Rehberg, Austria.

PISTOLS: SEMI-AUTO

KOLIBRI PISTOL - 2.7 or 3mm centerfire cal., unrifled barrel, 5 shot box mag., world's smallest semi-auto centerfire pistol.

$2,250	$1,950	$1,750	$1,500	$1,350	$1,175	$1,000

Add approx. $300 for original case.

Add approx. 20% for nickel finish (rare).

Individual rounds of 2.7 or 3mm (more rare) ammunition are currently trading in the $75 range as it has the distinction of being the world's smallest centerfire shell (shooting a 3 grain bullet at approx. 475 fps and generating 1.75 ft./lbs. of muzzle energy!).

KONGSBERG

Previous manufacturer circa 1814-1998 located in Kongsberg, Norway. Previously imported and distributed 1996-98, by Kongsberg America L.L.C. located in Fairfield, CT, and by Lew Horton Distributing Co., Inc. until 1996, located in Westboro, MA.

RIFLES: BOLT ACTION

Add $50 for iron sights on models listed below.

393 SERIES - .22-250 Rem., .243 Win., .270 Win., .30-06, .308 Win., 6.5x55 Swedish, 7mm Rem. Mag., .300 Win. Mag., or .338 Win. Mag. cal., available in either Classic, De Luxe, Thumbhole (.22-250 Rem. or 308 Win. only), or Select (Standard) configuration, checkered pistol grip, forend mounted recoil lug which connects to stock, 3-position rear safety, fixed rotary mag., fully adj. trigger. Imported 1994-98.

✳ *Classic Model*

$875	$750	$675	$575	$495	$440	$385

Last MSR was $995.

Add $114 for Mag. cals.

Add $138 for left-hand action.

✳ *Select Model (Standard Model in Europe)*

$860	$735	$660	$560	$495	$440	$385

Last MSR was $980.

Add $113 for Mag. cals.

Add $138 for left-hand action.

GRADING - PPGS™	100%	98%	95%	90%	80%	70%	60%

✳ De Luxe Model

	$940	$795	$700	$595	$515	$450	$395

Last MSR was $1,124.

Add $112 for Mag. cals.

Add $137 for left-hand action.

✳ Thumbhole Model - .22-250 Rem. or .308 Win. cal., features thumbhole stock. Mfg. 1996-98.

	$1,350	$1,175	$1,000	$875	$750	$625	$500

Last MSR was $1,580.

Add $138 for left-hand action.

KORA BRNO

Current revolver trademark manufactured by Kroko a.s., located in Brno, Czech Republic. No current U.S. importation.

To date, the Kora Brno revolver/revolver carbine line has had little or no importation into the U.S. Models include many configurations of both .22 LR, .22 Mag., and .38 Spl. cals. Please contact the factory directly for more information (see Trademark Index).

KORRIPHILA

Previous trademark manufacturered until 2004 by Intertex, located in Eislingen, Germany. Previously imported 1999-2004 by Korriphila, Inc., located in Pineville, NC., and by Osborne's located in Cheboygan, MI until 1988.

PISTOLS: SEMI-AUTO

Less than 30 Korriphila pistols were made annually.

HSP 701 - 7.65 Luger (disc.), .38 Spl. (disc.), 9mm Para., 9mm Police (disc.), 9mm Steyr (disc.), .45 ACP, or 10mm Norma (disc.) cal., double action, Budischowsky delayed roller block locking system assists in recoil reduction, 40% stainless steel parts, 4 or 5 in. barrel, blue or satin finish, walnut grips, 7 or 9 shot mag., approx. 2.6 lbs, very limited production.

	$6,500	$5,500	$3,750	$2,950	$2,150	$1,850	$1,675

✳ HSP 701 Odin's Eye (Damascus) - similar to HSP 701, except is completely made from one block of Damascus stainless steel, rosewood grips with Manta skin inlays, custom order only.

	$12,250	$10,250	$8,500

KORTH

Current manufacturer established 1954, and located in Ratzeburg, Germany. Currently imported beginning 2000 by Korth USA, a division of Earl's Repair Service, Inc., located in Tewksbury, MA. Previously imported 1997-99 by Keng's Firearms Specialty, Inc. located in Atlanta, GA. Previously imported by Mandall Shooting Supplies, Inc. located in Scottsdale, AZ, Beeman Precision Arms, located in Santa Rosa, CA and by Osborne's in Cheboygan, MI.

Korth handguns are very high quality and are literally manufactured one-at-a-time, resulting in limited mfg. (less than 100 annually) and importation. 7,140 revolvers in 10 different configurations were manufactured between 1964-1981.

Retail values listed below reflect the most recent U.S. pricing from Korth USA.

GRADING - PPGS™	100%	98%	95%	90%	80%	70%	60%

PISTOLS: SEMI-AUTO

KORTH SEMI-AUTO - 9mm Para., .357 SIG (disc. 2002), .40 S&W (disc. 2004), .45 ACP (Tactical Model, mfg. 2003-2004) or 9x21mm IMI cal., double action, 4, 4 1/2 threaded, or 5 in. barrel, all steel construction, 8 (.45 ACP cal.), 9 (.40 S&W and .357 SIG) or 10 (9mm Para. or 9x21mm IMI) shot mag., adj. sights, checkered walnut grips, top quality manufacture throughout. Introduced 1986 with first guns shipped 1988.

Current MSR on this model is $6,495.

Add $587 for .45 ACP Tactical Model. Add $705 for Model Schalldampfer (9mm Para cal. only, threaded barrel, new 2003). Add $285 for silver matte plasma finish. Add $740 for silver polished plasma finish. Add $845 for polish blue plasma finish. Add $1,440 per interchangeable barrels. Add $180 for extra mag.

Base values are for high polish blue finish.

JAEGER MODEL - 9mm Para. cal., 4 in. barrel, ivory grips with hunting scene, left side has hunter and dog, right side has deer in forest, gold inlaid, grey "pickled" finish, fully engraved in Arabesque style.

Current MSR on this model is $19,200.

WILLIE KORTH "JUBILEE" 50th ANNIVERSARY MODEL - 9mm Para cal., 4 in. barrel, combat trigger guard, gold inlaid with head of Willie Korth and dates (1954-2004), 50 Jahre oak leaf, and acorn engraving in high polish blue, deluxe hand engraved wood grips. Only 5 to be mfg. during 2004.

Current MSR on this model is $18,000.

A special case which holds both the anniversary pistol and the revolver, as well as a matching commemorative knife is also available.

REVOLVERS

The crane of the main cylinder and of the extra cylinder (.22 LR/.22 Mag. or .357 Mag./9mm Para.) are cut from the same billet of steel, and for reasons of smallest tolerance that Korth guarantees, once a gun is made with a single cylinder, the extra convertible cylinder cannot be ordered at a later date. Korth currently produces the world's most expensive revolver.

Add $255 for silver matte plasma finish. Add $520 for silver polished plasma finish. Add $620 for bright blue polished plasma finish.

Subtract approx. $550-$700 if w/o interchangeable different cal. cylinder on Combat, Sport, and Target Models.

TROJA MODEL - .22 LR, .22 Mag., or .357 Mag. cal., 3, 4, 5 1/4, or 6 in. barrel, matte finish, smooth oversized walnut finger groove grips. New 2003.

Current MSR on this model is $4,795.

Add $1,500 for bright blue finish.

COMBAT MODEL - .22 LR, .22 Mag., .38 Spl., or .357 Mag. cal., 3 (solid only), 4 VR, 5 1/4 VR, 6 VR, or 8 in. barrel, steel or stainless steel (disc., limited mfg.) construction, 6 shot, combat sights fully adj., full length shrouded ejector rod, adj. trigger, checkered and oil finished walnut grips, 2.6 lbs. Introduced 1967.

Current MSR on this model is $6,880.

Used specimens of this model are infrequently encountered, and secondary values are difficult to determine.

SPORT MODEL - .22 LR, .32 S&W Long, .38 Spl., or .357 Mag. cal., 2 1/2 (disc., scarce), 4, 5 1/4, 6 VR, or 8 in. barrel, 5 (early mfg.) or 6 shot, micro adj. sights, full length shrouded ejector rod, adj. trigger, checkered and oil finished walnut grips, 2.6 lbs. Introduced 1967.

Current MSR on this model is $7,000.

Subtract approx. 10%-15% for 5 shot, depending on condition.

Used specimens of this model are infrequently encountered, and secondary values are difficult to determine.

GRADING - PPGS™	100%	98%	95%	90%	80%	70%	60%

TARGET MODEL - .22 LR, .32 S&W Long, .38 Spl., or .357 Mag. cal., 5 1/4 or 6 VR in. barrel, 6 shot, micro adj. sights, adj. trigger, stippled oversized target walnut grips, 2.6 lbs.

Current MSR on this model is $7,240.

Used specimens of this model are infrequently encountered, and secondary values are difficult to determine.

WECHSEL MODEL - centerfire and .22 LR/.22 Mag. cals., both cylinder and barrel can be changed. New 2003.

Current MSR on this model is $7,800.

> **Revolvers: Special/Limited Editions**

MODEL EVEREST 40 YEARS KORTH SPECIAL EDITION - .357 Mag., 5 1/4 in. barrel only, deeply engraved frame and barrel with gold inlays, smooth select walnut grips, cased, only 25 mfg. 1994 only.

$8,950 $6,350 $4,500

Last MSR was $8,500.

WILLIE KORTH "JUBILEE" 50th ANNIVERSARY MODEL - .357 Mag., 4 in. barrel, gold inlaid with head of Willie Korth and dates (1954-2004), 50 Jahre oak leaf, and acorn engraving in high polish blue, deluxe hand engraved wood grips. Only 5 to be mfg. beginning 2004.

Current MSR on this model is $18,000.

A special case which holds both the anniversary pistol and the revolver, as well as a matching commemorative knife is also available.

ANNO DOMINI 2000 - 357 Mag., 4 in. combat model, PVD gold plasma coating, deep relief engraving featuring thorns, only 10 mfg. during 2000.

Extreme rarity precludes accurate pricing on this model – manufacturer's suggested retail was $10,000.

PLATINUM MODEL - .357 Mag. cal., 6 shot, 4 in. barrel, platinum engraved model with deluxe grips, includes black leather briefcase. New 2002.

Current MSR on this model is $9,600.

ARABESQUE MODEL - .357 Mag. cal., 6 shot, 4 in. barrel, arabesque engraved model with deluxe grips, includes black leather briefcase. New 2003.

Current MSR on this model is $9,600.

EICHENLAUB MODEL - .357 Mag. cal., 6 shot, 4 in. barrel, oak leaf engraved model with deluxe grips, includes black leather briefcase. New 2003.

Current MSR on this model is $9,600.

JAEGER MODEL - .357 Mag. cal., 4 in. barrel, ivory grips with hunting scene, left side has hunter and dog, right side has deer in forest, gold inalid, grey "pickled" finish, fully engraved in Arabesque style.

Current MSR on this model is $19,200.

MODEL BELLEZZA - .357 Mag. cal., 6 in. barrel, ruby and diamonds with palladium finish, special female figured grips, Arabesque engraving, includes case, very limited mfg.

Current MSR on this model is $150,000.

"Bellezza" comes from a Handel opera, and means "the triumph over sorrow and disappointment."

CUSTOM PRESENTATION MODEL - deluxe variation of Sport/Combat model.

This variation is available with engraving and other special options that are priced per individual quotation from the importer.

GRADING - PPGS™	100%	98%	95%	90%	80%	70%	60%

KRAG-JORGENSEN (30/40 KRAG)

Previous U.S. magazine fed military rifle. Official government designation is United State Magazine Rifle and Carbine, Caliber 30. First U.S. (.30-40 Krag) military repeating rifle to shoot smokeless powder ammunition. Approx. 475,000 mfg. 1894-1904.

There have been many conversions of Krag-Jorgensen rifles - many of which are hard to identify. As a rule, these conversions are not as desirable as the specific models listed below. Since prices for upper condition (95%+), original Krag-Jorgensens have increased significantly in recent years, beware of non-original guns, conversions, and in some cases, fakes.

RIFLES: BOLT ACTION

MODEL OF 1892 RIFLE (DATED 1894) - traditionally, these models have been categorized as either Type I (solid upper band) or Type II (double strap upper band), but this is too simple a definition - there were many variations. Ordnance documents list approx. 14 changes that were made during the production run, and examination of original rifles have found many more. 24,562 mfg.

$12,000	$10,000	$7,500	$5,000	$3,000	$2,000	$1,200

It is essential that anyone considering purchasing this model thoroughly research the sequence and scope of the changes.

Early rifles in original condition will have numbered bolt parts (below S/N 500) and magazine parts (below S/N 11,500) - they will command a premium.

Only one rifle that has all the appropriate bolt and magazine parts numbered to the reciever is known.

❋ *Model of 1892 Carbine* - rare, only 2 known - one in a government museum, and the other in a private collection.

Extreme rarity precludes accurate pricing on this model.

MODEL 1892/1896 RIFLE (ARSENAL ALTERED) - numerous variations of Model 1892 rifles arsenal altered to Model 1896. 21,264 altered.

$1,000	$875	$775	$675	$600	$525	$375

Add a small premium for models upgraded in 1897 by being restocked but retaining the Model 1892 extractor, and a receiver with no notch.

MODEL 1892 CADET RIFLE - rare, 2 variations - 400 in the 18-19,000 serial number range, with 1894 dated receiver, 4 in the 35,XXX serial number range with 1896 receiver, both have 1896 dated cartouches, three of the 400 were surveyed or condemned, and the remainder were converted to service rifle configuration. 3 of the group of 4 are known - 2 are in private collections and one is at West Point. 404 mfg.

Extreme rarity precludes accurate pricing on this model.

MODEL 1895/1896 TRANSISTION RIFLE - these rifles were produced prior to the official introduction of the Model 1896, receiver dates 1895 or 1896 with the MODEL prefix, cartouche dates will be 1896. 1,368 mfg.

$3,000	$2,500	$1,000	$700	$600	$500	$400

MODEL OF 1896 RIFLE - receivers marked Model 1896, cartouche dates are 1896, 1897, and 1898. 60,528 mfg.

$3,000	$2,500	$1,000	$700	$600	$500	$400

Add a premium for rifles with 1897 dated cartouches impressed sideways.

Add a premium for rifles with 1901 dated cartouches.

❋ *Model 1895/1896 Transistion Carbine* - a "crash" program was started in the spring of 1895 and completed in May, 1896 to arm the regular cavalry, receivers dated 1894 (rare) 1895, or 1896 with no MODEL prefix, 1896 cartouche date. 7,111 mfg.

$4,500	$3,800	$1,800	$1,200	$1,000	$800	$600

Add a premium for rare early version with two cleaning rod holes in the butt, stacked one above the other.

GRADING - PPGS™	100%	98%	95%	90%	80%	70%	60%

✱ *Model 1896 Carbine* - receivers stamped "MODEL 1896", with 1896, 1897, 1898, or 1901 dated cartouches (rare), rear leaf sight is calibrated to 20 and will be stamped at the top right with a "C" and the base will have a "C" on the right side. 14,942 mfg.

	$4,500	$3,800	$1,800	$1,200	$1,000	$800	$600

Buyer beware - some models may have fake sights.

MODEL OF 1898 RIFLE - some 25 variations exist in this model. 342,526 mfg.

	$3,000	$2,500	$1,000	$700	$600	$500	$400

Subtract 20%-40% for "as modified" guns.

Collectors must be aware of the correct combination of serial number, sight variation, and cartouche date of a rifle in original "as made" condition.

✱ *Model of 1898 Carbine* - scarce and rare in authentic original condition. 5,002 mfg.

	$5,000	$4,500	$3,500	$1,800	$1,500	$1,200	$1,000

Beware of fakes.

✱ *Model 1898 Rifles w/Parkhurst Device* - scarce/rare, most were destroyed. 100 modified.

Extreme rarity precludes accurate pricing on this model.

MODEL OF 1899 CARBINE - numerous variations, sight and hand guard changes. 36,052 mfg.

	$4,500	$3,800	$1,800	$1,200	$1,000	$800	$600

Subtract 20% - 40% for "as modified" or parts guns.

Collectors must be aware of the correct combination of serial number, sight variation, hand guard, and stock cartouche date.

✱ *Model 1899 Rifles w/Parkhurst Device* - scarce/rare, most were destroyed. 100 modified.

Extreme rarity precludes accurate pricing on this model.

BOARD OF ORDNANCE RIFLE - 26 in. barrel, rare. 100 mfg.

Extreme rarity precludes accurate pricing on this model.

PHILLIPINE CONSTABULARY RIFLE - records from the Bureau of Insular Affairs show that the civil government of the Phillipines purchased Model of 1899 carbines, and had them modified by the U.S. military at the Manila Ordnance Facility. 4,980 converted.

The absence of an authenticated example of this model precludes accurate pricing.

SCHOOL GUN - officially known as the United States Magazine Carbine, Model of 1899, Modified for Use with Knife Bayonet and Gun Sling, these were carbines and stocks modified between 1906-1916 at both Springfield and Rock Island, examples of Springfield modification have been observed with a block J.F.C. cartouche. 3,371 carbines and 6,118 stocks converted.

	$4,500	$3,800	$1,800	$1,200	$1,000	$800	$600

DCM/NRA CARBINE - original carbines and cut down rifles were sold by the DCM to NRA members and others during the 1930s-40s, widely imitated by commercial vendors.

	$1,500	$1,200	$1,000	$800	$600	$500	$400

Buyer beware - this gun should have original documentation before considering a purchase.

KRICO

Current trademark manufactured by Kriegeskorte Handels GmbH, located in Pyrbaum, Germany. Previously distributed by Precision Sales, Int'l, located in Westfield, MA, beginning in 1999-2002. Previously manufactured in Vohburg-Irsching, Germany 1996-1999, and in Fürth-Stadeln, Germany by Sportwaffenfabrik Kriegeskorte GmbH pre-1996.

During 2000, Krico was purchased by Marocchi. Krico has been imported/distributed by over ten U.S. companies/individuals. Krico manufactures high quality rifles, and to date, has mostly sold their guns in Europe. Many of the discontinued models listed below may still be current within the European marketplace.

RIFLES: BOLT ACTION

Values and information below reflect the most current information available to the publisher. Please contact the factory directly for current pricing and model availability.

SPORTING RIFLE - .22 Hornet or .222 Rem. cal., miniature Mauser action, 4 shot, 22, 24, or 26 in. barrel, single or double set triggers, open sights, checkered walnut stock, pistol grip. Mfg. 1956-62.

	$605	$550	$495	$440	$400	$360	$305

CARBINE - similar to Sporting Rifle, except 20 or 22 in. barrel, full length stock.

	$635	$580	$415	$470	$420	$375	$320

SPECIAL VARMINT RIFLE - similar to Sporting Rifle, except heavy barrel, no sights.

	$605	$550	$495	$440	$400	$360	$300

MODEL 300 SPORTER - .22 LR, .22 Mag., or .22 Hornet cal., select walnut with straight, checkered stock and fuller forearm, 23 1/2 in. barrel, 5 shot mag., grooved receiver, 6 1/2 lbs. Importation disc. 1999.

	$550	$495	$450	$410	$380	$350	$320

Last MSR was $595.

> Add $30 for .22 Mag. cal.
> Add $155 for .22 Hornet cal.
> This model was designated Model 302 Sporter until 1986.

> ✹ *Model 300 Deluxe* - similar to Model 300 Standard, except has deluxe wood and checkering. Imported 1991-99.

	$625	$550	$480	$430	$385	$350	$320

Last MSR was $695.

> Add $25 for .22 Mag. cal.
> Add $200 for .22 Hornet cal.

MODEL 311 SMALL BORE RIFLE - .22 LR cal. only, bolt action, 5 or 10 shot, 22 in. barrel, single or double set trigger, open sights, checkered stock. Disc.

	$330	$275	$250	$220	$195	$165	$155

> Add 30% for Kahles 2 1/2 power scope.

MODEL 320 MANNLICHER SPORTER - .22 LR, .22 Mag., or .22 Hornet cal., full stock sporter, 19 1/2 in. barrel, 5 shot mag., double set triggers, 6 lbs. Importation disc. 1999.

	$650	$575	$500	$460	$430	$395	$370

Last MSR was $750.

> Add $25 for .22 Mag. cal.
> Add $150 for .22 Hornet cal.
> This model was designated Model 304 Mannlicher Sporter until 1986. In 1991, it was redesignated the Model 320 Stutzen.

MODEL 340 S ST - .22 LR cal. only, silhouette model, 21 in. bull barrel, match trigger, no sights, 5 shot mag., stippled pistol grip and forearm, 7 1/2 lbs. Importation disc. 1999.

	$750	$625	$550	$500	$450	$375	$325

Last MSR was $795.

> ✹ *Model 340 Kricotronic* - similar to above, except with Krico electronic trigger. Importation disc. 1988.

	$1,295	$995	$900	$800	$690	$600	$550

Last MSR was $1,450.

GRADING - PPGS™	100%	98%	95%	90%	80%	70%	60%

⚹ Model 340 Mini-Sniper - non-glare wood and metal finish, military style barrel with muzzle brake, vent. forearm, no sights, match trigger (interchangeable), 5 shot, raised cheekpiece. Importation disc. 1988.

	$1,050	$825	$725	$600	$550	$500	$450

Last MSR was $1,200.

BIATHLON MODEL 360 S - .22 LR cal., standard biathlon configuration with conventional straight pull bolt. Importation disc. 1999.

	$1,375	$1,075	$925	$750	$625	$550	$500

Last MSR was $1,695.

BIATHLON MODEL 360 S2 - .22 LR cal., biathlon competition rifle featuring unique pistol grip operated rapid fire action, includes 5 mags., aperture sights, snow guards, and black stock. Importation disc. 1999.

	$1,300	$1,050	$900	$750	$625	$550	$500

Last MSR was $1,595.

MODEL 400 SPORTER - .22 LR or .22 Hornet cal., 23 1/2 in. barrel, select checkered walnut with European style curved cheekpiece, 5 shot mag., open sights, 6.8 lbs. Importation disc. 1999.

	$840	$750	$625	$550	$500	$450	$375

Last MSR was $895.

Add $55 for .22 Hornet cal.

⚹ Model 400 Match Single Shot - .22 LR only, match rifle configuration. Importation disc. 1999.

	$875	$750	$625	$550	$500	$450	$375

Last MSR was $950.

⚹ Model 400 Silhouette - .22 LR only, designed for silhouette shooting, no sights. Importation disc. 1999.

	$725	$615	$550	$500	$450	$375	$325

Last MSR was $775.

MODEL 420 L ST MANNLICHER SPORTER - .22 Hornet only, full stock sporter, 19 1/2 in. barrel, double set triggers, 5 shot, 6 1/2 lbs.

	$875	$750	$625	$550	$500	$450	$375

MODEL 440 - .22 Hornet, otherwise similar to Model 340. Importation disc. 1988.

	$900	$725	$575	$525	$450	$400	$360

Last MSR was $1,025.

MODEL 600 HUNTING - .222 Rem., .223 Rem., .22-250 Rem., .243 Win., .308 Win., or 5.6x50 Mag. cal., 23 1/2 in. barrel, select checkered walnut with curved European style cheekpiece and vent. forend, 3 or 4 shot mag., open sights, single set trigger, 7 lbs. Importation disc. 1999.

	$1,100	$975	$850	$750	$625	$550	$500

Last MSR was $1,295.

Add $55 for Model 600 SC.

Add $300 for Model 600 Benchrest.

Add $355 for Model 600 in sniper configuration.

This model was also available in single shot configuration at no extra charge as well as in a Match Model Group I & II - add $100 for Group II.

MODEL 620 MANNLICHER SPORTER - same cals. as Model 600, full stock sporter, 20 3/4 in. barrel, double set triggers, 3 shot mag., 6.8 lbs. Importation disc. 1988.

	$1,165	$965	$875	$760	$695	$650	$590

Last MSR was $1,300.

MODEL 640 S ST VARMINT

.22-250 Rem., .222 Rem., or .223 Rem. cal., 23 3/4 in. heavy barrel, high Monte Carlo comb and full cheekpiece, rosewood forearm tip and grip cap, Wundhammer hand swell, double set triggers, 4 shot mag., 9.6 lbs. Importation disc. 1990.

	100%	98%	95%	90%	80%	70%	60%
	$875	$750	$625	$550	$500	$450	$375

Last MSR was $950.

* **Model 640 Sniper** - similar to Model 640, except has non-adj. cheekpiece. Importation disc. 1988.

	100%	98%	95%	90%	80%	70%	60%
	$1,325	$1,075	$965	$875	$760	$695	$650

Last MSR was $1,500.

MODEL 640 DELUXE/SUPER SNIPER

.223 Rem. or .308 Win. cal., 23 in. barrel, select walnut stock has stippled hand grip, adj. cheekpiece and vent. forearm, engine turned bolt assembly, 3 shot mag., match trigger, 10 lbs. Importation disc. 1988.

	100%	98%	95%	90%	80%	70%	60%
	$1,495	$1,175	$1,025	$875	$760	$695	$650

Last MSR was $1,725.

This model was known as the 650 Sniper/Match until 1986.

MODEL 700A ECONOMY

.222 Rem., .243 Win., or .308 Win. cal. (Group I) or 6.5x55mm, 7x64mm, .270 Win., or .30-06 cal. (Group II), without sights, single trigger. Imported 1991-99.

	100%	98%	95%	90%	80%	70%	60%
	$900	$775	$650	$550	$500	$450	$375

Last MSR was $995.

Add $70 for Group II cals.

MODEL 700 SERIES

.17 Rem., .22-250 Rem., .222 Rem., .222 Rem. Mag., .223 Rem., 5.6x50mm Mag., .243 Win., .308 Win., or 5.6x57 RWS cal. (Group I), 6.5x55mm, 7x57mm, .270 Win., 7x64mm, .30-06, or 9.3x72 cal. (Group II), or 6.5x68mm, 7mm Rem. Mag., .300 Win. Mag., 8x68S, 7.5mm Swiss, or 6x62mm Freres (Group III) cal., matte black metal finish, open sights, approx. 7 lbs. Imported 1991-99.

* **Model 700 Hunting** - available in Group I or II cals. only, walnut hunting stock with Bavarian cheekpiece, recoil pad, and palm swell grip. Importation disc. 1999.

	100%	98%	95%	90%	80%	70%	60%
	$1,075	$950	$850	$750	$625	$550	$500

Last MSR was $1,249.

Add $50 for Group II cals.

* **Model 700 DeLuxe** - similar to Model 700 Hunting, except has better grade walnut and is available in Group III cals. also. Importation disc. 1999.

	100%	98%	95%	90%	80%	70%	60%
	$1,150	$1,000	$875	$750	$625	$550	$500

Last MSR was $1,379.

Add $20 for Group II cals.
Add $71 for Group III cals.
Add $150 for left-hand action.
Add $346-$516 for repeating variation in Groups I-III.

* **Model 700 Stutzen** - full stock variation (Mannlicher) of the Model 700 DeLuxe. Importation disc. 1999.

	100%	98%	95%	90%	80%	70%	60%
	$1,200	$1,025	$895	$750	$625	$550	$500

Last MSR was $1,450.

Add $39 for Group II cals.
Add $160 for Group III cals.
Add $275 for DeLuxe variation (includes better wood and finish).

KRICO®

GRADING - PPGS™	100%	98%	95%	90%	80%	70%	60%

MODEL 700 DL R SPORTER - .270 Win. or .30-06 cal., 23 1/2 in. barrel, curved European cheekpiece, select walnut, 3 shot Mag., single set trigger, open sights, 7 lbs. Importation disc. 1990.

	$925	$800	$650	$575	$500	$450	$375

Last MSR was $1,025.

> **Subtract $30 for Model 700 DM ST.**
> **Add $470 for Model 700 DLM.**

MODEL 720 MANNLICHER SPORTER - similar to Model 700, only has 20 3/4 in. barrel, double set triggers, 6.8 lbs. Importation disc. 1990.

	$1,100	$975	$850	$750	$625	$550	$500

Last MSR was $1,295.

✳ *Model 720 Limited Edition* - .270 Win. cal. only, 24Kt. gold scroll work on bolt handle, receiver, barrel, and mounts. Trigger and front sight are gold plated. Serial numbered in gold. Disc. 1986.

	$2,310	$1,990	$1,700	$1,450	$1,200	$1,050	$950

Last MSR was $2,659.

MODEL 902 DELUX GRADE I - .222 Rem., .243 Win., .270 Win., .30-06, 6.5x55mm, 7x64mm, 8x68mm, 9.3x64mm, or 7mm Rem. Mag. cal., 22 1/4 or 24 1/4 in. barrel, Oxidal deep black or satin finish, various grades, checkered walnut stock and forend. Importation began late 1999.

	MSR N/A	$1,650	$1,400	$1,200	$995	$875	$750	$625

✳ *Grade II*

	MSR N/A	$3,100	$2,750	$2,375	$2,050	$1,750	$1,450	$1,150

✳ *Grade III*

	MSR N/A	$3,950	$3,500	$3,100	$2,750	$2,375	$2,050	$1,750

✳ *Grade IV*

	MSR N/A	$4,950	$4,450	$3,800	$3,200	$2,600	$2,250	$1,875

✳ *Grade V* - custom model, individually built per customer specifications, POR.

RIFLES: SEMI-AUTO

MODEL 260 SPORTER - .22 LR cal. only, standard features. Importation began 1991.

	MSR N/A	$550	$495	$450	$410	$380	$350	$320

H. KRIEGHOFF GUN CO. (SHOTGUNS OF ULM)

KRIEGHOFF

Current manufacturer located in Ulm, Germany since circa 1954. Previous manufacture was in Suhl, Germany 1886-1947. Currently imported and distributed by Krieghoff International, Inc. located in Ottsville, PA. Dealer direct sales only.

Currently, Krieghoff manufacturers 2,000 guns annually, in all configurations.

WWII Krieghoff Lugers will appear in the Luger section of this text.

DRILLINGS

H. Krieghoff drillings can be ordered with a variety of cals. (.222 Rem., .243 Win., .270 Win., or .30-06) and special order features. The universal trigger system (UAS) and Combi-cocking device are standard on all Plus, Steingass, and Quadro drillings. Prices shown below are for standard guns with no options. Better models will have a finer grade walnut and exhibit more elaborate deep relief engraving.

> **Add $450 for free floating rifle barrels on Trumpf and Neptun Models listed below (both regular steel frame and Dural variations).**
> **Add $1,290 for 3-claw scope mount system (disc.).**

GRADING - PPGS™	100%	98%	95%	90%	80%	70%	60%

PLUS MODEL - 12, 16, or 20 ga. over rifle barrel (.222 Rem., .243 Win., .270 Win., or .30-06 cal.), boxlock action, includes universal trigger system (UAS) as standard, light engraving, choice of soldered or free floating rifle barrel with adj. point of impact (Thermo TS Stabil - Model Plus TS). Mfg. 1988-2004.

	$5,125	$3,650	$2,800	$2,200	$1,825	$1,525	$1,200

Last MSR was $6,275.

Add $1,700 for full length stock (Model Steingass, 20 ga. only).

QUADRO TS MODEL - 12 or 20 ga. over 21.5 in. rifle barrel (various rifle cals.), features Thermo Stabil barrels, standard engraving is small arabesque, includes soft case. New 2003.

MSR $8,995	$7,750	$6,500	$5,000	$3,850	$3,000	$2,500	$2,000

Add $1,995 for Quadro 20 Model with double rifle and single shotgun barrel configuration.

Add $1,795 - $1,995 for KS full length rifled barrel insert, depending on caliber (up to .380).

Add $1,795 for pivot mount for instqalled and sighted in pivot mount.

Add $800 for single trigger, or $1,195 for single/double trigger.

✳ *Quadro African Drilling* - 20 ga. under rifle barrels (.375 H&H, .500/.416 NE or .470 NE), 20 ga. drilling frame with reinforced sidewalls, hinged front trigger, similar sights as the Classic Big 5 double rifle. New 2003.

This gun is available by custom order only - pricing starts at $17,850.

TRUMPF MODEL - 12, 16, or 20 ga. O/U, or rifle shotgun combo., various cals., boxlock, 25 in. barrels, 7 1/2 lbs. Disc. 2003.

	$8,300	$6,300	$5,350	$4,250	$3,300	$2,750	$2,200

Last MSR was $9,950.

Add $1,850 for single trigger.

✳ *Trumpf Dural* - Dural aluminum frame variation of the Trumpf, 6.8 lbs., cased. Disc. 2003.

	$8,300	$6,300	$5,350	$4,250	$3,300	$2,750	$2,200

Last MSR was $9,950.

NEPTUN MODEL - 12 or 20 ga., variety of cals., elaborate engraving, sidelocks. Disc. 2003.

	$13,250	$10,400	$9,000	$7,550	$6,200	$5,100	$4,150

Last MSR was $16,500.

✳ *Neptun Dural* - Dural aluminum frame variation of the Neptun, cased. Disc. 2003.

	$13,250	$10,400	$9,000	$7,550	$6,200	$5,100	$4,150

Last MSR was $16,500.

NEPTUN PRIMUS MODEL - similar to Neptun Model, only hand detachable sidelocks and elaborate deep relief engraving. Disc. 2003.

	$18,500	$13,650	$10,450	$8,400	$7,100	$5,850	$4,950

Last MSR was $24,500.

✳ *Neptun Primus Dural* - Dural aluminum frame variation available at no extra charge. Disc. 2003.

	$18,500	$13,650	$10,450	$8,400	$7,100	$5,850	$4,950

Last MSR was $24,500.

RIFLES: DOUBLE, O/U & SxS

Various grades differ in style and amount of engraving, choice of walnut and various options that can be special ordered. N/As listed below indicate limited importation currently, and do not have current MSRs.

Add $1,950 for 4-claw scope mount (standard or European).

GRADING - PPGS™	100%	98%	95%	90%	80%	70%	60%

TECK O/U - .30-06, .300 Win. Mag. (disc. 1994), .308 Win., 7x56R (disc. 1994), 7x65R (new 1995), 8x57JRS, 8x75RS (new 1995), 9.3x74R, .375 H&H (disc. 1988), or .458 Win. Mag. cal., 25 in. barrels, boxlock action, cocking indicators, hard case included.

MSR N/A	$8,725	$6,475	$5,200	$4,300	$3,650	$3,300	$3,000

Add $1,400 for .375 H&H or .458 Win. Mag. cal.
Add $990 for DTs with front set trigger.

* *Teck-Handspanner* - 7x65R, .30-06, or .308 Win. cal. on 16 ga. receiver frame, manual cocking.

MSR N/A	$10,200	$7,950	$6,675	$5,175	$4,375	$3,950	$3,200

ULTRA TS O/U - various cals. up to 9.3x74R, features unique manual cocking/self cocking device and interchangeable muzzle wedge for adjustable point of impact. New 1993.

MSR $7,450	$6,600	$5,700	$4,950	$4,250	$3,500	$2,950	$2,250

CLASSIC O/U - same standard cals. as Teck O/U, boxlock action, light engraving. New 1995.

MSR N/A	$6,975	$5,900	$5,150	$4,300	$3,500	$2,950	$2,250

* *Classic Big Five O/U (Big Bore)* - .375 H&H, .375 Flanged Mag. NE, .500/.416 NE, .458 Win. Mag., .470 NE, or .500 NE/3 in. cal. New 1995.

MSR N/A	$8,250	$6,925	$5,950	$5,000	$4,150	$3,350	$3,150

ULM O/U - similar to Teck Double Rifle, except has any combination of cals., with sidelocks and more elaborate engraving.

MSR N/A	$14,300	$10,350	$8,550	$6,900	$6,100	$5,500	$4,950

Add $695 for hand detachable sidelocks.
Add $1,775 with single/double trigger.

* *Ulm Dekor* - sidelock with light scroll engraving. Importation disc. 1991.

	$10,450	$9,150	$8,000	$6,750	$5,600	$5,000	$4,400

Last MSR was $12,500.

* *Ulm Primus* - deluxe sidelock.

MSR N/A	$19,750	$13,000	$10,250	$8,100	$6,550	$5,700	$5,300

TRUMPF SxS - boxlock action, similar to Teck model, except in .30-06, 8x57JRS, or 9.3x74R cal. Disc. 1994.

	$13,200	$9,700	$8,350	$6,900	$6,100	$5,500	$4,950

Last MSR was $16,150.

CLASSIC SxS STANDARD - same standard cals. as Teck O/U, boxlock action, 21.5 (optional) or 23.5 in. regulated barrels, DTs, Combi cocking device, removable wedge and integrated front sight in cals. up to .375 H&H, extractors, choice of standard or bavarian style stock, light engraving, with or w/o sideplates, various engraving options, 7.5-11 lbs. New 1995.

MSR $8,475	$7,400	$6,250	$5,250	$4,400	$3,500	$2,950	$2,250

Add $3,750 for a set of 20 ga./3 in. barrels.
Add $4,950 per set of interchangeable rifle barrels.
Add $3,250 for sideplates with standard scroll engraving or $1,575 for boxlock standard engraving.

* *Classic SxS Big Five (Big Bore)* - .375 H&H (disc. 1999), .375 Flanged Mag. NE (new 1996), .416 Rigby (disc. 1999), .458 Win. Mag. (disc. 1999), .470 NE, .500/.416 NE (new 1996) or .500 NE cal., hinged front trigger, non-removable muzzle wedge, 23.5 in. barrel with express style quarter rib, 9.5-10.5 lbs. New 1995.

MSR $10,975	$9,475	$7,900	$6,450	$5,250	$4,250	$3,400	$3,150

Add $3,750 for a set of 20 ga./3 in. barrels.
Add $7,450 per set of interchangeable rifle barrels.
Add $3,250 for sideplates with standard scroll engraving or $1,575 for boxlock standard engraving.

GRADING - PPGS™	100%	98%	95%	90%	80%	70%	60%

NEPTUN SxS - sidelock double rifle, same features as the Ulm model. Importation disc. 1991.

	$12,750	$10,400	$8,700	$7,350	$6,000	$5,450	$4,995

Last MSR was $15,500.

RIFLES: SINGLE SHOT

HUBERTUS RIFLE - available in .22-250 Rem., .222 Rem., .243 Win., .270 Win., .30-06, .308 Win., .270 Wby. Mag. (disc.), .300 Win. Mag., 7mm Rem. Mag., and in 12 metric cals. between 5.6x50R Mag. - 9.3x74R, single shot stalking rifle with Kickspanner (unique manual cocking device), engraved boxlock action, 23.5 in. barrel with quarter rib, fast lock time, double underlugs, approx. 6.5 lbs. Importation began circa 1997.

MSR $5,950	$5,450	$4,700	$4,000	$3,450	$2,950	$2,575	$1,850

Add $1,000 for Mag. cals.
Add $3,250 for sideplates with standard scroll engraving.

SHOTGUNS: O/U

N/As listed below indicate limited importation currently, and do not have current MSRs.
Subtract 15% for 26 in. barrels.
Subtract 25% for 26 in. barrels on higher grades.

MODEL 32 STANDARD - 12, 20, 28 ga., or .410 bore, O/U, 28-32 in. high rib barrels, ejectors, boxlock, single trigger, select wood. Disc. 1983.

	100%	98%	95%	90%	80%	70%	60%
Standard	$2,500	$2,250	$2,000	$1,900	$1,700	$1,500	$1,250
San Remo	$5,250	$4,500	$3,750	$3,000	$2,250	$1,950	$1,650
Monte Carlo	$6,750	$5,625	$4,875	$4,125	$3,000	$2,250	$1,875
Crown	$7,500	$6,000	$5,250	$4,500	$3,375	$2,625	$2,250
Super Crown	$9,000	$7,500	$6,000	$5,250	$3,750	$3,000	$2,625

✱ **Low Rib** - 28 ga. or .410 bore.

	$3,950	$3,575	$2,875	$2,650	$2,200	$1,900	$1,600

Add approx. 20% for two-barrel set.

MODEL 32 4-BARREL SKEET SET - 12, 20, 28 ga., or .410 bore, O/U, matched barrels in case, grades differ in engraving and wood quality. Disc. 1983.

	100%	98%	95%	90%	80%	70%	60%
Standard	$8,450	$7,450	$6,500	$5,600	$4,650	$3,725	$2,775
München Grade	$9,950	$8,450	$7,450	$6,500	$5,600	$4,650	$3,725
San Remo Grade (unmarked)	$12,750	$10,350	$8,250	$6,750	$5,850	$4,950	$4,750
Monte Carlo (Silver Crown, 50 mfg.)	$18,750	$16,000	$13,750	$11,000	$9,000	$7,800	$6,600
Crown Grade (400 mfg.)	$24,995	$21,000	$17,750	$14,750	$12,100	$10,350	$9,650
Super Crown Grade (48 mfg.)	$29,995	$25,750	$20,750	$16,750	$14,775	$12,650	$10,350

K-20 SPORTING AND FIELD - 20, 28 ga., or .410 bore, compact 20 ga. frame, incorporates all of the technical refinements of the K-80, nickel plated receiver with satin grey finish and classic scroll engraving, 28 or 30 in. separated barrels (28 ga. and .410 bore barrels can be purchased separately but must be fitted) with tapered flat rib, SST, AE, checkered walnut stock and Schnabel forearm, includes 5 choke tubes, approx. 7.25 lbs., includes fitted aluminum case. Importation began 2000.

MSR $9,395	$7,375	$6,500	$5,750	$5,200	$4,750	$4,000	$3,150

Add $150 for 28 ga. or .410 bore.
Add $3,845 for extra set of 20 ga. barrels, or $3,995 for 28 ga. or .410 bore.
Add $795-$3,300 for wood upgrades, depending on quality.
A 20/28 ga. set with 10 choke tubes and hard case is also available for $13,390. A 3 gauge set (20, 28 ga. and .410 bore) with 15 choke tubes and hard case is also available for $17,405.
Additional options for the K-20 include case colors ($1,995), and K-20 models with engraving options include Super Scroll ($13,195 MSR), Suhl Scroll ($14,645 MSR), Parcours Special

GRADING - PPGS™	100%	98%	95%	90%	80%	70%	60%

($14,365 MSR), Gold Super Scroll (coin or blue finish, $15,995 MSR), Bavaria (disc. 2004 or Bavaria Royale (new 2005, $16,295 MSR), Gold Uplander (coin or blue finish, $19,395 MSR), Gold Plantation Scroll (coin or blue finish, $18,195 MSR), Plantation Scroll/Uplander (nickel or blue finish, $15,095 MSR), Millennium ($18,895 MSR, new 2005), Waterfowl Medallion Nitride ($21,895, new 2005), and Bavaria Suhl ($21,995 MSR).

K-80 TRAP

12 ga. only, available in O/U, Unsingle, Top Single (single top barrel), and Combo (O/U with extra trap barrel) configurations, standard model has silver finished receiver, adj. rib allowing variable points of impact (new 1993). In O/U configuration the barrels are separated, about 8.5 lbs. A wide variety of custom order options can be ordered on this model.

For the Model K-80 Trap, MSRs on extra barrels (fixed chokes) are $3,145 for O/Us, $2,950 for top single (disc. 1999), and $4,125 for unsingle barrel.

Beginning 2000, options for the K-80 Trap include case colors ($1,995), and K-80 models with engraving options include: Super Standard (new 2005, $10,690 MSR), Super Scroll ($12,495 MSR), Suhl Scroll ($13,945 MSR), Parcours Special ($13,665 MSR), Gold Super Scroll (coin or blue finish, $15,295 MSR), Gold Uplander (coin or blue finish, $18,695 MSR), Gold Plantation Scroll (coin or blue finish, $17,495 MSR), Plantation Scroll/Uplander (nickel or blue finish, $14,395 MSR), and Bavaria Suhl ($21,295 MSR).

Additonal custom engraving options (must be added to the Standard Grade price) include: Bavaria/Bavaria Royale ($6,900), Millenium ($9,500), Waterfowl Medallion ($12,500), Gold Bavarian Royale ($14,900), Danube ($25,500), Gold Target ($29,500).

Add $700 for O/U barrel screw-in chokes capability (5 tubes).

Add $470 for 3 screw-in chokes capability (single barrel guns only).

Add $3,095 (O/U) or $4,125 (unsingle) per extra barrel(s), w/o choke tubes.

Add $495 for single release trigger or $850 for double release trigger.

Subtract 20% for old style receiver with "K-80" on side.

* *Standard Unsingle* - 32 or 34 in. lower barrel with either fixed choke or choke tubes.

MSR $9,675	$7,000	$5,400	$4,400	$3,550	$3,200	$2,850	$2,500

Add approx. 30% for Combo (includes unsingle and O/U barrels), or approx. 35%-75% for Trap Special Combo CTIII (new 2005), depending on grade.

* *Standard O/U* - 30 or 32 in. barrels with either fixed chokes or choke tubes.

MSR $8,695	$6,250	$5,200	$4,200	$3,300	$2,900	$2,600	$2,295

Add 40% for Combo Standard K-80 variations.

Subtract 20% for top single variation (very limited mfg.).

* *Centennial Model* - 12 ga. only, available in combo configuration only, 100 only mfg. 1986 to commemorate Krieghoff's centennial year, ser. no. 14501-14600, H. Krieghoff's signature inlaid in gold on frame sides.

	$6,000	$5,000	$4,400				

Last MSR was $5,995.

K-80 SKEET/SKEET SPECIAL

12 ga. only, available in Standardweight (8mm rib) or International (12mm rib) configuration, 28 or 30 in. barrels, approx. 8.75 lbs.

Beginning 2000, options for the K-80 Skeet include case colors ($1,995),and K-80 models with engraving options include: Super Standard (new 2005, $10,215 MSR), Super Scroll ($12,020 MSR), Suhl Scroll ($13,470 MSR), Parcours Special ($13,190 MSR), Gold Super Scroll (coin or blue finish, $14,820 MSR), Gold Uplander (coin or blue finish, $18,220 MSR), Gold Plantation Scroll (coin or blue finish, $17,020 MSR), Plantation Scroll/Uplander (nickel or blue finish, $13,920 MSR), and Bavaria Suhl ($20,820 MSR).

Additonally, custom engraving options (added to the Standard Grade price) are also available. Add $6,900 for Bavaria Royale, $9,500 for Millenium, $12,500 for Waterfowl Medallion, $14,900 for Gold Bavaria, $18,500 for Monarch, $25,500 for Danube, and $29,500 for Gold Target. Crown, Majestic, and San Remo Bulino engraving are POR.

* *Standard Model* - available in Standardweight frame, hard case optional.

MSR $8,220	$5,800	$4,400	$3,250	$2,700	$2,250	$2,000	$1,800

Add $3,145 per extra set of barrels with fixed chokes, $3,845 with choke tubes (Skeet Special), or $3,395 for heavy Skeet barrels.

Subtract 20% for receivers with "K-80" on side.

GRADING - PPGS™	100%	98%	95%	90%	80%	70%	60%

✶ *Skeet Special Model* - similar to Standard Model, except includes 5 choke tubes and tapered flat rib.

   MSR $8,920   **$6,300**   **$4,800**   **$3,600**   **$2,900**   **$2,500**   **$2,125**   **$1,900**

   Subtract 20% for receivers with "K-80" on side.

✶ *Centennial Skeet* - available in skeet configuration - special features as noted above on Centennial Model description listed under K-80 Trap. Mfg. 1986 only.

                $3,675   **$3,150**   **$2,700**

                                      Last MSR was $3,980.

K-80 2-BARREL LIGHTWEIGHT SKEET SET - 12 ga., includes one set of 28 in. barrels with Tula chokes and one set of carrier barrels allowing use of sub-gauge tubes (carrier barrels cannot be used for 12 ga.), 8mm rib, hard case standard. Mfg. 1988-99.

✶ *Standard Grade*

                $9,400   **$7,000**   **$5,150**   **$4,300**   **$3,875**   **$3,300**   **$3,000**

                                        Last MSR was $11,840.

   Subtract $1,845 for heavy barrel variation, which does not include sub-gauge tubes.
   Retail price for 2 barrel heavy set with choke tubes was $9,995.

✶ *Bavaria Model* - game scene engraved silver receiver with light perimeter scroll work, select walnut. Imported 1988-99.

               $14,975   **$11,250**   **$8,575**   **$7,200**   **$6,200**   **$5,250**   **$4,800**

                                        Last MSR was $16,990.

   Subtract $1,845 for heavy barrel variation, which does not include sub-gauge tubes.
   Retail price for 2 barrel heavy set with choke tubes was $15,145.

✶ *Danube Model* - fine English scroll work on receiver sides and floor plate. Imported 1988-99.

               $22,945   **$15,250**   **$17,750**   **$9,400**   **$7,750**   **$7,000**   **$6,650**

                                        Last MSR was $28,090.

   Subtract $1,845 for heavy barrel variation, which does not include sub-gauge tubes.
   Retail price for 2 barrel heavy set with choke tubes was $26,245.

✶ *Gold Target Model* - deep chiseled scroll engraving with gold line accents, 100% coverage finest quality walnut. Importation disc. 1999.

               $25,975   **$20,500**   **$15,950**   **$12,375**   **$9,950**   **$8,700**   **$7,500**

                                        Last MSR was $31,635.

   Subtract $1,845 for heavy barrel variation.
   Retail price for 2 barrel heavy set with choke tubes was $29,790.

K-80 4-BARREL SKEET SET - 1 barrel each of 12, 20, 28 ga., and .410 bore, 12 ga. is Tula choked (even patterning), 8mm tapered flat or standard VR, includes hard case. Since most shooters prefer different gauge insert tubes (Briley, etc.) rather than barrel sets, values have gone down considerably recently for these 4 gauge sets.

✶ *Standard Grade* - satin finished receiver with skeet scroll engraving. Importation disc. 1999.

               $11,000   **$7,625**   **$6,275**   **$5,350**   **$4,500**   **$4,000**   **$3,650**

                                        Last MSR was $16,950.

✶ *Bavaria Model* - game scene engraved silver receiver with light perimeter scrollwork, select walnut. Importation disc. 1999.

               $15,000   **$12,500**   **$9,750**   **$8,250**   **$6,900**   **$5,400**   **$4,350**

                                        Last MSR was $22,100.

✶ *Danube Model* - fine English scroll work on receiver sides and floor plate. Importation disc. 1999.

                $22,500   **$17,000**   **$13,000**   **$10,500**   **$8,700**   **$7,500**   **$6,250**

                                        Last MSR was $33,200.

GRADING - PPGS™	100%	98%	95%	90%	80%	70%	60%

✷ *Gold Target Model* - deep chiseled scroll engraving with gold line accents, 100% coverage finest quality walnut. Importation disc. 1999.

	$29,650	$17,350	$13,000	$10,500	$8,700	$7,500	$6,250

Last MSR was $36,745.

K-80 PIGEON - 12 ga. only, available with 28 or 30 in. barrels, standard tapered step rib, IM/F choking, available in Standardweight configuration.

Beginning 1992, the K-80 Pigeon Model is available by special order only. Rather than list the various Pigeon models separately, their current values will be approximately the same as the corresponding K-80 Trap/Skeet Models listed.

K-80 SPORTING CLAYS - 12 ga. only, 28, 30 (new 1991), 32 (new 1993), or 34 (new 2003) in. barrels with 5 choke tubes, choice of 8mm VR skeet, tapered flat (broadway) or step rib (special order), sporting clay stock dimensions. New 1988.

For options on the Model K-80 Sporting, please refer to the options on the K-80 Skeet, as they are similar in price.

✷ *Standard Grade* - satin finished receiver with sporting scroll engraving.

MSR $9,395	$7,100	$6,250	$5,650	$5,050	$4,300	$3,450	$2,650

Add $3,845 for extra set of O/U barrels with 5 choke tubes.
Subtract $250 for 34 in. barrels w/o choke tubes.
Subtract 10% for 28 in. barrels.

ULM-P LIVE PIGEON - 12 ga. only, live pigeon gun with hand detachable sidelocks, 28 or 30 in. VR barrels, standard grade has light scrollwork engraving.

MSR N/A	$12,000	$9,175	$7,700	$6,000	$5,450	$4,995	$4,300

✷ *Bavaria Grade* - similar to Ulm-P, only with elaborate game scene engraving.

MSR N/A	$15,000	$11,750	$8,750	$6,750	$5,700	$5,300	$4,750

KS-2 SERIES - any ga., full H&H type sidelocks, priced by individual special order. Prices started at $24,000. Disc. 1988.

SHOTGUNS: O/U OR COMBINATION GUNS

N/As listed below indicate limited importation currently, and do not have current MSRs.

Add $695 for hand detachable sidelocks (Ulm only).
Add $1,290 for 4-claw scope mount system (disc.).
Add $1,150 for pivot mount system.

TECK MODEL - 12 and 16 ga., O/U shotgun or rifle/shotgun combo., various cals. (7x57R, 7x64mm, 7x65R, .30-06, or .308 Win.), boxlock action, Kersten double crossbolt, auto ejectors, 7 1/2 lbs.

MSR N/A	$6,650	$5,100	$4,400	$3,550	$3,000	$2,600	$2,295

✷ *Teck Dural* - dural aluminum frame variation of the Teck, 6.8 lbs.

MSR N/A	$6,625	$5,100	$4,400	$3,550	$3,000	$2,600	$2,295

ULM - similar to Teck, except sidelock and fully engraved with leaf arabesques.

MSR N/A	$11,700	$8,975	$7,600	$6,350	$5,250	$4,400	$3,500

✷ *Ulm Dural* - dural aluminum frame variation of the Ulm.

MSR N/A	$11,700	$8,975	$7,600	$6,350	$5,250	$4,400	$3,500

ULM PRIMUS - similar to Ulm, except game scene engraved with English arabesques.

MSR N/A	$18,100	$12,850	$9,000	$7,000	$5,975	$5,450	$4,995

✷ *Ulm Primus Dural* - dural aluminum frame variation of the Ulm Primus.

MSR N/A	$18,100	$12,850	$9,000	$7,000	$5,975	$5,450	4,995

ULTRA TS COMBINATION GUN - 12 ga. only, combination O/U, various calibers (lower barrel), 25 in. barrels, "Kickspanner" mechanism allows manual cocking from thumb safety, satin finish receiver, VR, 6 lbs. New 1985.

MSR $6,250	$4,950	$3,975	$2,600	$1,950	$1,500	$1,250	$1,050

GRADING - PPGS™	100%	98%	95%	90%	80%	70%	60%

✳ **Ultra-B** - similar to Ultra, except features a selector to switch the front set trigger to the top shotgun barrel. Disc. 1995.

	$4,050	$2,675	$1,925	$1,550	$1,350	$1,150	$1,000

Last MSR was $4,990.

SHOTGUNS: SxS

ESSENCIA - 20 ga., 3 in. chambers, round body back action sidelock, 26.5, 28, or 30 in. barrels choked IC/Mod., ejectors, DTs, color case hardened receiver with fine English scroll engraving, gold plated cocking indicators and Krieghoff engraved in gold on receiver sides, Turkish walnut straight grip stock with semi-beavertail forearm, Americase or Krieghoff leather case, 6.25-6.5 lbs. New 2003.

MSR $23,950		$20,950	$17,750	$15,000	N/A	N/A	N/A	N/A

Add $750 for Briley thin wall choke tubes.

Add $6,450 for extra set of 20 ga. barrels (w/o extra forearm) or $8,450 for extra set of 16 ga. or 28 ga. barrels with extra forearm.

SHOTGUNS: SINGLE BARREL TRAP

MODEL 32 - 12 ga., same action as Model 32 O/U, 32-34 in. barrel, VR, mod., imp. mod., or full choke.

	$1,800	$1,700	$1,600	$1,500	$1,400	$1,300	$1,200

KS-5 - 12 ga. only, 32 or 34 in. barrel, adj. point of impact, innovative trigger configuration, optional choke tubes, redesigned streamlined receiver (new 1993). Mfg. 1985-99.

	$2,500	$2,250	$2,100	$2,000	$1,875	$1,625	$1,400

Last MSR was $3,675.

Add $2,100 per additional barrel.

Add $200 for screw-in choke option.

Add $200 for factory adj. comb stock.

Subtract $250 if w/o factory aluminum case.

Subtract 20% for blued receiver.

Subtract 15% for receiver with "KS-5" engraved on sides.

Adj. point of impact on this model is achieved by means of different, optional front hangers.

✳ **KS-5 Special** - 12 ga. only, 32 or 34 in. barrel, features adj. rib and comb stock, cased. Mfg. 1990-99.

	$3,700	$3,500	$2,975	$2,475	$2,050	$1,750	$1,500

Last MSR was $4,695.

Add $2,750 per additional barrel.

Add $200 for screw-in choke option.

KX-5 - 12 ga. only, 2 3/4 in. chamber, 32 or 34 in. barrel, adj. point of impact, innovative adj. trigger (pull or release type), adj. stock comb, light scroll engraving, includes choke tubes and aluminum case. New 2002.

MSR $5,195		$3,800	$3,600	$3,300	$2,850	$2,650	$2,400	$2,000

Add $275 for factory release trigger.

Subtract 10% for 32 in. barrel.

KUFSTEINER WAFFENSTUBE

Current rifle manufacturer located in Kufstein, Austria. No current U.S. importation.

RIFLES

Kufsteiner rifles are essentially built per individual order. In addition to his unique bolt action, he also makes other bolt action designs and O/U rifles as well. It is recommended that Mr. Kepplinger of Kufsteiner Waffenstube be contacted for more information, including price quotations on his quality, custom order rifles (please refer to the Trademark Index).

Additionally, Kepplinger also manufactures an entire range of set triggers for many popular domestic rifles - these are distributed through Brownell's, located in Montezuma, IA. The company also makes double stage triggers for Mauser M-98 rifles.

KAISERBUCHSE 3-S SYSTEM BOLT ACTION RIFLE - various cals. inlcuding Magnum calibers, unique short action allows for straight on cartridge loading, high strength alloy main parts, grip safety on lower pistol grip, unique uncocking device allowing manual cocking/decocking of the firing pin spring, 23.6 in. standard barrel, 3 shot detachable mag., iron sights, receiver drilled for scope mounts, best quality wood, available in either Schnabel forearm or Mannlicher configuration, many styles of engraving are optional, 7.14 lbs.

    Please contact the factory directly regarding a price quotation for this model.

JAGERBUCHSE REPEATING RIFLE - various cals., bolt action, 3 front locking lugs, firing pin safety, ST, removable 5 shot mag., European walnut stock with Bavarian cheekpiece and Schnabel forearm, 5.8-10 lbs.

    Please contact the factory directly regarding a price quotation for this model.

L SECTION

L.A.R. MANUFACTURING, INC.

Current rifle manufacturer located in West Jordan, UT.
Dealer sales.

GRADING - PPGS™	100%	98%	95%	90%	80%	70%	60%

PISTOLS: SEMI-AUTO

GRIZZLY WIN. MAG. MARK I - .357 Mag., .357/.45 Grizzly Win. Mag. (new 1990), .45 ACP, 10mm, or .45 Win. Mag. cal., single action, based on the Colt 1911 design, 5.4 in. (new 1986), 6 1/2 in., 8 in. (new 1987), or 10 in. (new 1987) barrel, parkerized finish, 7 shot mag., ambidextrous safeties, checkered rubber grips, adj. sights, 48 oz. empty. Also can be converted to .45 ACP, 10mm (new 1988), .357 Mag., or .30 Mauser (disc.). Mfg. 1984-99.

✴ *Short Barrel Lengths* - 5.4 or 6.5 in. barrel.

$875	$675	$625	$525	$495	$475	$450

Last MSR was $1,000.

Add $14 for .357 Mag. cal.
Add $150 for hard chrome or nickel frame.
Add $260 for full hard chrome or nickel frame.
Add $233-$248 for cal. conversion units.
Conversion units include .357 Mag., 10mm, .40 S&W (1991-1993 only), and .45 ACP cals.

✴ *Long Barrel Lengths* - .357 Mag., .45 Win. Mag., or .357/.45 Grizzly Win. Mag. (new 1990) cal., 8 or 10 in. barrel, extended slides. Disc. 1995.

$1,195	$975	$895	$800	$725	$650	$575

Last MSR was $1,313.

Add $62 for 10 in. barrel.
Add $24 for .357 Mag.
Add $143 for scope mounts (disc.).
Add $110 for muzzle compensator.

✴ *Grizzly State Special Edition* - .45 Grizzly Win. Mag., 50 mfg. beginning 1998 to commemorate each state (ser. numbers match the order each state was admitted to the union), features gold etchings on frame, gold small parts, faux mother-of-pearl grips, cased. Limited mfg. 1998-99.
Regional demand/interest preclude accurate pricing on this model.

GRIZZLY .44 MAG. MARK 4 - .44 Mag. cal., choice of lusterless blue, parkerized, chrome, or nickel finish, 5.4 or 6 1/2 in. barrel, adj. sights. Mfg. 1991-99.

$875	$715	$635	$550	$495	$475	$450

Last MSR was $1,014.

GRIZZLY .50 MARK 5 - .50 Action Express cal., single action semi-auto, 5.4 or 6 1/2 in. barrel, 6 shot mag., checkered walnut grips, 56 oz. Mfg. 1993-99.

$1,025	$865	$720	$615	$525	$495	$475

Last MSR was $1,152.

Add $178-$189 per coversion unit (new 1996).

GRIZZLY WIN. MAG. MARK II - similar to Mark I, except has fixed sights, standard safeties, and different metal finish. Mfg. 1986 only.

$625	$550	$525	$495	$475	$450	$425

Last MSR was $550.

Add $25 for .357 Mag.

GRADING - PPGS™	100%	98%	95%	90%	80%	70%	60%

RIFLES: BOLT ACTION

GRIZZLY BIG BOAR COMPETITOR RIFLE - .50 BMG cal., single shot, bolt action design in bullpup configuration, alloy steel receiver and bolt, 36 in. heavy barrel with compensator, thumb safety, match or field grade, includes bipod, scope mount, leather cheek pad and hard carry case, 30.4 lbs. New 1994.

	MSR $2,295	$2,125	$1,700	$1,450	$1,300	$1,125	$995	$895

    Add $100 for parkerizing.

    Add $250 for nickel frame.

    Add $350 for full nickel.

    Add $250 for stainless steel barrel.

    Add $522 for redesigned (2002) tripod and pintle mount.

RIFLES: SEMI-AUTO

GRIZZLY 15 - .223 Rem. cal., patterned after the AR-15, available in either A2 or A3 configuration, limited edition beginning 2004.

	MSR $795	$725	$650	$575	$525	$475	$425	$375

    Add $85 for detachable carry handle.

L E S INCORPORATED

Previous manufacturer located in Morton Grove, IL.

PISTOLS: SEMI-AUTO

P-18 ROGAK - 9mm Para. cal., double action, 18 shot, 5 1/2 in. barrel, stainless steel, black plastic grips with partial thumb rest. Disc.

	$350	$295	$265

High polish finish

	$395	$330	$295

    This pistol was patterned after the Steyr Model GB. Approx. 2,300 P-18s were mfg. before being disc.

LABANU INCORPORATED

Labanu, Inc. SKSs were manufactured by Norinco in China, and imported exclusively until 1998 by Labanu, Inc., located in Ronkonkoma, NY.

RIFLES: SEMI-AUTO

MAK 90 SKS SPORTER RIFLE - 7.62x39mm cal., sporterized variation of the SKS with thumbhole stock, 16 1/2 in. barrel, includes accessories, 5 lbs. Importation began 1995, banned 1998.

	$200	$175	$150	$135	$120	$100	$90

                      Last MSR was $189.

LAHTI PISTOL

Previous manufacturer located in Husqvarna, Sweden. Also mfg. by Vkt (state rifle factory) in Jyvaskyla, Finland.

PISTOLS: SEMI-AUTO

SWEDISH MODEL 40 - 9mm Para. cal., 4 3/4 in. barrel, blue finish, fixed sights, plastic grips, mfg. 1940-44.

	$450	$375	$300	$275	$260	$250	$240

    Add 10% for Holster-Rig.

    Note: It is important to note that there are diversely marked variations of this pistol, such as RPLT (Danish State Police); such police markings reduce value by about 10%.

GRADING - PPGS™	100%	98%	95%	90%	80%	70%	60%

FINNISH L-35 - 9mm Para., 4 basic variations - only the first 2 types have the more desirable shoulder stock lug. Military pistols are usually "SA" marked, approx. 9,100 mfg. 1938-1954.

* ✳ *1st Variation* - can be identified by "hump" for yoke locking piece and loaded indicator, ser. no. range 1001-3700.

	$2,500	$2,250	$2,000	$1,650	$1,400	$1,100	$800

* ✳ *2nd Variation* - does not have the "hump" for yoke locking piece, scarcer than 1st Variation, ser. no. 3701-4700.

	$2,500	$2,250	$2,000	$1,650	$1,400	$1,100	$800

* ✳ *3rd Variation* - can be identified by small changes in loaded indicator, most are marked "Valmet," ser. no. range 4701-6800.

	$1,350	$1,100	$850	$750	$700	$650	$600

* ✳ *4th Variation* - w/o loaded indicator, marked "Valmet," and sold commercially, ser. no. range 6801-9100.

	$1,100	$900	$850	$750	$700	$650	$600

* ✳ *Shoulder Stocks* - the shoulder stock for this model (w/o serial numbers) features a sheet metal compartment which contains a cleaning rod and extra magazine. Original stocks (only 50 mfg.) are currently selling in the $3,000-$3,500 range, while more recently manufactured stocks utilizing original hardware are currently priced in the $1,800-$2,250 range.

LAKE FIELD ARMS LTD.

Previous manufacturer located in Ontario, Canada. Lake Field Arms Ltd. was acquired by Savage Arms, Inc. during late 1994. Distributor sales only through most major U.S. distributors.

Lake Field rifles manufactured after the Savage acquisition are marked Savage - please refer to the Savage section for current mfg.

RIFLES: .22 RIMFIRE

MARK I - .22 LR cal., single shot bolt action, 20 3/4 in. rifled or smooth bore barrel, adj. rear sight, thumb rotary safety, walnut finish hardwood stock, 5 1/2 lbs. Disc.

	$110	$75	$65	$55	$50	$40	$30

Last MSR was $135.

    Add $14 for left-hand variation.

This model was also available in youth dimensions (19 in. barrel) at no extra charge (Model Mark I-Y).

MARK II - .22 LR cal., bolt action, 10 shot mag., 20 3/4 in. barrel, adj. rear sight, thumb rotary safety, walnut finish hardwood stock, 5 1/2 lbs. Disc.

	$120	$80	$70	$60	$50	$40	$30

Last MSR was $140.

    Add $15 for left-hand variation (mfg. 1993-95).

This model was also available in youth dimensions (19 in. barrel) at no extra charge (Model Mark II-Y).

MODEL 64B - .22 LR cal., semi-auto, side ejection, 10 shot mag., 20 1/4 in. barrel, adj. rear sight, thumb rotary safety, walnut finish hardwood stock, 5 1/2 lbs. Disc.

	$120	$85	$75	$65	$55	$45	$40

Last MSR was $143.

MODEL 90B (BIATHLON) - .22 LR cal., biathlon rifle, includes five 5-shot mags., 21 in. barrel, aperture sights, one-piece natural finish hardwood stock, 8 1/4 lbs. Mfg. 1991-95.

	$430	$300	$225	$195	$170	$150	$130

Last MSR was $570.

    Add $55 for left-hand variation (new 1993).

GRADING - PPGS™	100%	98%	95%	90%	80%	70%	60%

MODEL 91T - .22 LR cal., target rifle, single shot, 25 in. barrel with aperture sights, dark hardwood finished stock, 8 lbs. Mfg. 1991-95.

	$340	$255	$215	$175	$150	$135	$115

Last MSR was $455.

Add $45 for left-hand variation (mfg. 1993-95).

✱ *Model 91TR* - repeater version of the Model 91T, 5 shot mag. Mfg. 1993-95.

	$360	$265	$215	$175	$150	$135	$115

Last MSR was $485.

Add $45 for left-hand variation (mfg. 1993-95).

MODEL 92S - .22 LR cal., 5 shot detachable mag., 21 in. barrel, hardwood stock with Monte Carlo cheekpiece, 8 lbs. Mfg. 1993-95.

	$300	$240	$200	$175	$160	$150	$135

Last MSR was $388.

Add $37 for left-hand variation.

MODEL 93M - .22 Mag. cal., 5 shot mag., thumb operated rotary safety, 20 3/4 in. barrel, hardwood stock, 5 3/4 lbs. Mfg. 1995 only.

	$140	$120	$100	$85	$75	$65	$55

Last MSR was $168.

LAKELANDER

Previous trademark circa 1976-1999. Manufacture was by MIPRO AB (c. 1946-1999) in Sweden. Previously imported and distributed 1996-98 by Lakelander U.S.A., Inc. located in Gulfport, MS.

RIFLES: BOLT ACTION

LAKELANDER 389 - .270 Win., .30-06, or .308 Win. cal., unique design with many shooter enhancements, 4 shot integrated mag. with rotary swing plate, 3 configurations including Premium (22 in. barrel with skip-line checkering and Monte Carlo stock), Classic (22 in. barrel, standard stock with checkering), Match-Maker (target model with 21.7 in. barrel and competition stock and adj. cheekpiece, .308 Win. only), 7.3-8.4 lbs. Mfg. 1996-98.

	$1,425	$1,225	$995	$850	$700	$600	$500

Last MSR was $1,599.

Add $500 for Match-Maker Model.

LAMBOY, S.R. & CO. INC.

Previous importer located in Victor, NY until 2003. S.R. Lamboy manufactured Ithaca Classic Doubles and imported Renato Caem and other high quality, low production long guns from Italy.

LAMES

Previous manufacturer located in Italy.

SHOTGUNS: O/U

FIELD MODEL - 12 ga., 26, 28, or 30 in. barrels, various chokes, VR, engraving, SST, auto ejectors, checkered pistol grip stock with pad.

	$400	$380	$365	$350	$325	$300	$275

Add 25% for separated barrels.

STANDARD TRAP - similar to Field, 30 or 32 in. various trap bore barrels, with wide VR, trap style Monte Carlo stock.

	$600	$575	$550	$525	$425	$400	$450

GRADING - PPGS™	100%	98%	95%	90%	80%	70%	60%

CALIFORNIA TRAP - similar to Standard Trap, with separated barrels.

	$700	$675	$650	$625	$525	$500	$450

SKEET MODEL - similar to Field, with 26 in. skeet bore barrels, skeet stock and separated barrels.

	$600	$575	$550	$525	$425	$400	$350

LANBER

Current shotgun (O/U and semi-auto only) trademark manufactured by ComLanber, S.A., located in Zaldibar, Spain, and established in 1973. Beginning 1999, O/U shotguns are imported by Wingshooting Adventures, located in Grand Rapids, MI. Previously imported 1996-99 by ITC International, Inc. located in Marietta, GA. Previously imported and distributed until 1994, by Eagle Imports, Inc. located in Wanamassa, NJ. Previously imported by Exel Arms of America, Inc., located in Gardener, MA, and by Lanber Arms of America located in Adrian, MI.

Lanber makes a wide range of quality O/U and semi-auto shotguns.

SHOTGUNS: O/U, DISC.

Please refer to 19th-21st Editions of the *Blue Book of Gun Values* for more information on those Lanber models imported until 1987.

SHOTGUNS: O/U, CURRENT IMPORTATION

MODEL 2077 - 12 ga. only, 2 3/4 in. chambers, boxlock action, SST, black receiver finish, 26 in. VR barrels with 5 choke tubes, ejectors, checkered walnut stock and forearm, 6.2 lbs. Importation began 2000.

MSR N/A	$750	$650	$575	$525	$475	$400	$350

MODEL 2087 - similar to Model 2077, except has 3 in. chambers, engraved receiver and 28 in. barrels, 7 lbs. Importation began 2000.

MSR N/A	$725	$625	$550	$495	$450	$375	$325

MODEL 2088 - 12 ga. only, 2 3/4 in. chambers, sporting clays configuration, 28 in. VR barrels with 5 choke tubes, oil finished top quality European walnut, 7 1/2 lbs. Importation began 2000.

MSR N/A	$1,350	$1,175	$950	$825	$750	$625	$500

MODEL 2097 - 12 ga. only, 3 in. chambers, sporting clays configuration, engraved receiver, 28 or 30 in. VR barrels with 5 choke tubes, 7 3/4 lbs. Importation began 2000.

MSR N/A	$800	$700	$600	$525	$465	$415	$365

MODEL 2098 - 12 ga. only, 2 3/4 in. chambers, top-of-the-line sporting clays model with engraved coin finished sideplates, 7 lbs., 10 oz. Importation began 2000.

MSR N/A	$1,650	$1,325	$1,075	$950	$825	$750	$625

LANG, JOSEPH

Current trademark established in 1821 and manufactured by Atkin, Grant & Lang, located in Hertfordshire, England. No current U.S. importation.

During 1925, the company of Joseph Lang & Sons amalgamated with Steven Grant & Son, forming the new company of Grant & Lang, Ltd.

Prices indicated are for manufacturer's suggested retail and 100% condition factors are listed in English pounds. All new prices do not include VAT. Values for used guns in 98%-60% condition factors are priced in U.S. dollars.

Please contact the factory directly for more information and model availability (see Trademark Index). Atkin, Grant & Lang provide a useful historical research service on older Joseph Lang shotguns and rifles. The charge for this service is £25 per gun, and the company will give you all pertinent factory information regarding the history.

GRADING - PPGS™	100%	98%	95%	90%	80%	70%	60%

RIFLES: SxS

JOSEPH LANG DOUBLE RIFLE - available in cals. between .300 H&H - .577 NE, best quality double rifle, individually made per customer specifications.

	MSR £19,000	£19,000	$21,950	$19,000	$16,250	$13,750	$11,750	$10,250

SHOTGUNS: SxS

IMPERIAL SIDELOCK EJECTOR - 12, 16, 20, 28 ga., or .410 bore, best quality sidelock ejector model, individually made per customer specifications.

	MSR £25,000	£25,000	$28,875	$24,750	$20,750	$17,250	$15,000	$13,250

LASALLE

Previous manufacturer located in France.

SHOTGUNS

SLIDE ACTION SHOTGUN - 12 or 20 ga., 26, 28, or 30 in. barrels, various chokes, alloy frame, checkered pistol grip stock.

		$250	$225	$200	$175	$150	$125	$100

SEMI-AUTO SHOTGUN - 12 ga., 26, 28, or 30 in. barrels, various chokes, gas operated, checkered pistol grip stock.

		$300	$275	$250	$225	$200	$175	$150

LASERAIM ARMS, INC.

Previous distributor located in Little Rock, AR. Previously manufactured until 1999 in Thermopolis, WY. Laseraim Arms, Inc. was a division of Emerging Technologies, Inc.

PISTOLS: SEMI-AUTO

SERIES I - .40 S&W, .400 Cor-Bon (new 1998), .45 ACP, or 10mm cal., single action, 3 3/8 (Compact Model), 5, or 6 in. barrel with compensator, ambidextrous safety, all stainless steel metal parts are Teflon coated, beveled mag. well, integral accessory mounts, 7 (.45 ACP) or 8 (10mm or .40 S&W) shot mag., 46 or 52 oz. Mfg. 1993-99.

		$325	$295	$265

Last MSR was $349.

Add $120 for wireless laser combo (new 1997).

✱ *Compact Series I* - .40 S&W or .45 ACP cal., features 3 3/8 in. non-ported slide and fixed sights. Mfg. 1993-99.

		$325	$295	$265

Last MSR was $349.

Series I Illusion and Dream Team variations were made during 1993-94. Retail prices respectively were $650 and $695.

SERIES II - .40 S&W (disc. 1994), .45 ACP, or 10mm cal., similar technical specs. as the Series I, except has non-reflective stainless steel finish, fixed or adj. sights, and 3 3/8 (Compact Model, .45 ACP only), 5, or 7 (.45 ACP only) in. non-compensated barrel, 37 or 43 oz. Mfg. 1993-96.

		$485	$385	$300

Last MSR was $550.

Series II Illusion and Dream Team variations were made during 1993-94. Retail prices respectively were $500 and $545.

SERIES III - .45 ACP cal., 5 in. ported barrel, serrated slide, Hogue grips. Mfg. 1994-disc.

		$595	$465	$415	$375	$345	$310	$275

Last MSR was $675.

GRADING - PPGS™	100%	98%	95%	90%	80%	70%	60%

SERIES IV - .45 ACP cal., 3 3/8 (Compact Model) or 5 in. ported barrel, serrated slide, diamond checkered wood grips. Mfg. 1994-disc.

	$550	$450	$400	$360	$330	$300	$265

Last MSR was $625.

LAURONA

Current trademark established in 1941, and manufactured by Armas Eibar, S.A.L., located in Eibar, Spain. No current U.S. importation. Previously imported until 1993 by Galaxy Imports located in Victoria, TX.

Laurona was founded in Eibar during 1941 by four craftsmen (hence the name Laurona, which in Basque means "of the four"), each a specialist in a discipline of shotgun mfg. Laurona made SxS guns until 1978, at which time they discontinued mfg. to concentrate on the O/U marketplace.

Laurona manufactures high quality O/U shotguns and O/U express rifles/combination guns. Beginning 1992, Laurona switched from a one-piece, demi-block type of fabrication to a monobloc system which has improved strength characteristics while reducing weight in their X-Series line of shotguns and express rifles.

Laurona long guns come standard with a Black Chrome metal finish that is extremely resistant to oxidation. Left hand stocks are available for the 83 MG Super Game, 85 MS Super Game, Trap, and Super Skeet, Silhouette Trap models, and Silhouette Sporting Clays.

Suffix designations on Laurona shotguns refer to the following: G - twin non-selective triggers, S - selective single trigger, M - multi-chokes, T - Tulip, BV - beavertail, U - single non-selected triggers.

All Super Game Models were available with a deluxe package which includes a recoil pad, mid-bead sight, and select wood for an additional $250. Special order dull matte finished barrels (with multi-chokes) were available for an additional $200 - extra barrels were priced between $635 (20 ga.) or $800 (12 ga.) per set.

If more information is required on an older Laurona model not listed in this publication (including ser. no. dating), please contact Galaxy Imports (see Trademark Index). For an accurate appraisal, please send a complete description of your specimen (including Laurona model name, serial number, and other pertinent data - include photos if possible). The charge for this service is $25 per serial number.

RIFLES: O/U CURRENT MFG.

MODEL 2000X EXPRESS RIFLE - .30-06, 8x57JRS, 8x57RS, 9.3x74R, or .375 H&H cal., monobloc construction, 24 in. separated barrels featuring quarter rib sight and convergency adjustment at muzzle, matte black chrome finish, open sights, ejectors or extractors, SST or DT, approx. 8.1 lbs. New 1992.

> This model must be custom ordered - please contact the factory for more information.
> This model accepts Leupold or European styled ring mounts.

* *Model 2000X Combo* - includes choice of cals. listed, except for .375 H&H cal. with 12 ga. under-barrel. New 1992.

> This model must be custom ordered.

SHOTGUNS: O/U, RECENT MFG.

The author wishes to express his thanks to Thomas E. Barker for making the following information available.

GRADING - PPGS™	100%	98%	95%	90%	80%	70%	60%

1967 Series (Earliest O/U Model)

MODEL 67 (VERSIONS G & U) - 12 ga., first O/U model mfg. with manual extractors, G designation stands for Gemini for twin select trigger system (triggers will function as single or double), front trigger is non-selective firing in bottom to top sequence, and back trigger in top to bottom sequence, U designation stands for non-selective single triggers, boxlock action and barrel bluing, light walnut stock, skip diamond checkering.

	$500	$400	$350	$300	$250	$200	$150

1971 Series

MODEL 71 (VERSIONS G & U) - similar to Model 67 with minor improvements, bright chrome receiver with rolled engraved game scene, earlier models had traditional solid center ribbed blue barrels, later models had solid ribbed barrels with Black Chrome finish. G & U designations are the same as Model 67.

This model was imported and sold by Sears & Roebuck in 1973-74.

	$500	$400	$350	$300	$250	$200	$150

1982 Series

12 ga. only, similar to Model 71 with auto-ejectors. (Manual extractors were disc.) Firing pins changed to traditional round type, many internal parts were improved for better reliability. Skip diamond and standard checkering. All SUPER Series barrels separated (w/o center rib) with Black Chrome finish and hard chrome bores with long forcing cones in chambers. In most respects, the 82 Models are representative to present day Laurona O/U shotguns and will share most internal parts. G & U designations are the same as Model 67.

MODEL 82 GAME (VERSIONS G & U) - 12 ga, 28 in. black chromed barrels, 2 3/4 or 3 in. chambers, long forcing cones, solid side ribs, hard chrome bores, 5mm vent. rib, chokes ****/** or ***/* (IC/IM/M/F), Imperial nickel receiver with Louis XVI style engraving, tulip forend, field stock drop 35/65mm with plastic buttplate, 7 lbs.

	$550	$475	$400	$350	$300	$250	$200

MODEL 82 TRAP COMBO (VERSIONS G & U) - 12 ga., similar to 82 Game, except has 28 (chokes ***/*) or 29 (chokes **/*) in. barrels, steel rib, 8mm trap buttstock drop 35/55mm with rubber special trap recoil pad, 8 lbs.

	$550	$475	$400	$350	$300	$250	$200

82 TRAP COMPETITION (VERSION U) - 12 ga., similar to 82 Trap Combo, except has 13mm aluminum rib with long white sight, engraved motif on receiver, beavertail fluted forend, Monte Carlo trap stock drop 35/55mm with black rubber special trap recoil pad, 8 lbs.

	$600	$550	$475	$400	$350	$300	$250

82 PIGEON COMPETION (VERSION U) - 12 ga., similar to 82 Trap Competition, except has 28 in. barrels choked ****/** or ***/*, special competiton Pachmayr recoil pad with imitation leather face, 7 lbs, 13 oz.

	$650	$600	$550	$475	$400	$350	$300

Model 82 Super Series

The Super Models listed have nickel finished receivers with full coverage, delicate scroll engraving with Black Chrome relief and forend iron. All barrels are split (w/o side ribs), and have very durable rust resistance Black Chrome finish.

82 SUPER GAME (VERSIONS G & U) - 12 ga., similar to 82 Game, except has more elaborate fine scroll engraving.

	$575	$475	$400	$350	$300	$250	$200

GRADING - PPGS™	100%	98%	95%	90%	80%	70%	60%

82 SUPER TRAP (VERSION U) - 12 ga., similar to 82 Trap Competition, except has special trap Pachmayr recoil pad with imitation leather face and fine scroll engraving.

	$675	$600	$550	$475	$400	$350	$300

82 SUPER SKEET - 12 ga., similar to 82 Super Trap, except has 28 in. barrels choked Skeet/Skeet, buttstock drop 35/65mm with plastic buttplate, 7 lbs.

	$600	$550	$475	$400	$350	$300	$250

82 SUPER PIGEON - 12 ga., similar to 82 Super Trap, except has 28 in. barrels choked ****/** or ***/*, 7 lbs, 9 oz.

	$675	$600	$550	$475	$400	$350	$300

Model 83 Super Series

83MG SUPER GAME - 12 or 20 ga., 3 in. chambers, 26 (20 ga. only) or 28 in. barrels, 8mm rib, similar to 82 Super Game, except had Laurona's new multi-choke, not compatible with any other brand of screw in chokes because of the Black Chrome plating of the metric threads, 7 lbs.

	$995	$675	$600	$550	$475	$400	$350

Model 84 Super Series

The Super Game Models listed were available with an extra set of 26 or 28 in. 20 ga. multi-choke barrels and cast-on stocks for left-handed shooters.

> Add $400 for multi-choke barrels.
> Add $50 for left-hand stock.

84S SUPER GAME - 3 in. chambers, similar to 82 Super Game, except for new single selective trigger, ejectors, 28 in. barrels choked IC/IM or M/F, 8mm rib, 7 lbs.

	$750	$675	$600	$550	$475	$400	$350

> Add $400 for extra set of 20 ga. multi-choke barrels.

84S SUPER SKEET - 12 ga. only, 2 3/4 in. chambers, with elongated forcing cones, 28 in. separated barrels choked Skeet/Skeet, 13mm aluminum rib, extensive fine scroll engraving, rust resistant Black Chrome finish, 7 lbs. Imported 1988-90.

	$995	$675	$600	$550	$475	$400	$350

84S SUPER TRAP - 12 ga., 29 in. barrels with 2 3/4 in. chambers and long forcing cones, chokes IM and full, 13mm aluminum rib, auto ejectors, nickel plated receiver with fine scroll engraving, Black Chrome relief, beavertail forearm, MC or standard trap stock, 7 lbs., 12 oz.

	$1,250	$975	$875	$750	$625	$550	$475

Model 85 Super Series

85MS SUPER GAME - 12 or 20 ga., 3 in. chambers, similar to 83MG Super Game, except for single selective trigger, 7 lbs.

	$995	$675	$600	$550	$475	$400	$350

85MS SUPER TRAP - similar to 84S Super Trap, except for multi-choke in bottom barrel with fixed full on top, 7 lbs., 12 oz.

	$1,250	$975	$875	$750	$625	$550	$475

85MS SUPER PIGEON - similar to 85MS Super Trap, except for 28 in. barrels with fixed IM choke on top with multi-choke on bottom, intended for live bird competition, 7 lbs., 4 oz.

	$1,250	$975	$875	$750	$625	$550	$475

85MS SPECIAL SPORTING - similar to 85MS Super Pigeon, except field buttstock with plastic buttplate, intended for upland game, 7 lbs., 4 oz.

	$1,250	$975	$875	$750	$625	$550	$475

GRADING - PPGS™	100%	98%	95%	90%	80%	70%	60%

Excel 300 Series

EXEL 300 SERIES - 12 or 20 ga. The Model 301 is basic field gun, and the Model 310 was the highest grade.

* **Models 301 and 302** - 12 ga., double selective trigger system, ejectors, pistol grip, vent. rib, lightly engraved chrome finish receiver, various chokes and barrel lengths. Importation disc. 1986.

	$485	$415	$380	$340	$300	$275	$250

Last MSR was $553.

* **Models 303 and 304** - 12 ga., similar to 301/302, except has better engraving on coin finish receiver, vent. barrels. Importation disc. 1987.

	$545	$470	$430	$385	$340	$315	$270

Last MSR was $623.

Previously designated Model 82G Super.

* **Models 305(A) and 306(A)** - 12 or 20 ga., similar to 303/304, except has better engraving on coin finish receiver, screw-in choke tubes. Importation disc. 1987.

	$625	$535	$470	$430	$390	$350	$315

Last MSR was $711.

Previously designated Models 83MG and 85MS.

* **Models 307 and 308** - 12 ga., trap model, 29 in. barrels, extensive engraving, Monte Carlo stock. Importation disc. 1987.

	$580	$500	$460	$420	$380	$340	$300

Last MSR was $668.

Previously designated Model 82U Trap.

* **Models 309 and 310** - super trap model, 29 in. vent. barrels, more extensive engraving than Models 307/308. Importation disc. 1987.

	$630	$545	$495	$460	$415	$385	$340

Last MSR was $726.

Previously designated Model 82 S. Trap.

Silhouette 300 Series

These shotguns are basically the same as the Super Series, with the following exceptions; this series was readily indentifiable by their white and black chrome striped receiver, with the model engraved on the receiver side. Barrels were multi-choked on both bores and had an 11mm steel rib. Two types of chokes were used. Some guns came with knurl head type as in the Super Models, and others were made with flush Invector style. A later option for ease of changing chokes was the knurl long choke, which is a flush type with the knurl head added. Both later type chokes (flush and knurl long), can be used in the early multi-choke models with some extension showing.

SILHOUETTE 300 TRAP - 12 ga., 2 3/4 in. chambers, 29 in. 11mm VR barrels with long forcing cones and hard chrome bores, beavertail forearm and straight comb trap stock with vent. black rubber recoil pad, 8 lbs.

	$1,250	$975	$875	$775	$700	$650	$595

SILHOUETTE 300 SPORTING CLAYS - 12 ga., 3 in. chambers, similar to 300 Trap, except has 28 in. barrels and butt stock is field type with plastic buttplate or hard rubber sporting clays pad, 7 1/2 lbs.

	$1,250	$975	$875	$775	$700	$650	$595

SILHOUETTE 300 ULTRA MAGNUM - 12 ga. 3 1/2 in. chambers, similar to 300 Sporting Clays, Black Chrome finish, 7 1/2 lbs.

	$1,300	$1,025	$875	$775	$700	$650	$595

GRADING - PPGS™	100%	98%	95%	90%	80%	70%	60%

SHOTGUNS: SxS, BOXLOCK

Shotguns mfg. after 1975 with "X" after the model number featured Black Chrome barrels and action with hard chrome bores. 28 ga. and .410 bore could be special ordered. SxS shotguns were disc. by Laurona during 1978 in an effort to concentrate on the O/U marketplace.

MODEL 11 - 12, 16, or 20 ga., triple Greener type round crossbolt with independent firing pins bushed into the face of the action, Bellota steel barrels.

	$400	$350	$315	$260	$210	$175	$140

MODEL 13 - 12, 16, or 20 ga., similar to Model 11, except utilizes Purdey type bolt system, extractors are of double radius, sold through Sears & Roebuck.

	$400	$350	$315	$260	$210	$175	$140

❋ *Model 13 E* - similar to Model 13, except has ejectors.

	$500	$450	$395	$350	$315	$260	$210

❋ *Model 13 X* - similar to Model 13, except has Black Chrome finished barrels and action with hard chrome bores.

	$500	$450	$395	$350	$315	$260	$210

❋ *Model 13 XE* - similar to Model 13 E, except has Black Chrome finish and hard chrome bores.

	$600	$525	$450	$395	$350	$315	$260

MODEL 15 ECONOMIC PLUMA - 12, 16, or 20 ga., similar to Model 13, except was first model to have hard chrome bores.

	$450	$395	$350	$315	$260	$210	$175

❋ *Model 15 E Economic Pluma* - similar to Model 15 Economic Pluma, except has ejectors.

	$550	$475	$400	$350	$315	$260	$210

❋ *Model 15 X* - similar to Model 15 Economic Pluma, except has Black Chrome finish and hard chrome bores.

	$500	$450	$395	$350	$315	$260	$210

❋ *Model 15 XE* - similar to Model 15 E, except has ejectors.

	$600	$525	$450	$395	$350	$315	$260

MODEL 52 PLUMA - 12, 16, or 20 ga., back of actions scalloped and engraved in fine English scroll, Churchill rib and double radius extractors, hard chrome bores, 6 lbs.

	$750	$675	$600	$525	$450	$395	$350

❋ *Model 52 E Pluma* - similar to Model 52 Pluma, except has ejectors, 6 lbs., 2 oz.

	$850	$750	$675	$600	$525	$450	$395

SHOTGUNS: SxS, SIDELOCK

Models listed were available in 12, 16, or 20 ga. 28 ga. and .410 bore were available by special order.

MODEL 103 - 12, 16, or 20 ga., blue sidelocks with light border engraving, triple Purdey type bolt system, double radius extractors, Bellota steel barrels with hard chrome bores.

	$895	$800	$675	$575	$525	$475	$425

❋ *Model 103-E* - similar to Model 103 except with ejectors.

	$995	$895	$800	$675	$575	$525	$475

MODEL 104 X - 12, 16, or 20 ga., case colored sidelock with Purdey type bolting system, double radius extractors, fine double safety sidelocks, gas relief vents, articulated trigger, hard chromed bore, demi-block barrels of special Bellota steel, Black Chrome barrels.

	$1,200	$1,075	$925	$825	$700	$600	$525

GRADING - PPGS™	100%	98%	95%	90%	80%	70%	60%

✳ *Model 104 XE* - same as Model 104 X, but with H&H style automatic selective ejectors.

	$1,350	$1,200	$1,075	$925	$825	$700	$575

MODEL 105 X FEATHER - 12, 16, or 20 ga., similar to Model 104 X, except has concave rib, approx. 6 lbs. 2 oz. (12 ga.).

	$1,250	$1,100	$950	$875	$800	$725	$650

✳ *Model 105 XE Feather* - similar to Model 105 X, except has H&H automatic selective ejectors.

	$1,400	$1,225	$1,075	$925	$850	$775	$700

MODEL 502 FEATHER - 12, 16, or 20 ga., Purdey type bolting system, hand detachable sidelocks, gas relief vents, H&H style automatic selective ejectors, articulated trigger, inside hard chromed demi-block barrels of special Bellota steel, Black Chrome finish, fine English scroll engraving, marble grey or Laurona Imperial finish, Churchill or concave type rib, 6.4 lbs. (12 ga.).

	$2,200	$2,050	$1,875	$1,650	$1,525	$1,400	$1,275

MODEL 801 DELUXE - 12, 16, or 20 ga., similar to Model 502 Feather, except engraving is true deluxe Renaissance style, fully handmade with Laurona Imperial finish, best qulaity checkered walnut stock and forearm.

	$4,400	$4,150	$3,650	$3,250	$2,900	$2,600	$2,250

MODEL 802 EAGLE - 12, 16, or 20 ga., similar to Model 801 Deluxe, except features highly artistic bas-relief engraving of hunting scenes, hand engraved with burin and chisel.

	$5,000	$4,400	$3,900	$3,375	$2,825	$2,375	$1,875

LAW ENFORCEMENT ORDNANCE CORPORATION

Previous manufacturer located in Ridgway, PA until 1990.

SHOTGUNS: SEMI-AUTO

STRIKER-12 - 12 ga. Mag., paramilitary design shotgun featuring 12 shot rotary mag., 18 1/4 in. barrel, semi-auto, alloy shrouded barrel with PG extension, folding or fixed paramilitary design stock, 9.2 lbs., limited mfg. 1986-90.

	$850	$750	$625	$550	$495	$450	$375

Last MSR was $725.

Add $150 for folding stock.

Add $100 for Marine variation ("Metal Life" finish).

Earlier variations were imported and available to law enforcement agencies only. In 1987, manufacture was started in PA and these firearms could be sold to individuals (18 in. barrel only). This design was originally developed in South Rhodesia.

HARRY LAWSON CO.

Current custom gun manufacturer and customizer established during 1965 and currently located in Tucson, AZ. Consumer direct sales.

Harry Lawson Co. is well-known for custom stock work. This company also manufactures their own line of sporting rifles, most feature an innovative thumbole stock design. Please contact the factory directly for more information regarding custom model availability/configuration and current pricing (see Trademark Index).

RIFLES: BOLT ACTION

LAWSON 650 SERIES - various Wby. Mag. cals., features Wby. Mark V barreled action with choice of Burris scope, mounts, custom stabilizer sling, and Doskocil hardshell case, prices include new Mark V .340 Wby. Mag. action with black fiberglass "Cochise" (disc. 2003) stock. Many wood stock options available.

MSR $2,995	$2,700	$2,225	$1,775	$1,525	$1,350	$1,225	$1,100

GRADING - PPGS™	100%	98%	95%	90%	80%	70%	60%

LAWSON 650 MOUNTAINEER & ULTRALITE SERIES - various cals., features Rem. Model 700 barreled action, otherwise similar to Lawson 650 Series, prices include new Rem. Model 700 action with black fiberglass "Cochise" (disc. 2003) stock. Many wood stock options available.

MSR $2,555	$2,275	$1,950	$1,625	$1,425	$1,250	$1,100	$995H

LAZZERONI ARMS COMPANY

Current manufacturer located in Tucson, AZ since 1995.
Direct/ dealer sales.

LAZZERONI

RIFLES: BOLT ACTION

Lazzeroni ammunition is precision loaded in Lazzeroni's Tucson facility under rigid tolerances. All ammunition is sealed for absolute weatherproofing. Lazzeroni proprietary calibers are already established as being extremely effective at long distances.

SAKO MODEL TRG-S - 7.21 Firebird (.284, new 2002) or 7.82 Warbird (.308) cal., features Sako TRG action with free floating 26 in. barrel, 3 shot detachable mag., fully adj. trigger, and scope rings, 7.9 lbs. Mfg. 1999-2004.

	$825	$700	$600

Last MSR was $900.

Add $400 for metal finish upgrade or $1,200 for metal finish upgrade with Burris 4-16x50mm mil-dot scope.

SAVAGE 16LZ - 7.21 Tomahawk (.284, disc. 2001) or 7.82 Patriot (.308) cal., stainless steel action with 2 locking lugs, 24 in. stainless barrel, detachable box mag., injection molded composite stock, 6.8 lbs. Mfg. 2001-2004.

	$475	$400	$350

Last MSR was $550.

Add $100 for left-hand action.
Add $400 for Cabela's 4.5-14x42mm scope.

MODEL 700ST - various Lazzeroni cals., Rem. M-700 action, features remachined bolt face, squared recoil lug and receiver, mag. and follower are replaced with Lazzeroni style units, steel (disc.) or stainless steel (new 1999) action, blue steel or stainless steel 24 in. barrel. Mfg. 1998-99.

	$2,150	$1,750	$1,425

Last MSR was $2,395.

MODEL 2000 SERIES - available in either Lazzeroni short magnum (6.17 Spitfire - .243 cal., 6.71 Phantom - .264 cal., 7.21 Tomahawk - .284 cal., 7.82 Patriot - .308 cal., 8.59 Galaxy - .338 cal., or 10.57 Maverick - .416 cal.) or Lazzeroni long magnums (6.53 Scramjet - .257 cal., 7.21 Firebird - .284 cal., 7.82 Warbird - .308 cal., 8.59 Titan - .338 cal., or 10.57 Meteor - .416 cal.), features precision machined steel (disc.) or stainless steel (new 1999) receiver, helically fluted bolt with heavy duty extractor, stainless steel match barrel with integral muzzle brake, adj. benchrest trigger, matte finish metal, 3 position firing pin safety on most models (new 1999), 2 or 3 (new 1999) shot internal mag., various stock configurations. New 1996.

✻ *Model L2000ST* - features 27 in. barrel with conventional fiberglass stock, 8.1 lbs.

MSR $5,899	$5,250	$4,100	$3,175

✻ *Model L2000ST-28* - .308 Warbird cal., shoots 130 grain BarnesX boattail at 4,000 fps, 28 in. stainless steel fluted barrel, includes Schmidt & Bender 4-16x50mm scope, stainless action, black synthetic stock, approx. 8.3 lbs. Mfg. 1999-2001.

	$5,875	$5,250	$4,750

Last MSR was $6,310.

This model was advertised as the flattest shooting hunting rifle currently manufactured, and is zeroed in at 100, 200, and 300 yards.

✳ *Model L2000ST-W* - features 27 in. barrel with conventional black wood laminate stock. Mfg. 1996 only.

	$4,400	$4,050	$3,600

Last MSR was $4,795.

✳ *Model L2000ST-WF Package* - features 27 in. barrel with one conventional fiberglass and one black wood laminate stock. Disc. 1997.

	$4,875	$4,450	$4,050

Last MSR was $5,295.

✳ *Model L2000DG* - .375 Saturn or .416 Meteor cal. only, features Fibergrain stock finish, removable muzzle brake, 3 shot mag., 24 in. barrel, includes sling swivels, 10.1 lbs. New 1998.

MSR $6,199	$5,575	$4,400	$3,350

✳ *Model L2000LLT* - .257 Scramjet, .284 Firebird, .308 Warbird, .338 Titan cal., lightweight variation with 26 in. barrel and detachable muzzle brake, 4 shot mag., right- or left-hand action, 7.4 lbs. New late 2004.

MSR $5,899	$5,400	$4,300	$3,250

✳ *Model L2000SA* - .243 Spitfire, .264 Phantom, .284 Tomahawk, .308 Patriot, .338 Galaxy, .358 Eagle, .375 Hellcat, or .416 Maverick cal., short action cals. only, lightweight mountain configuration with 24 in. fluted barrel, 6.8 lbs. Mfg. 1998-2004.

	$4,750	$3,875	$3,050

Last MSR was $5,499.

✳ *Model L2000SLR* - features 28 in. extra heavy fluted barrel and conventional fiberglass stock, not chambered in .338 Titan. Disc. 1999.

	$3,775	$3,400	$2,975

Last MSR was $4,195.

✳ *L2000SP* - 25 in. fluted barrel, thumbhole fiberglass stock, 7.8 lbs. Disc. 2004.

	$4,750	$3,875	$3,050

Last MSR was $5,499.

✳ *L2000SP-W* - 23 in. barrel, thumbhole black wood laminate stock.

	$4,400	$4,050	$3,600

Last MSR was $4,795.

✳ *L2000SP-FW Package* - features 23 in. barrel with one thumbhole fiberglass and one black wood laminate thumbhole stock. Disc. 1997.

	$4,875	$4,450	$4,050

Last MSR was $5,295.

MODEL 2005 GLOBAL HUNTER SERIES - available in various Lazzeroni proprietary cals., variouos configurations including Short Magnum Lite, Long Magnum Lite, Long Magnum Thumbhole, Long Magnum Special Long Range, Short Magnum Dangerous Game and Long Magnum Dangerous Game, features stainless steel receiver, match grade fluted or unfluted barrel with muzzle brake and Jewell competition trigger, diamond fluted or helical cut bolt shaft, titanium firing pin, Limbsaver recoil pad, slim line graphite composite stock, approx. 6.1-7 lbs. New 2005.

MSR $5,899	$5,400	$4,300	$3,250

Add $300 for Mag. cals.

LEBEAU-COURALLY

Current manufacturer established during 1865 and located in Liege, Belgium. Currently imported by William Larkin Moore, located in Scottsdale, AZ. Previously imported until 1998 by New England Arms Co. located in Kittery Point, ME.

Lebeau-Courally manufactures only best quality rifles and shotguns. Approximately 50 are manufactured annually. Prices do not include engraving. Please contact the importer directly for a firm quotation on a Lebeau-Courally rifle or shotgun (see Trademark Index).

GRADING - PPGS™	100%	98%	95%	90%	80%	70%	60%

RIFLES: SxS

BOXLOCK EJECTOR - 8x57JRS or 9.3x74R cal., Anson & Deeley boxlock, ejectors, select French walnut stock, quarter rib with ramp front sight, about 8 lbs. Importation disc. 1988, resumed 1993.

> The importer or manufacturer should be contacted directly for current information and prices regarding this model (see Trademark Index).

SIDELOCK EJECTOR EXPRESS RIFLE - 7x65R, 8x57JRS, 9.3x74R, .30-06, .375 H&H, .458 Win. Mag., .470 NE (new 1991), or .577 NE (new 1992) cal., chopper lump barrels, reinforced action, select French walnut stock, quarter rib with ramp front sight, engraving not included, approx. 8 lbs.

> Current MSR on this model is $60,000 - the importer or manufacturer should be contacted directly for current information and availability regarding this model (see Trademark Index).

RIFLES: SINGLE SHOT

SINGLE SHOT - 6.5x57R, 7x65R, or other metric cals., best quality, boxlock or sidelock action.

> The importer should be contacted directly (see Trademark Index) for current information and prices regarding this model.

SHOTGUNS: O/U

SIDELOCK - 12, 20, or 28 ga., Greener locking system.

MSR N/A	$33,800	$29,000	$24,500	$20,750	$17,500	$14,500	$11,850

BOSS-VEREES - 12 or 20 ga., Boss pattern sidelock with low profile action, prices do not include engraving, top-of-the-line O/U individually made to customer specifications.

> Current MSR on this model is $96,000 - the importer or manufacturer should be contacted directly for current information and availability regarding this model (see Trademark Index).

SHOTGUNS: SxS

For currently manufactured shotguns - add $2,500 for single trigger. Older mfg. Lebeau-Courally shotguns have a completely different action and locking system than the newer models.

SOLOGNE - 12, 16, or 20 ga., Anson & Deeley boxlock action, various chokes and barrel lengths, select walnut, no engraving.

MSR N/A	$13,250	$11,250	$9,350	$7,500	$6,250	$5,150	$4,350

GRAND RUSSE MODEL - grade up from Sologne Model.

MSR N/A	$16,480	$13,000	$10,750	$8,475	$7,375	$5,250	$4,450

BOXLOCK EJECTOR - 12, 16, or 20 ga., choice of classic or rounded action, with or without sideplates, select French walnut stock, choice of numerous engraving patterns (optional), 26, 28, or 30 in. barrels, double trigger.

MSR N/A	$23,250	$14,000	$11,500	$9,950	$8,500	$7,250	$6,000

Subtract approx. 15%-20% w/sideplates.

SIDELOCK EJECTOR - 12, 16, 20, 28 ga., or .410 bore, choice of classic or rounded action, chopper lump barrels, select French walnut stock, choice of numerous engraving patterns (optional), 26, 28, or 30 in. barrels, double triggers.

> Current MSR on this model is $56,000 - the importer or manufacturer should be contacted directly for current information and availability regarding this model (see Trademark Index).

LEFEVER ARMS COMPANY

Previous shotgun manufacturer located in Syracuse, NY circa 1885-1948.

SHOTGUNS: SxS

The Lefever was the first commercially successful hammerless double barrel shotgun made in America. They were made in Syracuse, NY from 1885-1916, at which time the company was acquired by Ithaca Gun Company. Ithaca made the Lefever after 1916. In 1921, the Box Lock

100%	98%	95%	90%	80%	70%	60%	50%	40%	30%	20%	10%

Nitro Special was introduced and in 1934, the Lefever Grade A was introduced. Production of Lefever guns ceased in 1948.

The practice of assigning new serial numbers to guns returned to the factory for alterations absorbed approximately 5,000 numbers. Also, the serial number series started with 5,000, so approx. 62,000 guns were built.

The following is a percentage breakdown of gauges made between 1885-1916 (totaling 100%): 8 ga.-1/2%, 10 ga.-25%, 12 ga.-60%, 14 ga.-1/2%, 16 ga.-8%, 20 ga.-6%. Total manufacture was approx. 72,000 during this period. Damascus specimens of this trademark are worth approximately the same if in 60% or better original condition as their fluid steel barrel counterparts because of the rarity and desirability factors. Hammer guns are valued the same as damascus hammerless guns (grade for grade). Subtract 10%-30% on values with respective condition factors 50%-10%. Prices shown for 90% and up condition are very difficult to evaluate and are meant as a guide only - any Lefever shotgun in over 95% is rare and hard to evaluate.

SIDELOCK MODELS - 10, 12, 16, or 20 ga., 26-32 in. barrels, any choke, boxlock action (even though model nomenclature referred to sidelock model), cocking indicators on all but DS and DSE grades, double triggers standard, checkered straight or pistol grip stock, auto ejectors designated by letter E after grade. Mfg. 1885-1919.

Add 50% for 16 ga.
Add 100% for 20 ga.
Add 10% for SST.

✳ I Grade

100%	98%	95%	90%	80%	70%	60%	50%	40%	30%	20%	10%
$1,375	$1,250	$1,025	$925	$850	$775	$700	$630	$565	$500	$425	$350

✳ DS Grade

| $1,375 | $1,250 | $1,025 | $925 | $850 | $775 | $700 | $630 | $565 | $500 | $425 | $350 |

✳ DSE Grade

| $1,800 | $1,525 | $1,250 | $1,100 | $950 | $850 | $775 | $715 | $650 | $600 | $540 | $475 |

✳ H Grade

| $1,975 | $1,650 | $1,300 | $1,200 | $1,100 | $1,000 | $950 | $900 | $800 | $750 | $650 | $550 |

✳ HE Grade

| $2,750 | $2,350 | $1,800 | $1,600 | $1,400 | $1,250 | $1,100 | $1,000 | $900 | $850 | $800 | $700 |

✳ G Grade

| N/A | $1,975 | $1,600 | $1,500 | $1,400 | $1,300 | $1,200 | $1,100 | $1,000 | $900 | $800 | $600 |

✳ GE Grade

| N/A | $2,850 | $2,200 | $1,800 | $1,700 | $1,500 | $1,400 | $1,300 | $1,200 | $1,100 | $1,000 | $900 |

✳ F Grade

| N/A | N/A | $2,150 | $1,700 | $1,600 | $1,500 | $1,400 | $1,100 | $1,000 | $900 | $800 | $700 |

✳ FE Grade

| N/A | N/A | $2,950 | $2,400 | $2,000 | $1,800 | $1,600 | $1,400 | $1,300 | $1,100 | $1,000 | $900 |

✳ E Grade

| N/A | N/A | $2,700 | $2,300 | $2,100 | $1,900 | $1,800 | $1,600 | $1,400 | $1,200 | $1,100 | $900 |

✳ EE Grade

| N/A | N/A | $3,800 | $3,200 | $3,000 | $2,700 | $2,500 | $2,300 | $2,100 | $1,900 | $1,800 | $1,600 |

✳ D Grade

| N/A | N/A | $3,300 | $2,500 | $2,200 | $2,000 | $1,800 | $1,600 | $1,500 | $1,400 | $1,200 | $1,100 |

✳ DE Grade

| N/A | N/A | $4,850 | $4,000 | $3,700 | $3,200 | $2,700 | $2,200 | $2,000 | $1,800 | $1,600 | $1,400 |

✳ C Grade

| N/A | N/A | $4,850 | $4,000 | $3,200 | $2,700 | $2,400 | $2,200 | $2,000 | $1,900 | $1,800 | $1,600 |

✳ CE Grade

| N/A | N/A | $7,000 | $5,500 | $4,700 | $4,200 | $4,000 | $3,400 | $3,000 | $2,500 | $2,100 | $1,750 |

100%	98%	95%	90%	80%	70%	60%	50%	40%	30%	20%	10%

❋ B Grade

| N/A | N/A | $7,000 | $5,500 | $4,700 | $4,200 | $4,000 | $3,400 | $3,000 | $2,500 | $2,100 | $1,750 |

❋ BE Grade

| N/A | N/A | $8,250 | $7,500 | $6,750 | $5,950 | $5,100 | $4,400 | $3,700 | $3,500 | $3,200 | $3,000 |

❋ A grade - auto ejectors standard.

| N/A | N/A | $15,500 | $13,750 | $11,250 | $9,250 | $8,150 | $7,200 | $6,300 | $5,400 | $4,700 | $4,200 |

❋ AA grade - auto ejectors standard.

| N/A | N/A | $21,750 | $18,750 | $15,500 | $12,750 | $10,250 | $8,250 | $7,150 | $6,500 | $6,000 | $5,500 |

❋ **Optimus Grade** - auto ejectors standard. Extreme rarity precludes accurate percentage pricing.

❋ **Thousand Dollar Grade** - auto ejectors standard. Extreme rarity precludes accurate percentage pricing.

GRADING - PPGS™	100%	98%	95%	90%	80%	70%	60%

NITRO SPECIAL - 12, 16, 20 ga., or .410 bore, 26-32 in. barrels, various chokes, boxlock, extractors, checkered pistol grip stock. Mfg. 1921-48.

	100%	98%	95%	90%	80%	70%	60%
12 ga.	$575	$450	$395	$350	$300	$250	$225
16 ga.	$725	$650	$575	$475	$400	$350	$300
20 ga.	$950	$875	$775	$675	$575	$450	$395
.410 bore	$2,750	$2,450	$2,150	$1,725	$1,400	$1,175	$950

Add 10% for ST.

GRADE A FIELD MODEL - 12, 16, 20 ga., or .410 bore, 26-32 in. barrels, various chokes, boxlock, checkered pistol grip stock. Mfg. 1934-42.

	100%	98%	95%	90%	80%	70%	60%
12 ga.	$950	$875	$800	$725	$650	$575	$475
16 ga.	$1,100	$950	$875	$775	$675	$600	$500
20 ga.	$1,450	$1,250	$995	$875	$775	$675	$575
.410 bore	$3,475	$3,100	$2,750	$2,450	$2,150	$1,725	$1,400

Add 33% for auto ejectors.
Add 10% for ST.

GRADE A SKEET MODEL - similar to Grade A, with 26 in. skeet bore barrels, auto ejector, single trigger and beavertail forearm standard.

	100%	98%	95%	90%	80%	70%	60%
12 ga.	$1,450	$1,275	$1,075	$925	$800	$675	$575
16 ga.	$1,750	$1,475	$1,250	$1,075	$950	$800	$675
20 ga.	$2,250	$1,975	$1,700	$1,500	$1,250	$995	$850
.410 bore	$3,950	$3,500	$2,750	$2,450	$2,150	$1,725	$1,400

SHOTGUNS: SINGLE BARREL

TRAP GUN - 12 ga. only, 30 or 32 in. VR barrel, full choke, boxlock, auto ejector, checkered pistol grip stock. Disc. 1942.

	100%	98%	95%	90%	80%	70%	60%
	$550	$440	$385	$330	$275	$250	$195

LONG RANGE FIELD - 12, 16, 20 ga., or .410 bore, 26-32 in. barrel, boxlock, extractor, checkered pistol grip stock. Disc. 1942.

	100%	98%	95%	90%	80%	70%	60%
	$330	$275	$250	$220	$165	$140	$120

LEFEVER, D.M. & SON

Previous manufacturer located in Bowling Green, OH, circa 1901-1906.

SHOTGUNS

"Uncle Dan" Lefever, founder of Lefever Arms, designed and manufactured the first breech loading double hammerless shotgun made in the U.S. Production started in 1872 and continued in the Syracuse, NY plant until he sold his interest in the Lefever Arms Company during the early

100%	98%	95%	90%	80%	70%	60%	50%	40%	30%	20%	10%

1900s. He then moved to Ohio and started another factory under the name D.M. Lefever & Son. After his death a few years later the Ohio factory was closed, while his old company (Lefever Arms Co.) continued manufacturing Lefevers until being sold to Ithaca Gun Company in 1916. From that point, Lefever Arms Co. was a branch of Ithaca and continued to make shotguns until shortly after WWII.

Total production on D.M. Lefever shotguns between 1901-1904 totaled less than 1,200. Because of their inherent rarity, values listed show only 10%-80% condition specimens. D.M. Lefever specimens are so rare in 80%+ condition that prices cannot be accurately ascertained.

SHOTGUNS: SxS

NEW LEFEVER MODEL - 12, 16, or 20 ga., boxlock action, any length barrel and choke on order, auto ejectors standard on all grades except O Excelsior, double triggers standard on all except Uncle Dan grade, optional single triggers available, checkered walnut pistol grip or straight stock, grades differ as to engraving, wood, checkering and overall quality. Mfg. 1904-06.

> Add 50% for 16 ga.
> Add 10% for SST.

✳ O Excelsior Grade

N/A	N/A	N/A	N/A	$2,365	$1,925	$1,650	$1,475	$1,350	$1,175	$950	$750

✳ Excelsior Grade w/ejectors

N/A	N/A	N/A	N/A	$2,640	$2,310	$1,925	$1,595	$1,450	$1,300	$1,045	$825

✳ F Grade, No. 9

N/A	N/A	N/A	N/A	N/A	$2,640	$2,310	$1,925	$1,725	$1,575	$1,300	$1,000

✳ E Grade, No. 8

N/A	N/A	N/A	N/A	N/A	$3,350	$2,875	$2,300	$2,075	$1,800	$1,575	$1,250

✳ D Grade, No. 7

N/A	N/A	N/A	N/A	N/A	$4,125	$3,850	$3,375	$2,975	$2,750	$2,500	$1,925

✳ C Grade, No. 6

N/A	N/A	N/A	N/A	N/A	$5,200	$4,400	$4,125	$3,850	$3,575	$3,175	$2,750

✳ B Grade, No. 5

N/A	N/A	N/A	N/A	N/A	$5,500	$4,600	$4,275	$3,975	$3,750	$3,450	$3,100

✳ AA Grade, No. 4

N/A	N/A	N/A	N/A	N/A	$7,700	$6,600	$5,500	$4,850	$4,400	$3,700	$3,350

UNCLE DAN GRADE - extreme rarity factor precludes accurate pricing.

SHOTGUNS: SINGLE BARREL TRAP

TRAP GUN - 12 ga., 26-32 in. full choke, auto ejector, boxlock, checkered pistol grip stock. Mfg. 1904-06.

> Extreme rarity factor precludes accurate pricing.

LE FORGERON

Previous manufacturer located in Belgium. Previously imported and distributed by Midwest Gun Sport in Zebulon, NC.

GRADING - PPGS™	100%	98%	95%	90%	80%	70%	60%

RIFLES: SxS

MODEL 6020 - 9.3x74R cal., boxlock action, beavertail forearm, pistol grip stock.

	$4,450	$4,025	$3,750	$3,475	$3,100	$2,800	$2,550

Last MSR was $4,900.

> Add $700 for sideplates (Model 6040).

GRADING - PPGS™	100%	98%	95%	90%	80%	70%	60%

MODEL 6030 - sidelock action, engraved action with deluxe French walnut stock and forearm.

	$8,475	$7,900	$7,100	$6,300	$5,500	$4,700	$4,000

Last MSR was $8,950.

SHOTGUNS: SxS

Prices represent the last import information available (1989).

BOXLOCK EJECTOR - 20 or 28 ga. only, with or without sideplates, select French walnut stock, choice of engraving patterns (optional), single trigger.

	$3,975	$3,650	$3,325	$2,995	$2,600	$2,250	$1,900

Last MSR was $4,400.

Add $1,000 for sideplates.

SIDELOCK EJECTOR - 20 or 28 ga. only, select French walnut stock, choice of engraving patterns (optional), rounded action, single trigger.

	$10,200	$9,250	$8,500	$7,900	$7,100	$6,300	$5,500

Last MSR was $11,600.

LE FRANCAIS PISTOLS

Previous trademark manufactured by Manufacture Francaise d'Armes et Cycles de Saint-Etienne, located in Saint Etienne, France. Trade name was MANUFRANCE.

PISTOLS: SEMI-AUTO

POCKET MODEL AUTOMATIC - .25 ACP cal., double action, 7 shot, 2 3/8 in. hinged barrel, blue, fixed sights, hard rubber grips. Mfg. 1914-1966.

	$300	$250	$210	$180	$150	$125	$100

Add 50%-100% for engraved models, depending on amount of coverage.

TYPE POLICEMAN MODEL AUTOMATIC - .25 ACP cal., similar to Pocket Model, except has 3 1/2 in. hinged barrel, some are marked "FRANCO." Mfg. 1922-1968.

	$350	$290	$250	$210	$180	$150	$125

Add 50%-100% for engraved models, depending on amount of coverage.

.32 AUTOMATIC MODEL - .32 ACP cal., double action, 8 shot, 3 1/4 in. hinged finned barrel, blue, fixed sights, rubber grips. 10,000 mfg. 1950-1969, very few imported into the U.S.

	$1,000	$875	$800	$700	$575	$435	$350

TYPE ARMY MODEL AUTOMATIC - 9mm Browning Long cal., double action, 8 shot, 5 in. hinged barrel, blue, fixed sights, checkered walnut grips, some are marked "FRANCO." 4,000 mfg. 1928-1938. Early model with plain tapered barrel (1928), later model with finned barrel (1931).

	$1,500	$1,100	$850	$700	$550	$425	$350

Add 10% for later model with finned barrel (1931).
Add 50%-100% for engraved models, depending on amount of coverage.

LEGACY SPORTS INTERNATIONAL.

Current importer located in Alexandria, VA.

Legacy Sports International imports a wide variety of shotgun and rifle trademarks, including Escort, Khan, Howa, Puma, and Silma. Please refer to these individual listings. Legacy also imports Mauser actions, with current MSRs ranging from $457-$3,485.

LEGEND

Current rifle trademark manufactured by D'Arcy Echols & Co. beginning 1996, and located in Millville, UT.

GRADING - PPGS™	100%	98%	95%	90%	80%	70%	60%

RIFLES: BOLT ACTION

Current Legend rifles utilize an extensively modified and refined Winchester Model 70 claw extractor action. Synthetic stocks are built by special order. Models include the Standard Sporter ($6,150 MSR), Dangerous Game Model ($6,750 MSR), and Long Range Model ($6,450 MSR). Additionally, many special orders and options are also available. Please contact the company for more information (see Trademark Index).

LEITNER-WISE RIFLE CO. INC.

Current manufacturer located in Alexandria, VA beginning 1999. Dealer sales.

RIFLES: SEMI-AUTO

LW 15.22 - .22 LR or .22 Mag. cal., paramilitary configuration patterned after the AR-15, forged upper and lower receivers, choice of carry handle or flattop upper receiver, forward bolt assist, last shot hold open, 16 1/2 or 20 in. barrel, 10 or 25 shot mag. New 2000.

MSR $850	$775	$675	$600	$550	$500	$450	$425

Add $50 for A2 carrying handle.

LW 15.499 - .499 (12.5x40mm) cal., receiver action patterned after the AR-15, mil spec standards, 16 1/2 in. steel or stainless steel barrel, flattop receiver, 5 or 10 shot mag., approx. 6.5 lbs. New 2000.

MSR $1,498	$1,350	$1,150	$995	$875	$750	$675	$600

Add $92 for stainless steel barrel.

LES BAER CUSTOM, INC.

Current manufacturer and customizer established in 1993, and located in Hillsdale, IL. Dealer sales only.

PISTOLS: SEMI-AUTO

Les Baer has been customizing and manufacturing M1911 type pistols for decades. The company should be contacted directly (see Trademark Index) for an up-to-date price sheet and catalog on their extensive line-up of high quality competition/combat pistols that range in price from $1,425-$2,748, except for Presentation Grades ($5,999-$6,186 MSR). A wide range of competition parts and related gunsmithing services are also available. Early guns with low ser. nos. have become collectible.

RIFLES: SEMI-AUTO

CUSTOM ULTIMATE AR .223 - .204 Ruger (new 2004) or .223 Rem. cal., individual rifles are custom built with no expense spared, everything made in-house ensuring top quality and tolerances, all models are guaranteed to shoot 1/2-3/4 in. MOA groups, various configurations include Varmint Model (disc.), Super Varmint Model, NRA Match Rifle, Super Match Model (new 2002), M4 Flattop Model, and IPSC Action Model. New 2001.

MSR $1,989	$1,850	$1,650	$1,450	$1,250	$1,050	$925	$800

Add $800-$1,100 for scope package (includes Leupold Vari-X III 4.5-14x40mm scope).
The $1,989 MSR represents the base price on the Super Varmint Model. Other variations are typically priced $100-$500 more, depending on the configuration.

Make/Model	Qty. Made	Year Issue	Retail Price

LEW HORTON DIST. CO.

Current firearms distributor located in Westboro, MA. While Lew Horton is not a manufacturer or an importer, this company has been responsible for many special and limited editions that are listed with quanities, but without prices, since they may vary greatly from region to region. Special/Limited Editions began in 1983.

SPECIAL/LIMITED EDITIONS

BERETTA

Make/Model	Qty. Made	Year Issue	Retail Price
Lady Beretta	100	1985	$285

COLT MODELS

Make/Model	Qty. Made	Year Issue	Retail Price
SAA Horse Pistol	100	1983	$1,100
Presidential - Gold SAA & Det. Spec. w/Gold Eye	600	1985	$525
Colt Boa (includes complete production run of 4 & 6 in. barrel)	600	1985	$525
Ultimate Officer's .45 ACP	500	1989	$777
Lt. Commander .45 ACP	800	1985	$590
Combat Cobra 2 1/2 in.	1,000	1987	$500
Lady Colt (MK IV .380 ACP)	1,000	1989	$547
Night Commander .45 ACP	250	1989	$725
El Presidente .38 Super Govt.	350	1990	$800
El Comandante .38 Super Govt.	500	1991	$800
El General .38 Super Govt.	500	1991	$850
El Capitan .38 Super	500	1991	$875
Detective Special	100	1992	$430
Elite Ten/Forty	100	1992	$900
El Patron	500	1992	$850
El Jefe	500	1992	$849
El Dorado	750	1992	$1,099
El Teniente	400	1992	$1,037
El Teniente	300	2001	N/A
El Coronel	750	1993	$900
Classic Gold Cup	300	1993	$1,285
Classic Single Action	180	1993	$680
Night Officer	350	1993	$680
El Presidente Premier Edition	10	1993	$3,000
Classic Government	300	1993	$965
Night Government	300	1993	$705
El Caballero	500	1994	$986
El Potro	500	1994	$1,025
Frontier Six Shooter	100	1994	$1,849
McCormick Factory Racer	500	1994	$1,149
Springfield Armory Bicentennial Edition	400	1994	$1,000
Springfield Armory Premier Bicentennial	200	1994	$1,213
Classic 45 Special Edition	500	1995	$960
Comp Commander .45 ACP Ported	350	1998	$889
Defender Custom .45 ACP 3in. w/4 Ports	100	1998	$900
Delta 98 10mm 5in. Matte SS	100	1998	$800
El Aquila Supreme .38 Sup. Engraved	20	1999	$3,000
El Aquila .38 Sup. 5 in. RB	350	1999	$1,000
El Cabo .38 Sup. 5 in. Bright SS	350	1999	$1,200
El Campcon .38 Super Blue	550	1997	$870
El Centauro .38 Sup. BTS	350	1997	$798
El Embajador .38 Sup. BTS/Gold	350	1998	$1,000
El General 5 Star Deluxe 38 Sup. Engr.	10	1997	$2,000
El Jefe Supremo Supreme 38 Sup. Engr.	20	1999	$3,000
El Jefe Supremo 38 Sup BSTS/Fire Bl.	350	1999	$1,410

Make/Model	Qty. Made	Year Issue	Retail Price
El Oficial .38 Sup R/Blue w/gold	450	1998	$1,003
El Sargento .38 Super 5 in. RB/SS	350	1999	$1,000
El Soldado 38 Super 5 in. Ryl Blue/Pearlite grips	350	2000	$1,020
El Soldado Supreme 38 Super A Engraved	20	2000	$2,996
El Soldado Supreme	20	2001	N/A
El Soldado Supreme Proposed	20	2001	N/A
El Senador	350	2001	N/A
El Senador Supreme	20	2001	N/A
El Toro 38 Super Bl w/jeweled parts	350	2000	$1,020
El Toro	350	2001	N/A
El Toro Supreme	20	2001	N/A
El Obra Maestra .38 Super Royal Blue/Gold	350	2001	$1,130
El Matadore .38 Super 5 in. Bright Stainless w/Gold	350	2001	$1,425
El Rey Hi Polish Stainless Steel Blue .38 Super	350	2001	$1,050
McCormick Combat Cmdr 45 Engr.	50	1995	$1,213
McCormick Combat Cmdr 45 Chrome	500	1995	$1,073
McCormick Officer Cmdr 45 Chrome	300	1995	$1,073
Night Officer II Chrm 45 Night Sight	100	1994	$829
Night Officer III SS/Matte 45	200	1996	$810
Officers Ultimate .45 ACP Bl/SS	500	1995	$900
Officers Ultimate .45 ACP Engr.	10	1995	$1,995
SAA CC/B Mop. Std. Eng.	15	1999	$5,345
SAA .45 LC Nickel Bird's Head Mother-of-Pearl, Std. C	30	2001	$5,715
U.S. Shooting Team .45 ACP	750	1995	$1,150

EUROPEAN AMERICAN ARMORY

Make/Model	Qty. Made	Year Issue	Retail Price
Witness Competitor 45 Ported	100	1998	$460
Witness Competitor Polymer 45 Ported	100	1998	$460
Witness Defender II 45 Ported	100	1998	$460
Witness Defender Polymer 45 Ported	100	1998	$496
Witness Tactical .40 S&W 12rd	300	1997	$400
Witness Tactical .45 ACP 10rd	300	1997	$400

H&R 1871, INC.

Make/Model	Qty. Made	Year Issue	Retail Price
999 Premier Edition	100 pr.	1993	$345

MOSSBERG

Make/Model	Qty. Made	Year Issue	Retail Price
Night Persuader Special Edition	300	1990	N/A

REMINGTON

Make/Model	Qty. Made	Year Issue	Retail Price
Model 541J Curly Maple	500	1994	$500
Model 700 Police .308 Win., 26 in. fluted	500	2004	$1,000
Model 700 Police .308 Win. w/spruce green stock	500	2004	$930

SIGARMS

Make/Model	Qty. Made	Year Issue	Retail Price
P220 Premium Edition .45 ACP	200	1994	$850

SMITH & WESSON - Lew Horton is a major distributor of S&W's Heritage Series and Performance Center models. Please contact Lew Horton directly to find out more information on this wide variety of handguns, including current availability and pricing.

Make/Model	Qty. Made	Year Issue	Retail Price
Model 25-3 Lew Horton Special	100	1977	$500
Model 29-3 Lew Horton Special	5,000	1984	$425
Model 629-3 Lew Horton Special	5,000	N/A	$400
Model 24-3 Lew Horton Special	5,000	1983-84	$380
Model 686 Lew Horton Special	N/A	1984	$450
Model 657-3 Lew Horton Special	5,000	1986	$410
Model 624-2 Lew Horton Special	7,000	1986-87	$395
Model 640 Carry Comp	250	1991	$750
.40 Compensated	150	1992	$1,699
.40 Tactical	200	1992	$1,499
Shorty Forty	N/A	1992	$950
Model 629 Hunter	200	1992	$1,234
Model 629 Carry Comp	300	1992	$1,000
Model 686 Carry Comp 4 in.	300	1992	$1,000
Model 657 Classic Hunter	350	1993	$545

Make/Model	Qty. Made	Year Issue	Retail Price
Model 356 Shorty	N/A	1993	$999
Model 356 Tactical	N/A	1993	$1,350
Model 629 Hunter II	200	1993	$1,234
Model 629 Carry Comp II	100	1993	$1,000
Model 686 Carry Comp 3 in.	300	1993	$1,000
Model 686 Competitor	400	1993	$1,100
Model 686 Hunter	200	1993	$1,153
Model 5906 Shorty Nine	200	1993	$999
Model 60 Carry Comp	300	1993	$800
Model 629 Unfluted	300	1993	$1,234
Model 629 Hunter III	300	1994	$1,234
Springfield Armory Bicentennial Edition	500	1994	$775
Model 640 Paxton Quigley	250	1994	$800
Model 625 Classic Snub	300	1994	$603
Model 629 Classic Hunter	500	1994	$1,234
Model 629 Quad-magnaported .44 Mag.	150	1994	$900
Shorty Forty Mark II	150	1995	$999
Shorty .40 Mark III	500	1997	$1,025
Shorty .45	225	1997	$1,096
Shorty .45 Mark II	N/A	1997	N/A
Model 625 Hunter .45 LC Fluted	150	1997	$1,234
Model 629 Hunter .44 Mag. Unfluted	500	1997	$1,234
Model 686 Hunter 7 Shot Unfluted	300	1997	$1,234
Model 640 Quadport .357 Mag. 2 in. Brl	500	1997	$836
Model 681 Quadport .357 Mag. 7 Shot	300	1997	$700
PC M627 357 2 5/8 in. 8 shot RRWO Unfluted	450	2000	$1,025
Model 686 7 Shot Night Sight	300	1997	$1,000
F Comp. 3 in. Comp. Barrel	500	1997	$800
Model 629 Classic Carry 3 in. Unfluted	300	1997	$590
M625 .45 LC 3 in. Rosewood Red ramp WO	400	1998	$755
M625 45 Colt 3 FL Rosewood RRWO	150	2000	$755
M627 Classic Hunter 41 Mg 6.5 in. wood flt.	150	1997	$614
M627 Classic Hunter 41 Mg 6.5 in. wood unfl	400	1997	$614
PC M629 44 6 in. Hunter w/barrel cut out, unfluted	350	2000	$1,300
PC M629 44 12 in. barrel FL w/sling, Bomar sights	400	2000	$1,059
PC M1006 Classic SER 10mm 5 9 shot	28	1998	$550
PC M27 .357 Mag. 5 in. fluted cyl. SB	16	1999	$670
PC M29 Classic SER .44 Mag. 7.5 wood c/s	19	1998	$1,060
PC M41 Classic Ser .22 LR 7 S&W sights	14	1998	$801
PC M4516 Classic Ser .45 ACP 3 3/4	7	1998	$866
PC M4563 CQB .45 ACP 4 Alloy Frame	100	1998	$1,235
PC M4563 CQB .45 ACP 4 two-tone	200	1998	$1,235
PC M4566 CQB .45 ACP 4 SS frame	100	1998	$1,235
PC M4567 Classic Ser .45 4.5 two-tone	14	1998	$1,010
PC M627 Htr .357 6 in. 8 shot unf. wood	200	1997	$1,060
PC M627 .357 Mg. 5 in 8 shot ported	100	1997	$1,050
PC M627 .357 2 5/8 8 shot RRWO unflt.	300	1999	$1,025
PC M627 .357 5 in. 8 shot unf. wood cmbt	1,200	1997	$1,000
PC M627 .357 5 in. 8 shot unf. rosewood	200	1998	$1,000
PC M627 .357 6.5 in. 8 shot fluted rosewood	200	1998	$1,025
PC M629 .44 Mg. 6 1/2 in. flt. 6 shot RMB	200	1998	$1,020
PC M629 .44 Mg. 2 5/8 in. 6 sht rosewood	300	1999	$1,026
PC M629 6 Htr w/bbl CO Unf port	100	1999	$1,060
PC M657 Classic Ser .41 Mg. 3 in.	7	1994	$550
PC M657 Classic Ser .41 Mg. 4 in.	25	1998	$550
PC M657 41 Mg. 6 1/2 in. FL 6 sht	200	1998	$1,020
PC M686 .357 3 in. 7 sht ss night sights	500	1996	$1,000
PC M686 .357 6 in. 7 sht Hntr w/port	175	1996	$1,024
PC M686 .357 Mg. 7 sht profile bbl	125	1998	$1,025
PC M9 Shorty 9 MKII 9mm Compact	150	1995	$1,050
PC M625 3 in.	N/A	2004	$1,110
PC M329 .44 cal., Clear Scandium frame, 3 in. Stainless bbl	100	2004	$1,200
PC M329 .44 cal., Black Scandium frame, 3 in. bl. bbl.	500	2004	$1,200

Make/Model	Qty. Made	Year Issue	Retail Price
PC M629 .44 Mag. cal., 7.5 in. bbl Compted Hunter TDA	500	2004	$1,171
M15 .38 Spl. 4 in. color case blue	200	2001	$770
M15 .38 Spl. 4 in. nickel	200	2001	$750
M15 .38 Spl. 5 in. nickel McGivern	150	2001	$1,070
M15 .38 Spl. 6 in. blue McGivern	150	2001	$1,040
M15 .38 Spl. 6 in. color case blue	100	2001	$1,070
M17 .22 LR 6 in. AS blue	200	2001	$1,040
M17 .22 LR 6 1/2 in. color case blue	150	2001	$1,070
M24 .44 Spl.6 1/2 in. color case frame	300	2001	$1,110
M24 .44 Spl.6 1/2 in. fluted blue	150	2001	$1,050
M25 (1917) .45 ACP 5 1/2 in. 6 shot	200	2001	$1,047
M25 .45 Colt 6 1/2 in. color case blue frame	150	2001	$1,111
M25 .45 Colt 6 1/2 in. fluted blue	150	2001	$1,050
M25 (1917) .45 ACP 5 1/2 in. color case blue	100	2001	$1,110
M25 (1917) .45 ACP 5 1/2 in. Military	150	2001	$1,050
M29 .44 Mag. 6 1/2 in. blue	250	2001	$1,045
M29 .44 Mag. 6 1/2 in. nickel	200	2001	$1,070
Schofield M3 .45 S&W	100	2001	$1,520
Schofield 7 in. bright nickel	100	2001	$1,520
Model SW1911 "United We Stand"	250	2005	$1,127

SPRINGFIELD

Make/Model	Qty. Made	Year Issue	Retail Price
Night Light Compact 1911-A1 Lightweight	500	1997	$749
Night Light Standard 1911-A1 Lightweight	300	1997	$749
M1911 Ltw Compact .45 ACP bi-tone 7rd	125	1998	$675
M1911 Ltw Std. .45 ACP bi-tone 8rd	300	1998	$675

SAVAGE

Make/Model	Qty. Made	Year Issue	Retail Price
10FP Tactical .223 Rem. Short Action	200	1999	$492
10FP Tactical .308 Win. HB 20	550	1999	$500
30 Joshua Stevens .22 LR	250	2001	$400

TAURUS

Make/Model	Qty. Made	Year Issue	Retail Price
Model PT-92AF	250	1990	N/A
Model 85 3 in. Ported Blue	500	1995	$229
Model 85 3 in. Ported Stainless	500	1995	$349

In addition to the special/limited editions listed, Lew Horton also subcontracted special editions that were sold from company flyers and other promotional materials. They include the following Smith & Wesson Models - Classic Hunter M29 (500 mfg. 1989), Model 63 2 in. (500 mfg. 1989), Model 36 2nd Amendment (200 mfg. 1989), Model 60 25th Anniversary (100 mfg. 1989), Model 629 Classic Hunter (mfg. 1986), Model 5967 (500 mfg. 1990), and the Model 3914 (200 mfg. 1990). There are two Remington models - the M1100 Special Field (200 mfg. 1987-88) and the M700 BDL .257 Roberts cal. (500 mfg. 1990). There are three Colt models - the Combat Python (750 mfg. 1987-88), the Pocketlite (350 mfg. 1989), and the Custom Cobra Stainless Sets (2 sizes, mfg. 1989).

LIBERATOR

Previously manufactured by the Guide Lamp Corporation (division of General Motors) circa 1942.

GRADING - PPGS™	100%	98%	95%	90%	80%	70%	60%

PISTOLS: SINGLE SHOT

LIBERATOR PISTOL - .45 ACP cal., simplistic design and action utilizing nonstrategic WWII materials, mfg. for European resistance movement during WWII, very limited number used in Europe, most used in Phillipines and China, each gun was individually packaged in a paraffin-coated cardboard box with wood ejector rod, wood spacer, and a smaller box containing 10 rounds of .45 ACP ammo with a graphics only instruction sheet on top, 4 in. smooth bore barrel, sheet steel stamping mfg. with welds, no ser. no., 1 million mfg. 1942 only.

$1,300	$1,200	$1,000	$900	$800	$700	$600

Add $1,300 if complete in original box with instructions.

GRADING - PPGS™	100%	98%	95%	90%	80%	70%	60%

An authentic instruction sheet will have a watermark reading "WHITING MUTUAL BOND RAG CONTENT," and all ammo will have a headstamp of "FA 42". This is the only pistol that could be mfg. (6.6 sec.) faster than it could be loaded (10 sec.). While the Liberator's appearance is crude, remember that the entire production run (1 million) was mfg. and ready for overseas shipment in 10-11 weeks.

Even though 1 million of these pistols were mfg., remaining specimens brought into the U.S. are rare. Complete pistols in original box are extremely rare.

LIBERTY

Previous trademark imported 1997-2003 by K.B.I., Inc. located in Harrisburg, PA.

REVOLVERS: SAA

FRONTIER MODEL - .38-40 Win. (disc. 1998), .357 Mag. (disc. 1998, reintroduced 2000 only), .44- 40 WCF (disc. 2000), or .45 LC cal., 4 3/4, 5 1/2, or 7 1/2 in. barrel, case hardened, bright nickel, or antique silver (new 1999) frame, choice of brass or steel backstrap and trigger guard, mfg. by Uberti. Imported 1997-2001.

$295	$250	$235	$210	$195	$175	$160

Last MSR was $339.

Add $45 for steel backstrap and trigger guard.
Add $80 for antique silver finish (new 1999).
Add $25 for bright nickel finish (.44-40 WCF or .45 LC only).

TARGET MODEL - similar to Frontier Model, except is not available in .357 Mag. cal., and has adj. rear sight. Imported 1997-98.

$300	$265	$240	$220	$200	$180	$165

Last MSR was $319.

BISLEY MODEL - .44-40 WCF or .45 LC cal., features Bisley grip configuration, 4 3/4, 5 1/2, or 7 1/2 in. barrel, case hardened or bright nickel finish, steel backstrap and trigger guard. Limited importation 1999 only.

$415	$365	$325	$295	$260	$230	$200

Last MSR was $459.

Add $60 for bright nickel finish.

LIBERTY I/II - .357 Mag., .44-40 WCF, or .45 LC cal., 4 3/4, 5 1/2, or 7 1/2 in. barrel, case hardened frame, blue finish, choice of brass or steel backstrap and trigger guard.

$275	$250	$235	$210	$195	$175	$160

Last MSR was $319.

Add $70 for steel backstrap and trigger guard.

This model changed nomenclature to Charles Daly Model 1873 during 2004 - please refer to the Charles Daly 1976-present section for current information on this model.

RIFLES: LEVER ACTION

MODEL 1892 CARBINE - .357 Mag. or .45 LC cal., choice of case hardened or brass plated receiver, 20 in. round barrel. Limited importation 2000 only.

$595	$525	$475	$425	$395	$360	$330

Last MSR was $665.

Add $15 for brass plated receiver.

MODEL 1892 RIFLE - .357 Mag., .44-40 WCF, or .45 LC cal., choice of case hardened, brass plated, or antique silver finished receiver, 24 in. octagon barrel. Limited importation 2000 only.

$610	$535	$485	$430	$400	$360	$330

Last MSR was $680.

GRADING - PPGS™	100%	98%	95%	90%	80%	70%	60%

RIFLES: REPRODUCTIONS

SHARPS TRAPDOOR CARBINE/RIFLE/BUSINESS - .45-70 Govt. cal., case hardened receiver finish, choice of 22 (Carbine), 28 (Rifle), or 32 (Business, limited importation 2000 only) in. round barrel, single or double set triggers. Imported from Pedersoli 2000-2001.

	$675	$575	$500	$450	$400	$350	$300

Last MSR was $769.

Add $20 for Hunter rifle.
Add $60 for Business Model (limited importation 2000 only).

ROLLING BLOCK CARBINE/RIFLE - .357 Mag., .45 LC, or.45-70 Govt. cal., case hardened receiver finish, 22 in. round (Carbine) or 28 in. octagon (Rifle) barrel. Imported from Pedersoli 2000-2001.

	$615	$550	$475	$425	$375	$325	$275

Last MSR was $689.

Add $10 for Rifle.

SPRINGFIELD TRAPDOOR CARBINE/RIFLE - .45-70 Govt. cal., case hardened receiver finish, 22 (Carbine) or 26 (Rifle) in. round barrel. Imported from Pedersoli 2000-2001.

	$725	$650	$600	$550	$475	$425	$375

Last MSR was $815.

Add $34 for rifle with 26 in. barrel.

RIFLES: SxS

LIGHTNING EXPRESS DOUBLE RIFLE - .44-40 WCF, .45 LC, or .45-70 Govt. cal., exposed hammers, 22 in. barrels, choice of case hardened, bright nickel (disc.) or antique silver (new 2000) finish. Limited importation 1999-2000.

	$750	$650	$550	$475	$425	$375	$325

Last MSR was $840.

Add $40 for antique silver finish.

SHOTGUNS: SxS

LIBERTY I/II COACH GUN - 12 ga. only, exposed hammers, 20 or 24 (disc. 2000, reintroduced 2002) in. barrels, choice of case hardened or antique silver finish, fixed chokes (cyl./cyl., 20 in. barrels only, or IC/M, 24 in. barrels only). Imported 1999-2003.

	$475	$435	$375	$345	$315	$285	$250

Last MSR was $559.

* *Liberty Coach Gun/Express Rifle Combination Set* - includes 20 in. 12 ga. barrels, and choice of 22 in. rifle barrels in any Lightning Express cal., blue finish only. Limited importation 1999 only.

	$1,025	$875	$750	$625	$550	$475	$425

Last MSR was $1,159.

LIBERTY ARMS WORKS, INC.

Previous manufacturer located in West Chester, PA circa 1991-1996.

PISTOLS: SEMI-AUTO

L.A.W. ENFORCER - .22 LR, 9mm Para., 10mm, .40 S&W (new 1994), or .45 ACP cal., patterned after the Ingram MAC 10, single action, 6 1/4 in. threaded barrel, closed bolt operation, manual safety, 10 (C/B 1994) or 30* shot mag., 5 lbs. 1 oz. Mfg. 1991-96.

	$575	$500	$450	$415	$385	$335	$295

Last MSR was $545.

GRADING - PPGS™	100%	98%	95%	90%	80%	70%	60%

LIEGEOISE D'ARMES

Previous manufacturer located in Belgium.

Small manufacturer that specialized in boxlock shotguns, normally engraved and with ejectors. Prices usually range from $600-$1,200, depending on condition and engraving.

LIGAMEC CORP.

Current rifle manufacturer located in Clearwater, FL.

RIFLES: BOLT ACTION

ULTRALITE 50 - .50 BMG cal., single shot with AR15/M16 lower receiver, 18.5, 22, 24, or 29 in. barrel with muzzle brake, Picatinny rail, 2 lug bolt head, M1 sling, approx. 11-15 lbs.

  MSR $1,350

$1,295	$1,150	$1,025	$925	$850	$800	$750

  Add $50 for 22 in. barrel, $100 for 24 iin. barrel, or $300 for 29 in. barrel.
  Add $160 for bipod.
  Add $150 for fluted barrel.
  Add $180 for iron sight.
  Add $130 for Ace stock with 1 in. recoil pad.

LIGNOSE (BERGMAN)

Previous manufacturer located in Suhl, Germany.

PISTOLS: SEMI-AUTO

EINHAND MODEL 2A POCKET AUTOMATIC - 6.35mm/.25 ACP cal., 6 shot, 2 in. barrel, blue, rubber grips, can be cocked by rearward pressure on triggerguard.

$350	$295	$225	$165	$140	$110	$85

MODEL 3 POCKET AUTOMATIC - similar to 3A, except without one hand cocking trigger guard.

$250	$220	$195	$165	$140	$110	$85

MODEL 3A POCKET AUTOMATIC - similar to 2A, except longer grip, 9 shot capacity.

$395	$325	$250	$200	$140	$110	$85

MODEL 2 POCKET AUTOMATIC - similar to 2A, without one hand cocking trigger-guard.

$325	$265	$215	$165	$90	$75	$55

LILIPUT

Previous trademark manufactured by August Menz, located in Suhl, Germany.

PISTOLS: SEMI-AUTO

4.25mm cal. - 4.25mm centerfire Liliput cal. (shoots 12 grain bullet), blue or nickel finish, limited 1920s mfg.

$700	$550	$425	$385	$340	$300	$280

6.35mm cal. - .25 ACP cal., mfg. in large quantities pre-WWII.

$250	$200	$140	$110	$90	$75	$55

LINDNER GUN COMPANY

Current manufacturer located in Sanbornville, NH.

Lindner Gun Company manufactures fine quality long arms per individual custom order. Please contact the company directly for more information, including model availability and pricing (see Trademark Index).

LINEBAUGH, JOHN

Current pistolsmith located in Cody, WY.

Mr. John Linebaugh has been making specialized, custom sixguns since 1980. He is the inventor of the .475 Linebaugh cartridge (introduced 1988), and the .500 Linebaugh caliber (the first successful .50 caliber revolver and cartridge introduced in 1986). Current pricing for a customer supplied Ruger Bisley model is $2,000-$3,500. Please contact him directly for more information, including a price quotation (see Trademark Index).

LITTLE SHARPS RIFLE MFG.

Current rifle manufacturer established in 1996, and located in Big Sandy, MT. Consumer direct sales.

RIFLES: SINGLE SHOT

LITTLE SHARPS RIFLE - various rimmed cals. between .22 LR and .38-55 WCF, features scaled down frame for smaller cals. (20% smaller than original Sharps), octagon barrel. New 1998.

MSR $3,250	$2,900	$2,600	$2,250	$1,850	$1,550	$1,275	$1,050

Add $100+ for English walnut wood upgrade.
Add $250 for set trigger.

LJUNGMAN

Previously manufactured by Carl Gustaf, located in Eskilstuna, Sweden.

RIFLES: SEMI-AUTO

AG 42 - 6.5x55mm Swedish cal., 10 shot mag., wood stock, tangent rear sight, hooded front, bayonet lug, designed in 1941. This was the first mass produced, direct gas operated rifle. This weapon was also used by the Egyptian armed forces and was known as the Hakim, and chambered in 8x57mm Mauser.

	$850	$700	$600	$495	$450	$400	$365

LJUTIC INDUSTRIES, INC.

Current shotgun manufacturer established circa 1955 and located in Yakima, WA. Dealer direct and retail sales.

Prior to 1960, Ljutic Industries, Inc. did business as Ljutic Gun Co.

SHOTGUNS: O/U

LM 6 - 12 ga. only, supplied with one set of O/U barrels, deluxe wood and checkering, separated barrels on O/U.

MSR $19,995	$19,995	$15,750	$11,000	$9,250	$8,400	$7,500	$6,600

Add $6,000 for extra set of O/U barrels.
Add $6,000 for top single barrel (includes 2 pull trigger groups, and 2 forearms).

DYNA BI GUN - 12 ga. only, includes one set of O/U barrels, deluxe wood and checkered stock and forearm. New 2000.

MSR $15,995	$15,995	$12,000	$9,250	$8,400	$7,500	$6,600	$5,700

Subtract $2,000 for stainless steel construction.

SHOTGUNS: SEMI-AUTO

BI MATIC AUTO LOADER - 12 ga., 2 shot, 26-32 in. barrels, low recoil, trap or skeet models available, stock and choking to customer specifications. Limited mfg. until 1999.

	$5,995	$4,450	$2,500	$2,100	$1,750	$1,250	$900

Last MSR was $5,995.

Add $2,000 for extra barrel.
Add $750 for extra release trigger.

GRADING - PPGS™	100%	98%	95%	90%	80%	70%	60%

SHOTGUNS: SINGLE BARREL TRAP

To date approx. 15,000 target shotguns have been manufactured total (all models).

DYNATRAP MODEL - 12 ga., 33 in. barrel, full choke, push button opening, extractor, trap stock.

	$2,500	$2,150	$1,600	$1,475	$1,300	$1,200	$1,100

Add $300 for release trigger.
Add $400 for extra release trigger.
Add $250 for extra pull trigger.

MODEL X-73 MODEL - 12 ga., 33 in. barrel. full choke, push button opening, high rib fancy Monte Carlo stock.

	$2,500	$2,250	$2,000	$1,850	$1,700	$1,600	$1,500

Add $300 for extra pull trigger.
Add $500 for extra release trigger.

DYNOKIC MODEL - 12 ga., 32 (disc.) or 33 in. barrel with 2 choke tubes, patented recoil reduction system reduces felt recoil by 50%, checkered walnut stock, many options available. Mfg. 1997-2003.

$4,795	$4,000	$3,450	$2,900	$2,500	$2,000	$1,650

Last MSR was $4,795.

Add $1,000 for stainless steel construction.

✳ **Dynokic Supreme** - similar to Dynokic Model, except has deluxe walnut stock with checkering. Mfg. 2000-2004.

$5,595	$4,250	$3,400	$3,000	$2,650	$2,300	$1,900

Last MSR was $5,595.

✳ **Dynokic Centennial Pro Stainless** - 12 ga., high grade walnut stock and forearm, 33 in. stainless steel barrel with 2 chokes, recoil reduction system reduces recoil by 50%.

MSR $7,995 $7,995 $6,250 $4,875

MONO GUN - 12 ga., 34 in. barrel, custom choked, custom stocked, pull or release trigger, a "built to customers specifications" trap gun. Also known as Standard Rib or Medium Rib.

✳ **Standard, Medium, or Olympic Rib Model**

MSR $6,495 $6,495 $4,900 $3,650 $3,325 $2,700 $2,300 $1,900

Add $400 for stainless choke tubes.
Add $1,000 for stainless steel construction.
Add $2,700 for stainless steel SLE Pro Model.
Add $1,000 for SLE Pro Package (includes Laib adj. comb, adj. alum. base plate with 2 pads, and Pro barrel with special bore).
Approximately 3,100 Mono Guns have been manufactured to date.

✳ **LTX (Deluxe Mono Trap)** - similar to Mono Gun except has 33 (disc.) or 34 in. medium rib barrel and exhibition wood and checkering.

MSR $7,995 $7,995 $6,800 $5,725 $4,750 $3,800 $2,900 $2,350

Add $500 for extra pull trigger.
Add $650 if with release trigger.
Add $300 for choke tube barrel with 2 chokes.
Add $850 for extra release trigger.
Add $2,499 for extra barrel.
Add $1,200 for stainless steel package.

GRADING - PPGS™	100%	98%	95%	90%	80%	70%	60%

✳ Pro 3 (Deluxe Mono Trap) - similar to Mono Gun except is lighter weight, 34 in. medium rib ported barrel, exhibition wood and checkering, Briley Series 12 choke tubes, pull trigger. New 2000.

MSR $7,995		$7,995	$6,800	$5,725	$4,750	$3,800	$2,900	$2,350

Add $1,000 for adj. comb.
Add $750 for extra pull trigger.
Add $650 if with release trigger.
Add $850 for extra release trigger assembly.
Add $2,599 for extra barrel with fixed chokes or $2,995 with SIC.
Add $1,000 for stainless steel Pro 3 Package.

SPACE GUN - 12 ga. only, single barrel, unusual design permits in-line round stock with recoil pad, circular forearm wraps around barrel, high post rib on muzzle half of barrel, patented recoil reduction system reduces recoil by 50%. Disc. 1999.

		$5,995	$4,150	$3,375	$2,825	$2,300	$2,000	$1,750

Last MSR was $5,995.

LLAMA - Fabrinor S.A.L.

Current manufacturer established during 1904, and located in Alava, Spain. Previously located in Vitoria, Spain until 1992. Currently distributed by Import Sports, Inc. located in Wanamassa, NJ. Previously imported and distributed by Stoeger Industries, Inc. located in South Hackensack, NJ until 1993. Previous company name was Llama - Gabilondo y Cia S.A.

During 1992, Llama Gabilondo/Vitoria went bankrupt. In January 2000, after arranging new financing, manufacture was taken over by approx. 60 employees of Gabilondo under the name Fabrinor S.A.L. - a cooperative.

PISTOLS: SEMI-AUTO

Most of the pistols listed below were imported by Stoeger, long time exclusive U.S. importer, and are so marked on the guns.

MODEL IIIA - .380 ACP cal., 7 shot, 3 in. barrel, adj. sights, blue, plastic grips., vent. rib slide. Mfg. 1951-disc.

	$235	$200	$180	$160	$140	$120	$110

MODEL XA - similar to Model IIIA, except .32 ACP.

	$235	$200	$180	$160	$140	$120	$110

MODEL XV - similar to Model XA, except .22 LR.

	$235	$200	$180	$160	$140	$120	$110

Add 50% for airweight.

MODEL XVII - .22 S cal.

	$235	$200	$180	$160	$140	$120	$110

Add 15%-30% for Deluxe Executive Model with choices of chrome or gold finish and engraving (choice of regular or gold damascened).

MODEL XVIII - .25 ACP cal., blue finish standard, available with optional chrome or gold finish and stag grips.

	$275	$225	$180	$160	$140	$120	$110

Add 15%-30% for Deluxe Executive Model with choices of chrome or gold finish and engraving (choice of regular or gold damascened).

MODELS C-IIIA, C-XA, C-XV - similar to Model C, except engraved chrome.

	$350	$300	$250	$205	$180	$155	$140

MODELS BE-IIIA, BE-XA, BE-XV - similar to Model CE, except engraved, blue.

	$365	$315	$250	$205	$180	$155	$140

Deluxe Models, all blue or chrome engraved with simulated pearl grips, add $20.

GRADING - PPGS™	100%	98%	95%	90%	80%	70%	60%

MODEL G-IIIA - similar to IIIA, except gold damascened, simulated pearl grips.

	$1,515	$880	$825	$660	$550	$440	$330

MODEL VIII - .38 Super cal., 9 shot, 5 in. barrel, fixed sights, wood grips. Mfg. 1952-disc.

	$305	$255	$220	$195	$180	$165	$140

MODEL IXA - similar to Model VIII, except .45 ACP, vent. rib slide.

	$305	$255	$220	$195	$180	$165	$140

MODEL XI - similar to Model IXA, except 9mm Para.

	$305	$255	$220	$195	$180	$165	$140

MODELS C-VIII, C-IXA, C-XI - similar to Model VIII, except satin chrome.

	$360	$315	$285	$260	$220	$195	$165

MODELS CE-VIII, CE-IXA, CE-XI

	$425	$350	$310	$285	$265	$220	$195

MODELS BE-VIII, BE-IXA, BE-XI - similar to Model CE, except blue, engraving.

	$495	$395	$295	$275	$250	$210	$180

Deluxe Models are similar, except simulated pearl grips - add $20.

OMNI - .45 ACP or 9mm Para. cal., double action, all steel construction, 2 sear bars, 3 safeties, 4 1/4 in. barrel, 7 shot mag. in .45 cal., 13 shot mag. in 9mm Para., blue finish. Importation disc. 1986.

9mm Para.	$440	$380	$330	$295	$260	$225	$200

Last MSR was $546.

.45 ACP Caliber	$395	$360	$320	$285	$250	$220	$195

Last MSR was $500.

SMALL FRAME MODEL - .22 LR (disc. 1994), .32 ACP (disc. 1993), or .380 ACP cal., Colt 1911A1 design, single action, 3 11/16 in. barrel, 7 shot mag., 23 oz. Also available in satin chrome, optional engraving patterns. Disc. 1997.

	$220	$180	$155	$135	$120	$110	$100

Last MSR was $259.

Add $60 for duo-tone finish (.380 ACP only, mfg. 1991-1993).
Add $33 for satin chrome finish (not avail. in .32 ACP cal.).

COMPACT FRAME MODEL (IX-D) - 9mm Para. (disc.) or .45 ACP cal., scaled down variation of the Large Frame Model, 4 1/4 in. barrel, 7 or 9 shot mag., 34 or 37 oz. Mfg. 1986-97.

	$325	$255	$200	$180	$160	$155	$150

Last MSR was $409.

Add $16 for satin chrome finish.
Add $90 for duo-tone finish (mfg. 1990-1993).

GOVERNMENT MODEL (IX-C) - 9mm Para. (disc.), .38 Super (mfg. 1988-1996), or .45 ACP cal., similar to Small Frame Model, 5 1/8 in. barrel, 36 oz., 9 shot mag. in 9mm Para., 7 shot mag. in .45 ACP. Engraved and deluxe models available also. Disc. 1997.

	$325	$255	$200	$180	$160	$150	$140

Last MSR was $409.

Add $16 for satin chrome finish (.45 ACP only).
Add $90 for duo-tone finish (.45 ACP only, mfg. 1991-1993).

MAX I MODEL - 9mm Para. or .45 ACP cal., patterned after the Colt Govt. Model, single action only, 4 1/4 (Compact Model) or 5 1/2 in. barrel, 3-dot combat sights, 7 (.45 ACP) or 9 (9mm Para.) shot mag., matte blue, satin chrome, or duo-tone finish, rubber grips, 34 or 36 oz. Mfg. 1995-99.

	$265	$225	$200	$180	$160	$150	$140

Last MSR was $299.

Add $10 for duo-tone finish (.45 ACP cal. only).
Add $16 for satin chrome finish (new 1996).

GRADING - PPGS™	100%	98%	95%	90%	80%	70%	60%

✳ *Max-I Compensated* - .45 ACP only, 7 or 10 shot mag., features compensated barrel. Disc. 1997.

	$445	$385	$330	$250	$200	$180	$160

Last MSR was $492.

Add $25 for 10 shot model.

MINI-MAX - 9mm Para. (disc. 1999), .40 S&W (disc. 2004), or .45 ACP cal., mini-compact variation featuring 6 or 8 shot mag., choice of matte, satin chrome, duo-tone (.45 ACP only), or stainless steel finish/construction, 34 oz. New 1996.

MSR $309	$265	$230	$190	$170	$150	$140	$130

Add $25 for satin chrome finish.
Add $7 for duo-tone finish (.45 ACP only).
Add $66 for stainless steel construction (disc.).

✳ *Mini-Max Sub Compact* - 9mm Para. (disc. 2000), .40 S&W (disc. 2000), or .45 ACP cal., 3.14 in. barrel, all steel construction, 3-dot combat sights, 10 shot mag., polymer grips, choice of matte, satin chrome, or duo-tone finish, 31 oz. New 1999.

MSR $316	$270	$235	$195	$175	$150	$140	$130

Add $26 for satin chrome finish.
Add $9 for duo-tone finish (.45 ACP cal. only).

MICRO-MAX - .32 ACP (mfg. 1999-2004, matte finish only) or .380 ACP cal., features standard or lightweight steel design, polymer grips, 7 or 8 shot mag., 3 dot combat sights, slimline slide and frame, non-glare matte or satin chrome finish, 23 oz. New 1998.

MSR $282	$250	$220	$200	$170	$160	$150	$140

Subtract $15 for Ultra Lite Model (disc.).
Add $18 for satin chrome finish (.380 ACP cal. only, beginning 1999).

MAX II - 9mm Para. or .45 ACP cal., 4.25 (Compact) or 5 1/8 (Government) in. barrel, 3-dot combat sights, anatomically designed polymer grips, 13 (.45 ACP) or 17 (9mm Para.) shot mag., 39-41 oz. New 2005.

MSR $325	$275	$240	$200	$180	$155	$140	$130

MODEL 82 - 9mm Para. cal., double action, 4 1/4 in. barrel, blue finish, 3-dot sighting system, 15 shot mag., ambidextrous safety, loaded chamber indicator, black polymer grips, 39 oz. Imported 1988-93.

	$550	$500	$450	$400	$350	$300	$275

Last MSR was $975.

MODEL 87 COMPETITION - 9mm Para. cal., competition variation of the Model 82, includes built in ported compensator, oversize magazine and safety release, fixed barrel bushing, beveled rapid load magazine well, 14 shot mag., extended and serrated triggerguard, and adj. trigger. Imported 1989-93.

	$995	$850	$750	$700	$625	$575	$500

Last MSR was $1,450.

REVOLVERS: DOUBLE ACTION

MARTIAL MODEL - .22 LR or .38 Spl. cal., 6 shot, 4 and 6 in. barrels, target sights, blue, checkered wood grips. Mfg. 1969-76.

	$220	$200	$180	$165	$140	$120	$100

DELUXE MARTIAL - similar to Martial, except finish as follows:

Satin chrome	$275	$250	$220	$195	$165	$140	$120
Chrome, engraved	$305	$275	$250	$220	$195	$165	$140
Blue, engraved	$290	$265	$235	$210	$180	$155	$120
Gold, damascened	$1,430	$880	$770	$660	$550	$495	$415

GRADING - PPGS™	100%	98%	95%	90%	80%	70%	60%

COMANCHE I - .22 LR cal., similar to Martial DA, mfg. 1977-82.

	$255	$220	$195	$165	$155	$140	$110

COMANCHE II - .38 Spl. cal., similar to Martial DA, mfg. 1977-82 and 1986 in .22 LR and .22 Mag. only.

	$240	$220	$195	$165	$155	$140	$110

Last MSR was $272.

COMANCHE III - .22 LR (disc.) or .357 Mag. cal., 6 shot, 4, 6, or 8 1/2 (disc. 1986) in. barrel, blue, adj. sights, checkered walnut grips. Mfg. 1975-95. Before 1977, it was called "Comanche."

	$280	$245	$200	$165	$155	$140	$130

Last MSR was $339.

❋ *Satin Chrome Finish (disc.)*

	$330	$270	$230	$205	$185	$170	$160

Last MSR was $395.

❋ *Gold Damacene Finish (disc.)*

	$1,100	$880	$825	$660	$550	$440	$330

SUPER COMANCHE IV - .44 Mag. cal., 6 or 8 1/2 in. VR barrel, adj. sights, blue only. Disc. 1998.

	$350	$285	$235	$220	$205	$185	$175

Last MSR was $440.

SUPER COMANCHE V - .357 Mag. cal., 6 shot, 4, 6, or 8 1/2 in. VR barrel, adj. sights, blue only. Importation disc. 1988.

	$335	$275	$230	$210	$200	$190	$180

Last MSR was $414.

LONE STAR ARMAMENT, INC.

Previous pistol manufacturer circa 1970-2004, and located in Stephenville, TX. During 2003, Lone Star Armament was absorbed by STI, located in Georgetown, TX.

PISTOLS: SEMI-AUTO

Lone Star Armament manufactured a lineup of M1911 style pistols. Models included: Ranger Match ($1,595 last MSR), Lawman Match ($1,595 last MSR), Lawman Series ($1,475 last MSR), Ranger Series ($1,475 last MSR), and the Guardian Series ($895 last MSR).

LONE STAR RIFLE CO., INC.

Current rifle manufacturer established 1992 and located in Conroe, TX, specializing in Remington Rolling Block rifle reproductions. Dealer and consumer direct sales.

RIFLES: REPRODUCTIONS

REMINGTON ROLLING BLOCK SERIES - various black powder cartridge cals., configurations, and options, case colored or nickel plated receiver, rust or nitre blue barrel, extra select checkered walnut, single or double set triggers.

❋ *Creedmoor* - features competition long range 34 in. full octagon or half octagon/ half round barrel with pistol grip and shotgun butt, single trigger set at 3 lbs., per Creedmoor rules, 10 lbs.

MSR $1,995	$1,850	$1,550	$1,250	$995	$875	$725	$600

❋ *Silhouette (Target)* - designed for silhouette competition, with 30, 32, or 34 in. full octagon or half octagon/half round barrel with pistol grip and shotgun butt.

MSR $1,995	$1,850	$1,550	$1,250	$995	$875	$725	$600

GRADING - PPGS™	100%	98%	95%	90%	80%	70%	60%

* **Silhouette Standard Rifle** - .40-65 or .45-70 Govt. cal., similar to #5 Sporting Standard Rifle, except has 32 or 34 in. barrel, steel shotgun butt plate, pistol grip stock, 11 lbs. New 1999.

MSR $1,595	$1,400	$1,150	$900	$750	$600	$550	$475

* **Cowboy Action Rifle** - .32-40 WCF, .38-55 WCF, .40-65 WCF, .44-77, .45 LC (disc. 2002), .45-70 Govt., or .50-70 cal., heavy 28 in. barrel, 8 1/2 lbs. New 1999.

MSR $1,595	$1,400	$1,150	$900	$750	$600	$550	$475

* **#5 Sporting Standard Rifle** - .25-35 WCF (new 2002), .30-30 Win. (new 2000) or .30-40 Krag cal., 26 in. round barrel, single trigger, case colored frame, standard American walnut stock and forearm, 6 lbs. New 1999.

MSR $1,595	$1,400	$1,150	$900	$750	$600	$550	$475

* **#7 Sporting Rifle** - .25-20 WCF, .32-20 WCF, or .22 Hornet cal. New 2002.

MSR $3,500	$3,000	$2,650	$2,350	$1,950	$1,725	$1,500	$1,200

* **Sporting Rifle** - various cals., standard sporting rifle designed for accuracy, 28, 30, or 32 in. barrel, straight grip stock.

MSR $1,995	$1,850	$1,550	$1,250	$975	$850	$725	$600

* **Deluxe Sporting Rifle** - deluxe variation of the Sporting Rifle with 28, 30, or 32 in. full octagon or half octagon/half round barrel with pistol grip and shotgun butt, buckhorn rear sight and choice of front sight.

MSR $1,995	$1,850	$1,550	$1,250	$975	$850	$725	$600

* **Custer Rifle** - .50-70 cal., an exact reproduction of Gen. G.A. Custer's original Remington Rolling Block, 28 in. octagon barrel with SST, straight grip, crescent buttplate, and Schnabel forearm tip.

MSR $3,500	$3,000	$2,650	$2,350	$1,950	$1,725	$1,500	$1,200

* **Buffalo Rifle** - various cal., features relic finish enabling a new gun to appear somewhat worn, double set triggers, exact copy of the original, 16 lbs. 100% refers to NIB condition, not finish.

MSR $2,900	$2,575	$2,225	$1,875	$1,625	$1,400	$1,200	$1,000

* **Take Down Model** - features take down action. Mfg. 2001-2002.

	$3,600	$3,150	$2,750	$2,300	$1,995	$1,700	$1,375

Last MSR was $4,000.

GOVE ROLLING BLOCK - various cals., new rolling block with underlever design by Carlos Gove. Mfg. 1998-2002.

	$2,650	$2,250	$1,875	$1,625	$1,400	$1,200	$1,000

Last MSR was $2,995.

LORCIN ENGINEERING CO., INC.

Previous handgun manufacturer located in Mira Loma, CA, 1989-1999.

DERRINGERS: O/U

STAINLESS MODEL - .357 Mag. or .45 LC cal., 3 1/2 in. barrel, synthetic grips, tip-up action, rebounding hammer, fixed sights. Mfg. 1996-98.

	$95	$80	$65

Last MSR was $110.

PISTOLS: SEMI-AUTO

During the height of production in the mid-90s, Lorcin was making 40,000 semi-auto pistols a month. One year, their production totalled 400,000 units.

GRADING - PPGS™	100%	98%	95%	90%	80%	70%	60%

L-22 MODEL - .22 LR cal., similar to L-25 Model, except 2.55 in. barrel and 9 shot mag., black or chrome finish, 16 oz. Mfg. 1992-99.

	$75	$60	$50	$45	$40	$35	$35

Last MSR was $89.

L-25 MODEL - .25 ACP cal., single action, 6 shot mag., 2.4 in. barrel, anatomically designed grips to fit hand better, choice of black and gold, chrome and pearl, satin chrome and pearl, Teflon camo finish (new 1992), or black and pearl finish, 13.5 oz. Mfg. 1989-99.

	$65	$50	$45	$40	$35	$35	$35

Last MSR was $79.

> **Add $20 for lightweight frame (Model LT 25, new in 1990).**

✳ *Lady Lorcin* - same specifications as the L-25 Model, except is available in chrome, satin chrome, or black exterior finish with pink grips. Mfg. 1990-99.

	$70	$60	$50	$45	$40	$35	$35

Last MSR was $79.

L-32 - .32 ACP cal., single action, 7 shot mag., 3.5 in. barrel, available in black or chrome finish, 23 oz. Mfg. 1992-99.

	$80	$70	$60	$50	$45	$40	$35

Last MSR was $89.

L-380 - .380 ACP cal., single action, 7 shot mag., 3.5 in. barrel, available in black or chrome finish, 23 oz. Mfg. 1992-99.

	$85	$75	$65	$55	$50	$45	$40

Last MSR was $100.

LH-380 - .380 ACP cal., similar to L9MM, 36 oz. Mfg. 1995-99.

	$125	$115	$100	$90	$85	$80	$75

Last MSR was $149.

L9MM - 9mm Para. cal., single action, 10 (C/B 1994) or 13* shot mag., 4 1/2 in. barrel, grip safety, black finish, 3-dot sights, 36 oz. Mfg. 1994-99.

	$125	$115	$100	$90	$85	$80	$75

Last MSR was $149.

> **Add $20 for disc. 13 shot mag. variation.**

LORENZO, CRESS

Current rifle manufacturer located in Minersville, UT.

Custom gunmaker Cress Lorenzo specializes in custom express rifles built to customer specifications. Many options are available, in addition to general gunsmithing services. Please contact Mr. Lorenzo directly for more information, including models, options, availability and pricing (see Trademark Index).

LUCCHINI, SANDRO

Current manufacturer located in Sarezzo (Brescia), Italy.

Lucchini manufactures high quality, made to order, double rifles and SxS shotguns (approx. 10-12 guns annually). Shotguns starting prices are as follows (does not include engraving – Purdey style rose and scroll is approx. $2,000, while elaborate work by a master engraver can exceed $25,000): $6,000 for Anson action without sideplates (add $1,000 for sideplates), $14,000 for standard sidelock, manual cocking extractor hammer guns starts at $11,000, self cocking ejectors are $14,000. Add 10% for 28 ga. or .410 bore, and 20% for matched pairs. All shotgun barrels are chopper lump construction. Double rifles start at $26,000 for calibers under .375 H&H, and are available up to .600 NE. All double rifles feature Ferlach barrels. Please contact the manufacturer directly for more current information (see Trademark Index).

LUGERS WITH VARIATIONS

Currently manufactured trademark of both pistol and shotgun configurations. Pistol design originated by Georg Luger, circa 1899. This trademarked name is currently manufactured/marketed by Stoeger Industries, located in Wayne, NJ. Previous post-WWII manufacture (through 1997) was by Mauser- Werke Oberndorf Waffensysteme, located in Oberndorf, Germany. Many previous manufacturers - see main text for more information.

Note: The Luger section in this book is arranged chronologically by year of manufacture (1900 models to Post-War production), under individual manufacturer headings.

Often times, year of production can be hard to nail down, especially on commercial models. An easier way to initially identify your Luger is to categorize by toggle marking first - then by chamber marking within groups (chronologically for dated chambers). Once you know period of manufacture, simply refer to the appropriate subheading in this section. While some rare variations will be excluded in this generalized overview, it will be very helpful to establish correct, basic knowledge about your particular Luger.

While many recently imported Lugers would make workable shooters, they have in no way lowered prices on 90%+ condition specimens due to normal collector activity in top quality only pistols. Recently imported Lugers should have the importer's name visibly stamped on an exterior surface. Most of these imports are in the 9mm Para. - 4 in. barrel configuration.

Every year more and more reblue, restrawed, regripped, reframed, rebarreled Lugers are sold to unknowing military handgun collectors as rare variations. On any expensive contract variation, careful inspection on all parts must be made before potentially purchasing. If in doubt, secure 2 or 3 additional appraisals/observations from qualified individuals. Lugers are a field in themselves and an experienced Winchester dealer would not be qualified to guesstimate the originality of these German handguns.

A final note on Lugers: Original pistols in 90%-100% condition have not been affected by the influx of recent imports as these newly imported guns are usually in 80% and lower condition or have been reblued.

It seems that every year the prices of top quality (98%+ condition) original Lugers get more expensive and less predictable. For this reason, the 100% values on some vintage Lugers have been omitted intentionally, since rarity precludes accurate price evaluation in this condition factor. In many cases, the value for a mint original military Luger can double the 98% price listed.

Values for all variations of Lugers listed assume a proper magazine and matching parts.

REFERENCE GUIDE BY TOGGLE MARKING

DWM TOGGLE IDENTIFICATION

DWM MODELS

- ✱ *DWM MODELS* - mfg. from 1900 to 1930 in Berlin, Germany.
- ✱ *1900 Models* - grip safety and "Dished" Toggles, ser. nos. 1-24,999.
- ✱ *1906 Models* - grip safety, many chamber markings, ser. nos. 25,000-74,000.
- ✱ *1908 Commercial Models* - no grip safety, 9mm Para., ser. nos. 39,000-74,000.
- ✱ *1908 Military Models* - no stock lug.
- ✱ *1914 Military Models* - stock lug, dated 1913-18.

✳ ***1920 Commercial Models*** - no grip safety, usually 3 7/8 in. barrel. Most common Luger, undated chamber, 7.65mm Para. or 9mm Para.

> Note: Lugers with 4 inch barrels are most frequently encountered in military and commercial models. 6 in. barrels usually denote "Navy" models. 8 in. barrels usually denote "Artillery" models. Guns with barrels over 8 inches are rare and should be checked carefully for originality.

DWM COMMERCIAL LUGERS

DWM MEANS DEUTSCHE WAFFEN & MUNITIONS FABRIKEN.

These are models manufactured from 1900-1923 found in the five digit serial range.

MODEL 1900 - ser. range 1-20,000. Configuration: 4 3/4 in. x .30 Commercial, American Eagle, Swiss.

MODEL 1900 - ser. range 20,001-21,000. Configuration: 4 3/4 in. x .30 Bulgarian.

MODEL 1902 - ser. range 21,001-25,000. Configuration: 9mm Para. x 4 in. "Fat Barrels" and 11 3/4 in. x 7.65mm Para. Carbine models, intermixed with 4 3/4 x 7.65mm Para. American Eagles and Commercials.

MODEL 1906 - ser. range 25,001-39,000. Configuration: Commercial American Eagle, Navy Commercial and Swiss, both 4 3/4 in. x 7.65mm Para. and 9mm Para. x 4 in. grip safety models.

MODEL 1908 - ser. range 39,001-71,000. Configuration: First 9mm Para. x 4 in. without grip safety, M1908 Commercials were interspersed with 7.65mm Para. and 9mm Para. Eagles, Commercials, Navy Commercials, and a few Carbines and Swiss.

MODEL 1914 - ser. range 71,001-74,000. Configuration: Last pre-WWI Commercial Lugers, made with stock lug, with a few 9mm Para. Commercials mixed in.

MODEL 1920 - ser. range 2,000i-9,999u. Configuration: Post-WWI Commercials, mostly 3 7/8 in. x 7.65mm Para. cal.

MODEL 1923 - ser. range 89,001-91,000. Configuration: The last thousand or so made have "safe" on lever and "loaded" on the extractor, 3 7/8 in. x 7.65mm Para. barrels.

ERFURT TOGGLE IDENTIFICATION

ERFURT MODELS - produced from 1911-1914 and 1916-1918 in Erfurt, Germany. Military Model - Chamber dated 1911-1914 and 1916-1918. Erfurt models exhibit the most proof marks and individual parts numbering. Walnut grips.

SIMSON & CO. TOGGLE IDENTIFICATION

SIMSON & CO. - manufactured 1922 to 1934 in Suhl, Germany. Most Simson Lugers are military models (9mm - 4 in. barrels). During this 12 year period, Simson supplied the German Army Lugers exclusively. Can be dated 1925-1928. Many reworks of WWI DWM Military Lugers were refurbished by Simson, and can be detected by the Simson "Eagle-over-6" proof on repaired parts. A very few Simsons made in 1934 have just an "S" on the toggle (very rare).

SWISS BERN MODELS - Manufactured 1924 to 1929 by WAFFENFABRIK Bern, Switzerland. Relatively rare - these Swiss models have "improved" changes (flat and curved front grip strap), 4 3/4 in. barrels, walnut or plastic grips, grip safety. 1929 model (flat front grip strap) has Swiss Cross in shield on front link.

MAUSER VARIATIONS - Manufactured 1934-1942 in Oberndorf, Germany. Between 1930 and 1934 Mauser Werke was primarily engaged in reworking older Lugers, since transfer of machinery and personnel to the DWM plant in Berlin was completed in 1931. Mauser "Banner" models were made from 1934 to 1942, many are dated from 1939-1942 on the chamber. S/42 models are MOSTLY MILITARY contract guns manufactured between 1934 and 1940, usually chamber marked. "42" toggle marked guns (Mauser code) were mfg. 1939 and 1940 and are dated. "byf" marked toggles indicate guns made for German military use after 1940 and are more common than other military models. The Mauser Werke trademark also appears on those Lugers made in the 1970s.

KRIEGHOFF MODELS - Manufactured between 1934-1946 in Suhl, Germany. Early Krieghoffs are side frame inscribed. The German Luftwaffe contracted with Krieghoff for military guns in 1935. Early military Krieghoffs have "S" marked chambers, most are chamber dated between 1936 and 1945. Krieghoff Lugers are prized for their quality fit and finish and command higher prices because of their rarity factor.

VICKERS - Manufactured by Vickers, Ltd., circa 1921, in England from DWM parts for military contract sale to the Netherlands. Added barrel date is a date of arsenal refinish or refurbishing. Distinguishable by Vickers toggle and "rust" marked safety. Serial range is 1-10,100. Grips can be finely checkered with shallow contour or very coarsely checkered. Configuration is 9mm Para., 4 in. barrel, and grip safety.

GRADING - PPGS™	100%	98%	95%	90%	80%	70%	60%

PISTOLS: SEMI-AUTO, LUGERS & VARIATIONS

Lugers: Pre-1900 & 1900 DWM Mfg.

Values on most 100% Lugers have been omitted intentionally since rarity precludes accurate price evaluation in this condition factor.

1898/99 BORCHARDT LUGER TRANSITIONAL - 7.65mm Para. cal., 5 in. barrel, this is perhaps one of the most desirable Lugers, only few mfg. Examples scarce, no reported sales, an original example would command a price in the 5-figure range.

1899/1900 SWISS TEST MODEL - 7.65mm Para. cal., 4 3/4 in. barrel, 100 or less mfg., the very first true Luger. Engraved "Swiss Cross" chamber marking.

	N/A	$36,000	$30,000	$22,000	$16,000	$12,000	$8,500

Approx. 50 pistols serial numbered in the 1-50 range.
Buyers should be very cautious when considering a purchase of this rare model, as good fakes do exist.

1900 COMMERCIAL DWM - 7.65mm Para. cal., 4 3/4 in. barrel, 5,500 mfg.

	N/A	$3,850	$2,625	$2,000	$1,650	$1,325	$950

1900 SWISS COMMERCIAL DWM - 7.65mm Para. cal., 4 3/4 in. barrel, 2,000 commercially mfg. and 3000 military mfg.

	N/A	$4,150	$3,250	$2,500	$2,000	$1,500	$1,200

Add 15% for wide trigger (found only in ser. no. range 4,000).

1900 AMERICAN EAGLE DWM - 7.65mm Para. cal., 4 3/4 in. barrel, approx. 12,000 mfg.

	N/A	$3,750	$2,450	$1,575	$1,200	$900	$750

Add 40% for U.S. Test Model (approx. ser. no. range 6,100-7,925).

1900 BULGARIAN DWM - 7.65mm Para. cal., 4 3/4 in. barrel, 1,000 mfg., very rare in U.S., most often seen in the 60% and lower condition.

	N/A	$9,000	$5,350	$3,750	$3,150	$2,650	$2,150

Subtract 30% if rebarreled.

Lugers: 1902-DWM Mfg.

1902 COMMERCIAL - 9mm Para. cal., 4 in. barrel, serial number range 22,300-22,400 and 22,900-23,500 (500-600 mfg.). Commonly called "Fat Barrel" model.

	N/A	$10,500	$7,150	$4,750	$3,950	$3,350	$2,750

1902 AMERICAN EAGLE - 9mm Para. cal., 4 in. barrel, 600-700 mfg., commonly called the "Fat Barrel." Same ser. range as 1902 Commercial Model.

	N/A	$14,250	$9,500	$7,600	$6,500	$5,500	$4,500

1902 CARTRIDGE COUNTER AMERICAN EAGLE - 9mm Para. cal., only 50 mfg. with the Powell Indication Device; be extremely wary of fakes. Ser. no. range 22,401- 22,450.

	N/A	$33,500	$20,000	$15,000	$10,250	$9,000	$7,500

1902 DANZIG TEST - 7.65mm Para. or 9mm Para. cal., blank toggle, 4 in. barrel, Crown D proofs.

	N/A	$6,750	$5,150	$4,250	$3,400	$2,950	$2,200

1902 CARBINE - 7.65mm Para. cal., 11 3/4 in. barrel, approx. 2500 mfg.

Gun w/matching stock	N/A	$15,000	$10,750	$8,250	$6,500	$5,250	$4,500
Gun only	N/A	$8,250	$6,250	$3,500	$2,700	$2,200	$1,800

Add approx. 40% for American Eagle variation.
Subtract 20% for non-matching stock.

GRADING - PPGS™	100%	98%	95%	90%	80%	70%	60%

1902/06 TRANSITIONAL CARBINE - 11 3/4 in. barrel, 50-100 mfg., may have new model frame. Ser. nos. start at 50,000.

	N/A	$9,500	$6,400	$4,500	$4,200	$4,000	$3,800

Subtract 30% if without matching stock.

1903 COMMERCIAL - 7.65mm Para. cal., 4 in. barrel, 50 mfg., extractor marked "charge," ser. range 25,000-25,050, with 90 degree toggle checkering.

	N/A	$6,900	$6,150	$5,500	$5,000	$3,000	$2,500

Lugers: 1904-DWM Mfg.

1904 NAVY DWM - 9mm Para. cal., 6 in. barrel, limited mfg., a Transitional Navy, "Fat Barrel" with 90 degree toggle checkering and toggle lock, should have 2-digit ser. no. Extreme rarity precludes pricing for individual condition factors. Good condition (70%-95%), no problem, original specimens are currently selling in the $28,000-$35,000 range. Most of these pistols available for sale are fakes - buyer beware!

Lugers: 1906-DWM Mfg.

1906 COMMERCIAL 7.65mm Para. W/"GESICHERT" MARKED SAFETY - 7.65mm Para. cal., 4 3/4 in. barrel, "GESICHERT" marked safety, long frame. Approx. 750 mfg.

	N/A	$3,250	$2,050	$1,500	$1,125	$900	$750

1906 COMMERCIAL 9mm Para. - 9mm Para. cal., 4 in. barrel, 3,500-4,000 mfg. Scarcer than 7.65mm Para.

	N/A	$3,350	$2,000	$1,200	$900	$775	$650

1906 COMMERCIAL 7.65mm Para. - 7.65mm Para. cal., 4 3/4 in. barrel, area under safety polished bright, 5,000 mfg.

	N/A	$2,750	$1,625	$950	$775	$625	$550

1906 AMERICAN EAGLE - 9mm Para. - 9mm Para. cal., 4 in. barrel, American Eagle stamped in front of breech, 3,000 mfg.

	N/A	$3,350	$2,175	$1,350	$975	$800	$650

1906 AMERICAN EAGLE - 7.65mm Para. - 7.65mm Para. cal., 4 3/4 in. barrel, 7,500- 8,000 mfg. Add 40% for long frame.

	N/A	$2,950	$2,150	$1,200	$850	$725	$600

1906 NAVY COMMERCIAL - 9mm Para. cal., 6 in. barrel, approx. 2,500 mfg.

	N/A	$4,250	$3,250	$1,800	$1,600	$1,200	$950

Add 50% for 7.65mm Para. cal. with 6 in. barrel.

1906 NAVY MILITARY FIRST ISSUE - 9mm Para. cal., 6 in. barrel, first issue, 19,000 mfg., mostly altered safety marking - "GESICHERT" in upper position. Ser. no. range 1-9,000a.

	N/A	$4,250	$3,150	$2,400	$1,200	$875	$600

Add 10% for Navy unit markings.
Add 25% for unaltered safety variation.

1906 NAVY MILITARY SECOND ISSUE - 9mm Para. cal., 6 in. barrel, second issue, 2,000 mfg. Ser. range 9,000a-1,000b.

	N/A	$4,750	$3,550	$2,000	$1,600	$1,200	$1,000

Add 10% for Navy unit markings.

Lugers: 1906-1918 DWM & Erfurt Mfg.

Most common variations in good supply within this section in 50% or less condition will approximate the 60% value. This reflects its value as a representative shooter rather than a higher priced collector's gun.

GRADING - PPGS™	100%	98%	95%	90%	80%	70%	60%

1906 SWISS COMMERCIAL - 7.65mm Para. or 9mm Para. cal., 4 3/4 in. barrel, less than 1,000 mfg., Swiss "Cross in Sunburst," short frame.

	N/A	$2,850	$1,950	$1,500	$1,350	$1,200	$1,100

Add 20% for "Cross in Shield".

1906 SWISS MILITARY - 7.65mm Para. cal., 4 3/4 in. barrel, long frame, Swiss Police has Cross in Shield. Either "Cross in Shield" or "Cross in Sunburst."

	N/A	$2,950	$2,050	$1,200	$900	$800	$700

1906/23 DUTCH - 9mm Para. cal., 4 in. barrel, approx. 4,000 mfg., often seen as arsenal rework.

	N/A	$2,250	$1,500	$900	$750	$600	$525

Add 200% for original finish and barrel.

1906 BRAZILIAN - 7.65mm Para. cal., 4 3/4 in. barrel, 5,000 mfg., extremely rare in fine condition.

	N/A	$2,950	$1,925	$1,000	$800	$700	$650

1906 BULGARIAN - 7.65mm Para. cal., 4 3/4 in. barrel, 1,500 mfg., most rebarrelled to 9mm Para. (deduct 60%).

	N/A	$5,250	$3,650	$2,775	$2,000	$1,850	$1,450

This is the rarest Bulgarian - most are fakes or have been restored.

1908 BULGARIAN - 9mm Para. cal., 4 in. barrel, DWM on chamber, 10,000 mfg., extremely rare in mint condition.

	N/A	$3,000	$1,975	$1,000	$825	$750	$675

1906 PORTUGUESE ARMY - 7.65mm Para. cal., 4 3/4 in. barrel, Manuel II crest on chamber. Approx. 5,000 mfg.

	N/A	$2,650	$1,750	$1,125	$700	$600	$500

1906 ROYAL PORTUGUESE NAVY - 9mm Para. cal., 4 in. barrel, Anchor & Crown on chamber, very rare. Most are fakes.

	N/A	$10,000	$6,250	$4,000	$2,500	$2,000	$1,500

1906 REPUBLIC OF PORTUGAL NAVY - 7.65mm Para. cal., Anchor R.P. on chamber, very rare. Most are fakes.

	N/A	$10,000	$6,250	$4,000	$2,500	$2,000	$1,500

1906 RUSSIAN - 9mm Para. cal., 4 in. barrel, approx. 1,000 mfg., only 7 reported.

	N/A	$16,500	$10,000	$8,100	$6,400	$5,500	$4,600

1906 VICKERS DUTCH - 9mm Para., 4 in. barrel, approx. 10,000 assembled by Vickers Ltd. from DWM supplied parts.

	N/A	$3,250	$2,150	$1,500	$1,200	$800	$700

1906 FRENCH COMMERCIAL - 7.65mm Para. cal., 4 3/4 in. barrel.

	N/A	$2,650	$1,875	$1,575	$1,400	$1,200	$995

Add 100% if cased with accessories.

1908 DWM COMMERCIAL AND MILITARY - 9mm Para. cal., 4 in. barrel, Test/Acceptance Model, approx. 500 mfg. Ser. no. range 69,000-71,200.

	N/A	$1,750	$1,000	$750	$575	$475	$400

1908 NAVY COMMERCIAL - 9mm Para. cal., 6 in. barrel.

	N/A	$5,750	$3,900	$2,500	$1,800	$1,500	$1,300

Add 50% for 7.65mm Para. with 6 in. barrel.

GRADING - PPGS™	100%	98%	95%	90%	80%	70%	60%

1908 DWM MILITARY - 9mm Para. cal., 4 in. barrel, undated 1st issue or dated 1910-1913, no stock lug, except for a few late 1913 mfg. guns.

	N/A	$1,650	$950	$600	$500	$450	$400

Add 20%+ for Imperial unit markings (depends on history of unit).
Add 20% for undated or for 1913 date w/stock lug.

Approx. 25,000 1st issue pistols were mfg., 20,000 dated 1910, 15,000 dated 1911, 10,000 dated 1912, 25,000 dated 1913.

1908 DWM COMMERCIAL - 9mm Para. cal., 4 in. barrel, no stock lug or hold open, blank chamber.

	N/A	$1,650	$950	$750	$650	$500	$400

1910-1914 DATED 1908 ERFURT MILITARY - 9mm Para. cal., 4 in. barrel (dated 1910-14), 1911, 1912, and most 1913 chamber dates do not have stock lugs.

	N/A	$1,575	$925	$725	$600	$500	$400

Add 20%+ for Imperial unit markings (depends on history of unit).
Add 20% for 1913 chamber date with stock lug.

WWI ERFURT MILITARY SERIAL RANGES

CHAMBER DATE	OBSERVED LOW SERIAL	OBSERVED HIGH SERIAL	APPROXIMATE QTY. MADE
1911	575	9548	10,000
1912	255	866b	22,000
1913	575	2563b	25,000
1914	2137	539A	25,000
1915	none observed		
1916	13	5764b	80,000
1917	844	2854n	150,000
1918	304	5816s	180,000

Production data appears courtesy of Jan C. Still.

1908 NAVY - 9mm Para. cal., 6 in. barrel, scarce. Ser. No. range 1,000B-10,000B, 9,000 mfg.

	N/A	$6,750	$3,650	$2,400	$1,750	$1,500	$1,350

1908 BOLIVIAN CONTRACT - 9mm Para. cal., 4 in. barrel.

	N/A	$3,250	$2,625	$1,700	$1,300	$1,100	$900

1913 COMMERCIAL DWM - 9mm Para. cal., 4 in. barrel, grip safety and stock lug, horizontal "N" proof mark, 71,000 ser. no. range, rare.

	N/A	$2,650	$1,725	$1,150	$900	$780	$700

1914 COMMERCIAL DWM - 9mm Para. cal., 4 in. barrel, undated, stock lug, horizontal crown-N proofed.

	N/A	$1,975	$1,450	$1,000	$875	$750	$600

1914 NAVY - 9mm Para. cal., 6 in. barrel, scarce. Dated 1916 and 1917.

	N/A	$3,950	$2,800	$1,850	$1,300	$1,150	$950

Add 20% for 16 date.

Watch for fakes made from 1920 Commercials with new barrels and rear toggles added. Crown M proofs and date will look "fresh" (16 date usually encountered).

GRADING - PPGS™	100%	98%	95%	90%	80%	70%	60%

1916-1918 DATED ERFURT MILITARY - 9mm Para. cal., 4 in. barrel, dated 1916-18, there are no known 1915 chamber dated Erfurts.

	N/A	$1,500	$925	$775	$625	$500	$450

Add 20% for 1914 date.
Add $150 for original holster in average+ condition.
Add 50% for matching mag.
Add 100% for 2 matching mags.
Add 20%+ for Imperial unit markings (depends on history of unit).
Note: Date stamped on top frame is date of production; thus dates could be 1914, 1916, 1917, or 1918. All are Military P.08s, however, 99%-100% Erfurts are rare.

1914 ERFURT ARTILLERY - 9mm Para. cal., 1914 date is only one seen, 8 in. barrel.

	N/A	$3,000	$2,050	$1,275	$995	$875	$750

Add 20%+ for Imperial unit markings (depends on history of unit).

1912-1918 DATED WWI DWM MILITARY - 9mm Para. cal., 4 in. barrel. 1912-1918 dated. Most frequently encountered WWI military Luger, stock lug.

	N/A	$1,675	$1,000	$800	$625	$500	$450

Add $150 for original holster in average+ condition.
Add 50% for matching mag.
Add 100% for 2 matching mags.
Add 20%+ for Imperial unit markings (depends on history of unit).
Note: Date stamped on top frame is date of production; thus, dates could be 1914, 1915, 1916, 1917, or 1918. All are Military P.08s, however.

WWI DWM MILITARY SERIAL RANGES

CHAMBER DATE	OBSERVED LOW SERIAL	OBSERVED HIGH SERIAL	APPROXIMATE QTY. MADE
1908	(undated) 34	2636b	25,000
1910	5095b	5358d	20,000
1911	1524c	4825e	13,000
1912	599	9974	10,000
1913	2617	3850d	25,000
1914	282	6212c	40,000
1915	1398	2557d	100,000
1916	287	5438q	180,000
1917	587	3521m	60,000
1918	3690	9018n	190,000

Production data appears courtesy of Jan C. Still.

1914-1918 DATED DWM ARTILLERY - 9mm Para. cal., 8 in. barrel. Dated 1914-18.

	N/A	$2,795	$2,395	$1,750	$1,350	$1,150	$875

Add $500-$750 for matching stock, depending on condition.
Add $350 for proper non-matching stock.
Add $450 for original leather holster with shoulder strap.
Add 200% for rare 1914 chamber date.
Add 20% for 1915 chamber date.
Add 20%+ for Imperial unit markings (depends on history of unit).

GRADING - PPGS™	100%	98%	95%	90%	80%	70%	60%

Lugers: 1920-1930 DWM

Most common variations in good supply within this section in 50% or less condition will approximate the 60% value. This reflects its value as a representative shooter rather than a higher priced collector's gun.

1920 DWM OR ERFURT - 9mm Para. cal., 4 in. barrel, military and police, reworked and issued to police units, many thousand reworked, double date also, 1920 and 1921 dated.

	N/A	$995	$750	$600	$500	$475	$450

1920 COMMERCIAL - 7.65mm Para. or 9mm Para. cal., 3 7/8-4 in. barrel, available in many configurations, since these guns were assembled using the parts of previously manufactured Lugers, including 1900-06 mfg. with the grip safety on the frame.

	N/A	$995	$700	$500	$400	$325	$285

Add 25% for 9mm Para. cal.

These prices reflect original condition, and are not to be confused with recent imports (with import markings).

1920 NAVY COMMERCIAL - 9mm Para. cal., 6 in. barrel, very rare rework, Navy rear sight.

	N/A	$2,850	$2,050	$1,250	$1,025	$800	$700

Add 20% for 7.65mm Para. with 6 in. barrel.

1920 COMMERCIAL ARTILLERY - 9mm Para. cal., 8 in. barrel, very rare rework.

	N/A	$2,800	$2,400	$1,800	$1,400	$1,200	$900

1920 "LONG BARREL" COMMERCIAL - 7.65mm Para. or 9mm Para. cal., 10-20 in. barrel, extremely rare.

	N/A	$3,250	$2,650	$1,400	$750	$655	$600

Watch for fakes - these guns have to be evaluated one at a time. Barrel should have matching nos. and Crown N proof.

1920 NAVY CARBINE - 7.65mm Para. cal., 11 3/4 in. barrel, long frame (if short frame, be wary of fakes, very few produced). Navy rear sight, no forearm under barrel.

	N/A	$3,650	$2,550	$1,500	$1,025	$950	$850

1920 CARBINE - 7.65mm Para. cal., 11 3/4 in. barrel, very rare.

Gun only	N/A	$5,800	$4,850	$4,000	$3,000	$2,500	$2,000
Gun with stock	N/A	$9,750	$7,500	$6,550	$5,500	$4,650	$3,650

1920 SWISS REWORK - 7.65mm Para. cal., 3 5/8-6 in. barrel, several hundred produced.

	N/A	$1,775	$1,325	$1,000	$750	$655	$600

ABERCROMBIE & FITCH COMMERCIAL - 7.65mm Para. or 9mm Para. cal., long frame, 4 3/4 in. barrel, 100 mfg., total for both cals.

	N/A	$4,500	$3,450	$2,650	$2,100	$1,750	$1,500

Add 30% for 6 in. barrels (rare).

Inspect barrel legend very carefully (as in beware of fakes) - must have reinforced frame (look for rib in rear frame well).

1920/21-DWM - 9mm Para. cal., 4 in. barrel.

	N/A	$950	$725	$475	$400	$350	$300

Subtract 20% if arsenal reworked.

GRADING - PPGS™	100%	98%	95%	90%	80%	70%	60%

1920/23 STOEGER AMERICAN EAGLE - 7.65mm Para. or 9mm Para. cal., 3 5/8-24 in. barrels, less than 1,000 mfg., made by DWM for Stoeger, sold in USA, longer barrel models have higher value.

3 7/8 - 6 in. barrels	N/A	$3,750	$2,650	$1,500	$1,050	$900	$775
8 in. barrel	N/A	$4,950	$3,500	$2,350	$1,650	$1,200	$995

Add 50% for Mauser mfg., safe and loaded extractor, or V ser. no. suffix.

Be extremely careful when examining the frame markings on this variation as there are many fakes in the marketplace.

1923 DWM COMMERCIAL - 7.65mm Para. cal., 3 5/8 in. barrel, 14,000 mfg. ser. range 74,000-89,000.

	N/A	$1,000	$750	$525	$425	$350	$295

1923 DWM "SAFE AND LOADED" COMMERCIAL - 7.65mm Para. cal., "safe and loaded" marked on frame and ejector, 7.65mm Para. cal., 3 7/8 in. barrel, safety and extractor marked in English, 2,000 mfg. ser. range 89,000-91,000.

	N/A	$1,650	$1,125	$875	$600	$500	$420

1923 FINNISH LUGER - 7.65mm Para. cal., approx. 5,000-7,000 units made for Finnish military contract (Army and Navy), marked "SA" surrounded by a rectangle, most have been recently imported into the U.S.

	N/A	$900	$675	$525	$425	$375	$325

Lugers: Krieghoff Mfg.

Add 20% for matching mag. on Krieghoff Models listed.

1923 DWM/KRIEGHOFF COMMERCIAL - 7.65mm Para. (3 7/8 in. barrel only) or 9mm Para. (4 in. barrel only), few mfg., reworked by Krieghoff, chamber dated 1921 or unmarked, most in "i" range, Krieghoff stamped on back of frame. Be wary of fakes.

	N/A	$1,800	$1,400	$1,100	$880	$770	$660

DWM/KRIEGHOFF COMMERCIAL - 7.65mm Para. or 9mm Para. cal., 4 in. barrel, a few hundred made, side frame marked Krieghoff. Most are fake.

	N/A	$2,950	$2,100	$1,650	$1,300	$1,000	$800

KRIEGHOFF COMMERCIAL SIDE FRAME - 7.65mm Para. or 9mm Para. cal., 4 or 6 in. barrel, 1500 mfg., 1,000 with side frame marking, and 500 without side frame marking.

	N/A	$3,850	$2,950	$2,150	$1,475	$1,175	$900

Add 30% for side frame marked 7.65mm Para.

Add approx. 30% if w/o side frame marking.

KRIEGHOFF S CODE EARLY - 9mm Para. cal., 4 in. barrel, 1,800 mfg., German Luftwaffe. Has fat walnut grips, "H-K Suhl" toggle.

	N/A	$3,650	$2,575	$1,750	$1,200	$995	$895

KRIEGHOFF S CODE MID SERIES - 9mm Para. cal., 4 in. barrel, 500-700 mfg., Luftwaffe, ser. no. range 1600-2500, fine-checkered plastic grips.

	N/A	$3,650	$2,575	$1,750	$1,200	$995	$895

KRIEGHOFF S CODE LATE - 9mm Para. cal., 4 in. barrel, 1,800 mfg., Luftwaffe, ser. no. range 2300-4200.

	N/A	$2,975	$1,975	$1,300	$1,000	$750	$600

KRIEGHOFF 36 DATE - 9mm Para. cal., 4 in. barrel, 500-700 made, Luftwaffe military, 2 digit date, coarse checkered plastic grips.

	N/A	$3,500	$2,750	$1,800	$1,300	$1,000	$800

GRADING - PPGS™	100%	98%	95%	90%	80%	70%	60%

KRIEGHOFF 1936-1945 DATED - 9mm Para. cal., 4 in. barrel, approx. 9,000 mfg., 4 digit chamber date, 1936, 1937, and 1940 most common.

1936-37 & 1940	N/A	$3,450	$2,825	$1,900	$1,320	$1,225	$1,100
1938-39	N/A	$3,700	$3,000	$2,150	$1,500	$1,350	$1,225
1941	N/A	$4,500	$3,625	$2,500	$1,850	$1,500	$1,350
1942-43	N/A	$6,500	$5,800	$4,600	$3,550	$2,950	$2,500
1944	N/A	$8,750	$6,625	$5,250	$3,500	$2,950	$2,500
1945	N/A	$9,750	$7,650	$6,000	$4,000	$3,000	$2,500

The 1941 "large date" is very rare - watch for fakes (re-dated frames) on this model in general.

POST-WAR KRIEGHOFF TYPE I - 9mm Para. cal., 4 in. barrel, 150 mfg. for occupation forces, H-K marked toggle link.

	N/A	$2,850	$1,825	$1,350	$1,050	$950	$850

POST-WAR KRIEGHOFF TYPE II - 9mm Para. cal., 4 in. barrel, 150 mfg., unmarked toggle link, many parts proofed "Eagle-over-2."

	N/A	$2,750	$1,775	$1,200	$995	$875	$775

POST-WAR KRIEGHOFF COMMERCIAL - 7.65mm Para. cal., 4 in. barrel, 100-200 mfg., unmarked toggle, many parts proofed "Eagle-over-2."

	N/A	$2,200	$1,650	$1,100	$900	$800	$775

Lugers: Mauser Mfg.

Most common variations in good supply within this section in 50% or less condition will approximate the 60% value. This reflects its value as a representative shooter rather than a higher priced collector's gun.

1935-06 PORTUGUESE GNR - 7.65mm Para. cal., 4 3/4 in. barrel, 564 mfg., GNR on chamber, Portuguese marked safety and extractor.

	N/A	$2,750	$1,650	$1,300	$1,050	$800	$525

1934/06 MAUSER SWISS COMMERCIAL - 7.65mm Para. cal., 4 3/4 in. barrel, a few hundred produced, "Cross in Sunburst" or blank chamber, grip safety.

	N/A	$3,375	$2,600	$2,000	$1,500	$1,250	$850

1934 MAUSER BANNER COMMERCIAL - 7.65mm Para. or 9mm Para. cal., 4 in. barrel, hundreds produced, unmarked chamber, "v" suffix to ser. no.

	N/A	$3,150	$2,075	$1,550	$1,150	$950	$725

Add 15% for "Kal. 7.65" barrel marking.

S/42 K DATE - 9mm Para. cal., 4 in. barrel, approx. 10,000 mfg. during 1934 only for military.

	N/A	$5,000	$3,925	$2,500	$1,800	$1,500	$1,200

Add 100% for "large eagle over M Navy" proofmark.

S/42 G DATE - 9mm Para. cal., 4 in. barrel, many thousand produced 1935 only.

	N/A	$1,750	$1,250	$1,000	$800	$700	$600

Add 20% for Navy markings.

S/42 DATED CHAMBER - 9mm Para. cal., 4 in. barrel, many thousands produced, "S/42" stamped rear toggle, chamber dated 1936-1940. One of the most frequently encountered WWII military Lugers.

	N/A	$1,550	$1,250	$1,000	$800	$700	$600

Add $150 for original holster in average+ condition.
Add 50% for matching mag.
Add 100% for 2 matching mags.
Add 100% for Navy markings.
Add 20% for 1936 date.
Add 30% for "strawed" 1937 date.

The last regular production S/42 Models were mfg. approx. April of 1939.

GRADING - PPGS™	100%	98%	95%	90%	80%	70%	60%

MAUSER PERSIAN (IRANIAN) CONTRACT - 9mm Para. cal., 4 and 8 in. barrels, approx. 1,000 mfg. with 8 in. barrel, and 2,000-3,000 mfg. in 4 in. barrel, Farsi numerals.

	100%	98%	95%	90%	80%	70%	60%
4 in. barrel	N/A	$3,750	$3,200	$2,750	$2,250	$2,000	$1,750
Artillery (8 in.)	N/A	$3,000	$2,500	$2,000	$1,800	$1,500	$1,200

Add 50% for Artillery with matching rig.

1936-1942 DATED MAUSER BANNER - 9mm Para. cal., 4 in. barrel, over 1,000 mfg., commercial and contract sales. No sear safety, often have strawed small parts.

	N/A	$1,975	$1,350	$1,000	$800	$700	$600

MAUSER BANNER DUTCH CONTRACT - 9mm Para. cal., 4 in. barrel, 1,000 mfg., safety marked "Rust." Dated 1936-40.

	N/A	$3,000	$1,800	$1,000	$600	$500	$400

Add 25% for 1936, 1937, 1938, or 1939 chamber date.

MAUSER BANNER SWEDISH CONTRACT - 275 mfg. in 9mm Para. cal., 4 3/4 in. barrels, dated 1938, 25 mfg. in 9mm Para. cal., dated 1939, 30 mfg. in 7.65mm Para. cal., dated 1939, very rare in 7.65mm Para. dated 1940.

	N/A	$3,250	$2,125	$1,325	$750	$600	$500

Add 15% for 7.65mm Para. cal. (4 3/4 in. barrel).

CODE "S/42" COMMERCIAL CONTRACT - 9mm Para. cal., 4 in. barrel, a few hundred produced, dated 1938. Commercial proof marks only.

	N/A	$1,650	$1,100	$800	$650	$550	$500

CODE "42" - 9mm Para. cal., 4 in. barrels, dated 1939-1940, rear toggle marked "42." One of the most frequently encountered WWII military Lugers.

	N/A	$1,500	$1,200	$1,000	$800	$700	$600

Add 100% for Navy markings.
Add $125+ for original holster in average condition.

MAUSER BANNER POLICE - 9mm Para. cal., approx. 30,000 mfg., dated 1939-1942, police contract, have sear safeties, blue small parts. A few observed dated 1938.

	N/A	$2,000	$1,425	$1,100	$850	$650	$500

Add 30% with 1938 chamber date (rare).

CODE "41-42" - 9mm Para. cal., 4 in. barrel, 2-digit date, approx. 7,000 mfg. in January of 1941, "41" dated chamber, "42" code, most 42 dates are reworks.

	N/A	$2,500	$2,000	$1,200	$850	$650	$500

Add $150+ for original holster in average condition.

CODE "byf" - 9mm Para. cal., 4 in. barrel, thousands made, chamber dated 41 and 42. Rear toggle is stamped "byf," standard magazine was "fxo" marked and had an un-numbered plastic bottom. One of the most frequently encountered WWII military Lugers.

	N/A	$1,500	$1,200	$1,000	$800	$700	$600

Add 30% for original black bakelite grips.
Add $150 for original holster in average condition.
Code "byf" Lugers with black bakelite grips are referred to as the "Black Widow" variation.

AUSTRIAN BUNDES HEER - 9mm Para. cal., 4 in. barrel, several hundred produced, Austrian Federal Army, no serial letter suffix-same ser. placement as KU. Rarely encountered in mint condition.

	N/A	$2,000	$1,325	$975	$825	$750	$650

MAUSER 1934 CODE BYF, S/42 AND 42 KU - 9mm Para. cal., 3,500 mfg. Post-1942 Luftwaffe subcontract.

	N/A	$2,500	$2,000	$1,200	$825	$750	$650

GRADING - PPGS™	100%	98%	95%	90%	80%	70%	60%

Lugers: Reworks

DEATH'S HEAD REWORK - 9mm Para. cal., 4 in. barrel, very rare, possible early SS unit issue. Most are fakes.

	N/A	$2,500	$1,800	$1,500	$1,400	$1,200	$1,000

SIMSON REWORK - 9mm Para. cal., 4 in. barrel, DWM toggles, Simpson Eagle proofs on reworked parts.

	N/A	$1,050	$775	$550	$475	$450	$400

DOUBLE DATED DWM/ERFURT - 9mm Para. cal., 4 or 8 in. barrel, very scarce. 1920 over 1910-18 chamber dates. Often with sear safety and mag. safety remnant.

	N/A	$975	$775	$550	$500	$425	$400

Add 100% for intact mag. safety.
Add 40% for 8 in. barrel.

KONZENTRATION LUGER REWORK - 9mm Para. cal., 4 in. barrel, 200-300 marked "KI 1933" and issued to guards working in the first concentration camps - most went to Dachau. Most are fakes.

	N/A	$1,925	$1,575	$1,200	$1,000	$700	$600

Lugers: Simson Mfg.

SIMSON & COMPANY - 7.65mm Para. or 9mm Para. cal., 3 7/8 or 4 in. barrel, military and limited commercial sales, many thousands produced, but rarely found.

	N/A	$1,875	$1,075	$725	$525	$450	$375

SIMSON MILITARY DATED - 9mm Para. cal., 4 in. barrel, 2,000 mfg., dated 1925.

	N/A	$2,950	$2,300	$1,300	$1,000	$800	$700

This model is most commonly encountered with a 1925 chamber date.

SIMSON S CODE - 9mm Para. cal., 4 in. barrel, less than 1,000 mfg. Rare.

	N/A	$2,150	$1,525	$975	$675	$550	$500

Lugers: Swiss Bern

1906 BERN - 7.65mm Para. cal., 4 3/4 in. barrel, "Waffenfabrik Bern" on toggle, Swiss military, bordered checkered walnut grips, exactly 17,874 mfg.

	N/A	$2,600	$1,825	$1,200	$900	$700	$600

1929 SWISS BERN - 7.65mm Para. cal., 4 3/4 in. barrel, 29,857 mfg., many machining changes to simplify production, straight front grip strap, P prefix designates commercial model, brown or black plastic grips.

	N/A	$2,000	$1,250	$950	$825	$600	$500

Add 20% for red plastic grips and mag. bottom.

Lugers: KDF, Interarms, Stoeger, & Recent Import

Note: Post-WWII Lugers have been manufactured by Mauser Werke in Oberndorf, W. Germany during the 1970s, and by both Stoeger Industries and Mitchell Arms (see separate listing under Mitchell Arms) in recent years. Earlier Mauser importation was by Precision Imports, Inc. located in San Antonio, TX and Interarms of Alexandria, VA (and so marked on these guns).

Prices for 100% condition Lugers assume NIB status. If without box and accessories, deduct 25%.

INTERARMS MAUSER P.08 - 7.65mm Para. or 9mm Para. cal., 4 or 6 in. barrel, fully-contoured front grip strap.

	$1,000	$750	$550	$425	$375	$350	$300

GRADING - PPGS™	100%	98%	95%	90%	80%	70%	60%

INTERARMS "SWISS-STYLE" MAUSER EAGLE - 7.65mm Para. or 9mm Para. cal., "straight" front grip strap, American eagle logo on top of frame.

| | $800 | $650 | $425 | $375 | $350 | $325 | $300 |

Add 10% for 6 in. barrel in 9mm Para.

STOEGER .22 CAL. LUGER - .22 LR cal., toggle action, all steel or aluminum construction, 4 1/2 or 5 1/2 in. barrel, right or left-hand safety, 10 shot mag. capacity, previously mfg. in the U.S. until 1985.

| | $180 | $150 | $125 | $100 | $85 | $70 | $60 |

Last MSR was $200.

✳ **"1 of 1,000"** - .22 LR cal., 1,000 mfg. in 1984-85, includes wooden box and extra mag.

| | $295 | $225 | $175 |

STOEGER LUGER - 9mm Para. cal., choice of 4 or 6 (Navy) in. barrel, stainless steel construction, choice of polished stainless or matte black (new 1996) upper frame finish, American eagle engraved on top of frame, curved front grip strap, 7 shot mag., plastic mag. bottom, approx. 30 oz. Mfg. 1994-disc.

| | $675 | $475 | $325 |

Last MSR was $720.

Add $79 for matte black finish.

NEW MODEL CARBINE WITH STOCK - 9mm Para. cal., authentic reproduction of the original Luger Carbine complete with matching stock, accessories, and case. Inventory was depleted during 1998.

| | $6,500 | $5,500 | $4,000 |

Last MSR was $7,431.

CARTRIDGE COUNTER - 9mm Para. cal., left grip is slotted and contains a numbered metal strip. Manufacture began 1983, and inventory was depleted during 1998.

| | $2,650 | $1,550 | $950 |

Last MSR was $3,865.

COMMEMORATIVE BULGARIAN - 9mm Para. cal., 100 available on U.S. market.

| | $1,800 | $1,200 | $800 |

COMMEMORATIVE RUSSIAN - 9mm Para. cal., 100 available on U.S. market.

| | $1,800 | $1,200 | $800 |

✳ *Matched pair of each*

| | $4,000 | $2,550 | $1,850 |

MAUSER SPORT PARABELLUM - 7.65mm Para. or 9mm Para. cal., imported target barrel and adj. sights. 10 mfg. of each cal.

| | $2,500 | $2,000 | $1,250 |

✳ *Mauser Sport Consecutive Pair* - 7.65mm Para. or 9mm Para. cal.

| | $4,250 | $3,175 | $1,950 |

Lugers: Special Interest

SPANDAU LUGER - be wary of originality on this model.

MO4/05 G.L. BABY LUGER - 7.65mm Para. or 9mm Para. cal., 3 1/4 in. barrel, G.L. proofed, hand made under Georg Luger's supervision, two known to exist. Made with shortened barrel, mag., and grip frame.

BABY LUGER 1925/26 - .380 ACP/.32 ACP cal., prototype, 4 mfg., only one known is .380. Only Luger documented by the manufacturer.

VONO REWORK - 7.65mm Para. or 9mm Para. cal., 4 in. barrel, commercial, rework by W.P. Von Nordheim, extremely rare variation.

| | $1,500 | $1,275 | $1,050 | $900 | $800 | $700 | $600 |

GRADING - PPGS™	100%	98%	95%	90%	80%	70%	60%

1900 DWM CARBINE - 7.65mm Para. cal., 11 3/4 in. barrel, 100 mfg., only one known to exist. Characterized by "Ski slope" sight on rear toggle.

> Extreme rarity precludes accurate pricing on this model.

1907 U.S. ARMY TEST TRIAL - .45 ACP cal., at least four originally mfg., serial numbered 1-4, plus an un-numbered prototype.

> Extreme rarity precludes accurate pricing on this model. Undoubtedly, this is the most desirable semi-auto pistol ever manufactured, and is priced accordingly.

CONVERSIONS: JOHN MARTZ - John Martz of Lincoln, CA has converted WWII P.38s (please refer to P.38 section) and WWI or WWII Lugers into various configurations since 1968. These conversions are known for their quality workmanship and functional accuracy. Below is a generalized listing of variations he has fabricated and their values to date with production totals.

❋ *.380 ACP Baby Luger* - 6 fabricated, disc.

	$6,000	$3,200	$2,400

❋ *7.65mm Para. Baby Luger (Grip Safety)* - 192 mfg. total, includes 9mm Baby Luger also.

	$3,000	$2,500	$1,900

❋ *9mm Para. Baby Luger* - 2 1/4, 2 1/2, or 2 5/8 in. barrel.

	$2,500	$2,000	$1,500

❋ *Big-Bore .45 ACP Luger* - 79 fabricated (5 are babies), .45 ACP cal., fixed sights, 2 3/4, 4, 6, or 8 in. barrel. Disc.

	$5,500	$3,350	$2,400

❋ *.45 ACP Luger Reproduction* - made to original 1907 U.S. Army test trial specifications by Mike Krause (limited mfg.).

> This variation typically sells in the $8,500-$12,500 range, depending on condition.

❋ *Navy Model* - .45 ACP cal., 6 or 8 in. barrel, adj. rear Navy sight, estimated mfg. is 25 pistols, disc.

	$6,000	$4,450	$3,300

Add 10% for Navy Model with 100-200 meter rear sight.

❋ *Navy Model Ltd. Edition* - .38 Super cal., 6 in. barrel, adj. rear Navy sight, 10 fabricated, disc.

	$5,000	$3,950	$3,100

Subtract 10% for fixed rear sight (standard model with 4 in. barrel).

❋ *Standard Model* - .38 Super cal., 4 to 8 in. barrel, fixed sight, 3 fabricated.

	$4,500	$3,150	$2,400

❋ *Target Luger* - .22 Mag. cal., 6 or 9 in. barrel, fixed sight, 11 fabricated, disc.

	$7,500	$5,400	$3,400

❋ *Luger Carbines (with shoulder stock)* - .22 Mag. (disc.), 7.65mm Para., 9mm Para., or .38 Super cal., 11-18 in. barrel with adj. rear sights. Disc.

	$7,900	$5,650	$3,600

Add 20% for .22 Mag. cal. (2 fabricated).

83 Luger carbines with 16 in. barrels were fabricated with shoulder stocks.

42 Luger carbines with 12 in. barrels were fabricated w/o shoulder stocks.

❋ *Experimental Lugers* - experimental pistols have been made in .40 S&W (disc.), .41 AE (disc.), .357 SIG (11 mfg., 7, 8, or 9 in. barrel) and .357 Mag. Most have 8 in. barrels (except for .40 S&W cal., disc.). Extreme rarity (and not for sale status) precludes accurate price evaluation.

> The .357 SIG model had a retail price of $2,800.

GRADING - PPGS™	100%	98%	95%	90%	80%	70%	60%

LUGERS: ACCESSORIES

CONVERSION UNITS - .22 cal.

ERMA - postwar-green cardboard box.

	100%	98%	95%	90%	80%	70%	60%
	$600	$450	$325	$300	$250	$225	$200

ERMA-PREWAR IN WOODEN BOX - Pre-war in wooden box - deduct 20% for mismatched.

	100%	98%	95%	90%	80%	70%	60%
	$1,975	$1,475	$1,100	$800	$600	$430	$400

Add 50% for Nazi Navy property numbered.

Detachable Stocks

ARTILLERY TYPE FLAT BOARD

	100%	98%	95%	90%	80%	70%	60%
	$475	$350	$250	$200	$165	$135	$120

ARTILLERY HOLSTER RIG, COMPLETE

	100%	98%	95%	90%	80%	70%	60%
	$2,150	$1,500	$800				

Subtract 20% if shoulder strap is missing.

NAVAL-TYPE FLAT BOARD

	100%	98%	95%	90%	80%	70%	60%
	$2,000	$1,500	$800	$600	$450	$410	$350

NAVAL HOLSTER RIG, COMPLETE

	100%	98%	95%	90%	80%	70%	60%
	$4,500	$4,000	$3,000	$2,500	$1,800	$1,500	$1,200

Subtract 20% if shoulder strap is missing.

CARBINE CONTOURED (ORIGINAL)

	100%	98%	95%	90%	80%	70%	60%
	$3,750	$3,150	$2,600	$1,800	$1,200	$900	$700

IDEAL TELESCOPING WITH GRIPS - mfg. U.S. by Ideal Corp.

	100%	98%	95%	90%	80%	70%	60%
	$2,150	$1,675	$1,000	$700	$600	$550	$500

"Snail" Drum Magazines

1ST ISSUE

	100%	98%	95%
	$1,500	$1,250	$900

2ND ISSUE

	100%	98%	95%
	$1,300	$1,000	$750

LOADING TOOL

	100%	98%	95%
	$950	$750	$550

SHOTGUNS: O/U

CLASSIC MODEL - 12 ga., 3 1/2 in. chambers, engraved boxlock action, 26, 28, or 30 in. vent. barrels with VR and 3 choke tubes, gold SST, AE, checkered walnut stock and forearm, approx. 7 1/2 lbs.

While advertised for $919 by Stoeger Industies during 2000, this model was never imported. However, it has had limited importation to date from domestic distributors.

SHOTGUNS: SEMI-AUTO

ULTRA-LIGHT MODEL - 12 ga. only, 3 in. chamber, gas operated, 26 or 28 in. VR barrel with 3 choke tubes, checkered walnut stock and forearm, approx. 6 1/2 lbs.

	100%	98%	95%	90%	80%	70%	60%
	$295	$260	$230	$210	$195	$180	$165

While advertised by Stoeger Industies during 2000, this model was never imported by Stoeger Industries. However, it has had limited importation to date from domestic distributors.

LU-MAR s.r.l.

Current shotgun manufacturer located in Gardone, Italy. No current U.S. importation.

Lu-Mar makes a wide variety of O/U shotguns. In addition to their fine O/U lineup, Lu-Mar also manufactures SxS shotguns. Please contact the factory directly (see Trademark Index) for more information on Lu-Mar's complete line of quality shotguns.

LUNA

Previous manufacturer located in Germany.

PISTOLS: SINGLE SHOT

MODEL 200 FREE PISTOL - .22 LR cal., 11 in. barrel, blue, target sights, checkered target grips, pre-WWII.

$1,100	$990	$855	$770	$660	$605	$525

RIFLES: SINGLE SHOT

TARGET RIFLE - falling block action, .22 LR or .22 Hornet cal., 20 in. barrel, adj. sights, target type stocks, pre-WWII.

$990	$880	$800	$690	$605	$550	$495

M SECTION

MAB

Please refer to listings under the French Military heading.

MAC (MILITARY ARMAMENT CORP.)

Please refer to FMJ and Ingram sections in this text. MAC is located in Ducktown, TN. Please refer to the FMJ listing in the Trademark Index for current information.

MAS

Previously manufactured by D'Armes St. Etienne (MAS) located in France.
Please refer to the French Military heading in this text.

MBA GYROJET

Previous manufacturer circa 1966-1969 located in San Ramon, CA.

GRADING - PPGS™	100%	98%	95%	90%	80%	70%	60%

PISTOLS: SEMI-AUTO

MARK I GYROJET PISTOL - 12mm or 13mm (no cartridge case) cal., uses spin-stabilized rocket projectiles that accelerate to 1,250 FPS in .12 seconds, 2 in. (rare) or 5 in. barrel, 6 shot semi-auto action drives rocket projectile (primer activated) into fixed firing pin, smooth walnut grips, black, antique nickel, or gold-plated finish, 13 or 16 oz., "A" prefix until ser. no. 49, "B" prefixes followed, there are also other variations and experimental models in addition to the production models listed. Not particularly accurate.

The rocket ammunition for this model is rare and typically sells in the $30-$35/round range per shell.

✱ *Mark I Model A Cased* - 13mm, black finish, smooth walnut grips, walnut cased with 10 rounds and medal.

	100%	98%	95%	90%	80%	70%	60%
	$1,750	$1,400	$1,125	$950	$875	$795	$700

✱ *Mark I Model B Cased* - 13mm, black, nickel, satin, or green finish, many variations with different grips, casings, and barrel lengths, wood cased.

	$1,500	$1,250	$975	$850	$725	$625	$525

Add approx. 25% for satin finish.

✱ *Mark I Model B Uncased or Cardboard* - either with cardboard case or no case, black finish.

	$850	$750	$625	$500	$400	$360	$330

✱ *Mark II Model C Uncased or Cardboard* - 12mm, black finish, walnut grips.

	$850	$750	$625	$500	$400	$360	$330

This variation was manufactured in 12mm to conform with the 1968 GCA, since any caliber over .50 was classified as a destructive device (i.e., 12mm = .49 cal. and 13mm =.51 cal.). In 1982, the 13mm guns were reclassified as curios and relics.

✱ *Mark I Presentation Model* - cased with 10 dummy/live rounds and bronze medal honoring rocket pioneers Robert H. Goddard and Joseph J. Stubbs.

	$2,250	$1,600	$995

RIFLES: SEMI-AUTO, CARBINES

MARK I MODEL A or B CARBINE - 13mm cal., same action as Mark I pistol, black (Model A) or satin (Model B) finish, full stock with pistol grip extension, 18 in. barrel, nickel finish, 4 1/2 lbs. Limited mfg.

	100%	98%	95%	90%	80%	70%	60%
Model A	$1,850	$1,700	$1,475	$1,350	$1,225	$1,100	$1,000
Model B	$1,395	$1,150	$950	$850	$750	$650	$550

MG ARMS INCORPORATED

Current manufacturer established in 1980, and located in Spring, TX. MG Arms Incoroporated was previously named Match Grade Arms & Ammunition. Consumer direct sales.

REVOLVERS

MGA CUSTOM BIG 5 - .45 LC+P, .454 Casull, .475 Linebaugh, .50 AE, or .500 Linebaugh cal., Ruger frame, stainless 5 shot cylinder, custom barrels. New 2000.

MSR $1,295	$1,175	$975	$875	$775	$700	$625	$525

MG Arms also offered a conversion package for $795 (customer supplies Ruger revolver).

RIFLES: BOLT ACTION

ULTRA-LIGHT MODEL - various cals., lightened and skeletonized Wby. Vanguard (disc. 2004) or Rem. 700 (new 2005) action, MGA button rifled barrel, Teflon metal finish, epoxy stock with Pachmayr decelerator pad, Super Eliminator muzzle brake, variety of camo finishes on stock, 5.5 lbs.

MSR $2,395	$2,200	$1,925	$1,675	$1,375	$1,100	$975	$800

Add $100 for Win. M70 action.

MGA VARMINTER - various cals., squared and lapped Rem. M700 action, stainless steel National Match barrel with Super Eliminator muzzle brake, black Teflon metal finish, camo epoxy stock.

MSR $2,195	$2,000	$1,800	$1,575	$1,300	$1,050	$925	$750

SIGNATURE CLASSIC - various cals., Nesika Hunter action, Hart stainless steel barrel, Jewell trigger, fiberglass or claro walnut stock. Limited mfg. (approx. 10 guns per year) beginning 2000.

MSR $4,500	$4,300	$3,900	$3,550	$3,200	$2,800	$2,400	$2,000

M-K SPECIALTIES INC.

Previous rifle manufacturer circa 2000-2002 located in Grafton, WV.

RIFLES: SEMI-AUTO

M-14 A1 - .308 Win. cal., forged M-14 steel receiver using CNC machinery to original government specifications, available as Rack Grade, Premier Match, or Tanker Model, variety of National Match upgrades were available at extra cost, base price is for Rack Grade. Mfg. 2000-2002.

$1,400	$1,200	$995	$875	$750	$625	$500

Last MSR was $1,595.

National Match upgrades ranged from $345-$955.

MK ARMS INC.

Previous manufacturer located in Irvine, CA circa 1992.

CARBINES

MK 760 - 9mm Para. cal., paramilitary design carbine configuration, steel frame, 16 in. shrouded barrel, fires from closed bolt, 14, 24, or 36 shot mag., parkerized finish, folding metal stock, fixed sights. Mfg. 1983-approx. 1992.

$675	$625	$575	$525	$475	$415	$375

Last MSR was $575.

MKE

Previous manufacturer located in Ankara, Turkey. Previously distributed by Mandall Shooting Supplies, Inc., located in Scottsdale, AZ.

PISTOLS: SEMI-AUTO

KIRIKKALE AUTOMATIC - 7.65mm Para. (disc.) or .380 ACP cal., double action, 7 shot, blue, fixed sights, checkered plastic grips, this is a close copy of Walther's PP and the Turkish Army's standard service pistol. Disc. 1987.

$365	$295	$240	$215	$185	$170	$155

Last MSR was $395.

M.O.A. CORPORATION

Current manufacturer located in Eaton, OH. Dealer direct sales only.

PISTOLS: SINGLE SHOT

Approx. 500-600 Maximum pistols are produced annually.

MAXIMUM - available in 30 standard chamberings between .22 Rimfire and .454 Casull cal., additional custom calibers are also available upon special order, single shot lever action pistol, falling block action, Chromoly receiver (disc. 1991), Armoloy coated Chromoly (disc. late 1992), or stainless steel (new 1991, standard 1992) receiver, 8 3/4 (new 1989), 10 1/2, or 14 in. interchangeable barrel, transfer bar safety, adj. open sights, walnut grips and forearm. New 1986.

MSR $823	$715	$585	$500	$450	$400	$375	$350

Subtract 10% for older steel receiver.

Add $60 for scope mounts.

Add $96 for stainless steel barrel on either receiver.

Add $125 for muzzle brake.

Add $269 per extra steel barrel.

Add $336 per extra stainless steel barrel.

Barrels must be fitted to individual receivers at the factory initially. Afterwards, they can be changed by the customer with the spanner wrench (included with extra barrels).

* ***Carbine Model*** - cals. up to .250 Sav., stainless receiver, otherwise similar to Maximum, except has 18 in. blue barrel. Mfg. began 1986, and production has been disc. several times.

MSR $938	$850	$750	$650	$575	$525	$475	$425

MTs ARMS

Current trademark manufactured by Sporting and Hunting Guns Central Design and Research Bureau, a subsidiary of the State Unitary Enterprise, Instrument Design Bureau, (GUP "KBP" - "TsKIB SOO"), located in Tula, Russia. No current U.S. importation.

MTs Arms manufactures a variety of firearms, including SxS and O/U shotguns, combination guns, self-loading shotguns, slide action shotguns, bolt action rifles, drillings, competition guns, and semi-auto rifles. TsKIB SOO is the only manufacturer of quality hunting guns in Russia and the countries of the CIS (Commonwealth of Independent States). Please contact the company directly for more information regarding this trademark and current domestic availability (see Trademark Index).

JAMES MacNAUGHTON & SONS

Current trademark owned and manufactured by Dickson & MacNaughton, located in Edinburgh, Scotland.

The firm of James MacNaughton was founded in Edinburgh, Scotland in 1864. During 1947, the company was acquired by John Dickson and during 1996, the ownership of the company changed again, having purchased the manufacturing rights from Dickson. In 1999, the directors of James MacNaughton & Sons acquired the whole share capital of John Dickson & Son, and the two companies now trade as one under the name of Dickson & MacNaughton. Please contact Dickson & MacNaughton directly for more information regarding this trademark, including current availability and pricing (see Trademark Index).

GRADING - PPGS™	100%	98%	95%	90%	80%	70%	60%

RIFLES: SxS

SIDELOCK RIFLE - .375 H&H or .470 NE cal., specifications per individual customer order.

Please contact the manufacturer directly regarding domestic availability and pricing.

SHOTGUNS

SxS SIDELOCK MODEL - 20 or 28 ga., lightweight construction.

Please contact the manufacturer directly regarding domestic availability and pricing.

MAADI-GRIFFIN CO.

Previous rifle manufacturer located in Mesa, AZ until 2003. Consumer direct sales.

RIFLES: SEMI-AUTO

MODEL MG-6 - .50 BMG cal., gas operated, bullpup configuration, one piece cast lower receiver, 5, 10, or 15 shot side mounted mag., 26-30 in. barrel, includes bipod, hard carrying case, and 3 mags. 23 lbs. Mfg. 2000-2003.

	$5,500	$4,750	$3,850	$3,250	$2,600	$2,200	$1,800

Last MSR was $5,950.

Add $450 for MK-IV tripod.

RIFLES: SINGLE SHOT

MODEL 89 - .50 BMG cal., one piece cast lower receiver, 36 in. barrel, felt recoil is less than 12 ga., tig-welded interlocking assembly, no screws, tripod optional, 22 lbs. Mfg. 1990-2003.

	$2,900	$2,600	$2,300	$2,000	$1,750	$1,500	$1,250

Last MSR was $3,150.

Add $600 for stainless steel.

MODEL 92 CARBINE - .50 BMG cal., 20 in. barrel, 5 lbs. trigger pull, 18 1/2 lbs. Mfg. 1990-2003.

	$2,800	$2,500	$2,200	$1,850	$1,650	$1,400	$1,200

Last MSR was $2,990.

Add $650 for stainless steel.

MODEL 99 - .50 BMG cal., similar to Model 89, except has 44 in. barrel, 28 lbs. Mfg. 1999-2003.

	$3,150	$2,725	$2,450	$2,050	$1,775	$1,500	$1,250

Last MSR was $3,350.

Add $650 for stainless steel.

MAGNUM RESEARCH, INC.

MAGNUM RESEARCH, INC.

Current trademark of pistols and rifles with company headquarters located in Minneapolis, MN.
Centerfire pistols (Desert Eagle Series) are again mfg. by IMI, located in Israel. Previously mfg. by Saco Defense located in Saco, ME during 1995-1998, and by TAAS/IMI (Israeli Military Industries) 1986-1995. .22 Rimfire semi-auto pistols (Mountain Eagle) were previously manufactured by Ram-Line. Single shot pistols (Lone Eagle) were manufactured by Magnum Research sub-contractors. Distributed by Magnum Research, Inc., in Minneapolis, MN. Dealer and distributor sales.

GRADING - PPGS™	100%	98%	95%	90%	80%	70%	60%

MRI CUSTOM SHOP

In addition to the models listed, Magnum Research can also provide a variety of special order options through their custom shop including a choice of eleven different Desert Eagle finishes listed, in addition to various sight systems and grips.

MRI's current custom shop finish options with MSRs are as follows (.357 Mag. and .50 AE cals., 6 in. barrel): Polished hard chrome (PC) - MSR is $1,489, matte chrome (MC) - MSR - $1,489, brushed hard chrome (BC) - MSR - $1,489, black chrome - MSR is $1,599, bright nickel (BN) - MSR is $1,489, satin nickel (SN) - MSR is $1,489, polished blue (PB) - MSR is $1,489, or gold accents (add $240). 24Kt. gold (GO) finish, titanium gold finish (TG, new 2000), titanium gold with tiger stripes (new 2005, .50 AE cal. only), or titanium carbon nitride (TCN, new 2002) - MSR is $1,749.

PISTOLS: SEMI-AUTO, RIMFIRE

THE MOUNTAIN EAGLE - .22 LR cal., single action, 6 (new 1995) or 6 1/2 (disc. 1994) in. polymer and steel barrel, features alloy receiver and polymer technology, matte black finish, adj. rear sight, 15 or 20 shot mag. 21 oz. Mfg. 1992-96.

	$185	$155	$135	$115	$100	$85	$75

Last MSR was $239.

* *Mountain Eagle Compact Edition* - similar to Mountain Eagle, except has 4 1/2 in. barrel with shortened grips, adj. rear sight, 10 or 15 shot mag., plastic case, 19.3 oz. Mfg. 1996 only.

	$165	$135	$120	$105	$95	$80	$70

Last MSR was $199.

* *Mountain Eagle Target Edition* - .22 LR cal., Target variation of the Mountain Eagle, featuring 8 in. accurized barrel, 2-stage target trigger, jeweled bolt, adj. sights with interchangeable blades, 23 oz. Mfg. 1994-96.

	$235	$185	$150	$135	$120	$105	$95

Last MSR was $279.

PISTOLS: SEMI-AUTO, CENTERFIRE

IMI SP-21 - 9mm Para., .40 S&W, or .45 ACP cal., DA or SA, traditional Browning operating system, polymer frame with ergonomic design, 3.9 in. barrel with polygonal rifling, 10 shot mag., finger groove grips, 3 dot adj. sights, reversible mag. release, multiple safeties, matte black finish, decocking feature, approx. 29 oz. Importation from IMI began late 2002.

MSR $499	$425	$375	$335	$300	$280	$260	$240

The IMI SP-21 uses the same magazines as the Baby Eagle pistols. This model is referred to the Barak SP-21 in Israel.

PISTOLS: SEMI-AUTO, CENTERFIRE - EAGLE SERIES

Magnum Research also offers a Collector's Edition Presentation Series. Special models include a Gold Edition (serial numbered 1-100), a Silver Edition (serial numbered 101-500), and a Bronze Edition (serial numbered 501-1,000). Each pistol from this series is supplied with a walnut presentation case, 2 sided medallion, and certificate of authenticity. Prices are available upon request by contacting Magnum Research directly.

Alloy frames on the Desert Eagle Series of pistols were discontinued in 1992. However, if sufficient demand warrants, these models will once again be available to consumers at the same price as the steel frames.

Beginning late 1995, the Desert Eagle frame assembly for the .357 Mag., .44 Mag., and .50 AE cals. is based on the .50 caliber frame. Externally, all three pistols are now identical in size. This new platform, called the Desert Eagle Pistol Mark XIX Component System, enables .44 Mag. and .50 AE conversions to consist of simply a barrel and a magazine - conversions to or from the .357 Mag. also include a bolt.

GRADING - PPGS™	100%	98%	95%	90%	80%	70%	60%

The slide assembly on the Mark I and Mark VII is physically smaller than the one on a Mark XIX. Also, the barrel dovetail on top is 3/8 in. on a Mark I or Mark VII, while on a Mark XIX, it is 7/8 in., and includes cross slots for scopes.

> **Individual Desert Eagle Mark XIX 6 in. barrels are $389-$564, depending on finish, and 10 in. barrels are $459-$634, depending on finish.**

THE BABY EAGLE - 9mm Para., .40 S&W, .41 AE (disc.), or .45 ACP (3.7 in. barrel only, new 2000) cal., double action, all steel or polymer (3.5 or 3.7 in. barrel, 9mm Para. or .40 S&W only) frame construction, 3.5 (new 2000), 3.62 (mfg. 1993-99), 3.7 (new 2000), or 4.52 in. barrel, short recoil operation, polygonal rifling, combat styled trigger guard, decocking slide safety or frame mounted safety (Model 9mmF), blued (disc. 1995), standard black (new 1996), or chrome (disc. 1999) finish, 10 (C/B 1994), 16* (9mm Para.), 11* (.41 AE), 10 (.40 S&W) or 15 (9mm Para. only, new 2005) shot mag., 38.5 oz. Imported 1991-96. Reintroduced mid 1999.

* *Baby Eagle Full Size* - 9mm Para. or .40 S&W cal., 4.52 in. barrel, steel frame only.

	MSR $499	$415	$350	$300	$265	$230	$210	$190

> **Add $239 for conversion kit (9mm Para. to .41 AE or .41 AE to 9mm Para., includes barrel, spring, and mag.), disc. 1996.**

> This model is also available in various optional finishes, including brushed or polished chrome - MSR is $719, titanium gold - MSR is $999, or titanium carbon nitride - MSR is $999.

* *Baby Eagle Semi-Compact* - 9mm Para, .40 S&W, or .45 ACP cal., same general specifications as Baby Eagle, except has 3.7 in. barrel, 36 oz. (steel) or 29 oz. (polymer).

	MSR $499	$415	$350	$300	$265	$230	$210	$190

> This model is also available in brushed or polished chrome finish - MSR is $719, titanium gold or titanium nitride (.45 ACP cal. only) - MSR is $999.

* *Baby Eagle Compact* - 9mm Para. or .40 S&W cal., same general specifications as Baby Eagle, except has 3.5 in. barrel, 27 oz. (polymer) or 34 oz (steel).

	MSR $499	$415	$350	$300	$265	$230	$210	$190

> This model is also available in brushed chrome finish - MSR is $719.

MARK I DESERT EAGLE - .357 Mag. cal., similar to Mark VII, except has standard trigger and safety lever is teardrop shaped, and slide catch release has single serration. Disc.

		$850	$650	$525	$475	$425	$395	$375

MARK XIX .357 MAG. DESERT EAGLE - features .50 cal. frame and slide, standard black finish, 6 or 10 in. barrel, 4 lbs., 6 oz. Mfg. by Saco 1995-98, and IMI again beginning 1998.

	MSR $1,249	$1,055	$895	$750	$575	$475	$400	$350

> Add $100 for 10 in. barrel.

MARK VII .357 MAG. DESERT EAGLE - .357 Mag. cal., gas operated, 6 (standard barrel length), 10, or 14 in. barrel length with 3/8 in. dovetail rib, steel (58.3 oz.) or alloy (47.8 oz.) frame, adj. trigger, safety lever is hook shaped, slide catch/release lever has three steps, adaptable to .44 Mag. with optional kit, 9 shot mag. (8 for .44 Mag.). Mfg. 1983-95, limited quantities were made available again during 1998 and 2001.

		$850	$650	$525	$475	$425	$395	$375

> *Last MSR was $929.*

> Add approx. $150 for 10 or 14 in. barrel (disc. 1995).
> Add $495 for .357 Mag. to .41 Mag./.44 Mag. conversion kit (6 in. barrel). Disc. 1995.
> Add approx. $685 for .357 Mag. to .44 Mag. conversion kit (10 or 14 in. barrel). Disc. 1995.

* *Whitetail Special .357 Mag.* - 14 in. barrel, includes scope mount, target walnut grips, and Desert Eagle premiums. Mfg. 1990-92.

		$925	$750	$650	$550	$450	$400	$375

> *Last MSR was $1,088.*

> Add $50 for stainless steel frame.

GRADING - PPGS™	100%	98%	95%	90%	80%	70%	60%

✻ *Stainless Steel .357 Mag.* - similar to .357 Mag. Desert Eagle, except has stainless steel frame, 58.3 oz. Mfg. 1987-95.

	$750	$650	$550				

Last MSR was $839.

Add approx. $150 for 10 or 14 in. barrel.

MARK VII .41 MAG. DESERT EAGLE - .41 Mag. cal., similar to .357 Desert Eagle, 6 in. barrel only, 8 shot mag., steel (62.8 oz.) or alloy (52.3 oz.) frame. Mfg. 1988-95, limited quanitites available during 2001.

	$785	$675	$565	$500	$465	$420	$390

Last MSR was $899.

Add $395 for .41 Mag. to .44 Mag. conversion kit (6 in. barrel only).

✻ *Stainless Steel .41 Mag.* - similar to .41 Mag. Desert Eagle, except has stainless steel frame, 58.3 oz. Mfg. 1988-95.

	$825	$700	$550				

Last MSR was $949.

MARK I DESERT EAGLE - .44 Mag. cal., similar to Mark VII, except has standard trigger and safety lever is teardrop shaped, and slide catch release has single serration. Disc.

	$925	$700	$565	$585	$430	$395	$375

MARK XIX .44 MAG. DESERT EAGLE - features .50 cal. frame and slide, standard black finish, 6 or 10 in. barrel, 4 lbs., 6 oz. Mfg. by Saco 1995-98, and by IMI again beginning 1998.

MSR $1,249	$1,055	$895	$750	$575	$475	$400	$350

Add $100 for 10 in. barrel.

MARK VII .44 MAG. DESERT EAGLE - .44 Mag. cal., similar to .357 Desert Eagle, 8 shot mag., steel (62.8 oz.) or alloy (52.3 oz.) frame. Originally mfg. 1986-95, re-released 1998-2000.

	$925	$700	$565	$585	$430	$395	$375

Last MSR was $1,049.

Add $100 for 10 (current) or 14 (disc. 1995) in. barrel.
Add $475 for .44 Mag. to .357 Mag. conversion kit (6 in. barrel). Disc. 1995.
Add $675 for .44 Mag. to .357 Mag. conversion kit (10 or 14 in. barrel). Disc. 1995.
Add $395 for .44 Mag. to .41 Mag. conversion kit (6 in. barrel). Disc. 1995.

✻ *Stainless Steel .44 Mag.* - similar to .44 Mag. Desert Eagle, except has stainless steel frame, 58.3 oz. Mfg. 1987-95.

	$825	$700	$550				

Last MSR was $949.

Add approx. $210 for 10 or 14 in. barrel.

HUNTER EDITION MARK VII - .357 or .44 Mag. cal., 6 in. barrel with extra 14 in. hunting barrel, includes Leupold 2X EER scope, scope mount. Mfg. late 1987-93.

	$1,200	$975	$825	$675	$550	$475	$425

Last MSR was $1,350.

Add $110 for .44 Mag. cal.

MARK VII .50 MAG. DESERT EAGLE - .50 AE cal., 6 in. barrel with 7/8 in. rib with cross slots for Weaver style rings, steel only, black standard finish, frame slightly taller than the Mark VII .357 Mag./.44 Mag., 7 shot mag., 72.4 oz. Mfg. 1991-95 by IMI, limited quantities were made available again during 1998 only.

	$950	$825	$700	$575	$500	$450	$400

Last MSR was $1,099.

This cartridge utilized the same rim dimensions as the .44 Mag. and was available with a 300 grain bullet. The .50 Action Express cal. has 60% more stopping power than the .44 Mag., with a minimal increase in felt recoil.

GRADING - PPGS™	100%	98%	95%	90%	80%	70%	60%

MARK XIX CUSTOM 440 - .440 Cor-Bon cal., similar to Mark XIX .44 Mag. Desert Eagle, 6 or 10 in. barrel, standard black finish, rechambered by MRI Custom Shop, limited mfg. 1999-2001.

	$1,175	$995	$850	$725	$575	$500	$450

Last MSR was $1,389.

Add $40 for 10 in. barrel.

MARK XIX .50 MAG. DESERT EAGLE - features .50 AE cal., larger frame, standard black finish, 6 or 10 in. barrel, 4 lbs., 6 oz. Mfg. by Saco 1995-98, and by IMI again beginning 1998.

MSR $1,249	$1,055	$895	$795	$700	$650	$600	$550

Add $100 for 10 in. barrel.

MARK XIX 3 CAL. COMPONENT SYSTEM - includes Mark XIX .44 Mag. Desert Eagle and 5 barrels including .357 Mag. (6 and 10 in.), .44 Mag., and .50 AE (6 and 10 in.) cals., .357 bolt assembly and ICC aluminum carrying case. Also available in custom finishes at extra charge. New 1998.

MSR $3,991	$3,525	$2,950	$2,450	$2,000	$1,700	$1,300	$1,050

✱ *Mark XIX Component System* - includes component Mark XIX system in 6 or 10 in. barrel only. New 1998.

MSR $2,575	$2,200	$1,800	$1,575	$1,275	$1,000	$850	$750

Add $240 for 10 in. barrels.

PISTOLS: SINGLE SHOT

LONE EAGLE (SSP-91) - .22 LR (disc. 1992), .22 Mag. (disc. 1992), .22 Hornet, .22-250 Rem., .223 Rem., .243 Win., .260 Rem. (new 1997), .30-30 Win., .30-06, .300 Win. Mag. (Ltd. ed., mfg. 1997-99), .308 Win., 6mmBR (disc. 1992), 7mm-08 Rem., 7mmBR, .35 Rem., .357 Max. (disc. 1997, reintroduced 2001), .358 Win., .44 Mag., .440 Cor-Bon (new 1999), .444 Marlin, or 7.62x39mm (new 1996) cal., circular rear breech action, quick change 14 in. barrels (drilled and tapped), black or chrome (new 1997) finish, black synthetic Valox ambidextrous pistol grip, 4 lbs. 3 oz.-4 lbs. 7 oz. Mfg. 1991-2001.

	$380	$315	$275	$230	$200	$185	$170

Last MSR was $438.

Add $40 for chrome finish.
Add $35 for adj. hunting sights.
Add $129 for adj. silhouette sights by RPM.
Add $319 for standard black finish barrel, $418 for standard barrel with muzzle brake, $359 for chrome barrel, and $469 for chrome barrel with muzzle brake.

The grip assembly ($119) and barreled actions were available individually on this model.

REVOLVERS

BFR LONG CYLINDER - .30-30 Win. (new 2004), .444 Marlin, .45 LC/.410 bore, .450 Marlin (new 2002, 10 in. barrel only), .45-70 Govt., or .500 S&W Mag. (new 2003) cal., single action, 5 shot, stainless steel, 7.5 (.45 LC/.410 bore and .45-70 Govt.) or 10 (.444 Marlin, .450 Marlin, or .45-70 Govt.) in. barrel, checkered rubber grips, 4 lbs.-4.36 lbs. New 1999.

MSR $899	$775	$650	$525

This model was originally advertised as the BFR Maxine, then was changed to BFR (Biggest Finest Revolver).

BFR SHORT CYLINDER - .22 Hornet, .45 LC+P (disc. 2001), .454 Casull, .475 Linebaugh/.480 Ruger (new 2002), or .50 AE (disc. 2001, reintroduced 2004) cal., similar to BFR Model, 6.5 (.45 LC+P, .454 Casull, .475 Linebaugh, or .480 Ruger cal.), 7.5, or 10 (not available in .50 AE or .45 LC+P cal.) barrel, 3.2-4.36 lbs. New 1999.

MSR $899	$775	$650	$525

This model was originally advertised as the BFR Little Max, then was changed to BFR (Biggest Finest Revolver).

GRADING - PPGS™	100%	98%	95%	90%	80%	70%	60%

RIFLES: BOLT-ACTION

MOUNTAIN EAGLE RIFLE - .223 Rem. (new 2000), 270 Win., .280 Rem., .30-06, 7mm STW (mfg. 1998-99), .300 Win. Mag., .300 Wby. Mag., .338 Win. Mag., .340 Wby. Mag. (disc. 1997), 7mm Rem. Mag., .375 H&H, or .416 Rem. Mag. cal., Sako action, adj. trigger, 4 or 5 shot mag., match grade Krieger barrel with cut rifling, H-S Precision composite stock with aluminum bedding block, includes carrying case. Mfg. 1994-2000.

	$1,325	$1,075	$900	$775	$625	$550	$495

Last MSR was $1,499.

Add $200 for muzzle brake.
Add $50 for left-hand action.
Add $300 for .375 H&H or .416 Rem. Mag. cal.

✱ *Varmint Mountain Eagle* - .222 Rem. or .223 Rem. cal., 26 in. stainless steel heavy fluted barrel, w/o sights, approx. 9 3/4 lbs. Mfg. 1996-2000.

	$1,425	$1,100	$925

Last MSR was $1,629.

MOUNTAIN EAGLE MAGNUM LITE - .223 Rem. (varmint only), .22-250 Rem. (varmint only), .280 Rem., .30-06, .300 Win. Mag., .300 WSM (new 2003), 7mm WSM (new 2003), or 7mm Rem. Mag. cal., custom-built Rem. short action (7mm WSM or .300 WSM cal. only) or Sako action with one-piece forged bolt, adj. trigger, 24 in. sport tapered or 26 in. varmint bull graphite barrel with stainless steel liner, no sights, black swirl H-S Precision Kevlar graphite or Hogue overmolded (7mm WSM or .300 WSM only) stock, 4 or 5 shot mag, 7 lbs., 2 oz.-9 lbs., 2 oz. New 2001.

MSR $2,295	$1,995	$1,700	$1,400	$1,100	$825	$700	$575

Magnum Lite graphite barrels are available in 3 configurations for $799.

MOUNTAIN EAGLE TACTICAL RIFLE - .223 Rem. (new 2002), .22-250 (new 2002), .308 Win., .300 Win. Mag., or .300 WSM (new 2002) cal., accurized Rem. M-700 action, 26 in. Magnum Lite barrel, H-S Precision tactical stock, adj. stock and trigger, 9 lbs., 4 oz. New 2001.

MSR $2,400	$2,075	$1,750	$1,425	$1,125	$850	$700	$575

Add $100 for .300 WSM cal.

RIFLES: SEMI-AUTO

Magnum Lite .22 graphite barrels are also available individually starting at $269. For the .17 Mach 2 barrel a bolt kit is also included.

Add $140 for Clark custom upgrade (includes Clark deluxe trigger kit, tuned extractor, and bolt release) on the models listed (.22 LR cal. only).

MAGNUM LITE RIFLE - .17 HMR (new 2004), .17 Mach 2 (new 2005), .22 LR or .22 Mag. (new 2000) cal., features Ruger 10/22 receiver with Acculite (disc.) or graphite (new 1999) barrel utilizing uni-directional graphite carbon fiber with stainless steel liner, barrel weighs 13 oz. New 1997.

✱ *Magnum Lite Rifle w/ Hogue or Fajen Stock* - choice of black Hogue Overmolded or Fajen high stock (disc. 1999) in either midnight or coffee color, 4.3 (.22 LR cal.) or 5.4 (.22 Mag. cal.) lbs. with Hogue stock. New 1997.

MSR $599	$525	$450	$395	$360	$330	$275	$250

Add $200 for .22 Mag. cal.
Add $110 for .17 Mach 2 cal.

✱ *Magnum Lite Rifle w/ Fajen Thumbhole Stock* - features choice of Fajen thumbhole sporter or thumbhole silhouette in midnight or coffee color. Mfg. 1997-99.

$625	$525	$450	$395	$360	$330	$275

Last MSR was $699.

Add $100 for thumbhole silhouette stock configuration.

GRADING - PPGS™	100%	98%	95%	90%	80%	70%	60%

✳ Magnum Lite Rifle w/ Turner Barracuda Stock - features skeletonized sporter stock in choice of green or coffee laminate, 4.4 (.22 LR cal.) or 5.4 (.22 Mag.) lbs. New 1997.

MSR $759	$650	$550	$475	$425	$375	$350	$325

Add $200 for .17 HMR or .22 Mag. cal.

MAGTECH

Current importer and distributor of CBC (Companhia Brasileria de Cartuchos) ammunition located in Centerville, MN. Previously located in Madison, CT 1999-2001 and in Las Vegas, NV until 1999. Magtech previously imported firearms manufactured by CBC located in Brazil.

RIFLES

MODEL 7022 SEMI-AUTO - .22 LR cal., Ruger 10/22 style action, 10 shot, 18 in. barrel, choice of hardwood or synthetic stock. New 2001.

	$120	$100	$85	$75	$70	$65	$60

MODEL 122 BOLT ACTION - .22 LR cal., 6 shot detachable mag., safety lever disconnects trigger from firing mechanism, uncheckered hardwood stock, 5.7 lbs. Imported 1992 only.

	$115	$95	$80	$70	$60	$50	$40

Last MSR was $131.

SHOTGUNS

MODEL 151 SINGLE SHOT - 12, 16, 20 ga., or .410 bore, 26, 28, or 30 in. barrel, exposed hammer, ejector, front triggerguard opening mechanism, some plastic used for buttons, levers, and bushings, 5-6 1/2 lbs. Imported 1992 only.

	$95	$80	$70	$60	$50	$40	$35

Last MSR was $109.

MODEL 199 - 12, 16, 20, 28 ga., or .410 bore, all steel construction, exposed hammer with underlever opening, unique hammer/firing pin safety, 24 or 28 in. barrel, uncheckered Brazilian stock and forearm, recoil pad supplied on Youth Models (20 ga. or .410 bore only), New 2001.

	$100	$85	$75	$70	$65	$60	$55

MODEL MT-586-2 SLIDE ACTION - 12 ga. only, 3 in. chamber, standard Field model shotgun, 28 in. barrel with fixed chokes, hardwood stock and forearm, double slide bars. Imported 1993-95.

	$190	$175	$160	$140	$130	$120	$110

Last MSR was $229.

The Model MT-586 preceded the MT-586-2. The MT-586 was disc. 1994.

✳ Model MT-586-2-VR Slide Action - similar to Model MT-586, except has choice of 26 or 28 in. VR barrel with interchangeable chokes. Imported 1993-95.

	$220	$185	$170	$155	$140	$130	$120

Last MSR was $259.

MODEL MT-586 SLIDE ACTION SLUG - 12 ga. only, slug gun featuring 24 in. cylinder bore barrel with rifle sights, matte finished metal parts, and special Monte Carlo stock. Imported 1993-95.

	$195	$180	$165	$145	$130	$120	$110

Last MSR was $239.

GRADING - PPGS™	100%	98%	95%	90%	80%	70%	60%

MODEL MT-586-2P - 12 ga. only, 3 in. chamber, slide action, 19 in. cylinder bore barrel, 7 shot mag., double slide bars, steel construction, hardwood stock, 7.3 lbs. Imported 1992-96.

	$185	$170	$155	$140	$130	$120	$110

Last MSR was $219.

MAJESTIC ARMS, LTD.

Current manufacturer established during 2000, and located on Staten Island, NY. Dealer sales only.

CARBINES: SEMI-AUTO

MA 2000 - .22 LR cal., Henry Repeating Arms Co. AR-7 take down action, fiberoptic sights, American walnut forearm, pistol grip, and buttplate, fixed tubular stock with butt bag, 16.25 in. Lothar Walther barrel with crown, black teflon or silver bead blast finish, 4 lbs. New 2000.

MSR $389		$350	$295	$250	$225	$195	$175	$150

MA 4 - .17 HMR, .17 Mach 2 (new 2005), .22 LR (new 2005), or .22 Mag. cal., take down action, traditional stock or wire frame, interchangeable barrel/bolt assembly. New 2004.

MSR $399		$355	$300	$250	$225	$195	$175	$150

Add $249-$299 per additional barrel/bolt assembly, depending on caliber (new mid-2005).

SHOTGUNS: SLIDE ACTION

BASE-TAC - 12 or 20 ga., 3 in. chamber, based on M870 Remington action, approx. 18 in. barrel with ghost ring sights, black synthetic (12 ga.) or hardwood stock and forearm, extended 6 shot tube mag., 6-7 lbs. New 2004.

MSR $729		$650	$575	$500	$450	$400	$350	$300

Add $40 for 20 ga.

MAKAROV

Pistol design originating from Russia. Russian mfg. Makarovs may be found under the "Russian Service Pistol and Rifle" heading in this text. Pistols listed have recently been imported by various companies, including Century International Arms, Inc. located in St. Albans, VT.

PISTOLS: SEMI-AUTO

MAKAROV COPIES - 9mm Makarov cal., patterned after the Soviet PM pistol, mfg. in eastern Germany, Bulgaria, and China, double action, blowback design, all steel, slide mounted safety that doubles as a decocking lever, 3.6 in. barrel, 8 shot mag., 25 oz.

No MSR		$185	$145	$125	$105	$95	$85	$75

Add approx. $35-$40 for polished blue or silver matte finish (Bulgarian mfg. only). The importation of this type of pistol increased beginning 1992.

MALIN, F.E.

Previous manufacturer located in England. Previously imported by Saxon Arms, Inc. located in Clearwater, FL. Charles Boswell purchased Malin shortly before manufacture stopped.

SHOTGUNS: SxS, CUSTOM

BOXLOCK - made to individual order, choice of game scene engraving, Anson & Deeley boxlock actions, select European hybrid walnut, double triggers, leather cased. Prices started at $3,750 and each shotgun was priced per individual special order.

GRADING - PPGS™	100%	98%	95%	90%	80%	70%	60%

SIDELOCK - made to individual order, choice of game scene engraving, H&H sidelock action, select European hybrid walnut, double triggers, leather cased. Prices started at $5,000 and each shotgun was priced per individual special order.

MAMBA

Previously manufactured by Viper Mfg. Co. (a division of Sandock Austral Boksburg) located in South Africa.

PISTOLS: SEMI-AUTO

AUTO PISTOL - 9mm Para. cal., double action, 5 in. barrel, 14 shot mag., designed in Rhodesia, manufacture was not successful due to the non-hardened steel used in the investment cast construction process, poor exterior finish, less than 80 imported into the U.S., and 25 prototypes were built for Navy Arms.

Rarity factor precludes accurate pricing and values vary greatly in different regions.

MANCHESTER ARMS INC.

Previous manufacturer located in Lenoir, TN.

PISTOLS: SEMI-AUTO

COMMANDO MARK 45 - .45 ACP cal., paramilitary type design with detachable mag., wood pistol grip, 5 in. barrel with muzzle brake. Disc.

	100%	98%	95%	90%	80%	70%	60%
	$525	$450	$395	$350	$300	$265	$235

MANDALL SHOOTING SUPPLIES, INC.

Current importer, distributor, and retailer located in Scottsdale, AZ.

Mandall Shooting Supplies distributes/imports various firearms including pistols, revolvers, rifles, and shotguns, as well as other models. Mandall Shooting Supplies, Inc. should be contacted directly for current pricing and special order questions (see Trademark Index).

MANNLICHER PISTOLS

Previously manufactured in Austria and Switzerland starting circa 1894.

PISTOLS: SEMI-AUTO

MODEL 1894 - 6.5mm or 7.6mm cal., unique blow forward design, fewer than 100 mfg. by Fabrique d' Armes in Neuhausen and OWG, Steyr.

	100%	98%	95%	90%	80%	70%	60%
	$13,500	$11,000	$9,500	$8,500	$7,500	$6,000	$5,000

Add 30% for 7.6mm cal.

MODEL 1897 - 7.63mm Mannlicher cal., first Mannlicher pistol with detachable mag. (matching), unique cocking lever on right frame, approx. 1,000 mfg.

	100%	98%	95%	90%	80%	70%	60%
	$7,500	$6,000	$5,000	$4,250	$3,750	$3,250	$2,750

Add 100% for extended barrel version with adj. sight and detachable shoulder stock.
Add 150% for Model 1896 prototype in similar configuration, but with fixed mag.
Subtract 15% for rifle (carbine).

MODEL 1899 - rear sight mounted on barrel, large safety lever on left frame, approx. 300 mfg.

	100%	98%	95%	90%	80%	70%	60%
	$7,500	$6,000	$5,000	$4,000	$3,500	$2,850	$2,500

MODEL 1901 - rear sight mounted on barrel, safety on rear of right slide, approx. 1,000 mfg.

	100%	98%	95%	90%	80%	70%	60%
	$3,250	$2,400	$1,600	$1,000	$600	$500	$400

GRADING - PPGS™	100%	98%	95%	90%	80%	70%	60%

MODEL 1905 - final and most common variation.

	100%	98%	95%	90%	80%	70%	60%
	$1,850	$1,300	$900	$500	$400	$350	$300

ARGENTINE MODEL 1905 - 7.65mm cal., Argentine crest on right panel is usually machined off. Values assume matching numbers but removed crest.

	$550	$475	$350	$300	$275	$250	$225

 ✹ *Argentine Model 1905* - with Original Military Crest.

	$2,250	$1,800	$1,350	$950	$700	$500	$400

MANNLICHER SCHOENAUER SPORTING RIFLES

Currently manufactured by Steyr, Mannlicher, A.G., in Austria from 1850s-present. Please refer to Steyr-Mannlicher in this text for currently manufactured rifles.

RIFLES: BOLT ACTIONS, PRE-WWII

Add approx. 25% for all takedown pre-war models.

MODEL 1903 CARBINE - 6.5x54mm Mannlicher Schoenauer cal., 5 shot, 17.7 in. barrel, rotary mag., two leaf rear sight, double set trigger, full length stock.

	N/A	$1,675	$1,500	$1,225	$950	$800	$650

This caliber may also be referred to as 6.5x53mm. This model is normally encountered in poor condition.

The Greek government ordered over 100,000 M1903 rifles, and many of these have been modified to a sporting configuration. These converted guns can be difficult to differentiate from true commercial Model 1903s, and values above are for original sporting carbines.

MODEL 1903 RIFLE - 6.5x54mm Mannlicher Schoenauer cal., 5 shot, various barrel lengths up to 23 inches, otherwise similar to Carbine.

	N/A	$1,675	$1,500	$1,225	$950	$800	$650

Full stocked rifles may be encountered.

The Greek government ordered over 100,000 M1903 rifles, and many of these have been modified to a sporting configuration. These converted rifles can be difficult to differentiate from true commercial Model 1903s, and values above are for original sporting rifles.

MODEL 1905 CARBINE - similar to Model 1903, except 9x56mm Mannlicher Schoenauer cal., 19.7 in. barrel.

	N/A	$1,275	$975	$850	$725	$600	$500

This model is normally encountered in poor condition. It is perhaps the least desirable of pre-war models because of the wide variation in bore diameters.

MODEL 1905 RIFLE - similar to Model 1905 Carbine, except available in various barrel lengths up to 25 inches.

	N/A	$1,275	$975	$850	$725	$600	$500

MODEL 1908 CARBINE - 8x56mm Mannlicher Schoenauer cal., 5 shot rotary mag., 19.7 in. barrel, two leaf rear sight, double set or single trigger, full length stock.

	N/A	$1,275	$975	$850	$725	$600	$500

This model is frequently noticed in better condition factors. Some exceptional takedown variations also exist within this model.

MODEL 1908 RIFLE - similar to Model 1908 Carbine, except available in various barrel lengths up to 24 inches.

	N/A	$1,275	$975	$850	$725	$600	$500

MODEL 1910 CARBINE - 9.5x56mm Mannlicher-Schoenauer (.375 Rimless Nitro Express or 9.5x57mm Mauser cal.), 7x57mm, 8x57mm, and other custom calibers, 19.7 in. barrel, 5 shot rotary magazine, two leaf rear sight, double set trigger, full length stock.

	N/A	$1,275	$975	$850	$725	$600	$500

GRADING - PPGS™	100%	98%	95%	90%	80%	70%	60%

MODEL 1910 RIFLE - 9.5x56mm Mannlicher-Schoenauer (standard cal.), may also be found in 7x57mm, 8x57mm, and other custom cals., similar to 1910 Carbine, except available in various barrel lengths up to 26 inches.

	N/A	$1,275	$900	$700	$600	$525	$475

Fully stocked rifles may be encountered.

MODEL 1924 (HIGH VELOCITY SPORTING RIFLE) - .30-06, 7x64mm, 8x60mm, 9.3x62mm, or 10.75x68mm cal., 23.6 in. barrel, three leaf rear sight, half stock, double set or single trigger.

	N/A	$1,675	$1,350	$1,195	$975	$850	$725

Add 100%-200% for 10.75x68mm cal.

Fully stocked rifles may be encountered.

RIFLES: BOLT ACTION, POST-WWII

Values below represent standard models with no engraving. Original engraving will add at least $500-$1,500 to prices listed with some heavily engraved Premier & Alpine models selling for large premiums. A variation of the 1950-1952 Series is called the "GK" because of its traditionally styled European stock, which is a variant of the pre-war style and approaches the design of the Model 1951 MCA. Of the calibers listed for post-WWII models, the 6.5x54mm is considered one of the most desirable, as well as the 9.3x62mm.

In 1951, Steyr (at Stoeger's request) made the following changes to the Model 1950 (named Improved Model 1950). These include: an ebony tip and fuller forend, left-side dummy plate cuts for side mount, left side of receiver was flattened to facilitate side scope mount, and flatter bolt handle requiring slot inside of stock.

In 1952, changes included a carved cheekpiece, change from 3/4 in. sling swivels to 1 in., swept back bolt handle, wood on left side of stock over the dummy sideplate cutout thickened to strengthen the stock with a side mount in place, and removal of loading ears and clip guides, thereby streamlining the receiver and enabling lower scope mounting.

At one time Stoeger listed 18 versions of the M1950-52 family, defined as #S-1 through #S-18, with three major differences existing within each block of Model 1950, Improved Model 1950, and Model 1952. The differences were: single and double set triggers (DST), rifle or carbine style, 6.5mm Carbine, single trigger or DST.

From the M1950 through the improved M1952, these rifles were in continuous change and parallel production, thus rifles can be found with 1950 characteristics and proofmarks as late as 1954. Some examples are found with "nonstandard" markings such as "Model 1952" and no reference to the "Improved" standard. After mid-1965, U.S. market rifles were drilled and tapped for the Redfield scope mount. Some rifles were chambered for 8x57mm and 7x64mm.

MANNLICHER-SCHOENAUER MAGNUM RIFLE - .257 Wby. Mag., 6.5x68mm, .264 Win. Mag., 8x68mm, .338 Win. Mag., or .458 Win. Mag., similar to Model 1956 MC, except has straight bolt handle, 5 shot rotary mag., 22 in. barrel with half stock, double set or single trigger.

	N/A	$2,700	$2,250	$1,800	$1,600	$1,075	$850

MODEL 1950 RIFLE - .270 Win., .30-06, 6.5x54mm, or 9.3x62mm Mauser, bolt action, 5 shot rotary mag., 24 in. barrel, straight style bolt handle, double or single set trigger, half stock.

$1,250	$1,125	$1,000	$850	$795	$675	$575

MODEL 1950 CARBINE - 6.5x54mm cal., similar to Model 1950, except has 18.25 in. barrel and full length stock.

$1,500	$1,375	$1,025	$875	$675	$525	$475

IMPROVED MODEL 1952 RIFLE - .257 Roberts, .270 Win., .30-06, 9.3x62mm cal., 24 in. barrel, 5 shot rotary mag., rear angled bolt handle, double set or single trigger, half stock.

$1,200	$1,000	$850	$725	$625	$550	$495

GRADING - PPGS™	100%	98%	95%	90%	80%	70%	60%

IMPROVED MODEL 1952 CARBINE - .257 Roberts, 6.5x54mm, .270 Win., 7x57mm, .308 Win. (new 1953), or .30-06 cal., 18.25 (6.5x54mm cal. only) or 20 in. barrel, rear angled bolt handle, double or single trigger.

	$1,500	$1,375	$1,025	$875	$675	$525	$475

MODEL 1956 MC RIFLE - .243 Win., 6.5x55mm, 6.5x57mm, 7x57mm, 7x64mm, 8x57mm, 8x60mm, 9.3x62mm, .244 Rem, .257 Rob, .270, .280, .308, .30-06, .358 WCF, .30-06 cals., similar to Model 1952, high comb stock design, 5 shot rotary mag., 22 in. barrel, half length stock, double set or single trigger. Mfg. 1956-1961.

	$1,350	$1,150	$900	$800	$625	$500	$450

MODEL 1956 MC CARBINE - .243 Win., 6.5x54mm, .257 Roberts, 6.5x55mm, 6.5x57mm, 7x64mm, 8x57mm, 8x60mm, .244 Rem, .280 Rem., 7x57mm, .270 Win., .30-06, .308 Win., or .358 Win. cal., similar to Model 1956 MC Rifle, except has 20 in. barrel with half stock, double set or single trigger. Mfg. 1956-1961.

	$1,500	$1,275	$975	$825	$650	$550	$450

During 1956, Steyr began to advertise "special order" calibers such as 8x57mm, 7x64mm, and 9.3x64mm.

MODEL 1961 MCA RIFLE - .243 Win., .270 Win., or .30-06 cal., similar to Model 1956 Rifle, except has Monte Carlo stock, 5 shot rotary mag., 22 in. barrel with half stock, double set or single trigger. Mfg. 1961-1971.

	$1,450	$1,200	$925	$775	$625	$525	$425

Subtract $250 for models with plastic tang safety.

MODEL 1961 MCA CARBINE - .243 Win., 6.5x54mm, .270 Win., .30-06, 7x57mm, .308 Win., or .358 Win. cal., 20 in. barrel with half stock, similar to Model 1956 Carbine, except has Monte Carlo stock. Mfg. 1961-1971.

	$1,500	$1,275	$975	$825	$650	$550	$450

Subtract $250 for models with plastic tang safety.

During production, the European market included the Model NO (Model MC/MCA) with GK stock and a straight pre-war bolt handle, produced in metric calibers such as 6.5x55mm Swedish, 7x64mm, and 8x57mm.

RIFLES: BOLT ACTION, CURRENT PRODUCTION

Current production guns are now called Steyr-Mannlicher models and can be located under this trademark in the S section.

MANU-ARM

Current rifle and airgun manufacturer located in Veauche, France. No current U.S. importation.

Manu-Arm manufactures good quality utilitarian .22 cal. bolt action and semi-auto rifles, in addition to an O/U in 9mm Para., .410 bore, and 32 ga. Please contact the factory directly for more information, including U.S. availability and pricing.

MANUFRANCE

Current manufacturer established circa 1887 and located in St. Etienne, France. No current U.S. importation.

Manufrance currently manufactures both SxS rifle and shotgun variations (the Robust Models being the most popular) that are not being currently imported into the U.S. Please contact the factory directly for more information, including model availability, parts, and domestic prices.

SHOTGUNS: DISC.

SEMI-AUTO MODEL - 12 ga., 26, 28, or 30 in. imp. cyl., mod. and full, 2 3/4 or 3 in. chamber, gas operated, walnut stock, black matte receiver, VR.

	$330	$305	$290	$275	$255	$240	$220

GRADING - PPGS™	100%	98%	95%	90%	80%	70%	60%

FALCOR O/U - 12 ga., VR, 26 in. imp. cyl. and mod., 28 in. mod. and full, SST, auto ejector, chrome lined barrel, walnut checkered stock.

	$715	$665	$635	$605	$550	$495	$470

MANURHIN

Current trademark manufactured by Manufacture d. Armes de tir Chapuis beginning in 1998, and located in Saint Bonnet Le Chateau, France. No current U.S. importation. During 1998, Chapuis Armes purchased Manurhin, and new revolvers are currently being manufactured in the new Manufacture d. Armes de tir Chapuis facility located in Saint Bonnet Le Chateau, France, utilizing the original production machinery. Previously manufactured by Manurhin Equipment 1972-1998, located in Mulhouse, France. Currently available by contacting the factory directly. Previously owned by Matra Manurhin Defense. Previously imported and distributed by Sphinx U.S.A. located in Meriden, CT. Previously imported (1984-86) directly by Matra-Manurhin International, Inc., located in Fort Lauderdale, FL.

Manurhin in France has been manufacturing models PP, PPK, and PPK/S since 1952. Previously, they were imported by Interarms out of Alexandria, VA. In 1984, Manurhin imported their new models directly and they were marked Manurhin on the left front slide assembly. This differs from the previous Walther stamped guns. Also, no Interarms logo appears on the right side.

PISTOLS: SEMI-AUTO, DISC.

P-1 - 9mm Para. cal., similar to W. German P-38, double action, 5 in. barrel.

	$350	$325	$300	$275	$230	$215	$200

MODEL P4 - 9mm Para. cal., P.38 variation issued to the French Police when in Berlin during post-WWII.

	$375	$340	$300	$245	$230	$215	$200

MODEL PP - .22 LR, .32 ACP, or .380 ACP cal., 3 7/8 in. barrel, 10 shot mag.-.22 LR, 8 shot mag.-.32 ACP, 7 shot mag.-.380 ACP, blue only, all steel construction, double action with positive steel hammer block safety, 24 oz. Add $10 for .22 LR cal., $46 for Durgarde finish. Imported 1984-86.

	$360	$320	$275	$230	$205	$185	$170

Last MSR was $419.

✳ *Collector Model* - blue finish, special engraving. Imported 1986 only.

	$465	$415	$350				

Last MSR was $529.

✳ *Presentation Model* - blue finish, special ornamentation. Imported 1986 only.

	$720	$650	$500				

Last MSR was $819.

Also available with various engraving options in either blue, nickel, or gold finish - prices range from $222-$540.

MODEL PPK/S - .22 LR, .32 ACP, or .380 ACP cal., 3 1/4 in. barrel, 10 shot mag.-.22 LR, 8 shot mag.-.32 ACP, 7 shot mag.-.380 ACP, blue only, all steel construction, double action with positive steel hammer block safety, 23 oz. Imported 1984-86.

	$360	$320	$275	$230	$205	$185	$170

Last MSR was $419.

Add $10 for .22 LR cal.

✳ *PPK/S Durgarde* - similar to PPK/S, only with bonded brushed chrome finish.

	$410	$365	$325	$290	$265	$250	$240

Last MSR was $465.

Add $14 for .22 LR cal.

GRADING - PPGS™	100%	98%	95%	90%	80%	70%	60%

✳ *Collector Model* - blue finish, special engraving. Imported 1986 only.

$465 **$415** **$350**

Last MSR was $529.

✳ *Presentation Model* - blue finish, special ornamentation. Imported 1986 only.

$720 **$650** **$500**

Last MSR was $819.

Also available with various engraving options in either blue, nickel, or gold finish - prices range from $222-$540.

PP SPORT - .22 LR cal. only, double action, 6.1 or 8.1 in. barrel, blue finish only, precision adj. sights, contoured plastic grips with thumb rest, 25 oz. New Manurhin design for 1985. Imported 1984-86.

$675 **$525** **$430** **$385** **$325** **$290** **$270**

Last MSR was $635.

Add 10% for 8.1 in. barrel.

✳ *PP Sport-C* - similar to PP Sport, except has single action with lightened trigger pull.

$650 **$500** **$415** **$370** **$310** **$280** **$260**

Last MSR was $635.

REVOLVERS

MODEL 73 DEFENSE - .357 Mag./.38 Spl. cal., 6 shot, 2 1/2, 3, or 4 in. barrel, checkered wood stocks, mfg. to precise tolerances, 31-33 1/2 oz. Importation began 1988.

MSR N/A **$1,200** **$1,000** **$850** **$725** **$600** **$500** **$425**

MODEL 73 GENDARMERIE - .357 Mag./.38 Spl. cal., 6 shot, similar to Model 73 Defense except has adj. sighting components and also is offered in 5 1/4, 6, or 8 in. barrel lengths. Manufactured for police requirements. Importation began 1988.

MSR N/A **$1,675** **$1,125** **$900** **$750** **$625** **$525** **$450**

MODEL 73 SPORT - .357 Mag./.38 Spl. cal., 6 shot, sport shooting features include minimized hammer stroke, micrometer rear sight, and free release trigger with fitted adj. sights. Importation began 1988.

MSR N/A **$1,675** **$1,125** **$900** **$750** **$625** **$525** **$450**

MODEL 73 CONVERTIBLE - includes choice of .22 LR/.38 Spl. or .22 LR/.32 Long cal. cylinders and barrels (5 3/4 in. for .38 Spl. and 6 in. for .22 LR/.32 Long). Imported 1988-95.

$1,925 **$1,675** **$1,325** **$1,125** **$950** **$800** **$700**

Last MSR was $2,200.

✳ *3 Cylinder Model 73 Convertible* - similar to Model 73 Convertible except includes 3 calibers (.22 LR, .32 Long, and .38 Spl.). Imported 1988-95.

$2,375 **$1,950** **$1,700** **$1,375** **$1,150** **$975** **$850**

Last MSR was $2,690.

MODEL 73 SILHOUETTE - .22 LR or .357 Mag. cal., Silhouette variation with fully adj. rear sight and either 10 (.22 LR) or 10 3/4 (.357 Mag.) in. heavy barrel with full shroud, contoured wooden target grips, approx. 4 lbs. Importation began 1988.

MSR N/A **$1,750** **$1,175** **$925** **$750** **$625** **$525** **$450**

Add $13 for .357 Mag. cal.

MODEL MR 88 - .357 Mag. cal., stainless steel, 4, 5, or 6 in. barrel, fixed sights, rubber grips. Importation began 1996.

MSR N/A **$775** **$625** **$450**

MODEL MR 96 - .357 Mag. cal., black finish, 3, 4, 5, or 6 in. VR barrel, adj. rear sight, ergonomic rubber grips. Importation began 1996.

MSR N/A **$750** **$615** **$425** **$375** **$350** **$325** **$295**

This model allows the user to unlock, swing the cylinder out, and eject the cases with one movement of the hand.

GRADING - PPGS™	100%	98%	95%	90%	80%	70%	60%

MARATHON PRODUCTS, INC.

Previously manufactured by Santa Barbara Armaments exclusively for Marathon Products, Inc. Most of the models listed were also available in kit form, but are not shown in this book.

PISTOLS: SINGLE SHOT

HOT SHOT MODEL - .22 LR cal., single shot, fixed sights, 14 3/4 in. barrel, hardwood stock with target grip configuration. Mfg. 1986-87.

	$55	$45	$40	$35	$35	$30	$30

Last MSR was $60.

RIFLES: BOLT ACTION

.22 FIRST SHOT - .22 LR cal., single shot, 16 1/2 in. barrel, hardwood stock, open sights, 31 in. total length, 3.8 lbs. Mfg. 1985-87.

	$55	$45	$40	$35	$35	$30	$30

Last MSR was $60.

✱ *.22 Super Shot* - similar to First Shot, except with 24 in. barrel and regular dimension stock. Mfg. 1985-87.

	$55	$45	$40	$35	$35	$30	$30

Last MSR was $60.

CENTERFIRE MODEL - .243 Win., .270 Win., 7x57mm, 7mm Rem. Mag., .30-06, .300 Win. Mag., or .308 Win. cal., Mauser type action, 5 shot fixed box mag., 24 in. barrel, select walnut with recoil pad, adj. trigger, open sights, 7.9 lbs. Available 1985-86 only.

	$295	$240	$215	$195	$180	$170	$160

Last MSR was $320.

MARBLE ARMS & MFG. CO.

Previous firearms manufacturer circa 1907-late 1950s, located in Gladstone, MI. Marble Arms is still in business, manufacturing sights, knives, and compasses.

In addition to axes and compasses, Marble Arms & Mfg. Co. also manufactured their Game Getter O/U combination gun from approx. 1907 to the early 1950s. During this period of production, the gun underwent quite a few changes including sights (an aperture sight mounted on the rear backstrap was optional in 1908), different configuration folding metal stock, and other changes.

GAME GETTER MODELS - starting manufacture in 1908, 2 variations of the model 1908 Game Getter were offered, the 1908A featured a flexible rear sight mounted behind the hammer and the 1908B had a filler blank in that space. The 1908s featured a .22 cal. rifled top barrel, and in standard configuration, a smooth bored bottom barrel chambered for the .44 round ball or .44 shot. Very late in production, chambering for the 2 in. .410 could be ordered. Standard barrel lengths were 12 in., 15 in., and 18 in., but Marbles was ready to please their customers, and on special order, 8 in., 10 in., 17 in., and 22 in. barrels were made, some were even shipped from the factory fitted with silencers, a very few guns ordered were not milled for the round tubular folding stock. A pivoting striker on the hammer was used to select the barrel to be fired, and the tip-up barrels were opened by pressing the trigger guard to the rear. The top frame featured a folding leaf sight, and the front barrel band incorporated the front sight, the grips were checkered black hard rubber with fleur-de-lis design. On very early 1908 guns, the buttplate was a separate piece secured to the tubing with 2 screws and later stocks were all one piece. A few guns were built with bottom barrels chambered for .25-20 & .32-20, but these are very rare. The gun was shipped in a dovetailed wooden box with sliding lid, and included a shoulder holster, cleaning rod, and directions for use. The first 1908 was shipped from the factory June 21, 1909, and serial letters A-M

GRADING - PPGS™	100%	98%	95%	90%	80%	70%	60%

were used. Then, starting with serial number 1, they continued through 9981, and the last gun was shipped from the factory May 22, 1918.

	$2,300	$2,100	$1,700	$1,400	$1,300	$1,100	$950

Add $250 for Model 1908A with original flexible tang sight.
Add $100-$150 for original holster, depending on condition of leather.
Add $600-$900 for correct original box, depending on condition.

✳ **1921 Model** - the 1921 was an entirely new gun, with similar barrel lengths (12, 15, or 18 in.), not nearly as pleasing in appearance as the 1908. The same barrel lengths were standard, but the bottom was chambered for the 2 in. .410. In 1924, the standard chamber was changed to 2 1/2 in. .410. It featured a bag style, oiled walnut grip, and a unique "Triple Combination Rear Sight," which was developed and made only for this model. A number of guns in the 14,000 to 16,000 serial number range can be found with brown plastic grips, conventional rear sight, and v notch with screw adjustment for elevation. The 1921 featured a folded and hinged 3 piece stock with an improved lock that eliminated wobble, but had no adjustment for drop. It also had a shorter action than the 1908, which was a faster action, and the hammer rebounded to a safety notch after firing. As with the 1908 Model, Marbles would accomodate the wishes of the customer, and barrels as short as 8 in. can be found. Some guns were ordered choke bored, some were chambered just for .44 Game Getter on the bottom barrel. A few had no provision for stock, at least 2 were shipped in .32-20, and as records are not complete, other calibers such as .25-20 and .38-40 may also exist. Supplied with a heavy cardboard box, shoulder holster, cleaning rod and instructions. First shipment was serial number 10,001 - shipped to William L. Marble, the west coast representative, on Oct. 4, 1921. Serial range 10,000-20,076.

	$1,900	$1,700	$1,500	$1,250	$1,100	$975	$900

Add $150 for original holster if in good condition.
Add $600-$900 for correct original box, depending on condition.

The first 200-300 of this model were shipped in 1908 boxes with 1921 yellow end label on the box. Values assume legal 18 in. barrels or correct registration. If not legal configuration, the gun is basically a black market item subject to BATF confiscation. The U.S. government and foreign countries continued to purchase 15 in. guns after the 1934 law was passed, and the last gun was shipped during the mid 1950s.

MARCEL THYS & SONS

Current SxS rifle and shotgun manufacturer established in 1960 and located in Crisnée, Belgium. The U.S. agent is currently Jean-Jacques Perodeau, located in Enid, OK.

Marcel Thys & Sons manufactures fine quality double rifles and shotguns, with many engraving options and special orders. Prices range from $12,000-$85,000, w/o engraving. Since these guns are custom-made per individual order, please contact the U.S. agent or the factory directly (see Trademark Index) for current information, availability, and a firm price quotation.

MARGOLIN

Original pistol design by M.V. Margolin developed after WWII as a training firearm for members of the Russian shooting team. The Margolin is currently manufactured at the Izhevsk mechanical plant located in Izhevsk, Russia as the "MTsN" sporting pistol. Limited importation.

PISTOLS: SEMI-AUTO

TARGET MODEL - .22 LR cal., originally developed from the TT (Tula Tokarev), manufactured to precise tolerances, many specimens are made to individual shooters' specifications, seldom encountered in the U.S., while rare, desirability to date has been limited, current mfg. - limited importation.

Margolin pistols are typically priced in the $475-$850 range, depending on features and assuming 95%+ original condition. While currently imported Chinese copies are considerably less expensive, they do not have the quality (or accuracy) of the Russian Margolins.

100%	98%	95%	90%	80%	70%	60%	50%	40%	30%	20%	10%

MARLIN FIREARMS COMPANY

Current manufacturer located in North Haven, CT. Marlin has been manufacturing firearms since 1870. Recent manufacture (1969-present) is in North Haven, CT. Previously, Marlin was manufactured (1870-1969) in New Haven, CT. Distributor sales only.

On Nov. 10th, 2000, Marlin Firearms Company purchased H&R 1871, Inc. This includes the brand names Harrington & Richardson, New England Firearms, and Wesson & Harrington (please refer to individual sections in this text).

PISTOLS: DERRINGERS AND REVOLVERS

Many of the more common variations in average condition sell in the $150-$250 range, while rarer specimens with 90%+ original condition will be priced in the $450-$1,750 range, depending on rarity and condition.

RIFLES: LEVER ACTION, ANTIQUE

Factory information by individual serial number may be available from the Cody Firearms Museum in Cody, WY on the following models: Models 1881, 1888, 1889, and 1892 (ser. no. range 4,001- 355,504 only), Models 1893, 1894, 1895, and 1897 may be researched. Marlin had only one series of serial numbers for all lever action repeating rifles from 1883-1906: therefore serial numbers do not reflect the place in production or sequence number of a gun within a model. Sometimes, a record shows two or even three guns with the same serial number from the same time period.

Values below are for standard models only without special order features. 98% and 100% prices have been intentionally replaced with N/As (not applicable), since these condition factors are seldom encountered and hard to accurately price, as their values have dramatically increased during the past 3-5 years.

Add a premium for all mint condition guns with strong, case colored frames.

MODEL 1881 - .32-40 WCF, .38-55 WCF, .40-60 WCF, .45-70 Govt., or .45-85 Marlin cal., tube mag., 28 in. octagonal barrel standard, top ejection, blued finish with case hardened hammer, lever, and buttplate. Approx. 20,000 mfg. between 1881-92.

N/A	N/A	$1,800	$1,425	$1,000	$900	$800	$650	$550	$500	$450	$400

This model came in 3 frame styles for various calibers.

Add approx. 15% for .45-70 cal.

Add 200-300% premium for rare First models (pre-ser. no. 600).

Add a premium for very early First models with hand engraved script barrel markings - approx. first 60 rifles mfg.

MODEL 1888 - .32-20 WCF, .38-40 WCF, or .44-40 WCF cal., 24 in. octagonal barrel most frequently encountered, top ejection, blued finish with case hardened hammer, lever, and buttplate, short throw lever action principle. Approx. 4,800 mfg. between 1888-89. Ser. range approx. 19,560-27,850.

N/A	N/A	$2,400	$2,000	$1,700	$1,475	$1,250	$1,000	$875	$750	$625	$500

Add 40% for half-round, half-octagon barrel (23 mfg.).

Add 20% for round barrel (266 mfg.).

Add 25% for half magazine (78 mfg.).

MODEL 1889 - .25-20 WCF (very rare), .32-20 WCF, .38-40 WCF, .38-55 WCF, or .44-40 WCF cal., 24 (approx. 39,300 mfg.) or 28 (approx. 2,260 mfg.) in. octagonal barrel most frequently encountered, side ejection with solid top frame, blued finish with case hardened hammer, lever, and buttplate, short throw lever action principle. Approx. 55,000 mfg. between 1889-1899. Ser. range approx. 25,000-100,000.

N/A	N/A	$1,100	$800	$600	$500	$400	$340	$295	$260	$230	$200

Add 300-500% for Musket.

Add 25% for carbine.

Add 15% for .44-40 WCF cal.

100%	98%	95%	90%	80%	70%	60%	50%	40%	30%	20%	10%

Factory special orders/features will add premiums, depending on the desirability of each option and the gun's original condition factor.

Also available as Carbine with either a 15 in. (only 367 mfg.) or 20 in. (approx. 10,000 mfg.) barrel or Musket (30 in. barrel - very rare).

MODEL 1891
- .22 Rimfire and .32 Rimfire/Centerfire cal., 24 in. octagonal barrel most often encountered, choice of side loading (1st variation) or tube loading (2nd variation), blued finish with case hardened hammer, lever, and buttplate, sear safety system on lever action. Approx. 18,650 mfg. between 1891-1897. Ser. no. range is approx. 37,500-118,000.

N/A	N/A	$1,700	$1,300	$1,100	$950	$875	$775	$695	$625	$550	$475

Add 50% for deluxe, pistol grip checkered model.

Subtract 40% for tube loading model (.32 Centerfire).

Add $100 each for special sights (including correct Lyman, Marbles, Beeches combo, etc.).

Factory special orders/features will add premiums, depending on the desirability of each option and the gun's original condition factor.

MODEL 1892
- .22 S, L, or LR, .32 S or L cal., 16, 24, 26, or 28 in. barrel, tubular mag., open sight, plain straight stock. Mfg. 1892-1916.

N/A	N/A	$1,350	$975	$775	$700	$600	$525	$475	$425	$385	$340

Add 10% for .22 cal.

Subtract 10% for .32 cal.

Add $100 each for special sights (including correct Lyman, Marbles, Beeches combo, etc.).

Factory special orders/features will add premiums, depending on the desirability of each option and the gun's original condition factor.

.22 cals. will bring a premium in this model.

MODEL 1893 RIFLE
- .25-36 Marlin, .30-30 Win., .32 Spl., .32-40 WCF, or .38-55 WCF cal., 20-32 in. round or octagonal barrels, blue (Model B) or case colored receiver, 10 shot tube mag., straight grip stock. Musket model also mfg. - 30 in. barrel and military style forearm. Mfg. 1893-1936.

N/A	N/A	$2,500	$1,800	$1,400	$1,050	$825	$625	$450	$400	$375	$350

Add 100% for Musket.

Add 1%5-20% for calibers other than .30-30 Win. or .32 Spl.

Add 15%-20% for takedown model, depending on condition.

Add approx. 20% for special Lightweight Model.

Subtract 50%-60% for the Model B with blue receiver.

Factory special orders/features will add premiums, depending on the desirability of each option and the gun's original condition factor.

Strong, original case colors over 95% condition can result in $2,500 asking prices.

Although incorrect, more than a few people refer to all 20 in. barrels as "Lightweight" models. Technically, the Lightweight variation has a 7 1/2 in. forearm rather than the standard 9 in.

Later production guns were marked "Model '93" and have less value. This model had two barrel variations - one was marked "special smokeless steel" while the other was marked "for Black Powder". The latter (also known as Model B) are 1st Models only and have blue receivers rather than case colored.

MODEL 1893 CARBINE
- .30-30 Win., .32 Spl., .32-40 WCF cal., or .38-55 WCF cal., 15 (only 61 mfg.) or 20 in. round barrel, case colored receiver, 7 shot tube mag., straight or pistol grip stock. Mfg. 1893-1935.

Add 15%-20% for calibers other than .30-30 Win. or .32 Spl.

Factory special orders/features will add premiums, depending on the desirability of each option and the gun's original condition factor.

✳ *1st Model* - with saddle ring. Mfg. 1893-1915.

N/A	N/A	$1,600	$1,300	$1,100	$900	$750	$600	$500	$400	$375	$350

Strong, original case colors over 95% condition can result in $2,500 asking prices.

100%	98%	95%	90%	80%	70%	60%	50%	40%	30%	20%	10%

✻ *2nd Model* - .30-30 Win. or .32 HPS cal., has "Bull's-eye" in stock, no saddle rings. Mfg. 1922-35.

N/A	N/A	$850	$725	$600	$475	$425	$385	$350	$325	$300	$285

✻ *Model 1893 Sporting Carbine* - .30-30 Win. or .32 Spl. cal., 20 in. round barrel, 2/3 mag., 5 shot, carbine style front sight, Rocky Mountain rear, straight stock, hard rubber buttplate, bull's-eye in stock. Mfg. 1923-35.

N/A	N/A	$1,375	$1,100	$900	$750	$700	$550	$475	$400	$375	$350

Subtract 40% for 2nd Model made in 1935 with "S" steel buttplate and ivory bead front sight.

MODEL 1894 - .25-20 WCF, .32-20 WCF, .38-40 WCF, or .44-40 WCF cal., case colored receiver, 10 shot tube mag., 24 in. round or octagon barrel, straight or pistol grip stock. Mfg. 1894-1934.

N/A	N/A	$2,500	$1,995	$1,650	$1,250	$875	$625	$450	$400	$375	$350

Add 25% for saddle ring carbine.

Add 10% for .44-40 WCF cal.

Add 40% for Baby Carbine with 18 in. barrel and 1/2 mag.

Add 15%-20% for takedown model, depending on condition.

Add 100% for Musket.

Factory special orders/features will add premiums, depending on the desirability of each option and the gun's original condition factor.

Strong, original case colors over 95% condition can result in $2,500 asking prices.

Later production guns were marked "Model '94" and have less value. This model was also available in both a Carbine and Musket variation.

MODEL 1895 - .33 WCF, .38-56 WCF, .40-65 WCF, .40-70 WCF, .40-82 WCF, .45-70 Govt. or .45-90 cal., case colored receiver, 9 shot tube mag., 24 or 26 in. round or octagon barrel standard, other lengths were available, open sights, plain straight or pistol grip stock. Mfg. 1895-1915.

N/A	N/A	$3,500	$3,000	$2,500	$2,000	$1,500	$1,200	$1,000	$750	$600	$550

Add 15%-25% for takedown model, depending on condition.

Premiums exist for .40-70 WCF (approx. 60 mfg.), .45-70 Govt., and .45-90 WCF cal.

Factory special orders/features will add premiums, depending on the desirability of each option and the gun's original condition factor.

Strong, original case colors over 95% condition can result in $3,500 asking prices.

In 1912, a lightweight variation was introduced with hard rubber buttplate and half-magazine, cals. were .33 WCF and .45-70 Govt. (commands a premium), and round barrels were either 22 or 24 in. A Carbine variation was also offered with approx. 200 mfg. - premiums may run as high as 150% over rifle values listed.

MODEL 1897 - .22 S, L, or LR cal., tube mag., 16, 24, 26, or 28 in. barrel, case colored receiver, takedown, open sights, plain straight or pistol grip stock. Mfg. 1897-1922.

N/A	N/A	$2,500	$1,750	$1,475	$1,250	$1,000	$850	$625	$450	$400	$375

Add 100% for 16 in. barrel "Bicycle Rifle."

Add 15%-20% for takedown model, depending on condition.

Add $100 each for special sights (including correct Lyman, Marbles, Beeches combo, etc.).

Factory special orders/features will add premiums, depending on the desirability of each option and the gun's original condition factor.

Strong, original case colors over 95% condition can result in $2,500 asking prices.

RIFLES: MODERN PRODUCTION

Year of manufacture can be determined from 1946-1968 by the following letter/numeral prefixes: 1946-C, 1947-D, 1948-E, 1949-F, 1950-G, 1951-H, 1952-J, 1953-K, 1954-L, 1955-M, 1956-N, 1957-P, 1958-R, 1959-S, 1960-T, 1961-U, 1962-V, 1963-W, 1964-Y,Z, 1965-AA, 1966-AB, 1967-AC, 1968-AD, 1969-69, 1970-70, 1971-71, 1972-72. Starting in 1973, the year can be determined by subtracting the first 2 numbers of the serial number from 100.

The models below are listed in numerical sequence for easy reference.

Machine cut checkering became standard on many Marlins beginning 1995. Safety locks have

GRADING - PPGS™	100%	98%	95%	90%	80%	70%	60%

been shipped with every new rifle/shotgun beginning 1999. In 2004, the T-900 fire control system became standard on all Marlin 900 Series rifles, except the Papoose and the Model 717M2. This improved trigger has a pull of 3-5 lbs., features a new safety mechanism with positive click positions for fire and safe, and a crisp let-off.

MODEL MR-7 BOLT ACTION - .22-250 Rem. (advertised in 1998, but never mfg.), .243 Win. (advertised in 1998, but never mfg.), .25-06 Rem. (new 1997), .270 Win., .280 Rem. (new 1998) .30-06, or .308 Win. (advertised in 1998, but never mfg.) cal., 4 shot box mag. with removable hinged floorplate, 3 position safety, adj. 3-6 lb. trigger, 22 in. barrel, checkered American walnut stock, cocking indicator, forged receiver, damascened bolt, includes sling swivels, with or without sights, approx. 7 1/2 lbs. Mfg. 1996-99.

	$495	$440	$375	$315	$275	$240	$215

Last MSR was $603.

Add $40 for open sights (.270 Win., .280 Rem., or .30-06).

✳ *Model MR-7B* - .270 Win. or .30-06 only, similar to Model MR-7, except has birch stock and forearm with cut checkering. Mfg. 1998-99.

	$380	$250	$185	$165	$150	$130	$125

Last MSR was $483.

Add $40 for open sights (mfg. 1998 only).

MODEL 9 CAMP CARBINE SEMI-AUTO - 9mm Para. cal. only, 16 1/2 in. barrel, 12 or 20 shot mag. (disc. 1989), 4 shot mag. became standard in 1990, sand blasted steel receiver, open sights, last shot automatic hold-open, 6 3/4 lbs. Mfg. 1985-99.

	$340	$230	$170	$150	$140	$130	$125

Last MSR was $443.

Add 10% for nickel plating (mfg. 1991-94, Model 9N).

A new high visibility orange front sight post with cutaway hood was added in 1989.

MODEL 15YN "LITTLE BUCKAROO" SINGLE SHOT - .22 S, L, or LR cal., single shot, 16 1/4 in. barrel, youth dimensions with 12 LOP, adj. rear sight, grooved receiver, pressed checkering, 4 1/4 lbs. Disc. 2003.

	$155	$135	$105	$80	$75	$70	$65

Last MSR was $209.

✳ *Model 15YS Stainless Steel* - similar to Model 15YN, except is stainless steel and has Fire Sights. Mfg. 2002-2003.

	$175	$150	$115				

Last MSR was $233.

MODEL 17V BOLT ACTION - .17 HMR cal., 7 shot detachable mag., 22 in. heavy barrel, walnut finished checkered hardwood Monte Carlo stock and forend, red cocking indicator, grooved receiver, includes scope mounts, 6 lbs. Mfg. 2002-2003.

	$220	$200	$180	$170	$160	$145	$130

Last MSR was $269.

✳ *Model 17VS* - similar to Model 17V, except has bead blasted stainless steel barrel and receiver, laminated black/grey hardwood Monte Carlo stock, 7 lbs. Mfg. 2002-2004.

	$330	$270	$225				

Last MSR was $402.

MODEL 18 SLIDE ACTION - .22 S, L, or LR cal., tube mag., 20 in. round or octagon barrel, open sight, exposed hammer, plain straight grip stock. Mfg. 1906-09.

	$450	$325	$225	$175	$135	$100	$85

MODEL 20 SLIDE ACTION - .22 S, L, or LR cal., 24 in. octagon barrel, open sight, exposed hammer, takedown, plain straight grip stock. Mfg. 1907-22.

	$395	$295	$200	$165	$125	$100	$85

GRADING - PPGS™	100%	98%	95%	90%	80%	70%	60%

MODEL 25 SLIDE ACTION - .22 Short cal. and CB cap., tube mag., 23 in. barrel, open sight, exposed hammer, takedown, plain straight grip stock. Mfg. 1909-10.

	$495	$450	$375	$325	$275	$225	$175

MODEL 25MB BOLT ACTION - .22 Mag. cal., bolt action, 16 1/4 in. micro-groove barrel, 7 shot mag., hardwood stock, takedown action, 6 lbs. Mfg. 1987-88 only.

	$145	$115	$95	$85	$75	$70	$65

Last MSR was $173.

This model included both a scope and gun case.

MODEL 25MG GARDEN GUN - please refer to the Marlin bolt action shotgun section for information on this model.

MODEL 25MN BOLT ACTION - .22 Mag. cal., bolt action, 7 shot mag., 22 in. barrel, choice of walnut finished hardwood or Mossy Oak Breakup camo (new 2001) stock (pressed checkering became standard 1994), grooved receiver, adj. rear sight (new 1995), 6 lbs. Mfg. 1989-2003.

	$185	$140	$105	$85	$75	$70	$65

Last MSR was $241.

Add $6 for 4X scope (disc. 2000).
Add $37 for Mossy Oak Breakup camo stock.

MODEL 25N BOLT ACTION - .22 LR cal., 7 shot mag., 22 in. barrel, press checkered Monte Carlo stock, 5 1/2 lbs. Disc. 2003.

	$155	$135	$110	$80	$75	$70	$65

Last MSR was $212.

Add $8 for 4X scope.

* ***Model 25NC Bolt Action*** - similar to Model 25N, except has Mossy Oak Breakup camo stock. Disc. 2003.

	$190	$145	$105	$85	$75	$70	$65

Last MSR was $248.

MODEL 27 SLIDE ACTION - .25-20 WCF, or .32-20 WCF cal., 2/3 tube mag., 7 shot, 24 in. octagon barrel, open sight, plain straight grip stock. Mfg. 1910-11.

	$425	$350	$250	$200	$165	$140	$125

Subtract 15% for .25RF cal.

MODEL 27S - .25RF, .25-20 WCF, or .32-20 WCF cal., similar to Model 27, except has safety button on right side of receiver, round or octagonal barrel added in 1913.

	$400	$350	$300	$250	$200	$150	$100

MODEL 29 SLIDE ACTION - similar to Model 20, with 23 in. round barrel, 1/2 tube mag. Mfg. 1913-16.

	$400	$325	$250	$200	$165	$140	$125

MODEL 30/30A LEVER ACTION - .30-30 Win. cal., 20 in. barrel, promotional Glenfield model with birch stock and pressed checkering. Mfg. 1964-83.

	$220	$185	$160	$135	$120	$110	$100

This model was replaced by the Model 30AS in 1983.

MODEL 336A/336AS (30AS) LEVER ACTION - .30-30 Win. cal. only, 20 in. barrel, 6 shot tube mag, walnut finished birch stock (pressed checkering became standard 1995, cut checkering became standard 1998), open sights (adj. rear sight became standard 1995), no frills version of the 336CS, 7 lbs. New 1983.

MSR $477	$355	$275	$175	$145	$125	$120	$115

Add $50 for 4X scope.

Prior to 2000, this was designated the Model 30AS. The Model 30AS was formerly part of the Glenfield line. During 2001, this model's nomenclature was changed from 336AS to 336A.

GRADING - PPGS™	100%	98%	95%	90%	80%	70%	60%

✴ *Model 336W (30AW)* - similar to Model 30AS, except has carbine style barrel band and gold trigger.

   MSR $482   **$360**   **$275**   **$175**   **$145**   **$130**   **$120**   **$115**

   Add $53 for 4X scope.

   This model was previously sold to Wal-Mart only. Model nomenclature was changed during 1998.

✴ *Model 336CC* - similar to Model 336W, except has Mossy Oak Breakup camo stock and forearm, 7 lbs. Mfg. 2001-2004.

              $365   **$285**   **$190**   **$155**   **$135**   **$125**   **$115**

                                       Last MSR was $503.

✴ *Model 336Y SpikeHorn* - similar to Model 336W, 5 shot tube mag, 16.5 in. barrel, shorter stock (12.5 in. LOP) with vent. recoil pad, 6.5 lbs. New 2003.

   MSR $566   **$410**   **$320**   **$210**   **$165**   **$135**   **$125**   **$115**

MODEL 32 SLIDE ACTION
- .22 S, L, or LR cal., 2/3 tube mag., 24 in. octagon barrel, open sight, plain pistol grip stock, hammerless. Mfg. 1914-15.

              $600   **$525**   **$425**   **$350**   **$300**   **$225**   **$150**

MODEL 1936
- .30-30 Win. or .32 HPS (High Power Special) cal., 6 shot, 20 or 24 in. barrel, tubular mag., open sights, pistol grip stock, barrel band, leaf mainspring, thinner "perch belly" forearm, case colored receiver, upper tang, buttstock has a fluted comb and flat hard rubber buttplate. Mfg. 1936-37.

              $750   **$650**   **$500**   **$350**   **$275**   **$200**   **$150**

   Add 10% for vivid case colors with strong greens, reds, and yellows.

   Add 10% for rifles and sporting carbines.

   Rifles have "A" suffix, sporting carbine has "SC" suffix, and regular and carbine has "RC" suffix. The Model 1936 has an upper tang inscription "Model 1936" and a case colored receiver. Also, the Model 1936 did not have a letter prefix in the ser. no.

MODEL 36 - 1ST VARIATION
- same as Model 1936 - called Model 36 in catalog only. Mfg. 1937-40.

              $600   **$550**   **$450**   **$375**   **$250**   **$200**   **$150**

   Add 10% for rifles and sporting carbines.

   The Model 36 - 1st Variation has an upper tang inscription "Model 1936" and a case colored receiver. Also, the Model 36 - 1st variation did not have a letter prefix in the ser. no.

MODEL 36 - 2ND VARIATION
- similar to Model 1936, still has case colored receiver with "Model 1936" on upper tang, coiled main spring, buttstock is heavier style and no longer has fluted comb, buttplate is a thicker, slightly curved style - hard rubber, forearm is a heavier beaver-tailed style, "B" prefix in ser. no. Mfg. 1941 only.

              $575   **$475**   **$375**   **$275**   **$250**   **$200**   **$165**

   Add 10% for rifles and sporting carbines.

MODEL 36ADL DELUXE RIFLE
- similar to Model 1936, case colored receiver, checkered pistol grip buttstock and forearm, pistol grip cap, Winchester quick detachable swivels with 1 in. sling, "B" prefix in ser. no., has "Model 1936" on upper tang. Less than 50 mfg. in 1941 only.

             $1,150   **$1,000**   **$800**   **$600**   **$400**   **$275**   **$250**

   Both the rear and front swivel bases are attached with two wood screws and are not inletted into the wood.

MODEL 36 - 3RD VARIATION
- .30-30 Win. or .32 SPEC cal., blued receiver, no upper tang markings, model no. and cal. marked on barrel, rifles have "A" suffix, Deluxe rifle has "ADL" suffix, Sporting Carbine has "SC" suffix, and regular carbine has "RC" suffix, small case "c" prefix in 1946, and large "D" prefix in 1947. Mfg. 1946-47.

              $500   **$425**   **$350**   **$225**   **$165**   **$150**   **$125**

   Add 10% for rifles and sporting carbines.

GRADING - PPGS™	100%	98%	95%	90%	80%	70%	60%

Deluxe rifles (ADL) had a checkered pistol grip stock and forearm with no pistol grip cap. Deluxe rifles also have swivel round studs in buttstock and forearm cap with quick detachable swivels and a 1 in. sling. Also, some standard rifles may have the "ADL" barrel markings in 1946-47. 1946 mfg. has a lowercase "c" prefix and 1947 mfg. has a capital "D" prefix in ser. no.

❋ *Model 36 ADL Deluxe* - similar to Model 36 3rd Variation, has checkered pistol grip stock and forearm, forearm has checkering on sides and underneath, round swivel stud in buttstock and on forearm cap, deluxe quick detachable swivels and 1 in. leather sling, does not have model designation on upper tang or pistol grip cap, hooded front ramp screw on front sight, Rocky Mountain rear, letter prefix in ser. no. is "C" or "D."

	100%	98%	95%	90%	80%	70%	60%
	$850	$700	$550	$450	$400	$375	$350

MODEL 37 SLIDE ACTION - similar to Model 29, with 24 in. barrel, full length tube mag. Mfg. 1913-16.

	$395	$325	$250	$200	$150	$125	$100

MODEL 38 SLIDE ACTION - .22 S, L, or LR cal., 2/3 tube mag., 24 in. octagon barrel, open sights, hammerless, takedown, plain pistol grip stock. Mfg. 1920-30.

	$350	$300	$225	$175	$125	$100	$85

MODEL 39 LEVER ACTION - .22 S, L, or LR cal., 24 in. octagon barrel with tube mag., open sights, takedown, case hardened receiver and lever, S-shaped pistol grip stock, bluing on barrel, forend tip, mag. tube, bolt, hammer, and screws, various qualities of walnut (X, 2X, or 3X), hard rubber buttplate. Approx. 40-50,000 mfg. 1922-38.

	N/A	N/A	$2,500	$2,100	$1,600	$1,300	$975

Early models with fancy 2X-3X wood will bring a considerable premium.

Excellent original condition in this model is extremely hard to find since most specimens were well used due to the 16/25 shell mag. capacity, reliability, and the fact that the balance point of the gun (the receiver) normally wore first due to carrying wear. Earlier guns without a prefix or with an "S" prefix are noted for their superior workmanship and fine finish. Later "HS" prefix (High Speed) are not quite as valuable as these earlier guns.

MODEL 39A - similar to Model 39, with case hardened receiver (mfg. 1939-1945), includes 1st and 2nd Models with round barrel. 3rd Model 1st Variation was introduced in 1946 and has blue receiver, 3rd Model 2nd Variation has flutes in buttstock comb and was introduced in 1951, and 3rd Model 3rd Variation has Micro-Groove rifling, no pistol grip cap, and was introduced in 1954.

❋ *1st Model* - case colored frame, no prefix. Mfg. 1939 only.

	N/A	$1,200	$1,000	$900	$775	$650	$500

The first variation of the Model 39A mfg. in 1939 is distinguishable by a buttstock and lever similar to those on earlier Model 39s.

❋ *2nd Model* - case colored frame, "B" prefix. Mfg. 1940-45.

	N/A	$800	$725	$650	$575	$450	$395

The second variation had a rounded lever like current production and no "S" shape to bottom of pistol grip.

❋ *3rd Model 1st Variation* - features blued receiver, new ramp front sight, hard rubber buttplate, and continued Ballard rifling. Mfg. 1946-50.

	N/A	$550	$500	$450	$400	$350	$300

❋ *3rd Model 2nd Variation* - similar to 3rd Model 1st Variation, except has flutes in buttstock comb, white plastic spacer next to buttplate, and pistol grip cap with white spacer and brass insert. Mfg. 1951-53.

	N/A	$400	$350	$300	$275	$250	$225

❋ *3rd Model 3rd Variation* - similar to 3rd Model 2nd Variation, except has Micro-Groove rifling, and no pistol grip cap. Mfg. 1954-57.

	N/A	$375	$325	$300	$250	$200	$175

GRADING - PPGS™	100%	98%	95%	90%	80%	70%	60%

GOLDEN 39A - similar to Model 39A, with gold-plated trigger, sling swivels. Mfg. 1957-87.

	$325	$300	$275	$250	$200	$175	$150

Add 30% to pre-1970 (oil finished stock) models.

GOLDEN 39M - similar to Golden 39A, except is carbine variation.

	$350	$325	$275	$250	$150	$125	$100

MODEL 39A "MOUNTIE" - straight grip stock, slim forearm, otherwise similar to 39A. Mfg. 1953-72.

	$450	$400	$350	$300	$250	$200	$175

❋ *Model 39A "MOUNTIE" with K prefix* - 24 in. barrel and slender forearm. 4,335 mfg. 1953 only.

	$750	$650	$550	$475	$425	$350	$300

90TH ANNIVERSARY 39A RIFLE - 24 in. chrome barrel and action, select checkered walnut stock, carved squirrel on side of buttstock. 500 mfg. in 1960.

	$1,200	$1,000	$750	$500	$425	$350	$250

Last MSR was $100.

90TH ANNIVERSARY MODEL 39M MOUNTIE CARBINE - similar to 90th Anniversary Model 39A, except 20 in. barrel, straight stock. 500 mfg. in 1960.

	$1,200	$1,000	$750	$600	$400	$350	$250

Last MSR was $100.

Add $50-$75 for original box and papers.

MODEL 39AWL - special model made exclusively for Wal-Mart, supporting the Wildlife Management Institution and Wildlife Forever, features similar to Marlin 1897CL CLassic, 24 in. half-round, half-octagon barrel, half mag., checkered black American walnut pistol grip stock, adj. semi-buckhorn rear sight, engraved receiver with scroll and "Wildlife for Tomorrow" and "Sportsmen Supporting Conservation". 2,000 mfg. 1997 only.

	$675	$600	$550	$500	$450	$400	$350

Last MSR was $729.

MODEL 39A-DL - similar to 90th Anniversary, with blue barrel and action, regular production. Mfg. 1960-63.

	$900	$800	$750	$500	$400	$300	$200

This model is also known as the "Marlin 39A Squirrel Gun."

MODEL 39 PRESENTATION - .22 cal., one of the pair in the "Brace of 1,000," engraved receiver, 20 in. tapered octagon barrel, select fancy walnut straight grip stock and forend. Mfg. 1970 only.

	$600	$450	$375

MODEL 39A OCTAGON - similar to Golden 39A, with octagon barrel, no pistol grip cap, 2,551 rifles and 2,140 carbines were produced. Mfg. 1973.

	$595	$550	$475	$425	$360	$295	$250

MODEL 39 CARBINE - similar to 39M, with light barrel, 3/4 tube mag. 9,695 mfg. 1963-67.

	$450	$400	$325	$275	$200	$150	$110

MODEL 39D - similar to 39M, with pistol grip stock. Mfg. 1971-73.

	$350	$300	$250	$190	$150	$125	$100

MODEL 39A/AS - .22 LR cal., current production model, lever action, 19-26 shot tube mag., 24 in. barrel, walnut stock (cut checkering became standard 1994), open sights, gold trigger, takedown, 6.5 lbs.

MSR $596	$425	$325	$250	$190	$150	$125	$100

This model was previously designated the Model 39A. In 1988, the Model 39AS became the standard production model and included a rebounding hammer and hammer block safety. In 2001, the model nomenclature was changed back to the Model 39A.

GRADING - PPGS™	100%	98%	95%	90%	80%	70%	60%

MODEL 39TDS - .22 LR cal., carbine variation of the Model 39AS, 16 1/2 in. barrel with open sights, 5 1/4 lbs. Mfg. 1988-95.

	$450	$350	$200	$175	$150	$125	$110

Last MSR was $443.

MODEL 39M - carbine version of Model 39A, 20 in. lightweight barrel, 16 shot tube mag., squared finger lever, 6 lbs. Disc. 1987.

	$350	$325	$295	$250	$200	$175	$150

Last MSR was $304.

MODEL 39M OCTAGON - similar to Model 39M, with octagon barrel. 2,140 mfg. 1973.

	$550	$495	$475	$425	$360	$295	$250

MODEL 39 CENTURY LTD - Marlin Centennial 1870-1970 Commemorative, 20 in. octagon barrel, select walnut straight stock, brass forearm cap and buttplate, name plate in butt. 35,388 mfg. 1970.

	$500	$450	$300	$200	$175	$150	$125

This model should have the original box for 100% values.

MODEL 39A ARTICLE II - NRA Centennial Commemorative 1871-1971, "Right to Bear Arms" medallion in receiver, 24 in. octagon barrel, fancy pistol grip stock, brass buttplate and forearm cap. 6,244 mfg. 1971.

	$450	$395	$375	$350	$295	$250	$195

MODEL 39M ARTICLE II CARBINE - similar to 39A Article II, with 20 in. barrel, straight grip stock. Mfg. 3,824.

	$450	$395	$375	$350	$295	$250	$195

MODEL 45 CARBINE - .45 ACP cal. only, 7 shot mag., sandblasted steel receiver, 16 1/2 in. barrel, last shot hold open device, press checkering, adj. rear sight, 6 3/4 lbs. Mfg. 1986-99.

	$340	$230	$175	$150	$140	$130	$125

Last MSR was $443.

A new high visibility orange front sight post with cutaway hood was added in 1989.

MODEL 56 - similar to Model 57 Levermatic, 22 or 24 in. barrel, with mag. Mfg. 1955-64.

	$300	$250	$200	$150	$125	$100	$85

MODEL 57 LEVERMATIC - .22 S, L, or LR cal., tube mag., 22 in. barrel, open sight, Monte Carlo pistol grip stock. Mfg. 1959-65.

	$375	$350	$300	$250	$200	$150	$125

MODEL 57M - .22 Mag. cal., similar to Model 57 Levermatic, except has 24 in. barrel.

	$350	$300	$225	$175	$135	$125	$110

MODEL 60 SEMI-AUTO - .22 LR cal., 14 shot (LR) tube mag., entry level rifle with 19 or 22 (disc. 2002) in. Micro-Groove barrel, aluminum receiver, walnut finished laminated hardwood stock (laminated now standard) with pressed checkering, adj. rear sight, crossbolt safety, last shot hold open, approx. 5.5 lbs. New 1960.

MSR $195	$155	$125	$95	$80	$75	$65	$60

Add $8 for 4X scope.

✳ *Model 60C* - similar to Model 60SS, except has full coverage Mossy Oak Breakup camo stock, 5.5 lbs. New 2000.

MSR $231	$175	$140	$110	$85	$75	$65	$60

✳ *Model 60DL* - similar to Model 60, except has Walnutone walnut patterned finish. New 2004.

MSR $231	$175	$140	$110	$85	$75	$65	$60

GRADING - PPGS™	100%	98%	95%	90%	80%	70%	60%

MODEL 60SS SEMI-AUTO STAINLESS
- .22 LR cal., 14 shot tube mag., stainless steel construction with laminated black/grey birch stock with Monte Carlo cheek-piece, Mar-Shield finish, 19 or 22 (disc. 2002) in. barrel, most recent mfg. has adj. semi-buckhorn folding rear with high visibility post and removable cutaway Wide-scan hood front sight, 5.5 lbs. New 1993.

MSR $312	$235	$190	$150	

* *Model 60SB* - similar to Model 60SS, except has uncheckered (mfg. 1998 only) or press-checkered (new 1999) birch Monte Carlo stock, laminated hardwood became standard 2004. New 1998.

MSR $247	$180	$160	$130	

Add $17 for 4X scope.

This model was previously sold to Wal-Mart only.

* *Model 60SSK* - similar to Model 60SS, except has black fiberglass stock with Monte Carlo cheekpiece. New 1998.

MSR $269	$215	$180	$140	

Add $15 for 4X scope (disc. 2001).

MODEL 62 LEVERMATIC
- .256 Mag. or .30 Carbine cal., 4 shot mag., 23 in. barrel, open sight, pistol grip Monte Carlo stock. Mfg. 1963-69.

	100%	98%	95%	90%	80%	70%	60%
.256 Mag.	$475	$375	$325	$275	$225	$195	$175
.30 Carbine	$375	$335	$300	$250	$200	$175	$150

MODEL 70P (PAPOOSE) SEMI-AUTO
- .22 LR cal. only, semi-auto, takedown carbine with 16.25 in. barrel, 7 shot mag., rustproof receiver, bolt hold open, is supplied with floating nylon carrying case. Mfg. 1986-94.

	100%	98%	95%	90%	80%	70%	60%
	$170	$125	$90	$75	$65	$60	$55

Last MSR was $225.

Subtract $25 if without 4X scope (became standard 1993).

* *Model 70PSS* - similar to Model 70P, except has stainless steel construction with black checkered synthetic stock with swing swivels, last shot hold-open became standard in 1996, includes blue nylon floatable case, 3.25 lbs. New 1995.

MSR $318	$240	$190	$140	

* *Model 70HC* - .22 LR cal., semi-auto, carbine with 18 in. barrel. Mfg. 1988-95.

	100%	98%	95%	90%	80%	70%	60%
	$185	$155	$130	$120	$110	$100	$90

MODEL 81TS BOLT ACTION
- .22 S, L, or LR cal., 22 in. barrel with 17-25 shot tube mag., black synthetic stock with molded checkering, adj. rear sight, 6 lbs. Disc. 2003.

	100%	98%	95%	90%	80%	70%	60%
	$165	$130	$100	$80	$75	$65	$60

Last MSR was $213.

MODEL 83TS BOLT ACTION
- .22 Mag. cal., 22 in. barrel, 12 shot mag., otherwise similar to Model 81TS, 6 lbs. Disc. 2003.

	100%	98%	95%	90%	80%	70%	60%
	$195	$150	$125	$95	$85	$75	$70

Last MSR was $259.

MODEL 322 BOLT ACTION VARMINT
- .222 Rem. cal., Sako Mauser type action, 3 shot mag., 24 in. medium weight barrel, 2 position aperture sight, checkered stock. Approx. 5,850 mfg. 1954-57.

	100%	98%	95%	90%	80%	70%	60%
	$550	$500	$475	$400	$325	$300	$250

MODEL 336A RIFLE
- improved 36A, .30-30 Win., .35 Rem., or .32 Spl. cal., round breech bolt, 24 in. barrel with 2/3 mag. Mfg. 1948-1962, re-introduced 1973-80.

	100%	98%	95%	90%	80%	70%	60%
	$350	$300	$250	$225	$195	$175	$150

Add 20% for 1st Model mfg. 1948-52.

Add 10% for 1953-62 mfg.

The .35 Rem. cal. was added in 1950, .32 Spl. was disc. in 1962.

GRADING - PPGS™	100%	98%	95%	90%	80%	70%	60%

* Model 336ADL Rifle - similar to Model 336A Rifle, except has deluxe checkered walnut stock and forearm, quick detachable swivels and 1 in. sling. Mfg. 1948-62.

	$500	$450	$375	$325	$275	$230	$200

Add 20% for 2nd Model.

The 336ADL 1st Model (mfg. 1948-56) did not have a raised comb or cheekpiece. The 2nd Model (mfg. 1957-62) is identifiable by a Monte Carlo buttstock with raised comb and cheekpiece. Wood was supplied by Bishop.

MODELS 336A/336AS/336CC/336W - these models are listed previously under the Model 30AS.

MODEL 336RC CARBINE - .30-30 Win., .32 Spl., or .35 Rem. cal., standard model carbine. Mfg. 1948-68.

	$300	$275	$200	$175	$155	$140	$120

Add 10% for 1st Model mfg. 1948-52.

MODEL 336C CARBINE - .30-30 Win., .32 Spl., or .35 Rem. cal., standard model carbine with 20 in. barrel. Mfg. 1969-83.

	$250	$210	$185	$160	$150	$135	$115

Add 10% for .35 Rem. cal.

MODEL 336SC SPORTING CARBINE - similar to Model 336C, with 20 in. barrel and 2/3 length mag. tube, raised comb buttstock (1957-63). Mfg. 1948-63.

	$350	$295	$250	$225	$195	$185	$165

Add 10% for 1st Model mfg. 1948-52.

MODEL 336SC .219 ZIPPER - similar to Model 336SC, in .219 Zipper cal., 5 shot mag. 3,230 mfg. 1955-60.

	$595	$550	$450	$350	$300	$250	$220

MODEL 336SD CARBINE (SPORTING DELUXE) - .30-30 Win., .32 Spl., or .35 Rem. cal., deluxe sporting carbine with 20 in. barrel, checkered stock and forearm, raised comb, no cheekpiece, quick detachable swivels and 1 in. sling. Mfg. 1954-62.

	$625	$550	$425	$275	$200	$185	$165

MODEL 336C (336CS) CARBINE LEVER ACTION - .30-30 Win. or .35 Rem. cal., 6 shot tube mag., 20 in. barrel, hammer block safety, American black walnut pistol grip stock (cut checkering became standard 1994), 7 lbs. Introduced 1984.

MSR $558	$375	$290	$225	$195	$175	$165	$150

During 2001, this model's nomenclature was changed from 336CS to 336C.

MODEL 336SS (336M) - .30-30 Win. cal. only, similar to Model 336W/30AW, except is stainless steel, 6 shot tube mag., 7 lbs. New 2000.

MSR $692	$500	$450	$385				

During 2001, this model's nomenclature was changed from 336M to 336SS.

MODEL 336 LTD - .35 Rem. cal., blue metal finish, 18 1/2 in. ported barrel with 5 shot tube mag., checkered straight grip walnut stock and forearm, includes letter of authenticity. 1,001 mfg. in 2000 only.

	$450	$300	$220	$200	$180	$170	$160

Last MSR was $515.

This model was distributed exclusively by Davidson's.

MODEL 336LTS CARBINE - .30-30 Win. cal. only, 16 1/4 in. barrel, 5 shot tube mag., 6 1/2 lbs. 2,671 mfg. 1988-89 only.

	$450	$400	$350	$200	$175	$165	$150

Last MSR was $346.

GRADING - PPGS™	100%	98%	95%	90%	80%	70%	60%

MODEL 336 COWBOY
- .30-30 Win. (disc. 2001) or .38-55 WCF cal., 8 shot tube mag., squared off finger lever, 24 in. tapered octagon barrel with deep cut Ballard-type rifling (6 grooves), cut checkered (disc. 2001) straight grip walnut stock and forearm, adj. Marbles semi-buckhorn rear and carbine front sight, ser. no. is on left side of receiver, instead of on tang, 7.5 lbs. Mfg. 1999-2004.

	$550	$475	$385	$310	$275	$250	$225

Last MSR was $735.

Add 10% for .30-30 Win. cal.

MODEL 336ER (EXTRA RANGE)
- .356 Win. cal., 5 shot tube mag., 20 in. barrel, walnut pistol grip stock, open sights, 7 lbs. 2,441 mfg. 1983-86.

	$550	$475	$325	$225	$200	$175	$150

Last MSR was $350.

Although advertised, the .307 cal. was never manufactured in this model.

MODEL 336T CARBINE "TEXAN"
- .30-30 Win., .35 Rem., or .44 Mag. (1965-1967 only) cal., similar to 336C, with straight stock, 18 1/2 (1983 only) or 20 in. barrel, saddle ring (1965-1971 only). Mfg. 1954-83.

	$350	$300	$250	$200	$165	$140	$120

MODEL 336DT CARBINE (DELUXE TEXAN)
- .30-30 Win. or .35 Rem. cal., select stock version of 336T, longhorn and map of Texas carved on buttstock. Mfg. 1962-63.

	$750	$625	$450	$300	$200	$150	$135

Add 10% for .35 Rem. cal.

MODEL 336TS TEXAN
- similar to 336 CS, except is .30-30 Win. cal., 18 1/2 in. barrel, straight grip stock and squared finger lever, crossbolt safety. Mfg. 1984-87.

	$300	$250	$200	$175	$150	$130	$120

Last MSR was $314.

MODEL 336 OCTAGON RIFLE
- .30-30 Win. cal. only, with 22 in. octagon barrel, standard model. 2,414 mfg. 1973 only.

	$500	$425	$300	$250	$200	$175	$150

MODEL 336 MARAUDER CARBINE
- .30-30 Win. or .35 Rem. cal., 16 1/4 in. barrel. 5,856 mfg. 1963-64.

	$475	$425	$350	$275	$235	$210	$185

Add 10% for .35 cal.

Approx. 65% were mfg. in .30-30 Win. cal., and 35% were mfg. in .35 Rem. cal.
Be careful of re-barreled examples of this model.

MODEL 336 MAGNUM CARBINE
- .44 Mag. cal., 20 in. standard carbine configuration, w/o saddle ring. 2,823 mfg. 1963-64 only.

	$375	$325	$295	$250	$200	$170	$160

MODEL 336T
- .44 Mag. cal., with saddle ring, 13,895 mfg. 1965-67.

	$375	$325	$295	$250	$200	$170	$160

MODEL 336 ZANE GREY CENTURY CARBINE
- .30-30 Win. cal., similar to 336 Octagon, 22 in. octagon barrel, Zane Grey medallion inlaid in receiver, select walnut stock, pistol grip, brass buttplate and forearm cap. 7,871 mfg. in 1971.

	$450	$350	$300				

This model was mfg. to commemorate the 100th anniversary of the birth of Zane Grey.

MODEL 336 PRESENTATION RIFLE
- .30-30 Win. cal., one of the pair in the "Brace of 1,000," 22 in. octagon barrel, engraved receiver, sold with Model 39 Presentation. Mfg. 1970 only.

	$600	$450	$375				

Add a premium for serial numbers under 100.

GRADING - PPGS™	100%	98%	95%	90%	80%	70%	60%

MARLIN CENTENNIAL MATCHED PAIR - Model 336 and Model 39 serial numbered the same, .30-30 Win. or .22 LR cal., engraved by Robert Kain and Winston Churchill, deluxe wood, inlaid medallions, cased. 1,000 mfg. sets in 1970.

	$1,500	$1,350	$900				

Last MSR was $750.

MODEL 375 - similar to Model 336 CS, except is .375 Win. cal. 16,315 mfg. 1980-83.

	$395	$350	$300	$250	$200	$175	$150

MODEL 444 LEVER ACTION - .444 Marlin cal., 4 shot tube mag., 24 in. barrel, open sights, straight grip, Monte Carlo stock, recoil pad, swivels, sling, 1st Model. Mfg. 1965-71.

	$425	$375	$275	$225	$200	$185	$160

✱ *Model 444S* - similar to Model 444, except has pistol grip stock. Mfg. 1972-83.

	$325	$265	$225	$200	$185	$165	$150

MODEL 444P OUTFITTER - .444 Marlin cal., 5 shot tube mag., 18 1/2 in. ported barrel with deep cut Ballard-type rifling (6 grooves), adj. semi-buckhorn folding rear sight with ramp front, checkered straight grip walnut stock and forearm, tapped for scope mount, approx. 7 lbs. Mfg. 1999-2002.

	$495	$395	$315	$245	$195	$180	$170

Last MSR was $631.

MODEL 444 (444SS) SPORTER - .444 Marlin cal., similar to Model 444, with 22 in. barrel and hammer block safety, pistol grip stock without Monte Carlo configuration (cut checkering became standard 1994), 7.5 lbs. Mfg. 1984-present.

MSR $654	$440	$315	$285	$230	$195	$180	$170

During 2001, this model's nomenclature was changed from 444SS to 444.

MODEL 455 BOLT ACTION SPORTER - .30-06, or .308 Win. cal., FN Mauser action with Sako trigger, 24 in. barrel, stainless steel barrel, Lyman aperture sight, checkered Monte Carlo pistol grip stock. 1,079 were mfg. in 30.06 cal., 59 in .308 Win. cal. Mfg. 1957-59.

	$650	$525	$375	$250	$220	$195	$165

Add 20% for .308 Win. cal.

MODEL 717M2 SEMI-AUTO - .17 Mach 2 cal., 7 shot detachable mag., 18 in. sporter barrel with open sights, walnut finished hardwood stock, 5.5 lbs. New 2005.

MSR $264	$200	$165	$150	$135	$120	$110	$100

MODELS 780, 781, 782, and 783 BOLT ACTION - .22 LR or .22 Mag. (Models 782 and 783) cal., tube or mag., 22 in. barrel. Disc. 1988.

	$110	$85	$75	$70	$65	$55	$50

Last MSR was $162.

Add $17-$25 for Models 782 and 783.

MODEL 795 SEMI-AUTO - .22 LR cal., 10 shot mag., 18 in. barrel, black synthetic Monte Carlo stock, grooved receiver, last shot bolt hold open, approx. 5 lbs.

MSR $168	$120	$95	$80	$75	$65	$60	$55

✱ *Model 795SS* - similar to Model 795, except has stainless steel barrel and nickel plated parts. New 2002.

MSR $247	$180	$150	$120				

MODELS 880/881 BOLT ACTION - .22 LR or .22 Mag. cal., replacement for Models 780, 781, Model 880 is .22 LR with 7 shot detachable mag. and 22 in. barrel, (cut checkering became standard 1994), Model 881 is .22 LR with 17 shot tube mag. and 22 in. barrel, 6 lbs. Mfg. 1989-97.

	$185	$145	$100	$85	$75	$70	$65

Last MSR was $251.

Add $10 for Model 881.

✻ *Model 880SS* - similar to Model 880, except is stainless steel, black fiberglass synthetic stock, approx. 6 lbs. Mfg. 1994-2003.

	100%	98%	95%
	$240	$175	$115

Last MSR was $316.

✻ *Model 880SQ (Squirrel Rifle)* - similar to Model 880, except has black fiberglass filled synthetic stock with checkering and heavy 22 in. barrel, without sights and grooved receiver, matte finish, 7 lbs. Mfg. 1996-2003.

100%	98%	95%	90%	80%	70%	60%
$245	$190	$135	$100	$80	$70	$65

Last MSR was $330.

MODELS 882/883 BOLT ACTION - .22 Win. Mag. cal., 7 shot detachable (Model 882) or 12 shot tube mag. (Model 883), 22 in. barrel, checkered (cut checkering became standard 1994), black walnut Monte Carlo stock with Mar-Shield finish, adj. semi-buckhorn rear sight and hooded front, thumb safety, 6 lbs. Mfg. 1989-2003.

100%	98%	95%	90%	80%	70%	60%
$240	$185	$130	$95	$85	$75	$70

Last MSR was $324.

Add $13 for Model 883.
Add $35 for nickel finish on Model 883N (disc. 1993).
The Models 882 and 883 are the replacements for Models 782 and 783.

✻ *Model 882SS* - .22 Win. Mag. cal., similar to Model 882, except is stainless steel and stock is black synthetic with molded-in checkering, fire sights (red fiberoptic inserts with cutaway hood) became standard 1998, approx. 6 lbs. Mfg. 1995-2003.

100%	98%	95%
$250	$190	$130

Last MSR was $345.

✻ *Model 882SSV* - .22 Win. Mag. cal., features 22 in. bead blasted stainless barrel and receiver with black fiberglass reinforced synthetic stock, 7 shot mag., grooved receiver, w/o sights, ring mounts included, 7 lbs. Mfg. 1997-2003.

100%	98%	95%
$245	$185	$125

Last MSR was $338.

✻ *Model 882L* - similar to Model 882, except has two-tone brown laminated hardwood stock, 6 1/4 lbs. Mfg. 1992-2003.

100%	98%	95%	90%	80%	70%	60%
$250	$200	$140	$100	$85	$75	$70

Last MSR was $342.

✻ *Model 883SS* - .22 Win. Mag. cal., 12 shot tube mag., similar to Model 883, except barrel is stainless steel and stock is laminated two-tone brown birch with Monte Carlo cheekpiece. Mfg. 1993-2003.

100%	98%	95%
$265	$205	$145

Last MSR was $358.

MODEL 915Y "LITTLE BUCKAROO" SINGLE SHOT - .22 S, L, or LR cal., 16.25 in. barrel, features T-900 fire control system, cocks on opening, youth dimensions, adj. rear sight, thumb safety, grooved receiver, walnut finished hardwood stock, 4.25 lbs. New 2004.

MSR $221	100%	98%	95%	90%	80%	70%	60%
	$165	$140	$110	$80	$75	$70	$65

Add $26 for front fiberoptic fire sight (Model 915YS, new 2004).

MODEL 917M2 BOLT ACTION - .17 Mach 2 cal., otherwise similar to Model 917V, 6 lbs. New 2005.

MSR $274	100%	98%	95%	90%	80%	70%	60%
	$210	$170	$150	$135	$115	$100	$90

✻ *Model 917M2S* - similar to Model 917M2, except has laminated grey/black hardwood Monte Carlo stock and stainless steel barrel, 7 lbs. New 2005.

MSR $410	100%	98%	95%	90%	80%	70%	60%
	$300	$225	$175	$150	$125	$110	$100

MODEL 917V BOLT ACTION - .17 HMR cal., 7 shot detachable mag., 22 in. heavy barrel, features T-900 fire control system, walnut finished checkered hardwood Monte Carlo stock, thumb safety, no sights, scope base included, 6 lbs. New 2004.

MSR $283	$215	$175	$155	$135	$115	$100	$90

* **Model 917VS** - similar to Model 917V, except has laminated grey/black hardwood Monte Carlo stock and stainless steel barrel. New 2004.

MSR $425	$310	$230	$180	$150	$125	$110	$100

Add $25 for fluted barrel (Model 917VSF, new 2005).

MODEL 922M SEMI-AUTO - .22 Win. Mag. cal., 7 shot detachable mag., 20 1/2 in. barrel, Garand style safety, alloy receiver, hold-open device, uncheckered or checkered (became standard 1994) walnut stock with solid pad, blue steel (hard coated on receiver), 6 1/2 lbs. Mfg. 1993-2001.

	$360	$295	$240	$200	$185	$175	$165

Last MSR was $454.

MODEL 925 BOLT ACTION - .22 LR cal., 7 shot detachable mag., features T-900 fire control system, 22 in. barrel, thumb safety, adj. rear sight, grooved receiver, walnut finished hardwood stock with swivel studs, 5.5 lbs. New 2004.

MSR $223	$165	$135	$110	$80	$75	$70	$65

Add $9 for 4x scope.

* **Model 925C** - similar to Model 925, except has Mossy Oak Break Up camo stock. New 2004.

MSR $263	$195	$160	$125	$95	$80	$70	$65

MODEL 925M BOLT ACTION - .22 Mag. cal., 7 shot detachable mag., features T-900 fire control system, 22 in. barrel, thumb safety, adj. rear sight, grooved receiver, walnut finished hardwood stock with swivel studs, 6 lbs. New 2004.

MSR $255	$195	$160	$130	$95	$85	$80	$75

Add $39 for Model 925MC with Monte Carlo stock.

MODEL 980S BOLT ACTION - .22 LR cal., 7 shot detachable mag., 22 in. stainless steel barrel, other metal parts stainless steel/nickel plated, T-900 fire control system, black fiberglass synthetic stock with molded checkering, thumb safety, adj. buckhorn rear sight, approx. 6 lbs. New 2004.

MSR $333	$250	$200	$155				

* **Model 980V** - similar to Model 980S, except has 22 in. heavy barrel with recessed muzzle, double bedding screws, swivel studs, no sights, grooved receiver with scope bases, drilled and tapped. New 2004.

MSR $349	$265	$210	$170	$145	$120	$100	$80

MODEL 981T BOLT ACTION - .22 S, L, or LR cal., 17-25 shot tube mag., 22 in. barrel, black fiberglass synthetic stock, features T-900 fire control system, thumb safety, adj. rear sight, approx. 6 lbs. New 2004.

MSR $225	$170	$135	$105	$85	$75	$65	$60

MODEL 982 BOLT ACTION - .22 Mag. cal., 7 shot detachable mag., 22 in. barrel, T-900 fire control system, checkered American Monte Carlo stock, adj. buckhorn rear sight, thumb safety, rubber buttplate, 6 lbs. New 2004.

MSR $341	$255	$210	$170	$145	$120	$100	$80

Add $20 for Model 982L with two-tone brown laminated stock (new 2004).

Add $23 for Model 982S with stainless steel barrel and nickel/stainless steel small parts (new 2004).

Add $16 for Model 982VS with 22 in. heavy stainless barrel and black synthetic stock (new 2004).

GRADING - PPGS™	100%	98%	95%	90%	80%	70%	60%

MODEL 983 BOLT ACTION - .22 Mag. cal., 12 shot tube mag., 22 in. barrel, features T-900 fire control system, checkered walnut Monte Carlo stock, adj. folding buckhorn sight, 6 lbs. New 2004.

MSR $356	$275	$215	$170	$150	$125	$105	$85

✳ *Model 983T* - .22 Mag. cal., 12 shot tube mag., 22 in. barrel, features T-900 fire control system, black fiberglass synthetic stock with molded-in checkering, adj. rear sight, 6 lbs. New 2004.

MSR $273	$215	$190	$160	$130	$110	$90	$75

✳ *Model 983S* - similar to Model 983T, except has stainless steel barrel and nickel plated/stainless steel parts, two-tone brown hardwood laminate stock, 6 lbs. New 2004.

MSR $377	$285	$225	$185

MODEL 990 SEMI-AUTO - .22 LR cal. only, 18 shot tube mag., 22 in. barrel, last shot automatic bolt hold-open, Monte Carlo American black walnut stock with pistol grip, 5 1/2 lbs. Disc. 1987.

	$115	$90	$75	$65	$60	$55	$50

Last MSR was $159.

MODEL 990L SEMI-AUTO - .22 LR cal., 14 shot tube mag., 22 in. barrel, laminated two-tone brown Monte Carlo stock, gold trigger, adj. rear sight, grooved receiver, 5 3/4 lbs. Mfg. 1993-94.

	$180	$160	$145	$130	$120	$110	$100

Last MSR was $223.

MODEL 995 SEMI-AUTO - .22 LR cal., 7 shot mag., 18 in. barrel, Monte Carlo walnut stock, 5 lbs. Disc. 1994.

	$160	$125	$85	$70	$65	$60	$55

Last MSR was $206.

✳ *Model 995SS* - .22 LR cal., stainless steel barrel and nickel-plated small parts, black fiberglass stock with molded-in checkering, adj. rear sight, last shot hold-open new 1996, 5 lbs. Mfg. 1995-99.

	$195	$145	$110

Last MSR was $255.

MODEL 1894 (1969-1984 MFG.) - .44 Spl. or .44 Mag. cal., 20 in. bbl., 10 shot tube mag., adj. sights, straight grip walnut stock and forearm, 6 lbs. Mfg. 1969-84.

	$375	$300	$250	$195	$165	$145	$130

MODEL 1894C CARBINE - .357 Mag. cal., 18 1/2 in. barrel, w/o hammer block safety, 6 lbs. Mfg. 1979-84.

	$350	$275	$225	$180	$160	$145	$130

MODEL 1894 SPORTER - .44 Mag. cal. only, 6 shot half mag. tube, crescent shaped hard rubber buttplate, 1,398 mfg. 1973 only.

	$500	$425	$360	$300	$250	$200	$175

MODEL 1894C CARBINE (1894CS) - copy of original Model 1894, .357 Mag./.38 Spl. cal., 9 shot mag., 18.5 in. round barrel, open sights (hooded front became standard 1999), straight grip stock (cut checkering became standard 1994), squared finger lever, 6 lbs. New 1984.

MSR $591	$465	$330	$235	$185	$150	$140	$130

During 2001, this model's nomenclature was changed from 1894CS to 1894C.

✳ *Model 1894CC41-LTD* - .41 Mag. cal., 20 in. tapered octagon barrel, blue finish, Marble sights, 10 shot full length tube mag., includes letter of authenticity. 1,001 mfg. in 1999.

	$575	$475	$400	$350	$300	$275	$250

Last MSR was $715.

This models was distributed exclusively by Davidson's.

GRADING - PPGS™	100%	98%	95%	90%	80%	70%	60%

✸ **Model 1894CP Carbine** - similar to Model 1894C, except has 16 1/4 in. ported round barrel, 8 shot mag., approx. 5 3/4 lbs. Mfg. 2001-2002.

	$440	**$320**	**$235**	**$185**	**$150**	**$140**	**$130**

Last MSR was $566.

✸ **Model 1894CL** - .32-20 Win. cal., 6 shot tube mag., 22 in. barrel with button rifling, Marble sights, American walnut stock and forearm with cut checkering. New 2005.

MSR $836	**$600**	**$525**	**$425**	**$350**	**$300**	**$250**	**$225**

MODEL 1894P CARBINE - .44 Mag./.44 Spl. cal., 16 1/4 in. ported barrel with deep-cut Ballard type 6 groove rifling, 8 shot tube mag., checkered straight grip walnut stock with vent. recoil pad, 5 3/4 lbs. Mfg. 2000-2002.

	$440	**$320**	**$235**	**$185**	**$150**	**$140**	**$130**

Last MSR was $566.

✸ **Model 1894S Limited** - .44 Mag./.44 Spl. cal., features 16 1/4 in. barrel with "The Marlin Limited" roll stamped on barrel, approx. 1,500 mfg. 1996 only.

	$450	**$400**	**$350**				

✸ **Model 1894SC 44/45 LTD** - .44 Mag./.44 Spl. or .45 LC cal., features 16 in. barrel, 8 shot tube mag., includes letter of authenticity, approx. 1,550 mfg. in .44 Mag. cal. 1996 only, 1,050 mfg. in .45 LC cal. 1997 only.

	$500	**$400**	**$350**	**$200**	**$160**	**$150**	**$140**

Last MSR was $460.

These models were distributed exclusively by Davidson's.

MODEL 1894FG - .41 Mag. cal., similar to Model 1894, except has pistol grip stock with cut checkering and 10 shot mag., 6.5 lbs. New 2003.

MSR $648	**$510**	**$350**	**$260**	**$195**	**$160**	**$145**	**$130**

✸ **Model 1894FG Limited Edition** - .41 Mag. cal., similar to Model 1894FG except is stainless steel, black and grey laminate stock. 251 mfg. beginning 2005.

MSR $1,450

MODEL 1894PG - .44 Mag. cal., similar to Model 1894FG. Mfg. 2003-2004.

	$490	**$340**	**$255**	**$190**	**$160**	**$145**	**$130**

Last MSR was $622.

MODEL 1894 (1894S) - .41 Mag. (disc. 1991), .44 Mag./.44 Spl., or .45 LC (mfg. 1988-91, reintroduced 2005) cal., Model 1894 with addition of cross bolt ("S" suffix) and hammer block safety, 20 in. barrel, 10 shot tube mag., adj. sights, straight grip walnut stock and forearm (cut checkering became standard 1994), 6 lbs. Disc. 2002, reintroduced 2005.

MSR $591	**$465**	**$375**	**$300**	**$225**	**$150**	**$140**	**$130**

During 2001, this model's nomenclature was changed from 1894S to 1894.

MODEL 1894SS - .44 Mag./.44 Spl. cal., stainless steel, 20 in. barrel, 10 shot tube mag., straight grip, checkered black walnut stock and forearm, offset hammer spur, approx. 6 lbs. New 2002.

MSR $716	**$560**	**$415**	**$310**				

MODEL 1894 COWBOY (COWBOY II) - .32 H&R Mag. (new mid-2004), .357 Mag. (new 1997), .44-40 WCF (mfg. 1997-99), .44 Mag. (new 1997), or .45 LC cal., 10 shot tube mag., incorporates "cowboy shooter" features, straight grip stock w/o or with checkering (disc. 2001), adj. Marbles-type rear sight, blued finish, 20 (new 2003, n/a in .45 LC cal.) or 24 in. tapered octagon barrel, 7 1/2 lbs. New 1996.

MSR $849	**$600**	**$515**	**$425**	**$325**	**$265**	**$225**	**$195**

Add $23 for .357 Mag., .44 Mag., or .45 LC cal.

The Model 1894 Cowboy II refers to the three new cals. introduced 1997. This model in .32 H&R Mag. cal. (new 2004) loads through a port in the front of the mag. tube, not a receiver port like the other cals.

GRADING - PPGS™	100%	98%	95%	90%	80%	70%	60%

❋ *Model 1894 Cowboy Competition* - .38 Spl. or .45 LC (new 2003) cal., 10 shot tube mag., 20 in. tapered octagon barrel with deep cut Ballard type rifling, hammer block safety, Marbles sights, case colored receiver, lever, and bolt, 6.5 lbs. New 2002.

	MSR $986	$765	$660	$505	$425	$375	$325	$295

❋ *Model 1894 Cowboy Carbine* - .44-40 WCF cal., 20 in. tapered octagon barrel with 10 shot full length tube mag., uncheckered straight grip walnut stock and forearm, adj. Marble rear sight, includes letter of authenticity. Only 325 mfg. in 2000.

	$580	$480	$400	$365	$310	$280	$260

Last MSR was $715.

This model was distributed exclusively by Davidson's.

❋ *Model 1894 Cowboy Carbine Limited* - .32-20 WCF cal., 20 in. tapered octagon barrel, blue finish, uncheckered straight grip walnut stock, Marble front and semi-buckhorn rear sight, drilled and tapped, 10 shot full length mag., includes letter of authenticy, 501 mfg.

	MSR $860	$700	$600	$475	$395	$350	$300	$275

This model is distributed exclusively by Davidson's.

MODEL 1894M (.22 MAG.) - .22 Mag. cal., with 20 in. barrel, 11 shot tube mag., straight grip walnut stock and forearm, 6 1/4 lbs. Disc. 1989.

	$450	$395	$350	$250	$200	$175	$150

Last MSR was $358.

MODEL 1894CL - .218 Bee (new 1990), .25-20 WCF or .32-20 WCF cal., 6 shot (two-thirds length) tube mag., 22 in. barrel, 6 1/4 lbs. Mfg. 1988-94.

	$450	$395	$350	$250	$200	$175	$150

Last MSR was $502.

Add 10% for .218 Bee cal.

MODEL 1894 CENTURY LIMITED (EMPLOYEE SPECIAL EDITION) - employee special edition featuring gold inlaid Marlin horse and rider logo. 100 mfg. 1994-95 in ser. no. range 1-100.

	$1,650	$1,450	$995

MODEL 1894 CENTURY LIMITED - .44-40 WCF cal., limited edition commemorative mfg. to celebrate the Model 1894's 100th Anniversary, 24 in. tapered octagon barrel with full 12 shot tube mag., features Giovanelli engraved receiver, bolt, and lever, receiver is case colored using traditional methods, checkered straight grip stock and forearm, crescent buttplate, 6 1/2 lbs. 2,500 mfg. 1994 only.

	$1,100	$900	$600

Last MSR was $1,088.

MODEL 1894 OCTAGON - similar to 1894 Carbine, with octagon barrel. Mfg. 1973.

	$475	$425	$350	$275	$225	$200	$185

MODEL 1895 LEVER ACTION - .45-70 Govt. cal., 4 shot tube mag., 22 in. barrel, open sights, straight grip stock with curved buttplate, forearm cap, sling and swivels. Mfg. 1972-1984.

	$395	$350	$300	$250	$200	$175	$160

Add 10% for guns mfg. between 1972-1978.

Add 10% for pre-micro-groove.

Early new Model 1895 Marlins had cut rifling suitable for cast bullets, while later mfg. was switched to Marlin's "Micro Groove" shallow rifling. Changes were also made from a straight stock to a pistol grip stock and from a traditional receiver to one with the newer hammer-block, push-button safety. Early guns with a straight grip stock, traditional receiver, and cut rifling command premiums over later mfg. Cut rifling occured during the first year of production only - these guns have a ser. no. prefix of "B.O." More recently mfg. models have pistol grip, Micro Groove rifling, and hammer-block safety - these newer guns are the least desirable from a collector's standpoint.

GRADING - PPGS™	100%	98%	95%	90%	80%	70%	60%

❋ *Model 1895S* - similar to Model 1895, except has pistol grip stock and straight butt-pad.

	$325	$300	$275	$200	$175	$150	$140

MODEL 1895 (1895SS)

- similar to Model 1895S only with hammer block safety, cut checkering became standard 1994, 7.5 lbs. New 1983.

MSR $654	$500	$365	$260	$190	$155	$140	$130

During 2001, this model's nomenclature was changed from 1895SS to 1895.

❋ *Model 1895SS Cody Stampede 75th Anniversary* - .45-70 cal., includes semi-fancy checkered walnut stock with medallion, serial numbered CS-001-CS-200, 200 mfg. 1994 only.

	$750	$500	$400				

Last MSR was $695.

❋ *Model 1895 LTD I/II* - .45-70 Govt. cal., 24 in. half round/half octagon (LTD I) or 24 in. full octagon (LTD II) barrel, uncheckered (LTD I) or checkered (LTD II) walnut pistol grip (LTD II) or straight (LTD I) stock and forearm. 1,001 of each model mfg. 1997-98.

	$525	$450	$375	$325	$290	$260	$230

Last MSR was $671.

These models were distributed exclusively by Davidson's.

❋ *Model 1895 LTD III* - .45-70 Govt. cal., 18 1/2 tapered octagon barrel, uncheckered straight grip walnut stock and forearm, Marble sights, 5 shot full length tube mag., includes letter of authenticity. 1,001 mfg. in 1991 only.

	$575	$475	$400	$350	$300	$275	$250

Last MSR was $715.

This model was distributed exclusively by Davidson's.

❋ *Model 1895 LTD IV* - .45-70 Govt. cal., 24 in. full octagon barrel with full length 8 shot tube mag., uncheckered straight grip walnut stock and forearm, Marble sights, includes letter of authenticity. Only 1,001 mfg. in 2000.

	$595	$495	$415	$365	$310	$280	$260

Last MSR was $729.

This model was distributed exclusively by Davidson's.

MODEL 1895M

- .450 Marlin Mag. cal. (belted), 4 shot tube mag., 18.5 in. ported barrel, checkered straight grip walnut stock and forearm, vent. recoil pad, adj. folding buckhorn rear sight, 7 lbs. New 2000.

MSR $719	$580	$465	$385	$320	$275	$250	$225

MODEL 1895MR

- similar to Model 1895M, except has 22 in. barrel, 7.5 lbs. Mfg. 2003-2004.

	$610	$485	$395	$325	$285	$255	$225

Last MSR was $761.

MODEL 1895 COWBOY

- .45-70 Govt., features 26 in. tapered octagon barrel and 9 shot tube mag., uncheckered straight grip walnut stock and forearm, marble front and rear (adj.) sights, 8 lbs. New 2001.

MSR $849	$625	$525	$450	$375	$325	$295	$260

MODEL 1895G GUIDE GUN

- .45-70 Govt. cal., features 18.5 in. ported barrel with Ballard style cut rifling, cut checkered American stock and forearm, adj. folding buckhorn rear sight, 4 shot tube mag., vent. recoil pad, approx. 7 lbs. 2,500 to be mfg. beginning 1998.

MSR $668	$520	$380	$260	$190	$155	$140	$130

❋ *Model 1895GS* - similar to Model 1895G, except is stainless steel. New 2001.

MSR $805	$610	$425	$295				

GRADING - PPGS™	100%	98%	95%	90%	80%	70%	60%

MODEL 1895RL - .480 Ruger/.475 Linebaugh cal., 6 (.480 Ruger) or 5 (.475 Linebaugh) shot tube mag., 18 1/2 in. barrel, walnut pistol grip stock, otherwise similar to Model 1895, 7 lbs. Limited mfg. 2004 only.

	$565	$455	$380	$315	$275	$250	$225

Last MSR was $695.

MODEL 1895 CENTURY LIMITED (CLTD) - .45-70 cal., commemorates Marlin's 125th Anniversary, engraving includes grizzly bear on left side, Marlin horse and rider logo on right, 24 in. half-round half-octagonal barrel, crescent buttplate, satin finished receiver, checkered walnut stock and forearm. Approx. 2,500 mfg. 1995 only.

	$1,100	$850	$550				

Last MSR was $1,104.

A Marlin Collector's Association Edition was also mfg. and was the same as the Model 1895 Century Limited.

* ***Model 1895 Century Limited (CLTD) Employee Edition*** - features 3 elk on left side and gold inlaid Marlin horse and rider logo on right. 100 mfg. 1995-96 in ser. no. range 1-100.

	$1,600	$1,100	$850				

MODEL 1897 COWBOY - .22 S, L, or LR cal., takedown action, 19 shot (.22 LR cal.), tube mag., rebounding hammer with block safety, 24 in. tapered octagon barrel with Micro-Groove (16 grooves) rifling, cut checkered walnut stock and forearm, adj. Marble semi-buckhorn rear and carbine front sight with brass bead, high polish blue, 6 1/2 lbs. Mfg. 1999-2001.

	$625	$495	$400	$350	$295	$265	$235

Last MSR was $708.

MODEL 1897T - .22 S, L, or LR cal., 14-21 shot mag., 20 in. tapered octagon barrel, hammer block safety, Marble front and rear sights, 6 lbs. Mfg. 2002-2003.

	$585	$430	$365	$330	$285	$240	$195

Last MSR was $748.

MODEL 1897 CENTURY LIMITED LEVER ACTION - .22 LR cal., 100th anniversary of the Model 1897, features extensive receiver engraving and gold accenting, 24 in. half round/half octagon barrel with open sights, checkered fancy walnut stock and forearm. Limited mfg. 1997 only, limited quantities remained through 1999.

	$950	$800	$650				

Last MSR was $1,055.

* ***Model 1897 Century Limited Employee Edition*** - .22 LR, features gold scroll work on lever, less than 100 mfg. 1997 only in ser. no. range 1-100.

	$1,500	$1,000	$850				

MODEL 1897 ANNIE OAKLEY - .22 LR cal., features 18 1/2 in. tapered octagon barrel with marble sights, blue receiver with rolled scroll engraving featuring gold Annie Oakley etched name on bolt, deluxe checkered walnut stock and forearm. Mfg. 1998 only.

	$750	$600	$500				

Last MSR was $1,054.

Add $100 for employee variation.

An employee variation of this model was made with gold inlays on finger lever, 100 mfg. total.

MODEL 2000 TARGET BOLT ACTION - .22 LR cal., single shot (can be converted), 22 in. heavy barrel with match chamber and Lyman adj. sights, 2 stage target trigger, molded synthetic stock made from fiberglass and Kevlar with twice baked blue enamel, adj. buttplate, aluminum forearm rail, 8 lbs. Mfg. 1991-95.

	$525	$410	$350	$300	$275	$250	$225

Last MSR was $602.

Add $34 for 5-shot conversion unit (for summer biathlon competition).

* *Model 2000A Target* - similar to Model 2000 Target, except has adj. comb, ambidextrous pistol grip, and molded-in logo. Mfg. 1994 only.

	$550	$425	$365	$315	$290	$260	$230

Last MSR was $625.

* *Model 2000L* - .22 LR cal., updated version of the Model 2000, featuring grey/black laminated stock, adj. aperture rear and aperture insert front sight, double bedding screws, factory test target supplied with each gun, 8 lbs. Mfg. 1996-2002.

	$600	$475	$380	$320	$280	$250	$225

Last MSR was $745.

MODEL 7000 SEMI-AUTO - .22 LR cal., 10 shot detachable mag., 18 in. heavy barrel without sights and recessed muzzle, black fiberglass, synthetic stock with molded-in checkering, grooved receiver, no sights, last shot hold open, scope mounts provided, 5.5 lbs. New 1997.

MSR $263	$210	$190	$165	$140	$130	$120	$110

* *Model 7000T* - .22 LR cal., target model with 18 in. heavy barrel, red, white and blue laminated hardwood stock with adj. pad, two stage target trigger with stop, aluminum forend rail with adj. stop, grooved receiver w/o sights, 7 1/2 lbs. Mfg. 1999-2001.

	$365	$300	$240	$200	$185	$175	$165

Last MSR was $465.

MARLIN PROMOTIONAL MODELS - Models 15 (disc.), 15Y (disc.), 15N (mfg. 1998- 99, last MSR $188), 15YN (refer to individual listing), 25 (disc.), 25M (disc.), 25N (refer to individual listing), 25NC (refer to individual listing), 70 (disc.), 70HC (mfg. 1989-95, last 1995 MSR was $167), 75C (disc.), 81TS (refer to individual listing), and 795 Semi-Auto (refer to individual listing), are inexpensive, utilitarian .22 LR or .22 Mag. cal. (Model 25M only), rifles designed for inexpensive shooting.

Series 15 and 25 Models designate bolt action, Series 60 and 70 designate semi-auto design.

RIFLES: .22 CAL.

From 1930 to date, Marlin has made a number of .22 cal. rimfire rifles, bolt action single shots, bolt action repeaters and auto loaders. These have normally been good quality, inexpensive weapons. In 1960, the name Glenfield was also used in connection with these guns. We will list these models for reference purposes with price ranges appearing at the end of each listing.

BOLT ACTION, SINGLE SHOT

Model 65 - 1932-1938. Price Range $35 - $65.
Model 65E - 1932-1938. Price Range $45 - $75.
Model 100 - 1936-1941. Price Range $45 - $75.
Model 100S Tom Mix Special - disc. Price Range $125 - $250.
Model 100SB - 1936-1941. Price Range $50 - $85.
Model 101 - 1941-1977. Price Range $45 - $75.
Model 101 DL - disc. Price Range $60 - $90.
Model 101 Crown Prince - 1959. Price Range $75 - $150.
Model 101G - 1960-1965, Marlin Glenfield. Price Range $40 - $70.
Model 10 - 1966-disc., Marlin Glenfield. Price Range $40 - $65.
Model 122 - 1966-disc. Price Range $40 - $65.

BOLT ACTION: REPEATING RIFLES

Model 80 - 1934-1939. Price Range $45 - $85.
Model 80E - 1934-1940. Price Range $50 - $90.
Model 80C - 1940-1970. Price Range $50 - $90.
Model 80DL - 1940-1965. Price Range $60 - $95.
Model 80G - 1960-1965, Marlin Glenfield. Price Range $40 - $70.
Model 20 - 1966-disc., Marlin Glenfield. Price Range $40 - $70.
Model 780 - 1971-1988. Price Range $45 - $75.

GRADING - PPGS™	100%	98%	95%	90%	80%	70%	60%

Model 781 - 1971-1988. Price Range $45 - $75.
Model 782 - 1971-1988, .22 WRM. Price Range $65 - $125.
Model 783 - 1971-1988, .22 WRM. Price Range $65 - $125.
Model 980 - 1962-1970, .22 WRM. Price Range $65 - $125.
Model 81 - 1937-1940. Price Range $45 - $85.
Model 81E - 1937-1940. Price Range $60 - $100.
Model 81C - 1940-1970. Price Range $60 - $100.
Model 81DL - 1940-1965. Price Range $65 - $90.
Model 81G - 1960-1965 Marlin Glenfield. Price Range $50 - $75.

AUTOLOADING RIFLES

Model 50 - 1931-1935. Price Range $75 - $140.
Model 50E - 1931-1934. Price Range $75 - $150.
Model A-1 - 1936-1940. Price Range $75 - $140.
Model A-1E - 1935-1946. Price Range $75 - $145.
Model A-1C - 1941-1946. Price Range $65 - $140.
Model A-1DL - 1941-1946. Price Range $65 - $140.
Model 88-C - 1948-1956. Price Range $65 - $135.
Model 88-DL - 1953-1956. Price Range $65 - $135.
Model 89-C - 1948-1961. Price Range $65 - $135.
Model 89-DL - 1950-1961. Price Range $65 - $135.
Model 98 - 1957-1959. Price Range $65 - $135.
Model 99 - 1959-1960. Price Range $65 - $135.
Model 99C - 1961-1978. Price Range $65 - $135.
Model 99G - 1960-1965, Marlin Glenfield. Price Range $65 - $135.
Model 60 - 1960-present, Marlin Glenfield (2000 MSR $172).
Model 99DL - 1960-1964. Price Range $65 - $135.
Model 49 - 1968-1970. Price Range $65 - $135.
Model 49DL - 1971-1978. Price Range $65 - $135.
Model 99M1 - 1964-1978. Price Range $65 - $135.
Model 989M2 - 1966-disc. Price Range $65 - $135.
Model 989 - 1962-1965. Price Range $65 - $135.
Model 70 (HC) - 1966-1995, Marlin Glenfield. Price Range $75 - $145.
Model 989G - 1962-1964, Marlin Glenfield. Price Range $65 - $135.
Model 990 - disc. Price Range $65 - $135.

SHOTGUNS: BOLT ACTION

MODEL 25MG GARDEN GUN - .22 Mag. shot shell, features 22 in. smooth bore barrel with high visibility bead front sight only, 7 shot detachable mag., black synthetic stock, thumb safety, 6 lbs. Mfg. 1999-2002.

$190	$155	$130	$110	$100	$90	$80

Last MSR was $245.

MODEL 50 DL - 12 ga. only, upland game model, 28 in. barrel bored M, black Rynite stock with molded-in checkering, 2 shot mag., 7 1/2 lbs. Mfg. 1997-99.

$255	$195	$150	$125	$115	$100	$90

Last MSR was $330.

MODEL 55 - 12, 16, or 20 ga., 2 shot detachable mag., 26 and 28 in. full choke barrel, plain pistol grip stock. Mfg. 1950-65.

	$90	$70	$55	$40	$35	$30	$25
With adj. choke	$100	$85	$65	$50	$45	$40	$30

GRADING - PPGS™	100%	98%	95%	90%	80%	70%	60%

MODEL 55 GOOSE GUN - similar to Model 55, except 12 ga. only, 36 in. full choke barrel, 3 in. chamber, 2 shot mag., leather carrying strap and detachable swivels, walnut stock with rubber recoil pad, 8 lbs. Mfg. 1962-96.

	$235	$185	$145	$125	$115	$100	$90

Last MSR was $308.

* **Model 55 GDL** - similar to Model 55 Goose Gun, except has black Rynite synthetic stock. Mfg. 1997-2000.

	$330	$240	$200	$180	$160	$145	$130

Last MSR was $396.

MODEL 55 SWAMP GUN - similar to Model 55, 12 ga., 20 in. adj. choke barrel, 3 in. mag. Mfg. 1963-65.

	$105	$90	$70	$55	$50	$45	$35

MODEL 55S SLUG GUN - 24 in. barrel, cylinder bore, rifle sights. Mfg. 1974-83.

	$140	$120	$110	$95	$85	$55	$40

MODEL 59 SINGLE SHOT - .410 bore, 2 1/2 or 3 in. chamber, 24 in. barrel bored F, walnut pistol grip stock and forearm, 48,447 mfg. 1956-1965.

	$150	$125	$110	$95	$85	$55	$40

MODEL 512 SLUGMASTER - 12 ga., 3 in. chamber, bolt action, 2 shot box mag., 21 in. rifled barrel, adj. rear sight, receiver is drilled and tapped for scope mount (included), walnut finished birch stock with pressed checkering and vent. recoil pad, 8 lbs. Mfg. 1994-99.

	$295	$220	$195	$175	$160	$145	$130

Last MSR was $361.

* **Model 512DL Slugmaster** - similar to Model 512 Slugmaster, except has black Rynite stock, Fire Sights (with red fiberoptic inserts) became standard 1998. Disc. 1998.

	$310	$230	$200	$180	$160	$145	$130

Last MSR was $372.

* **Model 512P Slugmaster** - 12 ga., 3 in. chamber, features 21 in. ported fully rifled barrel with front and rear Fire Sights (high visibility red and green fiberoptic inserts), 2 shot detachable box mag., black fiberglass synthetic stock with molded-in checkering, receiver is drilled and tapped, 8 lbs. Mfg. 1999-2001.

	$315	$235	$200	$180	$165	$155	$145

Last MSR was $388.

MODEL 5510 - 10 ga., 3 1/2 in. mag., 2 shot mag., 34 in. barrel, leather carrying strap and detachable swivels, rubber recoil pad, 10 1/2 lbs. Mfg. 1976-85.

	$220	$170	$160	$150	$140	$130	$120

Last MSR was $282.

SHOTGUNS: LEVER ACTION

MODEL .410 LEVER ACTION (1929-1932 MFG.) - .410 bore, 22 or 26 in. barrel, full choke, lever action, similar to 1893, exposed hammer, plain pistol grip stock. Mfg. 1929-32 as a stockholders' promotional firearm.

	$1,400	$1,200	$950	$750	$600	$550	$475

Add 20% for 22 in. barrel.

* **Model .410 Deluxe** - includes deluxe checkered walnut stock and forearm.

	$1,800	$1,600	$1,350	$1,100	$900	$800	$700

Deluxe forearm does not have flute in it.

NEW MODEL .410 LEVER ACTION - .410 bore, 2 1/2 in. chamber, 4-5 shot tube mag., 22 in. cylinder bore barrel, hammer bloc safety, checkered black American walnut stock and forend, folding rear with green fiberoptic front sight, 9.5 lbs. New 2004.

MSR $614	$475	$400	$360	$320	$285	$255	$225

GRADING - PPGS™	100%	98%	95%	90%	80%	70%	60%

SHOTGUNS: O/U

MODEL 90 SHOTGUN - 12, 16, 20 ga., or .410 bore shotgun or combination gun configuration (12 ga. over .30/30 barrels), 26, 28, or 30 in. barrels, boxlock, extractors, checkered pistol grip stock. Mfg. 1937-1958. Guns made from 1937-49 had vent. separated barrels, after 1949, solid barrels.

	100%	98%	95%	90%	80%	70%	60%
✳ *w/ double triggers*	$475	$425	$375	$330	$290	$265	$230
Add 15% for 16 or 20 ga.							
.410 bore	$1,175	$1,000	$875	$775	$675	$600	$525
✳ *w/ single trigger*							
	$625	$575	$525	$475	$440	$400	$375
.410 bore	$2,950	$2,600	$2,300	$2,000	$1,700	$1,500	$1,350
✳ *Combination Gun*	$1,350	$1,125	$950	$825	$725	$625	$550

✳ *Combination Gun* - shotgun over .22 LR, .22 Hornet, .218 Bee, or .30-30 Win. cal., very rare, approx. 500 mfg. Mfg. 1937-1959.

SHOTGUNS: SxS

Please refer to the L.C. Smith section for both older and newly manufactured L.C. Smith shotguns.

SHOTGUNS: SINGLE SHOT

MODEL 60 - 12 ga., 30 or 32 in. barrel, full choke, top lever, break open, exposed hammer, pistol grip stock. Approx. 3,000 mfg. 1923.

	100%	98%	95%	90%	80%	70%	60%
	$150	$135	$110	$90	$80	$70	$60

SHOTGUNS: SLIDE ACTION, 1898-1963 PRODUCTION

During 1998, Marlin issued a service bulletin recommending that slide action exposed hammer Models 1898, 16, 17, 19, 19S, 19G, 19N, 21, 24, 24G, 26, 30, 42, 49, and 49N, in addition to hammerless Models 28, 31, 43, 44, 53, and 63 should not be fired, as many of these guns are 70-100 years old, and system failures can and do happen.

MODEL 1898 - 12 ga., 5 shot tube mag., 26-32 in. barrels, various chokes, exposed hammer, pistol grip stock, grades differ in quality of wood and engraving on C and D. Mfg. 1898-1905.

	100%	98%	95%	90%	80%	70%	60%
Grade A	$325	$275	$225	$200	$165	$150	$140
Grade B	$580	$495	$440	$415	$360	$305	$275
Grade C	$880	$715	$635	$580	$525	$495	$440
Grade D	$1,760	$1,540	$1,320	$1,210	$1,045	$965	$880

Factory information by individual ser. no. from the Cody Firearms Museum may be available for this model in the ser. range 19,601-67,000.

MODEL 16 - 16 ga. only, 26 or 28 in. barrel, various chokes, takedown, pistol grip stock. Mfg. 1904-10.

	100%	98%	95%	90%	80%	70%	60%
Grade A	$325	$275	$225	$200	$165	$150	$140
Grade B	$495	$415	$360	$330	$305	$275	$250
Grade C	$635	$525	$495	$440	$415	$385	$330
Grade D	$1,320	$1,100	$990	$825	$715	$635	$550

MODEL 17 - 12 ga., 30 or 32 in. full choke barrel, solid frame, straight stock. Mfg. 1906-08.

	100%	98%	95%	90%	80%	70%	60%
	$335	$275	$235	$200	$165	$150	$140

MODEL 17 BRUSH GUN - similar to Model 17, with 26 in. cylinder bore barrel. Mfg. 1906-08.

	100%	98%	95%	90%	80%	70%	60%
	$325	$275	$235	$200	$165	$150	$140

GRADING - PPGS™	100%	98%	95%	90%	80%	70%	60%

MODEL 17 RIOT GUN - similar to Model 17, with 20 in. barrel. Mfg. 1906-08.

	100%	98%	95%	90%	80%	70%	60%
	$325	$275	$235	$200	$165	$150	$140

MODEL 19 - improved lightened version of Model 1898, matte top surface on barrel. Mfg. 1906-07.

	100%	98%	95%	90%	80%	70%	60%
Grade A	$325	$275	$235	$200	$165	$150	$140
Grade B	$495	$415	$360	$330	$305	$275	$250
Grade C	$635	$525	$495	$440	$415	$385	$330
Grade D	$1,320	$1,100	$990	$825	$715	$635	$550

MODEL 21 - straight grip version of Model 19.

	100%	98%	95%	90%	80%	70%	60%
Grade A	$325	$275	$235	$200	$165	$150	$140
Grade B	$495	$415	$360	$330	$305	$275	$250
Grade C	$635	$525	$495	$440	$415	$385	$330
Grade D	$1,320	$1,100	$990	$825	$715	$635	$550

MODEL 24 - improved 21, takedown, automatic recoil lock on slide, solid matte rib. Mfg. 1908-15.

	100%	98%	95%	90%	80%	70%	60%
Grade G	$295	$265	$225	$195	$165	$150	$140
Grade A	$325	$275	$235	$200	$165	$150	$140
Grade B	$525	$440	$385	$360	$330	$305	$275
Grade C	$660	$550	$525	$470	$440	$415	$360
Grade D	$1,375	$1,155	$1,045	$880	$770	$660	$580

MODEL 26 - similar to Model 24 Grade A, with solid frame, 30 or 32 in. full choke barrel. Mfg. 1909-15.

	100%	98%	95%	90%	80%	70%	60%
	$275	$230	$210	$195	$165	$150	$140

MODEL 26 BRUSH GUN - 26 in. cylinder bore barrel. Mfg. 1909-15.

	100%	98%	95%	90%	80%	70%	60%
	$275	$230	$210	$195	$165	$150	$140

MODEL 26 RIOT GUN - 20 in. cylinder bore barrel. Mfg. 1909-15.

	100%	98%	95%	90%	80%	70%	60%
	$250	$195	$180	$165	$150	$140	$120

MODEL 28 HAMMERLESS - 12 ga., 26-32 in. barrels, various chokes, takedown, matte top barrel, pistol grip stock. Mfg. 1913-22.

	100%	98%	95%	90%	80%	70%	60%
Grade A	$295	$265	$235	$200	$165	$150	$140
Grade B	$495	$415	$360	$330	$305	$275	$250
Grade C	$635	$525	$495	$440	$415	$385	$330
Grade D	$1,320	$1,100	$990	$825	$715	$635	$550

MODEL 28TS TRAP GUN - similar to Model 28, with 30 in. matte rib barrel, full choke, high comb straight grip stock. Mfg. 1915.

	100%	98%	95%	90%	80%	70%	60%
	$415	$330	$275	$250	$220	$195	$165

MODEL 28T - similar to Model 28TS, with fancy wood, checkering, better finish. Mfg. 1915.

	100%	98%	95%	90%	80%	70%	60%
	$605	$525	$495	$470	$415	$360	$305

MODEL 30 - similar to Model 16, with automatic recoil lock on slide, also mfg. in 20 ga. 1915-1917 (Model 30-20). Mfg. 1910-14.

	100%	98%	95%	90%	80%	70%	60%
Grade A	$325	$275	$235	$200	$165	$150	$140
Grade B	$495	$415	$360	$330	$305	$275	$250
Grade C	$635	$525	$495	$440	$415	$385	$330
Grade D	$1,320	$1,100	$990	$825	$715	$635	$550

MODEL 30 FIELD GRADE - similar to Model 30 Grade B, with 25 in. mod. barrel, straight stock. Mfg. 1913-17.

	100%	98%	95%	90%	80%	70%	60%
	$335	$275	$220	$180	$160	$130	$115

GRADING - PPGS™	100%	98%	95%	90%	80%	70%	60%

MODEL 31 - scaled down small ga. (16 and 20 ga.) version of the Model 28, has 26 and 28 in. barrels, various chokes, Model 31-16 was mfg. 1914-17, Model 31-20 was mfg. 1911-23.

	100%	98%	95%	90%	80%	70%	60%
Grade A	$385	$305	$250	$220	$195	$165	$140
Grade B	$495	$415	$360	$330	$305	$275	$250
Grade C	$636	$525	$495	$440	$415	$385	$330
Grade D	$1,320	$1,100	$990	$825	$715	$635	$550

MODEL 31F FIELD GUN - 25 in. mod. barrel. Mfg. 1915-17.

	$395	$350	$325	$295	$265	$225	$200

MODEL 42A - similar to Model 24, but lesser quality finishing. Mfg. 1922-34.

	$250	$220	$195	$165	$140	$120	$100

MODEL 43 HAMMERLESS - similar to Model 28, with lesser quality finish. Mfg. 1923-30.

	$275	$225	$200	$175	$150	$125	$100

MODEL 43TS - similar to Model 28T, lower quality.

	$525	$440	$415	$385	$360	$305	$275

MODEL 44A - similar to Model 31 Grade A, 20 ga. only. Mfg. 1923-35.

	$360	$275	$250	$220	$195	$165	$140

MODEL 44S - select checkered stock.

	$470	$385	$360	$330	$195	$165	$140

MODEL 49 - lower priced version of Model 42A. They were given to purchasers of 4 shares of Marlin stock. 3,000 mfg. in 1925-28.

	$440	$360	$305	$275	$220	$195	$165

MODEL 53 - similar to Model 43 Hammerless. Mfg. 1929-30.

	$330	$275	$250	$220	$195	$165	$140

MODEL 63 - similar to Model 43 Hammerless, later model. Mfg. 1931-35.

	$330	$250	$220	$195	$165	$140	$110

MODEL 63TS - similar to Model 43TS, with trap style stock.

	$385	$305	$250	$220	$195	$165	$140

MODEL 120 MAGNUM - slide action, 12 ga., 3 in. chamber, 26-40 in. barrel, takedown, various chokes, checkered pistol grip stock. Mfg. 1971-85.

	$290	$225	$215	$205	$195	$180	$165

Last MSR was $370.

Add 10%-15% for Model 120 MXR with 40 in. barrel (mfg. 1974-75).
Subtract $35 if without VR.

MODEL 778 - 12 ga. Mag. slide action, 20-38 in. barrels, 7 3/4 lbs. Disc. 1984.

	$225	$190	$175	$155	$140	$125	$110

PREMIER MARK I - 12 ga. only, aluminum receiver, takedown, manufactured in France for Marlin.

	$200	$180	$160	$150	$140	$120	$95

PREMIER MARK II - similar to Mark I, except with engraved receiver and checkering. Mfg. 1960-63 in France.

	$275	$235	$200	$175	$150	$125	$100

PREMIER MARK IV - similar to Mark II, only deluxe grade with better wood, more engraving. Mfg. 1960-63 in France.

	$305	$250	$220	$195	$165	$140	$110
With VR	$330	$275	$250	$220	$195	$165	$140

GRADING - PPGS™	100%	98%	95%	90%	80%	70%	60%

MAROCCHI

Current trademark established in 1922, and currently manufactured by CD Europe SRL, located in Sarezzo, Italy. Currently imported by GSI, located in Trussville, AL. Previously distributed by Precision Sales International, Inc. located in Westfield, MA.

Marocchi O/U shotguns are high quality, and currently have limited U.S. importation. Discontinued Frigon guns (manufactured by Marocchi) appear under the F section in this text.

COMBINATION GUNS

VALLEY COMBO - 12 ga. over .222 Rem. cal., 23 1/2 in. separated barrels with VR, 3 in. chamber, fold down rear sight and will accept claw scope mounts, fixed cylinder choke, DTs, engraved silver receiver, satin finish walnut Monte Carlo stock with checkering and recoil pad, 8 1/4 lbs. Disc. 1994.

	$585	$480	$415	$375	$325	$295	$275

Last MSR was $700.

SHOTGUNS: O/U, 1995 & EARLIER

FIELD MASTER I - 12 ga. only, 26 or 28 in. VR barrels and rib with choke tubes, engraved coin finished receiver, extractors, SNT, checkered walnut stock and forearm. Disc. 1994.

	$455	$350	$295	$260	$225	$210	$190

Last MSR was $530.

This model was imported exclusively by Sile Distributors.

* *Field Master II* - similar to Field Master I except has SST and choke tubes. Disc. 1994.

	$475	$395	$325	$275	$240	$215	$200

Last MSR was $550.

SKEET MODEL - 12 ga. only, 26 in. barrels bored SK/SK. Disc. 1994.

	$445	$395	$325	$275	$240	$215	$200

Last MSR was $520.

This model was imported exclusively by Sile Distributors.

TRAP MODEL - 12 ga. only, 30 in. barrels bored M/F, ejectors. Disc. 1994.

	$560	$485	$415	$360	$300	$260	$230

Last MSR was $630.

This model was imported exclusively by Sile Distributors.

AVANZA - 12 or 20 (disc. 1993) ga., 3 in. chambers, monobloc boxlock action, 26 or 28 in. vent. barrels with VR (with or without choke tubes), SST, ejectors, deluxe checkered walnut stock and forearm with vent. recoil pad, high polish bluing with gold accents, all steel lightweight mfg., 6 lbs. 5 oz.-6 lbs. 13 oz. Imported 1990-95.

	$775	$675	$575	$525	$475	$425	$375

Last MSR was $829.

Add $45 for 20 ga. (disc. 1993).

Subtract 10% if without choke tubes (3).

This model was imported exclusively by Precision Sales International, Inc.

* *Avanza Sporting Clays* - 12 ga. only, 3 in. chambers, built on 20 ga. frame, 28 in. vent. barrels with VR and choke tubes, select checkered walnut stock with deluxe recoil pad and forearm, gold-plated trigger, 7 lbs. Mfg. 1991-95.

	$825	$725	$600	$550	$495	$450	$400

Last MSR was $889.

Add $99 for Premier Grade (disc., included select walnut and gold etched triggerguard).
This model features a trigger that is adjustable for length and pull without special tools.

SHOTGUNS: O/U, RECENT PRODUCTION

In the U.S., Conquista shotguns are identical in specifications and features to the Marocchi Classic Doubles sold in Europe, with the exception of Classic Doubles U.S.A.

GOLDEN SNIPE III FIELD - 12 ga. only, 3 in. chambers, field configuration with 28 in. VR barrels and choke tubes. Mfg. 1998-2003.

$725	$675	$625	$575	$525	$475	$425

Last MSR was $800.

GOLDEN SNIPE III SPORTING - 12 ga. only, entry level sporting clays model with 28 or 30 in. VR barrels with choke tubes, checkered walnut stock and forearm. Imported 1999-2003.

$850	$750	$675	$625	$575	$525	$450

Last MSR was $950.

CONQUISTA FIELD MAGNUM GRADE I - 12 ga. only, 3 in. chambers, features 28 in. 8mm VR barrels with choke tubes, nickel finished receiver, SST, checkered walnut stock and forearm with smooth rosewood buttplate, approx. 7 1/4 lbs. Imported 1999-2001.

$1,275	$1,025	$900	$800	$700	$625	$550

Last MSR was $1,490.

CONQUISTA USA SPORTING - 12 ga. only, 3 in. chambers, features 30 in. vent. barrels with 10mm VR, muzzle porting, back boring, and lengthened forcing cones, blued barrels and receiver with gold accents, checkered standard or adj. walnut stock and forearm, approx. 8 lbs. Mfg. 1999-2003.

$1,275	$1,025	$900	$800	$700	$625	$550

Last MSR was $1,490.

Add $100 for adj. stock.

CONQUISTA SPORTING CLAYS - 12 ga. only, boxlock action with brushed coin finish, SST, ejectors, adj. trigger, choice of 28, 30, or 32 in. 10mm VR barrels with choke tubes, right- or left-hand (Grade I only) action, checkered walnut stock and forearm with recoil pad, 7 7/8 lbs. Imported 1994-2000.

✳ *Grade I* - features coin finished receiver with perimeter line engraving.

$1,725	$1,450	$1,200	$1,000	$850	$700	$550

Last MSR was $1,995.

Add $125 for left-hand variation.
Add $151 for adj. stock (new 1999).

✳ *Lady Sport* - 12 ga. only, features lighter weight specialized stock designed to fit women, cased, 7 1/2 lbs. Mfg. 1995-99.

$1,800	$1,525	$1,250	$1,000	$850	$700	$550

Last MSR was $2,120.

Add $180 for left-hand variation (Sport Spectrum only).
Add $79 for Lady Sport Spectrum (partially colored receiver).

✳ *Grade II* - features better walnut and game scene engraving on receiver.

$1,995	$1,675	$1,425	$1,200	$1,000	$850	$700

Last MSR was $2,330.

Add $355 for left-hand variation.

✳ *Grade III* - features more elaborate game scene engraving on receiver sides and fine scrollwork throughout rest of action, includes hard gun case and stock wrench.

$3,225	$2,650	$2,250	$1,875	$1,650	$1,400	$1,175

Last MSR was $3,599.

Add $396 for left-hand variation.

GRADING - PPGS™	100%	98%	95%	90%	80%	70%	60%

* *Grade IV* - top-of-the-line Sporting Clays model. Importation began 1997. Price available by request only.

CONQUISTA TRAP MODEL - 12 ga. only, Trap configuration, 30 or 32 (disc. 1997, reintroduced 2000) in. 10mm VR barrels with fixed chokes, 8 1/4 lbs. Imported 1994-2000.

* *Grade I* - features coin finished receiver with perimeter line engraving.

	$1,725	$1,475	$1,225	$1,000	$850	$700	$550

Last MSR was $1,995.

Add $151 for adj. stock (new 1999).

* *Grade II* - features better walnut and game scene engraving on receiver.

	$1,995	$1,675	$1,450	$1,200	$1,000	$850	$700

Last MSR was $2,330.

* *Grade III* - features more elaborate game scene engraving on receiver sides and fine scrollwork throughout rest of action, includes hard gun case and stock wrench.

	$3,225	$2,650	$2,250	$1,875	$1,650	$1,400	$1,175

Last MSR was $3,599.

* *Grade IV* - top-of-the-line Trap model. Importation began 1997. Price available by request only.

CONQUISTA SKEET MODEL - 12 ga. only, Skeet configuration, 28 in. 10mm VR barrels with fixed Skeet chokes, 7 3/4 lbs. Imported 1994-2000.

* *Grade I* - features coin finished receiver with perimeter line engraving.

	$1,725	$1,475	$1,225	$1,000	$850	$700	$550

Last MSR was $1,995.

* *Grade II* - features better walnut and game scene engraving on receiver.

	$1,995	$1,675	$1,450	$1,200	$1,000	$850	$700

Last MSR was $2,330.

* *Grade III* - features more elaborate game scene engraving on receiver sides and fine scrollwork throughout rest of action, includes hard gun case and stock wrench.

	$3,225	$2,650	$2,250	$1,875	$1,650	$1,400	$1,175

Last MSR was $3,599.

* *Grade IV* - top-of-the-line Skeet model. Importation began 1997. Price available by request only.

CLASSIC DOUBLES MODEL 92 - 12 ga. only, 3 in. chambers, sporting clays configuration featuring 30 in. vented barrels with VR, back-boring, elongated forcing cones, and three screw-in chokes, low profile blued receiver, checkered walnut stock, and Schnabel forearm, adj. trigger, gold receiver accents and trigger. Imported 1996-98.

	$1,450	$1,175	$950	$850	$775	$700	$650

Last MSR was $1,598.

MODEL 99 - 12 ga. only, 2 3/4 in. chambers, boxlock action with Boss locking system, silver grey reciever finish, SST, ejectors, adj. trigger, choice of 28 (Sporting or Skeet), 30, or 32 in. 10mm VR barrels with 5 extended choke tubes, choice of Sporting, Trap, or Skeet configuration, right-hand action only, deluxe checkered walnut stock and Schnabel forearm with recoil pad, approx. 7 1/2-8 lbs. New 2000.

* *Grade I*

MSR $2,995	$2,700	$2,475	$2,050	$1,750	$1,500	$1,250	$1,000

Add $1,600 per extra set of barrels.

* *Grade II* - features better walnut and engraving on receiver. Disc. 2003.

	$2,475	$2,125	$1,725	$1,400	$1,100	$925	$800

Last MSR was $2,870.

Add $155 for gold inlays.

GRADING - PPGS™	100%	98%	95%	90%	80%	70%	60%

✳ *Grade III* - features more elaborate engraving with gold inlays and wood upgrade, flush choke tubes.

	MSR $4,595	$3,950	$3,500	$3,000	$2,500	$2,100	$1,700	$1,525

Subtract approx. $250 if w/o gold inlays.

MODEL 99 CUSTOM GRADES - 12 ga. only, 2 3/4 in. chambers, available in either Sporting, Trap, or Skeet configuration, deluxe Model 99 with best quality walnut and elaborate engraving options per model - base model is the Blackgold (non-engraved with gold line frame accents), 28, 30, or 32 in. barrels. Importation began 2000.

Please contact GSI directly for more information regarding available options and pricing for the Maroccchi custom shop.

SHOTGUNS: SINGLE SHOT

MODEL 2000 - 12 ga. only, 3 in. chamber, hammer, 28 in. barrel, ejector, lightly engraved receiver. Importation disc. 1991.

	$80	$70	$60	$50	$45	$40	$35

Last MSR was $94.

MARTIN, ALEX

Current trademark owned and manufactured by Dickson & MacNaughton, located in Edinburgh, Scotland.

Please contact Dickson & MacNaughton directly for more information regarding this trademark, including current availability and pricing.

MARTINI

Please refer to individual listings in the BSA Guns, Limited section.

MASTERPIECE ARMS, INC.

Previous manufacturer of derringers located in Carrollton, GA from 2000-2004.

Masterpiece Arms manufactured derringers in both steel and stainless steel configuration.

MASQUELIER S.A.

Previous manufacturer located in Belgium. Previously distributed (until 1986) by Ambel Ltd., Inc. located in Sugarland, TX.

RIFLES: SxS

CARPATHE - .243 Win., .270 Win., .30-06, 7x57R, or 7x65R cal., single shot, hair trigger, push-down cocking system. Importation disc. 1986.

	$3,500	$3,200	$2,900	$2,600	$2,300	$2,100	$1,850

Last MSR was $3,850.

EXPRESS - .270 Win., .30-06, 8x57JRS, or 9.3x74R cal., O/U configuration, SST, ejectors. Add $800 for extra set of 20 ga. barrels. Importation disc. 1986.

	$3,300	$3,000	$2,800	$2,600	$2,300	$2,100	$1,850

Last MSR was $3,600.

ARDENNES MODEL - top-of-the-line model, custom order only. Importation disc. 1986.

	$6,600	$6,000	$5,400	$4,800	$4,300	$3,900	$3,450

Last MSR was $7,250.

SHOTGUNS: SxS

BOXLOCK - 12 ga. only, 2 3/4 in. chambers, Anson & Deeley boxlock action, ejectors, fine scroll engraving with French walnut. Importation disc. 1986.

	$4,400	$4,000	$3,650	$3,300	$2,995	$2,600	$2,200

Last MSR was $4,780.

GRADING - PPGS™	100%	98%	95%	90%	80%	70%	60%

SIDELOCK - 12 ga. only, 2 3/4 in. chambers, H&H style sidelocks, auto ejectors, English style fine scroll engraving with French walnut. Importation disc. 1986.

	$12,500	$10,000	$8,750	$7,600	$6,700	$5,800	$5,000

Last MSR was $15,850.

MATCHGUNS srl

Current manufacturer established during 2001, and located in Parma, Italy. No current U.S. importation.

During 2001, Cesare Morini left Morini Competition Arm S.A. of Switzerland and started a new company, Matchguns srl, with headquarters in Parma, Italy.

PISTOLS

MG2 - .22 LR cal., innovative new semi-auto action with patented compact mechanism allowing recoil reduction of up to 50% w/o the use of counterweights or muzzle brakes, 6 in. barrel, fully adj. rear sight, fully adj. anatomical walnut grips, 5 shot mag., blue only, adj. trigger from 60 grams - 950 grams, includes case and tools, approx. 2 lbs. New mid-2002.

MSR N/A	$1,295	$1,125	$975	$850	$725	$650	$575

MG3 - .22 Short cal., otherwise similar to MG2. New 2004.

MSR N/A	$1,295	$1,125	$975	$850	$725	$650	$575

MG5 - free pistol, single shot, limited importation. New 2004.

Please contact the company directly for more information on this gun, including pricing and domestic availability.

MATCH GRADE ARMS & AMMUNITION

Please refer to MG Arms, Inc. listing.

MATEBA

Current trademark manufactured by Mateba srl, located in Brescia, Italy. Previously located in Pavia, Italy. Limited U.S. importation and distribution until 2004 by American Western Arms, located in Delray Beach, FL. Previously imported 2000-2001 by Keisler's Wholesale, located in Jeffersonville, IN, and by American Arms, Inc. until late 1999. Previously manufactured by Macchine Termo Balistiche located in Italy. Older mfg. has had little domestic importation.

PISTOLS: SEMI-AUTO

MATEBA M1911 - .45 ACP cal., choice of dual tone blue or hard chrome, 8 shot mag. New 2003.

MSR N/A	$1,375	$1,150	$895	$800	$675	$525	$450

REVOLVERS

MATEBA REVOLVER - various cals. (older mfg.), most recent mfg is .357 Mag./.38 Spl., .44 Mag., or .454 Casull cal., combination semi-auto pistol and revolver, action allows cylinder and slide assembly to move back when fired, causing the cylinder to rotate, unique design permits barrel to fire lowest shell in cylinder (6 o'clock position), mechanism to rear of cylinder, single or double action, 6, 7 (older mfg.), or 8 (older mfg.) shot, 4, 6 (mfg. 1998-2000), or 8 (mfg. 1998-2000) in. barrel, steel/alloy frame, blue finish, flared ergonomic walnut grips, interchangeable barrels, 2.75 lbs.

MSR N/A	$995	$875	$775	$675	$525	$450	$400

Add $70 for frame mounted scope mount, or $150 for .454 Casull cal. with scope mount.
Add $170 for polished nickel finish.
Add $250 for carbine variation.

MATHELON ARMES

Current SxS double rifle and drilling manufacturer located in Rumilly, France. Currently, imported by Rocky Mountain Armoury, located in Silverthorne, CO.

Currently, Mathelon Armes manufactures a boxlock drilling (2 rifle barrels either 8x57JRS or 9.3x74R and 20 ga.), and SxS double rifle in 8x57JRS, 30R Blaser, and 9.3x74R cal. Please contact the importer directly (see Trademark Index) for more information and current pricing.

MATRA MANURHIN DEFENSE

Please refer to the Manurhin heading in this section.

MAUNZ

Previous manufacturer located in Maumee, OH until 1987.

RIFLES: SEMI-AUTO

MATCH SERVICE RIFLE - .308 Win. cal., 22 in. barrel, M1A configuration with M1 and M14 G.I. parts, fiberglass stock, NM sights, M1 trigger assembly, 10 lbs., approx. 200 mfg.

	100%	98%	95%	90%	80%	70%
	$2,000	$1,800	$1,500	$1,250	$1,050	$925	$800

MODEL 77 - .308 Win. cal., utilized M1A Springfield receiver initially, followed by Valley Ordnance mfg., receiver has removable lug under the barrel, red, white and blue laminated stock, ser. no. 000011-005040.

$1,800	$1,500	$1,250	$1,050	$925	$800	$600

MODEL 87 - various cals., 26 in. medium weight barrel, synthetic stock, G.I. parts with TRW bolts, satin black finish, open sights, ser. nos. 00001-03030, 11 lbs. Mfg. 1985-89.

$2,000	$1,800	$1,500	$1,250	$1,050	$925	$800

MAUSER JAGDWAFFEN GmbH

Current trademark established during 1871, and currently owned by San Swiss Arms AG beginning late 2000. Mauser Model 98 Magnum bolt action rifles are currently manufactured by Mauser Jagdwaffen GmbH, located in Isny, Germany. Currently imported by SIG Arms, located in Exeter, NH. Current handgun production is manufactured by SIG, located in Switzerland. The former transistion name was Mauser Jagd-und Sportwaffen GmbH. On January 1, 1999, Mauser transferred all production and distribution rights of both hunting and sporting weapons to SIG-Blaser. SIG Arms AG was purchased by San Swiss Arms AG in 2000. Mauser-Werke Oberndorf Waffensysteme GmbH continues to manufacture military defense contracts (including making small bore barrel liners for tanks), in addition to other industrial machinery.

Previously imported exclusively by Brolin Arms, located in Pomona, CA during 1997-98 only. During 1998, the company name was changed from Mauser-Werke Oberndorf Waffensysteme GmbH. During 1994, the name was changed from Mauser-Werke to Mauser-Werke Oberndorf Waffensysteme GmbH. Previously imported by GSI located in Trussville, AL, until 1997, Gibb's Rifle Co., Inc. until 1995, Precision Imports, Inc. located in San Antonio, TX until 1993, and KDF located in Seguin, TX (1987-89).

HANDGUNS: EARLY PRODUCTION

MODEL 1877 SINGLE SHOT - 9mm cal., single shot, barrel release in usual hammer position and safety on left side, examples are rare.

$12,500	$9,500	$7,000	$6,000	$5,000	$4,000	$3,000

GRADING - PPGS™	100%	98%	95%	90%	80%	70%	60%

MODEL 1878 "ZIG-ZAG" REVOLVER - 7.6mm, 9mm (most common) or 10.6mm cal., Zig-Zag refers to Z-pattern grooves cut into cylinder, earliest revolvers were solid frame, gate loaded, and chambered in 9mm, most were designed with a hinged frame, third and last version had an "improved" sliding release on the forward frame, most revolvers had a rust blue frame and barrel complementing a fire blue cylinder, grips were checkered or hard rubber with a floral pattern.

	100%	98%	95%	90%	80%	70%	60%
7.6mm	$4,500	$3,750	$2,500	$2,000	$1,850	$1,700	$1,400
9mm	$5,250	$4,250	$3,500	$3,000	$2,250	$1,900	$1,500
10.6mm	$7,500	$6,500	$5,000	$4,000	$3,000	$2,000	$1,600

Add 10% for earliest pistols with "midnight blue" finish. Premiums exist for solid frame, late improved model, and factory cased guns.

PISTOLS: SEMI-AUTO, DISC.

The Models 1906-08, 1912-14, and HSv are very rare and only infrequently encountered. A competent appraisal is advisable before buying or selling these models.

MODEL 1906-08 - 9mm Export (9x25mm) cal., detachable mag., incorporates features of both the pocket pistols and Model 1896 Broomhandle. Ser. range 1-100 (est.).

	N/A	$40,000	$32,500	$27,500	$22,500	$17,500	$12,500

MODEL 1912-14 - generally chambered for 9mm Para. cal., similar to pocket pistol configuration, but considerably larger, earliest specimens have inscribed slide legend. Those under serial number 100 (approx.) are not slotted for shoulder stock while those over 100 are generally slotted. Ser. range 1-175 (est.).

	N/A	$25,000	$22,500	$20,000	$17,500	$13,500	$10,000

Add 50% if slotted with matching shoulder stock.

This variation is very rare in .45 ACP cal. or with a tangent rear sight.

WTP MODEL I VEST POCKET AUTOMATIC - 6.35mm cal., 6 shot, 2 1/2 in. barrel, blue, rubber grips. Mfg. 1922-37.

	$550	$425	$300	$275	$250	$225	$200

WTP MODEL II - similar to Model I, but 2 in. barrel. Mfg. 1938-40.

	$700	$600	$500	$400	$300	$250	$200

POCKET MODEL 1910 - 6.35mm or 7.65mm cal., 9 shot, 3 in. barrel, blue fixed sights, checkered walnut or hard rubber grips. Mfg. 1910-34.

	$550	$350	$225	$175	$150	$140	$130

Add 30% for sidelatch variation.

POCKET MODEL 1914 - similar to Model 1910, but 7.65mm cal., 3.4 in. barrel. Mfg. 1914-34.

	$500	$350	$225	$175	$150	$140	$130

Add 10% for military acceptance proof by rear sight (Prussian eagle WWI proofs and/or crown D).

Add 500% for the "humpback" model.

POCKET MODEL 1934 - similar to Model 1914, but reshaped grip. Mfg. 1934-39.

	$550	$350	$225	$195	$150	$140	$130

Add 50% for Waffenamt or Nazi Police.

Add 100% for Nazi Navy marked.

MODEL HSv - 9mm Para. cal., limited mfg., similar features to Model HSc, except has larger dimensions.

	N/A	$15,000	$10,000	$8,500	$7,000	$6,500	$5,500

Mauser Pistols: HSc Models

MODEL HSc DOUBLE ACTION - 7.65mm (8 shot) or .380 ACP (7 shot) cal., 3.4 in. barrel, blue or nickel, fixed sights, checkered walnut grips. Mfg. 1938-disc. (most recent mfg. was by R. Gamba in Italy circa 1996).

GRADING - PPGS™	100%	98%	95%	90%	80%	70%	60%

Mauser Pistols: HSc WWII Military Mfg.

✳ Low Grip Screw - very rare, first variation with ser. numbers starting at 700,000, less than 2,000 mfg.

	$5,000	$4,000	$3,000	$2,000	$1,500	$1,000	$800

Add 20% if Navy marked.

✳ Early Nazi Army - proofed 655 and 135.

	$900	$700	$500	$300	$250	$200	$185

Add 50% for small 655 additionally test-proofed on left tang.

✳ Early Nazi Navy - marked on front grip strap.

	$1,000	$800	$540	$500	$440	$395	$350

✳ Early Nazi Police - Eagle L proof only.

	$750	$500	$400	$350	$300	$250	$200

✳ Wartime Nazi Army - proof 135 and WaA 135. Eagle N proofed also.

	$450	$350	$290	$250	$200	$180	$150

✳ Wartime Nazi Navy - proofed on left side of triggerguard.

	$850	$600	$500	$400	$350	$300	$250

✳ Wartime Nazi Police - proofed Eagle L.

	$500	$395	$360	$320	$285	$245	$200

Add 10% if Eagle F.

✳ Wartime Commercial - standard WWII Commercial Model.

	$450	$350	$300	$275	$250	$225	$200

✳ Swiss Commercial - ser. range 800,000-900,000. Very rare.

	$1,400	$1,250	$1,125	$995	$900	$850	$600

✳ Cutaways - mfg. to visibly show mechanism. Should not be proofed.

	$1,495	$1,000	$900	$850	$800	$750	$700

Mauser Pistols: HSc Post-WWII Mfg.

✳ French Manufacture - frequently encountered in poor condition - post-WWII production.

	$400	$350	$300	$250	$200	$175	$150

✳ Mauser Production - .32 or .380 cal., 15 shot, mfg. 1968-81.

	$400	$350	$300	$250	$200	$175	$150

Deduct 20% if not boxed or in .32 cal.

✳ Interarms Import - imported by Interarms from 1983-1985 (Mauser and Italian mfg. by Gamba).

	$350	$300	$250	$220	$180	$150	$125

Last MSR was $415.

✳ One of Five Thousand Edition - American Eagle edition (marked on gun), 5,000 total mfg. (serial numbered 1-5000).

	$450	$350	$300

✳ Armes De Chasse Import - previously imported by Armes De Chasse located in Chadds Ford, PA on a limited basis.

	$475	$425	$330	$300	$260	$240	$220

Last MSR was $695.

Add $195 for Limited Series.
Add $58 For G15 variation (9 shot).

✳ E.A.A. Import - imported by European American Armory, distributed by RSR Wholesale.

	$265	$225	$195	$175	$150	$125	$110

GRADING - PPGS™	100%	98%	95%	90%	80%	70%	60%

* **Recent Gamba Mfg.** - .32 ACP or .380 ACP cal., steel construction, double action, double safety, stippled walnut grips, recently imported by Gamba, USA until approx. 1996, and reintroduced during 2005.

MSR $783	$675	$375	$315	$265	$240	$220	$200

Mauser Pistols: Luger Mfg.

The original Mauser Luger P.08 is still currently mfg. at the factory, with very limited domestic importation. Both pre-war and post-war Mauser manufactured Lugers will be found in the Luger section of this book.

PISTOLS: SEMI-AUTO, RECENT IMPORTATION

MODEL 80 SA - .380 ACP or 9mm Para. cal., semi-auto single action patterned after the Browning Hi-power, 4 2/3 in. barrel, blue finish with checkered walnut grips, round hammer, steel construction, 10 (C/B 1994) or 13* shot mag., 1.95 lbs. Mfg. by FEG in Hungary, imported 1992-96.

	$450	$325	$275	$240	$215	$185	$165

Last MSR was $520.

MODEL 90 DA - similar to Model 80 SA, except is double action, spur hammer, and has 10 (C/B 1994) or 14* shot mag., 2.15 lbs. Mfg. by FEG, imported 1992-96.

	$445	$325	$275	$240	$215	$185	$165

Last MSR was $516.

* **Model 90 DAC** - similar to Model 90 DA, except is compact model with 4 1/8 in. barrel, 2.05 lbs. Imported 1992-96.

	$450	$325	$275	$240	$215	$185	$165

Last MSR was $520.

M-2 - .357 SIG (disc. 2001), .40 S&W, or .45 ACP cal., short recoil operation, striker fired operating system, rotating 3.54 in. barrel lockup, manual safety, 8 (.45 ACP) or 10 shot, DAO, hammerless, aluminum alloy frame with nickel chromium steel slide, black finish, includes case and trigger lock, approx. 29 or 32.5 oz. Mfg. by SIG in Europe, importation began 2000.

MSR N/A	$430	$380	$340	$300	$275	$250	$225

PISTOLS: SEMI-AUTO, MODEL 1896 BROOMHANDLES

Note: Manufactured in Oberndorf, Germany between 1897 & 1938.

While many variations of the famous 1896 Broomhandle exist, most common Broomhandles are pre-war Commercials, Model 1930 Commercials, Red 9s, and Bolos. They can be found in chronological order in this section. Holster stocks are a very popular accessory in this model. Commercial stocks may be matching or may not be serial numbered to gun (proper stock). Add $300+ for stock depending on overall original condition and if matching/non-matching.

In 1984, Federal legislation once again allowed importation of non-domestic WWI and WWII military handguns. While many of these newer imports would make workable shooters, they have in no way lowered prices on 90%+ condition specimens due to normal collector activity in top quality only pistols. Recently imported Broomhandles should have the importer's name visibly stamped on an exterior surface.

Mauser Broomhandles: Conehammer Variations

STANDARD CONEHAMMER - 7.63 Mauser cal., distinguishable by circular machined upper hammer with concentric rings. 5.5 in. barrel, 23 groove wooden grips, rear adjustable sight available in 1-10, 50-500, 100-300, 50-300, 50-700 meter configurations, 10 shot mag.

	$4,000	$3,000	$2,250	$1,800	$1,500	$1,250	$1,000

Add 40% for matching stock.

GRADING - PPGS™	100%	98%	95%	90%	80%	70%	60%

FIXED SIGHT CONEHAMMER - 7.63 Mauser cal., similar to Standard Conehammer, except has fixed rear sight.

	100%	98%	95%	90%	80%	70%	60%
	$4,500	$3,250	$2,500	$2,000	$1,500	$1,250	$1,000

6 SHOT CONEHAMMER - FIXED SIGHT - 7.63 Mauser cal., 4 3/4 in. barrel, 6 shot mag., rare.

	$8,500	$6,500	$4,500	$3,500	$3,000	$2,500	$2,000

 ✴ *6 Shot Conehammer w/adjustable sight* - 7.63 Mauser cal., 5.5 in. barrel, very rare.

	$13,500	$10,000	$7,500	$5,000	$4,000	$3,000	$2,500

 Sales of this variation are extremely limited.

TURKISH CONEHAMMER - 7.63 Mauser cal., 5.5 in. barrel, 10 shot mag. Approx. 1,000 mfg. for Turkey in 1898, Farsi serial numbers.

	$6,500	$4,500	$3,000	$2,400	$2,100	$1,800	$1,500

"SYSTEM MAUSER" CONEHAMMER - 7.63 Mauser cal., "SYSTEM MAUSER" marked on top of chamber, improved 5.5 in. tapered barrel, 10 shot mag.

	$15,000	$11,000	$6,000	$5,000	$4,000	$3,500	$3,000

 ✴ *Stepped barrel variation* - similar to System Mauser variation, except has older 5.5 in. stepped barrel with no taper.

	$27,500	$22,500	$15,000	$10,000	$9,000	$8,000	$7,000

 Add 40% for "SYSTEM MAUSER" stock.

20 SHOT CONEHAMMER - 7.63 Mauser cal., 20 shot non-detachable mag., frame can either be flatside or have milled panels, 5.5 in. tapered barrel, extremely rare.

	$30,000	$25,000	$15,000	$12,000	$9,000	$8,000	$7,000

 Add 20% for milled panel variation.
 Add 40% for matching stock cut for 20 shot mag.
 Several restored guns have recently sold in the $10,000 range.
 Many fake 20 shot pistols (especially flat side) have surfaced over the last few years. Use extreme caution when considering purchase.

EARLY TRANSITIONAL LARGE RING HAMMER - 7.63 Mauser cal., distinguishable by large, open centered ring, 10 shot mag., 5.5 in. barrel.

	$3,000	$2,250	$1,550	$1,200	$1,050	$925	$700

 This variation is normally found in the 12,000-15,000 serial range only.

Mauser Broomhandles: Flatside Variations

 Add approximately $500 for a matching shoulder stock on the following models, $350 for non-matching.

ITALIAN CONTRACT FLATSIDE - 7.63 Mauser cal., distinguishable by flatside frame and DV/AV proofmarks, 10 shot mag., 5.5 in. barrel.

	$4,000	$3,000	$2,250	$1,700	$1,250	$900	$700

 This variation is found in the 1-5,000 serial range only.

FLATSIDE COMMERCIAL - 7.63 Mauser cal., 5.5 in. barrel, 23 groove walnut grips, adj. rear sight typically marked 1-10 or 50-1,000.

	$3,500	$2,700	$2,000	$1,500	$1,000	$750	$500

 Early specimens may have pinned rear sights. Found in serial range 20,000-30,000.

Mauser Broomhandles: Post-1900 Variations

 Add approximately $400 for a matching shoulder stock on the following models, $325 for non-matching. This assumes excellent condition - exceptions are noted.

PRE-WAR LARGE RING BOLO - 7.63 Mauser cal., 3.9 in. barrel, floral grips, usually found in 29,000 and 40,000 serial range.

	$4,500	$3,000	$2,000	$1,450	$1,000	$700	$450

 Add $850 for short pre-war bolo stock, $1,500 if stock matches pistol.

LARGE RING SHALLOW MILLING - 7.63 Mauser cal., 5.5 in. barrel, 23 groove walnut or hard rubber grips, normally found in the 30,000-33,000 ser. range.

	100%	98%	95%	90%	80%	70%	60%
	$2,750	$1,600	$1,000	$750	$700	$500	$400

LARGE RING DEEP MILLING - 7.63 Mauser cal., 5.5 in. barrel, 35 groove walnut or hard rubber grips, normally found in the 34,000 ser. range.

	$2,650	$1,650	$1,000	$750	$625	$500	$400

PRE-WAR SMALL RING BOLO - 7.63 Mauser cal., 3.9 in. barrel, floral/checkered rubber or 31-36 groove walnut grips, usually found in 40,000-44,000 serial range.

	$3,750	$2,750	$1,800	$1,250	$800	$575	$400

Add $850 for short pre-war bolo stock, $1,500 if stock matches pistol.

6-SHOT BOLO - 7.63 Mauser cal., distinctive 6 shot mag., 3.9 in. barrel, either fixed rear sight (more common) or adjustable, could have either large ring or small ring hammer.

	$6,500	$5,000	$3,500	$3,000	$2,600	$2,200	$1,500

Add $850 for short pre-war bolo stock, $1,500 if stock matches pistol.

STANDARD PRE-WAR COMMERCIAL - 7.63 Mauser cal., 5.5 in. barrel, 10 shot mag., 34 groove walnut or checkered black rubber grips, typically 50-1,000 meter adj. rear sight.

	$1,800	$1,350	$850	$725	$600	$500	$400

This variation is the most commonly encountered of all M1896 broomhandles. It can be encountered in the 39,000-274,000 serial range. Early guns below serial no. 100,000 are often Von Lengerke and Detmold marked and can be encountered with hard rubber grips. Rifling changed from 4 groove to 6 groove at approx. serial no. 100,000.

Note: This model is once again being imported by domestic distributors/dealers. Condition is somewhat poor, and prices usually start in the $250 range. These specimens usually have been reblued in addition to other reworking because the original condition has generally been very poor.

MAUSER BANNER CHAMBER MARKED - 7.63 Mauser or 9mm Export/9mm Mauser (rare) cal., 5.5 in. barrel, distinguishable by Mauser banner trademark on top of chamber, 32 groove walnut grips. Approx. 10,000 mfg. in serial range 84,000-94,000.

	$3,750	$2,750	$1,600	$1,100	$800	$650	$500

This model is very similar in appearance to the Pre-War Commercial.

PERSIAN CONTRACT - 7.63 Mauser cal., 5.5 in. barrel, distinguished by Persian lion crest in left rear frame panel, must be in the 154,000 serial range, 50-1,000 meter adj. rear sight.

	$4,500	$3,250	$2,500	$1,800	$1,250	$850	$700

This variation is frequently faked - pay close attention to serial no. and Persian crest.

STANDARD WARTIME COMMERCIAL - 7.63 Mauser cal., 5.5 in. barrel, 10 shot mag., 30 groove walnut grips, adj. 50-1,000 meter rear sight.

	$1,650	$1,100	$750	$650	$550	$450	$350

This variation is encountered almost as frequently as the Standard Pre-War Commercial. It is usually found in the 290,000-440,000 serial range. It was the first model to utilize the "new safety" design, and can be noticed by the "NS" marking on the back of hammer. Similar features as the Pre-War Commercial, except finish and polishing exhibit more machine and tooling marks.

Note: This model is once again being imported by domestic distributors/dealers. Condition is somewhat poor, and prices usually start in the $250 range. These specimens usually have been reblued in addition to other reworking because the original condition has generally been very poor.

GRADING - PPGS™	100%	98%	95%	90%	80%	70%	60%

RED-9 ADJ. SIGHT - 9mm Para. cal., 5.5 in. barrel, 10 shot mag., 24 groove walnut grips usually marked with large red no. 9, adj. 50-500 meter rear sight, standard WWI military contract model with separate serial range 1-150,000, generally poorly finished. Mfg. 1916-1918.

	$2,500	$2,000	$1,600	$1,100	$850	$750	$650

> **Add $800 for matching stock.**
> **Add $450 for non-matching stock.**
> **Add $300 for original leather.**
> **Add 10% if Prussian Eagle proofed on front of magazine well.**
> The Red-9 may be the most popular Commercial Broomhandle whose value far outstrips its rarity. Note: Be cautious for originality since metal refinishing is prevalent in this model. The last 10,000 guns of this German military contract are not military proofed, are better polished, and will command a slight premium.

RED-9 FIXED SIGHT - 9mm Para. cal., 3.9 in. barrel, this is a 1920 commercial rework of the Red-9 military, may be dated 1920 and/or have police markings on front grip strap.

	$1,500	$1,350	$900	$750	$625	$500	$400

> Because of the Treaty of Versailles following WWI, barrels had to be shortened to less than 4 inches and the adj. rear sight removed.

FRENCH GENDARME - 7.63 Mauser cal., 3.9 in. barrel, distinguished by Bolo barrel length on large frame, hard rubber or walnut (rare) grips, found in the serial range 431,000-434,000, adj. 50-500 meter rear sight.

	$3,500	$2,700	$1,750	$1,250	$800	$600	$500

EARLY POST-WAR BOLO - 7.63 Mauser cal., 3.9 in. barrel, shot extractor, small ring hammer, usually found in the 440,000-500,000 serial range. Fit with full-size stock.

	$2,500	$1,750	$1,100	$725	$600	$500	$375

> **Add 50% for long barrel Bolos in approx. the 475,000 serial range.**

LATE POST-WAR BOLO - 7.63 Mauser cal., 3.9 in. barrel, similar features of Early Post-War Bolo except has Mauser banner trademark on left rear frame panel, usually encountered in the 500,000-700,000+ serial range. Fit with full-size stock.

	$2,750	$2,250	$1,500	$1,000	$800	$600	$400

> **Add 10% for late pistols with high polish salt blue finish.**

Mauser Broomhandles: Post-1930 Variations

> **Add approximately $500 for a Mauser banner marked stock. These late stocks were not marked with a serial number.**

EARLY MODEL 1930 COMMERCIAL - 7.63 Mauser cal., 5.2 (common) or 5.5 in. stepped barrel, 12 groove walnut grips, adj. 50-1,000 meter rear sight, usually found in the 800,000-890,000 serial range.

	$2,750	$1,750	$950	$750	$625	$500	$375

> This broomhandle variation had a high polish, salt blue finish. Small parts are still fire blue and milling grooves were machined in receiver rails.

LATE MODEL 1930 COMMERCIAL - 7.63 Mauser cal., 5.5 in. stepped barrel, similar appearance to early 1930 Commercial except has solid receiver rails and various small parts are salt blued. Ser. range 890,000-921,000 with production ending in late 1930s.

	$2,500	$1,750	$950	$750	$625	$500	$375

> This model is serial numbered on rear top of barrel extension assembly.

MODEL 1930 REMOVABLE MAG. - 7.63 Mauser cal., 5.5 in. stepped barrel, 12 groove walnut grips, adj. 50-1,000 meter rear sight, very rare.

	$18,000	$15,000	$9,000	$5,000	$4,000	$3,200	$2,500

> Original specimens of this variation have frames without the extra cuts required for the selector switch. Fakes are usually welded up Schnellfeuers made to look original. Only a very few are known in the 84,000-88,000 serial range.

GRADING - PPGS™	100%	98%	95%	90%	80%	70%	60%

SCHNELLFEUER (MODEL 712) - 7.63 Mauser cal., 5.5 in. stepped barrel, 12 groove walnut grips, adj. 50-1,000 meter rear sight, switchable full auto variation generally with selector switch, separate serial range 1-100,000, 10 or 20 shot detachable mag. 712 stock is internally grooved for selector switch.

	$8,500	$6,500	$4,500	$3,250	$2,300	$1,500	$1,200

Add $750-$1,200 for correct stock.

Subtact 60% if Class III transferable (Pre 1986 Gun Control Act).

The Model 712 is classified as a machine gun and is subject to registration and payment of a $200 transfer tax.

Broomhandle Carbines

FLUTED BARREL MODEL - marked "July 1897".

	$28,000	$16,000	$12,000	$8,000	$6,000	$5,000	$4,000

FLATSIDE CONE HAMMER - 7.63mm cal., 11 3/4 in. barrel, experimental variation.

	$25,000	$20,000	$15,000	$9,500	$7,500	$6,000	$5,000

FLATSIDE TRANSITIONAL - 7.63mm cal., 11 3/4 in. barrel.

	$20,000	$14,000	$10,000	$8,000	$7,000	$6,000	$5,000

LARGE RING HAMMER TRANSITIONAL - 7.63mm cal., 11 3/4 in. barrel.

	$17,500	$13,500	$10,000	$8,500	$7,000	$6,000	$5,000

LARGE RING HAMMER - 7.63mm cal., 14 1/2 in. barrel.

	$17,500	$13,500	$10,000	$8,500	$7,000	$6,000	$5,000

SMALL RING HAMMER - 7.63mm cal., 14 1/2 in. barrel.

	$17,000	$12,000	$9,500	$8,000	$7,000	$6,000	$5,000

Broomhandles: Copies from Other Countries

These pistols are Chinese manufactured copies of the original German design.

HAND-MADE MAUSER CHINESE MARKED AND OTHERS - 9mm Para. or .45 ACP cal., copies of the Mauser Broomhandle, many thousands made, fixed (.45 ACP cal.) or detachable (9mm Para.) mag., quality can vary significantly, recent imports will have import markings. IAR, Inc. imported these recently.

	100%	98%	95%	90%	80%	70%	60%
9mm Para.	$625	$550	$475	$400	$325	$275	$250
.45 ACP	$1,200	$950	$740	$680	$600	$500	$400

Add $100 for reproduction shoulder stock holster (with or w/o leather).

Subtract 25% for poor quality (QC with slave labor only goes so far).

HAND-MADE UNMARKED - poor quality.

	$400	$360	$330	$300	$275	$250	$225

ASIATIC FLATSIDE UNMARKED - better quality, not exceedingly rare.

	$1,200	$950	$740	$680	$600	$500	$400

TAKU-NAVAL DOCKYARD FLATSIDE - machine-made, better quality, not exceedingly rare, approx. 6,000 mfg.

	$1,750	$1,200	$800	$700	$600	$500	$400

Add 30% with correct stock.

Add 5% if with holster.

SHANSEI ARSENAL .45 CAL. - .45 ACP cal., approx. 8,500 mfg., scarce and desirable in excellent condition, as most remaining original pistols are in rough condition, original stripper clips for this model are rare.

	N/A	$4,500	$3,500	$2,500	$2,000	$1,600	$1,475

Recently, a small number of currently manufactured pistols have been marketed as "restorations." Buyer beware! These newly made guns are currently priced in the $1,000-$1,500 range. Also, fake stocks have recently surfaced.

GRADING - PPGS™	100%	98%	95%	90%	80%	70%	60%

Broomhandles: Spanish Copies

VERY EARLY ASTRA-900 - Bolo grips, frame has single-line address, approx. 1,200 mfg.

	$3,500	$2,750	$2,200	$2,000	$1,750	$1,600	$1,475

EARLY ASTRA-900 - single-line address, approx. ser. range 1,200-12,000.

	$3,000	$2,200	$1,500	$1,100	$800	$625	$500

LATE ASTRA-900 - two and three-line address, two-line address ser. range is approx. 12,000-20,000, three-line address ser. range is approx. 20,000-34,400.

	$2,750	$1,850	$1,350	$850	$700	$525	$425

Add 20% for Japanese character variation in the 27,000 serial range or if in Nazi procurement range.

ROYAL SEMI-AUTO - early Royals are mostly seen in semi-auto with round bolts.

	$3,000	$2,450	$1,900	$1,300	$850	$700	$600

There were many variations of the Royals and values assume standard variation.

ROYAL SELECTIVE FIRE - 7.63mm cal., most of approx. 25,000 Royals manufactured were selective fire, several variations, Class III transferable only.

Class III	$2,500	$2,200	$2,000	$1,800	$1,700	$1,600	$1,475

Add 20% if detachable mag.

Add 400% if MM34 with pneumatic rate retarder (production under 1,000 pistols).

This model had either a fixed mag. or detachable mag. May have been fit with pneumatic rate retarder.

RIFLES: BOLT ACTION, MILITARY PRODUCTION

Subtract 30% if bolt is not matching or contract crests have been removed.
Add 20%-25% if with matching bayonet.

ARGENTINA

	100%	98%	95%	90%	80%	70%	60%
Model 1891 Rifle Argentine pattern	$750	$600	$550	$400	$300	$200	$150
Model 1891 Carbine	$600	$550	$500	$400	$300	$200	$150
Model 1909 Rifle	$700	$650	$600	$500	$425	$350	$250
Model 1909 Sniper Rifle w/scope	$1,800	$1,600	$1,500	$1,300	$1,200	$1,000	$900
Model 1909 Cavalry Carbine	$600	$575	$500	$450	$400	$300	$200
Model 1909 Mountain Carbine	$600	$575	$500	$450	$400	$300	$200
FN Mle 24 Short Rifle	$550	$500	$450	$400	$300	$200	$150
FN Mle 30 Short Rifle	$550	$500	$450	$400	$300	$200	$150
Model 1933 Mauser Banner	$600	$575	$500	$450	$400	$300	$200
Model 1935 Mauser Banner	$600	$575	$500	$450	$400	$300	$200

AUSTRIA

	100%	98%	95%	90%	80%	70%	60%
Model 1914 Rifle	N/A	N/A	$1,500	$1,300	$1,100	$700	$500

BELGIUM

	100%	98%	95%	90%	80%	70%	60%
Model 1889 Rifle FN mfg.	$950	$800	$750	$600	$400	$400	$350
Model 1889 Rifle Hopkins & Allen	$750	$650	$550	$450	$325	$300	$250
Model 1889 Carbine (pre-WWI)	$600	$550	$500	$375	$275	$225	$200
Model 1889 Carbine (lightened)	$700	$650	$600	$475	$350	$300	$275
Model 1916 Carbine (all WWI makes)	$500	$475	$425	$325	$250	$200	$175
Model 1935 Short Rifle (FN receiver)	$550	$475	$400	$350	$300	$225	$175
Model 1935 Short Rifle (other receiver)	$500	$425	$350	$300	$250	$200	$125
Model 1889/36 Short Rifle (FN receiver)	$550	$475	$400	$350	$300	$200	$150

GRADING - PPGS™	100%	98%	95%	90%	80%	70%	60%
Model 1889/36 Short Rifle							
(other receiver)	$500	$425	$350	$300	$250	$150	$125
Model 50 "L" Crest	$550	$475	$400	$325	$275	$175	$150
Model 50 "B" Crest	$450	$400	$375	$300	$200	$150	$125
Model 50 Belgian Congo "FP" Crest	$700	$600	$500	$400	$350	$200	$175
Model 50 .22 cal. single shot trainer	$550	$500	$450	$375	$325	$250	$200

BOLIVIA

	100%	98%	95%	90%	80%	70%	60%
Model 1895 Rifle							
(Argentine M1891 Rifle)	$600	$550	$450	$350	$225	$175	$100
Model 1907 Rifle	$700	$600	$500	$350	$250	$150	$100
Model 1907 Short Rifle	$700	$600	$500	$350	$250	$150	$100
Czech marked Model VZ							
24 Short Rifle	$700	$600	$500	$300	$225	$150	$100
Standard Model Mauser							
Banner Short Rifle	$600	$500	$450	$350	$250	$175	$100
Model 1950 Rifle Series B-50	$600	$525	$450	$350	$250	$175	$100

BRAZIL

	100%	98%	95%	90%	80%	70%	60%
Model 1894 Rifle	$800	$650	$500	$400	$325	$250	$200
Model 1894 Carbine	$600	$500	$400	$300	$225	$175	$100
Model 1904 Mauser Vergueiro Rifle	$600	$500	$400	$300	$225	$175	$100
Model 1907 Rifle	$600	$500	$400	$300	$225	$175	$100
Model 1907 Carbine	$600	$500	$400	$300	$200	$175	$100
Model 1908 Rifle	$800	$700	$600	$500	$400	$200	$100
Model 1908 Short Rifle	$600	$550	$450	$375	$250	$150	$100
Model 1922 Carbine	$600	$425	$250	$175	$125	$80	$70
Model 1924 VZ 24 Carbine	$700	$550	$450	$375	$250	$150	$100
Model 1924/34 Czech Carbine	$700	$550	$450	$375	$250	$150	$100
Model 1908/34 Rifle .30-06 cal.	$700	$550	$450	$375	$250	$150	$100
Model 1935 Mauser Banner Rifle	$1,000	$950	$850	$700	$600	$300	$200
Model 1935 Mauser Banner Carbine	$1,000	$950	$850	$700	$600	$300	$200
Model M954 Rifle .30-06 cal.	$700	$550	$425	$400	$300	$200	$100

CHILE

	100%	98%	95%	90%	80%	70%	60%
Model 1893 Rifle -							
Bent bolt handle	$600	$550	$475	$350	$250	$175	$100
Model 1895 Rifle - Army	$525	$425	$240	$200	$140	$115	$90
Model 1895 Rifle - Anchor crest	$525	$425	$240	$200	$140	$120	$100
Model 1895 Short Rifle	$550	$450	$275	$200	$140	$120	$95
Model 1895 Carbine	$500	$425	$265	$220	$180	$150	$100
Model 1912 Rifle	$650	$500	$350	$225	$160	$120	$100
Model 1912 Rifle (7.62 NATO)	$650	$500	$350	$225	$160	$120	$100
Model 1912 Short Rifle	$650	$500	$350	$225	$160	$120	$100
Model 1912 Short Rifle (7.62 NATO)	$650	$500	$350	$225	$160	$120	$100
Model 1935 Carbine (7.62 NATO)	$525	$425	$285	$225	$160	$120	$100
Mauser Banner	$900	$800	$675	$600	$500	$300	$200

CHINA

	100%	98%	95%	90%	80%	70%	60%
Gew 1871 Rifle - Chinese marked	$800	$650	$500	$400	$290	$275	$250
Kar 1871 Carbine - Chinese marked	$800	$650	$500	$400	$300	$275	$250
Kar 98a Carbine	$700	$600	$500	$390	$300	$275	$250
Model 1907 Rifle - China contract	$900	$800	$650	$500	$300	$275	$250
Model 1907 Carbine	$900	$800	$650	$500	$300	$275	$250
Model 98/22 Rifle	$650	$500	$400	$300	$260	$225	$195

GRADING - PPGS™	100%	98%	95%	90%	80%	70%	60%
Model 24/30 FN Short Rifles	$600	$500	$350	$190	$160	$125	$90
Model 21 Chinese-made VZ 24	$500	$425	$325	$300	$250	$195	$160
Std. Modell 1933 Mauser Banner Rifle	$800	$700	$550	$400	$300	$225	$120
Std. Model 1933 Mauser Banner Carbine	$800	$700	$550	$400	$300	$225	$120
Chiang Kai-Shek Rifle - Chinese copy	$700	$600	$450	$250	$160	$100	$80
Chinese VZ 24 P prefix - "1937" SH. Rifle	$600	$450	$350	$225	$175	$140	$110
Chinese copy VZ 24 w/Jap. folding byt.	$900	$750	$650	$500	$400	$300	$275

COLOMBIA

	100%	98%	95%	90%	80%	70%	60%
Model 1891 Rifle - Argentine pattern	$600	$500	$350	$180	$160	$120	$95
Model 1912 Rifle - Steyr	$600	$475	$350	$225	$185	$150	$120
Model 1912 Short Rifle - Steyr	$600	$490	$375	$275	$220	$180	$150
Model 24 FN Short Rifle	$600	$500	$350	$160	$125	$90	$65
Model 30 FN Short Rifle	$600	$500	$350	$160	$125	$90	$865
Model VZ 24 Short Rifle	$600	$500	$350	$200	$160	$110	$90
Model 29 Short Rifle - Steyr	$750	$650	$500	$350	$225	$175	$120
Model 1950 Rifle - FN .30-06 cal.	$600	$450	$350	$200	$160	$120	$100

COSTA RICA

	100%	98%	95%	90%	80%	70%	60%
Model 1895 Rifle	$700	$600	$400	$300	$140	$110	$90
Model 1910 Rifle	$700	$600	$400	$300	$225	$180	$90
Model 24 FN Short Rifle	$600	$500	$400	$300	$175	$110	$95

CZECHOSLOVAKIA

	100%	98%	95%	90%	80%	70%	60%
Model 1919 Mauser - Jelen Rifle	N/A	N/A	$3,500	$3,000	$2,500	$1,800	$1,600
Model 1921 Mauser - Jelen Rifle	N/A	N/A	$3,000	$2,600	$2,200	$1,800	$1,600
Model 98/22 Rifle	$500	$375	$320	$295	$220	$150	$90
Model VZ 23 Short Rifle	$500	$375	$320	$280	$210	$160	$120
Model VZ 23A Short Rifle	$500	$375	$320	$280	$210	$160	$120
Model VZ 24 Short Rifle	$500	$350	$275	$180	$135	$90	$70
Model 98/29 Rifle	$600	$475	$325	$270	$200	$140	$100
Model VZ 08/33 Carbine	$600	$550	$450	$300	$200	$125	$80
Model VZ 12/33 Carbine - light VZ 24	$600	$550	$450	$300	$200	$150	$90
Model VZ 16/33	$700	$650	$450	$350	$300	$225	$145
Model "JC" Short Rifle	$700	$575	$450	$400	$350	$300	$250
Model "L" SH. Rifle cal., .303, Lithuania	N/A	$1,500	$1,200	$900	$675	$600	$550

DOMINICAN REPUBLIC

	100%	98%	95%	90%	80%	70%	60%
M1953 Rifle - Ex-Brazil M1908	$600	$475	$275	$190	$125	$90	$70
M1953 SH. Rifle - Ex-Brazil M1908 SHR.	$600	$475	$275	$190	$125	$90	$70

ECUADOR

	100%	98%	95%	90%	80%	70%	60%
Model 71/84 Rifle	$600	$475	$275	$180	$125	$80	$50
Model 1891 Rifle - Argentine pattern	$500	$425	$270	$220	$180	$130	$80
Model 1907 Rifle	$500	$425	$325	$275	$250	$195	$150
Model VZ 23 Short Rifle	$500	$425	$340	$290	$250	$190	$150
Model VZ 24 Short Rifle	$500	$425	$300	$250	$180	$135	$90

GRADING - PPGS™	100%	98%	95%	90%	80%	70%	60%
Model VZ 12/33 Carbine	$500	$425	$290	$200	$175	$100	$80
Model 24/30 FN Short Rifle	$500	$425	$230	$160	$125	$90	$65
EL SALVADOR							
Model 1895 Rifle - Chilean pattern	$500	$425	$225	$180	$140	$110	$90
Model VZ 12/33 Carbine	$500	$425	$330	$260	$200	$100	$80
Standard Model 1935 Export	$500	$425	$325	$290	$250	$195	$150
FN M50 Israeli Short Rifle	$500	$425	$320	$260	$200	$125	$90
ESTONIA							
Czech Model "L"							
Short Rifle - .303 cal.	N/A	$1,200	$900	$775	$675	$600	$550
ETHIOPIA							
Model 24 FN Short Rifle	N/A	N/A	$1,100	$850	$750	$650	$550
Model 24 FN Carbine	N/A	N/A	$1,200	$900	$800	$700	$600
Model 1933 Standard Model Rifle	$1,100	$900	$800	$600	$500	$450	$350
svwMB | ☆ **FRANCE**							
Modified 98K							
Carbine - Hex. stacking rod	$600	$500	$400	$325	$250	$200	$100
GERMANY							
Model 1871 Rifle - Gew 71	$1,150	$950	$850	$750	$600	$400	$295
Model 1871 Carbine - Kar 71	$1,150	$975	$900	$825	$750	$600	$295
Model 1871 Short Rifle - Jaeger 71	$1,300	$1,100	$900	$800	$750	$600	$295
Model 1871/84 Rifle	$1,000	$875	$700	$550	$425	$275	$150
Model 1888 Commission Rifle	$800	$650	$400	$300	$250	$150	$70
Model 1888/05 Commission Rifle	$800	$650	$400	$300	$225	$125	$70
Model 1888/14 Commission Rifle	$800	$650	$400	$300	$225	$125	$70
Model 1888 Commission Carbine	$800	$650	$400	$300	$225	$175	$140
Model 1891 Comm.							
Carbine w/stacking hook	$800	$650	$400	$300	$225	$175	$140
Model 1888/97 Rifle	N/A	N/A	N/A	$5,000	$4,500	$3,200	$2,800
Model 1898 Rifle - Gew 98	$850	$725	$650	$500	$350	$225	$100
Model 1898 Carbine -							
Kar. 98, 16.9 in. bbl.	N/A	$6,000	$4,500	$4,000	$3,500	$3,200	$2,800
Model 1898/17 RifleExp.	N/A	N/A	N/A	$4,500	$4,000	$3,200	$2,800
Model 1898/18 RifleExp.	N/A	N/A	N/A	$4,500	$4,000	$3,200	$2,800
Model 1909 Self Loading Carbine	N/A	$7,000	$5,000	$4,500	$4,200	$3,800	$3,500
Model 1898A Carbine	$775	$675	$500	$400	$290	$150	$100
Model 1898AZ Carbine							
(also Model 98a)	$775	$675	$500	$400	$290	$150	$100
Model 1898b Carbine	$975	$850	$675	$500	$350	$290	$175
Model Gew. 98 (Transitional)	$700	$575	$450	$300	$250	$180	$130
Model K98k Carbine							
(1936-45, coded mfg.)	$875	$775	$650	$400	$350	$290	$175
Model K98k, Para-troop model	$3,000	$2,800	$2,400	$1,800	$1,200	$800	$700
Model K98k "Kriegsmodell"	$600	$525	$400	$295	$195	$140	$110
Model 33/40 Carbine ("945" 1940)	$1,200	$1,000	$900	$700	$650	$500	$450
Model 33/40 Carbine							
("DOT" 1941-43)	$1,200	$1,000	$900	$700	$650	$500	$400
Model 24 (T) Rifle	$700	$575	$450	$350	$275	$200	$175
Model 98/40	$700	$575	$500	$400	$300	$200	$175
Model 29 (0) Rifle L/W issue	$950	$850	$750	$675	$550	$500	$460
Model VG-1	N/A	NA/	N/A	$1,000	$950	$850	$500
G 43 Semiautomatic Rifle	$2,250	$1,800	$1,500	$1,200	$1,000	$850	$750
G 43 Sniper Rifle	$5,500	$4,750	$4,250	$3,650	$3,100	$2,650	$2,250
G 41M Semiautomatic Rifle	$5,500	$4,500	$3,750	$3,250	$2,600	$2,300	$2,000
G 41W Semiautomatic Rifle	$5,000	$4,250	$3,250	$2,750	$2,100	$1,800	$1,500

GRADING - PPGS™	100%	98%	95%	90%	80%	70%	60%
GREECE							
Model 1930 FN Short Rifle	$600	$500	$375	$290	$200	$150	$90
GUATEMALA							
Czech VZ 24 Short Rifle	$725	$600	$500	$325	$190	$135	$90
M1895 Rifle	$500	$425	$275	$200	$150	$110	$80
HAITI							
Model 1930 FN Short Rifle	$650	$500	$400	$275	$200	$125	$90
IRAN (PERSIA)							
Model 1895 Rifle	$600	$500	$410	$300	$220	$150	$90
Model 98/29 Rifle	$900	$750	$600	$475	$380	$300	$200
Model 98/29 Short Rifle	$900	$750	$600	$475	$380	$300	$200
MVZ 24 Short Rifle	$900	$750	$600	$450	$375	$275	$200
Model 49 Carbine	$800	$700	$550	$420	$310	$250	$175
IRAQ							
Model 1948 98k Carbine	$500	$400	$350	$280	$225	$185	$90
ISRAEL							
German 98k with Israeli marks	$600	$500	$400	$300	$200	$150	$90
Czech 98k w/ large triggerguard	$600	$500	$400	$275	$210	$120	$90
Model 1950 Short Rifle FN mfg.	$600	$500	$400	$295	$250	$150	$100
Model 1954 Short Rifle	$625	$525	$380	$325	$250	$180	$130
Model 50 FN .22 cal. single shot trainer	$550	$500	$450	$375	$325	$250	$200
LATVIA							
Czech VZ 24 Short Rifle	$800	$700	$630	$550	$275	$225	$160
LIBERIA							
Model 24 FN Short Rifle	N/A	N/A	$395	$325	$275	$225	$160
LITHUANIA							
Czech "L" Model Short Rifle (.303)	N/A	N/A	$900	$750	$700	$550	$500
Model VZ 24 Short Rifle	N/A	N/A	$800	$725	$600	$495	$425
Model 30 FN Short Rifle	N/A	N/A	$1,100	$850	$700	$600	$500
Model 1900 Rifle	$700	$600	$495	$450	$395	$325	$275
MANCHURIA							
Mukden Arsenal Rifle	$1,500	$1,400	$1,200	$1,000	$850	$700	$400
MEXICO							
Model 1895 Rifle	$500	$450	$225	$190	$145	$110	$60
Model 1895 Carbine	$500	$450	$225	$190	$145	$110	$60

GRADING - PPGS™	100%	98%	95%	90%	80%	70%	60%
Model 1902 Rifle	$1,400	$1,200	$1,000	$800	$500	$250	$85
Model 1907 Rifle	$500	$425	$250	$210	$145	$115	$90
Model 1910 Rifle	$500	$425	$250	$200	$140	$110	$85
Model 1910 Carbine	$500	$425	$250	$200	$140	$110	$85
Model 1912 Rifle	$600	$500	$400	$300	$200	$110	$85
Model 1912 Short Rifle	$600	$500	$400	$300	$200	$110	$85
Model 1924 FN Short Rifle	$600	$475	$250	$185	$125	$100	$80
Model 1924 Carbine	$600	$475	$250	$190	$145	$110	$85
Model 1936 Short Rifle	$600	$475	$325	$275	$200	$150	$80
Model 1954 Short Rifle	$500	$425	$325	$275	$200	$150	$80

MOROCCO

	100%	98%	95%	90%	80%	70%	60%
Model 1950 FN Carbine (.308 Win. or .30-06)	$600	$500	$425	$350	$300	$250	$200

NETHERLANDS

	100%	98%	95%	90%	80%	70%	60%
Model 1950 Carbine "W" Wilhelmina crest	$600	$500	$425	$375	$350	$300	$275
Model 1950 Carbine "J" Juliana crest	$700	$600	$450	$400	$375	$325	$300

NICARAGUA

	100%	98%	95%	90%	80%	70%	60%
Model VZ 12/33 Short Rifle	$700	$600	$375	$295	$220	$120	$100
Model VZ 24 Short Rifle	$550	$450	$350	$295	$225	$190	$150

ORANGE FREE STATE

	100%	98%	95%	90%	80%	70%	60%
Model 1896 Rifle (OVS marked), DWM	$1,100	$950	$800	$600	$300	$175	$125
Model 1896 Rifle (OVS marked), Loewe & Sons	$1,100	$950	$750	$600	$300	$175	$125
Model 1896 Rifle, Chile overmark	$700	$500	$350	$280	$210	$175	$125
Model 1895 Short Rifle	$700	$500	$350	$280	$210	$175	$125
Model 1895 Carbine	$700	$550	$350	$280	$210	$175	$125

PARAGUAY

	100%	98%	95%	90%	80%	70%	60%
Model 1895 Rifle	$500	$425	$295	$210	$160	$110	$90
Model 1907 Rifle (DWM)	$600	$475	$400	$350	$250	$125	$90
Model 1907 Carbine (Full-stocked)	$600	$475	$425	$375	$275	$150	$120
Model 1927 Rifle (Oviedo)	$500	$425	$230	$195	$150	$90	$75
Model 1927 Short Rifle	$500	$425	$230	$195	$150	$90	$75
Model 1927 Carbine (Full-stocked)	$500	$425	$325	$220	$185	$140	$100
Model 1933 Standard Model Rifle	$550	$450	$380	$320	$230	$120	$95
M24 "Model 1935" FN Short Rifle	$550	$450	$380	$320	$230	$125	$100

PERU

	100%	98%	95%	90%	80%	70%	60%
Model 1891 Rifle (Lange sight)	$500	$425	$300	$250	$175	$100	$60
Model 1891 Carbine (Lange sight)	$500	$425	$300	$250	$175	$100	$60
Model 1909 Rifle	$1,000	$875	$825	$750	$290	$195	$120
Model VZ 24 Short Rifle (Model 32)	$600	$500	$400	$290	$195	$150	$125
Model VZ 32 Short Rifle (Model 32)	$575	$450	$400	$320	$250	$150	$125
Model 1935 FN Short Rifle (7.65mm/.30-06)	$600	$500	$425	$350	$250	$150	$120

GRADING - PPGS™	100%	98%	95%	90%	80%	70%	60%
POLAND							
Model 1898 Rifle	$600	$500	$420	$340	$280	$200	$150
Model 1898 Carbine (Kar 98a)	$600	$500	$320	$250	$190	$120	$80
Model 1929 Short Rifle (Wz 29)	$700	$600	$550	$450	$300	$200	$125
PORTUGAL							
Model 1904 Mauser-Verguiero Rifle	$700	$600	$520	$420	$300	$200	$100
Model 1937 Short Rifle	$600	$500	$350	$295	$220	$160	$110
Model 937a Short Rifle	$700	$600	$450	$395	$360	$280	$150
Model 1941 Short Rifle	$700	$600	$550	$480	$390	$300	$200
ROMANIA							
Model VZ 24 Short Rifle, "M" or "C" Crest	$700	$600	$540	$420	$300	$180	$120
SAUDI ARABIA							
Model 1950 FN Short Rifle	N/A	$500	$450	$400	$375	$325	$275
SERBIA							
Model 1878/80 Rifle	$1,400	$1,200	$1,000	$850	$600	$400	$250
Model 1885 Cavalry Carbine	$1,150	$1,100	$1,000	$850	$600	$400	$250
Models 1886/6C and 1880/7C	$1,200	$1,100	$1,000	$850	$350	$280	$225
Model 1899 Rifle	$650	$550	$475	$390	$275	$200	$110
Model 1889/07 Rifle	$600	$525	$430	$325	$250	$125	$90
Model 1899/08 Rifle	$600	$525	$430	$325	$250	$125	$90
Model 1899C Short Rifle	$600	$525	$430	$325	$250	$125	$80
Model 1899/08 Carbine	$700	$600	$540	$450	$350	$280	$150
Model 1910 Rifle	$525	$450	$390	$300	$225	$160	$125
SIAM (THAILAND)							
Model 1902 Rifle (Type 45)	$550	$450	$400	$360	$270	$175	$100
Model 1923 Short Rifle (Type 66)	$550	$450	$400	$360	$270	$175	$100
SLOVAK REPUBLIC							
Model VZ 24 Short Rifle	$775	$675	$600	$500	$375	$300	$180
SOUTH AFRICAN REPUBLIC							
Model 1896 Rifle "ZAR" marked	N/A	$600	$475	$400	$300	$195	$150
SPAIN							
Model 1891 Rifle	$700	$600	$500	$400	$290	$195	$100
Model 1892 Rifle	$1,150	$950	$800	$650	$500	$350	$200
Model 1892 Carbine	$600	$500	$425	$360	$290	$185	$120
Model 1893 Rifle	$500	$425	$350	$300	$240	$175	$110
Model 1895 Carbine (Full-stocked)	$550	$450	$380	$300	$195	$110	$80
Model 1916 Short Rifle	$500	$425	$220	$180	$140	$115	$95
Model 1943 Short Rifle	$500	$425	$350	$285	$190	$130	$95

GRADING - PPGS™	100%	98%	95%	90%	80%	70%	60%
SWEDEN							
Model 1894 Carbine	$700	$600	$550	$420	$360	$190	$120
Model 1896 Rifle	$500	$425	$340	$300	$220	$185	$120
Model 1938 Short Rifle	$500	$400	$220	$190	$130	$100	$80
Model 1940 Short Rifle (8mm)	$700	$600	$500	$450	$375	$325	$275
SYRIA							
Model 1948 Carbine	$500	$425	$340	$290	$190	$120	$80
TURKEY							
Model 1887 Rifle	$1,400	$1,200	$1,000	$750	$600	$375	$250
Model 1887 Carbine	$1,400	$1,200	$1,000	$750	$600	$375	$250
Model 1890 Rifle	$900	$850	$700	$600	$450	$380	$290
Model 1893 Rifle	$1,200	$1,000	$850	$700	$600	$450	$300
Model 1903 Rifle 7.65mm	$1,000	$700	$650	$600	$450	$380	$200
Model 1905 Carbine	$1,200	$1,050	$900	$700	$600	$400	$225
Model VZ 98/22 Rifle	$550	$450	$380	$300	$200	$140	$90
Model 1888 Rifle (Turkish marked)	$500	$425	$250	$200	$150	$110	$70
Model 1888/38 Rifle (improved)	$500	$425	$250	$200	$150	$110	$70
Model 1938 Rifle 8mm	$500	$425	$250	$200	$150	$90	$60
Model 1938 Short Rifle	$500	$425	$250	$200	$150	$90	$60
URUGUAY							
Model 1895 Rifle	$700	$600	$425	$375	$295	$125	$95
Model 1904 Rifle	$675	$600	$450	$395	$325	$260	$210
Model 1908 Rifle	$700	$600	$500	$450	$400	$300	$250
Model 1980 Short Rifle	$700	$600	$500	$450	$400	$300	$250
Czech VZ 32 Short Rifle (Model 1934)	$700	$600	$500	$400	$290	$200	$120
Czech VZ 24 Short Rifle (Model 1934)	$700	$600	$550	$500	$390	$300	$260
Mle 24 FN Short Rifle	$500	$425	$350	$280	$225	$175	$120
VENEZUELA							
Model 1910 Rifle	$500	$425	$350	$290	$240	$130	$90
Czech VZ 24/26 Short Rifle	$600	$500	$440	$385	$300	$250	$180
Mle 24/30 FN Short Rifle	$900	$800	$700	$625	$475	$385	$275
Mle 24/30 FN Carbine	$800	$700	$650	$625	$475	$385	$275
YEMEN							
Mle 30 Short Rifle (Markings unknown)	N/A	N/A	$400	$375	$300	$250	$190
YUGOSLAVIA							
M90T Short Rifle (ex-Turkish M1890)	N/A	$600	$500	$400	$325	$275	$190
Model M24B Rifle (ex-Mexican M1912)	N/A	$600	$500	$390	$300	$250	$200
Mle 22 FN Short Rifle	$650	$600	$500	$400	$350	$250	$200
Mle 24 FN Short Rifle	$550	$450	$390	$300	$200	$150	$120

GRADING - PPGS™	100%	98%	95%	90%	80%	70%	60%
Czech VZ 24 Short Rifle	$600	$500	$450	$360	$250	$160	$135
Model 1924 Short Rifle							
(Kragujevac)	$600	$500	$450	$380	$300	$220	$150
Model 30 FN Short Rifle	$550	$450	$390	$310	$240	$190	$130
Model 30 FN Carbine	$550	$450	$390	$310	$240	$190	$130
M24B Carbine	$800	$650	$550	$400	$300	$250	$200

RIFLES: BOLT ACTION, 1898-1946 COMMERCIAL MFG.

Approx. 125,000 commercial sporting Mausers were built between 1898 and 1946. Three action lengths; overall measurements: Short (Kurz) 8 1/4 in., Standard 8 3/4 in., and Magnum 9 1/4 in. Optional squarebridge receiver rings for custom sight mounting. Innumerable variations of triggers, barrels, sights and checkering.

Add $350-$550 for conversion unit.

Add 50% for single square bridge action.

Add 100% for double square bridge action.

Add 100% for Short (Kurz) action, except on Type K below.

Add 100% for Magnum action, except on African Type below.

SPECIAL RIFLE, TYPE A - expressly made for English market, superior finish, with round tapered barrel, silver-bead front sight on sleeved-on block with matted surface, hinged floorplate, pear shaped bolt knob, horn forend tip and PG cap, sling eyes.

$4,000	$3,500	$3,000	$2,000	$1,100	$750	$575

NORMAL RIFLE, TYPE B - 24 in. barrel, steel-capped PG, Schnabel forend, sling swivels, pear shaped bolt knob, hinged floorplate.

$2,750	$2,400	$1,650	$1,300	$900	$700	$500

LIGHT SHORT RIFLE, TYPE K - 6.5x54 Mauser, 8x51mm, or .250-3000 Savage cal., short action, 22 in. barrel, steel PG cap, sling swivels, pear shaped bolt knob, hinged floorplate, hard rubber buttplate.

$4,250	$3,675	$3,100	$2,550	$1,500	$1,250	$1,250

CARBINE, TYPE S - 20 or 24 in. barrel stocked to muzzle, steel PG cap, horn buttplate, sling swivels, pear shaped bolt knob, hinged floorplate.

$3,750	$2,875	$2,200	$1,650	$1,100	$750	$575

CARBINE, TYPE M - 20 in. barrel stocked to muzzle with steel forend cap, steel PG cap, trapdoor steel buttplate holding sectional cleaning rod, butterknife bolt handle, hinged floorplate.

$3,750	$2,875	$2,200	$1,650	$1,100	$750	$575

MILITARY SPORTING RIFLE, TYPE C - stepped round barrel, round bolt knob, half grip, banner Mauser imprint in side of buttstock.

$750	$600	$500	$450	$400	$350	$295

AFRICAN TYPE - 28 in. round barrel, stocked to 4 in. from muzzle, Magnum action, pear shaped bolt knob.

$5,000	$4,000	$3,000	$2,500	$2,250	$2,000	$2,000

RIFLES: BOLT ACTION, RECENT PRODUCTION

During April, 2001, SIG-Blaser completed the purchase of the production and distribution rights for Mauser sporting and hunting weapons.

Add $150 for double set triggers on all current models.

MODEL 03 - various cals. between .222 Rem. - .375 H&H, Mauser square bridge action with safety/cocking lever on rear of breech bolt, interchangeable barrels, manual cocking, Combi-trigger can be used as single stage or set trigger, choice of stock wood, 60 degree bolt lift, detachable mag., open sights standard, Mauser double square bridge scope mount, approx. 7.75 lbs. New 2005. Mfg. by Blaser in Isny, Germany.

MSR $2,995	$2,750	$2,400	$2,100	$1,800	$1,500	$1,275	$1,050

GRADING - PPGS™	100%	98%	95%	90%	80%	70%	60%

Add $200 for Mag. cals.

Add $1,000 for Arabesque grade with engraving.

Add $2,500 for Deluxe grade with elaborate engraving with animal motifs.

Add $400 for match grade rifle.

Add $1,200 for match rifle in Africa grade.

Add $800 per interchangeable standard cal. barrel, or $1,400 per Mag. cal. barrel.

MODEL 66A
similar to Model 66S except has American configured laminate stock (wood grain), cals., action, and features are the same as the Model 66S. Imported 1988-89 only.

* **Standard Calibers**

	$1,900	$1,425	$1,150	$925	$800	$700	$650

Last MSR was $2,100.

Add $630 per interchangeable barrel.

The "A" suffix on this model denotes American.

* **Magnum Calibers** - includes Weatherby Mag. cals. also.

	$2,050	$1,500	$1,200	$975	$825	$700	$650

Last MSR was $2,270.

Add $670 per interchangeable barrel.

* **Big Game Calibers** - includes most popular Mag. cals. up to .458 Win. Mag.

	$2,350	$1,900	$1,425	$1,150	$950	$825	$750

Last MSR was $2,700.

MODEL 66S STANDARD
telescoping short action, 5.6x57mm, 6.5x57mm, 7x57mm Mauser (disc. 1992), 7x64mm, 9.3x62mm, .243 Win., .270 Win., .30-06, or .308 Win. cal., 24 in. barrel, standard interchangeable barrels, single or double set triggers, adj. and detachable sights, Monte Carlo walnut stock with checkering, swivels, new safety, rosewood tipped forearm and pistol grip, rubber recoil pad, 7 1/2 lbs. Mfg. 1974-95.

	$2,350	$1,275	$995	$875	$775	$695	$625

Last MSR was $2,722.

* **Model 66 Magnum** - 28 in. barrel, 6.5x68mm, 8x68S, 9.3x64mm, 7mm Rem. Mag., .300 Win. Mag., or .300 Wby. Mag. cal., 7.9 lbs. Disc. 1995.

	$2,500	$1,325	$1,050	$900	$795	$695	$625

Last MSR was $2,925.

* **Model 66 Carbine (Stutzen-Mannlicher)** - .243 Win., .270 Win., .30-06, 7x64mm, or 9.3x62mm cal., 21 in. barrel, full-stock (Mannlicher only) and half-stock (disc. in 1989), double or single triggers, 7.5 lbs. Disc. 1995.

	$2,500	$1,325	$1,050	$900	$795	$695	$625

Last MSR was $2,925.

This model was available in a half-stock "Ultra" variation until 1989. Values are similar to those listed.

* **Model 66S Diplomat** - similar cals. as the Model 66S Standard, except not available in 5.6x57mm, similar features, except includes selected walnut and special engraving including deer and wild boar game scenes. Disc. 1995.

	$4,650	$3,850	$3,350	$2,750	$2,250	$1,850	$1,400

Last MSR was $5,317.

Add $390 for Mag. cals. (similar to Model 66S Magnum).

* **Safari/Big Game Model 66** - .375 H&H or .458 Win. Mag. cal., single trigger, 9.3 lbs. Disc. 1995.

	$2,950	$1,850	$1,350	$1,025	$875	$775	$650

Last MSR was $3,487.

GRADING - PPGS™	100%	98%	95%	90%	80%	70%	60%

MODEL 66SM - telescoping short action, .243 Win. (disc.), .270 Win., 7x57mm Mauser (disc.), 7x64mm, .308 Win., .30-06, or 6.5x57mm cal. (disc.), 24 in. barrel, standard interchangeable barrels, set trigger, adj. and detachable sights, Monte Carlo walnut stock with checkering, swivels, new safety, anatomical gripped select walnut stock with Mauser-nose, cocking lever on tang, rubber recoil pad, 7 1/4 lbs. Importation 1981-95.

	$2,875	$1,800	$1,325	$1,025	$875	$775	$650

Last MSR was $3,398.

* *Model 66SM Ultra* - all standard cals., 21 in. barrel, 7 1/4 lbs.

	$1,625	$1,325	$1,140	$920	$760	$650	$550

Last MSR was $1,903.

* *Model 66SM Magnum* - cals. similar to Model 66S Magnum, except not available in 9.3x64mm cal., 26 in. barrel, 8.4 lbs. Disc. 1995.

	$3,025	$1,925	$1,375	$1,025	$875	$775	$650

Last MSR was $3,578.

* *Model 66SM Diplomat* - similar cals. as the Model 66SM Standard, similar features, except includes selected walnut and special engraving including deer and wild boar game scenes. Disc. 1995.

	$5,075	$3,975	$3,450	$2,775	$2,250	$1,850	$1,400

Last MSR was $5,943.

Add $382 for Mag. cals. (similar to Model 66SM Magnum).

* *Model 66SM Carbine (Mannlicher type full stock)* - .30-06 cal., 21 in. barrel, 7 lbs. Disc. 1995.

	$3,025	$1,925	$1,375	$1,025	$875	$775	$650

Last MSR was $3,578.

These models were previously available on a custom order only basis through KDF, Inc. located in Seguin, TX.

MODEL 66SL - similar to Model 66SM, except features extra select walnut with special graining, 7 1/4 lbs. Disc. 1985.

	$1,370	$1,275	$890	$720	$580	$475	$420

Last MSR was $1,470.

* *Model 66SL Ultra* - 7x64mm or .30-06 cal., 21 in. barrel, 7 1/4 lbs. Disc. 1985.

	$1,475	$1,325	$940	$750	$600	$450	$400

Last MSR was $1,520.

* *Magnum Calibers* - similar to Model 66 S, 8.4 lbs. Disc. 1985.

	$1,475	$1,325	$940	$750	$600	$450	$400

Last MSR was $1,520.

* *Mannlicher Type Full Stock* - 21 in. barrel, 7 lbs. Disc. 1985.

	$1,475	$1,325	$940	$750	$600	$450	$400

Last MSR was $1,520.

MODEL 66SL DIPLOMAT - same specifications as Model 66SM, except includes selected walnut and special engraving including deer and wild boar game scenes.

Add $93 for Mannlicher full-stock (21 in. barrel).

Add $387 for Mag. cals.

This model was available on an individual custom order basis only. The last published retail price (1988) for a standard model without options was $3,167.

MODEL 660 - U.S. designation of 66S. Imported 1971-73.

	$925	$820	$720	$600	$500	$450	$400

MODEL 66S DELUXE - special order engraved and inlaid, select wood. Priced per individual customer order. All guns are custom made only.

MODEL 66P - imported 1995 only.

	$4,250	$3,575	$3,075	$2,600	$2,075	$1,700	$1,375

Last MSR was $4,888.

GRADING - PPGS™	100%	98%	95%	90%	80%	70%	60%

MODEL 66SP SUPER MATCH - .300 Win. Mag. or .308 Win. cal., telescoping short action, 27 1/2 in. heavy barrel with muzzle brake, no sights, match trigger, 3 shot mag., select European walnut stock with stippling and thumbhole, adj. cheekpiece and buttplate, includes premium scope, 12 lbs. Never imported domestically.

	$4,150	$3,500	$3,050	$2,600	$2,075	$1,700	$1,375

Last MSR was $4,737.

MODEL 77 - .243 Win., .270 Win., 6.5x57mm, 7x64mm, .308 Win., or .30-06 cal., 24 in. barrel, set trigger on tang, adj. and detachable sights, walnut stock with European cheekpiece and hand checkering, swivels, new safety, steel detachable box mag., rubber recoil pad, 7 1/4 lbs. Disc.

	$1,130	$950	$875	$810	$750	$675	$595

Last MSR was $1,331.

✳ *Model 77 Ultra* - 6.5x57mm, 7x64mm or .30-06 cal., 20 in. barrel, 7.7 lbs. Disc.

	$1,175	$975	$895	$835	$760	$675	$595

Last MSR was $1,394.

✳ *Magnum Calibers* - similar to Model 66S, 8 1/8 lbs. Disc.

	$1,175	$975	$895	$835	$760	$675	$595

Last MSR was $1,394.

✳ *Mannlicher type full stock* - 20 in. barrel, Mauser-set trigger, 7.7 lbs. Disc.

	$1,175	$975	$895	$835	$760	$675	$595

Last MSR was $1,394.

✳ *Big Game Model* - .375 H&H cal., 26 in. barrel, 8 1/8 lbs. Disc.

	$1,075	$1,000	$900	$795	$675	$575	$475

Last MSR was $1,150.

MODEL 77 SPORTSMAN - .243 Win. or .308 Win. cal., sports version of the Model 77, set trigger on tang, no sights, 24 in. barrel, 9 lbs. Disc.

	$1,495	$1,230	$1,075	$985	$895	$820	$740

Last MSR was $1,754.

Add $430 for Zeiss 2 1/2-10X scope and mounts.

MODEL 83 MATCH SINGLE SHOT - .308 Win. cal. only, cylinder locking action with 3 locking lugs in rear, match trigger, anatomical match stock with select walnut, adj. comb and buttplate. Disc.

	$2,170	$1,815	$1,660	$1,545	$1,400	$1,195	$925

Last MSR was $2,594.

This model is a UIT standard rifle for 300-meter competition.

MODEL 83 MATCH UIT FREE RIFLE - .308 Win. cal. only, cylinder locking action with 3 locking lugs in rear, match trigger, anatomical match stock with select walnut, adj. comb and buttplate. Disc.

	$2,320	$1,940	$1,760	$1,600	$1,430	$1,195	$925

Last MSR was $2,771.

MODEL 83 STANDARD RIFLE - similar to Model 83 Match, except has removable 10 shot steel mag., 26 in. barrel. Disc.

	$2,320	$1,950	$1,800	$1,625	$1,460	$1,250	$1,000

Last MSR was $2,766.

MODEL 86 LAMINATED/FIBERGLASS (SR) - .308 Win. cal., updated version of the Model 83 action, 25.6 (disc.) or 28 3/4 (new 1997) in. fluted barrel with muzzle brake, black laminate wood (with thumbhole) or fiberglass (disc.) stock with rail in forearm, adj. trigger, 9 shot detachable mag., cased, 10.8 lbs. Imported 1989-1996, recent mfg. included a 2 1/2-10X power Zeiss tactical scope with detachable mount.

	$10,750	$8,900	$7,700	$6,500	$5,500	$4,500	$3,500

Last MSR was $11,795.

MODEL SR 93

- .300 Win. Mag. cal., precision rifle employing skeletonized cast magnesium/aluminum stock, combination right-hand/left-hand bolt, adj. ergonomics, 27 in. fluted barrel with muzzle brake, integrated bipod, 4 or 5 shot mag., approx. 13 lbs. without accessories. Disc. 1996.

| | $20,000 | $17,250 | $14,750 | $11,950 | $8,700 | $6,500 | $5,000 |

Last MSR was $21,995.

MODEL 94

- .243 Win., .270 Win., .30-06, .308 Win., .300 Win. Mag., 7x64mm, 7mm Rem. Mag., 8x68S (disc. 1996), 9.3x62 Mag. cal., 22 or 24 in. interchangeable barrel, aluminum block in stock bedding system, 60 degree bolt, 6 lug locking system, checkered walnut stock and forearm, 3 or 4 shot mag., lateral slide safety, approx. 7 1/4 lbs. Mfg. began 1994, U.S. importation was disc. 1995, resumed 1997 only.

| | $1,925 | $1,550 | $1,325 | $1,100 | $925 | $850 | $775 |

Last MSR was $2,295.

Add $799 per interchangeable barrel assembly.

MODEL 96

- .25-06 Rem. (new 1997), .270 Win., .30-06, .308 Win. (new 1997), 7x64mm (new 1997), .300 Win. Mag. (new 1997), or 7mm Rem. Mag. (new 1997) cal., 16 lug bolt slides straight back allowing for low scope mounts, 22 or 24 (Mag. cals., new 1997) in. barrel, safety mechanism in bolt in addition to rear 3-position tang safety, checkered walnut stock, 4 (Mag. cals., new 1997) or 5 shot top loading mag., w/o sights, 6 1/4 lbs. Imported 1996-97.

| | $625 | $550 | $500 | $450 | $400 | $360 | $330 |

Last MSR was $699.

MODEL 98 COMMERCIAL

- various cals., features original breech mechanisms refurbished to new condition, barrel, trigger system, and stock are new from factory.

This model was mostly distributed in Europe with no domestic MSR.

MODEL 1898 COMMEMORATIVE

- 8x57mm Mauser cal., special limited edition model mfg. to commemorate the 100th anniversary of the original M-98, bright royal blue on most major metal parts, bolt and receiver have silver satin finish, checkered select European walnut. 1,998 mfg. 1998 only.

| | $2,175 | $1,775 | $1,500 |

Last MSR was $2,300.

MODEL 98 STANDARD/MAGNUM SAFARI

- various cals. from .22-250 Rem-9.3x64mm, Safari cals include .375 H&H (disc. 2002, reintroduced 2004), .338 Lapua (new 2004), .416 Rigby, .450 Dakota (new 2001), .458 Lott (new 2001), or .500 Jeffrey (new 2001) cal., 3-5 shot mag., original M-98 Magnum square bridge action with 3 lugs, Model 70 style wing safety, folding express sights (Safari model only), 24 in. barrel, features custom workmanship, extra select checkered walnut stock, 8.8 lbs. Limited mfg. beginning 1998.

| MSR $12,400 | $10,800 | $9,000 | $7,750 | $5,850 | $4,500 | $3,750 | $3,000 |

Add $1,400 for Magnum Safari, or $2,400 for Magnum Safari in .500 Jeffrey.

MODEL 99

- 5.6x57mm, 6.5x57mm, 7x57mm, 7x64mm, .243 Win., .25-06 Rem., .270 Win., .30- 06 or .308 Win. cal., bolt action with 60 degree throw, 24 in. freefloating barrel, jeweled bolt, available in either hand-rubbed oil or high-luster lacquer finish for stock, mini-claw extractor, adj. single stage trigger, 4 shot detachable mag., no sights, 8 lbs. Imported 1989-disc.

❋ *Classic Lacquer Finish* - high-luster lacquer finish for stock.

| | $1,110 | $925 | $850 | $775 | $700 | $625 | $550 |

Last MSR was $1,272.

This model was available with either a Schnabel forearm with regular stock or rosewood capped forearm with American Monte Carlo stock.

❋ *Classic Oil Finish* - hand rubbed oil finish for stock. Disc.

| | $1,130 | $995 | $875 | $775 | $700 | $625 | $550 |

Last MSR was $1,130.

This model was available with either a Schnabel forearm with regular stock or rosewood capped forearm with American Monte Carlo stock.

GRADING - PPGS™	100%	98%	95%	90%	80%	70%	60%

MODEL 99 MAGNUM - 8x68S, 9.3x64mm, 7mm Rem. Mag., .257 Wby. Mag., .270 Wby. Mag., .300 Wby. Mag., .300 Win. Mag., .338 Win. Mag., or .375 H&H cal., similar specifications as Model 99, except has 26 in. barrel and 3 shot mag. Imported 1989-disc.

✳ *Classic Lacquer Finish* - high-luster lacquer finish for stock.

	$1,135	$950	$875	$775	$700	$625	$550

Last MSR was $1,322.

This model was available with either a Schnabel forearm with regular stock or rosewood capped forearm with American Monte Carlo stock.

✳ *Classic Oil Finish* - hand-rubbed oil finish for stock.

	$1,025	$895	$795	$725	$625	$550	$495

Last MSR was $1,180.

This model is available with either a Schnabel forearm with regular stock or rosewood capped forearm with American Monte Carlo stock.

MODEL 225 - available in 13 cals. between .243 Win. and .300 Wby. Mag., bolt action, 60 degree bolt lift with 3 locking lugs, ultra fast lock time, adj. trigger, 24 or 26 (Mag. only) in. barrel, 3 or 5 shot mag., no sights, guaranteed 1/2 in. accuracy at 100 yards, many stock options available at extra cost.

✳ *Deluxe Standard Sporter* - standard model available in 6 regular cals. and 9 Mag. cals. Importation disc. 1989.

	$1,275	$1,000	$875	$750	$625	$550	$495

Last MSR was $1,400.

Add $90 for Mag. cals.

This model was formerly the KDF Model K-15.

MODEL 226 - left-handed variation of the Model 225 with slight changes. Disc. 1989.

	$1,275	$1,000	$875	$750	$625	$550	$495

Last MSR was $1,400.

MODEL 2000 (DISC.) - .270 Win., .308 Win., or .30-06 cal., 5 shot mag., 24 in. barrel, leaf rear sight, checkered walnut stock. Mfg. by F.W. Heym for Mauser, 1969-71.

	$495	$475	$450	$400	$375	$350	$325

MODEL 2000 CLASSIC - .270 Win., .30-06, .308 Win., .300 Win. Mag., or 7mm Rem. Mag. cal., features new design allowing interchangeable calibers from standard to standard and Magnum to Magnum models, bolt locks directly into barrel, detachable mag., deluxe walnut stock with checkering and rosewood forend, double function set trigger, high polish blue, includes studs. Limited importation 1998 only.

	$1,595	$1,375	$1,125	$950	$825	$700	$575

Last MSR was $1,800.

✳ *Model 2000 Varmint* - .22-250 Rem. or .243 Win. cal., choice of black synthetic or special varmint wood stock with accessory rail, heavy fluted barrel. Limited importation 1998 only.

	$1,900	$1,550	$1,350	$1,100	$900	$775	$650

Last MSR was $2,200.

✳ *Model 2000 Sniper* - .300 Win. Mag. or .308 Win. cal., features heavy fluted barrel, special set trigger system, bipod rail, and other special shooting performance features, satin blue metal finish, custom built with individual certificate. Limited importation 1998 only.

	$1,900	$1,550	$1,350	$1,100	$900	$775	$650

Last MSR was $2,200.

✳ *Model 2000 Professional* - .300 Win. Mag. or .308 Win. cal., features recoil reduction compensator, camo all-weather special pistol grip stock, satin blue metal finish, custom built with individual certificate. Limited importation 1998 only.

	$3,175	$2,725	$2,400	$2,100	$1,800	$1,500	$1,250

Last MSR was $3,500.

GRADING - PPGS™	100%	98%	95%	90%	80%	70%	60%

MODEL 3000 - .243 Win., .270 Win., .308 Win., or .30-06 cal., 5 shot mag., 22 in. barrel, no sights, walnut Monte Carlo style stock, rosewood forearm and pistol grip, skipline checkering, recoil pad and swivels. Mfg. 1971-74.

	$525	$475	$450	$425	$395	$335	$285

MODEL 3000 MAGNUM - similar to 3000, except 7mm Rem. Mag., .300 Win. Mag., or .375 H&H cal., 3 shot mag., 26 in. barrel.

	$575	$525	$475	$450	$415	$350	$295

This model was mfg. by Heym for Mauser.

MODEL 4000 VARMINT RIFLE - similar to 3000, except smaller action, .222 Rem. or .223 Rem. cal., folding leaf rear sight, rubber buttplate.

	$425	$400	$375	$350	$300	$260	$225

This model was mfg. by Heym for Mauser.

LIGHTNING MODEL - .308 Win. or 7.62x39mm cal., slide-bolt action, locking bolt similar to M-16 enabling locking directly onto free floating short barrel, fixed internal mag., specially bedded receiver, satin blue finish or stainless steel, open sights, synthetic stock available in black, light grey, blue, or NATO green. Limited importation 1998 only.

	$495	$425	$375	$325	$295	$275	$250

Last MSR was $550.

LIGHTNING HUNTER MODEL - .243 Win., .270 Win., .30-06, .308 Win., .300 Win. Mag., or 7mm Rem. Mag. cal., slide-bolt mechanism, detachable mag., choice of satin blue or bright blue metal finish, checkered satin or high gloss walnut stock, with or w/o sights, free floating barrel, bedded receiver. Limited importation 1998 only.

	$650	$575	$500	$450	$400	$360	$330

Last MSR was $730.

Add $50 for open sights.
Add $20 for bright blue metal finish with high gloss stock.

✳ *Lightning Hunter Stainless Steel Model* - similar to Lightning Hunter Model, except has satin finish stainless steel receiver and barrel, checkered satin finished walnut stock. Limited importation 1998 only.

	$665	$585	$500

Last MSR was $750.

Add $50 for open sights.

LIGHTNING HUNTER ALL-WEATHER MODEL - similar to Lightning Hunter, except has black synthetic stock, satin blue metal finish, scope mounts included, with or w/o sights. Limited importation 1998 only.

	$625	$550	$475	$400	$350	$325	$295

Last MSR was $700.

Add $50 for open sights.

✳ *Lightning All-Weather Stainless Steel* - similar to Lightning Hunter All-Weather Model, except is satin stainless steel. Limited importation 1998 only.

	$650	$575	$500

Last MSR was $730.

Add $50 for open sights.

LIGHTNING VARMINT MODEL - .22-250 Rem., .243 Win., features slide-bolt action, free floating heavy fluted barrel, satin blue metal finish, choice of special varmint wood or synthetic stock. Limited importation 1998 only.

	$895	$775	$675	$600	$525	$475	$425

Last MSR was $1,000.

＊ *Lightning Varmint Model Stainless* - similar to Lightning Varmint Model, except is satin stainless steel. Limited importation 1998 only.

	$895	$775	$675				

Last MSR was $1,000.

LIGHTNING SNIPER MODEL - .300 Win. Mag. or .308 Win. cal., slide-bolt action, features free floating heavy fluted barrel w/o sights, special wood or synthetic stock with built-in bipod rail, detachable mag., satin blue metal finish. Limited importation 1998 only.

	$895	$775	$675	$600	$525	$475	$425

Last MSR was $1,000.

＊ *Lightning Sniper Model Stainless* - similar to Lightning Sniper Model, except is satin stainless steel. Limited importation 1998 only.

	$895	$775	$675				

Last MSR was $1,000.

LIGHTNING PROFESSIONAL MODEL - .300 Win. Mag. or .308 Win. cal., slide-bolt action, features special black or camo synthetic adj. stock with pistol grip, special tuned trigger system, free floating heavy fluted barrel, recoil reduction compensator. Limited importation 1998 only.

	$1,595	$1,375	$1,125	$950	$825	$700	$575

Last MSR was $1,800.

RIFLES: BOLT ACTION, .22 CAL.

MODEL 20/22 - .22 LR or .22 Mag. cal., bolt action, features free floating barrel, precision trigger, standard or deluxe checkered walnut stock with stock. Limited importation 1998 only.

	$625	$550	$475	$400	$350	$325	$295

Last MSR was $700.

Add $100 for Deluxe Model.

MODEL 107 STANDARD - .22 LR cal. only, bolt action, 19 1/2 in. barrel, 5 shot mag., adj. iron sights, 6 lbs. Imported 1988-89, reintroduced 1993 only.

	$300	$260	$215	$185	$170	$155	$140

Last MSR was $356.

This model is the same as KDF's previous Model 2107 mfg. by Voere.

＊ *Model 107 Deluxe* - .22 LR or .22 Mag. cal., similar to Model 107, except has deluxe checkered walnut. Imported 1988-89 only.

	$290	$240	$210	$175	$150	$135	$120

Last MSR was $320.

Add $90 for .22 Mag. cal.

This model is the same as KDF's previous Model 2107 Deluxe mfg. by Voere.

MODEL 201 - .22 LR or .22 Mag. cal., bolt action, free-floating 21 in. barrel, 5 shot mag., adj. trigger, scaled-down version of the K-15, unusual action incorporates two front-located locking lugs on bolt face that engage Stellite inserts on the front receiver portion, blue only, no sights, beechwood stock with cheekpiece, 6 1/2 lbs. Disc. 1997.

	$635	$515	$465	$415	$365	$315	$260

Last MSR was $716.

Add $19 for sights (disc.).
Add $77 for .22 Mag. cal. (Model 201-SM).

This model is the same as KDF's disc. Model K-22 mfg. by Voere. Before 1989, this model came standard with a walnut stock.

GRADING - PPGS™	100%	98%	95%	90%	80%	70%	60%

✹ **Model 201 Luxus** - similar to the Model 201 except has walnut stock with rosewood forend. Disc. 1997.

	$710	$650	$550	$475	$425	$375	$295

Last MSR was $809.

Add $27 for sights (disc.).
Add $67 for .22 Mag. cal.

This model is the same as KDF's previous Model K-22 Deluxe mfg. by Voere.

MODEL DSM34 - .22 LR cal., bolt action, 25.98 in. barrel. "Deutsches Sportmodell" lightweight trainer, side sling, no bayonet lug.

$625	$375	$325	$300	$260	$225	$200

MODEL MS 420B - .22 LR Sporter cal., bolt action, pre-war, 5 shot mag.

$1,425	$875	$725	$625	$525	$450	$395

Add 15%-25% for double set triggers (rare).

MODEL ES340 - .22 LR cal., single shot, bolt action, 25 1/2 in. barrel, adj. sights, checkered pistol grip, grooved forearm, pre-1935.

$725	$425	$350	$325	$295	$260	$230

MODEL ES350 - .22 LR cal., single shot, bolt action, 27 1/2 in. barrel, championship rifle, micrometer rear sight, ramp front sight, checkered full target stock, swivels, pre-1935.

$925	$550	$500	$460	$430	$400	$375

Add 15%-25% for double set triggers (rare).

MODEL M410 - .22 LR cal., bolt action, repeating, 5 shot detachable mag., 23 1/2 in. barrel, adj. sights, sporter stock, checkered pistol grip, swivels, pre-1935.

$1,425	$875	$725	$625	$525	$450	$395

Add 15%-25% for double set triggers (rare).

MODEL M420 - .22 LR cal., bolt action, repeating, 5 shot detachable mag., 25 1/2 in. barrel, adj. sights, sporter stock, checkered pistol grip, swivels, pre-1935.

$1,425	$875	$725	$625	$525	$450	$395

Add 15%-25% for double set triggers (rare).

MODEL EN310 - .22 LR cal., single shot, bolt action, 19 3/4 in. barrel, fixed sights, plain pistol grip stock, pre-1935.

$625	$365	$315	$280	$260	$225	$200

MODEL EL320 - .22 LR cal., single shot, bolt action, 23 1/2 in. barrel, fixed sights, checkered pistol grip stock.

$695	$395	$330	$295	$275	$250	$225

MODEL KKW - .22 LR cal., single shot, bolt action, target, 26 in. barrel, tangent rear sight, military style stock with bayonet lug. This weapon was also produced by Walther, Gustloff, and Anschütz. It was used as a training rifle in addition to commercial sales. Deduct 15% for 4mm KKW Models.

$625	$375	$325	$300	$260	$225	$200

MODEL MS350B - .22 LR cal., bolt action, repeating, 5 shot mag., 26 3/4 in. barrel, grooved receiver for scope or sight, micrometer rear sight, ramp front sight, target stock, checkered pistol grip and forearm, swivels.

$1,200	$725	$650	$550	$495	$450	$395

MODEL ES350B - .22 LR cal., bolt action, single shot, 5 shot mag., 26 3/4 in. barrel, grooved receiver for scope or sight, micrometer rear sight, ramp front sight, target stock, checkered pistol grip and forearm, swivels.

$750	$425	$350	$325	$295	$260	$230

GRADING - PPGS™	100%	98%	95%	90%	80%	70%	60%

MODEL ES340B - .22 LR cal., bolt action, single shot, 26 3/4 in. barrel, adj. sight, plain pistol grip stock.

	$650	$375	$325	$300	$260	$225	$200

MODEL MM410BN - .22 LR cal., bolt action sporter, 5 shot mag., 23 1/2 in. barrel, adj. sights, lightweight stock, checkered pistol grip, swivels.

	$1,295	$775	$675	$575	$475	$400	$375

MODEL MS420B - .22 LR cal., bolt action target, 5 shot mag., 26 3/4 in. barrel, adj. sights, target style stock, checkered pistol grip, swivels.

	$1,100	$650	$575	$500	$450	$400	$365

RIFLES: SEMI-AUTO, .22 LR

MODEL 105 STANDARD - .22 LR cal. only, 10 shot mag., approx. 5 lbs. Imported 1995-97.

	$285	$250	$205	$180	$170	$155	$140

Last MSR was $330.

SHOTGUNS

Mauser shotguns were sub-contracted to various European firms and were made in various O/U (including field and target), SxS (both boxlock and sidelock), and single shot configurations. While they are relatively rare (these shotguns had limited importation into the U.S. by Bauer located in Michigan - models included the 496 single shot, 496 SxS, 580 SxS, 610 O/U, 620 O/U, 71E O/U, and others), collectability to date has been minimal. Values will depend on the grade, configuration, features, engraving, and overall desirability. Most of these shotguns have been priced in the $395-$1,350 range, depending on the configuration's desirability.

MAVERICK ARMS, INC.

Currently manufactured by Maverick Arms, Inc. located in Eagle Pass, TX. Administrative offices are at O.F. Mossberg & Sons, located in North Haven, CT. Distributor sales only.

SHOTGUNS

Beginning 1992, all Maverick slide action shotguns incorporate twin slide rails in the operating mechanism.

MODEL 60 SEMI-AUTO - while advertised, this model was never manufactured.

MODEL 88 FIELD SLIDE ACTION - 12 ga. only, 3 in. chamber, slide-action, 24 (Deer Model with iron sights), 28, or 30 in. plain or VR barrel, wood (disc.) or black synthetic stock and forearm with recoil pad, fixed or Accu-chokes (disc. 1997, reintroduced 2002), 6 shot (w/ two 3/4 in. shot shells), aluminum alloy receiver, crossbolt safety, approx. 7 1/4 lbs. New 1989.

MSR $249	$195	$160	$140	$125	$115	$105	$100

  Add $14 for Deer Model (24 in. cyl. bore barrel, disc. 1996).

  Subtract 10% if w/o Accu-choke barrel.

Maverick 88 barrels are compatible with Mossberg Model 500 barrels within gauge and capacity.

✳ *Model 88 Slug* - 12 ga., 3 in. chamber, 24 in. fully rifled or cylinder bore barrel with adj. rifle sights, blue finish, black synthetic stock and forearm.

MSR $201	$165	$135	$115	$110	$105	$100	$95

  Add $20 for fully rifled barrel.

GRADING - PPGS™	100%	98%	95%	90%	80%	70%	60%

✳ *Model 88 Deer Combos* - includes various combinations of extra Deer barrels with rifle sights, 28 in. plain or VR barrel, or extra 18 1/2 in. cyl. bore barrel. Mfg. 1990-95.

	$245	$190	$160	$130	$120	$110	$105

Last MSR was $294.

Add $10 for VR barrel.

Add $17 for Accu-choke barrel.

Add $29 for wood stock and forearm (mfg. 1992 only).

✳ *Model 88 Security* - 12 ga., 18 1/2 (6 shot) or 20 (8 shot) in. barrel with cyl. bore fixed choke, regular or pistol grip (disc. 1997) synthetic stock, 6 or 8 shot, plain synthetic forearm. New 1993.

MSR $199		$165	$135	$115	$110	$105	$100	$95

Add $7 for 8 shot model with 20 in. barrel.

Add $98 for Bullpup configuration (6 or 9 shot) (disc. 1994).

Add $47-$65 for combo package (disc.).

✳ *Model 88 Combat* - 12 ga. only, combat design featuring pistol grip stock and forearm, black synthetic stock is extension of receiver, 18 1/2 in. cyl. bore barrel with vented shroud with built-in carrying handle, open sights. Mfg. 1990-92.

	$375	$335	$285	$250	$225	$200	$185

Last MSR was $282.

MODEL 91 SLIDE ACTION - 12 ga. only, 3 1/2 in. chamber, 18 1/2 cyl. bore or 28 in. VR barrel with 1 choke tube, otherwise similar to Model 88. Mfg. 1991-95.

	$230	$190	$170	$160	$150	$140	$130

Last MSR was $269.

Add $2 for VR barrel.

MODEL 95 BOLT ACTION - 12 ga. only, 3 in. chamber, synthetic stock with recoil pad, 25 in. barrel bored mod., cross-bolt triggerguard safety. Mfg. 1995-97.

	$155	$135	$115	$100	$90	$80	$70

Last MSR was $184.

McMILLAN BROS. RIFLE CO.

MᴄBRᴏS

Current manufacturer located in Phoenix, AZ since 1993.
Dealer and consumer direct sales. During 1998, the company name changed from McBros Rifles to McMillan Bros. Rifle Co.

RIFLES: BOLT ACTION

AMERICAN HUNTER - available in 16 cals. between .22-250 Rem. and .416 Rem. Mag. (disc. 1997), camoflauged fiberglass stock, match grade stainless steel barrel, choice of MCRT (Rem. Model 700 custom type action mfg. to aerospace standards) or MCR (disc., Rem. Model 700 BDL action that has been trued). New 1993.

MSR $3,400		$2,925	$2,450	$2,100	$1,825	$1,550	$1,375	$1,100

✳ *Yukon Hunter* - available in 6 Mag. cals. between .300 Wby. Mag. and .458 Win. Mag., built to aerospace tolerances for any hunting situation, barrel band sling swivel, folding leaf sight, black synthetic stock. New 1993.

MSR $3,700		$3,350	$2,800	$2,400	$2,050	$1,775	$1,500	$1,350

✳ *Outdoorsman* - .30-378 Wby. Mag., .338 Lapua (new 2004), or .338-378 Wby. Mag. (disc. 1997) cal., RT action only. New 1996.

MSR $3,700		$3,350	$2,800	$2,400	$2,050	$1,775	$1,500	$1,350

MCR TACTICAL - .308 Win. or .300 Win. Mag. cal. New 1993.

MSR $3,100		$2,700	$2,250	$1,825	$1,500	$1,250	$1,050	$925

This model was formerly designated the MCR Sniper Model.

GRADING - PPGS™	100%	98%	95%	90%	80%	70%	60%

✳ MCRT Tactical - .300 Win. Mag. or .338 Lapua (new 1998), similar to MCR Tactical. New 1993.

	100%	98%	95%	90%	80%	70%	60%
MSR $3,400	$2,925	$2,450	$2,100	$1,825	$1,550	$1,375	$1,100

Add $600 for .338 Lapua Mag (muzzle brake is standard).

This model was formerly designated the MCRT Sniper Model.

BENCHREST COMPETITOR - .222 Rem., 6mm PPC, 6mm BR, 7mm BR, or .308 Win. cal., benchrest configuration. Mfg. 1993-99.

			95%	90%	80%	70%	60%
	$2,400	$1,925	$1,575	$1,275	$1,050	$900	$775

Last MSR was $2,800.

1000 YARD BENCHREST (NATIONAL MATCH COMPETITOR) - .300 Win. Mag. (new 1996), .30-378 Wby. Mag. (new 1996), 7.82 Warbird (new 1996), .308 Win. (disc. 1995) or .338-378 Wby. Mag. (mfg. 1996-97) cal. Mfg. 1993-99.

			95%	90%	80%	70%	60%
	$2,450	$1,950	$1,575	$1,275	$1,050	$900	$775

Last MSR was $2,875.

TUBB 2000 - .243 Win., .260 Rem., 7mm-08 Rem., 6mm, or .308 Win. cal., target rifle featuring metal 4 way adj. stock, Picatinny rail, hand lapped Schneider match barrel, Anschütz 2 stage trigger, state-of-the-art action, vent. handguard, 12 lbs. New 2000.

	100%	98%	95%	90%	80%	70%	60%
MSR $3,000	$2,700	$2,375	$1,925	$1,525	$1,250	$1,025	$875

Add $300 for Tubb 2000 C (includes four 10 shot mags., cleaning rod guide, etc.).

Add $500 for Schneider custom stainless steel match barrel.

BIG MAC/BOOMER - .50 BMG cal., available as either single shot sporter, repeater sporter, light benchrest, or heavy benchrest variation. New 1993.

	100%	98%	95%	90%	80%	70%	60%
MSR $4,800	$4,250	$3,650	$3,050	$2,550	$2,125	$1,825	$1,525

Add $200 for repeating action.

Add $400 for Tactical 50 variation.

Add $100 for Tactical single shot.

Add $100 for heavy benchrest variation.

Subtract $100 for light benchrest variation.

McMILLAN, G. & CO., INC.

Previous trademark established circa 1988, located in Phoenix, AZ.

G. McMillan & Co., Inc. had various barrel markings from 1988-1995 including G. McMillan, Harris - McMillan, and Harris Gunworks.

HANDGUNS

WOLVERINE - available in 9mm Para., 10mm, .38 Super, .38 Wad Cutter, .40 S&W, .45 ACP, or .45 Italian cal., interchangeable barrels, competition ready handgun patterned after the Colt 1911. Imported 1992-95.

✳ Combat Wolverine - combat features including 5 1/2 in. compensated barrel.

	100%	98%	95%	90%	80%	70%	60%
	$1,600	$1,350	$1,025	$875	$750	$625	$550

Last MSR was $1,700.

✳ Competition Match Wolverine - competition features including 6 in. non-compensated barrel.

	100%	98%	95%	90%	80%	70%	60%
	$1,600	$1,350	$1,025	$875	$750	$625	$550

Last MSR was $1,700.

SIGNATURE JR. BOLT ACTION - available in a variety of cals., utilizes Signature benchrest short action, choice of stainless steel barrel lengths, right- or left-hand action, single shot or repeater, McMillan design fiberglass stock, choice of electroless nickel or Teflon finish, 5 lbs. Mfg. 1992-95.

	100%	98%	95%	90%	80%	70%	60%
	$2,175	$1,775	$1,350	$995	$895	$800	$700

Last MSR was $2,400.

This model was also available in all titanium.

GRADING - PPGS™	100%	98%	95%	90%	80%	70%	60%

RIFLES: BOLT ACTION

The models listed were also available with custom wood stocks at varying prices. McMillan also manufactured a custom rifle from a supplied action. Features included new barreling, a fiberglass stock, matte black finish, and range testing to guarantee 3/4 M.O.A. Prices started at $1,400.

Add $150 for stainless steel receiver on most models.

TALON SPORTER - available in various cals. between .22-250 Rem. and .416 Rem., receiver available in either 4340 chrome molybdenum or 17-4 stainless steel, drilled and tapped, match grade barrel. Mfg. 1992-95.

	$2,375	$1,950	$1,650	$1,325	$1,000	$895	$800

Last MSR was $2,600.

The Talon action was patterned after the Winchester pre-64 Model 70. It features a cone breech, controlled feed, claw extractor, and 3 position safety.

SIGNATURE CLASSIC SPORTER - various cals. available between .22-250 Rem. and .416 Rem., premium wood stock, matte metal finish, 22 or 24 in. stainless steel barrel with button rifling, McMillan action made from 4340 chrome moly steel (either left- or right-handed), 3 or 4 shot mag. supplied with 5 shot test target. Mfg. 1988-95.

	$2,250	$1,850	$1,350	$950	$850	$750	$675

Last MSR was $2,400.

SIGNATURE VARMINTER - similar to Signature Model, except is available in 10 cals. between .22-250 Rem. and .350 Rem. Mag., hand bedded fiberglass stock, adj. trigger, 26 in. heavy contour barrel. Mfg. 1988-95.

	$2,250	$1,850	$1,350	$995	$895	$800	$700

Last MSR was $2,400.

SIGNATURE TITANIUM MOUNTAIN RIFLE - .270 Win., .280 Rem., .30-06, .300 Win. Mag., .338 Win. Mag., or 7mm Rem. Mag. cal., lighter weight variation with shorter barrel. Mfg. 1990-95.

	$2,750	$2,195	$1,850	$1,450	$1,100	$925	$825

Last MSR was $3,000.

Add $605 for titanium alloy light contour match grade barrel.

SIGNATURE ALASKAN - available in 11 cals. between .270 Win. and .416 Rem. Mfg. 1990-95.

	$3,050	$2,475	$2,100	$1,575	$1,200	$1,000	$900

Last MSR was $3,300.

TALON SAFARI - available in 15 cals. between .300 Win. Mag. and .460 Weatherby, hand-bedded fiberglass stock, 4 shot mag., 24 in. stainless steel barrel, matte black finish, 9 1/2 lbs. Mfg. 1988-95.

	$3,275	$2,675	$2,300	$1,675	$1,300	$1,100	$950

Last MSR was $3,600.

Add $600 for .300 Phoenix, .338 Lapua, .378 Wby. Mag., .416 Wby. Mag. or Rigby, or .460 Wby. Mag. cal.

The Talon action was patterned after the Winchester pre-64 Model 70. It featured a cone breech, controlled feed, claw extractor, and 3-position safety. Older Signature action rifles did not have this new Talon action.

M-40 SNIPER RIFLE - .308 Win. cal., Remington action with McMillan match grade heavy contour barrel, fiberglass stock with recoil pad, 4 shot mag., 9 lbs. Mfg. 1990-95.

	$1,675	$1,375	$1,050	$895	$800	$700	$600

Last MSR was $1,800.

GRADING - PPGS™	100%	98%	95%	90%	80%	70%	60%

M-86 SNIPER RIFLE - .300 Phoenix, .30-06 (new 1989), .300 Win. Mag. or .308 Win. cal., fiberglass stock, variety of optical sights. Mfg. 1988-95.

	$1,725	$1,400	$1,075	$925	$825	$725	$625

Last MSR was $1,900.

> Add $550 for .300 Phoenix cal.
> Add $200 for takedown feature (new 1993).
> * *M-86 Sniper System* - includes Model 86 Sniper Rifle, bipod, Ultra scope, rings, and bases. Cased. Mfg. 1988-92.

	$2,460	$2,050	$1,825	$1,600	$1,350	$1,100	$950

Last MSR was $2,665.

M-87 LONG RANGE SNIPER RIFLE - .50 BMG cal., stainless steel bolt action, 29 in. barrel with muzzle brake, single shot, camo synthetic stock, accurate to 1500 meters, 21 lbs. Mfg. 1988-95.

	$3,350	$2,750	$2,350	$2,000	$1,850	$1,700	$1,575

Last MSR was $3,735.

> * *M-87 Sniper System* - includes Model 87 Sniper Rifle, bipod, 20X Ultra scope, rings, and bases. Cased. Mfg. 1988-92.

	$3,950	$3,400	$3,000	$2,750	$2,450	$2,200	$2,000

Last MSR was $4,200.

> * *M-87R* - same specs. as Model 87, except has 5 shot fixed box mag. Mfg. 1990-95.

	$3,750	$2,950	$2,550	$2,200	$2,000	$1,850	$1,700

Last MSR was $4,000.

> Add $300 for Combo option.

M-89 SNIPER RIFLE - .308 Win. cal., 28 in. barrel with suppressor (also available without), fiberglass stock adj. for length and recoil pad, 15 1/4 lbs. Mfg. 1990-95.

	$2,075	$1,675	$1,375	$1,050	$895	$800	$700

Last MSR was $2,300.

> Add $425 for muzzle suppressor.

M-92 BULLPUP - .50 BMG cal., bullpup configuration with shorter barrel. Mfg. 1993-95.

	$3,750	$2,950	$2,550	$2,200	$2,000	$1,850	$1,700

Last MSR was $4,000.

M-93SN - .50 BMG cal., similar to M-87, except has folding stock and detachable 5 or 10 shot box mag. Mfg. 1993-95.

	$3,950	$3,250	$2,750	$2,300	$2,000	$1,850	$1,700

Last MSR was $4,300.

.300 PHOENIX LONG RANGE RIFLE - .300 Phoenix cal., special fiberglass stock featuring adj. cheekpieces to accommodate night vision optics, adj. buttplate, 29 in. barrel, conventional box mag., 12 1/2 lbs. Mfg. 1992 only.

	$2,700	$2,195	$1,850	$1,450	$1,100	$925	$825

Last MSR was $3,000.

.300 Phoenix was a cartridge developed to function at ranges in excess of 800 yards. It produces muzzle velocities of 3100 ft. per second with a 250 grain bullet.

COMPETITION MODELS - available in Metallic Silhouette (.308 Win. or 7mm-08 Rem. cal. - disc. 1989), National Match (.308 Win. cal. only), Long Range (.300 Win. Mag. only), or Bench Rest (shooter's choice). Each model made specifically for individual competition events. Mfg. 1988-95.

	$2,325	$1,775	$1,450	$1,100	$895	$800	$700

Last MSR was $2,600.

> Add $200 for Benchrest Model.
> Subtract $300 for Metallic Silhouette model (disc. 1989).

GRADING - PPGS™	100%	98%	95%	90%	80%	70%	60%

MEDWELL & PERRETT LIMITED

Current long gun manufacturer located in Suffolk, England. Consumer direct sales.

Medwell & Perrett manufactures best quality bolt action and double rifles, in addition to O/U shotguns. Delivery time is approx. 6-18 months, depending on caliber and configuration.

RIFLES

MEDWELL & PERRETT BOLT ACTION - various cals. up to .505 Gibbs, Medwell & Perrett action, Timney adj. trigger, select checkered walnut stock and forend, custom order only.

MSR $9,480	$9,480	$8,600	$7,500	$6,500	$5,500	$4,500	$3,500

Add $820 for Mag. length action.
Add $2,340 for .500 Jeffrey or .505 Gibbs cal.
Add $1,770 for takedown action.

MEDWELL & PERRETT SQUARE BRIDGE BOLT ACTION - various cals. up to .505 Gibbs, square bridge action, integral telescopic mount system, barrel quarter rib, adj. trigger, deluxe checkered walnut stock and forend.

MSR $15,320	$15,320	$12,950	$9,950	$8,500	$7,250	$6,000	$5,500

Add $815 for Mag. length action.
Add $1,530 for .500 Jeffrey or .505 Gibbs cal.

DOUBLE RIFLE SxS - most cals. up to .600 NE, back action, sidelock, ejectors, reinforced bolsters, DT, 22-26 in. chopper lump barrels with folding express sights, oil finished checkered walnut stock and forearm, 8 lbs., 14 oz.-14 lbs., 4 oz.

MSR $42,000	$42,000	$38,000	$32,000	$26,500	$21,000	$16,000	$12,000

Add $525 for detachable sidelocks.
Add $3,750 for cals over .375 H&H - .470 NE.
Add $9,180 for cals. over .470 NE - .577 NE.
Add $12,500 for .600 NE cal.

SHOTGUNS

O/U SIDELOCK - 12, 16, 20, 28 ga. or .410 bore, back action, sidelock, ejectors, ST, 25-30 in. barrels, oil finished deluxe walnut stock and forearm, house engraving pattern is standard, 5 lbs., 6 oz.-7 lbs., 4 oz.

MSR $39,420	$39,420	$35,000	$30,000	$25,000	$20,000	$16,000	$13,500

Add $4,560 for 28 ga. or .410 bore.
Add $7,200 for an extra set of interchangeable barrels (if ordered with new gun).
Add $630 for Teague choke tubes.

SxS SIDELOCK - 12, 16, 20, 28 ga. or .410 bore, ejectors, best quality SxS. New 2001.

MSR $34,750	$34,750	$31,000	$26,000	$22,000	$18,000	$14,000	$11,000

Add $4,440 for 28 ga. or .410 bore.

MENZ, AUGUST

Previous manufacturer located in Suhl, Germany.

Please refer to listings in the Liliput section of this text.

MERCURY

Previous importer of Spanish manufactured shotguns.

SHOTGUNS: SxS

MAGNUM MODEL - 10, 12, or 20 ga. Mag., 28 and 32 in. barrels, full and mod., boxlock, extractors, double triggers, engraved frame, checkered pistol grip stock.

	100%	98%	95%	90%	80%	70%	60%
12 or 20 ga.	$300	$275	$250	$225	$200	$180	$150
10 ga.	$400	$375	$325	$300	$275	$225	$200

GRADING - PPGS™	100%	98%	95%	90%	80%	70%	60%

MERCURY

Previous manufacturer located in Belgium. Previously imported 1962-68 by Tradewinds, Inc. located in Tacoma, WA.

PISTOLS: SEMI-AUTO

MERCURY MODEL - .22 LR cal., 7 shot mag., steel frame, fixed sights.

	100%	98%	95%	90%	80%	70%	60%
	$400	$375	$325	$300	$275	$225	$200

MERKEL

Current trademark manufactured by Suhler Jagd-und Sportwaffen GmbH located in Suhl, Germany since circa 1898. Currently imported exclusively beginning 2004 by Heckler & Koch, located in Sterling, VA. GSI located in Trussville, AL is a distributor. Previously imported (until 1992) by Armes De Chasse located in Chadds Ford, PA.

Merkel

For many years Merkel shotguns had an unfair disadvantage in this country because of the politics of importing firearms from communist bloc countries (goods were subject to a 65% non-favored nation tax). With the reunification of Germany in 1991, this trademark has become more competitive domestically. Merkel continues to manufacture high quality guns in Suhl, Germany. Merkel was purchased by the Steyr Group circa 2001.

Beginning in 1995, Merkel serialization employed an alphanumeric date code for year of manufacture, making it difficult to determine year of manufacture by serial number. Higher grade models (including the 300 Series) continue to be manufactured one at a time by hand, with less than 30 being mfg. annually.

Many Merkel collectors are now categorizing older production guns into three different categories. The first is guns made before 1962, when the Berlin Wall was created. The second is the GDR guns (German Democratic Republic). The last is after the Berlin wall came down (post-1991). Premiums are paid on pre-WWII manufacture and some GDR guns. All pre-war guns may have different actions such as square, half round, and square reinforced, etc. These older production models should be appraised by a knowledgeable person, since there are a lot of things to consider when evaluating these earlier Merkels. Some guns made up for the Nürnberg and Leipzig trade shows have top quality workmanship, especially the engraving.

On all factory engraved Merkels manufactured since 1992, the engraver's signature will appear.

COMBINATION GUNS

O/U MODEL - 12, 16, or 20 ga. (2 3/4 in. chamber) over 5.6x50R, 5.6x52R, 6.5x55mm, 6.5x57R, 7x57R, 7x65R, 8x57JRS, 9.3x74R, .22 Hornet (disc. 1997), .222 Rem., .243 Win., .30-06, .308 Win., or .375 H&H (disc. 1994) cal., 25.6 in. barrels, various chokes. Disc. 1999.

* **Model 210E**

	100%	98%	95%	90%	80%	70%	60%
	$5,700	$4,600	$3,700	$3,150	$2,600	$2,100	$1,800

Last MSR was $6,195.

* **Model 211E**

	100%	98%	95%	90%	80%	70%	60%
	$6,650	$4,750	$3,900	$3,300	$2,775	$2,275	$1,925

Last MSR was $7,495.

* **Model 213E** - disc. 1997.

	100%	98%	95%	90%	80%	70%	60%
	$13,000	$10,750	$8,250	$6,975	$5,825	$4,600	$3,550

Last MSR was $14,795.

* **Model 240E-1** - 20 ga. over .22 Rem., 7x57R, or .30-06 cal. Importation began 2003.

MSR $7,195	100%	98%	95%	90%	80%	70%	60%
	$6,175	$5,150	$3,900	$3,400	$2,900	$2,400	$2,125

GRADING - PPGS™	100%	98%	95%	90%	80%	70%	60%

✷ Model 313E - disc. 1997.

	$19,350	$14,950	$12,500	$9,950	$8,350	$7,100	$5,900

Last MSR was $22,795.

MODEL 314 - 12 ga. over 8x60mm Mag. cal., detachable H&H sidelock system, elaborate scroll engraving. Disc. pre-WWII.

	$21,250	$15,750	$13,000	$10,000	$8,500	$7,200	$6,200

SxS MODEL - similar gauges and cals. to O/U Combination Gun, boxlock models included 8EI and 9EI, 10EI is a sidelock, boxlock models ranged in MSRs from $5,500-$7,000 and the Model 10EI MSR was $9,500. Importation disc. 1990.

DRILLINGS

Previously, the Drilling Models 90 (disc. 1994), 90S (disc. 1997), 90K (disc. 1997), 95 (disc. 1994), 95K (disc. 1998), and 95S (disc. 1997) were also imported. Models differ in the amount of engraving, cocking systems, and quality of wood.

MODEL 96K - choice of 12, 16, or 20 ga., with the rifle barrel being bored in most popular U.S. and metric cals. between .22 Hornet and 9.3x74R (disc.), 23.6 in. barrels, current models are boxlocks with Greener crossbolt and double under barrel locking lugs, extractors, tang mounted cocking for rifle, case hardened receiver with arabesque scroll engraving, DT, fitted leather case.

MSR $8,095	$7,325	$5,900	$4,750	$3,650	$3,000	$2,500	$1,995

Add $1,200 for hunting scene engraving (Model 96K Engraved).

MERKEL ANSON DRILLING - 12, 16, or 20 ga., calibers 7x57R, 8x57JR, and 9.3x74R cals. most common, others noted, usually 2 shotguns over rifle, although 2 rifles over shotgun have been noted, 25.6 in. or 21.6 in. barrels, boxlock, Anson & Deeley system, double triggers, extractors, checkered pistol grip stock, pre-WWII.

MODEL 142 - engraved.

	$5,000	$4,000	$3,000	$2,750	$2,500	$2,200	$2,000

MODEL 142 - less ornamentation.

	$4,000	$3,500	$3,000	$2,500	$2,250	$2,100	$2,000

MODEL 145 - least ornamentation.

	$3,000	$2,800	$2,700	$2,600	$2,500	$2,100	$1,900

RIFLES: BOLT ACTION

MODEL 190 - various cals., Mauser M-98 system, checkered walnut stock and extended forend, values depend on caliber and action size. Disc. pre-WWII.

	$7,500	$6,500	$5,275	$4,200	$3,200	$2,350	$1,500

Premiums exist for Magnum or Kurz (short) action.

RIFLES: SINGLE SHOT

MODEL K1 LIGHTWEIGHT STALKING RIFLE - available in 9 cals. between .243 Win. - 9.3x74R, Franz Jaeger break open action, cocking/uncocking slide type safety, matte silver receiver, adj. trigger pull, 23.6 in. barrel, pistol grip, includes 1 in. or 30mm quick detachable mounts, silver border engraving is standard, 5 lbs., 5 oz. Importation began 2002.

MSR $3,395	$3,050	$2,725	$2,275	$1,900	$1,600	$1,300	$1,100

Add $300 for Premium Model with light arabesque scroll engraving.
Add $600 for Jagd Model with fine hunting scene engraving.
Add $900 for Swarovski scope combo (new 2005).

MODEL 180 - various cals., with (Model 180E) or w/o ejector, double triggers, checkered walnut stock and extended forend, values depend on caliber and action size. Disc. pre-WWII.

	$8,500	$7,250	$5,775	$4,600	$3,750	$3,000	$2,500

GRADING - PPGS™	100%	98%	95%	90%	80%	70%	60%

MODEL 183E - various cals., top-of-the-line rifle with elaborate engraving. Disc. pre-WWII.

	$12,500	$10,750	$8,250	$6,975	$5,825	$4,600	$3,550

RIFLES: DOUBLE

O/U MODEL - same cals. as the O/U Combination Gun, various actions, engraving options, and other special orders.

❋ **Model 220E Boxlock** - boxlock Blitz action, scroll engraved case hardened receiver, DTs, pistol grip with cheekpiece. Importation disc. 1994.

	$9,575	$8,250	$7,150	$6,100	$5,100	$4,250	$3,500

Last MSR was $10,795.

❋ **Model 221E Boxlock** - similar to 220E, except has silver-grey receiver with hunting scene engraving. Disc. 1998.

	$9,975	$8,450	$7,450	$6,300	$5,100	$4,250	$3,350

Last MSR was $10,895.

❋ **Model 223E Sidelock** - sidelock action with scroll or game scenes, removed without tools. Disc. 1997.

	$16,250	$13,650	$11,000	$9,750	$8,500	$7,400	$6,250

Last MSR was $17,895.

❋ **Model 323E Sidelock** - similar to 223E Sidelock, except has scrollwork or game scene engraving, top-of-the-line O/U double rifle. Disc. 1997.

	$23,300	$20,000	$17,500	$13,500	$11,250	$9,750	$8,350

Last MSR was $27,195.

MODEL 324 O/U - 8x60mm Mag. cal., premium quality pre-WWII double rifle, elaborate scroll engraving and best quality walnut. Disc. pre-WWII.

	$26,500	$23,000	$20,000	$17,500	$13,500	$11,250	$9,750

SxS MODELS - same cals. as listed for the O/U Combination Gun.

❋ **Model 128** - various cals., scalloped Anson & Deeley action featuring engine turned removable locks and hinged floorplate, elaborate scroll and game scene engraving (including scrollwork on barrels), deluxe checkered walnut stock and forearm, pre-WWII mfg.

	N/A	$25,000	$21,000	$18,000	$15,500	$13,250	$11,000

❋ **Model 140-1** - Anson & Deeley boxlock action with cocking indicators, double triggers, engraved case hardened receiver. Importation began 1994.

MSR $7,195		$6,100	$4,450	$3,300	$2,625	$2,100	$1,825	$1,675

Subtract approx. $400 if w/o H&H ejectors (pre-2002).

Add approx. $200 for set front trigger.

Add $1,100 for engraved hunting scenes on silver/grey receiver (Model 140-1.1).

❋ **Model 140-2** - .375 H&H, .416 Rigby, or .470 NE cal., similar to Model 140-1, except has scroll engraved silver grey receiver and positive extractors, includes fitted leather luggage case. Importation began 2000.

MSR $10,195		$8,600	$7,100	$5,700	$4,550	$3,700	$3,100	$2,600

>**Model 140-2.1** - similar to Model 140-2, except has Africa game scene engraving. Importation began 2000.

MSR $11,395		$9,625	$7,575	$5,650	$4,725	$3,850	$3,350	$2,850

❋ **Model 141-1** - .30-06, .308 Win. or 9.3x74R cal., Greener crossbolt Anson & Deeley boxlock action with double underbarrel locking lugs, petite frame, scroll engraved silver grey finish, ejectors, DT, deluxe checkered pistol grip walnut stock with cheekpiece and forearm, includes fitted leather case. Importation began 2004.

MSR $7,195		$6,100	$4,750	$3,950	$3,300	$2,750	$2,250	$1,950

GRADING - PPGS™	100%	98%	95%	90%	80%	70%	60%

>**Model 141-1.1** - similar to Model 141-1, except has hunting scene engraving. Importation began 2004.

MSR $8,295	$6,850	$5,150	$4,350	$3,600	$3,000	$2,500	$2,175

Add $1,700 for Leupold scope combo (new 2005).

* *Model 150-1* - Anson & Deeley boxlock action with cocking indicators and side-plates, double triggers, silver grayed receiver with arabesque engraving. Imported 1994-98.

	$6,500	$5,275	$4,375	$3,750	$3,250	$2,675	$2,100

Last MSR was $7,495.

Add $385 for H&H ejectors.
Add approx. $200 for set front trigger.

>**Model 150-1.1** - similiar to Model 150-1, except has elaborate hunting scene engraving. Importation disc. 2000.

	$7,750	$5,350	$4,250	$3,550	$2,900	$2,400	$2,000

Last MSR was $8,995.

* *Model 160S-1* - sidelock action with Greener crossbolt featuring fine arabesque engraving, H&H ejectors, DTs, pistol grip stock with cheekpiece. Disc. 1998.

	$11,400	$9,350	$7,675	$6,500	$5,300	$4,400	$3,550

Last MSR was $13,295.

Add $415 for H&H ejectors.
Add approx. $500 for set front trigger.
Add approx. $1,000 for single non-selective trigger.

>**Model 160-1.1** - similiar to Model 150-1, except has elaborate hunting scene engraving on silver-grey receiver. Importation disc. 2000.

	$13,250	$11,000	$9,000	$7,775	$6,600	$5,400	$4,750

Last MSR was $14,995.

>**Model 160-2.1** - .375 H&H, .416 Rigby, or .470 NE cal., features octagon barrels, African game scene engraving with gold wire inlays on silver receiver, includes fitted leather luggage case, special order only. Importation began 2002.

MSR $25,995	$23,500	$19,000	$15,250	$12,500	$10,000	$8,950	$7,750

MODEL 132 SxS - various cals., boxlock action with triple Greener cross bolt system, barrels, mfg. from Bohler steel, extractors (Model 132) or H&H system ejectors (Model 132E), DT, elaborate engraving and premium checkered walnut stock and forearm, pre-WWII mfg.

	$12,000	$10,500	$8,500	$6,500	$5,750	$4,900	$4,150

Add 20% for ejectors (Model 132E).

SHOTGUNS: O/U, DISC.

MODEL 100 - 12, 16, or 20 ga., various barrel lengths and chokes, boxlock, Greener cross bolt, double triggers, extractors, checkered pistol grip or English style stock, pre-WWII.

Plain	$1,850	$1,675	$1,450	$1,250	$1,000	$925	$850
Ribbed	$1,950	$1,775	$1,550	$1,300	$1,050	$950	$875

MODEL 101 - similar to 100, except selective extractors, rib barrel, some English style scroll engraving, pre-WWII.

	$2,050	$1,850	$1,600	$1,325	$1,100	$1,000	$900

MODEL 101E - similar to 100, except auto ejectors, pre-WWII.

	$2,200	$2,000	$1,750	$1,425	$1,250	$1,150	$1,000

MODEL 400 - similar to 101, except arabesque engraving and Kersten double cross bolt, pre-WWII.

	$2,075	$1,875	$1,650	$1,350	$1,200	$1,100	$975

MODEL 400E - similar to 400, except auto ejector, pre-WWII.

	$2,250	$2,050	$1,800	$1,450	$1,325	$1,175	$1,025

GRADING - PPGS™	100%	98%	95%	90%	80%	70%	60%

MODEL 410 - similar to 400, except more engraving and fancier wood, pre-WWII.

	$2,200	$2,000	$1,750	$1,425	$1,250	$1,150	$1,000

MODEL 410E - similar to 410, except auto ejectors, pre-WWII.

	$2,325	$2,175	$1,900	$1,600	$1,450	$1,225	$1,100

MODEL 200 - 12, 16, 20, 24, 28, or 32 ga., ribbed barrels in various lengths, Kersten double cross bolt, scalloped frame, boxlock, double triggers, extractors, cocking indicators, either pistol grip or English style checkered stock.

	$2,750	$2,475	$2,225	$2,000	$1,750	$1,400	$1,175

Add 10%-15% for 28 ga., depending on condition.

MODEL 210 - similar to 200, except engraved and better grade wood, pre-WWII.

	$3,000	$2,750	$2,475	$2,250	$2,000	$1,650	$1,325

Add 10%-15% for 28 ga., depending on condition.

MODEL 201 - 12, 16, or 20 ga., Greener crossbolt, hunting engraving or fine arabesque, dark walnut.

	$3,250	$3,000	$2,625	$2,400	$2,200	$1,825	$1,500

MODEL 201E - similar to 201, except with auto ejectors, pre-WWII.

	$3,750	$3,375	$3,050	$2,650	$2,400	$2,200	$1,825

MODEL 202 - similar to 201, except with false sideplates, higher quality wood, more profuse engraving, pre-WWII.

	$3,950	$3,625	$3,300	$2,850	$2,600	$2,300	$1,900

MODEL 202E - similar to 202, with auto ejectors, pre-WWII.

	$4,650	$4,100	$3,675	$3,200	$2,800	$2,485	$2,050

MODEL 203E - similar to 202E, except better engraving and wood.

	$6,000	$5,500	$4,900	$4,300	$3,800	$3,250	$2,650

MODEL 204E - similar to 203E, but fine English scroll engraving and Merkel sidelocks, ejectors, pre-WWII.

	$6,950	$6,500	$5,650	$4,900	$4,300	$3,850	$3,300

MODEL 300 - 12, 16, 20, 24, 28, or 32 ga., various lengths and choke ribbed barrels, Merkel-Anson boxlock, Kersten double cross bolt, two underlugs, scalloped frame, either English or pistol grip style stock, cocking indicators, pre-WWII.

	$5,150	$4,600	$4,100	$3,600	$3,100	$2,650	$2,400

Add 10%-15% for 28 ga.

This model is usually encountered without engraving and has standard wood.

MODEL 300E - similar to Model 300, with auto ejectors, pre-WWII.

	$5,750	$5,150	$4,600	$4,100	$3,600	$3,100	$2,650

This model is usually encountered without engraving and has standard wood.

MODEL 301 - similar to Model 300, but more profusely engraved and better grade wood, pre-WWII.

	$6,750	$6,100	$5,250	$4,250	$3,995	$3,500	$3,000

MODEL 310E - similar to Model 300, with auto ejectors, pre-WWII.

	$7,950	$7,200	$6,250	$5,300	$4,450	$3,900	$3,400

MODEL 302 - similar to Model 301, but has auto ejectors and more elaborate ornamentation, false sideplates and better grade wood.

	$14,000	$12,000	$10,500	$8,500	$6,500	$5,750	$4,900

MODEL 304E - special order version of Model 303E, higher quality and more ornamentation, game scene engraving similar to Model 303 EL Luxus, top of Merkel O/U line.

	$22,500	$18,750	$15,750	$12,000	$10,500	$8,750	$7,500

SHOTGUNS: O/U, RECENT PRODUCTION

MODEL 200E BOXLOCK - 12, 16, or 20 ga., case hardened scalloped boxlock action with minor scroll engraving, 26 (disc.), 26 3/4, or 28 in. barrels, checkered European walnut stock and forearm, ejectors, SST or DT, pistol grip or English style stock, solid rib, 6-7 lbs. Importation disc. 1994, quantities remained until 1998.

	$3,600	$2,750	$2,150	$1,900	$1,600	$1,300	$1,100

Last MSR was $3,995.

❋ *Model 200ES Skeet* - 12 ga. only, 26 3/4 in. VR barrels bored skeet/skeet. Imported 1993-94.

	$4,550	$3,950	$3,500	$3,000	$2,500	$2,100	$1,625

Last MSR was $4,995.

❋ *Model 200ET Trap* - 12 ga. only, 30 in. VR barrels bored full/full (other choke configurations available upon request). Importation disc. 1994.

	$4,400	$3,750	$3,300	$2,800	$2,300	$2,000	$1,550

Last MSR was $5,195.

MODEL 2000EL - 12, 20, 28 (new 1999) ga. or .410 bore (new 2004), Kersten double cross-bolt lock, scroll engraved, silver receiver, modified Anson & Deeley boxlock action, 26 or 28 in. fixed choke barrels, ejectors, ST or DT, select checkered walnut with pistol grip or English style stock, 3 piece forearm, 6.4-7 lbs. Importation began 1998.

MSR $6,495	$5,700	$4,450	$3,750	$2,975	$2,400	$1,775	$1,600

❋ *Model 2000EL Sporter* - 12, 20, or 28 ga., similar to Model 2000EL, except chokes are SK/IC only. Importation began 1999.

MSR $6,495	$5,700	$4,450	$3,750	$2,975	$2,400	$1,775	$1,600

MODEL 2001EL (201E) - 12, 16 (disc. 1997), 20, 28 (new 1995) ga. or .410 bore (new 2004), similar to Model 200E, except has coin finished action with light game scene engraving, three piece forearm, current mfg. includes fitted luggage case.

MSR $8,295	$7,100	$5,600	$4,250	$3,600	$3,100	$2,500	$2,250

This model's nomenclature was changed from 201E to 2001EL during 1998.

❋ *Model 2001EL Sporter* - 12, 20, or 28 ga., similar to Model 2001EL, except chokes are SK/IC only. Importation began 1999.

MSR $8,295	$7,100	$5,600	$4,250	$3,600	$3,100	$2,500	$2,250

❋ *Model 201ES Skeet* - 12 ga. only, 26 3/4 in. VR barrels bored skeet/skeet. Imported 1993-97.

	$7,850	$6,675	$5,400	$4,300	$3,450	$2,900	$2,250

Last MSR was $8,495.

❋ *Model 201ET Trap* - 12 ga. only, 30 in. VR barrels bored full/full (other choke configurations available upon request). Importation disc. 1997.

	$7,850	$6,675	$5,400	$4,300	$3,450	$2,900	$2,250

Last MSR was $8,495.

MODEL 2002EL (202E) - similar to Model 201E/2001EL, except has fine hunting scenes with arabesque engraving on silver false sideplates, 3 piece forearm, choice of pistol grip or English straight grip stock, includes fitted luggage case. Imported 1993-2003.

	$10,625	$8,000	$6,000	$5,000	$4,000	$3,500	$3,150

Last MSR was $12,395.

This model's nomenclature was changed from 202E to 2002EL during 1998.

GRADING - PPGS™	100%	98%	95%	90%	80%	70%	60%

MODEL 203E SIDELOCK - 12, 16 (disc. 1997), or 20 ga. (24, 28, and 32 gauges were once available but are now disc.), 26 (disc.), 26 3/4, or 28 in. barrels, VR, H&H ejectors, SST (current) or DT, elaborate scroll engraving on coin finished receiver, sidelock screws are H&H style but the removable sidelocks are not, choice of English or pistol grip stock, 6-7 lbs. Disc. 1998.

		$9,750	$6,450	$4,950	$3,900	$3,400	$2,550	$2,150

Last MSR was $11,995.

* **Model 203ES Skeet** - 12 ga. only, 26 3/4 in. VR barrels bored skeet/skeet. Imported 1993-97.

		$12,050	$9,100	$7,300	$5,975	$4,950	$3,950	$3,500

Last MSR was $14,595.

* **Model 203ET Trap** - 12 ga. only, 30 in. VR barrels bored full/full (other choke configurations available upon request). Importation disc. 1997.

		$12,050	$9,100	$7,300	$5,975	$4,950	$3,950	$3,500

Last MSR was $14,595.

MODEL 2016EL SIDELOCK - 16 ga., scroll engraved case hardened receiver, action similar to Model 2001EL, three piece forearm. Importation began 2004.

MSR $6,495		$5,700	$4,450	$3,750	$2,975	$2,400	$1,775	$1,600

Add $3,200 for 2 barrel set (16 and 20 ga. bored IC/Mod.).

MODEL 2116EL SIDELOCK - 16 ga., similar to Model 2016EL, except has upgraded wood and more engraving. Importation began 2004.

MSR $8,295		$7,100	$5,600	$4,250	$3,600	$3,100	$2,500	$2,250

Add $3,200 for 2 barrel set (16 and 20 ga. bored IC/Mod.).

MODEL 303EL (LUXUS) - 12, 20, or 28 (new 1998) ga., similar to Model 203EL, except has H&H type sidelock action with hidden thumbnail detachable sidelocks, double underlugs, more ornamentation and better wood, DT with articulated front.

MSR $22,995		$19,750	$16,250	$13,000	$10,250	$9,000	$7,750	$7,000

Luxus variations are also encountered in the 201 and 203 series in addition to older pre-war models.

SHOTGUNS: SxS, PRE-WWII PRODUCTION

Merkel began manufacturing SxS shotguns during 1914.

MODEL 126E - 12, 16, or 20 ga., similar action as the Model 127, except features game scene and other engraving patterns, H&H style system ejectors, pre-WWII mfg.

		N/A	$24,725	$21,500	$16,500	$12,500	$10,000	$8,800

MODEL 127E - 12, 16, or 20 ga., various barrel lengths and chokes, H&H style hand detachable sidelocks, auto ejectors, double triggers, pistol or English style stock, elaborate scroll engraving only, this is a best grade gun, pre-WWII mfg.

		N/A	$24,725	$21,500	$16,500	$12,500	$10,000	$8,800

MODEL 128E - 12, 16, or 20 ga., scalloped Anson & Deeley action featuring engine turned removable locks and hinged floorplate, DT, H&H system ejectors, elaborate scroll and game scene engraving (including scroll work on barrels), deluxe checkered walnut stock and forearm, pre-WWII mfg.

		N/A	$20,000	$16,500	$14,000	$12,000	$10,000	$8,000

MODEL 130 - 12, 16, or 20 ga., various barrel lengths and chokes, Anson & Deeley action with false side plates, boxlock, auto ejectors, English style or pistol grip stock, elaborate game scenes and arabesque engraving, pre-WWII mfg.

		N/A	$13,800	$12,000	$9,500	$7,500	$6,350	$5,400

SHOTGUNS: SxS, RECENT PRODUCTION

Add $895 for left-hand stocking on models.

GRADING - PPGS™	100%	98%	95%	90%	80%	70%	60%

MODEL 8 - 12, 16 (disc.), or 20 ga., case hardened scalloped boxlock action with light engraving, Greener crossbolt with chopper lump extension, extractors, SST (current) or DT, standard walnut with checkering, pistol grip or English style stock, sling swivels (disc. 1992). Disc. 1994.

	$1,150	$950	$795	$700	$625	$550	$475

Last MSR was $1,695.

MODEL 47E - 12, 16 (disc. 2001), or 20 ga., case hardened scalloped boxlock action with chopper lump extension and Greener crossbolt, 26 (disc.), 26 3/4, or 28 in. barrels with fixed chokes, SST (current) or DT, ejectors, deluxe checkered walnut, pistol grip or English style stock, sling swivels (disc. 1992), 5.9-6.8 lbs.

MSR $3,795	$3,025	$2,150	$1,500	$1,175	$900	$800	$700

MODEL 47SL - 12, 16 (disc. 2001), 20, 28 (disc.) ga., or .410 (disc.) bore, coin finished sidelock action with scroll engraving, Greener crossbolt, ST (current) or DT, deluxe walnut stock (with cheekpiece) and forearm, sling swivels (disc. 1992).

MSR $6,595	$5,650	$4,650	$3,800	$2,975	$2,400	$1,975	$1,625

Add approx. $600 for 28 ga. or .410 bore (mfg. 1992 only).

MODEL 76E - top-of-the-line boxlock shotgun. Importation disc. 1992.

	$2,600	$2,100	$1,850	$1,600	$1,325	$995	$775

Last MSR was $3,500.

MODEL 147 - 12, 16, 20, or 28 (new 1995, 147E only) ga., 26 3/4 or 28 in. barrels, Anson & Deeley boxlock, any choke, SST (current) or DT, extractors, straight or pistol grip stock, hunting scene engraved. Disc. 1998, some inventory remained until 1999.

	$2,400	$1,875	$1,425	$1,100	$875	$750	$650

Last MSR was $2,995.

Add $200 for H&H style auto ejectors (Model 147E).

✱ *Model 147E* - 12 or 20 ga., similar to Model 147, except has ejectors, 5.8-6.8 lbs.

MSR $4,495	$3,700	$2,950	$2,375	$1,975	$1,600	$1,325	$1,150

✱ *Model 147EL* - similar to Model 147E, except has luxury grade wood upgrade. Importation began 1999.

MSR $5,695	$4,800	$3,850	$3,150	$2,700	$2,300	$1,875	$1,500

MODEL 122 - 12, 16, or 20 ga., Anson & Deeley boxlock action with silver greyed false sideplates, H&H ejectors, SST or DT, fine hunting scenes with arabesque engraving, pistol grip or English style stock. Imported 1993-99.

	$3,750	$3,375	$3,000	$2,600	$2,300	$2,000	$1,600

Last MSR was $4,495.

MODEL 122E - 12, 16, or 20 ga., coin finished sidelock action with Greener crossbolt and chopper lump extension, cocking indicators, ejectors, DTs, deluxe game scene engraving. Importation disc. 1991.

	$4,100	$3,650	$3,200	$2,800	$2,250	$1,950	$1,650

Last MSR was $3,500.

MODEL 147SL - 12, 16 (disc. 2001), 20, 28 ga. (disc. 2003), or .410 (mfg. 1992 only) bore, coin finished sidelock action with Greener crossbolt and chopper lump extension, 25 1/2 (disc.), 26 (disc.), 26 3/4, or 28 in. barrels, ejectors, ST (current) or DT, deluxe game scene engraving, 6-7 lbs.

MSR $8,895	$7,650	$5,350	$4,300	$3,500	$2,925	$2,400	$2,000

Add $750 for .410 bore (mfg. 1992 only).

✱ *Model 147SSL* - similar to Model 147SL, except has luxury wood upgrade. Imported 1999-2003.

	$8,600	$7,000	$6,000	$5,000	$4,450	$3,650	$3,150

Last MSR was $9,995.

28 ga. had limited availability during 2001.

GRADING - PPGS™	100%	98%	95%	90%	80%	70%	60%

MODEL 247SL - 12, 16 (disc. 2001), 20, or 28 ga., similar to Model 147SL, except has deluxe scroll engraving. Importation disc. 1991, resumed 1993-2003.

	$7,700	$5,300	$4,250	$3,425	$2,900	$2,500	$2,150

Last MSR was $8,995.

MODEL 280 PETITE FRAME - 28 ga. only, Anson & Deeley boxlock action with Greener crossbolt and double under barrel locking lugs, scroll engraving, case hardened receiver, H&H ejectors, DT, English style stock, 28 in. barrels bored IC/M, includes fitted luggage case. Importation began 2002.

MSR $4,195	$3,525	$2,350	$1,675	$1,250	$950	$875	$750

✳ *Model 280/360 2 Barrel Set* - includes 28 in. 16 and 20 ga. barrels bored IC/M. Importation began 2002.

MSR $6,495	$5,500	$4,750	$4,250	$3,650	$3,100	$2,650	$2,250

MODEL 280E PETITE FRAME - similar to Model 280 Petite Frame, except has fine hunting scenes engraved on silver receiver. Importation began 2002.

MSR $4,995	$4,125	$3,650	$3,100	$2,700	$2,350	$1,950	$1,500

MODEL 280EL PETITE FRAME - 28 ga. only, Anson & Deeley boxlock action with Greener crossbolt and double underbarrel locking lugs, fine hunting scene engraving, ejectors, DT, pistol grip or English style stock, 28 in. barrels bored IC/M, includes fitted luggage case, 5.2 lbs. Importation began 2000.

MSR $6,495	$5,500	$4,400	$3,700	$3,000	$2,500	$2,150	$1,750

MODEL 280EL/360EL COMBO - consists of both 28 ga. and .410 bore barrels with fitted luggage case. Importation began 2000.

MSR $9,395	$8,050	$6,950	$6,250	$5,700	$5,000	$4,200	$3,500

MODEL 280SL PETITE FRAME - 28 ga. only, H&H style sidelock action with Greener crossbolt and double under barrel locking lugs, English style arabesque engraving featuring small scrolls, ejectors, DT, pistol grip or English style stock, 28 in. barrels bored IC/M, includes fitted luggage case, 5.2 lbs. Importation began 2000.

MSR $9,395	$8,050	$6,850	$6,150	$5,600	$4,950	$4,100	$3,500

✳ *Model 280SSL Petite Frame* - similar to Model 280SL Petite Frame, except has quick detachable sideplates. Imported 2002-2003.

	$8,900	$7,450	$6,250	$5,100	$4,300	$3,600	$3,200

Last MSR was $10,495.

MODEL 347SL - 12, 16, or 20 ga., similar to Model 247S, except has more elaborate engraving and better walnut. Importation disc. 1991, resumed 1993-97.

	$7,000	$4,850	$3,950	$3,350	$2,775	$2,275	$1,925

Last MSR was $7,895.

MODEL 360 PETITE FRAME - .410 bore, 28 in. barrels bored IC/F, otherwise similar to Model 280 Petite Frame. Importation began 2002.

MSR $4,195	$3,625	$2,350	$1,875	$1,500	$1,125	$875	$750

MODEL 360E PETITE FRAME - similar to Model 360 Petite Frame, except has fine hunting scenes engraved on silver receiver. Importation began 2002.

MSR $4,995	$4,125	$3,650	$3,150	$2,650	$2,300	$1,900	$1,600

MODEL 360EL PETITE FRAME - .410 bore, otherwise similar to Model 280EL, 5.5 lbs. Importation began 2000.

MSR $6,495	$5,625	$4,400	$3,700	$3,250	$2,700	$2,200	$1,850

MODEL 360SL PETITE FRAME - .410 bore, otherwise similar to Model 280SL, 5.5 lbs. Importation began 2000.

MSR $9,395	$8,100	$7,000	$6,150	$5,250	$4,600	$4,100	$3,500

GRADING - PPGS™	100%	98%	95%	90%	80%	70%	60%

✳ *Model 360SSL Petite Frame* - similar to Model 360SL Petite Frame, except has quick detachable sideplates. Imported 2002-2003.

	$8,950	$7,500	$6,350	$5,400	$4,700	$4,200	$3,500

Last MSR was $10,495.

MODEL 280SL/360SL 2 BARREL SET - consists of both 28 ga. and .410 bore barrels with fitted luggage case. Importation began 2000.

MSR $13,195	$11,650	$10,250	$9,250	$8,500	$7,200	$5,900	$4,900

MODEL 280SSL/360SSL 2 BARREL SET - similar to 280SL/360SL 2 barrel set, except has quick detachable sideplates. Imported 2002-2003.

	$12,450	$11,000	$9,950	$8,950	$7,500	$6,250	$5,000

Last MSR was $14,395.

MODEL 447SL - similar to Model 347S, except is also available in 28 ga. and has more delicate scroll engraving. Importation disc. 1991, resumed 1993-2003.

	$9,250	$8,350	$7,500	$6,500	$5,500	$4,500	$3,500

Last MSR was $10,995.

MODEL 1620 - 16 ga. only, Anson & Deely boxlock action, Greener crossbolt with double underbarrel locking lugs, 28 in. barrels with IC/Mod. fixed chokes, case hardened receiver with scroll engraving, H&H style ejectors, DT, English straight grip stock, includes fitted luggage case. Importation began 2002.

MSR $4,195	$3,525	$2,950	$2,500	$2,150	$1,850	$1,500	$1,275

✳ *Model 1620 2 Barrel Set* - includes 28 in. 16 and 20 ga. barrels bored IC/M. Importation began 2002.

MSR $6,495	$5,500	$4,750	$4,200	$3,650	$3,100	$2,650	$2,150

MODEL 1620EL - similar to Model 1620, except has finely engraved hunting scenes on silver receiver and luxury wood upgrade. Importation began 2002.

MSR $6,495	$5,500	$4,750	$4,200	$3,650	$3,100	$2,650	$2,150

✳ *Model 1620EL 2 Barrel Set* - includes 28 in. 16 and 20 ga. barrels bored IC/M. Importation began 2002.

MSR $9,395	$8,150	$7,250	$6,500	$5,750	$5,000	$4,250	$3,500

MODEL 1620SL - similar to Model 1620EL, except has sidelock action. Importation began 2002.

MSR $9,395	$8,150	$7,250	$6,500	$5,750	$5,000	$4,250	$3,500

✳ *Model 1620SL 2 Barrel Set* - includes 28 in. 16 and 20 ga. barrels bored IC/M. Importation began 2002.

MSR $13,195	$11,600	$10,000	$8,750	$7,500	$6,250	$5,100	$4,450

SHOTGUNS: SPORTING CLAYS

MODEL 47LSC SxS SPORTING CLAYS - 12 ga. only, features Anson & Deeley boxlock action with scroll engraved case hardened receiver, 28 in. barrels with Briley screw-in chokes, H&H style ejectors, SST adj. for length of pull, select grade checkered walnut stock with pistol grip and beavertail forearm, competition recoil pad. Disc. 1994.

	$2,725	$2,400	$2,050	$1,725	$1,450	$1,125	$925

Last MSR was $2,995.

MODEL 200SC O/U SPORTING CLAYS - 12 ga. only, 3 in. chambers, 30 in. VR fixed choke barrels with lengthened forcing cones, Kersten double cross-bolt lock, color case hardened receiver, Blitz action, SST, fitted luggage case. Imported 1995-96.

	$6,750	$4,600	$3,750	$3,200	$2,625	$2,175	$1,850

Last MSR was $7,495.

Add $500 for Briley choke tubes (5 total).

GRADING - PPGS™	100%	98%	95%	90%	80%	70%	60%

MERRILL

Previous manufacturer located in Tucson, AZ. This original pistol design was by Jim Rock, who then joined R.P.M.

A newer variation of the Sportsman, now designated the XL and Hunter Model XL was offered by R.P.M. Please refer to the R.P.M. listing for more information.

PISTOLS: SINGLE SHOT

SPORTSMAN MODEL - .22 S, L, or LR, .22 Mag., .22 Rem. Jet., .22 Hornet, .30 Herrett, .30 Merrill, .38 Spl., .357 Mag., .357 Herrett, 7mm Merrill, 7mm Rocket, .256 Win. Mag., .45 LC, .44 Mag., or .30-30 Win. cal., 9, 10 3/4, or 14 in. barrel, hinged break open action, smooth walnut grips.

	100%	98%	95%	90%	80%	70%	60%
	$650	$575	$525	$450	$395	$350	$300

Add $70 for interchangeable barrels.

Add $25 for wrist support.

MERWIN HULBERT & CO.

Previous company with headquarters located in New York, NY circa 1874-1891.

Merwin Hulbert offered very high quality revolvers which were serious competitors with the Colt, Smith & Wesson, and Remington large frame single actions during this era. Their guns are believed to have been manufactured in a separate section of the Hopkins & Allen plant. Most will have both Merwin Hulbert and Hopkins & Allen markings on the barrel.

Merwin revolvers have a unique twist-open mechanism. The latch on the bottom of the frame is pushed towards the rear, while barrel & cylinder are twisted clockwise and pulled forward. This design was intended to allow selective ejection of empty cases while leaving unfired cartridges in the cylinder.

Merwins will often be found with a distinctive, colorful, and unusual "punch dot" style engraving, often with some sort of simple panel scene (an animal, bird, flowers, etc.) on one or (rare) both sides of the frame. These will usually bring perhaps a 50% premium in lower grades, while in higher condition may bring double or triple what an undecorated gun will bring.

100%	98%	95%	90%	80%	70%	60%	50%	40%	30%	20%	10%

REVOLVERS: LARGE FRAME

All chambered for either .44 Merwin Hulbert (usually no caliber markings), .44 Russian (usually marked "Russian Model"), or .44-40 (marked "Calibre Winchester 1873"). Blue finish is rare and will being a premium.

The Merwin Hulbert system was copied by various Spanish & possibly other makers. These foreign copies will bring significantly less than original Merwins.

FIRST MODEL FRONTIER ARMY SA - .44 cal., square butt, open-top, scoop flutes on cylinder, 7 1/2 in. barrel, 2 screws above triggerguard.

100%	98%	95%	90%	80%	70%	60%	50%	40%	30%	20%	10%
N/A	N/A	$3,500	$2,750	$1,800	$1,600	$1,400	$1,200	$1,050	$950	$875	$750

SECOND MODEL FRONTIER ARMY SA - similar to First Model, except has only one screw above triggerguard.

100%	98%	95%	90%	80%	70%	60%	50%	40%	30%	20%	10%
$5,500	$4,650	$3,250	$2,500	$1,700	$1,500	$1,250	$1,100	$995	$900	$800	$700

SECOND MODEL POCKET ARMY SA - similar to Second Model Frontier Army, except has birdshead butt instead of square butt, 3 1/2 in. or 7 (scarce) in. barrel, may be marked "POCKET ARMY".

100%	98%	95%	90%	80%	70%	60%	50%	40%	30%	20%	10%
$5,000	$4,250	$3,000	$2,500	$1,250	$1,100	$1,000	$900	$800	$700	$600	$500

Add 10% for 7 in. barrel.

There are no First Model Pocket Army models.

100%	98%	95%	90%	80%	70%	60%	50%	40%	30%	20%	10%

THIRD MODEL FRONTIER ARMY SA - .44 cal., square butt, top strap, usually has conventional fluting on cylinder, but some have scoop flutes, 7 in. round barrel with no rib.

| $5,000 | $4,250 | $3,000 | $2,500 | $1,250 | $1,100 | $1,000 | $900 | $800 | $700 | $600 | $500 |

THIRD MODEL FRONTIER ARMY DA - similar to Third Model Frontier Army SA, except is double action.

| $4,750 | $3,950 | $2,750 | $2,250 | $1,150 | $1,000 | $900 | $800 | $700 | $625 | $550 | $450 |

There are no First or Second Model Army double action models.

THIRD MODEL POCKET ARMY SA - .44 cal., single action, bird's head butt, top strap, 3 1/2 in. or 7 in. round barrel with no rib.

| $4,750 | $3,950 | $2,750 | $2,250 | $1,150 | $1,000 | $900 | $800 | $700 | $625 | $550 | $450 |

THIRD MODEL POCKET ARMY DA - similar to Third Model Pocket Army SA, except is double action.

| $4,750 | $3,950 | $2,750 | $2,250 | $1,150 | $1,000 | $900 | $800 | $700 | $625 | $550 | $450 |

FOURTH MODEL FRONTIER ARMY SA - .44 cal., 3 1/2, 5 (most common), or 7 in. unique ribbed barrel, square butt, top strap, conventional flutes.

| $6,500 | $5,750 | $5,000 | $4,250 | $3,500 | $2,500 | $1,750 | $1,250 | $1,050 | $925 | $850 | $750 |

FOURTH MODEL FRONTIER ARMY DA - similar to Fourth Model Frontier Army SA, except is double action.

| $6,000 | $5,250 | $4,750 | $3,500 | $2,750 | $2,150 | $1,650 | $1,150 | $975 | $875 | $725 | $625 |

FOREIGN COPIES OF LARGE FRAME REVOLVERS - .44 cal.

These models may be based on any configuration, but 2nd & 3rd Frontier Army styles are probably the most commonly found. The words "Merwin Hulbert" (such as "Sistema Merwin Hulbert") may appear somewhere on the revolver, but are rarely, if ever, found with the Hopkins & Allen marking. These will usually bring half or less what a comparable genuine Merwin will bring.

REVOLVERS: MEDIUM & SMALL FRAME

Medium frame revolvers were usually 5 shot in .38 cal., or 7 shot in .32 cal. The small frame was a 5 shot in .32 cal. Models chambered for .38 MH or .32 MH cal. are very similar to the black powder loadings of the .38 S&W and .32 S&W cal.

FIRST POCKET MODEL SA - .38 cal., 5-shot, spur-trigger, w/ cyl. pin exposed at the front of the frame, distinguishing feature is round loading hole in recoil shield, with no loading gate.

| $1,500 | $1,200 | $825 | $750 | $625 | $550 | $495 | $450 | $375 | $325 | $275 | $225 |

SECOND POCKET MODEL SA - .38 cal., 5-shot, similar to First Model, except has sliding loading gate.

| $1,350 | $1,100 | $750 | $675 | $600 | $500 | $460 | $425 | $360 | $315 | $260 | $215 |

THIRD POCKET MODEL SA - .38 cal., 5-shot, similar to First Model, except has enclosed cylinder pin.

| $1,250 | $1,000 | $700 | $650 | $575 | $475 | $440 | $415 | $350 | $300 | $255 | $210 |

THIRD POCKET MODEL SA WITH TRIGGERGUARD - .38 cal., 5-shot, similar to Third Pocket Model, except has conventional triggerguard.

| $1,250 | $1,000 | $700 | $650 | $575 | $475 | $440 | $415 | $350 | $300 | $255 | $210 |

MEDIUM FRAME DA POCKET MODEL - .38 cal., 5 shot, double action, may have folding hammer spur.

| $950 | $775 | $500 | $450 | $415 | $365 | $335 | $300 | $275 | $250 | $225 | $200 |

Add 10% for folding hammer spur.

MEDIUM FRAME DA POCKET MODEL - .32 cal., 7 shot, double action.

| $1,100 | $875 | $675 | $625 | $550 | $450 | $425 | $395 | $340 | $295 | $250 | $210 |

SMALL FRAME DA POCKET MODEL - .32 cal., 5 shot, double action.

| $950 | $775 | $500 | $450 | $415 | $365 | $335 | $300 | $275 | $250 | $225 | $200 |

100%	98%	95%	90%	80%	70%	60%	50%	40%	30%	20%	10%

TIP-UP .22 MODEL - .22 rimfire cal., 7 shot, spur trigger, closely patterned after the S&W Model One. Very scarce.

100%	98%	95%	90%	80%	70%	60%	50%	40%	30%	20%	10%
$1,100	$875	$675	$625	$550	$450	$425	$395	$340	$295	$250	$210

RIFLES: SINGLE SHOT

These rifles were generally patterned after the Hopkins & Allen single shots.
The Merwin Hulbert name marking may bring a 25%-50% over models that do not have this marking.

MICHIGAN ARMS

Previous manufacturer located in Michigan until circa 1981.

GRADING - PPGS™	100%	98%	95%	90%	80%	70%	60%

PISTOLS: SEMI-AUTO

GUARDIAN - SS - .380 ACP cal., patterned after the Walther PPK, bears close resemblance to the Indian Arms .380 semi-auto, 3 1/4 in. barrel, checkered walnut grips with medallion, 6 shot finger extension mag., fixed sights. Limited mfg.

100%	98%	95%	90%	80%	70%	60%
$375	$295	$225	$210	$190	$170	$150

This model was mfg. by using Indian Arms tooling.

M1911 A1 - .45 ACP cal., patterned after the Colt M1911 A1, fixed sights, 7 shot mag. Disc.

100%	98%	95%	90%	80%	70%	60%
$450	$395	$350	$275	$225	$210	$190

MIDLAND RIFLES

Previous trademark of rifles manufactured by Gibbs Rifle Co. (please refer to the G section for previous models and pricing) and older models mfg. by Parker-Hale, Ltd. (please refer to the P section).

MIIDA

Previously manufactured by Nikko Firearms, Ltd. in Tochigi, Japan. Previously imported by Marubeni America Corp. located in New York, NY circa 1972-1974.

SHOTGUNS: O/U

MODEL 612 FIELD - 12 ga., 26 or 28 in. barrels, VR, various chokes, boxlock, auto ejectors, single selective trigger, checkered pistol grip stock. Mfg. 1972-1974.

100%	98%	95%	90%	80%	70%	60%
$800	$725	$650	$575	$510	$440	$400

MODEL 2100 SKEET GUN - similar to Model 612, with 27 in. VR, skeet bore barrels, more elaborate engraving. Mfg. 1972-1974.

100%	98%	95%	90%	80%	70%	60%
$875	$775	$700	$615	$550	$465	$425

MODEL 2200T TRAP GUN - similar to Model 2100, except with 29 3/4 in. imp. mod. and full choke barrels, wide VR, 60% engraved coverage and select wood. Mfg. 1972-1974.

100%	98%	95%	90%	80%	70%	60%
$925	$825	$750	$665	$595	$500	$450

MODEL 2200S SKEET GUN - similar to Model 2200T, except with 27 in. skeet bore barrels.

100%	98%	95%	90%	80%	70%	60%
$925	$825	$750	$665	$595	$500	$450

MODEL 2300 SERIES TRAP OR SKEET - similar to Model 2200 Trap/Skeet but with more engraving. Mfg. 1972-1974.

100%	98%	95%	90%	80%	70%	60%
$975	$875	$800	$715	$630	$550	$500

GRADING - PPGS™	100%	98%	95%	90%	80%	70%	60%

MODEL GRT GRANDEE TRAP GUN - 12 ga., 29 3/4 in. full choke barrels, single selective trigger, auto ejector, boxlock with side plates, receiver fully engraved as well as breech ends of barrel, triggerguard and locking lever, gold inlaid, extensive silver line inlays, high grade select walnut stock. Mfg. 1972-1974.

	$2,500	$2,200	$1,900	$1,575	$1,250	$1,000	$850

MODEL GRS GRANDEE SKEET GUN - similar to Model GRT, with 27 in. skeet bored barrels.

	$2,500	$2,200	$1,900	$1,575	$1,250	$1,000	$850

MILLER ARMS

Current trademark owned by Dakota Arms, and located in Sturgis, SD.

RIFLES: LEVER ACTION

SINGLE SHOT RIFLE - various cals. between .17 Dakota - .416 Rem. Mag., XXX English style checkered walnut stock and Schnabel forend, falling block action. New 2004.

❋ *Miller Standard* - various centerfire cals. up to .375 H&H, 24 in. round barrel, Hi-Wall falling block action with curved Farquharson lever, plain matte receiver, 7.5 lbs.

MSR $4,500	$4,150	$3,650	$3,175	$2,725	$2,350	$1,975	$1,500

❋ *Miller Low Boy* - various centerfire cals., 24 in. half round, half octagon barrel, falling block action, case colored receiver with gold Miller banner, jeweled block, 7 lbs.

MSR $5,000	$4,575	$4,050	$3,550	$3,100	$2,600	$2,300	$1,800

❋ *Miller Model F* - various centerfire cals. up to .45-110, 26 in. octagon barrel, lever style falling block action, perch belly buttstock, Queen Anne grip, cheekpiece, stainless steel receiver, tang sight with front globe, checkered steel buttplate or black recoil pad, 6 lbs.

MSR $6,000	$5,450	$4,750	$3,950	$3,500	$3,100	$2,750	$2,250

MILLER, DAVID CO.

See David Miller Co. listing.

MIL-SPEC INDUSTRIES CORP.

Current pistol manufacturer and related components supplier located in Roslyn Heights, NY since 1996. Dealer sales.

PISTOLS: SEMI-AUTO

MIL-SPEC 1911 A1 - 9mm Para., 9x21mm, 9x22mm, .40 S&W, .45 HP, or .45 ACP cal., high tech polymer and stainless steel frame, beavertail grip safety, aluminum trigger, 10 shot mag., 3 15/16 (Compact), 5 5/16 (Combat with compensator), or 5 (Government) in. barrel, choice of wood, plastic, or rubber grips, 39 1/2-46 oz. New late 1996.

MSR $690	$625	$550	$500	$450	$400	$360	$330

Add $5 for parkerized finish.
Add $45 for electroless nickel finish.
Add $50 for hard chrome finish.

MILTEX, INC.

Previous handgun importer located in La Plata, MD. Miltex imported commercial Makarovs until approx. 2000.

MIROKU FIREARMS MFG. CO.

Current manufacturer established during 1893 and located in Kochi, Japan. Miroku currently manufactures long arms for Browning and Winchester (please refer to individual sections), in addition to their own line of firearms mostly distributed in Europe.

Shotguns marked Miroku only without another trademark listing represent that period of manufacture before Miroku began manufacturing shotguns for other companies (i.e. Charles Daly, Browning, and others). Most guns marked Miroku only were made on a limited basis and although somewhat rare, collector desirability to date has been minimal. Since model notations were not specified in most instances (many shotguns were made to test market demand), a model rundown is virtually impossible. Values can be approx. ascertained by comparing a Miroku shotgun of similar gauge, features, engraving/wood, and condition to an equivalent Japanese Charles Daly model. Miroku also manufactured revolvers up until approx. 1964 which may be designated Liberty Chief - limited importation into the U.S.

MITCHELL ARMS, INC.

Previous manufacturer, importer, and distributor located in Fountain Valley, CA.

DERRINGERS: O/U

GUARDIAN ANGEL - .22 LR or .22 Mag. cal., double action, hammerless, choice of blue, satin, nickel, or gold finish. Mfg. 1996-97.

	$125	$105	$95	$85	$80	$75	$70

Last MSR was $150.

Add $10 for .22 Mag. cal.
Add $20 for blue or nickel finish.
Add $40 for gold finish.
Add $10 for Deluxe Model with case and angel charm.

PISTOLS: SEMI-AUTO

AMERICAN EAGLE LUGER - 9mm Para. cal., 4 in. barrel, stainless steel with toggle action, checkered American walnut grips, American Eagle version, contoured front grip strap. Disc. 1994.

$590	$475	$400

Last MSR was $695.

ROLLING BLOCK PISTOL - .22 LR, .22 Mag., .223 Rem., .357 Mag., or .45 LC cal., reproduction of the Remington Rolling Block design, 10 in. barrel. Mfg. 1991-92 only.

$340	$285	$240	$210	$185	$170	$150

Last MSR was $395.

Mitchell .22 Cal. Target Pistols

Mitchell Arms manufactured High Standard marked pistols during 1993-94. Due to litigation, the High Standard logo was dropped in 1994, and High Standard model nomenclature was dropped in 1996. These guns feature push button barrel takedown and usually, a choice between stainless steel or royal blue steel construction. Mitchell Arms is not responsible for the older High Standard pistols manufactured in New Haven and East Hartford, CT, even though Mitchell parts are interchangeable with original High Standard pistols.

MONARCH (CITATION II) - .22 LR cal., 5 1/2 bull or 7 1/4 in. fluted barrel, frame mounted bridge rear sight, checkered walnut grips with thumbrest, push button takedown, stippled front and rear grip straps, adj. trigger, travel, and weight, stainless steel or royal blue finish. Mfg. 1993-2000.

$395	$295	$245	$215	$190	$170	$150

Last MSR was $490.

GRADING - PPGS™	100%	98%	95%	90%	80%	70%	60%

MEDALIST (OLYMPIC I.S.U.) - .22 S or LR (new 1994) cal., military grip style, 6 3/4 in. special barrel with internal stabilizer, adj. barrel weights, other features similar to Citation II, stainless steel or blue finish. Mfg. 1993-2000.

	$625	$550	$425	$375	$325	$275	$22

Last MSR was $700.

BARON (SHARPSHOOTER II) - .22 LR cal., 5 1/2 in. bull barrel, standard trigger, adj. rear sight, smooth grip frame, stainless steel or blue (disc.) finish. Mfg. 1993-2000.

	$320	$280	$240	$210	$185	$160	$135

Last MSR was $400.

SPORTSTER (SPORT KING II) - .22 LR cal., 4 1/2 or 6 3/4 in. tapered barrel, military black checkered plastic grips, stainless steel only, adj. rear sight. Mfg. 1993-2000.

	$270	$220	$185	$160	$135	$120	$110

Last MSR was $330.

MEDALLION (TROPHY II) - .22 LR cal., 5 1/2 in. bull or 7 1/4 in. fluted barrel, military grips with full checkering and thumbrest, bridge rear sight, gold-plated trigger safety and mag. release, stippled front and rear grip straps, stainless steel or royal blue (disc. 1997) finish. Mfg. 1993-2000.

	$425	$350	$275	$225	$190	$170	$150

Last MSR was $500.

SOVEREIGN (VICTOR II) - .22 LR cal., 4 1/2 or 5 1/2 in. full length VR or black rib barrel, checkered walnut grips with thumbrest, stainless steel became standard 1998, gold-plated trigger, safety, mag. release, and side lock, rib mounted sights. Mfg. 1993-2000.

	$500	$425	$375	$325	$275	$225	$195

Last MSR was $600.

Add $80 for Weaver style base built into VR.

HIGH STANDARD COLLECTORS ASSOCIATION SPECIAL EDITIONS

✳ *HSCA-SE Trophy II* - .22 LR cal., 100 mfg. 1993 only, cased.

	$450	$375	$300

✳ *HSCA-SE Victor II*

	$495	$400	$325

✳ *HSCA-SE Citation II*

	$435	$365	$285

✳ *HSCA-SE Three Gun Set* - includes Trophy II, Olympic II, and Victor II.

	$1,495	$1,295	$1,050

✳ *HSCA-SE Six Gun Set* - includes 6 3/4 in. I.S.U. Olympic (.22 Short), 4 1/2 in. Victor, 7 1/4 in. Citation, 5 1/2 in. Sharpshooter, 4 1/2 in. Sport King, and Trophy Model. Special engraving, cased, HSCA prefix with 2-digit serial number, 19 sets total mfg. 1994 only.

	$2,650	$2,100	$1,675

Last MSR was $2,995.

Mitchell Centerfire Pistols

MODEL 57A (TOKAREV DESIGN) - .30 Mauser cal., single action semi-auto, 9 shot mag., hammer block and mag. safety, all steel construction. Imported from Yugoslavia 1990 only.

	$240	$215	$180	$160	$145	$135	$120

Last MSR was $280.

GRADING - PPGS™	100%	98%	95%	90%	80%	70%	60%

MODEL 70A (TOKAREV DESIGN) - 9mm Para. cal., otherwise similar to Model 57A. Imported from Yugoslavia 1990 only.

	$240	$215	$180	$160	$145	$135	$120

Last MSR was $280.

88A OFFICERS MODEL (TOKAREV DESIGN) - 9mm Para. cal., newer slenderized variation issued to the Officers Corps., short slide and frame, finger extension mag. Imported from Yugoslavia 1990 only.

	$255	$225	$190	$165	$145	$135	$120

Last MSR was $300.

SKORPION - while advertised during 1987, this model never went into production.

SPECTRE - while advertised during 1987, this model never went into production.

1911 GOLD/SIGNATURE SERIES (STANDARD) - .45 ACP cal., features new tapered barrel slide lock-up, wide body accepts staggered mag., full length guide rod recoil buffer assembly, beveled mag. well, blue (disc. 1995) or stainless steel, 8 shot mag., walnut checkered grips, fixed or adj. sights. New 1994-disc.

* *Blue Finish*

	$465	$395	$350	$325	$295	$270	$250

Last MSR was $535.

* *Stainless Steel* - disc. 1997.

	$675	$585	$525

Last MSR was $675.

* *Tactical Model* - stainless steel, features elongated grip safety and serrated front slide, fixed or adj. rear sight. Mfg. 1996-97.

	$640	$550	$500

Last MSR was $735.

    Add $40 for adj. rear sight.

* *Bullseye Model* - similar to Tactical Model, except has fully adj. rear sight. Mfg. 1996-97.

	$850	$700	$575

Last MSR was $950.

* *IPSC Limited Model* - choice of ghost ring or adj. rear sight. Mfg. 1996-97.

	$1,075	$875	$675

Last MSR was $1,195.

    Add $45 for ghost ring sight.

1911 GOLD/SIGNATURE SERIES (WIDE BODY) - .45 ACP cal., features new tapered barrel slide lock-up, full length guide rod recoil buffer assembly, beveled mag. well, blue (disc. 1995) or stainless steel, 10 (C/B 1994) or 13* shot mag., walnut checkered grips, fixed or adj. sights. Mfg. 1994-97.

* *Blue Finish*

	$595	$525	$475	$425	$375	$335	$295

Last MSR was $685.

* *Standard Model* - stainless steel, fixed sights, smooth grips. Mfg. 1996-97.

	$765	$650	$550

Last MSR was $840.

* *Tactical Model* - stainless steel, features elongated grip safety and serrated front slide, adj. rear sight. Mfg. 1996-97.

	$795	$675	$575

Last MSR was $895.

MITCHELL .44 - .44 Mag. cal., 5 1/2 in. barrel, blue finish, 7 shot mag., checkered walnut grips, adj. rear sight. Mfg. 1996-97.

	$1,050	$900	$800	$725	$650	$575	$495

Last MSR was $1,190.

GRADING - PPGS™	100%	98%	95%	90%	80%	70%	60%

JEFF COOPER SIGNATURE/COMMEMORATIVE MODEL - .45 ACP cal., blue finish. Mfg. 1996-97.

* *Signature Model*

	$725	$625	$560	$500	$450	$415	$375

Last MSR was $795.

* *Commemorative Model* - 1,000 mfg. 1996-97.

	$1,650	$1,400	$1,200	$1,000	$800	$675	$550

Last MSR was $1,895.

ALPHA SERIES - while advertised in 1995, this model never went into production.

REVOLVERS: SINGLE ACTION

SINGLE ACTION ARMY - .22 LR (disc.), .357 Mag., .44-40 WCF (new 1998), .44 Mag. (disc.), .45 ACP (disc.), or .45 LC cal., 4 3/4, 5 1/2, 6 (disc. 1993), or 7 1/2 in. barrel lengths, hammer block safety mechanism, steel construction, case hardened frame, one-piece walnut stock. Imported 1986-94, re-introduced 1997. Disc.

* *Cowboy Model* - .357 Mag., .44-40 WCF, .45 ACP (disc.), or .45 LC cal., 4 3/4 in. barrel.

	$395	$350	$315	$275	$260	$245	$230

Last MSR was $450.

Add $50 for nickel finish.
Add $50 for adj. rear sight (disc.).
Add $150 for dual cylinder (.357 Mag./9mm Para., .45 LC/.45 ACP, or .44-40 WCF/.44 Spl.).
Add $95 for steel back strap and triggerguard (disc.).
This model is also available in a Bat Masterson variation.

* *U.S. Army Model* - similar to Cowboy Model, except has 5 1/2 in. barrel.

	$395	$350	$315	$275	$260	$245	$230

Last MSR was $450.

Add $50 for nickel finish.
Add $150 for dual cylinder (.357 Mag./9mm Para., .45 LC/.45 ACP, or .44-40 WCF/.44 Spl.).

* *U.S. Cavalry Model* - similar to Cowboy Model, except has 7 1/2 in. barrel.

	$395	$350	$315	$275	$260	$245	$230

Last MSR was $450.

Add $150 for dual cylinder (.357 Mag./9mm Para., .45 LC/.45 ACP, or .44-40 WCF/.44 Spl.).
Add $50 for nickel finish.

* *.44 Mag.* - .44 Mag. cal., fully adj. target sights. Disc. 1992.

	$425	$350	$295	$250	$200	$180	$165

Last MSR was $495.

* *Rimfire Model* - .22 LR cal. Importation disc. 1989.

	$230	$200	$180	$160	$145	$130	$120

Last MSR was $280.

Add $30 for adj. rear sight.

* *Silhouette Model* - available with 10, 12, or 18 in. barrel in .44 Mag. or .45 LC cal. Importation disc. 1991.

	$395	$325	$260	$220	$195	$170	$155

Last MSR was $450.

Add $175 for shoulder stock (available with 18 in. barrel only).
The shoulder stock is available with .44 Mag./.44-40 WCF cals. only.

GRADING - PPGS™	100%	98%	95%	90%	80%	70%	60%

✱ **Dual Cylinder** - available in either .22 LR/.22 Mag. (disc.), .22 LR/.22 Mag. stainless (disc. 1988), .357 Mag./9mm Para. (disc. 1993), .44 Mag./.44-40 WCF (disc. 1991), or .45 LC/.45 ACP (new 1990) cal. Imported 1986-94.

	$475	$415	$365	$335	$300	$275	$250

Last MSR was $549.

Add $50 for adj. rear sight (disc.).
Add $39 for nickel finish.
Add $93 for for steel backstrap.

✱ **Stainless Model** - available in .22 LR or .357 Mag. (disc. 1987) cal. only, adj. sights. Imported 1986-88 only.

	$260	$225	$195				

Last MSR was $301.

Add $25 for .357 Mag.

BAT MASTERSON MODEL - .45 LC cal., 4 3/4 , 5 1/2 or 7 1/2 in. barrel with full ejector rod housing, nickel-plated, one-piece walnut stocks, hammer-block safety, rear sight is square notch in frame, two-piece backstrap. Imported 1989-94.

	$375	$285	$240	$210	$185	$170	$150

Last MSR was $450.

Add $156 for extra .45 ACP cylinder.

MODEL 1875 REMINGTON - .357 Mag. or .45 LC cal., royal blue finish with color case hardened frame, walnut grips. Imported 1990-91.

	$345	$285	$245	$210	$185	$170	$150

Last MSR was $399.

Add $76 for nickel finish.
Add $51 for extra convertible .45 ACP cylinder.

REVOLVERS: DOUBLE ACTION

TITAN II - .357 Mag. cal., 6 shot, 2, 4, or 6 in. barrel, blue or stainless, fixed sights, shrouded ejector rod, target hammer. Mfg. 1995 only.

	$285	$250	$220	$190	$170	$150	$135

Last MSR was $339.

TITAN III - similar to Titan II, except has adj. rear sight. Mfg. 1995 only.

	$340	$285	$245	$200	$175	$150	$135

Last MSR was $429.

GUARDIAN II - .38 Spl. cal., 6 shot, 3 or 4 in. barrel, fixed sights, blue only, target or combat grips. Mfg. 1995 only.

	$240	$215	$185	$165	$145	$130	$120

Last MSR was $275.

GUARDIAN III - similar to Guardian II, except has adj. rear sight, and 6 in. barrel. Mfg. 1995 only.

	$260	$230	$195	$175	$155	$140	$130

Last MSR was $305.

RIFLES: BOLT ACTION, RECENT MAUSER IMPORT

Beginning 1999, Mitchell Arms imported a sizeable quantity of WWII Mauser 98Ks manufactured in Yugoslavia during/after WWII. These guns are basically in new condition, having been only test fired over the past 50 years. They are supplied with bayonet and scabbard, military leather sling, original field cleaning kit, and leather ammo pouch. Caliber is 8mm Mauser (7.9x57mm), and all parts numbers match on these rifles. Basic retail on the Standard Grade is $225, w/o accessories. Additionally, a Collector Grade is $395, and a premium grade rifle is available for $495 (both include accessories).

RIFLES: DISC.

MODEL 15/22 OR 20/22 SEMI-AUTO CARBINE - .22 LR cal., American walnut stock, high polish blue, detachable 10 shot mag. Mfg. 1994-95.

	$155	$125	$105	$95	$85	$75	$65

Last MSR was $179.

Subtract $40 for 20/22 Special.

Add $20 for Deluxe model (includes deluxe walnut, rosewood accents, and fine line checkering).

LW22 SEMI-AUTO - .22 LR cal., 10 shot mag., composite or skeleton stock, patterned after Feather Industries semi-auto. Limited mfg. 1996-97.

	$240	$220	$195	$175	$160	$145	$130

Last MSR was $275.

Add $30 for composite stock.

LW9 SEMI-AUTO - 9mm Para. cal., semi-auto, blowback action, composite or skeleton stock, patterned after Feather Industries 9mm Para. semi-auto. Limited mfg. 1996-97.

	$450	$395	$360	$330	$300	$270	$240

Last MSR was $500.

Add $35 for composite stock.

MODEL 9303/9304/9305 STANDARD BOLT ACTION - .22 LR (9303) or .22 Mag. (9304, new 1995) cal., standard or deluxe variation, 10 shot mag. Mfg. 1994-95.

	$240	$195	$180	$160	$145	$130	$120

Last MSR was $275.

Add $14 for .22 Mag. cal.

Subtract $76 for special bolt action (9305).

MODEL 9301/9302 DELUXE BOLT ACTION - similar to 9304/9305, except includes deluxe walnut, rosewood accents, and fine line checkering. Mfg. 1994-95.

	$265	$220	$190	$170	$150	$135	$125

Last MSR was $313.

Add $12 for .22 Mag. cal.

M-16A3 - .22 LR, .22 Mag. (disc. 1987), or .32 ACP cal., patterned after Colt's AR-15. Mfg. 1987-94.

	$235	$195	$175	$160	$145	$130	$120

Last MSR was $266.

Add $100 for .22 Mag. cal. or .32 ACP (disc. 1988).

CAR-15/22 - .22 LR cal., carbine variation of M-16 with shorter barrel and collapsible stock. Mfg. 1990-94.

	$235	$195	$175	$160	$145	$130	$120

Last MSR was $266.

GALIL - .22 LR or .22 Mag. cal., patterned after Galil semi-auto paramilitary design rifle, choice of wood stock or folding stock (new 1992). Mfg. 1987-93.

	$285	$240	$195	$160	$150	$140	$130

Last MSR was $359.

MAS - .22 LR or .22 Mag. cal., patterned after French MAS rifle. Mfg. 1987-93.

	$285	$240	$195	$160	$150	$140	$130

Last MSR was $359.

Add $75 for .22 Mag. cal. (disc. 1988).

GRADING - PPGS™	100%	98%	95%	90%	80%	70%	60%

PPS-30/50 - .22 LR cal., patterned after the Russian WWII PPS military rifle, full length barrel shroud, 20 shot banana mag., adj. rear sight, walnut stock. Mfg. 1989-94.

	$235	$195	$175	$160	$145	$130	$120

Last MSR was $266.

Add $100 for 50 shot drum magazine.

SPECTRE CARBINE - while advertised during 1987, this model never went into production.

AK-22 - .22 LR or .22 Mag. (new 1988) cal., copy of the famous Russian AK-47, fully adj. sights, built-in cleaning rod, high quality European walnut or folding stock, 20 shot mag. Mfg. 1985-94.

	$235	$195	$175	$160	$145	$130	$120

Last MSR was $266.

Add $40 for folding stock.

AK-47 - 7.62x39 cal., copy of the original Kalashnikov AK-47, semi-auto, teak stock and forend, 30 shot steel mag., last shot hold open. Mfg. Yugoslavia. Imported 1986-89.

	$1,295	$1,150	$925	$850	$775	$700	$650

Last MSR was $675.

Add $23 for steel folding buttstock.
Add $150 for 75 shot steel drum mag.

.308 WIN. NATO AK-47 (M77B1) - .308 Win. cal., milled receiver, adj. gas port, otherwise similar to AK-47 except has scope rail, day/night Tritium sights, and 20 shot mag. Imported 1989 only.

	$1,150	$1,025	$900	$775	$675	$600	$550

Last MSR was $775.

Add $600 for military issue sniper scope and rings.

M76 - similar to AK-47, except is 7.92mm cal. and has longer barrel and frame set up for scope mount, counter sniper design, 10 shot mag., mfg. to mil. specs. Imported 1986-89.

	$1,875	$1,650	$1,475	$1,200	$950	$850	$760

Last MSR was $1,995.

SKS-M59 - 7.62x39 cal., copy of the SKS-M59 standard rifle, full walnut stock, fully adj. sights, gas operated. Mfg. in Yugoslavia. Imported 1986-89.

	$725	$600	$525	$450	$400	$350	$300

Last MSR was $699.

R.P.K. - 7.62x39mm or .308 Win. cal., forged heavy barrel with cooling fins, teak stock, detachable bipod, mil. specs. Importation disc. 1992.

	$1,100	$975	$850	$750	$650	$550	$500

Last MSR was $1,150.

Add $845 for .308 Win. cal.

MODEL M-90 - 7.62x39mm or .308 Win. cal., AK-47 type action, in various configurations (heavy barrel, folding or fixed stock, finned barrel, etc.), plastic thumbhole stock, 5 shot mag., limited importation from Yugoslavia 1991-92.

	$750	$650	$550	$495	$450	$395	$350

Last MSR was $829.

Add 20% for folding stock.
Add 10% for .308 Win. cal. (wood stock only).

This model was subjected to modification due to ATF regulations after arrival in the U.S.

GRADING - PPGS™	100%	98%	95%	90%	80%	70%	60%

RIFLES: REPRODUCTIONS

HENRY RIFLE - .44-40 WCF cal., polished brass frame, octagonal barrel, original loading system. Imported 1990.

	$840	$650	$585	$520	$465	$415	$375

Last MSR was $999.

Iron frame also available at extra charge.

MODEL 1866 - .22 LR (disc.), .38 Spl. (disc.), or .44-40 WCF cal., patterned after the Winchester Model 1866 rifle, solid brass frame, octagon barrel. Imported 1990-93.

	$715	$535	$465	$415	$375	$335	$295

Last MSR was $829.

This model was also available in a carbine variation.

MODEL 1873 - .22 LR (disc.), .38 Spl.(disc), .357 Mag. (disc.), .44-40 WCF (disc.), or .45 LC cal., patterned after the Winchester 1873 rifle, octagon barrel, solid steel frame. Imported 1990-93.

	$810	$640	$550	$515	$465	$415	$375

Last MSR was $950.

This model was also available in a carbine variation until 1992.

SHOTGUNS: SLIDE ACTION

MODEL 9104/9105 - 12 ga. only, features 20 in. barrel with bead sights, 5 shot mag. tube, uncheckered walnut stock and forearm. Mfg. 1994-96.

	$240	$195	$175	$160	$145	$130	$120

Last MSR was $279.

Add $20 for adj. rear rifle sight (Model 9105).
Add $20 for interchangeable choke tube (Model 9104 only).

MODEL 9108/9109 - 12 ga. only, all-purpose self-defense model featuring 20 in. barrel with 7 shot mag., choice of military green (special order), brown walnut, or black regular or pistol grip stock and forearm. Mfg. 1994-96.

	$240	$195	$175	$160	$145	$130	$120

Last MSR was $279.

Add $20 for adj. rear rifle sight (Model 9109).
Add $20 for interchangeable choke tube (Model 9108 only).

MODEL 9111/9113 - 12 ga. only, 18 1/2 in. barrel with bead sights, 6 shot mag., choice of brown or green synthetic (special order), brown walnut or black regular or pistol grip stock and forearm. Mfg. 1994-96.

	$240	$195	$175	$160	$145	$130	$120

Last MSR was $279.

Add $20 for adj. rear rifle sight (Model 9113).
Add $20 for interchangeable choke tube (Model 9111 only).

MODEL 9114 - 12 ga. only, designed for police and riot control, choice of synthetic pistol grip or top folding (disc. 1994) buttstock, 20 in. barrel with iron sights, 6 shot mag. Mfg. 1994-96.

	$295	$255	$210	$180	$160	$145	$130

Last MSR was $349.

MODEL 9115 - 12 ga. only, design based on Special Air Services riot gun, 18 1/2 in. barrel with vent. heat shield, parkerized finish, 6 shot mag., stealth grey stock featuring 4 shell storage. Mfg. 1994-96.

	$295	$255	$210	$180	$160	$145	$130

Last MSR was $349.

Add $20 for interchangeable choke tube.

GRADING - PPGS™	100%	98%	95%	90%	80%	70%	60%

MITCHELL'S MAUSERS

Current importer located in Fountain Valley, CA.

Additionally, Mitchell's Mausers imports centerfire ammunition, including the .50 BMG cal. Please refer to the Escalade and Sabre sections for currently imported semi-auto and slide action shotguns.

PISTOLS: SEMI-AUTO

Mitchell's Mausers also imports older Luger pistols in many variations. Current MSRs range from $3,500-$6,500. All have been restored and are cased with accessories. Additionally, the company also imports a restored WWII P.38, cased with accessories - current MSR is $1,995.

GOLD SERIES - 9mm Para., .40 S&W, or .45 ACP cal., M1911 design, blue finish or stainless steel construction, front and rear slide serrations, extended thumb and grip safeties, adj. rear sight, checkered walnut grips.

MSR $795	$695	$625	$550	$495	$450	$400	$350

REVOLVERS

CENTURION - .357 Mag. cal., blue finish or stainless steel construction, 6 shot, target trigger, hammer and grips, adj. rear sight, laminated one piece wood grip with medallion.

MSR $695	$625	$550	$500	$450	$400	$350	$300

VALKYRIE - .44 Mag. cal., red ramp front sight, laminated one piece wood grip with medallion.

MSR $895	$775	$650	$575	$500	$450	$400	$350

RIFLES: BOLT ACTION

Mitchell's Mausers also imports WWII rifles in many variations. Current MSRs range from $2,500-$10,000. All have been restored and are cased with accessories.

MAUSER SPORTERS (K98/M98) - 8mm Mauser cal., sporterized military Mauser action with choice of black laminate, brown laminate or American walnut stock with rollover cheekpiece and recoil pad, adj. rear sight, adj. trigger, controlled round feeding. Importation began 2003.

MSR $495	$440	$395	$375	$345	$295	$265	$235

> The above price is for the Premium rifle, with bayonet, scabbard, belt hanger and other accessories. Other grades include the Collector Grade - $295 MSR (includes bayonet and accessories), Service Grade - $175 MSR, Trucker Grade - $149 MSR.

MODEL 98 NORTH AMERICAN - .270 Win., .270 WSM, .30-06, .308 Win., .300 Rem. Ultra Mag., .300 Win. Mag., or 7mm Rem. Mag. cal., Mauser 98 double square bridge receiver. Importation began 2003.

MSR $4,900	$4,500	$3,850	$3,250	$2,650	$2,000	$1,500	$995

MODEL 98 VARMINTER - .220 Swift, .22-250 Rem., .223 Rem., or .223 WSM cal., features double square bridge receiver, varmint stock with Turkish walnut and fluted barrel, fully adj. trigger, 3 position side safety. Importation began 2003.

MSR $6,500	$5,950	$5,250	$4,500	$3,750	$3,000	$2,250	$1,500

MAUSER MAGNUM M98 - various big game cals. from .375 H&H - .500 Jeffries, double square bridge, magnum receiver, deluxe checkered walnut stock with forend cap, folding iron sights. Importation began 2003.

MSR $6,900	$6,450	$5,750	$4,950	$4,275	$3,600	$3,000	$2,400

> Add $1,000 for .500 Jefferies cal.

BLACK ARROW - 50 BMG cal., Mauser action, 5 shot detachable box mag., fluted and compensated barrel, includes bipod and quick detachable scope mount, shock absorbing buttstock. Importation began 2003.

MSR $6,500	$5,750	$4,950	$4,275	$3,600	$3,000	$2,400	$2,150

MOLL, M.F.

Current custom rifle manufacturer and gunsmith located in Moenchengladbach, Germany. Consumer direct sales.

M.F. Moll manufactures high quality reproductions of the Sharps Model 1874 rifle. He also provides many gunsmithing services, including his own proprietary color case hardening process. Please contact him directly for more information, including an individual price quotation and U.S. availability.

MONTANA ARMORY, INC.

Current distributor of C. Sharps Arms Co., Inc. rifles located in Big Timber, MT. Please refer to the C. Sharps Arms Co. listing in the S section for more information.

MONTGOMERY WARDMONTGOMERY WARD, cont.

Catalog sales/retailer that has subcontracted various domestic and international manufacturers to private label various brand names under the Montgomery Ward conglomerate.

Montgomery Ward shotguns and rifles have appeared under various labels and endorsers, including Western Field and others. There have literally been hundreds of various models (shotguns and rifles) sold through the Montgomery Ward retail network. Most of these models were manufactured through subcontracts with both domestic and international firearms manufacturers. Typically, they were "spec." guns made to sell at a specific price to undersell the competition. Most of these models were derivatives of existing factory models with less expensive wood and perhaps missing the features found on those models from which they were derived. Please refer to the Store Brand Crossover Section in the back of this book under Western Field for converting Montgomery Ward models to the respective manufacturer.

To date, there has been very little interest in collecting Montgomery Ward guns, regardless of rarity. Rather than list Montgomery Ward models, a general guideline is that values generally are under those of their "1st generation relatives." As a result, prices are ascertained by the shooting value of the gun, rather than its collector value.

MORINI COMPETITION ARM SA

Current target pistol manufacturer located in Bedano, Switzerland. Currently imported by Pilkington Competition Equipment, LLC, located in Monteagle, TN. Previously imported and distributed by Nygord Precision Products located in Prescott, AZ, and by Osborne's, located in Cheboygan, MI.

For more information and current pricing on both new and used Morini airguns, please refer to the *Blue Book of Airguns* by Dr. Robert Beeman & John Allen (also online).

PISTOLS: .22 CAL. TARGET

Morini was one of the first companies to develop a sophisticated anatomical grip for handgun target shooting, and continues to be a leader in grip design.

CM-22 - .22 LR cal., design for NRA or ISSF "standard pistol" competition, split trigger guard, direct bullet feed, fully adj. rear sight and trigger, 6 shot mag., 5.1 in. barrel, alloy and steel construction, adj. anatomical wood grips. New 2000.

MSR N/A	$1,450	$1,295	$1,150	$925	$825	$725	$625

CM-32 - .32 S&W Wadcutter cal., otherwise similar to CM-22. New 2000.

MSR N/A	$1,550	$1,395	$1,225	$995	$875	$775	$675

GRADING - PPGS™	100%	98%	95%	90%	80%	70%	60%

CM-80 STANDARD SINGLE SHOT - .22 LR cal. only, adj. grips, frame, and sights. Importation disc. 1989.

| | $925 | $825 | $725 | $650 | $585 | $520 | $465 |

Last MSR was $1,015.

     Add $50 for left-hand model.

✱ *CM-80 Super Competition* - similar to CM-80 Standard, except has deluxe finish, and unique plexiglass front sighting system. Importation disc. 1989.

| | $1,085 | $920 | $800 | $690 | $590 | $520 | $450 |

Last MSR was $1,196.

     Add $50 for left-hand model.

CM-84E FREE PISTOL - .22 LR cal., single shot, anatomical grips, unique electronic trigger features optic beam safety, cased.

| **MSR N/A** | $1,650 | $1,325 | $1,100 | $925 | $800 | $675 | $575 |

MODEL CM-102E SEMI-AUTO - .22 LR cal., advanced rapid fire competition pistol featuring updated ergonomic grips and flared trigger guard, first target pistol to utilize an electronic trigger. Mfg. 1992-97.

| | $1,525 | $1,250 | $995 | $895 | $795 | $695 | $595 |

Last MSR was $1,695.

MORTIMER, THOMAS

Current trademark owned and manufactured by Dickson & MacNaughton, located in Edinburgh, Scotland.

Please contact Dickson & MacNaughton directly for more information regarding this trademark, including current availability and pricing.

MOSSBERG, O.F. & SONS, INC.

Current manufacturer located in North Haven, CT, 1962-present and New Haven, CT, 1919-1962.

Oscar Mossberg developed an early reputation as a designer and inventor for the Iver Johnson, Marlin-Rockwell, Stevens and Shattuck Arms companies. In 1915, he began producing a 4-shot, .22 palm pistol known as the "Novelty," with revolving firing pin. After producing approx. 600 of these pistols, he sold the patent to C.S. Shattuck, which continued to manufacture under the name "Unique." The first 600 had no markings except serial numbers, and were destined for export to South America. Very few of these original "Novelty" pistols survived in this country, and are extremely rare specimens.

Since 1985, O.F. Mossberg & Sons, Inc. has produced only shotguns and accessories. Mossberg acquired Advanced Ordnance Corp. during 1996, a high quality manufacturer utilizing state-of-the-art CNC machinery.

DERRINGERS

BROWNIE - .22 LR cal., top break open action, rotating firing pin, 4-bbl. derringer, double action, 4-shot, approx. 32,000 mfg. 1919-32.

| | $400 | $325 | $275 | $250 | $205 | $175 | $150 |

RIFLES: DISC.

The models listed appear alphabetically first, followed by numerical models in sequence. Mossberg also has made several .22 bolt action and semi-auto sporters that are in the $115-$130 price range. While they are good shooting models, they are not covered in this section, as they are not collectible.

MODEL K - .22 S, L, or LR cal., tube mag., hammerless, 22 in. bbl., takedown, open sights, plain straight stock. Mfg. 1922-31.

| | $250 | $225 | $200 | $175 | $150 | $100 | $85 |

GRADING - PPGS™	100%	98%	95%	90%	80%	70%	60%

MODEL M - similar to Model K, except has 24 in. octagonal bbl. Mfg. 1928-31.

	$285	$250	$200	$175	$150	$100	$85

MODEL S - similar to Model K, except has shorter mag. tube and 19 3/4 in. bbl., very rare. Mfg. 1927-31.

	$350	$275	$225	$200	$175	$150	$135

MODEL L - .22 S, L, or LR cal., falling block action, single shot, 24 in. takedown bbl., open sights, pistol grip stock. Mfg. 1929-32.

	$450	$350	$300	$275	$200	$185	$165

MODEL L-1 - rare target version of Model L with Lyman 2A tang sight and factory sling.

> **Add $100 to Model L values.**

MODEL R - .22 S, L ,and LR cal., bolt action, 24 in. round bbl., first tube feed, ivory bead front sight, open sporting bbl. sight. Mfg. 1930-32.

	$250	$225	$200	$175	$150	$100	$85

MODEL RM-7 - .30-06 or 7mm Rem. Mag. cal., bolt action, 22 inch (.30-06) or 24 inch (7mm Rem. Mag.) round barrel, three-position safety, folding leaf rear sight, gold bead front sight, hand-checkered American walnut with grip cap, built on imported Swedish rotary magazine action, cartridge release lever for unloading magazine from top. 3 (7mm Rem. Mag.) or 4 (.30-06) shot mag. Mfg. approx. 1979-80.

	$325	$290	$265	$245	$230	$215	$200

MODEL B - .22 S, L, or LR cal., single shot, bolt action, 22 in. round tapered bbl. Mfg. 1930-32.

	$200	$150	$100	$75	$60	$50	$35

MODEL C - .22 S, L and LR cal., single shot, 24 in. bbl., ivory bead front sight, open sporting rear sight. Mfg. 1931-32.

	$200	$150	$100	$75	$60	$50	$35

MODEL C-1 - target version of Model C, Lyman front and rear sights, leather sling and swivels, special walnut stock, rare.

> **Add $100 to Model C values.**

MODELS 10, 14, 20, 21, 25, 25A, 125 - .22 S, L, or LR cal., single shot models. Mfg. 1933-38.

	$200	$150	$100	$75	$60	$50	$35

> **Add 25% to prices for models equipped with aperture sights.**

MODEL 26B - .22 S, L, or LR cal., entirely new design in single shot rifles, easily identified by bolt handle at extreme rear of bolt, 26 in. tapered bbl., hooded ramp front sight, No. 4 rear peep, open bbl. sight, swivels. Mfg. 1938-41.

	$200	$150	$100	$75	$60	$50	$35

MODEL 26-C - similar to Model 26B with less expensive sights. Mfg. 1938-41.

	$200	$150	$100	$70	$55	$45	$35

MODEL 26M (OR B26M) - rare version of 26 series model with two-piece Mannlicher-style stock. Mfg. 1938.

	$350	$300	$265	$200	$175	$150	$100

MODEL 30 - .22 S, L, or LR cal., single shot, 24 in. bbl., rear peep and ramp front sights, swivels. Mfg. 1933-35.

	$200	$150	$100	$75	$65	$55	$45

MODEL 34 - similar to Model 30, except with heavy stock, target style. Mfg. 1934-35.

	$225	$175	$125	$85	$70	$55	$45

GRADING - PPGS™	100%	98%	95%	90%	80%	70%	60%

MODEL 35 - .22 S, L, LR cal., single shot, first full target model, 26 in. heavy target bbl., walnut stock, hooded front ramp, No. 4 rear peep with adj. aperture, approx. 9 1/2 lbs. Mfg. 1935-37.

	$325	$275	$250	$225	$200	$150	$110

MODEL 35A - revised version of Model 35, with all-new "master action," approx. 8 1/4 lbs. Mfg. 37.

	$325	$275	$250	$225	$200	$150	$110

Add 50% for Model 35A-LS with Lyman sights.

MODEL 40 - .22 S, L, or LR cal., repeater with tube mag., 16 shot, 24 in. bbl., No. 3 Mossberg aperture sight, hooded ramp front sight, swivels, approx. 5 lbs. Mfg. 1933-35.

	$200	$150	$125	$90	$70	$65	$60

MODEL 44 - similar to Model 40, but with heavier target stock, approx. 6 lbs. Mfg. 1934-35.

	$300	$250	$200	$150	$90	$80	$75

MODEL 42 - .22 S, L, or LR cal., first model with 7 rd. magazine, 24 in. bbl., front ramp, sporting bbl., rear aperture sights, 42 in. overall length, approx. 5 lbs. Mfg. 1935-37.

	$200	$150	$100	$80	$70	$65	$60

MODEL 42A - redesign of Model 42, new master action with shorter bolt and receiver. Mfg. 1937-38.

	$200	$150	$100	$90	$80	$70	$65

MODEL 42B - same basic specs. as Model 42A, approx. 6 lbs. Mfg. 1938-41.

	$200	$150	$100	$90	$80	$70	$65

MODEL 42C - similar to Model 42B, with open bbl. and bead front sights. Mfg. 1938-41.

	$175	$150	$90	$80	$65	$55	$45

MODEL 42M - .22 S, L, or LR cal., 7-shot magazine, bolt action, two-piece Mannlicher-style stock, 23 in. bbl., 40 in. overall length, 6 3/4 lb., front ramp, open bbl., receiver aperture sights, trapdoor buttplate for extra mag. in buttstock. Mfg. 1940-44.

	$200	$150	$135	$110	$100	$75	$50

Add $40 for extra magazine in buttstock.

MODELS 42M(a), 42M(b), 42M(c) - similar to Model 42M with minor changes in extractors and sights. Mfg. 1944-50.

	$200	$150	$135	$110	$100	$75	$50

MODEL 42MB - military version of the Model 42M, approx. 50,000 mfg. for U.S. and British troops as a training rifle. "US Property" marked with serial number, usually found w/o bbl. sight. Mfg. 1942-43.

	$225	$200	$175	$150	$110	$100	$75

Add $50 for Lend-Lease models with British proofs.

MODEL L42A - left-handed version of Model 42A with true left-handed aperture sight, walnut stock, 1 1/4 in. swivels. Mfg. 1937-38.

	$350	$300	$250	$150	$135	$125	$100

MODEL 43 - .22 S, L, or LR cal., target rifle, 7-round magazine, external trigger adjustment, 13/16 in. diameter barrel, 26 in. long walnut stock with four-position 1 1/4 in. swivels in front, Lyman 17A front sight, Lyman 57 MS receiver peep sight, rare. Mfg. 1937-38.

	$300	$250	$200	$185	$175	$150	$135

Add $50 for 43S Model and $100 for 43SS Model.

MODEL L43 - left-handed version of Model 43 target rifle with left-handed Lyman 57 MS rear aperture sight, rare. Mfg. 1937-38.

	$400	$350	$300	$275	$250	$225	$200

Add $75 for models with true left-handed Mossberg scope.

MODEL 44B - .22 S, L, LR cal. target model, mag. fed, 26 in. heavy bbl., 43 in. overall length, approx. 8 lbs., front ramp and No. 4 receiver aperture sights, four-position front swivels, walnut stock. Mfg. 1938-41.

	$250	$225	$200	$185	$175	$150	$135

MODEL 44US - .22 S, L, or LR cal. target model, 7 round magazine, bolt action, 26 in. heavy bbl., overall length 43 in., approx. 8 1/2 lbs., ramp front sight with hood, rear aperture sight, detachable swivels. Mfg. 1943-45.

	$300	$275	$175	$165	$150	$135	$125

MODEL 44US (US PROPERTY MARKED) - used by all branches of military for target training, approx. 53,000 mfg. 1943-44.

	$350	$300	$250	$175	$150	$125	$100

MODELS 44US(a), 44US(b), 44US(c), 44US(d) - same rifle as 44US with minor changes in sights and extractors. Mfg. 1944-49.

	$250	$200	$175	$165	$150	$135	$125

MODEL 45 - .22 S, L, or LR cal., tube fed, bolt action, 24 in. heavy target bbl., overall length 42 1/2 in., approx. 6 3/4 lbs., hooded front sight, sporting bbl. sight, receiver aperture sight. Mfg. 1935-37.

	$200	$150	$135	$125	$100	$85	$65

MODEL 45-A - similar to Model 45 with newer, master action. Mfg. 1937-38.

	$200	$150	$135	$125	$100	$85	$65

MODEL L45-A - similar to Model 45-A, true left-handed version. Mfg. 1937-38.

	$400	$300	$250	$200	$150	$125	$100

MODEL 46 - .22 S, L, or LR cal., tube fed, bolt action, 26 in. heavy bbl., overall 44 1/2 in., beavertail walnut stock, hooded ramp front, rear aperture sight, 7 1/2 lbs. Mfg. 1935-37.

	$200	$150	$135	$125	$100	$85	$65

MODEL 46T - similar to Model 46 with heavier bbl. and stock. Mfg. 1936-37.

	$225	$175	$150	$135	$125	$100	$75

MODEL 46A - similar to Model 46 with master action. Mfg. 1937-38.

	$200	$150	$135	$125	$100	$85	$65

MODEL 46-ALS - similar to Model 46-A with Lyman 17A front sight and 57 MS rear aperture, rare. Mfg. 1937-38.

	$250	$225	$200	$175	$150	$125	$100

MODEL L46-ALS - similar to Model 46-ALS with true left-handed action and left-handed Lyman rear sight, very rare. Mfg. 1937-38.

	$400	$300	$275	$250	$225	$200	$175

MODEL 46B - .22 S, L, or LR cal., tube fed, new streamlined design, 43 1/3 in. overall, walnut stock, 7 lbs. Mfg. 1938-45.

	$200	$150	$110	$100	$85	$75	$65

MODEL 46B-T - heavy barrel and stock, target version of Model 46-B, rare. Mfg. 1938.

	$225	$175	$150	$135	$110	$95	$85

GRADING - PPGS™	100%	98%	95%	90%	80%	70%	60%

MODEL 46M - .22 S, L, or LR cal., bolt action, tube fed, with two-piece Mannlicher-style walnut stock, 23 in. bbl., overall 40 in., hooded front, sporting bbl., rear aperture sight, 7 lbs. Mfg. 1940-45.

	$200	$175	$150	$125	$110	$95	$80

MODELS 46M(a), 46M(b) - similar to Model 46M with minor changes in sights. Mfg. 1945-52.

	$200	$175	$150	$125	$110	$95	$80

MODEL 50 - .22 S, L, or LR cal., semi-auto, tube fed through buttstock, 24 in. bbl., overall 43 3/4 in., hooded front sight, open bbl. sight, no swivels, 6 3/4 lbs. Mfg. 1939-42.

	$175	$150	$135	$125	$110	$85	$65

MODEL 51 - similar to Model 50 with receiver aperture sight, heavier, beavertail stock, q.d. swivels, 7 1/4 lbs. Mfg. 1939.

	$175	$150	$135	$125	$110	$85	$65

MODEL 51M - similar to Model 51 with two-piece Mannlicher style walnut stock, 20 in. bbl, 40 in. overall, front ramp, rear aperture, sporting bbl. sights, 7 lbs. Mfg. 1939-46.

	$200	$150	$135	$125	$110	$95	$80

MODEL 140B - .22 S, L, or LR cal., bolt action, mag. fed, 24 1/2 in. bbl., 42 in. overall, walnut stock, front ramp, sporting bbl., rear aperture sight, 5 3/4 lbs. Mfg. 1957-58.

	$200	$150	$135	$125	$110	$85	$65

MODEL 140K - similar to Model 140B with post front and no aperture sight. Mfg. 1955-58.

	$175	$125	$100	$80	$70	$60	$50

MODEL 142A - .22 S, L, or LR cal., bolt action, 7 round mag., carbine model with fold down forearm, walnut stock with sling, 18 in. bbl., 27 in. overall length, rear aperture sight and military front sight, no bbl. sight, early models had "T" shaped bolt handles and wood forearms, later models had round knob bolt handle and black plastic forearm, 5 lbs. Mfg. 1949-57.

	$200	$160	$140	$125	$110	$85	$65

MODEL 142K - similar to Model 142A with less expensive sights, sporting barrel and post front type. No aperture sight. Mfg. 1953-57.

	$180	$150	$125	$100	$80	$75	$55

MODEL 144 - .22 S, L, or LR cal., full target rifle, heavy 26 in. bbl., 43 in. overall length, 8 lbs., QD swivels, four-position front swivels, rear aperture, front ramp sights, "T" shaped bolt handle. Mfg. 1949-54.

	$225	$185	$165	$150	$135	$125	$110

MODEL 144LS - similar to Model 144, with round knob handle, Lyman 57 MS rear aperture and 17A front sight. Mfg. 1954-60.

	$250	$235	$220	$200	$185	$165	$150

MODEL 144LS-A - similar to Model 144LS, with Mossberg S 130 rear aperture in place of Lyman 57 MS. Mfg. 1960-79.

	$275	$250	$220	$200	$185	$165	$150

MODEL 144LS-B - last generation of 144 series, 27 in. bbl., 15/16 in. diameter, 44 in. overall length, new Mossberg S 331 aperture, Lyman 17A front sight, 8 1/2 lbs. Mfg. 1979-85.

	$300	$250	$235	$210	$190	$175	$165

GRADING - PPGS™	100%	98%	95%	90%	80%	70%	60%

MODEL 146-B - .22 S, L, or LR cal., bolt action, tube fed, capacity of 30S, 23L, 20LR, 26 in. bbl., overall length 43 1/4 in., ramp front sight, leaf bbl. and rear aperture sight, walnut Monte Carlo stock with cheekpiece, QD swivels, adj. trigger, Schnabel forend, 7 lbs. Mfg. 1949-54.

	$200	$150	$135	$125	$100	$85	$65

MODEL 146B-A - similar to Model 146-B, with different bbl. sight. Mfg. 1954-58.

	$200	$150	$135	$125	$100	$85	$65

MODEL 151-K - .22 S, L, or LR cal., semi-auto, butt fed, 24 in. bbl., overall 44 in., open sights, walnut Monte Carlo stock with cheekpiece and Schnabel forend, 6 lbs. Mfg. 1950-51.

	$200	$150	$135	$100	$80	$70	$60

MODEL 151(M) - .22 S, L, or LR cal., semi-auto butt fed, capacity 15LR, 20 in. bbl., overall 40 in., two-piece Mannlicher-style walnut stock, QD swivels, steel buttplate, hooded ramp front, sporting rear, micro-click aperture sights, 7 lbs. Mfg. 1946-47.

	$200	$150	$135	$125	$100	$85	$65

MODELS 151M(a), 151M(b), 151M(c) - similar to Model 151M with minor changes in buttplate and sights. Mfg. 1947-58.

	$200	$150	$135	$125	$100	$85	$65

MODEL 152 - .22 S, L, or LR cal., semi-auto, mag. fed with 7 round capacity, carbine model with hinged, fold-down forend, Monte Carlo stock with adj. sling, 18 in. bbl., 27 in. overall, receiver aperture and military post front sights, 5 lbs. Mfg. 1948-52.

	$200	$150	$135	$125	$100	$85	$65

MODEL 152K - similar to Model 152 with open sights. Mfg. 1950-57.

	$180	$130	$110	$100	$90	$75	$50

MODEL 320B - .22 S, L, or LR cal., single shot, junior target model, bolt action, new closed breech design, 24 in. bbl., overall 43 1/2 in., 5 3/4 lbs., walnut finish Monte Carlo stock with swivels and pistol grip, front ramp, rear aperture and sporting bbl. sights. Mfg. 1960-71.

	$200	$150	$125	$110	$85	$75	$55

MODELS 320K, 320K-A - similar to Model 320B with open sights, no swivels, later models marked 321, 321K. Mfg. 1960-80.

	$175	$135	$90	$70	$60	$55	$50

MODELS 340B, 340B-A - .22 S, L, or LR cal., bolt action, 7 round magazine, 24 in. bbl., 43 1/2 in. overall length, walnut, Monte Carlo stock with cheekpiece and pistol grip, front ramp, sporting bbl., rear aperture sights, 6 1/2 lbs. Mfg. 1958-80.

	$200	$150	$125	$110	$85	$75	$55

At least one example of a Model 340B smoothbore gun is known. This particular specimen was factory fitted with a stock that lacked a magazine cut-out, so the gun could only be fired as a single shot. The muzzle was not threaded to accept any sort of barrel adaptor.

MODELS 340K, 340K-A - similar to Model 340B with open sights, later models marked 341. Mfg. 1958-80.

	$150	$100	$80	$70	$60	$55	$50

MODEL 340M - .22 S, L, or LR cal. bolt action, mag. fed, same operating design as other 340 series, with one-piece, walnut Mannlicher-style Monte Carlo stock with pistol grip and swivels, 18 1/2 in. bbl., 38 1/2 in. overall, open rear and bead front sights, rare, 5 1/4 lbs. Mfg. 1970-72.

	$350	$300	$250	$200	$185	$175	$165

MODEL 342 - .22 S, L, or LR cal., bolt action, mag. fed, carbine model with hinged, black plastic, fold-down forend, walnut Monte Carlo stock with swivels and sling, 18 in. bbl., 38 in. overall, military post front and rear aperture sight, 5 lbs. Mfg. 1957-59.

	$200	$150	$125	$110	$85	$75	$55

MODELS 342K, 342K-A - similar to Model 342 with open sights. Mfg. 1958-71.

	$175	$150	$100	$75	$60	$55	$50

MODELS 344, 344K - .22 S, L, or LR cal., bolt action, mag. fed, walnut finish, checkered stock, 344K is carbine length. Mfg. 1985.

	$175	$150	$125	$110	$85	$75	$55

MODEL 346B - .22 S, L, or LR cal., bolt action tube feed, closed-breech design, walnut Monte Carlo stock with cheekpiece, QD swivels, capacity 25S, 20L, 18LR, 24 in. bbl., 42 1/2 in. overall, rear aperture, sporting bbl., hooded front ramp sights, 6 1/2 lbs. Mfg. 1958-60.

	$175	$150	$125	$110	$85	$75	$55

MODELS 346K, 346K-A - similar to Model 346B w/ open sights. Mfg. 1958-68.

	$150	$125	$110	$100	$80	$70	$55

MODEL 350K - .22 LR cal., semi-auto, LR only, mag. fed, walnut Monte Carlo stock with pistol grip and cheekpiece, 23 1/2 in. bbl., overall 43 1/2 in., open sights, 6 lbs. Mfg. 1958-60.

	$150	$125	$100	$65	$60	$50	$40

MODEL 350 K-A - similar to Model 350K with dovetail bbl. sight. Mfg. 1960-68.

	$150	$125	$100	$65	$60	$50	$40

MODEL 351K - .22 LR cal., semi-auto, tube fed through stock, walnut Monte Carlo stock with pistol grip, 24 in. bbl., 43 in. overall, 6 lbs. Mfg. 1958-60.

	$150	$125	$100	$65	$60	$50	$40

MODEL 351K-A - similar to Model 351K with dovetail bbl. sight. Mfg. 1960-68.

	$150	$125	$100	$65	$60	$50	$40

MODEL 352 - .22 LR cal., mag. fed, carbine model with fold-down black plastic forend, walnut Monte Carlo stock, pistol grip, swivels, web strap, 18 in. bbl., overall 38 in., rear peep, post front sights, 5 lbs. Mfg. 1957-59.

	$150	$125	$100	$85	$75	$65	$55

MODELS 352K, 352 K-A, 352K-B - similar to Model 352 with open sights. Mfg. 1960-71.

	$140	$120	$90	$75	$70	$65	$55

MODEL 377, "PLINKSTER" - .22 LR cal., semi-auto, tube fed, synthetic stock with thumbhole, capacity 15 rds., 20 in. bbl., overall 40 in., 6.25 lbs., equipped with 4X scope. Mfg. 1977-79.

	$200	$150	$135	$100	$85	$75	$65

MODELS 380, 380S - same basic design as Model 377, only with solid wood stock, open sights. Model 480 same in 1985. Mfg. 1980-85.

	$175	$150	$100	$85	$75	$65	$55

MODEL 400 "PALAMINO" - .22 S, L, and LR cal., lever action, tube fed, walnut, beavertail stock and forearm, crossbolt safety, 24 in. bbl., overall length, 41 in., bead front, open rear sights, 5 1/2 lbs. Mfg. 1959-64.

	$275	$225	$175	$150	$135	$100	$85

Model 400-A similar to in specs and value, dovetail.

MODEL 402 - carbine version of Model 400, bbl. 20 in. Mfg. 1961-71.

	$275	$225	$175	$150	$135	$100	$85

MODEL 430 - .22 LR cal., semi-auto, tubular mag. under bbl. with capacity of 18 LR,

GRADING - PPGS™	100%	98%	95%	90%	80%	70%	60%

walnut checkered Monte Carlo stock and checkered forend, 24 in. bbl., overall length 43 1/2 in., open sights, 6.25 lbs. Mfg. 1970-71.

	$200	$150	$100	$85	$75	$65	$55

MODEL 432 - similar to Model 430 with 20 in. bbl., straight grip, smooth stock and forend, walnut finish. Mfg. 1970-71.

	$200	$150	$100	$75	$65	$60	$50

MODEL 472 CARBINE - .30-30 Win. or .35 Rem. cal., lever action carbine, 20 in. barrel, open sights, pistol grip or straight stock, saddle ring on straight model. Mfg. 1972-disc.

	$250	$200	$145	$130	$120	$110	$90

MODEL 472 RIFLE - similar to Carbine, except 24 in. barrel, pistol grip stock. Mfg. 1974-76.

	$250	$200	$155	$145	$130	$120	$100

MODEL 472 BRUSH GUN - similar to Carbine, except 18 in. barrel, straight stock only. Mfg. 1974-76.

	$275	$225	$175	$145	$130	$120	$100

MODEL 472 ONE IN FIVE THOUSAND - similar to Brush Gun, except Indian scene etched on receiver, brass buttplate, saddle ring and barrel bands, select stock, only 5,000 mfg., 1974.

	$415	$300	$225	$175	$165	$145	$120

MODEL 479 PCA - .30-30 Win. cal., lever action, 20 in. barrel, 6 shot capacity.

	$250	$200	$150	$110	$95	$85	$75

MODEL 479 RR - limited edition "Roy Rogers" signature model, gold trigger, barrel bands, 5,000 total mfg. New 1983.

	$400	$300	$250				

MODEL 479 - .30-30 Win. cal. only, lever action, 6 shot tube mag., 20 in. barrel with adj. sights, 7 lbs. Mfg. 1985 only.

	$250	$200	$160	$150	$145	$140	$135

Last MSR was $232.

MODEL 480 - similar to Models 380 and 380S.

	$150	$125	$100	$85	$75	$65	$55

MODEL 620K - .22 Mag. cal., single shot, bolt action, walnut Monte Carlo stock, pistol grip, cheekpiece, sling swivels, 24 in. bbl., overall 44 3/4 in., open rear, post front sights, 6 lbs. Mfg. 1959-60.

	$200	$150	$115	$100	$85	$75	$65

MODEL 620K-A - similar to Model 620K with change in bbl. sight. Mfg. 1960-68.

	$200	$150	$115	$100	$85	$75	$65

MODELS 640K, 640K-S - similar to 620 series, but 5 shot mag. repeater. Mfg. 1959-84.

	$250	$200	$135	$125	$105	$90	$75

MODEL 640KS - similar to Model 640K with deluxe checkered stock and gold trigger. Mfg. 1960-68.

	$260	$200	$185	$150	$135	$120	$110

MODEL 640M - full length, Mannlicher-styled stock, version of 640, checkered stock, Monte Carlo, cheekpiece, pistol grip, swivels and leather strap, heavy receiver, jeweled bolt, 20 in. bbl., overall 40 3/4 in., open rear sights, bead front, 6 lbs. Mfg. 1971.

	$350	$275	$225	$200	$175	$165	$150

GRADING - PPGS™	100%	98%	95%	90%	80%	70%	60%

MODEL 642K - .22 Mag. cal., carbine style, bolt action, 5 rd. mag., fold-down forend, walnut stock with web sling, 18 in. bbl., overall 38 1/4 in., open bbl. and bead front sights, 5 lbs. Mfg. 1960-68.

	$250	$200	$185	$150	$135	$120	$110

MODEL 800 - .222 Rem., .22-250 Rem., .243 Win., or .308 Win. cal., bolt action, 22 in. barrel, folding sight, checkered pistol grip stock. Mfg. 1967-disc.

	$275	$225	$200	$150	$100	$75	$50

MODEL 800VT - similar to 800, except .222 Rem., .22-250 Rem., or .243 Win. cal., 24 in. heavy barrel, no sights. Mfg. 1968-disc.

	$300	$250	$200	$150	$100	$75	$50

MODEL 800M - similar to 800, except 20 in. barrel, full length stock, spoon bolt handle. Mfg. 1969-72.

	$300	$250	$220	$205	$175	$160	$145

MODEL 800D - similar to 800, with roll-over combination and cheekpiece, checkered stock with rosewood forearm tip and pistol cap, no .222 Rem. available. Mfg. 1970-73.

	$325	$300	$275	$250	$225	$200	$165

MODEL 810 - .270 Win., .30-06, 6.5mm Rem. Mag., or .338 Win. Mag. cal., bolt action, 22 or 24 in. barrel, rear leaf sight, checkered Monte Carlo stock. Mfg. 1970-disc.

	$300	$275	$250	$225	$200	$175	$150

RIFLES: BOLT ACTION, RECENT PRODUCTION

In 1985, Mossberg purchased the parts inventory and importing rights for those rifles that Smith & Wesson imported from Howa of Japan. These new models were identical to those models which S&W disc.

MODEL 100ATR (ALL TERRAIN RIFLE) - .270 Win. or .30-06 cal., 22 in. free floating barrel, matte blue or stainless (synthetic stock only), synthetic, Dura-Wood synthetic or 100% Mossy Oak Break Up camo coverage stock. New 2005.

MSR $348	$275	$220	$185	$150	$135	$125	$115

Add $34 for Dura-Wood synthetic stock.

Add $43 for stainless steel (synthetic stock only).

Add $50 for camo.

MODEL 1500 MOUNTAINEER GRADE I - .223 Rem., .243 Win., .270 Win., .30-06, or 7mm Rem. Mag. cal., bolt action, 22 or 24 (7mm Rem. Mag. only) in. barrel, 5 or 6 shot mag., available with or without sights, hardwood stock is satin finished, blued finish, about 7 lbs. 10 oz. Imported 1986-87 only.

	$300	$250	$225	$195	$180	$165	$150

Last MSR was $335.

Add $15 for 7mm Rem. Mag. cal., $25 for iron sights.

✱ *Model 1500 Varmint* - .22-250 Rem., .223 Rem., or .308 Win. cal., similar to Model 1500 Grade I, except has 24 in. heavy barrel only, Monte Carlo stock. Imported 1986-87 only.

	$360	$300	$270	$235	$205	$190	$175

Last MSR was $457.

Add $10 for parkerized finish (oil finished stock with swivels - not available in .22-250 Rem. cal.).

Blue finish and high gloss wood finish available with .22-250 Rem. or .223 Rem. cal. only. Parkerized variation is available in .223 Rem. or .308 Win. cal. only (matte wood finish, includes swivels).

GRADING - PPGS™	100%	98%	95%	90%	80%	70%	60%

MODEL 1500 MOUNTAINEER GRADE II

- similar to Grade I Mountaineer, except has select checkered American walnut stock. Also available in .300 Win. Mag. or .338 Win. Mag. cal. Imported 1986-87 only.

	$325	$270	$235	$205	$190	$175	$160

Last MSR was $368.

>   **Add $15 for Mag. cals.**
>   **Add $25 for iron sights.**

MODEL 1550

- similar to Model 1500, except has detachable mag. and available in standard cals. (.243 Win., .270 Win., or .30-06), with or without sights. Imported 1986-87 only.

	$330	$280	$245	$210	$190	$175	$160

Last MSR was $391.

>   **Add $24 for iron sights.**

MODEL 1700 LS

- .243 Win., .270 Win., or .30-06 cal., no sights, jeweled bolt body and knurled bolt handle, detachable mag., Schnabel forend, deluxe checkering, 7 lbs. Imported 1986-87 only.

	$405	$365	$310	$275	$240	$205	$190

Last MSR was $492.

Mossberg "Targo" Smoothbore Models

These dual-purpose smoothbore rifles were designed to fire both .22 RF bullets and shotshell ammunition. Targo barrels are threaded either externally (Models 26T, 42TR, 42T, B42T) or internally (Models 320TR, 340TR) at the muzzle for attachment of rifled and smoothbore adapters which enable the shooter to use the gun as a standard rifle, or (with the smoothbore adapter installed) as a miniature shotgun. Mossberg produced a line of Targo accessories including a barrel-mounted miniature clay target launcher, a pistol grip hand trap frame, a hand thrower (three known variations), a target carrier, clay targets, hard rubber "practice" targets, and a target catching net. The presence of one or more of these accessories augments the value of any model Targo gun. Prices quoted below are for guns with all listed features exclusive of Targo accessories.

MODEL 26-T SINGLE SHOT

- .22 RF/shotshell cal., bolt action, thumb lever safety located at rear of bolt, black plastic buttplate and contoured black plastic triggerguard (#R413), rifle-style open rear sight with screw adjustments for windage and elevation, shotgun style elevated front bead sight with removable sight hood, smoothbore and rifled screw-on barrel adapters and spanner wrench for adapter removal and installation, stock generally provided with sling swivels, forend necks down toward muzzle, takedown screw has retaining bail to facilitate removal by hand. Mfg. 1940-42 (only 873 mfg.).

	$600	$450	$375	$335	$280	$245	$220

100% price is estimated since an example would be extremely rare.

MODEL 42T BOLT ACTION REPEATER

- .22 RF/shotshell cal., box magazine (7-round) fitted with adapter screw to enable firing of .22 Short cartridges, same safety, buttplate, optional stock swivels, and shotgun style front sight as Model 26T, #R145 contoured black plastic triggerguard, supplied with the smoothbore barrel adapter only (rifled adapter, open rear sight, and front sight hood were not provided), produced 1940-42 (906 guns made), examples in 95% or better condition are uncommon.

	$440	$325	$310	$295	$260	$235	$200

MODEL 42TR BOLT ACTION REPEATER

- .22 RF/shotshell cal., produced before and after WWII until roughly 1949. Pre-war (1940-42) guns identical to Model 42T except rifled adapter, open rear sight, and front sight hood were provided, and no stock swivels. The earliest pre-war 42TRs were marked using a 42T barrel stamp and a separate "R" (stamped to the right of the "T"). Post-war (1946-49) guns have slotted takedown screw, magazine plate, shorter unnecked forend, and (frequently) a blue bolt knob. The most common of all Targo guns. A total of 6,577 guns were

GRADING - PPGS™	100%	98%	95%	90%	80%	70%	60%

produced during the period 1940-42 (post-war production figures are not available). Both early and late versions of this model are comparably priced.

	$415	$345	$295	$280	$245	$190	$175

Add $250 for cased gun with clay targets and Targo accessories.

Cased Targo guns with all accessories have been seen for $1,000+.

Note: A very small number of 42TRs were supplied with fitted cases and Targo accessories and may have been used as dealer displays. Several variations in the internal compartmentalization of these cases have been noted. The pre-war 42TR display guns came in a hard (plywood) luggage case. The post-war guns were supplied in a semi-hard (fiberboard) luggage case.

MODEL B42T BOLT ACTION REPEATER

- .22 RF/shotshell cal., identical to the Model 42TR, except stock has sling swivels and metal buttplate with trapdoor for magazine storage. Gun was supplied with extended 15-round box magazine in addition to the standard 7-round mag. A comparatively scarce model marketed exclusively through mail order stores (e.g., Spiegel) in the early 1940s. According to factory records, only 250 guns were made, all in 1940.

	$465	$385	$350	$325	$285	$250	$210

The 15 round magazine originally supplied with this model is scarce – good specimens are currently selling for approx. $85-$120 (may exceed legal capacity limits, depending on state).

MODEL 320TR SINGLE SHOT BOLT ACTION

- .22 RF/shotshell, automatic safety with thumb lever located on right side of receiver, black plastic buttplate and contoured black plastic triggerguard. Rifle-style ("U" notch) rear sight adjustable for elevation (via sliding wedge) and windage (by deflecting sight arm laterally by hand). Sporting type vertical blade front sight. Gun supplied with rifled and smoothbore screw-in barrel adapters. A wire target carrier and a hand thrower for launching miniature clay targets were included with each gun. Limited mfg. 1961-62.

	$320	$240	$225	$190	$150	$135	$115

Factory records indicate that only 962 guns were sold during the production period.

MODEL 340TR BOLT ACTION REPEATER

- .22 RF/shotshell cal., 7-round box magazine featuring adjustable top bar to accommodate feeding of .22 S, L, or LR cartridges. Two known variations of thumb lever safety markings (words "OFF"/"ON" and red dot). Other features identical to Model 320TR. Limited mfg. 1961-62.

	$345	$265	$240	$215	$165	$145	$125

Factory records indicate that only 2,026 guns were sold during the production period.

RIFLES: LEVER ACTION

MODEL SSi-ONE INTERCHANGEABLE RIFLE/SHOTGUN

- .22-250 Rem., .223 Rem., .243 Win., .270 Win., .30-06, or .308 Win. cal., also available in 12 ga., design allows interchangeable rifle/shotgun barrels, single shot, satin finished or Mossy Oak Breakup camo (new 2003, available in shotgun configuration only) checkered walnut stock and forearm, matte blue metal, 24 in. regular or heavy (.22-250 Rem. or .223 Rem. cal.) rifle barrel with ejector or 12 ga. (3 in. chamber with rifled bore for Slug, 3 1/2 in. chamber for Turkey) ported barrel, break open action, cocking indicator, drilled and tapped intergral scope base, automatic safety, approx. 8 (regular) or 10 (heavy) lbs. Mfg. 2001-2004.

	$400	$315	$255	$225	$200	$180	$160

Last MSR was $483.

Add $240 per interchangeable rifle barrel and $298 for SSi-One Slug Model barrel.

Add $55 for Mossy Oak Breakup stock and forearm (Turkey Model) or $77 for Mossy Oak Breakup stock and forearm (Slug Model).

Add $22 for heavy bull barrel or 12 ga. Slug (fully rifled bore) variation.

SHOTGUNS: BOLT ACTION - DISC.

MODELS G-4, 70, 73, 73B

- .410 bore, single shot, mfg. 1932-40.

	$150	$100	$85	$70	$60	$50	$40

GRADING - PPGS™	100%	98%	95%	90%	80%	70%	60%

MODELS 80, 83, 83B, 83D - .410 bore, 3 or 4 shot, internal top-loading mag., mfg. 1933-46.

	$150	$110	$95	$75	$60	$50	$40

MODELS 75, 75A, 75B - 20 ga., bolt action, single shot, mfg. 1933-40.

	$150	$100	$85	$70	$60	$50	$40

MODELS 85, 85A, 85B, 85D - 20 ga., 2 or 3 shot mag., mfg. 1934-40.

	$150	$100	$85	$70	$60	$50	$40

MODELS 173, 173A, 173Y - .410 bore, single shot, "Y" designates youth model, mfg. 1957-73.

	$150	$100	$85	$70	$60	$50	$40

MODELS 183, 183D, 283D(a), 183D-B, 183D-C, 183D-D, 183D-E, 183D-F, 183K, 183K-B, 183K-C, 183T, 184T, 184TY, 283T, 284T, 284TY - .410 bore, bolt action shotgun, 2 or 3 shot mag., various screw-on or C-Lect choke on some models, mfg. 1948-85.

	$150	$110	$95	$75	$60	$55	$50

MODELS 185, 185D, 185D-A, 185D-B, 185D-C, 185K, 185K-A, 185K-B - 20 ga., 2 shot 2 3/4 in. mag., various screw-on or C-Lect chokes, mfg. 1947-59.

	$150	$110	$95	$75	$60	$55	$50

MODELS 190, 190D, 190D-A, 190K-A, 190K-B - 16 ga., bolt action, 2 shot 2 3/4 in. mag., various screw-on or C-Lect choke, mfg. 1955-58.

	$150	$110	$95	$75	$60	$55	$50

MODELS 195, 195A, 195K-A, 195D - same as model 185 Series, only 12 ga. version, mfg. 1954-68.

	$150	$110	$95	$75	$60	$55	$50

MODELS 385, 385K, 385KA, 385T, 485A, 485B - 20 ga., bolt action, 3 in. chamber, detachable box mag., mfg. 1960-86.

	$150	$110	$95	$75	$60	$55	$50

MODELS 390, 390K-A, 390K-B, 490A - 16 ga., 3 in. chamber, detachable box mag., mfg. 1971-76.

	$150	$110	$95	$75	$60	$55	$50

MODELS 395, 395K, 395KA, 395S, 395 SPL., 495A, 495B - 12 ga., 3 in. chamber, detachable box mag., mfg. 1963-83.

	$150	$110	$95	$75	$60	$55	$50

Add $40 for slug barrel ("S" designation) or 38 in. barrel (Spl.).

MODELS 595, 595K - 12 ga., bolt action, special police stock, 4 shot mag., mfg. 1983-85.

	$175	$150	$135	$110	$95	$85	$75

Add $40 for 38 in. barrel (Spl.).

SHOTGUNS: RECENT PRODUCTION

In 1985, Mossberg purchased the parts inventory and manufacturing rights for the shotguns that Smith & Wesson discontinued in 1984. These new models (manufactured in Japan) are identical to those models which S&W discontinued. Parts and warranties are not interchangeable. Beginning 1989, all Mossbergs sold in the U.S. and Canada have been provided with a Cablelock which goes through the ejection port, making the gun's action inoperable.

To celebrate its 75th anniversary, Mossberg released a new Crown Grade variation within most models during 1994, including the slide action 500 and 835 Series. These can be differentiated from previous manufacture by cut checkering, redesigned walnut or American hardwood stocks and forearms, screw-in choke tubes, and 4 different camo patterns. The Crown Grade was discontinued in 2000.

GRADING - PPGS™	100%	98%	95%	90%	80%	70%	60%

MODEL 200K SLIDE ACTION - slide action shotgun, 12 ga., 28 in., select choke, plain pistol grip stock, black nylon slide handle. Mfg. 1955-59.

	$200	$150	$125	$90	$65	$55	$40

MODEL 200D - similar to 200K, except interchangeable choke tubes (2). Mfg. 1955-59.

	$200	$150	$125	$90	$65	$55	$40

MODEL 500 SLIDE ACTION FIELD (1962-1998 MFG.) - 12, 20 ga., or .410 bore, slide action, 24 in. (with rifle sights) or 20-28 in. barrel (with various chokes), upper receiver slide safety, C-Lect (disc.) & Accu-choke (became standard 1994) choke system, checkered hardwood pistol grip stock after 1973. Mfg. 1962-98.

	$250	$200	$165	$135	$120	$110	$100

Last MSR was $309.

Subtract 10% if without VR (disc.).

Subtract 10% for fixed choke barrel in 12 or 20 ga.

For recent Model 500 information and values, please refer to Model 500 Field – Current Mfg. later in this section.

✳ *Model 500 Slugster* - 12, 16, or 20 (disc. 1997) ga., 24 in. cyl. (disc. 1997) or rifled bore (became standard 1998) barrel, barrel porting became standard in 1998, choice of sights, walnut finished hardwood stock and forearm. Disc. 1998.

	$270	$220	$175	$145	$125	$110	$100

Last MSR was $336.

Subtract $75 if w/o barrel porting or rifled bore.

✳ *Model 500 Bantam* - 20 ga. or .410 bore (new 1991) only, 22 in. (20 ga.), 24 in. fixed choke barrel (.410 bore), or 26 in. VR barrel with Accu-choke(s), blue or blue matte (disc.), Bantam Jake with Realtree Camo finish in 20 ga./22 in. VR barrel only (disc.), 20 ga. has walnut finish stock and .410 bore has synthetic stock (both stocks are tailored for youth dimensions), 6.9 lbs. Mfg. 1990-96, reintroduced 1998 only.

	$200	$195	$165	$135	$120	$110	$100

Last MSR was $312.

Subtract $12 for .410 bore.

Add $45 for Bantam Jake configuration (disc. 1993).

✳ *Model 500 Turkey* - 12 or 20 (new 1995) ga., 22 (20 ga. only), or 24 in. barrel, Woodlands metal/wood camo finish. Disc. 1997.

	$265	$195	$150				

Last MSR was $324.

Subtract $15 for 20 ga.

Add $60 for 24 in. VR barrel with Ghost Ring Sight (12 ga. only).

✳ *Model 500 Muzzleloader Combo* - 12 ga. only, includes 24 in. (rifled bore only, new 1993) or 28 in. VR Accu-choke barrel and additional 24 in. .50 cal. muzzleloader conversion barrel with rifled bore and iron sights, walnut finished hardwood stock and forearm, 7.2 lbs. Mfg. 1991-96.

	$335	$280	$240	$200	$180	$160	$145

Last MSR was $385.

✳ *Model 500 Quail Unlimited* - 20 ga. only, 26 in. VR barrel with Accu-II chokes (3), engraved receiver and hand selected stock and forearm, 3,500 mfg. in 1991 to commemorate the 10th anniversary of Quail Unlimited.

	$300	$240	$195				

Last MSR was $359.

✳ *Model 500 Sporting Steel Shot* - 12 ga. only, 3 in. chamber, 28 in. VR Accu-choke barrel with special Accu-steel tube for shooting steel shot. Mfg. 1987-90.

	$250	$200	$175	$165	$155	$145	$135

Last MSR was $295.

Add $29 for camo stock (disc. 1989).

This model was phased out of production in 1990 since all Mossberg shotguns currently manufactured are capable of shooting steel shot safely.

GRADING - PPGS™	100%	98%	95%	90%	80%	70%	60%

MODEL 500 REGAL SERIES - 12 or 20 ga., slide action, 26 or 28 in. barrel, select checkered walnut, VR. Disc. 1987.

	$240	$195	$175	$165	$155	$145	$135

Last MSR was $286.

Add $39 for Combo pack (includes 1 extra 24 in. slugster barrel).
Add $19 for Accu-choke.

MODEL 500 CAMPER - 12, 20 ga., or .410 bore only, 18 1/2 in. barrel, synthetic pistol grip (no stock), camo carrying case optional, blued finish. Mfg. 1986-90 only.

	$250	$190	$175	$165	$155	$145	$135

Last MSR was $276.

Add $25 for .410 bore.
Add $30 for camo case.

MODEL 500 HI-RIB TRAP - 12 ga. only, high post trap rib, 28 or 30 in. barrel. Disc. 1986.

	$325	$280	$230	$200	$175	$155	$140

Last MSR was $334.

Add $20 for Accu-choke.

MODEL 500 SUPER GRADE - similar to Model 500 Field, except VR and checkered, no 16 ga. Mfg. 1965-76.

	$250	$215	$180	$170	$160	$140	$130

MODEL 500 ATR SUPER GRADE - similar to Model 500 Field, except 12 ga., VR, 30 in. full, checkered Monte Carlo. Mfg. 1968-71.

	$295	$260	$230	$200	$175	$155	$140

MODEL 500 PIGEON GRADE - similar to 500 Super Grade, except etched and scroll engraving, select wood, floating VR. Mfg. 1971-75.

	$385	$330	$305	$250	$210	$185	$165

MODEL 500 APTR PIGEON GRADE TRAP - similar to 500 ATR, except trap style stock. Mfg. 1971-75.

	$440	$415	$330	$250	$220	$200	$175

MODEL 500 DSPR DUCK STAMP COMMERCIAL - similar to Pigeon Grade, except wood duck etching. 1,000 mfg. 1975.

	$525	$330	$310	$285	$260	$220	$195

MODEL 500L SERIES - similar to 500 Field Grade, except no 16 ga., etched receiver, new style stock and slide. Mfg. 1977-83.

	$250	$220	$210	$200	$175	$165	$140

MODEL 500 BULLPUP - 12 ga., 18 1/2 (6 shot) or 20 (9 shot) in. barrel, bullpup configuration, 6 or 9 shot mag., includes shrouded barrel, carrying handle, ejection port in stock, employs high impact materials. Mfg. 1986-90.

	$500	$425	$385	$350	$320	$290	$260

Last MSR was $425.

Add $15 for 8 shot mag. (disc.).

MODEL 500 SPECIAL HUNTER - 12 or 20 ga., 3 in. chamber, 26 or 28 in. VR barrel with or w/o porting and Accu-chokes set, parkerized metal finish, black synthetic stock and forearm. Mfg. 1999-2002.

	$260	$210	$170	$140	$120	$110	$100

Last MSR was $327.

GRADING - PPGS™	100%	98%	95%	90%	80%	70%	60%

MODEL 500 VIKING

12 or 20 ga., 24 (12 ga. only, with rifled barrel and sights, porting became standard in 1997), 26 (20 ga. only) or 28 (12 ga. only, porting became standard in 1997) in. ported (new 1997, 12 ga. only) or unported VR barrel with one Accu-choke and twin bead sights, matte finish with green synthetic stock and forearm, approx. 7 lbs. Mfg. 1996-98.

	$230	$190	$155	$135	$120	$110	$100

Last MSR was $287.

Add $40 for 12 ga. rifled barrel.

Add $108 for Slug Shooting System with ported barrel.

✳ *Model 500 Viking Turkey* - 12 ga. only, 24 in. ported VR barrel, green synthetic stock, matte finish, Accu-choke. Mfg. 1997-98.

	$230	$190	$155	$135	$120	$110	$100

Last MSR was $286.

MODEL 500 FIELD – CURRENT MFG.

12, 20 ga., or .410 bore, 3 in. chamber, 24, 26, or 28 in. ported (new 1997, 12 ga. only, 26 or 28 in. barrel) or unported VR (unless with rifle sights) barrel, Slug model offers choice of 12 ga. with 24 in. ported barrel and rifle sights (mfg. 2001-2004) or .410 bore (new 2003) with adj. fiberoptic sights and vent. rib, matte (12 or 20 ga. only, new 2005) or blue finish, walnut finished or synthetic (.410 bore only) stock, safety on back of receiver top, Accuchokes except for Slug Model and .410 bore, supplied with 1 Accu-choke, 6-7.5 lbs.

MSR $316	$255	$205	$175	$150	$145	$140	$135

Add $14 for Slug Model in .410 bore with adj. fiberoptic sights and VR barrel (disc. 2004).

Add approx. $39-$88 for various combo packages, depending on configuration.

This model also includes the Crown Grade, manufactured 1994-2000.

✳ *Model 500 Field Bantam* - 12 (new 2001), 20 ga. or .410 bore, 3 in. chamber, similar to Model 500 Field, except has shortened, specially contoured stock and forearm (13 in. LOP), and 22 (20 ga. only) or 24 in. ported (12 ga. only, with VR) or unported barrel.

MSR $316	$255	$205	$175	$150	$145	$140	$135

>*Model 500 Super Bantam* - 20 ga. only, 22 (Accu-Set or X-full chokes) or 24 (fully rifled bore with porting) in. barrel, short LOP, adj. synthetic stock and forend, matte blue finish or 100% Mossy Oak New Break-Up (Slug model only) or Realtree Hardwoods HD Green camo coverage. New 2005.

MSR $316	$255	$205	$175	$150	$140	$130	$120

Add $48 for Turkey model or Slug model with Mossy Oak New Break-Up finish.

✳ *Model 500 Slugster* - 12 or 20 ga., 24 in. ported (standard 1997) or unported (disc. 1996) barrel with choice of cyl. (disc. 2000) or rifled (standard 2001) bore, blue or Marinecote (mfg. 1995-97) finish, choice of rifle (Bantam Model in 20 ga.), Truglo fiberoptic sights (12 ga. only, disc. 2004), or Trophy Slugster integral scope base, press checkered hardwood stock and forearm or 100% Mossy Oak New Break Up camo coverage (new 2004), 6.5-7.25 lbs.

MSR $316	$255	$205	$175	$150	$145	$140	$135

Add $23 for Truglo fiberoptic sights (mfg. 1998-2004).

Add $22 for dual comb stock and integral scope base (new 2003, includes extra synthetic cheekpiece).

Add $48 for 100% camo coverage (new 2004).

Add $125 for Marinecote finish (with synthetic stock, disc.).

This model also includes the Crown Grade Slugster, manufactured 1994-2000.

✳ *Model 500 Synthetic* - 12, 20 ga. or .410 bore, 3 in. chamber, 24 (slug model with ported barrel with cylinder bore choke and adj. rifle sights, new 2001), 26 (20 ga. only), or 28 (12 ga. ported only) in. VR barrel, black parkerized metal finish, black synthetic stock and forearm, 7-7.5 lbs. Disc. 2004.

	$255	$205	$175	$150	$145	$140	$135

Last MSR was $316.

Add $14 for .410 bore Bantam Slug Model.

GRADING - PPGS™	100%	98%	95%	90%	80%	70%	60%

* ✳ *Model 500 Camo* - 12 or 20 ga., 100% camo finishes include parkerized camo (disc.), OFM Camo (standard, mfg. 1991-96), Mossy Oak Shadowgrass (new 2004), Mossy Oak New Break Up (new 2004, 12 ga. only) or Woodlands (mfg. 1995-2003) metal and synthetic stock coverage, 24 (disc.), 26 (disc.), 28, or 30 (disc.) in. ported (standard 1997) or unported (disc. 2000) VR barrel (choice of cylinder bore with rifle sights or Accu-II chokes), front fiberoptic sight, includes swivels, camo sling, and drilled and tapped receiver, older Speedfeed stock (disc. 1990) holds 4 extra shells, 7.5 lbs. New 1986.

  Subtract 10% if without Accu-II choke system.

  Add $30 for Speedfeed in synthetic stock (disc. 1990).

  Accu-chokes became standard in 1991. Current models are supplied with 2 choke tubes.

* ✳ *Model 500 Camo All Purpose* - 12 or 20 ga. (disc. 2004), 26 in. barrel, fiberoptic sights, 100% Mossy Oak New Break Up (12 ga. only) or Mossy Oak Shadowgrass (20 ga. only) camo coverage.

MSR $364	$290	$235	$185

* ✳ *Model 500 Camo Waterfowl* - 12 ga. only, 28 in. VR ported barrel with Accu-Set choke tubes, synthetic stock and forearm, 100% Woodlands (disc.), Advantage Max-4 (new 2004), or Mossy Oak Shadowgrass (new 2004) camo coverage.

MSR $364	$290	$235	$185

* ✳ *Model 500 Flyway Series Waterfowl 835* - 12 ga. only, 3 1/2 in. chamber, 28 in. VR barrel with X-factor ported barrel and choke tube, fiberoptic sights, synthetic stock and forearm with Advantage Max-4 camo, includes padded sling and embossed logo. New 2005.

MSR $419	$345	$285	$235	$195	$165	$145	$125

* ✳ *Model 500 Camo Turkey* - 12 or 20 ga., 20 (features ported turkey tube, new 2004) or 24 in. ported barrel with fiberoptic sights and XX-full choke tube only, synthetic stock and forearm with Woodlands (disc. 2003), Realtree Hardwoods HD Green (new 2004), Mossy Oak New Break Up (new 2004), or Mossy Oak Obsession (mfg. 2004) camo treatment, 7.25-7.5 lbs. New 1999.

MSR $364	$290	$235	$185

  Add $11 for Grand Slam Turkey model with X-factor ported turkey tube.

* >*Model 500 Camo Turkey Bantam* - 20 ga. only, 22 in. VR barrel with fiberoptic sights and Accu-II X-full choke only, available in Woodlands (100% coverage), Mossy Oak Realtree Hardwoods HD Green (new 2004) or Mossy Oak Treestand camo (mfg. 2003 only) stock and forearm only, 6.5 lbs. Mfg. 1997-2004.

$290	$235	$185

  Last MSR was $364.

* ✳ *Model 500 Camo Combo* - 12 or 20 ga., includes a wide variety of extra barrel combinations including slug barrel options, prices vary slightly depending on the configuration (gauge/barrel/choke set-up). Rifled bores, VR barrels, and Accu-chokes became standard in the combo package late 1994. Disc. 1998.

$375	$295	$250	$200	$180	$160	$145

  Last MSR was $434.

MODEL 500 HOME SECURITY - 20 (1996 only) ga. or .410 bore, 3 in. chamber, 18.5 in. barrel with spreader choke, Model 500 slide-action, 5 shot mag., blue metal finish, synthetic field stock with pistol grip forearm, 6.25 lbs. New 1990.

MSR $360	$285	$235	$205	$175	$150	$125	$110

* ✳ *Laser Home Security .410* - includes laser sighting device in right front of forearm. Mfg. 1990-93.

$400	$350	$315	$280	$250	$225	$195

  Last MSR was $451.

GRADING - PPGS™	100%	98%	95%	90%	80%	70%	60%

MODEL 500 PERSUADER

12 or 20 (new 1995) ga., 6 or 8 shot, 18.5 in. plain barrel, cyl. bore or Accu-chokes (new 1995), optional rifle (12 ga./20 in. cyl. bore barrel only) or ghost ring (new 1999) sights, blue or parkerized (12 ga. with ghost ring sights only) finish, Speedfeed stock was disc. 1990, optional bayonet lug, plain pistol grip wood (disc. 2004) or synthetic stock, approx. 6.75 lbs.

MSR $345	$270	$210	$175	$155	$145	$135	$120

Add $12 for pistol grip stock kit.

Add $127 for parkerized finish and ghost ring sights (disc. 2004).

Add $40 for combo with pistol grip (disc.).

Add $23 for rifle sights (disc., 12 ga. only).

❋ *Night Persuader Special Edition* - 12 ga. only, includes synthetic stock and factory installed Mepro-Light night sight bead sight, only 300 mfg. for Lew Horton Distributing in 1990 only.

	$295	$250	$200	$175	$150	$130	$115

Last MSR was $296.

MODEL 500 SPECIAL PURPOSE

12 ga. only, 18 in. cylinder bored barrel, choice of blue or parkerized finish, synthetic stock with or without Speedfeed. Disc. 1996.

	$330	$270	$240	$220	$200	$175	$160

Last MSR was $378.

Add $21 for Speedfeed stock.

Add $76 for ghost ring sight (parkerized finish only).

MODEL 500 CRUISER

12, 20, or .410 (new 1993) ga., 14 (12 ga. only, Law Enforcement Model, disc. 1995), 18.5, 20, or 21 (20 ga. only - mfg. 1995-2002) in. cylinder bore barrel, shroud is available in 12 ga. only, 6 or 8 shot mag., pistol grip forearm only. New 1989.

MSR $350	$275	$210	$180	$150	$145	$135	$120

Add $11 for heat shield around barrel (12 ga. only).

Add $96 for 14 in. barrel (disc.).

Add approx. $34 for camper case (1993-96).

❋ *Mil-Spec Cruiser* - 12 ga. only, 20 in. cylinder bored barrel with bead sights, built to Mil-Specs., parkerized finish. Mfg. 1997 only.

	$395	$350	$325	$295	$275	$250	$225

Last MSR was $478.

MODEL 500 GHOST RING SIGHT

12 ga. only, 3 in. chamber, 18 1/2 or 20 in. cyl. bore or Accu-choke (20 in. only - new 1995) barrel, 6 or 9 shot tube mag., blue or parkerized finish, synthetic field stock, includes ghost ring sighting device. Mfg. 1990-97.

	$270	$225	$180	$160	$150	$140	$130

Last MSR was $332.

Add $53 for parkerized finish.

Add $49 for 9 shot mag. (20 in. barrel only).

Add $123 for Accu-choke barrel (parkerized finish only).

Add $134 for Speedfeed stock (new 1994 - 9 shot, 20 in. barrel only).

MODEL 500 MARINER

12 ga. only, 3 in. chamber, 18.5 or 20 in. cyl. bore barrel, 6 or 9 shot, Marinecote finish on all metal parts (more rust-resistant than stainless steel), black synthetic stock and forearm, fixed or ghost ring (mfg. 1995-99) sights, approx. 6.75 lbs.

MSR $512	$420	$310	$230

Add $16 for 9 shot model.

Add $68 for ghost ring sights (disc. 1999).

Add $23 for Speedfeed stock (mini-combo only - disc.).

GRADING - PPGS™	100%	98%	95%	90%	80%	70%	60%

MODEL 505 YOUTH ALL PURPOSE FIELD - 20 ga. or .410 bore, slide action, 20 in. barrel with Accu-Set or F/Mod. chokes, vent. rib, brass mid-bead and white front bead sights, wood stock, blue metal finish, short 12 in. LOP. New 2005.

MSR $316	$255	$205	$175	$150	$145	$140	$135

Model 505 Youth barrels are not interchangeble with any Mossberg slide action shotgun.

MODEL 535 - 12 ga. only, 3 in. chamber, various configurations. New 2005.

* *Model 535 All Purpose Field* - 12 ga. only, 28 in. barrel with Accu-set chokes, vent. rib, blue metal, walnut stock, white bead front sight. New 2005.

MSR $332	$275	$215	$180	$150	$145	$140	$135

* *Model 535 Turkey* - 12 ga. only, 22 in. barrel with XX-Full choke, vent. rib, fiberoptic sights, matte blue, Mossy Oak New Break-Up or Realtree Hardwoods HD Green finish, synthetic stock. New 2005.

MSR $332	$275	$215	$180	$150	$145	$140	$135

Add $57 for camo.

* *Model 535 Waterfowl* - 12 ga. only, 28 in. barrel with Accu-set choke, vent. rib, synthetic stock, matte blue, Mossy Oak New Break-Up or Advantage Max-4 camo, fiberoptic sights. New 2005.

MSR $332	$275	$215	$180	$150	$145	$140	$135

Add $57 for camo.

* *Model 535 Slugster* - 12 ga. only, 24 in. fully rifled bore barrel, synthetic stock, rifle sights, matte blue metal or Mossy Oak New Break-Up camo. New 2005.

MSR $332	$275	$215	$180	$150	$145	$140	$135

Add $57 for camo.

Add $37 for Field/Deer combo or $96 for Turkey/Deer or Turkey/Waterfowl combo package.

MODEL 500/590 INTIMIDATOR LASER - 12 ga. only, 3 in. chamber, 18 1/2 (Model 500) or 20 (Model 590) in. cyl. bore barrel, 6 (Model 500) or 9 (Model 590) shot tube mag., blue or parkerized finish, synthetic field stock, includes laser sighting device. Mfg. 1990-93.

* *Model 500 Intimidator*

	$440	$375	$340	$295	$260	$230	$195

Last MSR was $505.

Add $22 for parkerized finish.

* *Model 590 Intimidator*

	$495	$440	$375	$340	$295	$260	$230

Last MSR was $556.

Add $45 for parkerized finish.

MODEL 590 SPECIAL PURPOSE SLIDE ACTION - 3 in. chamber, similar to Model 500, except has 9 shot mag., 20 in. cyl. bore barrel with or w/o 3/4 shroud, and bayonet lug, blue or parkerized finish, regular black synthetic stock, with or w/o Speedfeed, 7.25 lbs. New 1987.

MSR $422	$345	$285	$230	$190	$165	$145	$125

Add $60 for parkerized finish.
Add $152 for heavy barrel with ghost ring sights, metal triggerguard and safety.
Add $127 for ghost ring sights.
Add $33 for Speedfeed (blue, disc. 1999) or $103 for Speedfeed (parkerized) stock.

* *Model 590 Mariner* - similar to Model 500 Mariner except is 9 shot and has 20 in. barrel. Mfg. 1989-93.

	$310	$250	$200	$185	$165	$145	$125

Last MSR was $353.

Add $17 for Speedfeed stock (disc. 1990).
Add $15 for pistol grip adapter (mini combo - disc.).

✴ *Model 590 Bullpup* - similar to Model 500 Bullpup except is 9 shot and has 20 in. barrel. Mfg. 1989-90 only.

| | $425 | $360 | $300 | $250 | $225 | $195 | $175 |

Last MSR was $497.

✴ *Model 590A1* - 12 ga., marked 590A1 on receiver, parkerized, ghost ring rear sight, synthetic stock and forend, ramp front sight. Disc. 1997.

| | $450 | $395 | $360 | $330 | $295 | $260 | $230 |

✴ *Model 590 Double Action* - 12 ga. only, 3 in. chamber, world's first double action shotgun (long trigger pull), 18 1/2 or 20 in. barrel, 6 or 9 shot, bead or ghost ring sights, black synthetic stock and forearm, top tang safety, parkerized metal finish, 7-7 1/4 lbs. Mfg. 2000-2003.

| | $450 | $415 | $360 | $330 | $295 | $260 | $230 |

Last MSR was $510.

Add $31 for 9 shot capacity.

Add $48 for ghost ring sights.

Add $124 for Speedfeed stock (20 in. barrel with ghost ring sights only).

MODEL 695 BOLT ACTION

MODEL 695 BOLT ACTION - 12 ga. only, with detachable 2 shot mag., 3 in. chamber, 22 in. barrel with fully rifled and ported (new 1999) or Accu-choke (disc. 1998) barrel, black synthetic or Woodlands camo (with bead sights, disc. 2001) on stock and forearm, rifle or Truglo fiberoptic sights, 7 1/2 lbs. Mfg. 1996-2002.

| | $275 | $220 | $185 | $150 | $135 | $120 | $115 |

Last MSR was $345.

Subtract approx. $50 for Accu-choke barrel.

Add $22 for Truglo fiberoptic sights (new 1998).

Add $52 for Truglo fiberoptic sights and Woodlands camo finish (disc. 2001).

MODEL 712 SEMI-AUTO

MODEL 712 SEMI-AUTO - 12 ga. only, gas operated, shoots 2 3/4 and 3 in. shells interchangeably, plain barrel or VR, top of receiver safety, checkered hardwood stock, rubber recoil pad, fixed or Accu-choke II choking. Mfg. 1986-88 only.

| | $285 | $250 | $220 | $200 | $190 | $175 | $160 |

Last MSR was $345.

Subtract $25 without Accu-II choking.

Add $90 for combo pack (includes 1 extra 24 in. slugster barrel).

✴ *Model 712 Steel Shot* - similar to Model 712, except has Accu-steel choking system for steel shot, 28 in. VR barrel. Mfg. 1988 only.

| | $290 | $250 | $220 | $200 | $190 | $175 | $160 |

Last MSR was $349.

✴ *Model 712 Camo/Speedfeed* - 12 ga. only, similar to Model 712, except has camo finished metal parts, stock, and forearm, 24 or 28 in. barrel. Mfg. 1986-87 only.

| | $340 | $295 | $240 |

Last MSR was $390.

Add $20 for Accu-II choke.

MODEL 712 REGAL SEMI-AUTO

MODEL 712 REGAL SEMI-AUTO - 12 or 20 ga., action same as Model 712, special bright bluing, VR only, deluxe checkered walnut stock and forearm, gold trigger, inlaid medallion on receiver, top of receiver safety. Mfg. 1986-87 only.

| | $310 | $280 | $250 | $225 | $200 | $185 | $170 |

Last MSR was $366.

Add $20 for Accu-II choke.

NEW HAVEN BRAND - similar to previous models, except plainer finish. Disc.

Values are 20% less per model.

GRADING - PPGS™	100%	98%	95%	90%	80%	70%	60%

MODEL 835 ULTI-MAG SLIDE ACTION - 12 ga. with 3 1/2 in. chamber (new 1988), slide action, 24 (Turkey Model - new 1990) or 28 in. VR barrel with Accu-mag choke tubes, 6 shot mag., safety on top rear of receiver, choice of camo synthetic or checkered hardwood stock. Introduced late 1988, disc. 1991.

		$375	$310	$265	$220	$190	$165	$150

Last MSR was $430.

Add $30 for synthetic camo field stock.

Various Combo packages were available in this model with prices ranging from $469-$534 depending on barrel chokings and scope base options.

This model was followed by the 835 Regal Series introduced in late 1991.

ULTI-MAG 835 FIELD GRADE SLIDE ACTION - 12 ga. only, 3 1/2 in. chamber, 24 in. cyl. bore (disc.), 24 in. VR (Turkey Special, disc. 1993), or 28 in. ported (new 1997) or unported VR barrel with 1 Accu-mag choke, walnut finish stock and forearm (pressed checkering became standard 1994), blue finish, approx. 7 1/2 lbs. Disc. 1998.

	$270	$230	$200	$185	$165	$145	$125

Last MSR was $331.

Add $40 for combo package (disc. 1993).

ULTI-MAG 835 SYNTHETIC (SPECIAL HUNTER) - 12 ga. only, 3 1/2 in. chamber, 26 (disc. 1999, reintroduced 2004) or 28 in. VR ported barrel with mod. Accu-mag choke, parkerized finish, black synthetic stock, 7.75 lbs. New 1998.

MSR $394	$315	$260	$220	$185	$165	$145	$125

ULTI-MAG 835 FIELD SLIDE ACTION (CROWN GRADE) - similar to Field Grade, except has gold trigger and cut checkering on walnut finished hardwood stock, blue or OFM Woodland camo (24 in. Turkey only) finish, ported (standard 1997) or unported (disc.) VR barrel, 7.75 lbs. New 1994.

MSR $394	$315	$260	$220	$185	$165	$145	$125

✳ *Model 835 Turkey* - 12 ga. only, 24 in. ported VR barrel, parkerized finish, walnut finished stock and forearm. Mfg. 1997-2000.

$320	$255	$215	$190	$165	$145	$125

Last MSR was $378.

✳ *Model 835 New Turkey* - 12 ga. only, 24 in. ported barrel with Ulti-full choke only, choice of Realtree Advantage Timber (new 2001), Realtree Hardwoods (mfg. 2000 only), Realtree Xtra brown (disc. 1999) or Woodlands (disc. 1999) 100% camo finish, fiberoptic sights, 7.5 lbs. Mfg. 1999-2001.

$450	$380	$345	$300	$270	$235	$210

Last MSR was $525.

✳ *Ulti-Mag 835 Crown Grade* - 12 ga. only, 3 1/2 in. chamber, 28 in. VR ported (standard 1997) or unported barrel, walnut stock and forearm, Accu-mag choke. Disc. 1998.

$365	$300	$260	$230	$200	$180	$160

Last MSR was $421.

Add $7 for duo-comb stock.

MODEL 835 VIKING - 12 ga. only, 28 in. VR ported (standard 1997) or unported (1996 only) barrel with one Accu-Choke and twin bead sights, matte blue finish with green synthetic stock and forearm, 7.7 lbs. Mfg. 1996-98.

$260	$225	$200	$185	$165	$145	$125

Last MSR was $316.

MODEL 835 CAMO TURKEY & WATERFOWL - 12 ga. only, 3 1/2 in. chamber, OFM Woodland Camo (all-purpose camo, combo. only mfg. 1997-99), Realtree (mfg. 1993-99), Realtree AP (all purpose grey, mfg. 1996-99), Realtree X-tra Brown (mfg. 2000-2002), Brown Leaf (disc. 1999), Woodlands (new 2000), Mossy Oak Shadow Grass (new 2000, Waterfowl only), Realtree Hardwoods (mfg. 2002, Turkey only), Mossy Oak New Break-up (new 2003), Mossy Oak Forest Floor (mfg. 2003 only),

GRADING - PPGS™	100%	98%	95%	90%	80%	70%	60%

Mossy Oak Obsession (mfg. 2004, Turkey model only), Advantage Max-4 (Waterfowl only, new 2004), Realtree Hardwoods HD Green (new 2003), Advantage Timber (mfg. 2001-2002), or Mossy Oak (mfg. 1994-99) finish, 20 (Grand Slam Turkey Model with X-factor ported turkey tube, new 2004), 24 (Turkey Special), 26 (Waterfowl, new 2004) or 28 (Waterfowl only) in. VR ported (new 1997) or unported (disc. 2000) barrel with 6 choke tubes, dual comb wood (Turkey/Deer combo only) or synthetic stock, approx. 7.5 lbs. New 1991.

	MSR $460	$390	$355	$300	$270	$235	$210	$190

Add $42 for Turkey/Deer or Turkey/Waterfowl combo.

Add $11 for Grand Slam Turkey Model with 20 in. barrel and X-factor ported turkey tube (new 2004).

Add $65 for 28 in. barrel with Mossy Oak Shadow Grass and hunter set of chokes (Waterfowl Model, disc.).

Subtract $22 for Waterfowl Model with Woodlands camo finish.

OFM Woodland camo finish on this model included a dual comb stock.

MODEL 835 WALNUT ULTI-MAG (REGAL) SLIDE ACTION - 12 ga., 3 1/2 in. chamber, 28 in. VR barrel with Accu-Mag chokes (disc. 1996) or 24 in. rifled slug barrel, single (new 1993) or dual comb (2 comb inserts are provided for the stock affording different shooting positions), aluminum receiver, back-bored barrel, double slide bars, high gloss walnut stock with recoil pad, approx. 7 1/2 lbs. Mfg. 1991-96.

	$350	$290	$260	$230	$200	$175	$160

Last MSR was $404.

Add $8 for dual comb stock.

Add $30 for 24 in. slug barrel with trophy scope base and dual comb stock.

Add $72-$83 for combo package (includes extra slug barrel with choice of sights).

MODEL 835 WILD TURKEY FED. LIMITED EDITION - 12 ga. with 3 1/2 in. chamber, 24 in. VR barrel with Accu-mag. chokes, camo finish, includes camo sling, medallion in stock, and 10-pack of Federal Turkey loads. Mfg. 1989 only.

	$425	$360	$295

Last MSR was $477.

MODEL 835 NWTF SPECIAL EDITION - 12 ga. only, 24 in. VR barrel with Accu-mag chokes, features Realtree camo finish, drilled and tapped receiver, 7 1/2 lbs. Mfg. 1991 only to commemorate the National Wild Turkey Federation.

	$380	$300	$225

Last MSR was $436.

MODEL 835 WATERFOWL LIMITED EDITION - 12 ga. with 3 1/2 in. chamber, 28 in. VR barrel with Accu-mag. chokes, camo finish, synthetic stock, camo sling. Mfg. 1990 only.

	$425	$360	$295

Last MSR was $480.

MODEL 835 FLYWAY SERIES WATERFOWL - 12 ga. only, 3 1/2 in. chamber, 28 in. VR with X-factor porting barrel and choke tubes, fiberoptic sights, synthetic stock and forearm with Advantage Max-4 camo, includes padded sling and embossed logo. New 2005.

	MSR $507	$415	$325	$265	$230	$200	$180	$160

MODEL 930 - 12 ga. only, 3 in. chamber, various configurations. New 2005.

✳ *Model 930 All Purpose Field* - 12 ga. only, 26 or 28 in. ported barrel with Accu-set chokes, vent. rib, blue metal, walnut stock, white bead front sight. New 2005.

	MSR $516	$420	$330	$270	$230	$200	$180	$160

✳ *Model 930 Turkey* - 12 ga. only, 24 in. ported barrel with XX-Full choke, vent. rib, fiberoptic sights, matte blue, Mossy Oak New Break-Up or Realtree Hardwoods HD Green finish, synthetic stock. New 2005.

	MSR $501	$410	$320	$260	$230	$200	$180	$160

Add $107 for camo.

GRADING - PPGS™	100%	98%	95%	90%	80%	70%	60%

* **Model 930 Waterfowl** - 12 ga. only, 26 or 28 in. ported barrel with Accu-set choke, vent. rib, walnut or synthetic stock, matte blue (wood stock only), Mossy Oak New Break-Up or Advantage Max-4 camo, fiberoptic sights. New 2005.

MSR $501	$410	$320	$260	$230	$200	$180	$160

   Add $15 for walnut stock and foream with matte blue metal finish.

   Add $107 for camo.

* **Model 930 Slugster** - 12 ga. only, 24 in. fully rifled bore barrel, choice of walnut, synthetic, or Monte Carlo synthetic, rifle sights or integral scope base, matte blue metal or Mossy Oak New Break-Up camo. New 2005.

MSR $516	$420	$330	$270	$230	$200	$180	$160

   Add $15 for walnut stock and forearm.

   Add $107 for camo.

MODEL 935 MAGNUM

- 12 ga. only, 3 1/2 in. chamber, choice of turkey or waterfowl configuration, 22 (Grand Slam Turkey model with X-factor ported turkey tube), 24 (turkey only), 26, or 28 VR barrel with choke tube(s) and fiberoptic front sight, matte or camo metal finish, wood (disc.) or synthetic stock and forearm, choice of full coverage Mossy Oak New Break Up, Advantage Max-4, Mossy Oak Shadowgrass, or Realtree Hardwoods HD Green camo, approx. 8 lbs. New 2004.

MSR $565	$465	$410	$370	$340	$300	$280	$260

   Add $109 for 100% camo coverage.

   Add $123 for Grand Slam Turkey model with 22 in. barrel and X-factor ported turkey tube.

   Add $178 for Turkey/Deer or Turkey/Waterfowl combo (new 2005).

MODEL 935 FLYWAY SERIES WATERFOWL

- 12 ga. only, 3 1/2 in. chamber, 28 in. VR with X-factor porting barrel and choke tubes, fiberoptic sights, synthetic stock and forearm with Advantage Max-4 camo, includes padded sling and embossed logo. New 2005.

MSR $718	$575	$475	$425	$375	$325	$300	$275

MODEL 1000 SEMI-AUTO

- 12 or 20 ga., gas semi-auto, 2 3/4 in. chamber, scroll engraved aluminum alloy receiver, plain or VR barrel, also available in trap and skeet configuration, checkered walnut stock and forearm. Imported 1986-87 only. VR became standard in 1987.

	$410	$345	$300	$270	$245	$220	$200

   Last MSR was $472.

   Add $28 for Multi-Choke II.

   Deduct $50 if without VR.

   Model 1000 barrels are not interchangeable with Model 1000 Super barrels.

   Manufactured by Howa, Mossberg took over this series after Smith & Wesson decided to drop the line.

* **Model 1000 Junior** - similar to Model 1000, except 20 ga. only, shortened stock, and 22 in. VR Multi-Choke barrel. Imported 1986-87 only.

	$425	$355	$310	$275	$250	$220	$200

   Last MSR was $499.

* **Model 1000 Slug** - 12 or 20 ga., 22 in. barrel with rifle sights, recoil pad. Imported 1986-87 only.

	$405	$340	$295	$270	$245	$220	$200

   Last MSR was $464.

* **Model 1000 Skeet** - 12 or 20 ga., steel receiver, 26 in. VR barrel bored skeet. Mfg. 1986 only.

	$395	$335	$295	$270	$245	$220	$200

   Last MSR was $439.

GRADING - PPGS™	100%	98%	95%	90%	80%	70%	60%

MODEL 1000 SUPER SEMI-AUTO
- 12 or 20 (Super 20) ga., gas semi-auto, 3 in. chambers, shoots 2 3/4 and 3 in. shells interchangeably, steel receiver, vent. recoil pad, select checkered walnut stock and forearm, Multi-Choke II is standard (except on slug barrel). Slug models are approx. the same price as values listed directly below. Imported 1986-87 only.

	$495	$405	$365	$330	$295	$270	$245

Last MSR was $577.

Model 1000 Super barrels are not interchangeable with Model 1000 barrels.

Manufactured by Howa, Mossberg took over this series after Smith & Wesson decided to drop the line.

❋ *Model 1000 Super Waterfowler* - 12 ga. only, matte finished wood and metal, includes swivels and camouflaged sling, 28 in. Multi-Choke barrel. Imported 1986-87 only.

	$510	$430	$370				

Last MSR was $605.

❋ *Model 1000 Super Skeet* - 12 or 20 ga., 25 in. barrel, jug choking. Imported 1986-87 only.

	$575	$495	$450	$410	$375	$330	$295

Last MSR was $658.

❋ *Model 1000 Super Trap* - 12 ga. only, 30 in. Multi-Choke II barrel with high VR, Monte Carlo stock, recoil pad. Mfg. 1986 only.

	$470	$380	$345	$320	$285	$270	$250

Last MSR was $560.

MODEL 3000 SLIDE ACTION
- 12 or 20 ga. only, 3 in. chamber, slide action, steel receiver, double action bars, various chokes and VR barrel lengths, checkered walnut stock and forearm, vent. recoil pad. This model was introduced in 1986 and the field version was disc. in 1987.

	$325	$275	$250	$220	$200	$185	$170

Last MSR was $360.

Add $25 for Multi-Choke II.

❋ *Model 3000 Waterfowler* - 12 ga. only, similar to Model 3000, except has dull matte finish on wood and metal, includes swivels and camouflaged sling, VR only. Mfg. 1986 only.

	$340	$295	$265				

Last MSR was $386.

Add $30 for Multi-choke II option, $70 for camo/speedfeed stock.

❋ *Model 3000 Law Enforcement* - 12 or 20 ga. only, 18 1/2 or 20 in. cylinder bore only, rifle or bead sights. Mfg. 1986-87 only.

	$325	$275	$250	$220	$200	$185	$170

Last MSR was $362.

Add $25 for rifle sights.

Add $33 for black speedfeed stock.

MODEL 5500 SEMI-AUTO
- 12 ga., 2 3/4 or 3 in. mag., gas operated, 18 1/2 - 30 in. barrels. Disc. 1985.

	$250	$235	$205	$185	$170	$155	$140

Last MSR was $307.

Add $20 for VR.

❋ *Model 5500 Mag.* - 12 ga. only, 3 in. chamber, 30 in. VR barrel. Disc. 1985.

	$275	$250	$225	$205	$190	$175	$160

Last MSR was $325.

GRADING - PPGS™	100%	98%	95%	90%	80%	70%	60%

MODEL 5500 MKII SEMI-AUTO
- 12 ga. only, supplied with 2 VR barrels - 26 in./2 3/4 in. chamber or 28 in./3 in. chamber VR barrel, includes choice of Accu-II choke tubes (lead shot only) or Accu-Steel choke tubes, blue or camo finish (new 1990), checkered hardwood stock and forearm, top receiver safety, recoil pad, 7 1/2 lbs. Mfg. 1989-92.

	$260	$225	$200	$180	$160	$140	$125

Last MSR was $294.

> **Add $10 for 24 in. rifled bore barrel.**
> **Add $43 for camo metal finish and synthetic stock.**
> **Add $30 for Turkey Model (24 in. barrel, camo finish, and synthetic stock).**
> This model was also available with different Combo options. Prices varied between $463-$484, depending on configuration of barrel choking.

✳ *Model 5500 U.S. Shooting Team* - 2 3/4 in. chamber, 26 in. non-Mag. barrel with VR and Accu-II chokes, blue finish, checkered walnut stock and forearm, 7 1/2 lbs. Mfg. 1991-92.

	$325	$250	$225	$200	$185	$170	$160

Last MSR was $376.

✳ *NWTF Special Edition* - 12 ga. only, 3 in. chamber, 24 in. VR barrel with 1 choke tube, Mossy Oak Camo finish with synthetic stock and forearm, 7.3 lbs. Mfg. 1991-92.

	$365	$300	$265	$235	$200	$175	$160

Last MSR was $428.

MODEL 6000 SEMI-AUTO
- 12 ga. only, 2 3/4 or 3 in. chamber 28 in. VR barrel with Accu-choke, economical model with walnut finish stock, blue finish, 7.7 lbs. Mfg. 1993 only.

	$280	$240	$215	$200	$185	$165	$145

Last MSR was $321.

MODEL 9200 CROWN SEMI-AUTO
- 12 ga. only, 3 in. chamber, gas operated, shoots any shell interchangeably, 18 1/2 (SP only), 22 (Bantam only), 24 in. rifled, 24 (Turkey), 26 (U.S. Shooting Team variation, new 1993), or 28 in. VR barrel with 3 Accu-chokes, engraved aluminum receiver, synthetic (18 1/2 in. barrel only) or walnut stained hardwood stock (1 in. shorter on Bantam Model) and forearm, top tang safety, approx. 7 1/2 lbs. Mfg. 1992-2001.

	$460	$335	$275	$225	$190	$170	$160

Last MSR was $574.

> **Add approx. $73-$95 for combo package.**
> **Add $33 for Truglo fiberoptic sights (mfg. 1998 only).**
> **Add $23 for 24 in. rifled bore barrel with trophy scope base.**
> **Subtract $90 for synthetic stock (Special Purpose with matte blue finish, 18 1/2 in. barrel).**

✳ *Model 9200 Viking* - 12 ga. only, 28 in. VR barrel with one Accu-Choke and twin bead sights, matte finish with green synthetic stock and forearm, 7.7 lbs. Mfg. 1996-98.

	$365	$310	$270	$230	$200	$175	$160

Last MSR was $429.

✳ *Model 9200 Special Hunter* - 12 ga. only, 28 in. VR barrel with Accu-II choke set, parkerized finish, black synthetic stock. Mfg. 1998-2001.

	$425	$345	$285	$245	$200	$175	$160

Last MSR was $491.

✳ *Model 9200 Camo* - 12 ga. only, similar to Model 9200, except is supplied with OFM (disc. 1996), Mossy Oak (disc. 1999), Realtree (mfg. 1994-95), Realtree AP (mfg. 1996-99) or Woodlands (new 1995) camo finish, 24 (Turkey) or 28 in. VR barrel. Mfg. 1992-99.

	$445	$320	$265	$230	$195	$170	$160

Last MSR was $556.

Subtract approx. $40 for Turkey Model with Woodlands camo and one choke tube.

>Model 9200 New Turkey Camo - 12 ga. only, 24 in. VR barrel with XX-full choke tube only and fiberoptic sights, choice of 100% Woodlands or Mossy Oak Shadow Branch camo treatment. Mfg. 1999-2001.

	$415	$300	$250	$225	$195	$170	$160

Last MSR was $517.

Add approx. $95 for Mossy Oak Shadow Branch camo coverage.

✴ *Model 9200 Jungle Gun* - 12 ga. only, 18 1/2 in. plain barrel with cyl. bore, parkerized metal, synthetic stock. Mfg. 1998-2001.

	$610	$500	$360	$300	$250	$225	$200

Last MSR was $704.

MOUNTAIN RIFLERY, INC.

Current custom rifle builder located in Pocatello, ID. Consumer direct sales.

John Bolliger has been producing top quality, custom made bolt action rifles for over 30 years. Currently, Mountain Riflery is concentrating on 3 series of rifles: the Signature Series, the Excalibur Series, and the Crown Series. Since almost all rifles are special ordered per customer specifications (with many options also available), please contact Mountain Riflery directly for more information, including pricing and options.

MOUNTAIN RIFLES INC.

Previous rifle manufacturer located in Palmer, AK 1995-98.

RIFLES: BOLT ACTION

MOUNTAINEER - various cals., choice of M-700 Rem. or M-70 Win. action, Chrome Moly barrel with ultra muzzle brake, Timney trigger, parkerized finish, fiberglass stock with decelerator pad, 5 1/2 lbs. Limited mfg. 1995-98.

	$1,825	$1,475	$1,100	$900	$750	$675	$550

Last MSR was $1,995.

SUPER MOUNTAINEER - similar to the Mountaineer, except has Kevlar epoxy bedded stock with steel crossbolts on Mag. cals., 4 1/4 lbs. Limited 1995-98.

	$2,575	$2,025	$1,475	$1,100	$900	$750	$675

Last MSR was $2,895.

PRO MOUNTAINEER K.S. - various cals., Winchester M-70 controlled feed action, choice of fiberglass pillar epoxy bedded, Kevlar, or KSDB (Kevlar Stock Drop Box mag.) stock with decelerator pad, parkerized finish. 6 lbs. Limited mfg. 1995-98.

	$2,395	$1,950	$1,425	$1,050	$875	$725	$650

Last MSR was $2,695.

Add $500 for KSDB stock with drop mag.

PRO SAFARI - various cals., Winchester M-70 controlled feed action, high gloss bluing, exhibition grade English walnut with decelerator pad, 4 shot detachable mag. 7-9 lbs. Limited mfg. 1995-98.

	$3,795	$3,350	$2,875	$2,350	$1,775	$1,450	$1,200

Last MSR was $3,995.

ULTRA MOUNTAINEER - various cals., features stainless steel match grade barrel with black Kevlar/Graphite thumbhole stock, approx. 5 lbs. New 1997.

	$2,650	$2,075	$1,500	$1,100	$900	$750	$675

Last MSR was $2,995.

Add $500 for Rigby length.

MUSGRAVE

Previous manufacturer located in the Republic of South Africa since 1951.

Musgrave had very limited importation into the U.S. Newer models manufactured by Musgrave (imported into Austria and Switzerland) included the Model 90 (features Musgrave action) Standard Rifle, Model 90 Light Rifle, Mini-90, Model 90 Varmint, Model 90 De Luxe Rifle, and Magnum Rifle, in addition to the same series in the Mauser 98 action.

RIFLES: BOLT ACTION

VALIANT BOLT ACTION RIFLE - .243 Win., .270 Win., .30-06, .308 Win., or 7mm Rem. Mag. cal., 24 in. barrel, leaf sight, skip checkered straight stock, pistol grip. Mfg. 1971-1976.

$375	$325	$275	$250	$220	$195	$175

PREMIER - similar to Valiant, with 26 in. barrel, select Monte Carlo stock, rosewood pistol grip cap and forearm tip.

$425	$365	$315	$275	$250	$225	$200

RSA SINGLE SHOT TARGET RIFLE - .308 Win. cal. only, 26 in. heavy barrel, target sights and stock. Mfg. 1971-1976.

$425	$365	$315	$275	$250	$225	$200

MUSKETEER RIFLES

Previous trademark of rifles previously imported by Firearms International Company (FIC), located in Washington, D.C.

RIFLES: BOLT ACTION

SPORTER - .243 Win., .25-06 Rem., .270 Win., .264 Win. Mag., .308 Win., .30-06, 7mm Rem. Mag., or .300 Win. Mag. cal., bolt action, FN Mauser action, 24 in. barrel, no sights, checkered Monte Carlo stock. Mfg. 1963-1972.

$375	$325	$275	$250	$220	$195	$175

SPORTER DELUXE - adj. trigger, select wood, tear drop pistol grip, skipline checkering.

$425	$365	$315	$275	$250	$225	$200

CARBINE - similar to Sporter, except 20 in. barrel and full length stock.

$375	$325	$275	$250	$220	$195	$175

NOTES

N SECTION

NS FIREARMS CORP.

Previous importer located in Atlanta, GA until 1994. NS Firearms was a division of KFS, Inc. located in Atlanta, GA. Previously manufactured in China.

GRADING - PPGS™	100%	98%	95%	90%	80%	70%	60%

RIFLES: SEMI-AUTO

MODEL 522 SPORTER - .22 LR cal., 21 in. cold hammer forged barrel, 5 shot detachable mag., grooved receiver, checkered walnut stock, 7 3/4 lbs. Imported 1994 only.

	100%	98%	95%	90%	80%	70%	60%
	$250	$215	$185	$165	$145	$125	$110

Last MSR was $299.

NAMBU PISTOLS

Previously manufactured in Japan for the Japanese military between 1902-1945.

PISTOLS: SEMI-AUTO

Please refer to Japanese Military Pistols for the Hamada variations.

TYPE 14 - 8mm Nambu cal., recoil operated, 4.7 in. barrel, blue, wood grips, 8 shot mag., a simply designed pistol used by Japanese armed forces from 1925-45.

Type 14 Nambus have a 3 or 4 digit number just forward of the lanyard ring on the right side of frame (on back of grip). Earliest Taisho era pistols are dated 15.11 or 15.12 from the Nagoya arsenal - can be identified by small trigger guard and other early features. Fewer than 100 mfg. To determine year and month of manufacture for most type 14 pistols, add "1925" to the first two digits and the last number will indicate the month (i.e. code 13.3 indicates a gun built in March of 1938).

Add 25% for 3.X date Tokyo.
Add 50% for 2.X date Nagoya.
Add 400% for early Taisho era pistols dated 15.11 or 15.12 from Nagoya arsenal.
Add 10% for matching mag. on models listed.

* *1925-1930 Mfg.*

	100%	98%	95%	90%	80%	70%	60%
	$900	$700	$475	$350	$300	$250	$225

* *1930-1939 Mfg.* - small trigger guard.

	100%	98%	95%	90%	80%	70%	60%
	$750	$600	$450	$350	$300	$250	$225

* *1939-1945 Mfg.* - large trigger guard.

	100%	98%	95%	90%	80%	70%	60%
	$425	$350	$300	$250	$225	$200	$175

Add 10% for strawed trigger and safety.

TYPE 94 - 8mm Nambu cal., recoil operated, 3.8 in. barrel, blue, and bakelite wood grips, 6 shot mag. Mfg. 1935-45.

	100%	98%	95%	90%	80%	70%	60%
	$325	$275	$225	$200	$185	$175	$165

Add 300% for 10.X date, 200% for 11.X date, 100% for 12.X date, 30% if pre-WWII, and 20% if late square back.

HAMADA NAMBU - .32 ACP or 8mm Nambu (scarce) cal., available with rough (early production, mostly prototypes) or polished (production) finish, very rare.

	100%	98%	95%	90%	80%	70%	60%
	$4,000	$3,500	$3,000	$2,500	$2,000	$1,600	$1,475

Add 30% for "in the white" 8mm Nambu, numbered 1-50.

BABY NAMBU - 7mm Nambu cal., 3 1/4 in. barrel, blue, wood grips, grip safety, one of the most desirable Japanese handguns.

	100%	98%	95%	90%	80%	70%	60%
	$3,500	$3,000	$2,500	$2,000	$1,700	$1,450	$1,200

Add 10% for matching mag.
Add 50% for chamber marked "TGE" (Tokyo Gas & Electric).

GRADING - PPGS™	100%	98%	95%	90%	80%	70%	60%

PAPA NAMBU (MODEL 1904) - 8mm Nambu cal., 4.7 in. barrel, wood grips, grip safety, 8 shot mag., essentially the same action as the Baby, but a larger version. Mfg. 1904-25.

	$2,000	$1,750	$1,500	$1,250	$1,000	$800	$700

    Add 10% for matching mag.

    Add 50% for chamber marked "TGE" (Tokyo Gas & Electric).

GRANDPA NAMBU - 8mm Nambu cal., similar to Papa Nambu, except has smaller trigger guard and fixed lanyard ring, cherry wood based mag., issued with 2 matching mags. Early Tokyo arsenal or later Thai issue, all Grandpa frames are slotted.

	$6,500	$4,500	$3,250	$2,600	$2,150	$1,850	$1,500

    Add 100% for matching shoulder stock.

    Add $3,500 for spare stock alone.

    Add 10% for second matching mag.

    Original stocks are rare and expensive.

1893 REVOLVER (MODEL 26) - 9mm Japanese cal., double action only, 4.7 in. barrel, blue, wood grips. Approx. 59,000 mfg. 1893-1925.

	$750	$600	$450	$300	$250	$200	$150

    Subtract 25% for arsenal rework.

    Add 100% for early mfg. with internal numbers (approx. first 300 revolvers), or final Kokura assembled pistols in 58,971-59,183 serial range.

NATIONAL WILD TURKEY FEDERATION

Current national conservation organization located in Edgefield, SC.

Although the National Wild Turkey Federation is not a manufacturer or importer, this organization has been responsible for many special and limited editions that are listed with quanities but without prices since they may vary greatly from region to region. Also, many are sold at auction, making pricing difficult to determine. "NWTF" suffix after model name indicates National Wild Turkey Federation gun of the year. Some of the models (and current values) may be listed under manufacturer listings in this text.

Manufacturer	Model	Quantity	Year	Issue Price
SHOTGUNS: AUCTION/TRADE EDITIONS				
Navy Arms	Black Powder 12 ga. NWTF	500	1983	$350
Winchester	Model 101	300	1985	$1,895
Browning	BPS 12 ga. NWTF	500	1986	$495
American Arms	SxS 10 ga. 3 1/2 in.	150	1985/86	$695
Winchester	Model 1300 Win-Cam 12 ga.	500	1987/88	$449
Winchester	Model 1300 12 ga. Trade Gun	N/A	N/A	$458
Beretta	Model A-303 12 ga. NWTF	500	1988/89	$695
Winchester	Model 1300 12 ga. Win-Cam NWTF	500	1989	$479
Winchester	Model 1300 12 ga. Trade Gun	N/A	N/A	$458
Browning	Model A5 12 ga. NWTF	500	1990	$925
Mossberg	Model 835 12 ga. Auction	500	1991	$567
Mossberg	Model 835 12 ga. Trade Gun	N/A	N/A	$436
Remington	Model 11-87 12 ga. Auction	N/A	1992	N/A
Remington	Model 11-87 12 ga. Trade Gun	N/A	N/A	$698
Winchester	Model 1300 12 ga. Auction	500	1993	$671
New England Firearms	SxS 20 ga. Auction	N/A	N/A	$167
New England Firearms	SxS 12 ga. Trade Gun	N/A	N/A	$200
New England Firearms	SxS 10 ga. Trade Gun	N/A	N/A	$240
American Arms	Model Turkey 12 ga. Auction	300	1993	N/A
Mossberg	Model 9200 12 ga. Auction	600	1994	$690

Manufacturer	Model	Quantity	Year	Issue Price
Mossberg	Model 9200 12 ga. Trade	N/A	1994	N/A
Luigi Franchi	Model 610 12 ga. Auction	600	1995	N/A
Fausti	O/U 12 ga. Auction	720	1996	N/A
New England Firearms	Topper Jr. 20 ga. Auction	N/A	1996	N/A
Fausti	O/U 12 ga. Auction	900	1997	N/A
New England Firearms	Jakes Topper Jr. 20 ga. Auction	N/A	1997	N/A
Remington	Model 870 12 ga. Auction	1200	1998	N/A
Beretta	Model AL390 12ga.	1400	1999	N/A
Ithaca	Model 37 12ga.	1700	2000	N/A
Browning	BPS 12 ga.	1900	2001	N/A
Winchester	Super X2	2100	2002	N/A
Winchester	Model 9410 .410 bore	2200	2003	N/A
Remington	Model 1100 20 ga.	2400	2004	N/A
Browning	BPS 12 ga.	2400	2005	N/A

NAVY ARMS COMPANY

Current importer established during 1958, and located in Union City, NJ, beginning 2001. Previously located in Ridgefield, NJ. Navy Arms imports are fabricated by various manufacturers including the Italian companies Davide Pedersoli & Co., Pietta & Co., and A. Uberti & C. Distributor and dealer sales.

Navy Arms has also sold a wide variety of original military firearms in used condition. Handguns included the Mauser Broomhandle, Japanese Nambu, Colt 1911 Government Model, Tokarev, Browning Hi-Power, S&W Model 1917, and others. Rifles included Mauser contract models, Japanese Type 38s, Enfields, FNs, Nagants, M1 Carbines, M1 Garands, Chinese SKSs, Egyptian Rashids, French MAS Model 1936s, among others. Most of these firearms are priced in the $75-$500 price range depending on desirability of model and condition.

For more information and up-to-date pricing regarding current Navy Arms black powder models, please refer to *Colt Blackpowder Reproductions and Replicas* by Dennis Adler and the *Blue Book of Modern Black Powder Arms* by John Allen & Dennis Adler (also online). These books feature hundreds of color photographs and support text of the most recent black powder models available, as well as complete pricing and a reference guide.

GRADING - PPGS™	100%	98%	95%	90%	80%	70%	60%

PISTOLS

TU-711 MAUSER - 9mm Para. cal., patterned after Mauser 711 (semi-auto version of the Model 712 Schnellfeuer), 5 1/4 in. barrel, 712 upper receiver that has been converted to 9mm Para. and mounted on new lower receiver, supplied with 10 and 20 shot detachable mag., mfg. in China, 2 lbs. 11 oz. Imported 1992 only.

	$575	$475	$425	$375	$325	$295	$275

Last MSR was $650.

TT-OLYMPIA - .22 LR cal., patterned after the Walther Olympia that won 1936 Olympics, 4 5/8 in. barrel, checkered walnut grips, mfg. in China, 27 oz. Imported 1992-98.

	$255	$225	$195	$175	$160	$150	$140

Last MSR was $290.

TU-90 PISTOL - .30 Tokarev or 9mm Para. cal., patterned after the rare Tokagypt variation (improved TT-33 Tokarev), 4 1/2 in. barrel, single action, wraparound synthetic grips, unique forward motion safety, mfg. in China, 30 oz. Imported 1992-98.

	$115	$100	$90	$80	$70	$60	$50

Last MSR was $130.

Add $15 for 9mm Para. cal.
Add $40 for pistol combo (includes both cals.).

GRADING - PPGS™	100%	98%	95%	90%	80%	70%	60%

LUGER MODEL - .22 LR cal. only, 10 shot mag., Luger toggle type action, available in blue or matte finish, 4, 6, or 8 in. barrel, checkered walnut stocks. Mfg. in U.S. 1986-87 only.

	$140	$120	$95	$85	$75	$70	$65

Last MSR was $165.

GRAND PRIX SILHOUETTE - .30-30 Win., 7mm Spl., .44 Mag., or .45-70 Govt. cal., 13 3/4 in. barrel, non-glare matte blue finish, walnut forearm and grips, adj. heat dispersing aluminum rib, adj. target sights, 4 lbs. Mfg. 1985 only.

	$320	$280	$240	$220	$195	$175	$150

Last MSR was $375.

REVOLVERS: REPRODUCTIONS

1872 OPEN TOP - .38 Spl. cal., 5 1/2 or 7 1/2 in. round barrel, case colored frame with blue cylinder and barrel, silver plated brass trigger guard and backstrap, 2 1/2-2 3/4 lbs. Limited importation 2000-2001 only.

	$335	$275	$220	$185	$165	$150	$135

Last MSR was $400.

1873 SAA - GUNFIGHTER SERIES & VARIATIONS - .32-20 WCF (mfg. 2002 only), .357 Mag. (new 1998), .44-40 WCF or .45 LC cal., reproduction of the Colt SAA, case hardened frame with blue or nickel (disc. 1998) finish, 3 (Sheriff's Model - mfg. 1992-98), 4 3/4, 5 1/2, or 7 1/2 in. barrel, the Gunfighter Series was introduced during 2003, approx. 36 oz.

MSR $479	$395	$325	$285	$225	$180	$160	$145

Add $65 for nickel finish (disc.).

Add $30 for Pinched Frame Model (7 1/2 in. barrel, .45 LC, disc. 2002).

Subtract $20 for brass trigger guard and backstrap (disc.).

The Gunfighter Series, introduced in 2003, is different than previous production in that it features a U.S. mfg. Wolff spring kit, German silver plated backstrap and trigger guard, and black checkered gunfighter grips.

✳ *Stainless Steel Model* - .357 Mag. or .45 LC cal., 4 3/4, 5 1/2, or 7 1/2 in. barrel, stainless steel construction. Importation began 2003.

MSR $569	$450	$350	$300				

✳ *Deluxe Model* - .32-20 WCF cal., deluxe model with color case hardened and charcoal blue finishes, high polish walnut grips, includes Wolff springs. Limited importation 2003.

	$365	$295	$230	$200	$180	$165	$140

Last MSR was $435.

This model is sold exclusively through AcuSport.

✳ *Economy Model* - .44-40 WCF or .45 LC cal., 3, 4 3/4, 5 1/2, or 7 1/2 in. barrel, brass trigger guard and backstrap, 2-piece walnut grips. Imported 1993-96.

	$295	$230	$185	$160	$145	$130	$120

Last MSR was $345.

✳ *Deputy Model* - .44-40 WCF or .45 LC cal., patterned after the Colt 1877 Thunderer double action, bird's head grips, 3, 3 1/2, 4, or 4 3/4 in. barrel, case colored frame. Imported 1997-98 only.

	$350	$275	$210	$180	$160	$145	$130

Last MSR was $405.

✳ *Flattop Target Model* - .45 LC cal. only, features flattop frame, 7 1/2 in. barrel only, adj. spring loaded front sight and dovetailed rear sight, 30 oz. Importation began 1999.

MSR $514	$425	$350	$285	$240	$205	$175	$150

GRADING - PPGS™	100%	98%	95%	90%	80%	70%	60%

✱ *Shootist Model* - .357 Mag., .44-40 WCF, or .45 LC cal., interchangeable parts with original Colt 1st and 2nd Generation SAAs, designed for Cowboy Action Shooting, 4 3/4, 5 1/2, or 7 1/2 in. barrel, case colored frame and hammer, blue cylinder barrel, trigger guard and backstrap. Limited importation 2000 only.

	$350	$275	$210	$180	$160	$145	$130

Last MSR was $385.

✱ *Bisley Model* - .44-40 WCF or .45 LC cal., patterned after the Colt Bisley, 4 3/4, 5 1/2, or 7 1/2 in. barrel, case colored frame, spur hammer, walnut grips. Importation began 1997.

MSR $502	$400	$325	$250	$195	$160	$145	$130

>Bisley Flattop Target Model - .44-40 WCF or .45 LC cal., features flattop frame, adj. front sight, and dovetailed rear sight, 40 oz. Importation began 1999.

MSR $526	$415	$340	$265	$200	$175	$150	$135

✱ *Cavalry Model* - .45 LC cal. only, exact replica of the original U.S. Government issue SAA, 7 1/2 in. barrel, arsenal stampings, inspector's cartouche on walnut stocks.

MSR $550	$475	$365	$320	$275	$230	$200	$175

✱ *Artillery Model* - similar specifications to the Cavalry Model, except has 5 1/2 in. barrel.

MSR $550	$475	$365	$320	$275	$230	$200	$175

✱ *Scout Small Frame Model* - .38 Spl. cal., scaled down variation of the SAA, 4 3/4 or 5 1/2 in. barrel only. Importation began 2003.

MSR $479	$395	$325	$285	$225	$180	$160	$145

1875 REMINGTON REVOLVER - .44-40 WCF or .45 LC cal., reproduction of the 1875 Remington revolver, 7 1/2 in. barrel, case colored frame, 41 oz. Importation disc. 1991, resumed 1994-2000.

	$360	$295	$260	$230	$200	$175	$150

Last MSR was $435.

1890 REMINGTON REVOLVER - .44-40 WCF or .45 LC cal., reproduction of the 1890 Remington revolver, 5 1/2 in. barrel, brass trigger guard and lanyard loop, 39 oz. Importation disc. 1991, resumed 1994-2000.

	$370	$295	$260	$230	$200	$175	$150

Last MSR was $445.

1875 SCHOFIELD SERIES - various cals., patterned after the original S&W Schofield Model, blued finish, smooth wood grips, case colored hammer, trigger guard and opening lever. Imported 1994-2003.

	$615	$535	$455	$375	$325	$250	$195

Last MSR was $716.

✱ *Cavalry Model* - .38 Spl. (new 2003), .44-40 WCF, or .45 LC cal., patterned after the original Schofield Cavalry Model, 7 1/2 in. barrel, 37 oz. New 1994.

MSR $811	$675	$575	$475	$385	$330	$250	$195

✱ *Wells Fargo Model* - .38 Spl. (new 2003), .44-40 WCF, or .45 LC cal., 5 1/2 in. barrel, 35 oz. New 1994.

MSR $811	$675	$575	$475	$385	$330	$250	$195

✱ *Hideout Model* - .44-40 WCF or .45 LC cal., similar to Wells Fargo Model, except has 3 1/2 in. barrel, 34 oz. New 1999.

MSR $811	$675	$575	$475	$385	$330	$250	$195

✱ *Founders Model* - .45 LC cal., charcoal blue barrel and cylinder, case colored receiver, backstrap, trigger guard, and trigger, 7 1/2 in. barrel, white ivory tex grips. Importation began 2003.

MSR $919	$775	$650	$500	$400	$350	$250	$195

GRADING - PPGS™	100%	98%	95%	90%	80%	70%	60%

* ***Engraved Model*** - .44-40 WCF or .45 LC cal., similar to Deluxe Schofield, except does not have gold inlays, extensive B or C coverage scroll engraving on both frame, cylinder, and barrel. Special order only beginning 1999.

MSR N/A	$1,425	$1,225	$1,000	$875	$750	$625	$525

    Add $215 for C engraving.

* ***Deluxe Model*** - .44-40 WCF or .45 LC cal., available in Cavalry, Wells Fargo, or Hideout configurations, with light scroll engraving on frame and cylinder with extensive frame, barrel, and cylinder gold line inlays and scroll motifs. Special order only beginning 1999.

MSR N/A	$1,675	$1,450	$1,250	$995	$875	$750	$625

NEW MODEL RUSSIAN - .44 Russian cal., patterned after the S&W Model 3 Russian Third Model Single Action, 6 1/2 in. barrel, blue metal with case colored trigger, trigger guard, and hammer, smooth walnut grips, 40 oz. Importation began 1999.

MSR $893	$750	$625	$500	$400	$350	$250	$195

REVOLVERS: REPRODUCTIONS, COLT CARTRIDGE CONVERSIONS

1851 NAVY RICHARDS-TYPE CONVERSION - .38 Spl. or .38 LC cal., patterned after the Colt 1851 Navy Conversion, 5 1/2 or 7 1/2 in. barrel, case colored frame and hammer, blue cylinder and barrel, brass back strap and trigger guard, 40 or 44 oz. Imported 1999-2001.

	$320	$255	$200	$175	$160	$145	$130

Last MSR was $375.

1860 ARMY RICHARDS-TYPE CONVERSION - .38 Spl. or .38 LC cal., patterned after the Colt 1860 Army Conversion, other specifications similar to 1851 Navy Conversion. Imported 1999-2001.

	$320	$255	$200	$175	$160	$145	$130

Last MSR was $375.

1861 NAVY RICHARDS-TYPE CONVERSION - .38 Spl. or .38 LC cal., patterned after the Colt 1861 Navy Conversion, other specifications similar to 1851 Navy Conversion. Imported 1999-2001.

	$320	$255	$200	$175	$160	$145	$130

Last MSR was $375.

REVOLVERS: PREMIUM BLUE REPRODUCTIONS, CARTRIDGE CONVERSIONS

During 2003, Navy Arms planned to introduce its line of Premium Blue custom guns. To date, these guns have not yet been manufactured. Models included were: 1860 Army Richards Type I ($1,995 MSR), Richards-Mason Colt Pocket Navy Model ($2,995 MSR), Richards-Mason Colt Police Model ($2,695 MSR), 1842 Paterson Conversion Model ($2,100 MSR), Remington Navy .38 Colt Cartridge Conversion, Remington Army 5 Shot Cartridge Conversion ($1,295 MSR), and the Remington 6 Shot Cartridge Conversion ($1,495 MSR).

RIFLES: REPRODUCTIONS

REVOLVING CARBINE - .357 Mag., .44-40 WCF, or .45 LC cal., 6 shot cylinder, 20 in. barrel, case hardened frame, straight stock. Mfg. 1968-1984.

	$575	$475	$425	$375	$325	$275	$225

REMINGTON ROLLING BLOCK BUFFALO RIFLE - .444 Marlin (disc.), .45-70 Govt., or .50-70 (disc.) cal., replica of Remington Rolling Block, 26 or 30 in. heavy octagon or 1/2 round/ 1/2 octagon barrel (disc. 2000), open sight, straight grip stock. Mfg. 1971-2003.

	$655	$465	$350	$260	$195	$160	$140

Last MSR was $850.

Brass fittings were disc. during 1998, and replaced with steel fittings.

GRADING - PPGS™	100%	98%	95%	90%	80%	70%	60%

✳ *Buffalo Carbine* - similar to Rifle, with 18 in. barrel. Disc. 1985.

	$385	$325	$280	$230	$180	$160	$140

Last MSR was $375.

✳ *Rolling Block Baby Carbine* - .22 LR, .22 Hornet, .357 Mag., or .44-40 WCF cal., replica of small frame Remington, 20 in. octagon or 22 in. round barrel, open sight, straight stock. Mfg. 1968-84.

	$215	$175	$140	$110	$90	$65	$55

REMINGTON ROLLING BLOCK BODINE RIFLE - single or double set triggers, 30 in. heavy matte finished octagon barrel, "Soule" target rear tang sight, and split level globe front sight, No. 2 configuration became available during 2003, 12 lbs.

MSR $1,640	$1,375	$1,100	$950	$800	$650	$500	$400

ROLLING BLOCK PLAINS RIFLE - .45-70 Govt. cal., features 30 in. tapered octagon barrel with straight grip stock, bright polished receiver with steel furniture, 9 lbs. Imported 1997-98 only.

	$650	$500	$400	$285	$195	$175	$150

Last MSR was $800.

✳ *Deluxe Rolling Block Plains Rifle* - similar to Plains Rifle, except has hand engraved coin finished receiver and trigger guard, rust blue barrel with German silver forearm tip. Imported 1997-98.

	$1,475	$1,250	$1,050	$850	$725	$600	$525

Last MSR was $1,625.

ROLLING BLOCK NO. 2 CREEDMOOR TARGET - similar to Buffalo Rifle, in .45-70 Govt. or .50-70 (disc.) cal., with Creedmoor tang sight, color case hardened receiver, checkered walnut.

MSR $1,097	$850	$625	$450	$325	$200	$175	$150

✳ *Deluxe Rolling Block No. 2 Creedmoor Target* - featured hand engraved coin finished receiver and trigger guard, rust blue barrel and German silver forearm tip. Imported 1997-98.

	$1,625	$1,400	$1,200	$1,000	$850	$725	$600

Last MSR was $1,875.

SHARPS NO. 2 SILHOUETTE - .45-70 Govt. cal., 30 in. octagon barrel, 10 3/4 lbs. Importation began 2003.

MSR $1,639	$1,375	$1,100	$975	$850	$750	$650	$575

SHARPS NO. 2 HUNTER - limited importation 2003 only.

	$750	$650	$575	$525	$475	$425	$375

Last MSR was $815.

1874 SHARPS PLAINS RIFLE - .45-70 Govt. cal., 32 in. octagon barrel, case hardened receiver, checkered stock and forearm, double set triggers, 9 1/2 lbs. Mfg. 1996-2002.

	$1,020	$900	$800	$725	$625	$575	$525

Last MSR was $1,175.

    Add $75 for vernier rear tang or $55 for globe sight.

✳ *Engraved Sharps Plains Rifle* - .45-70 Govt. cal., features hand engraved coin finished receiver. Imported 1997-98.

	$2,325	$2,000	$1,800	$1,600	$1,400	$1,200	$995

Last MSR was $2,500.

    Add $700 for gold inlays (Deluxe Model).

1874 SHARPS BUFFALO RIFLE - .45-70 Govt. or .45-90 (disc. 2000) cal., 28 in. octagon heavy barrel, case colored receiver, checkered stock, 10 lbs. 10 oz. Mfg. 1996-2002.

	$1,035	$925	$825	$725	$625	$575	$525

Last MSR was $1,200.

    Add $75 for vernier rear tang or $55 for globe sight.

|---|---|---|---|---|---|---|---|

✱ Engraved Sharps Buffalo Rifle - .45-70 Govt. or .45-90 cal., features hand engraved coin finished receiver. Imported 1997-98.

	$2,325	$2,000	$1,800	$1,600	$1,400	$1,200	$995

Last MSR was $2,515.

Add $700 for gold inlays (Deluxe Model).

SHARPS SPORTING RIFLE - .45-70 Govt. cal., similar to Plains Rifle, except has pistol grip stock, No. 2 configuration became available during 2003. Importation began 1997.

MSR $1,603	$1,325	$1,150	$950	$825	$700	$625	$550

1874 SHARPS QUIGLEY - .45-70 Govt. cal., 34 in. octagon barrel, exact reproduction of rifle used in "Quigley Down Under," with patchbox. Importation began 2002.

MSR $1,703	$1,425	$1,175	$975	$850	$700	$625	$550

1874 SHARPS NO. 2 CREEDMOOR - .45-70 Govt. cal., 30 in. thin tapered round barel, polished nickel frame and action, "Soule" rear tang sight with front globe, 9 lbs. Importation began 2002.

MSR $1,603	$1,325	$1,150	$950	$825	$700	$625	$550

1874 SHARPS NO. 3 LONG RANGE - .45-70 Govt. cal., 34 in. medium weight octagon barrel with globe front target sight, shotgun buttplate, double set triggers, German silver forearm cap, 10 lbs. 14 oz. Importation began 2000.

MSR $2,206	$1,825	$1,500	$1,250	$1,075	$925	$725	$600

1874 SHARPS SNIPER/INFANTRY RIFLE - .45-70 Govt. cal., patterned after the 3-band military sniper rifle, 30 in. barrel, color case hardened frame, hammer, and furniture, ST or DST (Sniper rifle, disc. 1995). Mfg. 1994-2000.

	$895	$780	$650	$475	$395	$350	$325

Last MSR was $1,060.

Add $55 for DST (Sniper).

✱ 1874 Sharps Cavalry Carbine - .45-70 Govt. cal., patterned after Sharps Cavalry carbine, 22 in. barrel, color case hardened frame, hammer, patchbox, and furniture. New 1994.

MSR $1,186	$925	$780	$650	$475	$395	$350	$325

1873 SPRINGFIELD INFANTRY RIFLE - .45-70 Govt. cal., 32 1/2 in. barrel, 8 lbs, 4 oz. Imported 1997-2000.

	$840	$750	$650	$475	$395	$350	$325

Last MSR was $995.

✱ 1873 Springfield Cavalry Carbine - similar to the 1873 Springfield Rifle, except has 22 in. barrel, 1 barrel band, 7 lbs. Importation began 1997.

MSR $1,475	$1,295	$1,025	$900	$775	$650	$550	$450

Subtract $378 for Springfield Officer's Model.

KODIAK MARK IV DOUBLE RIFLE - .45-70 Govt. cal., patterned after the Colt Double rifle, semi-regulated barrels, hammers, folding leaf rear sight, 24 in. barrels, color cased hardened receiver, 10 lbs. 3 oz. Mfg. 1996-2000.

	$2,450	$2,250	$2,000	$1,800	$1,600	$1,400	$1,200

Last MSR was $2,815.

✱ Deluxe Kodiak Mark IV - similar to Kodiak Mark IV Double rifle, except has brown barrels and hand engraved satin finished receiver. Mfg. 1996-2000.

	$3,300	$2,900	$2,600	$2,375	$2,000	$1,750	$1,500

Last MSR was $3,690.

HENRY RIFLE - .44-40 WCF, .44 Rimfire (disc. 1989), or .45 LC (new 1998) cal., reproduction of Winchester's famous Henry Rifle, brass or iron frame. New 1985.

GRADING - PPGS™	100%	98%	95%	90%	80%	70%	60%

✳ *Military Rifle* - 24 in. barrel, brass frame, blue barrel, walnut stock, original style sling swivels, 9 1/4 lbs. New 1985.

MSR $1,165	$895	$700	$575	$450	$325	$250	$225

✳ *Union Pacific Railroad Commemorative* - .44-40 WCF cal., only 100 mfg.

	$795	$575	$475				

Last MSR was $695.

✳ *Engraved Rifle* - limited mfg., extensive engraving on brass frame. Disc. 1988.

	$1,510	$1,275	$1,100	$900	$750	$650	$550

Last MSR was $1,850.

Add $100 for steel frame.

✳ *Carbine* - 24 in. barrel, limited edition of 1,000 units including 50 engraved specimens, no swivels, 8 1/4 lbs. Importation disc. 2002.

	$685	$540	$450	$350	$275	$225	$195

Last MSR was $875.

✳ *Engraved Carbine* - limited production, only 50 mfg. Disc. 1988.

	$1,450	$1,225	$1,075	$900	$750	$650	$550

Last MSR was $1,750.

✳ *Trapper Model* - 16 1/2 in. barrel, 7 1/4 lbs., 34 1/4 in. overall length. Disc. 2000.

	$685	$540	$450	$350	$275	$225	$195

Last MSR was $875.

✳ *Iron Frame Model* - with steel frame and buttplate, 24 in. blue barrel, select walnut, 9 1/4 lbs.

MSR $1,222	$975	$800	$650	$550	$450	$375	$325

This model is available with either blue (.44-40 WCF cal. only) or color case hardened receiver.

MODEL 1866 YELLOWBOY CARBINE/RIFLE - .22 LR (disc.), .357 Mag. (disc.), .38 Spl. (new 1998), .44-40 WCF, or .45 LC (new 1998) cal., choice of rifle (24 1/4 in. octagon barrel), short rifle (20 in. octagon barrel), or carbine (19 in. round barrel), brass (disc.) or case hardened receiver, replica of the Winchester Model 1866. Mfg. 1972-84, reintroduced.

MSR $915	$745	$600	$450	$350	$250	$225	$200

Subtract $33 for carbine variation.

✳ *Model 1866 100th Anniversary Indian Victory in Little Big Horn* - quantity unknown.

	$725	$625	$525				

YELLOWBOY TRAPPER - .44-40 WCF cal., 16 1/2 in. barrel. Disc.

	$675	$575	$475	$425	$375	$325	$275

MODEL 1873 STANDARD CARBINE/RIFLE - .357 Mag. (new 1998), .44-40 WCF or .45 LC cal., choice of rifle (24 in. octagon barrel) or carbine (19 in. round barrel), replica of the Winchester Model 1873.

MSR $1,025	$865	$700	$575	$450	$350	$295	$250

Add $23 for rifle variation.

✳ *Model 1873 Trapper* - .44-40 WCF cal., similar to Carbine, with 16 1/2 in. barrel. Disc.

	$700	$600	$500	$425	$375	$325	$275

✳ *Model 1873 Border Model Rifle* - .357 Mag., .44-40 WCF, or .45 LC cal., features 20 in. short octagon rifle barrel, case hardened receiver with blue barrel, 7 lbs. 6 oz. Importation began 1999.

MSR $1,047	$880	$715	$575	$450	$350	$295	$250

✳ *Model 1873 Deluxe Border Model Rifle* - similar to Model 1873 Deluxe Sporting Rifle, except has 20 in. barrel. Importation began 2001.

MSR $1,183	$975	$800	$625	$500	$400	$300	$225

GRADING - PPGS™	100%	98%	95%	90%	80%	70%	60%

✳ *Model 1873 Deluxe Sporting Rifle* - deluxe variation of the Model 1873 featuring case hardened receiver, lever, and hammer, checkered pistol grip stock, and choice of 24 1/4 or 30 (not available in .357 Mag. cal., disc. 2002) in. barrel, 8 lbs. 4 oz. or 8 lbs., 14 oz. New 1992.

	100%	98%	95%	90%	80%	70%	60%
MSR $1,183	$975	$800	$625	$500	$400	$300	$225

    Add $30 for 30 in. barrel (disc. 2002).

✳ *Model 1873 Deluxe Sporting Rifle Long Range* - .44-40 WCF cal., 30 in. barrel with rear tang sight. Imported 2003 only.

			95%	90%	80%	70%	60%
		$995	$800	$625	$475	$350	$300	$250

                                           Last MSR was $1,140.

✳ *Model 1873 1 of 1,000* - only 1,000 mfg., deluxe wood, special engraving.

		98%	95%
	$1,000	$775	$550

MODEL 1892 STANDARD CARBINE/RIFLE - .357 Mag., .44-40 WCF, or .45 LC cal.,
features 20 (carbine, w/o forearm cap, disc. 2001) or 24 (rifle) in. octagon barrel, choice of brass (disc.), blue, or case hardened receiver and crescent buttplate, uncheckered straight grip walnut stock and forearm, 5 lbs. 14 oz. or 7 lbs. Imported 1999-2003.

		98%	95%	90%	80%	70%	60%
	$465	$385	$335	$280	$240	$210	$185

                                         Last MSR was $561.

    Subtract approx. $65 for carbine configuration (disc. 2001).

✳ *Model 1892 Stainless Carbine/Rifle* - similar to Standard Model 1892, except is stainless steel, not available in .44-40 WCF cal. Imported 2000-2003.

		98%	95%
	$435	$360	$300

                                         Last MSR was $530.

    Add $73 for rifle configuration.

✳ *Model 1892 Short Rifle* - also available in .32-20 WCF cal. (new 2002), similar to Model 1892 Standard Rifle, except has 20 in. short barrel, not available with brass frame, approx. 6 1/4 lbs. Imported 1999-2003.

		98%	95%	90%	80%	70%	60%
	$465	$385	$335	$280	$240	$210	$185

                                         Last MSR was $561.

✳ *Model 1892 Stainless Short Rifle* - similar to Model 1892 Short Rifle, except is stainless steel. Imported 2000 only.

		98%	95%
	$485	$360	$300

                                         Last MSR was $603.

MODEL 1885 HIGH WALL RIFLE - .45-70 Govt. cal., available with 30 in. medium
heavy octagon barrel with crescent buttplate or 28 in. round barrel with shotgun style buttplate, standard or open target sights, case hardened frame and lever, uncheckered European walnut stock and forearm, 9 1/4 or 10 lbs. Importation began 1999.

	100%	98%	95%	90%	80%	70%	60%
MSR $1,049	$900	$700	$600	$475	$375	$300	$275

    Add $85 for 30 in. octagon barrel.
    Add $117 for rear tang sight.

RIFLES: MODERN PRODUCTION

In addition to the models listed, Navy Arms in late 1990 purchased the manufacturing rights of the English firm Parker-Hale. In 1991, Navy Arms built a manufacturing facility, Gibbs Rifle Co., located in Martinsburg, WV and produced these rifles domestically 1991-1994 (see Gibbs Rifle Co. listing for more info on models the company currently imports).

TU-KKW TRAINING RIFLE - .22 LR cal., replica of the German "KKW" Gewehr training rifle, full sized Mauser 98K action with military sights, 26 in. barrel, detachable 5 shot mag., mfg. in China, 8 lbs. Imported 1992-94.

		98%	95%	90%	80%	70%	60%
	$210	$180	$150	$135	$120	$105	$90

                                         Last MSR was $310.

    Add $125 for 2 3/4 power Type 89 quick mount scope (Sniper Trainer).

GRADING - PPGS™	100%	98%	95%	90%	80%	70%	60%

TU-33/40 CARBINE - .22 LR or 7.62x39mm cal., based on WWII Mauser G33/40 mountain carbine, 20 3/4 in. barrel, includes sling, adj. rear sight, mfg. in China, 7 lbs. 7 oz. Imported 1992-94.

	$180	$150	$135	$120	$105	$90	$75

Last MSR was $210.

JW-15 RIFLE - .22 LR cal., sporter bolt action based on Brno Model 5 action, 24 in. barrel, detachable 5 shot mag., receiver top is dove-tailed, mfg. in China, 5 lbs. 12 oz. Imported 1992-94.

	$85	$70	$60	$50	$40	$35	$30

Last MSR was $100.

MARTINI TARGET RIFLE - .444 Marlin or .45-70 Govt. cal., single shot, 26 or 30 in. octagon barrel, tang sight, pistol grip stock. Mfg. 1972-84.

	$480	$420	$350	$250	$195	$175	$150

RPKS-74 - .223 Rem. or 7.62x39mm (new 1989) cal., semi-auto version of the Chinese RPK Squad Automatic Weapon, Kalashnikov action, 19 in. barrel, integral folding bipod, 9 1/2 lbs. Imported 1988-89 only.

	$525	$445	$350	$250	$195	$175	$150

Last MSR was $649.

MODEL 1 CARBINE/RIFLE - .45-70 Govt. cal., action is sporterized No. 1 MKIII Enfield, choice of 18 (carbine) or 22 (rifle) in. barrel with iron sights, black Zytel Monte Carlo (rifle) or straight grip walnut (carbine) stock, 7 (carbine) or 8 1/2 (rifle) lbs. Limited importation 1999 only.

	$325	$255	$200	$175	$160	$145	$130

Last MSR was $375.

MODEL 4 CARBINE/RIFLE - .45-70 Govt. cal., action is sporterized No. 4 MKI Enfield, choice of 18 (carbine) or 22 (rifle) in. barrel, blue metal, choice of checkered walnut Monte Carlo (rifle) or uncheckered straight grip (carbine, disc. 1999) stock, 7 or 8 lbs. Mfg. 1999-2001.

	$325	$255	$200	$175	$160	$145	$130

Last MSR was $375.

✳ *Deluxe No. 4 Enfield Sporter* - .303 British cal., synthetic Zytel Monte Carlo stock, 25 in. barrel with original military sights, approx. 8 1/2 lbs. Mfg. 1999-2001.

	$115	$95	$85	$75	$65	$55	$50

Last MSR was $125.

2A HUNTER CARBINE/RIFLE - .308 Win. cal., action is sporterized 2A Enfield, 18 (carbine) or 22 (rifle) in. barrel with Parker-Hale style muzzle brake, includes scope mount, 12 shot mag., black enamel synthetic Zytel stock, 6 3/4 or 10 1/4 lbs. Mfg. 1999-2001.

	$240	$210	$190	$175	$160	$145	$130

Last MSR was $275.

Add $50 for rifle variation.

✳ *Deluxe 2A Enfield Sporter* - .308 Win. cal., 25 in. barrel, black Zytel Monte Carlo stock, original 2A Enfield military sights, approx. 8 1/2 lbs. Mfg. 1999-2001.

	$130	$110	$95	$85	$75	$65	$55

Last MSR was $150.

SHOTGUNS: O/U, RECENT IMPORTATION

Importation of the models listed was disc. in 1990.

MODEL 83 - 12 or 20 ga., manufactured in Italy by R. Luciano, 3 in. chambers, extractors, double triggers, engraved chrome receiver, vent. barrels (bored M/F or IC/M) and rib. Introduced 1985.

	$280	$240	$215	$195	$170	$160	$150

Last MSR was $320.

GRADING - PPGS™	100%	98%	95%	90%	80%	70%	60%

MODEL 93 - 12 or 20 ga., manufactured in Italy by R. Luciano, 3 in. chambers, ejectors, double triggers, engraved chrome receiver, vent. barrels (bored M/F or IC/M) and rib. Introduced 1985.

	$325	$285	$250	$220	$200	$185	$160

Last MSR was $380.

MODEL 95 - similar to Model 93, except with single trigger and multi-chokes (includes 5 tubes), extractors.

	$375	$330	$295	$265	$235	$210	$190

Last MSR was $420.

MODEL 96 SPORTSMAN - 12 ga. only, 3 in. chambers, vent. barrels and rib, engraved chrome receiver, gold-plated receiver, multi-choked with 5 choke tubes, ejectors. Introduced 1985.

	$470	$425	$375	$330	$295	$260	$230

Last MSR was $530.

MODEL 100 - 12, 20, 28 ga., or .410 bore, 3 in. chambers, 26 in. VR barrels, photo engraved hard chrome receiver, single trigger, extractors, checkered walnut stock and forearm, approx. 6 1/4 lbs. Introduced 1985.

	$225	$205	$190	$170	$160	$150	$140

Last MSR was $250.

SHOTGUNS: SxS, RECENT IMPORTATION

MODEL 100 - 12 or 20 ga., 3 in. chambers, 27 1/2 in. barrels, checkered European walnut, double triggers, extractors, 6 1/2 or 7 lbs. Imported 1985-87 only.

	$380	$330	$290	$260	$230	$200	$170

Last MSR was $475.

MODEL 150 - similar to Model 100, except with ejectors. Imported 1985-87 only.

	$455	$395	$350	$310	$280	$250	$220

Last MSR was $574.

SHOTGUNS: SINGLE SHOT

MODEL 105 SINGLE BARREL - 12, 20 ga., or .410 bore, 26 or 28 in. full choke barrel only, folding action, engraved chrome receiver, checkered hardwood stock and forearm. New 1985.

	$80	$70	$65	$60	$55	$50	$45

Last MSR was $90.

This model was designated the Model 600 before 1988.

✳ *Model 105 Deluxe* - similar to Model 105, except has European walnut stock and VR.

	$95	$85	$75	$65	$60	$55	$50

Last MSR was $105.

This model was designated the Model 600 Deluxe before 1988.

P.V. NELSON, (GUNMAKERS)

Current manufacturer located in Bucks, England.

P.V. Nelson manufactures best quality shotguns and double rifles per individual customer order. Double rifles feature back action locks, and bolsters for extra strength. Side-by-side and over/under shotguns are available in most gauges, with a choice of rounded or regular action. Please contact the company directly (see Trademark Index) to find out more information about this quality English manufacturer.

NESIKA

Current trademark of rifles and actions manufactured by Nesika Bay Precision, Inc., located in Sturgis, SD. Currently distributed by Dakota Arms. Previously located in Poulsbo, WA until 2003. Dealer and consumer sales.

GRADING - PPGS™	100%	98%	95%	90%	80%	70%	60%

RIFLES: BOLT ACTION

Nesiak also sells its propriety actions in Classic, Round, and Hunter configuration and in a variety of cals. Current prices range from $900 MSR - $1,605 MSR.

CLASSIC HUNTER - various cals., stainless Nesika action and barrel, adj. trigger, composite, laminated or Turkish walnut stock, hinged floorplate, various options. New 2004.

MSR $3,710	$3,450	$2,950	$2,650	$2,325	$2,000	$1,600	$1,250

Add $60 for Model V or $450 for Model M.

NESIKA VARMINT - various varmint cals., single shot or repeater, stainless Nesika action and helical fluted bolt, stainless barrel, composite or wood laminated stock, various options. New 2004.

MSR $3,440	$3,050	$2,650	$2,375	$2,000	$1,750	$1,500	$1,250

Add $60 for Model K.

URBAN TACTICAL - various tactical cals., heavy duty receiver with Picatinny rail and fluted 24 or 28 in. barrel, detachable box mag., black synthetic stock with adj. recoil pad. New 2004.

MSR $5,040	$4,500	$4,000	$3,500	$3,000	$2,500	$2,000	$1,650

Add $160 for heavy .308 Win. cal. or $520 for Lapua or Lazzeroni Warbird or Patriot cals.

NEW ADVANTAGE ARMS, INC.

Previous handgun manufacturer located in Tucson, AZ, circa mid-1990s.

DERRINGERS

4 BARREL DERRINGER - .22 LR or .22 Mag. cal., 4 barrel, double action with rotating hammer, 4 shot mag., high grade alloy, 2 1/2 in. barrel, blue steel alloy or stainless steel, fixed sights, walnut grips, 15 oz. Disc.

	$175	$150	$120	$110	$100	$90	$80

NEW DETONICS MANUFACTURING CORPORATION

Previous manufacturer located in Phoenix, AZ 1989-1992. Formerly named Detonics Firearms Industries (previous manufacturer located in Bellevue, WA 1976-1988). Detonics was sold in early 1988 to the New Detonics Manufacturing Corporation, a wholly owned subsidiary of "1045 Investors Group Limited."

PISTOLS: SEMI-AUTO, STAINLESS

MARK I - .45 ACP cal., matte blue. Disc. 1981.

	$550	$450	$395

MARK II - .45 ACP cal., satin nickel finish. Disc. 1979.

	$495	$375	$300

MARK III - .45 ACP cal., hard chrome finish. Disc. 1979.

	$520	$390	$325

MARK IV - .45 ACP cal., polished blue. Disc. 1981.

	$539	$410	$360

COMBATMASTER MC1 (FORMERLY MARK I) - .45 ACP, 9mm Para., or .38 Super cal., 3 1/2 in. barrel, two-tone (slide is non-glare blue and frame is matte stainless) finish, 6 shot mag., fixed sights, 28 oz. Disc. 1992.

	$775	$575	$450

Last MSR was $920.

Add $15 for OM-3 model (polished slide - disc. 1983).
Add $100 for 9mm Para. or .38 Super cal. (disc. 1990).
This model was originally the MC1, then changed to the Mark I, then changed back to the MC1.

GRADING - PPGS™	100%	98%	95%	90%	80%	70%	60%

COMBATMASTER MARK V - .45 ACP, 9mm Para., or .38 Super cal., matte stainless finish, fixed sights, 6 shot mag. in .45 ACP, 7 shot in 9mm Para. and .38 Super, 3 1/2 in. barrel, 29 oz. empty. This model was disc. 1985.

$620 $550 $495

Last MSR was $689.

Add $100 for 9mm Para. or .38 Super cal.

COMBATMASTER MARK VI - .45 ACP, 9mm Para., or .38 Super cal., 3 1/2 in. barrel, 6 shot mag., adj. sights and polished stainless slide sides. Disc. 1989.

$685 $575 $450

Last MSR was $795.

Add $100 for 9mm Para. or .38 Super cal.

✳ *.451 Detonics Mag. Cal.* - limited mfg. 1,000. Disc. 1985.

$1,000 $900 $775

Last MSR was $1,165.

COMBATMASTER MARK VII - similar to Mark VI, only no sights, special order only, 25 oz.

$895 $775 $600

Add $100 for 9mm Para. or .38 Super cal.
Add $350 for .451 Detonics Mag., (disc. 1982).

MILITARY COMBAT MC2 - .45 ACP, 9mm Para., or .38 Super cal., dull, non-glare combat finish, fixed sights. Comes with camouflaged pile-lined wallet, and Pachmayr grips. Disc. 1984.

$621 $560 $500

Add $55 for 9mm Para. or .38 Super.

O.S. MODEL - .45 ACP cal. only, emergency backup pistol, similar to Combatmaster, 6 shot mag., choice of satin stainless or all black finish. 2 mfg. 1991 only.

Extreme rarity precludes accurate price evaluation.

SCOREMASTER - .45 ACP or .451 Mag. cal., match gun with closer tolerances, 5 or 6 in. barrel. Millett adj. sights, grip safety, 7 or 8 shot mag., 42 oz. Disc. 1992.

$995 $850 $695

Last MSR was $1,178.

Add $40 for 6 in. barrel.

COMPMASTER - .45 ACP cal. only, similar to Scoremaster, except is fully compensated. Mfg. 1988-92.

$1,995 $1,575 $1,250

Last MSR was $1,550.

This model was called the Janus Competition Scoremaster in 1988-1989.

COMPETITION MASTER T.F. - .45 ACP cal., competition model with dual port compensator, rotational torque compensating vents, patented coned barrel system, hand tuned trigger, includes all competition modifications. Disc. 1992.

$1,995 $1,575 $1,250

Last MSR was $1,550.

SERVICEMASTER - .45 ACP cal. only, shortened version of the Scoremaster, non-glare combat finish, 4 1/4 in. barrel, coned barrel system, 8 shot mag., interchangeable front and adj. rear sights, 39 oz. Disc. 1986.

$825 $675 $575

Last MSR was $686.

✳ *Servicemaster II* - similar to Servicemaster, except has polished stainless steel finish. Mfg. 1986-92.

$925 $750 $625

Last MSR was $998.

GRADING - PPGS™	100%	98%	95%	90%	80%	70%	60%

POCKET 9 - 9mm Para. cal., double action, 3 in. barrel, 6 shot mag., soft matte sheen finish, 26 oz. Limited mfg. 1985-86 only.

	$495	$400	$335				

Last MSR was $458.

The entire Pocket 9 series was disc. 1986.

✳ *Pocket 9 LS* - similar to Pocket 9, except has 4 in. barrel. Limited mfg. 1986 only.

	$575	$450	$375				

Last MSR was $458.

✳ *Pocket .380* - similar to Pocket 9, except is .380 ACP cal., 23 oz. Limited mfg. 1986 only.

	$575	$450	$375				

Last MSR was $458.

POWER 9 - 9mm Para. cal., similar to Pocket 9, except has polished slide sides and is supplied with 2 mags. Disc. 1986.

	$575	$450	$375				

Last MSR was $509.

New Detonics Ladies Escort Series

This series was designed specifically to suit a woman's shooting requirements.

ROYAL ESCORT - .45 ACP cal., action similar to Combatmaster, 3 1/2 in. barrel, 6 shot mag., black frame, slide and grips are iridescent purple, hammer and trigger are 24Kt. gold-plated. Less than 25 were mfg. 1990-92.

	$1,000	$850	$650				

Last MSR was $990.

MIDNIGHT ESCORT - similar to Royal Escort, except is stainless with a black slide and smooth black grips. Less than 30 were mfg. 1990-92.

	$1,150	$925	$750				

Last MSR was $1,090.

JADE ESCORT - similar to Midnight Escort, except has stainless frame, jade colored slide and grips. Less than 10 were mfg. 1990 only.

	$1,200	$950	$600				

Last MSR was $918.

NEW ENGLAND ARMS CORP.

Previous importer, distributor, and retailer from 1975-2004, and located in Kittery Point, ME.

New England Arms Corp. imported, distributed, or retailed the following trademarks: Arrieta, P. Arrizabalaga, Bertuzzi, Luciano Bosis, Cosmi, Henri Dumoulin, Fair Techni-Mec (I. Rizzini), Antonio Gil, Lebeau-Courally, F.lli Rizzini, B. Rizzini, Luciano Rota, S.I.A.C.E., and Fabio Zanotti. These trademarks may be found under their own headings in this text.

New England Arms Corp. should not be confused with New England Firearms.

NEW ENGLAND CUSTOM GUN SERVICE, LTD.

Current company importing and/or selling Heym long arms from Germany, AYA shotguns from Spain, Krieghoff double rifles, and custom-made guns from small makers in Suhl, Germany, including Adamy-Jagdwaffen.

NECG, Ltd. specializes in custom gun services including checkering, stock fitting/alterations, claw mount scope installation and repair, detachable rifle scope mounts, and other gunsmithing services. Please contact the company directly regarding more information on their extensive line of products and services.

NEW ENGLAND FIREARMS

Current trademark established during 1987, and located and manufactured in Gardner, MA. Distributor sales only.

During 2000, Marlin Firearms Co. purchased the assets of H&R 1871, Inc., and the name was changed to H&R 1871, LLC. Brand names include Harrington & Richardson, New England Firearms, and Wesson & Harrington. Production will remain at the Gardner, MA plant.

All NEF firearms utilize a transfer bar safety system and have a $10 service plan which guarantees lifetime warranty.

New England Firearms should not be confused with New England Arms Corp.

REVOLVERS: DOUBLE ACTION

Ultra Models listed were available in blue finish only. All Ultras were supplied with a lockable storage case beginning 1993.

STANDARD REVOLVER .22 (MODEL R92) - .22 S, L, and LR cal., 9 shot, swing out cylinder, 2 1/2 (disc. 1997), 3 (new 1998) or 4 in. barrel, blue or nickel finish, hardwood stocks, fixed rear sight, 25-28 oz. Mfg. 1988-99.

| $125 | $95 | $85 | $70 | $60 | $55 | $40 |

Last MSR was $144.

Add $10 for nickel finish.

✱ **Standard Revolver .32 H&R Mag. (Model R73)** - .32 H&R Mag. cal. similar to Standard Revolver .22, except has 5 shot cylinder, 2 1/2 (disc.), 3, or 4 in. barrel, choice of blue or nickel finish (not available with 4 in. barrel), 23-26 oz. Mfg. 1988-99.

| $125 | $95 | $85 | $70 | $60 | $55 | $40 |

Last MSR was $144.

Add $10 for nickel finish (2 1/2 or 3 in. barrel only).

ULTRA MODEL - .22 S, L, and LR cal., 9 shot, swing-out cylinder, 4 or 6 in. solid rib target-grade barrel with rebated muzzle and fully adj. rear sight, blue finish, smooth hardwood grips, 36 oz. Disc. 1999.

| $150 | $115 | $95 | $80 | $70 | $60 | $55 |

Last MSR was $180.

ULTRA MAG (MODEL R22) - .22 Mag. cal., 6 shot, 4 (disc. 1997) or 6 in. solid rib barrel, adj. rear sight, swing-out cylinder, blue finish, 36 oz. Mfg. 1988-99.

| $150 | $115 | $95 | $80 | $70 | $60 | $55 |

Last MSR was $180.

LADY ULTRA - .32 H&R Mag. cal., swing-out cylinder, 5 shot, blue finish, 3 (disc. 1997, reintroduced 1999) or 4 (mfg. 1998 only) in. barrel with rib, adj. sights, thinner contoured grips, 31 oz. Mfg. 1991-99.

| $150 | $115 | $95 | $80 | $70 | $60 | $55 |

Last MSR was $180.

RIFLES: SEMI-AUTO

SPORTSTER SL - .22 LR cal., 19 in. barrel, 10 shot mag., unchecked hardwood stock, grooved steel receiver, 5.5 lbs. Mfg. 2004 only.

| $125 | $105 | $90 | $80 | $70 | $60 | $55 |

Last MSR was $157.

RIFLES: SINGLE SHOT

HANDI-RIFLE - .204 Ruger (new 2005), .22 Hornet, .22-250 Rem. (mfg. 1992-94, reintroduced 2004), .223 Rem., .243 Win. (new 1992), .25-06 Rem. (new 2004), .270 Win. (new 1993), .280 Rem. (new 1996), .30-30 Win., .30-06 (new 1992), .308 Win. (new 1998), .357 Mag. (mfg. 1999-2003), .44 Rem. Mag. (new 1996), .45-70 Govt.,

GRADING - PPGS™	100%	98%	95%	90%	80%	70%	60%

7mm-08 Rem. (new 2003), .500 S&W (new 2005), 7x57mm Mauser (mfg. 1998-2003), or 7x64mm Brenneke (mfg. 1998-2003) cal., break open single shot action, 22 or 26 (.280 Rem. only) in. regular or bull (.223 Rem., .243 Win., or .22-250 Rem.) barrel, blue receiver, regular or Monte Carlo walnut stained hardwood stock, scope mount rail or ramp front and adj. rear sights, sling swivels, 7 lbs. New 1989.

MSR $284	$230	$180	$130	$110	$80	$70	$60

Add $20 for Handi-Rifle .243 Win./Huntsman .50 cal. black powder muzzleloader rifle combo (disc. 2002).

This model in .22-250 Rem., .223 Rem., or .243 Win. cal. is supplied with heavy barrel, scope mount, and no sights.

✱ *Handi-Rifle Synthetic* - .22 Hornet, .223 Rem., .243 Win., .270 Win., .280 Rem., .30-30 Win. (disc. 2003), .30-06, .357 Mag. (mfg. 2002-2003), .44 Rem. Mag. (disc. 2003), or .45-70 Govt. cal., 22 or 26 (.280 Rem. only) in. barrel, blue finish, features black synthetic stock and forearm, adj. sights on some cals., scope base mount only on others, 7 lbs. New 1998.

MSR $296	$235	$185	$140	$115	$85	$80	$75

✱ *Handi-Rifle Synthetic Stainless* - .22-250 Rem. (new 2004), .223 Rem., .243 Win., .270 Win., or .30-06 (new 2004) cal., similar to Handi-Rifle Synthetic, features 22 in. matte stainless steel barrel with matte nickel finished receiver, 7 lbs. New 2003.

MSR $354	$275	$210	$160	$130	$100	$85	$75

✱ *Handi-Rifle Youth* - .223 Rem., .243 Win., or 7mm-08 Rem. (new 2005) cal, features 22 in. barrel and shortened stock dimensions (13 1/2 in. LOP), blue finish, supplied with scope rail mount and hammer extension, no iron sights. New 1998.

MSR $284	$230	$180	$130	$110	$85	$70	$60

✱ *10th Anniversary Handi-Rifle* - same cals. as Handi-Rifle, limited edition features scroll engraving by Ken Hurst, deep bluing on receiver, steel trigger guard and forearm spacer, select hand checkered walnut, less than 100 mfg. 1997 only.

	$695	$475	$350

Last MSR was $750.

✱ *Handi-Rifle NTA Anniversary Edition* - .223 Rem. only, 24 in. heavy barrel w/o sights, features checkered black/grey laminate stock and forearm with NTA (National Trapper's Association) medallion in stock. Limited production 1999 only.

	$225	$200	$175	$160	$145	$135	$125

Last MSR was $272.

SUPER LIGHT HANDI-RIFLE - .22 Hornet, .223 Rem., or .243 Win. cal., break open single shot, black synthetic stock and forearm, recoil pad, 20 in. special contour barrel with rebated muzzle, .22 Hornet has sights (Model SB2-SL4), .223 Rem. has scope base and hammer extension (Model SB2-SL3), approx. 5.5 lbs. New 1997.

MSR $296	$235	$185	$140	$115	$85	$80	$75

This model is also available as a Youth Model with shorter stock dimensions (11.75 in. LOP).

SPORTSTER - .17 HMR (new 2002), .17 Mach 2 (new 2005), .22 LR or .22 Mag. (new 2001) cal., 20 (mid-weight) or 22 (.17 HMR cal. only, heavy) in. barrel with Weaver style scope rail, no iron sights, available in either adult or youth dimensions, black polymer stock and forearm. New 1999.

MSR $157	$120	$100	$85	$75	$60	$50	$45

Add approx. $30 for .17 HMR or .17 Mach 2 cal.

SURVIVOR - .223 Rem., .308 Win. (new 1999), .357 Mag. (disc. 1998) cal., similar in design to the Survivor Series shotgun, removeable forearm for ammo storage, thumbhole design with storage compartment, no iron sights, 22 in. barrel, blue or nickel (disc. 1998) finish, .357 Mag. cal. has open sights, .223 Rem. and .308 Win. cal. have heavy barrels and scope mount rail, 6 lbs. New 1996.

MSR $296	$235	$190	$150	$115	$90	$80	$70

Add approx. $15 for nickel finish (disc.).

GRADING - PPGS™	100%	98%	95%	90%	80%	70%	60%

SHOTGUNS: SINGLE SHOT

PARDNER - 12, 16 (new 1989), 20, 28 ga. (new 1991), or .410 bore, 2 3/4 or 3 in. chamber (12, 20 ga., and .410 bore), single shot, break open action, safety transfer bar mechanism on hammer, side lever release, color case hardened receiver, 14 in. LOP, 24 (disc.), 26, 28, or 32 in. fixed choke barrel, extractor, walnut stained hardwood stock and forearm, 5-6 lbs. New 1987.

	MSR $137	$110	$90	$75	$65	$55	$45	$40

Add $15 for 32 in. barrel (12 ga. only).
Add $65 for Pardner 12 ga. Shotgun/Huntsman .50 cal. black powder muzzleloader combo (disc. 2002).

✳ *Pardner Youth* - 12 (new 1998), 20, 28 ga., or .410 bore, similar to Pardner, except has 22 in. barrel and straight grip stock with recoil pad, 12 1/2 in. LOP.

	MSR $145	$115	$95	$80	$70	$55	$45	$40

Add $92 for Pardner Youth .22 cal. barrel/.410 bore Versa-Pack combo (disc. 2004).

✳ *Pardner Youth Turkey* - 20 ga. only, features 22 in. full choke barrel and camo painted wood. New 1999.

	MSR $195	$155	$120	$95	$80	$65	$55	$50

✳ *Pardner Turkey Gun* - 10 or 12 ga. only, 3 (disc.) or 3 1/2 in. chamber, 24 in. barrel with fixed or full choke tube, camo or matte black wood finish, 6 or 9 (10 ga.) lbs. New 1999.

	MSR $187	$150	$120	$100	$80	$70	$60	$50

Add $8 for Mossy Oak Break-Up camo in 12 ga. with full choke bore.
Add $72 for 10 ga. in black matte wood finish.
Add $99 for 10 ga. with camo wood finish.

✳ *Pardner Special Purpose* - 10 or 12 (new 2002) ga., 3 1/2 in. chamber, 28 or 32 (10 ga. only, new 1996) in. barrel, blue barrel and receiver, walnut or Mossy Oak Break Up camo (new 2002) finish on stock and forearm, recoil pad, 9.5 lbs. New 1988.

	MSR $221	$175	$150	$125	$100	$80	$65	$55

Add $59 for 10 ga. with walnut finish.

✳ *Pardner NRA Foundation Youth* - 20, 28 (disc. 2001) ga. or .410 bore, 22 in. barrel, high luster bluing, features "NRA Foundation Youth Endowment Edition" laser etched in black on stock, approx. 5 1/2 lbs. Mfg. 1999-2002.

	$130	$105	$90	$75	$65	$55	$45

Last MSR was $161.

✳ *National Wild Turkey Federation (NWTF)* - 10 or 20 (new 1993) ga., 22 (20 ga. only) or 24 in. barrel with full screw-in choke, full Mossy Oak camo treatment, includes swivels and sling. Mfg. 1992-96.

	$190	$160	$135	$110	$95	$80	$70

Last MSR was $230.

Subtract $80 for 20 ga.
This model was drilled and tapped for scope mounts.

SURVIVOR SERIES - 12 (disc. 2003), 20 ga. (disc. 2003), or .410/.45 LC (new 1995) bore, 3 in. chamber, 20 (.410/.45 LC) or 22 in. barrel with Mod. choke, blue or electroless nickel finish, synthetic thumbhole designed hollow stock with pistol grip, removable forend holds additional ammo, sling swivels, and black nylon sling, 13.25 in. LOP, 6 lbs. Mfg. 1992-93, reintroduced 1995.

	MSR $213	$170	$150	$120	$100	$85	$75	$65

Add $19 for electroless nickel finish.
Subtract 20% for 12 or 20 ga.

GRADING - PPGS™	100%	98%	95%	90%	80%	70%	60%

TRACKER SLUG MODEL - 10 ga. (mfg. 1994 only), 12, or 20 ga., 3 (12 or 20 ga.) or 3 1/2 (10 ga. only) in. chamber, 24 in. cylinder bore barrel, case colored receiver, includes recoil pad and adj. sights, 6 lbs. Mfg. 1992-2001.

	$120	$90	$75	$60	$50	$45	$40

Last MSR was $143.

✳ *Tracker II* - 12 or 20 ga., 3 in. chamber, similar to Tracker Slug Model except has 24 in. rifled bore barrel, 14 in. LOP, 5.25 lbs. New 1995.

MSR $192	$150	$120	$90	$70	$60	$50	$45

Add $44 for Tracker II 12 ga. Slug Gun/Huntsman .50 cal. black powder muzzleloader (disc. 2002).

SHOTGUNS: SLIDE ACTION

PARDNER PUMP - 12 ga. only, 3 in. chamber, steel reciever, crossbolt safety, double action bars, 28 in. VR barrel with choke tube, black synthetic (new 2005) or uncheckered walnut stock with recoil pad and forearm, matte black metal finish, 7.5 lbs. New 2004.

MSR $208	$160	$135	$115	$100	$90	$80	$70

Add $17 for walnut stock and forearm.

✳ *Pardner Turkey* - includes 100% Mossy Oak Breakup camo coverage, 22 in. barrel with Truglo front and rear sights, one Turkey choke tube. New 2005.

MSR $314	$245	$215	$180	$155	$130	$115	$100

✳ *Pardner Combo* - 12 ga. only, 3 in. chambers, includes 22 in. rifled slug and 28 in. barrel with modified choke tube. New 2005.

MSR $305	$240	$210	$175	$150	$125	$115	$100

NEW ULTRA LIGHT ARMS LLC

Current rifle manufacturer located in Granville, WV. Dealer sales.

RIFLES: BOLT ACTION

Add approx. $75-$100 for left-hand action, depending on the model.

ULTRA LIGHT RIFLE - caliber to customer specs., various actions, 2-position 3-function safety in top of stock, Timney trigger, Douglas barrel, no sights, Kevlar stock reinforced with graphite, recoil pad, Dupont Imron epoxy finish, designed to customer specifications, includes hard case, 5 1/4-5 3/4 lbs.

MODEL 20 - various short action centerfire cals. available between .17 Rem. and .358 Win, 5 1/4 lbs.

MSR $2,780	$2,425	$1,800	$1,325	$975	$850	$750	$650

✳ *Model 20 RF* - .22 LR cal., single shot or repeater, 5 1/4 lbs.

MSR $1,100	$975	$875	$775	$650	$425	$300	$250

Add $50 for repeater action.

MODEL 24 - various cals. between .25-06 Rem. - .338-06 cal., long action, 5 1/4 lbs.

MSR $2,900	$2,525	$1,875	$1,375	$1,025	$875	$775	$675

MODEL 28 MAGNUM - various Mag. cals. between .264 Win. Mag. - .338 Win. Mag., 5 3/4 lbs.

MSR $3,200	$2,850	$2,100	$1,625	$1,250	$975	$800	$700

MODEL 40 MAGNUM - .300 WSM or .416 Rigby cal., otherwise similar to Model 28 Magnum.

MSR $3,200	$2,850	$2,100	$1,625	$1,250	$975	$800	$700

GRADING - PPGS™	100%	98%	95%	90%	80%	70%	60%

NEWTON ARMS CO.

Previous manufacturer located in Buffalo, NY circa 1913-1932.

RIFLES: BOLT ACTION

NEWTON-MAUSER - .256 Newton - .30 Adolph Express cals., Oberndorf 98 bolt action, 24 in. barrel, sporting style stock, various grades and variations, some with double set triggers. A small number of these commercial rifles were built in Germany in 1914, and shipped to the U.S.

	100%	98%	95%	90%	80%	70%	60%
	$1,200	$1,050	$950	$850	$750	$650	$550

1922 NEWTON MAUSER - .256 Newton cal., commercial Mauser 98 action, double set triggers opposed in guard, stock and/or barrels marked "Made in Germany", some barrels marked "Chas. Newton Rifle Corp., Buffalo, NY", leaf type rear sight. Approx. 100 rifles imported.

	100%	98%	95%	90%	80%	70%	60%
	N/A	$1,250	$1,050	$875	$775	$675	$575

This model can can vary quite a bit from specimen to specimen.

FIRST TYPE STANDARD - .22 Newton, .256 Newton, .30 Newton, .33 Newton, .35 Newton, or .30-06 cal., 24 in. standard barrel, open barrel sight, bolt peep sight was optional, checkered pistol grip stock, segmentally rifled barrels are marked "Newton Arms Co., Buffalo, NY", double set triggers. Approx. 4,000 mfg. 1917-19.

	100%	98%	95%	90%	80%	70%	60%
	$1,200	$950	$850	$750	$600	$550	$500

SECOND TYPE STANDARD - prototype only, this model never went into production.

BUFFALO NEWTON - .256 Newton, .30-06, .30 Newton, or .35 Newton cal., checkered sporting stock, reversed double set triggers, Enfield style bolt handle, open sights, 24 in. parabolically rifle barrel marked "Buffalo Newton Rifle Corp., New Haven Conn". Approx. 1,000 mfg. 1923-29 in New Haven, CT.

	100%	98%	95%	90%	80%	70%	60%
	$750	$675	$625	$575	$525	$450	$385

There is little collector interest in this model.

NEWTON SPRINGFIELD - kit consisting of a Marlin-made sporting stock and .256 Newton barrel, customer supplied Springfield 1903 action and sights, original kit guns will have conventional square cut rifled barrels marked "Newton Arms Co. Buffalo, NY". Mfg. 1914-17.

	100%	98%	95%	90%	80%	70%	60%
	$595	$540	$495	$450	$410	$375	$330

Due to the low numbered Springfield receivers and the fact that many of these barrels were customer fitted, it is not advisable to fire these rifles until a competent gunsmith has performed an inspection.

NIGHTHAWK CUSTOM

Current manufacturer located in Berryville, AR. since 2004.

PISTOLS: SEMI-AUTO

Nighthawk Custom offers a complete line of high quality 1911 style semi-auto pistols. Models include: the Enforcer (MSR $1,750), Enforcer II (MSR $1,800), Talon (MSR $2,100), Talon Recon Rail (MSR $2,200), Talon II (MSR $2,150), Talon III (MSR $2,200), Predator (MSR $2,600), Predator Recon Rail $2,700), Predator II (MSR $2,650), and the Predator III (MSR $2,700). Please contact the company directly for more information on custom pistols, a wide variety of options, gunsmithing services and availability.

NIKKO FIREARMS CO., LTD.

Previous manufacturer located in Tochigi, Japan circa 1958-1989.

NIKKO HISTORY AND GENERAL INFORMATION

The publisher wishes to thank the Golden Eagle Collectors Association for providing this publication with the information listed. Please refer to the Golden Eagle heading in this text for information on Nikko manufactured Golden Eagle firearms.

Both Nikko Firearms Co., Ltd. and Nikko Arms Co., Ltd. were trade names used by the Kodensha Co., Ltd. of Tochigi, Japan on products they manufactured and distributed worldwide. Nikko is the name of the Prefecture, or district, in which Tochigi City is located, about 50 miles north of Tokyo. The word Nikko translates to English as "sunshine." Kodensha first manufactured or distributed under the Nikko name in April 1955, and exported out of Japan beginning in August 1958. Nothing is known of the origin of the Kodensha Co.

Kodensha first approached the American shotgun market in about 1958 or '59 using the Japanese export marketing firm of Kyowa-Boeki-Bussan. They contacted various U.S. distributors, and in about 1959 or '60, Continental Arms Co. of New York City began importing the Nikko "Grade 5." Continental imported these Nikko over/unders, in various models and configurations, until about 1972.

In 1962, the Kodensha Co., Ltd. formed a joint venture with Olin/Winchester of New Haven, CT to produce the Winchester Model 101 over/under shotgun. This venture was known as the Olin-Kodensha Co. Ltd. Added a little later was the side-by-side Model 23, and the Model 96 Xpert (a budget priced 101). The "pre-Olin" Kodensha factory was considerably outdated, and the joint venture began a complete modernization process, with the financial and technical assistance of Olin. Millions of dollars of machinery and technology were brought in, and the entire manufacturing process was upgraded to the then current standards.

One of the conditions of the joint venture was that Kodensha restrict their own products (made in the same factory, but recorded separately from the joint venture) to sale in Japan only. At the outset of the 25 years that the joint venture existed, Kodensha was probably amenable to this, as they were reaping huge financial and technical benefits from Olin. But, by the mid '60s, when the factory was in place and running smoothly, Kodensha essentially ignored that condition of the agreement, leaving Olin at somewhat of a disadvantage, not wanting to jeopardize their investment or production source. Additionally, Olin/Winchester was allowed only two permanent personnel, hardly enough to monitor the activities of a factory which employed up to 400 people. As an example, when walnut stock blanks arrived from France, Kodensha took first pick, and Olin got what was left over.

Kodensha converted an existing building near the manufacturing plant into an assembly area for Nikko and other brands of guns. This building was probably the "true" Nikko Firearms Co., Ltd. Manufactured components from the Olin-Kodensha factory were carted to the Nikko plant for final assembly and fitting. This "dual-factory" arrangement continued until the mid 1980s. In 1981, for an unknown reason, the Olin-Kodensha name was changed to OK Firearms Co. Ltd. In October 1987, Olin/Winchester sold their interest in OK Firearms to Classic Doubles International, which continued making the 101 style shotgun under their own name. For reasons unknown, Classic Doubles went out of business in December 1988. Shortly thereafter, the entire factory was torn down, and all that remains today is a vacant lot.

During the "dual-factory" days, Nikko produced firearms for the following distributors or retailers: 1) Kanematsu Gosho of Arlington Heights, IL approx. 1974-1982 - distributed Nikko brand shotguns, Golden Eagle brand shotguns and rifles (1975 through March 1977 only); 2) Golden Eagle Firearms, Houston, TX March 1977 through early 1981 - Golden Eagle shotguns and rifles; 3) Tradewinds, Inc. of Tacoma, WA exported from Japan by Caspoll International, Tokyo January 1971 through December 1972 - Shadow Seven; Shadow Indy (Model 707); Gold, Silver, and Black Shadow over/under shotguns; 4) Marubeni America, Inc. of New York City 1972-1974 - Miida brand over/under shotguns; 5) Winchester GMBH of West Germany, manufactured by Olin-Kodensha (dates unknown - early '80s) - Winchester Model 777 rifle (Golden Eagle look-alike); 6) Parker Reproduction shotguns, distributed in the US by Reagent Chemical & Research, Inc. 1984-1988; 7) International Star Commerce Corp. (ISCC) of Salt Lake City, Utah approx. 1982 - distributor of Nikko brand shotguns; 8) Moore Supply Co. of Salt Lake City, UT beginning mid-1981 - distributor of Nikko brand shotguns; 9) USA Nikko, Inc. of Los Angeles, CA (factory reps and distributors of Nikko shotguns), initial date unknown, through December 1981; 10) Weatherby, Inc. of Los Angeles, CA May 1972 to 1981. Centurion semi-auto and Patrician pump shotguns, some Mark 22 rifles. Olympian O/U shotgun and possibly other O/Us from 1978-81. Model 82 semi-auto and Model 92 pump shotguns; 11) Savage Industries of Hamden, CT 1981-1982 - Savage/Fox FA-1 and FP-1 shotguns; 12) Charles Daly "Automatic" distributed by Sloan's (Japanese made only) mid-1980s; 13) Sears, Roebuck Co. Ted Williams Model 400 and possibly others; 14) Churchill semi-auto, imported by Kassnar mid-1980s; 15) High Standard of Hamden, CT 1974-75 - Supermatic Shadow Indy (Model 707, an O/U), Supermatic Shadow Seven (also O/U), and Supermatic Shadow semi-auto.

GRADING - PPGS™	100%	98%	95%	90%	80%	70%	60%

NOTE: ALL of the semi-auto shotguns used essentially the same design. Each distributor may have made a few cosmetic or dimensional embellishments to differentiate their gun. Differences exist in barrel/breech fit, magazine caps, pistol grip caps, checkering pattern, piston size, ejector location, fluted bolt. Use caution if interchanging parts. Generally, the same statement can be made about the pump versions also.

NOBLE MFG. CO.

Previous manufacturer and importer of Spanish SxS shotguns located in Haydenville, MA 1953-1971.

Noble manufactured both semi-auto, lever, and slide action rifles and slide action shotguns, in addition to importing Spanish SxS shotguns. Shotgun models included the Model 420, 420 EK, and 450 E. While most models were relatively inexpensive, good working, utilitarian guns, there has been little collectibility to date and most rifles are seen priced in the $45-$150 price range while the shotguns are priced in the $75-$300 range, depending on gauge and features.

NOR-CAL PRECISION

Current manufacturer and riflesmith established in 1989 and located in American Canyon, CA.

Nor-Cal Precision manufacutures custom rifles based on the Rem. M700 action, in addition to a variety of gunsmithing services. Please contact the company directly for more information, including availability and pricing (see Trademark Index).

NORINCO

Current manufacturer located in China. Currently imported and distributed exclusively by Interstate Arms Corp., located in Billerica, MA. Previous importers have included: Norinco Sports U.S.A., located in Diamond Bar, CA, Century International Arms, Inc. located in St. Albans, VT; China Sports, Inc. located in Ontario, CA; Interarms located in Alexandria, VA; KBI, Inc. located in Harrisburg, PA; and others. Dealer and distributor sales only.

Norinco pistols, rifles, and shotguns are manufactured in the People's Republic of China by Northern China Industries Corp. (Norinco has over 100 factories). Please refer to the Interstate Arms Corp. for currently imported models.

PISTOLS: SEMI-AUTO

MODEL 213 - 9mm Para. cal., single action, satin blue finish. Imported 1988 only.

	100%	98%	95%	90%	80%	70%	60%
	$185	$150	$135	$125	$115	$105	$100

Last MSR was $200.

TYPE 54-1 TOKAREV STANDARD - 7.62x25mm Tokarev or .38 Super cal., single action semi-auto, 4.5 in. barrel, 8 shot mag., fixed sights, blue finish, 29 oz. Imported 1989-95.

	$125	$100	$80	$70	$65	$60	$55

Last MSR was $145.

＊ **Type 54-1 Double Column** - similar to Standard Model, except is also available in 9mm Para. cal. and has 10 (C/B 1994) or 13* shot mag., 35 oz. Imported 1991-95.

	$155	$135	$120	$110	$100	$90	$80

Last MSR was $185.

＊ **Type 54-1 Compact** - .38 Super, 9mm Para., or 7.62x25mm Tokarev cal., 3.8 in. barrel, 8 shot mag., 27 oz. Imported 1991-95.

	$155	$135	$120	$110	$100	$90	$80

Last MSR was $185.

GRADING ~ PPGS™	100%	98%	95%	90%	80%	70%	60%

TYPE 59 MAKAROV - 9x18mm Makarov or .380 ACP cal., double action semi-auto, 3.5 in. barrel, 8 shot bottom release mag., checkered plastic grips, PPK design with additional features, adj. rear sight, 24 oz. Imported 1989-95.

	$150	$135	$125	$115	$95	$85	$75

Last MSR was $185.

TYPE 77B - 9mm Para. cal., semi-auto single action, action patterned after the older German Lignose (unique design permits one handed operation utilizing "trigger guard cocking" enabling the slide to be moved backward cocking the hammer), 5 in. barrel, 8 shot mag., adj. rear sight, 34 oz. Limited importation 1991-95.

	$350	$295	$250	$225	$195	$165	$135

Last MSR was $285.

MODEL 1911 A1 - .45 ACP cal. only, patterned after the Colt 1911 A1, 5 in. barrel, 7 shot mag., fixed sights, blue or parkerized finish, wood grips, 39 oz. Imported 1991-95.

	$275	$245	$220	$195	$180	$165	$150

Last MSR was $320.

RIFLES: SEMI-AUTO

TYPE 84S AKS RIFLE - .223 Rem. cal., semi-auto Kalashnikov action, 16.34 in. barrel, hardwood stock and pistol grip, 30 shot mag., 1,000 meter adj. rear sight, includes bayonet and sheath, 8.87 lbs. Imported 1988-89 only.

	$1,050	$975	$900	$800	$700	$625	$550

Last MSR was $350.

* ***Type 84S-1*** - similar to Type 84S AKS except has under-folding metal stock. Imported 1989 only.

	$1,200	$1,000	$925	$825	$725	$625	$550

Last MSR was $350.

* ***Type 84S-3*** - similar to Type 84S AKS except has composite fiber stock (1 1/2 in. longer than wood stock). Imported 1989 only.

	$1,050	$975	$900	$800	$700	$625	$550

Last MSR was $365.

* ***Type 84S-5*** - similar to Type 84S AKS except has side-folding metal stock. Imported 1989 only.

	$1,275	$1,075	$900	$775	$675	$575	$500

Last MSR was $350.

NHM-90/91 (AK-47 THUMBHOLE) - .223 Rem. or 7.62x39mm cal., features new thumbhole stock for legalized import, 5 shot mag. Imported 1991-1993, configuration was restyled and renamed NHM-90/91 in 1994.

	$650	$575	$475	$400	$360	$330	$285

Last MSR was $375.

NHM-90/91 SPORT - 7.62x39mm cal., choice of 16.34 (NHM-90) or 23.27 (NHM-91) in. barrel, hardwood thumbhole stock, NHM-91 has bipod, 5 shot mag., 9-11 lbs. Imported 1994-95.

	$450	$400	$360	$330	$285	$250	$225

The .223 Rem. cal. was also available for the Model NHM-90. Each Model NHM-90/91 was supplied with three 5 shot mags., sling, and cleaning kit.

MODEL B THUMBHOLE - 9mm Para. cal., patterned after the Uzi, features sporterized thumbhole wood stock, 10 shot mag. Importation 1995 only.

	$550	$485	$440	$400	$360	$330	$295

Last MSR was $625.

R.P.K. RIFLE - 7.62x39mm cal., includes bipod. Importation disc. 1993.

	$1,100	$900	$800	$700	$625	$550	$500

Last MSR was $600.

GRADING - PPGS™	100%	98%	95%	90%	80%	70%	60%

TYPE SKS - .223 Rem. or 7.62x39mm cal., SKS action, 20.47 in. barrel, 10 (C/B 1994) or 30* shot mag., 1,000 meter adj. rear sight, hardwood stock, new design accepts standard AK mag., with or w/o folding bayonet, 8.8 lbs. Imported 1988-1989, reintroduced 1992-95 with Sporter configuration stock.

	$225	$200	$185	$165	$145	$130	$115

Last MSR was $150.

Add $100 for synthetic stock and bayonet.
Subtract 15% if refinished.

TYPE 81S AKS RIFLE - 7.62x39mm cal., semi-auto Kalashnikov action, 17.5 in. barrel, 5, 30, or 40 shot mag., 500 meter adj. rear sight, fixed wood stock, hold open device after last shot, 8 lbs. Imported 1988-1989.

	$1,100	$900	$775	$700	$600	$500	$450

Last MSR was $385.

* **Type 81S-1** - similar to Type 81S AKS except has under-folding metal stock. Imported 1988-89.

	$1,200	$975	$850	$750	$650	$525	$475

Last MSR was $385.

TYPE 56S-2 - 7.62x39mm cal., older Kalashnikov design with side-folding metal stock. Importation disc. 1989.

	$1,300	$1,150	$975	$875	$775	$675	$575

Last MSR was $350.

TYPE 86S-7 RPK RIFLE - 7.62x39mm cal., AK action, 23.27 in. heavy barrel with built-in bipod, in-line buttstock, 11.02 lbs. Imported 1988-1989.

	$1,500	$1,275	$1,075	$950	$850	$750	$650

Last MSR was $425.

TYPE 86S BULLPUP RIFLE - 7.62x39mm cal., bullpup configuration with AK action, under-folding metal stock, 17 1/4 in. barrel, ambidextrous cocking design, folding front handle, 7 lbs. Imported 1989 only.

	$1,400	$1,225	$995	$850	$725	$650	$575

Last MSR was $400.

DRAGUNOV (MODEL 350 NDM-86) - 7.62x54mm Russian, sniper variation of the AK-47, features 24 in. barrel with muzzle brake, special laminated skeletonized wood stock with vent. forearm, detachable 10 shot mag., 8 lbs. 9 oz. Importation disc. 1995.

	$1,900	$1,750	$1,625	$1,500	$1,250	$1,150	$1,000

Last MSR was $3,080.

This model was also imported by Gibbs Rifle Co. located in Martinsburg, WV.

* **Dragunov Carbine** - similar to Dragunov rifle, except shorter barrel, various accessories including a lighted scope were also offered, plastic furniture.

	$1,200	$1,000	$875	$775	$675	$600	$550

OFFICERS NINE - 9mm Para. cal., 16.1 in. barrel, action patterned after the IMI Uzi, 32 shot mag., black military finish, 8.4 lbs. Limited 1988-89.

	$1,100	$995	$850	$725	$650	$575	$500

Last MSR was $450.

RIFLES: .22 CAL.

MODEL EM-321 - .22 LR cal., slide action, 19.5 in. barrel, 10 shot tube mag., hardwood stock and forearm, fixed sights, 6 lbs. Importation began 1989-90, resumed 1994-disc.

	$135	$115	$95	$85	$75	$65	$55

GRADING - PPGS™	100%	98%	95%	90%	80%	70%	60%

TYPE EM-332 - .22 LR cal., bolt action, 18 1/2 in. barrel with adj. rear sight, mag. holder on stock holds two extra 5 shot mags., Monte Carlo stock with cheekpiece and recoil pad, 4 1/2 lbs. Imported 1991-93.

	$225	$195	$165	$140	$120	$95	$80

SHOTGUNS: O/U

TYPE HL12-203 - 12 ga. only, 2 3/4 in. chambers, boxlock action, ejectors, 30 in. vent. barrels and rib, single trigger, multi-chokes, checkered stock and forearm, 7 1/2 lbs. Imported 1989-1993.

	$400	$350	$300	$265	$225	$200	$185

SHOTGUNS: SEMI-AUTO

MODEL 2000 FIELD - 12 ga. only, 2 3/4 in. chamber, steel receiver and aluminum alloy trigger guard, 26 or 28 in. VR barrel with M choke tube, choice of black synthetic or checkered hardwood stock and forearm, approx. 7 1/2 lbs. Limited importation 1999 only.

	$260	$230	$200	$185	$170	$160	$150

Last MSR was $299.

 Add $8 for wood stock and forearm.
 Choke tubes are interchangeable with the WinChoke system.

 * ***Model 2000 Defense*** - 12 ga. only, 2 3/4 in. chamber, 18 1/2 in. barrel with cyl. choke tube and choice of bead, rifle, or ghost ring sights, matte black metal finish, black synthetic stock and forearm with recoil pad. Limited importation 1999 only.

	$245	$225	$190	$175	$160	$155	$145

Last MSR was $282.

 Add $5 for rifle sights.
 Add $17 for ghost ring sights.

SHOTGUNS: SLIDE ACTION

TYPE HL12-102 - 12 ga. only, 2 3/4 in. chamber, 28.4 in. barrel, 3 shot mag., crossbolt safety on rear trigger guard, fixed chokes, 9.3 lbs. Imported 1989-93.

	$230	$200	$175	$165	$150	$135	$120

MODEL 98 FIELD - 12 ga. only, 3 in. chamber, 26 or 28 in. VR barrel with M choke tube, choice of black synthetic or uncheckered hardwood stock and forearm with recoil pad, approx. 7 lbs. Limited importation 1999 only.

	$185	$160	$140	$125	$110	$100	$90

Last MSR was $205.

 Add $8 for wood stock and forearm.
 Add $55 for Field Combo (includes extra 18 1/2 in. barrel) or $82 for Field Combo with 22 in. slug or turkey barrel.

 * ***Model 98 Turkey*** - similar to Model 98 Field, except has 22 in. VR barrel with extra full choke tube, black synthetic stock and forearm only. Limited importation 1999 only.

	$190	$165	$140	$125	$110	$100	$90

Last MSR was $216.

 * ***Model 98 Defense*** - 12 ga. only, 3 in. chamber, 18 1/2 in. barrel with cyl. choke tube and choice of bead, rifle, or ghost ring sights, matte black metal finish, black synthetic stock and forearm with recoil pad. Limited importation 1999 only.

	$170	$150	$130	$115	$100	$90	$80

Last MSR was $190.

 Add $15 for ghost ring sights.

GRADING - PPGS™	100%	98%	95%	90%	80%	70%	60%

MODEL 983 - 12 ga. only, 22 in. barrel with external rifled choke tube and adj. rifle sights, synthetic black stock. Limited importation 2002 only.

	$215	$170	$155	$135	$125	$105	$95

Last MSR was $230.

MODEL 984/985/987 - 12 ga. only, 3 in. chamber, field series with 26 or 28 in. VR barrel and M choke tube, black synthetic or uncheckered hardwood stock and fore-arm, matte black metal finish. Limited importation 2001-2002.

	$200	$170	$155	$135	$125	$105	$95

Last MSR was $235.

Add $10 for hardwood stock (Models 985 & 987).

NORSMAN SPORTING ARMS

Current rifle manufacturer/customizer located in Havre, MT since 1999. Previously located in Bismarck, ND until 1999. Consumer direct sales.

Norsman specializes in both wood and synthetic take-down rifles and multiple barrel/caliber configurations, along with a complete line of built-to-order custom double rifles. Please contact the factory directly (see Trademark Index) for additional information and prices.

RIFLES: BOLT ACTION

VIKING GRADE - most standard cals., unique NSA takedown action, many options, including left-hand models, custom orders also available.

MSR N/A	$5,750	$5,250	$4,500	$3,750	$3,000	$2,500	$2,000

Add $1,500 per interchangeable barrel.

VIKING GRADE MAGNUM - most standard Mag. cals., unique NSA takedown action, many options and custom orders available, including left-hand.

MSR N/A	$8,600	$8,000	$7,000	$6,000	$5,000	$4,000	$3,000

Add $2,000 per interchangeable barrel.

FIELD GRADE SYNTHETIC - most standard cals., unique NSA takedown action, many options and custom orders available.

MSR N/A	$3,250	$2,850	$2,500	$2,100	$1,850	$1,500	$1,250

Add $1,200 per interchangeable barrel.

ODIN GRADE - .223 Rem. - .505 Gibbs cal., available in right- or left-hand Mauser style action, presentation grade walnut stock, match grade barrel, competition trigger, three position wing safety, quarter rib with banded ramped front sights, barrel band swivel, gold monogram stock oval, metal pistol grip cap, leather covered recoil pad, hand cut checkering, quick detachable scope bases and rings, engraving with gold inlays. New 2003.

MSR N/A	$10,000	$8,000	$6,000

THOR GRADE - .223 Rem. - .416 Rem. cal., right- or left-hand Mauser style action, extra fancy grade walnut stock, premium match grade barrel, competition trigger, three position wing safety, quarter rib with banded ramped front sights, barrel band swivel, metal pistol grip cap, rubber recoil pad, hand cut checkering, quick detachable scope bases and rings. New 2003.

MSR N/A	$8,000	$6,000	$4,250

TYR GRADE - .223 Rem. - .416 Rem. cal., right- or left-hand Mauser style action, fiber core or kevlar wrapped composite stock, premium match grade barrel, competition trigger, teflon all-weather coating on metal and stock, adj. rear and banded ramped front sights, three position wing safety, swivel studs, rubber recoil pad, quick detachable scope bases and rings. New 2003.

MSR N/A	$6,000	$5,000	$3,750

GRADING - PPGS™	100%	98%	95%	90%	80%	70%	60%

VOYAGER GRADE - .223 Rem. - .416 Rem. cal., Mauser style titanium action, fiber core or kevlar wrapped composite stock, premium match grade barrel, competition trigger, teflon all-weather coating on metal and stock, adj. rear and banded ramped front sights, three position wing safety, swivel studs, rubber recoil pad, quick detachable scope bases and rings. New 2003.

    MSR N/A $10,000 $8,000 $6,000

RIFLES: SxS

VIKING GRADE - most standard cals. including .30-30 WCF, .30-40 Krag, .375 Win., .444 Marlin, .45-70 Govt., as well as traditional European NE cals. up to .600 NE, built per individual custom order. New 2000.

    MSR N/A $19,600 $16,400 $14,000 $12,000 $10,000 $8,500 $7,250

NORTH AMERICAN ARMS, INC.

Current manufacturer established circa 1976, and currently located in Provo, UT. Distributor and dealer sales.

North American Arms was originally founded under the name Rocky Mountain Arms circa 1974-1975 by noted handgun entrepreneur Dick Casull. During 1976-1977, the company's name was changed to North American Arms, and it became part of the Tally Corp. of Newbury Park, CA. North American Arms was relocated from Salt Lake City to Provo, UT in 1978, and moved again in 1984 to Spanish Fork, UT. During 1986-1987, Teleflex Corp., an aerospace company, bought North American Arms' parent company, the Tally Corp. In 1992, Teleflex decided to sell off the gunmaking company, and North American Arms was purchased by Sandy Chisholm, a Teleflex employee. The company relocated again in 1994 to Provo, UT.

PISTOLS: SEMI-AUTO

In addition to many accessories being available for the Guardian Pistol Series, there is also a Guardian Custom Shop that offers consumers a customized Guardian model, with a wide variety of finish, slide, sight, grips, and serialization options. Please contact the company directly for more information on these custom shop special orders and options.

NAA .32 GUARDIAN - .32 ACP cal., double action only, hammerless, stainless steel construction, 6 shot mag., 2.185 in. barrel, fixed low profile sights, dimpled black synthetic grips, 13 1/2 oz. New 1999.

    MSR $402 $355 $285 $245

    Add $28 for ILS option.

NAA .32 NAA GUARDIAN - .32 NAA cal. (.380 ACP casing necked down to .32 cal.), double action only, larger version of the NAA .32 Guardian, 2.49 in. barrel, 6 shot mag., dimpled black grips, 18.7 oz. New 2002.

    MSR $449 $385 $300 $250

NAA .380 GUARDIAN - .380 ACP cal., double action only, larger version of the NAA .32 Guardian, 2.49 in. barrel, 6 shot mag., dimpled black grips, mfg. in partnership with Kahr Arms, 18.7 oz. New 2001.

    MSR $449 $385 $300 $250

    Add $30 for ILS option.

REVOLVERS: MINI SERIES

All NAA mini revolvers are manufactured to highest quality control standards and have halfway notches cut on the front cylinder face allowing the hammer to lock up the cylinder between cartridges. This allows the gun to be carried fully loaded without the danger of accidental discharge.

GRADING - PPGS™	100%	98%	95%	90%	80%	70%	60%

NAA .22 S/LR - .22 Short (new 1994) or .22 LR cal., 5 shot, single action, spur trigger, 1 1/8, 1 5/8, or 2 1/2 (disc.) in. barrel, stainless steel, plastic (disc.) or laminated rosewood grips, approx. 4 1/2 oz. Mfg. 1975-present.

    MSR $193   **$155**   **$120**   **$95**

    Add $15 for 2 1/2 in. barrel (disc.).

    Add $22 for holster grip accessory.

    Add $39 for quick-release belt buckle option.

    The optional holster grip allows the pistol to fold forward allowing concealability, safety, and has a clip which allows it to be attached to a belt.

NAA .17 - .17 HMR or .17 Mach 2 cal., otherwise similar to NAA .22 Model. New 2005.

    MSR $193   **$155**   **$120**   **$95**

    Add $22 for holster grip accessory.

    Add $15 for .17 HMR cal.

    Add $43 for .17 HMR cal. with extra .17 Mach 2 conversion cylinder.

NAA .22 MAGNUM - similar to .22 LR, except in .22 Mag. cal.

    MSR $208   **$170**   **$130**   **$110**

    Add $18 for 2 1/2 in. barrel (disc.).

    Add $21 for holster grip accessory.

    Add $34 for quick-release belt buckle option.

NAA .22 MAGNUM CONVERTIBLE - similar to NAA .22 Mag., except has extra LR cylinder in pouch.

    MSR $236   **$200**   **$170**   **$120**

    Add $18 for 2 1/2 in. barrel (disc.).

    Add $22 for holster grip accessory.

MINI-MASTER TARGET REVOLVER - .17 HMR (new 2003), .17 Mach 2 (new 2005), .22 LR, or .22 Mag. cal., 5 shot, 4 in. heavy vent. barrel, unfluted bull cylinder, spur trigger, fixed or adj. white outline rear sight, oversize black rubber Mini-master grip, 10.7 oz. New 1990.

    MSR $272   **$235**   **$200**   **$170**

    Add $29 for extra combo cylinder.

    Add $29 for adj. rear sight (elevation only).

    This model was also available in hot fuschia colored oversized grips.

MINI-MASTER BLACK WIDOW - .17 HMR (new 2003), 17 Mach 2 (new 2005), .22 LR or .22 Mag. cal., 2 in. heavy VR barrel, full size black rubber grip, fixed or adj. rear sight, unfluted cylinder, 8.8 oz. New 1991.

    MSR $258   **$215**   **$170**   **$130**

    Add $29 for extra combo cylinder.

    Add $29 for adj. rear sight (elevation only).

    This model was also available in hot fuschia colored oversized grips.

NAA STANDARD SET - 3 gun set (.22 Short, .22 LR, and .22 Mag. cals.) in walnut display case with matching serial numbers, high polish finish with matte contours.

    MSR $719   **$525**   **$455**   **$365**

NAA DELUXE SET - 3 gun set (.22 Short, .22 LR, and .22 Mag. cals.) in walnut display case with matching serial numbers, high polish finish on entire gun.

    MSR $863   **$725**   **$575**   **$425**

CASED .22 MAG. - includes .22 Mag. cal. model in walnut display case with high polish finish with matte contours.

    MSR $330   **$275**   **$200**   **$160**

GRADING - PPGS™	100%	98%	95%	90%	80%	70%	60%

NAA SINGLE ACTION REVOLVER - .45 Win. Mag. or .450 Mag. Express cal., polished stainless steel, transfer bar safety inside the hammer, 5 shot, 7 1/2 in. barrel, walnut grips, includes presentation case. Disc. 1984.

Matte finish	$1,200	$950	$700
High polish finish	$1,400	$1,100	$850
Both cylinders	$1,650	$1,275	$975

Last MSR was $650.

This model was also available by special order with 10 1/2 in. barrel and optional scope. Extra cylinders were also available at $75-$100 and were fitted to the gun. A set including 2 cylinders could also be ordered. North American Arms cannot perform any repair work on .450 Mag. Express revolvers.

NORTH AMERICAN SAFARI EXPRESS

Previous trademark for those rifles (SxS) assembled by A. Francotte of Belgium for exclusive importation by Armes De Chasse located in Chadds Ford, PA.

NORTHWEST ARMS

Please refer to Wilkinson Arms listing.

NOSLER, INC.

Current rifle manufacturer located in Bend, OR.

John Nosler founded Nosler, Inc. in 1948, and is responsible for the development of numerous ammunition lines specializing in accuracy and dangerous game.

RIFLES: BOLT ACTION

Nosler, Inc. builds high quality limited edition bolt action rifles. Each Nosler rifle features a new caliber every year, fancy checkered walnut stock with ebony forearm tip, cheekpiece, and Pachmayr Decelerator pad, 24 in. stainless steel Wiseman barrel with all-weather coating, and Leupold Custom Shop scope and rings. Rifles are individually serial numbered 1-500 per year, and include an aluminum travel case. Current MSR is $3,995. Please contact the company directly for more information, including delivery time and availability (see Trademark Index).

NOWLIN MFG., INC.

Current custom handgun and components manufacturer established in 1982, and located in Claremore, OK. Dealer or consumer direct sales.

Nowlin Mfg., Inc. manufactures a complete line of high quality M1911 A1 styled competition and defense pistols, available in 9mm Para., 9x23mm, .38 Super, .40 S&W, or .45 ACP cal. Various frame types are available, including a variety of Nowlin choices. Recent models (available in blue or nickel finish) include the NRA Bianchi Cup (approx. 1997 retail was $2,750 - disc.), 007 Compact ($1,395 - disc.), Compact X2 ($1,436 - disc.), Match Classic ($1,495), Crusader ($1,799), Avenger w/ STI frame ($2,079), Challenger ($1,849), World Cup PPC ($2,019), STI High Cap. Frame ($1,595 - disc. 1999), Mickey Fowler Signature Series ($2,087), Compact Carry ($1,695 - disc. 1999), Compact 4 1/4 in. ($1,750, .45 ACP, disc. 2002), Gladiator ($1,447 in .45 ACP cal., disc. 2002), Match Master ($2,595), Bianchi Cup Master Grade ($4,999 MSR, .38 Super cal.) and the Custom Shop Excaliber Series ($2,829). Please contact the factory directly for more information, including specific pricing (see Trademark Index).

NOTES

_____

_____

_____

_____

_____

_____

_____

_____

_____

_____

_____

_____

_____

_____

_____

_____

_____

_____

_____

_____

_____

_____

_____

_____

_____

_____

_____

_____

O SECTION

O.D.I. (OMEGA DEFENSIVE INDUSTRIES)

Previous manufacturer located in Midland Park, NJ circa 1981-82.

Essex Arms, located in Island Pond, VT, aquired the remaining O.D.I. Viking inventory of parts for the Viking pistol (see Trademark Index), in addition to being a components supplier (slides and receivers) for M-1911 styled pistols. Previously, Randco Manufacturing, located in Monrovia, CA, was providing service (and had parts) for these older O.D.I. pistols.

GRADING - PPGS™	100%	98%	95%	90%	80%	70%	60%

PISTOLS: SEMI-AUTO

VIKING & VIKING COMBAT - .45 ACP or 9mm Para. (advertised, but never mfg.) cal., Viking Model is Government size and the Combat Model is Commander size. All stainless steel construction, the design utilizes the Seecamp double action, teakwood grips. 5 in. barrel on the Viking Model and 4 1/4 in. barrel on the Viking Combat Model, 7 shot mag., 39 oz. Approx. 200-300 Viking Combat Models were made from kits.

$495	$385	$295	

Last MSR was $579.

Add $100 for slide with crossbolt safety.

OBREGON

Previously manufactured by Fabrica de Armas Mexico located in Mexico City, Mexico.

PISTOLS: SEMI-AUTO

OBREGON - 11.43mm cal., patterned somewhat after the Colt Model 1911A1, features tubular slide and Savage/Steyr type action, 1,000 pistols mfg. in Mexico for commercial sale during and after WWII, slide marked "Sistema Obregon Cal 11.43mm".

$4,750	$4,250	$3,750	$3,250	$2,750	$2,250	$1,750

OHIO ORDNANCE WORKS, INC.

Current rifle manufacturer established in 1997, and located in Chardon, OH.

RIFLES: SEMI-AUTO

MODEL BAR 1918A3 - .30-06 cal., patterned after the original Browning BAR (M1918A2) used during WWI, all steel construction utilizing original parts except for lower receiver, 24 in. barrel, original folding type rear sight, 20 shot mag., matte metal and wood finish, Bakelite or American walnut stock and forearm, 20 lbs. Limited mfg.

MSR $2,850	$2,600	$2,350	$1,975	$1,650	$1,425	$1,100	$875

Add $200 for American black walnut stock and forearm.

MODEL BAR A1918 SLR - .30-06 cal., similar to Model BAR 1918A3, except does not have A3 carry handle, mfg. by Ohio Ordnance Works, Inc. New 2005.

MSR $4,300	$3,975	$3,500	$3,000	$2,500	$2,150	$1,800	$1,625

MODEL 1928 BROWNING - .30-06, 7.65mm, .308 Win., or 8mm cal., semi-auto action patterned after the 1928 Browning watercooled machine gun, blue or parkerized finish, includes tripod, water hose, ammo can, 3 belts, and belt loader. Production began late 2001.

MSR $5,950	$5,450	$4,850	$4,450	$4,000	$3,650	$3,450	$3,150

Add $200 for .308 Win. or 8mm cal., or $250 for 7.6mm cal.
Subtract $2,100 for parkerized finish.

GRADING - PPGS™	100%	98%	95%	90%	80%	70%	60%

OLD-WEST GUN CO.

Previous importer and distributor that took over the inventory of Allen Firearms after they went out of business in early 1987. Old-West Gun Co. changed their name to Cimarron Arms in late 1987. Please refer to Cimarron Arms in this text for approximate prices on similar models from Old-West Gun Co.

OLLENDORFF, PHILIPP

Current manufacturer established during 1986, and located in Scharnitz, Austria.

Philipp Ollendorff manufactures best quality double rifles, O/U shotguns, stalking rifles, and other configurations. All guns are made to custom order, and there are many options available. Please contact the manufacturer directly for more information, including model availability and a price quotation (see Trademark Index).

OLYMPIC ARMS, INC.

Current manufacturer established during 1976, and located in Olympia, WA. Dealer direct sales.

In late 1987, Olympic Arms, Inc. acquired Safari Arms of Phoenix, AZ. As of Jan., 2004, the Safari Arms product name was discontinued, and all 1911 style products are now being manufactured in the Olympic Arms facility in Olympia, WA. Schuetzen Pistol Works is the in-house custom shop of Olympic Arms.

PISTOLS: SEMI-AUTO

Please refer to the Safari Arms section for previously manufactured pistols made under the Safari Arms trademark.

ENFORCER - .45 ACP cal., 3.8 in. barrel, 6 shot mag., shortened grip, available with max hard finish aluminum frame, parkerized, electroless nickel or lightweight anodized finishes, flat or arched mainspring housing, adj. sights, ambidextrous safety, neoprene or checkered walnut grips, 27 oz. (lightweight model).

MSR $625	$575	$500	$450	$425	$400	$375	$350

This model was originally called the Black Widow. After Safari Arms became Schuetzen Pistol Works, this model was changed extensively to include stainless construction, beavertail grip safety, and combat style hammer.

MATCHMASTER - similar to the Enforcer, except has 5 or 6 in. barrel and 7 shot mag., approx. 40 oz.

MSR $595	$550	$475	$425	$395	$375	$350	$325

Add $50 for 6 in. barrel.

BLAK-TAC MATCHMASTER - .45 ACP cal., 5 in. National Match barrel, 7 shot mag., widened and lowered ejection port, Blak-Tac treated frame and slide, low profile combat sights, adj. trigger, approx. 40 oz. New 2003.

MSR $729	$650	$575	$500	$450	$400	$350	$325

BIG DEUCE - .45 ACP cal., 6 in. longslide version of the MatchMaster, matte black slide with satin stainless steel frame, smooth walnut grips, 40.3 oz. Mfg. 1995-2004.

	$775	$625	$575	$500	$450	$400	$350

Last MSR was $835.

COHORT PISTOL - .45 ACP cal., features Enforcer slide and MatchMaster frame, 3.8 in. stainless steel barrel, beavertail grip safety, extended thumb safety and slide release, commander style hammer, smooth walnut grips with laser etched Black Widow logo, 37 oz. New 1995.

MSR $649	$595	$525	$475	$425	$375	$335	$300

GRADING - PPGS™	100%	98%	95%	90%	80%	70%	60%

STREET DEUCE - .45 ACP cal., M1911A1 styled frame, 5.2 in. stainless steel National Match bushingless barrel, stainless frame, steel slide, lowered and widened ejection port, 7 shot mag., diamond pattern checkered rosewood grips. New 2001.

MSR $995	$875	$775	$675	$575	$475	$400	$325

JOURNEYMAN - similar to Street Deuce, except has 4.2 in. barrel. New 2001.

MSR $995	$875	$775	$675	$575	$475	$400	$325

WESTERNER - .45 ACP cal., 100% case colored finish on frame and slide, fitted barrel bushing, wide beavertail grip safety, shaped and tensioned extractor, fully adj. LPA rear sight, dovetail front blade sight, custom made laser etched smooth holly grips. New 2003.

MSR $695	$625	$560	$495	$450	$395	$350	$315

✳ *Trail Boss Westerner* - similar to Westerner, except has 6 in. bull barrel, 7 shot mag., laser engraved grips. New 2005.

MSR $799	$700	$625	$550	$500	$450	$400	$350

✳ *Constable Westerner* - similar to Trail Boss, except has 4.25 in. bull barrel, compact frame. New 2005.

MSR $779	$685	$610	$550	$500	$450	$400	$350

OA-93 PISTOL - .223 Rem. (most common, current mfg.) or 7.62x39mm (very limited mfg., disc.) cal., semi-auto, gas operated without buffer tube stock, or charging handle, 6 (most common, disc.), 6.5 (new 2005), 9 (disc.), or 14 (disc.) in. free-floated match threaded barrel with flash suppressor, upper receiver utilizes integral scope mount base, 30 shot mag., 4 lbs. 3 oz., approx. 500 mfg. 1993-94 before Crime Bill discontinued production, reintroduced late 2004.

MSR $850	$850	$800	$750	$700	$650	$600	$550

Last MSR in 1994 was $2,700.

Add $800 for 7.62x39mm cal.

OA-96 AR PISTOL - .223 Rem. cal., 6 in. barrel only, similar to OA-93 Pistol, except has pinned (fixed) 30 shot mag. and rear takedown button for rapid reloading, 5 lbs. Mfg. 1996-2000.

$860	$775	$650	$575	$495	$450	$395

Last MSR was $860.

OA-98 PISTOL - .223 Rem. cal., skeletonized, lightweight version of the OA-96, 6.5 in. non-threaded barrel, 10 shot fixed mag., denoted by perforated appearance, 3 lbs. Mfg. 1998-2003, reintroduced 2005.

MSR $850	$775	$700	$625	$550	$500	$450	$400

RIFLES: BOLT ACTION

In 1993, Olympic Arms purchased the rights, jigs, fixtures, and machining templates for the Bauska Big Bore Magnum Mauser action. Please contact Olympic Arms (see Trademark Index) for more information regarding Bauska actions both with or without fluted barrels.

ULTRA MAG BBK-01 - various cals. between .300 Win. Mag.-.505 Gibbs, custom order rifle available with many barrel options and other special order features, price on request from the factory.

This model was formerly the Bauska BBK-02.

BOLT ACTION SAKO - various cals. between .17 Rem.-.416 Rem. Mag., 26 in. fluted barrel, various stock configurations, values represent base price with no options. Disc. 2000.

$660	$575	$500	$450	$400	$360	$330

Last MSR was $660.

GRADING - PPGS™	100%	98%	95%	90%	80%	70%	60%

ULTRA CSR TACTICAL RIFLE - .308 Win. cal., Sako action, 26 in. broach cut heavy barrel, Bell & Carlson black or synthetic stock with aluminum bedding, Harris bipod, carrying case. Mfg. 1996-2000.

	$1,140	$900	$740	$625	$550	$500	$450

Last MSR was $1,140.

COUNTER SNIPER RIFLE - .308 Win. cal., bolt action utilizing M-14 mags., 26 in. heavy barrel, camo-fiberglass stock, 10 1/2 lbs. Disc. 1987.

	$1,100	$900	$775	$695	$550	$440	$410

Last MSR was $1,225.

SURVIVOR I CONVERSION UNIT - .223 Rem. or .45 ACP cal., converts M1911 variations into carbine, bolt action, collapsible stock, 16 1/4 in. barrel, 5 lbs.

	$275	$225	$195

This kit was also available for S&W and Browning Hi-Power models.

RIFLES: SEMI-AUTO

Olympic Arms is currently shipping high capacity mags. with its rifles/carbines to those states where legal.

The PCR (Politically Correct Rifle) variations listed below refer to those guns manufactured after the Crime Bill was implemented from September 1994-2004. PCR rifles have smooth barrels (no flash suppressor), a 10 shot mag., and fixed stocks. Named models refer to the original, pre-ban model nomenclature.

COMPETITOR RIFLE - .22 LR cal., Ruger 10/22 action with 20 in. barrel featuring button cut rifling, Bell & Carlson thumbhole fiberglass stock, black finish and matte stainless fluted barrel, includes bipod, 6.9 lbs. Mfg. 1996-99.

	$575	$500	$450	$400	$360	$330	$300

Last MSR was $575.

ULTRAMATCH/PCR-1 - .223 Rem. cal., AR-15 action with modifications, 20 or 24 in. match stainless steel barrel, Picatinny flattop upper receiver, Williams set trigger optional, scope mounts, 10 lbs. 3 oz. New 1985.

* *PCR-1* - disc. 2004.

	$800	$725	$675	$625	$575	$525	$475

Last MSR was $1,074.

* *PCR-1P* - .223 Rem. cal., premium grade ultramatch rifle with many shooting enhancements, including Maxhard treated upper and lower receiver, 20 or 24 in. broach cut Ultramatch bull barrel, 1x10 in. or 1x8 in. rate of twist. Mfg. 2001-2004.

	$1,050	$900	$800	$700	$600	$550	$500

Last MSR was $1,299.

* *UM-1 Ultramatch* - 20 in. stainless Ultramatch barrel with non-chromed bore, approx. 8.5 lbs. Disc. 1994, reintroduced late 2004.

MSR $895	$850	$775	$700	$650	$600	$550	$500

Last MSR in 1994 was $1,515.

* *UM-1P Ultramatch* - similar to UM-1 Ultramatch, except has 20 or 24 in. Ultramatch bull barrel, premium grade ultramatch rifle with many shooting enhancements. New 2005.

MSR $1,299	$1,075	$925	$800	$700	$600	$550	$500

INTERCONTINENTAL - .223 Rem. cal., features synthetic wood-grained thumbhole buttstock and aluminum handguard, 20 in. ultra match barrel (free floating). Mfg. 1992-93.

	$1,650	$1,350	$1,050	$875	$750	$600	$550

Last MSR was $1,371.

GRADING - PPGS™	100%	98%	95%	90%	80%	70%	60%

INTERNATIONAL MATCH - .223 Rem. cal., similar to Ultramatch, except has custom aperture sights. Mfg. 1991-93.

	$1,475	$1,150	$950	$800	$675	$575	$525

Last MSR was $1,240.

SERVICE MATCH/PCR SERVICE MATCH - .223 Rem. cal., AR-15 action with modifications, 20 in. SS Ultramatch barrel, carrying handle, standard trigger, choice of A1 or A2 flash suppressor (Service Match only), 8 3/4 lbs.

✳ *Service Match* - disc. 1994, reintroduced late 2004.

MSR $916	$850	$775	$700	$625	$550	$500	$450

Last MSR in 1994 was $1,200.

✳ *SMP Premium Grade Service Match* - .223 Rem. cal., Maxhard upper and lower receiver, 20 in. broach cut Ultramatch super heavy threaded barrel (1 turn in 8 in. is standard), flash suppressor, 2-stage CMP trigger, Blak-Tak Armour bolt carrier assembly, Bob Jones NM interchangable rear sight system, AC4 pneumatic recoil buffer, Turner Saddlery competition sling, GI style pistol grip. New 2005.

MSR $1,344	$1,125	$975	$825	$725	$625	$550	$475

✳ *PCR Service Match* - disc. late 2004.

	$825	$750	$675	$625	$550	$500	$450

Last MSR was $1,062.

✳ *PCR- SMP Premium Grade Service Match* - .223 Rem. cal., Maxhard upper and lower receiver, 20 in. broach cut Ultramatch super heavy barrel (1 turn in 8 in. is standard), 2-stage CMP trigger, Blak-Tak Armour bolt carrier assembly, Bob Jones NM interchangable rear sight system, AC4 pneumatic recoil buffer, Turner Saddlery competition sling, GI style pistol grip. Mfg. 2004 only.

	$1,100	$950	$800	$700	$600	$550	$475

Last MSR was $1,613.

MULTIMATCH ML-1/PCR-2 - .223 Rem. cal., tactical short range rifle, 16 in. Ultramatch barrel with A2 upper receiver, aluminum collapsible (Multimatch ML-1) or fixed (PCR-2) stock, carrying handle, stealth vortex flash suppressor (Multimatch ML-1 only), 5 lbs. 14 oz. New 1991.

✳ *Multimatch ML-1*

MSR $799	$775	$700	$650	$600	$550	$500	$450

Last MSR in 1994 was $1,200.

✳ *PCR-2* - disc. late 2004.

	$750	$675	$600	$525	$450	$425	$400

Last MSR was $958.

MULTIMATCH ML-2/PCR-3 - .223 Rem. cal., features Picatinny flattop upper receiver with stainless steel 16 in. Ultramatch bull (new 2005) barrel, carrying handle (disc.), 5 lbs. 14 oz. New 1991.

✳ *Multimatch ML-2* - disc. 1994, reintroduced late 2004.

MSR $799	$725	$650	$575	$500	$450	$400	$350

Last MSR in 1994 was $1,200.

✳ *PCR-3* - disc. late 2004.

	$700	$625	$550	$500	$450	$350	$300

Last MSR was $958.

AR-15 MATCH/PCR-4 - .223 Rem. cal., patterned after the AR-15 with 20 in. barrel and solid synthetic stock, 8 lbs. 5 oz. Mfg. 1975-2004.

✳ *PCR-4*

	$730	$650	$575	$525	$475	$425	$395

Last MSR was $803.

GRADING - PPGS™	100%	98%	95%	90%	80%	70%	60%
✷ *AR-15 Match*							
	$995	$875	$775	$650	$575	$495	$450

Last MSR was $1,075.

CAR-15/PCR-5 - modified AR-15 with choice of 11 1/2 (disc. 1993) or 16 in. barrel, stow-away pistol grip and collapsible stock (CAR-15 only), 7 lbs. Mfg. 1975-1998, PCR-5 reintroduced 2000-2004.

   ✷ *PCR-5* - .223 Rem., 9mm Para. (new 1996), .40 S&W (new 1996), or .45 ACP (new 1996) cal. Disc. 1998, reintroduced 2000-2004.

	$695	$650	$550	$475	$450	$400	$375

Last MSR was $755.

   Add $45 for 9mm Para., .40 S&W, or .45 ACP cal.

   ✷ *CAR-15* - .223 Rem., 9mm Para., .40 S&W, .45 ACP, or 7.62x39mm cal.

	$960	$860	$775	$650	$575	$495	$450

Last MSR was $1,030.

   Add $170 for pistol cals.

PCR-6 - 7.62x39mm cal., 16 in. barrel, post-ban only, A-2 stowaway stock, carrying handle, 7 lbs. Mfg. 1995-2002.

	$795	$725	$650	$500	$475	$425	$375

Last MSR was $870.

PCR-7 ELIMINATOR - .223 Rem. cal., similar to PCR-4, except has 16 in. barrel, 7 lbs. 10 oz. Mfg. 1999-2004.

	$650	$575	$525	$485	$440	$410	$380

Last MSR was $844.

PCR-8 - .223 Rem. cal., same configuration as the PCR-1, except has standard 20 in. stainless steel heavy bull barrel with button rifling. Mfg. 2001-2004.

	$625	$575	$540	$500	$450	$425	$400

Last MSR was $834.

   ✷ *PCR-8 Mag.* - .223 WSSM or .243 WSSM cal., otherwise similar to PCR-8. Mfg. 2004.

	$825	$750	$675	$600	$550	$500	$450

Last MSR was $1,074.

   This model was also scheduled to be available in .308 Olympic Mag. and 7mm Olympic Mag. cals.

PCR-9/10/40/45 - 9mm Para., 10mm, .40 S&W, or .45 ACP cal., similar to PCR-5 Carbine except for pistol cals, A2 upper standard, 16 in. barrel, A2 buttstock, Mil-Spec lower. Mfg. 2001-2004.

	$650	$585	$535	$485	$435	$400	$375

Last MSR was $835.

PCR-16 - .223 Rem. cal., 16 in. match grade bull barrel, two-piece aluminum free-floating handguard, Picatinny receiver rail, 7 1/2 lbs. Mfg. 2003-2004.

	$550	$500	$465	$435	$400	$375	$350

Last MSR was $714.

PCR-30 - .30 Carbine cal., forged aluminum receiver with matte black anodizing, parkerized steel parts, A-2 adj. rear sight, accepts standard GI M1 .30 Carbine mags., 16 in. barrel with 1 turn in 12 in. twist, 7.15 lbs. Mfg. 2004.

	$625	$575	$525	$475	$425	$395	$350

Last MSR was $899.

PLINKER - .223 Rem. cal., similar to PCR-5, except has 16 in. button rifled barrel standard, A1 sights, cast upper/lower receiver, 100% standard Mil-Spec parts, 7 lbs. Mfg. 2001-2004.

	$550	$495	$460	$420	$400	$385	$370

Last MSR was $598.

PLINKER PLUS - .223 Rem. cal., similar to Plinker, except has 16 or 20 in. button rifled threaded barrel with flash suppressor, A1 sights, cast upper/lower receiver, 100% standard Mil-Spec parts, 7-8.4 lbs. New 2005.

	MSR $589	$560	$515	$475	$425	$400	$385	$370

Add $35 for 20 in. barrel.

CAR-97 - .223 Rem., 9mm Para., 10mm, .40 S&W, or .45 ACP cal., similar to PCR-5, except has 16 in. button rifled barrel, A2 sights, fixed CAR stock, standard with post-ban muzzle brake, approx. 7 lbs. Mfg. 1997-2004.

		$695	$650	$585	$530	$490	$460	$430

Last MSR was $780.

Add approx. $65 for 9mm Para., .40 S&W, or .45 ACP cal.

✴ **CAR-97 M4** - .223 Rem. cal., M4 configuration with contoured barrel, fixed carbine tube stock, factory installed muzzle brake, oversized shortened handguard. Mfg. 2003-2004.

		$695	$650	$600	$550	$500	$450	$400

Last MSR was $839.

Add $95 for detachable carrying handle (new 2004).

FAR-15 - .223 Rem. cal., featherweight model with lightweight 16 in. barrel, fixed collapsible stock, A1 contour lightweight button rifled barrel, 9.92 lbs. Mfg. 2001-2004.

		$625	$575	$525	$475	$425	$395	$375

Last MSR was $822.

GI-16 - .223 Rem. cal., forged aluminum receiver with black matte finish, parkerized steel parts, A1 adj. rear sights, 16 in. button rifled match grade barrel, 7 lbs. Mfg. 2004.

		$585	$525	$475	$440	$410	$375	$350

Last MSR was $699.

GI-20 - .223 Rem. cal., similar to GI-16, except has 20 in. heavy barrel and A-2 lower receiver, 8.4 lbs. Mfg. 2004.

		$595	$540	$495	$450	$425	$400	$375

Last MSR was $749.

OA-93 CARBINE - .223 Rem. cal., 16 in. threaded barrel, design based on OA-93 pistol, aluminum folding stock, flattop receiver, Vortex flash suppressor, 7 1/2 lbs. Mfg. 1995 - civilian sales disc. 1998, reintroduced 2004.

	MSR $895	$875	$825	$750	$675	$600	$550	$500

Last MSR in 1994 was $1,550.

✴ **OA-93PT Carbine** - .223 Rem. cal., aluminum forged receiver, black matte hard anodized finish, no sights, integral flattop upper receiver rail system, match grade 16 in. chromemoly steel barrel, push button removable stock attaches to left front side of vent. forearm, vertical pistol grip, 8 lbs. Mfg. 2004 only.

		$850	$800	$725	$650	$575	$525	$475

Last MSR was $1,074.

LIGHTWEIGHT TACTICAL RIFLE - .223 Rem. cal., available in LTF (fluted) or LT-MIL4 configuration, black matte anodized receiver, parkerized steel parts, adj. flip-up sight system, Picatinny rail, 16 in. non-chromed fluted or MIL4 threaded barrel with flash suppressor, tube style Ace FX buttstock. New 2005.

	MSR $942	$895	$825	$750	$675	$600	$525	$475

Add $68 for fluted barrel (LTF).

K3B CARBINE - .223 Rem. cal., 16 in. match grade chromemoly steel rifled threaded barrel with flash supressor, adj. A2 sight, A2 buttstock, adj. front post sight, optional A3 flattop receiver.

	MSR $629	$595	$550	$500	$465	$435	$400	$375

Add $79 for A3 flattop receiver.

GRADING - PPGS™	100%	98%	95%	90%	80%	70%	60%

✵ K3B-CAR - similar to K3B Carbine, except has carbine length handguard and collapsible stock. New 2005.

MSR $675	$650	$600	$550	$500	$450	$425	$400

Add $79 for A3 upper receiver.

✵ K3B-FAR - similar to K3B Carbine, except has smaller barrel diameter and is lightweight, 4.92 lbs. New 2005.

MSR $685	$655	$600	$550	$500	$450	$425	$400

Add $79 for A3 upper receiver.

✵ K3B-MIL4 - similar to K3B Carbine, except has MIL4 handguard, collapsible stock, and MIL4 barrel. New 2005.

MSR $699	$660	$610	$555	$500	$450	$425	$400

Add $79 for A3 upper receiver.

✵ K3B-MIL4-TC - similar to K3B-MIL4, except is tactical carbine version with FIRSH handguard, flattop upper receiver, and Picatinny rail. New 2005.

MSR $843	$795	$750	$700	$650	$600	$550	$500

K4B CARBINE - .223 Rem. cal., 20 in. match grade button chromemoly steel rifled threaded barrel with flash supressor, adj. A2 rear sight, A2 buttstock, adj. front post sight, A2 upper receiver and handguard.

MSR $669	$640	$585	$540	$500	$450	$425	$400

Add $79 for Picatinny flattop receiver and A3 detachable carry handle.

K7 ELIMINATOR - .223 Rem. cal., 16 in. stainless steel threaded barrel with flash suppressor, adj. A2 rear sight, A2 buttstock, adj. front post sight, 4.92 lbs. New 2005.

MSR $703	$670	$600	$550	$500	$450	$425	$400

Add $118 for A3 upper flattop receiver and detachable carry handle.

K8 - .223 Rem. cal., 20 in stainless steel button rifled bull barrel, A2 buttstock, Picatinny flattop upper receiver, 8.5 lbs. New 2005.

MSR $669	$640	$585	$540	$500	$450	$425	$400

✵ K8-MAG - similar to K8, except available in WSSM cals., and has 24 in. barrel. New 2005.

MSR $895	$825	$750	$675	$600	$550	$500	$450

K9/K10/K40/K45 - 9mm Para. (K9), 10mm Norma (K10), .40 S&W (K40), or .45 ACP (K45) cal., blow back action, adj. A2 rear sight, 16 in. threaded barrel with flash suppressor, A2 buttstock, bayonet lug. New 2005.

MSR $695	$650	$585	$535	$485	$435	$400	$375

✵ K9GL/K40GL - similar to K9 Series, except available only in 9mm Para. or .40 S&W cal., Glock style lower receiver, 16 in. straight or 17 in. barrel with flash suppressor, collapsible stock. New 2005.

MSR $770	$735	$675	$600	$550	$500	$465	$440

K16 - .223 Rem. cal., 16 in. free floating button rifled barrel, A2 buttstock, Picatinny flattop upper receiver, 4.92 lbs. New 2005.

MSR $595	$550	$500	$465	$435	$400	$375	$350

K30 - .30 Carbine cal., similar to K16, except has A2 upper receiver, collapsible stock, and threaded barrel with flash suppressor, 7.15 lbs. New 2005.

MSR $749	$675	$600	$550	$500	$450	$400	$350

OMEGA

Previous trademark manufactured by Armero Specialistas Reunidas, located in Eibar, Spain, circa 1920s.

GRADING - PPGS™	100%	98%	95%	90%	80%	70%	60%

PISTOLS: SEMI-AUTO

SEMI AUTOMATIC PISTOL - 6.35mm or 7.65mm cal., "Eibar" type action, marked Omega on slide, 6 shot mag.

	100%	98%	95%	90%	80%	70%	60%
6.35 cal.	$225	$180	$130	$110	$70	$55	$40
7.65 cal.	$250	$195	$135	$115	$80	$70	$55

OMEGA FIREARMS

Previous manufacturer located in Flower Mound, TX circa 1965-1969.

RIFLES: BOLT ACTION

SINGLE SHOT RIFLE - various cals., premium walnut. Disc. late 1960s.

$775	$650	$575	$495	$425	$360	$295

OMEGA PISTOL

Previously manufactured and distributed by Springfield Armory located in Geneseo, IL. Omega conversion kits only were available until 1996 from Safari Arms located in Olympia, WA under license from Peters-Stahl in Germany.

PISTOLS: SEMI-AUTO

OMEGA - .38 Super, 10mm Norma, or .45 ACP cal., single action, ported slide, 5 or 6 in. interchangeable ported or unported barrel with Polygon rifling, special lock-up system eliminates normal barrel link and bushing, Pachmayr grips, dual extractors, adj. rear sight. Mfg. 1987-90.

$625	$560	$495	$425	$360	$295	$265

Last MSR was $849.

   Add $663 for interchangeable conversion units.

   Add $336 for interchangeable 5 or 6 in. barrel (including factory installation).

   Each conversion unit includes an entire slide assembly, one mag., 5 or 6 in barrel, recoil spring guide mechanism assembly, and factory fitting.

OMEGA RIFLES/SHOTGUNS

Previous trademark of select rifles/shotguns imported by K.B.I., Inc. located in Harrisburg, PA, until 1994.

RIFLES

To date, there has been little collector interest for Omega rifles. Values are mostly determined by the shooting value rather than collector value.

SHOTGUNS

STANDARD O/U - 12, 20 (disc.), 28 (disc.) ga., or .410 (disc) bore, boxlock action, folding design, SNT, 26 or 28 in. VR barrels, extractors, checkered walnut stock and forearm, 5 1/2-7 lbs. Disc. 1994.

$425	$330	$295	$260	$230	$200	$180

* **Deluxe O/U** - 12 ga. only, similar to Standard Model except has better walnut. Importation disc. 1990.

$335	$290	$255	$220	$185	$160	$140

Last MSR was $379.

STANDARD SxS - 20, 28 ga., or .410 bore, boxlock action, folding design, double triggers, hardwood stock and forearm, 26 in. barrels, extractors, 5 1/2 lbs. Disc. 1989.

$190	$165	$140	$120	$110	$100	$90

Last MSR was $229.

   Add $40 for 28 ga. or .410 bore.

GRADING - PPGS™	100%	98%	95%	90%	80%	70%	60%

✱ **Deluxe SxS** - .410 bore only, similar to Standard Model except has better walnut. Disc. 1989.

	$200	$185	$170	$155	$140	$130	$120

Last MSR was $249.

SINGLE BARREL - 12, 20 ga., or .410 bore, various barrel lengths, matte blue finish, extractor. Importation disc. 1987.

	$85	$75	$65	$55	$45	$40	$35

Last MSR was $95.

STANDARD FOLDING SINGLE BARREL - 12, 16, 20, 28 ga., or .410 bore, 28 or 30 in. barrel, checkered hardwood stock, matte chrome receiver, approx. 5 1/2 lbs. Importation disc. 1987.

	$160	$135	$115	$100	$85	$70	$65

Last MSR was $180.

DELUXE FOLDING SINGLE BARREL - 12, 16, 20, 28 ga., or .410 bore, similar to Standard Model, except has checkered walnut stock and forearm, blue receiver. Importation disc. 1987.

	$195	$160	$135	$115	$100	$85	$70

Last MSR was $220.

OMEGA WEAPONS SYSTEMS INC.

Current shotgun manufacturer established circa 1998, and located in Tucson, AZ. Distributed by Defense Technology, Inc., located in Lake Forest, CA.

SHOTGUNS: SEMI-AUTO

OMEGA SPS-12 - 12 ga. only, 2 3/4 in. chamber, features gas operation and 5 shot detachable mag., 20 in. barrel, protected ghost ring sights, synthetic stock (with or w/o pistol grip) and forearm, 9 lbs. New 1998.

MSR N/A	$450	$400	$360	$330	$300	$275	$250

OMNI

Previous manufacturer located in Riverside, CA 1992-1998. During 1998, Omni changed its name to E.D.M. Arms. Previously distributed by First Defense International located in CA.

RIFLES: BOLT ACTION

LONG ACTION SINGLE SHOT - .50 BMG cal., competition single shot, chromemoly black finished receiver, 32-34 in. steel or stainless steel barrel with round muzzle brake, benchrest fiberglass stock, designed for FCSA competition shooting, 32 lbs. Mfg. 1996-98.

	$3,200	$2,800	$2,500	$2,150	$1,800	$1,500	$1,250

Last MSR was $3,500.

Add $400 for painted stock (disc. 1996).

SHELL HOLDER SINGLE SHOT - similar to Long Action Single Shot, except has fiberglass field stock with bipod, 28 lbs. Mfg. 1997-98.

	$2,525	$2,150	$1,800	$1,500	$1,250	$1,100	$925

Last MSR was $2,750.

MODEL WINDRUNNER - .50 BMG cal., long action, single shot or 3 shot mag., 1-piece I-beam receiver, chromemoly black finish, 36 in. barrel with round muzzle brake, fiberglass tactical stock, 35 lbs. Mfg. 1997-98.

	$6,950	$6,425	$5,875	$5,325	$4,750	$4,175	$3,500

Last MSR was $7,500.

Add $750 for 3 shot repeater.

GRADING - PPGS™	100%	98%	95%	90%	80%	70%	60%

MODEL WARLOCK - .50 BMG or 20mm cal., single, 3 (20mm), or 5 (.50 BMG) shot fixed mag., massive receiver design, fiberglass field stock, chromemoly black finished receiver, muzzle brake, 50 lbs. Mfg. 1997-98.

	$10,750	$8,950	$7,750	$6,750	$5,500	$4,750	$3,950

Last MSR was $12,000.

E.D.M. ARMS MODEL 97 - available in most cals. up to .308 Win., single shot or repeater (cals. .17 Rem. through .223 Rem. only), wire-cut one-piece design, black tactical stock with pillar-bedded chromemoly barrel, black finished receiver, unique trigger with safety, 9 lbs. Mfg. 1997-98.

	$2,525	$2,150	$1,800	$1,500	$1,250	$1,100	$925

Last MSR was $2,750.

E.D.M. ARMS WINDRUNNER WR50 - .50 BMG cal., sniper rifle, 5 shot mag., removable tactical adj. stock, take-down removable barrel, wire-cut one-piece receiver, titanium muzzle brake, blackened chromemoly barrel, approx. 29 lbs. Mfg. 1998 only.

	$11,750	$10,250	$9,500	$8,250	$7,000	$5,750	$4,500

Last MSR was $12,900.

OPUS SPORTING ARMS, INC.

Previous manufacturer located in Long Beach, CA.

RIFLES: BOLT ACTION

OPUS ONE - .243 Win., .270 Win., or .30-06 cal., U.S.R.A. Co. Model 70 action, 24 in. barrel, deluxe checkered walnut stock with ebony forend cap, 6 3/4 lbs., Halliburton cased. Mfg. 1987-88 only.

	$2,350	$1,995	$1,675	$1,250	$1,000	$875	$795

Last MSR was $2,700.

OPUS TWO - similar to Opus One, except in 7mm Rem. Mag. or .300 Win. Mag. cal., 7 1/4 lbs., cased. Mfg. 1987-88 only.

	$2,350	$2,050	$1,705	$1,300	$1,000	$875	$795

Last MSR was $2,700.

OPUS THREE - similar to Opus Two, except in .375 H&H or .458 Win. Mag. cal., 10 1/4 lbs., cased. Mfg. 1987-88 only.

	$2,600	$2,275	$1,800	$1,375	$1,050	$900	$825

Last MSR was $2,850.

OREGON ARMS

Please refer to the Chipmunk Rifles, Inc. section.

ORTGIES PISTOLS

Previous trademark of pistols manufactured by Deutsche Werke A.G. located in Erfurt, Germany.

PISTOLS: SEMI-AUTO

VEST POCKET AUTOMATIC - .25 ACP cal., 6 shot, 2 3/4 in. barrel, blue or nickel finish, fixed sights, wood grips. Mfg. 1921-28.

	$325	$225	$175	$150	$130	$115	$100

POCKET AUTOMATIC - .32 ACP cal. (8 shot) mfg. 1920-1928 or .380 ACP cal. (7 shot) mfg. 1922-1926, 3 1/4 in. barrel, blue or nickel finish, fixed sights, wood grips.

	$300	$225	$175	$150	$130	$115	$100

Add 20% for .380 ACP cal. or double safety variation.

ORVIS

Current catalog retailer and importer of private label subcontracted shotguns located in Manchester, VT and many other locations.

Orvis imports various shotguns under subcontract with various international manufacturers. Typical custom order delivery time is 2-8 months. Most of these private label models will approximate the values of the equivalent model manufactured by the subcontractor unless there are additional features and/or options which will add to the value.

SHOTGUNS: O/U

SKB GREEN MOUNTAIN UPLANDER (MODEL 555) - 12, 20, 28 ga., or .410 bore, 25-27 in. barrels, blue frame, straight stock with leather covered recoil pad. Disc.

$750	$675	$600	$550	$500	$450	$400

Last MSR was $995.

Add 15% for 28 ga. or .410 bore.

UPLANDER SERIES - 12 (disc. 1998), 20, or 28 ga., boxlock action, 26 in. barrels with choke tubes (except 28 ga.), SST, straight grip, select American black walnut with 24 LPI checkering, leather covered recoil pad since 1992, 6-7 lbs. Mfg. by P. Beretta of Italy.

MSR N/A	N/A	$2,450	$2,000	$1,550	$1,200	$995	$875

Add $1,250 for 28/20 ga. combo with case.

WATERFOWLER - 12 ga. only, 3 in. chambers, matte metal finish, 28 in. barrels with choke tubes, steel shot compatible, 7 1/2 lbs. Mfg. by P. Beretta of Italy.

MSR N/A	N/A	$2,650	$2,150	$1,650	$1,250	$1,025	$900

SPORTING CLAYS - 12 ga. only, 30 in. vented barrels with VR and choke tubes, adj. trigger, oil finished checkered walnut stock and forearm. New 1994.

MSR N/A	N/A	$2,550	$2,000	$1,550	$1,175	$995	$875

This model is also available in a women's configuration in 20 ga. with lightweight frame - includes carrying case.

SUPER FIELD - 12 or 20 ga., 26 (Uplander 20 ga. only), 28 (All Rounder), or 30 (Sporting Clays) in. VR barrels, configurations include Uplander 20 ga. with straight grip stock, All Rounder 12 ga. with 28 in. barrels and pistol grip stock, and Sporting Clays 12 ga. with 30 in. barrels, wide rib, and pistol grip stock, blue receiver, choke tubes, mfg. in Italy. Limited importation 1995 only.

$1,495	$1,250	$1,000	$875	$750	$625	$500

Last MSR was $2,150.

PREMIER GRADE - 12 or 20 ga., 3 in. chambers, 20 ga. features 28 in. barrels with straight grip stock, 12 ga. features pistol grip stock, select oil-finished European stock and forearm, choke tubes, blue frame with scrolled engraving, adj. trigger, cased, mfg. in Belgium 1995-98.

$6,450	$5,875	$5,250	$4,675	$4,000	$3,450	$2,675

Last MSR was $6,450.

Add $100 for Premier Grade Sporting.

This model is also available as a 20 ga. Superlight with straight grip stock and 26 in. barrels.

ORVIS DELUXE GRADE - similar to Uplander and Waterfowler, except has engraved bird scenes and scroll work on antique coin-finished receiver, deluxe checkered walnut stock and forearm, case. Imported 1993-94 only.

$4,250	$3,575	$2,950	$2,300	$1,900	$1,500	$1,275

Last MSR was $4,950.

GRADING - PPGS™	100%	98%	95%	90%	80%	70%	60%

RUGER/ORVIS MODEL - 12 or 20 ga., 3 in. chambers, Red Label Ruger action with customized Orvis features including blue receiver and straight grip English checkered stock. Importation disc. 1993.

	$1,295	$975	$850	$725	$600	$495	$450

Last MSR was $1,295.

SHOTGUNS: SxS

WATERFOWLER - 12 ga. only, 3 in. chambers, matte metal finish, 28 in. barrels with choke tubes, 7 3/4 lbs. Mfg. by P. Beretta of Italy until 1993.

	$1,950	$1,725	$1,475	$1,125	$950	$825	$700

Last MSR was $1,950.

CUSTOM UPLANDER - 12, 16, 20, 28 ga., or .410 bore, traditional frame, 25 or 27 in. barrels only, case colored or blue sidelock action with light engraving, DT, custom ordered gun, mfg. by Arrieta located in Spain.

MSR N/A	N/A	$2,525	$2,250	$1,950	$1,650	$1,450	$1,025

Add $950 for SNT.
Add $1,200 for extra set of barrels (same ga.).

FINE GRADE - 12, 16, 20, 28 ga., or .410 bore, custom ordered gun, custom order barrel lengths, sidelock action, DT, mfg. by Arrieta located in Spain. Disc. 1999.

	$4,650	$3,775	$3,150	$2,500	$1,995	$1,500	$1,150

Last MSR was $4,650.

Add $950 for SNT.
Add $1,950 for extra set of barrels (same ga.).

ROUNDED ACTION - similar to Fine Grade, except sidelock action has rounded corners and finer engraving (100% coverage) and wood upgrade, leather cased, mfg. by Arrieta located in Spain.

MSR N/A	N/A	$5,550	$4,250	$3,775	$3,300	$2,550	$1,995

＊ *Rounded Action Uplander* - similar to Rounded Action, except has less engraving, blue or case hardened frame. New 2000.

MSR N/A	N/A	$4,450	$3,950	$3,500	$3,000	$2,500	$2,000

NOTES

P SECTION

P.A.F.

Previous manufacturer located in S. Africa. P.A.F. stands for Pretoria Arms Factory.

GRADING - PPGS™	100%	98%	95%	90%	80%	70%	60%

PISTOLS: SEMI-AUTO

.25 ACP PISTOL - .25 ACP cal., patterned after the Baby Browning, blue finish. Approx. 10,000 mfg.

	100%	98%	95%	90%	80%	70%	60%
	$300	$275	$250	$235	$225	$200	$180

P.A.W.S., INC.

Current manufacturer located in Salem, OR. Distributor and dealer sales. Previously distributed by Sile Distributors, Inc. located in New York, NY.

CARBINES

ZX6/ZX8 CARBINE - 9mm Para. or .45 ACP cal., semi-auto paramilitary design carbine, 16 in. barrel, 10 or 32* shot mag., folding metal stock, matte black finish, aperture rear sight, partial barrel shroud, 7 1/2 lbs. New 1989.

MSR N/A	$715	$635	$550	$475	$375	$300	$250

The ZX6 is chambered for 9mm Para., while the ZX8 is chambered for .45 ACP.

PGW DEFENCE TECHNOLOGIES, INC.

Current manufacturer established in 1992, and located in Winnipeg, Manitoba, Canada. Previous company name was Prairie Gun Works until 2003. Currently imported by LBVG, located in Glasgow, MT.

RIFLES: BOLT ACTION

PGW manufactures approx. 50-60 guns annually. They also sell their actions separately for $900-$1,800, depending on caliber and configuration.

M-15 Ti ULTRA LITE - various cals., titanium (denoted by "Ti" model suffix) or re-machined Rem. 700 (disc.) short action, 20 in. barrel, Kevlar stock with glass bedding, matte metal finish, approx. 4 1/2-6 1/4 lbs. New 1996.

MSR $2,800	$2,650	$2,300	$2,000	$1,750	$1,750	$1,525	$1,375

Subtract $300 for benchrest or varmint single shot.
Add $100 for tactical stainless.
Add $200 for stainless steel (disc.).
Add $120 for Ultra Lite muzzle brake (disc.).
Add $200 for teflon black finish.
Add $100 for electroless nickel plating (disc.).

This model is also available in a hunter tactical configuration (Model M-15 Ti/HT) at no extra charge.

M-18 Ti ULTRA LIGHT - most long action cals. to .340 Wby. Mag., titanium or re-machined Rem. Model 700 long (disc.) action, 22 in. barrel, matte metal finish, approx. 4 3/4 lbs. New 1996.

MSR $2,800	$2,650	$2,300	$2,000	$1,750	$1,750	$1,525	$1,375

Subtract $300 for single shot.
Add $100 for stainless steel.
Add $200 for teflon black finish.
Add $120 for Ultra Lite muzzle brake (disc.).
Add $100 for electroless nickel plating (disc.).

GRADING - PPGS™	100%	98%	95%	90%	80%	70%	60%

TIMBERWOLF - .338 Win. or .408 Cheyenne cal., titanium or stainless steel construction, adj. trigger, 5 shot mag., custom teflon finish, single shot or repeater, various barrel lengths and stock configurations.

	MSR $6,300	$5,850	$5,400	$4,950	$4,500	$4,000	$3,500	$3,000

COYOTE - .308 Win. cal., titanium or stainless steel construction, adj. trigger, 5 shot mag., custom teflon finish, single shot or repeater, match grade fluted barrel, various barrel lengths and stock configurations.

	MSR $3,700	$3,450	$3,100	$2,800	$2,500	$2,250	$1,950	$1,750

LRT-2 (PGW/GIBBS) - various large cals. starting with .378, designed for dangerous game, 4 1/2 in. mag. box, one piece bolt, Sako type extraction, choice of Safari style or A-2 stock, 10-18 lbs. New 1999.

	MSR $2,975	$2,625	$2,350	$1,950	$1,750	$1,500	$1,250	$1,000

Add $100 for A-2 stock.

LRT-3 (PGW/GIBBS) - .50 BMG cal., single shot action, Big Mac stock. New 1999.

	MSR $4,500	$4,150	$3,700	$3,400	$3,100	$2,800	$2,500	$2,250

PKP, INC.

Previous manufacturer and distributor located in Tempe, AZ. Dealer or consumer direct sales.

PISTOLS

POWELL KNIFE PISTOL MR-38 - .38 Spl., unique knife-pistol design allows barrel to be incorporated into the upper rear portion of the break-action blade assembly, 1 3/4 in. barrel, stainless steel with wood handles, 17 oz. Limited mfg. 1997-98.

	$415	$350	$275

Last MSR was $450.

P.S.M.G. GUN COMPANY

Previous manufacturer located in Arlington, MA.

PISTOLS: SEMI-AUTO

SIX IN ONE SUPREME - .22 LR, 7.65mm Luger, .38 Super, .38 Spl., 9mm Para., or .45 ACP cal., single action, 3 1/4, 5, or 7 1/2 in. barrel with solid cooling rib, adj. rear sight, limited mfg. Mfg. 1988-89.

	$700	$600	$500	$450	$400	$365	$330

Last MSR was $895.

Add $20-$55 for caliber options.
Add $25 for 7 1/2 in. barrel.
Add $35 for satin nickel plating.
Add $225 per extra barrel.
Add $450 per individual conversion unit.

P.V. NELSON, (GUNMAKERS)

Please refer to the N section for this manufacturer.

PTK INTERNATIONAL, INC.

Previous distributor located in Atlanta, GA.
Please refer to listing under Poly-Technologies in this section.

P.38s

Standard German military 9mm Para. handgun beginning 1938. On older WWII German models, please refer to the German WWII Military Pistols section of this text.

GRADING - PPGS™	100%	98%	95%	90%	80%	70%	60%

PISTOLS: SEMI-AUTO

P.38 - JOHN MARTZ CONVERSIONS

✴ *Baby P.38* - 9mm Para. cal., shortened barrel (3 in.) grip, and two 7 shot mags., 62 fabricated.

	$2,500	$2,000	$1,500

✴ *P.38* - .38 Super (4 or 6 in. barrel, 9 fabricated) or .45 ACP (4 or 7 1/2 in. barrel, 24 fabricated) cal. Disc.

	$4,500	$2,750	$1,950

✴ *P.38 Carbine* - 9mm Para. cal., 16 in. barrel, adj. rear sight, 30 fabricated w/ shoulder stocks. Disc.

	$7,900	$5,950	$3,925

PALMETTO ARMS CO.

Current manufacturer located in Brescia, Italy. No current importation.

REVOLVERS

OUTLAW MODEL - .38 Spl./.357 Mag. or .45 LC cal., 4 3/4, 5 1/2, or 7 1/2 in. barrel, color case hardened finish, blue barrel, triggerguard and backstrap, walnut grips, blade front sight, notch rear sight. Limited mfg. beginninig 2003.

MSR N/A	N/A	$315	$285	$260	$240	$220	$200

RIFLES: SLIDE ACTION

LIGHTNING CARBINE - .44-40 WCF or .45 Colt cal., blue finish, 20 in. round barrel, blade front sight, elevated adj. semi-buckhorn rear sight, walnut stock with curved buttplate. Limited mfg. beginning 2004.

MSR N/A	N/A	$525	$450	$400	$350	$300	$250

LIGHTNING RIFLE - .32-20 WCF, .38 Spl., .38-40 WCF cal., 24 in. round or octagon barrel, blade front sight, elevated adj. semi-buckhorn rear sight, walnut stock with curved buttplate. Limited mfg. 2004.

Retail pricing in America has not yet been established on this model.

PARAMOUNT

Previous trademark manufactured by Imperial Gun Co., Ltd. located in Surrey, England. Actions were previously imported by O.K. Weber, Inc. located in Eugene, OR and Olympic Arms, Inc. located in Olympia, WA.

RIFLES: SINGLE SHOT

THE IMPERIAL - .308 Win. cal., single shot target rifle featuring thumbhole stock and CPE aperture rear sight, fully adj. trigger, vent. forearm. Disc. 1994.

	$3,250	$2,700	$2,250	$1,850	$1,400	$1,000	$795

Last MSR was $3,400.

RANGEMASTER - various cals., single shot design, steel frame, contoured walnut grips, satin chrome finish, 8 1/2 lbs. Limited importation 1992-94.

	$1,600	$1,400	$1,200	$995	$895	$795	$695

Last MSR was $1,800.

GRADING - PPGS™	100%	98%	95%	90%	80%	70%	60%

PARA-ORDNANCE MFG. INC.

Current manufacturer established in 1988, and located in Scarborough, Ontario, Canada. Various U.S. distributors. Distributor sales only.

Para-Ordnance.

PISTOLS: SEMI-AUTO

Previous Para-Ordnance model nomenclature typically listed the alphabetical letter of the series, followed by a one or two digit number indicating magazine capacity, followed by the number(s) of the caliber. Hence, a Model P14.45 is a P Series model with a 14 shot mag. in .45 ACP cal., and a 7.45LDA indicates a .45 ACP cal. with a 7 shot mag.

In 1999, Para-Ordnance introduced their LDA trigger system, originally standing for Lightning Double Action. During 2002, all alloy frame pistols were discontinued, and the abbreviation LDA became Light Double Action. Beginning 2003, all Para-Ordnance models are shipped with two magazines. Beginning Jan. 1, 2004, all Para-Ordnance models were replaced for the general market (except California) with the introduction of the new Power Extractor (PXT) models.

Currently, Para-Ordnance offers the following finishes on its pistols: Regal, Stealth, Black Watch, Spec Ops, or Sterling.

6.45 LDA/LLDA - Models 6.45 LDA (changed to Para-Companion, marked Para-Companion on left side of slide and C7.45LDA on right side of slide) and 6.45 LLDA were advertised in the 2001 Para-Ordnance catalog (became the Para-Carry, marked Para-Carry on left side of slide and 6.45 LLDA on right side of frame), the 6.46 LLDA was never manufactured. Mfg. 2001-2003.

C SERIES MODELS - .45 ACP cal., DAO, 3 (Carry), 3 1/2 (Companion or Companion Carry), 4 1/2 (CCW or Tac-Four), or 5 in. barrel, stainless steel only, single or double (Tac-Four only) stack mag., 6 (Carry), 7, or 10 (Tac-Four only) shot mag., approx. 30-34 oz. Mfg. 2003.

        $775   **$595**   **$495**

Last MSR was $939.

    Add $70 for Companion Carry Model.

D SERIES MODELS - 9mm Para., .40 S&W, or .45 ACP cal., DAO, 3 1/2 or 5 in. barrel, 7 or 10 shot single stack mag., steel receiver, matte black finish or stainless steel. Mfg. 2003.

        $715   **$575**   **$475**   **$425**   **$350**   **$325**   **$295**

Last MSR was $859.

    Add $80 for stainless steel.

P SERIES MODELS - 9mm Para. or .45 ACP cal., single action, 3 1/2, 4 1/4, or 5 in. barrel, 10 shot mag., matte black (5 in. barrel only) or stainless steel finish.

   ✱ **P10** - 9mm Para. (new 1998), .40 S&W, .45 ACP, 10mm (mfg. 1998 only, stainless steel) cal., single action, super compact variation featuring 3 in. barrel and shortened grip, 10 shot double column mag., 3-dot sights, choice of alloy (matte black), steel (matte black), or stainless (duo-tone – disc. 2000, or bright finish) frame, 31 oz. with steel frame or 24 oz. with alloy frame. Mfg. 1997-2002.

        $625   **$500**   **$435**   **$390**   **$350**   **$325**   **$295**

Last MSR was $740.

    Add $10 for steel frame.
    Add $49 for stainless steel.
    Add $45 for stainless steel with duo-tone finish (disc. 2000).

GRADING - PPGS™	100%	98%	95%	90%	80%	70%	60%

❋ **P12** - .40 S&W (disc. 2002) or .45 ACP cal., compact variation of the P14 featuring 10 (C/B 1994) or 11* shot mag. and 3 1/2 in. barrel, 33 oz. with steel frame (disc. 2002) or 24 oz. with alloy frame (disc. 2002) or stainless steel (standard beginning 2003, duo-tone stainless was disc. 2000). Mfg. 1990-2003.

	$750	$575	$475	$425	$375	$325	$295

Last MSR was $899.

Subtract 10% for steel frame (disc. 2002).

❋ **P13** - .40 S&W (disc. 2000) or .45 ACP cal., similar to P14, except has 10 (C/B 1994) or 12* shot mag., 4 1/4 in. barrel, 35 oz. with steel frame (disc. 2002) or 25 oz. with alloy frame (disc. 2002), stainless steel became standard 2003 (duo-tone stainless was disc. 2000). Mfg. 1993-2003.

	$750	$575	$475	$425	$375	$325	$295

Last MSR was $899.

❋ **P14** - .40 S&W (mfg. 1996-2000) or .45 ACP cal., patterned after the Colt Model 1911A1 except has choice of alloy (matte black, disc. 2002), steel (matte black), or stainless steel (stainless or duo-tone finish) frame that has been widened slightly for extra shot capacity (13* shot), 10 shot (C/B 1994) mag., single action, 3-dot sight system, rounded combat hammer, 5 in. ramped barrel, 38 oz. with steel frame or 28 oz. with alloy frame (disc. 2002), duo-tone stainless steel was disc. 2000. Mfg. 1990-2003.

	$685	$550	$475	$425	$375	$325	$295

Last MSR was $829.

Add $70 for stainless steel.

❋ **P15** - .40 S&W cal., otherwise similar to P13, 36 oz. with steel frame or 28 oz. with alloy frame. Mfg. 1996-99.

	$625	$500	$435	$390	$350	$325	$295

Last MSR was $740.

Add $10 for steel frame.
Add $59 for stainless steel.
Add $45 for stainless steel with duo-tone finish.

❋ **P16** - .40 S&W cal., otherwise similar to P14, steel or stainless steel (new 1997) frame only. New 1995-2002.

	$640	$515	$435	$385	$350	$325	$295

Last MSR was $750.

Add $49 for stainless steel.
Add $35 for duo-tone stainless steel (disc. 2000).

❋ **P18** - 9mm Para. cal., 5 in. ramped barrel, stainless steel, solid barrel bushing, flared ejection port, quadruple safety, adj. rear sight, 40 oz. Mfg. 1998-2003.

	$800	$625	$495				

Last MSR was $960.

PXT SERIES MODELS - 9mm Para., .40 S&W, or .45 ACP cal., features new power extractor design with larger claw (PXT), three markings on the left side of slide include: Para PXT 1911 (single action, single stack), Para PXT Hi-Cap (single action, high capacity), and Para PXT LDA (light double action, single stack and high capacity), right side marked with model name. New 2004.

❋ **PXT 1911** - .45 ACP cal. only, single action, single stack 7 shot mag., available in 3 1/2 (stainless only), 4 1/4 (steel or alloy frame), or 5 (steel frame) in. barrel, matte black finish or stainless steel.

MSR $749	$650	$575	$500	$450	$400	$350	$300

Add $219 for stainless steel.

GRADING - PPGS™	100%	98%	95%	90%	80%	70%	60%

PXT HIGH CAPACITY - 9mm Para. or .45 ACP cal., single action, 10 shot or high capacity mag., 3 (alloy), 3 1/2 (stainless steel), 4 1/4 (steel or stainless steel), or 5 (steel or stainless steel) in. barrel, various finishes.

	MSR $749	$650	$575	$500	$450	$400	$350	$300

Add $91 for 5 in. barrel with stealth finish.
Add $166 for 3 1/2 or 5 in. stainless steel.
Add $181 for 4 1/4 in. stainless steel or $91 for 4 1/4 in. steel barrel.
Add $226 for 9mm Para cal. (5 in. stainless only).

✴ *PXT High Capacity Limited* - .40 S&W or .45 ACP cal., single action, 10 shot or high capacity mag., 3 1/2 (stainless steel), 4 1/4 (stainless steel), or 5 (steel or stainless steel) in. barrel, stealth or sterling finish.

	MSR $1,020	$925	$800	$700	$600	$500	$400	$350

Add $75 for 3 1/2 or 4 1/4 in. barrel or stainless steel.

PXT LDA (CARRY OPTION SERIES) - .45 ACP cal., DAO, single stack 6 or 7 shot mag., stainless steel construction, 3, 3 1/2, or 4 1/4 in. barrel, features Griptor grips (grooved front grip strap).

	MSR $968	$835	$715	$600	$525	$450	$375	$325

Add $30 for stealth finish (3 in. barrel only).
Add $60 for Novak adj. rear sight and stealth finish (new mid-2004).
Add $15 for 3 1/2 in. barrel.

✴ *PXT LDA* - .45 ACP cal., DAO, single stack 7 shot mag., steel or stainless steel construction, 3 1/2, 4 1/4, or 5 in. barrel.

	MSR $878	$775	$675	$575	$500	$450	$375	$325

Add $75 for stainless steel with 5 in. barrel or $90 for stainless steel with 3 1/2 in. barrel.

✴ *PXT LDA Limited* - .45 ACP cal., DAO, single stack 7 shot mag., steel or stainless steel, 5 in. barrel.

	MSR $1,035	$935	$800	$700	$600	$500	$400	$350

Add $75 for stainless steel.

PXT LDA HIGH CAPACITY (CARRY OPTIONS SERIES) - .45 ACP cal., DAO, 10, 12 or 13 shot mag., stainless steel construction, 3 1/2 or 4 1/4 in. barrel, 3-dot or night sights.

	MSR $968	$835	$700	$600	$525	$450	$375	$325

Add $60 for 3 1/2 in. barrel.

✴ *PXT LDA High Capacity* - 9mm Para., .40 S&W, or .45 ACP cal., DAO, 10, 14, 16, or 18 shot mag., steel or stainless steel construction, 4 1/4 or 5 in. barrel.

	MSR $878	$775	$675	$575	$500	$450	$375	$325

Add $75 for stainless steel.
Add $37 for light rail (5 in. barrel only, new mid-2004).

✴ *PXT LDA Limited High Capacity* - 9mm Para., .40 S&W, or .45 ACP cal., DAO, 10, 14, 16, or 18 shot mag., steel or stainless steel, 5 in. barrel.

	MSR $1,035	$935	$800	$700	$600	$500	$400	$350

Add $75 for stainless steel.

PXT OPS - .45 ACP cal., 3 1/2 in. ramped barrel, 7 shot mag., white low-mount 3-dot fixed sights, stainless steel frame, spur competition hammer, match grade trigger, checkered cocobolo grips with gold medallions, extended slide lock, beavertail grip and firing pin safeties, 32 oz. New 2005.

	MSR $988	$850	$725	$615

PXT LTC - .45 ACP cal., 4 1/4 in. ramped barrel, 7 shot mag., white low-mount 3-dot fixed sights, stainless steel frame, spur competition hammer, match grade trigger, checkered cocobolo grips with gold medallions, extended slide lock, beavertail grip and firing pin safeties, 35 oz. New 2005.

	MSR $988	$850	$725	$615

GRADING - PPGS™	100%	98%	95%	90%	80%	70%	60%

⁑ **PXT LTC High Capacity** - .45 ACP cal., 4 1/4 in. barrel, 10 or 14 shot mag., 3-dot fixed sights, stainless steel frame, match grade trigger, black polymer grips with medallions, green spec. ops. finish, three safeties, 37 oz. New 2005.

MSR $855	$750	$650	$550

PXT S12-45 LIMITED - .45 ACP cal., 3 1/2 in. ramped barrel, 10 or 12 shot mag., stainless steel frame with black slide, Novak adj. rear sight, spur competition hammer, checkered cocobolo grips with gold medallions, 34 oz. New 2005.

MSR $1,105	$995	$850	$725

S SERIES MODELS - .40 S&W or .45 ACP cal., single action, 3 1/2, 4 1/4, or 5 in. barrel, 10 shot mag., matte black (5 in. barrel only) or stainless steel finish.

⁑ **S10 Limited** - similar to P10, except has competition shooting features, including beavertail grip safety, competition hammer, tuned trigger, match grade barrel, front slide serrations, choice of steel or alloy frame with matte black finish or stainless steel, 40 oz. Mfg. 1999-2002.

$765	$650	$525	$450	$395	$350	$325
						Last MSR was $865.

Add $10 for steel receiver.
Add $24 for stainless steel.

⁑ **S12 Limited** - .40 S&W (disc. 2002) or .45 ACP cal., similar to P12, except has competition shooting features, including beavertail grip safety, competition hammer, tuned trigger, match grade barrel, front slide serrations, choice of steel or alloy (disc. 2002) frame, matte black (disc. 2002) or stainless steel finish, 40 oz. Mfg. 1999-2003.

$895	$750	$650	$525	$450	$395	$350
						Last MSR was $1,049.

Subtract 10% for steel frame (disc. 2002).

⁑ **S13 Limited** - .40 S&W (disc. 2002) or .45 ACP cal., similar to P13, except has competition shooting features, including beavertail grip safety, competition hammer, tuned trigger, match grade barrel, front slide serrations, choice of steel or alloy (disc. 2002) frame, matte black (disc. 2002) or stainless steel finish, 40 oz. Mfg. 1999-2003.

$895	$750	$650	$525	$450	$395	$350
						Last MSR was $1,049.

⁑ **S14 Limited** - .40 S&W (disc. 2002) or .45 ACP cal., similar to P14, except has competition shooting features, including beavertail grip safety, competition hammer, tuned trigger, match grade barrel, front slide serrations, matte black or stainless steel, 40 oz. Mfg. 1998-2003.

$850	$725	$625	$525	$450	$395	$350
						Last MSR was $989.

Add $60 for stainless steel.

⁑ **S16 Limited** - .40 S&W cal., similar to P16, except has 5 in. barrel and competition shooting features, including beavertail grip safety, competition hammer, tuned trigger, match grade barrel, front slide serrations, matte black steel or stainless steel, 40 oz. Mfg. 1998-2003.

$850	$725	$625	$525	$450	$395	$350
						Last MSR was $989.

Add $60 for stainless steel.

COLONEL - .45 ACP cal., 4 1/4 in. ramped barrel, white low mount 3-dot fixed sights, steel frame, 10 or 14 shot mag., spur competition hammer, LDA trigger, black polymer grips with medallions, green spec. ops. finish, 37 oz. New 2005.

MSR $899	$795	$700	$600	$500	$450	$375	$325

GRADING - PPGS™	100%	98%	95%	90%	80%	70%	60%

STEALTH CARRY - .45 ACP cal., lightweight, compact design, 3 in. ramped barrel, 6 shot mag., stainless steel frame, Para Kote Stealth finish, Novak adj. rear sight, LDA trigger, spurless hammer, black polymer grips with medallions, 30 oz. New 2005.

MSR $1,075	$955	$825	$725				

STEALTH WARTHOG - .45 ACP cal., lightweight, compact design, 3 in. ramped barrel, alloy frame, 10 shot mag., tritium night sights, spur competition hammer, match grade trigger, extended slide lock, beavertail grip and firing pin safeties, black polymer grips, Para-Kote Stealth black finish, 24 oz. New 2004.

MSR $945	$825	$700	$600	$525	$450	$375	$325

This model is also supplied with an extra magazine with grip extension. It is also referred to as the "Nite Hawg."

T SERIES MODELS - 9mm Para., .40 S&W (stainless steel only), or .45 ACP cal., DAO, 5 in. barrel, 7 (.45 ACP cal. only, single stack mag.) or 10 shot mag., steel or stainless steel, matte black finish or stainless steel. Mfg. 2003.

	$825	$615	$500	$450	$385	$335	$295

Last MSR was $1,009.

Add $80 for stainless steel.

PARDINI, ARMI S.r.l.

Current manufacturer located in Lido di Camaiore, Italy. Currently imported by Larry's Guns, located in Portland, ME. Previously imported until 2004 by Nygord Precision Products located in Prescott, AZ, and distributed until 1996 by Mo's Competitor Supplies & Range, Inc. located in Brookfield, CT and until 1990 by Fiocchi of America, Inc., located in Ozark, MO.

For more information and current pricing on both new and used Pardini airguns, please refer to the *Blue Book of Airguns* by Dr. Robert Beeman & John Allen (also online).

PISTOLS: SEMI-AUTO

PC45 - .40 S&W, .45 ACP, or 9x21mm cal., single action mechanism designed for stock competition category, adj. trigger pull. Limited importation by Nygord 2000-2004.

	$1,295	$1,050	$840	$715	$575	$500	$440

Add $75 for 6 in. barrel and slide.

* **PC45S** - similar to PC, except has compensator and optic sight with scope mount.

	$1,500	$1,250	$1,100	$950	$850	$725	$600

* **PCS-Open** - similar to PCS, except w/o scope and frame mount, top-of-the-line semi-auto.

	$1,650	$1,400	$1,250	$1,100	$950	$850	$725

GT9/40/45 - 9mm Para., .40 S&W, or .45 ACP cal. 5 or 6 in. barrel, single action, diamond wood grips, matte silver, black or two-tone finish. Importation began late 2004.

No MSR	$1,245	$1,100	$975	$875	$775	$650	$550

Add $95 for 6 in. barrel.

PISTOLS: TARGET

Pardini pistols have always been known for their technological improvements developed from ongoing design research. During 1991, the entire Pardini pistol line was modified both internally and externally to improve function and reliability - these changes included the addition of grooves on the barrel shroud to accept scope mounts directly.

GRADING - PPGS™	100%	98%	95%	90%	80%	70%	60%

MODEL SP/MODEL SP NEW (STANDARD PISTOL)

- .22 LR cal. only, target grips, adj. sights, 4.92 in. barrel, interchangeable grips, detachable mag., SP New features mechanical trigger, SP features second generation electronic trigger, approx. 2.4 lbs. New 1991.

MSR $1,329	$1,299	$1,125	$995	$875	$775	$650	$550

Add $145 for SP Master Model.

MODEL SP1

- .22 LR cal., features electronic trigger, blue/silver two-tone finish, adj. anatomic target wood grips, includes six Tungsten weights. New 2005.

MSR $1,379	$1,325	$1,150	$1,000	$900	$800	$675	$575

MODEL SP1/SP1 NEW RAPID FIRE

- .22 LR cal., similar to Model SP1, SP1 has second generation electronic trigger, SP1 New has mechanical trigger, developed for rapid fire discipline, includes six Tungsten weights. New 2005.

As this edition went to press, U.S. pricing had yet to be established on this model.

LADIES PISTOL

- similar to Model SP, except grips are suitable for smaller hands. Importation disc. 1999.

$850	$700	$600	$520	$460	$410	$380

Last MSR was $995.

MODEL GP/GP E (RAPID FIRE PISTOL)

- .22 Short cal., features enclosed style grip assembly, adj. sights, choice of electronic (GP E, new 2004) or mechanical (GP) trigger, 5.12 in. barrel. Imported 1991-2004.

$1,425	$1,250	$1,050	$875	$775	$675	$575

Add $500 for "Schumann" Model (wraparound grip, special muzzle ports, sights, weights, etc.).

MODEL HP/HP E/HP NEW (CENTERFIRE PISTOL)

- .32 S&W Wadcutter cal., similar to Model SP Pistol, 4.92 in. barrel, beginning 2004, HP has second generation electronic trigger, HP E has electronic trigger, HP New has mechanical trigger, includes 4 (HP) or 6 (HP E & HP New) weights. New 1991.

MSR $1,449	$1,399	$1,250	$1,050	$875	$775	$675	$575

MODEL K22

- .22 LR cal., top-of-the-line target pistol, mechanical trigger, toggle bolt pushes cartridge into chamber, unique ventilated front sight assembly that also supports counterweights, cocking lever action. Importation began 2000.

No MSR	$1,699	$1,500	$1,325	$1,125	$975	$850	$725

MODEL K50 (FREE PISTOL)

- .22 LR cal., single shot, sliding rotating bolt, 9.06 in. barrel, tilted anatomical grip, top-of-the-line match pistol. Mfg. 1991-99.

$925	$750	$600	$500	$450	$420	$395

Last MSR was $1,050.

PARDINI/NYGORD MASTER

- .22 LR cal., designed for NRA bullseye shooting, micrometer rear sight and red-dot sight, includes small Adco sight, anatomical target grips. Imported 2000-2004.

$1,325	$1,145	$875	$750	$650	$550	$450

PARKER BROTHERS

Previously manufactured in Meriden, CT from 1866-1934. Remington took over production in 1934, and in 1938, the plant was moved to Ilion, NY. Over 4,500 "Transition Guns" (exhibiting Meriden and Ilion characteristics) were produced in Meriden between 1934-1937 and about 1,600 Parkers were manufactured at the Ilion location before production stopped circa 1942. Total production reached approx. 242,487.

95% of the original Parkers bought and sold each year are in 30% or less condition (referring to original case colors). Percentages on following pages refer to the amount of original case colors remaining on frame.

SHOTGUNS, SxS, DAMASCUS BARRELS

Parker damascus barreled shotguns (hammer or hammerless) are very collectible if original condition is over 40%. Specimens in 90% or better condition with strong case colors can approximate values of the steel barrel models if the bores are in excellent condition (no pitting). Values for under 40% specimens fall off rapidly and are no longer comparable to steel barrel guns. As an example, a 12 ga. steel "D" Grade (without ejectors) might range from $1,500 to $7,000 (10%-100%) with a rather even downward progression of values in between the high and low ranges. A 100% damascus hammer "D" Grade could have a $12,000-$15,000 price tag hanging from the trigger guard, while a 5%-15% condition specimen is typically seen priced in the $750-$1,500 range. A truly 95%-100% original damascus barreled, hammer Parker is more rare and desirable than a similar grade damascus hammerless Parker or a steel barreled hammerless Parker. Remember, the guns are not rare but their condition is.

SHOTGUNS, SxS, FLUID STEEL BARRELS

Values listed in the 95%-100% condition columns can vary a lot as there is very little supply and strong demand for these high condition "cream puffs."

Note: Values below are for guns without ejectors, unless otherwise indicated. An "E" suffix indicates ejectors. Skeet models with ejectors, beavertail forearm, and single selective trigger are valued at approx. 50%-75% higher than values shown. Higher grade Parkers typically had ejectors, and ejectors typically add 50%-100% value to a Parker in all grades. Also, lower condition, high grade models sometimes have their values established by the potential gain in refurbishing these specimens. Remember, it only cost a few hundred dollars more to refinish an A1 Special compared a VH Grade. Due to the extremely high value of Parker Guns, extreme care should be taken in their purchase. There are many upgraded and refinished guns represented as original; expert advice should always be sought. Many collectors would rather own a specimen with 30% original case colors than a refinished gun that is 100% (regardless who did the work). Many advanced collectors will discount a refinished Parker's value 40%-60% off the price for an original gun. Misrepresentation of refinished or upgraded Parkers is rampant today - especially case colors. Also, beware of fake boxes and hanging tags - if the box and Parker shotgun are an original "pair," the value is enhanced tremendously. If the box/hanging tag is fake, you could pay as much as $1,500 to learn this lesson! In other words, do your homework, be careful, shop carefully, and above all, get a receipt for exactly what it is that you are purchasing.

Frame size on Parker shotguns is determined by the number on the bottom of the rear barrel lug on breech. Frame sizes (from largest to smallest) include 7, 6, 5, 4, 3, 2, 1 1/2, 1, 1/2, 0, 00, and 000. 8 ga. guns typically are framed 6 or 7. 10 ga. guns typically are 3 or 4. 12 ga. guns typically range from 2 through 1 (more desirable). "1/2" frame 12 ga. guns are very rare and desirable. 20 and 16 gauges range from 2 through 0 (more desirable, rare in 16 ga.). 28 ga. guns are either 0 or 00 (more desirable and twice as expensive). .410 bore shotguns are 00 or 000 (most common and most desirable). 8 and 10 ga. steel barreled shotguns are very rare, and prices can equate .410 bore values if the original condition is there.

The grade on Parker shotguns is a number or initials located on the water table of the frame. An alphabetical designation would indicate the grade immediately. For numerals, a "2" would indicate a GH, while an "8" would specify an A-1 Special - interpolate for the others (numbers 3 through 7). Parker shotguns manufactured by Remington will have date codes stamped on left barrel flat that correspond to the month and the year (see Remington serialization in the Serialization Section). Also, if a Parker gun was returned to Remington for repair, alteration, or refinishing, it will usually have the date code stamped with a suffix of 3 (i.e., OK3 represents some type of rework completed in either July of 1941 or 1963). There is some ambiguity with the year as the year codes repeat.

A note about Parker condition: Percentages of condition indicate the amount of original case colors remaining on the frame, but sometimes these colors are faded and the rest of the gun is excellent - hence, all the separate condition factors must be considered when determining overall condition. A Parker IS NOT 60% if the barrel bluing and stock/forearm varnish are 60% but case colors are only 10%. Typically, a 60% case color Parker shotgun will have 90%+ blue and varnish, yet this does not mean the gun is 90% overall. Similarly, a 20% case color Parker will probably have 90% barrel bluing remaining. Strong, original case colors are the key in determining Parker condition and subsequent values. However, for shotguns under 30% condition, the overall condition

100%	98%	95%	90%	80%	70%	60%	50%	40%	30%	20%	10%

of the gun should determine value.

The Parker Story, Vol. I was published in late 1998. This book has production statistics derived from factory records, and the quantities manufactured listed in this text for steel-barreled hammerless Parker guns are taken from this book. This new publication also has more detailed production statistics on Parker guns produced from 1869-1942, including a breakdown by action type (lifter, top lever, and hammerless), grade, barrel steel, gauge, and barrel length. Some grades, gauges, etc., are fewer in number than previously estimated. All the grades are pictured in color, including the Invincible. Parker Reproductions are also covered in detail, including production statistics. Vol. II was published in late 2000.

Parker Gun Identification & Serialization was published in late 2002. Compiled by using records from The Parker Story, Vols. I & II, this title features more than 100 detailed images and over 155,000 serial numbers to help verify an original Parker configuration. If interested in Parkers, these publications will be invaluable. The author wishes to thank Mr. Charles Price, William Mullins, Roy Gunther, Louis C. Parker III, and Daniel Cote for sharing the following Parker production statistics with this publication.

The Parker Gun Collectors Association can also provide research letters on certain Parkers. Please refer to their listing under Firearms Organizations in the back of this text for contact information.

SHOTGUNS, PARKER MODELS & PRICING

The desirability of older Parker shotguns in today's marketplace can be greatly enhanced if the stock dimensions fit today's potential owner (typically 13 1/2 in. - 14 1/2 in. LOP), adding value due to the shootability.

Add 20% for SST.
Add 20% for beavertail forearm.
Add 40%-50% for VR (rare on smaller gauges).
Add 20% for straight English stock.
Add 20% for skeleton steel buttplate.
Add 20% for short barrels (26 in. with open chokes).

TROJAN - Parker's lowest-priced gun, single or double triggers, but no auto ejectors available, very rarely found in mint condition because they were used a lot, a genuine utility gun, introduced 1912-13 with approx. 33,000 total mfg.

✳ *12 ga.*

100%	98%	95%	90%	80%	70%	60%	50%	40%	30%	20%	10%
N/A	$2,000	$1,500	$1,175	$950	$850	$750	$650	$600	$575	$525	$500

✳ *16 ga.*

100%	98%	95%	90%	80%	70%	60%	50%	40%	30%	20%	10%
N/A	$2,950	$2,150	$1,825	$1,500	$1,200	$1,050	$950	$750	$700	$650	$600

✳ *20 ga.*

100%	98%	95%	90%	80%	70%	60%	50%	40%	30%	20%	10%
N/A	$3,750	$2,750	$2,250	$1,900	$1,600	$1,500	$1,400	$1,300	$1,200	$1,100	$900

VH - Parker's biggest selling model, offered with all options, the most commonly found Parker. Approx. 79,000 mfg. 10 ga. is very rare in this model.

Add 50%-100% for ejectors, depending on original condition (VHE Model).

✳ *12 ga.*

100%	98%	95%	90%	80%	70%	60%	50%	40%	30%	20%	10%
N/A	$3,150	$2,375	$1,750	$1,450	$1,200	$1,100	$1,000	$900	$800	$750	$700

✳ *16 ga.*

100%	98%	95%	90%	80%	70%	60%	50%	40%	30%	20%	10%
N/A	$3,150	$2,375	$1,750	$1,450	$1,200	$1,100	$1,000	$925	$850	$775	$700

✳ *20 ga.*

100%	98%	95%	90%	80%	70%	60%	50%	40%	30%	20%	10%
N/A	$4,150	$3,600	$3,250	$3,025	$2,800	$2,500	$2,300	$2,150	$2,000	$1,850	$1,700

✳ *28 ga.*

100%	98%	95%	90%	80%	70%	60%	50%	40%	30%	20%	10%
N/A	$8,150	$6,800	$6,000	$5,300	$4,750	$4,250	$3,850	$3,500	$3,250	$3,000	$2,850

✳ *.410 bore.*

100%	98%	95%	90%	80%	70%	60%	50%	40%	30%	20%	10%
N/A	N/A	$19,500	$17,750	$15,000	$12,250	$10,000	$9,000	$8,250	$7,750	$7,375	$7,000

100%	98%	95%	90%	80%	70%	60%	50%	40%	30%	20%	10%

PH - offered for a very short time, most had twist barrels, prices here are for fluid steel barrels only. Approx. 1,400 mfg. A very few .410 bores were mfg. 10 ga. with fluid steel barrels is very rare in this model.

Add 50%-100% for ejectors, depending on original condition (PHE Model).

✳ *12 ga.*

100%	98%	95%	90%	80%	70%	60%	50%	40%	30%	20%	10%
N/A	$3,150	$2,375	$1,750	$1,450	$1,200	$1,100	$1,000	$900	$800	$750	$700

✳ *16 ga.*

N/A	$3,150	$2,375	$1,750	$1,450	$1,200	$1,100	$1,000	$900	$800	$750	$700

✳ *20 ga.*

N/A	$5,750	$5,300	$4,850	$4,450	$4,075	$3,750	$3,525	$3,200	$3,000	$2,750	$2,500

✳ *28 ga.*

Extreme rarity precludes accurate pricing on this model.

GH - very popular model, barrels marked "Parker Special Steel", engraved moderately with all options available. 10 ga. with fluid steel barrels is very rare in this model, approx. 4,300 mfg.

Add 50%-100% for ejectors, depending on original condition (GHE Model).

✳ *12 ga.*

N/A	$3,950	$3,350	$2,600	$2,275	$1,850	$1,625	$1,500	$1,300	$1,100	$950	$900

✳ *16 ga.*

N/A	$4,400	$3,750	$2,800	$2,400	$2,150	$1,850	$1,600	$1,450	$1,250	$1,050	$975

✳ *20 ga.*

N/A	$5,750	$5,250	$4,750	$4,250	$3,750	$3,400	$3,100	$2,875	$2,650	$2,475	$2,300

✳ *28 ga.*

N/A	N/A	$9,250	$8,450	$7,750	$6,950	$6,450	$5,750	$5,300	$4,950	$4,600	$4,300

✳ *.410 bore*

N/A	N/A	N/A	$17,500	$15,250	$12,950	$10,750	$9,650	$8,700	$8,200	$7,700	$7,000

DH - the most popular higher grade gun, very tastefully engraved and flawlessly finished, approx. 9,400 mfg.

Add 50%-100% for ejectors, depending on original condition (DHE Model).

✳ *12 ga.*

N/A	$5,750	$5,250	$4,700	$4,250	$3,600	$3,150	$2,550	$2,050	$1,700	$1,500	$1,250

✳ *16 ga.*

N/A	$6,600	$5,450	$4,900	$4,375	$3,700	$3,250	$2,600	$2,100	$1,750	$1,550	$1,325

✳ *20 ga.*

N/A	$7,850	$7,100	$6,350	$5,850	$5,400	$5,000	$4,700	$4,475	$4,150	$3,750	$3,250

✳ *28 ga.*

N/A	$13,750	$11,250	$9,950	$9,175	$8,650	$8,200	$7,600	$7,150	$6,700	$6,350	$6,000

✳ *.410 bore*

N/A	N/A	N/A	$33,500	$28,250	$24,000	$20,000	$17,000	$15,500	$13,500	$11,750	$10,000

CH - scarce because they were only slightly more decorative than the DH, Acme steel barrels. Approx. 1,100 mfg. 10 ga. is very rare in this model.

Add 50%-100 for ejectors, depending on original condition (CHE Model).

✳ *12 ga.*

N/A	N/A	$5,250	$4,775	$4,000	$3,350	$2,750	$2,475	$2,200	$2,000	$1,800	$1,650

✳ *16 ga.*

N/A	N/A	$5,650	$5,250	$4,400	$3,600	$3,100	$2,650	$2,400	$2,150	$1,875	$1,700

✳ *20 ga.*

N/A	N/A	$8,250	$7,600	$6,850	$6,175	$5,550	$4,950	$4,500	$4,250	$4,000	$3,750

100%	98%	95%	90%	80%	70%	60%	50%	40%	30%	20%	10%

✳ 28 ga.

| N/A | N/A | $20,000 | $17,000 | $13,500 | $10,750 | $9,500 | $8,750 | $8,000 | $7,300 | $6,500 | $5,950 |

✳ .410 bore - very rare, approx. 6 are known to exist.

This model/gauge is very rare, and prices typically start in the $25,000-$50,000 range, depending on original condition.

BH - quite popular and decorative, 4 styles of engraving available, Acme steel barrels. Approx. 700 mfg. 10 ga. is very rare in this model.

Add 50%-100% for ejectors, depending on original condition (BHE Model).

✳ 12 ga.

| N/A | N/A | $7,750 | $6,950 | $6,375 | $5,650 | $4,950 | $4,300 | $3,850 | $3,450 | $3,000 | $2,750 |

✳ 16 ga.

| N/A | N/A | $8,450 | $7,500 | $6,850 | $6,100 | $5,350 | $4,500 | $3,950 | $3,550 | $3,100 | $2,850 |

✳ 20 ga.

| N/ | N/A | $16,000 | $14,000 | $12,000 | $10,250 | $9,300 | $8,275 | $7,500 | $6,850 | $6,100 | $5,500 |

✳ 28 ga.

| N/A | N/A | N/A | $24,750 | $22,000 | $18,950 | $16,000 | $14,000 | $11,750 | $10,000 | $9,000 | $8,000 |

✳ .410 bore - only 2 guns are known in this grade. Extreme rarity precludes accurate price evaluation, but will be VERY expensive.

AH - a scarce gun, extremely decorative and flawlessly executed, Acme steel barrels. Approx. 300 mfg. 10 ga. is very rare in this model.

Add 50%-100% for ejectors, depending on original condition (AHE Model).

✳ 12 ga.

| N/A | N/A | $19,250 | $16,100 | $12,250 | $10,000 | $9,000 | $8,000 | $7,250 | $6,750 | $6,350 | $5,995 |

✳ 16 ga.

| N/A | N/A | $21,000 | $17,000 | $13,000 | $10,500 | $9,150 | $8,150 | $7,350 | $6,850 | $6,450 | $6,250 |

✳ 20 ga.

| N/A | N/A | $25,000 | $21,000 | $17,500 | $14,250 | $12,750 | $10,750 | $9,950 | $9,250 | $8,800 | $8,400 |

✳ 28 ga.

| N/A | N/A | N/A | $37,500 | $31,500 | $25,650 | $22,000 | $19,950 | $18,500 | $17,250 | $16,000 | $15,000 |

✳ .410 bore - It is believed that only one gun was mfg. in this grade/bore.

AAH - very elaborate model, early AAs have Whitworth barrels, late ones have Peerless. Approx. 240 mfg.

Add 50%-100% for ejectors, depending on original condition (AAHE Model).

✳ 12 ga.

| N/A | N/A | $31,000 | $27,000 | $23,500 | $21,000 | $19,000 | $18,000 | $17,000 | $16,000 | $15,000 | $14,000 |

✳ 16 ga.

| N/A | N/A | $35,000 | $29,500 | $25,000 | $22,500 | $20,000 | $19,000 | $18,000 | $17,000 | $16,000 | $15,000 |

✳ 20 ga.

| N/A | N/A | $57,000 | $48,000 | $43,000 | $37,000 | $33,500 | $31,000 | $29,000 | $27,250 | $25,000 | $23,000 |

✳ 28 ga.

| N/A | N/A | N/A | $68,500 | $63,250 | $58,750 | $53,475 | $49,000 | $44,000 | $41,000 | $38,000 | $35,000 |

A-1 SPECIAL GRADE - 100% engraved, all were special ordered, each one inspected by the company president before being shipped. Approx. 80 mfg.

✳ 12 ga.

| N/A | N/A | $75,000 | $68,750 | $61,000 | $55,000 | $50,000 | $46,000 | $42,000 | $38,750 | $35,750 | $32,750 |

✳ 16 ga.

| N/A | N/A | $80,000 | $72,000 | $64,000 | $56,000 | $51,000 | $47,000 | $43,000 | $39,000 | $36,000 | $33,000 |

✳ 20 ga.

| N/A | N/A | N/A | $110,000 | $100,000 | $90,000 | $80,000 | $74,000 | $69,000 | $63,000 | $59,000 | $55,000 |

100%	98%	95%	90%	80%	70%	60%	50%	40%	30%	20%	10%

* **28 ga.** - extreme rarity and desirability factors preclude accurate price evaluation by condition factors. 70% original condition A-1 Specials HAVE sold for over $125,000.

INVINCIBLE GRADE - only 3 documented mfg. $1,250 MSR circa 1930, extreme rarity and desirability factors preclude accurate price evaluation on this model.

SHOTGUNS: SINGLE BARREL TRAP

12 or 20 (rare) ga., 26 (20 ga. only, rare), 28 (very rare), 30 (rare), 32, or 34 (rare) in. barrels, any boring was available, as was stock configuration, boxlock, auto ejector. The grades differ only in engraving, checkering and wood finish.

It should be noted that single barrel trap guns cannot be compared to the SxS models, as they are not as desirable, even though they are more rare. Approximately 1,900 Parker single barrel trap guns were manufactured, mostly in SC Grade. Most SxS collectors are not that interested in single barrel trap models and very few collectors specialize in single barrels.

Add 15% for 30 or 34 in. barrel.

S.C. GRADE

100%	98%	95%	90%	80%	70%	60%	50%	40%	30%	20%	10%
$4,000	$3,600	$3,100	$2,700	$2,350	$1,875	$1,625	$1,400	$1,150	$995	$900	$825

S.B. GRADE

100%	98%	95%	90%	80%	70%	60%	50%	40%	30%	20%	10%
$4,825	$4,300	$3,750	$3,475	$3,100	$2,700	$2,350	$1,875	$1,625	$1,400	$1,150	$995

S.A. GRADE

100%	98%	95%	90%	80%	70%	60%	50%	40%	30%	20%	10%
N/A	$5,000	$4,375	$3,875	$3,425	$3,050	$2,675	$2,275	$1,875	$1,550	$1,200	$1,050

S.A.A. GRADE

100%	98%	95%	90%	80%	70%	60%	50%	40%	30%	20%	10%
N/A	N/A	$5,500	$4,750	$4,000	$3,575	$3,050	$2,675	$2,375	$1,850	$1,575	$1,350

S.A.-1 SPECIAL GRADE

100%	98%	95%	90%	80%	70%	60%	50%	40%	30%	20%	10%
N/A	N/A	N/A	$13,000	$10,000	$9,150	$8,350	$7,425	$6,375	$5,550	$4,950	$4,300

PARKER PISTOLS

Refer to the Wyoming Arms section in this text.

PARKER REPRODUCTIONS

Previously imported by the Parker Reproduction Division of Reagent Chemical & Research, Inc., located in Middlesex, NJ. Previously distributed by Parker Reproductions located in Webb City, MO. These shotguns were manufactured in Japan to original Parker specifications by Winchester until the factory closed in January, 1989.

In 1984, Winchester was contracted by Reagent Chemical & Research, Inc. to manufacture a new Parker shotgun. The new SxS was a DHE model, available in 20 and 28 ga. initially. These models were fabricated in Japan to original Parker specifications, and the reproduction was so authentic that most parts are interchangeable with the late Parkers made by Remington in Ilion, NY. In 1993, a 16/20 ga. combo was introduced in some models. On Sept. 17, 1999, a flood destroyed all remaining inventory including parts.

During 2004, Connecticut Shotgun Manufacturing Company offered a limited quantity of A1 Specials in-the-white w/o metal finish and engraving in 12 or 20 ga. only, without cases or accessories. MSRs were $5,850 for one set of barrels and $6,750 for a 2 barrel set.

SHOTGUNS: SxS

Because of the high quality and limited mfg. of these reproductions, they have become very collectible, as they offer the shooter the only realistic alternative to using an original Parker Bros. shotgun. Currently, higher grade Parker Reproductions in smaller gauges are very desirable, and 95%-100% values are getting harder to accurately determine.

GRADING - PPGS™	100%	98%	95%	90%	80%	70%	60%

DHE GRADE - 12 (new 1986), 20, or 28 (new 1984) ga., 26 or 28 in. barrels, boxlock action, ejectors, single selective or double triggers, beavertail or splinter forend, straight or pistol grip stock, skeleton steel buttplate, engraving in original DH style, case hardened frame, rust blue barrels. Supplied with leather trunk case, canvas and leather cover, and snap caps. Disc.

	100%	98%	95%	90%	80%	70%	60%
12 ga.	$3,450	$3,150	$2,750	$2,500	$2,250	$2,000	$1,800

Last MSR was $3,370.

	100%	98%	95%	90%	80%	70%	60%
20 ga.	$3,750	$3,450	$3,050	$2,750	$2,500	$2,250	$2,000
28 ga.	$3,950	$3,650	$3,274	$3,000	$2,750	$2,500	$2,250

Add $150 for beavertail forend.

Add $650 for Sporting Clays Model w/ choke tubes.

Add $700-$1,150 per extra set of barrels, depending on gauge, configuration, and condition.

Quantities mfg. for this model are as follows: 12 ga. - 2,137 mfg., 20 ga. - 6,050 mfg., 28 ga. - 4,203 mfg.

* **DHE Steel Shot Special** - similar to 12 ga. D Grade, except has strengthened No. 1 1/2 barrels, 3 in. chambers, and 28 in. chrome lined barrels, 7 1/4-7 1/2 lbs. Approx. 350 mfg. 1987-89.

	100%	98%	95%	90%	80%	70%	60%
	$4,350	$3,650	$3,100	$2,675	$2,250	$1,850	$1,700

Last MSR was $3,370.

Add $100 for beavertail forend.

* **DHE Small Gauge Combo** - available in either 28 ga./.410 bore (disc.) or 16/20 ga. (mfg. 1993-97) combo with 2 barrels and 2 forends. Less than 160 mfg. of the 28 ga./.410 bore combo. Disc.

>28 ga./.410 bore Combo

	100%	98%	95%	90%	80%	70%	60%
	$7,000	$5,750	$4,500	$4,000	$3,625	$3,150	$2,900

Last MSR was $4,970.

>16/20 ga. Combo - new 1994 - disc.

	100%	98%	95%	90%	80%	70%	60%
	$6,250	$4,750	$4,000	$3,600	$3,300	$2,950	$2,600

Last MSR was $4,870.

* **DHE 3-Barrel Set** - includes two 28 ga. and one .410 bore barrels, cased. Disc.

	100%	98%	95%	90%	80%	70%	60%
	$8,000	$6,750	$5,500	$5,000	$4,500	$3,750	$3,500

Last MSR was $5,630.

BHE GRADE LIMITED EDITION - 12, 20, 28 ga. or 410 bore, original Parker BH specifications, single selective or double trigger(s), 26 or 28 in. barrels, straight or pistol grip stock, engraved skeleton buttplate, bank note scroll engraving around game scenes, cased. Only 100 manufactured in each gauge during late 1987-89. Disc.

	100%	98%	95%	90%	80%	70%	60%
	$5,000	$4,650	$4,150	$3,750	$2,750	$2,150	$1,800

Last MSR was $3,970.

Add $1,000 for 20 ga.

Add $4,000 for 28 ga. or .410 bore.

Add $1,500 per extra set of barrels, if in mint condition.

Add $150 for beavertail forend.

A 28 ga./.410 bore combo was also available with 2 forends. Only seven 28 gauges were mfg. in this model.

GRADING - PPGS™	100%	98%	95%	90%	80%	70%	60%

A-1 SPECIAL - 12, 16/20 ga. combo (introduced 1993), 20, or 28 ga., original Parker A-1 specifications, 26 or 28 in. barrels, single selective or double trigger(s), fine scroll engraving with game scenes, 32 lines/in. checkering, cased with accessories. Limited mfg. 1988-89.

	$10,500	$8,500	$7,250	$6,000	$5,475	$4,800	$4,350

Last MSR was $11,200.

Add $3,000+ for 28 ga.
Add $1,000 for extra set of barrels.
Add $200 for beavertail forend.
Add $1,700 for 16 ga. barrel (splinter model only).
Fourteen 3 barrel sets were mfg. in this grade. Rarity factor precludes accurate pricing.

* **A-1 Special Custom Engraved** - custom (per individual special order) engraving, available with two sets of barrels only, cased with accessories. Limited mfg. 1988-89. Prices started at $11,000 and go up according to individualized special features.

* **Federal Duck Stamp Collector's Series** - available in 12 or 20 ga., A-1 Special specifications, authorized by U.S. Department of Interior. Mfg. was limited to 10 per year in 1988-89 only.

	$13,500	$10,000	$8,000				

Last MSR was $14,000.

This model included special case and 2 barrels per buyer's specifications.

PARKER-HALE LIMITED

Previous gun manufacturer located in Birmingham, England. Rifles were manufactured in England until 1991 when Navy Arms purchased the manufacturing rights and built a plant in West Virginia for fabrication. This new company is called Gibbs Rifle Company and they manufactured models very similar to older Parker-Hale rifles during 1992-94. Shotguns were manufactured in Spain and imported by Precision Sports, a division of Cortland Line Company, Inc. located in Cortland, NY until 1993.

Parker-Hale Ltd. continues to make a wide variety of high quality firearms cleaning accessories for both rifles and shotguns, including their famous bipod.

RIFLES: BOLT ACTION

All Parker-Hale rifle importation was discontinued in 1991. Parker-Hale bolt action rifles utilize the Mauser K-98 action and were offered in a variety of configurations. A single set trigger option was introduced in 1984 on most models, which allows either "hair trigger" or conventional single stage operation - add $85.

MODEL 81 CLASSIC - available in 11 cals. between .22-250 Rem., and 7mm Rem. Mag., 24 in. barrel, open sights, 4 shot mag., select checkered walnut with sling swivels, 7 3/4 lbs. New 1985.

	$715	$565	$475	$395	$340	$300	$280

Last MSR was $860.

* **Model 81 African** - .375 H&H or 9.3x62mm Mauser cal., similar specifications as Model 81 Classic and has engraved action. New 1986.

	$875	$700	$600	$500	$425	$360	$330

Last MSR was $1,110.

MODEL 84 TARGET - .308 Win. cal., match rifle with special sights, adj. cheekpiece on stock. Importation disc. 1990.

	$1,080	$875	$760	$680	$610	$530	$465

Last MSR was $1,300.

GRADING - PPGS™	100%	98%	95%	90%	80%	70%	60%

MODEL 85 SNIPER RIFLE - .308 Win. cal., bolt action, extended heavy barrel, 10 shot mag., camo green synthetic stock with stippling, built in adj. bipod, enlarged contoured bolt, adj. recoil pad. Importation began 1989.

	$1,750	$1,425	$1,275	$1,050	$875	$750	$625

Last MSR was $1,975.

MODEL 86 TARGET - .308 Win. cal., 27 1/2 in. barrel, 5 shot mag., stippled stock and forend, aperture front and rear sights, 11 1/4 lbs. Distributed 1986 only by North American Precision.

	$980	$830	$760	$690	$610	$530	$465

Last MSR was $1,149.

MODEL 87 TARGET - .243 Win., 6.5x55mm Swedish, .308 Win., .30-06, or .300 Win. Mag. cal., target stock, aperture sights. Importation began 1987.

	$1,375	$1,100	$900	$775	$650	$550	$495

Last MSR was $1,525.

MODEL 1000 STANDARD - available in 9 cals. between .22-250 Rem. and .308 Win., 22 in. barrel, 4 shot mag., walnut stock with cheekpiece, 7 1/4 lbs. Disc. 1988.

	$400	$330	$285	$255	$230	$215	$195

Last MSR was $500.

MODEL 1100 LIGHTWEIGHT - available in 9 cals. between .22-250 Rem. and .30-06, 22 in. barrel, open sights, 4 shot mag., 6 1/2 lbs. New 1985.

	$495	$400	$350	$325	$285	$270	$255

Last MSR was $595.

* ***Model 1100M African*** - .375 H&H, .404 Jeffery, or .458 Win. Mag. cal., 24 in. barrel, 4 shot mag., 9 1/2 lbs.

	$800	$650	$575	$500	$450	$425	$400

Last MSR was $960.

MODEL 1200 SUPER - bolt action, Mauser type action, .22-250 Rem., .243 Win., 6mm Rem., .25-06 Rem., .270 Win., .30-06, .300 Win. Mag., 7mm Rem. Mag., or .308 Win. cal., 24 in. barrel, folding sight, skip checkered walnut stock, sling swivels, rosewood pistol grip cap and forend tip. New 1968-disc.

	$540	$450	$375	$330	$295	$275	$260

Last MSR was $680.

This model in Magnum cals. was called the 1200 M Super Magnum.

* ***Model 1200 C (Super Clip)*** - similar to Model 1200 Super, except has detachable 4 shot box mag.

	$590	$500	$400	$350	$300	$280	$265

Last MSR was $740.

MODEL 1200P PRESENTATION - similar to 1200, except .243 Win. or .30-06 cal., scroll engraved, no sights. Mfg. 1969-75.

	$495	$425	$395	$340	$315	$305	$275

MODEL 1200 SUPER VARMINT - similar to 1200, except .22-250 Rem., 6mm Rem., .25-06 Rem., or .243 Win. cal., 24 in. heavy barrel, no sights. Disc. 1988.

	$525	$425	$365	$325	$285	$270	$255

Last MSR was $660.

MODEL 1300 C SCOUT - shorter barrel variation.

	$695	$550	$450	$385	$330	$300	$275

Last MSR was $785.

MODEL 2100 MIDLAND (HYBRID ACTION) - available in 11 cals. between .22-250 Rem. - .300 Win. Mag. cal., 22 in. barrel, 4 shot mag., open sights, 7 lbs.

	$325	$270	$230	$200	$190	$180	$170

Last MSR was $365.

GRADING - PPGS™	100%	98%	95%	90%	80%	70%	60%

✹ *Model 2100 Midland Magnum* - .300 Win. Mag., or 7mm Rem. Mag. cal., 24 in. barrel, 4 shot mag., 9 1/2 lbs. Imported 1989-90 only.

	$380	$325	$295	$270	$260	$250	$240

Last MSR was $430.

MODEL 2600 MIDLAND SPECIAL - .243 Win., .270 Win., .308 Win., or .30-06 cal., Midland Gun Co. action, iron sights. New 1989.

	$295	$250	$225	$200	$190	$180	$170

Last MSR was $330.

MIDLAND 2700 LIGHTWEIGHT - lightweight variation of the Model 2600.

	$340	$285	$240	$200	$190	$180	$170

Last MSR was $390.

SHOTGUNS: SxS

Parker-Hale shotguns were manufactured by Ugartechea in Eibar, Spain and imported as Parker-Hale models by Precision Sports located in Cortland, NY until 1994.

PASTUSEK INDUSTRIES

Previous manufacturer located in Fort Worth, TX 1993-2000.

PISTOLS: SEMI-AUTO

HSK (SPORT KING) - .22 LR cal., 4 1/2 or 5 1/2 in. barrel. Mfg. 1995-2000.

	$275	$250	$225	$195	$175	$150	$135

Last MSR was $312.

HSS (SHARPSHOOTER) - .22 LR cal., 5 1/2 in. bull barrel. Mfg. 1995-2000.

	$315	$275	$240	$210	$190	$165	$150

Last MSR was $379.

HSC (SUPERMATIC CITATION) - .22 LR cal., 5 1/2 bull or 7 1/4 in. fluted barrel. Mfg. 1995-2000.

	$340	$295	$265	$230	$210	$180	$165

Last MSR was $388.

Add $22 for 7 1/4 in. fluted barrel.
This model was also available with an 8, 10, or 12 in. bull barrel.

HST (SUPERMATIC TROPHY) - .22 LR cal., 5 1/2 bull or 7 1/4 in. fluted barrel. Mfg. 1995-2000.

	$400	$340	$275	$240	$220	$180	$165

Last MSR was $494.

This model was also available with an 8, 10, or 12 in. bull barrel. Left-hand ejection is also an option on this model.

HSV (VICTOR) - .22 LR cal., 3 7/8, 4 1/2, 5 1/2, 8 (optional), or 10 (optional) in. VR barrel. Mfg. 1995-2000.

	$475	$375	$300	$250	$230	$185	$165

Last MSR was $569.

Add $30 for dove tail rib on 5 1/2 in. barrel only.
Add $79 for Weaver rib on 5 1/2 in. barrel only.

HSO (OLYMPIC) - .22 S or .22 LR cal., 6 3/4 in. barrel only. Mfg. 1995-2000.

	$495	$395	$325	$265	$245	$195	$170

Last MSR was $599.

PAUZA SPECIALTIES

Previously manufactured by Pauza Specialties circa 1991-96, and located in Baytown, TX. Previously distributed by U.S. General Technologies, Inc. located in South San Francisco, CA.

GRADING - PPGS™	100%	98%	95%	90%	80%	70%	60%

Pauza currently manufactures the P50 semi-auto rifle for Firearms International, Inc. — please refer to that section for current information.

RIFLES

P50 SEMI-AUTO - .50 BMG cal., semi-auto, 24 (carbine) or 29 (rifle) in. match grade barrel, 5 shot detachable mag., one-piece receiver, 3-stage gas system, takedown action, all exterior parts Teflon coated, with aluminum bipod, 25 or 30 lbs. Mfg. 1992-96.

	$5,950	$5,250	$4,600	$4,100	$3,650	$3,200	$2,800

Last MSR was $6,495.

PEACE RIVER CLASSICS

Previous manufacturer located in Bartow, FL until 2001. Peace River Classics was a division of Tim's Guns.

RIFLES: SEMI-AUTO

PEACE RIVER CLASSICS SEMI-AUTO - .223 Rem. or .308 Win. (new 1998) cal., available in 3 configurations including the Shadowood, the Glenwood, and the Royale, hand-built utilizing Armalite action, patterned after the AR-15, matched parts throughout, special serialization, laminate thumbhole stock. Mfg. 1997-2001.

	$2,575	$2,275	$2,000	$1,775	$1,525	$1,250	$995

Last MSR was $2,695.

Add $300 for .308 Win. cal.

PEDERSEN CUSTOM GUNS

Previously manufactured circa 1973-1975 by O.F. Mossberg located in North Haven, CT. Pedersen Custom Guns was a division of O.F. Mossberg.

RIFLES: BOLT ACTION

MODEL 3000 - .270 Win., .30-06, 7mm Rem. Mag., or .338 Win. Mag. cal., Mossberg Model 810 action, 22 or 24 in. barrel, open sights, checkered Monte Carlo stock.

✱ *Grade III* - no engraving.

	$550	$495	$470	$440	$420	$385	$330

✱ *Grade II* - moderately engraved.

	$660	$580	$525	$495	$440	$420	$385

✱ *Grade I* - heavily engraved and inlaid, with select wood.

	$990	$770	$745	$690	$635	$560	$495

✱ *Presentation Model* - top-of-the-line model.

	$1,250	$1,000	$895	$800	$745	$690	$635

MODEL 4700 - .30-30 Win. or .35 Rem. cal., custom deluxe lever action, (Model 472 Mossberg), 5 shot, tube mag., 24 in. barrel, open sight, black walnut stock.

	$250	$195	$165	$155	$145	$130	$120

SHOTGUNS: O/U

MODEL 1500 HUNTING GUN - 12 ga., 2 3/4 or 3 in. chambers, 26 in. imp. cyl. and mod., 28 in. mod. and full, 30 in. mod. and full barrels, boxlock, auto ejectors, selective or non-selective single trigger, checkered pistol grip stock. Mfg. 1973-75.

	$700	$575	$500	$440	$415	$385	$365

MODEL 1500 SKEET - similar to Hunting Gun, except 27 in. skeet barrel, skeet stock. Mfg. 1973-75.

	$725	$600	$525	$450	$425	$400	$385

GRADING - PPGS™	100%	98%	95%	90%	80%	70%	60%

MODEL 1500 TRAP - similar to Hunting Gun, except 30 and 32 in. full barrels, trap Monte Carlo stock. Mfg. 1973-75.

	100%	98%	95%	90%	80%	70%	60%
	$650	$550	$475	$435	$410	$375	$350

MODEL 1000 HUNTING GUN - 12 or 20 ga., 26, 28, or 30 in. barrels, various chokes, boxlock, auto ejectors, SST, checkered select walnut stock, silver inlays, more engraving. Mfg. 1973-75.

	100%	98%	95%	90%	80%	70%	60%
Grade I	$2,200	$1,980	$1,870	$1,700	$1,540	$1,460	$1,375
Grade II	$1,815	$1,540	$1,430	$1,265	$1,185	$1,100	$1,045

MODEL 1000 TRAP GUN - similar to Hunting Gun, but 12 ga., 30 or 32 in. mod. and full barrels, Monte Carlo trap stock. Mfg. 1973-75.

	100%	98%	95%	90%	80%	70%	60%
Grade I	$2,100	$1,800	$1,650	$1,500	$1,350	$1,200	$995
Grade II	$1,650	$1,500	$1,375	$1,200	$1,050	$900	$725

MODEL 1000 SKEET - similar to Hunting Gun, except 26 or 28 in. barrels, bored skeet. Mfg. 1973-75.

	100%	98%	95%	90%	80%	70%	60%
Grade I	$2,255	$2,145	$2,035	$1,870	$1,705	$1,625	$1,540
Grade II	$1,980	$1,705	$1,595	$1,430	$1,350	$1,265	$1,210

SHOTGUNS: SxS

MODEL 200 - 12 or 20 ga., 26 in. imp. cyl. and mod., 28 in. mod. and full, 30 in. mod. and full barrels, boxlock, auto ejectors, SST. Mfg. 1973-74.

	100%	98%	95%	90%	80%	70%	60%
Grade I	$2,420	$2,175	$2,090	$1,955	$1,790	$1,705	$1,625
Grade II	$2,200	$1,955	$1,815	$1,735	$1,625	$1,540	$1,485

MODEL 2500 - 12 or 20 ga., 26 in. imp. cyl. and mod., 28 in. mod. and full barrels, auto ejectors, boxlock, checkered pistol grip stock and forearm.

	100%	98%	95%	90%	80%	70%	60%
	$470	$385	$360	$305	$275	$260	$240

SHOTGUNS: SLIDE ACTION

MODEL 4000 - custom Mossberg Model 500, 12, 20 ga., or .410 bore, 3 in. chamber, 26 in. imp. cyl. or skeet, 28 in. full or mod. barrel, 30 in. full, vent. rib, floral engraved, checkered select walnut stock. Mfg. 1975.

	100%	98%	95%	90%	80%	70%	60%
	$460	$375	$330	$305	$265	$230	$220

MODEL 4000 TRAP - similar to 4000, except 12 ga., 30 in. full barrel, Monte Carlo trap stock and pad. Mfg. 1975.

	100%	98%	95%	90%	80%	70%	60%
	$485	$395	$350	$325	$285	$255	$240

MODEL 4500 - similar to 4000, less engraving.

	100%	98%	95%	90%	80%	70%	60%
	$420	$330	$305	$275	$240	$200	$175

MODEL 4500 TRAP - similar to 4000 Trap, less engraving.

	100%	98%	95%	90%	80%	70%	60%
	$440	$350	$310	$280	$240	$210	$200

PEDERSOLI, DAVIDE & C. Snc.

Current manufacturer of modern, black powder, and older historically significant firearms located in Brescia, Italy. Currently, full-line distributors include Flintlocks, Etc., located in Richmond, MA, Cherry's Fine Guns, located in Greensboro, NC, and Dixie Gun Works, Inc., located in Union City, TN. Current importers include Cabela's, located in Sidney, NE, Cimarron, FA Co., located in Fredricksburg, TX, and Navy Arms, located in Martinsburg, WV. Previously imported by E.M.F., located in Santa Ana, CA.

D. Pedersoli manufactures top quality black powder replicas and other high quality firearms reproductions.

For more information and up-to-date pricing regarding current Pedersoli black powder models, please refer to *Colt Blackpowder Reproductions and Replicas* by Dennis Adler

GRADING - PPGS™	100%	98%	95%	90%	80%	70%	60%

and the *Blue Book of Modern Black Powder Arms* by John Allen & Dennis Adler. These books feature hundreds of color photographs and support text of the most recent black powder models available, as well as complete pricing and a reference guide.

RIFLES: REPRODUCTIONS

Pedersoli reproduction rifles are listed separately under Dixie Gun Works and the importers listed above (except Cabela's) - please refer to the individual listings. Current models include: Remington Rolling Block (8 variations), 1859 Sharps (3 variations), 1863 Sharps, 1874 Sharps (12 variations), Springfield Trapdoor Rifle/Carbine (6 variations), and the Kodiak SxS double rifle (4 variations). For current pricing on older Pedersoli marked reproductions, please refer to similar model/configurations under the importer's listings.

PENTHENY de PENTHENY

Current manufacturer and gunsmith established in 1987, and located in Santa Rosa, CA.

RIFLES: BOLT ACTION

The rifles listed include ebony forend tips, old English style black recoil pads, steel skeleton grip caps, four panels of 22 LPI checkering, and other custom features. These models are built on a U.S.R.A. Model 70 action.

THE INVADER - small and medium bore cals., classic styled Claro walnut stock, blue finish.

MSR $3,850	$3,850	$2,975	$2,400	$1,975	$1,500	$1,150	$875

THE NORMAN - Mag. cals., classic styled English walnut stock, blue finish.

MSR $3,850	$3,850	$2,975	$2,400	$1,975	$1,500	$1,150	$875

THE CONQUEROR - large bore cals., classic styled English walnut stock, blue finish, rifle has secondary recoil lug, dual steel reinforcing bolts, and express sights including fixed and folding leaves.

MSR $4,700	$4,700	$3,650	$3,000	$2,400	$1,975	$1,500	$1,150

PERAZZI

Current manufacturer established in 1957, and located in Brescia, Italy. Imported and distributed by Perazzi USA, Inc. located in Azusa, CA. Previously located in Monrovia, CA until 2002, and in Rome, NY.

Ivo Fabbri and Daniel Perazzi were partners in the shotgun manufacturing business beginning in 1960 - these guns are ser. no. 5001-5339.

Note: Previously, Perazzi shotguns were imported by both Winchester and Ithaca during the 1960s and 1970s. The company now has its own distribution network and its current model line-up is extensive. Perazzi shotguns are well known for their quality control standards and reliability in clay target championships and in-field conditions.

SHOTGUNS

Perazzi shotguns have incorporated many improvements during their manufacture. One of the most important changes has been the modification of the forearm design. Basically, there have been 4 different types: Type 1 has a serial range of 30,000-33,250, Type 2 is serial numbered 33,251- 35,450, Type 3 has a range of 35,451-51,242, Type 4 started at 51,243 and is still current as of this writing. Differences include changes in the forearm iron and barrel lug attachment. Because of these forearm changes (and other parts modifications), the desirability factor on a Type 4 forearm shotgun as opposed to a Type 1 is much greater. Competition shooters prefer Types 3 or 4 as they are the current design. If a Type 1 or 2 competition gun develops problems, they are automatically retrofitted to the Type 4 design - and these modifications are expensive. For these reasons, the serial number of a Perazzi competition gun will determine its type. Since Types 1 through 3 are discontinued, Types 1 and 2 will be less desirable (and less expensive) than the values listed for Type 3.

Domestic prices on currently manufactured Perazzis have softened recently due to the availability of grey market guns from overseas.

As a final note on older Perazzi shotguns, the most collectible models will be those specimens which exhibit the highest quality and are equally rare. Older SCO grades on small frames with older style "V" springs are at the top for desirability. Also, any older SPECIAL GUNS were all custom made - usually engraved by master engravers with Angelo Galeazzi being considered the best.

Perazzi Shotguns Information

Not until 1988 did most single barrel trap guns have a "Special" option package which includes an adjustable trigger group (designated P4).

Models listed in the following sections assume a Type 4 forearm attachment design and are serial numbered 51,243 and above. Models that are serial numbered below 51,243 are an older design and will be priced less than the newer Type 4 models.

Rather than describe all the following models individually, descriptions will appear only once and are listed. The various grades have similar features and engraving (i.e., an SCO Grade Sideplate in American Skeet would appear similar to an American Trap SCO Grade Sideplate, except for stock dimensions of course).

Older SHO (Type 3s) and DHO models with rebounding hammers (disc.) are perhaps the most collectible Perazzi shotguns currently.

SC3 and other higher grade models have not been listed due to space consideration. The 14th edition does include all pertinent information (including 1993 pricing) pertaining to Perazzi higher grade models.

Recently, some Model MX8s have been modified by adding sideplates and other markings of the Extra Gold and SCO Models. These forgeries usually have the original markings polished off and have not been reproofed. Perazzi will verify any gun suspected of upgrading.

Perazzi discontinued "Mirage" model nomenclature during 1998.

Perazzi Grades and Descriptions

Due to space considerations and relative low manufacture, the higher grade Perazzis have been described but not individually priced. Please contact Perazzi, USA for more information and prices on these higher grades (see Trademark Index).

GRADES AND DESCRIPTIONS

* **Special Model** - introductory level model with high polished blue on barrels and receiver, normally listing model name on lower frame sides in gold letters and numerals. Checkered walnut stock (interchangeable) and forearm, all have adjustable trigger assembly.

* **Gold Outline Model** - similar to Standard Model, except has gold line engraving around perimeter of frame, also features better grade of walnut. This configuration is very rare.

* **SC3 Model** - features coin finished receiver with different styles of scroll engraving and different patterns of game scene engraving (snipe, grouse, pointing bird dog, or woodcock). Better grade of walnut than the Gold Outline Model.

* **SCO Model** - more elaborate than SC3 Model in that it features different styles of scroll engraving (deep relief "gargoyles" or fine English scroll) and different game scene engraving patterns. Again, a better grade of walnut (in addition to finer checkering) is utilized.

* **SCO Gold Grade Model** - differentiated from SCO Model in that it has engraving patterns featuring multiple gold inlays on receiver sides (including different duck scenes, separate grouse scenes, woodcock, and deep relief "gargoyle").

* **SCO Grade Sideplate Model** - includes coin finished receiver with game scene engraved sideplates (with boxlock action). Game scene engraving choices include different duck scenes, grouse, "Chisel" relief scroll, and Diana Goddess of the Hunt pattern.

GRADING - PPGS™	100%	98%	95%	90%	80%	70%	60%

* ***SCO Gold Grade Sideplate Model*** - similar to SCO Grade Sideplate Model, except has game figures on sideplates in relief gold. Patterns include different grouse scenes, separate ducks patterns, and dogs flushing upland game. This model can also be ordered with detachment lever for sideplates.

* ***Extra Grade Model*** - denoted by top-of-the-line fine bank note style game scene engraving with elaborate scroll and relief work on metal perimeters. Game scene choices include different dog scenes, grouse, and duck. Top quality Circassian walnut finely checkered.

* ***Extra Gold Grade Model*** - top-of-the-line boxlock model that differs from Extra Grade Model in that birds/dogs are in gold relief. This model can also be ordered with detachment lever for sideplates.

* ***SHO Over & Under Model*** - features sidelock action with coin finished receiver and intricate bank note game scene engraving with choices including different duck patterns and pheasant. Top quality walnut and checkering. Type One SHOs have non-rebounding firing pins, while Type Two guns have rebounding firing pins (since 1985).
  This model is individually handmade per customer's specifications. Currently, no orders are being taken for this series.

* ***SHO Gold Over & Under Model*** - similar to SHO Over & Under Model, except features game scene of wildlife in relief gold. This model is the best sidelock special order grade that Perazzi currently offers for sale.
  This model is individually handmade per customer's specifications. Currently, no orders are being taken for this series.

* ***DHO SxS Models*** - top-of-the-line sidelock model in 12 ga. only for DHO and DHO Gold grades. DHO Extra and DHO Gold Extra grades have similar engraving to Extra Grade and Extra Gold Grade models and are available in all gauges. The DHO Gold Extra is the most elaborate, highly finished SxS shotgun that an individual can currently special order from any company. The DHO model is exceedingly rare, and specimens should be appraised individually.
  This model is entirely handmade per customer's specifications. Currently, no orders are being taken for this series.

SHOTGUNS: RECENT MFG.

Perazzi manufactures approx. 2,000 O/U and single barrel shotguns annually, yet there are nearly 200 models! Because of this, and due to space considerations, only the Standard Grade models are listed and priced separately below, with discipline(s) listed in either O/U or single barrel configurations. Current models listed below have a removable trigger group, fixed ribs, chokes, and stocks unless otherwise noted.

Higher grade Perazzi models, including the SC3 Grade, SCO Grade, SCO Gold Grade, SCO Grade w/ sideplates, and SCO Gold w/sideplates have current MSRs only, and are listed under the individual discipline category names.

The MX-3, MX-3 Special, MX-5, MX-6, MX-7, MX-11, MX-14, MX-15, and the MX-16 models all have plain receivers, not sea shell scalloped. The MX-3, MX-5, MX-6, and the MX-7 models all have rounded monobloc barrels.

Important - retail values are for models with fixed chokes and selective/removable trigger group.
    Add $771 (MSR) for multichokes on O/U configurations, $510 (MSR) for single barrel.
    Subtract 5% if w/o selective trigger group.
    Subtract approx. 20% for single barrel (unsingle or top single) Trap model.
    Subtract 20% for Skeet model with fixed SK/SK chokes.

MIRAGE - similar features as the MX-8, in all configurations.

	100%	98%	95%	90%	80%	70%	60%
	$5,200	$4,500	$4,000	$3,500	$3,000	$2,750	$2,500

    Subtract 25% for older Ithaca and Winchester imports.

GRADING - PPGS™	100%	98%	95%	90%	80%	70%	60%

MT-6 - introduced for the 1976 Montreal Olympics, silver strips on receiver, fixed trigger group.

	$3,000	$2,500	$2,200	$2,000	$1,800	$1,600	$1,400

MS 80 SINGLE BARREL TRAP - introduced for the 1980 Moscow Olympics, fixed trigger group.

	$3,100	$2,700	$2,400	$2,100	$1,900	$1,700	$1,500

MX-1 O/U - same type of receiver as the MX-8, live pigeon gun, top firing, removable trigger group.

MSR $10,841	$4,800	$4,200	$3,900	$3,400	$3,000	$2,700	$2,400

Currently, live pigeon guns that fire the top barrel first are not as desirable as bottom first, since chokes are reversed.

MX-3 - plain receiver, same removable trigger group as MX-8, top firing, rounded monobloc.

	$3,500	$3,000	$2,700	$2,400	$2,100	$1,800	$1,600

Add 5% for "Special" model with adj. trigger group and square monobloc.

MX-5 - plain side receiver, fixed trigger group, rounded monobloc, entry level model introduced in 1985.

	$3,200	$2,800	$2,500	$2,200	$2,000	$1,700	$1,500

Add 10% for 20 ga. Field.

MX-6 - plain side receiver, same removable trigger group as the MX-8, rounded monobloc, entry level model.

	$3,500	$3,200	$2,800	$2,500	$2,200	$1,900	$1,700

MX-7 - plain side receiver, fixed trigger group, rounded monobloc, entry level model introduced in 1992.

	$3,400	$3,000	$2,600	$2,300	$2,100	$1,800	$1,600

MX-8 - 12, 20, 28 ga. or .410 bore, single or O/U barrels, standard of all current Perazzi models, removable trigger group with flat or coil spring, made in all configurations and disciplines, introduced in 1968 as the model for the Mexico City Olympics.

MSR $10,841	$6,600	$5,800	$5,200	$4,600	$4,000	$3,500	$3,000

Subtract 20%-25% for older Ithaca and Winchester imports.

✳ *MX-8L* - similar to MX-8, except has engraved action, this model is not available as a pigeon gun.

MSR $12,757	$7,775	$6,250	$5,500	$4,850	$4,250	$3,750	$3,250

Add $1,406 for seven choke tubes and engraving (Model MX-8LC, Sporting configuration only).

✳ *MX-8 Special* - similar to MX-8, except has ramped rib and adj. trigger. New 2004.

MSR $10,490	$6,200	$5,500	$5,000	$4,400	$3,800	$3,250	$2,850

MX-9 - similar to MX-8, except has changeable sight and adj. comb.

	$6,000	$5,500	$4,900	$4,400	$3,800	$3,300	$2,800

MX-10 SINGLE BARREL TRAP - similar to the MX-8 Single Barrel Trap, except has very high adj. rib and comb, top single.

MSR $11,567	$6,950	$5,900	$5,300	$4,700	$4,000	$3,500	$3,000

MX-11 - plain side receiver with square monobloc, removable trigger group, entry level model.

	$4,400	$3,900	$3,500	$3,100	$2,800	$2,600	$2,200

MX-12/MX-20 - 12 or 20 ga., non-removable trigger group, border engraving standard, available in only Sporting or Field configuration.

MSR $10,841	$6,000	$5,500	$4,800	$4,300	$3,800	$3,300	$3,000

Add approx. $400 ($771 MSR) for seven choke tubes (Model MX-12C - MX-20C, Sporting configuration only).

Subtract 20% for 26 in. barrels.

GRADING - PPGS™	100%	98%	95%	90%	80%	70%	60%

MX-14 SINGLE BARREL TRAP - unsingle combo with fixed rib, adj. comb, same receiver as the MX-15.

	$6,500	$5,900	$5,200	$4,600	$4,000	$3,500	$3,000

MX-15 SINGLE BARREL TRAP - unsingle only, with adj. rib, adj. comb, plain side receiver with removable trigger group.

MSR $9,230	$5,000	$4,500	$4,000	$3,600	$3,200	$2,700	$2,200

✳ *MX-15L Single Barrel Trap* - similar to MX-15, except has engraved action.

MSR $11,146	$6,650	$5,700	$5,100	$4,600	$4,000	$3,500	$3,000

MX-28 - 28 ga., Field Grade only, otherwise similar to MX-12.

MSR $21,682	$12,000	$10,000	$8,500	$7,500	$6,600	$5,800	$5,200

Add approx. $400 for choke tubes.
Subtract 20% for 26 in. barrels.

MX-410 - .410 bore, Field Grade only, otherwise similar to MX-28.

MSR $21,682	$12,995	$10,000	$8,500	$7,500	$6,600	$5,800	$5,200

MX-2000 - 12, 20, 28 ga. or .410 bore, single or O/U barrels, all disciplines and configurations, similar features as the MX-8, with MX-2000 style engraving and gold letter on receiver, fixed or adj. (Trap Model only) rib.

MSR $12,167	$7,200	$6,400	$5,700	$5,000	$4,400	$3,800	$3,300

Add $1,441 for multi-choke barrel with seven chokes.
Subtract 20% for single barrel models.
Subtract 20% for fixed SK/SK choke Skeet models.
Subtract 10% for fixed choke Trap models with non-selective trigger group.

TM1 SINGLE BARREL TRAP - low rib barrel.

	$2,900	$2,500	$2,100	$1,800	$1,500	$1,200	$1,100

TMX SINGLE BARREL TRAP - newer production, similar features as TM1, except has high rib.

	$3,600	$3,000	$2,500	$2,100	$1,800	$1,500	$1,200

SHOTGUNS: O/U, AMERICAN COMBO SETS (TRAP, SKEET, AND SPORTING)

Perazzi offers a wide variety of combination sets in Trap, Skeet, and Sporting configurations. These combination sets include a choice of either 29 1/2 or 31 1/2 in. O/U VR barrels with or w/o choke tubes and one VR barrel (chooice of top single or bottom single) with or w/o choke tubes. There are numerous configurations available, including many engraving, rib, and stock options. All shotguns, except the MX12, are equipped with a removable trigger group and flat springs. Currently, Perazzi offers the following Trap, Skeet, and Sporting combination sets:

Standard Grade Combo Models: MX8 Trap ($15,127 MSR), MX10 Trap ($18,007 MSR), MX10RS Trap ($18,007 MSR), MX200/8 Trap ($16,556 MSR), MX2000/10 Trap ($19,493 MSR), MX2000/RS ($19,493 MSR), MX8 Skeet ($12,384 MSR), MX8L Skeet ($14,300 MSR), MX2000/ 8 Skeet ($13,778 MSR), MX14 Trap ($12,916 MSR), MX12 Sporting ($13,381 MSR), MX2000S Sporting ($14,719 MSR), MX2000/8 Sporting ($14,719 MSR), MX14L Trap ($14,833 MSR), DB81 Trap ($16,023 MSR), MX2000/8 Gold Trap ($26,467 MSR), MX2000 Gold Trap ($24,4000 MSR), MX2000/8 Gold Skeet ($23,701 MSR), and the MX2000S Gold Sporting ($21,296 MSR).

SC3 Grade Models: MX8 SC3 Trap ($23,043 MSR), SC3 Trap ($25,935 MSR), MX8 SC3 Skeet ($20,299 MSR), and the MX12 SC3 Sporting ($18,780 MSR).

SCO Grade Models: MX8 SCO Trap ($38,057 MSR), SCO Gold Trap ($40,937 MSR), MX8 SCO Skeet ($39,452 MSR), and the MX12 SCO Sporting ($40,450 MSR).

SCO Gold Grade: MX8 SCO Gold Trap ($42,196 MSR), SCO Gold Trap ($45,088 MSR), MX8 SCO Gold Skeet ($34,790 MSR), and the MX12 SCO Gold Sporting ($35,670 MSR).

SCO Grade Models w/sideplates: MX8 SCO Trap ($54,659 MSR), SCO Trap ($57,550 MSR), MX8 SCO Skeet ($51,914 MSR), and the MX12 Gold Sporting ($52,913 MSR).

SCO Gold Grade Models w/sideplates: MX8 SCO Gold Trap ($60,624 MSR), SCO Gold Trap ($63,424 MSR), MX8 SCO Gold Skeet ($57,879 MSR), and the MX12 SCO Gold Sporting ($58,878 MSR).

Perazzi

SHOTGUNS: O/U, COMPETITON - OLYMPIC & DOUBLE TRAP

12 or 20 ga. Current barrel lengths include 29 1/2, 30 3/4, or 31 1/2 in.

The MX2/MX2L configuration is available mainly for the European marketplace. Values for this model represent recent pricing - Perazzi U.S.A. should be contacted directly for an up-to-date price quotation.

Perazzi offers a wide variety of competition style shotguns. Current Olympic Trap and Double Trap models include: Standard Trap w/ adj. rib ($23,100 MSR), and the MX2000S/20S Gold Sporting ($21,659-$22,430 MSR).

SC3 Grade: MX8 SC3 ($18,394 MSR), MX8/20 SC3 ($18,394 MSR), SC3/12 ($19,833 MSR), SC3/20 ($19,833 MSR), MX8/20 SC3 ($18,394 MSR), MX8/20C Sporting ($18,394-$19,800 MSR), MX12C SC3 and MX20C SC3 Sporting ($18,394-$19,165 MSR).

SCO Grade: MX8 SCO ($31,275 MSR, w/ adj. rib $32,716 MSR), and the MX8/20 SCO ($31,275 MSR, w/adj. rib $32,716 MSR).

SCO Gold Grade: MX8 SCO Gold ($31,160 MSR), MX8/20 Gold ($31,160 MSR), SCO Gold/12 ($32,220 MSR), and the SCO Gold/20 ($32,220 MSR).

SCO Grade w/sideplates: MX8 SCO ($42,300 MSR), MX8/20 SCO ($42,300 MSR), SCO/12 ($43,360 MSR), and the SCO/20 ($43,360 MSR).

SCO Gold Grade w/sideplates: MX8 SCO Gold ($47,740 MSR), MX8/20 SCO Gold ($47,740 MSR), SCO Gold/12 ($48,800 MSR), and the SCO Gold/20 ($48,800 MSR).

O/U SIDELOCK MODELS - older models without rebounding hammers are not as desirable. The most desirable configurations in this model are the Skeet, Pigeon, and Sporting variations (pricing follows new SHO Gold values). All SHO sidelock models were disc. 1992.

* ***SHO Older Mfg.***

	100%	98%	95%	90%	80%	70%	60%
	$12,000	$11,000	$10,000	$9,000	$8,500	$7,600	$6,800

Add $6,000 for game scene engraving.

* ***SHO Newer Mfg.***

	100%	98%	95%	90%	80%	70%	60%
	$28,500	$25,000	$21,500	$18,000	$16,500	$14,000	$12,000

Last MSR was $43,000.

* ***SHO Gold Older Mfg.***

	100%	98%	95%	90%	80%	70%	60%
	$17,000	$15,000	$13,000	$11,000	$9,950	$8,750	$7,000

* ***SHO Gold Newer Mfg.***

	100%	98%	95%	90%	80%	70%	60%
	$34,000	$29,500	$25,000	$21,250	$17,750	$14,000	$12,000

Last MSR was $48,000.

* ***SHO Extra*** - while advertised, none were sold.

Last MSR was $80,000.

* ***SHO Gold Extra*** - while advertised, none were sold.

Last MSR was $86,000.

SHOTGUNS: O/U, COMPETITION SKEET

12 or 20 ga., 26 3/4, 27 9/16, 28 3/8, 29 1/2, or 34 in. barrels.

Subtract $250-$500 on older Mirage Models (without the "Special" designation) that do not have the adjustable 4 position trigger.

Perazzi offers a wide variety of competition style shotguns. Current Skeet models include:

SC3 Grade: MX8 SC3 ($16,220 MSR), MX8/20 SC3 ($16,220 MSR), SC3/12 ($17,490 MSR), and the SC3/20 ($17,490 MSR).

SCO Grade: MX8 SCO ($31,275 MSR), MX8/20 SCO ($31,275 MSR), SCO/12 ($28,850 MSR), and the SCO/20 ($28,850 MSR).

SCO Gold Grade: MX8 SCO Gold ($31,160 MSR), MX8/20 Gold ($31,160 MSR), SCO Gold/12 ($32,220 MSR), and the SCO Gold/20 ($32,220 MSR).

SCO Grade w/sideplates: MX8 SCO ($42,300 MSR), MX8/20 SCO ($42,300 MSR), SCO/12 ($43,360 MSR), and the SCO/20 ($43,360 MSR).

SCO Gold Grade w/sideplates: MX8 SCO Gold ($47,740 MSR), MX8/20 SCO Gold ($47,740 MSR), SCO Gold/12 ($48,800 MSR), and the SCO Gold/20 ($48,800 MSR).

GRADING - PPGS™	100%	98%	95%	90%	80%	70%	60%

O/U SIDELOCK MODELS - older models without rebounding hammers are not as desirable.

* *SHO Older Mfg.*

| | $15,000 | $12,000 | $9,500 | $8,500 | $7,600 | $6,800 | $5,900 |

* *SHO Newer Mfg.*

| | $35,850 | $30,000 | $25,000 | $20,000 | $17,000 | $14,500 | $12,750 |

Last MSR was $43,000.

* *SHO Gold Older Mfg.*

| | $18,000 | $15,750 | $12,000 | $9,500 | $8,500 | $7,600 | $6,800 |

* *SHO Gold Newer Mfg.*

| | $45,000 | $34,500 | $27,250 | $22,000 | $18,500 | $15,950 | $13,750 |

Last MSR was $48,000.

* *SHO Extra* - imported 1985-92.

| | $68,750 | $54,700 | $38,100 | $32,000 | $26,500 | $21,250 | $18,000 |

Last MSR was $80,000.

* *SHO Gold Extra* - similar to SHO Extra, except has gold inlays. Imported 1992 only.

| | $72,750 | $56,500 | $39,500 | $33,000 | $27,000 | $22,000 | $18,500 |

Last MSR was $86,000.

SHOTGUNS: O/U, 4-GAUGE SKEET SETS

STANDARD GRADE MODELS

* *MX3 Special*

| | $5,200 | $4,875 | $4,650 | $4,500 | $4,150 | $3,650 | $3,150 |

Last MSR was $15,400.

* *Mirage Special* - disc. 1994.

| | $5,850 | $5,500 | $4,850 | $4,600 | $4,200 | $3,700 | $3,200 |

Last MSR was $17,500.

SHOTGUNS: O/U, COMPETITION SPORTING

12 or 20 ga.

Perazzi offers a wide variety of competition style shotguns. Current Sporting models include:
SC3 Grade: MX8 SC3 ($16,220 MSR), MX8/20 SC3 ($16,220 MSR), SC3/12 ($17,490 MSR), SC3/20 ($17,490 MSR), MX8C SC3 and MX8/20C SC 3 ($17,460 MSR), MX12 SC3 and MX20 SC3 ($16,220 MSR), and the MX12C SC3 and MX20C SC3 ($16,900 MSR).
SCO Grade: MX8 SCO ($27,580 MSR), MX8/20 SCO ($27,580 MSR), SCO/12 ($28,850 MSR), SCO/20 ($28,850 MSR), MX8C SCO and MX8/20C SCO $28,820 MSR), MX12 and MX20 SCO (27,580 MSR), and the MX12C and MX20C SCO ($28,260 MSR).
SCO Gold Grade: MX8 SCO Gold ($35,336 MSR), MX8/20 Gold ($35,336 MSR), SCO Gold/12 ($36,742 MSR), SCO Gold/20 ($32,220 MSR), MX8C SCO Gold and MX8/20 C Gold ($31,160 MSR), MX12 SCO Gold and MX20 SCO Gold ($31,160 MSR), MX12C SCO and MX20 SCO Gold ($31, 840 MSR), and the MX8 SCO Gold ($31,160 MSR).
SCO Grade w/sideplates: MX8 SCO ($47,968 MSR), MX8/20 SCO ($47,968 MSR), SCO/12 ($43,360 MSR), SCO/20 ($48,739 MSR), MX8C SCO and MX8/20 C SCO ($42,980 MSR), MX12 SCO and MX20 SCO ($42,300 MSR) and the MX12C SCO and MX20C SCO ($42,980 MSR).
SCO Gold Grade w/sideplates: MX8 SCO Gold ($54,137 MSR), MX8/20 SCO Gold ($55,543 MSR), SCO Gold/12 ($54,137 MSR), SCO Gold/20 ($54,908 MSR), MX8C SCO Gold and MX8/20 C SCO Gold ($48,980 MSR), MX12 SCO Gold and MX20 SCO Gold ($48,980 MSR), and the MX12C SCO Gold and the MX20C SCO Gold ($48,420 MSR).

SHOTGUNS: O/U, PIGEON-ELECTROCIBLES

Perazzi offers a wide variety of Pigeon shotguns. Current models include:
SC3 Grade: MX8 SC3 ($18,393 MSR).
SCO Grade: MX8 SCO ($31,275 MSR).
SCO Gold Grade: MX8 SCO Gold ($35,336 MSR).

GRADING - PPGS™	100%	98%	95%	90%	80%	70%	60%

SCO Grade w/sideplates: MX8 SCO ($47968,300 MSR).
SCO Gold Grade w/sideplates: MX8 SCO Gold ($54,137 MSR).

SHOTGUNS: O/U, GAME/HUNTING - BOXLOCK ACTION

Available in 12, 20, 28 ga., or .410 bore, 26 (disc. on MX8/12 ga. and MX12 1994), 26 3/4, 27 9/16, 28 3/8, or 29 1/2 in. barrels. Perazzi offers a wide variety of game/hunting configurations. Current models include: SC3 Grade Models: MX8 SC3 and MX8/20 SC3 ($18,394 MSR), MX12 SC3 and MX20 SC3 ($18,394 MSR), MX28 SC3 and MX410 SC3 ($29,189 MSR).
SCO Grade Models: MX8 SCO and MX/820 SCO ($31,275 MSR), MX12 SCO and MX20 SCO ($31,275 MSR), MX28 SCO and MX410 SCO ($42,196 MSR).
SCO Gold Grade: MX8 SCO Gold and MX8/20 Gold ($35,336 MSR), MX12 SCO Gold and MX20 SCO Gold ($35,336 MSR), MX28 SCO Gold and MX410 SCO Gold ($46,142 MSR).
SCO Grade w/sideplates: MX8 SCO and MX8/20 SCO ($47,968 MSR), MX12 SCO and MX20 SCO ($47,968 MSR), and the MX28 and MX410 SCO ($58,888 MSR).
SCO Gold Grade w/sideplates: MX8 SCO Gold and MX8/20 SCO ($54,137 MSR), MX12 SCO Gold and MX20 SCO Gold ($54,137 MSR), MX12 SCO and MX20 SCO Gold ($54,137 MSR), MX28 SCO and MX410 SCO Gold ($64,683 MSR).

SHOTGUNS: O/U, HUNTING - SIDELOCK MODELS

All SHO models were disc. in 1992 (they were available through special order only).

SHO MODELS

* **SHO Older Mfg.** - older models without rebounding hammers are not as desirable.

| | $15,000 | $12,000 | $9,500 | $8,500 | $7,600 | $6,800 | $5,950 |

* **SHO Newer Mfg.** - 12 ga. only, introductory sidelock O/U model with bank note game scene engraving on coin finished receiver.

| | $35,500 | $29,950 | $25,000 | $20,000 | $17,000 | $14,500 | $12,750 |

Last MSR was $43,000.

* **SHO Gold Older Mfg.** - older models without rebounding hammers are not as desirable.

| | $18,000 | $15,750 | $12,000 | $9,500 | $8,500 | $7,600 | $6,800 |

* **SHO Gold Newer Mfg.** - similar to SHO, except has game scenes in gold relief.

| | $38,650 | $31,500 | $26,500 | $21,250 | $18,000 | $15,500 | $13,750 |

Last MSR was $48,000.

* **SHO Extra** - importation began 1992.

| | $68,750 | $54,700 | $38,100 | $32,000 | $26,500 | $21,250 | $18,000 |

Last MSR was $80,000.

* **SHO Gold Extra** - similar to SHO Extra, except has gold inlays. Importation began 1992.

| | $72,750 | $56,500 | $39,500 | $33,000 | $27,000 | $22,000 | $18,500 |

Last MSR was $86,000.

SHOTGUNS: SxS, HUNTING - SIDELOCK MODELS

DHO Models have not been included within the scope of this text due to the extreme rarity factor. Please contact Perazzi, USA for more information on these models and current pricing.

Subtract 40% without rebounding hammers on older DHO models.

PEREGRINE INDUSTRIES, INC.

Previous company located in Huntington Beach, CA circa 1991.

While advertised, Peregrine Industries, Inc. never manufactured the Falcon Model.

GRADING - PPGS™	100%	98%	95%	90%	80%	70%	60%

PERUGINI-VISINI

Current manufacturer established during 1968 and located in Nuvolera, Brescia, Italy. No current importation. Previously imported 2002-2004 by Old Friends Hunting & Shooting Co., located in Livingston, MT. Rifles were previously imported and distributed until 1992 by William Larkin Moore & Co., previously located in Westlake Village, CA. All other models listed were previously imported and distributed by Armes De Chasse located in Chadds Ford, PA until 1988. Please contact the company directly for more information, including pricing and availability (see listing in Trademark Index).

Perugini-Visini makes best quality boxlock and sidelock rifles and shotguns. including bolt action and single shot rifles. Annual production is approx. 55 guns on a custom order basis only.

RIFLES

STANDARD MODEL: BOLT ACTION - available in most U.S. and metric cals., Mauser 98K action, 24 or 26 in. barrel, 3 shot mag.(non-detachable), matte finished European walnut, high polish bluing, no sights. Importation disc. 1987.

	$4,250	$3,800	$3,400	$2,950	$2,500	$2,000	$1,800

Last MSR was $4,250.

DELUXE MODEL: BOLT ACTION - similar to Standard Model, except has finely checkered oil finished walnut stock, sights, knurled bolt handle, and is cased. Importation disc. 1987.

	$4,250	$3,800	$3,400	$2,950	$2,500	$2,000	$1,800

Last MSR was $4,250.

MODEL EAGLE SINGLE SHOT - available in most U.S. and metric cals., Anson & Deeley type action, ejector, sights, adj. trigger, oil finished finely checkered European walnut stock, 24 or 26 in. Hämmerli barrel. Importation disc. 1987.

	$5,255	$4,500	$3,800	$3,400	$2,950	$2,500	$2,000

Last MSR was $5,255.

EAGLE MODEL SINGLE SHOT (CURRENT MFG.) - available in cals. up to .375 H&H, best quality single shot, built on patented Perugini-Visini sideplated action with border engraving standard, set trigger optional, supplied with Perugini-Visini claw mounts and Zeiss optics, engraving is optional, and quoted per individual order.

This model has a current price range of 15,000-20,000 euros.

Subtract $3,000 if w/o sideplates.

"PROFESSIONAL" BOLT ACTION MAGAZINE RIFLE - built on Perugini & Visini Mauser action for cals. up to .375 H&H, claw mounts and Zeiss optics included, quarter rib optional.

MSR N/A	N/A	$9,250	$8,450	$7,600	$6,800	$5,700	$4,900

"PROFESSIONAL" BOLT ACTION MAGNUM RIFLE - available in calibers from .375 H&H to .505 Gibbs, dedicated Perugini-Visini magnum Mauser action, includes quarter rib, express sights and sling swivels, unique takedown feature. Claw mounts, optics, and engraving are optional.

This model has a current MSR of 16,500 euros.

"SELOUS" EXPRESS DOUBLE RIFLE - available in cals. up to .600 NE, best quality H&H back action sidelock with Perugini-Visini patented ejectors for rimless cartridges, best quality English rose and scroll engraving is standard.

This model has a current MSR of 50,000 euros.

❉ *Selous SxS* - 9.3x74R, .375 H&H, .458 Win. Mag., .470 NE, or .500 3 in. NE cal., H&H style detachable sidelock action, ejectors, folding leaf rear sight, border engraving with best quality checkered walnut, top-of-the-line model, leather cased. Importation disc. 1992.

	$23,000	$18,500	$15,000	$12,000	$10,000	$9,000	$8,150

Last MSR was $26,000.

GRADING - PPGS™	100%	98%	95%	90%	80%	70%	60%

❋ *Sidelock Super Express SxS* - choice of 9 different cals. including .470 Nitro Express, H&H patterned sidelocks, chopper lump barrels, third lever fastener, multi-leaf express sights, coin finished or case hardened receiver, engraving patterns optional. Importation disc. 1989.

	$9,500	$8,400	$7,400	$6,850	$6,100	$5,600	$5,000

Last MSR was $10,500.

VICTORIA MODEL D EXPRESS DOUBLE RIFLE - available in calibers up to .500 NE, best quality A&D boxlock action with Perugini-Visini patented ejectors, chopper lump barrels with quarter rib and express sights, claw mounts are optional, best quality English rose and scroll engraving is standard.

This model has a current MSR of 25,000 euros.

❋ *Model Victoria D Mag. SxS* - similar to Model Victoria, except in .375 H&H, .458 Win., .470 NE, or .500-3 in. NE cal., demi-bloc barrels, and has elaborate engraving. Importation disc. 1992.

	$10,950	$9,150	$8,200	$7,400	$6,600	$5,800	$5,100

Last MSR was $13,750.

VICTORIA MODEL M EXPRESS DOUBLE RIFLE - available in cals. up to 9.3x74R cal., similar to Victoria Model D, except has monobloc barrel construction.

This model has a current MSR of 25,000 euros.

❋ *Model Victoria M SxS* - .30-06, 7x57R, 7x65R or 9.3x74R cal., Anson & Deeley boxlock action, border engraving, ejectors, folding leaf rear sight, DT, 24 or 26 in. monobloc barrels with chopper lumps, leather cased. Importation disc. 1992.

	$7,000	$5,700	$4,600	$3,500	$2,950	$2,500	$2,000

PRINCESS MODEL D EXPRESS O/U DOUBLE RIFLE - available in all cals. up to traditional express calibers, best quality Boss style boxlock action with automatic ejectors, chopper lump barrels with quarter rib and express sights, optional claw mounts, best quality English rose and scroll engraving is standard.

MSR N/A	N/A	$22,000	$18,750	$15,000	$12,250	$10,000	$8,750

PRINCESS MODEL M EXPRESS O/U DOUBLE RIFLE - available in cals. up to 9.3x74R cal., similar to Princess Model D, except has monobloc barrel construction.

MSR N/A	N/A	$18,500	$16,000	$13,750	$11,000	$9,000	$7,000

BOXLOCK EXPRESS SxS - .444 Marlin or 9.3x74R cal., Anson & Deeley boxlock action, ejectors, color case hardened frame, iron sights. Importation disc. 1989.

	$3,150	$2,800	$2,500	$2,200	$1,950	$1,700	$1,475

Last MSR was $3,500.

BOXLOCK MAGNUM O/U - .270 Win., .375 H&H, or .458 Win. Mag. cal., Anson & Deeley boxlock action, ejectors, monobloc barrels, select walnut. Importation disc. 1989.

	$5,500	$4,900	$4,300	$3,750	$3,100	$2,600	$2,200

Last MSR was $6,100.

SHOTGUNS

AUSONIA SxS - 12 or 20 ga., exposed hammers with double Purdey type sidelock action, various engraving options, demibloc barrels. Disc.

	$7,140	$6,500	$5,750	$4,950	$4,200	$3,500	$2,550

Last MSR was $7,140.

LIBERTY MODEL SxS - 12, 16, 20, 28 ga., or .410 bore, scalloped Anson & Deeley boxlock ejector with chopper lump barrels, Purdey lock, light rose and scroll engraving, oval for initials and factory gold crest on forearm, leather cased.

MSR N/A	N/A	$10,750	$9,000	$7,750	$6,500	$5,250	$4,350

GRADING - PPGS™	100%	98%	95%	90%	80%	70%	60%

CLASSIC MODEL SxS - 12, 16, 20, 28 ga. or .410 bore, best quality H&H style sidelock action with chopper lump barrels, exhibition wood stock with gold crest in forearm and stock oval, every refinement incorporated, supplied with Nizzoli leather case, engraving by master engraver.

	MSR N/A	N/A	$24,000	$20,500	$16,500	$13,000	$10,250	$9,350

REGINA MODEL SxS - 12 ga., heavy frame competition and hunting model, features removeable trigger group with chopper lump barrel construction, border engraving is standard, supplied with extra trigger group and Nasco case, engraving upgrade and sideplates optional.

	MSR N/A	N/A	$11,500	$9,950	$8,700	$7,600	$6,500	$5,150

ROMAGNA HAMMER GUN - 12,16, 20, 28 ga. or .410 bore, best quality Zanotti style bar action hammer gun, includes every refinement, engraved by master engraver in traditional style, available in heavy frame pigeon configuration for competition.

	MSR N/A	N/A	$19,500	$16,000	$13,000	$10,000	$8,500	$7,250

Add $1,850 for ejectors and self-cocking mechanism.

MAESTRO O/U - Boss style scalloped receiver with removable trigger group, monobloc barrels are standard, with chopper lump barrels optional, sideplated versions available in various competition and hunting style models.

Perugini-Visini uses advanced CNC fabrication and hand finishing with all Maestro models. Maestro models are also available with a 20 ga. receiver, and in 28 ga. and .410 bore barrel sets.

✳ *Maestro Traveling Hunter Model* - coin finished receiver with mirror polished internal parts, custom Briley chokes and Nasco case, best finish with exhibition wood stock, entry level engraving and adj. trigger standard.

This model has a current MSR of 12,500 euros.

Add 800 euros for sideplates or extra trigger group.

✳ *Maestro Lusso Model* - sideplated version with exhibition wood stock, adj. trigger group, English rose and scroll engraving standard, best quality, gold oval and factory gold crest, supplied with extra trigger group and Nizzoli leather case, ornamental engraving optional.

	MSR N/A	N/A	$16,750	$13,350	$10,250	$8,700	$7,800	$6,900

✳ *Maestro Reale Piccione Model* - ultimate competition O/U, designed with particular MOI for Flyer and Helice shooting, adj. trigger and English rose and scroll engraving standard, Boss side ribs and Anson plunger forearm, custom choked or Briley chokes provided, supplied with extra trigger group and Nizzoli leather case, ornamental engraving optional.

	MSR N/A	N/A	$18,000	$15,000	$12,500	$10,000	$8,750	$7,800

NOVA O/U - best quality Boss pattern sidelock with back action locks, Boss style forend iron and side ribs, best quality English rose and scroll engraving is standard, ornamental engraving is optional.

	MSR N/A	N/A	$38,500	$32,750	$26,500	$20,000	$17,000	$14,750

PETERS STAHL GmbH

Current pistol manufacturer located in Paderborn, Germany. No current U.S. importation. Previously distributed by Swiss Trading GmbH, located in Bozeman, MT. Previously imported 1998-1999 by Peters Stahl, U.S.A. located in Delta, UT, and by Franzen International Inc. located in Oakland, NJ until 1998. Dealer direct sales only.

PISTOLS: SEMI-AUTO

Peters Stahl manufactures high quality semi-auto pistols based on the Model 1911 design, but to date, has had limited U.S. importation. Current models include the Multicaliber, 92-Sport, O7-Sport, HC-Champion and variations, 1911-Tactical/Classic, PLS, and a .22 LR. Peters-Stahl also manufactures multicaliber conversion kits of the highest quality. Recent models previously imported (until 2000) included the Model Millennium (MSR was $2,195), Match 22 LR (MSR was $1,995), Trophy Master (MSR was $1,995), Omega Match (MSR was $1,995), High Capacity Trophy Master (MSR was $1,695), O7 Multicaliber (MSR was $1,995), and the 92 Multicaliber (MSR was $2,610-$2,720). In the past, Peters Stahl has manufactured guns for Federal Ordnance, Omega, Schuetzen Pistol Works, and Springfield Armory. The factory should be contacted directly (see Trademark Index) for current model information, U.S. availability, and pricing.

PHELPS MFG. CO.

Previous manufacturer located in Evansville, IN circa 1978-1996.

Phelps Manufacturing Company began shipping guns in early 1978. Phelps guns were invest-ment cast in 4140 steel, with basic single action simplicity, using a transfer bar in the action.

REVOLVERS

HERITAGE I - .45-70 cal., single action revolver, incorporates transfer bar hammer safety, blue finish (standard), nickel (optional), adj. rear sight, 8 in. barrel standard, other barrel lengths up to 20 in. available, 6 lbs. Disc. 1996.

	$2,050	$1,675	$1,425

Last MSR was $2,250.

Add $20 for each additional in. of barrel.

EAGLE I - .444 Marlin cal., single action revolver, blue finish, adj. rear sight, barrel options same as Heritage I, 6 lbs. Disc. 1996.

	$2,050	$1,675	$1,425

Last MSR was $2,250.

PATRIOT - .375 Win. cal., single action revolver, blue finish, adj. rear sight, barrel options are the same as Heritage I. Limited mfg. 1993-94.

	$1,925	$1,550	$1,350

Last MSR was $2,225.

GRIZZLY .50-70 - .50-70 cal., otherwise similar to Heritage I. Mfg. 1992-96.

	$2,300	$1,875	$1,500

Last MSR was $2,580.

Add $20 for each additional in. of barrel.

PHILLIPS & ROGERS, INC.

Previous manufacturer 1992-2003, and located in Huntsville, TX since 1997. Previously located in Conroe, TX circa 1992-1997.

In addition to manufacturing the firearms listed, Phillips & Rogers also made a multi-cali-ber conversion cylinder for all Ruger, .357 Mag., new model Blackhawk revolvers (disc. 1996) - the retail price was $145. Multi-caliber conversion cylinders are also available for the Ruger new Model Blackhawk (allows shooting .45 LC, .45 Win. Mag., or .45 ACP - retail price is $185) and the Ruger Super Blackhawk (converts .44 Mag. to .50 AE - $550). A new version of the Ruger .50 AE conversion was also available for $995.

REVOLVERS

MEDUSA MODEL 47 REVOLVER - multi-caliber, over 25 cals. in the .355 - .380 diameter range (including .357 Mag., .38 Super, .38 Spl., 9mm Para., etc.), unique design does not utilize half-moon clips or cylinder/barrel changes, 2 1/2, 4, 5, 6, or 8 in. barrel, 6 shot, double action, matte blue finish, rubber or wood grips. Mfg. 1993-2003.

$525	$475	$435	$400	$375	$350	$325

Last MSR was $599.

Add $95 for 8 in. barrel.

GRADING - PPGS™	100%	98%	95%	90%	80%	70%	60%

RIFLES: BOLT ACTION

WILDERNESS EXPLORER - .218 Bee, .22 Hornet, .44 Mag., or .50 AE cal., bolt action, features 18 in. match grade barrel, quick change bolt face and barrel allowing interchangeable calibers, white speckled black synthetic stock, side safety, 5 1/2 lbs. Mfg. 1997 only.

	$925	$825	$725	$650	$575	$500	$425

Last MSR was $995.

PHOENIX ARMS

Current manufacturer located in Ontario, CA since 1992. Distributor sales only.

PISTOLS: SEMI-AUTO

RAVEN - .25 ACP cal., single action, 2 7/16 in. barrel, 6 shot mag., alloy frame, choice of finishes and grips. Disc. 1998.

	$69	$50	$45	$40	$35	$30	$25

Last MSR was $79.

This model was supplied with a magazine disconnect lock.

HP MODEL - .22 LR or .25 ACP cal., single action, 3 in. VR barrel, 10 (.25 ACP), 10 (C/B 1994), or 11* (.22 LR) shot staggered mag., alloy frame, firing pin block safety, adj. rear sight, choice of polished blue or satin nickel finish, keyed mag. lock and safety cable lanyard, 20 oz. New 1994.

MSR $130	$100	$80	$70	$60	$50	$45	$40

Add $99 for laser sight and mount (new 1998).

Add $45 for 2-in-1 target barrel and magazine conversion kit.

✻ **HP Range Kit** - includes HP Model in .22 LR with 5 in. extended barrel, extended mag., locking plastic storage case (compartmentalized during 2000), and cleaning kit. New 1998.

MSR $171	$140	$115	$100	$90	$75	$65	$55

✻ **HP Deluxe Range Kit** - similar to HP Range Kit, except has 3 and 5 in. barrels and extended mag. New 1999.

MSR $210	$185	$165	$135	$110	$100	$90	$80

PHOENIX ARMS CO.

Previous importer located in Lowell, MA.

PISTOLS: SEMI-AUTO

PHOENIX - .25 ACP cal., Belgian semi-auto, previously manufactured by Robar et DeKerkhove located in Liege, Belgium.

	$495	$450	$400	$350	$300	$250	$200

PIETTA, F.LLI

Current black powder and firearms manufacturer established in 1960, and located in Gussago, Italy. Firearms are currently imported by Navy Arms and E.M.F. Black powder reproductions and replicas are currently imported by Cabela's, Navy Arms, Dixie Gun Works, Taylor's and E.M.F.

Pietta manufactures good quality black powder and modern firearms reproductions in many configurations for various American companies. During 2000-2001, Pietta developed its own proprietary centerfire bottleneck cartridge - the .30-357 AeT, manufactured by Lapua. The company also completed a modern SAA revolver during 2003, in cals. .357 Mag., .44-40 WCF, and .45 LC. Additionally, Pietta plans on producing the SAA in their new .30-357 AeT cartridge. Please visit their web site for current information or to request a comprehensive catalog listing of the wide assortment of firearms this company manufactures (see Trademark Index).

GRADING - PPGS™	100%	98%	95%	90%	80%	70%	60%

For more information and up-to-date regarding current Pietta black powder models, please refer to *Colt Blackpowder Reproductions and Replicas* Dennis Adler, and the *Blue Book of Modern Black Powder Arms*, by John Allen & Dennis Adler. These books feature hundreds of color photographs and support text of the most recent black powder models available, as well as a complete pricing and reference guide.

Pietta firearms are listed separately under Navy Arms and E.M.F. - please refer to the individual listings.

PIOTTI

Current manufacturer located in Brescia, Italy. Currently imported and distributed exclusively by William Larkin Moore & Co. located in Scottsdale, AZ.

Fratelli Piotti is one of Italy's premier gunmakers. These shotguns meet the highest standards of craftsmanship and are made to customer specifications. Variety of gauges, engraving, styles, chokes, etc.

SHOTGUNS: O/U

PIOTTI BOSS - 12, 16, 20, or 28 ga., 26-32 in. barrels, single or double triggers, standard with King 2 engraving, Turkish Circassian walnut, various engraving patterns available, 6 lbs - 20 ga., approx. 7 1/2 lbs. 12 ga. New 1995.

MSR $51,300	$48,000	$34,000	$28,750	$23,650	$18,950	$15,450	$12,950

Add $3,500 for single trigger.
Add $3,500 for 16 or 20 ga.
Add $9,500 for 28 ga.

SHOTGUNS: SxS

For the following models - add $2,900 for single trigger, $11,000 for H&H type self-opening mechanism, $1,250-$2,000 for hand-detachable locks, $950 for pinless action or $650 for rounded action, approx. $1,400-$2,200 for leather case, $5,950 for 10 ga., $975 for 16 or 20 ga., $1,350 for 28 ga. or .410 bore boxlock, $2,600 for 28 ga. or .410 bore sidelock.

HAMMER GUN - 12 ga. only, self cocking ejector model, DT, exposed hammers, back action with fine scroll engraving. Importation began 2001.

MSR $35,400	$33,000	$25,000	$19,250	$12,250	$10,000	$8,700	$6,800

Add $3,300 for ejectors and self-cocking mechanism.

PIUMA (BSEE) - 10, 12, 16, 20, 28 ga., or .410 bore, Anson & Deeley boxlock ejector double with chopper lump barrels, level file-cut rib, light scroll and rosette engraving, scalloped frame.

MSR $15,900	$14,950	$10,900	$9,500	$8,400	$7,000	$5,750	$4,500

WESTLAKE - 12, 16, 20, 28 ga., or .410 bore, H&H sidelock action, moderate scroll engraving. Mfg. disc. 1989.

$8,500	$7,500	$6,050	$5,300	$4,700	$4,200	$3,750

Last MSR was $8,400.

MONTE CARLO - 12, 16, 20, 28 ga., or .410 bore, best-quality H&H pattern sidelock ejector double with chopper lump barrels, Purdey style scroll and rosette engraving. Importation disc. 1990.

$10,500	$9,250	$8,200	$7,100	$6,000	$5,000	$4,500

Last MSR was $11,400.

KING NUMBER 1 - 12, 16, 20, 28 ga., or .410 bore, best-quality H&H pattern sidelock ejector double with chopper lump barrels, level file-cut rib, very fine, full coverage scroll engraving with small floral bouquets, gold crest in forearm, gold crown in top lever, name in gold and finely figured wood.

MSR $31,900	$29,600	$20,900	$17,750	$13,500	$10,050	$7,750	$6,600

GRADING - PPGS™	100%	98%	95%	90%	80%	70%	60%

LUNIK - 12, 16, 20, 28 ga., or .410 bore, best-quality H&H pattern sidelock ejector double with lump (demi-bloc) barrels, level file-cut rib, Renaissance style large scroll engraving in relief, gold crown in top lever, gold name, and gold crest in forearm, finely figured wood.

	MSR $33,200	$30,950	$21,900	$18,750	$14,250	$11,250	$8,700	$6,950

KING EXTRA - 12, 16, 20, 28 ga., or .410 bore, best-quality H&H pattern sidelock ejector double with chopper lump barrels, level file-cut rib, choice of either Bulino game scene engraving or standard cameo game scene engraving with gold inlays, engraved and signed by a master engraver, exhibition grade wood.

	MSR N/A	$35,000	$25,900	$22,000	$16,250	$12,000	$9,250	$7,250

MONACO NUMBER 1 OR 2 - 12, 16, 20, 28 ga., or .410 bore, best-quality H&H pattern sidelock ejector double with lump (demi-bloc) barrels, level file-cut rib, Renaissance style large scroll engraving in relief, gold crown in top lever, gold name, and gold crest in forearm, finely figured wood.

	MSR $40,400	$37,750	$27,000	$22,350	$17,000	$12,500	$9,500	$7,500

MONACO NUMBER 3 - next to top-of-the-line model.

	MSR $43,000	$41,000	$29,000	$24,000	$18,500	$13,250	$9,750	$7,750

MONACO NUMBER 4 - top-of-the-line model with every refinement incorporated. Custom order only and extremely rare.

	MSR $51,600	$48,300	$35,000	$31,500	$25,250	$20,750	$16,000	$13,750

PIRANHA

Previous trademark of a recoilless semi-auto 9mm Para. cal. pistol that was advertised circa 1996, but never manufactured by Recoilless Tech, Inc. located in Phoenix, AZ.

PLAINS RIFLE

A Plains rifle is a modification of the Kentucky rifle. Its original purpose was for use on the western frontier. The Plains rifle is often referred to as a half stock, and first appeared around the end of the first quarter of the 19th century, with production ending by 1880. There was a demand for shorter rifles to be carried on horseback and larger bores for bigger game. Bores ranged from .50 to .60 caliber, and barrel lengths were 36 to 40 inches. Plains rifles are generally found with percussion ignition systems.

Like the Kentucky rifle, Plains rifles were all handmade. Jacob and Samuel Hawken are considered the originators of the Plains rifle. They were the sons of Christian Hawken, Kentucky rifle maker of Hagerstown, MD. The popularity of Jacob and Samuel's guns spread rapidly. Gunmakers from across the country began to copy the Plains style rifle. In addition to the Hawken brothers, other well-known makers were Horace Dimick, J.P. Gemmer, James Henry, and Henry Leman.

Like Kentucky rifles, values for Plains rifles differ greatly, depending on the maker, condition and style. Values can range anywhere from $350-$25,000! Flintlock Plains rifles are scarce.

The publisher would like to thank Mr. Jim Buelow for making the above information available to the *Blue Book of Gun Values*.

GRADING - PPGS™	100%	98%	95%	90%	80%	70%	60%

POLI, ARMI F.LLI

Current manufacturer established in 1966, and located in Gardone, Italy. Currently imported by Cole Gunsmithing, located in Harpswell, ME.

F.lli Poli Armi

Armi F.lli Poli manufactures high quality, SxS and single barrel hammer shotguns in 12, 16, 20, 28 ga. or .410 bore. Current models include the Ivory (hammerless, boxlock action), Opal (hammerless, boxlock action with sideplates), Lapis (lightweight, scalloped boxlock action, hammerless), Onix (scalloped boxlock action, hammerless), Coral (sidelock back action w/hammers), Ruby (petite sidelock back action w/hammers), Emerald (sidelock back action w/hammers), and the Ametist (sidelock, hammerless). Please contact the importer for more information, including pricing and availability (see Trademark Index).

POLY TECHNOLOGIES, INC.

Previously distributed by PTK International, Inc. located in Atlanta, GA. Previously imported by Keng's Firearms Specialty, Inc., located in Riverdale, GA. Manufactured in China by Poly Technologies, Inc.

Poly Technologies commercial firearms are made to Chinese military specifications and have excellent quality control.

These models were banned from domestic importation due to 1989 Federal legislation.

RIFLES: SEMI-AUTO

Add 10% for NIB.

POLY TECH AKS-762 - 7.62x39mm or .223 Rem. cal., 16 1/4 in. barrel, semi-auto version of the Chinese AKM (Type 56) paramilitary design rifle, 8.4 lbs., wood stock. Imported 1988-89.

	$1,250	$1,150	$1,000	$925	$850	$795	$750

Last MSR was $400.

Add $100 for side-fold plastic stock.
This model was also available with a downward folding stock at no extra charge.

CHINESE SKS - 7.62x39mm cal., 20 9/20 in. barrel, full wood stock, machine steel parts to Chinese military specifications, 7.9 lbs. Imported 1988-89.

	$425	$350	$275	$225	$200	$180	$160

Last MSR was $200.

RUSSIAN AK-47/S (LEGEND) - 7.62x39mm cal., 16 3/8 in. barrel, semi-auto configuration of the original AK-47, fixed, side-folding, or under-folding stock, with or w/o spike bayonet, 8.2 lbs. Imported 1988-89.

	$1,550	$1,400	$1,275	$1,100	$995	$925	$850

Last MSR was $550.

Add $50 for folding stock.
The "S" suffix in this variation designates third model specifications.

✸ National Match Legend - utilizes match parts in fabrication.

	$1,700	$1,500	$1,225	$1,050	$975	$900	$825

RPK - 7.62x39mm cal. Disc.

	$1,300	$1,150	$1,025	$925	$850	$775	$700

U.S. M-14/S - .308 Win. cal., 22 in. barrel, forged receiver, patterned after the famous M-14, 9.2 lbs. Imported 1988-89.

	$950	$850	$775	$725	$650	$575	$500

Last MSR was $700.

GRADING - PPGS™	100%	98%	95%	90%	80%	70%	60%

POWELL, WILLIAM & SON (GUNMAKERS) LTD.

Please refer to the W Section for this trademark.

PRAIRIE GUN WORKS

Please refer to PGW Defence Technologies listing.

PRANDELLI-GASPERINI

Previous manufacturer located in Brescia, Italy. Previously imported by Richland Arms located in Blissfield, MI.

Prandelli-Gasperini made both O/U and SxS shotguns in either sidelock or boxlock. Currently, older boxlock models start at approx. $550 (assuming 80% or better original condition). Sidelock models in similar condition usually start at $1,450, depending on gauge, embellishments, and condition.

Approx. 250 specimens of this trademark were imported during Richland Arms importation.

PRECISION SMALL ARMS, INC. ("PSA")

Current manufacturer established in 1979, and made under F.N. license in Montrose, CO beginning in 2005. Previously manufactured in Irvine, CA until 2002, and in Charlottesville, VA until 1999.

PISTOLS: SEMI-AUTO

The PSP pistol was not in full scale production from 1995-2005, but approx. 1,000 nickel plated units were sold to various dealers between 1996-97. The new model manufactured in Montrose, CO is now called the PSA-25, and will be produced on a limited run basis.

(PSP) PSA-25 PISTOL - .25 ACP, single action, Baby Browning design mfg. in the U.S., 2 1/8 in. barrel, 6 shot mag., checkered black polymer grips, all steel construction with choice of polished blue (new 1999), black oxide (disc. 1999), brushed satin white nickel (Nouveau satin), or highly polished white nickel finish (Nouveau mirror), dual safety system, 7 1/4-9 1/2 oz. Mfg. 1989-2002, reintroduced 2005.

MSR $361	$315	$285	$255	$225	$200	$175	$160

Add $28 for Nouveau-Satin finish or $57 for Nouveau-Mirror finish.

This pistol is mfg. in the U.S. under license from Fabrique Nationale.

✳ *PSP-25 Stainless Steel* - features stainless steel construction. Mfg. 1996 only.

				$285	$230	$195	

Last MSR was $327.

✳ *PSP-25 Featherweight* - features aircraft aluminum frame with high polish nickel slide and mag., gold-plated trigger, smooth pearlescent polymer grips. Mfg. 1996-2002, reintroduced 2005.

MSR $545	$475	$425	$375	$335	$300	$275	$250

✳ *PSP-25 Diplomat* - features blue, high polish frame and slide, 24Kt. gold plated external components, ivory grips. Mfg. 1999-2002, reintroduced 2005.

MSR $838	$750	$675	$575	$475	$400	$325	$275

✳ *PSP-25 Montreux* - high polish 24Kt. gold plated frame, slide, and external components, ivory grips. Mfg. 1999-2002, reintroduced 2005.

MSR $928	$850	$750	$625	$525	$425	$350	$300

✳ *PSP-25 Presidential* - features highly polished 24Kt. gold plated slide, frame, magazine, and trigger, Dendrite ivory grips. Disc. 1999.

				$600	$475	$375	

Last MSR was $725.

GRADING - PPGS™	100%	98%	95%	90%	80%	70%	60%

✳ *PSP-25 Renaissance* - features chrome receiver with full coverage scroll engraving. Mfg. 1996-2002, reintroduced 2005.

MSR $1,495	$1,350	$1,175	$995	$875	$775	$675	$575

✳ *PSP-25 Imperiale* - features hand inlaid 24Kt. gold scroll pattern on frame and slide by Angelo Bee, black oxide finish, ivory grips. Limited mfg.

MSR $4,825	$4,400	$3,950	$3,500	$2,950	$2,500	$2,000	$1,650

✳ *PSP Signature Editions* - similar to Imperiale, except has "Michael B. Kassnar" signature on left slide top in gold. Mfg. 1989-91.

	$325	$295	$260	$230	$200	$175	$160

Last MSR was $385.

There were also two Limited Signature Editions (less than 10 mfg.) which retailed for $1,458 and approx. $2,150.

PREMIER

Previous trademark manufactured in Italy and Spain by various companies.

SHOTGUNS: SxS

Note: Premier is a trade name for guns that have been produced in both Spain and Italy for various importers.

REGENT MODEL - 12, 16, 20, 28 ga., or .410 bore, 26, 28, or 30 in. barrels, various chokes, checkered pistol grip stock and beavertail forearm. Mfg. 1955-disc.

	$275	$250	$220	$195	$140	$110	$100

REGENT MAGNUM EXPRESS - 12 ga., 3 in. chambers only, 30 in. full barrel, recoil pad. Mfg. 1957-disc.

	$305	$275	$250	$220	$165	$140	$110

REGENT 10 GAUGE MAGNUM - similar to 12 ga. Mag., but 10 ga., 3 1/2 in. chamber, 32 in. full and full barrel. Mfg. 1975-disc.

	$330	$305	$275	$250	$195	$165	$140

BRUSH KING - 12 or 20 ga., 22 in. imp. cyl. and mod. barrels, straight grip stock. Mfg. 1959-disc.

	$275	$250	$220	$195	$140	$110	$100

MONARCH SUPREME GRADE - 12 or 20 ga., 26 or 28 in. barrels, various chokes, boxlock, auto ejectors, select stock. Mfg. 1959-disc.

	$440	$385	$360	$330	$275	$250	$200

PRESENTATION CUSTOM GRADE - custom-made, gold and silver game scene. Mfg. 1959-disc.

	$1,100	$990	$880	$825	$715	$605	$495

AMBASSADOR MODEL - 12, 16, 20 ga., or .410 bore, 26 or 28 in. barrels, mod. and full choke, checkered pistol grip stock. Mfg. 1957-disc.

	$385	$360	$330	$305	$250	$220	$195

PRINZ

Previous manufacturer of bolt action rifles, single shot rifles, and combination guns. Previously imported and distributed by Helmut Hofmann Inc. located in Placitas, NM.

RIFLES

GRADE 1 BOLT ACTION - .243 Win., .30-06, .308 Win., .300 Win. Mag., or 7mm Rem. Mag. cal., single or double set trigger(s), oil finished walnut stock.

	$495	$440	$385	$360	$330	$275	$250

GRADING - PPGS™	100%	98%	95%	90%	80%	70%	60%

✳ *Grade 1 Carbine* - similar to Grade 1 except has carbine barrel.

	$570	$495	$435	$390	$360	$330	$275

GRADE 2 BOLT ACTION - similar to Grade 1 except has rosewood forend cap.

	$545	$485	$425	$385	$360	$330	$275

TIP-UP RIFLE - available in 8 cals. between .222 Rem. and .30-06, high quality and limited mfg. Importation began 1989.

	$2,175	$1,900	$1,675	$1,375	$1,100	$950	$775

PRINCESS MODEL 85 - combination gun available in 12 ga. (2 3/4 in. chamber) and choice of 8 cals. between .222 Rem. and .30-06.

	$1,450	$1,275	$1,100	$925	$800	$775	$650

This model came standard with a leather case.

PROFESSIONAL ORDNANCE, INC.

Previous manufacturer located in Lake Havasu City, AZ 1998-2003. Previously manufactured in Ontario, CA circa 1996-1997. Distributor sales only.

During 2003, Bushmaster bought Professional Ordnance and the Carbon 15 trademark. Please refer to the Bushmaster section for currently manufactured Carbon 15 rifles and pistols (still manufactured in Lake Havasu City).

PISTOLS: SEMI-AUTO

CARBON-15 TYPE 20 - .223 Rem. cal., Stoner type operating system with recoil reducing buffer assembly, carbon fiber upper and lower receiver, hard chromed bolt carrier, 7 1/4 in. unfluted stainless steel barrel with ghost ring sights, 30 shot mag. (supplies limited), also accepts AR-15 type mags., 40 oz. Mfg. 1999-2000.

$800	$725	$650	$575	$525	$475	$425

Last MSR was $1,500.

CARBON-15 TYPE 21 - .223 Rem cal., ultra lightweight carbon fiber upper and lower receivers, 7 1/4 in. "Profile" stainless steel barrel, quick detachable muzzle compensator, ghost ring sights, 10 shot mag., also accepts AR-15 type mags., Stoner type operating sytem, tool steel bolt, extractor and carrier, 40 oz. Mfg. 2001-2003.

$750	$675	$600	$550	$500	$450	$395

Last MSR was $899.

CARBON-15 TYPE 97 - similar to Carbon 15 Type 20, except has fluted barrel and quick detachable compensator, 46 oz. Mfg. 1996-2003.

$795	$725	$625	$575	$525	$475	$425

Last MSR was $964.

RIFLES: SEMI-AUTO

CARBON-15 TYPE 20 - .223 Rem. cal., same operating system as the Carbon-15 pistol, 16 in. unfluted stainless steel barrel, carbon fiber buttstock and forearm, includes mil spec optics mounting base, 3.9 lbs. Mfg. 1998-2000.

$850	$795	$725	$650	$550	$475	$425

Last MSR was $1,550.

CARBON-15 TYPE 21 - .223 Rem. cal., ultra light weight carbon fiber upper and lower receivers, 16 in. "Profile" stainless steel barrel, quick detachable muzzle compensator, Stoner type operating system, tool steel bolt, extractor and carrier, optics mounting base, quick detachable stock, 10 shot mag., also accepts AR-15 type mags., 3.9 lbs. Mfg. 2001-2003.

$850	$775	$675	$575	$500	$450	$400

Last MSR was $988.

GRADING - PPGS™	100%	98%	95%	90%	80%	70%	60%

CARBON-15 TYPE 97/97S - .223 Rem. cal., ultra lighweight carbon fiber upper and lower receivers, Stoner type operating system, hard chromed tool steel bolt, extractor and carrier, 16 in. fluted stainless steel barrel, quick detachable muzzle compensator, optics mounting base, quick detachable stock, 30 shot mag. (limited quantities), also accepts AR-15 type mags., 3.9 lbs. Mfg. 2001-2003.

			$900	$825	$750	$675	$600	$550	$500

Last MSR was $1,120.

Add $165 for Model 97S (includes Picatinny rail and "Scout" extension, double walled heat shield foregrip, ambidextrous safety, and multi-carry silent sling).

PUMA RIFLES

Current trademark of rifles imported by Legacy Sports International LLC, located in Alexandria, VA.

RIFLES: LEVER ACTION

MODEL 92 - .357 Mag./.38 Spl., .44 Mag., .45 LC, .454 Casull (new 2002, carbine only), or .480 Ruger (new 2004) cal., 9 (.454 Casull) or 10 shot tube mag., 20 in. round or 24 in. octagon barrel, choice of blue, brass, case colored frame, or stainless steel receiver and barrel, regular or large loop (.357 Mag. or .45 LC cal. only, new 2005), unchecked walnut stock and forearm. Importation began 2001.

✻ *Round Barrel Carbine* - .357 Mag./.38 Spl., .44 Mag., .45 LC, .454 Casull (new 2002), or .480 Ruger (new 2004) cal., blue, brass, case colored, or stainless steel, 20 in. ported (.44 Mag. or .454 Casull cal. only, new 2005) or unported barrel, 6.1 lbs.

MSR $450	$380	$315	$275	$235	$200	$175	$155

Add $116 for stainless steel construction.
Add $37 for HiViz sights.
Add $65 for HiViz sights and ported barrel (not available on .357 Mag. or .45 LC cal.).
Add $58 for .454 Casull or $34 for .480 Ruger cal.
Add $7 for brass (.357 Mag./.38 Spl. or .45 LC cal. only).

✻ *Octagon Barrel Rifle* - .357 Mag./.38 Spl., .44 Mag., or .45 LC cal., choice of blue/case colored, stainless steel, or stainless steel/brass (not available in .44 Mag. cal.), 24 in. octagon barrel, 7.7 lbs.

MSR $552	$430	$375	$315	$275	$235	$200	$180

Add $7 for blue/case colored finish.
Add $7 for brass.
Add $29 for buckhorn sights and saddle ring (new 2002).
Add $58 for stainless steel construction.
Add $65 for stainless steel/brass construction.

✻ *Model 92 Limited Edition* - .454 Casull (new 2002), or .480 Ruger (new 2004) cal., stainless steel, satin walnut straight grip stock, 16 in. barrel, 7 shot tube mag., 6 lbs. New 2004.

MSR $603	$495	$395	$335	$280	$240	$215	$195

This model is available exclusively from Davidson's.

PURDEY, JAMES & SONS, LTD.

Current manufacturer established in 1814, and located in London, England. Annual production is approximately 75 guns.

Purdey guns have long been regarded as among the finest in the world. They have typically been made to customer specifications, and as such, should be appraised individually for purposes of evaluation. Values vary with gauge, barrel length, chamber length and age. Listed are the modern models and approximate values for reference purposes.

GRADING - PPGS™	100%	98%	95%	90%	80%	70%	60%

Prices indicated are for manufacturer's suggested retail and 100% condition factors are listed in English pounds. All new prices do not include VAT. Values for used guns in 98%-60% condition factors are priced in U.S. dollars.

RIFLES: CUSTOM ORDER & OLDER PRODUCTION

New rifle prices represent the base price with standard fine scroll and bouquet engraving.

PURDEY DOUBLE RIFLE - various English Nitro Express cals., 25 1/2 in. barrels, folding leaf sight, checkered pistol grip stock, recoil pad, sidelock, auto ejectors. Mfg. pre-WWII and post-war.

* *Smaller calibers* - .300 H&H or .375 H&H cal.

	100%	98%	95%	90%	80%	70%	60%
MSR £77,500	£77,500	$75,000	$62,000	$45,000	$33,750	$26,500	$21,500

* *Large calibers*

>.416 Rigby - .500 NE

	100%	98%	95%	90%	80%	70%	60%
MSR £85,200	£85,200	$86,000	$72,000	$50,000	$38,750	$30,250	$26,500

>577 NE & .600 NE

	100%	98%	95%	90%	80%	70%	60%
MSR £94,000	£94,000	$105,500	$89,500	$70,000	$52,000	$48,500	$40,250

The values represent base price only. Since each Purdey is basically a special order, new gun pricing is calculated per individual customer work order.

MAGAZINE RIFLE - cals. up to .375 H&H are built on a Purdey or Mauser action, 24 in. barrel, folding leaf sight, checkered best quality walnut pistol grip stock, individually built per customer specifications.

	100%	98%	95%	90%	80%	70%	60%
MSR £17,500	£17,500	$19,500	$16,000	$13,500	$9,750	$8,500	$7,000

Add £2,300 for Purdey rail mount (for scopes).

MAGNUM MAGAZINE RIFLE - .375 H&H, .416/450, and .500 cal., built on Purdey's dedicated Magnum action, individually built per customer's specifications.

	100%	98%	95%	90%	80%	70%	60%
MSR £18,750	£18,750	$23,500	$18,000	$14,500	$11,250	$9,650	$8,500

Add £2,300 for Purdey rail mount (for scopes).

SHOTGUNS: CUSTOM ORDER & OLDER PRODUCTION

New shotgun prices represent the base price with standard fine scroll and bouquet engraving.

BEST QUALITY GAME GUN SxS - 10, 12, 16, 20, 28 ga., or .410 bore, best quality sidelock action. 26-30 in. barrels, any choke and style of rib, checkered straight or pistol grip stock. Mfg. 1880-present, auto ejector gun, best quality only.

	100%	98%	95%	90%	80%	70%	60%
MSR £46,500	£46,500	$47,000	$38,500	$31,750	$22,000	$17,500	$14,250

Add £2,000 for 28 ga., or £5,500 for .410 bore or 10 ga. on new mfg.

Add £9,400-£9,600 for extra set of barrels depending on gauge.

* *Older mfg.*

>Game gun

	98%	95%	90%	80%	70%	60%	
$23,450	$19,750	$16,750	$13,000	$10,750	$9,250	$7,950	

>Heavy Duck gun

	98%	95%	90%	80%	70%	60%	
	$20,500	$17,000	$14,000	$11,000	$9,500	$8,750	$7,500

Add 50% for 20 ga.

Add 35%-50% for 28 ga. or .410 bore, depending on condition.

Subtract 10%-15% if not cased with accessories.

Add $1,000 for SST.

GRADING - PPGS™	100%	98%	95%	90%	80%	70%	60%

O/U GUN - 12, 16, 20, 28 ga., or .410 bore best quality sidelock action. 26-30 in. barrels, any choke, auto ejectors, ST, checkered straight or pistol grip stock. Since WWII, Purdey has taken over the Woodward Company, and later guns have the Woodward O/U action. Very few early actions.

	MSR £55,000	£55,000	$57,000	$43,000	$30,000	$25,000	$21,000	$18,500

Add £3,000 for 28 ga. or £7,200 for .410 bore.

Add £14,300 (same ga.) or £16,975 (different ga.) for extra set of barrels.

❋ *Older mfg.*

	$37,500	$33,000	$30,000	$26,000	$21,500	$17,750	$15,000

Add $3,000 for Woodward action.

Add 25% for 20 ga.

Add 60%+ for 28 ga.

Add 10% for SST.

HAMMER EJECTOR GAME GUN - 12 or 20 ga., special order only. Mfg. began 2002.

	MSR£48,500	£48,500	$47,000	$35,000	$27,000	$21,000	$15,000	$10,000

SINGLE BARREL TRAP GUN - 12 ga. Purdey action only, similar to O/U specifications. Mfg. prior to WWII.

	$11,250	$10,000	$8,750	$7,900	$7,200	$6,750	$5,950

Q SECTION

QFI (QUALITY FIREARMS INC.)

Previous manufacturer located in Opa Locka, FL circa December 1990-1992.

GRADING - PPGS™	100%	98%	95%	90%	80%	70%	60%

PISTOLS: SEMI-AUTO

MODEL LA380 - .380 ACP cal., single action, 6-shot, magazine disconnect, hammer, trigger, and firing pin block safety, 3 1/4 in. barrel, blue or chrome finish. Mfg. 1991-92.

	$125	$100	$90	$80	$70	$60	$55

Last MSR was $147.

Add $23 for chrome finish.

✳ *Model LA380SS* - stainless steel variation of the Model LA380. Mfg. 1992 only.

	$195	$165	$135

Last MSR was $220.

MODEL SA 25 - .25 ACP cal., single action, 2 1/2 in. barrel, 6-shot, includes inertial firing pin, external exposed hammer with half cock, and trigger blocking thumb safety, blue, Dynachrome, or blue/gold finish, smooth walnut grips. Mfg. 1991 only.

	$55	$45	$40	$35	$30	$25	$25

Last MSR was $55.

Add $50 for blue/gold finish.
Add $10 for chrome finish with pearlite plastic grips.

TIGRESS MODEL - .25 ACP or .380 ACP cal., single action, 2 1/2 (.25 ACP) or 3 1/4 (.380 ACP) in. barrel, blue frame with gold-plated slide, 6-shot with finger extension on mag., white polymer grips with a red rose scrimshawed on both sides, designed for women, supplied with zippered gold pouch, 14 or 25 oz. Mfg. 1991 only.

	$130	$100	$90	$80	$70	$60	$55

Last MSR was $155.

Add $85 for .380 ACP cal.

REVOLVERS: DOUBLE ACTION

All revolvers under this heading are 6-shot.

RP SERIES STANDARD REVOLVER - .22 LR, .22 Mag., .32 S&W Long, .32 H&R Mag or .38 Spl. cal., 2 or 4 in. barrel, blue or chrome finish, fixed sights, hammer block safety, without ejector assembly, composition grips. Mfg. in U.S. 1990-disc.

	$85	$70	$65	$60	$55	$50	$45

Last MSR was $105.

Add $15-20 for chrome finish.
Add approx. $5 for 4 in. barrel.

MODEL SO 38 - .38 Spl. cal., swing out cylinder, 6-shot, 2 in. SR or 4 in. VR barrel, hammer block safety, composition grips. Mfg. 1991 only.

	$175	$135	$115	$95	$80	$75	$65

Last MSR was $175.

REVOLVERS: SINGLE ACTION

SAA WESTERN RANGER - .22 LR cal., 6-shot, 3, 4 (disc. 1991), 4 3/4 (new 1992), 6 (disc. 1991), 6 1/2 (new 1992), 7 (disc. 1991), or 9 in. barrel, blue finish with gold accenting, walnut grips. Mfg. 1991-92.

	$85	$70	$65	$60	$55	$50	$45

Last MSR was $105.

GRADING - PPGS™	100%	98%	95%	90%	80%	70%	60%

Add approx. $5 for 7 (disc.) or $7 for 9 in. barrel.

Add approx. $15-$35 for .22 Mag. extra cylinder (combo).

SAA PLAINS RIDER - similar to Western Ranger, except has black composition grips and no gold accenting. Mfg. 1991-92.

	$80	$65	$55	$50	$45	$40	$35

Last MSR was $100.

Add $11 for 9 in. barrel.

Add approx. $26 for .22 Mag. extra cylinder (combo).

SAA HORSEMAN SERIES - .357 Mag., .44 Mag., or .45 LC cal., 6-shot, 6 1/2 or 7 1/2 in. barrel, color case hardened or blue (Dark Horseman only) finish, walnut or black composition grips, hammer block safety. Mfg. 1991 only.

$250	$220	$190	$170	$150	$130	$115

Last MSR was $250.

The Dark Horseman had an extended grip frame with black composition grips and an adj. rear sight.

QUACKENBUSH, H.M.

Previous rifle manufacturer circa 1886-1922, and located in Herkimer, NY. Quackenbush also manufactured airguns 1871-1943.

For more information on Quackenbush airguns, including the combination rimfire/airgun, please refer to the *Blue Book of Airguns*, by Dr. Robert Beeman & John Allen (also online).

RIFLES: .22 CAL., RIMFIRE

Only one breech mechanism was used on all H.M. Quackenbush .22 cal. rimfire rifles, the company's only rifle configuration. They used a swing breech and were all single shot. These models were supplied in several different boxes, and often came with a cleaning rod. These and other accessories will significantly add to the value of the firearms prices listed. No serial numbers were applied to Quackenbush guns. Many variations of these models are encountered, which can also add premiums to the values listed. Quackenbush also manufactured heavy metal targets for these rifles 1884-1931.

SAFETY RIFLE - single shot, swinging breech, walnut stock, 18 or 22 in. barrel. Mfg. 1886-1922.

	$600	$500	$425	$375	$350	$325	$300

Add 10% for each of the following with heavy cast iron buttplate, original factory blue finish, optional Town & Country combination rear and front sights, or for barrel and optional sights where rear sight is approx. 1 in. forward of the breech end of the barrel.

JUNIOR SAFETY RIFLE - similar to Safety Model, except smaller and has tubular receiver, wire stocked, swinging breech, 18 in. barrel only. Mfg. 1890-1920.

	$800	$700	$600	$500	$400	$375	$350

Add 10% for original factory blue finish.

BYCYCLE RIFLE - similar to Safety Model, retractable wire stock, smaller, and has a wire pistol grip, fixed rear sight, nickel finish, 12 in. barrel. Mfg. 1896-1919.

	$1,800	$1,750	$1,550	$1,300	$1,150	$1,000	$700

Add 10% for original factory blue finish.

Subtract 50% if retractable shoulder stock is missing.

Manufacturer	Model	Quantity	Year	Issue Price

QUAIL UNLIMITED, INC.

Current national conservation organization with national headquarters located in Edgefield, SC.

Although Quail Unlimited, Inc. is not a manufacturer or importer, this organization has been responsible for many special and limited editions. These are listed below with quantities, but without secondary market prices, since they may vary greatly from region to region. Some of the models (and current values) may be listed under manufacturer listings in this text. Because of the relatively low quantities involved with these special editions, most of the models listed below have premiums currently being asked over issue prices, and the amount will vary with the region and acceptance by Quail Unlimited members. Quail Unlimited designated their special editions as follows: 1986 - Grand Slam I - Bobwhite Edition, 1987 - Grand Slam II - California Edition, 1988 - Grand Slam III - Gambel Edition, 1989 - Grand Slam IV - Mountain Quail Edition, 1990 - Grand Slam V - Scaled Quail Edition, 1992 - Gun Dog I - Pointer Edition, 1993 - Gun Dog II - Setter Edition, 1994 - Gun Dog III - Brittany Edition, 1995 - Gun Dog IV - German Shorthair Edition, 1996 - Gun Dog V - Belgian Edition. 1994 - Golden Covey I - Full Covey Edition, 1995 - Golden Covey II - Bobwhite Edition, 1997 - Upland I - Ruffed Grouse Edition.

Manufacturer	Model	Quantity	Year	Issue Price
Browning	Superposed 20 ga.	100	1986	$2,850
Winchester	Model 101 28 ga.	100	1987	$2,195
Browning	Sweet 16 16 ga.	100	1988	$1,895
Winchester	Model 23 12 ga.	100	1989	$2,885
Browning	Citori Lightning .410 bore	100	1990	$2,295

Add $500 to issue price for silver finish (standard finish was nickel).
Add $700 to issue price for gold finish (standard finish was nickel).

Manufacturer	Model	Quantity	Year	Issue Price
Browning	Model A-5 20 ga.	100	1992	$1,795
Browning	Citori Lightning 28 ga.	100	1993	$2,395
Browning	Model A-5 20 ga.	100	1993	$1,795
Browning	Citori Lightning .410 bore	100	1994	$2,395
Browning	Citori Lightning German Shorthair 20 ga.	100	1995	$2,395
Belgian Browning	Model A-5 20 ga. 3 in. GRIII (15th Anniv.)	75	1996	$2,195
Belgian Browning	Model A-5 20 ga. 3 in. GRV (15th Anniv.)	25	1996	$3,995
Rizzini	SxS 20 ga. (15th Anniv.)	34	1996	$2,850
Rizzini	SxS 20 ga. (Gold) (15th Anniv.)	15	1996	$4,250
Browning	Citori Superlight 20 ga.	100	1997	$2,495
Winchester	Model 12 20 ga.	100	1997	$995
Winchester	Model 12 20 ga.Chevy/QU Exclusive	298	1997	$995
Browning	Citori Superlight 28 ga.	100	1998	$2,495
Browning	Model A-5 Chevrolet	299	1998	$1,495
Franchi	620 VS 20 ga.	100	1999	$1,195
Browning	Citori Upland 12 ga.	100	1999	$2,495
Beretta	Whitewing TWRA Executive Ed. 12 or 20	72	1999	$1,595
Beretta	AL390 TWRA Reg. Ed. 12 or 20 ga.	40	1999	$995
Beretta	AL390 TWRA Youth Ed. 12 or 20 ga.	25	1999	$995
Browning	Citori Superlight 20 ga.	100	2000	$2,495
Sturm Ruger	Red Label 28 ga. Chevrolet	259	2000	$1,995
Franchi	Feniche 28 ga. 20th Anniversary	125	2000	$1,195
Ithaca Gun	Model 37 16 ga. 20th Anniversary	150	2000	$995
Franchi	620 VS 20 ga. Chevrolet	400	2001	$1,395
Browning	Citori Superlight .410 bore	100	2001	$2,495
Franchi	Feniche 28 ga. Encore	100	2001	$1,295
Franchi	620VS 20 ga. Chevrolet	252	2001	$1,395
Browning	Triton Upland Special 20 ga.	50	2002	$1,695

Manufacturer	Model	Quantity	Year	Issue Price
Browning	Citori Feather 20 ga.	100	2002	$2,595
Browning	Gold Auto 20 ga. Heritage I Ed. (GR2)	75	2002	$1,895
Browning	Gold Auto 20 ga., Heritage I Ed. (GR3)	25	2002	$2,195
Charles Daly	Superior Hunter 20 ga. 20th Anniversary	100	2002	$789
Browning	Gold Auto 12 ga. Heritage I Ed. (GR2)	75	2003	$1,895
Browning	Gold Auto 12 ga., Heritage I Ed. (GR3)	25	2003	$2,195
Franchi	620VS 20 ga. Dinner Gun	150	2003	$1,295
Charles Daly	Superior Hunter II 28 ga.	50	2003	$799

QUALITY PARTS CO./BUSHMASTER

Quality Parts Co. is a division of Bushmaster Firearms, Inc. located in Windham, ME that manufactures AR-15 type paramilitary rifles and various components and accessories for them. Distributor and dealer sales. Please refer to the Bushmaster section in this text for model listings and values.

R SECTION

RAF

Previous manufacturer of shotguns and rifles located in St. Etienne, France circa 1994-96. RAF manufactured superposed rifles, shotguns, combination guns, and semi-auto rimfire rifles.

RBA

Current competition pistol manufacturer located in Granarolo Emilia, Italy. No current U.S. importation.

Renzo Bonora Armi (RBA) currently manufactures high quality competition pistols in both .22 LR and .32 S&W Wadcutter. Please contact the factory directly for more information, including pricing and U.S. availablility (see Trademark Index).

RND MANUFACTURING

Current manufacturer located in CO. Previously distributed by Mesa Sportsmen's Association, L.L.C. located in Delta, CO. Dealer or consumer direct sales.

GRADING - PPGS™	100%	98%	95%	90%	80%	70%	60%

RIFLES: SEMI-AUTO

THE EDGE SERIES - .223 Rem. (RND 400), .300 WSM (new 2003), .300 RSM (new 2003), .338 Lapua Mag. (RND 2000, new 1999) or 7.62x39mm cal., patterned after the AR-15, CNC machined, 18, 20, or 24 in. barrel, choice of synthetic (Grade I), built to individual custom order, handmade laminated thumbhole (Grade II, disc. 1998), or custom laminated thumbhole with fluted barrel (Grade III, disc. 1998) stock, vented aluminum shroud, approx. 11 1/2-16 lbs., custom order only, values represent base model. New 1996.

MSR N/A	$2,275	$2,075	$1,775	$1,575	$1,375	$1,200	$1,075

Add $355 for Grade II.
Add $605 for Grade III or .308 Win. cal.
Add $1,855 for .338 Lapua Mag. cal.

R.F.M.

Please refer to Rota, Luciano listing.

R.G. INDUSTRIES

Previous importer located in Miami, FL. Operations ceased in January of 1986.

HANDGUNS

R.G. Industries manufactured and imported plain utilitarian revolvers and semi-auto pistols. Unfortunately, because of a product liability situation, R.G. Industries was litigated out of business during 1986. Although their models represent good values, they are not collectible, and so a generalized listing is provided.

RG 14 S, RG 23, RG 31

	$95	$80	$70	$60	$55	$50	$45

RG 40, RG 74, & HIGHNOON S.A.

	$125	$115	$95	$80	$70	$60	$55

RG 26 SEMI-AUTO - .25 ACP cal., 6 shot mag., 2 1/4 in. barrel, plastic grips, single action, 12 oz.

	$65	$55	$50	$40	$35	$30	$25

Last MSR was $66.

RPB INDUSTRIES

Current company located in Avondale, GA. RPB Industries' guns are made by Masterpiece Arms. Consumer and dealer sales.

CARBINES: SEMI-AUTO

RPB CARBINE - .45 ACP cal., closed bolt blowback action, 16 1/4 in. barrel, fixed skeletonized stock and forearm pistol grip, accepts M-3 mags., black finish, 9 1/2 lbs. New 2000.

	No MSR	$450	$375	$325	$285	$260	$235	$210

Add $75 for Deluxe Model with EZ cocker and installed scope mount.

RPM

Previous manufacturer located in Affton, MO 2002-2003. Previously located in Tuscon, AZ.

During 2004, RPM changed the name of the company to Gateway Precision Arms. Please refer to this listing for current information.

PISTOLS: SINGLE SHOT

XL PISTOL - many cals. available, tip-up action, 8, 10 3/4, 12, or 14 in. barrel, positive thumb safety, steel frame, cocking indicator, right- or left-hand action. Disc.

	$785	$675	$600	$550	$500	$450	$395

Last MSR was $858.

XL HUNTER - please refer to Gateway Precision Arms for current information on this model.

RWS

Current trademark of Dynamit Nobel GmbH which has been manufacturing firearms and airguns in Nuremberg, Stadeln, and Troisdorf, Germany since 1865. Dynamit Nobel is now a division of RUAG AmmoTec GmbH, located in Furth, Germany. RWS firearms were imported until 1995 by Dynamit Nobel of America, Inc. located in Closter, NJ. Other trademarks (including Rottweil) by Dynamit Nobel can be located under individual heading names in this text.

For more information and current pricing on both new and used RWS airguns produced by Dianawerk, Mayer, and Grammelspacher, please refer to the *Blue Book of Airguns* by Dr. Robert Beeman & John Allen (also online).

RIFLES: BOLT ACTION, TARGET

MODEL 820 L - .22 LR cal. only, 24 (disc.) or 26 in. barrel, no. 100 aperture sight, oil polished stock for 3 position match, stippled pistol grip and forearm, recoil pad, adj. trigger, 10.6 lbs. Disc. 1994.

	$1,275	$1,000	$850	$700	$575	$475	$400

Last MSR was $1,500.

Previous to 1986 this model was designated the 820 S and was supplied with a no. 75 aperture rear sight.

✻ *Model 820 S* - with Model 82 aperture sight.

	$1,100	$895	$795	$650	$560	$480	$420

Last MSR was $995.

MODEL 820 F MATCH - similar to Model 820 L, except has heavy match barrel, 15.4 lbs. Disc. 1994.

	$1,750	$1,400	$1,275	$1,000	$850	$700	$575

Last MSR was $2,000.

GRADING - PPGS™	100%	98%	95%	90%	80%	70%	60%
✳ *Model 820 SF* - with Model 820 L aperture sight. Disc.							
	$1,125	$900	$795	$650	$560	$480	$420

Last MSR was $1,010.

MODEL 820 K - .22 LR cal. only, made for running boar competition, 24 in. barrel, stock similar to Model 820 SF, no sights, 9 1/2 lbs. without barrel weight or scope. Importation disc. 1986.

	$900	$775	$695	$615	$540	$470	$420

Last MSR was $870.

RADOM

Currently manufactured by Z.M. Lucznik (Radom Factory) in Radom, Poland. Currently imported by Dalvar of USA, located in Seligman, AZ. Previously located in Richardson, TX and Henderson, NV. 1931-1939 production also by the Polish Arsenal, located in Radom, Poland.

REVOLVERS

RADOM REVOLVER - Nagant design, dated 1931-36.

	$1,500	$1,200	$1,000	$800	$600	$500	$400

PISTOLS: SEMI-AUTO, 1935-1939 PRODUCTION

P-35 AUTOMATIC - 9mm Para. cal., 8 shot, 4 3/4 in. barrel, blue, fixed sights, plastic grips. Mfg. 1935-WWII.

✳ *Polish Eagle* - dated 1936, 1937 (scarcest date), 1938, or 1939.

	$2,500	$1,600	$1,000	$700	$500	$400	$300

Add 15% for 1937 mfg.

Add 10% for 1936 mfg.

✳ *Polish Eagle Nazi Capture*

	N/A	$1,825	$1,200	$900	$700	$600	$500

Beware of fakes!

✳ *Nazi Type I Slotted*

	$1,000	$800	$600	$450	$300	$250	$200

✳ *Nazi Type II No Slot w/ Takedown Lever*

	$650	$475	$325	$225	$200	$185	$150

✳ *Nazi Type III No Slot, No Takedown Lever*

	$475	$350	$240	$200	$180	$160	$140

✳ *Nazi Type III* - parkerized with wood grips, small parts blue.

	$1,250	$1,000	$750	$550	$400	$300	$250

Note: Certain Radoms with German acceptance marks will bring a premium.

PISTOLS: SEMI-AUTO, RECENT PRODUCTION

VIS P-35 - 9mm Para. cal., patterned after the 1937 P-35, large Polish eagle stamped on left side of slide, with or w/o slotted rear grip strap for shoulder stock, 4 1/2 in. barrel, 36 oz. Limited mfg. 1997 only.

	$2,600	$1,425	$850	$625	$450	$375	$300

Last MSR was $2,999.

VANAD P-83 - 9x18mm Makarov cal., 8 shot mag., available in Standard Military Issue or Special Eagle Limited Edition, loaded chamber indicator, firing pin block safety, steel receiver with external hammer, 3 1/2 in. barrel, drift adj. target sights, checkered composition grips, 26 oz. Importation began 1994 (Standard Military Issue) or 1997.

MSR $390	$350	$290	$265	$235	$210	$190	$170

Add $46 for Standard Military Issue.

MAG 95 - 9mm Para. cal., single or double action with firing pin block, external hammer, ambidextrous hammer drop safety, 4 1/2 in. barrel, 37 oz. Limited importation 1997 only.

	$650	$550	$450	$400	$350	$300	$275

Last MSR was $749.

RAM-LINE, INC.

Previous manufacturer located in Grand Junction, CO until 1995.

In addition to the Ram-Tech pistol, Ram-Line, Inc. also manufactured a complete line of synthetic and wood stocks for a variety of firearms. Ram-Line continues to manufacture a complete line of magazines for most popular pistols and rifles.

PISTOLS: SEMI-AUTO

EXACTOR PISTOL - .22 LR cal., single action, aircraft alloy receiver with 5 1/2 in. polymer VR barrel and steel liner, unique two-motion safety featuring blocks on hammer, trigger, and sear, 15 shot mag., matte finish, easy disassembly, injected molded grip, fixed sight, 20.3 oz., supplied with case. Mfg. 1990-93.

	$195	$165	$135

Last MSR was $225.

✱ **Target Exactor** - similar to above, except has 7 1/2 in. barrel, 23 oz. Disc. 1993.

	$265	$230	$195

Last MSR was $300.

RAM-TECH PISTOL - similar to Exactor pistol, except 4 1/2 in. barrel w/o VR. Mfg. 1994-95.

	$175	$145	$125

Last MSR was $200.

RAMO DEFENSE SYSTEMS

Previous rifle manufacturer 1999-2003 and located in Nashville, TN.

RIFLES: BOLT ACTION

TACTICAL .308 - .308 Win. cal., Rem. M-700 long action, match grade stainless steel barrel, skeletonized black synthetic stock with cheekpad, matte black metal finish, 4 shot mag., 16 lbs. Mfg. 1999-2003.

	$2,495	$2,100	$1,850	$1,600	$1,400	$1,200	$995

Last MSR was $2,495.

M91/M91A2 - .308 Win. or .300 Win. Mag. cal., Rem. M-700 long action, black Kevlar and fiberglass stock, matte black metal finish, 4 shot mag., 14 lbs. Mfg. 1999-2003.

	$2,695	$2,250	$1,950	$1,675	$1,475	$1,250	$995

Last MSR was $2,695.

Add $200 for .300 Win. Mag. cal.

M600 SINGLE SHOT - .50 BMG cal., single shot, twin tube skeletonized stock with pistol grip and cheekpiece, 32 in. barrel with fins at breech and muzzle brake, 23 lbs. Mfg. 1999-2003.

	$4,195	$3,700	$3,200	$2,750	$2,250	$1,950	$1,675

Last MSR was $4,195.

M650 REPEATER - .50 BMG cal., repeater action with 6 shot detachable rotary mag., stock and barrel (30 in.) similar to M600, approx. 30 lbs. Mfg. 1999-2003.

	$6,395	$5,750	$5,150	$4,500	$3,750	$3,000	$2,250

Last MSR was $6,395.

GRADING - PPGS™	100%	98%	95%	90%	80%	70%	60%

RANDALL FIREARMS COMPANY

Previously manufactured in Sun Valley, CA. Manufactured between June 7, 1983 and December 15, 1984 - final plant closing was June 15, 1985.

Before manufacturing ceased in May of 1985, 24 models with 12 variations in 3 different calibers had been produced. In some instances, production on certain models was very limited and premiums for these low volume niches are starting to develop. Between June of 1983 and May of 1984, 9,968 handguns were manufactured with 75% of all 9mm Para. pistols being exported to Europe and 35% of 9mm Para. production employing a 10 groove barrel. Models manufactured after 1984 came equipped with an extended slide stop, long trigger, and beavertail grip safety. Production ser. nos. started at 02000 for right-hand models and 02100 for left-hand models. All but the first 200 (approx.) serial numbers started with "RF" and ended with "C" or "W." A few rare mismarks are in circulation. Total mfg. for all models and variations was 9,968. Randall prototype serialization starts with a "T" - less than 45 were manufactured and these specimens command up to a 50% premium. In addition, 78 serial numbers under 2,000 were manufactured by special order.

Models listed are generally described with values per specific variations listed afterward.

PISTOLS: SEMI-AUTO

The following is a complete listing for Randall Firearms variations including production statistics. Values shown represent recent aftermarket prices, but it should be noted that regional interest can change these prices significantly.

All original Randall pistols had no blue parts. Only the front and rear sights were finished in black oxide.

> **100% Randall prices assume NIB condition with paperwork.**
> **Add 50% for prototypes with "T" serial numbers.**

COMBAT MODEL - same size as Service Model, ribbed top fixed sight slide, Pachmayr grips on right-hand model only, left-hand models had Herrett walnut grips. While this model was advertised as having a flat mainspring housing, it never went into production.

Last MSR was $549.

RAIDER/SERVICE MODEL-C - 9mm Para. or .45 ACP cal., Colt Commander Model design, 4 1/4 in. barrel, 36 oz., total stainless steel construction. Add $130 for adj. sights/ribbed slide, available in either right-hand or left-hand (only 2 mfg.) model. Roll-marked Service Model-C in 1983 and Raider in 1984.

Last MSR was $460.

✱ *Raider/Service Model-C Featherweight* - .45 ACP cal. only, alloy receiver, stainless steel slide, roll-marked Service Model-C, T-type serial numbers, 29 oz. Disc. 1984, only 4 mfg.

FULL SIZE SERVICE MODEL - .38 Super, 9mm Para., or .45 ACP cal., Colt Model 1911 A1 design, 5 in. barrel, total stainless steel construction, 38 oz. Available in either right-hand or left-hand model.

Last MSR was $460.

CURTIS E. LEMAY 4-STAR MODEL - 9mm Para. or .45 ACP cal., Gen. Curtis E. LeMay design, 4 1/4 in. barrel, 6 (.45 ACP) or 7 (9mm Para.) shot mag., total stainless steel construction, 35 oz. Available in either right-hand or left-hand model, left-hand models are a true mirror image with over 17 major parts changes.

Last MSR was $533.

This model was 1/2 in. shorter in magazine well and had a cast, squared-off triggerguard compared to the Colt 1911A1 design.

GRADING - PPGS™	100%	98%	95%	90%	80%	70%	60%

✸ **Curtis E. LeMay Featherweight Model** - .45 ACP cal. only, alloy receiver, stainless steel slide, T-type serial numbers, 28 oz. Disc. 1984 (only one mfg.).

RANDALL MATCHED SETS - .45 ACP cal. only, each set consisted of a right-hand and a left-hand Service Model with matching serial numbers. Only 4 sets were mfg. on a special order basis. A111/B111 model configuration.

Last MSR was $1,250.

Randall Variations & Identification

Randall pistols are denoted by a four-character model notation, starting with an alphabetical prefix followed by three digits. The alphabetical prefix will be either A, B, or C. A designates right-hand configuration only, B designates left-hand configuration only, and C designates right-hand light-weight model. The first numerical digit will be 1, 2, or 3. 1 denotes Service Model, 2 denotes Service Model - C or Raider, and 3 represents the C.E. LeMay Model. The second numerical digit will be either 1, 2, or 3. 1 designates round top and fixed sight slide, 2 denotes flattop fixed sight slide, and 3 represents adj. sights, flattop frame. The third numerical digit will also be either 1, 2, or 3. 1 denotes .45 ACP cal., 2 designates 9mm Para., and 3 represents .38 Super. Hence, if you had a left-hand Randall in the service model size with a flattop adj. sight slide, and in .45 ACP cal., your model would be a B131. These model codes are not marked on the pistols.

A111 - 3,421 mfg.

$680	$595	$510	$465

Five A111s were mfg. with Austrian proofmarks with premiums existing.

A112 - 301 mfg.

$895	$795	$650	$525

A121 - 1,067 mfg.

$700	$625	$510	$465

A122 - 19 mfg.

$1,325	$1,125	$940	$795

A131 - 2,083 mfg.

$725	$640	$535	$495

A211 - 992 mfg.

$750	$660	$535	$480

A212 - 76 mfg.

$925	$815	$600	$500

A231 - 574 mfg.

$850	$750	$535	$505

A232 - 5 mfg.

$1,500	$1,075	$990	$775

A311 - 361 mfg.

$1,100	$950	$725	$575

Most LeMay models (4 1/4 in. barrel) were shipped in gun rugs without a factory box. Original factory LeMay boxes are rare - add 10% premium. Beware of Randall LeMay and service model pistols made from parts kits. There were 226 LeMay receivers and 322 service model receivers (all right-hand) sold that could be parts guns.

A312 - 1 mfg.

Rarity precludes accurate price evalution.

A331 - 293 mfg.

$1,200	$1,075	$700	$595

The note that appears for the Model A311 also applies to this variation.

A332 - 9 mfg.

$1,450	$1,275	$975	$825

GRADING - PPGS™	100%	98%	95%	90%	80%	70%	60%
B111 - 297 mfg.							
	$1,250	$1,100	$850	$750			
B121 - 110 mfg.							
	$1,500	$1,325	$1,075	$895			

B122 - 2 mfg.

Rarity precludes accurate price evaluation.

B123 - 2 mfg.

Rarity precludes accurate price evaluation.

B131 - 225 mfg.							
	$1,450	$1,250	$925	$775			
B311 - 52 mfg.							
	$1,575	$1,325	$895	$750			

B312 w/ .45 ACP FACTORY CONVERSION - 1 mfg.

Rarity precludes accurate price evaluation.

B312 - 9 mfg.							
	$2,750	$2,300	$1,800	$1,550			

B321 - 1 mfg.

Rarity precludes accurate price evaluation. The B321 was the only factory 3-slide set. It was fitted with the 3 different LH LeMay slides available (B311, B321, & B331). This model was mirror polished, engraved, and had ivory grips with the Randall logo.

B331 - 45 mfg.							
	$1,775	$1,495	$1,050	$875			

B2/321 - 1 mfg.

Rarity precludes accurate price evaluation. This was the only factory model variation to leave Randall Firearms. This was a left-hand Raider with the C.E. LeMay slide.

C211 - 5 mfg.

Rarity precludes accurate price evaluation.

C331 - 1 mfg.

Rarity precludes accurate price evaluation.

C332 - 4 mfg.

Rarity precludes accurate price evaluation.

* *Matched Sets* - large premiums exist for different models with the same serial number if NIB condition. Only 4 were mfg.

RANGER ARMS INC.

Previous manufacturer located in Gainesville, TX until the early 1970s.

Ranger Arms Inc. manufactured good quality, bolt action rifles in various calibers and configurations. Although somewhat rare in that there were not a large number manufactured, collectibility to date has been limited with specimens in 90%+ condition, typically priced in the $375-$500 range.

RAPTOR ARMS CO., INC.

Previous rifle manufacturer located in Shelton, CT, approx. 1997-mid 1999. Previously distributed by Davidson's and Jerry's Sport Centers.

GRADING - PPGS™	100%	98%	95%	90%	80%	70%	60%

RIFLES: BOLT ACTION

RAPTOR SPORTING RIFLE - .243 Win., .25-06 Rem., .270 Rem., .30-06, or .308 Win. cal., features "Taloncote" or blue (mfg. 1998 only) finished barreled action, black checkered fiberglass reinforced synthetic stock, adj. trigger, with or w/o sights. Mfg. 1997-99.

	100%	98%	95%	90%	80%	70%	60%
	$230	$195	$175	$160	$150	$140	$130

Last MSR was $259.

Add $30 for sights (disc.).
Add $15 for blue finish (disc.).
Add $36 for heavy barrel.
Add $50 for stainless steel barreled action with sights (new 1999).

✱ **Peregrine Deluxe Sporting Rifle** - similar to Raptor Sporting Rifle, except has deluxe checkered or plain hardwood stock. Mfg. 1998 only.

	$265	$225	$195	$175	$160	$150	$140

Last MSR was $309.

Subtract $10 for plain hardwood stock and no sights (blue finish only).

RAVELL

Previous manufacturer located in Barcelona, Spain.

RIFLES: SxS

MAXIM DOUBLE RIFLE - .375 H&H or 9.3x74R cal., H&H type sidelock action with automatic ejectors, Purdey scroll engraving, 23 in. barrels, deluxe walnut with full pistol grip and rubber buttplate, double articulated triggers. Importation disc. circa 1998.

	$6,600	$6,100	$5,000	$4,000	$3,500	$2,950	$2,600

Last MSR was $7,000.

Add 10% for .375 H&H cal.

RAVEN ARMS

Previous manufacturer located in Industry, CA circa 1970-1991. Approximately 2 million were mfg.

PISTOLS: SEMI-AUTO

P-25 - .25 ACP cal., single action, 2 7/16 in. barrel, 6 shot mag., walnut grips, available in nickel, blue, or chrome finish, 15 oz. Disc. 1984.

	$70	$60	$50	$40	$30	$25	$25

MP-25 - similar to Model P-25, except die-cast slide serrations are slightly different. Disc. 1992.

	$60	$50	$45	$40	$35	$30	$25

Last MSR was $70.

Walnut, slotted plastic, or ivory colored grips were available for this model. In 1987, a new sear - block safety was incorporated into manufacture.

RECORD-MATCH

Previously manufactured by Anschütz, located in Zella-Mehlis, Germany circa pre-WWII.

PISTOLS: SINGLE SHOT, TARGET

MODEL 210 FREE PISTOL - .22 LR cal., Martini action, 11 in. barrel, single shot, blue, carved and checkered walnut grips and forearm, set trigger (button release), micrometer rear sight, deluxe target pistol, pre-WWII.

	$1,320	$1,265	$1,210	$1,100	$880	$745	$550

GRADING - PPGS™	100%	98%	95%	90%	80%	70%	60%

MODEL 210A - similar to Model 210, except alloy frame.

	$1,265	$1,210	$1,155	$1,045	$825	$690	$495

MODEL 200 FREE PISTOL - similar to Model 210, except less deluxe features and spur trigger guard, pre-WWII.

	$990	$935	$770	$660	$525	$440	$360

GARY REEDER CUSTOM GUNS

Current custom pistol manufacturer located in Flagstaff, AZ. Consumer direct sales.

For over 25 years, Gary Reeder has specialized in customizing revolvers from various manufacturers, and is now building several series of custom revolvers on his own frames. These revolvers include the large caliber BMF (MSR $2,395), the new Western Classic, a smaller framed revolver designed for cowboy action shooting (MSR $1,295), in addition to the new Improved #5, a version of the Elmer Keith Classic #5 (MSR $1,295). Gary's son Kase also manufactures several series of custom 1911s built to customer specifications. Reeder currently produces over 60 different series of custom hunting handguns, cowboy guns, custom 1911s, and large caliber hunting rifles. For more information on on his extensive range of custom guns, please contact the factory directly (see Trademark Index).

REISING ARMS COMPANY

Previous manufacturer originally located in Hartford, CT and later in New York, NY.

PISTOLS: SEMI-AUTO

TARGET AUTOMATIC PISTOL - .22 LR cal., 12 shot, 6 3/4 in. barrel, blue, brown hard rubber grips, hinged frame, outside hammer. Mfg. 1921-24.

	$475	$395	$340	$315	$265	$220	$195

This model was mfg. in Hartford, CT from serial number 1,001-4,000. The New York, NY address occurs in the serial range 10,000-12,000.

Warning: This pistol's slide may crack if modern high speed .22 ammo is used.

REMINGTON ARMS COMPANY, INC.

Current manufacturer established in 1816, with factories currently located in Ilion, NY, and Mayfield, KY.

Remington®

Founded by Eliphalet Remington II and originally located in Litchfield, Herkimer County, NY circa 1816-1828. Remington established a factory in Ilion, NY next to the Erie Canal in 1828, and together with his sons Philo, Samuel, and Eliphalet III pioneered many improvements in firearms manufacture. Corporate offices were moved to Madison, NC in 1996. DuPont owned a controlling interest in Remington from 1933-1993, when the company was sold to Clayton, Dubilier & Rice, a New York City based finance company. The Mayfield, KY plant opened in 1997.

For current information on shotguns imported by Spartan Gun Works, a Remington subsidiary, please refer to the Spartan Gun Works section in this text.

REMINGTON TRADEMARKS - 1816-PRESENT

1816-1847 - Remington (mostly barrel and lock markings)
1847-1856 - E. Remington & Son
1856-1888 - E. Remington & Sons
1888-1911 - Remington Arms Company
1911-1916 - Remington Arms & Ammunition Company, Inc.
1916-1920 - Remington Arms - Union Metallic Cartridge Co., Inc.
1920 to date - Remington Arms Company, Inc.

100%	98%	95%	90%	80%	70%	60%	50%	40%	30%	20%	10%

HANDGUNS: 1857-1945 PRODUCTION

BEALS' FIRST MODEL POCKET REVOLVER - percussion .31 cal., 5 shot, smooth cylinder, 3 in. octagon barrel, blue finish, 1-piece hard rubber grip, brass or iron trigger guard. Approx. 3,000 produced, 1857-58.

N/A	N/A	$3,000	$2,750	$2,000	$1,500	$1,000	$800	$600	$500	$400	$300

BEALS' SECOND MODEL POCKET REVOLVER - percussion .31 cal., 5 shot, smooth cylinder, 3 in. octagon barrel, blue finish, 2-piece hard rubber grips, spur trigger. Less than 1,000 produced 1858-61. Quite rare.

N/A	N/A	$6,000	$5,000	$4,500	$4,000	$3,500	$3,000	$2,500	$2,250	$2,000	$1,850

BEALS' THIRD MODEL POCKET REVOLVER - percussion .31 cal., 5 shot, smooth cylinder, 4 in. octagon barrel, blue finish, 2-piece hard rubber grips, spur trigger, first Remington revolver with loading lever. Less than 1,000 mfg. between 1859-61.

N/A	N/A	$3,000	$2,750	$2,100	$1,550	$1,250	$1,000	$900	$800	$700	$600

BEALS' NAVY REVOLVER - percussion .36 cal., 6 shot, smooth cylinder, 7 1/2 in. octagon barrel, blue finish, 2-piece walnut grips, some martially marked with inspector's initials and cartouche on grips. Approx. 15,000 produced, 1861-62. Barrel address is "Beals' Patent, Sept. 14, 1858 - Manufactured by Remingtons', Ilion, N.Y."

* *Commercial Model* - single wing base pin (very rare), less than 400 mfg. Serial range under 200, very desirable.

N/A	N/A	$4,750	$4,500	$4,000	$3,000	$2,500	$2,000	$1,750	$1,500	$1,250	$1,200

* *Commercial Model* - several variations with serialization 1-15,500, most were purchased by military but were not inspected.

N/A	N/A	$4,000	$3,750	$3,000	$2,500	$2,000	$1,750	$1,500	$1,250	$1,000	$850

Subtract 20% for cartridge conversion.

* *Martially marked* - serial range 13,500-15,500.

N/A	N/A	$5,000	$4,500	$3,500	$3,000	$2,750	$2,500	$2,000	$1,250	$1,000	$800

BEALS' ARMY REVOLVER - percussion .44 cal., 6 shot, smooth cylinder, 8 in. octagon barrel, blue finish, 2-piece walnut grips. Barrel address is "Beals' Patent, Sept. 14, 1858 - Manufactured by Remingtons', Ilion, N.Y."

N/A	N/A	$4,500	$4,000	$3,500	$3,000	$2,500	$2,000	$1,500	$1,250	$1,000	$850

Subtract 20% for cartridge conversions.

* *Martially marked* - serial range is 850-1,900 inspected by "WAT" or "CGC," very desirable.

N/A	N/A	$6,000	$5,500	$4,750	$4,500	$4,000	$3,500	$3,000	$2,250	$1,750	$1,500

RIDER'S DOUBLE-ACTION POCKET REVOLVER - percussion .31 cal., 5 shot, unusual "mushroom-shaped" cylinder, 3 in. octagon barrel, blue finish, 2-piece hard rubber grips, brass triggerguard, no loading lever. One of the earliest double action handguns produced. Approx. 20,000 produced, 1860-70.

N/A	N/A	$1,500	$1,250	$1,000	$750	$600	$500	$425	$375	$350	$300

Subtract 30% for cartridge conversion.

RIDER'S SINGLE-SHOT DERRINGER - percussion .17 cal., all brass construction, grips included. Fewer than 1,000 produced, 1859-1860. MANY FAKES, caveat emptor.

N/A	N/A	$6,000	$5,500	$5,000	$4,250	$3,750	$3,250	$2,750	$2,500	$2,300	$2,100

MODEL 1861 NAVY REVOLVER - percussion .36 cal., 6 shot, unfluted cylinder, 7 1/2 in. octagon barrel, blue finish, 2-piece walnut grips. Loading lever has slot allowing cylinder pin to be pulled forward without lowering lever. Approx. 6,000 produced 1862-63 in serial range 15,000-21,000. Barrel address "Patented Dec. 17, 1861, 1858 - Manufactured by Remingtons', Ilion, N.Y."

100%	98%	95%	90%	80%	70%	60%	50%	40%	30%	20%	10%

✳ *Commercial Model*

| N/A | N/A | $4,000 | $3,750 | $3,250 | $2,750 | $2,000 | $1,750 | $1,500 | $1,100 | $900 | $800 |

Subtract 30% for cartridge conversion.

✳ *Martially Marked* - over 4,000 martially inspected "CGC".

| N/A | N/A | $4,500 | $4,000 | $3,500 | $3,000 | $2,500 | $2,000 | $1,750 | $1,500 | $1,250 | $1,000 |

MODEL 1861 ARMY REVOLVER - percussion .44 cal., 6 shot, unfluted cylinder, 8 in. octagon barrel, blue finish, 2-piece walnut grips. Majority are martially inspected "CGC". Loading lever has slot allowing cylinder pin to be pulled forward without lowering lever. Approx. 10,000 produced 1862-63 in serial range 1,900-12,000. Barrel address "Patented Dec. 17, 1861, 1858 - Manufactured by Remingtons', Ilion, N.Y."

| N/A | N/A | $4,000 | $3,750 | $3,250 | $2,750 | $2,000 | $1,750 | $1,500 | $1,100 | $900 | $800 |

Subtract 30% for cartridge conversion.

NEW MODEL ARMY REVOLVER - percussion .44 cal., 6 shot, unfluted cylinder, 8 in. octagon barrel, blue finish, 2-piece walnut grips. Approx. 135,000 produced 1863-1888 in serial range 12,000-148,000. Barrel address "Patented Sept. 14, 1858 - Manufactured by Remingtons', Ilion, N.Y. - New Model." Early models lack "New Model" markings on barrel and have transition features from "1861" model. Erroneously called the "Remington Model 1858 Revolver."

| N/A | N/A | $4,000 | $3,750 | $3,250 | $2,750 | $2,000 | $1,750 | $1,500 | $1,100 | $900 | $800 |

Subtract 25% for cartridge conversion (most are in .46 rimfire).

Add 25% for martially inspected.

NEW MODEL NAVY REVOLVER - percussion .36 cal., 6 shot, unfluted cylinder, 7 1/2 in. octagon barrel, blue finish, 2-piece walnut grips. Approx. 18,000 produced in percussion from 1863-1878 with serial range 21,000-48,000. None were martially marked at time of mfg. Approx. 4,000 were purchased by U.S. Navy during 1863-65 in serial range 21,000-32,000. Barrel address "Patented Sept. 14, 1858 - Manufactured by Remingtons', Ilion, N.Y. - New Model." Early specimens lack "New Model" markings on barrel and have transition features from "1861" model.

| N/A | N/A | $3,750 | $3,500 | $3,000 | $2,250 | $2,000 | $1,750 | $1,500 | $1,250 | $1,000 | $800 |

Subtract 25% for cartridge conversion (most are in .38 rimfire).

No premium for martial markings.

NEW MODEL BELT REVOLVER, SINGLE ACTION - percussion .36 cal., 6 shot, unfluted or fluted cylinder, 6 1/2 in. octagon barrel, blue or nickel finish, 2-piece walnut grips. Approx. 5,000 produced 1863-72.

| N/A | N/A | $2,500 | $2,000 | $1,750 | $1,250 | $1,200 | $1,100 | $900 | $800 | $600 | $500 |

Add 30% for fluted cylinder (cylinder numbered to the gun).

Subtract 25% for cartridge conversion (mfg. 1870-1886).

NEW MODEL BELT REVOLVER, DOUBLE ACTION - percussion .36 cal., 6 shot, smooth or fluted cylinder, 6 1/2 in. octagon barrel, blue or nickel finish, 2-piece walnut grips. Approx. 2,500 produced 1863-72.

| N/A | N/A | $2,500 | $2,000 | $1,750 | $1,250 | $1,200 | $1,100 | $900 | $800 | $600 | $500 |

Add 30% for fluted cylinder (most not numbered to the gun).

Subtract 25% for cartridge conversion.

NEW MODEL POLICE REVOLVER - percussion .36 cal., 5 shot, smooth cylinder, 3 to 6 1/2 in. octagon barrels, blue or nickel finish, 2-piece walnut grips. Approx. 18,000 produced 1863-72.

| N/A | N/A | $2,500 | $2,000 | $1,750 | $1,250 | $1,200 | $1,100 | $900 | $800 | $600 | $500 |

Add 10% for 6 1/2 in. barrel.

Subtract 40% for cartridge conversion.

100%	98%	95%	90%	80%	70%	60%	50%	40%	30%	20%	10%

NEW MODEL POCKET REVOLVER
- percussion .31 cal., 5 shot, smooth cylinder, spur trigger, 3 to 4 1/2 in. octagon barrel, blue or nickel finish, 2-piece walnut grips. Approx. 25,000 produced, 1863-88.

N/A	N/A	$2,500	$2,000	$1,750	$1,250	$1,200	$1,100	$900	$800	$600	$500

Add 25%-50% for brass frame and/or trigger sheath.
Subtract 25% for cartridge conversion.

ZIG-ZAG DERRINGER
- .22 short rimfire cartridge, 6 shot, 6 barrel cluster (rotating), ring trigger, 3 in. barrel cluster, blue finish, 2-piece hard rubber grips. Fewer than 1,000 produced, 1861-63. Reputed to be Remington's first cartridge handgun. William Elliot's patent.

N/A	N/A	$3,000	$2,500	$2,100	$1,800	$1,500	$1,300	$1,100	$975	$900	$800

ELLIOT'S FIVE SHOT DERRINGER
- .22 short rimfire cartridge, 5 shot, 5 barrel cluster (fixed), 3 in. barrel cluster, blue finish, 2-piece hard rubber, walnut, ivory or pearl grips, ring trigger. Approx. 25,000 produced (combined production total with .32 cal.).

N/A	N/A	$1,900	$1,500	$1,250	$1,000	$900	$800	$700	$600	$500	$425

ELLIOT'S FOUR SHOT DERRINGER
- cartridge .32 rimfire cal., 4 shot, 4 barrel cluster (fixed), ring trigger, 3 3/8 in. barrel cluster, blue finish, 2-piece hard rubber, walnut, ivory or pearl grips. Approx. 25,000 produced (combined production with .22 cal.).

N/A	N/A	$1,750	$1,400	$1,250	$1,100	$975	$850	$750	$625	$525	$450

VEST POCKET DERRINGER
- rimfire cartridge .22, .30, .32, or .41 cal., single shot, various barrel lengths, blue or nickel (post 1870) finish, 2-piece walnut grips, spur trigger. Rider's patent.

* *.22 Rimfire* - approx. 25,000 produced, 1865-88.

N/A	N/A	$1,300	$1,200	$1,050	$900	$800	$700	$600	$500	$400	$300

Subtract 25% for guns lacking company name.

* *.30 or .32 Rimfire* - number produced unknown, 1865-1888.

N/A	N/A	$1,500	$1,400	$1,300	$1,150	$900	$800	$700	$600	$500	$400

* *41 Rimfire* - approx. 25,000 produced, 1865-88.

N/A	N/A	$1,400	$1,300	$1,200	$1,050	$850	$750	$650	$550	$450	$350

OVER AND UNDER DERRINGER
- cartridge .41 Rimfire cal., 2 shot, 3 in. superimposed barrels, oscillating firing pin, spur trigger, blue and/or nickel finish, hard rubber, walnut, ivory or pearl 2-piece grips. Approx. 150,000 produced, 1866-1934. AKA Double Derringer or Model 95. William Elliot's patent.

* *Type One, Early Variation* - maker's name and patent data stamped between the barrels, made without extractor. 1866-88.

N/A	N/A	$2,500	$2,000	$1,750	$1,500	$1,200	$1,000	$900	$750	$600	$500

* *Type One, Late Variation* - maker's name and patent data stamped between the barrels, made with extractor. 1866-88.

N/A	N/A	$2,400	$2,200	$2,150	$1,750	$1,400	$1,100	$975	$775	$650	$550

* *Type Two* - two line markings atop barrels, maker's name and patent data. 1866-88.

N/A	N/A	$1,500	$1,400	$1,250	$1,100	$1,000	$900	$800	$700	$600	$500

* *Type Three* - marked on top of barrel, single line, "REMINGTON ARMS CO., ILION, N.Y." 1888-1911.

N/A	N/A	$1,500	$1,400	$1,250	$1,100	$1,000	$900	$800	$700	$600	$500

* *Type Four* - marked on top of barrel, single line, "REMINGTON ARMS-U.M.C. CO. ILION, N.Y."

N/A	N/A	$1,500	$1,400	$1,250	$1,100	$1,000	$900	$800	$700	$600	$500

100%	98%	95%	90%	80%	70%	60%	50%	40%	30%	20%	10%

MODEL 1866 NAVY ROLLING BLOCK PISTOL - cartridge .50 rimfire cal., single shot, 8 1/2 in. round barrel, spur trigger, walnut grip and forearm, blue finish. Approx. 6,500 produced, 1866-67. Erroneously designated as, "Model of 1865 Navy."

❋ *Martially Marked*

100%	98%	95%	90%	80%	70%	60%	50%	40%	30%	20%	10%
N/A	N/A	$5,750	$5,000	$4,500	$4,000	$3,500	$3,000	$2,500	$2,000	$1,750	$1,500

> **Subtract 30% if not martially marked (Commercial Model mfg. 1866-1868).**
> **Subtract 25% for centerfire breech block.**
> Fewer than 150 remain in original condition.

COMBINATION PISTOL-SHOTGUN - 20 ga., 11 3/4 in. single barrel with smooth bore, rolling block action, designed as a pistol or shotgun (with detachable shoulder stock). Mfg. circa mid-1920s by an unknown manufacturer (possibly Bannerman's). Rolling block receivers appear to have been from foreign made military rifles.

> Extreme rarity factor precludes accurate pricing information.
> In either configuration, this model is an NFA firearm that cannot be legally owned unless registered with the BATF.

MODEL 1870 NAVY ROLLING BLOCK PISTOL - cartridge .50 centerfire cal., single shot, 7 in. round barrel, standard trigger with triggerguard, walnut grip and forearm, blue finish. Approx. 6,400 produced 1870-75. Modified by Remington for the Navy from Model 1866 pistols.

100%	98%	95%	90%	80%	70%	60%	50%	40%	30%	20%	10%
N/A	N/A	$3,150	$2,550	$2,050	$1,800	$1,500	$1,300	$1,200	$1,100	$1,000	$900

> **Add approx. 20% for 8 in. commercial version (approx. 200-400 mfg.) without inspector's marks.**

MODEL 1871 ARMY ROLLING BLOCK PISTOL - cartridge .50 centerfire cal., single shot, 8 in. round barrel, standard trigger with triggerguard, walnut grip and forearm, blue finish. Approx. 5,000 produced, 1871-72.

100%	98%	95%	90%	80%	70%	60%	50%	40%	30%	20%	10%
N/A	$4,000	$3,500	$3,000	$2,500	$2,000	$1,750	$1,500	$1,400	$1,100	$1,000	$900

> **Subtract 10% for Commercial Model.**

MODEL 1887 TARGET ROLLING BLOCK PISTOL - cartridge .22, .25 rimfire and .32, .50 centerfire cals., single shot, 8 in. round barrel, standard trigger with triggerguard, walnut grip and forearm, blue finish. Approx. 900 produced 1887-91. AKA "Plinker Model of 1887."

100%	98%	95%	90%	80%	70%	60%	50%	40%	30%	20%	10%
N/A	$2,500	$2,250	$2,000	$1,750	$1,500	$1,250	$1,000	$900	$800	$700	$600

> **Add 10% for Navy framed.**
> Navy framed 1887s are discernible by military proofs on right side of frame, Remington altered from original Navy Model 1870. Estimated mfg. of 100.

MODEL 1891 TARGET MODEL ROLLING BLOCK PISTOL - cartridge .22, .25 rimfire and .32 centerfire cals., single shot, 10 in. part octagon, part round barrel, standard trigger with triggerguard, smooth walnut grip and forearm, blue finish. Limited mfg. 1891-1900.

100%	98%	95%	90%	80%	70%	60%	50%	40%	30%	20%	10%
N/A	$2,500	$2,250	$2,000	$1,750	$1,500	$1,250	$1,000	$900	$800	$700	$600

> Removing the grips on this model may reveal a 4-digit number, indicating a refurbished military action.

MODEL 1901 TARGET ROLLING BLOCK PISTOL - cartridge .22 S and L, .25 rimfire, .32 centerfire, or .44 S&W Russian cal., single shot, 10 in. part octagon, part round barrel, standard trigger with trigger guard, checkered walnut grip and forearm, blue finish. Limited mfg. 1900-09.

100%	98%	95%	90%	80%	70%	60%	50%	40%	30%	20%	10%
N/A	$2,500	$2,250	$2,000	$1,750	$1,500	$1,250	$1,000	$900	$800	$700	$600

> **Add $200 for .44 S&W Russian cal.**
> Removing the grips on this model may reveal a 4-digit number, indicating a refurbished military action.

100%	98%	95%	90%	80%	70%	60%	50%	40%	30%	20%	10%

RIDER'S MAGAZINE PISTOL
- .32 rimfire cal., 5 shot, 3 in. octagonal barrel, spur trigger, walnut, rosewood, ivory or pearl grips. Limited mfg. 1871-1888.

N/A	$2,000	$1,800	$1,600	$1,300	$1,200	$1,000	$900	$800	$700	$600	$500

Add 75% for original case hardened receiver.

Most of this model were engraved, and a non-engraved specimen, while rare, is not necessarily more desirable.

ELLIOT'S SINGLE SHOT DERRINGER
- .41 rimfire cartridge cal., single shot, 2 1/2 in. round barrel, spur trigger, walnut 2-piece grips, blue and/or nickel finish. Approx. 10,000 produced, 1867-1888. AKA "Mississippi Derringer."

N/A	$1,500	$1,400	$1,300	$1,000	$900	$750	$675	$600	$500	$400	$300

NO. 1 (SMOOT PATENT) REVOLVER
- cartridge .30 Rimfire cal., 5 shot, 2 3/4 in. octagon barrel, spur trigger, walnut, hard rubber, pearl or ivory 2-piece grips. Number produced debatable, 1873-1888.

N/A	$1,200	$900	$800	$700	$550	$500	$400	$300	$250	$200	$150

Add 100% on early #1s with revolving recoil shield.

On Number 1 through Number 4 Revolvers, ivory grips refer to Remington Celluloid, not genuine ivory. Only in rare instances does ivory appear.

NO. 2 (SMOOT PATENT) REVOLVER
- cartridge .30 or .32 Rimfire cal., 5 shot, 2 3/4 in. octagon barrel, spur trigger, hard rubber, pearl or ivory 2-piece grips. Number produced debatable, 1873-88.

N/A	$1,200	$900	$800	$700	$550	$500	$400	$300	$250	$200	$150

NO. 3 (SMOOT PATENT) REVOLVER
- cartridge .38 Rimfire or Centerfire cal., 3 3/4 in. octagon barrel with or without barrel rib, spur trigger, hard rubber, ivory or pearl 2-piece grips, "Bird-Head and SawHandle" grip frame with Remington logo "R" on the "saw-handle" hard rubber grips, Bird-Head referred to models with or without a barrel rib. Number produced debatable, 1875-88.

N/A	$1,200	$900	$800	$700	$550	$500	$400	$300	$250	$200	$150

Add a small premium for Centerfire calibers.

NO. 4 REVOLVER
- cartridge .38 and .41 Rimfire or Centerfire cals., 5 shot, 2 1/2 in. round barrel, hard rubber, pearl or ivory 2-piece grips. Number produced debatable, 1877-88.

N/A	$1,200	$900	$800	$700	$550	$500	$400	$300	$250	$200	$150

Add a small premium for Centerfire calibers.

IROQUOIS REVOLVER
- .22 rimfire cartridge cal., 7 shot, 2 1/4 in. round barrel, spur trigger hard rubber, pearl or ivory 2-piece grips, nickel finish, fluted or non-fluted cylinder. Approx. 10,000 produced between, 1878-88.

N/A	$1,200	$1,100	$1,000	$800	$700	$550	$350	$300	$250	$200	$175

Subtract 25% if unmarked.

Add 25% for fluted cylinder.

MODEL 1875 SINGLE ACTION REVOLVER
- .44 Rem., .44-40 Win., or .45 Colt centerfire cal., 6 shot, 7 1/2 or 5 3/4 (scarce) in. round barrel, standard trigger with triggerguard, blue or nickel finish, walnut, ivory, or pearl 2-piece grips. Approx. 25,000 produced, 1875-88.

N/A	$7,500	$6,000	$5,000	$3,500	$3,000	$2,500	$2,000	$1,750	$1,500	$1,250	$1,000

Add 25% for blue finish.

Add 50% for U.S.I.D. "Indian Police" markings.

Add 10% for .45 cal.

There is some debate over originality of the 5 3/4 in. barrel - some are known, but many were altered post-factory.

100%	98%	95%	90%	80%	70%	60%	50%	40%	30%	20%	10%

MODEL 1888 SINGLE ACTION REVOLVER - cartridge .44 Centerfire cal., resembles 1890 SA, has "E. Remington & Sons" barrel address, 5 3/4 in. barrel, nickel finish with walnut grips.

N/A	$7,500	$6,000	$5,000	$3,500	$3,000	$2,500	$2,000	$1,750	$1,500	$1,250	$1,000

This model was never listed in a Remington catalog or price list. Rather, it first appeared in a Hartly Graham ad in late 1888. This revolver was made from parts of Models 1875 & 1890 pistols. Model nomenclature has been created by collectors, not the factory.

MODEL 1890 SINGLE ACTION REVOLVER - .44-40 WCF cal., 6 shot, 7 1/2 or 5 3/4 in. round barrel, standard trigger with trigger guard, hard rubber 2-piece grips with Remington monogram, ivory or pearl grips on special order, blue or nickel finish. Approx. 2,000 produced, 1891-94.

✳ *Blue Finish*

N/A	$9,000	$8,500	$8,000	$7,000	$6,000	$5,000	$4,000	$3,000	$2,000	$1,500	$1,000

✳ *Nickle Finish*

N/A	$8,000	$7,500	$7,000	$6,000	$5,000	$4,000	$3,500	$3,000	$2,000	$1,500	$1,000

MODEL 51 SEMI-AUTO - .32 ACP or .380 ACP cal., 8 shot (7 in mag., 1 in chamber), hard rubber 2-piece grips with company's name, black finish. Approx. 65,000 mfg. 1918-1926.

$725	$650	$550	$450	$350	$300	$275	$225	$200	$175	$165	$150

Add 25% for original box, brochure, oiler, and cleaning rod.

Note: .380 ACP cal. much more common than .32 ACP cal., but commands a slight premium.

MODEL 1911 REMINGTON - UMC - .45 ACP cal., WWI M1911 military contract, over 21,500 mfg. (ser. numbered 1-21,676) in 1918-19 only, blue finish.

N/A	$3,500	$2,500	$1,500	$975	$725	$600	$525	$475	$425	$375	$350

The cutoff serial number for 1918 mfg. is 13,152.

MODEL 1911A1 REMINGTON RAND - approx. 1,086,624 mfg. 1943-1945 in Syracuse, NY, ser. no. ranges 916,405-1,041,404, 1,279,649-1,441,430, 1,471,431-1,609,528, 1,743,847-1,816,641, 1,890,504-2,075,103, 2,134,404-2,244,803, and 2,380,014-2,619,013, parkerized finish. Mfg. by Remington Rand Corp, and not a true Remington product.

$1,400	$1,200	$900	$700	$600	$550	$450	$415	$375	$350	$325	$300

Add 20% with original shipping carton.

MARK III SIGNAL PISTOL - 10 ga., single shot, brass frame, 9 in. round steel barrel, spur trigger, walnut 2-piece grips. Approx. 25,000 produced, 1915-18.

N/A	N/A	$500	$300	$230	$210	$190	$175	$160	$145	$130	$110

GRADING - PPGS™			100%	98%	95%	90%	80%	70%	60%

HANDGUNS: POST-WWII PRODUCTION

Model XP-100 & Variations

Manufacture stopped on the XP-100 at the end of 1994, and resumed briefly during 1998-99 (Model XP-100R).

MODEL XP-100 - .221 Rem. Fireball cal., single shot bolt action pistol, one-piece Dupont Zytel (nylon) pistol grip stock, adj. sights, drilled and tapped for receiver sight and scope, 4-digit ser. no., 3 3/4 lbs. Mfg. 1963-85.

$595	$550	$475	$425	$375	$325	$275

MODEL XP-100 VARMINT SPECIAL - single shot bolt action pistol, .223 Rem. (new 1986) cal., 14 1/2 in. barrel, drilled and tapped for receiver sights and scope, one-piece pistol grip nylon stock, 4 1/8 lbs. Mfg. 1986-92.

$595	$550	$475	$425	$375	$325	$275

Last MSR was $419.

Add $100 for original hard zipper case.

GRADING - PPGS™	100%	98%	95%	90%	80%	70%	60%

XP-SILHOUETTE - .35 Rem. (mfg. 1987-92) or 7mm BR Rem. (mfg. 1980-92) cal., bench rest model, 14 1/2 in. barrel, drilled and tapped, nylon (disc. 1992) or walnut (new 1992) stock, 3 7/8 lbs. Disc. 1992.

		$650	$575	$500	$450	$400	$350	$300

Last MSR was $427.

Add $15 for .35 Rem. cal.

MODEL XP-100 HUNTER - .223 Rem., 7mm BR Rem., 7mm-.08 Rem., or .35 Rem. cal., 14 1/2 in. barrel, drilled and tapped for sights, laminated wood stock, 4 3/8 lbs. New 1993-94.

		$675	$575	$500	$450	$400	$350	$300

Last MSR was $548.

MODEL XP-100 WALNUT - 7mm BR Rem. cal., 10 1/2 in. barrel, solid American walnut stock and target sights, 3 7/8 lbs. Mfg. 1993-94.

		$695	$600	$525	$475	$425	$375	$325

Last MSR was $625.

XP-100R KS - .22-250 Rem. (new 1992), .223 Rem., .250 Savage (new 1991), 7mm-08 Rem., .308 Win. (new 1992), .35 Rem., or .350 Rem. Mag. (new 1991) cal., repeater variation, Kevlar synthetic stock, right-hand action only, open sights (except for .223 Rem. and .250 Savage) 4 1/8 lbs. Mfg. 1990-94.

		$950	$875	$775	$675	$595	$495	$400

Last MSR was $840.

This model was available through Remington's Custom Shop only.

MODEL XP-100R - .22-250 Rem., .223 Rem., .260 Rem., or .35 Rem. cal., right-hand repeater with 4 or 5 shot blind mag., fiberglass composite stock, 14 1/2 in. barrel, drilled and tapped receiver, approx. 4 1/2 lbs. Mfg. 1998-99.

		$675	$575	$500	$450	$400	$350	$300

Last MSR was $665.

XP-100 CUSTOM - .22-250 Rem. (new 1992), .223 Rem., .250 Savage, 6mm BR Rem., 7mm BR Rem., .308 Win. (new 1992), .35 Rem., or 7mm-08 Rem. cal., choice of standard or heavy barrel, available through custom gun shop only, choice of right- or left-hand action, wood stock with contoured pistol grip, without sights. Mfg. by Custom Shop 1986-94.

		$1,000	$925	$800	$700	$600	$500	$400

Last MSR was $945.

100%	98%	95%	90%	80%	70%	60%	50%	40%	30%	20%	10%

RIFLES: DISC.

REVOLVING PERCUSSION RIFLE - .36 or .44 (rare) cal., 6 shot unfluted cylinder, 24 or 28 in. octagon barrel, walnut stock with crescent butt, scroll triggerguard, blue with case hardened frame. Fewer than 1,000 mfg. 1866-72.

N/A	N/A	$18,000	$12,000	$6,000	$5,000	$4,000	$3,500	$3,000	$2,500	$2,250	$2,000

Receivers were made especially for this model, and are not altered New Model revolvers. .38 R.F. factory conversions will be serial numbered on the recoil plate and cylinder. The ultimate in rarity in Remington Revolving Rifles is the .46 rimfire cal. Only three of this model are presently known.

MODEL 1862 "ZOUAVE RIFLE" - .58 cal., muzzle loading percussion, 33 in. round barrel, two barrel bands, blue barrel, case hardened lock, brass furniture. Mfg. 12,501, 1862-65.

N/A	$4,500	$4,250	$4,000	$3,500	$2,750	$2,250	$2,000	$1,750	$1,500	$1,250	$1,000

Add $450 for correct sword type bayonette in excellent condition.

Most models are in excellent condition, as few, if any, were distributed to the troops during the Civil War.

100%	98%	95%	90%	80%	70%	60%	50%	40%	30%	20%	10%

U.S. NAVY M1867 ROLLING BLOCK CARBINE - .50-45 centerfire cal., 23 1/4 in. barrel, open sight, blue with case hardened frame, bar and ring on frame, walnut straight grip stock. Mfg. 5,000, 1868-69. Mfg. by Springfield Armory from receivers made by E. Remington & Sons in Ilion, NY.

N/A	N/A	$4,000	$3,000	$2,500	$2,000	$1,750	$1,500	$1,250	$1,000	$750	$500

U.S. NAVY "ANNAPOLIS CADET" MILITARY RIFLE - .50-45 centerfire cal., Mfg. by Springfield Armory utilizing rolling block receivers supplied by E. Remington & Sons in Ilion, NY. Mfg. 1868.

N/A	N/A	$4,000	$3,000	$2,500	$2,000	$1,750	$1,500	$1,250	$1,000	$750	$500

Add $150 for correct angular bayonet in excellent condition.

U.S. ARMY MODEL 1870 "EXPERIMENTAL" CARBINE - .50-70 Govt. cal., single shot, rolling block action with sling ring on left side of receiver, mfg. by Springfield Armory under license from E. Remington & Sons. 331 mfg. 1870.

N/A	N/A	$12,000	$10,000	$9,000	$8,000	$7,000	$6,000	$5,000	$4,000	$3,500	$3,000

This model is extremely rare, and fewer than six are known to be in private hands.

U.S. ARMY MODEL 1870 "EXPERIMENTAL" MILITARY RIFLE - .50-70 Govt. cal., single shot, rolling block action, mfg. by Springfield Armory under license from E. Remington & Sons. Mfg. 1870.

N/A	N/A	$6,000	$5,500	$5,000	$4,500	$4,000	$2,750	$2,250	$1,750	$1,250	$1,000

Approx. 1,041 were mfg. 1870 and issued to infantry troops on the frontier for trial. This is a rarely encountered Springfield firearm.

U.S. NAVY MODEL 1870 (TYPES 1 & 2) MILITARY RIFLE - mfg. by Springfield Armory under license from E. Remington & Sons. Mfg. 1870.

N/A	$5,000	$4,500	$4,000	$3,000	$2,000	$1,500	$1,250	$1,000	$800	$1,000	$600

Add $300-$600 for correct Ames sword bayonet.

10,000 of these models were mfg. in 1870, but were not accepted by the U.S. Navy, reputedly because of the "unsafe" location of the rear sight (too close to the chamber). These "Type 1" Navy rifles were sold to Poultney & Trimble, who sold them to France. Springfield Armory subsequently manufactured 14,000 "Type 2" rifles with the rear sight moved up the barrel, and these models were accepted by the U.S. Navy. Values are the same for both types.

U.S. ARMY MODEL 1871 MILITARY RIFLE - .50-70 Govt. cal., single shot, rolling block action, mfg. by Springfield Armory under license from E. Remington & Sons. Mfg. 1872.

N/A	$3,500	$3,250	$2,750	$2,000	$1,750	$1,500	$1,200	$900	$700	$500	$400

Add $50-$75 for angular bayonet.

10,101 of these models were mfg., but there is no evidence to suggest that they were ever issued to the troops. As a result, many of these models can be found in excellent or above average condition.

NO. 1 LONG RANGE "CREEDMOOR" - .44-77, .44-90, or .44-100 cal., rolling block, barrel 1/3 octagon, case hardened receiver, long range tang sight, globe front sight, checkered pistol grip stock, blue. Approx. 500 mfg., 1873-1878.

N/A	N/A	$10,000	$8,500	$6,250	$4,475	$3,875	$3,175	$2,700	$2,475	$2,150	$1,800

Add premiums for higher grade guns with select wood, additional checkering, and other deluxe features.

Factory cased guns are rarely encounted.

NO. 1 SPORTING RIFLE - rolling block, .40-50, .40-70, .44-70, .44-77, .45-70, .50-45, or .50-70 centerfire, .38 or .46 rimfire cal., 28 or 30 in. octagon barrels, folding leaf sight, straight grip stock. Approx. 10,000 mfg., 1868-86.

N/A	$6,000	$5,000	$3,500	$3,000	$2,500	$2,000	$1,500	$1,000	$750	$500	$300

Subtract 25% for rimfire cals.

Add 20% for .44-77, .45-70, or .50-70 cal. (primary buffalo hunting cals.).

100%	98%	95%	90%	80%	70%	60%	50%	40%	30%	20%	10%

NO. 1 1/2 SPORTING RIFLE
- .22, .25 Stevens, .25 Long, .32, and .38 Long & Extra Long rimfire cal., also in .32-20 WCF, .38-40 WCF, and .44-40 WCF, 24-28 in. octagon medium weight barrel, straight grip walnut stock, somewhat lighter than the No. 1 Sporting. Several thousand mfg., 1888-97.

| N/A | $3,500 | $3,000 | $2,500 | $1,750 | $1,250 | $900 | $800 | $650 | $550 | $450 | $300 |

Add 20% for centerfire cals.

NO. 2 SPORTING RIFLE
- available in many rimfire cals. between .22 and .38 as well as several centerfire cals. between .22 and .38-40 WCF, blue barrel finish with case hardened frame, perch belly style walnut stock, many special orders available, smaller size action than the No. 1 and rear of frame is curved, mfg. 1873-1909.

| N/A | $3,000 | $2,750 | $2,000 | $1,000 | $750 | $700 | $600 | $400 | $300 | $200 | $150 |

LIGHT BABY CARBINE
- rolling block, .44-40 WCF cal., 20 in. lightweight round blue barrel with band, straight stock, nickel or case colored receiver. Several thousand mfg., 1892-1902, a few are known to exist in .44 Long rimfire cal.

| N/A | $5,000 | $4,750 | $4,000 | $3,500 | $2,750 | $2,250 | $1,750 | $1,500 | $1,000 | $750 | $600 |

Add 25% for blue barrel with color case hardened receiver.

REMINGTON - HEPBURN NO. 3
- falling block, single shot, side lever actuated, blue barrel, case hardened actions, patented 1879, first introduced 1880, many custom features were offered, variations as follows:

* *No. 3 Sporting & Target* - various cals. from .22 rimfire to .50-90 Sharps, 26, 28, or 30 in. round or octagon barrel, open sight, semi-pistol grip stock. Mfg. 1880-1907.

| N/A | $4,000 | $3,500 | $2,750 | $2,250 | $1,750 | $1,500 | $1,000 | $900 | $800 | $700 | $600 |

* *No. 3 Match Rifle A Quality* - similar to Sporting and Target, with target match sights (tang), and Schuetzen stock. Fewer than 1,000 mfg., 1883-1907.

| N/A | $5,000 | $4,500 | $3,500 | $3,000 | $2,250 | $1,800 | $1,500 | $1,250 | $1,000 | $850 | $700 |

>B Quality - select grade wood and vernier rear tang sight.

| N/A | $6,000 | $5,000 | $4,200 | $3,600 | $2,700 | $2,150 | $1,800 | $1,500 | $1,200 | $1,000 | $850 |

* *No. 3 Long Range Creedmoor* - .44-77, .44-90, or .44-105 centerfire cal., 32 or 34 in. octagon barrel, tang sight, otherwise similar to Target Model. A few hundred mfg., 1880-1907.

| N/A | $10,000 | $9,500 | $8,825 | $6,250 | $4,475 | $3,875 | $3,175 | $2,700 | $2,475 | $2,150 | $1,800 |

* *No. 3 Mid Range Creedmoor* - similar to Long Range, in .40-65 WCF and other cals., 28 in. barrel.

| N/A | $6,000 | $5,750 | $5,000 | $4,000 | $3,000 | $2,500 | $2,000 | $1,750 | $1,500 | $1,250 | $1,000 |

* *No. 3 Long Range Military* - similar to Creedmoor, with 34 in. full musket stock, in .44-75-520 Rem. cal., military sights, rarely encountered. Mfg. circa 1880s.

| N/A | N/A | $9,800 | $8,825 | $6,250 | $4,475 | $3,875 | $3,175 | $2,700 | $2,475 | $2,150 | $1,800 |

* *No. 3 Walker-Hepburn Schuetzen Match* - under-lever action, 30 or 32 in. barrel, tang sight, palm rest, target stock, approx. 23 mfg. in 1903, perhaps the rarest single shot American rifle.

Extreme rarity factor precludes accurate price evaluation but a few have been observed with price tags in the $15,000-$60,000+ range, depending on condition.

* *With False Muzzle*

Add a premium according to condition - very rare.

NO. 4 ROLLING BLOCK RIFLE
- .22 S-L-LR, .25 Stevens (barrels marked "25-10"), or .32 Short or Long cal. rimfire, 22 1/2 octagon barrel standard with round barrels available late in the series, smooth bore barrel was introduced approx. 1911, blue finish with case hardened frame, solid frame initially followed by takedown in 2 different types (lever release introduced approx. 1901, screw in approx. 1926), this model was Remington's smallest rolling block. Approx. 350,000 mfg. 1890-1933.

| N/A | $1,000 | $800 | $700 | $500 | $400 | $275 | $200 | $175 | $150 | $100 | $75 |

Solid frame variations will command a premium, especially if over 90% original condition.

	100%	98%	95%	90%	80%	70%	60%	50%	40%	30%	20%	10%
✳ **Model 4-S "Boy Scout"**												
N/A	$2,200	$2,000	$1,500	$1,100	$900	$800	$750	$600	$500	$400	$300	

✳ *Model 4-S Military* - .22 S-L-LR cal., either marked "MILITARY MODEL" (most common) or "AMERICAN BOY SCOUT" (rare), 28 in. round barrel with musket type forend (1 barrel band), thought to have been used by military academies to train their young cadets.

N/A	N/A	$1,500	$1,400	$1,000	$750	$700	$600	$450	$300	$275	$250	

Bayonets are an extremely rare accessory for this model, and values can exceed that of the rifle.

NO. 6 FALLING BLOCK RIFLE

- .22 S-L-LR or .32 short or long rimfire cal., 20 in. round barrel, boy's gun with small dimensions, takedown action, case hardened (early mfg.) or blue finish, also available in smooth bore, 497,000 mfg. 1901-33.

N/A	$600	$500	$450	$300	$275	$250	$175	$150	$125	$100	$75	

Add 10% for smooth bore barrel.

Original case colors will bring a premium on this model.

NO. 7 ROLLING BLOCK RIFLE

- .22 S, .22 LR, or .25-10 Stev. rimfire cal., constructed on Rem. Model 1871 SS pistol action frame, 24, 26, or 28 in. 1/2 round, 1/2 octagon tapered barrels, marked "REMINGTON ARMS CO. ILION, NY USA" on barrel top flat, dinstictive long tang pistol grip stock, checkered pistol grip and forearm, hard rubber buttplate, available in Target or Sporting configurations, with or w/o special Lyman tang mounted sight, ser. no. range 300,000. Last of the Rolling Block Rifles. Approx. 350 mfg. 1903-10.

N/A	$8,500	$7,000	$6,250	$5,500	$4,900	$4,300	$3,700	$3,100	$2,650	$2,250	$1,750	

Add $300 for Lyman folding tang sight.

REMINGTON KEENE MAGAZINE BOLT RIFLE

- .45-70 Govt., .40, or .43 cal. Approx. 5,000 mfg. 1880-1888.

✳ *Frontier Model* - those made for U.S. Dept. of Interior (Indian Police), marked U.S.I.D. will command a 75% premium.

N/A	N/A	$3,500	$3,000	$2,500	$2,000	$1,500	$1,000	$750	$500	$300	$250	

✳ *Full Stock Carbine Model* - 22 in. barrel, full stock.

N/A	N/A	$3,500	$3,000	$2,500	$2,000	$1,500	$1,000	$750	$500	$300	$250	

✳ *Half Stock Carbine Model* - 20 in. barrel, half stock, very limited mfg.

Extreme rarity precludes accurate pricing on this model.

✳ *Army Rifle* - 32 1/2 in. barrel, full stock.

N/A	N/A	$3,250	$2,750	$2,500	$1,750	$1,250	$900	$700	$500	$300	$250	

✳ *Sporter Rifle* - 1/2 oct. barrel, full or "BUTTON" mag. Add for pistol grip and select wood variations.

N/A	N/A	$3,250	$2,750	$2,500	$1,750	$1,250	$900	$700	$500	$300	$250	

✳ *Navy Rifle* - 29 1/2 in. barrel, full stock.

N/A	N/A	$3,250	$2,750	$2,500	$1,750	$1,250	$900	$700	$500	$300	$250	

GRADING - PPGS™	100%	98%	95%	90%	80%	70%	60%

RIFLES: ROLLING BLOCK, RECENT MFG.

The following models are manufactured in limited quantities by the Remington Custom Shop.

NO. 1 ROLLING BLOCK CREEDMOOR

- .45-70 Govt. cal., rolling block action, patterned after the original Remington No. 1 mid-range Creedmoor-style configuration, 30 in. half-round half-octagon tapered 30 in. barrel, includes rear tang aperture and front globe sight with four interchangeable inserts, checkered walnut stock and forearm, SST, case colored receiver, cased, 9 7/8 lbs. Mfg. 1997-98.

$2,800	$2,500	$1,900

Last MSR was $2,799.

GRADING - PPGS™	100%	98%	95%	90%	80%	70%	60%

NO. 1 ROLLING BLOCK MID-RANGE SPORTER

- .30-30 Win. (disc. 1998), .444 Marlin (disc. 1998), or .45-70 Govt. cal., 30 in. round barrel, checkered pistol grip sporter stock and forearm, blue barrel end and receiver, adj. buckhorn rear sight, 8.75 lbs. New 1998.

MSR $1,450		$1,200	$1,035	$925	$775	$675	$600	$550

NO. 1 ROLLING BLOCK SILHOUETTE

- .45-70 Govt. cal., meets BPCR silhouette requirements, similar to No. 1 Rolling Block Mid-Range Sporter, except has 30 in. round heavy barrel w/o sights and single set or double triggers, blue or case colored receiver. New 2000.

MSR $1,560		$1,275	$1,085	$950	$825	$675	$600	$550

Add $200 for case colored receiver.
Add $167 for single set trigger.

RIFLES: SEMI-AUTO - CENTERFIRE

The models have been listed in numerical sequence for quick reference.

MODEL FOUR

- 6mm Rem., .243 Win., .270 Win., .280 Rem. (mfg. 1984-87), .30-06, .308 Win. (disc. 1984), or 7mm Express (mfg. 1981-83) cal., cartridge "head" imbedded in bottom of receiver, gas operation with metering system, 22 in. barrel, 4 shot detachable mag., deluxe Monte Carlo stock and forend, detachable sights. Mfg. 1981-87.

		$395	$360	$325	$275	$250	$225	$195

Last MSR was $475.

* *Special Model Four Diamond Anniversary* - .30-06 cal. only, less than 1,500 mfg. in 1981 only to commemorate 75th anniversary of the Model 8, laser engraved with gold and premium checkered walnut stock and forearm. One grade only.

		$1,000	$795	$600

MODEL 8

- .25 Rem., .30 Rem., .32 Rem., or .35 Rem. cal., 22 in. barrel, open sights, 5 shot non-detachable box mag., plain stock. Approx. 60,000 mfg. 1906-36.

		$700	$600	$500	$250	$200	$150	$140

Add 15% for .25 cal.
Add substantial premiums for higher grades C through F.

MODEL 74 SPORTSMAN

- .30-06 cal. only, 22 in. barrel, 4 shot mag., uncheckered hardwood stock and forearm, open sights, 7 1/2 lbs. Mfg. 1984-87.

	$295	$260	$235	$210	$190	$175	$160

Last MSR was $353.

MODEL 81 "WOODSMASTER"

- .30 Rem., .32 Rem., .35 Rem., or .300 Savage cal., semi-auto, takedown action, 5 shot, non-detachable box mag., 22 in. round barrel, notched elevator rear sight. An improvement of the Model 8; was available in 5 grades. Better grades bring higher prices. 56,091 mfg. 1936-50.

	$500	$400	$300	$250	$200	$175	$150

The .32 Rem. cal. was dropped after WWII and the .300 Savage was added in 1940. A few specimens have been observed in .25 Rem. cal., but this was not a production caliber.

MODEL 740 WOODMASTER & 740A

- .244 Rem. (mfg. 1957-59), .280 Rem. (mfg. 1957-59), .30-06 (first caliber, introduced 1955) or .308 Win. (introduced 1956) cal., 22 in. barrel, open sight, box mag., gas operated, plain pistol grip stock. Mfg. 1955-59.

.244 Rem. or .30-06 cal. $295	$250	$225	$210	$200	$190	$180
.280 Rem. or .308 Win. cal.$295	$250	$225	$210	$200	$190	$180

Add 15% for carbine version.

GRADING - PPGS™	100%	98%	95%	90%	80%	70%	60%

MODEL 740ADL - similar to 740A, with checkered stock, grip cap and swivels. Mfg. 1955-59.

	100%	98%	95%	90%	80%	70%	60%
.244 Rem. or .30-06 cal. $375	$325	$280	$250	$225	$200	$180
.280 Rem. or .308 Win. cal. $415	$350	$300	$275	$250	$225	$200

Add 15% for carbine version.

MODEL 740BDL - similar to 740ADL, with select wood.

	100%	98%	95%	90%	80%	70%	60%
.244 Rem. or .30-06 cal. $395	$340	$295	$250	$225	$200	$180
.308 Win. cal. $425	$375	$350	$325	$275	$225	$200

Add 15% for carbine version.

BDLs were not listed in the 1958 or 1959 Remington price list.

MODEL 742 (A) "WOODSMASTER" - 6mm Rem. (mfg. 1963), .243 Win. (mfg. 1968), .280 Rem. (marked 7mm Express 1979-1980), .30-06, or .308 Win. cal., 22 in. barrel, open sights, 4 shot box mag., gas operated, checkered pistol grip stock. Mfg. 1960-80.

$325	$290	$275	$250	$235	$210	$185

Add 10% for .280 Rem. cal.

MODEL 742ADL DELUXE - similar to the Model 742A, except has fine checkering, sling swivels and engraved game scenes on receiver.

$350	$300	$275	$260	$235	$215	$195

MODEL 742 CARBINE - similar to 742, except .280 Rem., .30-06, or .308 Win. cal. only, 18 1/2 in. barrel. Mfg. 1961-80.

$450	$400	$350	$300	$275	$260	$235

MODEL 742BDL - similar to Model 742, except .30-06 or .308 Win. cal., step receiver, right-hand action with choice of right-hand or left-hand cheekpiece, Monte Carlo basket weave stock and forend, black pistol grip cap and forend tip. Mfg. 1966-80.

$350	$300	$275	$260	$235	$215	$195

MODEL 742D PEERLESS GRADE - similar to Model 742, with scroll engraving and fancy wood. Mfg. 1961-80.

$2,000	$1,870	$1,200

MODEL 742F PREMIER GRADE - similar to Model 742, with extensive hand engraved game scenes and scroll work, best grade wood.

$4,200	$3,860	$2,650

MODEL 742F PREMIER GRADE (WITH INLAYS) - gold inlaid model.

$6,500	$5,785	$4,180

MODEL 742 150TH YEAR ANNIVERSARY - .30-06 cal. only. 11,409 Mfg. 1966 only.

$395	$325	$300

MODEL 742 CANADIAN CENTENNIAL - 1,000 mfg. in 1967. Issue price was $200.

$395	$325	$300

REMINGTON/RUGER CANADIAN CENTENNIAL SET - please refer to the Sturm Ruger section of this text.

MODEL 742 BICENTENNIAL - similar to 742, with inscription on receiver. 10,108 Mfg. 1976 only.

$400	$325	$300	$275	$225	$200	$185

GRADING - PPGS™	100%	98%	95%	90%	80%	70%	60%

MODEL 7400 - 6mm Rem. (disc. 1987), .243 Win., .270 Win., 7mm Express (mfg. 1981-83), .280 Rem. (introduced 1984, disc. 2000), .30-06, .308 Win., or .35 Whelen (mfg. 1993-95) cal., modified Model 742 action, gas operation, 22 in. barrel, 4 shot detachable mag., pressed checkered Monte Carlo walnut stock, 7.5 lbs. Mfg. 1981 to date.

	100%	98%	95%	90%	80%	70%	60%
MSR $651	$515	$410	$325	$260	$230	$210	$185

Add 15% for .35 Whelen cal.

Beginning in 1991, a high gloss wood finish became available in cals. .270 Win. and .30-06 (Model 7400 High Gloss). Beginning 1997, receiver panels have photo etched game scene engraving.

* **Model 7400 Carbine** - .30-06 cal. only, similar to Model 7400 Rifle, except has 18.5 in. barrel, 7.25 lbs. New 1988.

	100%	98%	95%	90%	80%	70%	60%
MSR $651	$515	$410	$325	$260	$230	$210	$185

* **Model 7400 SP (Special Purpose)** - .270 Win. or .30-06 cal., similar to Model 7400, except has non-reflective matte finish on both wood and metalwork. Mfg. 1993-94.

	$435	$370	$300	$255	$230	$210	$185

Last MSR was $524.

* **Model 7400 Weathermaster** - .270 Win. or .30-06 cal., features matte nickel plated receiver, barrel, and magazine, black synthetic stock and forearm, 22 in. barrel with open sights, 7.5 lbs. Mfg. 2003-2004.

	$495	$400	$315	$255	$230	$210	$185

Last MSR was $624.

* **Model 7400 Synthetic** - same cals. as Model 7400, features black fiberglass reinforced synthetic stock and forend, matte black metal finish, 22 in. barrel only. New 1998.

	100%	98%	95%	90%	80%	70%	60%
MSR $547	$435	$365	$320	$280	$260	$240	$220

>**Model 7400 Synthetic Carbine** - .30-06 cal., similar to Model 7400 Synthetic, except has 18.5 in. barrel. 7.25 lbs. New 1998.

	100%	98%	95%	90%	80%	70%	60%
MSR $547	$435	$365	$320	$280	$260	$240	$220

* **Model 7400 175th Anniversary** - .30-06 cal. only, Anniversary Model with light engraving and high gloss finish. 4890 Mfg. in 1991 only.

	$435	$365	$300

Last MSR was $515.

A limited quantity of .270 Win. cal. were specially made in this 175th Anniversary Model for distributor Bill Hicks in MN. Pricing varies, since these rifles are a special edition.

* **Model 7400 ADF Limited Edition** - .30-06 cal. only, special edition 1997 only featuring Buckmaster's American Deer Foundation, special ADF engraving. Mfg. 1997 only.

	$495	$400	$315

Last MSR was $600.

* **Model 7400 Engraved** - the engraved Model 7400s were introduced 1988.

* **D Grade (Peerless)**

MSR $3,723	$2,900	$2,075	$1,425

* **F Grade (Premier)**

MSR $7,245	$6,000	$4,400	$2,850

* **F Grade w/gold inlays (Premier Gold)** - top-of-the-line Custom Shop model.

MSR $10,663	$9,030	$5,150	$3,425

RIFLES: SLIDE ACTION, CENTERFIRE

MODEL SIX - 6mm Rem. (disc. 1985), .243 Win., .270 Win., .30-06, or .308 Win. (disc. 1984) cal., pump action, laser engraved, detachable sights, cartridge "head" imbedded in bottom of receiver, 4 shot mag. Mfg. 1981-87.

	$400	$360	$290	$265	$235	$215	$195

Last MSR was $439.

GRADING - PPGS™	100%	98%	95%	90%	80%	70%	60%

✳ D Peerless Grade - custom shop hand engraved.

| | $1,975 | $1,870 | $1,200 |

Last MSR was $2,291.

✳ F Premier Grade

| | $4,150 | $3,835 | $2,650 |

Last MSR was $4,720.

✳ F Premier Gold Grade - with gold inlays.

| | $6,420 | $5,735 | $4,000 |

Last MSR was $7,079.

MODEL 14/14A RIFLE - .25 Rem., .30 Rem., .32 Rem., or .35 Rem. cal., 22 in. barrel, 5 shot mag., open sight, plain pistol grip stock, 22 in. steel barrel, 6 lbs. Mfg. 1912-35.

| | $600 | $500 | $400 | $300 | $200 | $130 | $110 |

> **Add 100% for "thumbnail" safety (introduced in 1918).**
>
> **Add 15% for .25 Rem.**
>
> This model was also manufactured in higher grades, including A, C, and F. Premiums vary according to originality and condition.

MODEL 14R CARBINE - similar to 14A, with 18 in. barrel, straight grip stock.

| | $700 | $600 | $550 | $500 | $450 | $400 | $350 |

> **Add 25% for .25 Rem. cal.**
>
> **Add 10% for .35 Rem. cal.**

MODEL 14 1/2 RIFLE - .38-40 WCF or .44-40 WCF cal., similar to 14A, with 10 shot mag., 22 1/2 in. barrel. Mfg. began Dec. 5, 1913-34.

| | $1,000 | $925 | $850 | $800 | $725 | $650 | $575 |

> **Add 10% for .44-40 WCF cal.**
>
> Quantities mfg. of this model are unknown, as serial numbers were intermixed with the Model 14. This model was also manufactured in higher grades, including A, C, and F. Premiums vary according to originality and condition.

MODEL 14 1/2 R CARBINE - similar to 14 1/2 Rifle, with 8 shot mag. and 18 in. barrel.

| | $1,600 | $1,450 | $1,300 | $1,200 | $995 | $850 | $725 |

> **Add 25% for "fingernail" safety (introduced in 1918).**

MODEL 25/25A SLIDE ACTION - .25-20 WCF or .32-20 WCF cal., 24 in. barrel, open sight, tube mag., plain pistol grip stock. Mfg. 1923-35.

| | $700 | $600 | $575 | $500 | $400 | $350 | $275 |

MODEL 25R CARBINE - similar to 25A, with 18 in. barrel and straight stock.

| | $700 | $650 | $600 | $550 | $500 | $450 | $400 |

MODEL 76 SPORTSMAN SLIDE ACTION - .30-06 cal. only, 22 in. barrel, 4 shot mag., uncheckered hardwood stock and forearm, open sights, 7 1/2 lbs. Mfg. 1984-87.

| | $255 | $225 | $195 | $180 | $170 | $160 | $150 |

Last MSR was $319.

MODEL 141/141A SLIDE ACTION RIFLE - .25 Rem. (very few mfg. during 1936 only), .30 Rem., .32 Rem., or .35 Rem. cal., 24 in. barrel, takedown, open sight, plain pistol grip stock. Mfg. 1936-50.

| | $425 | $350 | $295 | $240 | $195 | $165 | $140 |

> **Add 60% for .25 Rem. cal.**
>
> **Add 10% for .35 Rem. cal.**

MODEL 141 CARBINE - mfg. 1936-42.

| | $750 | $700 | $650 | $600 | $550 | $500 | $450 |

GRADING - PPGS™	100%	98%	95%	90%	80%	70%	60%

MODEL 760 "GAMEMASTER" RIFLE - .222 Rem. (mfg. 1958-61), .223 Rem. (limited mfg. 1964-68), 6mm Rem. (introduced 1969), .243 Win. (introduced 1968), .244 (mfg. 1957-61), .257 Roberts (mfg. 1955-61), .270 Win., .280 Rem. (marked 7mm Express 1979-80), .30-06, .300 Sav., .308 Win., or .35 Rem. (mfg. 1952-67, and 1980) cal., 22 in. barrel, detachable mag., unchecked pistol grip stock. Mfg. 1952-80.

	100%	98%	95%	90%	80%	70%	60%
	$375	$325	$275	$250	$225	$200	$175
.222 Rem. cal.	$1,150	$900	$800	$725	$650	$575	$500
.223 Rem. cal.	$1,350	$995	$850	$775	$700	$625	$575
.257 Roberts cal.	$850	$695	$575	$450	$400	$350	$300

Add 10% for .300 Savage or .35 Rem. cal.

The Model 760 seems to have regional pricing differences in the rare calibers. Values in the Eastern U.S. seem to be quite a bit higher than prices encountered in the Midwest and West. Hence, values on the .222 Rem., .223 Rem., and .257 Roberts cals. reflect a nationalized average rather than one region's high or another's low. A few Model 760s were also mfg. in .244 cal. (before going to 6mm Rem.) - very rare with pricing unpredictable.

MODEL 760 CARBINE - .270 Win. (introduced 1969), .280 Win., .30-06, .308 Win., or .35 Rem. cal., 18 1/2 in. barrel.

$450	$400	$375	$325	$300	$275	$250

Subtract 10% for .30-06 cal.

MODEL 760D PEERLESS GRADE - similar to 760, with hand engraving and fancy wood. Mfg. 1953-80.

$1,100	$935	$825	$770	$690	$605	$525

MODEL 760F - similar to Model 760, with extensive hand engraved game scenes, best grade wood.

$2,420	$1,980	$1,760	$1,650	$1,485	$1,375	$1,100

✳ *Gold Inlaid Model*

$5,500	$4,675	$4,180	$3,960	$3,300	$2,750	$2,200

MODEL 760 150 YEAR ANNIVERSARY - .30-06 cal. only. 4610 Mfg. 1966 only.

$395	$325	$300	$275	$225	$200	$185

MODEL 760 BICENTENNIAL - similar to Model 760, with commemorative inscription engraved on receiver. 3,800 Mfg. 1976 only.

$395	$325	$300	$275	$225	$200	$185

MODEL 760ADL - .30-06 cal., similar to Model 760A, except with checkered pistol grip, deluxe wood and sling swivels. Mfg. 1953-63.

$395	$350	$325	$300	$275	$250	$225

MODEL 760BDL - similar to Model 760, except .270 Win., .30-06, or .308 Win. cal. only, step receiver, available with right- or left-hand cheekpiece on Monte Carlo stock (basket weave checkering pattern became standard mid-'70s), black pistol grip and forend tip. Mfg. 1953-82.

$425	$375	$350	$300	$275	$250	$225

Add 20% for .308 Win. cal.

MODEL 7600 - 6mm Rem. (disc. 1984), .243 Win., .270 Win., .280 Rem. (mfg. 1988-2000), .30-06, .308 Win., or .35 Whelen (mfg. 1988-96) cal., modified 760 action, 22 in. barrel, 4 shot detachable mag., pressed checkered pistol grip stock and forearm, 7.5 lbs. Mfg. 1981 to date.

MSR $615	$490	$400	$300	$240	$205	$185	$165

Add 10% for .35 Whelen cal.

Subtract $27 for limited edition laminated stock (Model 7600 LS, mfg. 2004 only).

Beginning in 1990, a high gloss wood finish became available in cals. .270 Win. and .30-06 (Model 7600 High Gloss). Beginning 1997, receiver panels have photo etched game scene engraving.

GRADING - PPGS™	100%	98%	95%	90%	80%	70%	60%

✳ *Model 7600 Carbine* - .30-06 cal. only, similar to Model 7600 Rifle, except has 18.5 in. barrel, 7.25 lbs.

	MSR $615	$490	$400	$300	$240	$205	$185	$165

✳ *Model 7600P Patrol Rifle* - .308 Win. cal., 16 1/2 in. barrel, synthetic stock, parkerized finish, Wilson Combat ghost ring sights, designed for police/law enforcement only.

Remington does not publish consumer retail pricing for this police/law enforcement model. Secondary prices for this model will be slightly higher than for current pricing on the Model 7600 Synthetic.

✳ *Model 7600 SP (Special Purpose)* - .270 Win. or .30-06 cal., similar to Model 7600, except has non-reflective matte finish on wood and metalwork. Mfg. 1993-94.

		$420	$360	$280	$230	$205	$185	$165

Last MSR was $496.

✳ *Model 7600 Synthetic* - same cals. as Model 7600, features black fiberglass reinforced synthetic stock and forend, matte black metal finish, 22 in. barrel only, 7.5 lbs. New 1998.

	MSR $511	$400	$340	$300	$275	$255	$240	$225

>**Model 7600 Synthetic Carbine** - similar to Model 7600 Synthetic, except has 18.5 in. barrel. 7.25 lbs. New 1998

	MSR $511	$400	$340	$300	$275	$255	$240	$225

✳ *Model 7600 175th Anniversary* - also available in 7mm-08 Rem. cal., 1,000 mfg. 1991 only.

		$625	$525	$375

✳ *Model 7600 ADF Limited Edition* - .30-06 cal. only, special edition 1997 only featuring Buckmaster's American Deer Foundation, special ADF engraving. Mfg. 1997 only.

		$460	$385	$295

Last MSR was $567.

✳ *Model 7600 Engraved* - hand engraved Model 7600s were introduced 1988.

✳ *D Grade (Peerless)*

	MSR $3,723	$2,900	$2,075	$1,425

✳ *F Grade (Premier)*

	MSR $7,245	$6,000	$4,400	$2,850

✳ *F Grade w/gold inlays (Premier Gold)* - top-of-the-line Custom Shop model.

	MSR $10,663	$9,030	$5,150	$3,425

MODEL 7615P PATROL RIFLE
- .223 Rem. cal., 16 1/2 in. barrel, 10 shot mag., synthetic stock, parkerized finish, extended mag., accepts AR-15 and M16 style magazines, Wilson Combat ghost ring sights, designed for police/law enforcement, 7 lbs.

Remington does not publish consumer retail pricing for this police/law enforcement model. Secondary prices for this model will be slightly higher than for current pricing on the Model 7600 Carbine.

RIFLES: RIMFIRE, DISC. & CURRENT PRODUCTION

From 1930-1960 Remington produced a number of bolt action .22 cal. Rimfire rifles, both single shot and repeaters. They were good quality, serviceable weapons with many slight variations upon a basic design. Whenever possible, models have been listed in numerical sequence.

On factory engraved E & F grade rifles, the ser. no. is usually engraved instead of stamped, and there is no standard factory engraving pattern on these grades.

	100%	98%	95%	90%	80%	70%	60%
Model 33	$200	$150	$125	$100	$85	$75	$60
Model 33 NRA	$400	$275	$250	$200	$150	$125	$100
Model 33-P	$250	$200	$175	$150	$125	$100	$75
Model 33 SB	$350	$325	$300	$290	$280	$260	$250

GRADING - PPGS™	100%	98%	95%	90%	80%	70%	60%
263,557 of the Model 33 were mfg. 1932-35.							
Model 34	$225	$175	$125	$100	$85	$75	$60
Model 34-P	$300	$225	$200	$175	$150	$125	$100
Model 34 NRA	$450	$400	$350	$300	$275	$250	$200
162,941 of the Model 34 were mfg. 1932-36.							
Model 341 A	$175	$125	$100	$90	$85	$80	$75
Model 341 P	$200	$150	$125	$100	$85	$75	$70
Model 341 SB	$375	$350	$300	$290	$280	$260	$250
131,604 of the Model 341 "Sportsmaster" were mfg. 1936-40.							
Model 41 A	$150	$125	$100	$75	$65	$60	$55
Model 41 AS							
(.22 Rem. Spec. cal.)	$300	$250	$175	$150	$140	$125	$110
Model 41 P	$175	$150	$100	$85	$65	$60	$55
Model 41 SB	$325	$275	$250	$240	$230	$220	$210
306,880 of the Model 41 "Targetmaster" were produced 1936-39.							
Model 411	$500	$450	$350	$300	$250	$225	$200

The Model 411 is similar to the Model 41 single shot, but in CB Cap or .22 Short and without safety on rear of bolt. Eye screw for gallery use. 1,316 mfg. 1937-39 (although never cataloged). Add 50% premium for .22 Short.

Model 510 A	$125	$110	$90	$75	$65	$60	$55
Model 510 C (Carbine)	$200	$175	$95	$85	$75	$65	$60
Model 510 P	$175	$150	$95	$85	$75	$65	$60
Model 510 Routledge/Smoothbore	$275	$260	$250	$240	$230	$220	$210

Add 15% for Mo-Skeet-O Bore

These models were mfg. 1939-62. Approx. 545,000 were mfg.

Model 511 A	$165	$135	$120	$100	$85	$80	$75
Model 511 P	$200	$165	$125	$110	$100	$90	$85

These models were mfg. 1939-62. Approx. 375,000 mfg.

Model 512 A	$175	$135	$120	$100	$85	$80	$75
Model 512 P	$200	$165	$125	$110	$100	$90	$85

These models were mfg. 1940-62. Approx. 395,000 mfg.

Model 510-X	$160	$140	$125	$100	$90	$80	$70
Model 510-X SB	$275	$260	$250	$240	$225	$210	$200
Model 511-X (29,120 mfg.)	$200	$175	$150	$125	$100	$85	$75
Model 512-X (30,670 mfg.)	$200	$175	$150	$125	$100	$85	$75

These models were mfg. 1964-66. 19,901 Model 510-Xs were mfg. and mixed with the Model 511-X and 512-X.

Model 514 (1948-1970)	$135	$110	$90	$75	$65	$55	$40
Model 514 P (1952-1971)	$175	$165	$145	$120	$85	$75	$65
Model 514 Boy's Rifle (1961-1970)	$155	$135	$120	$100	$85	$75	$65
Model 514 Routledge/Smoothbore	$240	$230	$220	$210	$200	$195	$190

The Routledge/Smoothbore was mfg. 1951-1969 - 5,557 were mfg.
Serialization began in 1968, approx. 780,000 mfg.

MODEL 12A SLIDE ACTION RIFLE - .22 S, L, and LR cal., hammerless, 22 in. round or octagon barrel, open sights, tube mag., plain grip stock, approx. 840,000 (all variations) were mfg. 1909-36.

	$600	$475	$350	$325	$300	$275	$250

Originally this model was designated "The New .22 Repeater," and did not have a model number. It was also available in Grades 1-6.

GRADING - PPGS™	100%	98%	95%	90%	80%	70%	60%

MODEL 12B (GALLERY SPECIAL) - similar to Model 12C, except in .22 Short cal., all had octagon barrels.

	$850	$700	$600	$525	$425	$375	$350

Add 15% for extended mag. tube.

MODEL 12C - similar to Model 12A, except 24 in. octagon barrel.

	$800	$650	$500	$400	$350	$325	$300

Add premiums for grades D, E, and F.

MODEL 12C NRA TARGET - limited manufacture.

	$1,100	$975	$800	$700	$550	$500	$450

MODEL 12CS - similar to Model 12C, chambered for .22 Rem. Spl. (.22 WRF) cal.

	$800	$650	$500	$400	$350	$325	$300

MODEL 16/16A AUTOLOADING RIFLE - .22 Rem. Autoloading cal., 22 in. barrel, open sight, tube mag. in buttstock, straight stock. 17,738 mfg. 1914-28.

	$600	$550	$450	$325	$300	$275	$250

Add premiums for higher grades C, D, and F.

MODEL 24/24A AUTOLOADING RIFLE - .22 S or LR cal., 19 in. barrel, open sights, Browning semi-auto design, bottom ejection, tube mag. through buttstock, take-down, plain pistol grip stock. Approx. 131,000 mfg. 1922-35.

	$400	$300	$250	$175	$150	$125	$115

Add premiums for higher grades C Special, D Peerless, E Expert, and F Premier.

MODEL 37 "RANGEMASTER" BOLT ACTION TARGET RIFLE - .22 LR cal., 5 shot with single shot adapter, 28 in. barrel, target sight and scope bases, target stock, 12 1/2 lbs. Mfg. 1937-40.

	$1,000	$850	$700	$600	$525	$475	$450

Add 50% for stock with original barrel band.

MODEL 37 - 1940 - improved trigger and stock design. Mfg. 1940-54.

	$1,000	$850	$700	$600	$525	$475	$450

Total manufacture of the Model 37 was 12,198.

MODEL 121A SLIDE ACTION RIFLE - hammerless, .22 S, L, or LR cal., 24 in. round barrel, tube mag., plain pistol grip stock. 201,000 were mfg. 1936-54.

	$450	$350	$275	$250	$225	$215	$200

Originally designated Model 121.

MODEL 121S - similar to Model 121A, except chambered for .22 Rem. Spl. (rare) cal.

	$600	$500	$400	$350	$325	$300	$275

MODEL 121SB/ROUTLEDGE - similar to Model 121A, except smooth bore for .22 shot, at least 5 different chamberings and barrel markings. Approx. 3,000 were mfg. pre-WWII-1952.

	$800	$750	$650	$600	$575	$550	$525

MODEL 241A SPEEDMASTER SEMI-AUTO - .22 S or LR cal., 24 in. barrel, replaced the Model 24, open sights, takedown, tube mag. through stock, non-checkered walnut stock and forearm. Approx. 132,000 mfg. 1935-49.

	$425	$375	$300	$200	$150	$125	$115

Add premiums for Special, Peerless, Expert, and Premier Grade models.

MODEL 504 BOLT ACTION - .17 Mach 2 (new 2005) or .22 LR cal., bolt action, drilled and tapped solid steel receiver, 20 in. barrel w/o sights, matte metal finish, features 5-R button rifling (same as the Model 40-XR), dual bedding points, fully adj. trigger group, dual extractors, 6 shot detachable mag., checkered American walnut stock, cocking indicator, approx. 6 lbs. New 2004.

MSR $710	$595	$475	$425	$365	$335	$295	$265

GRADING - PPGS™	100%	98%	95%	90%	80%	70%	60%

✳ *Model 504-T Bolt Action* - .17 HMR or .22 LR cal., similar to Model 504, except has 20 in. heavy free floating barrel, Eley match chamber, 5 (.17 HMR) or 6 shot mag., brown laminate Monte Carlo stock with palm swell and beavertail forend, satin blue metal, approx. 6.5 lbs. New 2005.

	MSR $799	$665	$525	$465	$395	$350	$315	$285

Add $26 for .17 HMR cal.

MODEL 513T (TARGET) "MATCHMASTER" BOLT ACTION - .22 LR cal., 27 in. barrel, Redfield aperture sight, target stock, 6 shot, sling swivels, approx. 166,000 were mfg. 1940-68.

	$395	$300	$250	$200	$175	$150	$125

A "TR" suffix on this gun indicated with sights, a "TX" indicated w/o sights, a "TS" indicated sporter. Most 513s are marked either 513T (Target) or 513S (Sporter).

MODEL 513S (SPORTER) - similar to Model 513T, with Marbles open sight and checkered sporter stock. 13,677 were mfg. 1941-56.

	$695	$650	$600	$550	$475	$400	$350

MODEL 521TL JR. BOLT ACTION - .22 LR cal., 25 in. barrel, Lyman target sights, takedown, 6 shot mag., target stock, approx. 67,000 were mfg. 1947-68.

	$350	$325	$300	$250	$200	$175	$150

These models had no ser. no. until 1954.

MODEL 522 VIPER SEMI-AUTO - .22 LR cal., semi-auto blowback action, 20 in. barrel, full-length black synthetic resin stock with beavertail forend, 10 shot mag., cocking indicator, adj. rear sight, grooved synthetic receiver, 4 5/8 lbs. Mfg. 1993-97.

	$150	$125	$110	$100	$90	$80	$70

Last MSR was $152.

MODEL 540X RIMFIRE - .22 LR cal., single shot bolt action, 26 in. heavy barrel, no sights, target stock, adj. butt, approx. 5,115. Mfg. 1969-74.

	$425	$400	$300	$250	$200	$185	$175

MODEL 540XR - similar to Model 540X, with large position style stock with adj. butt-plate. Mfg. 1974-83.

	$350	$325	$300	$250	$200	$185	$175

✳ *Model 540XR JR* - similar to Model 540X, except 1 1/2 in. shorter stock. Mfg. 1974-83.

	$350	$325	$300	$250	$200	$185	$175

MODEL 541S CUSTOM BOLT ACTION - .22 S, L, or LR cal., bolt action, 24 in. barrel, no sights, 5 shot mag., scroll engraved receiver and triggerguard, checkered walnut stock with rosewood pistol grip cap and forend tip. Mfg. 1972-84.

	$650	$575	$500	$425	$375	$325	$275

MODEL 541T BOLT ACTION - .22 LR cal. only, 5 shot mag., 24 in. standard or heavy (new 1993) barrel, checkered American walnut stock with satin finish, barrel is drilled and tapped, 5 7/8 lbs. Mfg. 1986-99.

	$380	$300	$235	$200	$180	$165	$150

Add $27 for heavy barrel.

Last MSR was $465.

MODEL 541X - .22 LR cal. only, bolt action, U.S. military training rifle, 27 in. barrel, 5 shot mag., ser. no. inscribed by hand on bolt, 9,077 mfg. 1984-86.

	$550	$450	$400	$375	$350	$325	$300

MODEL 550A SEMI-AUTO - .22 S, L, or LR cal., 24 in. barrel, open sight, shell deflector, 2 extractors, tube mag., plain one piece pistol stock. 34,577 Mfg. 1941-46.

	$195	$150	$110	$90	$80	$70	$60

GRADING - PPGS™	100%	98%	95%	90%	80%	70%	60%

Add 100% if w/o shell deflector (not tapped).

MODEL 550-1 - similar to Model 550A, except has single extractor. Approx. 730,000 mfg. 1946-70.

	$175	$140	$110	$90	$75	$65	$55

MODEL 550P - similar to Model 550-1, with aperture (peep) sight.

	$250	$200	$175	$150	$135	$120	$100

MODEL 550-2G - .22 Short cal., similar to Model 550-1, except 22 in. barrel and eye screw for counter chain in shooting gallery.

	$250	$225	$200	$160	$135	$120	$100

MODEL 552A SPEEDMASTER SEMI-AUTO - .22 S, L, or LR cal., 23 in. barrel, semi-auto open sight, tube mag., pistol grip stock. Mfg. 1957-disc.

	$160	$135	$120	$100	$85	$75	$65

This model was also mfg. in a 150th Anniversary Model (1966 only) and a 175th Anniversary (1991 only). Slight premiums are being asked if condition is 98% or better.

MODEL 552C - similar to Model 552A, with 21 in. barrel. Mfg. 1961-77.

	$170	$145	$130	$110	$95	$85	$75

✳ *Model 552 BDL Deluxe Speedmaster* - similar to Model 552C, except checkered gloss finished walnut Monte Carlo stock and forearm, 21 in. barrel, approx. 5.5 lbs. Mfg. 1966 to date.

MSR $413	$315	$230	$170	$130	$105	$90	$75

MODEL 552 175th ANNIVERSARY - 1,000 mfg. 1991 only.

	$395	$275	$200				

MODEL 572 LIGHTWEIGHT SLIDE ACTION - .22 S, L, LR cal., slide action, anodized alloy receiver and barrel, steel sleeved, checkered "Sun-Grain" stock and forend, 4 lbs. Offered in 3 colors. Approx. 34,785 mfg., 1958-62.

	100%	98%	95%	90%	80%	70%	60%
Buckskin Tan	$275	$250	$200	$150	$120	$110	$100
Crow-Wing Black	$375	$345	$295	$195	$150	$125	$100
Teal-Wing Blue	$700	$600	$425	$300	$250	$225	$200

MODEL 572SB/ROUTLEDGE - similar to Model 572A, except smooth bore.

	$400	$375	$350	$340	$330	$320	$310

MODEL 572 FIELDMASTER SLIDE ACTION - .22 S, L, or LR cal., slide action, 21 in. barrel, walnut stock and forearm, tube mag., 5 1/2 lbs. Mfg. 1955-88.

	$160	$145	$125	$105	$90	$75	$65

Last MSR was $176.

This model was also mfg. in a 150th Anniversary Model (1966 only). 20% premiums if condition is 98% or better.

✳ *Model 572 BDL Deluxe Fieldmaster* - similar to Model 572, except with checkered gloss finished walnut Monte Carlo stock and forearm. Mfg. 1966 to date.

MSR $427	$325	$235	$175	$130	$105	$90	$75

This model has also been available in several limited production runs. Prices are usually slightly higher than the standard pricing listed above.

MODEL 572 175th ANNIVERSARY - 300 mfg. 1991 only.

	$425	$295	$225				

MODEL 580 SINGLE SHOT - .22 S, L, or LR cal., bolt action, 24 in. barrel, open sights, Monte Carlo stock. Mfg. 1967-78.

	$150	$125	$105	$100	$90	$80	$75

Add 50% for smooth bore (Model 580SB).

GRADING - PPGS™	100%	98%	95%	90%	80%	70%	60%

MODEL 580BR - Boy's Model, 1 in. shorter stock. Mfg. 1971-78.

	100%	98%	95%	90%	80%	70%	60%
	$175	$150	$125	$100	$75	$65	$50

MODEL 581 BOLT ACTION - .22 LR cal., bolt action, 6 shot mag., converts to single shot. Mfg. 1967-83.

	$175	$160	$135	$115	$100	$90	$80

MODEL 581 SPORTSMAN - .22 LR cal., bolt action, 5 shot mag., 24 in. barrel, hardwood uncheckered stock, 4 3/4 lbs. Mfg. 1986-99.

	$175	$160	$135	$115	$100	$90	$80

Last MSR was $239.

MODEL 582 BOLT ACTION - similar to 581, with tube mag. Mfg. 1967-83.

	$175	$150	$125	$115	$100	$85	$75

MODEL 591 BOLT ACTION - 5mm Rimfire Mag. cal., 24 in. barrel, open sight, 5 shot mag., Monte Carlo stock. Approx. 27,000 mfg. 1970-74.

	$175	$125	$100	$85	$75	$65	$50

5mm rimfire ammo has been disc. for some time, and as a result, collectibility on this model is mostly for 95% or better condition. There is little shooter utility in lower conditions, so the discontinued ammo has become too expensive. Original 5mm ammo is selling for $50 or more per box.

MODEL 592 BOLT ACTION - similar to 591, with tube mag. Approx. 25,000 mfg. 1970-74.

	$175	$125	$100	$85	$75	$65	$50

MODEL 597 SEMI-AUTO - .22 LR cal., alloy receiver with nickel plated bolt, matte black metal finish, one-piece dark grey smooth synthetic stock, 20 in. free-floating barrel, 10 shot staggered detachable mag., adj. iron sights, new trigger design, 5.5 lbs. New 1997.

MSR $156	$130	$115	$100	$90	$80	$70	$60

This model has also been available in several limited production runs. Prices are usually slightly higher than the standard pricing listed above.

✳ *Model 597 Sporter* - similar to Model 597, except has hardwood stock, includes sling swivel studs. Mfg. 1998-2000.

	$160	$135	$115	$100	$90	$80	$70

Last MSR was $199.

✳ *Model 597 Stainless Sporter* - similar to Model 597 Sporter, except has stainless steel barrel and hardwood stock. Mfg. 2000 only.

	$190	$155	$130

Last MSR was $239.

✳ *Model 597 SS* - similar to Model 597, except is stainless synthetic with satin finished receiver and barrel, beavertail style forend. New 1998.

MSR $240	$190	$155	$125

✳ *Model 597 LSS* - similar to Model 597, except has stainless steel barrel with matching alloy receiver, and satin finished brown wood laminate stock, 5 1/2 lbs. New 1997.

MSR $295	$245	$195	$160

✳ *Model 597 HB LS* - similar to Model 597 LSS, except has 20 in. heavy steel barrel. New 2001.

MSR $288	$240	$190	$160

MODEL 597 CUSTOM TARGET - .22 LR cal., 20 in. custom contoured satin finish heavy stainless free floating barrel w/o sights, match chamber, special green laminated stock with Monte Carlo profile and beavertail forend. Mfg. 1998-2000.

	$495	$400	$300

Last MSR was $599.

GRADING - PPGS™	100%	98%	95%	90%	80%	70%	60%

✳ Model 597 Custom Target - .22 Mag. cal. Disc. 2000.

	$600	$450	$350				

Last MSR was $745.

MODEL 597 MAGNUM SYNTHETIC
- .17 HMR (new 2003) or .22 Mag. cal., similar in appearance to Model 597, 8 shot mag., 20 in. barrel, black synthetic stock with sling swivel studs, 6 lbs. New 1997.

MSR $351	$285	$240	$190	$170	$140	$125	$110

Add $26 for .17 HMR cal.

✳ Model 597 Magnum LS - .17 HMR (mfg. 2002-2003 only) or .22 Mag. (disc. 2003) cal., features brown laminate stock with sling swivel studs and steel barrel. Mfg. 1998-2003.

	$315	$265	$230	$190	$160	$140	$125

Last MSR was $377.

✳ Model 597 Magnum LS Heavy Barrel - .17 HMR or .22 Mag. cal., similar to Model 597 Magnum LS, except has 20 in. heavy barrel, 6 lbs. New 2001.

MSR $428	$350	$290	$245	$200	$165	$140	$125

Add $27 for .17 HMR cal.

RIFLES: RIMFIRE - "NYLON SERIES"

These models can be identified by the markings on the grip cap.

NYLON 10 SINGLE SHOT
- .22 S, L, or LR cal., bolt action. 8,606 were mfg. 1962-64.

	$275	$220	$165	$120	$90	$75	$60

✳ Nylon 10-SB - similar to Nylon 10, except smooth bore barrel used for .22 shot cartridges. 2,064 mfg.

	$1,000	$800	$500	$300	$175	$155	$135

This model is infrequently encountered.

MOHAWK 10-C
- similar to Model 77, renamed after changing to a 10 shot mag, approx. 129,000 were mfg. 1971-78.

	$200	$175	$125	$115	$110	$105	$100

MODEL 11 NYLON
- .22 S, L, or LR cal., bolt action repeater, 6 or 10 shot mag., 4 1/2 lbs. 22,423 were mfg. 1962-64.

	$325	$275	$250	$200	$150	$100	$75

MODEL 12 NYLON
- similar to 11, with tube mag. 27,551 were mfg. 1962-64.

	$325	$275	$250	$200	$150	$100	$75

NYLON 66 AUTOLOADER
- .22 LR cal., 19 5/8 in. barrel, open sights, buttstock tube mag. holds 14 shells, 4 lbs. Stock made from Zytel plastic in black, brown, or green. 1,050,336 were mfg. 1959-90.

	$200	$175	$125	$115	$110	$105	$100

Add 25% for Black Diamond (56,000 mfg.).
Add 40% for Apache black or chrome finish (221,000 mfg.).
Add 50% for Seneca green (45,000 mfg.).
Add 100% for Gallery Special (.22 Short cal. only).

Last MSR was $124.

NYLON 66 150TH ANNIVERSARY
- 3,792 mfg. in 1966 only with 150th Anniversary Remington logo on receiver.

	$500	$475	$350	$250	$175	$165	$150

NYLON 66 BICENTENNIAL
- inscription on receiver, 10,268 mfg. 1976 only, brown nylon stock only.

	$450	$400	$300	$250	$225	$200	$150

GRADING - PPGS™	100%	98%	95%	90%	80%	70%	60%

NYLON 76 LEVER ACTION - similar appearance to Nylon 66 with brown or black stock, short throw lever action, 25,312 mfg. in standard finish, 1,615 mfg. in black chrome finish 1962-64 only.

	100%	98%	95%	90%	80%	70%	60%
Standard finish (25,312 mfg.)	$500	$425	$350	$300	$250	$225	$200
Apache Black/chrome finish (1,615 mfg.)	$700	$625	$550	$500	$425	$400	$350

The Nylon 76 "Trail Rider" is the only lever action repeating rifle ever mfg. by Remington.

NYLON 77 - similar to Nylon 66, except with 5 shot mag. 15,327 were mfg. 1970-71 only.

	100%	98%	95%	90%	80%	70%	60%
	$300	$250	$200	$150	$125	$115	$100

NYLON APACHE 77 - similar to Model 10-C, but bright green stock. Mfg. for K-Mart in 1987-89.

	100%	98%	95%	90%	80%	70%	60%
	$135	$100	$65	$55	$50	$45	$40

RIFLES: BOLT ACTION, CENTERFIRE

The models in this section have been listed in numerical sequence for quick reference.

Remington has manufactured many limited production runs for various distributors and wholesalers over the years. These rifles are usually built to a specific configuration (caliber, stock, barrel length, finish, etc.), and are usually available until supplies run out. While these models are not included in this section, pricing in most cases will be similar to the base models from which they were derived.

MODEL SEVEN LIGHTWEIGHT - .17 Rem. (mfg. 1993-95), .222 Rem. (disc. 1984), .223 Rem. (new 1984), .243 Win., .260 Rem. (new 1997), 6mm Rem. (disc. 1994), 7mm-08 Rem., or .308 Win. cal., short action, 18 1/2 in. barrel, 4 or 5 shot mag., individually test fired, oil finished American walnut, adj. rear and ramp front sight (w/o sights on .17 Rem.), 6 1/4 lbs. Mfg. 1983-1999.

	100%	98%	95%	90%	80%	70%	60%
	$475	$370	$275	$225	$205	$180	$165

Last MSR was $585.

Add 5%-10% for .17 Rem. cal.

Add 10% for .222 Rem. cal.

All steel Model Sevens (including floor plate and triggerguard) are currently commanding a small premium.

✳ *Model Seven LS Lightweight* - .223 Rem., .243 Win., .260 Rem. (disc. 2001), .308 Win., or 7mm-08 Rem. cal., features brown laminated stock, 20 in. steel barrel, matte barrel and satin wood finish, 6 1/2 lbs. New 2000.

MSR $735	$590	$455	$325	$260	$225	$200	$180

✳ *Model Seven LS Magnum* - .300 Rem. SAUM or 7mm Rem. SAUM cal., short action, 22 in. barrel, blue action and barrel, 3 shot mag. with detachable floor plate, brown laminated stock, sling swivel studs, 7 1/8 lbs. New 2002.

MSR $775	$615	$455	$350

✳ *Model Seven LSS* - .22-250 Rem., .243 Win. (disc. 2001), or 7mm-08 Rem. cal., similar to Model Seven LS, except has stainless steel barrel w/o sights. Mfg. 2000-2003.

	$610	$445	$325

Last MSR was $770.

✳ *Model Seven SS* - .223 Rem. (mfg. 1997-2002), .243 Win., .260 Rem. (new 1997), .308 Win., or 7mm-08 Rem. cal., features stainless steel construction, 20 in. barrel w/o sights, and synthetic stock, 6.25 lbs. New 1994.

MSR $763	$600	$445	$320

GRADING - PPGS™	100%	98%	95%	90%	80%	70%	60%

* ✳ *Model Seven SS Magnum* - .300 Rem. SAUM or 7mm Rem. SAUM cal., short action, satin finished stainless steel action and 22 in. barrel, 3 shot mag. with detachable floor plate, black synthetic stock, sling swivel studs, 7 1/8 lbs. New 2002.

	MSR $803	$635	$475	$360			

* ✳ *Model Seven Youth* - .204 Ruger (limited mfg. 2004 only), .223 Rem. (new 2000), .243 Win., 6mm Rem. (disc. 1994), .260 Rem. (new 1998), .308 Win. (disc.), or 7mm-08 Rem. (new 1994) cal., also available in 20 in. barrel beginning 2000, uncheckered hardwood (.260 Rem. cal.) or synthetic (new 2004) stock shortened 1 in., 6 lbs. New 1993.

MSR $580	$460	$380	$310	$245	$205	$180	$165

Subtract $33 for limited edition synthetic model in .204 Ruger cal.

* ✳ *Model Seven FS* - .243 Win., 7mm-08 Rem., or .308 Win. cal., 18 1/2 in. parkerized blue barrel, grey or grey camo Kevlar fiberglass stock, adj. rear sight, 5 1/4 lbs. Mfg. 1987-89 only.

$525	$455	$415	$375	$335	$310	$285

Last MSR was $600.

* ✳ *Model Seven Custom MS (Mannlicher Stock)* - .222 Rem., .22-250 Rem., .223 Rem., .243 Win., .250 Savage, .257 Roberts, .260 Rem. (new 1997), .308 Win., .35 Rem., .350 Rem. Mag., 6mm, or 7mm-08 Rem. cal., features 20 in. custom shop barrel with Model 7 action bedded to a Mannlicher style laminate full stock, 6.5 lbs. New 1993.

MSR $1,332	$1,130	$835	$610	$495	$425	$385	$340

This model is available from the Custom Shop only (special order).

* ✳ *Model Seven Custom KS* - .223 Rem. (new 1989), .260 Rem. (new 1998), 7mm BR Rem. (mfg. 1989-1990), 7mm-08 Rem. (new 1989), .308 Win. (new 1991), .35 Rem., or .350 Rem. Mag. cal., 20 in. barrel with (.35 Rem. or .350 Rem. Mag.) or w/o sights, synthetic Kevlar stock with solid recoil pad, 5.75 lbs. New 1987.

MSR $1,314	$1,095	$825	$580	$485	$425	$385	$340

This model is available from the Custom Shop only (special order).

* ✳ *Model Seven AWR (Alaskan Wilderness Rifle)* - .300 Rem. SAUM or 7mm Rem. SAUM cal., short action, stainless steel action and 22 in. barrel with matte black Teflon satin finish, 3 shot mag. with detachable floor plate, fiberglass matte black stock, sling swivel studs, 6 1/8 lbs. New 2002.

MSR $1,546	$1,365	$1,160	$810	$650	$550	$450	$375

This model is available from the Custom Shop only (special order).

MODEL 30A RIFLE

- .25 Rem., .30 Rem., .30-06 (original cal.), .32 Rem., .35 Rem., or 7x57mm Mauser (introduced 1931), Enfield M/1917 type action, 22 in. barrel, checkered pistol grip stock. Mfg. 1921-40.

	$550	$475	$400	$350	$300	$260	$200

MODEL 30R CARBINE

- .25 Rem., .30 Rem., .32 Rem., .35 Rem., or .30-06 cal., similar to Model 30A, with 20 in. barrel. Introduced 1927.

	$575	$500	$450	$375	$325	$275	$225

MODEL 30 EXPRESS

- .25 Rem., .30 Rem., .32 Rem., .35 Rem., or .30-06 cal. Introduced 1926.

	$550	$475	$400	$350	$300	$260	$200

MODEL 30S (SPECIAL GRADE)

- .25 Rem. rimless (introduced 1931), .257 Roberts (new 1934), 7x57mm Mauser (introduced 1931), or .30-06 (original cal.) cal., deluxe version of Model 30A, 22 or 24 in. barrel, Lyman receiver sight, special stock, 7 1/2 lbs. Mfg. 1930-40.

	$675	$550	$500	$450	$375	$300	$250

The Model 30S Express Rifle was introduced in 1934 in .257 Roberts cal.

GRADING - PPGS™	100%	98%	95%	90%	80%	70%	60%

MODEL 78 SPORTSMAN - .223 Rem., .243 Win., .270 Win., .30-06, or .308 Win. cal., 22 in. barrel, 4 shot mag., uncheckered hardwood stock, open sights, 7 lbs. Mfg. 1984-89.

	$300	$250	$210	$190	$170	$160	$150

Last MSR was $333.

MODEL XR-100 RANGEMASTER - .204 Ruger, .22-250 Rem., or .223 Rem., features XP-100 sinigle shot target pistol action with Model 40-XP target adj. trigger, 26 in. barrel, laminate thumbhole stock with vent. beavertail forend. New 2005.

MSR $879	$735	$620	$555	$490	$445	$395	$365

MODEL 600 - .222 Rem., .223 Rem. (very rare), 6mm Rem., .243 Win., .308 Win., or .35 Rem. cal., 18 1/2 in. VR barrel, dog leg bolt handle, checkered pistol grip stock. 94,086 were mfg. 1964-68.

	100%	98%	95%	90%	80%	70%	60%
Reg. cals.	$450	$350	$275	$210	$195	$175	$155
.35 Rem.	$575	$495	$350	$320	$295	$270	$250
.222 Rem.	$495	$465	$425	$385	$350	$325	$295
.223 Rem.	$995	$825	$700	$500	$400	$350	$325

315 Model 600s in .223 Rem. cal. were mfg.

✳ *Model 600 Montana Centennial* - 6mm Rem., 1,020 mfg. in 1964 only.

	$900	$700	$600				

Last MSR was $125.

MODEL 600 MAGNUM - 6.5mm Rem. Mag. or .350 Rem. Mag. cal., laminated walnut/beech stock with or without recoil pad (early mfg. walnut stocks did not have recoil pad). Mfg. 1965-68.

	$975	$875	$775	$675	$575	$475	$425

MODEL 600 MOHAWK - .222 Rem., 6mm Rem., .243 Win., or .308 Win. cal., this variation was a promotional model, 18 1/2 in. barrel with no rib. 94,920 were mfg. 1971-79.

	$395	$325	$285	$265	$240	$225	$200

MODEL 660 STANDARD - .222 Rem., 6mm Rem., .243 Win., or .308 Win. cal., 20 in. barrel, open sight, dog leg bolt handle, checkered pistol grip stock, black pistol grip cap and forend tip. 50,536 were mfg. 1968-71.

	$495	$465	$425	$385	$350	$325	$295

Add 10% for .222 Rem. cal.

✳ *.223 Rem. cal.* - 227 total mfg. This cal. was never listed in a Remington catalog.

	$1,100	$875	$725	$600	$500	$400	$350

MODEL 660 MAGNUM - 6.5mm Rem. Mag. or .350 Rem. Mag. cal., laminated stock and recoil pad.

	$875	$700	$600	$450	$400	$350	$300

MODEL 673 GUIDE RIFLE - .300 Rem. Ultra Mag., .350 Rem. Mag., 6.5mm Rem. Mag. (new 2004) or .308 Win. (new 2004) cal., patterned after the Model 600 Magnum and features the Model Seven action, 22 in. contoured barrel with VR and iron sights, drilled and tapped, two-tone tan wide striped checkered laminate stock with solid recoil pad, 3 shot hidden mag., polished blue metal, 7.5 lbs. New 2003.

MSR $859	$720	$610	$545	$485	$440	$395	$365

MODEL 710 SPORTSMAN - .270 Win., .30-06, 7mm Rem. Mag. (new 2004) or .300 Win. Mag. (new 2004) cal., unique bolt to barrel lockup design utilizing 3 locking lugs on bolt face that lock directly in an integrated rear barrel design (as opposed to locking into the receiver), long action, steel (became standard 2005) or polymer receiver sleeve (disc. 2004), adj. trigger, detachable 4 shot box mag, 60 degree bolt throw, 22 in. ordnance grade steel barrel with matte finish, grey synthetic stock with solid

GRADING - PPGS™	100%	98%	95%	90%	80%	70%	60%

pad, supplied with bore sighted 3-9x40mm Bushnell Sharpshooter scope and mounts, ISS (Integrated Security System) locking bolt safety, 7 1/8 lbs. New 2001.

	MSR $426	$350	$315	$290	$260	$250	$240	$230

Add $39 for limited edition Skyline Excel camo (mfg. 2004 only).

MODEL 720A - Enfield type action, .257 Roberts, .270 Win., or .30 - 06 cal., 22 in. barrel, open sights, 5 shot, checkered pistol grip stock, 2,500 mfg. 1941-44.

	$1,200	$995	$850	$700	$600	$500	$400

Add 50%+ for .270 Win. cal.

Add 100%+ for .257 Roberts cal.

920-1,000 Model 720As were purchased by the Dept. of Navy during 1942 and used as trophies - these are discernible by crossed cannon proofs on wood.

Most of this model was chambered for .30-06 cal. Approx. 100 were chambered for .270 Win. and 20 or less were chambered for the .257 Roberts.

MODEL 720R - similar to 720A, except with 20 in. barrel.

	$1,400	$1,100	$900	$750	$650	$550	$450

This is the rarest variation in the Model 720 Series.

MODEL 720S - similar to 720A, except with 24 in. barrel.

	$1,475	$1,125	$900	$750	$600	$500	$400

MODEL 721 - .270 Win., .280 Rem. (new 1960), or .30-06 cal., 24 in. barrel, open sights, 4 shot, plain pistol grip stock. Mfg. 1948-62.

	$395	$300	$225	$200	$165	$155	$145

.280 Rem. (688 mfg.) and .264 Win. Mag. (1,115 mfg.) are rare in this model. 100% condition on these calibers could bring $700+.

MODEL 721ADL - similar to Model 721A, except has deluxe checkered stock.

	$465	$415	$375	$335	$280	$240	$200

This model's suffix does not appear on the gun. ADL features will determine the model.

MODEL 721BDL - similar to 721ADL, except has extra select wood.

	$525	$465	$415	$365	$330	$300	$275

This model's suffix does not appear on the gun. BDL features will determine the model.

MODEL 721A MAGNUM - .264 Win. Mag. or .300 H&H cal., 26 in. heavy barrel, recoil pad, 3 shot mag., 8 1/4 lbs.

	$495	$450	$360	$320	$295	$275	$260

Add 15% for .264 Win. Mag. cal.

MODEL 721ADL MAGNUM - 264 Win. Mag., similar to 721A Mag., checkered. 1,115 mfg. 1961-62, not cataloged.

	$550	$495	$400	$350	$315	$290	$275

MODEL 721BDL MAGNUM - similar to 721ADL Mag., select wood.

	$675	$600	$525	$465	$415	$390	$360

MODEL 722(A) - short action version of 721A, .222 Rem. (mfg. 1950-62), .222 Rem. Mag. (mfg. 1958-62), .243 Win. (mfg. 1960-62), .244 Rem. (mfg. 1957-62), .257 Roberts (disc. 1960), .300 Savage (disc. 1959), or .308 Win. (mfg. 1956-62) cal., 7 lbs. Mfg. 1948-62.

	$350	$300	$275	$250	$225	$200	$180

Subtract 10% for .300 Savage cal.

Add 20% for .257 Roberts or .308 Win. cal.

.222 Rem. Mag. (3,803 mfg.) and .243 Win. (2,186 mfg.) are rare in this model. Add approx. 25% to values for these cals.

MODEL 722ADL - similar to Model 722(A), except with deluxe checkered wood.

	$500	$425	$300	$275	$225	$200	$180

This model's suffix does not appear on the gun. ADL features will determine the model.

GRADING - PPGS™	100%	98%	95%	90%	80%	70%	60%

MODEL 722BDL - similar to Model 722ADL, except features extra select wood.

	100%	98%	95%	90%	80%	70%	60%
	$650	$550	$450	$375	$330	$300	$275

This model's suffix does not appear on the gun. BDL features will determine the model.

MODEL 725ADL - .222 Rem., .243 Win., .244 Rem., .270 Win., .280 Rem., or .30-06 cal., 22 in. barrel, open sights, 4 shot, checkered Monte Carlo stock. 16,635 mfg. 1958 - 61.

	100%	98%	95%	90%	80%	70%	60%
.30-06 cal.	$575	$450	$375	$350	$325	$300	$280
.270 Win.	$700	$575	$450	$400	$375	$350	$325
.280 Rem.	$900	$700	$525	$450	$400	$350	$325
.222 Rem.	$750	$625	$500	$450	$400	$350	$325
.244 Rem.	$800	$675	$500	$450	$400	$350	$325
.243 Win.	$800	$675	$500	$450	$400	$350	$325

Caliber mfg. breakdown is as follows: 7,657 in .30-06; 2,784 in .280 Rem.; 2,818 in .270 Win.; 840 in .244 Rem.; 1,478 in .222 Rem.; 998 in .243 Win.

MODEL 725 KODIAK - .375 H&H Mag. or .458 Win. Mag. cal., 26 in. barrel, 3 shot, recoil reducer in muzzle, deluxe checkered Monte Carlo stock, black pistol grip cap and forend tip. 52 mfg. 1961 only.

	100%	98%	95%	90%	80%	70%	60%
	$4,000	$3,200	$2,700	$2,250	$2,000	$1,800	$1,650

Only 24 rifles in .458 Win. Mag. were mfg. and 28 rifles in .375 H&H Mag.

MODEL 788 - .222 Rem. (disc. 1979, reintroduced 1982-83), .22-250 Rem., .223 Rem. (new 1975), 6mm Rem. (mfg. 1969-1979), .243 Win. (new 1969), .308 Win. (new 1969), .30-30 Win. (disc. 1972), 7mm-08 Rem. (new 1980), or .44 Mag. (disc. 1970) cal., 18 1/2 (Carbine, .243 Win., .308 Win., or 7mm-08 Rem. cal.), 22 (6mm Rem., .243 Win., and .308 Win. cal.), or 24 (.222 Rem., .22-250 Rem., .223 Rem. cal. 1967-1979, .223 Rem. and .22-250 Rem. cal. 1980-83) in. barrel, short action, open sight, plain pistol grip Monte Carlo stock. Mfg. 1967-1983.

	100%	98%	95%	90%	80%	70%	60%
Rifle	$375	$275	$250	$225	$210	$200	$185
Carbine (18 1/2 in. barrel)	$375	$275	$250	$225	$210	$200	$185

Add 10% for .30-30 Win. cal.

Add 15% for 7mm-08 Rem. cal.

Add 30% for .44 Mag. cal.

Add 10% for left-hand action (6mm Rem. and .308 Win. cal. only, mfg. 1969-1979).

In 1970, this gun was also manufactured with a 4X scope as a promotion, but was a non-Remington catalog item.

RIFLES: BOLT ACTION, MODEL 700 & VARIATIONS

MODEL 700 TITANIUM ULTIMATE LIGHTWEIGHT - .260 Rem., .270 Win., .30-06, .300 Rem. SAUM (new 2004), .308 Win. (new 2002), 7mm Rem. SAUM (new 2004), or 7mm-08 Rem cal., titanium receiver (drilled and tapped), spiral cut breech bolt with flutes and skeleton handle, 22 in. stainless steel barrel, satin stainless finish on receiver and barrel, ultra lightweight carbon-fiber matte finished Kevlar reinforced stock, 3-4 shot fixed mag., sling swivel studs, 5.25-5.5 lbs. New 2001.

MSR $1,272	$925	$865	$715

Add $40 for Rem. SAUM cals.

MODEL 700 AS - .22-250 Rem., .243 Win., .270 Win., .280 Rem., .30-06, .308 Win., 7mm Rem. Mag., or .300 Wby. Mag. cal., synthetic stock is made from Arylon resin, matte black finished stock and metal, 22 or 24 in. barrel, 6 1/2 lbs. Mfg. 1989-91 only.

$475	$370	$310	$275	$250	$220	$195

Last MSR was $528.

Add $21 for 7mm Rem. Mag. or .300 Wby. Mag. cal.

GRADING - PPGS™	100%	98%	95%	90%	80%	70%	60%

MODEL 700 FS - .243 Win., .270 Win., .30-06, .308 Win., or 7mm Rem. Mag. cal., 22 in. polished blue barrel, grey or grey camo Kevlar fiberglass stock with solid recoil pad, iron sights, 6 1/4 lbs. Mfg. 1987-88 only.

	100%	98%	95%	90%	80%	70%	60%
	$530	$460	$415	$375	$335	$310	$285

Last MSR was $613.

Add $20 for 7mm Rem. Mag. cal. (24 in. barrel).

MODEL 700P & VARIATIONS - various cals., long or short action, various barrel lengths, designed for police/law enforcement and military, current configurations include: 700P, 700P TWS (Tactical Weapons System, includes scope, bipod and case), 700P LTR (Light Tactical Rifle), 700P LTR TWS (Light Tactical Rifle/Tactical Weapons System, includes scope, bipod, and case), and the Model M-24 (combination of Model 700 and Model 40-XB design, sniper weapon system with scope, case, and bipod).

Remington does not publish consumer retail pricing for these police/law enforcement models. Secondary prices for base models w/o scopes and other options will be slightly higher than for current pricing on the Model 700BDL Custom Deluxe. Prices for rifles with scopes and other features will be determined by how much the individual options and accessories add to the base value.

MODEL 700 RS - .270 Win., .280 Rem., or .30-06 cal., 22 in. polished blue barrel, grey or grey camo DuPont Rynite synthetic stock with smooth cheekpiece and solid recoil pad, iron sights, 7 1/4 lbs. Mfg. 1987-88 only.

	100%	98%	95%	90%	80%	70%	60%
	$550	$475	$425	$385	$350	$310	$285

Last MSR was $547.

Add 30% for .280 Rem. cal.

In 1987 less than 500 rifles were dual barrel marked - 7mm EXP REM .280 REM. These specimens will command a 40% premium.

MODEL 700 CAMO SYNTHETIC - .22-250 Rem. (disc. 1993), .243 Win., .270 Win. (disc. 1993), .280 Rem. (disc. 1993), 7mm-08 Rem. (disc. 1993), 7mm Rem. Mag., .30-06, .308 Win. (disc. 1993), or .300 Wby. Mag. (disc. 1993) cal., 22 or 24 (Mag. only) in. barrel, features synthetic stock and is fully camouflaged in Mossy Oak Bottomland pattern, iron sights, approx. 7 1/4 lbs. Mfg. 1992-94.

	100%	98%	95%	90%	80%	70%	60%
	$490	$425	$350	$315	$285	$265	$250

Last MSR was $581.

Add $27 for Mag. cals.

MODEL 700ADL DELUXE RIFLE - .22-250 Rem. (disc. 1991), .222 Rem. (disc.), .222 Rem. Mag. (disc.), .25-06 Rem. (disc. 1991), 6mm Rem. (disc.), .243 Win. (disc. 1997), .270 Win., .280 Rem. (disc. 1997 - marked 7mm Express 1979-82), .30-06, .308 Win. (disc. 2001), or 7mm Rem. Mag. (disc. 2002) cal., 20 (disc.), 22, or 24 in. barrel, open sights, 4 shot mag., checkered Monte Carlo stock or brown laminated stock (new 1988). Mfg. 1962-2005.

	100%	98%	95%	90%	80%	70%	60%
	$460	$360	$280	$230	$175	$165	$155

Last MSR was $580.

Add 5% for 7mm Rem. Mag. cal. (disc. 2002).
Add 20% for 20 in. barrel (mfg. 1962-63).
Add 50% for .222 Rem. Mag. or .280 Rem. cal. 20 in barrel.
Add 15% for 7mm Rem. Mag., .264 Win. Mag., or .300 Win. Mag. cal. with stainless steel barrel (mfg. 1962-1970).

During 1962-63, the 20 in. barrel was standard on .222 Rem., .222 Rem. Mag., .243 Win., .270 Win., .280 Rem., .30-06, or .308 Win. cal. In 1964, these cals. had a standard barrel length of 22 in.; 24 in. barrels were standard on 7mm Rem. Mag. and .264 Win. Mag. cal.

Remington, in 1987-89, introduced a Model 700 Gun Kit that enabled the owner to assemble the stock to the barreled action. All metal work is completely finished and wood finishing is all that is required. This kit was available in most popular cals. - last MSR price was $333 (1989).

✳ *Model 700ADL Synthetic* - .22-250 Rem. (new 1999), .223 Rem., .243 Win., .270 Win., .30-06, .308 Win., .300 Win. Mag. (new 1999), or 7mm Rem. Mag., features fiberglass reinforced synthetic stock with positive checkering, black matte finish on metal, open sights, approx. 7 3/8 lbs. Mfg. 1996-2005.

	100%	98%	95%	90%	80%	70%	60%
	$395	$315	$260	$215	$185	$170	$155

Last MSR was $500.

Add $27 for .300 Win. Mag. or 7mm Rem. Mag. cal.

✳ *Model 700ADL Synthetic Youth* - .243 Win., .270 Win. (new 2004), .30-06 (new 2004), or .308 Win. cal., similar to Model 700ADL Synthetic, except has 20 in. barrel and 1 in. shorter LOP. Disc. 2005.

	100%	98%	95%	90%	80%	70%	60%
	$395	$315	$260	$215	$185	$170	$155

Last MSR was $500.

✳ *Model 700ADL/LS* - .243 Win. (mfg. 1989-1993), .270 Win. (new 1989), .30-06, or 7mm Rem. Mag. (mfg. 1988-1993) cal., brown laminate stock with checkering. Mfg. 1988-1993, reintroduced 2002-2004.

	100%	98%	95%	90%	80%	70%	60%
	$460	$360	$280	$230	$175	$165	$155

Last MSR was $580.

Add $27 for 7mm Rem. Mag. cal. (disc.).

This model was available through selective distributors only.

MODEL 700BDL CUSTOM DELUXE - .17 Rem., .22-250 Rem., .222 Rem., .223 Rem., .243 Win., .25-06 Rem., .264 Win. Mag. (disc.), .270 Win., .280 Rem. (mfg. 1992-95, resumed 2000-2002), .300 Savage (mfg. 1992 only), .30-06, .308 Win. (disc. 1995), .35 Whelen (mfg. 1989-94), 6mm Rem. (disc. 1994), 7mm-08 Rem. (disc. 1994, reintroduced 2000-2002), 7mm Rem. Mag., .308 Win. (left-hand only, disc. 2004), .300 Win. Mag., .300 Rem. Ultra Mag (new 1999), .338 Win. Mag. (mfg. 1988-94, resumed 1997-2002), .338 Rem. Ultra Mag. (mfg. 2000-2002, mfg. 2004 in left-hand only), .375 Rem. Ultra Mag. (mfg. 2001-2002), 7mm Rem. Ultra Mag. (new 2001), or 8mm Mag. (disc.) cal., 22, 24 (Magnum), or 26 (SAUM cals.) in. barrel, similar to 700ADL Deluxe, except with hinged floorplate, cut skipline checkering, black pistol grip cap and forend tip, receiver and floorplate fine line engraving was standard 1997-2001, supplied with iron sights first year, approx. 7 1/4-7 5/8 lbs.

MSR $716		$570	$440	$355	$295	$255	$220	$195

Add $27-$67 for left-hand model (available in certain cals. only, short action .22-250 Rem. and .243 Win. cals. are scarce in left-hand, disc. 2004).

Add $27 for .17 Rem., 7mm Rem. Mag., .300 Win. Mag., .338 Win. Mag. (disc.), .300 Rem. Ultra Mag. or 7mm Rem. Ultra Mag. cal.

Add 15% for 7mm Rem. Mag., .264 Win. Mag., or .300 Win. Mag. cal. with stainless steel barrel (mfg. 1962-1970).

In 1962, the 20 in. barrel was standard on .222 Rem., .222 Rem. Mag., .243 Win., .270 Win., .280 Rem., .30-06, or .308 Win. cal. In 1964, these cals. had a standard barrel length of 22 in. 24 in. barrels were standard on 7mm Rem. Mag. and .264 Win. Mag. cals.

Remington mfg. the Model 700BDL in .350 Rem. Mag. and 6.5mm Rem. Mag. (1,584 mfg. between 1969-75). 1,558 were assembled in 1969, and sold through 1975. The .350 Rem. Mag. mfg. in 1969 is 3 times rarer than the 1985 Model 700 Classic chambered for .350 Rem. Mag.

	100%	98%	95%	90%	80%	70%	60%
.222 Rem. Mag.	$575	$500	$425	$340	$300	$280	$260
.350 Rem. Mag.	$750	$575	$450	$350	$325	$300	$275
6.5mm Rem. Mag.	$750	$575	$450	$350	$325	$300	$275

MODEL 700BDL 200th ANNIVERSARY SPECIAL EDITION - .30-06 cal., features curly maple stock with ebony forend cap and pistol grip, 200th Anniversary and Remington cameo/caption laser etched on floorplate. Limited mfg. 1993 only.

	100%	98%	95%	90%	80%	70%	60%
	$725	$650	$575	$500	$400	$300	$200

GRADING - PPGS™	100%	98%	95%	90%	80%	70%	60%

MODEL 700BDL CLASSIC (LTD EDITION)

MODEL 700BDL CLASSIC (LTD EDITION) - similar to 700BDL, except has classic straight stock, high polish bluing, has been offered in .17 Rem., .220 Swift, .221 Fireball (new 2002), .222 Rem., .22-250 Rem. (Classic only), .223 Rem., .250 Savage (250/3000), 6.5x55mm Swedish, 6mm Rem. (Classic only), 7x57mm Mauser, 8mm Rem. Mag., 8mm Mauser, .243 Win. (Classic only), .25-06 Rem., .257 Roberts, .264 Win. Mag., .270 Win. (Classic only), .280 Rem., .300 Savage (new 2003), .300 Win. Mag., .300 Wby. Mag., .30-06 (Classic only), .308 Win. (new 2005), 7mm-08 Rem., 7mm Wby. Mag., .338 Win. Mag., .350 Rem. Mag., .35 Whelen, .300 H&H, or .375 H&H cal. The original Model 700 Classic was mfg. 1978-1985. Limited edition calibers were introduced during 1981 (see listings), and continue to be produced annually, receiver and floorplate fine line engraving was standard 1997-2001.

MSR $716	$580	$465	$375	$290	$255	$220	$195

Add 10% for 7x57mm Mauser, .220 Swift, .338 Win. Mag., or .350 Rem. Mag. cal.

The Model 700 Classic was originally introduced in 1978 in .22-250 Rem., 6mm Rem., .243 Win., .270 Win., .30-06, and 7mm Rem. Mag., and was part of the standard Remington product lineup until 1985. Limited editions were introduced during 1981, and are still being produced today.

This model is produced in limited quantities of a different caliber each year. Add premiums for several calibers in NIB condition only (including 7x57mm Mauser, .257 Roberts, .300 H&H, and .375 H&H).

The following is a list of annual Limited Classic calibers offered previously with year of manufacture: 7x57mm Mauser (1981), .257 Roberts (1982), .300 H&H (1983), .250 Savage (1984), .350 Rem. Mag. (1985), .264 Win. Mag. (1986), .338 Win. Mag. (1987), .35 Whelen (1988), .300 Wby. Mag. (1989), .25-06 Rem. (1990), 7mm Wby. Mag. (1991), .220 Swift (1992), .222 Rem. (1993), 6.5x55mm Swedish (new 1994), .300 Win. Mag. (1995), .375 H&H Mag. (1996), .280 Rem. (1997), 8mm Rem. Mag. (1998), .17 Rem. (1999), .223 Rem. (2000), 7mm-08 Rem. (2001), .221 Fireball (2002), .300 Savage (2003), 8mm Mauser (2004), and .308 Win. (2005).

MODEL 700BDL DM (DETACHABLE MAG.)

MODEL 700BDL DM (DETACHABLE MAG.) - .243 Win. (disc. 1999), .25-06 Rem. (disc. 1997), .260 Rem., .270 Win., .280 Rem. (disc. 1999), 6mm Rem. (disc. 1996), 7mm Rem. Mag., 7mm-08 Rem. (disc. 1999), .30-06, .308 Win. (disc. 1996), .300 Win. Mag. (disc. 2002), or .338 Win. Mag. (disc. 1996) cal., 22 or 24 in. barrel, Monte Carlo walnut stock with 20 LPI skip-line checkering, high polish bluing, black forend cap, receiver and floorplate fine line engraving was standard 1997-2001, open sights, 3-4 shot detachable mag. Mfg. 1995-2004.

	$600	$480	$390	$330	$285	$265	$250

Last MSR was $749.

Add $27 for .300 Win. Mag. and 7mm Rem. Mag. cals.

Left-hand actions on this model were disc. in 1999. Their last retail prices ranged from $665 - $692, depending on caliber.

✳ *Model 700BDL Lew Horton Special Edition* - .257 Roberts cal., 500 mfg. in 1990 only, first time the 700BDL has been offered in .257 Roberts cal.

	$575	$525	$450	$395	$360	$325	$280

Last MSR was $580.

MODEL 700BDL SS (STAINLESS SYNTHETIC)

MODEL 700BDL SS (STAINLESS SYNTHETIC) - .223 Rem. (mfg. 1993-94), .243 Win. (mfg. 1993-94), .25-06 Rem. (disc. 1994), .270 Win., .280 Rem. (disc. 1995), .30-06, .308 Win. (disc. 1994), 7mm Rem. (mfg. 1993-94), 7mm-08 Rem. (mfg. 1993-94), .300 Win. Mag. (new 1993), .300 Rem. Ultra Mag. (new 1999), .300 Rem. SA Ultra Mag. (new 2003), .300 Wby. Mag. (mfg. 1993-94), .338 Win. Mag. (mfg. 1993-94, resumed 1997-2002), .338 Rem. Ultra Mag. (new 2000), 7mm Rem. Mag., 7mm Rem. Ultra Mag. (new 2001), 7mm Rem. SA Ultra Mag. (new 2003), 7mm Wby. Mag. (scarce, disc. 1994), .375 Rem. Ultra Mag. (mfg. 2001-2002), or .375 H&H (mfg. 1997-2002) cal., features matte finished 416 stainless steel barrel, receiver, and bolt, black synthetic stock with checkering, R3 recoil pad became standard during 2004, drilled and tapped, hinged floorplate mag., 24 or 26 (Rem. Ultra Mag. cals.) in. barrel, no sights, 6.25-7 lbs. Mfg. 1992-2004.

	$585	$470	$355				

Last MSR was $735.

Add $26 for Mag. cals., except 7mm Rem. Mag.
Add $40 for Ultra Mag. or SA Ultra Mag. cals.
Add approx. $100 for .223 Rem. cal., $150 for 7mm Wby. Mag. cal.

GRADING - PPGS™	100%	98%	95%	90%	80%	70%	60%

✳ *Model 700BDL LSS* - .270 Win. (left-hand only, disc. 2000), .300 Win. Mag., .300 Rem. Ultra Mag. (new 1999), .338 Rem. Ultra Mag. (new 2000), .30-06 (left-hand only, disc. 2000), 7mm Rem. Ultra Mag., 7mm Rem. Mag., or .375 Rem. Ultra Mag. cal., stainless steel barreled action, grey tinted laminate Monte Carlo wood stock, 24 or 26 (Rem. Ultra Mag. cals.) in. barrel, w/o sights, 7.5 lbs. Mfg. 1996-2004.

	$660	$510	$390

Last MSR was $827.

Add $13 for Rem. Ultra Mag. cal.

Add $40 for Mag. cals. in left-hand action.

✳ *Model 700BDL SS DM (Detachable Mag.)* - .243 Win. (disc. 1997), .25-06 Rem. (disc. 2002), .260 Rem. (mfg. 1997-2000), .270 Win., .280 Rem. (disc. 2002), 6mm Rem. (disc. 1995), 7mm Rem. Mag., 7mm-08 Rem. (disc. 1998, resumed 2000-2001), .30-06, .308 Win. (disc. 1999), .300 Win. Mag., .300 Wby. Mag. (disc. 2000), or .338 Win. Mag. (disc. 1996) cal., features 3-4 shot detachable mag., stainless steel, 24 in. barrel, satin finish metalwork, R3 recoil pad became standard during 2004, black non-reflective stock with checkering, receiver and floorplate fine line engraving was standard in 1997-2001, w/o sights, 7 3/8 lbs. Mfg. 1995-2004.

	$670	$560	$460

Last MSR was $801.

Add $27 for Mag. cals.

Add $89 for muzzle brake (Model 700BDL SS DM-B, mfg. 1996-2001, available in 7mm STW, 7mm Rem. Mag. [disc. 1999] or .300 Win. Mag. cals. only).

MODEL 700BDL VARMINT SPECIAL - .22-250 Rem., .222 Rem., .223 Rem., .25-06 Rem.(disc.), 6mm Rem., .243 Win., .308 Win., or 7mm-08 Rem. cal., 24 in. heavy barrel, checkered walnut stock, no sights. Mfg. 1967-94.

	$480	$420	$350	$315	$285	$265	$250

Last MSR was $565.

✳ *Model 700VS (Varmint Synthetic)* - .220 Swift (disc. 1996), .22-250 Rem., .223 Rem., .243 Win. (mfg. 1997-98), or .308 Win. cal., short action, composite, textured black and grey synthetic stock features Kevlar, fiberglass, and graphite, matte metal finish, 26 in. heavy barrel w/o sights, 9 1/8 lbs. Mfg. 1992-2004.

	$650	$470	$410	$330	$295	$265	$250

Last MSR was $811.

Add $26 for left-hand action.

The right-hand model was disc. 1998, but resumed in 2000.

✳ *Model 700VSF* - .22-250 Rem., .223 Rem., or .308 Win. cal., updated Model 700VS with VS SFII stock design in desert tan with black webbing, 26 in. fluted heavy blue barrel, blue receiver, available in right- or left-hand action, 9 lbs. New 2005.

MSR $932	$750	$585	$455	$330	$290	$265	$250

Add $27 for left-hand action.

✳ *Model 700VS SF/SF-P (Varmint Synthetic Stainless Fluted/Ported)* - .220 Swift (ported barrel only until 2000), .22-250 Rem., .223 Rem. (w/o porting), .308 Win. (ported barrel only, disc. 1999) or .338 Rem. Ultra Mag. (mfg. 2000 only) cal., stainless steel action with 26 in. barrel with flutes, 2 barrel ports became an option in some cals. during 1998-99 only (Model SF-P), 8.5 lbs. Mfg. 1994-2004.

	$820	$600	$475

Last MSR was $976.

Add 5% for ported barrel (Model 700VS SF-P, disc. 1999).

✳ *Model 700VS SF-II* - .204 Ruger, .220 Swift, .22-250 Rem., or .223 Rem. cal., updated Model 700 VS SF with reconfigured H-S Precision composite stock, palm swell and contoured beavertail forend, 26 in. heavy barrel with black fluting, black synthetic stock with spruce green webbing, 8.5 lbs. New 2005.

MSR $1,025	$855	$625	$485

GRADING - PPGS™	100%	98%	95%	90%	80%	70%	60%

✳ ***Model 700VLS (Varmint Laminated Stock)*** - .204 Ruger (new 2005), .222 Rem. (mfg. 1995 only), .22-250 Rem., .223 Rem., .243 Win., 6mm Rem. (new 1998), .260 Rem. (disc. 1999), .308 Win., or 7mm-08 Rem. (mfg. 1997-99) cal., 26 in. heavy barrel, blue metalwork, w/o sights, brown laminated stock with (disc. 2001) or w/o skip line checkering, beavertail shaped forend became standard 1998, 9 3/8 lbs. New 1995.

	MSR $759	$615	$490	$385	$330	$290	$265	$250

✳ ***Model 700LV SF (Laminated Varmint Stainless Fluted)*** - .204 Ruger (new 2005), .17 Rem., .221 Rem. Fireball, .223 Rem., or .22-250 Rem. cal., short action, 22 in. fluted barrel w/o sights, black composite stock with R3 recoil pad, stainless action and barrel, jeweled bolt, blind box mag., 6.75 lbs. New 2004.

	MSR $952	$765	$590	$460

MODEL 700VS COMPOSITE
- .22-250 Rem., .223 Rem., or .308 Win. cal., similar to Model 700 Sendero Composite, except is available in short action only. Mfg. by Custom Shop 1999-2000.

$1,550	$1,225	$825	$700	$600	$550	$500

Last MSR was $1,912.

MODEL 700BDL SS CAMO RMEF
- .300 Rem SA Ultra Mag. (mfg. 2003), .300 Rem. Ultra Mag. (mfg. 2001), .300 Win. Mag. (new 2004), or 7mm Rem. Ultra Mag. (mfg. 2002) cal., Realtree Hardwoods camo stock treatment, satin finished receiver and round barrel, laser engraved floorplate including RMEF logo, limited special edition for the Rocky Mountain Elk Foundation, approx. 7.5 lbs. New 2001-2004.

$680	$525	$405

Last MSR was $835.

MODEL 700BDL DALE EARNHARDT JR.
- .30-06 cal., 22 in. blue barrel, 4 shot mag., synthetic stock with Dale Earnhardt Jr. signature #8 logo, special ser. no. (DEJ8xxx), R3 recoil pad, no sights, drilled and tapped. Limited mfg. 2004 only.

$675	$525	$425

Last MSR was $735.

MODEL 700 MOUNTAIN RIFLE DM (DETACHABLE MAG.)
- .243 Win. (disc. 1997), .260 Rem. (new 1998), .25-06 Rem. (disc. 2002), .270 Win., .280 Rem., 7mm-08 Rem., or .30-06 cal., detachable mag., 22 in. barrel, satin finished American walnut stock, R3 recoil pad became standard on Mag. cals., during 2004, satin bluing, without sights, approx. 6.5 lbs. New 1995.

	MSR $783	$625	$495	$395	$335	$290	$265	$250

✳ ***Model 700 Mountain LSS*** - .260 Rem., .270 Win., .30-06, or 7mm-08 Rem. cal., features stainless action and 22 in. barrel w/o sights, brown laminate stock, approx. 6.5 lbs. New 1999.

	MSR $833	$675	$525	$410

MODEL 700BDL MOUNTAIN RIFLE (FIXED MAG.)
- .243 Win. (new 1988), .25-06 Rem. (new 1992), .257 Roberts (new 1991), .270 Win., 7mm-08 Rem. (new 1988), .280 Rem., .30-06, .308 Win. (new 1988), or 7x57mm Mauser (new 1990) cal., 22 in. tapered barrel, checkered satin finished American walnut stock with cheekpiece and ebony forend, 4 shot mag., without sights, 6 3/4 lbs. Mfg. 1986-94.

$445	$380	$315	$275	$250	$220	$195

Last MSR was $532.

✳ ***Model 700BDL Mountain Stainless*** - .25-06 Rem., .270 Win., .280 Rem., or .30-06 cal., 22 in. barrel, black synthetic stock with pressed checkering, blind mag., 7 1/4 lbs. Mfg. 1993 only.

$450	$385	$315

Last MSR was $532.

GRADING - PPGS™	100%	98%	95%	90%	80%	70%	60%

MODEL 700BDL EUROPEAN - .243 Win., .270 Win., .280 Rem., 7mm-08 Rem., 7mm Rem. Mag., .30-06, or .308 Win. cal., Monte Carlo stock with hand-rubbed oil finish, 22 or 24 (Mag. cals. only) in. barrel, hinged floorplate, iron sights, approx. 7 1/4 lbs. Disc. 1994.

	100%	98%	95%	90%	80%	70%	60%
	$445	$375	$325	$280	$250	$220	$195

Last MSR was $532.

Add $27 for 7mm Rem. Mag. cal.

MODEL 700CDL - .243 Win., .25-06 Rem. (new 2005), .270 Win., .30-06, .35 Whelen (new 2005), .300 Win. Mag., 7mm-08 Rem., 7mm Rem. Mag., 7mm Rem. Ultra Mag., or .300 Rem. Ultra Mag., classic style checkered walnut stock with satin finish, black forend tip and pistol grip cap, satin blue metal finish, R3 recoil pad standard, 24 or 26 (Mag. cals.) in. barrel w/o sights, hinged floorplate, approx. 7.5 lbs. New 2004.

MSR $743	$605	$490	$385	$330	$290	$265	$250

Add $26 for Mag. cals.

Add $26 for left-hand action (select cals. only, new 2005).

MODEL 700 SENDERO SPECIAL - .25-06 Rem., .270 Win. (disc. 2001), .300 Win. Mag., or 7mm Rem. Mag. cal., similar to Model 700 VS, except has long action for Mag. cals., 24 (non-cataloged) or 26 in. barrel, 9 lbs. Mfg. 1994-2002.

	$635	$510	$420	$335	$295	$265	$250

Last MSR was $788.

Add $27 for Mag. cals.

Add approx. $100 for fluted barrel (not cataloged).

✳ *Model 700 Sendero SF (Stainless Fluted)* - .25-06 Rem. (disc. 2002), .300 Win. Mag., .300 Wby. Mag. (mfg. 1997-2001), .300 Rem. Ultra Mag. (new 1999), .300 Rem SA Ultra Mag. (new 2003), .338 Rem. Ultra Mag. (new 2000), 7mm STW (mfg. 1997-2002), 7mm Rem. Mag., 7mm Rem. Ultra Mag. (new 2001), or 7mm Rem. SA Ultra Mag. (new 2003) cal., 26 in. varmint type fluted barrel, approx. 8 1/2 lbs. Mfg. 1996-2004.

	$835	$640	$475				

Last MSR was $1,003.

MODEL 700 SENDERO COMPOSITE - .25-06 Rem., .300 Win. Mag., or 7mm STW cal., features 26 in. composite barrel, matte black finished steel action, Kevlar reinforced black synthetic stock, 7 7/8 lbs. Mfg. 1999 only.

	$1,395	$1,125	$750	$650	$575	$525	$475

Last MSR was $1,665.

MODEL 700 ETRONX VS SF - .220 Swift (electronic primer), .22-250 Rem. (electronic primer), or .243 Win. (electronic primer) cal., features patented Etronx technology utilizing an electronic discharge for virtually instant cartridge ignition, CPU located in stock incorporates standard 9V battery, and allows electric signal to be passed through a ceramic coated firing pin, which in turn activates the specially designed electronic primer. There are no moving parts in this system, and therefore, nothing to delay ignition. Electronic trigger mechanism enables almost zero lock time. LED on top of grip indicates system status (fire or safe mode), chamber status (loaded or not loaded), low battery indicator, and any possible system malfunction. 26 in. heavy stainless steel barrel with black flutes, alumiunum bedding, Kevlar reinforced composite stock with matte black finish, 8 7/8 lbs. Mfg. late 1999-2003.

	$1,150	$950	$750				

Last MSR was $1,332.

This model can fire only Etronx ammunition which used an electronic primer. Remington discontinued manufacture of Etronx ammunition during 2003.

Because the Etronx ignition system used an electronic primer the same size as a standard rifle primer, reloading was no different than using standard cases, powder, and bullets. The only thing that has changed is the electronic primer.

GRADING - PPGS™	100%	98%	95%	90%	80%	70%	60%

MODEL 700 SPS (SPECIAL PURPOSE SYNTHETIC)

- .204 Ruger, .22-250 Rem., .223 Rem., .243 Win., .270 Win., .270 WSM, .30-06, 7mm-08 Rem., 308 Win., .300 WSM, 7mm Rem. Mag., .300 Win. Mag., or .300 Rem. Ultra Mag. cal., standard or Youth synthetic stock with R3 recoil pad. New 2005.

MSR $520	$425	$385	$360	$325	$290	$260	$230

This model is available in a Youth variation in cals. .243 Win., .270 Win., .30-06 or .308 Win. at no extra charge.

* *Model 700 SPS DM* - .243 Win., .270 Win., .30-06, 7mm-08 Rem., 7mm Rem. Mag. or .300 Win. Mag. cal., features detachable mag., otherwise similar to Model SPS. New 2005.

MSR $547	$440	$395	$365	$330	$295	$260	$230

* *Model 700 SPS Stainless* - same cals as Model SPS DM, features stainless steel barreled action, synthetic stock with R3 recoil pad. New 2005.

MSR $613	$480	$425	$385

MODEL 700 XCR (XTREME CONDITIONS RIFLE) -

.270 Win., .270 WSM, .30-06, 7mm Rem. Mag., .300 WSM, .300 Win. Mag., 7mm Rem. Ultra Mag., .300 Rem. Ultra Mag., .338 Rem. Ultra Mag., .338 Win. Mag., .375 H&H, or .375 Rem. Ultra Mag., stainless steel with TriNyte corrosion control, patented Hogue overmolded stock with R3 recoil pad. New 2005.

MSR $867	$700	$535	$410

Add $27 for Mag. cals.

MOREINFO

* *Model 700 XCR RMEF* - 7mm Rem. Mag. cal., features RMEF camo Realtree Hardwood HD camo overmolded stock with R3 recoil pad. New 2005.

MSR $868	$700	$535	$410

MODEL 700 CUSTOM KS MOUNTAIN RIFLE

- .270 Win., .280 Rem., .300 Win. Mag., .300 Wby. Mag. (new 1989), .300 Rem. Ultra Mag. (new 1999), .30-06, .338 Win. Mag. (new 1986), .338 Rem. Ultra Mag. (new 2000), .35 Whelen (new 1989), 7mm STW (new 1999), 7mm Rem. Mag., 7mm Rem. Ultra Mag. (new 2001), 8mm Rem. Mag. (new 1986), .375 Rem. Ultra Mag. (new 2001), or .375 H&H cal., 22 in. barrel, features extra lightweight Kevlar fiber-reinforced stock, available in either right- or left-hand action. Mfg. 1986-2004.

$1,025	$850	$675	$550	$450	$385	$350

Last MSR was $1,314.

Add $79 for left-hand action.

This model is available from the Custom Shop only (special order).

* *Model 700 Custom KS Mountain Rifle Stainless* - similar to Model 700 Custom KS Mountain Rifle, except has stainless steel action and barrel, not available in .35 Whelen or 8mm Rem. Mag. cal., not available in left-hand action. Mfg. 1995-2004.

$1,250	$950	$730

Last MSR was $1,500.

Add $80 for left-hand action.

* *Model 700 Mountain Rifle Custom KS Wood Grained Kevlar* - similar to Model 700 Custom KS Safari Grade, except has wood grained Kevlar stock. Mfg. 1992-93.

$1,000	$875	$750	$650	$550	$485	$430

Last MSR was $1,109.

Add $63 for left-hand action.

MODEL 700 SAFARI GRADE

- .375 H&H, 8mm Rem. Mag. (new 1986), .416 Rem. Mag. (new 1989), or .458 Win. Mag. cal., heavier 700BDL barrel, 3 shot mag., 24 in. barrel, available with either Classic or Monte Carlo stock configuration, custom shop special order only, 9 lbs. Mfg. 1962-2000.

$1,015	$800	$595	$440	$415	$385	$330

Last MSR was $1,225.

Add $73 for left-hand model (Classic stock only).

GRADING - PPGS™	100%	98%	95%	90%	80%	70%	60%

✳ *Model 700 Custom KS Safari Grade* - 8mm Rem. Mag., .375 H&H, .416 Rem. Mag., or .458 Win. Mag. cal., stock made from Kevlar and fiberglass, 24 in. barrel. Mfg. 1989-2004.

	$1,275	$985	$765	$660	$575	$500	$450

Last MSR was $1,520.

Add $81 for left-hand model.

✳ *Model 700 Custom KS Safari Stainless* - .375 H&H, .416 Rem. Mag., or .458 Win. Mag. cal., features fiberglass and Kevlar stock and stainless steel action. Mfg. 1993-2004.

	$1,385	$1,060	$730

Last MSR was $1,697.

MODEL 700 ABG (AFRICAN BIG GAME) - .375 H&H, .375 Rem. Ultra Mag., .416 Rem. Mag., or .458 Win. Mag. cal., straight line 3 shot detachable box mag., checkered brown lamniate stock with right-hand cheekpiece, matte finished steel receiver, 26 in. barrel, custom shop special order only, 9 1/2 lbs. Mfg. 2001-2004.

	$1,475	$950	$750	$525	$475	$425	$395

Last MSR was $1,726.

MODEL 700 APR (AFRICAN PLAINS RIFLE) - .300 Win. Mag., .300 Wby. Mag., .300 Rem. Ultra Mag. (new 1999), .338 Win. Mag., .338 Rem. Ultra Mag. (new 2000), .375 H&H, 7mm Rem. Mag, 7mm Rem. Ultra Mag. (new 2001), or .375 Rem. Ultra Mag. (new 2001) cal., custom shop variation with 26 in. custom shop barrel, satin finish metal and brown, pressure laminated, checkered wood stock with satin finish and buttpad, machined steel triggerguard and floor plate. Mfg. 1994-2004.

	$1,445	$1,135	$960	$785	$650	$550	$485

Last MSR was $1,716.

MODEL 700 AWR (ALASKAN WILDERNESS RIFLE) - .300 Win. Mag., .300 Wby. Mag., .300 Rem. Ultra Mag. (new 1999), .338 Win. Mag., .338 Rem. Ultra Mag. (new 2000), .375 H&H, 7mm STW (new 1998), 7mm Rem. Mag., 7mm Rem. Ultra Mag. (new 2001), or .375 Rem. Ultra Mag. (new 2001) cal., black synthetic fiberglass with Kevlar stock, black stainless steel action. Mfg. 1994-2004.

	$1,415	$1,110	$955

Last MSR was $1,593.

Add $80 for left-hand action.

MODEL 700C GRADE (CUSTOM SHOP) - from custom shop, no engraving, deluxe checkered wood with rosewood forearm cap. Mfg 1964-83. Reintroduced 2003-2004.

	$1,465	$1,150	$960	$785	$650	$550	$485

Last MSR was $1,733.

MODEL 700D PEERLESS GRADE (CUSTOM SHOP) - scroll engraving, best wood. Mfg. 1962-83.

	$2,000	$1,625	$1,400	$1,175	$900	$800	$700

MODEL 700F PREMIER GRADE (CUSTOM SHOP) - elaborate engraving, best wood. Mfg. 1962-83.

	$3,450	$2,850	$2,500	$2,200	$2,035	$1,870	$1,760

MODEL 700 CUSTOM GRADE - special order only, grades differ in amount of engraving and type of walnut. Available as a custom order only through Remington. Values reflect 1991 information. The Remington Custom Shop should be contacted for a current price quotation and the availability of options.

Special order Model 700s mfg. between early '60s-1982 were designated C Grade, D Grade, or F Grade. Values will approximate Custom Grade Models I-III listed. In 1991, Remington discontinued Custom Grade Model designations.

✳ *Model 700 Custom Grade Model I* - mfg. 1983-91.

	$1,200	$1,000	$795

Last MSR was $1,314.

✳ *Model 700 Custom Grade Model II* - mfg. 1983-91.

	100%	98%	95%
	$1,995	$1,675	$1,295

Last MSR was $2,335.

✳ *Model 700 Custom Grade Model III* - mfg. 1983-91.

	100%	98%	95%
	$2,900	$2,150	$1,750

Last MSR was $3,650.

✳ *Model 700 Custom Grade Model IV* - mfg. 1983-91.

	100%	98%	95%
	$4,875	$4,100	$2,950

Last MSR was $5,695.

MODEL 700 CUSTOM RIFLE - the Remington Custom Shop should be contacted directly (see Trademark Index) for current information regarding this model. New 1992.

MSR $3,297	$2,650	$2,150	$1,475	$1,125	$900	$750	$625

Beginning 1992, Remington stopped Custom Grade Model designations in favor of individualized quotations per work order. The suggested retail price for this model is the starting price with the minimum number of options. The Custom Shop should be contacted directly regarding special order pricing (see Trademark Index).

RIFLES: BOLT ACTION, MODEL 40X & VARIATIONS

MODEL 40X SPORTER - .22 LR cal. only, sporterized version of the 40X Target Rifle, 5 shot mag., custom 700 stock, a special order only gun from the factory. Rare, less than 700 mfg. 1969-77, parts clean-up to 1980.

	$3,000	$2,300	$1,800	$1,700	$1,600	$1,475	$1,300

Add 10% if NIB.

This model was last listed in the 1977 Remington catalog - retail was $525.

MODEL 40X TARGET RIFLE (RANGEMASTER) - .22 LR cal., 28 in. heavy barrel, Redfield Olympic sights, scope bases, target stock, rubber butt, first production rifle with built in bedding device and adjustment screws, 12 3/4 lbs. Mfg. 1956-64.

	$800	$700	$600	$525	$450	$375	$325
No sights	$750	$650	$550	$475	$400	$350	$300

MODEL 40X STANDARD BARREL (RANGEMASTER) - similar to 40X Target Rifle, with lighter barrel, 10 3/4 lbs.

	$550	$475	$380	$310	$250	$220	$190
No sights	$495	$450	$360	$295	$240	$200	$180

MODEL 40X CENTERFIRE (RANGEMASTER) - similar to Model 40X Rim Fire, except in .222 Rem., .222 Rem. Mag., .30-06, or .308 Win. cal. Mfg. 1961-64.

	$550	$475	$380	$310	$250	$220	$190
No sights	$495	$450	$360	$295	$240	$200	$180

MODEL 40-XB RANGEMASTER RIMFIRE - .22 LR cal., bolt action single shot, 28 in. light or heavy barrel, no sights, target stock with guide rail, rubber butt. Mfg. 1964-74.

	$575	$525	$420	$335	$275	$220	$195

Add a premium for this model equipped with a mag.

MODEL 40-XB RANGEMASTER CENTERFIRE - available in 18 cals. between .22 BR Rem. and .300 Rem. Ultra Mag., custom made, 27.25 in. barrel (current production is stainless steel action and barrel), single shot or repeater (5 shot mag.), walnut stock, test fired, right- or left-hand action, 10.5-11 lbs. Mfg. 1964-present by Custom Shop.

MSR $1,636	$1,325	$1,030	$735	$550	$450	$375	$325

Add $125 for repeater model.
Add $73 for left-hand action.

An International Free Rifle was also offered - only 107 were mfg. with premiums being paid.

GRADING - PPGS™	100%	98%	95%	90%	80%	70%	60%

MODEL 40-XBBR - similar to Model 40-XB Rangemaster Centerfire, except single shot only, 20 or 24 in. barrel.

	$675	$625	$575	$525	$475	$295	$250

MODEL 40-XB KS (KEVLAR STOCK) - 15 short action cals. between .220 Swift and .300 Win. Mag., 27.25 in. bright finished stainless steel barrel, single shot or repeater, black finish Kevlar stock, right- or left-hand action, no sights, 9.75 lbs. Mfg. 1987-present by Custom Shop.

MSR $1,848	$1,595	$1,100	$765

Add $28 for bench rest model (Model 40-XBBR KS).
Add $123 for repeater model.
Add $73 for left-hand action.
Add $197 for 2 oz. trigger.

MODEL 40-XC KS - .223 Rem. (mfg. 1995-99) or .308 Win. cal., National Match Course repeater rifle, adj. trigger pull, wood (disc. 1989) or fiberglass with Kevlar (standard 1990) stock. Disc. 2004.

	$1,545	$1,060	$755

Last MSR was $1,821.

Subtract approx. $120 for wood stock.

MODEL 40-XB TACTICAL - .308 Win. cal., repeater action with adj. 40-X trigger, aluminum bedding block, 27.25 in. button rifled fluted stainless barrel, Teflon coated metal, matte black HS Precision synthetic tactical stock with vertical pistol grip, 10.25 lbs. New 2004.

MSR $2,108	$1,695	$1,225	$825

MODEL 40-XB/XS - .308 Win. cal., 27 1/4 in. stainless steel barrel, repeater action, Teflon coated synthetic H-S Precision stock, XS Model includes Leuplod scope, Harris bipod, and case, mfg. by the Custom Shop.

Remington does not publish consumer retail pricing for these police/law enforcement models. Secondary prices for base models w/o scopes and other options will be similar to the Model 40-XB Tactical listed above. Prices for rifles with scopes and other features will be determined by how much the individual options and accessories add to the base value.

MODEL 40-XRBR/KS RIMFIRE SINGLE SHOT - .22 LR cal., 24 in. heavy barrel, no sights, adj. buttplate and palm stop, target wood (disc. 1989) or fiberglass with Kevlar (became standard 1990, now available only in benchrest configuration) stock. Mfg. 1974-2004.

	$1,600	$1,110	$775

Last MSR was $1,894.

Subtract 20% for wood stock.

MODEL 40-XR KS SPORTER - .22 LR or .22 Mag. cal., Model 40-XR action, match chambered, custom sporter contoured 24 in. barrel, fiberglass with Kevlar stock, drilled and tapped receiver, w/o sights, special order. Mfg. 1994-99.

	$1,375	$1,100	$750	$625	$550	$500	$450

Last MSR was $1,638.

MODEL 40-XB THUMBHOLE - available in 18 centerfire cals. between .22 BR Rem. - .300 Rem. Ultra Mag, 27.25 in. heavy stainless barrel, laminated thumbhole stock. New 1999.

MSR $1,848	$1,555	$1,110	$795

Add $122 for repeater action (new 2000).

MODEL 40-XR CUSTOM SPORTER - .22 LR or .22 Win. Mag. (new 2000) cal., repeating action, top-of-the-line sporter from the custom shop, individually made per customer's specifications.

MSR $3,383	$2,960	$2,425	$1,910	$1,600	$1,325	$1,100	$925

MODEL 40-XR CUSTOM SPORTER HIGH GRADES

MODEL 40-XR CUSTOM SPORTER HIGH GRADES - .22 LR cal. only, single shot, available on special order from Remington's Custom Shop only, Grades I-IV (disc. 1991) increase by amount of engraving, quality of wood, and other special order options and features. Mfg. 1986-1991.

Values for Custom Grades listed reflect 1991 (the year of discontinuance) price information. The Remington Custom Shop should be contacted directly regarding current values and options.

* *Model 40-XR Custom Grade Model I* - mfg. 1986-91.

	100%	98%	95%
	$1,100	$925	$795

Last MSR was $1,314.

* *Model 40-XR Custom Grade Model II* - mfg. 1986-91.

	100%	98%	95%
	$1,995	$1,675	$1,295

Last MSR was $2,335.

* *Model 40-XR Custom Grade Model III* - mfg. 1986-91.

	100%	98%	95%
	$2,900	$2,150	$1,750

Last MSR was $3,650.

* *Model 40-XR Custom Grade Model IV* - mfg. 1986-91.

	100%	98%	95%
	$4,875	$4,100	$2,950

Last MSR was $5,695.

SHOTGUNS: O/U

Values listed for Model 3200s assume NIB condition - subtract 10%-15% if without box, warranty card, and original shipping container (with packing materials).

MODEL 32 - 12 ga., double lock action, SST, separated barrels, 26, 28, or 30 in. barrels without rib, SR, or VR. Approx. 6,050 mfg. (ser. range approx. 0001-6,053) 1931-1947. There is a discrepancy as to when serialization started on this model.

	100%	98%	95%	90%	80%	70%	60%
	$1,950	$1,675	$1,425	$1,275	$925	$825	$795

Add 10% for SST.
Add 10% for vent. or solid rib.
Add 20% for VR on 28 in. barrels.

MODEL 32 serialization is as follows: 1931 - 0001-1,009; 1932 - 1,010-1,903; 1933 - 1,904-1,948; 1934 - 1,949-2,727; 1935 - 2,728-3,610; 1936 - 3,611-4,259; 1937 - 4,260 - 4,755; 1938 - 4,756-4,958; 1939 - 4,959-5,202; 1940 - 5,203-5,425; 1941 - 5,426-5,741; 1942 - 5,742 - 6,020; 1943 - 6,021-6,031; 1944 - 6,032-6,049; 1945 to 1947 - 6,050-6,053.

MODEL 32D TOURNAMENT

	100%	98%	95%	90%	80%	70%	60%
	$3,750	$3,000	$2,500	$2,000	$1,750	$1,400	$1,175

MODEL 32E EXPERT - less than 35 mfg.

	100%	98%	95%	90%	80%	70%	60%
	$4,500	$3,950	$3,500	$2,975	$2,650	$2,200	$1,875

MODEL 32F PREMIER

	100%	98%	95%	90%	80%	70%	60%
	$6,500	$5,500	$5,000	$4,500	$3,520	$2,750	$2,300

Note: Grades differ in quality, grade of wood, and amount of engraving.

MODEL 32 SKEET - similar to 32A, with 26 or 28 (more desirable) in. skeet bored barrels, SST. Mfg. 1932-42.

	100%	98%	95%	90%	80%	70%	60%
	$1,600	$1,400	$1,200	$1,000	$950	$875	$800

Add 10% for VR.
Add 10%-15% for 28 in. barrels.

MODEL 32TC TARGET - similar to 32A, with 30 or 32 in. VR full choke barrels, trap style stock. Mfg. 1932-42.

	100%	98%	95%	90%	80%	70%	60%
	$3,000	$2,300	$1,800	$1,700	$1,600	$1,475	$1,300

Add 10% for 30 in. VR barrels.

MODEL 300 IDEAL
12 ga. only, 3 in. chambers, boxlock action, features unique forearm latching system that incorporates barrel selector switch, 26, 28, or 30 in. 8mm VR barrels with twin beads and Rem. chokes (3), engraved receiver sides, gold SST, high polish blue, checkered satin finished American walnut stock and forearm with English style solid recoil pad, 7 3/8 - 7 7/8 lbs. Mfg. 2000-2001.

	100%	98%	95%	90%	80%	70%	60%
	$1,150	$995	$875	$800	$750	$700	$650

Last MSR was $1,332.

MODEL 332
12 ga. only, 3 in. chambers, new modified boxlock action with under-lock custom shop design, low profile receiver with Model 32 type styling, engraved frame panels, 26, 28, or 30 in. 8mm VR light contour barrels with Remchokes, glass-bead blasted black oxide metal finish with resembles Model 32 rust bluing, satin finished checkered walnut stock and slim forearm with solid rubber recoil pad, mechanical SST, ejectors, 7.5 - 8 lbs. Mfg. in Ilion beginning late 2001.

MSR $1,691	$1,375	$1,050	$900	$775	$625	$550	$475

✳ *Model 332 Engraved* - introduced 2004.

>D Grade (Peerless)

MSR $4,184	$3,150	$2,200	$1,500

>F Grade (Premier)

MSR $7,706	$6,300	$4,550	$2,975

>F Grade w/gold inlays (Premier Gold) - top-of-the-line Custom Shop model.

MSR $11,122	$9,375	$5,300	$3,575

MODEL 396 SKEET/SPORTING CLAYS
12 ga. only, satin finished boxlock action with engraved sideplates, 28 or 30 in. barrels with 10mm VR and Rem. chokes, select checkered walnut stock and target style forend, Sporting Clays Model has ported barrels, SST, ejectors, approx. 7 1/2 lbs. Mfg. 1996-98.

✳ *Model 396 Skeet*

	$1,750	$1,475	$1,250	$1,075	$925	$800	$700

Last MSR was $1,993.

✳ *Model 396 Sporting Clays*

	$1,875	$1,575	$1,300	$1,100	$950	$825	$725

Last MSR was $2,126.

MODEL 3200 FIELD
12 ga., 26, 28, or 30 in. barrels, VR, various chokes, boxlock, auto ejectors, single selective trigger, checkered pistol grip stock, separated barrels. Mfg. 1973-77.

	$1,100	$1,000	$950	$900	$850	$800	$750

During 1998-2000, the custom shop once again manufactured a limited amount of the Model 3200 from existing parts (parts cleanup).

Model 3200s with shorter barrels (26 or 28 in.) and open choking are more desirable than 30 in. tubes bored F/M.

MODEL 3200 serialization is as follows: 1973 - 4,200-16,667; 1974 - 16,668-27,393; 1975 - 27,394-35,303; 1976 - 35,304-39,216; 1977 - 39,217-41,432; 1978 - 41,433-42,813; 1979 - 42,814-44,278; 1980 - 44,279-45,504; 1981 - 45,505-45,974; 1982 - 45,975-47,200; 1983 - 47,201-47,308.

MODEL 3200 MAGNUM
12 ga., 3 in. chambers, 30 in. heavy wall barrels (steel shot compatible), less than 1,000 mfg. 1975-77.

	$1,695	$1,575	$1,475	$1,200	$1,050	$950	$850

MODEL 3200 SKEET
similar to 3200 Field, with 26 or 28 in. skeet bored barrels, skeet style stock. Mfg. 1973-80.

	$1,295	$1,050	$950	$850	$750	$650	$575

28 in. barrels will command a premium on this model.

This model was also mfg. in a 28 in. IM/F configuration with gold pigeon on bottom for live pigeon shooting. Since less than 300 were mfg., prices in the $2,700 range are being asked if

GRADING - PPGS™	100%	98%	95%	90%	80%	70%	60%

NIB condition. This model generally had a trap style rib, but there have been some field ribs as well. Originally, it was called the "Competition Live Pigeon" and was mfg. with a competition receiver and trap grade style wood.

* **Model 3200 Competition Skeet Four Ga. Set** - includes 12, 20, 28 ga., or .410 bore, cased. Mfg. 1980-83.

	100%	98%	95%	90%	80%	70%	60%
	$5,500	$5,000	$4,600	$4,200	$4,000	$3,800	$3,500

Add 10%-15% for 28 in. barrels.

28 in. barrels will command a premium on this model.

MODEL 3200 COMPETITION SKEET - similar to 3200 Skeet, with scroll engraved frame and trigger guard, select wood. Mfg. 1976-83.

	$1,700	$1,450	$1,250	$995	$950	$850	$750

Add 10%-15% for 28 in. VR barrels.

MODEL 3200 TRAP - similar as 3200 Field, with 30 or 32 in. barrels choked IM/F or F/F, stock and rib. Mfg. 1973-77.

	$1,375	$1,100	$950	$875	$800	$750	$700

30 in. barrels are more desirable than 32 in.

MODEL 3200 SPECIAL TRAP - similar to 3200 Trap, except fancy wood. Mfg. 1973-80.

	$1,450	$1,300	$1,200	$1,000	$875	$800	$750

MODEL 3200 COMPETITION TRAP - similar to 3200 Trap, with scroll engraving. Mfg. 1976-83.

	$1,950	$1,800	$1,675	$1,450	$1,200	$950	$875
Pigeon Grade	$2,450	$2,150	$1,850	$1,500	$1,250	$995	$900

The Pigeon Grade featured a gold pigeon on receiver bottom - approx. 250 mfg. 1979-83. There was a special production of this model during 1991-92 which was limited to approx. 100 guns.

MODEL 3200 PREMIER - 12 ga., sold through Remington's International Division, 500 mfg. 1975 only, patterned after "One of 1000" series, regular or Monte Carlo stock.

	$2,900	$2,500	$2,150	$1,800	$1,500	$1,200	$1,025

Add 125% for engraving (only 116 mfg., engraving was done in Belgium).

MODEL 3200 "ONE OF 1000" - limited edition, elaborate engraving, fancy wood, supplied with hard case, made in both skeet and trap models. Mfg. 1,000 each model: 1973 (Trap) and 1974 (Skeet).

	100%	98%	95%	90%	80%	70%	60%
Trap (30 IM/F or F/F)	$2,150	$1,750	$1,475	$1,325	$1,200	$1,075	$875
Skeet (26 or 28 in. SK/SK)	$1,925	$1,675	$1,475	$1,325	$1,200	$1,075	$875

Add 10% for 28 in. barrels on the Skeet Model.

PEERLESS FIELD GRADE - 12 ga. only, 3 in. chambers, 26, 28, or 30 in. VR barrels with Rem. chokes, boxlock with engraved sideplates, SST, ejectors, high-gloss checkered walnut stock and forearm with vent. recoil pad, 3.28 milliseconds lock time, blue metal, approx. 7 1/2 lbs. Mfg. 1993-98.

	$1,000	$900	$850	$800	$750	$700	$650

Last MSR was $1,172.

This model is an entirely new design not sharing any parts with either the Models 32 or 3200.

SHOTGUNS: SxS

The author wishes to express thanks to Charles Semmer for once again updating the following section on older Remington SxS Shotguns.

Because E. Remington & Sons shotguns are classified as antique, it may be helpful to consult the "NRA Antique Condition Standards" section in the front of this text to convert to the Percentage Grading System listed.

For Remington serialization, please refer to the Serialization section.

100%	98%	95%	90%	80%	70%	60%	50%	40%	30%	20%	10%

MODEL 1873 "HAMMER LIFTER"

MODEL 1873 "HAMMER LIFTER" - 10 or 12 ga., also known as Whitmore Hammer Lifter, 28 or 30 in. decarbonized, twist, or damascus barrels, top "thumb lever" action activated by pushing upward to open, rib top marked "E. REMINGTON & SONS, ILION, N.Y.", patented "AUG. 8, 1871, APRIL 16, 1872", steel buttplate, pistol grip was optional, grades above 3 were made to order. Approx. 5,000 mfg. from 1873-78, starting with ser. no. 1.

* **Grade 1** - decarbonized steel barrels, no checkering or engraving.

100%	98%	95%	90%	80%	70%	60%	50%	40%	30%	20%	10%
$1,800	$1,500	$1,200	$1,000	$950	$800	$600	$500	$375	$300	$250	$225

* **Grade 2** - twist steel barrels, checkering, no engraving.

$2,500	$2,200	$2,000	$1,700	$1,500	$1,200	$1,000	$900	$750	$650	$500	$350

* **Grade 3** - twist or damascus steel barrels, checkering and engraving.

$3,700	$3,500	$3,200	$2,200	$1,750	$1,500	$1,200	$1,100	$1,000	$750	$650	$450

Add 10%-20% to Grade 3 prices for higher grades (extra fine engraving).

MODEL 1875 AND 1876 "LIFTER" (WHITMORE LIFTER)

MODEL 1875 AND 1876 "LIFTER" (WHITMORE LIFTER) - 10 or 12 ga., 28 or 30 in. decarbonized, twist, or damascus barrels, top "thumb lever" action activated by pushing upward to open, rib top marked "E. REMINGTON & SONS, ILION, N.Y.", patented "AUG. 8, 1871, APRIL 16, 1872", steel buttplate, pistol grip was optional, the Model 1875 started with ser. no. 1, and went to approx. 3,350, the Model 1876 started with ser. no. 3,350 and went to approx. 5,900. Approx. 5,900 Model 1875s and 1876s were mfg. from 1875-82.

* **Grade 1** - decarbonized steel barrels, no checkering or engraving.

$1,800	$1,500	$1,200	$1,000	$950	$800	$600	$500	$375	$300	$250	$225

* **Grade 2** - twist steel barrels, checkering, no engraving.

$2,000	$1,800	$1,500	$1,200	$1,000	$900	$750	$650	$550	$500	$350	$275

* **Grade 3** - twist or damascus steel barrels, checkered and engraving.

$3,500	$3,200	$2,200	$1,500	$1,200	$1,000	$900	$750	$650	$550	$400	$300

* **Grade 4** - twist or damascus steel barrels, checkered and extra fine engraving.

$4,000	$3,500	$3,000	$2,100	$1,500	$1,200	$1,000	$900	$750	$650	$475	$350

* **Grade 5** - damascus steel barrels, checkered and superior engraving.

$4,500	$4,000	$3,500	$2,600	$2,300	$1,800	$1,200	$1,000	$900	$800	$550	$400

Add 100% to the few Model 1873s and 1875s that are rib marked "NEW YORK & LONDON".

Add 100% for double rifles and combination guns in Models 1873, 1875, and 1876. There were very few double rifles and combination guns made in Models 1873, 1875, and 1876 - they are very rare, and be aware of fake double rifles.

MODEL 1878 HAMMER (HEAVY DUCK GUN)

MODEL 1878 HAMMER (HEAVY DUCK GUN) - 10 ga., called the Heavy Duck Gun, 30-32 in., 9 3/4 and 10 lbs., "thumb-lever" action, thick bolsters, top extension rib, no flash fences, steel buttplate. Approx. 2,500 mfg. from 1878-82, starting with ser. no. 1.

* **Grade 1** - decarbonized steel barrels, no checkering, no engraving.

$1,800	$1,500	$1,200	$1,000	$950	$800	$600	$500	$375	$300	$250	$250

* **Grade 2** - twist steel barrels, checkered, no engraving.

$2,100	$1,800	$1,500	$1,200	$1,000	$900	$750	$650	$550	$500	$375	$375

* **Grade 3** - laminated steel barrels, checkered, engraved.

$4,000	$3,500	$3,000	$2,100	$1,500	$1,200	$1,000	$900	$750	$650	$475	$475

* **Grade 4** - damascus steel barrels, checkered, engraved.

$4,500	$4,000	$3,500	$3,000	$2,500	$2,000	$1,500	$1,200	$1,000	$900	$650	$600

MODEL 1879 SxS HAMMER

MODEL 1879 SxS HAMMER - usually 12 ga., top extension rib, no flash fences, steel buttplate, only Whitmore model with Deeley & Edge forend catch. Ser. nos. within the Model 1878.

Add 40% for this scarce variation to Model 1878 listed prices.

100%	98%	95%	90%	80%	70%	60%	50%	40%	30%	20%	10%

MODEL 1882 SxS HAMMER

(includes the unique Model 1883), 10 or 12 ga., 30 or 32 in. decarbonized, twist or damascus steel barrels, rib marked "E. REMINGTON & SONS, ILION, N.Y.," typical top lever, all grades have checkered pistol grip and forend with various designs according to grade. All contain Deeley & Edge forend catch. Approx. 16,000 Model 1882s, possibly 1,000 Model 1883s were mfg. from 1882-88. Started with ser. no. 1,000.

* **Grade 1** - decarbonized steel barrels, no enraving, steel buttplate.

100%	98%	95%	90%	80%	70%	60%	50%	40%	30%	20%	10%
$1,500	$1,300	$1,200	$1,000	$750	$650	$550	$450	$350	$275	$250	$200

* **Grade 2** - twist steel barrels, no engraving, steel buttplate.

$1,400	$1,200	$1,100	$900	$750	$650	$550	$450	$350	$275	$250	$200

* **Grade 3** - laminated steel barrels, engraved, steel buttplate.

$1,800	$1,600	$1,400	$1,200	$1,000	$875	$750	$650	$550	$400	$350	$250

* **Grade 4** - damascus steel barrels, engraved, steel buttplate.

$2,500	$2,000	$1,500	$1,400	$1,200	$1,000	$800	$700	$600	$500	$400	$300

* **Grade 5** - fine damascus steel, finely engraved, superior rubber buttplate.

$3,500	$3,000	$2,600	$2,200	$2,000	$1,700	$1,400	$1,000	$800	$700	$600	$500

* **Grade 6** - extra fine damascus, fine scroll engraved, superior rubber buttplate.

$5,500	$5,000	$4,500	$3,700	$3,200	$2,700	$2,500	$2,000	$1,500	$1,200	$1,000	$800

Add 25% for optional auxiliary rifle barrel insert.

MODEL 1883

identified by its hammer shape which is different that the Model 1882.

Add 50% to the values for this model.

MODEL 1885/1887 SxS HAMMER

10, 12, or 16 ga., different hammer style variation of the Model 1882, 28, 30, or 32 in. decarbonized, twist or damascus steel barrels, rib marked "E. REMINGTON & SONS, ILION, N.Y.," top lever, all grades are checkered pistol grip and forend with various designs according to grade, Deeley & Edge forend catch, rubber buttplate with ERS logo. Approx. 7,000 mfg. from 1885-88. Ser. nos. started at 16,700. Guns before ser. no. 20,200 are considered Model 1885s, ser. nos. after are Model 1887s.

* **Grade 1** - decarbonized steel barrels, no engraving.

$1,800	$1,600	$1,400	$1,200	$1,000	$700	$600	$500	$400	$300	$275	$225

* **Grade 2** - twist steel barrels, no engraving.

$1,700	$1,500	$1,300	$1,000	$850	$750	$650	$550	$450	$375	$300	$225

* **Grade 3** - damascus steel barrels, no engraving.

$1,800	$1,600	$1,400	$1,200	$1,000	$875	$750	$650	$550	$400	$350	$250

* **Grade 4** - damascus steel barrels, engraved.

$2,000	$1,800	$1,600	$1,400	$1,200	$1,000	$800	$700	$600	$500	$400	$300

* **Grade 5** - fine damascus steel barrels, finely engraved.

$3,500	$3,000	$2,600	$2,200	$1,700	$1,500	$1,200	$900	$750	$650	$500	$400

* **Grade 6** - extra fine damascus barrels, fine scroll engraved.

$5,500	$5,000	$4,500	$3,700	$3,200	$2,700	$2,500	$2,000	$1,500	$1,200	$900	$700

* **Grade 7** - superior damascus barrels, extra fine scroll engraved, game scene.

$8,000	$7,500	$7,250	$6,500	$6,000	$5,500	$5,000	$4,000	$3,500	$3,000	$2,000	$1,000

Add 25% for optional auxiliary rifle barrel insert.

Add 30% for 16 ga.

MODEL 1889 SxS HAMMER

10, 12, or 16 ga., 28, 30, or 32 in., a few 26 in. are known. Decarbonized, twist, or damascus barrels, exposed "circular" hammers, rib marked "REMINGTON ARMS CO. ILION, N.Y. U.S.A.," top lever, all grades have checkered pistol grip and forend with various designs according to grade, Deeley & Edge forend catch. Grade number is stamped on water table left of the ser. no. Rubber buttplate with RACo logo. 134,200 mfg. 1889-1908. Ser. range from 30,000 to 100,000. After the year 1900, ser. nos. are in the 200,000 range.

* **Grade 1** - decarbonized steel barrels, no engraving.

$1,500	$1,300	$1,200	$1,000	$750	$650	$550	$450	$350	$300	$275	$225

100%	98%	95%	90%	80%	70%	60%	50%	40%	30%	20%	10%

✳ Grade 2 - twist steel barrels, no engraving.

| $1,600 | $1,400 | $1,300 | $1,000 | $750 | $750 | $650 | $550 | $450 | $350 | $300 | $225 |

✳ Grade 3 - damascus steel barrels, no engraving.

| $1,700 | $1,500 | $1,400 | $1,100 | $950 | $850 | $750 | $650 | $500 | $400 | $350 | $250 |

✳ Grade 4 - damascus steel barrels, engraved.

| $3,500 | $3,000 | $2,600 | $2,200 | $2,000 | $1,700 | $1,400 | $1,000 | $800 | $700 | $600 | $500 |

✳ Grade 5 - damascus steel barrels, finely engraved.

| $5,500 | $5,000 | $4,500 | $3,700 | $3,200 | $2,700 | $2,500 | $2,000 | $1,500 | $1,200 | $1,000 | $800 |

✳ Grade 6 - extra fine damascus barrels, fine scroll engraved.

| $8,000 | $7,500 | $7,300 | $6,500 | $6,000 | $5,500 | $5,000 | $4,000 | $3,500 | $3,000 | $2,000 | $1,000 |

✳ Grade 7 - superior damascus barrels, extra fine scroll engraved, game scene.

| $16,000 | $15,000 | $12,000 | $9,000 | $8,000 | $7,000 | $6,000 | $5,000 | $4,000 | $3,500 | $2,500 | $1,500 |

Add 20% for 16 ga.

Grades 4 through 7 may command higher values. To date, there are only 15 examples known of these engraved Model 1889 hammer guns - five Grade 4s, three Grade 5s, four Grade 6s, and three Grade 7s.

MODEL 1894 SxS HAMMERLESS - 10, 12, or 16 ga., 26 to 32 in. "Remington," "Ordnance," or Damascus steel barrels, auto ejectors, boxlock, double triggers, checkered pistol grip or straight stock, Purdey forend snap. Grades A, B, F, and C have RACo hard rubber butt, Grade D, horn butt, Grade E, horn or heel and toe plates. Grade is usually stamped on the water table. 16 and especially 10 ga., are considered scarce and will command a higher value. 41,194 mfg. between 1894-1910 in the 100,000 block serial range.

✳ Grade AE - no engraving.

| $1,500 | $1,300 | $1,200 | $1,100 | $1,000 | $850 | $700 | $600 | $500 | $400 | $300 | $200 |

✳ Grade BE - scroll and line engraving.

| $3,000 | $2,800 | $2,500 | $2,200 | $2,000 | $1,700 | $1,400 | $1,000 | $700 | $500 | $400 | $300 |

✳ Grade FE Trap - scroll and line engraving.

| $3,000 | $2,800 | $2,500 | $2,200 | $2,000 | $1,700 | $1,400 | $1,000 | $700 | $500 | $400 | $300 |

✳ Grade CE - extra scroll engraving, silver name plate.

| $4,500 | $4,300 | $4,000 | $3,600 | $3,300 | $3,000 | $2,500 | $2,000 | $1,500 | $1,000 | $600 | $500 |

✳ Grade DE - fine scroll and game engraving, silver name plate.

| $9,000 | $8,000 | $7,500 | $7,000 | $6,500 | $6,000 | $5,000 | $4,000 | $3,000 | $2,000 | $1,500 | $1,000 |

✳ Grade EE - finest quality scroll, bird and game engraving, gold name plate.

| $18,000 | $17,000 | $15,000 | $12,000 | $10,000 | $8,000 | $7,000 | $6,500 | $5,000 | $3,500 | $2,500 | $2,000 |

Subtract 20% for non-ejector guns.

Add 25% for "Ordnance" barrels.

A few Remington SPECIAL grade guns were produced; they are so rare, it is not practical to attempt a value.

MODEL 1900 SxS HAMMERLESS - 12 or 16 ga., 28 or 30 in. "Remington" or damascus steel barrels, lower priced gun to meet market competition, quality a cut below the Model 1894, but mechanically the same, snap forend. No engraving was offered on this model. 98,475 mfg. between 1900-10 in the 300,000 block serial range.

✳ Grade K and KD - Remington or Damascus steel barrels, non-ejector.

| $1,000 | $900 | $825 | $750 | $675 | $625 | $575 | $525 | $475 | $295 | $250 | $200 |

✳ Grade KE and KED - Remington or Damascus steel barrels, ejectors.

| $1,300 | $1,200 | $1,100 | $1,000 | $900 | $800 | $700 | $600 | $500 | $300 | $250 | $200 |

PARKER AHE - while advertised, the Remington re-issue of the original Parker AHE Model was never mfg. due to product liability considerations. Older Remington manufactured Parkers may be found in the Parker section of this text.

GRADING - PPGS™	100%	98%	95%	90%	80%	70%	60%

SHOTGUNS: SEMI-AUTO, DISC.

REMINGTON AUOLOADING SHOTGUN (PRE-MODEL 11) - 12 ga. only, original Remington mfg. of the Browning A-5, 5 shot, various grades, 20 (riot), 26, or 28 in. plain or matted rib barrel. Mfg. 1905-10.

	100%	98%	95%	90%	80%	70%	60%
	$350	$275	$225	$175	$160	$135	$110

Add 20% for matted rib.

MODEL 11A AUTOLOADER 5-SHOT - 12, 16 (introduced 1931), or 20 (introduced 1930) ga., 26-32 in. barrels, takedown, various chokes, Browning type, checkered pistol stock. Approx. 300,000 mfg., 1911-48.

	100%	98%	95%	90%	80%	70%	60%
Plain barrel	$295	$240	$215	$185	$165	$150	$120
Solid rib	$395	$315	$235	$200	$185	$165	$140
Vent. rib	$440	$360	$335	$305	$275	$220	$165

Add 35% for barrels marked "Long Range" - beware of fakes.

This model was mfg. under patent agreement with John Browning.

MODEL 11B SPECIAL - higher grade wood with hand checkered stock and forearm.

	100%	98%	95%	90%	80%	70%	60%
	$1,200	$1,075	$950	$825	$700	$650	$600

MODEL 11D TOURNAMENT

	100%	98%	95%	90%	80%	70%	60%
	$1,200	$1,075	$950	$825	$700	$650	$600

MODEL 11E EXPERT

	100%	98%	95%	90%	80%	70%	60%
	$2,500	$2,250	$2,000	$1,800	$1,600	$1,400	$1,200

MODEL 11F PREMIER

	100%	98%	95%	90%	80%	70%	60%
	$3,000	$2,750	$2,500	$2,250	$2,000	$1,850	$1,650

Note: Grades differ in quality, grade of wood, and amount of engraving.

MODEL 11R - 12 ga. only, similar to Model 11A, except has 20 in. cylinder bore barrel, 4 shot mag. Mfg. circa 1920s.

	100%	98%	95%	90%	80%	70%	60%
	$325	$265	$235	$200	$150	$120	$100

SPORTSMAN MODEL SEMI-AUTO - 12, 16, or 20 ga., 26 (3 shot only) in. barrel, skeet choke, beavertail forend. Mfg. 1931-49.

	100%	98%	95%	90%	80%	70%	60%
Plain barrel	$325	$275	$250	$195	$165	$140	$120
Solid rib	$400	$350	$300	$250	$200	$180	$150
Vent. rib	$470	$415	$360	$330	$275	$250	$220

This model was manufactured in Field, Riot, and Skeet configurations.

MODEL 48 MOHAWK (SPORTSMAN) - 12, 16, or 20 ga., 26, 28, or 32 in. barrels, 3 shot, mechanical (solid breech) ejection system, various chokes, rounded receiver, checkered pistol grip stock with cap. Approx. 275,000 mfg., 1949-60.

	100%	98%	95%	90%	80%	70%	60%
	$300	$225	$200	$185	$175	$165	$140
VR barrel	$325	$275	$250	$200	$175	$165	$140

MODEL 48B SELECT

	100%	98%	95%	90%	80%	70%	60%
	$420	$360	$310	$290	$245	$220	$195

MODEL 48D TOURNAMENT

	100%	98%	95%	90%	80%	70%	60%
	$1,200	$1,075	$950	$825	$700	$650	$600

MODEL 48F PREMIER

	100%	98%	95%	90%	80%	70%	60%
	$3,000	$2,750	$2,500	$2,250	$2,000	$1,850	$1,650

MODEL 48A RIOT GUN - 12 ga. only, 20 in. plain barrel.

	100%	98%	95%	90%	80%	70%	60%
	$275	$220	$195	$165	$150	$140	$110

MODEL 48SA SKEET - 26 in. barrel, skeet bore, ivory bead. Mfg. 1949-60.

	100%	98%	95%	90%	80%	70%	60%
	$305	$275	$255	$230	$210	$195	$165
With VR barrel	$395	$350	$300	$260	$230	$210	$195

GRADING - PPGS™	100%	98%	95%	90%	80%	70%	60%

MODEL 48SC SKEET - "C" suffix designates C-grade wood.

	100%	98%	95%	90%	80%	70%	60%
	$385	$360	$330	$305	$275	$250	$220

MODEL 48SD TOURNAMENT - custom shop engraved.

	$1,200	$1,075	$950	$825	$700	$650	$600

MODEL 48SF PREMIER - custom shop engraved.

	$3,000	$2,750	$2,500	$2,250	$2,000	$1,850	$1,650

MODEL 11-48 SEMI-AUTO - 12, 16, 20, 28 (introduced 1952) ga., or .410 (introduced 1954) bore, recoil operated action, walnut stock. Approx. 429,000 mfg., 1949-68.

	100%	98%	95%	90%	80%	70%	60%
Plain barrel	$300	$225	$200	$185	$175	$165	$140
VR barrel	$325	$275	$250	$200	$175	$165	$140

Add 15% - 40% for 28 ga. or .410 bore, depending on condition.

MODEL 58ADL "SPORTSMAN - 58" SEMI-AUTO - 12, 16, or 20 ga., 26, 28, or 30 in. barrel, gas operation, various chokes, 3 shot, checkered pistol grip stock, scroll game scene engraved. Approx. 271,000 mfg., 1956-63.

	100%	98%	95%	90%	80%	70%	60%
Plain barrel	$275	$250	$220	$195	$140	$120	$110
VR barrel	$360	$305	$275	$250	$220	$165	$140

Add 5% for Magnum in 12 ga.

MODEL 58 X-SERIES (SUNGRAIN) - similar to Model 58ADL semi-auto, except has blonde stock, available in Field (special order only), Skeet, or Trap configuration.

	$275	$250	$220	$195	$160	$140	$120

MODEL 58BDL - similar to 58ADL, with select wood.

	100%	98%	95%	90%	80%	70%	60%
Plain barrel	$295	$275	$250	$225	$210	$195	$165
VR barrel	$375	$335	$300	$275	$250	$200	$175

MODEL 58SA SKEET GUN - similar to 58ADL, with 26 in. skeet bore VR barrel, skeet stock.

	$360	$330	$305	$275	$250	$200	$175

MODEL 58SC SKEET - "C" suffix designates C-grade wood.

	$495	$440	$415	$385	$330	$305	$275

MODEL 58D TOURNAMENT - custom shop engraved.

	$1,200	$1,075	$950	$825	$700	$650	$600

MODEL 58F PREMIER - custom shop engraved.

	$3,000	$2,750	$2,500	$2,250	$2,000	$1,850	$1,650

Note: Models differ in grade of wood, amount of engraving, and gold inlays.

MODEL 878A "AUTOMASTER" - 12 ga. gas operated semi-auto, 26, 28, or 30 in. barrels, action similar to Model 58. Approx. 62,000 mfg., 1959-62. Add 15% for VR.

	$235	$200	$185	$170	$160	$150	$135

Barrels on this model are interchangeable with those on the Model 58.

SHOTGUNS: SEMI-AUTO, CURRENT/RECENT PRODUCTION

MODEL SP-10 - 10 ga., 3 1/2 in. chamber, semi-auto stainless steel gas system operation, lighter recoil than most 12 ga. Mags., 30 in. barrel with 3/8 in. VR and Rem. chokes (2), checkered stock and forearm with low gloss satin finish, matte metal finish, crossbolt safety, R3 recoil pad became standard 2004, supplied with camo sling, approx. 11 lbs. Introduced 1989.

MSR $1,387	$1,025	$900	$800	$675	$575	$550	$475

Add $317 (factory MSR) per extra Model SP-10 barrel.

The first 5,000 SP-10s were assigned special serialization (LE89 prefix) - no premiums exist at this time, however.

This model is NOT a re-designed Ithaca Mag-10 and the parts are NOT interchangeable. The SP-10 is a new design.

GRADING - PPGS™	100%	98%	95%	90%	80%	70%	60%

✸ **Model SP-10 Camo** - 23 (Turkey Model, mfg. 1999-2000), or 26 in. VR barrel, choice of Mossy Oak (disc. 1996), full coverage Mossy Oak Break-Up (mfg. 1997-2004), full coverage Mossy Oak Obsession and R3 recoil pad (became standard 2005), or Bottomland (mfg. 1994-96) camo finish. New 1993.

MSR $1,524	$1,115	$900	$800	$675	$585	$550	$475

Subtract 5% for disc. camo finishes.

✸ **Model SP-10 Magnum Synthetic** - features lightweight black synthetic stock and forearm, matte non-reflective metal finish, 26 in. barrel only, 10.75 lbs. Mfg. 2000-2004.

	$995	$875	$785	$675	$575	$550	$475

Last MSR was $1,331.

✸ **Model SP-10 Turkey Camo NWTF 25th Anniversary** - 12 ga., limited mfg. to commemorate the 25th Anniversary of the NWTF during 1998, Truglo fiberoptic sights. Mfg. 1998 only.

	$1,050	$925	$775				

Last MSR was $1,225.

✸ **Model SP-10 Turkey Combo** - includes choice of either 26 or 30 VR regular barrel and extra 22 in. deer barrel with rifle sights. Mfg. 1991-94.

	$1,295	$1,125	$925	$775	$700	$650	$625

Last MSR was $1,132.

Remington Shotguns: Semi-Auto, Model 1100 & Variations

3 in. shells (12 or 20 ga.) may be shot in Magnum receivers only, regardless of what the barrel markings may indicate (the ejection port is larger in these Magnum models with "M" suffix serialization).

Add $667 for custom shop Etchen stock and forearm installed on new Model 1100s (new 2000).

SPORTSMAN 12 AUTO - 12 ga. only, 2 3/4 in. chamber, 28 or 30 in. VR barrel, similar to Model 1100 action, hardwood stock and forearm, 7 3/4 lbs. Mfg. 1985-86 only.

	$300	$260	$220	$195	$170	$160	$150

Last MSR was $405.

Add 10% for Rem. chokes (mfg. 1986 only).

MODEL 1100 FIELD - 12 (disc. 1987), 16 (disc. 1980), or 20 ga., 26, 28, or 30 in. barrels, various chokes, gas operated, checkered pistol grip stock, Rem. chokes became standard 1987 (introduced 1986 as $40 option), VRs became standard in 1985 on this model, 20 ga. lightweight frame became standard 1972, prices assume VR and Rem. chokes. Mfg. 1963-88.

	$350	$295	$265	$225	$200	$185	$170

Last MSR was $545.

Subtract $40 if without VR.
Subtract $45 if without Rem. chokes.

The Model 1100 20 ga. Standard (12 ga. frame) was disc. in 1969 (mahogany wood stock and forearm – advertised as a Lightweight), except for Skeet A & B grades. This model was produced only in a Lightweight or Mag. 20 (3 in. chamber), 28 ga., or .410 bore, before the release of the Model 11-87.

The Model 1100 left-hand, with the ejection port on the left side of the receiver was introduced in 1972 in both 20 and 12 ga., with either VR or plain barrels. The 20 ga. left-hand model was disc. in 1977.

MODEL 1100 SPECIAL FIELD - 12, 20 ga., or .410 (limited mfg., disc.) bore, 21 (disc. 1993) or 23 (new 1994) in. VR barrel, various chokes, gas operated, checkered straight grip stock, VR standard, high gloss wood finish (1991 only) or satin wood finish. Rem. chokes became standard in 1987. Mfg. 1983-99.

	$510	$415	$325	$265	$230	$210	$180

Last MSR was $665.

Subtract 10% if without Rem. chokes.
Add 15%-20% for .410 bore.

Two hundred .410 bores were mfg. for National Shooting Supplies in Houston, TX.

GRADING - PPGS™	100%	98%	95%	90%	80%	70%	60%

MODEL 1100 CLASSIC FIELD - 16 or 20 (new 2004) ga., 2 3/4 in. chamber, 26 or 28 in. VR light contoured barrel with Remchoke, non-embellished receiver with blue finish, satin (disc.) or gloss finished American walnut stock and forearm, 7 lbs. New 2003.

MSR $799	$620	$495	$425	$380	$340	$300	$275

MODEL 1100 "1 OF 3,000" FIELD - 12 ga. only, limited edition, serial numbered 1-3,000, deluxe walnut, gold washed etched hunting scenes on receiver, 28 in. modified VR barrel. Mfg. 1980.

	$1,100	$900	$600	$500	$425	$350	$300

MODEL 1100 SMALL GAUGE - 28 ga. or .410 bore, 25 in. barrel, scaled down receiver, skeet and field fixed choke, VR standard. Mfg. 1969-94.

	$550	$475	$425	$365	$300	$275	$250

Last MSR was $647.

MODEL 1100 LW-20 (LIGHTWEIGHT) - 20 ga. only, 2 3/4 in. chamber, lightweight scaled down receiver, mag. tube, and barrel, similar to 28 ga./.410 bore frame, standard length ejection port, with mahogany stock, 26 or 28 in. barrel, 6 1/2 lbs. Mfg. 1970-76.

	$510	$415	$325	$265	$230	$210	$180

Subtract 10% if w/o VR.

Remington introduced a lightweight 20 ga. Model 1100 in 1961, with standard frame, mahogany stock and forearm. This model was disc. in Dec., 1969.

MODEL 1100 LT-20 - 20 ga. only, variation of Model 1100 LW-20, 2 3/4 in. chamber, has opened ejection port and barrel extension similar to 12 ga. (long), lightened receiver, 23, 26 (disc., gloss wood only) or 28 (disc., satin wood only) in. barrel, VR became standard 1985, hi-gloss (disc.) or satin finish walnut stock and forearm, 6 1/2 lbs. Mfg. 1977-95.

	$510	$415	$325	$265	$230	$210	$180

Last MSR was $665.

Subtract 10% if without VR.

Subtract $34 for gloss walnut.

Please refer to the Model 1100 Synthetic for currently manufactured LT-20 values/information. Rolled scroll receiver engraving became standard on 20 ga. in 1998.

MODEL 1100 LT-20 YOUTH - 20 ga. only, similar to Model 1100 Lightweight, except stock is 1 in. shorter and 21 in. barrel only. Disc. 1998.

	$500	$415	$325	$265	$230	$210	$180

Last MSR was $659.

＊ *Model 1100 LT-20 Youth Camo NWTG* - 20 ga. only, features 100% Mossy Oak break up camo finish, Truglo fiberoptic sights, 6 1/2 lbs. Mfg. 1998 only.

	$495	$415	$325	$265	$230	$210	$180

Last MSR was $652.

MODEL 1100 LT-20 MAG. (LIGHTWEIGHT MAGNUM) - chambered for 3 in. 20 ga. Mag., 20 (disc.), 26 (disc.), or 28 in. barrel, Rem. chokes became standard 1987. Introduced 1977, disc. 1998.

	$500	$415	$325	$265	$230	$210	$180

Last MSR was $659.

Subtract 10% if without VR.

MODEL 1100 MAGNUM DUCK GUN - similar to 1100, in 12 (disc. 1987) or 20 ga., 3 in. chamber, recoil pad, VR became standard 1984, Rem. chokes became standard 1987. Mfg. 1963-88.

	$400	$325	$280	$260	$220	$200	$180

Last MSR was $533.

Add $80 for left-hand model (disc. 1986).

Subtract $40 if without VR.

Subtract $45 if without Rem. chokes.

✳ *Model 1100 Magnum Special Purpose (SP)* - 12 ga. only, low luster finish on stock and forearm, sand blasted metal parts. Mfg. 1985-86 only.

	$395	$350	$295	$265	$235	$200	$180

Last MSR was $550.

Add $40 for Rem. chokes

MODEL 1100 SYNTHETIC (INCLUDING LT-20)

- 12, 16 (new 2003), or 20 (LT-20) ga., 2 3/4 in. chamber, 26 (20 ga. only) or 28 (12 ga. only) in. VR barrel with Rem. choke, checkered black synthetic stock and forearm, matte metal finish, 7-7.5 lbs. Mfg. 1996-2004.

	$430	$340	$275

Last MSR was $549.

Add $157-$296 (factory MSR) per extra barrel (2 3/4 in. chamber only), depending on configuration.

✳ *Model 1100 LT-20 Synthetic Youth* - features 21 in. VR barrel, matte black synthetic stock and forearm. Mfg. 1999-2004.

	$430	$340	$275

Last MSR was $549.

Add $63 for Youth Turkey Camo - includes 3 in. chamber and 100% Realtree Advantage or Skyline Excel (new 2003) camo on stock and forearm.

✳ *Model 1100 Synthetic Deer* - 12 or 20 (LT-20) ga., 21 in. fully rifled barrel with choice of cantilever scope mount (12 ga. only, became standard 2004 in 12 ga.) or rifle sight (20 ga. only), 7 or 7.5 lbs. New 1997-2004.

	$495	$375	$300

Last MSR was $629.

Subtract approx. $50 for rifle sights.

MODEL 1100 COMPETITION MASTER

- 12 ga. only, 2 3/4 in. chamber, designed for 3 gun matches in practical shooting, 22 in. VR barrel with fiberoptic front sight and Rem. choke, 8 shot mag., grey synthetic stock and forearm, features R3 recoil pad, matte black finish, 8 lbs. Mfg. 2003-2004.

	$775	$600	$525	$465	$435	$395	$350

Last MSR was $932.

MODEL 1100 DEER GUN

- 12 (disc. 1987) or 20 ga., 20 (disc.), 21 in. (20 ga. only) or 22 (disc.) in. imp. cyl. barrel with rifle sights. Disc. 1996.

	$435	$345	$270	$225	$200	$185	$165

Last MSR was $584.

Add $80 for left-hand model (disc. 1986).
Add $117 for 21 in. fully rifled cantilever deer barrel.

✳ *Model 1100 Special Purpose Deer (SP)* - similar to Model 1100 Deer Gun, except has low luster finish on stock and forearm, sandblasted metal parts. Mfg. 1986 only.

	$335	$295	$275	$255	$220	$200	$180

Last MSR was $495.

MODEL 1100 TOURNAMENT SKEET

- 12 or 20 (LT-20, disc.) ga., 26 in. skeet bored or Rem. choke barrel, optional Cutts Compensator available from Jan. 1964 to Dec. 1976. Mfg. 1963-1994, mfg. 1996-97, reintroduced 2003 in 12 ga. only, 8 lbs.

MSR $901		$740	$560	$480	$380	$325	$275	$225

Add 5% for left-hand model (disc. 1986).

MODEL 1100 SMALL GAUGE SKEET

- 28 ga. or .410 bore, 25 or 26 (disc.) in. VR barrel, 6 1/2-7 1/4 lbs. Mfg. 1969-94.

	$550	$450	$415	$375	$300	$265	$230

Last MSR was $692.

2 1/2 in. chamber is standard on the .410 bore (Skeet only).

GRADING - PPGS™	100%	98%	95%	90%	80%	70%	60%

MODEL 1100 SKEET MATCHED PAIR - 28 ga. and .410 bore, walnut stock and forearm. 5,067 cased Skeet sets were mfg. 1969 and 1970 only.

	$1,250	$995	$875				

MODEL 1100 SPORTING - 12 (new 2000), 20 (new 1998), 28 ga., or .410 bore (new 2004), 25 (28 ga. only, disc. 2003) 27 (small gauge only, new 2004) or 28 (20 ga. only) in. VR barrel with Rem. chokes, 12 ga. has lightweight 28 in. VR target barrel, high gloss checkered deluxe walnut stock and forearm, 6 1/2 - 8 lbs. New 1996.

MSR $901	$740	$560	$480	$380	$325	$275	$225

Add $34 for 28 ga. or .410 bore.

MODEL 1100 TA TRAP - 12 ga., 30 in. barrel, recoil pad on regular stock, available in left- or right-hand. Mfg. 1979-86.

	$410	$330	$295	$270	$230	$210	$190

Last MSR was $570.

Add 5% for Monte Carlo stock.
Add $50 for left-hand model.

MODEL 1100 TB TRAP - 12 ga., 30 in. VR full choke barrel, special trap stock, select wood. Mfg. 1963-81.

	$475	$400	$325	$300	$245	$210	$190
Monte Carlo stock	$495	$415	$340	$310	$280	$235	$220

MODEL 1100 TOURNAMENT TRAP - 12 ga., 30 in. VR full choke barrel, special trap stock, extra select wood. Mfg. 1979-86.

	$550	$495	$425	$365	$325	$285	$250

Last MSR was $675.

Add 5% for Monte Carlo stock.

MODEL 1100 CLASSIC TRAP - 12 ga. only, features 30 in. VR light contour target barrel, high gloss checkered walnut Monte Carlo stock and forearm, high polish blue, receiver features fine line engraving and gold inlays, 8.25 lbs. New 2000.

MSR $935	$760	$585	$495	$395	$330	$275	$225

MODEL 1100 150TH ANNIVERSARY - limited mfg. in 1966 only.

	$400	$340	$290				

MODEL 1100 BICENTENNIAL - 12 ga. only, configurations include Trap, Skeet, and Trade, mfg. to commemorate U.S. Bicentennial (1776-1976).

Trap or Skeet	$450	$375	$325				
Trade	$375	$295	$225				

In 1976, the 1100 Bicentennial Trap retailed for $320 ($330 w/Monte Carlo stock), the Skeet retailed for $285, and the Trade retailed for $270.

MODEL 1100 DUCKS UNLIMITED - "DU" in serial number.

Remington has offered many variations of the Model 1100 specifically manufactured according to individual DU chapter specifications. The price of a DU 1100 varies substantially from the "DU point of purchase" to real market conditions. When contemplating a DU gun it is always important to know how many of that particular variation were manufactured. The Remington factory normally has this information unless the special DU work was subcontracted elsewhere.

While most DU guns are good vehicles for fund raising, their collectibility to date has been minimal. Actual market conditions indicate that unless production is truly limited, most DU firearms sell very close to the models they were derived from. Also, any collectibility that does exist is for 100% guns new in the box with warranty papers. Used DU guns have values comparable to the standard model from which they were derived.

In addition to regular DU guns, Remington has also produced special editions including the 1982 Atlantic Flyway (dinner gun) and a 1981 DU Lt. 20 ga. and 12 ga. (dinner gun - 2,400 mfg. each), and a 1973 dinner gun (600 mfg.). These were rarer DU shotguns, and current values could vary significantly.

GRADING - PPGS™	100%	98%	95%	90%	80%	70%	60%

MODEL 1100 D-GRADE (TOURNAMENT) - custom order only, any gauge. Mfg. 1963-present.

MSR $3,723 · $2,900 · $2,075 · $1,425

MODEL 1100 F-GRADE (PREMIER) - custom order only, any gauge. Mfg. 1963-present.

MSR $7,245 · $6,000 · $4,400 · $2,850

MODEL 1100 F-GRADE W/GOLD (GOLD PREMIER) - with gold inlay, custom order only. Mfg. 1963-present.

MSR $10,663 · $9,030 · $5,150 · $3,425

Note: Grades differ in quality, grade of wood, amount of engraving, and gold inlays.

Remington Shotguns: Semi-Auto, Model 11-87 & Variations

Add $667 for custom shop Etchen stock and forearm installed on new Model 11-87s (new 2000).

Remington MSRs on extra barrels (3 in. chamber standard) for the following currently manufactured models range from $192-$324 per barrel, depending on configuration.

MODEL 11-87 SPORTSMAN - 12 or 20 ga., 3 in. chamber, black synthetic stock, vent. rib, 21 (fully rifled with cantilever, 12 ga. only), 26 or 28 in. barrel with Rem. Chokes. New 2005.

MSR $625 · $495 · $450 · $375 · $315 · $265 · $230 · $200

Add $80 for 21 in. fully rifled barrel with cantilever scope mount.

This model is available in a 20 ga. Youth configuration with 21 in. barrel at no extra charge.

MODEL 11-87 PREMIER - 12 or 20 (new 1999, LT-20) ga. (3 in. chamber), 26, 28, 30 (12 ga. only, new 2000) or 32 (disc. 1996) in. VR Rem. choked barrel, successor to Model 1100, gas compensating action adaptable to all loads, stainless steel magazine tube, polished blue finish, high gloss or satin (current mfg. is in 12 ga./28 in. barrel only) finished and checkered walnut stock and forearm, a high gloss wood finish option became available in 1991 at N/C, and is now standard, fine line receiver engraving (referred to as embellished receiver) became standard during 1999, solid recoil pad, 8 1/8-8 3/8 lbs. Introduced 1987.

MSR $827 · $635 · $500 · $420 · $375 · $315 · $275 · $250

Add $81 for 21 in. fully rifled cantilever deer barrel.

Add $66 for left-hand action (12 ga. only).

Note: Model 11-87 Premier barrels are not interchangeable with Model 1100 barrels.

* **Model 11-87 Premier Upland Special** - 12 or 20 ga., 3 in. chamber, 23 in. (light contour barrel on 12 ga.) VR barrel, straight grip satin finished checkered walnut stock and forearm, high polish metal with engraving, 6.5 or 7.25 lbs. New 2000.

MSR $827 · $635 · $500 · $420 · $375 · $315 · $275 · $250

MODEL 11-87 PREMIER 3 1/2 IN. SUPER MAGNUM - 12 ga. only, 3 1/2 in. chamber, 28 in. VR barrel with Rem. chokes, blue high polish non-embellished receiver and barrel, checkered high gloss walnut stock and forearm or 100% Mossy Oak Break-Up camo (disc. 2004) coverage, 8.25 lbs. New 2001.

MSR $899 · $720 · $510 · $445 · $375 · $325 · $300 · $280

Add approx. 10% for camo (disc. 2004).

MODEL 11-87 SP (SPECIAL PURPOSE) - 12 ga. only, 3 in. chamber, 26, 28, or 30 (disc.) in. VR Rem. choked barrel, parkerized metal with satin finish wood stock and forearm, vent. recoil pad, included camouflaged nylon sling, 8 1/4 lbs. Mfg. 1987-2003.

$590 · $465 · $395 · $350 · $315 · $275 · $250

Last MSR was $765.

MODEL 11-87 SP (SPECIAL PURPOSE) 3 1/2 IN. SUPER MAGNUM - 12 ga.
only, 3 1/2 in. chamber, non-reflective black matte finish on barrel and receiver, 26 or 28 in. VR barrel with Rem. choke, satin finished stock and forearm, approx. 8 1/8 lbs. New 2000.

	100%	98%	95%	90%	80%	70%	60%
MSR $912	$725	$525	$450	$375	$325	$300	$280

MODEL 11-87 POLICE - 12 ga. only, 18 in. barrel, improved cylinder choke, synthetic stock, parkerized finish, choice of bead or rifle sights, 7 shot extended mag., designed for police/law enforcement.

> Remington does not publish consumer retail pricing for this police/law enforcement model. Secondary prices for this model will be slightly higher than for current pricing on the Model 11-87 SPS.

MODEL 11-87 SPS (SPECIAL PURPOSE SYNTHETIC) - see individual sub-models listed below.

✳ Model 11-87 SPS 3 in. Magnum - similar to Model 11-87 SP 3 in. Mag., except is supplied with black synthetic stock and forearm. Disc. 2004.

		98%	95%	90%	80%	70%	60%
	$610	$475	$400	$360	$315	$275	$250

Last MSR was $791.

✳ Model 11-87 SPS Camo (Special Purpose Synthetic Camo) - 12 ga. only, 3 in. chamber, 21 (new 1999), 26 or 28 (disc. 1998) in. VR barrel with Rem. choke, available in Mossy Oak Bottomland (disc. 1996) or Mossy Oak Break-Up (new 1997) finish. New 1994.

	100%	98%	95%	90%	80%	70%	60%
MSR $925	$735	$525	$445	$365	$325	$300	$280

✳ Model 11-87 SPS Waterfowl - 12 ga., 3 in. chamber, 100% Mossy Oak New Shadow Grass camo coverage, 28 in. VR barrel with Hi-Viz front sight (interchangeable), includes sling and swivels, 8.25 lbs. New 2004.

	100%	98%	95%	90%	80%	70%	60%
MSR $960	$760	$540	$460	$375	$330	$300	$280

✳ Model 11-87 SPS-BG Camo (Special Purpose Synthetic Big Game) - 12 ga. only, 21 in. plain barrel with rifle sights and Rem. choke. Mfg. 1994 only.

		98%	95%	90%	80%	70%	60%
	$555	$425	$350	$290	$250	$225	$200

Last MSR was $692.

✳ Model 11-87 SP/SPS (Special Purpose Deer Gun) - 12 ga. only, 3 in. chamber, 21 in. IC or Rem. choked (Model SP, mfg. 1989-2003) or fully rifled (new 1993, became standard 2004) barrel with iron sights, parkerized metal with matte finished wood or black synthetic (Model SPS, new 1993) stock and forearm, vent. recoil pad, includes camouflaged nylon sling, 7.25 lbs. New 1987.

	100%	98%	95%	90%	80%	70%	60%
MSR $908	$695	$525	$450	$395	$350	$300	$250

Subtract 10% for fixed choke barrel or if w/o cantilever (became standard 2005) scope mount.

Rem. chokes were standard on this model between 1989-1992.

✳ Model 11-87 SPS-T (Special Purpose Turkey) - 12 ga. only, 3 in. chamber, 21 in. VR barrel with Rem. choke, available in flat black (disc. 2000) or 100% camo treatment in Mossy Oak (disc. 1996), Mossy Oak Break Up (new 1999), Realtree X-tra Brown (mfg. 1997 only), or Greenleaf (disc. 1996), TruGlo rifle sights became standard in 2002 (Model SPS-T Turkey Gun RS/TG). Disc. 2003.

		98%	95%	90%	80%	70%	60%
	$765	$550	$460	$385	$335	$300	$280

Last MSR was $963.

Add $324 for Leupold Gilmore red dot sights, Monte Carlo stock and superfull choke tube (mfg. 2000 only).

Subtract approx. $20 if w/o TruGlo rifle sights.

>Model 11-87 SPS Turkey Camo NWTF - 20 ga. only, features 100% Mossy Oak Break-Up camo finish, TruGlo fiberoptic sights, 6 1/2 lbs. Mfg. 1998 only.

		98%	95%	90%	80%	70%	60%
	$675	$575	$450	$395	$325	$290	$265

Last MSR was $832.

GRADING - PPGS™	100%	98%	95%	90%	80%	70%	60%

MODEL 11-87 SPS 3 1/2 IN. SUPER MAGNUM - choice of 26 or 28 in. VR barrel
with Rem. choke, black synthetic or 100% Mossy Oak Break-Up camo covered stock and forearm, approx. 8 1/8 lbs. New 2000.

	MSR $912	$725	$515	$445	$375	$325	$300	$280

Add $84 for camo coverage.

✸ *Model 11-87 SPS-T 3 1/2 in. Super Magnum Turkey Camo* - 12 ga. only, 3 1/2 in. chamber, full coverage Mossy Oak Break-Up (disc. 2003) or Obsession (new 2005) camo treatment, 23 in. barrel with TruGlo rifle sights and Rem. choke tube, 8 1/8 lbs. New 2001.

	MSR $1,016	$810	$585	$495	$450	$385	$340	$300

MODEL 11-87 SPORTING CLAYS - 12 ga. only, 26 (disc. 1996) or 28 in. VR barrel
with extended Rem. chokes (knurled extension chokes allow for no-wrench field changes), specially balanced, satin finished walnut, top metal surfaces have fine matte finish, radiused recoil pad, twin bead sights on 5/16 wide VR, 7 1/2 lbs. Mfg. 1992-99.

		$675	$575	$450	$395	$325	$290	$265

Last MSR was $833.

✸ *Model 11-87 Sporting Clays NP* - 12 ga. only, features matte nickel plated receiver with engraving, satin finished checkered stock and forearm, 28 (new 1998) or 30 in. VR ported barrel with extended choke tubes, 7 3/4 lbs. Mfg. 1997-2001.

		$775	$650	$525	$450	$375	$325	$295

Last MSR was $948.

MODEL 11-87 PREMIER SKEET - 12 ga. only, 26 in. VR Rem. choked barrel, deluxe
walnut with quality cut checkering, 7 3/4 lbs. Mfg. 1987-99.

		$650	$550	$475	$425	$375	$325	$275

Last MSR was $799.

Add approx. $70 for left-hand action.
Subtract 10% if without Rem. chokes.

MODEL 11-87 PREMIER TRAP - 12 ga. only, 30 in. raised VR Rem. choked barrel,
deluxe walnut stock (Monte Carlo became standard in 1996) with quality cut checkering, 8 1/4 lbs. Mfg. 1987-99.

		$660	$565	$440	$385	$300	$275	$260

Last MSR was $833.

Subtract $30 if without Monte Carlo stock.
Add approx. $40 for left-hand action (disc. 1994).
Subtract 10% if without Rem. chokes.

MODEL 11-87 175TH ANNIVERSARY - 12 ga. only, 28 in. barrel with Rem -
chokes, 175th Anniversary Model (1816-1991) with light engraving and high gloss wood finish. 4,606 1991 mfg. only.

		$515	$425	$335				

Last MSR was $618.

MODEL 11-87 DALE EARNHARDT COMMEMORATIVE - 12 ga. only, features "7
Time Winston Cup Champion" tributary banner on right side with gold letters, 28 in. light contoured VR barrel, select checkered American walnut stock and forearm, serialization starts with DE3, 7.75 lbs. Mfg. 2003-2004.

		$800	$650	$575				

Last MSR was $972.

MODEL 11-87 D-GRADE (TOURNAMENT) - custom order only, any gauge. Mfg.
1963-present.

	MSR $3,723	$2,900	$2,075	$1,425				

MODEL 11-87 F-GRADE (PREMIER) - custom order only, any gauge. Mfg. 1963-
present.

	MSR $7,245	$6,000	$4,400	$2,850				

GRADING - PPGS™	100%	98%	95%	90%	80%	70%	60%

MODEL 11-87 F-GRADE W/GOLD (GOLD PREMIER) - with gold inlay, custom order only. Mfg. 1963-present.

	100%	98%	95%
MSR $10,663	$9,030	$5,150	$3,425

Note: Grades differ in quality, grade of wood, and amount of engraving.

Remington Shotguns: Semi-Auto, Model 11-96

MODEL 11-96 EURO LIGHTWEIGHT - 12 ga. only, steel receiver with distinctive slight hump over chamber, 26 or 28 in. 6mm VR Rem. choked barrel, checkered walnut stock and forearm, receiver panel engraving, approx. 7 lbs. Mfg. 1996 only.

$715	$615	$550	$475	$395	$335	$295

Last MSR was $852.

100%	98%	95%	90%	80%	70%	60%	50%	40%	30%	20%	10%

SHOTGUNS: SINGLE BARREL

MODEL NO. 3 RIDER SINGLE BARREL - 12 ga., single barrel, 30 or 32 in. barrels, top lever break open, button release forend, plain pistol grip stock. Approx. 87,850 mfg. 1893-1903.

$325	$290	$260	$230	$200	$170	$140	$110	$85	$65	$50	$35

MODEL NO. 9 RIDER SINGLE BARREL - similar to No. 3, screw release forend, auto ejector. 65,698 mfg. 1902-10.

$375	$325	$290	$260	$230	$200	$170	$140	$110	$85	$65	$50

GRADING - PPGS™	100%	98%	95%	90%	80%	70%	60%

MODEL 90-T (TRAP) - 12 ga., 32 (disc. 1993) or 34 in. full choke VR barrel with fixed full choke, matte black receiver and wood around tang area, deluxe checkered stock and forearm, short throw top-lever release, elongated forcing cone, approx. 8 3/4 lbs. Mfg. 1992-97.

$1,850	$1,550	$1,375	$1,175	$1,025	$925	$850

Last MSR was $3,199.

Add $50 for factory porting.

* *Model 90-T HPAR (High Post w/ adj. Rib)* - features high post, adj. rib. Mfg. 1994-97.

$2,300	$1,875	$1,700	$1,550	$1,450	$1,325	$1,075

Last MSR was $3,992.

MODEL 310 SKEET - .32 Rimfire case loaded with No. 12 leadshot, break open single shot, .310 bore shotgun, used in conjunction with a self-operated trap set which threw half-size clay targets, entire set-up included gun, shooting booth, ammunition, and trap thrower, 5 1/2 lbs., mfg. circa late '60s.

Gun only	$425	$350	$300	$250	$195	$175	$150

Add 25%-75% depending on the amount of original accessories included.

This model was mfg. by CBC in Brazil, and imported into the U.S. as the .310 Skeet. This model was never mass produced, but test marketed for approx. 5 years in CT, NJ, PA, and TX primarily at amusement parks. It failed commercially due to lack of sales.

SHOTGUNS: SLIDE ACTION, DISC.

REMINGTON REPEATING SHOTGUN - 12 ga., hammerless, bottom ejection, takedown, plain barrel only, blue finish, sight notch on receiver top, marked "REMINGTON ARMS CO." with February 3rd, 1903 and May 18th, 1905 patent dates, walnut pistol grip stock and short forearm, hard rubber buttplate, 7 1/2 lbs., approx. 10,000 mfg. 1908-10.

$295	$225	$200	$175	$150	$125	$110

Add 10% for 32 in. barrel.

There were 7 grades of this model (Numbers 0-6) that were originally priced from $27 to approx. $140. This model was renamed the Model 10 in 1911.

GRADING - PPGS™	100%	98%	95%	90%	80%	70%	60%

MODEL 10A SLIDE ACTION - 12 ga., 26-32 in. barrels, various chokes, takedown, plain pistol grip stock. Mfg. 1911-29.

	$300	$275	$200	$175	$150	$125	$110

Add 10% for 32 in. full choke barrel.

Add 35% for guns marked "Long Range" - beware of fakes.

MODEL 17A SLIDE ACTION - 20 ga., 26-32 in. barrel, various chokes, takedown, bottom ejection, 4 shot mag., plain grip stock. Approx. 48,000 mfg., 1917-33.

	100%	98%	95%	90%	80%	70%	60%
Plain barrel	$350	$275	$220	$195	$165	$140	$110
Solid. rib	$450	$375	$325	$290	$270	$250	$210

Grades range from "A" - "F" in suffix form, "F" being the highest. Large premiums are paid for mint condition, higher grade models.

MODEL 17R - 20 ga. only, security configuration, 20 in. cylinder bore barrel, 4 shot mag. Mfg. circa 1920s.

	$325	$265	$235	$200	$150	$120	$100

MODEL 29A SLIDE ACTION - 12 ga., 26-32 in. barrel, bottom ejection, various chokes, takedown, 5 shot mag., checkered pistol grip stock. Approx. 24,000 mfg., 1929-33.

	$325	$265	$235	$200	$150	$120	$100

Add 15% for solid rib, 25% for VR.

✳ *32 in. Long Range barrel* - should be marked "Long Range" - beware of fakes.

	$525	$475	$425	$350	$250	$200	$180

Grades range from A - C and TA - TF, lowest to highest. Premiums exist for finer condition upper grades. The Model 29 was similar in appearance to the Model 10.

MODEL 29R - 12 ga. only, security configuration, 20 in. cylinder bore barrel, 5 shot mag. Mfg. circa 1920s.

	$375	$325	$265	$235	$200	$150	$120

MODEL 29S - "Trap Special" with trap style straight grip stock, matted or VR rib.

	$500	$450	$425	$375	$350	$325	$300

Add 20% for VR rib.

MODEL 31A SLIDE ACTION - 12, 16, or 20 ga., side ejection, 2 or 4 shot mag., 26-32 in. barrels, various chokes, takedown, pistol grip stock. Approx. 160,000 mfg., 1931-49.

	100%	98%	95%	90%	80%	70%	60%
Plain barrel	$395	$345	$300	$265	$225	$185	$150
Solid rib	$455	$385	$345	$300	$270	$230	$190
Vent. rib	$475	$415	$375	$320	$290	$250	$210

Add 15% for 20 ga.

Grades range from A - F suffixes. Higher grades will bring considerable premiums in excellent condition. TC suffix is Target Model. A Model 31L (lightweight) was mfg. 1948-1950 and while rare, demand dictates to subtract 20% for this variation. Early models will command a small premium in this model.

MODEL 31B "SPECIAL" - higher grade wood and hand checkered pistol grip stock and forearm.

	$650	$550	$440	$385	$360	$305	$275

MODEL 31R "RIOT" GRADE - features shortened barrel.

	$425	$365	$325	$295	$270	$230	$190

MODEL 31D TOURNAMENT - features scroll engraving.

	$1,100	$880	$715	$580	$525	$495	$470

MODEL 31E EXPERT - features scroll engraving with game scene on left side of receiver.

	$1,320	$1,100	$935	$880	$770	$660	$605

GRADING - PPGS™	100%	98%	95%	90%	80%	70%	60%

MODEL 31F PREMIER - features scroll engraving and game scenes on both sides of receiver. Introduced 1942.

	$2,100	$1,800	$1,600	$1,500	$1,300	$1,050	$875

Add 20% for 20 ga.

Note: Grades differ in quality, grade of wood, and amount of engraving.

This model was also available with a Cutts compensator 1940-49, or a Poly Choke on special order from 1941-49.

MODEL 31TC TRAP - similar to 31A, with 12 ga. only, 30 or 32 in. VR barrel milled out of one piece of steel, full choke, trap stock and beavertail forend, pad.

	$875	$795	$675	$575	$450	$375	$300

Subtract 10% for lightweight receiver.

TC stands for Trap with C Grade wood.

MODEL 31S TRAP SPECIAL - solid rib barrel, plainer wood.

	$550	$500	$450	$400	$365	$345	$325

MODEL 31H HUNTER - similar to 31S, with sporter stock. Mfg. 1941-disc.

	$395	$350	$300	$275	$250	$220	$195

MODEL 31L LIGHTWEIGHT - features an alloy receiver, available in both field and skeet, introduced 1941.

	$350	$325	$300	$275	$250	$225	$200

MODEL 31 SKEET - similar to 31A, with 26 in. skeet bored barrel, standard solid rib, beavertail forend.

	100%	98%	95%	90%	80%	70%	60%
Plain barrel	$495	$450	$395	$365	$335	$265	$220
Vent. rib	$650	$550	$495	$425	$375	$340	$295

Subtract 10% for lightweight receiver.

Add 20% for 20 ga. with VR barrel.

SHOTGUNS: SLIDE ACTION, MODEL 870 & VARIATIONS

3 in. shells (12 or 20 ga.) may be shot in Magnum receivers only regardless of what the barrel markings may indicate (the ejection port is larger in these Magnum models with M suffix serialization).

Remington has manufactured many limited production runs for various distributors and wholesalers over the years. These shotguns are usually built to a specific configuration (gauge, stock, barrel length, finish, etc.), and are usually available until supplies run out. While these models are not included in this section, pricing in most cases will be similar to the base models from which they were derived.

Add $667 for custom shop Etchen stock and forearm installed on new Model 870s (mfg. 2000-2002).

Add 25%-35% for 16 ga. on older mfg., if original condition is 95%+.

Remington MSRs on extra barrels (3 in. chamber is standard, except for Skeet barrel) for the following currently manufactured models range from $148-$321 per barrel, depending on configuration.

MODEL 870AP SLIDE ACTION - "Wingmaster," 12, 16, or 20 ga., 26, 28, or 30 in. barrel, 5 shot, various chokes, plain pistol grip stock. Mfg. 1950-63.

	100%	98%	95%	90%	80%	70%	60%
Plain barrel	$220	$195	$175	$165	$140	$120	$110
Vent. rib	$250	$220	$200	$195	$165	$150	$140

Add 15% for "Sungrain" blonde maple wood (mfg. 1959-1961).

MODEL 870ADL - deluxe checkered version of 870AP. Mfg. 1950-63.

	100%	98%	95%	90%	80%	70%	60%
Plain barrel	$250	$220	$200	$180	$165	$140	$120
Matted top barrel	$275	$250	$220	$210	$195	$165	$140
Vent. rib	$300	$275	$250	$225	$200	$175	$150

GRADING - PPGS™	100%	98%	95%	90%	80%	70%	60%

MODEL 870BDL - select walnut stock.

	100%	98%	95%	90%	80%	70%	60%
Plain barrel	$275	$250	$220	$200	$180	$165	$140
Vent. rib	$315	$290	$260	$240	$210	$195	$165

SPORTSMAN 12 PUMP - 12 ga. only (3 in. chamber), 28 or 30 in. barrel, recoil pad, VR standard, hardwood stock and forearm, Model 870 type action, 7 1/2 lbs. Mfg. 1984-86.

	$275	$235	$195	$175	$160	$150	$140

Last MSR was $270.

Add $35 for Rem. chokes.

MODEL 870 EXPRESS - 12, 16 (new 2002), 20 (new 1991), 28 ga. (disc., reintroduced 2002-2004), or .410 bore (disc., reintroduced 2002-2004), 3 in. chamber, 20, 25 (28 ga. or .410 bore only), 26, or 28 in. VR Rem. choked (12 or 20 ga., supplied with Mod. Rem. choke) barrel, parkerized metal, matte finished hardwood stock and forearm, solid recoil pad, 7.25 lbs. New 1987.

MSR $332	$265	$215	$180	$160	$145	$135	$130

Add $27 for 28 ga. or .410 bore.

Add $27 for left-hand action (12 ga., 28 in. barrel only, new 1998).

Various combination Express packages are available in both 12 and 20 ga. Retail prices range from $455-$489.

✱ *Model 870 Synthetic Express* - 12 or 16 ga., 26 or 28 in. VR barrel with one Rem. choke, features black synthetic stock and forearm. New 1994.

MSR $332	$265	$215	$180	$160	$145	$135	$130

Add $13 for 7 shot tube mag.

>**Model 870 Synthetic Express Deer** - 12 or 20 ga., features 20 in. fully rifled barrel with rifle sights. New 2002.

MSR $372	$295	$225	$185	$165	$145	$135	$130

✱ *Model 870 Express Deer Gun* - 12 or 20 ga., 20 in. IC choked barrel or fully rifled barrel with rifle sights, Monte Carlo stock. Introduced in 1991.

MSR $332	$265	$215	$180	$160	$145	$135	$130

Add $87 for fully rifled cantilever barrel with Bushnell scope (12 or 20 ga., new 2005).

Add $78 for cantilever scope system and IC Rem. choke (disc. 1991).

✱ *Model 870 Turkey Express* - 12 ga. only, choice of wood with flat finish or Realtree Advantage (new 1998) or Skyline Excel (new 2003) camo stock and forearm, 21 in. VR barrel with Rem. turkey choke, 7 1/4 lbs.

MSR $345	$270	$215	$185	$160	$145	$135	$130

Add $54 for camo stock and forearm (Skyline Excel pattern new 2003).

✱ *Model 870 Youth* - 16 (new 2004) or 20 ga. only, 21 in. VR barrel with Rem. choke, 13 in. LOP with recoil pad, choice of RealTree Advantage (new 1998) or Skyline Excel (new 2003) camo or regular wood finish on stock and forearm, 6 lbs.

MSR $332	$265	$215	$180	$160	$140	$130	$125

Add $33 for Youth Deer Gun (fully rifled 20 in. barrel). New 1994.

Add $87 for Youth Turkey with choice of NWTF Jake's Skyline Excel.

Add $67 for Youth Turkey with RealTree Advantage (disc. 2003) or Skyline Excel (new 2003) camo.

✱ *Model 870 Express Synthetic HD (Home Defense)* - 12 ga. only, 18 in. cyl. choked barrel with bead sights, black synthetic stock and forend. New 1991.

MSR $319	$250	$205	$170	$155	$140	$130	$125

MODEL 870 EXPRESS SUPER MAGNUM - 12 ga., 3 1/2 in. chamber, choice of checkered natural hardwood, black synthetic, or 100% RealTree Advantage camo stock and forearm, 23 (camo only), 26 (synthetic only), or 28 (wood only) in. VR barrel, matte or 100% camo finish metal, recoil pad, approx. 7.25 lbs. New 1998.

MSR $376	$295	$230	$190	$165	$145	$135	$130

Add $13 for synthetic Turkey Model with 23 in. barrel (new 1999).

Add $124 for 100% Skyline Fall Flight camo coverage (new 2005).

Add $147 for combo package (includes 26 in. regular and 20 in. fully rifled deer barrel).

GRADING - PPGS™	100%	98%	95%	90%	80%	70%	60%

✳ **Model 870 Express Super Magnum Turkey Camo** - features 100% RealTree Advantage or Skyline Excel (new 2003) camo on metal and stock/forearm, 23 in. VR barrel only with Turkey extra full Rem. choke. New 1998.

MSR $500	$395	$315	$250	$210	$175	$160	$145

✳ **Model 870 Express Super Magnum Synthetic Camo** - 12 ga., 3 1/2 in. chamber, 23 or 26 in. VR barrel with Rem. choke, 100% Mossy Oak Break Up camo coverage, wood or synthetic stock and forearm. Mfg. 1999 only.

	$385	$320	$265	$240	$220	$200	$180

Last MSR was $532.

MODEL 870 FIELD WINGMASTER

- 12, 16 (disc. 1980, reintroduced late 2001), 20 (LW-20), 28 (disc. late 1994, reintroduced 1999) ga., or .410 (disc. late 1994, reintroduced 1999) bore, various barrel lengths (26, 28, and 30 are current mfg.), incorporates twin slide rails, 3 in. chamber in 12 ga. became standard in 1985, Rem. chokes became standard in 1987, lightweight frame on 20 ga. was introduced 1972, checkered walnut stock and forearm, a choice of high gloss or satin (28 in. barrel only) wood finish became available in 1991. Mfg. 1964-present.

Plain barrel	$250	$225	$205	$190	$175	$160	$150

✳ **Model 870 w/Vent. rib** - became standard in 1985.

MSR $625	$440	$365	$310	$260	$215	$190	$175

Subtract 10% without Rem. chokes.

Add $48 for left-hand model (12 ga. only, disc. 1994).

Add $80 for 20 in. fully rifled cantilever deer barrel (12 ga. - mfg. 1992-99 or 20 ga. - mfg. 1992-95).

Beginning 1998, rolled scroll engraving started to appear on 20 ga. guns only. During 2005, a Wingmaster Jr. was released in a LW-20 in 20 ga. with 12 in. LOP and 18.75 in. barrel at no extra charge.

✳ **Wingmaster Small Gauge** - 28 ga. or .410 bore, scaled down 870 on lightweight smaller frame, 25 in. fixed (F or M, .410 bore only) or Rem. choke (28 ga. only, new 1999) barrel, VR became standard 1984, 6-6 1/2 lbs. Mfg. 1969-94, reintroduced 1999.

MSR $655	$560	$460	$395	$330	$295	$260	$240

Add $54 for 28 ga.

Subtract 10% if w/o VR.

✳ **Wingmaster Fiftieth Anniversary Classic Trap** - 12 ga. only, 2 3/4 in. chamber, features high polish blue fine line receiver engraving with gold inlays, 30 in. low profile light contour barrel, checkered high gloss semi-fancy walnut stock and forearm with cut checkering, 8 lbs. New 2000.

MSR $819	$710	$575	$475	$400	$345	$300	$265

✳ **Wingmaster Dale Earnhardt Tribute** - 12 ga. only, 28 in. VR barrel with Remchokes, special embellishments featuring Dale Earnhardt. New 2005.

MSR $820	$710	$575	$475	$400	$345	$300	$265

WINGMASTER 3 1/2 IN. SUPER MAGNUM

- 12 ga. only, 28 in. VR barrel with choke tubes, high polish blue with receiver engraving, high gloss walnut stock and forearm with cut checkering, 7.5 lbs. New 2000.

MSR $692	$580	$485	$400	$350	$300	$265	$250

MODEL 870 MAGNUM DUCK GUN

- 3 in. chamber, 12 or 20 ga., 26, 28, or 30 in. full or mod. barrel, recoil pad. Mfg. 1964-present. 3 in. chambers became standard on all Model 870s starting in 1985. Rem. chokes became standard 1987 (introduced 1986 as $40 option).

Please refer to Model 870 Field Wingmaster prices.

GRADING - PPGS™	100%	98%	95%	90%	80%	70%	60%

MODEL 870 SPECIAL PURPOSE

12 ga. only, differs only in that metal parts are sand blasted, choice of Mossy Oak Camo (new 1992), black synthetic, or checkered wood stock with low luster finish, 21 (Turkey barrel), 26, or 28 in. VR barrel. Rem. chokes were introduced 1986.

> **Add $75 for wood stock and forearm (disc. 1992).**
>
> **Subtract 10% without Rem. chokes.**

* *Model 870 Special Purpose Super Magnum Synthetic Camo* - 12 ga. only, 3 1/2 in. chamber, 26 or 28 in. VR barrel with Rem. choke, available in either Mossy Oak (disc. 1995) Bottomland (disc. 1996), full coverage Mossy Oak Break Up (new 1997) finish. New 1994.

MSR $617	$460	$365	$285	$250	$215	$180	$170

* *Model 870 SPS-T (Turkey) Super Magnum* - 12 ga. only, features 3 1/2 in. chamber, choice of 23, 26 (disc. 2004), or 28 (mfg. 2001-2004) in. VR barrel with Rem. chokes, fully camouflaged in Mossy Oak Break-Up or Obsession (new 2005) pattern, choice of standard wood, thumbhole (new 2005), or synthetic (26 in. barrel only) stock. New 2000.

MSR $617	$460	$365	$285	$250	$215	$180	$170

> **Add $33 for thumbhole stock with TruGlo rifle sights and 100% Mossy Oak Obsession coverage (new 2005).**
>
> **Add $18 for cantilever scope mount (new 2001) with Turkey super full choke tube.**
>
> **Add approx. $330 if with Leupold Gilmore red dot sights and Turkey super full choke tube - 23 in. barrel only (mfg. 2000 only).**

* *Model 870 SPS-BG Camo (Special Purpose Synthetic Big Game)* - 12 ga. only, 20 in. plain barrel with rifle sights and Rem. choke. Mfg. 1994 only.

	$350	$285	$235	$200	$170	$150	$130

Last MSR was $442.

* *Model 870 Special Purpose Turkey (SPS-T)* - 12 (disc. 2004) or 20 ga., 20 (new 2002) or 21 in. VR barrel with Rem. choke, available in flat black, Mossy Oak (disc. 1996, reintroduced 2002), Greenleaf (disc. 1996), or Realtree X-tra Brown (full SPS-T-camo, mfg. 1997 only) finish. Disc. 1999, reintroduced 2002.

MSR $621	$460	$365	$285	$250	$215	$180	$170

This model was also available 2002-2003 in a Youth Model with 1 in. shorter LOP.

* *Model 870 Special Purpose Deer Gun (SPS-Deer)* - 12 ga. only, 3 in. chamber, 20 in. Rem. choke barrel (disc. 1992) or fully rifled barrel with iron sights (new 1993), satin finished (disc. 1992) or black synthetic (new 1993) stock and forearm, matte black metal, 7 1/4 lbs. Mfg. 1989-99.

	$345	$275	$225	$195	$175	$160	$145

Last MSR was $436.

> **Add $28 for Cantilever deer barrel with Rem. choke (disc. 1996).**
>
> **Add $60 for fully rifled Cantilever deer barrel.**
>
> **Add $65 for Cantilever scope mount system (disc. 1992).**

* *Model 870 Special Purpose Super Slug Deer (SPS Super Slug Deer)* - 12 or 20 (new 2004) ga., 3 in. chamber, 23 in. fully rifled cantilever barrel, matte black metal finish, black synthetic Monte Carlo stock and forearm, approx. 8 lbs. Mfg. 1999-2004.

	$470	$375	$310	$255	$225	$195	$175

Last MSR was $580.

MODEL 870 LIGHTWEIGHT

20 ga. only, lighter and shorter mahogany stock than magnum model, 23 in. barrel. Mfg. 1972-83.

	$270	$230	$210	$190	$175	$165	$155

> **Add $30 for VR.**

GRADING - PPGS™	100%	98%	95%	90%	80%	70%	60%

MODEL 870 LIGHTWEIGHT (MAGNUM)
20 ga., 3 in. chamber, 26 or 28 in. barrel, 6 lbs. Mfg. 1972-1994. Rem. chokes became standard 1987.

	100%	98%	95%	90%	80%	70%	60%
	$365	$320	$260	$225	$200	$175	$160

Last MSR was $460.

Subtract 10% without Rem. chokes.
Subtract $40 without VR.

MODEL 870 SPECIAL FIELD
12 or 20 (LW-20) ga., lighter straight grip stock with solid recoil pad, 21 (disc. 1993) or 23 (new 1994) in. VR barrel, 6 1/4 or 7 lbs. New 1984. Rem. chokes became standard 1987 (introduced 1986 as $40 option). Disc. 1995.

	100%	98%	95%	90%	80%	70%	60%
	$380	$320	$265	$230	$210	$190	$175

Last MSR was $473.

Subtract 10% without Rem. chokes.

MODEL 870 BRUSHMASTER
12 or 20 (disc.) ga., 20 in. barrel with imp. cyl. (disc.) or Rem. choke and rifle sights, 3 in. chamber standard for 1985, normal bluing with satin finished wood. Disc. 1994.

	100%	98%	95%	90%	80%	70%	60%
	$355	$310	$255	$225	$200	$175	$160

Last MSR was $452.

Add $43 for left-hand model.

MODEL 870 MARINE MAGNUM
12 ga. only, 3 in. chamber, 18 in. plain barrel bored cyl., features electroless nickel plating on all metal parts, supplied with 7 shot mag., R3 recoil pad became standard during 2004, sling swivels and Cordura sling, 7.5 lbs.

	100%	98%	95%	90%	80%	70%	60%
MSR $600	$445	$365	$280	$245	$210	$185	$175

MODEL 870 POLICE
12 ga. only, 18 or 20 in. plain barrel, choice of blue (18 in. barrel only) or parkerized finish, bead or rifle (disc. 1995, 20 in. barrel only) sights, Police cylinder (disc.) or IC choke. New 1994.

	100%	98%	95%	90%	80%	70%	60%
MSR $461	$355	$295	$235	$195	$175	$160	$145

Add $14 for parkerized finish.
Add $44 for rifle sights (disc. 1995).

Remington also offers a Model 870P, 870P MAX, and 870P Synthetic for police/law enforcement, featuring Speedfeed, extended capacity magazines and improved cylinder chokes. While Remington does not publish consumer retail pricing for these police/law enforcement models, secondary prices for these guns will be slightly higher than for current pricing on the Model 870 Police.

MODEL 870 RIOT
12 ga. only, 18 or 20 in. barrel, choice of blue or parkerized metal finish. Disc. 1991.

	100%	98%	95%	90%	80%	70%	60%
	$295	$265	$225	$200	$170	$150	$130

Last MSR was $355.

Add $40 for police rifle sights (20 in. barrel only).

MODEL 870 D-GRADE (TOURNAMENT)
custom order only, any gauge. Mfg. 1950-present.

	100%	98%	95%
MSR $3,723	$2,900	$2,075	$1,425

MODEL 870 F-GRADE (PREMIER)
custom order only, any gauge. Mfg. 1950-present.

	100%	98%	95%
MSR $7,245	$6,000	$4,400	$2,850

MODEL 870 F-GRADE W/GOLD (GOLD PREMIER)
with gold inlays, custom order only. Mfg. 1950-present.

	100%	98%	95%
MSR $10,663	$9,030	$5,150	$3,425

Note: Grades differ in quality, grade of wood, and amount of engraving. Prices also vary accordingly.

MODEL 870 DUCKS UNLIMITED
"DU" in serial number, disc.

	100%	98%	95%
	$335	$270	$195

Remington has offered many variations of the Model 870 specifically manufactured according to individual DU chapter specifications. The price of a DU 870 varies substantially from the "DU

GRADING - PPGS™	100%	98%	95%	90%	80%	70%	60%

point of purchase" to real market conditions. When contemplating a DU gun it is always important to know how many of that particular variation were manufactured. The Remington factory normally has this information unless the special DU work was subcontracted elsewhere.

While most DU guns are good vehicles for fund raising, their collectibility to date has been minimal. Actual market conditions indicate that unless production is truly limited, most DU firearms sell very close to the model which they were derived from. Also, any collectability that does exist is for 100% guns new in the box with warranty papers. Used DU guns have values comparable to the standard model from which they were derived.

In addition to regular DU guns, Remington has also produced special editions including the 1982 Mississippi Edition (dinner gun) and a 1974 DU (dinner gun - first 500 mfg.).

MODEL 870 "WILDLIFE FOR TOMORROW" - 12 ga. only, side panels fine line laser etched with gold engraving, special wood, 2,000 mfg. for Wildlife Forever fundraiser 1996.

	100%	98%	95%
	$325	$250	$175

MODEL 870 150TH ANNIVERSARY - 12 ga. only, 2,534 mfg. 1966 only.

	100%	98%	95%
	$400	$325	$275

MODEL 870 BICENTENNIAL - 12 ga. only, configurations include Trap, Skeet, and Trade, mfg. to commemorate U.S. Bicentennial (1776-1976).

	100%	98%	95%
Trap or Skeet	$425	$350	$295
Trade	$375	$295	$225

In 1976, the 870 Bicentennial Trap retailed for $255 ($265 w/Monte Carlo stock), and the Skeet retailed for $220.

MODEL 870 SC SKEET - 12, 16 (disc. 1960), or 20 ga., 26 in. VR skeet bore barrel, C grade hand checkered wood stock. Mfg. 1950-79.

	100%	98%	95%	90%	80%	70%	60%
	$600	$445	$365	$280	$245	$210	$185

MODEL 870 SKEET MATCHED PAIR - includes .410 bore and 28 ga., 1,503 cased sets mfg. 1969 only.

	100%	98%	95%
	$1,150	$995	$895

MODEL 870 TA TRAP - 12 ga. trap model, deluxe walnut, VR. Add $15 for Monte Carlo stock. Mfg. 1978-86.

	100%	98%	95%	90%	80%	70%	60%
	$425	$375	$325	$275	$250	$225	$200

Last MSR was $430.

MODEL 870 TB TRAP - similar to 870, with 28 or 30 in. VR full choke barrel, trap stock, recoil pad. Mfg. 1950-81.

	100%	98%	95%	90%	80%	70%	60%
	$425	$375	$325	$275	$250	$225	$200

MODEL 870 TC TRAP - higher grade walnut and special VR, Rem. chokes became standard 1987. Mfg. 1950-79, reintroduced 1996-99.

	100%	98%	95%	90%	80%	70%	60%
	$600	$475	$400	$350	$275	$240	$220

Last MSR was $680.

Subtract 5% if w/o Monte Carlo stock.
Add 20% for early Model 870 TC Trap guns with hand cut checkering.

MODEL 870 COMPETITION TRAP - 12 ga. single shot competition model, reduced recoil, competition walnut stock with cut checkering, VR. 5,300 mfg. 1980-86.

	100%	98%	95%	90%	80%	70%	60%
	$550	$475	$395	$350	$315	$275	$250

Last MSR was $680.

MODEL 870 ALL AMERICAN TRAP - 30 in. full choke barrel, engraved receiver, triggerguard and barrel, deluxe trap stock. Approx. 1,000 mfg., 1972-76.

	100%	98%	95%	90%	80%	70%	60%
	$795	$700	$650	$605	$495	$440	$385

RENATO GAMBA
Please refer to the Gamba section in this text.

RENETTE, GASTINNE

Please refer to the Gastinne Renette section of this text.

REPUBLIC ARMS, INC.

Previous manufacturer 1997-2001, and located in Chino, CA.

PISTOLS: SEMI-AUTO

THE PATRIOT - .45 ACP cal., double action only, ultra compact with 3 in. barrel, 6 shot mag., black polymer frame with stainless steel slide (either brushed or with black Melonite coating, new 2000), locked breech action, checkered grips, 20 oz. New 1997.

100%	98%	95%	90%	80%	70%	60%
$265	$230	$210	$185	$175	$165	$155

Last MSR $299.

REPUBLIC ARMS OF SOUTH AFRICA

Previous manufacturer located in Jeppestown, Union of South Africa. Previously imported until 2002 by TSF Ltd., located in Fairfax, VA.

PISTOLS: SEMI-AUTO

RAP 401 - 9mm Para. cal., 8 shot mag., otherwise similar to Rap-440. Importation 1999-circa 2002.

100%	98%	95%	90%	80%	70%	60%
$495	$425	$375	$350	$325	$300	$275

RAP-440 - .40 S&W cal., compact double action, 3 1/2 in. barrel with high contrast 3 dot sights, last shot hold open, hammer drop safety/decocking lever, firing pin block safety, 7 shot mag., all steel construction, 31 1/2 oz., includes case, spare magazine, and lock. Imported 1998-circa 2002.

100%	98%	95%	90%	80%	70%	60%
$545	$475	$425	$395	$375	$330	$300

Add $50 for Trilux tritium night sights.

SHOTGUNS: SLIDE ACTION

MUSLER MODEL - 12 ga., lightweight shotgun, polymer reinforced stock and forearm, action opening release lever, action locks open after the last round. Imported 1998-circa 2002.

100%	98%	95%	90%	80%	70%	60%
$549	$475	$425	$395	$375	$330	$300

REXIO

Previous trademark of guns manufactured in Argentina beginning late 1999. Previously imported and distributed until 2002 by VAM Distribution Company, LLC, located in Wooster, OH.

PISTOLS: SINGLE SHOT

OUTFITTER RC-SERIES - various cals., including .45 LC/.410 bore, tip-up action, 6 or 10 in. barrel, synthetic SAA style grip and full forearm, opening release lever in front of triggerguard, transfer bar safety, with or w/o (.45 LC/.410 bore only) sights, manual locking safety, 2.2-3 lbs. Imported 2000-2002.

100%	98%	95%	90%	80%	70%	60%
$185	$165	$145	$130	$120	$110	$100

Last MSR was $205.

REVOLVERS

RJ-22 SERIES - .22 LR cal., 9 shot, 4 or 6 in. VR barrel with full shroud, choice of wood or synthetic grips with finger grooves, adj. sights, 2.1-2.6 lbs. Imported 2000-2002.

100%	98%	95%	90%	80%	70%	60%
$150	$135	$125	$115	$105	$100	$95

Last MSR was $170.

GRADING - PPGS™	100%	98%	95%	90%	80%	70%	60%

RJ-38 SERIES - .38 Spl. cal., 6 shot, 3 or 4 in. VR barrel with full shroud, choice of wood or synthetic grips with finger grooves, 1.8-2 lbs. Imported 2000-2002.

	$150	$140	$125	$115	$110	$105	$100

Last MSR was $170.

RS-22 SERIES - .22 LR or .22 Mag. cal., 8 (.22 Mag.) or 9 (.22 LR) shot, alloy or steel frame, blue finish, rubber grips with finger grooves, 4 or 6 in. VR barrel with full shroud, fixed or adj. sights, supplied with plastic case. Imported 2000-2002.

	$155	$140	$125	$115	$110	$105	$100

Last MSR was $175.

Add $12 for adj. sights.

* *RS-22 Series Stainless* - similar to RS-22 Series, except is stainless steel. Imported 2000-2002.

	$175	$150	$130				

Last MSR was $200.

Add $12 for adj. sights.

RS-357 SERIES - .357 Mag. cal., 6 shot, alloy or steel frame, 3, 4, or 6 in. VR barrel with full shroud, fixed or adj. sights, supplied with plastic case. Imported 2000-2002.

	$155	$140	$125	$115	$110	$105	$100

Last MSR was $175.

Add $12 for adj. sights.

* *RS-357 Series Stainless* - similar to RS-357 Series, except is stainless steel. Imported 2000-2002.

	$175	$150	$130				

Last MSR was $200.

Add $12 for adj. sights.

RHODE ISLAND ARMS COMPANY

Previous manufacturer located in Hope Valley, RI.

SHOTGUNS: O/U

MORRONE MODEL - 12 or 20 ga., 26 or 28 in. plain barrels, boxlock, extractors, single trigger, checkered straight or pistol grip stock. Mfg. 1949-1953, only 500 of these guns were mfg., 450 in 12 ga., and 50 in 20 ga., very few with VR, they are quite rare although collector interest is not overwhelming.

	$1,100	$880	$770	$660	$550	$495	$440

Add 20% for 20 gauge.
Add 20% for VR.

RIB MOUNTAIN ARMS, INC.

Previous rifle manufacturer circa 1992-2000, and located in Beresford and Sturgis, SD.

RIFLES: BOLT ACTION

MODEL 92 - .50 BMG cal., match grade barrel with muzzle brake, long action, walnut thumbhole stock, Timney trigger, approx. 28 lbs. Mfg. 1997-2000.

	$3,175	$2,725	$2,275	$2,000	$1,750	$1,575	$1,300

Last MSR was $3,475.

MODEL 93 - similar to Model 92, except has short action with removable shell holder bolt, approx. 25 lbs. Mfg. 1997-2000.

	$3,175	$2,725	$2,275	$2,000	$1,750	$1,575	$1,300

Last MSR was $3,475.

RICHLAND ARMS COMPANY

Previous importer (until 1986) located in Blissfield, MI. The models listed were made by various manufacturers located in either Italy or Spain.

SHOTGUNS

MODEL 80 LS SINGLE SHOT - 12, 20 ga., or .410 bore, 26 or 28 in. full choke barrel. Mfg. 1986 only.

	100%	98%	95%	90%	80%	70%	60%
	$140	$120	$110	$100	$90	$80	$70

Last MSR was $162.

MODEL 711 MAGNUM SxS - 10 ga., 3 1/2 in. chamber, 12 ga., 3 in. chamber, 32 in. full and full, 30 in. full and full, 20, 28 ga., and .410 bore also available on special order, hammerless, boxlock, extractors, checkered, walnut stock, recoil pad. Mfg. 1963-85 in Spain.

	100%	98%	95%	90%	80%	70%	60%
10 gauge	$400	$325	$275	$250	$230	$210	$190
12 gauge	$340	$295	$265	$250	$230	$210	$190
20 gauge	$450	$340	$295	$260	$230	$210	$195

MODEL 707 DELUXE SxS - 12 or 20 ga., 3 in. chambers, 26, 28, or 30 in. barrels, various chokes, boxlock, extractors, double triggers, checkered stock and forend. Mfg. 1963-1972 in Spain.

	100%	98%	95%	90%	80%	70%	60%
	$330	$300	$275	$250	$230	$210	$190

MODEL 200 FIELD GRADE SxS - 12, 16, 20, 28 ga., or .410 bore, 22, 26, and 28 in. barrels, various chokes, Anson & Deeley boxlock, extractors, double triggers, checkered stock, 6 lbs. 2 oz. - 7 lbs. 4 oz. Mfg. 1963-85 in Spain.

	100%	98%	95%	90%	80%	70%	60%
	$330	$300	$275	$250	$230	$210	$190

Last MSR was $379.

Add 20% for 20 ga., or 50% for 28 ga. or .410 bore.

MODEL 202 ALL PURPOSE SxS - similar to Field, except 2 sets of barrels, 12 and 20 ga. only. Mfg. 1963-disc. in Spain.

	100%	98%	95%	90%	80%	70%	60%
	$450	$400	$350	$300	$275	$250	$225

Add 20% for 20 ga., or 50% for 28 ga. or .410 bore.

MODEL 41 ULTRA O/U - 20, 28 ga., or .410 bore, 3 in. chambers (.410 bore only), single non-selective trigger, 26 or 28 in. barrels, extractors, VR, engraved silver finished receiver, select checkered walnut stock and forearm, 6 lbs. 2 oz. Importation disc. 1986.

	100%	98%	95%	90%	80%	70%	60%
	$395	$350	$300	$260	$230	$200	$180

Last MSR was $298.

MODEL 747 O/U - 12 or 20 ga. only, 3 in. chambers, Greener crossbolt, boxlock action, VR and barrels, SST, extractors. Importation disc. 1986.

	100%	98%	95%	90%	80%	70%	60%
	$475	$425	$350	$325	$310	$295	$280

Last MSR was $464.

MODEL 757 O/U - 12 ga., 3 in. chambers, boxlock action with Greener crossbolt, vent. barrels and rib, double triggers, extractors, walnut stock and forearm, 7 lbs. 4 oz. New 1986. Importation disc. 1986.

	100%	98%	95%	90%	80%	70%	60%
	$325	$275	$225	$200	$185	$170	$155

Last MSR was $325.

Add 20% for multi-chokes (Model 7570).

MODEL 787 O/U - 12 ga. only, 3 in. chambers, boxlock action with silver finish, single trigger, vent. barrels and rib, extractors, walnut stock with recoil pad, is supplied with 5 interchangeable choke tubes, 7 1/4 lbs. Made 1986 only.

	100%	98%	95%	90%	80%	70%	60%
	$495	$440	$380	$340	$310	$280	$250

Last MSR was $471.

GRADING - PPGS™	100%	98%	95%	90%	80%	70%	60%

MODEL 808 O/U - 12 ga., 26, 28, or 30 in. barrels, various chokes, boxlock, extractors, checkered stock. Mfg. 1963-1968 in Italy.

	$425	$375	$330	$315	$290	$270	$230

MODEL 810 O/U - 10 ga., 3 1/2 in. chambers, ST, extractors.

	$600	$550	$500	$460	$430	$395	$360

MODEL 828 O/U - 28 ga., single non-selective trigger, extractors, engraved, only 250 imported.

	$650	$550	$500	$450	$400	$350	$325

RIEDL RIFLE COMPANY

Previous single shot rifle manufacturer.

RIFLES: SINGLE SHOT

SINGLE SHOT RIFLE - many cals., 22-30 in. barrel, rack and pinion action, lever trigger guard activated, fully adj. trigger, select walnut stock, basically custom made.

	$495	$470	$440	$415	$385	$330	$305

✳ *Stainless barrel*

	$560	$535	$505	$480	$450	$395	$370

RIFLES, INC.

Current rifle manufacturer located in Pleasanton, TX. Previously located in Cedar City, UT. Dealer or direct consumer sales.

Riflemaker and custom gunsmith Lex Webernick has been manufacturing lightweight sporting rifles for 20 years.

RIFLES: BOLT ACTION

CLASSIC - various cals., features Remington or Winchester stainless steel controlled round action, stainless lapped barrel, matte stainless finish, laminated fiberglass stock with pillar glass bedding, approx. 6 1/2 lbs. New 1996.

MSR $2,500	$2,275	$1,650	$1,225

Add $100 for left-hand action.

LIGHTWEIGHT STRATA STAINLESS - various cals., lightened stainless Remington action, match grade barrel with slimbrake, matte stainless finish, 5 lbs. New 1996.

MSR $2,850	$2,625	$2,025	$1,650

Add $150 for left-hand action.

TITANIUM STRATA - various cals., based on lightened and blue printed Rem. 700 action, titanium receiver, 4 1/2 lbs. New 2002.

MSR $3,850	$3,450	$2,750	$2,000

LIGHTWEIGHT 70 - most cals. up to .375 H&H, features Winchester Model 70 stainless controlled round feeding blue printed action, match grade stainless steel barrel with muzzle brake, matte stainless finish, laminated Kevlar/boron/graphite stock with glass bedding, approx. 5 1/2 lbs. New 1997.

MSR $2,750	$2,525	$1,950	$1,600

Add $150 for left-hand action.

VARMINT/TARGET - similar to Classic, except has different stock design and dimensions, different barrel contour. Mfg. 1998-99.

	$1,800	$1,375	$1,075

Last MSR was $1,900.

Add $250 for Varmint brake.

GRADING - PPGS™	100%	98%	95%	90%	80%	70%	60%

MASTER SERIES - various cals. up to .300 Wby. Mag., designed for long range accuracy, blue printed Rem. Model 700 action, fiberglass stock, guaranteed to shoot 1/2 MOA. New 1998.

	MSR $2,950	$2,725	$2,075	$1,650

SIGNATURE SERIES - .300 Rem. Ultra Mag. cal., blue printed, Rem. M-700 stainless receiver, honed trigger assembly, 27 in. fluted match grade stainless steel barrel with matte finish, w/o sights, synthetic McMillan sporter stock, each gun is signed by Lex Webernick on the floorplate, guaranteed 1/2 in. MOA. Limited mfg. beginning 2000.

	MSR $2,800	$2,600	$2,050	$1,700

Add $175 for slimbrake.
Add $150 for left-hand action.

SAFARI - .375 H&H, .416 Rem., or .458 Lott cal., features Winchester Model 70 controlled round feeding action, match grade barrel with slimbrake, matte stainless or black Teflon finish, various options are available. New 1996.

	MSR $2,700	$2,525	$1,975	$1,650

RIGANIAN, RAY (RIFLEMAKER)

Current custom riflemaker and gunsmith established in 1988 and located in Glendale, CA. Consumer direct sales.

RIFLES: BOLT ACTION

PEERLESS I - various cals., various blueprinted actions, McMillan fiberglass stock with Pachmayr decelerator recoil pad, various barrel lengths, matte black metal finish, custom order only.

	MSR $3,500	$3,500	$3,150	$2,750	$2,400	$2,100	$1,850	$1,600

PEERLESS II - various cals., various blueprinted actions, features California English XXX walnut stock, various barrel lengths, matte black metal finish, custom order only.

	MSR $6,500	$6,500	$5,750	$5,000	$4,300	$3,750	$3,150	$2,500

Add $1,400 for .375 H&H cal.
Add $2,100 for .416 Rem., .458 Lott, or .470 Capstick.
Other calibers such as .416 Rigby, .505 Gibss, and .500 Jeffery are quoted on an individual basis.

SPORTER - various cals., Win. Mod. 70 or Mauser 98 action, features California English XXX handcheckered walnut stock, ebony forend tip, steel grip cap, and cheekpiece, various match grade barrel lengths, matte black metal finish, custom order only.

	MSR $9,500	$9,500	$8,250	$7,300	$6,400	$5,500	$4,600	$3,700

Add $1,000 for Mag. cals.

EXPRESS RIFLE - .375 H&H, .416 Rem., or .458 Lott cals., similar features as the Sporter, extra deep Blackburn steel trigger guard and floorplate, 5 shot, custom made box mag. (.416 or .458 cal. only), quick detachable scope mount system, barrel band swivel base, front sight and bead, quarter rib with one standing leaf, custom order only.

	MSR $12,500	$12,500	$11,000	$9,250	$8,100	$7,200	$6,350	$5,500

Add $700 for .416 Rem. or .458 Lott cal.

RIGBY, JOHN & CO. (GUNMAKERS), INC.

Current manufacturer established during 1735 in Dublin, Ireland. Currently manufactured in Paso Robles, CA since 1997. Previously manufactured in London, England. Currently and distributed domestically by John Rigby & Co. (Gunmakers), Inc., located in Paso Robles, CA. Previously imported by Griffin & Howe until 1998.

Original trade name was W. & J. Rigby circa 1820-1865, during the percussion era. Rigby has always been well-known for its dueling pistols. The first London Branch of J. Rigby was opened in 1865, and the Dublin Premises were closed during 1895. The firm became a company in 1900, and has been responsible for many of the large caliber developments in both rifles and ammunition. During 1997, Rigby was acquired by an American investment group located in Paso Robles, CA.

Rigby is one of the world's finest weapons makers. A good portion of the guns they manufacture were custom built to customer specifications. They were chambered for the large black powder express cartridges used for dangerous game in Africa and Asia. The modern Rigby guns follow this same tradition.

Please contact the company directly for more information on the currently manufactured models listed, including delivery time.

We will list the modern Rigby Guns with approximate values but strongly urge that if purchase or sale is contemplated, a professional appraisal be utilized.

RIFLES

Current delivery time on the current rifles is approx. 10-12 months on sidelocks, and 6 months on boxlocks.

SINGLE SHOT STALKING RIFLE - .22 Hornet - .500 NE cals., Farquharson lever actuated falling block action, 24 in. barrel, extractor, checkered pistol grip stock, deluxe finish and engraving. Reintroduced 2000-2003.

$9,250	$8,500	$7,500	$6,500	$5,500	$4,500	$3,500

Last MSR was $9,750.

.350 MAGNUM MAGAZINE RIFLE - .350 Magnum cal. originally, most were rechambered to .375 H&H Mag. cal.

$3,995	$3,400	$2,950	$2,600	$2,300	$2,000	$1,700

AFRICAN (HEAVY) EXPRESS MAGAZINE RIFLE - various cals. include .300 H&H, .375 H&H, .416 Rigby, .458 Win. Mag., .500 Jeffrey (new 2003), or .505 Gibbs (disc. 2002), other calibers are available upon request, new double square bridge Mauser action (pre-1939), claw extraction bolt action, 3-5 shot mag., 20-28 in. barrel, exhibition grade checkered walnut, full pistol grip stock.

MSR $23,500	$20,000	$14,500	$10,250	$8,000	$6,750	$5,950	$4,800

Many options include wood upgrades, engraving, express sights, telescopic sight, case, or other details.

LIGHT STANDARD MAGAZINE RIFLE - similar to Heavy Express Magazine rifle, except in small cals.

MSR $14,500	$13,250	$11,250	$9,750	$8,500	$7,000	$6,000	$5,000

Many options include wood upgrades, engraving, express sights, telescopic sight, case, or other details.

BEST QUALITY SIDELOCK EJECTOR DOUBLE RIFLE - currently mfg. cals. include .375 H&H Flanged, .416/500 Flanged, .470 NE, .500 NE, or .577 NE, 3 leaf express sights, older cals. have included .22 LR, .275 Mag., .350 Mag., .416 Rigby, .458 Win. Mag., .465, or .470 NE cal., 24-28 in. barrels, case colored contoured and reinforced Greener sidelock action with cross bolt, deluxe finish and engraving.

MSR $45,500	$41,750	$37,500	$33,000	$27,250	$22,500	$18,500	$14,000

Many options include wood upgrades, engraving, express sights, telescopic sight, case, or other details.

BEST QUALITY BOXLOCK EJECTOR DOUBLE RIFLE - current production cals. include .375 H&H Flanged, .416/500 Flanged, .470 NE, .500 NE, or .577 NE cal., 22-26 in. barrels, Greener cross bolt Anson & Deeley action.

MSR $28,500	$25,500	$22,250	$18,250	$16,450	$13,250	$10,750	$8,750

Add $1,500 for .500 NE cal.
Add $3,000 for .577 NE cal.

GRADING - PPGS™	100%	98%	95%	90%	80%	70%	60%

SECOND QUALITY BOXLOCK EJECTOR DOUBLE RIFLE - similar to Best Quality, with less select wood and engraving. Disc.

	100%	98%	95%	90%	80%	70%	60%
	$12,750	$10,750	$9,750	$8,750	$7,350	$6,350	$5,000

Subtract 35% without ejectors.
Values are for larger calibers, smaller cals. could have less value than listed.

SHOTGUNS: O/U

BEST QUALITY SIDELOCK - 12, 20, 28 ga. or .410 bore, true sidelock action with double safety sears, configured for clay pigeon sports, live bird, or field use, all working parts are titanium nitrate coated, various length vent. barrels with VR, exhibition grade English walnut and various stock configurations, case colored, rust blue, or coin finished is standard, 100% small English scroll engraved. New 2000.

	100%	98%	95%	90%	80%	70%	60%
MSR $47,500	$43,000	$36,500	$32,000	$28,000	$25,000	$22,000	$18,500

SHOTGUNS: SxS

HAMMER SHOTGUN - 12, 16, 20, 28 ga. or 410 bore, manual cocking hammers, rebounding firing pins and hammers, extractors only, exhibition grade English walnut, 70% English scroll engraving coverage, special order only.

	100%	98%	95%	90%	80%	70%	60%
MSR N/A	$15,750	$13,250	$11,000	$9,000	$7,500	$6,250	$5,000

BOXLOCK SHOTGUN - all gauges, barrel lengths and chokes to order, checkered stock to order, auto ejectors, double triggers.

* *Chatsworth Grade*

	100%	98%	95%	90%	80%	70%	60%
	$4,500	$3,500	$3,000	$2,500	$2,000	$1,600	$1,200

* *Sackville Grade* - deluxe engraved.

	100%	98%	95%	90%	80%	70%	60%
	$5,900	$5,000	$4,500	$3,750	$3,100	$2,650	$2,200

Add 20% for 20 ga.
Add 40% for 28 ga.
Add 60% for .410 bore.

SIDELOCK SHOTGUN - PRE-1997 PRODUCTION - all gauges, barrel lengths and chokes to specifications, double triggers, auto ejectors stocked to order.

* *Sandringham Grade*

	100%	98%	95%	90%	80%	70%	60%
	$9,500	$7,500	$6,000	$5,000	$4,450	$3,775	$2,950

* *Regal Grade* - deluxe engraved.

	100%	98%	95%	90%	80%	70%	60%
	$12,500	$10,000	$8,750	$7,500	$6,400	$5,250	$4,250

Add 20% for 20 ga.
Add 40% for 28 ga.
Add 60% for .410 bore.

BEST QUALITY SIDELOCK - CURRENT MFG. - 12, 16 (disc.), 20, 28 ga. or 410 bore, case colored or coin finished contoured hand detachable sidelock action, Krupp steel barrels, current engraving includes fine frame and border English scroll, also available with optional game scene engraving on both sidelocks.

	100%	98%	95%	90%	80%	70%	60%
MSR $39,950	$36,250	$32,150	$26,750	$22,000	$18,000	$14,000	$12,000

RIZZINI, BATTISTA

Current manufacturer established during 1965, and located in Marcheno, Italy. Currently imported beginning 2004 by Rizzini USA, located in West Chester, PA. Previously located in Harpswell, ME. Previously imported in the U.S. 2002-2003 by SIG Arms, located in Exeter, NH, William Larkin Moore & Co. located in Scottsdale, AZ, and New England Arms Corp. located in Kittery Point, ME. Dealer direct sales.

In 2002, San Swiss AG purchased Battista Rizzini.

GRADING - PPGS™	100%	98%	95%	90%	80%	70%	60%

RIFLES: O/U

The models listed below are available in 7x65R, 8x57 JRS, 9.3x74 R, .30-06, .308 Win., or .444 Marlin cal.

EXPRESS 90L - ST, ejectors, deluxe wood and features, includes case.

MSR $4,725	$4,225	$3,800	$3,175	$2,700	$2,300	$1,950	$1,625

EXPRESS 92EL - similar to Express 90, except has sideplates with more elaborate engraving, includes Nizzoli case, custom dimensions available.

MSR $10,500	$9,500	$7,850	$6,700	$5,600	$4,700	$3,900	$3,300

WILD EXPRESS - various cals., low profile boxlock action, ejectors, ST, coin finished receiver with relief game scene engraving. Importation began 2004.

MSR $4,850	$4,325	$3,850	$3,225	$2,700	$2,300	$1,950	

SHOTGUNS: O/U

Add 20% for small scale frame on 28 ga. or .410 bore.

ROUND BODY GAME GUN - all gauges, 29 in. solid rib barrels, case colored or alloy receiver, straight grip Turkish walnut stock and checkered forearm, five screw in choke, scroll engraving.

MSR $5,900	$5,350	$4,500	$3,500	$2,850	$2,300	$1,725	$1,425

Add $590 for 16, 28 ga. or .410 bore.

OMNIUM EM - 12 or 20 ga., blued receiver with basic scroll engraving, SST, ejectors, 28 or 29 1/2 in. VR barrels with choke tubes, cased. New 2004.

MSR $1,650	$1,350	$1,125	$975	$775	$650	$550	$450

AURUM CLASSIC - 12, 16, 20, 28 ga. or .410 bore, boxlock action, SST, ejectors, 28 or 29 1/2 in. barrels with choke tubes (except 16 ga.), case hardened receiver with light engraving, cased. New 1996.

MSR $2,350	$1,975	$1,625	$1,250	$975	$775	$650	$525

Add $400 for Aurum small action in 28 ga. or .410 bore.
Add $1,300 for Aurum small action combo.
Add $825 for Aurum Classic 20/28 ga. combo.

❋ *Aurum Light* - 16 ga. only, standard dimensions only, engraving with gold inlays, cased. Imported 2000-2004.

	$1,675	$1,475	$1,225	$975	$825	$675	$550

Last MSR was $1,900.

❋ *Aurum Teutonic* - similar to Aurum Light, except has different engraving, cased. Importation began 2004.

MSR $2,575	$2,225	$1,700	$1,350	$1,025	$875	$700	$575

ARTEMIS CLASSIC - similar to Aurum, except has sideplates, better engraving and wood, cased. New 1996.

MSR $2,950	$2,500	$2,000	$1,675	$1,375	$1,050	$850	$750

Add $600 for Artemis small action in 28 ga. or .410 bore.

ARTEMIS DELUXE FIELD - all gauges, game scene engraving.

MSR $5,400	$4,750	$4,100	$3,250	$2,750	$2,225	$1,725	$1,425

❋ *Artemis Deluxe Sporting* - 12 ga., coin finished action, sideplates with hand finished game scenes, SST, ejectors, extra select walnut stock, 28, 29 1/2, 30, or 32 in. barrels, 10mm rib, 5 extended chokes, cased. Importation began 2004.

MSR $5,475	$4,850	$4,400	$3,350	$2,850	$2,400	$1,900	$1,550

ARTEMIS EL - top-of-the-line gun with hand engraving. Importation disc. 2000, reintroduced 2004.

MSR $16,500	$14,250	$11,250	$9,500	$8,350	$7,100	$6,000	$5,000

GRADING - PPGS™	100%	98%	95%	90%	80%	70%	60%

780 FIELD SERIES - 10, 12, or 16 ga., boxlock action, DTs, extractors, checkered walnut stock and forearm. Importation disc. 1998.

	$1,075	$875	$750	$675	$595	$525	$450

Last MSR was $1,225.

> Add $550 for 10 ga.
> Add $150 for ejectors (Model S780 E).
> Add $200 for SST with ejectors (Model S780 EM).
> Add $350 for SST, ejectors, and upgraded wood (Model S780 EML).
> A Model S780 EMEL is also available that is entirely hand-finished and engraved for $5,995.

✳ *780 Competition Series* - includes Skeet, Trap, and Sporting Clays configuration. Importation disc. 1998.

	$1,375	$1,050	$925	$825	$725	$625	$525

Last MSR was $1,600.

✳ *780 Small Gauge Series* - includes 20, 28, or 36 ga., DTs, ejectors. Importation disc. 1998.

	$1,275	$975	$875	$800	$725	$625	$525

Last MSR was $1,500.

> Add $50 for SST (Model 780 EM).

S 780 EMEL - 12, 16, 20, 28 ga. or .410 bore, highly polished coin finish, 28 or 29 1/2 in. barrels, hand engraved ornamental motifs and game scenes, SST, ejectros, extra select hand checkered and polished walnut stock, includes Nizzoli case.

MSR $12,750	$11,000	$9,250	$7,800	$6,450	$5,200	$4,200	$3,400

782 EM FIELD SERIES - 12 or 16 ga., boxlock action with sideplates, SST ejectors, extractors, checkered walnut stock and forearm. Importation disc. 1998.

	$1,450	$1,150	$995	$875	$750	$675	$550

Last MSR was $1,700.

> Add $450 for Slug variation (Model 782 EM Slug).
> Add $350 for better engraving and wood (Model 782 EML).
> A Model S7820 EMEL was also available that was entirely hand-finished and engraved for $12,000.

✳ *S 782 EMEL Deluxe* - all gauges, individually made per customer specifications, 27 1/2 in. VR barrels with choke tubes (except .410 bore), coin finished receiver with side plates featuring elaborate Bulino game scene engraving with gold inlays and fine scroll borders, deluxe English walnut, Nizzoli best leather case. Importation began 1994.

MSR $13,750	$11,900	$10,350	$8,900	$7,500	$6,500	$5,500	$4,250

790 SERIES COMPETITION - 12 or 20 ga., choice of Trap, Skeet, or Sporting Clays configuration, features black frame outlined with gold line engraving. Importation disc. 1999.

	$1,975	$1,575	$1,300	$1,050	$925	$825	$695

Last MSR was $2,275.

> Subtract $150 for 20 ga. Trap.
> Subtract $50 for 20 ga. Skeet.
> Add $1,050 for 20 ga. Sporting (includes sideplates and quick detachable stock).
> A Model 790 Trap EL was also available that was entirely hand-finished with 18Kt. gold and hand engraving - prices begin at $5,650 in 12 ga., $5,200 in 20 ga.

✳ *790 Small Gauge Series* - similar to 790 Competition Series, except in 20, 28, or 36 ga., SST and ejectors standard. Importation disc. 2000.

	$1,475	$1,150	$995	$875	$750	$675	$550

Last MSR was $1,750.

> A Model 790 EMEL was also available that was entirely hand-finished with 18Kt. gold and hand engraving - prices began at $9,600.

✳ *S 790 EL Sporting* - includes multichokes and case. Importation disc. 2000, reintroduced 2004 by special order only.

MSR $6,600	$5,750	$4,750	$3,950	$3,400	$2,750	$2,100	$1,775

GRADING - PPGS™	100%	98%	95%	90%	80%	70%	60%

✴ **S 790 EMEL Deluxe** - all gauges, individually made per customer specifications, 27 1/2 in. VR barrels with choke tubes (except .410 bore), color case hardened or coin finished receiver with ornate ornamental engraving and Rizzini crest, deluxe English walnut, Nizzoli best leather case. Importation began 1994.

MSR $11,000	$9,650	$7,650	$6,500	$5,400	$4,350	$3,400	$2,600

792 SMALL GAUGE MAG. SERIES - 20, 28, or 36 ga., Mag. chambers, SST, ejectors, includes engraved sideplates. Importation disc. 1998.

	$1,850	$1,400	$1,100	$895	$750	$675	$595

Last MSR was $2,000.

A Model 792 EMEL was also available that was entirely hand finished with 18Kt. gold and hand engraving - prices begin at $8,250.

✴ **S 792 EMEL Deluxe** - all gauges, individually made per customer specifications, 27 1/2 in. VR barrels with choke tubes (except .410 bore), coin finished receiver with side plates featuring upgraded Bulino game scene engraving and fine scroll borders, deluxe English walnut, Nizzoli leather case. Importation began 1994.

MSR $10,500	$9,500	$7,750	$6,300	$5,150	$4,300	$3,700	$3,000

MODEL 2000 TRAP - 12 ga. only, includes nickel finished receiver with sideplates, gold trigger, VR barrels and rib. Importation disc. 1998.

	$1,900	$1,500	$1,275	$1,025	$925	$825	$695

Last MSR was $2,200.

A Model 2000 Trap EL was also available that was entirely hand finished with 18Kt. gold and hand engraving - prices began at $5,290.

MODEL 2000-SP - 12 ga. only, 26, 28, 30, or 32 in. overbored barrels with choke tubes, includes engraved sideplates, semi-fancy select walnut with quick detachable stock, cased. Imported 1994-98.

	$3,250	$2,800	$2,400	$1,975	$1,600	$1,300	$1,000

Last MSR was $3,650.

PREMIER SPORTING - 12 or 20 ga., 28, 29 1/2, 30, 32 or 34 in. multi-choke (5 extended chokes) barrels, hard cased, custom dimensions upon application. Importation began 1994.

MSR $2,995	$2,600	$2,050	$1,650	$1,375	$1,100	$900	$750

PREMIER II - similar to Premier Sporting, except has blued receiver, European target style stock and beavertail foream, extra select walnut. Limited importation 2004 only.

	$3,400	$2,800	$2,275	$1,775	$1,450	$1,300	$1,075

Last MSR was $4,050.

VERTEX SPORTING - 12 ga., chromium finished action, 28, 29 1/2, 30 or 32 in. barrels, SST, 10mm rib, long forcing cones, 5 extended chokes, cased. Importation began 2004.

MSR $1,995	$1,750	$1,400	$1,150	$950	$850	$675	$525

S 2000 SPORTING - 12 ga., chromium finished action, 28, 29 1/2, 30 or 32 in. barrels, SST, 10mm rib, long forcing cones, 5 extended chokes, sideplates with English scroll and border engraving, extra select walnut stock, cased. Importation began 2004.

MSR $3,550	$3,150	$2,550	$1,900	$1,500	$1,350	$1,100	$950

SPORTING EL - includes multichokes and case. Importation disc. 2000.

	$3,425	$2,850	$2,500	$2,225	$1,950	$1,675	$1,500

Last MSR was $3,750.

UPLAND EL - all gauges, 27 1/2 in. VR barrels with choke tubes (except .410 bore), case hardened receiver, deluxe walnut, hard case. Imported 1994-2003.

	$2,800	$2,400	$2,100	$1,800	$1,500	$1,200	$995

Last MSR was $2,800.

RIZZINI, EMILIO

Current shotgun manufacturer established during 1974, and located in Brescia, Italy. Currently imported by Tristar Sporting Arms, Ltd., (models are listed below) located in N. Kansas City, MO, and by Traditions, located in Old Saybrook, CT. (see Traditions section for listings). Some models were also previously imported by Armsport, Inc, located in Miami, FL.

All Emilio Rizzini shotguns are equipped with a patented Four Locks locking system. Models listed were introduced during 1999. Most Emilio Rizzini field shotguns are available with internal choke tubes.

SHOTGUNS: O/U

CLASS MODEL - 12, 16, 20, 28 ga., or 410 bore, boxlock action with reinforced frame, hand engraving, select wood, ejectors, SST. Importation disc. 2000.

$1,625	$1,400	$1,125	$975	$875	$750	$675

Last MSR was $1,870.

Add $70 for sideplates and case (Class SL Model).

CLASS DE LUXE MODEL - 12, 16, 20, 28 ga., or 410 bore, boxlock action with reinforced frame, hand finished game scene engraving with gold inlays, ejectors, SST, cased. Importation disc. 2000.

$3,675	$3,325	$2,975	$2,625	$2,300	$1,950	$1,675

Last MSR was $4,185.

Add $170 for sideplates (Class SL De Luxe Model).

BRIXIAN DE LUXE - all gauges, top-of-the-line model, boxlock action with reinforced frame, master fine scroll engraving, ejectors, SST, deluxe English wood, individually made per customer's specifications, leather cased. Importation disc. 2000.

$8,350	$7,600	$6,950	$5,700	$4,500	$3,650	$2,950

Last MSR was $8,975.

Add $1,986 for sideplates and best leather case (Brixian SL DE Luxe).

TR-I FIELD (NOVA I) - 12 or 20 ga., blue boxlock action, SST, extractors, 26 or 28 vent. barrels with 7mm VR and fixed chokes, checkered standard grade walnut stock and forearm, gold trigger, approx. 7 1/4 lbs. Imported 1998-2001.

$585	$485	$430	$375	$330	$300	$275

Last MSR was $687.

* ***TR-I Plus*** - 12 or 20 (disc. 2004) ga., 3 in. chambers, includes choke tubes, 7mm vent. rib, Importation began 2000.

MSR $779	$650	$575	$485	$435	$375	$330	$300

TR-II FIELD (NOVA II) - 12, 16 (fixed chokes, disc. 2004), 20 (disc. 2004), 28 (disc. 2004) ga. or .410 bore (fixed chokes, disc. 2004), similar to Nova I, except has choke tubes and ejectors. New 1998.

MSR $919	$795	$675	$575	$475	$415	$355	$300

Add $50 for 20, 28 ga., or .410 bore (disc. 2004).

TR-MAG. (NOVA MAG.) - 10 (mfg. 2000-2002) or 12 ga. only, 3 1/2 in. chambers, SST, ejectors or extractors (10 ga. only), 24 or 28 in. vent. barrels with 7mm VR and choke tubes, matte finished wood and metal or Mossy Oak/Shadowgrass camo wood finish (new 2000), 7.25-9.25 lbs. Impoprted 1998-2004.

$665	$585	$475	$435	$375	$330	$300

Last MSR was $799.

Add $170 for camo (new 2000).
Add $368 for 10 ga. with camo (mfg. 2000-2002).

SHOTGUNS: O/U, COMPETITION SERIES

The following models are available in either Trap, Skeet, or Sporting Clays configuration. Sporting Clays models have 5 internal multichokes.

GRADING - PPGS™	100%	98%	95%	90%	80%	70%	60%

COMPACT MODEL - 12, 16, or 20 ga., boxlock action with reinforced frame, ejectors, SST, model and company name inlaid on black finished action, select checkered walnut stock and forearm, cased. Importation disc. 2000.

	$1,900	$1,750	$1,450	$1,100	$900	$775	$700

Last MSR was $2,135.

GARA MODEL - similar to Compact, except has hand engraving and wood upgrade. Importation disc. 2000.

	$3,325	$2,975	$2,600	$2,200	$1,800	$1,400	$1,250

Last MSR was $3,765.

Add $351 for Gara Cup Model (company logo inlaid in gold).
Add $1,022 for Gara SL Model (includes engraved sideplates).

GARA DE LUXE - top-of-the-line competition model, ornamental pattern engraved by master engraver, deluxe wood, best leather case. Importation disc. 2000.

	$6,600	$5,750	$5,250	$4,400	$3,500	$2,750	$2,450

Last MSR was $7,375.

SHOTGUNS: O/U, PREMIER SERIES

Last MSRs for the models listed below are as follows: Premier - $1,599, Premier Deluxe - $2,199, Premier SL - $1,899, Premier SL Deluxe - $2,399, Premier EL - $1,999, Premier EL Gold - $2,699, Premier ELX Gold - $3,199.

PREMIER SERIES - 12 or 20 ga., various configurations, oil finished stock and forearm, ST or DT, includes 3 choke tubes. Limited importation by Traditions 2003 only.

The Premier Series had limited importation during 2003 only, and MSRs ranged from $1,599-$3,199. Current values for these models range from 35%-75% of the MSRs listed above, depending on condition.

SHOTGUNS: O/U, SPORTING CLAYS

TR-SC (NOVA SC) - 12 or 20 (mfg. 1999-2003) ga. only, 3 in. chambers, sporting clays model, silver finished boxlock action, gold SST, 28 or 30 in. vent. barrels with 10mm VR and mid-rib sight beads, fancy checkered walnut stock and forearm, approx. 7 1/2 lbs. Importation began 1998.

MSR $1,047	$885	$775	$675	$575	$475	$395	$350

Add $80 for 20 ga. (mfg. 1999-2003).

TR-L - similar to Nova SC, except has stock dimensions for female shooter (13 1/2 LOP), was also available in 20 ga. until 2004, approx. 7.75 lbs. Imported 1999-2004.

	$890	$780	$680	$575	$450	$395	$350

Last MSR was $1,063.

TR-ROYAL - 12, 20 (disc. 2004), or 28 (disc. 2004) ga., 3 in. chambers, similar to the TR-SC, except has special dimension stock designed to reduce recoil, 28 or 30 in. VR barrels with 7mm-10mm tapered rib and rhino ported extended choke tubes, ejectors, silver finished boxlock action, deluxe checkered walnut stock and forearm, silver frame with gold accents, approx. 7.5 lbs. Importation began 1999.

MSR $1,319	$1,075	$935	$825	$700	$600	$500	$400

TR-CLASS SL - 12 ga. only, 2 3/4 in. chambers, features select materials, silver finished boxlock action with engraved sideplates, ejectors, SST, 28 or 30 VR barrels with choke tubes, 7 3/4 lbs. Imported 1999-2002.

	$1,525	$1,275	$1,025	$900	$800	$700	$575

Last MSR was $1,775.

GRADING - PPGS™	100%	98%	95%	90%	80%	70%	60%

RIZZINI, F.LLI

Current manufacturer located in Magno V.T., Italy. Currently imported and distributed by William Larkin Moore & Co. located in Scottsdale, AZ, Some models have been imported by New England Arms Corp. located in Kittery Point, ME, and by L. Michael Weatherby, located in Laguna Niguel, CA. Please contact the importer directly for more information (see Trademark Index).

SHOTGUNS: SxS, CUSTOM, OLDER MFG.

In the past the Rizzini brothers collaborated with Rinaldo Zoli to make "spec" guns that were usually imported by Abercombie & Fitch. These guns are normally marked on the water table "Zoli Rizzini ".The Zoli Rizzini gun factory closed in 1971. These guns are not to be confused with the quality of current Rizzini F.lli mfg. Normally these older Field Grade models (non-ejector, boxlock action in 12, 16, 20, 28 ga. or .410 bore) sell in the $500-$1,200 range, with a 25% premium for 28 ga. or .410 bore. Deluxe Field Models with scalloped boxlock action ad ejectors are currently valued in the $1,500-$2,500 range with a 30% premium for 28 ga. or .410 bore. The Extra Lusso Model (top-of-the-line) currently sells in the $3,500 range in 12 ga., $4,750 in 28 ga., and $4,250 in .410 bore.

SHOTGUNS: SxS, CUSTOM, RECENT MFG.

Today's F.lli Rizzini Shotguns are made to individual custom order only (about 20 are made a year). Prices do not include engravings (engraving prices range from $8,700-$21,700, substantially more for famous name engravers such as Fracassi, Torcoli, etc) and may be subject to fluctuation in exchange rates. F.lli Rizzini make their own barrels in house, and use their patented mechanisms.

Add approx. $17,500 for fine English scroll or ornamental engraving with swans.
Please contact the importer directly for a quotation on special engraving options.

R2-E BOXLOCK EJECTOR - 12, 16, or 20 ga., select walnut, detachable bottom inspection plate, various barrel lengths, without engraving. Disc. 1995.

		$11,500	$9,000	$8,000	$7,000	$6,200	$5,500	$4,750

Last MSR was $25,000.

✳ 28 ga. or .410 bore. - otherwise similar to above. Disc. 1995.

		$15,000	$12,250	$10,000	$8,750	$7,500	$6,250	$5,000

Last MSR was $27,500.

RI-E SIDELOCK EJECTOR - 12, 16, 20, 28 ga. or .410 bore, F.lli Rizzini patented sidelocks, select Circassian walnut, various barrel lengths, without engraving.

MSR $70,000	$66,900	$50,000	$40,000	$33,000	$28,000	$24,500	$21,250

Add $9,000 for 28 ga. or .410 bore.

R3-E - patented boxlock ejector model w/o engraving, Importation began 2000.

MSR $55,000	$52,250	$40,000	$33,000	$27,500	$21,750	$17,500	$14,750

RIZZINI, I.

Please refer to the Fair Tecni-Mec listing.

THE ROBAR COMPANIES, INC.

Current customizer established during 1986, and located in Phoenix, AZ.

Robar is a leader in custom metal finishing, including combination finishes. These include the Roguard black finish, NP3 surface treatment, and additional finishes including bluing, electroless nickel, Polymax camoflauge, and Polymax finish. Please contact Robar directly (see Trademark Index) for more information, including current prices on their lineup of firearms, custom metal and wood finishes, and customizing services, including shotguns.

GRADING - PPGS™	100%	98%	95%	90%	80%	70%	60%

PISTOLS: SEMI-AUTO

Robar offers customizing services on new Colt-style semi-auto .45 ACP pistols. Various configurations include the Super Deluxe Pistol Package ($2,200), Robar Combat Master ($1,250), or Basic Carry ($850). These guns are built up from other makers including Springfield and Colt to provide the configuration/modifications necessary.

RIFLES

Robar also offers customizing services, mainly on the Remington 700, and Ruger M-77 actions. Various configurations include: the SR60 ($2,900), SR90 ($3,500), QR2 ($3,200), QR2-F ($3,800), Robar RC 50 BMG ($7,000), Hunter, Precision Hunter, and Varminter (POR).

SHOTGUNS

Defensive shotguns are also customized from the Remington Model 870, and include the Robar Elite ($1,200), Robar Defender ($575), Robar S.O.F. ($870), and Thunder Ranch model ($700).

ROBERT HISSERICH COMPANY

Current custom rifle manufacturer located in Mesa, AZ. Previous company name was Stockworks. Consumer direct sales only.

RIFLES: BOLT ACTION

ROBERT HISSERICH BOLT GUN - various cals., features Weatherby Vanguard action, Pac-Nor stainless steel barrel, Pachmayr decelerator pad, hinged floor plate, black synthetic stock. New 2003.

MSR $1,795	$1,795	$1,500	$1,250	$1,050	$875	$750	$625

LIGHTWEIGHT RIFLES SLR - various cals., Rem. long or short action, Kevlar/fiberglass MPI stock, match grade Pac-Nor barrel, straight flutes in bolt body, Timney trigger, straight line muzzle brake, pillar bedded action floating barrel, "window" cuts in action for lightening, black oxide finish on blue or stainless steel, English or Claro deluxe checkered stock, custom order only - allow 3-4 months. Approx. 4 3/4-5 lbs.

MSR $2,600	$2,600	$2,300	$2,000	$1,800	$1,600	$1,400	$1,200

Add $200 for stainless steel.

SHARPSHOOTER - various cals., Win. Model 70 action with controlled feeding, precision long range hunting rifle with Schnieder stainless steel fluted barrel, laminated stock with ebony forend tip, titanium firing pin, pillar glass bedded with free floating barrel, includes Leupold 6.5-20x40mm scope, custom order only.

MSR $5,950	$5,950	$5,100	$4,500	$3,900	$3,400	$2,850	$2,150

ROBERTS, J. & SON (GUNMAKERS) LTD.

Current manufacturer, import agent, and dealer established during 1950, and located in London, England.

Please contact J. Roberts & Son (Gunmakers) Ltd. directly for more information on their current inventory and other services (see Trademark Index).

RIFLES

J. Roberts & Son new boxlock SxS ejector rifles are currently priced in the £14,000-£16,000 range, depending on caliber. New Roberts magazine rifles are currently priced from £6,500-£10,400, depending on caliber.

SHOTGUNS

Please contact the company directly for a quotation on a new shotgun (boxlock or sidelock).

ROBERTSON

Current trademark manufactured by Boss & Co., Ltd. Manufacture is in Birmingham, England.

Please contact the company directly for more information on this trademark, including current model availability and pricing.

ROBINSON ARMAMENT CO.

Current rifle manufacturer located in Salt Lake City, UT. Currently distributed by ZDF Import/Export, Inc., located in Salt Lake City, UT. Dealer and consumer direct sales.

RIFLES: SEMI-AUTO

Please refer to the Vepr. Rifle section for more information on Vepr. Rifles.

M96 EXPEDITIONARY RIFLE/CARBINE - .223 Rem. cal., paramilitary modular design, unique action allows accessory kit to convert loading from bottom to top of receiver (available later in 2000), 16.2 (Recon Model, new 2001), 17 1/4 (carbine, new 2000) or 20.25 in. barrel with muzzle brake, stainless steel receiver and barrel, matte black finish metal, black synthetic stock and forearm, adj. sights, gas operated with adjustment knob, last shot hold open, rotating bolt assembly, 8.5 lbs. New 1999.

MSR $1,600	$1,495	$1,300	$1,100	$925	$850	$775	$700

Add $750 for rifle/carbine with top feed.

ROCHE, CHRISTIAN

Current manufacturer located in Veauche, France.

Christian Roche manufactures quality side-by-side shotguns and double rifles. Since all orders are per individual specifications, the factory must be contacted directly to obtain a current price quotation and information (see Trademark Index).

ROCK RIVER ARMS, INC.

Current handgun and rifle manufacturer located in Colona, IL beginning 2004. Previously located in Cleveland, IL until 2003. Dealer and consumer direct sales.

PISTOLS: SEMI-AUTO

Rock River Arms makes a variety of high quality M-1911 based semi-autos. They specialize in manufacturing their own National Match frames and slides. Current models (standard cal. is .45 ACP, but most models are also available in .38 Super, 9mm Para. and .40 S&W) include the Standard Match (disc. 2003, last MSR was $1,150), National Match Hardball (MSR $1,490), Bullseye Wadcutter (MSR $1,625), Basic Limited Match (MSR $1,700), Limited Match (MSR $2,065), Ultimate Match Achiever (disc. 2003, last MSR was $2,255), Matchmaster Steel (disc. 2001, last MSR was $2,355), Elite Commando (MSR $1,725), Basic Carry (MSR $1,525), Tactical Pistol (MSR $1,925), Limited Police Competition (MSR $2,310), Unlimited Police Competition (MSR $2,310), Hi-Cap Basic Limited (disc. 2003, last MSR was $1,895), and the Doug Koenig Signature Series (disc. 2003, last MSR was $5,000, .38 Super cal.). Rock River Arms also offers additional options and parts. Please contact the factory for additional information and availability.

RIFLES: SEMI-AUTO

Rock River Arms makes a variety of paramilitary style rifles/carbines patterned after the AR-15 in .223 Rem. cal. Current models include the CAR UTE (disc. 2004, last MSR was $850), Standard A2 (MSR $890), CAR A2 (MSR $865), CAR A4 Flattop (MSR $875), Standard A4 Flattop (MSR $850), Tactical Carbine A2 (disc.) and Tactical Carbine A4 (MSR $950), Elite CAR A4 (MSR $950), Elite CAR UTE A2/A4 (MSR $935), Entry Tactical (MSR $950), TASC rifle (MSR $890), M4 Entry (disc. 2003, last MSR was $875), Varmint A4 (MSR $1,000), Varmint EOP (MSR $1,025), NM A2-DCM Legal (MSR $1,265), and the Government Model (MSR $2,250).

ROCKY MOUNTAIN ARMS CORP.

Previous manufacturer of mini revolvers circa mid-1960s, and located in Salt Lake City, UT.

REVOLVERS

MINI REVOLVER - .22 Short cal., 5 shot, stainless steel, locking bolt is in top strap, bolt cam on left side of hammer, supplied with black velveteen case.

$275 $225 $150

> When RMAC went out of business, production was resumed by North American Arms Corp., then after another company change, Freedom Arms started production.

ROCKY MOUNTAIN ARMS, INC.

Previous firearms manufacturer located in Longmont, CO 1991-2002.

Rocky Mountain Arms was a quality specialty manufacturer of rifles and pistols. All firearms were finished in a Dupont Teflon-S industrial coating called Bear Coat.

PISTOLS: SEMI-AUTO

BAP (BOLT ACTION PISTOL) - .308 Win., 7.62x39mm, or 10mm Rocky Mountain Thunderer (10x51mm) cal., features 14 in. heavy fluted Douglas Match barrel, Kevlar/graphite pistol grip stock, supplied with Harris bipod and black nylon case. Mfg. 1993 only.

$1,425 $1,275 $1,100 $950 $825 $700 $575

Last MSR was $1,595.

1911A1-LH - .40 S&W or .45 ACP cal., specifically designed for left-handed shooters, featuring left side ejection port and right side controls, gold cup size, stainless steel construction, hand fitted parts, integral ramp barrel, Millett adj. sights, test target. Mfg. 1991-93.

$1,295 $995 $750

Last MSR was $1,395.

Add $100 for Bo-Mar sights.

BACKUP PLUS - .45 ACP cal., hand tuned AMT Back-up pistol, black DuPont Teflon-S finish, Tritium front night sight. Mfg. 1995-97.

$575 $515 $450 $400 $360 $330 $300

Last MSR was $650.

22K PISTOLS - .22 LR cal., AR style pistols featuring 7 in. barrel, choice of matte black or NATO Green Teflon-S finish, will use Colt conversion kit, choice of carrying handle or flattop upper receiver, 10 or 30 shot mag., includes black nylon case. Mfg. 1993 only.

$475 $425 $375 $350 $325 $295 $275

Last MSR was $525.

Add $50 for flattop receiver with Weaver style bases.

PATRIOT PISTOL - .223 Rem. cal., AR style pistol featuring 7 in. match barrel with integral Max Dynamic muzzle brake, 21 in. overall, available with either carrying handle upper receiver and fixed sights or flattop receiver with Weaver style bases, fluted upper receiver became an option in 1994, accepts standard AR-15 mags, 5 lbs. Mfg. 1993-94 (per C/B).

$2,295 $1,975 $1,625 $1,425 $1,250 $1,075 $950

Last MSR was $1,795.

Add $200 for black milled upper and lower receiver w/o carrying handle.

GRADING - PPGS™	100%	98%	95%	90%	80%	70%	60%

KOMRADE - 7.62x39mm cal., includes carrying handle upper receiver with fixed sights, floating 7 in. barrel, Teflon red or black finish, 5 lbs., 5 shot mag. Mfg. 1994-95.

	$1,825	$1,650	$1,425	$1,200	$975	$850	$775

Last MSR was $1,995.

RIFLES: BOLT ACTION

PROFESSIONAL SERIES - .223 Rem., .30-06, .308 Win., or .300 Win. Mag. cal., bolt action rifle utilizing modified Mauser action, fluted 26 in. Douglas premium heavy match barrel with integral muzzle brake, custom Kevlar-Graphite stock with off-set thumbhole, test target. Mfg. 1991-95.

	$2,050	$1,650	$1,275	$995	$850	$725	$600

Last MSR was $2,200.

Add $100 for .300 Win. Mag. cal.
Add $300 for left-hand action.

PRAIRIE STALKER - .223 Rem., .22-250 Rem., .30-06, .308 Win., or .300 Win. Mag. cal., choice of Remington, Savage, or Winchester barreled action, includes Choate ultimate sniper stock, lapped bolt and match crown, "Bear Coat" all-weather finish, includes factory test target. Limited mfg. 1998 only.

	$1,595	$1,350	$1,150	$950	$875	$775	$675

Last MSR was $1,795.

* **Ultimate Prairie Stalker** - similar to Prairie Stalker, except custom barrel and caliber specifications are customer's choice. Limited mfg. 1998 only.

	$2,200	$1,875	$1,625	$1,400	$1,200	$1,000	$895

Last MSR was $2,495.

PRO-VARMINT - .22-250 Rem., or .223 Rem. cal., RMA action, 22 in. heavy match barrel with recessed crown, Bear Coat metal finish, Choate stock with aluminum bedding. Mfg. 1999-2002.

	$995	$875	$800	$725	$650	$575	$450

Last MSR was $1,095.

POLICE MARKSMAN - .308 Win. or .300 Win. Mag. cal., similar to Professional Series, except has 40X-C stock featuring adj. cheekpiece and buttplate, target rail, Buehler micro-dial scope mounting system. Mfg. 1991-95.

	$2,325	$1,995	$1,650	$1,325	$1,100	$900	$700

Last MSR was $2,500.

Add $100 for .300 Win. Mag. cal.
Add $400 for left-hand action.
Add $400 for illuminated dot scope (4-12x56mm).

* **Police Marksman II** - .308 Win. cal., RMA action, 22 in. heavy match barrel with recessed crown, Bear Coat metal finish, Choate stock with aluminum bedding. Mfg. 1999-2002.

	$995	$875	$800	$725	$650	$575	$450

Last MSR was $1,095.

PRO-GUIDE - .280 Rem., .35 Whelen, .308 Win., 7x57mm Mauser, or 7mm-08 Rem. cal., Scout Rifle design with 17 in. Shilen barrel, "Bear Coat" finish, approx. 7 lbs. Mfg. 1999-2002.

	$2,025	$1,800	$1,600	$1,425	$1,200	$1,000	$825

Last MSR was $2,295.

NINJA SCOUT RIFLE - .22 Mag. cal., takedown rifle based on Marlin action, black stock, 16 1/2 in. match grade crowned barrel, forward mounted Weaver style scope base, adj. rear sight, 7 shot mag. Mfg. 1991-95.

	$640	$575	$525	$460	$430	$390	$360

Last MSR was $695.

Add $200 for illuminated dot scope (1.5-4X) w/extended eye relief.

GRADING - PPGS™	100%	98%	95%	90%	80%	70%	60%

SCOUT SEMI-AUTO - .22 Mag. cal., patterned after Marlin action. Mfg. 1993-95.

	$650	$575	$495	$395	$350	$295	$260

Last MSR was $725.

Add $200 for illuminated dot scope (1.5-4X) w/extended eye relief.

RIFLES: SEMI-AUTO

M-SHORTEEN - .308 Win. cal., compact highly modified M1-A featuring 17" match crowned barrel, custom front sight, mod. gas system, hand honed action and trigger, custom muzzle brake. Mfg. 1991-94.

	$1,650	$1,425	$1,175	$995	$850	$725	$600

Last MSR was $1,895.

Add $200 for Woodland/Desert camo.

VARMINTER - .223 Rem. cal. only, AR-15 styled rifle with 20 in. fluted heavy match barrel, flattop receiver with Weaver style bases, round metal National Match hand guard with floating barrel, choice of NATO green or matte black Teflon-S finish, supplied with case and factory test target (sub-MOA). Mfg. 1993-94.

	$2,195	$1,800	$1,600	$1,400	$1,200	$1,000	$875

Last MSR was $2,495.

PATRIOT MATCH RIFLE - .223 Rem. cal., 20 in. Bull Match barrel, regular or milled upper and lower receivers, two-piece machined aluminum hand guard, choice of DuPont Teflon finish in black or NATO green, 1/2 MOA, hard case. Mfg. 1995-97.

	$2,375	$1,975	$1,650	$1,400	$1,200	$1,000	$895

Last MSR was $2,500.

Add approx. $325 for milled upper receiver.
Add approx. $650 for milled upper and lower receivers.

SHOTGUNS: SLIDE ACTION

870 COMPETITOR - 12 ga., 3 in. chamber, security configuration with synthetic stock, hand-honed action, ghost ring adj. sights, "Bear Coat" finish, high visibility follower. Mfg. 1996-97.

	$695	$625	$550	$500	$450	$400	$360

Last MSR was $795.

ROCKY MOUNTAIN ELK FOUNDATION

Current national conservation organization with national headquarters located in Missoula, MT.

RIFLES: BOLT ACTION

RUGER NO. 1-A LIGHT SPORTER - .35 Whelen cal., features gold inlaid elk on right side of receiver and mountain scene with gold accents on left side, engraved by Adams & Son, blue finish, deluxe wood, 50 mfg. 1995 only.

	$2,395	$1,850	$1,475

Last MSR was $2,395.

SAUER MODEL 90 - .270 Win. or .30-06 cal., banquet offering only, total mfg. unknown.

	$1,375	$1,100	$925

ROGAK

Please refer to the L E S Incorporated listing in this text for more information on the Rogak Pistol.

GRADING - PPGS™	100%	98%	95%	90%	80%	70%	60%

ROGUE RIVER RIFLEWORKS

Current manufacturer located in Paso Robles, CA. Dealer and consumer direct sales.

RIFLES

Please contact the manufacturer directly, including current MSRs on these models.

BOLT ACTION MODEL - 7mm STW, .300 Win. Mag., .30-378 Wby. Mag., 8mm Rem. Mag., .375 H&H, .416 Rem. Mag., or .458 Win. Mag. cal., choice of Remington M-700 or Winchester M-70 action, Pac-Nor match grade barrel (with cryogenic treatment), engraved receiver, floorplate, and grip cap, jewelled bolt, exhibition grade checkered walnut stock with ebony forend cap. Limited mfg. beginning 1998.

MSR N/A	$9,500	$8,500	$7,500	$6,500	$5,500	$4,500	$3,250

LEVER ACTION MODEL - .243 Win., .260 Rem., 7mm-08 Rem., .308 Win., or .358 Win. cal., features rebuilt Winchester Model 88 action, match grade chrome moly barrel, exhibition grade walnut, choice of American classic or Mannlicher stock design. Limited mfg. beginning 1998.

MSR N/A	$4,650	$4,125	$3,675	$3,100	$2,600	$2,000	$1,700

SxS MODEL - .470 NE, .500 NE, or .577 NE cal., Anson & Deely action, Purdey double locking lugs, Greener crossbolt, Southgate selective ejectors, quarter rib with rear sights, exhibition grade wood, case colored or coin finished receiver. Limited mfg. 1998-2000.

Prices started at $12,500 for .470 NE cal. A 12, 16, or 20 ga. shotgun barrel conversion kit was also available for $3,800.

RÖHM

Previous firearms manufacturer located in Sontheim an der Brenz, Germany. Limited importation into the U.S. Röhm still manufactures gas alarm pistols, mostly for European sales.

Röhm produced inexpensive revolvers for the U.S. marketplace during the late 1960s-1970s. Most of these guns were built as sub-contracts for U.S. companies and/or distributors (i.e., Hy-Score, a previous distributor located in Brooklyn, NY). Some of the models included are RG-7 through RG-88 (21 variations), Romo, Thalco, Valor, Vestpocket, Western Style, Zephyr, and others. Röhm also manufactured a few semi-auto pistols (RG-25 and RG-26) at approx. the same time. Currently, these guns are seen priced in the $35-$125 range, as the shooting value determines the price tag, not collector interest.

DERRINGERS

DERRINGER - .22 LR cal., blue, copy of Remington O/U derringer. Excellently made, but half-cock safety is old design and could fail if dropped.

	$150	$115	$95	$85	$75	$65	$55

ROHRBAUGH FIREARMS CORP.

Current manufacturer located in Deer Park, NY.

PISTOLS: SEMI-AUTO

R-9 - 9mm Para cal., DAO, 2.9 in. barrel, free bored to reduce felt recoil, frame is 7075-T651 aluminum, stainless steel slide, 6 shot mag., parts cut from solid billets, all internal parts are stainless, short recoil locked breech with cam operated tilting barrel locking system, recessed hammer, carbon fiber grips, no sights, 12.8 oz. New 2003.

MSR $945	$800	$700	$600

✳ *Model R9S* - similar to Model R-9, except has fixed iron sights. New 2004.

MSR $945	$800	$700	$600

GRADING - PPGS™	100%	98%	95%	90%	80%	70%	60%

ROSS RIFLE COMPANY

Previous manufacturer located Quebec, Canada circa 1900-1917.

The Ross rifle was the design of prolific figure Sir Charles Ross (1872-1942) born in Scotland. Known for his "straight pull" action design, as a college student, Ross took out his first patent for a straight pull rifle in 1893. This rifle was never produced, but in 1896, Ross patented another version which ultimately became the Model 1897 ("hammer model") Magazine Sporting Rifle. This rifle was produced and marketed by Charles Lancaster of London. These rifles had receivers made in Hartford, CT with some rifles completed in Connecticut and some completed by Lancaster in London. Production spanned less than 20 years with early rifle production occurring in England and Hartford, CT. The bulk of rifle production occurred in Canada from 1900 - 1917. Ross rifles have been known for their unique design and their tremendous accuracy in match competition. Like many manufacturers of the time, Ross also made custom and presentation rifles to order.

Note: many military .303 rifles had their chambers made oversized for smoother chambering. In some cases, the chambers will be found to be substantially oversized. Also, like many military rifles, Ross rifles found today have often been altered in various ways.

The author wishes to express his thanks to Mr. Barry DeLong & Mr. Steve Engleson for making the following information available.

RIFLES: BOLT ACTION

The values listed below are for specimens that have been unaltered except where noted.

MODEL 1897 SPORTER - .303 Brit. cal., 26 inch barrel, 5 round magazine, known as the "hammer model" because the bolt cocked the hammer as it traveled over it, clip loaded Mannlicher type magazine, bolt head design of solid, opposing locking lugs with vertical travel and horizontal locking. Hartford, CT version checkered walnut straight stock and a two leaf rear sight, Lancaster version has checkered walnut pistol grip stock, V notch rear sight and tang mounted peep sight. Mfg. 1897-1900.

> This variation is encountered with such low frequency that consistent market pricing cannot be established.

MODEL 1900 SPORTER - similar to the Model 1897, except has no hammer and a coil mainspring and internal bolt striker. Mfg. 1900-01.

> This variation is encountered with such low frequency that consistent market pricing cannot be established.

RIFLES: BOLT ACTION, CANADIAN PRODUCTION

Canadian production of Ross Rifles consisted of three basic centerfire actions and one rimfire. All four were produced in sporting and military configurations. Commerical rifles typically have a serial number on the left side of the barrel immediately ahead of the receiver. Military rifles are numbered on the right side of the stock - a three digit number from 1-999 over the year manufactured/accepted, followed initially by one letter, then two letters.

MARK I (MILITARY)/MODEL 1903 (SPORTING) - a modification of the Model 1900, "Patented 1903" on left side of receiver, slide button safety, slimmed and completely knurled bolt piece and thumbpiece mag. lifter, enclosed mag.

* ✱ *Mark I* - .303 Brit. cal., 28 in. barrel, walnut stock, overall length of 45 and 5/8th inches, H-type hinged rear sight adjustable to 2,200 yards with adjustments for windage and elevation.

$2,000	$1,750	$1,500	$1,250	$1,000	$900	$800

> In 1905, the first 1000 rifles were delivered to the Royal Northwest Mounted Police in Regina, Saskatchewan. The early Mk Is used the Ross Mk I and Mk I* rear sight. Most were retrofitted with the Ross Mk II sight. The early nosecaps were formed from sheet metal. Those specimens with the original Mk I or Mk I* sight and original nosecap would bring a premium with values up to $2,500 for a top condition specimen.

GRADING - PPGS™	100%	98%	95%	90%	80%	70%	60%

✱ *Model 1903 Sporter* - .303 British (most common), .256 Mannlicher, or .370 Express cal., 26 or 28 in. barrel, walnut checkered stock, two leaf English style rear sight, 5 round magazine. Very scarce with manufacture in Hartford, CT, London, and Quebec. Slight variations based on manufacture location.

	$1,500	$1,350	$1,200	$950	$800	$650	$500

Add 20% for .256 Mannlicher cal.
Add 50% for .370 Express cal.

MARK II (MILITARY)/MODEL 1905 (SPORTING) - "1905 Patented" on left side of receiver, action is cocked on opening, bolt action camming to initiate cartridge extraction, did not have bolt knurled thumbpiece, improved extractor added to later Model 1905 variations. Mfg. beginning 1906.

✱ *Mark II (Not Including MKII**)* - .303 Brit. cal., 28 in. round barrel, walnut stock, same basic rifle design with modifications, identified by Roman numeral and number on left of star stamped above serial number in stock.

	$750	$675	$600	$550	$500	$450	$425

✱ *Mark II Original (No Star)* - .303 Brit. cal., Ross MKII or MKIII sight, early model with flat buttplate and "stepped" nosecap (similar to MKI rifles).

	$1,000	$900	$800	$700	$600	$550	$500

✱ *Mark II 2** - .303 Brit. cal., 30 1/2 in. heavy barrel and receiver bridge mounted rear sight, military issue, but primarily a target rifle, final military model had no barrel sight and one piece top wood, scarce variation and seldom seen.

	$1,700	$1,500	$1,325	$1,175	$950	$850	$750

✱ *Mark II 3** - .303 Brit. cal., 28 in. barrel, most common example, includes 20,000 sold to U.S. and marked with flaming bomb proof.

	$850	$750	$650	$600	$550	$500	$450

The scarce U.S. sub-variation is shortened by 7/8 in. and has rechambered barrel. This model is seldom seen and commands a premium.

✱ *Mark II 4** - .303 Brit. cal., 28 in. barrel, similar to MKII 3*, except has earlier Ross MKIII sight fitted (flattop sight), many were converted to a 3*.

	$650	$625	$600	$550	$500	$450	$400

✱ *Mark II 5** - .303 Brit. cal., 28 in. barrel, seldom encountered variation that has the Sutherland "H" type sight variation with short wood between receiver and sight.

	$850	$750	$650	$600	$525	$475	$400

✱ *Model 1905 M Sporter* - .303 Brit. cal., 28 in. barrel, illustrated in 1906 catalog only, Enfield barrel sight. Very few known.

	$1,250	$1,100	$950	$850	$775	$700	$625

✱ *Model 1905 R Sporter* - .303 Brit. cal., 26 or 28 in. barrel, no checkering on stock, originally fitted with Winchester semi-buckhorn sight.

	$750	$675	$625	$575	$525	$475	$400

✱ *Model 1905 E Sporter* - .303 Brit. or .35 WCF cal., 22, 24, 26 or 28 in. barrel, built up on MKII** receiver, fine-thread heavy barrel, checkered pistol grip wood. Several different multi-leaf "express" sights found on this model.

	$1,000	$900	$800	$700	$625	$550	$500

Add 25% for .35 WCF cal.

✱ *Mark II** Commercial Target Model* - .303 Brit. cal., 30 1/2 in. barrel, identical to the Military 2* rifle but typically found with commercial finish on wood and no sling swivels, target sight on bridge over receiver and serial number on barrel.

	$1,650	$1,400	$1,175	$1,000	$900	$850	$800

This model won almost all rifle matches from 1908 to 1913.

MODEL 1907 & 1905/1910 MATCH TARGET RIFLE - between the MKII (1905) and the MKIII (1910), two important and scarce rifles were built and sold on a modified MKII action with threaded, not solid, locking lugs.

GRADING - PPGS™	100%	98%	95%	90%	80%	70%	60%

❋ *Model 1907 "Scotch Deer Rifle Stalking Pattern"* - .280 Ross cal., 26 or 28 in. barrel, 4 shot mag., walnut pistol grip checkered stock, finely finished for Canadian/U.S. market, usually fitted with steel buttplate. For British/Colonial market, many were supplied "in the white" to British gunmakers for completion, usually found UK proofed, finer finish on steel and wood with checkered walnut butt.

	$1,850	$1,650	$1,400	$1,200	$1,050	$925	$800

❋ *Model 1905/Model 1910 Match Target Model* - .280 Ross cal., single-shot with 30 1/2 in. barrel, tangent rear sight on heel of butt and optical hooded front sight, free-floated barrel, can be found in early (deep forend with finger grooves) and later (tapered forend) versions. Very scarce and none found blued (left in the white).

	$2,750	$2,500	$2,250	$2,000	$1,900	$1,800	$1,750

MKIII (MILITARY)/MODEL 1910 (SPORTER) RIFLE - replaced the previously used solid lugs which traveled vertically, has the "triple thread, interrupted-screw, double-bearing cam bolt" with the bolt head traveling horizontally.

It is these models where the report of "bolt blowbacks" have occurred. The bolt on these models, could, with some difficulty be rotated 180 degrees and hence not close completely. If fired in this situation, the bolt could blow back and potentially injure the shooter. Sporters were produced in three grades: R (economy), E (military box magazine and checkered wood) and the top of the line - the M-10.

❋ *MKIII/MKIII B Military* - .303 Brit. cal., 30 1/2 in. barrel, slight changes only through the production run, early models had stamped sheet metal nosecaps, later ones were forged, models found with British proofs were likely in the trenches in France and WWII Homeguard. For the Mk III B, the only change from Canadian issue is the front and rear sight.

	$995	$925	$850	$775	$700	$625	$575

❋ *Military Match Target Model* - .280 Ross cal., 26 in. barrel, box mag. (same as M-10 Sporter with flat floorplate), light walnut stocks with a commercial finish and a Ross MK III battle sight, recalibrated for .280 Ross cal. Mfg. circa 1912.

	$5,000	$4,500	$3,750	$3,000	$2,500	$2,000	$1,500

In 1912, Ross built what he considered the perfect military rifle. A suspected total of 25 rifles were built on the commercial line and all known examples are serial numbered in the 10,200 range.

❋ *Model R-10* - .303 Brit. cal., 26 or 28 in. barrel, no checkering, Winchester semi-buckhorn rear sight, miltary five shot box mag., plain steel uncheckered rifle buttplate.

	$700	$650	$600	$550	$500	$425	$400

There is the possibility that Ross used previously rejected military components in these rifles. This is a fairly plain rifle, but seldom encountered.

❋ *Model E-10* - .303 Brit. or .35 WCF cal., 26 or 28 in. barrel, checkered straight grain walnut stock, M-10 pattern checkering on bottom of pistol grip, military box mag, several different express sights can be found on this model. Scarce.

	$800	$750	$700	$650	$600	$550	$500

Add 25% for .35 WCF cal.

❋ *Model M-10* - .280 Ross cal., 24, 26 or 28 in. barrel, enclosed four shot double row mag., beautifully finished, pistol grip checkered walnut, grip cap screwed to pistol grip, flat floorplate, 0 to 500 yard sight on barrel, some are equipped with Porter "pop up" sight on the rear receiver bridge.

	$1,250	$1,100	$925	$800	$700	$600	$500

Add $50-$100 for rifles with Porter apeture sight.

❋ *Homeguard Model Mark III* - .303 Brit. cal., identical to the Canadian issued Mk III Military Model but appear to have superior finish and fit on wood and metal, serial number will be found on the barrel just ahead of the receiver, issue stamps may (or may not) be stamped in the stock. Less than 1,000 mfg.

	$1,250	$1,100	$950	$850	$750	$650	$575

GRADING - PPGS™	100%	98%	95%	90%	80%	70%	60%

MODEL 1912 CADET - .22 rimfire cal., single shot, 21 1/2 in. barrel, full stocked walnut, usually found in three variations.

* *Commercial Model* - serial number on the left side of the barrel, ahead of the receiver.

	$500	$475	$450	$400	$375	$350	$300

* *Military Model* - serial number stamped in stock over year of acceptance, preceeded by a letter, usually multiple "CC" (Cadet Corps) stamps also.

	$500	$475	$450	$400	$375	$350	$300

* *"Leftovers" Model* - so called because models were assembled after factory expropriation, no serial numbers, proofs, or stamps in metal or wood.

	$400	$375	$350	$325	$300	$275	$250

ROSSI

Current trademark manufactured by Amadeo Rossi S.A., located in Sao Leopoldo, Brazil. Currently imported exclusively by BrazTech, International beginning late 1998, located in Miami, FL. Previously imported by Interarms, located in Alexandria, VA.

PISTOLS: SINGLE SHOT

ROCKET SINGLE SHOT - .22 LR, .22 Hornet, .22-250 Rem., .220 Swift, .223 Rem., .30-30 Win., .357 Mag., .44 Mag., or .45 LC cal., break open single shot action. Limited importation 2000 only.

	$135	$120	$110	$100	$90	$80	$75

Last MSR was $149.

Add $36 for stainless steel.

REVOLVERS: DOUBLE ACTION

All discontinued models in this section were only imported by Interarms, not Braztech. Braztech is the exclusive North American importer for Rossi firearms.

MODEL 31 - .38 Spl., 5 shot, 4 in. medium barrel, target trigger and hammer, 22 oz. Disc. 1985.

	$120	$105	$95	$85	$75	$70	$65

Last MSR was $139.

Add $5 for nickel.

MODEL 51 - .22 LR cal., 6 shot, 6 in. barrel, blue only, adj. sights. Disc. 1985.

	$125	$110	$100	$90	$85	$80	$75

Last MSR was $149.

* *Sportsman 511 Stainless* - .22 LR cal. only, stainless steel, 4 in. barrel, with matted rib, adj. rear sight, 6 shot, hardwood stocks, 30 oz. Imported 1986-90 only.

	$190	$160	$125				

Last MSR was $235.

MODEL 68 - .38 Spl. cal., 5 shot, 2 or 3 in. barrel, blue or nickel (3 in. barrel only), choice of wood or rubber grips with 2 in. barrel. Disc. 1998.

	$165	$135	$100	$90	$80	$70	$65

Last MSR was $225.

MODEL 69 - .32 S&W cal., 6 shot, 3 in. barrel, walnut grips. Disc. 1985.

	$120	$105	$95	$85	$75	$70	$65

Last MSR was $139.

Add $5 for nickel finish.

GRADING - PPGS™	100%	98%	95%	90%	80%	70%	60%

MODEL 70 - .22 LR cal, 6 shot, 3 in. barrel. Disc. 1985.

	$120	$105	$95	$85	$75	$70	$65

Last MSR was $139.

Add $5 for nickel finish.

MODEL 84 STAINLESS - .38 Spl. cal., 6 shot, 3 or 4 in. solid raised rib barrel, standard service sights, checkered hardwood grips, 27 1/2 oz. Imported 1985-86 only.

	$190	$155	$125

Last MSR was $205.

MODEL 88 STAINLESS - .38 Spl. cal., 5 shot, stainless steel construction, 2 or 3 in. barrel, hardwood or rubber (2 in. barrel only) grips, 21 oz. Disc. 1998.

	$195	$145	$110

Last MSR was $255.

✳ *Model 88 Lady Rossi* - .38 Spl., 2 in. barrel, stainless steel, slim round grips. Imported 1995-98.

	$215	$175	$150

Last MSR was $285.

MODEL 89 STAINLESS - .32 S&W cal. only, 6 shot, 3 in. barrel. Imported 1985-86. Reintroduced 1989-90.

	$175	$135	$115

Last MSR was $215.

MODEL 94 - .38 Spl. cal., 6 shot, 3 or 4 in. barrel, blue finish only, 27 1/2 oz. Imported 1985-1988.

	$160	$140	$120	$110	$95	$85	$75

Last MSR was $185.

MODEL R351 - .38 Spl.+P cal., 5 shot, 2 in. barrel, blue finish, combat rubber grips, supplied with key lock, 24 oz. Importation began 1999.

MSR $298	$240	$185	$165	$145	$130	$115	$105

MODEL R352 - similar to Model R351, except is stainless steel. Importation began 1999.

MSR $345	$275	$220	$165

MODEL R461 - .357 Mag.+P cal., 6 shot, 2 in. barrel, blue finish, combat rubber grips, supplied with key lock, 26 oz. Importation began 1999.

MSR $298	$240	$185	$165	$145	$130	$115	$105

MODEL R462 - similar to Model R461, except is stainless steel. Importation began 1999.

MSR $345	$275	$220	$165

MODEL 515(M) STAINLESS - .22 LR or .22 Mag. (Model 515M) cal., double action, 6 shot, classic kit gun design, stainless steel with shrouded ejector rod, adj. rear sights, checkered custom wood grips, 4 in. barrel, 30 oz. Imported 1992 only.

	$195	$145	$110

Last MSR was $248.

MODEL 515 STAINLESS - .22 Mag. cal., similar to 515(M), supplied with 2 pairs of grips (checkered wood and rubber wraparound). Imported 1994-98.

	$210	$165	$140

Last MSR was $270.

MODEL 518 STAINLESS - .22 LR cal., otherwise similar to Model 515 Stainless. Disc. 1998.

	$195	$155	$135

Last MSR was $255.

GRADING - PPGS™	100%	98%	95%	90%	80%	70%	60%

MODEL 677 FS - .357 Mag. cal., 6 shot, 2 in. heavy barrel, enclosed ejector rod, rubber combat grips, matte blue finish, 26 oz. Imported 1997-98.

	$215	$160	$135	$110	$95	$80	$70

Last MSR was $260.

MODEL 720 STAINLESS - .44 Spl. cal., choice of hammer or hammerless (new 1994) design, 3 in. ribbed barrel, double action, 5 shot with fluted or unfluted cylinder, full ejector rod shroud, adj. rear sight, rubber combat grips, stainless, 27 1/2 oz. Imported 1992-98.

	$220	$180	$155				

Last MSR was $290.

✸ **Model 720C** - similar to Model 720 Stainless, except hammerless.

	$220	$180	$155				

Last MSR was $290.

MODEL 851 - .38 Spl.+P cal., 4 in. barrel, 6 shot, integral key lock, rubber grips. Importation began 2001.

MSR $298		$240	$185	$165	$145	$130	$115	$105

MODEL 851 STAINLESS - .38 Spl. cal., 3 (disc. 1994) or 4 in. VR barrel, 6 shot, walnut grips, adj. rear sight, 27 1/2 oz. Mfg. 1985-98.

	$195	$155	$135				

Last MSR was $255.

This model was previously designated the Model 85 Stainless.

MODEL 877 FS STAINLESS - .357 Mag. cal., 6 shot, small frame, 2 in. barrel with full ejector rod housing, rubber combat grips, 26 oz. Mfg. 1996-98.

	$220	$175	$150				

Last MSR was $290.

MODEL 951 - .38 Spl. cal., 6 shot, 3 or 4 in. VR barrel, blue finish only, 27 1/2 oz. Imported 1985-90.

	$190	$155	$135	$120	$110	$100	$90

Last MSR was $233.

This model was previously designated the Model 95.

MODEL 971 - .357 Mag. cal., 4 in. solid rib barrel with internal ejector shroud, 6 shot, adj. rear sight, blue only, hardwood grips, 36 oz. Imported 1988-98.

	$200	$160	$145	$135	$125	$115	$105

Last MSR was $255.

✸ **Model 971 Stainless** - .357 Mag. cal., 2 1/2 (new 1992), 4, or 6 in. solid rib barrel with full shroud, 6 shot, combat style rubber grips, adj. rear sight, 35.4-40.5 oz. Imported 1989-98.

	$220	$175	$145				

Last MSR was $290.

✸ **Model 971 Compensated** - .357 Mag. cal., stainless steel, 3 1/4 in. compensated barrel, 32 oz. Imported 1993-98.

	$220	$175	$145				

Last MSR was $290.

MODEL 971 VRC STAINLESS - .357 Mag. cal., stainless steel, 6 shot, choice of 2 1/2, 4, or 6 in. barrel with 8-port vented rib compensator and full-length ejector shroud, combat rubber grips, adj. rear sight, 30-39 oz. Mfg. 1996-98.

	$295	$220	$175				

Last MSR was $340.

MODEL 971 (NEW MFG.) - .357 Mag. cal., 4 in. barrel, 6 shot, rubber grips, adj. sights, integral key lock. Importation began 2001.

MSR $345		$275	$220	$165	$150	$135	$125	$115

GRADING - PPGS™	100%	98%	95%	90%	80%	70%	60%

MODEL 972 - similar to Model 971, except is stainless steel, 6 in. barrel only. Importation began 2001.

MSR $391	$325	$265	$195

CYCLOPS (MODEL 988 STAINLESS) - .357 Mag. cal., 6 or 8 shot, 8 or 10 3/4 (ported or unported, new 1998) in. full shroud barrel with 8 compensation ports, black rubber grips, 51 oz. Imported 1997-98.

$385	$300	$230

Last MSR was $429.

Add $50 for unported 10 3/4 in. barrel.
Add $60 for ported 10 3/4 in. barrel.

RIFLES

For current information on Rossi mfg. Puma rifles imported by Legacy, please refer to the Puma section.

MODEL 65/92 SRC LEVER ACTION - .38 Spl./.357 Mag., .44 Spl./.44 Mag., .44-40 WCF (mfg. 1995-98), or .45 LC (mfg. 1995-98) cal., patterned after Win. Model 92, 16 (.38 Spl./.357 Mag. only), 20 (blue or stainless) or 24 (new 1997, half round/half octagon) in. barrel, 5-5.75 lbs. Importation disc. 1998.

$285	$220	$165	$125	$110	$100	$90

Last MSR was $360.

Add approx. $70 for 24 in. half-round, half-octagon barrel.

This model in .44 Spl./.44 Mag., .44-40 WCF, or .45 LC cal. is sometimes known as the Model 65. This model was also available in matte blue finish at no extra charge.

MODEL 62 SA SLIDE ACTION - .22 LR cal., copy of Win. 1890 "gallery" model, rifle (23 in. barrel) or carbine (16 1/2 in. barrel) available, takedown action, blue or nickel finish, round or octagon barrel, 12 or 13 shot tube mag. Importation disc. 1998.

$185	$145	$115	$95	$85	$80	$75

Last MSR was $240.

Add $10 for nickel finish.
Add $10 for octagon barrel.

❊ **Model 62 SA Stainless** - similar to regular model, except is stainless steel. Imported 1986 only.

$165	$145	$120

Last MSR was $192.

MODEL 62 SAC CARBINE - similar to Model 62 SA, except has 16 1/2 in. carbine barrel with full length mag. tube (12 shot), 4 1/4 lbs. Imported 1988-98.

$185	$145	$115	$95	$85	$80	$75

Last MSR was $240.

Add $10 for nickel finish.

❊ **Model 62 SAC Carbine Stainless** - similar to Model 62 SAC Carbine, except is stainless steel. Imported 1998 only.

$215	$165	$125

Last MSR was $280.

MODEL 59 - .22 Mag. version of Model 62 SA, 10 shot mag., 5.5 lbs. Importation disc. 1998.

$220	$170	$130	$120	$110	$100	$90

Last MSR was $280.

ROCKET SINGLE SHOT - .22 LR, .22 Hornet, .22-250 Rem., .220 Swift, .223 Rem., .30-30 Win., .357 Mag., .44 Mag., or .45 LC cal., action and other specifications similar to Model S12 shotgun. Limited importation 2000 only.

$160	$145	$130	$115	$100	$90	$80

Last MSR was $179.

Add $30 for stainless steel.

GRADING - PPGS™	100%	98%	95%	90%	80%	70%	60%

FIELD GRADE SINGLE SHOT - .17 HMR cal. (new 2003), .22-250 Rem. (new 2005), .22 LR (disc. 2003), .22 Mag. (disc. 2003), .223 Rem. (new 2002), .243 Win. (new 2002), .270 Win. (new 2004), .30-06 (new 2004), .308 Win. (new 2004), .357 Mag./.38 Spl. (disc. 2003), .44 Mag. (disc. 2003), 7.62x39mm (new 2005), or .410/ .45 LC (disc. 2003) cal., 23 in. lightweight tapered or heavy (new 2005) barrel with fully adj. sights, choice of matte blue with natural wood or matte stainless steel (disc. 2004, except for Youth Model) with black wood finish, manual safety, extractor (centerfire) or ejector (rimfire), Monte Carlo stock became an option in 2002, 4.75-6.25 lbs. Importation began 2001.

* *Field Grade Rimfire* - .17 HMR, 18.5 (Youth) or 23 in. matte finished blue or stainless steel barrel, natural (matte blue) or black (stainless steel) finished wood.

MSR $175	$140	$115	$95	$80	$70	$60	$60

  Add $47 for stainless steel.
  Subtract $11 for Youth Model.

* *Field Grade Centerfire* - centerfire cals., 22 (Youth) or 23 in. barrel, matte blue metal, natural wood finish.

MSR $224	$175	$145	$125	$110	$95	$80	$65

  Add $8 for heavy barrel.

SHOTGUNS: SxS

OVERLUND - 12, 20 ga., or .410 bore, exposed hammers, 20 (Coach Model), 26, or 28 in. barrels, double triggers. Importation disc. 1988.

$275	$230	$185	$155	$140	$125	$115

Last MSR was $332.

SQUIRE - 12, 20 ga., or .410 bore, hammerless, 20, 26 or 28 in. barrels, double triggers, raised matted rib, beavertail forearm, pistol grip, hardwood stock, 3 in. chambers. Imported 1985-90.

$300	$245	$195	$160	$150	$140	$130

Last MSR was $350.

SHOTGUNS: SINGLE SHOT

MODEL S12/S20/S41 - 12, 20 ga., or .410 bore, 3 in. chamber, lightweight break open action with exposed hammer, ejector, uncheckered hardwood stock and forearm with sling swivels, blue action and 22 (Youth) or 28 (Standard) in. barrel, supplied with trigger lock, 4 lbs. 13 oz Importation began 1999.

MSR $115	$95	$85	$75	$65	$60	$50	$45

  Add $75 for 12 ga. Slug gun with 23 in. fully rifled barrel with adj. TruGlo sights (new 2004).

  This model is also available as a Youth Model in .20 ga. or .410 bore (.410 bore weighs approx. 4 lbs.) - prices are the same as listed.

MATCHED PAIR RIMFIRE/CENTERFIRE - includes choice of 12, 20 ga., or .410 bore single shotgun barrel and interchangable .22 LR, .223 Rem. (new 2002), .243 Win. (new 2002), .270 Win. (new 2003), .30-06 (new 2003), .308 Win. (new 2003) cal. rifle barrel with fully adj. front sight, manual safety. Importation began 2000.

* *Matched Pair Rimfire*

MSR $154	$125	$105	$90	$80	$70	$60	$60

  Add $46 for .17 HMR cal.
  Add $41 for stainless steel (.410 bore and .22 LR or .17 HMR cal. only).
  Add $6 for 12 ga. in full size.
  Add $89 for .410 bore and .17 HMR rifle barrel.
  Add $30 for matched pair carrying case.

✳ *Matched Pair Centerfire* - includes 12 or 20 ga. barrel and choice of .22-250 Rem. (new 2005, Youth only), .223 Rem., .243 Win., .270 Win., .30-06, or .308 Win. cal., 22 (Youth only) or 28 in. shotgun barrel, 22 (Youth only) or 23 (full size) in. rifle barrel.

MSR $272	**$215**	**$185**	**$165**	**$145**	**$130**	**$115**	**$100**

Add $30 for matched pair carrying case.

This model is also available in Youth Model in 20 ga. with.22-250 Rem., .223 Rem., .243 Win., or .308 Win. cal. rifle barrel.

ROTA, LUCIANO

Current manufacturer located in Brescia, Italy. Currently imported and distributed beginning 2002 by Tristar, located in N. Kansas City, MO. Previously imported by New England Arms Corp., located in Kittery Point, ME.

SHOTGUNS: SxS

The Models 105 and 106 were imported exclusively by New England Arms, and the Model 411 is imported exclusively by Tristar.

MODEL 105 - most gauges, 26-32 in. barrels, boxlock action with sideplates, floral scroll engraving, choice of case colored or coin finished receiver, fixed chokes (any combination), extractors, Circassian checkered walnut stock and forearm. Importation disc. 2004.

	$1,325	**$1,075**	**$875**	**$750**	**$650**	**$550**	**$500**

Last MSR was $1,595.

Add $100 for 28 ga. or .410 bore.
Add $50 for ST, or $175 for multichokes.
Add $500 for hand engraving.

MODEL 106 - all gauges, Anson & Deeley type engraved boxlock action, DT or ST, ejectors, extractors, Circassian checkered walnut stock and forearm, case colored action. Importation disc. 2004.

	$1,225	**$950**	**$775**	**$675**	**$550**	**$500**	**$450**

Last MSR was $1,395.

Add $100 for 28 ga. or .410 bore.
Add $155 for 10 ga.
Add $50 for ST, or $175 for multichokes.
Add $300 for hand engraving.

✳ *Model 106 Slug Gun* - 12 or 20 ga., similar to Model 106, except has 25 in. barrels with express rib and folding leaf sights, with or w/o sideplates, tapered front ramp sight, choke tubes. Importation disc. 2004.

	$1,325	**$1,075**	**$875**	**$750**	**$650**	**$550**	**$500**

Last MSR was $1,595.

Add $200 for hand engraving.
Add $400 for sideplates.

MODEL 411 SERIES - various configurations, all models include boxlock action, checkered walnut stock and forearm, and have either color case hardened or coin finished frame. Importation by Tristar began 2003.

✳ *Model 411 Field* - 12, 16, 20, 28 ga. or .410 bore, DTs, splinter forearm, 3 choke tubes included except for fixed chokes on 16, 28 ga. and .410 bore, extractors, 6 1/4-7 1/4 lbs.

MSR $849	**$775**	**$675**	**$550**	**$500**	**$450**	**$400**	**$350**

✳ *Model 411 D Field* - 12, 20, 28 ga. or .410 bore, straight grip English stock with ST, ejectors, 6 1/4-7 1/4 lbs.

MSR $1,110	**$995**	**$875**	**$775**	**$650**	**$525**	**$400**	**$350**

GRADING - PPGS™	100%	98%	95%	90%	80%	70%	60%

✳ *Model 411 F Field* - 12, 20, 28 ga. or .410 bore, engraved coin finished action with sideplates, gold ST, ejectors, straight grip English stock, 6 1/4-7 1/4 lbs.

MSR $1,608	$1,475	$1,250	$995	$875	$775	$650	$525

✳ *Model 411 R Field* - 12 or 20 ga., 20 in. fixed choke barrels bored cyl./cyl., DTs, extractors, designed for cowboy competiton, approx. 6 1/2 lbs. Disc. 2003.

	$675	$550	$500	$450	$400	$350	$295

Last MSR was $745.

ROTTWEIL

Current manufacturer located in Rottweil, Germany. No current U.S. importation. Previously imported by Rottweil Competition, located in Orange, CA.

SHOTGUNS

PARAGON - 12 ga. only, new design featuring boxlock action, 11 different stock configurations, detachable and interchangeable trigger action, trigger and sear safety, ejectors (switchable to extractors), various barrel lengths (30 in. standard) and rib combinations, cased. Limited importation 1993-99.

	$6,950	$6,500	$5,750	$4,850	$3,950	$3,000	$2,500

Last MSR was $7,500.

Add $850 for Trap Model.
Add $3,150 per extra set of barrels.

✳ *Paragon Sporting Clays Deluxe* - 30 in. barrels only, features better quality wood and engraving. Limited importation.

	$6,950	$6,500	$5,750	$4,850	$3,950	$3,000	$2,500

Last MSR was $7,500.

MODEL 650 FIELD O/U - 12 ga. only, 28 in. barrels with VR, ejectors, single trigger, select checkered walnut, multi-choked with 6 choke tubes, lightly engraved, coin finished receiver. Importation disc. 1986.

	$750	$650	$595	$550	$500	$460	$435

Last MSR was $850.

MODEL 72 FIELD O/U - 12 ga. only, 28 in. vent. barrels and rib, sand blasted receiver, select walnut with checkered stock and forearm, single trigger, ejectors. Importation disc. 1987.

	$1,850	$1,650	$1,450	$1,200	$1,000	$850	$700

Last MSR was $2,295.

MODEL 72 AMERICAN SKEET O/U - 12 ga. only, 26 3/4 in. barrels, VR, ejectors, select French walnut, marginal engraving on sand blasted receiver, single trigger, 7 1/2 lbs. Importation disc. 1987.

	$1,850	$1,650	$1,450	$1,200	$1,000	$850	$700

Last MSR was $2,295.

This model was distributed exclusively by Paxton Arms, located in Dallas, TX.

MODEL 72 AAT SINGLE BARREL TRAP - 12 ga. only, adj. American trap (AAT), barrel features adj. point of impact, 34 in. barrel bored full, high VR. Importation disc. 1986.

	$1,400	$1,200	$1,000	$850	$700	$650	$600

Last MSR was $2,295.

MODEL 72 AT O/U - 12 ga. only, 32 in. IM & F barrels, VR, sand blasted receiver, checkered select walnut stock and forearm, non-adj. point of impact, single trigger, ejectors. Importation disc. 1987.

	$1,850	$1,650	$1,450	$1,200	$1,000	$850	$700

Last MSR was $2,295.

GRADING - PPGS™	100%	98%	95%	90%	80%	70%	60%

MODEL 72 AAT COMBINATION - 12 ga. only, comes with 2 single barrels (32 and 34 in.) that have adj. impact points. Importation disc. 1986.

| | $2,450 | $2,100 | $1,850 | $1,600 | $1,450 | $1,250 | $995 |

Last MSR was $2,850.

* **72 AAT Combination** - supplied with 1 single adj. barrel and 32 in. O/U barrels.

| | $2,450 | $2,100 | $1,850 | $1,600 | $1,450 | $1,250 | $995 |

Last MSR was $2,850.

MODEL 72 AAT 3-BARREL SET - 12 ga. only, supplied with 2 single barrels (32 and 34 in.) with adj. impact points and 1 set of 32 in. O/U barrels bored IM & F. Importation disc. 1986.

| | $2,850 | $2,600 | $2,300 | $2,000 | $1,800 | $1,600 | $1,400 |

Last MSR was $3,250.

MODEL 72 INTERNATIONAL TRAP - 12 ga. only, O/U 30 in. barrels bored IM & F with extra high rib. Importation disc. 1987.

| | $1,850 | $1,650 | $1,450 | $1,200 | $1,000 | $850 | $700 |

Last MSR was $2,295.

MODEL 72 INTERNATIONAL SKEET - 12 ga. only, 26 3/4 in. barrels, VR, select walnut stock and forearm. Importation disc. 1987.

| | $1,850 | $1,650 | $1,450 | $1,200 | $1,000 | $850 | $700 |

Last MSR was $2,295.

ROYAL AMERICAN SHOTGUNS

Previously imported by Royal Arms International, located in Woodland Hills, CA circa 1985-87.

SHOTGUNS

MODEL 100 O/U - 12 or 20 ga., 2 3/4 in. chambers, double triggers, extractors, vent. rib and barrels. Imported 1985-87 only.

| | $325 | $265 | $240 | $220 | $200 | $180 | $170 |

Last MSR was $390.

Add $40 for 3 in. chambers, single trigger, and auto ejectors.

MODEL 600 BOXLOCK SxS - 12, 20, 28 ga., or .410 bore, sideplates, silver finished receiver, 3 in. chambers, single trigger, auto ejectors. Imported 1985-87 only.

| | $365 | $295 | $265 | $235 | $210 | $195 | $180 |

Last MSR was $420.

Subtract 25% for double triggers and 2 3/4 in. chambers.

MODEL 800 SIDELOCK SxS - 12, 20, 28 ga., or .410 bore, sidelocks with sideplates, silver finished receiver, 3 in. chambers, single trigger, checkered straight grip stock with select walnut, auto ejectors. Imported 1985-87 only.

| | $775 | $650 | $595 | $550 | $500 | $460 | $435 |

Last MSR was $899.

RUBY

Previous trademark manufactured by Gabilondo, located in Eibar, Spain.

RUGER

See Sturm, Ruger, & Co. section in this text.

RUKO SPORTING GOODS, INC.

Previous importer (non-exclusive) located in Buffalo, NY that imported Arms Corp. of the Philippines firearms circa 1990-95. Ruko Sporting Goods, Inc. (previously Ruko Products) firearms were manufactured by the Arms Corporation of the Philippines. In

1991, Ruko Products, Inc. became the exclusive domestic importer for arms manufactured by Arms Corp. of the Philippines. These firearms were marked "Ruko-Armscor" on the barrels.

Please refer to the Armscor section for current importation, as well as previous importation by Armscorp Precision, Inc. and Ruko Products, Inc.

RUSSIAN SERVICE PISTOLS AND RIFLES

Previously manufactured at various Russian military arsenals (including Tula).

HANDGUNS

MODEL TT30 & TT33 TOKAREV AUTOMATIC - 7.62mm Russian cal., design borrowed from Colt 1911, Petter-type unitized trigger/hammer assembly, 8 shot, 4 1/2 in. barrel, blue. Mfg. 1930-54.

	100%	98%	95%	90%	80%	70%	60%
	$325	$290	$250	$225	$165	$145	$110

Add 20% for matching mag.
Add 100% for TT30 Model.
Values listed assume original condition - no recent imports with importer markings.

✳ *TT Recent Import* - 7.62x25mm Tokarev cal., must be stamped by importer, Russian Arsenal mfg., currently imported by Century Arms International, Inc. and others.

	100%	98%	95%	90%	80%	70%	60%
No MSR	$140	$110	$90	$80	$70	$60	$50

NAGANT REVOLVER - 7 shot, cylinder comes forward to seal barrel.

	$260	$225	$185	$165	$135	$115	$100

Add 10% for pre-communist Imperial marked.
"GRU" marked gun (Armed Forces Intelligence) has shorter barrel and grip frame. While rarer, there is a slight premium being asked.

MAKAROV MD - 9mm Makarov cal., mag. fed double action, post-war manufacture.

	$450	$400	$350	$300	$250	$200	$150

Recent imports or commercial models with adj. rear sight are currently selling in the $175 range.

RIFLES

Original Soviet Mosin-Nagant bolt action rifles/carbines include: M1891 rifle, M1891 Dragoon, M1891/30 Rifle, M1891/30 Sniper Model, M1910 Carbine, M1938 Carbine, and the M1944 Carbine. Values for these older original military configurations will approximate values listed for the original mfg. Mosin-Nagant.

TOKAREV M38 & M40 BOLT ACTION - semi-auto Russian issue.

	100%	98%	95%	90%	80%	70%	60%
Original mfg.	$365	$310	$270	$250	$230	$210	$195

Add 20% for M38, 100% for scoped sniper.

MOSIN-NAGANT BOLT ACTION - various cals., bolt action, many produced under various military contracts, including Remington, New England Westinghouse, and Sako, prices assume recent importation.

	100%	98%	95%	90%	80%	70%	60%
Original mfg.	$250	$225	$185	$165	$145	$130	$120
Recent imports	$125	$100	$90	$80	$70	$65	$60

Add $40% for laminate stock.

RPD SEMI-AUTO - 7.62x39mm cal., converted from belt fed to semi-auto only, closed bolt, milled receiver, includes 50 shot mag., recent importation.

	$3,795	$3,495	$2,950	$2,600	$2,300	$2,000	$1,750

GRADING - PPGS™	100%	98%	95%	90%	80%	70%	60%

RUTTEN HERSTAL

Previous firearms manufacturer of O/U shotguns located in Herstal, Belgium. Previously imported by Labanu, Inc. located in Ronkonkoma, NY.

For more information and current pricing on both new and used Rutten airguns, please refer to the *Blue Book of Airguns* by Dr. Robert Beeman & John Allen (also online).

SHOTGUNS: O/U

MODEL RM 100 - 12 ga., 3 in. chambers, VR multi-choke barrels, ejectors, checkered walnut stock and forearm, hard case. Imported 1995-98.

	100%	98%	95%	90%	80%	70%	60%
	$875	$775	$675	$575	$500	$450	$400

Last MSR was $1,095.

MODEL RM 285 - similar to Model RM 100, except has engraved side plates and silver engraved receiver, select walnut with Schnabel forearm, hard case. Imported 1995-98.

	100%	98%	95%	90%	80%	70%	60%
	$1,025	$850	$725	$600	$500	$450	$400

Last MSR was $1,295.

NOTES

S SECTION

S.A.C.M.

Previous company located in Cholet, France. S.A.C.M. stands for Societe Alsacienne de Construction Mechanique.

GRADING - PPGS™	100%	98%	95%	90%	80%	70%	60%

PISTOLS: SEMI-AUTO

FRENCH MODEL 1935A - 7.65mm Long cal., 8 shot, 4.3 in. barrel, blue, fixed sights, checkered stocks, used by French troops in WWII and Indochina 1945-1954. Mfg. 1935-45.

	$250	$220	$205	$180	$165	$150	$140

Add 50% for Nazi WWII mfg. (Waffenamt proofed).

SAE

Previous importer located in Miami, FL. SAE stands for Spain America Enterprises Inc. SAE imported Felix Sarasqueta shotguns from Spain until circa 1988.

SHOTGUNS: O/U

MODEL 70 - 12 or 20 ga., 3 in. chambers, boxlock action, single trigger, ejectors, 26 in. VR barrel, European checkered walnut stock and forearm, standard finish is blue, Model 70 multi-choke has silver finished action with Florentine engraving and low gloss stock finish. Imported 1988 only.

	$400	$275	$260	$245	$230	$215	$195

Last MSR was $598.

Add $120 for multi-chokes (27 in. barrel).

MODEL 66C - 12 ga. only, 26 in. Skeet or 30 in. F&M VR barrels, boxlock with engraved sideplates including 24Kt. gold inlays, Monte Carlo deluxe stock and beavertail forearm. Imported 1988 only.

	$950	$725	$650	$575	$495	$450	$395

Last MSR was $1,544.

SHOTGUNS: SxS

MODEL 210S - 12, 20 ga., or .410 bore, 3 in. chambers, boxlock action, double triggers, extractors, silver finished receiver with light engraving, approx. 7 lbs. Imported 1988 only.

	$420	$280	$260	$245	$230	$215	$195

Last MSR was $638.

MODEL 340X - 12 or 20 ga., sidelock action, 26 in. barrels with 2 3/4 in. chambers, H&H boxlock action, case hardened finish with moderate scroll engraving, straight grip select walnut stock and forearm with high gloss finish. Imported 1988 only.

	$700	$550	$495	$460	$430	$395	$375

Last MSR was $1,170.

MODEL 209E - 12, 20 ga., or .410 bore, H&H type sidelock action, 26 or 28 in. barrels with 2 3/4 in. chambers, hand engraved coin finished receiver, select checkered walnut stock and forearm, double triggers. Imported 1988 only.

	$925	$700	$650	$575	$495	$450	$395

Last MSR was $1,490.

S.A.M.

Please refer to Shooter Arms Manufacturing Incorporated.

S.I.A.C.E.

Current shotgun manufacturer located in Gardone V.T., Italy. No current U.S. importation. Previously imported by New England Arms Corp., located in Kittery Point, ME.

RIFLES: SxS

MODEL ALASKA - 7x65R, 9.3x74R, .30-06, .45-70 Govt., or .444 Marlin cal., scalloped boxlock with hand engraving, figured Turkish walnut. Imported 2002-2004.

MSR N/A		N/A	$3,995	$3,650	$3,125	$2,700	$2,250	$1,850

MODEL YUKON - 8x57JRS, .30-06, .45-70 Govt., or .444 Marlin cal., exposed hammers, sidelock action, Bulino style hand engraving, figured Turkish walnut. Limited importation 2002, and no U.S. MSRs were ever established.

SHOTGUNS: SxS, HAMMERGUN

MODEL GARDONE - 12, 16, 20, 28 ga., or .410 bore, scalloped boxlock with different round frame sizes for each gauge, ejectors, DT, full coverage best hand engraving, checkered deluxe Turkish walnut and custom dimensions. Imported 2000-2004.

MSR N/A		N/A	$3,125	$2,700	$2,250	$1,850	$1,450	$1,250

MODEL VINTAGE - 12, 16, or 20 ga., sidelock, case hardened or coin finished receiver with border edged engraving, top tang safety, DT, extractors, monobloc barrels.

MSR N/A		N/A	$1,850	$1,475	$1,100	$850	$700	$550

MODEL ETON - 12, 16, 20, 28 ga., or .410 bore, 2 3/4 in. chambers standard, DT, extractors, monobloc barrels, case colored or coin finished receiver with scroll engraving, Turkish walnut, straight or pistol grip stock with splinter or semi-beavertail forearm. Imported 2000-2004.

MSR N/A		N/A	$3,125	$2,700	$2,250	$1,850	$1,450	$1,250

Add $1,250 for ejectors and self cocking system (Model Eton Deluxe).

MODEL 350G AURORA SUPER LUSSO - 24, 28, 32 ga., or .410 bore, back action sidelock, case hardened or coin finished receiver with finely engraved rose and scroll patterns, DT, extractors, top tang safety. Disc. 2000.

$5,500	$4,750	$3,950	$3,150	$2,450	$1,875	$1,450

Last MSR was $5,950.

This model became part of the Juno Series.

MODEL 370B CONCORDIA - 12, 16, 20, 24, 28 or 32 ga., or .410 bore, scalloped frame back action sidelock, silver or case hardened receiver with fine scroll engraving, top tang safety., select checkered Turkish walnut, prices include custom dimensions.

MSR N/A		N/A	$4,750	$3,950	$3,150	$2,450	$1,875	$1,450

MODEL 371Q JUNO - 12, 16, 20, 24, 28, 32 ga., or .410 bore, sidelock, available with self cocking and ejectors, silver or case colored receiver, best quality rose and scroll engraving, DT or ST, top tang safety, select checkered Turkish walnut, prices include custom dimensions.

MSR N/A		N/A	$4,750	$3,950	$3,150	$2,450	$1,875	$1,450

SKB SHOTGUNS

Currently manufactured by the new SKB Arms Company located in Tokyo, Japan. Currently imported and distributed by G.U. Inc. located in Omaha, NE. SKB has been manufacturing firearms since 1855. Dealer sales.

Previously imported by Ithaca. In 1987, importation resumed on most SKB models. While the model numbers have changed, quality is similar to those models imported previously by Ithaca. In most cases, the newer models are derived closely from their previous counterparts. Listings below will differentiate older, disc. models from currently imported models.

SHOTGUNS: O/U

MODEL 85 TARGET SUPER SPORT (TSS) - 12, 20, 28 ga. or .410 bore, monobloc barrel construction, 2 different frame sizes, Greener crossbolt, non-detachable trigger assembly, silver nitride receiver finish, polished blue barrels, available in Sporting Clays, Skeet, or Trap configuration (including sets), Mag-na-ported barrels, Hi-Viz competition front sight, available with or w/o adj. comb stock (Graco CTS systems), matte wood finish. New 2002.

✳ *Model 85 TSS Sporting Clays* - choice of fixed or adj. comb stock, 28, 30, or 32 in. VR barrels, 8.5mm (28 ga. or .410 bore) or 12mm (12 or 20 ga.) stepped VR, 7 1/2-8 1/2 lbs. New 2002.

MSR $1,999	$1,685	$1,425	$1,175	$950	$875	$800	$725

Add $50 for .410 bore.
Add $200 for adj. comb on stock.
Add $190 for pigeon porting by Mag-na-port.
Add $390 for high grade wood (12 ga. only, limited availability, new 2003).

>**Model 85 TSS Sporting Clays 2 Gauge Set** - includes 2 sets of barrels in different gauges. New 2002.

MSR $3,249	$2,725	$2,250	$1,825	$1,550	$1,275	$1,050	$875

Add $200 for adj. comb on stock.
Add $380 for pigeon porting by Mag-na-port.

>**Model 85 TSS Sporting Clays 3 Gauge Set** - includes 20 ga., 28 ga. and .410 bore and 30 in. barrels, includes aluminum case. New 2002.

MSR $4,829	$4,075	$3,325	$2,900	$2,475	$2,150	$1,850	$1,600

Add $549 for high grade wood (limited availability, new 2004).

✳ *Model 85 TSS Skeet* - choice of fixed or adj. comb stock, 28, 30, or 32 in. VR barrels, 8.5mm (28 ga. or .410 bore) or 9.5mm (12 ga.) sloped VR, 7 lbs. 6 oz.-8 lbs. 6 oz. New 2002.

MSR $1,999	$1,685	$1,425	$1,175	$950	$875	$800	$725

Add $50 for .410 bore.
Add $200 for adj. comb on stock.
Add $390 for high grade wood (12 ga. only, limited availability, new 2003).

>**Model 85 TSS Skeet 3 Gauge Set** - includes 20 ga., 28 ga. and .410 bore and 28 in. barrels, includes aluminum case. New 2002.

MSR $4,829	$4,075	$3,325	$2,900	$2,475	$2,150	$1,850	$1,600

Add $549 for high grade wood (limited availability, new 2004).

✳ *Model 85 TSS Trap O/U* - choice of 30 or 32 in. barrels, fixed or adj. comb standard or Monte Carlo stock. New 2002.

MSR $1,999	$1,685	$1,425	$1,175	$950	$875	$800	$725

Add $200 for adj. comb.
Add $190 for pigeon porting by Mag-na-port.

✳ *Model 85 TSS Trap Un-Single* - 12 ga. only, bottom un-single, adj. rib, 32 or 34 in. barrel with adj. rib, fixed or adj. comb stock, standard or Monte Carlo stock. New 2002.

MSR $2,269	$1,975	$1,650	$1,400	$1,150	$995	$875	$775

Add $200 for adj. comb on stock.
Add $390 for high grade wood (limited availability, new 2003).
Add $114 for pigeon porting by Mag-na-port.

GRADING - PPGS™	100%	98%	95%	90%	80%	70%	60%

>**Model 85 TSS Un-Single Combo** - includes bottom un-single barrel and extra 30 or 32 in. VR O/U barrels. New 2002.

	MSR $3,189	$2,650	$2,200	$1,825	$1,550	$1,275	$1,050	$875

Add $200 for adj. comb on stock.

Add $390 for high grade wood (limited availability, new 2003).

Add $300 for pigeon porting by Mag-na-port.

MODEL 500 - 12, 20, 28 ga., or .410 bore, field grade, selective ejectors, VR, SST, 26 in. imp. cyl. and mod., 28 in. full and mod., and 30 in. full and mod. barrels, checkered stock. Prices below assume 50% engraving coverage and gold SST. Mfg. in Japan by SKB 1966-79.

		$525	$440	$395	$365	$330	$300	$275

Add 15% for 20 ga.

Add 25% for 28 ga. or .410 bore.

Add 10%-15% for fully engraved frame with pheasant, or duck/quail and dog game scene if in 98%+ condition.

Subtract 10% if w/o gold trigger.

Subtract 15%-25% if less than 50% engraving coverage.

The Model 500 varied quite a bit during the course of production in the amount of factory engraving (engraved animals or not), the quality of wood, style of checkering, and also had either silver or gold trigger. This model should also be checked carefully for hairline cracks in the buttstock, where it joins the receiver. Also, beware of bluing wear on frame bottom, and on the front and back of the triggerguard.

✳ *Model 500 Magnum* - 12 ga., 3 in. Mag., field grade, similar to Model 500, except 3 in. Mag. chambers.

		$625	$455	$410	$385	$355	$320	$290

MODEL 505 DELUXE FIELD - 12, 20, or 28 (disc.) ga., blue (new 1998) or silver nitride engraved frame (disc. 1997), 3 in. chambers, 26 or 28 in. barrels (supplied with choke tubes), single selective trigger, ejectors, matte finished (new 2004) or checkered walnut stock with recoil pad and forearm.

	MSR $1,269	$1,115	$900	$750	$625	$500	$460	$420

Add $500 for combo package (disc.).

The combo package included either 12/20 ga. barrels with Inter-chokes or 28 ga./.410 bore barrels.

✳ *Model 505 Sporting Clays* - 28 or 30 in. multi-choke barrels, blue frame with light engraving, dimensioned for Sporting Clays competition, 1997 importation features Schnabel forearm, semi-wide channeled rib, and lengthened forcing cones, approx. 8 1/4 lbs. Older importation, in addition to new model imported 1997-2002.

	$1,100	$885	$765	$650	$525	$460	$420

Last MSR was $1,299.

✳ *Model 505 Trap* - 12 ga., 30 or 32 in. choke tube barrels with or without Monte Carlo stock, high rib.

	$875	$725	$650	$525	$475	$430	$395

Last MSR was $995.

Add $400 for O/U Trap Combo.

The above Combo includes one set of O/U Trap barrels and a top single Trap barrel.

✳ *Model 505 Skeet* - 12, 20, 28 ga., or .410 bore, 28 in. barrels with multi-chokes.

	$875	$725	$650	$525	$475	$430	$395

Last MSR was $995.

✳ *Model 505 3-Ga. Skeet Set* - includes 20, 28 ga., and .410 bore extra Skeet barrels, aluminum case.

	$1,925	$1,575	$1,350	$1,200	$1,125	$950	$875

Last MSR was $2,195.

GRADING - PPGS™	100%	98%	95%	90%	80%	70%	60%

MODEL 585 DELUXE FIELD - 12, 20, 28 ga., or .410 (new 1995) bore, silver nitride engraved receiver, 3 in. chambers, 26 or 28 in. barrels (supplied with choke tubes), similar to 505 Series, except has .735 diameter bore on 12 ga. models and includes lengthened forcing cones with extended length "Competition Series" Inter-Choke System designed to improve shot patterns and reduce recoil, SST, ejectors, matte finished (new 2004) or checkered walnut stock with recoil pad and forearm (Youth model is also available with shortened dimensions), 6 lbs. 10 oz.-7 lbs. 11 oz. Importation began 1992.

MSR $1,549	$1,285	$975	$775	$625	$525	$475	$425

Add $70 for 28 ga. or .410 bore.

Add $190 for Gold Package featuring choice of silver or blue receiver, gold plated trigger, and 2 gold game scenes with Schnabel forearm - new 1998.

✳ *Model 585 Field Set* - includes 12/20 ga., 20/28 ga., 28 ga./.410 bore, 26 or 28 (new 1994) in. VR barrels with SKB Inter-choke system (on 12, 20, and 28 ga.), silver nitride receiver with finely engraved scroll game scenes, low profile receiver, crossbolt locking system, SST, ejectors, manual safety, checkered high gloss American walnut stock and forearm.

MSR $2,479	$2,175	$1,825	$1,500	$1,225	$995	$895	$800

Add $70 for 20/28 ga. set or 28 ga./.410 bore set.

Add $300 (12/20 ga.) or $360 (20 ga. and smaller) for Gold Package featuring choice of silver or blue receiver, gold plated trigger, and 2 gold game scenes with Schnabel forearm - new 1998.

✳ *Model 585 Medallion* - 12 or 20 ga., 3 in. chambers, features two inlaid medallions in gold or bronze finish (medallion artwork by Ron Van Gilder and Rocky Capece), very limited production. New 2000.

MSR $1,819	$1,610	$1,275	$1,025	$900	$800	$700	$600

✳ *Model 585 Upland* - 12, 20, or 28 ga., 3 in. chambers for 12 and 20 ga., features straight grip stock with recoil pad and 26 in. VR barrels, Schnabel forearm, 6 lbs. 10 oz.-7 lbs. 10 oz. New 1997.

MSR $1,549	$1,285	$975	$775	$625	$525	$475	$425

Add $70 for 28 ga.

Add $190 for Gold Package featuring choice of silver or blue receiver, gold plated trigger, and 2 gold game scenes with Schnabel forearm - new 1998.

✳ *Model 585 Trap* - 12 ga., 30 or 32 in. choke tube barrels with or w/o Monte Carlo stock, high rib. Disc. 2002.

		$1,310	$975	$800	$600	$500	$450	$395

Last MSR was $1,619.

Add $200 for Gold Package featuring choice of silver or blue receiver, gold plated trigger, and 2 gold game scenes with Schnabel forearm - mfg. 1998-2002.

Add $800 for O/U Trap Combo or $1,100 for O/U Trap Combo with Gold Package.

The above Combo includes one set of O/U Trap barrels and a top single Trap barrel.

✳ *Model 585 Skeet* - 12, 20, 28 ga., or .410 bore, 28 or 30 (12 ga. only - new 1994) in. barrels with multi-chokes. Disc. 2002.

		$1,310	$975	$800	$600	$500	$450	$395

Last MSR was $1,619.

Add $60 for 28 ga. or .410 bore.

Add $200 for Gold Package featuring choice of silver or blue receiver, gold plated trigger, and 2 gold game scenes with Schnabel forearm - mfg. 1998-2002.

✳ *Model 585 3-Ga. Skeet Set* - includes 20, 28 ga., and .410 bore extra Skeet barrels, aluminum case. Disc. 2002.

		$3,175	$2,550	$2,000	$1,700	$1,525	$1,400	$1,300

Last MSR was $3,779.

Add $450 for Gold Package featuring choice of silver or blue receiver, gold plated trigger, and 2 gold game scenes with Schnabel forearm - mfg. 1998-2002.

GRADING - PPGS™	100%	98%	95%	90%	80%	70%	60%

✳ *Model 585 Sporting Clays* - 12, 20, or 28 ga., 3 in. chambers (12 and 20 ga.), 28 in. (all gauges), 30 in. (12 or 20 ga.), or 32 in. (12 ga. only) multi-choke barrels, dimensioned for Sporting Clays competition, narrow rib (3/8 in.) became available 1994. Disc. 2002.

	100%	98%	95%	90%	80%	70%	60%
	$1,410	$1,050	$850	$635	$530	$475	$425

Last MSR was $1,679.

Add $50 for 28 ga.

Add $170 for Gold Package featuring choice of silver or blue receiver, gold plated trigger, and 2 gold game scenes with Schnabel forearm - mfg. 1998-2002.

>*Model 585 Sporting Clays Set* - includes 2 sets of barrels (12 ga. - 30 in., 20 ga. - 28 in.), cased. Mfg. 1996-2002.

	$2,135	$1,775	$1,495	$1,200	$1,050	$925	$825

Last MSR was $2,419.

Add $300 for Gold Package featuring choice of silver or blue receiver, gold plated trigger, and 2 gold game scenes with Schnabel forearm - mfg. 1998-2002.

✳ *Model 585 Waterfowler* - 12 ga. only, 3 in. chambers, oil finished stock and forearm, matte blue finish. Imported 1995-2000, reintroduced 2005.

MSR $1,549	$1,285	$975	$775	$625	$525	$475	$425

✳ *Model 585 Youth/Ladies* - 12 or 20 ga., 26 or 28 (12 ga. only) in. VR barrels, features 13 1/2 in. LOP, barrels have .735 in. bores with lengthened forcing cones. New 1994.

MSR $1,549	$1,285	$975	$775	$625	$525	$475	$425

Add $190 for Gold Package featuring choice of silver or blue receiver, gold plated trigger, and 2 gold game scenes with Schnabel forearm - new 1998.

MODEL 585 150th ANNIVERSARY - 12 or 20 ga., 3 in. chambers, silver nitride engraved receiver with gold game scenes, matte finished metal, 26 or 28 in. barrels, matte finish high grade black American walnut stock with finger groove forend, 6 lbs. 12 oz. - 7 lbs. 14 oz. Very limited production beginning 2005.

MSR $1,999	$1,685	$1,425	$1,175	$950	$875	$800	$725

MODEL 600 FIELD GRADE - similar to Model 500, except silver-plated frame and select wood and fully engraved.

	$995	$850	$700	$525	$475	$430	$395

Add 20% for 20 ga.

An unknown quantity of Model 600s were mfg. with blue receivers - a small premium may be asked.

MODEL 600 MAGNUM - similar to Model 600 Field, except chambered for 3 in. Mag., 12 ga. Mfg. 1969-72 by SKB.

	$1,050	$875	$700	$525	$475	$430	$395

MODEL 600 TRAP GRADE - similar to Model 600 Field Grade, except 12 ga. only, trap stock, recoil pad, select wood.

	$995	$850	$700	$525	$475	$430	$395

MODEL 600 DOUBLES GUN - similar to Model 600 Trap, except choked for 21 yd. and 30 yd. targets. Mfg. 1973-75.

	$995	$850	$700	$525	$475	$430	$395

MODEL 600 SKEET GRADE - 12, 20, 28 ga., or .410 bore, 26 or 28 in. barrels, bored S&S, otherwise similar to Model 600 Trap.

	$995	$850	$700	$525	$475	$430	$395
28 ga. or .410 bore.	$1,425	$1,175	$900	$750	$650	$550	$450

MODEL 600 SKEET GRADE COMBO SET - similar to Model 600 Skeet, except fitted with matched set of 20, 28 ga., and .410 bore barrels, in fitted case.

	$2,650	$2,250	$1,875	$1,550	$1,325	$1,175	$1,025

GRADING - PPGS™	100%	98%	95%	90%	80%	70%	60%

MODEL 605 FIELD - similar to Model 505 Deluxe Field except has silver finished engraved receiver with better walnut. Importation disc. 1992.

	$1,075	$850	$750	$675	$575	$500	$450

Last MSR was $1,195.

Add $500 for extra set of barrels (Combo).

* ✳ *Model 605 Trap* - 12 ga., 30 or 32 in. choke tube barrel with or without Monte Carlo stock, high rib.

	$1,075	$850	$750	$675	$575	$500	$450

Last MSR was $1,195.

Add $400 for O/U Trap Combo.

The above Combo includes one set of O/U Trap barrels and a top single Trap barrel.

* ✳ *Model 605 Skeet* - 12, 20, 28 ga., or .410 bore, 28 in. barrels with multi-chokes.

	$1,100	$850	$750	$675	$575	$500	$450

Last MSR was $1,195.

* ✳ *Model 605 3-Ga. Skeet Set* - includes 20, 28 ga., and .410 bore extra Skeet barrels, aluminum case.

	$2,175	$1,650	$1,400	$1,250	$1,125	$950	$875

Last MSR was $2,395.

* ✳ *Model 605 Sporting Clay* - 28 or 30 in. multi-choke barrels, dimensioned for Sporting Clay competition.

	$1,110	$850	$750	$675	$575	$500	$450

Last MSR was $1,245.

* ✳ *Model 605 DU Sponsor Gun* - mfg. for DU chapters - dinner auction gun, 850 mfg. in 12 ga. (1990) and 850 mfg. in 20 ga. (1991). Features gold inlays and presentation case.

DU sponsor gun values are usually hard to ascertain in the secondary marketplace. Currently, prices seem to range between $1,200-$1,400.

MODEL 680 ENGLISH - similar to Model 600 Field, except English style stock, select walnut and fine scroll engraving. Mfg. 1973-76.

	$1,300	$1,150	$975	$850	$725	$650	$600

Add 20% for 20 ga.

MODEL 685 FIELD - similar to Model 585 Deluxe Field, except has silver finished engraved receiver with gold inlays and better walnut, engine turned monobloc.

	$1,325	$950	$795	$675	$575	$500	$450

Last MSR was $1,549.

* ✳ *Model 685 Field Set* - includes 12/20, 20/28 ga., 28 ga./.410 bore 26 or 28 (new 1994) in. VR barrels with SKB Inter-choke system (on 12, 20, and 28 ga.), silver nitride receiver with finely engraved scroll game scenes, low profile receiver, crossbolt locking system, SST, ejectors, manual safety, checkered high gloss American walnut stock and forearm.

	$1,850	$1,650	$1,500	$1,350	$1,275	$1,100	$1,000

Last MSR was $2,149.

* ✳ *Model 685 Trap* - 12 ga., 30 or 32 in. choke tube barrels with or w/o Monte Carlo stock, high rib.

	$1,365	$975	$825	$700	$600	$525	$450

Last MSR was $1,595.

Add $600 for O/U Trap Combo.

The above Combo includes one set of O/U Trap barrels and a top single Trap barrel.

* ✳ *Model 685 Skeet* - 12, 20, 28 ga., or .410 bore, 28 or 30 (12 ga. only - new 1994) in. barrels with multi-chokes.

	$1,365	$975	$825	$700	$600	$525	$450

Last MSR was $1,595.

GRADING - PPGS™	100%	98%	95%	90%	80%	70%	60%

✳ **Model 685 3-Ga. Skeet Set** - includes 20, 28 ga., and .410 bore extra Skeet barrels, aluminum case.

	$2,550	$2,175	$1,875	$1,675	$1,450	$1,275	$1,125

Last MSR was $2,949.

✳ **Model 685 Sporting Clays** - 28 (all gauges), 30 (12 ga. only), or 32 (12 ga. only) in. multi-choke barrels, dimensioned for Sporting Clays competition, 3/8 in. narrow rib became available 1994. Importation disc. 1995.

	$1,365	$975	$825	$700	$600	$525	$450

Last MSR was $1,595.

✳ **Model 685 Sporting Clays Set** - includes one set of 12 ga. (28, 30, or 32 in. VR barrels) and 20 ga. (28 in. only) or one set of 32 and 28 in. barrels in 12 ga only. Imported 1994-95.

	$2,000	$1,675	$1,500	$1,350	$1,200	$1,025	$895

Last MSR was $2,295.

MODEL 700 TRAP GRADE - 12 ga., similar to Model 600 Trap, except more engraving, better grade wood, wide rib. Mfg. 1969-75.

	$820	$770	$740	$685	$630	$595	$565

MODEL 700 DOUBLES GUN - 12 ga., similar to Model 700 Trap, except choked for 21 yd. and 30 yd. targets. Mfg. 1973-75.

	$795	$770	$740	$685	$630	$595	$565

MODEL 700 SKEET GRADE - 12 ga., similar to Model 700 Doubles, only bored S&S, available in 12 or 20 ga.

	$840	$770	$740	$685	$620	$585	$555

MODEL 785 DELUXE FIELD - 12, 20, 28 ga., or .410 bore, silver nitride engraved receiver, 3 in. chambers, 26 or 28 in. barrels (supplied with choke tubes), similar to 585 Series, except has chrome lined bores on all models and also includes lengthened forcing cones with extended length "Competition Series" Inter-Choke System designed to improve shot patterns and reduce recoil, SST, ejectors, checkered walnut stock with recoil pad and forearm, 6 lbs. 10 oz.-7 lbs. 11 oz. Imported 1995-2002.

	$1,900	$1,650	$1,400	$1,150	$1,000	$900	$800

Last MSR was $2,119.

Add $80 for 28 ga. or .410 bore.

✳ **Model 785 Field Set** - includes 12/20, 20/28 ga., 28 ga./.410 bore, 26 or 28 in. VR barrels with SKB inter-choke system (on 12 and 20 ga.), silver nitride receiver with finely engraved scroll game scenes, low profile receiver, crossbolt locking system, SST, ejectors, manual safety, checkered high gloss American walnut stock and forearm. Importation disc. 2002.

	$2,680	$2,300	$1,925	$1,600	$1,500	$1,375	$1,275

Last MSR was $3,019.

Add $100 for 20/28 ga. set or 28 ga./.410 bore set.

✳ **Model 785 Medallion** - 12 or 20 ga., 3 in. chambers, features three inlayed medallions in gold or bronze finish (medallion artwork by Ron Van Gilder and Rocky Capece), very limited production. New 2000.

MSR $2,389	$2,075	$1,750	$1,450	$1,175	$1,050	$925	$825

✳ **Model 785 Trap** - 12 ga., 30 or 32 in. choke tube barrels with or w/o Monte Carlo stock, high rib. Importation disc. 2002.

	$1,940	$1,625	$1,365	$1,125	$995	$895	$800

Last MSR was $2,199.

Add $880 for O/U Trap Combo.
The above Combo includes one set of O/U Trap barrels and a top single Trap barrel.

GRADING - PPGS™	100%	98%	95%	90%	80%	70%	60%

* *Model 785 Skeet* - 12, 20, 28 ga., or .410 bore, 28 or 30 (12 ga. only) in. barrels with multi-chokes. Importation disc. 2002.

	$1,940	$1,625	$1,365	$1,125	$995	$895	$800

Last MSR was $2,199.

Add $40 for 28 ga. or .410 bore.

* *Model 785 3-Ga. Skeet Set* - includes 20, 28 ga., and .410 bore extra Skeet barrels, aluminum case. Importation disc. 2002.

	$3,835	$2,975	$2,350	$2,000	$1,600	$1,400	$1,295

Last MSR was $4,439.

* *Model 785 Sporting Clays* - 12, 20, or 28 ga., 28 in. (all gauges), 30 in. (12 ga. only), or 32 in. (12 ga. only) multi-choke barrels, dimensioned for Sporting Clays competition with 3/8 in. narrow rib. Importation disc. 2002.

	$2,000	$1,675	$1,375	$1,150	$995	$895	$800

Last MSR was $2,269.

Add $80 for 28 ga.

>**Model 785 Sporting Clays Set** - includes 2 sets of barrels (12 ga. - 30 in., 20 ga. - 28 in.). Imported 1996-2002.

	$2,775	$2,450	$2,125	$1,825	$1,625	$1,400	$1,200

Last MSR was $3,149.

MODEL 800 TRAP GRADE
- 12 ga., similar to Model 700 Trap, except more engraving, better grade wood, wide rib. Limited mfg. 1969-1975.

	$1,150	$875	$775	$675	$575	$500	$425

MODEL 800 SKEET GRADE
- 12 or 20 ga., skeet chokes. Mfg. 1969-1975.

	$1,200	$1,000	$895	$795	$680	$595	$565

MODEL 880 CROWN GRADE
- 12, 20, 28 ga., or .410 bore, coin finished receiver, extensively engraved with sideplates, SST, ejectors, select walnut with fleur-de-lis scroll style checkering, double crossbolt action. Limited mfg. Disc. 1980.

	$2,000	$1,825	$1,625	$1,300	$1,150	$975	$890

Add 25% for 28 ga. or .410 bore.

MODEL 885
- available in either Field, Skeet, or Trap configuration, coin finished receiver featuring fine scroll engraving with game scenes, boxlock action with sideplates, beginning 1992, the 885 Series in 12 ga. features lengthened forcing cones, .735 bore, and a competition series of extended length multi-chokes. Imported 1988-94.

* *Model 885 Field* - 12, 20, 28 ga., or .410 bore, field dimensions, barrels include choke tubes. Imported 1989-94.

	$1,600	$1,200	$975	$825	$725	$650	$595

Last MSR was $1,895.

* *Model 885 Trap* - 12 ga., 30 or 32 in. barrels with multi-chokes, standard or Monte Carlo stock.

	$1,650	$1,200	$975	$850	$750	$650	$595

Last MSR was $1,949.

Add $700 for O/U Trap Combo.
The above Combo includes one set of O/U Trap barrels and a top single Trap barrel.

* *Model 885 Skeet* - 12, 20, 28 ga., or .410 bore, 28 or 30 (12 ga. only - new 1994) in. barrels with multi-chokes.

	$1,650	$1,200	$975	$850	$750	$650	$595

Last MSR was $1,949.

* *Model 885 Field Set* - includes 12/20, 20/28 ga., 28 ga./.410 bore 26 or 28 (new 1994) in. VR barrels with SKB Inter-choke system (on 12 and 20 ga.), silver nitride receiver with finely engraved scroll game scenes, low profile receiver, crossbolt locking system, SST, ejectors, manual safety, checkered high gloss American walnut stock and forearm.

	$2,450	$2,150	$1,750	$1,500	$1,250	$1,075	$925

GRADING - PPGS™	100%	98%	95%	90%	80%	70%	60%

✳ *Model 885 3-Ga. Skeet Set* - includes 20, 28 ga., and .410 bore extra Skeet barrels, aluminum case.

	$3,200	$2,700	$2,300	$1,975	$1,725	$1,500	$1,400

Last MSR was $3,595.

✳ *Model 885 Sporting Clays* - 28 (all gauges), 30 (12 ga. only), or 32 (12 ga. only) in. multi-choke barrels, dimensioned for Sporting Clays competition, 3/8 in. narrow rib became available 1994.

	$1,650	$1,200	$975	$850	$750	$650	$595

Last MSR was $1,949.

MODEL 5600 - 12 ga. only, available as Trap or Skeet model only, VR (Trap only) and vent. barrels (Skeet only), no engraving, select walnut. Disc. 1980.

	$575	$495	$450	$420	$390	$360	$330

✳ *Model 5700* - available as Trap or Skeet model only, light engraving, select walnut, VR. Disc. 1980.

	$750	$625	$540	$495	$460	$430	$400

✳ *Model 5800* - available as Trap or Skeet model only, more deluxe engraving, select walnut. Disc. 1980.

	$950	$800	$695	$595	$500	$450	$425

SHOTGUNS: SxS

Models 100, 150, 200, 280, 300, 400, and 480 were available in 12 and 20 ga. only, featured 25-30 in. barrels, and all had boxlock actions. More expensive models differ in the amount of engraving, grade of walnut, and style of checkering, beavertail forearm, 6 1/4-7 lbs. Disc. 1980.

MODEL 100 - 12 or 20 ga., Mag. model also, SST, extractors, blue only.

	$695	$595	$490	$395	$350	$300	$250

Add 20% for 20 ga.

Add 10%-15% for fully engraved receiver with pheasant, or duck/quail and dog game scene if in 98%+ condition.

Subtract 15%-25% if w/ less than 50% engraving coverage.

The Model 100 varied quite a bit during the course of production in the amount of factory engraving (engraved animals or not), the quality of wood, style of checkering, and also had either silver or gold trigger. This model should also be checkered carefully for hairline cracks in the buttstock, where it joins the receiver. Also, beware of bluing wear on receiver bottom, and on the front and back of the triggerguard.

MODEL 150 - similar to Model 100, except scroll engraving, beavertail forearm. Mfg. 1972-74 by SKB.

	$695	$550	$485	$395	$350	$300	$275

Add 20% for 20 ga.

MODEL 200 - 12 or 20 ga., Mag. model also, SST, ejectors, boxlock, scalloped frame, lightly engraved coin finished receiver.

	$995	$895	$795	$695	$650	$490	$425

Add 20% for 20 ga.

MODEL 200 (RECENT MFG.) - similar to original Model 200, SST, ejectors, pistol grip stock, recoil pad. Imported 1987-1988 only.

	$995	$895	$795	$695	$650	$490	$425

Last MSR was $895.

Add 20% for 20 ga.

This model was supplied with 3 factory choke-tubes.

✳ *Model 200E (English)* - similar to New Model 200, except has straight grip stock. Importation disc. 1988.

	$995	$895	$795	$695	$575	$485	$395

Last MSR was $895.

Add 30% for 20 ga.

GRADING - PPGS™	100%	98%	95%	90%	80%	70%	60%

MODEL 280 ENGLISH - 12 or 20 ga., Mag. model also, SST, AE, lightly engraved blue receiver, straight grip.

	$1,095	$995	$885	$775	$675	$585	$495

Add 30% for 20 ga.

MODEL 300 - 12 or 20 ga., Mag. model also, SST, AE, lightly engraved coin finished receiver.

	$995	$895	$795	$685	$575	$485	$425

Add 30% for 20 ga.

MODEL 385 FIELD - 12 (new 1998), 20 or 28 ga., scalloped boxlock action with silver nitride receiver, engraved scroll and game scene designs, SST, ejectors, automatic safety, semi-fancy gloss finished American walnut, English or pistol grip stock, beavertail or satin finished splinter forearm, limited quantities. Imported 1992-2004.

	$1,750	$1,425	$1,050	$850	$725	$600	$525

Last MSR was $2,049.

* *Model 385 Sporting Clays* - 12, 20 (new 2000), or 28 (new 2000) ga., 3 in. chambers (12 ga.), 28 or 30 (new 2003) in. barrels with raised VR and double bead sights, pistol grip stock, approx. 7 1/2 lbs. Imported 1998-2004.

	$1,850	$1,425	$1,050	$875	$750	$650	$550

Last MSR was $2,159.

>Model 385 Sporting Clays Set - includes a pair of 20 and 28 ga., 28 or 30 (new 2003) in. barrels. Imported 1999-2004.

	$2,575	$2,100	$1,750	$1,475	$1,200	$1,050	$975

Last MSR was $3,059.

* *Model 385 Field Set* - includes a pair of 20 and 28 ga., 26 in. barrels, choice of pistol grip or English straight stock. Imported 1997-2004.

	$2,475	$2,100	$1,750	$1,475	$1,200	$1,050	$975

Last MSR was $2,929.

* *Model 385 DU Commemorative* - features gold inlaid mallards on both receiver sides and gold inlaid DU duck head on receiver bottom, includes hard shell case, and signed letter from SKB president, DU proofmarks, limited mfg. - 200 sets in 1992.

	$3,950	$2,750	$1,950				

Last MSR was $5,000.

This model is a DU "Collectors Series" gun.

MODEL 400 - 12 or 20 ga., Mag. model also, boxlock, SST, AE, moderately engraved coin finished receiver with sideplates.

	$1,395	$1,295	$1,195	$950	$795	$695	$585

Add 30% for 20 ga.

MODEL 400 (RECENT MFG.) - similar to original Model 400, SST, ejectors, recoil pad, choke tube system. Imported 1987-88 only.

	$1,395	$1,295	$1,195	$950	$795	$695	$585

Last MSR was $1,195.

Add 30% for 20 ga.

* *Model 400E (English)* - similar to New Model 400, except has engraved sideplates and straight grip stock. Importation disc. 1989.

	$1,595	$1,495	$1,395	$1,195	$995	$795	$675

Last MSR was $1,195.

Add 30% for 20 ga.

MODEL 480 ENGLISH - 12 or 20 ga., Mag. model also, SST, AE, moderately engraved coin finished receiver, straight grip. Limited mfg.

	$1,675	$1,525	$1,395	$1,195	$995	$795	$675

Add 30% for 20 ga.

GRADING - PPGS™	100%	98%	95%	90%	80%	70%	60%

MODEL 485 FIELD - 12 (new 1998), 20, or 28 ga., coin finished boxlock action with engraved upland game scene side plates, 26 or 28 in. barrels with raised VR, checkered gloss finished American walnut stock and beavertail forearm, ejectors, SST, satin finish and splinter forearm became available in 20 or 28 ga. during 2002, approx. 7 lbs. Imported 1997-2004.

	$2,400	$2,050	$1,725	$1,425	$1,250	$995	$850

Last MSR was $2,769.

✳ *Model 485 Field Set* - includes a pair of 20 and 28 ga., 26 or 28 in. barrels, choice of pistol grip or English straight stock. Imported 1998-2004.

	$3,400	$2,825	$2,300	$2,000	$1,675	$1,375	$1,150

Last MSR was $3,949.

SHOTGUNS: SEMI-AUTO

MODEL 300 STANDARD - 12 or 20 ga., 3 in. chamber, recoil operated, 26 in. imp. cyl., 28 in. mod. or full plain barrel, 30 in. full, checkered pistol grip stock. Mfg. 1968-72.

	$295	$255	$205	$165	$155	$145	$140

MODEL XL-300 - 12 or 20 ga., 2 3/4 (12 ga.) or 3 (20 ga.) in. chamber, gas operated, white alloy receiver with light game scene etching, 4 shot mag., 26-30 in. plain barrel.

	$325	$285	$235	$200	$185	$165	$150

MODEL 1300 UPLAND - 12 or 20 ga., 3 in. chamber, 22, 26, or 28 in. VR barrel with multi-chokes, matte black receiver, checkered walnut stock and forearm. Importation resumed 1988-96.

	$450	$385	$340	$300	$270	$240	$210

Last MSR was $495.

This model was previously designated the Model XL-300. The new Model 1300 was available in Slug configuration with 22 in. barrel/iron sights at no extra charge. Recent Model 1300s have a magazine cutoff system on front left side of frame.

MODEL 900 STANDARD - 12 or 20 ga., 3 in. chamber, similar to Model 300 standard, except has vent. rib. barrel. Mfg. 1968-1972.

	$325	$285	$235	$200	$185	$165	$150

XL 900 - similar to XL 300, except has vent. rib barrel and no recoil pad, 6 1/4 lbs.

	$365	$325	$275	$250	$230	$190	$175

XL 900 MR - 12 ga. only, gas operated, 26-30 in. barrel, 5 shot, alloy receiver, engraved game bird scroll work on receiver, shoots both 2 3/4 and 3 in. shells by interchanging barrels. Disc. 1980.

	$325	$280	$260	$240	$225	$190	$175

XL 900 TRAP GRADE - similar to XL 900 MR, 12 ga. only, scroll engraved black chrome receiver, 30 in. imp. mod. or full barrel, trap style stock, straight or Monte Carlo, recoil pad. Mfg. 1980-disc.

	$395	$350	$320	$305	$275	$265	$260

XL 900 SKEET GRADE - similar to XL 900 MR, except scroll engraved black chrome receiver, 26 in. barrel, skeet stock. Mfg. 1972-disc.

	$400	$350	$320	$305	$275	$265	$260

XL 900 SLUG GUN - similar to XL 900 MR, except 24 in. slug barrel, rifle sights, no rib. Mfg. 1972-disc.

	$350	$310	$280	$265	$250	$220	$200

GRADING - PPGS™	100%	98%	95%	90%	80%	70%	60%

MODEL 1900 - 12 or 20 ga., 3 in. chamber, 22, 26, or 28 in. VR barrel with multi-chokes, deluxe outdoor field scene etched on receiver, gold trigger, approx. 1,000-2,000 mfg. per year. Importation disc. 1996.

	$485	$430	$395	$360	$330	$295	$260

Last MSR was $545.

This model was previously designated the Model XL 900. The Model 1900 was available in Slug configuration with 22 in. barrel and iron sights or Trap Model at no extra charge. Recent Model 1900s have a magazine cutoff system on front left side of frame.

MODEL 3000 - 12 or 20 ga., 3 in. chamber, gas operated, (shoots both 2 3/4 and 3 in. shells interchangeably) with semi-squareback styling, elaborate game scenes etched on both sides of receiver, deluxe checkered walnut stock and forearm. Imported 1988-90.

	$545	$475	$415	$380	$350	$315	$285

Last MSR was $597.

Add $125 for Trap model (2 3/4 in. chamber).

This model has not previously been imported in this configuration.

SHOTGUNS: SINGLE BARREL, TRAP

MODEL 505 TRAP - 12 ga., 32 or 34 in. barrel with multi-chokes, regular or Monte Carlo stock.

	$875	$725	$650	$525	$475	$430	$395

Last MSR was $995.

MODEL 605 TRAP - 12 ga., 32 or 34 in. barrel with multi-chokes.

	$1,075	$850	$750	$675	$575	$500	$450

Last MSR was $1,195.

CENTURY TRAP - 12 ga., 32 or 34 in. VR barrel, engraved, auto ejector, full choke, checkered walnut stock. Mfg. 1973 and 1976.

	$550	$525	$470	$440	$385	$360	$320

This model was imported by Ithaca.

CENTURY II TRAP - improved trap stock version of Century, Monte Carlo stock.

	$600	$550	$495	$470	$415	$385	$350

This model was imported by Ithaca.

SHOTGUNS: SLIDE ACTION

MODEL 7300 - 12 or 20 ga., 2 3/4 or 3 in. chambers, blue only, French walnut stock-hand checkered, twin action slide bars. Disc. 1980.

	$295	$250	$225	$200	$180	$165	$150

MODEL 7900 - trap or skeet variation of the Model 7300.

	$350	$310	$265	$235	$200	$180	$160

SKS

SKS designates a semi-auto rifle design originally developed by the Russian military, and manufactured in Russia 1949-1956. No current domestic importation. Currently manufactured in Russia, China, and many other countries. Previously manufactured in Russia, China (largest quantity), N. Korea, East Germany, Romania, Albania, Yugoslavia, and North Vietnam.

SKS DEVELOPMENT & HISTORY

SKS (Samozaryadnyi Karabin Simonova) - developed by Sergei Gavrilovich Simonov in the late 1940s to use the 7.62 cartridge of 1943 (7.62x39mm). The SKS is actually based on an earlier design developed by Simonov in 1936 as a prototype self-loading military rifle. The SKS was adopted by the Soviet military in 1949, two years after the AK-47, and was originally intended as a complement to the AK-47's select-fire capability. It served in this role until the mid- to late

1950s, when it was withdrawn from active issue and sent to reserve units and Soviet Youth "Pioneer" programs. It was also released for use in military assistance programs to Soviet Bloc countries and other "friendly" governments. Much of the original SKS manufacturing equipment was shipped to Communist China prior to 1960. Since then, most of the SKS carbines produced, including those used by the Viet Cong in Vietnam, have come from China.

Like the AK-47, the Simonov carbine is a robust military rifle. It, too, was designed to be used by troops with very little formal education or training. It will operate reliably in the harshest climatic conditions, from the Russian arctic to the steamy jungles of Southeast Asia. Its chrome-lined bore is impervious to the corrosive effects of fulminate of mercury primers and the action is easily disassembled for cleaning and maintenance.

The SKS and a modified sporter called the OP-SKS (OP stands for Okhotnichnyj Patron) are the standard hunting rifles for a majority of Russian hunters. It is routinely used to take everything from the Russian saiga antelope up to, and including, moose, boar, and brown bear. The main difference between the regular SKS and the OP variant is in the chamber dimensions and the rate of rifling. The OP starts as a regular SKS, then has the barrel removed and replaced with one designed to specifically handle a slightly longer and heavier bullet.

Prior to the ban, hundreds of thousands of SKS carbines were imported into the U.S. The SKS was rapidly becoming one of the favorites of American hunters and shooters. Its low cost and durability made it a popular "truck gun" for those shooters who spend a lot of time in the woods, whether they are ranchers, farmers, or plinkers. While the Russian-made SKS is a bonafide curio and relic firearm and legal for importation, the Clinton administration suspended all import permits for firearms having a rifled bore and ammunition from the former Soviet Union in early 1994. In order to get the ban lifted, the Russian government signed a trade agreement, wherein they agreed to deny export licenses to any American company seeking SKS rifles and a variety of other firearms and ammunition deemed politically incorrect by Clinton & Gore. The BATF then used this agreement as a reason to deny import licenses for any SKS from any country.

Most of the SKS carbines imported into the U.S. came from the People's Republic of China. They were a mix of refurbished military issue, straight military surplus, and even some new manufacture. Quality was rather poor. Compared to the SKS Chinese carbines, only a few Russian made SKSs ever made it into the U.S. All are from military stockpiles and were refurbished at the Tula Arms Works, probably the oldest continuously operating armory in the world. Recently, more SKS carbines have been imported from the former Yugoslavia by Century International Arms. These carbines carry the former Soviet Bloc designation of "Type 58" and feature milled receivers. Quality is generally good, and values are comparable to other Russian/European SKS imports. Values for unmodified Russian and Eastern European made SKS carbines (those with the original magazines and stock) are higher than the Chinese copies.

The most collectible SKS is East German mfg., and SKS rifles mfg. in N. Korea and N. Vietnam are also quite rare in the U.S.

Over 600 million SKS carbines have been manufactured in China alone, by over 45 different manufacturers, in addition to the millions manufactured in other former Soviet Bloc countries. The Simonov carbine was the best selling semi-auto rifle in America (and other countries) during 1993-94, and remains a popular choice for plinking, hunting, and protection in the new millennium.

RIFLES: SEMI-AUTO

SKS - 7.62x39mm Russian cal., Soviet designed, original Soviet mfg. as well as copies mfg. in China, Russia, Yugoslavia, and many other countries, gas operated weapon, 10 shot fixed mag., wood stock (thumbhole design on newer mfg.), with or w/o (newer mfg.) permanently attached folding bayonet, tangent rear and hooded front sight, no current importation from China, Russia, or the former Yugoslavia.

Original Mfg.	$175	$150	$120	$100	$85	$75	$70
Recent Chinese Mfg.							
w/ thumbhole stock	$195	$175	$140	$120	$100	$85	$70

From late 1993 until the Crime Bill was enacted during September of 1994, runaway demand escalated SKS prices on recent Chinese exports to the $195-$250 range. Earlier Russian manufacture at the time was selling for $250-$325, but prices fell once the glut of Chinese imports arrived. However, as supply began equaling demand, prices fell off to their current levels. With

GRADING - PPGS™	100%	98%	95%	90%	80%	70%	60%

interest waning and a current stable marketplace, SKS pricing has become more predictable, and knowledgeable shooters and collectors are now seeking out earlier Russian-made SKSs, as these guns have the most quality and best fit/finish (not Chinese overall poor quality). Lately there have been a rash of lawsuits over recently imported SKS semi-auto models going full auto, and as a result, prices have gone down slightly.

This model may also be listed under those importers/distributors who import this model and are listed in this text.

SOG INTERNATIONAL INC.

Current importer located in Lebanon, OH.

SOG International Inc. imports a wide variety of surplus military firearms, in addition to currently manufactured guns. Please contact the company directly for more information regarding current model availability and pricing (see Trademark Index).

SSK INDUSTRIES

Previous Class II manufacturer located in Wintersville, OH.

SSK Industries is no longer manufacturing complete guns, but maintains a wide variety of gunsmithing services.

SSK Industries previously manufactured complete rifles and suppressors for police, military, and civilian use (where legal in accord with ATF regulations). Their custom shop worked on virtually anything 20mm or smaller.

SSK Industries used Thompson Center flatside frames and applies an industrial hard chrome finish. Most SSK handguns and rifles were extensively customized in exotic calibers, finishes, and various engraving options. Receivers and barrels could be purchased separately - values below are for complete assembled pistols.

SSK has also manufactured various limited editions including the Handgun Hunters International (HHI) Models 1, 2, and 3. Issue prices on these guns were $1,100 (Model 3), $1,200 (Model 2), and $1,300 (Model 1). Only 50 were mfg. total in 1987. SSK also customized a Ruger Super Redhawk (.44 Mag. or .45 LC cal.). This variation came with either a scoped 7 1/2 in. octagon barrel (Beauty Model) or a 6 in. bull barrel with muzzle brake (Beast Model). Prices started at $1,430 - add $245 extra for .45 LC cal.

PISTOLS: SINGLE SHOT

Values listed are for basic models with no options or special features.

SSK-CONTENDER - over 150 cals. available from .17 Bee to .50-70, various custom barrels available, basically, this is a custom order only gun.

	$1,500	$1,375	$1,250	$1,125	$1,000	$900	$825

Individual barrels were available starting at $268.
An arrestor muzzle brake was available on special order.
This model included barrel, frame, stocks, and sights as standard equipment.

SSK-XP100 - various cals. between .17 and .50, includes TSOB mount and rings.

	$1,700	$1,500	$1,300	$1,150	$1,025	$925	$850

The .50 cal. XP100 (12.9 X 50.8 JDJ) came with SSK muzzle brake, scope, dies, and new reinforced fiberglass stock - retail price was $1,700.

RIFLES

Values listed are for basic models with no options or special features. In addition, SSK also custom manufactured a bolt action rifle available in almost any caliber and configuration - prices started at approx. $2,000 and can go as high as $6,000, depending on the customer's individual special orders. SSK also has developed a 6.5mm, 7mm, or .30 cal. upper unit conversion for AR-15s and M-16s utilizing heavy sub-sonic bullets designated "whispers." SSK also manufactured a line of .50 BMG cal. rifles available in either Brown or Sako action.

GRADING - PPGS™	100%	98%	95%	90%	80%	70%	60%

SSK TCR 87 - .14 through .600 cals., Nitro Express cals. are also available, features Thompson Center TRC 87 receiver, and SSK custom barrels, muzzle brakes, and exotic finishes were available at extra cost.

		$1,700	$1,500	$1,300	$1,150	$1,025	$925	$850

SSK RUGER NO. 1 - many cals. including .577 NE (optional), custom order rifle based on a Ruger No. 1 frame.

		$2,000	$1,800	$1,600	$1,400	$1,250	$1,100	$1,000

SSK BOLT ACTION - various cals., ground up custom order rifle.

		$2,500	$2,250	$1,800	$1,600	$1,400	$1,250	$1,100

STI INTERNATIONAL

Current manufacturer established during 1993, and located in Georgetown, TX. Distributor and dealer sales.

In addition to manufacturing the pistols listed, STi International also makes frame kits in steel, stainless steel, aluminum, or titanium - prices range between $405-$717.

PISTOLS: SEMI-AUTO

The beginning numerals on all STi pistols designate the barrel length, and most of the following models are listed in numerical sequence.

LSA LAWMAN - .45 ACP cal., 1911 Govt. style, 5 in. barrel, hammer forged carbon steel frame, designed for IPSC, USPSA and IDPA, 36 oz. New 2005.

MSR $1,344	$1,150	$950	$825	$700	$575	$500	$450

3.4 BLS9/BLS40 - 9mm Para. or .40 S&W cal., blue finish, Govt. length grips, Heine low mounted sights, single stack mag., 30 oz. New 1999.

MSR $889	$765	$650	$565	$460	$400	$360	$330

3.4 LS9/LS40 - 9mm Para. or .40 S&W cal., blue finish, Commander length grips, single stack mag., Heine low mounted sights, 28 oz. New 1999.

MSR $789	$665	$575	$525	$450	$400	$350	$325

3.9 FALCON - .38 Super, .40 S&W, or .45 ACP cal., STi standard frame, 3.9 in. barrel, size is comparable to Officers Model, adj. rear sight. Limited mfg. 1993-98.

	$1,875	$1,375	$1,175	$925	$850	$775	$675

Last MSR was $2,136.

RANGER II (3.9 RANGER) - .45 ACP cal. only, Officer's Model with 3.9 (Ranger, disc. 2004) or 4.15 (Ranger II, new 2005) in. barrel and 1/2 in. shortened grip frame, 6 shot mag., blue steel frame with stainless steel slide, single stack mag., low mount STI/Heine sights, 29 oz. New 2001.

MSR $1,029	$885	$750	$640	$550	$450	$400	$350

3.9 STINGER - 9mm Para. or .38 Super cal., black frame, designed for IPSC and USUSA shooting, 38 oz. New 2005.

MSR $2,773	$2,500	$2,225	$1,975	$1,750	$1,575	$1,375	$1,150

3.9 V.I.P. - .45 ACP cal. only, aluminum frame, STi modular polymer grip, stainless steel slide, 3.9 in. barrel with STi Recoilmaster muzzlebrake, 10 shot double stack mag., STi fixed sights, 25 oz. New 2001.

MSR $1,653	$1,450	$1,275	$1,025	$950	$850	$750	$650

4.1 TACTICAL - 9mm Para., .40 S&W, or .45 ACP cal., blue steel, fixed sights, short trigger, ambidextrous safety, 34.5 oz. New 2004.

MSR $1,922	$1,725	$1,475	$1,250	$1,000	$875	$800	$675

GRADING - PPGS™	100%	98%	95%	90%	80%	70%	60%

4.3 HAWK - various cals., 4.3 in. barrel, STi standard frame (choice of steel or aluminum), 27 or 31 oz. Mfg. 1993-1999.

	$1,725	$1,275	$1,075	$875	$800	$700	$600

Last MSR was $1,975.

4.3 NIGHT HAWK - .45 ACP cal., 4.3 in. barrel, STi wide extended frame, blue finish, 33 oz. Limited mfg. 1997-99.

	$1,875	$1,375	$1,175	$925	$850	$775	$675

Last MSR was $2,136.

5.0 SPARROW - .22 LR cal. only, breech blow back mechanism, STi standard extended frame, 5.1 in. ramped bull barrel, fixed sights, blue finish, 30 oz. Limited mfg. 1998-99 only.

	$1,025	$900	$800	$700	$600	$500	$400

Last MSR was $1,090.

5.0 EDGE - 9mm Para., 10mm Norma, .40 S&W, or .45 ACP cal., designed for limited/standard IPSC competition, STi wide extended frame, wide body with stagger stack mag., blue finish, 39 oz. New 1998.

MSR $1,874	$1,650	$1,400	$1,200	$950	$850	$750	$625

5.0 DUTY ONE - 9mm Para., .40 S&W, or .45 ACP cal., ramped bull barrel, checkered wood grips, 38 oz. New 2005.

MSR $1,648	$1,450	$1,275	$1,025	$950	$850	$750	$650

5.0 EXECUTIVE - .40 S&W cal. only, STi long/wide frame, 10 shot double stack mag., stainless construction, grey nylon polymer grips and square triggerguard, hard chrome finish with black inlays, fiberoptic front and STi adj. rear sights, approved for IPSC standard and USPSA limited edition, 38 oz. New 2001.

MSR $2,389	$2,075	$1,775	$1,500	$1,300	$1,050	$900	$800

✳ **5.0 IPSC 30th Commemorative** - 9mm Para., .40 S&W, or .45 ACP cal., ramped bull barrel, two-tone hard chrome finish, special engraved slide with "IPSC 30th Anniversary" on side, 39 oz. New 2005.

MSR $2,775	$2,500	$2,225	$1,975	$1,750	$1,575	$1,375	$1,150

✳ **5.0 Special Edition** - 9mm Para., .40 S&W, or .45 ACP cal., ramped bull barrel, 24Kt. gold on all steel surfaces, checkered black grips, "Special Edition" engraved on slide, 39 oz. New 2005.

MSR $2,930	$2,625	$2,325	$2,000	$1,775	$1,600	$1,400	$1,200

5.0 TROJAN - 9mm Para., .40 S&W, .40 Super, or .45 ACP, standard Govt. length grips, single stack mag., 36 oz. New 1999.

MSR $1,024	$885	$750	$625	$550	$450	$400	$350

Add $288 for .40 Super with .45 ACP conversion kit.

5.0 RANGEMASTER - 9mm Para. or .45 ACP cal., black frame, ramped bull barrel, STI Recoilmaster guide rod, 38 oz. New 2005.

MSR $1,440	$1,275	$1,050	$875	$750	$625	$525	$475

5.0 EAGLE - various cals., 5.1 in. barrel, STi standard frame (choice of steel or aluminum) govt. model full-size, wide body with stagger stack mag., adj. rear sight, 31 or 35 oz.

MSR $1,794	$1,550	$1,325	$1,065	$850	$825	$725	$600

Add $266 for .40 Super with .45 ACP conversion kit.

5.0 TACTICAL - 9mm Para., .40 S&W, or .45 ACP cal., blue steel, fixed sights, short trigger, ambidextrous safety, 39 oz. New 2004.

MSR $1,922	$1,725	$1,475	$1,250	$1,000	$875	$800	$675

✳ **Tactical Lite** - similar to 5.0 Tactical, except stainless slide, alloy frame, fixed sights, 34.5 oz. New 2004.

MSR $2,002	$1,800	$1,525	$1,300	$1,050	$900	$825	$700

GRADING - PPGS™	100%	98%	95%	90%	80%	70%	60%

5.1 LIMITED - while advertised during 1998, this model never went into production.

Last MSR was $1,699.

5.5 EAGLE - various cals., features STi standard frame, 5 1/2 in. compensated barrel, 44 oz. Limited mfg. 1994-98.

	$2,100	$1,750	$1,475	$1,200	$995	$895	$775

Last MSR was $2,399.

5.5 TRUBOR COMPETITOR (COMPETITOR) - .38 Super cal. only, standard frame, classic slide with front and rear serrations, square hammer, compensator, double stack, match sear, STi "Alchin" style blast deflector mount, TruBor compensator became standard 2005, C-more rail scope, wide ambidextrous and grip safeties, 42.5 oz. New 1999.

MSR $2,639	$2,275	$1,925	$1,700	$1,450	$1,200	$995	$875.

5.5 GRANDMASTER - .38 Super cal. standard, custom order gun with any variety of options available, double stack mag., 42 oz. New 2001.

MSR $3,296	$2,995	$2,600	$2,250	$1,900	$1,650	$1,425	$1,200

6.0 HUNTER - 10mm cal. only, 6 in. barrel, STi super extended heavy frame with single stack mag., blue finish, 51 oz. Only 2 mfg. 1998, disc. 2000.

	$2,250	$1,875	$1,650	$1,425	$1,200	$995	$895

Last MSR was $2,485.

Add $350 for Leupold 2X scope with terminator mount.

6.0 EAGLE - various competition cals., features STi super extended heavy frame, 6 in. barrel, blue finish, wide body with stagger stack mag., 42 oz. New 1998.

MSR $1,894	$1,700	$1,450	$1,275	$1,025	$875	$800	$725

Add $267 for .40 Super with .45 ACP conversion kit.

6.0 TROJAN - similar to Trojan 5.0, except has 6 in. barrel and single stack mag., 36 oz. New 2000.

MSR $1,344	$1,150	$950	$825	$700	$575	$500	$450

Add $143 for .40 Super with .45 ACP conversion kit.

6.0 TARGETMASTER - 9mm Para. or .45 ACP cal., black frame, ramped bull barrel, two piece steel guide rod, 40 oz. New 2005.

MSR $1,440	$1,275	$1,050	$875	$750	$625	$525	$475

6.0 .450 XCALIBER - .450 cal., single stack mag., V-10 barrel and slide porting, stainless grip and thumb safeties, adj. rear sight. Limited mfg. 2000-2002.

	$1,000	$850	$750	$650	$525	$450	$395

Last MSR was $1,122.

6.0 .450+ XCALIBER - .450+ cal., otherwise similar to Xcaliber 6.0 .450, except has 6 in. frame with patented polymer grip and stagger stack mag. Limited mfg. 2000-2002.

	$1,775	$1,575	$1,350	$1,175	$995	$875	$775

Last MSR was $1,998.

RIFLES: SEMI-AUTO

STi 10/22 FORCE - .22 LR cal., aluminum receiver, 21 in. barrel, black synthetic Hogue stock, 7 lbs. New 2003.

MSR $1,050	$925	$800	$700	$600	$500	$400	$350

S.W.D., INC.

Previous manufacturer located in Atlanta, GA.

Similar models have previously been manufactured by R.P.B. Industries, Inc. (1979-82), and met with BATF disapproval because of convertibility into fully automatic operation. "Cobray" is a trademark for the M11/9 semiautomatic pistol.

GRADING - PPGS™	100%	98%	95%	90%	80%	70%	60%

CARBINES

SEMI-AUTO CARBINE - 9mm Para. cal., same mechanism as M11, 16 1/4 in. shrouded barrel, telescoping stock.

	$550	$495	$450	$400	$325	$275	$235

PISTOLS: SEMI-AUTO

COBRAY M-11/NINE mm - 9mm Para. cal., fires from closed bolt, 3rd generation design, stamped steel frame, 32 shot mag., parkerized finish, similar in appearance to Ingram Mac 10.

	$350	$315	$235	$200	$175	$160	$150

This model was also available in a fully-auto variation, Class III transferable only.

REVOLVERS

LADIES HOME COMPANION - .45-70 Govt. cal., double action design utilizing spring wound 12 shot rotary mag., 12 in. barrel, steel barrel and frame, 9 lbs. 6 oz. Mfg. 1990-94.

	$650	$525	$400	$360	$335	$310	$290

SHOTGUNS: SINGLE SHOT

TERMINATOR - 12 or 20 ga., paramilitary design shotgun with 18 in. cylinder bore barrel, parkerized finish, ejector. Mfg. 1986-88 only.

	$95	$80	$70	$60	$55	$50	$45

Last MSR was $110.

SABATTI s.p.a.

Current manufacturer located in Gardone, Italy with history tracing back to 1674. No current U.S. importation. Previous limited importation by European American Armory located in Sharpes, FL.

In 1960, the sons of Antonio Sabatti formed the current company, and manufacture currently includes good quality O/U and SxS shotguns, O/U combination and double rifles, bolt action and semi-auto rifles, and slide action and single shot shotguns. Sabatti should be contacted directly (see Trademark Index) regarding more information and domestic availability on their extensive firearms lineup.

SABRE

Current trademark of shotguns imported by Mitchell's Mausers, located in Fountain Valley, CA.

SHOTGUNS: SEMI-AUTO

SABRE - 12 ga. only, gas operated, 18 1/2 (w/o VR), 22, or 28 in. VR barrel with choke tubes, choice of black fiberglass or checkered walnut stock and forearm, configurations include Hunting, Turkey, Deer Hunter, and Police, mfg. in Turkey.

MSR $495		$435	$375	$325	$275	$235	$210	$190

Add $55 for Police model.

SABRE DEFENCE INDUSTRIES LLC.

Current manufacturer located in Nashville, TN.

RIFLES: SEMI-AUTO

Sabre Defence Industries manufactures 16 variations of the AR-15 paramilitary design rifle for civilians, law enforcement, and military. Please contact the company directly for more information, including civilian models and current pricing (see Trademark Index).

SACO DEFENSE INC.

Previous firearms manufacturer located in Saco, ME. Saco Defense was purchased by General Dynamics in July of 2000, and continues to produce guns for military defense contracts. This company was previously owned by Colt's Manufacturing Company, Inc. during late 1998-2000.

In the past, Saco Defense utilized their high-tech manufacturing facility to produce guns for Magnum Research, Weatherby (contract ended Sept., 2001), and others.

SAFARI ARMS

Previous trademark manufactured in Olympia, WA. M-S Safari Arms was started in 1978 as a division of M-S Safari Outfitters. In 1987, Safari Arms was absorbed by Olympic Arms. Safari Arms manufactured 1911 style pistols since the acquisition of M-S Safari Arms in 1987.

In Jan. 2004, the Safari Arms name was discontinued and all 1911 style pistols are now being manufactured by Olympic Arms. Please refer to the Olympic Arms section for currently manufactured models.

Safari Arms previously made the Phoenix, Special Forces, Camp Perry, and Royal Order of Jesters commemoratives in various configurations and quantities. Prices average in the $1,500 range except for the Royal Order of Jesters ($2,000).

Schuetzen Pistol Works

Schuetzen Pistol Works is the current custom shop of Olympic Arms. Some of the pistols made by Safari Arms had the "Schuetzen Pistol Works" name on them (c. 1994-96). Until Jan. 2004, all pistols were are marked with the Safari Arms slide marking. All pistols, however, have been marked "Safari Arms" on the frame. The pistols formerly in this section have been moved to the PISTOLS: SEMI-AUTO category.

PISTOLS: SEMI-AUTO

Safari Arms manufactured mostly single action, semi-auto pistols derived from the Browning M1911 design with modifications. Please refer to Olympic Arms listing for currently manufactured pistols.

GI SAFARI - .45 ACP cal., patterned after the Colt Model 1911, Safari frame, beavertail grip safety and commander hammer, parkerized matte black finish, 39.9 oz. Mfg. 1991-2000.

$500	$455	$395	$350	$295	$275	$250

Last MSR was $550.

CARRYCOMP - similar to MatchMaster, except utilizes W. Schuemann designed hybrid compensator system, 5 in. barrel, available in stainless steel or steel, 38 oz. Mfg. 1993-99.

$1,030	$875	$750	$600	$500	$425	$375

Last MSR was $1,160.

✳ Enforcer CarryComp - similar to Enforcer, except utilizes W. Schuemann designed hybrid compensator system, available in stainless steel or steel, 36 oz. Mfg. 1993-96.

$1,175	$1,025	$875	$750	$600	$500	$425

Last MSR was $1,300.

CARRIER - .45 ACP cal. only, reproduction of the original Detonics ScoreMaster, except has upgraded sights, custom made by Richard Niemer from the Custom Shop. New 1999-2001.

$750	$625	$575	$500	$450	$400	$350

Last MSR was $750.

GRADING - PPGS™	100%	98%	95%	90%	80%	70%	60%

RENEGADE - .45 ACP cal., left-hand action (port on left side), 4 1/2 (4-star, disc. 1996) or 5 (new 1994) in. barrel, 6 shot mag., adj. sights, stainless steel construction, 36-39 oz. Mfg. 1993-98.

	$955	$800	$700	$600	$525	$450	$395

Last MSR was $1,085.

Add $50 for 4-star (4 1/2 in. barrel, disc.).

RELIABLE - similar to Renegade, except has right-hand action. Mfg. 1993-98.

	$730	$620	$525	$450	$425	$400	$375

Last MSR was $825.

Add $60 for 4-star (4 1/2 in. barrel, disc.).

GRIFFON PISTOL - .45 ACP cal., 5 in. stainless steel barrel, 10 shot mag., standard govt. size with beavertail grip safety, full-length recoil spring guide, commander style hammer, smooth walnut grips, 40 1/2 oz. Disc. 1998.

	$855	$725	$650	$575	$500	$450	$395

Last MSR was $920.

BLACK WIDOW - .45 ACP cal., 3.9 in. barrel, hand contoured front gripstrap, schrimshawed ivory Micarta grips with Black Widow emblem, 6 shot mag., 27 oz. Inventory was depleted 1988.

	$565	$510	$460	$430	$400	$375	$350

Last MSR was $595.

BILL OF RIGHTS BICENTENNIAL MATCHED SET - includes the MatchMaster Pistol and ServiceMatch Rifle, features beryllium receivers and special engraving. Disc.

	$8,950	$6,500	$4,750

Last MSR was $7,400.

PARTNER - .22 LR cal., formerly the Whitney Wolverine, 8 shot mag., black plastic grips, non-adj. sights. Advertised beginning late 1997.

While advertised since 1997, this gun was not manufactured commercially.

MODEL 81 TARGET PISTOL - .38 Spl. or .45 ACP cal., 5 in. barrel, hand contoured front gripstrap, 2 lbs. 10 oz. Disc. 1987.

	$775	$695	$550	$440	$410	$375	$350

Last MSR was $875.

Add $50 for Deluxe Model (with Herrett adj. grips).

* *Model 81L* - .38 Spl. or .45 ACP, 6 in. barrel, 2 lbs. 13 oz. Disc. 1987.

	$850	$775	$695	$550	$440	$410	$375

Last MSR was $975.

Add $50 for Deluxe Model (with Herrett adj. grips).

* *Model 81 NM* - .38 Spl. or .45 ACP cal., similar frame as Model 81, except has flat front gripstrap, 5 in. barrel, 2 lbs. 5 oz. Disc. 1987.

	$775	$695	$550	$440	$410	$375	$350

Last MSR was $875.

* *Model 81BP* - .38 Spl. or .45 ACP cal., 6 in barrel, contoured front gripstrap, faster cycle time, 2 lbs. 9 oz. Disc. 1987.

	$875	$775	$695	$550	$440	$410	$375

Last MSR was $995.

* *Silueta* - .45 ACP or .38/.45 Wildcat cal., 10 in. extended barrel, designed for silhouette shooting, 2 lbs. 14 oz. Disc. 1987.

	$875	$775	$695	$550	$440	$410	$375

Last MSR was $1,050.

GRADING - PPGS™	100%	98%	95%	90%	80%	70%	60%

PISTOLS: SINGLE SHOT

ULTIMATE/UNLIMITED - various cals., bolt action target pistol, 14 15/16 in. barrel, black finished metal, laminated stock. Disc. 1987.

	100%	98%	95%	90%	80%	70%	60%
	$850	$775	$695	$550	$440	$410	$375

Last MSR was $975.

SAFARI CLUB INTERNATIONAL

SCI is an international hunting and conservation organization with headquarters located in Tucson, AZ.

Although Safari Club International (SCI) is not a manufacturer or importer, this organization is responsible for special and limited editions similar to the one listed. Additionally, SCI also has one custom-built rifle manufactured for each annual SCI convention with an auction determining the price of the rifle.

Manufacturer	Model	Quantity	Year	Issue Price
SPECIAL/LIMITED EDITIONS				
Winchester	Super Grade 25th Anniversary	200	1997	$1,395

SAIGA

Current trademark manufactured by Izhmash, located in Izhevsk, Russia. No current U.S. importation. Previously imported by European American Armory Corp., located in Sharpes, FL.

GRADING - PPGS™	100%	98%	95%	90%	80%	70%	60%

RIFLES: SEMI-AUTO

SAIGA RIFLE - .223 Rem. or .308 Win. cal., Kalashnikov type action, black synthetic or hardwood (new 2003, only available in .308 Win. cal.) stock and forearm, 16.3-22 in. barrel length, matte black metal, 7-8 1/2 lbs. Imported 2002-2004.

	100%	98%	95%	90%	80%	70%	60%
	$275	$230	$200	$180	$160	$140	$120

Last MSR was $329.

    Add $20 for .308 Win. cal.
    Add $40 for wood stock.

* *Saiga Rifle 7.62x39mm Cal.* - 7.62x39mm cal., 16.3 or 20 1/2 in barrel, otherwise similar to Saiga Rifle. Imported 2002-2004.

	$240	$210	$190	$170	$150	$130	$120

Last MSR was $299.

SHOTGUNS: SEMI-AUTO

SAIGA SHOTGUN - 12 or 20 ga., 3 in. chamber, 5 shot detachable box mag., Kalashnikov type action, black synthetic stock and forearm, 19-22 in. barrel length, matte black metal, 6.7-7.8 lbs. Imported 2002-2004.

	$340	$300	$275	$260	$245	$230	$215

Last MSR was $389.

    Add $20 for 12 ga.
    Add $40 for choke tubes (12 ga. only).

* *Saiga Shotgun .410 Bore* - .410 bore, 19 or 21 in barrel, 4 shot detachable box mag., otherwise similar to Saiga Shotgun, approx. 6.6 lbs. Imported 2002-2004.

	$240	$210	$190	$170	$150	$130	$120

Last MSR was $299.

GRADING - PPGS™	100%	98%	95%	90%	80%	70%	60%

SAKO, LTD.

Current rifle manufacturer established circa 1921 and located in Riihimäki, Finland. Current models are presently being imported by Beretta USA, located in Accockeek, MD. Previously imported by Stoeger Industries, Inc. located in Wayne, NJ, Garcia, and Rymac.

During 2000, Sako, Ltd. was purchased by Beretta Holding of Italy. All currently produced Sakos are imported by Beretta USA Corp. located in Accokeek, MD.

Beginning 2000, most Sako rifles (except the Action I in .223 Rem. cal.) are shipped with a Key Concept locking device. This patented system uses a separate key to activate an almost invisible lock which totally blocks the firing pin and prevents bolt movement.

PISTOLS: SEMI-AUTO

Less than 200 Triace pistols were imported into the United States.

TRIACE - .22 Short, .22 LR, or .32 S&W Wadcutter cal., target pistol incorporating unique action, competition walnut grips with thumbrest and adj. heel, blue finish with chrome accents. Imported 1985-86 only.

$1,300	$1,150	$950	$825	$700	$600	$500

Last MSR was $1,395.

✳ *Triace Pistol Kit* - consists of Triace frame, .22 Short, .22 LR, and .32 S&W barrels. Cased with accessories. Imported 1985-86 only.

$2,500	$2,200	$2,000	$1,500	$1,300	$1,175	$1,025

Last MSR was $2,385.

RIFLES: BOLT ACTION, DISC.

Add 10%-15% for popular Mag. cals. on rifles listed.
Note: Prices are for pre-1972 Sako rifles, unless stated otherwise. Pre-1972 Sakos utilize the L-46, L-461, L-579, L-57, and L-61 R actions.
Subtract approx. 25% for post-1972 models.

DELUXE - various cals., Monte Carlo stock, skipline checkering, long, medium, or short actions, contrasting pistol grip cap and forend tip, engraved floorplate.

$1,045	$925	$775	$625	$450	$425	$385

STANDARD SPORTER - long, medium, and short actions.

$850	$725	$625	$500	$450	$410	$375

HEAVY BARREL MODEL - long, medium, and short actions.

$850	$725	$625	$500	$450	$410	$375

FULL STOCK MODELS - 20 in. carbine barrel (all actions), 23 1/2 in. barrel on rifle (short & medium actions).

✳ *Finnbear* - long action.

$1,100	$975	$800	$725	$550	$475	$425

✳ *Forester* - medium action.

$1,050	$925	$775	$700	$525	$450	$400

✳ *Vixen* - short action.

$1,050	$925	$775	$700	$525	$450	$400

L-46 action pre-Vixen Sakos had detachable mags.

MAUSER ACTION (FN) - .270 Win. or .30-06 cal., long action. Mfg. 1950-57.

$695	$500	$400	$345	$310	$280	$260

MAGNUM MAUSER (FN) - 8x60S, 8.2x57mm, .300 H&H, or .375 H&H cal.

$745	$635	$580	$495	$450	$410	$375

GRADING - PPGS™	100%	98%	95%	90%	80%	70%	60%

MODEL 74 - various cals.

	$650	$575	$450	$375	$340	$320	$290

MODEL 78 - .22 LR, .22 Mag., or .22 Hornet cal., detachable mag., same size as short action Standard Model. Importation disc. 1986.

	$480	$395	$340	$310	$280	$265	$250

Last MSR was $647.

Add $30 for .22 Hornet cal.

FINNSPORT MODEL 2700 - available in long (AIII) action only, .270 Win., .300 Win. Mag. cals., select checkered walnut. Disc. 1985.

	$750	$675	$600	$560	$510	$475	$430

Last MSR was $910.

FINNWOLF - .243 Win. or .308 Win. cal., lever action, 4 shot mag. early model, 3 shot mag. later model. Mfg. 1962-74.

	$895	$775	$550	$500	$440	$410	$375

Add 15% for early model with 4 shot mag.

* **Finnwolf Sako Collectors Association** - .243 Win. or .308 Win. cal., gold lettering on left side of breech, approx. 175 mfg. in 1982.

	$2,995	$1,750	$1,050

The 100% value on this model refers to NIB unfired condition with factory papers.

ANNIVERSARY MODEL - 7mm Rem. Mag. cal. only, 1,000 mfg.

	$2,750	$1,625	$975

The 100% value on this model refers to NIB unfired condition with factory papers.

RIFLES: BOLT ACTION, RECENT PRODUCTION

Beginning late 2001, Sako established a custom shop, which allows the consumer to select from a wide variety of finishes, options, and special orders, including individual stock dimensions. Please contact Beretta USA for more information regarding the Sako custom shop.

All Sako left-handed models are available in medium or long action only.

During 2003-2004, about three thousand rifles sold under the Sako label were recalled following catastrophic failures, but a small number remain in the hands of American consumers who have not heard about the recall. A weakness in the stainless steel used to manufacture the rifles has led to ruptured barrels. Consumers are asked to contact the Sako Recall Center at 800-503-8869 with your rifle's serial number to find out if your firearm is affected.

FINNFIRE - .22 LR cal., 22 in. regular or heavy (new 1996) or 23 (Sporter/Varmint and Target) in. cold-hammer forged free-floating barrel, single stage adj. trigger, 50 degree bolt lift, 2 position safety, European walnut pistol grip or adj. Target competition (new 2003) stock, cocking indicator, available in Hunter, Target (new 2003)/Sporter (new 1999), or Varmint configuration, 5 or 10 shot mag., integral 11mm dovetail (for scope mounting), with (new 1996) or w/o open sights, 5.75 (Target/Sporter) lbs. Importation began 1994.

MSR $1,044	$850	$725	$625	$525	$450	$400	$350

Add $45 for Varmint Model with heavy barrel.

Add $125 for Target/Sporter Model with 10 shot mag. and adj. competition stock.

QUAD - .17 HMR, .17 Mach 2, .22 LR, or .22 Mag. cal., 22 in. barrel. New 2005.

MSR $948	$775	$675	$575	$500	$425	$375	$325

* **Quad Combo** - includes four rimfire barrels in cals. .17 HMR, .17 Mach 2, .22 LR, or .22 Mag. New 2005.

MSR $1,739	$1,475	$1,200	$975	$850	$775	$700	$625

GRADING - PPGS™	100%	98%	95%	90%	80%	70%	60%

HUNTER LIGHTWEIGHT RIFLE - available in short action (AI) in .17 Rem., .222 Rem., or .223 Rem. cal., medium action (AII) in .22-250 Rem., .243 Win., .308 Win., or 7mm-08 Rem. cal., or long action (AIII) in .25-06 Rem., .270 Win., .280 Rem., .30 - 06, .270 Wby. Mag. (disc. 1996), 7mm Wby. Mag. (disc. 1996), 7mm Rem. Mag., .300 Win. Mag., .300 Wby. Mag., .338 Win. Mag., .340 Wby. Mag. (disc. 1996), .375 H&H, or .416 Rem. Mag. (new 1991) cal., 21 1/4, 21 3/4, or 22 in. barrel, classic styled stock with choice of oil (disc. 1996) or matte lacquer finish, finely checkered French walnut. Disc. 1997.

	$850	$685	$550	$490	$460	$430	$410

Last MSR was $1,050.

> Add $35 for long action.
>
> Add $50-$70 for Mag. cals.
>
> Add approx. $80 for left-hand action (available in all Mag. cals. - mfg. 1994-96).

> ✴ *Hunter Carbine (Handy)* - available in medium action in .22-250 Rem. (disc. 1990), .243 Win. (new 1991), .308 Win. (new 1991) cal. or long action in .25-06 Rem. (disc. 1990), 7mm Rem. Mag. (disc. 1990), .338 Win. Mag. cal., or .375 H&H (new 1990) cal., 18 1/2 in. barrel with iron sights, oil or lacquer finished deluxe walnut stock with checkering, approx. 7 lbs. Mfg. 1986-91.

	$725	$650	$600	$490	$460	$430	$410

Last MSR was $945.

> Add $50-$65 for long action (Mag. cals.).

FINNLIGHT - .243 Win., .25-06 Rem., .270 Win., .270 WSM (new 2004), .280 Rem., .30-06, .308 Win., .300 Win. Mag., .300 WSM (new 2003) 6.5x55mm, 7mm-08 Rem., 7mm WSM (new 2005) or 7mm Rem. Mag. cal., stainless steel action with four sizes, 20 1/4, 20 7/8 or 24 3/8 in. stainless steel free-floating fluted barrel, alloy triggerguard/mag. bottom, black synthetic stock, 4 or 5 shot detachable mag., no sights, 6.5 lbs. Importation began 2001.

MSR $1,584		$1,275	$950	$750			

LONG RANGE HUNTING MODEL - available in long action in .25-06 Rem., .270 Win., .300 Win. Mag., or 7mm Rem. Mag. cal., 26 in. heavy barrel only w/o sights. Mfg. 1996-97.

	$1,030	$785	$625	$545	$495	$465	$440

Last MSR was $1,275.

> Add $15 for Mag. cals.

FIBERCLASS MODEL - available in medium action (disc. 1992) in .22-250 Rem., .243 Win., .308 Win., or 7mm-08 cal., or long action in .25-06 Rem., .270 Win., .280 Rem., .30-06, 7mm Rem. Mag., .300 Win. Mag., .338 Win. Mag., .375 H&H, or .416 Rem. Mag. (new 1991) cal., has black fiberglass stock. Disc. 1996.

	$1,170	$930	$785	$725	$630	$560	$510

Last MSR was $1,388.

> Add $17-$37 for Mag. cals.
>
> Subtract $40 for medium action cals. (disc. 1992).
>
> Add $80 for left-hand action (disc. 1989).

> ✴ *FiberClass Carbine (Handy)* - available in medium action in .243 Win. or .308 Win. cal. and long action in .25-06 Rem. (disc.), .270 Win. (disc.), .30-06, 7mm Rem. Mag. (disc.), .300 Win. Mag. (disc.), .338 Win. Mag., or .375 H&H (new 1991) cal., 18 1/2 in. barrel with fiberglass stock. Mfg. 1986-91.

	$995	$895	$775	$725	$630	$560	$510

Last MSR was $1,239.

> Add $50-$65 for Mag. cals.

GRADING - PPGS™	100%	98%	95%	90%	80%	70%	60%

LAMINATED RIFLE - available in short action (disc. 1989), medium action in .22-250 Rem., .243 Win., .308 Win., or 7mm-08 Rem. cal., or long action in .25-06 Rem., .270 Win., .280 Rem., .30-06, 7mm Rem. Mag., .300 Win. Mag., .338 Win. Mag., .375 H&H, or .416 Rem. Mag. (new 1991) cal., features laminated wood stock. Mfg. 1988-95.

	$985	$790	$635	$550	$495	$460	$430

Last MSR was $1,200.

Add $35 for short action.
Add $55 for long action.
Add $75-$95 for Mag. cals.
Add approx. $100 for left-hand action (disc.).
The left-hand action was available in .270 Win., .280 Rem., .30-06, 7mm Rem. Mag., .300 Win. Mag., .338 Win. Mag., .375 H&H, or .416 Rem. Mag. cal.

MODEL TRG-21 - .308 Win. cal., bolt action, 25 3/4 in. barrel, new design features modular synthetic stock construction with adj. cheekpiece and buttplate, stainless steel barrel, cold hammer forged receiver, and resistance free bolt, 10 shot detachable mag., 10 1/2 lbs. Imported 1993-99.

	$2,300	$2,000	$1,800	$1,600	$1,400	$1,200	$975

Last MSR was $2,699.

MODEL TRG-22 - .308 Win. cal., bolt action, 26 in. barrel, updated TRG-21 design featuring adj. modular synthetic stock (green or all black) construction with adj. cheekpiece and buttplate, competition trigger, choice of blue (disc. 2002) or phosphate (new 2002) metal finish, stainless steel barrel, cold hammer forged receiver, and resistance free bolt, 10 shot detachable mag., approx. 10.25 lbs. Importation began 2000.

MSR $3,589	$2,950	$2,300	$1,925	$1,750	$1,500	$1,225	$875

Add $2,260 for folding stock.

MODEL TRG-41 - .338 Lapua Mag. cal., similar to Model TRG-21, except has long action and 27 1/8 in. barrel, 7 3/4 lbs. Imported 1994-99.

	$2,700	$2,425	$2,150	$1,850	$1,625	$1,400	$1,200

Last MSR was $3,099.

MODEL TRG-42 - .300 Win. Mag. or .338 Lapua Mag. cal., updated TRG-41 design featuring long action and 27 1/8 in. barrel, choice of black composite/blue finish or green composite/phosphate (new 2002) finish, 5 shot mag., 11.25 lbs. Importation began 2000.

MSR $3,589	$2,950	$2,300	$1,925	$1,750	$1,500	$1,225	$875

Add $410 for green stock with phosphate metal finish.

MODEL TRG-S - available in medium action (disc. 1993) in .243 Win. or 7mm-08 cal., or long action in .25-06 Rem. (Mfg. 1994-98), .270 Win. (disc. 2000), 6.5x55mm Swedish (disc. 1998), .30-06 (disc.), .308 Win. (disc. 1995), .270 Wby. Mag. (disc. 1998), 7mm Wby. Mag. (Mfg. 1998), 7mm Rem. Mag. (disc.), .300 Win. Mag. (disc.), .300 Wby. Mag. (mfg. 1994-99), .30-378 Wby. Mag. (new 1998, 26 in. barrel only), .338 Win. Mag. (disc. 1999), .338 Lapua Mag. (new 1994), .340 Wby. Mag. (disc. 1998), 7mm STW (26 in. barrel only, disc. 1999), .375 H&H (disc. 1998), or .416 Rem. Mag. (disc. 1998) cal., black synthetic stock, Sporter variation derived from the Model TRG - 21, 22 (disc.), 24 (Mag. cals. only, disc.), or 26 in. barrel, 3 or 5 shot detachable mag., fully adj. trigger, 60 degree bolt-lift, matte finish, 8 1/8 lbs. Imported 1993-2004.

	$765	$615	$525	$475	$440	$415	$380

Last MSR was $896.

GRADING - PPGS™	100%	98%	95%	90%	80%	70%	60%

MANNLICHER CARBINE - available in short action (disc. 1989), medium action in .243 Win. or .308 Win. cal., or long action in .25-06 Rem. (disc. 1991), .270 Win., .30 - 06, 7mm Rem. Mag. (disc. 1991), .300 Win. Mag. (disc. 1991), .338 Win. Mag., or .375 H&H cal., 18 1/2 in. barrel, two-piece full Mannlicher style stock, open sights. Disc. 1996.

	$1,030	$785	$625	$545	$495	$465	$440

Last MSR was $1,275.

Add $35 for long action.
Add $60-$75 for Mag. cals.

PPC MODEL - 22 PPC or 6 mm PPC cal., 21 3/4 or 23 3/4 (Benchrest Model) in. barrel, single shot in Benchrest Model, 4 shot mag. in Hunter or Deluxe Model, checkered walnut stock, Deluxe Model has rosewood pistol grip and forearm caps plus skip line checkering, matte lacquer finish on Hunter and Deluxe, oiled finish on Benchrest, 6 1/4 or 8 3/4 (Benchrest Model with heavy barrel) lbs. Imported 1989-97.

	$1,250	$950	$750	$650	$600	$540	$500

Last MSR was $1,535.

Add $320 for Deluxe Hunter Model (disc. 1993).
Add $85 for Benchrest Model (disc. 1993).

VARMINT RIFLE - available in short action (AI) in .17 Rem., .222 Rem., or .223 Rem., and medium action (AII) .22-250 Rem., .243 Win., .308 Win., or 7mm-08 cal., 22 3/4 in. heavy barrel, no sights. Disc. 1997.

	$1,025	$795	$615	$545	$475	$430	$400

Last MSR was $1,240.

CLASSIC GRADE - .243 Win., .270 Win., .30-06, or 7mm Rem. Mag. cal., short (AI, disc. 1992), medium (AII), or long (AIII) action, classic styled stock, finely checkered French walnut with matte lacquer finish. Disc. 1985, reintroduced 1992-97.

	$895	$745	$600	$545	$475	$430	$400

Last MSR was $1,050.

Add $50 for Mag. cal.
Add $35 for long action.
Add $120-$135 for left-hand action (disc. 1994) (.270 Win. or 7mm Rem. Mag cal. only).

In 1992, the Classic Grade was once again imported into the U.S. in .243 Win., .270 Win., .30-06, or 7mm Rem. Mag. cal.

DELUXE LIGHTWEIGHT RIFLE - available in short action (AI) in .17 Rem., .222 Rem., or .223 Rem. cal., medium action (AII) in .22-250 Rem., .243 Win., .308 Win., or 7mm-08 Rem. cal., or long action (AIII) in .25-06 Rem., .270 Win., .280 Rem., .30 - 06, 7mm Rem. Mag., .300 Win. Mag., .300 Wby. Mag., .338 Win. Mag., .375 H&H, or .416 Rem. Mag. (new 1991) cal., 21 1/4, 21 3/4, or 22 in. barrel, deluxe quality skipline checkered walnut stock with rosewood forend tip. Disc. 1997.

	$1,185	$965	$750	$650	$595	$540	$500

Last MSR was $1,475.

Add $35 for long action.
Add $50-$70 for Mag. cals.
Add $150-$175 for left-hand action (disc. 1994, available in long action only).

SAFARI GRADE - available in long (AIII) action only, .300 Win. Mag. (disc. 1989), .338 Win. Mag., .375 H&H, or .416 Rem. Mag. (new 1991) cal., deluxe walnut with sculptured cheekpiece, 22 in. barrel, 4 shot mag., open sights, sling swivels. Disc. 1996.

	$2,235	$1,785	$1,475	$1,250	$1,050	$900	$795

Last MSR was $2,765.

GRADING - PPGS™	100%	98%	95%	90%	80%	70%	60%

SUPER DELUXE - a limited edition rifle available on special order only, various cals. are available in the short (AI), medium (AII), and long (AIII) actions, presentation grade walnut with both checkering and carving, rosewood forend tip. Disc. 1997.

	100%	98%	95%	90%	80%	70%	60%
	$2,400	$1,825	$1,475	$1,250	$1,050	$900	$795

Last MSR was $3,100.

SAKO 75 HUNTER - available in 5 action sizes, .17 Rem. (mfg. 1998-2002), .222 Rem. (mfg. 1998-2002), .223 Rem. (new 1998), .22-250 Rem., .243 Win., .308 Win., 7mm-08 Rem., .25-06 Rem., .260 Rem. (new 2005), .270 Win., .270 WSM (new 2004), .280 Rem. (disc. 2004), .30-06, .270 Wby. Mag. (disc. 2001), 6.5x55mm (new 2005), 7mm Rem. Ultra Mag. (mfg. 2002-2003), 7mm Wby. Mag. (disc. 2003), 7mm STW (disc. 2003), 7mm WSM (new 2005), 7mm Rem. Mag., .300 WSM (new 2004), .300 Win. Mag., .300 Wby. Mag. (disc. 2003), .300 Rem. Ultra Mag. (mfg. 2000-2003), .338 Win. Mag., .340 Wby. Mag. (disc. 2003), .375 H&H, or .416 Rem. Mag. (disc. 2001) cal., hammer forged 22-24 3/8 in. barrel, utilizes 3 locking lugs, mechanical ejector, 5 bolt sliding guides with 70 degree bolt lift, 3-position rear tang safety, available with top loading fixed mag. (hinged floorplate, .300 Rem. Ultra Mag., .416 Rem. Mag., and 7mm Rem. Ultra mag. cals. only), or detachable staggered 4-6 shot mag., checkered walnut stock, no sights, approx. 7.75 lbs. New 1997.

MSR $1,419	$1,150	$900	$725	$625	$550	$500	$450

Add $80 for .375 H&H cal.

This model is also available in left-hand action in .25-06 Rem., .270 Win., or .30-06 cal. at no extra charge.

✷ *Sako 75 Deluxe* - similar cals. as Sako 75 Hunter, features hinged floorplate and deluxe walnut stock with gloss finish, skipline checkering, and rosewood forend and pistol grip caps, custom stock bedding and iron sights available on .375 H&H or .416 Rem. Mag. cals., approx. 7.75 lbs. New 1997.

MSR $2,044	$1,700	$1,450	$1,200	$925	$750	$625	$550

Add $374 for .416 Rem. Mag.

✷ *Sako 75 Stainless Synthetic* - available in .22-250 Rem., .243 Win., .25-06 Rem., .260 Rem. (new 2005), .270 Win., .270 WSM (new 2004), .30-06, .308 Win., .300 Win. Mag., .300 Wby. Mag. (mfg. 1999-2003), .300 WSM (new 2004), .300 Rem. Ultra Mag. (mfg. 2000-2003), 7mm-08 Rem. (new 1998), 7mm STW (mfg. 1998-2003), 7mm Rem. Mag., 7mm Rem. Ultra Mag. (mfg. 2002-2003), .338 Win. Mag., or .375 H&H cal., 3-4 shot detachable mag. (except for floorplate with Rem. Ultra Mag. cals.), features black composite stock with soft rubber grip inserts in pistol grip and forearm area, matte stainless steel metal, 7.75 lbs. New 1997.

MSR $1,499	$1,195	$925	$750				

✷ *Sako 75 Stainless Walnut* - .270 Win., .30-06, .300 Win. Mag., .300 Wby. Mag., .338 Win. Mag., 7mm STW, or 7mm Rem. Mag. cal., features checkered walnut stock and forearm. Imported 1999-2002.

		$1,050	$840	$685			

Last MSR was $1,239.

Add $35 for Mag. cals.

✷ *Sako 75 Greywolf* - .22-250 Rem., .223 Rem., .243 Win., .25-06 Rem., .260 Rem., .270 Win., .30-06, .308 Win., .270 WSM, .300 WSM, 7mm WSM, or 7mm-08 Rem., available in 4 frame sizes and 3 barrel lengths. New 2005.

MSR $1,549	$1,225	$925	$800	$700	$600	$525	$450

✷ *Sako 75 Varmint* - .17 Rem. (disc. 2003), .22-250 Rem., .222 Rem. (disc. 2002), .223 Rem., 22PPC (mfg. 1999-2003), or 6mmPPC (mfg. 1999-2003) cal., 23 5/8 in. heavy barrel w/o sights and beavertail forend, 5 or 6 shot detachable mag., 8 5/8 lbs. New 1998.

MSR $1,628	$1,400	$1,000	$850	$725	$650	$575	$500

GRADING - PPGS™	100%	98%	95%	90%	80%	70%	60%

✳ *Sako 75 Varmint w/ Set Trigger* - similar to Sako 75 Varmint, except is also available in .204 Ruger, .243 Win., .260 Rem. or .308 Win. cal., set trigger. New 2005.

MSR $1,864	$1,575	$1,275	$975	$800	$700	$600	$500

✳ *Sako 75 Stainless Varmint Laminated* - .22-250 Rem., .222 Rem. (disc. 2002), .223 Rem., 22PPC (disc. 2003), 6mmPPC (disc. 2003), or 7mm-08 Rem. (new 2002), similar to Sako 75 Varmint, features stainless steel action and barrel, brown laminated wood stock, 9 lbs. New 1999.

MSR $1,794	$1,475	$1,175	$875

✳ *Sako 75 Stainless Varmint Laminated w/ Set Trigger* - similar to Sako 75 Stainless Varmint Laminated, except is also available in .204 Ruger, .243 Win., .260 Rem. or .308 Win. cal., set trigger. New 2005.

MSR $1,959	$1,675	$1,375	$1,025	$850	$725	$600	$500

✳ *Sako 75 Custom Deluxe* - .270 Win. or .30-06 cal., extra grade deluxe oil finished walnut stock with rosewood forend tip and pistol grip cap, 7.75 lbs. Importation began late 2003.

MSR $4,344	$3,750	$3,250	$2,575	$2,175	$1,850	$1,550	$1,350

This model is available through Sako showcase dealers only.

✳ *Sako 75 Single Shot* - .22-250 Rem., .243 Win., 7mm-08 Rem., 6mmPPC, .308 Win. cal., medium III action, stainless steel action and barrel, heavy free floating fluted barrel w/o sights, 9 lbs. New 2004.

MSR $3,448	$2,850	$2,375	$2,125	$1,850	$1,550	$1,350	$1,150

✳ *Sako 75 80th Anniversary Model* - .375 H&H cal., limited edition rifle featuring Mauser style claw extractor, premium grade checkered walnut with ebony forend tip, cold hammer forged match grade barrel has 1/4 rib with open sights, 5 shot internal mag. with hinged floorplate, includes Swarovski PV-1 scope and case, only 80 rifles (serial numbered 200101-200180) mfg. beginning 2001.

MSR $20,038	$16,500	$14,000	$11,000	$9,000

✳ *Sako 75 Super Deluxe* - a limited edition rifle available on special order only, presentation grade walnut with both checkering and carving, rosewood forend tip.

Please contact Beretta USA Corp. directly for a price quotation on this special order model.

SALERI, W.R. di SALERI WILLIAM & C. snc

Current longun manufacturer established in 1998 located in Gardone, Italy. Currently imported by MacGregor Wing and Clay, located in Cary, North Carolina. Previously imported by S.R. Lamboy, located in Victor, NY.

W.R. Saleri manufactures high quality boxlock O/U shotguns (Continental model, in both a standard and round scalloped frame with detachable locks) and single barrel rifles (Viper model). Please contact the importer directly for more information, including pricing and availability (see Trademark Index).

SAMCO GLOBAL ARMS, INC.

Current importer and distributor located in Miami, FL. Dealer sales.

Samco Global Arms currently imports a variety of foreign and domestic surplus military rifles (including various contract Mausers, Loewe, Steyr, Czech, Lee Enfield, etc.). Most of these guns are in the $95-$1,500 range and they offer excellent values to both shooters and collectors. Samco also sold newly remanufactured sporting rifles (German or Spanish) in .308 Win. or 7x57mm cal. These sporters ranged in value from approx. $225-$325. During 2000, Samco also received some older Schmidt-Rubin carbines and rifles chambered in 7.5mm Swiss (Model 11 cartridge) - these are valued in the $200-$575 range, depending on configuration and condition.

GRADING - PPGS™	100%	98%	95%	90%	80%	70%	60%

SAN SWISS ARMS AG

Current company established during late 2000, with headquarters located in Neuhausen, Switzerland. SAN Swiss firearms/trademarks are currently imported into the U.S. by SIG Arms, except for B.R. Rizzini.

**swiss
arms**
SAN Swiss Arms AG

During the end of 2000, SIG Arms AG was purchased by SAN Swiss Arms AG, a newly formed company. Unchanged are the 140 years of expertise in the development and manufacture of firearms for the military, law enforcement, and civilian market. Also firmly in place is the group of companies that represent numerous renowned brands and products. This new group currently includes six independently operational companies – Blaser Jadgwaffen GmbH located in Isny, Germany, Hämmerli AG located in Lenzburg, Switzerland, B.R. Rizzini (acquired in 2002), J.P. Sauer & Sohn GmbH located in Eckernförde, Germany, SIG Arms, Inc. (U.S.A.) located in Exeter, NH, and SAN Swiss Arms AG, located in Neuhausen, Switzerland. Current trademarks include: Aurora shotguns (mfg. by B. Rizzini), Blaser, Hämmerli, Mauser Magnum rifles (current mfg. by Blaser), B.R. Rizzini, Sauer rifles, and Sig-Sauer pistols. Please refer to these individual listings for current information and pricing.

SARASQUETA, FELIX

Previous manufacturer located in Eibar, Spain. Previously imported and distributed by SAE (Spain America Enterprises), Inc. located in Miami, FL.

SHOTGUNS: O/U

MODEL MERKE - 12 ga. only, boxlock action, 22 or 27 in. separated barrels, single non-selective trigger, blue only, extractors, recoil pad. Imported 1986 only.

$255	$215	$200	$190	$180	$170	$160

Last MSR was $291.

SARASQUETA, J.J.

Previous manufacturer located in Eibar, Spain. Imported until 1984 by American Arms, Inc. located in Overland Park, KS.

SHOTGUNS: SxS

MODEL 107 E - 12, 16, or 20 ga., ejectors, various barrel lengths, checkered walnut stock and forearm, double triggers.

$360	$290	$270	$255	$240	$215	$200

Last MSR was $435.

MODELS 119E-132E-1882E - more deluxe versions of Model 107E.

$470	$375	$340	$315	$285	$255	$230

Last MSR was $570.

MODEL 130 E - more deluxe version of Model 119 E.

$800	$635	$590	$555	$515	$480	$450

Last MSR was $960.

MODEL 131 E - action similar to Model 107 E, except has deluxe engraving.

$1,050	$845	$770	$710	$665	$620	$585

Last MSR was $1,250.

MODEL 1882 E LUXE - double triggers, moderate engraving, otherwise similar to Model 107 E.

$825	$660	$615	$565	$520	$480	$450

Last MSR was $990.

✱ **Model 1882 E Luxe w/ gold inlays** - SST, extensive engraving.

$1,120	$920	$850	$790	$740	$695	$650

Last MSR was $1,320.

GRADING - PPGS™	100%	98%	95%	90%	80%	70%	60%

✳ *Model 1882 E Luxe w/silver inlays* - SST, extensive engraving.

	100%	98%	95%	90%	80%	70%	60%
	$1,055	$855	$795	$740	$700	$660	$630

Last MSR was $1,260.

MODEL 150 E - 12 or 16 ga., single trigger, ejectors, select walnut and extensive engraving.

	$1,285	$1,035	$960	$895	$835	$770	$695

Last MSR was $1,500.

✳ *Model 150 E Trap* - similar to Model 150 E, except trap dimensions on stock.

	$1,360	$1,125	$1,010	$940	$875	$790	$720

Last MSR was $1,600.

SARASQUETA, VICTOR

Previous manufacturer located in Eibar, Spain. Trademark was sold to Diarm S.A. circa 1986.

SHOTGUNS:SxS

MODEL 3 BOXLOCK - 12, 16, or 20 ga., all standard barrel lengths and chokes, boxlock, double triggers, checkered English style stock and forearm.

	100%	98%	95%	90%	80%	70%	60%
Extractors	$445	$395	$350	$295	$250	$215	$185
Auto ejectors	$575	$515	$450	$375	$300	$250	$225

HAMMERLESS SIDELOCK - 12, 16, 20, 28 ga., or .410 bore, SxS, barrel length and choke to order, straight English style stock, models differ as to amount of engraving, grade of wood, and overall quality as follows:

> **Add 25% for 28 ga.**
> **Add 30% for .410 bore.**

MODEL 4 - extractors.

	$620	$550	$525	$495	$450	$415	$360

MODEL 4E - auto ejectors.

	$680	$605	$580	$550	$505	$470	$415

MODEL 203 - extractors.

	$650	$570	$545	$515	$475	$435	$380

MODEL 203E - auto ejectors.

	$710	$625	$600	$570	$530	$490	$435

MODEL 6E

	$800	$715	$690	$660	$615	$580	$525

MODEL 7E

	$855	$770	$745	$715	$670	$635	$580

MODEL 10E

	$1,735	$1,595	$1,485	$1,405	$1,320	$1,240	$1,100

MODEL 11E

	$1,870	$1,680	$1,595	$1,515	$1,430	$1,350	$1,265

MODEL 12E

	$2,145	$1,900	$1,790	$1,705	$1,570	$1,430	$1,375

SARDIUS

Please refer to the Sirkis Industries section in this text.

SARRIUGARTE, FRANCISO S.A.

Previous manufacturer located in Elgoibar, Spain. Previously part of the Diarm S.A. Group which was imported and distributed by American Arms, Inc. located in North Kansas City, MO.

SARSILMAZ

Current manufacturer established during 1880, and located in Istanbul, Turkey. Pistols currently imported by Adco Sales, located in Woburn, MA. Previously distributed 2000-2003 by PMC, located in Boulder City, NV. Previously imported and distributed until 2000 by Armsport, Inc. located in Miami, FL.

PISTOLS: SEMI-AUTO

Sarsilmaz offers a wide range of semi-auto pistols in many configurations. The Model 2000 Convertible pistol is currently imported by Adco Sales, and the MSR is $439. Please contact the importer directly for more information about this model (see Trademark Index).

SHOTGUNS

Sarsilmaz manufactured a variety of shotguns in O/U, semi-auto, and slide action configurations. Some of these models have been imported in the past in limited quantities. Currently, Sarsilmaz is manufacturing some models for Bernardelli. Please contact the factory directly for more information regarding availability and U.S. pricing (see Trademark Index).

SAUER, J.P., & SOHN

Current manufacturer located in Eckernförde, Germany since 1751 (originally Prussia). Currently imported by SIG Arms located in Exeter, NH since 1995. Previously manufactured in Suhl pre-WWII. Rifles were previously imported until 1995 by the Paul Company Inc. located in Wellsville, KS and until 1994 by G.U., Inc. located in Omaha, NE.

In 1972, J.P. Sauer & Sohn entered into a cooperative agreement with SIG. During 2000, SAN Swiss Arms AG purchased SIG Arms AG, including the J.P. Sauer & Sohn trademark. Production remains in Eckernförde, Germany.

DRILLINGS & COMBINATION GUNS

SAUER MODEL 3000 DRILLING - available in either 16 ga./.30-06, 6.5x57R, 7x57R, 7x65R or 12 ga./.222 Rem. (disc.), .243 Win., .30-06, 6.5x57R, 7x57R, 7x65R, or 9.3x74R cal., Greener crossbolt and double barrel lug locking, cocking indicators, front set trigger, automatic safety, walnut pistol grip stock with hog-back and cheekpiece, Grade III scroll engraving, 7 1/4 lbs. Importation disc. 1999.

$4,300	$3,600	$3,100	$2,675	$2,200	$1,800	$1,400

Last MSR was $4,600.

This model was also previously imported by Weatherby and Colt - please refer to separate listings for more information.

* *Luxury Grade* - similar to Model 3000 standard, except select root timber and extensive engraving featuring two animals. Importation disc. 1999.

$5,550	$4,875	$4,400	$3,875	$3,475	$3,000	$2,575

Last MSR was $6,100.

COMBO BBF 54 O/U - standard grade combination gun, 16 ga./.222 Rem., .243 Win., 6.5x57R, 7x57R, 7x65R, and .30-06 cals., ejectors, double triggers with front set trigger, moderate engraving on coin finished receiver, Greener crossbolt with double barrel lugs, 6 lbs. Importation disc. 1986.

$2,200	$2,060	$1,760	$1,565	$1,380	$1,250	$1,125

Last MSR was $2,495.

* *Luxury Grade* - similar to Combo BBF 54, except game scene engraved and deluxe crotch walnut.

$2,450	$2,200	$2,000	$1,785	$1,600	$1,475	$1,300

Last MSR was $2,745.

GRADING - PPGS™	100%	98%	95%	90%	80%	70%	60%

LUFTWAFFE SURVIVAL DRILLING - 12 or 16 ga. (65mm) SxS over 9.3x74R, 28 in. barrels, large eagle swastika on stock and breech end of right barrel. Originally mfg. for Luftwaffe pilots during WWII.

	$13,500	$11,000	$8,000	$7,000	$6,000	$5,000	$4,000

Subtract 40% if w/o original aluminum case or accessories.

SAUER MODEL 3000E DRILLING - see listing under Colt Sauer Drilling.

PISTOLS: SEMI-AUTO

MODEL 1913 POCKET AUTOMATIC - .32 ACP cal., 7 shot, 3 in. barrel, fixed sights, blue, black rubber grips. Mfg. 1913-30.

	$295	$225	$185	$165	$155	$145	$135

MODEL 1913 25 AUTOMATIC - .25 ACP cal., 7 shot, 2 1/2 in. barrel, fixed sights, blue, black rubber grips. Mfg. 1913-30.

	$325	$250	$200	$175	$150	$140	$135

MODEL 28 - .25 ACP cal., 7 shot, 3 in. barrel, fixed sights, blue, black rubber grips. Mfg. 1930-38.

	$300	$240	$185	$170	$155	$145	$135

BEHÖRDEN "AUTHORITY" M1930 MODEL - .32 ACP cal., 3 in. barrel, blue only, black plastic grips.

	$325	$240	$200	$175	$150	$145	$135

Add $1,000 for very rare alloy frame example.

MODEL 38 H DOUBLE ACTION AUTOMATIC - .22 LR (extremely rare), .32 ACP, or .380 ACP (rare) cal., 3 1/4 in. barrel, fixed sights, blue, plastic grips. Mfg. 1938-45.

	100%	98%	95%	90%	80%	70%	60%
.32 ACP	$500	$425	$375	$325	$275	$250	$225
.380 ACP	$3,500	$2,750	$2,000	$1,500	$1,250	$995	$775
.22 LR	$4,500	$3,000	$2,200	$1,600	$1,250	$995	$775

Add 100% for early high polish guns.
Add 10% for Waffenamt proofing.
Add 15%-25% for police markings.
Add 60% for alloy frame.

REVOLVERS: DA

Sauer manufactured .38 cal. double action revolvers circa 1960-1985, and also licensed other manufacturers, including Armi San Paolo. Most had blue finish and walnut grips. Current values range from $125-$275, depending on condition.

RIFLES: BOLT ACTION

SAUER PRE-WWII BOLT ACTION RIFLE - most popular European cals. and .30 - 06, 22 or 24 in. barrel, raised solid rib, Krupp steel, double-set triggers, folding 3 leaf express sight, checkered sporter stock. Mfg. pre-WWII.

	$715	$550	$495	$440	$360	$330	$305

MODEL 90 STANDARD - .22-250 Rem., .222 Rem. (only 3 mfg.), .243 Win., .25-06 Rem., 6.5x55mm, .270 Win., .30-06, .308 Win. (late mfg.), .300 Win. Mag., .300 Wby. Mag., 7mm Rem. Mag., .375 H&H, or .458 Win. Mag. cal., 24 in. barrel, 3 or 4 shot detachable mag., satin, oil finished checkered walnut stock with Monte Carlo cheekpiece and rosewood forend cap, 2 stage set trigger, free floated barrel, approx. 7 1/2 lbs. Importation disc.

	$1,000	$875	$750	$625	$550	$500	$450

Last MSR was $1,175.

Early importation rifles came standard with a half stock and barrel band, and also had European sling swivels with milled stops in 1989, this model's design changed to look more like the Colt Sauer rifle (w/o sights, gloss finished stock and set trigger was removed). During 1985-1989, Sauer exported to Sigarms 2,300 Model 90 rifles, 1,100 of these were in Mag. cals.

GRADING - PPGS™	100%	98%	95%	90%	80%	70%	60%

* **Model 90 Stutzen** - .22-250 Rem., .222 Rem. (3 mfg.), or .243 Win., Mannlicher style full stock, not available in European or Mag. cals. Importation disc. 1989.

	$1,200	$995	$850	$750	$650	$475	$500

Last MSR was $1,225.

* **Safari Model** - .458 Win. Mag cal., 23.62 in. barrel, 10 1/2 lbs. Imported 1986-88 only.

	$1,250	$950	$850	$750	$650	$575	$500

Last MSR was $1,675.

MODEL 90 SUPREME (LUX)
- .243 Win., .25-06 Rem., 6.5x55 Swedish, .270 Win., .30 - 06, .300 Win. Mag., .300 Wby. Mag., 7mm Rem. Mag., .338 Win. Mag., or .375 H&H cal., similar to Model 90, satin finished deluxe stock with Monte Carlo cheek-piece and rosewood forearm and pistol grip caps, gold trigger, no sights, 7.1-7.7 lbs. Importation 1987-98.

	$1,300	$1,050	$875	$775	$650	$475	$500

Last MSR was $1,350.

Add $32 for Mag. cals.

On Models 90 Lux and Supreme add 69% for Grade I engraving, 105% for Grade II, 128% for Grade III, and 164% for Grade IV.

* **Safari Model (Lux)**

While advertised, this model was never imported. MSR was set at $1,795.

* **Model 90 Stutzen (Lux)**

While advertised, this model was never imported. MSR was set at $1,200.

MODEL 200 BOLT ACTION
- available in 15 cals. between .243 Win. and .375 H&H, short and medium actions only, 23.62 in. unique interchangeable barrels, 6 lug bolt, easily detachable stock and forearm, optional set trigger, detachable mag. with hidden release button, 7.7 lbs. Production disc. 1993.

	$1,225	$925	$800	$700	$600	$525	$450

Last MSR was $1,395.

Add $100 for 7mm Rem. Mag. or .300 Win. Mag. cal.

Add $300 for extra interchangeable barrel.

During 1986-89, Sauer exported to Sigarms 4,170 Model 200 rifles, 1,370 of these were in Mag. cals.

* **Model 200 Lightweight** - similar to Model 200, only with alloy receiver, 6.6 lbs.

	$1,225	$925	$800	$700	$600	$525	$450

Last MSR was $1,395.

Add $150 for left-hand version.

* **Model 200 Lux** - similar to Model 200, except has deluxe walnut, rosewood forend tip and pistol grip cap, marmorized bolt and gold trigger.

	$1,395	$1,175	$925	$800	$700	$600	$525

Last MSR was $1,595.

* **American 200 Lux** - similar to Model 200 Lux, except has high gloss Monte Carlo stock, 24 in. barrel, jeweled bolt, and gold trigger.

	$1,395	$1,175	$925	$800	$700	$600	$525

Last MSR was $1,595.

Add $150 for left-hand version.

* **European 200 Lux** - similar to Model 200 Lux, except has European configured stock with Schnabel forearm, 26 in. barrel.

	$1,395	$1,175	$925	$800	$700	$600	$525

Last MSR was $1,595.

Add $95 for left-hand version.

GRADING - PPGS™	100%	98%	95%	90%	80%	70%	60%

✱ *Model 200 Carbon Fiber* - similar to Model 200, except has carbon fiber stock. Imported 1987-88 only.

	$800	$700	$625	$565	$500	$465	$430

Last MSR was $1,200.

MODEL 202 SUPREME (LUX) - .22-250 Rem. (new 2001), .243 Win. (disc. 1998, resumed 2000), .25-06 Rem., .270 Win., .30-06, .308 Win., 6.5x55mm Swedish (disc. 2000), or 7x64mm (disc. 1997) cal., steel receiver, modular design allowing barrel change within 2 minutes, dual safety, 2 piece figured walnut stock, cocking indicator, detachable 3-5 shot mag., takedown with interchangeable barrels, right- or left-hand action, 7.5 lbs. Imported 1994-2004.

	$2,950	$1,500	$1,225	$975	$800	$700	$600

Last MSR was $3,400.

Add $300 for left-hand action (.30-06 cal. only).

Add $900 per extra barrel in non-Mag. cals.

Also available in left-hand action in .270 Win. (disc. 2000) or .30-06 cal.

✱ *Model 202 Supreme Magnum (Lux)* - .300 Win. Mag., .300 Wby. Mag., .338 Win. Mag. (disc. 1997), .375 H&H, 7mm Rem. Mag., 6.5x68mm (importation disc. 1997), or 8x68mm (inportation disc. 1997) cal., converts to 7 cals., 7.7 lbs. Imported 1994-2004.

	$3,100	$1,750	$1,375	$1,075	$900	$800	$700

Last MSR was $3,600.

Add $200 for .375 H&H cal.

Was also available until 2000 in left-hand action in .300 Win. Mag. or 7mm Rem. Mag. cal.

MODEL 202 CLASSIC (STANDARD) - similar to Model 202 Synthetic, except has checkered walnut stock and forearm, 7.7 lbs. Importation began 2001.

MSR $2,399	$2,075	$1,300	$1,050	$900	$775	$675	$600

Add $200 for Mag. cals., $400 for .375 H&H cal.

Add $900 for interchangeable standard cal. barrel, or $1,000 for Mag. cal. barrel.

MODEL 202 SYNTHETIC - .22-250 Rem. (new 2001), .243 Win. (new 2001), .25-06 Rem., .270 Win., .30-06, .308 Win., .300 Win. Mag., 7mm Rem. Mag. (new 2000), .300 Wby. Mag., .375 H&H (disc. 2005), or 6.5x55mm Swedish (disc. 2000) cal., features black synthetic stock, 24 or 26 in. barrel w/o sights, 7.7 lbs. Importation began 1999.

MSR $1,999	$1,750	$1,200	$995	$875	$750	$675	$600

Add $200 for Mag. cals., $400 for .375 H&H cal.

Add $900 for interchangeable standard cal. barrel, or $1,000 for Mag. cal. barrel.

MODEL 202 LIGHTWEIGHT - .22-250 Rem., .243 Win., .25-06 Rem., .270 Win., .30-06, .308 Win., and various metric cals., 24 in. fluted barrel w/o sights, aluminum alloy receiver with integral Weaver rail, Ilaflon (disc.) or Teflon coated metal, black synthetic stock, 6 1/2 lbs. Importation began 2001.

MSR $2,995	$2,600	$1,500	$1,225	$975	$800	$700	$600

MODEL 202 VARMINTER - .22-250 Rem., .243 Win., or .25-06 Rem. cal., 24 in. match grade fluted bull barrel with no sights, 3 shot mag., matte black finish, adj. cheekpiece on checkered Turkish walnut stock, 9.5 lbs. Importation began 2001.

MSR $3,400	$2,950	$1,500	$1,225	$975	$800	$700	$600

MODEL 202 TAKEDOWN - available in many standard and Mag. cals., 2 or 4 shot mag., takedown action allows disassembly within seconds, point of impact remains constant, open sights on .375 H&H Mag. cal., 6 bolt connect forend with action, and can be detached by pressing a button, deluxe checkered walnut, round or flat bolt handle, approx. 8.8 lbs. Importation began 2003.

MSR $4,999	$4,500	$3,500	$2,600	$2,225	$1,875	$1,550	$1,300

Add $200 for Mag. cals.

GRADING - PPGS™	100%	98%	95%	90%	80%	70%	60%

MODEL 202 SUPER GRADE

While advertised in 1994, this model was never imported. MSR was set at $1,020.

MODEL 202 HUNTER MATCH

While advertised in 1994, this model was never imported. MSR was set at $1,495.

MODEL 202 ALASKA

While advertised in 1994, this model was never imported. MSR was set at $1,335.

MODEL 205 TR TARGET

- 6.5x55mm or .308 Win. cal., true left-hand variation, 200 meter diopter sights, modular design allows changing single components including caliber, free floating barrel with vent. forearm, 5 shot mag., interchangeable barrel systems, 12.1 lbs. Imported 1994-97.

$1,775	$1,575	$1,400	$1,250	$1,100	$950	$825

Last MSR was $1,900.

SSE 3000 PRECISION RIFLE

- .308 Win. cal., very accurate, law enforcement counter Sniper Rifle, built to customer specifications.

$4,845	$3,655	$3,200	$2,850	$2,500	$2,275	$2,000

SSG 2000

- available in .223 Rem., 7.5mm Swiss, .300 Wby. Mag., or .308 Win. (standard) cal., bolt action, 4 shot mag., no sights, deluxe sniper rifle featuring thumbhole style walnut stock with stippling and thumbwheel adj. cheekpiece, 13 lbs. Importation disc. 1986.

$2,480	$2,260	$1,950	$1,700	$1,500	$1,300	$1,100

Last MSR was $2,850.

This model was available in .223 Rem., .300 Wby. Mag., or 7.5mm cal. by special order only.

SSG 3000

- .223 Rem., 22 1/2 in. barrel, Parker-Hale bipod, 2-stage match trigger, includes 2 1/2-10x52mm Zeiss scope, 200 mfg. for Swiss police.

$12,000	$10,000	$8,500	$7,000	$6,750	$5,500	$4,250

SSG 3000 PRECISION TACTICAL RIFLE (CURRENT MFG.)

- .308 Win. cal., modular design, ambidextrous McMillan tactical stock with adj. comb, 23.4 in. barrel with muzzle brake, 5 shot detachable mag., supplied in 3 different levels, Level I does not have bipod or scope, cased, 12 lbs. New 2000.

MSR $3,999	$3,600	$2,400	$1,850	$1,550	$1,100	$975	$850

Add $1,500 for Level II (includes Leupold Vari-X III 3.5-10x40mm duplex scope and Harris bipod).

Add $2,300 for Level III (includes Leupold Mark 4 M1 10x40mm Mil-Dot scope and Harris bipod).

Add $1,500 for .22 conversion kit.

SHOTGUNS

MODEL 60 SXS

- various gauges, boxlock action, DT, extractors, checkered walnut stock and forearm, this model was the standard model of its period.

$975	$875	$750	$650	$550	$450	$395

Add 20% for 20 ga.

ROYAL MODEL SXS

- 12, 16 or 20 ga., 26, 28, or 30 in. barrels, various chokes, boxlock, scalloped engraved frame, cocking indicators, SST, auto ejectors, Krupp steel barrel, checkered pistol grip stock. Mfg. 1955-77.

$1,650	$1,375	$1,210	$1,100	$880	$770	$660

Add 20% for 20 ga.

ARTEMIS SXS

- 12 ga., 28 in. barrels, mod. and full choke, H&H type sidelock, SST, auto ejector, Krupp steel, checkered pistol grip stock. Mfg. 1966-77.

* *Grade I* - fine line engraved.

$5,500	$4,620	$3,850	$3,520	$3,080	$2,640	$2,200

GRADING - PPGS™	100%	98%	95%	90%	80%	70%	60%
✳ *Grade II* - extensive engraving.							
	$6,600	$5,500	$4,840	$4,235	$3,850	$3,300	$3,080

GRADE 380 SXS

	100%	98%	95%	90%	80%	70%	60%
	$4,500	$4,000	$3,500	$3,000	$2,500	$2,200	$1,500

GRADE F-40 SXS

Rarity factor precludes accurate price evaluation.

MODEL F-45 SXS

	100%	98%	95%	90%	80%	70%	60%
	$12,000	$10,500	$9,000	$8,000	$6,500	$5,000	$3,200

MODEL F-60 SXS

	100%	98%	95%	90%	80%	70%	60%
	$23,000	$20,000	$17,000	$14,000	$12,000	$9,000	$5,000

MODEL 66 O/U FIELD GUN - 12 ga., 28 in. mod. and full, Krupp steel barrels, H&H type sidelocks, SST, auto ejectors, checkered pistol grip stock, available in three grades of engraving. Mfg. 1966-75.

	100%	98%	95%	90%	80%	70%	60%
Grade I	$2,200	$1,760	$1,540	$1,320	$1,100	$880	$770
Grade II	$3,080	$2,420	$1,980	$1,650	$1,430	$1,210	$990
Grade III	$3,850	$3,300	$2,860	$2,420	$1,980	$1,650	$1,320

MODEL 66 O/U SKEET GUN - similar to Field Gun, with 26 in. VR skeet bored barrel and vent. forearm. Mfg. 1966-75.

MODEL 66 O/U TRAP GUN - similar to 66 Skeet, with 30 in. barrels, full and full, or mod. and full choke, trap style stock.

	100%	98%	95%	90%	80%	70%	60%
Grade I	$2,090	$1,760	$1,540	$1,320	$1,100	$880	$770
Grade II	$3,080	$2,420	$1,980	$1,650	$1,430	$1,210	$880
Grade III	$3,850	$3,300	$2,860	$2,420	$1,980	$1,650	$1,320

SAUER/FRANCHI STANDARD GRADE O/U - 12 ga. only, double triggers, checkered walnut stock and forearm, SST, blue finish only, sling swivels, VR. Importation disc. 1986.

	100%	98%	95%	90%	80%	70%	60%
	$375	$340	$315	$290	$275	$260	$245

Last MSR was $785.

✳ *Regent Grade* - similar to Standard grade, except has single trigger and lightly engraved silver finished receiver. Importation disc. 1986.

	100%	98%	95%	90%	80%	70%	60%
	$475	$395	$350	$310	$290	$275	$265

Last MSR was $825.

✳ *Favorit Grade* - similar to Regent Grade, except has elaborate scroll engraving on coin finished receiver, gold-plated trigger. Importation disc. 1986.

	100%	98%	95%	90%	80%	70%	60%
	$550	$495	$450	$420	$385	$350	$300

Last MSR was $875.

✳ *Diplomat Grade* - similar to Favorit Grade, except has more elaborate scroll engraving and with model name gold filled on receiver sides and barrel, extra grain French walnut, cased.

	100%	98%	95%	90%	80%	70%	60%
	$875	$750	$625	$550	$495	$460	$435

Last MSR was $1,520.

SAUER/FRANCHI SPORTING S O/U - 12 ga. only, 28 in. barrels, ejectors, SST, select European walnut with checkered stock and forearm, 10mm VR, plain silver finished receiver with model name gold filled on both sides. Importation disc. 1986.

	100%	98%	95%	90%	80%	70%	60%
	$800	$700	$600	$500	$450	$420	$395

Last MSR was $1,375.

SAUER/FRANCHI MODEL TRAP O/U - similar to Sporting S, except has 29 in. barrels, trap chokes and stock dimensions. Importation disc. 1986.

	100%	98%	95%	90%	80%	70%	60%
	$875	$750	$625	$550	$495	$460	$435

Last MSR was $1,375.

GRADING - PPGS™	100%	98%	95%	90%	80%	70%	60%

SAUER/FRANCHI MODEL SKEET O/U - similar to Sporting S, except has skeet chokes. Importation disc. 1986.

	$875	$750	$625	$550	$495	$460	$435

Last MSR was $1,375.

SAVAGE ARMS, INC.

Current manufacturer located in Westfield, MA since 1959, with sales offices located in Suffield, CT. Previously manufactured in Utica, NY - later manufacture was in Chicopee Falls, MA. Distributor sales only.

This company originally started in Utica, NY in 1895. The Model 1895 was initially manufactured by Marlin between 1895-1899. The company was renamed Savage Arms Co. in 1899. After WWI, the name was again changed to the Savage Arms Corporation. Savage moved to Chicopee Falls, MA circa 1946 (to its J. Stevens Arms Co. plants). In the mid-1960s the company became The Savage Arms Division of American Hardware Corp., which later became The Emhart Corporation. This division was sold in September 1981, and became Savage Industries, Inc. located in Westfield, MA (since the move in 1960). On November 1, 1989, Savage Arms Inc. acquired the majority of assets of Savage Industries, Inc.

Savage Arms, Inc. will offer service and parts on their current line of firearms only (those manufactured after Nov. 1, 1989). These models include the 24, 99, and 110 plus the imported Model 312. Warranty and repair claims for products not acquired by Savage Arms, Inc. will remain the responsibility of Savage Industries, Inc. For information regarding the repair and/or parts of Savage Industries, Inc. firearms, please refer to the Trademark Index in the back of this text. Parts for pre-1989 Savage Industries, Inc. firearms may be obtained by contacting the Gun Parts Corporation located in West Hurley, NY (listed in Trademark Index). Savage Arms, Inc. has older records/info. on pistols, the Model 24, older mfg. Model 99s, and Model 110 only. A factory letter authenticating the configuration of a particular specimen may be obtained by contacting Mr. John Callahan (see Trademark Index for listings and address). The charge for this service is $20.00 per gun, and $25.00 per gun for Models 1895, 1899, and 99 rifles. Please allow 2-4 weeks for an adequate response.

For more Savage model information, please refer to the Serialization section in the back of this text.

Please refer to the *Blue Book of Modern Black Powder Values* by John Allen & Dennis Adler (also online) for more information and prices on Savage's lineup of modern black powder models. For more information and current pricing on both new and used Savage airguns, please refer to the *Blue Book of Airguns* by Dr. Robert Beeman & John Allen (also online).

COMBINATION GUNS

All Model 24s are under the domain of Savage Arms, Inc.

Add 20% for .22 Mag. cal. on models listed below, where applicable.

MODEL 24 O/U - .22 LR over .410 bore, open rifle sight, visible hammer, break open, plain pistol grip stock. Mfg. 1950-65.

	$395	$325	$275	$230	$210	$180	$155

This model featured top lever opening, except on the Models 24S and 24MS.

MODEL 24B-DL - 22 LR or .22 Mag. over .410 bore.

.22 LR cal.	$475	$435	$375	$325	$265	$215	$165

MODEL 24S - similar to Model 24, with 20 ga. or .410 bore barrel, side lever, dovetail for scope. Mfg. 1964-71.

	$350	$315	$275	$250	$225	$190	$160

MODEL 24MS - similar to Model 24S, with .22 Mag. barrel. Mfg. 1964-71.

	$575	$525	$450	$400	$350	$275	$225

GRADING - PPGS™	100%	98%	95%	90%	80%	70%	60%

MODEL 24DL - similar to Model 24S, with top lever, satin chrome frame and checkered stock. Mfg. 1962-69.

	$350	$315	$275	$250	$225	$190	$160

MODEL 24MDL - similar to Model 24DL, with .22 Mag. barrel and chrome frame. Mfg. 1962-69.

	$525	$450	$400	$350	$275	$225	$185

MODEL 24FG - similar to Model 24D, w/o Monte Carlo stock, with top lever. Mfg. 1972-disc.

	$350	$315	$275	$250	$225	$190	$160

MODEL 24 FIELD - .22 LR or .22 Mag. over 20 ga. or .410 bore, lightweight field version, 24 in. separated barrels, 3 in. chambers, 6 3/4 lbs. Disc. 1989.

	$350	$315	$275	$250	$225	$190	$160

Last MSR was $209.

MODEL 24F (PREDATOR) - choice of .17 HMR (new 2004), .22 LR, .22 Hornet, .222 Rem. (disc. 1989), .223 Rem., or .30-30 Win. (12 ga. only) cal., over 12, 20 ga., or .410 bore (mfg. 1998-2000), 3 in. chamber, 24 in. barrels, 12 ga. barrel is available either with fixed choke or choke tube, wood (disc.) or matte black Dupont Rynite synthetic stock, hammer block safety, DTs, approx. 8 lbs. New 1989.

MSR $628	$535	$415	$325	$275	$230	$200	$180

Add $33 for 12 ga.

Add $55 for .410 bore adaptor (12 ga. only, disc. 2000).

Add $14 for Camo Rynite stock (disc., Model 24F-T, Turkey Model-12 ga./.22 Hornet or .223 Rem. cal. only).

The .22 LR cal. is available with 20 ga. barrel only.

MODEL 24V - similar to Model 24, with .22 Hornet (disc. 1984), .222 Rem. (1967 only), .223 Rem., .30-30 Win., .357 Max., or .357 Mag.(disc.), 20 ga., 3 in. chamber, 24in. barrels, single trigger, 7 lbs. Mfg. 1971-89.

	$425	$375	$325	$275	$250	$225	$200

MODEL 24D - .22 LR or .22 Mag. over .410 bore or 20 ga., black or case hardened frame, game scene decoration was eliminated in 1974, forearm not checkered after 1976. Introduced 1971.

	$350	$315	$275	$250	$225	$190	$160

MODEL 24C CAMPER'S COMPANION - nickel finish, .22 LR over 20 ga., 20 in. barrel cylinder bore, buttplate opens to store ten .22 LR cartridges and one 20 ga. shell in buttstock, carrying case, 5 3/4 lbs. Mfg. 1972-88.

	$525	$450	$400	$325	$275	$235	$200

Last MSR was $239.

Add 10% for nickel finish (Model 24CS - shipped with pistol grip stock also).

MODEL 24 VS - similar to Model 24CS, only .357 Mag. over 20 ga., nickel finish, accessory pistol grip stock is included.

	$575	$525	$450	$400	$350	$275	$225

MODEL 2400 O/U - 12 ga. full choke barrel over .222 Rem. or .308 Win. rifle barrel, 23 1/2 in. barrels, folding leaf sight, solid rib, dovetailed for scope mount, checkered Monte Carlo stock. Mfg. by Valmet between 1975-80.

	$625	$575	$525	$495	$440	$415	$385

MODEL 389 - 12 ga. with 3 in. chamber over choice of .308 Win. or .222 Rem., choke tubes standard, hammerless, double triggers, checkered walnut stock and forearm with recoil pad. Mfg. 1988-90 only.

	$800	$640	$550	$495	$435	$365	$300

Last MSR was $919.

GRADING - PPGS™	100%	98%	95%	90%	80%	70%	60%

PISTOLS: BOLT ACTION

MODEL 501F SPORT STRIKER - .22 LR cal., left-hand bolt, right side ejection, 10 in. button rifled barrel with scope blocks, 10 shot mag., grey fiberglass/graphite composite stock, 4 lbs. New 2000.

	MSR $245	$200	$180	$165	$145	$130	$125	$120

Add $46 for XP package (Model 501FXP, includes scope and mounts).

MODEL 502F SPORT STRIKER - similar to Model 501F Sport Striker, except is .22 Mag. cal., and 5 shot mag. New 2000.

	MSR $269	$220	$195	$180	$160	$140	$130	$125

MODEL 503F SPORT STRIKER - similar to Model 501F Sport Striker, except available in .17 HMR cal., 4 lbs. New 2003.

	MSR $295	$250	$210	$185	$165	$155	$140	$135

* *Model 503FSS Striker* - similar to Model 503F Sport Striker, except is stainless steel. Mfg. 2003-2004.

	$290	$230	$200

Last MSR was $335.

MODEL 510F STRIKER CENTERFIRE - .22-250 Rem. (disc. 2002), .223 Rem. (new 1999), .243 Win., .260 Rem. (mfg. 1999-2000), .308 Win., or 7mm-08 Rem. cal., left-hand short bolt action with right-hand ejection, 14 in. free floating unported barrel, 2 shot internal box mag., blue barrel action, black composite stock with grooved forend and wide bottom swell, drilled and tapped, 5 lbs. Mfg. 1998-2003.

$405	$345	$290	$245	$215	$180	$165

Last MSR was $469.

MODEL 516FSS STRIKER - similar to 510F Striker, except has stainless steel barreled action. Mfg. 1998-2000.

$410	$365	$320

Last MSR was $462.

* *Model 516FSAK Striker* - .243 Win., .270 WSM (mfg. 2003-2004), .300 WSM (new 2003), .308 Win., 7mm WSM (disc. 2004), or 7mm-08 Rem. cal., similar to 516FSS Striker, except has adj. muzzle brake (AMB), 14 in. ported barrel. New 1998.

	MSR $621	$535	$425	$355

* *Model 516FSAK Striker Camo* - .300 WSM cal., similar to 516FSAK Striker, except has camo treatment stock. Mfg. 2002 only.

$480	$395	$335

Last MSR was $538.

MODEL 516BSAK/BSS SUPER STRIKER - similar cals. to Model 510F Striker, features dual pillar bedded short action and custom designed thumbhole laminate grey stock, stainless steel frame and fluted 14 in. barrel with adj. muzzle brake (AMB), new ESP (Engineered Step Performance) adj. two-stage trigger, approx. 5 lbs. Mfg. 1999-2001.

$535	$430	$350

Last MSR was $618.

Subtract approx. $50 if w/o muzzle brake (Model 516BSS, disc. 2000).

PISTOLS: SEMI-AUTO

MODEL 1907 AUTO PISTOL - .32 ACP or .380 ACP cal., 9 (.380 ACP) or 10 (.32 ACP) shot mag., 3 13/16 (.32 ACP) or 4 5/16 (.380 ACP) in. barrel, blue, fixed sights, metal (early mfg. on .32 ACP only until serial no. 10,980) or hard rubber grips, exposed cocking piece. Mfg. 1910-17.

	.32 ACP	$550	$425	$300	$200	$150	$125	$100
	.380 ACP	$650	$525	$400	$300	$250	$200	$150

GRADING - PPGS™	100%	98%	95%	90%	80%	70%	60%

Add 40% for original box with instructions (beware of recent reproductions).

Add large premiums for factory nickel, silver, or gold finish (rare).

There were three different types of pearl grips: the early variation was a snap-on with an S/A logo, screw-on with an indian head logo, and the flared 1917 with no logo. Asking prices for the grips alone are in the $250-$1,000 range (this also applied to the Model 1915 Hammerless and Model 1917 Automatic).

MODEL 1915 HAMMERLESS - similar to Model 1907, with grip safety and no visible cocking piece. Mfg. 1915-17.

	100%	98%	95%	90%	80%	70%	60%
.32 ACP	$700	$600	$500	$400	$300	$225	$200
.380 ACP	$850	$700	$600	$450	$300	$250	$200

Add 40% with original box and instruction manual.

MODEL 1917 AUTOMATIC - similar to Model 1907, with spur cocking piece and trapezoidal grips. Mfg. 1920-28.

	100%	98%	95%	90%	80%	70%	60%
.32 ACP	$425	$300	$200	$150	$130	$110	$100
.380 ACP	$500	$400	$350	$300	$250	$200	$150

Add 40% with original box and instruction manual.

M1907 U.S. ARMY TEST TRIAL .45 ACP - .45 ACP cal., large version of Model 1907, exposed hammer. Approx. 400 mfg. 1907-11 for military trials.

100%	98%	95%	90%	80%	70%	60%
$9,000	$7,000	$6,000	$5,000	$4,000	$3,500	$3,000

Add 250% for experimental M1910 and M1911.

Add 100% if in original condition.

Most pistols were repurchased from the government, reconditioned (many reblued), and resold to the public as commercial models.

PISTOLS: SINGLE SHOT

MODEL 101 - .22 LR cal., 5 1/2 in. barrel, single action, adj. sight, swing out barrel, blue, wood grips. Mfg. 1960-68.

100%	98%	95%	90%	80%	70%	60%
$225	$200	$135	$100	$80	$70	$60

RIFLES: DISC, CENTERFIRE & RIMFIRE

Savage made a wide variety of inexpensive, utilitarian rifles that, to date, have attracted mostly shooting interest, but little collector interest. A listing of these models may be found in the back of this text under "Serialization."

MODEL 1895 - .303 Savage cal. only, lever action, mfg. in either carbine (22 in.), rifle (26 in.), or musket (30 in.) variations, round (scarce) or octagon barrel that has Marlin proofmark under the forend, open top, solid breech, side ejecting, 6 shot rotary mag., some had unfired shots indicator. Originally mfg. by Marlin, marked "Savage Repeating Arms Co. Utica, N.Y. U.S.A. Pat. Feb. 7, 1893", approx. 6,000 mfg. 1895-99, early models had hole in top of bolt - later ones were smooth.

100%	98%	95%	90%	80%	70%	60%
$1,500	$1,250	$995	$880	$770	$660	$495

Values assume rifle configuration - add a 150%+ premium for the carbine (rare) and musket (rare) and for unfired shots indicator.

MODEL 1899 - improvement of Model 1895 with squared-off front end of breech bolt and cocking indicator as opposed to viewing hole indicator. Early Model 1899s have oblong cocking indicator located on the top of the breech bolt. In approx. 1908, this was changed to a pin on the upper tang. A wide variety of special order features were available including special length barrels (up to 30 in.), pistol grip stocks, checkering, woods, plating, grades of engraving, sights, etc., all of which can command a moderate to sizeable premium.

Add 20% for .25-35 WCF, .32-40 WCF, or .38-55 WCF cal.

In 1905 Savage broadened the variety of this model and added the 1899A2, CD, BC, AB, Excelsior, Leader, Crescent, Victor, Rival, Premier, and Monarch (top-of-the-line model). Prices at the time ranged from $21 to $250 - quite a range. Any factory engraved Savage 99 is rare

GRADING - PPGS™	100%	98%	95%	90%	80%	70%	60%

(less than 1,000 mfg. to date) with values having to be computed one gun at a time. Engraved Model 1899s range from $2,000-$40,000, depending on the level of engraving and original condition. Because of this, the above values assume standard rifle with no engraving options (Grades A through G).

All Model 1899s and 99s fall within the domain of Savage Arms, Inc.

Rifles under ser. no. 90,000 should be inspected before firing for possible receiver cracking at rear left corner.

From 1899-circa 1950, Model 1899s had serial numbers stamped on buttplate, buttstock, and forearm. A factory drilled and tapped Model 1899 has the model nomenclature moved to the left side.

✳ *Model 1899A Rifle* - .303 Savage, .30-30 Win., .25-35 WCF, .32-40 WCF, .38-55 WCF, or .300 Sav., 26 in. round barrel, straight grip stock, cresent or steel shotgun butt, takedown added 1909. Mfg. 1899-1927, Short rifle (22 in.) mfg. 1899-1922.

	$950	$750	$600	$500	$450	$400	$350

✳ *Model 1899B Rifle* - .303 Savage, .30-30 Win., .25-35 WCF, .32-40 WCF, or .38 - 55 WCF, 26 in. octagon barrel, straight grip stock, cresent or steel shotgun butt. Mfg. 1899-1915.

	$995	$800	$650	$550	$450	$400	$350

✳ *Model 1899C Rifle* - .303 Savage, .30-30 Win., .25-35 WCF, .32-40 WCF, or .38 - 55 WCF, 26 in. half octagon barrel, straight grip, cresent or steel shotgun butt. Mfg. 1899-1915.

	$1,050	$950	$750	$600	$500	$450	$400

✳ *Model 1899-D Military Rifle (Musket)* - .30-30 Win. or .303 Savage cal., 28 or 30 in. round barrel with two barrel bands, straight grip stock with bayonet lug.

	$3,500	$3,200	$2,800	$2,400	$2,000	$1,600	$1,200

✳ *Model 1899-F Carbine* - various cals., 3 different variations, the first variation was made approx. 1899-1905 with small barrel band and receiver ring (scarce), the second and third variations are more frequently encountered.

	$1,500	$1,275	$1,100	$925	$800	$700	$600

Add approx. 25% for Winchester calibers.

Add 75% for small barrel band variation.

✳ *Model 1899H Rifle* - .22 Hi-Power, .25-35 WCF, .30-30 Win., or .303 Savage cal., 20 in. featherweight barrel, straight grip, steel or hard rubber shotgun butt, takedown added in 1909. Mfg. 1905-15.

	$950	$750	$650	$600	$500	$400	$300

Add 10% for .22 Hi-Power.

Add 20% for .25-35 WCF.

✳ *Model 1899 .250-3000 Rifle* - takedown frame only, pistol grip checkered stocks with corrugated steel butt, fine cross-checkered trigger (unique to this model). Mfg. 1914-21.

	$995	$800	$650	$550	$450	$400	$350

MODEL 99A - .30-30 Win., .300 Sav., or .303 Sav. cal., lever action, 24 in. barrel, open sight, hammerless, straight grip stock, crescent butt. Mfg. 1920-36.

	$795	$650	$500	$400	$325	$300	$250

MODEL 99A RECENT PRODUCTION - similar to original, with .243 Win., .250 Sav., .300 Sav., .308 Win., or .375 Win. (1981 only, approx. 1,500 mfg.) cal., 20 or 22 in. barrel, tang safety, conventional butt. Mfg. 1971-81.

	$450	$400	$350	$325	$300	$275	$250

Add 10% for .375 Win. or .250 Sav. cal.

MODEL 99B - takedown version of original Model 99A, 24 (introduced 1926-27) or 26 (initial standard barrel length) in. barrel. Mfg. 1920-34.

	$995	$800	$650	$550	$450	$400	$350

GRADING - PPGS™	100%	98%	95%	90%	80%	70%	60%

MODEL 99H CARBINE - .250-3000 Sav., .30-30 Win., .300 Sav. (scarce) or .303 Sav. cal., solid frame, carbine type stock. Mfg. 1923-40.

	$950	$750	$600	$500	$400	$350	$300

　　Add 30% for .250 Sav. and .300 Sav. cal.

　　There were four variations of this model - the latter three had barrel bands. This variation did not have a saddle ring.

MODEL 99E - .22 Hi Power, .250-3000 Sav., .30-30 Win., .300 Sav., or .303 Sav. cal., 20, 22 or 24 in. barrel, solid frame, straight stock. Mfg. 1922-34.

	$850	$700	$600	$475	$400	$350	$300

　　Add 15% for .22 Hi Power or .250 Sav. cal.

MODEL 99E CARBINE - .243 Win., .250 Sav., .300 Sav., or .308 Win. cal., 22 in. barrel, checkered pistol grip stock, 5 shot rotary mag. Mfg. 1960-82.

	$375	$340	$300	$270	$250	$200	$175

　　　　　　　　　　　　　　　　　　　Last MSR was $343.

　　Add 25% for early Schnabel forearm.

MODEL 99F FEATHERWEIGHT - similar to pre-war Model 99E, except takedown and 1/2 pound lighter, also mfg. with .410 bore shotgun barrel. Mfg. 1920-40.

	$900	$700	$650	$575	$450	$400	$300

　　Add 35% for .410 bore shotgun barrel.
　　Add 10% for cut checkering.
　　Add 10% for .22 HP or .250 Sav. cal.

MODEL 99F - .243 Win., .250-3000 Sav., .284 Win., .300 Sav., .308 Win., or .358 Win. cal., solid frame, checkered pistol grip stock. Mfg. 1955-73.

	$700	$600	$500	$450	$400	$300	$250

　　Add 35% for .250-3000 Sav. cal.
　　Add 20% for .358 Win. cal.
　　Add 20% for .284 Win. cal.

　　This model, in many cases, had the receiver marked "99M".

MODEL 99G - similar to Model 99E pre-war, with checkered pistol grip stock and takedown. Mfg. 1922-41.

	$900	$750	$600	$500	$400	$350	$300

　　Add 10% for .250 Sav. cal.

MODEL 99EG - similar to Model 99G, with solid frame and no checkering. Mfg. 1935-41.

	$750	$650	$575	$500	$400	$350	$300

MODEL 99EG POST-WAR - .243 Win., .250 Sav., .300 Sav., .308 Win., or .358 Win. cal., checkered stock. Mfg. 1946-60.

	$500	$450	$400	$350	$300	$275	$250

　　Add 20% for .358 Win. cal.
　　Add 10% for .250 Sav. cal.

MODEL 99R PRE-WAR - .250-3000 Sav., .303 Sav., or .300 Sav. cal., 22 or 24 in. barrel, large pistol grip stock and forearm. Mfg. 1932-42.

	$650	$600	$500	$400	$350	$325	$300

　　Add 35% for .250-3000 Sav. cal.

MODEL 99R POST-WAR - .250-3000 Sav., .300 Sav., .308 Win., .358 Win., or .243 Win. cal., similar to Pre-War, 24 in. barrel only, swivel studs. Mfg. 1946-60.

	$600	$500	$450	$400	$350	$325	$300

　　Add 10% for .250-3000 Sav. cal.
　　Add 30% for .358 Win. cal.

MODEL 99RS PRE-WAR - similar to Model 99R Pre-War, with Lyman aperture sight, swivels and sling. Mfg. 1932-42.

	$850	$700	$600	$500	$450	$400	$350

GRADING - PPGS™	100%	98%	95%	90%	80%	70%	60%

MODEL 99RS POST-WAR - similar to Model 99R Post-War, with Redfield receiver sight. Mfg. 1946-58.

	$700	$600	$500	$400	$350	$325	$300

MODEL 99T - 20 or 22 in. barrel, solid frame, lightweight, checkered pistol grip stock. Mfg. 1935-40.

	$995	$800	$650	$500	$400	$300	$275

MODEL 99K - engraved receiver and fancy wood stock, Lyman aperture sight and folding middle sight. Mfg. 1926-40.

	$3,000	$2,500	$1,800	$1,500	$1,200	$800	$500

MODEL 99DL - .243 Win., .250-3000 Sav., .284 Win., .300 Sav., .308 Win., or .358 Win. cal., Monte Carlo stock and sling swivels. Post-war mfg. 1960-73.

	$700	$600	$500	$400	$350	$325	$300

Add 10% for cut checkering.
Add 35% for .250-3000 Sav. cal.
Add 20% for .284 Win. or .358 Win. cal.

MODEL 99C - similar to Model 99F Post-War, available in .22-250 Rem. (rare), .243 Win., .284 Win. (disc.), 7mm-08 (disc.), or .308 Win. cal., 22 in. barrel, Monte Carlo stock with cut checkering and recoil pad, top tang safety, cocking indicator, open sights, detachable 4 shot mag., 7 3/4 lbs. Mfg. 1965, 1995-97.

	$500	$450	$400	$350	$300	$275	$250

Last MSR was $629.

Add 10% for .22-250 cal.
Add 15% for .284 Win.
Add 25% for 7mm-08 cal.

MODEL 99CD - similar to Model 99C, with Monte Carlo cheekpiece stock. Mfg. 1975-81.

	$550	$500	$400	$325	$300	$275	$250

MODEL 99-358 (BRUSH GUN) - .358 Win. cal., recoil pad. Mfg. 1977-80.

	$700	$600	$550	$500	$450	$400	$350

MODEL 99-375 (BRUSH GUN) - .375 Win. cal., recoil pad, fluted forearm. Mfg. 1980 only.

	$800	$725	$650	$600	$550	$500	$450

MODEL 99PE - elaborately engraved and plated receiver, tang, and lever, fancy wood with hand cut checkering. Mfg. 1966-70.

	$1,500	$1,200	$950	$800	$600	$500	$400

This model had the receiver marked "99M".

MODEL 99DE CITATION - similar to Model 99PE, except with less engraving and pressed checkering. Mfg. 1968-70.

	$885	$660	$495	$330	$250	$220	$195

This model had the receiver marked "99M".

MODEL 99M - while the receivers on Models 99F, 99PE, and 99DE were marked "99M" this is not a model designation. Rather, the "M" barrel designation indicated Monte Carlo stock.

SAVAGE 1895 ANNIVERSARY - a replica of the original M1895, .308 Win. cal., 24 in. octagon barrel, engraved receiver, brass-plated lever, straight stock, Schnabel forend, medallion in stock, brass crescent buttplate. Mfg. 9,999 in 1970 only, to commemorate Savage's 75th year.

	$550	$400	$300				

Last MSR was $195 and mfg. by Savage Arms, Division of Emhart.

GRADING - PPGS™	100%	98%	95%	90%	80%	70%	60%

MODEL 1903 STANDARD SLIDE ACTION - .22 S, L, or LR cal., 24 in. barrel, open sights, box mag., pistol grip stock. Mfg. 1903-22.

	$375	$315	$200	$150	$120	$100	$85

❋ *Model 1903 Grade EF* - features "B" grade checkering on fancy English walnut stock, Savage #22B front sight, and #21B micrometer open rear sight.

	$1,150	$1,000	$850	$750	$650	$550	$450

❋ *Model 1903 Expert Grade* - features "A" grade engraving on receiver, "B" grade checkering on fancy American walnut stock, standard sights.

	$850	$750	$650	$550	$475	$400	$350

❋ *Model 1903 Grade GH* - features "A" grade checkering on plain American walnut stock, no engraving, #22B front sight, and #21B micrometer open rear sight.

	$395	$325	$250	$200	$160	$120	$90

❋ *Model 1903 Gold Medal* - features animal ornamentation on receiver, less elaborate checkering on plain American walnut stock, standard sights.

	$650	$550	$475	$400	$350	$275	$200

MODEL 1909 SLIDE ACTION - similar to Model 1903, with 20 in. round barrel. Mfg. 1909-1915.

	$220	$180	$160	$145	$110	$90	$75

MODEL 1904 SINGLE SHOT - .22 S, L, or LR cal., bolt action, 18 in. barrel, straight stock. Mfg. 1904-17.

	$175	$140	$125	$100	$85	$65	$50

MODEL 1905 SINGLE SHOT - similar to Model 1904, except 24 in. barrel, take-down. Mfg. 1905-19.

	$175	$140	$125	$100	$85	$65	$50

MODEL 1911 - .22 S only, bolt action, 20 shot tubular mag. in buttstock, 20 in. barrel. Limited mfg. 1911-12.

	$400	$325	$295	$240	$195	$150	$115

MODEL 1912 AUTOLOADER - .22 LR cal., semi-auto, 20 in. barrel, takedown, straight stock. Mfg. 1912-16.

	$350	$295	$235	$190	$150	$115	$80

MODEL 1914 SLIDE ACTION - .22 S, L, and LR cal., 24 in. octagon barrel, plain pistol grip stock. Mfg. 1914-26.

	$250	$225	$195	$135	$110	$75	$65

MODEL 19 NRA BOLT ACTION - .22 LR cal., 25 in. barrel, adj. aperture sight, 5 shot, military stock. Approx. 50,000 mfg. 1919-32.

	$220	$140	$110	$100	$90	$75	$65

> Between 1943-45 approx. 6,000 Model 19s were made under military contract - add 15%.

MODEL 19 BOLT ACTION TARGET - .22 LR cal., 25 in. barrel, speed lock, adj. aperture sight, target stock. Mfg. 1933-46.

	$250	$165	$140	$110	$100	$90	$70

MODEL 19L - similar to Model 19, with Lyman receiver sight. Mfg. 1933-42.

	$330	$275	$195	$140	$120	$110	$100

MODEL 19M - similar to Model 19, with 28 in. heavy barrel and scope bases. Mfg. 1933-42.

	$330	$275	$195	$165	$140	$120	$110

MODEL 19H - similar to Model 19, except .22 Hornet. Mfg. 1933-42.

	$550	$495	$330	$220	$175	$165	$155

GRADING - PPGS™	100%	98%	95%	90%	80%	70%	60%

MODEL 1920 BOLT ACTION - Mauser type action, .250-3000 Sav. or .300 Sav. cal., 22 or 24 in. barrel, open sights, 5 shot, checkered pistol grip, Schnabel forend. Mfg. 1920-31.

	$450	$395	$360	$330	$300	$265	$230

    Add 10% for .250-3000 Sav. cal.

MODEL 1920-1926 - similar to Model 1920, with 24 in. barrel, Lyman aperture sight, Mfg. 1926-31.

	$425	$375	$340	$310	$285	$265	$245

    Add 10% for .250-3000 cal.

MODEL 1922 - .22 LR cal., predecessor of the Model 23A, mfg. 1922.

	$250	$220	$165	$140	$110	$95	$85

MODEL 23A BOLT ACTION RIFLE - .22 LR cal., 23 in. barrel, open sights, plain pistol grip stock, Schnabel forend. Mfg. 1923-33.

	$250	$200	$185	$140	$100	$85	$70

MODEL 23AA - improved version of Model 23A, with speedlock and checkered stock. Mfg. 1933-42.

	$300	$250	$195	$150	$130	$100	$80

MODEL 23B - .25-20 WCF cal., same configuration as Model 23A, 25 in. barrel, full forearm. Mfg. 1923-42.

	$300	$250	$200	$175	$140	$125	$100

MODEL 23C - .32-20 WCF, similar to Model 23B. Mfg. 1923-42.

	$350	$300	$225	$175	$150	$125	$100

MODEL 23D - with .22 Hornet, similar to Model 23B. Mfg. 1933-47.

	$375	$325	$275	$240	$225	$185	$140

MODEL 25 SLIDE ACTION - .22 S, L, or LR cal., 24 in. octagon barrel, open sight, takedown, hammerless, tube mag., plain pistol grip stock. Mfg. 1925-29.

	$350	$300	$250	$200	$175	$125	$75

MODEL 40 BOLT ACTION RIFLE - .250-3000 Sav., .300 Sav., .30-30 Win., or .30-06 cal., 22 or 24 in. barrel, open sight, 4 shot mag., plain pistol grip stock, Schnabel forend. Mfg. 1928-40.

	$350	$300	$250	$225	$200	$175	$150

    Add 10% for .250-3000 Sav. cal.

MODEL 45 SUPER - similar to Model 40, with Lyman receiver sight and checkered stock. Mfg. 1928-40.

	$385	$325	$275	$225	$200	$175	$150

MODEL 29 SLIDE ACTION - .22 S, L, or LR cal., 22 in. barrel, octagon until 1940, round on post-WWII, open sights, checkered pistol grip stock on pre-war, plain on late model. Mfg. 1929-67.

Pre-war	$350	$275	$225	$200	$175	$150	$125
	$300	$250	$200	$165	$150	$135	$125

MODEL 3 SINGLE SHOT - .22 S, L, or LR cal., bolt action, 26 in. barrel, 24 in. barrel on post-war, open sights, plain grip stock. Mfg. 1930-47.

	$85	$65	$55	$40	$30	$30	$30

MODEL 3S - similar to Model 3, with aperture sight. Mfg. 1930-47.

	$100	$85	$70	$55	$40	$30	$30

MODEL 3ST - similar to Model 3S, with swivels and sling. Mfg. 1930-47.

	$110	$90	$85	$70	$45	$35	$30

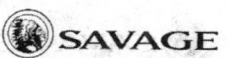

GRADING - PPGS™	100%	98%	95%	90%	80%	70%	60%

MODEL 4 BOLT ACTION REPEATER - .22 S, L, or LR cal., 24 in. barrel, open sight, takedown, 5 shot, checkered pistol grip stock on pre-war, plain stock on post-war. Mfg. 1933-65.

	100%	98%	95%	90%	80%	70%	60%
	$110	$85	$70	$55	$40	$30	$30
Pre-war	$120	$95	$85	$65	$50	$40	$30

MODEL 4S - similar to Model 4, with aperture sight. Mfg. 1933-42.

	$120	$90	$75	$65	$55	$40	$30

MODEL 4M - similar to Model 4, except .22 Mag. Mfg. 1961-65.

	$110	$85	$70	$55	$45	$30	$30

MODEL 5 - similar to Model 4, with tubular mag. Mfg. 1938-64.

	$110	$85	$70	$55	$45	$30	$30

MODEL 5S - similar to Model 5, with aperture sight. Mfg. 1936-42.

	$120	$95	$85	$65	$55	$40	$30

MODEL 6 AUTOLOADER - .22 S, L, or LR cal., 24 in. barrel, tubular mag., takedown, checkered pistol grip stock on pre-war, plain stock on post-war. Mfg. 1938-68.

	$140	$110	$95	$85	$65	$55	$40
Pre-war	$150	$120	$105	$95	$75	$65	$50

MODEL 6S - similar to Model 6, with aperture sight. Mfg. 1938-42.

	$150	$120	$105	$95	$75	$65	$45

MODEL 7 AUTOLOADER - similar to Model 6, with box mag. Mfg. 1939-51.

	$140	$110	$95	$65	$55	$55	$40
Pre-war	$150	$120	$105	$95	$75	$65	$50

MODEL 7S - similar to Model 7, with aperture sight. Mfg. 1938-42.

	$150	$120	$105	$95	$75	$65	$45

MODEL 60 AUTOLOADER - .22 LR cal., 20 in. barrel, leaf sight, tubular mag., checkered Monte Carlo walnut stock. Mfg. 1969-72.

	$95	$85	$70	$55	$45	$35	$30

MODEL 90 AUTOLOADING CARBINE - similar to Model 60, with 16 1/2 in. barrel, plain carbine stock, with barrel band.

	$95	$85	$70	$55	$45	$35	$30

MODEL 88 AUTOLOADER - similar to Model 60, except has walnut finished hardwood stock. Mfg. 1969-72.

	$85	$65	$55	$45	$40	$35	$30

MODEL 63/63K SINGLE SHOT - .22 S, L, or LR cal., bolt action, 18 in. barrel, open sights, trigger locks with key (only on Model 63K), full length pistol grip walnut finished hardwood stock, Model 63s were mfg. 1964-69, Model 63Ks were mfg. 1970-72.

	$80	$65	$55	$45	$40	$35	$30

MODEL 63KM - .22 Mag. cal., similar to Model 63K.

	$115	$90	$80	$70	$60	$50	$40

MODEL 219 SINGLE SHOT - .22 Hornet, .25-20 WCF, .32-20 WCF, or .30-30 Win. cal., 26 in. barrel, open sight, hammerless, break open, top lever, plain pistol grip stock. Mfg. 1938-65.

.30-30 Win. cal.	$195	$160	$135	$110	$100	$90	$80

Add 15% for all other cals.

MODEL 219L - similar to Model 219, with side lever. Mfg. 1965-67.

	$135	$85	$70	$55	$45	$35	$30

GRADING - PPGS™	100%	98%	95%	90%	80%	70%	60%

MODELS 221, 222, 223, 227, 228, AND 229 - single shot, similar to Model 219, only supplied with additional shotgun barrel, interchangeable, different model numbers are for different cals., gauges, and barrel lengths, all have been disc.

	$130	$100	$85	$75	$65	$50	$45

SAVAGE/STEVENS MODEL 65 - please refer to listing under Stevens section.

MODEL 34M - similar to Model 34, chambered for .22 Mag. Mfg. 1969-73.

	$90	$70	$55	$45	$35	$30	$30

MODEL 35 - .22 LR cal., bolt action, 22 in. barrel, 5 shot detachable mag., open sights, hardwood Monte Carlo stock. Disc. 1985.

	$90	$80	$65	$50	$35	$30	$30

Last MSR was $100.

MODEL 36 - .22 LR cal., single shot, otherwise similar to Model 35. Mfg. 1983-84.

	$90	$80	$65	$50	$35	$30	$30

MODEL 46 - similar to Model 34, with tubular mag. Mfg. 1969-73.

	$90	$70	$55	$45	$35	$30	$30

MODEL 65M - .22 Mag. cal., similar to Model 65.

	$95	$75	$65	$55	$45	$35	$30

SAVAGE/FOX MODEL FB-1 - .22 LR cal., bolt action, 24 in. barrel, hooded front sight, Williams adj. rear, premium walnut stock with rollover cheekpiece, rosewood tip and forend cap, fancy cut checkering. Mfg. 1981 only.

	$225	$185	$165	$140	$120	$100	$80

SAVAGE/STEVENS MODEL 72 "CRACKSHOT" - please refer to listing under Stevens section.

SAVAGE/STEVENS MODEL 73 - similar to Model 63, w/o Monte Carlo stock. Mfg. 1964-69.

	$125	$100	$85	$65	$55	$40	$35

SAVAGE/STEVENS MODEL 89 SINGLE SHOT - please refer to listing under Stevens section.

MODEL 340 BOLT ACTION - .22 Hornet, .222 Rem., .223 Rem., or .30-30 Win. cal., 22 and 24 in. barrel, open sights, 4 or 5 shot mag., 7 1/2 lbs., plain pistol grip stock. Mfg. 1950-85.

	$225	$195	$170	$160	$150	$140	$130

Last MSR was $257.

EL 340C - similar to Model 340, with aperture sight, checkered stock, and sling swivels. Mfg. 1952-60.

	$235	$205	$180	$165	$155	$145	$135

MODEL 340V - .225 Win. cal., varmint configuration, 24 in. barrel. Limited mfg. in late 1960s.

	$295	$265	$235	$205	$180	$165	$150

MODEL 340S DELUXE - similar to Model 340, with aperture sight, checkered stock, sling swivels. Mfg. 1952-60.

	$260	$225	$205	$190	$175	$160	$150

MODEL 342 AND 342S - .22 Hornet cal., similar to Model 340. Mfg. 1950-55.

	$250	$215	$200	$185	$170	$160	$150

MODEL 982DL/MDI - .22 LR (DL) or .22 Mag. (MDI) cal., bolt action, 22 in. barrel, ramp front sight, folding leaf rear sight, checkered American walnut stock with Monte Carlo comb, matte receiver finish. Mfg. 1981 only.

	$195	$175	$150	$125	$100	$85	$65

    Add 20% for .22 Mag. cal.

GRADING - PPGS™	100%	98%	95%	90%	80%	70%	60%

RIFLES: RIMFIRE, CURRENT PRODUCTION

CUB (G) - .17 Mach 2 (new 2005), .22 LR cal., single shot Youth Model with 16 1/8 in. barrel and shortened hardwood stock, traditional safety, aperture rear sight. New 2003.

MSR $156	$125	$105	$85	$80	$70	$65	$60

Add $9 for .17 Mach 2 cal.

MARK I-G SERIES BOLT ACTION - .22 S-L-LR, or LR shot (Mark I - GSB) cal., single shot, self-cocking, 19 (Mark I-GY, Youth Model) or 20 3/4 in. barrel, checkered hardwood stock, approx. 5 lbs. New 1996.

MSR $152	$125	$105	$85	$80	$70	$65	$60

Add $35 for Youth Color (new 2002) or $31 for Camo Youth (mfg. 2002-2004).

Add $7 for scope (Model Mark I-GYXP only, mfg. 2002-2004).

This Model is also available with left-hand action (Mark I-GL, disc. 2003), Youth Model (Mark I-GY), Youth Color (Mark I-GLY, features blue/green/grey laminate stock, new 2002), Camo Youth (Mark I-Y Camo, mfg. 2002-2004), or with smooth bore barrel (Mark I-GSB).

* *Mark I-GFVT* - similar to Mark I-G, except has synthetic stock, 20 3/4 in. heavy barrel and aperture rear sight. New 2005.

MSR $289	$230	$180	$135	$115	$100	$90	$80

MARK II-F SERIES BOLT ACTION - .17 Mach 2 (new 2004) or .22 LR cal., features checkered black synthetic stock, 20 3/4 in. barrel, blue barrel, 10 shot mag., 5 lbs. New 1998.

MSR $151	$120	$100	$85	$75	$70	$65	$60

Add $7 for Mark II-FXP package (includes 4x15mm scope).

Add $43 for .17 Mach 2 cal.

* *Mark II Camo* - .22 LR cal. only, similar to Mark II-F, Realtree Hardwoods HD full camo stock treatment. New 2002.

MSR $184	$145	$125	$105	$85	$80	$75	$65

* *Mark II FSS* - .17 Mach 2 (new 2004) or .22 LR cal., 20 3/4 stainless steel barrel with sights, black graphite/polymer stock with checkering, dovetailed receiver, 5 lbs. New 1997.

MSR $213	$165	$130	$100				

Add $28 for .17 Mach 2 cal.

* *Mark II-FV* - .17 Mach 2 (new 2004) or .22 LR cal., features 21 in. heavy barrel w/o sights, black synthetic stock, 5 shot detachable mag., Weaver style bases included, 6 lbs. New 1998.

MSR $216	$175	$140	$115	$100	$90	$80	$70

Add $38 for Mark II-FVXP package (includes 4x32mm scope, disc. 2004).

Add $4 for .17 Mach 2 cal.

Add $60 for Mark II-FVSS (stainless) in .17 Mach 2 cal., new 2005.

* *Mark II-G* - .17 Mach 2 (new 2004) or .22 LR cal., similar to Mark I-G Series, except has detachable 10 shot mag., approx. 5 lbs. New 1996.

MSR $169	$140	$120	$95	$75	$70	$65	$60

Add $64 for Mark II-GV (new 2005).

Add $7 for Mark II-GXP package (includes 4x15mm scope, disc. 2004).

Add $7 for Mark II-GLXP package (left-hand, includes 4x15mm scope, disc. 2004).

This Model is also available with left-hand action (Mark II-GL), Youth Model (Mark II-GY), Youth Model Left-Hand (Mark II-GLY), Varmint Left Hand (Mark II GLV) at no additional charge.

* *Mark II BV/LV* - .17 Mach 2 (new 2005) or .22 LR cal., features 21 in. blue heavy barrel, 5 shot mag., no sights, grey or brown laminated hardwood stock with (Mark II LV, disc. 2004) or w/o (Mark II BV) cut checkering, 6.5 lbs. New 1997.

MSR $264	$215	$180	$150	$125	$115	$105	$100

Add $60 for Mark II BVSS (stainless) in .17 Mach 2 cal. - grey finish only, new 2005.

SAVAGE

MODEL 64G SEMI-AUTO
- .22 LR cal., 20 1/4 in. barrel with adj. rear sight, 10 shot detachable mag., checkered hardwood stock, thumb operated rotary safety, 5.5 lbs. New 1996.

MSR $162	$135	$115	$90	$75	$70	$65	$60

Add $9 for Model 64-GXP package (includes 4x15mm scope).

* *Model 64F/64FV* - .22 LR cal., similar to Model 64G, except has black graphite/polymer checkered stock, 20 1/4 regular or 21 (Model 64FV, mfg. 1998-2004) heavy barrel, 5 or 6 lbs. New 1997.

MSR $135	$110	$95	$85	$75	$70	$65	$60

Add $48 for Model 64FV with heavy barrel (disc. 2004).

Add $7 for Model 64-FXP package (includes 4x15mm scope).

* *Model 64FSS* - similar to Model 64F, except has stainless steel barrel and action with checkered black synthetic graphite/polymer stock, 5 lbs. New 2002.

MSR $202	$155	$130	$100

* *Model 64FVSS* - similar to Model 64FSS, except has 21 in. heavy barrel, 6 lbs. Mfg. 2002-2004.

	$190	$150	$115

Last MSR was $240.

* *Model 64F Camo* - similar to Model 64F, except has Realtree Hardwoods HD, camo finish and 20 in. barrel, 5 lbs. New 2003.

MSR $175	$135	$115	$95

MODEL 93G/GL MAGNUM BOLT ACTION
- .22 Win. Mag. cal., 20 3/4 in. barrel with adj. rear sight, 5 shot detachable mag., checkered right- or left-hand (Model 93 GL) hardwood Monte Carlo stock, 5.75 lbs. New 1996.

MSR $195	$155	$130	$105	$85	$75	$70	$65

* *Model 93F* - features 20 3/4 blue barrel with checkered black synthetic graphite polymer stock, 5 lbs. New 1998.

MSR $187	$145	$120	$95	$85	$75	$70	$65

* *Model 93FSS* - similar to Model 93G, except has stainless steel barrel and action with checkered black synthetic graphite/polymer stock, 5 lbs. New 1997.

MSR $236	$190	$160	$120

* *Model 93FVSS* - similar to Model 93FSS, except has 21 in. heavy barrel with recessed crown and button rifling, drilled and tapped, Weaver bases included, 6 lbs. New 1998.

MSR $267	$215	$170	$130

Add $38 for Model 93FVSSXP package (includes 4x32mm scope and mounts).

* *Model 93F Camo* - similar to Model 93G, except has Realtree Hardwoods HD camo finish. Mfg. 2003-2004.

	$180	$150	$110

Last MSR was $211.

MODEL 93R17F BOLT ACTION
- .17 HMR cal., black synthetic or hardwood stock and forearm, 20 3/4 or 21 in. barrel, otherwise similar to Model 93 Series, 5 lbs. New 2003.

MSR $194	$155	$125	$100	$85	$75	$70	$65

* *Model 93R17BVSS* - similar to Model 93R17F, except has laminated hardwood stock and stainless steel action, 6 lbs. New 2003.

MSR $324	$265	$195	$155

* *Model 93R17 Camo* - similar to Model 93R17F, except has Realtree Hardwoods HD camo finish. New 2003.

MSR $227	$190	$160	$120

GRADING - PPGS™	100%	98%	95%	90%	80%	70%	60%

✳ *Model 93R17FSS* - similar to Model 93R17F, except has stainless steel barrel and action with checkered black synthetic graphite/polymer stock, 5 lbs. New 2003.

    MSR $241   **$200**   **$170**   **$120**

✳ *Model 93R17FV* - similar to Model 93R17F, except has heavy stainless steel barrel. New 2003.

    MSR $220   **$175**   **$145**   **$115**

✳ *Model 93R17FVSS* - similar to Model 93FSS, except has 21 in. heavy barrel with recessed crown and button rifling, drilled and tapped, Weaver bases included, 6 lbs. New 2003.

    MSR $276   **$220**   **$175**   **$135**

✳ *Model 93R17GV/GLV* - similar to Model 93R17 F, except has checkered hardwood stock with varmint barrel, GLV is left-hand model, 6 lbs. New 2003.

    MSR $233   **$190**   **$160**   **$120**

MODEL 900 SERIES

MODEL 900 SERIES - .22 LR cal., single (Target/Silhouette Model) or 5 shot (Biathlon Model), 21 or 25 (Target Model) in. free floated barrel, uncheckered hardwood stock, right- or left-hand action, approx. 8 lbs. Mfg. 1996-2001.

✳ *900B Biathlon* - blonde stock, supplied with five 5-shot mags., includes shooting rail and barrel snow cover, aperture rear sight. Mfg. 1996-97.

         $445   **$395**   **$350**   **$300**   **$265**   **$230**   **$200**

                                         Last MSR was $498.

This model was also available with left-hand action (Model 900B-LH, new 1997).

✳ *900S Silhouette* - brown hardwood stock, heavy 21 in. barrel with muzzle crown, scope bases installed, w/o sights. Mfg. 1996-97.

         $300   **$265**   **$230**   **$200**   **$180**   **$160**   **$140**

                                         Last MSR was $346.

This model was also available with left-hand action (Model 900S-LH, mfg. 1997).

✳ *900TR Target* - features aperture sights, shooting rail with hand stop, 25 in. barrel. Disc. 2001.

         $395   **$325**   **$280**   **$235**   **$200**   **$180**   **$160**

                                         Last MSR was $448.

This model was also available with left-hand action (Model 900TR-LH, new 1997).

RIFLES: CENTERFIRE, CURRENT/RECENT PRODUCTION

The 110 Series was first produced in 1958. Beginning in 1992, Savage Arms, Inc. began supplying this model with a master trigger lock, earmuffs, shooting glasses (disc. 1992), and test target. Beginning 1994, all Savage rifles employ a laser etched bolt featuring the Savage logo. During 1996, Savage began using pillar bedded stocks for many of their rifles. Savage introduced a new line of Rimfire rifles during 1996.

Recent Savage nomenclature usually involves alphabetical suffixes which mean the following: B - Brown laminated wood stock, C - detachable box mag., F - composite/synthetic stock, G - hardwood stock, K - standard muzzle brake, AK - adj. muzzle brake with fluted barrel, L - left-hand, LE - Law Enforcement, NS - no sights, P - police (tactical) rifle, SE - safari express, SS - stainless steel, SS-S - stainless steel single shot, T - Target (aperture rear sight), U - high luster blue, blue metal finish and/or stock finish, V - Long Range (Varmint w/ heavy barrel), XP - package gun (scope, sling, and rings/base), Y - Youth/Ladies Model. Hence, the Model 116-FCSAK designates a 116 series firearm with composite stock, detachable stainless steel mag., and adj. muzzle brake on barrel. Likewise, a Model 93FVSS-XP indicates a Model 93 with heavy varmint barrel, stainless steel construction, and scope package. A 2 digit model number (10) designates new short action. A 3 digit model number (110) indicates long action.

During 2003, Savage released its new patented AccuTrigger, which allows the consumer to adjust the trigger pull from the outside of the rifle from 1 1/2 lbs. - 6 lbs. using a proprietary tool. The AccuTrigger also has almost no trigger creep and is infinitely adjustable. Initially, it was released in all Varmint, LE, and heavy barrel long range rifles, and during 2004, the AccuTrigger became stan-

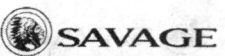

GRADING - PPGS™	100%	98%	95%	90%	80%	70%	60%

dard on all Savage centerfire rifles, except for the Model 40 and the Model 111 FCXP3 Package. Whenever possible, the models within this category have been listed in numerical sequence.

> **Subtract approx. 10% on models listed below w/o AccuTrigger (became standard on all centerfire rifles in 2004).**

MODEL 10FCM SCOUT - .308 Win., or 7mm-08 Rem. (disc. 2002) cal., 20 in. barrel with removable ghost ring rear sight, one-piece barrel mount (allows long scope eye relief), 4 shot detachable mag., satin blue action with large ball bolt handle, black synthetic dual pillar bedded stock, includes swivel set and sling, 6 1/8 lbs. Mfg. 1999-2003.

	$500	$430	$375	$335	$300	$280	$265

Last MSR was $581.

MODEL 10FM (SIERRA) - .243 Win., .308 Win., .270 WSM (new 2003), .300 WSM (new 2002), or 7mm-08 Rem. (new 1999) cal., short action, lightweight, features black synthetic stock with dual pillar bedding, button rifling and recessed crown, 20 (Sierra, standard weight, new 1999) or 24 (heavy only, disc. 1998) in. barrel, w/o sights, 6 lbs. Mfg. 1998-2004.

	$435	$360	$290	$245	$210	$175	$160

Last MSR was $511.

This model was also available in left-hand action (disc.).

MODEL 10FCM (SIERRA) - .243 Win., .270 WSM, .300 WSM, .308 Win., or 7mm-08 Rem cal., 20 in. barrel, synthetic stock, short action, detachable box mag., no sights. New 2005.

MSR $552	$450	$350	$295	$265	$225	$190	$165

MODEL 10FP - .223 Rem., .260 Rem. (mfg. 1999-2001), .308 Win., or 7mm-08 (mfg. 1999-2001) cal., short action, tactical/law enforcement model, checkered black synthetic stock, features 24 in. heavy barrel w/o sights, AccuTrigger became standard 2003, 8 lbs. New 1998.

MSR $601	$490	$385	$315	$275	$230	$190	$165

This model is also available in left-hand action (Model 10FLP).

> ✳ *Model10FP Duty* - similar to Model 10FP, except has open iron sights. Mfg. 2002 only.

	$435	$355	$290	$250	$215	$180	$165

Last MSR was $525.

> ✳ *Model10FP-LE1/LE1A* - .223 Rem. (LE1A only) or .308 Win. cal., similar to Model 10FP, except has 20 in. heavy barrel with no sights, choice of standard (LE1) or Choate (LE1A) stock. New 2002.

MSR $601	$490	$385	$315	$275	$230	$190	$165

Add $128 for Choate stock.

> ✳ *Model10FP-LE2/LE2A* - .223 (LE2A only) or .308 Win. cal., similar to Model 10FP-LE1/LE1A, except has 26 in. heavy barrel and choice of standard (LE2) or Choate stock (LE2A). New 2002.

MSR $601	$490	$385	$315	$275	$230	$190	$165

Add $128 for Choate stock (LE2A).

> ✳ *Model10FP-LE2B* - .308 Win. cal., short action, features McMillan tactical fiberglass stock with stippled grip areas, 4 shot mag., 26 in. heavy barrel. New 2003.

MSR $984	$825	$700	$600	$500	$400	$325	$265

> ✳ *Model10FPXP-LE/LEA* - .308 Win. cal. only, short action, features skeletonized synthetic stock, 26 in. barrel w/o sights, LEA has Choate stock, LE has standard stock, includes Burris (disc.) or Leupold (new 2004) 3.5-10x50mm scope with flip covers and sling, 4 shot mag., Harris bipod, aluminum case, 10.5 lbs. New 2002.

MSR $1,805	$1,475	$1,150	$925	$825	$675	$550	$450

Add $144 for Choate stock (Model 10FPXP-LEA package).

GRADING - PPGS™	100%	98%	95%	90%	80%	70%	60%

MODEL 10GY - .223 Rem., .243 Win., or .308 Win. cal., ladies/youth model with shorter wood stock and 22 in. barrel with open sights.

MSR $496	$415	$335	$275	$230	$195	$175	$160

MODEL 11F HUNTER - .22-250 Rem., .223 Rem., .243 Win., .260 Rem. (mfg. 1999-2000), .270 WSM (new 2003), .308 Win., .300 RSUM (mfg. 2003), .300 WSM (new 2002), 7mm RSUM (mfg. 2003), 7mm WSM (new 2003), or 7mm-08 Rem. (new 1999) cal., short action, dual pillar bedding, checkered black synthetic stock, 22 or 24 (.300 WSM cal. only) in. blue barrel with open sights, 6.75 lbs. New 1998.

MSR $486	$415	$335	$280	$235	$195	$175	$160

Subtract $9 if w/o sights (Model 11FNS, disc. 2004).

This model is also available in left-hand action (Model 11FL).

MODEL 11FCNS (11FC) - .22-250 Rem. .243 Win., .260 Rem. (disc. 2000), .270 WSM (new 2005), .308 Win., .300 WSM (new 2005), 7mm WSM (new 2005), or 7mm-08 Rem. cal., 22 in. blue barrel and action, fixed (disc. 2004) or detachable box mag. (new 2005, Model FCNS), dual pillar bedded black synthetic stock, 6 3/8 lbs. Mfg. 1999-2001, reintroduced 2003.

MSR $507	$425	$345	$285	$235	$200	$175	$160

This model was also available in left-hand action (Model 11FLC, disc. 2001).

MODEL 11FYXP3 - .223 Rem. (new 2003), .243 Win., 7mm-08 Rem. (new 2003) cal., similar to 11F Hunter, except is Youth Model with 12 1/2 LOP, includes 3-9x40mm scope, 6.5 lbs. New 2002.

MSR $501	$420	$335	$285	$230	$195	$175	$160

MODEL 11G/11GCNS HUNTER - similar to 11F Hunter, except has wood stock with pressed fleur-de-lis checkering, detachable box mag became standard in 2005 (Model 11GCNS). New 1998.

MSR $496	$420	$335	$280	$225	$195	$175	$160

Add $22 for Model 11GCNS (new 2005).

Subtract $10 if w/o sights (Model 11GNS, disc. 2004).

This model is also available in left-hand action (Model 11GL).

MODEL 11GC - .22-250 Rem., .243 Win., .260 Rem. (disc. 2000), .308 Win. or 7mm-08 Rem. cal., detachable mag., hardwood stock, open sights, 22 in. barrel, blue finish, 6 3/8 lbs. Mfg. 1999-2001.

	$375	$310	$270	$230	$200	$175	$160

Last MSR was $441.

This model is also available in left-hand action (Model 11GLC).

MODEL 12 VARMINTER LOW PROFILE - .204 Ruger (new 2005), .22-250 Rem. or .223 Rem. cal., choice of repeater or single shot, 26 in. fluted stainless heavy barrel and action, AccuTrigger standard, low profile brown laminated stock with extra wide beavertail forend, short action, 10 lbs. New 2004.

MSR $778	$640	$535	$430

During 2005, this model became available in left-hand action at no extra charge.

MODEL 12BVSS - .22-250 Rem., .223 Rem., .243 Win. (new 2002), .300 WSM (new 2003), or .308 Win. (disc. 1999, reintroduced 2001) cal., short action, 26 in. heavy fluted stainless barrel w/o sights, dual pillar bedding, brown laminated wood stock with flat beavertail forend, AccuTrigger became standard 2003, 9 lbs. New 1998.

MSR $721	$600	$490	$395

This model is also available in left-hand action in cals. .22-250 Rem. and .223 Rem. at no extra charge (mfg. 2004, Model 12BLVSS).

✳ *Model 12BVSS-S* - .220 Swift (new 2004), .22-250 Rem., .223 Rem. or .308 Win. cal., similar to Model 12BVSS, except is single shot, AccuTrigger became standard 2003. Mfg. 1998-2001, reintroduced 2002.

MSR $721	$600	$490	$395

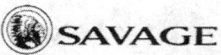
GRADING - PPGS™	100%	98%	95%	90%	80%	70%	60%

✳ Model 12BVSS-SXP - similar to Model 12BVSS, except not available in .243 Win. cal., target style heavy prone laminate stock with Wundhammer palm swell and black forend cap, 26 in. fluted stainless barrel w/o sights, includes 6-18x37mm scope and black aluminum hard case, 12 lbs. Mfg. 2002-2004.

$1,050	$895	$775	

Last MSR was $1,225.

MODEL 12FV/FVY - .204 Ruger (new 2005), .22-250 Rem., .223 Rem., .243 Win. (new 2002), .308 Win. (new 1999) cal., short action, features 26 in. regular barrel with low luster bluing, black synthetic stock with dual pillar bedding, 5 shot top loading mag., drilled and tapped, AccuTrigger became standard 2003, 9 lbs. New 1998.

MSR $549	$450	$365	$300	$250	$210	$175	$160

This model is also available with a Youth Model (Model 12FVY, available in .22-250 Rem. and .223 Rem. cal. only, mfg. 2003-2004). This model is also available in left-hand action (Model 12FLV, disc. 2001, reintroduced during 2004, not available in .243 Win. cal.).

MODEL 12FVSS - .22-250 Rem., .223 Rem., .270 WSM (new 2003), .300 WSM (new 2003) or .308 Win. cal., short action, features 26 in. fluted heavy stainless free floating barrel w/o sights, black checkered synthetic stock with dual pillar bedding, drilled and tapped, AccuTrigger became standard 2003, 9 lbs. New 1998.

MSR $667	$565	$450	$360

This model was also available in left-hand action (Model 12FLVSS, not available in WSM cals., disc. 2004).

✳ Model 12FVSS-S - similar to Model 12FVSS, except is single shot and not available in .308 Win. cal. Mfg. 1998-2001.

$480	$405	$335	

Last MSR was $549.

✳ Model 12VSS/12VSS-S - .22-250 Rem., .223 Rem., or .308 Win. cal., available in long (12VSS) or short (12VSS-S, mfg. 2003-2004, not available in .308 Win. cal.) action, semi-skeletonized Choate adj. black synthetic stock with cheekpiece, 24 in. fluted stainless barrel, blue stainless steel receiver, 4 shot mag., drilled and tapped receiver, AccuTrigger became standard 2003, 15 lbs. New 2000.

MSR $934	$805	$680	$565

MODEL 14 AMERICAN CLASSIC - .22-250 Rem., .243 Win., .270 WSM, .300 WSM .308 Win., or 7MM-08 Rem. cal., 22 or 24 in. barrel, detachable box mag., no sights. New 2005.

MSR $616	$525	$425	$350	$295	$245	$225	$200

MODEL 16BSS WEATHER WARRIOR - .270 WSM (new 2003), .300 WSM, .300 RSUM (disc. 2002), 7mm WSM (new 2003), or 7mm RSUM (disc. 2002) cal., 24 in. barrel w/o sights, 2 or 3 shot mag., brown laminated stock with cut checkering, stainless action and barrel, 7 3/4 lbs. Mfg. 2002-2003.

$560	$460	$355	

Last MSR was $668.

MODEL 16FCSS WEATHER WARRIOR - .243 Win., .260 Rem. (disc. 2000), .308 Win., or 7mm-08 Rem. cal., stainless steel barreled action with 22 in. barrel, detachable mag., dual pillar bedded black synthetic stock, 6 3/4 lbs. Mfg. 1999-2001.

$460	$395	$325	

Last MSR was $532.

Also available in left-hand action at no additional charge (Model 16FLCSS).

MODEL 16FCSAK WEATHER WARRIOR - .243 Win., .270 WSM, .300 WSM, .308 Win., 7mm-08 Rem., or 7mm WSM cal., short action, 22 or 24 in. fluted barrel with adj. muzzle brake, detachable box mag., no sights. New 2005.

MSR $661	$560	$495	$415	$350	$315	$275	$245

GRADING - PPGS™	100%	98%	95%	90%	80%	70%	60%

MODEL 16FSS
- .204 Ruger (new 2005), .22-250 (new 2003), .223 Rem., .243 Win., .260 Rem. (mfg. 1999-2000), .270 WSM, .308 Win., .300 WSM (new 2002), .300 RSUM (mfg. 2002-2003), 7mm WSM (new 2003), 7mm RSUM (mfg. 2002-2003), or 7mm-08 Rem. (new 1999) cal., short action, stainless steel 22 or 24 (WSM and RSUM cals only) in. barreled action w/o sights, checkered black synthetic stock with dual pillar bedding, 6 3/4 lbs. New 1998.

	MSR $552	**$460**	**$400**	**$310**			

Also available in left-hand action at no additional charge (Model 16FLSS).

✴ *Model 16FCSS* - similar to Model 16FSS, except features detachable box mag., not available in .204 Ruger or .223 Rem. New 2005.

	MSR $573	**$475**	**$410**	**$315**			

MODEL 16FXP3 PACKAGE
- .204 Ruger (new 2005), .22-250 Rem. (new 2003), .223 Rem., .243 Win., .270 WSM (new 2003), .300 RSUM (mfg. 2003), .308 Win., .300 WSM, 7mm WSM (new 2003), or 7mm RSUM (mfg. 2003) cal., short action, stainless action and 22 or 24 in. stainless barrel w/o sights, checkered black synthetic stock, includes nickel finished 3-9x40mm scope and mounts, supplied with sling, approx. 6.5 lbs. New 2002.

	MSR $601	**$510**	**$410**	**$335**			

MODEL 40 SINGLE SHOT
- .22 Hornet or .223 Rem. (disc. 2004) cal., single shot action, varmint configuration featuring 24 in. heavy contour barrel and brown laminate stock with full beavertail forend, AccuTrigger is not available in this model, 7.75 lbs.

	MSR $436	**$360**	**$290**	**$250**	**$225**	**$200**	**$175**	**$155**

MODEL 99C LEVER ACTION
- .243 Win. or .308 Win. cal., detachable box mag., checkered Monte Carlo stock and forearm, high gloss bluing, 22 in. barrel with adj. rear sight, drilled and tapped, 7 3/4 lbs. Reintroduced 1996-97 only.

		$585	**$500**	**$450**	**$400**	**$360**	**$330**	**$300**

Last MSR was $665.

MODEL 99-CE (CENTENNIAL EDITION)
- .300 Sav. cal. only, limited edition featuring fully engraved nickel receiver and lever, 24Kt. gold-plated receiver figures, trigger, and safety, deluxe hand checkered walnut stock and forearm, 1,000 mfg. 1996-97 only, serial numbered AS0001-AS1000.

		$1,500	**$1,100**	**$750**			

Last MSR was $1,660.

MODEL 110 SPORTER BOLT ACTION
- .243 Win., .270 Win., .308 Win., or .30-06 cal., 22 in. barrel, open sight, 4 shot, checkered pistol grip stock. Mfg. 1958-63.

	$375	**$325**	**$275**	**$250**	**$225**	**$200**	**$185**

MODEL 110-MC
- similar to Model 110, with Monte Carlo stock. Mfg. 1959-69.

	$385	**$325**	**$275**	**$250**	**$225**	**$200**	**$185**

MODEL 110-M
- similar to Model 110MC, except 7mm Rem. Mag., .264 Win. Mag., .300 Win. Mag., or .338 Win. Mag. cal., recoil pad. Mfg. 1963-69.

	$395	**$335**	**$285**	**$250**	**$225**	**$200**	**$185**

MODEL 110-C/CL
- various cals., push-button detachable mag., walnut stock. Mfg. 1966-85.

	$425	**$365**	**$325**	**$295**	**$275**	**$250**	**$225**

MODEL 110-D
- .22-250 Rem. (disc.), .223 Rem., .243 Win., .25-06 Rem. (disc.), .270 Win., .308 Win. (disc.), .30-06, 7mm Rem. Mag., .300 Win. Mag. (disc.), or .338 Win. Mag. cal., similar to Model 110B, hinged floorplate (1972-75 only), checkered walnut stock, removable and adj. rear sight, 7 1/2 lbs. Mfg. 1966-88.

	$350	**$300**	**$275**	**$250**	**$225**	**$190**	**$170**

Last MSR was $409.

Add $80 for left-hand version.

GRADING - PPGS™	100%	98%	95%	90%	80%	70%	60%

MODEL 110-E - .22-250 Rem., .223 Rem., .243 Win., .270 Win., 7mm Rem. Mag., .308 Win., or .30-06 cal., 22 or 24 (Mag. only) in. barrel, open sights, uncheckered hardwood Monte Carlo stock, blind internal floorplate, 7 lbs. Mfg. 1963-88.

	$350	$300	$275	$250	$225	$190	$170

Last MSR was $325.

Subtract $16 without sights.

MODEL 110-F - .22-250 Rem., .223 Rem., .243 Win., .250 Sav. (new 1993), .25-06 Rem. (new 1993), .308 Win., .30-06, .270 Win., 7mm-08 Rem. (new 1993), 7mm Rem. Mag., .300 Sav. (new 1993), .300 Win. Mag., .338 Win. Mag. (new 1991) cal., 22 or 24 (Magnum) in. barrel, black DuPont Rynite stock with swivel studs and recoil pad, adj. rear sight, drilled and tapped for scope mounts, 4 or 5 shot mag., 6 3/4 lbs. Mfg. 1989-93.

	$335	$300	$265	$235	$210	$195	$180

✳ **Model 110-FNS** - similar to Model 110-F, except has no sights. Mfg. 1991-93.

	$325	$285	$250	$225	$200	$190	$175

✳ **Model 110-FXP3** - .22-250 Rem. (new 1992), .223 Rem. (new 1992), .243 Win., .270 Win., .30-06, .308 Win. (new 1992), 7mm Rem. Mag., or .300 Win. Mag. cal., similar to Model 110-F except is without sights and has integral Weaver type scope bases. Mfg. 1989-93.

	$415	$370	$325	$285	$250	$225	$195

MODEL 110-GY - .223 Rem. (Mfg. 1993-99), .243 Win. (disc. 1999), .270 Win. (new 1994), .300 Sav. (disc. 1995), or .308 Win. (mfg. 1994-99) cal., 22 in. barrel, youth/ladies variation with shortened classic stock, open sights, 6 1/2 lbs. Mfg. 1991-2000.

	$350	$300	$260	$220	$195	$175	$160

Last MSR was $395.

MODEL 110-WLE - .250-3000 Sav., .300 Sav., or 7x57mm Mauser cal. Mfg. 1991-93.

	$425	$390	$360	$320	$280	$250	$225

Approx. 1,000 of each cal. were mfg. in this model.

✳ **Model 110-WLE 1 of 1,000** - 7x57mm Mauser, features select walnut stock with Monte Carlo cheekpiece, high luster blue finish with laser etched Savage logo on bolt body, drilled and tapped, 1,000 mfg. beginning 1992, 7 3/4 lbs. Mfg. 1992-93 only.

	$415	$370	$325	$285	$250	$225	$195

MODEL 110-FM SIERRA ULTRA LIGHT - .243 Win. (disc. 1998), .270 Win., .30 - 06, or .308 Win. (disc. 1998) cal., features 20 in. high gloss barrel w/o sights, black graphite/fiberglass - filled stock with non-glare finish, drilled and tapped, 6 1/4 lbs. Mfg. 1996-2000.

	$380	$325	$270	$230	$205	$175	$160

Last MSR was $449.

MODEL 110-FP TACTICAL POLICE RIFLE - .223 Rem. (disc. 1998), .25-06 Rem. (new 1995), .300 Win. Mag. (new 1995), .30-06 (new 1996), .308 Win. (disc. 1998), or 7mm Rem. Mag. (new 1995) cal., long action, 24 in. heavy barrel pillar bedded tactical rifle, all metal parts are non-reflective, 4 shot internal mag., black Dupont Rynite stock, right- or left-hand (new 1996) action, tapped for scope mounts, AccuTrigger became standard 2003, 8.5 lbs. Mfg. 1990-2001, reintroduced 2003.

MSR $601	$515	$420	$340	$300	$265	$240	$210

Also available in left-hand action at no additional charge (mfg. 1996-2001, Model 110-FLP).

MODEL 110-G - .22-250 Rem., .223 Rem., .243 Win., .250 Sav. (new 1992), .25-06 Rem. (new 1992), .300 Sav. (new 1993), .308 Win., .30-06, .270 Win., 7mm-08 Rem. (new 1992), 7mm Rem. Mag., or .300 Win. Mag. cal., top loading internal box mag., 22 or 24 in. barrel, adj. iron sights, checkered hardwood stock, approx. 7 lbs. Mfg. 1989-93.

	$325	$285	$250	$225	$200	$190	$175

Subtract $10-$20 if without sights (Model 110-GNS).

GRADING - PPGS™	100%	98%	95%	90%	80%	70%	60%

⁕ Model 110-GC - .270 Win., .30-06, 7mm Rem. Mag., or .300 Win. Mag. cal., features detachable 3 or 4 shot mag., 22 or 24 in. barrel, checkered hardwood stock, adj. sights, 6 3/4 lbs. Mfg. 1992-93.

	$410	$325	$275	$240	$210	$180	$165

Add $20 for Mag. cals.

⁕ Model 10GXP3/110-GXP3 Package - .22-250 Rem., .223 Rem., .243 Win., .250 Savage (disc. 1995), .25-06 Rem., .270 Win., .270 WSM (new 2003), .300 Sav. (disc. 1995), .30-06, .300 RSUM (mfg. 2002-2003), .308 Win., 7mm-08 Rem. (disc. 1995, reintroduced 1999), 7mm WSM (new 2003), 7mm Rem. Mag., 7mm RSUM (mfg. 2003), .300 WSM (new 2005), .300 Rem. Ultra Mag. (new 2002), or .300 Win. Mag. cal., short (10GXP3) or long (110-GXP3) action, similar to Model 110-G, except has no sights, includes 3-9x32 scope, rings, bases, QD swivels, and deluxe rifle sling, includes integral Weaver type scope bases. New 1989.

MSR $539	$450	$375	$300	$250	$210	$175	$160

Also available in left-hand action at no additional charge (Model 10GLXP3/110-GLXP3, not available in short action).

⁕ Model 110-GCXP3 Package - .270 Win., .30-06, .300 Win. Mag., or 7mm Rem. Mag. cal., 22 or 24 in. barrel, checkered hardwood stock, detachable box mag., package includes 3-9x32 scope, rings, bases, QD swivels, and deluxe rifle sling, 7 1/4 lbs. Disc. 2001.

	$445	$375	$315	$275	$235	$190	$175

Last MSR was $524.

Was also available in left-hand action at no additional charge (Model 110-GLCXP3 – disc. 2000).

⁕ Model 110-GL - .30-06, .270 Win., or 7mm Rem. Mag. cal., left-hand variation of the Model 110 - G. Mfg. 1989-93.

	$325	$265	$225	$200	$180	$165	$150

⁕ Model 110-GLNS - similar to Model 110-GL, except has no sights. Mfg. 1991-1993.

	$320	$260	$220	$200	$180	$165	$150

MODEL 110-K - .243 Win., .270 Win., or .30-06 cal., incorporates laminated camouflage stock. Mfg. 1986-88.

	$335	$280	$240				

Last MSR was $399.

MODEL 110-S - .308 Win. or 7mm-08 Rem. (disc.) cals., silhouette model, 22 in. heavy barrel, Wundhammer swell pistol grip with stippling, no sights, 4 shot mag., 8 lbs. 10 oz. Disc. 1985.

	$340	$290	$255	$225	$205	$190	$175

Last MSR was $385.

MODEL 110-V - .22-250 Rem. or .223 Rem. cal. only, varmint model, 26 in. heavy barrel, no sights, 5 shot mag., stippled walnut Wundhammer pistol grip stock, 9 1/4 lbs. Disc. 1989.

	$370	$315	$265	$230	$205	$190	$175

Last MSR was $439.

MODEL 110-GV - .22-250 Rem. or .223 Rem. cal., varmint variation, 24 in. medium barrel, no sights, checkered hardwood stock with rubber rifle pad, drilled and tapped for scope, 8 1/4 lbs. Mfg. 1989-93.

	$380	$285	$250	$225	$200	$190	$175

MODEL 110-B - similar to Model 110E, except available in .243 Win., .270 Win. or .30-06 cal., select stock and pistol grip cap, features blind mag, walnut Monte Carlo stock. Reintroduced 1989 with laminate stock (Model 110-B Laminate). Mfg. 1978-79.

	$360	$300	$265	$235	$205	$190	$175

This model was also available in left-hand action (Model 110-BL).

GRADING - PPGS™	100%	98%	95%	90%	80%	70%	60%

MODEL 110-B LAMINATE - similar to Model 110-B, except is available in .300 Win. Mag. or .338 Win. Mag. cal. also, has brown laminate hardwood stock with iron sights, approx. 7 1/2 lbs. Mfg. 1989-91.

	100%	98%	95%	90%	80%	70%	60%
	$385	$310	$250	$225	$200	$190	$180

Last MSR was $477.

MODEL 110-P PREMIER GRADE - similar to Model 110B, with select French walnut stock, skip checkered, rosewood forend and pistol grip cap, sling swivels, 7mm Mag. has recoil pad. Mfg. 1964-70.

	100%	98%	95%	90%	80%	70%	60%
	$440	$330	$310	$275	$250	$220	$195
7mm Mag.	$460	$350	$330	$305	$275	$240	$220

MODEL 110-PE PRESENTATION GRADE - similar to Model 110P, with engraved receiver, floorplate and triggerguard. Mfg. 1968-70.

	100%	98%	95%	90%	80%	70%	60%
	$660	$550	$525	$470	$440	$415	$385
7mm Mag.	$690	$580	$550	$495	$470	$440	$415

MODEL 111 CHIEFTAIN ACTION - .243 Win., .270 Win., 7x57mm, 7mm Mag., or .30-06 cal., 22 in. barrel, 24 in. barrel (Mag. cals.), leaf sight, 4 shot detachable mag., checkered walnut Monte Carlo stock, pistol grip cap, sling swivels. Mfg. 1974-78.

	100%	98%	95%	90%	80%	70%	60%
	$375	$350	$300	$250	$225	$200	$175
Magnum	$395	$375	$325	$295	$275	$225	$195

MODEL 111-F - similar to Model 111-G, except has black graphite/fiberglass stock (with non-glare finish) and also available in .338 Win. Mag. cal., long action, 22, 24, or 26 (disc. 2003) in. barrel, solid recoil pad, 6.5 lbs. New 1994.

	100%	98%	95%	90%	80%	70%	60%
MSR $486	$420	$345	$290	$235	$195	$175	$160

Subtract $8 if w/o sights (Model 111-FNS, not available in .300 Rem. Ultra Mag. or 7mm Rem. Ultra Mag. cals., disc. 2002).

This model is also available in left-hand (Model 111-FL).

✱ **Model 111-FC** - .270 Win., .30-06, .300 Win. Mag., or 7mm Rem. Mag. cal., 22 or 24 in. barrel, detachable box mag., black graphite/fiberglass stock, 6 1/2 lbs. Mfg. 1994-2003.

	100%	98%	95%	90%	80%	70%	60%
	$400	$340	$285	$230	$195	$175	$160

Last MSR was $468.

This model was also available with left-hand action (Model 111-FLC).

✱ **Model 111-FCNS** - .25-06 Rem., .270 Win., .30-06, .300 Win. Mag., .338 Win. Mag., or 7mm Rem. Mag. cal., features detachable box mag., no sights. New 2005.

	100%	98%	95%	90%	80%	70%	60%
MSR $507	$435	$355	$295	$240	$200	$175	$160

MODEL 111-FAK EXPRESS - .270 Win., .30-06, .300 Win. Mag., .338 Win. Mag., or 7mm Rem. Mag. cal., 22 in. barrel with adj. muzzle brake, black or black matte graphite/fiberglass-filled stock, w/o sights, 6 3/4 lbs. Mfg. 1996-98.

	100%	98%	95%	90%	80%	70%	60%
	$390	$340	$285	$240	$200	$180	$165

Last MSR was $450.

MODEL 111-FCXP3 PACKAGE - .270 Win., .30-06, .300 Win. Mag. (disc. 2001, reintroduced 2005), or 7mm Rem. Mag. (disc. 2001, reintroduced 2005) cal., 4 shot detachable box mag., checkered black syntetic stock, 22 or 24 in. barrel, package includes bore sighted 3-9x32mm scope, rings, bases, QD swivels, and deluxe rifle sling, AccuTrigger not available on this model, 6 1/2 lbs. New 1994.

	100%	98%	95%	90%	80%	70%	60%
MSR $411	$355	$295	$265	$230	$200	$175	$160

Add approx. $60 for Mag. cals. (disc. 2001).

This model was also available with left-hand action (Model 111-FLCXP3 – disc. 2000).

MODELS 11FXP3 & 111-FXP3 PACKAGES - .204 Ruger (new 2005), .22-250 Rem., .223 Rem., .243 Win., .250 Savage (disc. 1996), .25-06 Rem., .270 WSM (new 2003), .270 Win., .300 Sav. (disc. 1996), .30-06, .308 Win., .300 Rem. Ultra Mag. (mfg. 2003-2004), .300 Win. Mag., .300 WSM (new 2002) .338 Win. Mag., 7mm

GRADING - PPGS™	100%	98%	95%	90%	80%	70%	60%

WSM (new 2003), 7mm RSUM (mfg. 2003), 7mm Rem. Mag., 7mm Rem. Ultra Mag. (mfg. 2002-2003), or 7mm-08 Rem. (disc. 1996, reintroduced 1999-2001) cal., short (11FXP3) or long (111-FXP3) action, 22 or 24 in. barrel, black graphite/fiberglass composite stock, non-glare finish, package consists of bore sighted 3-9x32 scope, rings, bases, QD swivels, and deluxe rifle sling, approx. 7.25 lbs. New 1994.

MSR $516	**$435**	**$370**	**$300**	**$250**	**$200**	**$180**	**$165**

This model was also available with left-hand action (Model 11FLXP3/111-FLXP3, disc. 2002).

MODEL 111-G - .22-250 Rem. (disc. 1998), .223 Rem. (disc. 1998), .243 Win. (disc. 1998), .250 Savage (disc. 1996), .25-06 Rem., .270 Win., .300 Sav. (disc. 1996), .30-06, .308 Win. (disc. 1998), .300 Win. Mag., .300 Rem. Ultra Mag. (mfg. 2002-2003), .338 Win. Mag. (disc. 1993 - not available with wood stock), 7mm-08 Rem. (disc. 1996), 7mm Rem. Ultra Mag. (mfg. 2002-2003), or 7mm Rem. Mag. cal., long action, walnut finished hardwood stock with cut checkering and vent. recoil pad, open sights, top tang safety with red dot indicator, 22, 24, or 26 in. barrel, drilled and tapped, 6 3/8 or 7 lbs. New 1994.

MSR $496	**$430**	**$340**	**$280**	**$235**	**$195**	**$175**	**$160**

Subtract $10 w/o sights (Model 111-GNS, not available in .300 Rem. Ultra Mag. or 7mm Rem. Ultra Mag. cals., disc. 2004).

This model is also available in left-hand (Model 111-GL, not available in 7mm Rem. Ultra Mag.).

✳ Model 111-GC - .270 Win., .30-06, .300 Win. Mag., or 7mm Rem. Mag. cal., 22 or 24 in. barrel, detachable box mag., walnut finished hardwood stock with cut checkering and vent. recoil pad. Mfg. 1994-2001.

	$385	**$325**	**$275**	**$240**	**$210**	**$175**	**$160**

Last MSR was $441.

This model was also available with left-hand action (Model 111-GLC – disc. 2000).

✳ Model 111-GCNS - .25-06 Rem., .270 Win., .30-06, .300 Win. Mag., or 7mm Rem. Mag. cal., features detachable box mag., no sights. New 2005.

MSR $518	**$440**	**$360**	**$300**	**$245**	**$200**	**$175**	**$160**

MODEL 112V VARMINT RIFLE - .220 Swift, .222 Rem., .223 Rem. (new 1976), .22-250 Rem., .243 Win., or .25-06 Rem. cal., single shot, bolt action, 26 in. heavy barrel, no sights, heavy select walnut stock, checkered, swivels. Mfg. 1975-78.

	$350	**$325**	**$300**	**$275**	**$250**	**$235**	**$225**

MODEL 112 R - .22-250 Rem., .25-06 Rem., or .243 Win. cal., similar to Model 112V, except has 4 shot mag. Disc. 1980.

	$340	**$305**	**$275**	**$250**	**$230**	**$210**	**$175**

MODEL 112-BV - .22-250 Rem. or .223 Rem. cal., alloy steel construction, 26 in. barrel with recessed muzzle, 4 shot mag., brown laminate stock with ambidextrous Wundhammer style pistol grip, 9 1/2 lbs. Mfg. 1993 only.

	$475	**$430**	**$365**	**$315**	**$285**	**$250**	**$215**

MODEL 112-BVSS LONG RANGE - .22-250 Rem. (disc. 1998), .223 Rem. (disc. 1998), .25-06 Rem. (new 1996), .30-06 (new 1996), .308 Win. (mfg. 1996-98), .300 Win. Mag. (new 1996), or 7mm Rem. Mag. (new 1996) cal., 4 shot, pillar bedded laminate wood stock with Wundhammer palm swell, 26 in. stainless steel fluted barrel, bolt handle and trigger guard, recessed muzzle, AccuTrigger became standard 2003, 10.5 lbs. New 1994.

MSR $721	**$595**	**$470**	**$390**	**$325**	**$280**	**$235**	**$200**

✳ Model 112-BVSS-S - .220 Swift, .223 Rem. (disc. 1998), .22-250 Rem. (disc. 1998), or .300 Win. Mag. (new 1996) cal., single shot, 26 in. stainless steel fluted barrel, with target features, 10 1/2 lbs. Mfg. 1994-2001.

	$510	**$420**	**$360**				

Last MSR was $595.

GRADING - PPGS™	100%	98%	95%	90%	80%	70%	60%

MODEL 112-BT COMPETITION GRADE - .223 Rem. or .308 Win. cal., laminated

pillar bedded wood stock with adj. cheek rest and Wundhammer palm swell, vent. forend, 5 shot internal mag., alloy steel receiver with 26 in. matte black finished heavy stainless steel barrel w/o sights, drilled and tapped receiver, approx. 10 7/8 lbs. Mfg. 1994-2001.

	$930	$810	$705	$625	$550	$495	$400

Last MSR was $1,049.

* ✻ *Model 112-BT-S* - .300 Win. Mag. cal., single shot, otherwise similar to Model 112 - BT Competition Grade. Mfg. 1995-2001.

	$930	$810	$705	$625	$550	$495	$400

Last MSR was $1,049.

MODEL 112-FV - .22-250 Rem. or .223 Rem. cal., varmint variation with 26 in. heavy

barrel, with or w/o iron sights, 4-shot mag., black Rynite synthetic stock with recoil pad, 8 7/8 lbs. Mfg. 1991-98.

	$360	$300	$260	$235	$200	$175	$160

Last MSR was $410.

* ✻ *Model 112-FVS* - similar to Model 112-FV, except is single shot with solid bottom receiver and is available in .220 Swift (new 1993) cal. Mfg. 1992-93 only.

	$375	$340	$295	$265	$235	$210	$195

* ✻ *Model 112-FVSS (Long Range)* - .22-250 Rem. (disc. 1998), .223 Rem. (disc. 1998), .25-06 Rem. (new 1995), .30-06 (new 1996), .308 Win. (mfg. 1996-98), .300 Win. Mag. (new 1995), or 7mm Rem. Mag. (new 1995) cal., alloy receiver with 26 in. fluted stainless steel barrel, 4 shot mag., black synthetic pillar bedded sporter stock w/o sights, 8 7/8 lbs. Mfg. 1993-2002.

	$495	$425	$360				

Last MSR was $569.

This model was also available with left-hand action (Model 112-FLVSS, mfg. 1996-2002, not available in .30-06 cal.).

* ✻ *Model 112-FVSS-S* - .220 Swift, .22-250 Rem. (disc. 1998), .223 Rem. (disc. 1998), or .300 Win. Mag. (new 1996) cal., single shot variation, pillar bedded stock, 8 7/8 lbs. Mfg. 1994-2001.

	$480	$415	$355	$300	$270	$230	$200

Last MSR was $549.

MODEL 114 AMERICAN CLASSIC - .270 Win., .30-06, .300 Win. Mag., or 7mm

Rem. Mag. cal., features detachable box mag., long action, no sights. New 2005.

MSR $616	$525	$425	$350	$295	$245	$225	$200

MODEL 114-C (CLASSIC) 114-CU (CLASSIC ULTRA) - .270 Win., .30-06, .300

Win. Mag., or 7mm Rem. Mag. cal., 22 or 24 in. barrel, features high gloss classic American black walnut stock with cut checkering, fitted grip cap, and recoil pad, removable 3 or 4 shot staggered box mag., available with deluxe adj. sights (Model 114-CU, disc. 1995) or w/o sights (Model 114-C, new 1996), approx. 7 1/8 lbs. Mfg. 1991-2000.

	$485	$410	$355	$300	$270	$230	$200

Last MSR was $556.

MODEL 114-U - similar to Model 114-C, except is also available in 7mm STW (disc.

2002) cal., 3 shot internal mag, no sights, approx. 7 lbs. Mfg. 1999-2004.

	$490	$415	$350	$285	$250	$230	$200

Last MSR was $569.

MODEL 114-CE (CLASSIC EUROPEAN) - same cals. as the Model 114-C, except

also available in 7x64mm Brenneke cal., features oil finished stock with Schnabel forend and skip-line checkering, high luster bluing, 22 or 24 in. barrel with adj. rear sight, 7 1/8 lbs. Mfg. 1996-2001.

	$480	$400	$350	$285	$260	$235	$200

Last MSR was $554.

MODEL 116-BSS WEATHER WARRIOR

- .270 Win., .30-06, .300 Win. Mag., .300 Rem. Ultra Mag., or 7mm Rem. Mag. cal., long action, brown wood laminate stock with cut checkering, stainless steel action and tapered barrel, 2-4 shot internal mag., 24 or 26 in. barrel, 7-7 3/4 lbs. Mfg. 2001-2002.

$560   **$480**   **$410**

Last MSR was $644.

MODEL 116-FSS

- .22-250 Rem. (mfg. 1992 only), .223 Rem. (mfg. 1992-98), .243 Win. (mfg. 1993-98), .270 Win., .30-06, .308 Win. (disc. 1998), 7mm Rem. Mag., 7mm STW (mfg. 2001-2002), 7mm Rem. Ultra Mag. (mfg. 2002-2003), .300 Win. Mag., .300 Rem. Ultra Mag. (new 2001), .338 Win. Mag., or .375 H&H (mfg. 2002 only) cal., short (disc.) or long (new 2001) action, features black Dupont Rynite synthetic stock, stainless steel metal parts, drilled and tapped for scope mounting, 22, 24, or 26 in. barrel, 3 or 4 shot mag., 6.75 lbs. New 1991.

MSR $552   **$470**   **$410**   **$345**   **$285**   **$245**   **$225**   **$200**

This model is also available with left-hand action (Model 116-FLSS, disc. 2002).

✳ *Model 116-FCSS* - .270 Win., .30-06, 7mm Rem. Mag., .300 Win. Mag., .338 Win. Mag. (new 2005) cal., otherwise similar to Model 116-FSS, except has removable 3 or 4 shot mag. with recessed push-button release, 22 or 24 in. barrel, 6 1/2 lbs. Mfg. 1992-2001, reintroduced 2005.

MSR $573   **$485**   **$425**   **$350**

Subtract $21 for left-hand action (Model 116-FLCSS).

✳ *Model 116-FSK (Kodiak)* - similar cals. as Model 116-FCSS, except also available in .338 Win Mag. cal., stainless steel construction, 22 in. barrel with recoil arrester, cocking indicator, 3 shot mag., black synthetic sporter stock, no sights, 6 1/2 lbs. Mfg. 1993-2000.

$495   **$430**   **$370**   **$325**   **$290**   **$260**   **$230**

Last MSR was $569.

This model was also available with left-hand action (Model 116-FLSK).

MODEL 116-US (ULTRA STAINLESS)

- .270 Win., .30-06, 7mm Rem. Mag., or .300 Win. Mag. cal., 24 in. barrel, checkered walnut stock and forearm with ebony tip, no sights, 7 1/8 lbs. Mfg. 1995-98.

$625   **$550**   **$500**   **$450**   **$400**   **$360**   **$330**

Last MSR was $700.

MODEL 116-SE (SAFARI EXPRESS)

- .300 Win. Mag. (disc. 2002), .300 Rem. Ultra Mag. (mfg. 2002), .338 Win. Mag. (disc. 2001), .375 H&H (mfg. 2000-2002), .425 Express (mfg. 1995 only), or .458 Win. Mag. cal., stainless steel receiver and 24 in. barrel with adj. muzzle brake, controlled round feeding, select grade checkered walnut stock with solid recoil pad and ebony forend, 3-leaf express sights, 8.5 lbs. Mfg. 1994-2004.

$895   **$775**   **$685**   **$625**   **$575**   **$535**   **$475**

Last MSR was $1,045.

MODEL 116-FSAK

- .270 Win., .30-06, .300 Win. Mag., .300 Rem. Ultra Mag. (new 2001), .338 Win. Mag., .375 H&H (mfg. 2002 only), 7mm STW (mfg. 2001-2002), 7mm Rem. Ultra Mag. (mfg. 2002 only), or 7mm Rem. Mag. cal., short (disc.) or long (new 2001) action, features 22 in. fluted stainless steel barrel with adj. muzzle brake, 6.5 lbs. Mfg. 1994-2004.

$530   **$465**   **$390**   **$340**   **$295**   **$265**   **$235**

Last MSR was $619.

This model was also available with left-hand action (Model 116-FLSAK, not available in 7mm STW, 7mm Rem. Ultra Mag., or .375 H&H cals.).

GRADING - PPGS™	100%	98%	95%	90%	80%	70%	60%

MODEL 116-FCSAK - .270 Win., .30-06, .300 Win. Mag., .338 Win. Mag. (new 2005), or 7mm Rem. Mag. cal., features push-button activated detachable box mag., 22 or 24 (new 2005) in. fluted barrel with adj. muzzle brake, 6 1/2 lbs. Mfg. 1994-2000, reintroduced 2005.

	100%	98%	95%	90%	80%	70%	60%
MSR $661	$560	$495	$415	$350	$315	$275	$245

This model was also available with left-hand action (Model 116-FLCSAK).

MODEL 116FXP3 PACKAGE - 270 Win., .30-06, .300 Rem. Ultra Mag. (disc. 2003), .300 Win. Mag., .338 Win. Mag., 7mm STW (disc. 2002), 7mm Rem. Mag., or 7mm Rem. Ultra Mag. (disc. 2003) cal., stainless long action 22, 24, or 26 in. stainless barrel w/o sights, checkered black synthetic stock, includes nickel finished 3-9x40 scope and mounts, supplied with sling, approx. 6.5-7 lbs. New 2002.

	100%	98%	95%				
MSR $601	$500	$410	$335				

MODEL 170 PUMP RIFLE - .30-30 Win. or .35 Rem. (rare) cal., 22 in. barrel, folding leaf sight, 3 shot tube mag., checkered pistol grip stock. Mfg. 1970-81.

		98%	95%	90%	80%	70%	60%
		$180	$155	$140	$110	$90	$65	$55

This model was mfg. by Emhart.

MODEL 170C - .30-30 Win. cal. only, similar to 170, 18 1/2 in. barrel. Mfg. 1974-81.

		98%	95%	90%	80%	70%	60%
		$195	$170	$150	$115	$90	$65	$55

SHOTGUNS

Most Savage shotguns (except the Model 312 Series) fall under the domain of Savage Industries, Inc. Savage made a wide variety of inexpensive, utilitarian shotguns that, to date, have attracted mostly shooting interest, but little collector interest. A listing of these models may be found in the back of this text under "Serialization."

The models listed are grouped by configuration, and are not in numerical sequence.

MODEL 420 O/U - 12, 16, or 20 ga., 26-30 in. barrel, various chokes, boxlock, double trigger, extractors, plain pistol grip stock. Mfg. 1937-43.

		98%	95%	90%	80%	70%	60%
		$385	$305	$275	$250	$210	$195	$155
Single trigger		$440	$360	$330	$305	$265	$220	$195

MODEL 430 O/U - similar to Model 420, with checkered stock and solid rib, recoil pad.

		98%	95%	90%	80%	70%	60%
		$440	$360	$305	$275	$240	$220	$195
Single trigger		$495	$415	$360	$320	$285	$265	$220

MODEL 220 SINGLE BARREL - 12, 16, 20, 28 ga., or .410 bore, 26-32 in. barrel, various chokes, hammerless, plain pistol grip stock. Mfg. 1938-65.

		98%	95%	90%	80%	70%	60%
		$125	$100	$85	$75	$65	$50	$40

MODEL 220P - similar to Model 220, with poly choke, not made in .410 bore.

		98%	95%	90%	80%	70%	60%
		$90	$65	$55	$45	$35	$30	$30

MODEL 220 AC - similar to Model 220, with Savage adj. choke.

		98%	95%	90%	80%	70%	60%
		$100	$85	$65	$55	$45	$35	$30

MODEL 220L - similar to Model 220, with sidelever. Mfg. 1965-72.

		98%	95%	90%	80%	70%	60%
		$90	$65	$55	$45	$35	$30	$30

MODEL 720 AUTOLOADER STANDARD - 12 or 16 ga., Browning A-5 style semi-auto action, 26-32 in. barrels, various chokes, checkered pistol grip stock. Mfg. 1930-49.

		98%	95%	90%	80%	70%	60%
		$225	$180	$165	$155	$140	$120	$110

MODEL 720 RIOT - see the "Trench/Riot Shotgun" category in the T section for more information and prices.

MODEL 726 SEMI-AUTO UPLAND SPORTER - similar to Model 720, except 2 shell mag. Mfg. 1931-49.

		98%	95%	90%	80%	70%	60%
		$275	$195	$165	$155	$140	$120	$110

GRADING - PPGS™	100%	98%	95%	90%	80%	70%	60%

MODEL 740C SKEET GUN - similar to Model 726, with Cutts Compensator and skeet stock, 24 1/2 in. barrel. Mfg. 1936-49.

| | $305 | $230 | $200 | $175 | $155 | $140 | $120 |

MODEL 745 LIGHTWEIGHT - similar to Model 720, with alloy receiver, 12 ga. only, 28 in. barrel. Mfg. 1940-49.

| | $275 | $195 | $165 | $155 | $140 | $120 | $110 |

MODEL 755 STANDARD SEMI-AUTO - 12 or 16 ga., 26, 28, or 30 in. barrel, various chokes, rounded-off receiver, checkered pistol grip stock. Mfg. 1949-58.

| | $265 | $180 | $160 | $150 | $140 | $120 | $110 |

MODEL 755SC - similar to Model 755, with Savage Super Choke.

| | $275 | $195 | $165 | $155 | $140 | $120 | $110 |

MODEL 775 LIGHTWEIGHT SEMI-AUTO - similar to Model 755, with alloy receiver. Mfg. 1950-65.

| | $275 | $195 | $180 | $165 | $150 | $140 | $120 |

MODEL 775SC - similar to Model 775, with Savage Super Choke.

| | $285 | $205 | $195 | $175 | $160 | $150 | $130 |

MODEL 750 SEMI-AUTO - 12 ga., Browning patterned semi-auto, 26 or 28 in. barrels, various chokes, checkered pistol grip stock. Mfg. 1960-69.

| | $275 | $195 | $165 | $155 | $140 | $120 | $110 |

MODEL 750SC - similar to Model 750, with Savage Super Choke.

| | $285 | $205 | $175 | $165 | $150 | $130 | $120 |

MODEL 750AC - similar to Model 750, with poly choke.

| | $285 | $205 | $175 | $165 | $150 | $130 | $120 |

MODEL 21 SLIDE ACTION - similar to Model 28, except stock has no checkering. Mfg. 1920-28.

| | $300 | $265 | $235 | $190 | $165 | $150 | $130 |

MODEL 28 SLIDE ACTION - 12, 16, or 20 ga., patterned after the Winchester Model 12. Mfg. 1927-34.

| | $300 | $265 | $235 | $190 | $165 | $150 | $130 |

This model was available in either standard configuration (Models 28A and 28B), Riot (28C), Trap (28D), or Special (28S).

MODEL 30 SLIDE ACTION - 12, 16, 20 ga., or .410 bore, 26, 28, or 30 in. barrels, various chokes, VR, plain pistol grip stock. Mfg. 1958-70.

| | $220 | $175 | $155 | $140 | $120 | $100 | $85 |
| Checkered Late Model | $230 | $185 | $165 | $150 | $130 | $110 | $95 |

MODEL 30AC - similar to Model 30, with adj. choke, checkered wood, 12 ga. only. Mfg. 1959-70.

| | $240 | $200 | $175 | $160 | $145 | $120 | $100 |

MODEL 30T TRAP AND DUCK GUN - similar to Model 30, with 30 in. full barrel, 12 ga. only, Monte Carlo stock and pad. Mfg. 1963-70.

| | $230 | $185 | $165 | $150 | $130 | $110 | $90 |

MODEL 30FG TAKEDOWN ACTION - 12, 20 ga., or .410 bore, 26, 28, or 30 in. barrel, various chokes, checkered pistol grip stock. Mfg. 1970-75.

| | $175 | $155 | $130 | $110 | $95 | $85 | $70 |

MODEL 30T TAKEDOWN TRAP - 12 ga. only, 30 in. full barrel, Monte Carlo stock with pad. Mfg. 1970-73.

| | $195 | $175 | $155 | $140 | $110 | $100 | $85 |

GRADING - PPGS™	100%	98%	95%	90%	80%	70%	60%

MODEL 30AC TAKEDOWN - similar to Model 30FG, with adj. choke, 12 or 20 ga., 26 in. barrel. Mfg. 1971-72.

| | $200 | $180 | $165 | $150 | $120 | $110 | $90 |

MODEL 30 TAKEDOWN SLUG GUN - similar to Model 30FG, with 32 in. cylinder bore barrel, rifle sights. Mfg. 1971-disc.

| | $195 | $175 | $160 | $140 | $110 | $100 | $85 |

MODEL 30D TAKEDOWN - similar to Model 30FG, with VR, engraved receiver and pad. Mfg. 1971-disc.

| | $200 | $180 | $165 | $150 | $120 | $110 | $90 |

MODEL 67 SLIDE ACTION - see listing under Stevens Section.

FOX MODELS B, B-SE, AND STEVENS 311 - see listing under Fox and Stevens Sections.

SAVAGE/FOX MODEL FA-1 - 12 ga., 2 3/4 in. chamber, semi-auto, gas operated, walnut stock and forend, cut checkering, 28 or 30 in. vent. rib barrel. Mfg. 1981-82 in Japan.

| | $250 | $215 | $185 | $160 | $140 | $120 | $100 |

SAVAGE/FOX MODEL FP-1 - 12 ga., similar to Model FA-1, except is slide action. Mfg. 1981-82 in Japan.

| | $175 | $150 | $125 | $100 | $85 | $70 | $60 |

MODEL 210F SLUG WARRIOR BOLT ACTION (MASTER SHOT) - 12 ga. only, 3 in. chamber, built on Model 100 action with controlled round feeding, 24 in. rifled barrel (1:35 twist), 2 shot detachable mag., 60 degree bolt lift, Realtree camo finished (new 2003) or black synthetic stock with checkering and recoil pad, top tang safety, no sights, 7.5 lbs. New 1997.

| MSR $475 | $400 | $335 | $290 | $245 | $215 | $195 | $180 |

Add $38 for camo finish (Model 210F Camo).

Add $76 for Turkey configuration with 24 in. barrel and camo coverage (Model 210FT Camo, new 2005).

✳ *Model 210FT* - similar to Model 210F, except has Advantage camo stock and mag., 24 in. smooth bore barrel accepts Win. style choke tubes. Mfg. 1997-2000.

| | $410 | $350 | $305 | $265 | $235 | $215 | $195 |

Last MSR was $466.

MODEL 242 O/U - .410 bore, single exposed hammer, single trigger, barrel selector lever, full chokes. Mfg. 1977-81.

| | $350 | $300 | $260 | $230 | $200 | $175 | $150 |

MODEL 440/440B O/U - 12 or 20 ga., 26, 28, or 30 in. barrels, various chokes, boxlock, ST (Model 440) or SST (Model 440B), extractors, checkered pistol grip stock, VR. Imported from Italy 1968-72.

| | $495 | $440 | $415 | $385 | $330 | $305 | $250 |

MODEL 440T - similar to Model 440, 12 ga., 30 in. barrel only, imp mod. or full choke, wide VR, trap style stock, pad. Mfg. 1969-72.

| | $550 | $470 | $440 | $415 | $385 | $360 | $330 |

MODEL 444 DELUXE - similar to Model 440, with auto ejectors, select walnut. Mfg. 1969-72.

| | $550 | $470 | $440 | $415 | $385 | $360 | $330 |

MODEL 550 SxS - 12 or 20 ga., 26, 28, or 30 in. barrels (made by Valmet - rare), various chokes, boxlock, auto ejectors, single trigger, checkered pistol grip stock. Mfg. 1971-73.

| | $275 | $220 | $195 | $165 | $150 | $130 | $110 |

GRADING - PPGS™	100%	98%	95%	90%	80%	70%	60%

KIMEL KAMPER SINGLE SHOT - 20 ga. or .410 bore, 3 in. chamber, 18 1/2 in. barrel, pistol grip hardwood stock and forearm, butt trap holds 3 shells, bottom opening, exposed hammer. Mfg. 1979-c.1981

	$175	$150	$135	$120	$105	$90	$75

MODEL 312 SERIES O/U - 12 ga. only, boxlock action, 3 in. chambers, vent. barrels, satin chrome finished receiver, checkered walnut stock and forearm, SST, choke tubes, approx. 7 lbs. Mfg. 1990-93.

> The Model 312 Series falls under the domain of Savage Arms, Inc.

✱ *312 Field* - 26 or 28 in. VR barrels with choke tubes.

	$585	$520	$485	$435	$395	$360	$330

✱ *312 Trap* - 30 in. barrels only, Monte Carlo stock with recoil pad.

	$615	$550	$500	$460	$415	$375	$330

✱ *312 Sporting Clays* - 28 in. barrels only with 7 choke tubes provided, recoil pad.

	$595	$530	$485	$435	$395	$360	$320

MODEL 330 O/U - 12 or 20 ga., 26, 28, or 30 in. barrels, various chokes, boxlock, SST, extractors, checkered pistol grip stock. Mfg. by Valmet between 1969-80.

	$495	$440	$385	$335	$275	$250	$220

> Add 25% for extra set of barrels.

MODEL 333T - similar to Model 330, with 30 in. VR barrels bored imp. mod. and full choke, trap stock with pad. Mfg. by Valmet between 1972-80.

	$550	$470	$415	$385	$360	$305	$275

MODEL 333 O/U - 12 or 20 (rare) ga., 26, 28, or 30 in. VR barrels, various chokes, boxlock, SST, auto ejectors, checkered pistol grip stock. Mfg. by Valmet between 1973-80.

	$650	$575	$500	$450	$400	$375	$330

> Add 25% for extra set of barrels.
> Add 30% for 20 ga.

SAVIN, J.C.

Current manufacturer located in St. Etienne, France. J.C. Savin manufactures only best quality shotguns and rifles per individual order. Annual production is approx. 25 long guns. Please contact the factory directly for domestic availability and current pricing.

RIFLES: DOUBLE, CUSTOM

Available in either O/U or SxS sidelock or Anson & Deeley boxlock. Available in various cals. (.30 - .577 NE), 24 or 26 in. barrels.

SHOTGUNS: DOUBLE, CUSTOM

Available in either O/U or SxS sidelock configuration, 12 or 20 ga., DT or ST, premier quality. A SxS round action Dixon model with trigger plate is also available in 12 or 20 ga.

SAXONIA

Current manufacturer located in Schwarzenberg, Germany. No current U.S. importation.

Saxonia makes semi-auto pistols, security/combat shotguns, and bolt action sniper rifles in various configurations. Please contact the company directly (see Trademark Index) to obtain model information and domestic availability.

SCATTERGUN TECHNOLOGIES INC. (S.G.T.)

Current manufacturer located in Berryville, AR since 1999. Previously located in Nashville, TN 1991-1999. Distributor, dealer, and consumer sales.

GRADING - PPGS™	100%	98%	95%	90%	80%	70%	60%

During 1999, Wilson Combat purchased Scattergun Technologies. S.G.T. manufactures practical defense, tactical, and hunting shotguns in 12 ga. only, utilizing Remington Models 870 and 11-87 (disc.) actions in various configurations as listed. All shotguns feature 3 in. chamber capacity and parkerized finish.

SHOTGUNS: SEMI-AUTO

Add $15 for short stock on models listed.
Add $125 for Armor-Tuff finish on models listed.

K-9 MODEL - 12 ga., 18 in. barrel, adj. ghost ring sight, 7 shot mag., side saddle, synthetic buttstock and forearm. Disc. 2003.

	$1,100	$875	$775			

Last MSR was $1,325.

SWAT MODEL - 12 ga., similar to K-9 Model, except has 14 in. barrel and forearm with 11,000 CP flashlight. Disc. 2003.

	$1,400	$1,150	$895			

Last MSR was $1,750.

This model was available for military and law enforcement only.

URBAN SNIPER MODEL - 12 ga., 18 in. rifled barrel, scout optics, 7 shot mag., side saddle, synthetic buttstock, forearm and bipod. Disc. 1999.

	$1,225	$1,075	$950			

Last MSR was $1,390.

SHOTGUNS: SLIDE ACTION

On the following models, Armor-Tuff finish became standard during 2003.

Add $15 for short stock on models listed.
Subtract approx. $100 if w/o Armor Tuff finish.

STANDARD MODEL - 12 or 20 ga., 18 in. barrel, adj. ghost ring sight, 7 shot mag., side saddle, synthetic buttstock and forearm with 11,000 CP flashlight.

MSR $1,150	$975	$875	$725			

PROFESSIONAL MODEL - 12 ga., similar to Standard Model, except has 14 in. barrel and 6 shot mag.

MSR $1,175	$995	$875	$725			

This model is available for military and law enforcement only.

EXPERT MODEL - 12 ga., 18 in. barrel with mod. choke, nickel/Teflon finished receiver, adj. ghost ring sight, forearm incorporates 11,000 CP flashlight. Mfg. 1997-2000.

	$1,200	$995	$775			

Last MSR was $1,350.

ENTRY MODEL - 12 ga., 12 1/2 in. barrel with mod. choke, adj. ghost ring sights, 5 shot mag., side saddle, synthetic buttstock and nylon strap assisted forearm with 5,000 CP flashlight. Disc.

	$995	$800	$600			

Last MSR was $1,125.

This model is available for military and law enforcement only.

COMPACT MODEL - 12 1/2 in. barrel with mod. choke, adj. ghost ring sight, 5 shot mag., synthetic buttstock and forearm. Mfg. 1994-99.

	$575	$510	$420			

Last MSR was $635.

This model was available for military and law enforcement only.

GRADING - PPGS™	100%	98%	95%	90%	80%	70%	60%

PRACTICAL TURKEY MODEL - 20 in. barrel with extra full choke, adj. ghost ring sight, 5 shot mag. for 3 in. shells, synthetic buttstock and forearm. Mfg. 1995-99.

| | $545 | $500 | $465 | | | | |

Last MSR was $595.

LOUIS AWERBUCK SIGNATURE MODEL - 18 in. barrel with fixed choke, adj. ghost ring sight, 5 shot mag., side saddle, wood buttstock with recoil reducer and forearm. Mfg. 1994-99.

| | $625 | $490 | $385 | | | | |

Last MSR was $705.

F.B.I. MODEL - similar to Standard Model, except has 5 shot mag. Disc. 1999.

| | $715 | $625 | $490 | | | | |

Last MSR was $770.

MILITARY MODEL - 18 in. barrel with vent. handguard and M-9 bayonet lug, adj. ghost ring rear sight, 7 shot mag., synthetic stock and grooved corncob forearm. Mfg. 1997-98.

| | $625 | $490 | $385 | | | | |

Last MSR was $690.

PATROL MODEL - 18 in. barrel, adj. ghost ring sight, 5 shot mag., synthetic buttstock and forearm. Disc. 1999.

| | $545 | $500 | $465 | | | | |

Last MSR was $595.

BORDER PATROL MODEL 20 - 12 or 20 ga., similar to Patrol Model, except has 7 shot mag., black synthetic stock and forearm, choice of 18 or 20 in. barrel.

| MSR $875 | | $750 | $650 | $550 | | | |

Add $35 for 20 ga.

BORDER PATROL MODEL 21 - similar to Border Patrol Model 20, except has 14 in. barrel and 6 shot mag.

| MSR $900 | | $775 | $675 | $550 | | | |

This model is available for military and law enforcement only.

CONCEALMENT MODEL 00 - 12 1/2 in. barrel with fixed choke, 5 shot mag., bead sight, grooved wood forearm and pistol grip. Disc. 1998.

| | $490 | $395 | $280 | | | | |

Last MSR was $550.

CONCEALMENT MODEL 01 - similar to Concealment Model 00, except has synthetic finger-grooved combat forearm and pistol grip. Disc. 1993.

| | $475 | $395 | $295 | | | | |

Last MSR was $525.

CONCEALMENT MODEL 02 - similar to Concealment Model 00, except has Pachmayr forearm and pistol grip. Disc. 1993.

| | $495 | $415 | $315 | | | | |

Last MSR was $555.

CONCEALMENT MODEL 03 - similar to Concealment Model 01, except has synthetic nylon strap assisted forearm with 5,000 CP flashlight. Disc. 1993.

| | $550 | $455 | $350 | | | | |

Last MSR was $625.

BREACHING MODEL - similar to Concealment Model 00, except has standoff device. Disc. 1998.

| | $450 | $390 | $340 | | | | |

Last MSR was $500.

GRADING - PPGS™	100%	98%	95%	90%	80%	70%	60%

SCHALL

Previous manufacturer located in Hartford, CT.

Schall provided parts and repair service for Fiala pistols, and produced additional repeating pistols with the Schall name between 1930-36.

REPEATING HANDGUN - .22 LR cal., 10 round mag. fed manual repeating action, tapered barrel 7 1/2 in. barrel with fixed sights and blue finish, walnut ribbed grips, usually marked "Schall & Co./New Haven, Conn. USA", some have no markings.

	$450	$425	$400	$375	$325	$250	$200

Subtract 50% if not in working order.

SCHEIRING GmbH

Current custom rifle manufacturer located in Ferlach, Austria.

H. Scheiring manufactures best quality rifles (including O/U, SxS, and Stalking variations) per individual customer special order. Scheiring was a member of the Ferlach Guild until it was dissolved in 2004. The factory should be contacted directly for more information regarding current models and domestic availability (see Trademark Index).

SCHELLER SPEZIALWAFFEN

Previous manufacturer located in Suhl, Germany that specialized in bolt action rifles.

SCHERZ, MICHAEL

Current custom rifle manufacturer located in Yuma, AZ.

Michael Scherz specializes in high-quality, bolt action rifles in .550 Magnum caliber. Please contact him directly for more information, including pricing and availability (see Trademark Index).

SCHILLING, FA. ALFRED

Current rifle manufacturer and gunsmith established in 1898, and located in Zella-Mehlis, Germany.

Current owner Jorg Schilling manufactures high quality target rifles, in addition to providing gunsmithing services, including color case hardening and bluing. All guns are custom order, and the standard Schilling breechblock rifle retails at $6,500, while the Aydt target model has an MSR of $5,000. Please contact the company for more information, including an individual price quotation, delivery time, and availability (see Trademark Index).

SCHMIDT-RUBIN RIFLES

Please refer to the Swiss Military listing in this section.

SCHMITT FRERES

Previous manufacturer located in Saint Etienne, France.

This manufacturer produced copies of 1894 patent Darne R model guns until 1956. While higher grades do exist, they do not command the prices given for the later patent (1909) Darne-produced guns. Lower grade guns will be priced in the same range as Soleihac and lower grade Darne R models.

SCHUERMAN ARMS., LTD.

Current bolt action rifle manufacturer located in Scottsdale, AZ. Consumer direct sales.

RIFLES: BOLT ACTION

MODEL SA40 - various cals., including WSMs, WSSMs, and Rem. Ultra Mags., right- or left-hand action features three rotating locking lugs in bolt, 70 degree bolt lift, 20-26 in. matte stainless steel barrel and action, controlled round feeding, fully enclosed case head, three-position safety, choice of detachable mag., hinged floorplate, or blind box mag., laminated fiberglass sporter style stock. New 2001.

MSR $3,450	$3,450	$3,075	$2,700	$2,400	$2,100	$1,800	$1,600

GRADING - PPGS™	100%	98%	95%	90%	80%	70%	60%

SCHUETZEN PISTOL WORKS

Schuetzen Pistol Works is the in-house custom shop of Olympic Arms. Schuetzen Pistol Works has been customizing Safari Arms and Olympic Arms 1911 style pistols since 1997. For currently manufactured pistols, please refer to the Olympic Arms listing. For discontinued models, please refer to the Safari Arms listing.

SCHUETZEN RIFLES

A Schuetzen Rifle is a special single-shot target rifle. During the time span 1875-1945 this target configuration rifle was very popular with competition shooters. Many of these guns had elaborate locking systems, top quality sights, double-set triggers, heavy barrels, palm and thumb rests, sculptured cheekpiece, Swiss style buttplate, etc. Rather than list all the various domestic and European makers (there are hundreds), it should be noted that, since there are so many combinations of options for this configuration, most guns have to be examined and appraised individually. Most non-major trademarks sell in the $650-$1,750 range, depending on features and condition. A famous trademark specimen (Ballard, Stevens, Winchester, etc.) in a rare model with superior original condition can bring over $10,000. Schuetzen Rifles are a field in themselves and a knowledgeable dealer/collector should be consulted before buying or selling one of these guns.

SCHULTZ & LARSEN

Previous manufacturer located in Otterup, Denmark circa 1911.

RIFLES: BOLT ACTION

NO. 47 MATCH RIFLE - .22 LR cal., single shot, 28 in. heavy barrel, target sights, set trigger, free rifle stock.

$660	$550	$495	$440	$385	$360	$330

M61 MATCH RIFLE - .22 LR cal., single shot, 28 in. heavy barrel, target sights, set trigger, free rifle stock, palm rest.

$895	$825	$740	$680	$600	$550	$500

M62 MATCH RIFLE - various cals., single shot, 28 in. heavy barrel, target sights, set trigger, free rifle stock, palm rest.

$995	$875	$780	$700	$620	$550	$500

MODEL 54 FREE RIFLE - any American centerfire standard caliber, plus 6.5x55mm, 27 in. heavy barrel, target sights, free rifle stock.

$825	$745	$690	$605	$550	$495	$440

MODEL 54J SPORTING RIFLE - .270 Win., .30-06, or 7x61 Sharpe and Hart cal., 3 shot, 24 in. barrel, checkered Monte Carlo stock, no sights.

$650	$550	$470	$415	$360	$330	$300

MODEL 68 DL - .22-250 Rem., .243 Win., 6mm Rem., .264 Win. Mag., .270 Win., .30-06, .308 Win., 7x61 S&H, 7mm Rem. Mag., 8x57JS, .300 Win. Mag., .308 Norma Mag., .338 Win. Mag., .358 Norma Mag., or .458 Win. Mag. cal., 24 in. barrel, Bofors Steel receiver, bolt has 4 rear locking lugs, select French walnut, adj. trigger, no sights except for .458 Mag.

$725	$650	$575	$525	$495	$460	$430

SHOTGUNS: O/U

Schultz & Larsen also manufactured a very limited quantity of O/U shotguns, including a 20 ga. boxlock. Current pricing reflects shooting value more than collectibility.

SCOTT, W.C., LTD.

Previous manufacturer established during 1834 and located in Birmingham, England. All operations ceased during 1991.

Established in 1834 by William Scott, located in Birmingham, England, and remained in the family until 1897. At this time, Scott merged with P. Webley & Son to form Webley & Scott Revolver and Arms Co., Ltd. (later changed to Webley & Scott Ltd.). Even though Scott family members were no longer associated with this new company, the Scott gun-line was continued with the trademark intact until 1935. Thereafter, only a few guns were marked Scott. In 1979, Webley & Scott ceased manufacture of all firearms. A new company, W. & C. Scott, was formed in 1980 utilizing mostly employees of Webley & Scott. W. & C. Scott remained part of its parent company, Harris & Sheldon (also had controlling interest in Hardy and Churchill trademarks), until 1985 when Scott was purchased by Holland & Holland. Manufacture of Scott guns decreased substantially after the merger, and in September 1991, W. & C. Scott ceased operation altogether. During its 157 years of production, Scott and Webley & Scott produced approximately, 150,000 double guns, 10,000 rifles (either double or bolt-action) and thousands of single guns and single rifles.

SHOTGUNS: SxS

All W.C. Scott Shotguns were discontinued in 1990. W.C. Scott also manufactured many hammer guns that vary in price from $250-$2,500, depending on grade and original condition.

KINMOUNT - 12, 16, 20, or 28 ga., boxlock action, ejectors, deluxe checkered walnut, scroll engraving.

$6,500	$5,750	$5,000	$4,500	$4,000	$3,000	$2,500

Last MSR was $11,000.

Add 20% for 28 ga. or .410 bore.
Add 10% for SNT.

BOWOOD - 12, 16, 20, or 28 ga., boxlock action, ejectors, deluxe checkered walnut, extensive scroll engraving.

$7,500	$6,500	$5,750	$5,000	$4,500	$4,000	$3,500

Last MSR was $12,500.

Add 20% for 28 ga. or .410 bore.
Add 10% for SNT.

CHATSWORTH - 12, 16, 20, or 28 ga., top-of-the-line boxlock action, ejectors, deluxe checkered walnut, extensive scroll engraving.

$8,750	$7,500	$6,500	$5,750	$5,000	$4,500	$4,000

Last MSR was $14,000.

Add 20% for 28 ga. or .410 bore.
Add 10% for SNT.

BLENHEIM - 12 bore only, upgraded models, custom-made to individual specifications, originally priced per individual order.

Specimen rarity precludes percentage grading pricing. Individual appraisals have to be secured on this model.

SEARCY, B. & CO.

Current rifle manufacturer established in 1975 and located in Boron, CA.

RIFLES: SxS

B. Searcy & Co. manufactures a unique stainless steel double rifle in a variety of calibers. Current models include: PH Boxlock Model w/ ejectors ($9,500 - MSR), Deluxe Grade ($15,000 - MSR), Under Lever Model ($16,500 - MSR), and the Back Action Sidelock ($18,000 - MSR). Previous models included the .577 NE Boxlock (last MSR was $18,000), .600 NE Boxlock (last MSR was $24,000), .700 NE Boxlock (last MSR was $50,000), .577 NE or .600 NE Sidelock (last MSR was $35,000), and the .700 NE Sidelock (last MSR was $50,000). Please contact the company directly (see Trademark Index) for current model information and availability.

GRADING - PPGS™	100%	98%	95%	90%	80%	70%	60%

SEARS ROEBUCK AND CO.

Catalog merchandiser that, in addition to selling major trademark firearms, also private labeled many configurations of firearms (mostly longarms) under a variety of trademarks and logos (i.e., J.C. Higgins, Ted Williams, Ranger, etc.). Sears discontinued the sale of all firearms circa 1980, and the Ted Williams trademark was stopped circa 1978.

A general guideline for Sears Roebuck and related labels (most are marked "Sears, Roebuck and Co." on left side of barrel) is that values are generally lower than those of the major factory models from which they were derived. Remember, 99% of Sears Roebuck and related label guns get priced by their shootability factor in today's competitive marketplace, not collectibility. An extensive crossover listing (see Storebrand Cross-Over List) has been provided in the back of this text for linking up the various Sears Roebuck models to the original manufacturer with respective "crossover" model numbers.

SECURITY INDUSTRIES

Previous manufacturer located in Little Ferry, NJ.

REVOLVERS

MODEL PSS 38 DOUBLE ACTION - .38 Spl. cal., 5 shot cylinder, 2 in. barrel, stainless steel, fixed sights, wood grips. Mfg. 1973-78.

	$175	$150	$140	$130	$125	$110	$100

MODEL PM357 - .357 Mag. cal., similar to Model PSS 38, 2 1/2 in. barrel. Mfg. 1975-disc.

	$225	$175	$165	$150	$140	$125	$110

MODEL PPM 357 - .357 Mag. cal., 5 shot, 2 in. barrel, spurless hammer until 1977, new models have spur. Mfg. 1965-disc.

	$225	$175	$165	$150	$140	$125	$110

SEDCO INDUSTRIES, INC.

Previous manufacturer located in Lake Elsinore, CA until 1991.

PISTOLS: SEMI-AUTO

MODEL SP-22 - .22 LR cal., single action, 2 1/2 in. barrel, rotary safety, serrated slide, nickel, satin nickel (new 1990), or black metal finish, simulated pearl grips in white, blue, grey, or pink, 11 oz. Mfg. 1989-90 only.

	$60	$55	$50	$45	$40	$35	$35

Last MSR was $69.

SEDGLEY, R.F., INC.

Previous manufacturer located in Philadelphia, PA.

RIFLES: BOLT ACTION

SPRINGFIELD SPORTING RIFLE - .218 Bee, .220 Swift, .22-3000, .22-4000, .22 Hornet, .25-35 WCF, .250-3000 Sav., .257 Roberts, .270 Win., 7x57mm Mauser, or .30-06 cal., '03 Springfield bolt action, 24 in. barrel, Lyman receiver sight, checkered pistol grip stock, pre-WWII.

	$1,250	$1,125	$995	$875	$750	$625	$495

SPRINGFIELD CARBINE SPORTER - similar to Rifle, with 20 in. barrel, and full length stock.

	$1,450	$1,250	$1,125	$995	$875	$750	$625

SEECAMP, L.W. CO., INC.

Current handgun manufacturer located in Milford, CT. Dealer direct sales only.

All Seecamp pistols are hand machined and hand fitted from stainless steel. Manufacture has always emphasized quality over quantity - this explains why values often exceed the company's retail prices. There is simply more demand than supply.

PISTOLS: SEMI-AUTO

LWS .25 ACP MODEL - .25 ACP cal., double action, 2 in. barrel, 7 shot mag., stainless steel, matte finish, no sights, 12 oz. Approx. 4,000 mfg. 1981-85.

$400	$325	$275

Last MSR was $275.

LWS 32 MODEL - .32 ACP cal., (mfg. recommends .32 ACP Win. Silvertip ammo only), double action, 2.06 in. barrel, stainless steel, 6 shot mag., no sights, extreme backorder situation coupled with high demand has resulted in elevated 100% values, 11 1/2 oz. Mfg. Jan. 1985-present.

MSR $425	$425	$375	$350

Add $100 for California edition (with trigger mounted safety).

This model is available in either a matte or polished finish. The polished finish carries a slight premium.

MATCHED PAIR - includes both .25 ACP and .32 ACP pistols with the same serial number, approx. 200 sets were mfg. before the BATF stopped this practice.

$1,200	$1,000	$850

This set contained a matte finished .25 ACP and a polished .32 ACP.

LWS-380 MODEL - .380 ACP cal. (mfg. recommends .380 ACP Win. Silvertip ammo only), identical in appearance to the LWS 32 Model, 2.06 in. barrel, double action only, delayed blowback mechanism, polished stainless steel, checkered black glass filled nylon grips, no sights, 11.5 oz. Very limited production beginning 2000.

MSR $850	$850	$775	$650

SEITZ

Previous manufacturer located in Portland, OR circa mid-1980s-1993.

SHOTGUNS: SINGLE BARREL TRAP

SINGLE BARREL TRAP GUN - 12 ga. only, single barrel, various barrel lengths, pull or release trigger, only 45 guns mfg.

$18,500	$16,000	$13,000	$10,000	$8,500	$7,700	$6,950

SEMMERLING

Current trademark owned by American Derringer Corp., located in Waco, TX. Previously manufactured by Semmerling Corporation, located in Boston, MA from 1978-1982.

Less than 600 LM-4 pistols were originally mfg. by the Semmerling Corporation.

PISTOLS: SLIDE ACTION

LM-4 PISTOL - .45 ACP cal., 2 in. barrel, blue, smallest .45 ACP repeater available, slide is worked manually with thumb on serrated slide-top, extremely high quality, hand fitted and choice of finishes include chrome, electroless nickel, or high polish blue.

Chrome	$2,950	$2,600	$2,300	$2,100	$1,950	$1,725	$1,600
Electroless nickel	$3,200	$2,950	$2,600	$2,300	$2,100	$1,950	$1,725
High polish blue	$4,950	$4,500	$4,000	$3,600	$3,200	$2,800	$2,500

The original U.S. Army contract pistol mfg. by Semmerling in Boston sold for $5,000. Earlier mfg. by Lichtman will also command a premium over values listed.

GRADING - PPGS™	100%	98%	95%	90%	80%	70%	60%

✳ **LM-4 (Current Mfg.)** - .45 ACP cal., 2 in. barrel, thumb activated slide mechanism, matte stainless steel (disc.) or blue finish, 24 oz. Limited mfg. by special order only since 1998.

The 2003 MSR on this model was $2,655.

Please contact American Derringer directly for a price quotation on this special order model.

SENTINEL ARMS

Previous importer of Arsenal Bulgaria pistols and rifles.

SERBU FIREARMS, INC.

Current manufacturer located in Tampa, FL.

RIFLES: SINGLE SHOT

SINGLE SHOT MODEL - .50 BMG cal., single shot bolt action, 22 (carbine) or 29 (rifle) in. match grade barrel with muzzle brake, AR-15 style trigger and safety, Picatinny rail, parkerized finish, 22 lbs.

MSR $2,195	$2,000	$1,850	$1,650	$1,450	$1,250	$1,175	$975

Add $25 for "Have a Nice Day" engraving on Shark muzzle brake.

SERENGETI RIFLES, INC.

Current custom rifle manufacturer and stock maker located in Kalispell, MT.

Serengeti Rifles Inc. manufactures a complete line of high-quality, custom-order bolt action rifles, in addition to its own line of proprietary actions and stocks. Please contact the company directly for more information, including pricing, availability and delivery time (see Trademark Index.)

C. SHARPS ARMS CO. INC.

Current manufacturer located in Big Timber, MT.

C. Sharps Arms Co. Inc. currently distributes smokeless powder replicas of C. Sharps rifles/carbines and the Winchester Model 1885 single shot. They are able to shoot both smokeless and black powder loads. Most models are available in the following cals.: .38-55, .40-50, .40-65, .40-70, .40-90, .45-70, .45-90, .45-100, .45-110, .45-120, .50-70, .50-90, .50-100, and .50-140. All models are authentically reproduced and high quality.

RIFLES: REPRODUCTIONS, SHARPS BLACK POWDER

Currently, C. Sharps Arms Co. Inc. is experiencing a back order situation on some of their models. New Models 1875 and 1885 are experiencing a 2-4 month wait, while the New Model 1874 and New Model 1877 are currently running over 2-3 years for delivery. However, C. Sharps currently has some models in stock - call for availability and pricing (see Trademark Index).

Because each rifle is a special order, there are many options available which would be added to the base price shown.

NEW MODEL 1874 BRIDGEPORT SPORTING RIFLE

MSR $1,570	$1,570	$1,450	$1,400	$1,350	$1,300	$1,200	$1,100

In addition to the 1874 Sporting Model, a custom long range target rifle or Schuetzen short range target rifle is available in this model. Because of the extended back order situation on this model, premiums will probably exist for those people who would rather pay a premium than wait.

NEW MODEL 1874 HARTFORD SPORTING RIFLE

	$1,700	$1,575	$1,475	$1,400	$1,350	$1,300	$1,200

Last MSR was $1,775.

NEW MODEL 1874 CARBINE HUNTER

	$1,450	$1,395	$1,300	$1,250	$1,200	$1,150	$1,100

Last MSR was $1,495.

CUSTOM NEW MODEL 1874 BOSS GUN - features 34 in. No. 1 heavy tapered octagon barrel, vernier tang sight, straight grip stock with cheekrest and steel shotgun butt.

This gun is custom order only. Please contact the factory to obtain a quotation on this model.

NEW MODEL 1875 SPORTING RIFLE - similar to New Model 1875 Classic, except has receiver with round crown.

MSR $1,385	$1,325	$1,225	$1,100	$975	$900	$825	$750

NEW MODEL 1875 TARGET SPORTING RIFLE - .38-55, .40-65, .40-70 Sharps Straight, .45-70 Govt., or .45-90 cal., 30 in. heavy tapered round barrel American walnut stock with pistol grip, black buttplate, color case receiver, drilled and tapped, single trigger, 11 lbs. Limited mfg. 2004 only.

$1,075	$975	$925	$850	$795	$725	$650

Last MSR was $1,137.

NEW MODEL 1875 CLASSIC RIFLE - receiver with octagon top, 26, 28, or 30 in. tapered full octagon barrel, straight grip stock with steel toe plate, 9 1/2 lbs. New 1992.

MSR $1,185	$1,125	$995	$900	$850	$750	$700	$650

NEW MODEL 1875 CARBINE - features 24 in. tapered round barrel. Mfg. 1996-98.

$875	$750	$675	$600	$500	$450	$375

Last MSR was $810.

NEW MODEL 1875 SADDLE RIFLE - receiver with octagon top, 26 in. barrel only. Disc. 1998.

$925	$850	$775	$700	$625	$550	$460

Last MSR was $910.

NEW MODEL 1875 BUSINESS RIFLE - receiver with round top, 28 in. heavy tapered round barrel. Disc. 1998.

$875	$775	$700	$625	$550	$500	$450

Last MSR was $810.

Add $50 for barrel sights.

CUSTOM NEW MODEL 1877 -.44-90, .45-70 Govt., .45-90, or .45-100 cal., 32 or 34 in. tapered round barrel, presentation grade American or English walnut stock, checkered pistol grip and forend, ebony forend tip, classic long range sights, 10 lbs. Limited production 2004 only.

$5,250	$4,750	$4,450	$4,100	$3,750	$3,450	$3,100

Last MSR was $5,500.

NEW MODEL 1885 HIGHWALL - .22 LR, .22 Hornet, .219 Zipper, .30-40 Krag, .32-40, .348 Win., .38-55 WCF, .40-65, .405 Win., .444 Marlin, or .45-70 cal., patterned after the Winchester Model 1885 single shot, falling block action, case colored receiver and small parts, 26-30 in. octagon barrel. New 1992.

MSR $1,350	$1,050	$900	$775	$650	$550	$475	$410

Add $200 for New Model 1885 Highwall Classic rifle (crescent buttplate and satin grey receiver finish).

SHARPS, CHRISTIAN

Previously manufactured by Sharps Rifle Manufacturing Company circa 1851-1855 and located in Windsor, VT. Also manufactured in Hartford, CT under same name between 1855-1874. Reorganized as Sharps Rifle Company in 1876 with production resuming in Hartford (1876 only) and Bridgeport, CT from 1877-1881.

100%	98%	95%	90%	80%	70%	60%	50%	40%	30%	20%	10%

HANDGUNS

REVOLVER, PERCUSSION - made 1850s in Philadelphia, production about 2000, 3 in. octagonal tip-up barrel with rib, .25 caliber, 6 shot.

$1,950	$1,750	$1,500	$1,275	$1,100	$1,000	$900	$800	$700	$600	$500	$400

PEPPERBOX PISTOL - also marked Sharps and Hankins, 4-shot breech-loading, .32, .30, or .22 rimfire cal., firing pin rotates, brass frame with silver plating, or case-hardening on iron frame.

  * *First Model* - 5 variations, 2 1/2 in. barrel. Scarcer variations can be worth up to 150% more.

$595	$550	$500	$465	$430	$400	$360	$330	$300	$275	$250	$225

  * *Second Model* - 5 variations, 3 in. barrel. Scarcer variations can be worth up to 150% more.

$595	$550	$500	$465	$430	$400	$360	$330	$300	$275	$250	$225

  * *Third Model* - Sharps and Hankins markings, .32 rimfire short, 4 variations, 3 1/2 in. barrel. Premium for scarcer variations.

$750	$700	$650	$600	$560	$520	$480	$440	$400	$360	$320	$280

  * *Fourth Model* - 4 variations, 2 1/2, 3, or 3 1/2 in. barrel, bird's head grip, .32 rimfire long. Premium for scarcer variations.

$650	$575	$525	$475	$430	$400	$360	$330	$300	$275	$250	$225

RIFLES: BREECH LOADING

The earliest Sharps rifles and carbines were made for Christian Sharps by A.S. Nippes, in Mill Creek, PA circa 1850, and a year later by Robbins and Lawrence Co. of Windsor, VT. Not until 1856 did the Sharps Rifle Co. of Hartford, CT begin to manufacture its own guns.

MODEL 1849 RIFLE - .36 or .44 cal., percussion breechloader, 30 in. barrels and brass patchboxes were standard, serial numbered 1 and up, very few examples exist, less than 100 mfg. These are the first of all Sharps long guns, there is no fixed value range. Depending on condition, they could range from $5,000 to $50,000+.

MODEL 1850 RIFLE - .36 or .44 cal., incorporated the Maynard tape primer on the right side of the breech, features similar to Model 1849, approx. 150 mfg. by A.S. Nippes, very rare. Values only slightly less than Model 1849.

MODEL 1851 CARBINE - .52 cal. percussion, 21 5/8 barrel, hammer mounted inside frame, Maynard tape primer. Approx. 1,800 mfg. by Robbins and Lawrence, 200 went to U.S. Government - these will bring a premium.

N/A	N/A	$11,000	$9,900	$8,800	$7,920	$7,100	$6,600	$6,050	$5,350	$4,840	$4,400

MODEL 1852 CARBINE - this design became standard for all the Sharps for the next two decades, first to be called "slant breech," established Christian Sharps as a major gun manufacturer. Approx. 5,000 mfg. by Robbins and Lawrence, U.S. military markings will command a premium.

N/A	N/A	$7,700	$6,930	$5,940	$5,170	$4,620	$4,180	$3,630	$3,300	$2,860	$2,420

MODEL 1853 CARBINE - .52 cal., very similar to Model 1852, with walnut stock and brass patchbox, Sharps patented pellet primer feed, ser. no. range 9,000-19,000.

N/A	N/A	$6,600	$5,720	$4,950	$4,180	$3,520	$2,750	$2,200	$1,980	$1,650	$1,320

  Approx. 10,000 mfg. by Robbins and Lawrence 1854-1858, an additional 3,000 rifles mfg. - subtract 25%.

MODEL 1855 CARBINE - .52 cal., U.S. military model, all with Maynard tape primer, this was the period that Robbins and Lawrence failed, and Sharps Rifle Co. took over production. 800 mfg.

N/A	N/A	$9,200	$8,580	$7,480	$6,270	$5,500	$4,400	$3,630	$3,080	$2,750	$2,420

100%	98%	95%	90%	80%	70%	60%	50%	40%	30%	20%	10%

Sharps "New Model"

Manufactured in Hartford, CT by Sharps Rifle Manufacturing Co. circa 1859-1866. Visibly different from earlier models because of straight breech and pellet priming feature built into lock plate. Approx. 115,000 were built, all in .52 cal. breechloading paper cartridge. Carbines had 22 in. barrels, rifles came standard with 30 in. round barrels. After ser. nos. reached 100,000, a "C" prefix was used in the number - i.e. C500 represents ser. no. 100,500.

MODEL 1859 CARBINE - standard with all-iron furniture and patchbox, first 3,000 had brass instead of iron, ser. no. range 30,000-75,000. Approx. 33,000 mfg.

N/A	N/A	$10,200	$9,000	$7,200	$6,000	$4,800	$4,200	$3,600	$3,000	$2,400	$1,800

MODEL 1863 CARBINE - made with and w/o iron patchbox, ser. no. range 75,000 - 140,000. Approx. 65,000 mfg. - those with patchbox will bring a premium.

N/A	N/A	$8,800	$7,700	$6,050	$4,950	$3,850	$3,300	$2,750	$2,200	$1,650	$1,325

MODEL 1865 CARBINE - made w/o patchbox, ser. no. range 140,000-145,000. Only 5,000 mfg.

N/A	N/A	$9,000	$8,000	$6,500	$5,500	$4,500	$4,000	$3,500	$3,000	$2,500	$2,000

MODEL 1859 RIFLE - iron patchbox only, long forearm fastened with three barrel bands, approx. 4,300 mfg. in carbine ser. range with lug on barrel for attachment of saber bayonet. Approx. 600 were mfg. with 36 in. long barrel - these will command a premium.

$14,000	$12,000	$10,500	$9,500	$7,800	$6,500	$5,000	$4,000	$3,000	$2,500	$2,000	$1,500

COFFEE MILL MODEL - experimental variation buttstock with a grinding device and detachable handle that was fitted to several Model 1859 & 1863 Carbines. Designed to provide a quick and easy method for cavalry troops in the field to process coffee beans or corn for meals. Field trials are believed to have been in Trenton, NJ circa 1863. Very few originals known - no official records indicating government acceptance. Originals are extremely rare and values could range from $10,000-$50,000.

> Buyer beware! Many fakes exist.

MODEL 1863 RIFLE - adapted for socket bayonet, shared ser. range with carbine. Approx. 6,000 mfg.

N/A	N/A	$9,500	$8,700	$6,800	$5,500	$4,500	$3,500	$2,700	$2,200	$1,800	$1,200

MODEL 1865 RIFLE - only 1,000 mfg. in carbine ser. range.

N/A	N/A	$11,500	$10,500	$8,600	$7,500	$6,000	$4,700	$3,700	$3,200	$2,800	$2,200

Sharps Cartridge Conversions

In 1867, the U.S. government decided to convert their percussion Sharps carbines and rifles to the new .50/70 metallic cartridge. Approx. 31,000 carbines and 1,000 rifles were converted by the Sharps Co. Any original, six groove barrels that were worn beyond specification had a groove liner installed. Those barrels meeting specs. remained unaltered. All buttstocks were stamped on the left side with "D.F.C." in a ribbon cartouche, the initials for the principal sub-inspector, David F. Clark. Damaged buttstocks were all replaced with the plain (no patchbox) Model 1865 buttstock, regardless of the model of the carbine; however, many of the old style buttplates with notches for patchboxes were retained.

.50/70 CARBINES - most had relined three groove barrels, approx. 31,000 remodeled. Those found with original six groove barrels will command a slight premium, as will those Model 1859s & Model 1863s with original patchbox buttstocks.

N/A	N/A	$4,900	$4,200	$3,300	$2,800	$2,300	$2,000	$1,800	$1,600	$1,400	$1,200

.50/70 RIFLES - all had three groove relined barrels, approx. 1,000 converted in 1867. More rare, but do not command any higher prices than their carbine counterparts.

100%	98%	95%	90%	80%	70%	60%	50%	40%	30%	20%	10%

SPRINGFIELD/SHARPS MODEL 1870-1871 - approx. 1,000 rifles and 300 carbines altered by Springfield Armory to fire .50/70 metallic cartridge, in addition to those done by Sharps Co., rifle barrels 35 1/2 in., carbine barrels 22 in., receivers color case hardened, all other metal parts bright finish, own ser. range, and numbered on receiver tang and left side of barrel.

* *Rifles*

N/A	N/A	$5,720	$4,950	$4,180	$3,630	$3,190	$2,860	$2,530	$2,200	$1,870	$1,650

* *Carbines*

N/A	N/A	$5,390	$4,730	$3,740	$3,300	$2,750	$2,530	$2,310	$1,980	$1,760	$1,540

Sharps Metallic Cartridge Models

MODEL 1874 - mfg. in several configurations and a variety of calibers, designed to fire metallic cartridges and was not a conversion from percussion parts, made famous for its deadly accuracy at long distances and became known as the "Buffalo Rifle" of its day. Mfg. in Hartford, CT circa 1874-76, and in Bridgeport, CT circa 1881.

* *Sporting Model* - .40, .44, .45 or .50 cal., variety of barrel lengths and weights, many special order features. Approx. 6,500 mfg.

N/A	N/A	$13,500	$11,000	$9,000	$7,500	$6,000	$5,000	$4,200	$3,500	$3,000	$2,500

* *Business Rifle* - no frills version of the 1874 Sporting, with shorter, round barrel and open sights.

N/A	N/A	$9,000	$8,200	$7,300	$6,600	$5,000	$4,200	$3,500	$2,700	$2,200	$2,000

* *Military Rifle* - .45/70 or .50/70 cal., long forearm and three barrel bands. Approx. 1,700 mfg.

N/A	N/A	$7,000	$6,500	$5,500	$4,500	$3,700	$3,200	$2,700	$2,300	$2,000	$1,700

* *Military Carbine* - most in .50/70 cal., very similar to previous Sharps carbines. Less than 500 mfg.

N/A	N/A	$8,000	$7,500	$6,000	$5,000	$4,000	$3,200	$2,800	$2,400	$2,000	$1,600

* *Meachan Type Conversion* - most in .45/70 cal., very similar to Business Rifle, with both round and octagon barrels, mfg. from Civil War Sharps carbine actions and surplus, as well as new parts by several commercial firms in the 1880s after Sharps Rifle Co. closed. Sharps Co. assembled several hundred of these from 1879-1881 from existing parts on hand.

N/A	N/A	$7,500	$6,800	$5,700	$4,500	$3,700	$3,200	$2,800	$2,200	$1,800	$1,500

While of lesser quality than the Model 1874, these rifles were widely used on the Western frontier and have become very desirable to today's firearms collectors.

MODEL 1878 SHARPS-BORCHARDT - many cals. and barrel lengths, single trigger, hammerless action designed by Hugo Borchardt, carbines, military, sporting, and target rifles were all mfg., but sales suffered from a bolt and lever action market glut. Less than 9,000 mfg. by Sharps Rifle Co. in Bridgeport, CT c. 1878-81.

N/A	N/A	$5,500	$5,000	$4,000	$3,200	$2,800	$2,500	$2,200	$1,900	$1,600	$1,300

Special order or deluxe models with other than standard features will command a premium.

GRADING - PPGS™	100%	98%	95%	90%	80%	70%	60%

SHERIDAN PRODUCTS INCORPORATED

Previous manufacturer located in Racine, WI.

PISTOLS: SINGLE SHOT

KNOCKABOUT - .22 S-L-LR cal., 5 in. barrel, checkered plastic grips, fixed sights. Mfg. 1953-60.

		$195	$150	$110	$100	$85	$75	$60

GRADING - PPGS™	100%	98%	95%	90%	80%	70%	60%

SHILEN RIFLES, INCORPORATED

Previous manufacturer located in Enis, TX circa 1975-mid 1980s.

RIFLES: BOLT ACTION

Older Shilen rifles have become very desirable for target shooters and other accuracy enthusiasts. Because of their small quantities of manufacture (approx. 3,350 mfg.) and new-found demand, prices have gone up considerably on this trademark. Originally, the Sporters retailed in the $600-$700 range, but at the end, prices were in the $3,500 range.

DGA SPORTER - .17 Rem., .223 Rem., .22-250 Rem., .220 Swift, 6mm Rem., .243 Win., .250 Savage, .257 Roberts, .284 Win., .308 Win., or .358 Win. cal., 3 shot mag., 24 in. barrel, no sights, claro walnut stock.

$1,475	$1,175	$950	$800	$675	$575	$495

DGA VARMINTER - similar to Sporter, except 25 in. medium heavy barrel.

$1,395	$1,100	$900	$775	$650	$575	$495

DGA SILHOUETTE RIFLE - similar to Varminter, .308 Win. cal. only.

$1,395	$1,100	$900	$775	$650	$575	$495

DGA BENCHREST RIFLE - single shot, choice of cals., 26 in. heavy or medium barrel, no sights, choice of fiberglass or walnut stock, thumbhole available.

$1,450	$1,200	$950	$800	$650	$575	$495

SHILOH RIFLE MFG. CO.

Current manufacturer located in Big Timber, MT since 1983. Previously manufactured by Shiloh Products, a division of Drovel Tool Company of Farmingdale, NY, 1976-1983. Dealer or consumer direct sales.

For more information on Shiloh's lineup of black powder reproductions and replicas, please refer to the *Blue Book of Modern Black Powder Arms* by John Allen & Dennis Adler (also online).

RIFLES: REPRODUCTIONS

The Shiloh Rifle Mfg. Co. is currently manufacturing quality replicas of Sharps rifles and carbines. Models include: 1874 #2 Creedmor Silhouette Rifle ($2,485 MSR), 1874 Military Carbine ($1,547 MSR), 1874 Business Rifle ($1,547 MSR), 1874 Creedmor Target Rifle ($2,485 MSR), 1874 Quigley Buffalo Rifle ($2,903 MSR), 1874 Long Range Express ($1,638 MSR), 1874 Sporter #3 ($1,547 MSR), 1874 Sporter #1 ($1,638 MSR), 1874 Montana Roughrider ($1,638 MSR), 1874 Saddle Rifle ($1,594 MSR), 1874 Hartford Model ($1,745 MSR), and the 1874 Military ($1,793 MSR). Please contact Shiloh Rifle Mfg. Co. directly regarding availability and the current waiting period (see Trademark Index.)

SHOOTERS ARMS MANUFACTURING INCORPORATED

Current manufacturer established in 1992, and located in Cebu, the Philippines. Currently imported by Century International Arms, located in Delray Beach, FL, and Pacific Arms Corp. in Modesto, CA.

Shooter Arms Manufacturing Inc. makes semi-auto pistols, including the Elite, Commodore, Military, GI, Chief, Scout, Falcon, Raven, Omega, and Alpha. Previous models have included the React, React-2, Military Enhanced, GI Enhanced, and Elite Sport. Shooters Arms Manufacuring Inc. also manufactures a revolver, the Protector, and previously manufactured slide action shotguns. Please contact the importers directly for more information, including pricing and U.S. availability.

GRADING - PPGS™	100%	98%	95%	90%	80%	70%	60%

SIDEWINDER

Previous trademark manufactured by D-Max, Inc. located in Bagley, MN circa 1993-96.
Dealer or consumer sales.

REVOLVERS

SIDEWINDER - .45 LC or 2 1/2/3 in. .410 bore shotshells/slugs, 6 shot, stainless
steel construction, 6 1/2 or 7 1/2 in. bull barrel (muzzle end bored for choke), Pachmayr grips, transfer bar safety, adj. rear sight, unique design permits one cylinder
to shoot above listed loads, cased with choke tube, 3.8 lbs. Mfg. 1993-96.

$695   **$575**   **$475**

Last MSR was $775.

SIG ARMS AG

Current Swiss company (SIG) established during 1860 in Neuhausen,
Switzerland. P 210 pistols are currently imported and distributed by
SIG Arms, established in 1985, located in Exeter, NH. Previously
located in Hordon, VA and Tysons Corner, VA.

During late 2000, SIG Arms AG was purchased by SAN Swiss Arms AG,
a newly formed company. This new group includes 6 independently operational companies – Blaser Jadgwaffen GmbH, Hämmerli AG, B.R. Rizzini (acquired 2002), J.P. Sauer &
Sohn GmbH, SIG Arms, Inc. (U.S.A.), and SAN Swiss Arms AG. Please refer to these
individual listings for current information and pricing.

PISTOLS: SEMI-AUTO

SIG Custom Shop variations of the P 210 were also available in three configurations - United We
Stand ($8,990 last MSR) and two variations of the 50 Year Jubilee ($4,995 or $5,999 last MSR).

Add $1,473 for .22 LR conversion kit on the following models (not available on the P 210-8).

TRAILSIDE/TRAILSIDE COMPETITION - please refer to the Hämmerli section for
more information and current pricing on these models.

P 210 - 9mm Para. or 7.65mm Para. (disc.) cal., single action, 4 3/4 in. barrel, 8 shot
mag., standard weapon of the Swiss Army, 2 lbs.

> Originally mfg. in 1947, this pistol was first designated the SP 47/8 and became the standard
> military pistol of the Swiss Army in 1949. Later designated the P 210, this handgun has been
> mfg. continuously for over 55 years.

✴ Danish Army M49 - Danish Army version of the Model P 210, approx. 25,000 mfg.

$1,675   **$1,375**   **$1,050**   **$900**   **$750**   **$625**   **$550**

✴ P 210-1 - polished finish, walnut grips, special hammer, fixed sights. Importation
disc. 1986.

$2,350   **$1,950**   **$1,500**   **$1,250**   **$975**   **$850**   **$750**

Last MSR was $1,861.

✴ P 210-2 - matte finish, field or contrast (recent mfg.) sights, plastic (disc.) or wood
grips. Limited importation 1987-2002.

$1,675   **$1,375**   **$1,050**   **$900**   **$750**   **$625**   **$550**

Last MSR $1,680.

Add 20% for early high polish guns.

**Add 20% for West German Police Contract models with unique loaded indicator on
slide. Approx. 5,000 mfg. in "D" prefix serial range.**

✴ P 210-5 - matte finish, heavy frame, micrometer target sights, 150mm or 180mm
(disc.) extended barrel, hard rubber (disc.) or wood (current mfg.) grips, bottom
(EU) or push-button side mounted (U.S.) mag. release, very limited mfg. Limited
importation since 1997.

MSR $3,032   **$2,250**   **$2,150**   **$1,675**   **$1,350**   **$1,125**   **$1,000**   **$895**

Add $124 for side mounted mag. release.

GRADING - PPGS™	100%	98%	95%	90%	80%	70%	60%

✳ *P 210-6* - matte blue finish, fixed (current importation) or micrometer sights, 120mm barrel, checkered walnut grips, bottom (EU) or push-button side mounted (U.S.) mag. release.

	MSR $2,696	$1,850	$1,700	$1,500	$1,300	$1,125	$1,000	$895

✳ *P 210-7* - .22 LR or 9mm Para. cal., regular or target long barrel, limited importation. Disc.

		$3,375	$2,950	$2,600	$2,300	$1,950	$1,600	$1,275

✳ *P 210-8* - features heavy frame, target sights, and wood grips. Special order only. Limited importation 2001-2003.

		$3,750	$3,250	$2,650	$2,300	$1,950	$1,600	$1,275

Last MSR was $4,289.

✳ *P 210 Deluxe Models* - various models differ in the amount of engraving, gold inlays, carved wood grips, presentation cases, and other special order features available from the factory.

Please contact SIG directly for more information, including availability and pricing.

RIFLES: BOLT ACTION

SHR 970 - .25-06 Rem., .270 Win., .280 Rem., .30-06, .308 Win., .300 Win. Mag. or 7mm Rem. Mag. cal., steel receiver, standard model featuring easy take-down (requires single tool) and quick change 22 or 24 (Mag. cals. only) in. barrel, detachable 3 or 4 shot mag., 65 degree short throw bolt, 3 position safety, standard medium gloss walnut stock with checkering, ultra-fast lock time, nitrided bore, no sights, includes hard carry case, approx. 7.3 lbs. Mfg. 1998-2002.

	$475	$395	$350	$325	$295	$275	$250

Last MSR was $550.

Add $395 for extra barrel.

✳ *SHR 970 Synthetic* - similar to SHR 970, except has checkered black synthetic stock with stippled grip. Mfg. 1999-2002.

	$445	$375	$325	$295	$275	$250	$230

Last MSR was $499.

STR 970 LONG RANGE - .308 Win. or .300 Win. Mag. cal., inlcudes stippled black McMillan composite stock with precision bedding blocks, 24 in. fluted heavy barrel with integral muzzle brake and non-reflective Ilaflon metal coating, cased, 11.6 lbs. Mfg. 2000-2002.

	$875	$795	$675	$575	$525	$475	$425

Last MSR was $899.

RIFLES: SEMI-AUTO

PE-57 - 7.5 Swiss cal. only, semi-auto version of the Swiss military rifle, 24 in. barrel, includes 24 shot mag., leather sling, bipod and maintenance kit. Importation disc. 1988.

	$5,125	$4,500	$3,950	$3,500	$2,950	$2,500	$2,000

Last MSR was $1,745.

The PE-57 was previously distributed in limited quantities by Osborne's located in Cheboygan, MI.

SIG-AMT RIFLE - .308 Win. cal., semi-auto version of SG510-4 auto paramilitary design rifle, roller delayed blowback action, 5, 10, or 20 shot mag., 18 3/4 in. barrel, wood stock, folding bipod. Mfg. 1960-present. Importation disc. 1988.

	$3,875	$3,250	$2,675	$2,300	$2,000	$1,750	$1,500

Last MSR was $1,795.

GRADING - PPGS™	100%	98%	95%	90%	80%	70%	60%

SG 550/551 - .223 Rem. cal. with heavier bullet, Swiss Army's semi-auto version of newest paramilitary design rifle (SIG 90), 20.8 (SG 550) or 16 in. (SG 551 Carbine) barrel, some synthetics used to save weight, 20 shot mag., diopter night sights, built-in folding bipod, 7.7 or 9 lbs.

Sig 550 (Rifle)	$8,500	$7,750	$7,000	$6,250	$5,500	$4,950	$4,500
Sig 551 (Carbine)	$10,500	$9,500	$8,875	$8,000	$7,250	$6,500	$5,600

Last MSR was $1,950.

This model has been banned from domestic importation due to 1989 Federal legislation.

SIG-HÄMMERLI

Previously manufactured by Hämmerli Ltd. in Lenzburg, Switzerland.

PISTOLS: SEMI-AUTO

P240 TARGET PISTOL - .32 S&W Long Wadcutter or .38 Mid-range (disc.) cal., single action, 5 shot mag., 5.9 in. barrel, blue finish, thumbrest walnut grips, adj. sights and trigger, 3 lbs. Importation mostly disc. 1986.

$1,475	$1,225	$1,000	$875	$775	$700	$660

Last MSR was $1,350.

Add $100 for Morini adj. grips.

.38 Mid-range cal. is very desirable in this model - healthy (and inconsistent) premiums are being asked.

❋ **.22 Conversion Unit**

$550	$495	$400

Last MSR was $595.

SIG SAUER

Current firearms trademark manufactured by SIG Arms AG (Schweizerische Industrie-Gesellschaft) located in Neuhausen, Switzerland. Currently imported, manufactured (some models), and distributed by SIG Arms, Inc., established in 1985, and located in Exeter, NH. Previously located in Hordon, VA and Tysons Corner, VA.

During late 2000, SIG Arms AG (including Sig Sauer) was purchased by SAN Swiss Arms AG, a newly formed company. This new group includes 6 independently operational companies – Blaser Jadgwaffen GmbH, Hämmerli AG, B.R. Rizzini (acquired in 2002), J.P. Sauer & Sohn GmbH, SIG Arms, Inc. (U.S.A.), and SAN Swiss Arms AG. Current trademarks include: Aurora, Blaser, Hämmerli, Mauser, Sauer rifles, and Sig Sauer pistols. Please refer to these individual listings for current information and pricing.

PISTOLS: SEMI-AUTO

Beginning 2001, add approx. $20 for all handguns that are MA compliant (include loaded chamber indicator). Pistols that are NY compliant (includes empty shell casing) are priced the same as the models listed.

The SIG Custom Shop, located in Exeter, NH, has recently been established, and offers a wide variety of Custom Shop services, including action enhancement, full servicing, DA/SA conversions, trigger and hammer modifications, barrel replacement, and many refinishing options. Please contact SIG Custom Shop directly for more information and current pricing on these services.

During 2005, the SIG Custom Shop plans on producing 12 limited editions, including the P229 Rail (January), P245 w/ Meprolight night sights (February), P220 Rail (March), P239 Satin Nickel (April), GSR 1911 Nitron (May), P229 Nitron (June), P232 Rainbow Titanium (July), P226 Rail (August), P220 Sport Stock (September), P239 w/ extra .40 S&W cal. barrel (October), P228 Two-Tone (November), and the P226 package w/ Oakley glasses (December). For current pricing and availability, please contact an authorized SIG dealer.

Early SIG Sauer pistols can be marked either with the Hordon or Tysons Corner, VA barrel

GRADING - PPGS™	100%	98%	95%	90%	80%	70%	60%

address, and can also be marked "W. Germany" or "Germany". Earlier mfg. had four proofmarks on the bottom front of the slide. Early guns with these barrel markings will command a slight premium over prices listed below, if condition is 98%+. Current mfg. has Exeter, NH barrel address.

P 210 - please refer to listing under SIG heading.

MODEL P220 - .22 LR (disc.), .38 Super (disc.), 7.65mm (disc.), 9mm Para. (disc 1991), or .45 ACP cal., 7 (.45 ACP) or 8 shot mag., full size, regular double action or double action only (.45 ACP cal. only), 4.4 in. barrel, decocking lever safety, choice of matte blue, stainless steel (new 2001), K-Kote (disc. 1999), electroless nickel (disc. 1991), two-tone with nickel finished slide, or Ilaflon (mfg. 2000 only) finish, lightweight alloy frame, black plastic grips, optional DAK trigger system (DAO with 6.5 lb. trigger pull) available beginning 2005, tactical rail became standard 2004 at no extra charge (blue or stainless only), approx. 30.4 or 41.8 (stainless steel) oz. Mfg. 1976-present.

	MSR $800	$665	$580	$490	$435	$395	$350	$310

Add $40 for DAK trigger system (new 2005).
Add $103 for Siglite night sights.
Add $56 for two-tone (nickel slide) finish (new 1992).
Add $61 for stainless steel frame & slide (new 2001).
Add $40 for Ilaflon finish (disc. 2000).
Add $45 for factory K-Kote finish (disc. 1999).
Add $70 for electroless nickel finish (disc. 1991).
Add $680 for .22 LR conversion kit (disc.).
Subtract 10% for "European" Model (bottom mag. release - includes 9mm Para. and .38 Super cals.).

Values are for .45 ACP cal. and assume American side mag. release (standard 1986).

This model was also available as a Custom Shop Limited Edition during July, 2004 (MSR was $800 and November, 2004 (MSR was $861).

❋ *P220 Sport* - .45 ACP cal., features 4.8 in. heavy compensated barrel, stainless steel frame and slide, 10 shot mag., target sights, improved trigger pull, single or double action, 46.1 oz. Imported 1999-2000, reintroduced 2003.

	MSR $1,600	$1,375	$975	$800

❋ *P220 NRALE* - .45 ACP cal., features NRA Law Enforcement logo and the words "NRA Law Enforcement" engraved in 24Kt. gold, cocobolo grips with NRA medallions, gold trigger and appointments. Limited production of 1,000, including P226 NRALE 2002-2003.

		$850	$650	$495

Last MSR was $911.

MODEL P225 - 9mm Para. cal., regular double action or double action only, similar to P220, shorter dimensions, 3.85 in. barrel, 8 shot, thumb actuated button release mag., fully adj. sights, 28.8 oz. Disc. 1998.

		$595	$525	$450	$425	$395	$350	$310

Last MSR was $725.

Add $45 for factory K-Kote finish.
Add $105 for Siglite night sights.
Add $45 for nickel finished slide (new 1992).
Add $70 for electroless nickel finish (disc. 1991).

This model was also available as a Custom Shop Limited Edition during March, 2004. MSR is $803.

MODEL P226 - .357 SIG (new 1995), 9mm Para. (disc. 1997, reintroduced 1999), or .40 S&W (new 1998) cal., full size, choice of double action or double action only (new 1992) operation, 10 (C/B 1994) or 15* shot mag., 4.4 in. barrel, alloy frame, currently available in blackened stainless steel (Nitron finish became standard 2000), two-tone, or nickel (disc. 2002) finish (stainless slide only), tactical rail

GRADING - PPGS™	100%	98%	95%	90%	80%	70%	60%

became standard 2004 (alloy frame with stainless steel slide or all stainless), choice of traditional DA or DAK trigger system (DAO with 6.5 lb. trigger pull) available beginning 2005, high contrast sights, automatic firing pin block safety, 31.7 or 34 oz. New 1983.

MSR $840	$730	$600	$540	$450	$400	$350	$310

Add $104 for Siglite night sights.

Add $126 for stainless steel frame and slide (new 2004).

Add $56 for two-tone finish (nickel finished stainless steel slide - new 1992).

Add $45 for K-Kote (Polymer) finish (mfg. 1992-97, 9mm Para. only).

Add $70 for electroless nickel finish (disc. 1991).

This model is also available in double action only (all finishes) at no extra charge.

This model was also available as a Custom Shop Limited Edition during Feb., 2004 (MSR was $1,085). A limited edition P226 America with blue titanium and gold finishes was also available from SIG's Custom Shop (MSR was $7,995).

✳ *Model P226 Jubilee* - 9mm Para. cal., limited edition commemorating SIG's 125th anniversary, features gold-plated small parts, carved select walnut grips, special slide markings, cased. Mfg. 1985 only.

	$1,495	$1,175	$950

Last MSR was $2,000.

✳ *P226 NRALE* - .40 S&W cal., features NRA Law Enforcement logo and the words "NRA Law Enforcement" engraved in 24Kt. gold, cocobolo grips with NRA medallions, gold trigger and appointments. Limited production of 1,000, including P220 NRALE, 2002-2003.

	$850	$650	$495

Last MSR was $911.

✳ *P226 Sport* - 9mm Para. cal., features 5.6 in. match or heavy compensated barrel, stainless steel frame and slide, 10 shot mag., target sights, improved trigger pull, single or double action, rubber grips, 48.8 oz. New 2003.

MSR $1,600	$1,375	$975	$800

MODEL P228 - 9mm Para., choice of double action or double action only (new 1992) operation, compact design, 3.86 in. (compact) barrel, 10 (C/B 1994) or 13* shot mag., automatic firing pin block safety, high contrast sights, alloy frame, choice of blue, nickel slide (new 1991), or K-Kote finish, 29.3 oz. Mfg. 1990-97.

	$675	$575	$500	$425	$395	$350	$310

Last MSR was $750.

Add $95 for Siglite night sights.

Add $45 for K-Kote (Polymer) finish.

Add $45 for nickel finished slide (new 1992).

Add $70 for electroless nickel finish (disc. 1991).

This model is also available in double action only (all finishes) at no extra charge.

This model was also available as a Custom Shop Limited Edition during April, 2004 (MSR was $800).

MODEL P229 - .357 SIG (new 1995), 9mm Para. (mfg. 1994-96, reintroduced 1999), or .40 S&W cal., compact size, similar to Model P228, except has blackened Nitron or satin nickel finished stainless steel slide with aluminum alloy frame, 10 (C/B 1994) or 12* shot mag., choice of traditional DA or DAK trigger system (DAO with 6.5 lb. trigger pull) available beginning 2005, tactical rail became standard in 2004 (Nitron finish only), includes lockable carrying case, 31.1 or 32.4 oz. New 1991.

MSR $840	$730	$600	$540	$450	$400	$350	$310

Add $104 for Siglite night sights.

Add $56 for two-tone satin nickel finished stainless steel slide.

This model is also available in double action only at no extra charge.

This model was also available as a Custom Shop Limited Edition during June, 2004 (MSR was $873), during August, 2004 (MSR was $916) and during Dec., 2004 (MSR was $844).

✴ *Model P229 Sport* - .357 SIG or .40 S&W (new 2003) cal., features 4.8 in. match or heavy (disc. 2000) compensated barrel, stainless steel frame and slide, target sights, improved trigger pull, single or double action, 43.6 oz. Mfg. 1998-2000, reintroduced 2003.

MSR $1,600 $1,375 $975 $800

✴ *Model P229 HE (Heritage Fund)* - .40 S&W cal., 10 shot, 3.9 in. barrel, slide marked "10th Anniversary P229", frame marked "1992-2002", gold engraving and accents, brushed stainless steel, gold trigger, cocobolo Hogue grips with NSSF Heritage Fund medallion, includes wood display case. Limited mfg. late 2001-2004.

$1,195 $750 $600

Last MSR was $1,299.

MODEL P230 - .22 LR (disc.)-10 shot, .32 ACP-8 shot, .380 ACP-7 shot, or 9mm Ultra (disc.) cal., 7 shot, 3.6 in. barrel, regular double action or double action only, blue, composite grips, 17.6 oz. Mfg. 1976-96.

$425 $375 $300 $270 $240 $215 $190

Last MSR was $510.

Add $35 for stainless slide (.380 ACP only).

✴ *Model P230 SL Stainless* - similar to Model P230, except stainless steel construction, 22.4 oz. Disc. 1996.

$480 $400 $375

Last MSR was $595.

MODEL P232 - .380 ACP cal., choice of double action or double action only, 3.6 in. barrel, 7 shot mag., aluminum alloy frame, compact personal size, blue or two-tone stainless slide, automatic firing pin block safety, composite grips. New 1997.

MSR $519 $450 $390 $315 $275 $240 $215 $190

Add $48 for Siglite night sights (new 2001).
Add $19 for stainless two-tone slide.

✴ *Model P232 Stainless* - similar to Model P232, except stainless steel construction, natural finish, 17.6 or 22.4 (stainless) oz. New 1997.

MSR $579 $500 $440 $365

Add $47 for Siglite night sights and Hogue grips.

MODEL P239 - .357 SIG, 9mm Para., or .40 S&W (new 1998) cal., compact personal size, double action or double action only, blackened or two-tone stainless steel slide and aluminum alloy frame, firing pin block safety, 3.6 in. barrel, 7 or 8 (9mm Para. only) shot mag., fixed sights, approx. 29 oz. New 1996.

MSR $702 $540 $460 $385 $310 $265 $220 $195

Add $103 for Siglite night sights.
Add $54 for two-tone stainless slide.

This model was also available as a Custom Shop Limited Edition during May, 2004 (MSR was $673).

MODEL P245 - .45 ACP cal., compact model featuring 3.9 in. barrel, traditional double action, 6 shot mag., blue, two-tone, Ilaflon (mfg. 2000 only), or K-Kote (disc. 1999) finish, approx. 30 oz. New 1999.

MSR $840 $695 $585 $495 $440 $400 $350 $310

Add $103 for Siglite night sights.
Add $56 for two-tone or K-Kote (disc.) finish.
Add $50 for Ilaflon finish (mfg. 2000 only).

GRANITE SERIES 1911 GSR - .45 ACP cal., single action, 5 in. match grade barrel, choice of white or blued stainless steel, 8 shot mag., under frame Picatinny rail, firing pin safety, 20 LPI grooved front and rear strap checkering, Novak sights, checkered wood (all stainless) or synthetic (blued stainless) grips, approx. 41 oz. Mfg. in Exeter, NH. New 2004.

MSR $1,077 $900 $800 $700 $600 $500 $400 $325

GRADING - PPGS™	100%	98%	95%	90%	80%	70%	60%

MODEL SIG PRO SP2009 - 9mm Para. cal., otherwise identical to SP2340, 28 oz. New 1999.

	MSR $640	$510	$450	$355	$290	$260	$220	$195

Add $60 for Siglite night sights.
Add $31 for two-tone finish.

MODEL SIG PRO SP2340 - .357 SIG, or .40 S&W cal., features polymer frame and one-piece Nitron finished stainless steel or two-tone (new 2001) finished slide, 3.86 in. barrel, includes two interchangeable grips, 10 shot mag., approx. 30.2 oz. New 1999.

	MSR $640	$510	$450	$355	$290	$260	$220	$195

Add $60 for Siglite night sights.
Add $31 for two-tone finish.

RIFLES: BOLT ACTION

Please refer to listing in J.P. Sauer & Sohn section.

SHOTGUNS: O/U

The following Aurora shotguns are mfg. by Battista Rizzini, located in Marcheno, Italy.

L.L. BEAN NEW ENGLANDER SERIES - 12, 20, 28 ga., or .410 bore. Importation began 2001.

	MSR $2,161	$1,895	$1,575	$1,325	$1,100	$950	$800	$675

AURORA TR20 FIELD (APOLLO) - 12, 20, 28 ga., or .410 bore, 3 in. chambers except for 28 ga., 26 or 28 in. VR barrels with choke tubes, satin finished low profile boxlock receiver, monobloc construction, removable hinge pins, gold SST, ejectors, deluxe checkered round pistol grip walnut stock and forearm, 6-7 lbs. New 2000.

	MSR $2,250	$1,995	$1,750	$1,475	$1,265	$1,050	$925	$800

⁕ *Aurora TR20U Field (Apollo)* - similar to Apollo/Aurora TR20 Field, except has straight English stock (Upland Model) and color case hardened receiver. New 2000.

	MSR $2,250	$1,995	$1,750	$1,475	$1,265	$1,050	$925	$800

AURORA TR30 FIELD (APOLLO) - similar to Apollo/Aurora TR20 Field, except has color case hardened receiver with sideplates. New 2000.

	MSR $2,650	$2,275	$1,900	$1,675	$1,375	$1,150	$975	$850

AURORA TR40 GOLD/SILVER (APOLLO) - similar to Apollo/Aurora TR30 Field, except receiver and sideplates are engraved and have multiple gold bird inlays, choice of color case hardened (Gold Series) or silver receiver (Silver Series) finish, deluxe checkered walnut stock and forearm. New 2000.

	MSR $3,050	$2,575	$2,125	$1,850	$1,575	$1,350	$1,100	$950

⁕ *Aurora TR40U (Apollo)* - similar to Apollo/Aurora TR40 Gold/Silver, except has straight English grip stock and silver finished receiver only. Imported 2000 only.

		$2,250	$1,950	$1,725	$1,500	$1,300	$1,000	$825

Last MSR was $2,595.

AURORA TT25 COMPETITION (APOLLO) - 12 or 20 ga., 3 in. chambers, features include polished 5 in. forcing cones and American stock dimensions with palm swell and Schnabel forearm, oil finished checkered walnut stock and forearm, matte finished 28, 30, or 32 (12 ga. only) in. VR barrels, 6 3/4 or 7 1/4 lbs. New 2000.

	MSR $2,950	$2,475	$2,000	$1,750	$1,500	$1,300	$1,075	$950

AURORA TT45 COMPETITION - 12 or 20 ga., 28, 30, or 32 (12 ga. only) in. VR barrels. Importation began 2001.

	MSR $3,350	$2,745	$2,250	$1,925	$1,700	$1,500	$1,300	$1,100

GRADING - PPGS™	100%	98%	95%	90%	80%	70%	60%

SA 3 - 12 or 20 (new 1998) ga., 3 in. chambers, scalloped coin finished monobloc box-lock action with game scene engraving, field or Sporting Clays (new 1998) configuration, 26, 28, or 30 (Sporting Clays only) in. separated barrels with VR and choke tubes, ejectors, SST, checkered walnut stock and forearm, approx. 7 lbs. Mfg. 1997-98 only.

	$1,175	$925	$775	$650	$550	$475	$400

Last MSR was $1,335.

SA 5 - 12 or 20 ga., 3 in. chambers, features coin finished boxlock action with hand engraved detachable side plates, ejectors, SST, select checkered walnut stock and forearm, field or Sporting Clays (new 1998) configuration, 26 1/2, 28, or 30 (Sporting Clays only) in. barrels with VR and choke tubes, supplied with lockable case, 6 or 7 lbs. Mfg. 1997-99.

	$2,175	$1,775	$1,450	$1,225	$1,075	$900	$775

Last MSR was $2,670.

Add $130 for Sporting Clays Model (12 ga. only, 28 or 30 in. barrels).

SILE DISTRIBUTORS

Previous distributor, importer, and previous manufacturer located in New York, NY.

In addition to distributing a wide variety of firearms and related accessories (including the mfg. of stocks and grips), Sile Distributors also had some firearms "private labeled" to their specifications.

SILMA SPORTING GUNS

Current manufacturer established during 1949 and located in Brescia, Italy. Currently distributed and imported beginning 2000 on a limited basis by Legacy Sports, International, LLC, located in Alexandria, VA **(Model 70 EJ variations only). All Silma shotguns, double rifles, and combination models are high quality and utilize premium materials in their manufacture.**

Please contact the importer directly (see Trademark Index) for current domestic model availability and pricing.

RIFLES

Currently, Silma offers one O/U double rifle (Model EX 70 N). This is also available in a combination gun (12 ga. x various cals.). Not currently imported.

SHOTGUNS

In addition to the Model 70 EJ and Superlight models listed, Silma also manufactures other Model 70 configurations. Models 70 and 80 are O/U hunting models available in either 12, 20 ga., or .410 bore. They are available with double triggers standard, extractors or ejectors (extra cost), with or without sideplates, or in superlight configuration - retail values range between $730-$980. Competition models (including T.J. 70, T.S. 81, Cobra T1, T2, or T3) are also available for trap, skeet, or sporting clays events. Values range between $1,000-$6,200 (with T.J. 70 being the least expensive, and Cobra T2 the most expensive). Two side-by-side models (AS/70 N and AS/70 EJ) are also available.

MODEL 70 EJ STANDARD O/U - 12 or 20 ga., 3 or 3 1/2 (12 ga. only) in. chambers, similar to Model 70 EJ Deluxe, except has standard grade walnut, 6.9-7.6 lbs. Importation began 2001.

MSR $944		$775	$625	$525	$475	$425	$375	$335

Add $72 for 12 ga. with 3 1/2 in. chambers.

GRADING - PPGS™	100%	98%	95%	90%	80%	70%	60%

MODEL 70 EJ DELUXE O/U - 12, 20, 28 ga., or .410 bore, 3 (12 and 20 ga. only) or 3 1/2 in. chambers, 28 in. VR barrels with either multichokes (12 ga. only) or fixed chokes, engraved coin finished boxlock receiver, gold ST (disc.) or SST (standard beginning 2004), deluxe checkered walnut stock and forearm, 6.9-7.6 lbs. Importation began 2001.

	MSR $1,016	$865	$775	$700	$625	$575	$525	$475

Add $73 for 12 ga. with 3 1/2 in. chambers.
Add $124 for 28 ga. or .410 bore.

MODEL 70 EJ SUPERLIGHT O/U - 12 or 20 ga., 3 in. chambers, similar to Model 70 EJ Deluxe, except has separated barrels and lightweight aluminum frame, 5.6 lbs. Importation began 2001.

	MSR $1,191	$1,025	$875	$750	$650	$550	$495	$450

MODEL 70 EJ CLAYS - 12 ga., 3 in. chambers, 28 in. vent. barrels with VR and three choke tubes, non-automatic safety, satin silver finish, competition style, oil finished checkered stock and forearm, mechanical SST, 7.9 lbs. Importation began 2003.

	MSR $1,387	$1,060	$925	$800	$675	$575	$495	$450

SIMILLION, GENE

Current custom rifle maker located in Gunnison, CO. Consumer direct sales.

RIFLES: BOLT ACTION, CUSTOM

EXTREME HUNTER RIFLE - various cals., customer supplied Winchester Model 70 Classic action, match grade barrel, McMillan fiberglass stock, 8 1/2-10 lbs. New 2003.

	MSR $5,000	$4,500	$3,450	$2,750	$2,175	$1,800	$1,500	$1,250

Add $1,400 for Mag. cals through .338.
Add $1,900 for heavy Mags. cals. .375 H&H and greater.

CLASSIC HUNTER RIFLE - various cals., new Winchester Model 70 Classic action, options include LOP, caliber, and barrel length, deluxe walnut, custom made to individual customer specifications. Disc. 2004.

		$6,950	$5,750	$5,150	$4,500	$3,750	$3,000	$2,500

Last MSR was $7,500.

Add $1,000 for Mag. cals. up to .375 H&H.
Add $1,500 for heavy Mag. cals. .375 H&H. and larger.

PREMIER MODEL 70 RIFLE - various cals., mostly Winchester new Model 70 action (others available), custom made to individual customer specifications, finest materials and workmanship, individually tested.

	MSR $12,800	$11,500	$9,250	$8,250	$7,250	$6,250	$5,250	$4,250

Add $1,400 for Mag. cals. up to .375 H&H.
Add $2,200 for heavy Mag. cals. .375 H&H and larger.

PREMIER MODEL 98 RIFLE - various cals., Granite Mountain Arms Model 98 short or long action, custom made to individual customer specifications, exhibition grade walnut, ebony forend tip, swivel bases, solid steel grip cap, wide variety of custom options. New 2005.

	MSR $14,500	$13,250	$11,750	$9,250	$8,150	$7,150	$6,150	$4,975

Add $1,000 for scope sighted rifle in standard action.
Add $4,500 for Mag. action.

SIMSEK

Previous shotgun manufacturer located in Turkey.

Simsek manufactured shotguns in O/U, SxS, and semi-auto configurations. They had very limited importation into the U.S.

GRADING - PPGS™	100%	98%	95%	90%	80%	70%	60%

SIMSON

Previous firearms and airgun manufacturer located in Suhl, Germany.

More research is underway regarding the various models and configurations made by this company, most of which had little U.S. importation.

SIRKIS INDUSTRIES, LTD.

Previous manufacturer located in Ramat-Gan, Israel. Previously imported and distributed by Armscorp of America, Inc. located in Baltimore, MD.

PISTOLS: SEMI-AUTO

S.D. 9 - 9mm Para. cal., double action mechanism, frame is constructed mostly of heavy gauge sheet metal stampings, 3.07 in. barrel, parkerized finish, loaded chamber indicator, 7 shot mag., plastic grips, 24 1/2 oz. Imported under the Sirkis & Sardius trademarks between 1986-90.

$375	$295	$250	$200	$190	$180	$170

Last MSR was $350.

RIFLES

MODEL 35 MATCH RIFLE - .22 LR cal. only, single shot bolt action, 26 in. full floating barrel, select walnut, match trigger, micrometer sights. Disc. 1985.

$650	$625	$595	$550	$510	$460	$420

Last MSR was $690.

MODEL 36 SNIPER RIFLE - .308 Win. cal. only, gas operated action, carbon fiber stock, 22 in. barrel, flash suppressor, free range sights. Disc. 1985.

$670	$580	$520	$475	$430	$390	$350

Last MSR was $760.

SKORPION

Please refer to Armitage International, Ltd. in the "A" section of this text.

SMITH, L.C.

Current trademark manufacture beginning late 2004 by Marlin Firearms Company, located in North Haven, CT. Previous trademark manufactured 1878-1888 by W.H. Baker & Co and L.C. Smith Maker located in Syracuse, NY., also manufactured 1890-1950 by Hunter Arms Company and L.C. Smith Gun Co. in Fulton, NY, and from 1968-1972 by Marlin Firearms Company, located in New Haven, CT.

The L.C. Smith shotgun is considered an "American Best" and is recognized as one of America's most prestigious and collectible sidelock shotguns. Recently released records indicate that L.C. Smith sold as many medium to high grade models as Parker Bros., and collector interest has been very high. The *Blue Book of Gun Values* strongly recommends an expert appraisal when contemplating a purchase of a higher grade L.C. Smith, particularly in 90%+ original condition.

Guns that are mechanically factory original, but have been expertly restored (barrels, receivers, and wood) have less collector interest. Therefore, these expertly restored guns should be valued up to 70%-80% of the highest value listed for a particular model in this section, assuming the restored gun has no wear.

Collector interest in Syracuse and Fulton damascus barreled models, both hammer and hammerless, is on the rise, and any damascus barrel gun should be examined closely by an expert gunsmith before use.

The L.C. Smith Collectors Association offers a variety of services as well as a collector newsletter. Readers may reach the organization through the website: www.lcsmith.org, or by phone: 513-777-1946.

100%	98%	95%	90%	80%	70%	60%	50%	40%	30%	20%	10%

The Cody Firearms Museum in Cody, WY, has the following L.C. Smith and Hunter Arms Co. records available: Hunter Arms Company factory records 1890-1919 (including Fulton and some single barrel guns), shipping records 1918-1946, and L.C. Smith Gun Company 1946-1950 ("FWS" prefix). Please contact the Cody Firearms Museum directly for historical research on these periods of manufacture (see Trademark Index).

SHOTGUN-RIFLES: BAKER 3-BARREL, HAMMER-DAMASCUS, SYRACUSE MFG. 1878-1888

The ser. no. range is 1-10,000, and estimated total guns produced is 1,186. Values are based on NRA Antique standards, converted to equivalent percentages of original condition.

QUALITY NO. 1

100%	98%	95%	90%	80%	70%	60%	50%	40%	30%	20%	10%
N/A	N/A	N/A	N/A	$1,200	$1,100	$1,025	$950	$775	$600	$475	$325

QUALITY NO. 2

N/A	N/A	N/A	N/A	$1,250	$1,125	$1,050	$1,000	$850	$700	$525	$350

QUALITY NO. 3

N/A	N/A	N/A	N/A	$1,500	$1,400	$1,325	$1,250	$1,100	$900	$675	$475

QUALITY NO. 4

N/A	N/A	N/A	N/A	$1,750	$1,650	$1,575	$1,500	$1,350	$1,150	$875	$600

QUALITY NO. 5

N/A	N/A	N/A	N/A	$2,500	$2,250	$2,000	$1,750	$1,625	$1,500	$1,250	$995

SHOTGUNS: SXS, BAKER HAMMER-DAMASCUS, SYRACUSE MFG. 1878-1884

The ser. no. range is 1-10,000, and estimated total guns produced is 8,305. Values are based on NRA Antique standards, converted to equivalent percentages of original condition.

QUALITY A

N/A	N/A	N/A	N/A	$450	$425	$375	$350	$275	$200	$150	$100

QUALITY B

N/A	N/A	N/A	N/A	$550	$525	$485	$450	$350	$250	$175	$125

QUALITY C

N/A	N/A	N/A	N/A	$750	$675	$625	$550	$425	$300	$200	$150

QUALITY D

N/A	N/A	N/A	N/A	$800	$725	$675	$600	$475	$350	$250	$175

QUALITY E

N/A	N/A	N/A	N/A	$900	$825	$750	$700	$550	$450	$325	$225

QUALITY F

N/A	N/A	N/A	N/A	$1,250	$1,125	$1,000	$900	$750	$600	$450	$325

SHOTGUNS: SxS, L.C. SMITH SIDELOCK, HAMMER-DAMASCUS, MFG. 1884-1898

Serial number range for Syracuse guns: 15,000-22,500. Serial number range for Fulton guns: 27,776-27,999 and 50,500-58,000. Values are based on NRA Antique standards, converted to equivalent percentages of original condition.

QUALITY F

N/A	N/A	N/A	N/A	$1,250	$1,050	$875	$700	$550	$400	$300	$200

QUALITY E

N/A	N/A	N/A	N/A	$1,350	$1,150	$925	$775	$600	$450	$325	$225

100%	98%	95%	90%	80%	70%	60%	50%	40%	30%	20%	10%
QUALITY D											
N/A	N/A	N/A	N/A	$1,400	$1,175	$950	$795	$625	$475	$350	$250
QUALITY C											
N/A	N/A	N/A	N/A	$1,450	$1,200	$1,000	$850	$675	$525	$375	$275
QUALITY B											
N/A	N/A	N/A	N/A	$1,600	$1,325	$1,100	$1,050	$800	$650	$450	$325
QUALITY A											
N/A	N/A	N/A	N/A	$2,500	$2,150	$1,925	$1,750	$1,500	$1,250	$900	$600
QUALITY AA											
N/A	N/A	N/A	N/A	$4,000	$3,650	$3,325	$3,000	$2,500	$2,000	$1,500	$900

SHOTGUNS: SxS, L.C. SMITH SIDELOCK, HAMMERLESS-DAMASCUS, MFG. 1886-1898

Serial number range for Syracuse guns: 15,000-22,500. Serial number range for Fulton guns: 30,000-46,000 and 500-3,173. Values are based on NRA Antique standards, converted to equivalent percentages of original condition.

100%	98%	95%	90%	80%	70%	60%	50%	40%	30%	20%	10%
QUALITY 2											
N/A	N/A	N/A	N/A	$1,450	$1,275	$1,050	$900	$750	$600	$450	$300
QUALITY 3											
N/A	N/A	N/A	N/A	$1,650	$1,400	$1,175	$975	$825	$650	$475	$325
QUALITY 4											
N/A	N/A	N/A	N/A	$1,850	$1,550	$1,275	$995	$850	$675	$500	$350
QUALITY 5											
N/A	N/A	N/A	N/A	$2,000	$1,750	$1,500	$1,300	$1,000	$750	$550	$375
QUALITY 6 - disc. 1892.											
N/A	N/A	N/A	N/A	$2,700	$2,450	$2,200	$1,950	$1,500	$1,000	$675	$425
MONOGRAM - new 1892.											
N/A	N/A	N/A	N/A	$2,850	$2,550	$2,300	$2,100	$1,625	$1,150	$750	$475
QUALITY 7											
N/A	N/A	N/A	N/A	$3,250	$2,950	$2,700	$2,500	$1,850	$1,350	$875	$550
QUALITY A2 - new 1892.											
N/A	N/A	N/A	N/A	$5,000	$4,650	$4,100	$3,500	$2,750	$2,200	$1,500	$875

SHOTGUNS: SxS, L.C. SMITH/HUNTER ARMS, SIDELOCK, HAMMERLESS, FLUID STEEL BARRELS, MFG. 1892-1913

All values listed are for hammerless 12 ga. guns with fluid steel barrels (except A-1 Grade). Guns were manufactured in the following gauges on regular weight frames in 8 ga. and 10 ga., and regular and light frames in 12, 16, and 20 ga. only. Hammer guns with either fluid steel or damascus barrels are of almost equal value if the damascus barrels are in 90% original condition, with the bores in excellent original condition without pitting, and have not been rebored or polished out. L.C. Smith shotguns are rare and were all made to exacting standards. Collector interest can be high, and guns in 90%+ original condition are very hard to evaluate and the values shown are meant as a guide only. It is important to note that 16 ga. guns are as rare as 20 ga., and that collector interest and values for these gauges are approaching parity.

Add 50% for 20 ga. on all grades.

Add 33% for 16 ga. on all grades.

100%	98%	95%	90%	80%	70%	60%	50%	40%	30%	20%	10%

Add $500 for auto ejectors on all grades with values of $1,500+, or 33% for values less than $1,500.

Add $500 for Hunter single selected one trigger on all grades with values of $1,500+, or 33% for values less than $1,500.

GRADE F HAMMER GUNS - fluid steel or damascus barrels.

100%	98%	95%	90%	80%	70%	60%	50%	40%	30%	20%	10%
N/A	N/A	$1,500	$1,250	$1,000	$750	$650	$550	$500	$450	$425	N/A

HAMMERLESS GRADES

00 - approx. 58,000 mfg.

N/A	N/A	$1,500	$1,250	$1,000	$750	$650	$550	$400	$350	$325	N/A

0 - approx. 30,000 mfg.

N/A	N/A	$1,600	$1,350	$1,050	$800	$700	$550	$450	$400	$350	N/A

1 - approx. 10,000 mfg.

N/A	N/A	$1,950	$1,600	$1,300	$1,050	$950	$850	$750	$500	$400	N/A

2 - approx. 13,000 mfg.

N/A	N/A	$2,500	$2,100	$1,750	$1,550	$1,450	$1,350	$1,250	$1,150	$1,050	N/A

3 - approx. 4,000 mfg.

N/A	N/A	$3,500	$2,750	$2,250	$1,950	$1,850	$1,750	$1,650	$1,550	$1,450	N/A

PIGEON - approx. 1,200 mfg.

N/A	N/A	$4,000	$3,250	$2,750	$2,450	$2,350	$2,050	$1,950	$1,850	$1,750	N/A

4 - approx. 455 mfg.

N/A	N/A	$6,000	$4,800	$3,780	$3,250	$3,000	$2,800	$2,600	$2,500	$2,400	N/A

A1 - damascus barrels only, approx. 740 mfg.

N/A	N/A	$3,750	$3,000	$2,500	$2,150	$2,000	$1,750	$1,650	$1,550	$1,450	N/A

5 - approx. 485 mfg.

N/A	N/A	$7,000	$5,500	$4,500	$4,150	$4,000	$3,600	$3,500	$3,400	$3,300	N/A

MONOGRAM - approx. 128 mfg.

N/A	N/A	$10,000	$8,500	$7,500	$6,000	$5,500	$4,700	$4,500	$4,300	$4,100	N/A

A2 - approx. 200 mfg.

N/A	N/A	$12,000	$10,000	$8,500	$7,000	$6,000	$5,200	$5,000	$4,800	$4,600	N/A

A3 - approx. 17 mfg.

Extreme rarity precludes accurate pricing.

SHOTGUNS: SxS, L.C. SMITH/HUNTER ARMS, SIDELOCK, HAMMERLESS, FLUID STEEL BARRELS, MFG. 1913-1950

Values shown are for hammerless 12 ga. guns with fluid steel barrels. Guns were manufactured in 12, 16, 20 ga. and .410 bore on either regular or lightweight frames. Hammer guns with fluid steel or damascus barrels are of almost equal value if the damascus barrels are in 90%+ original condition, with bores in excellent original condition without pitting, and have not been rebored or polished out. L.C. Smith shotguns are rare and were all made to exacting standards. Collector interest can be high, and guns in 90%+ original condition are very hard to evaluate and the values shown are meant as a guide only. It is important to note that 16 ga. guns are as rare as 20 ga., and that collector interest and values for these gauges are approaching parity.

Add 50% for 20 ga. on all grades.

Add 33% for 16 ga. on all grades.

Add 300% for .410 bore on Field Grades.

Add 400% for .410 bore on all grades except Skeet.

Add $500 for auto ejectors on all grades with values of $1,500+, or 33% for values less than $1,500.

100%	98%	95%	90%	80%	70%	60%	50%	40%	30%	20%	10%

Add $500 for Hunter selective one trigger on all grades with values of $1,500+, or 33% for values less than $1,500.

Add $500 for vent. rib. on all grades with values of $1,500+, or 33% for values less than $1,500.

GRADE F HAMMER GUNS - fluid steel or damascus barrels, damascus barrels were disc. 1918, hammer guns were disc. 1932.

100%	98%	95%	90%	80%	70%	60%	50%	40%	30%	20%	10%
N/A	N/A	$1,500	$1,250	$1,000	$750	$650	$550	$500	$450	$425	N/A

HAMMERLESS GRADES

FIELD - approx. 195,000 mfg.

N/A	N/A	$1,250	$1,000	$750	$650	$600	$550	$500	$450	$425	N/A

IDEAL - approx. 26,000 mfg.

N/A	N/A	$1,750	$1,500	$1,200	$950	$850	$700	$600	$550	$500	N/A

SKEET SPECIAL - includes AE, SST, and BTF, approx. 770 mfg.

N/A	N/A	$2,800	$2,500	$2,300	$2,100	$2,000	$1,900	$1,800	$1,700	$1,600	N/A

PREMIER SKEET - includes AE, SST, and BTF, approx. 510 mfg.

N/A	N/A	$2,800	$2,500	$2,300	$2,100	$2,000	$1,900	$1,800	$1,700	$1,600	N/A

TRAP - approx. 3,400 mfg.

N/A	N/A	$2,000	$1,700	$1,400	$1,150	$1,050	$950	$850	$750	$700	N/A

SPECIALTY - approx. 6,700 mfg.

N/A	N/A	$2,500	$2,100	$1,800	$1,600	$1,500	$1,400	$1,300	$1,200	$1,100	N/A

EAGLE - approx. 580 mfg.

N/A	N/A	$5,000	$4,000	$3,500	$3,100	$2,800	$2,600	$2,500	$2,400	$2,300	N/A

CROWN - approx. 890 mfg.

N/A	N/A	$7,000	$5,500	$4,500	$4,150	$4,000	$3,600	$3,500	$3,400	$3,300	N/A

MONOGRAM - approx. 138 mfg.

N/A	N/A	$10,000	$8,500	$7,500	$6,000	$5,500	$4,700	$4,500	$4,300	$4,100	N/A

PREMIER - approx. 28 mfg.

Extreme rarity precludes accurate pricing.

DELUXE - approx. 30 mfg.

Extreme rarity precludes accurate pricing.

SHOTGUNS: SINGLE BARREL TRAP, BOXLOCK, HAMMERLESS, MFG. 1917-1950

The L.C. Smith single barrel trap is considered one of America's best made guns, and awards for both the guns and shooters are legendary, including Olympic medals and world titles. Collector interest can be high, and an expert appraisal is recommended on guns in 80%+ condition.

Single barrel trap models were 12 ga. only, with 32 or 34 in. barrel, boxlock, auto ejector, checkered pistol grip stock and recoil pad. Approx. 2,650 were mfg. between 1917-1951.

OLYMPIC

N/A	$1,500	$1,350	$1,200	$950	$850	$800	$750	$725	$700	$600	N/A

SPECIALITY

N/A	$2,000	$1,850	$1,700	$1,300	$1,200	$1,150	$1,100	$1,050	$1,000	$800	N/A

CROWN

N/A	$3,500	$3,250	$3,000	$2,250	$2,000	$1,900	$1,800	$1,650	$1,500	$1,250	N/A

MONOGRAM

N/A	$6,500	$6,000	$5,500	$3,800	$3,500	$3,200	$2,900	$2,700	$2,600	$1,750	N/A

PREMIER

N/A	$12,000	$11,000	$10,000	$7,000	$6,300	$6,000	$5,700	$5,350	$5,000	$3,000	N/A

100%	98%	95%	90%	80%	70%	60%	50%	40%	30%	20%	10%
DELUXE											
N/A	$16,000	$14,000	$13,000	$10,500	$9,500	$9,000	$8,700	$8,350	$8,000	$4,500	N/A

SHOTGUNS: SxS, HUNTER ARMS, FULTON BOXLOCK, HAMMERLESS, FLUID STEEL, MFG. 1915-1945

These models have been unduly maligned over the years, being referred to as cheap boxlocks, and are not to be confused with actual L.C. Smith sidelock shotguns. In reality, these models are high quality, inexpensive boxlocks built with quality similar to field grade L.C. Smiths. The receiver, forend iron, trigger guard and triggers were all machined (not stamped) from forgings. These models have excellent durability and there is collector interest.

Manufactured in 12, 16, 20 ga. and .410 bore with 26, 28, 30, or 32 in. barrels.

>   Add 50% for 20 ga.
>   Add 33% for 16 ga.
>   Add 250% for .410 bore.
>   Add $150 for non-selective single trigger.

FULTON - plain stock with half pistol grip.

N/A	$500	$450	$400	$350	$300	$275	$250	$225	$200	$150	N/A

FULTON SPECIAL - checkered stock with full pistol grip, decorated frame.

N/A	$625	$575	$525	$475	$425	$400	$375	$350	$325	$275	N/A

HUNTER SPECIAL - similar to Fulton Special, except has L.C. Smith rotary locking bolt system.

N/A	$650	$600	$550	$500	$450	$425	$400	$375	$350	$300	N/A

SHOTGUNS: SxS, L.C. SMITH/MARLIN, SIDELOCK, HAMMERLESS, FLUID STEEL, MFG. 1968-1973

The Marlin Firearms Company reintroduced the L.C. Smith trademark in 1968. These models are considered real L.C. Smiths, not copies, and collector interest is increasing. The following Marlin-manufactured shotguns with an "FWM" prefix that were manufactured through 1971 can be researched by the Cody Firearms Museum.

FIELD - 12 ga., 28 in. barrels, aluminum vent. rib, F/M chokes, extractors, double triggers, checkered pistol grip stock.

N/A	$700	$650	$600	$550	$500	$475	$450	$425	$400	$300	N/A

DELUXE - 12 ga., 28 in. barrels, Simmons floating vent. rib, F/M chokes, extractors, double triggers, select walnut PG stock, beavertail forearm.

N/A	$1,000	$925	$850	$750	$700	$675	$650	$625	$550	$400	N/A

GRADING - PPGS™	100%	98%	95%	90%	80%	70%	60%

SHOTGUNS: O/U, L.C. SMITH/MARLIN, CURRENT MFG. BEGINNING 2005

MODEL LC12 - 12 ga., 28 in. vent. rib barrels with choke tubes, SST, ejectors, checkered walnut pistol grip stock with fluted comb, recoil pad, bead front sight, approx. 7.25 lbs. Mfg. for Marlin in Italy beginning 2005.

MSR $1,394		$1,095	$975	$850	$725	$600	$525	$450

MODEL LC20 - 20 ga., 26 in. vent. rib barrels with choke tubes, otherwise similar to LC12, approx. 6.75 lbs. Mfg. for Marlin in Italy beginning 2005.

MSR $1,394		$1,095	$975	$850	$725	$600	$525	$450

GRADING - PPGS™	100%	98%	95%	90%	80%	70%	60%

SHOTGUNS: SxS, L.C. SMITH/MARLIN, CURRENT MFG. BEGINNING 2005

MODEL LC12-DB - 12 ga., action patterned after the first generation L.C. Smith action, 28 in. vent. rib barrels with choke tubes, single trigger, ejectors, checkered walnut pistol grip stock with fluted comb, recoil pad, bead front sight, approx. 6.25 lbs. Mfg. for Marlin in Italy beginning 2005.

MSR $1,884	$1,495	$1,250	$1,100	$875	$750	$625	$550

MODEL LC20-DB - 20 ga., 26 in. vent. rib barrels with choke tubes, otherwise similar to Model LC12-DB, approx. 6 lbs. Mfg. for Marlin in Italy beginning 2005.

MSR $1,884	$1,495	$1,250	$1,100	$875	$750	$625	$550

SMITH & WESSON

Current manufacturer located in Springfield, MA, 1857 to date. Partnership with H. Smith & D.B. Wesson 1856-1874. Family owned by Wesson 1874-1965. S&W became a subsidiary of Bangor-Punta from 1965-1983. Between 1983-1987, Smith & Wesson was owned by the Lear Siegler Co. On May 22, 1987, Smith & Wesson was sold to Tomkins, an English holding company. During 2001, Tomkins sold Smith & Wesson to Saf-T-Hammer, an Arizona-based safety and security company.

Smith & Wessons have been classified under the following category names - TIP-UPS, TOP-BREAKS, SINGLE SHOTS, EARLY HAND EJECTORS (Named Models), NUMBERED MODEL REVOLVERS (Modern Hand Ejectors), SEMI-AUTOS, RIFLES, and SHOTGUNS.

Each category is fairly self-explanatory. Among the early revolvers, Tip-ups have barrels that tip up so the cylinder can be removed for loading or unloading, whereas Top-breaks have barrels & cylinders that tip down with automatic ejection.

Hand Ejectors are the modern type revolvers with swing out cylinders. In 1958, S&W began a system of numbering all models they made. Accordingly, the Hand Ejectors have been divided into two sections - the Early Hand Ejectors include the named models introduced prior to 1958. The Numbered Model Revolvers are the models introduced or continued after that date, and are easily identified by the model number stamped on the side of the frame, visible when the cylinder is open. The author wishes to express his thanks to Mr. Jim Supica, Mr. Rick Nahas, and Mr. Roy Jinks, the S&W Historian, for their updates and valuable contributions.

For more information and current pricing on both new and used Smith & Wesson airguns, please refer to the *Blue Book of Airguns* by Dr. Robert Beeman & John Allen (also online).

Factory special orders, such as ivory or pearl grips, special finishes, engraving, and other production rarities will add premiums to the values listed. After 1893, all ivory and pearl grips had the metal S&W logo medallions inserted on top.

TIP-UPS

Spur-trigger rimfires, these include the earliest S&W revolvers, made 1857-1881. A latch at the bottom front of the frame allows the hinged barrel to be tipped up and the cylinder removed for loading and unloading. These pistols are listed in order of model number (1, 1 1/2, 2).

MODEL NO. 1 FIRST ISSUE TIP-UP - .22 Short cal., single action, 7 shot non-fluted cylinder, 3 3/16 in. octagon barrel, bottom break, spur trigger, silver-plated brass frame, blue barrel and cylinder, square rosewood grips, circular sideplate, cross-section of frame is oval with rounded frame sides. Approx. 11,500 mfg. 1857-60.

＊ *First Type* - serial range approx. 1-200.

Extreme rarity factor of this model precludes accurate pricing - a nice condition model can easily exceed $10,000.

＊ *Second Type* - serial range approx. 200-1130.

Extreme rarity factor of this model precludes accurate pricing - a nice condition model can easily exceed $10,000.

100%	98%	95%	90%	80%	70%	60%	50%	40%	30%	20%	10%

❋ Third Type - serial range approx. 1130-3000.

| N/A | N/A | $8,000 | $7,000 | $5,500 | $5,000 | $4,500 | $3,000 | $2,500 | $2,000 | $1,500 | $1,000 |

❋ Fourth Type - serial range approx. 3000-4200.

| N/A | $3,500 | $3,000 | $2,000 | $1,800 | $1,650 | $1,600 | $1,500 | $1,350 | $1,200 | $1,000 | $900 |

❋ Fifth Type - serial range approx. 4200-5500.

| N/A | $3,500 | $3,000 | $2,000 | $1,800 | $1,650 | $1,600 | $1,500 | $1,350 | $1,200 | $1,000 | $900 |

❋ Sixth Type - serial range approx. 5,500-11,500.

| N/A | $2,000 | $1,900 | $1,800 | $1,600 | $1,500 | $1,400 | $1,300 | $1,100 | $900 | $800 | $750 |

MODEL NO. 1 SECOND ISSUE TIP-UP

 - similar to First Issue, except flat-sided frame and irregular-shaped sideplate. 114,900 mfg. 1860-1868. Serial range approx. 11,500 - approx. 126,000.

| $1,500 | $1,000 | $700 | $650 | $600 | $575 | $550 | $500 | $450 | $400 | $350 | $300 |

An early sideplate variation with 2 patent dates on cylinder occurred in the serial range 11,500-12,100. The second sideplate variation with 2 patent dates occurred in the serial range 12,100-20,000.

❋ Second Quality

Extreme rarity precludes accurate pricing on this model. May bring double or triple values over the Model No. 1 Second Issue Tip-Up. Beware of fakes!

MODEL NO. 1 THIRD ISSUE TIP-UP

 - similar to Second Issue, except fluted cylinder, round barrel, and birdshead grip. 131,163 mfg. 1868-82. This model has its own serial range no. 1-131,163. Mfg. 1868-1882.

❋ 3 3/16 in. Barrel Model. - will have markings on top of barrel.

| $1,500 | $1,000 | $600 | $500 | $425 | $375 | $350 | $300 | $250 | $225 | $200 | $175 |

❋ Short Barrels 2 11/16 - 2 3/4 in. - will have markings on side of barrel.

| $900 | $850 | $775 | $720 | $680 | $640 | $600 | $560 | $520 | $480 | $440 | $400 |

MODEL NO. 1 1/2 OLD MODEL (MODEL 1 1/2 FIRST ISSUE)

 - .32 rimfire, single action, 3 1/2 or 4 (rare) in. octagon barrel, 5 shot non-fluted cylinder, bottom break, spur trigger, blue or nickel, rosewood grips, square butt. 26,300 mfg. 1865-68. Serial range 1-approx. 26,300.

| $1,200 | $800 | $600 | $500 | $425 | $350 | $275 | $250 | $225 | $210 | $195 | $185 |

Early production had 2 patent dates with the barrel markings (approx. serial range 1-15,500). Later production had 3 patent dates (approx. serial range 15,501-26,300).

❋ 4 in. Barrel

Extreme rarity precludes accurate pricing on this model. May bring double or triple values over the Model No. 1 1/2 Old Model. Watch for fakes (i.e. stretched barrels).

❋ Model 1 1/2 Transitional Model - octagon barrel with birdshead grips, serial range 27,200-28,800, rare.

| $3,000 | $2,500 | $1,800 | $1,500 | $1,350 | $1,275 | $1,200 | $1,125 | $1,075 | $1,000 | $950 | $900 |

MODEL NO. 1 1/2 NEW MODEL (MODEL 1 1/2 SECOND ISSUE)

 - similar to First Issue, with birdshead grips and round barrel, fluted cylinder. 100,800 mfg. 1868-75. Serial range 26,301-127,100.

❋ Short Barrel Model - barrel markings on side, length varies from 2 1/2-2 3/4 in. (scarce).

Extreme rarity precludes accurate pricing on this model. May bring double or triple values over the Model No. 1 1/2 New Model. Beware of fakes!

❋ 3 1/2 in. Barrel Model

| $900 | $750 | $500 | $400 | $350 | $300 | $225 | $200 | $180 | $165 | $150 | $135 |

MODEL NO. 2 ARMY TIP-UP

 - .32 rimfire long, similar in appearance to No. 1 1/2 First Issue, except 6 shot cylinder, different barrel lengths, used as a sidearm during Civil War. 77,155 mfg. 1861-74. Serial number range 1-77,155.

100%	98%	95%	90%	80%	70%	60%	50%	40%	30%	20%	10%

❋ 5 or 6 in. Standard Model

| $3,000 | $2,500 | $1,500 | $1,000 | $900 | $800 | $700 | $625 | $525 | $450 | $400 | $375 |

Premiums exist for early 2 pin models under ser. no. 3,000. Large premiums will be asked for 4 in. barrel - beware of fakes!

TOP-BREAKS

These revolvers have a latch just in front of the hammer, which locks the barrel to the frame. When the action is opened, the barrel & cylinder tip down, with an automatic extractor ejecting the shells. Mfg 1870-1940, they include single action (spur-trigger or trigger guard), double action, and safety hammerless designs. They are listed in order of frame size. Model 1 1/2 is the smallest or .32 cal. pocket sized frame; Model 2 is the medium or .38 cal. belt sized frame; Model 3 is the large holster or .44 cal. frame. Within each frame size, they are listed by action type - SA, DA, or Hammerless, as applicable.

Changes from one Top-Break model type to another are not necessarily definitive at a specific serial number. Therefore, an overlap of serial numbers from one model to another may be observed.

.32 SINGLE ACTION (MODEL 1 1/2 CENTERFIRE) - .32 S&W cal., spur trigger, top break, rebounding hammer, auto extraction. 97,599 mfg. 1878-1892. Serial range 1-97,599.

❋ Later Model - with strain screw, remainder of serial range.

| $750 | $500 | $400 | $350 | $300 | $275 | $250 | $225 | $210 | $200 | $190 | $150 |

Early models under ser. no. 6,000 w/o strain screw will bring a slight premium. Original 2, 8, or 10 in. barrel models with bring a large premium - watch for fakes!

.32 DOUBLE ACTION FIRST MODEL - .32 S&W cal., 5 shot fluted cylinder, 3 in. round barrel, square edged side plate, blue or nickel finish, black rubber grips, one of the rarest of all S&Ws. Only 30 mfg. 1880. Serial range 1-30.

Extreme rarity precludes accurate pricing on this model.

.32 DOUBLE ACTION SECOND MODEL - similar to First Model, except irregular shaped sideplate, 3, 3 1/4, 4, 5, or 6 in. barrel, 22,142 mfg. 1880-82. Serial range 31-22,172.

| $475 | $425 | $380 | $340 | $300 | $260 | $220 | $180 | $150 | $120 | $100 | $90 |

.32 DOUBLE ACTION THIRD MODEL - similar to Second Model, except without groove around cylinder. 22,232 mfg. 1882-83. Serial range 22,173-43,405.

| $475 | $425 | $380 | $340 | $300 | $260 | $220 | $180 | $150 | $120 | $100 | $90 |

.32 DOUBLE ACTION FOURTH MODEL - similar to Third Model, except rounded triggerguard, pinned front sight. 239,600 mfg. 1883-1909. Serial range 43,406-approx. 282,999.

| $345 | $305 | $270 | $240 | $210 | $185 | $160 | $135 | $115 | $100 | $90 | $85 |

An 8 or 10 in. barrel on this model will command a premium.

.32 DOUBLE ACTION FIFTH MODEL - similar to Fourth Model, except integral front sight. 44,641 mfg. 1909-19. Serial range approx. 282,300-327,641.

| $375 | $335 | $300 | $270 | $240 | $215 | $190 | $165 | $135 | $120 | $105 | $90 |

.32 SAFETY HAMMERLESS FIRST MODEL (LEMON SQUEEZER) - .32 S&W cal., double action only, 5 shot fluted cylinder, 2, 3 (most common), 3 1/4, 3 1/2, or 6 (rare) in. round barrel, blue or nickel, black rubber grips. This model was officially called the New Departure. 91,417 mfg. 1888-1902. Serial range 1-91,417.

Short 2 in. barrel versions known as "Bicycle model" will bring 25% to 50% premium on all Safety Hammerless models. Six inch barrels will bring a premium as well.

❋ Standard Model - 2, 3, 3 1/4, or 3 1/2 in. barrel.

| $500 | $475 | $450 | $425 | $400 | $375 | $350 | $325 | $275 | $235 | $185 | $150 |

100%	98%	95%	90%	80%	70%	60%	50%	40%	30%	20%	10%

.32 SAFETY HAMMERLESS SECOND MODEL - 2, 3, 3 1/4, 3 1/2, or 6 in. barrel,
similar to First Model with pinned front sight and T-shaped latch. 78,500 mfg. 1902-09.
Serial range 91,418-170,000.

$450	$425	$400	$375	$350	$325	$300	$275	$235	$200	$165	$130

.32 SAFETY HAMMERLESS THIRD MODEL - 2, 3, 3 1/4, 3 1/2, or 6 in. barrel,
usually has forged front sight. 73,000 mfg. 1909-37. Serial range 163,082-242,981
(with some overlap from the Second Model).

$450	$425	$400	$375	$350	$325	$300	$275	$235	$200	$165	$130

.38 SINGLE ACTION FIRST MODEL (BABY RUSSIAN) WITH SPUR TRIGGER - .38
S&W cal., 5 shot fluted cylinder, 3 1/4, 4, 5, or 6 in. barrel, blue with wood grips, nickel with
"S&W" monogram hard black or red rubber grips. 25,548 mfg. 1876-77. Serial range 1-
25,548.

✳ *Standard Model*

$1,750	$700	$600	$500	$400	$350	$325	$300	$275	$250	$225	$200

Substantial premiums will be asked for "Aldrich" safety models (first 50-100 guns). Add a
slight premium for ser. nos. under 1,500 with filler screws on right side of frame.

.38 SINGLE ACTION SECOND MODEL - similar to above, except very short ejec-
tor housing under barrel, cal. and cylinder same as above, 3 1/4, 4, 5, 6, 8, or 10 in.
barrel, grips same as above. 108,225 mfg. 1877-1891. Serial range 1-108,255.

✳ *Standard Model*

$700	$500	$375	$285	$250	$225	$210	$200	$190	$185	$180	$150

✳ *8 or 10 in. Barrel*

Extreme rarity precludes accurate pricing on this model.

.38 SINGLE ACTION THIRD MODEL (MODEL OF 1891) - similar to above,
except has trigger guard, cal. and cylinder same as above, 3 1/4, 4, 5, or 6 in. barrel (also accepts the single shot barrel), blue or nickel finish with "S&W" monogram,
hard black rubber grips. 26,850 mfg. 1891-1911. Serial range 1-28,107 which also
includes the serial number range of the Single Shot First Model in .22 LR, .32 S&W,
.38 S&W cal. and the .38 S.A. Mexican Model described below. Barrel marked "Model
of 1891".

$2,300	$1,650	$1,425	$1,250	$1,075	$950	$850	$775	$700	$625	$550	$475

Add 50%-75% for single shot barrel with matching serial number.

.38 SINGLE ACTION MEXICAN MODEL - essentially same as above, except has
inserted spur trigger, .38 S&W cal., 5 shot fluted cylinder, 3 1/4, 4, 5, or 6 in. barrel,
blue or nickel finish, "S&W" monogram checkered hard rubber or walnut grips. Features unique to this model are flat sided hammer, half cock notch, and "inserted"
spur trigger assembly (not integral with frame). This model would also accept the
single shot barrel, limited mfg. 1891-1911. Approx. 2,000 mfg. in ser. no. range 1-
28107. Watch out for fakes (and conversions)!

N/A	$4,000	$3,500	$2,750	$2,000	$1,650	$1,400	$1,250	$1,150	$1,050	$975	$950

Add 50%-75% for single shot barrel with matching serial number.

.38 DOUBLE ACTION FIRST MODEL - .38 S&W cal., 5 shot fluted cylinder, 3 1/4 or
4 in. barrel, blue or nickel finish, "S&W" monogram checkered hard rubber grips.
4,000 mfg. 1880. Serial range 1-4,000.

$900	$850	$750	$650	$550	$475	$400	$325	$250	$200	$175	$150

.38 DOUBLE ACTION SECOND MODEL - .38 S&W cal., cylinder same as above, 3
1/4, 4, 5, or 6 in. barrel, blue or nickel finish, "S&W" monogram checkered hard
rubber grips in black or red. 115,000 mfg. 1880-84. Serial range approx. 4,001-
approx. 119,000.

$500	$350	$250	$225	$200	$185	$170	$165	$160	$145	$135	$125

100%	98%	95%	90%	80%	70%	60%	50%	40%	30%	20%	10%

.38 DOUBLE ACTION THIRD MODEL - .38 S&W cal., cylinder same as above, 3 1/4, 4, 5, 6, 8, or 10 in. barrel, blue or nickel finish, "S&W" monogram hard rubber grips. 203,700 mfg. 1884-95. Serial range approx. 119,001-322,700.

$500	$350	$225	$200	$190	$175	$160	$155	$150	$140	$125	$115

✳ *8 or 10 in. Barrel*
  Extreme rarity precludes accurate pricing on this model.
  A 2 in. variation, while extremely rare, was manufactured in the Third Model, Fourth Model, Fifth Model, and Perfected Models listed. Large premiums do exist ($850-$1,500) - watch for fakes!

.38 DOUBLE ACTION FOURTH MODEL - .38 S&W cal., cylinder same as above, 3 1/4, 4, 5, or 6 in. barrel, blue or nickel finish, "S&W" monogram checkered hard rubber grips, also offered in an extended square butt target style. 216,300 mfg. 1895-1909. Serial range 322,701-539,000.

$450	$300	$230	$200	$185	$170	$155	$150	$145	$135	$120	$110

.38 DOUBLE ACTION FIFTH MODEL - .38 S&W cal., cylinder, barrel, and grip specifications same as above with the additional availability of an extended square butt target style walnut grip as an accessory. 15,000 mfg. 1909-11. Serial range approx. 539,001-554,077.

$500	$465	$425	$375	$325	$285	$250	$225	$200	$180	$150	$125

.38 DOUBLE ACTION PERFECTED MODEL - .38 S&W cal., 2 (extremely rare – watch for fakes), 3 1/4, 4, 5, or 6 in. barrel, cylinder change in frame incorporates rolled I frame revolver and lockwork, trigger guard is integral part of frame, and side plate is on right side, not left side. The last of the S&W break open revolvers. 59,400 mfg. 1909-20. Serial range 1-59,400. Identified by having both top latch and side latch.

$800	$500	$425	$375	$325	$285	$250	$225	$200	$180	$150	$125

✳ *.38 Double Action Perfected Model Top Latch Only* - as above, except no side latch - rare.
  Extreme rarity precludes accurate pricing on this model.
  Add a substantial premium for triggerguard with integral frame.

.38 SAFETY HAMMERLESS FIRST MODEL (.38 NEW DEPARTURE) - .38 S&W cal., 5 shot fluted cylinder, 3 1/4, 4, 5, or 6 in. barrel, blue or nickel finish, "S&W" monogram checkered hard rubber grips, features "Z-Bar" latch. Approx. 5,000 mfg. in 1887. Serial range 1-5,001.

$1,200	$800	$700	$550	$485	$435	$375	$325	$275	$250	$225	$150

  Add 25% for blue finish.

✳ *6 in. Barrel*
  Extreme rarity precludes accurate pricing on this model.

.38 SAFETY HAMMERLESS SECOND MODEL - .38 S&W cal., cylinder same as above, 3 1/4, 4, 5, or 6 in. barrel, finish and grips same as above. 37,350 mfg. 1887-90. Serial range approx. 5,001-42,483.

$600	$465	$425	$375	$325	$285	$250	$225	$200	$180	$150	$125

U.S. MARTIALLY MARKED - 100 purchased by Govt. in 1890, serial range 41,333 - 41,470, serial numbers in Second Model range, but are true Third Models.
  Extreme rarity precludes accurate pricing on this model. Beware of fakes!

.38 SAFETY HAMMERLESS THIRD MODEL - .38 S&W cal., cylinder same as above, 3 1/4, 4, 5, or 6 in. barrel, finish and grips same as above. 73,500 mfg. 1890-1898. Serial range 24,284-116,002.

$500	$375	$330	$300	$275	$250	$225	$200	$175	$150	$135	$110

.38 SAFETY HAMMERLESS FOURTH MODEL - .38 S&W cal., cylinder, barrel lengths, finishes and grips same as above. 104,000 mfg. 1898-1907. Serial range 116,003 to approx. 220,000.

$375	$280	$240	$205	$190	$165	$155	$145	$135	$125	$115	$100

  A 2 in. barrel in this variation is rare (Bicycle Model).

100%	98%	95%	90%	80%	70%	60%	50%	40%	30%	20%	10%

.38 SAFETY HAMMERLESS FIFTH MODEL - .38 S&W cal., cylinder same as above, 2, 3 1/4, 4, 5, or 6 in. barrel, blue or nickel finish, "S&W" monogram checkered hard rubber or checkered walnut grips. 41,500 mfg. 1907-40. Serial range 220,000-261,493.

| $450 | $350 | $240 | $205 | $190 | $165 | $155 | $145 | $135 | $125 | $115 | $100 |

❋ *2 in. Barrel*

Extreme rarity precludes accurate pricing on this model - will bring a premium.

MODEL 3 AMERICAN FIRST MODEL (SINGLE ACTION) - .44 S&W American or .44 rimfire Henry cal., single action, 6 shot fluted cylinder, 6, 7, or 8 in. round barrel, blue or nickel finish, walnut grips. 8,000 mfg. 1870-72. Serial range 1-approx. 8,000. Serial number overlaps on the variations below are known to exist.

Slight premiums will be asked for models with vent. hole in bottom rear barrel (approx. first 1,500).

Original barrel lengths other than 8 in. are worth a premium - beware of cut barrels.

❋ *Standard Model* - without hole in extractor.

| N/A | $8,000 | $4,500 | $3,500 | $3,000 | $2,500 | $2,150 | $1,850 | $1,650 | $1,450 | $1,250 | $1,100 |

❋ *Transitional Model* - includes locking notch on hammer, with small trigger pin, serial range 6,700-8,000.

| N/A | $8,000 | $4,600 | $3,600 | $3,100 | $2,650 | $2,250 | $2,150 | $1,850 | $1,650 | $1,450 | $1,200 |

❋ *.44 Rimfire Henry* - limited mfg. Watch for fakes!

| N/A | $8,250 | $7,000 | $6,000 | $5,000 | $4,000 | $3,750 | $3,500 | $3,250 | $3,000 | $2,750 | $2,500 |

❋ *U.S. Marked* - approx. 1,000 mfg., 800 in blue, and 200 in nickel finish. All nickel plated revolvers are serial numbered above 1,950 – watch for fakes.

| N/A | $15,000 | $10,750 | $9,100 | $8,100 | $7,250 | $6,500 | $5,900 | $5,375 | $4,850 | $4,450 | $4,000 |

❋ *Nashville Police* - very rare, only 32 manufactured. Scarcity precludes accurate pricing – beware of fakes.

MODEL 3 AMERICAN SECOND MODEL - .44 S&W American or .44 rimfire Henry cal., single action, 6 shot fluted cylinder, mechanism allows the hammer to lock the barrel latch in place, larger trigger pin, 5 1/2, 6, 6 1/2, 7, or 8 in. barrel, blue or nickel, walnut grips. 19,635 mfg. 1872-1874, serial range approx. 8,000-32,800 which includes commercial version of Model 3 Russian First Model.

❋ *Standard Model* - .44 S&W American cal., 8 in. barrel.

| N/A | $7,000 | $3,750 | $3,250 | $2,750 | $2,250 | $2,150 | $1,850 | $1,650 | $1,450 | $1,250 | $1,100 |

Add 35% for 5 1/2, 6, 6 1/2, or 7 in. barrel.

❋ *Standard Model .44 Rimfire Henry* - 6, 7, or 8 in. barrel, non-locking hammer below approx. serial number 25,000. 3,014 mfg.

| N/A | $8,000 | $4,750 | $3,750 | $3,525 | $3,050 | $2,650 | $2,250 | $2,150 | $1,850 | $1,650 | $1,450 |

MODEL 3 FIRST MODEL RUSSIAN (OLD OLD MODEL RUSSIAN) - .44 S&W Russian, 5 1/2, 6, 7, or 8 in. barrel, Russian contract revolvers had 8 in. barrels, blue finish, and Cyrillic barrel markings, commerical mfg. had blue or nickel finish, walnut grips, looks similar to First and Second Model American. 5,165 mfg. 1871-1874 for commercial sale and 20,014 for Russian Contract (separate ser. no. range). Serial range 6,000-32,800, see Model 3 Second Model American.

❋ *Commercial Version* - 4,665 mfg.

| N/A | $5,000 | $4,000 | $3,250 | $2,750 | $2,250 | $2,150 | $1,850 | $1,650 | $1,450 | $1,250 | $1,100 |

❋ *Reject Russian Contract* - approx. 500 mfg., can be determined by the barrel, latch, and cylinder having a full serial number, rather than assembly numbers.

| N/A | $5,000 | $4,000 | $3,250 | $2,750 | $2,250 | $2,150 | $1,850 | $1,650 | $1,450 | $1,250 | $1,100 |

❋ *Russian Contract* - 20,014 mfg., rare, most sent to Russia, Cyrillic marked. Serial range 1-approx. 20,014.

| N/A | N/A | $6,750 | $5,975 | $5,125 | $4,450 | $3,800 | $3,350 | $2,950 | $2,600 | $2,250 | $2,000 |

100%	98%	95%	90%	80%	70%	60%	50%	40%	30%	20%	10%

MODEL 3 SECOND MODEL RUSSIAN (OLD RUSSIAN) - 2nd and 3rd Model Russians have an extreme knuckle at the top of backstrap and trigger guard spur, 85,200 mfg. in all variations between 1873-78, 7 in. barrel, small screw in top-strap of frame, features longer ejector housing and "Russian Model" marking on top of barrel. Ser. nos. started at 32,800.

* *Commercial Version* - 6,200 mfg.

N/A	$3,750	$3,000	$2,375	$2,000	$1,750	$1,500	$1,300	$1,100	$995	$895	$795

* *.44 Rimfire Henry* - approx. 500 mfg.

N/A	$5,000	$4,500	$4,000	$3,525	$3,050	$2,650	$2,250	$2,150	$1,850	$1,650	$1,500

* *Russian Contract* - approx. 70,000 mfg. for Russian Military contract, cryllic marked, rare in U.S.

N/A	N/A	$3,150	$2,850	$2,525	$2,275	$2,100	$1,950	$1,800	$1,650	$1,500	$1,350

* *Turkish Model* - 1,000 mfg. in their own serial number range in .44 Rimfire, features rimfire hammer, but the cylinder is chambered for .44 Russian. This is probably the rarest and most valuable variation.

N/A	N/A	$5,000	$4,500	$4,000	$3,600	$3,250	$2,900	$2,675	$2,475	$2,250	$2,000

This model was converted to rimfire from .44 S&W Russian cal.

* *Japanese Contract* - may be marked with an anchor.

N/A	N/A	$3,200	$2,600	$2,300	$2,050	$1,825	$1,650	$1,500	$1,375	$1,250	$1,175

MODEL 3 THIRD MODEL RUSSIAN - commonly called the "New Model Russian" and is similar to old model, except has shorter extractor housing, 6 1/2 in. barrel, large knurled screw in top-strap of frame, shorter ejector housing, butt is usually marked with an 1874 in a square, approx. 60,600 mfg. 1874-78. Values are similar to old model for comparable variations. In addition, the Tula Arsenal in Russia also mfg. 300,000-400,000 pistols for domestic use and Ludwig & Loewe in Germany mfg. 100,000.

* *Commercial Version* - approx. 13,500 mfg.

N/A	$3,750	$3,000	$2,375	$2,000	$1,750	$1,500	$1,300	$1,100	$995	$895	$795

* *.44 Rimfire Henry*

N/A	$5,000	$4,500	$4,000	$3,525	$3,050	$2,650	$2,250	$2,150	$1,850	$1,650	$1,500

* *Russian Contract* - 41,138 mfg. Cyrillic lettering.

N/A	$3,500	$3,200	$2,900	$2,650	$2,400	$2,200	$2,000	$1,775	$1,575	$1,325	$1,100

* *Ludwig & Loewe, & Tula Copies* - copies mfg. for the Russian government.

N/A	$2,800	$2,500	$2,250	$2,000	$1,800	$1,625	$1,475	$1,350	$1,225	$1,100	$950

Add 30% for Tula copies.

* *Turkish Contract* - 5,000 mfg., utilizes .44 Russian cylinder - chambered for .44 Rimfire.

N/A	$4,000	$3,700	$3,425	$3,100	$2,850	$2,575	$2,325	$2,025	$1,700	$1,425	$1,200

* *Japanese Contract* - 1,000 made.

N/A	$3,800	$3,150	$2,300	$2,000	$1,750	$1,500	$1,300	$1,225	$1,100	$950	$800

MODEL 3 SCHOFIELD FIRST MODEL - .45 S&W cal., single action, 7 in. barrel, 6 shot fluted cylinder, blue finish only, walnut grips, ser. no. range 1-3035. 3,035 mfg. 1875.

* *U.S. Issue* - 3,000 mfg.

N/A	$15,000	$9,000	$6,000	$4,500	$4,000	$3,600	$3,400	$3,200	$3,000	$2,600	$2,250

* *Commercial Model (not U.S. marked)* - 35 were produced without U.S. markings, very rare - beware of fakes - there could be more phony ones than real ones.

Extreme rarity factor of this model precludes accurate pricing.

100%	98%	95%	90%	80%	70%	60%	50%	40%	30%	20%	10%

* *Wells Fargo and Company* - barrel cut to approx. 5 in. with Wells Fargo markings.

| N/A | N/A | N/A | N/A | $7,000 | $5,100 | $4,550 | $4,175 | $3,750 | $3,350 | $3,050 | $2,750 |

Warning - Beware of fakes! There may be more fake Wells Fargo Schofields than authentic ones. While most fakes are usually poor quality, others may be quite impressive.

Many Schofields are found with cut 5 in. barrels and no Wells Fargo marking - these will bring approx. 66% of uncut values, or if they have fake WF markings, then their value is 1/2 of the uncut values.

MODEL 3 SCHOFIELD SECOND MODEL - ser. no. range 3036-8969. Mfg. 1876-1877.

* *Standard Model* - "U.S." on butt.

| N/A | $14,000 | $8,000 | $5,500 | $4,500 | $4,000 | $3,600 | $3,400 | $3,200 | $3,000 | $2,600 | $2,250 |

* *Commercial Model* - blue or nickel finish, 650 mfg.

| N/A | $9,500 | $7,000 | $5,000 | $4,500 | $4,000 | $3,600 | $3,400 | $3,200 | $3,000 | $2,600 | $2,250 |

* *Wells Fargo and Company* - barrel cut to 5 in. with Wells Fargo markings.

| N/A | N/A | N/A | N/A | $7,000 | $5,100 | $4,550 | $4,175 | $3,750 | $3,350 | $3,050 | $2,750 |

Warning - Beware of fakes! There may be more fake Wells Fargo Schofields than authentic ones. While most fakes are usually poor quality, others may be quite impressive. Many Schofields are found with cut 5 in. barrels and no Wells Fargo marking - these will bring approx. 66% of uncut values, or if they have fake WF markings, then their value is 1/2 of the uncut values.

NEW MODEL NO. 3 - features very short extractor housing under the barrel, knuckle on backstrap is less pronounced than Russian Models, single action, round butt. 35,796 mfg. between 1878-1912.

Slight premiums will be asked for cut shoulder stock ($750-$1,250), target sights (standard non-target models only).

Add a premium for barrel lengths other than 6 1/2 in. (beware of .44 DA barrels!), and for calibers other than .44 Russian.

Early production had rack and gear extractor (serial number range 1-13,500), and will bring a slight premium over the later mfg. Also, premiums do exist for all but 6 and 6 1/2 in. barrel lengths; premiums for unusual chamberings.

* *Commercial Version*

| $8,500 | $5,000 | $2,850 | $2,000 | $1,800 | $1,625 | $1,475 | $1,325 | $1,175 | $995 | $795 | $695 |

* *Japanese Navy Model* - Japan purchased approx. 1/3 of total production.

Add 50% for Japanese characters on ejector housing. Japanese anchor brings only a small premium, if any.

* *Australian Model* - 7 in. barrel, detachable stock, for Australian Colonial Police, broad arrow marking on both pistol and stock, stocks were originally numbered to the matching pistol, but are seldom seen with matching numbers today, approx. 250 mfg., usually found in the low 12,000-low 13,000 ser. no. range.

Add a substantial premium if with shoulder stock.

* *Argentine Model* - unknown total production, marked "Ejercito Argentina" (very rare).

Add a premium over the Commercial Version.

* *State of Maryland Model* - "U.S." marked, serial number range 7,126-7,405.

Add a premium over the Commercial Version.

Add a premium for Revenue Cutter Service (Coast Guard) model, identifiable only by ser. no.

NEW MODEL NO. 3 FRONTIER - .44-40 WCF cal., single action, 4, 5, or 6 1/2 in. barrel, blue or nickel finish, walnut or hard rubber grips, ser. no. range 1-2072. 2,072 mfg. 1885-1908.

* *Japanese Purchase* - 786 converted to .44 Russian cal., cylinder should measure 1 9/16 in., in the Frontier serial range of 1-2,072.

| N/A | $5,000 | $3,000 | $2,250 | $1,800 | $1,625 | $1,475 | $1,325 | $1,175 | $995 | $795 | $695 |

100%	98%	95%	90%	80%	70%	60%	50%	40%	30%	20%	10%

✴ *Standard Model* - .44-40 WCF cal.

100%	98%	95%	90%	80%	70%	60%	50%	40%	30%	20%	10%
$9,000	$6,000	$3,500	$3,000	$2,500	$2,250	$2,000	$1,850	$1,600	$1,400	$1,250	$1,100

NEW MODEL NO. 3 - .38-40 WCF. - separate ser. range, only 74 mfg., ser. no. 1-74. Mfg. 1900-1907.

Extreme rarity factor of this model precludes accurate pricing.

NEW MODEL NO. 3 TARGET MODEL - .32-44 S&W or .38-44 S&W cal., target sights, ser. no. range 1-4333. 4,333 mfg. between 1887-1910.

100%	98%	95%	90%	80%	70%	60%	50%	40%	30%	20%	10%
$6,500	$3,250	$2,500	$2,250	$1,925	$1,700	$1,500	$1,350	$1,100	$950	$800	$700

NEW MODEL NO. 3 TURKISH - .44 rimfire cal., 5,461 mfg. between 1879-88, in separate serial number series.

100%	98%	95%	90%	80%	70%	60%	50%	40%	30%	20%	10%
N/A	$7,000	$4,675	$4,350	$4,050	$3,750	$3,450	$3,150	$2,850	$2,550	$2,275	$1,950

.44 CAL. DOUBLE ACTION FIRST MODEL - .32-44 (rare), .38-44 (rare), .38 Military (rare), .44 S&W Russian (most common), and .455 (rare) cal., caliber markings on later production for .44 S&W Russian is ".44 Smith & Wesson", 6 shot fluted cylinder, 4, 5, 6, or 6 1/2 in. barrel, blue or nickel finish, "S&W" monogram checkered hard rubber or walnut grips. Walnut grips with "S&W" inlays will be found after 1900. 53,668 mfg. 1881-1913. Serial range 1-54,668.

Add 100% for cals. other than .44 S&W Russian with target sights on sub-models listed.

✴ *Standard Model*

100%	98%	95%	90%	80%	70%	60%	50%	40%	30%	20%	10%
$4,500	$1,900	$1,500	$1,275	$1,000	$925	$825	$695	$650	$575	$475	$375

✴ *.44 Double Action Wesson Favorite* - similar to Standard Model, but in 5 in. barrel only with special front sight, blue nickel finish, patent markings are on the cylinder rather than on the barrel, grooved barrel rib, external and internal lightening cuts to reduce weight. Approx. 1,000 mfg. 1882-83. Ser. range included with .44 Double Action First Model, between approx. 8,900-10,100.

100%	98%	95%	90%	80%	70%	60%	50%	40%	30%	20%	10%
N/A	$10,000	$8,000	$7,000	$5,500	$4,500	$3,600	$3,200	$2,825	$2,500	$2,275	$2,000

Add 30-40% for blue finish.

.38 WIN. DOUBLE ACTION - .38-40 WCF cal., 4, 5, 6, or 6 1/2 in. barrel, only 276 mfg. in separate ser. range 1-276. Mfg. 1900-1910.

100%	98%	95%	90%	80%	70%	60%	50%	40%	30%	20%	10%
N/A	$6,000	$5,000	$4,000	$3,000	$2,500	$2,000	$1,750	$1,500	$1,300	$1,225	$1,125

.44 DOUBLE ACTION FRONTIER - .44-40 WCF cal., 4, 5, 6, or 6 1/2 in. barrel, only 15,340 mfg. in separate ser. range 1-15,340. Mfg. 1886-1913.

100%	98%	95%	90%	80%	70%	60%	50%	40%	30%	20%	10%
$4,500	$1,900	$1,500	$1,275	$1,000	$925	$825	$695	$650	$575	$475	$375

Add 100% for factory target sights.

.44 DOUBLE ACTION WESSON FAVORITE - .44 S&W Russian cal., ser. no. range 8900-10100. Approx. 1,000 mfg. 1882-1883.

100%	98%	95%	90%	80%	70%	60%	50%	40%	30%	20%	10%
N/A	N/A	$10,000	$8,200	$7,500	$6,500	$6,000	$5,000	$4,000	$2,500	$2,000	$1,500

SINGLE SHOTS

FIRST MODEL - .22 LR (862 mfg.), .32 S&W (229 mfg.), or .38 S&W (160 mfg.) cal., 6, 8, or 10 in. barrel marked "Model of 1891", blue or nickel, hard rubber extension grips, single action trigger. 1,251 mfg. 1893-1905, ser. range (same as Third Model 38 Single Action) 1-28,107. Serial number is located on the front strap.

✴ *.22 LR* - approx. 862 mfg.

100%	98%	95%	90%	80%	70%	60%	50%	40%	30%	20%	10%
$1,500	$800	$650	$575	$525	$475	$425	$375	$350	$325	$300	$285

Add a premium for .32 S&W or .38 S&W cals.

SECOND MODEL .22 LR - similar to First Model, but will not accommodate a revolver cylinder, flatsided frame (does not have recoil shield) 6 (rare) or 10 in. barrel, single action trigger, black hard rubber extension grips, 4,617 mfg. 1905-09. Ser. range 1-4,617 (ser. no. located on front gripstrap).

100%	98%	95%	90%	80%	70%	60%	50%	40%	30%	20%	10%
$1,100	$750	$625	$575	$525	$475	$425	$375	$325	$280	$250	$225

100%	98%	95%	90%	80%	70%	60%	50%	40%	30%	20%	10%

THIRD MODEL .22 (PERFECTED MODEL) - similar to Second Model, except is built on "I" solid frame with integral trigger guard, side plate on right side, made in both single or double action, checkered walnut extension grips. 6,949 mfg. 1909-1923. Serial range 4,618-11,641 (ser. no. located on front gripstrap).

$1,100	$750	$600	$550	$500	$450	$400	$350	$300	$265	$235	$210

   Add 30% for Olympic Model in extra short .22 LR rifle chamber.

STRAIGHT LINE TARGET SINGLE SHOT - .22 LR cal., single shot, 10 in. barrel, sideswing barrel, blue, target sights, smooth walnut grips, shaped like an auto-loader. 1,870 mfg. 1925-36. Ser. range 1-1,870. Values below assume steel case and accessories.

$1,850	$1,200	$950	$850	$750	$650	$550	$450	$415	$350	$335	$315

   Subtract 30% w/o case and accessories.

EARLY HAND EJECTORS (NAMED MODELS)

Named Models. 1896-1958. Listed in order by caliber, except where newer mfg. might also include model number. These will NOT have any model number stamped on the frame. Several were continued after 1958 as Numbered Models, so be sure to check that section as well.

MODEL .22 HAND EJECTOR (LADYSMITH) - originally chambered for .22 S&W (same as .22 Long) cal., 7 shot fluted cylinder, small frame, available in blue or nickel finish, nicknamed "Ladysmith" due to its small size. Over 26,000 mfg. between 1902-21.

  ✳ *First Model* - .22 L cal., 3, or 3 1/2 in. barrel length, serial numbered 1-4,575, checkered hard rubber grips, round butt. 4,575 mfg. 1902-1906. Serial range 1-4,575. Identifiable by frame mounted cylinder release lever.

$2,500	$1,800	$1,500	$1,250	$975	$800	$650	$550	$475	$435	$390	$350

  ✳ *Second Model* - .22 L cal., 3, or 3 1/2 in. barrel, distinguishable from first model in that cylinder locking device was placed on barrel bottom, locking both ends. 9,400 mfg. 1906-10. Serial range 4,576-13,950.

$2,000	$1,500	$1,275	$950	$800	$700	$600	$525	$475	$425	$375	$325

  ✳ *Third Model* - .22 L cal., 2 1/2, 3, 3 1/2, or 6 in. barrel, smooth walnut grips with "S&W" medallion inlays, square butt. 12,200 mfg. 1910-21. Serial range 13,951-26,154.

$2,000	$1,475	$1,250	$900	$750	$650	$550	$475	$425	$375	$325	$325

   Add 85% for 6 in. barrel with target sights.
   Add 95% for 6 in. barrel with plain sights.

.22/.32 HAND EJECTOR (ALSO KNOWN AS .22/32 BEKEART MODEL) - .22 LR cal., 6 shot fluted cylinder, 6 in. barrel, blue, checkered walnut grips with "S&W" medallions, extension style square butt, there were several hundred thousand of the standard .22/.32 Hand Ejector mfg. The first 3,000 mfg. will be found with a separate ser. no. (1-3,000) stamped into the bottom of the wood grips. This model was cataloged as the .22/.32 heavy frame target unit in 1931. Mfg. 1911-1941.

  ✳ *Bekeart Model* - will be found with separate identification number on bottom of wooden grip. Serial numbers for early Bekeart models start at 138,226.

$1,075	$875	$750	$650	$550	$450	$350	$275	$200	$150	$135	$110

   Slight premiums are charged over the values listed for early production in lower ser. no. range 1,001-3,000.
   This model was specifically mfg. for a San Francisco retailer, Philip Bekeart. Originally, Mr. Bekeart ordered 1,000 guns to his specifications, S&W mfg. 5,000. While the first 1,000 revolvers in ser. no. range 138,226 with grip numbered 1-1,000 are accepted as "True Bekearts," only 292 were actually delivered to Philip Bekeart.

  ✳ *Standard .22/.32 Hand Ejector Model* - mfg. approx. 1913-53, continued as the Model 35.

$750	$600	$500	$425	$350	$325	$275	$225	$175	$135	$115	$100

100%	98%	95%	90%	80%	70%	60%	50%	40%	30%	20%	10%

.22/32 KIT GUN - similar to Standard .22/32 Hand Ejector Model, except has 2 or 4 in. barrels, round or square butt. Mfg. 1935-53, serial number overlaps occur within this model, continued as the Model 34.

$800	$700	$575	$500	$450	$400	$350	$300	$260	$230	$200	$175

Pre-war kit guns in ser. no. range approx. 525670 to 536684 will bring a 300%-400% premium over above values, if in better condition. Mfg. 1935-1941.

Early post-war kit guns in ser. no. range approx. 536684 to 59000 will bring a 200% premium over above values, if in better condition. Mfg. 1946-1952.

✴ *1953-1957 "Pre-Model 34" Production* - improved I or J frame, continued in 1957 as the Model 34.

$500	$385	$300	$275	$225	$200	$175	$160	$140	$120	$110	$100

Early alloy frame airweight kit guns (pre-Model 43), will bring values similar to the steel frame pre-Model 34.

GRADING - PPGS™	100%	98%	95%	90%	80%	70%	60%

K-22 OUTDOORSMAN - .22 LR cal., 6 shot, 6 in. round barrel, K frame, blue, adj. target sights, walnut grips, serial numbers are in the 600,000 range of the .38 M&P. Mfg. 1931-40.

	$700	$575	$500	$450	$375	$330	$285

PRE-WAR K-22 MASTERPIECE - similar to K-22 Outdoorsman, but has micro click rear sight, short action, round barrel w/o rib. 1,067 mfg. in 1940 with serial range 682,420-696,952 in .38 Hand Ejector range.

	$1,800	$1,400	$1,050	$875	$750	$675	$600

POST-WAR K-22 MASTERPIECE - similar to pre-war K-22, ribbed barrel, ser. no. started with "K" prefix, pre-Model 17, mfg. 1946-1957, then continued as the Model 17.

	$485	$400	$325	$285	$250	$225	$235

100%	98%	95%	90%	80%	70%	60%	50%	40%	30%	20%	10%

.32 HAND EJECTOR FIRST MODEL (MODEL OF 1896) - .32 S&W Long cal., 6 shot fluted cylinder, 3 1/4, 4 1/4 or 6 in. barrel, blue or nickel, black rubber grips, round butt, cylinder stop is mounted in frame top-strap, patent markings are on cylinder, rather than on barrel. 19,712 mfg. 1896-1903. Serial range 1-19,712.

$850	$650	$550	$500	$465	$435	$400	$370	$340	$310	$285	$250

Add 10% for short hammer variation.

.32 HAND EJECTOR SECOND MODEL (MODEL OF 1903) - .32 S&W Long cal., 6 shot fluted cylinder, 3 1/4, 4 1/4 or 6 in. barrel, blue or nickel, black rubber grips. 19,425 mfg. 1903-04. Serial range 1-19,425.

$400	$340	$300	$275	$250	$225	$200	$175	$150	$130	$115	$100

✴ *.32 Hand Ejector (Model of 1903 - 1st Change)* - rubber grips. 31,700 mfg. 1904-06. Serial range 19,426-51,126.

$395	$340	$300	$275	$250	$225	$200	$175	$150	$130	$115	$100

✴ *.32 Hand Ejector (Model of 1903 - 2nd Change)* - rubber grips. 44,373 mfg. 1906-09. Serial range 51,127-95,500.

$395	$340	$300	$275	$250	$225	$200	$175	$150	$130	$115	$100

✴ *.32 Hand Ejector (Model of 1903 - 3rd Change)* - rubber grips. 624 mfg. 1909-10. Serial range 95,501-96,125.

$650	$500	$450	$385	$350	$320	$290	$265	$240	$220	$205	$190

✴ *.32 Hand Ejector (Model of 1903 - 4th Change)* - rubber grips. 6,374 mfg. 1910. Serial range 96,126-102,500.

$400	$340	$300	$275	$250	$225	$200	$175	$150	$130	$115	$100

✴ *.32 Hand Ejector (Model of 1903 - 5th Change)* - rubber grips.

$355	$315	$280	$250	$225	$200	$175	$150	$125	$110	$100	$90

100%	98%	95%	90%	80%	70%	60%	50%	40%	30%	20%	10%

.32 HAND EJECTOR THIRD MODEL - .32 S&W Long cal., 6 shot fluted cylinder, 3 1/4, 4 1/4, or 6 in. barrel, blue or nickel finish, grips of checkered hard rubber with "S&W" monogram, round butt. 271,531 mfg. 1917-1942. Serial range approx. 263,001-534,532.

100%	98%	95%	90%	80%	70%	60%	50%	40%	30%	20%	10%
$350	$310	$275	$250	$225	$200	$175	$150	$125	$110	$100	$90

Add 50% for pre-war mfg.

GRADING - PPGS™	100%	98%	95%	90%	80%	70%	60%

.32 HAND EJECTOR POST WWII (PRE-MODEL 30) - .32 S&W Long cal., 6 shot, 2, 3, 4, or 6 in. barrel, blue or nickel, fixed sights, walnut or rubber grips. Mfg. 1946-76.

100%	98%	95%	90%	80%	70%	60%
	$300	$275	$200	$150	$125	$100	$100

This model was designated Model 30 after 1958.

.32 REGULATION POLICE - .32 S&W cal., 6 shot, 2, 3, 4, or 6 in. barrel, square butt, walnut grips, fixed sights, blue or nickel. Mfg. 1917-57.

	100%	98%	95%	90%	80%	70%	60%
Pre-war	$450	$300	$250	$200	$150	$135	$125
Post-war	$325	$275	$225	$170	$145	$135	$115

Add 300% for Regulation Police Target (6 in. barrel only, blue).

100%	98%	95%	90%	80%	70%	60%	50%	40%	30%	20%	10%

.32-20 WCF HAND EJECTOR FIRST MODEL - .32-20 WCF cal., 6 shot fluted cylinder, 4, 5, 6, or 6 1/2 in. barrel, blue or nickel, case hardened trigger and hammer, hard rubber with "S&W" monogram or non-monogrammed walnut grips, round butt style.

100%	98%	95%	90%	80%	70%	60%	50%	40%	30%	20%	10%
$520	$475	$450	$425	$400	$375	$350	$325	$305	$290	$260	$230

.32-20 WCF HAND EJECTOR SECOND MODEL (MODEL OF 1902) - .32-20 WCF cal., 6 shot fluted cylinder, 4, 5, or 6 1/2 in. barrel, blue or nickel, grips of hard rubber with "S&W" monogram or walnut, round butt style. 4,499 mfg. 1902-05. Serial range 5,312-9,811.

100%	98%	95%	90%	80%	70%	60%	50%	40%	30%	20%	10%
$500	$450	$350	$300	$250	$200	$150	$125	$110	$95	$85	$75

✳ *.32-20 WCF Hand Ejector Second Model (Model of 1902 - 1st Change)* - grip also available in checkered walnut. 8,313 mfg. 1903-05. Serial range 9,812-18,125.

100%	98%	95%	90%	80%	70%	60%	50%	40%	30%	20%	10%
$500	$450	$340	$290	$240	$190	$140	$120	$105	$90	$80	$75

.32-20 WCF HAND EJECTOR (MODEL OF 1905) - .32-20 WCF cal., (revolvers manufactured until approx. 1916 were marked .32 Winchester, .32 WCF between 1916-1928, and late production was marked .32/20), cylinder and barrel specifications same as above, with round or square grip. 4,300 mfg. 1905-06. Serial range 18,126-22,426.

100%	98%	95%	90%	80%	70%	60%	50%	40%	30%	20%	10%
$475	$400	$350	$300	$250	$200	$150	$125	$110	$95	$85	$75

Add 75% for Target Models.

✳ *.32-20 WCF Hand Ejector (Model of 1905 - 1st Change)* - 4, 5, 6, or 6 1/2 barrel, blue or nickel, grips same as above, round or square butt. 11,073 mfg. 1906-07. Serial range 22,427 to approx. 33,500.

100%	98%	95%	90%	80%	70%	60%	50%	40%	30%	20%	10%
$465	$390	$340	$290	$240	$190	$140	$120	$105	$90	$80	$75

✳ *.32-20 WCF Hand Ejector (Model of 1905 - 2nd Change)* - caliber, cylinder, barrel and grip specifications same as above. 11,699 mfg. 1906-07. Serial range 33,501-45,200.

100%	98%	95%	90%	80%	70%	60%	50%	40%	30%	20%	10%
$465	$390	$340	$290	$240	$190	$140	$120	$105	$90	$80	$75

✳ *.32-20 WCF Hand Ejector (Model of 1905 - 3rd Change)* - caliber and cylinder same as above, 4 or 6 in. barrel, finish and grips same as above. 20,499 mfg. 1909-15. Serial range approx. 45,201-65,700.

100%	98%	95%	90%	80%	70%	60%	50%	40%	30%	20%	10%
$455	$380	$330	$280	$230	$180	$140	$120	$105	$90	$80	$75

✳ *.32-20 WCF Hand Ejector (Model of 1905 - 4th Change)* - caliber and cylinder same as above, 4, 5, or 6 in. barrel, finish and grips same as above. 78,983 mfg. 1915-40. Serial range 65,701-144,684.

100%	98%	95%	90%	80%	70%	60%	50%	40%	30%	20%	10%
$375	$325	$280	$235	$200	$175	$135	$115	$100	$85	$80	$75

100%	98%	95%	90%	80%	70%	60%	50%	40%	30%	20%	10%

.38 MILITARY & POLICE FIRST MODEL (MODEL OF 1899)

.38 S&W Special cal., early Army & Navy models were marked "S&W .38 MIL.", civilian guns and standard models are 2-line barrel marked ".38 S&W SPECIAL & U.S. SERVICE CTG'S" with the "Maltese Cross" emblem stamped both before and after the caliber, these models are also referred to as .38 Hand Ejectors, 6 shot fluted cylinder, 4, 5, or 6 1/2 in. barrel, blue or nickel finish, "S&W" monogram checkered hard rubber or checkered walnut grips with walnut grips exhibiting an impressed circle at top, left plain for civilian issue, marked with inspector's initials for military issue. 20,975 mfg. 1899-1902. Serial range 1-20,975.

> On these models, barrel markings are somewhat confusing, generally marked .38 S&W Spl. & U.S. Service cartridge, Military Issue is typically marked .38 Military. Fixed sights are referred to as Military & Police Models while target sights are referred to as .38 Hand Ejectors.

* *Standard Model* - Civilian Issue

$850	$700	$475	$425	$375	$325	$275	$240	$205	$190	$180	$170

> Add 75% for target sights.

* *U.S. Navy Model* - 1,000 revolvers in .38 S&W Spl. cal. with 6 in. barrel, blue, checkered walnut grips, delivered in 1900. Stamped on butt "U.S.N." with an anchor and inspector's initials. All in S&W serial range 5,001-6,000. U.S. Navy serial range 1-1,000.

$1,900	$1,600	$1,375	$1,200	$1,050	$925	$825	$725	$625	$525	$435	$375

* *U.S. Army Model* - 1,000 revolvers in .38 Military cal. with 6 in. barrel, blue, checkered walnut grips, inspector's initials "K.S.M." on right grip panel with "J.T.T.1901" on left grip panel. Stamped on butt "U.S. ARMY/MODEL 1899". S&W serial range 13,001-14,000.

$1,900	$1,600	$1,375	$1,200	$1,050	$925	$825	$725	$625	$525	$435	$375

.38 MILITARY & POLICE SECOND MODEL (MODEL OF 1902)

.38 S&W Special and .38 Military cal., civilian guns and standard models are barrel 2-line marked ".38 S&W SPECIAL & U.S. SERVICE CTG'S" with the "Maltese Cross" emblem stamped both before and after the caliber, 6 shot, fluted cylinder, 4, 5, 6, and 6 1/2 in. barrels, blue or nickel, "S&W" monogram checkered hard rubber or checkered walnut grips. 12,827 mfg. 1902-03. Serial range 20,976-33,803.

* *Standard Model* - civilian issue, all in .38 S&W Special cal.

$600	$470	$425	$390	$335	$320	$290	$260	$235	$210	$200	$185

> Add 75% for target sights.

* *U.S. Navy Model* - 1,000 revolvers in .38 United States Service caliber with 6 in. barrel, delivered in 1902. Stamped on butt "U.S.N." with "J.A.B.", anchor, and arrow through horizontal "S" and "No." (Naval Ser. No. designation).

$1,800	$1,575	$1,400	$1,250	$1,125	$1,000	$900	$800	$750	$700	$650	$610

.38 MILITARY & POLICE SECOND MODEL - 1ST CHANGE

.38 S&W Special cal., 6 shot fluted cylinder, 4, 5, or 6 1/2 in. barrel, blue or nickel, "S&W" monogram checkered hard rubber or checkered walnut grips, rounded butt style. 28,645 mfg. 1903-05. Serial range 33,804-62,449.

> Add 75% for target sights.

* *Standard Model Round Butt* - hard rubber grips, round butt.

$550	$450	$350	$275	$250	$210	$175	$150	$135	$125	$115	$100

* *Standard Model Square Butt* - checkered walnut grips or square butt to frame style. All will have serial numbers over the 58,000 range.

$475	$355	$335	$300	$275	$235	$200	$175	$160	$145	$130	$115

.38 MILITARY & POLICE (MODEL OF 1905)

.38 S&W Special cal., 6 shot fluted cylinder, 4, 5, or 6 1/2 in. barrel, blue or nickel finish, "S&W" monogram checkered hard rubber (round butt) or checkered walnut (square butt) grips. 10,800 mfg. 1905-06. Serial range 62,450-73,250.

$550	$450	$375	$310	$275	$240	$205	$175	$150	$125	$110	$100

> Add 50% for Target Model.

100%	98%	95%	90%	80%	70%	60%	50%	40%	30%	20%	10%

.38 MILITARY & POLICE (MODEL OF 1905 - 1ST CHANGE) - .38 S&W Special cal., 6 shot fluted cylinder, 4, 5, 6, or 6 1/2 in. barrel, blue or nickel finish, grips same as above. 73,648 mfg. (including Model 1905 2nd change), exact quantity of both models has not been determined. The first change mfg. in 1906-08. Serial range 73,251 - unknown.

| $400 | $275 | $250 | $225 | $200 | $175 | $155 | $135 | $115 | $100 | $90 | $80 |

Add 50% for Target Model.

.38 MILITARY & POLICE (MODEL OF 1905 - 2ND CHANGE) - .38 S&W Special cal., cylinder barrel lengths, finishes and grip styles same as above. 73,648 (including Model 1905 1st change) mfg. Exact quantity unknown. The second change mfg. in 1908-09. Serial range unknown-146,899.

| $400 | $275 | $250 | $225 | $200 | $175 | $155 | $135 | $115 | $100 | $90 | $80 |

Add 50% for Target Model.

.38 MILITARY & POLICE (MODEL OF 1905 - 3RD CHANGE) - .38 S&W Special cal., 6 shot fluted cylinder, 4, 5, or 6 in. barrel, finishes and grip styles as above. 94,803 mfg. 1909-15. Serial range 146,900-241,703.

| $400 | $275 | $250 | $225 | $200 | $175 | $155 | $135 | $115 | $100 | $90 | $80 |

Add 50% for Target Model.

.38 MILITARY & POLICE (MODEL OF 1905 - 4TH CHANGE) - .38 S&W Special cal., 6 shot fluted cylinder, 2, 4, 5, or 6 in. barrel, finishes and grip styles same as above. 458,296 mfg. 1915-42. Serial range 241,704-approx. 1,000,000.

| $400 | $255 | $230 | $205 | $180 | $165 | $140 | $125 | $110 | $100 | $90 | $80 |

Add 50% for Target Model.

GRADING - PPGS™		100%	98%	95%	90%	80%	70%	60%

.38 REGULATION POLICE - .38 S&W cal., 6 shot, 2, 3, 4, or 6 in. barrel, square butt, walnut grips, fixed sights, blue or nickel. Mfg. 1917-57.

	100%	98%	95%	90%	80%	70%	60%
Pre-war	$450	$300	$250	$200	$150	$135	$125
Post-war	$325	$275	$225	$170	$145	$135	$115

Add 300% for Regulation Police Target (6 in. barrel only, blue).

VICTORY MODEL - .38 Spl. (post-WWII commercial sales only), .38 S&W Spl. (U.S. government sales only), or .38 S&W (Lend-Lease arms to Allied Forces only) cal., mfg. in accordance with British/American Lend-Lease agreement of WWII, parkerized finish, most with "V" prefix, mfg. 1942-44.

	100%	98%	95%	90%	80%	70%	60%
U.S. Govt. Models	$500	$450	$400	$350	$325	$300	$275
Lend-lease mfg.	$350	$300	$250	$210	$190	$180	$170
Post-WWII Commercial sales	$325	$300	$250	$200	$190	$175	$160

Post-WWII Victorys sold commercially went through the Defense Supply Commission, and had no U.S. markings. These models will bring a premium. Be careful of fake markings.

U.S. AIR FORCE LIGHTWEIGHT (U.S. MODEL M 13) - .38 Spl. cal., aluminum cylinder and frame, "USAF" marked back strap, K frame, 6 shot. Most were destroyed by the government. Perhaps S&W's most faked revolver!

			100%	98%	95%	90%	80%	70%	60%
			$950	$850	$675	$525	$475	$425	$350

The 5 shot, J-frame, "Baby Aircrewman" will bring a premium, depending on condition, (usually $5,000 when documented as an original.)

This model was purchased in large quantities from 1951 to 1957 only. While S&W never assigned a model number to this variation, M 13 is marked on the top strap and thus misnomered as the Model 13. In 1954, a conventional steel cylinder replaced the aluminum cylinder on the civilian model only because of cracking.

This model was based on the S&W .38 Military & Police Airweight (later became the Model 12).

GRADING - PPGS™	100%	98%	95%	90%	80%	70%	60%

.357 MAGNUM FACTORY REGISTERED - .357 Mag. cal., this model could be custom ordered with any barrel length from 3 1/2 - 8 3/4 in., adj. sights, checkered walnut grips, hand fitted and registered to the buyer by a number found on the inside of the yoke, ser. no. with "REG" prefix. This practice was disc. 1939 (approx. 5,500 were mfg.) due to the tremendous demand for the .357 Mag. revolver. Mfg. 1935-39.

	100%	98%	95%	90%	80%	70%	60%
	$1,950	$1,700	$1,500	$950	$850	$700	$650

Add 40% for rare registration certificate.
Add 20% for non-standard barrel lengths.
Common barrel lengths were 3 1/2, 4, 5, 6 1/2, and 8 3/4 in.

.357 MAGNUM PRE-WAR NON-REGISTERED - similar to above, but not registered. 1,142 mfg. 1938-41.

	100%	98%	95%	90%	80%	70%	60%
	$1,500	$1,200	$850	$725	$650	$525	$470

.357 MAGNUM POST-WAR (PRE-MODEL 27) - ser. no. had "S" prefix.

	100%	98%	95%	90%	80%	70%	60%
	$650	$525	$425	$350	$325	$240	$200

100%	98%	95%	90%	80%	70%	60%	50%	40%	30%	20%	10%

.44 HAND EJECTOR FIRST MODEL (.44 HAND EJECTOR NEW CENTURY OR .44 TRIPLE LOCK) - .38-40 WCF, .44 S&W Special cal. (standard), .44-40 WCF, .44 S&W Russian, .45 LC, or .455 Mark II cal., 4, 5, 6 1/2, or 7 1/2 in. barrel, non-monogrammed checkered walnut grips and square butt on early production, gold monogram inlay on later production. 15,375 mfg. 1908-17. Serial range 1-15,375 (overlapping occurs between the 1st and 2nd models, and there is some ser. no. duplication with the .455 Mark II).

✳ *Special Caliber Model* - .38-40 WCF, .44 Russian, .44-40 WCF, .45 LC (marking, only 21 mfg.), or .455 Mark II (commercial) cal.

Due to the rarity of these calibers, prices could be 200% or more above Standard Model values.

✳ *Conversion Model* - .455 Mark II cal.

100%	98%	95%	90%	80%	70%	60%	50%	40%	30%	20%	10%
$2,000	$1,075	$975	$885	$765	$675	$600	$540	$480	$420	$365	$325

Only 808 factory conversions of .44 Special to .455 cal. were mfg. and sold to the British government.

✳ *Standard Model* - .44 S&W Special cal.

100%	98%	95%	90%	80%	70%	60%	50%	40%	30%	20%	10%
$2,750	$1,525	$1,325	$1,100	$1,000	$900	$800	$715	$630	$545	$460	$400

Add 100% for factory target sights.

✳ *British Target Model Triple Lock* - .455 cal., 6 1/2 or 7 1/2 in. barrel, with drift adj. sights (not screw operated) for shooting at Bisley, England, typically unmarked for cal., very few mfg.

100%	98%	95%	90%	80%	70%	60%	50%	40%	30%	20%	10%
$3,200	$2,950	$2,675	$2,350	$1,875	$1,650	$1,450	$1,275	$1,130	$985	$840	$695

.44 HAND EJECTOR 2ND MODEL - .44 S&W Special cal. as standard, .38-40 WCF, .44-40 WCF, or .45 LC cal., 4, 5, 6, or 6 1/2 in. barrel, blue or nickel finish, checkered walnut grips of square butt style, with or w/o "S&W" monogram inlays. 34,624 mfg. 1914-37. Ser. range 15,376-approx. 60,000.

✳ *Standard Caliber* - .44 S&W Special cal.

100%	98%	95%	90%	80%	70%	60%	50%	40%	30%	20%	10%
$1,200	$800	$575	$475	$430	$385	$365	$340	$275	$250	$225	$200

Add 50% for factory target sights.

✳ *Special Calibers* - .38-40 WCF, .44-40 WCF, or .45 LC cal.

Due to the rarity of these calibers, prices could be 200% or more above Standard Model values.

100%	98%	95%	90%	80%	70%	60%	50%	40%	30%	20%	10%

.44 HAND EJECTOR THIRD MODEL (MODEL 1926 HAND EJECTOR THIRD MODEL) - .44 S&W Special cal., very rare in .44-40 WCF or .45 LC cal., 6 shot fluted cylinder, 4, 5, or 6 1/2 in. barrel, finishes and grips same as above, same ser. range as the Second Model .44 Hand Ejectors, approx. 4,976 mfg. pre-war. Ser. range 28,358-S62,489.

* ❋ *Standard Model* - .44 S&W Special Cal.

100%	98%	95%	90%	80%	70%	60%	50%	40%	30%	20%	10%
$2,500	$1,600	$850	$675	$600	$550	$450	$425	$365	$325	$300	$250

There is also a post-war variation of this model mfg. 1946-49 in the ser. range S62,490-S74,000 (approx. 1,432 mfg. 1946-49). These transitional guns have hammer block safeties but long actions. The values are about 2/3 of the pre-war models.

* ❋ *.44 Hand Ejector 1926 Target Model* - pre-war, target sights, blue only, otherwise same as above. Mfg. 1926-41.

Values will bring a significant premium over Standard Model.

There is also a post-war variation of this model mfg. 1946-49 in the ser. range S62,490-S74,000. These transitional guns have hammer block safeties but long actions. The post-war Target Model has a barrel rib and 1950s style micrometer rear sight. The values are similar to those listed.

GRADING - PPGS™	100%	98%	95%	90%	80%	70%	60%

.44 MAGNUM PRE-MODEL 29 (5 SCREW) - .44 Mag. cal., 5 screw, can be discerned by 4 screws on right sideplate, 1 located under grip, and 1 in front of the trigger guard. Approx. 6,500 mfg. during 1956-58.

	100%	98%	95%	90%	80%	70%	60%
	$2,500	$2,150	$1,800	$1,550	$1,200	$995	$775

This model was cataloged in 4 and 6 1/2 in. barrel. The 4 in. is rare, and commands a premium. Also, a rare variation in this model is a 5 in. barrel. Only 500 were mfg. in 5 screw Pre-Model 29 variation with bright blue finish, diamond target stocks, and wood case. In NIB condition the value is $2,800 - add 25% for nickel finish.

.45 HAND EJECTOR (MODEL OF 1917) - .45 Auto Rim, or .45 ACP (in half moon clip) cal., 6 shot, 5 1/2 in. barrel, fixed sights, satin blue on military - high gloss blue on commercial, smooth walnut on military, checkered walnut on commercial models. Early military revolvers have concentric groove cut inside of hammer (approx. serial range 1-15,000).

* ❋ *Military* - 175,000 mfg., 1917-19.

			100%	98%	95%	90%	80%	70%	60%
			$900	$650	$475	$350	$300	$275	$250

Add 25% for early military mfg. with concentric groove cut inside of hammer.

* ❋ *Commercial* - mfg. 1920-41.

Due to extreme rarity, this model will bring 200% over values for the Military Model.

Add 200% for factory target sights.

* ❋ *Brazilian Contract of 1937* - Brazilian shield on right side, 25,000 originally sold to Brazil, 14,000 were imported.

			100%	98%	95%	90%	80%	70%	60%
			$350	$285	$260	$240	$250	$220	$210

Add 100% for older "non-import."

Post-war Commercial Model 1917s will bring similar values as the pre-war Commercial models.

There was also a "1917 Army" commercial mfg. May 14, 1946-July 25, 1947 (approx. 991 mfg.). Denoted by hammer block safety and ser. no. "S" prefix.

100%	98%	95%	90%	80%	70%	60%	50%	40%	30%	20%	10%

.455 HAND EJECTOR FIRST MODEL - .455 Mark II cal., ser. range 1-5,000 in its own range, English or Canadian proofed.

100%	98%	95%	90%	80%	70%	60%	50%	40%	30%	20%	10%
$1,250	$1,100	$975	$885	$765	$675	$600	$540	$480	$420	$365	$325

Add 25% for commerically sold revolvers.

Subtract 20%-40% for conversion to American caliber.

100%	98%	95%	90%	80%	70%	60%	50%	40%	30%	20%	10%

.455 HAND EJECTOR SECOND MODEL - ser. range 5,001-74,755, generally British or Canadian proofed.

$850	$500	$420	$360	$325	$285	$260	$250	$240	$230	$220	$200

Add 25% for commerically sold revolvers.

Subtract 20%-40% for conversion to American caliber.

GRADING - PPGS™	100%	98%	95%	90%	80%	70%	60%

NUMBERED MODEL REVOLVERS (MODERN HAND EJECTORS)

Smith & Wesson handguns manufactured after 1958 are stamped with a model number on the frame under the cylinder yoke. The number is visible when the cylinder is open. All revolvers manufactured by S&W from 1946-58 were produced without model numbers.

To determine which variation a particular revolver is in the following section, simply swing the cylinder out to the loading position and notice the model number inside the yoke. The designation Mod. and a two- or three-digit number followed by a dash and another number designates which engineering change was underway when the gun was manufactured. Hence, a Mod. 48-3 is a Model 48 in its 3rd engineering change (and should be indicated when ordering parts). Usually, earlier variations are the most desirable to collectors unless a particular improvement is rare. The same rule applies to semi-auto pistols, and the model designation is usually marked on the outside of the gun.

Beginning 1994, S&W started providing synthetic grips and drilled/tapped receiver for scope mounting on certain models.

S&W revolvers are generally categorized by frame size. Frame sizes are as follows: J-frame (small), K-frame (medium), L-frame (medium), N-frame (large), and X-frame (extra large).

All currently manufactured S&W revolvers chambered for .38 S&W Spl. cal. will also accept +P rated ammunition.

Add 10%-15% for those models listed that are pinned and recessed (pre-1981 mfg.).

MODEL 10 M & P - .38 Spl. +P cal., 6 shot, K-frame, round or square butt (4 in. barrel only starting 1992), fixed sights, 2 (disc. 1996), 3 (disc.), 4 (standard – disc. or heavy), 5 (disc.), or 6 (disc.) in. barrels, current mfg. utilizes Uncle Mike's combat grips, 36 oz.

MSR $544		$400	$275	$210	$160	$130	$115	$100

Add $12 for nickel finish (disc. 1991, 4 in. barrel only).

The Model 10 is currently available in 4 in. heavy barrel only (a 4 in. heavy barrel nickel square butt variation was disc. in 1992).

To date, there have been 14 engineering changes in this model.

MODEL 11 38/200 M & P - .38 S&W cal. only, similar to Model 10, limited production.

	$500	$425	$325	$250	$200	$150	$100

There were 4 engineering changes in this model.

MODEL 12 M & P AIRWEIGHT - similar to Model 10, only alloy frame, 2 or 4 in. barrel. Disc. 1986.

	$350	$275	$210	$200	$185	$175	$150

Last MSR was $320.

Add $40 for nickel finish (disc.).

There were 4 engineering changes in this model.

MODEL 13 M & P - .357 Mag. cal., 6 shot, fixed sights, 3 (round butt, disc. 1996) or 4 (square butt) in. heavy barrel. Disc. 1998.

	$310	$260	$200	$185	$175	$165	$160

Last MSR was $411.

Add $20 for nickel finish (disc. 1986).

There were 5 engineering changes in this model.

GRADING - PPGS™	100%	98%	95%	90%	80%	70%	60%

✳ *Model 13 - N.Y. State Police* - .357 Mag. cal., 4 in. barrel, blue, fixed sights, 1,200 were mfg. for the N.Y. State Police and are marked 10-6. All 1,200 were recalled by S&W and exchanged for Model 28s.

	$375	$300	$250	$200	$175	$150	$140

MODEL 14 (K-38 TARGET MASTERPIECE) - .38 Spl. cal., 6 or 8 3/8 (new 1959) in. barrel, target model, blue only. Mfg. 1947-1981.

	$300	$250	$215	$200	$185	$175	$160

Add $20 for 6 in. barrel single action (mfg. 1961-1981).
There were 4 engineering changes on this model.

MODEL 14 K-38 FULL-LUG - .38 Spl. cal., 6 in. full lug barrel, adj. rear sight, combat style Morado wood square butt grips, blue finish, 47 oz. Mfg. 1991-1999.

	$350	$310	$260	$225	$200	$185	$165

Last MSR was $498.

There were 3 engineering changes on this model.

MODEL 15 (K-38 COMBAT MASTERPIECE) - .38 Spl. cal., adj. sights, 6 shot, square butt, 2 (disc.), 4, 6 (mfg. 1986-91), or 8 3/8 (new 1986, disc.) in. barrel. Disc. 1999.

	$340	$260	$215	$190	$180	$160	$150

Last MSR was $450.

Add $31 for TT or TH (disc. 1991).
Add $11 for 8 3/8 in. barrel (disc.).
Add $20 for nickel finish (disc. 1987).
Add 300% for USAF marked (mfg. 1965).
There were 9 engineering changes on this model.

MODEL 16 (K-32 MASTERPIECE) - .32 S&W Long cal., 6 in. barrel, adj. sights, checkered walnut, blue. Only 3,630 mfg., 1947-74.

	$1,350	$1,150	$995	$875	$750	$625	$525

There were 3 engineering changes to this model.

✳ *Pre-War K-32 Target*

	N/A	$3,700	$2,000	$1,650	$1,450	$1,250	$995

✳ *Pre-War K-32* - only 104 mfg. pre-war, scarce.

	$2,250	$1,950	$1,700	$1,475	$1,250	$1,050	$875

✳ *Post-War K-32 Target (Pre-Model 16)*

	$1,300	$1,000	$850	$725	$650	$575	$500

✳ *K-32 M&P* - K frame, fixed sights.

	$1,600	$1,200	$900	$850	$750	$650	$550

MODEL 16-4 (FULL LUG) - .32 cal./.32 Mag. cal., 6 shot, 4 (mfg. 1990-91 only), 6, or 8 3/8 (disc. 1991) in. barrel, square butt, blue finish only, TH and TT. Mfg. 1990-92.

	$335	$280	$225	$210	$200	$190	$180

Last MSR was $419.

Add 5%-10% for 8 3/8 in. barrel.

MODEL 17 (K-22 MASTERPIECE) - .22 LR cal., blue only, 6 shot, 4 (mfg. 1986-93), 6 (current mfg.), or 8 3/8 (disc. 1992) in. barrel. Disc. 1993, reintroduced 1996, disc. 1998.

	$400	$300	$260	$235	$210	$200	$185

Last MSR was $508.

Add $39 for full lug 6 in. long barrel (w/ TT & TH, disc.).
Add $50 for full lug 8 3/8 in. long barrel (w/ TT & TH, disc. 1992).
There were 5 engineering changes in this model.

GRADING - PPGS™	100%	98%	95%	90%	80%	70%	60%

MODEL 17 FULL LUG - .22 LR cal., 6 (mfg. 1990-95) or 10 (mfg. 1996-99) shot, 4, 6, or 8 3/8 full lug barrel, steel (6 shot) or alloy (10 shot) cylinder.

	$475	$425	$360	$325	$265	$235	$180

There were 3 engineering changes in this model.

MODEL 17-2 PROTOTYPE MERCOX DART PROJECTILE GUN - .530 Dart Projectile, .22 Ramset blank gas generator, 12 in. barrel, blue finish only, 25 prototype units mfg. 1966 only.

	$3,950	$3,250	$2,750

Add $500 for handmade Safariland holster.

Add $100-$500 depending on variation of projectile (six known).

MODEL 18 .22 COMBAT MASTERPIECE - .22 LR cal., combat style adj. sights, 4 in. barrel, blue only. Disc. 1985.

	$350	$350	$250	$200	$180	$175	$165

Last MSR was $352.

Add $30 for TT and TH.

There were 4 engineering changes to this model.

MODEL 19 .357 COMBAT MAGNUM - .357 Mag. cal., K frame, adj. sights, 2 1/2 (round butt, disc. 1998), 4 (square butt), or 6 (square butt, disc. 1996) in. barrel, bright blue or nickel (disc. 1992) finish, drilled/tapped receiver and synthetic grips became standard 1994. Disc. 1999.

	$345	$265	$210	$190	$180	$170	$160

Last MSR was $457.

Add $9 for 4 in. or $14 for 6 in. (disc. 1996) barrel.

Add $35 for white outline rear sight (disc. 1994).

Add $20 for nickel finish - disc. 1991.

Add $60 for TS, TT, TH, RR, and WO - disc. 1991 (6 in. barrel only).

This model was supplied with a round butt on 2 1/2 in. barrel. The 2 1/2 and 6 in. barrels (blue finish) were disc. in 1991 along with the 4 and 6 in. nickel variations.

There were 8 engineering changes to this model.

MODEL 20 HEAVY DUTY - .38 Spl. cal., 6 shot, 4, 5, or 6 1/2 in. barrel lengths, N frame, fixed sights, walnut grips, blue or nickel, walnut grips. Mfg. 1930-1941 and re-introduced 1946 (with "S" prefix starting at serial 62,930), became the Model 20 in 1957.

	100%	98%	95%	90%	80%	70%	60%
Pre-war	$850	$650	$450	$415	$385	$340	$300
Post-war (pre-Model 20)	$775	$585	$375	$350	$300	$250	$200

Add 40% for 6 1/2 in. barrel.

Early post-war models had pre-war long action (ser. range S62,489-approx. S74,000).

There were two engineering changes in this model.

MODEL 21 (.44 HAND EJECTOR FOURTH MODEL - MODEL OF 1950 MILITARY) - .44 S&W cal., 6 shot, 4, 5, or 6 1/2 in. barrel, large frame, blue, walnut grips, fixed sights, 1,200 mfg. scattered throughout serial range S75,000-S263,000. Mfg. 1950-1966.

	$2,500	$2,000	$1,200	$950	$750	$600	$500

Add 50% for 6 1/2 in. (rare).

There were 3 engineering changes for this model.

MODEL 21-4 "THUNDER RANCH" - .44 Spl., 4 in. barrel, 24Kt. gold plated Thunder Ranch insignia. New 2004.

MSR $958		$750	$675	$600	$525	$450	$375	$300

MODEL 22 (.45 HAND EJECTOR MODEL OF 1950 MILITARY) - .45 Auto Rim or .45 ACP cal., same specifications as 1917 Army, except redesigned hammer block, short action, fixed sights. Approx. 1,200 mfg. 1950-1966.

	$1,500	$1,100	$900	$800	$700	$600	$500

There were 2 engineering changes for this model.

GRADING - PPGS™	100%	98%	95%	90%	80%	70%	60%

MODEL 23 (.38-44 OUTDOORSMAN) - .38 Spl. cal., similar to Model 20 in .38 Spl., except with adj. sights, blue only, featured ribbed 6 1/2 in. barrel standard. Mfg. 1930-67.

	100%	98%	95%	90%	80%	70%	60%
Pre-war	$800	$650	$550	$450	$375	$300	$280
Post-war pre-Model 23	$700	$500	$400	$375	$300	$250	$200
Numbered Models	$1,000	$700	$475	$375	$300	$280	$270

Early post-war models had long action with barrel rib and micrometer sights (ser. range S62,489-approx. S74,000). There were 4,761 pre-war revolvers, 2,036 post-war transitional, and 6,039 styled after the 1950 model.

The "44" in this model's name refers to the size frame, not the caliber. This variation became designated the Model 23 after 1958.

There were 2 engineering changes for this model.

MODEL 24 (.44 HAND EJECTOR FOURTH MODEL - 1950 TARGET) - .44 Spl., redesigned hammer, short action, 6 1/2 in. ribbed barrel standard, satin blue or bright blue, micrometer sights, serialization begins at approx. S75,000. 5,050 mfg. 1950-67.

$2,000	$1,200	$695	$575	$500	$400	$375

Add 20% for bright blue.

Add 40% for 4 in. barrel.

Add 50% for 5 in. barrel.

There were 2 engineering changes for this model.

MODEL 24-3 - .44 Spl., reintroduction, 4 or 6 1/2 in. barrel, bright blue only, checkered Goncalo Alves target grips (without speedloader cutout), barrel and frame not pinned, 7,500 mfg. 1983 only.

✳ *4 in. barrel.* - 2,625 mfg.

$450	$425	$400	$375	$325	$275	$225

✳ *6 1/2 in. barrel.* - 4,875 mfg.

$400	$375	$350	$325	$275	$225	$175

Last MSR was $359.

This model's serialization is triple alpha - 4 numeric (i.e. ABC0123).

✳ *Model 24 Lew Horton Special* - .44 Spl., 3 in. barrel, round butt, adj. sights, blue finish, includes special fitted holster.

$380	$325	$250

Subtract 10% without holster.

MODEL 25/25-2 (1955 TARGET MODEL) - .45 ACP, .45 Auto Rim or .45 LC (earlier mfg.) cal., N frame, blue finish only, target grips, 6 (later mfg.) or 6 1/2 (earlier mfg.) in. barrel. Disc. approx. 1985.

$450	$400	$350	$300	$235	$200	$190

Last MSR was $347.

Add $150 for 6 1/2 in. barrel (early mfg. with pinned barrel).

Add 300% for .45 LC cal.

After 1957, the Model 25 in .45 ACP cal was designated Model 25-2, with trigger guard screw eliminated.

There were 13 engineering changes to this model.

✳ *Model 25 Lew Horton Special* - .45 ACP cal., 3 in. barrel, adj. sights, blue finish, only 100 mfg.

$500	$450	$375

MODEL 25-5 - .45 LC cal., 4, 6, or 8 3/8 in. barrel, blue or nickel finish (no extra charge - disc. 1987). Disc. 1991.

$375	$315	$250	$215	$200	$190	$180

Last MSR was $429.

Add 5%-10% for 8 3/8 in. barrel.

GRADING - PPGS™	100%	98%	95%	90%	80%	70%	60%

MODEL 26 (.45 HAND EJECTOR MODEL OF 1950 TARGET) - .45 ACP, or .45
LC cal., adj. sights, thin ribbed barrel, 2,768 mfg. 1950-1960.

	$2,000	$1,200	$650	$550	$440	$350	$300

✳ *Model 26-1 Georgia Highway Patrol Commemorative* - .45 Colt cal., blue finish, 5 in. barrel, marked "1937 Georgia State Patrol 1987", mfg. 1988.

	$550	$500	$450				

MODEL 27 - .357 Mag. cal., N-frame, 3 1/2 (disc. 1977), 4 (disc. 1991), 5 (disc. 1977),
6, 6 1/2, or 8 3/ 8 (disc. 1991) in. barrel, blue or nickel (disc. 1987) finish. Disc. 1994.

	$400	$375	$300	$220	$205	$190	$180

Last MSR was $486.

> **Add 10% for pinned barrel and recessed cylinder.**
> **Add $28 for white outline rear sight - (disc. 1991).**
> **Add $8 for 8 3/8 in. barrel - (disc. 1991).**
> There were 7 engineering changes to this model.
> ✳ *3 1/2 and 5 in. barrel* - disc.

	$425	$365	$275	$265	$240	$230	$180

MODEL 28 HIGHWAY PATROLMAN - .357 Mag. cal., "Highway Patrol" utility
model, dull or brushed nickel (very rare) finish, adj. sights, standard grips, blue only, 4 or 6 in. barrel, mfg. 1954-86.

	$325	$260	$210	$200	$190	$180	$150

Last MSR was $306.

> **Add $20 for TS.**
> **Add 30% for 5 screw variation (pre-Model 28).**
> **Add 300% for brushed nickel finish (beware of fakes).**
> There were 3 engineering changes to this model.

MODEL 29 .44 MAGNUM (4 SCREW) - .44 Mag. cal., 4 screw, can be discerned by
2 exposed screws on lower right sideplate (one is concealed by the right grip, and one in front of the trigger guard). Mfg. began 1957 after approx. ser. no. S175,000 and was disc. 1961.

	$995	$875	$775	$675	$575	$475	$375

MODEL 29/29-2 (3 SCREW) - .44 Mag. cal., 4, 6 1/2, or 8 3/8 in. barrel, eliminated
top screw on sideplate and 1 screw in front of trigger guard. Disc. 1999.

	$495	$440	$395	$360	$325	$295	$275

Last MSR was $574.

> **Add $12 for 8 3/8 in. barrel.**
> **Add $11 for nickel finish (disc. 1991).**
> **Add 10%-15% for pinned barrel and recessed cylinder, depending on condition.**
> **Add $45 for combat grips with scope mount - disc. 1991 (8 3/8 in. barrel only).**
> **Subtract $40 if without case.**
> Older .44 Magnum Pre-Model 29 mfg. (5 screw variations) will appear under the previous subheading: "EARLY HAND EJECTORS (NAMED MODELS)."
> The "S" serial number prefix was used on this model until 1968, at which time the law required a new numbering system, and the serial number prefix was changed to "N". The "S" prefix originally designated the additional hammer block safety.
> There were 9 engineering changes to this model.

MODEL 29 CLASSIC - .44 Mag. cal., 5, 6 1/2, or 8 3/8 in. full lug barrel, blue only,
round butt with Hogue conversion square butt grips, interchangeable front sights with white outline rear sight, frame is drilled and tapped to accept scope mounts, blue finish only. Mfg. 1990-94.

	$475	$400	$380	$340	$325	$300	$285

Last MSR was $591.

> **Add $8 for 8 3/8 in. barrel.**

GRADING - PPGS™	100%	98%	95%	90%	80%	70%	60%

✳ *Model 29 Classic DX* - similar to Model 29 Classic, except supplied with 2 sets of grips, 6 1/2 or 8 3/8 in. barrel, 5 interchangeable front sights, numbered test target, 51-54 oz. Mfg. 1991-92.

	$550	$500	$450	$400	$375	$300	$250

Add $8 for 8 3/8 in. barrel.

MODEL 29 SILHOUETTE - .44 Mag. cal., 10 5/8 in. barrel, adj. front and rear sights, bright blue only, Goncalo Alves target stocks. Mfg. 1983-91.

	$550	$475	$395	$335	$290	$260	$240

Last MSR was $536.

MODEL 29 MAGNACLASSIC - .44 Mag. cal., 7 1/2 in. full lug, ported barrel, high polish bright bluing, round butt, interchangeable front sight, supplied with cherry wood display case mfg. in England, 3,000 mfg. in 1990 only.

	$850	$725	$600	$500	$450	$395	$360

Last MSR was $999.

MODEL 30 - .32 S&W cal., improved I frame and J frame, 6 shot, 2, 3, 4, or 6 in. barrel, square butt, walnut grips, fixed sights, blue or nickel finish. Mfg. 1948-1976.

	$300	$260	$220	$190	$175	$165	$150

There was one engineering change to this model.

MODEL 31 - .32 S&W Long cal., improved I frame and J frame, fixed sights, 2, 3 or 4 (disc.) in. barrel, blue only. Disc. 1991.

	$290	$235	$195	$185	$175	$165	$150

Last MSR was $365.

Add 25% for early flatlatch models.
There were 3 engineering changes to this model.

MODEL 32 (.38 TERRIER) - .38 S&W cal., 5 shot, 2 in. barrel, walnut or rubber grips, blue or nickel, fixed sights, built on .32 frame. Mfg. 1948-1974.

	$365	$275	$175	$150	$135	$125	$115

✳ *Model 032* - .32 Mag. cal., 6 shot, alloy J frame, blue, scarce, mfg. 1992 only.

	$525	$450	$325	$250	$200	$150	$75

MODEL 33 (.38 REGULATION POLICE) - .38 S&W cal., 5 shot, 2, 3, 4 in. barrel, square butt, walnut grips, fixed sights, blue or nickel finish, improved I frame and J frame. Mfg. 1949-1974.

	$325	$275	$225	$170	$145	$135	$125

MODEL 34 - .22 LR cal., adj. sights in J frame, improved I frame and J frame, 6 shot, 2 or 4 in. barrel, round or square butt, blue or nickel (disc. 1986) finish. Disc. 1991. This model was reissued for 2-3 years.

	$325	$285	$225	$185	$175	$165	$150

Last MSR was $366.

Add $25 for nickel finish.
Add 25% for early flatlatch models.
There were 2 engineering changes to this model.

MODEL 35 (.22/32 TARGET MODEL OF 1953) - similar to Standard .22/.32 Hand Ejector Model, except micrometer rear sight, 6 in. barrel, improved I and J frame, target grips. Mfg. 1953-74.

	$500	$350	$265	$230	$200	$180	$160

GRADING - PPGS™	100%	98%	95%	90%	80%	70%	60%

MODEL 36 (.38 CHIEFS SPECIAL) - .38 Spl. cal., 5 shot, J frame, round or square (disc. 1991) butt, 1 7/8 in. regular or 3 in. (heavy only, disc. 1994) barrel, blue or nickel (disc. 1992) finish. Disc. 1999.

| | $325 | $290 | $225 | $200 | $185 | $180 | $175 |

Last MSR was $406.

Add $12 for nickel finish (disc., round butt - 2 in. barrel only).

Add 25% for early small trigger guard and grips (below ser. no. 2,500).

Note: 1st models with high polish blue and diamond grips will bring premiums when mint in original box.

There were 10 engineering changes to this model.

MODEL 36 TARGET - similar to Model 50, 2 in. barrel, square butt, usually marked 36-1 with target sights, mfg. started 1955.

| | $850 | $725 | $650 | $575 | $500 | $400 | $350 |

MODEL 36 LADYSMITH (36LS) - .38 Spl. +P cal., 5 shot, J-frame, 1 7/8 in. standard or 3 (disc. 1991) in. standard or heavy barrel, blue finish only, Combat Dymondwood grips are anatomically designed for women (round butt on 1 7/8 in., wood combat grips on 3 in.), fixed sights, redesigned double action, 20-23 oz., Morocco grained (disc. 1991) or soft side jewelry case. New 1990.

| MSR $568 | $420 | $325 | $270 | $215 | $185 | $180 | $175 |

MODEL 37 CHIEFS SPECIAL AIRWEIGHT - similar to Model 36 Chiefs Special, except alloy frame and 1 7/8 in. barrel only, J-frame, blue or nickel (disc. 1995) finish, barrels are marked "Airweight", no internal lock.

| MSR $573 | $360 | $310 | $240 | $200 | $185 | $180 | $175 |

Add $16 for nickel finish (disc.).

There were 3 engineering changes to this model.

MODEL 38 BODYGUARD AIRWEIGHT - .38 S&W Spl. cal., 5 shot, alloy frame, round butt, shrouded hammer, 2 in. barrel, blue or nickel (disc. 1996) finish. Disc. 1998.

| | $350 | $300 | $250 | $200 | $185 | $180 | $175 |

Last MSR was $462.

Add $15 for nickel finish (disc. 1996).

There were 3 engineering changes for this model.

MODEL 40 CENTENNIAL - .38 S&W Spl. cal., 2 in. barrel, double action only, fully concealed hammer, grip safety, smooth walnut grips, blue or nickel. Mfg. 1953-74.

| | $425 | $395 | $325 | $290 | $250 | $240 | $220 |

This model commands a premium for the first series with no letter prefix. After 1968, "L" prefix series began.

MODEL 42 CENTENNIAL AIRWEIGHT - .38 S&W Spl. cal., aluminum variation of Model 40 Centennial, mfg. began 1953. Disc. 1974.

| Blue | $475 | $425 | $395 | $325 | $300 | $265 | $240 |
| Nickel | $1,100 | $950 | $875 | $775 | $675 | $550 | $475 |

✸ *Model 042* - .38 Spl. cal., 5 shot, blue finish, alloy frame. Mfg. 1992 only.

| | $450 | $350 | $300 | $275 | $225 | $175 | $100 |

MODEL 43 (.22/32 KIT GUN AIRWEIGHT) - .22 LR cal., 3 1/2 in. barrel, round or square butt, adj. sights, aluminum frame and cylinder, mfg. 1955-74.

| | $350 | $300 | $265 | $240 | $185 | $165 | $150 |

MODEL 45 (.22 MILITARY & POLICE) - .22 LR cal. only, originally mfg. as training gun, not cataloged. Mfg. 1948-1978.

| | $850 | $775 | $675 | $550 | $450 | $375 | $300 |

There were 3 engineering changes to this model.

GRADING - PPGS™	100%	98%	95%	90%	80%	70%	60%

MODEL 48 (K-22 MRF MASTERPIECE) - .22 Mag cal., 4, 6 or 8 3/8 in. barrel, blue only. Disc. 1986.

	$350	$300	$250	$220	$210	$200	$180

Last MSR was $320.

> Add $15 for 8 3/8 in. barrel.
> Add $15 for TT, TH, and TS (disc.).
> There were 4 engineering changes to this model.

MODEL 49 BODYGUARD - similar to Model 38, only steel frame, 2 in. barrel, blue or nickel (disc.) finish. Disc. 1996.

	$325	$275	$225	$210	$200	$175	$150

Last MSR was $409.

> Add $25 for nickel finish (disc.).
> There were 3 engineering changes to this model.

MODEL 50 (.38 CHIEFS SPECIAL TARGET) - .38 S&W Spl. cal., Chiefs Special Target, mfg. from 1955 in 2 in. (see Model 36 Target listing) or 3 (211 mfg. beginning 1973) in. barrels, target sights, most were unmarked for model number, approx. 1,100 mfg. The other variation was designated Model 36 Target.

	$600	$450	$400	$350	$300	$250	$225

> The Model 50 designation was not used until 1970.

MODEL 51 - .22 Mag. cal. only, variant of the .22/32 kit gun, 3 1/2 in. barrel, 6 shot, adj. rear sight, blue or nickel, walnut stocks. Disc. 1974.

	$400	$350	$300	$275	$250	$225	$200

MODEL 53 .22 REM. JET - .22 Jet cal. with S, L, or LR inserts, 6 shot, 4, 6, or 8 3/8 in. barrel, blue, walnut grips, adj. sights. Mfg. 1960-74.

	100%	98%	95%	90%	80%	70%	60%
4 screw	$735	$650	$550	$470	$385	$360	$330
3 screw	$600	$550	$500	$425	$375	$350	$300

> Add 10% for 8 3/8 in. barrel.
> Add $200 for extra matching .22 LR cylinder.
> There was one engineering change to this model.

MODEL 56 "USAF" - .38 Spl. cal., 2 in. barrel marked "U.S." on backstrap. 15,205 mfg. 1963 only.

	$7,500	$5,750	$5,000	$4,500	$3,500	$2,900	$2,200

MODEL 57 - .41 Mag. cal., N Target frame, 6 shot, 4 (disc. 1991), 6 or 8 3/8 (disc. 1991) in. barrel, blue or nickel finish, micrometer rear sight, special oversize Goncalo Alves grips, shrouded extractor rod, "S" ser. no. prefix 1964-68, changed to "N" prefix during 1969, 44-52 oz. Mfg. 1963-1993.

	$475	$415	$340	$300	$265	$240	$220

Last MSR was $466.

> Add 10-20% for "S" prefix serialization.
> Add 10% for nickel finish if NIB.
> Add $20 for 8 3/8 in. barrel.
> Add 10% for pinned barrel and recessed cylinder.
> There were 4 engineering changes to this model.

MODEL 58 - .41 Mag cal., M&P, fixed sights, 4 in. barrel, blue or nickel finish. Mfg. 1964-1977.

	$400	$350	$300	$275	$250	$225	$200

> Add $25 for nickel finish or "S" serial number prefix.

GRADING - PPGS™	100%	98%	95%	90%	80%	70%	60%

MODEL 60 .38 SPL. CHIEFS SPECIAL - .38 S&W Spl., stainless version of Chiefs Special, 2 or 3 in. full lug barrel. Disc. 1996.

         $350 $295 $250

Last MSR was $458.

> **Subtract $25 for 2 in. barrel.**
>
> **Add 30% for early Model 60s without letter prefix and bright satin finish.**
>
> The full lug barrel option began in 1990 with limited mfg. It had been tested for +P ammo and features an adj. rear sight - 24 1/2 oz.
>
> There were 16 engineering changes to the base model in two calibers.

MODEL 60 .357 MAG. CHIEFS SPECIAL - .357 Mag. cal., 2 1/8, 3 (new 1997), or 5 (new 2005) in. barrel, round butt, stainless steel, J-frame, Uncle Mike's Combat or wood (5 in. barrel only) grips, 22.5-24 oz. New 1996.

   MSR $594 $435 $320 $270

> Add $36 for 3 in. full lug barrel with adj. sight (new 1997) or $77 for 5 in. barrel (new 2005).

MODEL 60LS (LADYSMITH) - .38 S&W Spl. +P or .357 Mag. (disc.) cal., 5 shot, 2 in. regular (disc. 1996), 2 1/8 (new 1997), or 3 in. heavy (disc. 1991) barrel, J-frame, frosted stainless steel finish, Combat Dymondwood grips are anatomically designed for women (round butt on 2 in., wood combat grips on 3 in.), fixed sights, redesigned double action, 20-23 oz, Morocco grained (disc. 1991) or soft side jewelry case. New 1990.

   MSR $621 $400 $325 $255

MODEL 63 .22/32 KIT GUN - .22 LR cal., J frame, stainless kit gun, 2 or 4 in. barrel, 19 oz. Disc. 1998.

         $365 $300 $225

Last MSR was $476.

> **Add $5 for 4 in. barrel.**
>
> There were three engineering changes to this model.

MODEL 64 M & P - .38 Spl. +P cal., satin stainless Model 10, 6 shot, 2, 3, or 4 in. barrel, K-frame, 3 (square butt disc. 1992) and 4 in. (square butt only) barrels are heavy, current production uses Uncle Mike's combat grips, 30.5-36 oz.

   MSR $583 $365 $285 $215

There have been 7 engineering changes to this model.

MODEL 65 - .357 Mag. cal., stainless version of Model 13, K-frame, has 3 (round butt, disc. 2000) or 4 (square butt) in. heavy barrels, satin stainless steel, current production uses Uncle Mike's grips, fixed sights, 35 oz. Disc. 2004.

         $360 $275 $210

Last MSR was $563.

There have been 7 engineering changes to this model.

MODEL 65 LADYSMITH - .357 Mag. cal., K-frame, 3 in. barrel with round butt, glass beaded stainless finish, soft side jewelry case, smooth Dymondwood combat grips, 32 oz. Mfg. 1992-2004.

         $390 $320 $230

Last MSR was $618.

MODEL 66 COMBAT MAGNUM - .357 Mag. cal., K-frame, satin stainless version of Model 19, has 2 1/2, 3 (disc., only 2,500 mfg.), 4, or 6 (disc.) in. barrel, current production uses Uncle Mike's Combat grips, 32-39 oz. Disc. 2004.

         $390 $320 $230

Last MSR was $614.

> **Add $11 for 2.5 in. barrel.**
>
> **Add $29 for 6 in. barrel (disc.).**
>
> **Add $48 for TH and TT with 4 (disc. 1991) or 6 in. barrel only (disc. 1999).**

GRADING - PPGS™	100%	98%	95%	90%	80%	70%	60%

Note: Several models of the Model 66 were made - such features as an all-stainless steel rear sight and a recessed cylinder will bring a slight premium if NIB. There have been 6 engineering changes to this model.

✳ *Model 66 Combat Magnum Special Edition* - .357 Mag. cal., 3.25 in. barrel, satin stainless steel, black rubber finger groove grips, adj. V-notch rear sight, Hi-Viz front sight, 6 shot, target trigger. Mfg. 2003-2004.

	$415	$350	$265

Last MSR was $641.

This model was available exclusively through Davidson's.

MODEL 67 COMBAT MASTERPIECE - .38 S&W Spl.+P cal., K-frame, stainless version of Model 15, has 4 in. barrel, current production uses Uncle Mike's Combat grips, 36 oz. Disc. 1988, reintroduced 1991.

MSR $642	$410	$330	$230

1991 mfg. included square butt and red ramp front sight insert.
There have been 5 engineering changes to this model.

MODEL 68 - .38 S&W Spl. cal., similar in appearance to the Model 66, except is in .38 Spl. cal., 6 in. barrel, approx. 7,500 mfg.

	$750	$625	$495

Add 10% for CHP markings.
This model was originally ordered by CA Highway Patrol (usually has "OHB" overstamp).

MODEL 73 - .38 Spl. cal., C frame.

Most copies of this model were destroyed by S&W in 1973. Few examples have survived. The last known traded price was $10,000!

MODEL 242 AIRLITE Ti CENTENNIAL - .38 Spl.+P cal., L-frame, 7 shot, similar to Model 296. Mfg. 1990 only.

	$500	$395	$300

MODEL 296 AIRLITE Ti CENTENNIAL - .44 S&W Spl. cal., L-frame, 5 shot, 2 1/2 barrel, similar to Model 242 in construction materials, alloy frame and titanium cylinder, Uncle Mike's Boot grips, 18.9 oz. Mfg. 1999-2002.

	$620	$490	$355

Last MSR was $754.

MODEL 317 AIRLITE/KIT GUN - .22 LR cal., J-frame, 8 shot, 1 7/8 or 3 (new 1998, Hi-Viz sights became standard in 2001, Model 317 Kit Gun) in. barrel, combination of aluminum alloy and stainless steel construction, brushed aluminum finish, round butt, choice of synthetic or Dymondwood Boot (disc. 1998) grips, fixed sights, 10.5 oz. New 1997.

MSR $603	$455	$325	$230

Add $55 for 3 in. barrel.
Add $33 for Dymondwood Boot grips (disc.).
There have been three engineering changes to this model.

✳ *Model 317 Airlite LadySmith* - .22 LR cal., 1 7/8 in. barrel only, includes Dymondwood Boot grips, 9.9 oz. Mfg. 1998-2002.

	$445	$320	$220

Last MSR was $596.

MODEL 325 PD-AIRLITE Sc - .45 ACP cal., 2.5 in. barrel, otherwise similar to Model 329 PD. New 2004.

MSR $939	$725	$585	$460	$380	$325	$300	$275

MODEL 329 PD-AIRLITE Sc - .44 Mag. cal., 4 in barrel, N-frame, 6 shot, Scandium frame with matte black metal finish, wood Ahrends grips with finger grooves, and Hogue rubber mongrip, Hi-Viz front sight, approx. 26 oz. New 2003.

MSR $960	$740	$600	$475	$395	$335	$300	$275

GRADING - PPGS™	100%	98%	95%	90%	80%	70%	60%

MODEL 331 AIRLITE Ti CHIEFS SPECIAL - .32 H&R Mag. cal., J-frame, 6 shot, 1 7/8 in. barrel with stainless steel liner, features titanium cylinder and aluminum alloy frame, barrel shroud, and yoke, fixed sights, Uncle Mike's or Dymondwood Boot (disc.) wood grips, two-tone matte stainless/grey finish approx. 12 oz. Mfg. 1999-2003.

	$565	$435	$370	$335	$300	$275	$250

Last MSR was $716.

Add $24 for Dymondwood Boot grips (mfg. 1999 only).

MODEL 332 AIRLITE Ti CENTENNIAL - .32 H&R Mag. cal., J-frame, similar Model 331 Airlite Ti, except is hammerless and double action only, current production uses Uncle Mike's Boot grips, 12 oz. Mfg. 1999-2003.

	$575	$455	$390	$345	$310	$280	$250

Last MSR was $734.

Add $24 for Dymondwood Boot grips (mfg. 1999 only).

MODEL 337 AIRLITE Ti CHIEFS SPECIAL - .38 S&W Spl.+P cal., J-frame, 5 shot, 1 7/8 in. barrel, similar design as the Model 331, 11.9 oz. Mfg. 1999-2003.

	$565	$435	$375	$335	$310	$280	$250

Last MSR was $716.

Add $24 for Dymondwood Boot grips (mfg. 1999 only).

MODEL 337 AIRLITE Ti KIT GUN - .38 S&W Spl.+P cal., J-frame, 5 shot, 3 1/8 in. barrel with Hi-Viz front sight (new 2001), choice of Dymondwood or Uncle Mike's combat grips, approx. 13 oz. Mfg. 2000-2003.

	$600	$460	$385	$345	$315	$285	$250

Last MSR was $779.

MODEL 337 PD AIRLITE Ti CHIEFS SPECIAL - .38 S&W Spl.+P cal., J-frame, 5 shot, 1 7/8 in. barrel, black/grey finish, black Hogue Bantam grips, 10.7 oz. Mfg. 2000-2003.

	$580	$450	$385	$340	$310	$280	$250

Last MSR was $740.

MODEL 340 AIRLITE Sc CENTENNIAL - .357 Mag. cal., J-frame, 5 shot, 1 7/8 in. barrel only, Scandium alloy frame, barrel shroud, and yoke, titanium cylinder, two-tone matte stainless/grey finish, hammerless, Hogue Bantam grips, 12 oz. New 2001.

MSR $838	$645	$495	$410	$360	$315	$280	$250

MODEL 340 PD AIRLITE Sc CENTENNIAL - similar to Model 340 Airlite Sc, black/grey finish, 12 oz. New 2000.

MSR $862	$645	$495	$410	$355	$315	$285	$250

Add $15 for Hi-Viz front sight.

MODEL 342 AIRLITE Ti CENTENNIAL - .38 S&W Spl.+P cal., similar to Model 337, except is hammerless and double action only, matte stainless/grey finish, Uncle Mike's Boot grips, 12 oz. Mfg. 1999-2003.

	$575	$445	$390	$345	$310	$280	$250

Last MSR was $734.

Add $24 for Dymondwood Boot grips (mfg. 1999 only).

MODEL 342 PD AIRLITE Ti CENTENNIAL - .38 S&W Spl.+P cal., J-frame, 5 shot, double action only, aluminum alloy frame with titanium cylinder and stainless steel 1 7/8 in. barrel, hammerless, black/grey finish, Hogue Bantam grips, 10.8 oz. Mfg. 2000-2003.

	$595	$460	$390	$340	$310	$280	$250

Last MSR was $758.

GRADING - PPGS™	100%	98%	95%	90%	80%	70%	60%

MODEL 351 PD AIRLITE Sc CHIEFS SPECIAL (CENTENNIAL) - .22 Mag. cal., J-frame, 1 7/8 in. barrel, 7 shot, black finish, Scandium alloy frame and cylinder, wood grips, 10.6 oz. New 2004.

	MSR $647	$410	$335	$235	$200	$185	$170	$155

MODEL 360 AIRLITE Sc CHIEFS SPECIAL - .357 Mag. cal., J-frame, 5 shot, 1 7/8 in. barrel, Scandium alloy frame with titanium cylinder, matte stainless/grey finish, Hogue Bantam grips, fixed sights, 12 oz. New 2001.

	MSR $818	$630	$480	$415	$360	$310	$280	$250

MODEL 360 PD AIRLITE Sc CHIEFS SPECIAL - similar to Model 360 Airlite Sc Chiefs Special, except has matte stainless/grey finish, 12 oz. New 2002.

	MSR $843	$645	$480	$400	$365	$330	$295	$260

Add $15 for Hi-Viz front sight.

MODEL 360 AIRLITE Sc KIT GUN - .357 Mag. cal., J-frame, 5 shot, 3 1/8 in. barrel with Hi-Viz front sight, Scandium alloy frame with titanium cylinder, matte stainless/grey finish, Uncle Mike's Combat grips, 14.5 oz. New 2001.

	MSR $865	$650	$510	$420	$365	$325	$295	$260

MODEL 386 AIRLITE Sc MOUNTAIN LITE - .357 Mag. cal., L-frame, 7 shot, 3 1/8 in. stainless barrel with Hi-Viz front sight, Scandium alloy frame with titanium cylinder, two-tone matte stainless/grey finish, Hogue Bantam grips, 18.5 oz. New 2001.

	MSR $876	$670	$495	$415	$360	$330	$295	$265

MODEL 386 PD AIRLITE Sc - .357 Mag. cal., L-frame, 7 shot, 2.5 in. stainless barrel with adj. black rear sight, Scandium alloy frame with titanium cylinder, black/grey finish, Hogue Bantam grips, 17 1/2 oz. New 2001.

	MSR $872	$665	$500	$415	$355	$315	$285	$250

Add $22 for Hi-Viz front sight (disc. 2005).

MODEL 396 AIRLITE Ti MOUNTAIN LITE - .44 S&W Spl. cal., L-frame, 5 shot, 3 1/8 in. barrel with stainless liner and Hi-Viz front sight, aluminum alloy frame with titanium cylinder, matte stainless/grey finish, Hogue Bantam grips, 18 oz. Mfg. 2001-2004.

		$625	$475	$400	$355	$315	$285	$250

Last MSR was $812.

There has been one engineering change to this model.

MODEL 431 CENTENNIAL AIRWEIGHT - .32 H&R Mag cal., J-frame, 6 shot, 2 in. barrel, blue finish. New mid-2004.

	MSR $450	$350	$300	$260	$230	$200	$180	$160

MODEL 432 CENTENNIAL AIRWEIGHT - .32 H&R Mag cal., J-frame, DAO, 6 shot, 2 in. barrel, blue finish. New mid-2004.

	MSR $469	$365	$310	$265	$235	$200	$180	$160

Add $263 for Crimson Trace laser grips (new 2005).

MODEL 442 CENTENNIAL AIRWEIGHT - .38 S&W Spl.+P cal., J-frame, 5 shot, double action only, 1 7/8 in. barrel only with fixed sights, hammerless, aluminum alloy/steel frame, blue or nickel (disc. 1995) finish, round butt, current production uses Uncle Mike's Boot grips, 15 oz. New 1993.

	MSR $600	$450	$320	$240	$200	$180	$170	$150

Add $15 for nickel finish (disc.).

There have been two engineering changes to this model.

MODEL 460 XVR - .460 Mag. cal., 5 shot, X-frame, SA/DA, 8.5 in. barrel with Hi-Viz sights, stainless steel frame with matte finish, similar in design to the Model 500, approx. 70 oz. New 2005.

	MSR $1,253	$1,050	$900	$775				

MODEL 500 - .500 S&W Mag. cal., X-frame, 5 shot, DA, two-piece 4 (new 2004) or 8 3/8 in. ported barrel and full shroud, stainless steel, recoil compensator, new Sorbathane Hogue wraparound rubber finger groove grips, micrometer click adj. rear sight, red ramp (4 in. barrel) or interchangeable front sight blades (8 3/8 in. barrel only), frame is drilled and tapped, 72.5 oz. (with 8 3/8 in. barrel). New 2003.

MSR $1,130	$895	$775	$675				

Add $66 for 4 in. barrel.

Add $104 for Hi-Viz sights (8 3/8 in. barrel only, new 2005).

✱ *Model 500 SCI "Big 5" Master's Edition* - features hand engraving by S&W master engraver Wayne D'Angelo, with 24Kt. gold inlays of the African Big 5 animals, ivory grips, includes presentation case, serial numbered SCI001-SCI005. Limited mfg. 2004.

	$10,000	$8,000	$6,000

Last MSR was $10,000.

✱ *Model 500 SCI "Big 5" Limited Edition* - features roll engraving, with 24Kt. gold inlays of the African Big 5 animals, ivory grips, includes presentation case, serial numbered SCI0006-SCI0300. Limited mfg. 2004.

	$3,000	$2,250	$1,500

Last MSR was $3,000.

MODEL 520 - .357 Mag. cal., 4 in. barrel, fixed sights, N-frame, originally ordered for N.Y. State Police but never purchased. Approx. 3,000 mfg. with box.

$350	$310	$250	$210	$185	$175	$165

MODEL 544 - please refer to the Commemorative section.

MODEL 547 M & P - 9mm Para. cal., 3 or 4 in. heavy barrel, 6 shot, round (3 in. barrel) or square (4 in. barrel) butt, blue only, 32 oz. Disc. 1985.

$295	$265	$240	$210	$195	$185	$175

Last MSR was $317.

MODEL 581 (DISTINGUISHED SERVICE MAGNUM) - .357 Mag. cal., L-Frame, fixed sights, 4 in. barrel, 6 shot, blue or nickel finish, 38 oz. Disc. 1992.

$335	$285	$250	$230	$220	$210	$200

Last MSR was $335.

Add $20 for nickel (mfg. 1980-88).

MODEL 586 (DISTINGUISHED COMBAT MAGNUM) - .357 Mag. cal., L-Frame, 4, 6, or 8 3/8 (disc. 1991) in. barrel, adj. sights, blue or nickel (disc. 1991) finish. Disc. 1999.

$370	$300	$250	$230	$220	$210	$200

Last MSR was $494.

Add 5%-10% for nickel finish (disc.).

Add $4 for white outlined rear sight (disc. 1994).

Add $5 for 6 in. barrel.

Add $22 for 8 3/8 in. barrel (disc. 1991).

Add $35 for adj. front sight - disc. 1991 (6 in. barrel only, new 1986).

There have been 7 engineering changes to this model.

MODEL 610 CLASSIC - 10mm/.40 S&W cal., N-frame, 6 shot, adj. sights, 4 (new 2001) 5 (disc. 2000) or 6 1/2 (disc. 2000) in. full lug barrel, stainless steel construction, fluted or unfluted (4 or 6 1/2 in. barrel only) cylinder, round butt, adj. rear sight, current production uses Hogue rubber grips, target hammer optional, 50 oz., approx. 5,000 mfg. 1990 only, reintroduced 1998-2004.

$670	$520	$405

Last MSR was $833.

There have been three engineering changes to this model.

MODEL 617 (K-22 MASTERPIECE STAINLESS) - .22 LR cal., K-frame, stainless steel variation of the Model 17 (K-22 Masterpiece), 6 (6 in. full lug barrel only beginning 1999) or 10 (new 1997) shot, 4, 6, or 8 3/8 (disc. 2002) in. full lug barrel, satin stainless finish, combat trigger and Hogue rubber grips are standard on current production, semi-target, 41-52.5 oz. New 1990.

MSR $686   **$445**   **$350**   **$235**

Add $21 for 4 in. barrel, add $48 for 6 in. barrel with 10 shot, or $54 for 8 3/8 in. barrel (disc. 2002).

In 2000, this model includes target hammer with 8 3/8 in. barrel. 4 and 6 in. barrels were standard during a limited production period in 1991.

MODEL 619 - .357 Mag. cal., 7 shot, two-piece 5 in. barrel, stainless steel with satin finish, rubber grips, fixed sights. New 2005.

MSR $615   **$385**   **$325**   **$240**

MODEL 620 - .357 Mag. cal., 4 in. barrel, similar to Model 619, except has white outline rear sight and red ramp front sight. New 2005.

MSR $817   **$650**   **$525**   **$400**

MODEL 624 .44 TARGET - .44 S&W Spl. cal., 6 shot, 4 or 6.5 in. barrel, 42 oz. Mfg. 1986-87 only.

                  $360   **$325**   **$250**

Last MSR was $449.

Add $14 for 6.5 in. barrel.

MODEL 625 - .45 ACP or .45 Colt (disc.) cal., N-frame, stainless variation of the Model 25-2, 6 shot, 3 (disc. 1991), 4 (disc. 1991, reintroduced 2002), or 5 in. barrel, round butt, choice of matte or satin (new 2005) stainless finish, ramp front (3 or 4 in. barrel) or Patridge front (5 in. barrel) sight, full lug barrel, Pachmayr (disc.) or Hogue rubber combat grips, 45 oz. New 1988.

MSR $817   **$545**   **$475**   **$335**

Add $28 for satin finish (4 in. barrel only).

Approx. 1,500 of the 5 in. barrel models had a frame stamped "625-2", roll engraved barrel with ".45 CAL MODEL OF 1988" barrel inscription, and a ramp front sight. Laser engraving replaced roll engraving in 1989.

There have been 10 engineering changes for this model.

MODEL 627 - .357 Mag. cal., also known as "Model of 1989" (stamped on barrel), N-frame, smooth combat grips, S&W medallion logo, round butt, unfluted cylinder, full underlug 5.5 in. barrel. Disc.

                  $500   **$425**   **$325**

This model evolved into a Performance Center model.

MODEL 629 - .44 Mag./.44 S&W Spl. cal., N-frame, 6 shot, similar to Model 29, available with 4, 6, or 8 3/8 (disc. 2002) in. barrel, satin stainless finish, current production uses Hogue rubber combat grips, 41.5-49.5 oz. New 1979.

MSR $787   **$550**   **$470**   **$335**

Add $23 for 6 in. barrel or $39 for 8 3/8 in. barrel (disc.).

Add $52 for combat grips with barrel scope mount (cut across barrel rib) - disc. 1991 (8 3/8 in. barrel only).

Add 10% for pinned barrel with recessed cylinder.

During 1978, approx. 100 pre-production revolvers were made with pinned barrels and recessed cylinders, serial range is N629,062-N629,200, includes wood box. Prices range from $650-$750, depending on condition.

✱ *Model 629 Classic* - satin stainless steel variation of the Model 29 Classic, 5, 6.5 (with or w/o PowerPort), or 8 3/8 in. barrel, current production uses Hogue rubber combat grips, 49.5-53.5 oz. New 1990.

MSR $843   **$575**   **$485**   **$355**

Add $16 for 6.5 in. barrel with white outline on rear sight.

Add $28 for 8 3/8 in. barrel.

Add $51 for Hi-Viz front sight, 6.5 in. barrel only.

✳ *Model 629 Classic DX* - similar to Classic, except is supplied with 2 sets of grips (Hogue combat square and Morado wood round buttstocks), 6 1/2 or 8 3/8 in. barrel, satin stainless finish, 5 interchangeable front sights, numbered test target, 51-54 oz. Mfg. 1992-2002.

$650	$550	$510

Last MSR was $986.

Add $32 for 8 3/8 in. barrel.

✳ *Model 629 Magna Classic* - .44 Mag. cal., similar to Model 29, 3,000 mfg. during 1990 only.

$900	$825	$750

Last MSR was $999.

MODEL 631 - .32 Mag. cal., 6 shot, 2 (fixed sight) or 4 (adj. sight) in. barrel, combat stocks, round butt only, approx. 5,500 mfg. 1990-92.

$340	$275	$200

Last MSR was $386.

✳ *631 Ladysmith* - 2 in. barrel only, rosewood stocks.

$365	$295	$225

Last MSR was $400.

MODEL 632 CENTENNIAL - .32 Mag. cal., 2 or 3 (mfg. 1991 only) in. barrel, stainless/alloy construction, fully concealed hammer, J frame, Santoprene combat grips, fixed sights, 15.5 oz. Mfg. 1991-92.

$450	$350	$250

Last MSR was $410.

Add 20% for 3 in. barrel.

MODEL 637 CHIEFS SPECIAL AIRWEIGHT - .38 S&W Spl.+P cal., J-frame, 5 shot, matte finish, alloy frame with 1 7/8 in. satin stainless steel barrel and cylinder, current production uses Uncle Mike's Boot grips, 15 oz., 560 mfg. during 1991, reintroduced 1996.

MSR $450	$325	$255	$215

Add $13 for Carry Combo configuration (new 2004).
Add $245 for Crimson Trace laser grips (new 2005).

MODEL 638 BODYGUARD AIRWEIGHT - .38 S&W Spl.+P cal., J-frame, 5 shot, alloy frame, 1 7/8 in. stainless steel barrel and cylinder, shrouded hammer, round butt, Uncle Mike's Boot grips, 15 oz. 1,200 mfg. during 1990 only, reintroduced 1998.

MSR $620	$460	$330	$265

MODEL 640 CENTENNIAL - .357 Mag./.38 S&W Spl.+P or .38 S&W Spl. (disc.) cal., J-frame, 5 shot, double action only, 1 7/8 (mfg. 1998-2001), 2 1/8 (new 1991), or 3 (disc. 1992) in. barrel, hammerless, current production uses Uncle Mike's Combat grips, satin stainless finish, round butt, 23 oz. New 1991.

MSR $658	$485	$340	$250

MODEL 642 CENTENNIAL AIRWEIGHT - .38 S&W Spl.+P cal., J-frame, 5 shot, 1 7/8, 2 (disc. 1997), or 3 (disc. 1991) in. barrel, alloy frame with stainless steel cylinder and barrel, combat grips, hammerless, satin stainless finish, fixed rear sight, 15 oz. Mfg. 1990-1992, reintroduced 1996.

MSR $469	$340	$265	$220

✳ *Model 642 CT* - similar Model 642 Centennial Airweight, except has Crimson Trace laser grips. New 2004.

MSR $695	$535	$355	$250

MODEL 642 LADYSMITH AIRWEIGHT - .38 S&W Spl.+P cal., J-frame, 5 shot, 1 7/8 in. barrel, stainless steel/alloy construction, smooth wood grips, satin stainless finish, includes soft side carry or jewelry case, 14.5 oz. New 1996.

MSR $633	$485	$330	$230

MODEL 646 - .40 S&W cal., 4 in. barrel, stainless steel, 6 shot, titanium cylinder. Limited mfg. during 2000 and 2003.

$575 $450 $365

MODEL 647 - .17 HMR cal., K-frame, 6 shot, stainless steel, 8 3/8 in. barrel with full lug, Hogue rubber grips with finger grooves, Patridge rear with adj. front sight, 52 oz. Mfg. 2003-2004.

$545 $365 $260

Last MSR was $697.

MODEL 648 - .22 Mag. cal., K-frame, 6 in. full lug barrel, combat grips, square butt, combat trigger, semi-target hammer. Mfg. 1989-1996.

$450 $325 $250

Last MSR was $464.

MODEL 648-2 - .22 Mag. cal., K-frame, 6 shot, stainless steel, 6 in. barrel with full lug, Hogue rubber grips with finger grooves, Patridge rear with adj. front sight, 45 oz. New 2003.

MSR $703 $525 $345 $240

MODEL 649 BODYGUARD - .357 Mag./.38 S&W Spl.+P or .38 S&W Spl. (disc.) cal., J-frame, otherwise similar to Model 49 Bodyguard, except is satin stainless steel, 1 7/8 (mfg. 1998 only), 2 (disc. 1997), or 2 1/8 (new 1998) in. barrel, shrouded hammer, current production uses Uncle Mike's Combat grips, 23 oz. New 1986.

MSR $651 $480 $320 $230

There have been five engineering changes to this model.

MODEL 650 - .22 Mag. cal., service kit gun, stainless steel, 3 in. heavy barrel, J-frame, fixed sights. Mfg. 1983-87.

$375 $300 $200

Last MSR was $305.

MODEL 651 KIT GUN - .22 Mag. cal., target kit gun, stainless steel, 4 in. barrel, J-frame, adj. sights. Mfg. 1983-87, re-released in late 1990, disc. 1998.

$400 $325 $225

Last MSR was $478.

This model could be ordered with a factory fitted optional .22 LR cylinder until 1987 (last mfg. sug. retail was $295 for the cylinder alone). This variation with the extra cylinder is very desirable.

MODEL 657 - .41 Mag. cal., N-frame, 4 (disc.), 6 (disc. 2000), 7.5 (new 2001), or 8 3/8 (disc. 1992) in. barrel, satin stainless steel, current production uses Hogue rubber combat grips, approx. 53 oz. New 1986.

MSR $774 $500 $400 $300

Add $17 for 8 3/8 in. barrel (disc. 1992).

There have been 5 engineering changes to this model.

MODEL 681 DISTINGUISHED SERVICE MAGNUM - .357 Mag. cal., stainless steel, 4 in. barrel, L-Frame. Mfg. 1980-1992.

$320 $270 $225

Last MSR was $412.

1991 mfg. includes square butt.

MODEL 686 DISTINGUISHED COMBAT MAGNUM - .357 Mag./.38 S&W Spl.+P cal., L-Frame, similar to Model 586, except 2.5 (new 1990), 4, 6 (with or w/o Power-Port), or 8 3/8 (disc. 2002) in. barrel, fixed (disc.) or adj. sights, current production uses Hogue rubber grips, 35-51 oz. New 1980.

MSR $667 $445 $380 $265

Add $27 for 4 in., $33 for 6 in. barrel, $80 for PowerPort 6 in. barrel, or $55 for 8 3/8 in. barrel (disc.).

GRADING - PPGS™	100%	98%	95%	90%	80%	70%	60%

✳ *Model 686 Plus* - .357 Mag./.38 S&W Spl.+P cal., L-frame, 7 shot, 2.5, 4, or 6 in. barrel, synthetic or Hogue rubber grips, stainless steel, round (2.5 in. barrel only) or square butt, white outline rear sight on 4 or 6 in. barrel, 34.5-43 oz. New 1996.

	MSR $692	$465	$355	$260

  Add $24 for 4 in. or $35 for 6 in. barrel.

MODEL 696 - .44 S&W Spl. cal., L-frame, 5 shot, 3 in. barrel with full shroud, Hogue rubber (disc. 2000) or Uncle Mike's Combat grips, satin stainless steel, adj. rear sight, 36 oz. Mfg. 1997-2002.

		$485	$315	$250

  Last MSR was $620.

MODEL 940 CENTENNIAL - 9mm Para. cal., fully concealed hammer, 2 or 3 (disc. 1992) in. barrel, fixed rear sight, Santoprene combat grips, 23-25 oz. Mfg. 1991-98.

		$390	$265	$220

  Last MSR was $493.

100%	98%	95%	90%	80%	70%	60%	50%	40%	30%	20%	10%

PISTOLS: SEMI-AUTO

Listed in order of model number (except .32 and .35 Automatic Pistols). Alphabetical models will appear at the end of this section.

To understand S&W 3rd generation model nomenclature, the following rules apply. The first two digits (of the four digit model number) specify caliber. Numbers 39, 59, and 69 refer to 9mm Para. cal. The third digit refers to the model type. 0 means standard model, 1 is for compact, 2 is for standard model with decocking lever, 3 is for compact variation with decocking lever, 4 is for standard with double action only, 5 designates a compact model in double action only, 6 indicates a non-standard barrel length, 7 is a non-standard barrel length with decocking lever, and 8 refers to non-standard barrel length in double action only. The fourth digit refers to the material(s) used in the fabrication of the pistol. 3 refers to an aluminum alloy frame with stainless steel slide, 4 designates an aluminum alloy frame with carbon steel slide, 5 is for carbon steel frame and slide, 6 is a stainless steel frame and slide, and 7 refers to a stainless steel frame and carbon steel slide. Hence, a Model 4053 refers to a pistol in .40 S&W cal. configured in compact version with double action only and fabricated with an aluminum alloy frame and stainless steel slide. This model nomenclature does not apply to 2- or 3-digit model numbers (i.e., Rimfire Models and the Model 52).

.32 AUTOMATIC PISTOL - .32 ACP cal., 7 shot mag., 3 1/2 in. barrel, blue with "S&W" monogram inlaid plain walnut grip. 957 mfg. 1924-36. Serial range starting with S/N 1.

$3,000	$2,500	$2,000	$1,750	$1,500	$1,250	$1,000	$800	$700	$600	$500	$400

.35 AUTOMATIC PISTOL (MODEL 1913) - .35 S&W Auto cal., 7 shot mag., 3 1/2 in. barrel, blue or nickel w/ "S&W" monogram inlaid in plain walnut grips. 8,350 mfg. 1913-21. Serial range starting with no. 1.

$775	$625	$525	$450	$375	$325	$275	$235	$200	$185	$175	$165

  A slight premium might exist for the first model (up to ser. no. 3,125).

GRADING - PPGS™	100%	98%	95%	90%	80%	70%	60%

MODEL 22A SPORT SERIES - .22 LR cal., single action, 10 shot mag., aluminum alloy frame, stainless steel slide, choice of 4 standard, 5.5 standard or bull, or 7 in. standard barrel with raised solid rib, adj. rear and Hi-Viz (5.5 in. bull barrel only, new 2001) sights, 2-piece black polymer (hard or soft) or Dymondwood (5.5 bull barrel only) grips, blue or camo (new 2004, 5.5 in. barrel only) finish, 28-39 oz. New 1997.

	MSR $293	$225	$195	$165	$135	$110	$95	$80

  Add $31 for 5.5 in. standard barrel with soft-touch grips.
  Add $74 for 7 in. standard barrel with thumbrest soft-touch grips or camo finish (new 2004).

GRADING - PPGS™	100%	98%	95%	90%	80%	70%	60%

Add $114 for 5.5 in. bull barrel with Dymondwood target grips.

Add $136 for 5.5 bull barrel with Hi-Viz sights (new 2001).

Add $71 for 5.5 in. bull barrel with 2 piece target grips and thumbrest (disc. 2000).

MODEL 22S SPORT SERIES - .22 LR cal., single action, 10 shot mag., aluminum alloy frame, stainless steel slide, choice of 5.5 standard/bull or 7 (disc. 2004) in. standard barrel with raised solid rib, adj. rear and Hi-Viz (5.5 in. bull barrel only, new 2001) sights, 2-piece black polymer (hard or soft) or Dymondwood (5.5 in. bull barrel only) grips, satin stainless finish, 41-48 oz. New 1997.

	MSR $396	$310	$250	$205	$170	$140	$125	$110

Add $40 for 7 in. standard barrel with thumbrest soft-touch grips (disc. 2004).

Add $83 for 5.5 in. bull barrel with Dymondwood target grips (disc. 2004).

Add $102 for 5.5 bull barrel with Hi-Viz sights (mfg. 2001-2004).

Add $44 for 5.5 in. bull barrel with 2 piece target grips and thumbrest (disc. 2000).

MODEL 39 STEEL FRAME - 9mm Para. cal., 8 shot, 4 in. barrel, long ejector, walnut stocks, blue, adj. rear windage only sight, double action, walnut grips, 927 mfg. during 1966 only in 3 ser. no. ranges.

		$1,200	$975	$850	$735	$650	$550	$475

MODEL 39 ALLOY FRAME - 9mm Para. cal., alloy frame, this model was unmarked up to ser. no. approx. 2,600, early guns had a short safety lever, checkered walnut grips, blue or nickel finish. Mfg. started 1954.

		$400	$350	$315	$260	$210	$175	$140

Add $35 for nickel finish.

Collectors report an approx. ser. no. range 1,001-105,000 with long ejector.

This model was the first commercially mfg. 9mm Para. double action semi-auto in the U.S.

✳ Early Mfg. (Pre 39) - short safety, first group of 298 were produced for military inspection, various markings include "Quantico, VA", approx. ser. no. range 1,001-2,600. Mfg. 1954-55.

		$1,495	$1,250	$995	$875	$750	$625	$500

Add 50% for early manufacture original military trial guns.

MODEL 39-2 ALLOY FRAME (LATER PRODUCTION) - 7.65mm (.30 Luger) or 9mm Para. cal., double action, 8 shot mag., 4 in. barrel, checkered walnut grips, adj. sight, alloy frame, approx. 1971, the 39-2 was introduced as an improved version. Mfg. 1970-82.

9mm Para.	$360	$325	$260	$240	$220	$200	$195

Add $35 for nickel finish.

7.65mm cal.	$1,250	$1,100	$950	$825	$700	$625	$550

The .30 Luger cal. (7.65mm) was mfg. for the European marketplace only. Very hard to find in the U.S.

MODEL 41/41-1 .22 RF - .22 S (disc., Model 41-1) or LR cal., match target pistol, single action, 10 shot mag., adj. Patridge sights, checkered walnut grips with thumbrest, 5 (disc.), 5.5 (heavy) 7 (standard) or 7 3/8 (disc. 2004) in. barrel, blue finish only, 41 oz. Mfg. 1957-present.

	MSR $1,062	$750	$600	$465	$375	$315	$285	$250

Add $100 for 5.5 in. barrel with extended sight (disc.).

Add $35 for 7 3/8 in. barrel with muzzle brake (disc.).

Add 125% for .22 Short cal. with counterweight and muzzle brake (disc.).

Add 15%-40% for early variations with cocking indicator (disc. 1978).

Note: there are several disc. barrels on the Model 41. They are the 5 in. standard weight with extended sight, 7 3/8 in. with muzzle brake, and 5 1/2 in. heavy barrel with extended sight.

MODEL 44 - 9mm Para. cal., single action design, S&W's rarest semi-auto pistol, approx. 10 mfg.

Extreme rarity precludes accurate price evaluation, but a specimen has recently been sold for over $10K.

GRADING - PPGS™	100%	98%	95%	90%	80%	70%	60%

MODEL 46 - .22 LR cal., 5, 5 1/2, or 7 in. barrel, blue, nylon grips, adj. sights. Mfg. 4,000, 1957-66.

	$450	$335	$300	$260	$225	$200	$195

This model is similar to the Model 41, but does not have high polish bluing, and has brown plastic grips.

MODEL 52-A - .38 AMU cal., same action as Model 39, 4 in. barrel. Originally mfg. for U.S. Army Marksman Training Unit, 87 mfg.

	$3,000	$2,500	$2,200	$1,950	$1,600	$1,300	$1,000

MODEL 52 - .38 S&W Spl. Wadcutter only, similar action to Model 39, except incorporates a set screw locking out the double action, 5 in. barrel, 5 shot mag. Approx. 3,500 mfg. 1961-63.

	$875	$775	$675	$575	$475	$395	$360

MODELS 52-1 & 52-2 - .38 Spl. Mid-Range Wadcutter cal. only, single action semi-auto, 5 in. barrel, adj. sights, checkered walnut grips, blue only, 5 shot mag.

	$675	$550	$450	$400	$350	$295	$265

Last MSR was $908.

The Model 52-1 was mfg. 1963-1971, and the Model 52-2 was mfg. 1971-93.

MODEL 59 - similar to Model 39, except has 14 shot mag., black nylon grips. Disc. 1981.

	$385	$340	$270	$250	$225	$215	$200

Add $35 for nickel finish.
Add $150 for smooth (ungrooved) grip frame.

MODEL 61 ESCORT - .22 LR cal., 5 shot, semi-auto, blue or nickel, 2 1/2 in. barrel, plastic grips, mfg. 1970-74.

	100%	98%	95%	90%	80%	70%	60%
Blue finish	$250	$210	$165	$150	$140	$110	$95
Nickel finish	$275	$230	$165	$150	$140	$110	$95

MODEL 147-A - 9mm Para. cal., 14 shot, steel frame, 4 in. barrel, black plastic grips, adj. sights for windage only, similar to Model 59, except has steel frame, 112 mfg. 1979 only.

	$1,375	$1,050	$875	$800	$725	$650	$575

This model was originally marked Model 47 for export, prefix and suffix were added. Ser. nos. were stamped, and are crude by today's standard.

MODEL 410 - .40 S&W cal., traditional double action, steel slide with alloy frame, blue finish, 4 in. barrel, 10 shot mag., single side safety, 3-dot sights, straight backstrap with synthetic grips, 28.5 oz. New 1996.

MSR $649	$500	$355	$265	$225	$195	$175	$165

Add $21 for Hi-Viz front sight (disc. 2003).

✱ *Model 410S* - similar to Model 410, except has stainless steel slide with alloy frame, 28.5 oz. New 2003.

MSR $669	$515	$365	$270	$240	$205	$175	$165

Add $264 for Crimson Trace laser grips (new 2005).

MODEL 411 - .40 S&W cal., 4 in. barrel, 11 shot mag., fixed sights, blue finish, aluminum alloy frame, manual safety. Mfg. 1993-95.

	$440	$375	$335	$310	$295	$280	$265

Last MSR was $525.

MODEL 422 .22 RF (FIELD) - .22 LR cal., single action, 4 1/2 or 6 in. barrel, aluminum frame with steel slide, 10 shot mag., fixed sights, black plastic or wood grips, matte blue finish, 22 oz. Mfg. 1987-96.

	$185	$150	$115	$110	$105	$100	$95

Last MSR was $235.

GRADING - PPGS™	100%	98%	95%	90%	80%	70%	60%

✱ Model 422 Target - .22 LR cal., single action, 4 1/2 or 6 in. barrel, aluminum frame with steel slide, 10 shot mag., adj. rear sight, checkered walnut grips, matte blue finish, 22 oz. Mfg. 1987-96.

	$225	$175	$140	$115	$110	$105	$95

Last MSR was $290.

MODEL 439 - 9mm Para. cal., double action, 4 in. barrel, blue or nickel finish, alloy frame, 8 shot mag., checkered walnut grips, 30 oz. Disc. 1988.

	$385	$315	$255	$240	$225	$210	$200

Last MSR was $472.

Add $34 for nickel finish (disc. 1986).
Add $26 for adj. sights.

MODEL 457 COMPACT - .45 ACP cal., traditional double action, alloy frame and steel slide, 3.75 in. barrel, single side safety, 3-dot sights, 7 shot mag., straight backstrap, blue finish only, black synthetic grips, 29 oz. New 1996.

MSR $649	$500	$355	$265	$225	$195	$175	$165

✱ Model 457S - similar to Model 457, except has stainless steel slide with alloy frame, 29 oz. New 2003.

MSR $676	$520	$375	$270	$240	$200	$175	$165

MODEL 459 - 9mm Para. cal., 14 shot version of Model 439, checkered nylon stocks, limited mfg. with squared-off triggerguard with serrations. Disc. 1988.

	$410	$345	$290	$270	$255	$240	$210

Last MSR was $501.

Add $26 for adj. sights.
Add $44 for nickel finish (disc. 1986).

✱ Model 459 Brushed Finish - 9mm Para. cal., 14 shot, 4 in. barrel, dull finish, fixed sights, special grips made to F.B.I. or police specs., 803 mfg.

	$650	$600	$550	$440	$385	$330	$300

MODEL 469 "MINI" - 9mm Para. cal., double action, alloy frame, 12 shot finger extension mag., short frame, bobbed hammer, 3 1/2 in. barrel, sandblast blue or satin nickel finish, ambidextrous safety standard (1986), molded Delrin black Grips, 26 oz. Disc. 1988.

	$370	$320	$265	$250	$235	$220	$210

Last MSR was $478.

MODEL 539 - 9mm Para. cal., double action, steel frame, 8 shot, 4 in. barrel, blue or nickel. Approx. 8,300 mfg. Disc. 1983.

	$450	$395	$375	$350	$325	$300	$275

Add $35 for nickel finish.
Add $30 for adj. rear sight.

MODEL 559 - 9mm Para. cal., double action, steel frame, 14 shot mag., 4 in. barrel, blue or nickel. Approx. 1,700 mfg. Disc. 1983.

	$485	$435	$375	$275	$250	$225	$200

Add $35 for nickel finish.
Add $30 for adj. rear sight.

MODEL 622 .22 RF (Field) - .22 LR cal., single action, 4 1/2 or 6 in. barrel, stainless/alloy construction, 10 shot mag., fixed sights, black plastic grips, 21 1/2 or 23 1/2 oz. Mfg. 1990-96.

	$220	$175	$160				

Last MSR was $284.

GRADING - PPGS™	100%	98%	95%	90%	80%	70%	60%

✱ *Model 622 Target* - .22 LR cal., single action, 4 1/2 or 6 in. barrel (VR was an option in 1996 only), stainless steel construction, 10 shot mag., adj. rear sight, checkered walnut grips, 21 1/2 or 23 1/2 oz. Mfg. 1990-96.

	$275	$225	$175

Last MSR was $337.

MODEL 639 STAINLESS - 9mm Para. cal., similar to Model 439-only stainless steel, 8 shot mag., ambidextrous safety became standard 1986, 36 oz. Disc. 1988.

	$420	$300	$275

Last MSR was $523.

Add $27 for adj. sights.

MODEL 645 STAINLESS - .45 ACP cal. only, 5 in. barrel, 8 shot mag., squared-off trigger guard, black molded nylon grips, ambidextrous safety, fixed sights, 37 1/2 oz. New 1986. Disc. 1988.

	$475	$365	$300

Last MSR was $622.

Add $27 for adj. sight.
Approx. 150 Model 645 "Interim" pistols were mfg. in 1988 only. Add $120 to values listed.

MODEL 659 STAINLESS - 9mm Para. cal., similar to Model 459-only stainless steel, 14 shot mag., ambidextrous safety became standard 1986, 39 1/2 oz. Disc. 1988.

	$445	$335	$300

Last MSR was $553.

Add $27 for adj. sights.
Approx. 150 Model 659 "Interim" pistols were mfg. in 1988 only. Add $150 to values listed.

MODEL 669 STAINLESS - 9mm Para. cal., smaller version of Model 659 with 12 shot finger extension mag., 3 1/2 in. barrel, fixed sights, molded Delrin grips, ambidextrous safety standard, 26 oz. Mfg. 1986-88 only.

	$425	$305	$275

Last MSR was $522.

Approx. 150 Model 669 "Interim" pistols were mfg. in 1988 only. Add $150 to values listed.

MODEL 745 IPSC - .45 ACP cal., single action, 5 in. barrel, stainless steel frame with steel slide, hammer, and trigger, checkered walnut stocks, fixed rear sight, 38 3/4 oz. Mfg. 1987-90.

	$575	$440	$335

Last MSR was $699.

Early guns had optional "IPSC" markings. Later, these markings became standard.

MODEL 908 COMPACT - 9mm Para. cal., compact variation of the Model 909/910, 3.5 in. barrel, 3-dot sights, 8 shot mag., straight backstrap, 24 oz. New 1996.

MSR $587	$455	$330	$260	$225	$190	$175	$165

✱ *Model 908S* - similar to Model 908, except has stainless steel slide with alloy frame, 24 oz. New 2003.

MSR $611	$475	$345	$265	$230	$200	$175	$165

Add $13 for carry combo variation (includes Kydex carry holster, new 2004).

MODEL 909 - 9mm Para. cal., 4 in. barrel, traditional double action, large frame, 9 shot mag., fixed sights, single side safety, alloy frame and steel slide, curved backstrap with black synthetic grips, 27 oz. Mfg. 1994-96.

	$360	$275	$225	$205	$190	$175	$165

Last MSR was $443.

MODEL 910 - similar to Model 909, except has 10 shot mag., 28 oz. New 1994.

MSR $587	$455	$330	$260	$225	$190	$175	$165

Add $22 for Hi-Viz front sight (disc. 2003).

✱ Model 910S - similar to Model 910, except has stainless steel slide with alloy frame, 28 oz. New 2003.

	100%	98%	95%	90%	80%	70%	60%
MSR $602	$465	$335	$265	$220	$195	$175	$165

MODEL 915 - 9mm Para. cal., 4 in. barrel, fixed sights, 10 (C/B 1994) or 15* shot mag., manual safety, aluminum alloy frame, blue finish. Mfg. 1993-94.

	$350	$255	$225	$205	$190	$175	$165

Last MSR was $467.

MODEL 1006 STAINLESS - 10mm cal., double action semi-auto, stainless steel construction, 5 in. barrel, exposed hammer, 9 shot mag., fixed or adj. sights, ambidextrous safety. Mfg. 1990-93.

	$635	$530	$400

Last MSR was $769.

Add $27 for adj. rear sight.

MODEL 1026 STAINLESS - 10mm cal., 5 in. barrel, traditional double action, features frame mounted decocking lever, 9 shot mag., straight backstrap. Mfg. 1990-91 only.

	$630	$525	$400

Last MSR was $755.

MODEL 1046 STAINLESS - 10mm cal., 5 in. barrel, fixed sights, double action only, 9 shot mag., straight backstrap. Mfg. 1991 only.

	$620	$515	$400

Last MSR was $747.

MODEL 1066 STAINLESS - 10mm cal., 4 1/4 in. barrel, 9 shot mag., straight backstrap, ambidextrous safety, traditional double action, fixed sights. Mfg. 1990-92.

	$610	$515	$395

Last MSR was $730.

Add $40 for Tritium night sights - disc. 1991 (Model 1066-NS).
Only 1,000 Model 1066-NSs were manufactured.

MODEL 1076 STAINLESS - similar to Model 1026 Stainless, except has 4 1/4 in. barrel. Mfg. 1990-93.

	$645	$530	$400

Last MSR was $778.

MODEL 1086 STAINLESS - similar to Model 1066 Stainless, except is double action only.

	$710	$515	$395

Last MSR was $730.

MODEL SW1911 - .45 ACP cal., patterned after the Colt M1911, large frame, 5 in. barrel, 8 shot, stainless steel or blue/black (new 2005) finish, patented S&W firing pin safety release activated by the grip safety, pinned-in external extractor, Wolff springs throughout, Texas Armament match trigger, Hogue rubber or wood (new 2004) grips, McCormick hammer and thumb safety, Briley barrel bushing, two Wilson magazines, full-length heavy guide rod, high profile Wilson beavertail safety, Novak Lo-Mount Carry sights, 39 oz. New 2003.

	100%	98%	95%	90%	80%	70%	60%
MSR $960	$775	$575	$425	$375	$325	$295	$275

Add $89 for adj. sights.
Add $69 for wood grips and adj. sights.
Add $253 for black blade front sights.

✱ Model SW1911 Stainless

	100%	98%	95%	90%
MSR $960	$775	$575	$425

Add $89 for adj. sights.
Add $69 for wood grips and adj. sights.
Add $321 for Crimson Trace laser grips (new 2005).

✷ *Model SW1911 PD (Sc)* - similar to Model SW1911, except has 4.25 in. barrel with small alloy frame, 8 shot, black finish, and wood grips. New 2004.

	100%	98%	95%	90%	80%	70%	60%
MSR $1,029	$825	$625	$450	$415	$385	$350	$325

Add $301 for Crimson Trace laser grips.

MODEL 2206 STAINLESS .22 RF (FIELD) - .22 LR cal., similar to Model 622 Field, except all stainless steel components, black plastic grips, 6 in. barrel with standard (disc. 1995) or adj. rear sight, 35 or 39 oz. Mfg. 1990-96.

	$290	$225	$175

Last MSR was $385.

Subtract $58 if w/o adj. sights.

✷ *Model 2206 Stainless Target* - similar to Model 2206 Stainless, except has adj. target sight, target stocks, and is drilled and tapped. Mfg. 1994-96.

	$360	$275	$225

Last MSR was $433.

MODEL 2213 STAINLESS .22 RF "SPORTSMAN" - .22 LR cal., single action, 3 in. barrel, alloy frame with stainless steel slide, 8 shot mag., 2 dot fixed rear sight, black plastic molded grips, 18 oz., includes holster/carry case. Mfg. 1992-99.

	$255	$200	$160

Last MSR was $340.

MODEL 2214 .22 RF "SPORTSMAN" - .22 LR cal., similar to Model 2213, except has alloy frame with blue carbon steel slide with matte black finish, and no case. Mfg. 1991-99.

	$230	$185	$160	$150	$140	$130	$120

Last MSR was $292.

MODEL 3904 - 9mm Para. cal., double action semi-auto, aluminum alloy frame, 4 in. barrel with fixed bushing, 8 shot mag., Delrin one piece wraparound grips, exposed hammer, ambidextrous safety, beveled magazine well, extended squared-off triggerguard, adj. or fixed rear sight, 3-dot sighting system, 28 oz. Mfg. 1989-91.

	$450	$385	$350	$325	$300	$280	$265

Last MSR was $541.

Add $25 for adj. rear sight.

MODEL 3906 STAINLESS - stainless steel variation of the Model 3904, 35 1/2 oz. Mfg. 1989-91.

	$510	$435	$375

Last MSR was $604.

Add $28 for adj. rear sight.

MODEL 3913 COMPACT STAINLESS - stainless steel variation of the Model 3914, 25 oz. Mfg. 1990-99.

	$535	$440	$365

Last MSR was $662.

✷ *Model 3913NL* - similar to Model 3913 Ladysmith, except does not have Ladysmith on the slide. Disc. 1994.

	$510	$425	$365

Last MSR was $622.

✷ *Model 3913 LS (LadySmith)* - similar to Model 3913 Stainless, except has white Delrin grips and mag. does not have finger extension, includes case, 25 oz. New 1990.

MSR $858	$680	$510	$395

MODEL 3913TSW TACTICAL - 9mm Para. cal., traditional double action, compact frame, 3.5 in. barrel, 7 shot mag., Novak low mount 2 dot sights, stainless steel slide, aluminum alloy frame, satin stainless finish, straight black backstrap synthetic grips, 24.8 oz. New 1998.

MSR $834	$660	$500	$395

GRADING - PPGS™	100%	98%	95%	90%	80%	70%	60%

MODEL 3914 COMPACT - 9mm Para. cal., double action semi-auto, aluminum alloy frame, 3 1/2 in. barrel, hammerless, 8 shot finger extension mag., fixed sights only, ambidextrous safety, blue finish, straight backstrap grip, 25 oz. Mfg. 1990-95.

	$465	$385	$340	$320	$295	$280	$265

Last MSR was $562.

This model was also available with a single side manual safety at no extra charge - disc. 1991 (Model 3914NL).

* *Model 3914 LadySmith* - similar to Model 3914, except has Delrin grips, 25 oz. Mfg. 1990-91 only.

	$485	$415	$365

Last MSR was $568.

MODEL 3953 COMPACT STAINLESS - 9mm Para. cal., double action only, aluminum alloy frame with stainless steel slide, compact model with 3 1/2 in. barrel, 8 shot mag. Mfg. 1990-99.

	$535	$440	$365

Last MSR was $662.

MODEL 3953TSW - similar to Model 3913TSW, except is double action only, 24.8 oz. Mfg. 1998-2002.

	$615	$475	$380

Last MSR was $760.

MODEL 3954 - similar to Model 3953, except has blue steel slide. Mfg. 1990-92.

	$445	$380	$340	$320	$295	$280	$265

Last MSR was $528.

MODEL 4003 STAINLESS - .40 S&W cal., traditional double action, 4 in. barrel, 11 shot mag., white dot fixed sights, ambidextrous safety, aluminum alloy frame with stainless steel slide, one piece Xenoy wraparound grips, straight gripstrap, 28 oz. Mfg. 1991-93.

	$585	$495	$395

Last MSR was $698.

* *Model 4003TSW* - similar to Model 4003 Stainless, but has aluminum alloy frame, 10 shot mag., stainless steel slide, S&W tactical features, including equipment rail and Novak Lo-Mount Carry sights, traditional double action only, satin stainless finish, 28.5 oz. Mfg. 2000-2004.

	$775	$665	$510	$445	$400	$360	$330

Last MSR was $940.

MODEL 4004 - .40 S&W cal., similar to Model 4003, except has aluminum alloy frame with blue carbon steel slide. Mfg. 1991-92.

	$540	$460	$375	$325	$295	$280	$265

Last MSR was $643.

MODEL 4006 STAINLESS - .40 S&W cal., 3 1/2 (Shorty Forty) or 4 in. barrel, 10 (C/B 1994) or 11* shot mag., satin stainless finish, exposed hammer, Delrin one piece wraparound grips, 3-dot sights, 38 1/2 oz. Mfg. 1990-99.

	$655	$545	$400

Last MSR was $791.

Add $31 for adj. rear sight.
Add $115 for fixed Tritium night sights (new 1992).
The bobbed hammer option on this model was disc. in 1991.

* *Model 4006TSW* - similar to Model 4006 Stainless, but has aluminum alloy frame and stainless steel slide, S&W tactical features, including equipment rail, traditional double action only, 37.8 oz. Mfg. 2000-2004.

	$785	$665	$510	$465	$410	$365	$330

Last MSR was $963.

Add $38 if w/o Novak Low Carry (NLC) mount sights.
Add $133 for night sights (disc.).

GRADING - PPGS™	100%	98%	95%	90%	80%	70%	60%

MODEL 4013 COMPACT STAINLESS - .40 S&W cal., semi-auto, standard double action, 3 1/2 in. barrel, 8 shot mag., fixed sights, ambidextrous safety, alloy frame. Mfg. 1991-96.

		$595	$485	$385	$330	$295	$280	$265

Last MSR was $722.

MODEL 4013TSW TACTICAL - .40 S&W cal., semi-auto, standard double action, 3.5 in. barrel, 9 shot mag. with reversible mag. catch, aluminum alloy frame with stainless steel slide, satin stainless finish, black synthetic grips, fixed 3-dot Novak Lo-Mount Carry sights, ambidextrous safety, 26.8 oz. New 1997.

MSR $973		$790	$615	$440

MODEL 4014 COMPACT - similar to Model 4013, except is steel with blue finish. Mfg. 1991-93.

		$510	$425	$375	$330	$300	$275	$250

Last MSR was $635.

MODEL 4026 STAINLESS - .40 S&W cal., traditional double action with frame mounted decocking lever, 10 (C/B 1994) or 11* shot mag., fixed sights, curved backstrap, 36 oz. Mfg. 1991-93.

		$620	$520	$400

Last MSR was $731.

MODEL 4040 PD - .40 S&W cal., compact frame using Scandium, 3.5 in. barrel, Hogue rubber grips, Novak Lo-Mount Carry 3-dot sights, matte black finish, 25.6 oz. New 2003.

MSR $840		$670	$510	$345

MODEL 4043 STAINLESS - .40 S&W cal., double action only, aluminum alloy frame with stainless steel slide, 4 in. barrel, 10 (C/B 1994) or 11* shot mag., one piece Xenoy wraparound grips, straight backstrap, white-dot fixed sights, 30 oz. Mfg. 1991-99.

		$635	$510	$390

Last MSR was $772.

✴ *Model 4043TSW* - double action only, similar to Model 4043 Stainless, but has S&W tactical features, including equipment rail, 28 1/2 oz. Mfg. 2000-2002.

		$740	$640	$495	$445	$400	$360	$330

Last MSR was $886.

MODEL 4044 - .40 S&W cal., similar to Model 4043, except has carbon steel slide. Mfg. 1991-92.

		$540	$460	$375	$325	$295	$280	$265

Last MSR was $643.

MODEL 4046 STAINLESS - similar to Model 4006 Stainless, except is double action only, 4 in. barrel only. Mfg. 1991-99.

		$655	$540	$400

Last MSR was $791.

Add $115 for Tritium night sights (new 1992).

✴ *Model 4046TSW* - double action only, similar to Model 4046 Stainless, but has S&W tactical features, including equipment rail, 37.8 oz. Mfg. 2000-2002.

		$755	$655	$500	$455	$400	$360	$330

Last MSR was $907.

Add $133 for night sights.

MODEL 4053 COMPACT STAINLESS - double action only variation of the Model 4013. Mfg. 1991-97.

		$600	$490	$380

Last MSR was $734.

MODEL 4053TSW (TACTICAL) - .40 S&W cal., double action only, 3 1/2 in. barrel, 9 shot mag. with reversible mag. catch, alloy frame with stainless steel slide, satin stainless finish, black synthetic grips, fixed sights, ambidextrous safety, 26.8 oz. Mfg. 1997-2002.

$730 $580 $425

Last MSR was $886.

MODEL 4054 - double action only variation of the Model 4014. Mfg. 1991-92.

$510 $425 $375

Last MSR was $629.

MODEL 4056TSW (TACTICAL) - .40 S&W cal., double action only, 3 1/2 in. barrel, 9 shot mag. with reversible mag. catch, alloy frame with stainless steel slide, satin stainless finish, black synthetic grips, fixed sights, ambidextrous safety, 37.5 oz Mfg. 1997-2000.

$700 $560 $415

Last MSR was $844.

MODEL 4505 - .45 ACP cal., carbon steel variation of the Model 4506, fixed or adj. rear sight. 1,200 mfg. 1991 only.

$575 $500 $450 $400 $350 $300 $265

Last MSR was $660.

Add $27 for adj. rear sight.

MODEL 4506 STAINLESS - .45 ACP cal., 5 in. barrel, 8 shot mag., combat trigger-guard, exposed hammer, fixed or adj. rear sight, straight backstrap (curved is optional), Delrin one-piece grips, 40.5 oz. Mfg. 1990-99.

$680 $550 $410

Last MSR was $822.

Add $33 for adj. rear sight.

Approx. 100 Model 4506s left the factory mismarked Model 645 on the frame. In NIB condition they are worth $700.

MODEL 4513TSW - 45 ACP cal., traditional double action, compact frame, 3 3/4 in. barrel, 7 shot mag., 3-dot Novak Lo-Mount Carry sights, stainless steel slide, aluminum alloy frame, satin stainless finish, 28.6 oz. Mfg. 1998-2004.

$785 $610 $460

Last MSR was $980.

MODEL 4516 COMPACT STAINLESS - .45 ACP cal., hammerless compact variation of the Model 4506, 3 3/4 in. barrel, 7 shot mag., ambidextrous safety, fixed rear sight only, 34 oz. Mfg. 1990-97.

$655 $535 $400

Last MSR was $787.

Original model is marked 4516 while later mfg. changed slide legend to read 4516-1. Original mfg. is more collectible and slight premiums are being asked.

MODEL 4526 STAINLESS - similar to Model 4506 Stainless, except has frame mounted decocking lever. Mfg. 1990-91 only.

$635 $530 $400

Last MSR was $762.

MODEL 4536 STAINLESS - similar to Model 4516 Compact, except has frame mounted decocking lever only. Mfg. 1990-91 only.

$635 $530 $400

Last MSR was $762.

MODEL 4546 STAINLESS - similar to Model 4506 Stainless, except is double action only. Mfg. 1990-91 only.

$620 $520 $400

Last MSR was $735.

GRADING - PPGS™	100%	98%	95%	90%	80%	70%	60%

MODEL 4553TSW - similar to Model 4513TSW, except is double action only. Mfg. 1998-2002.

     $755 $595 $450

Last MSR was $924.

MODEL 4556 STAINLESS - .45 ACP cal., features double action only, 3 3/4 in. barrel, 7 shot mag., fixed sights. Mfg. 1991 only.

     $620 $520 $400

Last MSR was $735.

MODEL 4563TSW - .45 ACP cal., traditional double action only, 4 1/4 in. barrel, 8 shot mag., aluminum alloy frame with stainless steel slide, satin stainless finish, includes S&W tactical features, including equipment rail and Novak 3-dot sights, synthetic black straight backstrap grips, 30.6 oz. Mfg. 2000-2004.

     $785 $615 $455

Last MSR was $977.

MODEL 4566 STAINLESS - .45 ACP cal., traditional double action with ambidextrous safety, 4 1/4 in. barrel, 8 shot mag. Mfg. 1990-99.

     $680 $550 $410

Last MSR was $822.

   ✳ *Model 4566TSW* - similar to Model 4566, except has ambidextrous safety, 39.1 oz. Disc. 2004.

     $800 $620 $455

Last MSR was $1,000.

MODEL 4567-NS STAINLESS - similar to Model 4566 Stainless, except has Tritium night sights, stainless steel frame and carbon steel slide. 2,500 mfg. in 1991 only.

     $620 $520 $400

Last MSR was $735.

MODEL 4576 STAINLESS - .45 ACP cal., features 4 1/4 in. barrel, frame mounted decocking lever, fixed sights. Mfg. 1990-92.

     $635 $535 $410

Last MSR was $762.

MODEL 4583TSW - similar to Model 4563TSW, except is double action only, 30.6 oz. Mfg. 2000-2002.

     $750 $595 $445

Last MSR was $921.

MODEL 4586 STAINLESS - .45 ACP cal., 4 1/4 in. barrel, double action only, 8 shot mag. Mfg. 1990-99.

     $680 $550 $410

Last MSR was $822.

   ✳ *Model 4586TSW* - similar to Model 4566TSW, except is double action only, 39.1 oz. Mfg. 2000-2002.

     $760 $600 $445

Last MSR was $942.

MODEL 5903 - 9mm Para. cal., double action semi-auto, 4 in. barrel, stainless steel slide and alloy frame, exposed hammer, 10 (C/B 1994) or 15* shot mag., adj. (disc. 1993) or fixed rear sight, ambidextrous safety. Mfg. 1990-97.

     $575 $470 $395 $365 $325 $300 $285

Last MSR was $701.

     Add $30 for adj. rear sight (disc).

GRADING - PPGS™	100%	98%	95%	90%	80%	70%	60%

✳ *Model 5903TSW* - 9mm Para. cal., traditional double action, aluminum alloy frame with stainless slide, satin stainless finish, includes S&W tactical features, such as equipment rail and Novak Lo-Mount Carry sights, black synthetic grips with curved backstrap, 28.9 oz. Mfg. 2000-2004.

	$725	$580	$430	$385	$330	$275	$250

Last MSR was $892.

MODEL 5904 - similar to Model 5903, except has steel slide and blue finish, 26 1/2 oz. Mfg. 1989-98.

	$535	$445	$360	$330	$300	$280	$265

Last MSR was $663.

Add $30 for adj. rear sight (disc. 1993).

MODEL 5905 - 9mm Para. cal., similar to Model 5904, except has carbon steel frame and slide. Approx. 5,000 mfg. 1990-91 only.

	$650	$575	$500	$440	$375	$335	$300

MODEL 5906 STAINLESS - stainless steel variation of the Model 5904, 37 1/2 oz. Mfg. 1989-99.

	$615	$500	$400				

Last MSR was $751.

Add $37 for adj. rear sight.
Add $115 for Tritium night sights.

✳ *Model 5906TSW* - traditional double action only, similar to Model 5906 Stainless, but has S&W tactical features, including equipment rail, 38.3 oz. Mfg. 2000-2004.

	$755	$655	$510				

Last MSR was $915.

Add $44 if w/o NLC sight.
Add $132 for night sights (disc.).

MODEL 5924 - 9mm Para. cal., 4 in. barrel, features frame mounted decocking lever, 15 shot mag., 37 1/2 oz. Mfg. 1990-91 only.

	$515	$440	$365	$330	$300	$280	$265

Last MSR was $635.

MODEL 5926 STAINLESS - stainless variation of the Model 5924. Disc. 1992.

	$580	$480	$395				

Last MSR was $697.

MODEL 5943 STAINLESS - 9mm Para. cal., double action only, 4 in. barrel, aluminum alloy frame with stainless steel slide, straight backstrap, 15 shot mag. Mfg. 1990-91 only.

	$550	$465	$390				

Last MSR was $655.

✳ *Model 5943-SSV Stainless* - similar to Model 5943 Stainless, except has 3 1/2 in. barrel, Tritium night sights. Mfg. 1990-91 only.

	$580	$485	$395				

Last MSR was $690.

✳ *Model 5943TSW* - double action only, aluminum alloy frame with stainless steel slide, includes S&W tactical features, equipment rail, and Novak Lo-Mount Carry sights, 28.9 oz. Mfg. 2000-2002.

	$695	$560	$420	$375	$325	$280	$265

Last MSR was $844.

MODEL 5944 - similar to Model 5943 Stainless, except has blue finish slide. Mfg. 1990-91 only.

	$510	$435	$360	$330	$300	$280	$265

Last MSR was $610.

GRADING - PPGS™	100%	98%	95%	90%	80%	70%	60%

MODEL 5946 STAINLESS - 9mm Para. cal., double action only, one piece Xenoy wraparound grips, all stainless steel variation of the Model 5943, 39 1/2 oz. Mfg. 1990-99.

	$615	$500	$400				

Last MSR was $751.

✱ *Model 5946TSW* - 9mm Para. cal., double action only, includes S&W tactical features, equipment rail, and Novak Lo-Mount Carry sights, 38.3 oz. Mfg. 2000-2002.

	$710	$570	$425				

Last MSR was $863.

MODEL 6904 COMPACT - 9mm Para. cal., compact variation of the Model 5904, 3 1/2 in. barrel, 10 (C/ B 1994) or 12* shot finger extension mag., fixed rear sight, 26 1/2 oz. Mfg. 1989-97.

	$510	$410	$350	$325	$300	$280	$265

Last MSR was $625.

MODEL 6906 COMPACT STAINLESS - stainless steel variation of the Model 6904, 26 1/2 oz. Mfg. 1989-99.

	$585	$470	$380				

Last MSR was $720.

Add $116 for Tritium night sights (new 1992).

MODEL 6926 STAINLESS - 9mm Para. cal., 3 1/2 in. barrel, standard double action, features frame mounted decocking lever, aluminum alloy frame with stainless slide, 12 shot mag. Mfg. 1990-91 only.

	$550	$455	$375				

Last MSR was $663.

MODEL 6944 - 9mm Para., double action only, 3 1/2 in. barrel, 12 shot mag., aluminum alloy frame with blue steel slide. Mfg. 1990-91 only.

	$480	$400	$350	$325	$300	$280	$265

Last MSR was $578.

MODEL 6946 STAINLESS - similar to Model 6944, except has stainless steel slide, semi-bobbed hammer, 26 1/2 oz. Mfg. 1990-99.

	$585	$470	$375				

Last MSR was $720.

MODEL CS9 CHIEFS SPECIAL - 9mm Para. cal., compact design with traditional double action, hammerless, 3 in. barrel, 7 shot mag., alloy frame/stainless slide or stainless steel construction (disc. 2000), Hogue wraparound rubber grips, 3-dot Novak low mount sights, 20.8 oz. New 1999.

MSR $747	$580	$450	$375	$320	$270	$230	$195

MODEL CS40 CHIEFS SPECIAL - .40 S&W cal., similar to Model CS9, except has 3 1/4 in. barrel, 24.2 oz. Mfg. 1999-2002.

	$575	$435	$375	$315	$275	$230	$195

Last MSR was $717.

MODEL CS45 CHIEFS SPECIAL - .45 ACP cal., similar to Model CS40, except has 6 shot mag., 23.9 oz. New 1999.

MSR $787	$630	$470	$395	$330	$280	$230	$195

SIGMA MODEL SW9F SERIES - 9mm Para. cal., double action only, 4 1/2 in. barrel, fixed sights, polymer frame and steel slide, striker firing system, blue finish only, 10 (C/B 1994) or 17* shot mag., 26 oz. Mfg. 1994-96.

	$485	$390	$345	$320	$295	$280	$265

Last MSR was $593.

Add $104 for Tritium night sights.

GRADING - PPGS™	100%	98%	95%	90%	80%	70%	60%

✳ *Compact Sigma Model SW9C* - similar to Sigma Model SW9F, except has 4 in. barrel, 25 oz. Mfg. 1996-98.

	$450	$355	$325	$295	$280	$265	$240

Last MSR was $541.

✳ *Compact Sigma Model SW9M* - features 3 1/4 in. barrel, 7 shot mag., fixed channel rear sight, grips integral with frame, satin black finish, 18 oz. Mfg. 1996-98.

	$300	$270	$240	$220	$195	$175	$160

Last MSR was $366.

SIGMA MODEL SW9VE/GVE (SW9E/SW9P/SW9G/SW9V) - features 4 in. standard or ported (SW9P, mfg. 2001-2003) barrel, 10 or 16 (new late 2004) shot mag., 3-dot sighting system, grips integral with grey (disc. 2000), Nato green (SW9G, disc. 2003) or black polymer frame, black (SW9E, mfg. 1999-2002) or satin stainless steel slide, 24.7 oz. New 1997.

MSR $379	$300	$265	$225

Add $48 for SW9P or SW9G with night sights (disc. 2003).

Add $210 for Tritium night sights (disc. 2000).

The Enhanced Sigma Series Model SW9VE was introduced during 1999, after the SW9V was discontinued.

SIGMA MODEL SW40F SERIES - .40 S&W cal., double action only, 4 1/2 in. barrel, fixed sights, polymer frame, blue finish only, 10 (C/B 1994) or 15* shot mag., 26 oz. Mfg. 1994-98.

	$450	$355	$325	$295	$280	$265	$240

Last MSR was $541.

Add $104 for Tritium night sights (disc. 1997).

✳ *Compact Sigma Model SW40C* - similar to Sigma Model SW40F, except has 4 in. barrel, 26 oz. Mfg. 1996-98.

	$450	$355	$325	$295	$280	$265	$240

Last MSR was $541.

SIGMA MODEL SW40VE/SW40P/SW40G/SW40GVE (SW40E/SW40V) - features 4 in. standard or ported (SW40P, new 2001) barrel, 10 or 14 (new mid-2004) shot mag., 3-dot sighting system, grips integral with grey (disc. 2000), Nato green (SW40G) or black polymer frame, black slide with melonite finish (SW40E, mfg. 1999-2002) or satin stainless steel slide, 24.4 oz. New 1997.

MSR $379	$300	$265	$225

Add $210 for Tritium night sights (disc.).

Add $145 for Model SW40P or SW40G (includes night sights).

The Enhanced Sigma Series Model SW40VE was introduced during 1999, after the SW40V was discontinued.

MODEL SW99 - 9mm Para., .40 S&W, or .45 ACP (new 2003) cal., traditional double action, 9 (.45 ACP cal.), 10 shot mag., similar to the Walther P99, black polymer frame with black stainless slide and barrel, 4, 4 1/8 (.40 S&W cal. only), or 4.25 (.45 ACP cal. only, new 2003) in. barrel, black finish, ambidextrous mag. release, frame equipment groove, interchangeable backstraps, decocking lever, cocking indicator, adj. 3-dot or night sights, 25.4 (9mm Para cal.) or 28.5 oz. Mfg. 2000-2004.

	$565	$485	$430	$380	$340	$300	$275

Last MSR was $667.

Add $123 for night sights.

Add $41 for .45 ACP cal. (new 2003).

✳ *SW99 Compact Model* - similar to SW99, except is compact version, not available in .45 ACP cal., 3.5 in. barrel, 8 (.40 S&W cal.) or 10 (9mm Para cal.) shot mag. with finger extension, approx. 23 oz. Mfg. 2003-2004.

	$565	$485	$430	$380	$340	$300	$275

Last MSR was $667.

GRADING - PPGS™	100%	98%	95%	90%	80%	70%	60%

SIGMA MODEL SW357 - .357 SIG cal., 4 in. barrel, 10 shot mag., black finish, stainless steel. Mfg. 1998 only.

	$375	**$325**	**$250**				

SIGMA MODEL SW380 - .380 ACP cal., double action only, 3 in. barrel, fixed sights, polymer frame and steel slide, striker firing system, blue finish only, 6 shot mag., shortened grip, 14 oz. Mfg. 1996-2000.

	$285	**$245**	**$210**	**$190**	**$180**	**$170**	**$160**

Last MSR was $358.

MODEL SW990L - 9mm Para., .40 S&W, or .45 ACP cal., DAO, 10 (all cals.), 12 (.40 S&W cal.) or 16 (9mm Para.) shot mag., similar to the Walther P99, black polymer frame with black stainless melonite slide and barrel, 4 (9mm Para. cal. only), 4 1/8 (.40 S&W cal. only), or 4.25 (.45 ACP cal. only) in. barrel, black finish. New 2005.

MSR $694	**$585**	**$500**	**$440**	**$400**	**$350**	**$300**	**$275**

Add $52 for .45 ACP cal.

✳ **SW990L Compact Model** - similar to SW990L, except is compact version with small polymer frame, not available in .45 ACP cal., 3.5 in. barrel, 8 (.40 S&W cal.) or 10 (9mm Para cal.) shot mag. with finger extension. New 2005.

MSR $694	**$585**	**$500**	**$440**	**$400**	**$350**	**$300**	**$275**

ENGRAVING OPTIONS FOR CURRENT PRODUCTION HANDGUNS

The prices listed are for original factory finished guns with no extra engraving. The listings below show most recent factory engraving costs. These prices should be added to the cost of each engraved production gun to determine the correct value.

CLASS "C" ENGRAVING - 1/3 METAL COVERAGE
Pistols - add $1,108.
For J Frame - add $876.
10 5/8 in. N Frame - add $1,343.
2-5 in. K, L, or N Frame - add $1,130.
6-8 3/8 in. K, L, or N Frame - add $1,285.

CLASS "B" ENGRAVING - 2/3 METAL COVERAGE
Pistols - add $1,448.
For J Frame - add $1,430.
10 5/8 in. N Frame - add $1,672.
2-5 in. K, L, or N Frame - add $1,477.
6-8 3/8 in. K, L, or N Frame - add $1,599.

CLASS "A" ENGRAVING - FULL COVERAGE
Pistols - add $1,761.
For J Frame - add $1,501.
10 5/8 in. N Frame - add $2,006.
2-5 in. K, L, or N Frame - add $1,814.
6-8 3/8 in. K, L, or N Frame - add $1,919.

SPECIAL ENGRAVING - Also available with custom artwork: inlays, seals, scenes, lettering - prices quoted on request. Please call 1-800-331-0852, ext. 2904 – a free color brochure on custom engraving services is available.

LASERSMITH ENGRAVING - laser etching was available 1989-90 only. This process involved a digitally-controlled laser producing a variety of designs, logos, commemorative messages, or autograph on the metal surface(s). Some of these designs were made exclusively for major firearms distributors. Others were custom designed for clubs or organizations. Retail prices started at just under $18 and went as high as $150+, depending on the amount and complexity of the laser etching. To date, premiums are not being paid for these "rarer" variations.

GRADING - PPGS™	100%	Issue Price	Qty. Made

S&W COMMEMORATIVES/SPECIAL EDITIONS

During the course of a year, I receive many phone calls and letters on special editions and limited editions that do not appear in this section. It should be noted that a commemorative issue is a gun that has been manufactured, marketed, and sold through the auspices of the specific trademark (in this case S&W). During the past several decades, hundreds of limited editions have been ordered through various police agencies, state highway patrol units, and other law enforcement organizations. Many of these variations do not have the special suffix serialization (and may not have had a retail price when issued). Since most of these special editions/commemoratives were made for a specific organization, regional demand has a lot to do with determining values (a Model 66 Montana HP Commemorative will not sell for a premium in Alabama). For this reason, most of these guns will not appear in this section and you should contact the factory to learn more about the provenance of these special editions. Remember - values on these models can vary A LOT from one region to another and an averaged "national" single price is almost impossible. While these guns do have special interest, they do not have the collectibility or desirability of many of the standard models listed.

The variations listed represent the only five factory S&W Commemoratives manufactured to date. Anything else will be a special or limited edition made for a organization, company, or special event.

MODEL 19 TEXAS RANGER - .357 Mag., with or without knife, approx. 8,000 with knife, approx. 2,000 without, cased. Mfg. 1973 only.

	$595	$250	10,000

✳ *Model 19 Texas Ranger Deluxe* - approx. 50 mfg. with a serial numbers divisible by 10, cased.

	N/A	N/A	50

125TH ANNIVERSARY COMMEMORATIVE - .45 LC cal., plain variation was called Model 25-3, 10,000 mfg. total in 1977, cased with nickel silver medallion, and Roy Jinks's book, "125th Anniversary of Smith & Wesson."

	$450	$350	10,000

✳ *125th Anniversary Commemorative Deluxe* - Model 25-4, approx. 50 mfg. with S&W prefix serial numbers divisible by 10, cased, sterling silver medallion, and a leatherbound "History of Smith & Wesson" book by Roy Jinks.

	N/A	N/A	50

MODEL 26-1 GEORGIA STATE PATROL COMMEMORATIVE - .45 ACP cal.

	$450	N/A	N/A

MODEL 29 ELMER KEITH COMMEMORATIVE - .44 Mag. cal., 4 in. barrel, standard and deluxe editions, approx. 2,500 total mfg.

	$850	N/A	2,500

50TH ANNIVERSARY OF THE .357 MAGNUM - Model 27, both standard and deluxe editions, 1987 mfg.

	$450	N/A	N/A

MODEL 544 TEXAS WAGON TRAIN COMMEMORATIVE - .44-40 WCF cal. only, 6 shot, 5 in. barrel, bright blue finish, adj. sights, 4,782 mfg. 1986 to commemorate the Texas Sesquicentennial (1836-1986). Special markings on frame and barrel, smooth Goncalo commemorative grips, ser. no. TWT0001-TWT7800 (estimated). Made 1986 only.

	$450	N/A	7,800

S&W PERFORMANCE CENTER HANDGUNS

The Performance Center (PC) of Smith & Wesson got its start in 1990 from the efforts of two Master Gunsmiths, Paul Liebenburg and John French. The Performance Center is today managed by Tom Kelly and has grown to about 26 employees, all of which are engaged in the handgun shooting sports, a condition of being in the Center. The Performance Center generally does not take production guns and improve them. These handguns are built from scratch. Using two CNC machines, the Performance Center turns out about 400+ guns a month. There is no inventory of PC products. They are pre-sold before they are made. Once a new design is made and prototyped, it is shown to distributors of speciality guns. The distributor is given an exclusive on a particular model and those handguns are sold through the distributor's network of retailers. Currently, the major distributors ordering PC products include: Lew Horton, RSR Group, Camfour, and Talo Dist. The Performance Center delivers limited production runs, unique design and special feature firearms, and also provides gunsmithing services to existing S&W standard products.

While we have tried to list all the Performance Center guns in this section, it is possible that you may find some models listed with their corresponding numbered model in the Semi-Auto Pistols and Numbered Model Revolvers section in this text. Models are listed in the general order of the model number upon which they are based, with descriptions of each gun. At the end of the model descriptions, you may find a collected listing of variations, changes, and/or product codes for PC guns based on a particular model. In the Serialization section in the back of this text, a listing of all Performance Center guns in order of Product Code number has been provided.

During the past 10 years, all PC guns have been marked with the Performance Center trademark on the frame. The product codes are only on the shipping container or box. The 170XXX Performance Center product code indicates a handgun that has been designed and made from scratch by the Performance Center, while the 178XXX code indicates an exisiting product/SKU that has been improved/changed.

Pricing of Performance Center Handguns

Whenever possible, original PC model MSRs have been provided. In some cases, the distributor never posted an MSR on a particular PC model. N/As designate that more research is under way to find out more about the original MSRs, if they exist, and will be included in future editions and our online services.

As a general rule, the easiest way to determine values for Performance Center handguns is to look at the current pricing of the models from which they are derived. In other words, on a PC Model 442 Ultralight, check the standard Model 442 pricing in this text, and use the MSR - 100% price range to establish a base price, assuming the condition is NIB. Depending on the desirability of the PC configuration, such as finishes, barrel lengths, styling, special orders/features (i.e., laser or hand engraving, precious metal inlays, ivory or exotic wood grips, etc.), special sights, and other production variances from the standard model, premiums may exist over the 100% or current MSR values listed for the standard model. If a particular PC model has an original MSR that's significantly higher than the standard model, the buyer and seller are going to have to interpolate a possible premium which both feel comfortable with.

It is important to note that PC models are essentially limited runs of custom guns, which sell out in a relatively short period of time, and only resurface sporadically in the secondary marketplace. Many can be found in NIB or Excellent condition. Also, dealer or retail pricing is very rarely published on these models, making values difficult to determine for the secondary marketplace.

PC gun values can form a bell curve, with the peak being around $1,000. Semi-auto pistols generally sell for more than revolvers. Elaborate engraving, custom shop options, and the desirability of the configuration make all the difference when determining the value of an S&W Performance Center handgun.

Heritage Series From Lew Horton & Performance Center Handguns

Beginning in 2001, Lew Horton Dist and the Performance Center manufactured a series of specials from Smith & Wesson called "The Heritage Series." These were produced over a period of 2 years which include case color Models (10 & 24) and other models no longer manufactured and were very popular over the last century. This series will include (but is not limited to) Models 10, 15, 17, 19, 24, 25, 29, the Model of 1917 in various finishes. Each will have a gold color antique style box unique to the Heritage series, with a picture of Horace Smith and Daniel Wesson on the top with blue metal corners and a modern end label. All guns were shipped with a fired case from the gun by ser. no. in a small sealed envelope signed by the shooter, along with a trigger lock or cable lock. Mfg. 2001-2003.

PERFORMANCE CENTER REVOLVER VARIATIONS

SCHOFIELD MODEL OF 2000 - .45 S&W (.45 Schofield) cal., 6 shot, 7 in. barrel, SA, this 3rd Model Schofield is a modern top break, features the design concepts of the original Model 3 Schofield and incorporates the technical and engineering advantages of the last 125 years, modern hammer block safety, case colored hammer, smooth case colored trigger, 1st edition latches, fixed notch rear and pinned half moon post front sights, walnut grips, carbon steel frame w/ polished blue finish, 40 oz., 12.5 in. overall, Serial prefix of "GWS" for "Col. George W. Schofield." Mfg. began in Jan., 2000.

Last MSR was $1,549.

Product Code: 170146.

✳ *Schofield Model of 2000 w/ Nickel Finish* - .45 S&W (.45 Schofield) cal., 7 in. barrel, nickel finish, "US" stamped on the butt with ser. no., black pinned round blade front sight with Mod 3 Schofield 1875" on the right side, case colored hammer, latch and trigger guard, shipped in the Heritage Series box. Mfg. began in Nov. 2001.

Last MSR was $1,520.

Product Code: 170209FC.

✳ *Schofield Model of 2000 Wells Fargo Editions* - .45 S&W (.45 Schofield) cal., 5 in. barrel, blue or nickel finish, black pinned round blade front sight, case colored hammer, latch and trigger guard, similar to other editions with "US" on butt with ser. no., marked ".45 S&W" on left side of barrel, and "Schofield Pat. Apr. 22d 1873" on right side, shipped in Heritage Series box. Mfg. beginning Nov. 2001.

Last MSR was $1,500.

Product Code: 170207FC (nickel), 170208FC (blue).

LEW HORTON MODEL 10 - .38 S&W Spl. cal., DA, case colored square butt frame and yoke, blue 4 1/4 in. tapered barrel, blue cylinder and thumb piece finish, brown laminated magna style wood grips with silver medallions, limited production from Lew Horton Dist. "Heritage Series," serial prefix of CRS0001-CRS0080, model stampings of 10-7 and 10-9 have been observed, 80 were scheduled for manufacture with a square butt frame and another 70 on a round butt frame with square butt grips, does not have Performance Center trademark, 1st shipments of square butt frames were in May 2001.

Last MSR was $790.

Product Code: 178006FC.

MODEL PC-13 - .357 Mag. cal., DA, 6 shot, 3 in. Magna ported barrel, fixed rear w/ ramp front sight, Eagle Secret Service boot or Uncle Mike's grips on a K-frame, matte blue finish with beveled cylinder latch, trigger, and charge holes, shrouded extractor rod, trigger has an overtravel stop, 400 mfg., distributed by Lew Horton during 1995.

Last MSR was $760.

Product Code: 170059 (eagle grips) or 170063 (Uncle Mike's grips).

MODEL 14 PPC - .38 Spl. cal., DA, 4 in. full lug barrel, precision crowned muzzle, custom duty action, polished forcing cone, shipped to a law enforcement distributor in Mississippi for the National Police Shooting Championships, received by the MS Highway Patrol and L.A.P.D. pistol teams, accurized by the Performance Center, not for retail trade. Limited production of less than 100 units 1995-96.

Last MSR was N/A.

Product Code: 170154.

LEW HORTON HERITAGE SERIES MODEL 15-8 - .38 Spl. cal., special case colored frame and yoke, 4 in. blue barrel, blue cylinder, ramp on ramp base front sight with micrometer click rear sight, drilled and tapped, smooth trigger with checked hammer spur, round butt frame with wood laminated checkered grips, marked ".38 Smith & Wesson Special CTG" on right side of barrel and "Smith & Wesson" on the left, Performance Center logo under the thumbpiece, ser. no. prefix CSC0164 (example), shipped in a Heritage Series box with metal corners. Mfg. Aug., 2001.

Last MSR was $922.

Product Code: 17009FC.

LEW HORTON HERITAGE SERIES MODEL 15-8 - .38 Spl. cal., similar to previous model, except has bright nickel finish, wood laminate grips on round butt 3 screw frame, ser. prefix NSC0170 (example). Mfg. Sept. 2001.

Last MSR was $922.

Product Code: 178008FC.

LEW HORTON HERITAGE SERIES MCGIVERN MODEL 15-9 - .38 S&W Spl. cal., 6 in. barrel, new Model 15-9 frame with integral frame lug, commemorates Ed McGivern's world speed records in 1934, commemorative plate details McGivern's records of 5 shots in 2/5 of a second and 5 shots in 9/20 of a second at the Armory in Lewiston, MT, 6 shot with Patridge front sight and McGivern gold bead, micrometer click rear sight, round butt frame, period Altamont fancy checkered service grips, color case hardened, nickel, or blue finish, McGivern speed record sideplate attached just like on McGivern's original gun, shipped in Heritage Series box. Mfg. 2001.

Last MSR was $1,059.

Product Code: 170217FC (nickel), 170216FC (case colored), or 170199FC (blue).

MODEL 17-8 KT22 - .22 LR cal., DA, 6 shot, all blue finish or case colored frame with blue barrel and cylinder, counter bored cylinder with a nominal length of 1.62 in., round butt frame built on new K-frame (-8) with CNC machining, built-in frame lug, floating firing pin, drilled and taped, Non-Magna Wood grips with the Diamond insert around the screw with S&W medallions held in place with RTV, Patridge front sight on a pinned raised boss with an adjustable rear sight on a round barrel, smooth trigger with a pinned stop, checked hammer, frame is fitted with a standard non-MIM thumbpiece and 4 screw sideplate, blue finish, serial numbers w/ LRM prefix on the butt and in two places on the frame under the grips, Performance Center logo under the thumbpiece, supplied with fired case serial numbered to the frame in a small manila envelope, shipped in "Heritage Series" box. Distributed by Lew Horton, 2003.

Last MSR was $1,040.

Product Code: 170198FC (blue) or 170212FC (case colored).

MODEL 19 PERFORMANCE CENTER K COMP - .38 Spl./.357 Mag. cal., DA, blue matte finish, Target K-frame w/ round butt, 6 shot fluted cylinder with counterbores, 3 in. full lug ported barrel, blue matte finish, smooth combat trigger, set back tritium night rear sight on post, black blade adjustable front sight, contoured thumbpiece, rubber combat grips, 36 oz. Mfg. 1994 and 2000.

Last MSR was $800.

Product Code: 170025 (1994 mfg.) and 170163 (2000 mfg.).

LEW HORTON HERITAGE SERIES MODEL 24-5 - 44 Spl. cal., case colored frame, blue 6 1/2 in. barrel, blue cylinder, 4 screw sideplate, round butt frame, ball detent lockup at yoke, traditional thumpiece, diamond checkered walnut grips with S&W monogram, PC trademark under thumbpiece, ser. prefix "CSH". 150 mfg. May 2001.

Last MSR was $1,110.

Product Code: 170185FC.

✱ *Lew Horton Heritage Series Model 24-5* - similar to previous model except has all blue finish, ser. prefix of BCBxx66. Mfg. Sept. 2001.

Last MSR was $1,050.

Product Code: 170189FC.

MODEL 25-10 "HAND EJECTOR" 2001 - .45 LC cal., 6 in. tapered barrel with shrouded extractor, pinned gold bead Patridge front sight with black blade micrometer click rear sight, 1955 Hand Ejector features built on the most modern N-frame design, yoke has a ball detent front lockup with the normal extractor rod lock, sideplate is made with 4 screws, traditional thumbpiece opening, cylinder modified with chambered charge holes, wood grips with S&W medallions, bright blue finish, supplied with

Certificate signed by the Performance Center manager, shipped with aluminum PC locking gun case, 42 oz., approx. 150 mfg. Distributed by Sports South, Inc. 2001.

Last MSR was N/A.

Product Code: 170179FC.

MODEL 25-11 - 45 LC cal., 6 1/2 in. blue barrel, case colored frame, adj. rear sight, 6 shot fluted cylinder, 4 screw frame stamped Model 25-11, ser. prefix "GBP", marked "45 Colt CTG" on right side of barrel, shipped in Heritage Series gold box. 150 mfg. July 2001.

Last MSR was $1,150.

Product Code: 170186FC.

MODEL 25-11 - 45 LC cal., 6 1/2 in. barrel, all blue finish, adj. rear sight, 6 shot fluted cylinder, 4 screw frame stamped Model 25-11, ser. prefix "BAK", marked "45 Colt CTG" on right side of barrel, shipped in Heritage Series gold box. Mfg. July 2001.

Last MSR was $1,150.

Product Code: 170196FC.

LEW HORTON HERITAGE SERIES MODEL OF 1917 - 45 ACP cal., 5 1/2 in. barrel, blue finish, fixed rear sight, lanyard ring and half moon clips, 4 screw frame, marked Model 25-12, 6 shot fluted cylinder, marked ".45 ACP" on right side of barrel and "S&W D.A. 45" on left, PC logo under thumbpiece, ser. no. prefix "NCS00", shipped in Heritage Series gold box. 150 mfg. Aug. 2001.

Last MSR was $1,050.

Product Code: 170197FC.

✳ *Lew Horton Heritage Series Model of 1917* - similar to Lew Horton Heritage Series Model of 1917, except has case colored finish. 150 mfg. Sept., 2001.

Last MSR was $1,050.

Product Code: 170211FC.

✳ *Lew Horton Heritage Series Military Model of 1917* - similar to Lew Horton Heritage Series Model of 1917, except has dull military-style finish.

Last MSR was $1,050.

Product Code: 170218FC.

MODEL 27-7 - .357 Mag. cal., 8 shot, 100 with 4 in. barrel with black ramp front sight, 100 with 6 1/2 in. barrel with black Patridge front sight, Magna combat grips, 42-45 oz. Distributed by Bangers.

Last MSR was N/A.

Product Code: 170166 (4 in.) or 170167 (6 1/2 in.).

"CLASSIC SERIES" MODEL 27 - .357 Mag. cal., the last 6 shot Model 27s were mfg. with frame and barrels from 50th Anniversary Commemoratives with recessed cylinder from "outnumbered," "AVU" ser. prefix. 14 were mfg. and sold through Lew Horton in June 1999.

Last MSR was N/A.

Product Code: 170151.

MODEL 29-9 HERITAGE SERIES - .44 Mag. cal., 6 1/2 in. barrel, blue finish, adj. rear sight, 6 shot fluted cylinder, 4 screw frame stamped "Model 29-9", extractor shroud, PC logo under thumbpiece, target grips, shipped in Heritage Series gold box. Mfg. 2002.

Last MSR was $1,045.

Product Code: 170213FC.

✳ *Lew Horton Heritage Series Model 29-9* - similar to Model 29-9 Heritage Series, except has nickel finish, serial prefix is BBR. Mfg. 2002.

Last MSR was $1,045.

Product Code: 170214FC.

MODEL 41 - "Classic 41," approx. 10 mfg.

Last MSR was N/A.

Product Code: 170108.

GRADING - PPGS™	100%	98%	95%	90%	80%	70%	60%

MODEL 60 ET COMP - .38 Spl.+P cal., 3 in. ported full lug barrel, dovetail front and adj. rear sight, round butt frame, contoured thumbpiece, rosewood laminate or pearl inlaid synthetic grips, blue hard case, approx. 300 mfg. Distributed by Lew Horton, 1993.

Last MSR was $795.

Product Code: 170029.

MODEL 66 F COMP - .357 Mag. cal., 3 in. full lug barrel w/ compensator, dovetailed tritium front night sight, tuned action, round butt w/ rubber grips, counterbored cylinder, contoured cylinder latch, "LHF" serial number prefix, approx. 300 mfg. Distributed by Lew Horton, 1993.

Last MSR was N/A.

Product Code: 170024.

MODEL 66 THE SUPER K - .357 Mag. cal., 3 in. specially contoured barrel with 2 port magna porting, white synthetic grip with S&W medallions, Performance Center Tuned action and overtravel trigger stop. Distributed by Lew Horton, 1997.

Last MSR was N/A.

Product Code: 170090.

MODEL 66 F-COMP - .357 Mag. cal., 3 in. full lug ported barrel with drift adj. dovetailed ramp front sight and micrometer click rear sight, 6 shot cylinder with chambered charge holes, front sight set behind ported barrel, glass bead finish, shipped with walnut combat grips and an additional Hogue Bantam monogrip, released during 2003 at the SHOT Show.

Last MSR was $798.

Product Code: 170024FC.

MODEL 327 Sc - .357 Mag., 8 shot, 2 in. barrel with titanium shroud, black finish with natural grey titanium cylinder, Scandium alloy N-frame, teardrop color case hammer and trigger with over travel stop, Ahrens cocobolo round butt grips with finger grooves, small lanyard pin, PC logo under thumbpiece, fixed sights, shipped with black PC marked gun rug made by Allen with internal pouch, 2 full moon clips, special ser. no. range, released during 2004 at the SHOT Show.

MSR $1,226	$955	$665	$560	$480	$425	$375	$335

Product Code: 170245FC (black) or 170251FC (clear).

MODEL 329-1 AIRLITE PD - .44 Mag. cal. DA, round butt Scandium alloy N-frame, 6 shot titanium cylinder, painted red ramp front sight, serrated and ported 3 in. barrel, adj. black blade front sight, Ahrends cocobolo finger groove wood grips, includes extra Hogue rubber grip, checked teardrop hammer and smooth combat trigger, marked ".44 MAGNUM" on left side of barrel and "PERFORMANCE CENTER" on right, clear or black matte finish, internal key lock, PC logo under thumbpiece, shipped with PC aluminum double lock carry case. Mfg. 2003.

Last MSR was $1,100.

Product Code: 170233 (clear) or 170232FC (black).
All Model 329-1 Airlites were recalled by S&W during July, 2004.

MODEL 442 THE ULTRALIGHT - .38 S&W Spl. cal., similar to Model 442 Centennial, it has been reported (and photographed) that a few (approx. 10) with an alloy cylinder were made for the U.S. Secret Service as prototypes but were never sold or released to the general public. These prototypes have no markings on the sideplate, and have a matte blue finish. One observed Ser. no. prefix is "BSS". Both fluted cylinders and non-fluted cylinders are reported to have been mfg. These cylinders passed the 5000 round test with no failures, using +P ammo. Built on the original "J" frame. This variation is actually lighter than the Ti series because of the all alloy cylinder. Mfg. 1997.

Last MSR was N/A.

This model was never offered for commercial sale.
Product Code: 170023.

GRADING - PPGS™	100%	98%	95%	90%	80%	70%	60%

MODEL 460 AIRWEIGHT - .38 S&W Spl. cal., DA only, alloy J-frame w/ round butt, 5-shot fluted steel cylinder, fully concealed hammer, 2 in. steel Magna Ported barrel, fixed sight, blue matte finish, Eagle Secret Service grips, smooth trigger, Performance Center logo laser etched on the sideplate, does not have the standard S&W trademark on the frame. Shipped in a Performance Center blue plastic case, ser. no. prefix "SDE", 15.8 oz. approx. 450 mfg. 1994.

Last MSR was $595.

Product Code: 170055.

MODEL 500 MAGNUM HUNTER (NEW 2004) - .500 S&W Magnum cal., X-frame, 5 shot, fluted cylinder, 6 (Compensated Hunter, mfg. 2004 only) or 10.5 in. tapered lug barrel, with recoil compensator and integral Weaver base, Houge mono-grip, stainless steel, glass bead finish with flas chromed hammer and trigger, adj. white outline rear sight, includes black nylon sling, swivels, and soft case, 82 oz.

MSR $1,391   **$1,125**   **$975**   **$850**

Product Code: 170231FC (10 1/2 in.) or 170246FC (6 1/2 in.).

MODEL 586 L COMP - .357 Mag. cal., 3 in. full lug ported barrel with Tritum Dot front and Micrometer click rear sight, Altamont Rosewood grips, 7 shot cylinder recessed for moon clips, black or blue finish, shipped with locking aluminum case & Master Gun Lock, first blue finish revolver in 7 shot offered by S&W, 37.5 oz. Distributed by Camfour, 2000 and 2004.

Last MSR was N/A.

Product Code: 170170 (2000 mfg.) or 170248FC (2004 mfg.).

MODEL 610 - 10mm cal., 6 1/2 in. barrel.

Last MSR was N/A.

Product Code: 170109.

MODEL 617 - .22 LR cal., new profile barrel for export, only 327 mfg. 1995 and 1999.

Last MSR was N/A.

Product Code: 170122 or 170066 (235 were mfg. in 1995 for export only).

MODEL 625-6 FLUTED HUNTER - .45 Colt cal., 6 in. ported barrel, chambered cylinder, Red Ramp dovetailed front sight, round butt frame, serrated backstrap & forestrap, will accept Weaver style scope mount on the integral rail system, removal of weights and spacers internal to the barrel with a small allen wrench, ser. no. prefix "LHD", most were sent to Germany with about 50 remaining in the U.S. Distributed by Lew Horton, 1997.

Last MSR was N/A.

Product Code: 170081.

MODEL 625-6 HUNTER - .45 Colt cal., 6 in. ported slabside barrel, non-fluted cylinder, marked "45 Colt CTG". Mfg. 1997.

Last MSR was N/A.

Product Code: 170085.

MODEL 625-6 "V COMP" - .45 ACP cal., 4 in. slabside barrel with a removable compensator or a replacement muzzle to protect the crown, 6 shot non-fluted cylinder has a ball-detent lockup in the yoke, Millett dovetailed red ramp front and micrometer click rear sight, Hogue Combat wood grips, semi-target hammer, smooth combat trigger w/ overtravel stop, shipped w/ double combo lock aluminum carry case, 43 oz. Distributed by RSR, 1999.

Last MSR was $925.

Product Code: 170136.

MODEL 625-7 LIGHT HUNTER - .45 Colt cal., 6 in. ported match grade barrel with integral Weaver style base rail, ball detent lockup, fluted cylinder w/ chambered charge holes, Millet dovetail front sight, forged and flash chromed trigger and hammer, satin stainless finish, Hogue wood combat grips, shipped with aluminum PC carry case, 43 oz. Distributed by RSR, 1999.

Last MSR was N/A.

Product Code: 170132.

MODEL 625-5 JERRY MICULEK DESIGN -.45 ACP cal., 5 1/4 in. barrel, Patridge front w/ gold bead and adj. black blade rear sight, reduced cylinder freebore, 6 shot fluted cylinder w/ chambered charge holes, deep cut broached rifling, hand honed bore, satin stainless finish, "Jerry Miculek" Hogue Laminate combat grips, lockable aluminum case, 42 oz. Distributed by Camfour, 2001.

Last MSR was $899.

Product Code: 170176.

MODEL 625-10 -.45 ACP cal., 6 shot, 2 in. barrel, Scandium N-frame, fixed V-notch rear sight with serrated and dovetailed ramp front sight, eagle wood and Hogue rubber grips, stainless steel cylinder, glass bead finish, barrel marked ".45 ACP", includes PC locking case, 24 oz. Distributed by Lew Horton Sept., 2003.

Last MSR was $925.

Product Code: 170266FC (clear) or 170252FC (black).

MODEL 627-2 STAINLESS - .357 Mag./.38 Spl. cal., DA, stainless steel version of the Model 27, 8 shot cylinder, 5 in. tapered barrel, interchangeable front sights, drilled & tapped for scope mount, chambered charge holes, flash chrome teardrop hammer, radiused smooth combat trigger with overtravel stop pin, Hogue hardwood combat grips, new thumbpiece, engraved ".357 Magnum 8 More" on barrel, floating firing pin, 44 oz. Distributed by Lew Horton, 1997-98.

Last MSR was $1,000.

Product Code: 170089.

MODEL 627 1998 LEW HORTON SPECIAL "HUNTER STYLE" - .357 Mag. cal., 6 1/2 in. magna ported slabside barrel, fluted cylinder w/ beveled edges, contoured thumb latch, integral scope mount and weight system, adj. sights, rosewood grips.

Last MSR was $1,025.

Product Code: 170102.

MODEL 627PC 1998 LEW HORTON SPECIAL - .357 Mag. cal., 8 shot, 6 in. barrel. ser. no. prefix "LHV", engraved ".357 Magnum 8 times" with floating firing pin.

Last MSR was N/A.

MODEL 627-2 1998 LEW HORTON SPECIAL - .357 Mag. cal., 8 shot cylinder, 6 1/2 in. tapered barrel, interchangeable front sights, flash chrome teardrop hammer, radiused smooth combat trigger with overtravel stop pin.

Last MSR was $1,025.

MODEL 627-3 "V-COMP JERRY MICULEK SPECIAL" - 8 shot cylinder, 5 in. barrel, removable compensator, removable/interchangeable cap to protect the rifling, smooth combat trigger w/ overtravel stop pin, TH, drift adj. red ramp front sight, micrometer click rear sight. "Jerry Miculek" design Hogue wooden grips, locking aluminum case, 47 oz. Distributed by RSR, 2000.

Last MSR was N/A.

On July 24th 1999 Jerry Miculek set a world record for firing an S&W 8 shot revolver. The results were: 8 Shots on 1 target in 1.00 seconds and 8 Shots on 2 targets in 1.06 seconds. Both records set using a Model 627 from the Performance Center. Product Code: 170142.

MODEL 627-3 HUNTER - .357 Mag. cal., 8 shot unfluted cylinder, ball detent lockup, 2 5/8 in. barrel, full length extractor, Millett red ramp drift adj. front sight, micrometer click white outline rear sight, Eagle wood boot grips, flash chromed custom teardrop hammer, smooth combat trigger, glass bead stainless steel finish, aluminum double lock carry case, 37.6 oz., 450 mfg. Distributed by Lew Horton, 1999-2000.

Last MSR was $1,025.

Product Code: 170095.

MODEL 627-PC - .357 Mag. cal., 8 shot, 2 5/8 in. barrel, Millet red ramp drift adj. front sight with micrometer click white outline rear sight, Eagle wood boot grips, flash chromed custom teardrop hammer, smooth combat trigger, full length extractor, stainless steel with glass bead finish, shipped with aluminum double lock carrying case, 37.6 oz. Approx. 302 mfg. 1999-2000.

Last MSR was $1,025.

Product Code: 170133.

GRADING - PPGS™	100%	98%	95%	90%	80%	70%	60%

MODEL 627-4 - .38 Super cal., 8 shot, black non-fluted cylinder, 5 1/2 in. barrel, angled cut removable compensator and cap, red/white/blue Jerry Miculek designed grip, Patridge front sight with adj. black outline rear sight, chrome teardrop hammer and chrome trigger with overtravel stop, stainless steel, glass bead finish, drilled and tapped. Mfg. for Banger's 2002.

Last MSR was N/A.

Product Code: 170205.

MODEL 627-5 - .357 Mag. cal., 5 in. tapered and countoured barrel with fluted cylinder, 8 shot, floating firing pin, interchangeable front sight with black blade rear sight, Hogue rubber grips, trigger stop, internal lock system, new frame design, shipped with black PC marked gun rug, released during 2003.

MSR $1,161	$920	$625	$530	$480	$430	$375	$335

Product Code: 170210.

✳ *Model 627-5* - .357 Mag. cal., 8 shot, 5 in. full lug barrel, removable cap and crown, wood grips with extra Hogue grip, fluted cylinder, black drift adj. front sight, black rear sight, marked ".357 Magnum-V8" on left side of barrel and "Performance Center" on right, floating firing pin, internal lock system, new frame design, ser. no. prefix "VCM". Limited mfg. 2004.

	$875	$600	$525	$475	$425	$375	$335

Last MSR was $1,106.

Product Code: 170237FC.

MODEL 629-3: CARRY COMP STAINLESS - .44 Mag. cal., 3 in. barrel, integral compensator, dovetailed interchangeable red ramp front sight, fixed rear sight, beveled cylinder, semi-target hammer, smooth combat trigger, N-frame, round butt, Goncalo Alves grips w/ finger grooves, contoured thumbpiece, 42 oz. Distributed by Lew Horton, 1992.

Last MSR was $1,000.

Product Code: 170012.

MODEL 629-3 CLASSIC HUNTER I - .44 Mag. cal., fluted cyl. Distributed by Lew Horton, 1992.

Last MSR was $1,234.

Product Code: 170008.

MODEL 629-3: THE CLASSIC HUNTER II - .44 Mag. cal., unfluted cyl., 6 in. slabside barrel, approx. 600 mfg. Distributed by Lew Horton, 1992.

Last MSR was $1,234.

Product Code: 170197.

MODEL 629-3: CARRY COMP II - .44 Mag. cal., 3 in. barrel, adj. rear sight, compensator system, unfluted Classic Hunter style cylinder, hard case, approx. 100 mfg. Distributed by Lew Horton, 1993.

Last MSR was $1,000.

Product code: 170026.

MODEL 629-4: .44 MAGNUM LIGHT HUNTER - .44 Mag. cal., 6 in. Magna ported slabside barrel, non-fluted cylinder, round butt frame, scope broaching, recessed crown, radiused smooth trigger w/ stop, serial number range RSR3500-RSR4000, 500 mfg. Distributed by RSR.

Last MSR was N/A.

May 1995. Two additional variations also made for Lew Horton Dist. Product Code: 170056.

MODEL 629-4: THE CLASSIC HUNTER III - .44 Mag. cal., 6 in. slab side barrel, integral variable weight system, Weaver scope mount rail system, Magna ported, non fluted chambered cylinder, red ramp dovetail front sight, ser. no. prefix "LHK". Distributed by Lew Horton, 1996.

Last MSR was $1,234.

Product Code: 170046.

MODEL 629 "THE AVENGER" - .44 Mag. cal., 3 in. Dual Magna-port barrel, unfluted cylinder, 26 Mfg.

Last MSR was N/A.

Product code: 170058.

MODEL 629 MAGNUM HUNTER PLUS - .44 Mag. cal., 7 1/2 in. slabside barrel, Magna ported, integral Weaver Scope Rail, unfluted cylinder. Distributed by RSR, 1996.

Last MSR was N/A.

Product Code: 170065.

MODEL 629-4 TROPHY WHITE TAIL - .44 Mag. cal., 6 1/2 in. ported barrel, dove-tailed front sight, adj. rear sight, target hammer, smooth trigger with stop, chambered cylinder, contoured thumbpiece, Hogue Grips with S&W trademark, two deer scene laser etched on the sideplate, with "Trophy Whitetail" etched on the barrels right side, drilled and tapped for scope mount, Performance Center logo on the frame, ser. no. range is ZAN0001-ZAN0200. 200 mfg. Distributed by Zanders Sports, 1997.

Last MSR was N/A.

Product Code: 170050.

MODEL 629-4 "SCOPE ONLY" MASTER HUNTER - .44 Mag. cal., 7 1/2 in. barrel, non-fluted cylinder, drilled and tapped for scope mount only w/ rear cutout for a standard rear sight, smooth barrel without a rib, satin stainless finish, Performance Center logo, ser. no. prefix "MHS". Mfg. 1997.

Last MSR was N/A.

Product Code: 170087.

MODEL 629-4 "COMPED HUNTER" - .44 Mag. cal., 6 in. barrel, Weaver integral base, fully adj. micrometer click rear sight, dovetailed Millett red ramp front sight, removable 4 port compensator, w/ replacement muzzle, glass bead finish, stainless steel, N-frame, round butt, Altamont wood grips, unfluted cylinder with chambered charge holes, ball detent lock up, flash chromed and radiused hammer, smooth combat trigger with stop, "CMH" ser. no. prefix, 58.9 oz. Distributed by RSR, 1998.

Last MSR was $1,080.

Product Code: 170100.

MODEL 629-4 "3" CARRY COMP" - .44 Mag. cal., dovetailed front sight w/ bright red stripe, unfluted cylinder, Magna ported, w/ trigger stop. Mfg. 1998.

Last MSR was N/A.

MODEL 629-4 - .44 Mag. cal., 6 1/2 in. barrel, removable muzzle brake with replaceable end cap, rosewood grips. Distributed by Lew Horton, 1998.

Last MSR was N/A.

Product code: 170124.

MODEL 629-5 "V-COMP" - .44 Mag. cal., 4 in. slabside barrel with removable compensator, muzzle cap, non-fluted cylinder, ball-detent lockup in the yoke, flash chromed semi-target hammer, smooth combat trigger w/ overtravel stop, dovetail red ramp front sight, micrometer click rear sight, Hogue wood combat grips w/ S&W Monogram, aluminum carry case, 43 oz. Distributed by RSR in 1999.

Last MSR was N/A.

Product code: 170137.

MODEL 629-5 DEFENSIVE REVOLVER - .44 Mag. cal., 2 5/8 in. barrel, ball detent lockup system in the yoke, 6 shot non-fluted cylinder, flash chromed teardrop hammer and smooth combat trigger, Millett dovetailed red ramp front sight, micrometer click rear sight, Hogue wood combat grips, glass bead stainless steel finish, aluminum carry case with the Performance Center logo, 39.6 oz. Distributed by Lew Horton, 1999-2000.

Last MSR was $1,026.

Product code: 170135.

GRADING - PPGS™	100%	98%	95%	90%	80%	70%	60%

MODEL 629-5 "THE EXTREME HUNTER"

- .44 Mag./.44 S&W Special cal., 12 in. barrel, 6 shot fluted cylinder, Wilson rubber combat grips, round butt frame, Uncle Mike's swivels and sling, long under extension to support the long barrel and front swivel mount, dovetailed Patridge front sight, Wilson Silhouette rear sight, glass bead stainless steel finish, new design frame with floating firing pin and MIM hammer and trigger, Waller 21 in. gun rug, ser. no. prefix "AMH", 65 oz. Distributed by Lew Horton, 2000.

Last MSR was $1,201.

Product code: 170157.

MODEL 629-5 "STEALTH HUNTER"

- .44 Mag. cal., 7 1/2 in. Magna ported Hunter style barrel, 6 shot unfluted flat black cylinder with ball detent lockup and chambered charge holes, integral Weaver style rib and counterbored muzzle, adj. Millett red ramp drift front sight, white outline micrometer adj. rear sight, Hogue black rubber monogrip with the S&W trademark, black smooth trigger with a rubber stop, black tapered hammer spur, NATO green stainless steel frame and barrel, black contrasting screws, grip, cylinder, thumbpiece, hammer, and trigger, Performance Center aluminum case, ser. no. prefix "FBS", approx. 50 oz. Distributed by Camfour, 2000-2001.

Last MSR was $1,200.

Product code: 170171.

MODEL 629-5 "COMPENSATED HUNTER"

- .44 Mag. cal., 7 1/2 in. ported barrel, glass bead finish, stainless steel, fixed compensator, 6 shot fluted cylinder w/ chambered charge holes, ball detent lock-up, adj. front sight w/ orange ramp insert, adj. micrometer black blade rear sight, removable stainless steel scope mount, rosewood laminate grips, extra Hogue monogrip, round butt frame, lockable Performance Center aluminum case, 52.2 oz. Distributed by Talo, 2001.

Last MSR was $1,104.

Product code: 170181.

MODEL 629-5 "44 MAGNUM LIGHT HUNTER"

- .44 Mag. cal., all black Birdsong finish, barrel is cut for scope mount with weaver rail, unfluted cylinder, gold bead front sight, Hogue monogrip, ser. no. prefix "DEL". Mfg. 2002.

Last MSR was N/A.

Product code: 170194.

MODEL 629 LIGHT HUNTER (NEW 2003)

- .44 Mag. cal., 7.5 in. barrel with integral muzzle brake, stainless steel, tapered ejector rod housing, wood combat grips, includes scope rail, released during 2003.

MSR $1,189	$975	$850	$700	$600	$500	$425	$375

MODEL 629-5 HUNTER

- .44 Mag. cal., DA, 8 3/8 in. heavy barrel, satin stainless steel, 6 shot, tapered ejector rod housing, orange fiberoptic and front blade sights, adj. rear sight, Weaver style scope base, includes Hogue rubber and rosewood combat grips. New 2004.

MSR $1,059	$875	$775	$675	$575	$475	$425	$375

This model is available exclusively through Davidson's. Product code: 170234FC.

CARRY COMP MODEL 640

- .38 Spl.+P cal., 2 in. ported barrel, adj. front sight, fixed rear sight, radiused hammer and trigger, 150 mfg. w/ rosewood grips, 150 mfg. w/ Bader mother-of-pearl inlaid finger grips, blue plastic case w/ Performance Center logo, 23 oz. Distributed by Lew Horton. Mfg. 1993.

Last MSR was $750.

Product code: 170042.

THE PAXTON QUIGLEY MODEL 640 - 38 Spl. cal., 2 5/8 in. barrel, integral compensator, dovetailed adj. front sight, tuned by the S&W Performance Center, laminated wood grips w/ mother-of-pearl inlaid heart, Boyt tapestry case and letter of authenticity from Paxton Quigley, author of *Armed & Female*. Limited production of 250. Distributed by Lew Horton, 1994.

Last MSR was $725.

Product codes: 170014 (3 in.) or 170043 (2 in.).

MODEL 640 RSR SPECIAL - .357 Mag. cal., 2 1/8 in. Magna-Ported barrel, 5 shot non-fluted cylinder, glass bead stainless steel finish, concealed hammer, J-frame, round butt, Heritage Walnut Grips, chrome smooth combat trigger, pinned black ramp front sight, square notch rear sight, 25 oz. Mfg. 1996.

Last MSR was N/A.

Product code: 170073.

MODEL 640 LEW HORTON - .357 Mag. cal., 5 shot, 2 1/8 in. ported barrel, dovetail front sight with Tritium insert on black post, matte stainless finish, Performance Center Tuned Action, Pachmayr Decelerator grips, chrome smooth combat trigger. Mfg. 1996.

Last MSR was $839.

At least one Model 640 is known to have been chambered in .38 Super caliber for test purposes by the Performance Center. Product code: 170068.

MODEL 640 "LEW HORTON .357 MAGNUM" - .357 Mag. cal., 2 1/8 in. Quad Port barrel, glass bead finish. Mfg. 1999.

Last MSR was $851.

Product code: 170078.

MODEL 646 - .40 S&W cal., 4 in. ribbed slabside barrel, SA/DA, 6 shot fluted titanium cylinder, adj. Patridge front sight, micrometer adj. rear sight, drilled and tapped for scope mount, smooth combat trigger, round butt, L-target frame, "Performance Center" on the left side and "40 S&W" on the right side, frosted glass bead stainless finish, Performance Center trademark on the frame, Altamont wood combat grips, 2 sets of half moon clips and extraction tool, Performance Center aluminum case with Performance Center trademark, ser. no. prefix "RDA", 36 oz. Mfg. 2000.

Last MSR was $845.

Product code: 170165.

MODEL 647-1 VARMINTER - .17 HMR cal., stainless steel K-frame, 12 in. Walther barrel, Weaver scope rail, includes bipod adapter, black Patridge front sight with adj. black blade rear sight, glass bead satin stainless finish, wood target square grips, internal trigger lock system, black Allen soft zipper case, distributed by Camfour and Hill Country.

Last MSR was $1,200.

Product code: 170229FC.

MODEL 657 DEFENSIVE REVOLVER - .41 Mag. cal., 2 5/8 in. barrel, 6 shot non-fluted cylinder, ball detent lockup, full length extractor, round butt, N-frame, adj. Millett red ramp front sight, micrometer adj. white outline rear sight, flash chromed teardrop hammer, chromed trigger with travel overstop, Hogue combat grips, glass bead stainless steel finish, aluminum carry case, 39.6 oz. Distributed by Lew Horton, 1999.

Last MSR was $1,001.

Product code: 170134.

MODEL 657 HUNTER - .41 Mag. cal., 6 in. Magna-Ported barrel, integral weaver base, N-frame, round butt, 6 shot unfluted cylinder, ball detent lockup, adj. Millett red ramp front sight, adj. rear sight, 48 oz. Distributed by RSR, 1995-99.

Last MSR was N/A.

Product code: 170062.

MODEL 657-5 HUNTER - .41 Mag. cal., DA, 8 3/8 in. barrel, N-frame, round butt, satin stainless steel, glass bead finish, 6 shot, unfluted cylinder, tapered ejector rod housing, interchangeable black Patridge or fluorescent red fiberoptic front sight with black adj. rear sight, smooth trigger, checked teardrop hammer, internal key lock system, Hogue rubber monogrip and rosewood fingergroove grips. Mfg. 2003-2004.

Last MSR was N/A.

This model was available exclusively through Davidson's. Product code: 170235FC.

MODEL 681-4 LEW HORTON SPECIAL - .357 Mag. cal., 3 in. Quadra-port barrel, 7 shot chambered cylinder, trigger overtravel stop, fixed sight, ser. no. prefix "LHB", 300 mfg. Distributed by Lew Horton, 1996.

Last MSR was $700.

Product code: 170080.

MODEL 681-5 SPECIAL FOR CAMFOUR - .357 Mag. cal., 3 in. or 4 in. full lug barrel, 7 shot fluted cylinder, adj. black ramp front sight, Quad Porting, glass bead stainless steel finish, laminate checkered wood and Hogue Bantam Monogrip, 7 shot moon clips, chambered cylinder charge holes, Performance Center case. Distributed by Camfour, 2001.

Last MSR was N/A.

Product code: 170172 (4 in.) or 170178 (3 in.).

MODEL 686 MAG COMP - .357 Mag. cal., 3 in. barrel, integral compensator, adj. front red ramp sight, white outline rear sight, radiused full lug barrel, radiused hammer, radiused combat trigger w/ overtravel stop, Uncle Mike's grips, Performance Center logo, contoured thumbpiece, full-length extractor rod, 350 mfg. Distributed by Lew Horton, 1992.

Last MSR was $1,000.

Product code: 170010.

MODEL 686 CARRY COMP - .357 Mag. cal., 4 in. barrel, integral compensator, dovetailed front sight w/ interchangeable post or red ramp, white outline rear sight, Uncle Mike's grips. Distributed by Lew Horton.

Last MSR was $1,000.

Product code: 170016.

MODEL 686 PPC REVOLVER - .357 Mag. cal., 6 in. barrel, custom underlug, integral barrel port.

Last MSR was N/A.

MODEL 686 CARRY COMP - .357 Mag. cal., 6 in. barrel, integral port, replaceable front sight, Hogue grips, semi-target hammer, smooth combat trigger, full underlug contour.

Last MSR was $1,099.

Product code: 170009.

MODEL 686 COMPETITOR - .357 Mag. cal., 6 in. barrel, fluted cylinder w/ radiused charge holes, integral scope base, 6 ounce variable underweight, dovetailed front post, black blade rear sight, Hogue grips, semi-target hammer, smooth combat trigger, 52-58 oz. Distributed by Lew Horton.

Last MSR was $1,100.

Product code: 170015.

MODEL 686 ACTION REVOLVER - .357 Mag. cal., 6 in. match grade barrel, barrel compensator.

Last MSR was N/A.

MODEL 686 HUNTER - .357 Mag. cal., similar to the Model 686 Competitor, except wood grips. 200 mfg.

Last MSR was $1,153.

Product code: 170021.

MODEL 686 PLUS - .357 Mag. cal., 6 in. tapered barrel, 7 shot fluted cylinder, machined for full moon clips w/ chambered charge holes, L-frame drilled and tapped for scope mount, round butt, Altamont wood grips, flash chromed semi-target hammer and smooth combat trigger, gold bead Patridge front sight, micrometer adj. white outline rear sight, satin stainless steel finish, 44 oz. Distributed by Lew Horton, 1998.

Last MSR was $929.

Product code: 170103.

MODEL 686-4 WITH ADJUSTABLE SIGHTS - .357 Mag. cal., 2 1/2 in. barrel, Magna Port, 7 shot cylinder, wood grips. Mfg. 1998.

Last MSR was N/A.

Product code: 170077.

MODEL 686 - .38 Super cal., 4 in. tapered lug barrel, interchangeable red ramp front sight, adj. black rear sight, Ahrend's cocobolo finger groove grips, stainless steel, glass bead finish, 6 shot, unfluted cylinder, L-frame, internal key lock system, accepts full moon clips, includes PC aluminum carry case, 37 oz. Distributed by Banger's 2003.

Last MSR was N/A.

Product code: 170225.

MODEL 940 SPECIAL - .356 TSW cal., ported barrel, dovetail front sight, barrel markings are ".356 TSW" on the right and "Smith & Wesson" on the left side. S/N prefix "APC". Limited Production of 300. Distributed by Lew Horton, 1994.

Last MSR was $575.

Product code: 170047.

This model has also been referred to as the "Pocket Rocket."

MODEL 942 AIRWEIGHT 9MM CENTENNIAL - 9mm cal., 2 in. ported barrel, one was made as a prototype using a Model 642-1 alloy frame, stainless steel cylinder, S/N CAN1706. Built as a T&E prototype, it was shipped to Firearms Journalist Wiley Clapp in 1999 for test and evaluation.

Last MSR was N/A.

PERFORMANCE CENTER SEMI-AUTO PISTOL VARIATIONS

MODEL 845 BULLSEYE - .45 ACP cal., full target version of the Model 745, Bo-Mar low-profile sights, beavertail, checkered front strap, fitted barrel bushing, Hi-Impact plastic grips, 8-round magazine, extra recoil spring, S/N prefix "MPC" (1995) "SDN" (1998). Distributed by Lew Horton.

Last MSR was $1,496.

Product code: 170064.

MODEL 945 PERFORMANCE CENTER .45 MATCH PISTOL - .45 ACP cal., 5 in. barrel, titanium coated spherical barrel bushing, 8 round mag., Performance Center markings, post front sight, adj. Bo-Mar rear sight, checkered two-piece laminated wood grips, bead blast stainless steel finish, ambidextrous frame mounted thumb safety, grip safety as part of the short beavertail, Master trigger lock, "Performance Center" marked foam-filled aluminum case starting in 1999, 43.5 oz. (1998) 42 oz. (1999 and later mfg.) Mfg. 1998-2000.

✱ *170104* - 5 in. barrel, stainless steel, 8 shot, 43.5 oz. Mfg. 1998.

Last MSR was $1,618.

✱ *170147* - 5 in. barrel, two-tone or blue finish, lightened trigger, grip safety, Bo-Mar rear sight, post front sight, stainless steel, ambidextrous frame mounted safety, 42 oz. Distributed by RSR. Mfg. 1998, 1999-2000.

Last MSR was N/A.

GRADING - PPGS™	100%	98%	95%	90%	80%	70%	60%

❋ **170152** - 4 in. barrel, black finish, 8 shot mag., post front and Novak 2 Dot Lo-Mount Carry rear sight, frame mounted safety, titanium coated spherical bushing, 20 Line checkering front and back strap, extended magazine catch, checkered two-piece wood grips, stainless steel, grip safety, S/N prefix "PCZ", 36 oz. Distributed by Camfour, 2000.

Last MSR was N/A.

❋ **170153** - 4 in. barrel, post front and Novak 2 Dot Lo-Mount carry rear sight, grip safety, checkered two piece wood grips, lightened trigger, bead blast stainless steel finish, frame mounted safety, S/N prefix "PCZ", 36 oz. Distributed by RSR, 2000.

Last MSR was N/A.

❋ **170169** - 3 3/4 in. barrel, white dot dovetail front and Novak 2 Dot Lo-Mount Carry rear sight, grip and single side mounted safety, 7 round mag., checkered laminate wood grips, lightened trigger, black finish alloy frame, stainless steel slide, S/N Prefix "CMF", 28 oz. Distributed by Camfour, 2000.

Last MSR was N/A.

❋ **170177** - 3 1/4 in. barrel, white dot dovetail front and Novak 2 Dot Lo-Mount Carry rear sight, beavertail grip and single-side mounted safety, 6 round mag., checkered Hogue laminated wood grips, alloy frame with clear glass bead stainless steel slide, Performance Center carry case, 2 mags., 24.5 oz. Distributed by Camfour, 2001.

Last MSR was N/A.

❋ **170180** - .40 S&W cal., 3 3/4 in. barrel, white dot dovetail front and Novak 2 Dot Lo-Mount Carry rear sight, beavertail grip and single-side mounted safety, 7 round mag., checkered Hogue laminated wood grips, alloy frame w/ glass bead finish stainless steel slide, Performance Center carry case, 2 mags., 25.7 oz. Distributed by Sports South, 2001.

Last MSR was N/A.

❋ **170184** - 3 1/4 in. glass bead black barrel, white dovetail front and Novak 2 Dot Lo-Mount Carry rear sight, grip and single side mounted safety, 6 round mag., checkered Hogue laminated wood grips, alloy frame with stainless steel slide, lightened trigger, S/N prefix "PCZ", 24 oz. Distributed by RSR, 2001.

Last MSR was N/A.

MODEL 945-1 - .45 ACP cal., 8 shot mag., SA, 5 in. barrel, features scalloped slide serrations and two-tone finish, checkered front and rear gripstrap, checkered wood panel grips, stainless steel, adj. rear sight, target trigger and bobbed hammer, released during 2003, reintroduced 2005.

MSR $2,159	$1,675	$1,200	$1,050

Product code: 170173.

MODEL 952 (MFG. 2000) - 9mm Para. cal., 5 in. match grade black finish stainless steel barrel, titanium coated spherical barrel bushing, 9 round mag., loaded chamber indicator, dovetail post front and adj. Wilson rear sight, carbon steel frame and slide, two-piece wood grip panels w/ alloy backstrap, slide mounted decocking lever, marked "Performance Center 952" with small "mm" in the curl of the 9, Performance Center case, 200 mfg., 41 oz. Distributed by Bangers, 2000.

Last MSR was N/A.

Product code: 170168.

MODEL 952-1 - 9mm Para. cal., 5 in. barrel, 9 shot mag., SA, checkered wood panel grips, black finish, steel frame with stainless steel barrel, released during 2003.

Last MSR was $1,515.

Product code: 170220.

GRADING - PPGS™	100%	98%	95%	90%	80%	70%	60%

MODEL 952-2 (NEW 2004)

9mm Para. cal., 5 or 6 (mfg. 2004 only) in. barrel, blue finish, 9 shot mag., checkered wood grips, stainless steel frame, wide spur hammer, firing pin block safety, wide smooth trigger with frame stop, adj. dovetailed black post front sight and Wilson adj. black rear sight, released during 2004.

	100%	98%	95%
MSR $2,032	$1,575	$1,150	$995

Product code: 170244 (5 in.) or 170247 (6 in.).

MODEL 1911 (NEW 2004)

.38 Super (new 2005) or .45 ACP cal., 5 in. barrel, single action, black finish, 8 or 10 (.38 Super cal.) shot mag., dovetailed black front sight with adj. micro-click black rear sight, checkered laminate wood grips, stainless steel or stainless melonite (new 2005) frame/barrel, glass bead finish, full length guide rod, ambidextrous frame mounted safety, 30 LPI front strap checkering, hand lapped and polished fitted barrel, frame and slide, unique front and rear serrations, includes two magazines, 41 oz., released during 2004.

	100%	98%	95%
MSR $2,272	$1,750	$1,250	$1,050

Add $48 for .38 Super cal. (stainless steel only, new 2005).

Subtract $160 for stainless steel frame/slide.

Product code: 170243.

MODEL 3566

.356 TSW (9x21.5 mm) cal., 3 1/2 (approx. 200 mfg. Compact), 4 1/4 (Tactical), or 5 in. (.356 TSW Limited) match grade barrel, titanium barrel bushing, stainless frame, matte blue and hand rubbed stainless finish, oversize frame rails, 12 shot (Compact) or 15 shot (Limited) mag., adj. trigger, fitted slide and barrel, adj. Bo-Mar sights, checkered front strap, extended mag. well, Hogue rubber grips w/ S&W logo or plastic panel grips, Performance Center trademark on the right side of the slide, S/N prefix "TSW". Distributed by Lew Horton, 1993.

Last MSR was $1,000-$1,350.

Product code: 170027 (3 1/2 in., 12 shot Compact), 170032 (5 in., 15 shot Limited), 170037/39 (exported models), or 170052(4 1/4 in., 12 shot Tactical).

THE SHORTY 9 MKIII

9mm cal., match grade barrel w/ hand fitted titanium bushing, over-size slide rails, ambidextrous safety, Performance Center action job, adj. Novak low mount sights, included Zippo lighter with Performance Center logo. Distributed by Lew Horton, 1997.

Last MSR was $1,024.

9 RECON

9mm cal., 3 1/2 in. match grade barrel, titanium coated spherical barrel bushing, double stack 12 + 1 mag., white dot front and Novak 2 Dot Lo-Mount rear sight, traditional DA trigger, hand lapped oversize rails, ambidextrous spring loaded decocker, 20 LPI checkering on the front strap, Hogue wraparound rubber grips, compact frame, two-tone finish with a clear anodized alloy frame and a carbon steel blue slide, aluminum carry case, 27.2 oz. Distributed by RSR, 1999-2000.

Last MSR was N/A.

Product code: 170140.

S&W 4006 SHORTY FORTY

.40 S&W cal., 3 1/2 in. Bar-Sto barrel, spherical bushing, bobbed hammer, Novak Lo-Mount carry sights, 9-round single stack magazine, alloy frame, grips and frame stamped with Performance Center logo, beveled trigger, adj. front dovetail sight, oversize slide rails, 500 mfg., 27 oz. Distributed by Lew Horton, 1992, 1993, and 1995.

Last MSR was $1,500.

✴ *S&W Tactical Forty* - .40 S&W cal., full size companion to Shorty Forty, 5 in. barrel. Distributed by Lew Horton, limited production 1993.

Last MSR was $1,500.

Product code: 170020.

✴ *S&W Compensated Forty* - .40 S&W cal., compensator mounted on ported barrel. Distributed by Lew Horton.

Last MSR was $1,700.

✳ ***Shorty Forty MK III*** - third variation S/N prefix "PCW". Mfg. 1995.

Last MSR was $949.

Product code: 170011.

✳ ***Shorty Forty MKIII 1997*** - ambidextrous safety, low mount adj. sights, hand fitted titanium barrel bushing, precision checkered front strap, hand honed double action S/N prefix "KPC". Distributed by Lew Horton.

Last MSR was $1,025.

Product code: 170061.

✳ ***Performance Center .40 S&W Tactical*** - .40 S&W cal., 5 in. match grade barrel, fixed tritium night front and Novak 2-dot rear sight, stainless steel frame w/ carbon steel slide materials, tactical black matte slide w/ satin stainless frame finish, 10 round mag., box cut frame and slide rails for 100% contact, balanced slide, ambidextrous decocker, 41.6 oz. Distributed by RSR, 1997.

Last MSR was $1,146.

Product code: 170091.

✳ ***Performance Center Compact*** - .40 S&W cal., 4 1/4 in. barrel. Mfg. August, 1994.

Last MSR was N/A.

Product code: 170054.

MODEL 4006 SHORTY FORTY Y2000 - .40 S&W cal., 3 1/2 in. barrel, white dove-tail front sight, Novak Lo-Mount Carry 2 Dot rear sight, aluminum frame with stainless slide, 9 round mag., two-tone black finish, Performance Center aluminum case. Distributed by Camfour 2000.

Last MSR was N/A.

Product code: 170164.

PERFORMANCE CENTER 40 RECON - .40 S&W cal., 4 1/4 in. match grade barrel w/ compensator, titanium coated spherical barrel bushing, white dot post front and all black Novak Lo-Mount rear sight, 7 round magazine, ambidextrous spring loaded decocker, Hogue wraparound rubber grip, stainless steel material with matte black finish, laser etched with "40 RECON Performance Center" on the left side. Distributed by RSR, 1998.

Last MSR was N/A.

Product code: 170099.

PERFORMANCE CENTER 45 RECON - .45 ACP cal., 4 1/4 in. match grade ported barrel, titanium coated spherical barrel bushing, white dot post front and black Novak Lo-Mount rear sight, ambidextrous spring loaded decocker, Hogue wraparound rubber grip, 7 round magazine, stainless steel construction, stainless or matte black finish, laser etched "45 RECON Performance Center" on the left side, aluminum carry case, S/N prefix "SFF", 27.8 oz. Distributed by RSR, 1998.

Last MSR was $1022.

Product code: 170098 (matte black), 170141 (stainless finish), or 170128 (includes Recon SWAT knife).

PERFORMANCE CENTER 45 CQB PISTOLS (CLOSE QUARTERS BATTLE) - .45 ACP cal., 4 in. match grade barrel, two variations offered in 1998, Novak Lo-Mount Dot front and Novak Lo-Mount 2 Dot rear sight, 7 round mag., straight back-strap grip, stainless steel slide, titanium coated spherical barrel bushing, alloy frame with a matte black finish (Model CQB-AL) or stainless steel frame with a matte stainless (Model CQB-SS) finish, ".45 C.Q.B. Performance Center" laser etched on the slide's left side. Distributed by Lew Horton, 1998-1999.

Last MSR was $1,235.

Product code: 170106 (alloy) or 170105 (stainless).

THE SHORTY .45 - .45 ACP cal., match grade barrel, ambidextrous safety, adj. sights, hand fitted titanium barrel bushing, oversize frame and slide rails, precision checked front strap, hand honed double action. Mfg. 1997.

Last MSR was $1,146.

Product code: 170075.

THE .45 LIMITED - 45 ACP cal., match grade barrel, SA trigger, oversize precision cut frame and side rails, hand fitted titanium barrel bushing, and slide lock, adj. sights, oversize mag. well, tuned action, Zippo lighter with Perf. Center logo. Distributed by Lew Horton, 1997.

Last MSR was $1,470.

MODEL 5906 PC-9 - 9mm cal., 3 1/2 in. titanium barrel, spherical bushing, 15 shot mag., blue slide with satin stainless frame, smooth trigger, bobbed hammer, dovetail front and Novak Lo-Mount fixed rear sight, 27 oz. Distributed by Lew Horton.

Last MSR was N/A.

100%	98%	95%	90%	80%	70%	60%	50%	40%	30%	20%	10%

RIFLES

S&W in 1984 disc. importation of all Howa manufactured rifles. Mossberg continued importation utilizing leftover S&W parts in addition to fabricating their own.

MODEL 320 REVOLVING RIFLE - .320 S&W cal., 6 shot cylinder, 16, 18, or 20 in. round barrel, hard rubber grips, detachable shoulder stock, blue or nickel (rare, add a premium) finish. 977 mfg. 1879-87.

✳ *16 or 20 in. barrel Model* - 239 mfg. with 16 in., and 224 with 20 in. barrel.

$12,000	$10,000	$8,700	$8,100	$7,675	$7,000	$6,375	$5,600	$4,800	$3,850	$2,950	$1,950

✳ *18 in. barrel Model* - 514 mfg.

$9,750	$9,350	$8,700	$8,100	$7,675	$7,000	$6,375	$5,600	$4,800	$3,850	$2,950	$1,950

GRADING - PPGS™	100%	98%	95%	90%	80%	70%	60%

MODEL A BOLT ACTION RIFLE - .22-250 Rem., .243 Win., .270 Win., .308 Win., .30 - 06, 7mm Mag., or .300 Win. Mag. cal., 23 3/4 in. barrel, folding leaf sight, checkered Monte Carlo stock with rosewood forend tip and pistol grip cap. Mfg. 1969-72.

	$385	$330	$305	$275	$220	$195	$165

MODEL B - similar to Model A, in .243 Win., .270 Win., or .30-06 cal., 20 3/4 in. barrel, Schnabel forend.

	$425	$305	$275	$250	$195	$165	$140

MODEL C - similar to Model B, with cheekpiece.

	$425	$305	$275	$250	$195	$165	$140

MODEL D - similar to Model C, with full length stock.

	$550	$385	$360	$305	$250	$220	$195

MODEL E - similar to Model D, with no cheekpiece.

	$550	$385	$360	$305	$250	$220	$195

Note: These rifles were made for S&W by Husqvarna in Sweden.

MODEL 1500 MOUNTAINEER - .222 Rem., .22-250 Rem., .223 Rem, .243 Win., .25-06 Rem, .270 Win, .30-06, or .308 Win. cal., bolt action, 22 in. barrel 5-6 shot mag., no sights, walnut stock, approx. 7 lbs. 10 oz. New 1983.

	$300	$250	$245	$210	$195	$175	$160

Add $27 for sights.

✳ *Model 1500 Mountaineer Magnum* - 7mm Rem. Mag. or .300 Win. Mag. cal.

	$325	$275	$260	$225	$200	$180	$160

MODEL 1500 DELUXE - same cals. as standard 1500, Monte Carlo stock, skip-line checkering, select walnut, no sights. New 1983.

	$350	$300	$260	$220	$200	$180	$160

Add $20 for 7mm Mag. and .300 Win. Mag.

GRADING - PPGS™	100%	98%	95%	90%	80%	70%	60%

MODEL 1500 DELUXE VARMINT - .222 Rem, .22-250 Rem., or .223 Rem. cal., heavy 24 in. barrel, skip-line checkering, no sights. New 1983-disc..

	$375	$325	$275	$225	$200	$180	$160

Add $15 for parkerized finish.

MODEL 1700 LS "CLASSIC HUNTER" - .243 Win, 270 Win, or .30-06 cal., 22 in. barrel, removable 5 shot mag., solid recoil pad, no sights, Schnabel forend, finely checkered. New 1983.

	$400	$350	$315	$265	$240	$220	$195

SHOTGUNS

S&W in 1984 disc. importation of all Howa manufactured shotguns. Mossberg continued importation utilizing leftover S&W parts in addition to fabricating their own.

MODEL 916 SLIDE ACTION SHOTGUN - 12, 16, or 20 ga., 20, 26, 28, or 30 in. barrels, various chokes, plain pistol grip stock, solid frame. Mfg. by S&W in Springfield, MA. 1972-disc.

	$175	$150	$140	$130	$120	$110	$100

✳ *Vent. rib and pad*

	$200	$175	$155	$145	$135	$130	$120

MODEL 916T SLIDE ACTION - similar to 916, except barrels can be interchanged.

	$195	$170	$155	$145	$135	$130	$125

✳ *Vent. rib and pad*

	$225	$200	$180	$170	$155	$145	$135

MODEL 96 SLIDE ACTION - various gauges, disc.

	$125	$110	$100	$90	$75	$70	$65

MODEL 1000 P SLIDE ACTION - 12 ga., various barrel lengths, chokes, VR.

	$350	$305	$270	$230	$210	$190	$170

This model is the same as the Model 3000.

MODEL 3000 SLIDE ACTION - 12 or 20 ga., 3 in. chambers, 22-30 in. barrels, walnut stock and forend, 6 1/4-7 1/2 lbs.

	$350	$305	$270	$230	$210	$190	$170

Add $30 for multi-choke tubes.
Subtract $40 for slug gun (rifle sights on 22 in. barrel).
This model was also available in a "Waterfowler" variation - values are approx. the same as listed.

MODEL 3000 POLICE - 12 ga. only, blue or parkerized finish, many combinations of finishes, stock types, and other combat accessories were available for this model, 18 or 20 in. barrel.

	$325	$255	$215	$185	$170	$155	$140

Add $125 for folding stock.

MODEL 1000 AUTOLOADER - 12 or 20 ga., 22-30 in. barrels, various chokes, gas operated, vent rib, engraved alloy receiver, checkered pistol grip stock. Mfg. 1972-1984.

	$350	$325	$295	$260	$240	$220	$200

Add $30 for multi-choke tubes.
Add approx. $125 for slug barrel.

✳ *Model 1000 Waterfowler* - 3 in. chamber, parkerized finish, Magnum 28 or 30 in. barrel, multi-chokes, steel receiver, "M" suffix, camo sling and swivels.

	$500	$450	$375	$340	$310	$275	$255

* **Model 1000 Super 12** - handles all loads interchangeably, top-of-the-line model during its time.

	100%	98%	95%	90%	80%	70%	60%
	$500	$450	$400	$360	$330	$300	$280

Add $50 for multi-choke.

* **Model 1000 Target** - 12 or 20 ga., skeet, super skeet, and trap models available. Super skeet has 15 barrel muzzle vents to reduce recoil. Trap model has multi-choke tubes, Monte Carlo select walnut stock and forend. Both alloy and steel receivers available in Skeet model, Trap is steel only.

	100%	98%	95%	90%	80%	70%	60%
Skeet/Super Skeet	$400	$390	$335	$260	$235	$215	$190
Trap (Model 1000T)	$595	$525	$450	$375	$325	$285	$235

Note: Shotguns made for S&W by Howa Machinery, Ltd., Japan. This line was picked up by Mossberg after S&W discontinued them - these models may be more desirable.

SMITHSON, J.P.

Current custom rifle manufacturer located in Orem, UT.

J.P. Smithson specializes in custom bolt action rifles. Please contact him directly for more information, including model availability and pricing (see Trademark Index).

SNAKE CHARMER

Currently manufactured by Verney-Carron USA, Inc. located in Clay Center, KS a joint venture of Verney-Carron SA located in Saint-Etienne, France (please refer to the separate Verney-Carron listing) and Y.B.E., Inc. located in Clay Center, KS (distributor of Hastings barrels and choke tubes). Distributor sales only.

SHOTGUNS: SINGLE SHOT

SNAKE CHARMER II - .410 bore only, stainless steel, break open single shot, black molded plastic stock and forend, shell holder in stock, also available as Night Charmer (disc. 1988) and Sea Charmer (disc. 1988), 3 1/2 lbs.

MSR $190		$155	$120	$95

Add $10 for Night Charmer (disc. 1988).

Add $18 for Sea Charmer (disc. 1988).

Subtract $18 for black carbon steel barrel (New Generation Model).

SOCIETA SIDERURGICA GLISENTI

Previous manufacturer located in Brescia, Italy. Also see the Italian Military Arms listing.

PISTOLS: SEMI-AUTO

GLISENTI MODEL 1910 - 9mm Glisenti cal., 7 shot, 4 in. barrel, fixed sights, blue, checkered wood, rubber or plastic grips, Italian service pistol. Mfg. 1910-WWII.

	$750	$625	$450	$325	$275	$225	$200

Warning: While some Glisentis may chamber and fire the 9mm Para. cartridge, it is extremely dangerous to do so.

SODIA, FRANZ

Previous manufacturer located in Ferlach, Austria until 1992.

Sodia arms are superb and are often excellently engraved and inlaid. Professional appraisal should be sought before purchase, since prices are high. Sodia was famous for double-barrel shotguns as well as two- and three-barrel combinations of rifles and shotguns.

DRILLING

BOCKDRILLING - various cals., 2 rifle barrels and 1 shotgun, top quality workmanship.

	$7,000	$6,500	$6,000	$5,000	$4,000	$3,000	$2,500

GRADING - PPGS™	100%	98%	95%	90%	80%	70%	60%

RIFLES: DOUBLE, CUSTOM

DOPPELBÜCHSE - various cals., SxS double rifle, top quality workmanship.

	$5,000	$4,500	$4,000	$3,000	$2,000	$1,800	$1,600

O/U RIFLE - various cals., top quality workmanship.

	$4,500	$4,250	$4,000	$3,500	$3,000	$2,000	$1,800

SHOTGUNS; O/U

TRAP SHOTGUN - 12 ga. only, boxlock action, various degrees of engraving and ornamentation.

	$2,500	$1,850	$1,475	$1,100	$900	$750	$600

SOKOLOVSKY CORPORATION SPORT ARMS (SCSA)

Previous manufacturer until 1990 located in Sunnyvale, CA.

PISTOLS: SEMI-AUTO

SOKOLOVSKY .45 AUTOMASTER - .45 ACP cal. only, stainless steel, single action, 6 in. barrel, 6 shot mag., adj. Millet sights, unique action, is free of external devices, 55 oz. Mfg. 1984-90.

	$2,700	$2,200	$1,850

Last MSR was $3,300.

Total production on this model is 50 pistols.

SOLEIHAC ARMURIER

Previous manufacturer located in Saint Etienne, France.

This manufacturer produced copies of 1894 patent Darne R model guns until 1950. The guns produced were generally simple and less expensive than other manufacturers' sliding breech guns. Most unmarked sliding breech guns were probably manufactured by Soleihac Armurier. Quality and pricing will be similar to low grade (Halifax and RIO model) Darne guns in average condition.

SOMMER + OCKENFUSS GmbH

Previous manufacturer located in Baiersbronn, Germany until 2002. Previously imported by Lothar Walther Precision Tool, located in Cumming, GA. Previously imported by Intertex Carousels Corporation during 1998-2000, and located in Pineville, NC.

Sommer + Ockenfuss also produced a bolt adapter to convert the Remington 700 bolt action into a straight pull repeater, enabling the addition of a firing pin safety and firing chamber lock.

PISTOLS: SEMI-AUTO

P21 - .224 HV, 9mm Para., or .40 S&W cal., 3.11 (Combat) or 3.55 (Police) in. rotating barrel, SA/DA operation, release grip safety uncocks the hammer, keyed slide lock blocks firing pin and slide, 10 shot mag., approx. 24 oz. Mfg. 2001.

	$550	$495	$450	$415	$375	$340	$310

Last MSR was $608.

Add approx. $320 for conversion slide assemblies.

RIFLES: SLIDE ACTION

SHORTY - most popular cals., unique slide action rifle in bullpup configuration featuring a straight line design with a grip safety pistol grip that also works the slide assembly, stainless or black coated barrel, compact 6-lug bolt with a locking surface of 0.263 sq. in., with or w/o sideplates inlet into walnut or black synthetic (new 1999) stock. Imported 1998-2002.

* *Shorty Wilderness Rifle* - match trigger, polymer stock, and stainless steel barrel.

$1,495	$1,275	$1,100	$995	$925	$850	$750

Last MSR was $1,660.

Add $310 for .375 H&H or .416 Rem. Mag. cal. (Shorty Safari).
Add $200 for walnut stock (Shorty American Hunter).
Add $210 for sight mounts.
Add $88 for recoil brake.

* *Shorty Marksman Rifle* - similar to Wilderness Rifle, except has choice of black coated or fluted heavy match barrel and recoil brake.

$1,875	$1,675	$1,450	$1,275	$1,100	$995	$850

Last MSR was $2,020.

Add $80 for .308 Win. or .300 Win. Mag. (fluted barrel), $420 for .338 Lapua Mag. with black coated barrel, or $710 for .338 Lapua Mag. with fluted stainless barrel.
Add $80 for stainless barrel.
Add $210 for sight mount, $168 for bipod, $210 for Spigot stock cap.

There were also deluxe variations, limited editions, and Marksman's packages ($4,100-$4,860 MSR) available in this model.

SPARTAN GUN WORKS

Spartan Gun Works is a subsidiary of Remington, and began importing select shotgun configurations from Russia beginning 2004.

SHOTGUNS

SPR100 SINGLE SHOT - 12, 20 ga., or .410 bore (Youth only), 3 in. chamber, 24 (Youth only), 26 (20 ga.) or 28 (12 ga.) in. barrel with fixed choke, trigger guard opening lever, steel action with selectable ejector or extractor, cocking indicator, crossbolt safety, hardwood stock and forearm, 5.8-6 lbs. Importation began 2004.

MSR $97	$85	$75	$65	$55	$45	$40	$35

Add $7 for Youth model (.410 bore only).

SPR210/220 SxS - 12, 16, 20, 28 ga., or .410 bore, 3 in. chamber except for 16 and 28 ga., boxlock action, choice of DT or SST, ejectors, 26 or 28 in. barrels with choke tubes (N/A on 28 ga. or .410 bore), tang safety, blued finish, checkered walnut stock and forearm, 6.8-7 lbs. Importation began 2004.

MSR $320	$265	$235	$200	$180	$160	$140	$120

Add $70 for SST or $99 for 28 ga. or .410 bore (fixed chokes only).

SPR310/320 O/U - 12, 16, 20, 28 ga., or .410 bore, 3 in. chamber except for 16 and 28 ga., boxlock action with monobloc barrels, choice of DT or SST, ejectors, 26 or 28 in. VR barrels with choke tubes (N/A on 28 ga. or .410 bore), tang safety, blued finish, checkered walnut stock and forearm with rubber recoil pad, 7.3-7.4 lbs. Importation began 2004.

MSR $419	$350	$295	$250	$215	$185	$165	$145

Add $70 for SST or $101 for 28 ga. or .410 bore (fixed chokes only).

SPECIAL WEAPONS LLC

Previous paramilitary rifle manufacturer 1999-2002, and located in Mesa, AZ. Previously located in Tempe, AZ.

Special Weapons LLC closed its doors on Dec. 31, 2002. Another company, Special Weapons, Inc., is handling the warranty repairs on Special Weapons LLC firearms (see Trademark Index).

CARBINES: SEMI-AUTO

OMEGA 760 - 9mm Para. cal., reproduction of the S&W Model 76, 16 1/4 in. partially shrouded barrel, fixed wire stock, 30 shot mag., 7 1/2 lbs. Limited mfg. 2002.

$495	$450	$425	$395	$375	$350	$325

Last MSR was $575.

SW-5 CARBINE - 9mm Para. cal., paramilitary configuration styled after the HK-94 (parts interchangeable), stainless steel receiver, plastic lower housing, 16 1/4 in. stainless steel barrel, A2 style black synthetic stock with wide forearm, 10 shot mag. (accepts high capacity HK-94/MP-5 mags also), approx. 6 3/4 lbs. Mfg. 2000-2002.

$1,475	$1,225	$1,025	$875	$800	$750	$695

Last MSR was $1,600.

SW-45 CARBINE - .45 ACP cal., otherwise similar to SW-5 Carbine. Mfg. 2000-2002.

$1,550	$1,275	$1,050	$895	$825	$775	$725

Last MSR was $1,700.

RIFLES: SEMI-AUTO

SW-3 - .308 Win. cal., paramilitary configuration styled after the HK-91 (parts interchangeable), tooled receiver, metal steel lower trigger housing, 17.71 stainless steel barrel, A2 style stock, approx. 10 lbs. Mfg. 2000-2002.

$1,425	$1,175	$995	$850	$800	$750	$695

Last MSR was $1,550.

* **SW-3 SP** - similar to SW-3, except has PSG-1 style trigger assembly, 22 in. custom target barrel and Weaver rail welded to top. Mfg. 2000-2002.

$2,250	$1,975	$1,700	$1,500	$1,250	$1,050	$895

Last MSR was $2,500.

SPENCER REPEATING RIFLES CO.

Manufactured by Spencer Repeating Rifle Company located in Boston, MA between 1860-1868. Spencer manufactured approximately 144,000 rimfire rifles and carbines, of which approximately 107,000 were contracted to the United States Government during the Civil War.

The brainchild of young Christopher Miner Spencer, more than 13,500 Spencer M1860 Army rifles, 800 M1860 Navy rifles, and 48,000 M1860 Army carbines saw action during the Civil War.

In late 1864, the Chief of Ordnance directed modifications, including reducing the bore from .52 to .50 caliber, and shortening the barrel from 22 inches to 20 inches. The new carbine was designated the Spencer M1865 carbine. Nearly 19,000 were produced by the Spencer Repeating Rifle Company, and another 30,500 by the Burnside Rifle Company, although all were delivered too late to see action in the Civil War. Model 1865 carbines and refurbished M1860 carbines became the mainstay of America's troops on the Western Frontier until replaced by "Trap-Door" Springfield carbines after 1873.

The author wishes to express his thanks to Mr. Roy Marcot for providing most of the information listed.

100%	98%	95%	90%	80%	70%	60%	50%	40%	30%	20%	10%

RIFLES: LEVER ACTION

SMALL-FRAME MILITARY CARBINES AND SPORTING RIFLES - fewer than four dozen prototype small-frame .38 rimfire cal. sporting rifles and .44 rimfire cal. military carbines were made by Christopher Spencer in Hartford between 1860 and 1861. They are exceedingly rare, and only a few are in private hands.

N/A	$15,000	$14,000	$12,000	$9,500	$8,500	$7,500	$6,500	$5,500	$4,500	$4,000	$3,500

MODEL 1860 NAVY RIFLES - the rarest of production Spencer firearms, 803 Spencer Model 1860 Navy rifles with sword-type bayonets were produced for the U.S. Navy Bureau of Ordnance between 1862 and 1863.

N/A	$12,000	$11,000	$9,000	$6,000	$4,000	$3,500	$3,250	$3,000	$2,750	$2,500	$2,000

Add $500-$1,000 for sword-type bayonets.

MODEL 1860 ARMY RIFLES - between 1863 and 1864, the Spencer factory in Boston produced 11,471 Spencer M1860 Army rifles for the Federal Ordnance Department, another 200 for the U.S. Navy, and approximately 2,000 for private purchase. All were issued with Pattern M1855 angular bayonets which fit only these rifles.

N/A	$10,000	$9,000	$7,000	$5,000	$3,750	$3,250	$2,800	$2,500	$2,200	$2,000	$1,800

Add $200-$450 for angular bayonets.

MODEL 1860 CARBINES - beginning in October 1863, the Spencer factory began delivering the first of 45,733 Spencer M1860 carbines to the Ordnance Department for use by Federal cavalrymen. As many as 3,000 additional M1860 carbines went to private purchasers, and also saw action in the war. Because Spencer carbines were so important to the Federal war effort, nearly all saw hard use during the last 18 months of fighting. This resulted in very few weapons available today in excellent condition, and fewer yet with case colors remaining on the receiver.

N/A	$10,000	$9,000	$7,000	$5,000	$3,750	$2,750	$2,500	$2,250	$1,750	$1,500	$1,200

Subtract 25% for Springfield Armory reconditioned Spencer Model 1860 carbines (after the war).

MODEL 1865 CARBINES - in 1865 and 1866, the Spencer factory delivered 18,959 Spencer M1865 carbines to the Federal Ordnance Department. Concurrently, the Burnside Rifle Company of Providence, Rhode Island manufactured and delivered 30,502 Spencer M1865 carbines to the Ordnance Department.

N/A	$6,000	$5,000	$4,000	$3,000	$2,750	$2,500	$2,000	$1,750	$1,500	$1,200	$1,000

MODEL 1865 ARMY RIFLES - as many as 3,000 Spencer M1865 Army rifles were made by the Spencer factory in 1865. While none were ordered by the U.S. Army Ordnance Department, 2,000 went to the Commonwealth of Massachusetts National Guard, and another 1,000 went to Canadian troops and to private purchasers.

N/A	$6,000	$5,000	$4,000	$3,000	$2,750	$2,500	$2,000	$1,750	$1,500	$1,200	$1,000

SPRINGFIELD ARMORY RIFLE MUSKET CONVERSION OF SPENCER CARBINES - in 1871, General Dyer, Chief of Ordnance, directed that 1,109 Spencer M1865 carbines be converted to two-band muskets. Each was fitted with Springfield .50 caliber barrels which held the standard M1855 pattern bayonet.

N/A	$5,000	$4,000	$3,000	$2,500	$1,750	$1,500	$1,250	$1,000	$900	$750	$625

MODEL 1867 ARMY RIFLES AND CARBINES - in 1867, the Spencer factory produced approx. 1,000 M1867 Army rifles and 12,000 carbines. All were intended for private domestic or foreign military sales.

N/A	$4,000	$3,000	$2,500	$2,000	$1,900	$1,750	$1,500	$1,400	$1,200	$1,000	$900

NEW MODEL ARMY RIFLES AND CARBINES - in their final year of production, 1868, the Spencer Repeating Rifle Company produced approx. 1,000 Army rifles and 5,000 carbines. These too, were intended for private domestic or foreign military sales.

N/A	$4,000	$3,000	$2,500	$2,000	$1,900	$1,750	$1,500	$1,400	$1,200	$1,000	$900

100%	98%	95%	90%	80%	70%	60%	50%	40%	30%	20%	10%

SPORTING RIFLES - between 1864-68, the Spencer factory produced approximately 2,000 sporting rifles for the civilian trade. The initial 200 or so were made from surplus military M1860 Army rifle receivers. Thereafter, approximately 1,800 sporting rifles were made expressly as such. The majority chambered the Spencer 56-46 bottleneck rimfire cartridge, but a small number were produced in .50 caliber, chambering 56-50 and the 56-52 cartridges. Spencer sporting rifles missing the rear tang sight are worth approximately 25% less than those listed.

N/A	$7,000	$6,000	$5,000	$4,000	$3,000	$2,500	$2,000	$1,500	$1,300	$1,250	$1,000

SPHINX SYSTEMS LTD.

SPHINX

Current manufacturer established in 1876, and presently located in Matten b. Interlaken, Switzerland. Currently distributed by Sabre Defence Industries, LLC, located in Nashville, TN. Currently imported by Rock Mountain Armoury, located in Silverthorne, CO. Previously manufactured by Sphinx Engineering S.A. located in Porrentruy, Switzerland. Previously imported by Sphinx U.S.A., located in Meriden, CT until 1996. Previously imported by Sile Distributors located in New York, NY.

GRADING - PPGS™	100%	98%	95%	90%	80%	70%	60%

PISTOLS

MODEL AT-380 - .380 ACP cal., semi-auto double action only, 3.27 in. barrel, stainless steel frame, two-tone finish, 10 shot mag. with finger extension, checkered walnut grips. Disc. 1996.

			$435	$375	$350	$325	$295	$275	$250

Last MSR was $494.

Add $20 for black finish.
Add $71 for N/Pall finish.

MODEL 2000S STANDARD - 9mm Para. or .40 S&W (new 1993) cal., semi-auto in standard double action or double action only, 4.53 in. barrel, stainless steel fabrication, 10 (C/B 1994), 15* (9mm Para.), or 11* (.40 S&W) shot mag., checkered walnut grips, fixed sights, 35 oz. Importation disc. 2002

		$965	$750	$625	$525	$450	$410	$375

Add $117 for .40 S&W cal.

✱ *Model 2000PS Police Special* - similar to Model 2000S, except has compact slide and 3.66 in. barrel.

		$850	$625	$525	$450	$410	$380	$350

Add $40 for .40 S&W cal.
Add $87 for N/Pall finish.

✱ *Model 2000P Compact* - similar to Model 2000 Standard, except has 3.66 in. barrel and 13 shot mag., 31 oz.

		$850	$625	$525	$450	$410	$380	$350

Add $40 for .40 S&W cal.
Add $87 for N/Pall finish.

✱ *Model 2000H Sub-Compact* - similar to Model 2000 Compact, except has 3.34 in. barrel and 10 shot mag., 26 oz. Disc. 1996.

		$850	$625	$525	$450	$410	$380	$350

Last MSR was $940.

Add $40 for .40 S&W cal.
Add $87 for N/Pall finish.

MODEL 2000 MASTER - 9mm Para., 9x21mm, or .40 S&W cal., single action only, two-tone finish only, designed for Master's stock class competition.

		$1,795	$1,350	$1,100	$995	$895	$775	$650

Last MSR was $2,035.

GRADING - PPGS™	100%	98%	95%	90%	80%	70%	60%

MODEL AT-2000 (NEW MODEL) - 9mm Para. or .40 S&W cal., 4.53 in. barrel, 10 shot mag., machined slide with electro deposited finish, decocking mechanism. Importation began 2004.

	MSR N/A	$1,825	$1,675	$1,450	$1,225	$1,000	$800	$675

MODEL AT-2000CS COMPETITOR - 9mm Para., 9x21mm, or .40 S&W cal., single or double action, competition model featuring many shooting improvements including 5.3 in. compensated barrel, 10 (C/B 1994), 11* (.40 S&W), or 15* shot mag., Bo-Mar adj. sights, two-tone finish. Imported 1993-96.

	$1,725	$1,275	$1,050	$950	$850	$750	$675

Last MSR was $1,902.

Add $287 for Model AT-2000C (includes Sphinx scope mount).
Add $1,538 for AT-2000K conversion kit (new 1995).
Add $1,490 for Model AT-2000CKS (competition kit to convert AT-2000 to comp. pistol, disc. 1994).

MODEL 2000 COMPETITION - similar to Model 2000 Master, except is SA only and includes more advanced competitive shooting features, Bo-Mar sights, top-of-the-line competition model. Imported 1993-96.

	$2,475	$1,925	$1,725	$1,500	$1,250	$1,050	$895

Last MSR was $2,894.

Add $78 for Model AT-2000GM (includes Sphinx scope mount).

MODEL 3000 SERIES - 9mm Para., 9x21mm (disc.), .40 S&W, or .45 ACP cal., SA/DA, available in standard (4.53 in. barrel) or tactical (3 3/4 in. barrel) configuration, titanium upper/lower frame with stainless slide, stainless steel slide with titanium lower frame or stainless steel frame/slide, front/rear gripstrap stippling, two-tone finish. New 2001.

	MSR N/A	$2,400	$2,150	$1,850	$1,525	$1,375	$1,050	$875

Add $300 for titanium frame with stainless steel slide.
Add $800 for stainless steel slide with titanium upper/lower frame.

SPHINX COMPETITION MODELS - currently available in either an Open (extended barrel with 3 port compensator and Aimpoint scope), Modified (2 port compensator and rear sight optics), or Standard.

Please contact the distributor directly for more information on these models, including U.S. availability and pricing.

SPIDER FIREARMS

Current rifle manufacturer located in St. Cloud, FL.

FERRET 50 - .50 BMG cal., single shot bolt action, A2 style buttstock and pistol grip, Picatinny rail, choice of 18, 29, or 36 in. barrel, matte black finish, perforated handguard with bipod, includes muzzle brake. New 2003.

	MSR $1,650	$1,575	$1,450	$1,300	$1,150	$995	$875	$750

Add $100 for 29 in. barrel or $150 for 36 in. barrel.
Add $270-$320 for stainless steel barrel, depending on length.
Add $330-$380 for stainless super match barrel.

SUPERCOMP FERRET 50 - similar to Ferret 50, except features solid steel construction, fixed scope rails, 29 or 36 Lothar Walther stainless Supermatch barrels, adj. 1 lb. competition style trigger, two-axis cheekrest, and detachable rear monopod. New 2004.

	MSR $3,210	$2,995	$2,600	$2,300	$2,000	$1,750	$1,600	$1,450

SPITFIRE

See listing under JSL (Hereford) in this text.

SPRINGFIELD ARMORY

America's first federal armory located in Springfield, MA. Production began in 1795 and an Act of Congress made it an official federal arsenal in 1872. Not associated with the private firm of the same name located in Geneseo, IL.

In recent years, collectors have realized that military specimens in 98%-100% original condition are very rare and desirable in most cases. Since the supply of these guns is so limited, values listed for these condition factors may not be indicative of current market conditions. As always, many collectors agree that it is hard to overpay for a mint, original, military specimen.

CARBINES/RIFLES

Please refer to the U.S. M1 Carbines/Rifles section for more information on previously manufactured military and commercial M1 carbines and Garands.

MODEL 1870 ROLLING-BLOCK RIFLE, U.S.N. - .50 cal. centerfire, 32 5/8 in. barrel, not serial numbered, 22,013 mfg.

	100%	98%	95%	90%	80%	70%	60%
	N/A	$2,200	$1,950	$1,500	$1,100	$900	$750

MODEL 1871 ROLLING-BLOCK RIFLE, U.S.A. - .50 cal. centerfire, 36 in. barrel, not serial numbered, 10,001 mfg.

	N/A	$1,750	$1,350	$1,000	$900	$750	$650

MODEL 1873 RIFLE "TRAPDOOR" - .45-70 Govt. cal., 32 5/8 in. barrel, 2 bands. Approx. 73,000 mfg. between 1873-77. Subtract 20% if stock cartouche faint or absent.

	$2,150	$1,800	$1,500	$1,150	$775	$650	$450

MODEL 1884 RIFLE "TRAPDOOR" - .45-70 Govt. cal., 32 5/8 in. barrel, 2 bands. Approx. 232,000 mfg. between 1885-90. Subtract 20% if stock cartouche faint or absent.

	$1,850	$1,450	$975	$725	$625	$525	$425

MODEL 1873 CARBINE - 22 in. barrel, half stock, single barrel band/stacking swivel, 20,000 made, but semi-scarce. Pre-Custer serial numbers below 43,700, add up to 50% (pre-1876 mfg.).

	N/A	$5,250	$4,250	$3,250	$2,750	$2,250	$2,000

MODEL 1873 CADET RIFLE - .45-70 Govt. cal., 29 1/2 in. barrel, stacking swivel, no sling swivels.

	$1,600	$1,300	$1,050	$900	$775	$650	$600

Subtract $100 for variation with sling-swivels.
Subtract 25-35% if restocked with buttplate and hole drilled for cleaning tools.

MODEL 1875 OFFICER'S RIFLE FIRST TYPE - .45-70 Govt. cal., 477 mfg. between 1875 and 1886, 26 in. barrel, single barrel band. Not serial numbered, some dated, non-issue.

	N/A	$35,000	$27,000	$23,000	$20,000	$15,000	$10,000

Subtract 15-20% for types 2 and 3.
Approx. 25 rifles were mfg. prior to the standardization of this model.

MODEL 1877 RIFLE - .45-70 Govt. cal., mfg. 3,943.

	N/A	$2,650	$2,250	$1,875	$1,625	$1,325	$1,175

MODEL 1877 CARBINE - .45-70 Govt. cal., 22 in. barrel, "C" rear sight to 1,200 yards. Mfg. 2,946.

	N/A	$4,250	$3,850	$3,300	$2,850	$2,450	$2,100

MODEL 1877 CADET RIFLE - .45-70 Govt. cal., 29 1/2 in. barrel. 1,050 mfg.

	N/A	$1,200	$1,000	$950	$900	$800	$700

MODEL 1879 RIFLE - .45-70 Govt. cal., approx. 140,000 mfg.

	$1,350	$1,150	$950	$850	$700	$650	$450

MODEL 1879 CARBINE - .45-70 Govt. cal., no stacking swivel. Approx. 15,000 mfg.

	N/A	$2,500	$2,150	$1,900	$1,500	$1,000	$850

GRADING - PPGS™	100%	98%	95%	90%	80%	70%	60%

MODEL 1879 CADET RIFLE - .45-70 Govt. cal., stacking swivel but no sling swivels. 5,000 mfg.

	$995	$850	$750	$650	$600	$550	$500

MODEL 1880 - .45-70 Govt. cal., combination triangular, sliding type, bayonet-ram-rod. 1,001 mfg.

	N/A	$2,900	$2,600	$2,400	$2,000	$1,800	$1,650

MODEL 1881 FORAGER - 20 ga., 1,376 mfg. 1881-85. Be cautious when purchasing.

	N/A	$2,250	$1,800	$1,500	$1,300	$1,150	$1,000

PISTOLS: SEMI-AUTO

M1911 MILITARY MFG. SPRINGFIELD ARMORY - approx. 30,000 mfg. between 1914-15, blue finish.

	N/A	$3,500	$2,500	$1,500	$975	$725	$600

Serialization is 72,751-83,855, 102,597-107,596, 113,497-120,566, and 125,567-133,186. Most mint/100% specimens encountered in this model have been refinished - be careful.

KRAG-JORGENSEN VARIATIONS MFG. BY SPRINGFIELD

Please refer to the Krag-Jorgensen section. Values listed for Model 1903s assume 100% original guns. Values listed for Model 1922s assume 100% original blued guns.

U.S. MODEL 1903 SPRINGFIELD - .30-06 cal., bolt action, mfg. by Springfield Armory and Rock Island Arsenal, 24 in. barrel. Mfg. 1903-30.

✱ **Pre-WWI Mfg.** - values below represent original rifles.

	$6,000	$4,800	$3,650	$3,000	$2,250	$1,850	$1,650

Subtract 80% if reworked.

✱ **Serialized 800,000 - 1,275,767** - double heat treated receiver.

	$3,950	$3,250	$2,750	$2,500	$2,100	$1,650	$1,300

✱ **Serialized 1,275,768 +** - nickel steel receiver.

	$3,950	$3,250	$2,750	$2,500	$2,100	$1,650	$1,300

U.S. MODEL 1903 MARK I - .30-06 cal., similar to U.S. Model 1903 Springfield, except altered for the Pedersen device, a slot is milled into the left side of receiver to act as an ejection port for use of the semi-auto bolt insert, value without device.

	$4,000	$3,500	$1,800	$1,200	$1,000	$850	$750

1903-A1 - .30-06 cal., similar to U.S. Model 1903 Springfield, except type C pistol grip stock. Mfg. 1930-39. In 1941 Remington mfg. approx. 350,000.

	$4,000	$3,500	$1,800	$1,200	$1,000	$850	$750

✱ **Remington produced**

	$4,000	$3,500	$1,800	$1,200	$1,000	$850	$750

1903-A1 NATIONAL MATCH

	$4,500	$3,500	$2,000	$1,200	$1,000	$850	$750

1903-A3 - .30-06 cal., similar to 1903, with production modifications, aperture rear sight, no finger groove in forestock, lower quality finish, stamped floorplate and barrel band. Mfg. WWII by Remington and Smith Corona.

	$800	$700	$500	$400	$330	$300	$275

Add 25% for Smith Corona mfg.

1903-A3 NATIONAL MATCH - 200 mfg., known as the "unmatched" match rifle.

	$1,800	$1,400	$1,000	$850	$750	$675	$600

1903-A4 SNIPER - .30-06 cal., with M73B1 or M84 scope in Redfield mount, no front sight.

	$4,500	$3,800	$2,500	$1,800	$1,000	$700	$500

Subtract 25% if reworked with parkerized small parts.

GRADING - PPGS™	100%	98%	95%	90%	80%	70%	60%

1903 MARINE SNIPER - .30-06 cal., includes 8X Unertl scope.

	$5,500	$3,950	$3,000	$2,500	$2,000	$1,800	$1,650

    If this model is verified as an original, large premiums (double or triple) are currently being asked on values listed.

1903 NRA NATIONAL MATCH - .30-06 cal., similar to 1903, with hand selected and custom fit parts, produced for target shooting. "NRA" and flaming bomb proofed on trigger guard. 1915 date.

	$4,500	$3,500	$2,400	$1,500	$995	$850	$725

1903 SPORTER - .30-06 cal., similar to National Match, with sporter stock and Lyman sight.

	$4,800	$3,500	$1,800	$1,200	$925	$825	$700

1903 MATCH STYLE T - .30-06 cal., similar to Sporter, with heavy barrel, globe sight, target bases, 26, 28, or 30 in. barrel.

    Because original specimens are extremely rare, pricing is very hard to determine. Excellent original condition specimens have been seen with asking prices in the $8,000-$9,000 range.

1903 FREE RIFLE TYPE A - .30-06 cal., similar to Style T, with 28 in. barrel, and Swiss hook butt.

    Because original specimens are extremely rare, pricing is very hard to determine. Excellent original condition specimens have been seen with asking prices in the $8,000-$9,000 range.

1903 FREE RIFLE TYPE B - .30-06 cal., similar to Type A, with double-set triggers, cheekpiece stock, modified firing pin.

    Because original specimens are extremely rare, pricing is very hard to determine. Excellent original condition specimens have been seen with asking prices in the $8,000-$9,000 range.

MODEL 1922-M1 - .22 LR cal., Target Rifle, 5 shot mag., 24 in. barrel, modified 1903, Lyman receiver sight, sporter stock, issued 1927.

	$2,500	$2,000	$1,500	$1,000	$625	$550	$495

MODEL 1922 NRA VARIATION - not tapped for scope, without forend grooves.

	$2,500	$2,250	$1,925	$1,725	$1,500	$1,250	$1,000

M2 .22 TARGET RIFLE - similar to 1922 M1, except improved lock time, adj. head space, bolt design.

	$1,500	$1,200	$1,000	$700	$600	$550	$500

SPRINGFIELD ARMORY (MFG. BY SPRINGFIELD INC.)

Current trademark manufactured by Springfield Inc., located in Geneseo, IL. Springfield Inc. has also imported a variety of models. This company was named Springfield Armory, Geneseo, IL until 1992.

Springfield Inc. manufactures commercial pistols and rifles, including reproductions of older military handguns and rifles.

SPRINGFIELD, INC.®

COMBINATION GUNS

M6 SCOUT RIFLE - .22 LR, .22 Mag. (disc.), or .22 Hornet cal. over smoothbore .410 bore w/ 3 in. chamber, O/U Survival Gun, 14 (legal transfer needed) or 18.25 in. barrels, parkerized or stainless steel (new 1995), approx. 4 lbs. Disc. 2004.

	$175	$145	$115	$90	$75	$70	$65

    Last MSR was $215.

    Add $34 for stainless steel.

    Add $24 for lockable Marine flotation plastic carrying case.

    Older mfg. does not incorporate a trigger guard while newer production has a trigger guard.

GRADING - PPGS™	100%	98%	95%	90%	80%	70%	60%

M6 SCOUT PISTOL/CARBINE - .22 LR or .22 Hornet cal. over .45 LC/.410 bore, 16 in. barrels, parkerized or stainless steel. Mfg. 2002-2004.

	100%	98%	95%	90%	80%	70%	60%
	$185	$160	$125	$95	$80	$70	$65

Last MSR was $223.

Add $24 for stainless steel.

Add $134-$149 per interchangeable 10 in. barrel assembly.

This model is also available with an optional detachable stock ($49-$59 MSR, not legal with a rifled barrel less than 16 in. or smoothbore less than 18 in.).

M6 SCOUT PISTOL - .22 LR or .22 Hornet cal. over .45 LC/.410 bore, 10 in. barrels, parkerized or stainless steel. Mfg. 2002-2004.

	100%	98%	95%	90%	80%	70%	60%
	$165	$135	$110	$85	$75	$70	$65

Last MSR was $199.

Add $24 for stainless steel.

Add $134-$149 per interchangeable 16 in. carbine barrel.

PISTOLS: SEMI-AUTO

OMEGA PISTOL - .38 Super, 10mm Norma, or .45 ACP cal., single action, ported slide, 5 or 6 in. interchangeable ported or unported barrel with Polygon rifling, special lockup system eliminates normal barrel link and bushing, Pachmayr grips, dual extractors, adj. rear sight. Mfg. 1987-90.

	$775	$650	$575	$495	$425	$360	$295

Last MSR was $849.

Add $663 for interchangeable conversion units.

Each conversion unit includes an entire slide assembly, one mag., 5 or 6 in barrel, recoil spring guide mechanism assembly, and factory fitting.

Add $336 for interchangeable 5 or 6 in. barrel (including factory installation).

OMEGA MATCH - same cals. as Omega, except has low profile combat sights, 8 shot mag., and beveled mag. well. Mfg. 1991-92 only.

	$925	$775	$660	$535	$460	$420	$385

Last MSR was $1,103.

Pistols: Semi-Auto - P9 Series

MODEL P9 - 9mm Para., 9x21mm (new 1991) .40 S&W (new 1991), or .45 ACP cal., patterned after the Czech CZ-75, selective double action design, blue (standard beginning 1993), parkerized (standard until 1992), or duotone finish, various barrel lengths, checkered walnut grips. Mfg. in U.S. starting 1990.

✱ *P9 Standard* - 4.72 in. barrel, 15 shot (9mm Para.), 11 shot (.40 S&W), or 10 shot (.45 ACP) mag., parkerized finish standard until 1992 - blue finish beginning 1993, 32.16 oz. Disc. 1993.

	$430	$375	$335	$295	$275	$240	$215

Last MSR was $518.

Add $61 for .45 ACP cal.

Add $182 for duotone finish (disc. 1992).

Subtract $40 for parkerized finish.

In 1992, Springfield added a redesigned stainless steel trigger, patented sear safety which disengages the trigger from the double action mechanism when the safety is on, lengthened the beavertail grip area offering less "pinch," and added a two-piece slide stop design.

✱ *P9 Stainless* - similar to P9 Standard, except is constructed from stainless steel, 35.3 oz. Mfg. 1991-93.

	$475	$425	$350

Last MSR was $589.

Add $50 for .45 ACP cal.

GRADING - PPGS™	100%	98%	95%	90%	80%	70%	60%

* **P9 Compact** - 9mm Para. or .40 S&W cal., 3.66 in. barrel, 13 shot (9mm Para.) or 10 shot (.40 S&W) mag., shorter slide and frame, rounded triggerguard, 30 1/2 oz. Disc. 1992.

	$395	$350	$300	$275	$250	$225	$200

Last MSR was $499.

> **Add $20 for .40 S&W cal.**
> **Add $20-$30 for blue finish depending on cal.**
> **Add $78 for duotone finish.**

* **P9 Sub-Compact** - 9mm Para. or .40 S&W cal., smaller frame than the P9 Compact, 3.66 in. barrel, 12 shot (9mm Para.) or 9 shot (.40 S&W) finger extension mag., squared-off triggerguard, 30.1 oz. Disc. 1992.

	$395	$350	$300	$275	$250	$225	$200

Last MSR was $499.

> **Add $20 for .40 S&W cal.**
> **Add $20-$30 for blue finish depending on cal.**

* **P9 Factory Comp** - 9mm Para., .40 S&W, or .45 ACP cal., 5 1/2 in. barrel (with compensator attached), extended sear safety and mag. release, adj. rear sight, slim competition checkered wood grips, choice of all stainless (disc. 1992) or stainless bi-tone (matte black slide), dual port compensated, 15 shot (9mm Para.), 11 shot (.40 S&W), or 10 shot (.45 ACP) mag., 33.9 oz. Mfg. 1992-93.

	$595	$525	$450	$420	$390	$360	$330

Last MSR was $699.

> **Add $36 for .45 ACP cal.**
> **Add $75-$100 for all stainless finish.**

* **P9 Ultra IPSC (LSP)** - competition model with 5.03 in. barrel (long slide ported), adj. rear sight, choice of parkerized (standard finish until 1992 when disc.), blue (disc. 1992), bi-tone (became standard 1993), or stainless steel (disc. 1992) finish, extended thumb safety, and rubberized competition (9mm Para. and .40 S&W cals. only) or checkered walnut (.45 ACP cal. only) grips, 15 shot (9mm Para.), 11 shot (.40 S&W), or 10 shot (.45 ACP) mag., 34.6 oz. Disc. 1993.

	$555	$475	$415	$350	$300	$275	$250

Last MSR was $694.

> **Add $30 for .45 ACP cal.**

* **P9 Ultra LSP Stainless** - stainless steel variation of the P9 Ultra LSP. Mfg. 1991-92.

	$675	$525	$425

Last MSR was $769.

> **Add $30 for .40 S&W cal.**
> **Add $90 for .45 ACP cal.**

* **P9 World Cup** - see listing under 1911-A1 Custom Models heading.

Pistols: Semi-Auto - R-Series

PANTHER MODEL - 9mm Para., .40 S&W, or .45 ACP cal., semi-auto single or double action, 3.8 in. barrel, hammer drop or firing pin safety, 15 shot (9mm Para.), 11 shot (.40 S&W), or 9 shot (.45 ACP) mag., Commander hammer, frame mounted slide stop, narrow profile, non-glare blue finish only, walnut grips, squared-off triggerguard, 29 oz. Mfg. 1992 only.

	$535	$450	$395	$350	$300	$275	$250

Last MSR was $609.

FIRECAT MODEL - 9mm Para. or .40 S&W cal., single action, 3.5 in. barrel, 3-dot low profile sights, all steel mfg., firing pin block and frame mounted ambidextrous safety, 8 shot (9mm Para.) or 7 shot (.40 S&W) mag., checkered combat style triggerguard and front/rear gripstraps, non-glare blue finish, 35 3/4 oz. Mfg. 1992-93.

	$495	$425	$375	$330	$295	$275	$250

Last MSR was $569.

GRADING - PPGS™	100%	98%	95%	90%	80%	70%	60%

BOBCAT MODEL - while advertised in 1992, this model was never mfg.

LINX MODEL - while advertised in 1992, this model was never mfg.

Pistols: Semi-Auto - Disc. 1911-A1 Models

MODEL 1911-A1 STANDARD MODEL - .38 Super, 9mm Para., 10mm (new 1990), or .45 ACP cal., patterned after the Colt M1911-A1, 5.04 (Standard) or 4.025 (Commander or Compact Model) in. barrel, 7 shot (Compact), 8 shot (.45 ACP), 9 shot (10mm), or 10 shot (9mm Para. and .38 Super) mag., walnut grips, parkerized, blue, or duotone finish. Mfg. 1985-90.

	$400	$360	$330	$300	$280	$260	$240

Last MSR was $454.

Add $35 for blue finish.

Add $80 for duotone finish.

This model was also available with a .45 ACP to 9mm Para. conversion kit for $170 in parkerized finish, or $175 in blue finish.

✳ *Defender Model* - .45 ACP cal. only, similar to Standard 1911-A1 Model, except has fixed combat sights, beveled mag. well, extended thumb safety, bobbed hammer, flared ejection port, walnut grips, factory serrated front strap and two stainless steel magazines, parkerized or blue finish. Mfg. 1988-90.

	$485	$435	$375	$340	$300	$280	$260

Last MSR was $567.

Add $35 for blue finish.

✳ *Commander Model* - .45 ACP cal. only, similar to Standard 1911-A1 Model, except has 3.63 in. barrel, shortened slide, Commander hammer, low profile 3-dot sights, walnut grips, parkerized, blue, or duotone finish. Mfg. in 1990 only.

	$450	$415	$350	$325	$285	$260	$245

Last MSR was $514.

Add $30 for blue finish.

Add $80 for duotone finish.

✳ *Combat Commander Model* - .45 ACP cal. only, 4 1/4 in. barrel, bobbed hammer, walnut grips. Mfg. 1988-89.

	$435	$385	$325	$295	$275	$250	$230

Add $20 for blue finish.

✳ *Compact Model* - .45 ACP cal. only, compact variation featuring shortened Commander barrel and slide, reduced M1911 straight gripstrap frame, checkered walnut grips, low profile 3-dot sights, extended slide stop, combat hammer, parkerized, blue, or duotone finish. Mfg. 1990 only.

	$450	$415	$350	$325	$285	$260	$245

Last MSR was $514.

Add $30 for blue finish.

Add $80 for duotone finish.

✳ *Custom Carry Gun* - .38 Super (special order only), 9mm Para., 10mm (new 1990), or .45 ACP cal., similar to Defender Model, except has tuned trigger pull, heavy recoil spring, extended thumb safety, and other features. Mfg. 1988-disc.

	$860	$725	$660	$535	$460	$420	$385

Last MSR was $969.

Add $130 for .38 Super Ramped, 10mm was POR.

✳ *National Match Hardball Model* - .38 Super (disc.), 9mm Para. (disc.), or .45 ACP cal., National Match barrel and bushing, specially fitted frame and slide, Bo-Mar adj. rear sight, Herrett walnut grips, plastic cased. Mfg. 1988-90.

	$780	$650	$565	$515	$460	$415	$385

Last MSR was $897.

This model was made specifically for DCM competition shooting.

GRADING - PPGS™	100%	98%	95%	90%	80%	70%	60%

* ***Bullseye Wadcutter Model*** - .45 ACP cal. only, designed for wadcutter loads only, 5 or 6 (ported or unported) in. barrel, Bo-Mar rib mounted on slide, checkered gripstraps, match trigger, beavertail grip safety, polished feed ramp and throated barrel. Mfg. 1989-disc.

	$1,415	$1,200	$1,025	$925	$825	$750	$675

Last MSR was $1,599.

Add $25 for 6 in. barrel.
Add $80 for 6 in. ported barrel.

* ***Trophy Master Competition Pistol*** - .38 Super, 9mm Para. (disc.), 10mm (new 1990), or .45 ACP cal., competition model which includes low profile combat sights, ambidextrous safety, long match trigger, bobbed hammer, Pachmayr wraparound grips. Mfg. 1988-90.

	$1,300	$1,100	$950	$875	$800	$730	$660

Last MSR was $1,443.

Add $130 for .38 Super with supported chamber, 10mm was POR.

* ***Trophy Master Competition Expert Model*** - .38 Super, 9mm Para. (disc.), 10mm (new 1990), or .45 ACP cal., mfg. for IPSC competition shooting, dual chamber compensator system on match barrel, blue finish, ambidextrous thumb safety, beveled and polished mag. well, lowered and flared ejection port, wraparound Pachmayr grips, shock buffer, includes 2 mags. and plastic carrying case. Mfg. 1988-90.

	$1,664	$1,450	$1,225	$1,025	$950	$890	$850

Last MSR was $1,664.

Add $130 for .38 Super with supported chamber, 10mm was POR.
This model was an improved variation of the Master Grade Competition Pistol "A."

* ***Trophy Master Competition Distinguished Model*** - similar to Expert Model, except has brushed hard chrome finish, checkered gripstraps and trigger guard, top-of-the-line competition model. Mfg. 1988-90.

	$2,000	$1,675	$1,450	$1,225	$1,025	$950	$875

Last MSR was $2,275.

Add $130 for .38 Super with supported chamber, 10mm was POR.
Subtract $130 for "B" Model.
This model was an improved variation of the Master Grade Competition Pistol "B-1."

Pistols: Semi-Auto - 1911-A1 (90s Series)

The initials "PDP" refer to Springfield's Personal Defense Pistol series.

Beginning in 2000, Springfield Armory started offering a Loaded Promotion package on their 1911-A1 pistol line. Many of these features and options are found on the FBI's Hostage Rescue Teams (HRT) pistol contract with Springfield Armory. Standard features of this Loaded Promotion package are hammer forged premium air-gauged barrel, front and rear cocking serrations, Novak patented low profile sights or Bo-Mar type adj. sights, extended thumb safety, tactical beavertail, flat mainspring housing, Cocobolo grips, High Hand grip, lightweight match trigger, full length guide rod, and machine beveled mag. well. This promotion includes all pistols except the Mil-Spec Model 1911 A-1.

In 2001, Springfield's Custom Loaded 1911-A1 Series pistols came equipped standard with Springfield's integral locking system, carry bevel, hammer forged premium air-gauged barrel, front and rear cocking serrations, Novak patented low profile sights (some models come equipped with Tritium sights or Bo-Mar type adj. sights), extended thumb safety, tactical beavertail, flat mainspring housing, cocobolo grips, high hand grip, lightweight adj. match trigger, full length guide rod, machine beveled magwell, and a "loaded" coupon ($600 consumer savings). These Custom Loaded features will vary by model. All models with less than a 5 in. and all alloy pistols supplied with ramped, fully supported barrels.

Beginning 2002, every Springfield pistol is equipped with a patented integral locking system (I.L.S., keyed in the rear gripstrap) at no extra charge.

GRADING - PPGS™	100%	98%	95%	90%	80%	70%	60%

PDP DEFENDER MODEL - .40 S&W (disc. 1992) or .45 ACP cal., standard pistol with slide and barrel shortened to Champion length (4 in.), tapered cone dual port compensator system, fully adj. sights, Videcki speed trigger, rubber grips, Commander style hammer, serrated front strap, parkerized (disc. 1992), duotone/bi-tone, or blue (disc. 1993) finish. Mfg. 1991-98.

	$850	$735	$630	$550	$495	$450	$425

Last MSR was $992.

❋ *PDP Factory Comp* - .38 Super (disc.) or .45 ACP cal. only, entry level IPSC gun, featuring 5 5/8 in. barrel with compensator attached, adj. rear sight, Videki speed trigger, checkered walnut grips, beveled mag. well, 10 shot (.38 Super) or 8 shot (.45 ACP) mag., blue finish only, 40 oz. Mfg. 1991-2000.

	900	$685	$585	$500	$450	$420	$390

Last MSR was $1,049.

❋ *PDP High Capacity Factory Compensated* - .38 Super (disc.) or .45 ACP cal. only, blue finish. Mfg. 1995-2000.

	$955	$795	$655	$575	$500	$450	$395

Last MSR was $1,109.

MODEL 1911-A1 90s EDITION (CUSTOM LOADED) - .38 Super, 9mm Para., 10mm (disc. 1991), .40 S&W, or .45 ACP cal., patterned after the Colt M1911-A1, except has linkless operating system, 5.04 (Standard) or 4 (Champion or Compact Model) in. barrel, 7 shot (Compact), 8 shot (.40 S&W or .45 ACP Standard), 9 shot (9mm Para., 10mm, or .38 Super), or 10 shot (.38 Super) mag., checkered walnut grips, parkerized (.38 Super beginning 1994 or .45 ACP beginning 1993), blue or duotone (disc. 1992) finish. New 1991.

❋ *1911-A1 Mil-Spec* - .38 Super or .45 ACP cal., blue (disc.), parkerized, bi-tone (new 2004), or OD Green (new 2004) finish, 3-dot Hi-Viz fixed combat sights, 35.6 oz.

MSR $640	$525	$410	$355	$315	$285	$265	$235

Add $17 for blue finish (disc. 2001).

Add $21 for OD Green or bi-tone finish (mfg. 2004 only).

Add $123 for .38 Super cal. (until 2003).

Add $561 for .38 Super cal. in High Polish Steel (Acusport exclusive beginning 2004).

>**1911-A1 Stainless Steel Mil-Spec** - similar to Mil-Spec Model, except is stainless steel. New 2003.

MSR $704	$565	$455	$365				

❋ *1911-A1 Mil-Spec Operator* - .45 ACP cal. only, similar to Mil-Spec 1911-A1, except has Picatinny light mounting system forged into lower front of frame, parkerized finish only. Disc. 2002.

	$615	$475	$425	$365	$325	$285	$255

Last MSR was $756.

❋ *1911-A1 Loaded Operator* - .45 ACP cal. only, similar to full size service model, except has Picatinny light mounting platform forged into lower front of frame, checkered hardwood (disc. 2003) or plastic grips, OD Green with black bi-tone Armory Kote finish, Novak low mount tritium sights. New 2002.

MSR $1,125	$900	$750	$600	$525	$450	$400	$350

❋ *1911-A1 Standard or Lightweight Model* - Standard model has parkerized, blue, or OD Green with Armory Kote (new 2002) finish, Custom Loaded features became standard in 2001, Lightweight Model was introduced 1995 with either matte (disc. 2002), bi-tone (new 2003) or blue (mfg. 1993-disc.) finish, current mfg. is w/ either Novak low mount or night sights, 28.6 or 35.6 oz.

MSR $845	$680	$515	$435	$370	$325	$285	$255

Add $63 for Lightweight Model (with Trijicon night sights).

Subtract approx. 10%-25% if w/o Custom Loaded features (new 2001), depending on condition.

GRADING - PPGS™	100%	98%	95%	90%	80%	70%	60%

* **1911-A1 Stainless Standard Model** - 9mm Para. (new 1994), .38 Super (disc.), .40 S&W (mfg. 2001-2002), or .45 ACP cal., 7 (.45 ACP cal.), 8 (.40 S&W), or 9 (9mm Para.) shot mag., Custom Loaded features became standard in 2001, wraparound rubber (disc.) or checkered hardwood grips, Novak low mount or Bo-Mar type (mfg. 1996-2001) sights, beveled mag. well, 39.2 oz. New 1991.

MSR $876	**$715**	**$545**	**$460**				

Add $72 for 9mm Para. cal., or $32 for .40 S&W cal. (disc.).
Add $1 for Tactical Model with combat features and black stainless steel (new 2005).
Add $50 for Bo-Mar type sights (disc. 2001).
Add $202 for long slide variation in .45 Super cal. with V16 porting and Bo-Mar sights (disc.).
Subtract $31 for parkerized finish with Novak tritium sights.

* **1911-A1 Stainless Super Tuned Standard** - .45 ACP cal. only, super tuned by the Custom Shop, 7 shot mag., 5 in. barrel, Novak fixed low mount sights, 39.2 oz. Mfg. 1997-99.

	$875	**$750**	**$600**

Last MSR was $995.

* **1911-A1 Target Model** - 9mm Para. or .45 ACP cal., includes Custom Loaded features, stainless steel or black stainless steel (new 2003), with (.45 ACP cal. only) or w/o V12 ported barrel, adj. sights, 38 oz. New 2001.

MSR $938	**$790**	**$585**	**$480**				

Add $142 for black stainless steel with adj. tritium sights.
Add $15 for 9mm Para. cal.
Subtract approx. $15 for non-ported V12 barrel and approx. $100 for stainless steel.

* **1911-A1 Trophy Match** - .40 S&W (new 2001) or .45 ACP cal. only, top-of-the-line pistol featuring improved trigger pull, adj. rear sight, match grade barrel and bushing, Custom Loaded features became standard in 2001, choice of Armory Kote (.40 S&W cal. only, new 2001), stainless steel, bi-tone (disc.), or blue finish, 35.6 oz. New 1994.

MSR $1,409	**$1,165**	**$910**	**$700**	**$600**	**$550**	**$475**	**$425**

Add $10 for bi-tone finish (disc.).
Add $8 for High Capacity Trophy Match (disc.).
Subtract $100 for blue finish (disc.).

* **1911-A1 Standard High Capacity** - 9mm Para. (disc.) or .45 ACP cal., 5 in. barrel, blue (disc. 2001) or matte parkerized (new 1996) finish with plastic grips, 3-dot fixed combat sights, 10 shot (except for law enforcement) mag. Mfg. 1995-2003.

	$635	**$540**	**$475**	**$425**	**$375**	**$335**	**$295**

Last MSR was $756.

Add $50 for blue finish (disc.).

* **1911-A1 Stainless High Capacity** - similar to Standard High Capacity, except is stainless steel. Mfg. 1996-2000.

	$675	**$540**	**$475**

Last MSR was $819.

* **1911-A1 XM4 High Capacity Model** - 9mm Para. or 45 ACP cal., features widened frame for high capacity mag., blue (mfg. 1993 only) or stainless finish only. Mfg. 1993-94.

	$595	**$550**	**$500**

Last MSR was $689.

MODEL 1911-A1 LONG SLIDE CUSTOM LOADED STAINLESS - .45 ACP or .45 Super (mfg. 2001 only) cal., 6 in. ported or unported barrel, 7 shot mag., checkered wood grips, adj. sights, 41 oz. New 2001.

MSR $1,064	**$880**	**$685**	**$555**

Add $72 for ported barrel (V16, disc. 2004).
Add $403 for Trophy Match Model (disc. 2004).

GRADING - PPGS™	100%	98%	95%	90%	80%	70%	60%

MODEL 1911-A1 GI - .45 ACP cal., 5 in. barrel, parkerized, OD Green Armory Kote finish or stainless steel, low profile military sights, checkered walnut grips, 36 oz. New 2004.

MSR $502	$440	$360	$320	$290	$260	$240	$220

Add $76 for stainless steel.

Add $57 for high capacity magazine (parkerized finish, new 2005).

1911-A1 TACTICAL RESPONSE (TRP SERIES) - .45 ACP only, 5 in. standard or bull (Operator Model only) barrel, 7 shot mag., matte Armory Kote finish or stainless steel, checkered rosewood grips, Novak or Hi-Viz (disc., Operator Model only) 3-dot Tritium (disc. 2001) sights, 36 oz. New 1999.

MSR $1,560	$1,275	$1,050	$850	$725	$625	$575	$500

Add $79 for Operator Model with integral light mounting rail and adj. night sights.

1911-A1 COMMANDER MODEL - .45 ACP cal. only, similar to Standard 1911-A1 Model, except has 3.63 in. barrel, shortened slide, Commander hammer, low profile 3-dot sights, walnut grips, parkerized, blue, or duotone finish. Mfg. 1991-92.

	$425	$365	$330	$300	$275	$250	$225

✴ *1911-A1 Combat Commander Model* - .45 ACP cal. only, 4 1/4 in. barrel, bobbed hammer, walnut grips. Mfg. 1991 only.

	$425	$365	$330	$300	$275	$250	$225

1911-A1 CHAMPION MODEL - .380 ACP (Model MD-1, mfg. 1995 only) or .45 ACP cal., similar to Standard Model, except has 4 in. barrel and shortened slide, blue (disc. 2000) or parkerized (Mil-Spec Champion, new 1994) finish, Commander hammer, checkered walnut grips, 3-dot sights (Novak night sights became standard 2001), 7 shot mag., 33 1/2 oz. Mfg. 1992-2002.

	$695	$500	$400	$350	$325	$295	$275

Last MSR was $856.

Add $30 for Ultra Compact slide (mfg. 1997-98).

Add $79 for ported Champion V10 with Ultra Compact slide (disc.).

Subtract approx. 10%-25% if w/o Custom Loaded features (new 2001), depending on condition.

Subtract approx. $150 for .380 ACP cal. (Model MD-1, disc.).

✴ *1911-A1 Champion Model (Custom Loaded)* - .45 ACP cal. only, stainless steel or Lightweight bi-tone with OD Green finish (new 2004). New 1992.

MSR $922	$740	$560	$430	$380	$350	$325	$295

Add $119 for Ultra Compact slide (mfg. 1997-98).

Add $52 for ported Champion V10 with Ultra Compact slide (disc. 2000).

Subtract $36 for Lightweight Champion with bi-tone OD Green finish (new 2004).

Subtract approx. 10%-25% if w/o Custom Loaded features (new 2001), depending on condition.

✴ *1911-A1 Champion GI Model* - .45 ACP cal., parkerized or blued slide with black anodized frame (Lightweight Model, new 2005), low profile military sights, 34 oz. New 2004.

MSR $502	$440	$360	$320	$285	$260	$240	$220

✴ *1911-A1 TRP Champion* - .45 ACP cal., 4 in. barrel, otherwise similar to TRP Tactical Response. Mfg. 1999-2001.

	$1,045	$875	$700	$600	$500	$450	$395

Last MSR was $1,249.

✴ *1911-A1 Champion Lightweight* - .45 ACP cal., aluminum frame, matte metal finish, night sights became standard during 2001. New 1999.

	$700	$495	$395	$345	$310	$275	$240

Last MSR was $867.

Subtract approx. 10%-25% if w/o Custom Loaded features (new 2001), depending on condition.

GRADING - PPGS™	100%	98%	95%	90%	80%	70%	60%

✻ *1911-A1 PDP Champion Comp* - .45 ACP cal. only, compensated version of the Champion Model, blue. Mfg. 1993-98.

	$780	$690	$600	$550	$500	$450	$395

Last MSR was $869.

✻ *1911-A1 Super Tuned Champion* - .45 ACP cal., super tuned by the Custom Shop, 7 shot mag., 4 in. barrel, blue or parkerized finish, Novak fixed low mount sights, 36.3 oz. Mfg. 1997-99.

	$850	$725	$575	$500	$450	$400	$365

Last MSR was $959.

Add $30 for blue finish.

✻ *1911-A1 Champion XM4 High Capacity* - 9mm Para. or .45 ACP cal., high capacity variation. Mfg. 1994 only.

	$615	$555	$500

Last MSR was $699.

1911-A1 COMPACT MODEL - .45 ACP cal. only, compact variation featuring shortened 4 in. barrel and slide, reduced M1911-A1 curved gripstrap frame, checkered walnut grips, low profile 3-dot sights, 6 or 7 shot mag., extended slide stop, standard or lightweight alloy (new 1994) frame, combat hammer, parkerized, blue, or duotone (disc. 1992) finish, standard or lightweight (new 1995) configuration, 27 or 32 oz. Mfg. 1991-96.

	$415	$355	$300	$275	$250	$225	$200

Last MSR was $476.

Add $66 for blue finish.
Add $67 for Compact Lightweight Model (matte finish only).

✻ *1911-A1 Stainless Compact Model* - stainless steel variation of the Compact Model. Mfg. 1991-96.

	$495	$420	$350

Last MSR was $582.

✻ *1911-A1 Compact Lightweight* - .45 ACP cal., forged alloy frame, matte metal finish, 6 shot mag., Novak night sights became standard 2001. Mfg. 1999-2003.

	$585	$495	$425	$375	$325	$295	$275

Last MSR was $733.

Subtract approx. 10%-25% if w/o Custom Loaded features (new 2001), depending on condition.

>**1911-A1 Compact Lightweight Stainless** - similar to Compact Lightweight, except is stainless steel. Disc. 2001.

	$725	$550	$475

Last MSR was $900.

Subtract approx. 10%-25% if w/o Custom Loaded features (new 2001), depending on condition.

✻ *1911-A1 Compact Comp Lightweight* - compensated version of the Compact Model, bitone or matte finish, regular or lightweight alloy (new 1994) frame. Mfg. 1993-98.

	$775	$685	$600	$550	$500	$450	$395

Last MSR was $869.

✻ *1911-A1 High Capacity Compact* - blue or stainless steel, 3-dot fixed combat sights, black plastic grips, 10 shot (except for law enforcement) mag. Mfg. 1995-96 only.

	$540	$465	$425	$395	$360	$330	$295

Last MSR was $609.

Add $39 for stainless steel.

GRADING - PPGS™	100%	98%	95%	90%	80%	70%	60%

✳ **1911-A1 PDP High Capacity Compact Comp** - .45 ACP cal. only, features compensated 3 1/2 in. barrel, 10 shot (except law enforcement) mag., blue finish only. Mfg. 1995-96 only.

	$830	$725	$625	$550	$495	$450	$425

Last MSR was $964.

ULTRA COMPACT 1911 A-1 (CUSTOM LOADED) - .380 ACP (lightweight only, mfg. 1995 only), 9mm Para. (new 1998, lightweight stainless only), or .45 ACP cal., 3 1/2 in. barrel, bi-tone (.45 ACP only, disc.), matte (.380 ACP, MD-1), or parkerized (Mil-Spec Ultra Compact) finish, 6, 7 (.380 ACP cal.) or 8 (9mm Para. cal.) shot mag., Custom Loaded features and night sights became standard in 2001, 24 or 30 oz. Mfg. 1995-2003.

	$680	$485	$380	$325	$295	$265	$235

Last MSR was $837.

Add $12 for V10 porting.

Add $12 for Novak Tritium sights (not available on 9mm Para cal.).

Add $110 for bi-tone finish (disc.).

Subtract $50 for MD-1 variation (.380 ACP only).

Subtract approx. 10%-25% if w/o Custom Loaded features (new 2001), depending on condition.

✳ **1911 A-1 Ultra Compact Mil-Spec** - .45 ACP cal., parkerized (disc.) or blued (new 2004) finish, similar to full size Mil-Spec Model, 6 shot mag., checkered grips, 3-dot fixed Hi-Viz combat sights. Mfg. 2001-2002, reintroduced 2004 only.

	$550	$475	$425	$375	$325	$275	$225

Last MSR was $641.

Subtract approx. 10%-25% if w/o Custom Loaded features (new 2001), depending on condition.

✳ **1911 A-1 Ultra Compact Stainless** - 9mm Para. (disc. 2004) or .45 ACP cal., stainless steel, Novak night sights became standard 2001. New 1998.

MSR $922	$775	$560	$455

Add $17 for 9mm Para cal. (lightweight, disc. 2004).

Subtract approx. 10%-25% if w/o Custom Loaded features (new 2001), depending on condition.

✳ **1911 A-1 Ultra Compact Lightweight** - .45 ACP cal., aluminum frame, matte metal finish, night sights became standard 2001. Mfg. 1999-2001.

	$695	$495	$395	$345	$310	$275	$240

Last MSR was $867.

Subtract approx. 10%-25% if w/o Custom Loaded features (new 2001), depending on condition.

✳ **1911 A-1 V10 Ultra Compact Lightweight Ported** - .45 ACP cal., bi-tone finish. Mfg. 1999-2001.

	$750	$550	$425	$365	$335	$300	$275

Last MSR was $737.

>**1911 A-1 V10 Ultra Compact Lightweight Stainless** - 9mm Para. or .45 ACP (exclusive) cal., similar to Ultra Combat Lightweight, except is stainless steel, Novak low mount sights. Mfg. 1999-2002.

	$725	$525	$425

Last MSR was $870.

Add $31 for night sights (.45 ACP cal. only).

Subtract approx. 10%-25% if w/o Custom Loaded features (new 2001), depending on condition.

GRADING - PPGS™	100%	98%	95%	90%	80%	70%	60%

❋ *1911 A-1 High Capacity Ultra Compact* - 9mm Para. (disc.) or .45 ACP cal., parkerized (Mil-Spec) or blue (disc.) finish, and stainless steel (disc.) construction, 10 shot mag., 3-dot fixed combat (disc.) or Novak low mount (new 2002) sights, black plastic grips. Mfg. 1996-2002.

	$735	$525	$425	$365	$325	$300	$275

Last MSR was $909.

> **Add $98 for stainless steel.**
> **Add $145 for stainless steel with V10 ported barrel (disc.).**
> **Subtract approx. 10%-25% if w/o Custom Loaded features (new 2001), depending on condition.**

❋ *1911 A-1 V10 Ultra Compact Ported* - .45 ACP cal. only, 3 1/2 in. specially compensated barrel/slide, blue (disc.), bi-tone, or parkerized (Mil-Spec Ultra Compact) finish, Novak low mount or 3-dot combat sights, 30 oz. Mfg. 1995-2002.

	$690	$485	$395	$345	$310	$275	$240

Last MSR was $853.

> **Subtract approx. 10%-25% if w/o Custom Loaded features (new 2001), depending on condition.**

❋ *1911 A-1 V10 Super Tuned Ultra Compact Ported* - .45 ACP cal. only, super tuned by the Custom Shop, 3 1/2 in. ported barrel, bi-tone finish or stainless steel (exclusive), Novak fixed low mount sights, 32.9 oz. Mfg. 1997-99.

	$925	$775	$600	$525	$475	$425	$385

Last MSR was $1,049.

> **Add $70 for stainless steel (exclusive).**

MICRO COMPACT 1911-A1 - .45 ACP cal. only, 3 in. tapered barrel w/o bushing, matte finish, checkered grips, 6 shot mag., Novak low mount Tritium sights. Mfg. 2002 only.

	$625	$475	$375	$325	$295	$265	$235

Last MSR was $749.

❋ *1911 A-1 Micro Compact Lightweight Custom Loaded* - similar to Micro Compact 1911 A-1, except also available in .40 S&W cal., bi-tone, OD Green (mfg. 2003 only), or black Armory Kote (mfg. 2003-2004) finish with forged steel slide (grey) and aluminum alloy frame (blue), checkered cocobolo grips, 24 oz. New 2002.

MSR $1,184	$975	$850	$750	$650	$550	$450	$375

Add $189 for Operator Model with XML X-treme mini light.

❋ *1911 A-1 Micro Compact Lightweight Stainless Custom Loaded* - .45 ACP cal. only, similar to Micro Compact 1911 A-1 Custom Loaded, except is stainless or black stainless steel slide. Mfg. 2003.

	$825	$725	$595				

Last MSR was $993.

❋ *1911 A-1 Micro Compact GI* - .45 ACP cal., parkerized finish, checkered walnut grips, 32 oz. New 2004.

MSR $578	$495	$425	$365	$335	$295	$265	$240

GULF VICTORY SPECIAL EDITION - .45 ACP cal., special edition featuring presentation grade blue finish, gold etching on slide and other gold-plated small parts, includes specially padded and embroidered storage case with jacket patch, window decal, and cloisonne medallion honoring all U.S. Armed Forces. Mfg. 1991-92.

	$750	$600	$475				

Last MSR was $869.

Pistols: Semi-Auto - 1911-A1 Custom Models

In addition to the models listed, Springfield also custom builds other configurations of Race Guns that are available through Springfield dealers. Prices range from $2,245-$2,990.

> **Add $100 for all cals. other than .45 ACP.**

GRADING - PPGS™	100%	98%	95%	90%	80%	70%	60%

CUSTOM CARRY GUN - .45 ACP (other cals. available upon request) cal., similar to Defender Model, except has tuned trigger pull, 7 shot mag., heavy recoil spring, extended thumb safety, available in blue or phosphate (disc.) finish. New 1991.

MSR $1,495	$1,300	$1,025	$875	$750	$650	$550	$475

CUSTOM OPERATOR - .45 ACP cal. New 2001.

MSR $2,495	$2,125	$1,725	$1,375	$1,075	$950	$825	$725

BASIC COMPETITION - .45 ACP (other cals. available upon request) cal., Bo-Mar adj. rear sight, blue finish, checkered walnut grips. New 1994.

MSR $1,600	$1,375	$1,065	$900	$775	$675	$550	$475

PROFESSIONAL MODEL - .45 ACP cal. New 1999.

MSR $2,395	$2,050	$1,675	$1,350	$1,075	$950	$825	$725

PPC TROPHY MATCH - 9mm Para. cal. New 2004.

MSR $1,395	$1,175	$975	$825	$700	$625	$525	$450

NRA PPC - .45 ACP (other cals. available upon request) cal., designed to comply with NRA PPC competitive rules/regulations, factory test target, custom carrying case. New 1995.

MSR $1,950	$1,700	$1,400	$1,050	$925	$775	$675	$575

1911-A1 CUSTOM COMPACT - .45 ACP cal. only, carry or lady's model with shortened slide and frame, compensated, fixed 3-dot sights, Commander style hammer, Herrett walnut grips, other custom features, blue only.

	$1,615	$1,325	$1,100	$950	$850	$750	$675

Last MSR was $1,815.

1911-A1 CUSTOM CHAMPION - similar to Custom Compact, except is based on Champion model with full size frame and shortened slide.

	$1,615	$1,325	$1,100	$950	$850	$750	$675

Last MSR was $1,815.

NATIONAL MATCH HARDBALL - .45 ACP cal. only, National Match barrel and bushing, specially fitted frame and slide, blue only, Bo-Mar adj. rear sight, Herrett walnut grips, plastic cased.

MSR $1,535	$1,350	$1,040	$900	$775	$650	$550	$475

This model is made specifically for DCM competition shooting.

BULLSEYE WADCUTTER - .45 ACP (other cals. available upon request) cal., specifically designed for wadcutter loads, Bo-Mar rib mounted on slide top, 5 or 6 in. barrel.

MSR $1,725	$1,525	$1,250	$995	$875	$750	$650	$575

ENTRY LEVEL WADCUTTER - .38 Super, .40 S&W, 10mm, or .45 ACP cal., 5 in. barrel, standard competition features.

	$925	$800	$700	$600	$550	$475	$425

Last MSR was $1,049.

Add $200 for .38 Super cal.
Add $391 for 10mm or .40 S&W cal.

This model features supported chamber in all cals. except .45 ACP.

TROPHY MASTER "COMPETITION" - .45 ACP (other cals. available upon request) cal., competition model which includes low profile combat sights, ambidextrous safety, long match trigger, bobbed hammer, Pachmayr wraparound grips. Disc. 1996.

	$1,420	$1,125	$950	$875	$800	$725	$650

Last MSR was $1,598.

GRADING - PPGS™	100%	98%	95%	90%	80%	70%	60%

EXPERT - .45 ACP (other cals. available upon request) cal., mfg. for IPSC competition shooting, dual chamber compensator system on match barrel, duotone finish.

MSR $1,985	$1,775	$1,500	$1,225	$995	$850	$750	$675

Subtract $160 for Limited Class variation.

This model is an improved variation of the Trophy Master Competition Model.

DISTINGUISHED - similar to Expert Model, except has brushed hard chrome finish, checkered gripstraps and triggerguard, top-of-the-line competition model.

MSR $2,825	$2,475	$2,050	$1,650	$1,275	$995	$850	$750

Subtract $170 for Limited Class variation.

CUSTOM HIGH CAPACITY LTD - new 2004.

MSR $2,395	$2,050	$1,675	$1,350	$1,075	$950	$825	$725

OPERATOR LIGHTWEIGHT - .45 ACP cal., 3 in. barrel, bi-tone finish, XML mini-light, includes Novak Trijicon night sights. New 2005.

MSR $1,247	$1,050	$925	$800	$700	$600	$500	$400

OPERATOR TACTICAL RESPONSE - .45 ACP cal., 5 in. barrel, black Armory Kote finish, adj. Trijicon night sights. New 2005.

MSR $1,639	$1,395	$1,075	$900	$775	$675	$575	$475

LOADED OPERATOR - .45 ACP cal., 5 in. barrel, OD Green or black Armory Kote finish and slide, Novak or Trijicon night sights. New 2005.

MSR $1,218	$1,025	$900	$800	$700	$600	$500	$400

LEATHAM TROPHY MATCH - .40 S&W cal., 5 in. barrel, high capacity model, Armory Kote finish. New 2005.

This model is available POR - please contact the company directly.

LEATHAM LEGEND SERIES TGO 1 SERVICE MODEL - .45 ACP cal., 5 in. stainless steel Nowlin match grade throated barrel, bi-tone finish, Bo-Mar low mount fully adj. rear sight, Dawson fiberoptic front sight, NM trigger High-Hand beavertail grip safety, ambidextrous thumb safety, includes two sets of grips - Leatham Legend signature series laser engraved cocobolo smooth wood and black micarta double diamond, extended mag. release, includes four mags., custom aluminum case, special markings and ser. no., 38 oz. New 2003.

MSR $2,999	$2,650	$2,375	$2,000	$1,625	$1,250	$995	$850

This model is available exclusively through Davidson's.

LEATHAM LEGEND SERIES TGO 2 SERVICE MODEL - .45 ACP cal., 5 in. stainless steel hammer forged throated match barrel, bi-tone finish, similar features as the TGO 1, 38 oz. New 2003.

MSR $1,899	$1,675	$1,450	$1,200	$995	$850	$750	$675

This model is available exclusively through Davidson's.

LEATHAM LEGEND SERIES TGO 3 SERVICE MODEL - similar to TGO 1, except has lightweight forged aluminum frame with black Armory Kote finish and stainless steel slide, 30 oz. New 2003.

MSR $1,295	$1,150	$975	$875	$775	$675	$575	$475

This model is available exclusively through Davidson's.

DISTINGUISHED BIANCHI/COMPETITION STEEL - new 2004.

MSR $2,995	$2,650	$2,375	$2,000	$1,625	$1,250	$995	$850

FULL HOUSE RACE GUN - .45 ACP cal., high capacity frame, chrome finish only. New 1998.

MSR $3,085	$2,700	$2,300	$2,000	$1,725	$1,500	$1,350	$1,200

Add $150 for STI/SV style frame.

GRADING - PPGS™	100%	98%	95%	90%	80%	70%	60%

P9 WORLD CUP - 9mmx21 or .40 S&W cal., state-of-the-art competition pistol, based on factory P9 Race gun, hard chrome finish only.

	100%	98%	95%	90%	80%	70%	60%
	$2,550	$2,100	$1,775	$1,500	$1,250	$975	$795

Last MSR was $2,935.

Pistols: Semi-Auto – XD Series

All XD pistols are shipped with two magazines. Beginning 2005, high capacity magazines are legal for civilian sales in those states that permit high cap. mags.

X-TREME DUTY (XD MODELS) - 5 IN. - 9mm Para., .357 SIG, .40 S&W, or .45 GAP (new 2005) cal., cold hammer forged 5 in. barrel, 10, 12 (.40 S&W or .357 SIG), or 15 (9mm Para.) shot mag., lightweight polymer frame, matte black, bi-tone, or OD Green finish, steel slide, single action striker fired with U.S.A. trigger system, firing pin and loaded chamber indicators, dual recoil spring system, integral accessory rails standard on frame, ambidextrous mag. release, grip safety, front and rear slide serrations, approx. 23 oz. New 2002.

MSR $542	$465	$410	$380	$340	$300	$265	$235

Add $29 for bi-tone finish (.45 GAP cal. only, new 2005).
Add $88 for Trijicon or Heine tritium slant pro sights (n/a in .45 GAP).

❋ XD Tactical Pro - limited mfg. 2003 only.

	$875	$775	$675	$575	$475	$400	$350

Last MSR was $1,099.

X-TREME DUTY (XD MODELS) - 4 IN. - 9mm Para., .357 SIG, .40 S&W, or .45 GAP (new 2005) cal., cold hammer forged 4 in. ported or unported barrel, 10, 12 (.40 S&W or .357 SIG), or 15 (9mm Para.) shot mag., lightweight polymer frame, matte black, bi-tone (new 2003) or OD Green finish, steel slide, single action striker fired with U.S.A. trigger system, firing pin and loaded chamber indicators, dual recoil spring system, integral accessory rails standard on frame, ambidextrous mag. release, grip safety, front and rear slide serrations, approx. 23 oz. New 2002.

MSR $514	$445	$390	$345	$300	$265	$235	$200

Add $28 for V10 ported barrel (black finish, not available in .45 GAP cal.).
Add $28 for bi-tone finish (only available in 9mm Para. and .40 S&W cal.).
Add $85 for Trijicon or Heine tritium slant pro sights.

X-TREME DUTY (XD MODELS) - 3 IN. SUB-COMPACT - 9mm Para. or .40 S&W (new 2004) cal., cold hammer forged 3 in. barrel, 9 (.40 S&W) or 10 (9mm Para.) shot mag., lightweight polymer frame, bi-tone (new 2004, 9mm Para. cal. only), matte black or OD Green finish, steel slide, single action striker fired with U.S.A. trigger system, firing pin and loaded chamber indicators, dual recoil spring system, integral accessory rails standard on frame, ambidextrous mag. release, grip safety, front and rear slide serrations. New 2003.

MSR $514	$445	$390	$345	$300	$265	$235	$200

Add $28 for bi-tone finish.
Add $71 for Heine tritium slant pro sights (disc. 2004).
Add $71 for X-treme mini light.

PISTOLS: SINGLE SHOT, 1911-A2 SASS SERIES

1911-A2 SASS - various cals., single shot break open action featuring interchangeable barrels, Pachmayr grips, adj. front and rear sights, blue finish only, 61-66 oz. Mfg. 1990-1992.

❋ 10 3/4 in. barrel - .22 LR, 7mm BR, .243 Win., .357 Mag., or .44 Mag. cal.

	$650	$560	$495	$450	$420	$390	$360

Last MSR was $749.

Add $399 per interchangeable conversion unit (includes barrel).

GRADING - PPGS™	100%	98%	95%	90%	80%	70%	60%

✱ **15 in. barrel** - .22 LR, .223 Rem., .243 Win. (new 1991), 7mm BR, 7mm-08 Rem., .308 Win., or .358 Win. cal.

	$650	$560	$495	$450	$420	$390	$360

Last MSR was $749.

Add $399 per interchangeable conversion unit (includes barrel).

RIFLES: BOLT ACTION

MAUSER M98 - 7x57mm Mauser cal., surplus rifles with standard military dimensions and features. Importation disc. 1989.

✱ **Hunting/Utility Grade**

	$70	$50	$45	$45	$40	$40	$35

Last MSR was $75.

✱ **Collector Grade**

	$105	$90	$80	$70	$60	$50	$40

Last MSR was $116.

✱ **Premium Grade**

	$170	$150	$130	$115	$100	$90	$80

Last MSR was $194.

CZ 98 HUNTER CLASSIC - .243 Win., .270 Win., .30-06, .308 Win., 6.5x55mm, 7x57 Mauser, 7x64mm, 7.29x57mm, .300 Win. Mag., or 7mm Rem. Mag. cal., features Mauser 98 Large Ring action, mfg. by CZ in the Czech Republic and Springfield Armory, controlled feeding, 24 in. hammer forged barrel, adj. trigger, choice of walnut or synthetic stock, 7.7 lbs. Limited mfg. 1995 only.

	$345	$315	$285	$260	$240	$220	$195

Last MSR was $411.

Add $38 for walnut stock.

RIFLES: SEMI-AUTO, MILITARY DESIGN

M1 CARBINE - .30 Carbine cal., features new receiver on older military M1 GI stocks. Disc.

	$375	$325	$285	$260	$240	$220	$195

M1 GARAND AND VARIATIONS - .30-06, .270 Win. (disc. 1987), or .308 Win. cal., semi-auto, 24 in. barrel, gas operated, 8 shot mag., adj. sights, 9 1/2 lbs.

✱ **Garand Rifle** - .30-06 or .308 Win. cal., mfg. with original U.S. government issue parts, with new walnut stock, 8 shot mag., 24 in. barrel. Limited mfg. beginning 2002.

MSR $1,348	$1,100	$975	$850	$725	$650	$575	$475

Add $30 for .308 Win. cal.

✱ **Standard Model** - supplied standard with camo GI fiberglass stock.

	$725	$650	$575	$525	$485	$450	$425

Last MSR was $761.

Subtract $65 if with GI stock.

✱ **National Match** - walnut stock, match barrel and sights.

	$850	$775	$700	$650	$600	$550	$495

Last MSR was $897.

Add $240 for Kevlar stock.

✱ **Ultra Match** - match barrel and sights, glass bedded stock, walnut stock standard.

	$950	$850	$725	$675	$610	$550	$500

Last MSR was $1,033.

Add $240 for Kevlar stock.

GRADING - PPGS™	100%	98%	95%	90%	80%	70%	60%

* **M1-D Sniper Rifle** - .30-06 or .308 Win. cal., limited quantities, with original M84 scope, prong type flash suppressor, leather cheek pad and slings.

	$950	$850	$725	$675	$610	$550	$500

Last MSR was $1,033.

* **Tanker Rifle** - similar to T-26 authorized by Gen. MacArthur at the end of WWII, 18 1/4 in. barrel, .30-06 or .308 Win. cal., GI stock standard.

	$725	$675	$600	$525	$460	$380	$335

Last MSR was $797.

Add $23 for walnut full stock.

* **D-Day M1 Garand Rifle** - .30-06 cal., 24 in. barrel, gas operated, military square post front sights, engraved stock, two 8 shot mags., leather sling, cleaning kit, includes wooden crate and limited edition lithograph print, 9.5 lbs. 1,944 mfg. beginning 2004.

MSR $1,490	$1,375	$1,250	$1,125	$900	$800	$700	$600

BM 59 - .308 Win. cal., mfg. in Italy and machined and assembled in the Springfield Armory factory, 19.32 in. barrel, 20 shot box mag., 9 1/2 lbs.

* **Standard Italian Rifle** - with grenade launcher, winter trigger, tri-compensator, and bipod.

	$1,750	$1,400	$1,200	$1,000	$895	$850	$800

Last MSR was $1,950.

* **Alpine Rifle** - with Beretta pistol grip type stock.

	$2,025	$1,625	$1,350	$1,150	$1,000	$925	$850

Last MSR was $2,275.

This model was also available in a Paratrooper configuration with folding stock at no extra charge.

* **Nigerian Rifle** - similar to BM 59, except has Beretta pistol grip type stock.

	$2,075	$1,650	$1,375	$1,150	$1,000	$925	$850

Last MSR was $2,340.

* **E Model Rifle**

	$1,975	$1,595	$1,325	$1,125	$975	$900	$825

Last MSR was $2,210.

M1A RIFLES - .243 Win. (disc.), .308 Win., or 7mm-08 Rem. (1991 mfg. only) cal., patterned after the original Springfield M14 - except semi-auto, walnut or fiberglass stock, 22 in. steel or stainless steel barrel, fiberglass handguard, "New Loaded" option (see separate listing) beginning 2001 includes NM air gauge barrel, trigger group, front and rear sights, and flash supressor or Springfield proprietary muzzle brake, 9 lbs.

* **M1A Standard/Basic Model** - above specifications, choice of Collector (original GI stock, disc. 2001), birch (disc. 2003), walnut (M1A Standard Model beginning 1993), Mossy Oak camo finished (new 2003), black fiberglass (M1A Basic Model), camo fiberglass (disc.), GI wood (disc. 1992), and brown (disc.) or black laminated (M1A Standard Model mfg. 1996-2000) stock, regular or National Match (disc.) barrel.

MSR $1,486	$1,250	$1,075	$925	$825	$725	$625	$525

Add $100 for new walnut stock.
Add $21 for Mossy Oak camo finished stock.
Add $12 for black fiberglass stock.
Add $59 for birch stock (disc. 2003).
Add $44 for stainless steel barrel (disc.), $74 for bipod and stabilizer (disc.) or $159 for brown laminated stock (disc.), $59 for National Match barrel (disc.), $155 for National Match barrel and sights (disc.), $200 for folding stock (disc. 1994).
Subtract $58 for camo fiberglass stock (disc.).
Standard (entry level model) stock configuration for 1996 was black or camo fiberglass.

GRADING - PPGS™	100%	98%	95%	90%	80%	70%	60%

✳ **M1A E-2** - standard stock is birch. Disc.

	$975	$825	$745	$650	$590	$550	$495

Last MSR was $842.

Add $30 for walnut stock.
Add $120 for Shaw stock with Harris bipod.

✳ **M1A Bush Rifle** - .308 Win. cal., 18 in. shrouded barrel, 8 lbs. 12 oz., collector GI, walnut, Mossy Oak camo finished (new 2003), black fiberglass folding (disc. 1994 per C/B), and black fiberglass (disc.) or laminated black (disc.) stock. Disc. 1999, reintroduced 2003 only.

	$1,300	$985	$845	$725	$625	$525	$475

Last MSR was $1,529.

Add $29 for walnut stock (disc.), $15 for black fiberglass stock (disc.), $86 for black laminated stock (disc.), $235 for National Match variation (disc.), and $525 for Super Match variation (disc.)

✳ **M1A National Match** - National Match sights, steel or stainless steel (new 1999) barrel, mainspring guide, flash suppressor, and gas cylinder, special glass bedded oil finished match stock, tuned trigger, walnut stock became standard in 1991, 9 lbs.

MSR $2,049		$1,735	$1,250	$975	$825	$725	$625	$550

Add $49 for stainless steel barrel.
Add $155 for heavy composition stock (disc.).
Add $250 for either fiberglass or fancy burl wood stock (disc.).
.243 Win. and 7mm-08 Rem. cals. are also available at extra charge.

✳ **M1A Super Match** - similar to National Match, except has air-gauged Douglas or Hart (disc.) heavy barrel, oversized walnut or fiberglass super match stock, and modified operating rod guide, rear lugged receiver beginning 1991, approx. 11.5 lbs.

MSR $2,550		$2,175	$1,550	$1,175	$975	$850	$750	$650

Add $168 for stainless steel Douglas barrel.
Add $250 for Krieger or Hart barrel (disc.).
Add $599 for McMillan black or Marine Corps camo fiberglass stock.
Add $200 for fancy burl walnut (disc.) stock.
.243 Win. and 7mm-08 Rem. cals. are also available at extra charge.

M21 TACTICAL - .308 Win. cal., Garand action, 22 in. barrel, tactical variation of the Super Match mfg. with match grade parts giving superior accuracy, adj. cheekpiece stock, 11.6 lbs. New 1990.

MSR $3,086		$2,650	$2,150	$1,800	$1,575	$1,275	$1,050	$875

Add $362 for Krieger barrrel.

M25 "WHITE FEATHER" TACTICAL - .308 Win. cal., Garand action, includes black fiberglass M3A McMillan stock, 22 in. Kreiger heavy carbon barrel standard, Rader trigger, White Feather logo and Carlos Hathcock II signature, 10 shot box mag., includes Harris bipod, 12 3/4 lbs. New 2001.

MSR $4,648		$4,100	$3,350	$2,850	$2,375	$1,900	$1,600	$1,250

M1A LOADED STANDARD - .308 Win. cal., 22 in. National Match steel or stainless steel barrel, features shooting upgrades such as National Match trigger assembly, front and rear sights, and National Match flash suppressor, 10 shot mag., black fiberglass, Collector GI walnut (disc. 2000), or new walnut stock, approx. 9.5 lbs. New 1999.

MSR $1,639		$1,395	$1,100	$900	$750	$650	$575	$525

Add $103 for new walnut stock.
Add $191 for stainless steel barrel and walnut stock.
Add $88 for stainless steel barrel.
Add $100 for Collector GI walnut (disc. 2000).

GRADING - PPGS™	100%	98%	95%	90%	80%	70%	60%

M1A "GOLD SERIES" - .308 Win. cal., heavy walnut competition stock, gold medal grade heavy Douglas barrel. Add $126 for Kevlar stock, add $390 for special Hart stainless steel barrel, add $516 for Hart stainless steel barrel with Kevlar stock. Mfg. 1987 only.

	100%	98%	95%	90%	80%	70%	60%
	$1,944	$1,750	$1,375	$1,150	$975	$850	$740

Last MSR was $1,944.

M1A SCOUT SQUAD - .308 Win. cal., 18 in. barrel, choice of GI Collector (disc. 1998), new walnut, black fiberglass, Mossy Oak camo finished, or black laminated (disc. 1998) stock, muzzle stabilizer standard, supplied with Scout mount and hand-guard, approx. 9 lbs. New 1997.

MSR $1,610	$1,375	$1,050	$900	$775	$650	$575	$500

Add $117 for walnut stock.
Add $43 for Mossy Oak camo finish.

M1A SOCOM - .308 Win. cal., 16.25 in. barrel with muzzle brake, black fiberglass stock with steel buttplate, upper handguard has been cut out for sight rail, 10 shot mag., tritium front sight with ghost ring aperture rear sight, two-stage military trigger, 8.9 lbs. New 2004

MSR $1,727	$1,495	$1,175	$975	$850	$750	$675	$600

Add $30 for urban camo stock (new 2005).
Add $221 for Generation II black fiberglass stock (new 2005).

SAR-8 - .308 Win. cal., patterned after the H & K Model 91, recoil operated delayed roller lock action, fluted chamber, rotary adj. rear aperture sight, 18 in. barrel, recent mfg. incorporated a cast aluminum receiver with integrated Weaver rail, pistol grip, slim forearm, and green furniture (for law enforcement only), supplied with walnut (disc. 1994) or black fiberglass thumbhole sporter stock, 10 (C/B 1994) or 20 (disc. 1994) shot detachable mag., 8.7 lbs. Mfg. in U.S. starting 1990, disc. 1998.

	$1,015	$835	$750	$675	$600	$550	$500

Last MSR was $1,204.

SAR-8 parts are interchangeable with both SAR-3 and HK-91 parts.

* **SAR-8 Tactical Counter Sniper Rifle** - .308 Win. cal., tactical sniper variation of the SAR-8. Mfg. 1996-98.

	$1,325	$1,000	$825	$725	$650	$575	$525

Last MSR was $1,610.

SAR-48 MODEL - .308 Win. cal., authentic model of the Belgian semi-auto FAL/LAR rifle, 21 in. barrel, adj. gas operation, 20 shot mag., walnut or stock, adj. sights, sling, and mag. loader. Mfg. 1985-89.

	$1,675	$1,475	$1,200	$1,050	$925	$850	$775

This model was available in the Israeli configuration with heavy barrel, bipod, flash hider, and flip-up buttplate - add approx. 20%. The SAR-48 was disc. in 1989 and reintroduced as the Model SAR-4800 in 1990.

* **SAR-48 Bush Rifle** - similar to SAR-48 model, except has 18 in. barrel.

	$1,750	$1,550	$1,250	$1,075	$950	$850	$775

SAR-4800 SPORTER MODEL - .223 Rem. (new 1997) or .308 Win. cal., authentic model of the Belgian semi-auto FAL/LAR rifle, 18 (.223 Rem. cal. only) or 21 in. barrel, adj. gas operation, 10 (C/B 1994) or 20 (disc.) shot mag., walnut (disc.) or black fiberglass thumbhole sporter stock, adj. sights, sling, and mag. loader. Mfg. 1990-98.

	$1,080	$915	$785	$675	$625	$575	$525

All SAR - 4800 parts are interchangeable with both SAR-48 and FN/FAL parts. This model is an updated variation of the pre-WWII FN Model 49.

* **SAR-4800 Bush Rifle Sporter Model** - similar to standard model, except has 18 in. barrel.

	$1,085	$900	$795	$695	$640	$595	$550

Last MSR was $1,216.

GRADING - PPGS™	100%	98%	95%	90%	80%	70%	60%

✱ *SAR-48 .22 Cal.* - .22 LR cal., variation of the Sporter Model. Disc. 1989.

	$725	$660	$595	$540	$495	$450	$400

Last MSR was $760.

DR-200 SPORTER RIFLE - while advertised, this model never went into production. ($687 was planned MSR).

STALLARD ARMS

Current manufacturer of 9mm Para. pistols located in Mansfield, OH since 1991. Distributed by MKS Supply, Inc. located in Dayton, OH.

Please refer to the Hi-Point listing in this text.

STANDARD ARMS & STANDARD ARMS MFG. CO.

Standard Arms started production in Wilmington, DE, in Sept., 1909, and the company folded in 1912. The company was restarted in 1913 as Standard Arms Mfg. Co., and closed in April, 1914.

Nearly 5,000 rifles were manufactured at the actual factory. At the time the plant closed, approx. 2,200 rifles were in various stages of production, and a supply of parts remained. These were primarily purchased by Numrich Arms, made into complete rifles, and sold. Total production (Standard Arms, Standard Arms Mfg. Co. & those assembled by Numrich Arms) reached approx. 7,000 rifles. The highest known serial number is 9012. Within serialization, it is noted that large blocks of numbers were abandoned, and this is thought to be due to changes and improvements made during production. In addition, as the factory folded with a large number of rifles in partial stages of production, it is often not possible to determine which rifles were actually made and completed at the factory, and which were completed outside the factory at a later date.

Many special order options were available, such as checkering, pistol grip, deluxe grades of woods, special sights, etc. Several grades of engraving were available, including Rocky Mountain, Adirondack, Sierra, and Selkirk. Lower priced "etched" models were also available and less frequently encountered than engraved models. A .50 caliber "Camp Carbine" was offered in smooth bore, slide action only. Approx. 25-30 were manufactured and utilized a special cartridge similar to the .50-70 shot cartridge. These are rarely encountered, although they are known to exist in collections.

RIFLES: SEMI-AUTO

MODEL G AUTOLOADER - .25-35 WCF, .30-30 Win., .25 Rem., .30 Rem., or .35 Rem. cal., bottom loading box mag., 22 in. barrel, open sight, straight stock. This was the first gas operated rifle in the U.S.A. Gas port can be closed and gun will function as a slide action. Mfg. 1910.

	$475	$400	$300	$275	$250	$225	$200

Subtract 10% for slide action only (Model M).

STANDARD ARMS OF NEVADA, INC.

Previous manufacturer 1999-2000, and located in Reno, NV.

PISTOLS: SEMI-AUTO

SA-9 - 9mm Para. cal., double action only, sub-compact design, 10 shot mag., 3.1 in. barrel, black polymer frame with matte black steel slide, 14 oz. Mfg. 1999-2000.

	$220	$190	$175	$165	$150	$140	$130

Last MSR was $249.

STANDARD 380 - while advertised, this model never went into production. MSR was $176.

GRADING - PPGS™	100%	98%	95%	90%	80%	70%	60%

STAR, BONIFACIO ECHEVERRIA S.A.

Previous manufacturer located in Eibar, Spain. Star, Bonifacio Echeverria S.A. closed its doors on July 28th, 1997, due to the intense financial pressure the Spanish arms industry experienced during the late 1990s. Previously imported by Interarms, located in Alexandria, VA.

PISTOLS: SEMI-AUTO

MODEL H - similar to Model HN, except 7.65mm, 7 shot.

$350	$250	$170	$120	$100	$90	$75

MODEL HN - .380 ACP cal., 6 shot, 2 3/4 in. barrel, blue, fixed sights, plastic grips. Mfg. 1934-41.

$375	$265	$180	$120	$100	$90	$75

MODEL I - .32 ACP cal., 9 shot, 4 3/4 in. barrel, blue, fixed sights, plastic grips. Mfg. 1934-36.

$350	$250	$170	$120	$100	$85	$70

MODEL IN - similar to Model I, except .380 ACP, 8 shot, 4 3/4 in. barrel, blue.

$395	$265	$180	$125	$105	$90	$75

MODEL 1920 - 9mm Bergmann Bayard or .38 Super cal., easily identified by unusual safety located on left rear slide. Issued to Spanish Guardia Civil.

$550	$400	$325	$280	$275	$185	$150

MODEL 1921 - 9mm Bergmann Bayard cal., this model was fitted with a grip safety that was later dropped when standardizing the Model A production. Issued to Spanish Guardia Civil.

$475	$350	$300	$250	$225	$185	$150

MODEL 1922 - designation for the early Model A. Issued to Spanish Guardia Civil.

$375	$285	$240	$215	$180	$145	$135

MODEL A - .38 Super cal., modified Government Colt, 5 in. barrel, no grip safety, blue, checkered wood grips. Mfg. 1934-disc.

$325	$275	$240	$215	$180	$145	$135

   Add 50% for Spanish Air Force issue if in original box.

MODEL A CARBINE - usually 7.63mm cal., unusual variation, slotted with tangent rear sight and extended barrel.

$1,750	$1,350	$1,050	$825	$700	$575	$450

   Add $500 for original stock (different from MB and MMS stock).

MODEL B - similar to Model A, but 9mm Para. cal. Mfg. 1934-75.

$295	$250	$205	$170	$150	$140	$115

   Add 50% for post-war German police if with 2 matching magazines.
   Add 150% if Waffenamt proofed (WaA251).

MODEL M - similar to Model A, except has large frame, available in 9mm Bergmann Bayard, 9mm Para., 8 shot, and .45 ACP, 7 shot, 5 in. barrel, blue, fixed sights, checkered wood or plastic grips.

$325	$275	$240	$215	$185	$160	$140

   Add 100% for early variation with ser. no. under 4,835.

MODEL P - .45 ACP cal. only, similar to Model A, except has large frame, 7 shot mag. Mfg. 1934-75.

$350	$285	$240	$215	$185	$160	$140

   Add 100% for early variation with ser. no. under 5,112.

GRADING - PPGS™	100%	98%	95%	90%	80%	70%	60%

MODELS SUPER A (9mm Largo), M (9mm Largo), & P (.45 ACP) - similar to Models A, M, & P, except has loaded chamber indicator, mag. safety, and easier takedown feature. Mfg. 1946-89.

	$395	$325	$215	$180	$160	$145	$125

Last MSR was $340.

Add 100% for Super M and Super P.

The Super A was a Spanish Service pistol. Recent imports in 80% condition were available in the $150 range.

MODEL SUPER B - 9mm Para. cal., similar to Model B, except has loaded chamber indicator, mag. safety and easier takedown feature, choice of blue or Starvel finish on Model B, late production models are poorly polished and have parkerized small parts. Importation disc. in 1990.

	$325	$250	$210	$185	$160	$140	$120

Last MSR was $330.

Add $30 for Starvel finish.

SUPER TARGET MODEL - similar to Star Super, but target sights, extended trigger guard, modified trigger. Rare.

	$1,250	$950	$800	$700	$600	$500	$400

MODEL MB - 9mm Para. cal., late production Model M cut for shoulder stock, mag. safety.

	$1,350	$1,000	$675	$565	$450	$365	$250

Add $300 for shoulder stock.
Add 20% to rig if matching stock.

MODEL MMS - 7.63mm cal., late production Model M cut for shoulder stock, mag. safety.

	$1,200	$900	$600	$400	$325	$260	$200

Add $300 for shoulder stock.
Add 20% for matching stock.

MODEL SI - .32 ACP cal., 8 shot, 4 in. barrel, blue, without grip safety, small version of Government .45 in appearance, plastic grips. Mfg. 1941-65.

	$200	$190	$160	$135	$115	$100	$80

MODEL S - similar to Model SI, except .380 ACP cal., 9 shot, mfg. 1941-1965. Importation of these Police contract models was disc. 1991.

	$235	$200	$160	$135	$115	$100	$80

Last MSR was $237.

Add $30 for Starvel finish.
Add 100% for guns issued to the Spanish Air Force with original box and 2 matching mags.

In 1989, Interarms imported factory reconditioned used Spanish Police Contract Model S pistols - these guns were available in either blue or Starvel finish and were supplied with a plastic box with accessories.

MODELS SUPER SI AND S - similar to Model S, with Super Star improvements. Mfg. 1946-1972.

	$250	$230	$210	$195	$165	$140	$120

MODEL SUPER SM - similar to Model Super S, except adjustable sight and wood grips. Mfg. 1973-81.

	$295	$250	$220	$200	$175	$145	$125

MODEL CO POCKET - .25 Auto cal., 2 3/4 in. barrel, blue, fixed sights, plastic grips. Mfg. 1929-56.

	$275	$195	$165	$145	$120	$110	$90

GRADING - PPGS™	100%	98%	95%	90%	80%	70%	60%

MODEL CU STARLET - .25 Auto cal., 2 3/8 in. barrel, alloy frame, fixed sights, plastic grips, blue, or chrome slide, frame anodized in black, blue, green, grey, or gold. Mfg. 1957-72.

	$235	$200	$165	$145	$120	$110	$90

Minor changes prompted a model redesignation as CK during 1973.

MODEL D - .380 ACP cal., small steel frame version of the Model A with several minor variations, 40,416 mfg. 1922-47.

	$550	$475	$400	$350	$300	$250	$200

MODEL DK (STARFIRE) - .380 ACP cal., 3 1/8 in. barrel, fixed sights, plastic stocks, finished in same color availability as Model CU. Mfg. 1957-1972, U.S. import ceased as of 1968 due to Federal GCA legislation.

	$400	$350	$295	$255	$225	$180	$155

Add 10% for unusual alloy colors.

Minor changes prompted a redesignation as DKL (.380 ACP) 1972 and DKI (.32 ACP) 1972.

MODEL HK LANCER - similar to Model Starfire, except .22 LR cal. Mfg. 1955-68.

	$245	$215	$180	$160	$140	$120	$110

MODEL F - .22 LR cal., 10 shot, 4 in. barrel, fixed sights, blue, plastic grips. Mfg. 1942-67.

	$325	$225	$140	$110	$95	$85	$55

MODEL FS - similar to Model F, except 6 in. barrel, adj. sights. Mfg. 1942-67.

	$325	$225	$150	$120	$100	$90	$65

MODEL F OLYMPIC RAPID FIRE - .22 Short cal., 9 shot, 7 in. barrel, adj. sight, aluminum slide, barrel weights and muzzle brake, blue, plastic grips. Mfg. 1942-67.

	$450	$325	$210	$175	$155	$140	$130

MODEL FR - restyled Model F, with "squared" barrel, adj. sight and slide stop. Mfg. 1967-72.

	$325	$225	$150	$120	$100	$90	$65

Add 15% for chrome finish.

MODELS FR SPORT AND MODEL FR TARGET - similar to Model FR, except FR Sport has 150mm barrel, and the Model FR Target has 180mm barrel, 65,534 mfg. 1967-83.

	$350	$250	$150	$120	$100	$90	$65

Add 15% for chrome finish.

MODEL FM - similar to Model FR, except heavier frame, web ahead of trigger guard, 4 1/2 in. barrel. 8,799 mfg. 1972-83.

	$300	$225	$150	$120	$100	$90	$65

MODEL BKS STARLIGHT - 9mm Para. cal., 8 shot, 4 1/4 in. barrel, plastic grips. Mfg. 1970-81.

Blue	$265	$230	$210	$180	$160	$145	$130

Add 10% for chrome finish.

MODEL BM SEMI-AUTO - 9mm Para. cal., single action, 8 shot mag., 4 in. barrel, steel frame, Colt 1911 action, blue, chrome (disc. 1989), or Starvel (new 1990) finish, plastic grips, 35 oz. Importation disc. 1991.

	$285	$245	$205	$180	$165	$155	$145

Last MSR was $415.

Add $30 for Starvel or chrome (disc. 1990) finish.
Add $150 for Navy issue with escutcheon grips.

GRADING - PPGS™	100%	98%	95%	90%	80%	70%	60%

MODEL BKM - identical to Model BM, except lightweight duraluminum frame, blue finish only, 26 oz. Importation disc. 1991.

	$310	$270	$225	$200	$180	$170	$155

Last MSR was $415.

MODEL PD - .45 ACP cal., 6 shot mag., single action, 4 in. barrel, adj. rear sight, blue or Starvel (new 1990) finish only, walnut grips, alloy frame, 25 oz. Mfg. 1975-importation disc. 1991.

	$345	$290	$250	$215	$195	$170	$160

Last MSR was $475.

Add $20 for Starvel finish (new 1990).
Add 20% for late variation with 30M rear sight.

MODEL 28 - 9mm Para. cal., double action, 15 shot mag., 4 1/4 in. barrel, blue finish only, advanced design, 40 oz. Mfg. 1983 and 1984 only.

	$400	$335	$325	$275	$250	$225	$200

Note: Model 28 is interesting since no screws are used in its manufacture. Hammer assembly (including spring, cocking lever, sear, disconnector and ejector) is housed under removable backstrap.

MODEL 30M - 9mm Para. cal. only, successor to the Model 28, double action, 4.33 in. barrel, 15 shot mag., blue finish only, adj. rear sight, checkered wraparound plastic grips, steel frame, 40 oz. New 1985. Importation disc. 1991.

	$350	$295	$275	$255	$235	$215	$195

Last MSR was $495.

MODEL 30 PK DURAL FRAME - similar to Model 30M, except slightly shorter duraluminum frame, 3.86 in. barrel, 30 oz. Disc. 1989.

	$350	$295	$270	$250	$225	$210	$195

Last MSR was $580.

MODEL 31P (STEEL FRAME)/31PK (DURAL FRAME) - 9mm Para. (disc. 1993) or .40 S&W (new 1990) cal., compact variation utilizing double action, features Acculine barrel (3.86 in.), 14 shot mag., ambidextrous safety with decocking lever, blue or Starvel finish, all steel construction, 39.4 oz. Imported 1990-94.

	$350	$295	$270	$250	$225	$210	$195

Last MSR was $398.

Add $30 for Starvel finish (disc. 1993).
Prices are the same for Model 31PK Dural Frame (imported 1990-93).

MODEL M40 FIRESTAR - .40 S&W cal., single action, 6 shot mag., 3.39 in. Acculine barrel, checkered rubber grips, compact design utilizing all steel construction, 3-dot sighting system with adjustable rear sight, blue, Starvel, or nickel (new 1997) finish, 30.35 oz. Mfg. 1990-disc.

	$295	$250	$200	$180	$165	$150	$135

Last MSR was $306.

Add $17 for nickel finish.
Add $20 for Starvel finish.

✳ *Model M40 Firestar Plus* - similar to M40 Firestar, except incorporates alloy frame, new grip design, ambidextrous easy-view safety, and fast button release 10 shot mag. Advertised initially during 1995.
This model was never released for commercial sale.

MODEL M43 FIRESTAR - 9mm Para. cal., 7 shot mag., otherwise similar to Model M40 Firestar. Disc.

	$295	$265	$235	$200	$185	$170	$155

Last MSR was $296.

Add $17 for nickel finish.
Add $20 for Starvel finish.

✳ *Model M43 Firestar Plus* - similar to M43 Firestar, except incorporates alloy frame, new grip design, ambidextrous easy-view safety, and fast button release 10 shot double stack mag. Mfg. 1995-97.

	$325	$265	$235	$200	$185	$170	$155

Last MSR was $351.

Add $12 for nickel finish.
Add $25 for Starvel finish.

MODEL M45 FIRESTAR - .45 ACP cal., single action, ultra compact design featuring 4 barrel lugs, steel frame and slide, 3.6 in. reverse taper Acculine barrel, 6 shot mag., black synthetic grips, blue or Starvel finish, 35 oz. Mfg. 1992-97.

	$325	$295	$250	$200	$185	$170	$155

Last MSR was $351.

Add $12 for nickel finish.
Add $20 for Starvel finish.

✳ *Model M45 Firestar Plus* - similar to M45 Firestar, except incorporates alloy frame, new grip design, ambidextrous easy-view safety, and fast button release 10 shot mag. Advertised during 1995.

This model was never released for commercial sale.

MEGASTAR - 10mm or .45 ACP cal., larger variation of the Firestar featuring 4.6 in. barrel and 12 (.45 ACP) or 14 (10mm) shot mag., 47.6 oz. Imported 1992-94.

	$450	$375	$350	$325	$295	$275	$250

Last MSR was $653.

Add $29 for Starvel finish.

ULTRASTAR - 9mm Para. or .40 S&W (new 1996) cal., compact double action design, 3.57 in. barrel, 9 shot mag., blue steel metal, triple dot sights, steel internal mechanism, polymer exterior construction, 26 oz. Mfg. 1994-97.

	$295	$250	$225	$200	$175	$165	$155

Last MSR was $296.

STEEL CITY ARMS, INC.

Previous manufacturer located in Pittsburgh, PA until 1990. In 1991, the name was changed to Desert Industries, Inc. and manufacture was moved to Las Vegas, NV. Very few guns exist with Steel City markings.

PISTOLS: SEMI-AUTO

DOUBLE DEUCE - .22 LR cal. only, double action, matte finish stainless steel, 2 1/2 in. barrel, 7 shot mag., unchecked rosewood grips, 18 oz. Mfg. 1984-90.

	$265	$230	$200

Last MSR was $290.

Various select hardwood stocks were also available at extra cost ($20-100).

STERLING

Previous manufacturer located in Gasport and Lockport (1978-1986), NY until 1986.

PISTOLS

Rather than list individual models, the following generalizations will help in ascertaining values for this trademark. Models 300, 302 and 402 will average between $75 and $150 if in 70%+ condition, Models 283, 284, 285 (Husky), and 286 (Trapper) are semi-auto .22 cal. pistols with various barrel lengths - values will range between $90-$150. Models 400 (.380 ACP), PPL (.380 ACP short barrel), and 450 (.45 ACP, prototype only - no mfg.) usually range between $150-$275.

STERLING ARMAMENT, LTD.

Previous manufacturer established c. 1900, and located in Dagenham, Essex, England. Previously imported and distributed by Cassi Inc. located in Colorado Springs, CO until 1990.

CARBINES: SEMI-AUTO

AR-180 - please refer to Armalite section for more information and pricing on this model.

STERLING MK 6 - 9mm Para. cal., blowback semi-auto with floating firing pin, shrouded 16.1 in. barrel, side mounted mag., folding stock, 7 1/2 lbs. Disc. 1989.

	N/A	$1,475	$1,300	$1,075	$875	$675	$550

Last MSR was $650.

PISTOLS: SEMI-AUTO

PARAPISTOL MK 7 C4 - 9mm Para. cal., 4 in. barrel, semi-auto paramilitary design pistol, crinkle finish, same action as MK. 6 Carbine, fires from closed bolt, 10, 15, 20, 30, 34 or 68 shot mag., 5 lbs. Disc. 1989.

	N/A	$1,400	$1,250	$1,075	$875	$675	$550

Last MSR was $600.

Add $50 per 30 or 34 shot mag., $125 for 68 shot mag.

PARAPISTOL MK 7 C8 - 9mm Para. cal., similar to C4, except has 7.8 in. barrel, 5 1/4 lbs. Disc. 1989.

	N/A	$1,400	$1,250	$1,075	$875	$675	$550

Last MSR was $620.

Add $50 per 30 or 34 shot mag., $125 for 68 shot mag.

STEVENS, J., ARMS COMPANY

J. Stevens Arms Company was founded in 1864 at Chicopee Falls, MA as J. Stevens & Co. In 1886 the name was changed to J. Stevens Arms and Tool Co. In 1916, the plant became New England Westinghouse, and tooled up for Mosin-Nagant Rifles. In 1920, the plant was sold to the Savage Arms Corp. and manufactured guns were marked "J. Stevens Arms Co." This designation was dropped in the late 1940s, and only the name "Stevens" has been used up to 1990. Beginning in 1999, Savage Arms, Inc. began manufacturing the Stevens Favorite again as the Model 30G.

Depending on the remaining Stevens factory data, a factory letter authenticating the configuration of a particular specimen may be obtained by contacting Mr. John Callahan (see Trademark Index for listings and address). The charge for this service is $15.00 per gun - please allow 2-4 weeks for an adequate response.

For more Stevens model information, please refer to the Serialization section in the back of this text.

COMBINATION GUNS

MODEL 22-410 - .22 LR cal. over .410 bore, selector on right side of frame, Tenite stock. Introduced mid-1939-disc.

	$250	$200	$165	$140	$120	$110	$100

PISTOLS

NO. 10 TARGET SINGLE SHOT - .22 LR cal., 8 in. barrel, blue, adj. sights, rubber grips, squared-off like an automatic pistol, tip up action. Mfg. 1919-39.

	$220	$200	$185	$165	$140	$120	$100

GRADING - PPGS™	100%	98%	95%	90%	80%	70%	60%

NO. 35 TARGET SINGLE SHOT - .22 LR or .25 Rimfire cal., 6, 8, 10, or 12 1/4 in. barrel, blue, walnut grips. Mfg. 1907-39.

	$350	$300	$265	$220	$200	$185	$165

NO. 35 "OFF-HAND" SHOTGUN - .410 smoothbore cal., 8 or 12 1/4 in. barrel. Mfg. 1923-35.

	$350	$300	$250	$225	$200	$150	$125

If this model is not currently registered with the ATF, it cannot be legally owned, and is subject to seizure.

NO. 35 "OFF-HAND" AUTOSHOT - similar to Off-Hand Shotgun. Mfg. 1929-34.

	$300	$250	$225	$200	$150	$125	$100

RIFLES

Stevens made a wide variety of inexpensive, utilitarian rifles that, to date, have attracted mostly shooting interest, but little collector interest. A listing of these models may be found in the back of this text under "Serialization."

TIP-UP RIFLES - .22 S, .22 LR, .25 Stevens, .32, .38, or .44 Long RF or CF, variations No. 1 - No. 15 feature various weights, wood styles, sights, and other differences, later series has full loop at rear triggerguard, circa 1870s-95.

* *Basic Model No. 1 without forearm*

	$500	$475	$425	$375	$300	$250	$200

* *Model 101* - .44 shot cartridge, built on the No. 12 Marksman action, lever action opening, straight grip stock, 26 in. barrel. Mfg. 1914-20.

	$250	$225	$195	$175	$150	$125	$100

NO. 12 MARKSMAN - .22 LR, .25 Long or .32 rimfire cal., boys type single shot with traditional Stevens profile, operated with underlever that allows barrel to tip up for loading, 22 in. round tapered barrel, walnut stock and forend, silver blade front sight and "V" block rear sight, knurled thumbscrew for take-down. Mfg. 1912-1933.

	$275	$240	$215	$185	$160	$135	$110

NO. 14 1/2 LITTLE SCOUT - .22 RF cal., 18 or 20 in. barrel, rolling breech block action, iron sights. Mfg. 1909-36.

	$250	$225	$195	$175	$150	$125	$100

STEVENS/SPRINGFIELD MODEL 15/120 - .22 S, L, or LR, bolt action single shot, one piece integral barrel and receiver, manually operated cocking piece at rear of bolt, birch hardwood stock, open rear and bead front sight, thousands mfg. for companies such as Sears, Montgomery Wards, J.C. Penny, Cotter & Co., etc. Mfg. 1936-1971.

	$200	$185	$165	$135	$115	$95	$80

POCKET RIFLES - detachable serially numbered nickel-plated stock, variations found within each frame size.

* *Small Frame* - .22 cal. (various issues).

	$450	$400	$350	$300	$275	$235	$200

* *Without Stock*

	$300	$250	$200	$150	$125	$100	$80

* *Medium Frame* - .22, .32, .38, .44 cals. (various issues).

	$500	$450	$400	$350	$300	$250	$200

* *Without Stock*

	$300	$250	$200	$150	$125	$100	$75

* *Large Frame* - .22 to .44 cals.

	$600	$550	$500	$450	$400	$350	$300

GRADING - PPGS™	100%	98%	95%	90%	80%	70%	60%
✳ **Without Stock**							
	$425	$375	$325	$275	$225	$200	$175

MODEL 44 IDEAL SINGLE SHOT - .22 LR through .44-40 WCF cals., rolling block, lever action, takedown, 24 or 26 in. barrels, straight grip stock and forearm. Mfg. 1894-1932.

	$650	$600	$550	$500	$425	$325	$300

Subtract 20% for Rimfire cals.

MODEL 44 1/2 IDEAL SINGLE SHOT - similar to Model 44, except .22 LR through .44-40 WCF cals., falling block, lever action, takedown, 24 or 26 in. barrels, straight grip stock and forearm, action redesigned 1903. Mfg. 1903-16.

	$950	$850	$750	$625	$500	$425	$350

Subtract 10% for rimfire cals.

MODELS 45-54 SINGLE SHOTS - .22 LR through .44-40 WCF cals., rolling and falling block receivers, lever action, takedown, deluxe versions of the Models 44 and 44 1/2, many special order features, including double-set triggers, types of finish, engraving, length and weight of barrels, stock configuration could be special ordered. The higher grade Schuetzens and Stevens-Pope are very collectible and command premiums. These models have to be taken one at a time for determining value. Therefore, no prices are shown. Mfg. 1896-1916.

MODEL 200 BOLT ACTION - .22-250 Rem., .223 Rem., .243 Win., .25-06 Rem., .270 Win., .30-06, .308 Win., .300 Win. Mag., 7mm-08 Rem., or 7mm Rem. Mag. cal., short or long action, no sights, Accutrigger not available on this model, 22 or 24 in. barrel, checkered stock and forend. New 2005.

MSR $316	$250	$220	$195	$180	$165	$150	$135

MODEL 322 BOLT ACTION (INCLUDING A, B, C, & S) - .22 Hornet cal., otherwise similar to Model 325. Mfg. 1947-50.

	$450	$395	$335	$275	$225	$185	$150

The Model 322S had an aperture sight.

MODEL 325 BOLT ACTION (INCLUDING A, B, C) - .30-30 Win. cal., 4 shot detachable mag. Introduced 1947. Disc. 1950.

	$375	$335	$275	$225	$185	$150	$135

NO. 414 ARMORY MODEL - .22 LR or .22 Short cal. only, lever action, 26 in. barrel, single shot, Lyman aperture sight. Mfg. 1912-32.

	$450	$400	$375	$330	$290	$250	$220

MODEL 416 - .22 LR cal., bolt action, 25 in. medium barrel, 5 shot mag. Disc.

	$140	$120	$110	$100	$90	$80	$70

This model was also mfg. as a U.S. military training rifle. Can be denoted by "U.S. Property" on rear of bolt housing. Healthy premiums exist for this variation. Originally, 10,000 were mfg. at a cost of $22.42 each.

NO. 417 WALNUT HILL MODEL - .22 LR, .22 Short, and .22 Hornet cal., lever action, 28 or 29 in. extra heavy barrel, target stock with full pistol grip, beavertail forend, made in 0-3 suffix variations (different sights). Mfg. 1932-47.

	$875	$675	$525	$475	$440	$395	$360

NO. 417 1/2 WALNUT HILL MODEL - similar to No. 417, except available in .25 rimfire also. Mfg. 1932-40.

	$875	$675	$525	$475	$440	$395	$360

NO. 418 WALNUT HILL MODEL - .22 LR or .22 Short only, 26 in. barrel, pistol grip stock, semi beavertail forearm. Mfg. 1932-40.

	$595	$400	$295	$260	$230	$200	$180

GRADING - PPGS™	100%	98%	95%	90%	80%	70%	60%

NO. 425 HIGH POWER LEVER ACTION RIFLE - .25, .30, .32, or .35 Rem. cals., 22 in. round barrel with 2/3 length mag. tube, side ejection, blue only, plain walnut stock and forearm, originally designed by John Redfield. Approx. 26,000 mfg. 1910-17.

	$650	$595	$535	$465	$400	$350	$295

Variations of the No. 425 include the No. 430 (deluxe checkered stock and forearm), No. 435 (extra fancy checkered stock and forearm with engraved designs on receiver borders and lever), or No. 440 (best quality checkered walnut with fully engraved game scenes, and engraved forearm tip and lever). Values range respectively from $450-$950, $650-$1,400, and $1,000-$2,950.

STEVENS FAVORITE NO.'S 17-29 - .22 LR, .25 RF or .32 RF cal., 24 in. barrel most common, other lengths available, Rocky Mountain front sight, straight grip stock, small tapered forearm. Mfg. 1894-1935. Octagonal barrels command a 33% premium.

	$450	$395	$300	$195	$165	$145	$125

STEVENS FAVORITE (CURRENT MFG.) - .17 HMR (Model 30R17, new 2004), .22 LR (Model 30G), or .22 Mag. (Model GM, new 2002) cal., choice of solid or takedown (new 2004) action, lever action falling block with inertia firing pin, 21 in. half octagon (Model 30G) or full octagon (Model GM) barrel, uncheckered wood stock and forearm, open sights, 4.25 lbs. New mfg. began in late 1998 by Savage Arms, Inc.

MSR $228	$185	$160	$135	$115	$100	$80	$65

Add $38 for .22 Mag. cal. (new 2002).
Add $64 for .17 HMR cal. (new 2004).
Add $21 for takedown action (.22 LR or .17 HMR cal. only).

STEVENS MODEL 65 - .22 LR cal., bolt action, 20 in. barrel, open sights, 5 shot mag., checkered walnut stock. Mfg. 1969-disc.

	$90	$70	$55	$45	$35	$30	$30

NO. 70 "VISIBLE LOADING" SLIDE ACTION RIFLE - .22 S, L, or LR cal., exposed hammer, 22 in. barrel, open sights, straight grip stock, tube mag., grooved slide handle. Other variations with different barrel lengths and sights will command slight premiums.

	$250	$175	$150	$130	$115	$100	$90

MODEL 71 "STEVENS FAVORITE" COMMEMORATIVE - .22 LR cal., replica of original, 22 in. octagon barrel, plain straight stock, medallion inlaid, crescent butt. 1,000 mfg. in 1971.

	$250	$195	$150

Last MSR was $75.

SIDE LEVER CRACKSHOT - .22 RF or .32 RF cal., boys type single shot rifle, breech block is operated by a small lever on the side of the frame, side lever opening, 20 in. round barrel with fixed sights. Mfg. 1900-1913.

	$250	$225	$195	$175	$150	$125	$100

NO. 26 CRACKSHOT - .22 RF or .32 RF cal., boys type single shot rifle, under lever opening, 18 in. round barrel, hardwood straight grip stock and forend, open sights. Mfg. 1913-41.

	$250	$225	$195	$175	$150	$125	$100

MODEL 72 CRACKSHOT - .22 LR cal., single shot falling block action, 22 in. octagon barrel, open sights, color case hardened frame, straight stock. Mfg. 1972-89.

	$145	$125	$110	$100	$90	$80	$70

Last MSR was $165.

MODEL 74 - similar to Model 72 Crackshot, except has round barrel. Mfg. 1972-89.

	$140	$120	$110	$100	$90	$80	$70

Last MSR was $165.

GRADING - PPGS™	100%	98%	95%	90%	80%	70%	60%

MODEL 987 - .22 LR cal. only, semi-auto, 15 shot tube mag., 20 in. barrel, hardwood Monte Carlo stock, adj. rear sight, 6 lbs. Disc. 1989.

	$95	$80	$70	$60	$50	$40	$45

Last MSR was $119.

MODEL 89 LEVER ACTION - .22 LR cal., single shot, 18 1/2 in. barrel, Martini type action, Western style lever, straight stock. Mfg. 1976-disc.

	$85	$65	$60	$50	$45	$40	$35

SHOTGUNS

Stevens made a wide variety of inexpensive, utilitarian shotguns that, to date, have attracted mostly shooting interest, but little collector interest. A listing of these models may be found in the back of this text under "Serialization."

NO. 20 FAVORITE - .22 RF or .32 RF smooth bore, 24 in. barrel, smooth bore variation of the No. 17 rifle.

	$250	$225	$200	$165	$125	$95	$75

NO. 26 1/2 CRACKSHOT - .22 RF or .32 RF smooth bore, smooth bore variation of the No. 26 rifle.

	$225	$200	$175	$135	$110	$85	$65

MODEL 67 SLIDE ACTION - 12, 20 ga., or .410 bore, all are 3 in. chambered, steel receiver, 5 shot, upper receiver safety, 6 1/4-7 1/2 lbs. Recent mfg. by Stevens. Disc. 1989.

	$200	$180	$170	$155	$145	$135	$125

Last MSR was $229.

Add $30 for choke tubes (with VR).
Add $10 for VR only.

✳ *Model 67 VTR-K Camo* - 12 or 20 ga., 28 in. VR barrel with choke tubes, laminated camo stock. Mfg. 1986-88.

	$250	$220	$190	$170	$155	$145	$135

Last MSR was $295.

✳ *Slug Model* - 12 ga. only, 21 in. barrel, rifle sights. Disc. 1989.

	$200	$165	$140	$110	$100	$90	$80

Last MSR was $245.

✳ *Model 67 VRT-Y* - 20 ga. only, 22 in. VR barrel with choke tubes, youth model with smaller stock dimensions. Mfg. 1987-88.

	$205	$170	$140	$110	$100	$90	$80

Last MSR was $259.

MODEL 69-RXL SLIDE ACTION - 12 ga. only, law enforcement version of the Model 67, 18 1/4 in. cylinder bore barrel with recoil pad, 6 1/2 lbs. Disc. 1989.

	$200	$165	$140	$110	$100	$90	$80

Last MSR was $245.

MODEL 77 SLIDE ACTION W/ J, K, M, OR SC SUFFIX - 12 ("J" suffix), 16 ("K" suffix), or 20 ("M" suffix) ga. or .410 bore, "SC" designates Super Choke. Mfg. 1955-1971.

	$175	$160	$140	$120	$100	$80	$60

MODEL 94 - 12, 16, 20, 28 ga., or .410 bore, single shot breakopen, hammer, 6 1/4 lbs. Mfg. 1929-disc.

	$95	$85	$75	$60	$50	$45	$40

Last MSR was $92.

GRADING - PPGS™	100%	98%	95%	90%	80%	70%	60%

MODEL 124 BOLT ACTION - 12 ga. only, straight pull action, 28 in. barrel, 3 shot, Tenite buttstock and forearm, circa 1950.

	$215	$190	$175	$155	$145	$135	$125

NO. 200 SLIDE ACTION - 20 ga., 3 in. chamber, tube mag., 26, 28, 30, or 32 in. barrel, take-down, 5 shot, 6 1/2 lbs., c. 1910.

	$225	$190	$180	$150	$125	$95	$85

MODEL 240 O/U - .410 bore, split hammers, double trigger.

	$350	$300	$250	$220	$190	$170	$155

MODEL 311 SxS - 12, 16, 20 ga., or .410 bore, 3 in. chambers, double triggers, extractors, VR. Disc. 1989.

	$245	$205	$185	$150	$140	$125	$115

Last MSR was $309.

Add 30% for .410 bore.
Add 20% for 16 or 20 ga.

✱ *Model 311-R* - 12 ga. only, similar to Model 311, except has 18 1/4 in. cylinder bore barrels for law enforcement use, 3 in. chambers, 6 3/4 lbs. Disc. 1989.

	$245	$205	$185	$150	$140	$125	$115

Last MSR was $309.

MODEL 315 SxS - 12, 16, 20 ga., or .410 bore, DT, extractors, hammerless, case colored frame, walnut stock and forearm, model identification is on top lever, this model also was mfg. under various trade names, including Riverside and Springfield.

	$225	$185	$150	$140	$125	$115	$100

MODEL 411 SxS - 12, 20 ga. (disc. 2004) or .410 bore (disc. 2004), 28 in. monobloc barrels with choke tubes, boxlock action with laser engraved sideplates, SST, checkered walnut stock and splinter forearm, approx. 6.25 lbs., mfg. in Russia. New 2004.

MSR $438	$380	$330	$280	$235	$200	$180	$160

MODEL 520 SLIDE ACTION - this model was designed by John M. Browning, slight humpback in receiver.

	$190	$180	$150	$125	$95	$85	$75

MODEL 520-30 TRENCH/RIOT MILITARY SHOTGUNS - see the "Trench/Riot Shotgun" category in the T section for more information and prices.

MODEL 620 SLIDE ACTION - an improved version of the Model 520 with streamlined receiver.

	$275	$240	$215	$180	$160	$135	$100

MODEL 620 TRENCH/RIOT MILITARY SHOTGUNS - see the "Trench/Riot Shotgun" category in the T section for more information and prices.

MODEL 675 SLIDE ACTION - 12 ga. only, 24 in. VR multi-choked barrel with iron sights (including removable rear ramp), hardwood stock with recoil pad, 6 1/2 lbs. Mfg. 1987-88.

	$250	$220	$190	$170	$155	$145	$135

Last MSR was $295.

MODEL 9478 - 10, 12, 20 ga., or .410 bore, single shot break open, inertia firing pin, external hammer. Mfg. 1978-85.

	$95	$85	$75	$60	$50	$45	$40

FOX/STEVENS MODEL B SxS - please refer to this listing in the A.H. Fox section.

FOX/STEVENS MODEL B-SE SxS - please refer to this listing in the A.H. Fox section.

GRADING - PPGS™	100%	98%	95%	90%	80%	70%	60%

STEYR AUSTRIAN MILITARY

Previously manufactured for the Austrian military in Steyr, Austria.

RIFLES: BOLT ACTION

MODEL 95 RIFLE - 8x56R Mannlicher cal., straight pull bolt action, 30 in. barrel, adj. sights, military full stock.

	$140	$110	$100	$85	$65	$55	$40

MODEL 90 CARBINE - similar to Model 95, except 19 1/2 in. barrel.

	$155	$125	$110	$95	$85	$65	$45

STEYR DAIMLER PUCH A.G.

Previous manufacturer located in Steyr, Austria 1911 to circa 1960.

PISTOLS

POCKET AUTO - .25 ACP or .32 ACP cal., tip up barrel, mag. fed. Disc.

	$325	$265	$200	$150	$140	$130	$120

Add 10% for .32 ACP cal.

ROTH STEYR AUTO (MODEL 1907) - 8mm Steyr cal.

	$850	$650	$475	$350	$300	$250	$200

Add 30% for "Budapest" markings.

STEYR-HAHN MODEL 1911 AUTOMATIC - 9mm Steyr cal., 8 shot, 5.1 in. barrel, fixed magazine top loaded by stripper clip, blue, checkered wood grips. Mfg. 1911-19. In 1938, the Germans confiscated and converted a quantity of these to 9mm Para., "08" was stamped on the left side of these guns.

	$450	$375	$325	$275	$225	$195	$175

Add 100% if marked "08" or with Rumanian Crest.

MODEL SP - .32 ACP cal., semi-auto, trigger cocking mechanism, very rare. Mfg. in 1959 only.

	$650	$595	$540	$495	$450	$400	$350

STEYR MANNLICHER

Currently manufactured by Steyr-Mannlicher AG & Co. KG in Austria. Founded in Steyr, Austria by Joseph Werndl circa 1864. Rifles are currently imported beginning 2004 by Steyr USA, located in West Point, MS. Previously imported 2002-2003 by Dynamit Nobel, located in Closter, NJ. Previously imported and distributed until 2002 by Gun South, Inc. (GSI) located in Trussville, AL.

Note: also see Mannlicher Schoenauer in the M section for pre-WWII models.

For more information and current pricing on both new and used Steyr airguns, please refer to the *Blue Book of Airguns* by Dr. Robert Beeman & John Allen (also online).

PISTOLS: SEMI-AUTO

MODEL GB - 9mm Para. cal., double action, 18 shot mag., gas delayed blowback action, non-glare checkered plastic grips, 5 1/4 in. barrel with Polygon rifling, matte finish, steel construction, 2 lbs. 6 oz. Importation disc. 1988.

Commercial	$600	$525	$475	$425	$375	$335	$300
Military	$550	$450	$395	$350	$300	$280	$260

Last MSR was $514.

In 1987, Steyr mfg. a military variation of the Model GB featuring a phosphate finish - only 937 were imported into the U.S.

GRADING - PPGS™	100%	98%	95%	90%	80%	70%	60%

MODEL SPP - 9mm Para. cal., single action semi-auto, delayed blow back system with rotating 5.9 in. barrel, 15 or 30 shot mag., utilizes synthetic materials and advanced ergonomics, adj. sights, grooved receiver for scope mounting, matte black finish, 44 oz. Limited importation 1992-93.

	$800	$675	$600	$550	$495	$450	$400

Last MSR was $895.

MODEL M SERIES - 9mm Para., .357 SIG, or .40 S&W cal., features first integrated limited access key lock safety in a semi-auto pistol, 3 different safety conditions, black synthetic frame, 10 shot mag., matte black finish, loaded chamber indicator, triangle/trapezoid sights, 28 oz. Limited importation 1999-2002.

	$440	$395	$360	$330	$300	$275	$250

Last MSR was $610.

Add $65 for night sights.

M-A1 SERIES - .357 SIG (M357 A-1), 9mm Para. (M9 A-1), or .40 S&W (M40 A-1) cal., updated Model M with Picatinny rail on lower front of frame, redesigned grip frame, lockable safety system, black polymer frame with matte black finished slide, 4 in. barrel, 12 (.40 S&W or .357 SIG) or 14 (9mm Para.) shot mag., triangle/trapezoid sights, approx. 27 oz. Importation began 2004.

MSR $589	$465	$425	$390	$355	$315	$285	$260

Add $23 for right angle sights with Trilux.

M-A1 SERIES SPECIAL EDITION - 9mm Para., or .40 S&W cal., matte black finish, advanced ultra-rigid synthetic frame, 4 in. barrel, triangle/trapezoid sights, three user-selectable safety features. New 2004.

MSR $610	$495	$450	$400	$360	$320	$290	$270

This model is available exclusively through Davidson's.

MODEL S - similar to Model M, except has 3.5 in. barrel and shorter grip frame, 10 shot mag., 22 1/2 oz. Limited importation 2000-2002.

	$475	$435	$385	$350	$325	$300	$280

Last MSR was $610.

S-SERIES SPECIAL EDITION - 9mm Para., or .40 S&W cal., matte black finish, advanced ultra-rigid synthetic frame, 3 1/2 in. barrel, traingle/trapezoid sights, three user-selectable safety features. New 2004.

MSR $610	$495	$450	$400	$360	$320	$290	$270

This model is available exclusively through Davidson's.

RIFLES: BOLT ACTION, RECENT PRODUCTION

Current production guns are now called Steyr-Mannlicher models. For models manufactured 1903 - 1971, please refer to the Mannlicher Schoenauer Sporting Rifles section in this text.

The recenty discontinued models SL, L, M, S, and S/T listed have 4 different action lengths and model designations stand for the following: SL=Super Light, L=Light, M=Medium, S=Magnum, S/T=Magnum with heavy barrel. These sporting rifles were available with left-hand stock - add $109 and with either single set or double-set triggers - add $125.

ZEPHYR 22 - .22 LR cal., features full length Mannlicher stock, single- or double-set triggers, open sights, checkered walnut stock with horn cap, sling swivels. Mfg. circa 1955-71.

	$1,350	$1,200	$1,000	$850	$725	$600	$525

MODEL M72 L/M RIFLE - .243 Win., .308 Win., .270 Win., .30-06, 7x57mm, and 7x64mm cals., 23 in. barrel, single- or double-set triggers. Mfg. 1972-80.

	$795	$725	$650	$575	$500	$460	$420

GRADING - PPGS™	100%	98%	95%	90%	80%	70%	60%

MODEL SL - .222 Rem., .222 Rem. Mag. (disc.), .223 Rem., .22-250 Rem. (disc. 1992), or 5.6x50mm (disc. 1991) cal., bolt action, 23.6 in. barrel, double-set triggers, rotary mag. Available in full stock (Carbine), half stock (rifle), or varmint version (vent. square forearm). Disc. 1996.

	$1,500	$1,200	$800	$725	$600	$495	$450

Last MSR was $2,250.

✳ *Carbine Model (Full Stock)* - skipline checkered full stock, 20 in. barrel. Disc. 1996.

	$1,600	$1,300	$850	$800	$650	$550	$450

Last MSR was $2,450.

✳ *Varmint Rifle* - .222 Rem. (disc.), .223 Rem. (new 1993), or .22-250 Rem. (disc. 1992) cal., 26 in. heavy barrel, stippled pistol grip, vent. forearm, no sights. Disc. 1996.

	$1,625	$1,325	$875	$800	$650	$550	$500

Last MSR was $2,450.

MODEL L - 5.6x57mm (disc. 1991), .243 Win., or .308 Win. cals., available in .22-250 and 6mm Rem. on special order only, otherwise same general specifications as Model SL. Disc. 1996.

	$1,500	$1,325	$950	$775	$675	$600	$540

Last MSR was $2,250.

✳ *Carbine Model (Full Stock)* - skip-line checkered full stock, 20 in. barrel. Disc. 1996.

	$1,650	$1,400	$995	$825	$700	$600	$540

Last MSR was $2,450.

✳ *Varmint Rifle* - .222 Rem. (disc. 1991), .22-250 Rem., .243 Win. (disc.), or .308 Win. (disc.) cal., 26 in. heavy barrel, stippled pistol grip, vent. forearm, no sights. Disc. 1996.

	$1,600	$1,325	$875	$800	$650	$550	$500

Last MSR was $2,450.

✳ *Model L Luxus* - 5.6x57mm, .243 Win., or .308 Win. cal., full or half stock only, .22-250 Rem. and 6mm Rem. available on special order, 3 shot mag. Disc. 1996.

	$1,700	$1,450	$1,100	$900	$800	$700	$650

Last MSR was $2,950.

✳ *Model L Luxus Carbine (Full Stock)* - similar to L Luxus rifle, except has full stock and 20 in. barrel. Disc. 1996.

	$1,800	$1,500	$1,200	$1,000	$800	$700	$650

Last MSR was $3,150.

MODEL M - 6.5x55mm, 6.5x57mm, 7x64mm, .270 Win., .30-06, or 9.3x62mm cal., bolt action, full stock or half stock, rotary mag., double-set triggers. Disc. 1996.

	$1,550	$1,325	$950	$775	$675	$600	$540

Last MSR was $2,250.

Add $400 for left-hand action.

✳ *Carbine Model (Full Stock)* - skipline checkered full stock, 20 in. barrel. Disc. 1996.

	$1,650	$1,400	$995	$825	$700	$600	$540

Last MSR was $2,450.

Add $400 for left-hand action.

✳ *Professional Rifle* - .270 Win., 7x57mm (disc. 1991), 7x64mm, .30-06, or 9.3x62mm cal., 23.6 in. barrel, Cycolac synthetic stock, 7 1/2 lbs. Disc. 1993.

	$1,200	$900	$800	$700	$600	$540	$495

Last MSR was $1,710.

Add $469 for left-hand action with half stock (rifle).
Add $625 for left-hand action with full stock (carbine).

This variation is also available in .270 Win. or .30-06 cal. with half stock and 20 in. barrel (carbine).

Model M Luxus - 6.5x55mm, 6.5x57mm (disc.), 7x64mm, .270 Win., or .30-06 cal., special order in 6.5x55mm and 7.5mm Swiss. Disc. 1996.

| | $1,750 | $1,500 | $1,200 | $900 | $800 | $700 | $650 |

Last MSR was $2,950.

Model M Luxus Carbine (Full Stock) - similar to Model M Luxus, except with full stock and 20 in. barrel. Disc. 1996.

| | $1,900 | $1,650 | $1,300 | $950 | $825 | $700 | $650 |

Last MSR was $3,150.

Carbine - 1000 Year Commemorative - 1984 only, .30-06 cal.

| | $4,200 | $3,620 | $2,835 |

M-III PROFESSIONAL - .25-06 Rem. (new 1996), .270 Win., .30-06, or 7x64mm cal., features black synthetic half stock, 23.6 in. barrel, no sights. Imported 1994-96.

| | $800 | $700 | $600 | $500 | $475 | $450 | $375 |

Last MSR was $995.

Add $130 for stippled checkered European wood stock.

JAGD MATCH - .222 Rem., .243 Win., or .308 Win. cal., features shortened action, 23.6 in. heavy barrel with iron sights, 5 shot rotary mag., laminated checkered half-stock, recoil pad, designed for European Match events limited to hunting rifles, double-set triggers, 8 1/2 lbs. Imported 1995-96.

| | $1,600 | $1,200 | $1,000 | $800 | $675 | $600 | $540 |

Last MSR was $2,450.

MODEL S (MAGNUM) - 6.5x68mm, 8x68S, .300 Win. Mag., .338 Win. Mag. (disc. 1992), .375 H&H, or 7mm Rem. Mag. cal., half-stock, 26 in. barrel, bolt action. Disc. 1996.

| | $1,600 | $1,200 | $1,000 | $800 | $725 | $625 | $550 |

Last MSR was $2,550.

MODEL S/T - available in 9.3x64 (disc. 1992), .300 H&H, .375 H&H, or .458 Win. Mag. cal., half-stock, 26 in. heavy barrel. Disc. 1996.

| | $1,750 | $1,500 | $1,000 | $900 | $775 | $675 | $595 |

Last MSR was $2,850.

Tropical Rifle - .300 H&H, .375 H&H and .458 Win. Mag. cals., 26 in. heavy barrel. Disc. 1985.

| | $1,150 | $900 | $810 | $730 | $660 | $600 | $550 |

Last MSR was $1,332.

Luxus S - available in 6.5x68mm, 8x68S, 7mm Rem. Mag., or .300 Win. Mag. cal., 26 in. barrel, half-stock only, 3 shot mag., 8 lbs. Disc. 1996.

| | $1,850 | $1,600 | $1,350 | $1,000 | $875 | $750 | $675 |

Last MSR was $3,250.

STEYR ULTRA LIGHT - .222 Rem., .223 Rem., .243 Win., .308 Win. or 7mm-08 Rem. cal., bolt has 4 locking lugs and a 70 degree bolt throw, 3-position roller tang safety, 19 in. fluted barrel, Weaver rail, 4 shot detachable mag., checkered European walnut stock with rosewood pistol grip and forend caps, approx. 6 lbs. Importation began 2004.

| MSR $1,780 | $1,550 | $1,325 | $1,050 | $900 | $875 | $675 | $550 |

STEYR SCOUT - .223 Rem. (new 2000), .243 Win. (mfg. 2000 only), .308 Win., 7mm-08 Rem. (new 2000), or .376 Steyr (mfg. 1999-2000, reintroduced 2005) cal., designed by Jeff Cooper, features grey, black synthetic Zytel or camo (.308 Win. cal. only beginning 2005) stock, 19.25 in. fluted barrel, Picatinny optic rail, integral bipod, Package (disc. 2004) included Leupold M8 2.5x28 IER scope with factory Steyr mounts, and luggage case. New 1998.

| MSR $1,942 | $1,695 | $1,450 | $1,200 | $1,050 | $900 | $775 | $650 |

Add $80 for camo.

Add approx. 15% for Steyr Scout Package with Leupold scope, mounts and luggage case (disc. 2004).

GRADING - PPGS™	100%	98%	95%	90%	80%	70%	60%

❋ **Steyr Scout Jeff Cooper** - .223 Rem., .308 Win. or .376 Steyr (disc. 2000, reintroduced 2005) cal., grey synthetic Zytel stock with Jeff Cooper logo and integral bipod, certificate of authenticity with test target, Package (disc. 2004) included Leupold M8 2.5x28 IER scope with factory Steyr mounts, and luggage case. New 1999.

MSR $2,303	$2,000	$1,750	$1,425	$1,175	$1,050	$900	$775

Add approx. 15% for Steyr Scout Package with Leupold scope, mounts and luggage case (disc. 2004).

❋ **Steyr Scout** - .243 Win. cal., similar to Jeff Cooper Package, except does not include scope, mounts, or case. Mfg. 1999-2002.

$1,525	$1,350	$1,200	$1,050	$900	$750	$625

Last MSR was $1,969.

Add $100 for .376 Steyr cal. (black stock only, disc. 2000).

Add $100 for Jeff Cooper grey stock.

❋ **Steyr Scout Tactical** - .223 Rem. (new 2000) or .308 Win. cal., similar to Steyr Scout, except has black synthetic stock with removable spacers, oversized bolt handle, and emergency ghost ring sights. Mfg. 1999-2002.

$1,600	$1,400	$1,250	$1,050	$900	$750	$625

Last MSR was $2,069.

>**Steyr Scout Tactical Stainless** - similar to Steyr Scout Tactical, except has stainless steel barrel. Mfg. 2000-2002.

$1,650	$1,425	$1,150

Last MSR was $2,159.

SBS PROHUNTER MODEL - .222 Rem. (new 2004), .223 Rem. (new 2004), .243 Win., .25-06 Rem., .260 Rem. (mfg. 2000-2004), .270 Win., .280 Rem. (new 2000), .30-06, .308 Win., 7mm-08 Rem., 6.5x55mm, 6.5x57mm (disc. 1999), 7x64mm (disc. 1999), or 9.3x62mm (disc. 1999) cal., features safe bolt system (SBS), detachable mag., black synthetic or camo (new 2000) stock, matte blue finish, 23.6 in. barrel without sights. New 1997.

MSR $899	$775	$650	$525	$465	$400	$350	$300

Add $129 for camo stock (new 2000, .270 Win. or .30-06 cal. only).

Add $152 for heavy barrel (.308 Win. cal. only).

❋ **SBS ProHunter Magnum** - .270 WSM (new 2004), .300 WSM (new 2004), .300 Win. Mag., 7mm WSM (new 2004), 7mm Rem. Mag., 6.5x68mm (disc. 1999), or 8x68S (disc. 1999) cal., similar to SBS ProHunter Model, except has 25.6 in. barrel. New 1997.

MSR $899	$775	$650	$525	$465	$400	$350	$300

Add $129 for camo stock (new 2000, .300 Win. Mag. or 7mm Rem. Mag. only).

Add $152 for heavy barrel (.300 Win. Mag. only).

Add $150 for metric cals (disc.).

❋ **SBS ProHunter SS** - similar to SBS ProHunter, except has stainless steel barrel with matte finish. New 2000.

MSR $1,001	$850	$700	$600

Add $129 for camo stock (.270 Win. or .30-06 cal.).

>**SBS ProHunter SS Magnum** - similar to SBS ProHunter Magnum, except has stainless steel barrel with matte finish. New 2000.

MSR $1,001	$850	$700	$600

Add $129 for camo stock (.300 Win. Mag. or 7mm Rem. Mag. cal. only).

Add $165 for black finish (7mm Rem. Mag. cal. only, new 2005).

❋ **SBS ProHunter .376 Steyr** - .376 Steyr cal. only, 20 in. barrel with iron sights, black synthetic or camo (new 2000) stock, matte blue finish. Mfg. 1999-2004.

$695	$600	$500	$450	$395	$350	$300

Last MSR was $799.

Add $60 for camo.

GRADING - PPGS™	100%	98%	95%	90%	80%	70%	60%

* **SBS ProHunter Compact (Youth/Ladies) Rifle** - .243 Win., .260 Rem. (new 2000) 7mm-08 Rem., or .308 Win. cal., shortened stock with 2 butt spacers for adj. length, 20 in. barrel with iron sights, matte blue finish. Mfg. 1999-2002.

	$710	$640	$570	$500	$450	$395	$350

Last MSR was $819.

* **SBS ProHunter Compact (Youth/Ladies) SS** - similar to ProHunter Compact, except has stainless steel barrel with matte finish. Mfg. 2000-2002.

	$780	$675	$600				

Last MSR was $909.

* **SBS ProHunter Mountain Rifle** - .243 Win., .25-06 Rem., .260 Rem. (new 2000), .270 Win., .270 WSM (mfg. 2004), .30-06, .300 WSM (mfg. 2004), .308 Win., .376 Steyr (new 2005), 7mm-08 Rem., 7mm WSM (mfg. 2004), or 6.5x55mm (new 2000) cal., 20 in. barrel, no sights, matte blue finish, black or camo (mfg. 2000-2002) synthetic stock, detachable mag. New 1999.

MSR $899		$775	$650	$525	$465	$400	$350	$300

Add $95 for 7mm-08 Rem. cal. with open sights.

* **SBS ProHunter Mountain Rifle SS** - similar to ProHunter Mountain Rifle, except has stainless steel barrel with matte finish. New 2000.

MSR $1,001		$850	$700	$600				

Add $129 for camo stock (.243 Win., .270 Win. or .30-06 cal. only).

* **SBS ProHunter Tactical** - .308 Win. cal., features 20 in. barrel and 10 shot mag. Importation began 2005.

MSR $983		$850	$700	$575	$500	$450	$400	$350

SBS FORESTER MODEL - similar to SBS Pro Hunter Model, except has wood stock and standard blue finish. Mfg. 1997-2002, reintroduced 2005.

MSR $1,051		$925	$800	$700	$600	$525	$425	$350

* **SBS Forester Mountain Rifle** - .243 Win. (disc. 2002), .25-06 Rem., .260 Rem. (new 2000), .270 Win. (disc. 2002, reintroduced 2005), .30-06 (disc. 2002), .308 Win. (disc. 2002), 7mm-08 Rem., 6.5x55mm (mfg. 2000-2002) cal., 20 in. barrel, no sights, matte blue finish, checkered walnut stock, detachable mag. Mfg. 1999-2002, reimported beginning 2004.

MSR $1,051		$925	$800	$700	$600	$525	$425	$350

* **SBS Forester Magnum** - .300 Win. Mag., 7mm Rem. Mag., 6.5x68mm (disc. 1999), or 8x68S (disc. 1999) cal., similar to SBS Forester Model, except has 25.6 in. barrel. Mfg. 1997-2002.

	$720	$635	$565	$510	$450	$395	$350

Last MSR was $829.

SBS CLASSIC MANNLICHER HALF STOCK (AMERICAN) - .243 Win., .25-06 Rem., .260 Rem. (disc. 2002), .270 Win., .280 Rem. (disc. 2002), .30-06, .308 Win., 7mm-08 Rem., 6.5x55mm, or 8x57JRS cal., features deluxe checkered walnut stock with full pistol grip and forend cap, deep blue finish, 23.6 in. barrel with exterior hammer forged swirls, no sights. New 2000.

MSR $1,795		$1,575	$1,225	$1,025	$875	$750	$650	$550

* **SBS Classic Mannlicher Half Stock Magnum** - .270 WSM (new 2004), .300 WSM (new 2004), .300 Win. Mag., 7mm WSM (new 2004) or 7mm Rem. Mag. cal., 25.6 in. barrel. New 2000.

MSR $1,795		$1,575	$1,225	$1,025	$875	$750	$650	$550

* **SBS Classic Mannlicher Full Stock** - similar to SBS Classic American, also available in 7x57mm Mauser (disc. 2002) cal., has deluxe full length stock and 20 in. barrel with sights. New 2000.

MSR $2,179		$1,875	$1,500	$1,150	$950	$825	$675	$575

GRADING - PPGS™	100%	98%	95%	90%	80%	70%	60%

✳ *SBS Classic Mannlicher Goiserer* - .270 Win., .30-06, or .308 Win. cal., similar to Classic Mannlicher Half Stock, except has iron sights and 20 in. barrel, 4 shot mag. New 2003.

MSR $2,014	$1,725	$1,325	$1,100	$950	$775	$675	$575

SBS TACTICAL

- .308 Win. cal. only, 20 in. barrel w/o sights, features oversized bolt handle and high capacity 10 shot mag. with adapter, matte blue finish. Mfg. 1999-2002.

	$840	$735	$625	$550	$500	$450	$395

Last MSR was $969.

✳ *SBS Tactical Heavy Barrel* - .300 Win. Mag. (new 2000) or .308 Win. cal., features 20 (carbine, new 2000, .308 Win. only) or 26 in. heavy barrel w/o sights and oversized bolt handle, matte blue finish or stainless steel (carbine only, new 2000). Mfg. 1999-2002.

	$865	$745	$635	$550	$500	$450	$395

Last MSR was $1,019.

Add $30 for .300 Win. Mag. cal.

Add $40 for stainless steel.

✳ *SBS Tactical McMillan* - similar to SBS Tactical Heavy barrel, except has custom McMillan A - 3 stock with adj. cheekpiece and oversized bolt handle, matte blue finish. Mfg. 1999-2002.

	$1,465	$1,245	$1,035	$850	$725	$600	$550

Last was $1,699.

Add $30 for .300 Win. Mag. cal.

✳ *SBS Tactical CISM* - .308 Win. cal., 20 in. heavy barrel w/o sights, laminated wood stock with black lacquer finish, adj. cheekpiece and buttplate, 10 shot detachable mag., vent. forend. Mfg. 2000-2002.

	$3,050	$2,650	$2,300	$1,950	$1,600	$1,300	$1,150

Last MSR was $3,499.

This model was also available as a Swiss contract CISM Match in 7.5x55mm cal. with match diopter sights and 23 1/2 in. barrel. Only 100 were imported. NIB Prices are in the $1,850 range.

SBS TACTICAL ELITE

- .223 Rem. or .308 Win. cal., 20 (carbine) or 26 in. barrel with full length Picatinny spec. mounting rail, oversize bolt handle, two 5 shot detachable mags. (with spare buttstock storage), adj. black synthetic stock, matte blue finish or stainless steel. New 2000.

MSR $2,405	$2,025	$1,625	$1,275	$1,050	$875	$775	$650

Add $112 for 26 in. stainless steel barrel (.308 Win. cal. only).

Add $1,100 for heavy barrel package (includes factory installed ZF optic, disc.).

MANNLICHER SBS EUROPEAN MODEL

- .243 Win., .25-06 Rem., .270 Win., .30-06 (disc. 1998), .308 Win., 7mm-08 Rem., 6.5x55mm, 6.5x57mm, 7x64mm, 7.5x55mm, or 9.3x62mm cal., features safe bolt system (SBS), 23.6 in. barrel with sights, checkered walnut stock and forearm. Mfg. 1997-99.

	$2,300	$1,850	$1,600	$1,325	$1,100	$925	$850

Last MSR was $2,795.

✳ *Mannlicher SBS Magnum European Model* - .300 Win. Mag., 7mm Rem. Mag., 6.5x68mm, or 8x68S cal., 25.6 in. barrel with sights, checkered walnut stock and forearm. Mfg. 1997-99.

	$2,375	$1,900	$1,625	$1,350	$1,100	$925	$850

Last MSR was $2,895.

✳ *Mannlicher SBS European Model* - "Goiserer" - similar to Mannlicher SBS European Model, except has 20 in. barrel. Mfg. 1997-99.

	$2,500	$2,000	$1,650	$1,350	$1,100	$925	$850

Last MSR was $2,995.

GRADING - PPGS™	100%	98%	95%	90%	80%	70%	60%

* Mannlicher SBS European Model - Full Stock - similar to Mannlicher SBS European Model, except has full-length Mannlicher stock. Mfg. 1997-99.

	$2,500	$2,000	$1,650	$1,350	$1,100	$925	$850

Last MSR was $2,995.

MODEL SSG - .243 Win. (disc., PII Sniper only) or .308 Win cal., for competition or law-enforcement use. Marksman has regular sights, detachable rotary mag., teflon coated bolt with heavy duty locking lugs, synthetic stock has removable spacers, parkerized finish. Match version has heavier target barrel and "match" bolt carrier, can be used as single shot. Extremely accurate.

* PI Rifle - 26 in. barrel with iron sights, 3 shot mag., black or green ABS Cycolac synthetic stock. Disc. 2004.

	$1,425	$1,200	$995	$850	$725	$600	$525

Last MSR was $1,597.

Add 15% for walnut stock (disc. 1992, retail was $448).

* PII/PIIK Sniper Rifle - .22-250 Rem. (new 2004), .243 Win. (disc.) or .308 Win. cal., 20 in. heavy (Model PIIK) or 26 in. heavy barrel, no sights, green or black synthetic Cycolac or McMillan black fiberglass stock, modified bolt handle, choice of single or set triggers.

MSR $1,795		$1,575	$1,300	$1,050	$875	$750	$625	$525

Add $91 for rifle sights.

Add 15% for walnut stock (disc. 1992, retail was $448).

* PIII Rifle - .308 Win. cal., 26 in. heavy barrel with diopter match sight bases, H-S Precision Pro-Series stock in black only. Importation 1991-93.

	$2,300	$1,875	$1,425	$1,050	$825	$700	$600

Last MSR was $3,162.

* PIV (Urban Rifle) - .308 Win. cal., carbine variation with 16.5 in. heavy barrel and flash hider (disc.), ABS Cycolac synthetic stock in green or black. Imported 1991-2002, reimported beginning 2004.

MSR $2,201		$1,975	$1,675	$1,325	$1,050	$875	$750	$625

* Jagd Match - .222 Rem., .243 Win., or .308 Win. cal., hunting rifle that features checkered wood laminate stock, 23.6 in. barrel, Mannlicher sights, double-set triggers, supplied with test target. Mfg. 1991-92.

	$1,550	$1,050	$950	$800	$675	$600	$540

Last MSR was $1,550.

* Match Rifle - .308 Win. only, 26 in. heavy barrel, brown ABS Cycolac stock, Walther Diopter sights, 8.6 lbs. Mfg. disc. 1992.

	$2,000	$1,500	$1,225	$925	$800	$700	$600

Last MSR was $2,306.

Add $437 for walnut stock.

* Model SPG-T - .308 Win. cal., Target model. Mfg. 1993-98.

	$3,225	$2,850	$2,550	$2,200	$1,850	$1,500	$1,200

Last MSR was $3,695.

* Model SPG-CISM - .308 Win. cal., 20 in. heavy barrel, laminated wood stock with adj. cheekpiece and black lacquer finish. Mfg. 1993-99.

	$2,995	$2,600	$2,300	$1,950	$1,700	$1,450	$1,200

Last MSR was $3,295.

* Match UIT - .308 Win. cal. only, 10 shot steel mag., special single set trigger, free floating barrel, Diopter sights, raked bolt handle, 10.8 lbs. Disc. 1998.

	$3,000	$2,500	$2,000	$1,800	$1,500	$1,200	$1,000

Last MSR was $3,995.

UIT stands for Union Internationale de Tir.

GRADING - PPGS™	100%	98%	95%	90%	80%	70%	60%

✻ **SSG 04** - .308 Win. or .300 Win. Mag. cal., 20 or 23.6 heavy hammer forged barrel with muzzle brake, two-stage trigger, matte finished metal, black synthetic stock, adj. bipod, 8 (.300 Win. Mag.) or 10 (.308 Win.) shot mag., Picatinny rail, adj. buttstock, 10.1 lbs. Importation began 2004.

	MSR $2,405	$2,050	$1,750	$1,350	$1,050	$875	$750	$650

HS-50 - .50 BMG cal., bolt action. Importation began 2004.

	MSR $5,234	$4,675	$4,200	$3,775	$3,250	$2,600	$2,250	$1,750

RIFLES: SEMI-AUTO

AUG S.A. - .223 Rem. cal., semi-auto paramilitary design rifle, design incorporates use of advanced plastics, integral Swarovski scope, 16, 20, or 24 in. barrel, bullpup configuration, 7.9 lbs.

	$2,950	$2,750	$2,450	$2,150	$1,750	$1,575	$1,400

Last MSR was $1,575.

This model was available in limited quantities only to law enforcement agencies until 2000, due to 1989 Federal legislation banning the importation for commercial sales.

✻ **AUG S.A. Commercial** - similar to AUG S.A., grey (3,000 mfg. circa 1997), green, or black finish.

		$2,750	$2,450	$2,150	$1,750	$1,575	$1,400
SP receiver (Stanag metal)	$2,950	$2,750	$2,450	$2,150	$1,750	$1,575	$1,400
Grey finish	$3,150	$2,875	$2,600	$2,250	$1,825	$1,625	$1,450
Green finish (last finish)	$3,400	$2,975	$2,700	$2,300	$1,875	$1,675	$1,500

Last MSR was $1,362 (1989).

Black finish	$4,125	$3,750	$3,300	$2,950	$2,750	$2,500	$2,250

STOCK, FRANZ

Previous manufacturer located in Berlin, Germany.

PISTOLS: SEMI-AUTO

.22 LR PISTOL - .22 LR cal. Mfg. in Germany 1920-40.

	$295	$250	$225	$175	$125	$100	$75

.25 ACP PISTOL - .25 ACP or .32 ACP cal. Mfg. in Germany 1920-40.

	$295	$225	$175	$150	$100	$90	$80

STOCKWORKS

Please refer to Robert Hisserich Co. section.

STOEGER INDUSTRIES, INC.

Current importer established in 1924, and currently located in Accokeek, MD. Previously located in Wayne, NJ, until 2000. Stoeger Industries, Inc. was purchased by Beretta Holding of Italy in 2000, and is now a division of Benelli USA. Please refer to the IGA listing for currently imported Stoeger shotgun models.

Stoeger has imported a wide variety of firearms during the past seven decades. Most of these guns were good quality and came from known makers in Europe (some were private labeled). Stoeger carried an extensive firearms inventory of both house brand and famous European trademarks - many of which were finely made with beautiful engraving, stock work, and other popular special order features. As a general rule, values for Stoeger rifles and shotguns may be ascertained by comparing them with a known trademark of equal quality and cal./ga. Certain configurations will be more desirable than others (i.e. a Stoeger .22 caliber Mannlicher with double-set triggers and detachable mag. will be worth considerably more than a single shot target rifle).

Perhaps the best reference works available on these older Stoeger firearms (not to mention the other trademarks of that time) are the older Stoeger catalogs themselves - quite

GRADING - PPGS™	100%	98%	95%	90%	80%	70%	60%

collectible in their own right. You are advised to purchase these older catalogs (some reprints are also available) if more information is needed on not only older Stoeger models, but also the other firearms being sold at that time.

PISTOLS: SEMI-AUTO

PRO SERIES 95 - .22 LR cal., target pistol with choice of either 5 1/2 or 7 1/4 VR, fluted, or bull barrel, adj. rear sight, adj. trigger, push-button takedown, Pachmayr rubber grips, gold accents, 10 shot mag., 45-47 oz. Mfg. 1995-96.

* **5 1/2 in. bull barrel**

$440	$375	$335	$300	$275	$250	$225

Last MSR was $495.

* **5 1/2 in. VR barrel**

$515	$425	$365	$325	$285	$255	$225

Last MSR was $595.

* **7 1/4 in. fluted barrel**

$455	$385	$340	$300	$275	$250	$225

Last MSR was $525.

SHOTGUNS: RECENT IMPORTATION

Please refer to the IGA section for currently imported Stoeger O/U, SxS, semi-auto, and single shot shotguns.

STONER RIFLE

Please refer to the Knight's Manufacturing Company listing in this text.

STRAYER TRIPP INTERNATIONAL

Please refer to the STI International listing in this section.

STRAYER-VOIGT, INC.

Current manufacturer of Infinity pistols located in Grand Prairie, TX. See the Infinity listing for more information.

STREET SWEEPER

Previously manufactured by Sales of Georgia, Inc. located in Atlanta, GA.

SHOTGUNS

STREET SWEEPER - 12 ga. only, 12 shot rotary mag., paramilitary configuration with 18 in. barrel, double action, folding stock, 9 3/4 lbs. Restricted sales following the ATF classification as a "destructive device." Mfg. 1989-approx. 1995.

$775	$675	$575	$475	$400	$360	$330

Unless this model was registered with the ATF before May 1st, 2001, it is subject to seizure with a possible fine/imprisonment.

STURM, RUGER & CO., INC.

Current manufacturer with production facilities located in Newport, NH (rifles and shotguns) beginning 1993 and Prescott, AZ (handguns) beginning 1986. Previously manufactured in Southport, CT 1949-1993 (office headquarters remain at this location).

On July 6, 2002, the legendary William B. Ruger, Sr. passed away in his home in Prescott, AZ. He will be remembered for his visionary efforts in firearms manufacturing and marketing, exceptional design skills, and his philanthropic donations in support of the firearms industry.

NOTE: In 1976, Ruger stamped "Made in the 200th year of American Liberty" on the side

GRADING - PPGS™	100%	98%	95%	90%	80%	70%	60%

of all of the guns they produced for this one year only. These Bicentennial or "Liberty Model" guns will bring a $50-$75 premium from collectors interested in acquiring them. In most cases, this is only true of 100% guns, unfired with the original box and papers.

Almost all the models in this section are factory variations, and non-factory limited or special editions are not included in this section because of the amount and price unpredictability.

> ALL VALUES FOR 100% CONDITION RUGERS ASSUME NIB UNFIRED. PRICES OF GUNS WITH ORIGINAL BOXES AND PAPERWORK CAN VARY GREATLY BECAUSE OF RARITY OF CERTAIN MODELS AND CONDITION OF BOX OR ACCESSORIES. INDIVIDUAL APPRAISALS NEEDED.

Beginning 1998, all handguns are supplied with a case and lock.

Please refer to the *Blue Book of Modern Black Powder Arms* by John Allen (also online) for more information and prices on Sturm Ruger black powder models.

PISTOLS: SEMI-AUTO, RIMFIRE

Many distributors and customizers have produced special/limited editions on this popular series of .22 cal. pistols. Individual companies should be contacted for current pricing and special order features/prices.

"RED EAGLE" - approx. 29,000 mfg. 1949-1952, distinguishable by recessed red enamel eagle in left-hand grip, most production occurred prior to Alexander Sturm's death (1951).

	100%	98%	95%	90%	80%	70%	60%
Standard Auto	$650	$550	$450	$350	$265	$235	$200

Add 100%+ in 100% condition factor only for early Red Eagle with wood "salt cod" box.

	100%	98%	95%	90%	80%	70%	60%
Target w/ 6 7/8 in. barrel	$675	$595	$525	$425	$375	$350	$300

Produced until early 1952. Serialized approx. 0001 - 35,000 with Mark I Auto occupying blocks from 15,000-17,000 and 25,000-25,300.

STANDARD MODEL - .22 LR cal., 9 shot, 4 3/4 in. or 6 in. barrel, blue, fixed sights, checkered wood or rubber grips. After ser. no. 29,000. Mfg. 1951-1982.

	100%	98%	95%	90%	80%	70%	60%
	$275	$225	$175	$145	$115	$95	$80

Variations marked "Hecho En Mexico" are rare. 98%+ condition specimens have sold for as much as $1,500.

✳ *Stainless Steel 1 of 5,000*

	100%	98%	95%
	$395	$350	$300

MARK I TARGET - similar to Standard, except has 5 1/2 in. heavy barrel, 5 1/4 in. tapered (scarce) barrel, or 6 7/8 in. heavy tapered barrel, adj. rear sights, target sight. Mfg. 1951-82.

	100%	98%	95%	90%	80%	70%	60%
	$375	$325	$275	$225	$185	$150	$135
U.S. Marked	$775	$675	$575	$450	$325	$200	$165
5 1/4 in. tapered barrel	$795	$700	$600	$475	$350	$225	$175

Add $100 for Ruger addressed muzzle brake.

MARK II STANDARD - .22 LR cal., 4 3/4 or 6 in. barrel, checkered black Delrin synthetic grips, blue finish, 10 shot mag., approx. 2.25 lbs. Mfg. 1982-2004.

	100%	98%	95%	90%	80%	70%	60%
	$225	$175	$135	$115	$110	$100	$95

Last MSR was $299.

✳ *Stainless Steel* - variation of the Mark II Standard. Disc. 2004.

	100%	98%	95%
	$295	$215	$175

Last MSR was $390.

Serial numbers start approx. at 18-00001.

RUGER

GRADING - PPGS™	100%	98%	95%	90%	80%	70%	60%

MARK II STANDARD 50TH ANNIVERSARY
.22 LR cal., features blue receiver machined to same contour as original production, stainless steel bolt with Ruger medallion on rear, 50th Anniversary Ruger crest on top of frame in front of ejection port, black grips with Ruger medallion in red background, lockable red case. Approx. 35,000 mfg. 1999 only.

	$250	$200	$150	$125	$115	$110	$100

Last MSR was $287.

RUGER ENDOWMENT SPECIAL NRA LIMITED EDITION MARK II
.22 LR cal., William B. Ruger signature rollmarked on receiver, Ruger crest with NRA logo, blue steel, checkered ivory colored grips, red Ruger medallions on grips and mags., includes Ruger commemorative case, certificate of authenticity signed by Bill Ruger, Jr. and Wayne LaPierre, special serialization (NRA-XXXX). New 2003.

MSR $334	$295	$260	$225

This model is available exclusively from Davidson's.

MARK II TARGET
.22 LR cal., 4 (mfg. 1996-99) bull, 5 1/4 (disc. 1994), 5 1/2 bull, 6 7/8 standard, or 10 in. bull barrel, single action, 2 5/8 - 3 1/4 lbs. depending on barrel. Disc. 2004.

	$295	$245	$205	$165	$130	$120	$110

Last MSR was $365.

Add $16 for 4 in. bull barrel.
Add $8 for 10 in. bull barrel.

* **Stainless Steel** - stainless variation of the Mark II Target, includes choice of 5 1/4 (disc. 1994), 5 1/2 bull, 6 7/8 standard, or 10 in. bull barrel. Disc. 2004.

	$355	$280	$210

Last MSR was $460.

Add $6 for 10 in. bull barrel.

* **Mark II Competition Target Special Edition** - .22 LR cal., blue finish, black polymer grips, 6 7/8 or 8 in. slab-side barrel, adj. sights, drilled and tapped, includes two magazines. Mfg. 2003-2004.

	$250	$200	$175	$150	$140	$125	$100

Last MSR was $339.

This model was available exclusively through Davidson's.

GOVERNMENT TARGET MODEL (MK678G)
commercial variation of the government training model without "U.S." markings, 6 7/8 in. bull barrel, adj. rear sight, blue finish, black plastic grips, 46 oz., individually test targeted. Mfg. 1987-2004.

	$350	$280	$210	$180	$155	$140	$125

Last MSR was $445.

* **Military "U.S." Marked** - issued to U.S. military personnel, must be factory verified. Disc. 1999.

	$600	$500	$450	$400	$360	$330	$300

Last MSR was $600.

* **Stainless Government Target Model** - 6 7/8 in. bull barrel only. Mfg. 1993-2004.

	$410	$320	$235

Last MSR was $535.

Add $20 for 6 7/8 in. slab side bull barrel with scope rings and base.

MARK III STANDARD
.22 LR cal., 4 3/4 or 6 in. barrel, the Mark III action is an evolution of the Mark II design, featuring a relocated mag. release button on the left side of the grip, behind the triggerguard, recontoured ejection port and tapered bolt ears, blue finish, loaded chamber indicator, 10 shot mag. with disconnect, checkered composition grip panels. New 2005.

MSR $322	$245	$195	$150	$120	$110	$100	$95

GRADING - PPGS™	100%	98%	95%	90%	80%	70%	60%

MARK III TARGET - .22 LR cal., 5 1/2 in. bull of 6 7/8 in. tapered barrel, adj. rear sight, operating mechanism is the same as the Mark III Standard, blue finish, checkered composition grip panels. New 2005.

MSR $382	$295	$235	$200	$180	$160	$140	$125

* ❋ *Stainless Mark III Target (KMKIII)* - stainless variation of the Mark III Target. New 2005.

MSR $483	$375	$295	$235				

* ❋ *Brown Laminate Mark III Target* - features 6 7/8 in. slab sided bull barrel and brown laminated grip panels. New 2005.

MSR $555	$430	$370	$315	$260	$230	$210	$195

MARK III HUNTER - .22 LR cal., stainless steel construction, 6 7/8 in. target crowned fluted barrel, checkered cocobolo grips, V-notch rear sight blade, Hi-Viz front sights with interchangeable LitePipes, drilled and tapped. New 2005.

MSR $567	$450	$375	$315	$180	$160	$140	$125

MODEL 22/45 -.22 LR cal. only, semi-auto single action, Zytel frame is patterned after the Model 1911 .45 ACP Gov't, 4 regular, 4 3/4 regular, 5 1/4 regular (Target, disc.), or 5 1/2 in. bull barrel, 10 shot mag. (push-button release), fixed (4 3/4 in. barrel only) or adj. sights, 28-35 oz. Mfg. 1993-2004.

* ❋ *Blue Finish* - 4 in. regular barrel with adj. sights (Model P4, new 1997) or 5 1/2 in. bull barrel with adj. sights (Model P512). Mfg. 1994-2004.

	$225	$190	$165	$135	$125	$115	$100

Last MSR was $290.

* ❋ *Stainless Steel* - 4 3/4 in. regular barrel with fixed sights (Model KP4, new 1997) or 5 1/2 in. bull barrel with adj. sights (Model KP512). Disc. 2004.

	$250	$210	$180				

Last MSR was $315.

Add $65 for adj. sights (5 1/2 in. bull barrel only).

MARK III 22/45 - .22 LR cal., Zytel frame is patterned after the Model 1911 .45 ACP Gov't, push button mag. release, 4 (regular or slab sided) or 5 1/2 in. bull barrel, fixed or adj. sights, blue finish. New 2005.

MSR $305	$230	$180	$145	$125	$115	$100	$95

PISTOLS: SEMI-AUTO, CENTERFIRE

P85 MARK II - 9mm Para. cal., double action, 4 1/2 in. barrel, aluminum frame with steel slide, 3-dot fixed sights, 15 shot mag., ambidextrous safety or decocking levers, oversized trigger, polymer grips, matte black finish, 2 lbs. Mfg. 1987-92.

	$350	$295	$265	$235	$215	$200	$185

Last MSR was $410.

Subtract $30 if without case and extra mag.

* ❋ *KP85 Mark II Stainless Steel* - stainless variation of the P85. Mfg. 1990-92.

	$375	$315	$280				

Last MSR was $452.

Subtract $30 if without case and extra mag.

Variants included a decocking or double action only version at no extra charge.

P89 - 9mm Para. cal., improved variation of the P85 Mark II, 10 (C/B 1994) shot mag., ambidextrous safety or decocker (Model P89D), blue finish, 32 oz. New 1992.

MSR $475	$380	$330	$280	$250	$215	$200	$185

Variants were available in a decocking (P89DC) or double action only (P-89DAO) version at no extra charge.

GRADING - PPGS™	100%	98%	95%	90%	80%	70%	60%

✳ *KP89 Stainless* - stainless variation of the P89, also available in double action only (disc.). New 1992.

MSR $525	$425	$360	$305

Add $45 for convertible 7.65mm Luger cal. barrel (disc).

P90 - .45 ACP cal., similar to KP90 Stainless, except has blue finish.

MSR $525	$425	$360	$305	$250	$215	$200	$185

P90 SPECIAL EDITION - 9mm Para., .40 S&W, or .45 ACP cal., features two-tone finish or stainless steel, polymer or Hogue grips, 4 1/2 in. barrel, manual safety, fixed sights, includes black plastic lockable case. New 2003.

MSR $448	$385	$325	$265	$230	$180	$150	$125

Add $51 for .45 ACP cal. or $9 for .40 S&W cal.

Add $14 for Hogue grips.

This model is available exclusively through Davidson's.

P90 GUNS & AMMO 45TH ANNIVERSARY SPECIAL EDITION - .45 ACP cal., DA, 4 1/2 in. barrel, two-tone finish with blue slide, Hogue grips, fixed 3-dot sights, special embellishments with either gold filled or non-gold filled laser engraving with "45 Years of Guns & Ammo" and "Deluxe Special Edition 1 of 45" on slide, special ser. no. beginning with GA45, 8 shot mag., includes two extra mags, mag loader, and black plastic lockable case.

MSR $560	$435	$375	$315	$250	$215	$200	$185

This model is available exclusively through Davidson's.

KP90 STAINLESS - .45 ACP cal., double action, 4 1/2 in. barrel, oversized trigger, aluminum frame with stainless steel slide, 7 shot single column mag., ambidextrous safety (KP90) or decocking (KP90D), polymer grips, 3-dot fixed sights. New 1991.

MSR $565	$440	$375	$315

This model was previously available in a double action only variation (KP90C, disc. 1992).

KP91 STAINLESS - .40 S&W cal., similar to Model KP90 Stainless, except is not available with external safety and has 11 shot double column mag. Mfg. 1992-94.

	$385	$335	$295

Last MSR was $489.

This model was available in a decocking variation (KP91D) or double action only (KP91DAO).

P93D BLUE - similar to KP93 Stainless, except has blue finish, ambidextrous decocker, 31 oz. Mfg. 1998-2004.

	$395	$330	$285	$240	$215	$200	$185

Last MSR was $495.

KP93 STAINLESS - 9mm Para. cal., compact variation with 3 9/10 in. tilting barrel - link actuated, matte blue or REM (new 1996) finish, 3-dot sights, 10 (C/B 1994) or 15* shot mag., available with ambidextrous decocking or double action only, 31 oz. Mfg. 1994-2004.

	$450	$370	$315

Last MSR was $575.

P94 BLUE - similar to KP94 Stainless, except has blue finish. Mfg. 1998-2004.

	$395	$330	$285	$240	$215	$200	$185

Last MSR was $495.

KP94 STAINLESS - 9mm Para. cal., available with ambidextrous safety, matte blue or REM (new 1996) finish, ambidextrous decocker, or double action only, 10 (C/B 1994), or 15* (9mm Para.) shot mag., 33 oz. Mfg. 1994-2004.

	$450	$370	$315

Last MSR was $575.

GRADING - PPGS™	100%	98%	95%	90%	80%	70%	60%

P95 BLUE - 9mm Para. cal., available in ambidextrous decocker (D suffix), ambidextrous safety (new 2001) or double action only configuration (DAO suffix, disc.), polymer frame, 3 9/10 in. barrel, fixed sights, blue finish, 10 shot mag., 27 oz. New 1997.

	100%	98%	95%	90%	80%	70%	60%
MSR $425	$345	$280	$230	$190	$165	$150	$135

✳ *KP95 Stainless* - stainless variation of Model P95. New 1997.

	100%	98%	95%
MSR $475	$380	$305	$245

P97D - .45 ACP cal., ambidextrous decocker, 8 shot mag., blue finish, 30 1/2 oz. Mfg. 2002-2004.

	100%	98%	95%	90%	80%	70%	60%
	$370	$315	$275	$235	$215	$200	$185

Last MSR was $460.

✳ *KP97 Stainless* - .45 ACP cal., similar to KP95 Stainless, except has 8 shot mag., 27 oz. Mfg. 1999-2004.

	100%	98%	95%
	$395	$315	$265

Last MSR was $495.

P345 - .45 ACP cal., ambidextrous safety or decocker, black polymer frame with matte stainless or blue stainless steel slide, 4.2 in. barrel with fixed sights, polyurethane grips, slimmer profile frame, 8 shot single column mag., with or w/o Picatinny rail, loaded chamber indicator. New 2005.

	100%	98%	95%	90%	80%	70%	60%
MSR $513	$415	$365	$315	$265	$225	$210	$195

Add $27 for stainless steel w/o Picatinny rail or $48 for stainless steel slide with Picatinny rail.

P944 - .40 S&W cal., similar to P93, ambidextrous safety, blue finish, 34 oz. New 1999.

	100%	98%	95%	90%	80%	70%	60%
MSR $495	$395	$330	$280	$235	$215	$200	$185

✳ *KP944 Stainless* - similar to P944, except is stainless steel. New 1999.

	100%	98%	95%
MSR $575	$450	$375	$320

REVOLVERS: SINGLE ACTION, OLD MODELS

Note: The following Rugers are known as "Old Models" (mfg. 1953-early 1973) and are instantly recognized by the three screws through the frame and the four clicks emitted upon cocking. They are now actively sought by collectors and some shooters who desire the smoother operation they afford.

SINGLE SIX REVOLVER - .22 LR cal., 4 5/8, 5 1/2, 6 1/2, or 9 1/2 in. barrel, smaller XR-3 grip frame disc. in 1962, fixed sights, rubber or wood grips, blue. Mfg. 1953-1962.

✳ *Flat loading gate* - 5 1/2 in. barrel only, approx. 60,000 mfg. from 1953-1957. Four variations.

	100%	98%	95%	90%	80%	70%	60%
	$700	$600	$475	$325	$200	$160	$150

✳ *5 1/2 in. barrel, XR-3 frame*

	100%	98%	95%	90%	80%	70%	60%
	$400	$300	$200	$130	$120	$110	$100

>**Early 4 5/8 in. Barrel, XR-3 frame** - single cylinder, ser. no. range 127,000-198,000.

	100%	98%	95%	90%	80%	70%	60%
	$550	$450	$350	$300	$250	$200	$175

An extra convertible cylinder will command a premium on this model (mfg. 1961-63, ser. no. range 164,000-198,000).

>**Early 9 1/2 in. Barrel, XR-3 frame** - single cylinder, ser. no. range 127,000-198,000.

	100%	98%	95%	90%	80%	70%	60%
	$500	$400	$350	$300	$250	$200	$175

An extra convertible cylinder will command a premium on this model (mfg. 1961-63, ser. no. range 164,000-198,000).

✳ *Factory Engraved Model RSSE*

Subtract $650 if w/o presentation case.

Approx. 250 factory cased, engraved Single Six models have been mfg. Seldom seen and among the rarest of Ruger revolvers, prices have been reported in the $4,000-$5,000 range. The Jerred engraved blue grip frame is currently valued in the $4,500 range, the Jerred engraved polished grip frame is currently valued at $3,500, and the Spanish engraved is currently valued at $6,500.

GRADING - PPGS™	100%	98%	95%	90%	80%	70%	60%

✸ .22 Mag. - 6 1/2 in. barrel only, mfg. only three years, serial numbered between 300,000-342,000. Frame stamped Mag. only.

	$400	$300	$200	$175	$165	$160	$150

Add a premium for extra convertible .22 LR cylinder.

SINGLE SIX CONVERTIBLE - similar to Single Six, except .22 LR and .22 Mag. interchangeable cylinders, redesigned grip frame (XR-3 red), wood grips, 4 5/8, 5 1/2, 6 1/2, or 9 1/2 in. barrel with 4 5/8 in. being the rarest. Mfg. 1963-1972.

✸ 5 1/2, 6 1/2 in. barrel

	$400	$300	$200	$170	$120	$110	$100

✸ 4 5/8 or 9 1/2 in. barrel

	$450	$350	$250	$200	$175	$160	$150

LIGHTWEIGHT SINGLE SIX - similar to Single Six, except alloy frame, 4 5/8 in. barrel, made 1956-1958. 200,000-212,000 serial range, can have alloy or steel cylinder.

	$600	$500	$400	$300	$200	$175	$150

✸ Tri-color - ser. no. range 200,000-205,8XX

	$850	$775	$675	$550	$425	$300	$225

✸ Blue - all blue with alloy cylinder, ser. no. range 205,8XX-206,000

	$1,000	$850	$750	$650	$525	$375	$275

✸ Blue - steel cylinder, ser. no. range 206,000-212,4XX

	$650	$550	$475	$400	$325	$250	$175

✸ Tri-color - "S" marked (verified).

	$1,350	$1,100	$875	$725	$600	$475	$350

SUPER SINGLE SIX CONVERTIBLE - similar to Single Six Convertible, except adj. sights. Mfg. 1964-72.

	$400	$300	$200	$155	$140	$120	$105

This model in 4 5/8 in. barrel is the rarest with prices ranging between $800-$1,000 in blue finish. Nickel finish 6 1/2 in. barrel specimens are trading for $1,200-$2,250.

BLACKHAWK SINGLE ACTION "FLATTOP" - .357 Mag. cal., 6 shot, 4 5/8, 6 1/2, and 10 in. barrel, flattop cylinder strap, adj. sight, blue, black rubber or walnut grips. Approx. 43,000 mfg. between 1955-63.

	100%	98%	95%	90%	80%	70%	60%
4 5/8 in. barrel	$800	$650	$475	$300	$250	$225	$200
6 1/2 in. barrel	$1,000	$750	$550	$375	$350	$300	$250
10 in. barrel	$1,650	$1,350	$995	$850	$700	$600	$500

BLACKHAWK SINGLE ACTION - .30 Carbine, .357 Mag., .41 Mag., or .45 LC cal., this model is the 1962 variation with protected rear sight, ramp in front of rear sight, and 4 5/8 (.357 Mag., .41 Mag. or .45 LC), 6 1/2 (.357 Mag. or .41 Mag.), or 7 1/2 (.30 Carbine or .45 LC) in. barrel.

	100%	98%	95%	90%	80%	70%	60%
.30 Carbine	$475	$400	$300	$215	$180	$160	$140
.357 Mag.	$450	$375	$275	$200	$170	$150	$130
.41 Mag.	$575	$475	$400	$300	$225	$185	$165
.45 LC	$625	$525	$425	$325	$250	$200	$175
.357 Mag. w/brass frame	$650	$550	$450	$350	$275	$225	$200
.41 Mag. w/brass frame	$895	$750	$650	$550	$450	$350	$250
.45 LC w/brass frame	$825	$700	$600	$500	$400	$300	$225

BLACKHAWK CONVERTIBLE - similar to Blackhawk, with extra cylinder, .357 Mag. and 9mm Para., and .45 LC and .45 ACP cals.

	100%	98%	95%	90%	80%	70%	60%
.357 Mag./9mm Para.	$550	$450	$300	$250	$225	$195	$175
.45 LC/.45 ACP	$800	$650	$500	$400	$325	$295	$275

This model did not feature a brass grip frame.

GRADING - PPGS™	100%	98%	95%	90%	80%	70%	60%

BLACKHAWK FLATTOP .44 MAGNUM - similar to Blackhawk Flattop, except heavier frame and cylinder, .44 Mag., 6 1/2, 7 1/2, and 10 in. barrels. Approx. 28,000 mfg. between 1956-1963.

	100%	98%	95%	90%	80%	70%	60%
6 1/2 in. barrel	$1,100	$800	$625	$500	$350	$300	$250
7 1/2 in. barrel	$1,325	$950	$725	$625	$550	$475	$400
10 in. barrel	$1,750	$1,375	$950	$825	$700	$600	$500

Distinguishable from Super Blackhawk by fluted cylinder and rounded triggerguard.

SUPER BLACKHAWK - .44 Mag. cal., 6 1/2 (rare) or 7 1/2 in. barrel, larger grip frame and square back triggerguard, unfluted cylinder, adj. sights, walnut grips. Mfg. 1959-72.

	100%	98%	95%	90%	80%	70%	60%
	$600	$500	$400	$300	$190	$185	$175
✱ *Super Blackhawk Early Variations*							
Brass grip frame	$800	$700	$650	$600	$500	$400	$300
Dragoon frame 6 1/2 bbl.	$850	$700	$650	$600	$500	$400	$300
Dragoon frame white cardboard case/sleeve	$1,200	$1,000	$800	$700	$600	$500	$400
Dragoon frame, mahogany cased	$1,000	$850	$750	$650	$500	$400	$300
Long frame, mahogany cased	$1,500	$1,200	$1,000	$900	$800	$700	$650

OLD MODEL BEARCAT - .22 LR cal., 6 shot, 4 in. barrel, alloy frame, brass anodized trigger guard, blue, simulated wood grips w/o medallion on early models, models mfg. after 1963 had oil filled walnut with insert eagle medallion, 17 oz. Mfg. 1958-1970.

	100%	98%	95%	90%	80%	70%	60%
	$450	$350	$275	$225	$200	$180	$170
w/ alphabetical prefix	$500	$400	$325	$275	$250	$230	$215

Add 100%+ for blue aluminum triggerguard variation (73,000-77,000 ser. no. range). Numerous variations exist within this model incorporating production changes.

OLD MODEL SUPER BEARCAT - similar to Bearcat, except steel frame, made with brass anodized aluminum trigger guard (early model), or blue steel guard, 25 oz. Mfg. 1971-74.

	100%	98%	95%	90%	80%	70%	60%
	$450	$350	$250	$225	$200	$180	$165

HAWKEYE SINGLE SHOT - .256 Mag. cal., single shot, round cylinder replaced by rectangular rotating breech block, 8 1/2 in. barrel, blue, walnut grips, adj. sight, very rare, 45 oz., approx. 3,300 mfg. Mfg. 1963-64 only.

	100%	98%	95%	90%	80%	70%	60%
	$2,000	$1,600	$1,200	$800	$600	$550	$500

REVOLVERS: SINGLE ACTION, NEW MODELS

The following single actions are known as "New Models." They have 2 pins through the frame and cock without the clicks associated with the single action. The changeover occurred as a result of desire for safety features. The "New Models" have a transfer bar similar to those found on modern double action revolvers and do not accidentally discharge if dropped. Manufacture started 1973. During certain years of manufacture, Ruger's changes in production on certain models (cals., barrel markings, barrel lengths, etc.) have created rare variations that are now considered premium niches. These areas of low manufacture will add premiums to the values listed on standard models. Beginning 1996, Ruger started supplying all New Model revolvers with a case and lock.

SINGLE SIX CONVERTIBLE - .22 S, L, or LR cal., includes interchangeable .22 Mag. cylinder, 5 1/2 or 6 1/2 in. barrel, fixed sights, blue finish, approx. 34 oz. New 1994.

	100%	98%	95%	90%	80%	70%	60%
MSR $399	$300	$230	$170	$140	$120	$110	$100

GRADING - PPGS™	100%	98%	95%	90%	80%	70%	60%

✱ *Single Six Convertible Stainless Steel* - similar to Single Six Convertible, except is stainless steel. Mfg. 1994-97, reintroduced 1999 only.

	$350	$255	$185				

Last MSR was $415.

✱ *Single Six Convertible 50th Anniversary* - similar to Single Six Convertible, 4 5/8 in. barrel only, cocobolo wood grips and 50th Anniversary 1953-2002 Ruger logo, includes red plastic case. Mfg. 2003 only.

	$325	$240	$190	$170	$155	$145	$135

Last MSR was $425.

SUPER SINGLE SIX
- .17 HMR cal., 6 shot, 6 1/2 in. barrel, blue finish with adj. barrel sights, smooth rosewood grips, 35 oz. New 2003.

MSR $399	$300	$230	$175	$140	$120	$110	$100

✱ *Super Single Six Stainless Steel Hunter* - similar to Super Single Six, except stainless steel, 7 1/2 in. barrel, black laminate grips, includes Ruger scope rings. New 2004.

MSR $599	$460	$335	$285				

SUPER SINGLE SIX CONVERTIBLE
- .22 LR cal., includes interchangeable .22 Mag. cylinder, 4 5/8, 5 1/2, 6 1/2, or 9 1/2 in. barrel, 6 shot, similar to old Super Single Six, except has new interlocking safety mechanism previously described, adj. rear sight, 33 oz (w/5 1/2 in. barrel). Mfg. 1973-present.

MSR $411	$325	$250	$200	$145	$120	$110	$100

✱ *Super Single Six Stainless Steel* - similar to Super Single Six, except stainless steel construction, 4 5/8 (disc. 1976), 5 1/2, 6 1/2, or 9 1/2 (disc.-rare) in. barrel.

MSR $485	$395	$300	$200				

Values for 4 5/8 or 9 1/2 in. barrel are approx. $575 if NIB.

✱ *Super Single Six Stainless Steel Hunter* - similar to Super Single Six Stainless Steel, except has 7 1/2 in. barrel, black laminate grips, includes Ruger scope rings. New 2004.

MSR $650	$500	$385	$310				

✱ *Super Single Six Hunter Convertible* - .17 HMR or .17 Mach 2 cal., includes .17 HMR or .17 Mach 2 cylinders, 6 shot, stainless steel, 7 1/2 in. barrel, black laminated wood grips, intergral scope mounts with one inch rings. New 2005.

MSR $675	$515	$400	$325				

✱ *Super Single Six "Star" Model* - .22 LR cal., so named because of star stamped on bottom of frame, blue or stainless, single cylinder (not convertible). Mfg. 1974-75 only.

	100%	98%	95%	90%	80%	70%	60%
Blue 5 1/2 or 6 1/2 in. bbl.	$450	$400	$350	$295	$275	$250	$225
Blue 9 1/2 in. bbl. (rare)	$550	$500	$450	$400	$350	$300	$250
Blue 4 5/8 in. bbl. (very rare)	$800	$750	$700	$625	$550	$475	$395
Stainless 5 1/2 or 1/2 in. bbl.	$400	$300	$250				
Stainless 9 1/2 in. bbl.	$500	$450	$400				
Stainless 4 5/8 in. bbl. (rare)	$600	$550	$500				

✱ *Super Single Six High Gloss Stainless* - 5 1/2 (disc. 1996) or 6 1/2 in. barrel, features high gloss stainless steel finish, simulated ivory grips became standard 1997. Mfg. 1994-97.

	$400	$300	$195				

Last MSR was $425.

Subtract approx. 8% if without simulated ivory grips.

GRADING - PPGS™	100%	98%	95%	90%	80%	70%	60%

* **Colorado Centennial Super Single Six** - 15,000 mfg. 1975 only, includes walnut case with medallion insert, stainless steel grip frame, 6 1/2 in. barrel, issue price was $250.

	$500	$350	$250				

* **New Model Super Single Six SSM** - .32 H&R Mag. cal., similar to .22 LR/.22 Mag. Super Single Six, 4 5/8, 5 1/2, 6 1/2 or 9 1/2 in. barrel, blue frame, 6 shot, adj. sights, wood grips, 32-35 oz. Disc. 1996.

	$550	$500	$450	$400	$350	$300	$250

Add 50% if cylinder and frame is marked "SSM".

NEW MODEL .32 H&R MAG. (SUPER SINGLE SIX SSM) - .32 H&R Mag. cal., 4 5/8, or 5 1/2 in. barrel, case colored frame or high gloss stainless steel (new 2001), 6 shot, fixed sights, choice of bird's head with black Micarta grips (new 2002) or regular grips (simulated ivory became standard 2001), 32-35 oz. Mfg. 2001-2004.

	$450	$330	$270	$240	$210	$175	$145

Last MSR was $576.

Subtract $41 for slim rosewood grips.

BLACKHAWK - .30 Carbine (disc. 1996, reintroduced 1998), .357 Mag., .41 Mag. (disc. 1996, reintroduced 1999), or .45 LC cal., similar to old Model Blackhawk, with new interlocking safety mechanism, 6 shot, 4 5/8, 6 1/2, or 7 1/2 in. (.30 Carbine and .45 LC only) barrel, 40-44 oz. Mfg. 1973-present.

MSR $468	$355	$260	$200	$165	$145	$135	$125

* **Blackhawk Convertible** - similar to New Model Blackhawk, except interchangeable cylinders, .357 Mag./9mm Para. (current), .44 Mag./.44-40 WCF (disc.), or .45 LC/.45 ACP (disc. 1985, reintroduced 1999) cal., 4 5/8, 5 1/2 (.45 LC/.45 ACP only), or 6 1/2 in. barrel.

MSR $530	$400	$320	$255	$205	$170	$160	$150

Add 30% for disc. convertible cals.

* **Buckeye Special** - .32-20 WCF/.32 H&R Mag. cal., 6 1/2 in. barrel. Mfg. 1989.

	$600	$500	$400	$250	$220	$200	$180

Subtract 10% for limited edition Buckeye Special in .38-40 WCF/10mm auto (mfg. for Buckeye Sports in 1990).

* **Blackhawk Stainless Steel** - .357 Mag. or .45 LC (new 1993) cal., 4 5/8, 6 1/2, or 7 1/2 (.45 LC only) in. barrel.

MSR $572	$480	$345	$280				

300 .357 Mag./9mm Para. convertible pistols were made in this model - NIB prices have ranged $500-$750.

New Model .357 Mag. Blackhawks are serial numbered 32-00001 on up. New Model .45 LC Blackhawks are serial numbered 46-00001 on up.

* **Blackhawk High Gloss Stainless Steel** - .357 Mag. or .45 LC cal., 4 5/8, 6 1/2 (.357 Mag. only), or 7 1/2 (.45 LC only) in. barrel, features high gloss stainless steel finish. Mfg. 1994-96.

	$395	$295	$250				

Last MSR was $443.

BLACKHAWK-SRM - similar to New Model Blackhawk, except is chambered for .357 Rem. Maximum, 7 1/2 or 10 1/2 in. barrels available, target sights, 53 oz., 11,500 mfg. 1982-84 - production suspended due to unresolvable engineering problems.

	$650	$500	$400	$325	$300	$250	$225

50th ANNIVERSARY BLACKHAWK - .357 Mag. cal., 4 5/8 in. barrel, flattop frame, smaller, pre-1962 XR-3 grip frame with checkered hard rubber grips with black Ruger medallions, cylinder indexing aligns loading gate cutout with cylinder borings, "50th YEAR BLACKHAWK 1955-2005" gold rollmark, supplied with red case. New 2005.

MSR $583	$455	$350	$315	$280	$260	$240	$220

RUGER

SUPER BLACKHAWK - .44 Mag. cal., 4 5/8 (new 1994), 5 1/2 (new 1987), 7 1/2 or 10 1/2 bull in. barrel, 6 shot, blue finish, walnut grips, similar to old model in appearance, but has new action, steel ejector housing was introduced in 2000. Mfg. 1973-present.

	MSR $562	$415	$310	$250	$200	$170	$160	$150

Add $10 for 10 1/2 in. bull barrel (not cased).

The new model started with serial number 81-00001.

* **Super Blackhawk Stainless Steel** - stainless variation of the Super Blackhawk.

	MSR $577	$450	$355	$250

Add $12 for 10 1/2 in. bull barrel (not cased).

Add $16 for hunter grip frame with laminate grip panels (disc.).

* **Super Blackhawk High Gloss Stainless Steel** - high gloss stainless steel finish, not available in 10 1/2 in. bull barrel. Mfg. 1994-96.

		$450	$350	$250

Last MSR was $450.

* **Super Blackhawk Stainless Hunter** - 7 1/2 in. ribbed barrel only, choice of standard or Bisley gripstraps, black laminated wood grips, includes scope rings and integral scope mounts (new 2002). Mfg. 1992-95, reintroduced 2002.

	MSR $676	$615	$510	$380

A special edition of this model with wood grain laminated grips and lockable plastic case was available through Davidson's - retail was $639.

VAQUERO - .357 Mag. (new 1997), .44-40 WCF (new 1994), .44 Mag. (new 1994), or .45 LC cal., 6 shot, 4 5/8, 5 1/2, or 7 1/2 (not available in .357 Mag.) in. barrel, color case hardened frame, blue steel frame, barrel, and cylinder, steel ejector housing became standard in 2000, transfer bar hammer safety, smooth rosewood, smooth bird's head (mfg. 2001 only) or black Micarta bird's head, (.45 LC cal. only, 4 3/4 in. barrel, new 2002), or simulated ivory (new 1996) grips, patterned after the Colt SAA, fixed sights, 39-41 oz. Mfg. 1993-2004.

	$475	$330	$265	$225	$195	$170	$160

Last MSR was $555.

Add $40 for simulated ivory grips (new 1996).

Add approx. $150 for simulated ivory grips and engraved cylinder (mfg. 1998-99).

* **Vaquero High Gloss Stainless Steel** - high gloss stainless steel finish, black Micarta bird's head grips became optional 2002. Mfg. 1994-2004.

	$475	$330	$265

Last MSR was $555.

Add $40 for simulated ivory grips (new 1996).

* **Vaquero Bird's Head** - .357 Mag. or .45 LC cal., 3 3/4 or 4 5/8 in. barrel, color case hardened frame or stainless steel bird's head frame, choice of black Micarta or simulated ivory (new 2003) grips. Disc. 2004.

	$475	$360	$295	$245	$210	$185	$165

Last MSR was $595.

* **Vaquero 45 Years of Guns & Ammo Special Limited Edition** - .45 LC cal., 5 1/2 in. barrel, blue steel with case colored finish, black Micarta grips, fixed front blade sights, 6 shot, gold filled or non-gold laser rollmarking with "45 Years of Guns & Ammo" on barrel, special ser. no. beginning with 45GA, includes black plastic lockable case. Mfg. 2003-2004.

	$465	$360	$295	$245	$210	$185	$165

Last MSR was $599.

This model was available exclusively from Davidson's.

GRADING - PPGS™	100%	98%	95%	90%	80%	70%	60%

✴ *Vaquero Dual Cylinder Special Limited Edition* - .45 LC or .45 ACP cal., single action with convertible cylinders, 4 5/8 or 5 1/2 in. barrel, bright stainless steel, rosewood grips, fixed sights, includes black plastic lockable case. Mfg. 2003-2004.

	$525	$450	$395	$350	$325	$295	$275

Last MSR was $600.

This model was available exclusively from Davidson's.

NEW VAQUERO - .357 Mag. or .45 LC cal., 4 5/8, 5 1/2, or 7 1/2 (.45 LC cal. only) in. barrel, 6 shot, redesigned using a slimmer pre-1962 XR-3 style grip frame, smaller cylinder frame allows loading gate cutout to align with cylinder borings, color case hardened frame with blued gripstraps, barrel, and cylinder, recontoured hammer, new hammerspring, beveled cylinder, checkered hard rubber grips, crescent-shaped ejector rod head. New 2005.

MSR $583	$455	$360	$295	$250	$225	$200	$175

✴ *New Vaquero High Gloss Stainless* - similar to New Vaquero, except is stainless steel. New 2005.

MSR $583	$455	$360	$295				

✴ *New Vaquero Limited Edition* - similar to New Vaquero, except is .32-20 WCF cal., includes extra .32 H&R Mag. cylinder, black Micarta grips. New 2004.

MSR $642	$475	$350	$260				

This model is available exclusively from Davidson's.

BISLEY VAQUERO - .357 Mag. (new 1999, 5 1/2 in. barrel only), .44 Mag. or .45 LC cal., 4 5/8 (new 1999) or 5 1/2 in. barrel, case colored frame with blue steel grips, barrel, and cylinder, steel ejector housing became standard in 2000, fixed sights, approx. 40 oz. Mfg. 1998-2004.

		$435	$340	$275	$230	$200	$180	$160

Last MSR was $555.

Add $40 for simulated ivory grips.

✴ *Bisley Vaquero Stainless* - similar to Bisley Vaquero, except is stainless steel. Disc. 2004.

	$440	$330	$265				

Last MSR was $575.

Add $40 for simulated ivory grips.

✴ *Bisley Single-Six Vaquero Special Edition* - .22 LR cal., single action, bright stainless steel, scroll engraving on cylinder, rosewood grips, fixed sights. Disc. 2004.

	$450	$395	$325				

Last MSR was $555.

This model was available exclusively through Davidson's.

BISLEY MODEL - .22 LR, .32 H&R Mag. (disc. 1996), .357 Mag., .41 Mag. (disc. 1996), .44 Mag., or .45 LC cal., 6 shot, incorporates Bisley features (flattop frame, raked hammer, longer grip frame), 6 1/2 (.22 LR or .44 Mag. only) or 7 1/2 in. barrel, fixed (disc. 1992, except for .32 H&R Mag.) or adj. sights, available with fluted/unfluted or roll-marked/unmarked (disc.) cylinders, satin blue finish only, Goncalo Alves smooth grips. New 1986.

✴ *.22 LR or .32 H&R Mag.*

MSR $461	$360	$265	$210	$180	$160	$150	$140

Add $50 for .32 H&R Mag. (disc. 1996).

✴ *Other cals.*

MSR $580	$450	$350	$285	$235	$200	$180	$160

✴ *Bisley Shootist* - .22 LR cal., special limited edition, stainless steel, 4 5/8 in. barrel, adj. sights, marked "In Memory of Our Friend, Tom Ruger, The Shootist", only 52 mfg. 1994.

	$1,500	$1,250	$995				

GRADING - PPGS™	100%	98%	95%	90%	80%	70%	60%

NEW BEARCAT - .22 LR cal., includes interchangeable .22 Mag. cyl. (disc. 1996), frame slightly longer than old Bearcat, 4 in. barrel, transfer bar hammer safety, blue finish, smooth walnut grips, fixed sights, 24 oz. New 1994.

MSR $398	$325	$260	$200	$140	$125	$115	$105

* **New Bearcat Convertible** - similar to New Bearcat, except has convertible cylinder, early production, recalled by the factory.

	$1,100	$1,000	$900

* **New Bearcat Bright Stainless Steel** - similar to New Bearcat, except is stainless steel. New 2002.

MSR $450	$390	$310	$205

REVOLVERS: DOUBLE ACTION

During certain years of manufacture, Ruger's changes in production on certain models (cals., barrel markings, barrel lengths, etc.) have created rare variations that are now considered premium niches. These areas of low manufacture will add premiums to the values listed on standard models.

SPEED SIX (MODELS 207, 208 and 209) - .38 Spl., .357 Mag., or 9mm Para. cal., 2 3/4 or 4 in. barrel, fixed sights, checkered walnut grips, round butt, blue finish, some guns have factory speed hammer (no hammer spur). Mfg. 1973-88. Model 207 and 208 disc. 1988.

	$300	$205	$190	$170	$160	$150	$140

Last MSR was $292.

Add $100 for 9mm Para. (Model 209 disc. 1984).

* **Models 737 and 738** - stainless steel versions of Models 207 and 208, .357 Mag and .38 Spl. cals., 2 3/4 or 4 in. barrel. Disc. 1988.

	$325	$245	$220

Last MSR was $320.

* **Model 739** - stainless steel, 9mm Para. Disc. 1984.

	$400	$250	$230

SECURITY SIX (MODEL 117) - .357 Mag. cal., 6 shot, 2 3/4, 4 (heavy), or 6 in. barrel, adj. sights, checkered walnut grips, square butt. Mfg. 1970-85.

	$300	$225	$195	$185	$160	$150	$140

Last MSR was $309.

Add $15 for target grips.

500 of this model were mfg. for the California Highway Patrol during 1983 (.38 Spl. cal.) in stainless steel only. They are distinguishable by a C.H.P. marking. Other Security Six Model 117 special editions have been made for various police organizations - premiums might exist in certain regions for these variations.

* **Model 717** - stainless steel version of Model 117. Disc. 1985.

	$300	$255	$230

Last MSR was $338.

POLICE SERVICE SIX - .357 Mag, .38 Spl., or 9mm Para. cal., blue finish only, square butt, fixed sights, checkered walnut grips.

* **Model 107** - .357 Mag, 2 3/4 or 4 in. barrel, fixed sights. Disc. 1988.

	$400	$300	$250	$190	$180	$170	$165

Last MSR was $287.

* **Model 108** - .38 Spl., 4 in. barrel, fixed sights. Disc. 1988.

	$300	$220	$200	$190	$180	$170	$165

Last MSR was $287.

* **Model 109** - 9mm Para., 4 in. barrel, fixed sights. Disc. 1984.

	$300	$230	$205	$195	$185	$180	$175

GRADING - PPGS™	100%	98%	95%	90%	80%	70%	60%

POLICE SERVICE SIX STAINLESS STEEL - stainless construction, 4 in. barrel only, fixed sights, checkered walnut grips.

❋ *Model 707* - .357 Mag., square butt. Disc. 1988.

	$300	**$235**	**$210**

Last MSR was $310.

❋ *Model 708* - .38 Spl., square butt. Disc. 1988.

	$300	**$235**	**$210**

Last MSR was $310.

GP-100 - .357 Mag. or .38 Spl. cal., 3 (new 1990, fixed sights and .357 Mag. cal. only), 4, or 6 (.357 Mag. cal. only) in. standard or heavy barrel, 6 shot, strengthened design intended for constant use with all .357 Mag. ammunition, rubber cushioned grip panels with polished Goncalo Alves wood inserts, fixed or adj. (.357 Mag. only) sights with white outlined rear and interchangeable front, 35-46 oz. depending on barrel configuration. New 1986.

MSR $536	**$435**	**$335**	**$275**	**$230**	**$200**	**$185**	**$170**

Add $5 for adj. rear sight (.357 Mag. cal., 4 or 6 in. barrel only).

❋ *GP-100 Stainless Steel* - similar to GP-100, .357 Mag. cal. only, stainless steel. New 1987.

MSR $580	**$455**	**$345**	**$280**

Add $17 for adj. sights.

❋ *GP-100 High Gloss Stainless Steel* - .357 Mag. only, high gloss stainless steel finish, 3 or 4 in. heavy barrel. Mfg. 1996 only.

	$375	**$295**	**$250**

Last MSR was $457.

❋ *GP-100 Special Limited Edition* - .357 Mag. cal., DA, 5 in. heavy barrel, satin stainless steel, black cushioned grips with wood insert panels, adj. sights, 6 shot, includes lockable plastic case, 43.5 oz. Mfg. 2003-2004.

	$440	**$350**	**$285**	**$240**	**$200**	**$180**	**$160**

Last MSR was $555.

This model was available exclusively from Davidson's.

SP-101 STAINLESS STEEL - .22 LR (6 shot - mfg. 1990-2004), .32 H&R (6 shot - new 1991), .38 Spl. (5 shot), 9mm Para. (5 shot – mfg. 1991-2000), or .357 Mag. (5 shot - new 1991) cal., 2 1/4, 3 1/16, or 4 (new 1990) in. barrel, small frame variation of the GP - 100 Stainless, fixed or adj. (new 1996) sights, 25-34 oz. New 1989.

MSR $515	**$415**	**$315**	**$250**

Ruger introduced adj. sights in 1996 available in .22 LR or .32 H&R cal. only.

Ruger introduced a .357 Mag./2 1/4 in. (new 1993) or .38 Spl./2 1/4 (new 1994) in. configuration featuring a spurless hammer, double action only.

SP-101 barrel lengths are as follows: .22 cal. is available in 2 1/4 or 4 in. standard or heavy barrel, .32 H&R is available in 3 1/16 or 4 (new 1994) in. heavy barrel, .38 Spl. is available in 2 1/4 or 3 1/16 in. length only, 9mm Para. is available in 2 1/4 (new 1992) or 3 1/16 in. only, and .357 Mag. is available in 2 1/4 or 3 1/16 in. only.

❋ *SP-101 High Gloss Stainless Steel* - .38 Spl. (disc. 1996), 9mm Para. (disc. 1996), or .357 Mag. cal., similar to SP-101 Stainless Steel, except has high gloss stainless steel finish. Mfg. 1996-97.

	$410	**$310**	**$250**

Last MSR was $443.

Ruger introduced adj. sights in 1996 available in .22 LR or .32 H&R cal. only.

REDHAWK - .357 Mag. (disc. 1985), .41 Mag. (disc. 1992), or .44 Mag. cal., 6 shot, this is a redesigned large frame handgun, 5 1/2 and 7 1/2 in. barrel, square butt, smooth hardwood grips, 49-54 oz.

MSR $633	**$515**	**$395**	**$320**	**$265**	**$215**	**$180**	**$165**

Add $40 for scope rings.

.357 Mag. and .41 Mag. cals. will bring collector premiums if NIB.

GRADING - PPGS™	100%	98%	95%	90%	80%	70%	60%

✳ **Redhawk Stainless Steel** - .44 Mag or .45 LC (new 1998) cal., stainless steel construction, 49–54 oz.

MSR $695	$550	$425	$335

Add $47 for scope rings.

This model was also available as a KRH-35, and is marked both "Redhawk" and ".357 Magnum". Mfg. was circa 1984-1991.

SUPER REDHAWK STAINLESS - .44 Mag., .454 Casull (new 1999), or .480 Ruger (new 2001) cal., 6 shot, 7 1/2 or 9 1/2 in. barrel, fluted (.44 Mag. cal. only) or non-fluted cylinder, choice of regular or high gloss (mfg. 1997-2004) stainless steel, adj. rear sight, cushioned grip panels (GP-100 style), stainless steel scope rings, 53-58 oz. New late 1987.

MSR $742	$590	$435	$310

Add $77 for .454 Casull or .480 Ruger (new 2001) cal.

✳ **Super Redhawk Stainless Alaskan** - .454 Casull or .480 Ruger, 6 shot, 2 1/2 in. barrel, includes Hogue monogrips, 42 oz. New 2005.

MSR $819	$650	$475	$375

RIFLES: BOLT ACTION, RIMFIRE

MODEL 77/17 - .17 Mach 2 (new 2005) or .17 HMR cal. only, 22 in. barrel, blue finish or stainless steel (new 2003), checkered walnut or black laminate (new 2003, .17 HMR cal. only) stock. New 2002.

MSR $613	$465	$375	$295	$245	$210	$190	$175

Add $72 for stainless steel.

Add $61 for .17 Mach 2 cal.

MODEL 77/22-R/RS - .22 LR cal. only, 10 shot rotary mag., 20 in. barrel, all steel construction, 3 position safety, checkered walnut stock, blue finish, non-adj. trigger, available with either optional iron sights or plain barrel (no sights) with scope rings (included), 2.7 millisecond lock time on trigger, 6 lbs. 2 oz. New 1984.

MSR $613	$465	$375	$295	$245	$210	$190	$175

Add $25 for iron sights (disc. 2004).

Add 125% if w/o 77/22 roll mark or with green laminated stock.

✳ **Model 77/22-RP/RSP All-Weather Stainless** - similar to Model 77/22, except has stainless steel metal with matte black DuPont Zytel synthetic stock, 5 lbs. 14 oz. New 1989.

MSR $613	$465	$375	$295

Add $25 for iron sights (disc. 2004).

✳ **Model 77/22-VBZ Varmint Stainless Laminated** - similar to Model 77/22, except stainless steel, heavy stainless barrel with dull finish, laminated brown hardwood stock. New 1995.

MSR $685	$525	$400	$320

MODEL 77/22-RM/RSM MAG. - similar to Model 77/22-R/RS, except in .22 Win. Mag. cal., 9 shot rotary mag., blue finish, checkered walnut stock. New 1990.

MSR $613	$465	$375	$295	$245	$210	$190	$175

Add $25 for iron sights (disc. 2004).

✳ **Model 77/22-RMP/RSMP Mag. All-Weather Stainless** - similar to Model 77/22 - RM/RSM Mag., except has stainless steel metal with matte black Dupont Zytel synthetic stock. New 1990.

MSR $613	$465	$375	$295

Add $25 for iron sights.

✳ **Model 77/22-VMBZ Mag. Varmint Stainless Laminated** - similar to Model 77/22 RM/RSM Mag., except stainless steel, heavy stainless barrel with dull finish, laminated brown hardwood stock. New 1993.

MSR $685	$525	$400	$320

GRADING - PPGS™	100%	98%	95%	90%	80%	70%	60%

RIFLES: BOLT ACTION, CENTERFIRE

During certain years of manufacture, Ruger's changes in production on certain models (cals., barrel markings, barrel lengths, etc.) have created rare variations that are now considered premium niches. These areas of low manufacture will add premiums to the values listed on standard models. Earlier flat-bolt models (pre-1972) are desirable in the rarer cals. and will command a 100% premium if in 98%+ original condition.

MODEL 77/22-RH/RSH HORNET - .22 Hornet cal., features lengthened receiver, detachable 6 shot rotary mag. (not interchangeable with other 77/22 mags.), 20 in. blue barrel, checkered American walnut stock, includes scope rings, 6 lbs. New 1994.

MSR $649	$505	$410	$320	$255	$225	$195	$180

     Add $20 for iron sights (disc. 2002).

* **Model 77/22-VHZ Hornet Varmint Stainless Laminated** - similar to Model 77/22 Hornet, stainless steel, 24 in. heavy stainless barrel with dull finish and no sights, laminated brown hardwood stock, 6 5/8 lbs. New 1995.

MSR $685	$525	$405	$320

MODEL 77/44 - .44 Mag. cal., 18 1/2 in. barrel, rotary mag., plain birch or checkered walnut stock, open sights, 6 lbs. Mfg. 1998-2004.

$510	$380	$310	$270	$245	$200	$200

                                      Last MSR was $635.

* **Model 77/44 Stainless** - .44 Mag. cal., black synthetic stock, stainless steel construction, open sights. Mfg. 1999-2004.

$510	$380	$310

                                        Last MSR was $635.

MODEL 77R - .22-250 Rem., .220 Swift, 6mm Rem. (disc.), .243 Win. (disc.), .250 Savage (disc.), .257 Roberts, .25-06 Rem., .270 Win., 7x57mm, 7mm-08 (disc.), 6.5mm Rem. Mag. (scarce), 7mm Rem. Mag., .280 Rem., .284 Win., .308 Win. (disc.), .30-06, .300 Win. Mag., .338 Win Mag., .350 Rem. Mag., or .358 Win. cal., long or short action, blue finish, 5 shot mag., 3 shot in Mag. cals., 22 or 24 in. barrel, available with integral bases or round top, some models supplied with sights, stock is checkered walnut with red rubber buttplate, approx. 7 lbs. Mfg. 1968-92.

$450	$395	$325	$265	$245	$200	$200

                                        Last MSR was $558.

     Add 10-15% for .284 cal.
     Add 20%-30% for .350 Rem. Mag. cal.

* **Model 77 RL** - .22-250 Rem. (disc.), .243 Win., .250 Sav., .257 Roberts, .270 Win., .30-06, or .308 Win. cal., ultra light variation weighing 6 lbs., black forearm tip. Disc. 1992.

$445	$375	$325	$270	$250	$225	$205

                                        Last MSR was $592.

* **Model 77 RS** - .243 Win., .250 Sav., 6mm Rem., 6.5mm Rem. Mag., 7x57mm, .25-06 Rem. (disc.), 270 Win., .280 Rem., .284 Win., .30-06, .308 Win., 7mm Rem. Mag., 300 Win. Mag., .338 Win. Mag, .35 Whelen, .350 Rem. Mag., or .358 Win. cal., similar to Model 77R, except has open sights. Disc. 1992.

$500	$425	$350	$300	$265	$230	$210

                                        Last MSR was $616.

     Add 30% for .284 Win.
     Add 50% for .35 Whelen, .358 Win., or .350 Rem. Mag. cal.

* **Model 77PL** - .25-06 Rem., .270 Win., .30-06, .300 Win. Mag., .338 Win. Mag., 7mm Rem. Mag., or 7x57mm cal., differs from R Model in that it has a round top, drilled to take Redfield scope mounts, w/o sights.

$420	$395	$325	$265	$245	$200	$200

GRADING - PPGS™	100%	98%	95%	90%	80%	70%	60%

* **Model 77ST** - .25-06 Rem., .257 Roberts, 7x57mm, .300 Win. Mag., .338 Win. Mag., 7mm Rem. Mag., .30-06, or .270 Win. cal., differs from RS Model in that is has round top drilled to take Redfield scope mounts with iron sights on barrel.

	$460	$425	$350	$300	$265	$230	$210

* **Model 77V Varmint** - .22-250 Rem., .220 Swift, .243 Win. (disc.), 6mm Rem. (disc.), .25-06 Rem., .280 Rem., .308 Win., or .30-06 cal., 24 in. heavy barrel (26 in. on .220 Swift), drilled and tapped for target bases, approx. 9 lbs. Mfg. 1968-92.

	$430	$395	$325	$265	$245	$210	$200

Last MSR was $574.

* **Model 77 RS African** - similar to Model 77R, except in .458 Win. Mag. cal. Disc. 1991.

	$600	$500	$400	$365	$335	$315	$300

Last MSR was $680.

This model was supplied standard with a steel triggerguard and steel floor plate.

* **Model 77 RSC** - similar to Model 77 RS African, except has Circassian walnut stock (C suffix). Mfg. 1976-78.

	$800	$650	$500	$450	$400	$365	$335

* **Model 77 RLS** - .243 Win. (disc. 1989), .270 Win., .30-06, or .308 Win. cal. (disc. 1989), ultra light, 18 1/2 in. barrel, open sights, 6 lbs. Mfg. 1987-93.

	$445	$395	$310	$280	$260	$230	$210

Last MSR was $592.

* **Model 77 RSI** - .22-250 Rem. (disc. 1991), .243 Win. .250-3000 Sav. (reintroduced 1990), .270 Win., .30-06, .308 Win. (disc. 1991), 7x57mm (rare), or 7mm-08 Rem. cal., International Mannlicher (full length stock) with 18 1/2 in. barrel and open sights (includes scope rings), approx. 7 lbs. Disc. 1993.

	$550	$400	$325	$295	$265	$230	$210

Last MSR was $623.

    Add 20% for 7mm-08 cal.

MODEL 77R MARK II SERIES

MODEL 77R MARK II SERIES - various cals. as listed in the submodels below, evolutionary design of the Ruger Model 77R featuring slenderized proportioning, 3 position swing-back safety, new trigger, trigger guard and floor plate latch, stainless steel bolt with Mauser extractor design, various barrel lengths, integral base receiver, hand checkered American walnut stock, includes scope rings, various weights. New 1989.

* **Model 77R** - .204 Ruger (new 2004), .220 Swift (new 1995), .22-250 Rem. (new 1993), .223 Rem. (new 1992), .243 Win., .25-06 Rem. (new 1993), .257 Roberts (new 1993), .260 Rem. (new 1999), .270 Win. (new 1993), .270 WSM (new 2004), .280 Rem. (new 1993), 6mm Rem., 6.5x55mm Swedish (new 1993), 7x57mm (mfg. 1993-2004), .30-06 (new 1993), .308 Win., 7mm WSM (new 2004), 7mm Rem. Mag. (new 1993), 7mm RSUM (new 2002), .300 Win. Mag. (new 1993), .300 WSM (new 2004), .300 RSUM (new 2002), .338 Win. Mag. (new 1993). or .350 Rem. Mag. (new 2004) cal., checkered walnut stock is standard, 22 or 24 in. barrel, standard model of the new Mark II Series, approx. 7 lbs.

MSR $716	$490	$395	$325	$285	$245	$200	$200

> **Model 77 LR** - .25-06 Rem., .270 Win., .30-06, .300 Win. Mag., or 7mm Rem. Mag. cal., left-hand variation of the Model 77R. New 1991.

MSR $716	$490	$395	$325	$285	$245	$200	$200

* **Model 77 RL** - .223 Rem., .243 Win., .257 Roberts (new 1993), .270 Win. (new 1993), .30-06 (mfg. 1993-2004), or .308 Win. cal., 20 in. barrel, black forend tip, ultra light variation weighing approx. 6 lbs. New 1990.

MSR $773	$530	$435	$335	$290	$255	$225	$205

GRADING - PPGS™	100%	98%	95%	90%	80%	70%	60%

※ Model 77 RLFP Stainless - .204 Ruger, .223 Rem. (new 2005), .243 Win., .270 Win. or .30-06 cal., 20 in. barrel, black synthetic stock, ultralight variation of the Model 77, w/o sights, 6 1/2 lbs. New 1999.

MSR $716	$490	$395	$325				

※ Model 77 RS - 6mm Rem., .243 Win., .25-06 Rem. (new 1993), .270 Win. (new 1993), .30-06 (new 1993), .308 Win., 7mm Rem. Mag. (new 1993), .300 Win. Mag. (new 1993), .338 Win Mag. (new 1993), or .458 Win. Mag. (mfg. 1994-98) cal., 22 or 24 in. barrel, similar to Model 77R, except has open sights. Mfg. 1990-2004.

MSR $780	$555	$435	$355	$310	$270	$230	$210

Last MSR was $780.

※ Model 77 CR Compact - .223 Rem., .243 Win., .260 Rem., .308 Win., or 7mm-08 Rem. cal., features 16.5 in. barrel, checkered walnut stock, includes scope rings, no sights, approx. 5 3/4 lbs. New 2002.

MSR $716	$490	$395	$325	$285	$245	$200	$200

>Model 77 CRBBZ Compact Stainless - stainless variation of the Model 77 CR Compact, black laminate stock. New 2002.

MSR $773	$530	$435	$335

※ Model 77 FRBBZ Frontier - .243 Win., .308 Win., .300 WSM, or 7mm-08 Rem. cal., compact design features 16.5 in. barrel, and shortened grey laminate stock, barrel cantilever allows scope to be mounted over barrel in front of action, blue finish, includes scope rings and Weaver style scope base adapter. New 2005.

MSR $799	$570	$445	$360	$315	$275	$230	$210

※ Model 77 RSI - .243 Win., .270 Win., .30-06, or .308 Win. cal., International Mannlicher (full length stock) with 18 1/2 in. barrel and open sights (includes scope rings), approx. 7 lbs. New 1993.

MSR $819	$580	$455	$370	$315	$270	$230	$210

※ Model 77 RLS - .243 Win. or .308 Win. cal., ultra light, 18 1/2 in. barrel, open sights. Mfg. 1990 only.

	$460	$375	$310	$280	$260	$230	$210

Last MSR was $564.

※ Model K77 RFP All-Weather Stainless - .204 Ruger (new 2005), .22-250 (new 1996), .223 Rem., .243 Win., .25-06 Rem. (new 1999), .260 Rem. (new 1999), .270 Win., .270 WSM (new 2004), .280 Rem. (new 1993), 7.62x39mm (disc. 2000), .30-06, .308 Win., 7mm-08 Rem. (new 2005), 7mm Rem. Mag., 7mm WSM (new 2004), 7mm RSUM (new 2002), .300 Win. Mag., .300 WSM (new 2004), .300 RSUM (new 2002), or .338 Win. Mag. (new 1992) cal., 22 or 24 in. barrel, similar to Model 77R Mark II except has stainless steel metal with matte black DuPont Zytel synthetic stock, no sights. New 1990.

MSR $716	$490	$395	$325				

※ Model K77 RSFP All-Weather Stainless - .223 Rem. (new 2002), .243 Win., .270 Win., .30-06, 7mm Rem. Mag., .300 Win. Mag., or .338 Win. Mag. cal., otherwise similar to Model K77 RFP All-Weather Stainless, except has open sights. Disc. 2004.

	$525	$425	$355				

Last MSR was $780.

※ Model K77 RBZ Satin Stainless - .22-250 Rem. (new 1999), .223 Rem., .243 Win., .270 Win., .280 Rem., .30-06, .308 Win., 7mm Rem. Mag., .300 Win. Mag., .338 Win. Mag., or .350 Rem. Mag. cal., features brown wood laminate stock with sling swivels, 22 or 24 in. barrel without sights, approx. 7 5/16 lbs. New 1997.

MSR $773	$530	$435	$335

GRADING - PPGS™	100%	98%	95%	90%	80%	70%	60%

❋ ***Model K77 RSBZ*** - .243 Win., .270 Win., .30-06, .300 Win. Mag., .338 Win. Mag., or 7mm Rem. Mag. cal., 22 or 24 in. barrel, laminated stock, open sights, includes scope rings, approx. 7 3/8 lbs. Disc. 2004.

		$515	$470	$355			

Last MSR was $825.

❋ ***Model K77 VT (VBZ)*** - .22 PPC (disc. 1996), .204 Ruger (new 2004), .220 Swift, .22-250 Rem., .223 Rem., .243 Win., .25-06 Rem., .308 Win., or 6mm PPC (disc. 1996) cal., 26 in. heavy barrel, features stainless steel construction, laminated stock, approx. 9.75 lbs. New 1993.

MSR $870		$550	$495	$375			

This model's nomenclature changed from VBZ to VT during 1994.

❋ ***Model 77 LRBBZ Stainless*** - .25-06 Rem. (new 2004), .270 Win., .30-06, 7mm Rem. Mag., or .300 Win. Mag. cal., 22 in. barrel, uncheckered grey laminated stock, includes scope rings. New 1999.

MSR $773		$515	$420	$355			

MODEL 77 RSM - .375 H&H, .416 Rigby, or .458 Lott (new 2002) cal., 23 in. barrel, premium grade Circassian walnut with hand cut checkering and ebony forend tip, integral barrel and sighting quarter rib, approx. 9 1/2 lbs. New 1990.

MSR $1,975		$1,575	$1,150	$975	$875	$775	$675	$595

MODEL 77 RS EXPRESS - .270 Win., .30-06, 7mm Rem. Mag., .300 Win. Mag., or .338 Win. Mag. (new 1994) cal., 22 or 24 in. barrel, 3 or 4 shot mag., similar construction to Model 77RSM with premium grade wood and other materials, 7 1/2 lbs. Mfg. 1991-2002.

	$1,250	$875	$815	$750	$700	$675	$595

Last MSR was $1,625.

RIFLES: LEVER ACTION

MODEL 96 CARBINE - .17 HMR (new 2002), .22 LR (disc. 2003), .22 Mag., or .44 Mag. cal., 18 1/2 in. barrel with single barrel band, uncheckered hardwood stock with curved buttplate, 10 (.22 LR), 9 (.22 Mag.), or 4 (.44 Mag.) shot detachable rotary mag., crossbolt safety on trigger guard, adj. rear sight, .44 Mag. has case hardened lever, rimfire receivers are drilled and tapped while the .44 Mag. has an integral base receiver with scope rings (became standard 1997), approx. 5 1/4-5 7/8 lbs. New 1996.

MSR $390		$305	$230	$195	$170	$150	$135	$125

Add approx. $40 for .44 Mag. cal. w/o scope rings (disc.).
Add $156 for .44 Mag. cal. with scope rings.

RIFLES: SEMI-AUTO

During certain years of manufacture, Ruger's changes in production on certain models (cals., barrel markings, barrel lengths, etc.) have created rare variations that are now considered premium niches. These areas of low manufacture will add premiums to the values listed on standard models. The Model 10/22 has been mfg. in a variety of limited production models including a multi-colored or green laminate wood stock variation (1986), a brown laminate stock (1988), a Kittery Trading Post Commemorative (1988), a smoke or tree bark laminate stock (1989), a Chief AJ Model, Wal-Mart (stainless with black laminated hardwood stock - 1990), etc. These limited editions will command premiums over the standard models listed, depending on the desirability of the special edition.

Note: All Ruger Rifles, except Stainless Mini-14, all Mini-30s, and Model 77-22s were made during 1976 in a "Liberty" version. Add $50-$75 when in 100% in the original box condition.

10/17 CARBINE - .17 HMR cal., steel receiver, birch stock only, 18 1/2 in. barrel, otherwise similar to 10/22 Standard Carbine. Mfg. 2004 only.

	$425	$335	$265	$225	$185	$165	$150

Last MSR was $510.

GRADING - PPGS™	100%	98%	95%	90%	80%	70%	60%

10/22 STANDARD CARBINE - .22 LR cal., 10 shot rotary mag., 18 1/2 in. barrel, birch, black synthetic (new 1999), or optional deluxe hand checkered walnut stock, folding rear sight. Mfg. 1964-present.

	MSR $258	$210	$170	$125	$100	$80	$60	$55

Add 10% for uncheckered walnut stock (mfg. 1964-1980 and 1987-1989).

Add $66 for deluxe checkered walnut sporter stock (Model 10/22 DSP).

✳ *10/22RB Standard Carbine Stainless* - similar to 10/22 Standard Carbine, except has stainless barrel and choice of birch or black synthetic (new 1997) stock. New 1992.

	MSR $304	$225	$185	$130

✳ *10/22 Standard Carbine 40th Anniversary* - similar to 10/22 Standard Carbine, except includes 40th Ruger anniversary medallion. Mfg. 2004 only.

		$225	$165	$125	$100	$85	$65	$55

Last MSR was $279.

10/22 RIFLE - similar to 10/22 Standard Carbine, except has 20 in. barrel with hardwood stock. New 2004.

	MSR $275	$220	$165	$125	$105	$80	$60	$55

10/22-T TARGET MODEL - .22 LR cal., features brown laminated American hardwood stock, blue hammer-forged spiral finish barrel, w/o sights. New 1996.

	MSR $445	$365	$290	$230

✳ *K10/22-T Target Model Stainless* - similar to 10/22T Target Model, except is stainless steel. New 1998.

	MSR $495	$405	$310	$250

✳ *K10/22-TNZ Target Stainless* - features 20 in. barrel w/o sights, stainless steel action and barrel, laminated thumbhole stock with slanted forend, 7 lbs. Mfg. 2001-2002.

		$450	$375	$300

Last MSR was $649.

10/22 FINGERGROOVE SPORTER - similar to 10/22 Standard, except Monte Carlo stock and beavertail forearm. Mfg. 1966-71.

		$475	$400	$325	$275	$225	$200	$175

Add 100% for checkered stock in NIB condition.

10/22 INTERNATIONAL (OLD PRODUCTION) - similar to 10/22 Standard, except walnut full stock Mannlicher style. Mfg. 1966-69.

		$650	$550	$475	$425	$375	$350	$325

Add 50% for checkered stock.

10/22RBI INTERNATIONAL (NEW PRODUCTION) - features Mannlicher style international birch full stock. Mfg. 1994-2003.

		$220	$180	$135	$105	$95	$80	$65

Last MSR was $279.

✳ *K10/22RBI Stainless* - stainless variation of the 10/22RBI International. Disc. 2003.

		$275	$190	$140

Last MSR was $299.

10/22 CANADIAN CENTENNIAL - 2,000 mfg. in 1967.

		$450	$400	$350

Last MSR was $100.

10/22 MAGNUM - .22 Mag. cal., steel receiver, longer and heavier bolt, 10 shot rotary mag., 18 1/2 in. barrel, uncheckered birch stock, blue metal, folding rear sight, 5 9/16 lbs. New 1999.

	MSR $536	$425	$365	$310	$265	$230	$200	$185

GRADING - PPGS™	100%	98%	95%	90%	80%	70%	60%

RUGER/REMINGTON CANADIAN CENTENNIAL MATCHED NO. 3 SET - includes a Remington Model 742 in .308 Win. cal. and a Ruger 10/22 Sporter with special commemorative appointments, cased. 1,000 sets mfg. 1967 only.

	$700	$525	$425				

❋ *Ruger Canadian Centennial Matched No. 2 Set* - 70 sets mfg. 1967 only.

	$950	$775	$550				

❋ *Ruger Canadian Centennial Matched No. 1 Special Deluxe Set* - 30 sets mfg. 1967 only.

	$1,150	$895	$675				

RUGER/LYMAN 1878 CENTENNIAL RIFLE - .45-70 Govt. cal., 101 sets mfg. in Grade I and 1,000 in Grade II. Grade I has hand engraving, custom stock, 28 in. D weight barrel, tubular 4X Lyman Century scope, ser. nos. L-001-1878 to L-101-1978. Grade II had photo engraved frame, ser. nos. L-78-0001 to L-101-1978. Mfg. 1978 only.

	$1,750	$1,425	$1,050	$850	$725	$600	$525

One William Lyman commemorative cased rifle was also mfg., preceeding Grades I & II. This model was auctioned off at the 1978 NRA Show.

MODEL 44 STANDARD CARBINE - .44 Mag. cal., 4 shot mag., 18 1/2 in. barrel, blowback action, folding sight, curved butt. Mfg. 1961-85.

	$500	$350	$325	$295	$275	$250	$225

Last MSR was $332.

❋ *Deerstalker Model* - approx. 3,750 mfg. with "Deerstalker" marked on rifle until Ithaca lawsuit disc. manufacture (1962).

	$925	$850	$725	$600	$550	$475	$400

❋ *25th Year Anniversary Model* - mfg. 1985 only, limited production, has medallion in stock.

	$550	$425	$375				

Last MSR was $495.

MODEL 44RS - similar to 44, but has aperture sight and swivels.

	$600	$550	$500	$450	$400	$350	$300

MODEL 44 FINGERGROOVE SPORTER - Monte Carlo stocked version of 44 Standard. Mfg. until 1971.

	$750	$650	$550	$500	$450	$400	$350

Add 100% for factory checkered stock.

MODEL 44 INTERNATIONAL - similar to Standard, except full length Mannlicher style stock. Mfg. until 1971.

	$825	$700	$625	$550	$475	$400	$350

Add 50% for factory checkered stock.

MODEL 99/44 DEERFIELD CARBINE - .44 Mag. cal., 4 shot rotary mag., 18 1/2 in. barrel with folding aperture rear sight, rotating bolt with dual front locking lugs, blue finish only, uncheckered hardwood stock, includes intergral scope mounts and rings, 6.25 lbs. New 2000.

MSR $702	$540	$450	$410	$375	$335	$300	$260

RUGER CARBINE - 9mm Para. (PC9) or .40 S&W (PC4) cal., 16.25 in. barrel, black synthetic stock, matte metal finish, with or w/o sights, with fully adj. rear sight or rear receiver sight, crossbolt safety, 6 lbs. New 1998.

MSR $623	$510	$415	$360	$310	$265	$240	$215

Add $24 for adj. rear receiver sight.

GRADING - PPGS™	100%	98%	95%	90%	80%	70%	60%

MINI-14 - .223 Rem. or .222 Rem. (disc.) cal., 5 (standard mag. starting in 1989), 10 (disc.), or 20* shot detachable mag., 18 1/2 in. barrel, gas operated, blue finish, aperture rear sight, military style stock, approx. 6.75 lbs. Mfg. 1974-2004.

	$535	$445	$365	$320	$275	$240	$215

Last MSR was $655.

Add 20% for .222 Rem. cal.

Add $125 for folding stock (disc. 1989).

Add 25% for Southport Model with gold bead front sight.

Due to 1989 Federal legislation and public sentiment, the Mini-14 was shipped with a 5 shot detachable mag. only. This model was also available as a Mini-14 GB (primarily used for law enforcement), and was equipped with a flash hider and bayonet lug (blue or stainless, current value is approx. $1,000 if in 95%+ original condition).

❊ *Mini 14 Stainless* - mini stainless steel version, choice of wood or black synthetic (new 1999) stock. Disc. 2004.

	$565	$445	$380				

Last MSR was $715.

Add 20% for .222 Rem. cal.

Add $125 for folding stock (disc. 1990).

MINI-14 RANCH RIFLE - .223 Rem. cal., 5 (standard mag. starting in 1989), 10 (disc.), or 20* shot detachable mag., 18 1/2 in. barrel, folding rear sight, receiver cut for factory rings, similar to Mini-14, supplied with scope rings, adj. ghost ring aperture rear sight and protected front sight became standard 2005, approx. 6.5 lbs. New 1982.

MSR $750	$580	$475	$425	$385	$340	$310	$275

Due to 1989 Federal legislation and public sentiment, the Mini-14 Ranch Rifle is now being shipped with a 5 shot detachable mag. only.

❊ *Stainless Ranch Rifle* - stainless steel construction, choice of wood or black synthetic (new 1999) stock. New 1986.

MSR $809	$630	$500	$400				

Add $125 for folding stock (disc. 1990).

MINI-THIRTY - 7.62x39mm Russian cal., 18 1/2 in. barrel, 5 shot detachable mag., hardwood stock, includes scope rings, 7 lbs. 3 oz. Mfg. 1987-2004.

	$540	$450	$405	$375	$335	$300	$260

Last MSR was $695.

❊ *Mini-Thirty Stainless* - stainless steel variation of the Mini-Thirty, adj. ghost ring aperture rear sight and protected front sight became standard 2005. New 1990.

MSR $809	$630	$500	$400				

XGI - while advertised, this model was never shipped commercially because it could not maintain Ruger accuracy standards.

MSR was originally targeted at $425.

RIFLES: SINGLE SHOT

During certain years of manufacture, Ruger's changes in production on certain models (cals., barrel markings, barrel lengths, etc.) have created rare variations that are now considered premium niches. These areas of low manufacture will add premiums to the values listed on standard models.

Pre-1969, non-prefix rifles with long action cals. will command a 30%-50% premium (ser. no. 1-8XXX).

NO. 1-A LIGHT SPORTER - similar to No. 1-B Standard, .204 Ruger (new 2005), .22 Hornet (disc., 355 mfg.), .243 Win., .270 Win., 7x57mm, or .30-06 cal., 22 in. barrel, folding sight on quarter rib, ramp front sight, no rings, Alexander Henry forearm, front swivel in barrel band, 7 1/4 lbs. Mfg. 1966-present.

MSR $966	$800	$575	$475	$385	$310	$260	$230

The "A" suffix designates an Alexander Henry classic forearm with light barrel.

GRADING - PPGS™	100%	98%	95%	90%	80%	70%	60%

NO. 1-B STANDARD - falling block action with curved Farquharson lever, popular cals. include .204 Ruger (new 2004), .218 Bee, .22 Hornet (new 1988), .22-250 Rem., .220 Swift, .223 Rem., .257 Roberts (disc. 2003), .243 Win., 6mm Rem (disc. 2003), .25-06 Rem., .270 Win., .280 Rem. (disc. 2003), .30-06, .308 Win. (new 2002), 6.5mm Rem. Mag. (disc.), 7mm Rem. Mag., .270 Wby. Mag. (new 1990), .300 Wby. Mag. (new 1990), .300 Win. Mag., or .338 Win. Mag., 22 or 26 in. barrel, quarter rib with integral scope bases, supplied with rings and no sights, checkered stock and semi beavertail forearm. Mfg. 1966-present.

	MSR $966	$800	$575	$475	$385	$310	$260	$230

The "B" suffix designates semi-beavertail forearm with medium barrel and is available in all cals. under .375 H&H except 7x57mm.

NO. 1-H TROPICAL RIFLE - similar to Medium Sporter, except .375 H&H, .404 Jeffery (mfg. 1993-95), .416 Rem. (mfg. 1993-2003), .416 Rigby (new 1991), .458 Lott (new 2004), .458 Win. Mag., or .405 Win. (new 2004) cal., 24 in. heavy barrel, open sights, approx. 9 lbs.

	MSR $966	$800	$575	$475	$385	$310	$260	$230

Add 100% for .404 Jeffrey cal. (rare).

NO. 1 K1-B-BBZ STAINLESS - various cals. and configurations, satin stainless steel action and barrel, grey laminate hardwood stock with black recoil pad, drilled and tapped rear quarter rib w/o sights. New 2001.

✳ *No. 1 K1-B-BBZ Standard* - .243 Win., .25-06 Rem., .270 Win. (new 2004), .30-06, .308 Win. (new 2002), .300 Win. Mag., 7mm STW (disc. 2004), or 7mm Rem. Mag. cal., 26 in. barrel, 8 lbs. New 2001.

	MSR $998	$775	$600	$525

✳ *No. 1 K1-H-BBZ Tropical* - .375 H&H, .416 Rigby (new 2002), .405 Win. (mfg. 2004), .458 Win. (new 2005), or .458 Lott (mfg. 2002-2004) cal., 24 in. barrel, 9 lbs. New 2001.

	MSR $998	$775	$600	$525

✳ *No. 1 K1-S-BBZ Sporter* - .45-70 Govt. cal. only, 22 in. barrel with iron sights, 7.25 lbs. New 2001.

	MSR $998	$775	$600	$525

✳ *No. 1 K1-V-BBZ Varmint* - .204 Ruger (new 2004), or .22-250 Rem. cal. only, 24 in. barrel, 9 lbs. New 2001.

	MSR $998	$775	$600	$525

NO. 1-RSI INTERNATIONAL - .243 Win., .270 Win., 7x57mm, or .30-06 cal., features 20 in. lightweight barrel with full length Mannlicher stock, includes swivels and open sights, 7 1/4 lbs.

	MSR $998	$800	$600	$525	$425	$375	$325	$295

NO. 1-S MEDIUM SPORTER - .218 Bee (disc. 2003), 7mm Rem. Mag. (disc. 2003), .45-70 Govt., .300 Win. Mag. (disc. 2003), or .338 Win. Mag. (disc. 2003) cal., similar to Light Sporter, 22 (.45-70 Govt. cal. only) or 26 in. medium barrel, open sights, 7 1/4-8 lbs.

	MSR $966	$775	$575	$475	$385	$310	$260	$230

✳ *No. 1-S 50th Anniversary* - .45-70 Govt. cal. only, engraved action with gold inlays, including the Ruger logo and 50 years, William B. Ruger signature on receiver bottom, checkered Circassian walnut stock and forearm. 1,500 mfg. 1999 only.

	$1,950	$1,700	$1,500	$1,250	$995	$850	$700

Last MSR was $1,950.

GRADING - PPGS™	100%	98%	95%	90%	80%	70%	60%

NO. 1-V VARMINT - similar to No. 1-B Standard, except .22 PPC (mfg. 1993-96), .22-250 Rem., .220 Swift, .223 Rem., .243 Win. (disc.), .25-06 Rem., 6mm Rem., 6mm PPC (mfg. 1993-96), or .280 Rem. (disc.) cal., 24 or 26 (.220 Swift only) in. heavy barrel, without rib, checkered walnut stock and forearm, target scope blocks, 9 lbs. Mfg. 1966-present.

MSR $966	$800	$575	$475	$385	$310	$260	$230

NO. 3 CARBINE - same basic action as No. 1, except simpler lever design, uncheckedered stock, available in .22 Hornet, .30-40 Krag, .45-70 Govt. (only cal. available 1986), .223 Rem., .44 Mag., or .375 Win. cal., 22 in. barrel, folding sight. Mfg. 1972-87.

	$600	$500	$400	$300	$250	$200	$150

Last MSR was $284.

SHOTGUNS: O/U

RED LABEL - 12, 20, or 28 (new 1994) ga., 3 in. chambers (except 28 ga.), various barrel lengths and choke (including skeet) combinations, boxlock, SST, 26 or 28 in. VR barrels, auto ejectors, choice of checkered pistol grip or English straight grip (new 1992, Red Label English Field) stock, stainless steel frame became standard on 12 ga. 1985 (not available in 20 ga.), choke tubes became optional in 1988, standard 1990. Mfg. 1977-present.

✳ Standard Grade

MSR $1,622	$1,225	$925	$775	$675	$575	$500	$450

Add $622 for .410 bore Briley conversion tube set for 28 ga. only.
Subtract 15%-20% without choke tubes.

During late 1994, some 12 and 20 ga. Red Label boxes were marked "EZ", indicating the new easy-opening feature (this is not mechanically spring-assisted, but rather works on tight machining tolerances). All Red Label shotguns have the "EZ"-opening feature beginning 1995. Earlier all-steel 12 ga. models (approx. 500 mfg.) with short field tubes could command 10%-15% premiums over values listed from collectors interested in acquiring this variation. 20 ga. models w/o choke tubes are blue only.

✳ Red Label All Weather Stainless - 12 ga. only, stainless steel (disc.) or target grey stainless steel (new 2003) receiver and barrels, checkered black synthetic stock and forearm, 26, 28, or 30 in. VR barrels with choke tubes, 7.5 lbs. New 1999.

MSR $1,622	$1,225	$925	$775				

✳ Red Label Sporting Clays - 12 or 20 (new 1994) ga., features 30 in. separated barrels, choice of walnut or synthetic stock, Briley chokes with forcing cones back bored to .744 in., 3/8 in. VR with middle bead, sporting clays recoil pad. New 1992.

MSR $1,622	$1,225	$925	$775	$675	$575	$500	$450

>Red Label Sporting Clays Engraved - available in 12 ga. only with 1/3 engraving pattern. Mfg. 1997.

	$2,500	$2,200	$1,900	$1,650	$1,300	$1,000	$850

Last MSR was $3,068.

✳ Red Label English Field - 12, 20, or 28 (new 1995) ga., similar to Red Label, except has English style straight grip stock. Mfg. 1992-2000.

	$965	$775	$685	$600	$550	$500	$450

Last MSR was $1,276.

✳ Red Label Engraved (Current Mfg.) - 12, 20, or 28 ga., 26, 28, or 30 (disc. 2004) in. barrels, 4 different gold inlay options (depending on ga.) with receiver scroll engraving, available in Standard Model, All Weather Stainless (disc. 2004), and Sporting Clays (disc. 2004) configurations. New 2001.

MSR $1,811	$1,350	$1,125	$850	$675	$575	$500	$450

GRADING - PPGS™	100%	98%	95%	90%	80%	70%	60%

✱ *Red Label Engraved (1997-2000 Mfg.)* - available in 12, 20, or 28 ga., available in 3 different engraving patterns (pattern engraving standard). Mfg. 1997-2000.

	$2,200	$1,900	$1,650	$1,300	$1,000	$850	$725

Last MSR was $2,552.

Add $190 for 1/3 engraving coverage.

Add $532 for 2/3 engraving coverage (12 ga. only, disc.).

RED LABEL "WOODSIDE" - 12 ga. only, 3 in. chambers, 26, 28, or 30 (Sporting Clays Model only with special chokes, new 1996) in. barrels, straight or pistol grip stock, features premium checkered walnut, satin nickel finish, unique stock design permitting wood to fill-in where frame boxlock action would normally be, hand-engraving available at extra cost, 7 1/2-8 lbs. Mfg. 1995-2002.

	$1,525	$1,250	$1,000	$800	$625	$550	$500

Last MSR was $1,889.

✱ *Red Label "Woodside" Engraved* - available with patterned engraving only with pistol grip and 26 or 28 in. barrels. New 1997-disc.

	$2,200	$2,050	$1,725	$1,350	$1,050	$875	$750

Last MSR was $2,805.

WILDLIFE FOREVER SPECIAL EDITION - 12 ga. only, limited edition to celebrate the 50th anniversary of Wildlife Forever, features Baron & Son engraving with gold pheasant and mallard inlays on receiver sides, 300 mfg. 1993 only.

	$1,595	$900	$775				

Last MSR was $1,595.

Add $125 for hard case.

SHOTGUNS: SxS

GOLD LABEL SxS - 12 ga. only, 3 in. chambers, 28 in. barrels with solid rib and choke tubes, rounded stainless boxlock action, SST, blue barrel finish, ejectors, choice of deluxe 22 LPI checkered English straight grip or pistol grip stock and splinter forearm, 6 1/3 lbs. New late 2002.

MSR $2,000		$1,600	$1,300	$1,025	$825	$625	$550	$500

SHOTGUNS: SINGLE BARREL

TRAP MODEL - 12 ga., 34 in. stainless barrel with straight grooves and 2 choke tubes, fully adj. high post rib, engraved stainless receiver with gold Ruger name, adj. deluxe checkered walnut stock, beavertail forearm, adj. trigger, 9 lbs. Approx. 300 mfg. 2000-2003.

	$3,000	$2,500	$2,000	$1,500	$1,300	$1,200	$1,000

Last MSR was $2,850.

SUHLER JAGDGEWEHR MANUFAKTUR GmbH

Previous manufacturer and firearms restorer located in Suhl, Germany.

Suhler Jagdgewehr manufactured a variety of SxS shotguns, in addition to restoring both antique and historical guns.

SUNDANCE INDUSTRIES, INC.

Previous manufacturer located in Valencia, CA.

DERRINGERS

POINT BLANK DERRINGER - .22 LR cal., O/U design, double action, 3 in. barrels, black matte finish, 8 oz. Mfg. mid-1994-2002.

	$80	$60	$50	$45	$40	$35	$30

Last MSR was $99.

GRADING - PPGS™	100%	98%	95%	90%	80%	70%	60%

PISTOLS: SEMI-AUTO

MODEL A-25 - .25 ACP cal., single action design, 2 7/16 in. barrel, 7 shot mag., rotary safety, lower grip push button mag. release, satin nickel (disc.), bright chrome, or black teflon finish, choice of simulated pearl with different colors or grooved black grips, serrated slide. Mfg. 1989-2002.

	$65	$55	$45	$40	$35	$30	$25

Last MSR was $79.

LADY LASER/LASER 25 - .25 ACP cal., similar to Model A-25, except has factory installed and sighted 5mW Laser sight with no exposed wiring or switch, polished chrome or black finish (Laser 25 only), dual safety switch. Mfg. 1995-2002.

	$195	$160	$135	$115	$95	$80	$70

Last MSR was $220.

The Laser Lady was disc. during 1998.

MODEL BOA - similar to Model A-25, except has patented squeeze grip safety. Mfg. 1990-2002.

	$75	$60	$50	$45	$40	$35	$30

Last MSR was $95.

SUPERIOR AMMUNITION

Current custom rifle manufacturer located in Sturgis, SD. Consumer direct sales only.

RIFLES: BOLT ACTION

SUPERIOR CLASSIC LIGHTWEIGHT - various cals. up to .375 H&H, Rem. Mod. 700, Win. Mod. 70 Classic, or Dakota Mod. 76 action, blind box mag. or hinged floorplate, approx. 5 3/4 lbs.

MSR N/A	N/A	$1,650	$1,350	$1,100	$900	$750	$625

SUPERIOR VARMINT MODEL - various smaller cals., Rem. Mod. 700, Dakota Varmint, or Searcy action, stainless match grade barrel, heavy or light variations.

MSR N/A	N/A	$1,725	$1,400	$1,125	$900	$750	$625

SUPERIOR PROFESSIONAL MODEL - various large cals. up to .470 Capstick, only available in Win. Mod. 70 Classic or Dakota Mod. 76 action, blind box mag. (optional) or hinged floorplate.

MSR N/A	N/A	$2,150	$1,850	$1,600	$1,350	$1,150	$900

SUPER SIX LIMITED

Previous manufacturer located in Brookfield, WI until 1992.

REVOLVERS

GOLDEN BISON SERIES - .45-70 Govt. cal., 6 shot revolver, 8 or 10 1/2 in. octagon barrel, large size (overall length 15-17 1/2 in.), manganese bronze frame, crossbolt manual safety, smooth hardwood grips, approx. 6 lbs. 177 total mfg. (including special/limited editions). Disc. approx. 1992.

	$1,675	$1,475	$1,275	$1,000	$875	$775	$675

Last MSR was $1,895.

Low serialization specimens (ser. nos. 1-15) have asking prices of $2,250-$2,950.

❋ *Centennial Limited Edition* - features special engraving and case. 20 total mfg.

	$2,950	$2,275	$1,675

Last MSR was $3,995.

SUPER SIX LLC

Current manufacturer established during 1999, and located in Milwaukee, WI. Consumer direct sales.

During late 1998, Super Six LLC purchased the previous trademark of Super Six Limited. Limited mfg. to date. Please contact the company directly (see Trademark Index) for current information, including model availability and pricing.

SURVIVAL ARMS, INC.

Previous manufacturer established in 1990 located in Orange, CT. Previously located in Cocoa, FL, until 1995.

In 1990, Survival Arms, Inc. took over the manufacture of AR-7 Explorer rifles from Charter Arms located in Stratford, CT.

RIFLES: SEMI-AUTO

AR-7 EXPLORER RIFLE - .22 LR cal., takedown or normal wood stock, takedown barreled action stores in Cycolac synthetic stock, 8 shot mag., adj. sights, 16 in. barrel, black matte finish on AR-7, silvertone on AR-7S, camouflage finish on AR-7C, 2 1/2 lbs. Disc.

$120	$100	$85	$75	$65	$55	$50

Last MSR was $150.

AR-20 SPORTER - similar to AR-22, except has shrouded barrel, tubular stock with pistol grip, 10 or 20 shot mag. Mfg. 1996-98.

$165	$140	$120	$105	$95	$80	$70

Last MSR was $200.

AR-22/AR-25 - .22 LR cal., 16 in. barrel, black rifle features pistol grip with choice of wood or metal folding* stock, includes 20 (1995 only) or 25 (disc. 1994) shot mag. Disc. 1995.

$155	$120	$95	$80	$70	$60	$55

Last MSR was $200.

Subtract $50 for wood stock model.

SVENDSEN, ERL, F.A. MFG. CO.

Previous manufacturer located in Itasca, IL.

DERRINGERS

LITTLE ACE - .22 S cal., patterned after the Ethan Allen "HIDE-A-WAY," bronze frame, blue steel barrel with case hardened hammer and spur trigger.

$85	$75	$70	$65	$60	$55	$50

4-ACES - .22 S cal., 4 barrel derringer with rotating firing pin and spur trigger, bronze frame with blue rifled steel barrels and case hardened parts.

$175	$150	$135	$120	$105	$90	$75

SWING

Previously manufactured by Schutzen Bohme GmbH located in Rintein, Germany.

RIFLES: BOLT ACTION

SWING BOLT ACTION - .308 Win. cal., target bolt action rifle with thumbhole stock and vented forearm, target sights, 30 in. barrel, 12.1 lbs. Mfg. 1994.

$850	$750	$650	$575	$500	$450	$395

GRADING - PPGS™	100%	98%	95%	90%	80%	70%	60%

SWISS MILITARY

Previously manufactured Swiss military rifles.

RIFLES: BOLT ACTION

The models below were manufactured by Schmidt-Rubin, unless otherwise indicated.

MODEL 1889 - usually encountered between 85%-95% condition.

	100%	98%	95%	90%	80%	70%	60%
	$350	$325	$285	$260	$230	$210	$185

MODEL 1911 - available in either carbine or rifle configuration.

	100%	98%	95%	90%	80%	70%	60%
	$450	$325	$200	$185	$170	$160	$150

Add 125% for carbine configuration.

MODEL 1931

	100%	98%	95%	90%	80%	70%	60%
	$650	$600	$525	$450	$285	$250	$225

Add 500% for sniper variations.
Subtract 30% if import marked.

VETTERLI - .41 Swiss or 10.4mm Swiss cal., not mfg. by Schmidt-Rubin.

	100%	98%	95%	90%	80%	70%	60%
	$450	$400	$360	$320	$285	$250	$225

SYMES & WRIGHT LTD.

Previous manufacturer located in London, England.

Symes & Wright Ltd. manufactured approx. 25 best quality shotguns and double rifles annually. Values must be determined after evaluating each firearm individually.

SZECSEI & FUCHS FINE GUNS GmbH

Current long gun manufacturer established in 1986, and located in Innsbruck, Austria. North American headquarters are located in Windsor, Canada.

Szecsei & Fuchs manufactures extremely high quality and unique long guns, including combination guns, drillings, bolt action and double rifles, and SxS shotguns. The company is well known for its unique magazine fed SxS double rifle, which utilizes a single bolt to load/unload both chambers. Many options are available, including a titanium bolt trigger system. At a recent European trade show, Szecsei & Fuchs exhibited a show stopper – a solid titanium O/U .700 NE double bolt rifle with side mount magazine! Please contact the North American office directly for more information on their current models (virtually anything is possible), including pricing, availability, delivery time, and U.S. pricing.

RIFLES: BOLT ACTION

DOUBLE BARREL REPEATER - various cals., unique action allows single bolt to chamber both barrels from one twin column detachable titanium mag., titanium bolt face, right- or left-hand, various engraving and wood options available. Base price is $33,900 w/o options, engraving, or other special orders. Base weight is approx. 13 lbs.

Add $2,100 for titanium.

NOTES

T SECTION

TNW, INC.

Current rifle manufacturer located in Vernonia, OR. Consumer direct sales.

RIFLES: SEMI-AUTO

TNW makes a belt-fed semi-auto variation of the original Browning M2 HB machine gun in .50 BMG cal. Current price is $7,400. They also make a semi-auto Model 1919 A4 in .30-06 or .308 Win. cal. Retail pricing is in the $2,050 range. TNW also manufactures a variation of the German MG-34 semi-auto. Current retail is is $3,595. Please contact the company directly for more information regarding these semi-auto working replicas (see Trademark Index).

TACONIC FIREARMS, LTD.

Current rifle manufacturer located in Cambridge, NY. Consumer direct sales.

GRADING - PPGS™	100%	98%	95%	90%	80%	70%	60%

RIFLES: BOLT ACTION, CUSTOM

TACONIC 98 ULTIMATE MOUNTAIN HUNTER - various cals., features double square bridge, titanium alloy M-98 action, XXX Grade English or Circassian walnut, stainless or chrome moly barrel, matte finished metal, available with a variety of options, base prices are listed below.

MSR $5,995	$5,750	$5,100	$4,500	$4,000	$3,500	$3,000	$2,500

TACTICAL RIFLES

Current rifle manufacturer located in Dade City, FL.

RIFLES

Tactical Rifles makes a complete lineup of bolt action and semi-auto tactical rifles. Current models include the Tactical Long Range ($2,550 MSR), Tactical Para w/ folding stock ($3,150 MSR), Tactical Long Range Magnum ($2,995 MSR), Tactical M40 ($2,375 MSR), Tactical M21 ($3,695 MSR, $4,395 MSR for .300 WSM), Dow Custom AR10 (disc. 2004, $2,695 last MSR), Dow FAL15 ($1,895 MSR), Tactical AR15 ($1,995 MSR), Tactical Special Varmint ($1,925 MSR), and the Tactical M4C ($1,885 MSR). Please contact the company for more information (see Trademark Index).

TACTICAL WEAPONS

Current law enforcement/military division of FNH USA, located in McLean, VA.

Tactical Weapons currently manufactures machine guns only for law enforcement/military.

TALON INDUSTRIES, INC.

Previous pistol manufacturer located in Ennis, MT until 2001.

PISTOLS: SEMI-AUTO

T100 - .380 ACP cal., double action only, 3.3 in. barrel, black polymer frame with choice of black (T100B) or satin (T100S) slide finish, alloy frame and slide, 10 shot mag., failsafe loaded chamber indicator positioned on top of slide in back of breech bolt, 3-dot sights, 20 1/2 oz. Mfg. 2000-2001.

$115	$95	$85	$75	$65	$55	$50

Last MSR was $135.

T200 - 9mm Para. cal., otherwise similar to Model T100. Mfg. 2000-2001.

$145	$125	$100	$90	$75	$65	$55

Last MSR was $170.

TANFOGLIO, FRATELLI, S.r.l.

Current pistol manufacturer located in Gardone, Italy. Currently imported by European American Armory, located in Sharps, FL, and by K.B.I., located in Harrisburg, PA. Previously imported by Excam, F.I.E., and others.

Tanfoglio manufactures a wide variety of high quality semi-auto pistols and these are currently being imported by European American Armory Corp. and K.B.I. (see individual listings). Tanfoglio also manufactures their own complete line which, to date, has been mostly distributed in Europe.

TANNER, ANDRÉ

Previous manufacturer located in Switzerland. Previously imported and distributed by Mandall Shooting Supplies, Inc. located in Scottsdale, AZ, and by Osborne's located in Cheboygan, MI.

Tanner rifles are noted for their superior accuracy and limited production - less than 150 were mfg. annually.

RIFLES: BOLT ACTION

300 METER MATCH RIFLE - 7.5 Swiss (special order) or 7.62mm cal. only, single shot, top-of-the-line 300 meter match rifle incorporating all match shooting features including deluxe palm rest, aperture sights. Importation disc.

100%	98%	95%	90%	80%	70%	60%
$4,650	$3,995	$3,400	$2,775	$2,250	$1,900	$1,600

Last MSR was $4,900.

Add $100 for adj. cheekpiece.
Subtract $190 for repeating model with similar features.

* **300 Meter UIT Standard** - similar to Model 300, except is without palm rest and adj. Swiss buttplate, 10 shot mag., aperture sights. Importation disc.

100%	98%	95%	90%	80%	70%	60%
$4,450	$3,850	$3,350	$2,750	$2,225	$1,925	$1,600

Last MSR was $4,700.

Add $100 for adj. cheekpiece.

SUPERMATCH MODEL 50 M - .22 LR cal. only, 50 meter free rifle, deluxe palm rest, adj. buttplate, thumbhole stock. Importation disc.

100%	98%	95%	90%	80%	70%	60%
$3,600	$3,200	$2,850	$2,450	$2,050	$1,800	$1,600

Last MSR was $3,900.

Add $100 for adj. cheekpiece.

TAR-HUNT CUSTOM RIFLES, INC.

Current custom rifled shotgun manufacturer established in 1990, and located in Bloomsburg, PA. Dealer and consumer direct sales.

SHOTGUNS: BOLT ACTION

The following models are available in left-hand action at no additional charge.

PROFESSIONAL MODEL RSG-12 - 12 (RSG-12) ga., 2 3/4 or 3 (new 2003) in. chamber, bolt action slug gun featuring 21 1/2 or 23 (new 2003) in. Shaw barrel and 2 lug bolt, 1 round down in mag. (new 1998), matte black finish, McMillan fiberglass stock with Pachmayr Decelerator rifle pad, receiver drilled and tapped for standard Leupold windage bases (included, new 1997), muzzle brake became standard 1994, various finish options, 7 3/4 lbs. New 1991.

MSR	$2,395	98%	95%	90%	80%	70%	60%
		$2,150	$1,875	$1,525	$1,275	$1,050	$900	$800

* **RSG-12 Combo Slug Gun** - includes standard Professional RSG-12 Slug Gun and a second benchrest McMillan heavy weight stock. Mfg. 1994-2004.

100%	98%	95%	90%	80%	70%	60%
$2,250	$1,900	$1,575	$1,250	$1,000	$850	$750

Last MSR was $2,175.

GRADING - PPGS™	100%	98%	95%	90%	80%	70%	60%

* **RSG-12/RSG-20 10th Anniversary** - 12 or 20 ga., hand selected actions and barrels, Jewell custom adj. trigger, NP-3 nickel/Teflon metal finish, black McMillan stock with Pachmayr Decelerator pad. Only 25 mfg. during 2000 only, reintroduced 2005.

MSR $2,395	$2,150	$1,875	$1,525	$1,275	$1,050	$900	$800

MATCHLESS MODEL RSG-12 - upgraded variation featuring 400 grit polished gloss metal finish and the McMillan regular or "Fiber" grain stock (wood grain finish, disc. 2000). Mfg. 1995-2004.

$2,175	$1,925	$1,600	$1,300	$1,100	$950	$850

Last MSR was $2,495.

PEERLESS MODEL RSG-12 - upgraded variation featuring NP-3 (nickel/Teflon) metal finish by Robar of Phoenix, AZ, McMillan regular or "Fiber" grain stock (wood grain finish, disc. 2000). Mfg. 1995-2004.

$2,725	$2,350	$1,900	$1,600	$1,400	$1,200	$1,000

Last MSR was $3,075.

ELITE MODEL RSG-16 - 12 ga., 2 3/4 in. chamber, 23 in. Shaw rifled barrel, and 2 lug bolt, 1 shot mag., matte black finish, black McMillan fiberglass stock with Pachmayr decelerator pad, drilled and tapped for Rem. 700 long action style bases. Mfg. 2003-2004.

$2,150	$1,875	$1,525	$1,275	$1,050	$900	$800

Last MSR was $2,395.

MOUNTAINEER MODEL RSG-20 - 20 (RSG-20) ga., 2 3/4 in. chamber, features 21 in. Shaw rifled barrel and 2 lug bolt, one shot mag., matte black finish only, McMillan fiberglass stock with Pachmayr Decelerator pad, receiver drilled and tapped for Rem. Mod. 700 long action style bases, muzzle brake standard, 6 1/2 lbs. Mfg. 1997-2004.

$2,150	$1,875	$1,525	$1,275	$1,050	$900	$800

Last MSR was $2,395.

RSG-TACTICAL (SNIPER) MODEL - 12 ga. only, similar to RSG-12, except has M-86 McMillan fiberglass black tactical stock with Pachmayr Decelerator pad and heavy barrel. Mfg. 1992-98.

$1,495	$1,250	$995	$875	$750	$700	$650

Last MSR was $1,595.

Add $150 for Bipod.

BLOCK CARD MODEL - 12 ga., 2 3/4 in. chamber, various barrel lengths, cartage type chokes, special McMillan fiberglass stock, Pachmayr Decelerator pad, fluted barrels optional, special chambers, weighted stocks optional, single shot actions. Disc.

$1,625	$1,425	$1,125	$900	$800	$750	$700

Last MSR was $1,775.

TATE GUNMAKERS LLC

Current shotgun manufacturer established 1995 and located in Ione, CA. Consumer direct sales.

SHOTGUNS: SxS

Dale Tate, formerly of J. Purdey & Sons, makes custom order shotguns per individual customer specifications in 10, 12, 16, 20, or 28 ga. Current SxS models include: Vintager Model w/ hammers - $8,500 MSR (add $700 for 28 or 10 ga.), Concours Model w/ hammers - $11,000 MSR, and the Tate Model w/ hammers - $18,000 MSR. Hammerless models include the Tate Model - $13,000 MSR, add $7,000 for Purdey rose and scroll engraving. Tate Gunmakers also specializes in gun repair and restoration. Prices are quoted per individual work order. Please contact the company directly for more information, including delivery time and pricing (see Trademark Index).

TAURUS INTERNATIONAL MFG., INC.

Currently manufactured by Taurus Forjas S.A., located in Porto Alegre, Brazil. Currently imported by Taurus International Mfg., Inc. located in Miami, FL since 1982. Distributor sales only.

All Taurus products are known for their innovative design, quality construction, and proven value, and are backed by a lifetime repair policy.

Taurus order number nomenclature is as follows: the first digit followed by a dash refers to type (1 = pistol, 2 = revolver, 3 = rifle/carbine, 5 = magazines, accessories, or grips, and 10 = scope mount bases), the next 2 or 3 digits refer to model number, the next digit refers to type of hammer (0 = exposed, 1 = concealed), the next digit refers to barrel length, the last digit refers to finish (1 = blue, 9 = stainless), and the suffix at the end refers to special features (T = total titanium, H = case hardened, M = matte finish, UL = Ultra-Lite, C = compensator [ported], G = gold accent, R = rosewood grips, PRL = mother-of-pearl grips, and NS = night sights). Hence, 2-454089M refers to a revolver in .454 Casull cal. with exposed hammer, and an 8 3/8 in. barrel in stainless steel with matte finish.

PISTOLS: SEMI-AUTO

From 1990-92, certain models became available with a Laser Aim LA1 sighting system that included mounts, rings (in matching finish), a 110 volt AC recharging unit, a 9 volt DC field charger, and a high impact custom case.

Taurus incorporated their keyed Taurus security system on most models during 2000, except the PT-22 and PT-25, and is now available with all models. When the security system is engaged (via a keyed button on the bottom of rear grip strap), the pistol cannot be fired, cocked, or disassembled, and the gun's manual safety cannot be disengaged. This security key also works for the revolver.

> **Add approx. $30 for the Deluxe Shooter's Pack option (included extra mag. and custom case) on the 92, 99, 100, and 101 Series (disc. 2000).**

PT-22 - .22 LR cal., double action only, tip-up 2 3/4 in. barrel, 8 shot mag., fixed sights, blue, nickel (new 1995), blue/nickel (mfg. 1997-2000), Duo-tone (new 2000), or deluxe blue/gold (new 1997) finish, wood (new 1999), mother-of-pearl (new 2000, deluxe blue/gold finish only), or rosewood grips, 12.3 oz. New 1992.

MSR $219	$175	$135	$115	$95	$80	$70	$60

> **Add $15 for blue/gold or nickel/gold finish with rosewood or $31 for blue/gold or nickel/gold finish with mother-of-pearl grips.**

PT-24/7 - 9mm Para., .40 S&W, or .45 ACP (new 2005) cal., DAO, large black polymer frame with blued steel or satin stainless steel slide, 4 in. barrel with 3-dot sights, grips have Ribber grip overlays, 10, 12 (.45 ACP cal.), 15 (.40 S&W cal.), or 17 (9mm Para. cal.) shot mag., built-in Picatinny rail system on bottom of frame, includes 3 safeties, 27.5 oz. New late 2004.

MSR $578	$450	$345	$275	$240	$215	$200	$190

> **Add $16 for stainless steel.**

PT-25 - .25 ACP cal., similar to PT-22, except has 9 shot mag., 12.3 oz. New 1992.

MSR $219	$175	$135	$115	$95	$80	$70	$60

> **Add $15 for blue/gold or nickel/gold finish with rosewood or $31 for blue/gold or nickel/gold finish with mother-of-pearl grips.**

PT-38 - .38 Super cal., 4.25 in. barrel, DA/SA utilizes Model PT-945 alloy frame, choice of blue, stainless steel, or stainless/gold finishes, 3-dot fixed sights, 10 shot mag., checkered rubber (standard) or smooth faux mother-of-pearl grips, 30 oz. New 2005.

MSR $563	$425	$365	$295	$275	$250	$225	$200

> **Add $15 for stainless steel slide.**
> **Add $78 for stainless steel slide, gold accents, and faux mother-of-pearl grips.**

GRADING - PPGS™	100%	98%	95%	90%	80%	70%	60%

PT-58 - .380 ACP cal., similar to PT-99AF, except in .380 ACP cal., 4 in. barrel, 10 (C/B 1994) or 12* shot mag. Mfg. 1988-96.

	$325	$275	$235	$215	$200	$190	$180

Last MSR was $429.

Add $32 for satin nickel finish (disc. 1994).

Beginning 1993, the PT-58 utilized the Taurus Tri-Position safety system which features a hammer-drop, "cocked-and-locked" option system.

✳ **PT-58SS (Stainless Steel)** - similar to PT-58, except is stainless steel. Mfg. 1992- 96.

	$385	$310	$260

Last MSR was $470.

PT-91AF - .41 Action Express cal., action similar to PT-92AF, except is in .41 AE cal., 10 shot mag., 34 oz. Imported 1990 only.

	$365	$300	$250	$225	$200	$190	$180

Last MSR was $446.

Add $36 for satin nickel finish.

Add $25 for shooter's pack (includes custom case and extra mag.).

PT-92(AF) - 9mm Para. cal., semi-auto double action, design similar to Beretta Model 92 SB-F, exposed hammer, ambidextrous safety, 5 in. barrel, 10 (C/B 1994), 15*, or 17 (new late 2004) shot mag., smooth Brazilian walnut (disc.) or checkered rubber (new 1999) grips, blue, nickel (disc.), or stainless steel finish, fixed or night (mfg. 2000-2004) sights, 34 oz.

MSR $578	$430	$340	$275	$235	$210	$195	$180

Add $40 for satin nickel finish (disc. 1994).

Add $415 for Laser Aim Sight (disc. 1991).

Add $78 for night sights (disc. 2004).

Add $266 for blue or stainless conversion kit to convert 9mm Para. to .22 LR (mfg. 1999-2004).

✳ **PT-92SS (Stainless Steel)** - similar to PT-92AF, except is fabricated from stainless steel. New 1992.

MSR $594	$440	$350	$280

Add $78 for night sights (disc. 2004).

✳ **PT-92 Deluxe** - choice of blue/gold (disc. 2004) or stainless steel with gold finish, rosewood, or mother-of-pearl (new 2000) grips. New 1999.

MSR $641	$500	$375	$295	$250	$225	$200	$190

Add $16 for mother-of-pearl grips.

Subtract approx. $15 for blue/gold finish (disc. 2004).

✳ **PT-92AFC** - compact variation of the Model PT-92AF, 4 in. barrel, 10 (C/B 1994) or 13* shot mag., fixed sights. Disc. 1996.

	$335	$285	$235	$225	$200	$190	$180

Add $38 for satin nickel finish (disc. 1993).

Last MSR was $449.

✳ **PT-92AFC (Stainless Steel)** - similar to PT-92AFC, except stainless steel. Mfg. 1993-96.

	$400	$310	$260

Last MSR was $493.

✳ **PT-92AF Lew Horton Special Edition** - 9mm Para. cal., matte satin finished frame with high polish stainless steel slide, blue barrel, hammer, trigger, mag. release, safety, and slide release. 250 mfg. in 1990 only.

	$395	$350	$295	$250	$225	$210	$190

Last MSR was $454.

PT-99 (AF) - similar to Model PT-92AF, except has adj. rear sight, 17 shot mag. became standard late 2004.

MSR $594	$465	$355	$290	$250	$215	$200	$190

Add $45 for satin nickel finish (disc. 1994).

Add $266 for blue or stainless conversion kit to convert 9mm Para. to .22 LR (mfg. 1999-2004) or .40 S&W (mfg. 2000-2004).

This action is similar to the Beretta Model 92SB-F.

✳ *PT-99SS (Stainless Steel)* - similar to PT-99, except is fabricated from stainless steel. New 1992.

MSR $609	$475	$385	$295

PT-100 - .40 S&W cal., semi-auto, standard double action, 5 in. barrel, 10 (C/B 1994), 11* (reintroduced late 2004) shot mag., safeties include ambidextrous manual, hammer drop, inertia firing pin, and chamber loaded indicator, choice of blue, satin nickel (disc. 1994), or stainless steel finish, smooth Brazilian hard wood (disc.) or rubber grips, 34 oz. Mfg. 1992-97, reintroduced 2000.

MSR $578	$450	$345	$275	$240	$215	$200	$190

Add $40 for satin nickel finish (disc. 1994).

Add $78 for night sights (mfg. 2000-2004).

Add $266 for blue or stainless conversion kit to convert .40 S&W to .22 LR cal. (disc. 2004).

✳ *PT-100SS (Stainless Steel)* - similar to PT-100, except is fabricated from stainless steel. Mfg. 1992-96, reintroduced 2000.

MSR $594	$465	$355	$285

Add $78 for night sights.

✳ *PT-100 Deluxe* - choice of blue/gold (disc. 2004) finish or stainless steel with gold, rosewood, or mother-of-pearl grips. New 2000.

MSR $641	$500	$375	$295	$250	$225	$200	$190

Add $15 for mother-of-pearl grips.

Subtract approx. $15 for blue/gold finish (disc. 2004).

PT-101 - similar to PT-100, except has adj. rear sight., 11 shot mag. became standard during late 2004. Mfg. 1992-96, reintroduced 2000.

MSR $594	$465	$355	$285	$245	$215	$200	$190

Add $266 for blue or stainless conversion kit to convert .40 S&W to .22 LR cal.

Add $45 for satin nickel finish (disc. 1994).

✳ *PT-101SS (Stainless Steel)* - similar to PT-101, except is stainless steel. Mfg. 1992-96, reintroduced 2000.

MSR $617	$475	$375	$295

PT-111 MILLENNIUM - 9mm Para. cal., double action only, 3.25 in. barrel with fixed 3-dot sights, black polymer frame with steel slide, striker fired, 10 shot mag. with push-button release, 18.7 oz. Mfg. 1998-2004.

	$355	$290	$235	$190	$155	$135	$120

Last MSR was $422.

Add $78 for night sights (new 2000).

Add $47 for pearl or burl walnut grips (limited mfg. 2003).

✳ *PT-111 Millennium Stainless* - similar to Model PT-111, except has stainless steel slide. Mfg. 1998-2004.

	$360	$290	$235

Last MSR was $438.

Add $78 for night sights (new 2000).

Add $46 for pearl or burl walnut grips (limited mfg. 2003).

GRADING - PPGS™	100%	98%	95%	90%	80%	70%	60%

✳ *PT-111 Millennium Titanium* - similar to Model PT-111, except has titanium slide and night or 3-dot (new 2004) sights. Mfg. 2000-2004.

	$415	**$330**	**$255**				

Last MSR was $508.

Add $78 for night sights.

PT-111 MILLENNIUM PRO - similar to Model PT-111 Millennium, 10 or 12 (new late 2004) shot mag., except has improved ergonomics, Posi-Traction slide serrations, recessed magazine release, manual safety lever, trigger block mechanism, firing pin block, and lightweight frame. New 2003.

MSR $422	**$355**	**$290**	**$235**	**$190**	**$155**	**$135**	**$120**

Add $78 for night sights (disc. 2004).

✳ *PT-111 Millennium Pro Stainless* - similar to Model PT-111 Millennium Pro, except has stainless steel slide. New 2003.

MSR $438	**$360**	**$290**	**$235**				

Add $78 for night sights (mfg. 2004).

✳ *PT-111 Ti Millennium Pro Titanium* - similar to Model PT-111 Millennium Pro, except has titanium construction. New 2005.

MSR $508	**$415**	**$330**	**$255**				

PT-132 MILLENNIUM - .32 ACP cal., double action only, 3.25 in. barrel, black polymer frame, manual safety, 10 shot mag., fixed 3-dot (disc. 2002) or adj. (new 2003) sights, blue steel slide, 18.7 oz. Mfg. 2001-2004.

	$355	**$290**	**$235**	**$190**	**$155**	**$135**	**$120**

Last MSR was $422.

✳ *Model PT-132 Millennium Stainless* - similar to Model PT-132, except has stainless steel slide. Mfg. 2001-2004.

	$360	**$290**	**$235**				

Last MSR was $438.

PT-132 MILLENNIUM PRO - similar to Model PT-132 Millennium, except has improved ergonomics, Posi-Traction slide serrations, recessed magazine release, manual safety lever, trigger block mechanism, firing pin block, and lightweight frame. Mfg. 2003, reintroduced 2005.

MSR $422	**$355**	**$290**	**$235**	**$190**	**$155**	**$135**	**$120**

✳ *PT-132 Millennium Pro Stainless* - similar to Model PT-132 Millennium Pro, except has stainless steel slide. Mfg. 2003, reintroduced 2005.

MSR $438	**$360**	**$290**	**$235**				

PT-138 MILLENNIUM - .380 ACP cal., double action only, 3.25 in. barrel, black polymer frame, manual safety, 10 shot mag., fixed 3-dot sights, blue steel slide, 18.7 oz. Mfg. 1999-2004.

	$355	**$290**	**$235**	**$190**	**$155**	**$135**	**$120**

Last MSR was $422.

Add $78 for night sights (mfg. 2000-2003).

✳ *Model PT-138 Millennium Stainless* - similar to Model PT-138, except has stainless steel slide. New 1999.

	$360	**$290**	**$235**				

Add $78 for night sights (mfg. 2000-2003).

PT-138 MILLENNIUM PRO - similar to Model PT-138 Millennium, 10 or 12 shot (new 2005) mag. except has improved ergonomics, Posi-Traction slide serrations, recessed magazine release, manual safety lever, trigger block mechanism, firing pin block, and lightweight frame. Mfg. 2003, reintroduced 2005.

MSR $422	**$355**	**$290**	**$235**	**$190**	**$155**	**$135**	**$120**

Add $78 for night sights (disc. 2003).

GRADING - PPGS™	100%	98%	95%	90%	80%	70%	60%

✴ **PT-138 Millennium Pro Stainless** - similar to Model PT-138 Millennium Pro, except has stainless steel slide. Mfg. 2003, reintroduced 2005.

MSR $438	$360	$290	$235				

PT-140 MILLENNIUM - .40 S&W cal., double action only, 3.25 in. barrel, black polymer frame, manual safety, 10 shot mag., fixed 3-dot sights, blue steel slide, 18.7 oz. Mfg. 1999-2004.

	$375	$295	$235	$190	$155	$135	$120

Last MSR was $461.

Add $78 for night sights (new 2000).
Add $47 for pearl or burl walnut grips (mfg. 2003).

✴ **PT-140 Millennium Stainless** - similar to Model PT-140, except has stainless steel slide. Mfg. 1999-2004.

	$380	$305	$245				

Last MSR was $476.

Add $78 for night sights (new 2000).
Add $46 for pearl or burl walnut grips (mfg. 2003).

PT-140 MILLENNIUM PRO - similar to Model PT-140 Millennium, except has improved ergonomics, Posi-Traction slide serrations, recessed magazine release, manual safety lever, trigger block mechanism, firing pin block, and lightweight frame. New 2003.

MSR $461	$380	$300	$250	$200	$160	$135	$120

Add $78 for night sights (disc. 2004).

✴ **PT-140 Millennium Pro Stainless** - similar to Model PT-140 Millennium Pro, except has stainless steel slide. New 2003.

MSR $476	$390	$320	$250				

Add $78 for night sights (disc. 2004).

PT-145 MILLENNIUM - .45 ACP cal., otherwise similar to Model PT-140 Millennium, 23 oz. Mfg. 2000-2003.

	$395	$320	$250	$200	$165	$145	$135

Last MSR was $484.

Add $79 for night sights (new 2000).

✴ **PT-145 Millennium Stainless** - similar to Model PT-140, except has stainless steel slide. Mfg. 1999-2003.

	$400	$325	$260				

Last MSR was $500.

Add $78 for night sights (new 2000).

PT-145 MILLENNIUM PRO - similar to Model PT-145 Millennium, except has improved ergonomics, Posi-Traction slide serrations, recessed magazine release, manual safety lever, trigger block mechanism, firing pin block, and lightweight frame. New 2003.

MSR $461	$380	$300	$250	$200	$160	$135	$120

Add $78 for night sights (disc. 2004).

✴ **PT-145 Millennium Pro Stainless** - similar to Model PT-145 Millennium Pro, except has stainless steel slide. New 2003.

MSR $476	$390	$320	$250				

Add $78 for night sights (mfg. 2000-2004).

PT-400 - .400 Cor-Bon cal., similar to Model PT-940, except has 4.25 in. ported barrel and 8 shot mag., 29 1/2 oz. Mfg. 1999 only.

	$415	$325	$270	$235	$210	$200	$190

Last MSR was $523.

GRADING - PPGS™	100%	98%	95%	90%	80%	70%	60%

✻ PT-400 Stainless - similar to Model PT-400, except has stainless steel slide. Mfg. 1999 only.

	$415	$330	$275				

Last MSR was $539.

PT-745 COMPACT MILLENNIUM PRO - .45 ACP cal., DAO, compact variation of Millennium Pro with 3.25 in. barrel, 6 shot mag. with finger extension, matte blue steel slide, loaded chamber indicator, black polymer grip frame, 20.8 oz. New 2005.

MSR $484	$395	$315	$260	$210	$165	$140	$120

✻ PT-745 Stainless - similar to PT-745 Compact Millennium Pro, except has stainless steel slide. New 2005.

MSR $500	$410	$325	$275				

PT-908 - 9mm Para. cal., compact version of the PT-92 with 3.8 in. barrel and 8 shot mag., fixed sights, blue or nickel finish. Mfg. 1993-97.

	$330	$285	$235	$215	$200	$190	$180

Last MSR was $435.

✻ PT-908D SS (Stainless Steel) - similar to Model PT-908, except is stainless steel. Mfg. 1993-97.

	$385	$310	$260				

Last MSR was $473.

PT-911 COMPACT - 9mm Para. cal., single or double action, 4 in. barrel, 10 or 15 (new late 2004) shot mag., checkered rubber grips, fixed sights, 28.2 oz. New 1997.

MSR $523	$415	$335	$275	$225	$200	$185	$170

Add $79 for night sights (disc. 2004).

✻ PT-911 SS (Stainless Steel) - stainless variation of the PT-911 Compact.

MSR $539	$420	$325	$275				

Add $78 for night sights (disc. 2004).

✻ PT-911 Deluxe - choice of blue/gold finish or stainless steel with gold, rosewood, or mother-of-pearl grips. New 2000.

MSR $570	$450	$365	$290	$255	$225	$210	$200

Add $16 for stainless steel with gold.
Add $16 for mother-of-pearl grips.

PT-922 - .22 LR cal., sport model with 10 shot mag., 6 in. tapered barrel and adj. sights, medium frame, blue finish, angled synthetic grip frame with Taurus medallions on bottom, 25 oz. Limited mfg. 2004.

	$285	$225	$195	$165	$130	$100	$90

Last MSR was $370.

PT-938 COMPACT - .380 ACP cal., DA/SA, 3.75 in. barrel, ambidextrous safety, 10 or 15 (new late 2004) shot mag., blue finish with alloy frame and steel slide, rubber grips, fixed sights, 34 oz. New 1997.

MSR $516	$410	$340	$270	$235	$200	$180	$170

✻ PT-938 SS (Stainless Steel) - stainless slide variation of the PT-938 Compact with matte stainless finish.

MSR $531	$420	$345	$285				

PT-940 - .40 S&W cal., compact version of the PT-100 with 3 5/8 in. barrel and 10 shot mag., fixed sights, 28.2 oz. New 1996.

MSR $523	$425	$355	$290	$240	$210	$190	$180

Add $79 for night sights (disc. 2004).

✻ PT-940 SS (Stainless Steel) - similar to PT-940, except is stainless steel. New 1996.

MSR $539	$435	$360	$295				

Add $78 for night sights.

GRADING - PPGS™	100%	98%	95%	90%	80%	70%	60%

✳ **PT-940 Deluxe** - choice of blue/gold or stainless steel with gold finish, rosewood, or mother-of-pearl grips. New 2000.

MSR $570	$465	$385	$310	$260	$230	$210	$200

Add $16 for stainless steel with gold.
Add $16 for mother-of-pearl grips.

PT-945 - .45 ACP cal., compact double action, 4.25 in. ported (mfg. 1997-2003) or unported barrel, 8 shot single stack mag., ambidextrous 3 position safety, chamber loaded indicator, 3-dot sights, 29.5 oz. New 1995.

MSR $563	$450	$365	$305	$260	$230	$210	$200

Add $78 for night sights (disc. 2004).
Add $39 for ported barrel (disc. 2003).

✳ **PT-945 SS (Stainless Steel)** - stainless steel variation of the PT-945. New 1995.

MSR $578	$475	$385	$310

Add $78 for night sights (disc. 2004).
Add $39 for ported barrel (disc. 2003).

✳ **PT-945 Deluxe** - choice of blue/gold (disc. 2004) or stainless steel finish, mother-of-pearl (new 2000), or rosewood grips. New 1999.

MSR $625	$500	$400	$325

Add $16 for mother-of-pearl grips.
Subtract approx. $15 for blue/gold finish.

PT-957 - .357 SIG cal., compact model with 3 5/8 in. ported (available only with night sights or in 957 Deluxe beginning 2002) or non-ported (new 2002) barrel and slide, 10 shot mag., ambidextrous 3-position safety, blue finish, checkered rubber grips, fixed sights, 28 oz. Mfg. 1999-2003.

		$425	$355	$290	$240	$210	$190	$180

Last MSR was $523.

Add $90 for night sights.
Add $40 for ported barrel (disc. 2002).

✳ **PT-957 SS (Stainless Steel)** - stainless steel variation of the PT-957. Mfg. 1999-2003.

		$430	$360	$295

Last MSR was $539.

Add $40 for ported (disc. 2001) barrel, or $130 for ported barrel and night sights (disc. 2003).

✳ **PT-957 Deluxe** - choice of blue/gold or stainless steel with gold finish, rosewood, or mother-of-pearl grips. Mfg. 2000-2002.

		$475	$385	$310	$260	$230	$210	$200

Last MSR was $610.

Add $15 for stainless steel.
Add $15 for mother-of-pearl grips.

REVOLVERS: RECENT PRODUCTION

From 1990-1992, certain models became available with a Laser Aim LA1 sighting system that included mounts, rings (in matching finish), a 110 volt AC recharging unit, a 9 volt DC field charger, and a high impact custom case.

The following Taurus revolvers have been listed in numerical order. All currently manufactured revolvers listed are rated for +P ammunition.

All currently manufactured Taurus revolvers are equipped with their patented Taurus Security System, introduced in 1998, which utilizes an integral key lock on the back of the hammer, locking the action.

Add $49 for scope base mount on currently produced models that offer this option.
Add $31 for carrying case on Raging Bull & Raging Hornet Models listed.

GRADING - PPGS™	100%	98%	95%	90%	80%	70%	60%

MODEL 17C - .17 HMR or .17 Mach 2 (new 2004) cal., small frame, 8 shot, 2, 4 or 5 in. barrel, blue only, adj. sights, full underlug on 4 and 5 in. barrels, soft rubber grips, 24-27.5 oz. New 2003.

MSR $359	$275	$210	$160	$135	$115	$100	$95

✳ *Model 17C Ultra-Lite* - ultra light hammer forged frame, 2 in. barrel, available in matte blue (disc. 2004) or bright stainless steel, 18.5 oz. New 2003.

MSR $438	$330	$240	$185	$155	$125	$105	$100

Subtract approx. $50 for matte blue finish.

✳ *Model 17CSS (Stainless Steel)* - similar to Model 17C, except is polished stainless steel. New 2003.

MSR $406	$305	$225	$170

MODEL 17 TRACKER - .17 HMR cal., compact frame, 7 shot, adj. sights, 6.5 or 8 3/8 (mfg. 2004 only) in. Tracker VR barrel, blue (new 2004), duo-tone (mfg. 2004 only, 6 1/2 in. barrel only) finish or matte stainless steel, 41 or 45 oz. New 2003.

MSR $406	$305	$225	$170

Subtract approx. $50 for matte blue finish.

MODEL 17-12 SILHOUETTE - .17 HMR cal., compact frame, features 12 in. barrel, adj. sights, includes scope mount. Mfg. 2003-2004.

	$320	$235	$175

Last MSR was $430.

MODEL 21T TRACKER - .218 Bee cal., compact frame, 7 shot, 6.5 in. Tracker barrel with VR, matte stainless steel, adj. sights. Mfg. 2003-2004.

	$325	$240	$180

Last MSR was $438.

MODEL 22H SS RAGING HORNET - .22 Hornet cal., large frame, 8 shot, stainless steel construction, 10 in. VR barrel with full shroud, fully adj. sights, scope mount bases included, contoured rubber grips, 50 oz. Mfg. 1999-2004.

	$795	$700	$600

Last MSR was $898.

MODEL 30C SS RAGING THIRTY HUNTER - .30 Carbine cal., large frame, 8 shot, 10 in. heavy VR barrel with full shroud and adj. sights, matte stainless steel, includes scope mounts and full moon clips, 50 oz. Mfg. 2003-2004.

	$795	$700	$600

Last MSR was $898.

MODEL 30S SILHOUETTE/HUNTER - .30 Carbine cal., large frame, 8 shot, double action, 12 in. VR barrel with partial shroud, matte stainless steel, adj. trigger tension and trigger stop, includes scope mounts, 50 oz. Mfg. 2003-2004.

	$625	$550	$475

Last MSR was $743.

MODEL 44 - .44 Mag. cal., 6 shot, large frame, integral porting compensator, exposed or concealed (3 in. barrel only, mfg. 1997-98) hammer, bright blue finish, adj. sights, rubber grips, 3 (mfg. 1997-98), 4, 6.5 (VR), or 8 3/8 (VR) in. ported or non-ported (disc. 2002) barrel, 45-57 oz. Mfg. 1994-2004.

	$400	$325	$265	$225	$190	$160	$130

Last MSR was $500.

Add $23 for 6.5 or 8 3/8 in. ported barrel.

Subtract approx. 10% for non-ported barrel.

✳ *Model 44SS (Stainless Steel)* - similar to Model 44, except matte finished stainless steel. New 1994.

MSR $563	$455	$365	$295

Add $15 for 6.5 or 8 3/8 in. ported barrel.

Add $46 for 3 in. ported barrel with fixed sights and round butt grips (mfg. 1996-97).

GRADING - PPGS™	100%	98%	95%	90%	80%	70%	60%

✳ Model 44 Silhouette - similar to Model 44, except has 12 in. VR non-ported barrel and adj. trigger tension and trigger stop, includes scope base mounts. Mfg. 2003-2004.

	$485	$395	$315	$260	$220	$195	$175

Last MSR was $602.

MODEL 44C TRACKER - .44 Mag. cal., 5 shot, blue or stainless steel, 4 in. ported barrel, adj. rear sight, Ribber grips, 34 oz. New 2005.

MSR $500	$400	$325	$265	$225	$190	$160	$130

Add $47 for stainless steel.

MODEL 45 RAGING BULL - .45 LC cal., 6 shot, 6 1/2 or 8 3/8 in. VR ported barrel, adj. sights, soft rubber grips, 53 or 63 oz. Mfg. 1999-2001.

	$475	$415	$375	$335	$300	$280	$260

Last MSR was $575.

✳ Model 45 .45 LC Raging Bull Stainless - similar to Model 45 Raging Bull, except is stainless steel. Disc. 2001.

	$530	$435	$360				

Last MSR was $630.

MODEL 45SA - .45 LC cal., SA Western style revolver, large frame, 5.5 in. barrel, fixed sights, four click action, choice of all blue, blue/color case hardened, matte stainless, or polished stainless steel. New 2005.

MSR $484	$400	$325	$285	$250	$225	$200	$175

Add $16 for stainless steel or blue/color case hardened finish.

MODEL 65 - .357 Mag./.38 Spl. cal., medium frame, double action, 6 shot, fixed sights, 2.5 (mfg. 1993-97), 3 (disc. 1992) or 4 in. full underlug barrel, blue finish, checkered walnut (disc.) or rubber (new 1999) grips, 38 oz. Disc. 1997, reintroduced 1999.

MSR $375	$285	$210	$150	$130	$100	$90	$85

Add $15 for satin nickel finish (disc.).

✳ Model 65SS (Stainless Steel) - similar to Model 65, except is matte finished stainless steel. Mfg. 1993-97, reintroduced 1999.

MSR $422	$325	$250	$200				

MODEL 66 - .357 Mag./.38 Spl. cal., medium frame, double action, 6 (disc. 2001) or 7 (new 1999) shot, 2 1/2 (mfg. 1993-97), 3 (disc. 1992), 4, or 6 in. barrel, checkered walnut (disc. 1999) or rubber (new 2000) grips, blue finish, adj. sights, 38-40 oz. Disc. 1997, reintroduced 1999.

MSR $422	$325	$250	$200	$165	$140	$120	$100

Add $15 for satin nickel finish (disc.).
Add $10 for 4 or 6 in. compensated (66CP) barrel (mfg. 1993-94).

✳ Model 66SS (Stainless Steel) - similar to Model 66, but in stainless steel. Mfg. 1987-97, reintroduced 1999.

MSR $469	$370	$260	$200				

Add $10 for 4 or 6 in. compensated (66CP) barrel (mfg. 1993-94).

✳ Model 66 Silhouette/Hunter - .357 Mag./.38 Spl. cal., 7 shot, 12 in. barrel with adj. sights, rubber grips, adj. trigger tension and stop became standard 2003, includes scope mount. Mfg. 2001-2004.

	$330	$240	$205	$165	$140	$120	$100

Last MSR was $430.

✳ Model 66 Silhouette/Hunter SS (Stainless Steel) - similar to Model 66 Silhouette/Hunter, except is matte finished stainless steel. Mfg. 2001-2004.

	$380	$305	$250				

Last MSR was $477.

GRADING - PPGS™	100%	98%	95%	90%	80%	70%	60%

MODEL 73 - .32 Long cal. only, double action, 6 shot, 3 in. heavy barrel only, checkered walnut grips, 20 oz. Disc. 1992.

	$175	$150	$125	$115	$105	$95	$85

Last MSR was $223.

Add $20 for satin nickel finish.

MODEL 76 - .32 H&R Mag. cal., double action, 6 shot, 6 in. heavy barrel with solid rib, fully adj. rear sight, transfer bar safety, checkered hard wood grips, blue only, 34 oz. Mfg. 1991-94.

	$240	$190	$155	$130	$115	$100	$90

Last MSR was $308.

MODEL 80 - .38 Spl. cal. only, double action, 6 shot, 3 or 4 in. barrel, checkered walnut grips, fixed sights, 30 oz. Disc. 1996.

	$190	$145	$115	$105	$95	$85	$80

Last MSR was $252.

Add $15 for satin nickel finish (disc. 1992).

* ***Model 80SS (Stainless Steel)*** - similar to Model 80, except stainless steel. Mfg. 1993-97.

	$245	$180	$135				

Last MSR was $313.

MODEL 82 - .38 Spl. cal. only, medium frame, double action, 6 shot, 3 (disc. 1998) or 4 in. heavy barrel, checkered walnut (disc.) or rubber (new 1999) grips, full underlug, fixed sights, 34 oz.

MSR $352	$255	$185	$140	$110	$95	$85	$80

Add $15 for satin nickel finish (disc.).

* ***Model 82SS (Stainless Steel)*** - similar to Model 82, except is polished stainless steel. New 1993.

MSR $398	$300	$210	$150				

MODEL 83 - .38 Spl. cal. only, double action, 6 shot, 4 in. heavy barrel, checkered walnut grips, adj. sights, 34 1/2 oz. Disc. 1998.

	$215	$155	$125	$115	$105	$95	$80

Last MSR was $278.

Add $13 for satin nickel finish.

* ***Model 83SS (Stainless Steel)*** - similar to Model 83, except stainless steel. Mfg. 1993-98.

	$250	$185	$135				

Last MSR was $324.

MODEL 85 - .38 Spl. cal. only, small frame, double action, 5 shot, 2 or 3 (disc. 2001) in. heavy ported (new 1997) or unported barrel, hammer forged frame, exposed hammer, checkered walnut (disc. 2000) or soft rubber boot grips, fixed sights, 21-24 1/2 oz.

MSR $375	$285	$215	$160	$130	$110	$95	$85

Add $16 for ported barrel (disc. 2003).
Add $20 for satin nickel finish (3 in. barrel only, disc. 1992).

* ***Model 85 Ultra-Lite*** - ultra-lightweight version of Model 85 using an alloy frame, 17 oz.

MSR $406	$310	$225	$175	$140	$110	$100	$90

>**Model 85SSUL Ultra-Lite Stainless** - matte stainless variation of the Model 85 Ultra-Lite, 17 oz.

MSR $430	$330	$235	$175				

>**Model 85 Ultra-Lite Deluxe** - ported barrel, choice of blue/gold or stainless/gold, mother-of-pearl (new 2000) or rosewood grips, 17 oz. New 1999.

MSR $414	$320	$230	$170				

Add $24 for stainless/gold.
Add $24 for mother-of-pearl grips with blue finish or $70 for mother-of-pearl grips in stainless/gold.

* **Model 85SS (Stainless Steel)** - stainless version of Model 85.

  MSR $422 $325 $235 $175

  Add $16 for ported barrel (mfg. 1997-2003).

* **Model 85CH (Blue or Stainless)** - similar to Model 85, except has Brazilian hardwood combat (disc. 2000) or soft rubber grips and spurless concealed hammer that fits flush with the frame, 2 in. barrel, double action only, 21 oz. Mfg. 1992-2004.

     $285 $210 $155 $125 $105 $95 $85

  Last MSR was $375.

  Add $16 for ported barrel (disc. 2003).

  Add $47 for polished stainless steel.

* **Model 85 Titanium Ultra-Lightweight** - features titanium barrel and cylinder and choice of matte aluminum or stainless steel (disc. 2001) small frame, fixed sight, rubber grips, choice of hammer or concealed hammer (Police Model 85). New 1999.

  MSR $531 $445 $370 $315

* **Model 85 Special Edition/Deluxe** - features blue finish with gold trim or stainless/gold trim, ported 2 in. barrel, rosewood or mother-of-pearl grips, includes integral key lock. New 1998.

  MSR $445 $325 $270 $195 $145 $130 $115 $105

  Add $24 for mother-of-pearl grips.

  Add $8 for stainless/gold trim.

* **Model 85T** - similar to Model 85, except 100% titanium construction, 2 in. ported barrel only, choice of bright spectrum blue, matte spectrum blue, matte spectrum gold, stealth grey (mfg. 2000 only), or shadow grey (new 2000) finish, 15.4 oz. New 1999.

  MSR $547 $470 $425 $355

  Add $39 for gold titanium finish and mother-of-pearl grips (disc. 2004).

MODEL 86 CUSTOM TARGET - .38 Spl. cal. only, double action target model, 6 shot, 6 in. barrel, specially contoured smooth walnut grips, adj. rear sight, blue only, 34 oz. Disc. 1994.

   $270 $200 $160 $150 $140 $130 $120

Last MSR was $352.

This model was available in either single or double action with adj. counterweight and interchangeable front sight inserts.

MODEL 94 - .22 LR cal., small frame, double action, 9 shot, 2 (new 1997), 3 (mfg. 1991-98), 4, or 5 (new 1996) in. barrel, full underlug on 4 or 5 in. barrel, blue finish, adj. rear sight, target features, 25 oz. New 1989.

MSR $328 $245 $180 $140 $120 $105 $95 $85

* **Model 94 Ultra-Lite** - ultra light hammer forged frame, 2 in. barrel, available in matte blue or bright stainless steel, 18 oz. New 1999.

  MSR $359 $270 $200 $155 $125 $105 $95 $85

  Add $47 for matte stainless steel construction.

* **Model 94SS (Stainless Steel)** - stainless version of Model 94. New 1990.

  MSR $375 $290 $210 $155

MODEL 96 TARGET SCOUT - .22 LR cal. only, double action, 6 shot, 6 in. barrel, checkered walnut grips, same features as Model 86, 34 oz. Disc. 1998.

   $275 $200 $160 $150 $140 $130 $120

Last MSR was $376.

GRADING - PPGS™	100%	98%	95%	90%	80%	70%	60%

MODEL 218 RAGING BEE - .218 Bee cal., large frame, 8 shot, 10 in. heavy VR barrel with full shroud and adj. sights, matte stainless steel, includes scope mounts, 50 oz. Mfg. 2003-2004.

	MSR $898	$795	$700	$600

Last MSR was $898.

MODEL 218 SILHOUETTE/HUNTER - .218 Bee cal., large frame, 7 shot, double action, 12 in. VR barrel with partial shroud, matte stainless steel, rubber boot grips, adj. trigger tension and trigger stop, includes scope mounts, 49.8 oz. Mfg. 2003-2004.

	$400	$335	$275

Last MSR was $461.

MODEL 415SS - .41 Mag. cal., compact frame, 5 shot, similar to Model 415T, except has matte stainless steel construction, Ribber grips, 30 oz. New 1999.

	$435	$355	$290

Last MSR was $508.

MODEL 415T - .41 Mag. cal., compact frame, 5 shot, all titanium construction, 2.5 in. ported barrel with fixed sights, choice of bright spectrum blue (disc. 2001), matte spectrum blue (disc. 2001), matte gold (mfg. 1999 only), stealth grey (mfg. 2000 only), or shadow grey (new 2000) finish, Ribber grips. Mfg. 1999-2003.

	$500	$440	$360

Last MSR was $602.

MODEL 416 SS RAGING BULL - .41 Mag., large frame, 6 shot, 6.5 in. ported heavy barrel with VR and adj. sights, matte stainless steel, rubber grips, 53 oz. New 2003.

	MSR $641	$530	$460	$370

MODEL 425 SS TRACKER - .41 Mag. cal., compact frame, 5 shot, similar to Model 415T, 4 in. ported barrel with full shroud, adj. sights with red inserts, Ribber grips, stainless steel with matte finish, 34.8 oz. New 2000.

	MSR $516	$440	$360	$295

MODEL 425T TRACKER - similar to Model 425 Tracker, except is all titanium construction, choice of stealth grey (mfg. 2000 only) or shadow grey finish, adj. sights, 24.3 oz. New 2000.

	MSR $688	$560	$465	$350

MODEL 431 - .44 Spl. cal., 5 shot, 2 (new 1995), 3, or 4 in. barrel, blue only, fixed sights. Mfg. 1993-97.

	$220	$170	$145	$130	$115	$100	$90

Last MSR was $286.

✳ *Model 431SS (Stainless Steel)* - similar to Model 431, except stainless steel. Mfg. 1993-97.

	$285	$215	$180

Last MSR was $368.

MODEL 441 - similar to Model 431, except has 3, 4, or 6 in. barrel, adj. sights. Mfg. 1993-97.

	$240	$180	$145	$130	$115	$100	$90

Last MSR was $313.

✳ *Model 441SS (Stainless Steel)* - similar to Model 441, except is stainless steel. Mfg. 1993-97.

	$350	$250	$195

Last MSR was $468.

MODEL 444 RAGING BULL - .44 Mag. cal. only, large frame, 6 shot, 6.5 or 8 3/8 in. VR ported barrel with full shroud, soft rubber grips, 53 or 63 oz. New 1999.

	MSR $578	$485	$415	$370	$335	$300	$280	$260

✳ *Model 444 Raging Bull Stainless* - similar to Model 444, except is matte stainless steel. New 1999.

	MSR $641		$535	$465	$365			

✳ *Model 444 Ultra-Lite* - .44 Mag. cal., 6 shot, blue alloy or stainless steel Raging Bull style frame with titanium cylinder, rubber grips with finger grooves, adj. rear sight, 28.3 oz. New 2005.

MSR $650	$535	$465	$375	$325	$285	$250	$225

Add $49 for stainless steel frame and barrel.

MODEL 445 - .44 Spl. cal., compact frame, 5 shot, 2 in. ported (new 1999) or standard barrel, fixed sights, blue or stainless, Ribber or rubber grips, 28 oz. Mfg. 1997-2003.

		$280	$210	$165	$145	$115	$100	$90

Last MSR was $359.

Add $16 for ported barrel (new 1999).

✳ *Model 445 Concealed Hammer* - similar to Model 445, except w/o hammer, ported or unported barrel. Mfg. 1999-2003.

		$280	$210	$165	$145	$115	$100	$90

Last MSR was $359.

Add $16 for ported barrel.

✳ *Model 445 Concealed Hammer Stainless* - similar to Model 445 Concealed Hammer, except is stainless steel. Mfg. 1999-2003.

		$310	$230	$160

Last MSR was $406.

Add $16 for ported barrel.

✳ *Model 445 SS (Stainless Steel)* - stainless variation of the Model 445. Mfg. 1997-2003.

		$310	$230	$160

Last MSR was $406.

Add $16 for ported barrel.

✳ *Model 445 Ultra-lite Stainless* - features ported 2 in. barrel and matte stainless steel. Mfg. 1999-2002.

		$370	$285	$230

Last MSR was $500.

✳ *Model 445 Ultra-lite Concealed Carry* - features stainless steel or titanium frame, ported 2 in. barrel, walnut combat grips. Mfg. 2002 only.

		$370	$285	$230

Last MSR was $500.

Add $100 for titanium construction.

MODEL 445T - .44 Spl. cal., 5 shot, all titanium construction, 2 in. ported barrel with fixed sights, choice of bright spectrum blue, matte spectrum blue, matte gold (mfg. 1999 only), stealth grey (new 2000), or shadow grey (new 2000) finish, Ribber grips. Mfg. 1999-2002.

		$500	$440	$360

Last MSR was $600.

MODEL 450 - .45 LC cal., 5 shot, compact frame, similar to Model 450T, except is matte stainless steel, also available in Ultra-Lite variation, Ribber grips, 20 (Ultra Lite) or 28 oz. New 1999.

MSR $492		$425	$350	$285

Add $31 for Ultra-Lite Model.

GRADING - PPGS™	100%	98%	95%	90%	80%	70%	60%

MODEL 450T - .45 LC cal., 5 shot, all titanium construction, 2 in. ported barrel with fixed sights, choice of bright spectrum blue, matte spectrum blue, matte gold (mfg. 1999 only), stealth grey (new 2000), or shadow grey (new 2000) finish, Ribber grips. Mfg. 1999-2002.

	$500	$440	$360				

Last MSR was $600.

MODEL 454 CASULL RAGING BULL - .454 Casull cal., large frame, single or double action, 5 shot, front and rear cylinder locks, bright blue or case colored (new 1999) finish, 5 (case colored, disc. 2000), 6.5 or 8 3/8 in. full lug ported barrel with integral VR, soft black rubber grips with recoil absorbing insert, micrometer adj. rear sight, transfer bar ignition, integral key lock, 53-63 oz. New 1998.

MSR $797	$730	$650	$590	$530	$475	$450	$425

Add $96 for case colored frame (disc. 2000).

* *Model 454 Casull Raging Bull Stainless* - similar to Model 454 Casull Raging Bull, except is stainless steel, with either satin (6 1/2 in. barrel only, disc. 2000) or matte (new 1999) stainless finish. New 1998.

MSR $859	$780	$710	$635				

* *Model 454 Casull Raging Bull Silhouette* - similar to Model 454 Casull Raging Bull Stainless, except has 12 in. non-ported barrel with adj. sights, adj. trigger tension and trigger stop. Mfg. 2003-2004.

MSR $859	$725	$625	$525				

Last MSR was $859.

MODEL 455 TRACKER - .45 ACP cal., compact frame, 5 shot, 2, 4 or 6 in. ported barrel, adj. rear sight, matte stainless steel, includes 5 Stellar full moon clips, Ribber grips. Mfg. 2002-2004.

	$450	$360	$295				

Last MSR was $523.

* *Model 455 Titanium Tracker* - similar to Model 455 Tracker, except has titanium construction with shadow gray finish. Mfg. 2004 only.

	$525	$435	$365				

Last MSR was $625.

MODEL 460 TRACKER - .45 LC cal., compact frame, 5 shot, 4 or 6.5 in. VR ported barrel, adj. sights, matte stainless steel. Mfg. 2003-2004.

	$445	$355	$295				

Last MSR was $516.

* *Model 460T Tracker* - similar to Model 460 Tracker, except has titanium construction, 4 VR or non-VR 6 1/2 in. barrel. Mfg. 2003-2004.

	$565	$480	$385				

Last MSR was $688.

MODEL 480 RUGER RAGING BULL - .480 Ruger cal., large frame, 5 shot, 5 (limited mfg.), 6.5, or 8 3/8 in. VR barrel, matte stainless finish only, otherwise similar to Model 454 Casull, 51-63 oz. New 2001.

MSR $641	$525	$450	$375				

MODEL 500 - .500 S&W Mag. cal., 5 shot, 10 in. ported barrel, soft rubber cushioned grips, stainless steel only. New mid-2005.

MSR $899	$800	$725	$650				

MODEL 605 - .357 Mag. cal., small frame, 5 shot, 2 in. unported (new 2002), 2.25 or 3 (mfg. 1996-98) in. barrel, blue steel, 4 port compensated barrel (2.25 in. only) with fixed sights, exposed or concealed (Model 605CH, new 1997, 2.25 in. barrel) hammer, full barrel shroud, oversized finger grooved rubber grips, 24.5 oz. New 1995.

MSR $375	$290	$215	$155	$130	$110	$95	$85

Add $16 for ported barrel (disc. 2003).

GRADING - PPGS™	100%	98%	95%	90%	80%	70%	60%

✴ Model 605 SS (Stainless Steel) - stainless variation of the Model 605.

    MSR $422   **$315**   **$235**   **$170**

    Add $16 for ported barrel (disc. 2003).

✴ Model 605T Titanium - similar to Model 605, except is titanium with shadow grey finish. New 2005.

    MSR $547   **$465**   **$375**   **$300**

MODEL 606 - .357 Mag. cal., 6 shot, 2 or 2.25 in. uncompensated or compensated barrel, exposed or concealed hammer, fixed sights. Mfg. 1997-98.

    $235   **$180**   **$140**   **$120**   **$105**   **$95**   **$85**

                                    Last MSR was $296.

    Add $19 for ported barrel (2 in. only).

✴ Model 606 SS (Stainless Steel) - stainless variation of the Model 606. Disc. 1998.

    $260   **$185**   **$140**

                                    Last MSR was $344.

    Add $20 for ported barrel (2 in. only).

MODEL 607 - .357 Mag. cal., 7 shot, 4 or 6.5 (VR) in. compensated barrel, adj. rear sight, Santoprene synthetic grips, 44 oz. Mfg. 1995-97.

    $335   **$280**   **$240**   **$205**   **$185**   **$160**   **$150**

                                    Last MSR was $447.

    Add $18 for 6 1/2 in. VR barrel.

✴ Model 607SS (Stainless Steel) - stainless variation of the Model 607. Mfg. 1995-97.

    $375   **$325**   **$265**

                                    Last MSR was $508.

    Add $20 for 6 1/2 in. VR barrel.

MODEL 608 - .357 Mag. cal., large frame, 8 shot, 3 (mfg. 1997-98), 4, 6.5 (VR), 8 3/8 (VR, new 1997) in. barrel with integral compensator, exposed or concealed (new 1997, 3 in. barrel) hammer, adj. sights, 44-56 oz. Mfg. 1996-2004.

    $355   **$295**   **$250**   **$210**   **$185**   **$160**   **$150**

                                    Last MSR was $469.

    Add $15 for 6.5 or 8 3/8 in. VR ported barrel.

✴ Model 608SS (Stainless Steel) - stainless variation of the Model 608. New 1996.

    MSR $523   **$390**   **$335**   **$275**

    Add $24 for 6.5 or 8 3/8 in. VR barrel.

MODEL 617 - .357 Mag. cal., compact frame, 7 shot, double action, 2 in. regular or ported barrel, fixed sights, exposed or concealed (Model 617CH) hammer, rubber grips, 28.3 oz. New 1998.

    MSR $391   **$320**   **$265**   **$225**   **$185**   **$150**   **$135**   **$120**

    Add $15 for ported barrel (disc. 2003).

✴ Model 617SS (Stainless Steel) - similar to Model 617, except is polished stainless steel. New 1998.

    MSR $438   **$335**   **$245**   **$185**

    Add $15 for ported barrel (disc. 2003).

✴ Model 617 ULT - similar to Model 617, except is 5 shot, aluminum alloy receiver and titanium cylinder, matte stainless finish, 2 in. regular or ported barrel, soft rubber grips. Mfg. 2001-2002.

    $455   **$365**   **$290**   **$260**   **$220**   **$185**   **$150**

                                    Last MSR was $530.

    Add $15 for ported barrel.

GRADING - PPGS™	100%	98%	95%	90%	80%	70%	60%

✳ *Model 617T* - .357 Mag. cal., compact frame, 7 shot, all titanium construction, 2 in. ported barrel with fixed sights, choice of bright spectrum blue, matte spectrum blue (disc. 2001), matte gold (mfg. 1999 only), stealth grey (mfg. 2000 only), or shadow grey (new 2000) finish, Ribber grips, 19.9 oz. New 1999.

	MSR $602	$500	$440	$360			

MODEL 627 SS TRACKER - .357 Mag. cal., compact frame, 7 shot, 4 or 6.5 (new 2001, VR) in. ported barrel with adj. sights, and heavy full underlug, stainless steel with matte finish, Ribber grips, 28.8 or 40 oz. New 2000.

	MSR $508	$400	$280	$210			

✳ *Model 627T Tracker* - .357 Mag. cal., 7 shot, all titanium construction, 4 or 6.5 (new 2001, non-VR) in. ported barrel with adj. sights, choice of stealth grey (disc. 2001) or shadow grey finish, Ribber grips, 24.3 or 28 oz. New 2000.

	MSR $688	$560	$475	$385			

MODEL 650 CIA - .357 Mag. cal., small frame, 5 shot, double action only, hammerless, 2 in. barrel with fixed sights, soft rubber grips, blue finish. New 2001.

	MSR $383	$320	$265	$225	$185	$150	$135	$120

✳ *Model 650 CIA SS (Stainless Steel)* - similar to Model 650 CIA, except is matte stainless steel. New 2001.

	MSR $430	$325	$235	$180			

MODEL 651 PROTECTOR - .357 Mag. cal., small frame, 5 shot, 2 in. barrel, single or double action, zero profile hammer, soft rubber grips, 25 oz. New 2003.

	MSR $383	$320	$265	$225	$185	$150	$135	$120

✳ *Model 651T Protector* - similar to Model 651 CIA Protector, except is shadow grey titanium construction, 17.3 oz. New 2004.

	MSR $547	$450	$325	$255			

✳ *Model 651 SS Protector (Stainless Steel)* - similar to Model 651 CIA Protector, except is matte stainless steel. New 2003.

	MSR $430	$325	$235	$180			

MODEL 669 - similar to Model 66 except has fully shrouded 4 or 6 in. barrel, blue finish, 37 oz. Disc. 1998.

		$260	$190	$145	$125	$115	$100	$90

Last MSR was $344.

Add $10 for VR barrel (mfg. 1989-1992).
Add $400 for Laser Aim Sight (offered 1990-1992).
Add $19 for compensated (669CP) barrel (new 1993).

✳ *Model 669SS (Stainless Steel)* - similar to Model 669, but in stainless steel. Disc. 1998.

		$325	$245	$190			

Last MSR was $421.

Add $21 for compensated (669CP) barrel (new 1993).

MODEL 689 - similar to Model 669, except has VR. Disc. 1998.

		$265	$195	$145	$125	$115	$100	$90

Last MSR was $358.

Add $390 for Laser Aim Sight (mfg. 1990-91 only).

✳ *Model 689SS (Stainless Steel)* - similar to Model 669, but in stainless steel. Disc. 1999.

		$340	$255	$190			

Last MSR was $435.

GRADING - PPGS™	100%	98%	95%	90%	80%	70%	60%

MODEL 731 SS ULTRA-LITE
- .32 H&R Mag. cal., small frame, double action, 6 shot, matte stainless steel, 2 in. ported barrel, fixed sights, rubber boot grips, 17 oz. New 1998.

	MSR $438	$335	$235	$175

✳ *Model 731T* - .32 H&R Mag. cal., small frame, 6 shot, all titanium construction, 2 in. ported barrel with fixed sights, bright blue (disc. 1999), matte blue, shadow grey (new 2003) or matte gold (disc. 1999) finish, rubber grips. Mfg. 1999, reintroduced 2003-2004.

		$455	$360	$295

Last MSR was $531.

Subtract $64 for matte blue finish.

MODEL 741
- .32 H&R Mag. cal., 6 shot, 3 or 4 in. barrel, blue only, adj. sights. Mfg. 1993-94.

	$205	$155	$125	$115	$100	$90	$85

Last MSR was $254.

✳ *Model 741SS (Stainless Steel)* - similar to Model 741, except is stainless steel. Mfg. 1993-94.

	$275	$215	$185

Last MSR was $342.

MODEL 761
- .32 H&R Mag. cal., 6 shot, 6 in. barrel, blue only, adj. sights. Mfg. 1993-94.

	$250	$185	$145	$125	$115	$100	$90

Last MSR was $326.

MODEL 817 ULTRA-LITE
- .38 Spl. cal., compact frame, 7 shot, 2 in. ported (disc. 2002) or unported solid rib barrel, soft rubber grips, bright blue finish, 21 oz. New 1999.

	MSR $391	$305	$220	$160	$135	$110	$100	$90

Add $20 for ported barrel (disc. 2002).

✳ *Model 817 Ultra-Lite Stainless* - similar to Model 817 Ultra-Lite, except is stainless steel. New 1999.

	MSR $438	$335	$255	$185

Add $20 for ported barrel (disc. 2003).

MODEL 827
- .38 Spl. cal., 7 shot, 4 in. heavy SR barrel, fixed sights, rubber grips, 36 1/2 oz. Mfg. 1999 only.

	$240	$215	$170	$130	$110	$100	$95

Last MSR was $317.

✳ *Model 827 Stainless* - similar to Model 827, except is stainless steel. Mfg. 1999 only.

	$280	$220	$170

Last MSR was $364.

MODEL 850 CIA
- .38 Spl. cal., small frame, 5 shot, hammerless, double action only, 2 in. barrel with fixed sights, rubber grips, blue finish, approx. 23 oz. New 2001.

	MSR $383	$295	$230	$165	$135	$110	$95	$85

✳ *Model 850 CIA SS (Stainless Steel)* - similar to Model 850 CIA, except is matte stainless steel. New 2001.

	MSR $430	$325	$245	$185

✳ *Model 850 CIA Ultra Lite* - similar to Model 850 CIA, except is ultralight variation with adj. sight. New 2005.

	MSR $414	$310	$225	$165	$125	$105	$95	$85

Add $47 for aluminum frame with stainless steel slide.

✳ **Model 850T CIA** - .38 Spl. cal., similar to Model 850 CIA, except has shadow grey finish and all titanium construction, spectrum blue/titanium gold finish and mother-of-pearl grips became standard 2005. New 2001.

MSR $594	$480	$390	$310				

Subtract approx. $40 for shadow grey finish.

MODEL 851 PROTECTOR - .38 Spl. cal., small frame, 5 shot, 2 in. full underlug barrel, double action only, shrouded hammer, rubber boot grips, 25 oz. New 2003.

MSR $383	$295	$230	$165	$135	$110	$95	$85

✳ **Model 851 Protector SS (Stainless Steel)** - similar to Model 851 Protector, except is matte stainless steel. New 2003.

MSR $430	$325	$245	$185				

✳ **Model 851 Protector Ultra-Lite** - similar to Model 851 Protector, except is Ultra-Lite model with blue finish and intergral adj. sight. New 2003.

MSR $414	$315	$230	$165	$140	$120	$105	$95

✳ **Model 851 Protector Ultra-Lite Aluminum/Titanium** - similar to Model 851 Protector Ultra-Lite, except is aluminum/stainless steel or aluminum/titanium. New 2003.

MSR $461	$400	$340	$275				

Add $78 for aluminum/titanium construction.

✳ **Model 851 Protector Titanium** - similar to Model 851 Protector, except is shadow grey titanium. Mfg. 2003-2004.

	$450	$375	$300				

Last MSR was $555.

Add $39 for spectrum blue/titanium gold finish and mother-of-pearl grips.

MODEL 905 - 9mm Para cal., small frame, 5 shot, rubber boot grips, exposed or concealed (CH Model) hammer, fixed sights, includes 5 Stellar full moon clips. New 2003.

MSR $383	$285	$210	$160	$125	$105	$95	$85

✳ **Model 905SS (Stainless Steel)** - similar to Model 905, except is stainless steel. New 2003.

MSR $430	$355	$260	$210				

✳ **Model 905 Ultra-Lite** - ultra light frame, blue finish. Mfg. 2003-2004.

	$310	$225	$165	$125	$105	$95	$85

Last MSR was $414.

>**Model 905 Ultra-Lite Stainless** - matte stainless variation of the Model 905 Ultra-Lite. Mfg. 2003-2004.

MSR $461	$380	$275	$220				

Last MSR was $461.

MODEL 941 - .22 Mag. cal., small frame, 8 shot, 2 (new 1997), 3 (disc. 1998), 4, or 5 in. barrel, blue only, adj. sights, full underlug on 4 and 5 in. barrels, soft rubber or wood (disc. 2000, 5 in. barrel only) grips, 24-27.5 oz. New 1993.

MSR $344	$260	$190	$145	$120	$105	$95	$85

✳ **Model 941 Ultra-Lite** - ultra light hammer forged frame, available in matte blue or bright stainless steel, 18.5 oz. New 1999.

MSR $375	$280	$205	$155	$125	$105	$95	$85

Add $47 for matte stainless steel construction.

✳ **Model 941SS (Stainless Steel)** - similar to Model 941, except is polished stainless steel. New 1993.

MSR $391	$295	$220	$160				

MODEL 970 TRACKER SS (STAINLESS STEEL) - .22 LR cal., compact frame, double action, 7 shot, 6.5 in. heavy barrel with VR and adj. rear sight, Ribber grips, matte stainless steel. New 2001.

MSR $391	$295	$220	$160				

GRADING - PPGS™	100%	98%	95%	90%	80%	70%	60%

MODEL 971 TRACKER SS (STAINLESS STEEL) - .22 Mag. cal., otherwise similar to Model 970 Tracker, 45.2 oz. Mfg. 2001-2004.

	$325	$240	$195

Last MSR was $406.

MODEL 980 SILHOUETTE/HUNTER SS (STAINLESS STEEL) - .22 LR cal., compact frame, 7 shot, double action, 12 in. heavy barrel with adj. rear sight, Ribber grips, adj. trigger tension and trigger stop, includes scope mount, 56.8 oz. Mfg. 2001-2004.

	$335	$245	$200

Last MSR was $414.

MODEL 981 SILHOUETTE/HUNTER SS (STAINLESS STEEL) - .22 Mag. cal., otherwise similar to Model 980 Silhouette SS, 56.2 oz. Mfg. 2001-2004.

	$350	$255	$205

Last MSR was $430.

RIFLES: SEMI-AUTO

MODEL 63 - 22 LR cal., patterned after the Winchester Model 63, 10 shot tube mag., blue finish, takedown design, 23 in. round barrel with adj. rear sight, 72 oz. Importation began 2003.

MSR $295	$260	$225	$195	$175	$155	$140	$125

Add $33 for tang sight (new 2005).

* *Model 63 Stainless* - similar to Model 63, except is stainless steel. New 2003.

MSR $311	$270	$235	$200

Add $33 for tang sight (new 2005).

MODEL 73 - .22 Mag. cal., similar to Model 63, except mag. has less capacity. Imported late 2003-2004.

	$270	$235	$200	$175	$155	$140	$125

Last MSR was $311.

* *Model 73 Stainless* - similar to Model 73, except is stainless steel. Imported 2003-2004.

	$290	$250	$210

Last MSR was $342.

MODEL 173 - .17 HMR cal., similar to Model 73. Imported late 2003-2004.

	$290	$250	$210	$180	$160	$140	$125

Last MSR was $342.

* *Model 173 Stainless* - similar to Model 173, except is stainless steel. Imported 2003-2004.

	$300	$260	$210

Last MSR was $358.

RIFLES: SLIDE ACTION

Add $28 for Weaver style scope base mount.

Add $12 for Taurus Rimfire Recharger (2 pack w/o ammo, new 2002).

MODEL 62 RIFLE/CARBINE - .22 LR or .22 Mag. (disc. 2000) cal., patterned after the Win. Model 62, 16 1/2 (carbine) or 23 (rifle) in. barrel with open adj. sights, 11 or 12 shot tube mag., includes switchable manual firing pin block on top of receiver bolt and integral Taurus Security System lock on hammer, uncheckered hardwood stock and grooved forearm, blue or case colored receiver, approx. 4.5 lbs. Importation began 1999.

MSR $280	$250	$220	$190	$170	$160	$140	$125

Add $33 for rear tang sight (new 2002).

GRADING - PPGS™	100%	98%	95%	90%	80%	70%	60%

❋ *Model 62 Rifle/Carbine Stainless* - similar to Model 62 Rifle/Carbine, except is stainless steel. New 2000.

MSR $295	$260	$230	$200				

Add $78 for rear tang sight (mfg. 2002-2004).

❋ *Model 62 Rifle/Carbine "Upstart" Youth/Adult Combo* - similar to Model 62 Rifle/Carbine, except is available with both youth (shortened LOP), and adult stocks. Imported 2002-2004.

	$270	$235	$200				

Last MSR was $311.

Add $16 for stainless steel.

MODEL 72 RIFLE/CARBINE - .22 Mag. cal., 10 or 11 shot tube mag., blue or case colored receiver, similar to Model 62 Rifle/Carbine, 72 oz. Importation began 2001.

MSR $295	$260	$225	$195	$175	$155	$140	$125

Add $33 for rear tang sight (new 2002).

Beginning 2001, this model's nomenclature changed from Model 62 to Model 72 (.22 Mag. cal. only).

❋ *Model 72 Rifle/Carbine Stainless* - similar to Model 72 Rifle/Carbine, except is stainless steel, 80 oz. Importation began 2001.

MSR $311	$270	$235	$200				

Add $33 for rear tang sight (new 2002).

MODEL 172 RIFLE/CARBINE - .17 HMR cal., 16.5 (carbine) or 23 (rifle) in. barrel with adj. sights, 72 oz. Importation began 2003.

MSR $327	$280	$240	$200	$175	$155	$140	$125

❋ *Model 172 Rifle/Carbine Stainless* - similar to Model 172 Rifle/Carbine, except is stainless steel. Importation began 2003.

MSR $342	$290	$245	$205				

TAYLOR, F.C. FUR CO.

Previous company which marketed animal trap guns circa 1921-1941.

PISTOLS: SINGLE SHOT

.22 CAL. TAYLOR FUR GETTER - .22 LR cal., designed to shoot animal at close range once trigger mechanism has been activated (usually with bait attached to a lever). Mfg. by O.F. Mossberg for Taylor, ser. range 1-3,100.

	N/A	$750	$650	$600	$560	$530	$500

Add 10%-15% for low ser. no. with two-piece swiveling stake.

.38 CAL. TAYLOR FUR GETTER - .38 cal., mfg. on 1914 patent of C.D. Lovelace, believed to have been mfg. by Hopkins & Allen, markings cast in top of frame (brass) with iron barrel - all bearing the 1914 patent date.

	N/A	$550	$500	$460	$430	$400	$375

Add 10%-15% premium for alloy frame with top plate attached with two screws and uncracked frame.

TAYLOR'S & CO., INC.

Current importer and distributor established during 1988, and located in Winchester, VA.

Taylor's & Co. is an Uberti importer and distributor of both black powder and firearms reproductions, in addition to being the exclusive U.S. distributor for Armi Sport, located in Brescia, Italy. Taylor's is also the exclusive distributor for Hartford Armory revolvers - please refer to the Hartford Armory section.

For more information and up-to-date pricing regarding current Taylor's & Co., Inc. black powder models, please refer to Colt Blackpowder Reproductions and Replicas by Dennis Adler, and the Blue Book of Modern Black Powder Arms by John Allen & Dennis Adler.

GRADING - PPGS™	100%	98%	95%	90%	80%	70%	60%

These books feature hundreds of color photographs and support text of the most recent black powder models available, as well as complete pricing and reference guides.

REVOLVERS: REPRODUCTIONS, SAA

CATTLEMAN VARIATIONS - available in .32-20 WCF, .357 Mag., .38-40 WCF, .44 Spl., .44-40 WCF, .45 ACP (new 2003), or .45 LC cal., 4 3/4, 5 1/2, and 7 1/2 in. barrel lengths, brass (New Model frame) or steel (Old Model frame) backstrap and trigger guard, mfg. by Uberti. New 2002.

* ✷ *Steel backstrap and trigger guard* - choice of new or old model frame, old model frame not available in .357 Mag. cal.

MSR $405	$345	$285	$225	$185	$165	$150	$135

  Add $44 for charcoal blue finish (.357 Mag. or .45 LC cal. only).
  Add $78 for convertible cylinder (.45 LC/.45 ACP in 5 1/2 in. barrel only).
  Add $10 for .45 ACP cal., or subtract $5 for .32-20 WCF cal.

* ✷ *Brass backstrap and trigger guard* - .357 Mag., or .45 LC cal.

MSR $495	$425	$335	$265	$225	$185	$165	$140

* ✷ *Cattleman Millenium* - .45 LC cal., 4 3/4 in. barrel, brass backstrap and trigger guard. New 2000.

MSR $320	$275	$245	$200	$180	$160	$145	$130

* ✷ *Cattleman Engraved* - .45 LC cal. only, 4 3/4 or 5 1/2 in. barrel, features unique photo engraving on frame, cylinder, and barrel (Taylor's exclusive), white heat treated finish with charcoal blue screws. New 2003.

MSR $662	$550	$450	$375	$315	$275	$240	$215

* ✷ *Cattleman "TR" Presidential* - .45 LC cal. only, 5 1/2 in. barrel, features unique photo engraving on frame, cylinder, and barrel (Taylor's exclusive), white heat treated finish with charcoal blue screws, simulated ivory, wood, or black hard rubber grips. New 2005.

MSR $685	$565	$450	$375	$315	$275	$240	$215

  Add $30 for black grips, or $100 for simulated ivory grips.

CATTLEMAN BIRDSHEAD - .357 Mag. or .45 LC cal., 3 1/2 or 4 3/4 in. barrel, patterned after the Colt 1877 Thunderer, case colored frame, smooth walnut birdshead grips. New 1997.

MSR $475	$395	$300	$235	$190	$170	$150	$135

  Add $70 for nickel finish (.357 Mag. cal. only, with 4 3/4 in. barrel).

CATTLEMAN BISLEY - .357 Mag., .38-40 WCF or .45 LC cal., patterned after the Colt Bisley Model, 4 3/4, 5 1/2, or 7 1/2 in. barrel, case colored frame, wood grips. New 1997.

MSR $485	$415	$315	$250	$210	$190	$170	$150

STALLION 1873 - .38 Spl. cal., 3 1/2, 4 3/4, or 5 1/2 in. barrel, scaled down SAA with small frame, standard or birdshead smooth grips, steel backstrap and trigger guard. Mfg. 1999-2004.

	$365	$275	$210	$180	$160	$150	$135

Last MSR was $420.

  Add $22 for birdshead grips.

OUTFITTER - .357 Mag. or .45 LC cal., solid stainless construction with two-piece walnut grips, 4 3/4, 5 1/2, or 7 1/2 in. barrel. New 2003.

MSR $599	$500	$425	$350				

NEW VAUQUERO "HANDLEBAR DOC SIGNATURE SERIES" - .357 Mag. or .45 LC cal., color case hardened blue or stainless steel frame, 4 5/8, 5 1/2, or 7 1/2 in. barrel, checkered black grips with "HD" medallions, "Handlebar Doc Series" etched on barrel, Taylor's exclusive. New 2005.

MSR $710	$595	$550	$495	$450	$400	$365	$335

GRADING - PPGS™	100%	98%	95%	90%	80%	70%	60%

RIFLES: REPRODUCTIONS, LEVER ACTION

The following models are manufactured by Uberti, except for the 1892 rifle, which is manufactured by Armi Sport.

HENRY RIFLE - .44-40 WCF or .45 LC cal., brass or steel frame, 24 1/2 in. barrel, 13 shot mag., available in brass, case colored, or in-the-white finish.

MSR $1,118	$925	$750	$650	$525	$425	$360	$320

Add $16 for charcoal blue barrel finish.
Add $27 for steel frame.
Add $89 for in-the-white finish.

1866 YELLOWBOY RIFLE/CARBINE - .32-20 WCF, .38 Spl., .44-40 WCF, or .45 LC cal., 19 (carbine), 20 (rifle) or 24 1/4 (rifle) in. barrel. New 2002.

MSR $823	$750	$650	$525	$425	$375	$325	$295

Add $19 for carbine.

1873 CARBINE - .32-20 WCF, .357 Mag. or .45 LC cal., steel receiver, 19 in. round barrel. New 2002.

MSR $967	$850	$725	$575	$450	$400	$350	$325

1873 SPORTING RIFLE - .32-20 WCF (disc. 2004), .357 Mag., .38-40 WCF (disc. 2004), .44-40 WCF, or .45 LC cal., case hardened receiver, 20 in. octagon (Short Rifle), 24 1/4 in. octagon or 30 (Deluxe) in. octagon barrel. New 2002.

MSR $980	$875	$750	$600	$475	$425	$375	$350

Add $100 for Special Sporting Rifle with 24 1/4 in. barrel, checkered pistol grips and stock (.45 LC cal. only).
Add $130 for Deluxe Model with 30 in. barrel.

1892 CARBINE/RIFLE - .32-20 WCF, .32 H&R Mag., .38-40 WCF, .38 Spl., .357 Mag., .44 S&W, .44-40 WCF, or .45 LC cal., choice of 20 (.32-20 WCF cal. only) or 24 1/2 round (new 2005) or octagon barrel, solid (.32-20 WCF, .38-30 WCF, or .44 S&W cal. only) frame or takedown action.

MSR $865	$795	$725	$625	$525	$450	$400	$350

Add $34 for octagon barrel.
Add $34 for rifle.
Add $124 for takedown action.

RIFLES: SINGLE SHOT

1865 SPENCER CARBINE/RIFLE (160 SERIES) - .44 Russian, .44-40 WCF (new 2005), .45 Schofield, or .56-50 (rifle only) cal., reproduction of the Civil War Spencer carbine, case colored receiver, lock, and hammer, 20 or 30 (rifle, new 2005) in. barrel, 7-9 shot mag., walnut stock and forearm, includes slings, mfg. by Armi-Sport. Importation began 2002.

MSR $1,275	$1,075	$950	$825	$700	$600	$500	$400

Add $235 for .44 Russian or .45 Schofield cal.

This model in .44-40 WCF cal. is POR, as well as the 1865 Spencer Rifle - please contact Taylor's for more information.

1874 SHARPS SPORTING RIFLE - .40-65, .45-70 Govt., .45-90, or .45-120 cal., 30, 32, or 34 in. barrel, single or double set triggers, case colored for white finished frame, with or w/o pewter accents.

MSR $985	$875	$750	$625	$525	$450	$375	$300

Add $145 for double triggers with Hartford style forearm tip.
Add $220 for 34 in. barrel.
Add $250 for pistol grip stock with buckhorn sight or $295 for pistol grip stock and heavy barrel.

Taylor's also imports engraved models of the 1874 Sporting Rifle in either .45-70 Govt. or .45-120 cal., including standard engraving ($1,945 MSR) and hand engraving with gold medallions ($2,840 MSR).

GRADING - PPGS™	100%	98%	95%	90%	80%	70%	60%

1874 SHARPS QUIGLEY - .45-70 Govt. or .45-120 cal., 32 or 34 in. octagon barrel, exact reproduction of rifle used in "Quigley Down Under," with patchbox, includes Hartford style pewter forearm tip.

	MSR $1,235	$1,025	$875	$775	$675	$575	$475	$400

Add $90 for 34 in. barrel or .45-120 cal.

1874 SHARPS CAVALRY CARBINE - .45-70 Govt. or .50-70 (new 2005) cal., patterned after Sharps Cavalry carbine, 22 in. barrel, color case hardened frame.

	MSR $990	$900	$760	$600	$525	$450	$375	$300

Add $60 for .50-70 cal.

1874 SHARPS INFANTRY/BERDAN MODEL - .45-70 Govt. cal., 30 in. barrel, musket configuration with 3 barrel bands and patchbox.

	MSR $1,135	$975	$825	$675	$575	$475	$375	$300

Add $30 for Berdan model with DT.

1885 LOW/HIGH WALL - .17 HMR (new 2005), .17 Mach 2 (new 2005), .22 LR, .32-20 WCF, .38-40 WCF or .45-70 Govt. (High Wall only) cal., 30 or 32 (High Wall only) in. octagon barrel, case colored receiver, straight (High Wall) or checkered pistol grip (Low Wall) walnut stock and forearm. New 1999.

	MSR $875	$760	$650	$575	$500	$450	$400	$350

Add $35 for High Wall.

TECHNO ARMS (PTY) LIMITED

Previous manufacturer located in Johannesburg, S. Africa circa 1994-1996. Previously imported by Vulcans Forge, Inc. located in Foxboro, MA.

SHOTGUNS: SLIDE ACTION

MAG-7 SLIDE ACTION SHOTGUN - 12 ga. (60mm chamber length), 5 shot detachable mag. (in pistol grip), 14, 16, 18, or 20 in. barrel, stock or pistol grip, matte finish, 8 lbs. Imported 1995-96.

	$795	$675	$625	$550	$500	$450	$400

Last MSR was $875.

TELO, RENATO

Current manufacturer located in Brescia, Italy. No current U.S. importation.

Renato Telo manufactures best quality long guns. To date, this trademark has had very little importation into the U.S. Please contact the factory directly for more information, including models, availability, delivery time and U.S. pricing.

TERRIER ONE

Previous trademark distributed by Serrifile located in Lancaster, CA.

REVOLVERS

TERRIER ONE - .32 S&W cal., double action, 2 1/4 in. barrel, 5 shot, nickel-plated, 17 oz. Mfg. 1984-87.

	$45	$35	$30	$25	$25	$25	$25

Last MSR was $55.

TEXAS ARMS

Previous manufacturer located in Waco, TX, until circa 1999.

DERRINGERS: O/U

DEFENDER - .357 Mag., .38 Spl., 9mm Para., .44 Mag., .45 ACP, or .45 LC/.410 bore shotshell, features 3 in. interchangeable SS octagon barrels, spur trigger, shell ejector for rimmed cartridges, rebounding hammer and retracting firing pins, crossbolt safety, bead blasted grey finish, 16-21 oz. Mfg. 1993-c.1999.

$275	$235	$200	$175	$160	$145	$130

Last MSR was $310.

Add $100 per interchangeable set of barrels.

TEXAS GUNFIGHTERS

Previous importer located in Irving, TX circa 1988-1990.

REVOLVERS: SINGLE ACTION

SHOOTIST EDITION - .45 LC cal., patterned after the Colt SAA, 4 3/4 in. barrel, nickel-plated black powder frame, one piece walnut grips, mfg. by A. Uberti of Italy. New 1988.

* **Standard Model** - 1,000 total mfg., cased.

$625	$525	$440

Last MSR was $649.

* **1 of 100 Edition** - 100 total mfg., fully engraved, genuine mother-of-pearl one-piece grips, cased.

$1,275	$1,050	$775

Last MSR was $1,395.

This model was also supplied with an extra set of walnut grips.

TEXAS LONGHORN ARMS, INC.

Previous manufacturer located in Richmond, TX circa 1988-1997.

REVOLVERS

SINGLE-ACTION - various cals., patterned after Colt's SAA, except the ejection port has been moved to left side of frame enabling left-hand loading, mfg. from 4140 steel, 1-piece grip, adj. trigger, case-hardened and blue, entirely handmade, supplied with lifetime warranty. Models included the Texas Border Patrol (last MSR was $1,595), South Texas Army (last MSR was $1,595), Texas Flattop (last MSR was $1,595), Grover's Northpaw (last MSR was $685), and Grover's Improved Number Five (last MSR was $1,195). Special editions and sets were also advertised (ranging from $1,500 MSR - $7,650 MSR), but very few were actually built. Mint examples are currently in the $1,350-$1,500 range, except for Grover's Northpaw, which is in the $650 range. While production plans called for 1,000 of each model to be manufactured, very few pistols were actually made.

THOMAS

Previous trademark manufactured by Alexander James Ordnance, Inc. located in Covina, CA.

Please refer to listing under A.J. Ordnance in this text.

THOMPSON & CAMPBELL

Current rifle manufacturer located in Rosshire, Scotland. No current U.S. importation. Consumer direct sales.

GRADING - PPGS™	100%	98%	95%	90%	80%	70%	60%

RIFLES: BOLT ACTION

Thompson & Campbell manufactures high quality bolt action rifles featuring the patented Inver action, which utilizes a rear extension plate and reinforcement rod that is inletted into the stock for additional strength. Individual models include the Inver, Cromie, the Islay, and Jura (Mannlicher configuration). Thompson & Campbell manufactures approx. 20-24 rifles annually. Please contact the factory directly for more information, current pricing, and delivery times.

THOMPSON CARBINES & PISTOLS

Auto-Ordnance Corporation

See Auto Ordnance Corp. section of this book.

THOMPSON/CENTER ARMS CO., INC.

Current manufacturer established during 1967, and located in Rochester, NH. Distributor and dealer sales.

Please refer to the *Blue Book of Modern Black Powder Arms* by John Allen & Dennis Adler (also online) for more information and prices on Thompson/Center's lineup of modern black powder models.

PISTOLS: SINGLE SHOT

Caution: older and newer TC components do not interchange safely. Although parts will fit, they may not function properly. Special ordering of barrels, frames, and calibers started in 1988. Values below are for complete guns - including frame and barrel.

G2 CONTENDER - various rimfire and centerfire cals., including .17 Mach 2 (new 2005), .204 Ruger (new 2004) and .375 JDJ (new 2004), 12 or 14 in. barrel with adj. sights, blued finish, walnut finger groove grip and forearm, replacement for the Contender model, will accept older Contender barrels w/o frame alteration, automatic hammer block safety with built-in interlock, hammer recocking w/o breaking open the gun, opening has been made easier, approx. 3.5 lbs. New late 2002.

MSR $562	$435	$365	$290	$255	$220	$195	$170

Add $7 for 14 in. barrel.
Add approx. $10 for 22 LR cal.
Add $22 for .17 HMR or 17 Mach 2 cal.
Add $44 for .45 LC/.410 bore.
Add $255-$324 per additional barrel, depending on length and caliber.
Currently, a G2 Contender frame assembly only retails for $313.

CONTENDER - .22 LR, .22 Rem., 5mm Rem., .218 Bee, .22 Hornet, .22 Jet, .221 Fireball, .222 Rem., .25-35 WCF, .256 Mag., .30 Carbine, .30-30 Win., .38 Spl., .357 Mag., .17 Ackley Bee, .17 Bumblebee, .17 Hornet, .17K Hornet, .17 Rem., .300 Whisper (new 1994), .30 Herrett, .357 Herrett, .357-44 B&D, 7x30 Waters, .32 H&R Mag., .32-20 WCF, 6mm TCU, 6.5mm TCU, or 9mm Para. cal., barrels are interchangeable, 8 3/4 (disc.), 10, or 14 in. barrel, hinged break open, triggerguard, action lever, blue, .44, .357 Mag., and .45 Colt available with detachable choke for hot shot cartridges, VR, 10 in. barrel available, 10 in. bull barrel, adj. sights, checkered walnut grip and forearm. Mfg. 1967-2000.

The Contender action was made in 3 variations, and a wide variety of changes were made to grips, stocks, sights, etc. during 1967-2000. These production variances do not necessarily add premiums to values listed.

GRADING - PPGS™	100%	98%	95%	90%	80%	70%	60%

❋ Bull Barrel - available in 13 cals. between .17 Rem. and .45 Win. Mag., 10 in. round barrel only.

	$380	$295	$220	$190	$170	$160	$150

Last MSR was $510.

Add $22 for .45 Colt/.410 bore with internal chokes.
Add $11 for .22 LR match grade chamber (new 1996).
Add approx. $230-$267 per additional barrel.

❋ Armour Alloy II Bull Barrel - 7 cals. between .22 LR and .30-30 Win., similar to regular Bull Barrel, except has Armour Alloy II satin finish which is harder than stainless steel. Mfg. 1986-89.

	$320	$285	$230

Last MSR was $415.

Add $5 for .45 Colt/.410 bore internal choke.

❋ Vent. Rib - .357 Mag. (disc.), .44 Mag. (disc.) or .45 Colt/.410 bore, 10 in. VR barrel only, adj. front and flip-up rear sight, internal choke became standard in 1985.

	$400	$300	$225	$185	$170	$160	$150

Last MSR was $533.

❋ Armour Alloy Vent. Rib - .45/.410 internal choke, has Armour Alloy II satin finish which is harder than stainless steel. Mfg. 1986-disc.

	$350	$295	$230

Last MSR was $435.

❋ Stainless Steel - various cals., 10 in. bull barrel. Mfg. 1993-2000.

	$435	$315	$220

Last MSR was $578.

Add approx. $240 per additional barrel.
Add $5 for .45/.410 with adj. sights.
Add $20 for .45/.410 with VR.

❋ Octagon Barrel - .22 LR, .22 Mag. (disc.), .22 Hornet (disc.), .22K Hornet (disc.), .222 Rem. (disc.), or .357 Mag. (disc.) cal., 10 in. barrel. Disc. 1998.

	$355	$260	$200	$180	$170	$160	$150

Last MSR was $474.

❋ Match Grade Barrel - .22 LR cal. only, choice of 10 or 14 in. match barrel. Mfg. 1992-98.

	$350	$265	$200	$180	$170	$160	$150

Last MSR was $460.

Add $10 for 14 in. barrel.

CONTENDER SHOOTERS PACKAGE - .22 LR Match, .223 Rem., .30-30 Win., or 7-30 Waters cal., includes blue frame and 14 in. barrel w/o sights, 2.5-7X scope, composite grips and forend, Weaver style base and rings, pistol case. Mfg. 1998-2000.

	$650	$575	$550	$450	$400	$360	$330

Last MSR was $754.

CONTENDER SUPER (14 & 16 IN.) - 13 cals. available from .17 Rem. - .45 Win. Mag. (disc.), 14 or 16 in. bull barrel only, special grips, beavertail forearm, adj. sight, 3 1/2 lbs. Disc. 1997.

	$360	$265	$200	$180	$170	$160	$150

Last MSR was $474.

Add $5 for 16 in. barrel.
Add $31 for .17 Rem. cal. (new 1992).
Add $10 for .45-70 Govt. cal. in 16 in. barrel only with muzzle brake (new 1992).
Add approx. $224 per additional barrel.
Add $31 for VR barrel (.45 LC/.410 bore only).

Thompson Center will also make special order guns in different cals. other than those listed above. If factory work, these pistols will be worth a premium.

GRADING - PPGS™	100%	98%	95%	90%	80%	70%	60%

✸ *Stainless Contender Super* - various cals., choice of 14 or 16 in. barrel. Mfg. 1993-97.

	$385	$275	$215				

Last MSR was $505.

Add $5 for 16 in. barrel.
Add $25 for .45-70 Govt. bull barrel with muzzle tamer.
Add $30-$35 for .45 LC/.410 bore with internal choke.
Add approx. $240 per additional barrel.

✸ *Armour Alloy II Super Contender* - 5 cals. between .22 LR and 7mm Rem. Mag., similar to regular Super Contender, except has Armour Alloy II satin finish which is harder than stainless steel. Mfg. 1986-89.

	$355	$295	$240				

Last MSR was $425.

SUPER CONTENDER (14 & 16 IN.)
various cals. between .22 LR - .45-70 Govt., wood grips with rear stippling, barrel configurations include 14 or 16 in. bull (with or w/o VR), adj. sights, blue finish only. Mfg. 1999-2000.

	$410	$345	$285	$255	$220	$195	$170

Last MSR was $520.

Add $35 for 14 in. VR barrel.
Add $5 for 16 in. tapered barrel.

✸ *Super Contender Stainless* - similar to Super Contender, except is only available in 14 in. barrel. Mfg. 1999-2000.

	$430	$320	$215				

Last MSR was $578.

Add $35 for VR barrel.
Add $22 for .45/.410 ga. barrel.

CONTENDER HUNTER PACKAGE
.223 Rem., .7-30 Waters, .30-30 Win., .35 Rem., .357 Rem. Max. (disc. 1994), .375 Win. Mag. (new 1992), .44 Mag., or .45-70 Govt. cal., special 12 (disc.) or 14 (new 1992) in. barrel with muzzle brake, 2.5 power scope with lighted reticle, walnut grip has nonslip rubber insert to cushion recoil, includes studs, swivels, sling, and deluxe carrying case, approx. 4 lbs. Mfg. 1990-97.

	$695	$575	$495	$430	$365	$315	$275

Last MSR was $798.

CONTENDER 25TH ANNIVERSARY
.22 LR cal. only, 10 in. octagon barrel, laser etched anniversary logo on receiver sides and barrel, checkered stock and forearm, limited mfg. in 1992 only.

	$610	$535	$465	$410	$360	$315	$275

Last MSR was $700.

✸ *Contender 25th Anniversary Cased Set* - cased set with 5 barrels including .22 LR, .22 Mag., .22 Jet, .22 Hornet, and .38 Spl. cal., 50 sets mfg. 1992 only.

	$1,850	$1,550	$1,225	$1,050	$900	$775	$650

Last MSR was $1,975.

ENCORE
various cals. between .22 LR and .480 Ruger (new 2002), features walnut grip with finger grooves and forend, blue finish, 10 (disc. 1999), 12 (new 1999), or 15 in. barrel with adj. sights, VR barrel on .45 LC/.410 bore, hammer block safety with bolt interlock, 4-4 1/2 lbs. New 1998.

MSR $592		$465	$390	$310	$265	$230	$200	$170

Subtract $8 for 12 in. barrel.
Add $228 for extra 10 in. (disc.), $263-$294 for extra 12 in. barrel, or $370-$332 for extra 15 in. barrel, depending on caliber.
Add $29 for .45 LC/.410 bore barrel, depending on barrel length.
Encore pistol barrels ARE NOT interchangeable with Contender pistol barrels.
Currently, an Encore frame assembly only retails for $328.

GRADING - PPGS™	100%	98%	95%	90%	80%	70%	60%

✽ Encore Stainless - .22-250 Rem., .223 Rem., .243 Win., .30-06, .308 Win., 7mm-08 Rem., .44 Mag., .45 LC/.410 bore, or .480 Ruger (mfg. 2003) cal., black synthetic finger groove grips and forearm. New 1999.

MSR $636	$500	$375	$265				

Add $23 for .480 Ruger cal. (mfg. 2003).
Add $9 for 15 in. barrel.

✽ Encore Hunter Package - .22-250 Rem., .270 Win., or .308 Win. cal., features 15 in. barrel w/o sights and 2.5-7X scope, Weaver base and rings, composite grip and forend, includes case. New 1998.

MSR $859	$730	$620	$575	$465	$400	$360	$330

RIFLES

ENCORE RIFLE - available in many rimfire and centerfire cals. between .17 Mach 2 (new 2005) and .45-70 Govt., interchangeable standard 24 or heavy 26 in. barrel, automatic hammer block, trigger guard opening lever, choice of black synthetic (new 1999), Realtree camo (new 2005), Realtree Hardwoods HD camo, or American walnut uncheckered forearm and Monte Carlo stock with pistol grip, adj. rear sight, approx. 7 lbs. New 1997.

MSR $605	$480	$365	$290	$240	$195	$180	$170

Add $43 for walnut stock and forearm.
Add $58 for camo.
Add $35 for .17 Mach 2 cal.
Add $277 per extra blue finish barrel.
Encore rifle barrels ARE NOT interchangeable with Contender Carbine barrels.
Currently, an Encore frame, including buttstock and forearm starts at $334 MSR.

✽ Encore Stainless - similar to Encore Rifle, except has black synthetic stock and forearm or Realtree/Realtree Hardwoods HD (new 2005) camo treatment, and is stainless steel. New 1999.

MSR $681	$535	$375	$265				

Add $311 per extra barrel.
Add $58 for camo.

✽ Encore Katahdin Carbine - .444 Marlin (disc. 2003), .450 Marlin, or .45-70 Govt. cal., 18 in. barrel with muzzle tamer, blue steel, black composite stock and forearm, fiber optic sights, drilled and tapped, 6 lbs., 10 oz. New 2002.

MSR $617	$490	$370	$255	$235	$195	$180	$170

Add $292 for extra barrel.

✽ Encore Hunter Package - .300 Win. Mag., or .308 Win. cal., includes 3-9x40mm scope, Weaver style base and rings, and hard case. New 2002.

MSR $905	$770	$640	$585	$475	$400	$360	$330

CONTENDER CARBINE - available in 15 cals. between .17 Rem. and .44 Rem. Mag., also .410 bore (3 in.), Contender action with pistol grip full stock and forearm, 21 in. interchangeable barrel, drilled for scope mounts, iron sights standard. Mfg. 1986-2000.

	$415	$315	$255	$215	$190	$175	$160

Last MSR was $540.

Add $31 for .17 Rem. cal. (disc. 1997).
Add $21 for .410 bore barrel. (disc. 1997).
Add approx. $244 per extra barrel.
Add $11 for match grade .22 LR barrel.
Subtract $36 for Youth Model (16 1/4 in. barrel w/o VR - disc. 1998).
Add $175 for Survival Carbine System (disc. - includes Rynite stock, 16 1/4 .223 Rem. barrel, extra .45 Colt/.410 barrel, and soft camo cordura case).

GRADING - PPGS™	100%	98%	95%	90%	80%	70%	60%

* *Rynite Contender Carbine* - similar to Contender Carbine, except has Rynite stock and forend. Mfg. 1990-93.

	$335	$270	$220	$195	$180	$165	$155

Last MSR was $425.

Add $30 for .17 Rem. cal.
Add $10 for match grade barrel.
Add $25 for 21 in. VR smooth bore .410 bore barrel.

* *Contender Carbine Stainless* - various cals., 21 in. barrel, choice of walnut (disc. 1993) or Rynite synthetic stock. Mfg. 1993-2000.

	$415	$310	$230				

Last MSR was $546.

Add $35 for walnut stock (disc.).
Add $11 for .22 LR match barrel (new 1995).
Add $26 for .410 smooth bore barrel with screw-in full choke (disc.).
This model was also available in a Youth Model with walnut stock at no extra charge (disc. 1993).

HUNTER RIFLE MODEL - single shot, top lever break open action w/ interchangeable barrels, .22 Hornet, .223 Rem., .22-250 Rem., .243 Win., .270 Win., 7x57mm, .30-06, .308 Win., .375 H&H (new 1992), or .416 Rem. Mag. (new 1992) cal., 23 in. barrel, 6 lbs. 14 oz., checkered walnut stock, choice of medium or light sporter weight barrel. New 1983 and improved in 1987. Available in left-hand at no extra charge. Disc. 1992.

	$500	$415	$350	$295	$265	$240	$220

Last MSR was $595.

Add $20 for .375 H&H or .416 Rem. Mag. cal.
Add approx. $275 per extra rifle barrel.

* *Hunter Deluxe Rifle Model* - similar to Hunter Model, except features double triggers and upgraded walnut stock and forearm. Mfg. 1992 only.

	$550	$450	$375	$325	$285	$250	$225

Last MSR was $675.

Add $20 for .375 H&H or .416 Rem. Mag. cal.

* *Hunter Shotgun Model* - same action as Hunter Rifle, except is supplied with 12 ga. barrel (field choke with 3 1/2 in. chamber or slug with 3 in. chamber and iron sights) or 10 ga. barrel (3 1/2 in. chamber). Disc. 1992.

	$500	$415	$350	$295	$265	$240	$220

Last MSR was $595.

Add $275 per additional shotgun barrel.

TCR '83 ARISTOCRAT - similar to Hunter Model, except stock has cheekpiece and forearm is checkered, stainless steel, double set triggers. Disc. 1986.

	$425	$370	$345				

Last MSR was $475.

Add $175 for each additional barrel(s) (including 12 ga. slug).

RIFLES: SEMI-AUTO

SILVER LYNX - .22 LR cal., 20 in. match grade barrel with adj. fiber optic open sights, 5 shot mag., stainless steel action and barrel, black composite stock with Monte Carlo cheekpiece, 5.5 lbs. New 2004.

MSR $423	$340	$295	$240	$200	$165	$145	$120

CLASSIC - .22 LR cal., blowback action, all steel construction, 5 (new 2003) or 8 (disc. 2002) shot mag., 22 in. match grade barrel with muzzle crown, adj. rear sight, blue finish, uncheckered Monte Carlo walnut stock, 5 1/2 lbs. New 2000.

MSR $396	$320	$275	$225	$195	$160	$140	$120

GRADING - PPGS™	100%	98%	95%	90%	80%	70%	60%

* **Classic Benchmark Target** - same action as Classic, 18 in. heavy target barrel, brown laminated hardwood Monte Carlo target stock, matte finish blue, 10 shot mag., no sights, receiver is drilled and tapped, 6.8 lbs. New 2003.

MSR $506	$415	$340	$270	$235	$215	$175	$150

MODEL R55 - .17 Mach 2 cal., blue or stainless steel, 20 in. barrel, brown laminate or black composite stock, fiberoptic sights. New 2005.

MSR $479	$395	$350	$275	$240	$220	$200	$175

Add $66 for stainless steel.

SHOTGUNS: SINGLE SHOT

ENCORE SHOTGUN - 12 (new 2004) or 20 ga., 3 in. chamber, action based on Encore pistol with trigger guard release for barrel opening, 26 in. VR barrel with three choke tubes, recoil pad. New 1998.

MSR $727	$600	$500	$400	$325	$250	$200	$175

Add $337 (20 ga.) or $358 (12 ga.) per additional shotgun barrel with choke tubes. Subtract $23 for 20 ga.

* **Encore Slug Gun** - 12 or 20 ga. only, 3 in. chamber, 24 or 26 (20 ga. only) in. rifled barrel with fiberoptic sights, walnut stock and forearm. New 2000.

MSR $684	$570	$475	$385	$315	$250	$225	$200

Subtract $27 for 20 ga.

* **Encore Turkey Gun** - 12 or 20 ga., 3 in. chamber, 24 in. smoothbore barrel with screw-in turkey choke tube, 100% Realtree Hardwoods (new 2003) or Advantage Timber (mfg. 2002 only) camo coverage, and fiberoptic sights. New 2002.

MSR $763	$600	$520	$415	$325	$275	$225	$200

Add $71 for muzzleloading barrel (disc. 2003).

* **Katahdin Encore Turkey Gun** - 12 ga., 3 in. chamber, 20 in. barrel with turkey choke tube, composite stock with Realtree Hardwoods HD camo pattern, fiberoptic sights. New 2005.

MSR $748	$590	$510	$410	$325	$275	$225	$200

THUNDER-FIVE

Current trademark manufactured by MIL Inc., located in Piney Flats, TN. Previous company name was Holston Enterprises, Inc. Various distributors. Previously manufactured by Mil, Inc. located in Piney Flats, TN. Previously distributed by C.L. Reedy & Associates, Inc. located in Jonesborough, TN.

While previously advertised as the Spectre Five (not mfg.), this firearm was re-named the Thunder Five.

REVOLVERS

THUNDER-FIVE - .45 LC cal./.410 bore with 3 in. chamber or .45-70 Govt. cal. (mfg. 1994-98), single or double action, unique 5 shot revolver design permits shooting .45 LC or .410 bore shotshells interchangeably, 2 in. rifled barrel, phosphate finish, external ambidextrous hammer block safety, internal draw bar safety, combat sights, hammer, trigger, and trigger guard, Pachmayr grips, includes padded plastic carrying case, 48 oz., serialization starts at 1,101. New 1992.

MSR $495	$450	$400	$375	$350	$325	$300	$275

Sub-caliber sleeve inserts were available until 1998 for 9mm Para., .357 Mag./.38 Spl., and .38 Super cals.

TIKKA

Current trademark imported by Beretta U.S.A. Corp., located in Accokeek, MD. Previously imported until 2000 by Stoeger Industries, located in Wayne, NJ. Tikka rifles are currently manufactured by Sako, Ltd. located in Riihimäki, Finland. Previously manufactured by Oy Tikkakoski Ab, of Tikkakoski, Finland (pre-1989).

During 2000, Tikka was purchased by Beretta Holding of Italy. All currently produced Tikkas are imported by Beretta U.S.A. Corp., located in Accokeek, MD.

Also see listings under Ithaca combination guns and bolt action rifles for older models.

COMBINATIONS GUNS: O/U

Previously manufactured in Jyvaskyla, Finland. In 1989, under a joint venture agreement, the 412 O/U shooting system was manufactured in Italy. Older models may be found in the Valmet trademark section of this text.

During 1993, the new models of the 512S series replaced the older 412S series. Separate listings have not been provided, since they are almost identical in most respects.

MODEL 512S SHOOTING SYSTEM - interchangeable barrel assemblies permit a double rifle, shotgun/rifle, and O/U shotgun configuration, user installed interchangeable barrels, monobloc locking, rifle barrel positioning by adjustment, SST, extractors or ejectors, checkered walnut stock and forend, cocking indicators, blue finish.

The 412S Model nomenclature was changed to 512S in late 1993.

✳ *Model 512S Field Grade* - 12 ga. only, 3 in. chambers, auto ejectors, screw-in choke tubes (includes 5), 26 or 28 in. barrels, matte nickel finish. New 1986-importation disc. 1997, reintroduced 2000 only.

$1,050	$750	$595	$550	$475	$440	$400

Last MSR was $1,134.

Subtract 10% for Standard Grade.
Add $45 for Sporting Clays Model (new 2000).
Add $659 per extra set of shotgun/rifle barrels.

The Premium Grade became standard issue beginning 1995. This model was reintroduced in 2000 only, and new features included back boring and ported barrels (Sporting Clays Model only).

✳ *Model 412ST Trap* - 12 ga., Monte Carlo stock, 30 in. barrels, screw-in chokes standard.

$1,125	$925	$725	$650	$580	$540	$475

Last MSR was $1,325.

This variation was made by Valmet in Finland.

✳ *Model 412ST Premium Grade Trap* - similar to Model 412ST Trap, except has better walnut and checkering.

$1,425	$1,000	$875	$750	$625	$580	$515

Last MSR was $1,665.

This variation was made by Valmet in Finland.

✳ *Model 512S Sporting Clays* - 12 ga. only, sporting clays configuration with 28 or 30 (new 1994) in. VR barrels and choke tubes. Imported 1992-97.

$1,160	$950	$735	$650	$580	$540	$475

Last MSR was $1,360.

✳ *Model 512S Combination Gun* - combination rifle/shotgun, 12 ga, 3 in. chambers, 24 in. barrels, under rifle barrel has choice of .222 Rem., .30-06, or .308 Win. cal., extractors. Importation disc. 1997.

$1,425	$1,025	$775	$675	$600	$525	$475

Last MSR was $1,770.

GRADING - PPGS™	100%	98%	95%	90%	80%	70%	60%

✳ *Model 512S Double Rifle* - .30-06 (new 1994), .308 Win. (new 1994), 9.3x74R cal., 24 in. barrels, extractors. Importation disc. 1997.

	$1,525	$1,125	$825	$750	$625	$550	$500

Last MSR was $1,890.

Add $745-$765 for extra shotgun barrels (includes screw-in chokes), $810 for extra shotgun/rifle combo, and $1,040 for double rifle barrels.

RIFLES: BOLT ACTION

About 3,000 rifles sold under the Tikka name have been recalled following catastrophic failures, but a small number of guns sold in the American market remain in the hands of consumers who have apparently not heard about the recall. A weakness in the stainless steel used to manufacture rifles during 2003-2004 has lead to ruptured barrels. Consumers are urged to contact the Tikka Recall Center at 800-503-8869 with your rifle's serial number to find out if your firearm is affected.

NEW GENERATION RIFLE (MODELS 595/695) - .22-250 Rem., .223 Rem., .243 Win., .270 Win., .30-06, .308 Win., 7mm Rem. Mag, .300 Win. Mag., or .338 Win Mag. cal., 22 1/2 (non-Mag.) or 24 1/2 (Mag. cals.) in. barrel, detachable 3 (standard) or 5 (optional) shot mag., forged and milled action in two lengths, checkered walnut stock, 7-7 1/2 lbs. Sako mfg. 1989-94.

	$725	$600	$550	$500	$450	$400	$360

Last MSR was $835.

Add $25 for Mag. cals.

Cals. .22-250 Rem., .308 Win., and .300 Win. Mag. were introduced in late 1989.

This model's nomenclature also included the Models 595 (short actions with cals. up to .308 Win. cal.) and 695 (long action, including Mag. cals.).

PREMIUM GRADE MODEL - same cals. as New Generation Rifle, stock is select walnut with rollover cheek-piece and rosewood pistol grip cap and forend tip, high polished barrel blue. Imported 1989-94.

	$860	$715	$600	$550	$500	$450	$400

Last MSR was $1,030.

Add $40 for Mag. cals.

VARMINT MODEL - .22-250 Rem., .223 Rem., .243 Win., or .308 Win. cal., 24 1/2 in. heavy barrel, no sights. Mfg. 1991-94.

	$895	$750	$625	$550	$500	$450	$400

Last MSR was $1,090.

T3 HUNTER - .22-250 Rem., .223 Rem., .243 Win., .25-06 Rem., .270 Win., .270 WSM, .30-06, .308 Win., 6.5x55mm Swedish, 7mm Rem. Mag., .300 WSM, .300 Win. Mag., or .338 Win. Mag. cal., cold hammer forged 22 7/16-24 3/8 in. barrel, similar action as the Whitetail Hunter, choice of checkered walnut or black synthetic stock (disc. 2003), 3-4 shot detachable mag., 2 position rear safety, designed by Giugiaro of Italy, approx. 6.25 lbs. Importation began mid-2003.

MSR $759	$625	$525	$475	$400	$350	$300	$275

Subtract 10% for synthetic stock.
Add $49 for Mag. cals.

✳ *T3 Lite* - similar to T3, except has TrueBody glass fiber reinforced polymer black stock, adj. buttplate, approx. 6.25 lbs. Importation began 2004.

MSR $674	$550	$495	$450	$400	$350	$295	$275

Add $35 for Mag. cals.

✳ *T3 Lite Stainless* - similar to T3, except has stainless action and barrel, available with black synthetic stock only. Importation began mid-2003.

MSR $759	$625	$525	$450

Add $39 for Mag. cals.

GRADING - PPGS™	100%	98%	95%	90%	80%	70%	60%

✳ **T3 Laminated Stainless** - .243 Win., .25-06 Rem., .270 Win., .270 WSM, .30-06, .300 WSM, .300 Win. Mag., .308 Win., 7mm Rem. Mag., or .338 Win. Mag., similar to T3, except has stainless action and barrel, available with grey matte laminated hardwood stock, approx. 6.75 lbs. Importation began 2004.

	MSR $908	$765	$625	$525			

Add $36 for Mag. cals.

✳ **T3 Big Boar Synthetic** - .30-06, .308 Win. or .300 WSM cal., synthetic stock, 19 in. barrel. Importation began 2005.

	MSR $719	$620	$550	$475	$400	$365	$330	$295

✳ **T3 Varmint** - .22-250 Rem., .223 Rem., or .308 Win. cal., choice of steel or stainless steel action/barrel, 23 3/8 in. heavy barrel, adj. stock mfg. from reinforced copolymer polypropylene, 3-6 shot detachable mag., 8 lbs. Importation began 2004.

	MSR $839	$775	$675	$575	$475	$400	$365	$330

Add $69 for stainless steel barrel.

✳ **T3 Super Varmint** - .22-250 Rem., .223 Rem. or .308 Win. cal., 23 3/8 in. heavy stainless barrel, 3 or 4 shot mag., laminated synthetic stock with adj. comb, Picatinny rail, extra swivel stud, adj. trigger. Importation began 2005.

	MSR $1,668	$1,425	$1,175	$925			

✳ **T3 Tactical** - .223 Rem. or .308 Win. cal., similar to T3, except has 20 or 24 in. barrel. Importation began 2004.

	MSR $1,584	$1,350	$1,075	$950	$825	$750	$650	$550

WHITETAIL HUNTER/SYNTHETIC (BATTUE) - .22-250 Rem. (new 1995), .223 Rem. (new 1995), .243 Win. (new 1995), .25-06 Rem.(new 1995), .270 Win., .30-06, .308 Win. (not available in synthetic), 6.5x55mm Swedish (new 2002), 7mm Rem. Mag., 7mm-08 Rem. (new 1999), .300 Win. Mag., or .338 Win. Mag. cal., 20 1/2 (disc. 1994), 22 1/2 (new 1995), or 24 1/2 (new 1995, Mag cals. only), in. barrel, 3 or 5 (optional) shot detachable mag., choice of wood or black synthetic (new 1996) stock, no sights (Hunter Model), or open sights on raised rib (disc., Battue Model), approx. 7 1/4 lbs. Mfg. 1991-2002.

		$525	$450	$390	$350	$325	$300	$275

Last MSR was $615.

Add $30 for Mag. cals.
Add $60 for carved elk or deer game scene stock (mfg. 1996-97).

✳ **Whitetail Hunter Left Hand** - similar cals. as Whitetail Hunter, left-hand action. Importation disc. 2003.

		$590	$530	$460	$395	$360	$325	$295

Last MSR was $680.

Add $30 for Mag. cals.

✳ **Whitetail Hunter/Battue Stainless** - similar cals. as Whitetail Hunter, except not available in 6.5x55mm Swedish cal., black synthetic stock only and satin finished stainless steel, 7 1/4 lbs. Mfg. 1997-2002.

		$590	$530	$460				

Last MSR was $680.

Add $30 for Mag. cals.

✳ **Whitetail Hunter Stainless Laminate** - .25-06 Rem., .270 Win., .30-06, .300 Win. Mag., or 7mm Rem. Mag. cal., similar to Whitetail Hunter Stainless, except has grey laminate wood stock and forend with checkering, satin finished stainless steel, 3 shot detachable mag., 7 1/4 lbs. Imported 2002-2003.

		$650	$565	$500				

Last MSR was $745.

Add $30 for Mag. cals.

GRADING - PPGS™	100%	98%	95%	90%	80%	70%	60%

✳ *Whitetail Hunter Deluxe* - similar cals. as Whitetail Hunter, gloss finished deluxe checkered walnut stock and forearm with rollover cheekpiece. Imported 1999-2003.

	$650	$565	$500	$460	$400	$360	$330

Last MSR was $745.

Add $30 for Mag. cals.

CONTINENTAL VARMINT MODEL - .17 Rem. (mfg. 2000-2002), .22-250 Rem., .223 Rem., or .308 Win. cal., heavy 26 in. barrel w/o sights, adj. trigger, quick release 3 shot detachable mag., integral scope mount rails, checkered walnut stock with beavertail forend, recoil pad spacer system, 8 1/8 lbs. Mfg. 1996-2003.

	$615	$520	$460	$400	$350	$325	$300

Last MSR was $720.

CONTINENTAL LONG RANGE HUNTER - .25-06 Rem. (disc. 2002), .270 Win. (disc. 2002), 7mm Rem. Mag., or .300 Win. Mag. cal., heavy 26 in. barrel w/o sights, checkered walnut stock and forend, 8 3/8 lbs. Mfg. 1996-2003.

	$640	$540	$475	$415	$365	$325	$300

Last MSR was $750.

Subtract 5% for non-Mag. cals. (disc. 2002).

TARGET (SPORTER) MODEL - .22-250 Rem., .223 Rem., .308 Win., 7mm-08 Rem. (new 2002), 6.5x55mm Swedish (new 2003) cal., 23 3/8 in. barrel w/o sights, competition style stock with adj. buttplate and cheekpiece, detachable 5 shot mag., stippled pistol grip and forend, 9 lbs. Mfg. 1998-2003.

	$845	$765	$660	$580	$515	$450	$395

Last MSR was $950.

This model was designated the Tikka Sporter until 2003.

TIMBERWOLF

Previous trademark manufactured by I.M.I. (Israel Military Industries) located in Israel. Previously imported and distributed by Action Arms located in Philadelphia, PA until 1994.

RIFLES: SLIDE ACTION

TIMBERWOLF - .357 Mag. or .44 Mag. (disc.) cal., slide action, straight grip shotgun style stock with adj. drop, blue or satin chrome finish, takedown, 18 1/2 in. barrel, 10 shot tube mag., sear locking and firing pin safeties, integral scope base, approx. 5 1/2 lbs. Imported 1989-93.

	100%	98%	95%	90%	80%	70%	60%
.357 Mag.	$260	$230	$195	$180	$160	$145	$130
.44 Mag. (blue only)	$425	$375	$335	$300	$275	$250	$225

Last MSR was $299.

Add $80 for satin chrome finish.

This model was designed by Evan Whilden, and imported/distributed by Action Arms Ltd. Springfield Armory imported 1,000 .44 Mag. Timberwolf models during 1990-91.

TIME PRECISION ARMS

Current custom riflemaker located in New Milford, CT. Previously located in Brookfield, CT. Consumer direct sales.

RIFLES: BOLT ACTION

Time Precision rifles feature SLV/ALV actions and are available in over 30 different types, in cals. from .22 LR - .416 Rigby, prices range from $834-$1,062. All guns are made per individual custom order, but are basically available in 3 different configurations - Hunting, Benchrest, and Target rifles. Base prices begin at $2,202 (add $120 for Mag. cals.), and $1,980 for .22 Sporter with a wide range of special order options. Please contact the company directly regarding delivery times and other information (see Trademark Index).

TIPPMAN ARMS CO.

Previous manufacturer located in Fort Wayne, IN.

Tippman Arms manufactured 1/2 scale semi-auto working models of famous machine guns. All models were available with an optional hardwood case, extra ammo cans, and other accessories. Mfg. 1986-1987 only.

RIFLES: REPRODUCTIONS, SEMI-AUTO

MODEL 1919 A-4 - .22 LR cal. only, copy of Browning 1919 A-4 Model, belt fed, closed bolt operation, 11 in. barrel, includes tripod, 10 lbs.

$3,125	$2,950	$2,700	$2,350	$2,000	$1,725	$1,500

Last MSR was $1,325.

MODEL 1917 - .22 LR cal. only, copy of Browning M1917, watercooled, belt fed, closed bolt operation, 11 in. barrel, includes tripod, 10 lbs.

$6,375	$6,000	$5,500	$5,000	$4,350	$3,750	$3,250

Last MSR was $1,830.

MODEL .50 HB - .22 Mag. cal. only, copy of Browning .50 cal. machine gun, belt fed, closed bolt operation, 18 1/4 in. barrel, includes tripod, 13 lbs.

$6,625	$6,400	$5,950	$5,400	$4,950	$4,500	$4,000

Last MSR was $1,929.

TOKAREV

See Russian Service Pistols and Rifles section.

TOLLEY, J & W

Current trademark manufactured by Premier English Shotguns, Ltd., located in Leicestershire, England.

RIFLES: SxS

J & W TOLLEY SIDELOCK - various cals. between .375 H&H - .600 NE, true H&H style action, approx. 12-18 months delivery time.

Prices in this model range from $55,000-$70,000, depending on caliber, options, and/or special orders.

TORNADO

Currently manufactured by AseTekno located in Helsinki, Finland.

RIFLES: BOLT ACTION

TORNADO MODEL - .338 Lapua Mag. cal., unique straight line design with free floating barrel, 5 shot mag., pistol grip assembly is part of frame, limited importation into the U.S.

The factory should be contacted directy regarding domestic availability and pricing (see Trademark Index).

TOZ

Current manufacturer established in 1712, and located in Tula, Russia. Limited U.S. importation by Larry's Guns, located in Portland, ME. Previously imported by Tula Firearms, located in San Diego, CA. TOZ is an abbreviation for Tulsky Oruzheiny Zavod. Dealer sales.

TOZ manufactures a wide variety of quality O/U, SxS, single shot, and semi-auto shotguns, in addition to both rifles and combination guns. TOZ also provides a complete line of custom services, including elaborate inlays (gold, silver, and platinum) and wood carving. Please contact the importer directly for more information regarding the TOZ trademark, including current U.S. model availability and pricing.

GRADING - PPGS™	100%	98%	95%	90%	80%	70%	60%

PISTOLS: SINGLE SHOT

TOZ-35 FREE PISTOL - .22 LR cal., employs virtually every shooting refinement possible in a single shot target pistol, fully adj. target grips (with or w/o Rink laminate grip and forestock), limited mfg.

No MSR	$995	$875	$795	$725	$650	$575	$475	$375

TRADEWINDS

Previous importer located in Tacoma, WA.

RIFLES

HUSKY MODEL 5000 - .22-250 Rem., .243 Win., .270 Win., .308 Win., or .30-06 cal., bolt action, 23 3/4 in. barrel, adj. sight, removable mag., hand-checkered walnut stock.

	$325	$310	$290	$250	$225	$200	$175

NORAHAMMER 900 SERIES - .270 Win., .308 Win., or .30-06 cal., similar to Husky Model, 20 1/2 in. barrel, 6 lbs., 8 oz.

	$325	$310	$290	$250	$225	$200	$175

MODEL 311-A - .22 LR cal., bolt action, 5 shot, 22 1/2 in. barrel, folding leaf rear sight, walnut checkered stock.

	$180	$170	$150	$130	$120	$100	$85

MODEL 260-A - .22 LR cal., semi-auto, 5 shot, 22 1/2 in. barrel, 3 leaf folding sight, checkered walnut stock.

	$200	$190	$175	$150	$130	$120	$100

SHOTGUNS: SEMI-AUTO

MODEL H-170 - 12 ga., 2 3/4 in. chamber, 26 in. mod. or 28 in. full, recoil operated action, alloy receiver, 5 shot, tube mag., VR, checkered walnut stock.

	$275	$265	$250	$225	$200	$180	$150

TRADITIONS PERFORMANCE FIREARMS

Current importer located in Old Saybrook, CT. Distributor and dealer sales.

Traditions Performance Firearms imports a wide variety of quality Stefano Fausti shotguns and a complete line of single shot (Pedersoli mfg.) rifles and accessories. Traditions previously imported Emilio Rizzini shotguns from Italy, a semi-auto shotgun, and a line of Uberti mfg. black powder models. Please contact the company directly for more information (see Trademark Index).

Please refer to the *Blue Book of Modern Black Powder Arms* by John Allen & Dennis Adler (also online) for more information and prices on Traditions' lineup of modern black powder models.

RIFLES

Traditions currently imports the Pedersoli 1874 Sharps rifle, Remington rolling block sporting rifle, and a Springfield Trapdoor carbine. Prices start from $689 for the Remington rolling block reproduction in .30-30 Win. or .45-70 Govt. cal. The Springfield Trapdoor carbine has a $1,109 MSR, with 22 in. barrel and blued frame/barrel. The 1874 Sharps Standard rifle has a MSR of $1,039, $1,299 for the Deluxe Sharps rifle, $2,359 for the Deluxe hand engraved Sharps rifle, and $1,799 for the Quigley model. Traditions also imported Uberti black powder guns until 2002, including the Henry, Model 1866, and Model 1873. Prices ranged from $669-$969, depending on the model.

GRADING - PPGS™	100%	98%	95%	90%	80%	70%	60%

SHOTGUNS: O/U

CLASSIC FIELD SERIES - 12, 16 (disc. 2002), 20, 28 ga., or .410 bore, boxlock action, vent. barrels, vent. recoil pad, various configurations. Mfg. by Fausti, importation began 2000.

* ***Field Hunter*** - 12 or 20 ga., 3 in. chambers, 26 or 28 in. VR barrels with 2 choke tubes included, blue (disc.) or silver finished frame, SST, extractors, checkered walnut stock and forearm, blue finish, 6 lbs. 7 oz. - 7 lbs. 4 oz.

MSR $899	$795	$675	$575	$500	$450	$400	$375

  Subtract 5% for blue finish.

* ***Field I*** - 12, 20, 28 ga., or .410 bore, 3 in. chambers (except for 28 ga.), 26 or 28 in. VR barrels with fixed chokes, gold SST, extractors, coin finished frame with etched engraving, checkered walnut stock and forearm, blue finish, 6 lbs. 5 oz. - 7 lbs. 4 oz.

MSR $849	$715	$615	$535	$500	$450	$395	$375

  Add $50 for 28 ga. or .410 bore.

* ***Field II*** - 12, 16 (mfg. 2001 only), 20, 28 ga., or .410 bore, 3 in. chambers (12 and 20 ga. only), 26 or 28 in. VR barrels with 3 choke tubes (except 28 ga. and .410 bore) included, coin finished frame with etched engraving, gold SST, ejectors, checkered walnut stock and forearm, blue finish, 6 lbs. 5 oz. - 7 lbs. 4 oz.

MSR $1,039	$875	$750	$650	$575	$525	$475	$425

* ***Field II Combo*** - 20 ga. frame, includes 20 ga. and .410 bore 26 in. barrels with extra forearm, cased. New 2004.

MSR $1,649	$1,365	$1,125	$925	$825	$750	$675	$575

* ***Field III Gold*** - 12 or 20 (new 2003) ga., 3 in. chambers, 26 or 28 in. VR barrels with 3 choke tubes included, gold SST, ejectors, coin finished frame with 3 gold engraved pheasants, deluxe checkered walnut stock and forearm, blue finish, protective gun sock and molded hard gun case became standard 2002, approx. 7 lbs. 5 oz.

MSR $1,299	$1,125	$925	$825	$700	$600	$550	$495

  Add $100 for 20 ga.

CLASSIC UPLAND SERIES - 12 or 20 ga., boxlock action, gold SST, vent. recoil pad, various configurations. Mfg. by Fausti, protective gun sock and molded hard gun case became standard 2002. Imported 2000-2004.

* ***Upland II*** - 3 in. chambers, 24 or 26 in. VR barrels with 3 choke tubes included, blue engraved frame, straight English grip walnut stock with Schnabel forearm, 6 lbs. 3 oz. - 7 lbs. 3 oz.

	$995	$850	$725	$650	$575	$500	$425

  Last MSR was $1,119.

* ***Upland III*** - 3 in. chambers, 26 in. VR barrels with 3 choke tubes included, blue engraved frame with gold pheasant inlays, checkered pistol grip walnut stock with Schnabel forearm, 7 lbs. 3 oz.

	$1,300	$1,075	$950	$825	$725	$625	$525

  Last MSR was $1,519.

CLASSIC SERIES SPORTING CLAYS II - 12 ga. only, 28, 30 or 32 (new 2005) in. wide VR ported barrels with 4 extended choke tubes, SST, ejectors, coin finished frame with perimeter engraving, checkered walnut stock with Schnabel forearm, approx. 8 lbs.

MSR $1,299	$1,115	$915	$800	$700	$600	$500	$400

GRADING - PPGS™	100%	98%	95%	90%	80%	70%	60%

* *Classic Series Sporting Clays III* - 12 or 20 ga., 28 or 30 in. wide VR ported barrels, SST, ejectors, extended choke tubes, hand finished silver engraved frame with gold inlays, premium checkered walnut stock with Schnabel forearm, protective gun sock and molded hard gun case, approx. 7.5-8 lbs. Importation began 2002.

	MSR $1,649	$1,400	$1,175	$1,025	$900	$775	$675	$575

Add $50 for 20 ga.

REAL 16 SERIES - 16 ga., features proportioned 16 ga. receiver, 26 in. VR barrels with choke tubes, gold ST, silver engraved frame with or w/o gold snipes on sides, ejectors, checkered walnut stock with shock absorbing recoil pad and forearm, 6.75 lbs. Mfg. by Fausti. Importation began 2004.

	MSR $1,249	$1,150	$900	$800	$700	$600	$500	$425

Add $250 for gold receiver inlays with hardshell case.

MAG. 350 SERIES - 12 ga. only, 3 1/2 in. chambers, SST, ejectors, vent. recoil pad, various configurations.

* *Mag. Hunter II* - 28 in. vent. barrels with VR, matte black metal finish, matte finished checkered walnut stock and forearm, 3 choke tubes, sling swivels, 7 lbs. 2 oz. Importation disc. 2002.

	$700	$630	$575	$530	$480	$425	$400

Last MSR was $799.

* *Mag. Hunter 350* - 28 in. barrels, checkered walnut stock and forearm with sling swivels, matte finished engraved black frame, SST, ejectors. Importation began 2005.

	MSR $1,039	$875	$775	$675	$575	$525	$475	$425

* *Waterfowl II* - 28 in. vent. barrels with VR, engraved matte black frame with Advantage Wetlands wood and barrel coverage, 3 choke tubes, sling swivels, 7.25 lbs.

	MSR $1,199	$1,015	$865	$725	$600	$500	$425	$375

* *Turkey II* - 24 or 26 in. vent. barrels with VR, engraved matte black frame with Mossy Oak Breakup wood and barrel coverage, 3 choke tubes, sling swivels, approx. 7 lbs.

	MSR $1,199	$1,015	$865	$725	$600	$500	$425	$375

GOLD WING SERIES - 12 ga. only, boxlock action with patented 4 lock system, 28 in. barrels with choke tubes, choice of case colored or silver finished frame, checkered oil finished pistol grip stock with recoil pad and forearm, ST, approx. 7.5 lbs. Mfg. by E. Rizzini. Imported 2004 only.

* *Gold Wing II Silver* - silver finished frame with engraving.

	$1,575	$1,350	$1,025	$900	$800	$700	$600

Last MSR was $1,759.

* *Gold Wing III Silver* - similar to Gold Wing II Silver, except has gold snipes inlaid on frame, upgraded walnut stock and forearm.

	$1,925	$1,650	$1,350	$1,025	$925	$825	$725

Last MSR was $2,289.

Add $220 for engraved silver finished sideplates (Gold Wing SL III Silver) with gold bird inlays.
Add $250 for engraved silver finished sideplates (Gold Wing SL III) case colored frame with gold inlays.

SHOTGUNS: SxS

ELITE SERIES - 12, 20, 28 ga., or .410 bore, boxlock action, 3 in. chambers (except 28 ga.), fixed or multichoke tubes. Mfg. by Fausti, importation began 2000.

* *Elite Field Hunter* - 12 or 20 ga. only, 26 in. barrels with 4 choke tubes, gold SST, blue finish with etched engraving, checkered walnut stock and forearm, approx. 6 or 6 1/2 lbs. Importation disc. 2002.

	$890	$785	$700	$575	$525	$475	$425

Last MSR was $999.

GRADING - PPGS™	100%	98%	95%	90%	80%	70%	60%

* **Elite Hunter** - 12 or 20 ga. only, 26 or 28 in. barrels with 3 screw-in chokes, ST, extractors, coin finished frame with engraving, checkered walnut stock and forearm. Importation began 2003.

MSR $1,399	$1,185	$975	$850	$750	$650	$550	$450

* **Elite Field I** - 12, 20, 28 ga. or .410 bore, 26 in. barrels with fixed chokes, DT or ST, extractors, coin finished frame with etched engraving, checkered walnut stock and forearm, 5 lbs. 12 oz.-6 lbs. 8 oz.

MSR $1,099	$950	$800	$700	$600	$550	$500	$425

Add $250 for 28 ga. or .410 bore.

Add $150 for ST.

* **Elite Field III** - 28 ga. or .410 bore only, 26 in. barrels with fixed chokes, DT or gold SST, ejectors, coin finished frame with multiple gold inlays, deluxe checkered straight grip walnut stock and forearm, approx. 6 1/4 lbs. Importation disc. 2002.

	$1,825	$1,550	$1,275	$1,000	$875	$750	$625

Last MSR was $2,099.

Subtract approx. $100 for DT.

UPLANDER SERIES

UPLANDER SERIES - 12 or 20 ga., 26 or 28 in. barrels with choke tubes, boxlock action with or w/o sideplates and engraving, DT or ST, checkered oil finished straight grip English stock and splinter forearm. Mfg. by E. Rizzini. Imported 2004 only.

* **Uplander II Silver** - silver finished frame with engraving, 6 3/4 lbs.

	$1,825	$1,575	$1,225	$975	$875	$775	$700

Last MSR was $2,129.

* **Uplander III Silver** - similar to Uplander II Silver, except has gold snipes inlayed on engraved frame, upgraded walnut stock and forearm, includes long trigger guard.

	$2,400	$1,975	$1,675	$1,375	$1,100	$975	$875

Last MSR was $2,889.

* **Uplander IV Silver** - similar to Uplander III Silver, except has gold game birds on engraved sideplates, includes long trigger guard.

	$2,995	$2,500	$2,150	$1,775	$1,500	$1,275	$1,100

Last MSR was $3,439.

SHOTGUNS: SEMI-AUTO

AL 2100 SERIES - 12 or 20 ga., 3 in. chamber, various VR barrel lengths, lightweight alloy receiver, gas operation, choke tubes in most models. Imported from Europe 2000-2004.

* **ALS Field Model** - checkered walnut stock and forearm, blue metal, multichokes, also available in Youth Model, 5 lbs. 10 oz. - 6 lbs. 5 oz.

	$295	$265	$235	$200	$185	$170	$155

Last MSR was $349.

* **ALS Hunter Model** - similar to ALS Field Model, except has black synthetic stock and forearm, not available in Youth Model, approx. 6.25 lbs.

	$275	$245	$215	$185	$170	$155	$140

Last MSR was $319.

* **ALS Hunter Combo** - includes 26 or 28 in. VR barrel and choice of 24 in. rifled slug barrel and walnut or synthetic stock and forearm. Importation began 2002.

	$435	$385	$340	$305	$275	$250	$225

Last MSR was $499.

Add $30 for cantilever scope mount.

Add $30 for walnut stock and forearm.

GRADING - PPGS™	100%	98%	95%	90%	80%	70%	60%

✴ **ALS Slug Hunter Model** - similar to ALS Hunter Model, except is 12 ga. only, 24 in. rifled barrel with choice of rifle sights or cantilever scope mount, Turkish walnut or black synthetic stock and forearm. Importation began 2002.

		$300	$270	$235	$200	$185	$170	$155

Last MSR was $359.

Add $30 for cantilever scope mount or walnut stock and forearm.

✴ **ALS Turkey/Waterfowl Hunter Model** - 21 (Turkey Model with Mossy Oak Breakup, disc. 2001), 26 (Turkey) or 28 (Waterfowl Model with Advantage Wetlands) in. barrel, 100% camo coverage.

		$315	$280	$240	$200	$185	$170	$155

Last MSR was $379.

✴ **ALS 2100 Home Security Model** - 12 ga. only, 20 in. barrel bored IC, black synthetic stock and forearm, bead sights, 6 lbs. Importation began 2002.

		$275	$245	$215	$185	$170	$155	$140

Last MSR was $319.

TRENCH/RIOT SHOTGUNS

The following is a chronological listing beginning with WWI of the various U.S. commercial Riot and military Trench and Riot shotguns mfg. to date.

The publisher wishes to express thanks to the late Pat Redmond and Rick Crosier for the information in this section.

Some 100% values have been intentionally omitted in this section as they are seldomly seen or sold.

All Trench/Riot shotguns listed are in 12 ga. only.

SHOTGUNS: MILITARY TRENCH, WWI

WINCHESTER MODEL 1897 MILITARY TRENCH GUN - high-polish commercial blue finish, solid frame with 6 row ventilated handguard for bayonet attachment, walnut high comb stock with hard rubber buttplate (no cartouches in stock). Guns used by the U.S. Army for trench warfare in WWI, originally did not have military markings. A "U.S." and ordnance bomb were hand stamped on the right side of the receiver on trench guns kept in the Army's inventory after the war. Military markings were added in the 1920s to about 10% of the total production. Serial range 650,000-695,000.

Trench Gun	N/A	$3,500	$2,400	$1,400	$1,000	$800	$700
Trench Gun w/ military markings	N/A	$5,800	$4,350	$3,000	$1,800	$1,500	$1,250

REMINGTON MODEL 10 MILITARY TRENCH GUN - high polish commercial blue finish with wood handguard on top of barrel, separate bayonet adaptor attaches to front of barrel for bayonet attachment. "U.S." and ordnance bomb marked on left side receiver, stock is unmarked. Extremely rare and hard to find complete and in original condition. Trench gun barrel length is 22 in. as compared to 20 in. Riot gun. Prices quoted only for complete guns with wood handguard and bayonet adaptor. Serial range 160,000-165,000.

Trench Gun	N/A	$10,000	$8,500	$4,800	$3,500	$2,000	$1,800
Riot Gun	N/A	$1,900	$1,500	$1,200	$650	$500	$400

SHOTGUNS: MILITARY RIOT/TRENCH, WWII

ITHACA MODEL 37 MILITARY SHOTGUNS - rarest of all Trench shotguns, high polish commercial blue finish, RLB and ordnance bomb on left side of receiver, ordnance bomb on barrel, stocks not proofed, blue vent. handguard for bayonet attach-

GRADING - PPGS™	100%	98%	95%	90%	80%	70%	60%

ment, only 1,420 Trench guns were ordered in 1941. Ithaca supplied mostly long barrel martially marked shotguns. Serial range 49,000-62,000.

Trench Gun	N/A	$12,000	$10,000	$7,500	$4,000	$3,250	$2,350
Riot Gun	N/A	$3,000	$2,500	$2,000	$1,000	$750	$600
Long Barrel	N/A	$1,850	$1,500	$1,000	$750	$600	$500

REMINGTON MODEL 31 MILITARY SHOTGUNS
- commercial blue finish (high polish and flat blue finishes noted). Can be marked "U.S. Property" on receiver and/or barrel. Some examples noted with only ordnance mark on stock. Serial range 39,500-60,500.

Riot Gun	N/A	$1,800	$1,500	$1,000	$750	$650	$500
Long Barrel	N/A	$1,200	$1,000	$650	$500	$400	$300
Trainer w/ comp.	N/A	$1,300	$1,100	$750	$600	$500	$400

REMINGTON MODEL 11 MILITARY SHOTGUNS
- this is the most commonly found military shotgun. Examples of 5 shot and 3 shot Sportsman Model. Examples with plain or engraved receivers and plain or fancy checkered wood. Military marked with "U.S." and ordnance bomb on receiver and barrel. Later models are marked "Military Finish". These shotguns all have highly polished commercial blue finish and ordnance marked stocks. Serial range 450,000-500,000 and 700,000-711,000.

Riot Guns	N/A	$1,000	$650	$450	$400	$350	$300
Long Barrel	N/A	$850	$500	$350	$300	$250	$200

✳ *Riot Gun* - this configuration was sold by the government as surplus as late as the 1970s and can occasionally be found NIB with packing materials and instruction manual. Mint in factory box - $2,000.

SAVAGE MODEL 720 MILITARY SHOTGUNS
- appears identical to Remington Model 11. This was mfg. by Stevens/Savage in very limited quantities, plain and engraved receivers noted with high quality commercial blue finish. Stocks are unmarked and must have ramp sights to be original. Watch for altered guns made into Riots. Serial range 69,000-90,000.

Riot Gun	N/A	$1,850	$1,500	$1,100	$900	$750	$600
Long Barrel	N/A	$1,000	$800	$750	$500	$350	$300

STEVENS MODEL 620 MILITARY SHOTGUNS
- this was the current model being sold by Stevens and has a commercial blue finish, but not of the same quality as the other companies. Trench guns are equipped with handguards that have a definite purple/reddish color to the front and dark blue vent. shaft. Model 620s are much rarer than 520s and have "U.S." and ordnance bomb on receiver, ordnance bomb on barrel and unmarked stock. Serial range 1,000-30,000.

Trench Gun	N/A	$3,500	$2,800	$1,700	$1,200	$800	$600
Riot Gun	N/A	$900	$750	$450	$400	$350	$250
Long Barrels	N/A	$500	$400	$250	$200	$175	$150

STEVENS 520-30 MILITARY SHOTGUNS
- this model was resurrected due to available machinery and is the most commonly found Trench gun. Riot guns in mint condition are hard to find. Same finish as Model 620, "U.S." and ordnance bomb on receiver, ordnance bomb on barrel and no proofing on stocks, except for reworks. Trench gun has same style handguard as Model 620. Serial range 30,000-70,000.

Trench Gun	N/A	$3,000	$2,000	$1,500	$800	$600	$500
Riot Gun	N/A	$1,000	$750	$350	$300	$250	$200
Long Barrels	N/A	$500	$400	$225	$175	$150	$125

STEVENS SINGLE & DOUBLE BARREL MILITARY SHOTGUNS
- these guns were procured by the government from distributors and gun dealers. "U.S." and oversized flaming bomb hand stamped on left side receiver.

Single Barrel	N/A	$750	$600	$400	$350	$300	$250
Double Barrel	N/A	$950	$800	$600	$400	$350	$300

GRADING - PPGS™	100%	98%	95%	90%	80%	70%	60%

WINCHESTER MODEL 97 MILITARY SHOTGUNS

- takedown model, high polish commercial blue finish, finger groove walnut stock with hard rubber buttplate. All early riot and trenchguns have "WB" and ordnance bomb cartouches on the left side of stock, left side of receiver is machined marked "U.S." with or w/o ordnance bomb. All WB trenchguns have a 6 row ventilated handguard. All 97s will have ordnance bomb on top of barrel. Around serial range 950,000, receivers were all marked on left side with a machined "U.S." and ordnance bomb proofs, ventilated handguard was changed to a 4 row, GHD and ordnance bomb cartouches on left side of stock. During this transition, a very few examples with 6 row handguards have been found. Serial range 920,000-960,000.

	100%	98%	95%	90%	80%	70%	60%
Riot Gun w/ WB	N/A	$1,800	$1,500	$800	$600	$500	$400
Trench Gun w/ WB	N/A	$5,000	$3,950	$2,850	$1,500	$1,200	$1,000
Trench Gun w/ GHD	N/A	$4,800	$3,550	$2,700	$1,800	$1,200	$1,000
Long Barrel	N/A	$1,500	$1,200	$800	$650	$500	$400

WINCHESTER MODEL 12 MILITARY SHOTGUNS

- takedown model with improved hammerless receiver. These were made to supplement Model 97 production. Riot guns and Trench guns share same serial range. Finished in high polished commercial blue, Trench guns (only) were the only WWII shotguns to have factory parkerized finishes. All Model 12s have "U.S." and ordnance bomb on right side of receiver, ordnance bomb on barrel and ordnance mark and inspector initials on left side of stock. Trench guns have 4 row vent. handguards.

✱ *Blue finish* - serial range 926,000-1,030,000.

	100%	98%	95%	90%	80%	70%	60%
Trench Gun	N/A	$5,000	$3,800	$2,200	$1,600	$1,400	$1,000
Riot Gun	N/A	$1,850	$1,500	$750	$650	$500	$400
Long Barrel	N/A	$1,200	$1,000	$750	$600	$450	$350

✱ *Parkerized finish* - serial range 1,030,000-1,040,000.

	100%	98%	95%	90%	80%	70%	60%
Trench Gun	N/A	$5,000	$3,800	$3,000	$2,000	$1,500	$1,200

WINCHESTER MODEL 37 MILITARY SHOTGUNS

- high polish, commercial blue, single barrel, procured from Winchester. "U.S." and ordnance bomb proofmarks were applied to left side of receiver. Winchester records show shipment of 5,410 guns to the military - very few examples of this model have ever been found.

	100%	98%	95%	90%	80%	70%	60%
Single Barrel	N/A	$2,000	$1,500	$1,200	$1,000	$750	$500

SHOTGUNS: MILITARY RIOT/TRENCH, VIETNAM

ITHACA MODEL 37

- parkerized finish with "U.S." marks on right side of receiver. Receiver and barrel are also marked "P". Serial range, applied on gun upside-down, is from S1,000-S23,500. Used in the Vietnam era. A very few original Trench guns with parkerized handguards have been noted.

	100%	98%	95%	90%	80%	70%	60%
Riot Gun	N/A	$2,000	$1,500	$800	$600	$500	$400
Trench Gun	N/A	$4,500	$3,500	$2,500	$2,000	$1,800	$1,200

SAVAGE 77E

- parkerized finish with sling swivels and red rubber buttpad. "U.S." marked on right side of receiver and military "P" proofmark on receiver and barrel. Hard to find in excellent condition.

	100%	98%	95%	90%	80%	70%	60%
Riot Gun	N/A	$1,000	$750	$400	$300	$250	$225

WINCHESTER MODEL 1200

- parkerized barrel, mag. tube, and bayonet adapter with U.S. marking on barrel. Aluminum receiver with black or matte type finish, "U.S." is marked under serial number. Very rare as few examples have been released by the government due to its continued use by military forces.

	100%	98%	95%	90%	80%	70%	60%
Trench Gun	N/A	$2,950	$2,500	$1,200	$800	$600	$500

SHOTGUNS: RIOT/TRENCH GUN, COMMERCIAL SALES

WINCHESTER MODEL 12 RIOT

- thousands mfg. between late 1930s-1960s.

	100%	98%	95%	90%	80%	70%	60%
	N/A	$550	$450	$395	$350	$295	$240

GRADING - PPGS™	100%	98%	95%	90%	80%	70%	60%

WINCHESTER MODEL 97 - commercial high polish blue, changed from solid frame to takedown in 1935. Trench guns made through 1945 and Riot gun mfg. continued until 1960s.

* *Solid Frame* - Serial range 700,000+.

	100%	98%	95%	90%	80%	70%	60%
Trench Gun	N/A	$2,500	$2,000	$1,500	$1,200	$1,000	$750
Riot Gun	N/A	$1,000	$900	$750	$600	$500	$300

* *Takedown* - Serial range 800,000+.

	100%	98%	95%	90%	80%	70%	60%
Trench Gun	N/A	$2,500	$2,000	$1,300	$1,100	$900	$600
Riot Gun	N/A	$800	$700	$600	$500	$400	$300

REMINGTON MODEL 10 - commercial high polish blue, sold in the 1920s to various government and banking agencies.

	100%	98%	95%	90%	80%	70%	60%
Riot Gun	N/A	$400	$350	$300	$275	$250	$200

REMINGTON MODEL 11 - made in 1930s for law enforcement use.

	100%	98%	95%	90%	80%	70%	60%
Riot Gun	N/A	$400	$350	$300	$275	$250	$200

MODEL 31R RIOT GUN - similar to 31A, with 20 in. barrel.

	100%	98%	95%	90%	80%	70%	60%
	N/A	$300	$200	$175	$150	$130	$110

ITHACA MODEL 37 - parkerized models made in 1960s for police agencies and commercial sales.

	100%	98%	95%	90%	80%	70%	60%
Trench Gun	N/A	$1,200	$900	$700	$600	$500	$400
Riot Gun	N/A	$275	$250	$225	$175	$150	$125

U.S. MILITARY SHOTGUN ACCESSORIES

WWI BAYONETS - military acceptance proofs, leather scabbards, and two variations of attachments to belt, two-toned blue handle and parkerized blade.

* *Winchester 1917 date*
Prices range from $150-$400, depending on original condition.
* *Remington 1917-1918 dates*
Prices range from $125-$300, depending on original condition.

LEATHER SLING - WWI dates, w/ brass hardware.
Prices range from $75-$150, depending on original condition. Mint condition will bring $250.

SHOTGUN SHELL POUCHES

* *32 round pouch w/ sling*
Prices range approx. $500, depending on original condition.
* *12 round pouches dated 1921-1922*
Prices range approx. $400, depending on original condition.

WWII BAYONETS - same as from WWI, but have plastic scabbard w/ large ordnance bomb, or orginal WWI leather scabbard.
Prices range approx. $125-$300, depending on original condition.

LEATHER SLING - WWII dates, w/ steel hardware.
Prices range from $50-$125, depending on original condition. Mint condition will bring $300.

SHOTGUN SHELL POUCHES - 12 round pouches with contract dates from 1960s-1990s.
Prices range from $50-$125.

SHOTGUN SHELL POUCHES - 12 round pouches dated 1942-45, various manufacturers, watch for recent 1943 JQMD fake pouches - they have extreme two-tone colors.
Prices range approx. $350, depending on original condition.

VIETNAM BAYONETS - new contracts to supplement large quantities of shotguns being sent to Vietnam, black plastic handles, green plastic scabbards, marked M-1917.
Gen. Cut - mfg. by General Cutlery prices range from $150-$250.
CA mfg. by Canadian Arsenal prices range from $150-$300.

TRIPLE ACTION LLC

Current handgun manufacturer located in Logan, UT.

PISTOLS: SINGLE SHOT

Triple Action LLC is planning to manufacture a .50 BMG single shot pistol with 13.2 in. barrel, with muzzle brake and nitrogen recoil controller. Construction materials include titanium and aircraft grade aluminum, and the weight is scheduled to be 10 or 12 lbs.

As this edition went to press, please contact the manufacturer directly regarding more information on this pistol, including availability and pricing.

TRISTAR SPORTING ARMS, LTD.

Current importer established in 1994, and located in N. Kansas City, MO. Distributor and dealer sales.

Tristar currently imports Australian International Arms (see A section), Breda (see B section), E. Rizzini (see R section), Valmet (see V section), the Turkish-made Diana TR Series and Spanish-made O/U (Silver Series) and SxS (Basque/411 Series), in addition to Uberti and Pedersoli reproductions.

REPRODUCTIONS: REVOLVER, SAA

REGULATOR - .357 Mag. or .45 LC cal., 4 3/4 or 5 1/2 in. barrel, choice of brass or steel backstrap/trigger guard, two-piece smooth walnut grips. Mfg. by Uberti.

MSR $389	$340	$295	$255	$235	$210	$190	$170

Add $36 for Regulator DLX with steel backstrap/trigger guard (.45 LC only).

STALLION - .17 HMR/.17 Mach 2 cal., 5 1/2, 7 1/2, or 9 in. barrel. Mfg. by Uberti. Importation began 2005.

MSR $465	$395	$350	$300	$265	$235	$200	$180

Add $94 for Stallion DLX with steel backstrap/trigger guard.

REPRODUCTIONS: RIFLES

HENRY LEVER ACTION - .44-40 WCF or .45 LC cal., brass frame only, 18 1/2 (Trapper) or 24 1/4 (rifle) in. barrel. Mfg. by Uberti.

MSR $1,176	$985	$825	$725	$625	$525	$425	$325

MODEL 1866 LEVER ACTION - .38 Spl., .44-40 WCF or .45 LC cal., 19 (Yellowboy), 20, or 24 1/4 in. barrel. Mfg. by Uberti.

MSR $911	$785	$675	$585	$500	$450	$400	$350

Add $46 for Sport configuration (20 or 24 in. barrel).

MODEL 1873 SPORT LEVER ACTION - .44-40 WCF or .45 LC cal., 24 1/4 or 30 in. barrel. Mfg. by Uberti.

MSR $1,090	$935	$775	$665	$585	$500	$425	$325

Add $45 for 30 in. barrel.

MODEL 1885 SINGLE SHOT HIGH WALL - .45-70 Govt. cal., 28 in. barrel. Mfg. by Uberti.

MSR $852	$725	$595	$535	$475	$400	$325	$250

MODEL 1874 SHARPS - .45-70 Govt. cal., 28, 32, or 34 in. barrel, double set triggers, adj. rear sight, case hardened frame, approx. 10 lbs. Mfg. by Pedersoli. Importation disc. 2004.

$735	$650	$575	$500	$450	$400	$350

Last MSR was $844.

Add $41-$67 for Bridgeport Model with higher sideplate.

GRADING - PPGS™	100%	98%	95%	90%	80%	70%	60%

RIFLES: BOLT ACTION

PEE-WEE .22 - .22 LR cal., single shot, manual cocking bolt, 16 1/2 in. barrel, steel construction, blue finish with adj. rear leaf sight, 12 in. LOP, uncheckered walnut stock with Monte Carlo, 2 3/4 lbs. Limited mfg. 1998 only.

	$170	$140	$130	$120	$110	$100	$90

Last MSR was $189.

SHOTGUNS: LEVER ACTION

Tristar also imports the ADI Model 1887. Please refer to the Australian International Arms listing for more information and current pricing.

MODEL 1887 - 12 ga. only, patterned after the Winchester Model 1887, "WRA Co." logo on left side of receiver, 30 in. barrel, 5 shot tube mag., blue finish, 2-piece walnut forearm and rounded pistol grip stock, 8 lbs. Limited importation 1997-98.

	$535	$475	$435	$400	$360	$330	$295

Last MSR was $599.

SHOTGUNS: O/U

Tristar also currently imports a wide variety of Emilio Rizzini O/U shotguns. Please refer to the Emilio Rizzini section for more information.

MODEL 300 - 12 ga. only, 3 in. chambers, under-lug action, double triggers, extractors, etched engraving, standard checkered Turkish walnut stock and forearm, 26 or 28. in. VR barrels with fixed chokes. Imported 1994-98 from Turkey.

	$375	$330	$300	$275	$250	$225	$200

Last MSR was $429.

MODEL 333 FIELD GRADE - 12 or 20 ga., 3 in. chambers, engraved boxlock frame with satin finish, SST, ejectors, fancy grade Turkish walnut with hand-cut checkering, 26 (12 ga. only), 28, or 30 in. VR barrels, supplied with 5 choke tubes, approx. 7 1/2 lbs. Imported from Turkey 1994-98.

	$735	$625	$550	$500	$450	$400	$360

Last MSR was $800.

✳ **Model 333 Sporting Clays** - similar to Model 333 Field Grade, except has sporting recoil pad, elongated forcing cones, 28 or 30 in. ported barrels with extended stainless steel choke tubes, 7 3/4 lbs. Imported from Turkey 1994-97.

	$825	$725	$625	$550	$500	$450	$400

Last MSR was $900.

✳ **Model 333SCL Ladies Sporting Clays** - similar to Model 333 Sporting Clays, except is fitted with special ladies stock, 28 in. barrels only with four choke tubes. Imported from Turkey. Disc. 1997.

	$825	$725	$625	$550	$500	$450	$400

Last MSR was $900.

MODEL 330 - 12 or 20 ga., 3 in. chambers, etched satin finished frame, SST, extractors, fixed chokes, checkered standard Turkish walnut stock and forearm, approx. 7 1/2 lbs. Imported from Turkey 1994-99.

	$475	$415	$375	$325	$295	$280	$265

Last MSR was $549.

✳ **Model 330D** - similar to Model 330, except has ejectors and three choke tubes. Imported from Turkey 1994-99.

	$615	$525	$495	$450	$400	$360	$330

Last MSR was $689.

GRADING - PPGS™	100%	98%	95%	90%	80%	70%	60%

SILVER HUNTER - 12 or 20 ga., 3 in. chambers, under-lug action, SST, extractors, silver receiver with etched engraving, standard checkered Turkish walnut stock and forearm, 26 or 28. in. VR barrels with choke tubes, 7 lbs. Imported from Spain 2002-2004.

	$615	$500	$450	$400	$365	$335	$300

Last MSR was $737.

SILVER II - 12, 16, or 20 ga., similar to Silver Hunter, except has ejectors. Importation from Spain began 2002.

MSR $825	$675	$535	$475	$410	$365	$335	$300

SILVER CLASSIC - 12 or 20 (new 2002) ga., similar to Silver II, except has case colored receiver and long forcing cones. Imported from Spain 2002-2004.

	$750	$625	$525	$465	$415	$365	$315

Last MSR was $899.

SILVER SPORTING - 12 ga., similar to Silver II, except has 3 in. chambers and 28 or 30 in. ported barrels with broadway VR, 7 lbs., 6 oz. Imported from Spain 2002-2004.

	$750	$625	$525	$465	$415	$365	$315

Last MSR was $899.

WS/OU MAGNUM - 12 ga., 3 1/2 in. chambers, ejectors, SST, 28 in. VR barrels with choke tubes, 100% Skyline Excel camo (new 2003) coverage (except frame) or matte black metal and checkered black finished walnut stock and forearm. 7 lbs. 2 oz. Imported 2002-2004.

	$650	$550	$475	$425	$395	$375	$350

Last MSR was $779.

Add $84 for Skyline Excel camo coverage.

SHOTGUNS: SxS

MODEL 311 - 12 or 20 ga., 3 in. chambers, Greener boxlock action, 26 or 28 in. barrels, standard checkered Turkish walnut stock and forearm, DTs, supplied with five choke tubes, white chrome frame finish, extractors. Imported 1994-97 from Turkey.

	$535	$475	$435	$400	$360	$330	$295

Last MSR was $599.

* **Model 311R** - 12 or 20 ga., 20 in. cylinder bore barrels designed for cowboy re-enactment shooting or home defense, other features similar to Model 311. Imported from Turkey. Disc. 1997.

	$375	$325	$300	$275	$250	$225	$200

Last MSR was $429.

MODEL 411 - 12, 16 (mfg. 1999-2004), 20 (disc. 2004), 28 (disc. 2004) ga., or .410 bore (disc. 2004), 3 in. chambers (except 28 ga.), 26 or 28 (12 ga. only) in. barrels with (12 and 20 ga.) or w/o (28 ga. or .410 bore) choke tubes, boxlock action, DT, extractors, steel shot compatible, case colored frame, checkered walnut stock and forearm with recoil pad, 6 1/2-7 1/4 lbs, mfg. by Luciano Rota (R.F.M.). Importation began 1998.

MSR $849	$710	$650	$575	$525	$450	$400	$350

* **Model 411D** - similar to Model 411, except not available in 16 ga., features engraved case colored frame, single trigger, ejectors, and English style stock, 6 1/2-7 1/4 lbs. New 1999.

MSR $1,110	$915	$800	$700	$600	$500	$400	$325

* **Model 411F** - 12, 20 (disc. 2004), 28 (disc. 2004) ga., or .410 bore (disc. 2004), 3 in. chambers (except 28 ga.), silver engraved sideplates, gold SST, English straight stock with cut checkering, ejectors, choke tubes (except for 28 ga. and .410 bore), 6 1/2-7 1/4 lbs. Importation began 2000.

MSR $1,608	$1,425	$1,200	$995	$850	$725	$650	$575

GRADING - PPGS™	100%	98%	95%	90%	80%	70%	60%

✱ **Model 411R Coach Gun** - 12 or 20 ga., 3 in. chambers, hammerless, 20 in. fixed choke (C/C) barrels, case colored frame, DT, extractors, 6-6 1/2 lbs. Imported 1999-2003.

	$650	$575	$525	$475	$425	$375	$325

Last MSR was $745.

This model was designed for both cowboy competition shooting and quail hunting.

GENTRY - 12, 16, 20, 28 ga. or .410 bore, 3 in. chambers, engraved coin finished boxlock action with sideplates, SST, extractors, 20 (Gentry Coach Model, 12 or 20 ga. only), 26, or 28 in. barrels with matted rib and three choke tubes (fixed chokes on 16, 20 ga. and .410 bore) checkered pistol grip stock and semi-beavertail forearm, approx. 6.5 lbs. Importation began 2003.

MSR $824	$685	$575	$485	$435	$380	$325	$275

Add $14 for 20, 28 ga. or .410 bore.
Subtract $14 for Gentry Coach Model (hammerless, disc. 2003).

BRITTANY - 12 or 20 ga., 3 in. chambers, boxlock action, case colored frame, SST, ejectors, 26 in. barrels with matted rib and three choke tubes, checkered straight grip stock and semi-beavertail forearm, approx. 6.5 lbs. Importation began 2003.

MSR $943	$775	$625	$550	$475	$425	$375	$325

BRITTANY SPORTING - 12 or 20 ga., 3 in. chambers, boxlock action with side-plates, engraved case colored frame, SST, ejectors, 28 in. barrels with matted rib and three choke tubes, checkered pistol grip stock and semi-beavertail forearm, approx. 6.75 lbs. Importation began 2003.

MSR $1,049	$875	$725	$625	$525	$475	$425	$375

DERBY CLASSIC - 12 or 20 ga., 3 in. chambers, true sidelock case colored action, DT, ejectors, checkered straight grip stock and splinter forearm, 7.75 lbs. Mfg. by Zabala Hermanos in Spain beginning 2002.

MSR $1,550	$1,300	$1,075	$900	$775	$675	$600	$525

SHOTGUNS: SEMI-AUTO

PHANTOM SERIES - 12 ga. only, 3 or 3 1/2 (Phantom Field/Synthetic Mag. only) in. chamber, various VR (except Phantom HP) barrel lengths with choke tubes, available in Field (blue metal finish, gold accents, and checkered walnut stock and forearm), Synthetic (black non-glare matte metal and flat black synthetic stock and forearm), or HP (home security with open sights, matte finished metal, and synthetic stock and forearm), 6 lbs. 13 oz.-7 lbs. 6 oz. Italian mfg., limited importation 2001-2002.

	$385	$350	$315	$285	$265	$245	$225

Last MSR was $425.

Subtract $44 for Phantom Synthetic.
Add $74 for 3 1/2 in. Mag. (Field).
Add $44 for Mag. Synthetic.

DIANA SERIES - 12, 20, or 28 (disc. 2003) ga., 3 or 3 1/2 in. chamber, various VR barrel lengths with choke tubes, available in Marine (19 in. barrel), Field (blue metal finish, gold accents, and checkered walnut stock and forearm), Synthetic (black non-glare matte metal and flat black synthetic stock and forearm), Slug (24 in. rifled barrel with iron sights), or camo model (100% camo coverage), 6.75-7 lbs. Importation began 2003.

MSR $385	$330	$300	$275	$250	$225	$200	$185

Add $14 for Field Grade.
Add $26 for 20 ga. or Youth Model.
Add $94 for Synthetic 3 1/2 in. chamber.
Add $150 for camo model (3 1/2 in. chamber).
Add $25 for Slug Model (24 in. rifled barrel, disc. 2004).
Add $34 for Marine Model with 19 in. barrel and choke tubes (mfg. 2004).

This model is designed by CD Europe of Italy and manufactured in Turkey.

GRADING - PPGS™	100%	98%	95%	90%	80%	70%	60%

SHOTGUNS: SLIDE ACTION

DIANA SERIES - 12 or 20 ga., 3 or 3 1/2 in. chamber, choice of Field, camo Mag., or black synthetic configuration, dual slide rails, 20, 24, or 28 (VR) in. barrel with choke tubes, 5 shot mag., crossbolt safety behind trigger, 6-7 lbs. Imported 2004 only.

	$160	$140	$120	$100	$90	$80	$70

Last MSR was $188.

Add $51 for Field or synthetic Mag.

Add $31 for synthetic stock/forearm.

Add $147 for Mag. camo in 12 ga., or $94 for Mag. w/o camo.

TROMIX CORPORATION

Current rifle manufacturer established in 1999, and located in Broken Arrow, OK. Dealer or consumer direct sales.

RIFLES: SEMI-AUTO

Tromix manufactures AR-15 style rifles. Tromix lower receivers bear no caliber designation. Serialization begins at TR-0001.

The models listed below are also available with many custom options - please contact the company.

TR-15 SLEDGEHAMMER - .44 Rem. Mag. (disc. 2001), .440 Cor-Bon Mag., .458 SOCOM, .475 Tremor, and .50 AE cal., 16.75 in. barrel, other lengths and weights available by custom order. New 1999.

MSR $1,350		$1,175	$975	$850	$775	$700	$650	$600

TR-15 TACKHAMMER - various cals., 24 in. bull barrel, other lengths and weights available by custom order. New 1999.

MSR $1,350		$1,175	$975	$850	$775	$700	$650	$600

TRUVELO ARMOURY

Current manufacturer located in Midrand, South Africa. Truvelo Armoury is a division of the Truvelo Manufacturers (Pty) Ltd. No current U.S. importation.

Truvelo Armoury manufactures a variety of firearms, including a shotgun, hunting and sporting rifles, and ADP pistols. Currently, they have several bolt action rifles available in the $700-$1,500 range. Sporting and hunting rifles are available in the $3,000-$4,800 range. The Neostead slide action shotgun retails for $1,450. Please contact the factory directly (see Trademark Index) for more information.

TULA ARMS PLANT

Current manufacturer located in Tula, Russia. Limited U.S. importation. Previously distributed by Tulsky Souvenir, LLC, located in San Diego, CA.

The Tula Arms Plant is one of the world's oldest and largest gun manufacturing facilities. Many millions of military weapons have been manufactured at this facility, and currently, Tula is getting more aggressive in providing sporting arms to western countries. For more information and current pricing on the wide variety of firearms produced by this world-famous manufacturing facility, please contact the factory directly (see Trademark Index).

TURKISH FIREARMS CORPORATION

Please refer to the Huglu section in this text.

DOUG TURNBULL RESTORATION, INC.

Current firearms restoration company located in Bloomfield, NY, that specializes in the accurate recreation of historic metal finishes on period firearms, from initial polishing to final finishing. These finishes include bone charcoal color case hardened, charcoal bluing, and Nitre bluing.

GRADING - PPGS™	100%	98%	95%	90%	80%	70%	60%

Turnbull Restoration has performed extensive restoration work on Colt 1911s, A.H. Foxes, Parkers, L.C. Smiths, and lever action Winchesters (including upgrades and antique finishes to duplicate natural aging). These guns have been provided with documentation.

Please contact the company directly for more information on the wide variety of services available (see Trademark Index).

REVOLVERS: SAA

Turnbull Restoration has reworked current Colt SAAs to look like a pre-1920 SAA. These guns have special, factory assigned serial numbers beginning with 000DT. The retail price is $2,200, not including many options. Additonally, the company produced a special run of Colt SAAs in .45 LC, 5 1/2 in. barrel configuration, that are serial numbered EHBM01-EHBM50. These guns have color case hardened frames with charcoal bluing, large flutes (1st Generation), beveled cylinder, and ejector housing. Retail price was $2,150.

GEORGE PATTON SERIES COLT SAA - .45 LC cal., patterned after Patton's original factory engraved SAA, 4.75 in. barrel, Helfricht style engraving by John Adams & Son, ivory grips with carved eagle on left and "GSP" monogram on right, silver plated finish, ser. nos. GP01-GP10. 10 mfg. 2003 - sold out early 2004.

$5,500 $4,250 $2,995

Last MSR was $5,500.

A portion of the proceeds benefited the Doug Turnbull Firearms Conservation Laboratory at the National Firearms Museum.

CATTLE BRAND COLT SAA - .45 LC cal., 5.5 in. barrel, two-piece ivory grips with blind screw hole, 3/4 engraving coverage by John Adams & Son, bone color case hardening and charcoal blue (ser. nos. CB01B-CB10B) or silver plated (ser. nos. CB01S-CB10S) finish, guns sold in sets of two, owner's personal cattle brand or initials can be scrimshawed on one side of grips, includes fitted hardwood case. New 2003.

Current MSR is $7,995.

A portion of the proceeds will benefit the Doug Turnbull Firearms Conservation Laboratory at the National Firearms Museum.

THEODORE ROOSEVELT COLT SAA - .44-40 WCF cal., 7.5 in. barrel, one-piece ivory grips with carved "TR" monogram on right grip and buffalo on left grip, black powder style frame, Nimschke style pattern engraving by John Adams & Son, gold-plated hammer, cylinder, and ejector rod housing, rest of gun silver plate, ser. nos. TR01-TR25, includes French style fitted monogrammed case and factory letter. 25 mfg. 2003.

Current MSR is $7,500.

A portion of the proceeds will benefit the Doug Turnbull Firearms Conservation Laboratory at the National Firearms Museum.

COWBOY CLASSIC SAA - .45 LC cal. standard, other cals. available, 4 3/4, 5 1/2, or 7 1/2 in. barrel, hard rubber grips standard with many options available, bone charcoal color case hardening and carbona bluing, ser. no. range 001DT-999DT. New 2004.

Current MSR is $1,150.

A portion of the proceeds will benefit the Doug Turnbull Firearms Conservation Laboratory at the National Firearms Museum.

RIFLES

Turnbull Restorations also announced the introduction of its Big Bore Classics line during late 2003, utilizing either new or original Winchester and Browning Model 1886 receivers. Chamberings include: .45-70, .45-90, .450 Alaskan (new 2005), .50-110 (.50 Express), and .50 Alaskan. Many metal options and wood choices are available - please contact the company directly for more information on these custom rifles.

U SECTION

U.S. ARMS COMPANY

Previous manufacturer located in Riverhead, NY.

GRADING - PPGS™	100%	98%	95%	90%	80%	70%	60%

REVOLVERS: SINGLE ACTION

ABILENE .357 MAG. - 6 shot, 4 5/8, 5 1/2, or 6 1/2 in. barrel, adj. sights, transfer bar ignition, smooth walnut grips, blue finish only. Mfg. 1976-83.

	$325	$275	$240	$200	$185	$170	$155

✻ *Abilene .357 Mag. Stainless Steel* - similar to Abilene, only in stainless steel.

	$350	$285	$240

ABILENE .44 MAG. - 7 1/2 and 8 1/2 in. barrel, unfluted cylinder blue finish only, otherwise similar to .357 Mag.

	$325	$265	$240	$220	$200	$165	$150

✻ *Abilene .44 Mag. Stainless Steel* - similar to Abilene .44 Mag., only stainless steel.

	$375	$330	$290

U.S. GENERAL TECHNOLOGIES, INC.

Previous manufacturer located in S. San Francisco, CA circa 1994-96.

RIFLES: SEMI-AUTO

P-50 SEMI-AUTO - .50 BMG cal., includes 10 shot detachable mag., folding bipod, muzzle brake, matte black finish. Mfg. 1995-96.

	$5,600	$4,950	$4,475	$3,975	$3,500	$3,050	$2,600

Last MSR was $5,995.

U.S. HISTORICAL SOCIETY

Previous organization which marketed historically significant firearms reproductions until April, 1994. Located in Richmond, VA. Most firearms were manufactured by the Williamsburg Firearms Manufactory and the Virginia Firearms Manufactory.

On April 1, 1994, the Antique Arms Divison of the U.S. Historical Society was acquired by America Remembers located in Mechanicsville, VA. America Remembers affiliates include the Armed Forces Commemorative Society, American Heroes & Legends, and the United States Society of Arms and Armor. Issues that were not fully subscribed are now available through America Remembers (please refer to listing in A section).

The information listed below represents current information up until America Remembers acquired the Antique Arms Division of the U.S. Historical Society.

Please refer to the *Blue Book of Modern Black Powder Arms* by John Allen & Dennis Adler (also online) for more information and prices on U.S. Historical Society's modern black powder models.

Manufacturer	Model	Quantity	Year	Issue Price
PISTOLS: SPECIAL EDITIONS				
Uberti	Secret Service Museum Edition	500	1988	$2,750
Uberti	Secret Service Investigator's Edition	1,000	1988	$1,250
N/A	George Jones SAA	950	1993	$1,675
N/A	Richard Petty Silver Edition SAA	1,000	1992	$1,675
Colt	King Richard Hand Engraved Colt .45 SAA	100	1993	$4,500
N/A	Charlton Heston SAA	500	1993	$1,850

Manufacturer	Model	Quantity	Year	Issue Price
N/A	Hopalong Cassidy Cowboy Edition SAA	950	1993	$1,675
Colt	Hopalong Cassidy Premier Colt Edition	100	1993	$4,500
Colt	Mel Torme Colt SAA	100	1992	$4,500
N/A	Roy Rogers Cowboy Edition SAA	2,500	1990	$1,350
N/A	Roy Rogers Premier Edition SAA	250	1990	$4,500
Armi San Marco	U.S. Marshals Wyatt Earp SAA	2,500	1991	$1,250
N/A	National Cowboy Hall of Fame SAA	1,000	1992	$1,600
Colt	Interpol Colt SAA	154	1991	$4,500
Springfield	Eisenhower .45 Auto	1,000	1992	$1,675
Colt	"Don't Give Up the Ship" Model .45 Auto	1,997	1993	$1,485
Colt	American Eagle Colt .45 Auto	2,500	1993	$1,950

REVOLVERS: MINIATURE SPECIAL EDITIONS

Manufacturer	Model	Quantity	Year	Issue Price
Uberti	SA Army Presidential Edition	1,500	1988	$1,550
Uberti	SA Army Classic Edition	1,500	1988	$575

SHOTGUNS: SPECIAL EDITIONS

Manufacturer	Model	Quantity	Year	Issue Price
Bertuzzi	Chuck Yeager Tribute	100	1989	$12,500
Reanto Telo	Arnold Palmer Tribute	100	1990	$9,750
Antonio Zoli	Christopher Columbus Tribute	200	1991	$12,500

U.S. M1 CARBINES/RIFLES

Previous manufacture for the military by various makers listed below.

GRADING - PPGS™	100%	98%	95%	90%	80%	70%	60%

CARBINES: SEMI-AUTO

U.S. M1 CARBINE (MILITARY & COMMERCIAL) - .30 Carbine cal., 18 in. barrel, 15 or 30 shot box mag., wood stocked, two- or four-position aperture rear, blade front sight with protective ears, with or without bayonet lug. This weapon was designed by Winchester for the U.S. government, over 6 million were produced by 10 different companies, while Plainfield was mfg. after the war for civilian sales. It is a gas operated lightweight carbine that was also used by other countries' armed forces. Makers and values as follows. Values are for original, unmodified carbines, with proper parts makers and stock cartouches. Some variations have the type III barrel band.

Values below are for original mfg. only, not recent imports (usually denoted by visible import markings and/or alterations to original finish).

Add 150% for Type I original guns with flip rear sight and no bayonet lug.

Add 120% for Type II original guns with adj. rear sight and no bayonet lug.

Add 100% for Type III original guns with adj. rear sight and bayonet lug.

Subtract 30% for original finish guns that have been changed back to the original configuration by switching parts.

Subtract 50% for modified guns with adj. sight and bayonet lug.

	100%	98%	95%	90%	80%	70%	60%
Underwood	$850	$675	$495	$400	$350	$300	$275
S.G. Saginaw	$825	$650	$475	$400	$350	$300	$275
Quality Hardware	$850	$675	$495	$415	$370	$325	$295
Nat'l Postal Meter	$950	$775	$525	$425	$375	$325	$295
IBM	$950	$775	$525	$425	$370	$325	$295
Standard Products	$800	$650	$495	$415	$370	$325	$295
Inland	$850	$675	$495	$415	$370	$325	$295

GRADING - PPGS™	100%	98%	95%	90%	80%	70%	60%

An Inland presentation carbine with white stock was also mfg. in limited quantities for military service organizations (i.e. V.F.W., American Legion, etc.). Values for original guns are currently in the $1,750-$2,000 range.

SG Grand Rapids	$950	$775	$525	$425	$375	$325	$295
Winchester	$1,150	$850	$750	$550	$425	$350	$325
Irwin Pedersen	$1,700	$1,400	$995	$850	$775	$675	$580
Rockola	$995	$925	$700	$525	$425	$350	$325
Plainfield							
(Commercial only)	$195	$175	$160	$150	$140	$130	$120

✹ *TI* - values assume original guns with flip rear sight and no bayonet lug.

	$4,000	$3,500	$3,000	$2,500	$2,150	$1,750	$1,450

✹ *TII* - values assume original guns with adj. rear sight and no bayonet lug.

	$3,200	$2,800	$2,400	$2,100	$1,750	$1,450	$1,150

✹ *TIII* - values assume original guns with adj. rear sight and bayonet lug.

	$2,600	$2,400	$2,000	$1,750	$1,500	$1,250	$1,000

M1 A1 PARATROOPER CARBINE - .30 Carbine cal., mfg. by Inland - WWII production, folding stock, crossed cannon proofed on bottom, 140,000 mfg. between 1942-45. Stock folds to 26 1/2 in. overall.

	$2,400	$2,000	$1,500	$1,250	$950	$750	$650

Beware of after-market fakes.

RIFLES: SEMI-AUTO

Add 50% for original early Type I guns (identified by gas trap barrels up to ser. no. 50,000 - all Springfield mfg.).

Add 10% for Type II guns (identified by gas port barrels and ser. nos. over 50,000).

M1 GARAND - .30-06 cal., semi-auto, 8 shot en bloc clip fed, gas operated, adj. aperture sight, wooden stock. Made 1937-57 by Springfield, Winchester, H&R, and International Harvester.

	$1,250	$1,050	$900	$800	$700	$600	$500

Add 200% for pre-WWII Winchester or Springfield mfg.

Add 100% for WWII date (serialization starts at approx. 400,000).

Subtract 50% if rewelded or 20% if mismatched.

✹ *M1-C or M1-D Sniper* - with scope and mounts (beware of fakes and rewelds with boxes and papers).

M1-D	$3,800	$3,400	$2,800	$2,200	$1,725	$1,350	$1,150
M1-C	N/A	N/A	$3,650	$3,250	$2,850	$2,500	$2,150

If verified original, asking prices may be considerably higher than values listed above. Top prices require original DCM shipping box, paperwork, and all listed accessories.

M1 GARAND NATIONAL MATCH - target version of the Garand, using National Match barrel and sights, glass bedding, etc. Must have serialized N.M. paperwork for prices listed below.

	$2,500	$2,000	$1,500	$1,250	$950	$750	$525

U.S. MILITARY

See listings under Colt, Springfield Armory, and Winchester. U.S. Military Trench and Riot guns may be found under the "Trench/Riot Shotguns" category in the T section of this text.

RIFLES: BOLT ACTION

Add 10% for Winchester mfg.

Add 10% for Type I guns.

GRADING - PPGS™	100%	98%	95%	90%	80%	70%	60%

U.S. MODEL 1917 ENFIELD RIFLE - .30-06 cal., bolt action, 5 shot, 26 in. barrel, original finish was high polish blue, adj. sights, military stock, derived from English P14 Enfield, over two million mfg. 1917-18, but original guns in 90%+ condition are rare.

* *Original high polish blue*

	$2,500	$1,800	$1,000	$875	$750	$525	$425

This model was manufactured primarily by Remington at the Eddystone plant in Eddystone, PA (Eddystone marked), the Ilion Remington plant, and by Winchester in New Haven, CT.

* *Matte blue or parkerized reworks* - most frequently encountered variation, many differences in the reworked matte blue and parkerized finishes.

	$700	$600	$500	$400	$350	$315	$265

U.S. ORDNANCE

Current rifle manufacturer located in Reno, NV.

RIFLES: SEMI-AUTO

U.S. Ordnance manufactures semi-auto reproductions (BATF approved) of the .303 Vickers (MSR was $4,500 w/o tripod), M-60/M-60E3 (MSR is $8,000), M60E4/Mk43 (MSR $8,900, new 2004), Browning M-1919 (MSR $1,995), and the M-1919A4 (MSR $2,095). These belt-fed variations are machined to military specifications, and have a 5-year warranty. Please contact the company directly for more information on these semi-auto reproductions (see Trademark Index).

USAS 12

Previous trademark manufactured by International Ordnance Corporation located in Nashville, TN circa 1992-95. Previously manufactured (1990-91) by Ramo Mfg., Inc. located in Nashville, TN. Previously distributed by Kiesler's Wholesale located in Jeffersonville, IN until 1994. Originally designed and previously distributed in the U.S. by Gilbert Equipment Co., Inc. located in Mobile, AL. Previously manufactured under license by Daewoo Precision Industries, Ltd. located in South Korea.

SHOTGUNS: SEMI-AUTO

USAS 12 - 12 ga. only, gas operated action available in either semi- or fully auto versions, 18 1/4 in. cylinder bore barrel, closed bolt, synthetic stock, pistol grip, and forearm, carrying handle, 10 round box or 20 drum (disc.) mag., 2 3/4 in. chamber only, parkerized finish, 12 lbs. Mfg. 1987-95.

	$1,050	$925	$850	$750	$650	$575	$500

Last MSR was $995.

Add $250+ for extra 20 shot drum magazine (banned by the BATF).

Values above are for a semi-auto model. This model is currently classified as a destructive device and necessary paperwork must accompany a sale.

U.S.R.A.

Previous organization (United States Revolver Association) that established certain rules for target pistol shooting. Target pistols were manufactured by Harrington & Richardson.

Readers interested in obtaining more information about specific U.S.R.A. pistols, or have information to share, are encouraged to contact Mr. L. Richard Littlefield (see Trademark Index).

PISTOLS: SINGLE SHOT

The author would like to express his thanks to Mr. Richard Littlefield for providing the following information.

MATCH TARGET PISTOL (MODEL 195) - .22 LR cal., many configurations, including 14 different stocks (including variations by Walter Roper), 5 trigger guards, 3 triggers, 2 hammers, 2 extractors, 3 barrel lengths (7, 8, or 10 inch), and 3 barrel rib designs, approx. 3,500 mfg. by H&R 1928-1941.

GRADING - PPGS™	100%	98%	95%	90%	80%	70%	60%

✳ *Variation 1 Pre-U.S.R.A.* - not marked "U.S.R.A.", known as the H&R Single Shot Pistol, no finger rest between the trigger guard and the front gripstrap, advertised with a "sawhandle" shape grip copied from the Model 1 or 2 smoothbore H&R Handy Gun, mfg. with a 10 in. barrel with deeply undercut rib. First 500 pistols mfg. 1928-1930.

	100%	98%	95%	90%	80%	70%	60%
	$400	$360	$330	$300	$270	$235	$200

✳ *Variation 2 U.S.R.A. Keyhole Barrel* - standard early model marked "U.S.R.A.", finger rest, non-sawhandle grips, optional grip shapes, grip screw goes from rear of grip into threaded hole in back grip strap. Mfg. 1930-31.

	100%	98%	95%	90%	80%	70%	60%
	$500	$450	$400	$350	$300	$250	$200

✳ *Variation 3 Modified Keyhole Barrel* - modification of Variation 2 to improve rear sight, barrel catch changed, reduced spent cartridge force by replacing cylindrical extractor with less powerful hinged type, hammer cocking spur and finger rest were wider, 8 in. optional or 10 in. standard barrel, optional grip shapes, transition model between early Variation 2 and final Variation 4 designs. Mfg. 1931.

	100%	98%	95%	90%	80%	70%	60%
	$500	$450	$400	$350	$300	$250	$200

✳ *Variation 4 Tapered Slabside Barrel* - new "truncated teardrop" barrel cross section shape, 7 in. standard or 10 in. optional barrel, adj. trigger, new sear, grips screw location was changed to front of grip, front sight was adj for elevation, trigger design changed from curved to straight beveled type with relocated cocking surfaces, 13 optional grip shapes, front sight protector standard, optional luggage style case. Mfg. 1931-1941.

	100%	98%	95%	90%	80%	70%	60%
	$550	$495	$450	$400	$350	$200	$250

This model was introduced circa 1931, the 1932 advertisements describe a fully redesigned gun, but pictured the Variation 2, indicating that H&R probably did not rephotogragh the new design. The final variation had a special, tight bore .217 inches in diameter, with bullet seating .03125 in (1-32 in.) into rifling, and is among the most accurate single shot .22 cal. pistols. The Model 195 U.S.R.A. was expensive, costing approx. $30 in 1932, and increased to more than $36 by the time production had ended in 1941, yet was the least expensive of all single shot quality .22 cal. target pistols during this time.

UBERTI, A. S.r.l.

Current firearms, black powder, and accessories manufacturer established in 1959 and located in Serezzo, Italy. Currently imported and distributed by Stoeger Industries (beginning 2003), located in Accokeek, MD, Taylor's & Co, located in Winchester, VA, Cimarron F.A. & Co, located in Fredricksburg, TX, E.M.F., located in Santa Ana, CA, Navy Arms, located in Martinsburg, WV, Tristar Sporting Arms, located in N. Kansas City, MO, Cabela's (certain models only), located in Sidney, NE, and Dixie Gun Works, located in Union City, TN. Previously imported until Dec. 31st, 2002 by Uberti USA, Inc., located in Lakeville, CT.

In late 1999, Beretta purchased Aldo Uberti & Co. S.r.l.

The current importers listed above import Uberti guns with their own importer stamp. However, all guns will also have the Uberti name listed as the manufacturer. Please refer to the individual importers for additional information on Uberti firearms.

For more information and up-to-date pricing regarding current Aldo Uberti black powder models, please refer to *Colt Blackpowder Reproductions and Replicas* by Dennis Adler and the *Blue Book of Modern Black Powder Values* by John Allen & Dennis Adler. These books feature hundreds of color photographs and support text of the most recent black powder models available, as well as complete pricing and reference guides.

GRADING - PPGS™	100%	98%	95%	90%	80%	70%	60%

REVOLVERS: REPRODUCTIONS, SAA & VARIATIONS

Factory engraving and other embellishments or finishes (including antique charcoal blue, white steel, nickel, etc.) may be special ordered by contacting the importer(s) directly.

Uberti also manufactured cartridge conversions exclusively for Cimarron F.A. Co. - please refer to the Cimarron section for information on these revolvers.

Values for finishes and special options reflect most recent pricing available.

    Add $85 for antique patina finish.

    Add $45 for antique charcoal blue finish on all Cattleman variations.

    Add $130 for silver plating.

    Add $40 for white finish.

    Add $85 for nickel plating (not available on Schofield).

    Add $85 for select grade walnut one-piece fitted grips (disc.), $250 or $575 (solid silver) for Army/Navy Tiffany grips.

    Add $45 for checkered grips.

    Add $50 for stag horn grips (disc.), $150 for black buffalo grips (disc.), or $350 for mother-of-pearl grips (disc.).

    Add $650-$1,450 for Cattleman engraving, depending on amount, and if with gold inlays.

1871 RICHARDS/MASON CONVERSION - .38 Spl., .38 LC, .44 Colt (8 in. barrel only), or .45 Schofield cal., choice of brass (New Model) or steel BS/TG (Old Model), 5 1/2, 7 1/2, or 8 in. round or octagon barrel, one-piece walnut grips, approx. 2.6 lbs. Imported 2002 only.

	$385	$350	$315	$275	$250	$225	$200

Last MSR was $450.

1871-1872 OPEN TOP EARLY/LATE MODEL - .38 Spl., .38 LC, .44 Russian, .44 Colt, .44 LC, .44 Spl., .45 Schofield, or .45 LC cal., open top frame, 5 1/2 (Early Model only) or 7 1/2 in. octagon barrel, Army (Late Model) or Navy (Early Model) size grips. Imported 2002 only.

	$385	$350	$315	$275	$250	$225	$200

Last MSR was $450.

    Add $25 for Late Model.

1873 CATTLEMAN VARIATIONS - available in .22 LR (disc. 1990), .22 Mag. (disc. 1990), .32-20 WCF (mfg. 2001-2003), .357 Mag., .38 Spl. (disc. 2003), .38-40 WCF (mfg. 1989-2003), .44 Spl. (disc. 2003), .44-40 WCF, or .45 LC cal., 3 3/4 (.45 LC only, disc.), 4 (.45 LC only, disc.), 4 3/4, 5 1/2, and 7 1/2 in. barrel lengths, brass or steel backstrap and trigger guard, Old Model (with cylinder pin retainer) or New Model (with plunger) frame. New 2002.

  ✳ ***Steel Backstrap and Trigger Guard*** - choice of New or Old Model frame, case colored or nickel finished, charcoal blue barrel/cylinder also available on Old Model.

MSR $410	$345	$275	$220	$180	$160	$150	$135

    Add $90 for nickel finish (New Model, .45 LC cal. only) or $85 for Old West (Old Model, not available in .44-40 WCF cal.) finish.

    Add $200 for nickel finish and faux ivory grips (new 2005, .45 LC cal. only).

    Add $185 for charcoal blue finish with pearl grips (new 2005, .45 LC only).

    Add $10 for Old Model.

    Add $70 for charcoal blue barrel, cylinder, and grip frame/trigger guard (.45 LC cal. onlu).

    Add $85 for stainless steel construction (.45 LC cal. only).

    Add $75 for convertible cylinder (.45 LC/.45 ACP, .22 LR/.22 Mag. in 5 1/2 in. barrel only, disc. 2002).

  ▸ **Sheriff's Model** - .44-40 WCF or .45 LC cal., 3 or 4 in. barrel. Importation disc. 2002.

	$345	$265	$210	$175	$160	$150	$135

Last MSR was $410.

GRADING - PPGS™	100%	98%	95%	90%	80%	70%	60%

❋ *Brass Backstrap and Trigger Guard* - .357 Mag., .38-40 WCF (mfg. 2001-2002), .44 Mag. (mfg. 2001-2002), .44 Spl. (mfg. 2001-2002), .44-40 WCF, or .45 LC cal., 3 3/4 (.45 LC only, disc.), 4 (.45 LC only, disc.), 4 3/4, 5 1/2, or 7 1/2 in. barrel.

MSR $355	$300	$260	$210	$175	$160	$150	$135

Add $51 for convertible cylinder (.45 LC/.45 ACP, disc. 2002).
Add $10 for .44 Spl. (disc. 2002) or .44-40 WCF cal.

>Sheriff's Model - .44-40 WCF or .45 LC cal., 3 or 4 in. barrel. Importation disc. 2002.

	$310	$240	$190	$165	$150	$140	$135

Last MSR was $359.

❋ *Target Model* - similar to standard Cattleman Model, only fully adj. rear blade sight, brass backstrap. Importation disc. 1990.

	$315	$245	$200	$185	$170	$150	$135

Last MSR was $335.

Add $25 for steel backstrap and trigger guard.
Add $60 for stainless steel construction (disc.).

CATTLEMAN U.S. CAVALRY - .45 LC cal. only, 7 1/2 in. barrel, Old Model frame, charcoal blue finish.

MSR $510	$415	$335	$260	$230	$200	$180	$160

CATTLEMAN ARTILLERY MODEL - .45 LC cal. only, 5 1/2 in. barrel, Old Model frame, charcoal blue finish.

MSR $510	$415	$335	$260	$230	$200	$180	$160

CATTLEMAN MILLENIUM - .357 Mag. or .45 LC cal., 4 3/4 in. barrel, New Model frame only. New 2000.

MSR $275	$235	$195	$175	$150	$140	$130	$120

CATTLEMAN GUNFIGHTER - .45 LC cal., 4 3/4, 5 1/2, or 7 1/2 in. barrel, New Model frame. New 2005.

MSR $360	$300	$260	$210	$175	$160	$150	$135

CATTLEMAN FLAT-TOP ("FIRST ISSUE") - .357 Mag. (mfg. 2001-2002), .38-40 WCF (disc. 2002), .44-40 WCF, or .45 LC cal., 4 3/4, 5 1/2, or 7 1/2 in. barrel, choice of regular (disc. 2002) or flattop receiver. Imported 1997-2004.

	$365	$310	$240	$195	$175	$160	$150

Last MSR was $430.

CATTLEMAN BIRD'S HEAD - .357 Mag. (new 2001), .44 Spl. (disc. 2002), .44-40 WCF (disc. 2004), or .45 LC cal., 3 (Sheriff's Model, .44-40 WCF or .45 LC cal. only, disc.), 3 1/2, 4, 4 3/4, or 5 1/2 in. barrel, patterned after the Colt 1877 Thunderer, case colored frame, checkered (disc.) or smooth walnut birdshead grips, choice of Old or New Model frame. New 1997.

MSR $460	$385	$320	$245	$195	$175	$160	$150

CATTLEMAN BISLEY - .357 Mag., .38-40 WCF (disc. 2002), .44 Spl. (disc. 2002), .44-40 WCF (disc. 2004), or .45 LC cal., patterned after the Colt Bisley Model, 4 3/4, 5 1/2, or 7 1/2 in. barrel, case colored frame, wood grips, New Model frame. New 1997.

MSR $460	$385	$320	$245	$195	$175	$160	$150

❋ *Cattleman Bisley Flattop* - similar to Cattleman Bisley, except has flattop frame with fixed or target (.44-40 WCF - disc. or .45 LC cal., 7 1/2 in. barrel only) sights. Importation disc. 2004.

	$365	$310	$240	$195	$175	$160	$150

Last MSR was $435.

Add $25 for target sights (disc.).

GRADING - PPGS™	100%	98%	95%	90%	80%	70%	60%

CATTLEMAN BUNTLINE - .22 LR/.22 Mag. combo (disc. 2000), .357 Mag., .44-40 WCF, .44 Mag. (mfg. 2001-2002), or .45 LC cal., 12 (mfg. 2001-2002, .45 LC only) or 18 in. barrel, New Model frame with steel or brass backstrap cut for shoulder stock. Importation disc. 1989, re-introduced 1993.

MSR $470	$385	$315	$245	$195	$175	$160	$150

Add $10 for target sights.

Subtract $56 for brass backstrap and trigger guard (disc. 2002).

✷ *Buntline Carbine* - similar to Cattleman Buntline, 18 in. barrel, includes non-detachable shoulder stock with brass hardware and lanyard ring. Importation disc. 1989, re-introduced 1993-95.

	$390	$310	$245	$200	$175	$160	$150

Last MSR was $475.

Add $34 for target sights.

Add $34 for .22 LR/.22 Mag. combo. (disc. 1989).

Add $175 for detachable shoulder stock.

CATTLEMAN SA REVOLVER CARBINE - .357 Mag. (disc. 2002), .44-40 WCF (disc. 2002), or .45 LC cal., 18 (new 2004) or 19 (disc. 2003) in. barrel, fixed stock with brass rifle buttplate, New Model frame, finger rest extension on trigger guard, choice of quick detachable mounts or target sights, 4.4 lbs. New 1997.

MSR $535	$445	$335	$260	$210	$175	$160	$150

Add $40 for target sights.

BUCKHORN - .44 Mag., .44 Spl. (disc.), or .44-40 WCF (disc.) cal., 4 3/4, 5 1/2 (new 2002) 6 (disc.), or 7 1/2 in. barrel, brass or steel backstrap. Importation disc. 2002.

✷ *Buckhorn New Model Frame* - steel or brass backstrap and triggerguard.

	$345	$265	$210	$175	$160	$150	$135

Last MSR was $410.

Add $69 for convertible cylinder.

Add $40 for Target Model (disc.).

Subtract $51 for New Model frame (brass BG & TG).

✷ *Buckhorn Buntline* - .44-40 WCF (disc.) or .44 Mag. cal., 18 in. barrel, includes non-detachable shoulder stock with brass hardware and lanyard ring. Importation disc. 1989, resumed 2001-2002.

	$375	$310	$240	$195	$175	$160	$150

Last MSR was $455.

Add $40 for target sights.

Add $40 for extra .44-40 WCF cylinder combo (disc.).

Add $122 for detachable shoulder stock (disc.).

Subtract $45 for New Model frame (brass BS & TG).

STALLION 1873 COLT - .22 LR/.22 Mag. cal. combo only, 4 3/4, 5 1/2, or 6 1/2 in. barrel, case hardened frame, 1-piece walnut grip, 2.4 lbs. Importation disc. 1989.

	$300	$210	$195	$170	$155	$140	$120

Last MSR was $325.

Add $27 for steel backstrap and trigger guard.

Add $26 for Target Model.

✷ *Stainless Stallion* - similar to standard Stallion, except is stainless steel. Importation disc. 1989.

	$370	$275	$225

Last MSR was $425.

GRADING - PPGS™	100%	98%	95%	90%	80%	70%	60%

STALLION 1873 STEEL BS/TG - .22 LR (new 2000) or .38 Spl. cal., 3 1/2 (disc. 2002), 4 3/4 (disc. 2002), or 5 1/2 in. barrel, smaller, scaled-down SAA case colored New Model frame, approx. 32 oz. New 1999.

	MSR $355	$300	$270	$240	$220	$195	$165	$150

Add $35 for .38 Spl. cal.
Add $30 for target sights.
Add $39 for Target Model (38 Spl. cal. only, not available with 3 1/2 in. barrel, disc. 2002).
Add $55 for .22 LR/.22 Mag. combo (disc. 2002).

✹ *Stallion 1873 Brass BS/TG* - .22 LR cal. only, 5 1/2 in. barrel.

	MSR $325	$285	$245	$220	$195	$165	$150	$135

Add $40 for target sights.
Add $39 for dual cylinder (.22 LR/.22 Mag., disc. 2002).
Add $39 for Target Model (disc.), or $90 for Target Model with dual cylinder (disc.).

1875 REMINGTON - .357 Mag. (disc. 2002), .44-40 WCF (disc. 2002), .45 ACP (mfg. 1992-2002, extra cylinder only), or .45 LC cal., 5 1/2 (Frontier configuration, disc. 1995, resumed 2001) or 7 1/2 (Outlaw configuration) in. barrel, brass (disc.) or steel (new 1993) trigger guard. Imported 2002, reimported beginning 2005.

	MSR $415	$350	$295	$245	$215	$180	$160	$140

Add $42 for convertible cylinder (.45 LC/.45 ACP, disc.).

✹ *Model 1875 Carbine* - same cals. as Outlaw 1875, 18 in. barrel, includes non-detachable shoulder stock with brass hardware and lanyard ring. Importation disc. 1989.

		$425	$285	$230	$200	$185	$180	$175

Last MSR was $440.

Add $110 for nickel plating.

1890 REMINGTON POLICE - .357 Mag., .44-40 WCF (disc. 2002), .45 ACP (mfg. 1993-2002, dual cylinder only), or .45 LC cal., 5 1/2, or 7 1/2 (disc. 1995) in. barrel, brass (disc. 2002) or steel (new 1993) trigger guard. Imported 2002, reimported beginning 2005.

	MSR $440	$365	$325	$275	$230	$200	$165	$130

Add $42 for dual cylinder (disc.).

PHANTOM MODEL - .357 or .44 Mag. cal. only, 10 1/2 in. barrel for silhouette use. Imported 1985-89.

		$475	$395	$325	$290	$260	$230	$215

Last MSR was $509.

1871 ROLLING BLOCK TARGET PISTOL - available in .22 LR, .22 Mag., .22 Hornet (disc. 2004), .357 Mag. (disc. 2002) or .45 LC (Navy Model with open sights only, mfg. 1992-95) cal., 9 1/2 in. barrel. New 2002.

	MSR $440	$355	$285	$235	$200	$175	$155	$135

1875 NO. 3 TOP BREAK - .44-40 WCF or .45 LC cal., 3 1/2, 5, or 7 in. barrel, available in First or Second Model. Importation began 2005.

	MSR $775	$650	$575	$500	$425	$350	$300	$250

REVOLVERS: DOUBLE ACTION

INSPECTOR MODEL - .32 S&W or .38 Spl. cal., 3, 4, or 6 in. barrels, double action, blue or chrome finish. Imported 1985-89.

		$390	$295	$245	$210	$170	$145	$125

Last MSR was $406.

Add $35 for target sights.
Add $25 for chrome plating.

GRADING - PPGS™	100%	98%	95%	90%	80%	70%	60%

REVOLVERS: REPRODUCTIONS

1874 SCHOFIELD RUSSIAN - .44 Russian cal., 6 shot, top-break, 6 (disc.), 6 1/2 (new 2002) or 7 (new 2002) in. barrel. Imported 2000-2002.

	$675	$585	$475	$425	$365	$300	$275

Last MSR was $800.

1875 SCHOFIELD - .44-40 WCF or .45 LC cal., 3, 5, or 7 in. barrel. Imported 2000-2002.

	$635	$550	$465	$400	$350	$300	$275

Last MSR was $750.

RUSSIAN NEW MODEL NO. 3 - .44 Russian cal., 6 1/2 in. barrel. Importation began 2005.

MSR $825	$675	$595	$525	$450	$375	$325	$275

RIFLES: REPRODUCTIONS

Values for finishes and special options reflect most recent pricing available.

- **Add $140 for antique patina finish.**
- **Add $80 for charcoal blue finish.**
- **Add $75 for white finish.**
- **Add $235 for silver plating.**
- **Add $210 for nickel plating.**
- **Add $90 for checkered wood, $210 for select wood, or $475 for deluxe wood.**
- **Add $850-$3,500 for hand-engraving options, depending on the amount of engraving and gold inlays.**

1860 HENRY RIFLE/CARBINE - .44-40 WCF or .45 LC (rifle only) cal., iron, brass or steel (.44-40 WCF only, disc. 2002) frame, 24 1/4 in. barrel on rifle, 22 1/2 in. barrel on carbine (disc. 2002), available in modern gun blue, charcoal blue, white, or chrome finish, approx. 9 lbs.

MSR $1,050	$900	$675	$550	$425	$360	$320	$260

Add $100 for steel frame.

The carbine was disc. in 1989, re-introduced 1992-2002.

* *Henry Trapper* - similar to above, except has 16 1/2 (disc. 2002) or 18 1/2 in. barrel. New 1990.

MSR $1,050	$900	$675	$550	$425	$360	$320	$260

* *Henry 1 of 1,000* - disc.

	$1,450	$1,150	$975	$850	$700	$575	$425

1866 YELLOWBOY CARBINE - .22 LR (disc. 1989), .22 Mag. (disc. 1989), .38 Spl., .44-40 WCF, or .45 LC cal., brass receiver, 19 in. round barrel, 7.4 lbs. Importation disc. 1995, resumed 2002.

MSR $805	$675	$550	$450	$360	$310	$275	$240

* *1866 Trapper Carbine* - .22 LR, .38 Spl., or .44-40 WCF cal., 16 in. barrel. Importation disc. 1989.

	$650	$475	$395	$340	$285	$260	$235

Last MSR was $686.

* *1866 Yellowboy Indian Carbine* - .22 LR, .22 Mag., .32-20 WCF (new 2002), .38 Spl., .44-40 WCF, or .45 LC (new 1996) cal., 19 in. barrel. Imported 2002 only.

	$670	$535	$430	$360	$310	$275	$240

Last MSR was $760.

Subtract $50 without brass tacks (disc.).

* *Red Cloud Commemorative Carbine* - same cals., special engraving and brass tacks in forearm and stock. Importation officially disc. 1989.

	$720	$600	$475	$400	$350	$330	$300

Last MSR was $850.

GRADING - PPGS™	100%	98%	95%	90%	80%	70%	60%

1866 SPORTING RIFLE - .22 LR (mfg. 2001-2002), .22 Mag. (mfg. 2001-2002), .32-20 WCF (mfg. 2002), .38 Spl., .38-40 WCF (mfg. 2002), .44-40 WCF, or .45 LC (new 1996) cal., brass receiver, 20 (new 2001) round (new 1993, carbine only) or 24 1/4 in. octagon barrel, 8.16 lbs.

MSR $825	$695	$550	$450	$375	$310	$275	$240

✳ *1866 Deluxe Uberti Model* - .44-40 WCF cal., features high polished receiver with fire-blue small parts, ladder rear sight. Imported 1995.

	$895	$675	$525

Last MSR was $895.

This model was sold exclusively by Cherry's, located in Greensboro, NC.

✳ *1866 "L.D. Nimschke" Special Edition* - .44-40 WCF cal., receiver, buttplate, and forend cap feature recreations of Nimschke scroll engraving by Giovanelli of Italy, silver plated, deluxe walnut, optional 2nd Edition of Nimschke pattern book by R.L. Wilson ($100), only 300 mfg. beginning 1995. Disc.

	$1,495	$1,000	$650

Last MSR was $1,495.

This model was sold exclusively by Cherry's, located in Greensboro, NC.

✳ *1866 Yellowboy Indian Rifle* - .22 LR (disc. 1989), .22 Mag. (disc. 1989), .38 Spl., or .44-40 WCF cal., 24 1/4 in. barrel. Importation disc. 1989, reintroduced 1993-95.

	$700	$560	$475	$385	$300	$260	$235

Last MSR was $800.

1866 MUSKET - .44-40 WCF or .45 LC cal., features 27 in. barrel with barrel bands. Imported 1999-2002.

	$810	$600	$500	$425	$360	$320	$280

Last MSR was $910.

1873 CARBINE - .22 LR (disc. 1991), .22 Mag. (disc. 1991), .32-20 WCF (new 2001), .357 Mag., .38 Spl. (disc. 1991) .38-40 (mfg. 2002), .44-40 WCF, or .45 LC (new 1992) cal., 10 shot mag., steel receiver, 19 in. round barrel with forearm barrel bands, 7.38 lbs.

MSR $945	$820	$650	$525	$425	$360	$320	$280

Add $35 for case colored frame (disc.).

✳ *1873 Trapper Carbine* - .357 Mag., .44-40 WCF, or .45 LC cal. only, 16 1/8 in. barrel. Importation disc. 1990.

	$750	$600	$500	$425	$360	$320	$280

Last MSR was $750.

1873 SPORTING RIFLE - .32-20 WCF (mfg. 2001-2002), .357 Mag. (new 1995), .38-40 WCF (mfg. 2002), .44-40 WCF (new 1995), or .45 LC cal., case hardened receiver, 20 in. octagon (new 1990, Short Rifle), 24 1/4 in. octagon, half-round/half-octagon, or 30 (mfg. 1990-2002) in. octagon barrel, can be drilled and tapped for Uberti rear tang aperture sight (new 1993), 8.16 lbs.

MSR $985	$850	$700	$550	$440	$375	$325	$280

Add $10 for half-octagon barrel.
Add $100 for Deluxe Model with hand-checkered pistol grip stock/forearm.
Add $115 for Deluxe Model with half-round, half-octagon barrel and hand-checkered pistol grip stock/forearm.
Add $17 for 30 in. barrel (.44-40 WCF or .45 LC cal. only, disc. 2002).
Add $77 for Deluxe Model with 30 in. barrel (disc. 2002).

MODEL 1873 125th ANNIVERSARY - .44-40 WCF cal., special anniversary offering featuring engraved gold plated metal with fire blue receiver and small parts, long rifle configuration with deluxe pistol grip and forearm. 125 mfg. 1998 only, marketed exclusively by Cherry's.

	$3,250	$2,500	$1,750

Last MSR was $3,500.

GRADING - PPGS™	100%	98%	95%	90%	80%	70%	60%

1873 MUSKET - .44-40 WCF or .45 LC cal., features 30 in. round barrel with barrel bands. Imported 1999-2002.

| | $875 | $700 | $575 | $450 | $375 | $325 | $300 |

Last MSR was $999.

RIFLES: SINGLE SHOT

1885 CARBINE/RIFLE - .22 Hornet (mfg. 2004), .30-30 Win. (disc. 2004), .38-55 WCF (disc. 2002), .40-65 WCF (disc. 2002), .44 Mag. (mfg. 2004), .44-40 WCF (disc. 2002), .45 LC (disc. 2004), .45-70 Govt., .45-90 WCF (disc. 2002, reintroduced 2005) or .45-120 (disc. 2002, reintroduced 2005) cal., Low Wall (disc. 2004) or High Wall, 28 (carbine, High Wall only, .45-70 Govt. cal. only) round or 30 (rifle) in. octagon barrel, case colored receiver, straight grip walnut stock and forearm, 7.7 or 9.9 lbs. New 1999.

| MSR $850 | $740 | $595 | $500 | $395 | $315 | $265 | $235 |

Add $165 for Deluxe Model with checkered pistol grip and aperture sights, depending on barrel lengths.

1871 ROLLING BLOCK TARGET CARBINE/RIFLE - available in .22 LR, .22 Mag., .22 Hornet (disc. 2004), or .357 Mag. (disc.) cal., 22 (carbine) or 26 in. barrel, approx. 5 lbs.

| MSR $535 | $440 | $350 | $295 | $240 | $200 | $175 | $155 |

Add $65 for rifle model.

SHOTGUNS: SxS

DOUBLE BARREL - 12 ga. only, 2 3/4, 3, or 3 1/2 in. chambers, 20, 21 1/2 , 24, or 26 in. barrels, exposed hammers, checkered walnut pistol grip stock and forearm. Imported 1999-2001.

| | $875 | $700 | $575 | $450 | $375 | $325 | $300 |

Last MSR was $999.

UGARTECHEA, ARMAS

Current manufacturer located in Eibar, Spain. Currently being imported by Aspen Outfitting Co., located in Aspen, CO, and by Lion Country Supply, located in Port Matilda, PA.

Currently, Aspen Outfitting Co. exclusively imports Models 116, 119, 1000, 1030, 1042, and the AOC/SG boxlock. Lion Country Supply exclusively imports Models 30, 40, 40 NEX, 75, 75NEX, and 110.

SHOTGUNS: SxS, BOXLOCK

MODEL AOC/SG - 12, 16, 20, 28 ga., or .410 bore, 2 3/4 in. chambers, Anson & Deeley boxlock action with extra polishing and fitting of parts, scalloped action shaping, 28 in. chopper lump barrels, IC/M choke, front bead sight, concave rib, DT w/ articulating front trigger, southgate auto ejectors, auto safety, free floating firing pins, engraved receiver with border scroll, upgraded European straight grip walnut stock and splinter forend with plunger release, inlaid forend screw escutcheon, hand-checkered buttstock, initial shield, case hardened action finish, long tang trigger guard with comfort roll, upgraded wood finish. Importation began in 1999.

| MSR $2,850 | $2,500 | $2,200 | $1,950 | $1,750 | $1,575 | $1,425 | $1,225 |

Add $400 for 28 ga. or $500 for .410 bore.

This model is imported exclusively by Aspen Outfitting Company.

GRADING - PPGS™	100%	98%	95%	90%	80%	70%	60%

UPLAND CLASSIC GRADE I (MODEL 30)

- 12, 16, 20, 28 ga., or .410 bore, Anson & Deeley boxlock action, DT, concave rib, extractors, case colored receiver, hand-checkered straight grip walnut stock and splinter forend.

MSR $995	$950	$875	$750	$600	$475	$400	$325

Add $100 for 28 ga.
Add $150 for .410 bore.

This model is imported exclusively by Lion Country Supply.

UPLAND CLASSIC GRADE II (MODEL 40)

- 12, 16, 20, or 28 ga., Anson & Deeley boxlock action, DT, coin finished and engraved receiver, hand-checkered straight grip walnut stock and splinter forend.

MSR $1,195	$1,075	$950	$875	$750	$600	$475	$400

Add $100 for 28 ga.

This model is imported exclusively by Lion Country Supply.

UPLAND CLASSIC GRADE III (MODEL 40 NEX)

- 12, 16, 20, or 28 ga., Anson & Deeley boxlock action, DT or SST, case colored and engraved receiver, hand-checkered straight grip walnut stock and splinter forend.

MSR $1,550	$1,400	$1,200	$1,000	$875	$750	$600	$500

Add $200 for SST.
Add $100 for 28 ga.

This model is imported exclusively by Lion Country Supply.

BILL HANUS BIRDGUN

- 16, 20, 28 ga., or .410 bore (6 mfg.), boxlock action, 26 in. barrels bored SK1/SK2, Churchill raised rib, SNT, ejectors, lightly engraved case colored receiver, tang and lever, checkered straight grip walnut stock and semi-beavertail forearm, oil finish, lifetime operational warranty, 5 1/4-6 1/2 lbs. Approx. 200 mfg. Imported 1989-circa 1992.

	$1,425	$1,250	$1,050	$880	$750	$635	$540

Last MSR was $1,695.

Add $100 for 28 ga.
Add $150 for .410 bore.
Add 15% for optional fitted luggage case.

BILL HANUS BIRDGUN CLASSIC

- 20, 28 ga., or .410 bore (4 mfg.), similar to Birdgun Model, except has double triggers with hinged front trigger, 27 in. barrels, splinter forearm and English leather handguard. Imported 1989-circa 1992.

	$1,355	$1,220	$1,035	$880	$750	$635	$540

Last MSR was $1,595.

Add 15% for optional fitted luggage case.
Add $100 for 28 ga.
Add $200 for .410 bore.

SHOTGUNS: SxS, SIDELOCK

Ugartechea sidelocks are best quality guns. Currently, Lion Country Supply stocks the Upland Classic Series. Additionally, custom orders are available through Aspen Outfitting and Lion Country Supply.

UPLAND CLASSIC GRADE IV

- 12, 16, or 20 ga., best quality true sidelock with intercepting sears, DT or SST with hinged front trigger, case colored or coin finished receiver with English style scroll engraving, auto ejectors, upgraded wood with hand rubbed oil finish.

MSR $2,195	$2,000	$1,700	$1,475	$1,200	$1,000	$875	$750

Add $200 for SST (20 ga. only).

This model is imported exclusively by Lion Country Supply.

GRADING - PPGS™	100%	98%	95%	90%	80%	70%	60%

UPLAND CLASSIC GRADE V (MODEL 110) - 12, 16, 20, or 28 ga., best quality round body game gun, true sidelock with intercepting sears, DT or SST with hinged front trigger, case colored or coin finished receiver with English style scroll engraving, auto ejectors, upgraded wood with hand rubbed oil finish.

MSR $2,995	$2,675	$2,300	$1,900	$1,600	$1,350	$1,100	$925

Add $200 for SST.
Add $100 for 28 ga.
This model is imported exclusively by Lion Country Supply.

MODEL 75/75EX - 12, 16, or 20 ga., case colored finish with minimal engraving, oil finished deluxe walnut stock and forearm. Importation began 1999.

MSR $1,995	$1,900	$1,750	$1,575	$1,425	$1,275	$1,150	$975

Add $200 for SST.

MODEL 116 - 12, 16, 20, 28 ga., or .410 bore, sidelock action, antique silver finish with elaborate floral engraving, deluxe oil finished walnut stock and forearm.

MSR $5,695	$5,250	$4,500	$3,875	$3,250	$2,600	$2,000	$1,500

Add $180 for 28 ga. or .410 bore.
This model is imported exclusively by Aspen Outfitting Company.

MODEL 119 - 12, 16, 20, 28 ga., or .410 bore, sidelock action with coin finish or case hardened frame, Purdey style engraving, deluxe oil finished walnut stock and forearm.

MSR $6,935	$6,500	$5,500	$4,550	$3,950	$3,250	$2,600	$2,000

Add $360 for 28 ga. or .410 bore.
This model is imported exclusively by Aspen Outfitting Company.

MODEL 1000 - 12, 16, or 20 ga., sidelock action with coin finish or case hardened frame, Churchill style deep relief engraving, deluxe oil finished walnut stock and forearm.

MSR $7,895	$7,425	$6,250	$5,250	$4,500	$3,750	$3,000	$2,350

This model is imported exclusively by Aspen Outfitting Company.

MODEL 1030 - 12, 16, or 20 ga., coin finished or case hardened frame, Woodward style scalloped fences and engraving. Importation began 1994.

MSR $8,965	$8,400	$6,950	$5,850	$5,150	$4,350	$3,750	$3,350

This model is imported exclusively by Aspen Outfitting Company.

MODEL 1042 - 12, 16, or 20 ga., sidelock action, coin finished or case hardened frame, exquisite full coverage fine scroll engraving, deluxe oil finished walnut stock and forearm.

MSR $10,495	$9,575	$8,000	$7,000	$6,000	$5,100	$4,200	$3,600

This model is imported exclusively by Aspen Outfitting Company.

SPECIAL MODELS - available in all gauges with game scene engraving and/or gold inlays to customer specifications. POR only. Please contact Aspen Outfitting Company (see Trademark Index).

UGARTECHEA, IGNACIO

Previous manufacturer located in Eibar, Spain. Previously imported exclusively by Aspen Outfitting Company, located in Aspen, CO.

Ignacio Ugartechea was founded in 1922 and is the oldest maker of side-by-side sidelock and boxlock shotguns in Spain (please refer to Armas Ugartechea for current information). From 1970 until the Parker-Hale name was sold in 1990 to Navy Arms, Ugartechea manufactured the popular line of Anson & Deeley boxlocks imported by Precision Sports in Cortland, NY. Precision Sports continued to import these guns under the Classic "600" name until 1994. Previously imported by Precision Sports, Inc. located in Cortland, NY until 1994. Previously imported by Exel Arms in Gardener, MA until 1987 as the Exel Model 200 series.

GRADING - PPGS™	100%	98%	95%	90%	80%	70%	60%

SHOTGUNS: SxS, BOXLOCK

Due to space considerations, the individual Ignacio Ugartechea models have not been listed in this edition. Please refer to older editions for more information on these previously imported models. The importation of Parker-Hale shotguns was disc. in 1993. Please contact Aspen Outfitting Company for accurate information on older Ignacio Ugartechea models.

ULTIMATE

Please refer to Camex-Blaser USA in the C section of this text.

ULTRA LIGHT ARMS, INC.

Previous manufacturer located in Granville, WV. Ultra Light Arms, Inc. was purchased by C.F. Holding Corp. in 1999.

PISTOLS: BOLT-ACTION

MODEL 20 HUNTERS PISTOL - various cals., 14 in. Douglas heavy barrel, 5-shot mag., Kevlar graphite reinforced stock in choice of 4 colors, Timney trigger, left- or right-hand bolt, approx. 4 lbs. Mfg. 1987-89.

	$1,295	$1,150	$975	$850	$700	$640	$575

Last MSR was $1,600.

MODEL 20 REB - popular cals. from .22-250 Rem. through .308 Win. (other cals. on request), 14 in. Douglas #3 barrel, 5 shot mag., composite Kevlar graphite reinforced stock, green, brown, black, or camo Dupont Imron paint, Timney adj. trigger, includes hard case, 4 lbs. Mfg. 1994-95, reintroduced 1998 only.

	$1,475	$1,200	$1,000	$875	$750	$625	$500

Last MSR was $1,600.

RIFLES: BOLT ACTION

ULTRA LIGHT RIFLE - caliber to customer specs., various actions, 2-position 3-function safety in top of stock, Timney trigger, Douglas 22 or 24 in. barrel, no sights, graphite reinforced stock with recoil pad, matte finish standard, other finishes at extra cost. Many special order features and services were available on these models, 4 3/4-5 3/4 lbs. Mfg. 1985-1999.

MODEL 20 - many cals. available between .17 Rem. and .358 Win., short action, Kevlar stock.

	$2,225	$1,675	$1,225	$950	$800	$700	$640

Last MSR was $2,500.

Add $100 for left-hand action.

✳ *Model 20 RF* - .22 LR cal., convertible from repeater to single shot, 22 in. Douglas premium barrel, DuPont composite stock with Imron paint (some color options available), no sights, drilled and tapped, 5 1/4 lbs. Mfg. 1983-1999.

	$750	$650	$550	$475	$400	$350	$300

Last MSR was $800.

Add $50 for repeater action.

The first 100 pre-production rifles in this model were marked "1-of-100" consecutively, with owner's initials.

MODEL 24 - .25-06 Rem., .270 Win., .280 Rem. (mfg. 1992 only), .30-06, or 7mm Exp. cal., long action, Kevlar stock, 5 1/4 lbs. Disc. 1999.

	$2,325	$1,775	$1,300	$995	$825	$700	$640

Last MSR was $2,600.

Add $100 for left-hand action.

GRADING - PPGS™	100%	98%	95%	90%	80%	70%	60%

MODEL 28 MAGNUM - .264 Win. Mag., .300 Win. Mag., .338 Win. Mag., 7mm Rem. Mag., or .416 Rigby (mfg. 1992 only) cal., Kevlar stock, 5 3/4 lbs. Disc. 1999.

	$2,625	$1,975	$1,550	$1,225	$950	$700	$600

Last MSR was $2,900.

Add $100 for left-hand action.

MODEL 40 MAGNUM - .300 Wby. Mag. or .416 Rigby cal., otherwise similar to Model 28 Series. Mfg. 1993-99.

	$2,625	$1,975	$1,550	$1,225	$950	$700	$600

Last MSR was $2,900.

Add $100 for left-hand action.

ULTRAMATIC

Previous trademark with manufacture located in Enzesfeld, Austria. Ultramatic Productions, GmbH, changed its name to Wolf Sporting Pistols in 1997.

PISTOLS: SEMI-AUTO

ULTRAMATIC PISTOL - 9mm Para. cal., double action semi-auto, various barrel lengths, competition model with muzzle brake. Disc. approx. 1996.

	$1,150	$975	$850	$700	$640	$575	$500

UMAREX SPORTWAFFEN GmbH & Co. KG.

Current firearms, airguns, and signal pistol manufacturer located in Arnsberg, Germany.

Umarex purchased Walther during 1996, and also manufactures ammunition, optics, and accessories.

Please refer to the Walther listing for currently imported Walther firearms. For more information on currently manufactured Umarex airguns, please refer to the *Blue Book of Airguns* by Dr. Robert Beeman & John Allen (also online).

UNERTL ORDNANCE COMPANY, INC.

Current pistol manufacturer beginning 2004 and located in Las Vegas, NV.

PISTOLS: SEMI-AUTO

As this edition went to press, Unertl Ordnance Company had plans to manufacture a MEU (SOC) .45 ACP cal. semi-auto pistol. Please contact the company for more information, including pricing and availability.

UNIQUE

Previous manufacturer located in Hendaye, France until 2001. Previously imported by Nygord Precision Products located in Prescott, AZ.

In addition to the current models listed below, Unique also manufactured additional models that were not imported into the U.S., but distributed mostly in Europe (Models I.S., DES 2000U, DES 69U, T3000 rifle, T/SM, T, and X51).

PISTOLS: SEMI-AUTO

All currently manufactured Unique pistols are supplied with leatherette case, weights are additional.

KRIEGSMODELL L - 7.65mm cal., 9 shot, 3.2 in. barrel, blue, plastic grips, fixed sights. Mfg. 1940-45, during German occupation of France, has German acceptance marks.

	$325	$250	$220	$200	$180	$160	$140

MODEL RR - post-war commercial version of Kreigsmodell, higher quality finish. Mfg. 1951-disc.

	100%	98%	95%	90%	80%	70%	60%
	$180	$170	$155	$130	$120	$110	$90

Add 15% for .22 LR.

MODEL B/CF - 7.65mm cal., 9 shot, or .380 auto cal., 8 shot, 4 in. barrel, blue, plastic thumbrest grips. Mfg. 1954-disc.

	$205	$195	$175	$155	$145	$130	$110

MODEL D6 - .22 LR cal., 10 shot, 6 in. barrel, adj. sights, blue, plastic grips. Mfg. 1954-disc.

	$300	$250	$200	$160	$145	$135	$120

MODEL D2 - similar to D6, except 4 1/2 in. barrel.

	$300	$250	$200	$160	$145	$135	$120

MODEL L - .22 LR cal., 10 shot, 7.65mm cal., 7 shot, and .380 ACP cal., 6 shot, 3.3 in. barrel, fixed sights, steel and alloy frame offered, plastic grips. Mfg. 1955-disc.

	$250	$200	$150	$130	$115	$100	$90

Add $500 for .22 LR cal. pistol-rifle combination.

MODEL MIKROS POCKET - .22 Short and .25 ACP cal., 6 shot, fixed sights, blue, plastic grips, steel or alloy frame. Mfg. 1957-disc.

	$200	$155	$140	$120	$100	$90	$75

MODEL DES/32U - .32 S&W Wadcutter cal., 5.9 in. barrel, dry firing device, ergonomically designed French walnut grips with adj. hand rest, 5 or 6 shot mag., 40.2 oz.

	$1,350	$1,225	$1,025	$900	$775	$625	$500

MODEL DES/69 MATCH - .22 LR cal. target pistol, wraparound grips, adj. features. Imported 1986-1988.

	$995	$850	$725	$625	$550	$490	$445

Last MSR was $1,198.

Add $62 for left-hand model.

MODEL DES/69U STANDARD MATCH - .22 LR cal., 5 shot mag., 5.9 in. barrel, adj. rear sight, adj. target stippled stocks, blue finish only. Imported 1969-1999.

	$1,150	$995	$875	$750	$625	$500	$450

Last MSR was $1,250.

Add $30 for left-hand model.

MODEL DES/96U - .22 LR cal., replacement for the Model DES/69U, top loading model, thinner grips, features gold-plated slide. Mfg. 1996-2002.

	$1,350	$1,225	$1,025	$900	$775	$625	$500

MODEL DES/823-U RAPID FIRE MATCH - .22 Short cal., 5 shot, 6 in. barrel, adj. sight, adj. trigger, adj. walnut target grips, squared barrel assembly, dry fire mechanism. Imported 1974-1988.

	$1,100	$850	$725	$625	$550	$490	$445

Last MSR was $1,300.

Add $60 for left-hand model.

MODEL 2000-U - .22 Short cal. only, specifically designed for rapid fire U.I.T. competition, 5.9 in. barrel, ergonomic styled grips with adj. hand rest, 5 shot mag. (inserted in top), 43.4 oz. Importation disc. 1995.

	$1,300	$1,050	$925	$775	$625	$500	$450

Last MSR was $1,450.

Add $30 for left-hand model.

GRADING - PPGS™	100%	98%	95%	90%	80%	70%	60%

RIFLES: BOLT ACTION

T66 MATCH RIFLE - .22 LR cal., single shot, bolt action, 25 1/2 in. barrel, micro rear and globe front sight, full target stock. Mfg. 1966-disc.

	$425	$410	$390	$350	$300	$280	$250

MODEL F 11 - .22 LR cal., military trainer, adj. sights, target walnut stock. Limited importation.

	$560	$435	$350	$285	$260	$240	$220

Last MSR was $695.

MODEL T DIOPTRA - .22 LR or .22 Mag. cal., bolt action Sporter with 23.6 in. barrel and adj. rear sight, 5 (.22 Mag. only) or 10 shot mag., grooved receiver for scope, checkered French walnut Monte Carlo stock, approx. 6.4 lbs. Importation disc. 1995.

	$795	$700	$600	$525	$450	$375	$300

Last MSR was $890.

MODEL T/SM - .22 LR or .22 Mag cal., bolt action Target variation with 20 1/2 in. barrel, no sights, 5 (.22 Mag. only) or 10 shot mag., stippled pistol grip stock and forearm, right- or left-hand action, 6.6 lbs. Importation disc. 1995.

	$850	$735	$625	$525	$450	$375	$300

Last MSR was $960.

Add $50 for left-hand action.

MODEL T/STANDARD UIT - .22 LR cal., designed for UIT competition, single shot, aperture sights, adj. cheekpiece and buttplate on stippled walnut stock, right- or left-hand action, 10.8 lbs. Importation disc. 1995.

	$1,350	$1,125	$975	$850	$725	$625	$525

Last MSR was $1,450.

Add $50 for left-hand action.

MODEL 2000 FREE RIFLE - .22 LR cal., Free Rifle variation of the Model T/Standard UIT.

	$2,600	$2,250	$1,875	$1,500	$1,250	$1,000	$850

UNITED SPORTING ARMS, INC.

Previous manufacturer located in Tucson, AZ. Manufacture ceased in early 1986.

REVOLVERS: SINGLE ACTION

SEVILLE - .357 Mag., .41 Mag., .44 Mag., or .45 LC cal., single action revolver, 4 5/8, 5 1/2, 6 1/2, or 7 1/2 in. barrels, adj. sights, smooth walnut grips.

	$395	$350	$315	$280	$260	$240	$220

Last MSR was $435.

* **Stainless steel** - all stainless version of the Seville.

	$395	$350	$315

Last MSR was $435.

* **Silver Seville** - similar to Seville, except has blue barrel, and high polish stainless steel grip frame.

	$425	$370	$330

Last MSR was $460.

* **Stainless .357 Maxi** - available in 5 1/2 or 7 1/2 in. barrel only.

	$575	$475	$395

Last MSR was $465.

* **Stainless .375 USA** - only in 7 1/2 in. barrel.

	$625	$525	$425

Last MSR was $490.

GRADING - PPGS™	100%	98%	95%	90%	80%	70%	60%

❋ *Stainless .454 Mag.* - only in 7 1/2 in. barrel, 5 shot.

	$700	$600	$500				

Last MSR was $595.

Note: In late 1986, some .454 Mags. were made up from parts purchased from the manufacturer. Unfortunately, while the exterior appearance might seem normal, they were not involved with any type of factory quality control program. As a result, shooting these non-factory revolvers could be dangerous, and careful inspection should be made before purchasing/ shooting this particular specimen.

❋ *Eldorado Stainless* - .44 Mag., 4 5/8, 5 1/2, 6 1/2, 7 1/2, or 10 1/2 in. barrel, adj. sights.

	$700	$600	$500				

SILVER SEVILLE SILHOUETTE - .357 Mag., .41 Mag., or .44 Mag. cal., single action revolver, 10 1/2 in. barrel, adj. sights, Pachmayr grips, blue barrel finish with stainless grip frame.

	$445	$370	$330	$295	$270	$250	$230

Last MSR was $485.

❋ *Stainless steel* - stainless version of the Silver Seville Silhouette.

	$425	$370	$330				

Last MSR was $460.

❋ *Stainless .357 Maxi* - available in 10 1/2 in. barrel only.

	$575	$475	$395				

Last MSR was $480.

❋ *Stainless .375 USA* - available in 10 1/2 in. barrel only.

	$625	$525	$425				

Last MSR was $515.

❋ *Stainless .454 Mag.* - available in 10 1/2 in. barrel only, 5 shot.

	$700	$600	$500				

Last MSR was $620.

SHERIFF MODEL - .357 Mag., .38 Spl., .44 Spl., .44 Mag., or .45 LC cal., single action revolver, 3 1/2 in. barrel, adj. sights, smooth walnut grips.

	$395	$350	$315	$280	$260	$240	$220

Last MSR was $435.

❋ *Stainless steel* - stainless version of the Sheriff Model.

	$395	$350	$315				

Last MSR was $435.

UNITED STATES FIRE ARMS MANUFACTURING COMPANY, INC.

Current manufacturer established during 1995 and located in Hartford, CT. Previously located at Colt's original old armory in Hartford, CT. Previous company name was United States Patent Firearms Manufacturing Company until 1997.

REVOLVERS: SAA

USFA also has a custom shop offering the following levels of engraving: Armory Grade A ($499 MSR), Armory Grade B ($725 MSR), Armory Grade C ($925 MSR), Armory Grade D ($1,100 MSR), Master Grade A ($865 MSR), Master Grade B ($1,905 MSR), Master Grade C ($2,772 MSR) or Master Grade D ($3,870 MSR).

COLT 1851 RICHARDS NAVY CONVERSION - .38 Spl. only, 7 1/2 in. barrel with ejector, Old Armoury Bone case hardened frame, gate, hammer, and conversion ring, Dome Blue barrel, cylinder, and ejector housing, smooth walnut grips.

	$1,175	$950	$825	$700	$600	$500	$400

Last MSR was $1,300.

GRADING - PPGS™	100%	98%	95%	90%	80%	70%	60%

SINGLE ACTION ARMY PREMIUM - .22 LR (mfg. 1996-2001), .22 Mag. (mfg. 1996-2001), .32-20 (new 1998), .357 Mag. (disc. 1998), .38 Spl. (new 2004), .38-40 WCF, .41 Colt (mfg. 1999-2003), .44 Spl. (new 2004), .44-40 WCF, .45 ACP, or .45 LC cal., 3 (no ejector), 4 (no ejector), 4 3/4, 5 1/2, 7 1/2, or 10 (new 1997) in. barrel, original screw cylinder release, white sided hammer standard beginning 2005, choice of Dome Blue, Dome Blue/Old Armoury Bone Case, or nickel finish, checkered U.S. hard rubber grips.

	MSR $949	$850	$725	$625	$525	$450	$375	$300

Add $271 for nickel finish.

The barrel marking for this revolver is "U.S.F.A. MFG. Co. HARTFORD CT. U.S.A."

✻ *Premium Flattop Target SAA* - similar to SAA, except has flattop receiver with target sights, full Dome Blue finish is standard. Mfg. 1997-2002, reintroduced 2004.

	MSR $1,020	$925	$775	$675	$550	$450	$400	$350

Add $55 for Dome Blue/Old Armory Bone Case finish.

Add $179 for Armory Blue/Old Armory Bone Case finish.

Add $219 for nickel finish.

Add $120 for full Armoury Blue finish.

✻ *U.S. Pre-War SAA* - similar cals. as the SAA Premium, except also available in .41 Colt, most historically correct and accurate pre-war SAA reproduction available. New 2000.

	MSR $1,195	$1,050	$850	$750	$600	$475	$425	$375

✻ *New Buntline Special* - .45 LC cal. only, 16 in. barrel, includes correct skeleton shoulder stock, ser. numbered 28,8xx and up. Mfg. 2000-2002.

		$1,850	$1,675	$1,500	$1,250	$1,000	$900	$800

Last MSR was $2,199.

Add $396 for nickel finish.

PATRIOT SERIES - .30 Carbine or .45 ACP cal., 5 1/2 (.45 ACP) or 7 1/2 (.30 Carbine) in. barrel with lanyard loop, Old Armory Bone case colored frame, Dome Blue (.30 Carbine) or Armory Blue (.45 ACP) finish, Automatic Colt Pistol rollmark. New 2005.

	MSR $1,545	$1,350	$1,175	$995	$875	$750	$625	$500

GOVERNMENT INSPECTOR SERIES - .45 LC cal., exact recreations of guns inspected by government inspectors, including Henry Nettleton, Orville Ainsworth, David Clark, and Rinaldo Carr, exact cartouche branding and hand-stamped markings, 5 1/2 or 7 1/2 in. barrel, historically correct, one-piece walnut grips, Old Armory Bone case color hardened frame, Armory Blue, antique, or nickel finish. New 2005.

	MSR $1,485	$1,325	$1,150	$950	$825	$700	$600	$500

Add $40 for antique finish.

Add $134 for nickel finish.

BISLEY MODEL SAA - same cals. as SAA, 4 3/4, 5 1/2, 7 1/2, or 10 (disc.) in. barrel, patterned after the Colt Bisley Model, smooth walnut grips, standard or target configuration, choice of bone case/Dome Blue, bone case/Armoury Blue, or nickel finish. Disc. 1998, reintroduced 2000-2002, again in 2004.

	MSR $1,099	$950	$850	$750	$625	$525	$450	$375

Add $130 for Armory Blue/Old Armory Bone Case finish.

Add $266 for nickel finish.

Add $230 for Target Model with adj. sights, or $381 for Target Model with nickel finish.

BIRDSHEAD MODEL SAA - same cals. as SAA, patterned after the Colt Model 1877 Thunderer, 3 1/2, 4, or 4 3/4 in. barrel with ejector, case colored frame. Mfg. 1997-2002.

	$975	$825	$725	$625	$525	$425	$325

Last MSR was $1,150.

Add $149 for nickel finish.

GRADING - PPGS™	100%	98%	95%	90%	80%	70%	60%

CHINA CAMP - various cals., designed for competition shooting, silver steel competition finish with two-piece hard rubber grips. Mfg. 2000-2003.

	$975	$850	$725	$625	$525	$425	$325

Last MSR was $1,200.

SHERIFF'S MODEL - similar cals. as the SAA, 2 1/2, 3, 3 1/2, or 4 in. barrel w/o ejector rod housing, U.S. hard rubber grips, choice of bone case/blue or nickel finish. New 2004.

MSR $949	$850	$750	$675	$600	$525	$450	$375

Add $271 for nickel finish.

RODEO - .32-20 WCF (new 2005), .38 Spl., .38-40 WCF (new 2005), .44-40 WCF, .44 Spl. (new 2005), or .45 LC, 4 3/4, 5 1/2, or 7 1/2 (new 2004) in. barrel, matte blue finish, fixed firing pin, square notch rear sight, hard rubber or Tru-Ivory grips, white sided hammer became standard 2005, entry level cowboy action shooting model. New 2002.

MSR $741	$660	$575	$500	$450	$400	$350	$315

Add $131 for Rodeo Heritage Model with Tru-Ivory grips (disc. 2005).

GUNSLINGER - .32-20 WCF, .38-40 WCF, .38 Spl., .44-40 WCF, .44 Spl., or .45 LC cal., 4 3/4, 5 1/2, or 7 1/2 in. barrel, cross-pin frame, cowboy action aged bluing, hard rubber grips, antique finish, square notch rear and front blade sights. New 2005.

MSR $968	$865	$725	$625	$525	$450	$375	$300

OMNI-POTENT SIX SHOOTER - various cals., 4 3/4, 5 1/2, or 7 1/2 in. barrel, choice of case colored, Old Armory Bone Case or Armory blue finish, checkered Bisley style walnut grips with round butt and lanyard loop. Mfg. 2000-2002, reintroduced 2004.

MSR $1,265	$1,075	$925	$825	$725	$625	$525	$425

Add $34 for nickel finish.
Add $60 for Omni-Target Model with raised adj. sights.

OMNI-POTENT SNUBNOSE - various cals., 2, 3, or 4 in. barrel, full Armory blue or nickel finish, checkered Bisley style walnut grips with round butt and lanyard loop. Mfg. 2000-2002, reintroduced 2004.

MSR $940	$850	$750	$650	$550	$475	$400	$325

Add $45 for nickel finish.

PLINKER - .22 LR or .22 Mag. cal., 4 3/4, 5 1/2, or 7 1/2 in. barrel, Old Armoury Bone Case/Dome Blue finish, U.S. hard rubber grips, square notch rear and square front blade sights, includes extra .22 Mag. cylinder. New 2004.

MSR $949	$850	$750	$650	$550	$475	$400	$325

Add $41 for Target Model with adj. sights.

HUNTER - .17 HMR cal., 7 1/2 in. barrel, matte blue finish, adj. rear sight, replaceable front blade sight, drilled and tapped, U.S. hard rubber grips, 3.5 lbs. Limited mfg. 2004-2005.

	$750	$650	$550	$475	$400	$325	$275

Last MSR was $839.

RIFLES: REPRODUCTIONS, LEVER ACTION

LIGHTNING PREMIUM GRADE RIFLE - .38-40 WCF, .44-40 WCF, or .45 LC cal., patterned after the Colt Lightning rifle, 26 in. round or octagon barrel, 15 shot mag., straight grip uncheckered walnut stock and small checkered forearm.

MSR $1,295	$1,100	$975	$875	$775	$650	$550	$425

Add $200 for half-round/half-octagon barrel.
Add $150 for nickel frame and blue barrel.

GRADING - PPGS™	100%	98%	95%	90%	80%	70%	60%

✳ *Deluxe Lightning Rifle* - similar to Premium Grade, except has deluxe checkered semi-pistol grip stock and forearm, choice of 26 in. octagon, round or half-round, half-octagon barrel with half mag.

MSR $1,995	$1,750	$1,500	$1,250	$1,000	$875	$750	$675

Add $280 for half-round, half-octagon barrel.
Add $200 for nickel frame/blue barrel.

LIGHTNING PREMIUM GRADE CARBINE - similar to Lightning Rifle, except has 20 in. round barrel and 12 shot mag.

MSR $1,295	$1,100	$975	$875	$775	$650	$550	$425

Add $255 for Lightweight Baby Carbine with special barrel taper and lightweight forearm.
Add $150 for nickel frame/blue barrel.

LIGHTNING COWBOY RIFLE/CARBINE - .38-40 WCF, .44-40 WCF, or .45 LC cal., 20 in. (carbine) or 26 (rifle) in. round barrel with ladder (carbine) or buckhorn rear sight, matte metal and wood finish.

MSR $995	$875	$775	$650	$575	$500	$425	$350

UNIVERSAL FIREARMS

Previous division of Iver Johnson's Arms, Inc. that was established during 1982. Formerly imported out of Hialeah, FL. Previously manufactured in Jacksonville, AR.

PISTOLS: SEMI-AUTO

MODEL 3000 ENFORCER PISTOL - .30 Carbine cal., walnut stock, 11 1/4 in. barrel, 17 3/4 in. overall, 15, and 30 shot. Mfg. 1964-83. Also see listing under Iver Johnson.

	100%	98%	95%	90%	80%	70%	60%
Blue finish	$325	$275	$235	$200	$185	$170	$160
Nickel-plated	$350	$295	$250	$235	$220	$200	$185
Gold-plated	$350	$275	$250	$225	$200	$185	$165
Stainless	$425	$350	$275				

Add $50 for Teflon-S finish.

RIFLES: SEMI-AUTO, CARBINES

MODEL 440 VULCAN - .44 Mag. cal., slide action, 18 1/4 in. barrel with adj. rear and front ramp sight, 5 shot detachable mag.

	$325	$275	$230	$195	$175	$150	$135

1000 MILITARY - .30 Carbine cal., "G.I." copy, satin blue, birch stock, 18 in. barrel. Disc.

	$300	$265	$235	$200	$180	$170	$160

MODEL 1003 - 16, 18, or 20 in. barrel, .30 M1 copy, blue finish, adj. sight, birch stock, 5 1/2 lbs. Also see listing under Iver Johnson.

	$300	$265	$235	$200	$180	$170	$160

Last MSR was $203.

✳ *Model 1010* - nickel finish, disc.

	$325	$275	$240	$210	$180	$155	$120

✳ *Model 1015* - gold electroplated, disc.

	$325	$275	$250	$215	$185	$160	$130

Add $45 for 4X scope.

1005 DELUXE - .30 Carbine cal., custom Monte Carlo walnut stock, high polish blue, oil finish on wood.

	$350	$315	$275	$250	$225	$200	$180

GRADING - PPGS™	100%	98%	95%	90%	80%	70%	60%

1006 STAINLESS - .30 Carbine cal., stainless steel construction, birch stock, 18 in. barrel, 6 lbs.

	$375	$300	$265				

Last MSR was $234.

1020 TEFLON - .30 Carbine cal., Dupont Teflon-S finish on metal parts, black or grey color, Monte Carlo stock.

	$350	$275	$250				

1256 "FERRET" - .256 Win. Mag. cal., M1 Action, satin blue, birch stock, 18 in. barrel, 5 1/2 lbs.

	$300	$265	$235	$200	$175	$165	$155

Last MSR was $219.

2200 LEATHERNECK - .22 LR cal., recoil operated action, birch stock, satin blue, 18 in. barrel, 5 1/2 lbs.

	$240	$190	$180	$170	$160	$145	$135

5000 PARATROOPER - .30 Carbine cal., metal folding extension, walnut stock, 16 or 18 in. barrel.

	$450	$375	$325	$285	$250	$225	$200

Last MSR was $234.

5006 PARATROOPER STAINLESS - similar to 5000, only stainless with 18 in. barrel only.

	$525	$425	$350				

Last MSR was $281.

1981 COMMEMORATIVE CARBINE - .30 Carbine cal., "G.I Military" model, cased with accessories. Mfg. for 40th Anniversary 1941-81.

	$650	$490	$400				

SHOTGUNS

All Universal shotguns were disc. after 1982.

MODEL 7312 O/U - 12 ga., 30 in. full and mod., VR barrel, boxlock, vent. barrel spacer, SST, auto ejectors, barrels ported to reduce recoil, engraved, color case hardened receiver, trap or skeet style, checkered select stock.

	$1,650	$1,540	$1,485	$1,430	$1,320	$1,210	$1,045

MODEL 7412 O/U - similar to 7312, without ejectors, blue and silver receiver.

	$1,430	$1,210	$1,155	$1,100	$9,900	$880	$825

MODEL 7712 O/U - 12 ga., 26 or 28 in. barrel, VR, non-selective single trigger, extractors, light engraving, checkered pistol grip stock.

	$440	$415	$385	$360	$330	$275	$220

MODEL 7812 O/U - similar to 7712, with auto ejectors and more engraving.

	$605	$580	$550	$525	$470	$415	$385

MODEL 7912 O/U - similar to 7812, with selective single trigger and gold damascene engraving.

	$1,210	$1,155	$1,100	$1,045	$965	$880	$825

MODEL 7112 SxS - 12 ga., 26 or 28 in. barrels, various chokes, boxlock, extractors, engraved case hardened frame, checkered pistol grip stock.

	$330	$305	$275	$250	$195	$165	$140

DOUBLE WING SxS - 10, 12, 20 ga., or .410 bore, 26, 28, or 30 in. barrels, various chokes, double triggers, boxlock, extractors, checkered pistol grip stock.

	$330	$305	$275	$250	$195	$165	$140
10 gauge	$385	$360	$330	$305	$250	$220	$165

GRADING - PPGS™	100%	98%	95%	90%	80%	70%	60%

MODEL 7212 SINGLE BARREL TRAP - 12 ga., 30 in. full, Simmons type VR, engraved case colored frame, vent. barrel to reduce recoil, boxlock, auto ejector, select checkered trap style stock.

	$1,100	$990	$935	$880	$770	$715	$605

USELTON ARMS INC

Current pistol manufacturer located in Goodlettsville, TN.

PISTOLS: SEMI-AUTO

Uselton Arms Inc. manufactures M1911-style semi-auto pistols. Current models include the Compact Classic Companion (MSR $2,249), Compact Classic (MSR $1,979), Carry Classic (MSR $1,989), Tactical Cobra Coat (MSR $1,925), Uselton National Match (MSR $1,749), and the Ultra Compact Classic (MSR $1,949-$3,250). Please contact the company for more information (see Trademark Index).

UZI

Currently manufactured by Israeli Military Industries (IMI). No commercial U.S. importation currently. During 1996-1998, Mossberg imported the Uzi Eagle pistols. These models were imported by UZI America, Inc., subsidiary of O.F. Mossberg & Sons, Inc. Previously imported by Action Arms, Ltd., located in Philadelphia, PA until 1994.

Serial number prefixes used on Uzi Firearms are as follows: "SA" on all 9mm Para. semi-auto carbines Models A and B; "45 SA" on all .45 ACP Model B carbines; "41 SA" on all .41 AE Model B carbines; "MC" on all 9mm Para. (only cal. made) semi-auto mini-carbines; "UP" on all 9mm Para. semi-auto Uzi pistols; "45 UP" on all .45 semi-auto Uzi pistols (disc. 1989). There are also prototypes or experimental Uzis with either "AA" or "AAL" prefixes - these are rare and will command premiums over values listed below.

CARBINES: SEMI-AUTO

CARBINE MODEL A - 9mm Para. cal., semi-auto, 16.1 in. barrel, parkerized finish, 25 shot mag., mfg. by IMI 1980-1983 and ser. range is SA01,001-SA037,000.

	$1,650	$1,475	$1,325	$1,125	$975	$875	$750

Approx. 100 Model As were mfg. with a nickel finish. These are rare and command considerable premiums over values listed above.

CARBINE MODEL B - 9mm Para., .41 Action Express (new 1987), or .45 ACP (new 1987) cal., semi-auto carbine, 16.1 in. barrel, baked enamel black finish over phosphated (parkerized) base finish, 16 (.45 ACP), 20 (.41 AE) or 25 (9mm Para.) shot mag., metal folding stock, includes molded case and carrying sling, 8.4 lbs. Mfg. 1983 - until Federal legislation disc. importation 1989 and ser. range is SA037,001-SA073,544.

	$1,500	$1,325	$1,200	$1,000	$950	$850	$750

Last MSR was $698.

Subtract approx. $150 for .41 AE or .45 ACP cal.
Add $150 for .22 cal. conversion kit (new 1987).
Add $215 for .45 ACP to 9mm Para./.41 AE conversion kit.
Add $150 for 9mm Para. to .41 AE (or vice-versa) conversion kit.
Add $215 for 9mm Para. to .45 ACP conversion kit.

MINI CARBINE - 9mm Para. cal., similar to Carbine except has 19 3/4 in. barrel, 20 shot mag., swing-away metal stock, scaled down version of the regular carbine, 7.2 lbs. New 1987. Federal legislation disc. importation 1989.

	$2,375	$2,175	$1,850	$1,600	1,350	$1,150	$995

Last MSR was $698.

GRADING - PPGS™	100%	98%	95%	90%	80%	70%	60%

PISTOLS: SEMI-AUTO

UZI PISTOL - 9mm Para. or .45 ACP cal. (disc.), semi-auto pistol, 4 1/2 in. barrel, parkerized finish, 10 (.45 ACP) or 20 (9mm Para.) shot mag., supplied with molded carrying case, sight adj. key and mag. loading tool, 3.8 lbs. Importation disc. 1993.

	$975	$850	$795	$750	$700	$650	$600

Last MSR was $695.

Add $285 for .45 ACP to 9mm Para./.41 AE conversion kit.
Add $100 for 9mm Para. to .41 AE conversion kit.
Add approx. 30%-40% for two-line slide marking "45 ACP Model 45."

UZI EAGLE SERIES - 9mm Para., .40 S&W, or .45 ACP cal., semi-auto double action, various configurations, matte finish with black synthetic grips, 10 shot mag. Mfg. 1997-1998. Imported by Magnum Research.

* *Full-Size Eagle* - 9mm Para. or .40 S&W cal., 4.4 in. barrel, steel construction, decocking feature, Tritium sights, polygonal rifling. Imported 1997-98.

	$485	$440	$400	$365	$335	$330	$275

Last MSR was $535.

* *Short Slide Eagle* - 9mm Para., .40 S&W, or .45 ACP cal., similar to Full-Size Eagle, except has 3.7 in. barrel. Imported 1997-98.

	$485	$440	$400	$365	$335	$330	$275

Last MSR was $535.

Add $31 for .45 ACP cal.

* *Compact Eagle* - 9mm Para. or .40 S&W cal., available in double action with decocking or double action only, 3 1/2 in. barrel. Imported 1997-98.

	$485	$440	$400	$365	$335	$330	$275

Last MSR was $535.

* *Polymer Compact* - similar to Compact Eagle, except has compact polymer frame. Imported 1997-98.

	$485	$440	$400	$365	$335	$330	$275

Last MSR was $535.

NOTES

V SECTION

VM HY-TECH LLC

Current rifle manufacturer located in Phoenix, AZ. Dealer and direct sales.

GRADING - PPGS™	100%	98%	95%	90%	80%	70%	60%

RIFLES

VM15 - .223 Rem. or 9mm Para. cal., AR-15 style, semi-auto, unique side charging on left side of receiver operated by folding lever allowing easy replacement of scopes, 16, 20, or 24 in. fluted and ported Wilson barrel, aluminum free-floating hand guard, forged lower receiver, A-2 style buttstock with pistol grip, black finish. New 2002.

	100%	98%	95%	90%	80%	70%	60%
MSR $865	$800	$750	$675	$600	$550	$500	$400

Add $34 for side-charging loading (new 2005).
Add $310 for 9mm Para. cal.

VM-50 - .50 BMG cal., single shot, 18, 22, 30, or 36 in. Lothar Walther barrel with muzzle brake, aluminum stock, includes bipod, black finish, 22-29 lbs. New 2004.

	100%	98%	95%	90%	80%	70%	60%
MSR $2,299	$2,000	$1,775	$1,600	$1,475	$1,350	$1,225	$1,075

Add $40 - $120 for 22-36 in. barrel.

VALKYRIE ARMS LTD.

Current manufacturer located in Olympia, WA. Dealer sales.

Valkyrie Arms Ltd. manufactures semi-auto copies of the M3A1, Browning 1919, and DeLisle Commando Carbine. Models include: M3-A1 SA Grease Gun ($750 MSR), Browning M1919-SA ($2,850 MSR), Delisle Commando Carbine ($1,795 MSR), DeLisle 2000 (bolt action, $1,695 MSR), Sten MKII/MKIII ($645 last MSR), and the DeLisle Sporter Carbine ($650 MSR). For more information, including availability, please contact the company directly (see Trademark Index).

VALMET

Current trademark manufactured in Brescia, Italy by Marocchi CD Europe, and imported beginning 2004 by Tristar, located in N. Kansas City, MO.

RIFLES: O/U

FINNCLASSIC 512 SC RIFLE/COMBO - .30-06, .308 Win. cal., 12 ga. (3 1/2 in. w/ choke tube) over .222 Rem. for combo, SST, rifle has cocking indicators, boxlock action, checkered Monte Carlo walnut stock and forearm, 7.7 (combo) or 8.25 lbs. Importation began 2004.

	100%	98%	95%	90%	80%	70%	60%
MSR $1,795	$1,575	$1,300	$1,050	$925	$825	$725	$625

Add $438 for double rifle configuration.

SHOTGUNS: O/U

FINNCLASSIC 512 - 12 or 20 ga., 3 in. chambers, boxlock action, blue (Field) or matte nickel finished receiver, choice of Sporting (12 ga. only, 28, 30, or 32 in. VR barrels with 11mm VR), Youth/Ladies (shorter LOP), or Field, 7.4 lbs. Importation began 2004.

	100%	98%	95%	90%	80%	70%	60%
MSR $1,185	$1,035	$900	$775	$675	$600	$525	$450

Add $22 for Sporting Clays configuration with 5 choke tubes.
Add $314 for Youth/Ladies model.

GRADING - PPGS™	100%	98%	95%	90%	80%	70%	60%

VALMET, INC.

Previous manufacturer located in Jyvaskyla, Finland. Previously imported by Stoeger Industries, Inc. located in South Hackensack, NJ.

The Valmet line was discontinued in 1989 and replaced by Tikka (please refer to the Tikka section in this text) in 1990.

RIFLES: SEMI-AUTO

HUNTER MODEL - .223 Rem., .243 Win., or .308 Win. cal., gas operated semi-auto, Kalashnikov action, 20 1/2 in. barrel, checkered walnut stock and forearm, matte finished metal, 5, 9, or 20 shot mag., 8 lbs. New 1986, Federal legislation disc. importation 1989.

$895	$795	$700	$625	$550	$500	$450

Last MSR was $795.

M-62S PARAMILITARY DESIGN RIFLE - 7.62x39 Russian, semi-auto version of Finn M-62, 15 or 30 shot mag., 16 5/8 in. barrel, gas operated, rotary bolt, adj. rear sight, tube steel or wood stock. Mfg. 1962-disc.

$1,800	$1,575	$1,375	$1,175	$975	$875	$775

M-71S - similar to M-62S, except .223 Rem. cal., reinforced resin or wood stock.

$1,450	$1,325	$1,175	$975	$875	$775	$675

MODEL 76 - .223 Rem., 7.62x39mm, or .308 Win. cal., gas operated semi-auto paramilitary design rifle, 16 3/4 in. or 20 1/2 (.308 only) in. barrel, 15 or 30 (7.62x39mm only) shot mag., parkerized finish. Federal legislation disc. importation 1989.

$1,950	$1,775	$1,550	$1,375	$1,175	$975	$875

Last MSR was $740.

Add $300 for folding, or $95-$125 for synthetic stock.

MODEL 78 - .308 Win. cal. only, similar to Model 76, except has 24 1/2 in. barrel, wood stock and forearm, and barrel bipod, 11 lbs. New 1987. Federal legislation disc. importation 1989.

$2,450	$2,225	$2,000	$1,825	$1,625	$1,475	$1,200

Last MSR was $1,060.

MODEL 82 BULLPUP - .223 Rem. cal., limited importation.

$2,500	$2,250	$2,000	$1,825	$1,625	$1,475	$1,200

SHOTGUNS/RIFLES: O/U

LION MODEL - 12 ga., 26, 28, or 30 in. barrels, various chokes, boxlock, SST, checkered stock. Mfg. 1947-68.

$415	$370	$340	$320	$305	$275	$240

MODEL 412 O/U SHOOTING SYSTEM - interchangeable barrel assemblies permit a double rifle, shotgun/rifle, and O/U shotgun configuration, user-installed interchangeable barrels, monobloc locking, rifle barrel positioning by adjustment, SST, extractors or ejectors, checkered walnut stock and forend, cocking indicators, blue finish. Importation on all models was disc. 1989.

Add $100 for synthetic stock on all 412 models.

* ✳ *Model 412S Field Grade* - 12 ga. was standard, auto ejectors, screw-in choke tubes, matte nickel finish. Imported 1986-89.

$855	$670	$580	$540	$475	$440	$400

Last MSR was $999.

Add 15% for 20 ga.

GRADING - PPGS™	100%	98%	95%	90%	80%	70%	60%

✳ *Model 412S Field and Target* - 12 ga. only, 2 3/4 and 3 in. chambers, ejectors. Disc. 1988.

	$775	$660	$580	$540	$475	$440	$400

Last MSR was $874.

✳ *Model 412ST Trap and Skeet* - 12 ga., Monte Carlo stock on Trap model, 28 in. barrels on Skeet model, screw-in chokes standard.

	$1,040	$875	$695	$650	$580	$540	$475

Last MSR was $1,215.

✳ *Model 412ST Premium Grade Target* - similar to Model 412ST Trap and Skeet, except has better walnut and checkering. Imported 1987-89.

	$1,355	$1,050	$865	$750	$640	$580	$515

Last MSR was $1,550.

✳ *Model 412S Combination Gun* - combination, 12 ga, 3 in. chamber over choice of .222 Rem., .223 Rem., .243 Win., .30-06, or .308 Win. cal., extractors.

	$1,025	$850	$675	$600	$550	$475	$440

Last MSR was $1,615.

✳ *Model 412S Double Rifle* - .243 Win. (disc. 1987), .30-06, .308 Win. (disc. 1987), .375 H&H Mag. (disc. 1987), or 9.3x73R cal., extractors, 24 in. barrels.

	$1,060	$895	$725	$650	$580	$540	$475

Last MSR was $1,275.

Add $100 for 9.3x74R cal. or .375 H&H Mag. cal.

This model in .30-06 cal. has extractors only while in 9.3x74R cal. ejectors are standard.

✳ *Model 412K Double Rifle* - .30-06 or .308 Win. cal. only, 24 in. separated barrels, extractors. Importation disc. 1986.

	$800	$660	$580	$540	$475	$440	$400

Last MSR was $899.

✳ *Model 412 Engraved* - satin finish, receiver extensively bank note engraved in choice of 4 patterns, select Triple-X wood hand-checkered - choice of field or target, available in any Valmet model.

This model had limited availability and prices were on request from the manufacturer.

✳ *Extra Barrel Assemblies (Model 412 O/U)* - $505-$605 each for shotgun (includes screw-in chokes), $579 each for shotgun/rifle combo, $660 each for double rifle (add $100 for ejectors).

VALTRO

Current manufacturer established during 1988 and located in Brescia, Italy. No current U.S. importation. Previously imported by Valtro USA, Inc., located in San Rafael, CA.

Valtro manufactures both excellent quality slide action and semi-auto shotguns, in addition to a semi-auto pistol, and a variety of signal pistols. Please contact the company directly for more product information and availability (see Trademark Index listing).

PISTOLS: SEMI-AUTO

1998 A1 .45 ACP - .45 ACP cal., forged National Match frame and slide, 5 in. barrel, deluxe wood grips, 8 shot mag., ambidextrous safety, blue finish, flat checkered mainspring housing, front and rear slide serrations, beveled mag. well, speed trigger, 40 oz. Limited importation beginning 1998.

MSR N/A	$1,095	$850	$675	$600	$500	$425	$375

GRADING - PPGS™	100%	98%	95%	90%	80%	70%	60%

SHOTGUNS: SLIDE ACTION

TACTICAL 98 SHOTGUN - 12 ga. only, 18 1/2 or 20 in. barrel featuring MMC ghost ring sights and integral muzzle brake, 5 shot mag., internal chokes, receiver side-saddle holds 6 exposed rounds, pistol grip or standard stock, matte black finish, lightweight. Limited importation beginning 1998.

MSR N/A	$790	$630	$525	$475	$425	$400	$360

VARBERGER

Previous rifle manufacturer located in Varberg, Sweden. Previously imported by Hill Country Wholesale, Inc. located in Austin, TX, and distributed by Paul & Associates, located in Wellsville, KS until late 1995.

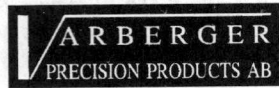

RIFLES: BOLT ACTION

MODEL 711 GRADE 1 - available in 19 cals. between .22 PPC and .358 Norma, bolt action design featuring specially designed and manufactured receiver, rotary mag., 6 lug engine-turned bolt, and stock featuring metal retainer plate, individually test-fired. Imported 1994-98.

	$950	$850	$750	$650	$550	$450	$375

Last MSR was $1,080.

MODEL 717 GRADE 1 MAGNUM - available in 11 Mag. cals. between .257 Wby. Mag. and .375 H&H. Imported 1994-98.

	$980	$875	$765	$650	$550	$450	$375

Last MSR was $1,130.

MODEL 757 GRADE 2 DELUXE - deluxe variation of the Model 711. Imported 1994-98.

	$1,775	$1,500	$1,250	$995	$895	$795	$695

Last MSR was $2,035.

Add $45 for Mag. cals.

MODEL 77 GRADE 3 PREMIER - top-of-the-line model. Imported 1994-98.

	$1,995	$1,675	$1,350	$1,050	$925	$795	$695

Last MSR was $2,375.

Add $65 for Mag. cals.

VARNER SPORTING ARMS, INC.

Previous manufacturer located in Marietta, GA circa 1988-1989.

RIFLES: SINGLE SHOT

VARNER FAVORITE HUNTER - .22 LR cal., patterned after J. Stevens Favorite Model, 1/2 round - 1/2 octagon 21 1/2 in. takedown barrel, blue frame, walnut stock and forearm, aperture rear sight, 5 lbs. Mfg. 1988-89.

	$325	$270	$220	$185	$150	$130	$110

Last MSR was $369.

* *Hunter Deluxe* - similar to Favorite Hunter, except has case colored frame and lever, and deluxe walnut stock and forearm. Mfg. 1988-89.

	$450	$375	$285	$225	$175	$150	$135

Last MSR was $500.

* *Presentation Grade* - includes target hammer and trigger, AAA quality checkered stock and forearm, includes takedown case. Mfg. 1988-89.

	$480	$400	$310	$250	$195	$170	$155

Last MSR was $569.

GRADING - PPGS™	100%	98%	95%	90%	80%	70%	60%

PRESENTATION ENGRAVED - previously available in a No. 1 Grade for $649, a No. 2 for $779, or a No. 3 for $1,099.

VECTOR ARMS, INC.

Current paramilitary rifle manufacturer located in N. Salt Lake, UT.

RIFLES: SEMI-AUTO

Vector Arms offers the following semi-auto paramilitary style rifles currently: V-53 (semi-auto version of the HK53 - $1,350 MSR), V-93 (semi-auto version of the HK33 - $1,100 MSR), Uzi full size post-ban ($595 MSR), and the RPD (drum of belt fed - $1,995 MSR). Please contact the company directly for more information on these rifles, including availability (see Trademark Index).

VEKTOR

Current trademark established during 1953 as part of LEW (Lyttelton Engineering Work). Currently manufactured in South Africa. In 1995, Vektor became a separate division of Denel.

Vektor has been manufacturing high quality and reliable firearms, including semi-auto and slide action rifles, for South African law enforcement for quite some time, in addition to having secured contracts with many foreign countries.

Since Vektor does not currently have any U.S. importation, values below reflect most recent importation, and last MSRs are based on 2001 pricing.

PISTOLS: SEMI-AUTO

All Vektor pistols feature polygonal rifling, excluding the Z88.

MODEL CP1 - 9mm Para. cal., 4 in. barrel, compact model with unique aesthetics and ergonomic design allowing no buttons or levers on exterior surfaces, hammerless, striker fire system, black or nickel finished slide, 10 shot mag., approx. 25 1/2 oz. Imported 1999-disc.

	$440	$400	$360	$330	$300	$280	$260

Last MSR was $480.

Add $20 for nickel slide finish.
This model was recalled due to design problems.

MODEL Z88 - 9mm Para. cal., double action, patterned after the M92 Beretta, 5 in. barrel, steel construction, black synthetic grips, 10 shot mag., 35 oz. Importation began 1999.

MSR N/A	$550	$495	$450	$400	$360	$330	$295

Last MSR was $620.

MODEL SP1 - 9mm Para. cal., double action, 5 in. barrel with polygonal rifling, wrap-around checkered synthetic grips, matte blue or normal black finish, 2.2. lbs. Importation began 1999.

MSR N/A	$535	$485	$445	$395	$360	$330	$295

Last MSR was $600.

Add $30 for natural anodized or nickel finish.
Add $230 for Sport Pistol with compensated barrel.

* **Model SP1 Compact (General's Model)** - similar to Model SP1, except is compact variation with 4 in. barrel, 25.4 oz. Importation began 1999.

MSR N/A	$575	$510	$460	$410	$360	$330	$295

Last MSR was $650.

* **Model SP1 Sport Pistol/Tuned** - similar to Model SP1, except has is available with tuned action or target pistol features. Importation began 1999.

MSR N/A	$1,050	$900	$775	$650	$525	$400	$350

Last MSR was $1,200.

Add $100 for Target Pistol with dual color finish.

GRADING - PPGS™	100%	98%	95%	90%	80%	70%	60%

MODEL SP2 - .40 S&W cal., otherwise similar to Model SP1. Importation began in 1999.

	MSR N/A	$575	$510	$460	$410	$360	$330	$295

Last MSR was $650.

Add $190 for 9mm Para. conversion kit.

✱ *Model SP2 Compact (General's Model)* - similar to Model SP2, except is compact variation. Importation began 1999.

	MSR N/A	$575	$510	$460	$410	$360	$330	$295

Last MSR was $650.

✱ *Model SP2 Competition* - competition variation of the Model SP2 featuring 5 7/8 in. barrel, additional magazine guide, enlarged safety levers and mag. catch, and straight trigger, 35 oz. Importation began 2000.

	MSR N/A	$850	$775	$675	$575	$510	$460	$395

Last MSR was $1,000.

STOCK GUN - 9mm Para. cal., normal black finish. Importation began 2000.

	MSR N/A	$850	$775	$675	$575	$510	$460	$395

Last MSR was $1,000.

ULTRA MODEL - 9mm Para. or .40 S&W (new 2000) cal., top-of-the-line double action with most performance features, optional Lynx (disc. 1999) or Tasco (new 2000) scope. Importation began 1999.

	MSR N/A	$1,950	$1,700	$1,500	$1,300	$1,100	$900	$700

Last MSR was $2,150.

Subtract $150 if w/o Tasco scope.

RIFLES: BOLT-ACTION

K98 - standard cals are .243 Win., .270 Win., .30-06, .308 Win., 7x57mm Mauser, 7x64 Bren., Mag. cals. include .300 Win. Mag., .300 H&H, .416 Rigby, .470 Capstick, .458 Win. Mag., or 9.3x62mm, 5 shot staggered mag., non-rotating long extractor, positive bolt stop, checkered walnut stock, hammer forged barrel, iron sights on Mag. cals. only. Importation began 2000.

	MSR N/A	$995	$850	$775	$675	$575	$510	$460

Last MSR was $1,149.

Add $100 for Mag. cals.

RIFLES: SLIDE ACTION

H5 - .223 Rem. cal., 18 or 22 in. barrel, rotating bolt, uncheckered forearm and thumb-hole stock with pad, includes 4X scope with long eye relief, 9 lbs., 7 oz.-10 1/4 lbs. Importation began 2000.

	MSR N/A	$775	$650	$575	$510	$460	$410	$350

Last MSR was $850.

VEPR. RIFLES

Currently manufactured by Molot JSC (Vyatskie Polyany Machine Building Factory) located in Russia. Previously imported during 2004 by European American Armory, located in Sharps, FL, and until 2003 by ZDF Import/Export, Inc., located in Salt Lake City, UT.

RIFLES: SEMI-AUTO

VEPR HUNTER (VEPR II) CARBINE/RIFLE - .223 Rem., .270 Win. (new 2004), .30-06 (new 2004), .308 Win., or 7.62x39mm (new 2001) cal., features Vepr.'s semi-auto action, 16 (.223 Rem. or 7.62x39mm cal.), 20 1/2 (carbine, .308 Win. only, disc.), 21.6 or 23 1/4 (disc.) in. barrel with adj. rear sight, scope mount rail built into receiver top, standard or optional thumbhole checkered walnut stock with

GRADING - PPGS™	100%	98%	95%	90%	80%	70%	60%

recoil pad and forend, paddle mag. release, 5 or 10 shot mag., approx 8.6 lbs. Imported 1999-2004.

	$430	$395	$360	$330	$300	$275	$250

Last MSR was $499.

Add $20 for .270 Win. or .30-06 cal.

SUPER VEPR - .308 Win. cal. Limited importation 2001-2003.

	$800	$725	$650	$600	$550	$500	$450

Last MSR was $900.

VERNEY-CARRON

Current manufacturer of shotguns and rifles established during 1820, and located in St. Etienne, France. Currently imported by Verney-

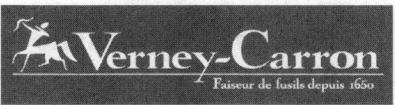

Carron USA, Inc., located in Clay Center, KS. Currently distributed by Process Solutions, Inc., located in Fayetteville, WV. Previously distributed until 2002 by the Graystone Group, located in Chicago, IL. Previously imported by Yellow Brick Entreprises, located in Clay Center, KS during 1998 only.

Established during 1820 by Claude Verney-Carron, whose ancestors were "Faiseur de fusils" - gunmakers - since at least 1650. Verney-Carron is proud to reflect on six generations of family ownership, and is the largest French manufacturer of hunting shotguns and rifles. Please contact the distributor directly for more information, including current model availability and domestic pricing regarding these fine firearms (see Trademark Index).

In 2000, Verney-Carron SA and Y.B.E., Inc. located in Clay Center, KS (distributor of Hastings barrels & choke tubes) established a joint venture, Verney-Carron USA, Inc., located in Clay Center, KS. This joint venture purchased Sporting Arms Manufacturing, Inc., the manufacturer of the Snake Charmer II shotgun. During 2001, Sporting Arms Manufacturing was dissolved, and the Snake Charmer II is now manufactured by Verney-Carron USA, Inc. Please refer to the separate Snake Charmer listing.

RIFLES

Current models include the Sagittaire NT O/U (with or w/o sideplates), the Impact Plus bolt action with vent. quarter rib, front and rear sight, as well as the semi-auto Impact Auto Rifle. All of these rifles are currently equipped for the easy mounting of an Optimum Infallible sight system.

SHOTGUNS

Verney-Carron makes a wide variety of shotgun models and configurations, including the Super 9III O/U (with or w/o sideplates, many options are available), Sagittaire NT O/U series, Alto 6 semi-auto, and the J.E.T. SxS.

VERONA

Current shotgun manufacturer located in Italy. Currently imported by B.C. Outdoors, located in Boulder City, NV.

COMBINATION GUNS

LX1001 EXPRESS COMBO - .223 Rem., .243 Win., .270 Win., .30-06. or .308 Win. over 20 ga., 2 3/4 in. chambers, 26 in. barrels, vent. rib, ejectors, sling swivel, checkered oil finished walnut stock with Bavarian cheekpiece, includes screw chokes, leather canvas hard case, approx. 6 lbs.

MSR $2,583	$2,250	$1,900	$1,500	$1,200	$975	$875	$800

GRADING - PPGS™	100%	98%	95%	90%	80%	70%	60%

SHOTGUNS: O/U

LX501 HUNTING MODEL - 12, 20, 28 ga. or .410 bore, 2 3/4 (28 ga.) or 3 in. chambers, 28 in. barrels, gold plated SST, ejectors, blue steel receiver with light engraving, checkered walnut stock, black rubber recoil pad, 6-7 lbs.

MSR $791	$725	$650	$575	$525	$475	$425	$375

Add $44 for 28 ga. or $23 for .410 bore.

* **LX501 Two Barrel Set** - includes choice of 20 and 28 ga., or 28 ga. and .410 bore, 28 in. barrels. New 2002.

MSR $1,379	$1,200	$1,050	$925	$850	$775	$700	$625

LX680 SERIES - 12 or 20 ga., 2 3/4 or 3 in. chambers, available in Sporting or Trap configuration, 29, 30, 32, or 34 in. ported or unported barrels, Interchokes, available in Sporting Clays, Skeet, or Competition Trap configurations, gold SST, silver alloy receiver with light engraving, vent. rib, adj. comb, 6 1/4-8 lbs.

MSR $1,043	$925	$825	$725	$650	$575	$500	$450

Add $468 for Gold Trap configuration.
Add $1,222 for Gold Trap combo.

LX692 SERIES - 12, 20, 28 ga. or .410 bore, 2 3/4 (28 ga.) or 3 in. chambers, available in Skeet, Sporting, or Trap configuration, 28 in. barrels, gold plated SST, ejectors, steel receiver with engraved sideplates and gold bird inlays, oil finished hand-checkered walnut stock and Schnabel forend, black rubber recoil pad, 6-7 lbs.

MSR $1,043	$925	$825	$725	$650	$575	$500	$450

Add $468 for Gold Trap configuration.
Add $1,222 for Gold Trap combo.

LX702 SERIES - 12 or 20 ga., 3 in. chambers, available in Skeet, Sporting, or Trap configuration, 28 in. barrels, hand-rubbed Turkish walnut stock and forend, color case hardened receiver and sideplates, engraving with gold inlaid bird hunting scenes, 6-7 lbs.

MSR $1,447	$1,300	$1,100	$900	$775	$650	$575	$500

LX980 SERIES - 12 ga., 2 3/4 in. chambers, available in Trap, Skeet or Sporting configuration, 30 or 32 in. ported barrels, oil finished Montecarlo Turkish walnut stock and forend with adj. comb, color case hardened receiver, wide competition rib, removable competition trigger assembly, includes deluxe case, 7 1/2 lbs.

MSR $3,527	$3,150	$2,700	$2,325	$2,000	$1,650	$1,325	$1,175

Add $249 for Gold Competition Skeet or Trap configuration.

SHOTGUNS: SxS

B.C. Outdoors was scheduled to begin importation of the SS662 and the SS772, manufactured by Bernardelli. There has been limited importation to date, with no U.S. retail pricing available. Please contact B.C. Outdoors directly for more information on these models.

SHOTGUNS: SEMI-AUTO

SX401 HUNTING SERIES - 12 ga. only, 3 in. chamber, 28 in. barrel, 5 shot mag., Turkish walnut stock, lightweight aluminum aircraft alloy reciever, sling swivels, approx. 6 3/4 lbs.

MSR $427	$375	$335	$300	$275	$250	$225	$200

GRADING - PPGS™	100%	98%	95%	90%	80%	70%	60%

SX405 HUNTING SERIES - 12 ga. only, 3 in. chamber, 22, 24, 26, or 28 in. barrel, 5 shot mag., black synthetic, Realtree Wetland or Hardwood camo finished stock, lightweight aluminum aircraft alloy reciever, sling swivels, approx. 6 1/2 lbs.

MSR $352	$315	$285	$265	$245	$225	$200	$175

Add $88 for camo finish.
Add $138 for 22 in. slug barrel.
Subtract $17 for 26 in. barrel.

✱ *SX405 Hunting Combo* - includes 22 in. slug and 26 in. barrels.

MSR $503	$450	$400	$360	$330	$300	$275	$250

SX801 SERIES - 12 ga. only, 2 3/4 in. chamber, 28 or 30 in. ported barrel, available in Sporting or Gold Sporting configuration, vent. rib, Hi-Viz front sight, black anodized receiver, gold trigger, includes four extended Trulock chokes, oil finished Turkish Montecarlo stock, mfg. by Bernardelli, approx. 6 3/4 lbs.

MSR $868	$775	$700	$625	$550	$500	$450	$395

Add $197 for Gold Sporting model with adj. comb.

VICKERS LIMITED

Previous manufacturer located in Crayford/Kent, England.

RIFLES: SINGLE SHOT, TARGET

JUBILEE SINGLE SHOT TARGET RIFLE - Martini type action, .22 LR cal., 28 in. heavy barrel, target sights, one-piece pistol grip, target stock, pre-WWII.

	$440	$330	$305	$275	$250	$220	$165

EMPIRE MODEL - similar to Jubilee, with 27 or 30 in. barrel, straight grip stock.

	$415	$310	$285	$260	$220	$195	$150

VICTOR ARMS CORPORATION

Previous manufacturer located in Houston, TX.

Victor Arms Corporation manufactured limited quantities of a .22 LR upper unit for the AR-15. It works by removing the standard .223 upper, and replacing it with the V22 upper assembly and magazine. Additionally, a complete protoype gun was also manufactured.

VICTORY ARMS CO. LIMITED

Previously manufactured in prototype format only by Modern Manufacturing Company located in Phoenix, AZ.

PISTOL: SEMI-AUTO

MODEL MC5 - while a few prototypes were mfg. for trade shows (circa 1991-92), this model was never commercially manufactured. Last advertised retail was $465.

VIERLINGS

The German word Vierling denotes a four barrel long arm configuration mostly manufactured in Germany and Austria.

This configuration of long arm has four barrels, usually a mixture of centerfire/rimfire caliber barrel(s) and shotgun barrel(s). Some Vierlings may also have all-shotgun barrels or all-rifle barrels (rare). Vierlings typically have two triggers, both single-set. Barrel selectors are usually on the top tang. This unusual configuration is mostly of German mfg., although there are a few Austrian specimens also (the gunmakers of Ferlach still custom-make this model). All Vierlings are mfg. one at a time, with fabrication being very complicated, lengthy, and expensive. As a result, every Vierling must be appraised individually - most

Vierling Configurations

older manufactured specimens, however, are priced in the $4,000-$9,500 range, depending on the desirability of the configuration, and overall condition. Recently and currently manufactured special order Vierlings are priced from $8,500-$40,000 range, depending on features, engraving, and other options.

VIRGIN VALLEY CUSTOM GUNS

Current manufacturer of custom bolt action rifles located in Hurricane, UT.

RIFLES: BOLT ACTION

Virgin Valley offers custom barrels, stocks, wildcat chamberings, and many other options and riflesmithing services. Please contact the company directly for more information on these services (see Trademark Index).

SAFARI RIFLE - various big game cals., choice of Dakota Mod. 76, Mauser, or Win. Mod. 70 action, individually custom ordered.

Please contact the company directly for a individual price quotation and delivery time for this model.

VIRGINIAN

This trademark can be located under the Interarms section in this text.

VIS

Currently manufactured by the F.B. Radom arsenal in Radom, Poland. Please refer to the Radom section in this text.

VOERE (AUSTRIA)

Current manufacturer established during 1965, and located in Kufstein, Austria. No current U.S. importation.

Voere of Austria is not associated with the Voere trademark of Germany that was taken over by Mauser-Werke after going bankrupt. Voere manufactures a complete line of quality rimfire semi-auto and centerfire bolt-action/semi-auto rifles. Their caseless ammunition released in 1991 was a unique step in the development of ammunition. More information on this trademark, including current models, U.S. availability, and U.S. pricing, can be obtained by contacting the company directly (see Trademark Index for information).

RIFLES

Values listed below are in euros, w/o tax.

MODEL K98 VOERE-KESSLER BOLT ACTION - various cals., Mauser 98 action, wing type, 3 position or cocking safety, 21.5 in. barrel, select hand-checkered walnut stock with bavarian cheekpiece, rosewood pistol grip cap. New 2004.

The current European MSR on this model, w/o tax, is 2,780 euros.

MODEL VEC 91 BOLT ACTION - 5.7 UCC or 6mm UCC caseless ammo, unique ignition system requires electrical impulse to activate semi-conducting primer that ignites propellant (2 small batteries are housed in the pistol grip capable of igniting

5,000 shots), 5 shot detachable mag., 20 in. free floating barrel, twin forward locking lugs, 2-stage electrical trigger adj. from 1/2 oz. to 7 lbs, 55 grain bullet achieves 3,300 fps with no loss in accuracy over normal mechanical primer ignited cartridges, 6 lbs. New 1992.

The current European MSR on this model, w/o tax, is 2,388 euros.

Last U.S. MSR was $2,540.

Unfortunately, BATF import certificates have made it very expensive to bring UCC caseless ammunition in small quantities into this country. This model is currently being distributed in Europe and other countries.

MODEL 20-02 XXL BOLT ACTION - various dangerous game cals., Magnum action, two locking lugs, checkered high grade walnut stock, iron sights, approx. 8 lbs. New 2003.

The current European MSR on this model, w/o tax, is 7,000 euros for the base model.

MODEL 20-03 LBW BOLT ACTION - various cals., interchangeable barrels, three lug fluted bolt, uncocking safety, walnut or rubber coated stock, 6.5 lbs. New 2003.

The current European MSR on this model, w/o tax, is 900 euros for the base model, 1,300 euros for the Luxus model, and 1,900 euros for the Deluxe Takedown.

MODEL 2155 BOLT ACTION - various cals., K-98 Mauser action, 20 in. barrel, tang safety, no sights.

The current MSR on this model, w/o tax, is 719 euros for the base model.

Last U.S. MSR was $780.

Add 59 euros for Mag. cals. (7mm Rem. Mag. or .300 Win. Mag.).

MODEL 2165 BOLT ACTION DELUXE - same cals. as Model 2155, European traditional style K-98 Mauser bolt action, 22 in. barrel, detachable 5 shot mag., hand-checkered deluxe walnut.

The current European MSR on this model, w/o tax, is 1,069 euros.

Last U.S. MSR was $1,110.

Add 59 euros for Mag. cals. (24 in. barrel).

MODEL 2185 SERIES MATCH/SPORTER SEMI-AUTO - .30-06, .308 Win. or 7x64mm cal., gas operated, free-floating barrel, 3 or 5 shot detachable mag., manual safety, iron sights, laminate wood, 11 lbs.

The current European MSR on this model, w/o tax, is 3,349 euros.

Last U.S. MSR was $2,715.

Add $1,500 for position style rifle (includes adj. cheekpiece, buttplate, and bottom sling rail, and Voere special scope base).

Other calibers are available on special order only. Sporter model has adj. aperture rear sight with post front sight.

MODEL 2185 SEMI-AUTO HUNTING RIFLE - 9.3x62mm, other cals. available upon special request, checkered stock and forend, iron sights.

The current European MSR on this model, w/o tax, is 1,731 euros.

Last U.S. MSR was $1,775.

Add 70 euros for Mannlicher full stock with 20 in. carbine barrel.

Add 86 euros for Europe model with hinged bottom plate.

AMERICAN CUSTOM CLASSIC BOLT ACTION - .22-250 Rem., .243 Win., .270 Win., 7x57mm, 7x64mm, .30-06, or .308 Win. cal., K-98 Mauser action, 3 position safety, hinged floorplate, deluxe walnut with hand-rubbed oil finish and checkering. Mfg. 1996 only.

	$1,575	$1,450	$1,300	$1,150	$995	$850	$675

Last MSR was $1,795.

Add $50 for Mag. cals. (.300 Win. Mag., .338 Win. Mag., 7mm Rem. Mag., or 9.3x64mm).

Add $100 for .375 H&H or .458 Win. Mag. cal.

GRADING - PPGS™	100%	98%	95%	90%	80%	70%	60%

.22 SEMI-AUTO - .22 LR cal., open (disc.) or closed bolt design, 10 shot mag., check-ered hardwood stock, adj. rear sight and trigger. Limited importation.

	100%	98%	95%	90%	80%	70%	60%
	$585	$535	$460	$400	$350	$300	$250

Last MSR was $645.

Add $50 for Deluxe Model.

VOERE (GERMAN)

Previous manufacturer located in Vohrenvach, Germany. Voere was absorbed by Mauser-Werke circa 1986, and most of the company machinery was moved to Oberndorf during that time. Voere of Germany should not be confused with the current Austrian firm of the same name.

Voere of Germany manufactured a wide variety of rifles in many configurations, including both bolt action and semi-auto (closed and open bolt) .22 cal. rifles. Bolt action centerfire rifles were also produced in many styles and calibers, including some private label contracts with such firms as Shikar, Frankonia, Akah, and others. While not considered as highly collectible today, most German Voere rifles were noted for their quality craftsmanship and above-average accuracy. Secondary values today depend on the desirability of the rifle configuration (stock design, finish, caliber, etc.) and original condition.

VOLQUARTSEN CUSTOM, LTD.

Current rifle customizer and manufacturer located in Carroll, IA. Dealer sales.

PISTOLS: SEMI-AUTO, CONVERSION

Volquartsen manufactures a wide variety of custom pistols based on the Ruger Mark II action. Prices range from $636-$1,173, depending on the configuration. Please contact the company directly for more information on these conversions.

CHEETAH - .17 HMR, .17 Mach 2, .22 LR, or .22 Mag. cal., titanium 7 in. (.22 LR cal. only) or 10 in. barrel, 9 or 10 shot mag., synthetic finger groove stock with ambidextrous grip, CNC aluminum frame, Weaver style mount, available in black, blue, red, green, or silver stock, 46 oz. New 2003.

MSR $844	$775	$700	$625	$575	$525	$475	$425

PREDATOR - .17 HMR or .22 Mag. cal., choice of brown laminate wood grips or black McMillian grips, 12 in. stainless steel bull barrel, wedge locking block system, includes scope mount. New 2005.

MSR $900	$825	$750	$675	$625	$550	$500	$450

Add $270 for black McMillian grips.

Add $215 for barrel only.

RIFLES: SEMI-AUTO

Current Volquartsen stock configurations include: brown synthetic, grey synthetic, Hogue, McMillan Sporter, and McMillan thumbhole stock. Base values below represent standard Hogue synthetic stock.

Add approx. $60 for grey/brown synthetic stock.

Add approx. $410 for McMillan Sport or thumbhole stock on the models listed below.

STANDARD 17 HMR - .17 HMR cal., similar to Standard 22 LR, similar configurations as the .22 Mag model, 18.5 (standard) or 20 in. fluted and compensated stainless steel bull barrel.

MSR $879	$775	$675	$575	$500	$425	$350	$300

Add $177 for Deluxe model with Hogue stock.

Add $106 for Lightweight model.

Add $185 for radial flute or Snake model.

Add $454 for VX5000 Lightweight.

Add $722 for VG-1 model with fluted and compensated barrel.

GRADING - PPGS™	100%	98%	95%	90%	80%	70%	60%

STANDARD 22 LR - .22 LR cal., similar to .22 Mag., stainless steel receiver, available in same configurations as .22 Mag, except not available in VG-1 or radial flute.

MSR $851	$750	$650	$550	$500	$425	$350	$300

Add $56 for Deluxe or Lightweight model with Hogue stock.
Add $176 for Snake model.
Add $496 for VX5000 Lightweight.

STANDARD 22 MAG. - .22 Mag. cal., choice of standard (18 1/2 in. stainless steel), deluxe (20 in. fluted), or lightweight (16 1/2 in. aluminum) barrel, Monte Carlo laminated wood or Hogue Overmolded composite stock, available in Standard, Lightweight, Snake, radial flute, Deluxe, Signature Series (top-of-the-line), VG-1, and VX5000 models. approx. 7 1/2 lbs.

MSR $879	$775	$675	$575	$500	$425	$350	$300

Add $177 for Deluxe model with Hogue stock.
Add $106 for Lightweight Model.
Add $185 for radial flute or Snake Model.
Add $454 for VX5000 Lightweight.
Add $722 for VG-1 model with fluted and compensated barrel.

SIGNATURE SERIES - .17 HMR or .22 Mag. cal., top-of-the-line model, many options are available.

MSR $3,686	$3,350	$3,000	$2,600	$2,300	$1,925	$1,675	$1,350

FUSION TAKE DOWN MODEL - .17 HMR or .22 Mag. cal., features interchangeable barrels between .17 HMR and .22 Mag. cals., black finished alloy receiver, 18 3/8 in. barrel with muzzle brake, Picatinny rails on top of receiver and bottom of barrel shroud, 9 shot rotary mag., 6 1/2 lbs. Limited mfg. 2004.

		$1,025	$900	$775	$675	$575	$500	$425

Last MSR was $1,127.

Add $206 for both barrels with gun or $296 per individual barrel.

EVOLUTION MODEL - .204 Ruger or .223 Rem. cal., gas operated, stainless steel receiver with Picatinny scope mount system machined into top of receiver, trigger guard and bolt, brown laminate stock with extended Monte Carlo checekpiece, 20 in. standard barrel, 10 shot AR-15 style mag., 10 lbs. New 2005.

MSR $1,930	$1,775	$1,500	$1,250				

VOLUNTEER ENTERPRISES

Previous manufacturer located in Knoxville, TN.

Volunteer Enterprises became Commando Arms after 1978.

CARBINES

COMMANDO MARK III CARBINE - .45 ACP cal., semi-auto, blowback action, 16 1/2 in. barrel, aperture sight, stock styled after the Auto-Ordnance "Tommy Gun." Mfg. 1969-1976.

	$425	$365	$315	$280	$225	$195	$160
Vertical grip	$440	$365	$320	$280	$225	$195	$160

COMMANDO MARK 9 - similar to Mark III in 9mm Para. cal.

	$440	$375	$325	$285	$230	$195	$160
Vertical grip	$440	$365	$320	$280	$225	$195	$160

VOUZELAUD

Previous manufacturer located in France. Previously imported by Waverly Arms Co. located in Suffolk, VA.

SHOTGUNS: SxS

MODEL 315 E - 12, 16 or 20 ga., boxlock, 28 in. barrels, auto ejectors, straight grip French walnut stock, double triggers, case colored receiver, light engraving. Importation disc. 1987.

    Values generally range between $1,350-$2,000 for this model.

MODEL 315 EL - similar to Model 315 E, except has satin finish receiver engraved with bouquets of fine English scrollwork, trigger guard and forearm also engraved. Importation disc. 1987.

    Values generally range between $1,475-$2,250 for this model.

    Add $600 for 28 ga. or .410 bore (Model 315 EL-S, special order only).

MODEL 315 EG - 12, 16 or 20 ga., sidelock, 28 in. barrels, selective ejectors, double triggers, extensive scroll engraving on coin finish receiver, English style stock of extra fancy French walnut. Importation disc. 1987.

    Values generally range between $1,750-$2,750 for this model.

MODEL 315 EGL-S - same general features as the Model 315 EGL, except monobloc barrel construction, extensive game scene engraving, and grand deluxe walnut stock and forearm with extra fine hand-checkering. Importation disc. 1987.

    Values generally range between $1,950-$2,950 for this model.

                                  Last MSR was $5,895.

VULCAN ARMAMENT, INC.

Current rifle manufacturer established in 2003 and located in Inver Grove Heights, MN.

RIFLES

Vulcan Arms makes a wide variety of bolt action and AR-15 styled semi-auto rifles, including configurations for military and low enforcement. Prices start at $499 for the V47 (AK-47 design), $1,450 for the V73 (Galil design), $799 for the V15 (AR-15 style design), and $1,699 for parkerized or $1,999 for laminated V50 (bolt action). Please contact the factory directly for more information, including a listing of various configurations, options, and availability (see Trademark Index).

W SECTION

WAFFENFABRIK HEIN

Current bolt action rifle manufacturer located in Tekoa, WA.

RIFLES: BOLT ACTION

Hein is known for its N-Series rifle action. Current bolt action rifles include Palouse Custom Trophy ($2,700 MSR) and the Palouse Custom Classic ($4,500 MSR). Please contact the company directly for more information, including availability and delivery time (see Trademark Index).

WAFFENSTUBE GUGGI

Current long gun manufacturer and custom order stock carver established during 1981, and located in Graz, Austria. No current U.S. importation.

Waffenstube Guggi manufactures custom order sidelock combination guns, single and SxS rifles, bolt action rifles, and shotguns. They also perform outstanding stock carving and checkering services. Please contact the company directly for more information and an individual price quotation (see Trademark Index).

WAFFEN JUNG GMBH

Current rifle manufacturer located in Lohmar, Germany. No current U.S. importation.

Waffen Jung GmbH manufactures a Stutzen style Rominten edition bolt action rifle. Please contact the company directly for more information, including U.S. availability and pricing.

WAFFEN VERATSCHNIG

Previous manufacturer located in Ferlach, Austria.

Waffen Veratschnig manufactured a variety of high grade, made to individual special order rifles, shotguns, combination guns, drillings, and vierlings. A wide variety of engraving scenes, wood carvings, and other special features were available at extra cost. Very few models were actually imported into the U.S.

WALTHER

Current manufacturer located in Ulm, Germany, 1953 to date. PPK/S, P99, and P22 pistols, in addition to the G22 carbine are currently distributed beginning 2002 by Smith & Wesson, located in Springfield, MA. Target, competiton and service pistols are also imported by Earl's Repair Service, Inc., located in Tewksbury, MA since 1984. Walther target pistols and target rifles are currently being imported by Champions Choice located in La Vergne, TN. Previously imported and distributed 1998-2001 by Walther USA LLC, located in Springfield, MA, and by Interarms located in Alexandria, VA. Previously manufactured in Zella-Mehlis, Germany 1886 to 1945. Walther was sold to Umarex Sportwaffen GmbH circa 1996, and company headquarters are located in Arnsberg, Germany.

The calibers listed in the Walther Pistol sections are listed in American caliber designations. The German metric conversion is as follows: .22 LR - 5.6mm, .25 ACP - 6.35mm, .32 ACP - 7.65mm, .380 ACP - 9mm kurz. The metric caliber designations in most cases will be indicated on the left slide legend for German mfg. pistols listed in the Walther section.

For more information and current pricing on both new and used Walther airguns, please refer to the *Blue Book of Airguns* by Dr. Robert Beeman & John Allen (also online).

GRADING - PPGS™	100%	98%	95%	90%	80%	70%	60%

PISTOLS: SEMI-AUTO, PRE-WAR

MODEL 1 - .25 ACP cal., 2.1 in. barrel, fixed sights, blue, checkered hard rubber grips, pre-WWI, 13.1 oz. Mfg. 1908-1909.

	$650	$525	$400	$300	$250	$225	$200

MODEL 2 - .25 ACP cal., 2.1 in. barrel, fixed sights, blue, hard rubber grips, pop-up rear sight on early models, fixed on late models, 9.75 oz. Mfg. 1902-1909.

	$550	$465	$400	$275	$185	$135	$125

   This model can usually be distinguished by its knurled barrel ring.

✴ *Early Model* - differentiated by its pop-up rear sight.

	$1,300	$1,025	$900	$775	$675	$550	$400

MODEL 3 - .32 ACP cal., 2.6 in. barrel, blue, fixed sights, hard rubber grips, ejection port on left side, 16.5 oz. Mfg. 1910-1913.

	$2,250	$1,850	$1,400	$1,100	$800	$650	$500

MODEL 4 - .32 ACP cal., 8 shot, 3 1/2 in. barrel, blue, hard rubber grips, ejection port on left side, 19.4 oz. Mfg. 1910-28.

	$475	$400	$325	$250	$200	$150	$100

   Add 10% for WWI "Eagle" proofs.

MODEL 5 - better quality version of Model 2, fixed rear sight, 9.71 oz. Mfg. 1913-1915.

	$525	$460	$415	$275	$145	$135	$125

MODEL 6 - 9mm Para. cal., 4 7/8 in. barrel, blue, hard rubber grips, ejection port on right side, 34 oz. Approx. 1,000 mfg. 1915-17. Some are Imperial proofed.

	$7,500	$5,250	$3,000	$3,000	$2,500	$2,000	$1,500

MODEL 7 - .25 ACP cal., 3 in. barrel, blue, fixed sights, hard rubber grips, ejection port on right side, 12 oz. Mfg. 1917-18.

	$675	$550	$465	$385	$285	$200	$125

MODEL 8 - .25 ACP cal., 2 7/8 in. barrel, blue or nickel finish, fixed sights, black checkered plastic grips with round medallions, 12.7 oz. Mfg. 1920-43.

	$700	$575	$475	$325	$240	$150	$125

   Add 20% for nickel.

   Add 10% for "Eagle N" proofing.

   Add 25% for engraved slide.

MODEL 9 VEST POCKET - .25 ACP cal., engineering revision of Model 1, 2 in. barrel, blue finish standard, upward ejection, 6 shot bottom release mag., fixed sights, black checkered plastic grips with round medallions, safety lever on left frame side behind trigger, 9 oz. Mfg. 1921-45.

	$650	$575	$495	$395	$285	$160	$140

   Add 40% for engraved slide, 20% for nickel.

   Add 10% for "Eagle N" proofing.

MODEL PP DOUBLE ACTION - .22 LR, .25 ACP, .32 ACP, or .380 ACP cal., PP designates "Polizei Pistole," 3 7/8 in. barrel, blue, fixed sights, plastic grips. Mfg. 1929-1945. Crown N proof until 1939. Eagle N Nazi commercial proof until 1945.

	100%	98%	95%	90%	80%	70%	60%
.22 LR cal.	$1,100	$895	$750	$650	$525	$450	$375
.25 ACP cal.	$3,500	$3,100	$2,650	$2,000	$1,500	$1,200	$1,000
.32 ACP cal.	$650	$550	$425	$350	$275	$225	$200
.380 ACP cal.	$1,250	$995	$750	$675	$600	$550	$500

   Add 15% for alloy frame.

   Original nickel finished Model PPs are very rare; this precludes accurate price evaluation. Values assume original guns without import markings. Recently imported WWII/surplus police used guns are stamped on the frame or receiver, indicating the current importer and address - subtract 20%-30% from values listed for these recent imports.

GRADING - PPGS™	100%	98%	95%	90%	80%	70%	60%
✱ *.32 ACP Bottom Release Magazine* - safety rotates 90 degrees.							
	$1,100	$900	$675	$625	$550	$425	$395
✱ *.380 ACP Bottom Release Magazine* - safety rotates 90 degrees.							
	$1,800	$1,450	$1,100	$900	$700	$600	$500
✱ *Pre-War Persian Proofed* - 9mm kurz BMR.							
	$2,000	$1,800	$1,600	$1,450	$1,250	$995	$825

Subtract 75% for recent imports which have been relisted.

✱ *Pre-War Verchromt .32 ACP cal.*							
	$2,500	$1,850	$1,400	$1,200	$800	$700	$600

Add 50% for .380 ACP cal.

✱ *Pre-War Stoeger* - .32 ACP cal. only.							
	$2,000	$1,450	$1,000	$750	$675	$525	$400
✱ *Nairobi* - Chas. Heyer.							
	$1,800	$1,450	$1,000	$750	$675	$525	$400
✱ *Aluminum Frame* - safety rotates 90 degrees.							
	$795	$675	$525	$400	$275	$235	$200
✱ *Allemagne* - French Comm.							
	$1,400	$1,075	$825	$720	$600	$425	$325

MODEL PP WARTIME PRODUCTION - mfg. 1940-1945, "Eagle N" Proof (Nazi commercial nitro proof after April 1940) or "Crown N" proof (German commercial proofmark used until April, 1940) found on pre-WWII military production. Variations are listed either by proofmarks or frame/slide markings.

✱ *"Waffenamt" Proofed* - .32 ACP or .380 ACP cal., "Eagle N," military acceptance marking.

	100%	98%	95%	90%	80%	70%	60%
.32 ACP cal. Milled finish	$750	$625	$450	$350	$250	$220	$200
.380 ACP cal.	$2,000	$1,400	$825	$700	$600	$550	$500

Add 25%-50% if Waffenamt proofed, depending on condition (late war PPs are sometimes encountered with Walther marked beechwood grips).

✱ *Eagle N Proofed* - .22 LR or .32 ACP cal., with lanyard loop.

	100%	98%	95%	90%	80%	70%	60%
.32 ACP cal.	$650	$550	$425	$350	$250	$200	$150
.22 LR cal.	$950	$850	$700	$650	$495	$450	$395

Add 50% to .32 ACP cal., Waffenamt proofed PPs that are hi-gloss finish (all .380s are hi-gloss).

In most cases, the .380 ACP cal. has the bottom mag. release.

After WWII, the French added a lanyard to the left side of the grip. Subtract 25% for this alteration.

✱ *Eagle C & F Marked (Nazi Police)* - .32 ACP cal., "Eagle F or C" proofed on left side of frame.

	$850	$725	$650	$525	$450	$380	$300

Add 25% if Eagle C marked. All hi-gloss are early productions.

✱ *RFV Marked* - .32 ACP cal., "Crown N." Mfg. for "Reichsfinanzverwaltung" Reich Finance Administration.

	$950	$750	$650	$500	$400	$325	$225

✱ *RJ Marked* - .32 ACP cal., "Crown N." Mfg. for "Reichsjustizministerium" Reich Justice Ministry.

	$1,200	$1,000	$800	$500	$450	$325	$225

✱ *SA Marked* - .22 LR or .32 ACP cal., "Crown N." Mfg. for SA (Sturm Abteilung - group leaders) of the Nazi party.

	$2,500	$1,975	$1,550	$1,200	$900	$600	$425

Add 20% for .22 LR.

Rare SA markings may bring as much as 50% more over values listed.

There are 28 SA groups.

GRADING - PPGS™	100%	98%	95%	90%	80%	70%	60%

❋ **NSKK Marked** - .32 ACP cal., "Crown N" or "Eagle N" proofed. Mfg. for "National-sozialistischer Kraftfahrkorps" Nazi Party Transport Corps, rare.

	100%	98%	95%	90%	80%	70%	60%
	$3,300	$2,250	$1,950	$1,250	$925	$750	$600

❋ **RRZ Proofed** - .32 ACP cal., mfg. for for "Reichsrundfunkzentrale" Reich Radio Broadcasting - only 3 known.

	$3,700	$3,100	$2,550				

❋ **PDM Marked** - .32 ACP cal., "Crown N," for "Polizeidirektion München" Munich Police Department, all have bottom mag. release.

	$1,750	$1,425	$1,050	$700	$550	$450	$400

❋ **AC Marked** - .32 ACP cal., replaced Walther Banner during 1945, "Eagle N."

	$500	$400	$300	$250	$200	$150	$125

Some are mismatched (assembled at factory by GIs after the factory was captured). Subtract 20% if mismatched.

❋ **Czech. Contract** - stamped "Rampant Lion".

	$1,125	$900	$800	$700	$600	$500	$400

❋ **Panagraph Slide**

	$850	$750	$695	$630	$550	$385	$275

❋ **Danish Rplt.**

	$995	$925	$825	$775	$700	$625	$400

MODEL PP LIGHTWEIGHT - aluminum alloy version.

Add 20% to Standard Model prices.
Add 20%-40% for original nickel finish (very rare).
Add 25% for early hi-gloss finish.

MODEL PPK PRE-WAR PRODUCTION - .22 LR, .25 ACP, .32 ACP, or .380 ACP cal., PPK designates "Polizei Pistole Kriminal," 3 1/4 in. barrel, blue, gold, nickel, or chrome silver, fixed sights, plastic grips. Mfg. 1931-40.

	100%	98%	95%	90%	80%	70%	60%
.22 LR cal.	$2,200	$1,300	$950	$750	$650	$525	$400
.25 ACP cal.	$7,500	$4,550	$3,800	$3,400	$2,800	$2,100	$1,475
.32 ACP cal.	$950	$700	$600	$500	$400	$300	$250
.380 ACP cal.	$4,500	$2,500	$1,750	$1,500	$900	$700	$500

Add 60% for bottom release mag (.32 ACP cal.).

MODEL PPK WARTIME PRODUCTION - mfg. 1940-1945, "Eagle N" proofed after April 1940, "Crown N" proofs appear on pre-1940 production with frame/slide markings. Variations are listed either by proof-marks, frame/slide markings, or type of finish.

❋ **Commercial "Eagle N" Proofed** - .22 LR, .32 ACP, or .380 ACP cal., Nazi Eagle over N (standard Nazi commercial acceptance proof).

	100%	98%	95%	90%	80%	70%	60%
.22 LR cal.	$1,800	$1,300	$900	$750	$525	$460	$420
.32 ACP cal.	$850	$650	$450	$350	$300	$250	$225
.380 ACP cal.	$3,750	$2,900	$2,200	$1,500	$1,000	$750	$550

This variation is normally encountered with semi-polished, exterior metal showing milling marks to various degrees.

❋ **Waffenamt Proofed With High Polish**

	$1,850	$1,450	$1,100	$650	$500	$400	$300

❋ **Eagle C Marked** - .32 ACP cal., "Crown N - Eagle C," mfg. for Nazi Police.

	$1,400	$1,000	$850	$600	$500	$400	$300

Add 25% for high polish finish.

❋ **Eagle F Marked** - .32 ACP cal., "Crown N - Eagle F," Nazi Police, all have the light weight aluminum frame.

	$1,650	$1,200	$900	$650	$500	$400	$300

GRADING - PPGS™	100%	98%	95%	90%	80%	70%	60%

✳ **RZM Marked** - .32 ACP cal., "Crown N," proof-marking for "Reichszeugmeisterei" Reich Party Purchasing Office.

	$2,500	$1,800	$1,300	$850	$500	$400	$300

✳ **Party Leader** - .32 ACP cal., named because grips (brown or black plastic) have the German eagle holding a Swastika, "Crown N" or "Eagle N" proofed, honor weapon awarded 3rd Reich political leaders, rare. Beware of fake grips (especially black color), as reproductions have been made recently. Unfortunately, the grips on a Party Leader (mfg. 1936-41) are the only distinguishing feature on this very desirable configuration.

	$4,750	$3,900	$2,450	$2,000	$1,600	$1,250	$1,000

✳ **RZM With Party Leader Grips** - .32 ACP cal., RZM marked, "Crown N" proofed.

	$6,000	$5,000	$3,000	$2,350	$1,650	$1,250	$1,000

✳ **RFV Marked** - .32 ACP cal., "Crown N." Mfg. for "Reichsfinanzverwaltung" Reich Finance Administration.

	$1,500	$1,250	$900	$750	$800	$700	$675

✳ **PDM Marked** - .32 ACP cal., "Crown N." Mfg. for "Polizeidirektion München" Police Dept. Munich. All have the bottom mag. release.

	$1,800	$1,400	$1,000	$800	$600	$500	$395

✳ **DRP Marked** - .32 ACP cal., "Crown N." Mfg. for "Deutsche Reichspost" German Postal Service.

	$1,250	$1,000	$800	$600	$420	$350	$260

✳ **Panagraph Slide**

	$875	$750	$675	$525	$450	$375	$300

✳ **Verchromt** - .32 ACP or 380 ACP cal., differentiated by dull silver satin type finish.

	$3,000	$2,500	$2,000	$1,000	$800	$650	$500

    Add 50% for .380 ACP cal.

✳ **"K" Suffix** - "K" beneath ser. no.

	$850	$650	$475	$375	$300	$275	$250

✳ **"W" Suffix** - .32 ACP cal., "Crown N" proofed, "W" suffix ser. no.

	$850	$650	$475	$375	$300	$275	$250

✳ **Early 90 Degree Safety**

	$950	$700	$525	$425	$325	$260	$195

✳ **Early Bottom Release Mag.**

	$1,500	$1,200	$900	$800	$700	$600	$500

✳ **PPK Marked PP**

	$2,650	$2,150	$1,850	$1,600	$1,400	$1,180	$900

✳ **7-Digit Ser. No.**

	$900	$800	$700	$600	$550	$400	$300

✳ **Dural Frame** - .22 LR, .32 ACP, or .380 ACP cal., chrome finish (very rare), "Eagle N."

	$950	$700	$600	$525	$400	$325	$275

    Add 200% for .380 ACP.
    Add 100% for .22 LR cal.
    Add 100% for early production with high-gloss finish (brown cast and green cast).

✳ **Czech. Contract** - Rampant Lion stamped.

	$1,250	$1,000	$750	$625	$550	$425	$325

✳ **Danish Rplt.**

	$1,250	$900	$750	$625	$550	$425	$325

✳ **Allemagne** - French Commercial - rare.

	$1,500	$1,200	$1,000	$800	$550	$425	$325

GRADING - PPGS™	100%	98%	95%	90%	80%	70%	60%

MODEL PPK LIGHTWEIGHT - aluminum alloy version.

     Add 20% to .32 cal. commercial price listing.

SPORT MODEL 1926 - .22 S or LR cal. (known as Standard Model in Germany).

	$1,275	$975	$850	$725	$600	$550	$495

1932 OLYMPIA MODEL - .22 S or LR cal., 10 shot, 6 or 9 in. barrel, target sights, one-piece grip, introduced in 1928 and used in 1932 Olympics. Marketed by Stoeger and Chas. Heyer-Nairobi.

	$2,200	$1,650	$1,250	$1,000	$800	$700	$600

     Add 20% for longer barrel.

OLYMPIA SPORT MODEL - .22 LR cal., 7.4 in. barrel, adj. target sights, blue, wood grips, 4 barrel weights available. Mfg. 1936-40.

	$1,500	$1,200	$1,000	$900	$800	$700	$600

     Add 20% for weight set.

1936 OLYMPIA "JÄGERSCHAFTS" HUNTING MODEL - similar to Sport, with 4 in. barrel. Mfg. 1936-40. Also seen with Eagle N proofs.

	$2,200	$1,650	$1,250	$1,000	$800	$700	$600

OLYMPIA RAPID FIRE MODEL - .22 Short cal. only, 7.4 in. barrel, blue, adj. sight, wood grip, has alloy slide. Mfg. 1936-40.

	$1,600	$1,200	$995	$600	$520	$460	$380

1936 OLYMPIA FÜNFKAMPF MODEL - .22 Short or LR cal., 9 1/4 in. barrel, blue, adj. sight, wood grips, barrel weights, circa 1936.

	$2,500	$2,200	$1,750	$1,500	$1,200	$900	$750

MODEL HP COMMERCIAL DOUBLE ACTION - 9mm Para. cal., pre-war version of P-38, 5 in. barrel, fixed sight, blue, wood or plastic grips. Mfg. 1937-44. Many variations, including several different finishes.

     See German WWII Military Pistols section for values on this model.

PISTOLS: SEMI-AUTO, POST-WAR

MODEL PP DOUBLE ACTION - .22 LR, .32 ACP, or .380 ACP cal., specifications similar to pre-war PP, 3 7/8 in. barrel. Imported 1963-2000. German manufacture.

     ✳ *.380 ACP cal.* - 7 shot mag.

	$750	$600	$450	$350	$300	$275	$250

                                   Last MSR was $999.

     ✳ *.32 ACP cal.* - 8 shot mag.

	$650	$500	$395	$295	$275	$250	$225

                                   Last MSR was $999.

     ✳ *.22 LR cal.* - 10 shot mag., disc. 1984.

	$800	$650	$425	$375	$325	$300	$275

                                   Last MSR was $783.

     ✳ *Blue Engraved* - .22 LR (disc.) or .380 ACP cal. Disc. 1984.

	$1,425	$1,125	$950

                                   Last MSR was $1,650.

         Add 5% for .22 LR cal.

     ✳ *Chrome Engraved* - .22 LR or .380 ACP cal. Disc. 1984.

	$1,450	$1,125	$900

                                   Last MSR was $1,600.

         Add $50 for .22 LR cal.

     ✳ *Silver Engraved* - .22 LR (disc.) or .380 ACP cal. Disc. 1984.

	$1,700	$1,175	$1,000

                                   Last MSR was $1,948.

GRADING - PPGS™	100%	98%	95%	90%	80%	70%	60%

✳ Gold Engraved - .22 LR (disc.) or .380 ACP cal. Disc. 1984.

	$1,850	$1,475	$1,150				

Last MSR was $2,053.

✳ Manurhin PP - .22 LR, .32 ACP, or .380 ACP cal. Disc. 1984.

	$525	$440	$350	$225	$180	$165	$150

Add 10% for .380 ACP cal.

✳ Model PP 50th Anniversary Commemorative - .22 LR., .32 ACP, or .380 ACP cal., gold-plated parts, hand-carved grips, presentation case. 500 imported to U.S. 1979. 800 mfg.

	$1,625	$1,175	$650				

Last MSR was $1,700.

✳ Model PP "100 Jahre" 1886-1986 - 7.65mm cal., 100th anniversary PP edition, primarily made for the German marketplace, inscription marked on right side of slide.

Plastic Grips	$995	$750	$625				
Extended Wood Grips	$1,095	$825	$675				

✳ PP Last Edition - supplied with fitted hard case, certificate; and video Walther history, 400 mfg. in .32 ACP cal., 100 mfg. in .380 ACP cal., 500 total mfg. in Germany 1999 only.

	$1,295	$1,050	$900				

Add $100 for .380 ACP cal.

This model was the last of the PP, PPK, PPK/S models to be manufactured when Germany stopped production in 1999.

PP SPORT - double action, thumbrest grips, round hammer with spur, adj. rear sight, 6.1 or 8.1 in. barrel, 25.6 or 27.2 oz. Mfg. 1953-70.

Manurhin Mfg.	$725	$650	$625	$550	$495	$425	$350
Mark II (1955-1957)	$825	$700	$650	$600	$545	$500	$450
Walther Mfg.	$925	$800	$700	$625	$575	$525	$450

Subtract 10% if not marked.

Add $75 for barrel weight, $100 for factory case, 20% for factory nickel, 5% for single action.

✳ PP Sport "C" Model C - mfg. for competition shooting, single action, 7 5/8 in. barrel, spur hammer.

	$950	$825	$725	$675	$575	$525	$450

MODEL PPK - similar to pre-war PPK, .22 LR, .32 ACP, or .380 ACP cal., 3.31 in. barrel. Mfg. post-war-1999, U.S. import stopped by GCA 68 on W. German and French production.

.32 ACP Cal.	$775	$550	$425	$350	$325	$295	$275
.22 LR Cal.	$1,075	$750	$600	$525	$450	$375	$325
.380 ACP Cal.	$1,075	$750	$600	$475	$425	$350	$300
Blue Engraved	$1,675	$1,300	$950				
Silver Engraved	$1,950	$1,400	$1,000				
Gold Engraved	$2,275	$1,675	$1,250				

100% column assumes NIB condition - subtract 15% if not boxed.

MODEL PPK LAST EDITION - similar to PP Last Edition, but was never imported into the U.S.

MODEL PPK LIGHTWEIGHT - similar to Standard, with dural frame, .22 LR or .32 ACP cal.

	$950	$700	$500	$375	$325	$295	$275

Add 20% for .22 LR cal.

GRADING - PPGS™	100%	98%	95%	90%	80%	70%	60%

MODEL PPK-1986 U.S. PRODUCTION

- .380 ACP cal. only, 3.35 in. barrel, similar specifications as previous W. German and French manufacture, blue or bright nickel (new 1997) finish, 7 shot finger extension mag., black plastic grips, 21 oz. Made in the U.S. Mfg. 1986-2001.

	100%	98%	95%	90%	80%	70%	60%
	$450	$365	$320	$295	$270	$250	$225

Last MSR was $543.

Manufacture in the U.S. was under an exclusive licensing agreement with Walther of Germany.

* **PPK Stainless** - .32 ACP (new 1998) or .380 ACP cal., stainless steel construction. Mfg. 1986-2001.

	100%	98%	95%
	$450	$400	$325

Last MSR was $543.

MODEL PPK/E

- .380 ACP cal., 3.4 in. barrel., high polish blue, 7 (.380 ACP) or 8 (.32 ACP) shot mag., 23 oz.

While advertised in America during 2000 with a MSR of $294, this model was distributed in Europe only, and was produced with the cooperation of F.E.G., located in Hungary. Only 6 were imported into the U.S. for the SHOT Show.

MODEL PPK/S

- .22 LR, .32 ACP, or .380 ACP cal., similar to PPK, except has larger PP frame to meet import requirements of 1968, 3 1/4 in. barrel, production in W. Germany, Manurhin of France (disc. 1986), and in the U.S. (mfg. under license from Walther by Interarms), 10 (.22 LR) or 8 (.32 ACP and .380 ACP) shot, double action, fixed sights.

* **American PPK/S** - .380 ACP cal. only, blue finish, 8 shot, one finger extension and one flat bottom mag. Disc. 2001.

	100%	98%	95%	90%	80%	70%	60%
	$450	$375	$320	$295	$270	$250	$225

Last MSR was $543.

* **Stainless PPK/S** - .32 ACP (new 1998) or .380 ACP cal., American manufacture, introduced July of 1983, disc. 2001, limited quantities available.

MSR $543	$425	$365	$320

* **W. German PPK/S** - .22 LR (disc. 1984), .32 ACP (disc. 1999), or .380 ACP (disc. 1999) cal.

	100%	98%	95%	90%	80%	70%	60%
.22 LR cal.	$850	$725	$595	$450	$375	$325	$300
.32 ACP cal.	$600	$525	$450	$400	$325	$295	$275
.380 ACP cal.	$750	$675	$550	$400	$325	$295	$275

* **American PPK/S** - blue engraved. Disc. 1985.

	100%	98%	95%
	$875	$850	$800

Last MSR was $990.

* **American PPK/S Gold-Engraved Commemorative** - 500 total mfg. Disc. 1987.

	100%	98%	95%
	$1,000	$875	$700

Last MSR was $1,200.

* **American PPK/S Gold-Engraved** - disc. 1985.

	100%	98%	95%
	$975	$850	$700

Last MSR was $1,070.

* **W. German PPK/S Blue Engraved** - inventory depleted 1990.

	100%	98%	95%
	$1,475	$1,050	$850

Last MSR was $1,550.

* **W. German PPK/S Chrome Engraved** - importation disc. 1991.

	100%	98%	95%
	$1,525	$1,075	$950

Last MSR was $1,700.

* **W. German PPK/S Silver Engraved** - disc. 1988.

	100%	98%	95%
	$1,675	$1,150	$975

Last MSR was $1,700.

GRADING - PPGS™	100%	98%	95%	90%	80%	70%	60%

✳ W. German PPK/S Gold Engraved - disc. 1985.

	$1,950	$1,250	$1,000

Last MSR was $1,800.

MANURHIN PPK/S - see listings under Manurhin section.

MODEL PP SUPER - .380 ACP cal., 3.6 in. barrel, 7 shot, fixed sights, plastic grips, blue, 1,000 mfg. in .380 ACP cal., 26.8 oz. Mfg. 1973-79.

$925	$725	$550	$395	$285	$250	$235

✳ PP Super Ultra/Police - 9x18mm cal., recently imported West German police trade-ins, approx. 4,000 mfg.

$425	$375	$335	$300	$275	$250	$225

✳ PP Super-Cutaway

$795	$650	$550

MODEL TP - .22 LR or .25 ACP cal., updated version of Model 9, 6 shot, 2.6 in. barrel, concealed hammer, 12 oz. Mfg. 1961-71.

.22 LR cal.	$800	$625	$435	$350	$300	$260	$210
.25 ACP cal.	$725	$500	$350	$300	$250	$220	$185

MODEL TPH - .22 LR or .25 ACP cal., double action 2.8 in. barrel, 6 shot, alloy frame, blue, fixed sights, plastic grips, 11.5 oz. Mfg. 1968-98 in W. Germany, U.S. import stopped by GCA of 1968.

.22 LR cal.	$825	$625	$550	$475	$350	$300	$250
.25 ACP cal.	$950	$725	$600	$500	$400	$325	$275

Subtract 10% on the 100% values if not boxed with all accessories.

TPH cutaways were also mfg. in small quantities for instructional use. Current pricing for a mint specimen is approx. $1,500.

100% price assumes NIB condition.

AMERICAN MODEL TPH - .22 LR or .25 ACP (new 1992) cal., blue finish or stainless steel, double action, black plastic grips, 6 shot mag., 2 1/4 in. barrel, 14 oz. Mfg. 1987-2000.

$400	$335	$280	$250	$225	$200	$185

Last MSR was $460.

✳ American Model TPH Stainless - stainless steel fabrication. Disc. 2000.

$400	$335	$280

Last MSR was $460.

MODEL P38 - post-war version of P38 Military, .22 LR (disc.), 7.65mm, or 9mm Para. cal., 5 in. barrel, 8 shot, alloy frame, matte black finish, 28 oz. W. German manufacture. Mfg. 1956-present, currently imported into the U.S. by Earl's Repair Service. See German WWII Military Pistols for wartime listings.

$800	$600	$500	$375	$325	$275	$225

Last MSR was $824.

Note: Due to the release of large numbers of W. German Police and Army trade-ins of P.38 9mm Para. and PP .32 ACP cal. models, the actual value of original models in 90% or less condition has decreased somewhat. The two models most affected are the P-1 variation of the P.38, and the German PP in .32 ACP cal.

✳ P38 Long Barrel Special Edition - 9mm Para. cal., steel frame, 6, 7, or 8, in. barrel, wood grips, 50 mfg. 1988.

$3,750	$3,200	$2,750

✳ Steel Frame P38 - .22 LR, 7.65mm Luger or 9mm Para. cal., similar to regular P.38, except has steel frame, 34 oz. Imported 1987-89 only, and in limited quantities.

$1,250	$900	$650

Last MSR was $1,400.

Add 30% for 7.65mm Luger cal.

Add 40% for German-marked frame with high polish finish.

GRADING - PPGS™	100%	98%	95%	90%	80%	70%	60%

✳ *P38 in .22 LR Cal.* - disc. 1989.

	$995	$675	$550	$475	$375	$325	$225

Last MSR was $1,050.

MODEL P38 II - similar to the Standard P.38, except has reinforced slide.

	$695	$550	$450	$375	$325	$275	$225

MODEL P38K - 7.65mm Luger or 9mm Para. cal., shortened 2.8 in. barrel variation of P.38, front sight on slide, adj. rear sight, 27.9 oz. 3,000 mfg. 1974-81.

	$800	$700	$600	$500	$425	$350	$275

Add 30% for 7.65mm Luger cal.

MODEL P38 SPECIAL EDITIONS/ENGRAVED

✳ *P38 50th Year Commemorative* - 9mm Para. cal., steel frame, carved grips, presentation engraved with deluxe walnut presentation case. Introduced 1987, inventory depleted 1992.

	$2,325	$1,750	$1,250

Last MSR was $950.

✳ *P38 HP 60th Year Commemorative* - 9mm Para. or 7.65mm (.30 Luger) cal., special production, steel frame, high polish, wood grips, includes wood presentation case. Approx. 100 mfg. in each caliber. Mfg. 1998.

	$2,325	$1,750	$1,250

Add 10% for 7.65mm cal.

✳ *P38 100th Year Commemorative* - 9mm Para. cal., alloy frame with slide engraving "100 Jahre Walther 1886-1986." Imported by Interarms.

	$825	$675	$475

✳ *Blue Engraved* - .22 LR, 7.65mm Luger, or 9mm Para. cal.

9mm Para.	$1,850	$1,325	$1,125
7.65mm Luger	$2,200	$1,875	$1,450
.22 LR	$2,000	$1,675	$1,350

Last MSR was $1,850.

✳ *Chrome Engraved* - .22 LR, 7.65mm Luger, or 9mm Para. cal., still imported.

	$1,475	$1,175	$925

Last MSR was $2,125.

✳ *Silver Engraved* - .22 LR, 7.65mm Luger, or 9mm Para. cal., still imported.

	$1,450	$1,175	$925

Last MSR was $2,100.

✳ *Gold Engraved* - .22 LR, 7.65mm Luger, or 9mm Para. cal., still imported.

	$1,800	$1,500	$1,000

Last MSR was $2,050.

MODEL P1 - 9mm Para. cal., post-war commercial variation of the P.38 with steel slide and alloy frame, 5 in. barrel, 8 shot mag., blue or phosphate finish, black plastic grips. Disc.

	$675	$550	$400	$300	$250	$215	$165
Imp. Police Trade-Ins	$325	$275	$250	$225	$200	$170	$135

MODEL P4 - 9mm Para. cal., modernized variation of the original P.38, 4 1/2 in. barrel, 8 shot mag., updates include reinforced steel slide and alloy frame, includes decocking lever and automatic safeties, rear sight, 29 oz. Mfg. 1975-81, importation disc. 1982.

	$725	$600	$525	$425	$300	$250	$200

Add 30% for commercial variation.

GRADING - PPGS™	100%	98%	95%	90%	80%	70%	60%

MODEL P5 - 7.65mm Luger, 9mm Para., or 9x21mm cal., double action, alloy frame, frame mounted decocking lever, 3 1/2 in. barrel, adj. rear sight, blue finish only, 8 shot mag., auto safeties, 28 oz. New 1977-currently imported by Earl's Repair Service.

	MSR $995	$850	$800	$700	$650	$525	$475	$450

P-5 cutaways were also mfg. in small quantities for instructional use. Current pricing for a mint specimen is approx. $2,000.

* *P5 Compact* - compact variation of P-5 with 3.1 in. barrel, 26 1/2 oz. Limited importation 1987- present.

		$995	$850	$600	$525	$450	$425	$375

* *P5 Long* - special edition, 5.3 in. barrel, wood grips, 29.6 oz. 50 mfg. 1988 only.

		$3,750	$2,750	$2,000

* *P5 100th Year Commemorative* - marked "1886-1986 100 Jahre" with Walther banner, elaborate grip carving, presentation walnut case. Imported 1986-91.

		$2,650	$1,750	$1,100

Last MSR was $2,890.

MODEL P88 - 9mm Para. or 9x21mm cal., double action, alloy frame, 4 in. barrel, 15 shot button release mag., fully ambidextrous, decocking lever, matte finish, adj. rear sight, internal safeties, plastic grips, 31 1/2 oz. Mfg. 1987-93.

		$1,000	$850	$700	$575	$490	$450	$400

Last MSR was $1,129.

P88 cutaways were also mfg. in small quantities for instructional use. Current pricing for a mint specimen is approx. $2,000.

* *P88 Compact* - 9mm Para. or 9x21mm cal., 3.93 in. barrel, 14* (disc.) or 10 (C/B 1994) shot mag., 29 oz. Imported 1993-2003.

		$925	$775	$625	$550	$500	$475	$450

Last MSR was $900.

Add 25% for 14 shot mag.

This model had a substantial price decrease beginning 1996 (1994 retail price was $1,725).

* *P88 Champion* - 9mm Para. only, 6 in. barrel, SA only, 14* shot mag., 30.9 oz. Very limited mfg. 1992-disc.

		$2,350	$1,850	$1,500	$1,250	$995	$775	$625

* *P88 Competition* - similar to P88 Champion, except has 4 in. barrel, SA only, 14* shot mag., 28.2 oz. Very limited mfg. 1992-disc.

		$1,875	$1,500	$1,250	$995	$775	$625	$550

* *P88 Sport* - .22 LR cal. only, 6 in. barrel, SA only, 10 shot mag. Very limited mfg. 1995-disc.

		$2,450	$1,900	$1,550	$1,250	$995	$775	$625

P99 - 9mm Para., 9x21mm (limited importation 1996), or .40 S&W (new 1999) cal., 4 in. barrel, polymer frame, 10, 12 (.40 S&W cal. only), or 16 (9mm Para. cal. only) shot mag., standard, anti-stress (traditional double action, AS Model, new 2004), or quick action (QA, allowing consistent SA trigger performance) trigger, decocking, and internal striker safeties, 10 shot mag., cocking and loaded chamber indicators, choice of matte black, QPQ (mfg. 1999-2003) finished (silver colored) slide, or titanium coated (new 2003) finish, ambidextrous mag. release, ergonomic black or green (Military model, new 1999) synthetic grips with interchangeable backstrap, adj. rear sight, 25 oz. Importation began 1995.

	MSR $611	$525	$450	$400	$360	$330	$300	$275

Add $31 for titanium finish.

Add $125 for 16 shot mag. (9mm Para. cal. only.)

* *P99 Compact* - 9mm Para. or .40 S&W cal., 3.5 in. barrel, 10 shot mag. with finger extension, available in QA, AS, or DAO, frame has Weaver rail, compact frame, blue finish only, 20 oz. New 2004.

	MSR $611	$525	$450	$400	$360	$330	$300	$275

GRADING - PPGS™	100%	98%	95%	90%	80%	70%	60%

❋ *P99 QSA* - 9mm Para. or .40 S&W cal., first introduced before the QA, slide marked with QSA inscription, large decocking plate. Very few mfg.

	$900	$750	$525				

❋ *P99 2000 Commemorative* - 9mm Para. or .40 S&W cal., features high polish blue slide with laser inscription "Commemorative for the year 2000." Limited mfg. 1,000 (only 500 for the U.S.) of each cal. in 2000 only, cased with Walther videotape.

	$850	$650	$495				

Last MSR was $840.

❋ *P99 La Chasse DU Engraved* - 9mm Para. or .40 S&W cal., similar to Model P-99 Military, except has laser engraved slide, luminescent sights, special case. Mfg. 1998-2000.

	$950	$800	$725				

Last MSR was $1,078.

❋ *P99 La Chasse Engraved* - features choice of elaborate oak leaf, arabesque, or English style hand scroll engraving on polished slide. Mfg. 1998-2000.

	$1,995	$1,600	$1,400				

Last MSR was $2,126.

❋ *P99 Canada Edition* - 9mm Para. cal. only, 105mm barrel, black finish only, scarce in the U.S.

	$1,000	$750	$600				

P990 - similar to P99, except is double action only, features Walther's constant pull trigger system, black, QPQ slide finish, or Military Model (green), 25 oz. Mfg. 1998-2003.

	$550	$475	$425	$385	$350	$325	$295

Last MSR was $644.

PISTOLS: SEMI-AUTO, TARGET

Walther target pistols, except the P22, are currently being imported by Champions Choice located in La Vergne, TN and Earl's Repair Service since 1984 located in Tewksbury, MA. Previously imported by Interarms until 1993 and Nygord Precision Products until 1996.

Add 10% to the values listed for left-hand stocks (available on most models).

P22 - .22 LR cal., 3/4 scale of the P99, hammer fired, black polymer frame with grooved and stippled grip, SA or DA, matte black, military green or nickel finish, internal trigger lock with loaded chamber indicator and mag. disconnect, 10 shot mag., firing pin drop safety, safety key lock on right side of frame, 3.42 (standard) or 5 in. (target) barrel, 15.2 or 18.5 (w/o mag.) oz. New 2001.

MSR $258	$225	$200	$180	$165	$155	$145	$125

Add $100 for target model with 5 in. barrel.

Add $46 for nickel finish.

Add $95 for laser sight (3.4 in. barrel in blue finish only).

Walther offered a limited P22 first edition that included two barrels, barrel extension, and was supplied with a blue plastic case. These were marked "Limited Edition P22" and 1,000 were mfg. Current value for a mint gun with all accessories is in the $325-$350 range.

A special edition two barrel set of this model is available exclusively through Davidson's - MSR is $370.

MODEL GSP TARGET STANDARD - .22 LR cal., 4 1/2 in. barrel, single action, 5 shot mag. standard, 8 or 10 shot mag. optional, adj. sights, nickel, two-tone, or blue finish, walnut target grips, 2-stage trigger became optional in 1995, optional carrying case, 42.3 oz. Mfg. 1969-2001.

	$1,425	$1,225	$995	$650	$550	$475	$425

Last MSR was $1,450.

This model also comes as a complete international package, including a GSP with .22 Short and .32 S&W Wadcutter conversion units, including triggers. MSR was approx. $3,100.

GRADING - PPGS™	100%	98%	95%	90%	80%	70%	60%

✳ **Model GSP Junior** - similar to GSP Target, except has slimmer 4 1/4 in. barrel design, smaller walnut grips, 40.1 oz. Importation disc. 1992.

	$1,450	$1,350	$995	$775	$600	$500	$425

Last MSR was $1,810.

✳ **Model GSP-C** - similar to Model GSP Target, except in .32 S&W Wadcutter, and 4 1/4 in. barrel, 49.4 oz. Mfg. 1971-2001.

	$1,475	$1,025	$800	$650	$550	$475	$425

Last MSR was $1,595.

Add $1,095 for OSP-2000 .22 Short conversion unit.

Add $895 for GSP .22 LR cal. conversion unit.

Add $1,195 for GSP-C .32 S&W Wadcutter conversion unit.

✳ **Model GSP Expert** - .22 LR cal. only, similar to GSP Standard, except for recoil compensation system located in barrel weight, sight radius has been changed, and sights are located further to the rear of the gun, modified frame (cut on an angle) behind the trigger area, stippled blonde/blue ergonomic laminated wood grips, 42.3 oz. New 2001.

MSR $1,595	$1,495	$1,025	$800	$650	$550	$475	$425

✳ **Model GSPC Expert** - similar to Model GSP Expert, except available in .32 S&W Wadcutter cal., 45.1 oz. New 2001.

MSR $1,695	$1,695	$1,100	$850	$675	$575	$495	$450

✳ **Model GSP 25th Year Commemorative Special Limited Edition** - .22 LR cal., aluminum carrying case, options included two-tone finish, laminated Canadian black birch grip, titanium plated bolt, special 70 g. barrel weight with "25 Jahre GSP" engraved, adj. front sight, two-stage trigger, 3 lbs. 1,000 mfg. 1994.

	$2,500	$2,150	$1,850

✳ **Model GSP Atlanta** - .22 LR cal., special edition for the 1996 Olympic Games, Atlanta inscribed on right side of bolt housing, black laminate grips, titanium plated bolt, otherwise same as GSP Target Standard.

	$1,800	$1,450	$1,000

✳ **Model GSP-C 25th Year Commemorative Special Limited Edition** - similar to GSP 25th Year Commemorative, except in .32 S&W Wadcutter, engraved 65 g. barrel weight, 1,000 mfg. as complete pistols or conversion units. Mfg. 1996 only.

	$1,995	$1,600	$1,250

✳ **Model GSP Special Anniversary Pistol/Rifle Combination** - only 50 pieces mfg. for 2000, includes scope, pistol, and rifle conversion kit.

MSR $5,500	$5,500	$3,750	$2,750

✳ **Model GSP Rifle Conversion Kit** - .22 LR cal., unique conversion allows taking a GSP action and inserting it into a rifle stock, includes 16 3/4 in. (18 1/4 with GSP compensator) stainless barrel, black, brown, camo, or Walther blue, laminate stock, right- or left-hand, 5, 8, or 10 shot mag. New 1996.

MSR $995	$995	$850	$725

Add $155 with Super Match stock.

Add $300 for Super Match Kit.

Add $75 for left-hand stock.

This rifle conversion kit is only available from Earl's Repair Service, Inc.

MODEL KSP 200 - .22 LR cal., Walther's semi-auto pistol with adj. laminated ergonomic grips, target trigger and sights, two-tone slide finish, mfg. in cooperation with Baikal. Mfg. 2000-2004.

	$500	$450	$415	$385	$350	$325	$295

Last MSR was $575.

GRADING - PPGS™	100%	98%	95%	90%	80%	70%	60%

MODEL OSP - similar to GSP, in .22 Short cal. Mfg. 1961-1994 for international competition (meets ISU and NRA regs.), 3.35 (1994-present, current model is OSP 2000) or 4 1/4 in. barrel, 44.4 oz.

	MSR $1,275	$1,275	$1,025	$800	$650	$550	$475	$425

Add $275 for extended sight radius and semi-wraparound grip (Model OSP 2000).

FREE PISTOL - .22 LR cal., single shot, electronic trigger, 11.8 in. heavy barrel, advanced target design with fully adj. grips and sights, 49.4 oz. Mfg. 1977-91.

		$1,450	$1,200	$1,000	$850	$675	$575	$500

Last MSR was $2,140.

P38 WWII MILITARY MFG. - see German Military for breakdown.

HÄMMERLI-WALTHER - see Hämmerli.

REVOLVERS

MODEL R99 - .357 Mag. cal., 6 shot, double action, 3 in. barrel, adj. rear sight, blue or stainless steel, unique Duo-grip allows for different hand sizes (2 grips included), 28 1/2 oz. Mfg. by Smith & Wesson 1999 only for the European market with no U.S. importation.

This model was basically a variation of the S&W Models 19 (blue) or 66 (stainless).

RIFLES: DISC.

MODEL B - .30-06 cal., bolt action, post-war mfg., 22 in. barrel. Disc.

	$450	$420	$380	$340	$300	$275	$250

Add 20% for double-set triggers.

MODEL 1 AUTOLOADING - .22 LR cal., Carbine model, autoloading, detachable mag., 20 1/2 in. barrel, 5 or 9 (optional) shot mag., could be used as bolt action or semi-auto, checkered pistol grip, walnut sporter stock, 5 1/2 lbs.

	$695	$600	$500	$400	$300	$250	$200

MODEL 2 AUTOLOADING - .22 LR cal., similar to Model 1, except has 24 1/2 in. barrel, finger grooved forearm, tangent sight, adj. trigger, checkered sporter stock, pre-war, 7 lbs.

	$775	$625	$500	$400	$300	$250	$200

MODEL V CHAMPION - similar to Model V Single Shot, with micrometer adj. sight and checkered pistol grip stock.

	$550	$495	$425	$385	$330	$305	$250

MODEL DSM 34 - .22 LR cal., single shot, military stock, tangent sight. Pre-war and wartime mfg.

	$1,000	$650	$550	$500	$450	$375	$300

Add 50% for stamp in stock.
Add 20% for AS stamp in stock.

MODEL KKM INTERNATIONAL MATCH - .22 LR cal., single shot bolt action, 28 in. heavy barrel, adj. aperture sight, adj. hook butt, thumbhole stock, accessory rail, post-war mfg.

	$880	$770	$715	$660	$550	$495	$440

MODEL KKM-S - similar to KKM, with adj. cheekpiece.

	$935	$825	$770	$715	$605	$550	$495

MODEL KKJ SPORTER - .22 LR cal., bolt action, 5 shot, 22 1/2 in. barrel, open sight, checkered sporter stock, post-war.

	$1,250	$995	$650	$550	$450	$385	$330

Add 20% for double-set triggers.

GRADING - PPGS™	100%	98%	95%	90%	80%	70%	60%

MODEL KKJ-MA - .22 Mag. cal.

	$1,250	$1,100	$775	$650	$550	$450	$385

MODEL KKJ-HO - .22 Hornet cal., repeater or single shot (Model KKJ-E).

	$1,450	$1,225	$825	$700	$575	$450	$385

Add 20% for double-set triggers.

MODEL KKW - .22 LR cal., single shot, military stock, tangent sight, pre-war and wartime mfg.

	$750	$600	$420	$300	$260	$220	$195

Add 50% for SA stamp on stock.

MODEL SSV VARMINT - .22 LR cal., single shot bolt action, 25 1/2 in. barrel, no sights, Monte Carlo pistol grip stock, post-war mfg.

	$700	$600	$525	$495	$415	$360	$330
.22 Hornet	$825	$725	$600	$550	$475	$415	$385

MODEL UIT BV UNIVERSAL - .22 LR cal., single shot bolt action, 25.6 in. heavy barrel, adj. aperture sight, target stock with palm rest, adj. butt, meets ISU regs., 11 lbs. Disc. 1990.

	$1,325	$1,050	$850	$700	$635	$580	$530

Last MSR was $1,700.

This model was previously known as the Model UIT Special.

GX-1 - similar to Model UIT Match, 25 in. barrel with fully adj. free rifle stock, all accessories included, 16 1/2 lbs. Importation disc. 1991.

	$1,895	$1,375	$1,125	$985	$860	$775	$680

Last MSR was $2,350.

MODEL KK/MS SILHOUETTE - .22 LR cal. only, designed for silhouette shooting with no sights, thumbhole stock with adj. butt, fully stippled forend and stock grip, front barrel weight, 23.6 in. barrel, 16.3 lbs. Imported 1984-91.

	$975	$795	$625	$560	$495	$435	$395

Last MSR was $1,175.

RUNNING BOAR MODEL 500 - similar to KK/MS, no sights, thumbhole stock with adj. wood buttplate and cheekpiece, 23.6 in. barrel, 8.4 lbs. Disc. 1990.

	$1,195	$900	$675	$575	$500	$435	$395

Last MSR was $1,300.

MODEL WA-2000 - .300 Win. Mag. (standard) or .308 Win. (optional) cal., ultra-deluxe semi-auto, 25.6 in. barrel, 5 or 6 shot mag., optional extras include aluminum case, spare mags., integral bipod, adj. tools and leather sling, regular or night vision scope, special order only, 16 3/4 lbs. Disc. 1988.

	$18,000	$12,500	$10,750	$9,000	$8,000	$7,000	$6,250

A 7.5 Swiss cal. conversion kit was also optional on this model.

MODEL UIT MATCH - similar to Model UIT, except with improved stock design which includes fully stippled lower forearm and pistol grip, 25.6 in. barrel, 8.6 lbs. Importation disc. 1993.

	$1,125	$925	$800	$660	$610	$555	$510

Last MSR was $1,400.

✳ **Model UIT-E** - electronic trigger, 25.6 in. barrel, 10.4 lbs. Disc. 1986.

	$1,350	$940	$860	$770	$670	$630	$560

Last MSR was $1,250.

MODEL PRONE 400 - similar to UIT Match, with Prone style competition stock and no sights. Disc.

	$750	$635	$580	$525	$415	$360	$305

GRADING - PPGS™	100%	98%	95%	90%	80%	70%	60%

RIFLES: CURRENT/RECENT MFG.

Except for the G22 and GSP rifles, the following models are available from Champion's Choice.

MODEL G22 SEMI-AUTO - .22 LR cal., bullpup design with thumbhole stock, fire control and mag. integrated in rear of stock, variable length stock, adj. sliding sights, right- or left-hand, blue or military green finish, Weaver style rails, 20 in. barrel, 10 shot mag., approx. 6 lbs. New 2004.

MSR $399	$340	$300	$260	$225	$200	$185	$170

Add $42 for scope or $70 for laser or red-dot sights.

MODEL KK200 - .22 LR cal., available in standard rifle laminated stock, power match, and sport configurations, top-of-the-line competition model, 19.7 in. barrel, 11.57 lbs.

MSR N/A	$1,490	$1,275	$1,000	$850	$725	$600	$550

Add $1,200 for machined KK200 Power Match Model with nickel plated stippled stock and forend, 25.5 in. barrel, 13 lbs. (limited mfg. 1995).
Add $420 for KK200 S (sport configuration).
Add $265 for electronic trigger on Power Match or Sport Models.

MODEL KK CLUB SPORT RIFLE - .22 LR cal. New 2000.

MSR N/A	$525	$450	$400	$350	$275	$260	$230

MODEL GSP RIFLE - .22 LR cal., utilizes GSP sport pistol action, 16 3/4 in. stainless fluted barrel, through engraved compensator, laminated "silhouette style" thumbhole stock, 5 shot standard, 8 or 10 shot optional, optics or scope optional, 8.55 lbs. Introduced 1996.

MSR $2,590	$2,400	$2,100	$1,800	$1,500	$1,250	$1,125	$1,000

This model is only available from Earl's Repair Service.

SHOTGUNS: SxS

MODEL WSF - 12 or 16 ga., checkered walnut stock, double triggers, boxlock, sling swivels, 28.4 in. barrel. Introduced 1932-disc.

	$725	$575	$425	$325	$275	$240	$200

MODEL WSFD - 12 or 16 ga., cheekpiece, checkered walnut stock, double triggers, boxlock, sling swivels, 6.3 (16 ga.) or 6.6 (12 ga.) lbs. Introduced 1932-disc.

	$925	$725	$575	$450	$400	$350	$300

SHOTGUNS: SEMI-AUTO

WALTHER SEMI-AUTO - 12 ga. only, 2 3/4 in. chamber, 25.5 in. barrel, crossbolt safety, checkered walnut stock and forearm. Mfg. in Zella-Mehlis 1921-31.

	$950	$875	$775	$650	$550	$450	$375

WALTHER, FRENCH-MADE BY MANURHIN

Previously manufactured in Mulhouse, France. Previously imported 1984-86 by Matra-Manurhin International, Inc. located in Alexandria, VA.

PISTOLS: SEMI-AUTO

Manufacture of these Walther PP type pistols commenced in Mulhouse, France in 1951. They were marked "MANURHIN" on the slide until 1954. Since then they were designated Walther MKII. They were imported into the USA by Interarms up to 1983.

In 1984, following a disagreement regarding the use of the Walther trademark, a few pistols were manufactured using the standard Walther slide legend, w/o the "under license of" above the legend. Additionally, the Manurhin name, logo, and the words "Made in France" were stamped on the heel of the gun in very small letters. Following this French production, pistols were made in Germany and marked Walther, or made in France and marked Manurhin. Manurhin briefly set

GRADING - PPGS™	100%	98%	95%	90%	80%	70%	60%

up an office in New York to do its own importation, and later moved to Florida.

In 1984, Manurhin was imported directly with no Interarms logo or Walther trademark appearing on Models PP and PPK/S. Importation was discontinued 1986, when all production resumed in Ulm, Germany.

MODEL PP - .22 LR, .32 ACP, or .380 ACP cal., 3 7/8 in. barrel, 10 shot mag. (.22 LR), 8 shot mag. (.32 ACP), 7 shot mag. (.380 ACP), blue only, all steel construction, double action with positive hammer block safety, 24 oz.

		$450	$350	$300	$230	$205	$185	$170

Last MSR was $419.

Add 20% for .22 LR or .380 ACP cal.
Add $46 for Durgarde finish.

✳ *Collector Model* - blue finish, special engraving. Imported 1986 only.

	$465	$415	$350

Last MSR was $529.

✳ *Presentation Model* - blue finish, special ornamentation. Imported 1986 only.

	$720	$650	$500

Last MSR was $819.

✳ *Interarms Import*

	$395	$325	$285

Also available with various engraving options in either blue, nickel, or gold finish - prices range from $222 - $540.

PP SPORT - .22 LR cal. only, double action, 6.1 or 8.1 in. barrel, blue finish only, precision adj. sights, contoured plastic grips with thumbrest, 25 oz. New Manurhin design beginning 1985-disc.

	$545	$485	$430	$385	$325	$290	$270

Last MSR was $635.

✳ *PP Sport-C* - similar to PP Sport, except is single action.

	$540	$475	$415	$370	$310	$280	$260

Last MSR was $635.

MODEL PPK - .22 LR, .32 ACP, or .380 ACP cal., 3 1/4 in. barrel, 10 shot mag.-.22 LR, 8 shot mag.-.32 ACP, 7 shot mag.-.380 ACP, blue only, all steel construction, double action with positive hammer block safety, 23 oz.

	$550	$475	$425	$375	$350	$325	$300

Add 20% for .22 LR or .380 ACP cal.

MODEL PPK/S - .22 LR, .32 ACP, or .380 ACP cal., 3 1/4 in. barrel, 10 shot mag.-.22 LR, 8 shot mag.-.32 ACP, 7 shot mag.-.380 ACP, blue only, all steel construction, double action with positive hammer block safety, 23 oz.

	$400	$350	$300	$230	$205	$185	$170

Last MSR was $419.

Add 20% for .22 LR cal.

✳ *PPK/S Durgarde* - similar to Model PPK/S, only with bonded brushed chrome finish.

	$450	$400	$350	$300	$275	$250	$240

Last MSR was $465.

Add 20% for .22 LR cal.

✳ *Collector Model* - blue finish, special engraving. Imported 1986 only.

	$465	$415	$350

Last MSR was $529.

✳ *Presentation Model* - blue finish, special ornamentation. Imported 1986 only.

	$720	$650	$500

Last MSR was $819.

GRADING - PPGS™	100%	98%	95%	90%	80%	70%	60%

✳ **Interarms Import**

       $395   **$340**   **$300**

Was also available with various engraving options in either blue, nickel, or gold finish - prices range from $222-$540.

WARNER ARMS CORPORATION

Previous manufacturer located in Norwich, CT.

PISTOLS: SEMI-AUTO

INFALLIBLE POCKET AUTO PISTOL - .32 ACP cal., 7 shot, 3 in. barrel, fixed sights, rubber grips. Mfg. 1917-19.

       $450   **$350**   **$250**   **$150**   **$125**   **$100**   **$90**

WATSON BROS.

Current long gun manufacturer established in 1885, and located in London, England.

Watson Bros. manufactures distinct round body actions with self-opening locks in both SxS and O/U shotgun configurations. Back action sidelock double rifles are also available. Please contact the factory directly (see Trademark Index) for more information including current pricing.

WEATHERBY

Current trademark manufactured and imported by Weatherby located in Atascadero, CA since 1995. Previously located in South Gate, CA, 1945-1995. Weatherby began manufacturing rifles in the U.S. during early 1995. Dealer and distributor sales.

Weatherby is an importer and manufacturer of long arms. Earlier production was from Germany and Italy, and German mfg. is usually what is collectible. Rifles are currently produced in the U.S., while O/U shotguns are made in Japan and semi-autos are mfg. in Italy. Workmanship in all instances is excellent. Weatherby is well-known for their high-velocity proprietary rifle calibers.

Weatherby offers a research authentication service for Weatherby firearms. The cost is $50 per serial number ($75 for custom rifles, $100 for special editions and commemoratives), and includes a certificate signed by Roy Weatherby Jr. and company historian Dean Rumbaugh. Please contact the company directly for more information regarding this service (see Trademark Index).

Early Weatherby rifles used a Mathieu Arms action in the 1950s - primarily since it was available in left-hand action. Right-handed actions were normally mfg. from the FN Mauser type.

DRILLINGS

WEATHERBY DRILLING - mfg. by J. P. Sauer during the late 1960s-early 1970s for Weatherby importation (marked Weatherby on right barrel), identical to Sauer Model 3000, except was not available in all metric cals. Disc.

    $2,850   **$2,450**   **$2,100**   **$1,800**   **$1,500**   **$1,250**   **$1,000**

PISTOLS: BOLT ACTION

SILHOUETTE PISTOL - .22-250 Rem. or .308 Win. cal., mfg. in Japan during late 1970s, 14 1/2 in. barrel, Lyman or Williams sights, fitted case. Only 50 were mfg. in .22-250 Rem. and 150 in .308 Win. cal. Disc. 1981.

    $3,750   **$3,300**   **$2,750**   **$2,450**   **$2,100**   **$1,850**   **$1,650**

GRADING - PPGS™	100%	98%	95%	90%	80%	70%	60%

MARK V CFP (CENTERFIRE PISTOLS) - .22-250 Rem., .223 Rem. (new 2000), .243 Win., 7mm-08 Rem., or .308 Win. cal., features 15 in. fluted stainless barrel with recessed crown, ambidextrous designed multi-layer brown laminate stock with finger grooves and swivel studs, blue Mark V lightweight action, no sights, 3 shot internal mag., 5 1/4 lbs. Mfg. 1997-2000.

	$935	$815	$735	$650	$600	$550	$500

Last MSR was $1,099.

* ✱ *Mark V Accumark CFP* - same cals. as Mark V CFP, features specially designed synthetic stock with Kevlar and other fibers, matte black finish with grey spider web pattern, 5 lbs. Limited mfg. 2000 only.

	$935	$815	$735	$650	$600	$550	$500

Last MSR was $1,099.

RIFLES: .22 LR CAL.

ACCUMARK CLASSIC & DELUXE BOLT ACTION - while these models were advertised in 1990 ($635 retail), they never went into production.

MARK XXII CLIP MAG OR TUBE FEED SEMI-AUTO - .22 LR cal., mag. feed, skip-line checkered walnut stock with rosewood forend and pistol grip cap, clip models have 5 or 10 shot detachable mag., 24 in. barrel, open V rear fold down sights, grooved alloy receiver, this model was originally mfg. in Italy by Beretta, followed by two different Japanese manufacturers, then production went to the U.S. briefly (Mossberg mfg.) and ended up back in Japan, slide selector changes operation from single shot to semi-auto, tube feed model weighs approx. 6 lbs., 10 oz., clip model weighs 5 lbs., 13 oz. Approx. 100,000 mfg. 1964-1989.

Japanese mfg.	$430	$395	$365	$320	$225	$160	$130

Last MSR was $454.

Subtract 10% for tube feed models.

There were three different Japanese manufacturers between 1967-1999 (not domestically imported after 1989). During this time, the type and quality of the wood and finish, safety switch, rear sight, trigger, trigger guard design, floorplate and magazines were just some of the many changes that occurred during this manufacturing period. Because of this, prices could fluctuate approx. 10%, depending on what features have become more desirable today. A slight premium may be asked for U.S. mfg. A Weatherby Mark XXII 4x50mm scope was also marketed during production, even though the lens is 25mm, not 50mm - current value is approx. $150 if in box.

Italian mfg. (W/ Clip)	$550	$495	$450	$400	$365	$265	$170

Subtract 20%-35% if w/o rosewood forend tip and/or discolored trigger guard/floorplate.

Subtract 10% for tube feed models.

The Mark XXII clip mag. was originally mfg. in Italy - a slight premium might be asked. This model featured a receiver slide-switch that allowed semi-auto operation to be converted to single shot mode. This model used an anodized aluminum alloy triggerguard and floorplate, which are prone to discoloration.

MARK XXII TUBE MAG SEMI-AUTO - .22 LR cal., same general specifications as Mark XXII Clip Mag. model, except tube-feed, 15 shot, 6 lbs. Disc. 1989.

	$395	$320	$265	$245	$215	$195	$180

Last MSR was $454.

RIFLES: BOLT ACTION, MARK V SERIES

In 1992, 24 in. barrels were disc. on most calibers of .300 or greater (including Models Mark V Deluxe, Fibermark, Lazermark, and Euromark). Since 1957, the Mark V Action has been manufactured in Germany, Japan, and the U.S. Early pre-Mark V Weatherby mfg. bolt actions utilized the FN Mauser and French Brevex Magnum Mauser actions rechambered for Weatherby Mag. cals. All Weatherby Magnums in .30-378, .338-378, .378, .416, and .460 cal. are equipped with an Accubrake.

MARK V DELUXE

MARK V DELUXE - .22-250 Rem. (mfg. 1999-2004), .240 Wby. Mag. (disc. 1996, reintroduced 1999-2004), .243 Win. (mfg. 1999-2004), .25-06 Rem. (mfg. 1999-2004), .257 Wby. Mag., .270 Win. (mfg. 1999-2004), .270 Wby. Mag., .280 Rem. (mfg. 1999-2004), 7mm Wby. Mag., 7mm-08 Rem. (mfg. 1999-2004), .30-06 (disc. 1996, reintroduced 1999-2004), .308 Win. (mfg. 1999-2004), .300 Wby. Mag., .340 Wby. Mag., .375 H&H (mfg. 1993 only), .378 Wby. Mag., .416 Wby. Mag. or .460 Wby. Mag. cal., bolt action, 3-5 shot mag., 24 or 26 in. barrel, current mfg. has 9 locking lugs (Mag. cals.) or 6 locking lugs (standard cals. and .240 Wby. Mag.), deluxe skip line checkered pistol grip walnut stock with rosewood tipped forearm and pistol grip, no sights, 8 lbs. Left-hand actions (.270 Wby. Mag. and .300 Wby. Mag.) were available at no extra charge through 1997. Mfg. began 1957.

Add 15%-25% for German manufacture (J.P. Sauer) in calibers under .35 if condition is 95% or better.

* *Short Action Cals.* - .22-250 Rem., .243 Win., .240 Wby. Mag., .25-06 Rem., .270 Win., .280 Rem., .30-06, .308 Win., or 7mm-08 Rem. short action cals. Mfg. 1999-2004.

	100%	98%	95%	90%	80%	70%	60%
	$1,550	$1,275	$995	$750	$625	$525	$475

Last MSR was $1,963.

* *Wby. Mag. Cals.* - includes cals. between .257 Wby. Mag. - .340 Wby. Mag., 8 1/2 lbs.

	100%	98%	95%	90%	80%	70%	60%
MSR $2,023	$1,595	$1,300	$1,025	$775	$650	$550	$500

Add approx. $200 for .375 H&H cal. (disc. 1993).

* *.378 Wby. Mag.* - 26 (disc.) or 28 (with muzzle brake) in. barrel, 8 1/2 lbs.

	100%	98%	95%	90%	80%	70%	60%
MSR $2,380	$1,875	$1,350	$1,050	$775	$650	$550	$500

* *.416 Wby. Mag.* - first new caliber (introduced 1989) since the .240 Mag. was released 1965, 26 (disc.) or 28 in. barrel, includes muzzle brake, 9 lbs.

	100%	98%	95%	90%	80%	70%	60%
MSR $2,380	$1,875	$1,350	$1,050	$775	$650	$550	$500

* *.460 Wby. Mag.* - 24 (disc.), 26 (disc.) or 28 (new 2004) in. barrel, includes custom stock, integral muzzle brake, 10 lbs. No extra charge for left-hand.

	100%	98%	95%	90%	80%	70%	60%
MSR $2,797	$2,225	$1,650	$1,250	$925	$775	$650	$575

ACCUMARK (MAG. CALS.)

ACCUMARK (MAG. CALS.) - .257 Wby. Mag., .270 Wby. Mag., .300 Win. Mag., .300 Wby. Mag., .30-378 Wby. Mag. (new 1997), .338-378 Wby Mag. (new 1998), 7mm STW (mfg. 1998-2004), 7mm Rem. Mag., 7mm Wby. Mag., or .340 Wby. Mag. cal., features Bell & Carlson hand laminated fiberglass stock with Pachmayr Decelerator pad, 2 or 3 shot mag., 26 or 28 (.30-378 or .338-378 Wby. Mag. cals. only) in. stainless steel fluted barrel, aluminum bedding plate, approx. 8 3/4 lbs. New 1996.

	100%	98%	95%	90%	80%	70%	60%
MSR $1,726	$1,400	$1,125	$925	$825	$725	$600	$550

Add $248 for .30-378 Wby. Mag. or .338-378 Wby. Mag. cals.
Add approx. $111 for left-hand action (available in most cals., mfg. 1999-2004).

* *Accumark (Reg. Cals.)* - .22-250 Rem., .223 Rem. (new 2000), .243 Win., .240 Wby. Mag., .25-06 Rem., .270 Win., .280 Rem., 7mm-08 Rem., .30-06, or .308 Win. cal., features hand laminated fiberglass stock with Pachmayr Decelerator pad, 24 in. fluted stainless barrel w/o sights, 7 1/4 lbs. Mfg. 1998-2004.

	100%	98%	95%	90%	80%	70%	60%
	$1,375	$1,075	$875	$800	$700	$600	$550

Last MSR was $1,666.

CLASSICMARK I

CLASSICMARK I - available in 9 Wby. Mag. cals. in addition to .270 Win., 7mm Rem. Mag., .30-06, or .375 H&H cal., oil finished American Claro walnut stock with no cheekpiece and ebony forend cap, 1 in. solid recoil pad, panel point checkering. Mfg. 1992-93.

	100%	98%	95%	90%	80%	70%	60%
	$1,075	$750	$625	$525	$475	$450	$410

Last MSR was $1,295.

Add $15 for 26 in. barrel.
Add $130 for .375 H&H cal.

GRADING - PPGS™	100%	98%	95%	90%	80%	70%	60%

❊ **.300 or .340 Wby. Mag.** - 26 in. barrel only, right- or left-hand action, 8 1/2 lbs.

	$1,095	$775	$625	$525	$475	$450	$410

Last MSR was $1,323.

❊ **.378 Wby. Mag.** - 26 in. barrel only, right- or left-hand action, 8 1/2 lbs.

	$1,125	$795	$625	$525	$475	$450	$410

Last MSR was $1,356.

❊ **.416 Wby. Mag.** - 26 in. barrel only, right- or left-hand action, integral muzzle brake.

	$1,150	$825	$650	$550	$495	$460	$430

Last MSR was $1,411.

❊ **.460 Wby. Mag.** - 26 in. barrel only, includes custom stock, integral muzzle brake, 10 lbs. No extra charge for left-hand.

	$1,250	$900	$675	$575	$525	$475	$430

Last MSR was $1,573.

CLASSICMARK II - available in 9 Wby. Mag. cals. in addition to .270 Win., 7mm Rem. Mag., or .30-06, similar to Classicmark I, except has deluxe American walnut with 22 LPI multiple point checkering, steel grip cap, satin finished wood and metal, guaranteed 1 1/2 in. or less 3 shot grouping at 100 yards, right-hand action only. Mfg. 1992 only.

	$1,525	$1,175	$975	$800	$650	$600	$550

Last MSR was $1,775.

Add $28 for 26 in. barrel.

❊ **.300 or .340 Wby. Mag.** - 26 in. barrel only.

	$1,550	$1,175	$975	$800	$650	$600	$550

Last MSR was $1,803.

❊ **.378 Wby. Mag.** - 26 in. barrel only.

	$1,700	$1,250	$1,000	$800	$650	$600	$550

Last MSR was $1,976.

❊ **.416 Wby. Mag.** - 26 in. barrel only, integral muzzle brake.

	$1,875	$1,375	$1,050	$825	$650	$600	$550

Last MSR was $2,128.

❊ **.460 Wby. Mag.** - 26 in. barrel only, includes custom stock, integral muzzle brake, 10 lbs.

	$1,925	$1,400	$1,050	$825	$650	$600	$550

Last MSR was $2,207.

❊ **Safari Classic** - .375 H&H cal., 24 in. barrel only, right-hand action, limited edition featuring custom action, quarter rib express and front ramp sights, barrel band swivel and engraved floor plate, stock similar to Classicmark II. Mfg. 1992 only.

	$2,300	$1,850	$1,650	$1,450	$1,300	$1,175	$995

Last MSR was $2,693.

EUROMARK - available in most cals. as the Sporter Model, also includes .378 Wby. Mag. and .416 Wby. Mag., differs from Mark V Deluxe in that it has an oil finished, hand checkered, deluxe American claro walnut stock with ebony pistol grip cap and forend tip, low luster bluing, and solid black recoil pad. Mfg. 1986-92, re-introduced 1995-2002.

	$1,410	$975	$740	$585	$475	$450	$410

Last MSR was $1,819.

Add $312 for either .378 Wby. Mag. or .416 Wby. Mag. cal.

❊ **.460 Wby. Mag.** - 24 or 26 in. barrel, includes custom stock, internal muzzle brake, no extra charge for left-hand. Disc. 1992.

	$1,450	$1,100	$925	$775	$650	$600	$550

Last MSR was $1,708.

FIBERMARK - available in .240 Wby. Mag., .257 Wby. Mag., .270 Wby. Mag., .30-06, 7mm Wby. Mag., .300 Wby. Mag., or .340 Wby. Mag. cal., black non-glare fiberglass with wrinkle finish stock, metal has non-glare matte finish, 24 or 26 in. barrel, available in right (disc. 1991) or left-hand action, 7 1/4 lbs. Mfg. 1983-92.

	100%	98%	95%	90%	80%	70%	60%
	$1,195	$875	$725	$600	$525	$475	$450

Last MSR was $1,376.

Add $118 for .300 or .340 Mag. cal.
This model was available in left-hand action (22 in. barrel) in .270 Win. or .30-06 cal. only.

FIBERMARK (CURRENT MFG.) - available in many cals. between .22-250 Rem. - .375 H&H, Mag. cals. only beginning 2005, pillar bedded black composite Monte Carlo stock of Aramid cross-directional fibers, matte blue metal, 24, 26 (Mag. cals. only), or 28 (.30-378 Wby. Mag. cal. only) in. steel barrel, 6 3/4-8 1/2 lbs. New 2001.

MSR $1,285	$1,025	$775	$650	$475	$400	$350	$325

Add $257 for .30-378 Wby. Mag. cal.

✱ *Mark V Fibermark Stainless* - similar to Mark V Fiberglass, except has stainless steel action and barrel with matte finish. Mfg. 2001-2004.

	$1,075	$775	$650

Last MSR was $1,334.

Add $98 for Mag. cals.
Add $301 for .30-378 Wby. Mag. cal.

LAZERMARK - various cals., differs from the Mark V Deluxe in that stock and forearm have been laser carved, 24 (disc.) or 26 in. barrel, 8 1/2 lbs. New 1985.

MSR $2,202	$1,800	$1,225	$875	$700	$575	$475	$450

✱ *.378 Wby. Mag. or .416 Wby. Mag.* - first new caliber (introduced 1989) since the .240 Mag. was released 1965, includes muzzle brake. Disc. 2002.

	$1,850	$1,300	$1,025	$825	$650	$575	$525

Last MSR was $2,266.

✱ *.460 Wby. Mag.* - 24 (disc. 2000), 26 (disc. 2000), or 28 in. barrel, includes custom stock, internal muzzle brake, no extra charge for left-hand. Disc. 2002.

	$2,150	$1,500	$1,200	$925	$650	$600	$550

Last MSR was $2,661.

✱ *Varmintmaster* - .22-250 Rem. or .224 Varmintmaster cal., 24 or 26 in. barrel. Disc. 1991.

	$1,085	$815	$675	$575	$500	$460	$425

Last MSR was $675.

Add $25 for 26 in. barrel.
Not available in left-hand action.

ULTRAMARK - .240 Wby. Mag., .257 Wby. Mag., .270 Wby. Mag., .30-06, 7mm Wby. Mag., .300 Wby. Mag., .378 Wby. Mag. (mfg. 1989 only), or .416 Wby. Mag. (mfg. 1989 only) cal., fancy American walnut, individually hand-bedded, high luster finish, customized action, 24 or 26 in. barrel, basket weave checkering (including pistol grip). Imported 1989-90 only.

	$1,125	$925	$800	$700	$630	$590	$550

Last MSR was $1,315.

Add $25 for 26 in. barrel.
Add $220 for .378 Wby. Mag. cal. (26 in. barrel only).
Add $325 for .416 Wby. Mag. cal. (26 in. barrel only).

WEATHERMARK - available in various Wby. Mag. cals. from .240 (disc. 1996) to .340 and .257 Roberts (disc. 1994), .270 Win., 7mm Rem. Mag., .300 Win. Mag., .30-06, .338 Win. Mag., or .375 H&H (disc.) cal., design is similar to Classicmark II, except is fitted with black checkered composite stock, satin finish black metal, 22 (disc. 1995, .270 Win. or .30-06 only), 24, or 26 in. barrel, right-hand only, 7 1/2 lbs. Mfg. 1992-94.

	$685	$540	$475	$400	$360	$330	$300

Last MSR was $799.

SYNTHETIC (MAG. CALS.) - .257 Wby. Mag., .270 Wby. Mag., .300 Wby. Mag., .30-378 Wby. Mag. (new 1998), .300 Win. Mag., .338 Win. Mag. (disc. 2004), .338-378 Wby. Mag. (new 2001), .340 Wby. Mag., 7mm Wby. Mag., 7mm Rem. Mag., 7mm STW (mfg. 2001-2004), or .375 H&H cal., 24, 26, or 28 in. barrel, features lightweight black synthetic stock, bead blasted matte metal finish, approx. 8 lbs. New 1997.

MSR $1,116	$900	$725	$575	$475	$375	$335	$300

Add $202 for .30-378 Wby. Mag. or .338-.378 Wby. Mag. cal. (28 in. barrel only).

* ❋ **Synthetic (Standard Cals.)** - .22-250 Rem., .243 Win., .240 Wby. Mag., .25-06 Rem., .270 Win., .280 Rem., .30-06, .308 Win., or 7mm-08 Rem. cal., features raised comb, matte black injection mold synthetic stock, no sights, 20 (carbine, .243 Win., .308 Win., or 7mm-08 Rem., disc. 2002) or 24 in. barrel, approx. 6 1/2 lbs. New 1997.

MSR $1,057	$850	$700	$550	$450	$350	$330	$300

* ❋ **Fluted Synthetic** - .257 Wby. Mag., .270 Wby. Mag., .300 Wby. Mag., .300 Win. Mag., 7mm Wby. Mag., or 7mm Rem. Mag. cal., features 24 or 26 in. fluted barrel, black synthetic stock with Monte Carlo cheekpiece, approx. 7 1/2 lbs. Mfg. 1997-98.

	$785	$635	$550	$495	$450	$395	$350

Last MSR was $949.

* ❋ **Weathermark Alaskan Model** - same cals. as Weathermark, similar to Weathermark, except has non-glare electroless nickel-plated metal parts, right- or left-hand (mfg. 1992 only) action. Mfg. 1992-94.

	$750	$635	$560	$495	$450	$400	$360

Last MSR was $875.

Add $37 for Wby. Mag. cals.
Add $164 for .375 H&H cal.
Add $375 for left-hand action (disc.).

SYNTHETIC STAINLESS MODEL (MAG. CALS.) - same cals. as Synthetic, except not available in .338-.378 Wby. Mag. or 7mm STW, features bead blasted matte stainless construction, synthetic Monte Carlo stock. Mfg. 1995-2004.

	$1,075	$775	$600

Last MSR was $1,282.

Add $200 for .30-378 Wby. Mag. (28 in. barrel only).

* ❋ **Synthetic Stainless (Standard Cals.)** - .22-250 Rem., .243 Win., .240 Wby. Mag., .25-06 Rem., .270 Win., .280 Rem., .30-06, .308 Win., or 7mm-08 Rem. cal., features raised comb, matte black injection molded synthetic stock, no sights, 20 (carbine, .243 Win., .308 Win., or 7mm-08 Rem. cal.) or 24 in. stainless barrel and action, approx. 6 1/2 lbs. Mfg. 1997-2004.

	$975	$725	$575

Last MSR was $1,166.

* ❋ **Fluted Stainless** - .257 Wby. Mag., .270 Wby. Mag., .300 Wby. Mag., .300 Win. Mag., 7mm Wby. Mag., or 7mm Rem. Mag., features 24 or 26 in. fluted stainless barrel and action, black synthetic stock with Monte Carlo cheekpiece, approx. 7 1/2 lbs. Mfg. 1997-98.

	$1,025	$925	$825

Last MSR was $1,149.

GRADING - PPGS™	100%	98%	95%	90%	80%	70%	60%

EUROSPORT - various cals., features hand-rubbed satin oil finished claro walnut stock with low luster blue metal work. Mfg. 1995-2002.

	$915	$695	$595	$510	$450	$395	$350

Last MSR was $1,143.

MARK V SLS (STAINLESS LAMINATE SPORTER) - .257 Wby. Mag., .270 Wby. Mag., .300 Wby. Mag., .300 Win. Mag., .338 Win. Mag., .340 Wby. Mag., 7mm Wby. Mag., or 7mm Rem. Mag. cal., 24 or 26 (Wby. Mag. cals. only) in. barrel, features grey laminate stock with recoil pad, stainless steel with matte blue finish, approx. 8 1/2 lbs. Mfg. 1997-2002.

	$1,125	$915	$700				

Last MSR was $1,393.

SPORTER (LONG ACTION) - .240 Wby. Mag. (mfg. 1996 only), .257 Wby. Mag., .270 Wby. Mag., 7mm Rem. Mag., .270 Win. (mfg. 1996 only), .30-06 (disc. 1996), .300 Wby. Mag., .300 Win. Mag., .338 Win. Mag. (disc. 2004), .340 Wby. Mag., or .375 H&H (disc. 2002) cal., 24 or 26 in. barrel, similar features as the Mark V, except has checkered walnut stock without forearm or pistol grip caps, low luster metalwork, vent. recoil pad, no sights, approx. 8 lbs. New 1993.

MSR $1,309	$1,050	$825	$675	$550	$450	$400	$375

❋ *Standard Action Sporter* - .22-250 Rem., .243 Win., .240 Wby. Mag., .25-06 Rem., .270 Win., .280 Rem., .30-06, .308 Win., or 7mm-08 Rem. cal., features raised comb, checkered walnut stock, 54 degree bolt lift, no sights, 24 in. barrel, approx. 6 3/4 lbs. Mfg. 1997-2004.

	$1,000	$775	$650	$525	$450	$400	$375

Last MSR was $1,249.

ULTRA LIGHT WEIGHT - .243 Win., .240 Wby. Mag., .257 Wby. Mag. (new 1999), .25-06 Rem., .270 Win., .270 Wby. Mag. (new 1999), .280 Rem., .300 Wby. Mag. (new 1999), .300 Win. Mag. (new 1999), 7mm-08 Rem., 7mm Rem. Mag. (new 1999), 7mm Wby. Mag. (new 1999), .30-06, .308 Win., or .338-06 A-Square (mfg. 2001-2003) cal., features 24 or 26 in. barrel and lightweight synthetic stock, 5 3/4 or 6 3/4 lbs. New 1998.

MSR $1,670	$1,395	$1,125	$950	$800	$700	$600	$550

Add $82 for long action Mag. cals. (new 1999).

Add $107 for left-hand action (.257 Wby. Mag., .270 Wby. Mag., .300 Wby. Mag., .300 Win. Mag., 7mm Rem. Mag. and 7mm Wby. Mag., mfg. 2000-2004).

WHITETAIL - .257 Sav. cal., limited edition features deluxe high grade Claro walnut, hand checkered bolt knob and engraved floorplate, 22 in. #1 contoured barrel, 6 lbs. Mfg. 1993 only.

	$1,150	$925	$775				

Last MSR was $1,366.

SVR (SPECIAL VARMINT RIFLE) - .22-250 Rem. or .223 Rem. cal., features 22 in. free-floating Kreiger barrel, 4 or 5 shot mag., black Monte Carlo composite stock with grey spider webbing, aluminum bedding block, Pachmayr decelerator pad, 7 1/4 lbs. New 2003.

MSR $1,176	$925	$675	$600	$500	$450	$395	$350

SPM (SUPER PREDATORMASTER) - .22-250 Rem., .223 Rem., .243 Win., .308 Win., or 7mm-08 Rem. cal., features 24 in. Criterion button rifled barrel with flutes, black spider webbing on tan Accumark type stock with slim fore end and CNC aluminum bedding block, Pachmayr Decelerator pad, 6 1/2 lbs. Mfg. 2001-2004.

	$1,375	$1,125	$925	$800	$650	$600	$550

Last MSR was $1,670.

GRADING - PPGS™	100%	98%	95%	90%	80%	70%	60%

SVM (SUPER VARMINTMASTER) - .220 Swift (single shot only, disc., reintroduced 2005), .22-250 Rem., .223 Rem., .243 Win., .308 Win. (disc. 2004), or 7mm-08 Rem. (disc. 2004) cal., features 26 in. Criterion button rifled fluted barrel with crown, 4 or 5 shot mag., available as repeater or single shot, black spider webbing on tan Accumark type stock with beavertail fore end and CNC aluminum bedding block, Pachmayr Decelerator pad, approx. 8 1/2 lbs. New 2000.

MSR $1,737	$1,425	$1,150	$950	$825	$675	$600	$550

SBGM (SUPER BIG GAME MASTER) - various cals. between .240 Wby. Mag. - .338-06 A-Square (disc.), 24 or 26 (Mag. cals. only) in. Criterion hand-lapped fluted Krieger barrel, barreled action is bed to a specially-designed, hand-laminated, raised comb, Monte Carlo composite stock (a combination of Aramid, graphite and unidirectional fibers, and fiberglass) with black spiderweb patterning, Pachmayr Decelerator pad, 6 3/4 lbs. New 2002.

	$1,375	$1,125	$925	$775	$650	$600	$550

Last MSR was $1,670.

Add $66 for Mag. cals.

TRR (THREAT RESPONSE RIFLE) - .223 Rem., .308 Win., .300 Win. Mag. (disc. 2002), .300 Wby. Mag. (disc. 2002), .30-378 Wby. Mag. (disc. 2002), or .338-.378 Wby. Mag. (disc. 2002) cal., 22 in. barrel, 5 shot mag., Mark V action with black finished metal and black hybrid composite stock, various barrel lengths, optional Picatinny style ring and base system, 8 1/2-10 1/2 lbs. New 2002.

MSR $1,737	$1,400	$1,150	$925	$800	$650	$600	$550

Add $52 for .300 Win. Mag. or .300 Wby. Mag. cals. (disc. 2002).

Add $208 for .30-378 Wby. Mag. or .338-378 Wby. Mag. cals. (disc. 2002).

VARMINTMASTER - .22-250 Rem. or .224 Varmintmaster (disc. 1994) cal., 24 (disc. 1991) or 26 in. barrel, 6 1/2 lbs. Disc. 1995.

	$1,075	$775	$625	$525	$475	$450	$410

Last MSR was $1,297.

Not available in left-hand action.

1976 BICENTENNIAL MARK V - .257 Wby. Mag., .270 Wby. Mag., 7mm Wby. Mag., or .300 Wby Mag. cal., 1,000 mfg. in 1976 only.

	$1,495	$1,150	$895				

Last MSR was $2,000.

1984 MARK V OLYMPIC COMMEMORATIVE - .257 Wby. Mag., .270 Wby. Mag., 7mm Wby. Mag., or .300 Wby. Mag. cal., special gold accenting, extra-fancy walnut stock with burnished brass oval depicting the Olympic "Star In Motion" emblem inlay. Mfg. 1984, only 1,000 mfg. at $2,000 retail.

	$1,000	$895	$700				

MARK V 35TH ANNIVERSARY COMMEMORATIVE - .257 Wby. Mag., .270 Wby. Mag., 7mm Wby. Mag., or .300 Wby. Mag. cal., limited mfg. 1980, 1,000 produced total.

	$1,000	$895	$700				

MARK V 40TH ANNIVERSARY COMMEMORATIVE - .257 Wby. Mag. (35 mfg.), .270 Wby. Mag. (35 mfg.), 7mm Wby. Mag. (35 mfg.), or .300 Wby. Mag. (95 mfg.) cal. Limited mfg. 1985, 200 produced total.

	$1,000	$895	$700				

RIFLES: BOLT ACTION, CUSTOM SHOP

OUTFITTER CUSTOM - various cals. between .243 Win. - .338-06 A-Square (disc.), 24 or 26 in. barrel, features ultra lightweight bolt action with titanium nitride hardcoating and a desert camo stock. New 2001.

MSR $2,583	$2,075	$1,725	$1,375	$1,075	$850	$700	$600

Add $60 for Mag. cals.

GRADING - PPGS™	100%	98%	95%	90%	80%	70%	60%

OUTFITTER KREIGER CUSTOM - same cals. as Outfitter Custom, 24 or 26 in. barrel, ultra lightweight action with Kreiger ultra lightweight contoured barrel with cut rifling, trued receiver and bolt face, lapped locking lugs, titanium nitride coating, desert camo stock. Mfg. 2001-2002.

	$2,995	$2,550	$2,175	$1,800	$1,500	$1,250	$995

Last MSR was $3,499.

Add $50 for Mag. cals.

DANGEROUS GAME RIFLE (CUSTOM) - .300 Win. Mag. (mfg. 2002-2004), .300 Wby. Mag. (new 2002), .338 Win. Mag. (mfg. 2002-2004), .340 Wby. Mag. (new 2002), .375 H&H, .375 Wby. Mag., .378 Wby. Mag., .416 Rem. Mag., .416 Wby. Mag., .458 Win. Mag., .458 Lott (new 2005), or .460 Wby. Mag. cal., 24 or 26 in. barrel with express sights (rear is adj.), black fiberglass stock with CNC machined aluminum bedding block and Pachmayr Decelerator pad, black oxide metal finish, 8 3/4 or 9 1/2 (.460 Wby. Mag.) lbs. New 2001.

MSR $3,095		$2,575	$2,100	$1,750	$1,375	$1,075	$875	$700

Add $171 for .378 Wby. Mag. or .416 Wby. Mag., and $265 for .460 Wby. Mag. cal.

Add $350 for snow or desert camo stock with titanium nitride coating.

CUSTOM GRADE - various cals. from .240 Wby. Mag. to .340 Wby. Mag., 24 or 26 in. barrel, super fancy walnut stock featuring No. 7 style inlays, floorplate is engraved "Weatherby Custom", 6-8 months delivery time. Disc. 2001.

	$4,250	$2,750	$2,050	$1,650	$1,450	$1,300	$1,175

Last MSR was $5,099.

TRCM (THREAT RESPONSE CUSTOM MAGNUM) - .300 Win. Mag., .300 Wby. Mag., .30-378 Wby. Mag., or .338-.378 Wby. Mag. cal., Mark V action with ergonomic, fully adjustable composite stock, black finished metal, various barrel lengths, optional Picatinny style ring and base system. New 2002.

MSR $2,888		$2,275	$1,675	$1,200	$950	$725	$650	$575

Add $173 for .30-378 Wby. Mag. or .338-378 Wby. Mag. cals.

Add $725 for desert camo stock with titanium nitride coating.

SAFARI GRADE CUSTOM - .257 Wby. Mag. (new 2000), .270 Wby. Mag. (new 2000), .300 Wby. Mag., .340 Wby. Mag., .375 H&H (new 2000), .375 Wby. Mag., .378 Wby. Mag., .416 Wby Mag., .460 Wby. Mag., or 7mm Wby. Mag. (new 2000) cal., custom order only, various options available, 6-8 month delivery.

MSR $6,050		$5,300	$3,200	$2,100	$1,725	$1,500	$1,300	$1,150

Add $239 for .378 Wby. Mag. or .416 Wby. Mag. cal.

Add $710 for .460 Wby. Mag. cal.

ROYAL CUSTOM - same cals. as Crown Custom, custom order only, features high grade fancy Claro walnut with checkering with rosewood pistol grip cap and forend, damascene bolt and follower, engraved receiver and floorplate, select 24Kt. gold and nickel plating, 26 in. barrel. New 2002.

MSR $6,239		$5,450	$3,350	$2,200	$1,800	$1,600	$1,575	$1,350

CROWN CUSTOM MODEL - .257 Wby. Mag., .270 Wby. Mag., .300 Wby. Mag., .340 Wby. Mag., or 7mm Wby. Mag. cal., custom order only, engraved barrel, receiver, and scope mount, top-of-the-line model.

MSR $7,757		$6,700	$4,000	$3,150	$2,550	$1,950	$1,600	$1,350

RIFLES: BOLT ACTION, VANGUARD SERIES

All currently manufactured Vanguard rifles are shipped with a factory three shot target, guaranteeing 1.5 in. accuracy at 100 yards.

VANGUARD - .243 Win., .25-06 Rem., .270 Win., .30-06, .308 Win., 7mm Rem. Mag., .264 Win. Mag., or .300 Win. Mag. cal., mfg. circa late 1960s-early 1970s.

	$435	$375	$325	$295	$260	$230	$200

Add 10% for .264 Win. Mag. cal.

GRADING - PPGS™	100%	98%	95%	90%	80%	70%	60%

VANGUARD SYNTHETIC (NEW MFG.)

- .22-250 Rem., .223 Rem., .243 Win., .257 Wby. Mag., .270 Win., .270 WSM (new 2005), .30-06, .308 Win., .300 WSM, .300 Win. Mag., .300 Wby. Mag., .338 Win. Mag., or 7mm Rem. Mag. cal., choice of matte black metal or satin stainless steel action/barrel, black synthetic stock, includes many Mark V features, including one-piece fluted bolt with 3 gas ports, 2 locking lugs, and 90-degree bolt lift, 3-5 shot mag., 24 in. barrel, adj. trigger, each gun supplied with 3 shot factory target, 7 3/4 lbs. Domestic mfg. beginning 1997.

MSR $476	$415	$375	$325	$295	$260	$230	$200

Add $120 for Vanguard package (includes Bushnell Banner 3-9x40mm scope mounted and bore sighted, Uncle Mike's nylon sling, and Plano molded case, new 2005).

Add $119 for stainless steel action/barrel.

Add $239 for Vanguard stainless package.

VANGUARD SPORTER

- same cals. as Vanguard Synthetic, features checkered walnut stock with rosewood forend tip, satin finish and checkering, matte blue metal, 24 in. barrel, 3 or 5 shot mag., 7.75 lbs. New 2005.

MSR $582	$495	$435	$395	$340	$310	$270	$240

Add $119 for matte stainless steel action/barrel (Sporter SS).

VANGUARD COMPACT

- .22-250 Rem., .243 Win., or .308 Win. cal., 20 in. barrel, shortened 12.5 LOP, 5 shot mag., matte black hardwood stock, 6.75 lbs. New 2005.

MSR $549	$475	$415	$375	$325	$295	$260	$230

VANGUARD SUB-MOA

- same cals. as Vanguard Synthetic, matte finished steel or stainless steel action and 24 in. barrel, choice of light tan or charcoal Monte Carlo Fiberguard stock with Pachmayr Decelerator pad, no sights, guaranteed to shoot a three shot .99 in. group at 100 yards, 3 or 5 shot mag., 7.75 lbs. New 2005.

MSR $799	$675	$600	$525	$475	$425	$375	$325

Add $120 for stainless steel action/barrel.

VANGUARD CLASSIC I

- .223 Rem., .243 Win., .270 Win., 7mm-08 Rem., 7mm Rem. Mag., .30-06, or .308 Win. cal., checkered walnut stock with satin finish, black buttpad, 24 in. barrel, 3 (7mm Rem. Mag.) or 5 shot mag., No. 1 barrel contour, approx. 7 lbs. 5 oz. Mfg. 1989-93.

	$480	$375	$325	$295	$260	$230	$200

Last MSR was $549.

This model was the replacement for the Vanguard VGS and VGL.

VANGUARD CLASSIC II

- .22-250 Rem., .243 Win., .270 Wby. Mag., .270 Win., 7mm Rem. Mag., .30-06, .300 Win. Mag., .300 Wby. Mag., or .338 Win. Mag. cal., 24 in. No. 2 barrel contour, 3 or 5 shot mag., custom checkered deluxe walnut stock with pistol grip cap and black forend cap, solid black recoil pad, matte finished metal, approx. 7 3/4 lbs. Mfg. 1989-92.

	$675	$550	$475	$425	$395	$360	$330

Last MSR was $750.

This model was also available in a No. 3 barrel contour in .22-250 Rem. cal. only.

VANGUARD VGD

- .22-250 Rem., .243 Win., .25-06 Rem., .270 Win., 7mm Rem. Mag., .30-06, or .300 Win. Mag. cal., bolt action, checkered deluxe walnut stock with rosewood tip forearm and pistol grip, 24 in. barrel, no sights, 5 shot mag. (except 3 shot for .300 Win. Mag.), high luster bluing, about 8 lbs. Disc. 1988.

	$525	$425	$365	$330	$300	$275	$255

Last MSR was $600.

Not available in left-hand action.

GRADING - PPGS™	100%	98%	95%	90%	80%	70%	60%

VANGUARD VGX DELUXE - .22-250 Rem., .243 Win., .270 Win., .270 Wby. Mag., .300 Win. Mag., .300 Wby. Mag., .30-06, .338 Win. Mag., or 7mm Rem. Mag. cal., 24 in. barrel, Monte Carlo stock with skipline checkering, high gloss wood and metal, rosewood grip cap and forend tip. Mfg. 1989-1993.

| | $625 | $550 | $475 | $425 | $395 | $360 | $330 |

Last MSR was $699.

VANGUARD VGS - same cals. as Vanguard VGX, bolt action, checkered satin finished walnut stock, 24 in. barrel, no sights, approx. 8 lbs. Disc. 1988.

| | $415 | $355 | $295 | $265 | $245 | $220 | $200 |

Last MSR was $467.

Not available in left-hand action.

VANGUARD VGL - .223 Rem., .243 Win., .270 Win., 7mm Rem. Mag., .30-06, or .308 Win. cal., lightweight bolt action, checkered walnut stock, 5 shot mag. (6 on .223 Rem.), 20 in. barrel, no sights, 6 1/2 lbs. Disc. 1988.

| | $415 | $355 | $295 | $265 | $245 | $220 | $200 |

Last MSR was $467.

Not available in left-hand action.

VANGUARD WEATHERGUARD - same cals. as Classic I, replacement for Fiberguard, wrinkle black finished synthetic stock, entry level Weatherby, similar specs. as Classic I, approx. 8 lbs. Mfg. 1989-1993.

| | $440 | $350 | $320 | $290 | $260 | $230 | $200 |

Last MSR was $499.

VANGUARD ALASKAN - same cals. as Classic I, features electroless nickel metal plating, no sights. Mfg. 1993-1994.

| | $625 | $550 | $475 | $425 | $395 | $360 | $330 |

Last MSR was $699.

VANGUARD FIBERGUARD - .223 Rem., .243 Win., .270 Win., 7mm Rem. Mag., .30-06, or .308 Win. cal., 20 in. barrel, green fiberglass stock, 3 to 6 shot mags., no sights, blue metal parts, approx. 6 1/2 lbs. Disc. 1988.

| | $500 | $450 | $395 | $355 | $285 | $255 | $220 |

Last MSR was $560.

Not available in left-hand action.

SHOTGUNS: O/U

Weatherby shotguns are currently mfg. by new SKB located in Japan. Current manufacture utilizes the IMC choke system (integral multi-choke), which allows interchangeability with Briley choke tubes.

REGENCY FIELD GRADE - 20 ga. Mag. (new 1968) or 12 ga., checkered stock, VR, engraved side plates, SST, early importation beginning in 1967 was from Italy, later mfg. was switched to Japan.

| | $1,250 | $895 | $800 | $700 | $600 | $550 | $500 |

Add 10-15% for early Italian mfg. (note proofmarks).

REGENCY TRAP GRADE - 12 ga., checkered trap stock, engraved, VR, SST. Imported from Italy.

| | $900 | $800 | $700 | $600 | $550 | $500 | $475 |

OLYMPIAN STANDARD - 12 and 20 ga., lightly engraved sideplates. Disc. 1980.

| | $850 | $775 | $725 | $625 | $525 | $450 | $400 |

OLYMPIAN SKEET - 26 or 28 in. barrel.

| | $885 | $775 | $725 | $625 | $525 | $450 | $400 |

OLYMPIAN TRAP - 30 or 32 in. barrel, VR.

| | $850 | $775 | $725 | $625 | $525 | $440 | $400 |

GRADING - PPGS™	100%	98%	95%	90%	80%	70%	60%

ATHENA GRADE III CLASSIC FIELD - 12, 20, or 28 (new 2001) ga., 2 3/4 (28 ga. only) or 3 in. chambers, 26 or 28 in. barrels, features oil finished Claro walnut stock with rounded pistol grip and slender forearm, gold SST, silver grey nitride sideplates with rose and scroll engraved gold pheasant and quail hunting scenes, gold "W" on opening lever, 6 1/2-8 lbs. New 1999.

MSR $2,173	$1,900	$1,550	$1,275	$1,050	$875	$750	$625

ATHENA GRADE IV FIELD - 12, 20, 28 (mfg. 1989-1993) ga., or .410 (mfg. 1989-1993) bore, 3 in. chambers, 26 or 28 in. VR barrels with or without choke tubes, boxlock with Greener Crossbolt, SST, ejectors, high luster finish on hand checkered claro walnut stock (full pistol grip with rosewood cap) and forearm, recoil pad, engraved sideplates with satin nickel finish, vent. barrels and rib, multi-chokes became standard (except .410 bore) 1986 and 1992 (28 ga.), 6 1/2-8 lbs. Mfg. 1982-2002.

	$2,085	$1,525	$1,150	$925	$750	$600	$525

Last MSR was $2,549.

Subtract 10% if without choke tubes.

This model was redesignated the Grade IV in 1989.

* **Skeet & Trap Models** - 12 (Trap only) or 20 ga., special stock dimensions, target sights. Disc. 1992.

	$1,675	$1,275	$1,000	$875	$725	$600	$525

Last MSR was $1,965.

Skeet models are available in fixed choke only.

* **Single Trap Model** - 12 ga., 32 or 34 in. barrel with multi-choke feature. Disc. 1992.

	$1,675	$1,275	$1,000	$875	$725	$600	$525

Last MSR was $1,975.

* **Trap Combo** - 12 ga., includes a set of O/U barrels and oversingle barrel with multi-choke feature. Disc. 1992.

	$2,300	$1,900	$1,605	$1,300	$995	$800	$675

Last MSR was $2,616.

* **Master Skeet Set** - 12 ga., includes 6 fitted full length Briley tubes with integral extractors (20, 28 ga., and .410 bore), cased. Imported 1988-91.

	$3,100	$2,650	$2,150	$1,900	$1,775	$1,625	$1,525

ATHENA GRADE V CLASSIC FIELD - 12 or 20 ga., 3 in. chambers, similar to Grade IV, except has more elaborate engraving w/o gold inlays, gold SST, and better walnut, 6.5-8 lbs. New 1989.

MSR $3,037	$2,500	$2,000	$1,550	$1,275	$950	$775	$675

In 1993, Weatherby changed the styling of this gun to incorporate European shooting features including an oil finished, round knob stock and slim forearm, tight rose-and-scroll engraving, and matted VR.

ORION UPLAND CLASSIC FIELD - 12 or 20 ga., 3 in. chambers, features high luster checkered Claro walnut stock and forearm, blue frame, gold SST, gold Weatherby flying W on triggerguard, rounded checkered pistol grip stock and slender forearm, ejectors, 26 or 28 in. VR barrels with choke tubes, 6.5-8 lbs. New 1999.

MSR $1,299	$1,095	$965	$800	$650	$550	$500	$450

ORION I FIELD - 12 or 20 ga., 3 in. chambers, 26, 28, or 30 (12 ga. only) in. VR barrels with multi-chokes, SST, ejectors, checkered walnut full pistol grip stock and forearm, recoil pad, blue receiver with engraved upland and waterfowl scenes, 6 1/2-8 lbs. Mfg. 1989-2002.

	$1,240	$1,040	$860	$675	$575	$525	$475

Last MSR was $1,539.

GRADING - PPGS™	100%	98%	95%	90%	80%	70%	60%

❋ Ducks Unlimited Orion - 12 ga. (sponsor gun in 1986) or 20 ga. (sponsor gun in 1987), deluxe walnut with gold duck scenes, blue frame, multi-chokes, includes presentation case.

	$1,395	$1,100	$875				

ORION II FIELD - 12, 20, 28 ga., or .410 bore, 3 in. chambers (except 28 ga.), box-lock with Greener Crossbolt, SST, ejectors, walnut with high-gloss finish, silver nitride receiver with light engraving. Multi-chokes became standard 1986. Field Grade disc. 1993.

	$1,075	$875	$750	$625	$550	$500	$450

Last MSR was $1,207.

Subtract 10% without choke tubes on older models.

Subtract $14 for Skeet grade (12 and 20 ga., fixed chokes only).

This model was redesignated Grade II in 1989. In 1993, the Standard Field Models in this variation were discontinued (Classic Grade took its place) - only Field and Sporting Clays variations are now available.

❋ Orion II Classic Field - 12, 20, or 28 ga., multi-choked barrels, features rounded pistol grip stock and oil finished Claro walnut stock and forearm, gold SST, ejectors, waterfowl and upland game scenes on silver grey nitride finish, matted VR, 6.5-8 lbs. New 1993.

MSR $1,622	$1,300	$1,095	$875	$700	$600	$550	$495

ORION II FIELD/CLASSIC SPORTING - 12 ga. only, Sporting Clays configuration, early mfg. was blue finish, current mfg. is silver nitride finish, choice of Field Sporting (with rosewood pistol grip cap and grooved upper forearm) or Classic Field Sporting (rounded pistol grip and smaller forearm), acid etched engraving, rounded recoil pad, matte finish VR, lengthened forcing cones. Mfg. 1991-2002.

	$1,400	$1,115	$925	$725	$625	$565	$515

Last MSR was $1,753.

SUPER SPORTING CLAYS (SSC) - 12 ga. only, 3 in. chambers, 28, 30, or 32 in. vented barrels with 12mm target VR and gas ports, choke tubes, fully adj. trigger, satin oil finished sporter style pistol grip stock with Schnabel forearm, Pachmayr Decelerator pad, approx. 8 lbs. New 1999.

MSR $2,059	$1,645	$1,350	$1,125	$875	$735	$650	$575

ORION III FIELD - 12 or 20 ga. only, similar to Grade II, except has silver grey receiver with custom engraving including mallard and pheasant game scenes, multi-chokes standard. Mfg. 1989-2002.

	$1,545	$1,225	$965	$795	$675	$600	$525

Last MSR was $1,917.

❋ Orion III Classic Field - 12 or 20 ga., multi-choked 26 or 28 in. VR barrels, features rounded pistol grip stock and oil finished Claro walnut stock and forearm, extensive engraving on silver grey nitride finish with gold game scene inlays, matted VR, 7 1/4-8 lbs. New 1993.

MSR $1,955	$1,565	$1,250	$975	$800	$675	$600	$525

❋ Orion III English Field - 12 or 20 ga., 3 in. chambers, features straight grip stock and silver grey nitride receiver with engraving and gold inlays, approx. 6 1/2 lbs. Mfg. 1997-2002.

	$1,595	$1,300	$1,075	$875	$700	$625	$550

Last MSR was $1,998.

SHOTGUNS: SxS

SxS manufacture utilizes the IMC choke system (integral multi-choke), which allows interchangeability with Briley choke tubes. Importation was disc. during 2003, and reintroduced during 2005.

GRADING - PPGS™	100%	98%	95%	90%	80%	70%	60%

ORION - 12, 20, 28 ga. or .410 bore, 3 in. chambers standard except for 28 ga., ejectors, case colored boxlock action, gold SST, 18 LPI checkered half-round pistol grip Turkish walnut stock and semi-beavertail forearm, 26 or 28 in. barrels, solid pad, 6 3/4-7 lbs., approx. 400 mfg. (including Athena) in Spain by Abolla 2002-2003.

	$960	$845	$735	$625	$525	$450	$395

Last MSR was $1,149.

ATHENA - 12 or 20 ga. 3 in. chambers, ejectors, case colored engraved boxlock action with sideplates, gold SST, 22 LPI checkered straight grip select Turkish walnut stock and splinter forearm, 26 or 28 in. barrels with IMC choke system (interchangeable with Briley), solid pad, 6 3/4-7 lbs., approx. 400 (including Orion) mfg. in Spain by Abolla 2002-2003.

	$1,285	$1,025	$865	$750	$650	$550	$475

Last MSR was $1,599.

ATHENA D'ITALIA - 12, 20, or 28 ga., 2 3/4 (28 ga. only) or 3 in. chambers, engraved coin finished Anson & Deeley boxlock action with sideplates, double locking system, monobloc barrels with ejectors and stainless steel choke tubes, DTs, oil finished English straight grip select walnut stock and slim forearm with new Scottish checkering, gold "W" on triggerguard, supplied with hardshell takedown case, 6.75-7.25 lbs. Mfg. in Italy. New 2005.

MSR $2,840	$2,400	$2,150	$1,850	$1,600	$1,350	$1,125	$875

Add $136 for 28 ga.

SHOTGUNS: SEMI-AUTO

Current manufacture utilizes the IMC choke system (integral multi-choke), which allows interchangeability with Briley choke tubes.

Add $359 for interchangeable SAS rifled 22 in. slug barrel (new 2004).

CENTURION FIELD GRADE - 12 ga., VR, checkered stock, gas operation, walnut full pistol grip stock. Mfg. 1972-81.

	$300	$280	$250	$240	$230	$210	$190

CENTURION TRAP GRADE - 12 ga., checkered stock, VR.

	$335	$300	$250	$240	$230	$210	$190

CENTURION DE LUXE - 12 ga., VR, checkered stock, lightly engraved.

	$375	$350	$310	$275	$250	$235	$210

Add 20% for deluxe wood.

* *Centurion DU* - mfg. 1980 for DU chapters.

	$550	$375	$325

MODEL 82 - 12 ga. only, 2 3/4 or 3 in. chamber, gas operation, alloy receiver, VR, deluxe walnut, multi-chokes became standard in 1985, Trap Grade was disc. 1984. Mfg. 1983-89.

	$395	$350	$315	$280	$250	$235	$210

Last MSR was $500.

Subtract $30 without multi-chokes.
Subtract $35 for Trap Grade (disc. 1984).

* *Model 82 Buckmaster* - 22 in. barrel choked skeet, rifle sights, 7 1/2 lbs. Disc. 1989.

	$395	$350	$315	$280	$250	$235	$210

Last MSR was $500.

SAS FIELD - 12 ga., 3 in. chamber, self-compensating gas operated mechanism, high grade satin oil finished checkered Claro walnut stock and forearm, includes stock shim system, Weatherby outlined in gold on right side of receiver, 26, 28 (disc. 2001, reintroduced 2005), or 30 (12 ga. only. disc. 2001) in. VR barrel with Briley choke tubes, 6 3/4-7 3/4 lbs., mfg. in Italy. New 1999.

MSR $899	$750	$625	$550	$475	$400	$350	$300

GRADING - PPGS™	100%	98%	95%	90%	80%	70%	60%

* **Model SAS Sporting Clays** - similar to SAS Field, except has choice of 26 (disc. 2004), 28, or 30 (new 2005) in. ported VR barrel with extended choke tubes, includes molded plastic case, 7-7.75 lbs. New 2002.

MSR $999	$850	$725	$625	$525	$425	$375	$325

* **Model SAS Synthetic** - similar to Model SAS Field, except has black synthetic stock and forearm. New late 2000.

MSR $849	$725	$600	$525	$465	$415	$350	$300

* **Model SAS Shadow Grass/Mossy Oak Breakup** - 12 ga. only, 24 (Mossy Oak Breakup only, new 2001) 26, or 28 (Shadow Grass only) in. VR barrel with 5 extended Briley choke tubes, Hi-Viz front sight, 100% camo coverage, 7.25-7.75 lbs. New late 2000.

MSR $949	$795	$675	$575	$475	$400	$350	$300

* **Model SAS Slug Gun** - 12 ga. only, 3 in. chamber, 22 in. rifled barrel w/o sights, includes cantilever base, checkered Monte Carlo walnut stock and forearm with sling swivels, 7.75 lbs. New 2003.

MSR $949	$795	$675	$575	$475	$400	$350	$300

SHOTGUNS: SLIDE ACTION

PATRICIAN FIELD GRADE - 12 ga., checkered stock, VR. Mfg. 1972-81.

	$275	$230	$210	$190	$180	$160	$140

PATRICIAN TRAP GRADE - 12 ga., checkered stock, VR.

	$295	$250	$225	$200	$185	$175	$165

PATRICIAN DE LUXE - 12 ga., checkered stock, lightly engraved, fancy wood, VR.

	$325	$275	$250	$215	$195	$175	$165

MODEL 92 - 12 ga. only, 2 3/4 and 3 in. chambers, ultra-short slide action w/ twin rails, 26-30 in. VR barrels, engraved black alloy receiver, checkered pistol grip walnut stock and forearm. Mfg. 1982-89.

	$325	$275	$250	$225	$200	$185	$175

Last MSR was $400.

Subtract 10% for Trap grade (disc. 1984).

Subtract 10% if fixed choke (multi-chokes became standard 1985) barrel.

* **Model 92 Buckmaster** - 22 in. skeet bore barrel, rifle sights, 7 1/2 lbs. Disc. 1987.

	$345	$285	$260	$240	$220	$200	$185

Last MSR was $400.

WEAVER ARMS CORPORATION

Previous manufacturer located in Escondido, CA circa 1984-1990.

CARBINES

NIGHTHAWK CARBINE - 9mm Para. cal., semi-auto paramilitary design carbine, fires from closed bolt, 16.1 in. barrel, retractable shoulder stock, 25, 32, 40, or 50 shot mag. (interchangeable with Uzi), ambidextrous safety, parkerized finish, 6 1/2 lbs. Mfg. 1987-90.

	$675	$600	$525	$450	$375	$325	$300

Last MSR was $575.

PISTOLS: SEMI-AUTO

NIGHTHAWK PISTOL - 9mm Para. cal., closed bolt semi-auto, 10 or 12 in. barrel, alloy upper receiver, ambidextrous safety, black finish, 5 lbs. Mfg. 1987-90.

	$800	$700	$625	$550	$475	$425	$350

Last MSR was $475.

GRADING - PPGS™	100%	98%	95%	90%	80%	70%	60%

WEBLEY & SCOTT, LIMITED

Previous firearms manufacturer located in Birmingham, England circa 1898 to 1979. Beginning 1980, Webley & Scott, Ltd. began manufacturing high quality weapons only. Currently, Webley & Scott manufactures airguns only.

Webley & Scott, Ltd. had the shotgun business re-established as a separate company named W & C Scott (Gunmakers) Ltd. in 1979. Shortly after being acquired by Holland & Holland, firearms manufacture was discontinued while airgun production resumed.

For more information and current pricing on both new and used Webley & Scott airguns, please refer to the *Blue Book of Airguns* by Dr. Robert Beeman & John Allen (also online).

PISTOLS: SEMI-AUTO

MODEL 1903 - .38 cal., experimental model.
  Extreme rarity precludes accurate pricing on this model.

MODEL 1904 - .455 cal., limited production, 10-15 mfg.
  Extreme rarity precludes accurate pricing on this model.

MODEL 1905 - 7.65mm-.32 cal., ser. no. range 1-22,309, approx. 13,000+ mfg. from 1906-1909.

100%	98%	95%	90%	80%	70%	60%
$1,500	$1,300	$1,100	$750	$600	$400	$300

MODEL 1906 - .45 cal., never reaches serial production.
  Extreme rarity precludes accurate pricing on this model.

MODEL 1907 - 6.35mm cal., .25 cal. hammer model, ser. no. range 7,060-163,109, approx. 50,000 mfg. from 1906-1939.

100%	98%	95%	90%	80%	70%	60%
$1,000	$900	$800	$700	$600	$500	$400

MODEL 1908 - .32 cal., ser. no. range 22,310-163,709, approx. 90,000 mfg. from 1909-1940.

100%	98%	95%	90%	80%	70%	60%
$750	$650	$550	$450	$350	$250	$200

MODEL 1909 - 9mm Browning Long cal., ser. no. range 16,0000-116,8873, approx. 1,700 mfg. from 1909-1915.

100%	98%	95%	90%	80%	70%	60%
$2,000	$1,900	$1,800	$1,700	$1,600	$1,500	$1,400

MODEL 1910 - .380 ACP cal., ser. no. range 55,047-156,175, less than 2,000 mfg. from 1910-1932.

100%	98%	95%	90%	80%	70%	60%
$2,000	$1,900	$1,800	$1,700	$1,600	$1,500	$1,400

MODEL 1910 - .38 ACP cal., ser. no. range 40,000-66,664, less than 1,000 mfg. from 1909-1911.

100%	98%	95%	90%	80%	70%	60%
$3,500	$3,000	$2,500	$2,000	$1,750	$1,500	$1,400

METROPOLITAN POLICE MODEL - .32 cal., ser. no. range 57,000-163,382, approx. 15,000 mfg. from 1911-1940.

100%	98%	95%	90%	80%	70%	60%
$1,500	$1,400	$1,300	$1,000	$750	$500	$400

MODEL 1911 - .22 LR cal., single shot target pistol, 4 1/2 or 9 in. barrel, ser. no. range 158,536-156,398, less than 1,500 mfg. from 1911-1932.

100%	98%	95%	90%	80%	70%	60%
$2,000	$1,900	$1,800	$1,700	$1,600	$1,500	$1,400

  Add 50% for shoulder stock.

GRADING - PPGS™	100%	98%	95%	90%	80%	70%	60%

MODEL 1912 - 6.35mm cal., .25 cal. hammerless version of the Model 1907, ser. no. range 41,000-161,859, approx. 15,000 mfg. from 1909-1938.

	$1,500	$1,400	$1,300	$1,000	$750	$500	$400

NAVY MODEL .455 MKI - .455 auto cal. version of the Model 1913, government contract, ser. no. range 1-8,000, approx. 500 were Australian contract, commercial production probably never reached 1,000 with number 158919 being finished in Dec. 1933. Mfg. 1913-1919.

	$2,000	$1,900	$1,800	$1,700	$1,600	$1,500	$1,400

ROYAL HORSE ARTILLERY MODEL .455 MKI - .455 Webley auto cal., ser. no. range 2,501-8,050, less than 500 mfg. 1913-1919.

	$5,000	$4,800	$4,600	$4,300	$4,000	$3,700	$3,600

    Add 50%+ for shoulder stock.

MODEL 1921 - .32 cal., Improved Model, Webley's final attempt at modernizing the .32 auto, ser. no. range 106,000-160,000, less than 4,500 mfg. from 1921-1940.

	$3,500	$3,300	$3,000	$2,500	$2,000	$1,800	$1,700

MODEL 1922 - 9mm cal., also known as the New Military & Police Model, the African Model, and the Romanian Model, ser. no. range 130,000-160,000, less than 1,900 mfg. from 1920-1932.

	$4,500	$4,000	$3,500	$3,000	$2,500	$2,000	$1,900

"HUMANE KILLER" MODEL - .32 cal., single shot variation based on the .32 auto cal. models, designed specifically for the humane put-down of livestock, used by vets, the Royal Society for the Prevention of Cruelty to Animals, and the Ministry of Agriculture and Fisheries, ser. no. range 100,000-200,000, less than 1,000 mfg. 1920-1940.

	$1,000	$900	$800	$700	$550	$450	$350

REVOLVERS

WEBLEY-FOSBERY AUTOMATIC MODELS - .455 cal., 6 shot, hinged frame, 4, 6, or 7 1/2 in. barrel, blue or nickel finish, walnut or hard rubber grips, ser. no. range 1-less than 5,000. Mfg. 1901-1924.

* ✹ *First Model 1901* - ser. nos. under 300, production prior to Dec. 1901.

	$6,000	$5,500	$5,000	$4,500	$4,000	$3,500	$3,000

* ✹ *Model 1902* - .38 Webley auto cal., 8 shot, ser. no. range mid 200-mid 1,300, extremely rare, less than 800 mfg. 1902-1903.

  This model is extremely rare, and values may exceed 200% - 400% of values for the Model 1901 or the Model 1903.

* ✹ *First Model 1903* - .455 cal., 6 shot, large and small frame, ser. nos. between 100 and 4930.

	$5,500	$5,000	$4,500	$4,000	$3,500	$3,000	$2,500

R.I.C. MODELS - .320, .380, .442, .450, .455, .476, .44 Win., .45 Colt, or .45 ACP cal., adopted by the Royal Irish Constabulary in Jan., 1868, recognized worldwide and produced in one variation or another from 1867-1939.

* ✹ *R.I.C. No. 1* - .442 or .455 cal., first of the series was offered .442 cal. with 4 1/2 barrel, later No. 1 New Model was offered in .455 cal., ser. nos. exceeded 60,300 by Oct., 1884.

	$1,000	$900	$800	$700	$600	$500	$400

* ✹ *R.I.C. No. 2* - .320, .380, .442, or .450 cal., 2 to 4 in. barrels, ser. nos. reached 100139 by 1914.

	$1,000	$900	$800	$700	$600	$500	$400

GRADING - PPGS™	100%	98%	95%	90%	80%	70%	60%

✳ *R.I.C. No. 3* - typically found in .442 cal., 2 to 4 in. barrels, ser. nos. range from single digits to 15,000, 16,000, 30,000 and 70,000, 4 in. barrel variation was chosen as the official police weapon of the Queensland Govt. in Australia.

	$1,000	$900	$800	$700	$600	$500	$400

✳ *R.I.C. Model 83* - .320, .380, .450, or .455 cal., 2 1/4, 2 1/2, 3, or 3 1/2 in. barrel, ser. no. 102,634. Mfg. until 1939.

	$900	$800	$700	$600	$500	$400	$300

✳ *M. P. Model* - .450 cal., introduced after the R.I.C. New Model No. 1, 6 shot, adopted by the London Metropolitan Police in 1883 and remained in service until 1911.

	$900	$800	$700	$600	$500	$400	$300

WEBLEY NO. 1 1/2 MODEL - .442 or .450 cal., 4 1/4 in. octagon barrel, limited examples of ser. nos. 28,000 and 60,000 have been observed.

	$1,000	$900	$800	$700	$600	$500	$400

WEBLEY NO. 2 BULL DOG PATTERN - .320, .380, .442, .450, or .500 cal., short (2-3 in.) barrel, designed and manufactured by Webley as pocket models for civilians, with model names such as British Bulldog, The Pug, The Ulster Bulldog, or The Tower Bulldog, all share same serial number range (exceeding 100,000).

	$900	$800	$700	$600	$500	$400	$300

WEBLEY NO. 5 EXPRESS MODEL - .360, .380, .450, .455, or .476 cal., include the large caliber military version and the small caliber civilian version, early military versions were based on the R.I.C. No. 1 frame with 6 in. barrel and came in .450 or .455 cal., New Model Express had new birdshead grip frame, .455 cal., and 5 1/2 in. barrel, military versions also included a single action in .476 cal., with 5 1/2 in. barrel issued to the Cape Mounted Rifles in 1881, civilian version offered in .360 or .380 cal., with a 2 1/2 - 4 1/2 in. barrel being the most common, ser. nos. range from the low 1000 to excess of 10000000.

	100%	98%	95%	90%	80%	70%	60%
Large Cals. (Military)	$2,000	$1,900	$1,800	$1,700	$1,200	$900	$600
Small Cals. (Civilian)	$1,000	$900	$800	$700	$600	$500	$400

Cased, engraved, or unusual examples will command a premium.

REVOLVERS: HINGED FRAME, CENTERFIRE

WOODS PATTERN - .450 cal., 6 shot, double action, 5 in. barrel, mfg. circa 1870.

Extreme rarity precludes accurate pricing on this model.

WEBLEY NO. 4 PRYSE PATTERN - .32, .38, .44, .450, .455, .476, or 7.577 cal., double action, 3 to 5 3/4 in. barrel, numerous makers produced this model from the mid 1870s, Webley production covered a ser. no. range from 364 to 81,035.

	$2,500	$2,000	$1,500	$1,000	$800	$700	$600

Webley-marked models may command premiums over other makers. Cased, engraved, or inscribed examples will also command a premium.

WEBLEY IMPROVED GOVT. - .455 cal., 5 3/4 in. barrel, 6 shot, birdshead grips, blue or nickel finish, identified as the "Kaufmann" pattern. Mfg. circa early 1880s.

✳ *First Pattern* - Kaufmann numbers 33-121.

	$2,500	$2,000	$1,500	$1,000	$800	$700	$600

✳ *Second Pattern* - Kaufmann numbers 165-1228.

	$2,500	$2,000	$1,500	$1,000	$800	$700	$600

✳ *Third Pattern* - Kaufmann numbers 1245-1316.

	$2,500	$2,000	$1,500	$1,000	$800	$700	$600

WEBLEY IMPROVED GOVT. MODEL 1886 - .455 or .476 cal., 6 shot "church steeple" cylinder, 6 in. barrel, birdshead grips, ser. no. range 1467-1876. Mfg. circa mid 1880s.

	$2,500	$2,000	$1,500	$1,000	$800	$700	$600

GRADING - PPGS™	100%	98%	95%	90%	80%	70%	60%

WEBLEY GOVT. MODEL 1889 - .455 or .476 cal., 6 shot "church steeple" cylinder, 6 in. barrel, flared or birdshead grips, ser. no. range 1982-3933. Mfg. circa late 1880s.

	$2,500	$2,000	$1,500	$1,000	$800	$700	$600

WEBLEY GOVT. MODEL 1891 - .450 or .476 cal., 6 shot "church steeple" cylinder, 7 1/2 in. barrel, flared grips, ser. no. range 4100-4200. Approx. 200 mfg. circa early 1890s.

	$3,500	$3,000	$2,500	$2,000	$1,500	$1,400	$1,300

WEBLEY GOVT. MODEL 1892 - .450, .455, or .476 cal., 6 shot "church steeple" cylinder, 7 1/2 in. barrel, flared grips, blue or nickel finish, ser. no. range 4197-6499. Mfg. circa early 1890s.

	$3,000	$2,500	$2,000	$1,500	$1,400	$1,300	$1,200

WEBLEY GOVT. MODEL 1893 - .450 or .455 cal., 6 shot "church steeple" cylinder, 7 1/2 in. barrel, flared grips, ser. no. range 5000-6000. Mfg. circa early 1890s.

	$3,300	$2,800	$2,300	$1,800	$1,700	$1,600	$1,500

WEBLEY GOVT. ARMY (TARGET) MODEL 1896 - .450, .455, or .476 cal., 6 (Army) or 7 1/2 (Target) in. barrel, birdshead (Army) or flared (Target) grips, ser. no. range 10000-23000. Mfg. circa late 1890s.

	$2,300	$2,000	$1,700	$1,500	$1,000	$700	$500

Cased, engraved, or inscribed examples will command a premium.

WEBLEY W.S. NEW MODEL ARMY - .455 cal., 4, 6, or 7 1/2 (Target) in. barrel, ser. no. range 88056-454229. Mfg. early 1900s to 1935.

	$1,800	$1,400	$1,000	$900	$800	$700	$600

Add 75%-100% for cased Target models with accessories.

WEBLEY WILKINSON MODELS - .450/.455, or .455/.476 cal., during production of the Webley No. 4 Model, Webley associated with Henry Wilkinson to produce the Wilkinson retailed revolvers that were well-made and finished, barrels were typically 5 3/4 or 6 in., with Target models in 7 1/2 in. Mfg. 1884-1914.

✱ *First Model 1884 Small Hinge Pattern* - Wilkinson numbers 7896-8301.

	$3,500	$3,000	$2,500	$2,000	$1,800	$1,600	$1,500

✱ *Second Model 1888 Large Hinge Pattern* - Wilkinson numbers 8357-8741.

	$3,500	$3,000	$2,500	$2,000	$1,800	$1,600	$1,500

✱ *Webley Wilkinson Model 1892* - Wilkinson numbers 8788-9385.

	$3,500	$3,000	$2,500	$2,000	$1,800	$1,600	$1,500

✱ *Webley Wilkinson Model 1900* - Wilkinson numbers W467-W967.

	$3,500	$3,000	$2,500	$2,000	$1,800	$1,600	$1,500

✱ *Webley Wilkinson Model 1905* - Wilkinson numbers W1102-W2977.

	$3,000	$2,500	$2,000	$1,500	$1,300	$1,100	$1,000

✱ *Webley Wilkinson Model 1910* - transitional model, Wilkinson numbers around 3000. Mfg. between 1905-1911.

	$4,500	$4,000	$3,500	$3,000	$2,500	$2,000	$1,500

✱ *Webley Wilkinson Model 1911* - Wilkinson numbers 3104-4400.

	$3,000	$2,500	$2,000	$1,500	$1,300	$1,100	$1,000

WEBLEY MARK II POCKET MODEL - .380 cal., 3 or 4 in. barrel, 6 shot, blue or nickel finish, folding trigger, ser. no. range 1-808. Mfg. circa early 1890s.

	$1,000	$900	$800	$700	$600	$500	$400

WEBLEY MARK III POCKET MODEL - .380 cal., 3, 4, 6 (Target) or 10 (Target) in. barrel, 6 shot, blue or nickel finish, ser. no. range 1656-55627. Mfg. circa mid-1890s.

	$1,000	$900	$800	$700	$600	$500	$400

GRADING - PPGS™	100%	98%	95%	90%	80%	70%	60%

WEBLEY MARK III POCKET MODEL - .320 cal., 3 in. barrel, 6 shot, blue or nickel finish, ser. no. range 10000-22000. Mfg. circa early 1900s.

	$1,000	$900	$800	$700	$600	$500	$400

WEBLEY W.P. - .32 S&W or .320 cal., 2 or 3 in. barrel, 6 shot, hammerless or hammer type, blue or nickel finish, ser. no. range 1000-8527. Mfg. circa early 1900s to mid-1930s.

	$1,000	$900	$800	$700	$600	$500	$400

WEBLEY MARK IV - .22 LR (scarce), .32 (scarce), .38 S&W, or .38 cal., 3, 4, 5 or 6 (Target) in. barrel, 6 shot, wartime production exceeded 125,000, commerical production approx. 50,000. Mfg. early 1920s to late 1970s.

	$450	$400	$350	$300	$250	$200	$150

Add 75%-100% for .22 LR or .32 cal.

REVOLVERS: SERVICE MODELS

Mark I-V Service Models were very similar, but some were made with longer barrels.

Many service Webleys were modified to use .45 ACP cal. ammo - this will decrease their value by 50% or more.

Cased, engraved, or inscribed examples have also been seen (usually in the commercial/non-military variation), and will bring a premium over values listed.

MARK I SERVICE - .455 cal., single/double action, 4 in. barrel, fixed sights, blue finish, top break 6 shot, service and commercial ser. no. range 4-39,436. Mfg. 1894-1897.

	$800	$750	$700	$625	$500	$400	$300

MARK II SERVICE - .455 cal., single/double action, 4 in. barrel, fixed sights, blue finish, top break 6 shot, service and commercial ser. no. range 41,675-63,584. Mfg. 1894-1897.

	$850	$800	$750	$675	$550	$450	$350

MARK III SERVICE - .455 cal., single/double action, 4 in. barrel, fixed sights, blue finish, top break 6 shot, ser. no. range 12-10,808 and 75,966-79,256. Mfg. 1894-1897.

	$900	$850	$800	$725	$600	$500	$400

MARK IV SERVICE - .455 cal., single/double action, 4 in. barrel, fixed sights, blue finish, top break 6 shot, "Boer War" model, ser. no. range 79,462-129,185. Mfg. 1899-1914.

	$750	$700	$650	$575	$500	$400	$300

MARK V SERVICE - .455 cal., single/double action, 4 in. barrel, fixed sights, blue finish, top break 6 shot, ser. no. range 129,942-159,724 and 173,015-193,025. Mfg. 1914-1915.

	$750	$700	$650	$575	$500	$400	$300

MARK VI SERVICE - .455 cal., single/double action, 6 in. barrel, fixed sights, blue finish, top break 6 shot, ser. no. range 214,000-445,999. Mfg. 1915-1919.

	$600	$550	$500	$425	$350	$250	$200

Add approx. 300% - 400% for rare shoulder stock and bayonet.

MARK VI SERVICE (LATER MFG.) - .455 cal., single/double action, 6 in. barrel, fixed sights, blue finish, top break 6 shot, ser. no. range 450,000-454,000. Mfg. by Enfield circa 1922-1935.

	$900	$800	$700	$600	$500	$300	$250

MARK VI TARGET - .22 cal., otherwise similar to Mark VI Service.

	$1,200	$1,000	$900	$800	$700	$600	$500

GRADING - PPGS™	100%	98%	95%	90%	80%	70%	60%

SHOTGUNS: SxS

MODEL 700 - 12 or 20 ga., boxlock, case hardened receiver, minimum engraving, single trigger. Mfg. 1949-80.

	100%	98%	95%	90%	80%	70%	60%
	$1,700	$1,625	$1,500	$1,250	$1,000	$750	$600

Subtract $50 for double trigger.

MODEL 701 - similar to Model 700 but fanciest walnut, most engraving. Mfg. 1949-80.

	100%	98%	95%	90%	80%	70%	60%
	$3,150	$2,500	$2,100	$1,800	$1,400	$1,150	$925

Subtract $100 for double trigger.
This model is hard to differentiate from the Model 702.

MODEL 702 - similar to Model 700 but middle grade. Mfg. 1949-80.

	100%	98%	95%	90%	80%	70%	60%
	$2,650	$2,200	$1,800	$1,500	$1,250	$950	$750

Subtract $75 for double trigger.

MODEL 712 - 12 ga., specifically designed for the American market.

	100%	98%	95%	90%	80%	70%	60%
	$1,700	$1,625	$1,500	$1,250	$1,000	$750	$600

MODEL 720 - 20 ga.

	100%	98%	95%	90%	80%	70%	60%
	$2,325	$1,875	$1,750	$1,650	$1,375	$1,100	$825

MODEL 728 - same action as the Model 700, except is 28 ga. and designed specifically for the American market, only 40 were mfg. 1966-68.

	100%	98%	95%	90%	80%	70%	60%
	$3,000	$2,600	$2,175	$1,850	$1,650	$1,375	$1,150

HERMANN WEIHRAUCH REVOLVER GmbH

Current manufacturer located in Mellrichstadt, Germany. Exclusive factory authorized U.S. distributor is European American Armory, located in Sharpes, FL.

Weihrauch also manufactures a compete line of single and double action revolvers, including target models. To date, they have had little importation into the U.S.

For more information and current pricing on both new and used Weihrauch airguns, please refer to the *Blue Book of Airguns* by Dr. Robert Beeman & John Allen (also online).

REVOLVERS: ARMINIUS

Currently manufactured Arminius revolvers are not individually listed, since they are not currently imported into the U.S. There are, however, many models, including combat, sport, and target variations. Calibers include .22 LR., .22 Mag., .32 S&W Wadcutter, .357 Mag., and .38 Spl. Please refer to Arminius listing for older models, or contact the company directly regarding U.S. availability and pricing (see Trademark Index).

RIFLES: BOLT ACTION

MODEL HW 60 TARGET - .22 LR cal., target rifle featuring adj. sights, 26 3/4 in. barrel, single shot, match walnut stock, and other match features, aperture sights, 10.8 lbs. Importation disc. 1995.

	100%	98%	95%	90%	80%	70%	60%
	$625	$550	$450	$395	$350	$295	$275

Last MSR was $705.

Add $220 for left-hand action (disc.).

MODEL HW 60J - .22 LR or .222 Rem. cal., sporter model with checkered walnut stock. Importation disc. 1992.

	100%	98%	95%	90%	80%	70%	60%
	$525	$465	$435	$395	$345	$300	$260

Last MSR was $585.

Add $304 for .222 Rem. cal.

GRADING - PPGS™	100%	98%	95%	90%	80%	70%	60%

MODEL HW 66 RIFLE - .22 Hornet or .222 Rem. cal., match grade bolt action rifle. Imported 1989-90 only.

	$575	$495	$395	$325	$285	$250	$215

Last MSR was $688.

Add $78 for double-set triggers.

Add $55 for stainless steel barrel (.22 Hornet).

MODEL HW 660 MATCH - .22 LR cal., match rifle variation featuring adj. stock comb with vent. forend, with or w/o aperture sights, 10.8 lbs. Importation began 1991.

MSR $999	$850	$725	$600	$500	$400	$350	$300

Add $160 for laminate stock (new 1998).

Subtract $160 if w/o Anschütz aperture sights.

WELLS

Current custom rifle manufacturer located in Prescott, AZ. Consumer direct sales.

RIFLES: BOLT ACTION

Fred Wells manufactures a custom rifle based on a Mauser double square bridge action, using the finest materials available. Action prices start at $5,000, and stocks are priced from $5,000 on up. Additionally, Wells also has a complete barrel manufacturing facility, specializing in cut rifle barrels in almost every caliber. Please contact the company directly for more information regarding complete rifle model and pricing (see Trademark Index).

WERNER BARTOLOT

Current custom gun manufacturer located in Hermagor, Austria. Direct sales only.

Werner Bartolot manufactures very high quality SxS and O/U double rifles, drillings, and single shot rifles. Please contact the company for more information, including availability and an individual price quotation (see Trademark Index).

WESSON, FRANK

Previous manufacturer located in Worcester, MA 1854 to 1865, and Springfield, MA circa 1865-1875.

100%	98%	95%	90%	80%	70%	60%	50%	40%	30%	20%	10%

PISTOLS: SINGLE SHOT

SMALL FRAME FIRST MODEL - .22 cal., tip up action, 3 1/2 in. 1/2 octagon barrel, brass frame, spur trigger, rosewood grips, round frame, irregular sideplate. Mfg. 2500, 1859-62.

$605	$550	$495	$440	$385	$330	$275	$220	$195	$165	$140	$110

SMALL FRAME SECOND MODEL - similar to First Model, with flat sided frame and circular sideplate. Mfg. 12,000, 1862-80.

$550	$495	$440	$385	$330	$305	$250	$195	$165	$110	$105	$85

MEDIUM FRAME FIRST MODEL - .30 S or L, .32 S rimfire cal., 4 in. 1/2 octagon barrel, iron frame, same as Small Frame in other respects, narrow hinge and short trigger. Mfg. 1000, 1859-62.

$525	$470	$415	$360	$305	$275	$220	$195	$165	$110	$105	$85

MEDIUM FRAME SECOND MODEL - similar to First Model Medium Frame, with wider hinge and longer trigger. Mfg. 1000, 1862-70.

$495	$440	$385	$330	$275	$250	$220	$195	$165	$110	$105	$85

100%	98%	95%	90%	80%	70%	60%	50%	40%	30%	20%	10%

RIFLES: SINGLE SHOT

NO. 1 LONG RANGE - .44-100 and .45-100 standard cal., side hammer, falling block lever actuated, 34 in. octagon barrel, aperture rear sight on upper tang, select checkered pistol grip stock. Less than 50 mfg., circa 1870-80.

| $4,950 | $4,675 | $4,400 | $3,850 | $3,575 | $3,080 | $2,860 | $2,475 | $2,200 | $2,035 | $1,760 | $1,540 |

NO. 2 HUNTING RIFLE - similar to No. 1, with finger loop lever. Less than 100 mfg.

| $4,400 | $4,180 | $3,850 | $3,520 | $3,025 | $2,750 | $2,420 | $2,255 | $2,035 | $1,925 | $1,760 | $1,540 |

NO. 1 SPORTING RIFLE - .38-100, .40-100, .45-100 standard cal., similar to No. 2, with center hammer, less than 25 mfg.

| $4,400 | $4,180 | $3,850 | $3,520 | $3,025 | $2,750 | $2,420 | $2,255 | $2,035 | $1,925 | $1,760 | $1,540 |

RIFLES: SINGLE SHOT, TIP UP

SMALL FRAME TIP UP - .22 Rimfire cal., 6 in. 1/2 octagon barrel, brass frame, spur trigger, rosewood grips. Approx. 500 mfg., 1865-75.

| $605 | $550 | $525 | $495 | $470 | $440 | $415 | $360 | $330 | $275 | $220 | $165 |

If without stock-subtract 25%.

MEDIUM FRAME TIP UP - .22, .30, or .32 rimfire cals, 10 or 12 in. barrel, same as small frame, with exceptions noted and larger frame. Approx. 1,000 mfg., 1862-70.

| $605 | $550 | $525 | $495 | $470 | $440 | $415 | $360 | $330 | $275 | $220 | $165 |

If without stock-subtract 25%.

MODEL 1870 SMALL FRAME FIRST TYPE - similar to Small Frame Tip Up, except barrel rotates on its axis to load, detachable stock. Approx. 3,000 mfg., 1870-90.

| $550 | $495 | $470 | $440 | $415 | $385 | $360 | $305 | $275 | $220 | $195 | $165 |

If without stock-subtract 25%.

MODEL 1870 SMALL FRAME SECOND TYPE - full octagon barrel.

| $525 | $470 | $440 | $415 | $385 | $360 | $330 | $275 | $250 | $195 | $165 | $140 |

MODEL 1870 SMALL FRAME THIRD TYPE - iron frame, push-button half cock.

| $495 | $440 | $415 | $385 | $360 | $330 | $305 | $250 | $220 | $165 | $140 | $110 |

MODEL 1870 MEDIUM FRAME FIRST TYPE - similar to Small Frame, except in size and availability of .32 cal. Approx. 5,000 mfg., 1870-93.

| $525 | $495 | $470 | $440 | $415 | $385 | $360 | $305 | $275 | $250 | $195 | $165 |

Subtract 25% if without stock.

MODEL 1870 MEDIUM FRAME SECOND TYPE - external push-button half cock and iron frame.

| $440 | $415 | $385 | $330 | $305 | $275 | $220 | $195 | $165 | $140 | $110 | $90 |

Subtract 25% if without stock.

MODEL 1870 MEDIUM FRAME THIRD TYPE - has three screws in frame, iron frame.

| $440 | $415 | $385 | $330 | $305 | $275 | $220 | $195 | $165 | $140 | $110 | $90 |

Subtract 25% if without stock.

MODEL 1870 LARGE FRAME FIRST TYPE - .32, .38, .42, or .44 rimfire cal., 15-24 in. barrels, similar to smaller frame models, auto extractor. Approx. 500 mfg., 1870-80.

| $825 | $770 | $715 | $660 | $605 | $550 | $525 | $495 | $440 | $385 | $305 | $275 |

Subtract 25% if without stock.

MODEL 1870 LARGE FRAME SECOND TYPE - similar to First Type, with standard sliding extractor.

| $825 | $770 | $715 | $660 | $605 | $550 | $525 | $495 | $440 | $385 | $305 | $275 |

Subtract 25% if without stock.

WESSON & HARRINGTON

Previous trademark of special/limited editions manufactured by H&R 1871, LLC 1995-2001. During 2000, Marlin Firearms Co. purchased the assets of H&R 1871, Inc., and the name was changed to H&R 1871, LLC. Production of Wesson & Harrington products was at the factory located in Gardner, MA.

RIFLES: SINGLE SHOT

Please refer to the H & R 1871 section for earlier Wesson & Harrington Buffalo Classic & Target Models.

SHOTGUNS: SINGLE SHOT

WESSON & HARRINGTON NWTF LONG TOM CLASSIC - 12 ga., top lever break open action, 32 in. FC barrel, case hardened frame, checkered straight grip walnut stock and forearm, 7 1/2 lbs. Mfg. 1995-2001.

	$300	$240	$195

Last MSR was $350.

DAN WESSON FIREARMS

Currently manufactured by New York International Corp. (NYI) located in Norwich, NY beginning 1997. Distributor and dealer sales.

PISTOLS: SEMI-AUTO

Dan Wesson currently manufactures a complete line of .45 ACP 1911 style semi-auto pistols. Previously manufactured models include: Seven (last MSR was $999), Seven Stainless (last MSR was $1,099), Guardian (last MSR was $799), the Guardian Deuce (last MSR was $799), the Dave Pruit Signature Series (last MSR was $899), and the Hi-Cap (last MSR was $689).

PATRIOT 1911 SERIES - .45 ACP or 10mm (Commander slide and frame only) cal., 4 1/4 (Commander) or 5 in. stainless steel match barrel, 1911 Series 70 action, features new external extractor, fitted parts, and many high-end components by McCormick, Ed Brown, Nowlin, etc., each gun shipped with test target, variations include Patriot Expert (blue or stainless, Bo-Mar style target sights), Patriot Marksman (blue or stainless, fixed sights), AAA cocobolo double diamond checkered grips with gold medallions, 2.3 lbs. New 2001.

MSR $929	$825	$750	$650	$550	$475	$425	$375

Add $20 for 5 in. Patriot with blued action.
Add $70 for 5 in. barrel in stainless steel.
Add $30 for checkered front grip strap.
Add $70 for bobtail frame.

KO3 PANTHER SERIES - .45 ACP cal., full size, 5 in. barrel, Series 70 pistol with cast alloy frame, features new external extractor, Chip McCormick beavertail with Commander style hammer, forged conventional round top slide, fixed rear sight, matte bead blasted frame and slide top, slide sides are polished, blue or stainless, Hogue rubber grips. Disc.

	$595	$525	$450	$415	$385	$350	$325

Add $20 for stainless steel.

PM POINTMAN SERIES - .45 ACP or 10mm cal., full size, 5 in. target barrel, features Chip McCormick beavertail with Commader style hammer, forged conventional round top slide, high target rib or low profile Clark style sights with adj. white outline or Bomar rear sight, blue or stainless, PM1-S is standard gun, checkered exotic hardwood grips.

MSR $809	$725	$650	$575	$500	$425	$385	$350

Add $50 for checkered front grip strap.
Add $50 for high or Ausi rib (Model PMA-S).
Add $100 for blue finish with Clark/Bo-Mar rib and sights (Model PMA-B, disc.).

GRADING - PPGS™	100%	98%	95%	90%	80%	70%	60%

PM3-P MINOR SERIES - .45 ACP cal., full size, 5 in. barrel, Series 70 pistol with cast alloy frame, Chip McCormick beavertail with Commander style hammer, forged conventional round top slide, fixed rear sight, matte bead blasted frame and slide top, slide sides are polished, blue or stainless, checkered exotic hardwood grips. Disc.

	100%	98%	95%	90%	80%	70%	60%
	$515	$450	$415	$385	$350	$325	$295

GLOBAL - .45 ACP or 10mm cal., 5 or 6 in. barrel, full size frame, steel or stainless steel, choice of accessory light rail or full length dust cover.

MSR $1,149	$1,000	$900	$800	$700	$600	$475	$350

RZ-10 RAZORBACK SPECIAL EDITION - 10mm cal., full size, 5 in. barrel, Series 70 pistol with forged stainless frame and slide, Bo-Mar adj. rear sight, match barrel, bushing, and link, match grade trigger, sear, hammer, and beavertail, checkered synthetic grips, limited mfg. beginning 2002.

MSR $999	$895	$825	$750	$675	$575	$500	$450

REVOLVERS: DOUBLE ACTION

Dan Wesson has also manufactured a variety of revolver packages that were available by special order only.

MODEL 715 SMALL FRAME SERIES - .357 Mag. cal., 6 shot, stainless steel, 2 1/2, 4, 6, 8, or 10 in. heavy barrel with VR and full ejector shroud, rubber wraparound finger groove grips, interchangeable barrels. New 2002.

MSR $709	$625	$550	$475	$425	$375	$325	$285

Add $50 for 4 in., $90 for 6 in., $150 for 8 in., or $190 for 10 in. barrel.

This model is also available as a pistol pack with 4 barrels and case. Current MSR is $1,699.

MODEL 741 LARGE FRAME SERIES - .44 Mag. cal., 6 shot, stainless steel, 4, 6, 8, or 10 in. heavy barrel with VR and full ejector shroud, rubber wraparound finger groove grips, raked hammer, interchangeable barrels. New 2002.

MSR $829	$725	$650	$575	$475	$400	$350	$300

Add $30 for 6 in., $110 for 8 in., or $170 for 10 in. barrel.

MODEL 7445 SUPERMAG FRAME SERIES - .445 SuperMag. cal., 6 shot, stainless steel, 4, 6, 8, or 10 in. heavy barrel with VR and full ejector shroud, rubber wraparound finger groove grips, interchangeable barrels. New 2002.

MSR $986	$875	$775	$675	$575	$475	$400	$350

Add $73 for 6 in., $133 for 8 in., or $183 for 10 in. barrel.

MODEL 44-AGS (ALASKAN GUIDE SPECIAL) - .445 SuperMag. cal., 6 shot, stainless steel, compensated 4 in. heavy barrel with VR and full ejector shroud, black Teflon metal finish, rubber wraparound finger groove grips, fully adj. sights. New 2002.

MSR $1,059	$895	$825	$750	$650	$550	$450	$350

RIFLES: BOLT ACTION

COYOTE CLASSIC - .22 LR or .22 Mag. cal., 22 3/4 in. tapered barrel, 6 or 10 shot mag., checkered hardwood stock and forend, adj. rear sight. Limited mfg. 2002 only.

	100%	98%	95%	90%	80%	70%	60%
	$200	$180	$160	$145	$130	$115	$100

Last MSR was $239.

COYOTE TARGET - .22 LR or .22 Mag. cal., 18 3/8 in. heavy bull barrel, 6 or 10 shot mag., uncheckered target hardwood stock with high cheekpiece, w/o sights. Limited mfg. 2002 only.

	100%	98%	95%	90%	80%	70%	60%
	$230	$200	$175	$155	$145	$135	$125

Last MSR was $279.

WESSON FIREARMS CO. INC.

Previous manufacturer located in Palmer, MA 1992-95. Previously located in Monson, MA until 1992. In late 1990, ownership of Dan Wesson Arms changed (within the family), and the new company was renamed Wesson Firearms Co., Inc.

REVOLVERS: DOUBLE ACTION

As a guideline, the following information is provided on Wesson Firearms frames. The smallest frames are Models 738P and 38P. Small frame models include 22, 722, 22M, 722M, 32, 732, 322, 7322, 8-2, 708, 9-2, 709, 14-2, 714, 15-2, and 715-2. Large frames include 41, 741, 44, 744, 45, and 745. SuperMag frame models include 40, 740, 375 (disc.), 414 (new 1995), 7414 (new 1995), 445, and 7445. Small frames are sideplate design, while large frames are solid frame construction. Dan Wesson revolvers were mfg. with solid rib barrels as standard equipment.

MODEL 11 - .357 Mag. cal., 6 shot, 2 1/2, 4, or 6 in. interchangeable barrels, fixed sights, blue, interchangeable grips, exposed barrel nut. Mfg. 1970-71 only.

$200	$175	$160	$150	$140	$130	$120

     Add $60 per extra barrel.

MODEL 12 - similar to Model 11, with adj. sights. Mfg. 1970-71 only.

$245	$200	$175	$160	$150	$140	$130

MODEL 14 - similar to Model 11, with recessed barrel nut. Mfg. 1971-75.

$225	$185	$170	$160	$150	$140	$130

MODEL 8 - similar to Model 14, except .38 Spl. cal.

$200	$170	$155	$145	$135	$125	$115

MODEL 15 - similar to Model 14, with adj. sights. Mfg. 1971-75.

$245	$200	$155	$145	$135	$125	$115

MODEL 9 - similar to Model 15, except .38 Spl. cal. Mfg. 1971-75.

$245	$200	$155	$145	$135	$125	$115

MODEL 22 - .22 LR cal., double action, 6 shot, adj. sights, 2 1/2, 4, 6, 8, or 10 in. (disc. 1987) barrel, disc. 1995.

$285	$225	$200	$190	$180	$170	$160

                               Last MSR was $357.

     Add approx. $9 for each additional barrel length, $21 for VR, $57 for vent. heavy rib shroud.

* ✳ *Model 22 Pistol Pac* - includes 2 1/2, 4, 6, and 8 in. barrel assemblies, extra grip, 4 additional front sight blades, and aluminum case. Disc. 1995.

$520	$400	$360	$330	$300	$275	$260

                               Last MSR was $653.

     Add $103 for full shroud VR barrels.
     Add $227 for heavy full shroud VR barrels.

* ✳ *Model 22 Silhouette* - .22 LR cal., choice of 10 in. vent. or heavy vent. barrel, single action only, combat style grip, narrow rear sight blade and Patridge front. Mfg. 1992-95.

$395	$325	$295	$275	$260	$245	$230

                               Last MSR was $474.

     Add $18 for vent. heavy barrel.

MODEL 22M - .22 Mag. cal., otherwise similar to Model 22. Disc. 1994.

$290	$230	$200	$190	$180	$170	$160

                               Last MSR was $349.

* **Model 22M Pistol Pac** - includes 2 1/2, 4, 6, and 8 in. barrel assemblies, extra grip, 4 additional front sight blades, and aluminum case. Disc. 1994.

	$500	$400	$360	$330	$300	$275	$260

Last MSR was $637.

Add $101 for full shroud VR barrels.
Add $191 for heavy full shroud VR barrels.

MODEL 32 - .32 H&R Mag. cal., 2 1/2, 4, 6, or 8 in. barrel, adj. rear sight, interchangeable colored front sight blades, blue finish, checkered target grips. Mfg. 1986-95.

	$285	$225	$200	$190	$180	$170	$160

Last MSR was $357.

Add $21 for VR barrel shroud (Model 32-V), $57 for VR heavy barrel shroud (Model 32-VH), approx. $9 for each additional barrel length over 2 1/2 in.

* **Model 32 Pistol Pac** - includes 2 1/2, 4, 6, and 8 in. barrel assemblies, extra grip, 4 additional front sight blades, and aluminum case. Disc. 1995.

	$520	$400	$360	$330	$300	$275	$260

Last MSR was $653.

Add $103 for full shroud VR barrels.
Add $227 for heavy full shroud VR barrels.

MODEL 38P - .38+P cal., 5 shot, 6 1/2 in. barrel, fixed sights, wood or rubber grips, 24.6 oz. Mfg. 1992-93.

	$230	$190	$170	$150	$135	$120	$110

Last MSR was $285.

MODEL 322 - .32-20 WCF cal., 2 1/2, 4, 6, or 8 in. barrel, adj. rear sight, interchangeable colored front sight blades, blue finish, checkered target grips. Mfg. 1991-95.

	$285	$225	$200	$190	$180	$170	$160

Last MSR was $357.

Add $21 for VR barrel shroud (Model 322-V), $57 for VR heavy barrel shroud (Model 322-VH), approx. $9-$30 for each additional barrel length over 2 1/2 in.

* **Model 322 Pistol Pac** - includes 2 1/2, 4, 6, and 8 in. barrel assemblies, extra grip, 4 additional front sight blades, and aluminum case. Disc. 1995.

	$520	$400	$360	$330	$300	$275	$260

Last MSR was $653.

Add $103 for full shroud VR barrels.
Add $227 for heavy full shroud VR barrels.

MODEL 14 - .357 Mag. cal., 2 1/2, 4, 6, or 8 (disc. 1994) in. interchangeable barrels, fixed sights, blue. Mfg. 1975-95.

	$215	$170	$150	$140	$130	$120	$110

Last MSR was $274.

Add approx. $7 for each additional barrel length.

* **Model 14 Fixed Barrel** - .357 Mag. cal., 2 1/2 or 4 in. (fixed sight Service Model) barrel, satin blue finish. Mfg. 1993-95.

	$225	$175	$150	$140	$130	$120	$110

Last MSR was $289.

Add $7 for 4 in. barrel.

* **Model 14 PPC** - .357 Mag. cal., extra heavy 6 in. bull shroud barrel with removable underweight, Hogue Gripper grips, Aristocrat sights. Mfg. 1992 only.

	$675	$550	$450	$375	$330	$300	$275

Last MSR was $780.

GRADING - PPGS™	100%	98%	95%	90%	80%	70%	60%

✳ *Model 14 Pistol Pac* - includes 2 1/2, 4, and 6 in. barrel assemblies, extra grip and aluminum case. Disc. 1994.

	$390	$325	$300	$275	$260	$245	$230

Last MSR was $463.

MODEL 8 - similar to Model 14, except .38 Spl. cal. Disc. 1995.

	$220	$170	$150	$140	$130	$120	$110

Last MSR was $274.

Add approx. $6 for each additional barrel length.

✳ *Model 8 PPC* - .38 Spl. cal., extra heavy 6 in. bull shroud barrel with removable underweight, Hogue Gripper grips, Aristocrat sights. Mfg. 1992 only.

	$675	$550	$450	$375	$330	$300	$275

Last MSR was $780.

MODEL 15 - similar to Model 14, except adj. sights, available with 2, 4, 6, 8, 10, 12, or 15 in. barrels. Disc. 1995.

✳ *2 in. barrel*

	$285	$225	$200	$190	$180	$170	$160

Last MSR was $346.

Add approx. $8-$13 for each additional barrel length over 2 inches, $22 for VR barrel (Model 15V), or $60 for VR heavy barrel shroud (Model 15HV).

✳ *Model 15 Target Fixed Barrel* - .357 Mag. cal., 3, 4, 5, or 6 in. barrel, high bright blue finish. Mfg. 1993-95.

	$270	$220	$190	$175	$150	$125	$110

Last MSR was $322.

Add approx. $9 for each barrel length over 3 in.
Add approx. $80 for compensated barrel (4, 5, or 6 in. - new 1994).

MODEL 15 GOLD SERIES - .357 Mag. cal., 6 or 8 in. VR heavy slotted barrel, "Gold" stamped shroud with Dan Wesson signature, smoother action (8 lb. double action pull), 18kt. gold-plated trigger, white triangle rear sight with orange-dot Patridge front sight, exotic hardwood grips. Mfg. 1989-94.

	$425	$380	$340	$300	$260	$225	$185

Last MSR was $544.

✳ *Model 15 Pistol Pac* - includes 2 1/2, 4, 6, and 8 in. barrel assemblies, extra grip, 4 additional front sight blades, and aluminum case. Disc. 1995.

	$500	$395	$360	$330	$300	$275	$260

Last MSR was $629.

Add $104 for full shroud VR barrels.
Add $214 for heavy full shroud VR barrels.

MODEL 9 - similar to Model 15, except .38 Spl. cal. Use same add-ons as in Model 15. Disc. 1995.

	$346	$285	$225	$200	$190	$180	$170

Last MSR was $346.

This model was also available in a Pistol Pac - same specifications and values as the Model 15 Pistol Pac.

MODEL 375 SUPERMAG - .375 Super Mag. cal., 4, 6, 8, or 10 in. VR barrel, adj. rear sight, interchangeable front and rear sight blades, bright blue finish, smooth target grips. Mfg. 1986-94.

	$410	$335	$285	$260	$240	$230	$225

Last MSR was $498.

Add approx. $15 for each barrel length after 6 in., $39 for slotted shroud (Model 375-V8S, 8 in. barrel only), $10-$12 for VR heavy shroud (Model 375-VH).

GRADING - PPGS™	100%	98%	95%	90%	80%	70%	60%

MODEL 40 (.357 SUPERMAG) - .357 Super Mag. cal. (.357 Max.), double action, 6 shot, 4, 6, 8, or 10 in. barrel VR. Disc. 1995.

	$410	$340	$285	$260	$240	$230	$225

Last MSR was $502.

Add $87 for slotted barrel shroud (8 in. barrel only), $22-$129 for heavy VR barrel, approx. $33 for each additional barrel length.

MODEL 41 - .41 Mag. cal., double action, 6 shot, 4, 6, 8, or 10 in. barrel VR. Disc. 1995.

	$375	$305	$265	$250	$230	$215	$200

Last MSR was $447.

Add approx. $20 for heavy barrel shroud, approx. $15 for each additional barrel length.

✳ *Model 41 Pistol Pac* - includes 6 and 8 in. VR barrel assemblies, extra grip, 2 additional front sight blades, and aluminum case. Disc. 1995.

	$555	$430	$380	$330	$300	$275	$260

Last MSR was $678.

Add $53 for full shroud VR barrels.

MODEL .414 SUPERMAG - .414 Super Mag. cal., 4, 6, 8, or 10 in. VR barrel, adj. rear sight, interchangeable front and rear sight blades (optional), bright blue finish, smooth target grips. Mfg. 1995 only.

	$425	$335	$290	$275	$250	$230	$225

Last MSR was $519.

Add approx. $14 for each barrel length after 4 in., $58 for slotted shroud (Model 414-V8S, 8 in. barrel only), approx. $23 for VR heavy rib shroud.

MODEL 44 - .44 Mag. cal., double action, similar to Model 41, adj. sights. Disc. 1995.

	$375	$305	$265	$250	$230	$215	$200

Last MSR was $447.

Add approx. $20 for heavy barrel shroud, approx. $15 for each additional barrel length.

✳ *Model 44 Target Fixed Barrel* - .44 Mag. cal., 4, 5, 6, or 8 in. barrel, high bright blue finish. Mfg. 1994-95.

	$375	$305	$265	$250	$230	$215	$200

Last MSR was $447.

Add approx. $4 for each barrel length over 3 in.

✳ *Model 44 Pistol Pac* - includes 6 and 8 in. VR barrel assemblies, extra grip, 4 additional front sight blades, and aluminum case. Disc. 1995.

	$555	$430	$380	$330	$300	$275	$260

Last MSR was $678.

Add $53 for full shroud VR barrels.

MODEL 45 - .45 LC cal., 4, 6, 8, or 10 in. VR barrel, same frame as Model 44V, blue finish. Mfg. 1988-95.

	$375	$305	$265	$250	$230	$215	$200

Last MSR was $447.

Add $20 for VR heavy barrel shroud, approx. $15 for each additional barrel length.

✳ *Model 45 Pistol Pac* - includes 6 and 8 in. VR barrel assemblies, extra grip, 2 additional front sight blades, and aluminum case. Disc. 1995.

	$555	$430	$380	$330	$300	$275	$260

Last MSR was $678.

Add $53 for full shroud VR barrels.

MODEL .45 PIN GUN - .45 ACP cal., competition pin gun model with 5 in. vent. or heavy vent. barrel configuration, blue steel, two stage Taylor forcing cone, 54 oz. Mfg. 1993-95.

	$575	$495	$440	$395	$350	$300	$250

Last MSR was $654.

Add $9 for VR heavy shroud barrel.

GRADING - PPGS™	100%	98%	95%	90%	80%	70%	60%

MODEL .445 SUPERMAG - .445 Super Mag. cal., 4, 6, 8, or 10 in. VR barrel, adj. rear sight, interchangeable front and rear sight blades (optional), bright blue finish, smooth target grips. Mfg. 1991-95.

	$425	$335	$290	$275	$250	$230	$225

Last MSR was $519.

Add approx. $14 for each barrel length after 4 in., $58 for slotted shroud (Model 445-V8S, 8 in. barrel only), approx. $23 for VR heavy rib shroud.

HUNTER SERIES - .357 Super Mag., .41 Mag., .44 Mag., or .445 Super Mag. cal., 7 1/2 in. barrel with heavy shroud, Hogue rubber finger grooved and wood presentation grips, choice of Gunworks iron sights or w/o sights with Burris base and rings, non-fluted cylinder, with or w/o compensator, approx. 4 lbs. Mfg. 1994-95.

	$750	$575	$475	$400	$360	$330	$300

Last MSR was $805.

Add $32 for compensated barrel.

Add $33 for scope mounts (w/o sights).

REVOLVERS: STAINLESS STEEL - Models 722, 722M, 709, 715, 732, 7322, 741V, 744V, and 745V were available in a pistol pack including 2 1/2, 4, 6, and 8 in. solid rib barrel assemblies, extra grip, 4 additional sight blades, and fitted carrying case. Last published retail prices were $712 and $785 for the standard and stainless steel models, respectively. VR or full shroud barrels were optional and were approx. priced $103 and $210, respectively.

MODEL 722 - stainless version of Model 22, use same add-ons for various barrel options. Disc. 1995.

	$335	$255	$205				

Last MSR was $400.

✻ *Model 722 Silhouette* - .22 LR cal., choice of 10 in. vent. or heavy vent. barrel, single action only, combat style grip, narrow rear sight blade and Patridge front. Mfg. 1992-95.

	$410	$340	$295				

Last MSR was $504.

Add $28 for heavy vent. barrel.

MODEL 722M - .22 Mag cal., otherwise similar to Model 722, use same add-ons for various barrel options. Disc. 1994.

	$320	$270	$230				

Last MSR was $391.

MODEL 708 - .38 Spl. cal., similar to Model 8. Add approx. $6 for each additional barrel length. Disc. 1995.

	$265	$200	$170				

Last MSR was $319.

✻ *Model 708 Action Cup/PPC* - .38 Spl. cal., extra heavy 6 in. bull shroud barrel with removable underweight, Hogue Gripper grips, mounted Tasco Pro Point II on Action Cup, Aristocrat sights on PPC. Mfg. 1992 only.

	$725	$650	$550				

Last MSR was $857.

Add $56 for Action Cup Model with Tasco Scope.

MODEL 709 - .38 Spl. cal., target revolver, adj. sights. Also available in special order 10, 12 (disc.), or 15 (disc.) in. barrel lengths. Disc. 1995.

	$310	$255	$205				

Last MSR was $376.

Add approx. $10 for each additional longer barrel length, approx. $19 for VR, approx. $56 for heavy VR.

GRADING - PPGS™	100%	98%	95%	90%	80%	70%	60%

MODEL 714 (INTERCHANGEABLE OR FIXED) - .357 Mag. cal., fixed sight Service Model with 2 1/2, 4, or 6 in. barrel, brushed stainless steel. Mfg. 1993-95.

	$260	$200	$160

Last MSR was $319.

Add approx. $6 for 4 or 6 in. barrel.
Subtract $6 for fixed barrel (2 1/2 or 4 in. barrel only).

* *Model 714 Action Cup/PPC* - .357 Mag. cal., extra heavy 6 in. bull shroud barrel with removable underweight, Hogue Gripper grips, mounted Tasco Pro Point II on Action Cup, Aristocrat sights on PPC. Mfg. 1992 only.

	$725	$650	$550

Last MSR was $857.

Add $56 for Action Cup Model with Tasco Scope.

MODEL 715 INTERCHANGEABLE - .357 Mag. cal., 2 1/2, 4, 6, 8, or 10 in. with adj. rear sight, brushed stainless steel. Mfg. 1993-95.

	$310	$255	$205

Last MSR was $376.

Add approx. $10 for each additional longer barrel length, approx. $19 for VR, approx. $56 for heavy VR.

* *Model 715 Fixed Target* - .357 Mag. cal., 3, 4, 5, or 6 in. fixed barrel, adj. rear sight. Mfg. 1993-95.

	$280	$210	$170

Last MSR was $345.

Add approx. $70 for compensated barrel (4, 5, or 6 in. - new 1994).

MODEL 732 - .32 H&R Mag. cal., similar to Model 32, except is stainless steel. Mfg. 1986-95.

	$335	$255	$205

Last MSR was $400.

Add $22 for VR barrel shroud (Model 732-V), $53 for VR heavy barrel shroud (Model 732-VH), approx. $9 for each additional barrel length over 2 1/2 in.

MODEL 738P - .38 +P cal., 5 shot, 6 1/2 in. barrel, fixed sights, wood or rubber grips, 24.6 oz. Mfg. 1992-95.

	$275	$210	$175

Last MSR was $340.

MODEL 7322 - .32-20 WCF cal., similar to Model 322, except is stainless steel. Mfg. 1991-95.

	$335	$255	$205

Last MSR was $400.

Add $22 for VR barrel shroud (Model 7322-V), $53 for VR heavy barrel shroud (Model 7322-VH), approx. $9 for each additional barrel length over 2 1/2 in.

MODEL 740V - .357 SUPERMAG - .357 Max. cal., 4, 6, 8, or 10 in. barrel, adj. rear sight with interchangeable front and rear blades, high polished finish, smooth target grips. Mfg. 1986-95.

	$460	$350	$315

Last MSR was $567.

Add approx. $20 for each additional barrel length after 4 in., $78 with vent. slotted shroud (only avail. with 8 in. barrel), $20 for VR heavy barrel shroud (Model 740-VH).

MODEL 741V - .41 Mag. cal., similar to Model 41V. Disc. 1995.

	$420	$325	$270

Last MSR was $524.

Add approx. $20 for heavy VR, approx. $13 for each barrel length over 4 in.

GRADING - PPGS™	100%	98%	95%	90%	80%	70%	60%

MODEL 744V - .44 Mag. cal., similar to Model 44V. Disc. 1995.

	$430	$345	$285

Last MSR was $524.

Add approx. $20 for heavy VR, $13 for each barrel length over 4 in.

* *Model 744V Target Fixed Barrel* - .44 Mag. cal., 4, 5, 6, or 8 in. barrel, brushed stainless steel. Mfg. 1994-95.

	$395	$315	$265

Last MSR was $493.

Add approx. $4 for each barrel length over 3 in.

* *Model 744 Commemorative* - limited mfg.

	$595	$475	$325

MODEL 745V - .45 LC cal., similar to Model 45, except in stainless steel. Disc. 1995.

	$430	$345	$285

Last MSR was $524.

Add $20 for heavy full shroud VR barrels, $13 for each additional barrel length.

MODEL .45 PIN GUN - .45 ACP cal., similar to Model .45 Pin Gun, except is stainless steel. Mfg. 1993-95.

	$625	$525	$425

Last MSR was $713.

Add $49 for VR heavy rib shroud.

MODEL 7414 SUPERMAG - .414 Super Mag. cal., 4, 6, 8, or 10 in. VR barrel, adj. rear sight, interchangeable front and rear sight blades (optional), bright blue finish, smooth target grips. Mfg. 1995 only.

	$475	$350	$295

Last MSR was $596.

Add approx. $14 for each barrel length after 4 in., $74 for slotted shroud (Model 7414-V8S, 8 in. barrel only), approx. $25 for VR heavy rib shroud.

MODEL 7445 SUPERMAG - .445 Super Mag. cal., 4, 6, 8, or 10 in. VR barrel, adj. rear sight, interchangeable front and rear sight blades (optional), high polished finish, smooth target grips. Mfg. 1991-95.

	$475	$350	$295

Last MSR was $596.

Add approx. $17 for each barrel length after 6 in., $74 for slotted shroud (Model 7445-VH8S, 8 in. barrel only), approx. $25 for VR heavy rib shroud, approx. $40 for VR heavy shroud and interchangeable sights (Model 7445-VH).

SUPER RAM SILHOUETTE - .357 Max., .414 Super Mag., or .44 Mag. cal., silhouette variation featuring modified Iron Sight Gun Works rear sight, Allen Taylor throated barrel, factory trigger job, 4 lbs. Mfg. 1995 only.

	$695	$550	$375

Last MSR was $807.

Add $43 for .414 Super Mag. cal.

HUNTER SERIES - .357 Super Mag., .41 Mag., .44 Mag., or .445 Super Mag. cal., 7 1/2 in. barrel with heavy shroud, Hogue rubber finger grooved and wood presentation grips, choice of Gunworks iron sights or w/o sights with Burris base and rings, non-fluted cylinder, with or w/o compensator, approx. 4 lbs. Mfg. 1994-95.

	$780	$595	$475

Last MSR was $849.

Add $32 for compensated barrel.
Add $32 for scope mounts (w/o sights).

WESTERN ARMS COMPANY

Previous manufacturer located in Ithaca, NY.

SHOTGUNS: SxS

WESTERN LONG RANGE - 12, 16, 20 ga., or .410 bore, 26-32 in. barrels, mod. and full choke, boxlock, extractors, double or single trigger, plain pistol grip stock, Western Arms Co. was a division of Ithaca Gun. Mfg. 1929-46.

	$275	$225	$200	$175	$150	$125	$100

* *Single trigger*

	$325	$275	$250	$225	$200	$150	$125

WESTERN FIELD

Previous trademark used on Montgomery Ward rifles and shotguns.

The Western Field trademark has appeared literally on hundreds of various models (shotguns and rifles) sold through the Montgomery Ward retail network. Most of these models were manufactured through subcontracts with both domestic and international firearms manufacturers. Typically, they were "spec." guns made to sell at a specific price to undersell the competition. Most of these models were derivatives of existing factory models with less expensive wood and perhaps missing the features found on those models from which they were derived. To date, there has been very little interest in collecting Western Field guns, regardless of rarity. Rather than list Western Field models, a general guideline is that values generally are under those of their "1st generation relatives." As a result, prices are ascertained by the shooting value of the gun, rather than its collector value. See Store Brand Crossover List located in the back of this text.

WESTLEY RICHARDS & CO. LTD.

Currently manufactured by Westley Richards and Co., Ltd., Birmingham, England 1812 to date. In 1995, Westley Richards opened their own agency in the US, which is currently located in Bozeman, MT. Previously located in Springfield, MO. Originally William Westley Richards was located in Birmingham, England.

There seems to be a lot of confusion regarding W. Richards, W. R. Richards, William Richards, and other generic derivatives of the famous English gunmaker, Westley Richards. Part of the problem is that there are seventeen registered firms in England, including several in London, who have made guns by the name of Richards. A genuine Westley Richards gun never has the first name abbreviated, and the London address is usually found on the rib panel. Further compounding the problem, a previous Belgian gunmaker, identifiable by W. Richards on the locks or rib, had many shotguns exported into the United States, which are commonly confused with the real London maker. These Belgian guns are commonly hammer guns with damascus twist barrels most frequently encountered in either 10, 12, or 16 ga. The easiest way to determine this maker is to recognize the Liege proofmarks on the barrel flats and chamber length given in millimeters. Most of these Belgian guns sell in the $100-$400 range, depending on condition and configuration.

Note: Westley Richards guns are essentially custom ordered - only 40-45 guns are made annually. They make many weapons that are impossible to list and evaluate, except on an individual basis. Professional appraisal is necessary upon purchase or sale.

To obtain a quotation for a new Westley Richards shotgun, an inquiry should be submitted to the manufacturer or importer (see Trademark Index).

RIFLES

MSR values for currently manufactured rifles are listed in English pounds. For used values, an appraisal/evaluation should be procured before buying.

GRADING - PPGS™	100%	98%	95%	90%	80%	70%	60%

FIXED LOCK (BOXLOCK) DOUBLE RIFLE - .470 NE or .500 NE; standard features include type 'C' doll's head, disc set strikers, two triggers, automatic ejectors, chopper lump barrels, quarter rib, express sights, ramp foresight, standard walnut stock, and traditional scroll engraving.

❋ *Current Mfg.*

MSR £23,500   **£23,500   N/A**

Add £3,250 for traditional scroll engraving.

The values listed represent the standard model without additional options (of which there are a wide array).

❋ *Older & Recent Mfg.*

	N/A	**$21,000**	**$18,750**	**$16,000**	**$13,750**	**$10,500**	**$9,250**

HAND DETACHABLE LOCK (DROPLOCK) DOUBLE RIFLE - nearly all calibers available; standard features include type 'C' doll's head, disk set strikers, hand detachable locks, two triggers, automatic ejectors, manual or automatic safety, chopper lump barrels, quarter rib, express sight.

❋ *Current Mfg.*

MSR £37,500   **£37,500   N/A**

Add £2,000 for .577 NE or .600 NE cal.

Add £1,500 for sideplates.

Add £4,000+ for game scene engraving.

The values listed represent the standard model without additional options (of which there are a wide array).

❋ *Older & Recent Mfg.*

	N/A	**$30,000**	**$25,000**	**$21,000**	**$18,750**	**$16,000**	**$13,000**

SIDELOCK DOUBLE RIFLE - nearly all calibers available; standard features include type 'C' doll's head, disk set strikers, two triggers, automatic ejectors, manual or automatic safety, chopper lump barrels, quarter rib, express sight.

MSR £44,500   **£44,50   N/A**

BOLT ACTION MAGAZINE RIFLE - nearly all calibers available; choice of standard, magnum, or Kurtz action, adjustable trigger, Model 70 safety, express sight, ramp foresight.

❋ *Current Mfg.*

MSR £8,200   **£8,200   N/A**

Add £750 for Magnum action, or £950 for short action.

The values listed represent the standard model without additional options (of which there are a wide array).

❋ *Older & Recent Mfg.*

	N/A	**$7,850**	**$6,950**	**$5,750**	**$4,750**	**$4,000**	**$3,300**

SHOTGUNS: PRE-WWII MFG.

Add 20% for 20 ga.

Add 30% for 28 ga.

Add $1,500 for cased extra set of locks.

OVUNDO O/U - detachable lock boxlock, optional sideplates. Disc.

$18,000	**$15,000**	**$12,500**	**$9,750**	**$8,500**	**$7,250**	**$6,000**

MODELE DE GRANDE LUXE - SxS - scalloped receiver, detachable locks, profuse scroll & game scene engraving. Disc.

$15,000	**$13,000**	**$11,000**	**$9,750**	**$8,500**	**$7,250**	**$6,000**

MODEL DE LUXE - SxS - scalloped receiver, detachable locks, fine scroll & game scene engraving. Disc.

$11,000	**$9,500**	**$8,500**	**$7,500**	**$6,000**	**$5,500**	**$5,000**

GRADING - PPGS™	100%	98%	95%	90%	80%	70%	60%

HAMMERLESS EJECTOR PLAIN QUALITY - SxS - scalloped receiver, Anson & Deeley fixed locks.

	$6,000	$5,000	$4,000	$3,500	$3,000	$2,500	$2,000

"B" QUALITY EJECTOR - SxS - boxlock with plain (unscalloped) receiver, light scroll engraving. Disc.

	$5,000	$4,000	$3,500	$3,000	$2,500	$2,250	$2,000

SHOTGUNS: O/U, RECENT MFG.

BEST QUALITY O/U - available in 20 ga. only. 2 1/2 or 2 3/4 in. chambers, standard features include Westley Richards top lever, automatic ejectors, automatic safety, two triggers or Westley Richards patent one trigger, hand detachable locks, hinged coverplate, sideplates with inspection port, chopper lump barrels.

MSR £37,500   £37,500   N/A

SHOTGUNS: SxS, RECENT MFG.

MSR values for currently manufactured rifles are listed in English pounds. For used values, an appraisal/evaluation should be procured before buying.

CONNAUGHT MODEL - 12, 20, or 28 ga., Anson & Deeley scalloped boxlock action, scroll engraving, 26 or 28 in. barrels, ejectors, about 6 1/2 lbs. Disc.

	$9,250	$8,000	$6,600	$5,600	$4,800	$4,000	$3,400

Last MSR was $10,900.

HAND DETACHABLE LOCK (DROPLOCK) - available in 12, 16, 20, 28 ga. or .410, 2 3/4 in. or 3 in. chambers, standard features include model 'C' doll's head, Westley Richards top lever, automatic ejectors, automatic safety, two triggers, hand detachable locks, hinged coverplate, chopper lump barrels.

* *Current Mfg.*

MSR £31,750   £31,750   N/A

Add £700 for 28 ga. or .410 bore.

Add £3,250 for SST.

Add £2,950 for spare detachable locks.

The values listed represent the standard model without engraving and additional options (of which there are a wide array).

* *Older & Recent Mfg.*

	N/A	$19,450	$14,000	$10,750	$8,750	$7,600	$6,400

Only six .410 Best Quality Boxlocks have been mfg. to date.

BEST QUALITY SIDELOCK - 12, 16, 20, 28 ga., or .410 bore, 2 3/4 in. or 3 in. chambers, standard features include Best London sidelock action, assisted opening system, automatic ejectors, automatic safety, two triggers, chopper lump barrels.

* *Current Mfg.*

MSR £31,750   £31,750   N/A

Add £750 for 28 ga. or .410 bore.

Add £2,100 for SNT or £3,250 for SST.

The values listed represent the standard model without engraving and additional options (of which there are a wide array).

* *Older & Recent Mfg.*

	N/A	$18,950	$14,000	$10,750	$8,750	$7,600	$6,400

Add 20% for 20 ga.

Add 40% for 28 ga.

Add 60% for .410 bore.

Add $1,000 for SST.

Most specimens in this model were custom ordered, so each gun should be evaluated individually.

100%	98%	95%	90%	80%	70%	60%	50%	40%	30%	20%	10%

WHITNEY ARMS COMPANY

Previous manufacturer located in New Haven, CT, 1798-1886.

Whitney Arms Company began firearms production in 1798. Eli Whitney Sr. & Eli Whitney Jr. were prominent figures and prolific producers in the arms manufacturing world for a great many years, and their production plant in New Haven is credited as being the first major manufacturer of commercial firearms in America. The Whitneys produced a tremendous variety of firearms under family ownership for approximately 90 years before selling the company to Winchester in 1888. Numerous long arms, starting with the Whitney 1798 U.S. Contract Musket, and moving forward through various other flintlock, percussion, rimfire, and centerfire rifles, handguns, and shotguns, contributed to the vast broadness of the Whitney line. The Whitney name saw collaboration with Burgess, Kennedy, Morse, Tiesing, Howard, Cochran, Scharf, and many others. Many of the early Whitney rifles, such as the historic 1798 Flintlock muskets, are rare and highly collectible, commanding substantial premiums when found in original configuration, and not converted to percussion. The Whitney lever action repeaters are also quite popular among collectors. A fair number remain in circulation.

The author wishes to express his thanks to Mr. Steve Engleson for providing the following information on Whitney Arms Company.

RIFLES: LEVER ACTION

WHITNEY-KENNEDY LEVER ACTION MAGAZINE RIFLES - a repeating rifle with loading port on right side, top ejection, approx. 15,000 mfg. between 1879-1886, barrels are typically marked "Whitney Arms Co." or "Whitneyville Armory" with some variations having the Kennedy name included, often referred to as the Kennedy rifle, two basic frame sizes were made (large & small), both frame sizes were also available in carbines and muskets, two other basic variations were the standard loop lever, a serpentine or "S" shaped finger lever, ser. nos. were sequential from 1-5,000, and from there a letter prefix was added, these appeared from "A" through "S", with numbers 1-999 following.

✳ *Large Frame* - .40-60 WCF, .45-60 WCF, .45-75 WCF, and .50-95 Express cal., 26 or 28 in. round or octagon barrels, walnut stocks, crescent steel buttplate, full magazine capacity of 9 rounds in standard rifle.

N/A	N/A	$2,500	$2,125	$1,900	$1,700	$1,475	$1,325	$1,100	$975	$850	$725

Add 300% for .50-95 Express cal. (extremely rare).
Add 10% for .45-75 cal. (rare).
Add 50% for carbine or musket.
Add 100% for half-round, half-octagon barrel.
Add 20% for nonprefix (early) serial numbers.
Add 10% for serpentine lever.

✳ *Small Frame* - .44-40 WCF, .38-40 WCF, and .32-20 WCF cal., 24 in. round or octagon barrel, walnut stock and crescent buttplate, full magazine capacity of 13 rounds in standard rifle.

N/A	N/A	$1,950	$1,675	$1,450	$1,225	$1,075	$950	$825	$700	$600	$500

Add 50% for carbine or musket (extremely rare).
Add 100% for half-round, half-octagon barrel.
Add 20% for half-magazine.
Add 20% for 26 or 28 in. barrel.

1878 BURGESS REPEATING RIFLE - .45-70 Govt. cal., standard sporting rifle, 28 in. octagon or round barrel, loading port on right side, serpentine shaped lever, walnut stock, blue receiver and full magazine capacity of 9 rounds, typically w/o Whitney markings, barrels marked "G.W. Morse Patented Oct. 28th 1856", and tangs are marked "A. Burgess Patented Jan. 7th 1873", several variations, including the first, second, and third models, as well as military carbines and muskets.

N/A	N/A	$3,300	$3,000	$2,700	$2,400	$2,100	$1,850	$1,600	$1,400	$1,250	$1,100

GRADING - PPGS™	100%	98%	95%	90%	80%	70%	60%

Add 300% for the first model top loader (few made and most converted by the factory to sideloader).

Add 100% for military carbine or musket (certain variations will command a higher premium).

Add 30% for first or second model.

Values shown are for the most typically encountered variation, the third model sporting rifle. This model was also known as the Whitney-Burgess-Morse lever action repeating rifle, mfg. through a license agreement with Andrew Burgess, total production of approx. 2,000 were made between 1878-82.

WHITNEY FIREARMS COMPANY

Previous manufacturer from 1956-1959 located in Hartford, CT.

PISTOLS: SEMI-AUTO

WOLVERINE OR LIGHTNING - .22 Auto cal., unique futuristic Jetsons appearance, 10 shot, 4 5/8 in. barrel, plastic grips, aluminum alloy frame and barrel shroud, blue model is more common (approx. 13,000 mfg.), nickel is rare (approx. 900 mfg.). Mfg. 1955-62.

	100%	98%	95%	90%	80%	70%	60%
Blue finish	$495	$425	$350	$300	$260	$230	$200
Nickel finish	$950	$850	$600	$500	$400	$350	$300

WHITWORTH

This trademark can be found in the Interarms section of this text.

WICHITA ARMS, INC.

Current manufacturer located in Wichita, KS. Distributor, dealer, and consumer direct sales.

PISTOLS

WICHITA INTERNATIONAL PISTOL (WIP) - available in 8 cals. between .22 LR and .357 Mag., single shot, break open action, stainless steel, adj. sights, 10 or 14 in. barrel, adj. sights or scope mounts, smooth walnut stocks and forearm. Disc. 1994.

$680	$465	$350	

Last MSR was $775.

Add $100 for 14 in. barrel.

WICHITA CLASSIC PISTOL - assorted cals. to .308 Win., 11 1/4 in. barrel, action has left-hand bolt for shooting with right hand, deluxe walnut, custom made, 3 lbs. 15 oz. Disc. 1997.

$3,280	$2,550	$2,150

Last MSR was $3,495.

✳ Wichita Classic Engraved - similar to Wichita Classic, except is extensively engraved.

MSR $5,250	$5,250	$3,750	$2,750

WICHITA SILHOUETTE PISTOL (WSP) - .308 Win. or 7mm/IHMSA cal., adj. trigger and sights, 14 15/16 in. barrel, center grip walnut stock, rear grip, 4 1/2 lbs. Left-hand action for shooting with right hand. Disc. 1994.

$1,520	$1,050	$850

Last MSR was $1,800.

WICHITA MAGAZINE PISTOL - .308 Win. or 7mm/IHMSA cal., fiberthane (disc. 1987) or walnut (new 1988) stock, choice of MK-40, Silhouette, or Classic configuration, 13 in. barrel, adj. trigger, multi-range sights, 4 1/2 lbs. Disc. 1994.

$1,250	$875	$700

Last MSR was $1,550.

GRADING - PPGS™	100%	98%	95%	90%	80%	70%	60%

* **Wichita Classic Pistol** - features octagon barrel, AAA walnut stock, 11 1/4 in. barrel, 3 lbs. 15 oz. Disc. 1994.

	$2,975	$2,450	$2,000

Last MSR was $3,400.

WICHITA BENCH PISTOL - .222 Rem., 6 PPC, or .22 Cheetah cal., uses WBR 1200 action, rear grip, 18 in. stainless steel Douglas barrel. Mfg. 1994-98.

	$1,875	$1,500	$1,250

Last MSR was $1,875.

RIFLES: BOLT ACTION

WICHITA CLASSIC RIFLE (WCR) - .17-222, .17-222 Mag., .222 Rem., .222 Mag., 223 Rem., 6x47mm, and other cals. up to and including .308 Win. cal., bolt action, single shot, select walnut, 21 in. octagon barrel, Canjar trigger, no sights, 7 lbs. Disc. 1997.

MSR $3,495		$3,275	$2,500	$2,150

Add $175 for left-hand action.

* **Wichita Varmint Rifle (WVR)** - similar to WCR, except available only in Varmint cals. (up to and including .308 Win.) and round barrel. Disc. 1997.

	$2,500	$1,795	$1,375

Last MSR was $2,695.

Add $175 for left-hand action.

* **Wichita Silhouette Rifle (WSR)** - available in most cals., grey fiberthane stock, 24 in. match grade barrel, 2 oz. Canjar trigger, no sights, 9 lbs. Disc. 1995.

	$2,475	$1,775	$1,375

Last MSR was $2,650.

Add $175 for left-hand action.

* **Wichita Magnum** - Mag. cals., stainless steel only. Disc. 1984.

	$1,725	$1,300	$1,175

WICKLIFFE RIFLES

Previously manufactured by Triple S Development located in Wickliffe, OH.

RIFLES: SINGLE SHOT

MODEL 76 STANDARD - falling block action, most popular cals., 22 or 26 in. barrel, no sights, select walnut pistol grip, 2 piece stock. Mfg. 1976-disc.

	$395	$350	$325	$300	$275	$250	$225

MODEL 76 DELUXE GRADE - similar to Standard, in .30-06 cal. only, 22 in. barrel, fancy wood, silver pistol grip cap.

	$460	$415	$385	$360	$320	$290	$250

MODEL 76 COMMEMORATIVE - similar to Deluxe, except etched receiver, U.S. silver dollar inlaid in stock, presentation case. Mfg. 100, 1976.

	$1,100	$825	$550	$495	$440	$330	$305

STINGER - similar to Model 76 Standard, in .22 Hornet or .223 Rem. cal., lightweight 22 in. barrel.

	$395	$350	$325	$300	$275	$250	$225

STINGER DELUXE - similar to 76 Deluxe, in .22 Hornet or .223 Rem. cal., lightweight 22 in. barrel.

	$460	$415	$385	$360	$325	$290	$250

TRADITIONALIST - similar to Standard 76, in .30-06 or .45-70 Govt. cal., 24 in. barrel.

	$395	$350	$325	$300	$275	$250	$225

GRADING - PPGS™	100%	98%	95%	90%	80%	70%	60%

KODIAK COMMEMORATIVE - similar to Model 76 Deluxe, .338 Win. Mag. cal., 26 in. barrel, etched receiver.

	$650	$550	$475	$425	$375	$325	$275

WIFRA
Please refer to W.R. Saleri listing in the S section.

WILD WEST GUNS
Current custom gunsmith and manufacturer located in Anchorage, AK. Dealer and consumer direct sales.

PISTOLS: SEMI-AUTO

Wild West Guns previously manufactured a customized M1911 style semi-auto model called the ShadowLite package - 1997 retail was $2,495.

RIFLES: BOLT ACTION

SUMMITLITE - various short action cals., Rem. or Win. action, fluted match grade barrel, lightweight configuration with scaled down synthetic stock, 4 1/2 lbs.

MSR $3,465	$3,100	$2,750	$2,400	$2,100	$1,800	$1,600	$1,200

Add $175 for stainless steel, $199 for thumbhole stock, or $220 for left-hand action.

PROGUIDE - .375 H&H, .416 Rem., .458 Win., or .458 Lott cal., Win. controlled feed action, slab side barrel with muzzle brake and quarter rib, parkerized finish, camo or black synthetic stock with Pachmayr decelerator pad.

MSR $3,465	$3,100	$2,750	$2,400	$2,100	$1,800	$1,600	$1,200

Add $175 for stainless steel or $220 for left-hand action.

RIFLES: LEVER ACTION

ALASKAN COPILOT RIFLE - .30-30 Win. (disc. 1999), .357 Mag. (disc. 1999), .44 Mag. (disc. 1999), .444 Marlin (disc. 1999), .45-70 Govt., .457 Mag. (new 2000), or .50 Alaskan (new 2000) cal., 16 1/2, 18 1/2, or 20 in. barrel with ghost ring rear sight, features customized Marlin lever action with takedown conversion, various finishes, ported barrel, matte blue or parkerized finish, includes soft case. New 1996.

MSR $1,980	$1,775	$1,425	$1,125	$900	$675	$625	$575

Add $200 for .50 Alaskan cal. package.
Subtract approx. 20% for older disc. cals.

* *Alaskan CoPilot Limited* - .457 Mag. or .45-70 Govt. cal., takedown action, features most of Wild West Guns custom shop options, includes hard case. Only 150 to be mfg. beginning 2001 with custom ser. nos.

	$2,995	$2,650	$2,150	$1,750	$1,500	$1,300	$1,100

Last MSR was $2,995.

ALASKAN GUIDE - .457 Mag. or .50 Alaskan cal., similar to Alaskan CoPilot, except is non-takedown, has 18 1/2 in. ported barrel with fiberoptic front sight, ghost ring rear sight, parkerized finish, straight style stock and recoil control porting. New 1997.

MSR $1,320	$1,175	$1,000	$875	$800	$700	$600	$495

Add $250 for .50 Alaskan cal. package.
Add $110 for stainless steel.

MASTER GUIDE - .457 Mag., .45-70 Govt., or .50 Alaskan cal., takedown action.

MSR $1,865	$1,675	$1,375	$1,100	$900	$675	$625	$575

Add $250 for .50 Alaskan cal. package.
Add $110 for stainless steel.

GRADING - PPGS™	100%	98%	95%	90%	80%	70%	60%

MODEL 04 - .454 Casull or .500 S&W cal., stainless steel CNC machined frame, take-down or solid rifle, 16.5, 18.5, or 20 in. barrel, walnut, laminate or synthetic stock, ghost ring sights, Pachmayr decelerator pad. New 2005.

> **MSR $1,499** $1,350 $1,150 $975
>
> Add $300 for synthetic stock.
> Add $400 for takedown.

WILDEY, INC.

Current manufacturer located in Warren, CT. Previously located in New Milford, CT until 1999.

Originally, the company was named Wildey Firearms Co., Inc. located in Cheshire, CT. At that time, serialization of pistols was 45-0000. When Wildey, Inc. bought the company out of bankruptcy from the old shareholders, there had been approximately 800 pistols mfg. To distinguish the old company from the present company, the serial range was changed to 09-0000 (only 633 pistols with the 09 prefix were produced). These guns had the Cheshire, CT address. Pistols produced by Wildey, Inc., New Milford, CT are serial numbered with 4 digits (no numerical prefix).

CARBINES: SEMI-AUTO

WILDEY CARBINE - .44 Auto Mag., .45 Wildey Mag., .45 Win. Mag., or .475 Wildey Mag. cal., features 18 in. barrel with forearm and detachable skeleton walnut stock, polished or matte stainless steel. New 2003.

> **MSR $3,020** $2,600 $2,175 $1,700
>
> Add $230 for matte stainless steel finish.

PISTOLS: SEMI-AUTO

> Add $585-$1,950 per interchangeable barrel assembly, depending on barrel length and finish.

WILDEY AUTO PISTOL - .45 Win. Mag., .45 Wildey Mag., or .475 Wildey Mag., gas operated, 5, 6, 7, 8, 10, or 14 in. VR barrel, selective single shot or semi-auto, 3 lug rotary bolt, fixed barrel (interchangeable), polished stainless steel construction, 7 shot, double action, adj. sights, smooth or checkered wood grips, designed to fire proprietary new cartridges specifically for this gun including the .45 Win. Mag. cal., 64 oz. with 5 in. barrel.

> Add $560-$1,148 per interchangeable barrel.

* *Survivor Model* - .44 Auto Mag. (new 2003), .45 Win. Mag., 45 Wildey Mag., or .475 Wildey Mag. cal., 5, 6, 7, 8, 10, 12, 14 (new 2000), or 18 (new 2003) in. VR barrel, polished stainless steel finish. New 1990.

> **MSR $1,525** $1,325 $975 $775
>
> Add $121 for 12 in. barrel.
> Add $561 for 14 in. barrel.
> Add $25 for 8 or 10 in. barrel.
> Add $1,171 for 18 in. barrel.
> Add $25 for .45 Wildey Mag. or .475 Wildey Mag. cal.
> The .475 Wildey cal. is derived from a factory case.

* *Survivor Guardsman* - similar to Survivor Model, except has squared-off trigger guard, same options apply to this model as for the Survivor model. New 1990.

> **MSR $1,525** $1,325 $975 $775

GRADING - PPGS™	100%	98%	95%	90%	80%	70%	60%

* *Hunter Model* - .45 Win. Mag., .45 Wildey Mag., or .475 Wildey Mag. cal., 5, 6, 7, 8, 10, 12, 14 (new 2000) or 18 (new 2003) in. VR barrel, matte finish on all metal parts, adj. sights. New 1990.

MSR $1,775	$1,500	$1,175	$925

Add $124 for 12 in. barrel.
Add $565 for 14 in. barrel.
Add $1,175 for 18 in. barrel.
Add $25 for 8 or 10 in. barrel.
Add $25 for .45 Wildey Mag. or .475 Wildey Mag. cal.
.475 Wildey Mag. is available in 8, 10, or 12 in. barrel only.

* *Hunter Guardsman* - similar to Hunter Model, except has squared-off trigger guard, same options apply to this model as for the Hunter model. New 1990.

MSR $1,775	$1,500	$1,175	$925

Add $100 for 12 in. barrel.
Add $625 for 14 in. barrel.
Add $1,175 for 18 in. silhouette barrel.

* *Presentation Model* - same specifications as Hunter Guardsman model, except is engraved with hand-checkered or smooth stocks.

	$2,500	$2,000	$1,600

Last MSR was $2,000.

* *Older Wildey Mfg.*
.475 Wildey Mag. cal. was available in 8 or 10 in. barrel only.

> SERIAL NOS. 1-200.

	$1,900	$1,700	$1,550

Last MSR was $2,180.

Add $20 for 8 or 10 in. barrel.
> SERIAL NOS. 201-400.

	$1,750	$1,550	$1,400

Last MSR was $1,980.

Add $20 for 8 or 10 in. barrel.
> SERIAL NOS. 401-600.

	$1,650	$1,375	$1,250

Last MSR was $1,780.

Add $20 for 8 or 10 in. barrel.
> SERIAL NOS. 601-800.

	$1,450	$1,200	$1,000

Last MSR was $1,580.

Add $20 for 8 or 10 in. barrel.
> SERIAL NOS. 801-1,000.

	$1,100	$925	$800

Last MSR was $1,275.

Add $25 for 8 or 10 in. barrel.
> SERIAL NOS. 1,001-2,489.

	$1,025	$850	$750

Last MSR was $1,175.

Add $20 for 8 or 10 in. barrel.

WILKES, JOHN GUNMAKERS LTD.

Current manufacturer established in 1833, and located in London, England. Currently imported and distributed beginning 2001 by First National Gun Banque, located in Colorado Springs, CO.

John Wilkes Gunmakers Ltd. has been manufacturing best quality guns for over 150 years. This trademark was reintroduced with the release of the new O/U sidelock ejector

GRADING - PPGS™	100%	98%	95%	90%	80%	70%	60%

model. Please contact the importer directly for more information, including available options, delivery times, and individual price quotations.

SHOTGUNS: O/U, SIDELOCK

O/U SIDELOCK BEST MODEL CLASSIC - 20 ga. only initially, unique sideplate locks w/o "V" springs (plungers instead), ST or DT, best quality wood and works-manship, Brazier "solid solid," mono solid (new 2004), monobloc or chopper lump barrels, lifetime warranty, special order only. Importation began 2001.

MSR $21,000	$21,000	$16,750	$14,250	$12,000	$11,000	$10,000	$9,250

Add $3,000 for "solid solid" barrels.
Add $2,500 per pair of additional locks.

✻ *O/U Sidelock Special Series*
Prices for the Special Series start at $28,950 with mono solid barrels, $31,500 with "solid solid" barrels.

SHOTGUNS: SxS

John Wilkes manufactures a sidelock model in all gauges - MSR is currently $40,700. Boxlock models are also available, with prices ranging from $2,760 - $6,000, depending on special orders/features.

WILKINSON ARMS

Current trademark manufactured by Northwest Arms, located in Parma, ID. Dealer direct sales.

CARBINES

LINDA CARBINE - 9mm Para cal., 16 3/16 in. barrel, aluminum receiver, pre-ban configuration (limited supplies), fixed tubular stock with wood pad, vent. barrel shroud, aperture rear sight, small wooden forearm, 18 or 31 shot mag., beginning 2002, this model came standard with many accessories, 7 lbs. New 2000.

MSR $1,800	$1,495	$750	$625	$550	$450	$395	$360

Only 2,200 Linda Carbines were marked "Luger Carbine" on the receiver. The last 1,500 distributed by Northwest Arms include a longer stock, and matched bolt and barrel (Rockwell 57).

✻ *Linda L2 Limited Edition* - mfg. from the last 600 of the original 2,200 pre-ban Linda Carbines, includes many upgrades and accessories. New 2002.

MSR $4,800	$4,350	$2,750	$1,900

TERRY CARBINE - 9mm Para. cal., blowback semi-auto action, 31 shot mag., 16 3/16 in. barrel, closed breech, adj. sights, 7 lbs. Disc.

With black P.V.C. stock	$475	$395	$325	$295	$260	$230	$200
With maple stock	$625	$525	$400	$350	$340	$325	$300

PISTOLS: SEMI-AUTO

SHERRY MODEL - .22 LR cal., 2 1/2 in. barrel, aluminum frame, fully machined steel slide, trigger group, and bolt insert, available in various colors, 9 1/4 oz. New 2000.

MSR $280	$245	$200	$160	$140	$125	$110	$100

Add $25 for gold anodized frame.
Add $20 for collector's edition.
Add $100 for Robar coating.

DIANE MODEL - .25 ACP cal., 6 shot, 2 1/8 in. barrel, fixed sight, matte blue, plastic grips. Disc.

	$150	$125	$95	$80	$65	$55	$50

LINDA MODEL - 9mm Para. cal., blowback action firing from closed bolt, 8.3 in. barrel, 31 shot mag., PVC pistol grip, maple forearm, Williams adj. rear sight. Disc.

	100%	98%	95%	90%	80%	70%	60%
	$675	$625	$550	$475	$425	$350	$295

WILLIAM & SON

Current manufacturer established in 1999, and located in London, England. Previous company name was William R. Asprey. William R. Asprey is the 7th generation of the renowned Asprey family who established their first business in 1781. William & Son continues the family tradition of building best quality English guns.

Prices indicated below for manufacturer's suggested retail and 100% condition factors are listed in English pounds. All new prices do not include English VAT. Values for used guns in 98%-60% condition factors are priced in U.S. dollars. Deluxe game scene engraving is available by quotation only.

RIFLES: BOLT ACTION

BOLT ACTION MAGAZINE RIFLE - standard cals. include .243 Win., .270 Win., .308 Win., or .375 H&H, Mauser or Mannlicher action, 3/4 rib with standard and two-folding leaf rear sight, best quality pistol grip walnut stock with traditional cheekpiece, custom order only - prices below reflect base model, and include leather case with accessories. Magnum or Kurtz action and scopes are priced upon individual quotation only.

	100%	98%	95%	90%	80%	70%	60%
MSR £10,500	£10,500	$14,000	$12,000	$9,500	$8,000	$7,200	$6,500

RIFLES: SxS, SIDELOCK

SxS DOUBLE RIFLE - various cals. up to .700, sidelock ejector with engraved reinforced action, pinless lockplates, best quality walnut, folding leaf rear sight on 3/4 rib, custom order only - prices below reflect base models, and include leather case with accessories. Limited mfg.

Add £2,250 for detachable scope mounts.

	100%	98%	95%	90%	80%	70%	60%
✱ Cals. up to .300							
MSR £45,000	£45,000	$68,250	$57,500	$47,500	$42,500	$36,500	$29,500
✱ Cals. up to .470							
MSR £50,000	£50,000	$74,000	$62,500	$50,000	$45,000	$38,500	$32,000
✱ Cals. up to .577							
MSR £55,000	£55,000	$80,000	$67,000	$52,500	$47,500	$40,000	$33,500

✱ .600 and .700 Bore - prices start at £60,000 and £70,000, respectively.

SHOTGUNS: O/U

SIDELOCK MODEL - 12, 16, or 20 ga., best quality sidelock ejector model, features pinless lockplates, DTs, best quality checkered walnut, custom order only - prices below reflect base model, and include leather case with accessories.

	100%	98%	95%	90%	80%	70%	60%
MSR £42,500	£42,500	$55,500	$46,500	$39,750	$34,250	$30,000	$26,500

Add £550 for pistol grip stock.
Add £2,200 for ST.

SHOTGUNS: SxS, SIDELOCK

SIDELOCK MODEL - available in 12 ga. - .410 bore, best quality sidelock ejector model, features pinless lockplates, DTs, best quality checkered walnut, custom order only - prices below reflect base model, and include leather case with accessories.

	100%	98%	95%	90%	80%	70%	60%
MSR £36,500	£36,500	$47,000	$41,000	$34,250	$30,000	$26,500	$21,050

Add £2,200 for ST.

GRADING - PPGS™	100%	98%	95%	90%	80%	70%	60%

WILLIAM DOUGLAS & SONS

Current manufacturer located in Staffordshire, England. No current U.S. importation. Previously imported and distributed by Cape Outfitters located in Cape Girardeau, MO.

Prices and MSRs listed reflect most recent U.S. importation.

RIFLES: SxS

EXPRESS RIFLE - .375 H&H cal., H&H type back action sidelock with bolster fences, DTs, ejectors, 24 in. regulated barrels, folding leaf rear sight, oil finished European walnut stock with 20 LPI checkering, light engraving, case hardened action.

MSR N/A	$19,750	$15,250	$11,000	$8,750	$7,400	$6,200	$5,300

BOXLOCK EXPRESS RIFLE - .470 NE or .500 NE (new 1998) cal., Anson & Deeley action with DT (front trigger is articulated), case colored action with deep blue small parts, 24 in. regulated barrels, checkered European walnut stock and forearm with oil finish, light border engraving.

MSR N/A	$12,975	$9,950	$9,000	$8,250	$7,500	$6,750	$6,000

Add $1,000 for .500 NE cal.

* *Deluxe Boxlock Express Rifle* - includes better walnut and fully engraved receiver.

MSR N/A	$15,650	$12,750	$10,750	$9,500	$8,750	$7,500	$6,750

SHOTGUNS: SxS

WILLIAM DOUGLAS BOXLOCK - 16, 20, or 28 ga., 2 3/4 in. chambers, case colored receiver, chopper lump barrels, DT, 26 or 28 in. barrels. Importation began 2000.

MSR N/A	$4,650	$4,200	$3,750	$3,250	$2,750	$2,250	$1,750

Add $800 for ST.

WILLIAM EVANS LIMITED

Current manufacturer of long arms established during 1883, and located in London, England.

William Evans Limited, Gun & Rifle Makers, have been manufacturing high quality shotguns and rifles for over 100 years. Most William Evans shotguns and double rifles must be appraised individually since they were all custom ordered initially. All new guns must be ordered from the factory directly. All prices are FOB England, less VAT. Please contact William Evans (refer to the Trademark Index) for more information, including any special orders.

RIFLES

MSR values for currently manufactured rifles are listed in English pounds, and used prices are not listed, since these models are only infrequently encountered in today's marketplace.

BEST QUALITY SIDELOCK DOUBLE RIFLE - various cals., traditional bold scroll-engraved sidelock action, many options available, custom order only.

* *Current Mfg.*

MSR £55,000	£55,000	N/A

Add £5,000 for .500 NE-.577 NE.

Cals. .600 NE and above are POR.

BOLT ACTION MAGAZINE RIFLE - various cals., Mauser standard or Magnum action, many options available, custom order only.

* *Current Mfg.*

MSR £8,500	£8,500	N/A

Add £7,000 for Mauser Magnum action.

GRADING - PPGS™	100%	98%	95%	90%	80%	70%	60%

SHOTGUNS: O/U & SxS

BEST QUALITY O/U SIDELOCK - 12, 16, 20, 28 ga. or .410 bore, best quality sidelock gun with DT, bold scroll engraving standard, custom order only.
* *Current Mfg.*

    MSR £45,000   **£45,000**   **N/A**
    Add £2,000 for 28 ga. or .410 bore.

BEST QUALITY SxS SIDELOCK - 12, 16, 20, 28 ga. or .410 bore, best quality sidelock gun with DT, bold scroll engraving standard, custom order only.
* *Current Mfg.*

    MSR £35,000   **£35,000**   **N/A**
    Add £2,000 for 28 ga. or .410 bore.

WILLIAM LARKIN MOORE

Current importer and dealer established in 1968, and located in Scottsdale, AZ.

William Larkin Moore imports a variety of high grade quality shotguns and double rifles. Currently, the company imports F.lli Rizzini, Famars, Art Manifattura Armi, Pedro Arrizabalga, Armas Garbi, Arrieta, Lebeau-Courally, Chapuis Armes, B. Rizzini, and is the sole U.S. importer for F.lli Piotti. Please refer to the individual listings for information on current models and pricing.

WILLIAM POWELL & SON (GUNMAKERS) LTD.

Current manufacturer established in 1802, and located in Birmingham, England. The company is still controlled by the descendants of William Powell I. No current U.S. importation. Previously imported 1999-2002 by John Higgins, located in Richmond Hill, GA, and by Bells Legendary Countrywear located in New York, NY, until 1999. The Heritage Series was introduced into the U.S. in 1984.

William Powell & Sons celebrated their 200th anniversary during 2002, and are one of England's oldest premier gunmakers. Please contact the factory directly for more information. They have a fine catalog, which, includes a lineup of accessories and clothing.

SHOTGUNS: SxS

Values listed are shown in pounds (£), and do not include VAT.

    Add 10% for 20, 28 ga. or .410 bore on models listed.

NO. 1 SIDELOCK EJECTOR - 12, 16, 20 ga., or .410 (disc.) bore, chopper lump barrels, extra choice French walnut, DTs, many special orders available. Gold inlays, deep relief carved action fences, can be obtained in self opener.
* *Current Mfg.*
    MSR £35,280   **£33,600**   **N/A**
    Add £3,310 for assisted opening action.
    Add £2,750 for SNT.
* *Recent & Older Mfg.*

	100%	98%	95%	90%	80%	70%	60%
	N/A	$39,500	$34,000	$28,750	$23,250	$17,500	$14,750

NO. 3 BOXLOCK EJECTOR - 12, 16, 20 ga., or .410 (disc.) bore, chopper lump barrels, scalloped boxlock action, extra choice French walnut, many special orders available.
* *Current Mfg.*
    MSR £21,015   **£20,016**   **N/A**

GRADING - PPGS™	100%	98%	95%	90%	80%	70%	60%

* *Recent & Older Mfg.*

	N/A	$27,000	$21,000	$16,000	$9,900	$7,500	$6,250

* *Model 4 Boxlock Ejector* - similar to Number 3, but has dovetail lump barrels and less engraving.
* *Current Mfg.*
  MSR £18,282   £17,412   N/A
  Add £1,934 for SNT.
* *Recent & Older Mfg.*

	N/A	$23,000	$16,500	$10,250	$7,950	$6,600	$5,400

* *Model 6 Boxlock Ejector* - disc. 1988.

	$2,750	$2,450	$2,050	$1,700	$1,400	$1,150	$900

HERITAGE NO. 1 SIDELOCK EJECTOR MKII - 12 or 20 ga., 2 3/4 in. chambers, chopper lump barrels, choice of game scene or bouquet and scroll engraving, DTs. Mfg. 1984-2000.

	$8,710	$12,750	$10,750	$9,000	$7,800	$6,700	$5,500

Last MSR was £8,710.

HERITAGE NO. 2 SIDELOCK MKII - similar to Heritage No. 1, except has less engraving and lesser grade walnut, easy opening action.

* *Current Mfg.*
  MSR £4,350   £4,255   N/A
  Add £1,325 for traditional scroll engraving.
* *Recent & Older Mfg.*

	N/A	$5,900	$5,200	$4,750	$4,375	$3,675	$3,100

HERITAGE "CONSORT" SIDELOCK EJECTOR - 12, 20, or 28 ga., 2 3/4 in. chambers chopper lump barrels, round body action, full bouquet and scroll engraving. New 1998.

* *Current Mfg.*
  MSR £7,395   £7,350   N/A
* *Recent & Older Mfg.*

	N/A	$8,200	$6,850	$6,000	$5,000	$4,250	$3,500

HERITAGE DE LUXE BOXLOCK DETACHABLE LOCK - features detachable locks, choice of traditional scroll or game scene engraving, ejectors. Disc. 1999.

	$21,485	$16,750	$13,750	$11,000	$8,500	$7,250	$5,950

Last MSR was $21,485.

HERITAGE ROUND ACTION EJECTOR - features unscalloped, rounded boxlock action with fine English scrollwork throughout, DTs. Disc. 1999.

	$15,785	$12,000	$9,600	$7,800	$6,600	$5,400	$4,500

Last MSR was $15,785.

WILSON COMBAT

Current firearms manufacturer, customizer, and supplier of custom firearms parts and accessories established in 1978, and located in Berryville, AR.

PISTOLS

Wilson Combat makes a complete range of high quality, semi-auto pistols styled after the M1911 Colt. Current models include: the CQB Series ($1,950-$2,045 MSR), Classic ($2,045-$2,080 MSR), Protector ($1,995-$2,045 MSR), KZ Series ($1,325-$1,410 MSR), Classic Super Grade ($3,595 MSR), Classic Stainless ($2,145-$2,180 MSR),

Tactical Super Grade ($3,495 MSR), Stealth ($2,895 MSR) and the Tactical Elite ($2,950 MSR). Please contact the company directly for more information, including a wide variety of options and features.

RIFLES

Wilson Combat makes three basic configurations patterned after the Colt AR-15. They include: the Urban Tactical Rifle ($1,599-$1,910 MSR), Tactical Carbine ($1,575-$1,884 MSR), and the Super Sniper Model ($1,799-$1,924 MSR). Please contact the company directly for more information, including a wide variety of options and features.

SHOTGUNS

Please refer to Scattergun Technologies for complete listing of shotguns and accessories.

WINCHESTER

Current manufacturer located in New Haven, CT from 1866 to date, and by Miroku of Japan since circa 1992. Also includes U.S. Repeating **WINCHESTER.** Arms, formed in 1981, with licensing agreement from Olin Corp. to manufacture shotguns and rifles domestically using the Winchester Trademark. Corporate offices are now located in Morgan, UT.

Olin Corp. previously manufactured shotguns and rifles bearing the Winchester Hallmark at the Olin Kodensha Plant (closed 1989) located in Tochigi, Japan and also in European countries. In 1992, U.S. Repeating Arms was acquired by GIAT located in France. In late 1997, the Walloon region of Belgium acquired controlling interest of both Browning and U.S. Repeating Arms.

For more information and current pricing on both new and used Winchester airguns and current black powder models, please refer to the *Blue Book of Airguns* by Dr. Robert Beeman & John Allen, and the *Blue Book of Modern Black Powder Arms* by John Allen & Dennis Adler (also online).

WINCHESTER OVERVIEW

Note: Winchester Rifles are a field in themselves. Models Henry, 1866, 1873, 1876, 1885, 1886, 1892, 1894, and 1895 were all produced with a multitude of special order options. Special orders included front and rear special sights, half or 2/3 magazines, takedown, various barrel lengths (barrel lengths from 14 to 36 inches could be special ordered for many models), configurations, and weights, special metal finishes, deluxe wood (either checkered or carved) in a variety of finishes, an impressive range of engraving options, different buttplates, etc. All of these special orders act independently and interdependently to determine the correct value of a particular Winchester. Some of the finest rifles ever made are special order Winchesters engraved by the Ulrichs, G. Young, L.D. Nimschke, and others. For these reasons, a Model 92 Winchester can range in price from $200 to over $500,000 - quite a price range for one model alone! When contemplating a purchase on the higher dollar range, qualified and professional opinions should be secured, preferably from at least 2 sources. Unfortunately, many fakes and upgraded (non-original) guns have surfaced in the last 10 years with the sudden increase in prices. Winchesters shown in this section are priced assuming a standard model with no special orders. Any special orders will further add to the prices shown. Caliber rarities must also be considered. Many of the early Winchesters are broken down by year of manufacture. Refer to the "Model Serialization" section in this book.

A factory letter specifying original shipping information by serial number will certainly help solidify values shown on older, out-of-production Winchester rifles and shotguns. A listing has been provided by model number with serialization range which can be historically researched by the Cody Firearms Museum now located in Cody, WY. To use this outstanding service, make sure the model and its serial number fall within the ranges listed. Simply mail in your request for information with serial number, model, and caliber to the Cody Firearms Museum, 720 Sheridan Ave. in Cody, WY, 82414. There is a $45 charge for this service, but this is subject to change, so please contact them directly for the most current rate. Research results will include (if available) specimen caliber, barrel length, any special orders or finishes, return(s) to the factory, as well as any additional provenance information obtained by examining existing factory shipping ledgers. I would recommend a trip to the Buffalo Bill Historical Center, as it contains the most comprehensive collection of projectile arms (including Chinese specimens that date back 2,000 years) and Americana housed under one roof in this country.

With the recent price appreciation on most upper condition Winchester rifles, excellent original condition has become so expensive that the many special order features Winchester offered currently do not cost that much more. However, on lesser condition guns that are much less expensive, these same special order features will cost more proportionally since the condition factor will not produce a premium.

Model 1866 Lever Action Rifle - ser. no. range 125,000-170,101.

Approx. 33 specimens have been researched outside of this ser. no. range.

Model 1873 Lever Action Rifle - ser. no. range 1-720,496.

Approx. 160 specimens have been researched outside of this ser. no. range.

Model 1876 Lever Action Rifle - ser. no. range 1-63,871.

Model 1883 Bolt Action Rifle (Hotchkiss Repeater) - ser. no. range 1-84,555.

May be referred to as Model 1879, 1880, or 1883.

Model 1885 Single Shot Rifle or Shotgun - ser. no. range 1-109,999.

Not available in ser. nos. 74,459-74,556. Also known as High and Low Wall.

Model 1886 Lever Action Rifle - ser. no. range 1-156,599.

Not available in ser. nos. 135,125-135,144 and 146,000-150,799.

Model 1887 & 1901 Lever Action Shotguns - ser. no. range 1-72,999.

Model 1890 Slide Action Rifle - ser. no. range 1-329,999.

Not available in ser. nos. 10,809-10,884, 20,000-29,999, 32,629-32,698, 37,599-37,627, 234,061- 234,140, and 234,142-234,160.

Model 1892 Lever Action Rifle - ser. no. range 1-379,999.

Not available in ser. nos. 374,851-376,100.

Model 1893 Slide Action Shotgun - ser. no. range 1-34,050.

Model 1894 Lever Action Rifle - ser. no. range 1-353,999.

Model 1895 Lever Action Rifle - ser. no. range 1-59,999.

Model "Lee" Bolt Action Rifle - ser. no. range 1-19,999.

Model 1897 Slide Action Shotgun - ser. no. range 34,051-377,999.

Model 1903 Semi-Auto .22 Cal. Rifle - ser. no. range 1-39,999.

Model 1905 Semi-Auto Rifle - ser. no. range 1-29,078.

Model 1906 Semi-Auto Rifle - ser. no. range 1-79,999.

Model 1907 Semi-Auto Rifle - ser. no. range 1-9,999.

Winchester factory data on models produced between approx. 1907-1961 is almost non-existent (except Custom Shop mfg.) since there was a fire at the Winchester factory in 1961.

A NOTE ON WINCHESTER FINISHES: It is very important to understand that there is a big value difference between a Model 1873 with 90% bright blue as opposed to a gun that has patina finish (turning brown). A bright blue specimen might bring several times more, because it is closer to the way it originally left the factory - with bright bluing. "Brown" guns are simply not as desirable as guns that show little or no use and retain bright blue finish.

GRADING EXPLANATION FOR WINCHESTER LEVER ACTIONS

A combination of grading systems is being used exclusively for Winchester Models Henry, 1873, and 1876 in this section to assist the reader in ascertaining the value of a particular specimen more accurately. They work as follows - the top line contains three value ranges (Above Average, Average, or Below Average) which have been created to encompass most of the specimens commonly encountered within this model.

Since there is a drastic value difference between 95%-50% bright blue and 30% dull patina/fading finish on older Winchesters, another grading/pricing line has been included to give you an

Above Average	Average	Below Average

example of the top end of the marketplace. Individual percentages of condition with corresponding values are listed here to give you a complete price range on older Winchester lever actions. While no grading system is perfect, it is hoped that this combination of pricing systems will be an advantage over previous attempts.

The three groupings include "Below Average Price Range," "Average Price Range," and "Above Average Price Range" (note the new grading line underneath specifying these condition factors). These ranges indicate the following:

BELOW AVERAGE PRICE RANGE - a specimen with no finish remaining, perhaps some parts have been replaced, deteriorated metal may be lightly pitted with faint barrel/frame markings, rounded edges of wood and metal, wood showing much wear with possible repairs or cracks, must be in working order.

AVERAGE PRICE RANGE - a specimen with all original parts, exhibits gun metal patina finish, metal mostly smooth (perhaps lightly pitted), principal lettering and markings legible throughout, wood showing honest wear with little finish remaining (may have small cracks and other imperfections), good working order.

ABOVE AVERAGE PRICE RANGE - a specimen featuring unpolished brass (on Henrys and Model 1866s) or plum brown patina with traces of bluing in protected areas (on all steel frame models), sharp corners, crisp barrel markings, traces of original finish remaining, metal should exhibit nice patina or older flaking finish, wood should have some original stock varnish remaining and minor handling marks and dings, good bore, perfect working order with no replacement parts.

VALUES FOR ABOVE AVERAGE CONDITION RANGE - this includes those specimens which are 50% bright blue or better condition - When this type of condition is encountered, refer to the grading/price line listing individual percentage of condition prices located underneath the Above Average, Average, or Below Average pricing line. You may notice a gap in prices between the Above Average high price and 50% price. This is normal, because in some cases, a rare 50% bright blue/bright brass specimen will be worth considerably more than one in Above Average condition.

PISTOLS: SINGLE SHOT

SINGLE SHOT PISTOL - .22 LR cal., bolt action, walnut, brass, or pot metal grips, 9 in. barrel with open sights, no two are exactly alike, and quality can run from very good to crude, ser. nos. under 20.

Prices on this model typically range from $3,250-$3,750, depending on original condition.

RIFLES: LEVER ACTIONS - 1860-1964

For the following lever action rifles, multiple special order features that add value are not cumulative (i.e., do not add 30% for an octagon barrel to a Deluxe rifle).

HENRY RIFLE - .44 rimfire, 15 shot, 24 in. barrel with integral slotted tube mag. and loading lever, blue barrel, brass or iron frame. Approx. 13,000 total production, mfg. 1860-1866.

Because almost all Henrys have little or no original finish left, values below are in ranges rather than in separate condition factors.

Add 25%+ for engraving, depending on amount and condition (these specimens should have fancy wood).

* **Iron Frame Model** - frame made of iron, round type buttplate, without lever latch, adj. sporting type rear leaf sight, serial numbers are in three digits only. Total production is believed to be less than 300.

$45,000 - $55,000	$30,000 - $35,000	$20,000 - $25,000

* **First Model** - approx. 3,500 mfg., generally serialized below 3,500, with or without lever latch, perch belly stock and slotted receiver for rear sight.

$20,000 - $25,000	$14,000 - $18,000	$8,000 - $12,000

* **Martial Marked** - contracted by U.S. military for Civil War use, denoted by "C.G.C." inspector markings on upper barrel breech and stock, approx. 1,900 with serialization scattered.

$25,000 - $35,000	$18,000 - $22,000	$12,000 - $15,000

This rifle was the most revolutionary shoulder weapon introduced in the Civil War.

Above Average	Average	Below Average

* **Late Model** - similar to first model, except buttplate heel has pointed profile, lever latch became standard and receiver is not slotted for rear sight, serial numbers over approx. 3,500, most commonly encountered Henry with approx. 8,000 mfg.

$12,000 - $18,000	$9,000 - $12,000	$6,000 - $9,000

MODEL 1866 LEVER ACTION - .44 rimfire or centerfire (4th Model only), 24 in. barrel, blue barrel with brass frame, differs from Henry in that it has a wood forearm, frame cartridge loading port, and separate tube mag. Total production reached 170,101 for all models, mfg. 1866-98.

* **Model 1866 First Model Rifle** - "Improved Henry" action, .44 cal. rimfire, without forend cap, serialization is concealed on lower tang inside buttstock, serial range is from mid-12,000 to mid-15,000 (in Henry serial range sequence).

$11,000 - $14,000	$8,000 - $11,000	$6,000 - $8,000
95% = $25,000	75% = $20,000	50% = $16,000

Buyer beware - watch for fakes!

* **Model 1866 Carbine First Model** - same action as Rifle, only with 20 in. barrel, 2 barrel bands and saddle ring.

$5,000 - $7,000	$3,000 - $5,000	$2,500 - $3,000
95% = $20,000	75% = $17,000	50% = $8,000

* **Model 1866 Rifle Second Model** - "New Model" with redesigned frame, with Henry barrel markings, serial number inside on the earlier guns after ser. no. 19,000, outside lower tang beneath lever (approx. after ser. no. 20,000).

$4,500 - $6,500	$3,000 - $4,500	$2,000 - $3,000
95% = $15,000	75% = $10,000	50% = $8,000

* **Model 1866 Carbine Second Model** - frame and other changes similar to Second Model Rifle.

$3,000 - $4,500	$2,000 - $3,000	$1,250 - $2,000
95% = $12,500	75% = $8,500	50% = $5,500

* **Model 1866 Rifle Third Model** - block style serial numbers usually located behind trigger, improved frame. Serial numbered approx. 25,000-149,000.

$3,500 - $4,750	$2,500 - $3,500	$1,500 - $2,500
95% = $10,000	75% = $8,000	50% = $6,500

* **Model 1866 Carbine Third Model** - same changes as Model 1866 Third Model Rifle, 20 in. barrel with 2 bands.

$2,500 - $3,750	$1,750 - $2,500	$1,250 - $1,750
95% = $8,500	75% = $7,000	50% = $5,000

* **Model 1866 Musket Third Model** - 27 in. round barrel, 24 in. magazine, 3 barrel bands.

$2,500 - $3,500	$1,750 - $2,500	$1,250 - $1,750
95% = $8,000	75% = $6,000	50% = $4,600

* **Model 1866 Rifle/Carbine/Musket Fourth Model** - .44 cal., twin rimfire and centerfire, script style serial number on lower tang near lever latch, improved frame, serial range approx. 149,000-170,101.

Values for these models are the same as for equivalent Third Model 1866s.

Subtract 20% for steel buttplate and forend cap on rifle.

This rifle is usually found with steel buttplate and forend cap.

MODEL 1873 LEVER ACTION - .32-20 WCF, .38-40 WCF, or .44-40 WCF cal., iron frame with sideplates, frame loading port, 20 or 24 in. round or octagon barrel, rifles have forearm caps and carbines have forearm bands, tube mag., blue finish with case hardened parts, oil finished stock, serial numbered on lower tang, 720,610 mfg. between 1873-1919.

Since early Model 1873s were only made in .44 cal., no caliber markings are present. After the introduction of additional calibers, the barrels were stamped just in front of the receiver and on the brass elevator with the caliber.

Model 1873s are serial numbered sequentially on the lower tang. On guns serial numbered 80,000 to 170,000, an "A" followed the number. From 170,000 to 190,000, either "A" or "B" may be found, while after 200,000, usually "B" was used. The letter does not seem to have any def-

Above Average	Average	Below Average

inite meaning. The earliest guns had no marking on the upper tang, but were marked "Model 1873" on the lower tang next to the ser. no. up to number 350, after which "Model 1873" is marked on the upper tang, where it remained through the model run.

Add 50%-75% for Deluxe Model 1873 with color case hardened frame, depending on original condition.

✳ *Model 1873 First Model Rifle* - serial numbers approx. 1-30,000, sliding thumbprint dust cover on 2 guides that are integral part of upper frame, absence of any cal. marking.

$1,950 - $2,500	$1,300 - $1,950	$700 - $1,300
95% = $11,000	75% = $6,000	50% = $3,500

✳ *Model 1873 Carbine First Model* - 20 in. round barrel with carbine style forearm band. Distinctive curved buttplate, with saddle ring.

$2,100 - $2,650	$1,500 - $2,100	$800 - $1,500
95% = $13,000	75% = $7,500	50% = $4,000

✳ *Model 1873 Musket First Model* - 30 in. round barrel, 27 in. mag. with 3 barrel bands, approx. 500 mfg.

$2,500 - $3,500	$2,000 - $2,500	$1,000 - $2,000
95% = $8,000	75% = $5,500	50% = $4,000

✳ *Model 1873 Rifle Second Model* - improved dust cover featuring slides on center rail on rear section of frame top which is held in place by two screws, serial range 31,000-90,000.

$1,000 - $1,500	$800 - $1,000	$400 - $800
95% = $4,500	75% = $3,500	50% = $2,500

✳ *Model 1873 Carbine Second Model* - changes similar to 1873 Second Model Rifle, with 20 in. round barrel and 2 barrel bands.

$1,000 - $1,500	$700 - $1,000	$300 - $700
95% = $8,500	75% = $5,500	50% = $4,000

✳ *Model 1873 Musket Second Model* - changes similar to 1873 Second Model Rifle, with 30 in. barrel and 3 barrel bands.

$1,200 - $1,500	$800 - $1,200	$400 - $800
95% = $3,650	75% = $2,750	50% = $1,875

✳ *Model 1873 Rifle Third Model* - dust cover rail integral with frame, serial 90,000-end of production.

$1,300 - $1,600	$800 - $1,300	$600 - $900
95% = $4,500	75% = $3,500	50% = $2,500

Add 20% for .44-40 WCF cal.

Add 30% for octagon barrel for .44-40 WCF cal. only.

✳ *Model 1873 Carbine Third Model* - changes similar to 1873 Rifle Third Model, with 20 in. barrel and 2 barrel bands.

$1,000 - $1,300	$800 - $1,000	$500 - $800
95% = $6,000	75% = $4,500	50% = $2,500

Add 10% for .32-20 WCF cal.

✳ *Model 1873 Musket Third Model* - 30 in. round barrel and 3 barrel bands.

$800 - $1,000	$600 - $800	$400 - $600
95% = $3,400	75% = $2,500	50% = $1,925

✳ *Model 1873 .22 Rimfire Rifle* - .22 S, L, or Extra L (very rare) cal., 24 in. barrel, no loading gate, the first .22 caliber repeater, 19,552 produced, mfg. 1884-1904. Made in rifle configuration only.

$900 - $1,200	$700 - $900	$500 - $700
95% = $6,000	75% = $4,000	50% = $2,250

Add 30% for takedown model.

The takedown mechanism is unique in that a pin is driven out of the receiver, and is very prone to wear.

Above Average	Average	Below Average

❋ **Model 1873 "One of One Thousand "** - special care taken in manufacture to guarantee better accuracy, markings on top of breech designate model, deluxe walnut, extremely rare, barrel marked "One of One Thousand" in most cases, 136 mfg. Original cost was $100.

Values can range from $30,000 - $200,000, depending on condition. A factory letter is a must for any "One of One Thousand" Winchester. Watch for fake letters.

Note: Rarity of the "One of One Thousand" and the "One of One Hundred" models makes upgrading to this model fairly common. Use extreme caution in purchasing.

❋ **Model 1873 "One of One Hundred "** - similar to "One of One Thousand" only rarer, 8 mfg. Sold new for $20 over the list price of a similarly equipped Model 1873.

Values can range from $40,000 - $225,000, depending on condition. A factory letter is a must for any "One of One Hundred" Winchester. Watch for fake letters.

MODEL 1876 LEVER ACTION
- .40-60 WCF, .45-60 WCF, .45-75 WCF(first caliber offered), or .50-95 Express cal., 22, 26, or 28 in. round or octagon barrel, similar but larger frame than Model 1873, tube mag., rifles have forearm caps while carbines have forearm bands, crescent butt, blue finish, straight grip stock, 63,871 mfg. between 1876-97.

The Model 1876 was also called the Centennial Model since its introduction coincided with the U.S. Centennial Exposition held in Philadelphia, PA in 1876. Popularity for this model decreased ten years later when the more powerful and advanced Model 1886 was introduced.

Add 50% for Deluxe Model 1876s with color case hardened frames to the values listed. Deluxe Models 1876 with 90%+ original case colors are rare.

❋ **Model 1876 Rifle First Model** - serial numbered approx. 1-5,000, distinguishable by no dust cover on frame top.

$2,000 - $2,500	$1,500 - $2,000	$1,000 - $1,500
95% = $10,000	75% = $7,500	50% = $5,000

❋ **Model 1876 Carbine First Model** - 22 in. round barrel, one barrel band, saddle ring, full-length forearm giving a musket appearance.

$2,500 - $3,500	$1,500 - $2,500	$1,000 - $1,500
95% = $12,500	75% = $9,500	50% = $6,000

❋ **Model 1876 Musket First Model** - 32 in. round barrel with 1 band, scarce model because no foreign military contracts.

$4,500 - $6,000	$3,000 - $4,500	$2,000 - $3,000
95% = $17,500	75% = $12,500	50% = $7,500

❋ **Model 1876 Rifle Second Model** - "Thumbprint" dust cover rail held on by screw, serial range 5,000-30,000.

$1,500 - $2,000	$1,200 - $1,500	$800 - $1,200
95% = $6,500	75% = $5,000	50% = $3,000

Add 35% for .50-95 WCF cal.

❋ **Model 1876 Carbine Second Model** - changes similar to Model 1876 Rifle Early Second Model, with 22 in. round barrel and full length forearm giving a musket appearance.

$1,800 - $2,950	$1,200 - $1,800	$900 - $1,200
95% = $10,000	75% = $6,250	50% = $4,000

❋ **Model 1876 Musket Second Model** - changes similar to Model 1876 Rifle Early Second Model, with 32 in. round barrel and carbine forend tip.

$3,500 - $5,500	$2,500 - $3,500	$1,500 - $2,500
95% = $13,000	75% = $9,000	50% = $7,500

❋ **Model 1876 Rifle Third Model** - dust cover rail integral with frame, serial range 30,000-end of production.

$1,500 - $2,000	$1,000 - $1,500	$700 - $1,000
95% = $6,500	75% = $4,000	50% = $2,500

Add 25% for .50-95 WCF cal.

Above Average	Average	Below Average

* **Model 1876 Carbine Third Model** - frame similar to Model 1876 Rifle Third Model, with 22 in. round barrel and full-length forearm giving a musket appearance.

$1,500 - $2,500	$1,100 - $1,500	$800 - $1,100
95% = $8,500	75% = $6,500	50% = $3,500

* **Model 1876 Musket Third Model** - frame similar to Model 1876 Rifle Third Model, with 32 in. round barrel.

$3,250 - $5,000	$2,250 - $3,250	$1,500 - $2,250
95% = $13,000	75% = $9,000	50% = $7,500

* **Model 1876 "One of One Thousand"** - special care taken in manufacture to guarantee better accuracy, markings on top of breech designate model, deluxe walnut, extremely rare, 54 mfg. Original cost was $100.

Values can range from $35,000 - $250,000, depending on condition. A factory letter is a must for any "One of One Thousand" Winchester. Watch for fake letters.

Values are not listed because too few original specimens are bought or sold to accurately establish pricing. A factory letter is a must for any "One of One Thousand" Winchester.

Note: Rarity of the "One of One Thousand" and the "One of One Hundred" models makes unethical upgrading to this model fairly common. Use extreme caution in purchasing.

* **Model 1876 "One of One Hundred"** - similar to "One of One Thousand" only rarer, 8 mfg. Sold new for $20 over the list price of a similarly equipped Model 1876.

Values can range from $45,000 - $500,000, depending on condition. A factory letter is a must for any "One of One Hundred" Winchester. Believe it or not, watch for fake letters.

Values are not listed because too few original specimens are bought or sold to accurately establish pricing. A factory letter is a must for any "One of One Hundred" Winchester.

* **Model 1876 Northwest Mounted Police Carbine** - .45-75 WCF cal. only, 22 in. barrel, "NWMP" or "MP" marking may appear on stock (with wear, this cartouche may not be visible - the majority were not marked) approx. 1,600 mfg., factory records can only verify 150.

$5,000 - $6,000	$4,000 - $5,000	$3,000 - $4,000
95% = $15,000	75% = $10,000	50% = $6,000

Above average specimens in this model should have traces of blue. Be very wary of the stock cartouche since these buttstocks were sold as surplus back in the 1920s. A letter of authenticity is a good idea on this model.

MODEL 1886 LEVER ACTION - .33 WCF, .38-56 WCF, .38-70 WCF (830 mfg.), .40-65 WCF, .40-70 WCF (629 mfg.), .40-82 WCF, .45-70 Govt., .45-90, .50-110 Express, or .50-100-450 (234 mfg.) cal. available, Browning's first high power lever action design distinguishable by vertical locking bars, .45-70 Govt. most popular cal., 26 in. round or octagon barrel, tube mag., steel forend cap, straight grip stock. Approx. 159,990 mfg. between 1886-1935.

The Model 1886 had case hardening standard on the frame, buttplate, and forend cap until 1901 (approx. 122,000 serial range) when the standard finish became blue.

On the Model 1886 variations listed, add the following percentages for special order features.

Add 20% for octagon barrel.

Add 25% for octagon barrel with takedown.

Add 20% for .45-70 Govt. or .45-90 cal.

Add 100% for .50-110 or 200% for .50-100-450 cal.

Add 100% for case colored receivers on standard guns only (pre-1902 mfg.).

Add 200% for Deluxe Model (pistol grip checkered walnut stock and case colored receiver).

100%	98%	95%	90%	80%	70%	60%	50%	40%	30%	20%	10%

* **Model 1886 Rifle**

100%	98%	95%	90%	80%	70%	60%	50%	40%	30%	20%	10%
N/A	N/A	$5,500	$5,000	$4,500	$3,950	$3,250	$2,250	$1,850	$1,550	$1,250	$850

100%	98%	95%	90%	80%	70%	60%	50%	40%	30%	20%	10%

✱ *Model 1886 Carbine* - same general specifications as Rifle, except 22 in. round barrel and saddle ring, solid frame only.

N/A	N/A	$15,000	$12,000	$9,950	$7,750	$6,350	$5,000	$3,750	$2,500	$2,000	$1,450

Add 40% for full stock carbine (very rare).

✱ *Model 1886 Musket* - 30 in. round barrel, full-length military style forearm, military sights, only 350 mfg., very rare.

N/A	N/A	$17,000	$15,000	$12,000	$9,950	$7,750	$6,350	$5,000	$3,950	$3,250	$2,500

Most specimens encountered in this variation are in very good condition - a pitted musket is almost never encountered.

✱ *Model 1886 Lightweight Rifle* - .45-70 Govt. or .33 WCF cal. only, 22 (.45-70 Govt. cal.) or 24 (.33 WCF cal.) in. round nickel steel tapered barrel, half mag., rubber shotgun buttplate.

✱ *.33 caliber*

N/A	N/A	$4,500	$4,000	$3,200	$2,600	$2,200	$1,800	$1,500	$1,250	$1,000	$600

✱ *.45-70 Govt. caliber*

N/A	N/A	$5,500	$5,000	$4,550	$3,750	$3,300	$2,975	$2,650	$2,300	$1,850	$1,450

Since lightweight rifles were fairly late production, all specimens are blue and in very good condition usually.

MODEL 1892 RIFLE

.25-20 WCF, .32-20 WCF, .38-40 WCF, or .44-40 WCF cal., 24 in. round or octagon barrel, blue, tube mag., forend cap, crescent butt. Mfg. 1,004,067 between 1892-1941.

N/A	N/A	$2,500	$2,000	$1,500	$1,300	$1,000	$900	$750	$600	$500	$400

Add 50% for .44-40 WCF cal.

Add 15% for .38-40 WCF cal.

Add 25% for Takedown Model.

Add 200% for fancy pistol grip checkered wood (Deluxe Model).

Add 30% for early antique ser. no. range under 168,000.

A short rifle configuration was also available in this model with special order short barrels under 16 inches, 14 in. being the rarest. These guns are very rare (most went to South America) and prices typically range $2,750-$8,000, depending on original condition.

MODEL 1892 CARBINE

20 in. round barrel, 2 barrel bands and saddle ring.

N/A	N/A	$2,750	$2,000	$1,600	$1,250	$1,050	$875	$775	$675	$550	$450

Add 40% for .44-40 WCF cal. or 15% for .38-40 WCF cal.

MODEL 1892 TRAPPER'S CARBINE

all features similar to standard SRC, except has a 14, 15, or 16 in. barrel, so called Trapper's Model because it was handy for trappers who had to carry a powerful but lightweight repeating rifle.

N/A	N/A	$8,000	$7,000	$5,500	$4,550	$3,650	$3,150	$2,550	$1,925	$1,550	$1,000

Most 1892 Trapper's Carbines are in the 15 in., .44-40 WCF cal. configuration. Most of the 1892 Trapper's Carbine were shipped to South America or Australia. This variation is almost never encountered over 30% condition - most are brown guns. Check federal laws regarding 14 and 15 inch barrels.

MODEL 1892 MUSKET

30 in. round barrel, full length military style forearm with military style rear sight.

N/A	N/A	$15,000	$13,500	$11,000	$9,250	$8,100	$7,000	$5,750	$4,350	$3,150	$2,000

MODEL 1894 RIFLE

.25-35 WCF, .30-30 Win. (.30 WCF), .32-40 WCF, .32 Spl., or .38-55 WCF cal., most common (and popular) is .30-30 Win. cal., tube mag., 24 or 26 in. round or octagon barrel was standard, blue, straight grip stock, Model 1894 nomenclature changed to Model 94 circa 1924-1936 between ser. range 990,000-1,100,000. Over 5,000,000 produced to date, mfg. 1894-1929, newer Model 94 mfg. may be found in the RIFLES: MODEL 94 LEVER ACTION - POST 1964 PRODUCTION section.

100%	98%	95%	90%	80%	70%	60%	50%	40%	30%	20%	10%

✳ *1894-1929 Mfg.* - Model 94s built post 1894-1929.

N/A	$1,950	$1,675	$1,350	$1,150	$925	$850	$675	$575	$500	$425	$350

Add 20% for takedown variation.

Add 30%-60% for deluxe models, depending on original condition.

Add 30% for 1894-1898 antique mfg. (pre-148,000 ser. no.).

Add approx. 20% for cals. other than .30-30 Win. or .32 Spl.

The Model 1894 Winchester has the distinction of being the world's most popular rifle. Deluxe models will command substantial premiums on models listed.

MODEL 1894 TRAPPER'S CARBINE - all features similar to the standard SRC, except with a 14, 15, or 16 in. barrel.

N/A	N/A	$6,500	$5,750	$4,650	$4,000	$3,400	$2,750	$2,150	$1,650	$1,350	$1,000

The large majority of this variation are encountered in .30-30 Win. cal. with 15 in. barrel. Any other caliber or barrel length will create a premium. Most of these carbines are brown and rusty. Rarely, if ever, encountered with very much finish remaining.

Note: Check federal laws on legality of 14 and 15 in. barrels.

MODEL 1894 SADDLE RING CARBINE - 20 in. round barrel.

N/A	N/A	$1,750	$1,500	$1,250	$975	$850	$750	$625	$500	$400	$350

Add 40% for 1894-1898 antique mfg. (pre-148,000 ser. no.).

Add 40% for any cal. other than .30-30 Win. or .32 Spl.

Carbines with special order features such as pistol grip, deluxe wood, checkering, etc. can bring even greater premiums than the rifle.

✳ *Eastern Carbine* - features long forearm, early stock design, early style carbine post front sight, and without saddle ring, mfg. late 1920s-early 1930s.

N/A	N/A	$1,350	$1,200	$975	$875	$775	$650	$550	$500	$450	$400

MODEL 1894 1940-1964 PRODUCTION CARBINE - 1940-1964 mfg. without saddle ring, barrel is marked Model 94.

$500	$450	$415	$385	$350	$300	$275	$250	$220	$195	$180	$165

Add 50% for .25-35 WCF cal.

Some WWII carbines with special U.S. markings will bring a premium over prices listed.

MODEL 1895 RIFLE FLATSIDE - .30 US (most common), .38-72, or .40-72 cal., early model, distinguishable in that frame does not have fluting or ridge contouring, serial range approx. 1-5000.

N/A	N/A	$4,400	$4,000	$3,600	$3,150	$2,750	$2,350	$1,925	$1,450	$1,000	$750

Add 25% for octagon barrel on cals. .38-72 or .40-72.

MODEL 1895 RIFLE - .30-03, .30-06, .30-40 Krag, .303 Brit., .35 Win., .38-72, .40-72, .405 Win., or 7.62mm Russian cal., 24-28 in. barrel, blue action, box mag., straight grip stock, 425,881 mfg. from 1896-1931.

N/A	N/A	$4,000	$3,600	$3,150	$2,750	$2,350	$1,925	$1,450	$1,000	$750	$500

Add 50%-150% for Deluxe Models, depending on condition.

Add 25% for octagon barrel.

Add 30% for .405 Win. cal.

Add 15% for takedown model.

The Model 1895 was a Browning design incorporating the first box type mag. in a lever action repeating rifle. .30 US is the most commonly encountered cal. in this model. A large Russian military contract was secured in 1915 with chambering for the 7.62mm Russian cartridge (over 293,000 mfg. or over 66% of total production).

MODEL 1895 CARBINE - .30 US (.30/40 Krag Army - most common cal.), .30-03, .30-06, or .303 Brit. cal., 22 in. round barrel, military style top handguard wood and military sights, with or without saddle ring.

N/A	N/A	$3,500	$3,150	$2,750	$2,450	$2,000	$1,650	$1,250	$900	$750	$525

Add 20% for caliber other than .30 U.S.

Add 50% for U.S. government marked.

100%	98%	95%	90%	80%	70%	60%	50%	40%	30%	20%	10%

MODEL 1895 FLATSIDE MUSKET - early models have serial range under 5,000, no flutes on frame, .30-40 Krag only.

Rarity on this model means only a few specimens in several museums.

MODEL 1895 MUSKET - .30-03, .30-06, or .30-40 Krag cal., 28 in. round barrel with hand guard over barrel, military sights.

100%	98%	95%	90%	80%	70%	60%	50%	40%	30%	20%	10%
N/A	N/A	$4,500	$4,000	$3,600	$3,150	$2,750	$2,350	$1,925	$1,450	$1,000	$750

Add 10%-15% if U.S. Govt. marked.

MODEL 1895 NRA MUSKET - .30-03, .30-06, or .30-40 Krag cal., similar to Standard Musket grade with 24 or 30 in. barrel, 1901 Krag style rear sight. NRA approved for official NRA competition.

100%	98%	95%	90%	80%	70%	60%	50%	40%	30%	20%	10%
N/A	N/A	$4,000	$3,600	$3,150	$2,775	$2,400	$2,000	$1,650	$1,275	$1,050	$800

Add 30% if U.S. government marked.

MODEL 1895 RUSSIAN MUSKET - 7.62mm Russian cal., over 293,000 mfg. for Imperial Russian Govt., mfg. 1915-16, various Russian Ordnance stamps should be present.

100%	98%	95%	90%	80%	70%	60%	50%	40%	30%	20%	10%
N/A	N/A	$3,250	$2,800	$2,400	$2,075	$1,650	$1,350	$1,075	$900	$750	$550

MODEL 53 RIFLE - .25-20 WCF, .32-20 WCF, or .44-40 WCF cal., 22 in. round barrel, 1/2 tube mag. holding 6 cartridges, solid frame or takedown, blue finish, pistol grip or straight grip stock, serial numbered both separately and within the Model 92 range. Mfg. 24,916 between 1924-32.

100%	98%	95%	90%	80%	70%	60%	50%	40%	30%	20%	10%
N/A	N/A	$1,850	$1,650	$1,450	$1,225	$1,075	$850	$675	$550	$475	$350

Add 30% for .44-40 WCF cal.

Add 20% for Takedown Model.

MODEL 55 RIFLE - .25-35 WCF, .30-30 Win., or .32 Win. Spl. cal., lever action design, solid frame and takedown, 24 in. round barrel, shotgun style buttstock with serrated steel buttplate, tube mag., holds 3 cartridges. Approx. 20,500 mfg. between 1924-1932. Serial numbered independently to approx. 2,865, then serialized with Model 1894 production on underside of receiver. Simply could not compete with the Model 1894.

100%	98%	95%	90%	80%	70%	60%	50%	40%	30%	20%	10%
N/A	$1,875	$1,500	$1,275	$1,150	$1,025	$900	$775	$650	$525	$425	$350

Add 75% for .25-35 WCF cal.

Add 100% for Deluxe Model.

Add 10% for Takedown Model.

MODEL 64 RIFLE - .219 Zipper, .25-35 WCF, .30-30 Win., or .32 Win. Spl. cal., 20 or 24 in. round barrel, with standard 26 in. on the .219 Zipper, blue metal, pistol grip stock, revamped Model 55 action with increased mag. capacity, 66,783 mfg. between 1933-1957 and 1972-73 (over 8,250 mfg. in .30-30 Win. cal. only - these last two years with minor changes).

100%	98%	95%	90%	80%	70%	60%	50%	40%	30%	20%	10%
N/A	$850	$700	$650	$600	$550	$500	$450	$400	$350	$300	$250

Add 30% for Deluxe Model, depending on condition.

Add 60% for 20 in. barrel (sometime referred to as Carbine).

Add 150% for .25-35 WCF cal.

Add 250% for .219 Zipper cal.

Many of this variation now have extra holes drilled on the top of the receiver to accept scope mounts - subtract 50% for this alteration. The Model 64 is usually found in excellent condition. Model 64 1972-73 mfg. may be found in the post-'64 section.

MODEL 65 RIFLE - .218 Bee (introduced 1939), .25-20 WCF, or .32-20 WCF cal., 22 in. round barrel (except .218 Bee - 24 in.), 1/2 tube mag. holding 7 cartridges, blue with pistol grip stock. Mfg. 5704 between 1933-47.

100%	98%	95%	90%	80%	70%	60%	50%	40%	30%	20%	10%
N/A	N/A	$3,600	$3,250	$2,850	$2,475	$2,100	$1,800	$1,500	$1,250	$1,000	$875

While the .25-20 WCF cal. is the rarest, the .218 Bee has the most demand.

100%	98%	95%	90%	80%	70%	60%	50%	40%	30%	20%	10%

The Model 65 was a design evolved from the Model 53. The Model 65 was not tapped on receiver side for scope mounts. As a rule, most specimens are in either pretty nice or refinished condition.

MODEL 71 RIFLE STANDARD - .348 Win. cal., 2/3 tube mag. holding 4 cartridges, improved Model 1886 frame, blue metal with pistol grip stock, 20 or 24 in. barrel, short or long tang. Mfg. 47,254 between 1935-57.

N/A	$1,100	$1,000	$900	$800	$700	$650	$600	$550	$500	$475	$450

Add 30%-40% for early variation long tang, depending on condition.
Add 50% for Deluxe Model, depending on condition.
Add 60% for short rifle with 20 in. barrel.

MODEL 88 RIFLE AND CARBINE - see listing under RIFLES: LEVER ACTION - POST-1964 PRODUCTION section.

RIFLES: SINGLE SHOT

MODEL 1885 - available in most popular cals. between .22-.50, falling block trigger guard activated action, John Browning's first high power single shot rifle design, many variations were made and we will list the standard types. Over 139,725 mfg. between 1885-1920.

This design was originally mfg. as the Model 1878 by the Browning Brothers in Ogden, UT, in the early 1880s. Fewer than 600 were mfg. - see the Browning section for values.

❋ *Sporting Rifle Low Wall* - 24 or 26 in. round or octagon barrel was standard, open sights, solid frame, standard trigger.

N/A	N/A	$1,400	$1,275	$1,100	$995	$875	$750	$625	$500	$350	$200

Add 20% for centerfire cal.
Add 30% for case colored frames, if in 95%+ original condition.

❋ *Sporting Rifle High Wall* - 30 in. barrel, standard trigger, open sights, solid frame. Available in various size and weight barrels numbered (in front of forearm) from lightest to heaviest: 1, 2, 3, 3 1/2 (introduced 1910), 4, and 5. Case hardened frames standard until 1901 when bluing became standard, three different frames depending on caliber. Heavier barrels in rare calibers will bring a premium.

N/A	N/A	$3,000	$2,650	$2,375	$2,100	$1,850	$1,625	$1,400	$1,250	$1,000	$800

Add 25% for 20 ga. shotgun.
Add 30% for Takedown Model.
Add 25% for No. 5 barrel.
Add 40% for Deluxe Model with case colored receiver, if in 95%+ original condition.
Add 10% for set trigger.

❋ *Schuetzen Rifle* - high wall, 30 in. octagon barrel, double-set triggers, spur lever, aperture sight, Schuetzen style stock, adj. palm rest and buttplate.

N/A	N/A	$5,500	$5,000	$4,650	$4,250	$3,800	$3,450	$3,125	$2,675	$2,250	$1,875

Add 20% for Takedown frame.
Add 30% for case colored frame, if in 95%+ original condition.

Prices are for factory original guns only. Since this model had many shooting alterations performed by various aftermarket suppliers of its time, perhaps only 10% of remaining specimens are unaltered (or 100% factory).

❋ *High Wall Musket* - usually found in .22 LR cal.

N/A	N/A	$1,400	$1,275	$1,100	$975	$850	$750	$650	$550	$475	$400

Add 50% for .45-70 Govt. or .45-90 cal.

❋ *Low Wall Musket (Winder Musket)* - low wall, 3rd model, .22 Short or LR (most common), 28 in. barrel, standard trigger and lever, military style stock and sights, grooved forearm, one barrel band.

N/A	N/A	$875	$800	$725	$675	$600	$525	$450	$375	$300	$250

100%	98%	95%	90%	80%	70%	60%	50%	40%	30%	20%	10%

MODEL 1885 (RECENT MFG.) - please refer to the RIFLES: SINGLE SHOT, POST 1964 MFG. section for these listings.

MODEL 1900 SINGLE SHOT - .22 S and L cal., 18 in. round barrel, blue metal, open sights, one-piece straight grip gumwood stock without fitted buttplate, takedown, not serial numbered. Approx. 105,000 mfg. between 1899-1902.

100%	98%	95%	90%	80%	70%	60%	50%	40%	30%	20%	10%
N/A	N/A	$900	$700	$525	$350	$275	$200	$165	$145	$125	$110

Add 100% for later models marked M1900 on barrel, and Win. stamped butt.
This model is usually encountered with flaked frames.

MODEL 1902 SINGLE SHOT - similar to 1900, with minor improvements. Distinguishable by specially shaped extended trigger guard. Not serial numbered. Approx. 640,299 mfg. between 1902-1931.

100%	98%	95%	90%	80%	70%	60%	50%	40%	30%	20%	10%
N/A	$450	$275	$200	$150	$120	$100	$90	$80	$75	$65	$60

Chambering included .22 cal. Extra Long in 1914 (interchangeable with S&L).

THUMB TRIGGER MODEL 99 - similar to 1902, with button behind cocking piece used to fire with thumb instead of trigger, not serial numbered. Approx. 75,433 were mfg. between 1904-23.

100%	98%	95%	90%	80%	70%	60%	50%	40%	30%	20%	10%
N/A	$2,000	$1,750	$1,500	$1,200	$1,000	$800	$700	$600	$400	$350	$300

MODEL 1904 SINGLE SHOT - improved version of 1902, 21 in. round barrel, chambering included .22 Extra Long in 1914, not serial numbered. Approx. 302,859 mfg. between 1904-31.

100%	98%	95%	90%	80%	70%	60%	50%	40%	30%	20%	10%
N/A	$400	$350	$300	$200	$175	$160	$150	$125	$100	$90	$80

✳ *Model 1904-A* - introduced 1927 with new sear bar and chambered for .22 LR.

100%	98%	95%	90%	80%	70%	60%	50%	40%	30%	20%	10%
N/A	$400	$275	$225	$200	$175	$160	$150	$125	$100	$90	$80

MODEL 47 - .22 S, L, or LR cal., single shot bolt action, 25 in. round barrel, unique bolt design, uncheckered walnut stock, 5 1/4 lbs., approx. 43,000 (not serial numbered) mfg. during 1948-54.

100%	98%	95%	90%	80%	70%	60%	50%	40%	30%	20%	10%
$300	$250	$200	$180	$150	$140	$130	$125	$120	$115	$110	$100

MODEL 52 - please refer to listings in the Rifles: Bolt Action section.

MODEL 55 - .22 cal. only, top loading single shot, bottom ejection, 22 in. round barrel, open sporting sights, not serial numbered. Over 45,000 mfg. between 1958-61.

100%	98%	95%	90%	80%	70%	60%	50%	40%	30%	20%	10%
$175	$135	$125	$115	$105	$95	$85	$75	$70	$65	$60	$60

GRADING - PPGS™

100%	98%	95%	90%	80%	70%	60%

MODEL 58 SINGLE SHOT - similar to Models 1902 and 1904, .22 LR cal., 18 in. round barrel, open sights, takedown. Approx. 38,992 mfg. between 1928-31.

100%	98%	95%	90%	80%	70%	60%
$800	$700	$600	$500	$250	$200	$150

MODEL 59 SINGLE SHOT - improved Model 58 with 23 in. round barrel and pistol grip stock with buttplate. Approx. 9,200 mfg. between 1930-31.

100%	98%	95%	90%	80%	70%	60%
$700	$600	$550	$450	$300	$250	$200

This model was disc. due to lack of sales.

MODEL 60 - .22 S, L, or LR cal., improved Model 59, 23 in. round barrel increased to 27 in. 1933. Approx. 160,754 mfg. between 1930-34.

100%	98%	95%	90%	80%	70%	60%
$315	$295	$225	$185	$160	$135	$110

Add 20% for 23 in. barrel.

MODEL 60A SPORTER - .22 S, L, or LR cal., sporter variation of Model 60, pistol grip walnut stock. Disc.

100%	98%	95%	90%	80%	70%	60%
$350	$295	$250	$200	$180	$160	$135

MODEL 60A TARGET - similar to Model 60 with Lyman 55W aperture rear sight, heavier target stock, and 27 in. round tapered barrel. Approx. 6,118 mfg. between 1932-39.

100%	98%	95%	90%	80%	70%	60%
$450	$400	$375	$325	$275	$235	$200

GRADING - PPGS™	100%	98%	95%	90%	80%	70%	60%

MODEL 67/67A - .22 S, L, LR or .22 WRF (authorized 1935) cal., 20 in. (Boys Rifle), 24 (miniature target boring), and 27 in. (sporting or smooth bore) round barrels, same basic action as the Model 60, not serial numbered. Approx. 383,000 mfg. between 1934-63.

	100%	98%	95%	90%	80%	70%	60%
	$225	$200	$130	$100	$70	$60	$50

Add 25% for Boys rifle.
Add 100% for .22 WRF cal.
Add 100%-150% for smooth bore, depending on condition.

MODEL 677 - same basic specifications as Model 67, except no iron sights or sight cuts in barrel, not serial numbered, supplied with Win. 5-A scope, .22 WRF is scarce. Approx. 2,240 mfg. between 1937-39.

	100%	98%	95%	90%	80%	70%	60%
	$1,750	$1,500	$1,400	$750	$600	$500	$350

MODEL 68 - .22 LR or .22 WRF cal., bolt action single shot, similar to Model 67, walnut stock, supplied with aperture sight (no rear sight), not serial numbered. Approx. 100,000 mfg. between 1934-46.

	100%	98%	95%	90%	80%	70%	60%
	$275	$225	$165	$125	$100	$65	$50

Add 200% for .22 WRF cal.

MODEL 121 SINGLE SHOT RIFLE - .22 LR cal., bolt action, 20 3/4 in. barrel, open sights, plain pistol grip stock. Mfg. 1967-73.

	100%	98%	95%	90%	80%	70%	60%
	$115	$85	$70	$55	$45	$35	$30

MODEL 121Y SINGLE SHOT RIFLE - similar to 121, with shorter stock.

	100%	98%	95%	90%	80%	70%	60%
	$115	$85	$70	$55	$45	$35	$30

MODEL 121 DELUXE - similar to 121, with ramp front sight and sling swivels.

	100%	98%	95%	90%	80%	70%	60%
	$125	$90	$75	$60	$50	$40	$35

MODEL 310 SINGLE SHOT - .22 LR cal., bolt action, 22 in. barrel, open sights, checkered pistol grip stock, swivels. Mfg. 1972-75.

	100%	98%	95%	90%	80%	70%	60%
	$200	$175	$140	$100	$80	$70	$60

100%	98%	95%	90%	80%	70%	60%	50%	40%	30%	20%	10%

RIFLES: BOLT ACTION

MODEL 1883 (HOTCHKISS REPEATER) - .45-70 Govt. cal., designed by Benjamin D. Hotchkiss, unique tube mag. located in buttstock attached to receiver, up-turn/pull-back bolt action, 26 in. round or octagon barrel standard on rifle. Over 84,000 mfg. between 1879-1889. Also available in carbine configuration (24 in. round barrel with one band), and musket (32 in. round barrel with cleaning rod and two barrel bands) - subtract 25%. Carbine extremely rare in Third Model (20 in. barrel).

* *First Style* - approx. 6,419 mfg. with magazine cut off and safety control incorporated into one unit.

100%	98%	95%	90%	80%	70%	60%	50%	40%	30%	20%	10%
$2,150	$1,750	$1,500	$1,325	$1,200	$1,100	$1,000	$900	$850	$800	$750	$725

* *Second Style* - approx. 16,102 mfg., magazine cut off on right receiver top, safety on left side.

100%	98%	95%	90%	80%	70%	60%	50%	40%	30%	20%	10%
$1,950	$1,750	$1,500	$1,300	$1,150	$1,050	$950	$850	$750	$650	$625	$600

* *Third Style* - most commonly encountered Hotchkiss, 2-piece stock, approx. 62,034 mfg. 1883-1899.

100%	98%	95%	90%	80%	70%	60%	50%	40%	30%	20%	10%
$1,650	$1,425	$1,250	$1,100	$900	$825	$750	$675	$625	$565	$525	$480

The Model 1883 Hotchkiss was the first bolt action designed for the U.S. military .45-70 Govt. cartridge. On the First and Second models, inspect wood directly below bolt and left frame side for cracks, breaks, or older repairs as it is frequently encountered on these early models with thin wrists.

100%	98%	95%	90%	80%	70%	60%	50%	40%	30%	20%	10%

LEE STRAIGHT PULL RIFLE

LEE STRAIGHT PULL RIFLE - 6mm Lee (.236 U.S.N. cal.), 5 shot non-detachable box mag., 24 (Sporting Rifle) or 28 (Musket) in. barrel, folding leaf sight, blue metal, military style full stock, mfg. 1897-1902, Navy Issue Model is the Musket with "236 U.S.N." on barrels. Approx. 20,000 mfg. (including 15,000 Muskets for the U.S. Navy military contract) between 1895-1902 with parts clean up occurring in 1916.

❋ *U.S.N. Military Musket*

$2,000	$1,750	$1,500	$1,250	$1,100	$1,000	$900	$800	$700	$650	$600	$550

❋ *Lee Sporting Rifle* - similar to Musket, with 24 in, barrel, sporter style stock. Approx. 1,700 mfg. 1897-1902.

$2,000	$1,800	$1,500	$1,300	$1,200	$1,100	$1,000	$900	$800	$700	$650	$600

This design was originally patented by James Paris Lee and assigned to the Lee Arms Company. Winchester obtained manufacturing rights to produce this model for the U.S Navy military contract 1895-1902.

MODEL 43

MODEL 43 - .218 Bee, .22 Hornet, .25-20 WCF, or .32-20 WCF cal., dubbed "Poor Man's Model 70," 24 in. round tapered barrel, box type mag. Approx. 62,617 mfg. between 1949-57.

$725	$600	$525	$450	$400	$350	$300	$250	$200	$175	$150	$125

Add 40% for Deluxe Model.

Premiums exist (in order of rarity) for .32-20 WCF, .25-20 WCF, or .218 Bee cals.

Subtract 60% if non-factory drilled and tapped (early models).

On Models 52, 54, 56, 57, 58, 59, 60, 60A, 67, 677, 68, 69, 69A, 697, and 70 values in 50% or less original condition have been omitted since values in those conditions will approximate the 60% price. This reflects the fact that while these lower condition specimens are not as desirable to collectors, they are still sought after as shooters.

GRADING - PPGS™	100%	98%	95%	90%	80%	70%	60%

MODEL 52 TARGET

MODEL 52 TARGET - .22 S (rare) or LR cal., 5 shot mag., 28 in. standard or heavy barrel (1st cataloged 1933), target sights and target style stock, speedlock trigger feature was introduced in 1929. Approx. 125,233 Model 52s in all variations were mfg. between 1919-79.

	$600	$550	$500	$450	$400	$350	$310
With speedlock	$625	$575	$525	$475	$425	$350	$310

Barrel drilling and tapping for scope blocks was not standard until ser. no. 5200.

❋ *Model 52A Target* - similar to Model 52, except all "A" suffix Model 52s have a speedlock action. Values are similar to Model 52 Target. In terms of rarity, it seems the "E" suffix is probably the scarcest (also the most poorly mfg.), followed by the "A" suffix variation.

MODEL 52A HEAVY BARREL

MODEL 52A HEAVY BARREL - similar to Standard Target, with heavy barrel.

	$800	$750	$650	$550	$450	$400	$350

MODEL 52-B TARGET

MODEL 52-B TARGET - extensively redesigned action, improved stock design, offered with a variety of sights. Approx. mfg. 1940-47.

	$1,100	$1,000	$900	$750	$650	$550	$450

MODEL 52-B HEAVY BARREL

MODEL 52-B HEAVY BARREL - similar to 52-B, with heavy barrel, with adj. sling swivel as to position of front swivel, and single shot adapter became available.

	$1,200	$1,100	$1,000	$900	$800	$700	$600

MODEL 52-B BULL GUN

MODEL 52-B BULL GUN - extra heavy weight barrel.

	$1,500	$1,300	$1,000	$900	$800	$650	$550

MODEL 52 SPORTER (SPORTING RIFLE)

MODEL 52 SPORTER (SPORTING RIFLE) - 24 in. round lightweight barrel with front sight cover, sporting type select walnut stock with cheekpiece, hard rubber pistol grip cap, black plastic tipped forearm, checkered steel buttplate, 5 shot mag. is standard, about 7 1/4 lbs. Mfg. 1934-1958. There is some controversy as to whether any of the Model 52 Sporters were drilled and tapped per factory worksmanship. Be cautious of "factory" drilled and tapped receivers on all model 52s, as there are many "gunsmith" Sporters that have been made with turned down, shortened target barrels.

GRADING - PPGS™	100%	98%	95%	90%	80%	70%	60%

* *Model 52* - advertised approx. 1936.

	$3,200	$2,900	$2,500	$2,000	$1,500	$1,300	$1,100

* *Model 52A* - introduced approx. 1937, receiver and locking lug were strengthened. Very rare.

	$4,000	$3,700	$3,250	$2,500	$2,250	$2,000	$1,500

* *Model 52B* - introduced approx. 1940.

	$3,500	$3,000	$2,800	$2,300	$1,900	$1,500	$1,200

* *Model 52B (1993 Re-issue)* - .22 LR cal., patterned after the original Model 52B and includes steel buttplate, 24 in. barrel w/o sights, Micro Motion trigger with adjustment screw on bottom plate, high-polish blue, 5 shot mag., checkered 52B style stock with ebony forend tip, 7 lbs. Mfg. by Miroku in Japan 1993-2002.

	$500	$460	$430	$395	$360	$330	$300

Last MSR was $662.

* *Model 52C* - introduced 1947 with adj. Micro Motion trigger, approx. 500-1,000 mfg., 2 screws in trigger guard.

	$3,750	$3,400	$3,100	$2,650	$2,150	$1,500	$1,250

A few Model 52 Sporters & Targets were mfg. with stainless steel barrels (17,XXX-27,XXX serial range) - these guns will command a premium over values shown. Stainless steel barrels were also offered by Winchester as after market parts.

MODEL 52-C STANDARD TARGET
- "Micro Motion" trigger and "Marksman" stock, single shot adaptor, 5 or 10 shot mag. was avail., standard barrel, otherwise similar to 52-B. Mfg. 1947-61.

	$1,300	$1,200	$1,100	$1,000	$800	$600	$500

MODEL 52-C HEAVY TARGET
- similar to Standard Target, with heavy barrel.

	$1,350	$1,250	$1,100	$1,000	$800	$700	$650

MODEL 52-C BULL TARGET
- extra heavy (bull) barrel model of Heavy Target 52-C. Mfg. approx. 1947-1961.

	$1,800	$1,500	$1,300	$1,200	$1,100	$1,000	$900

MODEL 52-D TARGET
- improved version of 52-C with free-floating standard or heavy barrel and adj. bedding device, all 52-Ds were single shot.

	$1,000	$900	$800	$700	$600	$500	$400

MODEL 52-D INTERNATIONAL MATCH
- similar to 52-D, with free rifle stock, accessory rail. Mfg. 1969-1975.

	$1,200	$1,000	$850	$750	$625	$525	$475

Previous Model 52s had ser. no. suffixes - either A, B, C, or D" After approx. 1975, rifles started appearing with an "E" serial prefix. Both Model 52 International and Prone could have factory stocks that were not Winchester mfg.

MODEL 52-D PRONE
- similar to International Match, with prone style stock. Mfg. 1960-75.

	$1,000	$800	$700	$600	$550	$500	$475

MODEL 52-E INTERNATIONAL PRONE
- similar to 52-D, with prone stock, removable roll over cheekpiece. Mfg. 1975-1980.

	$1,000	$800	$700	$600	$500	$400	$300

MODEL 54 HIGH POWER SPORTER
- .270 Win., 7x57mm, 7.65x57mm Mauser (rare), .30-30 Win., .30-06, 9x57mm Mauser (rare) cal., 5 shot mag., 24 in. barrel, open sights, checkered pistol grip stock. Mfg. 1925-30. Approx. 50,145 Model 54s were mfg. in all variations between 1925-36.

	$1,000	$900	$800	$700	$600	$500	$400

Rare cals. will add premiums to the values listed. This model was also mfg. with a stainless steel barrel during the late 1920s-early '30s with premiums also being asked.

GRADING - PPGS™	100%	98%	95%	90%	80%	70%	60%

MODEL 54 CARBINE - introduced 1927, similar to Rifle, with 20 in. barrel, plain stock.

	$1,500	$1,200	$1,000	$900	$800	$650	$500

MODEL 54 IMPROVED SPORTER - .22 Hornet, .220 Swift, .250-3000, .257 Robts., .270, 7x57mm, or .30-06 cal., 5 shot mag., 24 or 26 in. barrel, one piece firing pin, checkered pistol grip stock. Mfg. 1930-36.

	$1,200	$1,000	$900	$800	$700	$600	$500

Rare cals. will add premiums to the values listed.

MODEL 54 CARBINE IMPROVED - similar to Rifle, with 20 in. barrel.

	$1,600	$1,200	$1,000	$900	$800	$700	$600

MODEL 54 SUPER GRADE - introduced 1934, similar to Sporter, with better wood and black forend tip and pistol grip cap.

	$2,500	$2,000	$1,500	$1,300	$1,200	$1,000	$850

Rare calibers will command considerable premiums (i.e. this variation in 7x57mm cal. will sell for $2,500 in mint condition).

MODEL 54 SPORTING SNIPER'S RIFLE - introduced 1929, similar to Sporter, with 26 in. heavy barrel, .30-06 only, aperture sight.

	$2,000	$1,500	$1,250	$1,100	$1,000	$900	$800

MODEL 54 NATIONAL MATCH - introduced 1935, similar to Standard, with Lyman sights and Marksman stock.

	$1,500	$1,200	$1,000	$900	$750	$700	$600

MODEL 56 SPORTER - .22 S or LR cal., 5 or 10 shot box mag., 22 in. round barrel, open sights, plain pistol grip stock. Approx. 8,297 mfg. between 1926-29.

	$1,000	$800	$700	$600	$500	$450	$400

Add 25% for .22 Short cal. (disc. 1929).

MODEL 57 - .22 S or LR cal., 22 in. barrel, open sights, stock cutaway for aperture sight on left side, drilled and tapped receiver, pistol grip walnut stock with barrel band, 5 or 10 shot mag., left side push-button mag. release, approx. 5 1/2 lbs.

	$575	$495	$450	$395	$350	$300	$250

Add 20% for .22 Short cal.

❋ *Model 57 Target* - similar to Model 56, except with aperture sight and heavier target stock. Approx. 18,600 were mfg. between 1926-36.

	$595	$525	$450	$375	$300	$260	$220

MODEL 69 & 69A - .22 S, L, or LR cal., 5 or 10 shot repeater, 25 in. barrel, aperture or open rear sight, not serial numbered. Approx. 355,000 mfg. between 1935-63.

	$425	$365	$300	$235	$150	$100	$85

Add 40% for Target Model.

Add 20% for grooved receiver (Model 69A only).

Add 5% for chrome plated bolt handle and trigger guard.

The Model 69 was cocked by the closing motion of the bolt and had a non-swept back bolt handle, whereas the 69A was cocked by the opening motion of the bolt and had a swept back bolt handle. Number 97B rear aperture sight and 80A hooded front target sights and standard open sights were offered on both the Model 69 and 69A.

MODEL 72/72A - .22 LR and Gallery Model (.22 short only), tube mag., bolt action, 25 in. round, tapered barrel, aperture or open rear sight, not serial numbered. Over 161,000 mfg. between 1938-59.

	$450	$375	$300	$250	$115	$100	$85

Add 30% for Target Model.

Add 100% for Gallery Model (mfg. 1939-1942) - rare.

Add 20% for grooved receiver (Model 72A only).

Add 5% for chrome plated bolt handle and trigger guard.

The Model 72 and 72A both cocked on opening. The Model 72A has a swept back bolt handle and some minor internal mechanical improvements. Same open sight options as Models 69/69A.

GRADING - PPGS™	100%	98%	95%	90%	80%	70%	60%

MODEL 75 TARGET - .22 LR, 5 or 10 shot mag., 28 in. barrel, target sights, slight variation used by Government in WWII. Approx. 88,715 Model 75 Target and Model 75s were mfg. between 1938-58.

	$550	$475	$425	$350	$300	$275	$250

Add 25% for Olympic sights.

Add 20% for original Winchester leather sling.

MODEL 75 SPORTER - similar to Target, except 24 in. tapered barrel, detachable mag., non-target sights and select checkered walnut.

	$900	$800	$650	$600	$500	$450	$375

Add 20%-25% for "grooved" receiver allowing "tip-off" scope mounts.

MODEL 131 BOLT ACTION - .22 S, L, and LR, 7 shot mag.

	$225	$200	$175	$150	$125	$95	$75

MODEL 141 BOLT ACTION - .22 S, L, and LR, butt loading tube mage.

	$225	$200	$175	$150	$125	$95	$75

MODEL 320 RIFLE - .22 LR cal., similar to Single Shot Model 310, with 5 shot mag. Mfg. 1972-74.

	$325	$325	$300	$265	$235	$185	$150

MODEL 325 RIFLE - .22 Mag. cal., otherwise similar to Model 320, limited mfg. 1972-74.

	$375	$350	$325	$300	$250	$200	$100

MODEL 670 BOLT ACTION RIFLE - another economy version of the model 70, .225 Win., .243 Win., .270 Win, .308 Win., or .30-06 cal., 22 in. barrel, open sights, no hinged floorplate, pistol grip stock. Mfg. 1967-73.

	$300	$250	$220	$195	$175	$165	$140

MODEL 670 CARBINE - similar to 670, with 19 in. barrel, not available in .308 Win. Mfg. 1967-70.

	$300	$250	$220	$195	$175	$165	$140

MODEL 670 MAGNUM - similar to 670, with reinforced stock, .264 Mag., 7mm Mag., or .300 Win. Mag. cal. Mfg. 1967-70.

	$330	$275	$255	$220	$205	$195	$165

MODEL 697 - .22 WRF cal., same general specifications as the Model 69, except no iron sights or sight cuts in barrel and no ramp or sight cover. Telescope bases attached to barrel were standard.

	$2,000	$1,800	$1,500	$1,250	$1,000	$800	$650

MODEL 770 BOLT ACTION - .22-250 Rem., .222 Rem., .243 Win., .270 Win., .30-06, or .308 Win. cal., 22 in. barrel, open sights, no floorplate or forend tip. Mfg. 1969-71.

	$325	$285	$275	$260	$250	$220	$195

MODEL 770 MAGNUM - similar to Standard, in .264 Mag., 7mm Mag., or .300 Win. Mag. cal., recoil pad. Mfg. 1969-71.

	$350	$310	$285	$275	$265	$250	$220

MODEL 777 - .30-06 cal., bolt action, 4 shot mag., mfg. by Nikko in Japan during 1979-80 for sale to Winchester subsidiaries in Australia, Germany, Italy, and Scandinavia, only 3 were shipped to the U.S., checkered Monte Carlo stock with Wundhammer swell grip, lightweight barrel, engraved action, "Winchester" is cast on the left side of the receiver near the top, approx. 1,000 mfg. with 250 in .30-06 cal. - 750 mfg. in different cal. and sold elsewhere, 8 1/2 lbs.

Extreme rarity factor precludes accurate price evaluation. Some specimens have been reported as sold in the $1,850+ range.

100%	98%	95%	90%	80%	70%	60%	50%	40%	30%	20%	10%

RIFLES: SEMI-AUTO

MODEL 1903 - .22 Win. Auto rimfire cal., 10 shot tube mag., 20 in. round barrel, open sights, straight grip stock cut out for partial magazine filling. Approx. 126,000 mfg. between 1903-32.

N/A	$1,275	$1,100	$900	$775	$650	$550	$475	$400	$325	$250	$175

Add 50% for deluxe checkered model.

First U.S. semi-auto rifle designed for a special .22 cal. rimfire cartridge. Regular .22 cal. rimfire will not function or chamber properly in this model. The earliest models up to around ser. no. 5,000 were mfg. w/o a safety.

MODEL 1905 - .32 Win. or .35 Win. cal., 5 or 10 shot box mag., 22 in. round barrel, open sights, straight or plain pistol grip stock. Approx. 29,113 mfg. between 1905-20.

N/A	$650	$575	$525	$465	$400	$365	$330	$300	$275	$250	$225

MODEL 1907 - .351 Win. cal., 5 or 10 shot box mag., 20 in. round barrel, open sights, plain pistol grip stock, an improved version of the Model 1905. Approx. 58,490 mfg. between 1907-57.

N/A	$595	$525	$450	$375	$325	$295	$265	$230	$195	$175	$160

MODEL 1910 - .401 Win. cal., 4 shot box mag., 20 in. barrel, open sight, plain pistol grip stock. Mfg. 20,786 between 1910-36.

N/A	$750	$625	$550	$500	$450	$400	$365	$330	$300	$275	$250

Add 25% for Fancy Sporting Rifle (special checkered walnut).

MODEL 55 - please refer to listing in Rifles: Single Shot.

MODEL 63 - .22 LR cal., styling similar to Model 1903, takedown, 10 shot tube mag., 20 (disc. 1936) or 23 in. barrel, open sights, plain pistol grip stock. Approx. 174,692 mfg. between 1933-58.

$850	$750	$675	$550	$425	$350	$300	$265	$235	$215	$190	$175

Add 20% for grooved receiver variation (WFF)
Add 50%-100% for 20 in. barrel (carbine) depending on condition.

The Model 63 was introduced to take advantage of the new .22 LR cartridge, which the older Model 1903 couldn't chamber.

Watch for fake boxes and hanging tags on this model, especially with rifles in over 95%+ original condition.

GRADING - PPGS™	100%	98%	95%	90%	80%	70%	60%

MODEL 63 GRADE I - RECENT PRODUCTION - .22 LR cal., similar to original Model 63, 10 shot mag., 23 in. barrel, checkered walnut stock and forearm, blue finish with engraved receiver, 6 1/4 lbs. Mfg. 1997-98.

	$610	$550	$500				

Last MSR was $678.

✳ *Model 63 High Grade - Recent Mfg.* - .22 LR cal., similar to original Model 63, 10 shot mag., deluxe checkered walnut stock and forearm, blue finish with engraved gold animals and accents on receiver, 6 1/4 lbs. 1,000 mfg. 1997 only.

	$950	$825	$700				

Last MSR was $1,083.

MODEL 74 - .22 S or LR (introduced in 1940) cal., tubular mag. in stock, pop-out bolt assembly. Approx. 406,574 mfg. between 1939-1955. Distinguishable by squared-off rear receiver.

	$295	$250	$215	$175	$150	$125	$70

Add 25% for .22 Short cal. (mfg. 1939-1952).
Add 25% for pre-WWII mfg.

GRADING - PPGS™	100%	98%	95%	90%	80%	70%	60%

MODEL 77 - .22 LR cal., detachable box mag. or tubular mag. under barrel. Over 217,000 mfg. between 1955-62.

	100%	98%	95%	90%	80%	70%	60%
	$250	$225	$200	$175	$110	$100	$70

Add $50 for tube mag.

MODEL 100 RIFLE - .243 Win., .284 Win., or .308 Win. cal., 4 shot detachable mag., 22 in. round barrel with open sights, gas operated, basket weave pattern impressed on stock, pistol grip cap. Over 262,000 mfg. 1961-73 with some production occurring in Japan.

	100%	98%	95%	90%	80%	70%	60%
	$500	$450	$400	$300	$250	$230	$215

The pre-1964 .284 Win. cal. with cut checkering was made for less than one year (WFF, ser. range 72,XXX with no letter suffix or prefix).

❋ *Pre-1964 production*
  Add $25 for .243 Win. cal.
  Add $150 for .284 Win. cal.

MODEL 100 CARBINE - similar to rifle, with 19 in. barrel, plain pistol grip stock, barrel band. Mfg. 1967-1973.

	100%	98%	95%	90%	80%	70%	60%
	$600	$500	$400	$350	$300	$250	$200

  Add $25 for .243 Win. cal.
  Add $150 for .284 Win. cal.

MODEL 190 RIFLE - .22 S, L, or LR cal., semi-auto, 15 shot LR tube mag., alloy receiver, uncheckered walnut finished hardwood stock, 20 1/2 (Carbine Model) or 24 (Rifle Model) in. barrel, approx. 2,150,000 (including the Model 290 listed also) during 1967-1980.

	100%	98%	95%	90%	80%	70%	60%
	$150	$125	$100	$85	$75	$65	$55

MODEL 290 DELUXE RIFLE - similar to 190, with select Monte Carlo stock. Mfg. 1965-1973.

	100%	98%	95%	90%	80%	70%	60%
	$200	$175	$150	$115	$100	$90	$80

MODEL 490 RIFLE - .22 LR cal., 5 shot mag., 22 in. barrel, folding sight, checkered one piece stock. Mfg. 1975-1980.

	100%	98%	95%	90%	80%	70%	60%
	$250	$215	$185	$155	$145	$130	$110

100%	98%	95%	90%	80%	70%	60%	50%	40%	30%	20%	10%

RIFLES: SLIDE ACTION, DISC.

MODEL 1890 SLIDE ACTION - .22 S, L, LR, or WRF rimfire, cals. are non-interchangeable (don't shoot a .22 S in a gun chambered for .22 L) and the barrel is marked for single cal. only, visible hammer, solid-frame (first 15,000) or takedown, 24 in. octagonal barrel, case hardened receivers until 1901, model nomenclature changed to Model 90 circa 1919 at approx. ser. no. range 640,000. Approx. 849,000 mfg. between 1890-1932.

❋ *Model 1890 First Model Solid Frame* - color case hardened receiver, mfg. 1890-1892.

	100%	98%	95%	90%	80%	70%	60%	50%	40%	30%	20%	10%
N/A	$10,000	$8,000	$7,000	$6,000	$4,500	$4,000	$3,500	$3,000	$2,500	$2,000	$1,250

❋ *Model 1890 Second Model Takedown Frame* - color case hardened receiver, takedown feature was added in 1892 after over 15,000 solid frames had been made, approx. ser. no. range 15,500-326,000. Mfg. 1892-1907.

	100%	98%	95%	90%	80%	70%	60%	50%	40%	30%	20%	10%
N/A	$4,250	$3,750	$3,000	$2,750	$2,250	$1,750	$1,500	$1,000	$800	$500	$350

❋ *Model 1890 Takedown w/ Blue Finish* - most commonly encountered Model 1890, post-1901 manufacture.

	100%	98%	95%	90%	80%	70%	60%	50%	40%	30%	20%	10%
N/A	$1,000	$900	$800	$700	$600	$500	$400	$350	$300	$275	$235

Add 50% for .22 LR cal. (mfg circa 1919-1932, starting at ser. no. approx. 610,000).
.22 LR cal. accounted for approx. 10% of the total production on this model.

	100%	98%	95%	90%	80%	70%	60%	50%	40%	30%	20%	10%

Deluxe model will bring premiums over values listed. There were also a limited amount of guns mfg. with stainless steel barrels which will add to values of post-1901 mfg.

The Model 1890 was Winchester's first slide action repeating rifle. It replaced the Model 1873 .22 cal. It was an excellent and inexpensive .22 rifle that rapidly became the universal firearm used in shooting galleries. Even though production reached approx. 849,000 units, most guns were heavily used and specimens existing today in 98%+ condition are rare. Check carefully for rebarreling (notice proofmarks on barrel).

MODEL 1906 - .22 S, L, or LR, 20 in. round barrel, tube mag., visible hammer, open sights, straight stock with shotgun buttplate. Approx. 848,000 mfg. between 1906-1932.

N/A	N/A	N/A	$800	$600	$500	$400	$325	$250	$225	$175	$150

This model is seldom encountered in over 90% original condition - original mint specimens can top $2,000.

* ✳ *Model 1906 Expert* - similar to Model 1906, except has a pistol grip stock and different shaped slide handle, finish choices included blue, nickel trimmed receiver, guard, and bolt, or full nickel trimmed, .22 S cal. only until approx. 70,000, mfg. 1917-1925.

N/A	N/A	$1,500	$1,200	$1,000	$800	$600	$500	$400	$300	$250	$200

MODEL 61 HAMMERLESS - .22 S, L, LR, or WRF cal., 24 in. round or octagonal barrel (with rifling or smooth bore, i.e. Routledge), tube mag., open sights, plain grip stock. Approx. 343,XXX mfg. between 1932-1963.

$700	$600	$500	$400	$325	$300	$275	$225	$200	$185	$170	$150

Add 75% for single cal. barrel marking.

Add 20% for grooved receiver.

Add 300% for Routledge bore (WFF).

Pre-war manufacture has small forearm. Pre-war octagon barrel in S or LR cals. will command a 100% premium. "WRF" marked round barrel is rare - front of receiver must be marked "W.R.F."

Watch for fake boxes and hanging tags on this model, especially with rifles in over 95%+ original condition.

* ✳ *Model 61 Octagon* - .22 S, LR, or WRF cal., octagon barrel variation of the Model 61. Disc. approx. 1943.

N/A	$2,000	$1,800	$1,700	$1,500	$1,000	$800	$700	$500	$500	$450	$400

Add 30% for .22 Short cal.

* ✳ *Model 61 Magnum* - similar to Standard 61, but chambered for .22 Win. Mag. Mfg. 1960-63.

N/A	$1,200	$1,075	$950	$825	$700	$600	$500	$400	$350	$300	$250

MODEL 62/62A VISIBLE HAMMER - modern version of 1890, will shoot calibers interchangeably, 23 in. round tapered octagon barrel. Over 409,000 mfg. between 1932-58.

$650	$600	$500	$400	$350	$300	$250	$200	$185	$170	$155	$130

Add 50% for Gallery model.

Pre-war model is 62, distinguishable by small forearm. The Model 62-A was introduced 1940 at serial number 99,200 with minor changes. Model 62A single cal. barrel markings do not add premiums. .22 Short only models without the Winchester roll die receiver marking are more scarce than the so-called "Gallery Rifle" - mint specimens without the roll die marking are approx. $1,000. Gallery variations of these models will also command sizable premium.

Watch for fake boxes and hanging tags on this model, especially with rifles in over 95%+ original condition.

GRADING - PPGS™	100%	98%	95%	90%	80%	70%	60%

MODEL 270 SLIDE ACTION - .22 LR cal., tube mag., 20 1/2 in. barrel, checkered walnut pistol grip stock. Mfg. 1963-73.

	$150	$135	$120	$100	$80	$70	$60

GRADING - PPGS™	100%	98%	95%	90%	80%	70%	60%
✳ *Plastic forearm variation*							
	$150	$135	$120	$100	$80	$70	$60
✳ *Model 270 Deluxe* - similar to 270, with select wood, Monte Carlo stock. Mfg. 1965-73.							
	$195	$150	$110	$80	$70	$60	$50
MODEL 275 - similar to 270, in .22 Mag.							
	$165	$150	$135	$100	$80	$70	$65
✳ *Model 275 Deluxe* - similar to 270 Deluxe, in .22 Mag.							
	$210	$160	$140	$110	$80	$70	$60

RIFLES: LEVER ACTION - POST 1964 PRODUCTION

Beginning in 1992, all Model 94s and variations (not including the 9422 models) received an engineering change utilizing a crossbolt in the upper rear of the receiver that prevents the hammer from contacting the firing pin.

MODEL 64 1972-1974 MODEL - .30-30 Win. cal., lever action, 5 shot, 2/3 tube mag., 24 in. barrel, open sight, plain pistol grip stock. Mfg. 1972-74.

	100%	98%	95%	90%	80%	70%	60%
	$400	$350	$300	$250	$200	$150	$125

MODEL 88 LEVER ACTION RIFLE - pre-'64 version with diamond cut checkering, no barrel band, 22 in. barrel. Mfg. 1955-63. Total production for all varieties of the Model 88 Lever Action was approx. 284,000 units.

	100%	98%	95%	90%	80%	70%	60%
.308 Win. (1955-1963)	$950	$850	$600	$500	$400	$350	$300
.243 Win. (1956-1963)	$1,000	$900	$750	$650	$500	$450	$400
.358 Win. (1956-1962)	$2,800	$2,500	$1,900	$1,625	$1,275	$1,000	$875
.284 Win. (Intro-1963)	$1,950	$1,700	$1,500	$1,000	$900	$800	$600

MODEL 88 LEVER ACTION RIFLE - 1964 model with impressed basket weave checkering, no barrel band, 22 in. barrel. Mfg. 1964-73.

	100%	98%	95%	90%	80%	70%	60%
.308 Win. (1964-N/A)	$750	$550	$400	$350	$300	$250	$200
.243 Win. (1964-N/A)	$850	$650	$450	$400	$350	$300	$250
.284 Win. (1964-N/A)	$1,300	$1,000	$800	$650	$600	$450	$400

MODEL 88 LEVER ACTION CARBINE - introduced 1968, no checkering, one-piece stock, barrel band, 19 in. barrel. Mfg. 1968-73.

	100%	98%	95%	90%	80%	70%	60%
.308 Win. (1968-1973)	$925	$800	$575	$500	$425	$350	$300
.243 Win. (1968-N/A)	$1,100	$995	$875	$775	$660	$550	$495
.284 Win. (1968-N/A)	$1,900	$1,650	$1,425	$1,200	$1,000	$775	$650

MODEL 150 LEVER ACTION - .22 LR, 20 1/2 in. barrel, tube mag., hammerless, uncheckered hardwood stock and forearm, sling swivels, approx. 47,400 mfg. 1967-74.

	100%	98%	95%	90%	80%	70%	60%
	$125	$110	$95	$70	$60	$50	$40

MODEL 250 LEVER ACTION - .22 LR, 20 1/2 in. barrel, tube mag., hammerless, checkered pistol grip stock. Mfg. 1963-73.

	100%	98%	95%	90%	80%	70%	60%
	$150	$125	$110	$95	$70	$60	$50

✳ *Model 250 Deluxe* - similar to Model 250, with select wood and sling swivels. Mfg. 1965-71.

	100%	98%	95%	90%	80%	70%	60%
	$195	$155	$110	$95	$70	$60	$50

MODEL 255 - .22 Mag., otherwise similar to Model 250. Mfg. 1964-70.

	100%	98%	95%	90%	80%	70%	60%
	$195	$175	$150	$135	$110	$85	$70

✳ *Model 255 Deluxe* - .22 Mag., with select wood and swivels. Mfg. 1965-73.

	100%	98%	95%	90%	80%	70%	60%
	$260	$210	$165	$150	$135	$100	$75

MODEL 1886 GRADE I - .45-70 Govt. cal., 26 in. octagon barrel. Mfg. 1997-98.

	100%	98%	95%	90%	80%	70%	60%
	$900	$850	$750	$650	$600	$500	$450

Last MSR was $996.

✱ Model 1886 High Grade - .45-70 Govt. cal., features gold-line receiver engraving with multiple gold animals, polished blue, deluxe checkered walnut stock and forearm with metal cap, 1,000 mfg. 1997 only.

$1,475 $1,200 $995

Last MSR was $1,588.

MODEL 1886 TAKEDOWN

- .45-70 Govt. cal., features original takedown action design, uncheckered semi-pistol grip walnut stock with crescent buttplate, 26 in. octagon barrel with buckhorn rear sight, forend has ebony cap, 9 1/4 lbs. Mfg. 1999 only.

$995 $875 $750 $625 $600 $500 $400

Last MSR was $1,140.

MODEL 1886 EXTRA LIGHT GRADE I

- .45-70 Govt. cal., 22 in. round tapered barrel, shotgun buttplate, half magazine, high polish receiver and barel bluing, open sights, uncheckered walnut stock and forearm, 7 1/4 lbs. 3,500 mfg. 2000-2001.

$1,025 $875 $750

Last MSR was $1,152.

✱ Model 1886 Extra Light High Grade - similar to Model 1886 Extra Light Grade I, except features engraved elk and whitetail deer and game scenes on blue receiver, extra fancy checkered walnut stock and forearm, 7 1/4 lbs. 1,000 mfg. 2000-2001.

$1,225 $915 $800

Last MSR was $1,440.

MODEL 1892 GRADE I

- .357 Mag. (new 1998), .44-40 WCF (new 1998), or .45 LC cal., similar to original Model 1892 Winchester, 24 in. round barrel, top tang mounted manual hammer stop, blue finish with etched receiver engraving, gold trigger, satin finished walnut straight grip stock and forend with metal cap, 6 1/4 lbs. Mfg. 1997-99.

$665 $560 $430

Last MSR was $744.

✱ Model 1892 Short Rifle - .44 Mag. cal., features 20 in. round barrel with full mag., uncheckered staight grip walnut stock with crescent buttplate, buckhorn rear sight, high polish blue finish only, 6 lbs. Mfg. 1999-2000.

$670 $560 $430 $400 $360 $330 $300

Last MSR was $752.

✱ Model 1892 High Grade - .45 LC cal., features gold accents and receiver game scene, 1,000 mfg. 1997 only.

$1,125 $995 $750

Last MSR was $1,285.

MODEL 1892 LIMITED SERIES

- .357 Mag., .32-20 WCF, .38-40 WCF, or .44 Mag. cal., 20 in. tapered octagon barrel, blue finish, uncheckered satin finished walnut straight grip stock, steel crescent buttplate, steel forend cap, full length mag. tube, rollmarked "LIMITED SERIES - 1 of 500", special ser. no., includes special limited series box and certificate of authenticity. New 2004.

MSR $1,075 $850 $750 $650 $500 $435 $400 $350

This model is available exclusively through Davidson's.

✱ Model 1892 Limited Series Trapper - .45 LC cal., similar to Model 1892 Limited Series, except has 16 in. round barrel, shotgun style buttstock, steel barrel bands, and saddle ring. New 2004.

MSR $1,075 $850 $750 $650 $500 $435 $400 $350

This model is available exclusively through Davidson's.

GRADING - PPGS™	100%	98%	95%	90%	80%	70%	60%

MODEL 1895 GRADE I

.270 Win. (disc. 1999), .30-06 (mfg. 1998-99), or .405 Win. (new 2000) cal., similar to original Model 1895 Winchester, checkered straight grip stock and Schnabel forearm, 24 in. round barrel, 4 shot mag., top tang safety, blue finish, 8 lbs. Mfg. 1997-2002, .405 Win. cal. reintroduced 2004.

	100%	98%	95%	90%	80%	70%	60%
.405 Win. cal.	$925	$800	$700	$600	$525	$475	$425

Last MSR was $1,116.

	100%	98%	95%	90%	80%	70%	60%
.270 Win. or .30-06 cal.	$875	$750	$650	$550	$500	$450	$395

Last MSR was $1,045 on .270 Win. and .30-06 cals.

MODEL 1895 LIMITED EDITION

.30-06, similar to original Model 1895 Winchester, blue receiver, 24 in. round barrel, 4 shot mag. (box mag.), uncheckered woodstock and forearm, rear buckhorn sight, 2 piece cocking lever, 8 lbs. 4,000 mfg. 1995-97.

$725	$550	$425

Last MSR was $853.

✳ *Model 1895 High Grade* - .30-06 (mfg. 1995-99) or .405 Win. (mfg. 2000-2002) cal., same general specifications as the Model 1895 Limited Edition, features older No. 3 engraving pattern with double scenes, gold borders with multiple gold inlays, deluxe checkered walnut stock and forearm. 4,000 mfg. 1995-2002.

$1,295	$950	$825

Last MSR was $1,532.

Add 15% for .405 Win. cal.

RIFLES: MODEL 94 LEVER ACTION - POST 1964 PRODUCTION

100th Anniversary Model 1894s (mfg. 1994) are marked "1894-1994" on the receiver. During 2003, Winchester discontinued the crossbolt receiver safety, and introduced the new top tang safety.

Add 20% for Model 94s w/o the crossbolt safety (pre-1992 mfg.) if original condition is 95%+.

MODEL 94 STANDARD RIFLE

.30-30 Win., .32 Win. Spl. (disc. 1973, reintroduced 1992), 7-30 Waters (new 1989), or .44 Mag. (mfg. circa late 1960s-1970s) cal., lever action, 6 or 7 (24 in. barrel only) shot tube mag., 20 or 24 (mfg. 1987-88 only) in. round barrel, open sights, straight walnut stock, barrel band on forearm. Angled ejection became standard 1982, 6 1/2 lbs. Mfg. 1964-97.

$275	$215	$180	$165	$150	$140	$135

Last MSR was $363.

Add $15 for 24 in. barrel (disc. 1990).
Add $16 for .44 Mag. cal. (disc. 1986).
Add 15% for 7-32 Waters cal.

MODEL 94 TRADITIONAL (DELUXE WALNUT)

.30-30 Win., .44 Mag. (new 1999), or .480 Ruger Big Bore (mfg. 2002-2003) cal., similar to Standard Rifle, except has plain (new 1998, not available in .44 Mag. cal.) or checkered walnut stock and forearm, 6 (.30-30 Win. cal.) 10 (.480 Ruger cal.), or 11 (.44 Mag. cal.) shot mag., 6 1/4 lbs. Mfg. 1988-2004.

$325	$250	$200	$165	$150	$140	$135

Last MSR was $436.

Add $34 for Traditional–CW Model (w/ checkered stock and forearm).
Add $57 for .44 Mag. cal. (Traditional-CW Model with checkered stock, mfg. 1999-2004).
Add for .480 Ruger Big Bore cal. (mfg. 2002-2003) - $43 (Traditional) or $105 (Traditional-CW).
Add $55 for 1.5 - 4.5X scope with low mounts (disc.).

MODEL 94 LEGACY ROUND

.30-30 Win., .357 Mag. (new 1997), .44 Mag. (new 1997), or .45 LC (new 1997) cal., 7 (.30-30 Win. cal. only) or 12 shot mag., features pistol grip checkered walnut stock and forearm, 20 (disc. 1999) or 24 (new 1997) in. round barrel, 6 3/4 lbs. New 1995.

MSR $485	$360	$265	$215	$175	$150	$140	$135

Subtract $15 for 20 in. barrel.

GRADING - PPGS™	100%	98%	95%	90%	80%	70%	60%

❊ *Model 94 Legacy Round 26 In.* - .30-30 Win. or .38-55 Win. cal., 7 shot mag., adj. Marbles rear tang sight, similar to Model 94 Legacy Round, except features blue or color case hardened receiver and 26 in. round barrel. New 2004.

	MSR $783	$600	$525	$400	$350	$315	$285	$260

Add $56 for case colored receiver.

MODEL 94 LEGACY OCTAGON - .30-30 Win. or .38-55 Win. cal., 7 shot mag., adj. Marbles rear tang sight, features crescent buttplate, blue or color case hardened receiver and 26 in. octagon barrel. New 2004.

	MSR $882	$675	$575	$450	$395	$325	$300	$275

Add $56 for case colored receiver.

MODEL 94 RANGER - .30-30 Win. only, 20 in. barrel, uncheckered hardwood stock and forearm, 6 shot mag., 6 1/4 lbs. New 1985.

	MSR $377	$290	$230	$170	$150	$140	$130	$120

Add $56 for 4x32 scope with see-through mounts (disc. 1999).

❊ *Model 94 Ranger Compact* - .30-30 Win. or .357 Mag. cal., 16 in. barrel, uncheckered hardwood stock with 12 1/2 LOP with recoil pad, post-style front sight, 5 (.30-30 Win. cal.) or 9 shot mag., 5 7/8 lbs. Mfg. 1998-2004.

	$310	$235	$180	$160	$140	$130	$120

Last MSR was $402.

MODEL 94 TRAILS END - .357 Mag., .44-40 WCF (mfg. 1998-99), .44 Mag., or .45 LC cal., similar to standard rifle, except has 11 shot tube mag., 20 in. barrel, choice of standard or large loop lever (disc. 1998), crossbolt safety, 6 1/2 lbs. New 1997.

	MSR $468	$355	$275	$215	$165	$150	$140	$135

Add approx. $20 for large loop lever (disc. 1998).

❊ *Model 94 Trails End Octagon* - similar to Model 94 Trails End, except has octagon barrel, choice of blue or case colored receiver finish, 6 3/4 lbs. New 2004.

	MSR $757	$585	$495	$375	$325	$295	$265	$245

Add $59 for case colored receiver.

MODEL 94 TRAILS END HUNTER ROUND - .25-35 Win., .30-30 Win., or .38-55 Win. cal., 20 in. round barrel, 6 shot mag., uncheckered walnut stock and forearm, shotgun buttplate, 6 1/2 lbs. New 2005.

	MSR $468	$355	$275	$215	$165	$150	$140	$135

❊ *Model 94 Trails End Hunter Octagon* - similar to Model 94 Trails End Hunter, except has case colored receiver and octagon barrel, crescent buttplate. New 2005.

	MSR $816	$625	$550	$425	$365	$325	$295	$275

MODEL 94 PACK RIFLE - .30-30 Win. or .44 Mag. cal., 18 in. barrel, 4 or 5 shot 3/4 mag., over-dimension walnut stock and forearm cap w/o checkering, removable hood sight, 6 1/4 lbs. Mfg. 2000-2001.

	$380	$280	$220	$180	$165	$150	$140

Last MSR was $496.

Add $10 for .44 Mag. cal.

MODEL 94 TIMBER CARBINE - .444 Marlin (disc. 2001) or .450 Marlin (new 2004) cal., 18 in. ported barrel with 4 (.450 Marlin cal. only) or 5 (disc. 2001) shot 2/3 mag., top tang safety, checkered semi-pistol grip stock and forearm, blue finish only, adj. XS ghost ring rear sight (new 2004), hooded front sight (disc. 2001) or ramp style front sight, 6 lbs. Mfg. 1999-2001, reintroduced 2004.

	MSR $610	$475	$350	$300	$250	$215	$190	$175

❊ *Model 94 Timber Scout* - .30-30 Win. or .44 Rem. Mag. cal., similar to Model 94 Timber Carbine, 18 in. non-ported barrel with rail base, XS ghost ring sights, uncheckered walnut stock and forearm, 6 lbs. New 2005.

	MSR $610	$475	$350	$300	$250	$215	$190	$175

GRADING - PPGS™	100%	98%	95%	90%	80%	70%	60%

MODEL 94 WIN-TUFF RIFLE - .30-30 Win. cal., similar to Model 94 Rifle, except has laminated hardwood stock and forearm with checkering. Drilled and tapped for scope mounts. Mfg. 1987-disc.

	$300	$230	$180	$165	$150	$140	$135

Last MSR was $404.

MODEL 94 BLACK SHADOW - .30-30 Win. or .44 Mag./.44 Spl. cal., 20 or 24 (.30-30 Win. cal. only) in. barrel, 4 or 5 shot mag., non-glare finish, features black composite synthetic stock with recoil pad and Fuller forearm, approx. 6 1/4 lbs. Mfg. 1998-2000.

	$300	$230	$190	$160	$150	$140	$130

Last MSR was $381.

Add $13 for .44 Mag./.44 Spl. cal.

❋ *Model 94 Black Shadow Big Bore* - .444 Marlin cal., 20 in. barrel only, otherwise similar to Model 94 Black Shadow, 6 1/2 lbs. Mfg. 1998-2000.

	$325	$240	$190	$160	$150	$140	$130

Last MSR was $394.

MODEL 94 TRAPPER - .30-30 Win., .357 Mag. (mfg. beginning 1992), .44 Mag./.44 Spl. (new 1985), or .45 LC (new 1985) cal., 16 in. barrel, side ejection, walnut stock, 5 (.30-30 Win. cal.) or 9 shot tube mag., blue finish, dovetailed front sight, 6 lbs.

MSR $458	$350	$270	$210	$170	$150	$140	$130

MODEL 94 BIG BORE - .308 Win. (disc. 1998), .356 Win. (disc. 1998), or .375 Win. (disc. 1987), or .444 Marlin (new 1998) cal., angled ejection port provides scope mounting, checkered walnut Monte Carlo stock with recoil pad, 20 in. barrel, 6 shot mag., sling swivels, 6 1/2 lbs. New 1983.

	$355	$255	$210	$175	$160	$150	$140

Last MSR was $465.

Add 25% for .356 Win. or .375 Win. cal.

Also mfg. in a top eject (pre-USRA). This model had an "XTR" suffix until 1989.

MODEL 94 HERITAGE CUSTOM 1 OF 100 - .38-55 WCF cal., special edition for the NSSF Heritage Fund, features Winchester's historic No. 2 pattern hand engraved with 24Kt. gold inlays and individually signed by the engraver, deluxe spade checkered straight grip stock and forearm with metal cap, 1/2 round, 1/2 octagon 26 in. barrel, 6 3/4 lbs. Mfg. 2002-2003.

	$4,750	$3,150	$1,600

Last MSR was $5,400.

MODEL 94 HERITAGE CUSTOM 1 OF 1000 - .38-55 WCF cal., special edition for the NSSF Heritage Fund, features Winchester's historic No. 3 engraving pattern with 24Kt. gold inlays, deluxe spade checkered straight grip stock and forearm with metal cap, 1/2 round, 1/2 octagon 26 in. barrel, 6 3/4 lbs. Mfg. 2002 only.

	$1,625	$1,350	$1,050

Last MSR was $1,883.

MODEL 94 CUSTOM LIMITED EDITION - .44-40 WCF (mfg. 2000 only) or .38-55 WCF (new 2001) cal., features case colored receiver and 24 in. octagon match (.44-40 WCF cal. only) or 1/2 round, 1/2 octagon (.38-55 WCF cal. only) barrel with satin bluing, full (.44-40 WCF only) or 3/4 mag. tube, spade checkered straight grip walnut stock and forearm with metal cap, 7 1/4 (.38-55 WCF cal.) or 7 3/4 lbs. Only 75 mfg. in .44-40 WCF cal. 2000-2002.

	$2,100	$1,775	$1,650

Last MSR was $2,393.

GRADING - PPGS™	100%	98%	95%	90%	80%	70%	60%

MODEL 94 NEW GENERATION CUSTOM

.30-30 Win. cal., fancy pistol grip stock and long forearm with spade checkering, high lustre bluing with custom scroll engraving and hand engraved gold moose on right side of frame and gold doe/buck on left, new tang safety, 20 in. barrel. Limited mfg. 2003-2004.

$2,550	$2,100	$1,775

Last MSR was $2,995.

MODEL 94 LIMITED EDITION CENTENNIAL

.30-30 Win. cal., crossbolt safety, manufactured to commemorate the 100th anniversary of the Model 94 in 1994.

* *Grade I Limited Edition* - features No. 9 style Winchester engraving pattern (rolled) on both sides of receiver, 26 in. half-round half-octagonal barrel, pistol grip stock and forearm with cut checkering, half mag., open sights, crescent buttplate, 12,000 mfg. 1994.

$725	$550	$425

Last MSR was $811.

* *High Grade Limited Edition* - features No. 6 style Winchester engraving pattern (rolled) on both sides of receiver with gold outlines and 2 gold animals (mountain sheep and deer), Lyman No. 2 tang mounted rear sight, F-style checkering and carving, deluxe walnut, 26 in. half-round half-octagonal barrel, half-mag., crescent buttplate, 3,000 mfg. 1994.

$1,200	$875	$625

Last MSR was $1,272.

* *Custom High Grade Limited Edition* - .30 WCF cal., features No. 5 style Winchester engraving pattern (hand-executed) on both sides of greyed receiver, gold outline panel scenes featuring caribou and pronghorns, Lyman No. 2 upper tang sight, F-style checkering and carving, 26 in. half-round half-octagonal barrel, half-mag., crescent buttplate, 94 mfg. in 1994.

$8,700	$7,750	$6,800

Last MSR was $4,684.

Currently, a complete set of Model 94 Limited Edition Centennial rifles with the same serial number is selling in the $10,000+ range. Since there were only 94 Custom High Grade Limited Editions mfg., demand has escalated prices radically for this model.

MODEL 94 XTR

.30-30 Win. or 7-30 Waters (new 1985) cal., 20 or 24 (7-30 Waters only) in. barrel, checkered select walnut, hooded front sight (except 7-30 Waters which has dovetailed front blade), 6 1/2 lbs. Disc. 1988.

$260	$225	$205	$185	$160	$150	$140

Last MSR was $285.

Add $100 for 7-30 Waters cal. rifle.

The XTR nomenclature was disc. 1988.

* *Model 94 XTR Deluxe* - .30-30 Win. cal. only, deluxe American walnut stock and lengthened forearm with fancy checkering, 20 in. barrel with deluxe script, rubber buttpad. Mfg. 1987-88 only.

$370	$310	$270	$235	$210	$190	$160

Last MSR was $426.

MODEL 94 .44 MAG. S.R.C.

.44 Mag., top eject, 20 in. barrel, SRC. Mfg. 1967-72.

$325	$275	$250	$225	$200	$175	$150

MODEL 94 CLASSIC SERIES

.30-30 Win. Win. cal., 20 or 26 in. octagon barrel. Approx. 47,000 mfg. 1967-70.

$325	$285	$235	$200	$185	$160	$150

MODEL 94 ANTIQUE CARBINE

similar to Standard, with scroll on receiver, case hardened, gold-plated saddle ring. Mfg. 1964-83.

$250	$225	$200	$175	$160	$150	$140

GRADING - PPGS™	100%	98%	95%	90%	80%	70%	60%

MODEL 94 WRANGLER - .32 Win. Special, top ejection, only 7,947 mfg. Disc.

	$350	$310	$270	$235	$210	$190	$160

MODEL 94 WRANGLER II - .32 Win. Special (disc. 1984) or .38-55 WCF cal., angle ejection, 16 in. barrel, oversized hoop-shaped lever, roll-engraved receiver, 5 shot mag., 6 1/8 lbs. Made 1983-85 only.

	$350	$220	$200	$185	$165	$150	$140

Last MSR was $275.

MODEL 94 WRANGLER LARGE LOOP - .30-30 Win., .44 Mag., or .45 LC (new 1999) cal., 16 in. barrel, has large loop lever, uncheckered walnut stock and forearm, blue finish, open sights, 6 lbs. Mfg. 1992-99.

	$350	$225	$180	$165	$150	$140	$135

Last MSR was $400.

    Add $21 for .44 Mag. or .45 LC cal.

MODEL 9417 TRADITIONAL - .17 HMR cal., 11 shot mag., 20 1/2 in. barrel, checkered straight grip stock and forearm, full mag., 6 lbs. Limited mfg. 2003-2004.

	$410	$335	$300	$265	$240	$215	$195

Last MSR was $515.

MODEL 9417 LEGACY - .17 HMR cal., 11 shot mag., 22 1/2 in. barrel, checkered pistol grip grip stock and longer forearm, 6 lbs. Limited mfg. 2003-2004.

	$435	$355	$315	$285	$250	$225	$200

Last MSR was $551.

MODEL 9417 LIMITED - .17 HMR cal., 11 shot tube mag., 20 1/2 in. barrel, blue finish, grey/black laminate stock and forend, two barrel bands, grooved receiver, hammer spur extension, hooded front and adj. rear sights, special ser. no. Limited mfg. 2004.

	$425	$335	$300	$275	$240	$215	$190

Last MSR was $530.

    This model was available exclusively through Davidson's.

MODEL 9422 XTR CLASSIC - same general specifications as Model 9422 XTR Standard, except has 22 1/2 in. barrel and non-checkered, satin finished, pistol grip walnut stock and extended forearm, stock also has fluted comb with crescent steel buttplate, curved finger lever, 6 1/2 lbs. Mfg. 1985-87.

	$450	$425	$400	$325	$250	$200	$175

Last MSR was $301.

MODEL 9422 XTR TRADITIONAL (STANDARD WALNUT) - .22 LR or .22 Mag. cal., takedown, 20 1/2 in. round barrel, 15 shot (LR) or 11 shot (Mag. cal.) mag., grooved forged steel receiver, checkered straight grip, checkered high gloss (disc.) or satin weather resistant finish (new 1988) walnut stock and forearm, regular or large loop (mfg. 1998-99) lever, sights, 6 lbs. Mfg. 1972-2004.

	$365	$285	$230	$190	$175	$160	$145

Last MSR was $479.

    Add $22 for .22 Mag. cal.
    Add $25 for large loop lever (disc. 1999).

    This model had an "XTR" suffix until 1989. Earlier mfg., including pre-XTR and early XTR rifles, had no checkering - these guns will command slight premiums over values listed.

MODEL 9422 LEGACY - .22 LR or .22 Mag. (new 1999) cal., features 22 1/2 in. barrel with deluxe checkered semi-pistol grip stock, 11 (.22 Mag.) or 15 shot non-full length mag., 6 lbs. Mfg. 1998-2004.

	$400	$325	$265	$210	$190	$175	$165

Last MSR was $512.

    Add $25 for .22 Mag. cal.

MODEL 9422 SPECIAL EDITION TRADITIONAL TRIBUTE

.22 LR or .22 WMR cal., 20 1/2 in. round barrel, features a Winchester horse and rider engraved on right side of receiver, and Model 9422 Tribute banner on left, checkered straight grip walnut stock and forearm, 6 lbs. 9,422 to be mfg. beginning 2005.

MSR $516	$415	$340	$275	$225	$195	$175	$165

Add $29 for .22 WMR cal.

* *Model 9422 Special Edition Legacy Tribute* - .22 LR or .22 WMR cal., similar to Model 9422 Special Edition Traditional, except has 22 1/2 in. barrel and pistol grip stock with crescent recoil pad, 9,422 to be mfg. beginning 2005.

MSR $551	$440	$365	$295	$250	$215	$190	$175

Add $28 for .22 WMR cal.

MODEL 9422 HIGH GRADE TRADITIONAL TRIBUTE

.22 LR or .22 WMR cal., 20 1/2 in. round barrel, features silver banner with Model 9422 Tribute on left receiver side and horse and rider on right side, etched engraving on blued receiver, checkered straight grip walnut stock and forearm, 6 lbs. 9,422 to be mfg. beginning 2005.

MSR $1,050	$800	$725	$650	$600	$500	$400	$300

Add $28 for .22 WMR cal.

MODEL 9422 HIGH GRADE LEGACY TRIBUTE

.22 LR or .22 WMR cal., similar to High Grade Traditional Tribute, except has 22 1/2 in. barrel and crescent recoil pad, pistol grip stock, 6 lbs. 9,422 to be mfg. beginning 2005.

MSR $1,085	$825	$740	$660	$600	$500	$400	$300

Add $28 for .22 WMR cal.

MODEL 9422 CUSTOM TRIBUTE

.22 LR cal., 20 1/2 in. barrel, features engraved silver plated receiver with gold inlaid Model 9422 Tribute banner on left side of receiver and gold horse and rider on right, engine turned bolt and extractor, gold plated trigger, select walnut with fleur-de-lis checkering on straight grip stock and forearm, 6 lbs. 222 to be mfg. by the Custom Shop beginning 2005.

MSR $2,313	$1,925	$1,600	$1,300

MODEL 9422 TRAPPER

.22 LR or .22 Mag. (new 1998), 16 1/2 in. barrel, checkered walnut stock and forearm, 11 (.22 LR) or 8 (.22 Mag.) shot tube mag., 5 3/4 lbs. Mfg. 1996-2000.

	$335	$265	$215	$190	$175	$160	$145

Last MSR was $437.

Add $20 for .22 Mag. cal.

MODEL 9422 WIN-CAM

.22 Win. Mag. only, similar to 9422 XTR Standard, except has checkered greenish laminated hardwood stock and forearm. Mfg. 1987-97.

	$330	$270	$225	$200	$185	$175	$165

Last MSR was $424.

MODEL 9422 WINTUFF

.22 LR or .22 Mag., 20 1/2 in. barrel, checkered laminated brown hardwood stock and forearm, 6 1/4 lbs. Mfg. 1988-99.

	$325	$260	$215	$190	$175	$160	$145

Last MSR was $423.

Add $21 for .22 Mag. cal.

MODEL 9422 HIGH-GRADE

.22 LR cal., features engraved receiver with raccoon and coonhound, deluxe checkered walnut stock and forearm. Mfg. 1995-96 only.

	$415	$340	$265

Last MSR was $489.

MODEL 9422 HIGH GRADE SERIES II

.22 LR cal., 20 1/2 in. barrel, features high grade walnut stock and forearm with cut checkering, engraved receiver includes dog and squirrels, 6 lbs. Mfg. 1998-99.

	$430	$325	$250

Last MSR was $504.

GRADING - PPGS™	100%	98%	95%	90%	80%	70%	60%

MODEL 9422 25TH ANNIVERSARY GRADE I - .22 LR cal., features deluxe checkered walnut stock and forearm, engraved receiver with Winchester Horse and Rider, 2,500 mfg. 1997 only, inventory remained through 1999.

$535 $425 $325

Last MSR was $606.

MODEL 9422 25TH ANNIVERSARY HIGH GRADE - .22 LR cal., features extra-deluxe checkered walnut stock and forearm, high gloss blue and engraved receiver with Winchester Horse and Rider, featuring silver borders and lever accents, 250 mfg. 1997 only.

$1,175 $995 $850

Last MSR was $1,348.

RIFLES: BOLT ACTION - PRE-1964 MODEL 70

The Pre-'64 Model 70 Bolt Action Rifle (advertised by Winchester throughout much of its production history as "The Rifleman's Rifle") was produced from 1936 through 1963. Collectors recognize three major manufacturing periods: "Pre-War" (1936-1941); "Transition" (1946-1948); and "Latter" (1949-1963). There were only eighteen (18) original chamberings, these are: .22 Hornet, .220 Swift, .243 Win., .250 Savage (.250-3000), .257 Roberts, .264 Win. Mag., .270 Win., 7x57mm Mauser, .300 Savage, .300 H&H, .300 Win. Mag., .30-06 (.30 Govt. '06 Springfield - approx. 80% of total mfg. by cal.), .308 Win. (standard in Featherweight Style only), .338 Win. Mag., .35 Rem., .358 Win. (in Featherweight Style only), .375 H&H, and .458 Win. Mag. (in Super Grade AFRICAN Style only). It is important to note that every caliber was not available during each manufacturing period. Any other caliber encountered (including 7.65mm Argentine and 9x57mm Mauser) may be regarded as either special ordered or non-original. Magazine capacities are as follows: "Standard Calibers" (including .22 Hornet) five (5) rounds; "H&H Magnums" (.300 & .375) four (4) rounds; and "Winchester Short Magnums" (.264, .300, .338, .458) three (3) rounds. The rifle was produced in a myriad of styles and variations - most of which are covered individually. Unfortunately, a veritable "cottage industry" has developed involving the alteration, "upgrading," and/or outright faking of these guns. Be careful when contemplating a purchase of any rare Model 70 (and get a receipt describing the purchase accurately).

MODEL 70 PRE-WWII PRODUCTION STANDARD GRADE - 12 standard cals., 5 shot mag., 4 shot mag. on Magnums, 24, 25, or 26 in. barrel, open sights, checkered walnut pistol grip stock, ser. range is 1-31,675. Mfg. 1937-1941.

Values listed assume original, unaltered specimens - modifications/alterations to either the metal or wood surfaces can reduce prices by large amounts. All pre-war Model 70s have only 2 holes drilled in the front of the receiver (none in the back). An extra set of "holes" can decrease value as much as 50%. Some pre-WWII Model 70s have a "D" suffix indicating a doubled up serial number - this variation will command a premium because of its rarity. The Model 70 is one gun for which caliber ranks before condition in terms of desirability. Specimens encountered in under 60% condition will not decrease in price substantially since almost any shooter is worth $350-$500.

	100%	98%	95%	90%	80%	70%	60%
Standard Cals.	$1,175	$1,050	$950	$800	$625	$550	$475
.22 Hornet	$2,225	$1,950	$1,700	$1,350	$1,100	$900	$725
.220 Swift	$1,550	$1,300	$1,000	$825	$700	$595	$500
.257 Roberts	$2,000	$1,800	$1,600	$1,300	$1,050	$800	$600
.270 Win.	$1,600	$1,400	$1,200	$900	$700	$595	$500
.300 H&H	$2,000	$1,800	$1,500	$1,250	$1,000	$800	$600
.375 H&H	$2,500	$2,250	$2,000	$1,650	$1,350	$1,150	$900
7x57mm Mauser	$4,000	$3,600	$3,000	$2,750	$2,250	$2,000	$1,600
.250-3000 Savage	$3,500	$3,200	$3,000	$2,750	$2,500	$2,000	$1,650

Add approx. 80% for Super Grades in common cals.

There are more fakes than legitimate specimens in cals. 7x57mm and .250-3000 Savage! Rare cals. such as the .300 Savage, .35 Rem., 7.65mm, and 9x57mm Mauser are seldom encountered, and their scarcity precludes accurate price evaluation. Cals. 7.65mm and 9x57mm Mauser were special order only and were made up from leftover Model 54 barrels. Also, the original factory box, papers, and hanging tag will add 25%-30% to the values listed.

GRADING - PPGS™	100%	98%	95%	90%	80%	70%	60%

Believe it or not, there are getting to be a lot of fake Model 70 boxes that have been intentionally aged. Carefully screen NIB (watch the hanging tag also) specimens in this model.

MODEL 70 CARBINE (MFG. 1936-1946)
- available in most cals. during its period, 20 in. barrel, short rifle variation of the Pre-'64 Model 70 (Winchester never officially used the "Carbine" terminology). If original, front sight base will be an integral part of the barrel. All carbines were disc. shortly after WWII. Beware of fakes.

Add 50%-75% for carbine variations mfg. 1936-1946 with 20 in. barrel in .22 Hornet (watch for fakes, examine the front sight carefully), .250-3000 Savage, .257 Roberts, .270 Win., 7mm, or .30-06 (most common) cal.

MODEL 70 TRANSITION (MFG. 1946-1948)
- several of the post-war Model 70s mfg. between 1946-48 exhibit the pre-war receiver characteristics and have a transition safety. This variation is more rare than normal models, ser. no. range is 60,000-100,000.

Add 10%-20% above values for post-Transitional models.

On this Transitional Model, the receiver bridge may or may not be factory drilled.

MODEL 70 STANDARD GRADE (1946-1963 PRODUCTION)
- 18 standard cals. including .22 Hornet, .220 Swift, .243 Win., .250 Savage (.250-3000), .257 Roberts, .264 Win. Mag., .270 Win., 7x57mm Mauser, .300 Savage, .300 H&H, .300 Win. Mag., .30-06, .308 Win., .338 Win. Mag., .35 Rem., .358 Win., and .375 H&H, 5 shot mag., 4 shot mag. on Magnums, 24, 25, or 26 in. barrel, open sights, checkered walnut pistol grip stock, ser. range is 52,549-581,471. Mfg. 1946-63.

Values listed assume original, unaltered specimens - modifications/alterations to either the metal or wood surfaces can reduce prices by large amounts. Most post-war Model 70s are drilled on top of the receiver (2 holes in front and 2 holes in back) to accept scope mounts (except early .300 and .375 H&H cals.). Pre-1962 mfg. Model 70s are desirable since Winchester implemented manufacturing techniques that lowered the quality beginning in 1964.

	100%	98%	95%	90%	80%	70%	60%
.22 Hornet	$1,750	$1,500	$1,400	$1,250	$995	$795	$695
.220 Swift	$1,500	$1,300	$1,200	$900	$700	$550	$500
.243 Win.	$1,250	$1,100	$1,000	$725	$625	$550	$500
.257 Roberts	$1,750	$1,500	$1,250	$1,000	$850	$600	$500
.270 Win.	$1,200	$1,000	$800	$575	$500	$475	$450
.30-06 cal.	$900	$800	$600	$500	$450	$415	$375
.300 H&H	$1,800	$1,600	$1,300	$925	$750	$575	$525
.300 Win. Mag.	$2,000	$1,800	$1,500	$1,250	$1,000	$800	$700
.338 Win. Mag.	$1,800	$1,575	$1,375	$1,100	$875	$750	$650
.375 H&H	$2,350	$2,075	$1,800	$1,600	$1,500	$1,200	$800

Add 10% for .300 H&H or .375 H&H if rear receiver is not drilled and tapped.

Add 20% for stainless steel barrel in .300 H&H or .270 Win. cal.

Rare cals. such as the .250-3000, .300 Savage, .308 Win. (extremely rare, so watch for fakes), .35 Rem., and 7x57mm Mauser are seldomly seen or sold. Premiums depend on the rarity of the caliber and original condition.

Believe it or not, there are getting to be a lot of fake Model 70 boxes that have been intentionally aged. Carefully screen NIB (watch the hanging tag also) specimens in this model.

MODEL 70 FEATHERWEIGHT
- lightened version of Standard, .243 Win., .264 Win. Mag. (Westerner), .270 Win., .308 Win., .30-06, or .358 Win. cal., 22 in. barrel, aluminum trigger guard and floorplate, ser. range is 206,626-581,471. Mfg. 1952-1963.

	100%	98%	95%	90%	80%	70%	60%
.243 Win, .30-06	$1,000	$900	$800	$650	$600	$550	$500
.264 Win. Mag.	$1,600	$1,400	$1,250	$1,100	$900	$800	$700
.270 Win.	$1,500	$1,300	$1,150	$900	$750	$650	$600
.308 Win.	$1,000	$900	$800	$650	$500	$450	$425
.358 Win.	$2,500	$2,200	$1,800	$1,700	$1,500	$1,250	$1,000

Add 400% for Super Grade Models.

Add 10% for .30-06, .308 Win., .243 Win., or .270 Win. cal. models with aluminum buttplate.

The .358 Win. cal. is rare because Winchester had problems with this cal. Many of them were exchanged for other calibers, and the result is that original guns are rare in this cal.

GRADING - PPGS™	100%	98%	95%	90%	80%	70%	60%

MODEL 70 SUPER GRADE - similar to Standard Model, except has deluxe wood, black pistol grip cap and forend tip, all Super Grades have a raised cheekpiece with deluxe wraparound checkering, and Super Grade marked floorplate. Disc. 1960.

> A general rule for Super Grades is that if you add 100% to the standard grade in similar cals., values should be rather close. For .375 H&H cal., values are listed.

	100%	98%	95%	90%	80%	70%	60%
.375 H&H	$4,000	$3,500	$3,000	$2,500	$2,000	$1,500	$1,250

Later Model 70 Super Grades have jeweled action components and rust blued barrels.

MODEL 70 SUPER GRADE FEATHERWEIGHT - .243 Win., .270 Win., .30-06, or .308 Win. cal. only, because of inconsistencies of Super Grade action component jeweling (i.e., engine turning), a simple stock and hinged floorplate change can create an "instant" Super Grade Featherweight (check stock carefully for wood filling near area of Standard Super Grade rear sight "boss" in barrel channel), all Super Grade Featherweights have a raised cheekpiece with wraparound "fish tail" checkering, all have rust blued barrels, less than 1,000 mfg.

> Original S.G. Featherweights will command 3 to 4 times the value of a Standard Featherweight Model.

This is perhaps the rarest variation of the Pre-'64 Model 70 - beware of fakes.

MODEL 70 SUPER GRADE AFRICAN - .458 Win. Mag. only, front swivel base relocated and attached to bottom of barrel, nearly all possess one or two visible stock crossbolts (usually covered with Bakelite). Most have all action components (bolt body, extractor, extractor ring and magazine follower) jeweled (i.e., engine turned), rust blued barrel. 1,226 mfg. 1956-63.

	100%	98%	95%	90%	80%	70%	60%
	$5,000	$4,500	$4,000	$3,750	$3,500	$3,000	$2,500

While other Super Grades were disc. approx. 1960, the "AFRICAN" continued in that style until the end of all production. Normal attrition and collectors owning more than one contribute to extreme rarity. Retains considerable "shooter" value in lesser external conditions. Watch for cracked and/or repaired stocks.

MODEL 70 NATIONAL MATCH - similar to Standard, with target stock and scope bases, .30-06 only. Disc. 1960.

	100%	98%	95%	90%	80%	70%	60%
	$2,250	$2,000	$1,800	$1,750	$1,500	$1,200	$1,000

MODEL 70 TARGET - similar to Model 70 Standard, in .243 Win. or .30-06 cal. (mfg. 1955-1963), earlier pre-'51 Target guns were available in virtually any cal. (i.e., .22 Hornet, .220 Swift, etc.), 24 in. medium weight barrel and target stock. Disc. 1963.

> Add 50%-75% over standard values if condition is over 90%. 60% condition will be priced the same.

MODEL 70 BULL GUN - similar to Standard Model 70, with 28 in. heavy barrel, .300 H&H or .30-06 cal. only, .30-06 cal is much rarer.

	100%	98%	95%	90%	80%	70%	60%
.300 H&H cal.	$3,500	$3,200	$3,000	$2,600	$2,200	$2,000	$1,600
.30-06	$3,800	$3,500	$3,200	$3,000	$2,700	$2,500	$2,150

MODEL 70 VARMINT - similar to Standard Model 70, in .220 Swift or .243 Win. cal., 26 in. heavy barrel, scope bases, varmint style stock. Mfg. 1956-63.

	100%	98%	95%	90%	80%	70%	60%
	$1,200	$1,050	$975	$850	$775	$675	$600

Add 50% for .220 Swift cal.

Less than 900 were mfg. in .220 Swift cal. Stainless steel barrels are also encountered in this model with 3 different types of finishes.

MODEL 70 ALASKAN - similar to Standard Model 70, in .300 Win. Mag. (mfg. 1963 only with 25 in. barrel - known as Alaskan), .338 Win. Mag., or .375 H&H cal., 25 in. barrel, recoil pad. Mfg. 1960-63.

	100%	98%	95%	90%	80%	70%	60%
	$2,000	$1,850	$1,700	$1,500	$1,250	$1,000	$850

RIFLES: BOLT ACTION - MODEL 70, 1964 - CURRENT MFG.

Beginning 1994, Winchester began using the Classic nomenclature to indicate those models featuring a pre-1964 style action with controlled round feeding.

GRADING - PPGS™	100%	98%	95%	90%	80%	70%	60%

MODEL 70 STANDARD - .22-250 Rem., .222 Rem., .225 Win., .243 Win., .25-06 Rem., .270 Win., .308 Win., or .30-06 cal., 5 shot, 22 or 24 in. heavy barrel, open sight, Monte Carlo stock, swivels. Mfg. 1964-80.

	$400	$350	$300	$275	$250	$200	$175

    Add 25% for .225 Win. cal.

MODEL 70 MAGNUM - .264 Win. Mag., 7mm Rem. Mag., .300 H&H Mag., .300 Win. Mag., .338 Win. Mag., .375 H&H, or .458 Win. Mag. cal., 24 in. barrel.

	$450	$400	$350	$325	$300	$250	$225

    Add 25-35% for .375 H&H or .458 Win. Mag. (African Model) cal.

MODEL 70 SUPER GRADE - various cals., deluxe wood with ebony forend cap, Super Grade appears on the floorplate. Disc.

	$575	$525	$475	$425	$400	$375	$350

MODEL 70 DELUXE - .243 Win., .270 Win., .30-06, or .300 Win. Mag. cal., 22 in. barrel, open sight, hand-checkered, black forend tip. Mfg. 1964-71.

	$475	$415	$360	$320	$285	$220	$180

    The Model 70 Deluxe was redesignated the Standard Model 70 in 1972.

MODEL 70 TARGET RIFLE 1964-1971 - .308 Win. or .30-06 cal., 24 in. heavy barrel, no sights, target bases, heavy target style stock with hand stop. Disc. 1971.

	$630	$550	$495	$440	$360	$330	$275

MODEL 70 INTERNATIONAL ARMY MATCH 1971 - .308 Win. cal., 5 shot, 24 in. heavy barrel, no sights, adj. trigger, ISU stock with forearm, accessory rail, adj. butt. Disc. 1971.

	$715	$660	$605	$550	$470	$440	$385

MODEL 70 MANNLICHER 1969-1971 - .243 Win., .270 Win., .30-06, or .308 Win. cal., 19 in. barrel, open sight, full-length Monte Carlo stock with steel forend cap. Disc. 1971.

	$700	$600	$550	$500	$450	$400	$350

MODEL 70A - economy version of 1972 type Model 70, same cals., no hinged floorplate or forend tip. Mfg. 1972-78.

	$325	$285	$265	$230	$200	$165	$140

MODEL 70A MAGNUM - similar to Model 70A, except in Mag. cals. but not .375 H&H or .458. Mfg. 1972-78.

	$340	$310	$275	$250	$220	$195	$165

MODEL 70 FEATHERWEIGHT - .22-250 Rem., .223 Rem., .243 Win., .25-06 Rem. (disc. 1993), .257 Robts. (disc.), .270 Win., .280 Rem., 6.5x55mm Swedish (new 1991), 7x57mm Mauser (disc.), .30-06, .308 Win., 7mm-08 Rem. (new 1992), 7mm Rem. Mag. (mfg. 1991-92 only), or .300 Win. Mag. (mfg. 1991-92 only) cal., bolt action, both short and medium action, 5 shot mag., 22 in. barrel (24 in. with .300 Win. Mag.), checkered walnut stock, with or w/o sights, approx. 6 1/2 lbs. Mfg. 1981-94.

	$435	$380	$325	$300	$280	$260	$240

                                  Last MSR was $562.

    In 1981, during U.S.R.A. takeover transition, guns were distinguishable by the U.S.R.A. trademark on the recoil pad. Some collectors will pay a premium for Win. marked pads. Cals. .257 Robts. and 7x57mm Mauser were disc. 1985.

    This model had an "XTR" suffix until 1989.

MODEL 70 CLASSIC FEATHERWEIGHT - .22-250 Rem. (new 1994), .223 Rem. (mfg. 1994 only), .243 Win. (new 1994), .270 Win., .280 Rem. (disc. 2000), .30-06, .308 Win. (new 1994), 6.5x55mm Swedish (new 1997), or 7mm-08 Rem. (new 1994) cal., 22 in. barrel, 5 shot mag., blue action, features claw-controlled round feeding action bedded into standard grade walnut stock, jewelled bolt, knurled bolt handle, includes rings and bases, approx. 7 lbs. New 1992.

MSR $762		$570	$460	$360	$315	$290	$260	$240

GRADING - PPGS™	100%	98%	95%	90%	80%	70%	60%

✳ *Model 70 Classic Featherweight WSM* - .270 WSM (new 2002), .300 WSM, .325 WSM (new 2005) or 7mm WSM (new 2002) cal., controlled round feeding, 24 in. round barrel, 3 shot internal mag., approx. 7 1/4 lbs. New 2001.

	MSR $792	$600	$495	$385	$330	$295	$265	$245

Add $39 for left-hand action (new late 2003, not available in .325 WSM cal.).

✳ *Model 70 Classic Featherweight Super Short WSSM* - similar to Model 70 Classic Featherweight, except available in .223 WSSM, .243 WSSM, and .25 WSSM (new 2004) cals., 22 in. barrel, 3 shot mag., 6 lbs. New 2003.

	MSR $814	$615	$500	$385	$330	$295	$265	$245

✳ *Model 70 Classic Featherweight BOSS* - similar to Model 70 Classic Featherweight, except has 22 in. barrel with BOSS. Mfg. 1996 only.

		$600	$500	$395	$350	$325	$295	$275

Last MSR was $735.

✳ *Model 70 Classic Featherweight Stainless (New 2005)* - same calibers as Classic Featherweight, WSM, and WSSM models, 22 or 24 in. stainless barrel and action, no sights, three position safety, controlled round feed, Pachmayr Decelerator pad on WSM models, 3 shot mag., cut checkering with Schnabel forend, 6-7 1/4 lbs. New 2005.

	MSR $806	$615	$500	$385	$330	$295	$265	$245

Add $31 for WSM cals. or $53 for WSSM cals.

✳ *Model 70 Classic Featherweight Stainless* - .22-250 Rem., .243 Win., .270 Win., .30-06, .308 Win., .300 Win. Mag. (disc. 1998), or 7mm Rem. Mag. cal., 22 or 24 (Mag. cals. only) in. stainless barrel, checkered walnut stock, 3 or 5 shot mag., approx. 7-7 1/2 lbs. Mfg. 1997-99.

	$615	$510	$390

Last MSR was $746.

✳ *Model 70 Classic Featherweight All-Terrain* - .270 Win., .30-06, .300 Win. Mag., or 7mm Rem. Mag. cal., 22 or 24 in. matte finish stainless steel barrel/receiver, black fiberglass/graphite stock with checkering, with (1996-1997 only) or without BOSS, 3 or 5 shot mag., 7 1/4 lbs. Mfg. 1996-98.

	$565	$475	$375

Last MSR was $672.

Add $100 for BOSS (disc. 1997).

✳ *Model 70 Win-Tuff Featherweight Rifle* - .22-250 Rem., .223 Rem., .243 Win., .270 Win., .30-06, or .308 Win. cal., features brown laminated, checkered stock with Schnabel forend, includes base and rings, pistol grip cap, 7 lbs. Mfg. 1988-90. Reintroduced 1992-93.

	$445	$385	$325	$300	$280	$260	$240

Last MSR was $572.

✳ *Model 70 Featherweight Special* - .243 Win. cal., features custom fitted stock, hand-honed action, barrel, and bolt/follower, custom shop proofstamp, select American walnut with rounded pistol grips, no sights. Only 50 mfg.

	$600	$525	$475	$425	$380	$340	$300

This model is distinguishable by the Super Grade floorplate marking.

MODEL 70 XTR EUROPEAN FEATHERWEIGHT - 6.5x55 Swedish Mauser cal., 22 in. barrel, 5 shot mag., rifle sights, 6 3/4 lbs. Made 1986 only.

	$390	$365	$330	$305	$280	$260	$240

Last MSR was $460.

MODEL 70 LIGHTWEIGHT RIFLE - .22-250 Rem. (disc. 1992), .223 Rem., .243 Win., .270 Win., .280 Rem. (mfg. 1988-92), .30-06, or .308 Win. cal., 22 in. barrel, checkered walnut stock, no sights, 6 1/2 lbs. Mfg. 1987-95.

	$420	$335	$290	$255	$230	$210	$190

Last MSR was $513.

✳ *Model 70 Lightweight Carbine* - .22-250 Rem., .222 Rem. (scarce), .223 Rem., .243 Win., .250 Savage (new 1986), .308 Win., .270 Win., or .30-06 cal., bolt action, 5 shot mag., both short and medium action, 20 in. barrel, checkered walnut stock, no sights, approx. 6 lbs. Mfg. 1984-87.

$355	$320	$285	$255	$230	$210	$190

Last MSR was $395.

   Add $15 for open sights.

✳ *Model 70 Win-Tuff Lightweight Rifle* - .22-250 Rem. (mfg. 1988-89), .223 Rem. (new 1989), .243 Win. (new 1988), .270 Win. .30-06 or .308 Win. (new 1989) cal., similar to Model 70 Lightweight Rifle, except has laminated brown hardwood stock with checkering. Mfg. 1987-92.

$395	$330	$290	$255	$230	$210	$190

Last MSR was $471.

✳ *Model 70 Win-Cam Lightweight Rifle* - .270 Win. or .30-06 cal., greenish laminated hardwood stock with checkering, 22 in. barrel. New 1987.

$395	$330	$290	$255	$230	$210	$190

Last MSR was $471.

   This model was previously designated Featherweight before 1989.

MODEL 70 SPORTER - .22-250 Rem. (mfg. 1989-1993), .223 Rem. (mfg. 1989-93), .243 Win. (mfg. 1989-93), .25-06 Rem. (mfg. 1985-87 and reintroduced 1990), .264 Win. Mag., .270 Win., .270 Wby. Mag. (new 1988), .30-06, .300 Win. Mag., .300 Wby. Mag. (new 1989), .300 H&H (mfg. 1989- 1992), .308 Win. (mfg. 1986-89), .338 Win. Mag., or 7mm Rem. Mag. cal., 24 in. barrel, 3 or 5 shot mag., custom Sporter styling, Monte Carlo cheek piece, detachable sling swivels, 7 3/4 lbs. Disc. 1994.

$435	$375	$325	$300	$280	$260	$240

Last MSR was $556.

   Add $34 for iron sights (.270 Win., .30-06, .300 Win. Mag., or 7mm Rem. Mag. only). This model had an "XTR" suffix until 1989.

✳ *Sporter Win-Tuff* - .270 Win., .30-06, 7mm Rem. Mag., .300 Win. Mag., .300 Wby. Mag., or .338 Win. Mag., similar to Model 70 Sporter, except has checkered brown laminate stock with sling swivels, solid recoil pad, 24 in. barrel, approx. 7 3/4 lbs. Mfg. 1992 only.

$445	$380	$325	$300	$280	$260	$240

Last MSR was $572.

MODEL 70 CLASSIC SPORTER (LT) - .25-06 Rem., .264 Win. Mag. (disc. 2000), .270 Win., .270 Wby. Mag. (disc. 1998), .270 WSM (new 2004), .30-06, .300 Win. Mag., .300 WSM (new 2004), .300 Wby. Mag. (disc. 2000), .325 WSM (new 2005), .338 Win. Mag., 7mm STW (mfg. 1997-2002), 7mm WSM (new 2004), or 7mm Rem. Mag. cal., similar to Model 70 Sporter, except features controlled round feeding, 3 (Mag. cals. only) or 5 shot internal mag., 24 or 26 in. barrel, checkered walnut stock, blue finish, stock was redesigned by David Miller in 1999 (denoted by "LT" Model suffix), approx. 7 3/4-8 lbs. New 1994.

MSR $742	$565	$450	$365	$320	$290	$265	$240

   Add $31 for Mag. cals.
   Add $36 for left-hand action (new 1997).
   Add $38 for iron sights - disc. 1998 (available in .270 Win., .30-06, .300 Win. Mag., .338 Win. Mag., or 7mm Rem. Mag.).
   Left-hand action is available in .270 Win., .30-06, .300 Win. Mag., .338 Win. Mag. (disc. 2000), 7mm STW (disc. 2000), or 7mm Rem. Mag.
   This model's nomenclature was changed from Model 70 Classic Sporter LT to Model 70 Classic Sporter III during 2005. Sporter III improvements include a trimmer forend and stock, Pachmayr Decelerator pad, and a more open pistol grip.

GRADING - PPGS™	100%	98%	95%	90%	80%	70%	60%

* **Model 70 Classic Sporter BOSS** - .25-06 Rem. (disc. 1996), .270 Win., .30-06, .264 Win. Mag. (disc. 1996), 7mm STW (new 1997), 7mm Rem. Mag., .270 Wby. Mag. (mfg. 1996 only), .300 Win. Mag., .300 Wby Mag. (mfg. 1996 only), or .338 Win. Mag. cal., 24 or 26 in. barrel with BOSS, 3 or 5 shot mag., checkered walnut stock, approx. 7 3/4 lbs. Mfg. 1995-98.

	$620	$535	$440	$350	$295	$275	$250

Last MSR was $728.

Add $28 for left-hand action (new 1997).

* **Model 70 Classic Sporter Stainless** - .270 Win., .30-06, .300 Win. Mag., .338 Win. Mag., or 7mm Rem. Mag. cal., 24 or 26 in. barrel with (1997 only) or without BOSS, checkered walnut stock, controlled round feeding, 3 or 5 shot mag., right- or left-hand action, approx. 7 3/4 lbs. Mfg. 1997-98.

	$615	$530	$440				

Last MSR was $716.

Add $80 for BOSS.
Add $29 for left-hand action.

* **Model 70 Classic Laredo** - .300 Win Mag., 7mm STW (mfg. 1997-98), or 7mm Rem. Mag. cal., features claw extraction and controlled round feeding, 26 in. round or fluted (new 1998) barrel with (.300 Win. Mag and 7mm Rem. Mag. disc. 1997) or without BOSS. Mfg. 1996-99.

	$665	$560	$450	$350	$295	$275	$250

Last MSR was $794.

Add $95 for BOSS on barrel (disc. 1998).
Add $130 for fluted barrel.

* **Model 70 Classic Safari Express** - .375 H&H, .416 Rem. Mag., or .458 Win. Mag. cal., features Express style rear sight with standing blade, redesigned stock with negative drop and Pachmayr decelerator recoil pad, trigger guard and floorplate are one assembly, 3 shot mag., controlled round feed, 24 in. barrel with barrel band swivel attachment, checkered walnut stock and forearm, 8 1/2 lbs. New 1999.

MSR $1,149	$925	$785	$670	$595	$535	$480	$430

Add $40 for left-hand action (.375 H&H cal. only).

* **Model 70 Classic Super Express Mag.** - .375 H&H, .416 Rem. Mag. (new 1994), or .458 Win. Mag. cal., 3 shot mag., claw extractor controlled round feeding (new 1993), open sights, 22 or 24 in. (.375 H&H or .416 Rem. Mag.) barrel, 8 1/2 lbs. Disc. 1998.

	$730	$585	$525	$495	$460	$430	$400

Last MSR was $865.

Add $29 for left-hand action (new 1997), .375 H&H cal. only.
This model had an "XTR" suffix until 1989.

MODEL 70 CLASSIC LAMINATED WSM - .270 WSM, .300 WSM, .325 WSM (new 2005) or 7mm WSM cals., claw extractor controlled round feed, brown laminate stock, 24 in. barrel w/o sights, one inch deluxe recoil pad, blued receiver and barrel, 3 shot mag., 7 3/4 lbs. New 2003.

MSR $810	$640	$485	$440	$395	$360	$330	$300

MODEL 70 DBM (DETACHABLE BOX MAGAZINE) - .22-250 Rem. (mfg. 1993 only), .223 Rem. (mfg. 1993 only), .243 Win. (new 1993), .270 Win., .30-06, .308 Win. (mfg. 1993 only), 7mm Rem. Mag., or .300 Win. Mag. cal., checkered walnut stock and forend, features 3 shot detachable box mag., 24 or 26 in. barrel with or without sights, includes bases and rings or iron sights (new 1993, optional) in .30-06, .300 Win. Mag., or 7mm Rem. Mag., 7 3/4 lbs. Mfg. 1992-94.

	$465	$390	$330	$300	$280	$260	$240

Last MSR was $598.

Add $36 for iron sights.

GRADING - PPGS™	100%	98%	95%	90%	80%	70%	60%

MODEL 70 CLASSIC DBM - .22-250 Rem., .243 Win., .270 Win., .284 Win., .30-06, .308 Win., .300 Win. Mag., or 7mm Rem. Mag. cal., similar to Model 70 DBM, except has controlled round feeding, 24 or 26 in. barrel. Mfg. 1994 only.

Most cals.	$475	$395	$330	$300	$280	$260	$240
.284 Win.							
(less than 200 mfg.)	$695	$650	$550	$495	$395	$350	$295

Last MSR was $619.

Add $52 for iron sights (.270 Win., .30-06, .300 Win. Mag., or 7mm Rem. Mag.).

✳ *Model 70 Classic DBM-S* - .270 Win., .30-06, .300 Win. Mag., or 7mm Rem. Mag. cal., similar to Model 70 DBM, except has black synthetic stock, this model became a Classic series in 1994 (featuring controlled round feeding). Mfg. 1993-94.

	$475	$395	$330	$300	$280	$260	$240

Last MSR was $619.

MODEL 70 STAINLESS - .270 Win., .30-06, 7mm Rem. Mag., .300 Win. Mag., or .338 Win. Mag., features matte finished stainless steel receiver barrel and bolt, black synthetic composite stock, 22 (.270 Win. or .30-06 only, disc. 1992) or 24 in. barrel, approx. 6 3/4 lbs. Mfg. 1992-94.

	$475	$390	$330				

Last MSR was $616.

MODEL 70 CLASSIC STAINLESS - .22-250 Rem. (disc. 1999), .223 Rem. (disc. 1994), .243 Win. (disc. 1998), .270 Win., .270 WSM (mfg. 2002), .30-06, .308 Win. (disc. 1998), .270 Wby. Mag. (mfg. 1997 only), .300 Win. Mag., .300 Wby. Mag. (disc. 2000), .300 Rem. Ultra Mag. (disc. 2002), .300 WSM (mfg. 2001-2003), .338 Win. Mag., .375 H&H, 7mm STW (mfg. 2001-2002), 7mm WSM (mfg. 2002) or 7mm Rem. Mag. (disc. 2003, reintroduced 2004) cal., features controlled round feeding, 22 (disc. 2001), 24, or 26 in. barrel, black synthetic composite stock, 3, 5, or 6 shot mag., without sights except for .375 H&H cal., 6 3/4-7 1/2 lbs. New 1994.

MSR $817	$610	$465	$360				

Add $30 for Mag. cals., or $126 for .375 H&H cal.

✳ *Model 70 Classic Stainless BOSS* - .22-250 Rem. (disc. 1996), .243 Win. (disc. 1996), .270 Win., .30-06, .308 Win. (disc. 1996), .270 Wby. Mag. (mfg. 1997 only), .300 Win. Mag., .300 Wby. Mag. (mfg. 1996-97), .338 Win. Mag., or 7mm Rem. Mag. cal., 22, 24, or 26 in. barrel with BOSS, black synthetic stock, 6 3/4-7 1/2 lbs. Mfg. 1995-98.

	$645	$535	$430				

Last MSR was $788.

MODEL 70 CLASSIC LAMINATED STAINLESS - .270 Win., .30-06, .300 Win. Mag., .338 Win. Mag., or 7mm Rem. Mag. cal., 24 or 26 (Mag. cals. only) in. barrel without sights, checkered grey/black laminate stock with sporter style dimensions, stainless action and barrel, 3 or 5 shot mag., approx. 8 lbs. Mfg. 1998-99.

	$640	$545	$440				

Last MSR was $753.

✳ *Model 70 Classic Camo Stainless* - similiar to Model 70 Classic Stainless, except has Mossy Oak Treestand stock finish composite stock, not available in .338 Win. Mag. cal. approx. 7 1/4 lbs. Mfg. 1998 only.

	$630	$540	$445				

Last MSR was $745.

MODEL 70 COYOTE STAINLESS LAMINATED - .22-250 Rem., .223 Rem. (disc. 2003, reintroduced 2005), .223 WSSM (new 2003), .243 Win. (disc. 2003), .243 WSSM (new 2003), .25 WSSM (new 2003), .270 WSM (new 2002), .300 WSM (new 2002), .308 Win. (new 2002), or 7mm WSM (new 2002) cal., push feed (non-WSM/WSSM cals.) or controlled round feed (WSM/WSSM cals. only) action, 24 in. medium heavy stainless steel sporter barrel, uncheckered brown laminate stock with reverse taper on forend, 3 (WSM cals. only), 5, or 6 (.223 Rem. only) shot mag., 8.75 lbs. New 2000.

MSR $734	$575	$460	$355				

Add $29 for WSM cals. or $53 for WSSM cals.

GRADING - PPGS™	100%	98%	95%	90%	80%	70%	60%

MODEL 70 COYOTE LAMINATED BLUE - .223 Rem., .270 WSM, .300 WSM, .325 WSM, 7mm WSM, .223 WSSM, .243 WSSM, or .25 WSSM cal., similar to Model 70 Coyote Laminated Stainless, except has blued barrel/receiver finish. New 2005.

MSR $689	$535	$435	$350	$310	$285	$260	$240

Add $30 for WSM cals. or $53 for WSSM cals.

MODEL 70 COYOTE LITE - similar cals. as Model 70 Coyote Laminated Blue, features 24 in. blued steel or stainless steel fluted barrel/action, controlled round feed action, floorplate, carbon fiber/fiberglass composite Bell & Carlson stock with vents and forend, Pachmayr Decelerator pad, 7 1/2 lbs. New 2005.

MSR $839	$665	$500	$450	$400	$365	$330	$300

Add $29 for WSM cals. or $50 for WSSM cals.

Add $42 for stainless steel barrel/action.

MODEL 70 CLASSIC SM (SYNTHETIC MATTE) - .22-250 Rem. (mfg. 1993 only), .223 Rem. (mfg. 1993 only), .243 Win. (mfg. 1993 only), .270 Win., .30-06, .308 Win. (mfg. 1993 only), 7mm Rem. Mag., .300 Win. Mag., .338 Win. Mag., or .375 H&H (new 1993) cal., features black composite stock with checkering and sling swivels, 22 (.22-250 Rem., .223 Rem., .243 Win., or .308 Win. - mfg. 1993 only), 24, or 26 in. barrel with matte metal finish, 3 or 5 shot, approx. 7 1/2 lbs. Mfg. 1992-96.

	$465	$395	$330	$300	$280	$260	$240

Last MSR was $620.

Add $52 for .375 H&H cal. (open sights only).

Until 1993, this model was called the Model 70 SSM. In 1994, this model became the Model 70 Classic SM featuring controlled round feeding.

MODEL 70 CLASSIC SM BOSS - .270 Win., .30-06, 7mm Rem. Mag., .300 Win. Mag., or .338 Win. Mag. cal., 24 or 26 in. barrel with BOSS, 3 or 5 shot, approx. 7 1/4 lbs. Mfg. 1995-96 only.

	$625	$525	$430	$350	$295	$275	$250

Last MSR was $735.

MODEL 70 CLASSIC COMPACT - .243 Win., .308 Win. (disc. 2003), or 7mm-08 Rem. cal., features 12 1/2 in. LOP, 20 in. barrel and shallow profile, pre-64 type action, 4 shot mag., checkered walnut stock and forearm, blue action and barrel, 6-6 1/2 lbs. New 1998.

MSR $762	$590	$455	$360	$320	$285	$260	$240

MODEL 70 VARMINT - same general specifications as standard Sporter, .22-250 Rem., .223 Rem., .225 Win., .243 Win., or .308 Win. cal., 26 in. heavy barrel with cold hammer forged rifling and counter-bored at muzzle, no sights, 5 shot mag., target scope bases, 7 3/4 lbs. Mfg. 1964-93.

	$470	$375	$325	$295	$280	$260	$240

Last MSR was $720.

Add 25% for .225 Win. cal.

This model had an "XTR" suffix 1978-89.

✱ **Model 70 Heavy Varmint (HBV)** - .220 Swift (mfg. 1994-98), .22-250 Rem., .222 Rem. (mfg. 1997-98), .223 Rem., .243 Win., or .308 Win. cal., push-feed style action, 26 in. heavy stainless fluted (new 1997) or plain barrel (countersunk muzzle) without sights, features black synthetic beavertail H&S Precision stock with aluminum bedding block, 10 3/4 lbs. Mfg. 1993-99.

	$645	$515	$410				

Last MSR was $795.

Add $137 for fluted barrel.

MODEL 70 SHB (SYNTHETIC HEAVY BARREL) - .308 Win. cal., features checkered black composite stock, 26 in. barrel with matte metal finish, jeweled bolt, 9 lbs. Mfg. 1992 only.

	$460	$375	$325	$300	$280	$260	$240

Last MSR was $563.

GRADING - PPGS™	100%	98%	95%	90%	80%	70%	60%

MODEL 70 WINLIGHT - .25-06 Rem., .270 Win., .280 Rem. (new 1987), .30-06, 7mm Rem. Mag., .300 Win. Mag., .300 Wby. Mag., or .338 Win. Mag. cal., McMillan fiberglass stock, thermoplastic receiver bedding, blue metal parts, 22 or 24 (Mag. cals. only) in. barrel, 3 or 4 shot mag., no sights, approx. 6 1/2 lbs. Mfg. 1986-90.

	$555	$490	$440	$395	$350	$310	$280

Last MSR was $637.

MODEL 70 RANGER RIFLE - .22-250 Rem. (new 1999), .223 Rem. (new 1992), .243 Win. (new 1991), .270 Win., .30-06, or 7mm Rem. Mag. cal., push-feed action, 22 or 24 in. barrel, 3 (7mm Rem. Mag.), 5, or 6 shot mag., plain hardwood stock without checkering, open sights, approx. 7 lbs. Disc. 1999.

	$375	$285	$220	$200	$180	$165	$155

Last MSR was $503.

✳ *Model 70 Ranger Compact (Ladies/Youth)* - .22-250 Rem. (mfg. 1999 only), .223 Rem. (disc. 1989, reintroduced 1997, disc. 1998), .243 Win., .308 Win. (new 1991), or 7mm-08 Rem. (mfg. 1997-98, reintroduced 2000) cal., push-feed action, 20 (disc. 1992) or 22 (new 1993) in. barrel, 5 or 6 shot mag., shorter hardwood stock dimensions, open sights, 6 1/2 lbs. Disc. 2000.

	$390	$295	$230	$200	$180	$165	$155

Last MSR was $528.

MODEL 70 STEALTH - .22-250 Rem., .223 Rem., .308 Win. cal., push-feed style action, 26 in. heavy barrel w/o sights, non-glare matte metal finish, Accu Block black synthetic stock with full length aluminum beeding block, 5 or 6 shot mag., 10 3/4 lbs. Mfg. 1999-2003.

	$685	$590	$480	$420	$360	$330	$300

Last MSR was $800.

MODEL 70 STEALTH II - .22-250 Rem., .223 WSSM, .243 WSSM, .25 WSSM, or .308 Win. cal., push-feed style action, 26 in. heavy barrel w/o sights, matte blue finish, redesigned black synthetic stock with aluminum pillar bedding, 3 or 5 shot mag., 10 lbs. New 2004.

MSR $886	$745	$635	$500	$440	$385	$340	$300

Subtract $54 for non-WSSM cals.

MODEL 70 BLACK SHADOW - .270 Win., .30-06, .300 Win. Mag., or 7mm Rem. Mag cal., push-feed action, 3 (Mag. cals.) or 5 shot internal mag., 24 or 26 (Mag. cals.) in. barrel w/o sights, matte receiver and barrel finish, black composite stock with conventional floorplate mag., 7 1/4 lbs. Mfg. 1998-2003.

	$395	$310	$235	$205	$185	$165	$155

Last MSR was $523.

Add $30 for Mag. cals.

CLASSIC/CAMO ULTIMATE SHADOW - .223 WSSM (new 2004), .243 WSSM (new 2004), .25 WSSM (new 2004), .270 WSM, .300 WSM, .325 WSM (new 2005) or 7mm WSM cal., features controlled round feed, black or Dura-Touch armor coated Mossy Oak New Break-Up camo finished molded synthetic stock with rubber grip inserts and new recoil pad, matte black metal, 3 shot mag., 24 in. blued steel or stainless steel barrel, 6 3/4 lbs. New 2003.

MSR $817	$700	$595	$485	$425	$365	$335	$300

Add approx. $21 for WSSM cals.

Add $44 for stainless steel action.

Add $97 Mossy Oak New Break-Up camo finish.

MODEL 70 SUPER SHADOW - similar to Classic Ultimate Shadow, except has oval dot texture gripping surface on pistol grip and forearm, blue finish, controlled round push feed action, available in either short or super short action, blind mag., 22 (.223 WSSM, .243 WSSM, or .25 WSSM cal.) or 24 in. barrel w/o sights, 6 (WSSM cals.) or 6 3/4 lbs. New 2003.

MSR $554	$420	$330	$270	$235	$200	$180	$165

Add $22 for WSSM cals.

GRADING - PPGS™	100%	98%	95%	90%	80%	70%	60%

MODEL 70 CLASSIC SUPER GRADE

- .25-06 Win. (new 2001), .270 Win. (mfg. 1991-2003), .270 WSM (new 2004), .30-06 (new 1991), 7mm STW (230 mfg. 1999 only), 7mm WSM (new 2004), 7mm Rem. Mag. (disc. 1998, reintroduced 2000-2003), .264 Win. Mag. (limited mfg. 2000 only), .300 WSM (new 2004), .300 Win. Mag. (disc. 2003, reintroduced 2005), .325 WSM (new 2005) or .338 Win. Mag. cal., 24 or 26 in. barrel, 3 (Mag. cals.) or 5 shot mag., jewelled bolt, stainless steel extractor for true claw controlled round feeding and ejecting, three-position safety, checkered satin finish walnut stock with wood cheekpiece, black forend tip, bases and rings included, approx. 7 3/4 - 8 lbs. New 1990.

MSR $1,036	$825	$595	$480	$410	$350	$300	$280

Add $31 for WSM cals.

This model was designated the Model 70 Super Grade until 1995. During 1999, this model was redesigned to include a new Express style rear sight with standing blade, negative stock drop, Pachmayr Decelerator pad, one-piece floorplate and full barrel band swivel attachment. This model is on its third generation of design improvements (now called the Super Grade III) with trimmer sporter style stock, steel stock crossbolt, and inlaid swivel studs.

* ***Model 70 Classic Super Grade RMEF*** - .300 WSM or .325 WSM (new 2005) cal., similar to Model 70 Classic Super Grade, except is Rocky Mountain Elk Foundation special edition, includes Super Grade Stock with ebony forend and Pachmayr decelerator pad, special RMEF emblem on grip cap, 26 in. barrel, 8 lbs. Limited mfg. beginning 2003.

MSR $1,183	$940	$635	$510	$430	$365	$315	$290

This model was redesignated the Super Grade III RMEF in 2005.

* ***Model 70 Classic Super Grade BOSS*** - similar to Model 70 Classic Super Grade, except has BOSS. Mfg. 1995-97.

	$810	$685	$555	$450	$375	$335	$300

Last MSR was $956.

MODEL 70 50TH ANNIVERSARY MODEL

- .300 Win. Mag., 24 in. barrel, deluxe walnut stock, engraving and special motifs on metal surfaces, serial numbered 50 ANV 1 - 50 ANV 500, 7 3/4 lbs. 500 mfg. 1987 only.

	$1,200	$1,050	$900

Last MSR was $939.

RIFLES: BOLT ACTION - POST 1964 MODEL 70 CUSTOM GRADES

MODEL 70 CUSTOM GRADE

- various cals., old style Model 70 action, semi-fancy American walnut checkered stock, engine turned bolt and follower, hand honed internal parts. Mfg. 1988-89 only.

	$1,100	$875	$700	$600	$525	$475	$425

Last MSR was $1,172.

MODEL 70 XTR FEATHERWEIGHT ULTRA GRADE "1 OF 1,000"

- .270 Win., bolt action, extensively engraved, finely checkered deluxe French walnut, with mahogany presentation case.

	$1,800	$1,450	$950

Last MSR was $5,000.

MODEL 70 CLASSIC CUSTOM GRADE

- .264 Win. Mag. (new 1994), .270 Win., .30-06, 7mm Rem. Mag., .300 Win. Mag., .300 Wby. Mag. (new 1994) or .338 Win. Mag. cal., 24 or 26 in. barrel, similar to Model 70 Super Grade, but must be special ordered through the Custom Gun Shop, and includes many custom features including semi-fancy walnut with satin finish and hand-honed internal parts. Mfg. 1990-94.

	$1,625	$1,250	$995	$875	$800	$725	$650

Last MSR was $1,757.

A Model 70 Collector Grade is also a variation of this model that is mfg. in the Custom Gun Shop - this model is priced on request only.

GRADING - PPGS™	100%	98%	95%	90%	80%	70%	60%

* ✸ *Model 70 Classic Custom Grade Featherweight* - .22-250 Rem. (new 1994), .223 Rem. (new 1994), .243 Win. (new 1994), .270 Win., .280 Rem., .30-06, .308 Win. (new 1994), 7mm-08 Rem. (new 1994) cal., 22 in. barrel, includes Featherweight features, controlled round feeding, higher grade wood. Mfg. 1992-94.

	$1,625	$1,250	$995	$875	$800	$725	$650

Last MSR was $1,757.

* ✸ *Model 70 Classic/Custom Sharpshooter I/II* - .22-250 Rem. (new 1993), .223 Rem. (mfg. 1993-94), .30-06, .308 Win., or .300 Win. Mag. cal., includes specially designed McMillan A-2 (disc. 1995) or H-S Precision heavy target stock, Schneider (disc. 1995) or H-S Precision (new 1996) 24 (.308 Win. cal. only) or 26 in. stainless steel barrel, choice of blue or grey finish starting 1996. Mfg. 1992-98.

	$1,795	$1,375	$1,000	$875	$800	$725	$650

Last MSR was $1,994.

Subtract $100 if without stainless barrel (pre-1995).

This model was designated the Sharpshooter II in 1996 (features H-S Precision stock and stainless steel barrel).

This model is also available in left-hand action beginning 1998 (.30-06 and .330 Win. Mag. cals. only).

* ✸ *Model 70 Classic/Custom Sporting Sharpshooter I/II* - .270 Win. (disc. 1994), 7mm STW, or .300 Win. Mag. cal., 1/2-minute of angle sporting version of the Custom Sharpshooter, custom shop only, Sharpshooter II became standard in 1996. Mfg. 1993-98.

	$1,725	$1,295	$975	$850	$775	$700	$625

Last MSR was $1,875.

This model was also available in left-hand action in 1998.

* ✸ *Model 70 Custom/Sporting Sharpshooter* - .220 Swift cal., 26 in. Schneider barrel, controlled round feeding, available with either McMillan A-2 or Sporting synthetic (disc. 1994) stock. Mfg. 1994-95 only.

	$1,650	$1,250	$975	$850	$775	$700	$625

Last MSR was $1,814.

* ✸ *Model 70 Classic Custom Express* - .300 Petersen (mfg. 1995 only), .375 H&H, .375 JRS (mfg. 1992-96), 7mm STW (mfg. 1993-94), .416 Rem. Mag., .458 Win. Mag., or .470 Capstick (disc. 1995) cal., 24 in. (22 in. on .458 Win. Mag.) barrel, features claw controlled round feeding, deluxe walnut with satin finish and checkering, 3-leaf express (disc. 1995) or pre-64 style adj. rear sight (new 1996), high luster metal finish, bolt and follower are engine turned, available by special order through the custom gun shop only. Mfg. 1990-98.

	$2,300	$1,825	$1,550	$1,300	$1,125	$1,000	$895

Last MSR was $2,512.

Subtract $200 for 7mm STW cal.

In 1994, the model nomenclature was changed from Model 70 Custom Grade Express, and in 1996 it was changed from Model 70 Classic Express.

MODEL 70 CUSTOM ULTIMATE CLASSIC - .25-06 Rem., 6.5x55mm Swedish (new 2001), .270 Win., .280 Rem. (mfg. 1996, reintroduced 1999), .30-06, 7mm STW, .264 Win. Mag., .270 Wby. Mag. (disc. 1996), .35 Whelen (new 1998), 7mm Rem. Mag., 7mm Rem. Ultra Mag., .300 Win. Mag., .300 Wby. Mag., .300 H&H (mfg. 1996-99), .300 Rem. Ultra Mag. (new 2000), .338 Win. Mag., .338-06 (mfg. 1999-2001), .338 Rem. Ultra Mag. (new 2001), .340 Wby. Mag. (mfg. 1998), .375 H&H (1995 only), .416 Rem. Mag. (1995 only), or .458 Win. Mag. (1995 only) cal., controlled round feeding, engine turned bolt, checkered fancy walnut stock, choice of 22 (.458 Win. Mag. only), 24 or 26 in. tapered round full-fluted, 1/2 round, 1/2 octagonal, or full octagonal tapered stainless barrel, one inch black decelerator recoil pad,

GRADING - PPGS™	100%	98%	95%	90%	80%	70%	60%

choice blue or stainless barreled action, 3 or 5 shot mag., includes bases/rings except on some Mag. cals., approx. 7 3/4 lbs., except for large disc. cals., includes hard case. New 1995.

	MSR $3,000	$2,575	$2,000	$1,550	$1,275	$995	$850	$750

Add $100 for stainless steel barrel, $110 for fluted round barrel, or $235 for full or half octagon barrel.

Add approx. 15% for .375 H&H and larger Mag. cals (disc. 1995).

This model was previously designated the Model 70 Ultimate Classic until 2000, and was changed to the Model 70 Classic Custom Ultimate Classic.

Left-hand action (new 1997) available in all current cals.

MODEL 70 CLASSIC CUSTOM SHORT ACTION

.243 Win. (disc. 2000, reintroduced 2002 only), .257 Roberts, .260 Rem., .270 WSM (new 2002), .308 Win., .358 Win., .300 WSM (new 2001), .325 WSM (new 2005), 7mm-08 Rem., 7mm WSM (new 2002), or .450 Marlin (mfg. 2001-2004) cal., 22 (disc. 2002) or 24 (new 2003) in. match grade tapered stainless or chrome-moly barrel with cut rifling, controlled round feed, no sights, deluxe high gloss checkered walnut stock and forend, one inch black decelerator recoil pad, satin matte blue finished action and barrel, 3-5 shot mag., approx. 7 1/2 lbs. New 2000.

	MSR $2,762	$2,315	$1,775	$1,450	$1,225	$1,050	$875	$750

Left-hand action is available in all current calibers.

MODEL 70 CLASSIC CUSTOM FEATHERWEIGHT

.223 WSSM (mfg. 2004), .243 WSSM (mfg. 2004), .25 WSSM (mfg. 2004), .270 Win., .280 Rem. (new 2004), .30-06, or 7mm-08 Rem. (mfg. 2003) cal., 5 shot mag., Featherweight stock with Schnabel forend, match grade 22 in. barrel w/o sights, matte blue or stainless action/barrel, 7 1/4 lbs. New 2003.

	MSR $2,762	$2,315	$1,775	$1,450	$1,225	$1,050	$875	$750

MODEL 70 CLASSIC CUSTOM CARBON

.25-06 Rem., .270 WSM, .300 WSM, .338 Win. Mag., or 7mm WSM cal., satin stainless action, features 24 or 26 in. carbon fiber barrel with Schilen stainless barrel liner, controlled round feed, reinforced black composite stock, 6 1/2 - 7 lbs. Mfg. 2003-2004.

		$2,775	$2,125	$1,650	$1,325	$1,050	$900	$800

Last MSR was $3,233.

MODEL 70 CLASSIC CUSTOM EXTREME WEATHER

.25-06 Rem. (disc. 2001), .270 Win. (disc. 2000), .270 WSM (new 2004), .30-06, .300 Win. Mag., .300 Rem. Ultra Mag. (new 2001), .300 WSM (new 2004), .308 Win. (new 2004), .325 WSM (new 2005), .338 Win. Mag., 7mm WSM (new 2004), 7mm Rem. Mag., or .375 H&H (new 2001) cal., controlled round feed, matte finished stainless action and match grade 22 lightweight (.375 H&H only), 24, or 26 in. fluted stainless barrel w/o sights, black McMillian fiberglass stock with cheekpiece and 1 in. decelerator pad, 3 or 5 shot mag., available in either right- or left-hand action, approx. 7 1/2 lbs. New 2000.

	MSR $2,576	$2,135	$1,725	$1,425

MODEL 70 CLASSIC CUSTOM MANNLICHER

.260 Rem., .308 Win., or 7mm-08 Rem. cal., features full length checkered walnut stock, smooth tapered barrel and blue action, 19 in. barrel w/o sights (sights optional), 4 shot internal mag., approx. 6 3/4 lbs. Mfg. 1999-2000.

		$2,250	$1,800	$1,400	$1,200	$950	$800	$700

Last MSR was $2,595.

This model was designated the Model 70 Custom Mannlicher until 2000.

MODEL 70 CLASSIC CUSTOM SAFARI EXPRESS

.340 Wby. Mag. (disc. 1999), .358 STA (disc. 2000), .375 H&H, .375 Rem. Ultra Mag. (new 2001), .404 Jeffrey (mfg. 2004), .416 Rem. Mag., .416 Rigby (mfg. 2001), .458 Win. Mag., .458 Lott, or .470 Capstick (new 2002) cal., features honed internal parts, engine turned bolt and follower, adj. Dietrich Apel Express rear and front sights, deluxe checkered walnut

GRADING - PPGS™	100%	98%	95%	90%	80%	70%	60%

stock and forend, 22 (.458 Win. Mag. & .458 Lott) or 24 in. barrel with sling stud, 3 shot mag., approx. 9 1/4 lbs. New 1999.

MSR $3,104	$2,650	$2,075	$1,550	$1,275	$975	$825	$725

Add $490 for .416 Rigby cal. (mfg. 2001 only).

Beginning in 2000, this model is available in left-hand action in all cals.

This model was designated the Model 70 Custom Safari Express until 2000.

MODEL 70 WSM CUSTOM NORTH AMERICAN BIG GAME SERIES - .270 WSM, .300 WSM, or 7mm WSM cal., controlled round feed, checkered XXX American walnut stock with Schnabel forend, Pachmayr decelerator recoil pad, engraved receiver, trigger guard, and floorplate, high lustre bluing. Only 125 of each edition (Whitetail Deer - .270 WSM, Elk - .300 WSM, and Antelope - 7mm WSM) to be mfg. beginning 2004 with matching serial numbers.

MSR $3,030	$2,600	$2,150	$1,600	$1,300	$995	$875	$775

This model is sold in sets only (all 3 calibers.)

MODEL 70 CLASSIC CUSTOM AFRICAN EXPRESS - .340 Wby. Mag. (disc. 1999), .358 STA (disc. 2000), .375 H&H, .416 Rem. Mag., .416 Rigby (mfg. 2001 only), .458 Win. Mag., .458 Lott, or .470 Capstick (mfg. 2001 only) cal., features drop down floorplate, increasing mag. capacity to 4, checkered fancy English walnut stock with black decelerator pad and ebony pistol grip and forend caps, adj. Dietrich Apel Express rear and front sights, 22 (.458 Win. Mag. only) or 24 in. barrel with sling stud, approx. 9 1/2 lbs. New 1999.

MSR $4,663	$4,000	$3,250	$2,800	$2,350	$1,875	$1,450	$1,250

Add $437 for .416 Rigby cal. (disc. 2001).

Beginning in 2000, this model is available in left-hand action in all cals.

This model was designated the Model 70 Custom African Express until 2000.

MODEL 70 CLASSIC CUSTOM TAKE-DOWN - .300 Rem. Rem. Ultra Mag., .300 Win. Mag. (new 2002), .375 H&H, .416 Rem. Mag., or 7mm Rem. Mag. cal., all stainless construction with blue Teflon finish, take-down receiver/barrel assembly, brown synthetic stock and forearm, .75 MOA guaranteed for take-down action assembly/reassembly, 24 (.375 H&H or .416 Rem. Mag. cal. only) or 26 (fluted only) in. barrel, 3 shot internal mag., 8 1/2 - 9 lbs. Limited mfg. beginning 2001.

MSR N/A	$3,150	$2,675	$2,300	

While advertised beginning in 1998 with a MSR of $2,495, this model was finally produced during 2001. Currently, this model is only available from the Bass Pro Shops.

MODEL 70 ULTRA GRADE - .270 Win. cal., gold line engraved, includes wood display case, 500 mfg.

$2,500	$1,975	$1,550	$1,200	$900	$600	$425

Last MSR was $5,000.

MODEL 70 COLLECTOR GRADE - various cals., this variation must be special ordered through the Winchester Custom Shop and prices vary individually per quotation.

MODEL 70 CUSTOM BUILT - various cals., this variation must be special ordered through the Winchester Custom Shop and prices vary individually per quotation.

MODEL 70 EXHIBITION GRADE - various cals., fancy checkered American walnut stock with hardwood forend tip. Mfg. 1988-89 only.

$1,850	$1,475	$975

Last MSR was $2,192.

GRADING - PPGS™	100%	98%	95%	90%	80%	70%	60%

RIFLES: O/U

DOUBLE XPRESS RIFLE - .30-06, .257 Roberts, .270 Win., 7x57M, 7x57R, 7x65R, or 9.3x74R cal., 23 1/2 in. O/U barrels, iron sights with claw scope mounts, ejectors, fully engraved satin finish receiver with game scene engraving, walnut specially hand checkered, sling swivels, 8 1/2 lbs. Mfg. 1984-85 only.

	$3,000	$2,750	$2,250	$1,900	$1,650	$1,450	$1,300

Last MSR was $2,995.

In 1984, Aero Marine located in Birmingham, AL special ordered 200 deluxe double rifles in 7x57mm Mauser cal. They featured better engraving and game scenes with bottom of receiver marked Jaeger. Of the 200, 100 were rifles with 90 being standard grade and 10 being deluxe. The other 100 were supplied with an extra set of O/U shotgun barrels. Sales were slow on these special guns and eventually they were liquidated to another wholesaler. Recently, prices are in the $2,250-$3,000 range for the rifle alone and $3,000-$3,750 for the Combo.

RIFLES: SINGLE SHOT, POST 1964 MFG.

MODEL 1885 LOW WALL GRADE I .22 LR CAL. - .22 LR cal., features 24 1/2 in. half-round, half-octagon barrel with buckhorn rear sights, uncheckered straight grip walnut stock and forearm, crescent buttplate, blue finish only, 8 lbs. 2,400 mfg. late 1999-2001.

	$735	$625	$525	$450	$400	$350	$300

Last MSR was $828.

✱ **Model 1885 Low Wall High Grade** - similar to Model 1885 Low Wall Grade I, except features frame engraving, 24Kt. squirrel/cottontail scenes, fancy walnut stock and forearm with cut checkering. 1,100 mfg. late 1999-2001.

	$1,050	$875	$750	$650	$550	$450	$350

Last MSR was $1,180.

MODEL 1885 LOW WALL - .17 HMR or .17 Mach 2 (new 2005) cal., 24 in. octagon barrel, checkered straight grip walnut stock and Schnabel forearm, open sights, 8 lbs. New 2003.

MSR $1,014	$875	$700	$575	$500	$450	$400	$350

MODEL 1885 HIGH WALL - .270 WSM, .300 WSM, or 7mm WSM cal., 28 in. full octagon barrel without sights, checkered walnut stock with recoil pad and Schnabel forearm, adj. trigger, Pachmayr Decelerator pad, blued receiver, 8.5 lbs. New 2005.

MSR $1,085	$915	$725	$600	$525	$475	$425	$375

MODEL 1885 LIMITED SERIES - .38-55 WCF, .405 Win., or .45-70 Govt. cal., 28 in. tapered octagon barrel with semi-buckhorn rear sight, blue finish, satin finished checkered walnut straight stock, Marble's front blade and rear tang mounted aperture sights, drilled and tapped, steel crescent buttplate with strap on top, includes special limited series box and certificate of authenticity. New 2003.

MSR $1,360	$1,075	$875	$750	$625	$500	$400	$300

This model is available exclusively from Davidson's.

SHOTGUNS: 1879-1963

BREECH LOADING SxS - 10 or 12 ga., imported from England for sales through the Winchester New York City office only, exposed hammers, available in 5 grades ranging from Class D - Class A and Match gun (lowest to highest). Higher grades were mfg. by W.C. Scott & Sons, C.G. Bonehill, W.C. McEntree, Richard Redmond, and H. & E. Hammond Gun Mfg.'s. Approx. 10,000 were imported between 1879-84. Prices vary greatly due to condition and grade. Prices can range from $300 (poor condition Class D) to over $4,000 (95%+ condition specimen in Class A or Match gun).

This side by side model was the first shotgun bearing the Winchester name sold in the U.S. Identifiable by "Winchester Repeating Arms Co., New Haven, Connecticut, USA" marking on barrel rib top.

100%	98%	95%	90%	80%	70%	60%	50%	40%	30%	20%	10%

MODEL 1887 LEVER ACTION - 10 or 12 ga., 4 shot tube mag., 30 or 32 in. full choke fluid steel barrels, plain pistol grip stock, first Browning patent shotgun mfg. by Winchester, first lever action repeating shotgun mfg. domestically. Mfg. 1887-1901. Approx. 64,855 mfg.

$3,500	$3,000	$2,700	$2,400	$2,000	$1,700	$1,200	$1,000	$800	$700	$600	$500

Standard frame finish on this model was color case hardening. Premiums exist for original bright case colored specimens. 10 ga. began production with serial number 22148. Also mfg. in Riot configuration (20 in. cylinder bore barrel). Gauges were chambered for 2 5/8 in. (12 ga.) and 2 7/8 in. (10 ga.). A very small amount was also made up in .70-150 cal. - add a significant premium.

* *Model 1887 Deluxe* - damascus barrel, checkered stock, and other special order features.

$7,500	$6,000	$5,000	$4,000	$2,800	$2,200	$1,800	$1,500	$1,200	$1,000	$800	$650

MODEL 1893 SLIDE ACTION - 12 ga., 30 (standard) and 32 in. barrel, black powder only. First Winchester shotgun with sliding forearm action, first Browning slide action patent, disc. 1897 after run of some 34,050. Note: chambered for 2 5/8 shells only, damascus barrels were available at extra cost, as were fancy stocks.

$950	$850	$750	$675	$600	$525	$485	$425	$375	$325	$275	$225

This gun had limited sales because mechanical weaknesses developed when shooting smokeless powder. Winchester offered a brand new shotgun of the customer's choice when they returned their Model 1893.

MODEL 1897 SLIDE ACTION - 12 or 16 ga. (introduced 1900), improved Model 1893 action, 26-32 in. barrels, visible hammer, various chokes, takedown or solid frame, plain pistol grip stock. Over 1,024,700 mfg. between 1897-1957.

$850	$725	$575	$500	$450	$350	$250	$225	$195	$175	$150	$125

Add 25% for 16 ga.

Early 16 ga. Model 1897s were chambered for 2 9/16 in. shotshells, and are not as valuable because of the 2 3/4 in. shell length currently manufactured. The Model 1897 was the first Winchester shotgun chambered for 2 3/4 in. smokeless ammunition. This model was also manufactured with a damascus barrel for a short period of time, and is rare.

MODEL 1897 RIOT GUNS - see the "Trench/Riot Shotgun" category in the T section for more information and prices.

MODEL 1897 TRENCH GUNS - see the "Trench/Riot Shotgun" category in the T section for more information and prices.

This model changed its stock configuration after WWI.

MODEL 1897 TRAP - higher grade version of Standard, checkered stock, could have black diamond inlay in stock until 1919 (Black Diamond Trap), breech block marked "Trap" until approx. 1926. Mfg. 1897-1931.

$2,250	$2,000	$1,800	$1,600	$1,300	$1,000	$750	$600	$450	$400	$350	$300

* *Model 1897 Black Diamond Trap* - distinguishable by diamond ebony inlays in stock pistol grip.

$2,000	$1,800	$1,600	$1,400	$1,200	$1,000	$900	$750	$600	$500	$400	$300

MODEL 1897 PIGEON - higher grade version of Standard 97, should have engraved pigeon behind hammer on frame, breech block marked "Pigeon", most exhibit black diamond stock inlays until 1919. Mfg. 1897-1939.

$10,000	$8,500	$7,500	$6,000	$4,500	$3,500	$3,000	$2,000	$1,500	$1,000	$800	$700

MODEL 1901 - 10 ga. only, strengthened Model 1887 action to accept smokeless powder, lever action, standard barrel 32 in., blue barrel and frame, 5 shot mag. 13,500 mfg. between 1901-1920, starting with serial number 64,856.

$3,500	$3,200	$3,000	$2,500	$2,000	$1,800	$1,500	$1,250	$800	$700	$500	$450

Add 50% for Deluxe Grade (checkered wood).

This shotgun was chambered for 2 7/8 in. smokeless powder ammunition.

100%	98%	95%	90%	80%	70%	60%	50%	40%	30%	20%	10%

MODEL 1911 SL AUTOLOADER
- 12 ga., recoil operated, 26 or 28 in. barrel, various chokes, pistol grip laminated birch stock. Mfg. 1911-1921, with some production occuring between 1921-1928, 103,246 produced, action had design problems, nicknamed "Head Buster."

$600	$550	$500	$450	$350	$275	$200	$150	$140	$130	$120	$110

Values assume original wood without splitting, repair, or replacement. The Model 1911 was Winchester's first semi-auto shotgun. It did not prove to be satisfactory partly because the design had to be exclusive of the patents for Browning's famous A-5 model. Interestingly enough, this was a design which Winchester originally had helped Browning patent.

MODEL 36 SINGLE SHOT
- 9mm Rimfire cal., long shot, short shot, and ball, 18 in. round barrel, single shot bolt action, guns were not serial numbered, one-piece plain stock and forearm, special shaped trigger guard, 2 3/4 lbs. Approx. 20,000 mfg. between 1920-27.

N/A	$1,700	$1,500	$1,300	$1,050	$895	$750	$595	$495	$395	$295	$195

GRADING - PPGS™	100%	98%	95%	90%	80%	70%	60%

MODEL 12 SLIDE ACTION
- 12 (introduced 1914), 16 (introduced 1914), 20 (initial ga., mfg. 1912, 2 1/2 in. chamber mfg. until 1927), or 28 (introduced 1937) ga., 25 (20 ga. only, mfg. 1912-14), 26, 28, 30, or 32 in. standard, nickel, or stainless steel (scarce) barrel with or without rib (matted, solid, or VR), 2 9/16 (early 16 or 20 ga., until 1927, at ser. no. 464,565), 2 3/4 (becmae standard 1927) or 3 in. chamber, 6 shot, blue metal, various chokes, hammerless, plain pistol grip or straight walnut stock and forearm, marked Model 1912 from 1912-1919, approx. ser. no. 172,000. Mfg. 1912-76.

Special order features on field guns have captured much collector interest in recent years. Combinations of these features can add a considerable percentage to the base values listed. Rare special orders on rare variations are very desirable and prices can double and more if the combination is right. As is the case with most other collectible shotguns at this time, Model 12s with open choked barrels in shorter lengths are A LOT more desirable (and expensive) than a specimen with a 30 in. full choke barrel (most common). Values listed are for standard configuration (28 or 30 in. full choke barrel with no rib). For most Model 12s, values for condition factors less than 60% will approximate the 60% price, because of shooter demand. Premiums must be added for the rarer open choked barrels in shorter length on all gauges.

Original gauge can be determined by removing the buttstock and observing the gauge marking on the stock screw boss.

The following add-ons DO NOT apply to 28 ga. values.

Add 40%-50% for Win. solid rib.

Add 50%-60% for Win. milled VR.

Add 60% for each extra barrel(s).

Add 40%-50% for Win. special VR (offset barrel proofmark).

"Donut" post Winchester VRs are more desirable than the rectangular post.

	100%	98%	95%	90%	80%	70%	60%
12 ga.	$600	$450	$350	$325	$250	$200	$175
16 ga.	$650	$500	$350	$325	$275	$225	$200
20 ga.	$900	$725	$600	$550	$500	$425	$400
28 ga.	$4,000	$3,750	$3,250	$3,000	$2,650	$2,100	$1,850

Subtract 50% if with factory Cutts compensator.

Recently, some non-original, re-stamped 28 ga. barrels have been added to 16 or 20 ga. frames "creating" a more desirable (and expensive) gun to unsuspecting buyers. Roll die markings are getting better and better so be very cautious when considering a non-Cutts 28 ga. (as in get a receipt specifying originality). 28 ga. ser. no. range is approx. 720,XXX to 1,857,XXX. 28 ga. Model 12s were available with both 2 3/4 (common) or 2 7/8 (infrequent) in. chamber. Believe it or not, there are getting to be a lot of fake Model 12 boxes that have been intentionally aged. Carefully screen NIB (watch the hanging tag also) specimens in this model.

Editor's Note: The Model 12 Winchester was produced continuously from 1912-1980. Over 2,027,500 were produced both in standard and deluxe (Pigeon) grades. Pigeon grades were first listed in 1914 and disc. during the war (1941). Reintroduced in 1948, they were disc. permanently in 1964, after which the Super Pigeon Grade became available only on a custom-order basis from Winchester's Custom Gun Shop. These guns are worth 50-300% premiums depending on gauge, barrel lengths, stock options, engraving patterns, etc.

With an attrition rate of 33%, Model 12s with rare features 50 years ago will only be much rarer today (and expensive). 28 ga. guns were built between 1934 and 1960. Gauge rarity in increasing order is 12 ga., 16 ga., 20 ga., .410 bore (Model 42), and 28 ga. Serialization breakdown by year of manufacture is provided under the "Model Serialization" section of this book. When collecting Model 12s, ser. nos. on the underside of receiver (forward end), should match ser. no. on bottom rear of Mag. tube. Stainless steel barrel Model 12s were mostly mfg. in the late 1920s - early 1930s (65X,XXX serial range). Values typically range between $1,000-$2,500.

"Y" prefix appears on Model 12s built 1964-1980 - see listing under Post-64 Models.

MODEL 12 FEATHERWEIGHT - similar to Standard, except with alloy guard and different takedown system. Mfg. 1959-62. "F" suffix after ser. no.

	100%	98%	95%	90%	80%	70%	60%
	$550	$500	$450	$400	$325	$275	$225

MODEL 12 RIOT GUNS - see the "Trench/Riot Shotgun" category in the T section for more information and prices.

MODEL 12 MILITARY TRENCH GUNS - see the "Trench/Riot Shotgun" category in the T section for more information and prices.

MODEL 12 HEAVY DUCK GUN - 12 ga., 3 in. chamber, 30 or 32 in. barrel, solid rubber recoil pad, 1/2 in. shorter pull than regular Model 12. Mfg. 1935-63.

	100%	98%	95%	90%	80%	70%	60%
	$900	$800	$700	$600	$500	$400	$350

Add 60% for solid rib.

Add 40% for 32 in. barrel.

✱ **Vent. rib** - factory Winchester or 2 different styles mfg. by Simmons, notice barrel proof marking - rare.

Win. VR	$2,000	$1,600	$1,500	$1,350	$1,100	$1,000	$900

MODEL 12 SKEET GUN - 12, 16, 20, or 28 ga., 26 in. barrel, skeet choke, checkered pistol grip stock, pre-WWII. Mfg. 1933-1976.

	100%	98%	95%	90%	80%	70%	60%
	$1,300	$1,050	$850	$725	$525	$475	$425

Add 30% for solid rib.

Add 75% for Win. Special VR.

Add 100% for Win. milled VR.

Subtract 50% for Factory-Cutts compensator.

16 gauge - rarity will command a premium.

Add 150% for 20 ga.

Add 500% for 28 ga.

Add approx. 20%-25% for brown plastic Hydrocoil stock, 12 ga. only.

Add approx. 40%-50% for white plastic Hydrocoil stock (approx. 50 mfg, 12 ga. only).

MODEL 12 TRAP GUN - various gauges, full choke barrel, deluxe straight or pistol grip stock, solid recoil pad. Mfg. 1938-64.

	100%	98%	95%	90%	80%	70%	60%
	$1,200	$900	$800	$700	$550	$485	$450

Add 60% for milled VR.

Add approx. 20% for brown plastic Hydrocoil stock.

Add approx. 50% for white plastic Hydrocoil stock (approx. 50 mfg).

While plain barreled variation is rare, it is not as desirable.

MODEL 12 SUPER FIELD GRADE - 12 or 20 ga. only, features 26, 28, or 30 in. matted rib barrel, deluxe walnut with checkered pistol grip stock and forearm, mfg. 1955-59.

	100%	98%	95%	90%	80%	70%	60%
	$1,500	$1,350	$1,150	$1,000	$800	$600	$500

Add 60% for 20 ga.

Add 40% for 16 ga.

GRADING - PPGS™	100%	98%	95%	90%	80%	70%	60%

MODEL 12 "BLACK DIAMOND" TRAP

- various configurations, straight or pistol grip stock, features a small ebony diamond inlaid on each side of the pistol grip, solid rib.

	100%	98%	95%	90%	80%	70%	60%
	$2,150	$1,850	$1,650	$1,350	$1,150	$900	$800

Add 25% for milled VR.

MODEL 12 TOURNAMENT GRADE

- 12 ga. only, straight grip stock, small checkered forearm, usually stamped "Tourn" in wood on buttstock under buttplate. Mfg. 1914-1930.

	100%	98%	95%	90%	80%	70%	60%
	$2,000	$1,800	$1,500	$1,200	$1,000	$800	$600

MODEL 12 PIGEON GRADE

- finer and more deluxe version of Model 12, many variations. Mfg. 1914-41 and 1948-64, engine turned breech block and shell follower, usually with engraved pigeon on bottom rear of mag. tube.

	100%	98%	95%	90%	80%	70%	60%
	$2,850	$2,650	$2,400	$2,000	$1,250	$1,100	$900
28 ga.	$6,000	$5,500	$5,000	$4,500	$4,000	$3,500	$2,800

Add 25% for VR.
Add 100% for 20 ga.

MODEL 20

- .410 bore, single shot, hammer, boxlock, 26 in. full choke (a few guns have been observed with cylinder choking), 6 pounds. Mfg. 23,616 between 1919-24.

	100%	98%	95%	90%	80%	70%	60%
	$750	$650	$500	$400	$300	$200	$175

While most Model 20s have 2 1/2 in. chambers, late parts cleanup guns could be chambered for 3 in. also.

* ***Winchester Model 20 Junior Trap Shooting Outfit*** - includes shotgun, midget hand trap, 150 .410 bore shells, 100 clay targets and accessories, cased.

	100%	98%	95%	90%	80%	70%	60%
	$3,500	$3,200	$3,000	$2,700	$2,500	$2,200	$2,000

Prices for this model assume all accessories are included - if not, subtract substantially. Just the shotshell boxes and accessories from this outfit are worth $2,500+ in nice condition.

MODEL 21

- 12, 16, 20, 28 ga., or .410 bore, boxlock action, after years in the design stage, production began in 1929 with guns being shipped to the warehouse in 1930 and first offered in Winchester's 1931 price list. Regular production continued for thirty years, through 1959. Approx. 32,500 mfg. 1931-1988. Approx. 1,100 were mfg. by the Custom Shop (including Custom, Pigeon, and Grand American Grades) during 1960-1982. Factory records for these models (early mfg. is sketchy) are available by contacting the Cody Firearms Museum located in Cody, WY.

The early guns were plain, standard 12 gauge models with double triggers and extractors. Later in 1931, 16 and 20 gauge chamberings became available, as did selective single trigger and automatic ejectors.

By the end of 1933 the Model 21 skeet gun had been introduced as had Tournament, Trap, and Custom Built grades. By about this time options included fancier wood, beavertail or semi-beavertail foreends, checkered butts (standard on skeet guns) or skeleton steel buttplates, recoil pads and almost any variation the customers might desire. Metal finishes on a Model 21 are unusual in that they have salt blue frames and rust blue barrels - this explains the difference in coloration between these metal surfaces.

The Tournament Grade was dropped in 1936 and the Trap Grade in 1940. A Standard Grade Trap Gun was added in 1941. The early Custom Built Grade was dropped in 1942 and the Deluxe Grade was added. This grade included as standard many of the previously available extra cost options.

Relatively few guns were produced in chamberings smaller than 20 gauge. 28 gauge first appeared in the 1936 catalog, although a few were probably produced before that. Winchester records are unclear as to the total but it is generally believed that fewer than 100 original factory guns were made. In addition, a number of original 20 gauge guns have been modified at the factory or elsewhere with factory 28 gauge barrels. These latter guns are just as valuable if the conversion was done at the Winchester Custom Gun Shop. Authenticity of the original guns should be established by factory letter.

.410 bore guns were first listed in 1955 but, again, some had been produced earlier, one having been built for John Olin in 1950. Throughout Winchester history all the rules seem to have had exceptions and nowhere is this more apparent than with respect to the Model 21 which, after all, has been pretty much a custom gun from the very beginning. Factory records and tallies among dealers indicate the existence of 40 to 50 original factory guns. As in the case of the 28 gauge, extra barrels were available and at least some of those have been added to original 20 gauge guns.

The 3 inch Magnum 12 gauge Duck gun (stamped "Duck" on floor plate) was offered in Winchester catalogs from 1940 through 1952. Selective single triggers and automatic ejectors were standard as were the solid red Winchester recoil pads and 30 in. or 32 in. barrels. Some cases of non-factory upgrading of 2 3/4 or 3 inch Magnum guns have been reported. If authenticity is important to the buyer, a factory letter should be requested.

With respect to such letters, in cases where records may be missing or incomplete, the resultant letters may be less conclusive than desired. In some instances, consultation with, or a written appraisal from an authoritative collector arms dealer might be helpful.

Six standard patterns of engraving and several stock checkering and carving styles evolved during the production years. Values added by these and other embellishments such as precious metal inlays are beyond the scope of this work.

The following retail prices are for a standard field gun with average wood, beavertail forearm, ejectors, and single selective trigger with no alterations.

12 ga.	$6,000	$5,500	$5,000	$4,500	$4,000	$3,700	$3,500
16 ga.	$7,500	$7,000	$6,500	$6,000	$5,500	$5,000	$4,500
20 ga.	$8,500	$7,500	$7,000	$6,500	$6,000	$5,500	$5,000

Add $1,000 for VR.

Add $10%-15% for 3 in. chambers (Duck Gun, 12 ga. only).

Subtract approx. 40% for double triggers w/ extractors.

Subtract 20% for double triggers with ejectors (normally encountered with splinter forearm).

* ***Skeet Gun*** - available in Standard, Tournament, and Trap grades. Introduced 1933.

  Add 10% depending on grade.

* ***Trap Gun*** - introduced 1940, Trap Grade disc. same year, unaltered specimens will bring premium - add 10-25%.

* ***3 Inch Duck Gun*** - introduced 1940, must be so stamped (observe the 3 in. marking very carefully).

As can be seen, values are partly based on a certain interdependence between options. Higher grade guns, of course, will bring somewhat higher prices, although much of their increased value results from the many "options" being included as standard features.

Buyers or sellers with limited experience should always seek expert advice or appraisals in dealing with a Model 21. This is especially true with regard to higher grade guns and those with extra ornamentation.

* ***Model 21 .410 Bore*** - retail prices for original guns may be expected to range between $25,000 and $45,000 for mechanically sound guns depending on quality of finish. These prices take into consideration the reported sale of a plain standard gun in recent years for $37,000. Non-original guns with add-on factory barrels would probably be reduced by one-third.

* ***Model 21 28 Ga.*** - factory original guns will probably bring from $15,000 to $25,000 and, as with the 410s, 20 gauge guns modified to 28 gauge with factory barrels would be worth approx. the same if done at the factory.

Refinishing or Restoration: There is disagreement as to the effects of refinishing a Model 21. Many shooters and at least some collectors prefer a well refinished gun to a badly worn one. Higher grade guns restored by a master craftsman may approach factory original guns in value.

MODEL 21: RECENT PRODUCTION - refer to listing under SHOTGUNS: RECENT PRODUCTION SxS.

MODEL 24 SxS - 12, 16, or 20 ga., boxlock, hammerless, double triggers. Introduced 1940, disc. 1957 after approx. 116,280 mfg.

	$650	$575	$425	$300	$225	$175	$150

Add 20% for 16 ga.

Add 40% for 20 ga.

GRADING - PPGS™	100%	98%	95%	90%	80%	70%	60%

MODEL 25 SLIDE ACTION - 12 ga. only, non-takedown version of the Model 12, 26 or 28 in. barrel. 87,937 mfg. between 1949-54.

	100%	98%	95%	90%	80%	70%	60%
	$450	$400	$325	$275	$225	$175	$150

MODEL 37 SINGLE SHOT - 12, 16, 20, 28 ga., or .410 bore, top-lever break-open action, all barrels are full choke. Note on pricing that there is a big difference between a 100% gun without a box and NIB condition. Not serial-numbered. Over 1,015,000 mfg. between 1936-63.

	100%	98%	95%	90%	80%	70%	60%
12 gauge	$300	$250	$200	$125	$100	$90	$75
16 gauge	$300	$250	$200	$125	$100	$90	$75
20 gauge	$350	$300	$250	$150	$110	$90	$75
28 gauge	$1,650	$1,200	$900	$650	$525	$400	$350
.410 bore	$400	$350	$300	$250	$150	$100	$90

If models are truly NIB, add $125-$175 to 100% condition values only, depending on gauge.
Add 20% for "Red Letter" models.
Add 15% for 32 in. barrel (12, 16, or 20 ga. only).
Most 28 ga. Model 37s have the "Red Letter."

✴ *Model 37 Youth/Boys/Red Dot* - 20 ga. only, 26 in. barrel marked Mod. Choke on barrel, solid red factory pad, identifiable by red dot inset into metal that is visible when hammer is cocked.

	100%	98%	95%	90%	80%	70%	60%
N/A	$350	$275	$225	$175	$130	$100	

MODEL 40 SEMI-AUTO - 12 ga. only, long recoil action, 28 or 30 in. barrel, walnut stock, skeet model also, poorly designed, many recalled by Winchester. Approx. 12,000 mfg. 1940-41.

	100%	98%	95%	90%	80%	70%	60%
	$750	$600	$525	$450	$400	$300	$225

MODEL 41 BOLT ACTION - .410 bore, 2 1/2 in. chamber until 1933 when it changed to 3 in., bolt action, single shot, 24 in. round barrel bored F, one-piece plain walnut stock and forearm, not serialized, approx. 22,145 were mfg. 1920-34.

	100%	98%	95%	90%	80%	70%	60%
	$575	$500	$450	$375	$300	$250	$200

This model is rarely encountered with over 80% original condition.

MODEL 42 SLIDE ACTION - first pump specifically designed for the .410 bore, hammerless, 2 1/2 (introduced 1935) or 3 in. chamber, 26 or 28 in. barrel, plain walnut pistol grip stock with circular grooved forearm (modified 1947), invented by William Roemer, approx. 6 1/2 - 7 lbs. Approx. 164,800 mfg. in 4 grades between 1933-63.

Special order features on field guns have captured much collector interest in recent years. Combinations of these features can add a considerable percentage to the base values listed. Special orders on rare variations are very desirable, and prices can double, or more than double, if the combination is right.

Add 25% to any Model 42 chambered for 2 1/2 in. shells.

✴ *Standard Grade* - 26 or 28 in. plain, solid rib or vent. rib barrel, plain walnut straight or pistol grip stock, walnut grooved forearm. Mfg. 1933-63.

	100%	98%	95%	90%	80%	70%	60%
	$1,250	$1,150	$1,050	$950	$850	$750	$650

Add 25% for pre-war.
Add 75% for solid rib.
Add 150% for factory vent. rib.

✴ *Skeet Grade* - 26 or 28 in. plain, solid rib or vent. rib barrel, select checkered walnut straight grip or pistol grip stock and checkered forearm extension, 4 different chokes (full, modified, skeet, or cylinder) during pre-war (approx. ser. no. 1-52,000), post-war (approx. ser. no. 52,000-164,000) had same chokes available through 1953, when cylinder choke was dropped, and improved cylinder was added.

	100%	98%	95%	90%	80%	70%	60%
	$3,000	$2,750	$2,400	$2,150	$2,000	$1,600	$1,400

Add 50% for vent. rib.
Values are for solid rib.

✳ *Trap Grade* - first variation had small checkered forearm with one diamond in center, field choke (full, modified, or cylinder), second variation has large checkered forearm with 2 diamonds in center, both variations had 26 or 28 in. plain or solid rib barrel, select checkered walnut straight grip (one closed diamond on underside of grip) or pistol grip (one closed diamond on each side of grip) stock, usually choked skeet, stamped "TRAP" at bottom of receiver under the ser. no. Only 231 mfg.

	100%	98%	95%	90%	80%	70%	60%
	$9,000	$7,500	$6,250	$5,750	$4,750	$3,750	$3,250

✳ *Deluxe Grade* - same configurations as Trap Grade, 20 LPI checkering, most are fitted with special vent. rib after 1954 in 3 styles: round post-donut base, round post, and rectangle post, pre-1954 mfg. had plain or solid rib barrel, 1946-1950 mfg. may have "DELUXE" stamp under ser. no. on receiver. Mfg. 1946-63.

>Solid Rib

	$6,000	$5,500	$4,700	$4,200	$3,500	$2,700	$2,000

>Vent. Rib (factory)

	$7,000	$6,500	$5,500	$4,500	$3,200	$2,500	$2,250

✳ *Pigeon Grade* - same configurations as Deluxe Grade, except has pigeon engraved on underside of mag. tube, most were factory engraved, very few mfg.

Must be appraised individually. Before purchasing any factory engraved Model 42, it is advised that a reputable dealer/collector be consulted.

MODEL 50 SEMI-AUTO - 12 or 20 ga., 3 shot, recoil-operated (non-recoiling barrel), 26-30 in. barrels, VR optional, steel frame or Feather Weight Model (aluminum receiver, FTW) introduced 1958. Over 196,000 mfg. between 1954-61, starting with serial number 1,000.

	$600	$500	$450	$400	$350	$300	$250

Add $50 for VR (Simmons installed).
Add $50 for Feather Weight Model (denoted by "A" suffix in ser. no.).
Add $150 for 20 ga.
Add 50% for Trap & Skeet Model.
Add 200%-350% for Pigeon Grade ("PIGEON" stamped on receiver, near ser. no.).

MODEL 59 SEMI-AUTO - 12 ga. only, 3 shot, short recoil operation, Win-lite (steel and fiberglass) ribless barrels, 26-30 in. barrel lengths, alloy receiver inscribed with hunting scenes, Versalite (first interchangeable choke tubes) option introduced 1961, 6 1/2 lbs. 82,085 mfg. between 1960-65.

	$600	$500	$400	$350	$300	$250	$200

Add 30% for barrel with all three choke tubes.

Inspect carefully for either cracked receiver (by bolt handle cutout and over serial numbers), or separating fiberglass on end of barrel.

✳ *Pigeon Grade* - mfg. 1962-65, add 200-350% (rare).

Winchester also mfg. 20 and 14 gauges experimentally in this model, which are extremely rare and expensive.

SHOTGUNS: POST-1964

Winchester introduced WinChokes in 1969.

Shotguns: Post-1964, Lever Action

MODEL 9410 TRADITIONAL - .410 bore, 2 1/2 in. chamber, lever action based on the Model 94 rifle, 24 in. round barrel with cylinder bore or standard Invector chokes (new 2003), 9 shot tube mag., iron sights with TruGlo front and modified V adj. rear, checkered straight grip walnut stock and forearm, top tang safety became standard in 2003, approx. 6 3/4 lbs. New 2001.

MSR $626	$500	$400	$345	$285	$240	$220	$190

Subtract approx. $50 if w/o Invector chokes.

GRADING - PPGS™	100%	98%	95%	90%	80%	70%	60%

✳ **Model 9410 Semi-Fancy Traditional** - similar to Model 9410 Traditional, except has checkered semi-fancy walnut stock and standard Invector choke system. Mfg. 2004.

	$660	$575	$475	$420	$360	$330	$300

Last MSR was $789.

✳ **Model 9410 Packer** - cylinder bored or standard Invector chokes (new 2003, includes 3 chokes), 20 in. barrel, 5 shot, 2/3 mag., open sights, checkered semi-pistol grip walnut stock and forearm with sling swivel studs, 6 1/2 lbs. New 2002.

MSR $583	$480	$380	$325	$280	$240	$215	$195

Add $64 for standard Invector chokes (includes 3).

Add $64 for Packer Compact Model (12 1/2 in. LOP, 6 1/4 lbs., new 2003).

✳ **Model 9410 Ranger** - similar to Model 9410 Traditional, except has uncheckered hardwood stock and forearm, 24 in. barrel with fixed cylinder bore barrel, 6 3/4 lbs. New 2003.

MSR $532	$440	$355	$300	$260	$230	$210	$185

✳ **Model 9410 TS Custom Case Colored** - similar to Model 9410 Traditional, features case colored recevier, lever, crescent buttplate, lower tang, and barrel bands, deluxe straight grip checkered walnut stock and extended forearm, matte bluing, 24 in. round barrel, gold trigger, top safety, 7 lbs. New 2005.

MSR $1,418	$1,200	$1,050	$875	$725			

Shotguns: Post-1964, Semi-Auto

Winchester introduced WinChokes in 1969.

MODEL 140 RANGER SEMI-AUTO - 12, 16, or 20 ga., entry level model. Disc.

	$275	$250	$220	$200	$175	$155	$140

MODEL 1400 SEMI-AUTO - 12, 16, or 20 ga., 26, 28, or 30 in. barrel, 2 3/4 in. chamber, alloy receiver, various chokes, gas operated, 2 shot mag., checkered pistol grip stock. Mfg. 1964-81.

	$275	$250	$220	$200	$175	$155	$140
Vent. rib	$315	$265	$240	$220	$195	$165	$150

Add 33% for Hydro-coil recoil system.

Note: In 1968 the model 1400 series was modified. The action release was improved and the checkering redesigned. From 1968-72, they were designated MKII, which was then dropped. The values for the later guns mfg. from 1968-73 may run approx. 10% higher - values shown are for guns mfg. from 1965-68. Left hand was also available, and was disc. in 1973.

NEW MODEL 1400 WALNUT - 12 or 20 ga., 2 3/4 in. chamber, 22 (disc.), 26 (mfg. 1991-93), or 28 in. VR barrel, checkered walnut stock and forearm, WinChokes standard, 3 shot mag., rotary bolt system, 7-7 1/2 lbs. Mfg. 1989-94.

	$350	$290	$260	$240	$220	$190	$165

Last MSR was $419.

Add $15 for limited mfg. 1993 Quail Unlimited Model (2,500 mfg. 1993).

MODEL 1400 CUSTOM HIGH GRADE - 12 ga. only, 28 in. VR WinChoke barrel, special order only through the Custom Gun Shop, features deluxe hand checkered walnut and special engraving. Mfg. 1991-92.

	$1,295	$995	$750				

Last MSR was $1,695.

MODEL 1400 SKEET GRADE - similar to 1400, 12 or 20 ga., with 26 in. VR barrel, skeet bore, select skeet style stock. Mfg. 1965-73.

	$425	$350	$300	$275	$220	$195	$165

MODEL 1400 TRAP GRADE - similar to 1400, with 30 in. full choke VR barrel, select trap style stock. Mfg. 1965-73.

	$360	$330	$305	$275	$220	$195	$165

GRADING - PPGS™	100%	98%	95%	90%	80%	70%	60%

MODEL 1400 DEER GUN - similar to 1400, with 22 in. barrel, rifle sights, 12 ga. only. Mfg. 1965-74.

	$265	$240	$220	$200	$175	$165	$140

MODEL 1400 SLUG HUNTER - 12 ga. only, 22 in. smooth bore cyl. or rifled Sabot choke-tubed barrel, drilled and tapped for scope, includes bases or iron sights, 7 1/4 lbs. Mfg. 1990-92.

	$355	$310	$270	$250	$225	$195	$165

Last MSR was $420.

MODEL 1400 RANGER - 12 or 20 ga., gas operation, alloy receiver, 22 cyl. deer, 26 (mfg. 1991-93), or 28 in. WinChoke barrel, checkered walnut finished hardwood stock and forearm, VR became standard 1985, 7 1/4 lbs. Disc. 1994.

	$285	$235	$200	$180	$160	$140	$120

Last MSR was $377.

Add $53 for deer combo. (includes extra 22 in. cyl. bore barrel).
Subtract $40 without VR.

MODEL 1500 XTR - 12 or 20 ga., 2 3/4 inch only, 28 inch barrel, plain or VR, Win-Choke tubes, gas operation. Mfg. 1978-82.

	$300	$260	$240	$220	$200	$180	$160

SUPER X MODEL 1 - 12 ga., 26, 28, or 30 in. VR barrel, various chokes, steel receiver, gas operated - self compensating, checkered pistol grip stock and forearm. Mfg. 1974-81.

	$500	$450	$400	$350	$300	$250	$225

SUPER X MODEL 1 SKEET - similar to Standard, with 26 in. skeet bore barrel, select skeet style stock. Mfg. 1974-81.

	$695	$595	$500	$475	$450	$425	$400

Add 20% if NIB condition.

SUPER X MODEL 1 TRAP - similar to Standard, with 30 in. barrel, imp. mod. or full choke, select trap style stock.

	$595	$550	$475	$425	$415	$395	$350

Add 20% if NIB condition.

SUPER X MODEL 1 CUSTOM TRAP OR SKEET - 12 ga. only, limited production from the Custom Shop, deluxe checkered walnut stock and forearm, extensive scroll engraving on receiver, built to custom order. Limited mfg. 1987-92.

	$1,295	$925	$725

✳ *Super X Model 1 Custom Engraved* - features number 5 engraving pattern with 7 gold inlays. Disc.

	$2,395	$1,900	$1,350

Last MSR was $1,295.

Add $700 for factory gold inlays (8 flying ducks).

SUPER X2 3 IN. MAGNUM FIELD - 12 ga. only, 3 in. chamber, self-adjusting gas operation, 26 or 28 in. VR back-bored barrel with Invector chokes, 5 shot mag., choice of checkered walnut or black synthetic stock and forearm with recoil pad, high gloss blue or matte metal finish, approx. 7 1/4 - 8 lbs. Mfg. 1999-2004.

	$750	$650	$575	$525	$465	$400	$325

Last MSR was $874.

✳ *Super X2 Light Field* - 26 or 28 in. VR back-bored barrel with Invector Plus chokes, alloy receiver, checkered pistol grip walnut stock and forearm, 6.5-6.75 lbs. New 2005.

MSR $945	$835	$710	$600	$560	$500	$450	$375

GRADING - PPGS™	100%	98%	95%	90%	80%	70%	60%

✴ **Super X2 Sporting Clays** - 28 or 30 in. VR back-bored barrel with Invector chokes, adj. stock using spacers, includes 2 gas pistons, checkered walnut or Signature Red Dura-Touch finished (new 2003) hardwood stock and forearm, approx. 8 lbs. New 2001.

MSR $998	$875	$730	$610	$560	$500	$450	$375

Add $17 for Signature Red Dura-Touch finish on stock and forearm.

✴ **Super X2 Sporting Clays Signature II** - features red anodized alloy receiver and forearm cap, black metallic paint on stock and forearm, two gas pistons provided, adj. stock spacers provided, 30 or 32 in. barrel, approx. 8 lbs. New 2005.

MSR $1,015	$885	$735	$625	$575	$500	$450	$375

✴ **Super X2 Composite** - features black composite stock and forearm with Dura-Touch armor coating, matte metal finish, includes sling swivel studs, 26 or 28 in. VR barrels with three Invector chokes, approx. 7 3/4 lbs. New 2004.

MSR $908	$775	$665	$585	$525	$465	$400	$325

✴ **Super X2 Rifled Deer** - 22 in. rifled barrel with cantilever scope base and Tru-Glo sights (rear sight folds down), black synthetic stock and forearm, 7 1/4 lbs. New 2002.

MSR $957	$800	$675	$585	$530	$455	$395	$325

✴ **Super X2 Practical MK I** - similar to Super X2 Practical MKII, except has regular Tru-Glo iron sights, and does not have Dura-Touch, cylinder standard Invector choke, 8 lbs. New 2003.

MSR $1,116	$960	$800	$675	$575	$500	$465	$435

✴ **Super X2 Practical MK II** - home defense configuration featuring black composite stock and forearm, black metal finish, 22 in. barrel with standard Invector choke system and removable LPA ghost ring sights, 8 shot extended mag., includes sling swivels, Dura-Touch armor coated composite finish became standard during 2003, 8 lbs. New 2002.

MSR $1,287	$1,075	$885	$715	$635	$550	$495	$440

Subtract 10% if w/o Dura-Touch finished stock and forearm.

SUPER X2 3 1/2 IN. MAG. COMPOSITE - 12 ga. only, 3 1/2 in. chamber, similar to Super X2, black synthetic stock and forearm with vent. recoil pad, Dura-Touch armor coated stock/forearm treatment became standard during 2003 for all models, 24 (disc. 2000), 26, or 28 in. VR back-bored barrel with Invector chokes, 7 1/2-8 lbs. New 1999.

MSR $1,027	$885	$725	$625	$565	$500	$450	$375

✴ **Super X2 3 1/2 In. Mag. Universal Hunter** - similar to Super X2 3 1/2 In. Mag., except has full coverage Mossy Oak Break-Up camo composite stock and forearm, 26 in. VR barrel with 3 Invector Plus chokes, including optional extended extra full, Tru-Glo sights, 7 3/4 lbs. New 2002.

MSR $1,185	$995	$825	$685	$595	$515	$455	$375

Add $67 for extended extra full choke (Universal Hunter Turkey Model).

✴ **Super X2 3 1/2 In. Mag. Greenhead** - similar to Super X2 3 1/2 In. Mag., except has green Dura-Touch stock and forearm for enhanced durability and feel during cold/wet conditions, 28 in. VR barrel, matte metal finish, 8 lbs. New 2002.

MSR $1,036	$900	$740	$620	$565	$500	$450	$375

✴ **Super X2 3 1/2 In. Mag. Turkey** - similar to Super X2 3 1/2 In. Mag., except has 24 in. VR barrel with TruGlo sights and extra full turkey choke tube, matte finish only, 7 1/2 lbs. Mfg. 1999-2002.

	$880	$730	$615	$555	$495	$450	$375

Last MSR was $1,018.

During 2001-2002, this model incorporated a "Team NWTF" logo on the stock.

GRADING - PPGS™	100%	98%	95%	90%	80%	70%	60%

❋ **Super X2 3 1/2 In. Mag. Camo Turkey (NWTF)** - similar configuration as regular Turkey, except has 100% Mossy Oak Break-Up camo treatment and TruGlo sights, 7 1/2 lbs. New 2000.

MSR $1,236	$1,035	$850	$700	$550	$495	$425	$375

Beginning in 2001, this model incorporates a "Team NWTF" logo on the stock.

❋ **Super X2 3 1/2 In. Mag. Camo Waterfowl** - similar to Super X2 3 1/2 In. Mag., except has 100% Mossy Oak Shadow Grass treatment, 28 in. VR back-bored barrel with Invector chokes, 8 lbs. New 1999.

MSR $1,185	$1,000	$840	$685	$565	$495	$425	$375

SHOTGUNS: SINGLE BARREL

MODEL 370 - 12, 16, 20, 28 ga., or .410 bore, 28-32 in. full choke plain barrel, replaced the Model 37, top lever break open, exposed hammer, plain pistol grip stock. Approx. 221,578 mfg. between 1968-73.

	$120	$100	$90	$85	$80	$75	$70

Add 20-60%+ for 28 ga. and .410 bore.

The Model 370 was mfg. in Winchester's Canadian plant in Cobourg, Ontario.

MODEL 370 YOUTH - similar to 370, with 26 in. barrel, 12 1/2 in. stock, with recoil pad.

	$145	$110	$95	$85	$80	$75	$70

MODEL 37A - replaced the Model 370, roll engraved receiver, gold trigger. Approx. 391,168 mfg. between 1973-80 in the Winchester plant in Cobourg, Ontario.

	$140	$110	$95	$85	$75	$65	$55

Add 10% for 36 in. goose barrel.

Add 50% for 28 ga. and 75% for .410 bore.

MODEL 37A YOUTH - similar to 37A, except 20 ga. or .410 bore with 12 1/2 in. LOP stock.

	$175	$145	$100	$85	$70	$55	$40

MODEL 840 - various gauges, mfg. in Canada until 1980.

	$140	$110	$95	$85	$75	$65	$55

MODEL 1370 SLAGBLASTER - 12 ga., 26 in. heavy barrel, commercial sale only - used to clean slag from steel kilns, 9 lbs. Mfg. in Canada, disc.

	$350	$300	$250	$225	$200	$175	$155

Shotguns: Slide Action

Winchester introduced WinChokes in 1969.

MODEL 12 SUPER PIGEON GRADE - 12 ga., slide action, 26, 28, or 30 in. barrel, VR, any choke, hand honed action, engine turned breech block and loading flap, "B" checkering and No. 5 engraving, custom order grade walnut stock. Limited production between 1964-72.

	$2,995	$2,500	$2,250	$2,100	$1,750	$1,500	$1,300

Subtract 20% for Super Pigeon Grades mfg. 1984-85 (480 total).

MODEL 12 FIELD GRADE - 12 ga., slide action, 26, 28, or 30 in. VR barrel, various chokes, jeweled bolt, hand checkered, checkered select walnut stock. Mfg. 1972-75, "Y" ser. no. prefix.

	$750	$650	$600	$550	$500	$450	$400

In 1984, Y series Model 12s were once again available through a private contract with U.S.R.A. Co. which included engraving on Grades 1A-1C and 2-5. These guns were available in either Field, Trap, or Skeet configurations. Since there was no manufacturer's suggested retail, Model 12 values shown are established by analyzing the sales of the two private contractors - no more of these variations are available.

GRADING - PPGS™	100%	98%	95%	90%	80%	70%	60%

✱ Grades 1-A, 1-B, & 1-C - light engraving depicting dogs or ducks. Disc.

	$1,300	$1,195	$1,000	$875	$785	$695	$600

Last MSR was $1,375.

✱ Grades 2 & 3 - engraving features large duck and dog game scenes on receiver flats. Disc.

	$1,600	$1,495	$1,295	$1,075	$950	$830	$725

Last MSR was $1,695.

✱ Grade 4 - more elaborate game scene engraving than Grades 2 & 3. Disc.

	$1,850	$1,695	$1,450	$1,225	$1,075	$950	$850

Last MSR was $1,995.

✱ Grade 5 - elaborate game scene engraving with style B checkering. Disc.

	$2,195	$1,995	$1,725	$1,500	$1,225	$1,095	$950

Last MSR was $2,450.

Also available with gold inlays - add $1,000 to values.

✱ 3 Barrel Set - grade 5 engraving with gold inlays and two extra barrels. Disc.

	$5,500	$4,995	$4,350	$3,750	$3,325	$2,750	$2,300

Last MSR was $6,000.

MODEL 12 SKEET GRADE - similar to Field Grade, with 26 in. VR skeet bore barrel, skeet style stock, with recoil pad. Mfg. 1972-75.

	$950	$800	$625	$550	$495	$450	$425

See listings under Model 12 Field Grade for engraved values.

MODEL 12 TRAP GRADE - similar to Field grade, with 30 in. VR full choke barrel, trap style stock, straight or Monte Carlo, recoil pad. Mfg. 1972-80.

	$750	$675	$575	$525	$495	$450	$425

See listings under Model 12 Field Grade for engraved values.

MODEL 12 DU - limited mfg. for Ducks Unlimited Chapters.

	$1,500	$1,250	$1,000

MODEL 12 LIMITED EDITION

✱ Grade I 20 Ga. - 20 ga. only, 2 3/4 in. chamber only, reproduction of the famous Winchester Model 12 with slight design improvements, 26 in. VR barrel bored modified, 5 shot mag., high post floating rib, walnut stock and forearm with semi-gloss finish, takedown, 7 lbs. 4,000 mfg. by Miroku 1993-95.

	$795	$625	$450

Last MSR was $879

✱ Model 12 Grade IV 20 Ga. - similar specifications to Grade I, except has select walnut checkered 22 lines per inch with high gloss finish, extensive game scene engraving including multiple gold inlays. 1,000 mfg. 1993-95.

	$1,175	$850	$650

Last MSR was $1,431.

MODEL 42 HIGH GRADE LIMITED EDITION - .410 bore, 26 in. full choke VR barrel, features Grade V-VI wood with special scroll and gold border engraving, 850 mfg. 1993 only.

	$1,400	$1,100	$895

Last MSR was $1,617.

MODEL 120 RANGER - 12, 16, or 20 ga., entry level model, VR and WinChokes. Disc.

	$200	$180	$165	$140	$110	$100	$90

GRADING - PPGS™	100%	98%	95%	90%	80%	70%	60%

MODEL 1200 SLIDE ACTION FIELD GRADE - 12, 16, or 20 ga., 26, 28, or 30 in. barrel, alloy receiver, various chokes, checkered pistol grip stock, pad. Mfg. 1964-81.

	100%	98%	95%	90%	80%	70%	60%
	$200	$180	$165	$140	$110	$100	$90
Vent. rib	$220	$205	$195	$165	$140	$110	$100
WinChoke	$240	$215	$200	$190	$180	$160	$140

Add 33% for Hydro-coil recoil system.

MODEL 1200 MAGNUM - similar to 1200, chambered for 12 or 20 ga., 3 in. magnum shells. Mfg. 1964-80.

	100%	98%	95%	90%	80%	70%	60%
	$210	$190	$175	$165	$140	$110	$100
Vent. rib	$240	$215	$200	$185	$150	$140	$110

MODEL 1200 SKEET GUN - similar to 1200, 12 or 20 ga., 26 in. VR barrel, skeet bore, 2 shot mag. and select style stock. Mfg. 1965-74.

100%	98%	95%	90%	80%	70%	60%
$325	$275	$235	$200	$165	$140	$120

MODEL 1200 TRAP GUN - similar to 1200, with 12 ga., VR, 30 in. full choke barrel, select trap style stock. Mfg. 1965-74.

	100%	98%	95%	90%	80%	70%	60%
	$295	$275	$300	$195	$165	$140	$120
WinChoke	$330	$305	$275	$250	$220	$165	$140

MODEL 1200 DEER GUN - similar to 1200, with 22 in. barrel, rifle sights, 12 ga. only. Mfg. 1965-74.

100%	98%	95%	90%	80%	70%	60%
$250	$200	$165	$110	$100	$85	$75

MODEL 1200 POLICE STAINLESS - 12 ga. only, 18 in. barrel, 7 shot mag. Disc.

100%	98%	95%
$250	$195	$165

MODEL 1200 DEFENDER - 12 ga. only, 18 in. cylinder bore barrel, 7 shot mag., 6 lbs. Disc.

100%	98%	95%	90%	80%	70%	60%
$250	$200	$180	$155	$140	$125	$110

MODEL 1300 FEATHERWEIGHT SLIDE ACTION - 12 or 20 ga., 3 in. chamber, takedown, 26 (new 1991) or 28 in. barrel, 5 shot, plain or VR (became standard 1990), WinChoke tubes, checkered walnut stock and grooved forearm, alloy frame, recoil pad, 6 3/4 - 7 1/8 lbs. Mfg. 1978-93.

100%	98%	95%	90%	80%	70%	60%
$300	$260	$230	$195	$175	$160	$145

Last MSR was $374.

Subtract $30 without VR.

This model had an "XTR" suffix until 1989. Older Model 1300 Featherweights had roll-engraving but no premiums are being asked at this time.

MODEL 1300 WALNUT FIELD - 12 or 20 (disc. 1994) ga., 3 in. chamber, 26 or 28 in. VR barrel with WinChokes (includes 3), checkered satin (disc. 2003) or gloss finished (new 2004) walnut stock and forearm, approx. 7 1/4 - 7 1/2 lbs. New 1994.

MSR $438	$345	$250	$200	$160	$140	$120	$110

Beginning 2003, Winchester started engraving "Speed Pump" on receiver on all Model 1300 variations.

* **Model 1300 Black Shadow Field** - 12 or 20 (new 1996) ga., 3 in. chamber, 26 or 28 in. (12 ga. only) VR WinChoke barrel, black composite stock and forearm, 6 3/4 - 7 1/4 lbs. New 1995.

MSR $351	$270	$210	$170	$135	$120	$110	$95

* **Model 1300 Sporting/Field** - 12 ga., 3 in. chamber, 24 (compact) or 28 in. VR barrel with 5 WinChokes, satin finished checkered walnut full length or compact (13 in. LOP) stock and forearm with radiused recoil pad, Tru-Glo front sight, matte metal finish, 6.75 or 7.5 lbs. New 2002.

MSR $438	$345	$255	$205	$165	$135	$120	$110

GRADING - PPGS™	100%	98%	95%	90%	80%	70%	60%

✳ *Model 1300 Advantage Camo* - 12 ga. only, 28 in. barrel with choke tubes, full coverage. Advantage Camo. Mfg. 1997.

	$340	$265	$235	$195	$165	$145	$125

Last MSR was $432.

✳ *Model 1300 New Shadow Grass* - 12 ga. only, 26 or 28 in. VR barrel with 3 WinChokes, features 100% Mossy Oak New Shadow Grass camo coverage, approx. 7 lbs. New 2004.

MSR $472	$365	$275	$215	$180	$150	$130	$115

MODEL 1300 UPLAND SPECIAL FIELD - 12 or 20 (new 2000) ga., 3 in. chamber, features gloss finished (new 2004) or satin finished (disc. 2003) checkered straight grip walnut stock and forearm, solid recoil pad, 24 in. VR barrel with choke tube, blue only, 6.75 lbs. New 1999.

MSR $438	$345	$255	$205	$165	$135	$120	$110

MODEL 1300 CUSTOM HIGH GRADE - while advertised, this model never went into production. Advertised retail was $1,395.

MODEL 1300 WATERFOWL - 12 ga. only, 3 in. chamber, 28 or 30 (disc.) in. VR barrel, matte finished metal, choice of low luster walnut finish or brown Win-Tuff wood, recoil pad, includes camo sling and swivels, WinChokes standard, 7 lbs. Mfg. 1984-91.

	$295	$260	$235	$200	$180	$165	$150

Last MSR was $367.

MODEL 1300 TURKEY GUN - 12 ga. only, 3 in. chamber, 22 in. VR barrel, Win-Choked, walnut stock and forearm with low luster finish, metal surfaces have matte finish, supplied with camouflaged fabric sling, 6 3/8 lbs. Mfg. 1985-88.

	$290	$265	$235	$200	$180	$165	$150

Last MSR was $348.

✳ *Model 1300 Win-Cam Turkey Gun* - similar to Model 1300 Turkey Gun, except has greenish laminated hardwood stock and forearm. Mfg. 1987-93.

	$350	$295	$250	$200	$180	$165	$150

Last MSR was $435.

✳ *Model 1300 Win-Cam Combo Pack* - 12 ga., supplied with 22 and 30 in. VR non-glare finished barrels, greenish laminated hardwood stock and forearm, camo sling, matte finished metal. Mfg. 1987-88 only.

	$375	$330	$290	$260	$230	$200	$185

Last MSR was $425.

✳ *Model 1300 Ladies-Youth Win-Cam Turkey Gun* - 20 ga. only, 3 in. chamber, 22 in. VR barrel, green camo laminate shortened stock and forearm, includes sling and National Wild Turkey Federation engraving, 6 lbs. Mfg. 1992 only.

	$340	$295	$250	$200	$180	$165	$150

Last MSR was $411.

✳ *Model 1300 Win-Cam NWTF Series I-IV* - 12 or 20 ga., Series I was released 1989 (12 ga. only) and included special receiver engraving featuring National Wild Turkey Federation motifs, Series II was released 1990 with a choice of either 12 (disc.) or 20 ga. Ladies/Youth model, Series III was released 1991-92, Series IV was released 1993. Disc. 1994.

	$365	$300	$250	$200	$180	$165	$150

Last MSR was $458.

MODEL 1300 TURKEY - SYNTHETIC STOCK - 12 or 20 (mfg. 1996-99, Black Shadow only) ga., 3 in. chamber, 22 in. VR barrel with choke tube, choice of 2 color Realtree camo patterns on synthetic stock and forearm, full camo coverage available in Realtree or Advantage (new 1996), or non-glare black (Black Shadow) finish on all surfaces, approx. 6 3/4 lbs. Mfg. 1994-2000.

GRADING - PPGS™	100%	98%	95%	90%	80%	70%	60%

❋ *Model 1300 Black Shadow Finish* - disc. 2000.

	$260	$195	$160	$135	$120	$110	$95

Last MSR was $328.

❋ *Model 1300 Mossy Oak Break-Up Turkey* - 12 ga. only, 3 in. chamber, 22 in. VR barrel with TruGlo sights, high density X-full turkey tube, 100% Mossy Oak coverage on wood and metal, 6 3/4 lbs. Mfg. 2000 only.

	$375	$295	$260	$225	$200	$185	$170

Last MSR was $459.

This model was also available with iron sights and rifled sabot choke tube for deer hunting - add approx. $30.

❋ *Model 1300 RealTree/Advantage Camo Finish* - available with stock and forearm, Real-Tree only or full coverage camo. Disc. 1998.

	$290	$240	$180	$150	$130	$115	$100

Last MSR was $370.

Add $62 for full coverage camo.
Add $40 for full coverage without sling (disc. 1997).
Add $40 for smoothbore barrel (Advantage full camo only).

MODEL 1300 UNIVERSAL HUNTER
- 12 ga. only, 3 in. chamber, 26 in. VR barrel with 3 WinChokes, full coverage standard or New Mossy Oak Break-Up (new 2003) camo, with or w/o Tru-Glo 3-dot sights, composite stock and forearm, 7 lbs. New 2002.

MSR $472	$370	$320	$285	$240	$195	$155	$135

Add $37 for TruGlo sights (Universal Hunter Turkey Model).

MODEL 1300 NWTF TURKEY MODELS
- 12 ga. only, 3 in. chamber, 18 (Short Turkey, new 2002) or 22 in. barrel, choice of Black Shadow (black synthetic stock and forearm with non-glare metal finish and extra full choke tube, mfg. 2001 only), Turkey Superflauge with full coverage TreBark Superflauge (mfg. 2001) or Mossy Oak Break-Up camo with TruGlo sights, Buck & Tom Superflauge with full coverage Tre-Bark Superflauge (mfg. 2001) or Mossy Oak Break-Up (new 2002) camo with 2 choke tubes including rifled sabot, or Short Turkey (18 in. barrel with rifled sights and full coverage Mossy Oak Break-Up camo) configurations, "Team NWTF" logo printed on stock, 6 3/4 lbs. New 2001.

MSR $507	$420	$360	$260	$225	$175	$150	$125

Subtract approx. $160 for Black Shadow configuration.
Add $42 for Buck & Tom Superflauge configuration.

MODEL 1300 LADIES-YOUTH
- 20 ga. only, 3 in. chamber, 22 in. VR barrel, shortened stock dimensions, walnut stock with recoil pad and rear positioned, grooved forearm, 6 1/4 lbs. Mfg. 1992 only.

	$315	$260	$220	$180	$165	$150	$135

Last MSR was $355.

MODEL 1300 SLUG HUNTER
- 12 ga. only, 3 in. chamber, 22 in. rifled or smooth bore barrel with iron sights, checkered stock and forearm, satin walnut finish or brown laminate stock (Win-Tuff). Supplied with camo fabric sling and rings and bases. Mfg. 1988-disc.

	$360	$300	$250	$200	$180	$165	$150

Last MSR was $445.

Add $10 for smooth bore barrel with Sabot rifled tubes (disc. 1992).
Add $4 for "Whitetails Unlimited" Model (new 1991).

MODEL 1300 WALNUT DEER
- 12 ga. only, 3 in. chamber, 22 in. rifled barrel, non-glare metal surfaces, rifle sights, checkered walnut stock with recoil pad and forearm, 7 1/4 lbs. Mfg. 1994-99.

	$350	$285	$255	$225	$200	$185	$170

Last MSR was $429.

GRADING - PPGS™	100%	98%	95%	90%	80%	70%	60%

❋ *Model 1300 Black Shadow Deer* - 12 or 20 (mfg. 1996-97, reintroduced 2000) ga., 3 in. chamber, 22 in. smoothbore (12 ga. only, disc. 2003) or rifled (new 1996) barrel with IC WinChoke, matte black stock, forearm, and metal parts, rifle sights, drilled and tapped receiver, approx. 6 3/4 lbs. New 1994.

	100%	98%	95%	90%	80%	70%	60%
MSR $376	$295	$225	$175	$150	$125	$115	$95

Add $44 for Cantilever scope mount, available in 12 ga. only (new 2000).

Add $77 for deer combo package that includes 22 in. cyl. bore (disc. 1998) or rifled (new 2000) barrel and 28 in. VR WinChoke barrels.

Subtract approx. $25 for smoothbore barrel (disc. 2003).

❋ *Model 1300 Deer Ranger* - 12 or 20 (Ranger regular or compact) ga., 3 in. chamber, 22 in. rifled barrel with rifle or TruGlo (12 ga. only) sights, smaller dimensions on 20 ga. Deer Ranger Compact (13 in. LOP), brown composite stock and forearm, non-glare finish, 6.75 lbs. New 2000.

	100%	98%	95%	90%	80%	70%	60%
MSR $390	$300	$230	$170	$145	$125	$110	$100

❋ *Model 1300 Full Advantage Camo* - 12 ga. only, 3 in. chamber, choice of 22 in. rifled or smoothbore barrel, entire gun is in Full Advantage camo pattern, drilled and tapped receiver, iron sights, 7 lbs. Mfg. 1995-98.

	98%	95%	90%	80%	70%	60%
	$350	$295	$260	$225	$200	$185	$170

Last MSR was $432.

Subtract $22 for smoothbore barrel.

MODEL 1300 RANGER SLIDE ACTION - 12 or 20 ga., 3 in. chamber, 22 cyl. or rifled (deer only, disc.), 24 1/8 cyl. (disc. deer barrel), 26 (mfg. 1991-98), 28, or 30 (disc. 1992) in. plain or VR barrel, walnut finished hardwood stock, alloy receiver, approx. 7 1/4 lbs. Mfg. 1983-2004.

	98%	95%	90%	80%	70%	60%
	$285	$215	$170	$135	$120	$110	$95

Last MSR was $367.

Subtract $40 without VR or WinChokes.

This model was also available in a deer combination package which included either a 22 in. rifled or smoothbore deer barrel and a 28 in. VR WinChoke barrel in either 12 or 20 ga. (disc.). - add approx. 25% to values listed.

❋ *Ranger Ladies/Youth Model* - 20 ga. only, 3 in. chamber, 22 in. VR barrel, shorter stock dimensions - 13 in. LOP and rearward positioned forearm. Disc. 1998.

	98%	95%	90%	80%	70%	60%
	$285	$235	$200	$170	$150	$125	$110

Last MSR was $309.

Subtract $40 if without WinChoke and VR.

❋ *Ranger Compact* - 12 or 20 ga., 3 in. chamber, features shorter dimensions (13 LOP), 22 (20 ga. only) or 24 (12 ga. only) in. VR barrel with WinChoke and Tru-Glo sights, uncheckered hardwood stock and grooved forearm, blue only, approx. 6 3/4 lbs. New 1999.

	100%	98%	95%	90%	80%	70%	60%
MSR $366	$285	$215	$170	$135	$120	$110	$95

MODEL 1300 CAMP DEFENDER - 12 ga. only, 3 in. chamber, 8 shot mag., 22 in. barrel with rifle sights and WinChoke, choice of black synthetic (disc. 2000) or hardwood (new 2001) stock and forearm, matte metal finish, 6 7/8 lbs. Mfg. 1999-2004.

	98%	95%	90%	80%	70%	60%
	$300	$230	$180	$150	$125	$110	$100

Last MSR was $392.

MODEL 1300 DEFENDER - 12 or 20 (disc. 1996, reintroduced 2001) ga., 3 in. chamber, available in Police (disc. 1989), Practical (new 2005), Marine, and Defender variations, 18 or 24 (mfg. 1994-98) in. cyl. bore barrel, 5 (disc. 1998), 7 (disc. 1998), or 8 shot mag., matte metal finish, choice of hardwood (disc. 2001), composite (matte finish), or pistol grip (matte finish, 12 ga. only) stock, TruGlo sights became standard 1999, 5 3/4 - 7 lbs.

	100%	98%	95%
MSR $341	$270	$210	$160

Add $13 for short pistol grip and full length stocks.

Add approx. $100 for Combo Package (includes extra 28 in. VR barrel - disc. 1998).

GRADING - PPGS™	100%	98%	95%	90%	80%	70%	60%

* ***Model 1300 Practical Defender*** - 12 ga. only, 3 in. chamber, 8 shot mag., 22 in. barrel with TruGlo sights, adj. open sights, designed for practical shooting events, black synthetic stock and forearm. New 2005.

MSR $392	$300	$230	$170	$145	$125	$110	$100

* ***Stainless Coastal Marine Defender*** - 12 ga. only, 18 in. cyl. bore stainless steel barrel and mag. tube, a Sandstrom 9A phosphate coating was released late 1989 to give long lasting corrosion protection to all receiver and internal working parts, Dura-Touch armor coating stock treatment added 2004, 6 shot mag., synthetic pistol grip (disc. 2001) or full black stock configuration, approx. 6 3/8 lbs.

MSR $575	$465	$380	$275				

* ***Model 1300 Lady Defender*** - 20 ga. only, 3 in. chamber, choice of synthetic regular or pistol grip stock, 4 (disc. 1996) or 7 shot mag., 18 in. cyl. bore barrel (new 1996), 5 3/8 lbs. Disc. 1998.

		$235	$190	$150			

Last MSR was $290.

SHOTGUNS: O/U - RECENT PRODUCTION

Model 101 dates of manufacture and serialization data can be found in the SERIALIZATION section in the back of this text.

In November of 1987 Olin/Winchester disc. the Model 101. Classic Doubles (listed separately in this text) imported this model under their own trademark until approx. 1990. With the discontinuance of the Model 101 and its many variations, both dealers and collectors have created a lot more demand for this model recently. As a result, prices have escalated and the scramble is on to try and pick off those rare and desirable variations. Since there have been a lot of limited editions and production changes in the 101 O/U series, it could very well be that this model might become very collectible in upcoming years (as happened to the Model 12).

Note: Model 101 and Model 96 Xpert guns were made by Olin Kodensha located in Tochigi, Japan.

Add 10% for the following Model 101s listed in this section, if in NIB condition.

MODEL 91 - 12 ga. only, mfg. by Laurona in Spain for international sales including Europe, SST, ejectors optional, VR, distinguishable by black chrome finish on metal parts. Disc.

Prices hard to evaluate because of limited importation domestically. In some regions they are bought as medium priced field guns ($550-$650), while in others they are sold as a rare Winchester O&U ($900-$1,100).

MODEL 96 XPERT FIELD GRADE - 12 or 20 ga., similar action to Model 101, 3 in. chambers, auto ejectors, SST, various barrel lengths and chokes, action similar to 101, no engraving, checkered pistol grip stock and forearm. Mfg. 1976-82.

		$875	$775	$650	$550	$475	$425	$375

Add 10% for 20 ga.
This model has become known as the "Poor Man's 101."

MODEL 96 XPERT SKEET GRADE - 2 3/4 in. chambers, similar to Field Grade, with 27 in. skeet barrels, skeet style stock. Mfg. 1976-82.

		$925	$850	$725	$600	$500	$450	$410

Add 10% for 20 ga.

MODEL 96 XPERT TRAP GRADE - 12 ga. only, 2 3/4 in. chambers, similar to Field, 30 in. imp. mod. and full or full and full choke, trap style stock. Mfg. 1976-82.

		$875	$775	$650	$550	$475	$425	$375

MODEL 99 - 12 ga., DT, no engraving. Disc.

		$700	$575	$525	$470	$430	$395	$360

GRADING - PPGS™	100%	98%	95%	90%	80%	70%	60%

MODEL 101 FIELD VARIATION

MODEL 101 FIELD VARIATION - 12, 20 ga., or .410 bore, 26, 28, or 30 in. barrels, various chokes, boxlock, auto ejectors, SST, engraved receiver, checkered American walnut pistol grip stock. Mfg. 1963-87. Values assume WinChokes (standard since 1983) - subtract $60 if without.

* **Older production** - checkered walnut stock and forearm, ejectors, SST, blue metal with light engraving on receiver, various barrel lengths, w/o choke tubes.

	$995	$850	$725	$625	$585	$550	$500

Add 50% for 28 ga. or .410 bore.
Add 20% for 20 ga.

* **25th Anniversary Model** - 12 ga., 32 in. F/M barrels, 2 3/4 in. chambers, engraved "1 of 101" with silver inlays, cased. Mfg. 1988.

	$3,195	$2,750	$2,300	$1,950	$1,600	$1,300	$1,200

Last MSR was $3,500.

* **Field Special** - 12 ga., 3 in. chambers, VR, 27 in. barrels with WinChokes, blue receiver with scroll engraved ejectors, 7 lbs. Disc. 1987.

	$1,350	$1,225	$995	$875	$775	$695	$600

Last MSR was $1,185.

* **Lightweight Field** - 12 or 20 ga., similar to regular Field Grade, except has coin finished receiver, vent. barrels, and solid rubber recoil pad, 6 1/2 - 7 lbs. Disc. 1987.

	$1,475	$1,295	$1,195	$975	$875	$675	$595

Last MSR was $1,425.

Add 20% for 20 ga.

* **Waterfowl Model** - 12 ga. only, 3 in. chambers, 30 or 32 (disc.) in. WinChoked barrels, VR, matte blue receiver with moderate engraving, low gloss walnut stock with vent. recoil pad, 7 3/4 lbs. Disc. 1987.

	$2,000	$1,775	$1,500	$1,250	$1,050	$800	$700

Last MSR was $1,570.

* **Model 101 Field Grade 2 Barrel Hunting Set** - 12 or 20 ga. barrels, both with WinChokes, 26 in. barrels - 20 ga., 28 in. barrels - 12 ga., scroll engraved, blue receiver with game scene engraving and borders, cased. Mfg. 1984-87.

	$2,795	$2,500	$2,395	$2,200	$1,795	$1,695	$1,595

Last MSR was $2,345.

* **Quail Special** - 12, 20 (disc.1984), 28 (new 1987) ga., or .410 bore (new 1987), 25 1/2 in. WinChoke barrels, 6 3/4 lbs. - 12 ga., straight grip stock, vent. barrels and rib, coin finished receiver with game scene engraving, 500 of each ga. were mfg. Imported 1984-86.

	100%	98%	95%	90%	80%	70%	60%
12 ga.	$2,495	$2,250	$1,995	$1,750	$1,550	$1,450	$1,350
20 ga.	$2,875	$2,500	$2,195	$1,850	$1,750	$1,650	$1,550
28 ga.	$4,250	$3,950	$3,650	$3,250	$2,700	$2,500	$2,400
.410 bore	$3,600	$3,150	$2,750	$2,350	$1,900	$1,800	$1,500

Last MSR was $1,950.

All 28 ga. models are baby frames.

* **National Wild Turkey Federation Commemorative** - features golden turkeys on receiver sides, 27 in. VR barrels with choke tubes, only 300 mfg.

	$2,595	$2,250	$1,795

Original issue price was $1,950.

GRADING - PPGS™	100%	98%	95%	90%	80%	70%	60%

✳ American Flyer Live Bird - 12 ga. only, 28 or 29 1/2 (new 1988) in. separated barrels with special competition VR, blue frame with gold wire borders and pigeon inlay, 8 - 8 1/2 lbs. Imported 1987 only.

	$2,595	$2,275	$1,950	$1,775	$1,600	$1,425	$1,300

Last MSR was $2,910.

Add $925 for Combo Model (with extra set of 28 & 29 1/2 in. barrels with WinChokes - 45 mfg.).
Add $265 for 29 1/2 in. barrel with WT4 choke tubes.
Approx. 200 of this model were mfg.

MODEL 101 MAGNUM - similar to 101 Field, 12 or 20 ga., 3 in. Mag. chambering, recoil pad, 30 in. barrels, full and mod., or full and full choke. Mfg. 1966-81.

	$1,000	$875	$725	$650	$575	$500	$460

Add 20% for 20 ga.

MODEL 101 SKEET VARIATION - similar to 101 Field, with 26 1/2 (12 or 20 ga.) or 28 (28 ga. or .410 bore) in. skeet bored barrels, skeet style stock. Mfg. 1966-84.

	$1,000	$825	$770	$700	$650	$595	$540

Add 50% for 28 ga. or .410 bore.
Add 30% for 20 ga.

MODEL 101 THREE GAUGE SKEET SET - similar to Skeet 101, with 20, 28 ga., and .410 bore barrels, cased. Mfg. 1974-84.

	$3,495	$3,195	$2,850	$2,600	$2,250	$1,900	$1,650

MODEL 101 TRAP VARIATION - 12 ga. only, 30 or 32 in. barrels with normal or wide VR, imp. mod. and full or full and full chokes, trap style stock. Mfg. 1966-84.

	$1,320	$1,100	$935	$825	$715	$660	$605

MODEL 101 SINGLE BARREL TRAP - similar to O/U Trap, with 32 or 34 in. F or IM choke barrel, Monte Carlo trap style stock. Mfg. 1967-71.

	$880	$660	$550	$495	$385	$360	$330

Add 100% for an extra O/U barrel (Trap Set).

MODEL 101 PIGEON GRADE (XTR) - 12, 20, 28 ga. or .410 bore (disc. 1986), vent. O/U barrels, deluxe engraved silver receiver version of 101, select checkered wood. Mfg. 1974-87.

✳ Lightweight Field Model - lightweight variation, WinChokes standard, 28 ga. baby frame has 27 in. barrels, 6 1/2 - 7 lbs. Disc. 1987.

	100%	98%	95%	90%	80%	70%	60%
12 ga.	$2,195	$1,995	$1,795	$1,450	$1,350	$1,250	$1,150
20 ga.	$2,495	$2,295	$1,995	$1,795	$1,695	$1,595	$1,495
28 ga. standard	$3,395	$3,195	$2,895	$2,495	$2,200	$2,100	$1,700
28 ga. baby frame	$4,195	$3,950	$3,650	$3,250	$2,700	$2,500	$2,400
.410 bore	$3,395	$3,195	$2,895	$2,495	$2,200	$2,100	$1,700

Last MSR was $1,950.

Subtract 5% if without WinChokes (available in all gauges).

✳ Lightweight recent mfg. - 20 ga. only, 27 in. barrels only with WinChokes, previously manufactured guns that have been photo-chemically engraved and gold plated, 101 (total mfg.) shotguns were sold by Guns Unlimited Inc. located in Omaha, NE 1995-96.

	$2,495	$2,195	$1,995	$1,795	$1,595	$1,495	$1,295

Last MSR was $1,795.

✳ Lightweight two barrel set - includes either 12/20 ga. with WinChokes (28 in. barrels on 12 ga. and 27 in. on 20 ga.) or 28 ga./.410 bore (27 in. barrels, 28 ga. has WinChokes; .410 bore has fixed M/F chokes), 250 sets mfg. serial numbered HS1-HS250. Disc. 1986.

	$3,595	$3,350	$2,950	$2,750	$2,295	$2,195	$1,995

Last MSR was $2,500.

Add 30% for 28 ga./.410 bore combo.

GRADING - PPGS™	100%	98%	95%	90%	80%	70%	60%

* **Pigeon Grade 3 barrel set** - coin finished Pigeon Grade frame, approx. 250 mfg.

	$4,395	$4,195	$3,895	$3,395	$2,995	$2,695	$2,395

* **Featherweight** - 12 or 20 ga., English straight stock, 25 1/2 in. barrels bored IC/IM, 6 1/2 - 6 3/4 lbs. Disc. 1987.

	$1,950	$1,750	$1,450	$1,275	$950	$850	$750

Last MSR was $1,580.

Add 20% for 20 ga.
Add 20% for WinChokes.

* **Skeet Grade** - 12, 20, 28 ga., or .410 bore.

	$1,275	$1,100	$995	$880	$770	$715	$660

Add 25% for 20 ga.
Add 50% for 28 ga. or .410 bore.

* **Trap Grade** - 12 ga. only, vent. barrels and rib, coin finish receiver with fine scroll engraving, engraved pigeon on floorplate, WinChoke standard, 8 1/4 lbs. Disc. 1985.

	$1,475	$1,275	$1,050	$900	$800	$725	$650

Last MSR was $1,475.

Subtract 15% if w/o WinChokes.

* **Super Pigeon Grade** - 12 ga. only, blue receiver with elaborate engraving including multiple gold inlays, extra select walnut with fleur-de-lis checkering on stock and forearm, WinChoke standard, 7 1/2 lbs. Imported 1985-87 only.

	$4,500	$4,150	$3,500	$2,900	$2,500	$2,150	$1,920

Last MSR was $4,590.

101 DIAMOND GRADE - Trap or Skeet O/U, 12 (Trap only), 20, 28 ga., or .410 bore, vent. barrels and rib, WinChoke standard on Trap - add $75 on Skeet model (disc.1986), select hand checkered walnut, engraved satin-finish receiver. Trap model has extra high VR. Skeet model has raised rib and muzzle vents.

* **Standard Trap** - 12 ga. only, 30 or 32 in. vent. barrels, 8 3/4 - 9 lbs. Disc. 1987.

	$1,620	$1,440	$1,230	$1,075	$900	$780	$640

Last MSR was $1,860.

* **Unsingle Trap** - 12 ga. only, lower single barrel, 32 or 34 in. barrel, extended rib. Add $60 for WinChoke. Disc. 1986.

	$1,700	$1,525	$1,250	$995	$895	$830	$740

Last MSR was $1,760.

* **Oversingle Trap** - 12 ga. only, WinChokes, 34 in. upper barrel only, 8 1/2 lbs. Imported 1986-87 only.

	$1,985	$1,695	$1,545	$1,395	$1,200	$995	$895

Last MSR was $2,145.

* **Oversingle Combo** - includes one set of O/U barrels and an oversingle barrel, cased. Imported 1987 only.

	$3,075	$2,750	$2,525	$2,300	$2,000	$1,750	$1,625

Last MSR was $3,550.

Add $275 for ATA Trap set.

* **Trap Combo** - 12 ga. only, includes a set of 30 or 32 in. vent. O/U barrels and a 32 or 34 in. high ribbed unsingle (lower) barrel, standard or Monte Carlo stock, approx. 9 lbs. Disc. 1987.

	$2,570	$2,320	$1,975	$1,800	$1,600	$1,400	$1,200

Last MSR was $2,940.

GRADING - PPGS™	100%	98%	95%	90%	80%	70%	60%

✴ *Standard Skeet* - 12, 20, 28 ga., or .410 bore, 27 1/2 in. vent. barrels and competition rib, 6 1/2 - 7 1/4 lbs. Disc. 1987.

| | $1,650 | $1,465 | $1,240 | $1,075 | $900 | $780 | $640 |

Last MSR was $1,950.

Add 30% for 28 ga. or .410 bore.

Add 20% for 20 ga.

Certain design features may increase/decrease the values of this model.

✴ *Four Gauge Skeet Set* - includes 12, 20, 28 ga., and .410 bore 27 1/2 in. separated barrel assemblies, cased. Imported 1985-87 only.

| | $4,850 | $4,025 | $3,650 | $3,200 | $2,800 | $2,500 | $2,150 |

Last MSR was $5,025.

✴ *Sporting Clays Grade* - 12 ga. only, marked Diamond Sporter, 28 in. barrels with WinChokes, designed for Sporting Clay competition. Disc. 1987.

| | $2,050 | $1,700 | $1,400 | $1,100 | $925 | $795 | $650 |

Last MSR was $1,965.

501 GRAND EUROPEAN - Trap or Skeet, 12 or 20 (Skeet only) ga., 27, 30, or 32 in. barrels, extra select hand checkered walnut with oil finish, Schnabel forearm, extensive scroll engraving on satin-finished receiver, vent. barrels and rib. Mfg. 1981-86.

| | $2,195 | $1,995 | $1,895 | $1,795 | $1,595 | $1,395 | $1,195 |

Last MSR was $1,720.

Add 20% for 20 ga. Skeet.

✴ *Grand European Featherweight* - 20 ga. only, straight grip stock, 25 1/2 in. VR barrels, 5 3/4 lbs. Disc. 1986.

| | $2,795 | $2,500 | $2,350 | $2,100 | $1,900 | $1,700 | $1,400 |

Last MSR was $1,720.

PRESENTATION GRADE - 12 ga. only, available in both Trap and Skeet models, blue action extensively engraved with gold inlays, special crotch walnut, 27 (Skeet) or 30 in. vent. barrels, hand checkered, silver wire borders on perimeter of receiver. Imported 1984-87 only.

| | $3,950 | $3,395 | $3,075 | $2,400 | $2,000 | $1,800 | $1,600 |

Last MSR was $3,840.

Subtract 10% for Trap Model.

SHOTGUN/RIFLE COMBINATION - combination 12 ga. and .222 Rem., .223 Rem., .243 Win., .270 Win., .30-06, .308 Win., .300 Win. Mag., 5.6x57R, 6.5x55mm, 7x65R, 7x57 Mauser, or 9.3x74R cal. rifle, O/U, 25 in. barrels, top barrel is Win-Choked, Grand European engraving and finish, 8 1/2 lbs. Mfg. 1983-85.

| | $2,495 | $2,295 | $1,995 | $1,795 | $1,595 | $1,495 | $1,395 |

Last MSR was $2,550.

Add 20% for .300 Win. Mag. or 6.5x55mm cal.

This model was advertised in .222 Rem., .223 Rem., 6.5x55mm, or .300 Win. Mag. cal., but very few 6.5x55mm or .300 Win. Mag. cals. have been encountered to date.

MODEL 1001 FIELD GRADE - 12 ga. only, 3 in. chambers, boxlock action, 28 in. VR (8mm) barrel with WinPlus chokes, blue metal featuring 40% engraving coverage, Grade I stock and forearm, high luster finish, mfg. in Italy by Marocchi 1993, disc. 1998.

| | $975 | $795 | $725 | $650 | $595 | $550 | $495 |

Last MSR was $1,099.

✴ *Model 1001 Sporting Clays* - 12 ga. only, 2 3/4 in. chambers, 28 or 30 in. VR (10mm) vent. barrels with WinPlus chokes, full engraving (includes scroll and flying W with clay bird), silver nitrate receiver with remaining parts blue, Grade II-III stock and forearm, satin finish, mfg. in Italy by Marocchi 1993, disc. 1998.

| | $1,075 | $925 | $795 | $725 | $650 | $595 | $550 |

Last MSR was $1,253.

✴ **Model 1001 Sporting Clays Lite** - 12 ga. only, 3 in. chambers, blue finish, 28 in. VR barrels with WinPlus chokes, checkered walnut stock and forearm, gold SST, 7 lbs. Mfg. 1995-98.

	$1,000	$795	$725	$650	$595	$550	$495

Last MSR was $1,153.

MODEL G5500 SPORTER - 12 ga. only, marked Sporter, 28 or 30 in. barrels with fixed chokes (bored IC/M, IM/F, or XF/F) or WinChokes.

	$1,795	$1,475	$1,275	$1,075	$900	$780	$640

Add 20% for WinChokes.

MODEL G6500 SPORTER - 12 ga. only, marked Sporter, barrels and chokes same as G5500.

	$2,295	$1,925	$1,625	$1,400	$1,225	$1,050	$900

Add 20% for WinChokes.

SELECT FIELD (SUPREME) - 12 ga. only, 3 in. chambers, low profile boxlock action with dual tapered locking lugs positioned between the barrels, SST, ejectors, game scene engraved receiver, 26 (new 2001) or 28 in. 6mm VR back-bored barrels with Invector Plus choking (high polish barrels became standard in 2005), redesigned barrels in 2003, checkered walnut stock and forearm, blue action and barrels, barrel selector on safety switch, approx. 7 lbs. New 2000.

MSR $1,498	$1,265	$1,025	$900	$800	$700	$600	$500

During 2004, this model's nomenclature was changed from Supreme Select Field to Select Field.

SELECT ELEGANCE (SUPREME) - 12 ga. only, 3 in. chambers, grey game scene engraved low profile receiver with dual locking pin design, choice of regular checkered (Traditional Elegance) or oval checkered (Extreme Elegance, new 2004) Grade III walnut stock and Schnabel forearm, 26 or 28 in. non-ported barrels with Invector Plus choke system (high polish barrels became standard in 2005), includes red hardshell case, approx. 7 lbs. New 2003.

MSR $2,320	$1,950	$1,625	$1,275	$995	$875	$775	$675

SUPREME SELECT SPORTING - 12 ga. only, 2 3/4 in. chambers, features satin finished bi-tone receiver w/o engraving, 28 or 30 in. 10mm VR back-bored barrels with porting, redesigned barrels in 2003, SST with adj. trigger shoe system, sharply checkered walnut stock and Schnabel style forearm, approx. 7 1/2 lbs. Mfg. 2000-2003.

	$1,200	$995	$900	$800	$700	$600	$500

Last MSR was $1,406.

SELECT ENERGY SPORTING - 12 ga. only, 2 3/4 in. chambers, 28, 30, or 32 in. ported and vented side rib high polish barrels with Invector Plus chokes (high polish barrels became standard in 2005), marked "Select Energy Sporting" on contrasting chrome finished receiver, 10mm VR, select American walnut stock with oval checkering and palm swell, with or w/o adj. cheekpiece, adj. trigger shoe, TruGlo front sight, approx. 7 3/4 lbs. New 2004.

MSR $1,950	$1,635	$1,425	$1,125	$965	$855	$750	$650

Add $165 for adj. comb stock.

SELECT ENERGY TRAP - 12 ga. only, 2 3/4 in. chambers, 30 or 32 in. VR barrels with Invector Plus chokes (high polish barrels became standard in 2005), similar features as the Select Energy Sporting, features oval checkering on stock and forearm, palm swell, TruGlo front sight, Monte Carlo or adj. comb stock with solid recoil pad, approx. 7 3/4 lbs. New 2004.

MSR $1,950	$1,635	$1,425	$1,125	$965	$855	$750	$650

Add $165 for adj. comb stock.

GRADING - PPGS™	100%	98%	95%	90%	80%	70%	60%

SHOTGUNS: RECENT PRODUCTION SxS

Values for recently manufactured side-by-sides assume NIB condition - subtract 10%-15% if without box, warranty card, and original shipping container (with packing materials).

MODEL 21: RECENT/CURRENT MFG. - between 1960-1987, Model 21 production was limited to high grades, built to special order only, and 1987 was the last year Winchester carried Model 21 pricing in its catalog. On custom shop guns mfg. 1960-1969, there is no Winchester name on the barrels, but the Winchester proofmark is on the water table, along with a designation "Model 21" or "New Haven, CT" plus the ser. no. On Model 21s produced from 1969-1988, the water tables are stamped as already noted, and the designation "Model 21 - Winchester" is stamped on the top of the left barrel adjacent to the rib, next to the receiver. Connecticut Shotgun Manufacturing Company is currently manufacturing a limited amount of Model 21 shotguns, including Grades 21-1, 21-5, 21-6, Grand American, and the Royal Exhibition. These guns are not marked "Winchester", are not finished in the Winchester custom shop, and will not letter from the Cody Firearms Museum. Please contact Connecticut Shotgun Manufacturing Company directly for more information regarding these newer custom Model 21s (see Trademark Index).

    Add 25% for 16 or 20 ga.

    Add $1,500 for vent. rib.

✳ *Custom Built* - standard model with no engraving.

                  $8,000   **$7,000**   **$5,000**

                                          Last MSR was $8,100.

✳ *Custom Grade* - includes No. 6 engraved receiver and VR.

                  $12,500   **$10,500**   **$9,000**

                                         Last MSR was $11,080.

✳ *Pigeon Grade* - single set of barrels, No. 6 engraved, w/o gold inlays, 37 mfg. total in 12, 16, and 20 ga.

                  $20,000   **$18,000**   **$15,000**

✳ *Grand American Grade* - includes 2 sets of barrels with forearms, No. 6 engraved with gold inlays, cased.

                  $27,500   **$22,000**   **$18,500**

                                         Last MSR was $22,745.

✳ *Grand American Small Gauge* - 28 ga. or .410 bore.

                  $37,500   **$29,500**   **$23,000**

                                         Last MSR was $34,460.

    Add 25% for 28 ga./.410 bore combo.

✳ *Grand American ("1 of 8" set)* - includes 20, 28 ga., and .410 bore VR barrels. Only 4 of 8 sets actually mfg.

                  N/A   **$65,000**   **$45,000**

                                         Last MSR was $55,000.

✳ *Grand Royal (2 barrel set)* - the highest grade of Model 21s ever produced, originally made in a .410 bore 2 barrel set for John Olin, only 4 others were ever manufactured, and all were 2 barrel sets.

Extreme rarity precludes accurate pricing on this model.

MODEL 22 - 12 ga. only, subcontracted by Winchester and manufactured in Spain by Laurona circa 1975 for international sales including Europe, field configuration only with 28 in. barrels, DT, oil finished checkered walnut stock and semi-beavertail forearm, matted rib, black-chrome finish on metal parts, hand engraved receiver, limited mfg.

        $1,200   **$995**   **$825**   **$700**   **$600**   **$525**   **$475**

GRADING - PPGS™	100%	98%	95%	90%	80%	70%	60%

MODEL 23 XTR - 12 or 20 ga., 3 in. chambers, 25 1/2, 26, 28, or 30 in. barrels, various chokes, single trigger, VR, auto ejectors, scroll engraved, silver grey satin finish, blue barrel, checkered select walnut stock and forearm, first commercial gun to employ interchangeable chokes. Mfg. 1978-disc.

Grade 1	$1,800	$1,650	$1,500	$1,250	$1,000	$850	$700

Add 20% for 20 ga.

Subtract 10% for fixed chokes.

✳ *Pigeon Grade* - standard weight model, 6 1/2-7 lbs, coin finished receiver with scroll engraving. WinChoke option became standard in 1986. Disc. 1986.

	$2,200	$2,000	$1,750	$1,500	$1,200	$1,000	$800

Last MSR was $1,460.

Add 20% for 20 ga.

Subtract 10% if w/o WinChokes.

✳ *Pigeon Grade Lightweight* - 25 1/2 in. barrels only bored IM/IC (12 ga.) or IC/M (20 ga.) or with WinChokes, 6 1/4 - 6 3/4 lbs., coin finished receiver with scroll engraving. English stock. Disc. 1986.

	$2,495	$2,150	$1,925	$1,750	$1,250	$1,000	$800

Last MSR was $1,420.

Add 15% for 20 ga.

Subtract 10% if w/o WinChokes.

✳ *Pigeon Grade Ducks Unlimited* - only 500 mfg. 1981, "SPO" serial no. suffix, cased.

	$2,195	$1,975	$1,650	$1,425	$1,150	$950	$850

✳ *Golden Quail Model Series* - 12 ga. (1986), 20 ga. (1984), 28 ga. (1985), or .410 bore (1987), 25 1/2 in. solid rib barrels bored IC/M, mono-blocks are marked "IC/M" but the barrels are marked "Q1/Q2", coin finished receiver with one gold inlay on floorplate, beavertail forearm, straight grip English stock with recoil pad. Only 500 mfg. each year per gauge. Disc. 1987.

12 ga.	$2,575	$2,300	$2,000	$1,750	$1,400	$1,250	$1,150
20 ga.	$2,850	$2,500	$2,150	$1,850	$1,650	$1,395	$1,295
28 ga. (20 ga. frame)	$4,050	$3,750	$3,450	$3,150	$2,750	$2,350	$1,950
410 bore (small frame)	$4,050	$3,750	$3,450	$3,150	$2,750	$2,350	$1,950

Last MSR was $1,950.

✳ *Model 23 Light Duck* - limited edition, 500 mfg., introduced 1985, blue receiver and barrels, select walnut, 20 ga., 28 in.- F&F, 8 1/2 lbs.

	$2,795	$2,300	$1,975	$1,675	$1,250	$1,000	$875

Last MSR was $1,660.

✳ *Model 23 Heavy Duck* - limited edition, 500 mfg. 1984 only, blue receiver and barrels, select walnut, 12 ga., 30 in.- F&F, 8 1/2 lbs.

	$2,450	$1,950	$1,600	$1,275	$975	$875	$795

✳ *Custom 2 Barrel Set* - interchangeable 20 and 28 ga. 26 in. barrels, blue engraved receiver with gold inlays, "B" checkering on stock and forearm, leather cased with accessories, only 500 sets mfg. 1986. Disc. 1987.

	$5,750	$4,900	$4,150	$3,550	$3,050	$2,800	$2,500

Last MSR was $4,625.

MODEL 23 GRANDE CANADIAN - 12 or 20 ga., 25 1/2 in. barrels with fixed chokes, coin finished receiver with oak leaf engraving and one gold leaf inlay on receiver bottom, English AAA select walnut stock with beavertail forearm, 51 mfg. in 12 ga., 450 mfg. in 20 ga., approx. 50 two-gun sets were also offered with cases (approx. ser. nos. 1-51).

	$2,650	$2,200	$1,750	$1,500	$1,300	$1,050	$925
Add 20% for 20 ga.							
Cased set	$6,500	$5,800	$4,900	$4,200	$3,750	$3,200	$2,750

GRADING - PPGS™	100%	98%	95%	90%	80%	70%	60%

MODEL 23 CUSTOM
- 12 ga. only, 27 in. WinChoke barrels, high luster bluing, no engraving, SST, ejectors, solid red rubber recoil pad, 7 lbs. Imported 1987 only.

	100%	98%	95%	90%	80%	70%	60%
	$2,600	$2,295	$1,950	$1,550	$1,275	$1,175	$995

Last MSR was $1,975.

MODEL 23 CLASSIC SERIES
- 12, 20, 28 ga., or .410 bore, 26 in. VR barrels, single trigger, deluxe hand-checkered walnut stock and beavertail forearm, solid recoil pad, brass nameplate, gold inlay on bottom of receiver, ebony inlay in forearm, 5 3/4-7 lbs. Imported 1986-87 only.

	100%	98%	95%	90%	80%	70%	60%
12 ga.	$2,650	$2,375	$2,100	$1,825	$1,400	$1,250	$1,150
20 ga.	$2,950	$2,550	$2,225	$1,900	$1,675	$1,395	$1,295
28 ga. (small frame)	$4,250	$3,900	$3,300	$2,950	$2,750	$2,400	$2,150
.410 bore (small frame)	$3,950	$3,600	$3,150	$2,950	$2,750	$2,350	$2,100

Last MSR was $1,975.

100% values assume NIB for this model.

The 28 ga. on this model features a smaller frame, and was the only 28 ga. small frame produced in the Model 23 Series.

WINCHESTER COMMEMORATIVES: U.S. PRODUCTION

During the course of a year, I receive many phone calls and letters regarding Winchester special editions and limited editions that do not appear in this section. It should be noted that a factory commemorative issue is a gun that has been manufactured, marketed, and sold through the auspices of the specific trademark. There have literally been hundreds of special and limited editions which, although mostly made by Winchester (some were subcontracted), were not marketed or retailed by Winchester. These guns are NOT Winchester commemoratives and for the most part, do not have the desirability factor that the factory commemoratives have. Special/limited editions are not listed in this text, because there is minimal collector interest. Remember, the least your special/limited edition can be worth is a little more than the standard edition value. Don't concentrate on the rarity, or you'll be disappointed.

Typically, special and limited editions are made for distributors (these sub-contracts are the most common), an organization, state, special event, personality, etc. and are typically sold and marketed through a distributor to dealers, or a company/individual to those people who want to purchase them. These special editions may or may not have a retail price and, often times, since demand is regional, values decrease rapidly in other areas of the country. Desirability is the key to determining values on these editions.

As a reminder on commemoratives, especially for the beginning collector, here are a few facts applicable to all manufacturers of commemoratives. Commemoratives are current production guns designed as reproductions of historically famous gun models, or as tie-ins with historically famous persons or events. They are generally of very excellent quality and often embellished with select woods and finishes such as silver, nickel, or gold plating. Obviously, they are manufactured to be instant collectibles and to be pleasing to the eye. As with firearms in general, not all commemorative models have achieved collector status, although most enjoy an active market - especially during the past three years. Consecutively numbered pairs, as well as collections based on the same serial number, will bring a premium. Remember that handguns usually are in some type of wood presentation case, and that rifles may be cased or in packaging with graphics styled to the particular theme of the collectible.

The original factory packaging and papers should always accompany the firearm as they are necessary to realize full value at the time of sale. All commemorative firearms should be absolutely new, unfired, and as issued since any obvious use or wear removes it from collector status and lowers its value significantly. Many owners have allowed their commemoratives to sit in their boxes and plastic bags for years without inspecting them for corrosion or oxidation damage (could be serious if there's moisture where storage occurs). Periodic inspection should be implemented to insure no damage occurs - this is important, since even light "freckling" created from touching the metal surfaces can reduce values significantly. A fired gun with obvious wear or without its original packaging can lose as much as 50% of its normal value. Many used com-

GRADING - PPGS™	100%	Issue Price	Qty. Made

memoratives get sold as "fancy shooters" with little, if any, premiums being asked. Additionally, while some commemoratives may be unfired, their actions may have been racked to the point where there could be some visible wear, and this will also lower the value, depending on the amount of wear. New is new - no excuses.

The values listed reflect actual prices paid recently in various areas of the U.S. In some regions, it is possible to purchase a Winchester 94 commemorative made in substantial quantity for almost no premium over a standard production Winchester 94. Because of this, prices could fluctuate over 25% depending on the geographic location of purchase or sale.

A final note on commemoratives: One of the characteristics of commemoratives/special editions is that over the years of ownership, most of the original manufactured guns stay in the same NIB condition. Thus, if supply always is constant and in one condition, demand has to increase before price appreciation can occur. Many commemorative dealers have told me that recent changes in overseas currency rates have made domestic guns less expensive to own - for Europeans especially. For this reason, more commemoratives are being sold overseas resulting in less supply for the domestic market. Coupled with this increased foreign demand is the recent increase of domestic support and sales. After 41 years of commemorative/special edition production, many models' performance records can be accurately analyzed and the appreciation (or depreciation) can be compared against other purchases of equal vintage. You be the judge.

U.S. Repeating Arms had announced in 1990 that they would once again resume the production of factory commemorative firearms.

1964 WYOMING DIAMOND JUBILEE 94 CARBINE
	$795	$100	1,501

1966 CENTENNIAL '66 RIFLE
	$450	$125	N/A

1966 CENTENNIAL '66 CARBINE - total mfg. of both the rifle and carbine was 102,309.
	$425	$125	102,309

Add $50-$75 over individual prices for consecutively serial numbered rifle and carbine set.

1966 NEBRASKA CENTENNIAL 94 RIFLE
	$795	$100	2,500

1967 CANADIAN '67 CENTENNIAL RIFLE
	$450	$125	N/A

1967 CANADIAN '67 CENTENNIAL CARBINE - total mfg. of both the rifle and carbine was 90,301.
	$425	$125	90,301

Add $50-$75 over individual prices for consecutively serial numbered rifle and carbine set.

1967 ALASKAN PURCHASE CENTENNIAL CARBINE
	$795	$125	1,501

1968 ILLINOIS SESQUICENTENNIAL 94 CARBINE
	$395	$110	37,468

1968 BUFFALO BILL RIFLE "1 OF 300" PRES.
	$2,750	$1,000	300

1968 BUFFALO BILL RIFLE
	$450	$130	N/A

1968 BUFFALO BILL CARBINE - total mfg. of both the rifle and carbine was 112,923.
	$425	$130	112,923

Add $50-$75 over individual prices for consecutively serial numbered rifle and carbine set.

1969 GOLDEN SPIKE CARBINE
	$495	$120	69,996

GRADING - PPGS™	100%	Issue Price	Qty. Made

1969 THEO. ROOSEVELT RIFLE

	$450	$135	N/A

1969 THEO. ROOSEVELT CARBINE - total mfg. of both the rifle and carbine was 52,386.

	$425	$135	52,386

1970 COWBOY COMMEMORATIVE CARBINE

	$450	$125	27,549

1970 COWBOY CARBINE "1 OF 300"

	$2,750	$1,000	300

1970 LONE STAR RIFLE

	$450	$140	N/A

1970 LONE STAR CARBINE - total mfg. of both the rifle and carbine was 38,385.

	$425	$140	38,385

1971 NRA CENTENNIAL MUSKET

	$425	$150	23,400

1971 NRA CENTENNIAL RIFLE

	$425	$150	21,000

1974 TEXAS RANGER CARBINE

	$695	$135	4,850

1974 TEXAS RANGER PRESENTATION

	$2,750	$1,000	150

1976 U.S. BICENTENNIAL CARBINE

	$595	$325	19,999

1977 WELLS FARGO

	$495	$350	19,999

1977 "LIMITED EDITION I"

	$1,395	$1,500	1,500

1977 LEGENDARY LAWMEN

	$495	$375	19,999

1978 ANTLERED GAME CARBINE

	$550	$375	19,999

1979 LEGENDARY FRONTIERSMAN RIFLE

	$550	$425	19,999

1979 "LIMITED EDITION II"

	$1,395	$1,750	1,500

1979 MATCHED SET OF 1000

	$2,250	$3,000	1,000

1980 BAT MASTERSON CARBINE

	$795	$650	8,000

1980 "OLIVER WINCHESTER"

	$695	$375	19,999

1981 U.S. BORDER PATROL

	$595	$1,195	1,000

1981 U.S. BORDER PATROL - MEMBERS MODEL

	$595	$695	800

GRADING - PPGS™	100%	Issue Price	Qty. Made

1981 JOHN WAYNE

	$1,195	$600	49,000

Optional accessories were also available for this model: the gun rack with leather insert is currently selling for approx. $300 and the leather scabbard is trading for $250.

1981 "DUKE"

	$3,500	$2,250	1,000

1981 JOHN WAYNE "1 OF 300" SET

	$6,500	$10,000	300

1982 GREAT WESTERN ARTIST I CANADIAN

	$1,295	$2,200	999

1982 GREAT WESTERN ARTIST II CANADIAN

	$1,295	$2,200	999

1982 ANNIE OAKLEY

	$795	$699	6,000

1982 OKLAHOMA DIAMOND JUBILEE

	$1,395	$2,250	1,001

1982 AMERICAN BALD EAGLE - SILVER

	$595	$895	2,800

1982 AMERICAN BALD EAGLE - GOLD

	$4,000	$2,950	200

1983 CHIEF CRAZY HORSE

	$595	$600	19,999

1984 WINCHESTER-COLT COMMEMORATIVE SET - 1 each of the Model 1894 Carbine and Colt Peacemaker, serial numbered 1 WC-4440 WC., .44-40 WCF cal., elaborate gold etching, cased.

	$2,250	$3,995	2,300

Approx. 2,300 sets were actually put together in this combination. Some sets were split up with individual prices being discounted (Colt SAAs have been trading in the $700-$800 range).

1985 BOY SCOUTS 75TH ANNIVERSARY - Model 9422 action, .22 cal., rifle configuration, 6 1/4 lbs.

* *Boy Scout* - 15,000 mfg., serial numbered BSA 1 - BSA 15,000, roll engraved, antique pewter receiver, hooded front sight.

	$750	$495	15,000

* *Eagle Scout* - 1,000 mfg., serial numbered Eagle 1 - Eagle 1,000, receiver has triple level gold etching, select American walnut stock and forearm, gold-plated lever, hammer, and forearm cap.

	$3,750	$1,710	1,000

1985 MODEL 94 TEXAS SESQUICENTENNIAL - .38-55 WCF cal., available in carbine or rifle.

* *Model 94 Rifle* - 24 in. round barrel, elaborate gold etching, includes Bowie knife, oak cased, 586 mfg.

	$2,400	$2,995	1,500

* *Model 94 Carbine* - 18 1/2 in. round barrel, gold finished receiver and barrel bands, roll engraved receiver, 2,600 mfg., serial numbered TEX 1 and up.

	$695	$695	15,000

* *Rifle/Carbine Set* - includes one each of the Model 94 rifle and carbine, Bowie knife, 150 mfg.

	$6,250	$7,995	150

GRADING - PPGS™	100%	Issue Price	Qty. Made

1986 120TH ANNIVERSARY MODEL 94 CARBINE - .44-40 WCF cal. only, 20 in. barrel, hoop-type finger lever, crescent buttplate, deluxe checkered walnut stock and forearm, extensive gold etching on barrel and framesides, 1,000 mfg. ser. no. WRA001-WRA1000.

	$895	$995	1,000

1986 STATUE OF LIBERTY MODEL 94 - Model 94 rifle in .30-30 Win. cal. with octagon barrel, extensive C. Giovanelli scroll engraving with multiple 22Kt. gold inlays, deluxe walnut with fine checkering, also includes 29 in. hand-carved wooden statue of the Statue of Liberty, serial numbered SL1-SL62. This model is a USRAC factory commemorative.

	$7,500	$6,500	62

1986 MODEL 94 DU - .30-30 Win. cal., approx. 2,800 rifles were mfg. in the U.S. Since each Model 94 DU was bid on for ownership, prices will vary from points of origin. An average bid price seems to be in the $700-$995 range with lower and completing set ser. nos. selling at premiums. Serial numbered DU-86 0001 on up.

> This model is not a factory commemorative, but rather a trade gun commissioned by Ducks Unlimited.

1987 U.S. CONSTITUTION 200TH ANNIVERSARY

	$14,000	$12,000	17

This model was distributed exclusively by Cherry's, located in Greensboro, NC.

1988 WINCHESTER ARMS COLLECTOR'S ASSOCIATION CASED SET - includes Colt SAA and Winchester Model 1894 in cased set, features special embellishments and W.A.C.A. emblems and medallions. 100 sets were advertised, but only 22 were sold.

	$2,995	$2,695	22 sets

1990 WYOMING CENTENNIAL .30-30

	$1,250	$895	500

This model was distributed exclusively by Cherry's, located in Greensboro, NC.

1991 125TH ANNIVERSARY .30-30

	$5,750	$4,995	61

This model was distributed exclusively by Cherry's, located in Greensboro, NC.

1992 KENTUCKY BICENTENNIAL .30-30 - Winchester Model 94 with true charcoal case coloring, engraving depicts important KY graphics, serial numbered KY001-KY500.

	$1,250	$995	500

This model was distributed exclusively by Cherry's, located in Greensboro, NC.

1992 ARAPAHO .30-30 - features gold-plated receiver with etched Indian scenes on both sides, checkered semi-fancy American walnut stock.

	$1,250	$895	500

This model is distributed exclusively by Cherry's, located in Greensboro, NC.

1993 NEZ PERCE MODEL 94 CARBINE - features nickel finished receiver and barrel bands, extensively etched receiver, checkered semi-fancy American walnut stock and forearm, serial numbered NEZ 001-NEZ 600.

	$1,250	$950	600

This model is distributed exclusively by Cherry's, located in Greensboro, NC.

1995 FLORIDA SESQUICENTENNIAL 94 CARBINE - features motifs from Florida, including alligator scene and space shuttle launch, 24kt. gold-plated receiver, 500 mfg. ser. numbered FL001-FL500 during 1995 only.

	$1,250	$1,195	500

This model is distributed exclusively by Cherry's, located in Greensboro, NC.

GRADING - PPGS™	100%	Issue Price	Qty. Made

1997 EARP BROTHERS MODEL 94 CARBINE - features engraving motifs with multi-colored cameos of the characters involved in the Tombstone OK Corral gunfight, gold-plated hammer, trigger, and barrel bands, crossbolt safety. 250 Mfg. 1997 only.

	$1,250	$1,195	250

This model was distributed exclusively by Cherry's, located in Greensboro, NC.

WINCHESTER COMMEMORATIVES: NON-DOMESTIC - 1970 TO DATE

1970 NORTH WEST TERRITORIES (CANADIAN)

	$850	$150	2,500

1970 NORTHWEST TERRITORIES DELUXE (CANADIAN)

	$1,100	$250	500

1973 YELLOW BOY (SOLD IN EUROPE ONLY)

	$1,150	$150	4,903

1973 M.P.X. (MADE ESPECIALLY FOR A MOVIE)

	$4,995	$78	32

1973 R.C.M.P. (CANADIAN)

	$795	$190	9,500

1973 R.C.M.P. MEMBERS ISSUE (CANADIAN)

	$795	$190	4,850

1973 R.C.M.P. PRESENTATION - (CANADIAN)

	$9,995	N/A	100

1974 APACHE (CANADIAN)

	$795	$150	8,600

1975 KLONDIKE GOLD RUSH (CANADIAN)

	$795	$230	10,200

1975 K.G.R. (DAWSON CITY ISSUE) - (CANADIAN)

	$8,500	N/A	25

1975 COMANCHE (CANADIAN)

	$795	$230	11,511

1976 SIOUX (CANADIAN)

	$795	$280	10,000

1976 LITTLE BIG HORN (CANADIAN)

	$795	$230	11,000

1977 CHEYENNE (CANADIAN) - .44-40 WCF Cal.

	$795	$300	11,225

1977 CHEYENNE (CANADIAN) - .22 LR Cal.

	$750	$320	5,000

1978 CHEROKEE (CANADIAN) - .30-30 Win. Cal.

	$795	$385	9,000

1978 CHEROKEE (CANADIAN) - .22 LR Cal.

	$750	$385	3,950

1978 ONE OF ONE THOUSAND (SOLD IN EUROPE ONLY)

	$7,995	$5,000	250

This model was not advertised in the U.S.

1980 ALBERTA DIAMOND JUBILEE (CANADIAN)

	$795	$650	2,700

GRADING - PPGS™	100%	Issue Price	Qty. Made

1980 A.D.J. DELUXE PRESENTATION (CANADIAN)

	$1,495	$1,900	300

1980 SASKATCHEWAN DIAMOND JUBILEE (CANADIAN)

	$795	$695	2,700

1980 S.D.J. DELUXE PRESENTATION (CANADIAN)

	$1,495	$1,995	300

1981 CALGARY STAMPEDE (CANADIAN)

	$1,250	$2,200	1,000

1981 CANADIAN PACIFIC CENTENNIAL (CANADIAN)

	$695	$800	2,700

1981 CANADIAN PACIFIC CENTENNIAL PRESENTATION (CANADIAN)

	$1,100	$2,200	300

1981 CANADIAN PACIFIC (EMPL.) - (CANADIAN)

	$695	$800	2,000

1981 JOHN WAYNE (CANADIAN)

	$1,295	$995	1,000

1986 SECOND SERIES EUROPEAN 1 OF 1,000 - mfg. for European sales only 1986.

	$6,500	$6,000	150

1992 ONTARIO CONSERVATION - this model was marketed in Canada only.

	$1,250	$1,195	400

WINSLOW ARMS COMPANY

Previous manufacturer located in Camden, SC.

GRADING - PPGS™	100%	98%	95%	90%	80%	70%	60%

RIFLES: BOLT ACTION

WINSLOW BOLT ACTION SPORTING RIFLE - offered with various actions, FN Supreme, Mark X Mauser, Rem. 700 and 788, Sako, and Win. 70, offered in all popular calibers from .17 Rem. to .458 Mag., standard calibers have 24 in. barrels and 3 shot magazines, magnum calibers have 26 in. barrels and 2 shot magazines, two style stocks, "Bushmaster Conventional," slender pistol grip and beavertail forearm, "Plainsmaster," full curl, hooked pistol grip and flat wide forearm, both are Monte Carlo with cheekpieces, recoil pads and swivels, walnut, maple, and myrtle are used with rosewood forend tip and pistol grip cap, rifle comes in 8 basic grades, custom embellishments can increase values greatly, discretion must be used, values are for basic models.

COMMANDER GRADE

	$1,750	$1,500	$1,275	$1,025	$850	$725	$600

REGAL GRADE

	$1,875	$1,625	$1,300	$1,050	$875	$750	$625

REGENT GRADE

	$1,995	$1,675	$1,350	$1,100	$925	$800	$675

REGIMENTAL GRADE

	$2,750	$2,350	$2,050	$1,750	$1,500	$1,250	$1,000

CROWN GRADE

	$3,000	$2,500	$2,175	$1,850	$1,575	$1,325	$1,100

ROYAL GRADE

	$3,450	$2,950	$2,500	$2,150	$1,750	$1,500	$1,250

GRADING - PPGS™	100%	98%	95%	90%	80%	70%	60%
IMPERIAL GRADE							
	$3,850	$3,500	$3,050	$2,700	$2,375	$2,000	$1,750
EMPEROR GRADE							
	$6,200	$5,650	$5,000	$4,400	$3,700	$3,000	$2,350

WISCHO JAGD-UND SPORTWAFFEN GmbH & CO. KG

Current firearms manufacturer located in Erlangen, Germany.

Wischo makes a complete line of shotguns, rifles, pistols, and revolvers. No current U.S. importation. Please contact the factory directly for more information regarding model lineup, availability, and pricing (see Trademark Index).

WISEMAN, BILL AND CO.

Current custom rifle and pistol manufacturer located in College Station, TX.

Wiseman/McMillan also manufactures rifle barrels and custom stocks.

PISTOLS

SILHOUETTE PISTOL - various cals., Sako action, 14 in. Wiseman/McMillan fluted stainless barrel, 5 or 7 shot magazine, laminate or fiberglass (new 1999) pistol grip stock, no sights, 4 1/2-5 1/2 lbs. Limited mfg. 1989-2002.

	$1,295	$1,000	$900	$800	$750	$700	$650

Last MSR was $1,295.

Subtract $200 for fiberglass stock.

RIFLES: BOLT ACTION

Add 11% excise tax to prices shown for new manufacture. Some models listed have very limited production.

HUNTER MODEL - available in various cals., Sako action, stainless steel barrel by Wiseman/McMillan, laminate stock, teflon finished metal parts, Pachmayr Decelerator pad, sling swivels, glass bedded action.

MSR $3,395	$3,395	$2,750	$2,350	$1,850	$1,425	$1,150	$925

HUNTER DELUXE - similar to Hunter Model except has custom checkering.

MSR $3,895	$3,895	$3,400	$2,925	$2,450	$1,900	$1,450	$1,100

Add $500 for detachable mag.

MAVERICK - similar to Hunter but with black fiberglass stock. Disc. 2003.

	$1,995	$1,575	$1,200	$1,050	$900	$775	$675

Last MSR was $1,995.

VARMENTER - similar to Hunter but with thumbhole stock. Disc. 2003.

	$2,395	$1,925	$1,500	$1,250	$1,025	$875	$775

Last MSR was $2,395.

TEXAS SAFARI RIFLE (TSR) - various cals., choice of hidden mag. (no floorplate), standard floorplate or 4 shot detachable mag., regular or 2/3 position tang safety, stainless steel fluted or non-fluted barrel with or w/o integral muzzle brake, synthetic stock. New 1996.

MSR $2,195	$2,195	$1,625	$1,150

Add $300 for 4 shot detachable mag. (TSR-I).
Add $375 for extra magazine concealed in stock.
Add $195 for 2 or 3 position tang safety.
Add $195 for fluted barrel or muzzle brake.
Add $175 for extra straight in-line feed magazine.

GRADING - PPGS™	100%	98%	95%	90%	80%	70%	60%

TSR TACTICAL - .300 Win. Mag., .308 Win., or .338 Lapua Mag., 5 shot inline, detachable mag., or standard floorplate, synthetic stock with adj. cheekpiece, stainless steel fluted barrel with integral muzzle brake, guaranteed 1/2 minute of angle. Mfg. 1996-2003.

$2,795 $2,200 $1,700

Last MSR was $2,795.

Add $195 for fluted barrel.
Add $195 for muzzle brake.
Add $150 for 3 position safety.

WOLF SPORTING PISTOLS

Previous trademark of pistols manufactured in Vienna, Austria. Previously imported and distributed by J R Distributing, located in Moorpark, CA until 1999.

Wolf pistols were noted for their features, quality construction, and were based on the M 1911 type action.

WOODWARD, JAMES AND SONS

Previously mfg. in London, England. Acquired by James Purdey & Sons in January 1949. In 1996, James Purdey & Sons once again started manufacturing a best quality Woodward shotgun.

SHOTGUNS: DOUBLE AND SINGLE BARREL

Woodward made one of the world's finest shotguns. They were formally acquired by J. Purdey and Sons on January 1, 1949. Most of the long guns they made were custom built and grading and pricing should be done individually. It is strongly recommended to get competent professional appraisals when contemplating a Woodward purchase or sale.

Prices indicated are for manufacturer's suggested retail and MSRs & 100% condition factors are listed in English pounds. All new prices do not include VAT. Values for used guns in 98%-60% condition factors are priced in U.S. dollars.

BEST QUALITY SxS SHOTGUN - custom-built in all gauges, barrel lengths and chokes, sidelock, auto ejectors, stocked to specifications, pre-WWII and new mfg. circa 1996-2003.

$26,000 $23,000 $19,950 $17,000 $14,250 $12,000 $10,000

Last MSR was £40,100 (20 ga. only).

Add 20% for 20 ga.
Add 40% for 28 ga.
Add 60% for .410 bore.
Add $1,000 for SST

BEST QUALITY O/U SHOTGUN - custom-built in all gauges, barrel lengths, and chokes, VR, sidelock, auto ejectors, stocked to customer specifications, pre-WWII and new mfg. beginning 1996.

✳ *Best Quality O/U - New Mfg.* - 12, 16, 20, 28 ga., or .410 bore.

MSR £55,000   £55,000   N/A

✳ *Best Quality O/U - Recent & Older Mfg.*

N/A $28,500 $23,000 $19,000 $16,000 $13,800 $12,000

Add 35% for 20 ga.
Add 75% for 28 ga.
.410 bore - 2 mfg., too rare to accurately predict.
Add $1,000 for ST.

BEST QUALITY SINGLE BARREL TRAP GUN - 12 ga. only, limited mfg. pre-WWII only.

$12,750 $10,000 $8,950 $7,725 $6,500 $5,750 $4,900

WYOMING ARMS MFG. CORP.

Previous manufacturer located in Thermopolis, WY. Very small quantities of Parker pistols were mfg.

PARKER PISTOLS: STAINLESS STEEL

STANDARD PISTOL - 9mm Para., 10mm, .40 S&W, or .45 ACP cal., 3 3/8, 5, or 7 in. barrel, 7 (.45 ACP), 8 (10mm & .40 S&W), or 9 (9mm Para.) shot mag., Millett adj. sights, grooved synthetic grips, 29-39 oz. Disc. 1992.

$350 $300 $250

Last MSR was $399.

Add $50 for 7 in. barrel.

.357 MAG. - .357 Mag. cal., single action semi-auto, 7 in. barrel, adj. sights, 8 shot mag., lifetime warranty, 44 oz. Disc. 1992.

$425 $350 $300

Last MSR was $479.

Z SECTION

Z-B RIFLE

Previous trademark of rifles manufactured by Brno & Uhersky Brod, located in Czechoslovakia.

GRADING - PPGS™	100%	98%	95%	90%	80%	70%	60%

RIFLES: BOLT ACTION

Z-B MAUSER VARMINT RIFLE - .22 Hornet cal., short Mauser bolt action, 23 in. barrel, double set triggers, 3 leaf sight, checkered pistol grip stock (also known as Brno Hornet).

		$825	$745	$690	$605	$550	$470	$415

ZDF IMPORT EXPORT INC.

Current importer located in Salt Lake City, UT, since 1995.

RIFLES: SEMI-AUTO

Please refer to Robinson Armament listing.

Z-M WEAPONS

Current rifle manufacturer and pistol components maker located in Bernardston, MA. Dealer and consumer direct sales.

PISTOLS: SEMI-AUTO

STRIKE PISTOL - .38 Super, .40 S&W, or .45 ACP cal., several configurations available, with or without compensator. Limited mfg. 1997-2000.

			$2,375	$1,825	$1,700	$1,400	$1,150	$995	$750

Last MSR was $2,695.

RIFLES: SEMI-AUTO

LR 300 & VARIATIONS - .223 Rem. cal., modified gas system using AR-15 style action, features pivoting skeletal metal stock, 16 1/4 in. barrel, flattop receiver, matte finish, aluminum or Nylatron handguard, 7.2 lbs. New 1997.

MSR $1,475		$1,350	$1,125	$900	$775	$650	$525	$450

Add $23 for Nylatron handguard.
Add $50 for Military/Law Enforcement model.
Add $75 for Military/Law Enforcement model with Nylatron handguard.

ZABALA HERMANOS, S.A.

Current manufacturer established in 1932 and located in Eibar, Spain. Z. Hermanos is currently private labeling shotguns for KBI, Inc. (Charles Daly SxSs only) and Tristar, located in N. Kansas City. Previously imported and distributed by American Arms located in Kansas City, MO, until 2000, and by Galef Shotguns.

Zabala Hermanos manufactures good quality boxlock SxS shotguns (Models 213, Kestrel, Berri, and Sporting Magnum), O/U shotguns (XL 90 Series, Suprema Magnum, and Century Classic Magnum) and sidelock SxS shotguns (Vencedor Model). To date, the company has produced over 600,000 long guns, and remains family owned. For more information regarding this trademark, (including current models and prices) please contact the manufacturer directly (see Trademark Index).

ZANARDINI

Current manufacturer established in 1946, and located in Brescia, Italy. Currently imported by S.O.G. Arms, located in Hacienda Heights, CA. Several U.S. firms have stocked a few Zanardini models in the past, but not the complete line.

All rifles and shotguns are custom-built. For current information and up-to-date pricing, please contact the importer directly (see Trademark Index).

The values listed represent older importation.

COMBINATION GUNS: O/U

Zanardini is currently offering the Model 2000 Deluxe Super Light (with or w/o new loading system), and the Boxer Model with H&H style sidelocks.

PRINCESS - super light variation.

	100%	98%	95%	90%	80%	70%	60%
	$2,200	$1,925	$1,675	$1,400	$1,200	$1,000	$800

Last MSR was $2,542.

BOXER MODEL - H&H styled sidelocks, top-quality engraving.

	$5,750	$5,150	$4,600	$4,000	$3,550	$3,000	$2,650

Last MSR was $6,246.

BOXER 4-LOCKS MODEL

	$3,900	$3,400	$2,975	$2,625	$2,300	$2,050	$1,750

Last MSR was $4,562.

402 STRAUSS - top-of-the-line combination gun with best quality engraving and wood.

	$9,000	$8,000	$7,000	$6,000	$5,000	$4,000	$3,000

Last MSR was $10,548.

RIFLES

FUCHS A FOLDING RIFLE - double lock system.

MSR N/A	$2,275	$1,850	$1,500	$1,250	$1,200	$800	$600

PRINZ A 401 SUPER DELUXE SINGLE SHOT - internal and external hammers.

MSR N/A	$15,250	$12,500	$9,950	$8,750	$7,500	$6,250	$5,000

✳ *Prinz B Deluxe*

MSR N/A	$8,950	$7,750	$6,500	$5,200	$4,200	$3,200	$2,200

✳ *Prinz C Deluxe Standard*

MSR N/A	$3,200	$2,800	$2,400	$2,000	$1,800	$1,600	$1,400

403 OXFORD SxS - 9.3x74R and smaller cals.

	$3,400	$3,000	$2,700	$2,425	$2,150	$1,875	$1,575

Last MSR was $3,835.

✳ *Larger cals.* - .375 H&H Mag., .458 Win. Mag., or .470 Nitro cal.

	$6,700	$6,000	$5,500	$5,000	$4,500	$3,950	$3,450

Last MSR was $7,555.

Add approx. 135% for .470 Nitro cal.

EXPRESS RIFLE SxS - .470 NE cal., boxlock action, ST, checkered walnut stock (with cheekpiece), express sights. Other cals. available upon special order.

	$8,400	$8,100	$7,450	$6,750	$6,000	$5,500	$5,000

Last MSR was $8,995.

409 BRISTOL SxS - H & H style sidelock, ejectors, ST or DT.

Prices on this model start at $26,995.

407 OXFORD SL SxS - Anson & Deeley scalloped reinforced boxlock action, ejectors, ST or DT.

Prices on this model start at $14,995.

GRADING - PPGS™	100%	98%	95%	90%	80%	70%	60%

KONIG SIDELOCK O/U - 7.65R or 9.3x74R cal., H&H style sidelock, ejectors.

MSR N/A	$23,000	$20,000	$17,000	$13,500	$11,000	$9,950	$8,600

KONIG BOXLOCK O/U - Anson & Deely boxlock.

MSR N/A	$13,500	$11,000	$9,000	$7,500	$6,250	$5,000	$4,000

SHOTGUNS: SxS

Models listed are available in 12, 16, 20, 28 ga. or .410 bore, magnum chambers in 20 and 12 ga.

HAMMER LONDON MODEL SxS - features external hammers.

	$9,150	$8,125	$7,100	$6,100	$5,050	$4,000	$3,050

Last MSR was $10,735.

HAMMERLESS LONDON MODEL SxS - 12 or 20 ga., external hammers.
Prices on this model range from $11,000-$15,000, depending on engraving.

DONAU STANDARD MODEL SxS - boxlock action.

	$9,000	$8,000	$7,000	$6,000	$5,000	$4,000	$3,000

Last MSR was $10,548.

DONAU SIDELOCK SxS - H&H style sidelock action.
Prices on this model range from $17,000-$23,000, depending on engraving.

PRESTIGE TRAP AND SKEET SxS

	$2,250	$1,950	$1,675	$1,400	$1,200	$1,000	$800

Last MSR was $2,598.

HASE CACCIA MONTECATINI SxS - boxlock action, double set triggers, extractors.

	$900	$800	$700	$600	$550	$495	$450

Last MSR was $1,027.

Add 30% for ejectors.

HORN MODEL SxS - boxlock action, double set triggers, extractors.

	$950	$850	$750	$625	$550	$495	$450

Last MSR was $1,102.

Add 40% for ejectors.

ZANOTTI 1625

Current manufacturer established during 1625, and located in Brescia, Italy. Previous company name was Fabio Zanotti. Previously imported and distributed by New England Arms Corp. located in Kittery Point, ME until 1999. Fabio Zanotti became part of the Renato Gamba Group in 1985.

Fabio Zanotti is one of the world's oldest quality shotgun manufacturers. Current domestic importation is often times done on a custom order only basis. For more information on current Zanotti models, please contact the U.S. service center or the factory directly. Values listed are for most recent importation (approx. 2000), and current MSRs may have gone up considerably due to the devaluation of the dollar against the euro.

SHOTGUNS: O/U

MODEL 725 - 28 ga. or .410 bore only, scalloped case hardened shallow frame, DT or ST, ejectors, game scene and scroll engraving, custom built to individual specifications.

MSR N/A	$6,000	$4,500	$3,650	$3,000	$2,450	$2,000	$1,875

CASSIANO - 12, 20, 28 ga., or .410 bore, Boss style shallow action, best quality gun built to individual specifications. Prices start at $27,500 and go up accordingly.

GRADING - PPGS™	100%	98%	95%	90%	80%	70%	60%

SHOTGUNS: SxS

Add $500 for ST.
Add $250 for beavertail forearm.
Add $650 for leather case.

MODEL 625 BOXLOCK

MSR N/A	$6,275	$5,500	$4,250	$3,150	$2,500	$2,000	$1,750

MODEL 626 BOXLOCK - scroll, game scene, or combination engraving.

MSR N/A	$7,000	$6,000	$4,450	$3,375	$2,750	$2,175	$1,900

MODEL GIACINTO - hammer gun.

MSR N/A	$5,875	$5,300	$4,000	$2,950	$2,400	$1,900	$1,650

MODEL MAXIM SIDELOCK

MSR N/A	$10,750	$8,600	$7,450	$6,200	$5,200	$4,600	$3,850

MODEL EDWARD SIDELOCK

MSR N/A	$13,000	$9,900	$8,700	$7,000	$5,875	$5,000	$4,000

MODEL CASSIANO I SIDELOCK

MSR N/A	$15,500	$13,250	$9,900	$8,700	$7,000	$5,875	$5,000

MODEL CASSIANO II

MSR N/A	$17,750	$15,500	$13,250	$9,900	$8,700	$7,000	$5,875

CASSIANO EXECUTIVE - prices vary per individual order, top-of-the-line model. Prices start at $20,000 and go up.

ZASTAVA ARMS

Current manufacturer located in Yugoslavia. KBI currently imports certain models and actions. Previously distributed by Advanced Weapons Technologies, located in Athens, Greece. Previously imported by T.D. Arms, followed by Brno U.S.A., circa 1990. Previously distributed by Nationwide Sports Distributors located in Southampton, PA.

Zastava Arms makes a wide variety of quality pistols, rifles, and sporting shotguns. Please contact KBI or the company directly for more information regarding model availability and prices (see Trademark Index).

HANDGUNS: SEMI-AUTO

MODEL CZ99 - 9mm Para. cal., double action, 15 shot, 4 1/4 in. barrel, short recoil, choice of various finishes, SIG locking system, hammer drop safety, ambidextrous controls, 3-dot Tritium sighting system, alloy frame, firing pin block, chamber indicator, squared-off trigger guard, checkered dark grey polymer grips, 32 oz.

	$450	$395	$365	$330	$300	$285	$265

Last MSR was $495.

While a latter Z9 was advertised, it was never commercially imported. All guns were CZ99 or CZ40.

Zastava CZ99 configurations (with finishes) included matte blue with synthetic grips (500 imported), commercial blue with synthetic grips (750 imported), military "painted finish" with synthetic grips (1,000 imported), matte blue finish with checkered wood grips (115 imported), high polish blue with checkered grips (115 imported), and military "painted finish" with wood grips (2 prototypes only).

MODEL CZ40 - .40 S&W cal., 55 prototypes were imported for testing, but most had a feeding problem due to improper magazine design, mag. design changes were planned, but were cancelled due to the Serbian/Croatian war. Suggested retail was $495.

	$450	$395	$365	$330	$300	$285	$265

GRADING - PPGS™	100%	98%	95%	90%	80%	70%	60%

RIFLES: BOLT ACTION

MODEL CZ22 - .22 LR, .22 Mag. or .22 Hornet cal., 35 of each cal. imported circa 1990. Suggested retail was $275.

	$225	$195	$175	$150	$135	$120	$110

Add 15% for .22 Mag. or .22 Hornet cal.

ZIEGENHAHN & SOHN OHG

Current custom gun manufacturer established in 1923, and located in Zella-Mehlis, Germany. Currently imported by New England Custom Gun Service, Ltd., located in Plainfield, NH.

Ziegenhahn & Sohn manufactures high quality, classic Anson & Deeley boxlock "Big Five" double rifles with Holland & Holland pattern sidelocks and ejectors, and sidelocks in calibers up to .500 NE., with larger calibers also available upon request. Ziegenhahn & Sohn also manufactures high quality shotguns, drillings, and combination guns with a variety of custom order options. Please contact the importer directly for current pricing, availability, and delivery time.

Ziegenhahn currently is building the Krieghoff Essencia SxS in 20 ga. with back action - please refer to the Krieghoff section for more information.

ZEPHYR

Previous Stoeger trademark of guns manufactured in Spain, and imported by Stoegers circa 1930s-1972.

RIFLES

Stoeger's has imported a wide variety of bolt action rifles during the past 60 years. Rather than list the many models individually, each Zephyr rifle should be compared to a gun of equal caliber, quality, and features to ascertain an approximate value range.

SHOTGUNS: SxS

WOODLANDER II - 12 or 20 ga., various chokes, boxlock, double triggers, extractors, engraved, checkered pistol grip stock.

	$495	$440	$385	$360	$305	$275	$250

UPLANDER (4E) - 12, 16, 20, 28 ga., or .410 bore, sidelock action, double triggers, ejectors, engraved.

	$775	$695	$640	$585	$570	$480	$440

STERLINGWORTH II - similar to Woodlander, with sidelock action.

	$825	$725	$660	$605	$580	$525	$495

VICTOR SPECIAL - 12 ga., 25, 28, or 30 in. barrels, various chokes, double triggers, extractors, checkered pistol grip stock.

	$440	$385	$330	$305	$250	$220	$195

UPLAND KING - 12 or 16 ga., sidelock, single trigger, VR, ejectors, fully engraved.

	$1,000	$900	$800	$725	$650	$600	$550

THUNDERBIRD - 10 ga. Mag, 32 in. barrels, double triggers, French walnut, engraved.

	$850	$750	$625	$550	$510	$490	$475

Add $175 for ejectors.

SHOTGUNS: SINGLE SHOT

HONKER - 10 ga. Mag., 36 in. VR barrel, lightly engraved.

	$500	$460	$420	$350	$310	$290	$270

GRADING - PPGS™	100%	98%	95%	90%	80%	70%	60%

VANDALIA TRAP - 12 ga. Trap Model, 32 in. barrel, engraved.

	$700	$620	$575	$525	$475	$425	$390

ZOLI, ANGELO

Previous manufacturer located in Brescia, Italy. Previously imported and distributed exclusively by Angelo Zoli USA located in Addison, IL. Mfg. 1985-87.

Angelo Zoli went out of business in December, 1987 and was taken over by the Italian Bank of Brescia in 1989. Many people tend to confuse the shotguns of Angelo and Antonio Zoli (it is hard to determine which manufacturer made a gun marked "A. Zoli"). There is no correlation between these trademarks and Antonio Zoli DOES NOT have parts for these earlier Angelo Zoli long arms. Even though both trademarks may indicate "A. ZOLI" for a barrel address, they are mostly discernable by the model listings under both headings in this section.

COMBINATION GUNS

AIRONE - 12 ga./.30-06 or .308 Win. cal., boxlock with false sideplates, double triggers, checkered walnut stock and forearm, swivels. Disc. 1987.

	$1,450	$1,275	$1,050	$900	$800	$700	$600

CONDOR - similar to Airone, except does not have false sideplates. Disc. 1987.

	$1,295	$1,050	$900	$800	$700	$600	$500

RIFLES: SxS

LEOPARD EXPRESS - .30-06, .308 Win., .375 H&H Mag., or 7x65R cal., boxlock action, double triggers, checkered walnut stock and forearm. Disc. 1987.

	$1,325	$1,150	$975	$900	$840	$775	$725

Last MSR was $1,529.

SHOTGUNS: O/U

SNIPE - .410 bore, 3 in. chambers, 26 or 28 in. barrels, single trigger. Disc. 1987.

	$230	$200	$185	$170	$155	$145	$135

Last MSR was $265.

TEXAS - all gauges, 26 or 28 in. barrels, double triggers, folding design, lever action. Disc. 1987.

	$250	$220	$200	$185	$170	$155	$145

Last MSR was $291.

DOVE - .410 bore only, 3 in. chambers, 26 or 28 in. barrels, single trigger. Disc. 1987.

	$260	$230	$200	$185	$170	$155	$145

Last MSR was $306.

FIELD SPECIAL - 12, 20, or 28 ga., 3 in. chambers, various barrel lengths and chokings, single trigger. Disc. 1987.

	$450	$400	$360	$330	$300	$270	$240

Last MSR was $699.

PIGEON MODEL - 12 or 20 ga., 3 in. chambers, various barrel lengths, single trigger. Disc. 1987.

	$350	$295	$270	$250	$220	$195	$175

Last MSR was $394.

Add $60 for 20 ga.

STANDARD MODEL - 12 or 20 ga., 3 in. chambers, various barrel lengths and chokings, single trigger. Disc. 1987.

	$395	$345	$320	$300	$280	$260	$245

Last MSR was $459.

SILVER SNIPE - 12 or 20 ga., 3 in. chambers on the 20 ga., single trigger, ejectors, light engraving. Disc. 1987.

	100%	98%	95%	90%	80%	70%	60%
	$675	$585	$530	$485	$440	$400	$375

Last MSR was $739.

Add $50 for multi-chokes (12 ga. only).

This model was distributed by Euroarms of America, Inc.

CONDOR MODEL - 12 ga. skeet model, 28 in. barrels, SST, ejectors, wide VR, engraved silver finished receiver, recoil pad. Disc. 1987.

	100%	98%	95%	90%	80%	70%	60%
	$795	$700	$640	$585	$530	$485	$440

Last MSR was $895.

This model was distributed by Mandall Shooting Supplies, Inc.

TARGET MODEL 208 - 12 ga. only, available in either Trap, Skeet, or Monotrap configuration. Disc. 1987.

	100%	98%	95%	90%	80%	70%	60%
	$895	$775	$695	$620	$575	$500	$450

Last MSR was $996.

Add $494 for Monotrap II 208 Model.

TARGET MODEL 308 - 12 ga. only, available in either Trap, Skeet, or Monotrap configuration. Disc. 1987.

	100%	98%	95%	90%	80%	70%	60%
	$1,375	$1,125	$950	$875	$795	$725	$650

Last MSR was $1,581.

Add $76 for multi-chokes.
Add $824 for Monotrap II 308 Model.

SPECIAL MODEL - 12 ga. only, 3 in. chambers, various barrel lengths and chokings, SST. Disc. 1987.

	100%	98%	95%	90%	80%	70%	60%
	$465	$395	$355	$325	$290	$270	$250

Last MSR was $528.

Add $120 for multi-chokes.

DELUXE MODEL - similar to Special Model, except better wood and engraving. Disc. 1987.

	100%	98%	95%	90%	80%	70%	60%
	$645	$550	$495	$450	$400	$360	$320

Last MSR was $730.

Add $80 for multi-chokes.

PRESENTATION MODEL - 12 ga. only, includes sideplates. Disc. 1987.

	100%	98%	95%	90%	80%	70%	60%
	$740	$630	$575	$495	$450	$395	$350

Last MSR was $842.

Add $42 for multi-chokes.

ANGEL MODEL - 12 ga. only, field grade, SST, ejectors, wide VR, engraved receiver, recoil pad. Disc. 1987.

	100%	98%	95%	90%	80%	70%	60%
	$850	$775	$700	$640	$585	$530	$485

This model was distributed by Mandall Shooting Supplies, Inc.

ST. GEORGE'S TARGET - 12 ga. only, trap or skeet gun, SST, fixed choke. Disc. 1987.

	100%	98%	95%	90%	80%	70%	60%
	$900	$730	$645	$550	$495	$450	$400

Last MSR was $1,024.

✱ *St. George's Competition* - 12 ga. only, includes 30 in. O/U barrels and single barrel multi-choke. Disc. 1987.

	100%	98%	95%	90%	80%	70%	60%
	$1,995	$1,750	$1,550	$1,250	$995	$875	$775

Last MSR was $1,627.

GRADING - PPGS™	100%	98%	95%	90%	80%	70%	60%

PATRICIA MODEL - .410 bore only, 3 in. chambers, 28 in. barrels, SST. Disc. 1987.

| | $1,175 | $1,010 | $900 | $895 | $820 | $740 | $650 |

Last MSR was $1,345.

Add $121 for case.

SHOTGUNS: SxS

QUAIL SPECIAL - .410 bore, 3 in. chambers, single trigger, 28 in. barrels. Disc. 1987.

| | $205 | $185 | $170 | $150 | $125 | $110 | $100 |

Last MSR was $243.

FALCON II - .410 bore, 3 in. chambers, 26 or 28 in. barrels, double triggers. Disc. 1987.

| | $205 | $185 | $170 | $150 | $125 | $110 | $100 |

Last MSR was $246.

SILVER HAWK - 12 or 20 ga., double trigger, engraved.

| | $420 | $395 | $360 | $330 | $300 | $280 | $260 |

SILVER SNIPE - 12 or 20 ga., various barrel lengths, VR, single trigger, engraved.

| | $485 | $440 | $400 | $360 | $330 | $300 | $280 |

PHEASANT - 12 ga. only, 3 in. chambers, 28 in. barrels only, single trigger. Disc. 1987.

| | $370 | $320 | $300 | $280 | $260 | $240 | $220 |

Last MSR was $428.

ALLEY CLEANER - 12 or 20 ga., 3 in. chambers, 20 in. barrels, riot configuration, SST. Disc. 1987.

| | $575 | $495 | $460 | $420 | $390 | $350 | $310 |

Last MSR was $649.

Add $65 for multi-chokes.

CLASSIC - 12 or 20 ga., 3 in. chambers, 26-30 in. barrels, ST. Disc. 1989.

| | $995 | $875 | $750 | $650 | $550 | $475 | $400 |

Last MSR was $706.

Add $80 for multi-chokes.

SHOTGUNS: LEVER ACTION

APACHE - 12 ga. only, 3 in. chambers, 20 in. barrel, SST. Disc. 1987.

| | $410 | $355 | $325 | $300 | $280 | $260 | $245 |

Last MSR was $473.

Add $80 for multi-chokes.

SHOTGUNS: SINGLE BARREL

DIANO I - 12, 20 ga., or .410 bore, 3 in. chambers, top lever single barrel action, folding configuration, VR. Disc. 1987.

| | $115 | $95 | $85 | $80 | $75 | $70 | $65 |

Last MSR was $129.

DIANO II - similar to Diano I, except has bottom lever opening. Disc. 1987.

| | $115 | $95 | $85 | $80 | $75 | $70 | $65 |

Last MSR was $129.

LONER I - similar to Diano I. Disc. 1987.

| | $95 | $80 | $75 | $65 | $55 | $45 | $35 |

Last MSR was $109.

LONER II - similar to Diano II. Disc. 1987.

| | $95 | $80 | $75 | $65 | $55 | $45 | $35 |

Last MSR was $109.

GRADING - PPGS™	100%	98%	95%	90%	80%	70%	60%

SHOTGUNS: SLIDE ACTION

PUMP ACTION - 12 ga. only, available in riot, field, or deer (slug) barrel configurations, 3 in. chamber, hunter model has multi-chokes standard. Disc. 1987.

	$290	$245	$205	$185	$170	$150	$125

Last MSR was $329.

ZOLI, ANTONIO

Current manufacturer established in 1945, and located in Brescia, Italy. No current U.S. importation. O/U rifles were previously imported by Cape Outfitters, located in Cape Girardeau, MO. Previously imported and distributed (1990-91 only) by European American Armory Corp. located in Hialeah, FL. Prior to 1990, A. Zoli was imported and distributed exclusively by Antonio Zoli U.S.A., Inc. located in Fort Wayne, IN.

Antonio Zoli firearms are totally unrelated to those guns of Angelo Zoli (guns marked "A. Zoli" make it hard to determine the correct manufacturer). Parts are not interchangeable and warranties from Antonio Zoli firearms DO NOT apply to Angelo Zoli guns. Please contact the factory directly for U.S. model availability and current pricing.

COMBINATION GUNS

COMBINATO - 12 or 20 ga. over .243 Win. or .222 Rem. cal., boxlock action, game scene engraved frame with silver finish, double triggers, folding rear sight, skipline checkering, with sling swivels. Importation disc. 1993.

	$1,750	$1,500	$1,300	$1,100	$950	$775	$600

Last MSR was $1,995.

✱ **Combinato Set** - includes one set of either 20 or 12 ga. barrels and an additional rifle/shotgun barrel set, same cals. as Combinato, cased. Importation disc. 1993.

	$2,400	$2,150	$1,850	$1,600	$1,400	$1,200	$995

Last MSR was $2,700.

SAFARI DELUXE - similar to Combinato, except has sideplates with elaborate game scene engraving. Importation disc. 1993.

	$4,850	$4,400	$3,950	$3,550	$3,175	$2,800	$2,400

Last MSR was $5,200.

Add approx. 50% for Safari Deluxe 2 (includes 2 sets of shotgun barrels).

EXPRESS ELE3 SET - includes one set of .30-06 cal. O/U barrels, one set of 20 ga./.243 Win. cal. barrels, one set of 20 ga./20 ga. barrels, special order, elaborate game scene engraving, includes German claw mount 4X scope and case. Disc.

	$7,950	$7,250	$6,500	$5,750	$5,000	$4,500	$3,950

RIFLES: BOLT ACTION

AZ 1900C - .243 Win., .270 Win., 6.5x55mm, .30-06, .308 Win., 7mm Rem. Mag., or .300 Win. Mag. cal., 21 or 24 (Mag. cals.) in. barrel, checkered walnut stock with weatherproof stock finish, sling swivels, iron sights, 7.4 lbs. Importation disc. 1993.

	$1,100	$850	$740	$660	$585	$500	$450

Last MSR was $1,295.

Add approx. 10% for AZ 1900 Deluxe (better walnut).
Add 60% for AZ 1900 Super Deluxe (select walnut and moderate engraving).
Add approx. 10% for Model AZ 1900 DL (photo engraved receiver and floorplate).

GRADING - PPGS™	100%	98%	95%	90%	80%	70%	60%

MODEL AZ 1900M - .243 Win., 6.5x55mm, .270 Win., .30-06, or .308 Win. cal., 21 in. barrel, composite stock is composed of fiberglass, Kevlar, and graphite and features baked on walnut wood grain finish with checkering, drilled and tapped receiver. Imported 1991 only.

	$725	$625	$550	$495	$450	$415	$375

Last MSR was $840.

Add approx. 10% for Model AZ 1900M DL (photo engraved receiver and floorplate).

RIFLES: O/U

Please contact Cape Outfitters (see Trademark Index) for more information and current domestic pricing on the models listed.

EXPRESS - 7x65R, 7x57mm, .30-06, .308 Win., or 9.3x74R cal., 25.6 in. barrels, hand checkered walnut stock with cheekpiece, set trigger for bottom barrel, extractors. Importation disc. 1993.

	$3,875	$3,250	$2,900	$2,600	$2,200	$1,950	$1,650

Last MSR was $4,400.

Add $600 for E Model (with ejectors).

EXPRESS EM - 7x65R, .30-06, .308 Win., or 9.3x74R cal., mechanical single trigger, ejectors. Importation disc. 1990, reintroduced 1992 only.

	$4,850	$3,975	$3,300	$2,900	$2,600	$2,200	$1,900

Last MSR was $5,300.

Add $2,395 for De Luxe Model (disc.).
Add $7,200 for E3 De Luxe Model (disc.).
The Express E3 De Luxe Model includes 2 extra sets of barrels - 1 set is shotgun (20 ga. - 2 3/4 or 3 in. chambers).

RIFLES: SxS

SAVANA E - 7x65R, .30-06, .308 Win., or 9.3x74R cal., boxlock action, ejectors. Importation disc. 1990.

	$5,850	$4,850	$3,975	$3,300	$2,800	$2,350	$2,000

Last MSR was $6,600.

Add $400 for Savana EM Model (single trigger).

✳ *Savana Deluxe* - similar to Savana E, except has elaborate game scene engraving. Importation disc. 1990.

	$7,750	$7,100	$6,500	$6,000	$5,500	$5,000	$4,600

Last MSR was $8,295.

SHOTGUNS: O/U, RECENT PRODUCTION

GOLDEN SNIPE - 12 or 20 ga, various barrel lengths, VR, single trigger, ejectors, engraved.

	$560	$520	$475	$430	$395	$360	$330

DELFINO - 12 or 20 ga., 3 in. chambers, 26 or 28 in. barrels, ejectors, VR, single non-selective trigger, blue frame with delicate engraving, walnut pistol grip stock and forearm. Disc.

	$500	$425	$375	$325	$295	$280	$265

RITMO HUNTING - 12 ga. only, 3 in. chambers, 26 or 28 in. vent. barrels and rib, SST, ejectors, select checkered walnut, blue frame and barrels with moderate engraving, recoil pad, 7 1/4 lbs. Disc.

	$575	$510	$465	$410	$370	$350	$335

RITMO PIGEON GRADE IV - 12 ga. only, live pigeon gun, 28 in. barrels, SST, ejectors, superbly engraved silver finished receiver, extra fine checkering on deluxe walnut, vent. barrels and rib, cased, 7 1/2 lbs. Disc.

	$1,600	$1,450	$1,200	$1,000	$875	$795	$725

GRADING - PPGS™	100%	98%	95%	90%	80%	70%	60%

M85 RITMO TRAP OR SKEET - 12 ga. only, 28 in. (Skeet only), 30, or 32 in. barrels, ejectors, SST, special stock dimensions, engraved blue receiver, select checkered walnut stock and forearm, cased, 7 3/4 lbs. Disc.

| | $595 | $500 | $465 | $440 | $415 | $395 | $370 |

This model was also available in a single barrel trap model at no extra charge.

* *M85 Ritmo Trap Combination* - 12 ga. only, supplied with O/U and single barrel sets, various barrel lengths, cased. Disc.

| | $995 | $895 | $800 | $700 | $620 | $575 | $500 |

SILVER FALCON - 12 or 20 ga., 3 in. chambers, boxlock action, SST, ejectors, 26 or 28 in. barrels with multi-chokes, coin finished receiver with engraving, checkered Turkish walnut stock and forearm with weatherproof finish. Importation disc. 1991.

| | $1,450 | $700 | $575 | $500 | $450 | $400 | $365 |

Last MSR was $1,695.

WOODSMAN - 12 ga. only, 3 in. chambers, 23 in. vent. barrels are designed to shoot rifle slugs at 55 yards and to accept 5 interchangeable choke tubes, SST, ejectors, quarter rib on barrels with pop-up rifle sights, checkered Circassian walnut stock and forearm with swivels (waterproof finish).

| | $1,650 | $1,150 | $950 | $800 | $700 | $600 | $500 |

Last MSR was $1,895.

* *Woodsman Combo* - includes 2 sets of barrels (3 in. chambers) with Zoli interchangeable choke system.

| | $2,050 | $1,700 | $1,475 | $1,200 | $1,050 | $925 | $800 |

Last MSR was $2,320.

MODEL Z-90 TARGET MODEL - 12 ga. only, boxlock action, adj. SST, black competition receiver, deluxe checkered Turkish walnut stock with recoil pad and forearm, vent. barrels and rib, SST, ejectors.

* *Trap Gun* - 29 1/2 or 32 in. barrels with screw-in chokes and raised VR, Monte Carlo stock, blue finish. Importation disc. 1993.

| | $2,150 | $1,450 | $1,200 | $995 | $850 | $700 | $600 |

Last MSR was $2,495.

* *Mono Trap Gun* - 32 or 34 in. barrel with screw-in chokes and raised VR, Monte Carlo stock. Importation disc. 1993.

| | $2,150 | $1,450 | $1,200 | $995 | $850 | $700 | $600 |

Last MSR was $2,495.

* *Z-90 Combo Trap Set* - includes O/U trap barrels as well as Mono trap barrel on same receiver, available as 30/32 in. sets or 32/34 in. sets. Imported 1991-92.

| | $2,350 | $1,900 | $1,650 | $1,400 | $1,150 | $950 | $825 |

Last MSR was $2,700.

* *Skeet Gun* - 28 in. barrels only with screw-in chokes. Importation disc. 1993.

| | $2,150 | $1,450 | $1,200 | $995 | $850 | $700 | $600 |

Last MSR was $2,495.

* *Sporting Clays Gun* - 28 in. barrels with screw-in chokes, coin finished receiver with engraved sideplates, separated barrels, Schnabel forend, solid recoil pad. Importation disc. 1990.

| | $2,150 | $1,450 | $1,200 | $995 | $850 | $700 | $600 |

Last MSR was $2,495.

SHOTGUNS: SxS, RECENT PRODUCTION

UPLANDER - 12 or 20 ga., 3 in. chambers, 25 in. barrels with fixed chokes (IC/M), ST, ejectors, color case hardened receiver, English style checkered Circassian walnut stock and forearm with oil or polyurethane finish. Importation disc. 1990.

| | $750 | $625 | $560 | $520 | $485 | $450 | $425 |

Last MSR was $1,295.

GRADING - PPGS™	100%	98%	95%	90%	80%	70%	60%

SILVER FOX - 12 or 20 ga., 3 in. chambers, 26 or 28 (12 ga. only) in. barrels with fixed chokes, ST, ejectors, hand engraved silver finished receiver with "AZ" in gold, straight grip checkered Circassian walnut stock and forearm. Importation disc. 1990.

	$1,650	$1,425	$1,200	$995	$875	$750	$625

Last MSR was $2,995.

ARIETE M3 - 12 ga. only, 26 or 28 in. barrels, matted rib, single non-selective trigger, ejectors, blue receiver with fine scroll engraving, cased. Disc.

	$550	$475	$400	$360	$330	$310	$285

EMPIRE - 12 or 20 ga. Mag., 27 or 28 in. barrels, moderate engraving, coin finished receiver. Disc.

	$1,425	$1,175	$975	$875	$795	$725	$650

Add $100 for 3 in. Mag. chambers.

This model was distributed by Euroarms of America, Inc.

VOLCANO RECORD - 12 ga. only, 28 in. barrels, H&H type sidelocks, ejectors, SST, treble Purdey locks, silver finished receiver with elaborate engraving, best quality fine checkered walnut, special order only. Disc.

	$5,300	$4,475	$3,950	$3,400	$2,950	$2,650	$2,300

❋ *Volcano Record ELM* - 12 ga. only, built to individual customer specifications, best quality H&H style sidelock. Disc.

	$13,250	$11,000	$9,750	$8,600	$7,400	$6,300	$5,450

This model was distributed by Euroarms of America, Inc.

CUSTOM SERIES - SxS, individual custom order only, every refinement is used in the construction of these extremely rare and expensive shotguns. The Volcano Extra Lusso shotgun is probably the most elaborate Antonio Zoli shotgun with the recent list price being $58,850.

TRADEMARK INDEX

Having originally made its humble beginning back in the 10th edition, published in 1989, the original Trademark Index section listed pertinent contact information for over 200 companies. At that time, most companies did not even have a fax number yet! The fax machine had just been introduced, and most companies wouldn't spend $1,100-$1,300 at the time to buy one. Up until then, it was either mail, telephone, telex, or smoke signals if there was no wind. The Trademark Index originally started because I was frustrated when trying to find contact information on the multitudes of firearms and related companies, both domestic and foreign, without having to go through a pile of brochures, business cards, and magazines. Back then, there was no Internet, no email, and no contact management programs, and a fax machine was considered a luxury. Finding good information was difficult.

The Trademark Index wasn't something that was planned. All of a sudden, one March afternoon, the light bulb came on, and it was approximated that this new section would initially take no more than 4-8 hours of computer time. Four days later, after a virtual non-stop frenzy of WP activity, it was decided that the section was finally good enough to publish.

Since then, the Trademark Index has grown significantly each year, and continues to be the only up-to-date and accurate contact information published for firearms manufacturers, trademarks, importers, distributors, repair and service centers, and auction houses. Gathering this information has required scouring every firearms booth at both domestic and foreign trade shows. Additionally, hundreds of hours have been spent updating this section, and we feel confident that the information listed below is the most up-to-date and accurate we can provide, especially with the ever-changing emails, website addresses, and area codes.

Previously published annually, this Trademark Index is now available online at no charge. Also, the Trademark Index information is now revised and updated monthly, and this Trademark Index online will now be the most up-to-date contact information available for the firearms industry. Since I always want to be better informed, if you have new or additional information that would be helpful to update this continually changing section, please send in your potential contributions to us by email or fax, and we will enter them into our database immediately. Creating and maintaining this Trademark Index database is a big job, and we only have one goal – to make it the best and most up-to-date available, and it is now updated continuosly.

Even more so than last year, you will note additions and substantial changes regarding website and email listings – this may be your best way of obtaining up-to-date model and pricing information directly from current manufacturers, importers, and/or distributors. When online with the various company's web sites, it's not a bad idea to look at the date of last web update, as this will tell you how current the online information really is.

Previous readers will note that contact information for the black powder and airgun industries is no longer included in this *Blue Book of Gun Values* Trademark Index (it's large enough the way it is). For a complete listing of companies and contact information for these two separate industries, please refer to the respective Trademark Indexes in the *Blue Book of Modern Black Powder Arms* and the *Blue Book of Airguns*, also available online at no charge.

If parts are needed for older, discontinued makes and models (even though the manufacturer/trademark is current), it is recommended you contact either Numrich Gun Parts Corp. located in West Hurley, NY, or Jack First, Inc. located in Rapid City, SD for domestic availability and prices. For current manufacturers, it is recommended that you contact an authorized warranty repair center or stocking gun shop, unless a company/trademark has an additional service/parts listing. In Canada, please refer to the Bowmac Gunpar Inc. listing. Remember, most of the people you come in contact with to request customer service questions or parts/service will probably be busy, so have patience and respect their time.

DIALING INTERNATIONAL PHONE/FAX NUMBERS:

It is important to note that international fax/phone numbers will require overseas and country/city coding, which we have tried to list as much as possible. It is standard practice to dial the area code after the country code when calling overseas from the U.S. Europe is in the process of introducing a new system that requires the user to always dial the area code, even if you are in the same area code. This means that the area codes will be considered at all times to be part of the telephone number during dialing. Current countries that have this new system are Italy and Spain – other European countries still have the old dialing system.

As an example, with the old system, if you had to phone or fax Rome, Italy from the U.S., you had to dial 011-39-6-123-4567 (international code, country code, city code, and phone number). With the new system, this has changed to: 011-39-06-123-4567 (international code, country code, city area code (06), and phone number).

For mobile phones, the new system will affect the dialing of a 0 after the country code. Previously, the user would have had to dial a 0 after the country code, when calling either from abroad or from the U.S. The new system eliminates the 0 – it is not necessary to dial it at all, either from the U.S. or Europe.

If you should require additional assistance in "tracking" any of the current companies listed in this publication (or perhaps, current companies that are not listed), please contact us and we will try to help you regarding these specific requests. Again, the most up-to-date Trademark Index for the firearms, black powder, and airguns industries will be posted on our website: **www.bluebookinc.com.** We hope you appreciate this service – no one else in the industry has anything like it.

ADC
Armi Dallera Custom
Via Michelangelo, 64
I-25063 Gardone, VT (BS) ITALY
Fax No.: 011-39-0308911562
Website: www.intred.com/adc

AMT
Crusader Gun Company, Inc.
5200 Mitchelldale, Ste. E17
Houston, TX 77092
Phone No.: 800-272-7816
Fax No.: 713-681-5665

AMOSKEAG AUCTION COMPANY, INC.
250 Commercial Street, Unit 3011
Manchester, NH 03101
Phone No.: 603-627-7383
Fax No.: 603-627-7384
Website: www.amoskeag-auction.com

AR-7 INDUSTRIES L.L.C.
Please refer to Armalite, Inc. listing.

AR-15 KIT GUNS
Model 1 Sales
P.O. Box 211
Fox River Grove, IL 60021
Phone No.: 847-639-3192
Fax No.: 847-639-3397
Website: www.model1sales.com

ATA ARMS
Factory - ATA AV Tufekleri San. Ve Tic. Ltd. STI.
Imes Sanayi Sitesi B-Blok 201 Sok.
No.: 8 Yukari Dudullu Umraniye
Istanbul, TURKEY
Fax No.: 011-90-216-466-4571
Website: www.ataarms.com
Email: info@ataarmsusa.com

AWA USA
2280 W. 80th Street, Ste. 2
Hialeah, FL 33016
Phone No.:305-828-1982
Fax No.: 305-828-1066
Website: www.awaguns.com
Email: rustyguns@nxs.net

Factory - AWA USA
Branch Office
Via De Gusperi
I-25013 Carpenedolo (BS) ITALY
Fax No.: 011-390-30-9966322

A-SQUARE COMPANY
205 Fairview Ave.
Jefferson, IN 47130
Phone No.: 812-283-0577
Fax No.: 812-283-0375
Website: www.a-squarecompany.com

AYA
Importer/Distributor – please refer to New England Custom Gun Service, Ltd. listing
Importer/Distributor - please refer to Fieldsport listing
Importer/Distributor and AYA Warranty Service & Repairs
John F. Rowe
4213 Oakcrest Ave.
Enid, OK 73702
Phone No.: 405-233-5942
Phone No.: 405-233-4038
Importer/Distributor - Anglo American Sporting Agency
P.O. Box 331
Corona del Mar, CA 92625
Phone No.: 949-644-9557
Fax No.: 949-644-9558
Website: www.angloamericansport.com
Email: angloamericansport@earthlink.net
Retailer - Bill Hanus Birdguns LLC
(Bill Hanus models only)
P.O. Box 533
Newport, OR 97365
Phone No.: 541-265-7433
Fax No.: 541-265-7400
Website: www.billhanusbirdguns.com
U.K. Importer/Distributor - A.S.I.
Alliance House, Snape, Saxmundham
Suffolk, ENGLAND IP17 1SW
Fax No.: 011-44-1728-688950
Email: info@a-s-i.co.uk

Factory - AYA – Aguirre Y Aranzabal, S.A.L.
Avda. Otaol, 25-3
P.O. Box 45
20600 EIBAR (Guipuzcoa) SPAIN
Fax No.: 011-34-943100133
Website: www.aya-fineguns.com
Email: aya@aya-fineguns.com

ABBIATICO & SALVINELLI (FAMARS)
Please refer to Famars di Abbiatico & Salvinelli listing.

ACCU-TEK
Factory - Excel Industries, Inc.
4510 Carter Court
Chino, CA 91710
Toll Free Phone No.: 888-442-6096
Phone No.: 909-627-2404
Fax No.: 909-627-7817
Website: www.accu-tekfirearms.com
Email: email@accu-tekfirearms.com

ACCURACY INTERNATIONAL LTD.
Importer and Distributor - Accuracy International North America Inc.
P.O. Box 5267
Oak Ridge, TN 37831
Phone No.: 423-482-0330
Fax No.: 423-482-0336
Website: www.accuracyinternational.com
Email: neatguns@aol.com
Factory - Accuracy International Ltd.
P.O. Box 81, Portsmouth
Hampshire, ENGLAND PO3 5SJ
Fax No.: 011-44-23-9269-1852

ACTION LEGENDS MFG., INC.
1200 Blalock, Ste. 107
Houston, TX 77055
Phone No.: 713-984-2196
Phone No.: 866-984-2196
Fax No.: 713-984-2319
Website: www.almcarbines.com

ADAMY, GEBR. JADGWAFFEN
Importer - please refer to New England Custom Gun Service, Ltd. listing.
Factory - Adamy-Jadgwaffen
Bochsenmacher-Handwerksbetrieb
Windeweg 3, Suhl D-98527 GERMANY
Fax No.: 011-49-3681-709076
Website: www.adamy-jagdwaffen.de
Email: info@adamy-jagdwaffen.de

ADCO SALES INC.
4 Draper Street
Woburn, MA 01801-4522
Phone No.: 781-935-1799
Fax No.: 781-935-1011
Website: www.diamondguns.com
Website: www.adcosales.com
Email: questions@adcosales.com

ADVANTAGE ARMS, INC.
Conversion Kits for Glocks & 1911 Pistols
25163 W. Stanford
Valencia, CA 91355
Phone No.: 888-617-4666
Website: www.advantagearms.com
Email: gunkits@advantagearms.com

ALEXANDER ARMS LLC
U.S. Army - Radford Arsenal
P.O. Box 1
Radford, VA 24143
Phone No.: 540-639-8356
Fax No.: 540-639-8353
Website: www.alexanderarms.com
Email: sales@alexanderarms.com

ALCHEMY ARMS CO.
P.O. Box 114
Port Orchard, WA 98366
Phone No.: 800-282-4664
Fax No.: 253-939-4114
Website: www.alchemyltd.com
Email: contact@alchemyltd.com

ALFA PROJ. spol. s.r.o.
Zabrdovicka 11
615 00 Brno CZECH REPUBLIC
Fax No.: 011-420-54521-4497
Website: www.alfa-proj.cz
Email: info@alfa-proj.cz

AMERICA REMEMBERS
10226 Timber Ridge Dr.
Ashland, VA 23005
Phone No.: 804-550-9616
Fax No.: 804-550-9603
Website: www.americaremembers.com
Email: america.remembers@verizon.net

AMERICAN CUSTOM GUNMAKERS GUILD
22 Vista View Dr.
Cody, WY 82414-9606
Phone/Fax No.: 307-587-4297
Website: www.acgg.org
Email: acgg@acgg.org

AMERICAN DERRINGER CORPORATION
127 N. Lacy Dr.
Waco, TX 76705
Phone No.: 254-799-9111
Fax No.: 254-799-7935
Website: www.ladyderringer.com
Website: www.amderringer.com
Email: amderr@aol.com

AMERICAN HISTORICAL FOUNDATION
1142 W. Grace St.
Richmond, VA 23220
Phone No.: 800-368-8080
Fax No.: 804-359-4895
Website: www.ahfrichmond.com
Email: ahfrichmond@aol.com

AMERICAN HUNTING RIFLES, INC.
P.O. Box 300
Hamilton, MT 59840
Phone No.: 406-961-4944
Fax No.: 406-961-1430
Website: www.hunting-rifles.com
Email: info@hunting-rifles.com

AMERICAN SPIRIT ARMS CORP.
15001 North Hayden Road, Ste. 112
Scottsdale, AZ 85260
Phone No.: 888-486-5487
Fax No.: 480-483-5301
Website: www.gunkits.com
Email: gunkits@gunkits.com

ANSCHÜTZ
Distributors - Sporting Rifles & Pistols
AcuSport Corporation
One Hunter Place
Bellefontaine, OH 43311-3001
Phone No.: 937-593-7010
Fax No.: 937-592-5625
Website: www.acusport.com
Zanders Sporting Goods, Inc.
7525 Hwy. 154 W.
Baldwin, IL 62217-9706
Phone No.: 618-785-2235
Fax No.: 618-785-2320
Website: www.gzanders.com
Email: jbe@egyptian.net
Ellett Brothers
267 Columbia Ave.
Chapin, SC 29036
Phone No.: 803-345-3751
Fax No.: 803-345-1820
Website: www.ellettbrothers.com
Jerry's Sport Center, Inc.
P.O. Box 121 Main St.
Forest City, PA 18421-0121
Phone No.: 800-234-2612
Fax No.: 800-388-8452
Website: www.jerryssportcenter.com
Bonitz Brothers
931 Dana Dr.
Harrisburg, PA 17109
Phone No.: 800-825-7060
Fax No.: 800-933-3285
Outdoor Sports Headquarters
967 Watertower Lane
Dayton, OH 45449-2445
Phone: 937-865-5855
Simmons Gun Specialties
20241 W. 207th Street
Spring Hill, KS 66083-8839
Phone: 913-592-3939
Distributor - Sporting Rifles, Pistols & Target Rifles
Please refer to Champion's Choice Inc. listing.
Distributors - Target Rifles
Please refer to Gunsmithing Inc. listing.
Champions Shooter's Supply
P.O. Box 303
New Albany, OH 43054
Phone No.: 614-855-1603
Fax No.: 614-855-1209
Website: www.championshooters.com
Creedmoor Sports
3052 Industry St. #103
Oceanside, CA 92054
Phone No.: 760-757-5529
Website: www.creedmorsports.com
Email: greg@creedmoorsports.com
Repair/Warranty/Gunsmithing Services
10-Ring-Service, Inc.
2227 West Lou Drive
Jacksonville, FL 32216
Phone No.: 904-724-7419
Fax No.: 904-724-7149
Factory - ANSCHÜTZ, J.G. GmbH & Co. KG
Daimlerstrasse 12
D-89079 Ulm, GERMANY
Fax No.: 011-49-731-40125-205
Website: www.anschuetz-sport.com
Email: anschuetz@anschuetz-sport.com

ANZIO IRONWORKS
1905 16th Street North
St. Petersburg, FL 33704
Phone No.: 727-895-2019
Fax No.: 727-827-4728
Website: www.anzioironworks.com
Email: anzioshop@hotmail.com

ARCUS
Importer - please refer to Century International Arms listing.

ARM SPORT LLC
Colt and Remington cartridge conversions
P.O. Box 254
Eastlake, CO 80614
Phone No.: 303-451-7212
Website: www.armsportllc.com
Email: RLMillington@armsportllc.com

ARMALITE, INC.
P.O. Box 299
Geneseo, IL 61254
Phone No.: 309-944-6939
Fax No.: 309-944-6949
Website: www.armalite.com
Email: info@armalite.com
Law Enforcement Support Only
P.O. Box 340
Campbellsburg, KY 40011
Phone No.: 502-532-0300
Fax No.: 502-532-0775
Email: toppc@armalite.com

ARMAMENT TECHNOLOGY
(Repair only - no current mfg.)
3045 Robie St., Suite 113
Halifax, N.S. CANADA B3K 4P6
Phone No.: 902-454-6384
Fax No.: 902-454-4641
Website: www.armament.com
Email: info@armament.com

ARMES DE CHASSE LLC
P.O. Box 86
Hertford, NC 27944
Phone No.: 252-426-2245
Fax No.: 252-426-1557

ARMES PIERRE ARTISAN (P. CHAPUIS)
Le Mont Mille B.P. 12
F-42380 Saint Bonnett Le Chateau FRANCE
Fax No.: 011-33-04-77-507027

ARMI SPORT SNC DI CHIAPPIA SILVIA & C.
Exclusive Importer - please refer to Taylor's & Co., Inc. listing.
Factory
via Milano 2
25020 Azzano Mella (BS) ITALY
Fax No.: 011-39-030-9749232
Website: www.armichiappa.com
Email: info@armisport.com

ARMINIUS
Please refer to Herman Weihrauch Revolver GmbH listing.

ARMORY USA, L.L.C.
7311 Galveston Road, Ste. 260
Houston, TX 77034
Phone No.: 713-944-3551
Fax No.: 713-944-3581
Website: www.globaltrades.com

ARMS MORAVIA LTD.
Factory
Nadrazni 22
Ostrava 2, CZ-70200
CZECH REPUBLIC
Fax No.: 011-420-69-611-2202
Website: www.arms-moravia.cz

ARMSCOR (ARMS CORPORATION OF THE PHILIPPINES)
Importer (rifles only) – please refer to the K.B.I., Inc. listing
Importer & Distributor - Armscor Precision International
5329 S. Cameron St., Ste. 110
Las Vegas, NV 89118
Phone No.: 702-362-7750
Fax No.: 702-362-5019
Email: apiusa@earthlink.com
Factory office - Arms Corp. of the Philippines
Parang Marikina 1800
Metro Manilla, PHILIPPINES
Phone No.: 632-942-5936
Fax No.: 632-942-0862
Website: www.armscor.com.ph
Email: armscor@info.com.ph
Executive office - Arms Corp. of the Philippines
6th Floor, Strat 100 Bldg., Emerald Ave.
Ortigas Center, Pasig City, 1600 The Phillipines
Fax No.: 632-634-3906
Email: squires@cnl.net

ARMSCORP USA, INC.
4424 John Avenue
Baltimore, MD 21227-1506
Phone No.: 410-247-6200
Fax No.: 410-247-6205
Website: www.armscorpusa.com
Email: info@armscorpusa.com

ARRIETA, S.L.
Importer & Distributor - please refer to Quality Arms listing.
Importer - please refer to Griffin & Howe listing.
Importer - please refer to William Larkin Moore listing.
Importer - please refer to Orvis listing.
Importer - Wingshooting Adventures
O-1845 West Leonard
Grand Rapids, MI 49544-9510
Phone No.: 616-677-1980
Fax No.: 616-677-1986
Factory - Arrieta, Manufacturas, S.L.
Morkaiko 5
E-20870 Elgoibar (Guipuzcoa) SPAIN
Fax No.: 011-34-943-743154
Email: marrietasl@euskalnet.net

ARRIZABALAGA, PEDRO
Importer - please refer to Harry Marx Hi-Grade Imports listing.
Importer - please refer to William Larkin Moore listing.
Factory - Arrizabalaga, Pedro, S.A.
Errekatxu, 5
E-20600 Eibar (Guipuzcoa) SPAIN
Fax No.: 011-34-943-11-1743

ARSENAL, BULGARIA
Please refer to Arsenal Inc. listing.

ARSENAL INC.
5015 West Sahara Ave., Ste. 125
Las Vegas, NV 89146-3407
Phone No.: 888-539-2220
Fax No.: 702-643-2088
Website: www.arsenalinc.com

ARSENAL USA LLC
Please refer to Armory USA LLC listing.

ART MANIFATTURA ARMI
Importer - please refer to William Larkin Moore listing.
Factory
Via Madonnina 89
Gardone, VT, Brescia
I-25063 ITALY
Fax No.: 011-030-861591
Email: armi.art@intred.it

ASPEN OUTFITTING CO.
315 East Dean St.
Aspen, CO 81611
Phone No.: 800-784-2140
Fax No.: 970-920-3706
Website: www.aspenoutfitting.com
Email: contact@aspenoutfitting.com

ATKIN, GRANT & LANG
Broomhill Leys, Windmill Road, Markyate
St. Albans, Hertfordshire AL3 8LP ENGLAND
Fax No.: 011-44-1582-842318
Website: www.atkingrantandlang.co.uk
Email: AtkinGrant.Lang@btinternet.com

ATKIN, HENRY
Factory - please refer to Atkin, Grant & Lang listing.

AUSTRALIAN INTERNATIONAL ARMS
Brisbane, AUSTRALIA

AUTO-ORDNANCE CORP.
Please refer to the Kahr Arms listing.
Website: www.tommygun.com
Website: www.tommygunshop.com

AXTELL RIFLE COMPANY
Distributor - The Riflesmith Inc.
353 Mill Creek Road
Sheridan, MT 59749
Phone/Fax No.: 406-842-5814
Website: www.riflesmith.com
Email: riflesmith@riflesmith.com

BSA IMPORTS
3911 SW 47th Ave., Ste. 914
Ft. Lauderdale, FL 33314
Phone No.: 954-581-2047
Fax No.: 954-581-0600

BAER, LES
Please refer to the Les Baer Custom listing.

BAIKAL
Baikal Factory
Izhevsky Mekhanichesky Zavod
8, Promyshlennaya str.
Izhevsk, 426063 RUSSIA
Fax No.: 011-95-007-341-2765830
Website: www.baikalinc.ru
Email: worldlinks@baikalinc.ru

BALLARD RIFLE, LLC
113 West Yellowstone Avenue
Cody, Wyoming 82414
Phone No.: 307-587-4914
Fax No.: 307-527-6097
Website: www.ballardrifles.com
E-mail: ballard@wyoming.com

BANSNER'S ULTIMATE RIFLES L.L.C.
P.O. Box 839
261 East Main Street
Adamstown, PA 19501
Phone No.: 717-484-2370
Fax No.: 717-484-0523
Website: www.bansnersrifle.com
Email: bansner@ptd.com

BARRETT FIREARMS MANUFACTURING, INC.
P.O. Box 1077
Murfreesboro, TN 37133
Phone No.: 615-896-2938
Fax No.: 615-896-7313
Website: www.barrettrifles.com
Email: mail@barrettrifles.com

BATTAGLIA, MAURO
Via Dismano, 181
Santo Stefano di Ravenna ITALY
Fax No.: 011-39-0544-497879
Website: www.maurobattaglia.armifini.com
Email: maurobattaglia@armifini.com

BECAS
Factory - Molot JSC
Vyatskie Polyany Machine Building Plant
135 Lenin St., Vyatski Polyany
612960 Krov Region, RUSSIA
Fax No.: 011-007-83334-61462
Email: admir@molot.kirov.ru

BEEMAN PRECISION AIRGUNS
5454 Argosy Dr.
Huntington Beach, CA 92649-1039
Toll Free Phone No.: 800-227-2744
Phone No.: 714-890-4800
Fax No.: 714-890-4808
Website: www.beeman.com

BEEMILLER
Please refer to Hi-Point Firearms listing.

BENELLI
Importer - Benelli USA
17603 Indian Head Highway
Accokeek, MD 20607-2501
Phone No.: 301-283-6981
Fax No.: 301-283-6988
Website: www.benelliusa.com
Email: benusa1@aol.com
Pistol/Airgun Importer - please refer to Larry's Guns listing.
Warranty Repair Address - Benelli USA Corp.
901 Eight Street
Pocomoke, MD 21851
Factory - Benelli Armi S.p.A.
Via della Stazione, 50
I-61029 Urbino (PS) ITALY
Fax No.: 011-39-0722-307207
Website: www.benelli.it

BERETTA, PIETRO
Importer - Beretta U.S.A. Corp
17601 Beretta Drive
Accokeek, MD 20607
Fax No.: 301-283-0435
Website: www.berettausa.com
Beretta Premium Grades
Beretta Gallery
718 Madison Avenue
New York, NY 10021
Phone No.: 212-319-3235
Fax No.: 212-207-8219
Beretta Gallery
41 Highland Park Village
Dallas, TX 75205
Phone No.: 214-559-9800
Fax No.: 214-559-9805
Beretta Gallery
1061 Capital Federal
Arendales 1654/56
Buenos Aires, ARGENTINA
Phone No.: 011-54-813.92558

Factory - Fabbrica d'Armi Pietro Beretta S.p.A
Via Pietro Beretta 18
25063 Gardone Val Trompia
Brescia, ITALY
Phone No.: 011-39-30-8341-1
Fax No.: 011-39-30-8341-421
Website: www.beretta.it

WAYNE BERGQUIST CUSTOM PISTOLS
5760 Shirley Street, Unit #21.
Naples, FL 34109
Phone No.: 239-594-1573
Fax No.: 239-597-8259

BERNARDELLI, VINCENZO
Via Grandi, 10
Torbole Casaglia
I-25030 Brescia, ITALY
Fax No.: 011-39-030-2150963
Website: www.bernardelli.com
Email: bernardelli@bernardelli.com

BERSA
Master Distributor - Eagle Imports, Inc.
1750 Brielle Ave., Unit B-1
Wanamassa, NJ 07712
Phone No.: 732-493-0333
Fax No.: 732-493-0301
Web Site: www.bersa-llama.com
Email: gsodini@aol.com
Factory - Bersa S.A.
Castillo 312
(1704) Ramos Mejia, ARGENTINA
Fax No.: 011-54-1-656-2093

BERTUZZI
Factory - Bertuzzi, F.lli
Via Alessandro Volta, 65
I-25063 Gardone V.T. (BS) ITALY
Fax No.: 011-39-030-8912188

BETTINSOLI, TARCISIO Srl
Via I Maggio, 116
Sarezzo, Brescia, I-25068 ITALY
Fax No.: 011-39-030-890-0240

BLAND, THOMAS & SONS GUNMAKERS LTD.
Woodcock Hill, Inc.
P.O. Box 363
192 Spencers Road
Benton, PA 17814
Phone No.: 570-864-3242
Fax No.: 570-864-3232
Website: www.woodcockhill.com
Email: bland@epix.net

BLASER
Importer & Distributor - please refer to SIG Arms listing.
Factory - Blaser Jagdwaffen GmbH
Ziegelstadel 1
D-88316 Isny im Allgau, GERMANY
Fax No.: 011-49-75-62702-43
Website: www.blaserrifles.com

H. BLEIKER FEINMECHANIK/SPORTWAFFEN
Neufeldstrasse 1
CH – 9606 Bütschwil, SWITZERLAND
Phone No.: 011.41.71.982.8210
Fax No.: 011.41.71.982.8219
Website: www.bleiker.ch
Email: hbleiker@bleiker.ch

BLUEGRASS ARMORY
P.O. Box 1293
Richmond, KY 40476
Phone/Fax No.: 859-625-0874
Website: www.bluegrassarmory.com
Email: support@bluegrassarmmory.com

BOBCAT WEAPONS INC.
P.O. Box 21017
Mesa, AZ 85277
Phone No.: 480-832-0844
Fax No.: 206-350-5274
Website: www.bobcatweapons.com
Email: info@bobcatweapons.com

BOND ARMS, INC.
P.O. Box 1296
204 Alpha Lane
Granbury, Texas 76048
Phone No.: 817-573-4445
Fax No.: 817-573-5636
Website: www.bondarms.com
Email: bondarms@shooters.com

BOSIS, LUCIANO
Importer - British Sporting Arms, Ltd.
3684 Route 44
Millsbrook, NY 12545
Phone No.: 845-677-8303
Fax No.: 845-677-5756
Website: www.bsaltd.com/bsa_home.html
Email: info@bsaltd.com
Factory
via G. Marconi 30
25039 Travagliato, Brescia, ITALY
Phone/Fax No.: 011-39-030-660413
Website: www.bosis.com
Email: info@bosis.com

BOSS & CO., LTD.
16 Mount Street
London, ENGLAND W1K 2RH
Phone No.: 011-44-020-7493-1127
Fax No.: 011-44-020-7493-0711
Website: www.bossguns.com
Email: mail@bossguns.com

BOWEN, BRUCE & COMPANY
3541 Mayer Ave.
Sturgis, SD 57785
Phone No.: 605-347-3133
Website: www.bbguns.net
Email: Bbowen999@aol.com

BOWMAC GUNPAR INC.
Canadian Parts Supplier
69 Iber Rd., Unit 101
Stittsville, Ontario CANADA K2S 1E7
Phone No.: 800-668-2509
Phone No.: 613-831-8548
Fax No.: 613-831-0530

BRAZIER, JOSEPH, LTD.
Please refer to First National Gun Banque listing.
Factory
10/12 Fitzalan Rd., Arundel
West Sussex BN18 9JS ENGLAND
Email: brazier@fngbcorp.com

BREDA MECCANICA BRESCIANA
Importer - please refer to Tristar listing.
Factory
Via Lunga, 2
I-25126 Brescia ITALY
Fax No.: 011-39-030-322115
Website: www.bredafucili.com

RYAN BREEDING CUSTOM RIFLES
3112 West Ave. N.
Palmdale, CA 93551
Phone No.: 661-266-1908
Website: www.rbbigbores.com
Email: ryan@rbbigbores.com

BRETTON-GAUCHER
Factory
46, rue Desjoyaux
42000 St. Etienne FRANCE
Fax No.: 011-33-477419572
Website: www.bretton-gaucher.com
Email: info@bretton-gaucher.com

BRILEY MANUFACTURING INC.
1230 Lumpkin Rd.
Houston, TX 77043
Phone No.: 713-932-6995 (Technical)
Phone No.: 800-331-5718 (Orders only)
Fax No.: 713-932-1043
Website: www.briley.com

BRNO ARMS
Factory - ZBROJOVKA BRNO, a.s.
Lazaretni 7
656 17 BRNO
CZECH REPUBLIC
Fax No.: 011-42-545-152772
Email: arms.sales@zbrojovka.com

BROCKMAN'S CUSTOM GUNSMITHING
445 Idaho St.
Gooding, Idaho 83330
Phone No.: 208-934-5050
Fax No.: 208-934-5284
Website: www.brockmansrifles.com
Email: Brockman@brockmansrifles.com

A.A. BROWN & SONS GUNMAKERS
1 Snake Lane, Alvechurch
Brimingham, B48 7NT ENGLAND
Fax No.: 011-44-1214452113
Website: www.aabrownandsons.com
Email: robin@aabrownandsons.com

DAVID MCKAY BROWN GUNMAKERS, LTD.
32 Hamilton Road, Bothwell
Glasgow, SCOTLAND (U.K.) G71 8NA
Fax No.: 011-44-141-1698-854207
Website: www.mckaybrown.com
Email: info@mckaybrown.com

ED BROWN CUSTOM, INC.
(Rifles Only)
P.O. Box 492
43825 Muldrow Trail
Perry, MO 63462
Phone No.: 573-565-3261
Fax No.: 573-565-2791
Website: www.edbrown.com
Email: rifles@edbrown.com

ED BROWN PRODUCTS, INC.
(Pistols only)
P.O. Box 492
43825 Muldrow Trail
Perry, MO 63462
Phone No.: 573-565-3261
Fax No.: 573-565-2791
Website: www.edbrown.com
Email: 1911@edbrown.com

BROWN PRECISION, INC.
P.O. Box 270 W
7786 Molinos Avenue
Los Molinos, CA 96055
Phone No.: 530-384-2506
Fax No.: 530-384-1638
Website: www.brownprecision.com

BROWNING
Administrative Headquarters
One Browning Place
Morgan, UT 84050-9326
Phone No.: 801-876-2711
Product Service: 800-333-3288
Fax No.: 801-876-3331
Website: www.browning.com or www.browningint.com
Custom Shop U.S. Representative
Mr. Ron McGhie
Email: ronm@browning.com
Browning Parts and Service
3005 Arnold Tenbrook Rd.
Arnold, MO 63010-9406
Phone No.: 800-322-4626
Fax No.: 636-287-9751
Historical Research (Browning Arms Co. marked guns only)
Browning Historian
One Browning Place
Morgan, UT 84050-9326
Fax No.: 801-876-3331
Website: www.browning.com

BRUCHET
Please refer to Darne listing.

BRYCO ARMS
Distributor - Jennings Firearms, Inc.
P.O. Box 20135
3680 Research Way
Carson City, NV 89721
Phone No.: 800-518-1666
Fax No.: 702-882-3129

BUL TRANSMARK LTD.
Importer – please refer to KBI listing.
Factory - Bul Transmark Ltd.
10 Rival Street
Tel-Aviv 67778, ISRAEL
Fax No.: 011-972-3-687-4853
Website: www.bultransmark.com
Email: info@bultransmark.com

BUTTERFIELD & BUTTERFIELD (AUCTIONS)
Main Gallery & Corporate Office
220 San Bruno Ave.
San Francisco, CA 94103
Phone No.: 415-861-7500
Fax No.: 415-861-8951
Website: www.butterfields.com

BUSHMASTER FIREARMS
P.O. Box 1479
999 Roosevelt Trail
Windham, ME 04062
Phone No.: 800-883-6229
Fax No.: 207-892-8068
Website: www.bushmaster.com
Email: info@bushmaster.com

C Z (CESKA ZBROJOVKA)
Firearms & Airguns Importer - CZ-USA
P.O. Box 171073
Kansas City, KS 66117-0073
Phone No.: 913-321-1811
Toll Free No.: 800-955-4486
Fax No.: 913-321-2251
Website: www.cz-usa.com
Email: info@cz-usa.com
Administration Offices - Ceska Zbrojovka
Svatopluka Cecha 1283
CZ-68827 Uhersky Brod
CZECH REPUBLIC
Fax No.: 011-420-63363-3811
Website: www.czub.cz
Email: info@czub.cz

CZ (STRAKONICE)
Importer - Please refer Adco Sales listing.
Factory - CZ Stojirna s.r.o.
Tovarni 202
CZ-386 01 Strakonice CZECH REPUBLIC
Email: cz_strojirna@pvtnet.cz

CBC
Av. Humberto de Campos 3220
09426 900 Ribeirao Pires SP BRAZIL
Fax No.: 011-55-11-4822-8323
Website: www.cbc.com.br

CABELAS INC.
One Cabela Dr.
Sidney, NE 69160
Phone No.: 800-237-4444
Fax No.: 800-496-6329
Web Site: www.cabelas.com

RENATO CAEM
Factory
via Indipendenza 55
25060 Marcheno, Brescia, ITALY
Phone/Fax No.: 011-39-030-861142

CAESAR GUERINI, s.r.l.
Importer - Caesar Guerini USA LLC
700 Lake Street
Cambridge, MD 21613
Phone No.: 410-901-1131
Fax No.: 410-901-1137
Website:www.gueriniusa.com
Email: info@gueriniusa.com
Factory
Via Parte, 33
I-25060 Marcheno VT Brescia, ITALY
Fax No.: 011-39-030-8966147
Website: www.caesarguerini.it
Email: info@caesarguerini.it

CASPIAN ARMS, LTD.
P.O. Box 465
Hardwick, VT 05843-0465
Phone No.: 802-472-6454
Fax No.: 802-472-6709
Website: www.caspianarms.com
Email: caspianarm@aol.com

CASULL ARMS CORPORATION
P.O. Box 1629
Afton, WY 83110
Phone No.: 307-886-0200
Fax No.: 307-886-0300
Website: www.casullarms.com
Email: email@casullarms.com

CAVARLY ARMS CORPORATION
723 W. Commerce Ave. Ste. A
Gilbert, AZ 85233
Phone No.: 480-833-9685
Fax No.: 480-497-4002
Website: www.cavalryarms.com
Email: scout@cavalryarms.com

CENTURY INTERNATIONAL ARMS, INC.
430 Congress Ave., Ste. 1
Delray Beach, FL 33445
Phone No.: 800-991-4867
Phone No.: 561-265-4530
Fax No.: 561-265-4520
Website: www.centuryarms.com
Email: support@centuryarms.com

CHAMPIONS CHOICE, INC.
201 International Blvd.
LaVergne, TN 37086
Phone No.: (Orders Only) 800-345-7179
Phone No.: 615-793-4066
Fax No.: 615-793-4070
Email: champchoice@nashville.com

CHAMPLIN FIREARMS, INC.
P.O. Box 3191
Enid, OK 73702
Phone No.: 580-237-7388
Fax No.: 580-242-6922
Website: www.champlinarms.com
Email: info@champlinarms.com

CHAPUIS ARMES
Importer - Please refer to William Larkin Moore listing.
Importer - Chadick's, Ltd.
P.O. Box 100
119 Moore Ave.
Terrell, TX 75160
Phone No.: 972-563-7577
Fax No.: 972-563-1265
Website: www.doubleguns.com
Email: chadicksltd@aol.com
Factory - Chapuis Armes
Z.I. La Gravoux, BP 15
F-42380 St. Bonnet le Chateau, FRANCE
Fax No.: 011-33-4-77-501070
Website: www.chapuis-armes.com
Email: info@chapuis-armes.com

CHAPUIS, P. ARMES ET FILS
Le Mont Mille, BP 12
F-42380 St. Bonnet le Chateau FRANCE
Fax No.: 011-33-47750-7027

CHARTER 2000, INC.
273 Canal St.
Shelton, CT 06484
Phone No.: 203-922-1652
Fax No.: 203-922-1469
Website: www.charterfirearms.com

CHERRY'S FINE GUNS
3402-A West Wendover Avenue
Greensboro, NC 27407
Phone No.: 336-854-4182
Fax No.: 336-854-4184
Website: www.cherrys.com
Email: fineguns@cherrys.com

CHEYTAC
185 Arco Ave.
Arco, ID 83213
Toll Free: 888-807-8611
Phone No.: 208-527-8614
Fax No.: 208-527-8613
Website: www.cheytac.com

CHIPMUNK RIFLES
Factory - Rogue Rifle Co., Inc.
1140 36th St. N Ste. B
Lewiston, ID 83501
Phone No.: 208-743-4355
Fax No.: 208-743-4163
Website: www.roguerifle.com
Email: customerservice@roguerifle.com

CHRISTENSEN ARMS
192 East 100 North
Fayette, UT 84630
Phone No.: 435-528-7999
Fax No.: 435-528-7494
Website: www.christensenarms.com
Email: sales@christensenarms.com

CHRISTIE'S (AUCTIONS)
Rockefeller Center
20 Rockefeller Plaza
New York, NY 10020
Phone No.: 212-636-2000
Fax No.: 212-636-2399
Website: www.christies.com

E.J. CHURCHILL (GUNMAKERS)
U.S. Agent - please refer to Fieldsport listing.
Factory
Park Lane, Lane End, High Wycombe
Buckinghamshire, HP14 3NS ENGLAND
Phone No.: 011-44-1494-883066
Fax. No.: 011-44-1494-883215
Website: www.ejchurchill.com
Email: info@ejchurchill.com

CIMARRON, F.A. CO., INC.
105 Winding Oaks
Fredericksburg, TX 78624-0906
Phone No.: 830-997-9090
Fax No.: 830-997-0802
Website: www.cimarron-firearms.com
Email: cimarron@fbg.net

CLARK CUSTOM GUNS, INC.
336 Shootout Lane
Princeton, LA 71067
Phone No.: 318-949-9884
Toll Free Order No.: 888-458-4126
Fax No.: 318-949-9829
Web Site: www.clarkcustomguns.com
Email: clarkguns@prysm.net

COBB MANUFACTURING, INC.
P.O. Box 88
Dallas, GA 30132
Phone No.: 770-505-3080
Fax No.: 770-505-3007
Website: www.cobb50.com
Email: sales@cobb50.com

COBRA ENTERPRISES OF UTAH, INC.
1960 S. Milestone Drive, Ste. F
Salt Lake City, UT 84104
Phone No.: 801-908-8300
Fax No.: 801-908-8301
Website: www.cobrapistols.com
Email: cobrapistols@networld.com

CODY FIREARMS MUSEUM
720 Sheridan Ave.
Cody, WY 82414
Historical Research Phone No.: 307-578-4031
$20 minimum research fee
Website: www.bbhc.org

COGSWELL & HARRISON LTD.
Heathcliffe, Parkers Lane
Maidens Green, Bracknell
Bershire, ENGLAND
Phone No.: 011-44-1344885091
Fax No.: 011-44-1344890906
Website: www.cogswell.co.uk
Email: cogswellandharrison@barclays.net

COLE GUNSMITHING
21 Bog Hollow Rd.
Harpswell, ME 04079
Phone No.: 207-833-5027
Fax No.: 207-833-5677

COLT'S MANUFACTURING CO., INC.
Factory
P.O. Box 1868
Hartford, CT 06144-1868
Phone No.: 800-962-COLT
Fax No.: 860-244-1449
Website: www.colt.com
Historical Research - Colt Archive Properties LLC
P.O. Box 1868
Hartford, CT 01644-1868
If mailing in a request, make sure the proper research fee is enclosed (please refer to appropriate Colt section for current fees and related information).
1st and 2nd Generation phone service only
Phone no: 800-962-COLT
(Ask for Historical Dept. Research fees start at $150.)
Colt Cavalry & Artillery Revolver Authentication Service
Mr. John Kopec, Historian
Phone: 530-222-4440
Email: coltauthenticity@aol.com

COMANCHE
Master Distributor – SGS Imports Int'l, Inc.
1750 Brielle Ave., Unit B-1
Wanamassa, NJ 07712
Phone No.: 732-493-0302
Fax No.: 732-493-0301
Email: gsodini@aol.com

COMPETITOR CORPORATION
26 Knight Street, Unit 3
P.O. Box 352
Jaffrey, NH 03452
Phone No.: 603-532-9483
Fax No.: 603-532-8209
Website: www.competitor-pistol.com
Email: Competitorcorp@aol.com

CONCO ARMS INTERNATIONAL
P.O. Box 159
Emmaus, PA 18049
Phone/Fax No.: 610-967-5477

CONNECTICUT SHOTGUN MANUFACTURING COMPANY
P.O. Box 1692
35 Woodland St.
New Britain, CT 06501-1692
Phone No.: 860-225-6581
Fax No.: 860-832-8707
Website: www.connecticutshotgun.com
Email: Galazan@msn.com

CONQUEST
MK Vertriebs-Gesellschaft
Am Tairnbacher Weg 14
Dielheim D-69234 GERMANY
Fax No.: 011-49-06222-7721-35
Website: www.mk-v.de
Email: conquest@mk-v.de

COOPER FIREARMS OF MONTANA, INC.
P.O. Box 114
4004 Hwy. 93 North
Stevensville, MT 59870
Phone No.: 406-777-0373
Fax No.: 406-777-5228
Website: www.cooperfirearms.com
Email: cooper@bigsky.net

CORSON'S BARRELS
(Shotgun barrels only)
2124 Pawnee Drive
Kingman, AZ 86401
Phone: 928-718-4282
Website: www.corsonbarrels.com
Email: dccorson@citlink.net

COSMI, AMERICO & FIGLIO s.n.c.
Factory
Via Flaminia 307
I-60020 Torrette di Ancona, ITALY
Fax No.: 011-39-071-887008
Website: www.cosmi.com
Email: cosmi@cosmi.net

CRICKETT RIFLE
Keystone Sporting Arms
RD2 Box 20
Milton, PA 17847
Phone No.: 570-742-2777
Fax No.: 570-742-1455
Website: www.crickett.com
Email: crickett@sunlink.net

DCI INDUSTRIES, INC.
Dan Coonan Inc.
Blaine, MN
Website: www.dancoonan.com
Email: slincoln@madmouse.com

DGS, INC.
404 N. Jackson
Casper, WY 82601
Phone No.: 307-237-2414
Email: dalest@trib.com

DPMS, INC.
3312 12th Street SE
St. Cloud, MN 56304
Phone No.: 3202584448
Fax No.: 320-258-4449
Website: www.dpmsinc.com
Email: dpmsinc@aol.com

DSA, INC.
P.O. Box 370
Barrington, IL 60011
Phone No.: 847-277-7258
Fax No.: 847-227-7259
Website: www.dsarms.com
Email: dsarms@earthlink.net

DAEWOO
Importer - please refer to Century International Arms listing.

DAKOTA ARMS, INC.
1310 Industry Road
Sturgis, SD 57785
Phone No.: 605-347-4686
Fax No.: 605-347-4459
Website: www.dakotaarms.com
Email: info@dakotarms.com

DAKOTA SINGLE ACTION REVOLVERS
Importer - please refer to E.M.F. Company listing.

DALVAR OF U.S.A.
Please refer to the Radom listing.

DALY, CHARLES: CURRENT MFG.
Importer - please refer to K.B.I., Inc. listing.
Website: www.charlesdaly.com

DARNE S.A.
Importer - The Drumming Stump, Inc.
P.O. Box 151
Circle Pines, MN 55014
Phone No.: 763-785-7083
Fax No.: 763-434-4897
Email: tedJS@usfamily.net
Factory - Bruchet Darne
4 ter, rue de la Convention
F-42100 Saint Etienne, FRANCE
Phone No.: 011-33-477-370096
Email: darne.fusil.bruchet@wanadoo.fr

DAVID MILLER CO.
3131 E. Greenlee Rd.
Tucson, AZ 85716
Phone No.: 520-326-3117
Fax No.: 520-327-7672

DEFOURNEY
No current information available.

DEMAS, Ets
Importer & Sales - please refer to Verney-Carron listing.
Factory - Atelier Demas
11, rue Agricol Perdiguier
F-42000 St. Etienne, FRANCE
Fax No.: 011-33-0477-813437
Website: www.demas.fr
Email: demas@demas.fr

DETONICS USA
(New mfg. only)
115 Enterprise Dr., Ste. B
Pendergrass, GA 30567
Phone No.: 866-759-1169
Fax No.: 706-693-2228
Website: www.detonicsusa.com
Email: info@detonicsusa.com

J.C. DEVINE, INC. (AUCTIONS)
P.O. Box 413
20 South Street
Milford, NH 03055
Phone No.:603-673-4967
Fax No.: 603-672-0328
Website: www.jcdevine.com
Email: jcdevine@empire.net

DICKSON & MACNAUGHTON
21 Frederick Street
Edinburgh, Scotland UK EH2 2NE
Fax No.: 011-44-131-225-3658
Website: www.gunandline.com
Email: b.wilcox@gunandline.com

JOHN DICKSON & SON
Please refer to the Dickson & MacNaughton listing.

DIXIE GUN WORKS
P.O. Box 130
Union City, TN 38281
Phone No.: 731-885-0700
Fax No.: 731-885-0400
Website: www.dixiegunworks.com
Email: info@dixiegunworks.com

DLASK ARMS CORP.
U.S. Office
P.O. Box 607
683 Peace Portal Dr.
Blaine, WA 98231-0607
Factory
202B 1546 Derwent Way
Delta, British Columbia, V3M 6M4 CANADA
Phone No.: 604-527-9942
Fax No.: 604-527-9982
Website: www.dlask.com
Email: dlask@attglobal.net

DOUBLESTAR CORPORATION
Box 430
Winchester, KY 40391
Phone No.: 859-745-1757
Fax No.: 859-745-4638
Website: www.star15.com
Website: www.jtdistributing.com
Email: sales@star15.com

DOWNSIZER CORPORATION
P.O. Box 710316
Santee, CA 92072-0316
Phone No.: 619-448-5510
Website: www.downsizer.com

DUCKS UNLIMITED, INC.
One Waterfowl Way
Memphis, TN 38120-2351
Phone No.: 901-758-3825
Fax No.: 901-758-3850
Web Site: www.ducks.org

DUMOULIN, ERNEST S.P.R.L.
Importer - please refer to Empire Rifle Company listing.
Factory
Rue du Bouxthay 41
B-4041 Vottem-Herstal, BELGIUM
Fax No.: 011-32-41-228-89-69
Website: www.dumoulin-herstal.com
Email: contact@dumoulin-herstal.be

DUMOULIN, HENRI & FILS
Factory - Dumoulin, Henri & Fils
60 rue Hubert Streel
Herstal 4432, BELGIUM
Fax No.: 011-32-49-252-3937
Email: aukesyh@hotmail.com

DUMOULIN HERSTAL S.A.
Importer - please refer to Empire Rifle Company listing.
Factory
Rue du Tige 13
B-4041 Herstal, BELGIUM
Fax No.: 011-32-41-228-89-69
Website: www.dumoulin-herstal.com
Email: contact@dumoulin-herstal.be

DYNAMIT NOBEL
A division of RUAG Ammotec GmbH
81 Ruckman Road
Closter, NJ 07624
Phone No.: 201-767-1995
Fax No.: 201-767-1589
Website: www.dnrws.com
Factory - Dynamit Nobel Ammo Tec GmbH
Kronacher Strasse 63
Furth D-90765 GERMANY
Fax No.: 011-49-180-279-7797
Email: info@ammotec@ruag.com

E.D.M. ARMS
421 Business Ctr. Ct.
Redlands, CA 92374
Phone No.: 909-798-2770
Fax No.: 909-798-2889
Website: www.edmarms.com
Email: windruner@hotmail.net

E.M.F. COMPANY
1900 E. Warner Ave., Suite 1-D
Santa Ana, CA 92705
Phone No.: 949-261-6611
Fax No.: 949-756-0133
Website: www.emf-company.com
Email: sales@emf-company.com

EAGLE ARMS INC.
P.O. Box 146
Geneseo, IL 61254
Phone No.: 309-944-6977
Fax No.: 309-944-6978
Website: www.eagle-arms.com
Email: info@eagle-arms.com

EFFEBI snc
Importer - American Outdoor Adventures
1335 US Hwy 82 W
Leesburg, GA 31763-5334
Phone No.: 229-434-0539
Fax No.: 229-434-4672
Website: www.aoaworld.com
Email: wayne@aoaworld.com
Factory
Via Rossa, 4
I-25062 Concesio (BS) ITALY
Fax No.: 011-39-030-2180414
Website: www.effebi.org
Website: www.effebisnc.it
Email: info@effebisnc.it

EGO ARMAS, S.A.
Victor Sarasqueta, 1-4
Apartado 56
E-20600 Eibar (Guipuzkoa) SPAIN
Fax No.: 011-34-43-120463
Website: www.artesanosego.com
Email: info@artesanosego.com

EMPIRE RIFLE COMPANY LLC
36 Jenney Road, P.O. Box 406
Meriden, NH 03770
Phone No.: 603-469-3152
Fax No.: 603-619-8918
Website: www.empirerifles.com
Email: info@empirerifles.com

ENTRÉPRISE ARMS INC.
15861 Business Center Dr.
Irwindale, CA 91706
Phone No.: 626-962-8712
Fax No.: 626-962-4692
Websites: www.entreprise.com

ERMA SUHL, GmbH
Schutzenstrasse 26
D-98527 Suhl, GERMANY
Fax No.: 011-49-3681-854-203

ESCALADE
Importer - please refer to Mitchell's Mausers listing.

ESCORT
Importer - please refer to Legacy Sports International listing.
Factory
Hatsan Arms Company
1. Sanayi Sitsei 2835 No. 3
Izmir, TURKEY
Fax No.: 011-09232-458-1999
Website: www.hatsan.com
Email: info@hatsan.com

ESSEX ARMS
(Parts)
Box 345
Island Pond, VT 05846
Phone No.: 802-723-4313
Fax No.: 802-723-6203

EUROARMS OF AMERICA
208 East Piccadilly Street
P.O. Box 3277
Winchester, VA 22604
Phone No.: 540-662-1863
Fax No.: 540-662-4464
Website: www.euroarms.net
Email: tell-us@euroarms.net
Factory - Euroarms Italia Srl (formerly Armi San Paolo)
via Europa 172/A
I-25062 Concesio, (BS) ITALY
Phone No.: 011-39-030-275-1725
Fax No.: 011-39-30-218-0365
Website: www.euroarms.net
Email: info@euroarms.net

EUROPEAN AMERICAN ARMORY CORP.
P.O. Box 1299
Sharpes, FL 32953
Phone No.: 321-639-4842
Fax No.: 321-639-7006
Website: www.eaacorp.com
Email: eaacorp@bv.net

EVOLUTION USA
P.O. Box 154
White Bird, ID 83554
Phone No.: 208-983-9208
Fax No. 208-983-0944
Website: www.evo-rifles.com
Email: evorifle@camasnet.com

EXCEL INDUSTRIES, INC.
4510 Carter Court
Chino, CA 91710
Phone No.: 909-627-2404
Fax No.: 909-627-7817
Website: www.excelarms.com
Email: info@excelarms.com

F.A.I.R. S.r.l.
Factory - Fabbrica Armi Isidoro Rizzini
Via Gitti, 41
I-25060 Marcheno (BS) ITALY
Fax No.: 011-39-030-861-0179
Website: www.fair.it
Email: info@fair.it

F.A.V.S.
Factory – Fabbrica Armi Valle Susa
Via Nazionale 35
10050 Villar Focchiardo (To) ITALY
Fax No.: 011-39-9645496
Website: www.favsarmi.com
Email: info@favsarmi.com

FAS
Factory
Domino via Galilei
1-20010 Cornaredo, ITALY
Fax No.: 011-39-0293649570
Website: www.fasdomino.com
Email: info@fasdomino.com

FEG
Importer - please refer to Century International Arms, Inc. listing.
Website: www.fegarms.com
Factory - FEGARMY
1095 Budapest, Soroksari ut 158
Levelcim: H-1440 Budapest Pf. 6 HUNGARY
Fax No.: 011-361-280-6669

FIAS
Please refer to the Sabatti Armi listing.

FN HERSTAL S.A.
Importer - FNH USA, Inc.
P.O. Box 697
McLean, VA 22101
Phone No.: 703-288-1292
Fax No.: 703-288-1730
Website: www.fnhusa.com
Email: info@fnhusa.com
Military Only
P.O. Box 869
McLean, VA 22101
Phone No.: 703-288-3500
Fax No.: 703-288-4505
Factory - F.N. Herstal S.A.
Voie de Liege, 33
Herstal, Belgium B4040
Fax No.: 011-324-240-8679
Website: www.fnherstal.com

FABARM S.p.A.
Importer - please refer to SIG Arms listing.
Factory - Fabbrica Breciana Armi
Via Averolda 31, Zona Industriale
I-25039 Travagliato, Brescia ITALY
Fax No.: 011-39-030-6863684
Website: www.fabarm.com

FABBRI s.n.c.
Factory
Via Dante Alighieri, 29
I-25062 Concesio (BS) ITALY
Fax No.: 011-39-030-218-7301
Website: www.fabbri.it
Email: info@fabbri.it

FABRIQUE NATIONALE
Factory - Browning S.A.
Fabrique Nationale Herstal SA
Parc Industriel des Hauts Sarts
3me Ave. 25
B-4040 Herstal, BELGIUM
Fax No.: 011-32-42-40-5212

FALCO, s.r.l.
Factory
via Gitti, 37
I-25060 Marcheno (Brescia) ITALY
Fax No.: 011-39-30-861-267
Website: www.falcoarms.com
Email: falco@intred.com

FAMARS di ABBIATICO & SALVINELLI srl
Distributor – Robin Hollow Outfitters
Addieville East Farm
200 B Pheasant Dr.
Mapleville, RI 02839
Phone No.: 401-568-0331
Fax No.: 401-568-0264
Website: www.robinhollow.com
Email: RHOAddieville@aol.com
Importer - please refer to William Larkin Moore listing.
Importer - please refer to Fieldsport listing.
Factory
Via Valtrompia 16/18
25063 Gardone, V.T. Brescia ITALY
Fax No.: 011-39-030-8912894
Website: www.famars.com
Email: info@famars.com

FANZOJ, JOHANN
Factory - Fanzoj Jagdwaffen GmbH
Greisgasse 1
9170 Ferlach, AUSTRIA
Fax No.: 011-43-4227-2867
Website: www.fanzoj.com
Email: jfanzoj@aon.at

FAUSTI, STEFANO SRL
Importer - please refer to Traditions Performance Firearms listing.
Factory
Via Martiri Dell'Indipendenza, 70
I-25060 Marcheno (Brescia) ITALY
Fax No.: 011-39-030-861-0155
Website: www.faustistefanoarms.com
Email: info@faustistefanoarms.com

FEATHER USA
600 Oak Avenue
P.O. Box 247
Eaton, CO 80615
Phone No.: 800-519-0485
Fax No.: 970-206-1958
Website: www.featherusa.com

FEINWERKBAU
Factory - Westinger & Altenburger GmbH
Neckarstrasse 43
D-78727 Oberndorf/Neckar GERMANY
Fax No.: 011-49-7423-814-223
Website: www.feinwerkbau.de
Email: info@feinwerkbau.de

FERLIB
U.S. Importer of SxS rifles - please refer to Dakota Arms listing.
Factory
via Parte 33
I-25060 Marcheno BS ITALY
Fax No. 011-39-030-8966882
Website: www.ferlib.com
Email: info@ferlib.com

FIELDSPORT
3313 W. South Airport Road
Traverse City, MI 49684
Phone No.: 616-933-0767 or 616-933-0768
Website: www.fieldsportltd.com

FIREARMS INTERNATIONAL INC.
5200 Mitchelldale, Suite E-17
Houston, TX 77092
Phone No.: 713-462-4200
Fax No.: 713-681-5665
Website: www.highstandard.com
Email: info@highstandard.com

FIRESTORM
Master Distributor – SGS Imports Int'l, Inc.
1750 Brielle Ave., Unit B-1
Wanamassa, NJ 07712
Phone No.: 732-493-0302
Fax No.: 732-493-0301
Website: www.firestorm-sgs.com
Email: firestormsgs@aol.com

FIOCCHI OF AMERICA, INC.
(Ammunition & Components)
5030 Fremont Rd.
Ozark, MO 65721
Phone No.: 417-725-4118
Fax No.: 417-725-1039
Factory - Fiocchi Munizioni S.P.A.
Via Santa Barbara, 4
I-22053 Lecco ITALY
Fax No.: 011-39-341/281-171

FLODMAN GUNS SWEDEN
Skullman Enterprise AB
640 60 Akers Styckebruk
Jarsta SWEDEN
Fax No.: 011-46-159-30061
Website: www.flodman.com
Email: virve@flodman.com

A.H. FOX
Current mfg. only – please refer to Connecticut Shotgun Manufacturing Co. listing.
Older A.H. Fox Historical Research
Mr. John Callahan
53 Old Quarry Rd.
Westfield, MA 01085
$25.00 - $30.00 gun research fee.

FRANCHI, LUIGI
Importer - please refer to Benelli USA listing.
Website: www.franchiusa.com

Factory - Franchi, Luigi, S.p.A.
Via del Serpente, 12
I-25131 Fornaci (Brescia) ITALY
Fax No.: 011-39-30-3581554
Website: www.franchi.com
Email: info@franchi.com

FRASER, DANL. & CO.
Please refer to the Dickson & MacNaughton listing.

FREEDOM ARMS
P.O. Box 150
314 Hwy. 239
Freedom, WY 83120
Phone No.: 307-883-2468
Fax No.: 307-883-2005
Website: www.freedomarms.com
Email: freedom@freedomarms.com

FULTON ARMORY
8725 Bollman Place #1
Savage, MD 20763
Phone No.: 301-490-9485
Fax No.: 301-490-9547
Website: www.fulton-armory.com

GALAZAN
Please refer to Connecticut Shotgun Manufacturing Co. listing.

GALIL
No current U.S. importation - semi-auto rifle configuration was banned April, 1998.

GAMBA, RENATO
Exclusive Importer and Distributor – Renato Gamba U.S.A. Corp.
P.O. Box 615
Walnut, CA 91788-0615
Website: www.renatogambausa.com
Email: info@renatogambausa.com
U.S. Service Center
33 Claremont Road
Bernardsville, NJ 07924
Phone No.: 908-766-2287
Fax No.: 908-766-1068
Factory - S.A.B. s.r.l. - Renato Gamba
Via Artigiani, 91/93
I-25063 Gardone V.T. (Brescia), ITALY
Fax No.: 011-39-030-8912-180
Website: www.renatogamba.it
Email: infocomm@renatogamba.it

GARBI
Importer - please refer to William Larkin Moore & Co. listing.
Factory - Armas Garbi
Urki, 12-14
E-20600 Eibar, SPAIN

GARRAY RIFLES, LTD.
P.O. Box 29099
OK Mission RPO
Kelowna, BC CANADA V1W 4A2
Phone No.: 250-764-0712
Fax No.: 250-764-0728
Website: www.GarRay.com

GATEWAY PRECISION ARMS
8301 Crest Industrial Drive, Ste. C
Affton, MO 63123
Phone No.: 314-832-4005
Fax No.: 314-832-4006
Email: gatehose@mindspring.com

GATLING GUN COMPANY
Manufacturer and distributor - Furr Arms
485 South Commerce Road
Orem, UT 84058
Phone No.: 801-226-3877

GAUCHER
Please refer to Bretton-Gaucher listing.
GAZELLE ARMS
Importer & Distributor - Ema Distributors LLC
10809 Southern Loop Blvd. #7
Pineville, NC 28134
Phone No.: 866-GAZELLE
Website: www.gazellearms.com
Email: sales@gazellearms.com
Factory - Hisar Avcilik & Doga Sporlasi San Ve Tic. Ltd. Sti.
Sokak No. 48
Konak/Izmir, 861
TR-35250 TURKEY
Fax No.: 011-90-0232-441-6667
Website: www.hisarexport.com
Email: hisaras@ixir.com
GENTRY, DAVID - CUSTOM GUNMAKER
314 N. Hoffman
Belgrade, MT 59714
Phone No.: 406-388-GUNS
Website: www.gentrycustom.com
GIANI, VITTORIO
Via Dante, 163
Ponte Zanano (BS), ITALY I-25068
Fax No.: 011-39-030-8908079
Website: www.mag.it
Email: info@mag.it
GIBBS RIFLE CO.
219 Lawn St.
Martinsburg, WV 25401
Phone No.: 304-2629870
Fax No.: 304-262-1658
Website: www.gibbsrifle.com
GIL, ANTONIO & CO.
Factory
C/Ibargain, 8-2
Eibar (Guipuzcoa), SPAIN 20600
Fax No.: 011-34-943-700699
GLOCK, INC.
Importer
6000 Highlands Pkwy.
Smyrna, GA 30082
Fax No.: 770-433-8719
Website: www.glock.com
Factory - Glock Ges.m.b.H.
Nelkengasse 3, POB 9
A-2232 Deutsch-Wagram AUSTRIA
Fax No.: 011-43-2247-90300312
GRANGER, G.
U.S. Agent - Jean-Jacques Perodeau
P.O. Box 3191
Woodring Municipal Airport
Enid, OK 73702
Phone No.: 580-237-7388
Fax No.: 580-242-6922
Factory
66 Cours Fauriel
F-42100 St. Etienne FRANCE
Fax No.: 011-33-0477-38-66-99
GRANITE MOUNTAIN ARMS, INC.
1725 W. Williams Drive, Ste. 23
Phoenix, AZ 85027
Phone No.: 623-434-3404
Email: GMAHUNTER@aol.com
GRANT, STEPHEN
Factory - please refer to Atkin, Grant & Lang listing.

GREG MARTIN AUCTIONS
298 San Bruno Ave.
San Francisco, CA 94103
Phone No.: 800-509-1988
Phone No.: 415-522-5708
Fax No.: 415-522-5706
Website: www.gmartin-auctions.com
Email: info@gmartin-auctions.com
GREENER, W. W.
Sales/Administration Offices
Poachers Pocket, Stoppers Hill, Brinkworth
Chippenham, Wiltshire, SN15 5AW ENGLAND
Fax No.: 011-44-1666-510898
Website: www.wwgreener.com
Email: sales@wwgreener.com
Factory
The Mews, Hagley Hall
Hagley DY9 9LG ENGLAND
GRIFFIN & HOWE
Store Location (Gunsmithing also)
33 Claremont Road
Bernardsville, NJ 07924
Phone No.: 908-766-2287
Fax No.: 908-766-1068
Website: www.griffinhowe.com
Email: prather@griffinhowe.com
Store Location
340 West Putnam Ave.
Greenwich, CT 06830
Phone No.: 203-618-0270
Fax No.: 203-618-0419
Website: www.griffinhowe.com
Shooting School & Events
270 Stanhope Rd.
Andover, NJ 07821
Phone No.: 973-398-4330
GRIFFON
European Distributor
Kung GmbH
Amtshausgasse 2
Liestal, Switzerland CH-4410
Fax No.: 011-41-061-922-1245
Manufacturer - Continental Weapons (Pty) Ltd.
322 15th St. Randjespark
Midrand 1685, Johannesburg, South Africa
Phone No.: 011-27-11-314-5088
Fax No.: 011-27-11-314-5050
GRULLA ARMAS, S.L.
Importer/Dealer - please refer to Fieldsport listing.
Importer/Dealer - please refer to GSI listing.
Importer /Dealer– please refer to Harry Marx Hi-Grade Import listing.
Importer/Dealer - please refer to Lion Country Supply listing.
Importer/Dealer - Dale Decoys Den
5474 State Street
Albany, OH 45710
Phone No.: 614-698-5060
Factory - Grulla Armas
P.O. Box 453
Avda. de Otaola, 12
E-20600 Eibar (Guipuzcoa) SPAIN
Fax No.: 011-34-9-43-702133
Website: www.grullarmas.com
Email: usobiaga@grullaarmas.com

GRÜNIG & ELMIGER AG
U.S. representative - please refer to Gunsmithing, Inc. listing.
U.S. representative - Brenzovich Firearms Training Center
22301 Old Texas
Ft. Hancock, TX 79839
Phone/Fax No.: 915-764-2030
Website: www.brenzovich.com
Email: GunChamp@aol.com
Factory
Industriestr. 22
CH-6102 Malters SWITZERLAND
Fax No.: 011-041-499-9049
Website: www.gruenel.ch
Email: gruenel@gruenel.ch

GUN SOUTH, INC. (GSI)
P.O. Box 129
7661 Commerce Lane
Trussville, AL 35173
Phone No.: 205-655-8299
Fax No.: 205-655-7078
Website: www.GSIfirearms.com
Email: info@GSIfirearms.com

G.U. INC.
Please refer to SKB Shotguns listing.

GUNSMITHING INC.
30 West Buchanan Street
Colorado Springs, CO 80907
Phone No.: 800-284-8671
Fax No.: 719-632-3493
Website: www.nealjguns.com
Email: neal@nealjguns.com

HHF
Please refer to Huglu listing.

H & R 1871, LLC
Harrington & Richardson (post-1991 mfg. only)
60 Industrial Rowe
Gardner, MA 01440
Phone No.: 978-632-9393
Fax No.: 978-632-2300
Website: www.hr1871.com
Email: hr1871@hr1871.com

H-S PRECISION, INC.
1301 Turbine Dr.
Rapid City, SD 57703
Phone No.: 605-341-3006
Fax No.: 605-342-8964
Website: www.hsprecision.com

HABSBURG, LINIE
Griesgasse 3
A-9170 Ferlach Austria
Fax No.: 011-43-4227-533630
Website: www.linie-habsburg.com
Email: ferlach@liniehabsburg.com

HAMBRUSCH JAGDWAFFEN GmbH
Importer - please refer to CONCO Arms International
Factory - Hambrusch Jagdwaffen Gesellschaft
Gartengasse 4
A-9170 Ferlach, AUSTRIA
Fax No.: 011-43-4227/4106
Website: www.ferlachguns.com
Email: hambrush@ferlachguns.com

HÄMMERLI AG
Importer - please refer to SIG Arms Inc. listing
Website: www.sigarms.com
Importer - please refer to Champion's Choice listing.
Importer, Sales & Service - please refer to
Larry's Guns Inc. listing.
Importer - please refer to Gunsmithing, Inc. listing.
Repair/Gunsmithing Services - HÄMMERLI AG
10-Ring-Service, Inc.
2227 West Lou Drive
Jacksonville, FL 32216
Phone No.: 904-724-7419
Fax No.: 904-724-7149
Factory - Hämmerli AG
Industrieplaz
8212 Neuhausen
a/Rheinfall, SWITZERLAND
Website: www.haemmerli.ch
Email: info@haemmerli.ch

HARRISON & HUSSEY
Please refer to Cogswell & Harrison listing.

HARRY MARX HI-GRADE IMPORTS
8707 Monterey Road
P.O. Box 519
Gilroy, CA 95021
Phone No.: 408-846-1111 or 408-846-8500
Fax No.: 408-842-7270 or 408-842-9323
Website: www.higradeimports.com
Website: www.harrymarx.com
Email: Hi-gradeimports@mindspring.com

HARTFORD ARMORY
Distributor - please refer to Taylor's & Co., Inc. listing.
100-B Main St.
Collinsville, CT 06019-3133
Phone No.: 860-693-8932
Website: www.hartfordarmory.com

HARTMANN & WEISS GmbH
Rahlstedter Bahnhofstr. 47
22143 Hamburg, GERMANY
Phone No.: 011-49-40-677-5585
Fax No.: 011-49-40-677-5592
Email: hartmannundweiss@t-online.de

HATFIELD'S
2028 Frederick Ave.
St. Joseph, MO 64501
Phone No.: 816-233-9106

KARL HAUPTMANN JAGDWAFFEN
Bahnhofstrasse 5
A-9170 Ferlach, AUSTRIA
Fax No.: 011-43-4227-3435
Website: www.hauptmann-rifles.com
Email: office@hauptmann-rifles.com

HASKELL MFG. INC.
Please refer to Hi-Point listing.

HECKLER & KOCH, INC.
U.S. Headquarters
21480 Pacific Blvd.
Sterling, VA 20166-8903
Phone No.: 703-450-1900
Fax No.: 703-450-8160
Website: www.hecklerkoch-usa.com
Factory - Heckler & Koch GmbH
Alte Steige 7
P.O. Box 1329
D-78727 Oberndorf Neckar GERMANY
Fax No.: 011-49-7423-7922-80
Website: www.heckler-koch.de

HEINIE SPECIALTY PRODUCTS
301 Oak Street
Quincy, IL 62301
Phone No.: 217-228-952
Fax No.: 217-228-9502
Website: www.heinie.com
Email: rheinie@heinie.com

HENDRY, RAMSAY & WILCOX
55/57 North Methven Street
Perth PH1 5PX, SCOTLAND
Phone No.: 01-738-623679
Fax No.: 01-738-443327

HENRY, ALEX
Please refer to the Dickson & MacNaughton listing.

HENRY REPEATING ARMS COMPANY
110 8th St.
Brooklyn, NY 11215
Phone No.: 718-499-5600
Fax No.: 718-768-8056
Website: www.henry-guns.com

HERITAGE MANUFACTURING, INC.
4600 NW 135th St.
Opa Locka, FL 33054
Phone No.: 305-685-5966
Fax No.: 305-687-6721
Website: www.heritagemfg.com
Email: infohmi@heritagemfg.com

HEYM WAFFENFABRIK GmbH
Importer - please refer to New England Custom Gun Service Ltd. listing.
Importer (Ivory Hunter SxS model only) - PSI
233 N. Court St.
Fayetteville, WV 25840
Phone No.: 304-574-1779
Fax No.: 304-574-1474
Email: truett@kapsoptik.com
Factory
Am Aschenbach 2
D-98646 Gleichamberg GERMANY
Fax No.: 011-49-368-75-63222
Website: www.heym-waffenfabrik.de
Email: heym-waffenfabrik@t-online.de

HI-POINT FIREARMS
U.S. Marketer - MKS Supply, Inc.
8611-A North Dixie Drive
Dayton, OH 45414
Phone No.: 877-425-4867
Fax No.: 937-454-0503
Website: www.hi-pointFirearms.com
Email: mkshpoint@aol.com

HIGH STANDARD MANUFACTURING CO.
5200 Mitchelldale, Ste. E17
Houston, TX 77092
Phone No.: 713-462-4200
Fax No.: 713-681-5665
Website: www.highstandard.com
Email: info@highstandard.com

HIGH TECH CUSTOMS
31 N. Cascade Ave., Ste. 102
Colorado Springs, CO 80907
Phone No.: 719-667-1090
Fax No.: 719-632-4505
Website: www.htcustoms.com
Email: htcustoms@pcisys.net

HILL COUNTRY RIFLE COMPANY
5726 Morningside Dr.
New Braunfels, TX 78132
Phone No.: 830-609-3139
Fax No.: 830-625-4020
Website: www.hillcountryrifles.com
Email: sales@hillcountryrifles.com

GEORGE HOENIG INC.
6521 Morton Dr.
Boise, ID 83704
Phone No.: 208-375-1116

HOFER-JAGDWAFFEN, PETER
Kirchgasse 24
A-9170 Ferlach, AUSTRIA
Phone No.: 011-43-4227-3683
Fax No.: 011-43-4227-3683-30
Website: www.hoferwaffen.com
Email: peterhofer@hoferwaffen.com

P.L. HOLEHAN, INC.
5758 E. 34th St.
Tucson, AZ 85711
Phone No.: 520-745-0622
Fax No.: 520-745-2248
Email: plholehan@theriver.com

HOLLAND & HOLLAND LTD.
H&H - New York
10 East 40th Street, Ste. 1910
New York, NY 10016
Phone No.: 212-752-7755
Fax No.: 212-752-6975
Website: www.hollandandholland.com
Email: gunroomny@hollandandholland.com
H&H - France
29 Avenue Victor Hugo
F-75116 Paris FRANCE
Phone No.: 011-133-450-22200
Factory
Attn: Customer Service-BB
31-33 Bruton Street
London, ENGLAND W1X 8JS
Phone No.: 011-44-71-499 4411
Fax No.: 011-44-71-499 4544
Email: gunroom@holland-holland.co.uk

HOLLOWAY & NAUGHTON
Please refer to Premier English Shotguns, Ltd. listing.

HORTON, LEW, DIST. CO.
Please refer to Lew Horton Dist. Co. listing.

HOWA
Importer – please refer to Legacy Sports International, LLC listing.

HUGLU
Importer – Armsco
1247 Rand Road
Des Plaines, IL 60016
Phone No.: 847-768-1000
Fax No.: 847-768-1001
Website: www.armsco.net
Email: info@armsco.net
Factory - Huglu Hunting Firearms
Oguzlar Mahallesi
Ceyhun Atif Kansu Cad
56 Sokak No.: 22/3
Balgat, Ankara TURKEY
Fax No.: 011-90-312-287-6747
Website: www.huglu.com.tr
Email: huglu@huglu.com.tr

Warranty & Service – (Huglu USA guns only)
H-Legacy Shotguns, Ltd. Co.
4660 E. 267 N.
Rigby, ID 83442
Phone No.: 208-538-6744
Website: www.h-legacy.com

I.A.B.
Importer - please refer to E.M.F. listing.
Importer - please refer to Dixie Gun Works listing.
Importer - please refer to Tristar listing.
Importer - Kiesler's Firearms
3300 Industrial Parkway
Jeffersonville, IN 47130
Phone No.: 812-288-5740
Factory - Industria Armi Bresciane
Via Matteotti, 311
I-25063 Gardone, Brescia ITALY
Phone/Fax No.: 011-39030-891-2366
Website: www.iabarms.com
Email: info@iabarms.com

IAR, INC.
33171 Camino Capistrano
San Juan Capistrano, CA 92675
Phone No.: 949-443-3642
Fax No.: 949-443-3647
Website: www.iar-arms.com
Email: sales@iar-arms.com

IGA SHOTGUNS
Importer - please refer to Stoeger Industries, Inc. listing.

IBERIA FIREARMS
Please refer to Hi-Point listing.

INFINITY FIREARMS
Distributor - please refer to JP Enterprises listing.
Manufacturer - Strayer Voight, Inc.
3435 Roy Orr Blvd., Ste. 200
Grand Prairie, TX 75050
Phone No.: 972-513-1911
Fax No.: 972-513-0575
Website: www.sviguns.com
Email: info@sviguns.com
Factory - INTERTEX-Maschinenbau GmbH & Co.
Ludwigstrasse 24-28
D-73054 Eislingen GERMANY
Fax no.: 011-49-7161-98-40-5-50
Email: intertex@t-online.de

INTERSTATE ARMS CORP.
6G Dunham Road
Billerica, MA 01821
Phone No.: 800-243-3006
Phone No.: 978-667-7060
Fax No.: 978-671-0023

INTRAC ARMS INTERNATIONAL L.L.C.
Importation & Distribution only - U.S. Headquarters
HS America
5005 Chapman Highway
Knoxville, TN 37920
Phone No.: 865-573-0833
Fax No.: 865-579-0937
European Headquarters
Schlossgasse 12
A-2540 Bad Vuslau, AUSTRIA
Fax No. 011-43-2252-78897

INVESTARM, s.p.a.
Distributor - please refer to Kimber listing.
Factory - Fabbrica D'Armi
via Zanardelli, 20
25060 Marcheno, Brescia ITALY
Fax No.: 011-39-030-861-285
Website: www.investarm.com
Email: info@investarm.com

INVESTMENT ARMS INC.
4631 South Mason, Ste. B3
Fort Collins, CO 80525
Phone No.: 888-708-4867
Fax No.: 970-377-8078
Website: www.investmentarms.com

ISRAELI MILITARY INDUSTRIES
U.S./Canadian importer & distributor - please refer to Magnum Research, Inc. listing
Factory
Website: www.imi-israel.com

ITHACA GUN COMPANY, LLC
901 Route 34B
King Ferry, NY 13081
Phone No.: 888-9-ITHACA
Fax No.: 315-364-5134
Website: www.ithacagun.com

IVER JOHNSON ARMS, INC.
1840 Baldwin Street, Unit 10
Rockledge, FL 32955
Phone No.: 321-636-3377
Fax No.: 321-632-7745

IZHMASH
Factory - Izhmash, Concern OJSC
R-426006. 3 Pr. Deryabinia
Izhevsk, RUSSIA
Website: www.izhmash.ru
Email: itc@izhmash.ru

J.L.D. ENTERPRISES, INC.
U.S. Representative - Vincent Pestilli & Associates
193 Sam Brown Hill Rd.
Brownfield, ME 04010
Phone No.: 207-935-3603
Fax No.: 207-935-3996
Email: vapame@pivot.net
Factory
P.O. Box 562
Unionville, CT 06085
Website: www.jldenter.com
Email: jldent@worldnet.att.net

JP ENTERPRISES, INC.
7605 N. 128th Street
White Bear Lake, MN 55110
Phone No.: 800-528-9886
Fax No.: 651-426-2472
Website: www.jprifles.com
Email: johnpaul@jprifles.com

J R DISTRIBUTING
15634 Tierra Rejada Rd.
Moorpark, CA 93021
Fax No.: 805-529-2368

JAGD-UND SPORTWAFFEN SUHL GmbH
Distributor - please refer to Gun South, Inc. listing.
Factory - please refer to Merkel listing.

JACK FIRST, INC.
Gun Parts/Accessories/Service
1201 Turbine Dr.
Rapid City, SD 57703
Phone No.: 605-343-9544
Fax No.: 605-343-9420

JAMES D. JULIA, INC. (AUCTIONS)
P.O. Box 830, Rte. 201
Skowhegan Rd.
Fairfield, ME 04937
Phone No.: 207-453-7125
Fax No.: 207-453-2502
Website: www.juliaauctions.com

JANZ GmbH
Importer - Rocky Mountain Armoury
591 Blue River Parkway
P.O. Box 1835
Silverthorne, CO 80498
Phone No.: 970-468-5001
Fax No.: 970-262-1499
Email: tekarms@yahoo.com
Factory - JANZ-Technik und Labor GmbH
Lutjenburger Str. 84
D-23714 Malente GERMANY
Fax No.: 011-49-04523-6968
Website: www.jtl.de/revolver
Email: info@jtl.de

JARRETT RIFLES, INC.
383 Brown Road
Jackson, SC 29831
Phone No.: 803-471-3616
Fax No.: 803-471-9246
Website: www.jarrettrifles.com
Email: info@jarrettrifles.com

JEFFERY, W.J. & CO., LTD.
Please refer to the J. Roberts & Son listing.

JENNINGS, B.L., INC.
Please refer to Bryco Arms listing.

JOHANNSEN RIFLES
Factory – Reimer Johannsen GmbH
Haart 49
D-24534 Neumunster GERMANY
Fax No.: 011-49-4321-29325
Website: www.johannsen-jagd.de
Email: info@johannsen-jagd.de

JUST, JOSEF
Hauptplatz 18
A-9170, Ferlach, AUSTRIA
Fax No.: 011-41-04227-4284
Website: www.jagdwaffen-just.at
Email: office@jagdwaffen-just.at

K.B.I., INC.
P.O. Box 6625
5480 Linglestown Road
Harrisburg, PA 17112-0625
Phone No.: 717-540-8518
Fax No.: 717-540-8567
Website: www.kbi-inc.com
Email: sales@kbi-inc.com

KDF, INC.
2485 Highway 46 North
Seguin, TX 78155
Phone No.: 800-KDF-GUNS
Phone No.: 830-379-8141
Fax No.: 830-379-5420
Email: kdfinc@hotmail.com

KAHR ARMS
P.O. Box 220
Blauvelt, NY 10913
Customer Service Phone No.: 508-795-3919
Sales Phone No.: 845-735-4500
Fax No.: 845-735-4610
Website: www.kahr.com
Website: www.kahrshop.com

KEL-TEC CNC INDUSTRIES, INC.
1485 Cox Road
Cocoa, FL 32926
Phone No.: 321-631-0068
Fax No.: 321-631-1169
Website: www.kel-tec.com
Email: aimkeltec@aol.com

KEMEN
Importer - please refer to Fieldsport listing.
Factory - Armas Kemen, S.L.
Ermuraranbide, 14 - Apartado n. 60
20870 Elgoibar (Guipuzcoa), SPAIN
Fax No.: 011-34-43-74-4401
Website: www.sport-kemen.com
Email: kemen@sport-kemen.com

KEPPELER TECHNISCHE ENTWICKLUNG GmbH
Friedrich-Reinhardt Strasse 4
D-74427 Fichtenberg, GERMANY
Fax No.: 011-49-7971-91-1243
Website: www.keppeler-te.de
Email: info@keppeler-te.de

KEYSTONE SPORTING ARMS
Please refer to Crickett Rifle listing.

KHAN
Importer - please refer to Legacy Sports International, LLC listing.

KIMAR SRL
Importer - please refer to IAR listing.
Importer - Valor Corporation
1001 Sawgrass Corporate Parkway
Sunrise, FL 33323
Phone No.: 954-377-4925
Website: www.valorcorp.com
Email: sales@valorcorp.com
Importer - Collector's Armoury
P.O. Box 59, Dept. 1
Alexandria, VA 22313-0059
Phone No.: 703-684-6111
Website: www.collectorsarmoury.com
Email: sales@collectorsarmoury.com
Factory
Via Milano 2
I-25020 Azzano, Mella (BS) ITALY
Fax No.: 011-39-030-9749232
Website: www.kimar.com
Email: info@kimar.com

KIMBER
Corporate Offices - Kimber Mfg., Inc.
1 Lawton St.
Yonkers, NY 10705
Phone No.: 800-880-2418
Fax No.: 406-758-2223
Custom Shop Phone No.: 914-964-0742
Website: www.kimberamerica.com
Email: info@kimberamerica.com

KING'S GUN WORKS INC.
1837 West Glenoaks Blvd.
Glendale, CA 91201
Phone No.: 818-956-6010
Fax No.: 818-548-8606
Website: www.kingsgunworks.com
Email: kngswks@earthlink.net

KNIGHTS MANUFACTURING CO. (KMC)
701 Columbia Blvd.
Titusville, FL 32780
Phone No.: 772-778-3700
Fax No.: 772-569-2955
Website: www.knightarmco.com

KOLAR ARMS
1925 Roosevelt Ave.
Racine, WI 53406
Phone No.: 262-554-0800
Fax No.: 262-554-9093
Website: www.kolararms.com
Email: info@kolararms.com

KORA BRNO
Factory - Kroko a.s.
Hybesova 46
CZ-60200 Brno, Czech Republic
Fax No.: 011-42-5-43321265
Website: www.korabrno.cz
Email: kroko@korabrno.cz

KORTH
Importer – Korth USA
A division of Earl's Repair Service, Inc. (ERS)
437R Chandler Street
Tewksbury, MA 01876
Phone No.: 978-851-8656
Fax No.: 978-851-9462
Website: www.korthusa.com
Email: info@korthusa.com
Factory - Korth Vertriebsgesellschaft GmbH
Robert Bosch Strasse 4
D-23909 Ratzeburg, GERMANY
Fax No.: 011-49-45-4182479
Website: www.korthwaffen.de
Email: info@korthwaffen.de

KRICO
Factory - Krico Jagd-und Sportwaffen GmbH
Nurnberger Strasse 6
Pyrbaum, D-90602 GERMANY
Fax No.: 011-49-091-80-2661
Website: www.krico.de
Email: info@krico.de

KRIEGHOFF, H., GUN CO.
Importer - Krieghoff Intl., Inc.
P.O. Box 549
7528 Easton Rd.
Ottsville, PA 18942
Phone No.: 610-847-5173
Fax No.: 610-847-8691
Website: www.krieghoff.com
Email: info@krieghoff.com
Factory - H. Krieghoff GmbH
Boschstrasse 22
D-89079 Ulm, GERMANY
Fax No.: 011-49-731-40-18270
Website: www.krieghoff.de

KUFSTEINER WAFFENSTUBE
Ing. Hannes Kepplinger
Carl-Wagner-Strasse 1
A-6330 Kufstein, AUSTRIA
Fax No.: 011-43-5372-61887

L.A.R. MANUFACTURING, INC.
4133 West Farm Road
West Jordan, UT 84088-4997
Phone No.: 801-280-3505
Fax No.: 801-280-1972
Website: www.largrizzly.com
Email: guns@largrizzly.com

LANBER ARMAS S.A.
Importer - Wingshooting Adventures
O-1845 West Leonard
Grand Rapids, MI 49544-9510
Phone No.: 616-677-1980
Fax No.: 616-677-1986
Factory - ComLanber, S.A.
Zubiaurre 3
E-48250 Zaldibar (Vizcaya) SPAIN
Fax No.: 011-34-94-6827999
Website: www.lanber.net
Email: lanber@euskalnet.net

LANG, JOSEPH
Please refer to the Atkin, Grant & Lang Ltd. listing.

LARRY'S GUNS INC.
Phone No: 207-657-4559
Fax No.: 207-657-3429
Website: www.larrysguns.com

LAURONA
Factory - Armas Laurona S.A.L.
P.O. Box 260, Avda de Otaola, 25
E-20600 Eibar (Guipuzcoa) SPAIN
Fax No.: 011-34-943-700616
Website: www.laurona.com
Email: laurona@laurona.com

HARRY LAWSON
3328 N. Richey Blvd.
Tucson, AZ 85716
Phone No.: 520-326-1117

LAZZERONI ARMS COMPANY
P.O. Box 26696
Tucson, AZ 85726-6696
Phone No.: 888-492-7247
Fax No.: 520-624-4250
Website: www.lazzeroni.com
Email: arms@lazzeroni.com

LEBEAU-COURALLY
Importer - please refer to William Larkin Moore & Co. listing.
Factory - Aug. Lebeau-Courally
386, rue Saint-Gilles
B-4000 Liege, BELGIUM
Fax No.: 011-32-41-52-2008
Website: www.lebeau-courally.com
Email: info@lebeau-courally.com

LEGACY SPORTS INTERNATIONAL LLC
206 South Union Street
Alexandria, VA 22314
Phone No.: 703-548-4837
Fax No.: 703-549-7826
Web Site: www.legacysports.com

LEGEND RIFLES
Factory - D'Arcy Echols & Co.
P.O. Box 421
98 West 300 South
Millville, UT 84326
Phone No.: 435-755-6842
Fax No.: 435-753-2367

LEITNER-WISE RIFLE CO.
3670 Wheeler Ave. #A
Alexandria, VA 22304-6403
Phone No.: 703-751-8500
Fax No.: 703-751-8733
Website: www.leitner-wise.com
Email: info@leitner-wise.com

LES BAER CUSTOM, INC.
29601 34th Avenue N.
Hillsdale, IL 61257
Phone No.: 309-658-2716
Fax No.: 309-658-2610
Website: www.lesbaer.com
Email: lesbaer@starband.net

LEW HORTON DISTRIBUTING CO.
Distributor Only
15 Walkup Dr., P.O. Box 5023
Westboro, MA 01581
Phone No.: 508-366-7400
Fax No.: 508-366-5332
Website: www.lewhorton.com
Email: 1horton@tiac.net

LIGAMEC CORP.
22119 US 10 North
Clearwater, FL 33765
Phone No.: 727-480-1711
Fax No.: 727-856-8357
Website: www.UltraLite50.com
Email: ligameccorp98@msn.com

LINDER GUN COMPANY
P.O. Box 580
Sanbornville, NH 03872
Website: www.lindnergun.com
Email: lindner@lindnergun.com

LINEBAUGH, JOHN
P.O. Box 455
Cody, WY 82414
Phone No.: 307-645-3332
Website: www.sixgunner.com

LION COUNTRY SUPPLY
P.O. Box 480
Port Matilda, PA 16870
Phone No.: 800-662-5202
Fax No.: 814-684-5900
Website: www.ugartechea.com

LITTLE JOHN'S AUCTION SERVICE
1740 W. LaVeta Ave.
Orange, CA 92868
Phone No.: 714-939-1170
Fax No.: 714-939-7955
Website: www.littlejohnsauctionservice.com
Email: info@littlejohnsauctionservice.com

LITTLE SHARPS RIFLE MFG.
Mr. Aaron Pursley
HC 76 Box 1037
Big Sandy, MT 59520
Phone No.: 406-378-3200
Mr. Ronald Otto
P.O. Box 336
Big Sandy, MT 59520
Phone No.: 406-378-3855
Website: www.littlesharps.com
Email: otto@ttc-cmc.net

LJUTIC INDUSTRIES, INC.
732 North 16th Ave., Ste. 22
Yakima, WA 98902
Phone No.: 509-248-0476
Fax No.: 509-576-8233
Website: www.ljuticgun.com
Email: ljuticgun@earthlink.net

LLAMA
Master Distributor - Import Sports, Inc.
1750 Brielle Ave., Unit B-1
Wanamassa, NJ 07712
Phone No.: 732-493-0302
Fax No.: 732-493-0301
Website: www.bersa-llama.com
Email: gsodini@aol.com
Factory - Fabrinor S.A.L.
San Barolome 26
Poligono Industrial de Gojain
01171 Legutiano, Alava, SPAIN
Fax No.: 011-34-945-466221
Email: fabrinor@xpress.es

LONE STAR RIFLE CO., INC.
11231 Rose Road
Conroe, TX 77303
Phone/Fax No.: 936-856-3363
Website: www.lonestarrifle.com
Email: dave@lonestarrilfe.com

LORENZO, CRESS
349 E. 100 S., Box 14
Minersville, UT 84752
Phone No.: 435-386-1428

LUCCHINI, SANDRO
North American Sales – Springbrook Manufacturing Ltd.
3809 Ninth St. SE
Calgary, AB T2G 3C7 CANADA
Phone No.: 403-243-3308
Fax No.: 403-243-3762
Website: www.sbm-mangrove.com
Email: sbm-info@sbm-mangrove.com
Factory - Armi Italia di Lucchini Sandro
Via Petrarca, 47
25068 Sarezzo (Brescia), ITALY
Fax No.: 011-39-030-89-11573

LU-MAR S.R.L.
Factory - Lu-Mar s.rl. ARMI
Via Artigiani 11
I-25063 Gardone, (BS) ITALY
Fax No.: 011-39-30-891-1185
Website: www.lu-mar.it
Email: info@lu-mar.it

M.O.A. CORPORATION
2451 Old Camden Pike
Eaton, OH 45320
Phone No.: 937-456-3669
Fax No.: 937-456-9331
Website: www.moaguns.com
Email: info@moaguns.com

MG ARMS, INC.
6030 Treaschwig
Spring, TX 77373
Phone No.: 281-821-8282
Fax No.: 281-821-6387
Website: www.mgarmsinc.com
Email: kerry@mgarmsinc.com

MTs ARMS
Factory - TsKIB SOO
Krasnoarmeyskiy Prospekt 17
R-300041 Tula, RUSSIA
Fax No.: 011-7-0872-31-5959
Website: http://home.tula.net/tularms
Email: tularms@tula.net

JAMES MacNAUGHTON & SONS
Please refer to the Dickson & MacNaughton listing.

MAGNUM RESEARCH, INC.
7110 University Ave. NE
Minneapolis, MN 55432
Phone No.: 763-574-1868
Fax No.: 763-574-0109
Website: www.magnumresearch.com

MAGTECH AMMUNITION CO., INC.
6845 20th Ave. S., Ste. 120
Centerville, MN 55038
Phone No.: 651-762-8500
Fax No.: 651-429-9485
Website: www.magtechammunition.com

MAJESTIC ARMS, LTD.
101A Ellis St.
Staten Island, NY 10307
Phone No.: 718-356-6765
Fax No.: 718-356-6835
Website: www.majesticarms.com

MAKAROV
Importer - please refer to Century International Arms listing.

MANDALL SHOOTING SUPPLIES
3616 N. Scottsdale Rd.
Scottsdale, AZ 85252
Phone No.: 480-945-2553
Fax No.: 480-949-0734
Website: www.mandallshooting.com
Email: mandallshooting@earthlink.net

MANU-ARM
43, avenue de la liberation
F-42340, Veauche, FRANCE
Fax No.: 011-33-0477-947936
Website: www.manuarm.fr
Email: manuarm@manuarm.fr

MANUFRANCE
6, Rue de Lodi
F-42000 St. Etienne 1 FRANCE
Fax No.: 011-33-0477-418830
Email: manufrance@wanadoo.fr

MANURHIN REVOLVERS
Factory – Manufacture d. Armes de tir Chapuis – M.A.T.C.H.
Z.I. La Gravoux, BP 15
F-42380 St. Bonnet le Chateau, FRANCE
Fax No.: 011-33-4-77-501070
Website: www.chapuis-armes.com
Email: info@chapuis-armes.com

MARCEL THYS & SONS
U.S. Agent - Jean-Jacques Perodeau
P.O. Box 3191
Woodring Municipal Airport
Enid, OK 73702
Phone No.: 580-237-7388
Fax No.: 580-242-6922
Factory
Rue de Villers, 8
B-4367 Crisne BELGIUM
Fax No.: 011-32-4-240-1718
Website: www.marcelthys.com
Email: info@marcelthys.com

MARLIN FIREARMS COMPANY
100 Kenna Drive
P.O. Box 248
North Haven, CT 06473-0905
Phone No.: 203-239-5621
Fax No.: 203-234-7991
Website: www.marlinfirearms.com

MAROCCHI SHOTGUNS
Importer - please refer to GSI listing.
Factory - C.D. Europe SRL
Via Galilei, 6
I-25068 Sarezzo (Brescia) ITALY
Fax No.: 011-39-030-890-08370
Website: www.classicdoubles.com
Email: info@classicdoubles.com

MARTIN, ALEX
Please refer to the Dickson & MacNaughton listing.

MASTERPIECE ARMS, INC.
217 Brumbelow Road
Carrollton, GA 30117
Phone No.: 770-832-9430
Fax No.: 770-832-3495
Email: vickyb@pencinc.com

MATCHGUNS srl
Factory
Via cartiera 6/d
I-43010 Vigatto, Parma ITALY
Fax No: 011-39-0521631973
Website: www.matchguns.com
Email: info@matchguns.com

MATCH GRADE ARMS & AMMUNITION
Please refer to MG Arms, Inc. listing.

MATEBA
Factory – Mateba srl
Via Sardegna 7
I-25069 Villa Carcina, Brescia, ITALY
Fax No.: 011-39-0308982981
Website: www.mateba-arms.com
Email: info@mateba-arms.com

MATHELON ARMES
Importer - Rocky Mountain Armoury
591 Blue River Parkway
P.O. Box 1835
Silverthorne, CO 80498
Phone No.: 970-468-5001
Fax No.: 970-262-1499
Email: tekarms@yahoo.com
Factory
Rue de l'Artisanat
F-74150 Rumilly FRANCE
Fax No.: 011-33-4-50-016786

MAUSER
Importer – please refer to SIG Arms listing.
Factory – Mauser Jagdwaffen GmbH
Ziegelstadel 1
D-88316 Isny, GERMANY
Fax No.: 011-490-368-4750794
Website: www.mauser.com
Email: info@mauser.com

MAVERICK ARMS, INC.
Please refer to Mossberg listing.

McMILLAN BROS RIFLE CO., INC.
1638 W. Knudsen Dr. #102
Phoenix, AZ 85027
Phone No.: 623-582-3713
Fax No.: 623-582-3930
Website: www.mcmfamily.com
Email: mcbros@mcmfamily.com

MEDWELL & PERRETT LIMITED
Nicks Lane, Brome, Eye
Suffolk, ENGLAND IP23 8AN
Fax No.: 011-44-01379-870777
Email: nicky@medwellandperrett.com

MERKEL
Importer - please refer to Heckler & Koch USA listing.
Distributor - please refer to Gun South Inc. listing.
Service & Repair - please refer to Gun South listing.
Factory - Suhler Jagd-und Sportwaffen GmbH
Schutzenstrasse 26
D-98527 Suhl, GERMANY
Fax No.: 011-49-3681-854-201
Website: www.merkel-waffen.de

MIL-SPEC INDUSTRIES CORP.
10 Mineola Avenue
Roslyn Heights, NY 11577
Phone No.: 516-625-5787
Fax No.: 516-625-0988
Website: www.milspecindustries.com
Email: info@mil-spec-industries.com

MILLER ARMS
Please refer to Dakota Arms listing.

MILLER, DAVID
Please refer to David Miller Co. listing.

MIROKU FIREARMS MFG. CO.
537-1 Shinohara
Nangoku City Kochi-Pref, JAPAN
Fax No.: 011-81-88-863-3317

MITCHELL'S MAUSERS
P.O. Box 9295
Fountain Valley, CA 92728 -9295
Phone No.: 714-444-2220
Fax No.: 714-444-2226
Website: www.mitchellsales.com

MOLL, M.F.
Steins Strasse 101
D-41199 Moenchengladbach GERMANY
Phone No.: 011-49-2166997091
Fax No.: 011-49-216642253

MONTANA ARMORY, INC.
Please refer to C. Sharps Arms Co. Inc. listing.

MOORE, W.L. & CO.
Please refer to William Larkin Moore & Co. listing.

MORAVIA
Please refer to Arms Moravia listing.

MORINI
Importer – please refer to Pilkington Competition Equipment LLC listing.
Factory - Morini Competition Arm SA
Casella Postale 92
CH-6930 Bedano SWITZERLAND
Fax No.: 011-41-91-9-45-1502
Website: www.morini.ch
Email: morini@bluewin.ch

MORTIMER, THOMAS
Please refer to the Dickson & MacNaughton listing.

MOSSBERG
O.F. Mossberg & Sons, Inc.
7 Grasso Ave., P.O. Box 497
North Haven, CT 06473-9844
Phone No.: 203-230-5300
Fax No.: 203-230-5420
Factory Service Center - OFM Service Department
Eagle Pass Industrial Park
Industrial Blvd.
Eagle Pass, TX 78853
Phone No.: 800-989-4867
Website: www.mossberg.com
Email: service@mossberg.com

MOUNTAIN RIFLERY, INC.
1775 North Elk Road
Pocatello, ID 83204
Phone No.: 208-234-7142

NATIONAL WILD TURKEY FEDERATION
P.O. Box 530
Edgefield, SC 29824
Phone No.: 803-637-3106
Fax No.: 803-637-0034
Website: www.nwtf.com

NAVY ARMS CO.
219 Lawn St.
Martinsburg, WV 25401
Phone No.: 304-2629870
Fax No.: 304-262-1658
Website: www.navyarms.com
Email: info@navyarms.com

NELSON, P.V., (GUNMAKERS)
Folly Meadow, Hammersley Lane
Penn, High Wycombe,
Buckinghamshire, ENGLAND HP10 8HF
Phone/Fax No.: 011-44-49-4812836

NESIKA
Please refer to Dakota Arms listing.

NEW ENGLAND CUSTOM GUN SERVICE LTD.
438 Willow Brook Rd.
Plainfield, NH 03781
Phone No.: 603-469-3450
Fax No.: 603-469-3471
Website: www.newenglandcustomgun.com
Email: bestguns@adelphia.net

NEW ENGLAND FIREARMS
60 Industrial Rowe
Gardner, MA 01440
Phone No.: 978-632-9393
Fax No.: 978-632-2300
Website: www.hr1871.com
Email: hr1871@tiac.net

NEW ULTRA LIGHT ARMS LLC
P.O. Box 340
214 Price Street
Granville, WV 26534
Phone No.: 304-292-0600
Fax No.: 304-292-9662
Website: www.newultralight.com

NIGHTHAWK CUSTOM
1306 W. Trimble Ave.
Berryville, AR 72616-4632
Phone No.: 877-268-4867
Fax No.: 870-423-4230
Website: www.nighthawkcustom.com
Email: info@nighthawkcustom.com

NOR-CAL PRECISION
2004 Elliot Dr.
American Canyon, CA 94503
Phone No.: 707-552-3810
Fax No.: 707-558-8977
Website: www.norcalprecision.com
Email: nor-cal@worldnet.att.net

NORINCO
Exclusive Importer - please refer to Interstate Arms Corp. listing.

NORSMAN SPORTING ARMS
P.O. Box 500
1028 Second Ave., Ste. A
Havre, MT 59501
Phone No.: 406-262-2403

NORTHWEST ARMS
Please refer to Wilkinson Arms listing.

NORTH AMERICAN ARMS, INC.
2150 South, 950 East
Provo, UT 84606-6285
Phone No.: 801-374-9990
Fax No.: 801-374-9998
Customer Service and Custom Shop: 800-821-5783
Website: www.naaminis.com

NOSLER, INC.
P.O. Box 671
Bend, OR 97709
Phone No.: 800-285-3701
Fax No.: 541-388-4667
Website: www.noslercustom.com

NOWLIN MFG. INC.
20622 4092 Rd., Unit B
Claremore, OK 74017
Phone No.: 918-342-0689
Fax No.: 918-342-0624
Website: www.nowlinguns.com
Email: nowlinguns@msn.com

NUMRICH GUN PARTS CORP.
Parts supplier only
226 Williams Lane
P.O. Box 299
W. Hurley, NY 12491
Phone No.: 866-686-7424
Fax No.: 877-486-7278
Website: www.e-gunparts.com
Email: info@gunpartscorp.com

OHIO ORDNANCE WORKS, INC.
P.O. Box 687
Chardon, OH 44024
Phone No.: 440-285-3481
Fax No.: 440-286-8571
Website: www.ohioordnanceworks.com
Email: OhioOrdn@aol.com

OLD TOWN STATION LTD. (AUCTIONS)
P.O.B. 14040
Lenexa, KS 66285
Phone No.: 913-492-3000
Fax No.: 913-492-3022
Website: www.armsbid.com
Email: armsbid@aol.com

OLLENDORFF, PHILIPP
Eisack 169
A-6108 Scharnitz AUSTRIA
Fax No.: 011-43-5213-20133
Website: www.jagdwaffen-ollendorff.com
Email: info@jagdwaffen-ollendorff.com

OLYMPIC ARMS, INC.
624 Old Pacific Hwy. S.E.
Olympia, WA 98513
Phone No.: 800-228-3471
Fax No.: 360-491-3447
Website: www.olyarms.com
Email: info@olyarms.com

OMEGA WEAPONS SYSTEMS, INC.
Distributor - Defense Technology, Inc.
P.O. Box 482
Lake Forest, CA 92630
Phone No.: 949-830-8540
Fax No.: 949-830-1103
Factory
2918 E. Ginter
Tucson, AZ 85706
Phone No.: 520-889-8895
Fax No.: 520-741-9466

OMNI
Please refer to E.D.M. Arms listing.

ORVIS
(Custom shotgun information only)
Historic Route 7A
Manchester, VT 05254
Phone No.: 802-362-2580
Fax No.: 802-362-3525
Website: www.orvis.com

P.A.W.S., INC.
Factory
8175 River Road N.E.
Salem, OR 97303
Phone No.: 503-393-0838
Fax No.: 503-390-6075

PGW DEFENCE TECHNOLOGIES
Importer - LBVG
527 2nd Ave. N.
Glasgow, MT 59230
Factory
1-761 Mairon St.
Winnipeg, Manitoba
R2J 0K6 CANADA
Phone No.: 204-231-2976
Fax No.: 204-231-8566
Website: www.pgwdti.com

PALMETTO ARMS CO.
Factory
via Oberdan 48
Brescia, ITALY I-25125
Fax No.: 011-39-0303700960
Website: www.palmetto.it
Email: info@palmetto.it

PARA-ORDNANCE MANUFACTURING INC.
980 Tapscott Rd.
Scarborough, Ontario
M1X 1C3 CANADA
Phone No.: 416-297-7855
Fax No.: 416-297-1289
Web Site: www.paraord.com
Email: info@paraord.com

PARDINI, ARMI S.r.l.
Importer - please refer to Larry's Guns listing.
Factory
154/A via Italica
I-55043 Lido di Camaiore, ITALY
Fax No.: 011-39-584-90122
Website: www.pardini.it
Email: info@pardini.it

PARKER REPRODUCTIONS
Parker Reproduction Div.
115 U.S. Hwy 202
Ringoes, NJ 08551
Phone No.: 908-284-2800
Fax No.: 908-284-2113

PEDERSOLI, DAVIDE & C. Snc
Distributor - please refer to Cherry's listing.
Distributor - please refer to Dixie Gun Works listing.
Importer - please refer to Cabela's listing.
Importer - please refer to Cimarron, F.A. & Co listing.
Importer - please refer to Navy Arms listing.
Service & Repair - VTI Gun Parts
P.O. Box 509
Lakeville, CT 06039
Phone No.: 860-435-8068
Fax No.: 860-435-8146
Website: www.vtigunparts.com
Factory
Via Artigiani 57
I-25063 Gardone V.T. (BS), ITALY
Fax No.: 011-39-030-8911019
Website: www.davide-pedersoli.com

PENTHENY de PENTHENY, INC.
2352 Baggett Ct.
Santa Rosa, CA 95401
Phone/Fax No.: 707-573-1390

PERAZZI
Importer - Perazzi USA, Inc.
1010 W. Tenth St.
Azusa, CA 91702
Phone No.: 626-334-1234
Fax No.: 626-334-0344
Email: perazziusa@aol.com
Factory - Armi Perazzi S.p.A.
Via Fontanelle, 1/3
I-25080 Botticino Mattina Brescia ITALY
Fax No.: 011-39-030-269-2594
Website: www.perazzi.it

PERUGINI & VISINI
Factory
Via Camprelle 126
Nuvolera, Brescia I-25080 ITALY
Fax No.: 011-39-030-689-7535
Website: www.intred.it/perugini-visini
Email: pervis@intred.it

PETERS STAHL GmbH
Factory
Stettiner Strasse 42
D-33106 Paderborn, GERMANY
Fax No.: 011-49-5251-75611
Website: www.peters-stahl.com
Email: info@peters-stahl.com

PHOENIX ARMS
4231 E. Brickell St.
Ontario, CA 91761
Phone No.: 909-937-6900
Fax No.: 909-937-0060

PIETTA, F.A.P. F.lli e C. Snc.
Various U.S. distributors and importers
Service & Repair - VTI Gun Parts
P.O. Box 509
Lakeville, CT 06039
Phone No.: 860-435-8068
Fax No.: 860-435-8146
Website: www.vtigunparts.com

Factory - PIETTA, F.A.P. F.lli e C. Snc.
Via Mandolossa 102
I-25064 Gussago (Brescia) ITALY
Fax No.: 011-39-030-3737100
Website: www.pietta.it
Email: info@pietta.it

PILKINGTON COMPETITION EQUIPMENT LLC
P.O. Box 97
#2 Little Tree's Ramble
Monteagle, TN 37356
Phone No.: 931-924-3400
Fax No.: 931-924-3489
Website: www.pilkguns.com
Email: info@pilkguns.com

PIOTTI
Importer - please refer to William Larkin Moore & Co. listing.
Factory - Piotti, F.lli, S.n.c.
Via Cinelli, 10-12
I-25063 Gardone V.T. Brescia, ITALY
Fax No.: 011-39-030-891-6532

POLI, ARMI F.LLI
Importer - see Cole Gunsmithing listing.
Factory
Casella Postale, 6
via Matteotti
I-25063 Gardone, VT (BS), ITALY
Fax No.: 011-39-030-8349413
Website: www.intred.it/poli
Email: poli@intred.it

PRECISION SMALL ARMS, INC.
Distributor - please refer to Acusport listing.
Factory
118 Apollo Road
Montrose, CO 81401
Phone No.: 415-269-6415
Website: www.precisionsmallarms.com
Email: sales@precisionsmallarms.com

PREMIER ENGLISH SHOTGUNS LTD.
Turners Barn Farm - Kibworth Road, Three Gates
Illston-on-the-Hill, Leicestershire
LE7 9ER ENGLAND
Phone No.: 011-441-16-259-6592
Fax No.: 011-441-16-259-6574
Website: www.hollowaynaughton.co.uk
Email: afharvison@hollowaynaughton.co.uk

PUMA RIFLES
Importer – please refer to Legacy Sports International, LLC listing.

PURDEY, JAMES, & SONS, LTD.
Showroom
57-58 South Audley Street
London, W1K 2 ED ENGLAND
Phone No.: 011-44-20-7499-1801
Fax No.: 011-44-20-7355-3297
Website: www.purdey.com
Email: sales@james-purdey.co.uk

QUAIL UNLIMITED, INC.
31 Quail Run
PO Box 610
Edgefield, SC 29824
Phone No.: 803-637-5731
Fax No.: 803-637-0037
Website: www.qu.org
Email: National@qu.org

QUALITY ARMS, INC.
P.O. Box 19477
Houston, TX 77224
Phone No.: 281-870-8377
Fax No.: 281-870-8524
Website: www.arrieta.com
Email: Arrieta2@excite.com

QUALITY PARTS CO.
Please refer to Bushmaster Firearms, Inc. listing.

R.F.M.
Please refer to Rota, Luciano listing.

RBA
Factory - Renzo Bonora Armi
via 2 Argosto 1980 nr. 25
I-40057 Granarolo Emilia ITALY
Fax No.: 011-39-0517-66262
Email: rbaarms@dada.it

RND MANUFACTURING
Phone/Fax No.: 970-535-4458
Website: www.rndedge.com
Email: info@rndedge.com

RPB INDUSTRIES
P.O. Box 367
Avondale, GA 30002
Phone No.: 800-858-0809
Fax No.: 404-297-0917

RPM PISTOLS
Please refer to the Gateway Precision Arms listing.

RWS
Disc. firearms only - please refer to Dynamit Nobel listing.

RADOM
Importer (Current mfg.) - Dalvar of U.S.A.
1175 Sierra Verde Ranch
P.O. Box 31
Seligman, AZ 86337-0031
Website: www.dalvar.net
Email: dalvar_usa@juno.com

RAMO DEFENSE SYSTEMS
Please refer to Sabre Defence Systems, LLC listing.

GARY REEDER CUSTOM GUNS
2601 E. 7th Ave.
Flagstaff, AZ 86004
Phone No.: 928-527-4100
Fax No.: 928-527-0840
Web Site: www.reedercustomguns.com
Email: gary@reedercustomguns.com

REMINGTON ARMS CO., INC.
Consumer Services
870 Remington Drive
P.O. Box 700
Madison, NC 27025-0700
Phone No.: 800-243-9700
Fax No.: 336-548-7801
Website: www.remington.com
Email: info@remington.com

Repairs
14 Hoefler Ave.
Ilion, NY 13357
Phone No.: 800-243-9700
Fax No.: 336-548-7801
Email: info@remington.com

RIFLES, INC.
3580 Leal Rd.
Pleasanton, TX 78064
Phone No.: 830-569-2055
Fax No.: 830-569-2297
Website: www.riflesinc.com
Email: rifles@ev1.net

RIGANIAN, RAY (RIFLEMAKER)
324 N. Central Ave., Unit B
Glendale, CA 91203
Phone No.: 818-502-2678

RIGBY, JOHN & CO. (GUNMAKERS), INC.
500 Linne Rd., Ste. D
Paso Robles, CA 93446
Phone No.: 805-227-4236
Fax No.: 805-227-4723
Website: www.johnrigbyandco.com
Email: jrigby@johnrigbyandco.com

RIZZINI, BATTISTA
Importer - Rizzini USA
1140 McDermott Drive, Ste. 103
West Chester, PA 19380
Phone No.: 610-344-7730
Fax No.: 610-344-7741
Website: www.rizziniusa.com
Factory - Rizzini srl
Via 2 Giugno, 7/7 bis
I-25060 Marcheno (Brescia), ITALY
Fax No.: 011-39-30/861319
Website: www.rizzini.it
Email: info@rizzini.it

RIZZINI, EMILIO, s.n.c.
Importer - please refer to Traditions listing.
Importer - please refer to Tristar listing.
Factory
Via Martiri Dell'Indipendenza, 70
I-25060 Marcheno (Brescia) ITALY
Fax No.: 011-39-030-861-0155
Website: www.emiliorizzini.com
Email: info@emiliorizzini.com

RIZZINI, F.LLI
Importer - please refer to William Larkin Moore listing.
Factory
Via X Giornate N. 9
I-25063, Magno, VT, ITALY
Fax No.: 011-39-030-8911400
Email: srizzini@libero.it

ROBAR COMPANIES, INC.
21438 N. 7th Avenue
Phoenix, AZ 85027
Phone No.: 623-581-2648
Fax No.: 623-582-0059
Website: www.robarguns.com
Email: info@robarguns.com

ROBERT HISSERICH COMPANY
183A S. Los Alamos
Mesa, AZ 85204
Phone No.: 480-545-2994
Fax No.: 480-507-7560
Email: bhisserich@earthlink.net

ROBERTS, J. & SON (GUNMAKERS) LTD.
22 Wyvil Road, Vauxhall
London SW8 2TG ENGLAND
Fax No.: 011-44-0207-627-4442
Website: www.jroberts-gunmakers.co.uk
Email: shop@jroberts-gunmakers.co.uk

ROBERTSON
Please refer to Boss & Co., Ltd. listing.

ROBINSON ARMAMENT CO.
ZDF Import/Export
P.O. Box 16776
Salt Lake City, UT 84116-0776
Phone No.: 801-355-0401
Fax No.: 801-355-0402
Website: www.robarm.com
Email: ZDF@robarm.com

ROCHE, CHRISTIAN
12 Lotissement les Eglantiers
42 340 Veauche, France
Phone No.: 011-33-77-93-35-33
Fax No.: 011-33-77-94-35-33

ROCK ISLAND AUCTION COMPANY
1050 35th Ave.
Moline, IL 61265
Phone No.: 309-797-1500
Fax No.: 309-797-1655
Website: www.mgnteam.com
Email: riauction@aol.com

ROCK RIVER ARMS, INC.
1042 Cleveland Road
Colona, IL 61241
Phone No.: 309-792-5780
Fax No.: 309-792-5781
Website: www.rockriverarms.com
Email: rockriverarms@revealed.net

ROCKY MOUNTAIN ELK FOUNDATION
2291 W. Broadway
Missoula, MT 59802
Phone No.: 406-523-4500
Fax No.: 406-523-4581
Website: www.rmef.org

ROGUE RIVER RIFLEWORKS
500 Linne Road, Ste. D
Paso Robles, CA 93446
Phone No.: 805-227-4236
Fax No.: 805-227-4723

ROHRBAUGH FIREARMS CORP.
P.O. Box 785
Bayport, NY 11705
Phone No.: 800-803-2233
Phone No.: 631-242-3175
Fax No.: 631-242-3183
Website: www.rohrbaughfirearms.com
Email: ecr@rohrbaughfirearms.com

ROOSEVELT AND DRAKE
418 Main Street
Murray, KY 42071
Phone No.: 270-436-5270
Fax No.: 270-436-5257
Website: www.drake.net

ROSSI
Importer – BrazTech International L.C.
16175 N.W. 49th Ave.
Miami, FL 33014
Phone No.: 305-474-0401
Fax No.: 305-624-3180
Website: www.rossiusa.com
Factory - Amadeo Rossi, S.A.
Rua Amadeo Rossi, 143
B-93030-220 Sao Leopoldo-RS BRAZIL
Email: rossi.firearms@pnet.com.br

ROTA, LUCIANO
Importer - please refer to Tristar listing.
Factory - R.F.M. di Rota Luciano
via Patrioti, 26
I-25068 Noboli di Sarezzo
V.T. (Brescia) ITALY
Fax No.: 011-49-30-801152

ROTTWEIL
Repair - Pylinski Arms
(Models 72, 720 & Paragon service)
967 Anderson Hwy.
Cumberland, VA 23040
Phone No.: 804-492-4082
Email: pylinskifarms@aol.com
Factory
Metzgasse 13
D-78628 Rottweil, GERMANY
Fax No.: 011-49-0741-949-4070
Website: www.schwabenarmsrottweil.de

S.I.A.C.E.
Factory
Via Matteotti 127
Gardone, VT, Brescia, ITALY I-25063
Fax No.: 011-39-030-8911518

SKB SHOTGUNS
Importer - Guns Unlimited, Inc.
4325 S 120th Street
Omaha, NE 68137
Phone No.: 402-330-4492
Fax No.: 402-330-8040
Website: www.skbshotguns.com
Email: skb@skbshotguns.com
Factory
J-113-0021 Bunkyo-ku
Tokyo, Pacico Bldg. 601
Honokomagome 6-15-8 JAPAN
Fax No.: 011-81-0339-430695
Website: www.shirstone.com/skb
Email: mail@shirstone.com

SOG INTERNATIONAL
P.O. Box 590
Lebanon, OH 45036-0590
Phone No.: 800-944-4867
Fax No.: 513-932-8928
Website: www.southernohiogun.com
Email: soginc@go-concepts.com

SSK INDUSTRIES
Gunsmithing services only
590 Woodvue Lane
Wintersville, OH 43953
Phone No.: 740-264-0176
Fax No.: 740-264-2257
Website: www.sskindustries.com
Email: info@sskindustries.com

STI INTERNATIONAL
114 Halmar Cove
Georgetown, TX 78628
Phone No.: 800-959-8201
Fax No.: 512-819-0465
Website: www.stiguns.com
Email: sales@stiguns.com

SABATTI s.p.a.
Factory - Armi Sabatti s.p.a.
Via Volta 90
I-25063 Gardone Valtrompia, (BS) ITALY
Fax No.: 011-39-030-89-12059
Website: www.sabatti.com
Email: info@sabatti.com

SABRE
Please refer to Mitchell's Mausers listing.

SABRE DEFENCE INDUSTRIES LLC
450 Allied Drive
Nashville, TN 37211
Phone No.: 615-333-0077
Fax No.: 615-333-6229
Website: www.sabredefence.com

SAFARI CLUB INTERNATIONAL
4800 West Gates Pass Road
Tucson, AZ 85745
Phone No.: 888-724-4868
Fax No.: 520-622-1205
Website: www.safariclub.org
Membership email: huntsci@safariclub.org

SAFETY HARBOR FIREARMS, INC.
(Upper Barrel Assembly Conversion Only)
P.O. Box 563
Safety Harbor, FL 34695
Phone No.: 727-725-4700
Fax No.: 727-724-1872
Website: safetyharborfirearms.com
Email: sales@safetyharborfirearms.com

SAIGA
Factory - please refer to Izhmash listing.

SAKO LTD.
Importer (USA) - please refer to Beretta USA listing.
Importer (CANADA) – Stoeger Canada Ltd.
1801 Wentworth St., Unit 16
Whitby, Ontario, L1N 8R6 CANADA
Phone No.: 905-436-9077
Fax No.: 905-436-9079
Email: stoeger@idirect.com
Factory - Sako, Limited
P.O. Box 149
FIN-11101 Riihimki, FINLAND
Fax No.: 011-358-19-720446
Website: www.sako.fi
Email: export@sako.fi

SALERI, W.R. di WILLIAM & C. snc
Importer - MacGregor Wing & Clay
107 Edinburgh South, Ste. 209
Cary, NC 27511
Toll Free Phone No.: 866-831-5888
Phone No.: 919-388-5888
Fax No.: 919-388-3881
Factory
Via Filipinni, 2
I-25063 Gardone, VT Brescia ITALY
Fax No.: 011-39-030-8916-168

SAMCO GLOBAL ARMS, INC.
6995 N.W. 43rd St.
Miami, FL 33166
Phone No.: 800-554-1618
Phone No.: 305-593-9782
Fax No.: 305-593-1014
Website: www.samcoglobal.com
Email: samco@samcoglobal.com

SAN SWISS ARMS AG
Industrieplatz
CH-8212 Neuhausen am Rheinfall SWITZERLAND
Fax No.: 011-41-052-674-6418
Website: www.swissarms.ch
Email: info@swissarms.ch

SARSILMAZ
Importer - please refer to Adco Sales listing.
Factory
Nargileci Sokak No. 4 Sarsilmaz 1s
Merkei Mercan, Istanbul, TURKEY
Fax No.: 011-90212-51119-99
Website: www.sarsilmaz.com.

SAUER, J.P. & SOHN
Importer - please refer to SIG Arms listing.
Factory – J.P. Sauer & Sohn GmbH
Sauerstrasse 2-6
D-24340 Eckernforde, GERMANY
Fax No.: 011-49-43-51-471-160
Website: www.sauer-waffen.de

SAVAGE ARMS, INC.
100 Springdale Road
Westfield, MA 01085
Phone No.: 413-568-7001
Fax No.: 413-562-7764
Website: www.savagearms.com
Older Savage Arms Historical Research
Mr. John Callahan
53 Old Quarry Rd.
Westfield, MA 01085
$20.00/gun research fee, $25.00 per gun for Models
1895, 1899, and 99 rifles.

SAVIN, J.C.
11 Place de la Cite
F-42220 Bourg Argental, FRANCE
Fax No.: 011-33-4-77-39-1855

SAXONIA SPEZIALWAFFENTECHNIK GbR
Am Wasserwerk 1
D-08340 Schwarzenberg GERMANY
Fax No.: 011-49-3774-1807424
Website: www.saxonia-waffen.de
Email: decker-schwarzenberg@t-online.de

SCATTERGUN TECHNOLOGIES INC.
Please refer to Wilson Combat listing.

SCHEIRING GmbH
Klagenfurter Strasse 19
A-9170 Ferlach AUSTRIA
Fax No.: 011-43-4227-287620
Email: waffen.scheiring@aon.at

SCHERZ, MICHAEL
1314 S. 4th Ave.
Yuma, AZ 85364
Phone: 928-580-0976
Website: www.gilarivergunworks.com
Email: gilagunwks@aol.com

FA. ALFRED SCHILLING
Peter-Haseney Strasse 32
D-98544 Zella-Mehlis, GERMANY
Fax No.: 011-49-0362-486706
Website: www.Alfred-Schilling.de
Email: schilling@alfred-schilling.de

SCHUERMAN ARMS, LTD.
9301 E. Adobe Dr.
Scottsdale, AZ 85255
Phone No.: 480-473-2980
Fax No.: 480-948-9704
Website: www.schuermanarms.com
Email: info@schuermanarms.com

SCHUETZEN PISTOL WORKS, INC.
Please refer to Olympic Arms listing.

SCHUTZEN BOHME GmbH
Muhlenstrasse 6-8
31737 Rintein, GERMANY
Phone No.: 011-49-5751-44770
Fax No.: 011-49-5751-42490

SCOTT, W. C., LTD.
Holland & Holland, Ltd. (Repairs)
Attn: Mr. P. C. Chismon
31-33 Bruton St.
London WiJ 6HH ENGLAND
Phone No.: 011-44-020-7499-4411
Fax No.: 011-44-020-7409-3283
Website: www.hollandandholland.com
Email: peter.chismon@holland-holland.co.uk

SEARCY, B. & CO.
P.O. Box 584
Boron, CA 93596
Phone No.: 760-762-6131
Fax No.: 760-762-0191
Website: www.searcyent.com
Email: searcy@ccis.com

SEECAMP, L.W. CO., INC.
301 Brewster Road
Milford, CT 06460
Phone No.: 203-877-7926

SEMMERLING
Please refer to American Derringer Corp. listing.

SERBU FIREARMS, INC.
6001 Johns Rd., Ste. 144
Tampa, FL 33634
Phone/Fax No.: 813-243-8899
Website: www.serbu.com

SERENGETI RIFLES, INC.
2860 Farm to Market
Kalispell, MT 59901
Website: www.serengetirifles.com
Email: larryt@serengetirifles.com

C. SHARPS ARMS CO. INC.
100 Centennial Dr.
P.O. Box 885
Big Timber, MT 59011
Phone No.: 406-932-4353
Fax No.: 406-932-4443
Website: www.csharpsarms.com
Email: csharps@ttc-cmc.net

SHILOH RIFLE MFG. CO.
P.O. Box 279
Big Timber, MT 59011
Phone No.: 406-932-4454
Fax No.: 406-932-5627
Website: www.shilohrifle.com

SHOOTERS ARMS MANUFACTURING INCORPORATED
Importer - please refer to Century International Arms listing.
Importer - Pacific Arms Corp.
4813 Enterprise Way, Unit K
Modesto, CA 95356-8736
Phone No.: 209-545-2800
Fax No.: 209-545-2528
Factory
National Highway, Wireless
Mandaue City, Cebu, Phillipines
Fax No.: 011-6032-346-2331
Website: www.shootersarms.com.ph
Email: rhonedeleon@yahoo.com

SIG ARMS, INC.
18 Industrial Park Drive
Exeter, NH 03833
Phone No.: 603-772-2302
Fax No.: 603-772-9082
Customer Service Phone No.: 603-773-2302
Customer Service Fax No.: 603-772-4795
Law Enforcement Phone No.: 603-772-2302
Law Enforcement Fax No.: 603-772-1481
Web Site: www.sigarms.com

SIG SAUER
Importer – please refer to SIG Arms, Inc. listing.
Factory - SIG - Schweizerische Industrie-Gesellschaft
Industrielplatz
CH-8212 Neuhausen am Rheinfall, SWITZERLAND
Fax No.: 011-41-153-216-601

SILMA s.r.l.
Distributor & Importer – please refer to Legacy Sports International, LLC listing.
Factory
Via I Maggio, 74
I-25060 Zanano di Sarezzo, (BS) ITALY
Fax No.: 011-39-030-8900712
Website: www.silma.net
Email: info@silma.net

GENE SIMILLION GUNMAKER
220 S. Wisconsin
Gunnison, CO 81230
Phone/Fax No.: 970-641-1126
Email: Gsimillion@hotmail.com

SMITH & WESSON
2100 Roosevelt Avenue
P.O. Box 2208
Springfield, MA 01102-2208
Phone No.: 413-781-8300
Fax No.: 413-731-8980
Website: www.smith-wesson.com
Service email only: qa@smith-wesson.com
Smith & Wesson Research
Attn: Mr. Roy Jinks, S&W Historian
P.O. Box 2208
Springfield, MA 01102-2208
Phone No.: 413-781-8300
Fax No.: 413-731-8980

SMITHSON, J.P.
1194 N. 240 E.
Orem, UT 84057
Phone No.: 801-224-2041

SNAKE CHARMER
Verney-Carron USA, Inc.
320 Court Street
Clay Center, KS 67432
Phone No.: 785-632-2184
Fax No.: 785-632-6554
Website: www.snake-charmer.net
Email: email@verney-carron.us

SOLD USA (AUCTIONS)
1418 Industrial Drive
Matthews, NC 28105
Phone No.: 704-815-1500
Website: www.soldusa.com
Email: support@soldusa.com

SOTHEBY'S (AUCTIONS)
U.S. Office
1334 York Ave. at 72nd St.
New York, NY 10021
Phone No.: 212-606-7000
Fax No.: 212-606-7107
Website: www.sothebys.com
U.K. Office
34-35 New Bond Street at Bloomfield Place
London, WIA 2AA ENGLAND
Phone No.: 011-44-20-7293-5000
Fax No.: 011-44-20-7293-5989
Website: www.sothebys.com

SPARTAN GUN WORKS
Please refer to the Remington listing.

SPECIAL WEAPONS INC.
Warranty service & repair for Special Weapons LLC
www.tacticalweapons.com

SPHINX SYSTEMS LTD.
Distributor - please refer to Sabre Defence Industries LLC listing.
Importer - Rocky Mountain Armoury
591 Blue River Parkway
P.O. Box 1835
Silverthorne, CO 80498
Phone No.: 970-468-5001
Fax No.: 970-262-1499
Email: sphinxusa@sphinx-systems.ch
Factory
Gsteigstrasse 12
CH-3800 Matten SWITZERLAND
Fax No.: 011-41-033-821-1006
Website: www.sphinxarms.com
Email: info@sphinxarms.com

SPIDER FIREARMS
2005-B Murcott Dr.
St. Cloud, FL 34771-5826
Phone No.: 407-957-3617
Fax No.: 407-957-0296
Website: www.ferret50.com

SPRINGFIELD ARMORY
Springfield Inc.
420 W. Main St.
Geneseo, IL 61254
Phone No.: 309-944-5631
Phone No.: 800-680-6866
Fax No.: 309-944-3676
Website: www.springfield-armory.com
Email: sales@springfield-armory.com
Custom Shop Email: customshop@springfield-armory.com

STALLARD ARMS
Please refer to Hi-Point listing.

STEVENS, J., ARMS COMPANY
Please refer to Savage Arms listing.
Older Stevens Historical Research
Mr. John Callahan
53 Old Quarry Rd.
Westfield, MA 01085
$15.00/gun research fee.

STEYR MANNLICHER
Importer - Steyr USA
311 Hwy. 45 Alt. South
West Point, MS 39773
Phonoe No.: 662-492-8924
Fax No.: 662-492-8996
Email: steyrmannlicher@bellsouth.net
Factory - Steyr Mannlicher A.G. & Co. KG
Box 1000, Mannlicher Str. 1
Steyr A-4400 AUSTRIA
Fax No.: 01143-7252-78621
Website: www.steyr-mannlicher.com
Email: office@steyr-mannlicher.com

STOEGER INDUSTRIES
17601 Indian Head Hwy.
Accokeek, MD 20607-2501
Phone No.: 301-283-6986
Fax No.: 301-283-6300
Website: www.stoegerindustries.com

STONER RIFLE
Factory – please refer to Knight's Manufacturing Co. listing.

STRAYER TRIPP INTERNATIONAL
Please refer to the STI Internation listing.

STURM, RUGER & CO., INC.
Headquarters
1 Lacey Place
Southport, CT 06490
Phone No.: 203-259-7843
Fax No.: 203-256-3367
www.ruger.com
Service Center for Pistols, PC4 & PC9 Carbines
200 Ruger Road
Prescott, AZ 86301-6181
Phone No.: 928-778-6555
Fax No.: 928-778-6633
Website: www.ruger-firearms.com
Service Center for Revolvers, Long Guns & Ruger Date of Manufacture
411 Sunapee Street
Newport, NH 03773
Phone No.: 603-865-2442
Fax No.: 603-863-6165

SUPERIOR AMMUNITION, INC.
1320 Cedar Street
Sturgis, SD 57785
Phone No.: 605-347-9192
Fax No.: 605-347-9392
Website: www.superiorammo.com
Email: superiorammo@dtgnet.com

SUPER SIX LLC
3806 W. Lisbon Ave.
Milwaukee, WI 53208
Phone No.: 414-344-3343
Fax No.: 414-344-0304

SZECSEI Et. FUCHS FINE GUNS GmbH
North America Office
450 Charles St.
Windsor, Ontario N8X 3Z1 CANADA
Phone No.: 519-966-1234

Factory
Bozner Platz 1
corner Wilhelm-Greil-Strasse
A-6020 Innsbruck AUSTRIA
Phone/Fax No.: 011-43-512-5872-67
Website: www.jagdwaffe.com
Email: fuchs@jagdwaffe.com

TNW INC.
P.O. Box 311
Vernonia, OR 97064
Phone No.: 503-429-5001
Fax No.: 503-429-3505
Email: tnwcorp@aol.com

TACONIC FIREARMS, LTD.
Perry Lane, P.O. Box 553
Cambridge, NY 12816
Phone No.: 518-677-2704
Fax No.: 518-677-5974

TACTICAL RIFLES
19250 Hwy. 301
Dade City, FL 33525
Phone No.: 352-999-0599
Website: www.tacticalrifles.net
Email: info@tacticalrifles.net

TACTICAL WEAPONS
Please refer to FNH USA listing.

TANFOGLIO, FRATELLI, S.r.l.
Importer - please refer to European American Armory listing.
Importer - please refer to K.B.I. listing.
Factory
Via Valtrompia 39/41
I-25063 Gardone V.T. (BS) ITALY
Fax No.: 011-39-030-8910183
Website: www.tanfoglio.it
Email: info@tanfoglio.it

TAR-HUNT CUSTOM RIFLES, INC.
101 Dogtown Rd.
Bloomsburg, PA 17815-7544
Phone/Fax No.: 570-784-6368
Website: www.tar-hunt.com

TATE GUNMAKERS LLC
2951 Curran Road
Ione, CA 95640
Phone No.: 949-644-9557 (office)
Phone No.: 209-763-9040 (workshop)
Fax No.: 949-644-9558
Website: www.angloamericansport.com
Email: angloamericansport@earthlink.net

TAURUS INTERNATIONAL MANUFACTURING INC.
16175 NW 49th Ave.
Miami, FL 33014-6314
Phone No.: 305-624-1115
Fax No.: 305-623-7506
Website: www.taurususa.com

TAYLOR'S & CO.
304 Lenoir Dr.
Winchester, VA 22603
Phone No.: 540-722-2017
Fax No.: 540-722-2018
Web Site: www.taylorsfirearms.com
Email: info@taylorsfirearms.com

TELO, RENATO
Via Goldoni, 8
Gardone, VT, Brescia, ITALY I-25063
Fax No.: 011-39-030-831109

THOMPSON & CAMPBELL
Cromarty the Black Isle
Ross-shire IV11 8YB SCOTLAND
Fax No.: 011-44-01381-600767
Website: www.rifle.co.uk
Email: info@rifle.co.uk

THOMPSON/CENTER ARMS CO., INC.
P.O. Box 5002
Rochester, NH 03866
Customer Service Phone No.: 603-332-2333
Repair Only Phone No.: 603-332-2441
Fax No.: 603-332-5133
Website: www.tcarms.com
Email: tca@tcarms.com

THUNDER 5
Factory - MIL Inc.
1345-B Enterprise Rd.
Piney Flats, TN 37686
Website: www.thunder5.com

TIKKA
Importer - please refer to Beretta U.S.A. Corp. listing.
Factory - please refer to Sako listing.
Website: www.tikka.fi

TIME PRECISION ARMS
4 Nicholas Square
New Milford, CT 06776
Phone No.: 860-350-8343
Fax No.: 860-350-6343
Website: www.benchrest.com
Email: timeprecision@aol.com

TOLLEY, J & W
Please refer to Premier English Shotguns Ltd. listing.

TORNADO
Factory - AseTekno OY
P.O. Box 94 Plkneentie 18
FIN-00511 Helsinki, Finland
Fax No.: 011-358-9-753-6463
Website: www.asetekno.fi
Email: jaakko.vottonen@asetekno.fi

TOZ
Importer - please refer to Larry's Guns listing.
Factory
Fax No.: 011-0872-27-3439
Website: www.toz.vpk.ru
Email: toz@tula.net

TRADITIONS PERFORMANCE FIREARMS
1375 Boston Post Road
P.O. Box 776
Old Saybrook, CT 06475
Phone No.: 860-388-4656
Fax No.: 860-388-4657
Website: www.traditionsfirearms.com
Email: info@traditionsfirearms.com

TRIPLE ACTION LLC
708 W. 1800 N., Ste. 1A
Logan, UT 84341
Phone No.: 435-755-7083
Fax No.: 435-755-7021
Email: tripleaction50@aol.com

TRISTAR SPORTING ARMS LTD.
1814 - 16 Linn St.
N. Kansas City, MO 64116
Phone No.: 816-421-1400
Fax No.: 816-421-4182
Website: www.tristarsportingarms.com
Email: tristar@blitz-it.net

TROMIX CORPORATION
405 N. Walnut Ave. #8
Broken Arrow, OK 74012
Phone/Fax No.: 918-251-5640
Website: www.tromix.com
Email: tonyr@tromix.com

TRUVELO MANUFACTURERS (PTY) LTD.
Factory – Truvelo Armoury
107 Packard Street
Randjespark, Ext. 22, Midrand
P.O. Box 14189
Lyttelton 0140 SOUTH AFRICA
Fax No.: 011-27-11-314-1409
Website: www.truvelo.co.za
Email: armoury@truvelo.co.za

TULA ARMS PLANT
Factory
1 a Sovetskaja Str.
RUS-300002 Tula, RUSSIA
Fax No: 011-70872-27-3439
Email: tozmarketing@home.tula.net

DOUG TURNBULL RESTORATION, INC.
6680 Rts. 5 & 20, Box 471
Bloomfield, NY 14469
Phone/Fax No.: 585-657-6338
Website: www.turnbullrestoration.com

U.S. HISTORICAL SOCIETY
Please refer to America Remembers listing.

U.S.R.A. PISTOLS
(Information Only)
Mr. L. Richard Littlefield
P.O. Box 9
Jaffrey, NH 0342
Phone No.: 603-532-8004

U.S. ORDNANCE
P.O. Box 70425
Reno, NV 89570-0443
Phone No.: 775-356-1303
Fax No.: 775-356-1313
Website: www.usord.com

UBERTI, A. & C., S.r.l.
Importer - please refer Stoeger Industries listing.
Importer - please refer to Taylor's listing.
Importer - please refer to Tristar listing.
Importer - please refer to Dixie Gun Works listing.
Importer - please refer to Cabela's listing.
Importer - please refer to Cimarron, F.A. & Co listing.
Importer - please refer to E.M.F. Co. Inc. listing.
Importer - please refer to Navy Arms listing.
Service & Repair - VTI Gun Parts
P.O. Box 509
Lakeville, CT 06039
Phone No.: 860-435-8068
Fax No.: 860-435-8146
Website: www.vtigunparts.com
Factory - A. Uberti & C., S.r.l.
Via Artigiani 1
I-25063 Gardone, VT (BS) ITALY
Fax No.: 011-39-030-8341801
Website: www.ubertireplicas.it
Email: info@ubertireplicas.it

UGARTECHEA, ARMAS
Importer - please refer to Aspen Outfitting Co. listing.
Importer - please refer to Lion Country Supply listing.
Factory
P.O. Box 21
E-20600, Eibar, SPAIN
Fax No.: 011-3443-121669

UMAREX SPORTWAFFEN GmbH & CO. KG
Donnerfeld 2
D-59757 Arnsberg GERMANY
Fax No.: 011-49-2932-638224
Website: www.umarex.de

UNERTL ORDNANCE COMPANY INC.
2900 S. Highland Dr., Bldg. 18-C
Las Vegas, NV 89109
Phone No.: 702-369-4092
Fax No.: 702-369-4571
Website: www.unertlordnance.com

UNITED STATES FIRE ARMS MANUFACTURING COMPANY, INC.
445 Ledigard Street
Hartford, CT 06114
Phone No.: 877-277-6901
Fax No.: 860-724-6809
Website: www.usfirearms.com
Email: Sales@usfirearms.com

USELTON ARMS INC.
842 Conference Drive
Goodlettsville, TN 37072
Phone No.: 615-851-4919
Fax No.: 615-851-8811
Website: www.useltons.com

UZI
Trademark of IMI - no commercial importation.
Repair & Service - please refer to Vector Arms, Inc. listing.

VM HY-TECH LLC
2701 W. Grovers Ave., Ste. 100A
Phoenix, AZ 85053
Phone No.: 602-944-3956
Fax No.: 602-944-3953
Website: www.vmhytech.com
Email: info@vmhytech.com

VALKYRIE ARMS LTD.
120 State Ave. NE, No. 381
Olympia, WA 98501
Phone/Fax No.: 360-482-4036
Website: www.valkyriearms.com
Email: info@valkyriearms.com

VALMET
Factory - please refer to Marocchi listing.
Importer - please refer to Tristar listing.

VALTRO
Factory - Valtro Europe s.r.l.
Via Capretti 12
I-25136 Brescia, ITALY
Fax No.: 011-39-030-2000869
Email: info@valtroeurope.it

VECTOR ARMS INC.
270 West 500 North
N. Salt Lake, UT 84054
Phone No.: 801-295-1917
Fax No.: 801-295-9316
Website: www.vectorarms.com
Email: vectorarms@att.net

VEKTOR
P.O. Box 5445
Pretoria 0001 South Africa
Fax No.: 011-27-12-620-2407

VEPR. RIFLES
Factory – MOLOT JSC
Vyatskie Polyany Machine Building Plant
135 Lenin St.
Vyatskie Polyani, Kirov Region, 612960 RUSSIA
Fax No.: 011-007-83334-62199
Website: www.molot.net
Email: molot@lenta.ru

VERNEY-CARRON
Distributor - Process Solutions, Inc.
233 N. Court Street
Fayetteville, WV 25840
Phone No.: 304-574-1779
Fax No.: 304-574-1474
Email: truett@psi-pumps-valves.com
Importer - Verney-Carron U.S.A., Inc.
320 Court Street
Clay Center, KS 67432-3169
Phone No.: 785-632-2184
Fax No.: 785-632-6554
Website: www.verney-carron.us
Email: email@verney-carron.us
Factory - Verney-Carron S.A.
54, Boulevard Thiers
Boite Postale 72
F-42002 St.-Etienne Cedex 1 FRANCE
Phone No.: 011-33-477-791500
Fax No.: 011-33-477-790702
Website: www.verney-carron.com
Email: email@verney-carron.com

VERONA
Importer - B.C. Outdoors
P.O. Box 61497
Boulder City, NV 89006
Phone No.: 702-294-3056
Website: www.pmcammo.com
Email: verona@pmcammo.com

VIRGIN VALLEY CUSTOM GUNS
2410 West 350 North
Hurricane, UT 84737
Phone No.: 435-635-8941
Fax No.: 435-635-8903
Website: www.virginvalleyguns.com
Email: sales@virginvalleyguns.com

VOERE
Factory - Voere Austria
Untere Sparchen 56
A-6330 Kufstein, AUSTRIA
Fax No.: 011-43-5372-65752
Website : www.voere.de
Email: voere@aon.at

VOLQUARTSEN CUSTOM LTD.
P.O. Box 397
24276 240th St.
Carroll, IA 51401
Phone No.: 712-792-4238
Fax No.: 712-792-2542
Website: www.volquartsen.com
Email: info@volquartsen.com

VULCAN ARMAMENT, INC.
P.O. Box 2473
Inver Grove Heights, MN 55076-8473
Phone No.: 651-451-5956
Website: www.vulcanarms.com

WAFFENFABRIK HEIN
P.O. Box 610
Tekoa, WA 99033
Phone No: 509-284-2215
Website: www.rifleactions.com
Email: karl@rifleactions.com

WAFFENSTUBE GUGGI
Wienerstrasse 9
A-8020 Graz AUSTRIA
Fax No.: 011-43-316-711878
Website: www.guggi-arms.com
Email: office@guggi-arms.com

WAFFEN JUNG GMBH
Am Alten Garten 7
53797 Lohmar, GERMANY
Fax No.: 011-0224618491

WALTHER
Importer – please refer to Smith & Wesson listing.
www.waltheramerica.com
*Target pistol importer - please refer to Champion's Choice Inc.
listing.*
*Select pistols and GSP/rifle conversion kit importer -
factory repair station - Earl's Repair Service, Inc.*
437 Chandler Street (rear)
Tewksbury, MA 01876
Phone No.: 978-851-2656
Fax No.: 978-851-9462
Website: www.carlwalther.com
Email: info@carlwalther.com
German Company Headquarters (Umarex)
Carl Walther Sportwaffen GmbH
Donnerfeld 2
D-59757 Arnsberg GERMANY
Fax No.: 011-49-29-32-638149
Website: www.carl-walther.de
Email: sales@carl-walther.de
Factory - Carl Walther, GmbH
Sportwaffenfabrik
Postfach 4325
D-89033 Ulm/Donau, GERMANY
Fax No.: 011-49-731-1539170

WATSON BROS.
39 Redcross Way
London Bridge, London
SE1 1HG ENGLAND
Phone/Fax No.: 011-44-20-7403-3367

WEATHERBY
3100 El Camino Real
Atascadero, CA 93422
Technical Support: 805-466-1767
Service/Warranty: 800-227-2023
Fax No.: 805-466-2527
Website: www.weatherby.com

HERMANN WEIHRAUCH REVOLVER GmbH
*Firearms Importer - please refer to European American Armory
listing.*
Factory - H. Weihrauch, Sportwaffenfabrik
Postfach 25
D-97638 Mellrichstadt, GERMANY
Fax No.: 011-49-9776-707679
Email: info@hermann-weihrauch-revolver.de

WELLS CUSTOM RIFLES
110 North Summit Street
Prescott, AZ 86301
Phone No.: 928-445-3655
Website: www.cutrifle.com

WERNER BARTOLOT
Haupstrasse 11
A-9620 Hermagor, AUSTRIA
Fax No.: 011-43-0428225205
Website: www.jagdwaffe.at
Email: w.bartolot@utanet.at

DAN WESSON FIREARMS
5169 Highway 12 South
Norwich, NY 13815
Phone No.: 607-336-1174
Fax No.: 607-336-2730
Website: www.danwessonfirearms.com
Email: info@danwessonfirearms.com

WESTLEY RICHARDS & CO., Ltd.
Importer - Westley Richards Agency USA
3810 Valley Commons Drive
Bozeman, MT 59718
Phone No.: 406-586-1916
Fax No.: 406-586-3326
Factory
40 Grange Road
Bournbrook, Birmingham, ENGLAND B29 6AR
Fax No.: 011-44-121-414-1138
Website: www.westleyrichards.com

WICHITA ARMS, INC.
923 E. Gilbert
Wichita, KS 67211
Phone No.: 316-265-0661
Fax No.: 316-265-0760

WIFRA
Please refer to W.R. Saleri listing.

WILD WEST GUNS, INC.
7521 Old Seward Hwy., Unit A
Anchorage, AK 99518
Phone No.: 800-992-4570
Fax No.: 907-344-4005
Website: www.wildwestguns.com
Email: wwguns@ak.net

WILDEY F.A. INC.
45 Angevine Road
Warren, CT 06754
Phone No.: 860-355-9000
Fax No.: 860-354-7759
Website: www.wildeyguns.com
Email: wildeyfa@optonline.net

WILKES, JOHN GUNMAKERS LTD.
Distributor & Importer - The First National Gun Banque
P.O. Box 60719
Colorado Springs, CO 80960
Phone No.: 719-444-0786
Fax No.: 719-444-0731
Website: www.fngbcorp.com
Email: karl@fngbcorp.com

WILKINSON ARMS
Factory - Northwest Arms
26884 Pearl Rd.
Parma, ID 83660
Phone No.: 208-722-6771

WILLIAM & SON
10 Mount Street
London, W1K 2TY ENGLAND
Phone No.: 011-44-020-7493-8385
Fax No.: 011-44-020-7493-8386
Website: www.williamandson.com
Email: info@williamandson.com

WILLIAM LARKIN MOORE & CO.
8340 East Raintree Dr., Suite B-7
Scottsdale, AZ 85260
Phone No.: 480-951-8913
Fax No.: 480-951-3677
Website: www.williamlarkinmoore.com
Email: info@williamlarkinmoore.com

WILLIAM DOUGLAS & SONS
No information currently available.

WILLIAM EVANS LIMITED
67 St. James's Street
London SW1A 1PH ENGLAND
Fax No.: 011-44-171-499-1912
Website: www.williamevans.com
Email: sales@williamevans.com

WILLIAM POWELL & SON (GUNMAKERS), Ltd.
Factory & Store
35-37 Carrs Lane
Birmingham B47SX ENGLAND
Phone No.: 011-44-121-643-8362
Fax No.: 011-44-121-631-3504
Website: www.william-powell.co.uk
Email: sales@william-powell.co.uk

WILSON COMBAT
2234 CR 719
P.O. Box 578
Berryville, AR 72616-0578
Phone No.: 800-955-4856
Fax No.: 870-545-3310
Website: www.wilsoncombat.com

WINCHESTER - U.S.REPEATING ARMS
Administrative Offices
275 Winchester Avenue
Morgan, UT 84050-9333
Customer Service Phone No.: 800-333-3288
Parts & Service Phone No.: 800-945-1392
Fax No.: 801-876-3737
Website: www.winchester-guns.com
Factory - U.S. Repeating Arms Company, Inc.
275 Winchester Ave.
P.O. Box 30-300
New Haven, CT 06511-1970
Winchester Custom Shop
344 Winchester Ave.
New Haven, CT 06511-1970
Phone No.: 203-789-5503
Fax No.: 203-789-5526
Website: www.winchesterguns.com

WINCHESTER/OLIN
Models 101 & 23 only (Disc.)
Attn: Shotgun Customer Service
427 N. Shamrock Street
East Alton, IL 62024
Fax No.: 618-258-3393
Website: www.winchester.com

WISCHO JAGD-UND SPORTWAFFEN
Dresdener Strasse 30,
D-91058 Erlangen, GERMANY
Fax No.: 011-4991-31-300930
Website: www.wischo.com
Email: info@wischo.com

WISEMAN, BILL & CO.
P.O. Box 3427
Bryan, TX 77805
Phone No.: 979-690-3456
Fax No.: 979-690-0156

WM. PETE HARVEY AUCTIONS
P.O. Box 280
Cataumet, MA 02534
Phone/Fax No.: 508-548-0660
Website: www.firearmsauctions.com

WOODWARD, JAMES AND SONS
Factory - please refer to Purdey, James, & Sons, Ltd. listing.

YILDIZ SILAH SANAYI
Factory
Organize Sanayi Blgesi 40 Sokak No. 13
Burdur TURKEY
Fax No.: 01190-0248-252-9569

ZDF IMPORT EXPORT INC.
Please refer to Robinson Armament listing.

Z-M WEAPONS
203 South St.
Bernardston, MA 01337
Phone No.: 413-648-9501
Fax No.: 413-648-0219
Website: www.zmweapons.com
Email: zm@zmweapons.com

ZABALA HERMANOS, S.A.
Apartado 97
20600 Eibar SPAIN
Fax No.: 011-34-943-768201
Website: www.zabalahermanos.com
Email: imanol@zabalahermanos.com

ZANARDINI
Importer - S.O.G. Arms
15902A Halliburton Road #267
Hacienda Heights, CA 91745
Phone No.: 626-968-3208
Email: SOGARMS@earthlink.net
Factory - Zanardini, P. & C., S.n.c.
Via C. Goldoni, 34
I-25063 Gardone V.T. (Brescia), ITALY
Fax No.: 011-39-030-8910590
Website: www.zanardini.com
Email: info@zanardini.com

ZANOTTI 1625
(formerly Fabio Zanotti)
U.S. Service Center
33 Claremont Road
Bernardsville, NJ 07924
Phone No.: 908-766-2287
Fax No.: 908-766-1068
Factory - c/o Renato Gamba
Via Artigiani, 93
I0-25063 Gardone Val Trompia
Brescia, ITALY
Fax No.: 011-39-030-891-2180

ZASTAVA ARMS
Importer – please refer to KBI listing (certain models only).
Factory
Kragujevac, Trg Topolivaca 4
34000 MONTENEGRO
Fax No.: 011-381-034-323683
Email: zasatavanp@ppt.yu

ZIEGENHAHN & SOHN OHG
Importer - please refer to New England Custom Gun, Ltd. listing.
Factory
Suhler Str. 9 A
D-98544 Zella-Mehlis GERMANY
Fax No.: 011-49-36-82-896-28
Website: www.ziegenhahn.de
Email: info@ ziegenhahn.de

ZOLI, ANTONIO
Not affiliated with Angelo Zoli.
Factory - Zoli Antonio S.p.A.
Via Zanardelli, 39
I-25063 Gardone V.T. (BS) ITALY
Fax No.: 011-39-030-8911165
Website: www.zoli.it
Email: world@zoli.it

GLOSSARY

ACCOUTREMENT
All equipment carried by a soldier on the outside of their uniform, such as buckles, belts, or canteens, but not weapons.

ACTION
The heart of the gun, receiver, bolt, or breechblock feeding and firearm mechanism See Boxlock, Rolling Block, or Sidelock.

ADJUSTABLE CHOKE
A device built into the muzzle of a shotgun enabling changes from one choke to another.

AIRGUN
A gun that utilizes compressed air or gas to launch the projectile.

APERTURE SIGHT
A rear sight assembly consisting of a hole or aperture located in an adjustable rear sight through which the front sight and target are aligned.

ASSAULT RIFLE
Definition usually depends on if you're pro-gun or anti-gun. If you're pro-gun, it generally refers to a paramilitary style semi-auto rifle with certain features. If you're anti-gun, it can include almost anything, including sporter rifles from the turn of the 20th century.

AUTO LOADING
See Semi-automatic.

BACKSTRAP
Those parts of the revolver or pistol frame that are exposed at the rear of the grip.

BARREL
The steel tube (may be a sleeve wrapped in a synthetic material) that a projectile travels through.

BARREL BAND
A metal band, either fixed or adjustable, around the forend of a gun that holds the barrel to the stock.

BARREL THROAT
The breech end of a barrel that is chambered and somewhat funneled for the passage of a bullet from cartridge case mouth into the barrel. Also known as a forcing cone.

BEAVERTAIL FOREND
A wider than normal forend.

BLUING
The chemical process of artificial oxidation (rusting) applied to gun parts so that the metal attains a dark blue or nearly black appearance.

BOLT
The removable stud that rises and falls from the frame to lock the cylinder with the firing chamber in correct alignment with the bore.

BORE
Internal dimensions of a barrel (smooth or rifled) that can be measured using the Metric system (i.e. millimeters), English system (i.e. inches), or by the Gauge system (see gauge). On a rifled barrel, the bore is measured across the lands. It is also a traditional English term used when referring to the diameter of a shotgun muzzle (gauge in U.S. measure).

BOXLOCK ACTION
Typified by Parker shotgun in U.S. and Westley Richards in England. Generally considered inferior in strength to the sidelock. Developed by Anson & Deeley, the boxlock is hammerless. It has two disadvantages. First the hammer pin must be placed directly below the knee of action, which is its weakest spot. Second, the action walls must be thinned out to receive the locks. These are inserted from below into large slots in the action body, which is then closed with a plate. Greener crossbolt, when made correctly, overcomes many of the boxlock weaknesses.

BREECH
That portion of a gun which contains the rear chamber portion of the barrel(s), action, the trigger or firing mechanism, and the magazine.

BREVETTE
In gun terminology, refers to a European copy (usually Belgian, French, or English), or a gun patterned after a more famous design (i.e., Colt Brevette refers to a Dragoon, Pocket Model or 1851 Navy Model manufactured in Belgium under patent licensing agreement).

BUCKHORN SIGHT
Open metallic rear sight with sides that curl upward and inward.

BULL BARREL
A heavier, thicker than normal barrel with little or no taper.

BUTTPLATE
A protective plate (usually steel) attached to the back of the buttstock.

BUTTSTOCK
See Stock.

CALIBER
The diameter of the bore (measured from land to land), usually measured in either inches or millimeters/centimeters. It does not designate bullet diameter.

CAMO (CAMOUFLAGE)
Refers to a patterned treatment using a variety of different colors/patterns that enables a gun to blend into a particular outdoor environment. In most cases, this involves a film or additional finish to be put on top of a gun's wood and/or metal parts (i.e. Mossy Oak Break-Up, Advantage Timber, Realtree Hardwoods, etc.).

CASE COLORS
See Color Case Hardening.

CENTERFIRE
Self-contained cartridge where the detonating primer is located in the center of the case head.

CHAMBER
Rear part of the barrel that has been reamed out so that it will contain a cartridge. When the breech is closed, the cartridge is supported in the chamber, and the chamber must align the primer with the firing pin, the bullet with the bore.

CHAMBER THROAT
Also called throat, this is the area in the barrel that is directly forward of the chamber, which tapers to bore diameter.

CHECKERING
A functional decoration consisting of pointed pyramids cut into the wood. Generally applied to the pistol grip and forend/forearm areas, affording better handling and control.

CHOKE
The muzzle constriction on a shotgun to control spread of the shot.

CHOKE TUBES
Interchangeable screw-in devices allowing different choke configurations (i.e., cylinder, improved cylinder, improved modified cylinder, modified, full). While most choke tubes fit flush with the end of the barrel, some choke tubes now also protrude from the end of the barrel. Most recently made shotguns usually include three to five choke tubes with the shotgun.

CLIP
See Magazine.

COCKING INDICATOR
Any device which the act of cocking a gun moves into a position where it may be seen or felt in order to notify the shooter that the gun is cocked. Typical examples are the pins found on some high-grade hammer-less shotguns, which protrude slightly when they are cocked, and also the exposed cocking knobs on bolt-action rifles. Exposed hammers found on some rifles and pistols are also considered cocking indicators.

COLOR CASE HARDENING
A method of hardening steel and iron while imparting colorful swirls as well as surface figures. Normally, the desired metal parts are put in a crucible packed with a mixture of charcoal and finely ground animal bone to temperatures in the 800°C-900°C range, after which they are slowly cooled, and then submerged into cold water, leaving a thin, colorful protective finish.

COMB
The portion of the stock on which the shooter's cheek rests.

COMBINATION GUN
Generally a break-open shotgun-type configuration fitted with at least one shotgun barrel and one rifle barrel. Such guns may be encountered with either two or three barrels, and less frequently with as many as four or five, and have been known to chamber for as many as four different calibers.

COMPENSATOR
A recoil-reducing device that mounts on the muzzle of a gun to deflect part of the powder gases up and rearward. Also called a muzzle brake.

CRANE
In a modern solid-frame, swing-out cylinder revolver, the U-shaped yoke on which the cylinder rotates, and which holds the cylinder in the frame. The crane/yoke is the weakest part of a revolver's mechanism.

CRIMP
A turning in of the case mouth to affect a closure or to prevent the bullet from slipping out of the case mouth. Various crimps include: roll crimp, pie crimp, star or folded crimp, and rose crimp.

CROWNING
The rounding or chambering normally done to a barrel muzzle to insure that the mouth of the bore is square with the bore axis and that the edge is countersunk below the surface to protect it from impact damage. Traditionally, crowning was accomplished by spinning an abrasive-coated brass ball against the muzzle while moving it in a figure-eight pattern until the abrasive had cut away any irregularities and produced a uniform and square mouth.

CROSSBOLT
A transverse locking rod/bar used in many SxS boxlock shotguns and a few rifles, which locks the standing breech and barrels. Originally designed by W.W. Greener, this term is also referred to as the Greener crossbolt.

CRYOGENIC TEMPERING
Computer-controlled cooling process that relieves barrel stress by subjecting the barrel to a temperature of 310oF for 22 hours.

CYLINDER
A rotating cartridge holder in a revolver. The cartridges are held in chambers and the cylinder turns, either to the left or the right, as the hammer is cocked, depending on the gunmaker's design.

CYLINDER ARM
See Crane.

DAMASCENE
The decorating of metal with another metal, either by inlaying or attaching in some fashion.

DAMASCUS BARREL
A barrel made by twisting, forming and welding thin strips of steel around a mandrel.

DERRINGER
Usually refers to a small, concealable pistol with one or two short barrels.

DOUBLE ACTION
The principle in a revolver or auto-loading pistol wherein the hammer can be cocked and dropped by a single pull of the trigger. Most of these actions also provide capability for single action fire. In auto loading pistols, double action normally applies only to the first shot of any series, the hammer being cocked by the slide for subsequent shots.

DOUBLE ACTION ONLY
Hammer no longer cocks in single action stage (many new DAO models are hammerless).

DOUBLE-BARRELED
A gun consisting of two barrels joined either side-by-side or one over the other.

DOUBLE-SET TRIGGER
A device that consists of two triggers. One cocks the mechanism which spring-assists the other trigger, substantially lightening trigger pull.

DOVETAIL
A flaring machined or hand-cut slot that is also slightly tapered toward one end. Cut into the upper surface of barrels and sometimes actions, the dovetail accepts a corresponding part on which a sight is mounted. Dovetail slot blanks are used to cover the dovetail when the original sight has been removed or lost; this gives the barrel a more pleasing appearance and configuration.

DRILLED & TAPPED
Refers to screw holes that are drilled into the top of a receiver/frame, allowing scope bases, blocks, rings, or other sighting devices to be rigidly attached to the gun.

DRILLING
German for triple, which is their designation for a three-barrel gun. This is usually two shotgun barrels and one rifle barrel.

EJECTOR
Automatic mechanical device used to eject empty cartridges from chamber(s) after firing.

ELECTROCIBLE
Unique reusable target designed like an aircraft propeller that causes it to spin and go in different directions. In competition, electrocibles come out of one of five boxes located 25 meters from the shooter, who must hit it before it crosses over the ring at 21 meters.

ENGINE TURNING
Overlapped spots of circular polishing.

ENGLISH STOCK
A straight, slender-gripped stock.

ENGRAVING
The art of engraving metal in decorative patterns. Scroll engraving is the most common type of hand engraving encountered. Much of today's factory engraving is rolled on, which is done mechanically. Hand engraving requires artistry and knowledge of metals and related materials.

ETCHING
A method of decorating metal gun parts, usually done by acid etching or photo engraving.

EXTRACTOR
A device which partially lifts the spent casing(s) from the breech area, allowing the empty shell(s) to be removed manually.

FALLING BLOCK
A single shot action where the breechblock drops straight down when the lever is actuated.

FIT AND FINISH
Terms used to describe overall firearm workmanship.

FIRE CONTROL
Modern term referring to trigger mechanism and operating system - sometimes detachable.

FIRING PIN
That part of a gun that strikes the cartridge primer, causing detonation.

FLOATING BARREL
A barrel bedded to avoid contact with any point on the stock.

FLOOR PLATE
Usually, a removable/hinged plate at the bottom of the receiver covering the magazine well.

FORCING CONE
Forward part of the chamber in a shotgun where the chamber diameter is reduced to bore diameter. The forcing cone aids the passage of shot into the barrel.

FOREARM

In this text, a separate piece of wood in front of the receiver and under the barrel used for hand placement when shooting. Forearms can get expensive - H&H currently prices a replacement forearm at £10,000 (that's $16,000!).

FOREND

Usually the forward portion of a one-piece rifle or shotgun stock (in this text), but can also refer to a separate piece of wood.

FRAME

The part of a firearm that the action (lock work), barrel, and stock/grip are connected to. Most of the time this is used when referring to a handgun or hinged frame long gun.

FREE RIFLE

A rifle designed for international-type target shooting. The only restriction on design is a maximum weight of 8 kilograms (17.6 lbs.).

FRONT STRAP

That part of the revolver or pistol grip frame that faces forward and often joins with the trigger guard. In target guns, notably the .45 ACP, the front strap is often stippled to give the shooter's hand a slip-proof surface.

GAUGE/GA.

A unit of measure used to determine a shotgun's bore. Determined by the amount of pure lead balls equaling the bore diameter needed to equal one pound (i.e., a 12 ga. means that 12 lead balls exactly the diameter of the bore weigh one pound). In this text, .410 is referenced as a bore (if it was a gauge, it would be a 68 ga.).

GAUGE VS. BORE DIAMETER

10-Gauge = Bore Diameter of .775 inches or 19.3mm
12-Gauge = Bore Diameter of .729 inches or 18.2mm
16-Gauge = Bore Diameter of .662 inches or 16.8mm
20-Gauge = Bore Diameter of .615 inches or 15.7mm
28-Gauge = Bore Diameter of .550 inches or 13.8mm
68-Gauge = Bore Diameter of .410 inches or 12.6mm

GRIP

The handle used to hold a handgun, or the area of a stock directly behind and attached to the frame/receiver of a long gun.

GRIPS

Can be part of the frame or components attached to the frame used to assist in accuracy, handling, control, and safety of a handgun. Many currently manufactured semi-auto handguns have grips that are molded with checkering as part of the synthetic frame.

GRIPSTRAP(S)

Typically refers to the front and back metal that attaches to a handgun frame and supports the grips/stocks.

GROOVES

The spiral cuts in the bore of a rifle or handgun barrel that give the bullet its spin or rotation as it moves down the barrel.

HAMMER

A part of a gun's mechanism that causes it to fire. May or may not have a firing pin attached.

HAMMERLESS

Some "hammerless" firearms do in fact have hidden hammers, which are located in the action housing. Truly hammerless guns, such as the Savage M99, have a firing mechanism that is based on a spring-activated firing pin.

HALF COCK

A position of the hammer in a hammer-activated firing mechanism that serves as a manual safety.

HEEL

Back end of the upper edge of the buttstock at the upper edge of the buttplate or recoil pad.

JUXAPOSED

See Side-by-Side listing.

LAMINATED STOCK

A gunstock made of many layers of wood glued together under pressure. Together, the laminations become very strong, preventing damage from moisture, heat, and warping.

LANDS

Portions of the bore left between the grooves of the rifling in the bore of a firearm. In rifling, the grooves are usually twice the width of the land. Land diameter is measured across the bore, from land to land.

MAGAZINE (MAG.)

The container (may be detachable) which holds cartridges under spring pressure to be fed into the gun's chamber.

MAGNUM (MAG.)

A modern cartridge with a higher-velocity load or heavier projectile than standard.

MAINSPRING

The spring that delivers energy to the hammer or striker.

MANNLICHER STOCK

A full-length, slender stock with slender forend extending to the muzzle (full stock), affording better barrel protection.

MICROMETER SIGHT

A finely adjustable target sight.

MONTE CARLO STOCK
A stock with an elevated comb used primarily for scoped rifles.

MUZZLE
The forward end of the barrel where the projectile exits.

MUZZLE BRAKE
A recoil-reducing device attached to the muzzle.

NEEDLE GUN
Ignition system invented by Johan Nikolas v. Dreyse in 1829. This ignition system, which uses a paper cartridge, became obsolete with the invention of the metallic cartridge.

OVER-UNDER (SUPERPOSED)
A two-barrel gun in which the barrels are stacked one on top of the other.

PARALLAX
Occurs in telescopic sights when the primary image of the objective lens does not coincide with the reticle. In practice, parallax is detected in the scope when, as the viewing eye is moved laterally, the image and the reticle appear to move in relation to each other.

PARAMILITARY
Typically refers to a gun's configuration/styling resembling some military configurations. In this text, it refers mostly to semi-auto rifles that are styled/patterned after popular military models (i.e., AR-15/M16, AK-47, Galil, Uzi, FALs, etc.).

PARKERIZING
Matted rust-resistant oxide finish, usually matte or dull gray, or black in color, found on military guns.

PATINA
A condition of metal surfaces created after the bluing has oxidized naturally over the course of time coupled with normal wear and usage. Patina can vary in color from a light grey to dark brown.

PEEP SIGHT
Rear sights consisting of a hole or aperture through which the front sight and target are aligned.

PEPPERBOX
An early form of revolving repeating pistol, in which a number of barrels were bored in a circle in a single piece of metal resembling the cylinder of a modern revolver. Functioning was the same as a revolver. The entire cylinder was revolved to bring successive barrels under the hammer for firing. Though occurring as far back as the 16th century, the pepperbox did not become practical until the advent of the percussion cap in the early 1800s. Pepperboxes were made in a wide variety of sizes and styles, and reached their popularity peak during the percussion period. Few were made after the advent of practical metallic cartridges. Both single and double action pepperboxes were made. Single-barreled revolvers after the 1840s were more accurate and easier to handle and soon displaced the rather clumsy and muzzle-heavy pepperbox.

PERCH BELLY
Refers to a rifle's stock configuration where the bottom portion is curved rather than straight between the buttplate and pistol grip.

PINFIRE
Self-contained cartridge that is detonated by striking a small pin sticking through the side wall of the cartridge casing.

PICATINNY
Refers to a flat rail on top, bottom, or sides of the frame/slide, allowing different optics/sights to be used on the gun.

POLYGONAL
Circular rifling without hard-edged lands and grooves.

POPE RIB
A rib integral with the barrel. Designed by Harry M. Pope, famed barrel maker and shooter, the rib made it possible to mount a target scope low over the barrel.

PROOF MARK
Proofmarks are usually applied to all parts actually tested, but normally appear on the barrel (and possibly frame), usually indicating the country of origin and circa of proof (especially on European firearms). In the U.S., there is no federalized or government proof house, only the manufacturer's in-house proofmark, indicating that a firearm has passed its internal quality control standards per government specifications.

PRIMER
Small detonating cap fitted in the head of a centerfire cartridge case that, when struck by a firing pin, ignites the powder charge.

PRIMER RING
Refers to a visible dark ring created by the primers in centerfire ammunition around the firing pin hole in the frame after much use.

RECEIVER
That part of a rifle or shotgun (excluding hinged frame guns) that houses the bolt, firing pin, mainspring, trigger group, and magazine or ammunition feed system. The barrel is threaded into the somewhat enlarged forward part of the receiver, called the receiver ring. At the rear of the receiver, the butt or stock is fastened. In semiautomatic pistols, the frame or housing is sometimes referred to as the receiver.

RELEASE TRIGGER
A trap shooting trigger that fires the gun when the trigger is released.

RIB
A raised sighting plane affixed to the top of a barrel.

RIFLING
The spirally cut grooves in the bore of a rifle or handgun. The rifling stabilizes the bullet in flight. Rifling may rotate to the left or the right, the higher parts of the bore being called lands, the cuts or lower parts being called the grooves. Many types exist, such as oval, polygonal, button, Newton, Newton-Pope, parabolic, Haddan, Enfield, segmental rifling, etc. Most U.S.-made barrels have a right-hand twist, while British gun makers prefer a left-hand twist. In practice, there seems to be little difference in accuracy or barrel longevity.

RIMFIRE
Self-contained metallic cartridge where the priming compound is contained inside the rim of the cartridge case. Detonated by the firing pin(s) striking the bottom edge of the outside rim.

RINGS
See Scope Rings.

ROLLING BLOCK ACTION
Single shot action, designed in the U.S. and widely used in early Remington arms. Also known as the Remington-rider action, the breechblock, actuated by a lever, rotates down and back from the chamber. Firing pin is contained in block and is activated by hammer fall.

SAFETY
A mechanism in/on a gun that prevents it from firing. Many different types and variations.

SAW HANDLE
Refers to distinctive squared-off type of pistol grip design where stock makes right angle at top and is then attached to the frame.

SCHNABEL FOREND/FOREARM
The curved/carved flared end of the forend/forearm that resembles the beak of a bird (Schnabel in German). This type of forend is common on Austrian and German guns, and it was popular in the U.S., but the popularity of the Schnabel forend/forearm comes and goes with the seasons. A Schnabel forend is often seen on custom stocks and rifles.

SCOPE RINGS (BLOCKS/BASES)
Metal mounts used to attach a scope to the top of a gun's frame/receiver.

SEAR
The pivoting part in the firing or lock mechanism of a gun. The sear is linked to the trigger, and may engage the cocking piece or the firing pin.

SEMI-AUTOMATIC
A pistol, rifle, or shotgun that is loaded manually for the first round. Upon pulling the trigger, the gun fires, ejects the fired round, cocks the firing mechanism, and feeds a fresh round from the magazine. The trigger must be released after each shot and pulled again to fire the next round.

SHORT ACTION
A rifle action designed for shorter cartridges.

SHOTSHELL
Self-contained round of ammunition used in shotguns, generally either brass and paper (older mfg.) or brass/steel and plastic (newer mfg.).

SIDE-BY-SIDE (JUXTAPOSED)
A two-barrel shotgun where the barrels are arranged side-by-side.

SIDE LEVER
Refers to opening mechanism lever on either left or right side of receiver/frame.

SIDELOCK
A type of action, usually long gun, where the moving parts are located on side of the lock plates, which in turn are inlet in the stock. Usually found only on better quality shotguns and rifles.

SIDEPLATES
Ornamental steel panels normally attached to a boxlock action to simulate a sidelock.

SINGLE ACTION
A firearms design which requires the hammer to be manually cocked for each shot. Also, an auto loading pistol design which requires manual cocking of the hammer for the first shot only.

SINGLE TRIGGER
One trigger on a double-barrel gun. It fires both barrels individually by successive pulls.

SLING SWIVELS
Metal loops affixed to the gun on which a carrying strap is attached.

SPUR TRIGGER
A trigger mounting system that housed the trigger in an extension of the frame in some old guns. The trigger projected only slightly from the front of the extension or spur, and no trigger guard was used on these guns.

STOCK
Usually refers to the buttstock of a long gun, or that portion of a rifle or shotgun that comes in contact with the shooter's arm, and is attached to the frame/receiver.

STOCKS
Older terminology used to describe handgun grips (see Grips).

SUICIDE SPECIAL
A mass-produced variety of inexpensive single action revolvers and derringers, usually with a spur trigger. Produced under a variety of trade names, these guns earned their nickname by being almost as dangerous to shoot as to be shot at.

SUPERPOSED
Refers to an O/U barrel configuration.

TAKEDOWN
A gun which can be easily taken apart in two sections for carrying or shipping.

TANG(S)
Usually refers to the extension straps (upper and lower) of a rifle or shotgun receiver/frame to which the stock/grips are attached.

TOP LEVER
Refers to the opening lever mechanism on top of the upper frame/tang.

TOP STRAP
The upper part of a revolver frame, which often is either slightly grooved - the groove serving as rear sight - or which carries at its rearward end a sight that may be adjustable.

TRAP STOCK
A shotgun stock with greater length and less comb drop (Monte Carlo, in many cases) used for trap shooting, enabling a built-in height lead when shooting.

TRIGGER
Refers to a release device in the firing system that starts the ignition process. Usually a curved, grooved, or serrated piece of metal that is pulled rearward by the shooter's finger, and then activates the sear or hammer.

TRIGGER GUARD
Usually a circular or oval band of metal, horn, or plastic that goes around the trigger to provide both protection and safety in shooting circumstances.

TWIST BARRELS
A process in which a steel rod (called a mandrel) was wrapped with skelps (ribbons of iron). The skelps were then welded in a charcoal fire to form one piece of metal, after which the rod was driven out to be used again. The interior of the resulting tube then had to be laboriously bored out by hand to remove the roughness. Once polished, the outside was smoothed on big grinding wheels, usually turned by waterpower.

UNDER-LEVER
Action opening lever that is usually located below or in trigger guard. It can also be side pivoting from forearm.

VENTILATED RIB
A sighting plane affixed along the length of a shotgun barrel with gaps or slots milled for cooling and lightweight handling.

VERNIER
Typically used in reference to a rear aperture (peep) sight. Usually upper tang mounted, and is adj. for elevation by means of a highly accurate vernier.

VIERLING
A German word designating a four-barrel gun.

WUNDHAMMER GRIP/SWELL
Originally attributed to custom gunsmith Louis Wundhammer, it consists of a bulge on the right side of the pistol grip that ergonomically fills the palm of a trigger hand.

YOKE
See Crane.

YOUTH DIMENSIONS
Usually refers to shorter stock dimensions and/or lighter weight enabling youth/women to shoot and carry a lighter, shorter firearm.

ABBREVIATIONS

*	Banned 1994-2004 due to Crime Bill (may be current again)	HP	Hollow Point	RKST	Round Knob Short Tang
		I	Improved	RR	Red Ramp
A	Standard Grade Walnut	IC	Improved Cylinder	RSM	Remington Short Magnum
A2	AR-15/M16 Style/Configuration	IM	Improved Modified	RSUM	Remington Short Ultra Magnum
		intro.	Introduced		
A3	AR-15/M16 Style/Configuration	IPSC	International Practical Shooting Confederation	S	Short
				S&W	Smith & Wesson
AA	Extra Grade Walnut			S/N	Serial Number
AAA	Best Quality Walnut	ISSF	International Shooting Sports Federation	SA	Single Action
ACP	Automatic Colt Pistol			SAA	Single Action Army
adj.	Adjustable	L	Long	SAE	Selective Automatic Ejectors
AE	Automatic Ejectors or Action Express	lbs.	Pounds		
		LC	Long Colt	SAHP	Stupid Auction High Prices!
appts.	Appointments	LOP	Length Of Pull		
AWB	Assault Weapons Ban	LPI	Lines Per Inch	SAUM	Short Action Ultra Magnum
B	Blue	LR	Long Rifle		
BAC	Browning Arms Company	LT	Long Tang or Light	SB	Shotgun Butt
		LTRK	Long Tang Round Knob	ser.	Serial
BBL	Barrel	M (MOD.)	Modified Choke	SG	Straight Grip
BMG	Browning Machine Gun	M-4	Newer AR-15/M16 Style/Configuration	SK	Skeet
BOSS	Ballistic Optimizing Shooting System			sq.	Square
		M&P	Military & Police	SMG	Submachine Gun
BP	Buttplate or Black Powder	Mag.	Magnum Caliber	SML	Short Magazine Lee Enfield Rifle
		mag.	Magazine or Clip		
BPE	Black Power Express	MC	Monte Carlo	SNT	Single Non-Selective Trigger
BR	Bench Rest	MFG. or Mfg.	Manufactured/Manufacture		
BT	Beavertail			SPEC	Special
C/B 1994	Introduced because of 1994 Crime Bill	MIL SPEC	Mfg. to Military Specifications	SPG	Semi-Pistol Grip
				Spl.	Special
c.	Circa	MK	Mark	SR	Solid Rib
cal.	Caliber	MOA	Minute of Angle	SRC	Saddle Ring Carbine
CB	Crescent Buttplate	MR	Matted Rib	SS	Single Shot or Stainless Steel
CC	Case Colors	MSR	Manufacturer's Suggested Retail		
CCA	Colt Collectors Association			SSA	Super Short Action
		N	Nickel	SST	Single Selective Trigger
CF	Centerfire	N/A	Not Applicable or Not Available	ST	Single Trigger
CH	Crosshair			SxS	Side by Side
COMP	Compensated/Competition	NE	Nitro Express	TBA	To Be Announced
		NIB	New In Box	TD	Takedown
C-R	Curio-Relic	NM	National Match	TGT	Target
CYL/C	Cylinder	no.	Number	TH	Target Hammer
DA	Double Action	NSST	Non-Selective Single Trigger	TS	Target Stocks
DAO	Double Action Only			TT	Target Trigger
DB	Double Barrel	O/U	Over and Under	UIT	Union Internationale de Tir
DCM	Director of Civilian Marksmanship	OA	Overall		
		OAL	Overall Length	UMC	Union Metallic Cartridge Co.
DISC. or Disc.	Discontinued	OB	Octagon Barrel		
DSL	Detachable Side Locks	OBFM	Octagon Barrel w/ Full Magazine	VG	Very Good
DST	Double Set Triggers			VR	Ventilated Rib
DT	Double Triggers	OBO	Or Best Offer	w/o	Without
DWM	DeutscheWaffen and Munitions Fabrik	OCT	Octagon	w/	With
		oz.	Ounce	WBY	Weatherby
		Para.	Parabellum	WC	Wad Cutter
EJT	Ejectors	PG	Pistol Grip	WCF	Winchester Centerfire
EXC	Excellent	POR/P.O.R.	Price On Request	WD	Wood
EXT	Extractors	POST-'89	Paramilitary mfg. after Federal legislation in Nov. 1989	WFF	Watch For Fakes
F	Full Choke			WIN	Winchester
F&M	Full & Modified			WO	White Outline
FA	Forearm	POST-BAN	Configuration mfg. from September 13, 1994 until September 14, 2004 per C/B 1994	WRA	Winchester Repeating Arms Co.
FBT	Full Beavertail Forearm				
FE	Fore End			WRF	Winchester Rimfire
FFL	Federal Firearms License			WRM	Winchester Rimfire Magnum
		PPD	Post Paid		
FK	Flat Knob	PRE-'89	Paramilitary mfg. before Federal legislation in Nov. 1989	WSM	Winchester Short Magnum
FKLT	Flat Knob Long Tang				
FM	Full Mag			WSSM	Winchester Super Short Magnum
FMJ	Full Metal Jacket	PRE-BAN	Mfg. before September 13, 1994 per C/B 1994		
FN	Fabrique Nationale			WSUM	Winchester Short Ultra Magnum
FPS	Feet Per Second	QD	Quick Detachable		
g.	Gram	RB	Round Barrel/Round Butt	WW	World War
ga.	Gauge			X (1X)	1X Wood Upgrade or Extra Full Choke Tube
gr.	Grain	REC	Receiver		
GCA	Gun Control Act	REM	Remington		
GOVT	Government	REM. MAG.	Remington Magnum	XX (2X)	2X Wood Upgrade or Extra Extra Full Choke Tube
H&H	Holland & Holland	RF	Rimfire		
HB	Heavy Barrel	RFM	Rimfire Magnum		
HC	Hard Case	RK	Round Knob	XXX (3x)	3X Wood Upgrade
HMR	Hornady Magnum Rim-	RKLT	Round Knob Long Tang		

FIREARMS/SHOOTING ORGANIZATIONS

Listed below are the names and addresses of various firearms organizations/associations throughout the U.S. You are encouraged to join those organizations that pertain to your region and area of interest. As thorough as we try to be, every year we get back quite a bit of mail back from individual firearms associations that is undeliverable. So, if your club does not appear on the following pages or doesn't have a current address, please forward the correct information to us for inclusion in the next edition.

For the past 40 years, the NRA's affiliated Gun Collecting clubs (identified in the following listings with an *) have been a vital part of NRA's educational outreach programs. With over 100 of these clubs, there is one for almost every collecting interest and area. Collector affiliates are leaders in firearms safety programs for gun shows, and they sponsor some of the most popular and successful shows in the country. They participate in the NRA's Annual Meetings and Exhibits with spectacular displays of rare and historically important arms. Affiliates also sponsor the annual National Gun Show and the annual National Gun Collecting Seminar. An annual awards ceremony for collector affiliates is held every year at the NRA's Annual Meetings.

Academics for the Second Amendment (A2A)
Prof. J.E. Olson, President
Hamline University
P.O. Box 131254
St. Paul, MN 55113
Email: jolson@gw.hamline.edu

* Alabama Gun Collectors
Harold Boyd
P.O. Box 70965
Tuscaloosa, AL 35407
Phone: 205-758-6922
$20 Annual Membership Fee

* Alamo Arms Collectors' Association
P.O. Box 680642
San Antonio, TX 78268-0642
Leslie W. Moch, Secretary
Phone: 830-980-4746
George O. Stenzel, Treasurer
Phone: 210-523-5540
Email: aacanews@satx.rr.com
$20 yearly membership, meetings first Tuesday of each month

*Alaska Gun Collectors Association
P.O. Box 242233
Anchorage, Alaska 99524
Phone: 907-346-1075
Website: www.agca.net

American Custom Gunmakers Guild
Jan Billeb, Executive Director
22 Vista View
Cody, WY 82414-9606
Phone: 307-587-4297
Website: www.acgg.org
Email: acgg@acgg.org
$75 Associate Membership Fee
$150 Commercial Associate Membership Fee

* American Single Shot Rifle Association
Rudi Prusok
625 Pine Street
Marquette, MI 49855
Phone: 906-225-1825

* American Society of Arms Collectors Assn.
J. Williams La Rue
P.O. Box 50400
Albuquerque, NM 87181-0400
Phone: 505-299-7950
Website: www.americansocietyo-farmscollectors.org
Invitation only
Dues: $200 annual

* Arizona Arms Association
Cynthia Hale
P.O. Box 46464
Phoenix, AZ 85063
Phone: 602-210-3959

* Arkansas Gun Cartridge Collectors Club
Joe Burnett
P.O. Box 1015
Little Rock, AR 72203
Phone: 501-682-6728

* Ark - La - Tex Gun Collectors
Thomas L. Baird, President
9601 Blom Blvd.
Shreveport, LA 71118
Phone: 318-686-7101

* Arms Collectors of Georgia
Robert Messner
1554 Bubling Creek Rd.
Atlanta, GA 30319
Phone: 770-740-4908
Dues: $45 annual
Meetings 2nd Monday of each month

* Arms Collectors of Southwest Washington
James Hoeflein
P.O. Box 2622
Vancouver, WA 98668
Phone: 360-263-3447

* Association of Ohio Longrifle Collectors
Robin D. (Dan) Smith
23003 St., Rt. 339
Beverly, OH 45715
Phone: 740-984-4896
$15 annual dues

* Bayou Gun Club of LA
Robert Eddy
P.O. Box 73402
Metairie, LA 70033
Phone: 504-455-7078

* Browning Collectors Association
Charles P. Wagner, Secretary
711 Scott Street
Covington, KY 41011
Phone: 859-331-0955
Website: www.browningcollectors.com

Buffalo Bill Historical Center
David Kennedy
Robert W. Woodruff Curator
Cody Firearms Museum
720 Sheridan Ave.
Cody, WY 82414
Phone: 307-587-4771
Website: www.bbhc.org

* C.A.D.A. (Collector Arms Dealer Association)
P.O. Box 427
Thomson, IL 61285

California Rifle & Pistol Association, Inc.
271 E. Imperial Highway, Suite #620
Fullerton, CA 92835
Phone: 714-992-2772

* Central Penn Antique Arms Association
John E. Holman Jr.
978 Thistle Road
Elizabethtown, PA 17022

* Central States Gun Collectors Association
Lois Schwade
633-3 Rd. Street SE
Mason City, IA 50401-4104
Phone: 641-424-9234

* Central Wisconsin Gun Collectors Association
Norman Miller
P.O. Box 2184
Oshkosh, WI 54903
Phone: 920-235-3672

Chisholm Trail Antique Gun Association
1906 Richmond
Wichita, KS 67203

* Colorado Gun Collectors Association
Mr. William E. Pittman, Secretary/Treasurer
8075 S. Harrison Way
Centennial, CO 80122-3620
Phone: 303-773-0238
Website: www.CGCA.com
Email: Secretary@CGCA.com
$25 Annual Dues

* Colt Collectors Association
Karen Green, Secretary
P.O. Box 2241
Los Gatos, CA 95031
Website: www.coltcollectorsassoc.com
$40 Annual Membership Fee
$70 Annual Membership Fee - Outside U.S.

Contemporary Longrifle Association
P.O. Box 2097
Stauton, VA 24402
Phone: 540-886-6189
Website: www.longrifle.ws

* Dakota Territory Gun Collectors Association
Vicki Sandvig, Executive Secretary
Sonny Pesicka, President
P.O. Box 5053
West Fargo, ND 58078
Phone: 701-361-9215

* Dallas Arms Collectors Association, Inc.
Richard Shea
P.O. Box 704
DeSoto, TX 75123
Phone: 972-223-3066
Fax: 972-223-3277
Website: www.dallasarms.com

* Delaware Antique Arms Collectors Association
Robert Howard
P.O. Box 2966
Wilmington, DE 19805

* Eastern Shores Arms Collectors
Rodney Schwarm
P.O. Box 1836
Easton, MD 21601
Phone: 410-822-1555

* Egyptian Collectors Association
Bob Leckrone
Box 138
Centralia, IL 62801
Phone: 618-896-5519

The Firearms Coalition of Colorado
Steve Schreiner, President
P.O. Box 1454
Englewood, CO 80150-1454
Phone: 303-296-4867
Email: FCCtalk@yahoogroups.com
$20 Annual Membership Fee

* Forks of the Delaware Historical Arms Society, Inc.
Mr. Howard A. Hoffman
3491 Linden St.
Bethlehem, PA 18017
Phone: 610-997-8613
Fax: 610-997-8614
$20 Annual Membership Fee

* Ft. Lee Arms Collectors
Walter Dubas
50 Second Street
Clifton, NJ 07011
Phone: 914-796-2300

* Garand Collectors Association
Frank Walter
P.O. Box 187
Angola, IN 46703
Phone: 219-668-0440

Georgia Arms Collectors
Michael Kindberg
P.O. Box 277
Alpharetta, GA 30009
Phone: 678-860-8600

German Gun Collectors Association
Dietrich Apel
438 Willow Brook Rd
P.O. Box 385
Plainfield, NH 03781
Phone: 603-469-3450
Fax: 603-469-3471
Website: www.germanguns.com
Email: jaeger@valley.net
$36 Annual Fee (U.S. & Canada)
$50 Annual Fee (Foreign)

Gibbs Military Collector's Club
211 Lawn St.
Martinsburg, WV 25401
Phone: 304-262-1651
Fax: 304-262-1658
Website: www.gibbsrifle.com
Email: support@gibbsrifle.com

* Glock Collectors Association
Colette Steck, Membership Secretary
P.O. Box 1063
Maryland Heights, MO 63043
Phone/Fax: 314-878-2061
Website: www.glockcollectors.com
Email: casteck@prodigy.net
$25 Annual Membership Fee, includes 3-4 journals

Golden Eagle Collectors Association
Chris Showler, Secretary
11144 Slate Creek Rd.
Grass Valley, CA 95945

Great Lakes Military Collectors Association
P.O. Box 401
Maumee, OH 43537

Gun Owners Civil Rights Alliance/ Concealed Carry Reform Now!
Joseph E. Olson, President
P.O. Box 131254
St. Paul, MN 55113
Phone: 651-636-4465
Website: www.mnccrn.org
$30 Annual Membership Fee

Gun Owners of America
Larry Pratt, Executive Director
8001 Forbes Pl., Suite 102
Springfield, VA 22151
Fax: 703-321-8408
Website: www.gunowners.org
Email: goamail@gunowners.org
$20 Annual Membership Fee

* **Hawaii Historic Arms Association**
Sheldon Tyau
Box 1733
Honolulu, HI 96806
Phone: 808-955-9552

* **High Standard Collectors Association**
John Hanks
P.O. Box 1578
Decatur, IL 62525-1578
Website: www.highstandard.org
$20 Annual Dues

* **Houston Gun Collectors Association**
P.O. Box 741429
Houston, TX 77274-1429
Phone: 713-981-6463
Website: www.hgca.org
$50 Annual Dues

Indianhead Firearms Association
13810 25th Ave.
Chippewa Falls, WI 54729
Phone: 715-723-0860

* **Indian Territory Gun Collectors Association**
David Sears, Secretary-Treasurer
P.O. Box 33201
Tulsa, OK 74153-1201

* **International Ammunition Association**
John Moss
1033 Gilman Drive
Colma, CA 94015
Phone: 650-992-2829

* **Iroquois Arms Collectors Association**
Kenneth Keller, Secretary
Susann Keller, Show Secretary
214 70th St.
Niagara Falls, NY 14304

Jersey Shore Antique Arms Collectors
Steve Cassidy
P.O. Box 100
Bayville, NJ 08721-0100
$25 Annual Membership Fee

Kansas Cartridge Collectors Association
Vic Suelter
2185 E. Iron Drive
Lincoln, KS 67455

Kentuckiana Arms Collectors Association
Sally Harper, Secretary
P.O. Box 1776
Louisville, KY 40201
Phone: 502-425-2460
$20 Annual Membership Fee

* **Kentucky Rifle Association**
Attn: Ruth Collis
2319 Sue Ann Dr.
Lancaster, PA, 17602.

* **Lancaster Muzzle Loading Rifle Association**
James H. Frederick, Jr.
700 Prospect Road
Columbia, PA 17512

Lee County Gun Collectors Association
P.O. Box 6168
Fort Myers Beach, FL 33932
Phone: 239-463-2840

* **Long Island Antique Gun Collectors Association**
Frederick R. Wilkens
35 Beach Street
Farmingdale, L.I., NY 11735
Phone: 516-249-5133
$40 Annual Membership Fee

* **Mahoning Valley Gun Collectors Association**
P.O. Box 86
Campbell, OH 44405
$15 annual dues

* **Mannlicher Collectors Association**
P.O. Box 10105
College Station, TX 77842
$25 Annual Dues
$34 Annual Foreign Dues
Website: www.mannlicher.org

* **Marlin Firearms Collectors Association, Ltd.**
P.O. Box 491
Clay Center, KS 67432-0491
$5 Initiation Fee
$15 Annual Membership Fee
$17 Canadian (U.S. funds)
$24 International (U.S. Funds)

* **Maryland Arms Collectors Association (MACA)**
Del Kuzemchak, Secretary
33 S. Main Street P.O. Box 206
Loganville, PA 17342-0206
$25 Annual Membership Fee

Maryland Licensed Firearms Dealers Association, Inc.
P.O. Box 10237
Baltimore, MD 21234-9998
Phone: 410-356-9485
Fax: 410-356-9486

* **Massachusetts Arms Collectors**
P.O. Box 111
Hingham, MA 02043
Phone: 781-749-2889

* **Maumee Valley Gun Collectors Association**
P.O. Box 492
Maumee, OH 43537
Website: www.mvgca.com

Memphis Antique Weapons Association
Mr. Rob Estes
P.O. Box 20
Somerville, TN 38068

* **Michigan Antique Arms Collectors**
2454 Dorchester N.
Troy, MI 48084
Phone: 248-649-2664

* **Midwest Gun Traders Inc.**
Walter Butler
1304 Inwood Drive
Ft. Wayne, IN 46815
Phone: 219-426-3562

* **Miniature Arms Collectors/ Makers Society, Ltd.**
Bill Adrian, President
2502 Fresno Ln.
Plainfield, IL 60544-8470
Phone: 815-254-8692

* **Minnesota Weapons Collectors**
Alvin Olson
P.O. Box 605
Waseca, MN 56093
Phone: 507-833-5615
Website: www.mwca.org

* **Missouri Valley Arms Collectors Association, Inc. (MVACA)**
Membership Secretary
P.O. Box 6013
Leawood, KS 66206
Phone: 913-649-4248
Website: www.mvacagunshow.com
$25 Annual Membership (age 21 and over)
$10 Annual Membership (under 21)

* **Montana Arms Collectors Association**
Dean E. Yearout
1516 - 21st Ave. S.
Great Falls, MT 59405
Phone: 406-761-7280
$20 Annual Membership Fee

* **Nat'l Automatic Pistol Collectors Association (N.A.P.C.A.)**
Thompson D. Knox
Box 15738
St. Louis, MO 63163
Phone: 314-638-6505
Website: www.napca.net
$45 annual dues U.S.
$50 annual dues Canada
$60 Elsewhere

* **National Mossberg Collectors Association**
Victor Havlin
P.O. Box 487
Festus, MO 63028
$10 Annual Membership Fee
Phone: 636-937-6401
Website: www.mossbergcollectors.org

National Rifle Association (NRA)
11250 Waples Mill Rd.
Fairfax, VA 22030
Phone: 888-JOIN-NRA/800-NRA-3888
Fax: 703-267-3970
Website: www.nra.org
Email: membership@nrahq.org
$35 Regular Annual Membership Dues
$30 Annual Senior Membership (65 years of age and older, also disabled vets)
$60 for two years
$85 for three years
$125 for five years
$750 Life Membership Dues
$375 Senior Life Membership (also disabled vets)
$15 Annual Junior Membership (18 years and younger)
$10 Annual Liberty Associate Membership (w/o magazine)

National Shooting Sports Foundation (NSSF)
11 Mile Hill Road
Newtown, CT 06470
Phone: 203-426-1320
Fax: 203-426-1245
Website: www.nssf.org

New Eastcoast Arms Collectors Associates, Inc., NEACA, Inc.
Cathy Petronis, Secretary
38 N. Main St.
P.O. Box 385
Mechanicsville, NY 12118
Phone: 518-664-9743
Website: www.neaca.com
$30 annual dues
Promoters of Saratoga Springs & NY arms fairs

* **New Mexico Gun Collectors**
Paul Lisle
P.O. Box 13687
Albuquerque, NM 87192

* **New York State Arms Collectors**
Jack Ackerman
24 S. Mountain Terrace
Binghamton, NY 13903
Phone: 607-723-5668

* **North Carolina Gun Collectors**
Scott Woller
P.O. Box 23570
Charlotte, NC 28227
Phone: 704-573-1686

* **North Eastern Arms Collectors Assoc., Inc.**
Thomas J. Mulligan
P.O. Box 306
Island Park, NY 11558
Email: Mulligun@aol.com
$20 Annual Membership Fee

* **Northern Florida Arms Collectors**
Danny Brady
4471 Loveland Pass Dr.
Jacksonville, FL 32210
Phone: 904-613-9280

* **Northern Indiana Gun Collectors**
William Best
15237 W. 12th Road
Plymouth, IN 46563
Phone: 219-936-4431

* **Northwest Montana Arms Collectors Association (NWMACA)**
Paul Willis, Treasurer
P.O. Box 653
Kalispell, MT 59903-0653
Phone: 406-755-3980
Email: pswillis@centurytel.net

* **Ohio Gun Collectors Association**
Laura Knotts, Business Manager
P.O. Box 670406
Sagamore Hills, OH 44067-0406
Phone: 330-467-5733
Fax: 330-467-5793
Website: www.ogca.com
Email: ogca@ogca.com
$30.00 Annual Membership Fee
$10.00 Application Fee
Members and guests of members only

* **Oregon Arms Collectors, Inc.**
2221 NE Hoyt St.
Portland, OR 97232-2858
Website: members.tripod.com/ ~oregonarmscollectors/index.html
$20 Annual Membership Fee

* **Palm Beach Historical Arms Association**
Adolph Stuffer
6304 Silver Moon Lane
Greenacres, FL 33463

Parker Gun Collectors Association
Ron Kirby, Executive Director
8825 Bud Smith Road
Wake Forest, NC 27587
Phone: 919-554-4556
Fax: 919-554-8120
Website: www.parkergun.org

* **Paso Del Norte Gun Collectors**
James Foran
P.O. Box 31613
El Paso, TX 79930
Phone: 915-566-7968

* **Penn Antique Gun Collectors Assn.**
Ronald Gabel
P.O. Box 97
Slatington, PA 18080
Phone: 610-767-0356
Website: www.pagca.com

* **Penn Gun Collectors Assn.**
Richard Vensel
5209 Norma Dr.
Pittsburgh, PA 15236
Phone: 412-655-3850

Peoples Rights Organization
4444 Indianola Ave.
Columbus, OH 43214-2226
Phone: 614-268-0122
Fax: 614-261-9981
Firearms Classes: 614-261-1601
Refuse to be a Victim Classes: 614-323-3102
Website: www.pro-training.info
Website: www.peoplesrights.org
Email: d-walker@juno.com
$30 Annual Membership Fee
$360 Lifetime Membership Fee

* **Pioneer Gun Collectors Assn.**
Jim Marten
4500 South Georgia
Amarillo, TX 79110
Phone: 806-352-5331

* **Potomac Arms Collectors Association**
Attn: Secretary
P.O. Box 1812
Wheaton, MD 20915
$25 Annual Membership Fee

* **Remington Society of America**
George Slatten, President
1440 Wallace Rd. NW
Salem, OR 97304
Phone: 503-588-2080
Website: www.remingtonsociety.com
Email: Creamer10@comcast.net
$45 New Annual Membership
$40 Renewal Membership
$400 Life Membership
Foreign Memberships Available

* **Ruger Collectors Association, Inc.**
P.O. Box 240
Green Farms, CT 06838
Phone: 203-259-9498, Ext. 124
$30 Annual Membership Fee

SAAMI (Sporting Arms & Ammunition Manufacturers' Institute)
380 Maple Ave. West, Ste. 101
Vienna, VA 22180
Phone: 703-255-9020
Fax: 703-255-9029
Website: www.saami.org

SASS (Single Action Shooting Society)
23255 La Palma Avenue
Yorba Linda, CA 92887
Phone: 714-694-1800
Fax: 714-694-1815
Website: www.sassnet.com
Email: SASS@sassnet.com

* **St. Louis Antique Arms Collectors**
11220 W. Florissant Ave.
Florissant, MO 63033

Sako Collectors Association
Konie Wheeler, President
57330 Walker Road
Scappoose, OR 97056
Phone: 503-543-4410

* **Santa Barbara Historical Arms Coll. Association**
P.O. Box 6291
Santa Barbara, CA 93160-6291
$35 Initiation
$25 Annual Membership Fee

San Bernardino Valley Arms Collectors
Robert Walter
18710 Cajon Blvd.
San Bernardino, CA 92407
Los Alamos, NM 87544

San Fernando Valley Arms Collectors Association
Tom Barrabee, Secretary
10655 Olive Grove Ave.
Sunland, CA 91040
$20 Annual Membership Fee

San Gabriel Valley Arms Collectors
Gerald C. Knight, Secretary/Treasurer
1140 Daveric Drive
Pasadena, CA 91107-1740
Phone: 818-351-9368
$20 Annual Dues

* **San Luis Obispo Historical Arms Society**
P.O. Box 3554
San Luis Obispo, CA 93403
Second Amendment Foundation

The New Gun Week
Womens & Guns Magazine
Gottlieb-Tartaro Report
Second Amendment Reporter
Alan Gottlieb, Founder
James Madison Building
12500 NE Tenth Place
Bellevue, WA 98005
Phone: 425-454-7012
Fax: 425-451-3959
Member Services: 800-426-4302
Website: www.saf.org
Email: info@saf.org
Tax deductible membership dues $15.00
Tax deductible life membership dues $150

* **Smith & Wesson Collectors Association**
Michael G. Speers, Administrative Assistant
P.O. Box 357
Larned, KS 67550-0357
Phone: 620-285-6880
Email: swca357@hotmail.com
$60 first year dues
$45 renewal dues

* **Smoky Mountain Gun Collectors Assn.**
Huhg Yarbro
244 Hi-Way Drive
Clinton, TN 37716
Phone: 865-457-0505

* South Carolina Arms Collectors Assn.
Bobbby Oshields
403 Wilton Street
Greenville, SC 29609
Phone: 863-233-8892

* South Jersey Arms Collectors
Ralph Fairley
6 Georgetown Road
Glassboro, NJ 08028
Phone: 609-881-0637

* Southeastern Antique Arms Collectors, Inc.
Donald Armstrong, Secretary
Doug Eberhart, President & Show Chairman
P.O. Box 1104
Alpharetta, GA 30009
One annual show per year the 3rd week in Feb.

* Southern California Arms Collectors Association, Inc.
Martin J. Miller, Jr.
P.O. Box 7432
Thousand Oaks, CA 91359-7432
$40 Annual Membership Fee
Phone: 805-373-0683

* Starke Gun Collectors
Robert Kramer
6275 Parks Road
Alliance, OH 44601
Phone: 330-875-9503

* Stratford Gun Collectors
Steve Varga
90 Meadow Park Drive
Milford, CT 06460

Swiss Gun Collectors Association
P.O. Box 98
St. Johnsbury, VT 05819
Phone: 802-751-8064
Fax: 802-751-8268
Website: www.swiss-guncollectors.com
Email: info@swiss-guncollectors.com

* Tennessee Military Collectors Assn.
William Price
P.O. Box 1006
Brentwood, TN 37024
$10 annual dues
Phone: 615-661-9379
Website: www.tmcaonline.org
Email: blake.wylie@puresafety.com

Texas Gun Collectors Association (TGCA)
Carolyn Mims
P.O. Box 701314
San Antonio, TX 78270

* The Thompson Center Association
P.O. Box 792
Northboro, MA 01532
Email: TCA@aol.com
$30 Annual Membership Fee

* Thompson Collectors Association
Tracie Hill
P.O. Box 8710
Newark, OH 43055
Phone: 740-345-9777

* Tri-State Gun Collectors, Inc.
Manette Sneary, Business Manager
P.O. Box 1201
Lima, OH 45802
Phone: 419-647-0067

Tulsa Arms Collectors Association
Mr. Joe Wanenmacher,
Secretary-Treasurer
P.O. Box 33201
Tulsa, OK 74153-1201

* Utah Gun Collectors
Carrol Cone
P.O. Box 711161
Salt Lake City, UT 84121
Phone: 801-944-9324

* VA Gun Collectors
William Hurst
38802 Charles Town Pike
Waterford, VA 22190
Phone: 703-882-3543

* Wabash Valley Gun Collectors
Roger Dorsett
2601 Willow Road
Urbana, IL 61801
Phone: 217-367-5452

Washington Arms Collectors, Inc.
Aimee Stambach, Office Manager
P.O. Box 389
Renton, WA 98057-0389
Phone: 425-255-8410
Fax: 425-255-8946
Website: www.washingtonarms collectors.org
Email: office@washingtonarms collectors.org
$25 Membership Dues
$500 Life Membership Dues

* Weapons Collectors Society of Montana
Mike Balko
3004 7th Ave. South
Great Falls, MT 59405
Phone: 406-727-1579

* Weatherby Collectors Association, Inc.
P.O. Box 478
Pacific, MO 63069
Phone: 636.271.3336
Website: www.weatherbycollec-tors.com
Email: WCAsecretary@aol.com
$30 Membership Fee
$500 Lifetime Membership Fee

* Westchester Collectors Club
Martin Fasack
54 Farm View Road
Pt. Washington, NY 11050
Phone: 516-627-8804

Williamette Valley Arms Collectors Association, Inc.
James Crudele, Executive Secretary
P.O. Box 5191
Eugene, OR 97405
Phone: 541-747-5271
$20 Membership Fee

* Winchester Arms Collectors Association
David P. Bichrest, Executive Secretary
P.O. Box 367
Silsbee, TX 77656-0367
Phone: 409-385-5768
Fax: 409-385-5726
Web site: www.winchestercollector.org
Email: davidwaca@msn.com
$40 annual dues U.S.A.
$50 annual dues Canada
$60 annual dues Foreign
$500 lifetime membership fee

Winchester Club of America
Karen Sellers
Box 151B Crane Brook Rd
Alstead, NH 03602
$35 U.S. Annual membership
$50 Foreign membership
$350 Life U.S. membership
$500 Life Foreign membership

* Wisconsin Gun Collectors Assn.
Robert Zellmer
N. 59 W. 27099 Ainsworth
Sussex, WI 53089
Phone: 262-538-1316

* Wmette Valley Arms Collectors Assn.
James Crudele
P.O. Box 5191
Eugene, OR 97405

* Wyoming Weapons Collectors
Pat Aldrich
P.O. Box 1784
Laramie, WY 82073
Phone: 307-742-4630

* Ye Conn Gun Guild
Peter Kuck
602 Park Road
W. Hartford, CT 06107

* Zumbro Valley Arms Collectors, Inc.
Floyd Baumler
P.O. Box 6621
Rochester, MN 55901
Phone: 507-289-9383

CONSERVATION ORGANIZATIONS

The following are not firearms associations, but are conservation organizations that may or may not have links to hunting/shooting sports. These organizations are dedicated to preserving wildlife and natural habitat. You are encouraged to contact these organizations to learn more.

Dove Sportsman's Society
31 Quail Run
P.O. Box 610
Edgefield, SC 29824
Phone: 803-637-5731
Fax: 803-637-0037
Website: www.dovesociety.org
Membership includes Dove Hunter magazine

Ducks Unlimited
One Waterfowl Way
Memphis, TN 38120
Phone: 901-758-3825
Fax: 901-758-3850
Website: www.ducks.org

Foundation for North American Wild Sheep
Raymond Lee, President
720 Allen Ave.
Cody, WY 82414-9981
Phone: 307-527-6261
Website: www.fnaws.org
1 Yr. Membership $45; 3 Yrs. $120

The Mule Deer Foundation
1005 Terminal Way, Ste. 170
Reno, NV 89502
$25 Annual Membership Fee

The National Wild Turkey Federation
P.O. Box 530
Edgefield, SC 29824
Phone: 800-843-6983
Call for membership details.

North American Bear Foundation
1159 Bedow Road SW
Fort Ripley, MN 56449
Phone: 218-828-7739
Website: www.nabf.org

North American Moose Foundation
P.O. Box 30
610 W. Custer, Ste. D
Mackay, ID 83251
Phone: 208-588-2939
Fax: 208-588-2980
Website: www.moosefoundation.org
Email: moose@atcnet.net

North American Pronghorn Association
P.O. Box 1977
Parker, CO 80134
Email: info@northamericanpronghorn.org

North American Pronghorn Foundation
P.O. Box 13813
Rawlins, WY 82301
Phone: 307-324-5238
Website: www.antelope.org

North American Wild Sheep Foundation
Minnesota-Wisconsin Chapter
P.O. Box 892
Hudson, WI 54016

Pheasants Forever
1783 Buerkle Circle
White Bear Lake, MN 55110
Phone: 651-773-2000
Fax: 651-773-5500
Website: www.pheasantsforever.org
Email: pf@pheasantsforever.org
$30 Annual Membership Fee includes five issues of Pheasants Forever magazine

Quail Unlimited
31 Quail Run
P.O. Box 610
Edgefield, SC 29824
Phone: 803-637-5731
Fax: 803-637-0037
Website: www.qu.org

Email: national@qu.org
$30 Annual Membership includes bimonthly subscription to Quail Unlimited

Rocky Mountain Elk Foundation
2291 W. Broadway
Missoula, MT 59802
Phone: 406-523-4500
Fax: 406-523-4581
$30 Membership Fee includes six issues of Bugle magazine

The Ruffed Grouse Society
Ronald P. Burkert
451 McCormick Rd.
Coraopolis, PA 15108
Phone: 888-564-6747
Website: www.ruffedgrousesociety.org
Email: rgs@ruffedgrousesociety.org
$25 Annual Membership Fee
$50 Conservation Membership Fee
$100 Sustaining Membership Fee
$250+ Various Sponsor Membership Fee
All memberships include a subscription to Ruffed Grouse Society magazine.

Safari Club International
4800 W. Gates Pass Rd.
Tucson, AZ 85745-9490
Phone: 520-620-1220
Website: www.safariclub.org
$55 Annual Membership Fee USA/ CAN/MEX

Whitetails Unlimited
P.O. Box 720
2100 Michigan Street
Sturgeon Bay, WI 54235
Phone: 800-274-5471
Fax: 920-743-4658
Website: www.whitetailsunlimited.com
Email: nh@whitetailsunlimited.com

REFERENCE SOURCES

Adler, Dennis. *Blue Book of Airguns*. 1st ed. Minneapolis, MN: Blue Book Publications, 2001.

Adler, Dennis. *Blue Book of Modern Black Powder Values*. 1st ed. Minneapolis, MN: Blue Book Publications, 2000.

Adler, Dennis. *Blue Book of Modern Black Powder Values*. 2nd ed. Minneapolis, MN: Blue Book Publications, 2002.

Adler, Dennis. *Colt Blackpowder Reproductions & Replicas*. Minneapolis, MN: Blue Book Publications, 1998.

Allen, John. *Blue Book of Modern Black Powder Values*. 3rd ed. Minneapolis, MN: Blue Book Publications, Inc., 2003.

Allen, John and Dennis Adler. *Blue Book of Modern Black Powder Arms*. 4th ed. Minneapolis, MN: Blue Book Publications, Inc., 2004.

Antaris, Dr. Leonardo. *Astra Automatic Pistols*. Sterling, CO: FIRAC Publishing Co., 1988.

Antaris, Dr. Leonardo. *Star Firearms*. Davenport, IA: Firac Publishing, 2002.

Bady, Donald B. *Colt Automatic Pistols*. Los Angeles, CA: Borden Publishing Co., 1973.

Baer, Larry L. *The Parker Book*. North Hollywood, CA: Beinfeld Publishing Co., 1974.

Ball, Robert. *Mauser Military Rifles of the World*. Iola, WI: Krause Publications, 1996.

Ball, Robert. *Remington Firearms: The Golden Age of Collecting*. WI: Krause Publications, 1995.

Barnes, Frank C. *Cartridges of the World*. Northbrook, IL: DBI Books, Inc., 1989.

Beeman, Dr. Robert, and John Allen. *Blue Book of Airguns*. 2nd ed. Minneapolis, MN: Blue Book Publications, Inc., 2002.

Beeman, Dr. Robert, and John Allen. *Blue Book of Airguns*. 3rd ed. Minneapolis, MN: Blue Book Publications, Inc., 2003.

Beeman, Dr. Robert, and John Allen. *Blue Book of Airguns*. 4th ed. Minneapolis, MN: Blue Book Publications, Inc., 2004.

Beeman, Dr. Robert, and John Allen. *Blue Book of Airguns*. 5th ed. Minneapolis, MN: Blue Book Publications, Inc., 2005.

Belford, James N., and Jack Dunlap. *Mauser Self Loading Pistol*. Alhambia, CA: Borden Publishing Co., 1969.

Bender, Roy G. III. *Mauser*. Houston, TX: Collector's Press, 1971.

Boothroyd, Geoffry & Susan M. *Boothroyd's Directory of British Gunmakers*. Amity, OR: Sand Lake Press, 1994.

Breathed and Schroeder. *System Mauser*. Chicago, IL: Handgun Press, 1967.

Brophy, William S. *L.C. Smith Shotguns*. North Hollywood, CA: Beinfeld Publishing Co., 1977.

Brophy, William S. *Marlin Firearms*. Harrisburg, PA: Stackpole Books, 1989.

Butzer, David F. *The American Shotgun*. Middlefield, CT: Lyman Publications, 1973.

Buxton, Warren H. *The P-38 Pistol*. Vols. 1-3. Los Alamos, NM: U.C. Ross Books.

Byron, David. *Gunmarks, Tradenames, Codemarks, and Proofs from 1870 to the Present*. New York, NY: Crown Publishers, 1979.

Carder, Charles. *Side by Sides of the World*. Delphos, OH: AVIL ONZE Publishing.

Carder, Charles. *Side by Sides of the World Y2K*. Delphos, OH: AVIL ONZE Publishing, 2000.

Condry, Ken, and Larry Jones. *The Colt Commemoratives*. 1961-1986. Dallas, TX: Taylor Publishing Co., 1989.

Costanza, Sam. *World of Lugers*. Vol. 1. Mayfield Heights, OH: World of Lugers, 1977.

Eastman, Matt. *Browning, Sporting Arms of Distinction*. Fitzgerald, GA: Published by author, 1994.

Ezell, Edward Clinton. *Handguns of the World*. Harrisburg, PA: Stackpole Books, 1981.

Ezell, Edward Clinton. *Small Arms of the World*. 12th ed. Harrisburg, PA: Stackpole Books, 1983.

Dance, Tom. *High Standard; A Collector's Guide to the Hamden & Hartford Target Pistols*. Lincoln, RI: Andrew Mobray Publishers, 1991.

Flayderman, Norm. *Flayderman's Guide*. 7th ed. Northbrook, IL: DBI Books, Inc., 1998.

Gardner, Col. Robert. *Small Arms Makers*. New York, NY: Bonanza Books, 1963.

Grant, James. J. *Boys' Single Shot Rifles*. Prescott, AZ: Wolfe Publishing Company, 1991.

Groenewold, John. *Quackenbush Guns*. Mundelein, IL: Published by author, 2000.

Gunther, Mullins, Price, and Cote. *The Parker Story*. Vol. 1. Knoxville, TN: Parker Story Joint Venture Group, 1998.

Gunther, Mullins, Price, and Cote. *The Parker Story*. Vol. 2. Knoxville, TN: Parker Story Joint Venture Group, 2000.

Hill and Anthony. *Confederate Long Arms and Pistols*. Charlotte, NC: Confederate Arms, 1978.

Jinks, Roy G. *History of Smith & Wesson*. North Hollywood, CA: Beinfeld Publishing Co., 1977.

Karr and Karr, Jr. *Remington Handguns*. 2nd ed. Stackpole Co., 1951.

Kenyon, Charles Jr. *Lugers at Random*. Chicago, IL: Handgun Press, 1969.

Kersten, Manfred. *Walther: A German Legend*. Long Beach, CA: Safari Press, Inc., 2001.

Kimmel, J. *Savage & Stevens Arms*. Portland, OR: Corey/Stevens Pub., Inc., 1990.

Kopel, Graham, and Moore. *A Study of the Colt Single Action Army Revolver*. La Puente, CA: Kopel, Graham, and Moore Publishers, 1978.

Krasne, Jerry A. *Enyclopedia and Reference Catalog for Auto Loading Guns*. San Diego, CA: Triple K Manufacturing, 1989.

Leithe, Frederick. *Japanese Handguns*. California: Borden Publishing Co., 1968.

Madis, George. *The Model 12*. Lancaster, TX: Published by author, 1981.

Madis, George. *The Winchester Book*. Lancaster, TX: Privately published by author, 1975.

Marcot, Roy. *Remington, America's Oldest Gunmaker*. Peoria, IL: Primedia Special Interest Publications, 1998.

Maxwell, Samuel L., Sr. *Lever Action Magazine Rifles*. Published by author, 1978.

Muderlak, Ed. *Parker Guns, The Old Reliable*. Long Beach, CA: Safari Press, 1997.

Murray, Douglas. *The Ninety-Nine*. Published by author, 1985.

Nonte, George C., Jr. *Firearms Encyclopedia*. Outdoor Life: New York, NY, 1973.

Olson, Ludwig. *Mauser Bolt Action Rifles*. Montezuma, IA: F. Brownell & Son Publishers, Inc., 1976.

Price, Charlie and Parker Story Joint Venture Group. *Parker Gun Identification & Serialization*. *Minneapolis*, MN: Blue Book Publications, Inc., 2002.

Rankin, James L. *Walther*. Vols. 1-3. Coral Gables, FL: Published by author, 1976.

Rule, Roger C. *The Rifleman's Rifle*. Northridge, CA: Alliance Books, Inc., 1982.

Sellers, Frank. *American Gunsmiths*. Highland Park, NJ: The Gun Room Press, 1983.

Sellers, Frank. *Sharp's Firearms*. North Hollywood, CA: Beinfeld Publishing Co., 1978.

Serven, Ed. *The Collecting of Guns*. Bonanza Books, 1964.

Sharpe, Phillip B. *The Rifle in America*. Funk and Wagnalls, 1947.

S. Hackensack. *Shooter's Bible*. NJ: Published annually by Stoeger Industries.

Skennerton, Ian. *British Small Arms of World War II*. Labrador, Australia: Self-published, 1988.

Skennerton, Ian. *The Lee Enfield Story*. Labrador, Australia: Self-published, 1992.

Skennerton, Ian & Stamps. *.380 Enfield Revolver*. Labrador, Australia: Self-published, 1992.

Skennerton, Ian. *Small Arms Identification Series*. Vols. 1-17. Labrador, Australia: Self-published, 1993-2003.

Steindler. *Steindler's New Firearms Dictionary*. Phoenix, AZ: Stackpole Books, 1985.

Still, Jan C. *Axis Pistols*. Marceline, MO: Walsworth Publishing Co., 1986.

Still, Jan C. *Imperial Lugers*. Marceline, MO: Walsworth Publishing Co., 1991.

Still, Jan C. *Third Reich Lugers*. Marceline, MO: Walsworth Publishing Co., 1988.

Supica, Jim and Nahas, Richard. *Standard Catalog of Smith & Wesson*. Iola, WI: Krause Publications, 1996.

Supica, Jim. *Standard Catalog of Smith & Wesson*. Vol. 2. Iola, WI: Krause Publications, 2001.

Tanner, Hans. *Guns of the World*. Bonanza Books, 1972, 1977.

Vanderlinden, Anthony. *Belgian Browning Pistols 1889-1949*. Greensboro, NC: Wet Dog Publications, 2001.

Vanderlinden, Anthony, & H.M. Shirley. *Browning Auto-5 Shotgun - The Belgian FN Production*. Greensboro, NC: Wet Dog Publications, 2003.

Webster, Donald B. Jr. *Suicide Specials*. Harrisburg, PA: Stackpole, Co., 1958.

West, Bill. *Browning Arms & History*. Santa Fe Springs, CA: Stockton Trade Press, Inc., 1972.

West, Bill. *Marlin and Ballard Firearms & History*. Norwalk, CA: Stockton Trade Press, Inc., 1977.

West, Bill. *Remington Arms & History*. Whittier, CA: Stockton Trade Press, Inc., 1970.

West, Bill. *Savage and Stevens Arms & History*. Whittier, CA: Stockton Trade Press, Inc., 1971.

Whitaker, Dean H. *Model 70 Winchester 1937-1964*. Dallas, TX: Taylor Publishing Co., 1978.

Wilkerson, Don. *Post-War Colt Single Action Army*. Published by author, 1978.

Wilkerson, Don. *Post-War Colt Single Action Revolver, 1976-1986*. Dallas, TX: Taylor Publishing, 1986.

Wilkerson, Don. *Colt Scouts, Peacemakers, and New Frontiers in .22 Caliber*. Marceline, MO: Walsworth Publishing Co., 1993.

Wilkerson, Don. *Colt Single Action Army Revolver, Pre-War/Post-War Model*. Minneapolis, MN: Broughton Printing Inc., 1991.

Wilson, R.L. *The Colt Engraving Book*. Vols. 1-2. New York, NY: Bannerman's Limited Edition, 2001.

Wilson, R.L. *The Book of Colt Firearms*. Minneapolis, MN: Blue Book Publications, Inc., 1993.

Wilson, R.L. *Colt, An American Legend*. New York, NY: Abbeville Press.

Wilson, R.L. *Colt Commemorative Firearms*. Geneseo, IL: Robert E.P. Cherry Publishing Co., 1973.

Wilson, R.L. *The Colt Heritage*. New York, NY: Simon and Schuster.

Wilson, R.L. *Silk & Steel*. New York: Random House, 2003.

Wilson, R.L. *Winchester: An American Legend*. New York: Random House, 1991.

Wilson, R.L. *The World of Beretta: An International Legend*. New York: Random House, 2000.

Wilson, R.L. *Ruger & His Guns*. New York: Simon and Schuster, 1996.

Wirnsberger, Gerhard. *The Standard Directory of Proofmarks*. Jolex, Inc.

Wood, J.B. *Beretta Automatic Pistols, The Collector's & Shooter's Comprehensive Guide*. Harrisburg, PA: Stackpole Books, 1985.

Zhuk, A.B. *The Illustrated Encyclopedia of Handguns*. London: Greenhill Books, 1995.

American Firearms Industry - 150 SE 12th Street, Suite #200, Ft. Lauderdale, FL 33316. Phone: 954-467-9994. Membership is $55 per year. Trade publications and related material.

PERIODICALS

America's First Freedom - Published by the NRA. 11250 Waples Mill Rd., Fairfax, VA 22030. Phone: 800-672-3888. Subscription included in price of NRA Membership ($35). Published monthly.

American Gunsmith - P.O. Box 540638, Merrit Island, FL 32954. Phone: 321-459-1558. Published monthly. Subscription is $60 per year.

American Handgunner - Published by FMG. 12345 World Trade Center Drive, San Diego, CA 92128. Phone: 858-605-0253. Published bi-monthly. Subscription is $16.95 per year.

American Hunter - Published by the NRA. 11250 Waples Mill Rd., Fairfax, VA 22030. Phone: 800-672-3888. Subscription included in price of NRA Membership ($35). Published monthly.

American Rifleman - Published by the NRA. 11250 Waples Mill Rd., Fairfax, VA 22030. Phone: 800-672-3888. Subscription included in price of NRA Membership ($35). Published monthly.

Australian Shooter - Published by the Sporting Shooters Association of Australia, Inc., P.O. Box 2520, Unley, SA 5061, AUSTRALIA. Fax: 011-61-8-8272-2945. Website: www.ssaa.org.au. Subscription is $50 per year in Australia, $60 per year elsewhere, published monthly.

Bear Hunting - P.O. Box 457, Becker, MN, 55308. Subscription is $20 for 6 issues.

Big Game Adventures - P.O. Box 29099, OK Mission RPO, Kelowna, BC, Canada, V1W 4A2. Phone: 866-944-8382. Subscription is $24.95 per year, published quarterly.

Big Show Journal - N7450 Aanstad Road, P.O. Box 217, Iola, WI, 54945. Subscription is $14.95 per year, published 6 times per year.

Black's Wing & Clay - Published by the Ehlert Publishing Group. 6420 Sycamore Lane, Maple Grove, MN 55369. Phone: 800-848-6247. Published annually, $14.95.

Boar Hunter - 865 GW Turner Road, Baxley, GA, 31515. Phone: 888-297-2627. Fax: 912-366-8085. Subscription is $14.97 for 6 issues.

Buckmaster's Whitetail Magazine - P.O. Box 244022, Montgomery, AL, 36124-4022. Phone: 334-215-3337. Subscription is $26 per year with membership, published 6 times per year.

The Clay Pigeon - P.O. Box 1022, Milford, PA 18337. Phone: 570-296-5768. Fax: 570-296-9298. Subscription is $18 per year (11 issues).

Combat Handguns - Published by Harris Publications. 1115 Broadway, 8th Floor, New York, NY 10010. Phone: 212-807-7100. Fax: 212-807-1479. Subscription rate: $35 for 1 year (8 issues).

Deer & Deer Hunting - Published by Krause Publications, 700 E. State St., Iola, WI 54990. Phone: 715-445-2214. $19.95 per year, published 9 times per year.

Deutsches Waffen Journal - DWJ Verlags GmbH, Schmollerstrasse 31, Schwabisch Hall, D-74523, GERMANY. Phone: 011-49-791-956690. Fax: 011-49-791-95669-19. Website: www.dwj.de Email: info@dwj.de

The Double Gun Journal - P.O. Box 550, East Jordan, MI 49727-9636. Phone: 231-536-7439. Fax: 231-536-7450. Published quarterly.

Ducks Unlimited - One Waterfowl Way, Memphis, TN 38120. Phone: 901-758-3825. Fax: 901-758-3850. Membership rate: $25 per year, includes 6 issues.

Eastman's Bowhunting Journal - P.O. Box 798, 1201 East 7th Street, Powell, WY, 82435. Subscription is $19.95 per year, published 6 times per year.

Eastman's Hunting Journal - P.O. Box 798, 1201 East 7th Street, Powell, WY, 82435. Subscription is $19.95 per year, published 6 times per year.

Field & Stream Magazine - P.O. Box 55652, Boulder, CO 80322. Phone: 800-289-0639 or 212-779-5000. Subscription rate $25 annually. Published monthly (12 issues).

Gray's Sporting Journal - Published by North American Publications, Inc. 735 Broad Street, Augusta, GA 30901. Phone: 706-722-6060. Subscription is $36.95 for 7 issues.

Gun Report - P.O. Box 38, Aledo, IL 61231. Phone: 309-582-5311. $33.00 per year (USA), published monthly.

Guns and Ammo - Published by Primedia. 6420 Wilshire Blvd., Los Angeles, CA 90048. Phone: 323-782-2000. Subscription is $25 per year, published monthly.

Gun List - Published by Krause Publications, 700 E. State St., Iola, WI 54990. Phone: 715-445-2214. $36.98 per year, published bi-weekly.

Gun Tests - 1510 Eldridge Parkway, Ste. 110-163, Houston, TX 77077. Phone: 800-829-9084. Subscription is $24 for 13 issues.

Gun Week - P.O. Box 488, Buffalo, NY 14209. Annual Subscription is $35. Published 3 times per month. Phone: 716-885-6408.

Gun World - Published by Y-Visionary Publishing, 265 S. Anita Drive, Ste. 120, Orange, CA. Phone: 800-999-9718. Subscription is $21.95 for 12 issues.

Guns Magazine - Published by FMG. 12345 World Trade Center Drive, San Diego, CA 92128. Phone: 858-605-0252. Subscription is $19.95 per year (12 issues).

Gun Hunter - P.O. Box 244022, Montgomery, AL, 36124-4022. Phone: 334-215-3337. Subscription is $18.95 per year with membership, published 6 times per year.

Handguns Magazine - Published by Primedia. 6420 Wilshire Blvd., Los Angeles, CA 90048. Phone: 323-782-2000. Subscription is $20 per year, published monthly.

Handloader - Published by Wolfe Publishing Company, 2625 Stearman Rd., Ste. A, Prescott, AZ 86301. Phone: 800-899-7810. Subscription is $19.97 per year.

Knight & Hale's Ultimate Team Hunting - Published by Grandview Media, 3535 Grandview Parkway, 5th Floor, Ste. 500, Birmingham, AL, 35243. Phone: 888-431-2877. Subscription is $5.95, published twice a year.

Man at Arms - P.O. Box 460, Lincoln, RI 02865. Published bimonthly ($32 yearly). Phone: 401-726-8011.

Mossy Oak's Hunting the Country - Published by Grandview Media, 3535 Grandview Parkway, 5th Floor, Ste. 500, Birmingham, AL, 35243. Phone: 888-431-2877. Subscription is $9.95 for 4 issues.

Muzzle Blasts - Published by the National Muzzle Loading Rifle Association. P.O. Box 67, Friendship, IN 47021. Phone: 812-667-5131. Subscription is $35 per year, published monthly.

North American Hunter - 12301 Whitewater Dr., Minnetonka, MN 55343. Phone: 952-936-9333. Published 8 times per year (subscription included in membership).

North American Whitetail - Dept. NAW, P.O. Box 741, Marietta, GA, 30061. Subscription is $14.97 for 8 issues.

Outdoor Guide Magazine - 505 S. Ewing, St. Louis, MO 63103. Phone: 314-535-9786. Subscription is $12 for 6 issues.

Outdoor Life Magazine - Two Park Ave., New York, NY 10016. Phone: 800-365-1580 or 212-779-5000. Subscription is $15.97 for 9 issues.

Petersen's Hunting - Published by Primedia. 6420 Wilshire Blvd., Los Angeles, CA 90048. Phone: 323-782-2000. Subscription is $25 per year, published monthly.

Pheasants Forever - 1783 Buerkle Circle, White Bear Lake, MN 55110. Phone: 651-773-2000. Fax: 651-773-5500. Membership is $25 per year, includes 5 issues.

Pointing Dog Journal/Retriever Journal - Published by the Village Press, 2779 Aero Park Dr., Traverse City, MI 49686. Phone: 231-946-3712, Fax: 231-946-3289. Subscription is $25.95 for 8 issues.

Predator Extreme Magazine - Published by the Vulcan Outdoor Group. 1 Chase Corp. Dr., Ste. 300, Birmingham, AL 35244.

Quail Unlimited - P.O. Box 610 Edgefield, SC 29824. Phone: 803-637-5731. Fax: 803-637-0037. Membership is $25 per year, published bimonthly.

Rack - P.O. Box 244022, Montgomery, AL, 36124-4022. Phone: 334-215-3337. Subscription is $18.95 per year with membership, published 6 times per year.

Rifle - Published by Wolfe Publishing Company, 2625 Stearman Rd., Ste. A, Prescott, AZ 86301. Phone: 800-899-7810. Subscription is $19.97 per year.

Rifle Shooter - Published by Primedia. 6420 Wilshire Blvd., Los Angeles, CA 90048. Phone: 323-782-2000. Subscription is $20 per year, published bimonthly.

Safari Club International - 4800 W. Gates Pass Rd., Tucson, AZ 85745. Website: www.safari-club.org. Publications: Safari Magazine, Safari Africa, Deer of the World, Sheep of the World, International Record Book of Trophy Animals, Record Book Field Edition.

Shoot Magazine - 1770 West State St. #340, Boise, ID, 83702. Phone: 800-342-0904. Subscription is $27.95, published 6 times per year.

Shooting Illustrated - Published by the NRA. 11250 Waples Mill Rd., Fairfax, VA 22030. Phone: 800-672-3888. Subscription included in price of NRA Membership ($35). Published monthly.

Shooting Industry - Published by FMG. 12345 World Trade Center Drive, San Diego, CA 92128. Phone: 858-605-0254. Subscription is $25 per year (USA). Published monthly.

Shooting Sports USA - Published by the NRA. 11250 Waples Mill Rd., Fairfax, VA 22030. Phone: 800-672-3888. Subscription included in price of NRA Membership ($35). Published monthly.

Shooting Sportsman - Published by Down East Enterprise, Inc., P.O. Box 1357, Camden, ME, 04843. Phone: 207-594-9544. Fax: 207-594-5144. Subscription is $30 for 6 issues.

Shooting Sports Retailer - 130 W. 42nd St., New York, NY 10036. Phone: 212-840-0660. Free to retailers. Published 6 times per year.

Shooting Times - Published by Primedia, Inc. 2 News Plaza, Peoria, IL 61614. Phone: 800-727-4353. Subscription is $28.

Shotgun News - Published by Primedia, Inc. 2 News Plaza, Peoria, IL 61614. Phone: 800-345-6923. Subscription is $30 yearly (36 issues).

Shotgun Sports Magazine - P.O. Box 6810, Auburn, CA 95604. Website: www.shotgunsportsmagazine.com. Phone: 800-876-8920, Fax: 530-889-9106. Subscription is $31 per year (11 issues).

Sporting Classics - P.O. Box 23707, Columbia, SC 29224. Phone: 803-736-2424.

Sporting Clays Magazine - 5211 S. Washington Ave., Titusville, FL 32780. Phone: 800-376-2237. Subscription is $29.95 per year (USA). Published monthly.

Sporting Goods Business - 1 Penn Plaza, New York, NY 10119. $65 per year.

Sports Afield Magazine - 15621 Chemical Lane, Huntington Beach, CA, 92649. Website: www.sportsafield.com. Phone: 714-373-4910. Fax: 714-894-4949. Subscription is $32.95 per year (9 issues).

Successful Hunter - Published by Wolfe Publishing Company, 2625 Stearman Rd., Ste. A, Prescott, AZ 86301. Phone: 800-899-7810. Subscription is $19.97 per year.

Turkey & Turkey Hunting - Published by Krause Publications, Inc. 700 E. State St., Iola, WI 54990. Phone: 715-445-2214. Published bimonthly for $14.95 (6 issues).

True West - Published by True West Publishing, Inc., P.O. Box 8008, Cave Creek, AZ, 85327. Phone: 888-687-1881. Subscription is $29.95 for 10 issues.

Varmint Hunter Magazine - Published by the Varmint Hunter's Association. 436 S. Pierre St., Pierre, SD, 57501. Phone: 605-224-6665. Fax: 605-224-6544. Subscription is $24 per year (4 issues).

Visier - International Waffen Magazine - Erich-Kastner-Strasse 2, D-56379, Singhofen, GERMANY. Phone: 011-49-2604-9780. Fax: 011-49-2604-978-703.

Waterfowl Magazine - Published by Waterfowl USA, P.O. Box 50, Edgefield, SC 29824. Phone: 803-637-5767. 6 issues per year.

Western Outdoors - 3197-E East Airport Dr., Costa Mesa, CA 92626. Phone: 714-546-4370. Published 9 times per year for $14.95.

Whitetail Journal - Published by Grandview Media, 3535 Grandview Parkway, 5th Floor, Ste. 500, Birmingham, AL, 35243. Phone: 888-431-2877. Subscription is $9.95 for 5 issues.

Wildfowl - Published by Primedia. 2 In-Fisherman Drive, Brainerd, MN 56425. Phone: 800-800-7724. Subscription is $25 for 6 issues. Published bimonthly.

Women & Guns - Published by Second Amendment Foundation, P.O. Box 488, Station C, Buffalo, NY 14209. $18 annual subscription. Published bimonthly.

Women's Outlook - Published by the NRA. 11250 Waples Mill Rd., Fairfax, VA 22030. Phone: 800-672-3888. Subscription included in price of NRA Membership ($35). Published monthly.

STORE BRAND CROSS-OVER LIST

The following listing is provided as a cross-reference of Store Brands to original manufacturer and model number. Although not exhaustive, this list covers most major stores and chains that have had their name put on guns by other manufacturers. The values for the firearms listed on these pages are approximately 15% – 40% less than the original manufacturers' model(s).
Our thanks goes out to Numrich Gun Parts Corp., West Hurley, NY. They can be reached at (914) 679-4867.

House Brand	Model No.	Orig. Mfgr.	Orig. Model	House Brand	Model No.	Orig. Mfgr.	Orig. Model
Aldens	670	Springfield	67	Cotter & Co	75-45	Glenfield	75
Aldens	670	Savage	67	Cotter & Co	842	Springfield	840
				Cotter & Co	911	Springfield	511
Belknap	964A	Stevens	87N	Cotter & Co	918	Springfield	18
Belknap	B63	Springfield	947	Cotter & Co	948	Stevens	940
Belknap	B63	Savage	947B	Cotter & Co	948E	Savage	948E
Belknap	B63E	Savage	940E	Cotter & Co	949	Springfield	944
Belknap	B64	Savage	67	Cotter & Co	949C	Savage	940
Belknap	B65C	Springfield	745	Cotter & Co	949Y	Savage	944Y
Belknap	865C	Savage	745				
Belknap	B68	Savage	94C	C.I.L.	125	Anschutz	184
Belknap	B68D	Savage	94D	C.I.L.	212	Savage	7J
Belknap	B963	Springfield	120	C.I.L.	221	Savage	7J
Belknap	B963	Savage	120	C.I.L.	227	Savage	871
Belknap	B964	Savage	87J	C.I.L.	233	Savage	85N
Belknap	B967	Savage	87N	C.I.L.	266	Savage	187
				C.I.L.	470	Anschutz	520/61
Coast to Coast	180	Savage	58	C.I.L.	607	Savage	67
Coast to Coast	1800	Savage	18D	C.I.L.	607 TD	Savage	30 FLD GR.
Coast to Coast	182	Savage	18S	C.I.L.	621	Savage	30
Coast to Coast	184	Savage	951	C.I.L.	621 TD	Savage	30D
Coast to Coast	267	Savage	77	C.I.L.	710	Savage	311
Coast to Coast	285	Savage	7J	C.I.L.	725	Savage	FOX BDE
Coast to Coast	286	Savage	46	C.I.L.	830	Savage	340
Coast to Coast	288	Savage	87J	C.I.L.	871	Savage	170
Coast to Coast	320	Savage	120	C.I.L.	950C.D	Savage	110C.D
Coast to Coast	367	Savage	30	C.I.L.	MKVII	H & R	865
Coast to Coast	40	Marlin	99C				
Coast to Coast	42	Marlin	70	Eastern Arms	101.1	Stevens	94B
Coast to Coast	650	Marlin	55	Eastern Arms	IOI.23	Savage	416
Coast to Coast	779	Mossberg	479				
Coast to Coast	843	Savage	340	Foremost See J.C.Penney			
Coast to Coast	843	Springfield	840				
Coast to Coast	843V2DS	Savage	340(.222)	Gamble Skogkmo, Hiawatha			
Coast to Coast	843V3DS	Savage	340(.30/30)				
Coast to Coast	946	Stevens	940	Gamble Skogkmo	130	Savage	30
Coast to Coast	946	Springfield	947	Gamble Skogkmo	1300-567 VR	Savage	67-VR
Coast to Coast	946E	Stevens	940E	Gamble Skogkmo	180N	Savage	87N
Coast to Coast	946Y	Stevens	940Y	Gamble Skogkmo	189J	Savage	87J
				Gamble Skogkmo	189N	Stevens	87N
Cotter & Co	10-40	Glenfield	10	Gamble Skogkmo	521	Savage	120
Cotter & Co	10-40	Marlin	101	Gamble Skogkmo	567	Savage	67
Cotter & Co	121	Stevens	120-15	Gamble Skogkmo	S87	Savage	187
Cotter & Co	167	Springfield	67	Gamble Skogkmo	594	Savage	944
Cotter & Co	167T	Savage	30	Gamble Skogkmo	594Y	Savage	944Y
Cotter & Co	168	Savage	30	Gamble Skogkmo	GU12-5517A	J.C.Higgins	60 & 66
Cotter & Co	168	Springfield	67VR				
Cotter & Co	287	Springfield	87J	Glenfield	10	Marlin	101
Cotter & Co	33	Marlin	336C	Glenfield	20	Marlin	80
Cotter & Co	410	Savage	110E	Glenfield	25	Marlin	80 W/swivels
Cotter & Co	424	Savage	24F	Glenfield	30A	Marlin	336
Cotter & Co	434	Savage	34	Glenfield	35	Marlin	336 .35 cal
Cotter & Co	474	Savage	170	Glenfield	50	Marlin	55
Cotter & Co	474	Springfield	174	Glenfield	60	Marlin	5
Cotter & Co	487T	Springfield	187	Glenfield	60	Marlin	99C
Cotter & Co	489	Savage	89	Glenfield	65	Marlin	99M1
Cotter & Co	60-50	Glenfield	60	Glenfield	70	Marlin	989M2
Cotter & Co	60-50	Marlin	99C	Glenfield	75	Marlin	989MI
Cotter & Co	645	Savage	745				
Cotter & Co	645C	Savage	745C	Globco	Mohawk	Russian	Tokarev
Cotter & Co	75-46	Marlin	99M1				

House Brand	Model No.	Orig. Mfgr.	Orig. Model	House Brand	Model No.	Orig. Mfgr.	Orig. Model
Hawthorn See Wards				Sears. Ranger. J.C. Higgins			
Hercules	50	Stevens	5100	J.C.Higgins	30	High Standard	30
Hiawatha See Gambles				J.C.Higgins	101.1	Savage	94
				J.C.Higgins	101.24	Savage	15-120
J.C. Higgins See Sears				J.C.Higgins	20	High Standard	200
				J.C.Higgins	42 DL	Marlin	80
J.C. Penney common name, F - Foremost				J.C.Higgins	52	Sako	L46
				J.C.Higgins	S4	Browning	FN-300
J.C.Penney	2025	Marlin	80C	J.C.Higgins	583.13 to.23	High Standard	10
J.C.Penney	2035	Marlin	80	J.C.Higgins	583.2078-79	High Standard	20ga pump
J.C.Penney	2035	Glenfield	20	J.C.Higgins	583.514-730	High Standard	20ga pump
J.C.Penney	2066	Marlin	49DL	J.C.Higgins	6670H	Stevens	67H
J.C.Penney	2935	Marlin	336	J.C.Higgins	80	High Standard	101
J.C.Penney	3040	Marlin	336				
J.C.Penney	3040	Glenfield	30A	Ranger	101.2	Savage	238
J.C.Penney	4011	High Standard	FLIGHT KING	Ranger	101.8	Stevens	83
J.C.Penney	6400	Savage	340	Ranger	104.7	H&R	120
J.C.Penney	6610	Savage	120	Ranger	105.20	H&R	120
J.C.Penney	6630	Glenfield	50	Ranger	120	Winchester	1200
J.C.Penney	6630	Marlin	66	Ranger	30	Stevens	520A
J.C.Penney	6647	Savage	944	Ranger	34A	Marlin	80.C,780
J.C.Penney	6647	Springfield	944	Ranger	34A	Marlin	50-50E
J.C.Penney	6660	Glenfield	60	Ranger	35A	Stevens	66A
J.C.Penney	6660	Marlin	99C	Ranger	36	Marlin	80 Adj. Trigger
J.C.Penney	6670	Springfield	67H	Ranger	400	Stevens	311
J.C.Penney	6670	Savage	67				
J.C.Penney	6870	Savage	30	Sears	101.1	Savage	94
J.C.Penney	6870H	Savage	30H	Sears	101.100	Savage	96/96Y
				Sears	101.10040	Savage	94
Katz	F-1282	Marlin	989M2	Sears	101.10041	Savage	94
Katz	F-1282	Glenfield	70	Sears	101.10080	Stevens	940
Katz	F-1287	Marlin	55	Sears	101.1120	Savage	51 and 951
Katz	F-1287	Glenfield	50	Sears	101.12	Stevens	39
				Sears	101.13	Stevens	86-7
Kresge	151	Boito	CBC	Sears	101.138	Savage	38A and 58A
				Sears	101.138	Springfield	18.410
K-Mart	151	Boito	CBC	Sears	101.1380	Springfield	18,18C
				Sears	101.1380	Stevens	58,C
Marlin/new	780	Marlin/old	80	Sears	101.1381	Springfield	18,951 E,F
Marlin/new	781	Marlin/old	81	Sears	101.1381	Stevens	58,51, E,F
Marlin/new	782	Marlin/old	980	Sears	101.16	Savage	6,87
				Sears	101.1610	Savage	540 DL
New Haven	220K	Mossberg	320K-A	Sears	101.1610	Savage	FOX BDL
New Haven	240K	Mossberg	340K	Sears	101.1610	Fox BST	EC,BD,BE,B-F
New Haven	246K	Mossberg	346K-A	Sears	101.1620-1670	Stevens	530,A;311,A,C
New Haven	250K	Mossberg	152K	Sears	101.1700	Savage	94
New Haven	250K8	Mossberg	350K-A	Sears	101.1701	Fox BSE	C,D,Ser F,H
New Haven	273	Mossberg	173	Sears	101.1701-C	Savage	BSE
New Haven	273A	Mossberg	173A	Sears	101.1710	Savage	FOX BDE
New Haven	283.D	Mossberg	183D	Sears	101.1710	Savage	540 BDE
New Haven	284	Mossberg	173	Sears	101.1750	Savage	94
New Haven	285	Mossberg	185D-C	Sears	101.1760	Savage	94
New Haven	290	Mossberg	190D-A	Sears	101.19	Stevens	827-7
New Haven	453	Mossberg	353	Sears	101.20	Stevens	15
New Haven	600AT	Mossberg	500A	Sears	101.22	Stevens	87M(MUSKET)
New Haven	600C	Mossberg	500C	Sears	101.25	Stevens	39A,59A,BandC
New Haven	600E	Mossberg	500E	Sears	101.2830	Savage	63-73
New Haven	679	Mossberg	472	Sears	101.2830	Savage	73
New Haven	740	Mossberg	640	Sears	101.3	Stevens	237
				Sears	101.3538830	Stevens	89
Otasco	30	Marlin	336	Sears	101.4	Stevens	38
Otasco	30	Glenfield	30A	Sears	101.40	Springfield	947,D,Y
Otasco	65	Glenfield	60	Sears	101.40	Stevens	940,D,Y,DY
Otasco	65	Marlin	99C	Sears	101.451	Marlin	336
				Sears	101.5	Stevens	37
Palmetto	11	Stevens	85,89	Sears	101.51004	Savage	94
				Sears	101.510070	Savage	94
Premier	Trail Blazer	Stevens	29A	Sears	101.51009	Springfield	944,Yseries A
				Sears	101.51013	Springfield	944,Yseries A
Revelation, see Western Auto				Sears	101.51024	Savage	94

House Brand	Model No.	Orig. Mfgr.	Orig. Model	House Brand	Model No.	Orig. Mfgr.	Orig. Model
Sears	101.510270	Savage	94	Sears	103.2850	Marlin	81
Sears	101.51044	Savage	94	Sears	103.2870	Marlin	56
Sears	101.510660	Stevens	9478	Sears	103.350	Marlin	M90
Sears	101.510660	Springfield	944,Y series A	Sears	103.360	Marlin	90
Sears	101.510670	Stevens	9478	Sears	103.4	Marlin	A1
Sears	101.510680	Stevens	9478	Sears	103.450	Marlin	336
Sears	101.512220	Stevens	5100,530,311	Sears	103.451	Marlin	336
Sears	101.512230	Stevens	5100,530,311	Sears	103.720	Marlin	59
Sears	101.51451	Springfield	67	Sears	103.740	Marlin	59
Sears	101.51452	Springfield	67	Sears	103.8	Marlin	100
Sears	101.51454	Springfield	67	Sears	10.19790	Marlin	80
Sears	101.51472	Springfield	67 Series B	Sears	11.2	Stevens	238
Sears	101.52701	Stevens	71,74 S/S	Sears	153.512350	Laurona	S/S
Sears	101.52772	Savage	34,65,34M.65M	Sears	153.512351	Laurona	S/S
Sears	101.52773	Savage	34,65,34M,65M	Sears	153.512360	Laurona	S/S
Sears	101.5350	Springfield	18.58	Sears	153.512361	Laurona	S/S
Sears	101.5350-D	Stevens	18D	Sears	153.512740	Laurona	71 O/U
Sears	101.53521	Savage	340	Sears	18	Mossberg	183K
Sears	101.53527	Savage	340	Sears	18AC	Savage	18C
Sears	101.5380	Savage	18/18AC.58	Sears	2C	Winchester	131
Sears	101.5380	Springfield	18,12,16,20ga.	Sears	20	High Standard	200
Sears	101.5380D	Stevens	18ADC	Sears	200	Winchester	1200
Sears	101.538840	Savage	34,65,34M,65M	Sears	200	Mossberg	G4
Sears	101.540	FOX	B-BST,BDL	Sears	201	Mossberg	80
Sears	101.5410	Springfield	18,58	Sears	202	Mossberg	80
Sears	101.5410D	Savage	18D	Sears	203	Mossberg	85
Sears	101.5410D	Springfield	18DS	Sears	204	Mossberg	83
Sears	101.54880	Stevens	80 Series A	Sears	205	Mossberg	73
Sears	101.54880	Springfield	187 Series A	Sears	206	Mossberg	70
Seem	101.64881	Marlin	980 DL,987	Sears	207	Mossberg	75
Sears	101.600	Stevens	39A,59A,B,C	Sears	209	Stevens	84-7
Sears	101.7	Stevens	311	Sears	21	High Standard	K2011
Sears	101.750	SpringField	18.410	Sears	210	Mossberg	85B
Sears	101.750	Savage	38A and 58A	Sears	211	Mossberg	83B
Sears	101.7C	Stevens	311-C	Sears	211	Stevens	86-7
Sears	101.8	Stevens	83	Sears	212	Mossberg	73B
Sears	102	Stevens	240	Sears	213	Mossberg	75B
Sears	102.25	Stevens	520A	Sears	215	Mossberg	85C
Sears	102.35	Savage	M521	Sears	216	Mossberg	83C
Sears	102.35	Savage	M29-D2	Sears	217	Mossberg	75C
Sears	103.13	Marlin	81	Sears	217	Stevens	87M (MUSKET)
Sears	103.16	Marlin	80	Sears	218	Mossberg	73C
Sears	103.18	Marlin	100	Sears	218	Stevens	22/410
Sears	103.181	Marlin	101	Sears	231	Stevens	83
Sears	103.1977	Marlin	101	Sears	232	Stevens	87-7
Sears	103.19770	Marlin	101	Sears	233	Stevens	87-7
Sears	103.19771	Marlin	101	Sears	234	Savage	234
Sears	103.19780	Marlin	101	Sears	238	Stevens	827-7
Sears	103.19790	Marlin	80	Sears	25	High Standard	A1041 .22 auto
Sears	103.19791	Marlin	80	Sears	273.2400	Winchester	190
Sears	103.19800	Marlin	80	Sears	273.27S10(2C)	Winchester	131
Sears	103.19801	Marlin	80	Sears	273.27520(2M)	Winchester	131
Sears	103.1981	Marlin	81	Sears	273.510770	Winchester	37A
Sears	103.19810	Marlin	81	Sears	273.510780	Winchester	37A
Sears	103.19811	Marlin	81	Sears	273.510790	Winchester	37A
Sears	103.1982	Marlin	81DL	Sears	273.53421	Winchester	100
Sears	103.19820	Marlin	81	Sears	277	Stevens	1S
Sears	103.19821	Marlin	81	Sears	278.28180	Cooey	64
Sears	103.19840	Marlin	56	Sears	281.512650	Antonio Zoli	O/U
Sears	103.19880	Marlin	57 LR-MAG.	Sears	281.512651	Antonio Zoli	O/U
Sears	103.19881	Marlin	57 LR-MAG.	Sears	281.512660	Antonio Zoli	O/U
Sears	103.19890	Marlin	57 LR-MAG.	Sears	281.512661	Antonio Zoli	O/U
Sears	103.2	Marlin	80	Sears	281.512750	Antonio Zoli	O/U
Sears	103.228	Marlin	80	Sears	282.510821	Boito	ERA Single Bbl
Sears	103.229	Marlin	81	Sears	282.510831	Boito	ERA Single Bbl
Sears	103.273	Marlin	782	Sears	282.510841	Boito	ERA Single Bbi
Sears	103.273	Marlin	980	Sears	282.5227740	CBC	122
Sears	103.274	Marlin	122	Sears	282.527740	FIE	122
Sears	103.275	Marlin	122	Sears	2C	Winchester	131
Sears	103.2751	Marlin	122	Sears	2T	Winchester	121,131,141
Sears	103.2840	Marlin	80	Sears	2/57	Stevens	66

House Brand	Model No.	Orig. Mfgr.	Orig. Model	House Brand	Model No.	Orig. Mfgr.	Orig. Model
Sears	2/58	Stevens	66	Sears 200	273.2160	Winchester	1200
Sears	30	High Standard	22 PUMP	Sears 200	273.2250	Winchester	1200
Sears	300	Winchester	1400	Sears 200	273.2251	Winchester	1200
Sears	31	J.C. Higgins	31	Sears 200	273.2280	Winchester	1200
Sears	33	J.C. Higgins	33	Sears 200	273.4310	Winchester	1200
Sears	34	J.C. Higgins	34	Sears 200	273.4320	Winchester	1200
Sears	340.530430	Ithaca	49SS	Sears 200	273.4340	Winchester	1200
Sears	35A	Stevens	66A	Sears 200	273.4350	Winchester	1200
Sears	36	Marlin	80	Sears 200	273.4410	Winchester	1200
Sears	375	Mossberg	45B	Sears 200	273.4420	Winchester	1200
Sears	377	Mossberg	42C	Sears 200	273.4450	Winchester	1200
Sears	381	Mossberg	46B	Seem 200	273.514010	Winchester	1200
Sears	382	Mossberg	46B	Sears 200	273.614010	Winchester	1200
Sears	384	Mossberg	45A	Sears 200	273.514011	Winchester	1200
Sears	385	Mossberg	45B	Sears 200	273.514020	Winchester	1200
Sears	387	Mossberg	42C	Seem 200	273.514040	Winchester	1200
Sears	388	Mossberg	42C	Sears 200	273.514050	Winchester	1200
Sears	389	Mossberg	42A OR 26C	Sears 200	273.514051	Winchester	1200
Sears	390	Mossberg	26C	Sears 200	273.514210	Winchester	1200
Sears	3T	Winchester	190	Sears 200	273.514220	Winchester	1200
Sears	41	Marlin	101	Sears 200	273,514250	Winchester	1200
Sears	41 DLA	Marlin	122	Sears 200	273.514251	Winchester	1200
Sears	42	Marlin	80	Sears 200	273.514810	Winchester	1200
Sears	42DL	Marlin	80	Sears 200	273.614820	Winchester	1200
Sears	42DLM	Marlin	980	Sears 200	273.514830	Winchester	1200
Sears	43	Marlin	81	Sears 200	273.514840	Winchester	1200
Sears	43DL	Marlin	81	Sears 200	273.515010	Winchester	1200
Sears	44DL	Marlin	57	Sears 200	273.515020	Winchester	1200
Sears	44DLM	Marlin	57M	Sears 200	273.515050	Winchester	1200
Sears	45	Marlin	336C	Sears 200	273.515051	Winchester	1200
Sears	46	Marlin	56	Sears 200	273.515080	Winchester	1200
Sears	46DL	Marlin	56	Sears 200	273.515090	Winchester	1200
Sears	4980	Stevens	94-2 W/PAD	Sears 200	273.515220	Winchester	1200
Sears	49.11830/30	Savage	99 A	Sears 200	273.515221	Winchester	1200
Sears	53	Winchester	70	Sears 200	273.515250	Winchester	1200
Sears	54	Winchester	94	Sears 200	273.515251	Winchester	1200
Sears	583.1	High Standard	N/A	Sears 200	273.515280	Winchester	1200
Sears	583,126	Sako	L46	Sears 200	273.515290	Winchester	1200
Sears	583.13	High Standard	N/A	Sears 200	273.515410	Winchester	1200
Sears	583.14	H & R	120	Sears 200	273.515420	Winchester	1200
Sears	583.15	H&R	121	Sears 200	273.515470	Winchester	1200
Sears	583.16	High Standard	10	Sears 200	273.515710	Winchester	1200
Sears	583.17	High Standard	N/A	Sears 200	273.515720	Winchester	1200
Sears	583.18	H & R	120	Sears 200	273.515920	Winchester	1200
Sears	583.2	H & R	M120	Sears 200	273.5310	Winchester	1200
Sears	583.20	High Standard	Flight King	Sears 200	273.5350	Winchester	1200
Sears	583.2085-87	High Standard	20ga pump	Sears 2T	273.27530	Winchester	141
Sears	583.21	H&R	M120	Sears 300	273.1310	Winchester	1400
Sears	583.25	H&R	M121	Sears 300	273.1320	Winchester	1400
Sears	583.3	H&R	M121	Sears 300	273.1350	Winchester	1400
Sears	583.4	High Standard	10	Sears 300	273.21550	Winchester	1400
Sears	583.7	High Standard	10	Sears 300	273.2500	Winchester	1400
Sears	583.91	H & R	121	Sears 300	273.2540	Winchester	1400
Sears	6C (Canada)	Winchester	Cooy 64,64B	Sears 300	273.32060	Winchester	1400
Sears	6C(American)	Winchester	490	Sears 300	273.32070	Winchester	1400
Sears	66	High Standard	66	Sears 300	273.521050	Winchester	1400
Sears	73	Savage	73	Sears 300	273.521051	Winchester	1400
Sears	870.528140	Voere	Clip .22	Sears 300	273.521080	Winchester	1400
Sears	92	Stevens	39	Sears 300	273.521090	Winchester	1400
Sears	93	Stevens	38	Sears 300	273.521160	Winchester	1400
Sears	94	Stevens	237	Sears 300	273.521161	Winchester	1400
Sears	95	Stevens	238	Sears 300	273.521250	Winchester	1400
Sears	97	Savage	94	Sears 300	273.521251	Winchester	1400
Sears	97AC	Savage	94AC	Sears 300	273.521260	Winchester	1400
Sears	98	Stevens	37	Sears 300	273.521280	Winchester	1400
Sears	98	Springfield	944	Sears 300	273.521290	Winchester	1400
Sears	M30	Stevens	M520	Sears 300	273.521580	Winchester	1400
Sears	mzm	Savage	34	Sears 300	273.521680	Winchester	1400
Sears 100	273.532141	Winchester	NM 94	Sears 300	273.521710	Winchester	1400
Sears 200	2732.5320	Winchester	1200	Sears 300	273.521770	Winchester	1400
Sears 200	273.2011	Winchester	1200	Sears 300	273.521780	Winchester	1400
Sears 200	273.21010	Winchester	1200	Sears 300	273.523251	Winchester	1400

House Brand	Model No.	Orig. Mfgr.	Orig. Model	House Brand	Model No.	Orig. Mfgr.	Orig. Model
Sears 300	273.52151	Winchester	1400	Western Auto	101.53521	Savage	340
Sears 3T-A	273.2390	Winchester	190-290	Western Auto	101.5380	Savage	18AC
Sears 3T-A	273.2400	Winchester	190-290	Western Auto	101.5380D	Savage	18DAC
Sears 3T-A	273.528110	Winchester	190-290	Western Auto	101.5410	Savage	18DS,S
Sears 3T-A	273.528111	Winchester	190-290	Western Auto	103	Savage	89
Sears 4T	273.2360	Winchester	270	Western Auto	103.13	Marlin	81
Sears 53A	273.532780	Winchester	70A	Western Auto	103.16	Marlin	80
Sears 54	273.2120	Winchester	NM 94	Western Auto	103.18	Marlin	80
Sears 54	273.532140	Winchester	NM 94	Western Auto	103.181	Marlin	101
Sears 54	273.53419	Winchester	NM 94	Western Auto	103.19780	Marlin	101
Sears 54	273.810	Winchester	NM 94	Western Auto	103.19790	Marlin	80
Sears 54	273.811	Winchester	NM 94	Western Auto	103.19800	Marlin	80
Sears 6C	273.28130	Winchester	490	Western Auto	103.1981	Marlin	81
Sears 6C	273.528131	Winchester	490	Western Auto	103.1982	Marlin	81DL
Sears 6C	273.528132	Winchester	490	Western Auto	103.19820	Marlin	81
Sears MI	273.27010	Winchester	121	Western Auto	103.19840	Marlin	56
Sears M5,M-5T	273.2340	Winchester	150-250	Western Auto	103.19880	Marlin	57
Sears M5,M-5T	273.2341	Winchester	150-250	Western Auto	103.19890	Marlin	57M
Sears M5,M-5T	273.2350	Winchester	150-250	Western Auto	103.1997	Marlin	101
Sears M5,M-5T	273.2351	Winchester	150-250	Western Auto	103.2	Marlin	80
Sears T.W. 73	273.532730	Winchester	670 Mag.	Western Auto	103.228	Marlin	80
Sears T.W. 73	23.31020	Winchester	New Mod 70	Western Auto	103.229	Marlin	81
Sears T.W. 73	273.1390	Winchester	MN 30-06	Western Auto	103.273	Marlin	980
Sears T.W. 73	273.1400	Winchester	MN 70 (.270)	Western Auto	103.274	Marlin	122
Sears T.W. 73	273.1830	Winchester	New Mod 70	Western Auto	103.2751	Marlin	122
Sears T.W. 73	273.1840	Winchester	New Mod 70	Western Auto	103.2840	Marlin	80
Sears T.W. 73	273.1850	Winchester	New Mod 70	Western Auto	103.2850	Marlin	81
Sears T.W. 73	273.1860	Winchester	New Mod 70	Western Auto	103.2870	Marlin	56
Sears T.W. 73	273.1870	Winchester	New Mod 70	Western Auto	103.360	Marlin	90
Sears T.W. 73	273.31010	Winchester	New Mod 70	Western Auto	103.450	Marlin	336
Sears T.W. 73	273.31060	Winchester	New Mod 70	Western Auto	103.451	Marlin	336
Sears T.W. 73	273.32020	Winchester	New Mod 70	Western Auto	103.720	Marlin	59
Sears T.W. 73	273.32030	Winchester	New Mod 70	Western Auto	103.740	Marlin	59
Sears T.W. 73	273.32040	Winchester	New Mod 70	Western Auto	105-2060	Marlin	780
Sears T.W. 73	273.532061	Winchester	New Mod 70	Western Auto	105-2060	Marlin	80
Sears T.W. 73	273.532071	Winchester	New Mod 70	Western Auto	107	Mossberg	640K
Sears T.W. 73	273.532081	Winchester	New Mod 70	Western Auto	107A	Mossberg	640
Sears T.W. 73	273.53403	Winchester	New Mod 70	Western Auto	110-2140	Marlin	81
Sears T.W. 73	273.53406	Winchester	New Mod 70	Western Auto	110-2140	Marlin	781
Sears T.W. 73	273.53409	Winchester	New Mod 70	Western Auto	115	Savage	46
Sears T.W. 73	273.32010	Winchester	Now Mod 70	Western Auto	115-2277	Marlin	57
				Western Auto	116-2276	Marlin	57M
Ted Williams	340.530430	Ithaca	49SS	Western Auto	117	Mossberg	402
				Western Auto	120-2220	Marlin	99
Shapleigh's	KING NITRO	Savage	15	Western Auto	125	Mossberg	353
				Western Auto	135	Savage	187
Simmons	411	Savage	540DL	Western Auto	135	Springfield	187A
Simmons	411	Savage	Fox BDE 20ga	Western Auto	150m	Marlin	49
				Western Auto	150-2225	Marlin	49
Simmons	411E	Savage	540 BDE	Western Auto	160	Springfield	187A
Simmons	411E	Savage	Fox BDE 20ga	Western Auto	160	Savage	80
				Western Auto	200-2280	Marlin	39A
Talo	12DL	Stevens	120	Western Auto	200-2282	Marlin	39A
Talo	176 VR	Springfield	67 VR	Western Auto	200-2550	Marlin	336
Talo	176DL	Springfield	67	Western Auto	200-2554	Marlin	336(.44MAG)
				Western Auto	205	Mossberg	472PCA
Western Auto,Revelation				Western Auto	210A	Mossberg	810AH
				Western Auto	220A	Mossberg	800A
Revelation	300	Savage	30 D,E,F	Western Auto	220AD	Mossberg	800AD
Revelation	394 Series P	Stevens	94P	Western Auto	220B	Mossberg	800B
Revelation	76	High Standard	Double Nine	Western Auto	220BD	Mossberg	800BD
Revelation	R310	Mossberg	500AB	Western Auto	220C	Mossberg	800C
				Western Auto	220CD	Mossberg	800CD
Western Auto	100	Mossberg	321	Western Auto	225	Savage	340
Western Auto	101Y	Savage	73Y	Western Auto	2280	Marlin	39A
Western Auto	101.1701	Savage	540BS	Western Auto	2282	Marlin	39A Mountie
Western Auto	101.171	Savage	540BD	Western Auto	230	Savage	340
Western Auto	101.2830	Savage	73	Western Auto	250	Savage	110E
Western Auto	101.52772	Savage	65M	Western Auto	250A	Savage	110D
Western Auto	101.535D	Savage	18	Western Auto	250D	Savage	110
Western Auto	101.53500	Savage	18D	Western Auto	260	Savage	170

House Brand	Model No.	Orig. Mfgr.	Orig. Model	House Brand	Model No.	Orig. Mfgr.	Orig. Model
Western Auto	260	Springfield	174	Western Field	151X	Kessler	N/A
Western Auto	300	Springfield	67	Western Field	155	Mossberg	173
Western Auto	300	Stevens	30	Western Field	15A	Mossberg	83
Western Auto	300A	Savage	30AC	Western Field	16	Mossberg	85
Western Auto	300F	Stevens	77C	Western Field	160	Mossberg	385K
Western Auto	300H	Savage	30,HAC	Western Field	16A	Mossberg	85
Western Auto	300-300AC	Springfield	67	Western Field	17	Mossberg	73
Western Auto	310	Mossberg	500	Western Field	170	Mossberg	395K
Western Auto	310A	Mossberg	500A	Western Field	172	Mossberg	395K
Western Auto	310AB	Mossberg	500AB	Western Field	173	Mosaberg	395
Western Auto	310B	Mossberg	500B	Western Field	175	Mossberg	385K
Western Auto	310C	Mossberg	500C	Western Field	17A	Mossberg	73
Western Auto	310E	Mossberg	500E	Western Field	I8	Mossberg	75
Western Auto	312	Mossberg	395	Western Field	20	Mossberg	9R
Western Auto	312AK	Mossberg	395K	Western Field	215A	Mossberg	85
Western Auto	312SB	Mossberg	395T	Western Field	24M,488A	Mossberg	51
Western Auto	316	Mossberg	390	Western Field	30	Stevens	520
Western Auto	316BB	Mossberg	390T	Western Field	31A	Mossberg	44
Western Auto	316BK	Mossberg	390K	Western Field	31A	Mossberg	40
Western Auto	325B	Mossberg	385T	Western Field	32	Mossberg	21
Western Auto	325BK	Mossberg	385K	Western Field	32	Mossberg	20
Western Auto	330	Mossberg	183 & 183K	Western Field	33	Marlin	336
Western Auto	330B	Mossberg	183T	Western Field	35A	Mossberg	30
Western Auto	335-3725	Marlin	59	Western Field	36	Stevens	521
Western Auto	336	Springfield	951	Western Field	36	Mossberg	10
Western Auto	350	Stevens	94	Western Field	36B	Mossberg	25A
Western Auto	350A	Savage	94D	Western Field	36B	Mossberg	10
Western Auto	350M	Stevens	94	Western Field	36C	Mossberg	25A
Western Auto	355	Stevens	947	Western Field	360	Mossberg	26C
Western Auto	355Y	Savage	94Y	Western Field	37	Mossberg	30
Western Auto	355YE	Springfield	947YE	Western Field	39	Mossberg	25
Western Auto	356Y	Springfield	944Y	Western Field	390A	Mossberg	26C
Western Auto	360	Savage	540	Western Field	40,D	Mossberg	44
Western Auto	360	Savage	FOX mod B	Western Field	40	Marlin	101
Western Auto	360C	Savage	540C	Western Field	40N	Noble	40NA
Western Auto	400	Stevens	745	Western Field	40M-215A	Mossberg	185
Western Auto	400C	Savage	745C	Western Field	41	Mossberg	45
Western Auto	420	High Standard	Supmatic C-011	Western Field	45	Marlin	989M2
Western Auto	425	High Standard	Supmatic C-120	Western Field	45	Mossberg	42
Western Auto	460	Springfield	511	Western Field	45B	Mossberg	26C
Western Auto	SD52A	Stevens	311	Western Field	45C	Mossberg	25A
West Point	45	Marlin	60	Western Field	46	Mossberg	42
				Western Field	466	Mossberg	RA1
Wards, Western Field, and Hawthorn				Western Field	469	Mossberg	RA1-Kit
				Western Field	46A	Mossberg	42
Hawthorn	110	Unknown	S shot SG	Western Field	46C	Moseborg	42A
Hawthorn	580 EJN	Colt	Colteer/bolt	Western Field	46D	Mossberg	42C
Hawthorn	814 EJN	Colt	Colteer/SS	Western Field	47	Mossberg	45A
Hawthorn	820B	Mossberg	340	Western Field	472	Noble	50
Hawthorn	880	Colt	Colteer/semi	Western Field	47A,L	Mossberg	45A
Hawthorn	880 EJN	Colt	Colteer/bolt	Western Field	48	Mossberg	45A
				Western Field	488A	Mossberg	51
Wards	24M 419A	Mossberg	9	Western Field	48A	Mossberg	45B
Wards	472	Noble	50	Western Field	48A	Mossberg	46MLB
Wards	850	Mossberg	353	Western Field	5-4	Mossberg	8-M4
Wards Triumph	52	Stevens	315	Western Field	50	Glenfield	60
				Western Field	502-26FR	Mossberg	500
Western Field	04M-489A	Mossberg	50	Western Field	505	Mossberg	500
Western Field	04M-218A	Mossberg	73C	Western Field	509	Mossberg	500
Western Field	04M-2117A	Mossberg	9	Western Field	524	Mossberg	500
Western Field	04M-217A	Mossberg	75C	Western Field	534	Mossberg	500
Western Field	04M-214A	Mossberg	85C	Western Field	536	Mossberg	500
Western Field	04M-216A	Mossberg	83C	Western Field	539	Mossberg	500
Western Field	I	Mossberg	RF-1	Western Field	550A	Mossberg	500A
Western Field	10-SD247A	Stevens	94B (Tenite)	Western Field	550AS	Mossberg	500AB
Western Field	14	Savage	39A	Western Field	550B	Mossberg	500B
Western Field	14	Savage	59A	Western Field	550C	Mossberg	500B
Western Field	14M-215A	Mossberg	85	Western Field	550E	Mossberg	500E
Western Field	14M-497B	Mossberg	M42	Western Field	550E	Mossberg	500E
Western Field	14M-488A	Mossberg	50	Western Field	60	Savage	620A
Western Field	15	Mossberg	80	Western Field	600ERI 12 GA	Remington	SPT 58
Western Field	150	Mossberg	183K	Western Field	60SB	Savage	620A

House Brand	Model No.	Orig. Mfgr.	Orig. Model	House Brand	Model No.	Orig. Mfgr.	Orig. Model
Western Field	679	Mossberg	472	Western Field	M051	Stevens	515
Western Field	710	Savage	110	Western Field	M059	Stevens	M87
Western Field	72	Noble	50	Western Field	M060	Stevens	620
Western Field	72C	Mossberg	472	Western Field	M080	Savage	29 & 75
Western Field	730	Mossberg	8I0AH	Western Field	M087	Stevens	M87
Western Field	732	Mossberg	810AH	Western Field	M10	Stevens	94 Short tang
Western Field	734	Mossberg	810A	Western Field	M150	Mossberg	183T
Western Field	740	Marlin	336	Western Field	M155	Mosaberg	183D
Western Field	765	Mossberg	810A	Western Field	M160	Mossberg	385T
Western Field	766	Mossberg	810B	Western Field	M170	Mossberg	395S
Western Field	767	Mossberg	800A				
Western Field	768	Mossberg	800A	Western Field	M172	Mossberg	395K
Western Field	771	Mossberg	472BA	Western Field	M175	Mossberg	385K
Western Field	772	Mossberg	472PCA	Western Field	M23 NH402A	Stevens	820
Western Field	775	Mossberg	800AD	Western Field	M35	Savage	520 POLY
Western Field	776	Mossberg	800BD	Western Field	M36	Savage	521
Western Field	778	Mossberg	472BAS	Western Field	M60	Savage	620 DELUX
Western Field	780	Mossberg	800A	Western Field	M61	Savage	621 DELUX
Western Field	782	Mossberg	800B	Western Field	M72	Mossberg	472 PRA
Western Field	79	Mossberg	472 PRA	Western Field	M734	Mossberg	810BH
Western Field	50	Savage	29	Western Field	M771	Moseberg	472SBA
Western Field	807A ECH	Colt	Colteer S.S.	Western Field	M772	Mossberg	472PCA
Western Field	808	Savage	87	Western Field	M7 75	Mossberg	800AD
Western Field	808C	Savage	87J	Western Field	M776	Mossberg	800BD
Western Field	815	Mossberg	321	Western Field	M778	Mossberg	472BAS
Western Field	820B	Mossberg	340	Western Field	M780	Mossberg	800A
Western Field	822	Mossberg	640K	Western Field	M782	Mossberg	800B
Western Field	828	Mossberg	353	Western Field	M808.C	Stevens	87,C,J
Western Field	830	Mossberg	340K	Western Field	M808N	Stevens	87N
Western Field	832	Mossberg	341	Western Field	M80A	Savage	M29-D1
Western Field	836	Savage	187N	Western Field	M815	Mossberg	320
Western Field	840	Mossberg	640	Western Field	M822	Mossberg	640K
Western Field	842	Mossberg	346K	Western Field	M85	Stevens	85
Western Field	846	Mossberg	351C	Western Field	M-SD57	Stevens	87
Western Field	850 855	Mossberg	353	Western Field	SS 94B	Stevens	94C
				Western Field	SB033	Savage	520 W/POLY
Western Field	852	Mossberg	341	Western Field	SB066	Savage	621 DELX POLY
Western Field	865	Mossberg	402	Western Field	SB067	Savage	621 DELX COMP
Western Field	880	Colt	Colteer Semi.	Western Field	S5112C	Savage	540C
Western Field	894	Mossberg	430-432	Western Field	SB115	Savage	115
Western Field	895	Mossberg	402	Western Field	SB300,C	Stevens	311,C
Western Field	9-2 3/4	Mossberg	9-2 1/2	Western Field	SB30A	Savage	520
Western Field	93M	Mossberg	26C	Western Field	SB311C	Savage	311C
Western Field	93M-213A	Mossberg	75B	Western Field	SB312	Savage	540D
Western Field	93M-2116A	Mossberg	9	Western Field	SB312	Savage-Fox	BDL
Western Field	93M-212A	Mossberg	738	Western Field	SB33	Savage	520 POLY
Western Field	93M-211A	Mossberg	83B	Western Field	SB60A	Savage	620 DELUX
				Western Field	SB61A	Savage	621 DELUX
Western Field	93M-210A	Mossberg	85B	Western Field	SB620A	Stevens	620A
Western Field	93M-497A	Mossberg	42C	Western Field	SB66	Savage	621 DELX POLY
Western Field	93M-491A	Mossberg	465	Western Field	SB712	Savage	840
Western Field	93M-495A	Mossberg	45B	Western Field	SB80A	Savage	29-DI
Western Field	EMN 171	Marlin	50	Western Field	SB85TA	Stevens	85
Western Field	EMN 176	Marlin	55	Western Field	SB87,TA	Stevens	M87
Western Field	M-SD57	Stevens	M87	Western Field	XNH 175	Marlin	55
Western Field	M025	Savage	520A	Western Field	XNH 565	Noble	60-66
Western Field	M040 O/U	Marlin	90				
Western Field	M040N	Stevens	820	Widgeon	SA 650	Marlin	55 12 GA

SERIALIZATION

This section is included to identify year of manufacture dates on Brownings, Colts (including 3rd generation Colt S.A. model numbers), High Standard, Mauser broomhandles, Parker shotguns, Remington (manufacture dates), Savage/Stevens model information, Savage M-1899, selected Winchesters, and others. To use these tables, simply locate the Ser. No. of the above mentioned trademarks, locate the proper bracket it falls into by model, and refer to the adjacent year to determine the year of manufacture. In several cases, caliber rarity can also be determined. The publisher wishes to thank Galazams and Dixie Gun Works for a portion of this serialization.

BOSS & CO., LTD. SERIALIZATION

Year Starting	Serial Number
1830	680
1850	1400
1857	1600
1900	4700
1920	6618
1930	7730
1945	8711
1951	8912
1953	8920
1963	9219
1970	9559

BROWNING SERIALIZATION PRE-1976

Since 1968-1969 was a transition period in Browning serialization, firearms manufactured at this time may be serialized with either 1968 or 1969 style markings.

A-5 (AUTOMATIC 5) SHOTGUN -12 ga.

Year	Ser. # Start	Ser. # End
1903	1	4121
1904	4122	15300
1905	15301	19920
1906	19921	22320
1907	22321	26970
1908	26971	30446
1909	30447	33431
1910	33432	35630
1911	35631	35925
1912	35926	38988
1913	38989	44250
1914	44251	47298
1915-1918	No Production	
1919	47719	47950
1920	47299	47718
1921	48951	53500
1922	53501	58150
1923	58151	62600
1924	62601	69300
1925	69301	79150
1926	79151	88000
1927	88001	106250
1928	106251	127650
1929	127651	154500
1930	154501	177100
1931	177101	182300
1932	182301	182788
1933	182789	183152
1934	183153	185560
1935	185561	191604
1936	191605	194535

Year	Ser. # Start	Ser. # End
1937	194536	199200
1938	199201	208400
1939	208401	218808
1940	218809	224596
1941-1943	No Production	
1944	Production limited to servicemen	
1945	Production limited to servicemen	
1946	228729	240950
1947	240951	256500
1948	256501	274100
1949	274101	288550
1950	288551	316750
1951	316751	352050
1952	352051	387499
1953	387500	437400
1954	437401	447750
1955	447751	454700
1956	454701	459900
1957	459901	463700

In 1954 Browning added an alpha prefix to the serial number to differentiate between Lightweight and Standardweight guns.

Year	Std.12	Lt.Wt. 12
1953	H1-H6600	L1-L4450
1954	H6601-H39700	L4451-L45250
1955	H39701-H83450	L45251-L83600
1956	H83451-H100000	L83601-L99877
1956	M1-M35250	G1-G35450
1957	M35251-M86300	G35451-G85950
1958	M86301-M99999	G85951-G99663

1958-1976 Ser. No. sequence changed to include a one or two digit numeral followed by an alpha character.

Year	Std. Wt.	Lt. Wt.	Magnum
1958	8M	8G	8V
1959	9M	9G	9V
1960	0M	0G	0V
1961	1M	1G	1V
1962	2M	2G	2V
1963	3M	3G	3V
1965	5M	5G	5V
1966	6M	6G	6V
1964	4M	4G	4V
1967	7M	7G	7V
1968	8M	8G	8V
1969	69M	69G	69V
1970	Disc.	70G	70V
1971	Disc.	71G	71V
1972	Disc.	72G	72V
1973	Disc.	73G	73V
1974	Disc.	74G	74V
1975	Disc.	75G	75V
1976	Disc.	76G	76V

A-5 (AUTOMATIC 5) SHOTGUN -16 ga.

Year	Ser. # Start	Ser. # End
1909	1	3200
1910-1912	3201	15000
1913	15001	19000
1914-1918	No Production	
1919	19671	20500
1920	20501	22237
1921	22238	24050
1922	24051	26000
1923	26001	28400
1924	28401	35650
1925	35651	40010
1926	40011	51600
1927	51599	57900
1928	57901	65100
1929	65101	82750
1930	82751	90500
1931	90501	94000
1932	94001	96072
1933	96073	96143
1934	96144	99500
1935	99501	103500
1936	103501	105850
1937	105851	111000
1938	111001	118200
1939	118201	126123
1940	126123	126175
1941-1943	No Production	
1944	Production limited to servicemen	
1945	Production limited to servicemen	
1946	128117	128646
1947	128647	130616
1947	X1001	X13666
1948	X13667	X23501
1949	X23502	X34600
1950	X34601	X43700
1951	X43701	X59400
1952	X59401	X77700
1953	X77701	X99999

In 1953 Browning changed the Ser. No. alphabetic character to differentiate between Lightweight (Sweet 16) & Standard weight guns.

Year	Std.16	Sweet 16
1953	R1-R3100	S1-S3700
1954	R3100-R20800	S3701-S24850
1955	R20801-R48750	S24851-S49350
1956	R48751-R74700	S49350-S72300
1957	R74701-R99999	S72301-S99908

1957-58 Prefix "T" for Standardweight and Prefix "A" for Sweet 16 numbers mixed, but range from 1-10900.
1958-1976 Ser. No. sequence changed to include a one or two digit numeral followed by an alpha character.

Year	Std.16	Sweet 16
1958	8R	8S
1959	9R	9S
1960	0R	0S
1961	1R	1S
1962	2R	2S
1963	3R	3S
1964	Disc.	4S
1965	Disc.	5S
1966	Disc.	6S
1967	Disc.	7S
1968	Disc.	8S
1969	Disc.	69S

Year	Std.16	Sweet 16
1970	Disc.	70S
1971	Disc.	71S
1972	Disc.	72S
1973	Disc.	73S
1974	Disc.	74S
1975	Disc.	75S
1976	Disc.	Disc.

A-5 (AUTOMATIC 5) SHOTGUN - 20 ga.

Year	Lt.Wt. 20	Magnum 20
1958	8Z	Introduced in
1959	9Z	1967
1960	0Z	
1961	1Z	
1962	2Z	
1963	3Z	
1964	4Z	
1965	5Z	
1966	6Z	
1967	7Z	7X
1968	68Z	68X
1969	69Z	69X
1970	70Z	70X
1971	71Z	71X
1972	72Z	72X
1973	73Z	73X
1974	74Z	74X
1975	75Z	75X
1976	76Z	76X

SUPERPOSED MODEL - O & U - 12 ga.

Year	Ser. # Start	Ser. # End
1931	1	2000
1932	2001	4000
1933	4001	6000
1934	6001	8000
1935	8001	10000
1936	10001	12000
1937	12001	14000
1938	14001	16000
1939	16001	17000
1939-1947	NO PRODUCTION	
1948	17001	17200
1949	17201	20000
1950	20001	21000
1951	21001	27000
1952	27001	33000
1953	33001	37000
1954	37001	43000
1955	43001	48000
1956	48001	54000
1957	54001	59000
1958	59001	68500
1959	68501	76500
1960	76501	86500
1961	86501	96500
1962	96501	99999
1962	1	6500
1962	S2 suffix after Ser. No.	
1963	S3 suffix after Ser. No.	
1964	S4 suffix after Ser. No.	
1965	S5 suffix after Ser. No.	
1966	S6 suffix after Ser. No.	
1967	S7 suffix after Ser. No.	
1968	S8 suffix after Ser. No.	
1969	S69 suffix after Ser. No.	
1970	S70 suffix after Ser. No.	
1971	S71 suffix after Ser. No.	
1972	S72 suffix after Ser. No.	
1973	S73 suffix after Ser. No.	
1974	S74 suffix after Ser. No.	

SUPERPOSED MODEL - O & U - 12 ga. cont.

Year	Ser. # Start	Ser. # End
1975	S75 suffix after Ser. No.	
1976	S76 suffix after Ser. No.	
1976 to 1984	"P" or Presentation Models only	

SUPERPOSED MODEL - O & U - 20 ga.

Year	Ser. # Start	Ser. # End
1949	201	1700
1950	1701	2800
1951	2801	3200
1952	3201	5300
1953	5301	6700
1954	6701	8400
1955	8401	9400
1956	9401	10500
1957	10501	11500
1958	11501	14180
1959	14181	17060
1960	17061	20640
1961	20641	23820
1962	23821	27300
1963	V3 suffix after Ser. No.	
1964	V4 suffix after Ser. No.	
1965	V5 suffix after Ser. No.	
1966	V6 suffix after Ser. No.	
1967	V7 suffix after Ser. No.	
1968	V8 suffix after Ser. No.	
1969	V69 suffix after Ser. No.	
1970	V70 suffix after Ser. No.	
1971	V71 suffix after Ser. No.	
1972	V72 suffix after Ser. No.	
1973	V73 suffix after Ser. No.	
1974	V74 suffix after Ser. No.	
1975	V75 suffix after Ser. No.	
1976	V76 suffix after Ser. No.	

SUPERPOSED MODEL - O & U - 28 ga. &.410 bore

Year	28 ga.	.410 bore
1960-1962	NOT AVAILABLE	
1963	F3	J3
1964	F4	J4
1965	F5	J5
1966	F6	J6
1967	F7	J7
1968	F8	J8
1969	F69	J69
1970	F70	J70
1971	F71	J71
1972	F72	J72
1973	F73	J73
1974	F74	J74
1975	F75	J75
1976	F76	J76

LIEGE O & U - Approximately 10,000 produced

Year		
1973	73J prefix before Ser. No.	
1974	74J prefix before Ser. No.	
1975	75J prefix before Ser. No.	

DOUBLE AUTOMATIC SHOTGUN

Year	Ser. # Start	Ser. # End
1952 -	N/A	
1959	N/A	
1960 -	N/A	
1971	N/A	

1st or both digits indicate last 2 digits in year of manufacture (i.e. - OA1947 - 1960 mfg., 70A245671 - 1970 mfg.)

HI-POWER (9mm) PISTOL

Year	Ser. # Start	Ser. # End
1955	72251	75000
1956	75001	77250
1957	77251	80000
1958	80001	85267
1959	85268	89687
1960	89688	93027
1961	93028	109145
1962	109146	113548
1963	113549	115822
1964	115823	T136538
1965	T136569	T146372
1966	T146373	T173285
1967	T173286	T213999
1968	T214000	T258000
1969	T258001	T261000+
	and 69C prefix before Ser. No.	
1970	70C prefix before Ser. No.	
1971	71C prefix before Ser. No.	
1972	72C prefix before Ser. No.	
1973	73C prefix before Ser. No.	
1974	74C prefix before Ser. No.	
1975	75C prefix before Ser. No.	
1976	76C prefix before Ser. No.	
1977 to date	New style serialization	

BROWNING .380

Year	Ser. # Start	Ser. # End
1955 -	N/A	
1964	N/A	
1965	500000	598804
1966	598805	603890
1967	603891	619474
1968	619475	N/A
1969 -	N/A	

1970 Discontinued due to GCA of 1968. New model has longer barrel, adj. rear sight, modified grip.

1971	71N prefix before Ser. No.	
1972	72N prefix before Ser. No.	
1973	73N prefix before Ser. No.	
1974	74N prefix before Ser. No.	
1975	75N prefix before Ser. No.	

.25 CAL. BABY BROWNING PISTOL

Year	Ser. # Start	Ser. # End
1955-1958	Records not available	
1959	181000	206349
1960	206350	230999
1961	231000	250999
1962	251000	278999
1963	279000	286099
1964	286100	308499
1965	308500	329999
1966	333000	367443
1967	367444	412999
1968	413000	479000
1969	Discontinued because of GCA of 1968	

.22 CAL. PISTOLS (Nomad-Challenger-Medalist)

Year	Nomad	Challenger	Medalist
1959	P9	U9	T9
1960	P0	U0	T0
1961	P1	U1	T1
1962	P2	U2	T2
1963	P3	U3	T3

.22 CAL. PISTOLS (Nomad-Challenger-Medalist)

Year	*Nomad*	*Challenger*	*Medalist*
1964	P4	U4	T4
1965	P5	U5	T5
1966	P6	U6	T6
1967	P7	U7	T7
1968	P8	U8	T8
1969	P69	U69	T69
1970	P70	U70	T70
1971	P71	U71	T71
1972	P72	U72	T72
1973	P73	U73	T73
1974	Disc.	U74	T74
1975	Disc.	Disc.	Disc.

BOLT ACTION RIFLES
(Safari, Medallion, & Olympian Models)

Year	
1959 -	N/A
1962	No prefix (numeral-letter) before Ser. No. (i.e., only digits)
1963	3-single letter prefix or suffix by Ser. No.
1964	4-single letter prefix or suffix by Ser. No.
1965	5-single letter prefix or suffix by Ser. No.
1966	6-single letter prefix or suffix by Ser. No.
1967	7-single letter prefix or suffix by Ser. No.
1968	8-single letter prefix or suffix by Ser. No.
1969	Single letter (Y, Z, or L) followed by last 2 digits of year of mfg. Prefix only.
1970	"Y70" prefix
1971	"L71" prefix
1972	"Z72" prefix
1973	"Y73" prefix
1974	"Z74" prefix
1975	"L75" prefix

B.A.R.

Year	
1967	"M7" suffix after Ser. No.
1968	"M8" suffix after Ser. No.
1969	"M69" suffix after Ser. No.
1970	"M70" suffix after Ser. No.
1971	"M71" suffix after Ser. No.
1972	"M72" suffix after Ser. No.
1973	"M73" suffix after Ser. No.
1974	"M74" suffix after Ser. No.
1975	"M75" suffix after Ser. No.
1976	"M76" suffix after Ser. No.
1976 to date	New sequence with "RT" appearing in middle of Ser. No.

.22 AUTO RIFLE (Grades I, II, and III)

Year	
1956-Mid. 1961	"T" prefix = LR, "A" prefix = short
Mid. 1961	"A" changed to "E" prefix 5 digits or less.
1961	"1T" or "1A" or "1E" prefix before Ser. No.
1962	"2T" or "2E" before Ser. No.
1963	"3T" or "3E" prefix before Ser. No.
1964	"4T" or "4E" prefix before Ser. No.
1965	"5T" or "5E" prefix before Ser. No.
1966	"6T" or "6E" prefix before Ser. No.
1967	"7T" or "7E" prefix before Ser. No.
1968	"8T" or "8E" prefix before Ser. No.
1969	"69T" or "69E" prefix before Ser. No.
1970	"70T" or "70E" prefix before Ser. No.
1971	"71T" or "71E" prefix before Ser. No.
1972	"72T" or "72E" prefix before Ser. No.
1973	Japan production

T-BOLT RIFLE (T1 and T2)

Year	
1965	"X5" suffix after Ser. No.
1966	"X6" suffix after Ser. No.
1967	"X7" suffix after Ser. No.
1968	"X8" suffix after Ser. No.

T-BOLT RIFLE (T1 and T2)

Year	
1969	"X69" suffix after Ser. No.
1970	"X70" suffix after Ser. No.
1971	"X71" suffix after Ser. No.
1972	"X72" suffix after Ser. No.
1973	"X73" suffix after Ser. No.
1974	"X74" suffix after Ser. No.
1975	"X75" suffix after Ser. No.

BROWNING SERIALIZATION 1976-CURRENT

In 1975 Browning began using the two (2) letter code system (located in the middel of the serial number) for determining the year of manufacture. For example "PN" would be "89" inditacting 1989.

LETTER	NUMBER
Z	1
Y	2
X	3
W	4
V	5
T	6
R	7
P	8
N	9
M	10

E.J. CHURCHILL GUNMACKERS SERIALIZATION

YEAR	GUN #
1891	156
1892	339
1893	384
1894	480
1895	569
1896	655
1897	761
1898	923
1899	1047
1900	1156
1924	2834
1957	6901

COLT'S FIREARMS SERIALIZATION
MODEL 1849 POCKET REVOLVER

Year	*Ser. # Start*	*Ser. # End*
1849	1	11999
1850	12000	15999
1851	16000	24999
1852	25000	54999
1853	55000	84999
1854	85000	99999
1855	100000	109999
1856	110000	129999

MODEL 1849 POCKET REVOLVER cont.

Year	Ser. # Start	Ser. # End
1857	130000	139999
1858	140000	149999
1859	150000	159999
1860	160000	183999
1861	184000	196999
1862	197000	222999
1863	223000	249999
1864	250000	269999
1865	270000	279999
1866	280000	289999
1867	290000	299999
1868	300000	309999
1869	310000	319999
1870	320000	324999
1871	325000	329999
1872	330000	330999
1873	331000	340000

MODEL 1849 POCKET REVOLVER -LONDON BARREL ADDRESS

Year	Ser. # Start	Ser. # End
1853	1	999
1854	1000	4999
1855	5000	8999
1856	9000	11000

MODEL 1851 NAVY

Year	Ser. # Start	Ser. # End
1850	1	2499
1851	2500	9999
1852	10000	19999
1853	20000	34999
1854	35000	39999
1855	40000	44999
1856	45000	64999
1857	65000	84999
1858	85000	89999
1859	90000	92999
1860	93000	97999
1861	98000	117999
1862	118000	131999
1863	132000	174999
1864	175000	179999
1865	180000	184999
1866	185000	199999
1867	200000	203999
1868	204000	206999
1869	207000	209999
1870	210000	211999
1871	212000	213999
1872	214000	214999
1873	215000	215348

MODEL 1851 NAVY - LONDON BARREL ADDRESS

Year	Ser. # Start	Ser. # End
1853	1	3999
1854	4000	14999
1855	15000	40999
1856	41000	42000

MODEL 1860 ARMY

Year	Ser. # Start	Ser. # End
1860	1	1999
1861	2000	24999
1862	25000	84999
1863	85000	149999
1864	150000	152999
1865	153000	155999
1866	156000	161999

MODEL 1860 ARMY cont.

Year	Ser. # Start	Ser. # End
1867	162000	169999
1868	170000	176999
1869	177000	184999
1870	185000	189999
1871	190000	197999
1872	198000	198999
1873	199000	200500

MODEL 1861 NAVY

Year	Ser. # Start	Ser. # End
1861	1	4599
1862	4600	9999
1863	10000	16999
1864	17000	24999
1865	25000	27999
1866	28000	29999
1867	30000	30999
1868	31000	32999
1869	33000	33999
1870	34000	34999
1871	35000	35999
1872	36000	36999
1873	37000	38843

MODEL 1862 POLICE

Year	Ser. # Start	Ser. # End
1861	1	8499
1862	8500	14999
1863	15000	25999
1864	26000	28999
1865	29000	31999
1866	32000	34999
1867	35000	36999
1868	37000	39999
1869	40000	41999
1870	42000	43999
1871	44000	44999
1872	45000	45999
1873	46000	47000

MODEL 1873 - SINGLE ACTION ARMY (SAA) - PRE-WAR

Year	Caliber	Ser. # Start
1873	.45 Colt Caliber, Standard	1
1874	.450 Boxer	200
1875	.44 Rimfire series (own serials, 1-1863 made through 1880)	15000
1876	.476 Eley introduced	22000
1877		33000
1878	.44-40 introduced in quantity	41000
1879		49000
1880		53000
1881		62000
1882	Sheriff's model introduced	73000
1883	.22 rimfire introduced	85000
1884	.32-20 and .38-40 introduced	102000
1885	.41 Colt introduced	114000
1886	.38 Colt introduced	117000
1887	.32 Colt and .32 S&W introduced	119000
1888	Flattop Target S.A.A. began; no.	125000 126530
1889	.32 rimfire; ,32-44 S&W, .38 S&W; and .44 Russian introduced	128000

MODEL 1873 - SINGLE ACTION ARMY (SAA) - PRE-WAR cont.

Year	Description	Serial
1890	.44 Smoothbore; .380 and .450 Eley; and .44 S&W introduced	130000
1891	.38-44 introduced	136000
1892	Transverse cylinder latch introduced, screw lock at front of frame dropped	144000
1893		149000
1894	Beginning of Bisley models	154000
1895		159000
1896		163000
1897		168000
1898		175000
1899		182000
1900	Revolvers built to handle smokeless powder	192000
1901		203000
1902		220000
1903		238000
1904		250000
1905		261000
1906		273000
1907		288000
1908		304000
1909		308000
1910		312000
1911		316000
1912	Discontinue Bisley model	321000
1913	S&W Special introduced	325000
1914		328000
1915	Long flute cylinders; range no. 330001 to 331480	329500
1916		332000
1917		335000
1918		337000
1919		337200
1920		338000
1921		341000
1922		343000
1923		344500
1924	.45 ACP introduced, requiring special cylinders	346400
1925		347300
1926		348200
1927		349800
1928		351300
1929		352400
1930	.38 Special introduced	353800
1931		354100
1932		354500
1933		354800
1934		355000
1935	.357 Magnum introduced	355200
1936		355300
1937		355400
1938		356100
1939		356600
1940	A few S.A.A. during and just after the war	357000 thru 357859

1ST GENERATION COLT SINGLE ACTION ARMY - CALIBER BREAKDOWN

Caliber	S.A.A	Flattop Target	Bisley	Bisley Target
.22 Rimfire	107	93	0	0
.32 Rimfire	1	0	0	0
.32 Colt	192	24	160	44
.32 S&W	32	30	18	17
.32-44	2	9	14	17

1ST GENERATION COLT SINGLE ACTION ARMY - CALIBER BREAKDOWN cont.

Caliber	S.A.A	Flattop Target	Bisley	Bisley Target
.32-20	29,812	30	13,291	131
.38 Colt (through 1914)	1,011	122	412	96
.38 Colt (post-1922)	1,365	0	0	0
.38 S&W	9	39	10	5
.38 Colt Special	82	7	0	0
.38 S&W Special	25	0	2	0
.38-44	2	11	6	47
.357 Magnum	525	0	0	0
.380 Eley	1	3	0	0
.38-40	38,240	19	12,163	98
.41	16,402	91	3,159	24
.44 Smoothbore	15	0	1	0
.44 Rimfire	1,863	0	0	0
.44 German	59	0	0	0
.44 Russian	154	51	90	62
.44 S&W	24	51	29	64
.44 S&W Special	506	1	0	0
.44-40	64,489	21	6,803	78
.45	150,683	100	8,005	97
.45 Smoothbore	4	0	2	0
.45 ACP	44	0	0	0
.450 Boxer	729	89	0	0
.450 Eley	2,697	84	5	0
.455 Eley	1,150	37	180	196
.476 Eley	161	2	0	0
Total Quantities	310,386	914	44,350	976

COLT SINGLE ACTION ARMY – POST-WAR PRODUCTION

Year	Ser. # Start	Ser. # End
"SA" suffix from 1956 to 1978, "SA" prefix 1978 to 1981		
1956	0001SA	8799SA
1957	8800SA	18499SA
1958	18500SA	23399SA
1959	23400SA	28499SA
1960	28500SA	33599SA
1961	33600SA	35649SA
1962	35650SA	37299SA
1963	37300SA	38499SA
1964	38500SA	39999SA
1965	40000SA	41499SA
1966	41500SA	43799SA
1967	43800SA	46299SA
1968	46300SA	48999SA
1969	49000SA	52599SA
1970	52600SA	59399SA
1971	59400SA	61699SA
1972	61700SA	64399SA
1973	64400SA	69399SA
1974	69400SA	73319SA
1975	NONE PRODUCED	
1976 (start of 3rd generation of production)	80000SA	82000SA
1977	82001SA	95999SA
1978	96000SA	99999SA
Mid-1978 Start of "SA" prefix on front of Ser. No.		
1978	SA01000	SA14808

COLT SINGLE ACTION ARMY –
POST-WAR PRODUCTION cont.

Year	Ser. # Start	Ser. # End
1979	SA14809	SA30254
1980	SA30255	SA46919
1981	SA46920	SA58627
1982	SA58628	SA65255
1983	SA65256	SA66495
1984	SA66496	C.S. PROD.

NEW FRONTIER SINGLE ACTION ARMY

Year	Ser. # Start	Ser. # End
1961	3000NF	3005NF
1962	3006NF	3849NF
1963	3850NF	4699NF
1964	4700NF	4974NF
1965	4975NF	5399NF
1966	5400NF	5674NF
1967	5675NF	5699NF
1968	5700NF	5899NF
1969	5900NF	5924NF
1970	5925NF	6874NF
1971	6875NF	7049NF
1972	7050NF	7074NF
1973	7075NF	7174NF
1974	7175NF	7264NF
1975	7265NF	7288NF
1978	7501NF	N/A
	REINTRODUCED IN SEPTEMBER	
1978	01001NF	04424NF
1979	04425NF	06274NF
1980	06275NF	11374NF
1981	11375NF	16584NF
1982	16584NF	DISC. 1982

MODEL 1911 AND 1911A1 – Commercial production
Capital "C" prefix - .45 cal.

Year	Ser. # Start	Ser. # End
1912	C1	C1899
1913	C1900	C5399
1914	C5400	C16599
1915	C16600	C27599
1916	C27600	C74999
1917	C75000	C98999
1918	C99000	C105999
1919	C106000	C120999
1920	C121000	C126999
1921	C127000	C128999
1922	C129000	C133999
1923	C134000	C134999
1924	C135000	C139999
1925	C140000	C144999
1926	C145000	C150999
1927	C151000	C151999
1928	C152000	C154999
1929	C155000	C155999
1930	C156000	C158999
1931	C159000	C160999
1932	C161000	C164799
1933	C164800	C174599
1934	C174600	C177999
1935	C178000	C179799
1936	C179800	C183199
1937	C183200	C188699
1938	C188700	C189599
1939	C189600	C198899
1940	C198900	C199299
1941	C199300	C208799
1942	C208800	C215018
1943-1945: Commercial production		
interrupted by WWII		
1946	C221001	C222000

MODEL 1911 AND 1911A1 – Commercial production
Capital "C" prefix - .45 cal. cont.

Year	Ser. # Start	Ser. # End
1947	C222001	C231999
1948	C232000	C238500
1949	C238501	C240000
1950	C240000	247701C
	"C" SUFFIX STARTED	
	WITH SER. NO. 240228	
1951	247701C	253179C
1952	253180C	259549C
1953	259550C	266349C
1954	266350C	270549C
1955	270550C	272549C
1956	272550C	276699C
1957	276700C	281999C
1958	282000C	283799C
1959	283800C	285799C
1960	285800C	287999C
1961	288000C	289849C
1962	289850C	291299C
1963	291300C	293799C
1964	293800C	295999C
1965	296000C	300299C
1966	300300C	308499C
1967	308500C	315599C
1968	315600C	324499C
1969	324500C	332649C
1970	332650C	336169C
Mid-1970 New	70G01001	70G05550
1971	70G05551	70G18000
1972	70G18001	70G34400
1973	70G34401	70G43000
1974	70G43001	70G73000
1975	70G73001	70G88900
1976	70G88901	70G99999
Mid-1976 New	01001G70	13900G70
1977	13901G70	45199G70
1978	45200G70	N/A

MODEL 1911 AND 1911A1 MILITARY PRODUCTION

Year	Ser. # Start	Ser. # End	Manufacturer
1912	1	500	COLT
	501	1000	COLT USN
	1001	1500	COLT
	1501	2000	COLT USN
	2001	2500	COLT
	2501	3500	COLT USN
	3501	3800	COLT USMC
	3801	4500	COLT
	4501	5500	COLT USN
	5501	6500	COLT
	6501	7500	COLT USN
	7501	8500	COLT
	8501	9500	COLT USN
	9501	10500	COLT
	10501	11500	COLT USN
	11501	12500	COLT
	12501	13500	COLT USN
	13501	17250	COLT USN
1913	17251	36400	COLT
	36401	37650	COLT USMC
	37651	38000	COLT
	38001	44000	COLT USN
	44001	60400	COLT
1914	60401	72570	COLT
	72571	83855	SPRINGFIELD-
(THESE NUMBERS RESERVED FOR SPRING-			
FIELD)			
	83856	83900	COLT
	83901	84400	COLT USMC
	84401	96000	COLT

MODEL 1911 AND 1911A1 MILITARY PRODUCTION

Year	Ser. # Start	Ser. # End	Manufacturer
	96001	97537	COLT USN
	97538	102596	COLT
	102597	107596	
SPRINGFIELD(RESERVED NO. RANGE)			
1915	107597	109500	COLT
	109501	110000	COLT USN
	110001	113496	COLT
	113497	120566	SPRINGFIELD-
(RESERVED FOR SPRINGFIELD)			
	120567	125566	COLT
	125567	133186	SPRINGFIELD-
(RESERVED FOR SPRINGFIELD)			
1916	133187	137400	COLT
1917	137401	151186	COLT
	151187	151986	COLT USMC
	151987	185800	COLT
	185801	186200	COLT USMC
	186201	209586	COLT
	209587	210386	COLT USMC
	210387	215386	COLT
FRAMES(RESERVED FOR RECEIVERS)			
	215387	216186	COLT USMC
	216187	216586	COLT
	216587	216986	COLT USMC
1918	216987	217386	COLT USMC
	217387	223952	COLT
	223953	223990	COLT USN
	223991	232000	COLT
	232001	233600	COLT USN
	233601	580600	COLT
	1	13152	REM. UMC
1919	13153	21676	REM. UMC
	580601	629500	COLT
	629501	717386	COLT
1924	700001	710000	COLT
1937	710001	712349	COLT USN
1938	712350	713645	COLT
1939	713646	717281	COLT USN
1940	717282	721977	COLT
1941	721978	756733	COLT
1942	756734	793657	COLT
	793658	797639	COLT USN
	797640	800000	COLT
	S800001	S800500	SINGER
	800501	801000	H&R
	801001	856100	COLT
1943	856101	958100	COLT
	**856101	856404	Replacement No
	**856405	916404	ITHACA
	**916405	1041404	REM. RAND
	1041405	1096404	US&S
	1088726	1208673	COLT
	1208674	1279673	ITHACA
	1279674	1279698	RE NO AA
	1279699	1441430	REM. RAND
	1441431	1471430	ITHACA
	1471431	1609528	REM. RAND
1944	1609529	1743846	COLT
	1743847	1816641	REM. RAND
	1816642	1890503	ITHACA
	1890504	2075103	REM. RAND
1945	2075104	2134403	ITHACA
	2134404	2244803	REM. RAND
	2244804	2380013	COLT
	2380014	2619013	REM. RAND
	2619014	2693613	ITHACA

** *Denotes double issue ranges.*

COLT SINGLE-ACTION MODEL NUMBERS

The author wishes to express thanks to Mr. Don Wilkerson for allowing the edited information published below from his 1986 Post-War Single-Action Revolver, 1976-1986 publication.

A working knowledge of model numbers for the various Colt single-action revolvers is a must for even a novice collector. Since the mid - 1970s Colt has placed the model number on the end label of the shipping cartons of virtually all their firearms. Many collectors and publications regularly use the model number to describe or differentiate between revolvers. Using the model number is an accurate and efficient method to delineate a particular variation. Example: .45 caliber revolver with a 4 3/4 in. barrel, blue and casehardened finish and eagle stocks can be described as a simple "P-1840."

Each Colt model is specified by an alphabetical letter and 4 numerical digits. The basic model number as it pertains to single-action revolvers can be broken down as follows:

MODEL P - basic type of frame. The letter "P" is used to delineate the single-action type of frame.

FIRST NUMERAL - "1" is the first model built on a particular type of frame. Numerals 2, 3, 4, etc. indicate later versions. These versions are not always numbered in numerical order and the same number has been used for different models at different times. A "1" denotes the basic standard single-action frame. A "2" denotes the new black powder frame available through the Colt Custom Gun Shop. A "3" has been used at various times to denote a non-standard frame or cylinder. The "4" is used to specify the New Frontier style of frame. Numbers such as "7" and "8" are frequently used to specify commemorative or special editions.

SECOND NUMERAL - specifies caliber. A "4" denotes a .32-20, a "6" denotes .357 Magnum, a "7" denotes .44 Special, an "8" denotes .45 caliber, and a "9" specifies .44-40 caliber.*

THIRD NUMERAL - denotes barrel length. "3" is used to denote both a 3 inch and a 4 inch barrel. "4" is 4 3/4 inch or 5 inch, "5" is 5 1/2 inch, "7" is 7 1/2 inch, and "1" is 12 inch.*

FOURTH NUMERAL - is used to denote several different variations of the standard model. Some of the most common examples are: "1," "2," or "6" for nickel finish, "1" for full blue finish in the case of P-1871, and "2," "3," and "4" as used for the Sheriff's Model series to denote blue and casehardened finish, nickel finish, and Royal Blue and casehardened finish, respectively. The fourth numeral can also denote the type of stocks as in P-1673. The fourth numeral in the basic model designation must be used in conjunction with the preceding three numerals to determine its exact meaning. The fourth numeral is kind of a "catch-all" number. Many times this number serves only to differentiate a later model from a similar model assembled years earlier.

The .32-20 caliber and the 5 inch barrel length are listed in the 1984 Colt Buyer's Guide, but as of this date neither have been produced.

STANDARD MODEL P REVOLVER CODES

The primary model numbers used by Colt for Model P revolvers produced since 1976 are as follows:

P-1640 - .357 Magnum, 4 3/4 in. barrel, blue finish, eagle stocks.

STANDARD MODEL P REVOLVER CODES cont.

P-1641 - .357 Magnum, 4 3/4 in. barrel, nickel finish, wood stocks.

P-1650 - .357 Magnum, 5 1/2 in. barrel, blue finish, eagle stocks.

P-1656 - .357 Magnum, 5 1/2 in. barrel, nickel finish, wood stocks.

P-1670 - .357 Magnum, 7 1/2 in. barrel, blue finish, eagle stocks.

P-1673 - .357 Magnum, 7 1/2 in. barrel, blue finish, wood stocks.

P-1676 - .357 Magnum, 7 1/2 in. barrel, nickel finish, wood stocks.

P-1740 - .44 Special, 4 3/4 in. barrel, blue finish, eagle stocks.

P-1746 - .44 Special, 4 3/4 in. barrel, nickel finish, wood stocks.

P-1750 - .44 Special, 5 1/2 in. barrel, blue finish, eagle stocks.

P-1756 - .44 Special, 5 1/2 in. barrel, nickel finish, wood stocks.

P-1770 - .44 Special, 7 1/2 in. barrel, blue finish, eagle stocks.

P-1776 - .44 Special, 7 1/2 in. barrel, nickel finish, wood stocks.

P-1716 - .44 Special, 12 in. barrel, nickel finish, wood stocks.

P-1840 - .45 Colt, 4 3/4 in. barrel, blue finish, eagle stocks.

P-1841 - .45 Colt, 4 3/4 in. barrel, nickel finish, wood stocks.

P-1850 - .45 Colt, 5 1/2 in. barrel, blue finish, eagle stocks.

P-1856 - .45 Colt, 5 1/2 in. barrel, nickel finish, wood stocks.

P-1870 - .45 Colt, 7 1/2 in. barrel, blue finish, eagle stocks.

P-1876 - .45 Colt, 7 1/2 in. barrel, nickel finish, wood stocks.

P-1813 - .45 Colt, 12 in. barrel, blue finish, eagle stocks.

P-1816 - .45 Colt, 12 in. barrel, nickel finish, wood stocks.

P-1940 - .44-40 caliber, 4 3/4 in. barrel, blue finish, eagle stocks.

P-1941* - .44-40 caliber, 4 3/4 in. barrel, nickel finish, wood stocks.

P-1950 - .44-40 caliber, 5 1/2 in. barrel, blue finish, eagle stocks.

P-1970 - .44-40 caliber, 7 1/2 in. barrel, blue finish, eagle stocks.

P-1976* - .44-40 caliber, 7 1/2 in. barrel, nickel finish, wood stocks.

P-1911 - .44-40 caliber, 12 in. barrel, nickel finish, wood stocks.

These model numbers were used primarily for engraved or special ordered revolvers as the two models indicated were never produced as a regular model. "Blue finish" in the above chart denotes the standard blue finish, i.e., blue with case-hardened frame.

NEW FRONTIER MODEL

P-4671 - .357 Magnum, 7 1/2 in. barrel, nickel finish, wood stocks.

P-4750 - .44 Special, 5 1/2 in. barrel, Royal Blue finish, wood stocks.

P-4770 - .44 Special , 7 1/2 in. barrel, Royal Blue finish, wood stocks.

P-4840 - .45 Colt, 4 3/4 in. barrel, Royal Blue finish, wood stocks.

NEW FRONTIER MODEL cont.

P-4850 - .45 Colt, 5 1/2 in. barrel, Royal Blue finish, wood stocks.

P-4870 - .45 Colt, 7 1/2 in. barrel, Royal Blue finish, wood stocks.

P-4940 - .44-40 caliber, 4 3/4 in. barrel, Royal Blue finish, wood stocks.

P-4970 - .44-40 caliber, 7 1/2 in. barrel, Royal Blue finish, wood stocks.

Note: The term "Royal Blue" in the New Frontier chart denotes a revolver with a casehardened frame and a Royal (high polish) Blue finish on the other major components.

SHERIFF'S MODELS

P-1932 - .44-40 caliber, 3 in. barrel, blue finish, eagle stocks.

P-1933* - .44-40/.44 Special, 3 in. barrel, nickel finish, wood stocks.

P-1934* - .44-40/.44 Special, 3 in. barrel, Royal Blue finish, wood stocks.

*Circa 1984 all Sheriff's Models are listed as single calibers: .44-40 or .45 caliber.

REVOLVERS WITH FULL BLUE FRAMES

Some of the "full blue" models have had more than one model number assigned to the same variation. As a result, a particular model may have been identified by different model numbers at different times. Following the model numbers and descriptions in this chart will be an approximate time frame during which that particular model was in use. No date following the description indicates that only one model number for that particular variation is known to the author (Don Wilkerson).

P-1640 - FB - .357 Magnum, 4 3/4 in. barrel, fluted cylinder, eagle stocks.

P-1650 - FB - .357 Magnum, 5 1/2 in. barrel, fluted cylinder, eagle stocks.

P-1740 - FB - .44 Special, 4 3/4 in. barrel, fluted cylinder, eagle stocks.

P-1750 - FB - .44 Special, 5 1/2 in. barrel, fluted cylinder, eagle stocks.

P-1770 - FB - .44 Special, 7 1/2 in. barrel, fluted cylinder, eagle stocks.

P-1770 - UB - .44 Special, 7 1/2 in. barrel, unfluted cylinder, eagle stocks.

P-3840 - .45 Colt, 4 3/4 in. barrel, both fluted and unfluted cylinders, eagle stocks (early to mid - 1982).

P-1840 - FB - .45 Colt, 4 3/4 in. barrel, fluted cylinder, eagle stocks (mid to late 1982 to date).

P-1840 - UB - .45 Colt, 4 3/4 in. barrel, unfluted cylinder, eagle stocks (mid to late 1982 to date).

P-1850 - FB - .45 Colt, 5 1/2 in. barrel, fluted cylinder, eagle stocks.

P-1850 - UB - .45 Colt, 5 1/2 in. barrel, unfluted cylinder, eagle stocks.

P-1871 - .45 Colt, 7 1/2 in. barrel, fluted cylinder, wood stocks (1977 to 1979).

P-1870 - FB - .45 Colt, 7 1/2 in. barrel, fluted cylinder, wood stocks (1982 to date).

P-1870 - UB - .45 Colt, 7 1/2 in. barrel, unfluted cylinder, wood stocks (1982 to date).

P-1871 - FB - .45 Colt, 12 in. barrel, fluted cylinder, eagle stocks.

FULL BLUE NEW FRONTIERS

P-4770 - FB - .44 Special, 7 1/2 in. barrel, fluted cylinder, wood stocks.

FULL BLUE NEW FRONTIERS cont.

P-4870 - FB - .45 Colt, 7 1/2 in. barrel, fluted cylinder, wood stocks.

P-4870 - UB - .45 Colt, 7 1/2 in. barrel, unfluted cylinder, wood stocks.

MISCELLANEOUS MODEL NUMBERS

1750 - AA - .44 Special, 5 1/2 in. barrel, blue finish with nickel cylinder, eagle stocks.

1750 - AB - .44 Special, 5 1/2 in. barrel, blue finish with nickel cylinder with blue flutes, eagle stocks.

1840 - UC - .45 Colt, 4 3/4 in. barrel, blue finish, unfluted cylinder, eagle stocks.

1850 - UC - .45 Colt, 5 1/2 in. barrel, blue finish, unfluted cylinder, eagle stocks.

1870 - UC - .45 Colt, 7 1/2 in. barrel, blue finish, unfluted cylinder, eagle stocks.

Note: The term "blue finish" in this chart is the standard blue finish with a casehardened frame.

BLACK POWDER MODEL P REVOLVERS

P-2830 - .45 Colt, 3 in. barrel, blue finish.
P-2833 - .45 Colt, 3 in. barrel, nickel finish.
P-2834* - .45 Colt, 3 in. barrel, Royal Blue finish.
P-2836 - .45 Colt, 4 in. barrel, Royal Blue finish.
P-2837 - .45 Colt, 4 in. barrel, nickel finish.
P-2840 - .45 Colt, 4 3/4 in. barrel, blue finish.
P-2841 - .45 Colt, 4 3/4 in. barrel, nickel finish.
P-2847* - .45 Colt, 5 in. barrel, nickel finish.
P-2870 - .45 Colt, 7 1/2 in. barrel, blue finish.
P-2871 - .45 Colt, 7 1/2 in. barrel, nickel finish.
P-2940 - .44-40 caliber, 4 3/4 in. barrel, blue finish.
P-2941 - .44-40 caliber, 4 3/4 in. barrel, nickel finish.
P-2970 - .44-40 caliber, 7 1/2 in. barrel, blue finish.
P-2971 - .44-40 caliber, 7 1/2 in. barrel, nickel finish.
P-2437* - .32-20 caliber, 4 in. barrel, nickel finish.
P-2474* - .32-20 caliber, 7 1/2 in. barrel, Royal Blue finish.

As of this writing these calibers have not been produced. The terms "blue finish" and "Royal" in this chart refer to Colt's standard single-action finish, i.e., casehardened frame with all components finished in either standard blue or Royal Blue.

MODEL 1877 LIGHTNING & THUNDERE DA

Year	Ser. # Start	Ser. # End
1877	1	2900
1878	3000	13499
1879	13500	18999
1880	19000	27999
1881	28000	33999
1882	34000	39999
1883	40000	47999
1884	48000	51499
1885	51500	52999
1886	53000	57499
1887	57500	62699
1888	62700	72499
1889	72500	73499
1890	73500	80499
1891	80500	85399
1892	85400	88999
1893	89000	94999
1894	95000	96999
1895	97000	101699
1896	101700	105199
1897	105200	107499
1898	107500	111499
1899	111500	115499
1900	115500	122699

MODEL 1877 LIGHTNING & THUNDERE DA cont.

Year	Ser. # Start	Ser. # End
1901	122700	130299
1902	130300	139999
1903	140000	148499
1904	148500	156199
1905	156200	158999
1906	159000	161999
1907	162000	163999
1908	164000	164999
1909	165000	166849

MODEL 1878 SxS HAMMER SHOTGUN

Year	Ser. # Start	Ser. # End
1878	1	99
1879	100	2249
1880	2250	7849
1881	7850	11799
1882	11800	14999
1883	15000	17399
1884	17400	18549
1885	18550	20349
1886	20350	21199
1888	22000	22499
1889	22500	22683

MODEL 1883 SxS HAMMERLESS SHOTGUN

Year	Ser. # Start	Ser. # End
1883	1	249
1884	250	849
1885	850	1399
1886	1400	2199
1887	2200	3055
1888	3056	4057
1889	4058	4449
1890	4450	5349
1891	5350	6249
1892	6250	6749
1893	6750	7249
1894	7250	7549
1895	7550	8366

LIGHTNING SLIDE ACTION - SMALL FRAME

Year	Ser. # Start	Ser. # End
1887	1	999
1888	1000	7999
1889	8000	11749
1890	11750	14299
1891	14300	14699
1892	14700	15399
1893	15400	16599
1894	16600	19799
1895	19800	22999
1896	23000	25999
1897	26000	29599
1898	29600	35299
1899	35300	42799
1900	42800	52299
1901	52300	63299
1902	63300	73699
1903	73700	81999
1904	82000	89912

LIGHTNING SLIDE ACTION - MEDIUM FRAME

Year	Ser. # Start	Ser. # End
1884	1	3074
1885	3075	12649
1886	12650	20499
1887	20500	24999
1888	25000	32999
1889	33000	40999

LIGHTNING SLIDE ACTION - MEDIUM FRAME

Year	Ser. # Start	Ser. # End
1890	41000	49999
1891	50000	63199
1892	63200	65999
1893	66000	70999
1894	71000	75999
1895	76000	78999
1896	79000	80499
1897	80500	82499
1898	82500	83999
1899	84000	85799
1900	85800	87799
1901	87800	89299
1902	89300	89777

LIGHTNING SLIDE ACTION - LARGE FRAME

Year	Ser. # Start	Ser. # End
1887	1	999
1888	1000	2399
1889	2400	3799
1890	3800	5199
1891	5200	5699
1892	5700	5999
1893	6000	6299
1894	6300	6496

AR-15 - SPORTER MODELS

Year	Ser. # Start	Ser. # End
1963	SP00001	SP00023
SP00024-SP00100 Specials		
1964	SP00101	SP02500
1965	SP02501	SP05599
1966	SP05600	SP08249
1967	SP08250	SP10749
1968	SP10750	SP13999
1969	SP14000	SP14653
1970	SP15001	SP15473
1971	SP16001	SP19400
1972	SP19401	SP24200
1973	SP24201	SP32600
1974	SP32601	SP43800
1975	SP43801	SP55300
1976	SP55301	N/A

COLT BLACKPOW-DER 2ND GENERATION SERIALIZATION

Model No.	Ser. # Range	Total	Start	End

MODEL1851 NAVY

C-1121	4201 25100 20900		1971	1978

C-1122
As above but at higher range of numbers Unk'n - 1978

MODEL 1851 NAVY, R. E. LEE

C-9001	251 REL 5000 REL	4750	-	1971

1851 NAVY, U. S. GRANT

C-9002	251 USG 5000 USG	4750	-	1971

MODEL 1851 GRANT-LEE PAIR

C-9003	01 GLP 250 GLP	250	-	1971

3rd MODEL DRAGOON

C-1770	20801 20826	25	1974	1978

3rd MODEL DRAGOON cont.

Model No.	Ser. # Range	Total	Start	End
Prototype	20901 24501	3601		
C-1770MN S/N As Above		20	1984	1984

MODEL 1851 NAVY

F-1100	24900 29150	4250	5/80	10/81
F-1101 S/N As Above W/Blank Cylinders		300	10/81	11/81
F-1110 29151 S 29640 S Stainless Steel		489	6/82	10/82

MODEL 1860 ARMY

F-1200 201000 212835 Rebated Cylinder		7593	11/78	11/82
F-1200 EBO S/N As Above Butterfield		500	1979	1979
F-1200 LNK S/N As Above Electroless Nickel		Unk'n	Unk'n	Unk'n
F-1200 MN S/N As Above Nickel/Ivory		12	1984	1984
F-1202 S/N As Above Limited Edition		500	1979	1979
F-1203 207330 211250 Fluted Cylinder		2670	7/80	10/81
F-1210 211263 S 212540 S Stainless Steel		1278	1/82	4/82

1861 NAVY

F-1300	40000 43165	3166	9/80	10/81

862 POCKET NAVY

F-1400 48000 58850 and skip odd no.		5765	12/79	11/81
F-1400MN S/N As Above Nickel/Ivory		25	1984	1984
F-1401 S/N As Above Limited Edition		500	1979	1980

1862 POCKET POLICE

F-1500 49000 57300 and skip even no.		4801	1/80	9/81
F-1500 MN S/N As Above Nickel/Ivory		25	1984	1984
F-1501 S/N As Above Limited Edition		500	1979	1980

1847 WALKER

F-1600	1200 4120	2573	6/80	4/82
	32256 32500	245	5/81	9/81

1st MODEL DRAGOON

F-1700	25100 34500	3878	1/80	2/82

2nd MODEL DRAGOON

F-172 S/N As Above and Mix at Random for 1st, 2nd & 3rd		2676	1/80	2/82

3rd MODEL DRAGOON

F-140 S/N As Above and Mix at Random for

Model No.	Ser. # Range	Total	Start	End
1st, 2nd & 3rd	2856	1/80	2/82	
	31401 31450	50	10/81	11/81
F-1740EGA	Unk'n Unk'n	200	1982	1982
(Garabaldi Model<- "GCA" prefix)				

BABY DRAGOON

F-1760	16000 17851	1852	2/81	4/81
F-1761	S/N As Above	500	1979	1980
Limited Edition				

1860 ARMY

F-9005	US 001/001 US to			
	US 3025/3025 US	3025	9/77	1/80
Cavalry Commemorative (Two Gun Set)				

HERITAGE WALKER

F-9006	01 1853	1853	6/80	6/81

JOHN DICKSON & SON SERIALIZATION

Year Starting	Serial Number
1812-1854	1-1500
1860	2000
1864	2500
1870	3000
1878	3500
1885	3933
1886	4000
1889	4889
1892	4500
1898	5000
1903	5500

A.H. FOX SERIALIZATION

GRADE A-F 12 GAUGE

Year Starting	Serial Number
1907	7500
1908	7600
1909	9900
1910	15000
1911	18700
1912	20000
1913	20700
1914	21500
1915	22000
1916	23200
1917	24300
1918	24700
1919	25000
1920	25900
1921	27000
1922	27900
1923	29000
1924	30000
1925	30900
1926	31600
1927	32000
1928	32900
1929	33850
1930	33900
1931	33999
1932	34100
1933	34200
1934	34300
1935	34400
1936	34500

GRADE A-F 16 GAUGE

Year Starting	Serial Number
1937	34750
1938	34900
1939	35150
1940	35280
1912	300075
1913	300200
1914	300400
1915	300600
1916	300700
1917	300750
1918	300800
1919	300900
1920	301100
1921	301300
1922	301500
1923	301800
1924	302000
1925	302300
1926	302500
1927	302650
1928	302800
1929	303000
1930	303050
1931	303100
1932	303200
1933	303300
1934	303350
1935	303400
1936	303500
1937	303650
1938	303800
1939	303850
1940	303870
Highest no.	303875

GRADE A-F 20 GAUGE

Year Starting	Serial Number
1912	200100
1913	200250
1914	200500
1915	200700
1916	200800
1917	200900
1918	201000
1919	201300
1920	201500
1921	201600
1922	201800
1923	202000
1924	202200
1925	202400
1926	202500
1927	202800
1928	202950
1929	203100
1930	203150
1931	203200
1932	203300
1933	203350
1934	203500
1935	203700
1936	203750
1937	203800
1938	203830
1939	203900
1940	203970
Highest no.	203974

STERLINGWORTH 12 GAUGE

Year Starting	Serial Number
1910	53800
1911	59000
1912	63500
1913	66500
1914	74200
1915	75600
1916	77500
1917	79000
1918	82000
1919	84500
1920	89500
1921	92300
1922	94500
1923	97500
1924	99000
1925	100600
1926	105500
1927	113500
1928	119000
1929	122600
1930	128500
1931	130000
1932	132000
1933	134000
1934	136000
1935	138000
1936	139000
1937	145000
1938	150000
1939	155000
1940	161500
Highest no.	161556

STERLINGWORTH 16 GA.

Year Starting	Serial Number
1913	351000
1914	351600
1915	352300
1916	353000
1917	353700
1918	354200
1919	355000
1920	356500
1921	357000
1922	357800
1923	358500
1924	359500
1925	359900
1926	360300
1927	362000
1928	364500
1929	366400
1930	367500
1931	368000
1932	368600
1933	369200
1934	369900
1935	372000
1936	373500
1937	374200
1938	374800
Highest no.	378481

STERLINGWORTH 20 GAUGE

Year Starting	Serial Number
1912	250100
1913	252000
1914	253000
1915	254500
1916	254600

STERLINGWORTH 20 GAUGE cont.

Year Starting	Serial Number
1917	254700
1918	255000
1919	255300
1920	255800
1921	256100
1922	256400
1923	256800
1924	257200
1925	257700
1926	258200
1927	259300
1928	260500
1929	262000
1930	263600
1931	263800
1932	264000
1933	264300
1934	264600
1935	266500
1936	268500
1937	270500
1938	270800
1939	271200
1940	271225
Highest no.	271304

SINGLE BARREL TRAP - GRADE J, K, L, M

Year Starting	Serial Number
1919	400090
1920	400250
1921	400275
1922	400300
1923	400325
1924	400350
1925	400375
1926	400385
1927	400395
1928	400400
1929	400410
1930	400415
1931	400425
1932	400500
1933	400525
1934	400540
1935	400568

STEPHEN GRANT SERIALIZATION

Year Starting	Serial Number
1867	2480
1870	3000
1875	3900
1880	4750
1885	5450
1890	6100
1895	6700
1896	6857
1900	7300

W. W. GREENER SERIALIZATION

Year Starting	Serial Number
1878	19304
1880	22860
1895	38917
1902	50911

W. W. GREENER cont.

Year Starting	Serial Number
1915	58536
1920	62621
1930	68635
1967	79259

HARRINGTON & RICHARDSON SERIALIZATION 1940 - 1982

The following serial numbered prefixes are related to the corresponding year of manufacture:

Year Starting	S.N. Prefix
1940	A
1941	B
1942	C
1943	D
1944	E
1945	F
1946	G
1947	H
1948	I
1949	J
1950	K
1951	L
1952	M
1953	N
1954	P
1955	R
1956	S
1957	T
1958	U
1959	V
1960	W
1961	X
1962	Y
1963	Z
1964	AA
1965	AB
1966	AC
1967	AD
1968	AE
1969	AF
1970	AG
1971	AH(Snap on forecap)
1972	AJ
1973	AL
1974	AM
1975	AN
1976	AP
1977	AR(Striker Mech. Intr.)
1978	AS
1979	AT
1980	AU
1981	AX
1982	AY

HIGH STANDARD SERIALIZATION

The author wishes to express thanks to Mr. John J. Stimson, Jr. for the following information.

The serial numbers listed represent the highest serial number shipped for the year. Regular serial numbers began with 5,000 which was shipped October 15, 1932. Although it appears the guns were generally assembled in numerical sequence, the shipments were not and some guns may have remained in inventory for weeks, monthes, or even years between assenbly and shipment.

Year	Serial Number
1932	5,102
1933	6,567
1934	8,313
1935	11,651
1936	18,751
1937	30,026
1938	39,430
1939	50,619
1940	70,715
1941	91,986
1942	104,520
1943	115,423
1944	135,659
1945	145,817
1946	174,194
1947	233,402
1948	301,349
1949	325,953
1950	335,693
1951	356,899
1952	408,862
1953	442,984
1954	475,186
1955	508,613
1956	652,405
1957	776,129
1958	913,111
1959	1,044,802
1960	1,147,641
1961	1,224,652
1962	1,285,049
1963	1,353,764
1964	1,418,870
1965	1,507,541
1966	1,610,707
1967	1,853,513
1968	2,030,404
1969	2,172,356
1970	2,232,503
1971	2,828,293
1972	2,356,207
1973	2,424,175
1974	2,469,497

1975 is the last year of the regular serial number series (except for Sr. No. 2,500,811 shipped August 28, 1976) and marks the beginning of the letter prefix serialization.

Year	Sr. No.	Sr. No.	Sr. No.
1975	2,500,810	G 04,566	ML 06,747
1976		G 13,757	ML 23,065
1977	G 18,298	G 162,590	ML 29,707
1978	G 20,223		ML 41,270
1979			ML 63,483
1980	MLG 20,408		ML 81,629
1981	SH 18,446		ML 90,000
1982	SH 25,964		
1983	SH 31,558		
1984	SH 34,034		

HOLLAND & HOLAND SERIALIZATION

PARADOX SERIES

Year Starting	Serial Number
1885	11500
1886	N/A
1887	N/A
1888	11691
1889	11788
1890	11865
1891	11948
1895	15036
1892	15075
1895	15347
1900	15558
1903	15655
1905	15750
1906	15825
1907	15860
1911	15900
1914	15950
1919	19560
1922	15970
1930	15980
1956	15979

RECORDED DATES

Year Starting	Serial Number
March 1856	565(First Recorded Date)
October 1868	580
February 1857	584
August 1859	700
A gap in records	728-1059
1864	1060
1865	1101
1868	1352
1869	1439
1870	1578
1871	1769
1872	2002
1873	2401
1874	2759
1875	3174
1876	3649
1877	4179
1878	4774
1879	5274
1880	5819
1881	6382
1882	7009
1883	7473
1884	7904
1885	8406
1886	8809
1887	8999
Unused	9000-10000
Missing	10000-10849
Rook Rifles	10850-10999
Normal Series	11000-11499
Paradox Guns	11500-11999
Normal Series	12000-12999
Rook Rifles	13000-13999
Normal Series	14000-14999
Paradox Guns	15000-15999
Normal Series	16000-16999
Normal Series	17000-17399
Rifles and Rook Rifles	17400-17999
Believed Unused	18000-18999
Rifles	19000-19999

RECORDED DATES cont.

Year Starting	Serial Number
Misc. Guns and Rifles	20000-21999
See separate lists	22000+

ROOK RIFLES

Year Starting	Serial Number
1887	10850-10999
Assumed 1888 records missing	11000-11499
1889	13106
1890	13465
1891	13566
1892	13674
1893	13885-13999
1894 Rrook/others rifles	17401
1899	17999

MAGAZINE RIFLES

Year Starting	Serial Number
1910	28000
1911	28100
1913	28199
1913	28300
1919	28399
1920-29	1-581
1930-33	582-880
1920-32	881-1181
1935-49	1182-1782
1949-60	1783-2179
1951-58	2180-2577
1952-62	2578-2977
1958-65	2978-3377
1964-74	3378-3783
1975-80	3784-4000
1981-87	4001-4250
1988-92	4251-4330

PLAIN GUNS

Year Starting	Serial Number
1907	26200
1908	26300
1909	26400
1909	26500
1910	26600
1911	26700
1912	26800
1913	26900
1913	26999
1913	28600
1914	28700
1914	28800
1915	28900
1915	28999
1915	29500
1915	29600
1916	29700
1919	29800
1919	29900
1919	30000
1920	30100
1922	30200
1924	30300
1925	30334
1925	31100
1926	31200
1928	31300
1929	31399
1929	32200
1931	32300
1933	32400
1935	32499
1935	34000

PLAIN GUNS cont.

Year Starting	Serial Number
1936	34100
1937	34200
1939	34300
1949	34400
1953	34500
1956	34600
1961	34700
1975	34800

ROYAL GUNS

Year Starting	Serial Number
1899	22000
1900	22500
1902	23000
1903	23500
1906	25000
1907	25500
1910	25599
1910	27000
1911	27250
1912	27500
1913	27750
1914	27999
1914	29000
1915	29100
1919	29200
1920	29300
1920	29400
1921	29499
1921	30500
1922	30600
1922	30700
1924	30800
1925	30900
1926	30999
1926	31500
1927	31600
1927	31700
1928	31800
1929	31900
1929	32900
1934	32999
1934	33000
1935	33100
1936	33200
1937	33300
1937	33400
1939	33500
1946	33600
1948	33700
1950	33800
1952	33900
1954	33999
1954	36251
1956	36300
1958	36400
1959	36500
1962	36600
1964	36700
1965	36800
1970	36900
1970	40006
1972	40100
1974	40200
1979	40300
1980	40400
1981	40500
1982	40530
1983	40560
1984	40590
1985	40650

ROYAL GUNS cont.

Year Starting	Serial Number
1986	40770
1987	40820
1988	40880
1989	40920
1990	41000
1991	41075
1992	41150
1993	41210

ROYAL OVER & UNDER GUNS

Year Starting	Serial Number
1950	36000
1952	36010
1954	36020
1958	36029
1993	51001

SPORTING OVER & UNDER GUNS

Year Starting	Serial Number
1993	50500

CAVALIER GUNS

Year Starting	Serial Number
1986	50001
1989	50150
1992	50250

ROYAL DOUBLE RIFLES - .450 & .465

Year Starting	Serial Number
1910	28200
1914	28299
1914	28500
1919	28535
1921	30335
1921	30415
1925	31042
1925	31049
1927	32000
1941	32099

ROYAL DOUBLE RIFLES - .375

Year Starting	Serial Number
1911	28400
1920	28499
1920	30416
1925	30499
1925	31050
1927	31099
1927	32100
1933	32199

ROYAL DOUBLE RIFLES - .240 & Small Bores

Year Starting	Serial Number
1920	28566
1923	28599
1923	31000
1926	31041
1926	31400
1931	31450
1955	31499

ALL CALIBRES

Year Starting	Serial Number
1933	35000
1939	35100
1950	35200
1953	35250
1956	35300
1963	35350
1968	35450
1975	35495
1977	35498
1980	35500
1981	35505
1984	35524

ALL CALIBRES cont.

Year Starting	Serial Number
1985	35527
1988	35540
1989	35542
1990	35552
1991	35590

ITALIAN YEAR OF MFG. DATE CODES

Additional information regarding Italian Proof marks, and dates of manufacture can be found in *THE WORLD OF BERETTA An International Legend* by R. L. Wilson.

All Dates Prior to 1943 Have Month and Year (i.e. IXXII = January 1922.) 1944 -1953 = I - IX

Code	Year
X =	1954
XI =	1955
XII =	1956
XIII =	1957
XIV =	1958
XV =	1959
XVI =	1960
XVII =	1961
XVIII =	1962
XIX =	1963
XX =	1964
XXI =	1965
XXII =	1966
XXIII =	1967
XXIV =	1968
XXV =	1969
XVI =	1970
XXVII =	1971
XXVIII =	1972
XXIX =	1973
XXX =	1974
AA =	1975
AB =	1976
AC =	1977
AD =	1978
AE =	1979
AF =	1980
AH =	1981
AI =	1982
AL =	1983
AM =	1984
AN =	1985
AP =	1986
AS =	1987
AT =	1988
AW =	1989
AZ =	1990
BA =	1991

Code	Year
BB =	1992
BC	1993
BD	1994
BF	1995
BH	1996
BI	1997
BL	1998
BM	1999
BN	2000
BP	2001
BS	2002
BT	2003
BW	2004
BZ	2005

ITHACA GUN CO. SERIALIZATION

BAKER MODEL ITHACA DOUBLES

Year Starting	Serial Number
1880-1885	2447
1886	4104
1887	7003
1888	8787
1889 (Jan.-Aug.)	10534

CRASS MODEL ITHACA DOUBLES

Year Starting	Serial Number
1892	17235-21999
1893	25421
1894	25759
1895	27762
1896	28713
1897	30222
1898	33026
1899	38399
1900	46627
1901	61609
1902	76599
1903	94108

FLUES MODEL ITHACA DOUBLE & SINGLE

Year Starting	Serial Number
1908	175000-182031
1909	192499
1910	205399
1911	216499
1912	230099
1913	242599
1914	256699
1915	268199
1916	276899
1917	289299
1918	299799
1919	315399
1920	343335
1921	356513
1922	361849
1923	372099
1924	390499
1925	398352
1926	398365

N.I.D. MODEL ITHACA DOUBLE

Year Starting	Serial Number
1925	425000-425299
1926	439199
1927	451099
1928	454530
1929	457299
1930	458399

N.I.D. MODEL ITHACA DOUBLE cont.

Year Starting	Serial Number
1931	459139
1932	459162
1933	459195
1935	459637
1936	459649
1935	460799
1936	462399
1937	464699
1938	464827
1939	464850
1940	464899
1938	465199
1939	465999
1940	466999
1941	467146
1946	467199
1941	468099
1946	468699
1947	468794
1948	468799
1947	469949
1948	469979
1948	470099

CHARLES LANCASTER SERIALIZATION

Year Starting	Serial Number
1826	100
1830	600
1840	1200
1850	2100
1860	3200
1861	3400
1862	3540
1863	3693
1864	3805
1865	3914
1866	3999
1867	4087
1868	4183
1869	4271
1870	4328
1871	4401
1872	4477
1873	4562
1874	4644
1875	4714
1876	4769
1877	4833
1878	4892
1879	4924
1880	4949
1881	4982
1882	5079
1883	5186
1884	5359
1885	5497
1886	5627
1887	5764
1888	5926
1889	6136
1890	6406
1891	6671
1892	6988
1893	7189

Year Starting	Serial Number
1894	7360
1895	7548
1896	7709
1897	7940
1898	8132
1899	8353
1900	8529
1901	8700

JOSEPH LANG SERIALIZATION

Year Starting	Serial Number
1858	2085
1860	2332
1865	2970
1870	3916
1875	5180
1880	6000
1885	7031
1890	7546
1895	8150
1900	9100

MARLIN FIREARMS COMPANY SERIALIZATION

Approximate serialization for Marlin rifles from 1883 to 1906 including Models 1881, 1888, 1889, 1891, 1892, 1893, 1894, and 1897. Marlin did not assign a specific block of Ser. No. to these models, rather the models being produced that time were mixed. Using this list will place the year of manufacture plus or minus one year.

For a factor letter on an older Marlin firearm, contact the Buffalo Bill Historical center, Cody Firearms Museum, 720 Sheridan Ave., Cody, WY 82414.   Web site www.bbhc.org or phone 307-587-4771. There is a $45 fee per serial number search.

Older Rifles Mfg.

Year	From #	To #
1883	4001	6700
1884	6701	8850
1885	8851	11300
1886	11301	15000
1887	15001	17800
1888	17801	21500
1889	21501	30000
1890	30001	45000
1891	45001	63250
1892	63251	80250
1893	80251	95750
1894	95751	115000
1895	115001	133000
1896	133001	144400

Older Rifles Mfg. cont.

Year	From #	To #
1897	144401	161200
1898	161201	175500
1899	175501	196000
1900	196001	213000
1901	213001	233300
1902	233301	262500
1903	262501	287300
1904	287301	310500
1905	310501	329000
1906	329001	355300

1948-1968 Mfg.

Year	Serial No. Prefix
1948	E
1949	F
1950	G
1951	H
1952	J
1953	K
1954	L
1955	M
1956	N
1957	P
1957-1958	R
1958-1959	S
1960	T
1960-Aug. 1961	U
1961-Aug. 1962	V
1963	W
1964	Y & Z
1965	AA
1966	AB
1967	AC
1968	AD

MAUSER BROOMHANDLES SERIALIZATION 1896 - late 1930

Ser. #	Date	Nature of Changes
before	1896	-The cone hammer used in place of spur hammer.
#25	1896	- "SYSTEM MAUSER" marked on top of the chamber.
before	1897	- The locking system changed from one to two lugs.
#200		- The barrel contour at the chamber is tapered instead of stepped.
#390	1897	- "WAFFENFABRIK MAUSER OBERNDORF A/N" marked on top of the chamber.
#975	1897	- The center section of the rear panel on the left side of the frame is not milled out (this feature appears earlier on a few 20-shot pistols). This area is sometimes used for special markings on contract pieces such as the Turkish and Persian.
#12,200 to #14,999		
	1898	- The large ring hammer replaces the cone hammer.
#21,000	1899	- There is no panel milling on either side of the frame.
		- A single lug bayonet type mount adopted for retaining the firing pin instead of the dovetail plate.
		- The trigger is mounted directly to the frame by two integral lugs rather than attached to a removable block.

Ser. #	Date	Nature of Changes
		- The position of the serial number moved from the rear of the frame above the stock slot to the left side of the chamber.
#22,000	1900	- Two integral lugs used to mount the rear sight instead of a pin.
#29,000	1902	- Very shallow panels milled into the frame on both sides.*
#31,200	1903	- "WAFFENFABRIK MAUSER OBERNDORF A NECKAR" added to the right rear frame panel.*
#34,000	1904	- The depth of the frame panel milling increased.*
#35,000	1904	- The barrel extension side rails lengthened about a half inch.*
		- An additional lug for mounting added to the firing pin.*
		- The hammer changed to the small ring pattern.*
		- The safety mechanism altered to require that the lever be pushed up to engaged it instead of down.*
		- The center of the safety lever knob is no longer milled out.*
#38,000	1905	- The short extractor with two ribs replaces the long thin extractor.*
#100,000	1910	- The rifling changed from four groove to six groove.
		to
#130,000	1911	
#270,000	1915	- "NS" (Neues Sicherung or New Safety) appears on the back of the hammer. The hammer must be moved back beyond the cocked position to engage the safety.
#440,000	1921	- The lanyard ring stud is rotated 90 degrees.
#501,000	1923	- The Mauser "banner" appears on the left rear frame panel.
#800,000	1930	- The Mauser banner is enlarged.
		- A step is added to the barrel contour just ahead of the chamber.
		- The safety is changed to allow the hammer to be dropped from a cocked position, without danger, by pulling the trigger (called Universal Safety).
		- The front of the grip frame widened to equal the rear part where the stock slot is.
#850,000	1932	- "D.R.P.u.A.P." (Deutsches Reich Patenten und Anderes Patenten) added below the inscription on the right rear frame panel.
#860,000	1932	- The lettering in the frame inscription is slanted forward.
#900,000	1934	- The serial number is moved to the rear of the barrel extension behind the sight.
		- The two grooves in each side of the barrel extension side rails are eliminated.

*These nine changes appear out of sequence on three small batches of guns (29,000 to 29,900, 40,000 to 41,000, and 42,600 to 43,900). Most of these pistols are of the "bolo" style, that is they have 3.9 inch barrels, small grips, six or 10-shot magazines and fixed or adjustable rear sights. A few of these pistols show non-standard barrel contours, barrel extension milling and hammer safety devices. Apparently the factory withheld these numbers from the regular production series and reissued them at later dates.

PARKER BROTHERS SHOTGUNS SERIALIZATION 1866 - 1942

Additional information regarding Parker shotgun is available in PARKER GUN IDENTIFICATION & SERIALIZATION compiled and edited by Charles E. Price & S.P. Fjestad available on www.bluebookinc.com.

Year Starting	*Serial Number*
1866-1868	0-6,800
1868-1877	9,700
1877-1879	15,700
1880	17,600
1881	22,700
1882	27,300
1883	34,900
1884	36,000
1885	46,450
1886	48,125
1887	56,650
1889	59,500
1890	61,350
1891	66,800
1892	71,600
1893	77,000
1894	80,300
1895	82,400
1896	85,200
1897	86,450
1898	89,350
1899	92,450
1900	97,300
1901	105,750
1902	113,100
1903	121,900
1904	129,200
1905	132,000
1906	138,300
1907	144,250
1908	148,250
1910	153,000
1911	157,050
1912	157,800
first year of Trojan grade	
1913	165,000
1914	168,200
1915	171,500
1916	173,450

PARKER BROTHERS cont.

Year Starting	*Serial Number*
1917	175,650
first single barrel trap gun	
1918	180,250
1919	184,900
1920	190,100
1921	195,000
1922	200,500
first Parker single trigger	
1923	205,150
1924	207,150
first beaver tail forend	
1925	214,400
1926	218,050
first ventilated rib, first .410	
1927	222,650
1928	228,200
PH grade dropped	
1929	230,700
1930	234,200
1931	235,950
1932	236,100
1933	236,300
1934	236,650
first skeet guns, takeover of factory by Remington	
1935	237,000
1936	239,900
last regular catalog	
1937	240,300
1938-1942	242,385

PIOTTI SERIALIZATION

Year Starting	*Serial Number*
1962	1
1962	515
1963	1285
1964	1913
1965	2594
1966	2988
1967	3351
1968	3954
1969	4787
1970	5018
1971	5499
1972	5815
1973	6180
1974	6437
1975	6650
1976	6839
1977	7025
1978	7236
1979	7388
1980	7524
1981	7663
1982	7797
1983	7918
1984	8038
1985	8179
1986	8318
1987	8465
1988	8605
1989	8753
1990	8878
1991	8978
1992	9063

JAMES PURDY & SONS, LTD. SERIALIZATION

Year Starting	Serial Number
1814	974
1826	1149
1827	1324
1828	1549
1829	1874
1830	1999
1831	2247
1832	2421
1833	2497
1834	2697
1835	2773
1836	2848
1837	3098
1838	3223
1839	3298
1840	3473
1841	3623
1842	3698
1843	3848
1844	3998
1845	4048
1846	4098
1847	4223
1848	4348
1849	4473
1850	4599
1851	4720
1852	4844
1853	4944
1854	5093
1855	5167
1856	5267
1857	5443
1858	5542
1859	5747
1860	5997
1861	6271
1862	6422
1863	6671
1864	6871
1865	7121
1866	7420
1867	7646
1868	7896
1869	8246
1870	8322
1871	8646
1872	8821
1873	9096
1874	9288
1875	9505
1876	9648
1877	10153
1878	10440
1879	10800
1880	10900
1881	11082
1882	11342
1883	11669
1884	12036
1885	12171
1886	12530
1887	12875
1888	13150
1889	13468

JAMES PURDY & SONS, LTD. cont.

Year Starting	Serial Number
1890	13662
1891	14000
1892	14520
1893	14851
1894	15134
1895	15362
1896	15726
1897	16095
1898	16420
1899	16736
1900	17078
1901	17227
1902	17547
1903	17849
1904	18148
1905	18400
1906	18686
1907	18987
1908	19272
1909	19546
1910	19813
1911	20147
1912	20400
1913	20770
1914	21086
1915	21332
1916	21465
1917	21541
1919	21574
1920	21892
1921	22111
1922	22312
1923	22491
1924	22896
1925	22937
1926	23283
1927	23284
1928	23551
1929	23854
1930	24139
1931	24387
1932	24567
1933	24647
1934	24743
1935	24920
1936	25130
1937	25325
1938	25526
1939	25711
1940	25783
1941	25793
1942	25813
1943	25844
1945	25851
1946	25901
1947	25990
1948	26051
1949	26128
1950	26206
1951	26275
1952	26349
1953	26423
1955	26531
1975	28003
1979	28546
1981	28569

REMINGTON DATE CODE DATA & SxS SHOTGUN

Firearms Identification (Code located on barrel, left side at frame) Month of Manufacture (Code letter corresponds to numeral underneath). Additional markings if present will indicate the following.

2	Part order replacement bbl.
3	Service section repair.
4	Returned as received.
5	Employee sale.

B	L	A	C	K	P	O	W	D	E	R	X
1	2	3	4	5	6	7	8	9	10	11	12

Year of Manufacture and letter code

Year	Code
1921	M
1922	N
1923	P
1924	R
1925	S
1926	T
1927	U
1928	W
1929	X
1930	Y
1931	Z
1932	A
1933	B
1934	C
1935	D
1936	E
1937	F
1938	G
1939	H
1940	J
1941	K
1942	L
1943	MM
1944	NN
1945	PP
1946	RR
1947	SS
1948	TT
1949	UU
1950	WW
1951	XX
1952	YY
1953	ZZ
1954	A
1955	B
1956	C
1957	D
1958	E
1959	F
1960	G
1961	H
1962	J
1963	K
1964	L
1965	M
1966	N
1967	P
1968	R
1969	S
1970	T
1971	U
1972	W
1973	X

Year of Manufacture and letter code

Year	Code
1974	Y
1975	Z
1976	I
1977	O
1978	Q
1979	V
1980	A
1981	B
1982	C
1983	D
1984	E
1985	F
1986	G
1987	H
1988	I
1989	J
1990	K
1991	L
1992	M
1993	N
1994	O
1995	P
1996	Q
1997	R
1998	S
1999	T
2000	U
2001	W
2002	X
2003	Y
2004	Z
2005	A

The author wishes to express thanks to Mr. Charles Semmer for the following Remington SxS shotgun serialization information.

E. REMINGTON & SONS
WHITMORE MODELS

Model	Years	Ser. Block	Est. Total
1873	1873-1878	1-5000	5000
1875	1875-1877	1-3350	3350
1876	1876-1882	3350-5900	2250
1878	1878-1882	1-2400	2400
1879	1879-1888	W/ 1878	N/A

E. REMINGTON & SONS
MODELS 1882, 1883, 1885 AND 1887

Model	Years	Ser. Block	Est. Total
1882	1882-1888	1000-17000	16000
1883	1882-1884	W/ 1882	N/A
1885	1885-1886	16700-202003500	
1887	1886-1888	20200-237003500	

REMINGTON ARMS COMPANY
MODEL 1889 TOTAL Mfg. 134200

Year Starting	Serial Number
1888	W/ 1887
1889	30000-32199
1890	32200-36949
1891	36950-43012
1892	43013-49844
1893	49845-58879
1894	58880-66016
1895	66017-73571
1896	73572-76980
1897	76981-80389
1898	80390-89123
1899	89124-97714
1900	EST. 97715-105000

MODEL 1889 cont.

Year Starting	Serial Number
1900	EST. 200000-205934
1901	205935-221450
1902	221451-234803
1903	234804-240530
1904	240531-247581
1905	247582-251192
1906	251193-254394
1907	254395-257745
1908	257746-259246
1909	N/A
1910	259247-259262

REMINGTON ARMS COMPANY
MODEL 1894 TOTAL Mfg. 41194

Year Starting	Serial Number
1900	300000-305000
1901	305001-317502
1902	317503-337038
1903	337039-343893
1904	343894-350207
1905	350208-354620
1906	354621-363060
1907	363061-372117
1908	372118-377925
1909	377926-382072
1910	382073-398507
1911	398508

REMINGTON ARMS COMPANY
MODEL 1894 REM. SPCL.
TOTAL Mfg. Aprox. 12, W/ 4 recorded

Year Starting	Serial Number
1902-1910	400000-400012

SAVAGE/STEVENS PRODUCTION DATA

The information below represents a listing of most Savage/Stevens rifles and shotguns mfg. in the past (some data has been approximated). Rather than list these models separately, they have been provided in this section for quick reference. Values on many of the models listed below typically range between $50-$175, depending on rarity and condition.

MODEL	DATES	APPROX. GUNS
1903	1912-20	13,000
1904	1912-32	62,000
1905	1912-15	6,500
1909	1912-15	3,500
1911	1912-15	22,500
1912	1913-15	12,000
1914	1914-26	49,500
19	1933-45	16,000
1920	1920-32	12,000
1922	1922-25	16,000
'23A	1924-45	88,000
'23B	1924-45	16,500
'23C	1924-42	14,500
'23D	1932-45	15,000
3	1931-45	121,000
4	1933-45	38,000
5	1936-45	22,000
6	1938-45	45,500
7	1939-45	6,000
40	1928-42	16,000

MODEL	DATES	APPROX. GUNS
45	1928-42	6,000
1925	1925-32	36,000
29	1933-45	23,500
CS22	1926-45	87,500
219	1938-45	12,500
220	1937-45	50,000
420	1937-42	13,500
430	1937-42	11,000
1921	1921-32	13,000
1928	1928-32	6,500
721	1930-32	12,000
FOX	1933-45	31,000
FX B	1940-45	20,000
No. 12	1912-35	166,500
14-1/2	1912-41	592,500
Fav.	1912-42	462,000
No. 26	1912-45	501,500
44+414	1912-35	23,000
No. 70	1912-31	295,500
No. 71	1930-34	10,000
No. 75	1928-34	19,000
15+425	1912-17	11,500
No. 35	1912-19	12,500
No. 35	1923-42	43,000
41-43	1912-18	18,500
No. 10	1919-34	9,500
85-89	1912-42	38,500
No. 93	1912-19	12,500
No. 97	1912-19	16,000
No. 101	1914-20	5,000
No. 105	1912-45	221,500
No. 107	1912-45	443,500
106-08	1916-35	56,500
No. 115	1912-31	23,000
No. 124	1949-55	----
No. 125	1912-23	5,000
180-85	1912-23	16,000
No. 958	1925-33	5,000
116-17	1926-35	5,000
946-48	1928-34	7,000
No. 215	1913-32	61,000
No. 235	1912-32	61,500
No. 315	1914-36	192,000
No. 335	1912-31	67,500
No. 345	1916-31	3,500
No. 311	1926-45	145,500
No. 330	1926-35	33,500
No. 335	1926-35	2,000
No. 520	1912-32	191,000
No. 521	1930-32	5,000
60&61	1930-34	6,500
620-21	1926-45	66,500
Mod. 30	1933-34	26,000
Mod. 31	1933-34	2,000
No. 15	1936-45	224,000
No. 11	1923-33	141,500
No. 95	1926-35	55,000
No. 52	1933-37	88,000
No. 55	1935-36	3,500
No. 54	1933-42	23,500
No. 56	1933-45	97,500
No. 57	1939-42	500
No. 58	1933-45	29,500
No. 37	1936-42	29,000
No. 38	1936-45	33,500
No. 39	1938-45	64,000
No. 59	1938-45	21,000
No. 76	1938-45	6,000
65-66	1929-45	174,000
No. 82	1936-37	35,500
No. 83	1936-42	159,000
No. 84	1936-45	99,500

SAVAGE/STEVENS PRODUCTION DATA cont.

MODEL	DATES	APPROX.GUNS
No. 85	1939-43	14,000
No. 86	1936-43	82,500
No. 87	1938-45	200,000
No. 872	1940-42	3,500
NO. 89	1926-37	12,000
No. 94	1926-45	934,000
No. 96	1926-33	3,500
No. 416	1937-42	2,000
No. 417	1932-42	1,000
No. 418	1932-42	1,500
No. 419	1932-36	1,000
No. 237	1936-43	16,000
No. 254	1936-42	1,000
No. 238	1936-45	40,000
No. 258	1936-45	11,000
102-04	1936-42	500
No. 116	1936-42	1,000
No. 944	1936-42	1,500
No. 600	1936-42	5,500
No. 900	1936-42	2,000
No. 515	1936-42	500
No. 5151	1936-42	95,000
No. 530	1936-42	8,000
No. 500	1936-42	500
22-410	1939-45	105,000
M.240	1940-45	20,500

SAVAGE MODEL NINETY-NINE SERIALIZATION

Serial Numbers At Year End:

10,000	1899
13,400	1900
19,500	1901
25,000	1902
35,000	1903
45,000	1904
53,000	1905
67,500	1906
73,500	1907
81,000	1908
95,000	1909
110,000	1910
119,000	1911
131,000	1912
146,500	1913
162,000	1914
175,500	1915
187,500	1916
193,000	1917
N/A	1918
212,500	1919
229,000	1920
237,500	1921
244,500	1922
256,000	1923
270,000	1924
280,000	1925
292,500	1926
305,000	1927
317,000	1928
324,500	1929
334,500	1930
338,500	1931
341,000	1932
344,500	1933
345,800	1934
350,800	1935
359,800	1936
N/A	1937

SAVAGE MODEL NINETY-NINE SERIALIZATION cont.

Serial Numbers At Year End:

381,351	1938
388,640	1939
398,400	1940
416,000	1941
438,000	1946
464,000	1947
494,000	1948
528,000	1949
566,000	1950

L.C. SMITH SERIALIZATION

Existing L.C. Smith shotgun records include: Hunter Arms Company factory records circa 1890-1919, Hunter Arms Company shipping records circa 1918-1946, L.C. Smith Gun Company, 1946-1950 (FWS prefix), Marlin Firearms Company, 1969-71 (FWS prefix).

For a factor letter on an older Marlin firearm, contact the Buffalo Bill Historical center, Cody Firearms Museum, 720 Sheridan Ave. Cody, WY 82414. Web site www.bbhc.org or phone 307-587-4771. There is a $45 fee per serial number search.

L.C. Smith (Manufactured by Hunter Arms Co. 1890-1918).

Hammer Shotguns

GAUGE	YEAR	GUN
20	1907	5000-5131
20	1908	5379
20	1909	5677
20	1910	6238
20	1911	6593
20	1912	7076
20	1913	7521
20	1914	7828
20	1915	7935
20	1916	8149
20	1917	8250
10, 12, & 16	1894	50000-50867
10, 12, & 16	1895	51735
10, 12, & 16	1896	52602
10, 12, & 16	1897	55301
10, 12, & 16	1898	58000
10, 12, & 16	1900	79000-84943
10, 12, & 16	1901	89999
10, 12, & 16	1902	125000-129700
10, 12, & 16	1903	133039
10, 12, & 16	1904	137445
10, 12, & 16	1905	144409
10, 12, & 16	1906	150221
10, 12, & 16	1907	156901
10, 12, & 16	1908	159519
10, 12, & 16	1909	163160
10, 12, & 16	1910	166705
10, 12, & 16	1911	168761
10, 12, & 16	1912	171415
10, 12, & 16	1913	173371
10, 12, & 16	1914	175483
10, 12, & 16	1915	176091

Hammer Shotguns cont.

GAUGE	YEAR	GUN
10, 12, & 16	1916	176576
10, 12, & 16	1917	178522
10, 12, & 16	1918	179841

Hammerless Shotguns

GAUGE	YEAR	GUN
20	1907	1000-1204
20	1908	1329
20	1909	1788
20	1910	2587
20	1911	3615
20	1912	4630
20	1913	4999
20	1913	10000-10786
20	1914	11451
20	1915	11873
20	1916	12361
20	1917	12666
20	1918	12753
10 & 12	1890	30000-32527
10 & 12	1891	34381
10 & 12	1892	36615
10 & 12	1893	37324
10 & 12	1894	38892
10 & 12	1895	40334
8, 10, 12, & 16	1896	40335-42219
8, 10, 12, & 16	1897	44104
8, 10, 12, & 16	1898	45999
16	1895	60000-60144
16	1896	60289
16	1897	60434
16	1898	60579
16	1899	60724
16	1900	60869
16	1901	61014
16	1902	61159
16	1903	61402
16	1904	61685
16	1905	62156
16	1906	62653
16	1907	63698
16	1908	64226
16	1909	65021
16	1910	65861
16	1911	66821
16	1912	67683
16	1913	68704
16	1914	69681
16	1915	69999
16	1915	400000-401758
10 & 12	1899	105210
10 & 12	1900	105917
10 & 12	1901	111681
10 & 12	1902	119035
10 & 12	1903	120767
10 & 12	1904	124419
10 & 12	1905	124999
10 & 12	1904	300000-300301
10 & 12	1905	305787
10 & 12	1906	311528
10 & 12	1907	318079
10 & 12	1908	322129

Hammerless Shotguns cont.

GAUGE	YEAR	GUN
10 & 12	1909	329476
10 & 12	1910	333081
10 & 12	1911	336572
10 & 12	1912	341717
10 & 12	1913	345493
10 & 12	1914	350857
10 & 12	1915	352431
10 & 12	1916	355068
10 & 12	1917	359624
10 & 12	1918	361071
10, 12, & 16	1891	500-559
10, 12, & 16	1898	3173
10, 12, & 16	1901	6959
10, 12, & 16	1902	9000
10, 12, & 16	1902	200000-200025
10, 12, & 16	1903	201758
10, 12, & 16	1904	203272
10, 12, & 16	1905	205098
10, 12, & 16	1906	207093
10, 12, & 16	1907	209368
10, 12, & 16	1908	210579
10, 12, & 16	1909	211885
10, 12, & 16	1910	213084
10, 12, & 16	1911	214246
10, 12, & 16	1912	215615
10, 12, & 16	1913	216939
10, 12, & 16	1914	218260
10, 12, & 16	1915	218829
10, 12, & 16	1916	219603
10, 12, & 16	1917	219750

1918-1950 (These serial numbers include all types of L.C. Smith, Fulton and Hunter Shotguns).

YEAR	GUN
1918	101-3850
1919	18252
1920	35228
1921	44566
1922	51985
1923	64187
1924	75897
1925	86695
1926	93841
1927	103900
1928	114817
1929	125347
1930	132827
1931	134242
1932	137779
1933	138371
1934	140146
1935	144296
1936	151123
1937	162670
1938	171179
1939	181701
1940	190280
1941	197124
1942	201794
1943	202959
1944	204084
1945	205423
1946	1-8595
1947	25661
1948	41825

1918-1950 (These serial numbers include all types of L. C. Smith, Fulton and Hunter Shotguns) cont.

YEAR	GUN
1949	55608
1950	56800

SMITH & WESSON PERFORMANCE CENTER PRODUCT CODE INFO.

The following Smith & Wesson Performance Center product code information appear courtesy of Mr. Jim Supica and Mr. Richard Nahas. I would like to thank them for making these product codes available. For additional information on Smith & Wesson firearms, the *Standard Catalog of Smith & Wesson* by Jim Supica and Richard Nahas is highly recomended. This book is available through www.armchairgunshow.com or 913-492-3000.

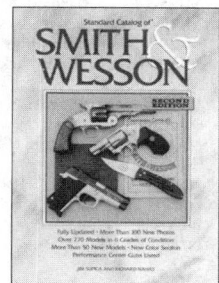

PERFOMANCE CENTER PRODUCT CODES

170 = Designed/made from scratch
178 = Used existing Product / and improved

Code	Configuration
170002	M-5906
170008	M-626 HUNTER
170009	M-686 C. C. 6"
170010	M-686 C. C. 3"
170011	SHORTY 40
170012	M-629 3" MAG.COMP.
170014	M-640 3" C. C.
170015	M-686 6" COMPETITOR
170016	M-686 4" C. C.
170020	Tactical Forty
170021	M-686 6" HUNTER
170023	M-442 ULTRALITE
170024	M-66 3" F-COMP.
170025	M-19 3" K-COMP.
170026	M-629 3" UNFLUTED
170027	M-356 COMPACT
170028	S/S SHORTY 40
I70029	M-60 3"FL ET-COMP.
170030	SHORTY 9mm
170032	M-356 LIMITED
170033	M-40 LIMITED
170034	M-686 6" HUNTER (BRAZIL)
170035	M-I9 3" K-COMP (BRAZIL)
170036	M-52 PERF. CTR.
170037	M-356 BRILEY CHASSIS

Code	Configuration
170038	M-845 WISCHO LIMITED
170039	M-356 PARKER HALE
170040	M-9mm WISCHO LIMITED
170042	M-640 2" Carry Comp.
170043	M-64O 2" Carry Comp.
170044	M-9mm WISCHO LTD. (2TONE)
170046	M-629 6" HUNTER (UNFLUTED)
170047	M-356 2" Carry Comp.
170048	M-629-4 3" Quad Port
170049	M-629 5" Carry Comp
170050	M-629 6.5" Carry Comp.
170052	356 TSW 4 1/4" Stocking Dealer
170053	9mm 4 1/4" Stocking Dealer
170054	40 S&W 4 1/4" Stocking Dealer
170055	M-460 Airweight
170056	M-629 Light Hunter: Duplicate PC
170056	M-625 V Comp 4" : Duplicate PC
170057	M-9mm Horton Limited
170058	M-629 3" DBL Magna Ported
170059	M-13 3" FS DBL Port (Eagle)
170060	Shorty 40 Mark II
170061	Shorty 40 MK III
170062	M-657 .41 Mag Light Hunter
170063	M-13 3" FS Dbl Port (Uncle Mikes)
170064	M-845 HORTON LIMITED
170065	M-629 7.5" HUNTER PLUS
170066	M-617 WISCHO Target
170067	M-9mm Compact
170068	M-640-.357 J-COMP
170069	not active
170070	M-625 5"
170071	not active
170072	M-625 HUNTER (PORTLESS)
170073	M-640-357 2 1/8 FL GB (RSR)
170074	M-686 7SH 3" FL CARRY COMP.
170075	SHORTY 45
170076	SHORTY 40 MARK III-S
170077	M-686 7SH 2.5" FL MAGPORT
170078	M-640.357 2 I/8 FL QUAD GB
170079	M-686 7SH 6" Hunter
170080	M-681 3" Quad Port
170081	M-625 45LC Flutted Hunter
170082	M-686 6" Supertarget
170083	PPC 9mm Limited
170084	M-629 7.5" Hunter
170085	M-625 6" GB Hunter
170086	M-686 7Shot 6" GB Hunter
170087	M-629 7.5" Master Hunter/Scope only
170088	Shorty 45 MKII
170089	M-627 5" 8SH Lew Horton GB
170090	M-66 3" Contour Frame/ bbl
170091	40 S&W Tactical-RSR
170092	M-627 5" 8 Shot Ported
170093	9mm 4" DA/SA FS
170094	M-629 7.5" Master Hunter
170095	M-627 6" 8 Shot Hunter
170098	45 RECON 45 ACP
170099	Shorty 4006 RECON 40 S&W
170100	M-629 6" Compensated Hunter
170102	M-627 6.5" 8 Shot
170103	M-686 6" 7 Shot Profile Bbl
170104	M-945 5" Stainless
170105	CQB Stainless 45 ACP
170106	CQB Alloy 45 ACP
170109	M-610 6 1/2"
170110	Not Used
170111	M-686 6" 6 Shot Profile Bbl
170116	M-627 5" 8 Shot unfluted
170117	M-5906 5" 9mm LTD CS Slide (Wischo)
170118	M-4563 CQB Two Tone
170119	M-5906 5" 9mm/356Mag SuperPC
170120	M-629 44 6" 6 shot Competitor
170121	M-686 6" 6 shot Fluted Competitor
170122	M-617 New Profile Barrel

Code	Configuration
170123	M-627 5" Profile Barrel 6 Shot Fluted
170124	M-629 44 6.5" 6 shot flutted full lug comp & cap
170125	M-657 41 6.5" 6 shot flutted full lug comp & cap
170126	M-629 Compensated Hunter- New Frame/Hammer
170128	.45 4515 RECON -RSR w/Knife
170129	M-4587 4.25"
170130	M-629 Classic 7 1/2" Barrel w/ Case
170131	M-29 Classic 7 1/2" Barrel w/Case
170132	M-625 6" 45 Long Colt Light Hunter Fluted GB
170133	M-627 2 5/8" 8 shot Defensive Revolver
170134	M-657 2 5/8" Defensive Revolver
170135	M-629 2 5/8" Defensive Revolver
170136	M-625 Light Hunter 6"
170137	M-629 V Comp 4" -RSR
170138	M-629 7 1/2" Light Hunter RSR
170139	M-4006
170140	9mm M-6906 RECON 3 1/2"
170141	45 RECON Black
170142	M-627-3 V-Comp Jerry Miculek Spcl. 5"
170143	M- 9mm Full Lug
170144	M-332 Never Made
170145	M-632 Never Made
170146	Schofield Model of 2000
170147	M-945 5" Blue 1998
170147	M-945 Two Tone 1999
170148	M-629 5" V-Comp RSR Special
170149	6" 629 Hunter Unfluted
170150	M-627 5 1/2" UnFluted RD
170151	M-27 Classic Series
170152	M-945 4" Black
170153	M-945 4" Stainless-RSR
170154	M-14 4"
170155	M-5906 5" 9mm 10 RDv Mag PPC
170156	M-945 3-3/4" RSR Special
170157	M-629 Extreme Hunter 12"
170158	M-629 12" w/sling
170159	M-629 8.5" Revolver w/sling
170160	M-657 12" Revolver w/sling
170161	M-657 12" Revolver w/sling
170162	M-657 8.5" Revolver w/sling
170163	M-19 K COMP Y2000
170164	M-4006 Shorty Forty -Y2000- Camfour
170165	M-646 4" 40 S&W
170166	M-27-7 8 Shot 4"
170167	M-27-7 8 Shot 6 1/2"
170168	M-952 9mm
170169	M-945 3 3/4" Black -Camfour
170170	M-586 L-Comp 3"
170171	M-629 7 1/2" Stealth Hunter
170172	M-681 4" Quad Port for Camfour
170173	M-945 5" RSR Special
170174	M-945 5" Two Tone RSR Special
170175	M-629 2 5/8" unfluted cyl
170176	M-625 5 1/4" 45 ACP for Camfour
170177	M-945 3 1/4" 45 ACP for Camfour
170178	M-681 3" Quad Port for Camfour
170179	M-25-10 6" for Sports South
170180	M-945 3 3/4" 40S&W for Sports South
170181	M-629 7 1/2" Compensated Hunter for TALO
170182	M-627 4" w/ Comp RSR Special
170183	M-627 4" w/ Comp RSR Special
170184	M-945 3 1/4" 45ACP for RSR
170185	M-24-5 6 1/2" Case Color Frame 44 Spl Heritage
170186	FC M-25-11 6 1/2" Case Color Frame 45 Colt Heritage
170187	M-25 44-40 6" 6 Sh AS WG Color Case Frame Heritage
170188	M-25 38-40 6" 6 Sh AS WG Blue
170189	M-24 44 Spl 6.5" AS WG All Blue Finish Heritage
170190	M-25 44-40 6" 6Sh AS WG Blue
170191	M-25 38-40 6" 6Sh AS WG Blue
170192	M-625 FL 5" 45 ACP 6 Sh AS IFS S
170193	M-629 7 1/2" Unfluted Green/ Black
170194	M-629 7-1/2" Black Unfluted
170195	M- 4006 4" SA/DA FS IDPA
170196	M-25 Colt 6" Taper Bbl 6 Sh Fluted Blue
170197	M-25-12 5 1/2" Fixed Sight Model of 1917 45ACP
170198	FC KT-22 6" 6 Sh Fluted Adj Blue Model 17-8 Heritage
170199	M-15-9 5" Blue
170200	M-681 357 3" FS WG 7 Sh Birdsong
170201	M-5906 6" Pistol
170202	M-952
170203	Mfg Purposes Only
170204	Mfg Purposes Only
170205	M-627 38 Super 8 shot
170206	M-586 357 GB 4-1/8"
170207	M-3 5" nickel
170208	M-3 5" blue
170209	M-3 Nickel Schofield 7" 45
170210	M-627-5 357 w/Internal Lock
170211	M-25-12 Case Colored, 45 ACP
170212	M-17-8 6" Heritage Series
170213	M-29 Heritage Series Blue
170214	M-29 Heritage Series Nickel
170215	M-29 Nickel ?
170216	M-15-9 Heritage Series 6" Blue (McGivern Model)
170217	M-15-9 Heritage Series 6" Nickel (McGivern Model)
170218	M-25 45ACP 5-1/2" 1917 w/Military Finish
170219	N/A
170220	N/A
170221	N/A
178001	N/A
178002	N/A
178003	N/A
178004	N/A
178005	M-29-5 8 3/8 RB TT TH RR WO B Wood Grips (SCR0002)
178006	FC M-10 4 1/4" Case Color Frame Square Butt w/FC
178007	N/A
178008	M-15-8 4" Nickel
178009	M-15-8 4" Heritage Series

PISTOL/REVOLVER FEATURE CODES

Code	Feature
A2D	Adj. 2-Dot Sight
AA	Aluminum Alloy Frame
AB	Adj. Black Sight
AMSF	Ambidextious Safety
AS	Adj. Rear Sight
ATS	Adj. Target Sight
AV	Adj. V-Notch Sight
AWO	Adj. White Outline Sight
B	Blue
BB	Bead Blast Finish
BBL	Barrel
B/G	Black/Gray Finish
BK	Black Finish
BK/M	Black/Melonite Finish
BP	Black Polymer Grip
BPF	Black Polymer Frame
BULL	Bull Barrel
CB	Curved Backstrap Grip
CC	Clear Cote™ Finish
CS	Carbon Steel
CWG	Checkered Wood Grip

Code	Feature
CWP	Checkered Wood Panel
DA	Double Action
DAO	Double Action Only
DBP	Dovetail Black Post
DFS	Dovetail Front Sight
DT	Drilled & Taped
ER	Equipment Rail
F2D	Fixed 2-Dot Sight
FN	Fixed Notch Sight
FNS	Fixed Tritium Night Sight (Fr. & Rr.)
FS	Fixed Sight
FV	Fixed V-Notch Sight
G	NATO Green
GB	Glass Bead Finish
GD	Green Dot
GY	Grey Finish
#SH	Magazine Capacity/Rds
HB	Heavy Barrel
HIVIS®	Light Gathering Sight
HR	Hogue Rubber Grip
HT	Hardwood Target Grip
HV	HIVIS® Front Sight
HWA	Hogue Wrap Around Rubber Grip
I	Integral or Interchangeable Sight
IB	Interchangeable Backstraps
IC	Integral Compensator
IFS	Interchangeable Front Sight
IL	Internal Lock
ISBR	Interchangeable Serrated Black Ramp Sight
LS	LadySmith®
M	Melonite Finish
MCA	Micrometer Click Adj.
MNSF	Manual Safety (Single Side)
MS	Matte Stainless
NG	Nato Green Polymer Grips
NLMC	Novak Lo-Mount Carry 2-Dot Sight
OD	Orange Dot
P	Partridge Sight
PBP	Pinned Black Partridge Sight
PBSR	Pinned Black Serrated Ramp Sight
PF	Polymer Frame
PP	PowerPort™ Ported Barrel
RB	Round Butt
RR	Red Ramp Sight
S	Stainless Finish
SA	Single Action
SB	Black Straight Backstrap Grip
SC	Scandium Alloy Frame
SG	Synthetic Grip
SNS	Satin Stainless Finish
SR	Serrated Ramp Sight
SS	Stainless Steel
STD	Standard Barrel
STG	Soft Touch Grip
T	Tritium
T2D	Tritium 2-Dot Rear Night Sight
TD	Tritium Dot Front Night Sight
TDA	Traditional Double Action
TR	Thumbrest
TS	Target Stock
UC	Unfluted Cylinder
UMB	Uncle Mike's Boot Grip
UMC	Uncle Mike's Combat Grip
UMR	Uncle Mike's Rubber Grip
VR	Vented Rib
WAS	Wilson Adj. Rear Sight
WC	Wood Combat Grip
WD	White Dot Sight
WG	Dymondwood® Grip
WO	White Outline Rear Sight
WT	Wooden Target Grip

SPANISH YEAR OF MFG. DATE CODES

The following Spanish year of manufacture information appears courtesy of Leonardo M. Antaris, M.D., author of Astra Automatic Pistols, and Star Firearms. For additional information regarding Spanish pistols, particularly Astras and Stars, see www.firac.us.

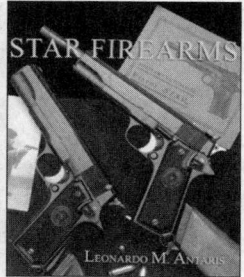

Code	Year
A	1927
B	1928
C	1929
CH	1930
D	1931
E	1932
F	1933
G	1934
H	1935
I	1936
J	1937
K	1938
L	1939
LL	1940
M	1941
N	1942
Ñ	1943
O	1944
P	1945
Q	1946
R	1947
S	1948
T	1949
U	1950
V	1951
X	1952
Y	1953
Z	1954
A1	1955
B1	1956
C1	1957
D1	1958
EI	1959
F1	1960
G1	1961
H1	1962
I1	1963
J1	1964
K1	1965
L1	1966
M1	1967
N1	1968
Ñ1	1969
O1	1970
P1	1971

SPANISH DATE CODES cont.

Code	Year
Q1	1972
R1	1973
S1	1974
T1	1975
U1	1976
V1	1977
X1	1978
Y1	1979
Z1	1980
A2	1981
B2	1982
C2	1983
D2	1984
E2	1985
F2	1986
G2	1987
H2	1988
I2	1989
J2	1990
K2	1991
L2	1992
M2	1993
N2	1994

A new coding system was implemented in January 1995. Requirements included: 1) all guns, irrespective of model, would be numbered in a new sequential series starting with the number 1 at the beginning of the year, 2) the serial number was to be followed by the last two digits of the producion year, 3) each manufacturer was assigned a code to be stamped on every pistol, and 4) guns were to be marked as to type: pistols 04; revolvers 05; rifles 06; shotguns 03; submachine guns 15; etc.

STURM, RUGER & CO., INC.

Additional information regarding Sturm, Ruger & Co., Inc. firearms (including serialization) can be found in Ruger &his Guns; A History of the Man, the Company and Their Firearms by R.L. Wilson.

WINCHESTER RIFLES SERIALIZATION

The following Winchester serial numbers appear courtesy of U.S. Repeating Arms, New Haven, CT. I would like to thank U.S. Repeating Arms and Mr. Pardee for making these production figures available. Records at the factory indicate the following serial numbers were assigned to guns at the end of the calendar year.

For additional information including factory letters contact the Cody Firearms Museum.

Buffalo Bill Historical Center
Attn: Cody Firearms Museum
720 Sheridan Ave.
P.O. Box 1000
Cody, WY 82414

MODEL 1866

Year	Approx. Last No.
1866	12476 to 14813
67	15578
68	19768
69	29516
70	52527
71	88184
72	109784
73	118401
74	125038
75	125965
76	131907
77	148207
78	150493
79	152201
80	154379
81	156107
82	159513
1883	162376
84	163649
85	163664
86	165071
87	165912
88	167155
89	167401
90	167702
91	169003
92	NONE
93	169007
94	169011
95	NONE
96	NONE
97	169015
98	170100
99	DISCONTINUED

MODEL 1873

Year	Approx. Last No.
1873	1 to 126
74	2726
75	11325
76	23151
77	23628
78	27501
79	41525
80	63537
81	81620
82	109507
83	145503
84	175126
85	196221
86	222937
87	225922
88	284529
89	323220
90	363220
91	405026
92	441625
93	466641
94	481826
95	499308

MODEL 1873 cont.

Year	Approx. Last No.
96	507545
97	513421
98	525922
99	541328
1900	554128
01	557236
02	564557
03	573957
04	588953
05	602557
06	613780
07	NONE
08	NONE
09	630385
10	656101
11	669324
12	678527
13	684419
14	686510
15	688431
16	694020
17	698617
18	700734
19	702042

No last # available
20, 21, 22, 23, 720609

MODEL 1876

Year	Approx. Last No.
1876	1 to 1429
77	3579
78	7967
79	8971
80	14700
81	21759
82	32407
83	42410
1884	54666
85	58714
86	60397
87	62420
88	63539
89	NONE
90	NONE
91	NONE
92	63561
93	63670
94	63678
95	NONE
96	63702
97	63869
98	63871

MODEL 1885 SINGLE SHOT

Year	Approx. last No.
1885 -	1 to 375
86 -	6841
87 -	18328
88 -	30571
89 -	45019
90 -	NONE
91 -	53700
92 -	60371
93 -	69534
94 -	NONE
95 -	73771
96 -	78253
97 -	78815
98 -	84700
99 -	85086
1900 -	88501

MODEL 1885 SINGLE SHOT cont.

Year	Approx. Last No.
01 -	90424
02 -	92031
03 -	92359
04 -	92785
05 -	93611
06 -	94208
07 -	95743
08 -	96819
09 -	98097
10 -	98506
11 -	99012
12 -	NONE
13 -	100352

No further serial numbers were recorded until the end of 1923.
Last No. known was: 139700

MODEL 1886

Year	Approx. Last No.
1886 -	1 to 3211
87 -	14728
88 -	28577
89 -	38401
90 -	49723
91 -	63601
92 -	73816
93 -	83261
94 -	94543
95 -	103708
96 -	109670
97 -	113997
98 -	119192
99 -	120571
1900 -	122834
01 -	125630
02 -	128942
03 -	132213
04 -	135524
05 -	138838
06 -	142249
07 -	145119
1908 -	147322
09 -	148237
10 -	150129
11 -	151622
12 -	152943
13 -	152947
14 -	153859
15 -	154452
16 -	154979
17 -	155387
18 -	156219
19 -	156930
20 -	158716
21 -	159108
22 -	159337

No further serial numbers were recorded until the discontinuance of the Model 1886 which was in 1935 - at - 159994.

MODEL 1887

Year	Approx. Last No.
1887 -	1 to 7431
88 -	22408
89 -	25673
90 -	29105
91 -	38541
92 -	49763
93 -	54367

MODEL 1887 cont.

Year	Approx. Last No.
94 -	56849
95 -	58289
96 -	60175
97 -	63952
98 -	64855

According to these records no guns were produced during the last few years of this model and it was therefore discontinued in 1901.

MODEL 1890

Records on the Model 1890 are somewhat incomplete. Factory records indicate the following serial numbers were assigned to guns at the end of the calendar year beginning with 1908. Actual records on the firearms which were manufactured between 1890 and 1907 will be available from the "Cody Firearms Museum", located at the "Buffalo Bill Historical Center".

Year	Approx. Last No.
1908 -	330000 to 363850
09 -	393427
10 -	423567
11 -	451264
12 -	478595
13 -	506936
14 -	531019
15 -	551290
16 -	570497
17 -	589204
18 -	603438
19 -	630801
20 -	NONE
21 -	634783
22 -	643304
23 -	654837
24 -	664613
25 -	675774
26 -	687049
27 -	698987
28 -	711354
29 -	722125
30 -	729015
31 -	733178
32 -	734454

The Model 1890 was discontinued in 1932, however, a clean up of the production run lasted another 8+ years and included another 14 to 15000 guns. Our figures indicate approximately 849,000 guns were made.

MODEL 1892

Year	Approx. Last No.
1892 -	1 to 23701
93 -	35987
94 -	73508
95 -	106721
96 -	144935
97 -	159312
98 -	165431
99 -	171820
1900 -	183411
01 -	191787
02 -	208871
03 -	253935
04 -	278546
05 -	315425

MODEL 1892 cont.

Year	Approx. Last No.
06 -	376496
07 -	437919
08 -	476540
09 -	522162
10 -	586996
11 -	643483
12 -	694752
13 -	742675
14 -	771444
15 -	804622
16 -	830031
17 -	853819
18 -	870942
19 -	903649
20 -	906754
21 -	910476
22 -	917300
23 -	926329
24 -	938641
25 -	954997
26 -	973896
27 -	990883
28 -	996517
29 -	999238
30 -	999730
31 -	1000727
32 -	1001324

MODEL 1894

Records at the factory, and in some years, estimates, indicate the following serial numbers were assigned to guns at the end of the calendar year.

Year	Approx. Last No.
1894 -	1 to 14579
95 -	44359
96 -	76464
97 -	111453
98 -	147684
99 -	183371
1900 -	204427
01 -	233975
02 -	273854
03 -	291506
04 -	311363
05 -	337557
06 -	378878
07 -	430985
08 -	474241
1909 -	505831
10 -	553062
11 -	599263
12 -	646114
13 -	703701
14 -	756066
15 -	784052
16 -	807741
17 -	821972
18 -	838175
19 -	870762
20 -	880627
21 -	908318
22 -	919583
23 -	938539
24 -	953198
25 -	978523
26 -	997603
27 -	1027571
28 -	1054465

MODEL 1894

Year	Approx. Last No.
29 -	1077097
30 -	1081755
31 -	1084156
32 -	1087836
33 -	1089270
34 -	1091190
35 -	1099605
36 -	1100065
37 -	1100679
38 -	1100915
39 -	1101051
40 -	1142423
41 -	1191307
42 -	1221289
43 -	No Record Available
44 -	No Record Available
45 -	No Record Available
46 -	No Record Available
47 -	No Record Available
48 -	1500000
49 -	1626100
50 -	1724295
51 -	1819800
52 -	1910000
53 -	2000000
54 -	2071100
55 -	2145296
56 -	2225000
57 -	2290296
58 -	2365887
59 -	2410555
60 -	2469821
61 -	2500000
62 -	2551921
63 -	2586000
*1964	2700000 - 2797428
65 -	2894428
66 -	2991927
67 -	3088458
68 -	3185691
69 -	3284570
70 -	3381299
71 -	3557385
72 -	3806499
73 -	3929364
74 -	4111426
75 -	4277926
75 -	4463553
76 -	4463553
77 -	4565925
78 -	4662210
1979 -	4826596
80 -	4892951
81 -	5024957
82 -	5103248

Model 1894 facts.

* The post-64 Model 94 began with serial number 2,700,000.

*Serial number 1,000,000 was presented to President Calvin Coolidge in 1927.

*Serial number 1,500,000 was presented to President Harry S. Truman in 1948.

*Serial number 2,500,000 and 3,000,000 were presented to the Winchester Gun Museum, now located in Cody, Wyoming.

Model 1894 facts.

*Serial number 3,500,000 was not constructed until 1979 and was sold at auction in Las Vegas, Nevada.

*Serial number 4,000,000 - whereabouts unknown at this time.

*Serial number 4,500,000 - shipped to Italy by Olin in 1978. Whereabouts unknown.

*Serial number 5,000,000 - in New Haven, not constructed as of March 1983.

MODEL 1895

Year	Approx. Last No.
1895 -	1 to 287
96 -	5715
97 -	7814
98 -	19871
99 -	26434
1900 -	29817
01 -	31584
02 -	35601
03 -	42514
04 -	47805
05 -	54783
06 -	55011
07 -	57351
08 -	60002
09 -	60951
10 -	63771
11 -	65017
12 -	67331
13 -	70823
14 -	72082
15 -	174233
16 -	377411
17 -	389106
18 -	392731
19 -	397250
20 -	400463
21 -	404075
22 -	407200
23 -	410289
24 -	413276
25 -	417402
26 -	419533
27 -	421584
28 -	422676
29 -	423680
30 -	424181
31 -	425132
32 -	425825

MODEL 1903

Year	Approx. Last No.
1903 -	# Not Available
04 -	6944
05 -	14865
1906 -	23097
07 -	31852
08 -	39105
09 -	46496
10 -	54298
11 -	61679
12 -	69586
13 -	76732
14 -	81776
15 -	84563
16 -	87148

MODEL 1903 cont.

Year	Approx. Last No.
17 -	89501
18 -	92617
19 -	96565
20 -	# Not Available
21 -	97650
22 -	99011
23 -	100452
24 -	101688
25 -	103075
26 -	104230
27 -	105537
28 -	107157
29 -	109414
30 -	111276
31 -	112533
32 -	112992

This model was discontinued in 1932, however, a clean up of parts was used for further production of approximately 2000 guns. Total production was approx. 126000 rifles through 1936.

MODEL 1905

Year	Approx. Last No.
1905 -	1 to 5659
06 -	15288
07 -	19194
08 -	20385
09 -	21280
10 -	22423
11 -	23503
12 -	24602
13 -	25559
14 -	26110
15 -	26561
16 -	26910
17 -	27297
18 -	27585
19 -	28287
20 -	29113

MODEL 1906

Year	Approx. Last No.
1906 -	1 to 52278
07 -	89147
08 -	114138
09 -	165068
10 -	221189
11 -	273355
12 -	327955
13 -	381922
14 -	422734
15 -	453880
16 -	483805
17 -	517743
18 -	535540
19 -	593917
20 -	NONE
21 -	598691
22 -	608011
23 -	622601
24 -	636163
25 -	649952
26 -	665484
1927 -	679892
28 -	695915
29 -	711202
30 -	720116
31 -	725978
32 -	727353

MODEL 1906 cont.

A clean up of production took place for the next few years with a record of production reaching approximately 729305.

MODEL 1907

Year	Approx. Last No.
1907 -	1 to 8657
08 -	14486
09 -	19707
10 -	23230
11 -	25523
12 -	27724
13 -	29607
14 -	30872
15 -	32272
16 -	36215
17 -	38235
18 -	39172
19 -	40448
20 -	No # Available
21 -	40784
22 -	41289
23 -	41658
24 -	42029
25 -	42360
26 -	42688
27 -	43226
28 -	43685
29 -	44046
30 -	44357
31 -	44572
32 -	44683
33 -	44806
34 -	44990
35 -	45203
36 -	45482
37 -	45920
38 -	46419
39 -	46758
40 -	47296
41 -	47957
42 -	48275
43 -	NONE
44 -	NONE
45 -	48281
46 -	48395
47 -	48996
48 -	49684
**49 -	50662
**50 -	51640
**51 -	52618
**52 -	53596
**53 -	54574
**54 -	55552
**55 -	56530
**56 -	57508
**57 -	58486

*** Actual records on serial numbers stops in 1948. The serial numbers ending each year from 1948 to 1957 were derived at by taking the last serial number recorded (58486) and the last number from 1948, (49684) and dividing the years of production (9), which relates to 978 guns each year for the nine year period.*

MODEL 1910

Year	Approx. Last No.
1910 -	1 to 4766
11 -	7695

MODEL 1910

Year	Approx. Last No.
12 -	9712
13 -	11487
14 -	12311
15 -	13233
16 -	13788
17 -	14255
18 -	14625
19 -	15665
20 -	No # Available
21 -	15845
22 -	16347
23 -	16637
24 -	17030
25 -	17281
26 -	17696
27 -	18182
28 -	18469
29 -	18893
30 -	19065
31 -	19172
32 -	19232
33 -	19281
34 -	19338
35 -	19388
36 -	19445

A cleanup of production continued into 1937 when the total of the guns was completed at approximately 20786

MODEL 1911 S.L.

Year	Approx. Last No.
1911 -	1 to 3819
12 -	27659
13 -	36677
14 -	40105
15 -	43284
16 -	45391
17 -	49893
18 -	52895
19 -	57337
20 -	60719
21 -	64109
22 -	69132
23 -	73186
24 -	76199
25 -	78611

The Model 1911 was discontinued in 1925. However, guns were produced for three years after that date to clean up production and excess parts. When this practice ceased there were approximately 82774 guns produced.

MODEL 52

Year	Approx. Last No.
1920 -	None indicated
21 -	397
22 -	745
23 -	1394
24 -	2361
25 -	3513
26 -	6383
27 -	9436
28 -	12082
29 -	14594
30 -	17253
31 -	21954
32 -	24951
33 -	26725

MODEL 52 cont.

Year	Approx. Last No.
34 -	29030
35 -	32448
1936 -	36632
37 -	40419
38 -	43632
39 -	45460
40 -	47519
41 -	50317
42 -	52129
43 -	52553
44 -	52560
45 -	52718
46 -	56080
47 -	60158
48 -	64265
49 -	68149
50 -	70766
51 -	73385
52 -	76000
53 -	79500
54 -	80693
55 -	81831
56 -	96869
57 -	97869
58 -	98599
59 -	98899
60 -	102200
61 -	106986
62 -	108718
63 -	113583
64 -	118447
65 -	120992
66 -	123537
67 -	123727
68 -	123917
69 -	E 124107
70 -	E 124297
71 -	E 124489
72 -	E 124574
73 -	E 124659
74 -	E 124744
75 -	E 124828
76 -	E 125019
77 -	E 125211
78 -	E 125315

This Model was discontinued in 1978. A small clean up of production was completed in 1979 with a total of - 125419.

MODEL 53

The Model 53 was serial numbered in both its own series (1 to slightly over 15,000) as well as within the Model 1892 series. Early guns predominate the Model 53 serial number series with Model 1892 series serial numbers appearing more frequently mid to late production.
This Model was discontinued in 1932, however, a clean up of production continued for 9 more years.

Year	Approx. Last No.
1924 -	1 to 1488
25 -	4350
26 -	6882
27 -	9180
28 -	11139
29 -	12873
30 -	13794

MODEL 53 cont.

Year	Approx. Last No.
31-	14416
32-	14623
33-	14727
34-	14817
35-	14976
36-	15047
37-	15078
38-	15092
39-	15099
1940-	15109
41-	15118

Total Production Approximately - 24,916.

Records at the factory indicate the following serial numbers were assigned to guns at the end of the calendar year.

MODEL 54

Year	Approx. Last No.
1925 -	1 to 3140
26 -	8051
27 -	14176
28 -	19587
29 -	29104
30 -	32499
31 -	36731
32 -	38543
33 -	40722
34 -	43466
35 -	47125
36 -	50145

MODEL 55

Year	Approx. Last No.
1924 -	1 to 836
25 -	2783
26 -	4957
27 -	8021
28 -	10467
29 -	12258
30 -	17393
31 -	18198
32 -	19204
33 -	Clean up 20580

MODEL 61

Year	Approx. Last No.
1932 -	1 to 3532
33 -	6008
34 -	8554
35 -	12379
36 -	20615
37 -	30334
38 -	36326
39 -	42610
40 -	49270
41 -	57493
42 -	59871
43 -	59872
44 -	59879
45 -	60512
46 -	71629
47 -	92297
48 -	115281
49 -	125461
50 -	135461
51 -	145821
52 -	156000

MODEL 61 cont.

Year	Approx. Last No.
53 -	171000
54 -	186000
55 -	200962
56 -	216923
57 -	229457
58 -	242992
59 -	262793
60 -	282594
61 -	302395
62 -	322196
63 -	342001

This Model was discontinued in 1963. For some unknown reason there are no actual records available from 1949 through 1963. The serial number figures for these years are arrived at by taking the total production figure of 342001, subtracting the last known # of 115281, and dividing the difference equally by the amount of remaining years available, (15).

MODEL 62

Year	Approx. Last No.
1932 -	1 to 7643
33 -	10695
34 -	14090
35 -	23924
36 -	42759
37 -	66059
38 -	80205
39 -	96534
40 -	116393
41 -	137379
42 -	155152
43 -	155422
44 -	155425
45 -	156073
46 -	183756
47 -	219085
48 -	252298
49 -	262473
50 -	272648
51 -	282823
52 -	293000
53 -	310500
54 -	328000
55 -	342776
56 -	357551
57 -	383513
58 -	409475

MODEL 63

Year	Approx. Last No.
1933 -	1 to 2667
34 -	5361
35 -	9830
36 -	16781
37 -	25435
38 -	30934
39 -	36055
40 -	41456
41 -	47708
42 -	51258
43 -	51631
44 -	51656
45 -	53853
46 -	61607
47 -	71714
48 -	80519
49 -	88889

MODEL 63 cont.

Year	Approx. Last No.
50 -	97259
51 -	105629
52 -	114000
53 -	120500
54 -	127000
55 -	138000
56 -	150000
57 -	162345
58 -	174692

MODEL 70

Year	Approx. Last No.
1935 -	1 to 19
36 -	2238
37 -	11573
38 -	17844
39 -	23991
40 -	31675
41 -	41753
42 -	49206
43 -	49983
1944 -	49997
45 -	50921
46 -	58382
47 -	75675
48 -	101680
49 -	131580
50 -	173150
51 -	206625
52 -	238820
53 -	282735
54 -	323530
55 -	361025
56 -	393595
57 -	425283
58 -	440792
59 -	465040
60 -	504257
61 -	545446
62 -	565592
63 -	581471

All post 64 Model 70s began with the serial number 700,000.

Year	Approx. Last No.
1964 -	740599
65 -	809177
66 -	833795
67 -	869000
68 -	925908
69 -	G941900
70 -	G957995
71 -	G1018991
72 -	G1099257
73 -	G1128731
74 -	G1175000
75 -	G1218700
76 -	G1266000
77 -	G1350000
78 -	G1410000
79 -	G1447000
80 -	G1490709
81 -	G1537134

MODEL 71

Year	Approx. Last No.
1935 -	1 to 4
36 -	7821
37 -	12988
38 -	14690
39 -	16155
40 -	18267

MODEL 71 cont.

Year	Approx. Last No.
41 -	20810
42 -	21959
43 -	22048
44 -	22051
45 -	22224
46 -	23534
47 -	25728
48 -	27900
49 -	29675
50 -	31450
51 -	33225
52 -	35000
53 -	37500
54 -	40770
55 -	43306
56 -	45843
57 -	47254

MODEL 74

Year	Approx. Last No.
1939 -	1 to 30890
40 -	67085
41 -	114355
42 -	128293
1943 -	NONE
44 -	128295
45 -	128878
46 -	145168
47 -	173524
48 -	223788
49 -	249900
50 -	276012
51 -	302124
52 -	328236
53 -	354348
54 -	380460
55 -	406574

MODEL 88

Year	Approx. Last No.
1955 -	1 to 18378
56 -	36756
57 -	55134
58 -	73512
59 -	91890
60 -	110268
61 -	128651
62 -	139838
63 -	148858
64 -	160307
65 -	162699
66 -	192595
67 -	212416
68 -	230199
69 -	H239899
70 -	H258229
71 -	H266784
72 -	H279014
73 -	H283718

MODEL 100

Year	Approx. Last No.
1961 -	1 to 32189
62 -	60760
63 -	78863
64 -	92016
65 -	135388
66 -	145239
67 -	209498

MODEL 100 cont.

Year	Approx. Last No.
68 -	210053
69 -	A210999
70 -	A229995
71 -	A242999
72 -	A258001
73 -	A262833

WINCHESTER SHOTGUNS

Records at the factory indicate the following serial numbers were assigned to guns at the end of the calendar year.

MODEL 1897

Year	Approx. Last No.
1897 -	1 to 32335
98 -	64668
99 -	96999
1900 -	129332
01 -	161665
02 -	193998
03 -	226331
04 -	258664
05 -	296037
06 -	334059
07 -	377999
08 -	413618
09 -	446888
1910 -	481062
11 -	512632
12 -	544313
13 -	575213
14 -	592732
15 -	607673
16 -	624537
17 -	646124
18 -	668383
19 -	691943
20 -	696183
21 -	700428
22 -	715902
23 -	732060
24 -	744942
25 -	757629
26 -	770527
27 -	783574
28 -	769806
29 -	807321
30 -	812729
31 -	830721
32 -	833926
33 -	835637
34 -	837364
35 -	839728
36 -	848684
37 -	856729
38 -	860725
39 -	866938
40 -	875945
41 -	891190
42 -	910072
43 -	912265
44 -	912327
45 -	916472
46 -	926409
47 -	936682
48 -	944085
49 -	953042
50 -	961999
51 -	970956

MODEL 1897 cont.

Year	Approx. Last No.
52 -	979913
53 -	988860
54 -	997827
55 -	1006784
56 -	1015741
57 -	1024700

Records on this Model are incomplete. The above serial numbers are estimated from 1897 thru 1903 and again from 1949 thru 1957. The actual records are in existence from 1904 through 1949.

MODEL 1897 TRENCH/RIOT SHOTGUN

This information is provided by Mr. Pat Redmond, after many years of research and collecting. Reference a Winchester Repeating Arms Co. Memorandum dated September 1945. Trench, Riot, and Long Barrel Contract Dates 1/31/42 - 3/23/43, Contract Shipments 24829 shotguns.

Year	Ser. Nos.	Type	Configuration
1937	902117-903762	Mil.	Long Barrel
1939	911788-911813	Mil.	Trench Gun
1940	914087	Com.	Trench Gun
1940	924312	Com.	Trench Gun
1941	920235-956126	Mil.	Trench Gun
1942	930537-956216	Mil.	Trench Gun
1943	956628	Mil.	Trench Gun
1944	965482	Com.	Trench Gun
1944	966144	Com.	Trench Gun
1944	967371	Com.	Riot Gun
1949	993750	Com.	Riot Gun

MODEL 1901

Year	Approx. Last No.
1904 -	64,856 to 64,860
05 -	66453
06 -	67486
07 -	68424
08 -	69197
09 -	70009
10 -	70753
11 -	71441
12 -	72167
13 -	72764
14 -	73202
15 -	73509
1916 -	73770
17 -	74027
18 -	74311
19 -	74872
20 -	77000

MODEL 1911

Year	Approx. Last No.
1911	1-3819
1912	27659
1913	36677
1914	40105
1915	43284
1916	45391
1917	49843
1918	52895
1919	57337
1920	60719
1921	64109
1922	69132
1923	73186
1924	76199
1925	78611
1926-28 parts clean-up ending at.	82744

MODEL 12

Year	Approx. Last No.
1912 -	5308
13 -	32418
14 -	79765
15 -	109515
16 -	136412
17 -	159391
18 -	183461
19 -	219457
20 -	247458
21 -	267253
22 -	304314
23 -	346319
24 -	385196
25 -	423056
26 -	464564
27 -	510693
28 -	557850
29 -	600834
30 -	626996
31 -	651255
32 -	660110
33 -	664544
34 -	673994
35 -	686978
36 -	720316
37 -	754250
38 -	779455
39 -	814121
40 -	856499
41 -	907431
42 -	958303
43 -	975640
44 -	975727
45 -	990004
46 -	1029152
47 -	1102371
48 -	1176055
49 -	1214041
50 -	1252028
51 -	1290015
52 -	1328002
53 -	1399996
54 -	1471990
55 -	1541929
56 -	1611868
57 -	1651435
58 -	1690999
59 -	1795500
60 -	1800000
61 -	1930999
62 -	1956990
63 -	1962001

A clean up of production took place from 1964 through 1966 with the ending serial # 1970875.

MODEL 12 TRENCH/RIOT SHOTGUN

This information is provided by Mr. Pat Redmond after many years of research and collecting. Reference a Winchester Repeating Arms Co. Memorandum dated September 1945. Trench/Riot and long barrel Contract Dates 4/1/42 - 3/21/44, Contract Shipments 61014 shotguns.

Blue Finish

Year	Ser. Nos.	Type	Configuration
1941 rel	926558--956504	Mil.	Riot & Long Barrel
1942	961934-1001014	Mil.	Trench/Riot/Long
1943	996899-1028856	Mil.	Trench & Riot

Parkerized Finish

Year	Ser. Nos.	Type	Configuration
1943	1030000-1035214	Mil.	Trench Gun

Parkerized Finish

Year	Ser. Nos.	Type	Configuration
1944	1035458	Mil.	Trench Gun
1944	1035525	Mil.	Trench Gun
1946	1071586	Com.	Riot Gun
1949	1740610	Com.	Riot Gun

NEW STYLE M/12

Year	Approx. Last No.
1972 -	Y200 011-Y2006396
73 -	Y2015662
74 -	Y2022061
75 -	Y2024478
76 -	Y2025482
77 -	Y2025874
78 -	Y2026156
79 -	Y2026399

MODEL 24

Year	Approx. Last No.
1939 -	1 to 8118
40 -	21382
41 -	27045
42 -	33670
43 -	NONE RECORDED
44 -	33683
45 -	34965
46 -	45250
47 -	58940
48 -	64417

There were no records kept on this model from 1949 until its discontinuance in 1958. The total production was approximately 116280.

MODEL 36

Approximately 20,000 Model 36 single shot 9mm shotguns were manufactured 1920-1927. These shotguns where not serial numbered.

MODEL 37

Approximately 1,000,000 Model 37 single shot shotguns were manufactured 1936-1963. These shotguns where not serial numbered.

MODEL 40

Year	Approx. Last No.
1939 -	1 to 2671
1940	10592
1941	13265
1942	18929

MODEL 42

Year	Approx. Last No.
1933 -	1 to 9398
34 -	13963
35 -	17728
36 -	24849
37 -	30900
38 -	34659
39 -	38967
40 -	43348
41 -	48203
42 -	50818
43 -	50822
44 -	50828
45 -	51168
46 -	54256
47 -	64853
48 -	75142
49 -	81107
50 -	87071
51 -	93038
52 -	99000
53 -	108201
54 -	117200
55 -	121883
56 -	126566

MODEL 42 cont.

Year	Approx. Last No.
57 -	131249
58 -	135932
59 -	140615
60 -	145298
61 -	149981
62 -	154664
63 -	159353

MODEL 50

Year	Approx. Last No.
1954 -	1 to 24550
55 -	49100
56 -	73650
57 -	98200
58 -	122750
59 -	147300
60 -	171850
61 -	196400

WINCHESTER MODEL 101 SERIALIZATION

12 gauge

Ser. No.	Mfg. Mo.	Year
50,000	10	1959
50,500	3	1960
51,000	5	1960
51,500	6	1960
52,000	9	1961
52,500	3	1962
53,000	4	1962
53,500	5	1962
54,000	8	1962
54,500	9	1962
55,000	10	1962
55,500	12	1962
56,000	1	1963
56,500	2	1963
57,000	3	1963
57,500	3	1963
58,000	4	1963
58,500	5	1963
59,000	6	1963
59,500	6	1963
60,000	7	1963
60,500	8	1963
61,000	8	1963
61,500	11	1963
62,000	11	1963
62,500	11	1963
63,000	12	1963
63,500	1	1964
64,000	1	1964
64,500	2	1964
65,000	3	1964
65,500	3	1964
66,500	3	1964
67,000	5	1964
67,500	5	1964
68,000	5	1964
68,500	5	1964
69,000	6	1964
69,500	6	1964
70,000	7	1964
70,500	7	1964
71,000	8	1964
71,500	9	1964
72,000	9	1964

12 gauge cont.

Ser. No.	Mfg. Mo.	Year
72,500	10	1964
73,000	10	1964
73,500	11	1964
74,000	11	1964
74,500	12	1964
75,000	12	1964
75,500	1	1965
76,000	2	1965
76,500	2	1965
77,000	3	1965
77,500	4	1965
78,000	4	1965
78,500	4	1965
79,000	4	1965
79,500	4	1965
80,000	5	1965
80,500	6	1965
81,000	6	1965
81,500	6	1965
82,000	6	1965
82,500	8	1965
83,000	8	1965
83,500	8	1965
84,000	9	1965
84,500	9	1965
85,000	10	1965
85,500	10	1965
86,000	10	1965
86,500	10	1965
87,000	10	1965
87,500	10	1965
88,000	11	1965
88,500	11	1965
89,000	11	1965
90,000	12	1965
90,500	12	1965
91,000	12	1965
91,500	1	1966
92,000	1	1966
92,500	2	1966
93,000	2	1966
93,500	2	1966
94,000	3	1966
94,500	3	1966
95,000	5	1966
95,500	5	1966
96,000	6	1966
96,500	7	1966
97,000	7	1966
97,500	7	1966
98,000	8	1966
98,500	8	1966
99,000	9	1966
99,500	9	1966
100,000	10	1966
100,500	10	1966
101,000	10	1966
101,500	11	1966
102,000	11	1966
102,500	12	1966
103,000	1	1967
103,500	1	1967
104,000	2	1967
104,500	3	1967
105,000	4	1967
105,500	5	1967
106,000	5	1967
106,500	5	1967
107,000	9	1967
107,500	10	1967
108,000	10	1967

12 gauge cont.

Ser. No.	Mfg.Mo.	Year
108,500	11	1967
109,000	11	1967
109,500	11	1967
110,000	12	1967
110,500	1	1968
111,000	2	1968
111,500	3	1968
112,000	3	1968
112,500	3	1968
113,000	3	1968
113,500	4	1968
114,000	5	1968
114,500	5	1968
115,000	6	1968
115,500	6	1968
116,000	7	1968
116,500	7	1968
117,000	9	1968
117,500	10	1968
118,000	1	1969
118,500	1	1969
119,000	2	1969
119,500	3	1969
120,000	4	1969
120,500	4	1969
121,000	4	1969
121,500	4	1969
122,000	5	1969
122,500	6	1969
123,000	6	1969
123,500	6	1969
124,000	7	1969
124,500	7	1969
125,000	7	1969
125,500	8	1969
126,000	8	1969
126,500	9	1969
127,000	9	1969
127,500	10	1969
128,000	11	1969
128,500	11	1969
129,000	11	1969
129,500	2	1970
130,000	2	1970
130,500	3	1970
131,000	3	1970
131,500	4	1970
132,000	4	1970
132,500	4	1970
133,000	4	1970
133,500	5	1970
134,000	5	1970
134,500	5	1970
135,000	6	1970
135,500	6	1970
136,000	6	1970
136,500	8	1970
137,000	8	1970
137,500	8	1970
138,000	8	1970
138,500	11	1970
139,000	12	1970
139,500	12	1970
140,000	12	1970
140,500	1	1971
141,000	2	1971
141,500	2	1971
142,000	2	1971
142,500	3	1971
143,000	3	1971
143,500	4	1971

Ser. No.	Mfg.Mo.	Year
144,000	4	1971
144,500	4	1971
145,000	4	1971
145,500	5	1971

20 gauge

Ser. No.	Mfg.Mo.	Year
200,000	3	1966
200,500	3	1966
201,000	3	1966
201,500	3	1966
202,000	4	1966
202,500	4	1966
203,000	4	1966
203,500	5	1966
204,000	6	1966
204,500	6	1966
205,000	7	1966
205,500	8	1966
206,000	8	1966
206,500	8	1966
207,000	9	1966
207,500	9	1966
208,000	9	1966
208,500	12	1966
209,000	2	1967
209,500	7	1967
210,000	10	1967
210,500	12	1967

28 ga. & .410 ga. added

Ser. No.	Mfg.Mo.	Year
211,000	1	1968
211,500	1	1968
212,000	10	1968
212,500	10	1968
213,000	10	1968
213,500	11	1968
214,000	12	1968
214,500	12	1968
215,000	1	1969
215,500	2	1969
216,000	5	1969
216,500	6	1969
217,000	9	1969
217,500	10	1969
218,000	11	1969
218,500	12	1969
219,000	12	1969
219,500	12	1969
220,000	12	1969
220,500	1	1970
221,000	1	1970
221,500	2	1970
222,000	3	1970
222,500	7	1970
223,000	9	1970
223,500	9	1970
224,000	9	1970
224,500	9	1970
225,000	10	1970
225,500	10	1970
226,000	11	1970
226,500	11	1970
227,000	11	1970
227,500	12	1970
228,000	12	1970
228,500	4	1971
229,000	4	1971
229,500	4	1971

PROOF MARKS

The proof marks shown below will assist in determining nationality of manufacturers when no other markings are evident. Since the U.S. has no proofing houses (as in England, France, Germany and other European countries), most U.S. manufacturers voluntarily proof their firearms with a specifed style of proofmark (i.e. the interlocked ©WPᵃ synonymous with the Winchester trademark can be fired using modern smokeless powder) shells. Pre-1850 European firearms oftentimes do not exhibit any commercial proof marks and, with the exception of an occasional barrel address, they represent the single hardest bracket of firearms one can research properly. Captured weapons from major wars occasionally show two different nationalities of proofmarks. This is acceptable since the gun was proofed in a national proof house after original manufacture and again when the gun was exported to a different country as a military acquisition. Please refer to the References section in this text for proofmark source information.

AUSTRIAN PROOF MARKS

PROOF MARK	CIRCA	PROOF HOUSE	TYPE OF PROOF and GUN
	since 1891	Vienna	provisional proof for multi barrel guns
	since 1891	Ferlach	provisional proof for multi barrel guns
	1829-1958	Vienna	black powder proof for multi barrel guns
	1829-1958	Ferlach	black powder proof for multi barrel guns
BH	since 1891	Bundesheer	preliminary proof for multi barrel guns
N$_B^P$	1891-1928	Budapest	smokeless powder proof for parabellum pistols
N$_F^P$	Since 1981	Ferlach	smokeless powder proof for parabellum pistols
N$_P^P$	1891-1931	Ferlach	smokeless powder proof for parabellum pistols
N$_V^P$	since 1891	Vienna	smokeless powder proof for parabellum pistols
N$_W^P$	1891-1931	Weipert	smokeless powder proof for parabellum pistols

BELGIAN PROOF MARKS

PROOF MARK	CIRCA	PROOF HOUSE	TYPE OF PROOF and GUN
	since 1852	Belgium	provisional black powder proof for breech loading guns and rifled barrels
	-	-	double proof marking for unfurnished barrels
	-	-	triple proof provisional marking for unfurnished barrels
	since 1893	-	definitive black powder proof for breech loading guns, small bore guns and handguns
	since 1853	Perron	View stamp and inspectors mark for parabellum pistols
P.V	since 1924	-	Nitro proof for rifled barrel and parabellum pistols
R	since 1852	-	rifled arms defense for smokeless proof parabellum pistols
PV	-	-	Superior nitro proof

BRITISH PROOF MARKS

PROOF MARK	CIRCA	PROOF HOUSE	TYPE OF PROOF and GUN
	since 1856	London	provisional proof for barrels
BP	since 1856	Birmingham	provisional proof for barrels
GP	since 1637	London	definitive black powder proof for shotguns, muzzle loader barrels
NP	since 1904	London	definitive nitro proof for all guns - parabellum pistols
BNP	since 1954	Birmingham	definitive nitro proof for barrel and action
BP	since 1904	Birmingham	black powder proof only for parabellum pistols

PROOF MARK	CIRCA	PROOF HOUSE	TYPE OF PROOF and GUN
	1868-1925	London	definitive special super power proof for parabellum pistols
	1868-1925	Birmingham	voluntary special black powder proof
	1868-1925	London	reproof marking for black powder rifles
	1868-1925	Birmingham	reproof marking for black powder rifles
	1868-1925	Birmingham	definitive black powder proof for shotguns
	since 1904	Birmingham	definitive nitro proof for all guns
	since 1670	London	view mark
	since 1904	Birmingham	view mark

FRENCH PROOF MARKS

PARIS HOUSE	ST ETIENNE HOUSE	CIRCA	TYPE OF PROOF and GUN
		since 1897	provisional proof unfinished short barreled guns
		1897	standard proof for finished guns
		1897	double proof finished and joined bar-
		1897	single barrel proof for non-assembled
		1897	finished black powder guns
		1897	special proof for finished guns
		1897	ordinary smokeless powder proof
		1897	superior smokeless powder proof

GERMAN PROOF MARKS

PROOF MARK	CIRCA	PROOF HOUSE	TYPE OF PROOF and GUN
	since 1952	Ulm	
	since 1968	Hannover	
	since 1968	Kiel (W. German)	
	since 1968	Munich	
	since 1968	Cologne (W. German)	
	since 1968	Berlin (W. German)	
FB	since 1952	W. German	voluntary proof for Flobert rifle
J	since 1952	W. German	repair proof for major gun parts
M	since 1952	W. German	provisional black powder for shotgun & multi barreled rifles
N	since 1952	W. German	definitive nitro proof for all guns
SP	since 1952	W. German	definitive black powder for smokeless ammo guns
	since 1952	W. German	Flobert for special purpose guns signal, flare, gas, & stun guns
N	since 1945	E. German, Suhl	smokeless powder proof
G	since 1950	E. German, Suhl	1st black powder proof for rifled barrels
N	since 1950	E. German, Suhl	nitro powder proof
R	since 1950	E. German, Suhl	repair proof
S	since 1950	E. German, Suhl	1st black powder proof for smooth bored barrels

PROOF MARK	CIRCA	PROOF HOUSE	TYPE OF PROOF and GUN
	since 1950	E. German, Suhl	inspection mark
	since 1950	E. German, Suhl	choke-bore barrel mark

ITALIAN PROOF MARKS

PROOF MARK	CIRCA	PROOF HOUSE	TYPE OF PROOF and GUN
	since 1951	Brescia	provisional proof for all guns
	since 1951	Gardone	provisional proof for all guns
	since 1951	Gardone & Brescia	definitive proof for guns with smokeless powder
	since 1951	Gardone & Brescia	finish proof for firearms ready for sale
	since 1951	Gardone & Brescia	1st black powder proof

SPANISH PROOF MARKS

PROOF MARK	CIRCA	PROOF HOUSE	TYPE OF PROOF and GUN
	since 1910	Eibar	provisional black powder proof for shotguns
	since 1910	Eibar	temporary black powder proof for shotguns
	since 1910	Eibar	final black powder proof for breech loading shotguns
	since 1910	Eibar	final smokeless powder proof for breech loading shotguns
	since 1910	Eibar	re-enforced smokeless powder proof for breech loading shotguns
	since 1910	Eibar	provisional proof for shotguns
	since 1910	Eibar	final black powder proof for breech loading shotgun

PROOF MARK	CIRCA	PROOF HOUSE	TYPE OF PROOF and GUN
	since 1923	Eibar	final and single black powder proof for double barreled muzzle loading shotun
	since 1923	Eibar	final and single black powder proof for single barrel smooth bored breechloading guns
	since 1923	Eibar	final black powder proof for double barreled breechloading rifles
	since 1923	Eibar	final black powder proof for single barrel breechloading rifles
	since 1923	Eibar	reinforced voluntary proof for single proof for single and double barrel shotguns
	since 1923	Eibar	final proof of military-style rifle
	since 1923	Eibar	single and final proof of non-self loading pistols
	since 1923	Eibar	single and final proof for self loading pistols and revolvers
	since 1929	Eibar	admission proof for guns with old marks
	since 1929	Eibar	proof used in Barcelona for guns with old marks
	since 1929	Eibar	final proof for revolver
	since 1929	Eibar	proof for semiautomatic pistols
	since 1929	Eibar	special manufacturer's mark for guns made for foreign sales
	since 1929	Eibar	smokeless proof for shotgun barrels
	since 1929	Eibar	reinforced smokeless proof for shotgun barrels

ATF GUIDE

A listing has been provided below of Field Division offices for the ATF. You are encouraged to contact them if you have any questions regarding the legality of any weapons or their interpretation of existing laws and regulations. Remember, ignorance is no excuse when it involves Federal firearms regulations and laws. Although these various offices may not be able to help you with state, city, county, or local firearms regulations and laws, their job is to assist you on a Federal level.

Atlanta Field Division
2600 Century Parkway
Atlanta, Georgia 30345
(404) 417-2600
Fax: (404) 417-2601

Baltimore Field Division
31 Hopkins Plaza
5th Floor
Baltimore, Maryland 21201
(410) 779-1700
Fax: (410) 779-1701

Boston Field Division
10 Causeway Street
Suite 253
Boston, Massachusetts 02222
(617) 557-1200
Fax: (617) 557-1201

Charlotte Field Division
6701 Carmel Road
Suite 200
Charlotte, North Carolina 28226
(704) 716-1800
Fax (704)716-1801

Chicago Field Division
525 West Van Buren Street
Suite 600
Chicago, Illinois 60607
(312) 846-7200
Fax: (312) 846-7201

Columbus Field Division
37 West Broad Street, Suite 200
Columbus, Ohio 43215-4167
(614) 827-8400
Fax: (614) 827-8401

Dallas Field Division
1114 Commerce Street
Room 303
Dallas, TX 75242
(469) 227-4300
Fax: (469) 227-4330

Detroit Field Division
1155 Brewery Park Boulevard
Suite 300
Detroit, Michigan 48207-2602
(313) 259-8050
Fax: (313) 393-6054

Houston Field Division
15355 Vantage Parkway West
Suite 200
Houston, Texas 77032-1960
(281) 372-2900
Fax: (281) 372-2919

Kansas City Field Division
2600 Grand Avenue
Suite 200
Kansas City, Missouri 64108
(816) 559-0700
Fax: (816) 559-0701

Los Angeles Field Division
350 South Figueroa Street
Suite 800
Los Angeles, California 90071
(213) 534-2450
Fax: (213) 534-2415

Louisville Field Division
600 Dr. Martin Luther King Jr.
 Place
Suite 322
Louisville, KY 40202
(502) 753-3400
Fax: (502) 753-3401

Miami Field Division
5225 NW 87 Avenue, Suite 300
Miami, FL 33178
(305) 597-4800
Fax: 305-597-4801

Nashville Field Division
5300 Maryland Way, Suite 200
Brentwood, Tennessee 37027
(615) 781-5364
Fax: 615-781-5371

New Orleans Field Division
111 Veterans Memorial BLVD.
Suite 1008
Heritage Plaza Building
Metairie, Louisiana 70005
(504) 841-7000
Fax: (504) 841-7039

New York Field Division
241 37th Street, 3rd Floor
Brooklyn, NY 11232
(718) 650-4000
Fax: (718) 650-4001

Philadelphia Field Division
United States Custom House
Suite 607
Philadelphia, Pennsylvania 19106
(215) 717-4700
Fax: (215) 717-4711

Phoenix Field Division
3003 N. Central Ave.
Suite 1010
Phoenix, AZ 85012
(602) 776-5400
Fax: (602) 776-5429

San Francisco Field Division
5601 Arnold Road
Suite 400
Dublin, CA 94568
(925) 479-7500
Fax: (925) 829-7612

Seattle Field Division
915 2nd Avenue
Room 790
Seattle, Washington 98174-1093
(206) 389-5800
Fax: (206) 389-582

St. Paul Field Division
30 East Seventh Street
Suite 1870
St. Paul, Minnesota 55101
(651) 726-0200
Fax: (651) 726-0201

Tampa Field Division
501 East Polk Street
Suite 700
Tampa, Florida 33602
(813) 202-7300
Fax: (813) 202-7301

Washington Field Division
607 14th Street, NW
Suite 620
Washington, DC 20005
(202) 927-8810
Fax: (202) 927-4024

SHOW TIME 2005

During the course of a year, we get many requests for information about which upcoming trade/gun shows we'll be attending. If you want to meet with Steve, John and related BBP road warriors during the next year, here's where we'll be hanging out. At these shows we will be displaying all of our publications and electronic products, including books, CD-ROMs, information downloads, and online subscriptions. Don't forget to check out the Show Time portion of our website after these shows are over for a potential photo recap, along with a little humor. It's always a pleasure to visit with our customers, and it also gives you a chance to see what's new, and to see whether we're aging gracefully.

April 2-3, 2005
Tulsa Gun & Knife Show
(consumer show, exhibiting)
Expo Center - Expo Square
Tulsa Fairgrounds
Sat. 8-7pm, Sun. 8-5pm
Contact: Tulsa Gun Show, Inc.
P.O. Box 33201
Tulsa, OK 74153-1201
Phone: 918-492-0401
www.tulsagunshow.com
mail@tulsagunshow.com

April 15-17, 2005
The 134th NRA Annual Meetings & Exhibits
 Show
(consumer show, exhibiting)
Brown Convention Center
Houston, TX
Contact: NRA
Phone: 800-694-9300
www.nra.org

April 16-19, 2005
EXA
(Italian trade show, attending)
Brixia Expo
Brescia, Italy

June 24-26, 2005
Duluth Gun Show
(consumer show, exhibiting)
Duluth Entertainment Convention Center
South Pioneer Hall
Sat. 9-5 p.m. Sun. 9-3 p.m.
$5.00 admission
Contact: Bob White
1920 Greysolon Rd
Duluth, MN 55812
Phone: 218-724-8387
Fax: 218-724-8740

July 29-31, 2005
35th Annual Kansas City National Summer Arms Show & 10th NRA Gun Collectors Show
(consumer show, exhibiting)
K.C.I. Expo-Center
Kansas City, MO
Contact: MVACA Show Committee
P.O. Box 33033
Kansas City, MO 64114
Phone: 913-642-2863
www.mvacagunshow.com

October 22-23, 2005
Tulsa Gun & Knife Show
(consumer show, exhibiting)
Expo Center - Expo Square
Tulsa Fairgrounds
Sat. 8-7pm, Sun. 8-5pm
Contact: Tulsa Gun Show, Inc.
P.O. Box 33201
Tulsa, OK 74153-1201
Phone: 918-492-0401
www.tulsagunshow.com
mail@tulsagunshow.com

Nov. 2-4, 2005
NASGW
(trade show, attending)
Reno Hilton
Reno, NV
www.nasgw.org

MUSEUMS

National Firearms Museum (NFM)
National Rifle Association
11250 Waples Mill Road
Fairfax, VA
www.nrahq.org/museum
Check website for special exhibits.
This is easily the best firearms museum east of the Mississippi, and if you are an NRA member, you have two major reasons to visit this well-appointed museum in the Washington, D.C. area. Blue Book Publications, Inc. is proud to be a sponsor.

Buffalo Bill Museum/Cody Firearms Museum
Cody, WY
www.bbhc.org
Check website for special exhibits.

Blue Book Publications, Inc. is also pleased to be a sponsor of The Buffalo Bill Historical Center. The BBHC is actually five museums, and by far one of the best places on earth to learn about the West, the Great Plains and early American History. Summer is the busiest time, so check their website for special events and exhibits.

INDEX

A

B

D

H

Q

R